Contents

Dictionary features

headwords in colour to find words more easily

word families show how words are related to each other; some entries include synonyms to increase

labels are given to encourage accurate use of language

example sentences from children's authors show headwords in use

word histories are given to increase language knowledge

words with different parts of speech are linked by being closer together

different meanings are numbered

pose *NOUN* **poses**

1 a position or posture of the body taken for a portrait or photograph
2 a way of behaving that someone adopts to give a particular impression

pose *VERB* **poses, posing, posed**

1 to take up a pose
2 to put someone into a pose
3 to pose as a person is to pretend to be that person
4 to put forward or present ◆ *Drug abuse poses a serious threat to the fabric of our society.*

WORD FAMILY *Pose* comes from the Latin word *ponere* meaning 'to place' or 'to put'. Other words to do with placing and putting (some only loosely) and having the same origin include *compose, depose, dispose, expose, interpose, propose, position, positive, purpose, suppose,* and *transpose.*

poser *NOUN* **posers**

1 a puzzling question or problem
2 a person who behaves in an affected way in order to impress other people

posh *ADJECTIVE* (*informal*)

1 very smart; high-class

Mum stopped outside this immensely posh French cake and coffee shop. 'Let's live dangerously,' she said, and went inside.
— *Jacqueline Wilson, Lola Rose*

2 typical of the upper classes ◆ *I heard a rather posh voice say 'Excuse me'.*

WORD HISTORY origin unknown: it is often thought to come from the first letters of the phrase *port out, starboard home*, which referred to the side of the ship where the most comfortable cabins were (because they were away from the heat of the sun) on the route between Britain and India; but this story is not the true origin

position *NOUN* **positions**

1 the place where something is or should be
2 the way a person or thing is placed or arranged ◆ *Hold your back in a straight upright position.*
3 a situation or condition ◆ *We were in no position to argue.*
4 a piece of paid employment; a job

▷ **positional** *ADJECTIVE*

position *VERB* **positions, positioning, positioned**

to place a person or thing in a certain position

positive *ADJECTIVE*

1 definite or certain ◆ *Are you positive the tank was full?* ◆ *I can only offer you a theory, since positive proof is impossible.*
2 a positive statement or reply is one that means 'yes'
3 a positive person or attitude looks at the best or most hopeful aspects of a situation
4 a positive test result indicates that there is a sign of what is being tested for

5 (*Mathematics*) a positive number or quantity is greater than zero; plus (SEE ALSO **negative**)
6 (*Science*) to do with the kind of electric charge that lacks electrons
7 (*Grammar*) the positive form of an adjective or adverb is its simple form, e.g. *fast* as distinct from *faster* (the comparative form) and *fastest* (the superlative form)

subject labels give context to meaning

▷ **positively** *ADVERB*

USAGE NOTE The opposite of meaning 1 is *uncertain*; for meanings 2–6, the opposite of *positive* is *negative*.

words that are derived from headwords are given at the end of entries

positive *NOUN* **positives**
a photograph or film in which the light and dark parts or colours appear as in the original scene or subject (SEE ALSO **negative**)

cross references link key words

positron *NOUN* **positrons**
(*Science*) a particle of matter with a positive electric charge

posse (*say* poss- ee) *NOUN* **posses**
a group of people recruited to help a sheriff

WORD HISTORY from Latin *posse comitatus* 'force of the county'

pronunciation guides help with words that cause difficulty

possess *VERB* **possesses, possessing, possessed**
1 to have or own something as your property
2 to control someone's thoughts or behaviour ◆ *What possessed his aunt to make such a crazy will?*

verb forms are given in full

▷ **possessor** *NOUN*

possessed *ADJECTIVE*
seeming to be controlled by strong emotion or an evil spirit ◆ *He ran down the street like a man possessed.*

definitions are clear and accurate

possession *NOUN* **possessions**
1 something that a person possesses or owns
2 the right or state of owning something

possessive *ADJECTIVE*
1 wanting to possess and keep things for yourself
2 (*Grammar*) a possessive word, e.g. *his* or *ours*, shows what or whom something belongs to

possessives

Possessive adjectives and **possessive pronouns** show to whom, or to what, something belongs or is connected.

The **possessive adjectives** are *my*, *your*, *his*, *her*, *its*, *our*, and *their*:
Is it okay to wear my trainers?
Our fate was in their hands.

The **possessive pronouns** are: *mine*, *yours*, *his*, *hers*, *ours*, and *theirs*:
Is that last slice of pizza mine or yours?
Theirs was the fastest finishing time.

Possessive pronouns can also be used after *of*:
That song is an old favourite of mine.

Note that there is no apostrophe in the possessive pronouns *hers*, *ours*, *yours*, and *theirs*, or in the possessive adjective *its*: *The shark opened its jaws.*

See also the panel on **determiners**.

special language panels focus on key topics to support reading and writing

Introduction

Vocabulary for today's needs

The *Oxford English Dictionary for Schools* has been written primarily for students at secondary school aged from 11 to 14 and has been designed so that it can be used across the curriculum. A key feature is the inclusion of the special vocabulary of subjects not normally given in dictionaries of this size but important from the perspective of school needs: for example *calligram, cinquain, digraph, grapheme, morpheme*; in the sciences, terms such as *cortex, genome, lesion, peptide*, and *xylem*; in the language of information technology, *applet, bandwidth, firewall, freeware, motherboard,* and *router*. This material has been carefully chosen from a study of information given in syllabuses and textbooks, supplemented by advice from teachers and specialist advisers.

The range of vocabulary is based on British English but explores varieties beyond this, in particular the English of Australia, New Zealand, and South Africa. Important differences between British and American English are also noted (e.g. the difference in form between *aluminium* and *aluminum*). In compiling this information, the editors have been able to draw on the expertise and experience of the overseas branches of Oxford University Press in the countries involved.

The treatment of vocabulary has been greatly enriched by access to language databases, primarily the British National Corpus, a database of 100 million words of printed and spoken language, and the Oxford English Corpus of over 1 billion words of selected and indexed machine-readable text. These sources have provided invaluable information at all levels of dictionary writing: in identifying the core vocabulary, in establishing the most common meanings and uses, and in recognizing usage based on actual practice rather than on compilers' intuitions. The definitions themselves have been written in straightforward language that strikes the right balance between accessibility and authority. In particular, formulaic 'dictionaryese' explanations have been avoided.

Real examples from children's literature

A key feature of a dictionary for schools is its use of example phrases and sentences to illustrate words in use. Readers of the dictionary will immediately notice a large number of quotations from the literature with which they will be familiar from their own reading: best-selling authors such as Philip Pullman, J. K. Rowling, and Jacqueline Wilson; the science fiction and fantasy writing of J. R. R. Tolkien, Eoin Colfer, Terry Pratchett, Ursula Le Guin, and others; British Asian writers including Bali Rai and Narinder Dhami; writers from India (Anita Desai), Nigeria (Chinua Achebe), South Africa (Beverley Naidoo), Australia (Joan Lindsay), and New Zealand (Witi Ihimaera); and classic works of fiction including those of John Buchan, Charles Dickens, H. G. Wells, as well as Edgar Allan Poe, L. M. Montgomery, Arthur Miller, J. D. Salinger, and other notable writers of North America. Non-fiction sources include famous autobiographies by Christy Brown, Helen Keller, Gerald Durrell, and Nelson Mandela, and the travel writing of Michael Palin, Joe Simpson, and Ellen MacArthur. All the works cited are likely to be on the reading lists of users, and the quotations will enable them not only to understand words and phrases in context but to draw on their knowledge of the literature to find a special resonance in the meanings and uses of words.

Word histories

The information on word histories (etymologies) has been chosen to illustrate the wide range of source languages that English has drawn on over many centuries; it concentrates on the anecdotal and interesting rather than the philological and formulaic, and provides historical background as well as dealing with the development of word forms: for example, there are colourful stories behind words such as *deadline*, *halibut*, and *trivial*.

Extra language information

The needs of language teaching today go beyond the explanation of individual words into the realms of understanding text and of language production at the level of phrase, sentence, and text. The notes on usage cover a broad range of issues to do with standards and sensitivities, and many of these deal with words that are often confused, for example the pairs *adverse* and *averse* and the trio *their, there,* and *they're*.

There are special language panels aimed specifically at this age group and covering key language topics that provide extra grammar and language support. These include the main word classes (*noun*, *verb*, etc.), structural features including *clauses, tenses,* and *punctuation*, and other major topics including terms for literature, terms for poetry, figurative language, and formal and informal language. These panels, which can be found at their alphabetical places in the main text of the dictionary (see the list on page ix), will enable students to develop more creative approaches to language use, helping them not just to understand their language but to use it imaginatively and effectively.

The Editors

Subject labels

Words and meanings that belong to special subjects are indicated by the following labels:

Art	ICT (information and communication technology)
Biology	Language
D & T (design and technology)	Mathematics
Drama	Medicine
Economics	Music
Geography	Politics
Grammar	Religion
History	Science

Usage labels

Some words and meanings are only used in certain types of speaking and writing. This is called *register*. The following labels are used to show a special register:

informal	chiefly used in more casual conversation and in other informal contexts, e.g. *scam*
formal	chiefly used in more formal writing and speaking, e.g. *mendacious*
literary	typically found in older fiction and other literature, e.g. *hark*
old use	a word or meaning that is no longer common but used to be, e.g. *chattel*
poetic	chiefly used in poetry, e.g. *isle*
humorous	used to produce a witty or amusing effect, e.g. *trusty*

Words that are registered as trademarks are shown with the label *trademark*.

Pronunciations

Pronunciation guides are given for words that cause difficulty. The guides use the ordinary English letters, and please note the following special groups of letters:

ah	as in *barn*, *rather*
oo	as in *moon*
ss	s sometimes used to avoid confusion with s pronounced as z (e.g. to show the difference between close in 'close (klohz) the door' and in 'a close (klohss) shave'
th	as in *thick*
th (italic)	as in *this*
uu	as in *book*
zh (italic)	as in *measure*
y (or, when clearer, eye)	as in *mine*, *item*

The stress, or main emphasis, on a word is shown in bold type, e.g. albino is given as al-**bee**-noh (with the stress on the second syllable, *-bee-*)

Where it is clearer, some pronunciations are given by showing a word that rhymes with the headword: for example, *aisle* 'rhymes with *mile*'.

Extra language information

The following special information on language topics will be found in panels at their alphabetical places in the dictionary:

abbreviations	active and passive	adjectives
adverbs	alliteration	alphabet
American spelling	apostrophes	Arabic words in English
brackets	clauses	colons
commas	comparative and superlative forms	compound words
confusable words	conjunctions and connectives	consonants
dashes	dates	definite and indefinite articles
determiners	direct and indirect speech	double negatives
eponyms	exclamation marks	figurative language
formal and informal language	French words in English	full stops
German words in English	Greek words in English	homographs and homophones
hyphens	Italian words in English	Latin words in English
non-European words in English	nouns	onomatopoeia
palindromes	paragraphs	place names
plurals	possessives	prefixes and suffixes
prepositions	pronouns	pronunciation
proper nouns	proverbs	punctuation
question marks	quotation marks	semicolons
sentences	simile and metaphor	singular and plural forms
Spanish words in English	spelling	synonyms and antonyms
tenses	varieties of English	verbs
vowels	word classes	terms for literature
terms for poetry		

Aa

a or **an** *DETERMINER* (called the indefinite article: **an** is used before a vowel)

1 one (when there are others as well)

'I'm going to be staying with a friend,' he said. 'I'll phone up as often as I can.' — *Philip Pullman, The Subtle Knife*

2 used to show how often something happens ◆ *She goes to the gym twice a week to do some weight training.*

aardvark (*say* **ahd**-vahk) *NOUN* **aardvarks**
an African mammal with a long snout, that eats ants

WORD HISTORY from Afrikaans, from *aarde* 'earth' and *vark* 'pig'

aback *ADVERB*
to be taken aback is to be alarmed or surprised ◆ *'What happened to your hair?' Lucy was taken aback. 'My hair?'*

WORD HISTORY from Old English *on bæc* 'backwards'. *Aback* was originally used to describe the sails of a ship when a wind blowing from the front pressed them back against the mast.

abacus (*say* **ab**-a-kus) *NOUN* **abacuses**
a device used for counting and adding, consisting of a frame with rows of wires, along which you slide beads

WORD HISTORY from Greek *abax*, a name for a board covered with grains of sand, used for counting. The Greek word came from a Hebrew word meaning 'dust'.

abandon *VERB* **abandons, abandoning, abandoned**

1 to leave someone or something without intending to return ◆ *He could not just return to England and abandon his family.*

2 to stop doing something when it becomes impossible ◆ *The rescuers had to abandon the search when the weather turned bad.*

▷ **abandonment** *NOUN*

abandon *NOUN*
to do something with abandon is to do it without any restraint or self-control ◆ *Both sides fought with abandon.*

abase *VERB* **abases, abasing, abased**
to make a person feel humble or humiliated

abashed *ADJECTIVE*
embarrassed

abate *VERB* **abates, abating, abated**
something strong or harmful abates when it becomes less or dies down

Towards dawn the storm had abated a little, and they had pushed on again until long past noon. — *Rosemary Sutcliff, The Eagle of the Ninth*

▷ **abatement** *NOUN*

abattoir (*say* **ab**-at-wahr) *NOUN* **abattoirs**
a place where animals are killed for food; a slaughterhouse

WORD HISTORY from French *abattre* 'to destroy'

abbey *NOUN* **abbeys**

1 a monastery or convent

2 a church that was once part of a monastery, for example Westminster Abbey in London

abbot *NOUN* **abbots**
the head of an abbey

WORD HISTORY from Greek *abbas* 'father', from Aramaic (an ancient language once spoken in the Middle East)

abbreviate *VERB* **abbreviates, abbreviating, abbreviated**
to shorten a word or phrase

WORD HISTORY from Latin *brevis* 'short', also the origin of our word *brief*

abbreviation *NOUN* **abbreviations**
(*Language*) a shortened form of a word or words

abbreviations

Abbreviations are shortened forms of words. There are several kinds of abbreviations:

- **shortenings**, in which part of the word is chopped off, e.g. *Mon.* for *Monday* and *sci-fi* for *science-fiction*.
- **contractions**, in which the middle of the word is left out, e.g. *Dr* for *Doctor* and *Rd* for *Road*.
- **initialisms**, in which the first letters of a group of words form the abbreviation, e.g. *BBC* for *British Broadcasting Corporation* and *pto* for *please turn over*. The abbreviations *e.g.* and *i.e.* are also initialisms, shortened from the Latin phrases *exempli gratia* (= 'for the sake of an example') and *id est* (= 'that is').
- **acronyms**, which are like initialisms but are pronounced as words in their own right rather than as a sequence of letters, e.g. *Aids* for *acquired immune deficiency syndrome*.

abdicate *VERB* **abdicates, abdicating, abdicated**
1 a queen or king abdicates if they give up the throne
2 to give up an important responsibility
▷ **abdication** *NOUN*

abdomen (*say* ab-do-men) *NOUN* **abdomens**
1 the lower front part of a person's or animal's body, containing the stomach, intestines, and other organs used for digesting food
2 the rear section of an insect's body
▷ **abdominal** (*say* ab-**dom**-in-al) *ADJECTIVE*

abduct *VERB* **abducts, abducting, abducted**
to take a person away by force and against their will; to kidnap someone
▷ **abduction** *NOUN*
▷ **abductor** *NOUN*

aberration *NOUN*
something unpleasant or bad that is not what people normally do or have
WORD HISTORY from Latin *aberrare* 'to stray'

abet *VERB* **abets, abetting, abetted**
to help or encourage someone to commit a crime
WORD HISTORY from Old French *abeter* 'to urge'

abeyance (*say* ab-**ay**-ans) *NOUN*
to be in abeyance is when something is not being used at the moment ◆ *Sadly the plan is in abeyance now as the country has more urgent problems to deal with.*

abhor *VERB* **abhors, abhorring, abhorred**
(*formal*) to hate or dislike something very much
WORD HISTORY from Latin *abhorrere* 'to shrink away in horror', from *horrere* 'to shudder'

abhorrent *ADJECTIVE*
hateful or disgusting
▷ **abhorrence** *NOUN*

abide *VERB* **abides, abiding, abided**
1 you can't abide something when you detest it or can't bear it ◆ *She couldn't abide convenience meals.*
2 to abide by a promise or agreement is to keep it and do what you said you would
WORD HISTORY from Old English *abidan* 'to wait'

abiding *ADJECTIVE*
lasting or permanent

ability *NOUN* **abilities**
1 ability is being able to do something
2 an ability is a skill or talent that you have

abject (*say* **ab**-jekt) *ADJECTIVE*
1 hopeless or pitiful ◆ *For the first three years he suffered abject misery.*
2 grovelling or humiliating ◆ *I owe you an abject apology.*
WORD HISTORY from Latin *abjectus* 'thrown down', related to *eject* and *trajectory*

ablaze *ADJECTIVE*
a building is ablaze when it is on fire and burning fiercely

able *ADJECTIVE* **abler, ablest**
1 having the power or skill or opportunity to do something

If you only had twelve of us instead of thirty-two you'd manage much better. You'd be able to keep order. — *K. M. Peyton, 'Who, Sir? Me, Sir?'*

2 skilful or clever
▷ **ably** *ADVERB*

able-bodied *ADJECTIVE*
fit and healthy; not disabled

abnormal *ADJECTIVE*
not normal; unusual ◆ *The poor television reception was due to abnormal weather conditions.*
▷ **abnormally** *ADVERB*
▷ **abnormality** *NOUN*

aboard *ADVERB, PREPOSITION*
on or into a ship or aircraft or train

abode *NOUN* **abodes**
(*formal*) the place where someone lives ◆ *He adorned his new abode with the finest furniture.*

abolish *VERB* **abolishes, abolishing, abolished**
to put an end to a law or custom
▷ **abolition** (*say* ab-ol-**ish**-on) *NOUN*
WORD HISTORY from Latin *abolere* 'to destroy'

abominable *ADJECTIVE*
very bad or unpleasant
▷ **abominably** *ADVERB*

abominate *VERB* **abominates, abominating, abominated**
(*formal*) to hate something very much
▷ **abomination** *NOUN*
WORD HISTORY from Latin *abominari* 'to regard as a bad omen'

aborigine (*say* ab-er-**ij**-in-ee) *NOUN* **aborigines**
one of the original inhabitants of a country. An **Aborigine** (with a capital A) is one of the original inhabitants of Australia who lived there before the Europeans arrived.
▷ **aboriginal** *ADJECTIVE, NOUN*
WORD HISTORY from Latin *ab origine* 'from the beginning'
WORD FAMILY Another word with the same meaning is aboriginal, which is also an adjective, as in *the aboriginal inhabitants.*

abort *VERB* **aborts, aborting, aborted**
to put an end to something before it has been completed ◆ *The pilot tried a landing but had to abort it.*
WORD HISTORY from Latin *aboriri* 'to miscarry'

abortion *NOUN* **abortions**
an operation to remove an unborn child from the womb before it has developed enough to survive

a b c d e f g h i j k l m n o p q r s t u v w x y z

abortive *ADJECTIVE*
unsuccessful or useless ◆ *He is remembered for his abortive attempt to swim the Irish Sea.*

abound *VERB* **abounds, abounding, abounded**
1 things abound when there are a lot of them ◆ *Rumours abound of another scandal.*
2 a place abounds in things when there are a lot of them there ◆ *The hills abound in magnificent forests.*

about *PREPOSITION, ADVERB*
1 used to show that something is approximate or not exact ◆ *The work was finished in about two months.* ◆ *Come at about two o'clock.*
2 used to show the subject or topic of talk or writing or thinking

He didn't want to think about her because it upset him. But he didn't want to not think about her either. — *Michael Hoeye, Time Stops for No Mouse*

3 used to show movement in several directions

Charlie's mother, and especially little Charlie himself, went about from morning till night with a horrible empty feeling in their tummies. — *Roald Dahl, Charlie and the Chocolate Factory*

4 used to show presence ◆ *At that time of night there were not many people about.*

to be about to do something is to be on the point of starting it

WORD HISTORY from an Old English word *butan* 'outside'

above *PREPOSITION, ADVERB*
1 used to show a higher place or position ◆ *A black cloud rose to twenty-five kilometres above the volcano.*
2 used to show a larger amount or number, with the meaning 'more than' ◆ *a crowd of above a thousand*

above board *ADJECTIVE, ADVERB*
things people do are above board when they are fair and honest

WORD HISTORY so called because card players could cheat by holding their cards under the table but not when they held them 'above board' (*board* = table)

abrasion *NOUN* **abrasions**
an area of skin that has been scraped

WORD HISTORY from Latin *radere* 'to scrape'

abrasive *ADJECTIVE*
1 something abrasive rubs or scrapes things
2 a person is abrasive when they are harsh or hurtful in what they say

abreast *ADVERB*
1 side by side ◆ *The men were sitting three abreast on a sofa.*
2 to keep abreast of a situation is to be aware of it and have enough information about it ◆ *It is important to keep abreast of the new technology.*

abridged *ADJECTIVE*
an abridged book or piece of writing is one that uses fewer words than the original and is therefore shorter ◆ *an abridged paperback edition*

▷ **abridgement** *NOUN*

abroad *ADVERB*
in or to another country

abrupt *ADJECTIVE*
1 sudden or hasty ◆ *He came to an abrupt stop when he saw Luke standing by the window.*
2 rather rude and unfriendly ◆ *Her voice was abrupt and she didn't thank him.*

▷ **abruptly** *ADVERB*

WORD HISTORY from Latin *abruptus* 'broken off' or 'steep'

abscess (*say* **ab**-sis) *NOUN* **abscesses**
an inflamed place where pus has formed in the body

abscond *VERB* **absconds, absconding, absconded**
to leave secretly, especially after doing something wrong ◆ *Catherine absconded after supper by climbing over the wall.*

abseil *VERB* **abseils, abseiling, abseiled**
to lower yourself down a steep cliff or rock by sliding down a rope that is fixed at the top

WORD HISTORY from German, from *ab* 'down' and *Seil* 'rope'

absent *ADJECTIVE*
not in the place you should be; not present ◆ *There was no mention of his absent wife.*

▷ **absence** *NOUN*

WORD HISTORY from Latin *absens*, from *abesse* 'to be away'

absent (*say* ab-**sent**) *VERB* **absents, absenting, absented**

to absent yourself is to stay away from somewhere you should be

absentee *NOUN* **absentees**
a person who is not present when they are expected to be

▷ **absenteeism** *NOUN*

absent-minded *ADJECTIVE*
having your mind on other things; forgetful

absolute *ADJECTIVE*
complete; not restricted ◆ *An Egyptian pharaoh had absolute power.*

absolutely *ADVERB*
1 completely ◆ *Maria was absolutely determined that her school wasn't going to be left behind.*
2 (*informal*) used as an answer meaning 'yes, I agree'

absolute zero *NOUN*
the lowest possible temperature, calculated as -273.15°C and represented by 0° in the Kelvin scale

absolution *NOUN*
in the Christian Churches, priests give absolution when they pronounce that a person's sins have been forgiven

absolve *VERB* **absolves, absolving, absolved**
1 to clear a person of blame or guilt
2 to release a person from a promise or obligation

WORD HISTORY from Latin *absolvere* 'to set free'

absorb *VERB* **absorbs, absorbing, absorbed**
1 (*Science*) to soak up a liquid or gas
2 to absorb a shock or impact is to take it and reduce its effects ◆ *Protective padding absorbed most of the blow.*
3 to take up a person's attention or time

WORD HISTORY from Latin *absorbere* 'to suck in'

absorbent *ADJECTIVE*
an absorbent substance or material is able to soak up liquids easily ◆ *Gently wipe the strawberries with absorbent kitchen paper.*

absorption *NOUN*
1 absorption is the soaking up of a liquid or gas
2 absorption is also being very interested in something you are doing, so that you ignore everything else

abstain *VERB* **abstains, abstaining, abstained**
1 to abstain from something is to stop yourself from doing it
2 to choose not to use your vote
▷ **abstention** *NOUN*

WORD HISTORY from Latin *abstinere* 'to keep something away', which was the original meaning in English

abstemious (*say* ab-**steem**-ee-us) *ADJECTIVE*
eating or drinking only small amounts; not greedy

WORD HISTORY from Latin *ab* 'from' and *temetum* 'alcoholic drink'

abstinence *NOUN*
going without something, especially alcohol

abstract (*say* **ab**-strakt) *ADJECTIVE*
1 concerned with ideas, not solid objects ◆ *Truth, hope, and danger are all abstract.*
2 (*Art*) an abstract painting or sculpture shows the artist's ideas or feelings rather than depicting a recognizable person or thing

WORD HISTORY from Latin *abstrahere* 'to draw off', related to our word *tractor*

abstract (*say* ab-**strakt**) *VERB* **abstracts, abstracting, abstracted**
(*formal*) to take something out or remove it ◆ *He abstracted a letter from the file.*
▷ **abstraction** *NOUN*

abstract (*say* **ab**-strakt) *NOUN* **abstracts**
a summary

absurd *ADJECTIVE*
ridiculous or foolish
▷ **absurdly** *ADVERB*
▷ **absurdity** *NOUN*

WORD HISTORY from Latin *absurdus* 'out of tune', related to *surdus* 'deaf'

a-bubble *ADJECTIVE*
very excited and lively

abundance *NOUN*
a large amount of something, often more than you need

WORD HISTORY related to *abound*

abundant *ADJECTIVE*
things are abundant when there are plenty of them
▷ **abundantly** *ADVERB*

abuse (*say* ab-**yooz**) *VERB* **abuses, abusing, abused**
1 to use something badly or wrongly; to misuse something
2 to hurt someone or treat them cruelly
3 to say unpleasant things about a person or thing

abuse (*say* ab-**yooss**) *NOUN* **abuses**
1 a misuse of something ◆ *Their action was a gross abuse of their authority.*
2 physical harm or cruelty done to someone
3 words that offend or insult a person

abusive *ADJECTIVE*
rude and insulting ◆ *He admitted letting down car tyres and making abusive phone calls.*

abysmal (*say* ab-**iz**-mal) *ADJECTIVE*
extremely bad ◆ *the abysmal ignorance of science in Britain*

abyss (*say* ab-**iss**) *NOUN* **abysses**
an extremely deep pit

WORD HISTORY from Greek *abyssos* 'bottomless'

AC *ABBREVIATION*
alternating current

acacia (*say* a-**kay**-sha) *NOUN*
a shrub with large thorns and yellow or white flowers

WORD HISTORY via Latin from Greek *akakia*

academic *ADJECTIVE*
1 to do with education or studying, especially at a school or college or university ◆ *Girls' academic achievements are at least as high as boys'.*
2 theoretical; having no practical use ◆ *The debate about public services is no longer just an academic one.*

academic *NOUN* **academics**
a university or college teacher

academy *NOUN* **academies**
1 a school or college, especially one that provides specialized teaching
2 a society of scholars or artists who meet regularly

WORD HISTORY from *Akademeia*, the name of a garden near Athens, where the Greek philosopher Plato taught his pupils. It was named after the legendary hero Academus.

accede (*say* ak-**seed**) *VERB* **accedes, acceding, acceded**
1 to accede to a request or suggestion is to agree to it ◆ *Eventually the government acceded to most of the demands.*
2 a person accedes to the throne when they become queen or king

accelerate *VERB* **accelerates, accelerating, accelerated**
1 a vehicle accelerates when it starts to go faster
2 to accelerate a vehicle is to make it go faster

WORD HISTORY from Latin *celer* 'swift'

acceleration *NOUN* **accelerations**
1 the rate at which the speed of something increases
2 (*Science*) the rate of change of velocity

accelerator *NOUN* **accelerators**
1 the pedal that a driver presses to make a motor vehicle go faster
2 (*Science*) a machine or device used to increase the speed of something

accent (*say* **ak**-sent) *NOUN* **accents** (*Language*)
1 the way a person pronounces the words of a language ◆ *He spoke with a strong Dutch accent.*
2 the emphasis or stress used in pronouncing a word ◆ *In 'cuckoo', the accent is on the first syllable.*
3 a mark placed over a letter to show how it is pronounced, e.g. in *resumé*

WORD HISTORY from Latin *cantus* 'song'

accentuate (*say* ak-**sent**-yoo-ayt) *VERB* **accentuates, accentuating, accentuated**
to emphasize something you say or make it more obvious
▷ **accentuation** *NOUN*

accept *VERB* **accepts, accepting, accepted**
1 to take a thing that is offered or presented to you
2 to say yes to an invitation or offer
▷ **acceptance** *NOUN*

USAGE NOTE Take care not to confuse this word with *except*.

acceptable *ADJECTIVE*
good enough to accept; pleasing
▷ **acceptably** *ADVERB*

access (*say* **ak**-sess) *NOUN*
1 a way to enter or reach a building or other place
2 the right to use or look at something

access *VERB* **accesses, accessing, accessed**
to read and use the data that has been stored in a computer

accessible *ADJECTIVE*
1 a place is accessible when you can reach it or go into it easily
2 a person is accessible when you can see them and talk to them without difficulty
▷ **accessibility** *NOUN*

accession *NOUN* **accessions**
1 a person's accession is when they reach a certain rank or position, especially when they become queen or king
2 an accession to a library is a new book that it has bought

accessory (*say* ak-**sess**-er-ee) *NOUN* **accessories**
1 a thing which can be added to something else to make it more useful or attractive
2 a person who helps someone else to commit a crime, without actually taking part in it

accident *NOUN* **accidents**
1 an unexpected happening, especially one causing injury or damage
2 something happens by accident when no one has planned it or meant it to happen

WORD HISTORY from Latin *accidere* 'to happen'

accidental *ADJECTIVE*
happening or done by accident
▷ **accidentally** *ADVERB*

acclaim *VERB* **acclaims, acclaiming, acclaimed**
to praise someone or something publicly or officially ◆ *Her poems have been highly acclaimed by many contemporary writers.*
▷ **acclamation** *NOUN*

WORD HISTORY from Latin *clamare* 'to shout'

acclaim *NOUN*
public or official praise for someone or something ◆ *He had won wide acclaim throughout the world for his kindness and humanity.*

acclimatize *VERB* **acclimatizes, acclimatizing, acclimatized**
to acclimatize, or to be acclimatized, to a new climate or new surroundings is to become used to them and find them comfortable
▷ **acclimatization** *NOUN*

USAGE NOTE This word can also be spelled acclimatise.

accolade (*say* **ak**-ol-ayd) *NOUN* **accolades**
a prize or piece of praise given to someone for something they have done

WORD HISTORY from Latin *collum* 'neck', so called because in the past when a man was knighted, the king put his arm round the man's shoulders

accommodate *VERB* **accommodates, accommodating, accommodated**
1 to provide somebody with a place to live, work, or sleep overnight
2 to help someone by providing them with what they need ◆ *The Centre is designed to accommodate the needs of all visitors.*

accommodating *ADJECTIVE*
willing to help or cooperate

accommodation *NOUN*
somewhere to live, work, or sleep overnight

accompaniment *NOUN*
a musical part that supports a singer or instrument

accompanist *NOUN* **accompanists**
a pianist or other musician who plays music to support a singer or another musician

accompany *VERB* **accompanies, accompanying, accompanied**
1 to go with somebody to a place ◆ *A tall fair-haired girl accompanied him to the hall.*
2 to happen or belong together with something else ◆ *Do you want a cold drink to accompany your meal?*
3 to play music, usually on a piano, to support a singer or another musician

accomplice (*say* a-**kum**-pliss) *NOUN* **accomplices**
a person who helps another in a crime or bad act

accomplish *VERB* **accomplishes, accomplishing, accomplished**
to do something completely and successfully
WORD HISTORY from Latin *complere* 'to complete'

accomplished *ADJECTIVE*
skilled or talented

accomplishment *NOUN* **accomplishments**
something you have achieved or are good at

accord *NOUN*
1 agreement or consent
2 to do something of your own accord is to do it when nobody else has asked you or told you to do it

accord *VERB* **accords, according, accorded**
1 to be consistent with something
2 (*formal*) to give or grant someone a power or privilege

accordance *NOUN*
to do something in accordance with a rule or principle is to follow the rule or principle when you do it

accordingly *ADVERB*
1 in a way that is suitable ◆ *You're grown up now, and must act accordingly.*
2 (as a linking word) because of what has just been said; therefore ◆ *Accordingly, the judges rejected the appeal.*

according to *PREPOSITION*
used to show where a piece of information comes from ◆ *According to Rose, the black cat was called Midnight*, or to show how one thing relates to another ◆ *Everyone arrived according to plan.*

accordion *NOUN* **accordions**
a portable musical instrument with bellows and a set of piano-type keys at one end, played by squeezing and stretching it and pressing the keys
WORD HISTORY from Italian *accordare* 'to tune an instrument'

accost *VERB* **accosts, accosting, accosted**
to approach a person and speak to them

account *NOUN* **accounts**
1 a statement of the money a person or organization owes or has received
2 an amount of money someone has in a bank or building society
3 a description or story about something that happened

on account of because of; for the reason that ◆ *The design is called a 'Butterfly Plan' on account of its shape.*

on no account certainly not; in no circumstances ◆ *On no account should you go near the weir.*

to take something into account is to consider it along with other things when making a decision or calculation

account *VERB* **accounts, accounting, accounted**
to account for something is to explain why it has happened

accountable *ADJECTIVE*
to be accountable for your actions is to have to explain why you have done them
▷ **accountability** *NOUN*

accountant *NOUN* **accountants**
a person whose job is to record and organize the money a person or organization spends and receives
▷ **accountancy** *NOUN*

accounting *NOUN*
the business of keeping financial accounts

accretion (*say* a-**kree**-shon) *NOUN* **accretions**
a growth or increase in which things are added gradually

accrue (*say* a-**kroo**) *VERB* **accrues, accruing, accrued**
to increase gradually over a period of time
▷ **accrual** *NOUN*

accumulate *VERB* **accumulates, accumulating, accumulated**
1 to collect things or pile them up
2 to increase in quantity
▷ **accumulation** *NOUN*
WORD HISTORY from Latin *cumulus* 'heap'

accumulator *NOUN* **accumulators**
a large battery that can be recharged

accurate *ADJECTIVE*
correct or exact; giving the right information

Atomic clocks are so accurate, they are even more accurate than the earth going round!
— *Kjartan Poskitt, Murderous Maths*

▷ **accurately** *ADVERB*
▷ **accuracy** *NOUN*

WORD HISTORY from Latin *cura* 'care', also the source of our words *curious* and *secure*

accusation *NOUN* **accusations**
a statement claiming that someone has committed a crime or done something wrong

accuse *VERB* **accuses, accusing, accused**
to accuse someone is to say that they have committed a crime or done something wrong

▷ **accuser** *NOUN*

WORD HISTORY from Latin *causa* 'cause'

accustom *VERB* **accustoms, accustoming, accustomed**
to make a person become used to something

ace *NOUN* **aces**
1 a playing card with one spot
2 a very skilful person or thing
3 (in tennis) a serve that is too fast or well aimed for the other player to return

WORD HISTORY from Latin *as* 'unit'

acerbic (*say* a-**serb**-ik) *ADJECTIVE*
having a sharp way of speaking

WORD HISTORY from Latin *acerbus* 'sour-tasting'

acetylene (*say* a-**set**-il-een) *NOUN*
a gas that burns with a bright flame, used in cutting and welding metal

ache *NOUN* **aches**
a dull continuous pain

ache *VERB* **aches, aching, ached**
to have an ache; to be painful

Every muscle ached to stop, to give up. It was only his brain that kept him going. — *Gillian Cross, On the Edge*

achieve *VERB* **achieves, achieving, achieved**
to succeed in doing or producing something

▷ **achievable** *ADJECTIVE*

achievement *NOUN* **achievements**
something good or worthwhile that you have succeeded in doing

acid *NOUN* **acids**
(*Science*) a chemical substance that contains hydrogen and neutralizes alkalis. The hydrogen can be replaced by a metal to form a salt.

▷ **acidic** *ADJECTIVE*
▷ **acidity** *NOUN*

acid *ADJECTIVE*
1 sharp-tasting; sour
2 looking or sounding bitter or unkind ◆ *'Not very successful, were you?' came the acid response.*

acid rain *NOUN*
rain made acid by mixing with waste gases from industrial burning of fossil fuels

acknowledge *VERB* **acknowledges, acknowledging, acknowledged**
1 to admit that something is true ◆ *Everyone acknowledges that the problem is complicated.*
2 to tell someone that you have received something they have sent ◆ *They wrote back to acknowledge my application.*
3 to express thanks or appreciation for something ◆ *Kevin raised his hands to acknowledge the applause.*

▷ **acknowledgement** *NOUN*

acme (*say* **ak**-mee) *NOUN*
the highest degree of something ◆ *The city was at the acme of its power.*

WORD HISTORY from Greek *akme* 'highest point'

acne (*say* **ak**-nee) *NOUN*
a skin condition causing inflamed red pimples on the face and neck

WORD HISTORY probably the same origin as *acme*

acorn *NOUN* **acorns**
the seed of the oak tree

WORD HISTORY from Old English *æcern*, which is related to our word *acre*

acoustic (*say* a-**koo**-stik) *ADJECTIVE*
1 to do with sound or hearing
2 an acoustic musical instrument is one that uses natural means, such as the hollow body of the instrument itself, to amplify the sound, and not electrical devices

▷ **acoustically** *ADVERB*

WORD HISTORY from Greek *akouein* 'to hear'

acoustics (*say* a-**koo**-stiks) *PLURAL NOUN*
1 the qualities of a hall or room that make it good or bad for carrying sound
2 the properties of sound

acquaint *VERB* **acquaints, acquainting, acquainted**
to acquaint someone with something is to tell them about it

to be acquainted with someone is to know them slightly

acquaintance *NOUN* **acquaintances**
1 a person you know slightly
2 a slight friendship ◆ *He had hardly got to know her in such a brief acquaintance.*

acquiesce (*say* ak-wee-**ess**) *VERB* **acquiesces, acquiescing, acquiesced**
to agree to something even though you may not like it completely
▷ **acquiescent** *ADJECTIVE*
▷ **acquiescence** *NOUN*
WORD HISTORY from Latin *quiescere* 'to rest'

acquire *VERB* **acquires, acquiring, acquired**
to get or be given something
WORD HISTORY from Latin *quaerere* 'to seek'

acquisition *NOUN*
1 an acquisition is something you have got or been given recently
2 acquisition is when you acquire something

acquisitive (*say* a-**kwiz**-it-iv) *ADJECTIVE*
eager to have more money and possessions

acquit *VERB* **acquits, acquitting, acquitted**
1 to decide that somebody is not guilty ◆ *He was acquitted of murder but found guilty of manslaughter.*
2 to acquit yourself well is to complete a task or piece of work well
▷ **acquittal** *NOUN*

acre (*say* **ay**-ker) *NOUN* **acres**
an area of land measuring 4,840 square yards or 4,047 square metres
▷ **acreage** *NOUN*
WORD HISTORY from Old English *æcer* the amount of land a pair of oxen could plough in a day

acrid *ADJECTIVE*
bitter ◆ *People were choking on the acrid fumes.*
WORD HISTORY from Latin *acer* 'sharp, bitter'

acrimonious (*say* ak-rim-**oh**-nee-us) *ADJECTIVE*
an acrimonious person or remark is one that is unpleasant or bad-tempered
▷ **acrimony** (*say* **ak**-rim-on-ee) *NOUN*
WORD HISTORY related to *acrid*

acrobat *NOUN* **acrobats**
a person who performs spectacular gymnastic feats to entertain an audience
▷ **acrobatic** *ADJECTIVE*
▷ **acrobatics** *PLURAL NOUN*
WORD HISTORY from Greek *akrobatos* 'walking on tiptoe', from *akron* 'tip' and *bainein* 'to walk'

acronym (*say* **ak**-ron-im) *NOUN* **acronyms**
(*Language*) a word or name that is formed from the initial letters of other words and pronounced as a word in its own right ◆ *NATO is an acronym of North Atlantic Treaty Organization.*
WORD HISTORY from Greek *akros* 'top' and *onyma* 'name'

across *PREPOSITION, ADVERB*
1 used to show movement from one side to the other

Daniel whipped a purple-spotted handkerchief from his pocket and handed it to his daughter across the table. — *Anne Fine, Mrs Doubtfire*

2 used to show that something is on the opposite side ◆ *She lived in the house across the street.*
WORD FAMILY Words which include 'across' in their meaning often begin with *trans-*: for example, *transatlantic* means 'across the Atlantic', and *transfer* means 'to move something across from one place to another'.

acrostic *NOUN* **acrostics**
(*Language*) a word puzzle or poem in which the first or last letters of each line form a word or group of words
WORD HISTORY from Greek *akros* 'top' and *stikhos* 'a line of verse'

acrylic (*say* a-**kril**-ik) *NOUN* **acrylics**
1 a kind of fibre, plastic, or resin made from an organic acid
2 (*Art*) a type of thick paint used by artists

act *NOUN* **acts**
1 something someone does
2 a pretence ◆ *She was putting on an act and laughing a lot.*
3 one of the main divisions of a play or opera
4 each of a series of short performances in a programme of entertainment ◆ *The next act was a juggler.*
5 a law passed by a parliament

act *VERB* **acts, acting, acted**
1 to do something; to behave in a particular way

Mr Dursley tried to act normally. When Dudley had been put to bed, he went into the living-room in time to catch the last report on the evening news. — *J. K. Rowling, Harry Potter and the Philosopher's Stone*

2 to perform a part in a film or drama
3 to function or have an effect ◆ *Religion acts as a restraining force on human nature.*

action *NOUN* **actions**
1 action is the process of doing something

Gerry was so deep in his plans he did not even hear… There were long lists of things to bring, and a detailed plan of the action. — *Raymond Briggs, Midnight Adventure*

2 an action is something someone does
3 an action is also a battle or fighting between armies ◆ *He was killed in action.*
4 in law, an action is a lawsuit
to be out of action is to be not working or functioning
to take action is to decide to do something

action replay *NOUN* **action replays**
an instant recording of part of a sports match or competition on television, played back immediately or in slow motion

activate *VERB* **activates, activating, activated**
to activate a plan or machine is to start it working

'Activate the tracking device as soon as you've found the dishes,' Blunt ordered. — *Anthony Horowitz, Scorpia*

▷ **activation** *NOUN*
▷ **activator** *NOUN*

active *ADJECTIVE*
1 taking part in many activities; energetic
2 functioning or working; in operation ◆ *You can take a boat trip to the active volcano.*
3 (*Grammar*) a form that verbs can have, in which the subject of the verb performs the action (SEE ALSO **passive**)
▷ **actively** *ADVERB*

active and passive

Verbs can be either **active** or **passive**, and these two choices are called **voice**.
A verb is active when the subject of the verb performs the action: *The sun rises in the East*, *My father wrote these words*. In these sentences, the verbs (*rises* and *wrote*) are active because their subjects (*the sun* and *my father*) are performing the actions. But when the verb takes an object (*these words* in the second sentence), you can turn the sentence round and say *These words were written by my father*. Now, the verb (*were written*) is passive, because the subject of the sentence is *these words*, and the subject and object are the other way round. You use the passive voice when you want the object to be the main topic of the sentence (i.e. in the previous example, when you are talking mainly about the words, and not about your father).
If a verb does not take an object (like *rises* in the first example), it can only be active; you cannot turn *The sun rises in the East* into a passive sentence because there is no object to make into the subject.
In passive sentences, the performer of the action often comes after the word *by*: *The mystery was solved by our neighbour*; *The penalty will be taken by the Welsh captain*. But sometimes the performer is unknown, or is not identified: *All the tickets have been sold*; *That file has been deleted*.
See also the panel on **formal and informal language**.

activist *NOUN* **activists**
a person who is active and energetic, especially in politics

activity *NOUN* **activities**
1 activity is being active or lively
2 an activity is an action or occupation ◆ *The charges include accommodation, entertainment, and leisure activities.*

actor *NOUN* **actors**
someone who acts a part in a film or drama

actress *NOUN* **actresses**
a woman who acts a part in a film or drama

actual *ADJECTIVE*
really happening or existing

actually *ADVERB*
really; for real

One of these days, Callum's going to forget himself and actually look pleased to see me. — *Malorie Blackman, Noughts and Crosses*

acumen (*say* ak-yoo-men) *NOUN*
the ability to make good judgements and take quick decisions

WORD HISTORY a Latin word meaning 'a point' or 'sharpness'

acupuncture (*say* ak-yoo-punk-cher) *NOUN*
a method of treating pain or illness by sticking fine needles into special points in the body

WORD HISTORY from Latin *acus* 'needle' and *puncture*

acute *ADJECTIVE*
1 an acute pain or illness is one that is serious or strong
2 an acute person is good at understanding things and making decisions
3 an acute remark is clever and shrewd
▷ **acutely** *ADVERB*
▷ **acuteness** *NOUN*

WORD HISTORY from Latin *acus* 'needle'

acute accent *NOUN* **acute accents**
a mark over a vowel that affects its sound, like the one over *é* in *resumé*

acute angle *NOUN* **acute angles**
an angle of less than 90° (SEE ALSO **obtuse angle**)

AD *ABBREVIATION*
used with dates to show that they are after the birth of Christ, e.g. AD2010

USAGE NOTE When you use AD with a year, it is better to put AD before the number, because it means 'in the year of Our Lord'. But it's common to say (for example) *the tenth century* AD.

WORD HISTORY from the first letters of Latin *anno Domini* 'in the year of Our Lord'

ad *NOUN* **ads**
(*informal*) an advertisement in a newspaper or on television

adage (*say* ad-ij) *NOUN* **adages**
a proverb or short statement expressing something true and wise

adamant (*say* ad-am-ant) *ADJECTIVE*
you are adamant when you refuse to let people persuade you about something or to let them change your mind

WORD HISTORY from Greek *adamas* 'unable to be tamed', from *daman* 'to tame'

adamant *NOUN*
a legendary rock or mineral associated at times with both diamond and lodestones

a b c d e f g h i j k l m n o p q r s t u v w x y z

Adam's apple *NOUN* **Adam's apples**
the lump at the front of a man's neck

WORD HISTORY from the Bible story that a piece of the forbidden fruit in the Garden of Eden became stuck in Adam's throat when he ate it

adapt *VERB* **adapts, adapting, adapted**
1 to adapt something is to change it so that it is suitable for a new purpose
2 to adapt, or to adapt yourself, is to become used to a new situation
▷ **adaptable** *ADJECTIVE*
▷ **adaptation** *NOUN*

WORD HISTORY from Latin *aptus* 'suitable', related to our word *apt*

adaptor *NOUN* **adaptors**
a device that connects pieces of electrical or other equipment

add *VERB* **adds, adding, added**
1 to add one thing to another is to put them together or make them into one
2 to add a remark is to say it during a conversation

'Simon,' his mother called from the kitchen. 'Is Jessica awake?' 'No,' Simon called back. 'But I could arrange it,' he added under his breath.
— *Theresa Breslin, Simon's Challenge*

to add up
1 you add up numbers, or the numbers add up, to give a total
2 (*informal*) something adds up when it makes sense, or seems reasonable

addenda *PLURAL NOUN*
extra text or other items that come at the end of a book

WORD HISTORY a Latin word meaning 'things to be added'

adder *NOUN* **adders**
a small poisonous snake

WORD HISTORY from Old English *nædre* 'serpent'. It was originally called *a nadder*, which later became *an adder*.

addict *NOUN* **addicts**
a person who does or uses something that they cannot give up
▷ **addicted** *ADJECTIVE*
▷ **addiction** *NOUN*

addictive *ADJECTIVE*
an addictive habit or drug is one that people cannot give up

addition *NOUN* **additions**
1 (*Mathematics*) addition is the process of adding
2 an addition is something added
in addition also; as an extra thing

additional *ADJECTIVE*
extra; as an extra thing
▷ **additionally** *ADVERB*

additive *NOUN* **additives**
a substance added to another in small amounts for a special purpose, e.g. as a flavouring

addled *ADJECTIVE*
1 an addled egg has become rotten and cannot produce a chick
2 an addled mind or brain is one that is muddled or confused

address *NOUN* **addresses**
1 the details of the place where someone lives or of where letters or parcels should be delivered to a person or firm
2 (*ICT*) the part of an instruction that shows where a piece of information is stored in a computer's memory
3 a speech to an audience

address *VERB* **addresses, addressing, addressed**
1 to write an address on a letter or parcel
2 to address somebody, or to address words to somebody, is to speak to them, usually in a formal way

addressee *NOUN* **addressees**
the person to whom a letter or packet is addressed

adenoids *PLURAL NOUN*
a piece of thick spongy flesh at the back of the nose and throat, which can make breathing difficult

WORD HISTORY from Greek *aden* 'gland'

adept (*say* a-**dept**) *ADJECTIVE*
to be adept at something is to be able to do it well

adequate *ADJECTIVE*
enough or good enough
▷ **adequately** *ADVERB*
▷ **adequacy** *NOUN*

adhere *VERB* **adheres, adhering, adhered**
1 to stick fast to something
2 to adhere to a belief or rule is to follow it
▷ **adhesion** *NOUN*

adherent (*say* ad-**heer**-ent) *NOUN* **adherents**
a person who supports a certain group or theory etc.
▷ **adherence** *NOUN*

adhesive *ADJECTIVE*
sticky; causing things to stick together

adhesive *NOUN* **adhesives**
a substance used to stick things together; glue

ad hoc *ADJECTIVE, ADVERB*
done or arranged only when necessary and not planned in advance ◆ *We had to make a number of ad hoc decisions.*

Adi Granth (*say* ah-di-**grunt**) *NOUN*
the holy book of the Sikhs

WORD HISTORY an ancient Sanskrit name meaning 'first book'

ad infinitum (*say* in-fin-y-tum) *ADVERB*
without limit; for ever

WORD HISTORY a Latin phrase meaning 'to infinity'

adjacent *ADJECTIVE*
1 one place is adjacent to another when it is near or next to it ♦ *The camp is on land adjacent to the parks.*
2 (*Mathematics*) adjacent angles are formed on the same side of a straight line when intersected by another line (SEE ALSO **alternate**)

WORD HISTORY from Latin *adjacere* 'to lie near to'

adjective *NOUN* **adjectives**
(*Grammar*) a describing word
▷ **adjectival** *ADJECTIVE*

WORD HISTORY from Latin *adjectum* 'something added', from *adicere* 'to add'

adjectives

Adjectives are words that describe a person, place, or thing, e.g. *tall, pale, delicious, jagged, unique, untrue*. They can come before a noun (e.g. *a tall giraffe, a jagged cliff*), or they can come after a verb like *be, become*, or *grow* (e.g. *The soup was delicious; My companion became pale; The weather grew cold*). Some adjectives can only be used in one position: *afraid* can only be used after a verb, and *utter* only before a noun. You can say *The crew were afraid* but not *an afraid crew*; and you can say *It was an utter disaster* but not *The disaster was utter.*
Non-gradable adjectives classify people and things, e.g. *Australian* (*an Australian actor*) or *square* (*a square envelope*). These are 'all-or-nothing' adjectives because actors are either Australian or not Australian, and things are either square or not.
Gradable adjectives describe a quality that people or things have, e.g. *tall* (*a tall teenager*) or *smelly* (*a smelly cheese*). These adjectives have variable meanings, because some teenagers are taller than others, and some cheeses are smellier than others.
See also the panel on **comparative and superlative forms.**

adjoining *ADJECTIVE*
buildings or rooms are adjoining when they are next to each other

adjourn (*say* a-**jern**) *VERB* **adjourns, adjourning, adjourned**
1 to break off a meeting until a later time
2 to break off and go somewhere else ♦ *The little group adjourned to the sitting room for coffee.*
▷ **adjournment** *NOUN*

WORD HISTORY from an earlier meaning 'to summon someone to appear on a named day', related to French *jour* 'day'

adjudicate (*say* a-**joo**-dik-ayt) *VERB* **adjudicates, adjudicating, adjudicated**
to act as judge in a competition or dispute
▷ **adjudication** *NOUN*
▷ **adjudicator** *NOUN*

WORD HISTORY from Latin *judex* 'judge'

adjunct (*say* **aj**-unkt) *NOUN* **adjuncts**
1 something extra that is useful but not essential
2 in grammar, a group of words added to a statement giving extra information rather like an adverb, e.g. *at a party* in the sentence *He met her at a party.*

WORD HISTORY from Latin *junctum* 'joined'

adjust *VERB* **adjusts, adjusting, adjusted**
1 to alter something so that it fits or is suitable
2 to put a thing into its proper position or order
▷ **adjustable** *ADJECTIVE*
▷ **adjustment** *NOUN*

ad lib *ADVERB*
to speak or act ad lib is to say or do things without any preparation

WORD HISTORY from Latin *ad libitum* 'according to pleasure'

ad-lib *VERB* **ad-libs, ad-libbing, ad-libbed**
to say or do things without any rehearsal or preparation

administer *VERB* **administers, administering, administered**
1 to give or provide something

Walter got me back into his lab and administered the antidote in a few seconds. — *John Wyndham, The Day of the Triffids*

2 to manage the affairs of a business or organization

WORD HISTORY from Latin *ministrare* 'to serve'

administrate *VERB* **administrates, administrating, administrated**
to manage public or business affairs
▷ **administrator** *NOUN*
▷ **administrative** *ADJECTIVE*

administration *NOUN* **administrations**
1 administration is the management of public or business affairs
2 an administration is the particular government of a country, or the set of people who manage a business or organization

admirable *ADJECTIVE*
worth admiring; excellent
▷ **admirably** *ADVERB*

admiral *NOUN* **admirals**
a naval officer of high rank

WORD HISTORY from Arabic *amir* 'commander'

admire *VERB* **admires, admiring, admired**
1 to think that someone or something is very good
2 to look at something and enjoy it
▷ **admiration** *NOUN*
▷ **admirer** *NOUN*
WORD HISTORY from Latin *mirari* 'to wonder at'

admissible *ADJECTIVE*
able to be allowed or accepted as being valid ◆ *admissible evidence*

admission *NOUN* **admissions**
1 admission is what you have to pay to go into a cinema, museum, or other public place
2 an admission is a statement admitting something; a confession

admit *VERB* **admits, admitting, admitted**
1 to allow someone or something to come in
2 to say reluctantly that something is true; to confess something ◆ *We admit that the task is difficult.* ◆ *He admitted his crime.*

admittance *NOUN*
being allowed to go in, especially to a private place

admittedly *ADVERB*
as an agreed fact; without denying it

admonish *VERB* **admonishes, admonishing, admonished**
to advise or warn someone firmly but mildly
▷ **admonition** *NOUN*
WORD HISTORY from Latin *monere* 'to warn or advise'

ad nauseam (*say* naw-see-am) *ADVERB*
to do or say something ad nauseam is to continue with it until people are sick of it
WORD HISTORY a Latin phrase meaning 'to sickness'

ado *NOUN*
without more or further ado without wasting any more time or trouble
WORD HISTORY originally as part of *much ado* meaning 'much action'

adolescence (*say* ad-ol-ess-ens) *NOUN*
the time between being a child and being an adult, from about 14 to 18
WORD HISTORY from Latin *alescere* 'to grow up'

adolescent *NOUN* **adolescents**
a young person at the age between being a child and being an adult, from about 14 to 18
▷ **adolescent** *ADJECTIVE*

adopt *VERB* **adopts, adopting, adopted**
1 to take a child into your family as your own child
2 to accept something; to take something and use it ◆ *They adopted new methods of working.*
▷ **adoption** *NOUN*
WORD HISTORY from Latin *optare* 'to choose'

adorable *ADJECTIVE*
lovable; deserving love and affection
▷ **adorably** *ADVERB*

adore *VERB* **adores, adoring, adored**
to love a person or thing very much
▷ **adoration** *NOUN*

adorn *VERB* **adorns, adorning, adorned**
to decorate something or make it pretty
▷ **adornment** *NOUN*

adrenalin (*say* a-**dren**-al-in) *NOUN*
a hormone produced when you are afraid or excited. It stimulates the nervous system, making your heart beat faster and increasing your energy and your ability to move quickly.
WORD HISTORY from Latin *renes* 'kidneys', because adrenalin is made by the adrenal glands, above the kidneys

adrift *ADJECTIVE, ADVERB*
a boat is adrift when it is drifting and out of control

adroit (*say* a-**droit**) *ADJECTIVE*
an adroit action or piece of work is clever and skilful
WORD HISTORY from a French phrase *à droit* 'by right, properly'

adulation *NOUN*
a lot of admiration or flattery

adult (*say* ad-ult) *NOUN* **adults**
a fully grown or mature person
WORD HISTORY from Latin *adultus* 'grown up'

adulterate *VERB* **adulterates, adulterating, adulterated**
to make a thing impure or less good by adding something to it
▷ **adulteration** *NOUN*

adultery *NOUN*
a married person commits adultery if they have sexual intercourse with someone other than their wife or husband
▷ **adulterer** *NOUN*
▷ **adulterous** *ADJECTIVE*

advance *NOUN* **advances**
1 a forward movement; a stage that marks progress
2 a development or improvement
3 a loan of money, or a payment made before it is due
in advance beforehand; ahead
WORD HISTORY from Old French *avancer*. The original meaning in English was 'to promote'.

advance *ADJECTIVE*
advance information or warning is given beforehand

advance *VERB* **advances, advancing, advanced**
1 to move forward or make progress
2 to lend or pay money ahead of the proper time ◆ *Can you advance me a month's pay?*
▷ **advancement** *NOUN*

advantage *NOUN* **advantages**
1 something useful or helpful ◆ *Larger bookshops can offer the advantage of a cafe or snack bar.*
2 (in tennis) the next point won after deuce
3 something is to your advantage when it will help you or benefit you
to take advantage of something is to make good use of it or benefit from it
to take advantage of someone is to use them unfairly to get some help or benefit
WORD HISTORY from French *avant* 'before', i.e. 'ahead of someone' and so enjoying an advantage

advantageous (*say* ad-van-**tay**-jus) *ADJECTIVE*
giving an advantage; helpful or beneficial

Advent *NOUN*
the period just before Christmas, when Christians celebrate the coming of Christ
WORD HISTORY from Latin *adventus* 'arrival'

advent *NOUN*
the first appearance of a new person or thing ◆ *It was the advent of television that really transformed sport.*
WORD HISTORY from Latin *venire, vent-* 'to come', which is the source of other English words including *adventure, convene, invent*, and *venture*

adventure *NOUN* **adventures**
1 an adventure is an exciting or dangerous experience

He was not, you would have thought, the sort of boy to plunge into an adventure of this sort. He was small and thin and shrinking. — *Gillian Avery, A Likely Lad*

2 adventure is doing exciting and daring things
WORD HISTORY from Latin *advenire* 'to arrive'. An *adventure* was originally just something that happened, and only later developed the meaning of something exciting or dangerous.

adventurer *NOUN* **adventurers**
someone who enjoys adventure; an explorer

adventurous *ADJECTIVE*
liking to do exciting and daring things

adverb *NOUN* **adverbs**
(*Grammar*) a word that adds to the meaning of a verb or adjective or another adverb
▷ **adverbial** *ADJECTIVE*
WORD HISTORY from Latin *ad-* 'added to' and *verbum* 'word'

adverbs

Adverbs answer questions such as *when?, where?, why?, how?*, and *how much?* Some adverbs go with adjectives: for example, *The map is very old* tells you how old the map is, and *a fairly expensive car* describes a car that is quite (but not very) expensive. Other adverbs go with verbs: for example, *The troll ate ravenously* tells you how the troll was eating, *It rains here frequently* tells you how often it rains, and *Hammering was heard downstairs* tells you where hammering was heard. Adverbs like these are often formed by adding *-ly* to an adjective, e.g. *ravenously, frequently*. Notice that adverbs can also go with other adverbs: *Sam smiled rather sheepishly*.

A groups of words that functions as an adverb is called an **adverbial**: for example, in the sentence *We email each other whenever we can*, the underlined phrase answers the question *when?* and is an adverbial (equivalent to *often* or *regularly*).

If an adverb tells you about a whole sentence, it usually comes at the beginning: *Honestly, I didn't know where to look; Clearly, we had a long wait ahead.*

See also the panel on **comparative and superlative forms**.

adversary (*say* **ad**-ver-ser-ee) *NOUN* **adversaries**
(*formal*) an opponent or enemy

adverse *ADJECTIVE*
adverse effects or conditions are bad or harmful
▷ **adversely** *ADVERB*
USAGE NOTE Take care not to confuse this word with *averse*.

adversity *NOUN* **adversities**
trouble or misfortune ◆ *The family had been brave in the face of adversity.*

advert *NOUN* **adverts**
(*informal*) an advertisement

advertise *VERB* **advertises, advertising, advertised**
1 to give out information about the good features of a product or service in order to get people to buy it or use it
2 to advertise a meeting or other occasion is to make it publicly known
3 to advertise a job is to publish information about it and invite people to apply for it
▷ **advertiser** *NOUN*

advertisement *NOUN* **advertisements**
a public notice or announcement, especially one advertising products or services in newspapers, on posters, or on television or radio

advice *NOUN*
1 words telling someone what they should do
2 a piece of information ◆ *We received advice that the goods had been sent.*
USAGE NOTE Take care not to confuse this word *advice* with the verb *advise*.

advisable *ADJECTIVE*
wise and sensible
▷ **advisability** *NOUN*

advise *VERB* **advises, advising, advised**
1 to give somebody advice
2 to inform somebody about something
▷ **adviser** *NOUN*
▷ **advisory** *ADJECTIVE*

advocate (*say* **ad**-vok-ayt) *VERB* **advocates, advocating, advocated**
to speak in favour of something; to recommend something ◆ *We advocate changing the law.*

advocate (*say* **ad**-vok-at) *NOUN* **advocates**
1 a person who recommends or speaks in favour of a policy or principle ◆ *They entered politics as advocates of economic reform.*
2 a lawyer presenting a case in a lawcourt

aegis (*say* **ee**-jiss) *NOUN*
to be under the aegis of someone is to have their protection or support ◆ *The scheme is under the aegis of the Scout Association.*

WORD HISTORY in ancient Greek the *aigis* was the magical shield of the god Zeus, traditionally made from a goatskin

aerate (*say* **air**-ayt) *VERB* **aerates, aerating, aerated**
1 to add air to something
2 to add carbon dioxide to a liquid

aerial *ADJECTIVE*
1 in the air or from the air
2 to do with aircraft or flying

WORD HISTORY from Greek *aer* 'air'

aerial *NOUN* **aerials**
a wire or rod that receives or transmits radio or television signals

aerobatics *PLURAL NOUN*
a spectacular display by flying aircraft
▷ **aerobatic** *ADJECTIVE*

aerobics *PLURAL NOUN*
exercises to improve your breathing and strengthen the heart and lungs
▷ **aerobic** *ADJECTIVE*

WORD HISTORY from Greek *aer* 'air' and *bios* 'life'

aerodrome *NOUN* **aerodromes**
an old word for an airfield or small airport

WORD HISTORY from Greek *aer* 'air' and *dromos* 'running track'

aerodynamic *ADJECTIVE*
designed to move through the air quickly and easily

aeronautics *PLURAL NOUN*
the study of aircraft and flying
▷ **aeronautical** *ADJECTIVE*

aeroplane *NOUN* **aeroplanes**
a flying vehicle with wings and powerful engines

aerosol *NOUN* **aerosols**
a container that holds a liquid under pressure and can let it out in a fine spray

aerospace *NOUN*
the technology and industry to do with flying and space flight

aesthetic (*say* iss-**thet**-ik) *ADJECTIVE*
(*D & T*) to do with the appreciation of beautiful things ◆ *They collected paintings and sculpture simply for their aesthetic qualities.*

WORD HISTORY from Greek *aisthesthai* 'to perceive'

afar *ADVERB*
far away ◆ *He had loved her from afar for many years.*

affable *ADJECTIVE*
polite and friendly

affair *NOUN* **affairs**
1 an event or matter ◆ *Dinner time was a very gloomy affair.*
2 a brief sexual relationship between two people who are not married to each other

WORD HISTORY from French *à faire* 'to do'

affairs *PLURAL NOUN*
the business and activities that are part of private or public life ◆ *Keep out of my affairs.* ◆ *a new series of current affairs programmes on breakfast-time radio*

affect *VERB* **affects, affecting, affected**
1 to have an effect on someone or something; to influence them
2 to pretend to have or feel something ◆ *I tried to affect a complete lack of concern, but my anxiety was obvious.*

USAGE NOTE Take care not to confuse this word, which is a verb, with the noun *effect*.

affectation *NOUN* **affectations**
unnatural behaviour that is intended to impress other people

affected *ADJECTIVE*
affected talk or behaviour is meant to impress people without being genuine or sincere

affection *NOUN* **affections**
a strong liking for a person

affectionate *ADJECTIVE*
showing affection; loving
▷ **affectionately** *ADVERB*

affidavit (*say* af-id-**ay**-vit) *NOUN* **affidavits**
a statement that someone has written down and sworn to be true, for use as legal evidence

WORD HISTORY a Latin word meaning 'he or she has stated on oath'

affiliated *ADJECTIVE*
a person or group is affiliated to a larger organization when they are officially connected with it
WORD HISTORY from Latin *affiliatus* 'adopted', from *filius* 'son'

affinity *NOUN* **affinities**
a similarity or relationship between two or more things ◆ *the search for affinities between art and science*

affirm *VERB* **affirms, affirming, affirmed**
to state something definitely or firmly
▷ **affirmation** *NOUN*
WORD HISTORY from Latin *firmus*, also the source of our word *firm*

affirmative *ADJECTIVE*
an affirmative statement or reply is one that says 'yes' (SEE ALSO **negative**)

affix (*say* a-**fiks**) *VERB* **affixes, affixing, affixed**
to affix something is to stick it on to something else

affix (*say* **aff**-iks) *NOUN* **affixes**
(*Grammar*) a prefix or suffix

afflict *VERB* **afflicts, afflicting, afflicted**
someone is afflicted with a disease or misfortune when it is making them suffer
▷ **affliction** *NOUN*

affluent (*say* **af**-loo-ent) *ADJECTIVE*
very wealthy or rich ◆ *The survey showed a contrast between poor and more affluent areas.*
▷ **affluence** *NOUN*
WORD HISTORY from Latin *affluens* 'overflowing'. In English *affluent* originally described water, and meant 'flowing freely'.

afford *VERB* **affords, affording, afforded**
1 to have enough money to be able to pay for or do something ◆ *They couldn't afford to live in the city any longer.* ◆ *Being unable to afford a bike each, they clubbed together for one to share between them.*
2 to have enough time or resources to do something
3 to be able to do something without suffering bad consequences ◆ *We can't afford to make any more mistakes.*

afforestation *NOUN*
the planting of trees to form a forest

affray *NOUN* **affrays**
(*formal*) an affray is a fight or riot that takes place in public

affront *VERB* **affronts, affronting, affronted**
to insult or offend someone
WORD HISTORY from Latin *ad frontem* 'to the face'

affront *NOUN* **affronts**
an insult

afield *ADVERB*
at or to a distance; away from home
◆ *Venturing further afield, you can plan a visit to India or China.*

afloat *ADJECTIVE, ADVERB*
floating; on the sea

afoot *ADJECTIVE*
happening or likely to happen

There's a plan afoot to send a deputation to the masters to state our grievances. — *Sue Reid, My Story: Mill Girl*

WORD HISTORY from the earlier form *on foot*

afraid *ADJECTIVE*
frightened or alarmed
I'm afraid is a way of saying you regret something ◆ *I'm afraid I was rather disappointed.*
WORD HISTORY the past participle of an old word *affray* 'to attack or frighten'
WORD FAMILY Words which include 'afraid' in their meaning often end in *-phobia* or *-phobic*: for example, *claustrophobic* means 'afraid of being in an enclosed space', and *xenophobia* means 'a fear of (and therefore dislike of) foreigners'.

afresh *ADVERB*
over again; in a new way ◆ *Tess decided to study the evidence afresh.*

African *ADJECTIVE*
to do with Africa or its people

African *NOUN* **Africans**
an African person

Afrikaans (*say* af-rik-**ahns**) *NOUN*
a language developed from Dutch, used in South Africa

Afrikaner (*say* af-rik-**ah**-ner) *NOUN* **Afrikaners**
a white person in South Africa who speaks Afrikaans

Afro-Caribbean *ADJECTIVE*
to do with Caribbean (especially West Indian) people whose ancestors came from Africa

aft *ADVERB*
at or towards the back of a ship or aircraft
WORD HISTORY from Old English, related to *after*

after *ADVERB, PREPOSITION, CONJUNCTION*
1 used to show that something is later or comes next in position ◆ *Some of the books were published after Tolkien's death.* ◆ *They met again the summer after.* ◆ *She left after she'd kissed him goodnight.* ◆ *The house is after the next traffic lights.*
2 used to show when someone is trying to reach or catch someone else

He heard Becky call, and her feet coming after him, but he could not wait. — *Philippa Pearce, Minnow on the Say*

3 to name a person or animal after someone or something is to use the same name as a kind of honour ◆ *She called her son William after the prince.*

4 to ask after someone is to enquire about how they are

after all something happens after all when you weren't expecting it to happen ◆ *They've decided to stay at home after all.*

WORD HISTORY from Old English *æfter*. It was probably originally a comparative form meaning 'further behind'.

WORD FAMILY Words which include 'after' in their meaning often begin with *post-*: for example, *postscript* means 'writing you add after the end of a letter', and *post-war* means 'after the war'.

afterbirth *NOUN*
the placenta and other membranes that come out of the mother's womb after she has given birth

afterlife *NOUN*
in some beliefs, another life that happens after death

aftermath *NOUN*
events or circumstances that come after something bad or unpleasant ◆ *He went to find his surviving relatives in the aftermath of the war.*

WORD HISTORY from *after* and *math*: *math* is a mowing of new grass, and an *aftermath* was originally the new grass that grew up after the old grass had been mowed

afternoon *NOUN* **afternoons**
the time from noon or lunchtime to evening

aftershave *NOUN*
a pleasant-smelling lotion that men put on their skin after shaving

afterthought *NOUN* **afterthoughts**
something you think of or add later, after you have done the main thinking about something

afterwards *ADVERB*
after that; at a later time

This is the story of a Polish family, and of what happened to them during the Second World War and immediately afterwards. — *Ian Serraillier, The Silver Sword*

again *ADVERB*

1 another time; once more

It'd be bacon and eggs again, or they'd go and have chips in Jubilee Road. — *Ann Pilling, Henry's Leg*

2 as before ◆ *You will soon be well again.*

WORD HISTORY from Old English *ongean*, which originally meant 'in the opposite direction'

against *PREPOSITION*

1 used to show that one thing touches or hits another

From time to time a stronger gust of wind would make one of the branches of a cedar or a fir move against another and groan like a cello. — *Philip Pullman, The Amber Spyglass*

2 used to show when someone is opposed to something ◆ *She was very much against spending all that money.*

3 used about preparation or taking precautions ◆ *She found him a huge jersey to protect him against the cold.*

WORD FAMILY Words which include 'against' in their meaning often begin with *anti-*: for example, *antifreeze* means 'something that is against (i.e. that prevents) freezing', and *anti-Semitic* means 'against (i.e. hostile to) Jews'.

agapanthus (*say* ag-a-**pan**-thus) *NOUN*
a South African lily with funnel-shaped blue flowers which grow in round clusters

age *NOUN* **ages**

1 the length of time a person has lived or a thing has existed

2 a special period of history or geology, such as the Bronze Age or an ice age

3 something takes ages, or lasts for ages, when it goes on for a long time

We didn't settle down to sleep for ages. — *Jacqueline Wilson, Sleepovers*

to come of age is to reach the age when you have an adult's legal rights and obligations (normally 18 years)

age *VERB* **ages, ageing, aged**
to become old, or to make someone old

Because I was a half-vampire I aged at only a fifth the rate of humans, which meant that though eighteen months had passed, my body was only three or four months older. — *Darren Shan, Tunnels of Blood*

aged *ADJECTIVE*

1 (*say* ayjd) having a particular age ◆ *He died in London aged 50.*

2 (*say* ay-jid) very old ◆ *Ian was visiting an aged aunt.*

age group *NOUN* **age groups**
all the people of a particular age ◆ *On average, people in their age group watch five hours of television daily.*

ageless *ADJECTIVE*
not ageing or appearing to age

agency *NOUN* **agencies**
an office or business that provides a special service ◆ *She got her next job through a recruitment agency.*

agenda (*say* a-**jen**-da) *NOUN* **agendas**
a list of things to be done or discussed at a meeting ◆ *The next year's budget came at the top of the agenda.*
WORD HISTORY a Latin word meaning 'things that have to be done', from *agere* 'to do'

agent *NOUN* **agents**
1 a person or business that organizes things for other people ◆ *Her agent negotiated a much bigger royalty on her next book.*
2 a spy acting for a country
WORD HISTORY from Latin *agens* 'doing things'

agglomeration *NOUN* **agglomerations**
a mass of things collected together
WORD HISTORY from Latin *glomus* mass

aggravate *VERB* **aggravates, aggravating, aggravated**
1 to make a thing worse or more serious
2 (*informal*) to annoy someone
▷ **aggravation** *NOUN*
WORD HISTORY from Latin *gravare* 'to make something heavy'

aggregate (*say* **ag**-rig-at) *ADJECTIVE*
combined or total ◆ *the aggregate amount*

aggregate *NOUN* **aggregates**
a total amount or score
WORD HISTORY from Latin *aggregare* 'to herd together', from *grex* 'flock'

aggression *NOUN*
being violent without being provoked, especially by starting an attack
WORD HISTORY from Latin *aggredi* 'to attack'

aggressive *ADJECTIVE*
1 violent and likely to attack people
2 very forceful
▷ **aggressively** *ADVERB*
▷ **aggressiveness** *NOUN*

aggressor *NOUN* **aggressors**
a person or nation that starts an attack or war without being provoked

aggrieved (*say* a-**greevd**) *ADJECTIVE*
resentful because you think you have been treated unfairly

aghast *ADJECTIVE*
shocked and horrified at something terrible or unpleasant

agile *ADJECTIVE*
moving quickly or easily
▷ **agilely** *ADVERB*
▷ **agility** *NOUN*

agitate *VERB* **agitates, agitating, agitated**
1 to make someone feel upset or anxious
2 to stir up public interest or concern; to campaign for something ◆ *They may agitate for shorter hours and longer holidays.*
3 shake something about
▷ **agitation** *NOUN*
▷ **agitator** *NOUN*
WORD HISTORY from Latin *agitare* 'to shake'

aglow *ADJECTIVE*
glowing

agnostic (*say* ag-**nost**-ik) *NOUN* **agnostics**
a person who believes that it is impossible to know whether God exists
▷ **agnosticism** *NOUN*
WORD HISTORY from *a-* 'not' and Greek *gnostikis* 'knowing'

ago *ADVERB*
in the past ◆ *I arrived in America two years ago.*
WORD HISTORY from Middle English *agone* 'gone by, past', from an old verb *ago* to pass

agog *ADJECTIVE*
eager and excited
WORD HISTORY from French *en gogues* 'in a happy mood'

agonize *VERB* **agonizes, agonizing, agonized**
1 to worry about something a great deal
2 to find it very difficult to decide about something
▷ **agonizing** *ADJECTIVE*
USAGE NOTE This word can also be spelled agonise.

agony *NOUN* **agonies**
very great pain or suffering
WORD HISTORY from Greek *agon* 'a struggle'

agoraphobia (*say* ag-er-a-**foh**-bee-a) *NOUN*
abnormal fear of being in open spaces
WORD HISTORY from Greek *agora* 'market place' and *phobia*

agrarian (*say* a-**grair**-ee-an) *ADJECTIVE*
to do with farm land or its cultivation
WORD HISTORY from Latin *ager* 'field'

agree *VERB* **agrees, agreeing, agreed**
1 to agree with someone is to think or say the same as they do ◆ *I agree that money is important.* ◆ *She had to work with him although she did not always agree with him about things.*
2 to agree to something or to do something is to say you will accept it or do it ◆ *We'll have to agree to a change of venue or the match will be cancelled.* ◆ *She agreed to meet him again.*
3 to suit a person's health or digestion ◆ *Spicy food didn't agree with him.*
4 (*Grammar*) to correspond in grammatical number, gender, or person. In the sentence *They are good players they* agrees with *players* (both are plural forms) and *are* agrees with *they*; *is* would be incorrect because it is singular.

agreeable *ADJECTIVE*
1 willing to agree to something ◆ *All three countries had to be agreeable to the terms of the agreement.*
2 pleasant or enjoyable ◆ *The exhibition is tiring but it is an agreeable experience.*
▷ **agreeably** *ADVERB*

agreement *NOUN* **agreements**
1 the process or state of agreeing
2 an arrangement that people have agreed to
3 (*Grammar*) the situation in which words 'agree' (have the right forms) in a sentence

agriculture *NOUN*
cultivating land on a large scale and rearing livestock; farming
▷ **agricultural** *ADJECTIVE*

aground *ADVERB, ADJECTIVE*
stranded on the bottom in shallow water

ah *EXCLAMATION*
a cry of surprise, pity, admiration, etc.

ahead *ADVERB*
1 further forward; in front
2 forwards ◆ *Full steam ahead!*

ahoy *EXCLAMATION*
a word used by seamen to attract attention

aid *NOUN* **aids**
1 help
2 something that helps or supports someone ◆ *By this time he was wearing a hearing aid.* ◆ *They would not be entitled to legal aid.*
3 money, food, etc. sent to another country to help it ◆ *A shipment of overseas aid will leave next week.*

in aid of for the purpose of; to help something

aid *VERB* **aids, aiding, aided**
to help or support someone

aide *NOUN* **aides**
an assistant

aide-de-camp (*say* ay-der-**kahm**) *NOUN* **aides-de-camp**
a military officer who is the assistant to a senior officer

Aids *NOUN*
a disease caused by the HIV virus, which weakens a person's ability to resist infections

WORD HISTORY from the initial letters of 'acquired immune deficiency syndrome'

ail *VERB* **ails, ailing, ailed**
(*old use*) to make a person ill or troubled ◆ *Medicine was no answer to the thing that ailed her.*

WORD HISTORY from an Old English word *egle* 'troublesome'

ailing *ADJECTIVE*
1 ill; in bad health ◆ *He returned to Scotland to attend to his ailing father.*
2 in difficulties; not successful ◆ *The government is trying to boost the ailing economy.*

ailment *NOUN* **ailments**
a slight illness

aim *VERB* **aims, aiming, aimed**
1 to point a gun or other weapon at a target
2 to throw or kick a ball or other object in a particular direction
3 to try or intend to do something

aim *NOUN* **aims**
1 aiming a gun or other weapon
2 a purpose or intention

aimless *ADJECTIVE*
without a purpose
▷ **aimlessly** *ADVERB*

air *NOUN* **airs**
1 the mixture of gases that surrounds the earth and which everyone breathes
2 the open space above the earth
3 a tune or melody
4 an appearance or impression of something ◆ *She has an air of someone who enjoys life very much.*
5 to have airs or put on airs is to adopt a grand or haughty manner

> He had never liked Queen Yolande with her haughty airs and fastidious manner.
> — *P. C. Doherty, Crown in Darkness*

by air in or by aircraft
on the air on radio or television

WORD FAMILY A word meaning 'in the air' or 'from the air' is aerial. Words which include 'air' in their meaning often begin with *aero-*: for example, *aerobics* means 'exercises to stimulate breathing' and *aeronautics* means 'the study of aircraft and flying'.

air *VERB* **airs, airing, aired**
1 to put clothes etc. in a warm place to finish drying
2 to allow air to cirulate round a room
3 to express an opinion or complaint ◆ *Several speakers aired their grievances and called for change.*

airborne *ADJECTIVE*
an aircraft is airborne when it has taken off and is in flight

air conditioning *NOUN*
a system for controlling the temperature, purity, etc. of the air in a room or building
▷ **air conditioned** *ADJECTIVE*

aircraft *NOUN* **aircraft**
an aeroplane, glider, or helicopter etc.

aircraft carrier *NOUN* **aircraft carriers**
a large ship with a long deck where aircraft can take off and land

airfield *NOUN* **airfields**
an area equipped with runways etc. where aircraft can take off and land

air force *NOUN* **air forces**
the part of a country's armed forces that is equipped with aircraft

airgun *NOUN* **airguns**
a gun in which compressed air shoots a pellet or dart

airline *NOUN* **airlines**
a company that provides a regular service of transport by aircraft

airliner *NOUN* **airliners**
a large aircraft for carrying passengers

airlock *NOUN* **airlocks**
1 a compartment with an airtight door at each end, through which people can go in and out of a pressurized chamber
2 a bubble of air that stops liquid flowing through a pipe

airmail *NOUN*
letters and parcels carried by air

airman *NOUN* **airmen**
a man who is a member of an air force or of the crew of an aircraft

airport *NOUN* **airports**
a place where aircraft land and take off, with passenger terminals and other buildings

air raid *NOUN* **air raids**
an attack by aircraft

airship *NOUN* **airships**
a large balloon with engines, designed to carry passengers or goods

airstrip *NOUN* **airstrips**
a strip of ground prepared for aircraft to land and take off

airtight *ADJECTIVE*
not letting air in or out

airworthy *ADJECTIVE*
an aircraft is airworthy when it is fit to fly
▷ **airworthiness** *NOUN*

airy *ADJECTIVE*
1 an airy room or space has plenty of light and fresh air
2 airy ideas or promises are vague and insincere
▷ **airily** *ADVERB*

aisle (*rhymes with* mile) *NOUN* **aisles**
1 a passage between rows of seats, pews in a church, or shelves in a supermarket
2 a side part of a church

ajar *ADVERB, ADJECTIVE*
a door is ajar when it is slightly open
WORD HISTORY from Old English *cerr* 'a turn'

akimbo *ADVERB*
arms akimbo with hands on hips and elbows out

akin *ADJECTIVE*
related or similar ◆ *a feeling akin to regret*

alabaster (*say* al-a-bast-er) *NOUN*
a kind of hard white stone

à la carte *ADJECTIVE, ADVERB*
ordered and paid for as separate items from a menu (SEE ALSO **table d'hôte**)

alacrity *NOUN*
speed and willingness ◆ *Richard accepted the task with alacrity.*

alarm *NOUN* **alarms**
1 a warning sound or signal; a piece of equipment for giving this
2 a feeling of fear or worry
3 an alarm clock

alarm *VERB* **alarms, alarming, alarmed**
to make someone suddenly frightened or anxious
▷ **alarming** *ADJECTIVE*
WORD HISTORY from Italian *all'arme!* 'to arms!' (a call to go and fight)

alarm clock *NOUN* **alarm clocks**
a clock that can be set to ring or bleep at a fixed time to wake someone who is asleep

alarmist *NOUN* **alarmists**
a person who makes people frightened and anxious about things that are not as bad as they make out

alas *EXCLAMATION*
a cry of sorrow

albatross *NOUN* **albatrosses**
a large seabird with very long wings
WORD HISTORY a mixture of Latin *albus* 'white' and Spanish *alcatraz* a name for various seabirds, ultimately from Arabic

albino (*say* al-bee-noh) *NOUN* **albinos**
a person or animal with no colouring pigment in the skin and hair (which are white)

album *NOUN* **albums**
1 a book with blank pages in which to keep a collection of photographs, stamps, autographs, etc.
2 a collection of songs on a CD, record, or tape
WORD HISTORY a Latin word meaning 'a white piece of stone' (for writing on)

albumen (*say* al-bew-min) *NOUN*
the white of an egg

alchemy (*say* al-kim-ee) *NOUN*
an early form of chemistry, the chief aim of which was to turn ordinary metals into gold
▷ **alchemist** *NOUN*
WORD HISTORY from Arabic *al-kimiya* 'the art of changing metals'

alcohol *NOUN*
1 a colourless liquid made by fermenting sugar or starch
2 drinks containing this liquid (e.g. wine, beer, whisky), that can make people drunk

alcoholic *ADJECTIVE*
containing alcohol

alcoholic *NOUN* **alcoholics**
a person who is seriously addicted to alcohol
▷ **alcoholism** *NOUN*

alcove *NOUN* **alcoves**
a section of a room that is set back from the main part
WORD HISTORY from Arabic *al-kubba* 'the arch'

alder *NOUN* **alders**
a kind of tree, often growing in marshy places

alderman (*say* awl-der-man) *NOUN* **aldermen**
a senior member of an English county or borough council
WORD HISTORY from Old English *aldor* 'elder, chief'

ale *NOUN* **ales**
beer
WORD HISTORY from Old English *alu*

alert *ADJECTIVE*
watching for something; ready to act
▷ **alertly** *ADVERB*
▷ **alertness** *NOUN*

alert *NOUN* **alerts**
a warning or alarm
to be on the alert is to be vigilant and watchful

alert *VERB* **alerts, alerting, alerted**
to warn someone of danger etc.; to make someone aware of something
WORD HISTORY from Italian *all' erta!* 'to the watchtower!'

A level *NOUN* **A levels**
advanced level in GCSE

alfresco *ADJECTIVE, ADVERB*
in the open air ◆ *an alfresco meal*

algae (*say* al-jee) *PLURAL NOUN*
plants that grow in water, with no true stems or leaves

algebra (*say* al-jib-ra) *NOUN*
mathematics in which letters and symbols are used to represent quantities
▷ **algebraic** (*say* al-jib-ray-ik) *ADJECTIVE*
WORD HISTORY from Arabic *al-jabr* 'putting together broken parts'

algorithm *NOUN* **algorithms**
(*ICT*) a process or set of rules a computer uses to make calculations or operations for solving problems

alias (*say* ay-lee-as) *NOUN* **aliases**
a false or different name

alias *ADVERB*
also named ◆ *Eric Blair, alias George Orwell*
WORD HISTORY a Latin word meaning 'at another time, otherwise'

alibi (*say* al-i-by) *NOUN* **alibis**
evidence that a person accused of a crime was somewhere else when it was committed

alien (*say* ay-lee-en) *NOUN* **aliens**
1 in stories, a being from another world
2 a person who is not a citizen of the country where he or she is living; a foreigner

alien *ADJECTIVE*
1 foreign
2 unnatural or unfamiliar ◆ *The notion of burial was alien to ancient Rome, where most individuals were cremated.*

alienate (*say* ay-lee-en-ayt) *VERB* **alienates, alienating, alienated**
1 to make a person become unfriendly or not willing to help you
2 to feel alienated is to feel alone and isolated from the people around you
▷ **alienation** *NOUN*
WORD HISTORY from Latin *alius* 'other'

alight ❶ *ADJECTIVE*
1 on fire
2 lit up

alight ❷ *VERB* **alights, alighting, alighted**
1 to get out of a vehicle or down from a horse etc. ◆ *We alighted, paid the driver, and then turned right.*
2 to fly down and settle ◆ *A lovely blue swallow alighted on a branch not far away.*

align (*say* al-yn) *VERB* **aligns, aligning, aligned**
1 to arrange things in a line
2 to align yourself with a country or group or organization is to agree with their principles or support them ◆ *The movement aligned itself with the working classes.* ◆ *A wide range of factors influence how people align themselves politically.*
▷ **alignment** *NOUN*

alike *ADJECTIVE, ADVERB*
two or more people or things are alike when they are the same or like one another

alimentary canal *NOUN* **alimentary canals**
the tube along which food passes from the mouth to the anus while it is being digested and absorbed by the body
WORD HISTORY from Latin *alimentum* 'food'

alimony *NOUN*
(*American*) money paid by someone to his or her wife or husband after they are separated or divorced; maintenance
USAGE NOTE The British word is *maintenance*.

alive *ADJECTIVE*
1 living; having life
2 you are alive to something when you are aware of it and ready to be influenced by it ◆ *Turner was always alive to new ideas in his paintings.*

alkali (*say* alk-al-y) *NOUN* **alkalis**
(*Science*) a chemical substance that neutralizes an acid to form a salt
▷ **alkaline** *ADJECTIVE*
▷ **alkalinity** *NOUN*
WORD HISTORY from Arabic *al-kali* 'the ashes' (because alkali was first obtained from the ashes of seaweed)

all *ADJECTIVE, NOUN, ADVERB*
1 the whole number or amount of something ◆ *She destroyed all Maud's letters.* ◆ *No one had seen her all week.*
2 everything or everyone ◆ *All we wanted was an apology.* ◆ *We all got the most terrible giggles.*
3 completely ◆ *She was dressed all in white.*
4 to each team or competitor ◆ *The score is fifteen all.*
to be all there is to have an alert mind
all the same in spite of this; making no difference ◆ *I like him, all the same.*
WORD FAMILY Words which include 'all' in their meaning often begin with *omni-* or *pan-*: for example, *omnipotent* means 'having all (i.e. unlimited) power', and a *pantechnicon* is 'a lorry that can carry everything (i.e. large loads)'.

Allah *NOUN*
the Muslim name of God

allay (*say* a-**lay**) *VERB* **allays, allaying, allayed**
to calm or relieve an unpleasant feeling ◆ *She breathed in deeply, hoping to allay her nervousness.* ◆ *This statement did little to allay their fears for the future.*

all-clear *NOUN*
a signal that a danger has passed

allegation (*say* al-ig-**ay**-shon) *NOUN* **allegations**
an accusation that someone has done wrong, without proof

allege (*say* a-**lej**) *VERB* **alleges, alleging, alleged**
to accuse someone of doing wrong without being able to prove it ◆ *They allege that we deserted the King because we were afraid.*
▷ **allegedly** (*say* a-**lej**-id-lee) *ADVERB*

allegiance (*say* a-**lee**-jans) *NOUN* **allegiances**
loyalty

allegory (*say* **al**-ig-er-ee) *NOUN* **allegories**
a story in which the characters and events represent or symbolize a deeper meaning, e.g. to teach a moral lesson
▷ **allegorical** (*say* al-ig-**o**-rik-al) *ADJECTIVE*
WORD HISTORY from Greek *allos* 'other' and *-agoria* 'speaking'

allele (*say* **al**-eel) *NOUN*
(*Biology*) each of two or more alternative forms of a gene that occur from mutation and are found at the same place on a chromosome

alleluia *EXCLAMATION*
praise to God

allergic *ADJECTIVE*
you are allergic to something that is normally safe, or suffer an allergic reaction to it, when it makes you feel ill or unwell ◆ *'Keep them,' she said. 'I'm allergic to roses. They make me sick.'*
WORD HISTORY from Greek *allos* 'other, different'

allergy (*say* **al**-er-jee) *NOUN* **allergies**
a condition of the body that makes you react badly to something that is normally safe

alleviate (*say* a-**lee**-vee-ayt) *VERB* **alleviates, alleviating, alleviated**
to alleviate a pain or difficulty is to make it less severe
▷ **alleviation** *NOUN*
WORD HISTORY from Latin *alleviare* 'lighten the weight of', from *levis* 'light'

alley *NOUN* **alleys**
1 (also **alleyway**) a narrow street or passage
2 a place where you can play bowls or skittles

alliance (*say* a-**ly**-ans) *NOUN* **alliances**
an association formed by countries or groups who wish to support each other

allied *ADJECTIVE*
1 joined as allies; on the same side
2 of the same kind

alligator *NOUN* **alligators**
a large reptile of the crocodile family
WORD HISTORY from Spanish *el lagarto* 'the lizard'

all-in *ADJECTIVE*
an all-in amount or price is one that includes everything

alliteration *NOUN*
(*Language*) the repetition of the same letter or sound at the beginning of several words for special effect
WORD HISTORY from Latin *littera* 'letter'

alliteration

Alliteration is a technique used by writers in which two or more words close to each other start with the same letter-sound:

*The **f**air **b**reeze **b**lew, the white **f**oam **f**lew,*
*The **f**urrow **f**ollowed **f**ree;*
*We were the **f**irst that ever **b**urst*
*Into that **s**ilent **s**ea.*
(from S. T. Coleridge, The Rime of the Ancient Mariner)

Alliteration has been used in many forms of poetry, from Old English verse to rap, and it is a popular technique in comic and nonsense verse:

*They went to **s**ea in a **S**ieve, they did,*
*In a **S**ieve they went to **s**ea;*
(from Edward Lear, The Jumblies)

Alliteration is mainly used in poetry, but some writers also use it for the names of characters, like *Bilbo Baggins* or *Phileas Fogg*. You can also hear it in everyday phrases, like *bed and breakfast* and *through thick and thin*.
See also the panel on **onomatopoeia**.

allocate *VERB* **allocates, allocating, allocated**
to give things to a number of people, especially tasks or resources
▷ **allocation** *NOUN*
WORD HISTORY from Latin *locus* 'a place'

a b c d e f g h i j k l m n o p q r s t u v w x y z

allot *VERB* **allots, allotting, allotted**
to give a number of things to different people

allotment *NOUN* **allotments**
1 a small rented piece of public land used for growing vegetables, fruit, or flowers
2 the process of allotting things, or the amount allotted

allow *VERB* **allows, allowing, allowed**
1 to permit someone to do something ♦ *It was kind of her to allow me to stay.*
2 to decide on a certain amount for a particular purpose ♦ *We have allowed £20 for travel expenses.*
▷ **allowable** *ADJECTIVE*

allowance *NOUN* **allowances**
1 an amount of money that is given regularly for a particular purpose
2 to make allowances for something is to consider it and excuse it ♦ *You must make allowances for their old age.*

alloy *NOUN* **alloys**
a metal formed by mixing two or more metals etc.

all right *ADJECTIVE, ADVERB*
1 satisfactory, permitted
2 unhurt; in good health
3 used as an alternative for 'yes, I agree'

SYNONYMS (meaning 1) satisfactory, acceptable, permitted, OK; (meaning 2) well, unhurt, unharmed, uninjured, safe

USAGE NOTE This word is also sometimes spelled alright, but some people consider this spelling incorrect.

all-round *ADJECTIVE*
general; not specialist ♦ *Anyone with these all-round abilities should be successful.*

all-rounder *NOUN* **all-rounders**
a person who is good at several things, especially sports

allude *VERB* **alludes, alluding, alluded**
to allude to something is to mention it briefly or indirectly ♦ *He alluded to an unpleasant experience in his childhood.*

USAGE NOTE Take care not to confuse this word with *elude*.

WORD HISTORY from Latin *ludere* 'to play'

allure *VERB* **allures, alluring, allured**
to attract or fascinate someone
▷ **allure** *NOUN*
▷ **alluring** *ADJECTIVE*

allusion *NOUN* **allusions**
a reference made to something without actually naming it

USAGE NOTE Take care not to confuse this word with *illusion*, which means 'something that seems to be real but is not'.

alluvium (*say* a-**loo**-vee-um) *NOUN*
sand and soil etc. deposited by a river or flood
▷ **alluvial** *ADJECTIVE*

WORD HISTORY from Latin *luere* 'to wash'

ally (*say* **al**-y) *NOUN* **allies**
1 a country that has agreed to support another country
2 a person who cooperates with another person

ally *VERB* **allies, allying, allied**
to form an alliance

almanac *NOUN* **almanacs**
an annual publication containing a calendar and other information

almighty *ADJECTIVE*
1 having complete power
2 (*informal*) very great ♦ *The most almighty storm blew up and the boat almost sank.*
the Almighty a name for God

almond (*say* **ah**-mond) *NOUN* **almonds**
an oval edible nut

almost *ADVERB*
near to being something but not quite ♦ *The answer is almost certainly no.* ♦ *A sudden gust of wind almost knocked him over.*

alms (*say* ahmz) *PLURAL NOUN*
(*old use*) money and gifts given to the poor

almshouse *NOUN* **almshouses**
a house set up as a charity to provide accommodation for poor people

aloft *ADVERB*
high up; up in the air

alone *ADJECTIVE, ADVERB*
without any other people or things; without help

along *ADVERB, PREPOSITION*
1 on or onwards ♦ *Push it along.*
2 accompanying somebody ♦ *I've brought a friend along.*
3 following the length of something

Billy changed direction and ran along the side of the wall. – *Barry Hines, A Kestrel for a Knave*

alongside *PREPOSITION, ADVERB*
next to something; beside

aloof *ADJECTIVE*
1 distant and unfriendly in manner ♦ *Michele seemed aloof and strangely tense.*
2 not taking part in something ♦ *He remained aloof from the king's marriage plans.*

aloud *ADVERB*
in a voice that can be heard

alpha *NOUN*
the first letter of the Greek alphabet, equivalent to Roman *A, a*

alphabet *NOUN* **alphabets**
the letters used in a language arranged in a set order
▷ **alphabetical** *ADJECTIVE*
▷ **alphabetically** *ADVERB*
WORD HISTORY from *alpha* and *beta*, the first two letters of the Greek alphabet

alphabet

An **alphabet** is a writing system which uses symbols (letters) to represent *sounds* (in contrast to systems which use symbols to represent *words*, such as Egyptian hieroglyphs or modern Chinese and Japanese). The first alphabet was used in the ancient Near East in the 2nd millennium BC. Its letters were named after words which began with the same sound: for example, the letter *D* was called *daleth*, meaning 'door'.
Symbols from the **Greek alphabet** (e.g. π, called *pi*) are often used in mathematics, and we still use the names of Greek letters in words such as delta and gamma rays. The Greek alphabet is the basis of both the **Cyrillic alphabet** (used for modern Russian) and the **Latin alphabet**, which we use for modern English. Many unrelated languages throughout the world also use the Latin alphabet, such as Turkish, Vietnamese, Quechua (spoken in parts of South America), and Swahili (spoken in central Africa).
Sometimes, languages which *are* related to each other use different alphabets for historical reasons. Although Hindi and Urdu are closely related, Hindi uses an alphabet derived from Sanskrit, while Urdu uses one derived from Arabic.
See also the panels on **consonants** and **vowels**.

alpine *ADJECTIVE*
alpine regions and plants are those in high mountain areas

already *ADVERB*
by now; before now ◆ *The term had already started.*

alright *ADJECTIVE, ADVERB*
another spelling of **all right**
USAGE NOTE See the note at *all right*.

Alsatian (*say* al-**say**-shan) *NOUN* **Alsatians**
a German shepherd dog
WORD HISTORY from *Alsace*, a region of north-eastern France: the name was adopted during the First World War, when British people disliked anything that was German

also *ADVERB*
in addition; besides

altar *NOUN* **altars**
a table or similar structure used in religious ceremonies
USAGE NOTE Take care not to confuse this word with the verb *alter*.

altarpiece *NOUN* **altarpieces**
a painting or other work of art placed above and behind an altar

alter *VERB* **alters, altering, altered**
to make or become different; to change
▷ **alteration** *NOUN*

altercation (*say* ol-ter-**kay**-shon) *NOUN* **altercations**
a noisy argument or quarrel

alternate (*say* ol-**tern**-at) *ADJECTIVE*
1 happening or coming one after the other ◆ *Put alternate layers of apple and crumbs in a glass bowl.*
2 one in every two ◆ *On alternate Sundays, Joanna walked across the moor to the village.*
3 (*Mathematics*) alternate angles are formed on the opposite sides of a line that crosses two parallel lines and between these two lines
▷ **alternately** *ADVERB*
USAGE NOTE See the note at *alternative*.

alternate (*say* **ol**-tern-ayt) *VERB* **alternates, alternating, alternated**
to use or come alternately
▷ **alternation** *NOUN*
▷ **alternator** *NOUN*
WORD HISTORY from Latin *alternus* 'every other one'

alternating current *NOUN* **alternating currents**
electric current that keeps reversing its direction at regular intervals

alternative *ADJECTIVE*
available instead of something else
▷ **alternatively** *ADVERB*
USAGE NOTE Take care not to confuse *alternative* with *alternate*. If there are *alternative colours* it means that there is a choice of two or more colours, but *alternate colours* means that there is first one colour and then the other.

alternative *NOUN* **alternatives**
one of two or more possibilities
to have no alternative is not to have any choice

alternative medicine *NOUN*
types of medical treatment that are not based on ordinary medicine. Acupuncture, homeopathy, and osteopathy are forms of alternative medicine.

although *CONJUNCTION*
though

altimeter *NOUN* **altimeters**
an instrument used in aircraft etc. for showing the height above sea level
WORD HISTORY from Latin *altus* 'high'

altitude *NOUN* **altitudes**
the height of something, especially above sea level

alto *NOUN* **altos** (*Music*)
1 an adult male singer with a very high voice
2 a female singer with a low voice

altogether *ADVERB*
1 with all included; in total ◆ *The factory employs five thousand people altogether.*
2 completely ◆ *The neighbours vanished altogether for several months.*
3 on the whole ◆ *Altogether, it was a good concert.*
USAGE NOTE Take care not to confuse *altogether* and *all together*.

altruistic (*say* al-troo-**ist**-ik) *ADJECTIVE*
unselfish; thinking about other people's welfare
▷ **altruist** *NOUN*
▷ **altruism** *NOUN*
WORD HISTORY from Italian *altrui* 'somebody else'

aluminium *NOUN*
a lightweight silver-coloured metal
USAGE NOTE The American spelling of this word is aluminum.

always *ADVERB*
1 at all times; for all the time in the past or future

The Grandpa she'd always known had been a man of vigour, energy, passion. — *Tim Bowler, River Boy*

2 often ◆ *They were always complaining about something.*
3 whatever happens ◆ *You can always sleep on the floor.*

Alzheimer's disease *NOUN*
a serious disease of the brain which affects some old people and makes them confused and forgetful
WORD HISTORY named after a German scientist, Alois Alzheimer

a.m. *ABBREVIATION*
before 12 o'clock midday
WORD HISTORY short for Latin *ante meridiem* 'before noon'

amalgam *NOUN* **amalgams**
1 an alloy of mercury
2 a mixture or combination

amalgamate *VERB* **amalgamates, amalgamating, amalgamated**
to mix or combine things
▷ **amalgamation** *NOUN*

amass *VERB* **amasses, amassing, amassed**
to heap up or collect something

amateur (*say* **am**-at-er) *NOUN* **amateurs**
a person who does something as a hobby, not as a professional
WORD HISTORY from Latin *amator* 'lover'

amateurish *ADJECTIVE*
not done or made very well; not skilful

amaze *VERB* **amazes, amazing, amazed**
to surprise somebody a lot; to fill somebody with wonder
▷ **amazement** *NOUN*

amazing *ADJECTIVE*
very surprising or remarkable

ambassador *NOUN* **ambassadors**
a person sent to a foreign country to represent his or her own government

amber *NOUN*
1 a hard clear yellowish substance used for making jewellery and ornaments
2 a yellow traffic light shown as a signal for caution, placed between red for 'stop' and green for 'go'
WORD HISTORY from Arabic *anbar*

ambidextrous *ADJECTIVE*
able to use either your left hand or your right hand equally well
WORD HISTORY from Latin *ambo* 'both' and *dexter* 'right hand'

ambiguous *ADJECTIVE*
(*Language*) having more than one possible meaning; unclear
▷ **ambiguously** *ADVERB*
▷ **ambiguity** *NOUN*
WORD HISTORY from Latin *ambiguus* 'doubtful, shifting'

ambition *NOUN* **ambitions**
1 ambition is a strong desire to do well and be successful
2 an ambition is strong desire to achieve a particular thing, or the thing itself ◆ *My one remaining ambition is to win a championship medal.*
WORD HISTORY from Latin *ambire* 'to go round' (to seek votes)

ambitious *ADJECTIVE*
1 wanting very much to achieve something, or to do well in life
2 an ambitious task or undertaking is one that is very demanding and difficult

ambivalent (*say* am-**biv**-al-ent) *ADJECTIVE*
having mixed feelings about something (e.g. both liking and disliking it)
▷ **ambivalence** *NOUN*
WORD HISTORY from Latin *ambo* 'both' and *valens* 'strong'

amble *VERB* **ambles, ambling, ambled**
to walk at a slow easy pace
WORD HISTORY from Latin *ambulare* 'to walk'

ambrosia (*say* am-**broh**-zee-a) *NOUN*
something delicious
WORD HISTORY a Greek word: in Greek mythology, *ambrosia* was the food of the gods

ambulance *NOUN* **ambulances**
a vehicle equipped to carry sick or injured people
WORD HISTORY from French *hôpital ambulant* 'mobile field hospital'; from Latin *ambulare* 'to walk'

ambush *NOUN* **ambushes**
a surprise attack from troops etc. who have concealed themselves

ambush *VERB* **ambushes, ambushing, ambushed**
to lie in wait for someone in order to attack them

ameliorate (*say* a-**mee**-lee-er-ayt) *VERB* **ameliorates, ameliorating, ameliorated**
(*formal*) to make something better
▷ **amelioration** *NOUN*

WORD HISTORY from Latin *melior* 'better'

amen *EXCLAMATION*
a word used at the end of a prayer or hymn, meaning 'may it be so'

amenable (*say* a-**meen**-a-bul) *ADJECTIVE*
to be amenable to a suggestion or idea is to be willing to accept it or try it out

WORD HISTORY from French *amener* 'to lead'

amend *VERB* **amends, amending, amended**
to alter something in order to improve it
to make amends is to make up for having done something wrong
▷ **amendment** *NOUN*

amenity (*say* a-**men**-it-ee or a-**meen**-it-ee) *NOUN* **amenities**
a pleasant or useful feature of a place ◆ *Ask about local amenities, and how far the hotel is from the beach.*

American *ADJECTIVE*
1 to do with the continent of America
2 to do with the United States of America
3 to do with the form of English used in America
▷ **American** *NOUN*

American spelling

The main features of **American spelling** are:
- the ending *-our*, as in *behaviour*, *colour*, and *humour*, is often spelled *-or*: *behavior*, *color*, *humor*.
- the ending *-re*, as in *centre*, *metre*, and *theatre*, is often spelled *-er*: *center*, *meter*, *theater*.
- the ending *-ogue*, as in *catalogue* and *dialogue*, is sometimes spelled *-og*: *catalog*, *dialog*.
- the combination *-ae-* or *-oe-*, as in *archaeology*, *manoeuvre*, is sometimes spelled *-e-*: *archeology*, *maneuver*.
- some verbs ending *-l*, e.g. *travel*, *compel*, do not double their final letter when endings are added: *Are you traveling to New York?* (British spelling, *Are you travelling to New York?*)

Other common American spellings (with their British equivalents) are: *analyze* (analyse), *favorite* (favourite), *gray* (grey), and *mold* (mould). American spelling is often preferred for computing terms like *disk* and *program*.

In American English, the verb *to practise* is spelled *to practice*, like the noun: *I've been practicing my guitar chords.* (The British spelling would be, *I've been practising.*) Conversely, *license* is used for both the noun and the verb: *Do I need a dog license?* (British spelling, *dog licence*.)

amethyst *NOUN* **amethysts**
a purple precious stone

WORD HISTORY from Greek *lithos amethystos* 'stone against drunkenness' (because people believed that they would not get drunk if there was an amethyst in their drink)

amiable *ADJECTIVE*
friendly and good-tempered
▷ **amiably** *ADVERB*

amicable *ADJECTIVE*
friendly
▷ **amicably** *ADVERB*

WORD HISTORY from Latin *amicus* 'friend'

amid or **amidst** *PREPOSITION*
in the middle of; among

amino acid (*say* a-**meen**-oh) *NOUN* **amino acids**
an acid found in proteins

amiss *ADJECTIVE*
wrong or faulty ◆ *He shone his torch inside and saw nothing amiss.*

amiss *ADVERB*
1 things go amiss when they go wrong or something bad happens. You say something would not go amiss when you would like it to happen. ◆ *She thought a cup of coffee would not go amiss, while she was waiting.*
2 to take something amiss is to be offended or upset by what someone says or does ◆ *They would take it amiss if they were left out of the group.*

ammonia *NOUN*
a colourless gas or liquid with a strong smell

ammunition *NOUN*
a supply of bullets, shells, grenades, etc. for use in fighting

amnesia (*say* am-**nee**-zee-a) *NOUN*
loss of memory

WORD HISTORY a Greek word meaning 'without memory'

amnesty *NOUN* **amnesties**
a general pardon for people who have committed a crime

WORD HISTORY from Greek *amnestia* 'forgetfulness' (because the crimes are legally 'forgotten')

amoeba (*say* a-**mee**-ba) *NOUN* **amoebas**
a microscopic creature consisting of a single cell which constantly changes shape and can split itself in two

WORD HISTORY from Greek *amoibe* 'change'

amok *ADVERB*
to run amok is to rush about wildly in a violent rage

WORD HISTORY a word in Malay (a language spoken in Malaysia), meaning 'fighting mad'

among or **amongst** *PREPOSITION*
1 surrounded by; forming part of ◆ *It was a great occasion, with the King and Queen among the guests.* ◆ *Nancy moved among them for a while.*
2 between ◆ *This document will be distributed among the people.*
WORD FAMILY Words which include 'among' in their meaning often begin with *inter-*: for example, *international* means 'among countries', i.e. 'belonging to more than one country'.

amoral (*say* ay-**mo**ral) *ADJECTIVE*
not based on moral standards; neither moral nor immoral

amorous *ADJECTIVE*
showing or feeling sexual love ◆ *She rejected his amorous advances.*
WORD HISTORY from Latin *amor* 'love'

amorphous (*say* a-**mor**-fus) *ADJECTIVE*
an amorphous mass of something has no definite shape or plan
WORD HISTORY from Greek *morphe* 'form'

amount *NOUN* **amounts**
1 a quantity
2 (*Mathematics*) a total

amount *VERB* **amounts, amounting, amounted**
to amount to something is to add up to it or be equivalent to it ◆ *Losses amounted to £1.2 million.* ◆ *His statement amounted to a confession.*
WORD HISTORY from Latin *ad montem* 'to the mountain, upwards'

amp *NOUN* **amps**
1 an ampere
2 (*informal*) an amplifier

ampere (*say* **am**-pair) *NOUN* **amperes**
(*Science*) a unit for measuring electric current
WORD HISTORY named after the French scientist André-Marie Ampère

ampersand *NOUN* **ampersands**
the symbol & (= and)
WORD HISTORY from the phrase *and per se and* '& by itself means and' (Latin *per se* 'by itself'). The symbol '&' was added to the end of the alphabet in children's school books. When they came to it, pupils reciting the alphabet would say the phrase, and so they thought it was the name of the symbol.

amphetamine (*say* am-**fet**-a-meen) *NOUN* **amphetamines**
a drug used as a stimulant

amphibian *NOUN* **amphibians**
1 (*Biology*) an animal able to live both on land and in water, such as a frog, toad, newt, and salamander
2 a vehicle that can move on both land and water
WORD HISTORY from Greek *amphi* 'around' and *bios* 'life'

amphibious *ADJECTIVE*
able to live or move both on land and in water

amphitheatre *NOUN* **amphitheatres**
an oval or circular building without a roof and with rows of seats round a central arena
WORD HISTORY from Greek *amphi* 'around' and *theatre*

ample *ADJECTIVE*
1 quite enough ◆ *a semi-detached cottage with ample parking*
2 large
▷ **amply** *ADVERB*
WORD HISTORY from Latin *amplus* 'large, plentiful'

amplifier *NOUN* **amplifiers**
a piece of equipment for making a sound or electrical signal louder or stronger

amplify *VERB* **amplifies, amplifying, amplified**
1 to make a sound or electrical signal louder or stronger
2 to give more details about something ◆ *They needed to amplify their ideas in a longer article.*
▷ **amplification** *NOUN*

amplitude *NOUN*
1 (*Science*) the greatest distance that a wave, especially a sound wave, vibrates
2 largeness or abundance

amputate *VERB* **amputates, amputating, amputated**
to cut off an arm or leg by a surgical operation
▷ **amputation** *NOUN*

amuse *VERB* **amuses, amusing, amused**
1 to make a person laugh or smile
2 to make time pass pleasantly for someone

amusement *NOUN* **amusements**
1 an amusement is a game or activity that makes time pass pleasantly
2 amusement is the state of being amused

amusement arcade *NOUN* **amusement arcades**
an indoor area where people can play on automatic game machines

amusement park *NOUN* **amusement parks**
a large outdoor area with fairground rides and other amusements

amusing *ADJECTIVE*
entertaining or pleasantly funny

an *DETERMINER* SEE **a**

anachronism (*say* an-**ak**-ron-izm) *NOUN* **anachronisms**
something wrongly placed in a particular historical period, or regarded as out of date ◆ *The talk of masters and slaves sounded like an anachronism.*
WORD HISTORY from Greek *ana* 'backwards' and *khronos* 'time'

anaemia (*say* a-**nee**-mee-a) ***NOUN***
a shortage of red blood cells that makes a person tired and pale
▷ **anaemic** ***ADJECTIVE***
WORD HISTORY from Greek *an-* 'without' and *haima* 'blood'

anaesthetic (*say* an-iss-**thet**-ik) ***NOUN*** **anaesthetics**
a substance or gas that makes you unable to feel pain
▷ **anaesthesia** ***NOUN***
WORD HISTORY from Greek *an-* 'without' and *aisthesis* 'sensation'

anaesthetist (*say* an-**ees**-thet-ist) ***NOUN*** **anaesthetists**
a person trained to give anaesthetics

anaesthetize ***VERB*** **anaesthetizes, anaesthetizing, anaesthetized**
to give an anaesthetic to a patient
USAGE NOTE This word can also be spelled anaesthetise.

anagram ***NOUN*** **anagrams**
a word or phrase made by rearranging the letters of another ◆ *'Strap' is an anagram of 'parts'.*
WORD HISTORY from Greek *ana* 'back' and *gramma* 'letter'

anal (*say* **ay**-nal) ***ADJECTIVE***
to do with the anus

analgesic (*say* an-al-**jee**-zik) ***NOUN*** **analgesics**
a substance that relieves pain
WORD HISTORY from Greek *an-* 'without' and *algesis* 'pain'

analogous (*say* a-**nal**-o-gus) ***ADJECTIVE***
to be analogous to something is to be like it in a specific way ◆ *Each part of the mechanism has a shape analogous to the head and tail of a tadpole.*

analogy (*say* a-**nal**-oj-ee) ***NOUN*** **analogies**
a comparison or similarity between two things that are alike in some ways ◆ *the analogy between the human brain and a computer*

analyse ***VERB*** **analyses, analysing, analysed**
1 to examine and interpret something ◆ *The report analyses the performance of the electronics industry.*
2 separate something into its parts

analysis ***NOUN*** **analyses**
1 a detailed examination of something
2 a separation of something into its parts
▷ **analytic** ***ADJECTIVE***
▷ **analytical** ***ADJECTIVE***

analyst ***NOUN*** **analysts**
a person who analyses things

anarchist (*say* **an**-er-kist) ***NOUN*** **anarchists**
a person who believes that all forms of government are bad and should be abolished

anarchy (*say* **an**-er-kee) ***NOUN***
1 lack of government or control, resulting in lawlessness
2 complete disorder
WORD HISTORY from Greek *an-* 'without' and *arkhos* 'ruler'

anathema ***NOUN***
something is anathema to you when you loathe or detest it ◆ *Foreign cars were anathema to him.*

anatomy (*say* an-**at**-om-ee) ***NOUN***
1 the study of the structure of the bodies of humans or animals
2 the structure of an animal's body
▷ **anatomical** ***ADJECTIVE***
▷ **anatomist** ***NOUN***
WORD HISTORY from Greek *ana-* 'up' and *tomia* 'cutting'

ancestor ***NOUN*** **ancestors**
anyone from whom a person is descended
▷ **ancestral** ***ADJECTIVE***
WORD HISTORY from Latin *antecedere* 'to go before'

ancestry ***NOUN*** **ancestries**
a person's ancestors or line of descent

anchor ***NOUN*** **anchors**
a heavy object joined to a ship by a chain or rope and dropped to the bottom of the sea to stop the ship from moving

anchor ***VERB*** **anchors, anchoring, anchored**
1 to fix or be fixed by an anchor
2 to fix something firmly

anchorage ***NOUN*** **anchorages**
a place where a ship can be anchored

anchovy ***NOUN*** **anchovies**
a small fish with a strong flavour

ancient ***ADJECTIVE***
1 belonging to the distant past ◆ *the remains of ancient cities in western Turkey*
2 very old

ancillary (*say* an-**sil**-er-ee) ***ADJECTIVE***
helping or supporting the people who do the main work ◆ *doctors, nurses, and ancillary staff*
WORD HISTORY from Latin *ancilla* 'servant'

and ***CONJUNCTION***
1 together with; in addition to ◆ *Thieves fled with her watch, camera, and handbag.*
2 so that; with this result ◆ *Ask them and they may be able to help.*
3 used instead of 'to' after the verbs *come, go,* and *try* ◆ *Go and bring another chair.*

android ***NOUN*** **androids**
(in science fiction) a robot that looks like a human being
WORD HISTORY from Greek *andros* 'man'

anecdote *NOUN* **anecdotes**
a short amusing or interesting story about a real person or thing
WORD HISTORY from Greek *anekdota* things that have not been published

anemone (*say* a-**nem**-on-ee) *NOUN* **anemones**
a plant with cup-shaped red, purple, or white flowers
WORD HISTORY from a Greek word meaning 'windflower' (from the belief that the flower opens when it is windy)

anew *ADVERB*
again; in a new or different way ◆ *Vietnam's programme to grow its forests anew*

angel *NOUN* **angels**
1 an attendant or messenger of God
2 a very kind or beautiful person
▷ **angelic** (*say* an-**jel**-ik) *ADJECTIVE*
WORD HISTORY from Greek *angelos* 'messenger'

angelica (*say* an-**jel**-i-ka) *NOUN*
a sweet-smelling plant whose crystallized stalks are used in cookery as a decoration

anger *NOUN*
a strong feeling that you want to quarrel or fight with someone

anger *VERB* **angers, angering, angered**
to make a person angry

angle *NOUN* **angles**
1 (*Mathematics*) the space between two lines or surfaces that meet; the amount by which a line or surface must be turned to make it lie along another
2 a point of view

angle *VERB* **angles, angling, angled**
1 to put something in a slanting position
2 to present news etc. from one point of view
WORD HISTORY from Latin *angulus* 'corner'

angler *NOUN* **anglers**
a person who fishes with a fishing rod and line
▷ **angling** *NOUN*

Anglican *ADJECTIVE*
to do with the Church of England
▷ **Anglican** *NOUN*

Anglo-Saxon *NOUN* **Anglo-Saxons**
1 an English person, especially of the time before the Norman conquest in 1066
2 the form of English spoken from about 700 to 1150; Old English

angry *ADJECTIVE* **angrier, angriest**
feeling that you want to quarrel or fight with someone
▷ **angrily** *ADVERB*

anguish *NOUN*
severe suffering or misery
▷ **anguished** *ADJECTIVE*

angular *ADJECTIVE*
1 having angles or sharp corners
2 an angular person is bony and not plump

animal *NOUN* **animals**
1 a living thing that can feel and move
2 a cruel or uncivilized person
WORD HISTORY from Latin *animalis* 'having breath'

animate *VERB* **animates, animating, animated**
1 to make a thing lively
2 to produce something as an animated film
▷ **animator** *NOUN*

animated *ADJECTIVE*
1 lively and excited
2 an animated film is one made by photographing a series of still pictures and showing them rapidly one after another, so they appear to move

animation *NOUN*
1 being lively or excited
2 the technique of making a film by photographing a series of still pictures

animosity (*say* an-im-**oss**-it-ee) *NOUN* **animosities**
a feeling of hostility

aniseed *NOUN*
a sweet-smelling seed used for flavouring things
WORD HISTORY from Greek *anison* 'dill' and *seed*

ankle *NOUN* **ankles**
the part of the leg where it joins the foot

annals *PLURAL NOUN*
a history of events, especially when written year by year
WORD HISTORY from Latin *annales* 'yearly books'

annex *VERB* **annexes, annexing, annexed**
1 to take possession of something and add it to what you have already
2 to add or join a thing to something else
WORD HISTORY from Latin *nexum* 'tied'

annexe *NOUN* **annexes**
a building added to a larger or more important building

annihilate (*say* an-**y**-il-ayt) *VERB* **annihilates, annihilating, annihilated**
to destroy something completely
▷ **annihilation** *NOUN*
WORD HISTORY from Latin *nihil* 'nothing'

anniversary *NOUN* **anniversaries**
a day when you remember something special that happened on the same day in a previous year
WORD HISTORY from Latin *annus* 'year' and *versum* 'turned'

annotate (*say* an-oh-tayt) ***VERB*** **annotates, annotating, annotated**
to add notes of explanation to something written or printed
▷ **annotation** ***NOUN***

announce ***VERB*** **announces, announcing, announced**
to make something known, especially by saying it publicly or to an audience
▷ **announcement** ***NOUN***
WORD HISTORY Latin *nuntius* 'messenger'

announcer ***NOUN*** **announcers**
a person who announces items in a radio or television broadcast

annoy ***VERB*** **annoys, annoying, annoyed**
1 to make a person slightly angry
2 to be troublesome to someone
▷ **annoyance** ***NOUN***
WORD HISTORY from Latin *in odio* 'hateful'

annual ***ADJECTIVE***
1 happening or done once a year ◆ *the annual countryside clean-up*
2 an annual income is what someone earns during one year
3 an annual plant is one that lives for one year or one season
▷ **annually** ***ADVERB***
WORD HISTORY from Latin *annus* 'year'

annual ***NOUN*** **annuals**
1 a book that comes out once a year
2 a plant that lives for one year or one season

annuity (*say* a-**new**-it-ee) ***NOUN*** **annuities**
a fixed annual allowance of money, especially from a kind of investment

annul ***VERB*** **annuls, annulling, annulled**
to cancel a law or contract; to end something legally ◆ *A woman who had not seen her husband since her wedding has had her marrige annulled.*
▷ **annulment** ***NOUN***

anode ***NOUN*** **anodes**
the electrode by which electric current enters a device (SEE ALSO **cathode**)

anoint ***VERB*** **anoints, anointing, anointed**
to put oil or ointment on someone or something, especially in a religious ceremony

anomaly (*say* an-**om**-al-ee) ***NOUN*** **anomalies**
something that does not follow the general rule or that is unlike the usual or normal kind
WORD HISTORY from Greek *an-* 'not' and *homalos* 'even'

anon ***ADVERB***
(*old use*) soon, or at some point in the vague future ◆ *I have a plane to catch. I'll see you anon.*
WORD HISTORY from Old English *on ane* 'in one, at once'

anon. ***ABBREVIATION***
anonymous

anonymous (*say* an-**on**-im-us) ***ADJECTIVE***
without the name of the person responsible being known or made public ◆ *The author wrote a reply to an anonymous review of his book.*
▷ **anonymously** ***ADVERB***
▷ **anonymity** (*say* an-on-**im**-it-ee) ***NOUN***
WORD HISTORY from Greek *an-* 'not' and *onyma* 'name'

anorak ***NOUN*** **anoraks**
a waterproof jacket with a hood
WORD HISTORY from Greenland Eskimo *anoraq*

anorexia (*say* an-er-**eks**-ee-a) ***NOUN***
an illness that makes a person so anxious to lose weight that they refuse to eat
▷ **anorexic** ***ADJECTIVE***
WORD HISTORY from Greek *an-* 'not' and *orexis* 'appetite'

another ***ADJECTIVE, PRONOUN***
a different or extra person or thing ◆ *One was killed and another seriously injured.* ◆ *Would you like another biscuit?* ◆ *We thought we were on another planet.*

answer ***NOUN*** **answers**
1 a reply
2 the solution to a problem

answer ***VERB*** **answers, answering, answered**
1 to give or find an answer to a question, or for a person asking it
2 to respond to a signal ◆ *Holly went to answer the phone.*
3 to answer to a name is to have that name ◆ *a well-dressed woman answering to the name of Suzanne*
4 to answer for something is to be punished for it or have to explain it
to answer back is to be rude or cheeky in replying to someone
WORD HISTORY from Old English

answerable ***ADJECTIVE***
to be answerable to someone is to be responsible to them for something

answering machine ***NOUN*** **answering machines**
a machine that records messages from people who telephone while you are out

answerphone ***NOUN*** **answerphones**
a telephone answering machine

ant ***NOUN*** **ants**
a very small insect that lives as one of an organized group

antagonism (*say* an-**tag**-on-izm) ***NOUN***
an unfriendly feeling; hostility
▷ **antagonist** ***NOUN***
▷ **antagonistic** ***ADJECTIVE***
WORD HISTORY from Greek *anti-* 'against' and *agon* 'struggle'

antagonize *VERB* **antagonizes, antagonizing, antagonized**
to make a person feel hostile or angry
USAGE NOTE This word can also be spelled antagonise.

anteater *NOUN* **anteaters**
an animal that feeds on ants and termites

antecedent (*say* an-ti-see-dent) *NOUN* **antecedents**
(*Grammar*) an earlier word, phrase, or clause to which a pronoun that comes later refers back. In the sentence *When the bus arrived, it was full, bus* is the antecedent of the pronoun *it*.

antediluvian (*say* an-tee-dil-oo-vee-an) *ADJECTIVE*
1 belonging to the time before Noah's Flood in the Old Testament
2 (*informal*) very old or out of date
WORD HISTORY from Latin *ante-* 'before' and *diluvium* 'deluge'

antelope *NOUN* **antelope** or **antelopes**
a fast-running animal like a deer, found in Africa and parts of Asia

antenatal (*say* an-tee-nay-tal) *ADJECTIVE*
(*Medicine*) to do with the period during pregnancy and before childbirth

antenna *NOUN*
1 (*plural* **antennae**) a feeler on the head of an insect or crustacean
2 (*plural* **antennas**) an aerial

anterior *ADJECTIVE*
1 at or near the front (SEE ALSO **posterior**)
2 (*formal*) to be anterior to a time or event is to exist or happen earlier than it

ante-room *NOUN* **ante-rooms**
a room leading to a more important room

anthem *NOUN* **anthems**
a religious or patriotic song, usually sung by a choir or group of people

anther *NOUN* **anthers**
the part of a flower's stamen that contains pollen
WORD HISTORY from Greek *anthos* 'flower'

anthill *NOUN* **anthills**
a mound of earth over an ants' nest

anthology *NOUN* **anthologies**
a collection of poems, stories, songs, etc. in one book
WORD HISTORY from Greek *anthos* 'flower' and *-logia* 'collection'

anthracite *NOUN*
a kind of hard coal

anthrax *NOUN*
a disease of sheep and cattle that can also infect people
WORD HISTORY from Greek *anthrax* 'carbuncle' (because of the carbuncles that the disease causes)

anthropoid *ADJECTIVE*
an anthropoid animal is one that is like a human being in form and posture

anthropology *NOUN*
the study of human beings and their customs
▷ **anthropological** *ADJECTIVE*
▷ **anthropologist** *NOUN*
WORD HISTORY from Greek *anthropos* 'human being'

anti-aircraft *ADJECTIVE*
used against enemy aircraft

antibiotic *NOUN* **antibiotics**
a substance (e.g. penicillin) that destroys bacteria or prevents them from growing
WORD HISTORY from Greek *anti-* 'against' and *bios* 'life'

antibody *NOUN* **antibodies**
a protein that forms in the blood as a defence against certain substances which it then attacks and destroys

anticipate *VERB* **anticipates, anticipating, anticipated**
1 to take action in advance about something you are aware of ◆ *He was always moving the goalposts so we could never anticipate what he wanted.*
2 to act before someone else does ◆ *Others may have anticipated Columbus in discovering America.*
3 to expect something ◆ *Telephone us if you anticipate any difficulties.*
▷ **anticipation** *NOUN*
▷ **anticipatory** *ADJECTIVE*
USAGE NOTE Many people regard meaning 3 as incorrect. It is better to avoid it and use *expect* or *foresee* for this meaning.

anticlimax *NOUN* **anticlimaxes**
a disappointing ending or result where something exciting had been expected

anticlockwise *ADVERB, ADJECTIVE*
moving in the direction opposite to clockwise

antics *PLURAL NOUN*
funny or foolish actions

anticyclone *NOUN* **anticyclones**
an area where air pressure is high, usually producing fine settled weather

antidote *NOUN* **antidotes**
something that acts against the effects of a poison or disease

antifreeze *NOUN*
a liquid added to water to make it less likely to freeze

a b c d e f g h i j k l m n o p q r s t u v w x y z

antihistamine *NOUN* **antihistamines**
a drug that protects people against unpleasant effects when they are allergic to something

WORD HISTORY from Greek *anti* and *histamine*, a substance in the body which is released as a reaction to an allergy

antimony (*say* **an**-ti-mo-ni) *NOUN*
a brittle silvery metal

antipathy (*say* an-**tip**-ath-ee) *NOUN*
to have an antipathy to something or someone is to dislike them

WORD HISTORY from Greek *anti* and *pathos* 'feeling'

antipodes (*say* an-**tip**-od-eez) *PLURAL NOUN*
places on opposite sides of the earth

the Antipodes Australia, New Zealand, and the areas near them, which are almost exactly opposite Europe

▷ **antipodean** *ADJECTIVE*

WORD HISTORY from a Greek word meaning 'having the feet opposite', from *podes* 'feet'

antiquarian (*say* an-ti-**kwair**-ee-an) *ADJECTIVE*
to do with the study of antiques

antiquated *ADJECTIVE*
old-fashioned or out of date

antique (*say* an-**teek**) *ADJECTIVE*
very old; belonging to the distant past

antique *NOUN* **antiques**
something that is valuable because it is very old

WORD HISTORY from Latin *antiquus* 'ancient'

antiquities *PLURAL NOUN*
objects that were made in ancient times

antiquity (*say* an-**tik**-wit-ee) *NOUN*
ancient times

anti-Semitic (*say* an-ti-sim-**it**-ik) *ADJECTIVE*
hostile or prejudiced towards Jews

▷ **anti-Semitism** (*say* an-ti-**sem**-it-izm) *NOUN*

antiseptic *ADJECTIVE*
1 able to destroy bacteria, especially those that cause things to become septic or to decay
2 thoroughly clean and free from germs

antiseptic *NOUN* **antiseptics**
a substance with an antiseptic effect

antisocial *ADJECTIVE*
unfriendly or inconsiderate towards other people

antistatic *ADJECTIVE*
counteracting the effects of static electricity

antithesis (*say* an-**tith**-iss-iss) *NOUN* **antitheses**
1 the exact opposite of someone or something ◆ *Joe was the antithesis of Leslie: big and blond and macho.*
2 a contrast of ideas

WORD HISTORY from Greek *anti* and *thesis* 'placing'

antitoxin *NOUN* **antitoxins**
a substance that neutralizes a toxin and prevents it from having a harmful effect

▷ **antitoxic** *ADJECTIVE*

antivivisectionist *NOUN* **antivivisectionists**
a person who is opposed to carrying out experiments on live animals

antler *NOUN* **antlers**
the branching horn of a deer

antonym (*say* **ant**-on-im) *NOUN* **antonyms**
(*Language*) a word that is opposite in meaning to another, e.g. *soft* and *hard*: see the language panel at **synonym**

WORD HISTORY from Greek *anti* and *onyma* 'name'

anus (*say* **ay**-nus) *NOUN* **anuses**
the opening at the lower end of the alimentary canal, through which solid waste matter is passed out of the body

WORD HISTORY from a Latin word, originally meaning 'ring'

anvil *NOUN* **anvils**
a large block of iron on which a blacksmith hammers metal into shape

WORD HISTORY from Old English *anfilte*, from *an* 'on' and *filt* 'to beat'

anxiety *NOUN* **anxieties**
1 anxiety is a feeling of being worried and slightly afraid
2 an anxiety is something you are worried about

anxious *ADJECTIVE*
1 worried and slightly afraid ◆ *He had become very anxious about her whereabouts.*
2 to be anxious to do something is to want to do it very much ◆ *There are a lot of people anxious to find out what happened.*

▷ **anxiously** *ADVERB*

WORD HISTORY from Latin *angere* 'to choke or squeeze'

any *ADJECTIVE, PRONOUN*
1 one or some

> He didn't have any particular expertise in the matter of curses, as far as Harry knew. — *J. K. Rowling, Harry Potter and the Goblet of Fire*

2 no matter which ◆ *You can upgrade the equipment at any time.* ◆ *As for information, any would be welcome.*

any *ADVERB*
at all; in some degree ◆ *Can you get them any smaller?*

anybody *NOUN, PRONOUN*
any person

anyhow *ADVERB*
1 anyway, in any case ◆ *They wouldn't have found us anyhow.* ◆ *Anyhow, it doesn't matter.*
2 (*informal*) carelessly, in no special way ◆ *Things had been put on the floor anyhow.*

anyone *NOUN, PRONOUN*
anybody

anything *NOUN, PRONOUN*
any thing

anyway *ADVERB*
whatever happens; whatever the situation may be or may have been

Skin would get him in the end anyway, so what difference did it make where he ran for sanctuary? — *Tim Bowler, Starseeker*

anywhere *ADVERB*
in or to any place

anywhere *PRONOUN*
any place ◆ *Anywhere will do.*

aorta (*say* ay-**or**-ta) *NOUN* **aortas**
the main artery that carries blood away from the left side of the heart
WORD HISTORY from a Greek word, from *aeirein* 'to raise'

apace *ADVERB*
quickly

apart *ADVERB*
1 away from each other; separately ◆ *Chang and Jamila sat apart.* ◆ *The buildings are all the same distance apart.*
2 into pieces ◆ *The little model fell apart in his hands.*
3 excluded ◆ *Joking apart, what do you think of it?*

apart from excluding, other than ◆ *No meals are provided apart from breakfast on the first morning.*
WORD HISTORY from Latin *a parte* 'at the side'

apartheid (*say* a-**par**-tayt) *NOUN*
the political policy that used to be practised in South Africa, of keeping people of different races apart
WORD HISTORY from an Afrikaans word, meaning 'being apart' (*-heid* is equivalent to English *-hood*)

apartment *NOUN* **apartments**
a set of rooms in a large house

apathy (*say* **ap**-ath-ee) *NOUN*
not having much interest in or caring about something
▷ **apathetic** (*say* ap-a-**thet**-ik) *ADJECTIVE*
WORD HISTORY from Greek *a-* 'not' and *pathos* 'feeling'

apatosaurus (*say* a-pat-o-**saw**-rus) *NOUN* **apatosauruses**
a large dinosaur with a long neck and tail, which fed on plants
USAGE NOTE This was formerly called *brontosaurus.*
WORD HISTORY from Greek *apate* 'deceit' (because its bones appeared to resemble other dinosaurs) and *sauros* 'lizard'

ape *NOUN* **apes**
any of the four kinds of monkey (gorillas, chimpanzees, orang-utans, and gibbons) that do not have a tail

ape *VERB* **apes, aping, aped**
to imitate or mimic someone in an exaggerated way
WORD HISTORY from Old English *apa*

aperitif (*say* a-**pe**-ri-teef) *NOUN* **aperitifs**
an alcoholic drink taken before a meal to stimulate the appetite
WORD HISTORY from a French word, from Latin *aperire* 'to open'

aperture *NOUN* **apertures**
an opening
WORD HISTORY from Latin *aperire* 'to open'

apex (*say* ay-peks) *NOUN* **apexes**
the tip or highest point
WORD HISTORY from a Latin word meaning 'peak or tip'

aphid (*say* ay-fid) *NOUN* **aphids**
a tiny insect (e.g. a greenfly) that sucks the juices from plants

aphis (*say* ay-fiss) *NOUN* **aphides** (*say* ay-fid-eez)
an aphid

aphorism (*say* **af**-er-izm) *NOUN* **aphorisms**
a short witty saying
WORD HISTORY from Greek *aphorizein* 'to define or limit'

apiary (*say* ay-pee-er-ee) *NOUN* **apiaries**
a place with a number of hives where bees are kept
▷ **apiarist** *NOUN*
WORD HISTORY from Latin *apis* 'bee'

apiece *ADVERB*
to, for, or by each ◆ *Each team had three wins apiece.*

aplomb (*say* a-**plom**) *NOUN*
dignity and confidence ◆ *She handled the crisis with great aplomb.*

apocryphal (*say* a-**pok**-rif-al) *ADJECTIVE*
not likely to be true; invented ◆ *The story is apocryphal but more interesting than the truth.*
WORD HISTORY from Greek *apokruptein* 'to hide away': the *Apocrypha* are books of the Old Testament that were not accepted by the Jews as part of the Hebrew Scriptures

apologetic *ADJECTIVE*
sorry and wanting to make an apology
▷ **apologetically** *ADVERB*

apologize *VERB* **apologizes, apologizing, apologized**
to make an apology
USAGE NOTE This word can also be spelled apologise.

apology *NOUN* **apologies**
1 a statement saying that you are sorry for

having done something wrong or badly

2 an apology for something is a very poor example of it ◆ *The landlady showed them into an apology for a bedroom.*

WORD HISTORY from Greek *apologia* 'a speech in your defence'

apoplectic (*say* ap-o-**plek**-tik) ***ADJECTIVE***
violently or fiercely angry

apoplexy (*say* **ap**-o-plek-see) ***NOUN***

1 sudden loss of the ability to feel and move, caused by the blocking or breaking of a blood vessel in the brain

2 (*informal*) rage or anger

WORD HISTORY from Greek *apoplexia* 'a stroke'

Apostle ***NOUN*** **Apostles**
any of the twelve men sent out by Christ to preach the Gospel

WORD HISTORY from Greek *apostellein* 'to send out'

apostrophe (*say* a-**poss**-trof-ee) ***NOUN*** **apostrophes**
(*Language*) the punctuation mark (') used to show that letters have been missed out (as in *didn't* = did not) or to show possession (as in *the boy's book; the boys' books*)

WORD HISTORY from Greek *apostrephein* 'to turn away'

apostrophes

Apostrophes have two distinct uses:

- to indicate a missing letter or letters in a shortened word, e.g. *didn't* (for *did not*) or *we'd* (for *we would*), or in a time, e.g. *six o'clock* (originally 'of the clock').
- to show what someone or something owns or possesses, e.g. *the extraterrestrial's toenails* (= the toenails of the extraterrestrial), or what something is associated with, e.g. *the day's news* (= the news of the day).

Where does the apostrophe go?

- For most nouns you add an apostrophe followed by an *s*: *the dragon's claw* (= the claw of the dragon), *the children's shoes* (= the shoes of the children), *the city's cathedral* (= the cathedral in the city), *the boss's desk* (= the desk belonging to the boss), *in a week's time* (= after a week).
- When the noun is plural and already ends in *s*, you add an apostrophe by itself: *the dragons' claws* (= the claws of the dragons), *the cities' cathedrals* (= the cathedrals in the cities), *the bosses' desks* (= the desks belonging to the bosses), *in three weeks' time* (= after three weeks).
- When a person's name ends in *s*, you add an apostrophe followed by *s* if you normally say an extra *s* in speaking: *Venus's orbit*; *St Thomas's Hospital*. But you just add an apostrophe when you don't say an extra *s* in speaking: *Achilles' armour*.

There is no apostrophe in ordinary plurals like *tomatoes* and *videos*. An apostrophe should only be used where there is possession: *the tomato's origins lie in ancient Mexico; the video's label has come off.*

You don't need an apostrophe for plurals of abbreviations, e.g. *CDs* and *DVDs*, or for plurals of decades, e.g. *in the 1990s*.

apothecary (*say* a-**poth**-ik-er-ee) ***NOUN*** **apothecaries**
(*old use*) a chemist who prepares medicines

WORD HISTORY from Latin *apothecarius* 'a storekeeper'

appal ***VERB*** **appals, appalling, appalled**
to fill a person with horror; to shock them very much

WORD HISTORY from Old French *apalir* 'to grow pale'

appalling ***ADJECTIVE***
shocking; very unpleasant

apparatus ***NOUN***
the equipment for a particular experiment or task

WORD HISTORY from Latin *apparare* 'to prepare or get ready'

apparel ***NOUN***
(*formal*) a person's clothes

apparent ***ADJECTIVE***

1 clear or obvious ◆ *The books were arranged in no apparent order.*

2 seeming; appearing to be true but not really so ◆ *The death had been an apparent suicide.*

▷ **apparently** ***ADVERB***

apparition ***NOUN*** **apparitions**

1 a ghost

2 something strange or surprising that appears

appeal ***VERB*** **appeals, appealing, appealed**

1 to ask for something that you badly need ◆ *He appealed to his friends for support.*

2 to ask for a decision to be changed ◆ *He's going to appeal against his prison sentence.*

3 something appeals to you when you like it or think it is attractive or interesting ◆ *The course will appeal to married women wishing to return to study.*

appeal ***NOUN*** **appeals**

1 an appeal is the act of asking for something you badly need, or for a decision to be changed

2 appeal is attraction or interest

appealing ***ADJECTIVE***
attractive or interesting

appear ***VERB*** **appears, appearing, appeared**

1 to come into sight; to begin to exist

2 to seem

3 to take part in a play, film, or show etc.

WORD HISTORY from Latin *ad* 'towards' and *parere* 'to come into view'

appearance ***NOUN*** **appearances**

1 appearing

2 what somebody looks like; what something appears to be

a b c d e f g h i j k l m n o p q r s t u v w x y z

appease *VERB* **appeases, appeasing, appeased**
to calm or pacify someone, especially by giving in to their demands
▷ **appeasement** *NOUN*

append *VERB* **appends, appending, appended**
to add something to the end of a document, report, etc.
WORD HISTORY from Latin *appendere* 'to hang on'

appendage *NOUN* **appendages**
something added or attached; a thing that forms a natural part of something larger

appendicitis (*say* a-pen-di-sy-tis) *NOUN*
inflammation of the appendix

appendix *NOUN*
1 (*plural* **appendixes**) a small tube leading off from the intestine
2 (*plural* **appendices**) a section added at the end of a book

appetite *NOUN* **appetites**
1 desire for food
2 an enthusiasm for something ◆ *Yesterday's fun has given you an appetite for excitement.*
WORD HISTORY from Latin *appetere* 'to seek after'

appetizer *NOUN* **appetizers**
a small amount of food eaten before the main meal
USAGE NOTE This word can also be spelled appetiser.

appetizing *ADJECTIVE*
food is appetizing when it looks and smells good to eat
USAGE NOTE This word can also be spelled appetising.

applaud *VERB* **applauds, applauding, applauded**
to show that you like something, especially by clapping your hands
WORD HISTORY from Latin *plaudere* 'to clap hands'

applause *NOUN*
a spell of clapping by the audience at the end of a performance

apple *NOUN* **apples**
a round fruit with a red, yellow, or green skin
the apple of your eye is a person or thing that you love and are proud of
WORD HISTORY from Old English

applet *NOUN* **applets**
(*ICT*) a minor computer application running within a larger program

appliance *NOUN* **appliances**
a device or piece of equipment ◆ *When was the last time you bought a kitchen appliance?*

applicable (*say* ap-lik-a-bul) *ADJECTIVE*
suitable or relevant

applicant *NOUN* **applicants**
a person who applies for a job or position

application *NOUN* **applications**
1 the action of applying
2 a formal request
3 the ability to apply yourself
4 (*ICT*) a computer program or piece of software designed for a particular purpose

applied *ADJECTIVE*
an applied subject such as applied maths or an applied science is one that has a practical use

appliqué (*say* a-**plee**-kay) *NOUN*
needlework in which cut-out pieces of material are sewn or fixed decoratively on another piece

apply *VERB* **applies, applying, applied**
1 to put one thing on another
2 to start using something
3 to apply for a job, grant, etc. is to make a formal request to be given it
4 something applies to a person or thing when it concerns them and they are affected by it ◆ *Our recommendations apply to children of all abilities.*
5 to apply yourself is to give all your attention to a task or piece of work
WORD HISTORY from Latin *applicare* 'to fold or fasten'

appoint *VERB* **appoints, appointing, appointed**
1 to choose a person for a job
2 an appointed time is one officially decided on for a meeting or deadline ◆ *You must submit your bid by 10.00 a.m. on the appointed day.*

appointment *NOUN* **appointments**
1 an arrangement to meet or visit somebody at a particular time
2 choosing somebody for a job
3 a job or position

apportion *VERB* **apportions, apportioning, apportioned**
to divide something into shares

apposite (*say* ap-o-zit) *ADJECTIVE*
an apposite remark or comment is suitable or relevant

apposition *NOUN*
(*Grammar*) nouns and phrases are in apposition to one another when they share the same role in the sentence and refer to the same person or thing. In the sentence *We've lost Albert, our cat*, *Albert* and *our cat* are in apposition.

appraise *VERB* **appraises, appraising, appraised**
to estimate the value or quality of a person or thing
▷ **appraisal** *NOUN*

appreciable *ADJECTIVE*
large or important enough to be noticed or felt
▷ **appreciably** *ADVERB*

appreciate *VERB* **appreciates, appreciating, appreciated**
1 to enjoy or value something
2 to understand something
3 to increase in value
▷ **appreciation** *NOUN*
▷ **appreciative** *ADJECTIVE*
WORD HISTORY from Latin *pretium* 'price'

apprehend *VERB* **apprehends, apprehending, apprehended**
1 to seize or arrest someone
2 to understand something
WORD HISTORY from Latin *prehendere* 'to grasp'

apprehension *NOUN* **apprehensions**
1 fear or worry
2 understanding
3 the arrest of a person

apprehensive *ADJECTIVE*
anxious or worried

apprentice *NOUN* **apprentices**
a person who is learning a trade or craft by a legal agreement with an employer
▷ **apprenticeship** *NOUN*

apprentice *VERB* **apprentices, apprenticing, apprenticed**
to give someone a position as an apprentice

approach *VERB* **approaches, approaching, approached**
1 to come near
2 to go to someone with a request or offer
◆ *They approached their friends for help.*
3 set about doing something or tackling a problem

approach *NOUN* **approaches**
1 the process of approaching
2 a way or road

approachable *ADJECTIVE*
friendly and easy to talk to

approbation *NOUN*
formal or official approval

appropriate (*say* a-**proh**-pree-at) *ADJECTIVE*
suitable
▷ **appropriately** *ADVERB*
WORD HISTORY from Latin *proprius* 'your own'

appropriate (*say* a-**proh**-pree-ayt) *VERB* **appropriates, appropriating, appropriated**
to take something and use it as your own
▷ **appropriation** *NOUN*

approval *NOUN*
the act of agreeing to a plan or proposal
on approval received by a customer to examine before deciding to buy

approve *VERB* **approves, approving, approved**
1 to approve of someone or something is to say or think that they are good or suitable
2 to approve a plan or decision is to agree formally that it should be put into effect
WORD HISTORY from Latin *probare* 'to try or test'

approximate (*say* a-**proks**-im-at) *ADJECTIVE*
almost exact or correct but not completely so
◆ *The approximate journey time from London is three hours.*

approximate (*say* a-**proks**-im-ayt) *VERB* **approximates, approximating, approximated**
to make or be almost the same as something
▷ **approximation** *NOUN*
WORD HISTORY from Latin *proximus* 'very near'

approximately *ADVERB*
roughly; almost exactly

apricot *NOUN* **apricots**
a juicy orange-coloured fruit with a stone in it

April *NOUN*
the fourth month of the year
WORD HISTORY from Latin *Aprilis*, a name that may be connected with the Greek goddess Aphrodite

apron *NOUN* **aprons**
1 a piece of clothing worn over the front of the body, especially to protect other clothes
2 a hard-surfaced area on an airfield where aircraft are loaded and unloaded
WORD HISTORY originally *a naperon*, from French *nappe* 'tablecloth'

apropos (*say* ap-rop-**oh**) *ADVERB*
you use **apropos** or **apropos of** to introduce a topic you are concerned with for the moment

Apropos Giles there's a bit of a crisis with the funds apparently. Nothing serious. A chum's let him down. — *Alan Bennett, Talking Heads*

WORD HISTORY from French *à propos* 'to the purpose'

apse *NOUN* **apses**
a domed semicircular part at the east end of a church
WORD HISTORY from Greek *apsis* 'arch or vault'

apt *ADJECTIVE*

1 to be apt to do something is to be likely to do it, or to do it a lot ◆ *Our memories are apt to play tricks on us.*

2 appropriate or suitable ◆ *He tried hard to think of an apt phrase.*

▷ **aptly** *ADVERB*

▷ **aptness** *NOUN*

WORD HISTORY from Latin *aptus* 'fitted'

aptitude *NOUN*

to have an aptitude for something is to be naturally good at it ◆ *He showed an aptitude for drawing and painting.*

aqualung *NOUN* **aqualungs**

a diver's portable breathing apparatus, with cylinders of compressed air connected to a face mask

aquamarine *NOUN* **aquamarines**

a bluish-green precious stone

WORD HISTORY from Latin *aqua marina* 'sea water'

aquarium *NOUN* **aquariums**

a tank or building in which live fish and other water animals are displayed

aquatic *ADJECTIVE*

to do with water, or living in water ◆ *A few aquatic plants will make the fish healthier.*

aquatint *NOUN* **aquatints**

an etching made on copper by using nitric acid

aqueduct (*say* **ak**-wee-dukt) *NOUN* **aqueducts**

a bridge carrying a water channel across low ground or a valley

aquiline (*say* **ak**-wi-lyn) *ADJECTIVE*

an aquiline nose is hooked like an eagle's beak ◆ *He had a thinnish face with an aquiline nose.*

WORD HISTORY from Latin *aquila* 'eagle'

Arab *NOUN* **Arabs**

a member of a Semitic people living in parts of the Middle East and North Africa

▷ **Arabian** *ADJECTIVE*

arabesque (*say* a-rab-**esk**) *NOUN* **arabesques**

1 (in dancing) a position with one leg stretched backwards in the air

2 an ornamental design of leaves and branches

WORD HISTORY a French word meaning 'Arabian' (because the leaf and branch designs were first used in Arabic art)

Arabic *ADJECTIVE*

to do with the Arabs or their language

Arabic *NOUN*

the language of the Arabs

Arabic words in English

English has borrowed many terms from **Arabic** in mathematics and astronomy. For example, *algebra* comes from an Arabic word meaning 'putting together broken parts'. The spelling of this word includes the Arabic article *al* 'the', as do other Arabic words in English, such as *alchemy* and *alkali*.

The words *cipher* and *zero* both come from *sifr*, the Arabic name for 0 or nought. During the 14th and 15th centuries, Arabic numerals (0, 1, 2, 3, etc.) began to be used throughout Europe in preference to Roman numerals (I, V, X, C, D, M), which did not include a zero.

The astronomical terms *zenith* and its opposite, *nadir*, are both Arabic in origin. Other words from Arabic are *monsoon*, *sirocco*, *admiral* (from *amir* 'commander'), and *arsenal* (a military storehouse), which comes from an Arabic word meaning 'workshop' or 'factory'.

arabic numerals *PLURAL NOUN*

the figures 1, 2, 3, 4, etc. (SEE ALSO **Roman numerals**)

arable *ADJECTIVE*

arable land is suitable for ploughing or growing crops

WORD HISTORY from Latin *arare* 'to plough'

arachnid (*say* a-**rak**-nid) *NOUN* **arachnids**

a member of the group of animals that includes spiders and scorpions

WORD HISTORY from Greek *arachne* 'spider'

arbiter *NOUN* **arbiters**

a person who has the power to decide what shall be done or used etc.

WORD HISTORY from a Latin word meaning 'judge or supreme ruler'

arbitrary (*say* **ar**-bit-rer-ee) *ADJECTIVE*

chosen or done on an impulse, not according to a rule or law ◆ *The country needs a coherent policy, not a series of arbitrary decisions.*

▷ **arbitrarily** *ADVERB*

arbitrate *VERB* **arbitrates, arbitrating, arbitrated**

to settle a dispute between other people when they cannot resolve it themselves

▷ **arbitration** *NOUN*

▷ **arbitrator** *NOUN*

arboreal (*say* ar-**bor**-ee-al) *ADJECTIVE*

to do with trees; living in trees

WORD HISTORY from Latin *arbor* 'tree'

arboretum (*say* ar-ber-**ee**-tum) *NOUN* **arboretums** or **arboreta**

a place where trees are grown for study and display

arbour (*say* **ar**-ber) *NOUN* **arbours**

a shady place among trees

arc *NOUN* **arcs**
1 a curve; part of the circumference of a circle
2 a luminous electric current passing between two electrodes
WORD HISTORY from Latin *arcus* 'a bow or curve'

arcade *NOUN* **arcades**
a covered passage or area, especially for shopping
WORD HISTORY from Latin *arcus* 'curve' (because early arcades had curved roofs)

arcane *ADJECTIVE*
secret or mysterious
WORD HISTORY from Latin *arcere* 'to shut up', from *arca* 'chest'

arch❶ *NOUN* **arches**
1 a curved structure that helps to support a bridge or other building etc.
2 something shaped like this

arch *VERB* **arches, arching, arched**
to form something into an arch or curve ◆ *The cat arched its back and spat at Gail.*

arch❷ *ADJECTIVE*
an arch manner is one that is self-consciously playful or mischievous
▷ **archly** *ADVERB*

archaeology (*say* ar-kee-**ol**-oj-ee) *NOUN*
the study of ancient civilizations by digging for the remains of their buildings, tools, etc. and examining them
▷ **archaeological** *ADJECTIVE*
▷ **archaeologist** *NOUN*
WORD HISTORY from Greek *archaios* 'old'

archaic (*say* ar-**kay**-ik) *ADJECTIVE*
belonging to former or ancient times
WORD HISTORY from Greek *arche* 'beginning'

archangel *NOUN* **archangels**
an angel of the highest rank

archbishop *NOUN* **archbishops**
the chief bishop of a region

archdeacon *NOUN* **archdeacons**
a senior priest ranking next below a bishop

arch-enemy *NOUN* **arch-enemies**
a person's or country's chief enemy

archer *NOUN* **archers**
a person who shoots with a bow and arrows
WORD HISTORY from Latin *arcus* 'a bow or curve'

archery *NOUN*
the sport of shooting at a target with a bow and arrows

archetype (*say* **ark**-i-typ) *NOUN* **archetypes**
1 the original form or model from which others are copied
2 a typical example of something
▷ **archetypal** *ADJECTIVE*

archipelago (*say* ark-i-**pel**-ag-oh) *NOUN* **archipelagos**
a large group of islands, or the sea containing these
WORD HISTORY Greek *pelagos* 'sea'

architect (*say* **ark**-i-tekt) *NOUN* **architects**
a person who designs buildings
WORD HISTORY from Greek *arkhos* 'chief' and *tekton* 'builder'

architecture *NOUN*
1 the process of designing buildings
2 a particular style of building ◆ *a fine example of genuine Tudor architecture*
▷ **architectural** *ADJECTIVE*

archive (*say* **ark**-yv) *NOUN*
1 (also **archives**) a collection of old documents and records belonging to a country or organization
2 (*ICT*) a set of computer files that are stored and no longer in active use

archive *VERB* **archives, archiving, archived**
(*ICT*) to put computer files into an archive

archives *PLURAL NOUN*
the historical documents etc. of an organization or community
WORD HISTORY from Greek *archeia* 'public records'

archivist (*say* **ar**-kiv-ist) *NOUN* **archivists**
a person trained to deal with archives

archway *NOUN* **archways**
an arched passage or entrance

arc lamp or **arc light** *NOUN* **arc lamps, arc lights**
a light using an electric arc

arctic *ADJECTIVE*
bitterly cold
WORD HISTORY from the *Arctic*, the area round the North Pole

ardent *ADJECTIVE*
enthusiastic or passionate
▷ **ardently** *ADVERB*
WORD HISTORY from Latin *ardens* 'burning'

ardour (*say* **ar**-der) *NOUN*
enthusiasm or passion

arduous *ADJECTIVE*
needing much effort; difficult and tiring
▷ **arduously** *ADVERB*
WORD HISTORY from Latin *arduus* 'steep'

area *NOUN* **areas**
1 the extent or measurement of a surface; the amount of space a surface covers, measured, for example, in square metres
2 a particular region or piece of land
3 a subject or activity
WORD HISTORY from a Latin word meaning 'a piece of ground'

arena (*say* a-**reen**-a) *NOUN* **arenas**
the level area in the centre of an amphitheatre or sports stadium
WORD HISTORY from a Latin word meaning 'sand' (because the floors of Roman arenas were covered with sand)

aren't
short for *are not*
aren't I? (*informal*) am I not?

argot (*say* **ah**-go) *NOUN*
(*Language*) the jargon or slang used by a particular group of people

arguable *ADJECTIVE*
1 able to be stated as a possibility
2 open to doubt; not certain
▷ **arguably** *ADVERB*

argue *VERB* **argues, arguing, argued**
1 to exchange angry comments with someone you disagree with
2 to state that something is true and give reasons

argument *NOUN* **arguments**
1 a disagreement or quarrel
2 a reason or series of reasons put forward

argumentative *ADJECTIVE*
fond of arguing

aria (*say* **ar**-ee-a) *NOUN* **arias**
a solo in an opera or oratorio

arid *ADJECTIVE*
having little or no rain; dry and barren

arise *VERB* **arises, arising, arose, arisen**
1 a situation or difficulty arises when it comes into existence and people notice it ◆ *There is a qualified doctor to call on if the need arises.*
2 (*old use*) to stand up ◆ *Arise, Sir Francis.*

aristocracy (*say* a-ris-**tok**-ra-see) *NOUN*
people of the highest social rank; members of the nobility
WORD HISTORY from Greek *aristos* 'best'

aristocrat (*say* a-ris-tok-rat) *NOUN* **aristocrats**
a member of the aristocracy
▷ **aristocratic** *ADJECTIVE*

arithmetic *NOUN*
the science or study of numbers; calculating with numbers
▷ **arithmetical** *ADJECTIVE*
WORD HISTORY from Greek *arithmos* 'a number'

ark *NOUN* **arks**
1 (in the Bible) the ship in which Noah and his family escaped the Flood
2 a wooden box in which the writings of the Jewish Law were kept
WORD HISTORY from Latin *arca* 'box'

arm ❶ *NOUN* **arms**
1 either of the two upper limbs of the body, between the shoulder and the hand
2 a sleeve
3 something shaped like an arm or jutting out from a main part
4 the raised side part of a chair
WORD HISTORY from an Old English word

arm ❷ *VERB* **arms, arming, armed**
1 to supply someone with weapons
2 to prepare for war
▷ **armed** *ADJECTIVE*
WORD HISTORY from Latin *arma* 'weapons'

armada (*say* ar-**mah**-da) *NOUN* **armadas**
a fleet of warships
the Armada or **Spanish Armada** a fleet of warships sent by Spain to invade England in 1588
WORD HISTORY from a Spanish word meaning 'navy', from Latin *armata* 'armed'

armadillo *NOUN* **armadillos**
a small burrowing South American animal whose body is covered with a shell of bony plates
WORD HISTORY from Spanish *armado* 'armed man'

armaments *PLURAL NOUN*
the weapons of an army etc.

armature *NOUN* **armatures**
the part of a dynamo or electric motor that carries the current

armchair *NOUN* **armchairs**
a large comfortable chair with arms

armed forces or **armed services** *PLURAL NOUN*
a country's army, navy, and air force

armful *NOUN* **armfuls**
the amount you can carry in your arms

armistice *NOUN* **armistices**
an agreement to stop fighting in a war or battle
WORD HISTORY from Latin *arma* 'weapons' and *sistere* 'to stop'

armour *NOUN*
1 a protective covering for the body, formerly worn in fighting
2 a metal covering on a warship, tank, or car to protect it from missiles
▷ **armoured** *ADJECTIVE*

armoury *NOUN* **armouries**
a place where weapons and ammunition are stored

armpit *NOUN* **armpits**
the hollow underneath the top of the arm, below the shoulder

arms *PLURAL NOUN*
1 weapons
2 a coat of arms
to be up in arms is to protest vigorously

a b c d e f g h i j k l m n o p q r s t u v w x y z

arms race *NOUN*
competition between nations in building up supplies of weapons, especially nuclear weapons

army *NOUN* **armies**
1 a large number of people trained to fight on land
2 an army of people or things is a large number of them having a powerful effect ◆ *An army of volunteers is needed to clear up the damage.*

WORD FAMILY A related adjective is military.

aroma (*say* a-**roh**-ma) *NOUN* **aromas**
a smell, especially a pleasant one
▷ **aromatic** (*say* a-ro-**mat**-ik) *ADJECTIVE*

WORD HISTORY from Greek *aroma* 'spice'

around *ADVERB, PREPOSITION*
all round; about

arouse *VERB* **arouses, arousing, aroused**
1 to stir up a feeling in someone ◆ *The sounds outside began to arouse their interest.*
2 to wake someone up

arpeggio (*say* ar-**pej**-ee-oh) *NOUN* **arpeggios**
(*Music*) the notes of a chord played one after the other instead of together

WORD HISTORY from Italian *arpa* 'a harp'

arrange *VERB* **arranges, arranging, arranged**
1 to put things into a certain order; to adjust them
2 to arrange something, or arrange to do something, is to make plans for it ◆ *We arranged to see them at the weekend.*
3 prepare music for a particular purpose
▷ **arrangement** *NOUN*

array *NOUN* **arrays**
a large display or choice of things ◆ *DIY stores offer a bewildering array of garden tools.*

array *VERB* **arrays, arraying, arrayed**
1 to arrange things in a special order
2 to be arrayed in fine or special clothes is to be wearing them very noticeably

arrears *PLURAL NOUN*
1 money that is owing and ought to have been paid earlier
2 a backlog of work etc.
to be in arrears is to be behind with payments

arrest *VERB* **arrests, arresting, arrested**
1 to seize a person by authority of the law
2 to stop a process or movement

arrest *NOUN* **arrests**
1 an act of arresting somebody ◆ *The police made several arrests.*
2 stopping something

arrive *VERB* **arrives, arriving, arrived**
1 to reach the end of a journey or a point on it

> Aunt Patsy arrived the morning after the accident. — *Honor Arundel, The High House*

2 to arrive at a decision or agreement is to make it
3 to come or happen ◆ *The day of the trial arrived at last.*
▷ **arrival** *NOUN*

WORD HISTORY from Latin *ad-* to and *ripa* 'shore'; the basic meaning is 'come to the shore'

arrogant *ADJECTIVE*
behaving in an unpleasantly proud way because you think you are better than other people
▷ **arrogantly** *ADVERB*
▷ **arrogance** *NOUN*

WORD HISTORY from Latin *arrogare* 'to claim or demand'

arrow *NOUN* **arrows**
1 a pointed stick to be shot from a bow
2 a sign with an outward-pointing V at the end, used to show direction or position
▷ **arrowhead** *NOUN*

WORD HISTORY from an Old Norse word

arsenal *NOUN* **arsenals**
a place where weapons and ammunition are stored or manufactured

WORD HISTORY from Arabic *dar-sinaa* 'workshop' or 'factory'

arsenic *NOUN*
a very poisonous metallic substance

WORD HISTORY from Greek *arsenikon*, ultimately from Arabic

arson *NOUN*
the crime of deliberately setting fire to a house or building
▷ **arsonist** *NOUN*

WORD HISTORY from Latin *ardere* 'to burn'

art *NOUN* **arts**
1 the production of something beautiful, especially by painting, drawing, or sculpture; things produced in this way
2 a skill ◆ *Mixing concrete is an art.*

WORD HISTORY from Latin *ars*

artefact *NOUN* **artefacts**
an object made by humans, especially one from the past that is studied by archaeologists

WORD HISTORY from Latin *arte factum* 'made by art'

artery *NOUN* **arteries**
1 one of the tubes that carry blood away from the heart to all parts of the body (SEE ALSO **vein**)
2 an important road or route
▷ **arterial** (*say* ar-**teer**-ee-al) *ADJECTIVE*

WORD HISTORY from Latin *arteria*

a b c d e f g h i j k l m n o p q r s t u v w x y z

artesian well *NOUN* **artesian wells**
a well that is bored straight down into a place where water will rise easily to the surface
WORD HISTORY from French *artésien* 'of Artois', a region of France where wells of this type were first made

artful *ADJECTIVE*
crafty or cunning
▷ **artfully** *ADVERB*

arthritis (*say* arth-**ry**-tiss) *NOUN*
a disease that makes joints in the body stiff and painful
▷ **arthritic** (*say* arth-**rit**-ik) *ADJECTIVE*
WORD HISTORY from Greek *arthron* 'joint'

arthropod *NOUN* **arthropods**
an animal of the group that includes insects, spiders, crabs, and centipedes
WORD HISTORY from Greek *arthron* 'joint' and *podes* 'feet' (because arthropods have jointed limbs)

artichoke *NOUN* **artichokes**
a kind of plant with a flower head used as a vegetable

article *NOUN* **articles**
1 an item or object
2 a piece of writing published in a newspaper or magazine
definite article (*Grammar*) the word 'the'
indefinite article (*Grammar*) the word 'a' or 'an'

articulate (*say* ar-**tik**-yoo-lat) *ADJECTIVE*
able to express things clearly and fluently

articulate (*say* ar-**tik**-yoo-layt) *VERB*
articulates, articulating, articulated
to say or speak clearly
▷ **articulation** *NOUN*
WORD HISTORY from Latin *artus* 'joint'

articulated *ADJECTIVE*
an articulated vehicle is one that has two or more sections connected by a flexible joint

artifice *NOUN* **artifices**
clever trickery

artificial *ADJECTIVE*
not natural; made by human beings in imitation of a natural thing
▷ **artificially** *ADVERB*
▷ **artificiality** *NOUN*

artificial intelligence *NOUN*
the use of computers to perform tasks normally requiring human intelligence, e.g. decision-making

artificial respiration *NOUN*
helping somebody to start breathing again after their breathing has stopped

artillery *NOUN*
1 large guns
2 the part of the army that uses large guns

artisan (*say* art-iz-**an**) *NOUN* **artisans**
a skilled worker

artist *NOUN* **artists**
1 a person who produces works of art, especially a painter
2 an entertainer
▷ **artistry** *NOUN*

artistic *ADJECTIVE*
1 to do with art or artists
2 having a talent for art
▷ **artistically** *ADVERB*

artless *ADJECTIVE*
simple and natural; not artful
▷ **artlessly** *ADVERB*

arts *PLURAL NOUN*
subjects (e.g. languages, literature, and history) in which opinion and interpretation are important, as opposed to sciences where measurements and calculations are used
the arts painting, music, and writing etc., considered together

artwork *NOUN*
pictures and charts prepared for inclusion in a publication

arum (*say* **air**-um) *NOUN*
a tall plant with small flowers and arrow-shaped leaves

as *ADVERB*
used in making a comparison ◆ *I got dressed as quickly as I could.*

as *PREPOSITION*
in the function or role of ◆ *Use it as a handle.*

as *CONJUNCTION*
1 when or while ◆ *She slipped as she got off the bus.*
2 because ◆ *As he was late, we missed the train.*
3 in a way that ◆ *Leave it as it is.*
as for with regard to ◆ *As for the money, you can keep it.*
as it were in a way ◆ *She became, as it were, her own enemy.*
as well also

A/S *ABBREVIATION*
advanced supplementary level in GCSE

asbestos *NOUN*
a fireproof material made up of fine soft fibres
WORD HISTORY from a Greek word meaning 'unquenchable'

Asbo (*say* **az**-boh) *ABBREVIATION*
anti-social behaviour order

ascend *VERB* **ascends, ascending, ascended**
to go up to a higher point
to ascend the throne is to become king or queen
WORD HISTORY from Latin *ascendere* 'to climb up'

ascendancy *NOUN*
a state of being in control over other people ◆ *Horses and chariots had helped the Hyksos pharaohs to gain ascendancy in Egypt.*

ascendant *ADJECTIVE*
rising; having more power or influence
to be in the ascendant is to have achieved great power or influence

ascender *NOUN* **ascenders**
(*Language*) a letter with an upward stroke that goes above the normal level of writing or printing, e.g. *b*, *d*, and *f*

ascension *NOUN*
the process of going up

ascent *NOUN* **ascents**
1 the process of going up
2 a way up; an upward path or slope

ascertain (*say* as-er-**tayn**) *VERB* **ascertains, ascertaining, ascertained**
to find something out by asking
▷ **ascertainable** *ADJECTIVE*

ascetic (*say* a-**set**-ik) *ADJECTIVE*
an ascetic life is simple and plain, not allowing yourself pleasure and luxuries
▷ **asceticism** *NOUN*

ascetic *NOUN* **ascetics**
a person who leads a simple life, often for religious reasons
WORD HISTORY from Greek *asketes* 'hermit'

ascribe *VERB* **ascribes, ascribing, ascribed**
to ascribe an event or situation to something is to regard that thing as the cause or source ◆ *They were bound to ascribe the disaster to sabotage.*
WORD HISTORY from Latin *ad-* and *scribere* 'to write'

aseptic (*say* ay-**sep**-tik) *ADJECTIVE*
clean and free from bacteria that cause things to become septic

asexual *ADJECTIVE*
(*Biology*) asexual reproduction is reproduction by methods other than sexual activity

ash❶ *NOUN* **ashes**
the powder that is left after something has been burned
▷ **ashy** *ADJECTIVE*
WORD HISTORY from Old English *aesce*

ash❷ *NOUN* **ashes**
a tree with silver-grey bark
WORD HISTORY from Old English *aesc*

ashamed *ADJECTIVE*
feeling shame and embarrassment at what you have done or are doing

Will searched his mother's bedroom first, ashamed to be looking through the drawers where she kept her underclothes. — *Philip Pullman, The Subtle Knife*

ashen *ADJECTIVE*
sickly grey or pale ◆ *His eyes were closed and his face was an ashen colour.*

ashore *ADVERB*
to or on the shore

ashtray *NOUN* **ashtrays**
a small bowl for tobacco ash

Asian *ADJECTIVE*
to do with Asia or its people

Asian *NOUN* **Asians**
an Asian person

Asiatic *ADJECTIVE*
to do with Asia

aside *ADVERB*
1 to or at one side ◆ *The men behind him moved aside.*
2 to put something aside is to keep it in case you need it later

aside *NOUN* **asides**
words spoken so that only certain people will hear

asinine (*say* **ass**-in-yn) *ADJECTIVE*
silly or stupid

ask *VERB* **asks, asking, asked**
1 to speak so as to find out or get something
2 to ask for something is to say that you want it
3 to ask someone to something is to invite them ◆ *Ask her to the party.*
WORD HISTORY from Old English *ascian*

askance (*say* a-**skanss**) *ADVERB*
to look askance at someone or something is to regard them with distrust or disapproval

askew *ADJECTIVE*
crooked; not straight or level

Chudleigh Pomeroy came storming in, his toupee askew and his round face red with indignation. — *Philip Reeve, Mortal Engines*

asleep *ADJECTIVE*
sleeping; not awake

asp *NOUN* **asps**
a small poisonous snake
WORD HISTORY from Greek *aspis*

asparagus *NOUN*
a plant whose young shoots are eaten as a vegetable

aspect *NOUN* **aspects**
1 one part of a problem or situation ◆ *The Prime Minister cannot control every aspect of government.* ◆ *For some, this is the most exciting aspect of the game.*

a b c d e f g h i j k l m n o p q r s t u v w x y z

2 a person's or thing's appearance ◆ *The tall shivering trees had a sinister aspect.*
3 the direction a house etc. faces ◆ *The living room has a southern aspect.*
WORD HISTORY from Latin *specere* 'to look'

aspen *NOUN* **aspens**
a tree with leaves that move in the slightest wind

asperity *NOUN*
harshness or severity
WORD HISTORY from Latin *asper* 'rough'

aspersions *PLURAL NOUN*
to cast aspersions on somebody is to attack their reputation or integrity
WORD HISTORY from an old word *asperse* 'to spatter with water or mud', from Latin *spergere* 'to sprinkle'

asphalt (*say* ass-falt) *NOUN*
a sticky black substance like tar, often mixed with gravel to surface roads etc.

asphyxia (*say* ass-**fiks**-ee-a) *NOUN*
a condition in which the body does not take in enough oxygen, causing unconsciousness or death
WORD HISTORY from a Greek word meaning 'stopping of the pulse', from *sphyxis* 'pulse'

asphyxiate (*say* ass-**fiks**-ee-ayt) *VERB* **asphyxiates, asphyxiating, asphyxiated**
to suffocate someone
▷ **asphyxiation** *NOUN*

aspic *NOUN*
a savoury jelly used for coating meat, eggs, etc.

aspidistra *NOUN* **aspidistras**
a house plant with broad leaves
WORD HISTORY from Greek *aspis* 'a shield' (because the plant's stigma has this shape)

aspirant (*say* asp-er-ant) *NOUN* **aspirants**
a person who tries to achieve something

aspirate (*say* asp-er-at) *NOUN* **aspirates**
the sound of 'h'

aspiration *NOUN* **aspirations**
ambition; strong desire

aspire *VERB* **aspires, aspiring, aspired**
to aspire to something important or ambitious is to want very much to achieve it ◆ *He even aspired to marry the king's daughter.*
WORD HISTORY from Latin *spirare* 'to breathe'

aspirin *NOUN* **aspirins**
a medicinal drug used to relieve pain or reduce fever

ass *NOUN* **asses**
1 a donkey
2 (*informal*) a stupid person
WORD HISTORY from Latin *asinus* 'donkey'

assail *VERB* **assails, assailing, assailed**
to attack someone, especially a large number of people
▷ **assailant** *NOUN*
WORD HISTORY from Latin *assilire* 'to leap on'

assassin *NOUN* **assassins**
a person who assassinates somebody
WORD HISTORY from Arabic *hashishi* 'hashish-takers'. This name was used at the time of the Crusades for a group of Muslims who were believed to take hashish before going out to kill Christian leaders.

assassinate *VERB* **assassinates, assassinating, assassinated**
to kill an important person deliberately and violently, especially for political reasons
▷ **assassination** *NOUN*

assault *NOUN* **assaults**
a violent or illegal attack

assault *VERB* **assaults, assaulting, assaulted**
to make an assault on someone

assay (*say* a-say) *NOUN* **assays**
a test made on metal or ore to discover its quality

assegai (*say* ass-ig-y) *NOUN* **assegais**
an iron-tipped spear used by South African peoples
WORD HISTORY from Arabic *az-zaghayah* 'the spear'

assemble *VERB* **assembles, assembling, assembled**
1 to bring or come together
2 to fit or put together the parts of something
▷ **assemblage** *NOUN*
WORD HISTORY from Latin *simul* 'together'

assembly *NOUN* **assemblies**
1 assembling
2 a regular meeting, such as when everybody in a school meets together
3 people who regularly meet for a special purpose; a parliament

assembly line *NOUN* **assembly lines**
a series of workers and machines along which a product passes to be assembled part by part

assent *VERB* **assents, assenting, assented**
to consent; to say you agree

assent *NOUN*
consent or approval
WORD HISTORY from Latin *sentire* 'to feel or think'

assert *VERB* **asserts, asserting, asserted**
1 to state something firmly
2 **to assert yourself** is to behave in a confident and forceful way

assertion *NOUN* **assertions**
a statement that you make confidently

assertive *ADJECTIVE*
acting forcefully and with confidence

assess *VERB* **assesses, assessing, assessed**
to decide or estimate the value or quality of a person or thing
▷ **assessment** *NOUN*
▷ **assessor** *NOUN*
WORD HISTORY from Latin *assessor* 'assistant judge', from *sedere* 'to sit'

asset *NOUN* **assets**
something useful or valuable to someone

assets *PLURAL NOUN*
a person's or company's property that could be sold to pay debts or raise money

assiduous (*say* a-**sid**-yoo-us) *ADJECTIVE*
working hard; persevering
▷ **assiduously** *ADVERB*
▷ **assiduity** *NOUN*

assign *VERB* **assigns, assigning, assigned**
1 to give a task or duty to someone
2 to appoint a person to perform a task
WORD HISTORY from Latin *signare* 'to mark out'

assignation (*say* ass-ig-**nay**-shon) *NOUN* **assignations**
1 an arrangement to meet someone
2 assigning something

assignment *NOUN* **assignments**
1 assigning
2 something assigned; a task given to someone

assimilate *VERB* **assimilates, assimilating, assimilated**
to take in and absorb something, e.g. nourishment into the body or knowledge into the mind
▷ **assimilation** *NOUN*
WORD HISTORY from Latin *similis* 'similar'

assist *VERB* **assists, assisting, assisted**
to help someone by doing a share of their work or task
▷ **assistance** *NOUN*
WORD HISTORY from Latin *assistere* 'to stand by'

assistant *NOUN* **assistants**
1 a person who assists another; a helper
2 a person who serves customers in a shop

assistant *ADJECTIVE*
helping a person and ranking next below him or her ◆ *the assistant manager*

associate (*say* a-**soh**-si-ayt) *VERB* **associates, associating, associated**
1 to associate one person or thing with another is to connect them in your mind ◆ *Many people associate hunting with upper class sports.*
2 to associate with people is to spend a lot of time with them or have a lot of dealings with them

associate (*say* a-**soh**-si-at) *NOUN* **associates**
a colleague or companion; a partner
▷ **associate** *ADJECTIVE*
WORD HISTORY from Latin *socius* 'an ally'

association *NOUN* **associations**
1 an organization of people; a society
2 associating
3 a connection or link in your mind

Association football *NOUN*
a form of football using a round ball that may not be handled during play except by the goalkeeper

assonance (*say* **ass**-on-ans) *NOUN*
(*Grammar*) a close similarity of the vowel sounds in two or more words, e.g. in *vermin* and *furnish*
WORD HISTORY from Latin *sonus* 'a sound'

assorted *ADJECTIVE*
of various kinds put together; mixed

assortment *NOUN* **assortments**
a mixed collection of things

assuage (*say* a-**swayj**) *VERB* **assuages, assuaging, assuaged**
to assuage a strong or uncomfortable feeling is to reduce it

Doubts assuaged, Butler returned to his copy of 'Guns and Ammo', leaving his employer to unravel the secrets of the universe — *Eoin Colfer, Artemis Fowl*

WORD HISTORY from Latin *suavis* 'pleasant'

assume *VERB* **assumes, assuming, assumed**
1 to accept without proof that something is true or sure to happen ◆ *Let's assume you are right.*
2 to assume a burden or responsibility is to agree to take it on
3 to assume a particular manner or expression is to show it

an assumed name is a false name someone uses for a special purpose
WORD HISTORY from Latin *sumere* 'to take'

assumption *NOUN* **assumptions**
something that you accept without proof that it is true or sure to happen

assurance *NOUN* **assurances**
1 a promise or guarantee that something is true or will happen
2 a kind of life insurance
3 confidence in yourself

assure *VERB* **assures, assuring, assured**
1 to tell somebody something confidently; to promise somebody
2 to make certain
WORD HISTORY from Latin *securus* 'secure'

aster *NOUN* **asters**
a garden plant with daisy-like flowers in various colours
WORD HISTORY from Greek *aster* 'star'

asterisk *NOUN* **asterisks**
(*Language*) a star-shaped sign (*) used to draw attention to something
WORD HISTORY from Greek *asteriskos* 'little star'

astern *ADVERB*
at the back of a ship or aircraft

asteroid *NOUN* **asteroids**
one of the small planets found mainly between the orbits of Mars and Jupiter

asthma (*say* ass-ma) *NOUN*
a disease that makes breathing difficult
▷ **asthmatic** *ADJECTIVE, NOUN*
WORD HISTORY from Greek *azein* 'to breathe hard'

astigmatism (*say* a-**stig**-mat-izm) *NOUN*
a defect that prevents an eye or lens from focusing properly
▷ **astigmatic** *ADJECTIVE*
WORD HISTORY from Greek *a-* 'not' and *stigma* 'a point'

astir *ADJECTIVE*
in a state of excited activity

At earliest dawn our camp was astir and an hour later we had started upon our memorable expedition. — *Sir Arthur Conan Doyle, The Lost World*

astonish *VERB* **astonishes, astonishing, astonished**
to surprise somebody a lot
▷ **astonishment** *NOUN*

astound *VERB* **astounds, astounding, astounded**
to astonish or shock someone a lot

astral *ADJECTIVE*
to do with the stars

astray *ADVERB, ADJECTIVE*
away from the right path or place or course of action
to go astray is to be lost or mislaid
to lead someone astray is to make them do something wrong

astride *ADVERB, PREPOSITION*
with one leg on each side of something

astringent *ADJECTIVE*
1 making the skin or body tissue contract
2 astringent criticism is harsh or severe
WORD HISTORY from Latin *stringere* 'to bind tightly'

astrology *NOUN*
the study of how the stars and planets may influence people's lives
▷ **astrologer** *NOUN*
▷ **astrological** *ADJECTIVE*
WORD HISTORY from Greek *astron* 'star'

astronaut *NOUN* **astronauts**
a person who travels in a spacecraft

astronomical *ADJECTIVE*
1 to do with astronomy
2 extremely large ◆ *The costs of the new building had reached an astronomical level.*

astronomy *NOUN*
the study of the stars and planets and their movements
▷ **astronomer** *NOUN*

astute *ADJECTIVE*
clever and good at understanding situations quickly; shrewd
▷ **astutely** *ADVERB*
▷ **astuteness** *NOUN*
WORD HISTORY from Latin *astus* 'cleverness or cunning'

asunder *ADVERB*
apart; into pieces
WORD HISTORY from Old English *on sundran* 'into a separate place'

asylum *NOUN* **asylums**
1 refuge and safety offered by one country to political refugees from another
2 (*old use*) an institution for the care of mentally ill people
WORD HISTORY from Greek *asylon* 'refuge'

asymmetrical (*say* ay-sim-**et**-rik-al) *ADJECTIVE*
not symmetrical
▷ **asymmetrically** *ADVERB*

at *PREPOSITION*
This word is used to show:
1 position ◆ *They stood at the top of the stairs.*
2 time ◆ *The film begins at eight o'clock.*
3 direction towards something ◆ *He fired at the target.*
4 cause ◆ *We were annoyed at having to leave.*
5 cost or level ◆ *Water boils at 100 °C.*
at all in any way
at it doing or working at something
at once
1 immediately
2 at the same time ◆ *It all seemed to happen at once.*

atheist (*say* ayth-ee-ist) *NOUN* **atheists**
a person who believes that there is no God
▷ **atheism** *NOUN*
WORD HISTORY from Greek *a-* 'not' and *theos* 'god'

athlete *NOUN* **athletes**
a person who is good at sport, especially athletics
WORD HISTORY from Greek *athlein* 'to compete for a prize'

athletic *ADJECTIVE*
1 physically fit and active
2 to do with athletes
▷ **athletically** *ADVERB*

athletics *PLURAL NOUN*
physical exercises and sports, e.g. running, jumping, and throwing

atlas *NOUN* **atlases**
a book of maps
WORD HISTORY named after Atlas, a giant in Greek mythology who was made to support the universe on his shoulders. His picture was put in the front of early atlases.

atmosphere *NOUN* **atmospheres**
1 the air around the earth
2 a feeling or mood given by surroundings ◆ *There was a holiday atmosphere in the house, which made it difficult for him to work.*
3 a unit of pressure, equal to the pressure of the atmosphere at sea level
▷ **atmospheric** *ADJECTIVE*
WORD HISTORY from Greek *atmos* 'vapour' and *sphere*

atoll *NOUN* **atolls**
a ring-shaped coral reef
WORD HISTORY from Maldivian (the language spoken in the Maldives) *atolu*

atom *NOUN* **atoms**
the smallest particle of a chemical element
WORD HISTORY from Greek *atomos* 'unable to be divided'

atom bomb or **atomic bomb** *NOUN* **atom bombs, atomic bombs**
a bomb using atomic energy

atomic *ADJECTIVE*
1 to do with an atom or atoms
2 to do with atomic energy or atom bombs

atomic energy *NOUN*
energy created by splitting the nuclei of certain atoms

atomic number *NOUN* **atomic numbers**
(*Science*) the number of protons in the nucleus of the atom of a chemical element

atomizer *NOUN* **atomizers**
a device for making a liquid into a fine spray
USAGE NOTE This word can also be spelled atomiser.

atonal *ADJECTIVE*
(*Music*) not written in any key

atone *VERB* **atones, atoning, atoned**
to make amends; to make up for having done something wrong
▷ **atonement** *NOUN*
WORD HISTORY from *at one*, because people who make amends are 'at one' (= on good terms again) with those they have wronged

atrocious (*say* a-**troh**-shus) *ADJECTIVE*
1 extremely wicked ◆ *atrocious behaviour*
2 very bad or unpleasant ◆ *The most atrocious storm developed.*
▷ **atrociously** *ADVERB*
WORD HISTORY from Latin *atrox* 'cruel'

atrocity (*say* a-**tross**-it-ee) *NOUN* **atrocities**
an extremely bad or wicked act

attach *VERB* **attaches, attaching, attached**
1 to fix or join one thing to something else
2 to attach (for example) importance to something is to make it clear that you think it is important ◆ *We attach great importance to healthy eating.*
3 to be attached to someone or something is to be very fond of them
WORD HISTORY from Old French *atachier* 'to fasten or fix'

attachment *NOUN* **attachments**
1 an extra part you add to a piece of equipment for a special purpose ◆ *The hose has an attachment for washing cars.*
2 (*ICT*) a file or piece of software sent with an email
3 fondness or friendship ◆ *They feel a strong attachment to the city they were born in.*

attaché (*say* a-**tash**-ay) *NOUN* **attachés**
a special assistant to an ambassador
◆ *a junior military attaché in the British Embassy*

attaché case *NOUN* **attaché cases**
a small case in which documents etc. may be carried

attack *NOUN* **attacks**
1 a violent attempt to hurt or overcome somebody
2 a piece of strong criticism
3 sudden illness or pain
4 the players in a team whose job is to score goals; an attempt to score a goal

attack *VERB* **attacks, attacking, attacked**
to act violently against someone, or to start a fight with them
▷ **attacker** *NOUN*

attain *VERB* **attains, attaining, attained**
to succeed in doing or getting something
▷ **attainable** *ADJECTIVE*
▷ **attainment** *NOUN*
WORD HISTORY from Latin *tangere* 'to touch'

attempt *VERB* **attempts, attempting, attempted**
to make an effort to do something

attempt *NOUN* **attempts**
an effort to do something; a try
WORD HISTORY from Latin *temptare* 'to try'

attend *VERB* **attends, attending, attended**
1 to be present somewhere; to go somewhere often
2 to look after someone
3 to attend to something is to spend time dealing with it
WORD HISTORY from Latin *tendere* 'to stretch'

attendance *NOUN* **attendances**
1 the act of attending or being present
2 the number of people present at an event
◆ *The attendance that day was small, because of the storms.*

attendant *NOUN* **attendants**
a person who helps or accompanies someone

attention *NOUN*
1 giving concentration and careful thought to something ◆ *She directed her attention to what was going on outside.*
2 to pay attention is to watch and listen closely
3 a position in which a soldier etc. stands with feet together and arms straight downwards

attentive *ADJECTIVE*
giving your attention to something
▷ **attentively** *ADVERB*
▷ **attentiveness** *NOUN*

attenuate *VERB* **attenuates, attenuating, attenuated**
to make a thing thinner or weaker
▷ **attenuation** *NOUN*
WORD HISTORY from Latin *tenuis* 'thin'

attest *VERB* **attests, attesting, attested**
to declare or prove that something is true or genuine
▷ **attestation** *NOUN*
WORD HISTORY from Latin *testari* 'to be a witness'

attic *NOUN* **attics**
a room in the roof of a house

attire *NOUN*
(*formal*) a person's clothes

attire *VERB* **attires, attiring, attired**
(*formal*) to be attired in particular clothes is to be wearing them
WORD HISTORY from Old French *atirer* 'to equip', from *a tire* 'in order'

attitude *NOUN* **attitudes**
1 the way you think about something or react to people
2 the position of the body or its parts; posture

attorney *NOUN* **attorneys**
1 a person who is appointed to act on behalf of another in business matters
2 (*American*) a lawyer
WORD HISTORY from Old French *a* 'towards' and *torner* 'to turn'

attract *VERB* **attracts, attracting, attracted**
1 to get someone's attention or interest; to seem pleasant to someone ◆ *The shop had no window to attract the public.*
2 to pull something by means of a physical force, as magnets attract metal (SEE ALSO **repel**)
WORD HISTORY from Latin *tractum* 'pulled'

attraction *NOUN* **attractions**
1 the process of attracting, or the ability to attract
2 something that attracts visitors ◆ *They are hoping to turn the old railway station into a major tourist attraction.*

attractive *ADJECTIVE*
1 pleasant or good-looking
2 an attractive idea or plan is one that is interesting or appealing
▷ **attractively** *ADVERB*
▷ **attractiveness** *NOUN*

attribute (*say* a-**trib**-yoot) *VERB* **attributes, attributing, attributed**
to regard something as belonging to or created by ◆ *Doctors attributed these symptoms to low blood pressure.*
▷ **attribution** *NOUN*

attribute (*say* **at**-rib-yoot) *NOUN* **attributes**
a quality or characteristic ◆ *Inspiration and foresight were his greatest attributes.*
WORD HISTORY from Latin *tribuere* 'to allot'

attributive (*say* a-**trib**-yoo-tiv) *ADJECTIVE*
(*Grammar*) an attributive adjective or noun is one that comes before the word it describes, e.g. *clever* in *the clever girl* and *expiry* in *expiry date* (SEE ALSO **predicative**)
▷ **attributively** *ADVERB*

attrition (*say* a-**trish**-on) *NOUN*
gradually wearing down an enemy by repeatedly attacking them
WORD HISTORY from Latin *atterere* 'to rub'

attuned *ADJECTIVE*
to be attuned to a situation or person is to have understood them or got used to them ◆ *filmmakers who are attuned to young audiences*

aubergine (*say* **oh**-ber-*zheen*) *NOUN* **aubergines**
a deep purple vegetable with thick flesh
WORD HISTORY from Catalan (a language of Spain) *alberginia*, from Arabic *al-badinjan*

auburn *ADJECTIVE*
auburn hair is reddish-brown

auction *NOUN* **auctions**
a public sale where things are sold to the person who offers the most money for them

auction *VERB* **auctions, auctioning, auctioned**
to sell something at an auction
▷ **auctioneer** *NOUN*
WORD HISTORY from Latin *augere* 'to increase'

audacious (*say* aw-**day**-shus) *ADJECTIVE*
bold or daring
▷ **audaciously** *ADVERB*
▷ **audacity** *NOUN*
WORD HISTORY from Latin *audax* 'bold'

audible *ADJECTIVE*
loud enough to be heard
▷ **audibly** *ADVERB*
▷ **audibility** *NOUN*
WORD HISTORY from Latin *audire* 'to hear'

audience *NOUN* **audiences**
1 people who have gathered to hear or watch something
2 a formal interview with an important person

audio *NOUN*
reproduced sounds

audio-visual *ADJECTIVE*
using both sound and pictures to give information

audit *NOUN* **audits**
an official examination of a company's financial accounts to see that they are correct

audit *VERB* **audits, auditing, audited**
to make an audit of accounts
▷ **auditor** *NOUN*

audition *NOUN* **auditions**
a test to see if an actor or musician is suitable for a part

audition *VERB* **auditions, auditioning, auditioned**
to give someone an audition

auditorium *NOUN* **auditoriums**
the part of a theatre or hall where the audience sits

au fait (*say* oh **fay**) *ADJECTIVE*
to be au fait with a subject or procedure is to know it well
WORD HISTORY from a French phrase meaning 'to the point'

augment *VERB* **augments, augmenting, augmented**
to increase or add to something
▷ **augmentation** *NOUN*
WORD HISTORY from Latin *augere* 'to increase'

au gratin (*say* oh **grat**-an) *ADJECTIVE*
cooked with a crisp topping of breadcrumbs or grated cheese
WORD HISTORY from a French phrase meaning 'by grating (cheese)', from *gratter* 'to grate'

augur (*say* **awg**-er) *VERB* **augurs, auguring, augured**
to augur well or augur badly is to be a good sign or a bad sign ◆ *She had come. That, at least, augured well.*
WORD HISTORY from Latin *augur* 'a prophet'

August *NOUN*
the eighth month of the year
WORD HISTORY named after *Augustus* Caesar, the first Roman emperor (ruled 31 BC–AD 14)

august (*say* aw-**gust**) *ADJECTIVE*
majestic or dignified
WORD HISTORY from Latin *augustus* 'majestic'

auk *NOUN* **auks**
a kind of seabird
WORD HISTORY from Old Norse *alka*

aunt *NOUN* **aunts**
the sister of your father or mother, or your uncle's wife
WORD HISTORY from Old French *ante*, from Latin *amita*

auntie or **aunty** *NOUN* **aunties**
1 (*informal*) a person's aunt
2 (*South African*) an informal form of address from a child to a woman

au pair (*say* oh **pair**) *NOUN* **au pairs**
a person from abroad, usually a young woman, who lives for a time with a family, helping to look after the children
WORD HISTORY from a French phrase meaning 'on equal terms'

aura (*say* **or**-a) *NOUN* **auras**
a general feeling surrounding a person or thing ◆ *His handmade shoes gave off an aura of wealth and power.*
WORD HISTORY from a Greek word meaning 'breeze'

aural (*say* **or**-al) *ADJECTIVE*
to do with the ear or hearing
▷ **aurally** *ADVERB*
USAGE NOTE Take care not to confuse this word with *oral*.
WORD HISTORY from Latin *auris* 'ear'

au revoir (*say* oh rev-**wahr**) *EXCLAMATION*
goodbye for the moment
WORD HISTORY from a French phrase, meaning literally 'to the seeing again'

aurora (*say* aw-**raw**-ra) *NOUN* **auroras**
bands of coloured light appearing in the sky at night, the **aurora borealis** (*say* bor-ee-**ay**-liss) in the northern hemisphere and the **aurora australis** (*say* aw-**stray**-liss) in the southern hemisphere
WORD HISTORY from Latin *aurora* 'dawn', *borealis* 'of the north', *australis* 'of the south'

auspices (*say* **aw**-spiss-eez) *PLURAL NOUN*
to be under the auspices of a country or organization is to be protected or supported by it ◆ *The investigation was set up under the auspices of the United Nations.*
WORD HISTORY from an earlier English meaning 'omens': from Latin *auspicium* 'the observation of birds (as a way of reading omens)' from *auspex* 'an observer of birds'

auspicious (*say* aw-**spish**-us) *ADJECTIVE*
fortunate or favourable ◆ *It was not an auspicious moment to ask for help.*
WORD HISTORY from Latin *auspicium* 'telling the future from the behaviour of birds', from *avis* 'bird'

austere (*say* aw-**steer**) *ADJECTIVE*
very simple and plain; without luxuries
▷ **austerely** *ADVERB*
▷ **austerity** *NOUN*
WORD HISTORY from Greek *austeros* 'severe'

authentic *ADJECTIVE*
genuine ◆ *a model of a Tudor house with authentic furniture*
▷ **authentically** *ADVERB*
▷ **authenticity** *NOUN*
WORD HISTORY from Greek *authentikos* 'genuine'

authenticate *VERB* **authenticates, authenticating, authenticated**
to confirm something as being authentic
▷ **authentication** *NOUN*

author *NOUN* **authors**
the writer of a book, play, poem, etc.
▷ **authorship** *NOUN*
WORD HISTORY from Latin *auctor* 'originator'

authoritarian *ADJECTIVE*
believing that people should be completely obedient to those in authority

authoritative *ADJECTIVE*
having proper authority or expert knowledge; official

authority *NOUN* **authorities**
1 authority is the right or power to give orders to other people
2 an authority is a person or organization with the right to give orders, in particular a department of local government
3 an authority on a subject is a person or book that gives reliable information about it ◆ *an authority on snakes*

authorize *VERB* **authorizes, authorizing, authorized**
to give official permission for something
▷ **authorization** *NOUN*
USAGE NOTE This word can also be spelled authorise.

autistic (*say* aw-**tist**-ik) *ADJECTIVE*
having a disability that makes someone unable to respond to their surroundings or communicate with other people
▷ **autism** *NOUN*
WORD HISTORY from Greek *autos* 'self'

autobiography *NOUN* **autobiographies**
the story of a person's life written by himself or herself
▷ **autobiographical** *ADJECTIVE*

autocracy (*say* aw-**tok**-ra-see) *NOUN* **autocracies**
rule by one person who has total and unlimited power

autocrat *NOUN* **autocrats**
a ruler with total and unlimited power
▷ **autocratic** *ADJECTIVE*
▷ **autocratically** *ADVERB*

autocue *NOUN* **autocues**
(*trademark*) a device that displays the script for a television presenter or public speaker to read

autograph *NOUN* **autographs**
the signature of a famous person

autograph *VERB* **autographs, autographing, autographed**
to sign something with an autograph

automate *VERB* **automates, automating, automated**
to make something work by an automatic process

automatic *ADJECTIVE*
1 working on its own without continuous attention or control by people
2 done without thinking
▷ **automatically** *ADVERB*
WORD HISTORY from Greek *automatos* 'self-operating'

automation *NOUN*
making processes automatic; using machines instead of people to do jobs

automaton (*say* aw-**tom**-at-on) *NOUN* **automatons**
1 a robot
2 a person who seems to act mechanically, without thinking

automobile *NOUN* **automobiles**
(*American*) a car

autonomy (*say* aw-**ton**-om-ee) *NOUN*
1 self-government
2 the right to act independently without being told what to do
▷ **autonomous** *ADJECTIVE*
WORD HISTORY from Greek *autos* 'self' and *nomos* 'law'

autopsy (*say* aw-top-see) *NOUN* **autopsies**
a post-mortem
WORD HISTORY from Greek *autopsia* 'seeing with your own eyes'

autumn *NOUN* **autumns**
the season between summer and winter
▷ **autumnal** *ADJECTIVE*
WORD HISTORY from Latin *autumnus*

auxiliary *ADJECTIVE*
giving help and support ◆ *auxiliary services*

auxiliary *NOUN* **auxiliaries**
a person who gives help and support
WORD HISTORY from Latin *auxilium* 'help'

auxiliary verb *NOUN* **auxiliary verbs**
(*Grammar*) a verb such as *do*, *have*, and *will*, which is used to form parts of other verbs, e.g. *have* in *I have finished*

avail *NOUN*
to or of no avail of no use; without success ◆ *Blake struggled, but to no avail. He was trapped.*

avail *VERB* **avails, availing, availed**
to avail yourself of something is to take it and use it
WORD HISTORY from Latin *valere* 'to be strong'

available *ADJECTIVE*
ready or able to be used
▷ **availability** *NOUN*

a b c d e f g h i j k l m n o p q r s t u v w x y z

avalanche *NOUN* **avalanches**
a mass of snow or rock falling down the side of a mountain

WORD HISTORY from French, from *avaler* 'to descend'

avant-garde (*say* av-ahn-**gard**) *NOUN*
people who use a very modern style in art or literature etc.

WORD HISTORY from a French word meaning 'vanguard'

avarice (*say* av-er-iss) *NOUN*
greed for money or possessions

▷ **avaricious** *ADJECTIVE*

WORD HISTORY from Latin *avarus* 'greedy'

avenge *VERB* **avenges, avenging, avenged**
to take vengeance for something done to harm you

▷ **avenger** *NOUN*

WORD HISTORY from Old French *avengier*, from Latin *vindicare* 'to vindicate'

avenue *NOUN* **avenues**
1 a wide street
2 a road with trees along both sides

WORD HISTORY from French *avenir* 'to approach'

average *NOUN* **averages**
1 (*Mathematics*) the value obtained by adding several quantities together and dividing by the number of quantities
2 the usual or ordinary standard

average *ADJECTIVE*
1 worked out as an average ◆ *Their average age is 10.*
2 of the usual or ordinary standard

average *VERB* **averages, averaging, averaged**
to work out, produce, or amount to as an average

WORD HISTORY from French *avarie* 'damage to a ship or its cargo', from Arabic *awar*. The modern meaning is based on the idea of losses at sea being shared between the owners of the ship and the owners of the cargo.

averse *ADJECTIVE*
to be averse to something is to dislike it or not want to do it; to be not averse to something is to be willing or even eager to do it ◆ *I was not averse to fighting with any boy who challenged me.*

USAGE NOTE Take care not to confuse this word with *adverse*.

WORD HISTORY from Latin *vertere* 'to turn'

aversion *NOUN*
to have an aversion to something is to dislike it very much

avert *VERB* **averts, averting, averted**
1 to turn something away ◆ *She thrust a piece of paper at him, averting her eyes as she did so.*
2 to prevent something ◆ *The government would take immediate steps to avert the danger.*

WORD HISTORY from Latin *vertere* 'to turn'

aviary *NOUN* **aviaries**
a large cage or building for keeping birds

WORD HISTORY from Latin *avis* 'bird'

aviation *NOUN*
the flying of aircraft

▷ **aviator** *NOUN*

avid (*say* **av**-id) *ADJECTIVE*
eager ◆ *My nephew is an avid reader, and all his books come to me.*

▷ **avidly** *ADVERB*

▷ **avidity** *NOUN*

WORD HISTORY from Latin *avere* 'to long for'

avocado (*say* av-ok-**ah**-doh) *NOUN* **avocados**
a pear-shaped tropical fruit

WORD HISTORY from Spanish, from Nahuatl (a Central American language) *ahuacatl*

avoid *VERB* **avoids, avoiding, avoided**
1 to avoid a person or place is to stay away from them
2 to avoid doing something is to make sure you don't do it ◆ *She was keen to avoid gossiping in the office.* ◆ *Stock up at a supermarket to avoid paying higher prices at your local resort.*

▷ **avoidable** *ADJECTIVE*

▷ **avoidance** *NOUN*

WORD HISTORY from Old French *evuider* 'to get rid of'

avoirdupois (*say* av-er-dew-**poiz**) *NOUN*
a system of weights using the unit of 16 ounces = 1 pound

WORD HISTORY from Old French *aveir de peis* 'goods of weight'

avuncular *ADJECTIVE*
kind and friendly towards someone younger

WORD HISTORY from Latin *avunculus* 'uncle on your mother's side'

await *VERB* **awaits, awaiting, awaited**
to wait for someone to come or something to happen

awake *VERB* **awakes, awaking, awoke, awoken**
to wake up

awake *ADJECTIVE*
not asleep

WORD HISTORY from Old English *awacian*

awaken *VERB* **awakens, awakening, awakened**
to wake up

▷ **awakening** *NOUN*

award *VERB* **awards, awarding, awarded**
to give something officially as a prize, payment, or penalty

award *NOUN* **awards**
something awarded, such as a prize or a sum of money

WORD HISTORY from Old French

aware *ADJECTIVE*
knowing or realizing something ◆ *Were you aware of the danger?*
▷ **awareness** *NOUN*
WORD HISTORY from Old English

awash *ADJECTIVE*
with waves or water flooding over it

away *ADVERB, ADJECTIVE*
1 to or at a distance; not at the usual place ◆ *The people had all gone away.*
2 out of existence
3 continuously or persistently ◆ *She worked away at it for days.*
4 an away game or match is played on the opposing team's ground
WORD HISTORY from Old English *aweg* 'on one's way'

awe *NOUN*
1 a feeling of great wonder and slight fear ◆ *They gazed down into the gorge, filled with awe.*
2 to be in awe of somebody is to respect and admire them a lot
▷ **awed** *ADJECTIVE*
▷ **awestricken** *ADJECTIVE*
▷ **awestruck** *ADJECTIVE*
WORD HISTORY from Old English *ege* 'terror or dread'

awesome *ADJECTIVE*
causing wonder and slight fear ◆ *the awesome silence of a deserted graveyard*

awful *ADJECTIVE*
1 very bad ◆ *I've got the most awful headache.*
2 (*informal*) very great ◆ *There seemed to be an awful lot of dogs around for her to play with.*
▷ **awfully** *ADVERB*
SYNONYMS (meaning 1) bad, severe, unpleasant, terrible, dreadful, horrible, nasty

awhile *ADVERB*
for a short time

awkward *ADJECTIVE*
1 difficult to use or deal with; not convenient
2 clumsy; not skilful
▷ **awkwardly** *ADVERB*
▷ **awkwardness** *NOUN*
WORD HISTORY from Old Norse *ofugr* 'turned the wrong way, upside down'

awl *NOUN* **awls**
a small pointed tool for making holes in leather, wood, etc.

awning *NOUN* **awnings**
a roof-like shelter made of canvas etc.

awry *ADVERB, ADJECTIVE*
1 twisted to one side; crooked
2 wrong; not according to plan ◆ *The President's foreign policies had started to go awry.*

axe *NOUN* **axes**
1 a heavy tool for chopping wood
2 (*informal*) a person or organization faces the axe when they are about to be made redundant or closed ◆ *Three factories in the north of England face the axe.*
to have an axe to grind is to have a personal reason for being involved in something

axe *VERB* **axes, axing, axed**
1 to cancel or abolish something
2 to reduce something by a lot
WORD HISTORY from Old English *aex*

axiom *NOUN* **axioms**
an established general truth or principle
▷ **axiomatic** *ADJECTIVE*
WORD HISTORY from Greek *axioma*, from *axios* 'worthy'

axis *NOUN* **axes**
1 a line through the centre of a spinning object
2 a line dividing a thing in half
3 (*Mathematics*) the horizontal or vertical line on a graph
WORD HISTORY from a Latin word meaning 'axle'

axle *NOUN* **axles**
the rod through the centre of a wheel, on which the wheel turns
WORD HISTORY from Old Norse

ayatollah (*say* eye-a-tol-a) *NOUN* **ayatollahs**
a Muslim religious leader in Iran
WORD HISTORY from Arabic *ayatu-llah* 'sign from God'

aye (*rhymes with* by) *ADVERB*
yes

azalea (*say* a-zay-lee-a) *NOUN* **azaleas**
a kind of flowering shrub
WORD HISTORY from Greek *azaleos* 'dry' (because the plant grows well in dry soil)

azure *ADJECTIVE*
sky-blue
WORD HISTORY from Old French *asur* from Persian *al lazaward* 'the lapis lazuli' (a bright blue rock used in jewellery)

Bb

baa *NOUN* **baas**
the natural cry of a sheep or lamb

babble *VERB* **babbles, babbling, babbled**
1 to talk very quickly without making sense

Frosya was beaming at the lost man, babbling into his ear and patting his hair as if he were her son, come back after twenty years away. — *Gillian Cross, Calling a Dead Man*

2 a river that babbles makes a gentle bubbling sound
▷ **babbler** *NOUN*

babe *NOUN* **babes**
1 (*poetic*) a baby
2 (*informal*) an attractive young woman

baboon *NOUN* **baboons**
a large African or Asian monkey with a long muzzle and short tail
WORD HISTORY from Old French word *babuin* which meant both 'an ape' and 'a gargoyle'

baby *NOUN* **babies**
1 a very young child or animal
2 (*informal*) someone's baby is a project that they are responsible for

babyish *ADJECTIVE*
like a baby or suitable for a baby; childish

My dress ... had embroidered teddy bears all across the chest. I'd liked them at first but now I felt sure Chloe would say I looked babyish. — *Jacqueline Wilson, Sleepovers*

babysitter *NOUN* **babysitters**
someone who looks after a child while its parents or guardians are out

baccalaureate (*say* bak-a-**law**-ri-at) *NOUN* **baccalaureates**
an examination taken by final-year school pupils in France and other European countries in preparation for entering university
WORD HISTORY from Latin *baccalaureatus*, from *baccalaureus* 'bachelor'

bach *NOUN*
(*New Zealand*) a small simply furnished holiday house

bachelor *NOUN* **bachelors**
a man who has not married

Bachelor of Arts or Science a person who has taken a first degree in arts or science
WORD HISTORY from French *bacheler* meaning 'squire, young knight', which was also the word's first meaning in English

bacillus (*say* ba-**sil**-us) *NOUN* **bacilli**
a rod-shaped bacterium
WORD HISTORY a Latin word meaning 'little stick', from Latin *baculus* 'stick, rod', which is related to *baguette*

back *NOUN* **backs**
1 the part of something that is furthest from the front; the rear
2 the back part of a person's or animal's body, from the shoulders to the base of the spine
3 the part of a seat that your back rests against
4 a defending player near the goal in sports like football and hockey
the back of beyond a very remote place
back to front with the back placed where the front should be
to get or put someone's back up is to annoy someone
to see the back of someone (*informal*) is to be rid of someone you don't like

back *ADJECTIVE*
1 placed at or near the back of anything ◆ *There's a road map on the back seat.*
2 to do with the back of your body ◆ *Would you like a back massage?*
3 a back street is a quiet street away from the centre of a town or city
4 a back number of a magazine is an old issue that is not the current one

back *ADVERB*
1 to or towards the back; backwards ◆ *Terry leaned back in his chair.*
2 in or to the place you have come from ◆ *It will be time to go back home soon.*
3 to an earlier time or memory ◆ *The spicy aroma of food took me back to my childhood.*
4 to a previous position

The wire sprang back and cut Hermux sharply across his cheek. — *Michael Hoeye, Time Stops for No Mouse*

5 to go back to an activity is to start doing it again ◆ *Mum curled up and went back to sleep.*
6 in return or in response ◆ *Can you email me back?*
7 in restraint, in check ◆ *He could hardly hold himself back.*

back *VERB* **backs, backing, backed**
1 to give someone support or help ◆ *Will you back me if I ask for more money?*
2 to move backwards, or drive a vehicle backwards
3 to bet on something ◆ *I'm sure we're backing a winner this time.*
4 to cover the back of something ◆ *My grandmother's quilt was backed with strips of faded tartan.*
to back off is to retreat or withdraw from danger
to back out of something is to refuse to carry out your part of an agreement or undertaking
to back someone up is to give them your support or help
to back something up (*ICT*) is to make a spare copy of a computer file to use if the original becomes damaged

backbencher *NOUN* **backbenchers**
a Member of Parliament who does not hold an important position

backbiting *NOUN*
unpleasant remarks said about someone who is not there

backbone *NOUN* **backbones**
1 the column of small bones down the centre of a person's or animal's back; the spine
2 someone who gives most support to an organization ◆ *But you can't leave! You're the backbone of the PTA.*
3 strength of character; courage

backdrop *NOUN* **backdrops**
a large painted cloth that is hung across the back of a stage

backer *NOUN* **backers**
someone who supports a project or plan by providing money

backfire *VERB* **backfires, backfiring, backfired**
1 a car backfires when an explosion in its exhaust pipe causes a loud bang
2 a plan backfires when it goes wrong ◆ *My plan to take over the world had backfired badly.*

backgammon *NOUN*
a game played with draughts and dice on a board marked with triangular points

WORD HISTORY from *back* and Old English *gamen* 'game', perhaps because pieces are sometimes put back on the table

background *NOUN*
1 (*Art*) the back part of a scene, picture, or view (SEE ALSO **foreground**)
2 the conditions leading up to and influencing a situation ◆ *I'm reading 'Gone with the Wind' to learn about the background to the American Civil War.*
3 a person's family, upbringing, and education
4 something that happens in the background is not noticeable or obvious

backhand *NOUN* **backhands**
a stroke made in tennis and other racquet sports with the back of your hand turned outwards

backhanded *ADJECTIVE*
a backhanded compliment is one that can also be understood as disapproving or slightly insulting

backing *NOUN*
1 support for an action or event ◆ *We've got the council's backing for a Blues festival next year.*
2 material that is used to cover the back of something
3 musical accompaniment

backlash *NOUN* **backlashes**
a violent reaction against a particular event or trend

backlog *NOUN* **backlogs**
an amount of work that should have been finished but is still waiting to be done

backpack *NOUN* **backpacks**
a bag with straps for carrying on your back; a rucksack

backpacking *NOUN*
travelling or hiking with your belongings in a rucksack
▷ **backpacker** *NOUN*

backside *NOUN* **backsides**
(*informal*) your buttocks; your bottom

backstage *ADVERB*
in or towards the parts of a theatre behind the stage

backstroke *NOUN*
a swimming stroke in which you lie on your back and move backwards by rotating your arms over your head

back-up *NOUN* **back-ups**
(*ICT*) a spare copy of a computer file for use if the original becomes damaged

backveld (*say* bak-felt) *NOUN*
remote country districts in South Africa

backward *ADJECTIVE*
1 going backwards ◆ *He propelled himself with powerful backward strokes of his arms.*
2 slow at learning or developing
▷ **backwardness** *NOUN*

backward *ADVERB*
backwards

USAGE NOTE The adverb backward is mainly used in American English. In British English, you would use backwards.

backwards *ADVERB*
1 to or towards the back

'Anything interesting?' yawned Pandora, slumping backwards onto Titus's bed. — *Debi Gliori, Pure Dead Wicked*

2 with the back end going first ◆ *The butler was practising walking out of the room backwards holding a tea tray.*
3 in reverse order ◆ *I can recite the twelve-times table backwards!*

backwards and forwards in each direction alternately; to and fro

WORD FAMILY Words which include 'backwards' in their meaning often begin with *retro-*: for example, *retrograde* means 'going backwards', and *retrospective* means 'looking backwards'.

backwater *NOUN* **backwaters**
1 a branch of a river that comes to a dead end where the water is stagnant
2 a quiet place that is not affected by progress or new ideas ◆ *Smallsville seemed almost proud of its reputation as a cultural backwater.*

bacon *NOUN*
smoked or salted meat from the back or sides of a pig

WORD HISTORY related to *back*

bacterium *NOUN* **bacteria**
a microscopic organism that can cause disease
▷ **bacterial** *ADJECTIVE*

USAGE NOTE Take care not to use the plural form *bacteria* when you are talking about a single organism. For example, you would say *this bacterium*, but *these bacteria*.

WORD HISTORY from Greek *baktērion* 'little stick', from *baktron* 'stick, rod', because the first ones discovered were rod-shaped

Bactrian camel *NOUN* **Bactrian camels**
an Asian camel with two humps

WORD HISTORY from *Bactria*, an ancient country in central Asia

bad *ADJECTIVE* **worse, worst**
1 of poor quality; not good ◆ *I'll read any detective book, good, bad, or indifferent.*
2 not skilled at something; incompetent ◆ *It was the final insult: accusing him of being a bad driver.*
3 unpleasant or upsetting ◆ *I'm afraid I've got some bad news.*
4 serious or severe ◆ *Reports are coming in of a bad accident on the motorway.*
5 ill or unhealthy; not strong ◆ *Don't put any pressure on your bad knee.*
6 harmful ◆ *Is eating chips bad for your complexion?*
7 decayed or rotten ◆ *There was a bad smell coming off the canals.*
8 wicked or evil ◆ *He was not a bad creature—but neither was he brave.*
9 a bad mood or temper is a feeling of being angry and irritated
10 to feel bad about doing something is to feel guilty or sorry about it
11 you describe something as not bad if it is quite good, or only good in parts
▷ **badness** *NOUN*

SYNONYMS (meaning 1) poor, awful, hopeless; (meaning 2) poor, incompetent, terrible, dreadful; (meaning 4) dreadful, terrible, appalling; (meaning 8) immoral, corrupt, villainous

WORD FAMILY Words which include 'bad' in their meaning sometimes begin with *dys-* or *caco-*: for example, *dysfunctional* means 'functioning badly', and a *cacophony* is 'a harsh unpleasant sound'.

baddy *NOUN* **baddies**
(*informal*) an evil or wicked character in a story

bade *an old past tense of* **bid** ❷

badge *NOUN* **badges**
a button or sign that you wear to show people who you are or what school or club you belong to

badger *NOUN* **badgers**
a grey animal with a black and white head, which lives underground and is active at night

badger *VERB* **badgers, badgering, badgered**
to keep asking someone to do something; to pester someone about something

If he badgered that pathetic librarian often enough, she'd find the hypnotism book. — *Georgia Byng, Molly Moon's Incredible Book of Hypnotism*

WORD HISTORY perhaps from *badge*, because of the markings on a badger's head. The word dates from the 16th century; the earlier Old English word for a badger was *brock*.

badly *ADVERB* **worse, worst**
1 in a bad way; not well ◆ *She wanted to complain about how badly she'd been treated.*
2 severely; causing serious injury ◆ *If you've hurt yourself badly you'll need medical attention.*
3 very much ◆ *We need that money badly.*

badminton *NOUN*
a game in which players use rackets to hit a light object called a shuttlecock across a high net

WORD HISTORY the name of a stately home in South-West England where the game was first played

bad-tempered *ADJECTIVE*
always angry and in a bad mood

baffle *VERB* **baffles, baffling, baffled**
to puzzle or confuse someone
▷ **bafflement** *NOUN*

bag *NOUN* **bags**
1 a container made of a soft material, for holding or carrying things
2 (*informal*) you say there is bags of something when there is plenty of it ◆ *Don't rush. We've got bags of time.*

a b c d e f g h i j k l m n o p q r s t u v w x y z

bag *VERB* **bags, bagging, bagged**
1 (*informal*) to catch or claim something
◆ *Someone had bagged all the best seats.*
2 to put something into bags
WORD HISTORY from Old Norse *baggi* 'bag, bundle'

bagatelle *NOUN*
a game played on a board in which small balls are struck into holes

bagel (*say* bay-gel) *NOUN* **bagels**
a ring-shaped bread roll

baggage *NOUN*
luggage

baggy *ADJECTIVE* **baggier, baggiest**
baggy clothes are large and loose-fitting
▷ **baggily** *ADVERB*
▷ **bagginess** *NOUN*

bagpipes *PLURAL NOUN*
a musical instrument played by squeezing air from an inflatable bag through a number of pipes

baguette (*say* ba-**get**) *NOUN* **baguettes**
a long thin loaf of French bread

Baha'i (*say* ba-**ha**-i) *NOUN*
a religion founded in Iran in the 19th century which advocates world peace
WORD HISTORY a Persian word, from Arabic *baha'* 'splendour'

bail[1] *NOUN*
money that is paid or promised as a guarantee that someone who is accused of a crime will return for trial if they are released in the meantime

bail *VERB* **bails, bailing, bailed**
to provide bail for someone
to bail someone out is to help them get out of trouble
WORD HISTORY an Old French word meaning 'custody, jurisdiction'

bail[2] *NOUN* **bails**
one of the two small pieces of wood placed on top of cricket stumps

bail[3] *VERB* **bails, bailing, bailed**
to bail out water is to scoop it out of a boat that has sprung a leak
WORD HISTORY from French *baille* 'bucket'

bailey *NOUN* **baileys**
1 the outer wall of a castle
2 a courtyard within this wall

bailiff *NOUN* **bailiffs**
1 an official who takes people's property when they owe money
2 a law officer who helps a sheriff by serving writs and carrying out arrests

Bairam (*say* by-**rahm**) *NOUN*
either of two Muslim festivals, one in the tenth month and one in the twelfth month of the Islamic year

bairn *NOUN* **bairns**
a Scottish word for a child
WORD HISTORY from Old English *bearn*, related to *bear*

Baisakhi (*say* by-**sa**-ki) *NOUN*
a major Sikh festival which commemorates the founding of the Khalsa order

bait *NOUN*
1 a piece of food that is put on a hook to catch a fish, or in a trap to catch an animal
2 something that is meant to tempt someone
◆ *We put a fake ad in the newspaper, thinking he'd take the bait.*

bait *VERB* **baits, baiting, baited**
1 to put bait on a hook or in a trap
2 to try to make someone angry by teasing them
WORD HISTORY related to *bite*

baize *NOUN*
the thick green cloth that is used for covering snooker tables
WORD HISTORY related to *bay* 'reddish-brown', because the cloth was originally that colour

bake *VERB* **bakes, baking, baked**
1 to make bread or cakes
2 to cook food in an oven with dry heat
3 someone says they are baking if they are feeling extremely hot
4 to make pottery hard by heating it in a kiln

baked beans *PLURAL NOUN*
cooked haricot beans, usually tinned with tomato sauce

baker *NOUN* **bakers**
a person who bakes or sells bread and cakes

bakery *NOUN* **bakeries**
a place where bread and cakes are baked, or a shop where they are sold

baking powder *NOUN*
a mixture of powders used to make bread and cakes rise when they are baked

baking soda *NOUN*
sodium bicarbonate

balaclava or **balaclava helmet** *NOUN* **balaclavas, balaclava helmets**
a close-fitting woollen hat which covers your head, neck, and sides of your face
WORD HISTORY the name of a village in the Crimea: balaclavas were worn by soldiers fighting near there during the Crimean War

balance *NOUN* **balances**
1 a steady position, with the weight or amount evenly distributed
2 to lose your balance is to be about to fall over
3 to be off balance is to have lost your balance

4 a device for weighing things, with two containers hanging from a bar; scales
5 the difference between money paid into an account and money taken out of it
6 the amount of money that someone owes

balance *VERB* **balances, balancing, balanced**
1 to balance on something is to make yourself steady on it
2 something is balanced when it is steady with its weight evenly distributed
3 a balanced argument or opinion is one that is fair and considers all sides

WORD HISTORY from Latin *libra bilanx* 'scales with two pans'

balcony *NOUN* **balconies**
1 a platform that sticks out from an outside wall of a building
2 the upstairs part of a theatre or cinema

bald *ADJECTIVE*
1 having no hair on the top of your head
2 a bald statement or description is one without any details or explanation
▷ **baldly** *ADVERB*
▷ **baldness** *NOUN*

bale❶ *NOUN* **bales**
a large bundle of hay, straw, or cotton, usually tied up tightly

WORD HISTORY related to *ball* 'sphere'

bale❷ *VERB* **bales, baling, baled**
to bale out of an aircraft is to jump out of it with a parachute in an emergency

baleful *ADJECTIVE*
menacing; threatening harm

Frodo and Sam, horror-stricken, began slowly to back away, their own gaze held by the dreadful stare of those baleful eyes. — *J. R. R. Tolkien, The Two Towers*

▷ **balefully** *ADVERB*

WORD HISTORY from Old English *balu* 'evil'

ball❶ *NOUN* **balls**
1 a solid or hollow round object that is kicked or thrown in many games and sports
2 something wound or gathered into a round shape, such as a ball of wool
3 the ball of your foot is the rounded part of your foot at the base of your big toe

ball❷ *NOUN* **balls**
a formal party where people dance with partners
to have a ball (*informal*) is to enjoy yourself very much

ballad *NOUN* **ballads**
1 a traditional song or poem that tells a story, often with a refrain
2 a slow romantic pop song

WORD HISTORY from Old French *balade* 'poem or song to dance to', related to our words *ball* 'dance' and *ballet*

ballast (*say* **bal**-ast) *NOUN*
heavy material that is carried in a ship or hot-air balloon to keep it steady

ball bearings *PLURAL NOUN*
small steel balls rolling in a groove on which machine parts can move easily

ballcock *NOUN* **ballcocks**
a floating ball that controls the water level in a cistern

ballerina (*say* bal-er-**een**-a) *NOUN* **ballerinas**
a female ballet dancer

ballet (*say* **bal**-ay) *NOUN* **ballets**
a stage entertainment that tells a story with dancing, mime, and music
▷ **balletic** (*say* ba-**let**-ik) *ADJECTIVE*

ballistic (*say* bal-**ist**-ik) *ADJECTIVE*
ballistic weapons are ones which are fired through the air

ballistic missile *NOUN* **ballistic missiles**
a missile that is powered and guided when it is launched and then falls under gravity on its target

balloon *NOUN* **balloons**
1 a bag made of thin rubber that can be inflated and used as a toy or decoration
2 a large round bag inflated with hot air or light gases to make it rise in the air, often carrying a basket in which passengers may ride
3 a speech balloon is a circle containing the words spoken by the characters in a cartoon

balloon *VERB* **balloons, ballooning, ballooned**
to swell outwards, or to make something swell outwards, like an inflating balloon

The troll ballooned its cheeks and howled. Scare tactics. — *Eoin Colfer, Artemis Fowl*

ballot *NOUN* **ballots**
1 a secret method of voting, usually by making a mark on a form
2 a piece of paper on which a vote is made

ballot *VERB* **ballots, balloting, balloted**
to send or give out forms to people so that they can vote on a particular issue

WORD HISTORY from Italian *balotta* 'small ball', after a secret method of voting by placing a ball of a chosen colour in a box (which is also the origin of the word *blackball*)

ballpark *NOUN* **ballparks**
1 an American baseball ground
2 (*informal*) a ballpark figure is one that is roughly correct

USAGE NOTE It is called a ballpark figure because it is at least 'in the right ballpark', i.e. in the right general range of figures.

ballpoint pen *NOUN* **ballpoint pens**
a pen with a tiny ball round which the ink flows

ballroom *NOUN* **ballrooms**
a large room where dances are held

balm *NOUN*
1 a sweet-scented ointment
2 something that soothes you

balmy *ADJECTIVE*
1 balmy weather is gentle and warm
2 sweet-scented like balm

balsa *NOUN*
a kind of very lightweight wood

balsam *NOUN* **balsams**
1 a sweet-smelling oily resin produced by certain trees, used to make perfumes and medicines
2 a tree that produces balsam

WORD HISTORY via Latin from Greek *balsamon*

balti *NOUN* **baltis**
a type of curry originally from Pakistan, traditionally cooked and served in a bowl-shaped pan

balustrade *NOUN* **balustrades**
a row of short posts or pillars that supports a rail or strip of stonework round a balcony or staircase

WORD HISTORY from Italian *balustra* 'pomegranate flower', because the pillars of a balustrade were the same shape as the flower

bamboo *NOUN* **bamboos**
1 a tall plant with hard hollow stems
2 a stem of the bamboo plant

bamboozle *VERB* **bamboozles, bamboozling, bamboozled**
(*informal*) to puzzle or trick someone

ban *VERB* **bans, banning, banned**
to forbid something or somebody officially

'Today is the one day in the year when all visitors are banned, on pain of death.' — *Mary Hoffman, Stravaganza: City of Masks*

ban *NOUN* **bans**
an order that bans something

banal (*say* ban-**ahl**) *ADJECTIVE*
ordinary and uninteresting ◆ *'Did you read the introduction?' 'No, it looked fairly banal.'*

banana *NOUN* **bananas**
a long curved fruit with a yellow or green skin

band❶ *NOUN* **bands**
1 a strip or loop of something
2 a range of values, wavelengths, etc.

band❷ *NOUN* **bands**
1 an organized group of people doing something together
2 a group of musicians who play rock, pop, or jazz music
3 a group of musicians who play brass, wind, and percussion instruments, sometimes while marching

band *VERB* **bands, banding, banded**
to band together is to form an organized group

bandage *NOUN* **bandages**
a strip of material tied round a wound

bandage *VERB* **bandages, bandaging, bandaged**
to tie a bandage round a wound

bandanna *NOUN* **bandannas**
a brightly coloured scarf worn round your head or neck

bandicoot *NOUN* **bandicoots**
an insect-eating marsupial animal of Australia and New Guinea

bandit *NOUN* **bandits**
a member of a gang of robbers who attack travellers

WORD HISTORY from Latin *bannire* 'banish'

bandstand *NOUN* **bandstands**
a platform for a band playing music outdoors, usually in a park

bandwagon *NOUN*
to jump on the bandwagon is to join other people in something that has become successful or popular

bandwidth *NOUN*
a range of frequencies used to transmit radio or television signals

bandy❶ *ADJECTIVE*
bandy legs are ones that curve outwards at the knees

WORD HISTORY from an old word *bandy* meaning 'a kind of curved hockey stick'

bandy❷ *VERB* **bandies, bandying, bandied**
a word or story is bandied about if it is mentioned or told by a lot of different people

bane *NOUN*
something is the bane of your life if it causes you a lot of trouble or worry

Kay was six years older than I was and the bane of my young life. — *Michael Morpurgo, Arthur, High King of Britain*

WORD HISTORY from Old English *bana*

bang *NOUN* **bangs**
1 a sudden loud noise like that of an explosion
2 a sharp blow or knock

bang *VERB* **bangs, banging, banged**
1 to hit or shut something noisily
2 to make a sudden loud noise
3 to bang on a surface is to hit it repeatedly and noisily
4 to bump part of your body against something

One last kiss, rushed and clumsy so that they banged cheekbones. — *Philip Pullman, The Amber Spyglass*

bang *ADVERB* (*informal*)
1 to be bang in the middle is to be exactly in the middle of something
2 to be bang on time is to be exactly on time
3 to be bang up to date is to be completely up to date or modern

banger *NOUN* **bangers**
1 a firework that makes a loud bang
2 (*informal*) a sausage
3 (*informal*) a noisy old car

bangle *NOUN* **bangles**
a bracelet or band worn round the wrist
WORD HISTORY from Hindi *bangli* 'glass bracelet'

banish *VERB* **banishes, banishing, banished**
1 to punish someone by ordering them to leave a place
2 to banish a thought or feeling is to drive it from your mind
▷ **banishment** *NOUN*

banisters *PLURAL NOUN*
a handrail with upright supports at the side of a staircase
WORD HISTORY related to *balustrade*

banjo *NOUN* **banjos**
a musical instrument with a round body and strings, played by plucking the strings like a guitar

bank❶ *NOUN* **banks**
1 a sloping piece of ground at either side of a river
2 a long, low mound of earth, sand, or snow
3 a long thick mass of cloud or fog
4 a series of similar things in a row ◆ *There was a bank of switches on the top of the desk.*

bank *VERB* **banks, banking, banked**
1 to pile up to form a bank
2 to tilt sideways while changing direction in the air

bank❷ *NOUN* **banks**
1 a business that looks after people's money
2 a supply of something ready for use if needed ◆ *a blood bank*
3 a public container in which you can leave articles for recycling ◆ *a bottle bank*

bank *VERB* **banks, banking, banked**
1 to put money in a bank
2 to bank on someone is to rely or depend on them
WORD HISTORY from Italian *banca* 'bench', referring to the table used by a money-lender

banker *NOUN* **bankers**
a person who manages a bank

bank holiday *NOUN* **bank holidays**
a public holiday, when banks are officially closed

banknote *NOUN* **banknotes**
a piece of paper money issued by a bank

bankrupt *ADJECTIVE*
to be bankrupt is to be unable to pay your debts
▷ **bankruptcy** *NOUN*
WORD HISTORY from *bank* 'business looking after money' and Latin *ruptum* 'broken'

banksia *NOUN*
an evergreen Australian shrub with yellow flowers like long thin brushes
WORD HISTORY named after the English botanist Sir Joseph *Banks*

banner *NOUN* **banners**
1 a flag
2 a strip of cloth with a design or slogan, which is fixed to a pole and carried in a procession or demonstration

banns *PLURAL NOUN*
an announcement in a church that the two people named are going to marry each other
WORD HISTORY the plural of *ban* 'proclamation'

banquet *NOUN* **banquets**
a formal meal for invited guests which includes several courses
▷ **banqueting** *NOUN*
WORD HISTORY an Old French word meaning 'little bench'

banshee *NOUN* **banshees**
in Irish legend, a female spirit who wails to warn of a death in a house
WORD HISTORY from Irish *ben síde* 'woman of the fairies'

bantam *NOUN* **bantams**
a breed of small hen
WORD HISTORY from the *Bantam* district in Java, from where it is thought the birds were imported

banter *NOUN*
playful teasing or joking

banter *VERB* **banters, bantering, bantered**
to joke in a good-humoured way

Bantu *NOUN* **Bantu** or **Bantus**
1 a member of a group of central and southern African peoples
2 the group of languages spoken by these peoples
WORD HISTORY a Bantu word meaning 'people'

banyan (*say* **ban**-yan) *NOUN* **banyans**
an Indian fig tree with roots which reach down from its branches to form new trunks
WORD HISTORY from a Sanskrit word meaning 'merchant', because merchants once met under one of these trees

baobab (*say* bay-o-bab) ***NOUN*** **baobabs**
a tropical tree found in Africa and Australia with a thick trunk and edible fruit

bap ***NOUN*** **baps**
a soft flat bread roll

baptism ***NOUN*** **baptisms**
(*Religion*) the ceremony in which a person is formally baptized and received into the Christian Church

Baptist ***NOUN*** **Baptists**
(*Religion*) a member of a group of Christians who believe that a person should not be baptized until he or she is old enough to understand what baptism means

baptize ***VERB*** **baptizes, baptizing, baptized**
(*Religion*) to receive a person into the Christian Church in a ceremony in which they are sprinkled with or dipped in water, and usually given a name

USAGE NOTE This word can also be spelled baptise.

WORD HISTORY from Greek *baptizein* 'to dip'

bar ***NOUN*** **bars**
1 a long solid piece of metal
2 a railing or strut in a cage or cot, or across a window
3 a solid block of soap or chocolate
4 a counter or room where refreshments, especially alcoholic drinks, are served
5 a barrier or obstruction
6 one of the small equal sections into which music is divided

the Bar the legal profession of barristers

bar ***VERB*** **bars, barring, barred**
1 to fasten something with a bar or bars
2 to bar someone's way or path is to block or obstruct them
3 to forbid or ban someone ◆ *Rude and aggressive passengers will be barred from flying.*

▷ **barred** ***ADJECTIVE***

barb ***NOUN*** **barbs**
1 a backward-pointing spike on a fish hook or harpoon, which makes it difficult to pull out
2 a deliberately hurtful remark

WORD HISTORY from Latin *barba* 'beard', related to *barber*

barbarian ***NOUN*** **barbarians**
an uncivilized or brutal person

WORD HISTORY from Greek *barbaros* 'babbling' (i.e. not speaking Greek)

barbaric or **barbarous** ***ADJECTIVE***
savage and cruel

▷ **barbarity** ***NOUN***
▷ **barbarism** ***NOUN***

barbecue ***NOUN*** **barbecues**
1 a metal frame for grilling food over an open fire outdoors
2 a party where food is cooked in this way

barbecue ***VERB*** **barbecues, barbecuing, barbecued**
to cook food on a barbecue

WORD HISTORY via Spanish from Arawak (a South American language) *barbacoa* 'wooden frame'

barbed ***ADJECTIVE***
1 having a barb or barbs
2 a barbed comment or remark is one that is deliberately hurtful

barbed wire ***NOUN***
wire with small spikes in it, used to make fences

barber ***NOUN*** **barbers**
a men's hairdresser

WORD HISTORY from Latin *barba* 'beard'

bar chart ***NOUN*** **bar charts**
a diagram that shows amounts as bars of equal width but varying height

bar code ***NOUN*** **bar codes**
a set of black lines that are printed on items for sale or loan, and which can be read by a computer to give information about the items

bard ***NOUN*** **bards**
(*literary*) a poet

WORD HISTORY from a Celtic word meaning 'travelling minstrel'

bare ***ADJECTIVE***
1 not covered with clothing; naked
2 bare ground is barren or not covered with vegetation
3 a bare room has no furniture or other contents
4 the bare facts are plain and simple information without any details
5 only just enough ◆ *the bare essentials*
6 to do something with your bare hands is to do it without the help of tools or weapons

bare ***VERB*** **bares, baring, bared**
an animal bares its teeth when it opens its mouth aggressively to reveal them

bareback ***ADJECTIVE, ADVERB***
to ride a horse bareback is to ride it without a saddle

barefaced ***ADJECTIVE***
a barefaced lie is one that is told boldly without any shame or guilt

bareheaded ***ADJECTIVE***
someone who is bareheaded is not wearing a hat or cap

barely ***ADVERB***
only just; scarcely

barest ***ADJECTIVE***
very small; slightest

bargain *NOUN* **bargains**
1 an agreement about buying, selling, or exchanging something
2 something that you buy cheaply which is worth more than you pay for it

bargain *VERB* **bargains, bargaining, bargained**
1 to argue over the price to be paid or what you will do in return for something
2 to bargain on something is to expect it to happen ◆ *They had not bargained on finding us there.*

more than you bargained for more than you planned for or expected ◆ *The insurance cost them more than they had bargained for.*

barge *NOUN* **barges**
a long flat-bottomed boat used on canals

barge *VERB* **barges, barging, barged**
1 to barge into someone or something is to push or knock against them roughly
2 to barge in or into a room is to rush into it carelessly and rudely

WORD HISTORY from Latin *barca* 'boat'

baritone *NOUN* **baritones**
a male singer with a voice between a tenor and a bass

WORD HISTORY from Greek *barus* 'heavy' and *tone*

barium (*say* **bair**-ee-um) *NOUN*
a soft silvery-white metal

WORD HISTORY from Greek *barus* 'heavy'

bark❶ *NOUN* **barks**
the short harsh sound made by a dog or fox

bark *VERB* **barks, barking, barked**
1 to make the sound of a bark
2 to speak loudly and harshly

to bark up the wrong tree is to have a mistaken impression or idea

bark❷ *NOUN*
the outer covering of a tree's branches or trunk

barley *NOUN*
a cereal plant from which malt is made

barley sugar *NOUN*
a hard clear sweet made from boiled sugar

bar mitzvah *NOUN* **bar mitzvahs**
a religious ceremony for Jewish boys aged 13, after which they take on the responsibilities of an adult under Jewish law

WORD HISTORY from a Hebrew phrase meaning 'son of the commandment'

barmy *ADJECTIVE*
(*informal*) crazy; mad

WORD HISTORY meaning literally 'full of froth', from *barm* 'froth, foam', related to *brew* and *broth*

barn *NOUN* **barns**
a farm building for storing hay or grain

WORD HISTORY from Old English *bere ern* 'barley house'

barnacle *NOUN* **barnacles**
a shellfish that attaches itself to rocks and the bottoms of ships

WORD HISTORY the word first referred to a kind of goose which was once believed to hatch from shellfish attached to rocks

barn dance *NOUN* **barn dances**
1 a kind of country dance
2 an informal gathering for dancing

barnyard *NOUN* **barnyards**
a farmyard next to a barn

barometer (*say* ba-**rom**-it-er) *NOUN* **barometers**
an instrument that measures air pressure, used in forecasting the weather

WORD HISTORY from Greek *baros* 'weight' and *meter*

baron *NOUN* **barons**
1 a member of the lowest rank of nobility
2 a powerful owner of an industry or business ◆ *a newspaper baron*

▷ **baronial** (*say* ba-**roh**-nee-al) *ADJECTIVE*

WORD HISTORY from Latin *baro* 'man, warrior'

baroness *NOUN* **baronesses**
a female baron or a baron's wife

baronet *NOUN* **baronets**
a member of the nobility with a knighthood inherited from his father

baroque (*say* ba-**rok**) *NOUN*
an elaborately decorated style of architecture used in Europe in the 17th and 18th centuries

WORD HISTORY a French word from Italian *barocco* 'irregular pearl'

barracks *NOUN*
a large building or group of buildings for soldiers to live in

WORD HISTORY from Spanish *barraca* 'soldier's tent'

barracuda (*say* ba-ra-**koo**-da) *NOUN* **barracudas**
a tropical sea fish with a long thin body and large jaws

WORD HISTORY from a Spanish word meaning 'overlapping tooth'

barrage (*say* **ba**-rahzh) *NOUN* **barrages**
1 a dam built across a river
2 heavy gunfire
3 an aggressive series of questions or remarks

Twig quaked under the barrage of insults and recriminations. — *Paul Stewart and Chris Riddell, Stormchaser*

barramundi *NOUN*
a large freshwater fish of Australia and South-East Asia

barrel *NOUN* **barrels**
1 a large rounded container for storing water or beer
2 the metal tube of a gun, through which the shot is fired
WORD HISTORY from Latin *barriculus* 'small cask'

barrel organ *NOUN* **barrel organs**
a musical instrument which you play by turning a handle

barren *ADJECTIVE*
1 a barren landscape is one without vegetation
2 a barren woman is not able to have children
3 a barren plant or tree is one that cannot bear fruit
▷ **barrenness** *NOUN*

barricade *NOUN* **barricades**
a barrier, especially one put up hastily across a street or door

barricade *VERB* **barricades, barricading, barricaded**
to block a street or door with a barricade
WORD HISTORY a French word from Spanish *barrica* 'barrel', because barricades were sometimes built from barrels

barrier *NOUN* **barriers**
1 a fence or wall that prevents people from getting past
2 something that stops you doing something

barrier reef *NOUN* **barrier reefs**
a coral reef close to the shore but separated from it by a channel of deep water

barrister *NOUN* **barristers**
a lawyer who represents people in the higher lawcourts in England and Wales (in Scotland, the equivalent is an *advocate*)
WORD HISTORY from an earlier meaning of a lawyer who was allowed to pass through the *bar*, a partition separating qualified lawyers from students

barrow❶ *NOUN* **barrows**
1 a wheelbarrow
2 a small cart that is pushed or pulled by hand
WORD HISTORY related to *bear* 'carry, support'

barrow❷ *NOUN* **barrows**
a mound of earth over a prehistoric grave
WORD HISTORY related to *burrow*

bartender *NOUN* **bartenders**
someone who serves drinks at a bar

barter *VERB* **barters, bartering, bartered**
to trade by exchanging goods for other goods rather than money

barter *NOUN* **barters**
the system of bartering

basalt (*say* bas-awlt) *NOUN*
a hard black volcanic rock
WORD HISTORY from a Greek word meaning 'hard stone, touchstone'

base❶ *NOUN* **bases**
1 the lowest part of something; the part on which a thing stands
2 a starting point or foundation; a basis
3 a headquarters
4 each of the four corners that must be reached by a runner in baseball
5 (*Science*) a substance that can combine with an acid to form a salt
6 (*Mathematics*) the number in terms of which other numbers can be expressed in a number system; 10 is the base of the decimal system and 2 is the base of the binary system

base *VERB* **bases, basing, based**
1 to be built on something
2 to use something as a starting point ◆ *The story is based on facts.*

base❷ *ADJECTIVE*
1 a base action or motive is one that shows no honour or moral principles
2 a base metal is one that has no great value
▷ **basely** *ADVERB*
▷ **baseness** *NOUN*
WORD HISTORY from French *bas* 'low'

baseball *NOUN* **baseballs**
1 a team game in which runs are scored by hitting a ball and running round a series of four bases, played mainly in North America
2 the ball used in this game

basement *NOUN* **basements**
a level of a house or building below ground level

bash *VERB* **bashes, bashing, bashed**
to hit something or someone hard

bash *NOUN* **bashes**
1 a hard hit
2 (*informal*) a try ◆ *Have a bash at it.*

bashful *ADJECTIVE*
shy and self-conscious
▷ **bashfully** *ADVERB*

basic *ADJECTIVE*
1 forming an essential part or starting point of something ◆ *Eggs are one of the basic ingredients of a cake mixture.*
2 very simple or plain ◆ *The accommodation was basic and very cheap.*

basically *ADVERB*
at the simplest or most fundamental level

basil *NOUN*
a Mediterranean herb used in cooking
WORD HISTORY from Old French *basile*, from a Greek phrase meaning 'royal herb' because it had so many uses in cooking and medicine

basilica (*say* ba-**zil**-ik-a) *NOUN* **basilicas**
a large oblong church with two rows of columns and an apse at one end

WORD HISTORY a Latin word meaning 'royal palace' from Greek *basileus* 'king', because basilicas were built to the same design as Roman palaces

basilisk (*say* **baz**-il-isk) *NOUN* **basilisks**
a mythical reptile said to be able to kill people just by looking at them

WORD HISTORY from Greek *basilikos* which originally meant 'little king' and is related to our words *basil* and *basilica*

basin *NOUN* **basins**
1 a deep bowl
2 a washbasin
3 a sheltered area of water for mooring boats
4 the area from which water drains into a river
◆ *the Amazon basin*

basis *NOUN* **bases**
something to start from or add to; the main principle or ingredient

bask *VERB* **basks, basking, basked**
to lie or sit comfortably in light or warmth

WORD HISTORY the original meaning of *bask* was 'to wallow in blood', but it changed to the current meaning in the 17th century

basket *NOUN* **baskets**
a container for holding or carrying things, made of strips of flexible material or wire woven together

basketball *NOUN* **basketballs**
1 a game in which goals are scored by putting a ball through high nets
2 the ball used in this game

basmati (*say* baz-**mah**-ti) *NOUN*
an Indian rice with long thin grains

WORD HISTORY from a Hindi word meaning 'fragrant'

Basque (*say* bask) *NOUN* **Basques**
1 a member of a people who live in north-east Spain and south-west France
2 the language spoken by the Basques, which is not related to any other known language

WORD HISTORY via French from Latin *Vasco*, which was the name the Romans gave to this people

bas-relief (*say* bas-ri-**leef**) *NOUN*
(*Art*) a style of sculpture in which a design is carved to project from a flat background

bass❶ (*say* bayss) *ADJECTIVE*
deep-sounding; the bass part of a piece of music is the lowest part

bass *NOUN* **basses** (*Music*)
1 a male singer with a very deep voice
2 a bass instrument or part

bass❷ (*say* bas) *NOUN* **bass**
a fish of the perch family

basset hound *NOUN* **basset hounds**
a short-legged dog with drooping ears, kept as a pet

WORD HISTORY from French *bas* 'low'

bassoon *NOUN* **bassoons**
a bass woodwind instrument

WORD HISTORY from Italian *basso* 'low'

bastard *NOUN* **bastards**
1 an old-fashioned word for an illegitimate child
2 (*informal*) an unpleasant or difficult person or thing

baste❶ *VERB* **bastes, basting, basted**
to moisten meat by spooning fat over it while it is cooking

baste❷ *VERB* **bastes, basting, basted**
to sew fabric together loosely with long stitches

bastion *NOUN* **bastions**
1 a part of a fortified building that sticks out from the rest, from which weapons could be fired
2 a person or institution that is a bastion of a particular belief or way of life is a strong supporter of it

WORD HISTORY from Italian *bastire* 'to build'

bat❶ *NOUN* **bats**
1 a shaped piece of wood used to hit the ball in sports like cricket, baseball, and table tennis
2 a batsman or batswoman
3 to do something off your own bat is to do it without help from other people

bat *VERB* **bats, batting, batted**
1 to strike a ball with a bat
2 to play as a batsman or batswoman

bat❷ *NOUN* **bats**
a flying animal that looks like a mouse with wings

bat❸ *VERB* **bats, batting, batted**
1 to bat your eyelashes is to flutter them
2 someone doesn't bat an eyelid if they appear not to be surprised or worried by something unusual

WORD HISTORY from an earlier word *bate* 'to flutter'

batch *NOUN* **batches**
a set of things or people dealt with together

WORD HISTORY related to *bake* because the original meaning was a number of loaves baked at the same time

bated *ADJECTIVE*
to wait or stand with bated breath is to do so anxiously and excitedly

bath *NOUN* **baths**

1 a large container for water in which to wash your whole body; this water ◆ *Your bath is getting cold.*

2 the process of washing your whole body while sitting in water

3 a liquid in which something is placed ◆ *an acid bath*

bath *VERB* **baths, bathing, bathed**

to wash yourself in a bath

bathe *VERB* **bathes, bathing, bathed**

1 to go swimming

> We never bathe in the moat until July or August—and even then we usually regret it.
> — *Dodie Smith, I Capture the Castle*

2 to wash something gently in water

3 to be bathed in light is to have light shining all over you

▷ **bathe** *NOUN*

▷ **bather** *NOUN*

▷ **bathing suit** *NOUN*

bathos (*say* **bay**-thos) *NOUN*

a sudden change from a serious subject or tone to a ridiculous or trivial one

WORD HISTORY a Greek word meaning 'depth'

bathroom *NOUN* **bathrooms**

a room containing a bath

baths *PLURAL NOUN*

1 a building with a public swimming pool

2 a public swimming pool

batik (*say* ba-**teek**) *NOUN*

a method of hand-dyeing fabric in which wax is applied to areas that will not be coloured

bat mitzvah *NOUN* **bat mitzvahs**

a religious ceremony for Jewish girls aged 13, after which they take on the responsibilities of an adult under Jewish law

WORD HISTORY from a Hebrew phrase meaning 'daughter of the commandment'

baton *NOUN* **batons**

1 a stick used by the conductor of an orchestra or choir to keep time

2 a short stick passed between runners in a relay race

3 a police officer's truncheon

batsman or **batswoman** *NOUN* **batsmen** or **batswomen**

a player who uses a bat in cricket or other sports

battalion *NOUN* **battalions**

an army unit containing two or more companies

WORD HISTORY from Italian *battaglia* 'battle'

batten *NOUN* **battens**

a strip of wood or metal that holds something in place

batten *VERB* **battens, battening, battened**

to batten down a door or lid is to fasten it firmly

batter *VERB* **batters, battering, battered**

to hit something hard and often

> There are guys so desperate or so crazy, they'll knife you or batter your head in for your sleeping bag and the coppers you've got in your pocket.
> — *Robert Swindells, Stone Cold*

batter *NOUN* **batters**

1 a beaten mixture of flour, eggs, and milk, used for making pancakes or coating food to be fried

2 a player who is batting in baseball

WORD HISTORY from Latin *battuere* 'to beat'

battering ram *NOUN* **battering rams**

a heavy pole that is used to break down walls or gates

battery *NOUN* **batteries**

1 a device consisting of one or more electric cells for storing and supplying electricity

2 a set of connected pieces of equipment

3 a series of cages in which poultry or farm animals are kept close together ◆ *I always buy free-range eggs. I hate the thought of battery farming.*

4 a group of heavy guns

WORD HISTORY related to *batter*, as the word's original meaning was 'hitting'

battle *NOUN* **battles**

1 a fight between two armies

2 a struggle

battle *VERB* **battles, battling, battled**

1 to fight in a battle

2 to make your way forcibly or roughly

WORD HISTORY related to *batter*

battlefield *NOUN* **battlefields**

a piece of ground on which a battle is or was fought

battlements *PLURAL NOUN*

the top of a castle wall, often with gaps from which the defenders could fire at the enemy

battleship *NOUN* **battleships**

a heavily armed warship

batty *ADJECTIVE* **battier, battiest**

(*informal*) crazy; mad

WORD HISTORY from the phrase *to have bats in the belfry* 'to be crazy'

bauble *NOUN* **baubles**

1 a bright and showy ornament that has little value

2 a decorative ball hung on a Christmas tree

WORD HISTORY from Old French *baubel* 'toy'

baulk *VERB* **baulks, baulking, baulked**

1 to stop and refuse to go on ◆ *The horse baulked at the fence.*

2 to frustrate someone; to prevent someone from doing or getting something

bauxite *NOUN*
the clay-like substance from which aluminium is obtained

WORD HISTORY from *Les Baux*, a place in France where it was first found

bawdy *ADJECTIVE* **bawdier, bawdiest**
a bawdy joke or story is one that refers to sex in a humorous way

▷ **bawdiness** *NOUN*

WORD HISTORY from an old word *bawd* meaning 'a brothel-keeper'

bawl *VERB* **bawls, bawling, bawled**
1 to shout loudly
2 to cry noisily

bay❶ *NOUN* **bays**
an area of the sea and coast where the shore curves inwards

bay❷ *NOUN* **bays**
an alcove or compartment

WORD HISTORY from Latin *batare* 'to gape'

bay❸ *NOUN* **bays**
a kind of laurel tree with leaves that are used to flavour sauces and stews

WORD HISTORY from Latin *bacca* 'berry', as the word originally meant 'laurel berry'

bay❹ *NOUN* **bays**
1 the long deep howl of a hunting dog or wolf
2 to keep someone or something harmful or unwanted at bay is to prevent them from threatening you

bay *VERB* **bays, baying, bayed**
to howl or cry, like a hunting dog chasing its prey

bay❺ *ADJECTIVE*
a bay horse is reddish-brown in colour

WORD HISTORY from Latin *badius* which was also used to describe this colour of horse

bayonet *NOUN* **bayonets**
a blade that can be fixed to the end of a rifle and used for stabbing

bay window *NOUN* **bay windows**
a rounded or three-sided window that sticks out from the main wall of a house

bazaar *NOUN* **bazaars**
1 a market place in a Middle Eastern country
2 a sale to raise money for charity

WORD HISTORY from Persian *bazar* 'market'

bazooka *NOUN* **bazookas**
a tube-shaped portable weapon for firing anti-tank rockets

WORD HISTORY from an earlier meaning 'a musical instrument like a trombone', because of the similar shape

BBC *ABBREVIATION*
British Broadcasting Corporation

BC *ABBREVIATION*
used with dates to show that they are before the birth of Christ

USAGE NOTE The abbreviation BC goes after the number of the year: *in 54 BC.*

BCE *ABBREVIATION*
before the Common Era, used with dates counting back from the year zero

be *VERB* **am, are, is; was, were; being, been**
1 to exist; to occupy a position ◆ *That is where we live.*
2 to happen; to take place ◆ *When is your birthday?*
3 used with a name or noun to state someone's identity, relationship, or occupation ◆ *I am Jeremiah Jones and this is my daughter.*
4 used with an adjective to state a quality or nature ◆ *They all promised to be good.*
5 used to form parts of other verbs ◆ *It is snowing.* ◆ *They were filming.* ◆ *I was asked.*

to have been somewhere is to have gone there as a visitor ◆ *He has been as far as Russia.*

beach *NOUN* **beaches**
the part of the seashore nearest to the water

beached *ADJECTIVE*
a beached whale or other animal is one that is stranded on a beach

beacon *NOUN* **beacons**
a light or fire used as a signal or warning

WORD HISTORY related to *beckon*

bead *NOUN* **beads**
1 a small pierced ball of glass, plastic, etc., for threading on string or wire to make jewellery, or for sewing on fabric
2 a drop of sweat or moisture

WORD HISTORY from Old English *gebed* 'prayer', because of the use of rosary beads while saying prayers

beady *ADJECTIVE*
beady eyes are small, bright, and piercing

▷ **beadily** *ADVERB*

beagle *NOUN* **beagles**
a small hound used for hunting hares

WORD HISTORY related to *bay* 'bark, howl'

beak *NOUN* **beaks**
the hard horny part of a bird's mouth

WORD HISTORY via Old French from Latin *beccus*; the earlier Old English word for a beak was *bile* which became our word *bill*

beaker *NOUN* **beakers**
1 a tall drinking mug, often without a handle
2 a glass container used for pouring liquids in a laboratory

WORD HISTORY from Old Norse *bikarr* 'cup', related to Greek *bikos* 'jug' and so to our word *pitcher*

beam *NOUN* **beams**
1 a long thick bar of wood or metal
2 a ray or stream of light or other radiation
3 a happy smile

beam *VERB* **beams, beaming, beamed**
1 to smile happily
2 to send out a ray of light

bean *NOUN* **beans**
1 a kind of plant with seeds growing in pods
2 its seed or pod eaten as food
3 the seed of a coffee plant

bean sprout *NOUN* **bean sprouts**
a sprout of a bean seed that can be eaten either cooked or raw

bear❶ *NOUN* **bears**
a large heavy animal with thick fur and large teeth and claws

WORD HISTORY from Old English *bera*, related to our word *brown*

bear❷ *VERB* **bears, bearing, bore, borne**
1 to carry or support something
2 to bear a mark or scar is to have one visible on your body
3 to bear a likeness or resemblance to someone is to look like them
4 to endure a difficult person or situation

A fortnight was all she thought she'd be able to bear of her aunt and uncle's hospitality. — *Meg Cabot, Victoria and the Rogue*

5 to move or turn in a particular direction
6 to give birth to a child or offspring
7 to produce fruit
8 something bears on a situation or issue when it is relevant to it or has an effect on it

to bear something in mind is to remember to consider it in the future

to bear something out is to support or confirm the truth of it

WORD HISTORY from Old English *beran* meaning both 'carry' and 'give birth'

bearable *ADJECTIVE*
able to be endured; tolerable

beard *NOUN* **beards**
hair that grows naturally on a man's chin

▷ **bearded** *ADJECTIVE*

bearer *NOUN* **bearers**
someone who carries or brings something important

bearing *NOUN* **bearings**
1 the way that you stand, walk, or behave

He knew he was a winner now; he had the bearing, the quiet arrogance of a winner. — *Roald Dahl, Taste*

2 the direction or position of one thing in relation to another
3 to have a bearing on something is to be relevant to it or to have an effect on it ◆ *Will this have any bearing on my exam results?*
4 to get your bearings is to work out where you are in a new place or situation
5 to lose your bearings is to become confused and disoriented

beast *NOUN* **beasts**
1 any large four-footed animal
2 (*informal*) a cruel or vicious person

WORD HISTORY via Old French from Latin *bestia*; the earlier Old English word for 'animal' was *deor* which became our word *deer*

beastly *ADVERB*
(*informal*) unpleasant; nasty

Matilda decided that every time her father or her mother was beastly to her, she would get her own back in some way or another. — *Roald Dahl, Matilda*

▷ **beastliness** *NOUN*

beat *VERB* **beats, beating, beat, beaten**
1 to hit someone repeatedly in order to hurt or punish them
2 to defeat an opponent in a contest
3 to shape or flatten something by hitting it repeatedly
4 to stir cooking ingredients vigorously
5 a heart beats when it makes regular movements
6 an animal or insect beats its wings when it flaps them repeatedly
7 to beat someone up is to attack them very violently

it beats me (*informal*) I don't understand it

beat *NOUN* **beats**
1 a regular rhythm or stroke ◆ *They could hear the beat of the eagle's wings high above them.*
2 a strong musical rhythm
3 the regular route patrolled by a police officer

beatific (*say* bee-a-**tif**-ik) *ADJECTIVE*
a beatific look or smile is one that expresses great happiness

WORD HISTORY from Latin *beatus* 'blessed'

beautiful *ADJECTIVE*
1 someone who is beautiful is very attractive to look at
2 giving pleasure to your senses or your mind
3 of a high standard; very expert or skilful ◆ *a beautiful header straight into the back of the net*

beautifully *ADVERB*
1 in a beautiful way
2 extremely well; in a very satisfactory way ◆ *Their ideas were developing beautifully.*

beautify *VERB* **beautifies, beautifying, beautified**
to make someone or something beautiful

▷ **beautification** *NOUN*

beauty *NOUN* **beauties**
1 a quality that gives pleasure to your senses or your mind
2 a person or thing that has beauty
3 an excellent example of something

4 an attractive feature or advantage ◆ *The beauty of living here is that it's so cheap.*

WORD FAMILY A related adjective is aesthetic.

beaver *NOUN* **beavers**
an animal with soft brown fur and strong teeth; beavers build their homes in deep pools which they make by damming streams

beaver *VERB* **beavers, beavering, beavered**
to beaver away at something is to work hard on it with concentration

becalmed *ADJECTIVE*
a ship that is becalmed is unable to move because there is no wind

The fishing fleet stood becalmed at the horizon as if it had come to the end of the world and could go no further. — *Anita Desai, The Village by the Sea*

because *CONJUNCTION*
used to show a reason for something or a cause of something ◆ *I did this because I was told to.* ◆ *We had to stay in because of the bad weather.*

WORD HISTORY from an earlier phrase *by cause*

beck *NOUN*
to be at someone's beck and call is to be always ready and waiting to do what they ask

beckon *VERB* **beckons, beckoning, beckoned**
to make a sign to someone asking them to come towards you

WORD HISTORY related to *beacon*

become *VERB* **becomes, becoming, became, become**
1 to begin to be ◆ *The village was becoming obscured by a blanket of fog.*
2 to come or grow to be ◆ *Within a few years he had become London's most famous archaeologist.*
3 a piece of clothing becomes someone if it makes them look attractive
4 to become of something is to happen to it ◆ *Whatever became of your plan to write a novel?*

bed *NOUN* **beds**
1 a piece of furniture for sleeping or resting, usually with a mattress and coverings
2 a plot of ground in a garden for growing plants
3 the bottom of the sea or of a river
4 a flat base; a foundation
5 a layer of rock or soil
to go to bed is to get into bed to go to sleep
to go to bed with someone (*informal*) is to have sexual intercourse with them

bed *VERB* **beds, bedding, bedded**
to bed down is to settle down to sleep, usually in a temporary bed

bedazzle *VERB* **bedazzles, bedazzling, bedazzled**
to astonish someone by being impressive ◆ *Images from the new space telescope have bedazzled astronomers.*

bedbug *NOUN* **bedbugs**
a tiny wingless insect that infests bedding

bedclothes *PLURAL NOUN*
sheets and blankets for covering a bed

bedding *NOUN*
items such as mattresses, pillows, and bedclothes that are put on a bed to make it comfortable

bedevil (*say* bi-**dev**-il) *VERB* **bedevils, bedevilling, bedevilled**
to trouble or cause continual problems for someone or something

WORD HISTORY from an earlier meaning of being possessed by a *devil* or evil spirit

bedfellow *NOUN* **bedfellows**
people or things that are bedfellows are temporarily connected or allied with each other ◆ *The country has made alliances with some unlikely bedfellows in the past.*

bedlam *NOUN*
noisy confusion; uproar

WORD HISTORY from *Bedlam*, the popular name of the Hospital of St Mary of Bethlehem, a London mental hospital in the 14th century

Bedouin (*say* **bed**-oo-in) *NOUN* **Bedouin**
a member of a nomadic Arab people living in the desert regions of Arabia and North Africa

WORD HISTORY via Old French from Arabic *badawi* 'desert dweller'

bedpan *NOUN* **bedpans**
a portable container for use as a toilet by someone who is bedridden

bedraggled (*say* bid-**rag**-eld) *ADJECTIVE*
looking untidy or messy, especially after getting very wet

At three o'clock on the afternoon of May 20, 1916, three bedraggled, hairy men staggered into Stromness. — *Paul Dowswell, True Polar Adventures*

WORD HISTORY from an old word *draggle* meaning 'to make dirty'

bedridden *ADJECTIVE*
someone who is bedridden is too ill or weak to get out of bed

bedrock *NOUN*
1 solid rock beneath soil
2 the fundamental facts or principles on which an idea or belief is based

bedroom *NOUN* **bedrooms**
a room for sleeping in

bedside *NOUN* **bedsides**
a space beside a bed

bedsitter or **bedsit** *NOUN* **bedsitters** or **bedsits**
a room used for both living and sleeping in

bedspread *NOUN* **bedspreads**
a covering spread over a bed during the day

bedstead *NOUN* **bedsteads**
the framework of a bed

bedtime *NOUN* **bedtimes**
the time for going to bed

bee *NOUN* **bees**
1 a stinging insect with four wings that produces wax and honey
2 a meeting or competition for a special purpose, e.g. a sewing bee or a spelling bee
to have a bee in your bonnet about something is to be obsessed with or continually thinking about it
WORD HISTORY from Old English *beo*

beech *NOUN* **beeches**
1 a tree with smooth grey bark and glossy leaves, which produces nuts in spiky cases
2 the light-coloured wood from a beech tree
WORD HISTORY from Old English *bece*

beef *NOUN*
meat from an ox, bull, or cow
WORD HISTORY from Old French *boef*, related to Latin *bos* 'ox', also the source of our word *bovine*

beef *VERB* **beefs, beefing, beefed**
to beef something up is to make it stronger or bigger and more impressive

beefeater *NOUN* **beefeaters**
one of the guards at the Tower of London who wear a uniform based on Tudor dress
WORD HISTORY originally a scornful word for a fat, lazy servant

beefy *ADJECTIVE*
solid or muscular
▷ **beefiness** *NOUN*

beehive *NOUN* **beehives**
a box or other container in which a colony of bees is kept

beeline *NOUN*
to make a beeline for something is to go straight and quickly towards it

Beelzebub *NOUN* (*say* bee-**el**-zi-bub)
the Devil; Satan
WORD HISTORY from a Hebrew phrase meaning literally 'Lord of the Flies'

been *past participle of* **be**

beep *VERB* **beeps, beeping, beeped**
1 an electronic device beeps when it gives out a short high-pitched sound as a signal
2 a car horn beeps when it sounds as a warning signal
3 to press a car horn as a signal

beeper *NOUN* **beepers**
(*informal*) an electronic pager

beer *NOUN* **beers**
an alcoholic drink made from malt and flavoured with hops
▷ **beery** *ADJECTIVE*
WORD HISTORY from Old English *beor*, related to Latin *biber* 'to drink' and to our word *beverage*

beeswax *NOUN*
a dark yellow substance produced by bees to build honeycombs, used in making candles and wood polish

beet *NOUN* **beet** or **beets**
1 a beetroot
2 a sugar beet is a root vegetable with sweet flesh used for making sugar
WORD HISTORY from Old English *bete*

beetle *NOUN* **beetles**
an insect with two pairs of wings, the front pair forming hard covers for the back pair
WORD HISTORY from Old English *bitula* from *bitan* 'to bite', because of its biting mouthparts

beetling *ADJECTIVE*
1 beetling eyebrows are bushy and stick out
2 a beetling cliff is overhanging

beetroot *NOUN* **beetroot**
a root vegetable with dark red flesh, eaten cooked

befall *VERB* **befalls, befalling, befell, befallen**
(*formal*) to happen to someone ◆ *The film is about a tragedy that befalls an American family.*

befit *VERB* **befits, befitting, befitted**
to be suitable or appropriate for an event or situation

before *ADVERB, PREPOSITION, CONJUNCTION*
1 used to show that something is in front or ahead in position ◆ *A vast landscape lay before them.*
2 used to show that something lies ahead in time ◆ *He had the whole afternoon before him.*
3 used to show that something occurs, or has occurred, at an earlier time ◆ *We've seen this film before.*
4 used to show that you prefer one thing over another ◆ *Death before defeat!*
5 to appear before a court or judge is to appear officially in their presence
WORD FAMILY Words which include 'before' in their meaning sometimes begin with *pre-*: for example, *preoccupied* means 'occupied before' (i.e. 'having your thoughts already busy with something') and a *preface* is a part of a book that comes before the main text.

beforehand *ADVERB*
earlier; in readiness ◆ *To save time, chop all the vegetables beforehand.*

befriend *VERB* **befriends, befriending, befriended**
to make friends with someone

beg *VERB* **begs, begging, begged**
1 to ask other people for money or food to live on
2 to ask someone to do something seriously or desperately ◆ *She begged them not to leave her.*
3 a dog begs when it sits up with its front paws off the ground
4 something that is going begging is available because no one else wants it
to beg the question is to argue in an illogical way by relying on the result that you are trying to prove
I beg your pardon
1 I apologize
2 I did not hear what you said

began *past tense of* **begin**

beget *VERB* **begets, begetting, begot, begotten** (*old use*)
1 to be the father of someone
2 to produce or cause something ◆ *Violence only begets more violence.*

beggar *NOUN* **beggars**
1 a person who lives by begging for food or money
2 (*informal*) a person ◆ *Aren't you dressed yet, you lazy beggar?*
▷ **beggary** *NOUN*

beggar *VERB* **beggars, beggaring, beggared**
to beggar belief is to be too extraordinary or unlikely to be believed

begin *VERB* **begins, beginning, began, begun**
1 to do the earliest or first part of something ◆ *I'll have to begin by explaining the Internet again.*
2 to start speaking
3 to come into existence ◆ *The programme begins at 8 p.m.*
4 to begin with something is to have it as the first part ◆ *The word 'ptarmigan' begins with a 'p'.*

beginner *NOUN* **beginners**
someone who is just beginning to learn a subject or skill

beginning *NOUN* **beginnings**
1 the first part of something
2 the starting point or origin of something

begone *EXCLAMATION*
(*old use*) go away immediately ◆ *Begone from my sight, you miserable worm!*

begonia (*say* big-**oh**-nee-a) *NOUN* **begonias**
a garden plant with brightly coloured flowers and jagged leaves

WORD HISTORY named after Michel Bégon, a Frenchman who encouraged the study of plants in the late 17th century

begot *past tense of* **beget**

begotten *past participle of* **beget**

begrudge *VERB* **begrudges, begrudging, begrudged**
1 to resent the fact that someone has something ◆ *Do you begrudge me my success?*
2 to resent having to do something ◆ *I don't begrudge paying that much for a ticket if it's a good concert.*

beguile (*say* big-**yl**) *VERB* **beguiles, beguiling, beguiled**
1 to amuse or fascinate someone
2 to trick someone into doing something ◆ *Stiff breezes and deserted sandy beaches beguiled us into believing we were heading in the right direction.*

begun *past participle of* **begin**

behalf *NOUN*
1 to act on behalf of a person or group is to be their representative
2 to do something on behalf of a charity is to do it for their benefit ◆ *a sponsored swim on behalf of whale conservation*

USAGE NOTE Take care not to say *on behalf of someone* when you mean simply 'by' someone: *This was a serious mistake on behalf of the government.* You can use *on the part of* instead: *This was a serious mistake on the part of the government.*

behave *VERB* **behaves, behaving, behaved**
1 to act in a particular way ◆ *He decided to behave as if nothing had happened.*
2 to behave or behave yourself is to show good manners

behaviour *NOUN*
the way that someone behaves or acts
▷ **behavioural** *ADJECTIVE*

behead *VERB* **beheads, beheading, beheaded**
1 to cut the head off someone or something
2 to execute someone by cutting their head off

behemoth *NOUN* (*say* bi-**hee**-moth) **behemoths**
an enormous beast or monster

WORD HISTORY from a Hebrew word meaning 'beast'

behest *NOUN*
(*formal*) to do something at someone's behest is to do it when they have asked you or ordered you to do it

behind *PREPOSITION, ADVERB*
1 used to show that someone or something is on the further side towards the back ◆ *He hid his bag behind a chair.*
2 used to show that something is immediately following ◆ *He set off and his family followed behind.*
3 used to show that something is in a place people have left ◆ *They had to leave a lot of their old furniture behind.*
4 used to show that someone is not keeping up in time or progress ◆ *We're already half an* ▶▶

a b c d e f g h i j k l m n o p q r s t u v w x y z

hour behind schedule. ◆ *By now she was behind with her work.*

5 used to show that something is the cause or reason for something ◆ *There is a simple idea behind this suggestion.*

6 used to show that someone is giving support for an idea or plan ◆ *I thought you said you'd be behind my proposal.*

to do something behind someone's back is to do it deceitfully without telling them

to be behind the times is to be old-fashioned or out of date

behind *NOUN* **behinds**
(*informal*) your buttocks; your bottom

behindhand *ADVERB, ADJECTIVE*
late or slow in doing something

behold *VERB* **beholds, beholding, beheld**
(*old use*) to see something in front of you
▷ **beholder** *NOUN*

beholden *ADJECTIVE*
to be beholden to someone is to be indebted to them for something they have done

behove *VERB* **behoves, behoving, behoved**
you say it behoves someone to do something when it is their duty to do it
WORD HISTORY from Old English *behofian* 'to need'

beige (*say* bayzh) *NOUN, ADJECTIVE*
a very light brown colour
WORD HISTORY a French word, perhaps related to Latin *bombax* 'cotton' which is the source of our word *bombastic*

being *NOUN* **beings**
1 being is existence or consciousness

'The dragons do not dream. They are dreams. They do not work magic: it is their substance, their being.' — *Ursula Le Guin, The Farthest Shore*

2 a being is a living creature

bejewelled *ADJECTIVE*
decorated with jewels

belabour *VERB* **belabours, belabouring, belaboured**
1 to attack someone with words or blows
2 to belabour a point or subject is to discuss it in too much detail

belated *ADJECTIVE*
coming very late or too late
▷ **belatedly** *ADVERB*

belay *VERB* **belays, belaying, belayed**
to fasten a rope by winding it round a peg or spike
WORD HISTORY from Dutch *beleggen*

belch *VERB* **belches, belching, belched**
1 to send out wind from your stomach through your mouth noisily
2 a machine or volcano belches smoke or fire when it has smoke or fire pouring out of it

belch *NOUN* **belches**
an act of belching
WORD HISTORY from Old English *bælcan*

beleaguered (*say* bil-eeg-erd) *ADJECTIVE*
1 experiencing a lot of difficulties or criticism
2 a beleaguered place is one under siege
WORD HISTORY from Dutch *belegeren* 'to camp around'

belfry *NOUN* **belfries**
1 a part of a church steeple in which bells are hung
2 a bell tower
WORD HISTORY from Old French *berfrei* 'siege tower', because the first part of the word became confused with *bell*

belie (*say* bi-ly) *VERB* **belies, belying, belied**
1 to give a false idea of something
2 to show that something is untrue ◆ *New research belies the idea that Mars was once a warm, wet planet.*
WORD HISTORY from Old English *beleogan*

belief *NOUN* **beliefs**
1 the feeling that something exists or is true
2 to have belief in someone is to have trust or confidence in them
3 something that a person believes
4 acceptance of the teachings of a particular religion

beyond belief too extraordinary or unlikely to be believed; absurd

believable *ADJECTIVE*
able to be believed ◆ *They changed their story to make it more believable.*
▷ **believably** *ADVERB*

believe *VERB* **believes, believing, believed**
1 to accept that something is true
2 to accept that someone is telling the truth
3 to think or suppose something ◆ *I believe it's starting to snow.*
4 to believe in a religious or mythological being is to think that they exist ◆ *When did you stop believing in Santa Claus?*
5 to believe in someone is to think that they are good or can be relied on
▷ **believer** *NOUN*

belittle *VERB* **belittles, belittling, belittled**
to talk about something as if it were unimportant or of little value
▷ **belittlement** *NOUN*

bell *NOUN* **bells**
1 a cup-shaped metal instrument that makes a ringing sound when struck by the clapper hanging inside it
2 a device that makes a ringing or buzzing sound to attract attention
3 a bell-shaped object

to ring a bell is to call up a memory, or to sound familiar

a b c d e f g h i j k l m n o p q r s t u v w x y z

belladonna *NOUN*
deadly nightshade (a poisonous plant)

WORD HISTORY from Italian *bella donna* 'beautiful woman', because a drug from the plant was used to dilate pupils, making eyes look brighter and more beautiful

bellbird *NOUN*
a New Zealand forest bird with a clear bell-like song

belle *NOUN* (*say* bel) **belles**
a beautiful girl or woman ◆ *You'll be the belle of the ball.*

WORD HISTORY a French word meaning 'beautiful'

bellicose (*say* **bel**-ik-ohs) *ADJECTIVE*
aggressive and eager to fight

WORD HISTORY from Latin *bellum* 'war', also the source of our word *rebel*

belligerent (*say* bil-**ij**-er-ent) *ADJECTIVE*
1 hostile and aggressive ◆ *The tone of his message was quite belligerent.*
2 belligerent groups or countries are fighting each other in a war

▷ **belligerently** *ADVERB*
▷ **belligerence** *NOUN*

WORD HISTORY from Latin *belligerare* 'to wage war', from *bellum* 'war'

bellow *NOUN* **bellows**
1 the loud deep sound made by a bull or other large animal
2 a loud deep shout

bellow *VERB* **bellows, bellowing, bellowed**
to give a loud deep shout

bellows *PLURAL NOUN*
a device with an air bag which is expanded and then squeezed to pump air into a fire

WORD HISTORY from Old English *belig* 'bag', also the source of our word *belly*

belly *NOUN* **bellies**
1 your stomach
2 a fat or protruding stomach

WORD HISTORY from Old English *belig* 'bag', related to our words *billow* and *bolster*

belly button *NOUN* **belly buttons**
(*informal*) your navel

bellyflop *NOUN* **bellyflops**
a dive into water in which you land flat on your front

belong *VERB* **belongs, belonging, belonged**
1 something that belongs to someone is owned by them
2 to belong somewhere is to have a proper place there

'I do not belong there, in the great cities among foreign men. I do not belong to any land.' — *Ursula Le Guin, The Tombs of Atuan*

3 people who belong to a club or organization are members of it

belongings *PLURAL NOUN*
a person's possessions

beloved *ADJECTIVE*
(*formal*) dearly loved

beloved *NOUN* (*say* bi-**luv**-id) **beloveds**
a much loved person

below *PREPOSITION, ADVERB*
used to show a lower place or position; underneath

WORD FAMILY Words which include 'below' in their meaning sometimes begin with *hypo-* or *sub-*: for example, *hypodermic* means 'under the skin', and a *submarine* is 'a ship that travels below the surface of the water'.

belt *NOUN* **belts**
1 a strip of material such as cloth or leather worn round your waist
2 a continuous moving band used in engines and machinery
3 a long narrow region ◆ *the asteroid belt*
4 an action or comment that is below the belt is unfair and often hurtful
5 to have an experience or qualification under your belt is to have successfully done or acquired it

belt *VERB* **belts, belting, belted**
1 to fasten something with a belt
2 (*informal*) to hit or beat someone
3 (*informal*) to run or travel very fast
4 rain is belting down when it is falling very heavily

to belt something out a singer belts out a tune when they sing it very strongly and loudly

to belt up
1 is to fasten your seatbelt in a car
2 (*informal*) is to stop talking

WORD HISTORY via Old English from Latin *balteus* 'girdle'

Beltane *NOUN* (*say* **bel**-tayn)
an ancient Celtic festival at the beginning of May in which bonfires were lit

WORD HISTORY from Gaelic *bealltainn*

bemused *ADJECTIVE*
puzzled or confused

WORD HISTORY from *muse* 'to wonder'

bench *NOUN* **benches**
1 a long seat made of wood or stone
2 a long table for working at in a workshop or laboratory
3 the seat where judges or magistrates sit
4 the judges or magistrates hearing a case

WORD HISTORY from Old English *benc*, related to our word *bank* 'sloping ground'

benchmark *NOUN* **benchmarks**

1 a standard or point of reference against which things can be compared or assessed ◆ *We set out to create a new benchmark for computer games.*

2 a surveyor's mark cut in a wall or stone to act as a reference point

WORD HISTORY so called because surveyors once used their marks to secure a bracket called a *bench*, on which they mounted their measuring equipment

bend *VERB* **bends, bending, bent**

1 to make something curved and no longer straight

2 to move your upper body downwards; to stoop ◆ *Can you bend and touch your toes?*

3 a road or path bends when it curves to take a new direction

bend *NOUN* **bends**

a place where something bends; a curve or turn

beneath *PREPOSITION, ADVERB*

1 under; underneath

2 an action or behaviour that is beneath someone is unworthy of them ◆ *Isn't reading other people's emails a bit beneath you?*

benediction *NOUN* **benedictions**

a prayer asking for blessing in a Christian church service

WORD HISTORY from Latin *benedicere* 'to say well to', from *bene* 'well' and *dicere* 'to say'

benefactor *NOUN* **benefactors**

someone who donates money to a person, cause, or institution

WORD HISTORY from Latin *bene facere* 'to do well to', from *bene* 'well' and *facere* 'to do'

beneficial *ADJECTIVE*

having a good or helpful effect ◆ *According to the packet, this tea is beneficial for headaches.*

WORD HISTORY from Latin *beneficium* 'favour, support'

beneficiary (*say* ben-if-**ish**-er-ee) *NOUN* **beneficiaries**

someone who benefits from another person's will

benefit *NOUN* **benefits**

1 an advantage that something brings

2 a payment to which someone is entitled from government funds or from an insurance policy

benefit *VERB* **benefits, benefiting, benefited**

1 to give an advantage to someone or something

2 to receive an advantage from something ◆ *We would all benefit from the introduction of regular training courses.*

WORD HISTORY via Old French from Latin *benefactum* 'good deed'

benevolent *ADJECTIVE*

1 a benevolent person is kind and helpful

2 a benevolent fund is one that collects money for charity

▷ **benevolently** *ADVERB*

▷ **benevolence** *NOUN*

WORD HISTORY via Old French from Latin *bene* 'well' and *volens* 'wishing'

benign (*say* bin-**yn**) *ADJECTIVE*

1 a benign expression or action is a kindly one

2 benign weather or a benign climate is mild or favourable

3 a benign tumour is not malignant or cancerous

▷ **benignly** *ADVERB*

WORD HISTORY from Latin *benignus* 'kind-hearted'

bent *ADJECTIVE*

1 curved or crooked

2 (*informal*) dishonest or corrupt

to be bent on doing something is to be determined to do it

bent *NOUN*

a natural inclination or talent

benzene *NOUN*

a colourless liquid obtained from coal tar and used as a solvent, motor fuel, and in the manufacture of plastics

WORD HISTORY via French from Arabic *lubanjawi* 'incense from Sumatra'

benzine *NOUN*

a colourless liquid obtained from petroleum and used as a solvent in dry cleaning

bequeath *VERB* **bequeaths, bequeathing, bequeathed**

to leave a possession to someone in your will

WORD HISTORY from Old English *becwethan* 'to speak about', from *cwethan* 'to say, speak', because a will is the expression of someone's words

bequest *NOUN* **bequests**

something left to a person in a will

berate *VERB* **berates, berating, berated**

to scold someone angrily ◆ *I was berating myself for sleeping so late.*

WORD HISTORY from an old word *rate* meaning 'to scold'

Berber *NOUN* **Berbers**

a member of a people living in North Africa

WORD HISTORY from Arabic *barbar*, also the origin of *Barbary Coast*, an old name for the Mediterranean coast of North Africa

bereaved *ADJECTIVE*

someone who is bereaved has recently suffered the death of a close relative

▷ **bereavement** *NOUN*

WORD HISTORY from an old word *reave* meaning 'to take by force'

bereft *ADJECTIVE*
to be bereft of something is to be deprived of it or be without it ◆ *We felt bereft of all hope.*
WORD HISTORY an old form of *bereaved*

beret (*say* **bair**-ay) *NOUN* **berets**
a round flat cap with no peak
WORD HISTORY a French word, related to Latin *birrus* 'hooded cloak'

bergamot (*say* **ber**-ga-mot) *NOUN*
1 a fragrant oil extracted from the rind of a type of orange, used to flavour tea
2 a fragrant Mediterranean herb
WORD HISTORY from *Bergamo*, a town in northern Italy where the oil was first produced and sold

beriberi (*say* berry-berry) *NOUN*
a tropical disease which affects the nervous system, caused by a vitamin deficiency
WORD HISTORY a Sinhalese word meaning 'weakness'. Sinhalese is the main language spoken in Sri Lanka.

Bermuda shorts *PLURAL NOUN*
loose-fitting knee-length shorts

berry *NOUN* **berries**
a small round juicy fruit without a stone
WORD HISTORY from Old English *berige*

berserk (*say* ber-**serk**) *ADJECTIVE*
to go berserk is to go into an uncontrollable and violent rage
WORD HISTORY an Old Norse name for a wild warrior that meant literally 'bear coat'

berth *NOUN* **berths**
1 a sleeping place on a ship or train
2 a place where a ship can moor
to give someone a wide berth is to avoid them by keeping at a safe distance

berth *VERB* **berths, berthing, berthed**
to moor in a berth
WORD HISTORY from *bear* 'to carry or support'

beryl *NOUN* **beryls**
a pale-green precious stone

beseech *VERB* **beseeches, beseeching, beseeched** or **besought**
to ask or beg someone earnestly to do something
WORD HISTORY related to *seek*

beset *VERB* **besets, besetting, beset**
to surround or attack a person or place from all sides

'The shadow of Mordor lies on distant lands,' answered Aragorn. 'Saruman has fallen under it. Rohan is beset.' — *J. R. R. Tolkien, The Fellowship of the Ring*

beside *PREPOSITION*
1 by the side of; near
2 compared with ◆ *My model looks rubbish beside yours.*
to be beside yourself is to be very excited or upset
WORD HISTORY from Old English *be sidan* 'by the side'

besides *PREPOSITION, ADVERB*
1 in addition to

Ransom had met other things in Mars besides the Martians. — *C. S. Lewis, Perelandra*

2 also; in addition

besiege *VERB* **besieges, besieging, besieged**
1 to surround a place in order to capture it
2 to crowd round a person or group

besotted *ADJECTIVE*
to be besotted with someone or something is to be too fond of them, or fond of them in a silly way ◆ *We're all besotted with the new puppy.*
WORD HISTORY from an old word *sot* 'to make stupid'

besought *past tense of* **beseech**

best *ADJECTIVE*
1 of the most excellent kind
2 most able to do something ◆ *Who is the best speaker here?*
at best in the most favourable interpretation

best *ADVERB*
1 in the greatest degree; most ◆ *Which one did they like best?*
2 most usefully; most wisely ◆ *We had best go.*

best *NOUN*
1 the best part or example of something ◆ *The best is yet to come.*
2 someone or something that is better than all others ◆ *We bought the best we could afford.*
3 to do your best to do something is to try as hard as you can to do it
4 a contest which is the best of a number of games is won by whoever wins most games ◆ *Let's make it the best of three.*

bestial (*say* best-ee-al) *ADJECTIVE*
savagely cruel or inhuman
▷ **bestiality** *NOUN*
WORD HISTORY from Latin *bestia* 'beast'

best man *NOUN* **best men**
the bridegroom's chief attendant at a wedding

bestow *VERB* **bestows, bestowing, bestowed**
to bestow a gift on someone is to present them with it formally
▷ **bestowal** *NOUN*

best-seller *NOUN* **best-sellers**
a book that has sold in large numbers

bet *NOUN* **bets**
1 an agreement that you will receive money if you are correct in choosing the winner of a race or game, or in saying something will happen, and will lose money if you are not correct
2 the amount of money you place on a bet

bet *VERB* **bets, betting, bet** or **betted**
1 to make a bet
2 (*informal*) to bet that something happens is to think that it is very likely to take place ◆ *I bet you he misses the start of the film.*

beta (*say* **beet**-a) *NOUN*
the second letter of the Greek alphabet, equivalent to Roman *B, b*

bête noire (*say* bayt **nwahr**) *NOUN*
someone or something you strongly dislike
WORD HISTORY a French phrase meaning literally 'black beast'

betide *VERB*
you say woe betide someone to warn them they will be in trouble if they do a particular thing
WORD HISTORY from Old English *tidan* 'to happen'

betoken *VERB* **betokens, betokening, betokened**
to be a sign of something

betray *VERB* **betrays, betraying, betrayed**
1 to be disloyal to someone you know, or to your country or beliefs
2 to reveal hidden information without meaning to
▷ **betrayal** *NOUN*
▷ **betrayer** *NOUN*
WORD HISTORY from Latin *tradere* 'to deliver'

betrothed *ADJECTIVE*
(*formal*) engaged to be married
▷ **betrothal** *NOUN*

better *ADJECTIVE*
1 more excellent; more satisfactory
2 recovered from illness ◆ *I'm feeling better now, thanks.*
to be better off than someone is to be more fortunate or richer than them
to get the better of someone is to defeat or outwit them
to go one better than someone is to improve on something they have done

better *ADVERB*
1 in a better way; more
2 to tell someone they had better do something is to advise or warn them to do it

'You'd better put on your moustache so as you get used to it.' — *Roald Dahl, The Great Automatic Grammatizator*

to think better of doing something is to change your mind and decide not to do it

better *VERB* **betters, bettering, bettered**
1 to better someone else is to do better than them
2 to better a score or achievement is to improve on it or surpass it
to better yourself is to improve your social position or status
▷ **betterment** *NOUN*

between *PREPOSITION, ADVERB*
1 used to show position or movement within two given limits ◆ *The house stood between two large oak trees.* ◆ *The train runs between London and Paris.*
2 used to show sharing ◆ *They divided the rest of the food between them.*
3 used to show a comparison or separation ◆ *It's hard to tell the difference between them.*
USAGE NOTE Take care to follow *between* with the object form of a pronoun (*me, her, him, them* or *us*). For example, you would say *'between you and me* (not *between you and I*).

betwixt *PREPOSITION, ADVERB*
(*old use*) between

bevel *VERB* **bevels, bevelling, bevelled**
to give a sloping edge to something

bevel *NOUN* **bevels**
a sloping edge

beverage *NOUN* **beverages**
a drink

bevy *NOUN* **bevies**
a large group of people or animals

bewail *VERB* **bewails, bewailing, bewailed**
to express great sorrow about something

beware *VERB*
to beware of someone or something is to be on your guard and watching out for them

bewilder *VERB* **bewilders, bewildering, bewildered**
to puzzle or confuse someone completely
▷ **bewilderment** *NOUN*
WORD HISTORY from an old word *wilder* 'to lose your way'

bewitch *VERB* **bewitches, bewitching, bewitched**
1 to put a magic spell on someone
2 to be bewitched by someone is to be fascinated and delighted by them

beyond *PREPOSITION, ADVERB*
1 used to show a position behind or further on ◆ *Beyond the garden wall was the street.*
2 used to show that something is greater or better

Their electronic machines were far beyond anything London's Engineers have been able to build. — *Philip Reeve, Mortal Engines*

3 a problem or activity that is beyond someone is one that is too difficult for them
WORD FAMILY Words which include 'beyond' in their meaning sometimes begin with *extra-* or *hyper-*: for example, *extraterrestrial* means 'beyond the limits of the earth', and a *hypermarket* is 'a supermarket that is beyond the normal size'.

Bhagavadgita (*say* bah-ga-vahd-**gee**-ta) ***NOUN***
the most famous religious text of Hinduism

WORD HISTORY a Sanskrit word meaning 'Song of the Lord'

bhaji ***NOUN*** **bhajis**
a ball of vegetables fried in batter, served as an appetizer in Indian cooking

bhangra (*say* **bahng**-gra) ***NOUN***
a style of music that combines traditional Punjabi music with rock music

WORD HISTORY from Punjabi (a language spoken in the Punjab)

biannual ***ADJECTIVE***
a biannual event happens twice a year
▷ **biannually** ***ADVERB***

USAGE NOTE Take care not to confuse this word with *biennial*. A biennial event happens once every two years.

bias ***NOUN*** **biases**
1 an opinion or feeling that strongly favours one side in preference to another; a prejudice
2 a distortion in statistical information because of a factor that has not been taken into account
3 a tendency of a ball or other object to swerve because of the way it is weighted
4 a dress or skirt that is made on the bias is cut so that the threads run diagonally across it

bias ***VERB*** **biases, biasing, biased**
to give a bias to something; to influence something unfairly

biased ***ADJECTIVE***
a biased opinion is one based on a person's likes or dislikes without examining the facts fairly

bib ***NOUN*** **bibs**
1 a cloth or covering put under a young child's chin to protect its clothes while eating
2 the front part of an apron, above the waist

WORD HISTORY probably from Latin *bibere* 'to drink'

Bible ***NOUN*** **Bibles**
1 (*Religion*) the sacred book of Judaism (the Old Testament) and of Christianity (the Old and New Testaments)
2 an indispensable manual or handbook ◆ *This should be every programmer's bible.*

WORD HISTORY from Greek *biblia* 'books' (originally rolls of papyrus from Byblos, a port now in Lebanon)

biblical ***ADJECTIVE***
to do with or mentioned in the Bible

bibliography (*say* bib-lee-**og**-ra-fee) ***NOUN*** **bibliographies**
1 a list of books about a subject or by a particular author
2 the study of books and their history
▷ **bibliographical** ***ADJECTIVE***
▷ **bibliographer** ***NOUN***

WORD HISTORY from Greek *biblion* 'book'

bicameral (*say* **by-kam**-er-al) ***ADJECTIVE***
a bicameral parliament has two legislative chambers

WORD HISTORY from Latin *camera* 'chamber'

bicarbonate ***NOUN***
a carbonate containing a double proportion of carbon dioxide

bicentenary (*say* by-sen-**teen**-er-ee) ***NOUN*** **bicentenaries**
a 200th anniversary
▷ **bicentennial** (*say* by-sen-**ten**-ee-al) ***ADJECTIVE***

biceps (*say* **by**-seps) ***NOUN*** **biceps**
the large muscle at the front of the the upper arm, which bends your elbow

WORD HISTORY a Latin word meaning 'two-headed', because its end is attached at two points

bicker ***VERB*** **bickers, bickering, bickered**
to quarrel constantly over unimportant things; to squabble

bicuspid ***NOUN*** **bicuspids**
a tooth with two points

WORD HISTORY from Latin *cuspis* 'sharp point'

bicycle ***NOUN*** **bicycles**
a two-wheeled vehicle driven by pedals

WORD HISTORY from Greek *kyklos* 'circle, wheel'

bid❶ ***NOUN*** **bids**
1 an offer of an amount you are willing to pay for something in a sale or auction
2 an effort to obtain or achieve something

bid ***VERB*** **bids, bidding, bid**
to make a bid
▷ **bidder** ***NOUN***

WORD HISTORY from Old English *beodan* 'to offer or command'

bid❷ ***VERB*** **bids, bidding, bid** or **bade, bid** or **bidden**
1 to bid a greeting or farewell to someone is to say hello or goodbye to them
2 to command someone to do something

'Truly,' said Aragorn ...'I would do as the master of the house bade me.' — *J. R. R. Tolkien, The Two Towers*

WORD HISTORY from Old English *biddan* 'to ask'

biddable ***ADJECTIVE***
meekly willing to obey

bidding ***NOUN***
to do someone's bidding is to do what they tell you to do

bide ***VERB*** **bides, biding, bided**
to bide your time is to wait for a good opportunity to do something

bidet (*say* bee-day) ***NOUN*** **bidets**
a low washbasin to sit on for washing the lower part of your body
WORD HISTORY a French word meaning 'pony', because you sit astride it like riding a pony

biennial (*say* by-**en**-ee-al) ***ADJECTIVE***
1 a biennial plant lives for two years, flowering and dying in the second year
2 a biennial event happens once every two years
▷ **biennially** ***ADVERB***
USAGE NOTE Take care not to confuse this word with *biannual*. A biannual event happens twice a year.

biennial ***NOUN*** **biennials**
a biennial plant
WORD HISTORY from Latin *biennis* 'of two years'

bier (*say* beer) ***NOUN*** **biers**
a movable stand on which a coffin or a dead body is placed before it is buried

bifocal (*say* by-**foh**-kal) ***ADJECTIVE***
bifocal lenses for glasses are made in two sections, with the upper part for looking at distant objects and the lower part for reading

bifocals ***PLURAL NOUN***
bifocal glasses

big ***ADJECTIVE*** **bigger, biggest**
1 large in size, amount, or intensity
2 important ◆ *We're staying in tonight to watch the big match.*
3 more grown-up; elder ◆ *I didn't know you had a big sister.*
4 (*informal*) kind or generous ◆ *That's big of you.*
SYNONYMS (meaning 1) large, great, high, tall, substantial, extensive, sizeable; (meaning 2) important, significant, major; (meaning 4) generous, considerate, kind, gracious

bigamy (*say* **big**-a-mee) ***NOUN***
the crime of marrying a person when you are already married to someone else
▷ **bigamous** ***ADJECTIVE***
▷ **bigamist** ***NOUN***
WORD HISTORY from Greek *gamos* 'married'

big bang ***NOUN***
the theory that the universe originated when a fireball of radiation expanded suddenly and then cooled

Big Brother ***NOUN***
a person or organization that supervises and controls people's lives in a sinister or frightening way
WORD HISTORY named after the tyrannical leader in George Orwell's novel *Nineteen Eighty-four* (1949)

big-head ***NOUN*** **big-heads**
(*informal*) a conceited person

bight ***NOUN*** **bights**
a long inward curve in a coastline

bigot ***NOUN*** **bigots**
someone who holds an opinion obstinately and is not willing to accept other people's beliefs
WORD HISTORY a French word

bigoted ***ADJECTIVE***
narrow-minded and unwilling to accept other people's beliefs
▷ **bigotry** ***NOUN***

big shot ***NOUN*** **big shots**
(*informal*) an important person

big toe ***NOUN*** **big toes**
the first and largest toe on your foot

big top ***NOUN*** **big tops**
the main tent at a circus

bigwig ***NOUN*** **bigwigs**
(*informal*) an important person
WORD HISTORY from the large wigs worn by distinguished men in the past

bijou (*say* **bee**-zhoo) ***ADJECTIVE***
small and elegant ◆ *a bijou flat*
WORD HISTORY a French word meaning 'jewel'

bike ***NOUN*** **bikes** (*informal*)
a bicycle or motorcycle

biking ***NOUN***
(*informal*) the sport of riding a bicycle or motorcycle
▷ **biker** ***NOUN***

bikini ***NOUN*** **bikinis**
a woman's two-piece swimsuit
WORD HISTORY from *Bikini*, an atoll in the West Pacific where an atomic bomb was tested in 1946, at about the time the bikini was first worn. Bikinis were supposed to have had an 'explosive' effect like the atomic bomb.

bilateral ***ADJECTIVE***
1 affecting both of two sides
2 a bilateral agreement or treaty is one between two people, groups, or countries

bilberry ***NOUN*** **bilberries**
a small dark-blue edible berry that grows on a shrub

bilby ***NOUN*** **bilbies**
an insect-eating marsupial animal of Australia, with long ears

bile ***NOUN***
1 a bitter yellowish liquid produced by your liver, which helps to digest fats
2 extreme anger and bitterness

bilge ***NOUN*** **bilges**
1 the bilges are the bottom of a ship, or the water that collects there
2 (*informal*) nonsense; worthless ideas
WORD HISTORY from an old spelling of *bulge*

bilingual (*say* by-**ling**-wal) *ADJECTIVE*
1 someone who is bilingual can speak two languages well
2 a bilingual text is written in two languages
WORD HISTORY from Latin *lingua* 'language'

bilious *ADJECTIVE*
1 feeling sick; nauseous
2 of a sickly colour ◆ *The queen was wearing a bilious green hat.*
3 spiteful or bad-tempered
▷ **biliousness** *NOUN*
WORD HISTORY from *bile*

bill❶ *NOUN* **bills**
1 a written statement of charges for goods or services that have been supplied ◆ *Can we have the bill, please?*
2 a poster or notice
3 a programme of entertainment at a cinema or theatre ◆ *Who's on the bill?*
4 the draft of a proposed law to be discussed by parliament
5 (*American*) a banknote ◆ *a ten-dollar bill*
bill of fare a menu
to fit or **fill the bill** is to be suitable for what is needed

bill *VERB* **bills, billing, billed**
1 to send a bill to someone
2 to announce or advertise something ◆ *This has been billed as the match of the century.*

bill❷ *NOUN* **bills**
a bird's beak

billabong *NOUN* **billabongs**
(*Australian*) a river branch that forms a backwater or a stagnant pool
The bush boy moved quickly. Skirting the outcrop of rock, he came to a place where a chain of billabongs went looping into the desert.
—*James Vance Marshall, Walkabout*
WORD HISTORY an Australian Aboriginal word

billboard *NOUN* **billboards**
a large board on which advertisements are displayed

billet *NOUN* **billets**
a temporary lodging for soldiers, especially in a private house

billet *VERB* **billets, billeting, billeted**
to house soldiers in a billet
WORD HISTORY from an earlier meaning 'an order to house troops', from Latin *bulla* 'seal, sealed letter'

billhook *NOUN* **billhooks**
a tool with a long handle and a curved blade, used for cutting branches off trees

billiards *NOUN*
a game in which three balls are struck with cues on a cloth-covered table
WORD HISTORY from French *billard* 'a cue'

billion *NOUN* **billions**
1 a thousand million (1,000,000,000)
2 (*old use*) a million million (1,000,000,000,000)
▷ **billionth** *ADJECTIVE, NOUN*
USAGE NOTE Most people now use *billion* to mean 'a thousand million'. In the past, though, this meaning was the one used in American English, while in British English the word was used for 'a million million'. Notice that you say *three billion* and *a few billion*, not *billions*.

billionaire *NOUN* **billionaires**
someone who possesses at least a billion pounds or dollars

billow *NOUN* **billows**
a large rolling mass of cloud, smoke, or steam

billow *VERB* **billows, billowing, billowed**
1 to fill with air and swell outwards
2 smoke or steam billows when it flows upwards and outwards

billycan *NOUN* **billycans**
a pot with a lid, used by campers as a kettle or cooking pot
WORD HISTORY from Australian Aboriginal *billa* 'water'

billy goat *NOUN* **billy goats**
a male goat (SEE ALSO **nanny goat**)

biltong *NOUN*
(*South African*) lean meat which is salted and dried in strips

bimbo *NOUN* **bimbos**
(*informal*) an attractive but unintelligent young woman
WORD HISTORY an Italian word meaning 'little child'

bimonthly *ADJECTIVE*
1 happening every two months
2 happening twice a month

bin *NOUN* **bins**
1 a container for rubbish or litter
2 a large container used for storing food or drink
WORD HISTORY via Old English from a Celtic word

bin *VERB* **bins, binning, binned**
to throw something away by putting it in a bin

binary (*say* **by**-ner-ee) *ADJECTIVE*
(*ICT*) involving sets of two; consisting of two parts
WORD HISTORY from Latin *bini* 'two together'

binary digit *NOUN* **binary digits**
(*ICT*) either of the two digits (0 and 1) used in the binary system

binary number *NOUN* **binary numbers**
(*ICT*) a number expressed in the binary system

binary star *NOUN*
two stars that revolve round each other

binary system or **binary notation** *NOUN*
(*ICT*) a system of expressing numbers by using the digits 0 and 1 only

bind *VERB* **binds, binding, bound**
1 to fasten a strip of material round something
2 to fasten the pages of a book into a cover
3 to tie someone up with a belt or strip of cloth
4 to bring people together or unite them ◆ *We are bound by ties of friendship.*
5 to make ingredients stick together in a solid mass ◆ *Now bind the mixture with egg yolk.*
6 to cover the edge of a piece of material in order to strengthen it or as a decoration
7 to make somebody agree to do something
to bind someone over is to make them agree not to break the law

bind *NOUN*
(*informal*) a difficult or annoying situation ◆ *It's such a bind having to change trains.*

binder *NOUN* **binders**
1 a cover for holding magazines or loose papers together
2 someone who binds books
3 a machine that binds harvested corn into sheaves or straw into bales

bindery *NOUN* **binderies**
a workshop where books are bound

bindi (*say* **bin**-dee) *NOUN* **bindis**
1 a coloured dot traditionally worn by Hindu girls and women on their forehead
2 a decorative jewel or tattoo worn on the forehead

binding *NOUN* **bindings**
1 the covering and glue which hold the pages of a book together
2 fabric used for binding the edges of a piece of material

binding *ADJECTIVE*
a binding agreement or promise is one that must be carried out or obeyed

bindweed *NOUN*
a twining plant with trumpet-shaped flowers

bine *NOUN*
the flexible stem of a climbing plant, especially a hop plant
WORD HISTORY from an old spelling of *bind*

binge (*say* binj) *NOUN* **binges**
(*informal*) a time spent eating or drinking too much

binge *VERB* **binds, binding, bound**
to spend time eating or drinking too much

bingo *NOUN*
a game using cards on which numbered squares are crossed out as the numbers are called out at random

binocular *ADJECTIVE*
for or using both eyes ◆ *binocular vision*

binoculars *PLURAL NOUN*
a device with lenses for both eyes, which makes distant objects seem nearer
WORD HISTORY from Latin *bini* 'two together' and *oculus* 'eye'

biochemistry *NOUN*
the study of the chemical composition and processes of living things
▷ **biochemical** *ADJECTIVE*
▷ **biochemically** *ADVERB*
▷ **biochemist** *NOUN*

biodegradable *ADJECTIVE*
biodegradable material can be broken down by bacteria in the environment
▷ **biodegradability** *NOUN*
▷ **biodegradation** *NOUN*

biodiversity *NOUN*
the variety of plant and animal life in a particular area

biography (*say* by-**og**-ra-fee) *NOUN* **biographies**
the published story of a person's life
▷ **biographical** *ADJECTIVE*
▷ **biographer** *NOUN*

biological *ADJECTIVE*
1 to do with biology
2 a child's biological parents are related to them by blood
3 a biological detergent is one that contains enzymes
▷ **biologically** *ADVERB*

biological clock *NOUN*
a natural mechanism that an organism has for controlling regular physical processes

biological warfare *NOUN*
the deliberate use of organisms to spread disease among an enemy

biology *NOUN*
the scientific study of the life and structure of living things
▷ **biologist** *NOUN*

bionic (*say* by-**on**-ik) *ADJECTIVE*
a bionic body part is operated by electronic devices

biopic (*say* **by**-oh-pik) *NOUN* **biopics**
(*informal*) a film about a person's life

biopsy (*say* **by**-op-see) *NOUN* **biopsies**
an examination of tissue from a living body

biorhythm *NOUN* **biorhythms**
a recurring cycle of physical, emotional, and intellectual activity said to occur in someone's life

bioscope *NOUN*
(*South African*) a cinema or cinema film

biosphere *NOUN* **biospheres**
all the parts of the Earth which contain living things

biotechnology *NOUN*
the use of living micro-organisms and biological processes in industrial and commercial production
▷ **biotechnological** *ADJECTIVE*
▷ **biotechnologist** *NOUN*

bipartisan (*say* by-parti-**zan**) *ADJECTIVE*
involving two political or other parties

bipartite (*say* by-**par**-tyt) *ADJECTIVE*
1 having two parts
2 involving two groups ◆ *a bipartite agreement*
WORD HISTORY from Latin *partitum* 'divided, parted'

biped (*say* by-ped) *NOUN* **bipeds**
a two-footed animal
WORD HISTORY from Latin *pedes* 'feet'

biplane (*say* by-playn) *NOUN* **biplanes**
an aeroplane with two sets of wings, one above the other

birch *NOUN* **birches**
1 a deciduous tree with smooth bark and slender branches
2 a bundle of birch twigs used in the past for flogging people

bird *NOUN* **birds**
1 a feathered animal with two wings and two legs
2 (*informal*) a young woman
WORD HISTORY from Old English *brid* 'young bird'

birdie *NOUN* **birdies**
1 (*informal*) a bird
2 a score in golf of one stroke under par for a hole

bird of paradise *NOUN* **birds of paradise**
a bird from New Guinea which has brightly coloured plumage

bird of prey *NOUN* **birds of prey**
a bird that feeds on animal flesh, such as an eagle or hawk

bird's-eye view *NOUN*
a view of something from above

biriani (*say* bi-ri-**ah**-ni) *NOUN*
an Indian dish made with highly seasoned rice and meat, fish, or vegetables
WORD HISTORY an Urdu word

Biro *NOUN* (*say* **by**-ro) **Biros**
(*trademark*) a ballpoint pen
WORD HISTORY named after its Hungarian inventor, László Biró (1900–85)

birth *NOUN* **births**
1 the process by which a baby or young animal comes out from its mother's body
2 a person's ancestry or parentage ◆ *He is of noble birth.*
3 the beginning of something ◆ *the birth of the Blues*
to give birth is to produce a baby or young animal
WORD FAMILY A related adjective (*technical*) is natal.

birth certificate *NOUN* **birth certificates**
an official document giving the date and place of a person's birth

birth control *NOUN*
using contraception and other ways of avoiding conceiving a baby

birthday *NOUN* **birthdays**
the anniversary of the day you were born
in your birthday suit completely naked

birthmark *NOUN* **birthmarks**
a coloured mark that has been on someone's skin since they were born

birth parent *NOUN* **birth parents**
someone's natural father or mother, as distinct from an adoptive parent

birthplace *NOUN* **birthplaces**
the house or district where you were born

birth rate *NOUN*
the number of children born in one year for every 1,000 people

birthright *NOUN*
a right or privilege to which someone is entitled through being born into a particular family or country

biscuit *NOUN* **biscuits**
1 a small flat kind of cake that has been baked until it is crisp
2 (*American*) a soft cake like a scone
3 a light brown colour
WORD HISTORY from Latin *bis* 'twice' and *coctus* 'cooked', because originally they were baked and then dried out in a cool oven to make them keep longer

bisect (*say* by-**sekt**) *VERB* **bisects, bisecting, bisected**
to divide something into two equal parts
▷ **bisection** *NOUN*
▷ **bisector** *NOUN*
WORD HISTORY from Latin *sectum* 'cut'

bisexual (*say* by-**sek**-shul) *ADJECTIVE*
1 a bisexual person is sexually attracted to both men and women
2 a bisexual flower has both male and female reproductive organs

bisexual *NOUN* **bisexuals**
a bisexual person

bishop *NOUN* **bishops**
1 a high-ranking member of the Christian clergy with authority over the work of the church in a city or district (called *diocese*)
2 a chess piece shaped like a bishop's mitre
WORD HISTORY via Old English from Latin *episcopus*

bishopric *NOUN* **bishoprics**
the position or diocese of a bishop

bismuth (*say* **biz**-muth) *NOUN*
1 a greyish-white metal
2 a compound of this used in medicine

bison (*say* **by**-son) *NOUN* **bison**
a wild ox found in North America and Europe, with a large shaggy head

bistro (*say* **bee**-stroh) *NOUN* **bistros**
a small restaurant
WORD HISTORY a French word

bit❶ *NOUN* **bits**
1 a small piece or amount of something
2 a moderate amount ◆ *He took a bit of persuading.*
3 a short distance or time ◆ *Wait a bit.*
4 to do your bit is to do your share of something
a bit slightly ◆ *By now she was feeling a bit tired.*
bit by bit gradually; little by little
quite a bit (*informal*) quite a lot; quite often
to bits
1 something falls or crumbles to bits when it breaks into small pieces
2 you love someone to bits when you love them very much
SYNONYMS (meaning 1) piece, chunk, morsel, scrap, fragment; (meaning 4) rather, fairly, slightly, somewhat, a little

bit❷ *NOUN* **bits**
1 the metal part of a horse's bridle that is put into its mouth
2 a detachable part of a drill used for boring
3 the part of a tool that cuts or grips things when twisted
to get the bit between your teeth is to begin to tackle a task in a determined way

bit❸ *NOUN* **bits**
(*ICT*) the smallest unit of information in a computer, expressed as 0 or 1

bit❹ *past tense of* **bite**

bitch *NOUN* **bitches**
1 a female dog, fox, or wolf
2 (*informal*) a spiteful and nasty woman

bitchy *ADJECTIVE*
spiteful and malicious
▷ **bitchily** *ADVERB*
▷ **bitchiness** *NOUN*

bite *VERB* **bites, biting, bit, bitten**
1 to cut or take something with your teeth
2 to pierce skin with a sting or teeth ◆ *I've been bitten all over by midges.*
3 to be in the habit of biting people ◆ *Does your dog bite?*
4 fish bite when they accept an angler's bait
5 to have an unpleasant effect ◆ *The pay cuts were beginning to bite.*
6 tyres bite when they grip or take hold on a surface
to bite off more than you can chew is to try to do more than you are capable of
to bite the dust (*informal*) is to die or be killed

bite *NOUN* **bites**
1 a mouthful cut off by biting ◆ *I'd only taken one bite of my sandwich.*
2 a wound or mark made by biting ◆ *They were covered in mosquito bites.*
3 a snack ◆ *Let's grab a bite to eat before the film.*

biting *ADJECTIVE*
1 a biting wind is very cold
2 a biting comment is sharp and critical

bitmap *NOUN* **bitmaps**
(*ICT*) a digital image made up of rows and columns of dots

bitmap *VERB* **bitmaps, bitmapping, bitmapped**
to make a bitmap image of something

bit part *NOUN* **bit parts**
a small part in a film or play

bitten *past participle of* **bite**

bitter *ADJECTIVE*
1 tasting sharp and unpleasant; not sweet
2 feeling hurt or resentful ◆ *He still feels bitter about the way he was treated.*
3 causing hurt or sorrow ◆ *a bitter disappointment*
4 bitter weather is extremely cold
▷ **bitterness** *NOUN*
WORD HISTORY related to *bite*

bitter *NOUN*
beer that is strongly flavoured with hops and has a bitter taste

bitterly *ADVERB*
1 sharply, unpleasantly
2 deeply or resentfully

Tom was bitterly disappointed that he was not allowed to climb the tower. — *Philippa Pearce, Tom's Midnight Garden*

bittern *NOUN* **bitterns**
a marsh bird related to the heron, known for the male's deep booming call

bitumen (*say* **bit**-yoo-min) *NOUN*
a black sticky substance obtained from petroleum, used for covering roads

bivalve (*say* **by**-valv) *NOUN* **bivalves**
a shellfish, such as an oyster or mussel, that has a shell with two hinged parts

bivouac (*say* **biv**-oo-ak) *NOUN* **bivouacs**
a temporary camp without tents

bivouac *VERB* **bivouacs, bivouacking, bivouacked**
to camp in a bivouac

biweekly *ADJECTIVE*
1 happening every two weeks
2 happening twice a week

bizarre (*say* biz-**ar**) *ADJECTIVE*
very odd in appearance or effect

WORD HISTORY from Italian *bizarro* 'angry'

blab *VERB* **blabs, blabbing, blabbed**
to let out a secret

black *ADJECTIVE*
1 of the very darkest colour, like coal or soot
2 having dark skin; of African or Australian Aboriginal ancestry
3 very dirty
4 dismal; not hopeful ◆ *The prospects for a quick recovery look black.*
5 a black look or mood is hostile or angry
6 involving tragedy or disaster ◆ *This has been a black day in our history.*
7 black tea or coffee has no milk added to it
8 black comedy presents a tragic theme or situation in comic terms

▷ **blackly** *ADVERB*
▷ **blackness** *NOUN*

black *NOUN* **blacks**
1 a black colour
2 black clothes ◆ *The mourners all wore black.*
3 a person with dark skin, especially a person with African or Australian Aboriginal ancestry

black *VERB* **blacks, blacking, blacked**
to make something black

to black out is to lose consciousness temporarily
to black something out is to cover it so that no light can penetrate
in black and white recorded in writing or print
in the black not owing any money; in credit

blackball *VERB* **blackballs, blackballing, blackballed**
to prevent someone from being elected as a member of a club by voting against them in a secret ballot

WORD HISTORY from the practice of voting against someone by placing a black ball in a ballot box

blackberry *NOUN* **blackberries**
a sweet dark purple berry which grows on a prickly bush

blackbird *NOUN* **blackbirds**
a European songbird, the male of which is black

blackboard *NOUN* **blackboards**
a dark board for writing on with chalk, used in classrooms

black box *NOUN* **black boxes**
a flight recorder of an aircraft, which records technical information about its flight

black economy *NOUN*
an unofficial system of employing and paying people without paying income tax and National Insurance contributions

blacken *VERB* **blackens, blackening, blackened**
1 to make something black, especially by burning

> A fire crackles in the hearth and a small, blackened cauldron hangs above the flames.
> — *Chris Priestley, Witch Hunt*

2 to blacken someone's name or reputation is to damage it
3 to become black

black eye *NOUN* **black eyes**
an eye with a bruise round it

blackguard (*say* **blag**-erd) *NOUN* **blackguards**
an old-fashioned word for a man who behaves in a wicked or dishonourable way

WORD HISTORY from an earlier phrase *black guard* 'the servants who did the dirty jobs'

blackhead *NOUN* **blackheads**
a small black spot blocking a pore in the skin

black hole *NOUN* **black holes**
a region in outer space with a gravitational field so intense that no matter or radiation can escape from it

black ice *NOUN*
hard thin transparent ice on roads

blackleg *NOUN* **blacklegs**
a person who continues to work while their fellow workers are on strike

WORD HISTORY from an earlier meaning of a disease that affected sheep

blacklist *NOUN* **blacklists**
a list of people who are disapproved of

blacklist *VERB* **blacklists, blacklisting, blacklisted**
to put someone on a blacklist

black magic *NOUN*
magic involving the summoning of evil spirits

blackmail *VERB* **blackmails, blackmailing, blackmailed**
to demand money from someone by threatening to reveal a secret which will damage their reputation

▷ **blackmailer** *NOUN*

WORD HISTORY from an old word *mail* meaning 'tax, tribute', because it was originally protection money paid to bandits

blackmail *NOUN*
the crime of blackmailing someone

black mark *NOUN*
a record of the fact that someone has done something that is disapproved of

black market *NOUN* **black markets**
the illegal buying and selling of goods or foreign currency

blackout *NOUN* **blackouts**
1 a period of darkness when no light must be shown
2 a temporary loss of consciousness
3 an order forbidding the release of information ◆ *There had been a total news blackout.*

black pudding *NOUN* **black puddings**
a large dark sausage made with pig's blood

black sheep *NOUN*
a member of a family or other group who is seen as a disgrace to it

blacksmith *NOUN* **blacksmiths**
a person who makes and repairs iron goods, especially someone who makes and fits horseshoes

WORD HISTORY so called because of the dark colour of iron

black spot *NOUN* **black spots**
a dangerous place where accidents often occur

black tie *NOUN*
formal dress for men which includes a black bow tie and a dinner jacket

black widow *NOUN*
a poisonous spider found in North America and the Far East. The female of one species eats its mate.

bladder *NOUN* **bladders**
1 the bag-like organ in your body in which urine collects
2 the inflatable bag inside a football

WORD HISTORY from Old English *blædr*, related to our word *blow*

bladderwrack *NOUN*
a type of seaweed with small air pockets on its strands

blade *NOUN* **blades**
1 the flat cutting edge of a knife, sword, or axe
2 the flat wide part of an oar, spade, or propeller
3 a long flat narrow leaf of grass
4 a broad flat bone ◆ *shoulder blade*

WORD HISTORY from Old English *blæd*, related to our words *bloom* and *blossom*

blame *VERB* **blames, blaming, blamed**
to blame someone is to say that they are responsible for something that is wrong

blame *NOUN* **blames**
responsibility for something that is wrong

WORD HISTORY from an Old French word, related to *blaspheme*

blameless *ADJECTIVE*
deserving no blame; innocent

blanch *VERB* **blanches, blanching, blanched**
1 if someone blanches, they turn pale with fear or fright
2 to make something white or pale
3 to blanch vegetables is to cook them quickly by plunging them in boiling water

WORD HISTORY from French *blanc* 'white'

blancmange (*say* bla-**monj**) *NOUN* **blancmanges**
a jelly-like pudding made with milk

WORD HISTORY from French *blanc* 'white' and *manger* 'to eat'

bland *ADJECTIVE*
1 having a mild flavour rather than a strong one ◆ *The chilli is a bit bland.*
2 not having any interesting features or qualities

Liz Finch, our student teacher, is bland, harmless and has no known habits. — *Nicky Singer, Feather Boy*

▷ **blandly** *ADVERB*
▷ **blandness** *NOUN*

WORD HISTORY from Latin *blandus* 'soothing'

blandishments *PLURAL NOUN*
flattering or coaxing words

WORD HISTORY related to *bland*

blank *ADJECTIVE*
1 not written or printed on; not showing any picture or words ◆ *The computer screen had gone blank.*
2 without interest or expression; not having or showing any thoughts

'Which way?' Buffy demanded, but Xander looked blank. 'I don't know.' — *Richie Tankersly Cusick, Buffy the Vampire Slayer: The Harvest*

▷ **blankly** *ADVERB*
▷ **blankness** *NOUN*

blank *NOUN* **blanks**
1 an empty space on a form or in a piece of writing
2 a blank cartridge

WORD HISTORY from French *blanc* 'white'

blank cartridge *NOUN* **blank cartridges**
a cartridge that makes a noise but does not fire a bullet

blank cheque *NOUN* **blank cheques**
a cheque with the amount not yet filled in

blanket *NOUN* **blankets**
1 a warm cloth covering for a bed
2 a thick soft layer covering something completely ◆ *There was a blanket of snow on the ground.*

blanket *VERB* **blankets, blanketing, blanketed**
to cover something completely with a thick soft layer

blanket *ADJECTIVE*
applying to all cases or circumstances ◆ *The authorities issued a blanket ban on traffic in the city centre.*

WORD HISTORY from an earlier meaning 'undyed woollen cloth', from French *blanc* 'white'

blank verse *NOUN*
(*Language*) unrhymed verse used in epic and dramatic poetry, usually in lines of ten syllables with five regular beats; for example, 'Friends, Romans, countrymen, lend me your ears'

blare *VERB* **blares, blaring, blared**
when a horn or trumpet blares it makes a loud harsh sound

blare *NOUN* **blares**
a loud harsh sound

blasé (*say* **blah**-zay) *ADJECTIVE*
not interested in or impressed by something because you are very familiar with it

WORD HISTORY a French word

blaspheme (*say* blas-**feem**) *VERB* **blasphemes, blaspheming, blasphemed**
1 to talk or write in a rude or disrespectful way about something that people consider holy or sacred
2 to swear or curse

WORD HISTORY from Greek *blasphēmos* 'evil-speaking'

blasphemy (*say* **blas**-fim-ee) *NOUN* **blasphemies**
rude or disrespectful talk about a holy or sacred person or thing
▷ **blasphemous** *ADJECTIVE*
▷ **blasphemously** *ADVERB*

blast *NOUN* **blasts**
1 a strong rush of wind or air
2 a loud noise ◆ *the blast of the trumpets*
3 to do something at full blast is to do it at full volume, strength, or speed

blast *VERB* **blasts, blasting, blasted**
1 to blow something up with explosives
2 to explode outwards

A bright red pall blasted from the cannon into the black sky. — *G. P. Taylor, Shadowmancer*

3 music or a sound blasts when it plays or sounds very loud

to blast off
1 a rocket or spacecraft blasts off when it is launched
2 to blast off a rocket or spacecraft is to launch it

WORD HISTORY from Old English *blest*, related to our words *blaze* 'to burn or shine' and *blow*

blast furnace *NOUN* **blast furnaces**
a furnace for smelting ore, which works by having hot air driven into it

blast-off *NOUN* **blast-offs**
the act of launching a rocket or spacecraft

blatant (*say* **blay**-tant) *ADJECTIVE*
very obvious ◆ *The excuse had been a blatant lie.*
▷ **blatantly** *ADVERB*

WORD HISTORY from an old word meaning 'noisy'

blaze ❶ *NOUN* **blazes**
a very bright flame, fire, or light

blaze *VERB* **blazes, blazing, blazed**
1 to burn or shine brightly
2 guns are blazing when they are being fired repeatedly
3 to be blazing with anger or fury is to feel extremely angry

WORD HISTORY from Old English *blæse* 'torch, flame'

blaze ❷ *NOUN* **blazes**
a white streak on a horse's face

blaze *VERB* **blazes, blazing, blazed**
to blaze a trail is to show the way for others to follow

blazer *NOUN* **blazers**
a light jacket, often with a badge or in the colours of a school or team

WORD HISTORY from *blaze* 'to burn or shine', because originally blazers were made in very bright colours

blazon *VERB* **blazons, blazoning, blazoned**
to announce something publicly and in a very noticeable way

bleach *NOUN*
a chemical substance used to remove colour from fabric or as a disinfectant

bleach *VERB* **bleaches, bleaching, bleached**
1 to remove colour from something using bleach
2 to take the colour out of something; to make something white or pale ◆ *Her hair had been bleached by hours in the sun.*
3 to become white or pale

WORD HISTORY from Old English *blæc* 'pale, shining', related to our word *bleak*

bleak *ADJECTIVE*
1 a bleak landscape is barren and cold
2 dreary or miserable ◆ *Things were looking a bit bleak.*
▷ **bleakly** *ADVERB*
▷ **bleakness** *NOUN*

WORD HISTORY from Old English *blæc* 'pale, shining', related to our word *bleach*

bleary *ADJECTIVE*
bleary eyes are tired and watery and make your vision blurred
▷ **blearily** *ADVERB*
▷ **bleariness** *NOUN*

bleat *NOUN* **bleats**
the natural cry of a lamb, goat, or calf

bleat *VERB* **bleats, bleating, bleated**
1 to cry with a bleat
2 to complain in an irritating way

bleed *VERB* **bleeds, bleeding, bled**
1 to lose blood
2 (in former times) to take blood or fluid from someone as a medical treatment
3 paint or dye bleeds when its colour runs

to bleed someone dry is to use up all their money or resources

my heart bleeds I am sorry for you, often said sarcastically with the meaning 'I don't care'

WORD HISTORY from Old English *bledan*, related to our words *blood* and *bless*

bleep *VERB* **bleeps, bleeping, bleeped**
when an electronic device bleeps it makes a short high-pitched sound as a signal

bleep *NOUN* **bleeps**
a bleeping sound

bleeper *NOUN* **bleepers**
a small electronic device that bleeps when the wearer is contacted

blemish *NOUN* **blemishes**
1 a mark or flaw that spoils a thing's appearance
2 something that spoils a person's character or reputation

WORD HISTORY from Old French *blemir* 'to make pale, to injure'

blemish *VERB* **blemishes, blemishing, blemished**
to spoil something with a blemish

blench *VERB* **blenches, blenching, blenched**
to back away in fear; to flinch

WORD HISTORY from Old English *blencan* 'to cheat or deceive'

blend *VERB* **blends, blending, blended**
1 to mix ingredients together ◆ *Blend the eggs and milk together.*
2 things blend when they combine well with each other ◆ *The colours blend well.*

to blend in is to fit in with your surroundings

blend *NOUN* **blends**
1 a mixture of different types of something ◆ *a smooth blend of coffee*
2 (*Language*) a word made from parts of other words and combining their meanings, e.g. *motel* from *motor* and *hotel*

blender *NOUN* **blenders**
an electric machine used to mix food or turn it into liquid

bless *VERB* **blesses, blessing, blessed**
1 to make something sacred or holy
2 to ask God to protect someone or something ◆ *The priest blessed the newly married couple.*
3 to give your approval or support to something

to be blessed with something is to be fortunate in having it ◆ *She is blessed with good health.*

WORD HISTORY from Old English *bletsian*, related to our words *bleed* and *blood*. The original meaning was 'to mark with blood'.

blessed (*say* **bles**-id) *ADJECTIVE*
1 holy or sacred
2 bringing happiness or relief ◆ *a few moments of blessed calm*

blessing *NOUN* **blessings**
1 a prayer that blesses a person or thing
2 something that you are grateful for ◆ *It's a blessing no one was hurt.*

blew *past tense of* **blow**[1]

blight *NOUN* **blights**
1 a disease that withers plants
2 something that spoils or damages something ◆ *Illness put a blight on all their holidays.*

blight *VERB* **blights, blighting, blighted**
1 to affect a plant with blight
2 to spoil or damage something ◆ *Knee injuries have blighted his career.*

blind *ADJECTIVE*
1 without the ability to see
2 without any thought or understanding ◆ *He was in a blind rage.*
3 a blind bend or corner is one where you cannot see clearly ahead

to turn a blind eye is to pretend not to notice something

▷ **blindly** *ADVERB*
▷ **blindness** *NOUN*

blind *ADVERB*
to do something blind is to do it without being able to see clearly

blind *VERB* **blinds, blinding, blinded**
1 to make someone blind
2 to dazzle someone with bright light
3 to prevent you from realizing something ◆ *Her loyalty blinded her to his faults.*

to blind someone with science is to confuse them with a display of knowledge they do not understand

blind *NOUN* **blinds**
1 a screen for a window, often on a roller
2 something used to hide your real intentions

blind alley *NOUN* **blind alleys**
1 an alley that is closed at one end
2 a course of action that leads nowhere

blind date *NOUN* **blind dates**
a date between people who have not met before

blindfold *NOUN* **blindfolds**
a strip of cloth tied round someone's eyes so that they cannot see

a b c d e f g h i j k l m n o p q r s t u v w x y z

blindfold *VERB* **blindfolds, blindfolding, blindfolded**
to cover someone's eyes with a blindfold
WORD HISTORY from an earlier word *blindfelled* 'struck blind', related to *fell* 'to cut down a tree'. The ending of the word became confused with *fold*, from the idea of a bandage being folded around someone's head.

blindfold *ADVERB*
to do something blindfold is to do it with a blindfold covering your eyes

blinding *ADJECTIVE*
a blinding light or flash is so bright that it hurts your eyes

blindingly *ADVERB*
blindingly obvious extremely obvious

blind man's buff *NOUN*
a game in which a blindfolded player tries to catch others
WORD HISTORY *buff* is a short form of *buffet* in the sense of 'to hit or knock'. The game is so called because the blindfolded player knocks against or touches the others.

blind spot *NOUN* **blind spots**
1 an area on the road that is not in a driver's line of vision
2 a subject that you do not understand or know much about ◆ *I've got a blind spot about modern art.*

blink *VERB* **blinks, blinking, blinked**
1 to shut and then open your eyes quickly
2 a light blinks when it shines unsteadily
WORD HISTORY from *blench*, but also influenced by Dutch *blinken* 'to glitter or shine'

blink *NOUN* **blinks**
a blink of an eyelid
in the blink of an eye very rapidly
on the blink (*informal*) not working properly

blinkered *ADJECTIVE*
very narrow or limited in outlook ◆ *a blinkered approach*

blinkers *PLURAL NOUN*
leather pieces fixed on a bridle to prevent a horse from seeing sideways

blip *NOUN* **blips**
1 an electronic bleep
2 a spot of light on a radar screen
3 a sudden and usually temporary change in a situation

bliss *NOUN*
extreme happiness
WORD HISTORY related to *blithe* 'happy'

blissful *ADJECTIVE*
1 feeling or causing extreme happiness ◆ *The spa bath was blissful.*
2 a state of blissful ignorance is when you are unaware of something unpleasant and are therefore not bothered by it
▷ **blissfully** *ADVERB*

blister *NOUN* **blisters**
1 a swelling like a bubble on the skin, filled with watery liquid
2 a bubble on a painted surface, filled with air or water

blister *VERB* **blisters, blistering, blistered**
to produce a blister or blisters on the skin or on a surface

blistering *ADJECTIVE*
1 blistering heat is very intense
2 blistering criticism is very severe

blithe (*say* blyth) *ADJECTIVE*
casual and carefree
▷ **blithely** *ADVERB*
WORD HISTORY related to *bliss* 'happiness'

blithering *ADJECTIVE*
(*informal*) used to show that you are annoyed with someone or something ◆ *What a blithering buffoon!*

blitz *NOUN* **blitzes**
1 a sudden violent attack from the air
2 a burst of busy activity
the Blitz the German bombing of London in 1940
WORD HISTORY short for German *Blitzkrieg*, meaning literally 'lightning war'

blitz *VERB* **blitzes, blitzing, blitzed**
1 to destroy a target by attacking it from the air
2 to do something with a lot of energy

blizzard *NOUN* **blizzards**
a severe snowstorm

bloated *ADJECTIVE*
1 swollen by liquid or air
2 full from overeating
WORD HISTORY from an earlier meaning 'soft, flabby', from Old Norse *blautr* 'soft'

bloater *NOUN* **bloaters**
a salted smoked herring

blob *NOUN* **blobs**
1 a soft lump of something thick and liquid ◆ *blobs of glue*
2 a small spot of colour

bloc *NOUN* **blocs**
a group of parties or countries who have formed an alliance
WORD HISTORY a French word meaning 'block'

block *NOUN* **blocks**
1 a solid piece of wood, stone, or other hard substance
2 an obstacle or obstruction ◆ *I've got a mental block about her name.*
3 a starting block in a race
4 a large building divided into flats or offices
5 a group of buildings with streets on all sides ◆ *I went for a walk round the block.*
6 a large piece of wood on which condemned people were beheaded in the past

block *VERB* **blocks, blocking, blocked**
1 to obstruct something so that nothing can get through ◆ *The pipe is blocked.* ◆ *A fallen tree was blocking the road.*
2 to prevent something happening ◆ *The opposition will try to block the new proposals.*
to block something in
1 to block in a vehicle is to park so that it cannot move out
2 to block in an area in drawing is to shade it in roughly

blockade *NOUN* **blockades**
a blocking of the entrance to a city or port in order to prevent people and goods from going in or out

blockade *VERB* **blockades, blockading, blockaded**
to set up a blockade of a place

blockage *NOUN* **blockages**
something that blocks a pipe or passageway

blockbuster *NOUN* **blockbusters**
(*informal*) a film or book that is extremely successful

blockhead *NOUN* **blockheads**
(*informal*) a stupid person

block letters *PLURAL NOUN*
plain capital letters

blog *NOUN* **blogs**
(*ICT*) a weblog, a personal website on which you can post your own messages and make links to other websites

bloke *NOUN* **blokes**
(*informal*) a man

blond or **blonde** *ADJECTIVE*
1 blond hair is yellow or gold in colour
2 having blond hair; fair-haired
WORD HISTORY from Latin *blondus* 'yellow'

blonde *NOUN* **blondes**
a girl or woman with blond hair

blood *NOUN*
1 the red liquid that flows through your veins and arteries carrying oxygen
2 family backgound or ancestry ◆ *Do you have any Irish blood?*
bad blood hatred between people
in cold blood deliberately and cruelly
WORD FAMILY Words which include 'blood' or 'bleeding' in their meaning sometimes begin with *haem-*: for example, *haemophilia* is 'a disease that causes people to bleed dangerously'.

blood bank *NOUN* **blood banks**
a place where supplies of blood and plasma for transfusions are stored

bloodbath *NOUN* **bloodbaths**
a massacre

blood count *NOUN*
the number of corpuscles in a specified amount of blood

blood-curdling *ADJECTIVE*
horrifying or terrifying

blood donor *NOUN* **blood donors**
a person who gives blood for use in transfusions

blood group *NOUN* **blood groups**
any of the classes or types of human blood

bloodhound *NOUN* **bloodhounds**
a large dog that was used to track people by their scent

blood money *NOUN*
money paid as compensation to the family of someone who has been killed

bloodshed *NOUN*
the killing or wounding of people

bloodshot *ADJECTIVE*
bloodshot eyes are streaked with red

blood sport *NOUN* **blood sports**
a sport that involves wounding or killing animals

bloodstained *ADJECTIVE*
stained with blood

bloodstream *NOUN*
the blood circulating in your body

bloodsucker *NOUN* **bloodsuckers**
1 an animal or insect that sucks blood
2 someone who ruthlessly exploits another person, especially for their money
▷ **bloodsucking** *ADJECTIVE*

bloodthirsty *ADJECTIVE*
eager to take part in or watch violence and bloodshed

blood vessel *NOUN* **blood vessels**
a tube that carries blood in the body; an artery, vein, or capillary

bloody *ADJECTIVE* **bloodier, bloodiest**
1 stained with blood
2 a bloody fight or battle is one that involves a lot of killing and bloodshed
3 (*informal*) used as a mild swear word
▷ **bloodily** *ADVERB*
▷ **bloodiness** *NOUN*

bloody-minded *ADJECTIVE*
deliberately awkward and not helpful

bloom *NOUN* **blooms**
1 a flower
2 a fine powder on the surface of leaves or fruit
to be in bloom is to be in flower

bloom *VERB* **blooms, blooming, bloomed**
1 to produce flowers
2 to be or look healthy and beautiful
WORD HISTORY from Old Norse *blómi* 'yellow'

bloomer *NOUN* **bloomers**
a long rounded load with slashes across the top

bloomers *PLURAL NOUN*
women's loose-fitting knickers reaching to the knees

blossom *NOUN* **blossoms**
a flower or mass of flowers on a fruit tree

blossom *VERB* **blossoms, blossoming, blossomed**
1 to produce flowers
2 to develop in a healthy or promising way ◆ *She will blossom into a fine actor.*

blot *NOUN* **blots**
1 a spot of ink
2 a flaw or fault
3 something ugly ◆ *a blot on the landscape*

blot *VERB* **blots, blotting, blotted**
1 to make a blot or blots on something
2 to dry with blotting paper

to blot your copybook is to spoil your good record

to blot something out
1 is to obscure it
2 to blot out a thought or memory is to make a deliberate effort to forget it

blotch *NOUN* **blotches**
a large irregular mark or patch of colour
WORD HISTORY related to *blot*

blotchy *ADJECTIVE*
1 marked with blotches of colour
2 blotchy skin is marked with uneven reddish patches

blotting paper *NOUN*
absorbent paper for soaking up ink from writing

blouse *NOUN* **blouses**
a loose-fitting women's shirt

blow ❶ *VERB* **blows, blowing, blew, blown**
1 wind or air blows when it is moving or flowing
2 to be moved or carried by air or the wind ◆ *Some papers blew across the road.*
3 to move something by sending out a current of air ◆ *A gust of wind blew his wig off.*
4 to send out a current of air from your mouth
5 to make or sound something by blowing with your mouth
6 a wind instrument blows when it makes the sound of being played
7 to break something open through the force of an explosion
8 a tyre blows when it is punctured and bursts suddenly
9 (*informal*) to blow an opportunity is to fail to take advantage of it

to blow a kiss is to kiss your hand and then blow across it towards someone

to blow away something blows you away when it makes a very strong impression on you

to blow in (*informal*) is to arrive casually or unexpectedly

to blow over
1 a storm blows over when it dies down
2 a difficult situation blows over when people lose interest in it

to blow up
1 is to explode
2 (*informal*) is to lose your temper

to blow something up
1 to blow up a balloon or tyre is to inflate it
2 to blow up something is to destroy it by an explosion
3 to blow up a photograph is to enlarge its image
4 to blow up a problem or situation is to exaggerate it
5 (*informal*) when someone blows up they become extremely angry

to blow your nose is to clear your nose by breathing out through it

to blow your own trumpet is to boast about yourself

to blow your top (*informal*) is to become extremely angry

blow *NOUN* **blows**
the action of blowing

blow ❷ *NOUN* **blows**
1 a hard knock or hit
2 a shock; a disaster

blow-by-blow *ADJECTIVE*
a blow-by-blow account tells you all the details of an event in the order in which they occurred

blow-dry *VERB* **blow-dries, blow-dried, blow-drying**
to dry hair after washing it using a hand-held dryer

blowhole *NOUN* **blowholes**
the nostril of a whale or dolphin on the top of its head

blowlamp *NOUN* **blowlamps**
a blowtorch

blown *past participle of* **blow** ❶

blowout *NOUN* **blowouts**
1 a burst tyre
2 a melted fuse
3 a rapid gush of oil or gas from a well

blowpipe *NOUN* **blowpipes**
a tube through which a dart or pellet is sent by blowing at one end

blowtorch *NOUN* **blowtorches**
a portable device which produces a very hot flame, used to burn off paint from a surface

blow-up *NOUN* **blow-ups**
an enlargement of a photograph

blowy *ADJECTIVE*
windy; breezy

blubber *NOUN*
insulating fat on a whale or other large sea mammal

WORD HISTORY from an earlier meaning of 'sea foam', probably related to *bubble*

blubber *VERB* **blubbers, blubbering, blubbered**
(*informal*) to cry noisily

bludgeon (*say* **bluj**-on) *NOUN* **bludgeons**
a short stick with a thickened end, used as a weapon

bludgeon *VERB* **bludgeons, bludgeoning, bludgeoned**
1 to beat a person or animal with a heavy stick or other object
2 to bludgeon someone into doing something is to bully them into doing it

blue *NOUN* **blues**
the colour of a cloudless sky
out of the blue unexpectedly

blue *ADJECTIVE*
1 of the colour blue
2 unhappy or depressed
3 (*informal*) a blue movie or video includes explicit sexual content
once in a blue moon very rarely
▷ **blueness** *NOUN*

bluebell *NOUN* **bluebells**
a plant with blue bell-shaped flowers

blueberry *NOUN* **blueberries**
1 a shrub with edible dark blue berries
2 a berry from this shrub, often baked in cakes and pies

blue blood *NOUN*
royal or aristocratic descent
▷ **blue-blooded** *ADJECTIVE*

bluebottle *NOUN* **bluebottles**
a large fly with a bluish body

blue cheese *NOUN*
cheese with veins of blue mould

blue-chip *ADJECTIVE*
a blue-chip company is one that is well established and successful and whose stock sells for a high price

WORD HISTORY so called because blue chips have a high value in gambling games like poker

bluegrass *NOUN*
a style of country music from the southern United States, often played on banjo, fiddle, and guitar

WORD HISTORY named after a type of bluish green grass that grows in the southern United States

Blue Peter *NOUN*
a blue flag with a white square, hoisted by a ship about to leave port

blueprint *NOUN* **blueprints**
1 a design plan or technical drawing
2 a detailed plan or scheme

WORD HISTORY so called because copies of plans were made on blue paper

blues *NOUN*
a style of music which developed from black American folk music, comprising mostly slow sad songs or tunes
the blues a very sad feeling; depression

WORD HISTORY short for *blue devils*, spiteful demons believed to cause depression

blue tit *NOUN* **blue tits**
a small European bird with blue feathers on the top of its head and a yellow breast

blue whale *NOUN* **blue whales**
a bluish-grey whale with grooves along its throat, the largest living animal

bluff❶ *VERB* **bluffs, bluffing, bluffed**
to try to deceive someone into believing that you can, or intend to, do something

bluff *NOUN* **bluffs**
1 an attempt to bluff someone
2 a threat that you make but do not intend to carry out

WORD HISTORY from Dutch *bluffen* 'to boast'

bluff❷ *ADJECTIVE*
frank and direct, but in a good-natured way
▷ **bluffness** *NOUN*

bluff *NOUN* **bluffs**
a cliff with a broad steep front

bluish *ADJECTIVE*
having a blue tinge

blunder *NOUN* **blunders**
a stupid mistake

blunder *VERB* **blunders, blundering, blundered**
1 to make a blunder
2 to move clumsily and uncertainly ◆ *I could hear him blundering about upstairs.*

blunderbuss *NOUN* **blunderbusses**
an old type of hand-held gun that fired many balls in one shot

WORD HISTORY from Dutch *donderbus* 'thunder-gun'

blunt *ADJECTIVE*
1 with no sharp edge or point; not sharp
2 speaking or said in plain terms ◆ *a blunt refusal*
▷ **bluntly** *ADVERB*
▷ **bluntness** *NOUN*

blunt *VERB* **blunts, blunting, blunted**
to make a point or edge blunt

blur *VERB* **blurs, blurring, blurred**
to make something less clear or distinct

blur *NOUN* **blurs**
something that you cannot see, hear, or remember clearly

The moon was almost complete, its outline well defined, except for the blur on the waxing curve. — *Barry Hines, A Kestrel for a Knave*

blurb *NOUN*
(*informal*) a short description promoting a book, printed on its back cover

WORD HISTORY a word invented by the American writer, Gelett Burgess, in the early 20th century

blurred *ADJECTIVE*
not clear in outline; out of focus

blurt *VERB* **blurts, blurting, blurted**
to say something suddenly or tactlessly ◆ *He blurted it out before he had time to think.*

blush *VERB* **blushes, blushing, blushed**
to become red in the face because you are ashamed or embarrassed

WORD HISTORY from Old English *blyscan* 'to turn red'

blush *NOUN* **blushes**
reddening in the face

blusher *NOUN*
a cosmetic used to add red or pink colour to the cheeks

bluster *VERB* **blusters, blustering, blustered**
1 the wind blusters when it blows strongly in gusts
2 someone who blusters is talking aggressively, making empty threats
▷ **blustery** *ADJECTIVE*

BMX *ABBREVIATION*
a kind of bicycle for use in racing on a dirt track

boa (*say* boh-a) or **boa constrictor** *NOUN* **boas, boa constrictors**
a large South American snake that squeezes its prey in order to suffocate it

WORD HISTORY from a Latin word meaning 'water snake'

boar *NOUN* **boars**
1 a wild pig
2 an uncastrated domestic male pig

board *NOUN* **boards**
1 a long flat piece of wood
2 a flat piece of stiff material for a special purpose ◆ *a chopping board* ◆ *a chess board* ◆ *a diving board*
3 daily meals given in return for payment or work ◆ *board and lodging*
4 a group of people who make the decisions in an organization

to go by the board is to be rejected
on board on or in a boat, ship, or aeroplane
to take something on board is to accept and act on a new idea or situation

board *VERB* **boards, boarding, boarded**
1 to go on to a boat, ship, or aeroplane
2 to receive meals and accommodation for payment

to board something up to board up a window or door is to block it up with fixed boards

WORD HISTORY from Old English *bord*. The meaning 'to receive meals' comes from the sense of eating at a *board* or table.

boarder *NOUN* **boarders**
1 a pupil who lives at a boarding school during the term
2 a lodger who receives meals

boarding house *NOUN* **boarding houses**
a private house where people are provided with rooms and meals for payment

boarding school *NOUN* **boarding schools**
a school where pupils live during the term

boast *VERB* **boasts, boasting, boasted**
1 to speak with great pride about yourself in order to impress people
2 to have something to be proud of

Born in 1848 and taken to the Great Exhibition as a toddling child—not many people still alive could boast a thing like that. — *James Hilton, Goodbye, Mr. Chips*

boast *NOUN* **boasts**
a boastful statement

boastful *ADJECTIVE*
a boastful person is someone who boasts a lot
▷ **boastfully** *ADVERB*
▷ **boastfulness** *NOUN*

boat *NOUN* **boats**
a vehicle built to travel on water, propelled by paddle, oars, sails, or an engine

in the same boat in the same situation; suffering the same difficulties
to rock the boat is to cause trouble

WORD HISTORY from Old English *bat*

boater *NOUN* **boaters**
a hard flat straw hat

WORD HISTORY so called because the hat was originally worn for boating

boathouse *NOUN* **boathouses**
a shed at the water's edge for housing boats

boating *NOUN*
going out in a rowing boat for pleasure

boat people *PLURAL NOUN*
refugees who leave a country by sea

boatswain (*say* boh-sun) *NOUN* **boatswains**
a ship's officer in charge of rigging, boats, and anchors

WORD HISTORY from *boat* and an old word *swain* which meant 'servant'

bob *VERB* **bobs, bobbing, bobbed**
to move quickly up and down

bob *NOUN* **bobs**
1 a quick movement up and down
2 a haircut for straight hair cut in an even line all round your head

bobbin *NOUN* **bobbins**
a small spool that holds thread to use in a sewing machine or for lacemaking
WORD HISTORY from French *bobine*

bobble *NOUN* **bobbles**
a small woollen ball used to decorate a jumper or woollen hat
▷ **bobbly** *ADJECTIVE*

bobsleigh or **bobsled** *NOUN* **bobsleighs, bobsleds**
a sledge with two sets of runners, used for racing down an ice-covered run
▷ **bobsleighing** *NOUN*

bode *VERB* **bodes, boding, boded**
to bode well is to be a sign that something good will happen or that something will be successful
WORD HISTORY from Old English *bodian* 'to announce', from *boda* 'messenger'

bodice *NOUN* **bodices**
the upper part of a woman's dress, down to the waist

bodily *ADJECTIVE*
to do with your body; physical

bodily *ADVERB*
by taking hold of someone's body ◆ *He was picked up bodily and bundled into the car.*

bodkin *NOUN* **bodkins**
a thick blunt needle with a large eye

body *NOUN* **bodies**
1 the complete physical structure which makes up a human being or animal
2 the main part of this structure apart from the head and limbs
3 a corpse
4 the main part of a vehicle or other large object
5 a group of people organized for a special purpose ◆ *The school's governing body meets this week.*
6 a quantity of something regarded as a unit ◆ *A large body of evidence has built up.*
7 a physical object ◆ *Stars and planets are heavenly bodies.*
WORD HISTORY from Old English *bodig*

bodybuilding *NOUN*
strengthening and enlarging your muscles by exercise such as weightlifting
▷ **bodybuilder** *NOUN*

bodyguard *NOUN* **bodyguards**
a guard whose job is to protect an important person

body language *NOUN*
movements by which you communicate your feelings or moods

body piercing *NOUN*
the piercing of parts of the body to wear decorative rings or studs

body shop *NOUN* **body shops**
a garage that deals with repairs to the bodywork of vehicles

bodysuit *NOUN* **bodysuits**
a tight-fitting piece of clothing worn by women on the upper part of the body

bodywork *NOUN*
the outer shell of a motor vehicle

Boer (*say* **boh**-er) *NOUN* **Boers**
1 an Afrikaner
2 (*History*) an early Dutch inhabitant of South Africa
WORD HISTORY a Dutch word meaning 'farmer'

boffin *NOUN* **boffins**
(*informal*) a person involved in scientific or technical research

bog *NOUN* **bogs**
an area of wet spongy ground
to be bogged down is to be stuck and unable to make any progress
▷ **boggy** *ADJECTIVE*
WORD HISTORY a Gaelic word meaning 'soft'

bogeyman *NOUN* **bogeymen**
an imaginary man feared by children, especially in the dark

boggle *VERB* **boggles, boggling, boggled**
to be amazed or puzzled ◆ *The idea set my mind boggling.*

bogus *ADJECTIVE*
not real; sham

Bohemian *NOUN* **Bohemians**
a person who does not live in a socially conventional way
WORD HISTORY from French *bohémien* 'gypsy', because gypsies were thought to come from Bohemia, a region of what is now the Czech Republic

Bohemian *ADJECTIVE*
not conventional in your way of living

boil[1] *VERB* **boils, boiling, boiled**
1 a liquid boils when it becomes hot enough to bubble and give off steam
2 to heat a liquid or its container so that the liquid boils
3 to cook or wash something in boiling water
4 to be extremely angry
5 (*informal*) to be boiling is to be very hot
to boil down a situation boils down to something that is its central issue or problem ◆ *It boils down to a question of money.*
to boil over
1 a liquid boils over when it overflows as it boils
2 to boil over with anger is to be so angry that you cannot control yourself

boil *NOUN*
the point at which a liquid starts to boil
◆ *Bring the milk to the boil.*
off the boil having just stopped boiling
on the boil boiling

boil ❷ *NOUN* **boils**
an inflamed swelling under the skin

boiler *NOUN* **boilers**
a large tank in which water is heated and stored

boiler suit *NOUN* **boiler suits**
a single long-sleeved piece of clothing worn to protect clothes during heavy or dirty work

boiling point *NOUN* **boiling points**
1 the temperature at which a liquid boils
2 a state of great anger or excitement

boisterous *ADJECTIVE*
1 noisy and lively ◆ *The children were in a boisterous mood.*
2 boisterous weather is wild and stormy

bold *ADJECTIVE*
1 brave and confident
2 cheeky or disrespectful
3 a bold colour or design is strong and vivid
4 printed in thick black type
▷ **boldly** *ADVERB*
▷ **boldness** *NOUN*
WORD HISTORY from Old English *bald*, related to our words *bull* and *boulder*

bold *NOUN*
thick black type on a printed page or word processor

bole *NOUN* **boles**
the trunk of a tree
WORD HISTORY from Old Norse *bolr*

bollard *NOUN* **bollards**
1 a short post for keeping traffic off a road
2 a short thick post on a quayside to which a ship's rope may be tied

bolshie *ADJECTIVE*
(*informal*) rebellious or uncooperative
▷ **bolshiness** *NOUN*
WORD HISTORY from *Bolsheviks*, the extremist faction of the Russian socialist party which was renamed the (Russian) Communist Party in 1918. Their name comes from a Russian word meaning 'big'.

bolster *NOUN* **bolsters**
a long pillow for placing across a bed under other pillows

bolster *VERB* **bolsters, bolstering, bolstered**
to add extra strength or support to something

So bolstering up his pride, he set his strong will on the work they gave him. — *Ursula Le Guin, A Wizard of Earthsea*

WORD HISTORY an Old English word meaning 'cushion', related to our words *bulge* and *belly*

bolt *NOUN* **bolts**
1 a sliding bar for fastening a door or window
2 a thick metal pin that screws into a nut, used for fastening things together
3 a sliding bar that opens and closes the breech of a rifle
4 a shaft of lightning
5 an arrow shot from a crossbow
a bolt from the blue a complete surprise
bolt upright sitting or standing with your back straight

bolt *VERB* **bolts, bolting, bolted**
1 to fasten a door or window with a bolt or bolts
2 to run away very quickly
3 to gulp down food quickly

bolt hole *NOUN* **bolt holes**
a place where someone can escape or hide

bolus (*say* **boh**-lus) *NOUN* **boluses**
1 a soft ball of chewed food
2 a large pill given to animals
WORD HISTORY from Greek *bolos* 'clod of earth'

bomb *NOUN* **bombs**
1 an explosive device which is set off by impact or by a timer
2 (*informal*) a large sum of money ◆ *He must be making a bomb these days.*
the bomb the nuclear bomb
to go like a bomb (*informal*) is to be very successful

bomb *VERB* **bombs, bombing, bombed**
1 to attack a place with bombs
2 (*informal*) to fail badly ◆ *The film bombed at the box office.*
WORD HISTORY probably from Greek *bombos* 'booming sound'

bombard *VERB* **bombards, bombarding, bombarded**
1 to attack a place with a continuous firing of guns or missiles
2 to direct a continuous flow of questions, criticisms, or information at someone
▷ **bombardment** *NOUN*

bombastic (*say* bom-**bast**-ik) *ADJECTIVE*
using pompous words
WORD HISTORY from an old word *bombast* 'stuffing, padding', which later came to mean pompous or 'padded-out' language

bomber *NOUN* **bombers**
1 someone who plants or sets off a bomb
2 an aeroplane from which bombs are dropped

bomber jacket *NOUN* **bomber jackets**
a short jacket gathered into a band at the waist and cuffs
WORD HISTORY so called because the crews of US bomber planes wore jackets in this style

bombproof *ADJECTIVE*
built to withstand the impact of a bomb

bombshell *NOUN* **bombshells**
something that comes as a great shock or disappointment

bona fide (*say* **boh**-na **fy**-dee) *ADJECTIVE*
genuine; not fraudulent ◆ *Are they bona fide tourists or spies?*
WORD HISTORY a Latin phrase meaning 'in good faith'

bonanza (*say* bon-**an**-za) *NOUN* **bonanzas**
something that brings you sudden wealth or luck
WORD HISTORY first used in American English, from a Spanish word meaning 'good weather, prosperity'

bond *NOUN* **bonds**
1 a close friendship or connection between two or more people ◆ *We hope to strengthen the bonds between our two countries.*
2 bonds are ropes or chains used to tie up a prisoner
3 a document containing a legal agreement
4 a document issued by a government or public company acknowledging that money has been lent to it and will be repaid with interest

bond *VERB* **bonds, bonding, bonded**
1 to become closely linked or connected
2 to establish a close relationship with someone ◆ *He has bonded well with his girlfriend's children.*
WORD HISTORY originally the same word as *band*

bondage *NOUN*
slavery; captivity

bone *NOUN* **bones**
1 one of the hard whitish parts that make up the skeleton of a person's or animal's body
2 the substance from which these parts are made
to have a bone to pick with someone is to have a reason to be annoyed with them
to make no bones about something is not to hesitate to do or say it

bone *VERB* **bones, boning, boned**
to remove the bones from meat or fish
WORD HISTORY from Old English *ban*

bone china *NOUN*
delicate china made of clay mixed with bone ash

bone dry *ADJECTIVE*
completely dry

bone idle *ADJECTIVE*
very lazy

bonemeal *NOUN*
crushed powdered bones used as a fertilizer

bonfire *NOUN* **bonfires**
an outdoor fire to burn rubbish or celebrate something
WORD HISTORY originally a *bone fire*, a fire to dispose of human or animal bones

bongo drums or **bongos** *PLURAL NOUN*
a pair of small drums held between the knees and played with the fingers
WORD HISTORY from a Latin American Spanish word

bonkers *ADJECTIVE*
(*informal*) mad; crazy

bonnet *NOUN* **bonnets**
1 a woman's or child's hat with strings that tie under the chin
2 a flat cap, often with a bobble, worn by Scottish men
3 the hinged cover over a car engine
WORD HISTORY from Latin *abonnis* 'hat'

bonny *ADJECTIVE* **bonnier, bonniest**
a Scottish and Northern English word meaning good-looking or pretty
▷ **bonnily** *ADVERB*
▷ **bonniness** *NOUN*
WORD HISTORY from French *bon* 'good'

bonsai (*say* **bon**-sy) *NOUN*
a tree or shrub grown in miniature form in a pot by artificially restricting its growth
WORD HISTORY a Japanese word meaning 'tray planting'

bonus (*say* **boh**-nus) *NOUN* **bonuses**
1 an extra payment in addition to a person's normal wages
2 an extra benefit
WORD HISTORY a Latin word meaning 'good'

bon voyage (*say* bawn voy-**yahzh**) *EXCLAMATION*
said to wish someone a good journey
WORD HISTORY a French phrase meaning 'good journey'

bony *ADJECTIVE* **bonier, boniest**
1 a bony person is thin so that their bones are noticeable
2 bony fish or meat is full of bones
3 looking or feeling like bone

boo *EXCLAMATION*
1 said to show disapproval for someone or something
2 said to take someone by surprise and startle them

boo *VERB* **boos, booing, booed**
to shout 'boo' in disapproval

boob *NOUN* **boobs**
(*informal*) an embarrassing mistake

boob *VERB* **boobs, boobing, boobed**
to make an embarrassing mistake

booby *NOUN* **boobies**
a babyish or stupid person

booby prize *NOUN* **booby prizes**
a prize given as a joke to someone who comes last in a contest

booby trap *NOUN* **booby traps**
something designed to hit or injure someone unexpectedly

booby-trap *VERB* **booby-traps, booby-trapping, booby-trapped**
to place a booby trap in or on something

boogie-woogie *NOUN*
a style of playing blues on the piano, marked by a strong fast beat

book *NOUN* **books**
a set of sheets of paper, usually with printing or writing on them, fastened together inside a cover

to be in someone's good (or bad) books is to be in favour (or not in favour) with them

to throw the book at someone is to punish them very severely

book *VERB* **books, booking, booked**
1 to reserve a place or ticket in advance
2 to engage a performer for an event in advance
3 to enter someone's name in a police record ◆ *The police booked him for speeding.*
4 to make a note of a player who has committed a foul in a football or other match

to book in is to register your arrival at a hotel

to be booked up a hotel or event is booked up when all its rooms or tickets have been reserved

WORD HISTORY from Old English *boc*, related to our word *beech*, because some early writings were carved on beechwood

bookcase *NOUN* **bookcases**
a piece of furniture with shelves for books

book club *NOUN* **book clubs**
1 a society for members who can buy books at a reduced price
2 a group of people who meet to discuss books

bookends *PLURAL NOUN*
a pair of supports for keeping a row of books upright

bookie *NOUN* **bookies**
(*informal*) a bookmaker

bookish *ADJECTIVE*
fond of books or reading

bookkeeping *NOUN*
the activity of keeping records of the money that is spent and received by a business
▷ **bookkeeper** *NOUN*

booklet *NOUN* **booklets**
a small thin book with paper covers

bookmaker *NOUN* **bookmakers**
a person whose business is taking bets

bookmark *NOUN* **bookmarks**
1 something placed between the pages of a book to mark a place
2 (*ICT*) a record of the address of a file or Internet page so that you can find it again quickly

bookmark *VERB* **bookmarks, bookmarking, bookmarked**
(*ICT*) to make a bookmark of an address

bookseller *NOUN* **booksellers**
a person whose business is selling books

bookshelf *NOUN* **bookshelves**
a shelf for holding books

bookshop *NOUN* **bookshops**
a shop that sells books

bookstall *NOUN* **bookstalls**
a stall or kiosk which sells books and newspapers

book token *NOUN* **book tokens**
a voucher for a specified amount which can be exchanged for books to that value

bookworm *NOUN* **bookworms**
a person who is fond of reading

WORD HISTORY originally a grub that eats holes in books

Boolean *ADJECTIVE*
(*ICT*) a Boolean query or operation is one which uses combinations of the logical operators AND, OR, and NOT

WORD HISTORY named after George *Boole* (1815–64), a British mathematician and logician who developed the system

boom ❶ *VERB* **booms, booming, boomed**
1 to make a deep hollow sound with the voice
2 to be growing and successful ◆ *The country was prosperous and business was booming.*

boom *NOUN* **booms**
1 a deep hollow sound
2 a period of increased growth or prosperity

boom ❷ *NOUN* **booms**
1 a long pole at the bottom of a sail to keep it stretched
2 a long pole carrying a microphone or film camera
3 a chain or floating barrier across a river or a harbour entrance

WORD HISTORY from a Dutch word meaning 'beam, tree'

boomerang *NOUN* **boomerangs**
a curved piece of wood that can be thrown so that it returns to the thrower, originally used by Australian Aborigines

WORD HISTORY an Australian Aboriginal word

boomslang *NOUN*
a large poisonous tree snake of southern Africa

boon *NOUN* **boons**
something very useful or practical ◆ *The corner shop down the road has been a real boon.*

WORD HISTORY from Old Norse *bon* 'prayer'

boon companion *NOUN* **boon companions**
a close friend

WORD HISTORY from French *bon* 'good'

boor *NOUN* **boors**
a rude, bad-mannered person
WORD HISTORY from an earlier meaning 'peasant farmer', from the same origin as *Boer*

boorish *ADJECTIVE*
rude and bad-mannered
▷ **boorishness** *NOUN*

boost *VERB* **boosts, boosting, boosted**
to help something to increase in strength or value ◆ *Winning last night boosted the team's morale.*

boost *NOUN* **boosts**
1 an increase in something ◆ *a boost in sales*
2 help or encouragement ◆ *That gave my confidence a boost.*

booster *NOUN* **boosters**
1 a second dose of a vaccine which renews the effect of an earlier one
2 the first section of a rocket or spacecraft, used to give initial acceleration, and then jettisoned

boot¹ *NOUN* **boots**
1 a shoe that covers your foot and ankle or lower leg
2 the compartment for luggage in a car
3 (*informal*) a hard kick
4 a procedure for starting up a computer
to get the boot (*informal*) is to be dismissed from your job
to give someone the boot (*informal*) is to dismiss them from their job

boot *VERB* **boots, booting, booted**
1 to kick something hard
2 to boot or boot up a computer is to switch it on and get it ready to use
WORD HISTORY from Old French *bote*. The sense 'luggage compartment' developed from an earlier meaning of an outside step for coach attendants to stand on.

boot² *NOUN*
to boot (*old use*) in addition, as well
WORD HISTORY from Old English *bot* 'advantage, remedy', related to our word *better*. This word is not related to *boot* meaning 'shoe'.

bootee *NOUN* **bootees**
a baby's knitted or crocheted boot

booth *NOUN* **booths**
an enclosed compartment for a public telephone, or for voting at elections
WORD HISTORY from Old Norse *buth*

bootleg *VERB* **bootlegs, bootlegging, bootlegged**
to make and sell something illegally
▷ **bootlegger** *NOUN*

bootleg *ADJECTIVE*
sold or distributed illegally ◆ *a bootleg CD*
WORD HISTORY so called from the smugglers' practice of hiding bottles in their boots

booty *NOUN*
valuable goods taken away by soldiers after a battle
WORD HISTORY from German *buite* 'exchange, sharing out'

booze *NOUN*
(*informal*) alcoholic drink

booze *VERB* **boozes, boozing, boozed**
(*informal*) to drink large quantities of alcohol
WORD HISTORY from Old Dutch *busen* 'to drink too much alcohol'

borage (*say* **bor**-ij) *NOUN*
a Mediterranean plant with thick edible leaves, sometimes used in salads

borax *NOUN*
a soluble white powder used in making glass and detergents
WORD HISTORY via Latin and Arabic from Pahlavi (an old form of Persian)

border *NOUN* **borders**
1 the line dividing two countries or other areas
2 an edge
3 something placed round an edge to strengthen or decorate it
4 a strip of ground round a garden or part of it

border *VERB* **borders, bordering, bordered**
to form a border around or along something

The cottage itself, though bordered by trees, occupied a small clearing. — *Tim Bowler, River Boy*

to border on something is almost to be it
◆ *Prices are bordering on the ridiculous.*

borderline *NOUN* **borderlines**
the line that marks a boundary, especially between two countries

borderline *ADJECTIVE*
only just belonging to a particular group or category ◆ *I got a borderline pass.*

bore¹ *VERB* **bores, boring, bored**
to make a hole with a drill or other tool

bore *NOUN* **bores**
the width of the inside of a pipe or gun barrel

bore² *VERB* **bores, boring, bored**
to make someone feel uninterested by being dull

During the lemon meringue pie, Uncle Vernon bored them all with a long talk about Grunnings, his drill-making company. — *J. K. Rowling, Harry Potter and the Prisoner of Azkaban*

bore *NOUN* **bores**
a dull and uninteresting person or thing
◆ *Doing the dishes is such a bore.*
▷ **boredom** *NOUN*

bore³ *past tense of* **bear²**

bored *ADJECTIVE*
weary and uninterested because something is so dull

USAGE NOTE Take care to say you are *bored with* something, and not *bored of* it: *I'm bored with this game.*

boring *ADJECTIVE*
dull and uninteresting

born *ADJECTIVE*
1 to be born is to have come into existence by birth
2 having a certain natural quality or ability ◆ *a born leader*

to be born of something is to exist as a result of something ◆ *Their courage was born of despair.*

borne *past participle of* **bear** ❷

USAGE NOTE The word *borne* is used as the past participle of *bear* when it comes before *by* or after *have, has,* or *had*: *She had borne him a son.* However, the word *born* is used in *A son was born.*

borough (*say* **bur**- ra) *NOUN* **boroughs**
a town or part of a city that has its own council

WORD HISTORY from Old English *burg* 'fortress, fortified town'

borrow *VERB* **borrows, borrowing, borrowed**
1 to get something to use for a time, with the intention of giving it back afterwards
2 to get money from a bank with an agreement to pay it back later
▷ **borrower** *NOUN*

USAGE NOTE Take care not to use *borrow* to mean *lend*, which means '*giving* something for someone to use for a time'.

borscht (*say* borsht) *NOUN*
a Russian soup made with beetroot

bosom *NOUN* **bosoms**
1 a woman's breast or chest
2 the centre of care or emotion ◆ *He returned to the bosom of his family.*

WORD HISTORY from Old English *bosm*

bosom *ADJECTIVE*
a bosom friend is a very close friend

boss ❶ *NOUN* **bosses**
(*informal*) a person who controls or gives orders to workers; a manager

boss *VERB* **bosses, bossing, bossed** (*informal*)
to boss someone around or **about** is to order them about

WORD HISTORY from Dutch *baas* 'master'

boss ❷ *NOUN* **bosses**
a round raised knob or stud

bossy *ADJECTIVE*
fond of ordering people about
▷ **bossily** *ADVERB*
▷ **bossiness** *NOUN*

botanical (*say* bo-**tan**-ik-al) *ADJECTIVE*
to do with botany

botany *NOUN*
the scientific study of plants
▷ **botanical** *ADJECTIVE*
▷ **botanist** *NOUN*

botch *VERB* **botches, botching, botched**
to spoil something by bad or clumsy work ◆ *a botched job*

botch *NOUN*
a piece of work that has been badly done ◆ *He made a botch of the tiling.*

both *ADJECTIVE, ADVERB, PRONOUN*
each of two people or things; not only one

both ... and not only ... but also ◆ *They have both power and ability.*

bother *VERB* **bothers, bothering, bothered**
1 to annoy or disturb someone
2 to make someone worried or concerned ◆ *Something was obviously bothering him.*
3 to take the time or trouble to do something

I don't bother to dress up or anything. I change out of my school uniform, obviously, but just into my black baggy trousers. — *Jacqueline Wilson, Girls Out Late*

4 a part of your body bothers you when it is painful or uncomfortable

bother *NOUN*
1 trouble or fuss ◆ *Don't go to a lot of bother.*
2 a person or thing that causes annoyance or trouble

'It seems to me,' said Wayne, 'that if people had the faintest idea what a bother they were, no one would ever have a baby.' — *Anne Fine, Flour Babies*

bothersome *ADJECTIVE*
causing bother; troublesome

bottle *NOUN* **bottles**
1 a narrow-necked container for liquids
2 (*informal*) courage ◆ *You've got bottle, I'll say that for you.*

bottle *VERB* **bottles, bottling, bottled**
1 to put or store something in bottles
2 to bottle up your feelings is to keep them to yourself

WORD HISTORY related to *butt* 'stub'

bottle bank *NOUN* **bottle banks**
a large container in which used glass bottles are collected for recycling

bottleneck *NOUN* **bottlenecks**
a narrow place where a flow of traffic or people cannot pass freely

bottom *NOUN* **bottoms**
1 the lowest part of something; the base
2 the lowest position in a group or series
3 the part furthest away; the end ◆ *We'll drop you off at the bottom of the road.*
4 your buttocks

to be at the bottom of something is to be its underlying cause or origin

to get to the bottom of something is to find out its cause or origin

bottom *ADJECTIVE*
lowest in position ◆ *the bottom shelf*
WORD HISTORY from Old English *botm*

bottomless *ADJECTIVE*
1 extremely deep
2 a bottomless fund or resource has no limit

boudoir (*say* boo-dwar) *NOUN* **boudoirs**
a woman's bedroom or other private room
WORD HISTORY a French word meaning 'place to sulk in'

bougainvillea (*say* boo-gan-**vil**-i-a) *NOUN*
a climbing plant with red or purple leaves which grows in warm climates
WORD HISTORY named after the French explorer, L. A. de *Bougainville* (1729–1811), who led the expedition in which the plant was discovered

bough (*rhymes with* cow) *NOUN* **boughs**
a large branch growing from the trunk of a tree

bought *past tense and past participle of* **buy**

bouillon (*say* **boo**-yawn) *NOUN*
clear soup; broth
WORD HISTORY a French word, from *bouiller* 'to boil'

boulder *NOUN* **boulders**
a large rock

boulevard (*say* **bool**-ev-ard) *NOUN* **boulevards**
a wide street, often with trees on each side
WORD HISTORY a French word, related to our word *bulwark*

bounce *VERB* **bounces, bouncing, bounced**
1 to spring back when thrown against something
2 make a ball or other object bounce
3 a cheque bounces when it is sent back by the bank because there is not enough money in the account
4 to move up and down repeatedly

bounce *NOUN* **bounces**
1 the action of bouncing
2 the ability to bounce ◆ *The ball has lost its bounce.*
3 a lively confident manner

bouncer *NOUN* **bouncers**
1 a person who stands at the door of a club and stops unwanted people coming in or makes troublemakers leave
2 a ball in cricket that bounces high

bouncing *ADJECTIVE*
a bouncing baby is strong and healthy

bouncy *ADJECTIVE* **bouncier, bounciest**
1 a bouncy person is confident and lively
2 able to bounce, or making something bounce

bouncy castle *NOUN* **bouncy castles**
an inflatable model castle for children to jump and play on

bound❶ *VERB* **bounds, bounding, bounded**
to move or run with large leaps

bound *NOUN* **bounds**
a large leap
WORD HISTORY from Old French *bondir*

bound❷ *past tense of* **bind**

bound *ADJECTIVE*
obstructed or hindered by something ◆ *The airport is fog-bound.*

to be bound to happen is to be certain or very likely to happen ◆ *They're bound to arrive late.*

to be bound up with something is to be closely connected with it

bound❸ *ADJECTIVE*
to be bound for a place is to be going towards it
WORD HISTORY from an earlier word *boun* 'ready', from an Old Norse word meaning 'to prepare'. The modern ending probably developed from confusion with *bound* (the past tense of *bind*), meaning 'fastened, agreed'.

bound❹ *VERB* **bounds, bounding, bounded**
1 land is bounded by something when it has it as a boundary
2 to be bounded by something is to be limited or restricted by it
WORD HISTORY from Old French *bonde*

boundary *NOUN* **boundaries**
1 a line that marks a limit
2 a hit to the boundary of a cricket field

boundless *ADJECTIVE*
without limits

bounds *PLURAL NOUN*
limits ◆ *This was beyond the bounds of possibility.*

to know no bounds is to have no limit or restriction

out of bounds outside the areas where you are allowed to go

bountiful *ADJECTIVE*
1 plentiful; producing a lot ◆ *a bountiful harvest*
2 giving generously

bounty *NOUN* **bounties**
1 a reward paid for capturing or killing someone
2 (*formal*) someone's generosity in giving things
WORD HISTORY from Latin *bonitas* 'goodness'

bouquet (*say* boo-**kay**) ***NOUN*** **bouquets**
1 a bunch of flowers
2 the special smell a type of wine has
WORD HISTORY a French word meaning 'group of trees'

bouquet garni (*say* boo-kay **gar**-nee) ***NOUN*** **bouquet garnis**
a bunch of herbs used to add flavour in cooking
WORD HISTORY a French phrase meaning 'garnished bouquet'

bourgeois (*say* **boor**-*zh*wah) ***ADJECTIVE***
to do with the middle class, especially in having conventional ideas and tastes
WORD HISTORY a French word meaning 'citizen of a borough', from Latin *burgus* 'castle'

bourgeoisie (*say* **boor**-*zh*wah-zi) ***NOUN***
the middle class in a society

bout ***NOUN*** **bouts**
1 a boxing or wrestling contest
2 a short period of activity or of an illness

boutique (*say* boo-**teek**) ***NOUN*** **boutiques**
a small shop selling fashionable clothes
WORD HISTORY a French word, related to our word *apothecary*

bovine (*say* **boh**-vyn) ***ADJECTIVE***
1 to do with or like cattle
2 dull and stupid

Claud's fat bovine face glimmered with a mawkish pride. — *Roald Dahl, Parson's Pleasure*

WORD HISTORY from Latin *bovis* 'of an ox'

bow❶ (*rhymes with* go) ***NOUN*** **bows**
1 a knot made with two loops and two loose ends
2 a strip of wood curved by a tight string joining its ends, used for shooting arrows
3 a wooden rod with horsehair stretched between its ends, used for playing a violin or similar string instrument
WORD HISTORY from Old English *boga*

bow❷ (*rhymes with* cow) ***VERB*** **bows, bowing, bowed**
1 to bend your body forwards to show respect or as a greeting
2 to bend a part of your body downwards
3 to bow to something is to submit or give in to it ◆ *We must bow to the inevitable.*
to bow out is to retire from a job or position

bow ***NOUN*** **bows**
a bending of your head or body in greeting or respect
WORD HISTORY from Old English *bugan*, also the source of our word *buxom*

bow❸ (*rhymes with* cow) ***NOUN*** **bows**
the front end of a ship

bowdlerize (*say* **bowd**-ler-ryz) ***VERB*** **bowdlerizes, bowdlerizing, bowdlerized**
to remove words from a book, document, etc. that are thought to be indecent or offensive
USAGE NOTE This word can also be spelled bowdlerise.
WORD HISTORY named after T. *Bowdler* (1754–1825) who in 1818 produced a censored version of Shakespeare's plays

bowels ***PLURAL NOUN***
your intestines
WORD HISTORY from Latin *botellus* 'little sausage'

bower ***NOUN*** **bowers**
a pleasant shady place under trees
WORD HISTORY from an earlier meaning of 'house, dwelling', from Old English *bur*, related to our words *byre* and the ending of *neighbour*

bowl❶ ***NOUN*** **bowls**
1 a round open container for food or liquid
2 the rounded part of a spoon or tobacco pipe
3 a stadium for sporting or musical events, such as the *Hollywood Bowl*

bowl❷ ***NOUN*** **bowls**
a ball used in the game of bowls, or in bowling

bowl ***VERB*** **bowls, bowling, bowled**
1 to send a ball to be played by a batsman in cricket
2 to get a batsman out by bowling
3 to send a ball rolling along the ground
to bowl someone over
1 is to knock someone down
2 is to surprise or impress someone very much

bow-legged ***ADJECTIVE***
having legs that curve outwards at the knees

bowler❶ ***NOUN*** **bowlers**
1 a person who bowls in cricket
2 a person who plays bowls or bowling

bowler❷ ***NOUN*** **bowlers**
(*informal*) a bowler hat

bowler hat ***NOUN*** **bowler hats**
a man's stiff felt hat with a rounded top
WORD HISTORY named after a 19th-century hat-maker, William *Bowler*

bowling ***NOUN***
1 the game of knocking down skittles with a heavy ball
2 the game of bowls

bowls ***NOUN***
a game in which heavy wooden balls are rolled towards a smaller target ball

bowsprit ***NOUN*** **bowsprits**
a spar which projects forward from the stern of a ship

bow tie *NOUN* **bow ties**
a tie worn by a man and tied into a bow at the front

bow window *NOUN* **bow windows**
a curved bay window

box ❶ *NOUN* **boxes**
1 a container with a flat base and usually a lid
2 a rectangular space to be filled in on a form or computer screen
3 a compartment for seating several people in a theatre
4 an enclosed area for the jury or witnesses in a law court

the box (*informal*) television

box *VERB* **boxes, boxing, boxed**
to put something into a box

to box someone in is to surround them so that they cannot move away

WORD HISTORY from Greek *puxis* 'wooden container', from *puxos* 'wood of the box tree'

box ❷ *VERB* **boxes, boxing, boxed**
to fight with your fists as a sport

to box someone's ears is to slap them on the side of the head

▷ **boxing** *NOUN*

box ❸ *NOUN* **boxes**
a small evergreen shrub, often grown as a hedge

WORD HISTORY from Latin *buxus*, related to *box* 'container'

boxer *NOUN* **boxers**
1 a person who boxes as a sport
2 a dog that looks like a bulldog

boxer shorts *PLURAL NOUN*
men's underpants with a gathered waist and loose-fitting legs

Boxing Day *NOUN*
the first weekday after Christmas Day

WORD HISTORY so called because presents used to be given to tradespeople and servants on that day

box number *NOUN* **box numbers**
a number identifying a box at a post office or newspaper office which receives replies to advertisements

box office *NOUN* **box offices**
an office for booking seats at a theatre or cinema

WORD HISTORY so called because theatre boxes could be reserved there

boxroom *NOUN* **boxrooms**
a small room in a house, often used for storage

boy *NOUN* **boys**
1 a male child
2 a young man

▷ **boyhood** *NOUN*

boycott *VERB* **boycotts, boycotting, boycotted**
to refuse to use or buy something because you disagree with something it represents
◆ *Customers have been boycotting these products.*

WORD HISTORY from the name of Captain *Boycott* (1832–97), a harsh landlord in Ireland whose tenants refused to deal with him

boycott *NOUN*
the process of boycotting something

boyfriend *NOUN* **boyfriends**
a person's regular male friend or lover

boyish *ADJECTIVE*
like a boy, or suitable for a boy

▷ **boyishly** *ADVERB*

▷ **boyishness** *NOUN*

bra *NOUN* **bras**
a piece of underwear worn by women to support their breasts

WORD HISTORY short form of French *brassière*

brace *NOUN* **braces**
1 a tool that clamps things together or holds them in place
2 a wire device fitted in your mouth to straighten your teeth
3 a pair of something ◆ *a brace of pheasants*

brace *VERB* **braces, bracing, braced**
to support something or make it firm

to brace yourself is to prepare yourself for something unpleasant

WORD HISTORY from Latin *bracchia* 'arms', also the source of our word *embrace*

bracelet *NOUN* **bracelets**
an ornamental band or chain worn round your wrist

WORD HISTORY a French word, from Latin *bracchium* 'arm'

braces *PLURAL NOUN*
straps to hold trousers up, which pass over your shoulders

brachiopod (*say* **brak-i-oh-pod**) *NOUN* **brachiopods**
a small sea creature with a hinged shell

WORD HISTORY a word coined in the 19th century meaning literally 'arm-foot', from Latin *bracchium* 'arm' and Greek *podos* 'foot'

brachiosaurus (*say* **brak-i-oh-saw-rus**) *NOUN* **brachiosauruses**
a dinosaur which had a long neck and very large forelegs

WORD HISTORY a word coined in the 20th century meaning literally 'arm-lizard', from Latin *bracchium* 'arm' and Greek *sauros* 'lizard'

bracing *ADJECTIVE*
bracing air or weather makes you feel refreshed and healthy

bracken *NOUN*
a large fern that grows in open country or on waste land

bracket *NOUN* **brackets**
1 a mark used in pairs to enclose words or figures
2 a support attached to a wall
3 a group or range that falls between certain limits ◆ *The new DVD players are all in the highest price bracket.*

bracket *VERB* **brackets, bracketing, bracketed**
1 to enclose words or figures in brackets
2 to group people or things together because they are similar

WORD HISTORY from Latin *bracae* 'breeches'

brackets

You use **brackets** to separate off a word or phrase from the main text, and you always use them in pairs. **Parentheses** (sometimes called **round brackets**) surround a comment or information which is not part of the main flow of the sentence, and which could be omitted without altering the meaning:

His stomach (which was never very quiet) began to gurgle alarmingly.
Mary Shelley (the daughter of Mary Wollstonecraft) wrote Frankenstein when she was only nineteen.

Square brackets are used by editors to add a short note (such as a translation of a foreign word) which is not part of the original text:

Is this what you call 'living la vida loca' [Spanish, literally 'crazy life']?

They are also used to enclose stage directions in the script of a play or film:

Gandalf [dropping the Ring into Frodo's palm]: What do you see?

brackish *ADJECTIVE*
brackish water tastes slightly salty

WORD HISTORY from German or Dutch *brac* 'salt water'

bradawl *NOUN* **bradawls**
a tool for boring a hole in wood or leather

WORD HISTORY from Old Norse *broddr* 'spike' and *awl*

brae (*say* bray) *NOUN* **braes**
a Scottish word for a hillside or slope

WORD HISTORY from Old Norse *brá* 'eyelash'

brag *VERB* **brags, bragging, bragged**
to boast

braggart *NOUN* **braggarts**
a person who brags

Brahmin *NOUN* **Brahmins**
a member of the highest Hindu class, originally priests

WORD HISTORY from Sanskrit *brahman* 'priest'

braid *NOUN* **braids**
1 a plait of hair
2 a strip of cloth with a woven decorative pattern, used as trimming

braid *VERB* **braids, braiding, braided**
1 to plait hair
2 to trim something with braid

WORD HISTORY from Old English *bregdan* meaning originally 'to move from side to side' and later 'to weave'

Braille (*rhymes with* mail) *NOUN*
a system of representing letters by raised dots which blind people can read by touch

WORD HISTORY named after its inventor, Louis *Braille* (1809–52)

brain *NOUN* **brains**
1 the organ inside the skull of a person or animal which controls the body
2 your mind or intelligence ◆ *My brain's feeling fuzzy today.*
3 the brain or brains of an organization is the person who has the ideas or does the planning

to have something on the brain is to be obsessed with it

WORD FAMILY A related adjective is (*technical*) cerebral.

brain *VERB* **brains, braining, brained**
to hit someone hard on the head

WORD HISTORY from Old English *brægen*

brainchild *NOUN*
someone's brainchild is their own invention or plan

brain drain *NOUN*
the loss of clever and skilled people who emigrate from a country

brainless *ADJECTIVE*
unintelligent or stupid

brainpower *NOUN*
mental ability or intelligence

brainstorm *NOUN*
1 a moment of mental confusion
2 a spontaneous group discussion to try to think of new ideas

brainstorm *VERB* **brainstorms, brainstorming, brainstormed**
to have a spontaneous group discussion to try to think of new ideas

brainwash *VERB* **brainwashes, brainwashing, brainwashed**
to force someone to give up one set of ideas or beliefs and accept new ones

brainwave *NOUN* **brainwaves**
a sudden clever or useful idea

brainy *ADJECTIVE* **brainier, brainiest**
(*informal*) clever; intelligent
▷ **braininess** *NOUN*

braise *VERB* **braises, braising, braised**
to cook food slowly in a little liquid in a closed container

WORD HISTORY a French word meaning 'coals, embers', also the source of our word *brazier*

brake *NOUN* **brakes**
a device for slowing down or stopping a moving vehicle

brake *VERB* **brakes, braking, braked**
to slow down a moving vehicle by using a brake

bramble *NOUN* **brambles**
a blackberry bush, or its fruit

WORD HISTORY from Old English *bræmbel*, related to our word *broom*

bran *NOUN*
ground-up husks of grain which have been sifted out from flour

branch *NOUN* **branches**
1 a woody arm-like part of a tree or shrub
2 a part of a railway, road, or river that leads off from the main part
3 a local shop, bank, or office that belongs to a large organization

branch *VERB* **branches, branching, branched**
1 a road or path branches when it divides into branches
2 to change direction by following a branch

They made the long circuit, past one false lead, to the passage that branched rightwards towards the Painted Room. — *Ursula Le Guin, The Tombs of Atuan*

3 a tree or plant branches when it grows branches

to branch off is to leave a main route and take a minor one
to branch out is to start something new

WORD HISTORY from Latin *branca* 'paw'

brand *NOUN* **brands**
1 a particular make of goods
2 a mark of identification made on cattle or sheep with a piece of hot iron
3 a piece of burning wood

brand *VERB* **brands, branding, branded**
1 to mark cattle or sheep with a piece of hot iron to identify them
2 to identify or class someone as something bad or undesirable ◆ *He will be branded for ever as a cheat.*
3 to sell goods under a particular trademark

brandish *VERB* **brandishes, brandishing, brandished**
to wave something about in a confident way ◆ *She came in brandishing her diploma.*

brand name *NOUN* **brand names**
a name given to a product or range of products

brand new *ADJECTIVE*
completely new

WORD HISTORY so called from the idea of something being newly made in a furnace

brandy *NOUN* **brandies**
a strong alcoholic drink made from wine or fermented fruit juice

WORD HISTORY from Dutch *brandewijn* 'burnt (distilled) wine'

brandy snap *NOUN* **brandy snaps**
a crisp gingerbread wafer that is rolled into a cylinder and often filled with cream

brash *ADJECTIVE*
assertive in a rude or aggressive way
▷ **brashly** *ADVERB*
▷ **brashness** *NOUN*

brass *NOUN* **brasses**
1 a yellow metal that is an alloy of copper and zinc
2 wind instruments made of brass, such as trumpets and trombones
3 an ornament made of brass

the top brass (*informal*) high-ranking officers or officials

brass *ADJECTIVE*
made of brass

to get down to brass tacks is to start to consider the practical details of a task or situation

brass band *NOUN* **brass bands**
a band made up of only brass and percussion instruments

brasserie (*say* **bras**-er-i) *NOUN* **brasseries**
a restaurant that serves simple inexpensive dishes

WORD HISTORY a French word meaning 'brewery'

brassière (*say* **bras**-ee-air) *NOUN* **brassières**
a woman's bra

WORD HISTORY a French word meaning 'child's vest'

brassy *ADJECTIVE* **brassier, brassiest**
1 sounding like a brass instrument
2 loud and vulgar
▷ **brassiness** *NOUN*

brat *NOUN* **brats**
(*informal*) a badly behaved child

bravado (*say* brav-**ah**-doh) *NOUN*
a display of boldness to impress people

WORD HISTORY from Spanish *bravata*

brave *ADJECTIVE*
having or showing courage

I wasn't that brave. In fact I was having enough difficulty staving off the dread which swamped through me as I descended. — *Joe Simpson, Touching the Void*

▷ **bravely** *ADVERB*

brave *VERB* **braves, braving, braved**
to face and endure something dangerous or unpleasant ◆ *Are you ready to brave the elements?*

brave *NOUN* **braves**
an old-fashioned word for a Native American warrior
WORD HISTORY from Latin *barbarus* 'barbarous'

bravery *NOUN*
courage

bravo (*say* brah-**voh**) *EXCLAMATION*
said to congratulate someone, or shouted by an audience to show their approval of a performance
WORD HISTORY an Italian word

bravura (*say* bra-**voor**-a) *NOUN*
great skill or artistic flair
WORD HISTORY an Italian word

brawl *NOUN* **brawls**
a noisy quarrel or fight

brawl *VERB* **brawls, brawling, brawled**
to take part in a brawl

brawn *NOUN*
muscular strength, as opposed to intelligence

brawny *ADJECTIVE* **brawnier, brawniest**
strong and muscular

bray *VERB* **brays, braying, brayed**
a donkey brays when it makes a loud harsh cry
WORD HISTORY from Old French *braire* 'to cry'

bray *NOUN* **brays**
a braying sound

brazen *ADJECTIVE*
1 bold and shameless ◆ *He was going to ask for more money, however brazen it seemed.*
2 made of brass

brazen *VERB* **brazens, brazening, brazened**
to brazen it out is to behave as if you have nothing to be ashamed of after doing something wrong
WORD HISTORY from an Old English word meaning 'made of brass'

brazier (*say* **bray**-zee-er) *NOUN* **braziers**
a metal basket in which coals can be burned to keep people warm outdoors
WORD HISTORY from French *braise* 'coals, embers'

breach *NOUN* **breaches**
1 the breaking of an agreement or rule or code of behaviour

> It was the grossest breach of etiquette imaginable to touch another person's dæmon.
> — *Philip Pullman, Northern Lights*

2 a gap made in a wall or barrier
to step into the breach is to offer your help in a crisis

breach *VERB* **breaches, breaching, breached**
1 to break an agreement or rule ◆ *She complained that he had breached the trust she had placed in him.*
2 to break through a barrier or defence, such as a wall or river bank
WORD HISTORY related to *break*

bread *NOUN* **breads**
1 a food made by baking flour and water, usually with yeast
2 (*informal*) money or wealth
WORD HISTORY an Old English word

breadcrumbs *PLURAL NOUN*
pieces of crumbled bread used to coat food before it is fried

breaded *ADJECTIVE*
coated with breadcrumbs

breadfruit *NOUN* **breadfruits** or **breadfruit**
the fruit of a tropical tree, the pulp of which looks like bread when it is cooked

breadline *NOUN*
on the breadline having barely enough money to live on

breadth *NOUN*
1 the distance or measurement across something, from one side to another
2 a wide range ◆ *She brings a breadth of experience to the job.*

breadwinner *NOUN* **breadwinners**
the member of a family who earns money to support the others

break *VERB* **breaks, breaking, broke, broken**
1 to divide something into pieces by hitting or pressing it
2 to fall into pieces because of being hit
3 to damage something so that it no longer works properly
4 to fail to keep a promise or law
5 to interrupt and stop something
6 to emerge or appear suddenly
7 to make a rush or dash ◆ *A player broke clear with only the goalkeeper to beat.*
8 to break information or news to someone is to reveal it to them
9 to break a record is to do better than it
10 weather breaks when it changes suddenly
11 waves break when they fall in foam on a shore
12 a boy's voice breaks when it becomes suddenly deeper at puberty
13 to break a code is to find the solution to it
14 to break someone is to destroy their spirit

to break down
1 a car or machine breaks down when it stops working properly
2 an agreement or discussion breaks down when the people involved stop talking or working together

to break even is to make gains and losses that balance exactly

to break in
1 a burglar breaks in when they force their way into a building

a b c d e f g h i j k l m n o p q r s t u v w x y z

2 someone breaks in when they say something to interrupt a conversation
3 to break in a horse is to make it used to being ridden

to break into something to break into an activity is to start doing it ◆ *He broke into a run.*

to break off
1 to break off a discussion is to bring it to a sudden end
2 when someone breaks off they suddenly stop speaking

break out
1 when something breaks out it begins suddenly
2 a prisoner breaks out when they escape

to break up
1 something breaks up when it breaks into small parts
2 a sound breaks up when it becomes difficult to hear
3 a school breaks up when it closes at the end of a term
4 people break up when they end a relationship with each other

Dad's band broke up after a year or so. Dad had a fight with the lead guitarist. — *Jacqueline Wilson, Lola Rose*

to break with something or someone
1 to break with a tradition or custom is to do something in a way that is different from it
2 to break with someone is to end your friendship with them

break *NOUN* **breaks**
1 a broken place; a gap
2 an escape; a sudden dash
3 a short rest from work or an activity

We were sitting on some steps that led up to the tennis courts during the afternoon break. — *Bali Rai, (Un)arranged Marriage*

4 (*informal*) a piece of luck; a fair chance ◆ *I never seem to get a break.*
5 a number of points scored continuously in snooker
6 the winning of a tennis game against your opponent's serve

break of day (*literary*) the dawn

breakable *ADJECTIVE*
able to be broken

breakage *NOUN* **breakages**
something that is broken ◆ *Breakages must be paid for.*

breakaway *ADJECTIVE*
a breakaway group is one that has split away from a larger group

break-dancing *NOUN*
an energetic style of street dancing

breakdown *NOUN* **breakdowns**
1 a sudden failure of a car or engine to work properly ◆ *We had a breakdown on the motorway.*
2 a collapse or failure in a system ◆ *the breakdown of law and order*
3 a period of mental illness caused by anxiety or depression
4 an analysis of accounts or statistics

breaker *NOUN* **breakers**
a large wave that breaks on the shore

breakfast *NOUN* **breakfasts**
the first meal of the day

WORD HISTORY from *break* and *fast*, because it is the first meal you eat after fasting overnight

breakfast *VERB* **breakfasts, breakfasting, breakfasted**
to have breakfast

break-in *NOUN* **break-ins**
a forcible entry into a building by a thief

breakneck *ADJECTIVE*
breakneck speed is dangerously fast

breakthrough *NOUN* **breakthroughs**
an important development or discovery

breakwater *NOUN* **breakwaters**
a wall built out into the sea to protect a coast from heavy waves

bream *NOUN* **bream**
a yellowish freshwater fish with an arched back

breast *NOUN* **breasts**
1 either of the two fleshy parts on the upper front of a woman's body that produce milk to feed a baby
2 a person's or animal's chest

WORD FAMILY Related adjectives are (*technical*) mammary and pectoral.

breastbone *NOUN* **breastbones**
the flat bone down the centre of your chest, which is joined to your ribs

breastfeed *VERB* **breastfeeds, breastfeeding, breastfed**
a mother breastfeeds a baby by feeding it with milk from her breasts

breastplate *NOUN* **breastplates**
(*History*) a piece of armour that covered a soldier's chest

breaststroke *NOUN*
a swimming stroke on your front in which you move your arms in a circular movement

breath (*say* breth) *NOUN* **breaths**
1 air that is drawn into your lungs and sent out again
2 a single taking in and letting out of breath

For a second, Mr. Sir's pain seemed to recede. He took several long, deep breaths. — *Louis Sachar, Holes*

3 a gentle blowing

in the same breath to say something in the same breath is to say it immediately after saying something else
out of breath panting
take your breath away something that takes your breath away is something that surprises or impresses you a lot
under your breath to say something under your breath is to whisper it

WORD FAMILY Related words are (*technical*) respiration and respiratory.

breathalyse *VERB* **breathalyses, breathalysing, breathalysed**
to test someone's alcohol level with a breathalyser

breathalyser *NOUN* **breathalysers**
a device for measuring the alcohol level in a person's breath

breathe (*say* breeth) *VERB* **breathes, breathing, breathed**
1 to take air into your body and send it out again
2 to say or speak about something ◆ *Don't breathe a word of this.*

breather (*say* **bree**-ther) *NOUN* **breathers**
(*informal*) a pause for rest ◆ *Let's take a breather.*

breathing space *NOUN*
a pause to recover from doing something or to decide what to do next

breathless *ADJECTIVE*
out of breath; panting
▷ **breathlessly** *ADVERB*
▷ **breathlessness** *NOUN*

breathtaking *ADJECTIVE*
very impressive or surprising ◆ *The view from the rim of the Grand Canyon was breathtaking.*

bred *past tense and past participle of* **breed**

breech *NOUN* **breeches**
the back part of a gun barrel, where the bullets are put in

WORD HISTORY from Old English *brec* 'hindquarters'

breech birth *NOUN*
a birth in which the baby's buttocks or feet appear first

breeches (*say* **brich**-iz) *PLURAL NOUN*
trousers which reach to just below your knees

breed *VERB* **breeds, breeding, bred**
1 to produce children or offspring
2 to keep animals in order to produce young ones from them
3 to be bred in a particular way is to be brought up or trained that way
4 to create or produce something ◆ *Poverty breeds illness.*
▷ **breeder** *NOUN*

breed *NOUN* **breeds**
a particular variety of animal that has been specially developed

WORD HISTORY related to *brood*

breeding *NOUN*
good manners thought of as resulting from a person's family background

breeze *NOUN* **breezes**
a gentle wind

breeze *VERB* **breezes, breezing, breezed**
to breeze in is to arrive or enter somewhere in a casual manner

breeze block *NOUN* **breeze blocks**
a lightweight building block made of sand, cinders, and cement

WORD HISTORY related to *brazier*

breezy *ADJECTIVE* **breezier, breeziest**
1 pleasantly windy
2 relaxed and cheerful
▷ **breezily** *ADVERB*
▷ **breeziness** *NOUN*

brethren *PLURAL NOUN*
an old-fashioned word meaning brothers

WORD HISTORY an old plural of *brother*

Breton (*say* **bret**-on) *NOUN* **Bretons**
1 a person who lives in, or was born in, Brittany in northern France
2 a Celtic language spoken in Brittany

breve (*say* breev) *NOUN* **breves**
a note in music, lasting eight times as long as a crotchet

WORD HISTORY related to *brief*

brevity *NOUN*
shortness; briefness

brew *VERB* **brews, brewing, brewed**
1 to make tea or coffee by mixing it with hot water
2 to make beer by boiling and fermentation
3 something undesirable is brewing when it is growing or developing ◆ *Trouble is brewing.*

brew *NOUN* **brews**
1 a variety of beer
2 (*informal*) a drink of tea or coffee

brewer *NOUN* **brewers**
a person who brews beer for sale

brewery *NOUN* **breweries**
a place where beer is brewed

briar *NOUN* **briars**
a thorny bush, especially the wild rose

bribe *NOUN* **bribes**
money or a gift offered to someone to influence them to do something to your advantage

bribe *VERB* **bribes, bribing, bribed**
to persuade someone to do something by offering them a bribe
▷ **bribery** *NOUN*
WORD HISTORY from Old French *briber* 'to beg'

bric-a-brac (*say* **brik**-a-brak) *NOUN*
small ornaments or pieces of furniture which are of no great value

brick *NOUN* **bricks**
1 a small hard block of baked clay used to build walls
2 (*informal*) someone who helps or supports you when you are in need

brick *VERB* **bricks, bricking, bricked**
to brick something up is to block an entrance or window with bricks

brickbat *NOUN* **brickbats**
1 a piece of brick used as a missile
2 a strongly critical remark

bricklayer *NOUN* **bricklayers**
a worker who builds with bricks

brick red *NOUN*
a deep brownish red

bride *NOUN* **brides**
a woman on her wedding day
▷ **bridal** *ADJECTIVE*
WORD HISTORY from Old English *bryd*

bridegroom *NOUN* **bridegrooms**
a man on his wedding day
WORD HISTORY from Old English *brydguma* 'bride's man'

bridesmaid *NOUN* **bridesmaids**
a woman or girl who accompanies a bride at her wedding

bridge❶ *NOUN* **bridges**
1 a structure built over and across a river, railway, or road to allow people or vehicles to cross it
2 a raised platform on a ship from which the captain and officers direct its course
3 the bony upper part of your nose
4 a part of a stringed instrument that holds the strings away from its body

bridge *VERB* **bridges, bridging, bridged**
make or form a bridge over something

bridge❷ *NOUN*
a card game rather like whist

bridle *NOUN* **bridles**
the part of a horse's harness that fits over its head
WORD HISTORY related to *braid*

bridle *VERB* **bridles, bridling, bridled**
1 to put a bridle on a horse
2 to show you are angry or offended by something

bridleway or **bridle path** *NOUN* **bridleways** or **bridle paths**
a road suitable for horses but not for vehicles

brief *ADJECTIVE*
1 lasting for a short time

Last week there was a brief interruption in our monotonous routine. — *Anne Frank, The Diary of a Young Girl*

2 using few words
in brief in a few words
▷ **briefly** *ADVERB*

brief *NOUN* **briefs**
1 (*D & T*) a set of instructions given to someone before they start a piece of work
2 a summary of the facts of a legal case, drawn up for a barrister or advocate

brief *VERB* **briefs, briefing, briefed**
1 to give someone the instructions and information they need to start a piece of work
2 to give a brief to a barrister or advocate
WORD HISTORY from Latin *brevis* 'short'

briefcase *NOUN* **briefcases**
a flat case for carrying documents

briefing *NOUN* **briefings**
a meeting to give someone instructions or information

briefs *PLURAL NOUN*
short knickers or underpants

brier *NOUN* **briers**
another spelling of **briar**

brigade *NOUN* **brigades**
1 a large unit of an army
2 an organized unit with a special purpose
3 a group of people with a common interest or belief ◆ *the anti-smoking brigade*
WORD HISTORY from Italian *brigata* 'a troop'

brigadier *NOUN* **brigadiers**
an army officer who commands a brigade, higher in rank than a colonel

brigand *NOUN* **brigands**
a member of a band of robbers
WORD HISTORY from Italian *brigante* 'foot soldier'

bright *ADJECTIVE*
1 giving a strong light

Bright sunlight was still pouring through the open hatch. — *Cornelia Funke, Dragon Rider*

2 filled with light or sunlight

It was a bright cold day in April, and the clocks were striking thirteen. — *George Orwell, Nineteen Eighty-four*

3 a bright colour is vivid and bold
4 a bright person is quick-witted and clever
5 a bright mood or expression is cheerful

to look on the bright side is to be optimistic in spite of difficulties

▷ **brightly** *ADVERB*

▷ **brightness** *NOUN*

brighten *VERB* **brightens, brightening, brightened**

1 to become brighter

2 to make something brighter

brilliant *ADJECTIVE*

1 shining very brightly

2 very clever or talented

3 excellent; marvellous

▷ **brilliantly** *ADVERB*

▷ **brilliance** *NOUN*

WORD HISTORY from Italian *brillare* 'to shine'

brim *NOUN* **brims**

1 the edge of a cup, bowl, or other container

2 the bottom part of a hat that sticks out

brim *VERB* **brims, brimming, brimmed**

to be full to the brim

Undaunted, Mrs McLachlan unlocked the cage door and edged inside, dragging the brimming cauldron behind her. — *Debi Gliori, Pure Dead Magic*

to brim over a container that is brimming over is overflowing with its contents

brimful *ADJECTIVE*

full to the brim

brimstone *NOUN*

an old-fashioned word meaning sulphur

WORD HISTORY from Old English *brynstan* 'burning stone'

brine *NOUN*

salt water

▷ **briny** *ADJECTIVE*

bring *VERB* **brings, bringing, brought**

1 to carry something with you

'Did you bring the sandwiches?' I interrupted, patting the bulging pockets of Mum's anorak. — *Anne Fine, Goggle-Eyes*

2 a road or path brings you somewhere when it leads you there

3 to bring someone a feeling or emotion is to cause them to feel it

4 to result in or cause something

Email can sometimes bring Internet users ginormous problems. — *Michael Cox, The Incredible Internet*

to bring something about to bring about a situation or event is to make it happen

to bring the house down is to get loud applause or laughter from an audience

to bring something in

1 to bring in a law or regulation is to introduce it

2 to bring in a sum of money is to produce that amount in sales or donations

3 to bring in a verdict is to announce it in court

to bring something off to bring off something you have planned is to carry it out successfully

to bring something out

1 to bring out a feature of something is to make it show more clearly

2 to bring out a book or new product is to publish it or launch it

to bring yourself to do something is to force yourself to do something unpleasant

to bring someone up to bring up children is to look after and train them as they grow

to bring something up

1 to bring up a subject is to mention it

2 to bring up food is to vomit

to bring up the rear is to come last in a line or contest

brink *NOUN* **brinks**

1 the edge of a steep place or of a stretch of water

2 the point beyond which something will happen

Haoyou struggled back from the brink of sleep to find his uncle kneeling over him. — *Geraldine McCaughrean, The Kite Rider*

WORD HISTORY from Old Norse *brekka* 'hill, slope'

brinkmanship *NOUN*

the tactic of continuing a dispute with another country until the brink of conflict or war, and then stopping it just in time

brioche (*say* bree-osh) *NOUN* **brioches**

a French bread roll made with sweet dough

briquette (*say* brik-et) *NOUN* **briquettes**

a block of compressed charcoal or coal dust, used as fuel

WORD HISTORY a French word meaning 'little brick'

brisk *ADJECTIVE*

1 a brisk walk or pace is quick and energetic

2 someone with a brisk manner deals with people quickly and rather abruptly

3 brisk business or trade is busy and going well

▷ **briskly** *ADVERB*

▷ **briskness** *NOUN*

bristle *NOUN* **bristles**

1 a short stiff hair

2 one of the stiff pieces of hair, wire, or plastic in a brush

▷ **bristly** *ADJECTIVE*

bristle *VERB* **bristles, bristling, bristled**

1 an animal bristles when it raises its bristles in anger or fear

2 someone bristles when they show clearly that they are angry or indignant about something

3 to bristle with something is to have a lot of that particular thing ◆ *The room bristled with computer screens.*

Britain *NOUN*
the island made up of England, Scotland, and Wales, with the small adjacent islands; Great Britain

USAGE NOTE Note the difference in use between the terms *Britain*, *Great Britain*, the *United Kingdom*, and the *British Isles*. Great Britain (or Britain) is used to refer to the island made up of England, Scotland, and Wales. The United Kingdom includes Great Britain and Northern Ireland. The British Isles refers to the whole of the island group which includes Great Britain, Ireland, and all the smaller nearby islands.

British Isles *PLURAL NOUN*
the island group which includes Great Britain, Ireland, and all the smaller nearby islands

USAGE NOTE See the note at *Britain*.

Briton (*say* **brit**-on) *NOUN* **Britons**
1 a person who lives in, or was born in, Britain
2 an inhabitant of southern Britain before the Roman conquest

brittle *ADJECTIVE*
hard but easy to break or snap
▷ **brittleness** *NOUN*

broach *VERB* **broaches, broaching, broached**
1 to start a discussion of something ◆ *We were unwilling to broach the subject.*
2 to make a hole in a container and draw out liquid

broad *ADJECTIVE*
1 large across; wide
2 broad tastes or interests are wide-ranging
3 a broad description or term is general and not detailed
4 to be in broad agreement is to be mainly or roughly in agreement
5 a broad hint is clear and unmistakable
6 a broad regional accent is very noticeable and strong

broad daylight full daylight; the daytime

broadband *NOUN*
(*ICT*) a broadband Internet connection is a continuous connection that uses signals over a wide range of frequencies

broad bean *NOUN* **broad beans**
a bean with large flat seeds

broadcast *VERB* **broadcasts, broadcasting, broadcast**
to send out a programme on television or the radio

broadcast *NOUN* **broadcasts**
a programme sent out on television or the radio
▷ **broadcaster** *NOUN*

WORD HISTORY from an earlier meaning 'to scatter seeds widely', from *broad* and *cast*

broaden *VERB* **broadens, broadening, broadened**
1 to make something broader
2 to become broader

broadly *ADVERB*
in a broad way

broadly speaking generally; on the whole

broad-minded *ADJECTIVE*
tolerant; not easily shocked

broadsheet *NOUN* **broadsheets**
a newspaper printed on large sheets of paper, thought of as more serious than the tabloids

broadside *NOUN* **broadsides**
1 an act of firing all the guns on one side of a ship
2 a strong spoken or written attack

WORD HISTORY from an earlier meaning 'the side of a ship, above the waterline'

broadsword *NOUN* **broadswords**
a sword with a broad blade, used for cutting rather than thrusting

brocade (*say* bro-**kayd**) *NOUN*
a rich fabric woven with raised patterns

WORD HISTORY from Italian *brocco* 'twisted thread'

broccoli *NOUN* **broccoli**
a kind of cauliflower with greenish flowerheads

WORD HISTORY an Italian word meaning 'cabbage-heads'

brochure (*say* **broh**-shoor) *NOUN* **brochures**
a booklet or pamphlet containing information

WORD HISTORY a French word meaning 'stitching', so called because the pages were originally stitched together

brogue ❶ (*rhymes with* rogue) *NOUN* **brogues**
a strong shoe with a decorative pattern of small holes

WORD HISTORY via Gaelic and Irish from an Old Norse word meaning 'leg covering'

brogue ❷ *NOUN* **brogues**
a strong regional accent ◆ *He spoke with an Irish brogue.*

broil *VERB* **broils, broiling, broiled**
1 to cook food using a direct heat such as a grill
2 to be broiling is to be very hot, usually because of the sun

WORD HISTORY from French *brûler* 'to burn'

broke ❶ *past tense of* **break**

broke ❷ *ADJECTIVE*
(*informal*) having no money left

WORD HISTORY an old past participle of *break*

broken *past participle of* **break**

broken-hearted *ADJECTIVE*
feeling great sadness or grief

broken home *NOUN* **broken homes**
a family in which the parents are divorced or separated

a b c d e f g h i j k l m n o p q r s t u v w x y z

broker *NOUN* **brokers**
a person who buys and sells things, especially shares, for other people

broker *VERB* **brokers, brokering, brokered**
to arrange or negotiate a deal or plan

brolly *NOUN* **brollies**
(*informal*) an umbrella

bromide *NOUN*
a substance used in medicine to calm the nerves

bronchial (*say* **bronk**-ee-al) *ADJECTIVE*
to do with the tubes that lead from your windpipe to your lungs
WORD HISTORY from Greek *bronchos* 'windpipe'

bronchitis (*say* bronk-**y**-tiss) *NOUN*
a disease causing inflammation of the bronchial tubes, which makes you cough a lot

bronco *NOUN* **broncos**
a wild or half-tamed horse of western North America

brontosaurus *NOUN* **brontosauruses**
an old name for *apatosaurus*
WORD HISTORY a word coined in the 19th century meaning literally 'thunder-lizard', from Greek *brontē* 'thunder' and *sauros* 'lizard'

bronze *NOUN* **bronzes**
1 a metal that is an alloy of copper and tin
2 something made of bronze
3 a bronze medal, awarded as third prize
4 a yellowish brown colour
WORD HISTORY probably from Persian *birinj* 'brass'

bronze *ADJECTIVE*
1 made of bronze
2 yellowish brown in colour

Bronze Age *NOUN*
the period in human history when tools and weapons were made of bronze

brooch *NOUN* **brooches**
an ornament with a hinged pin for fastening it onto clothes
WORD HISTORY from an old spelling of *broach*

brood *NOUN* **broods**
1 young birds or other animals that were hatched or born together
2 (*informal*) all the children of a family

brood *VERB* **broods, brooding, brooded**
1 to keep thinking and worrying about something
2 to sit on eggs to hatch them

brooding *ADJECTIVE*
looking or seeming dangerous or threatening

broody *ADJECTIVE*
1 a broody hen is ready to sit on her eggs
2 a woman who feels broody is eager to have children
3 a person is broody when they are quietly worried and unhappy about something

brook[1] *NOUN* **brooks**
a small stream
WORD HISTORY from Old English *broc*

brook[2] *VERB* **brooks, brooking, brooked**
to allow or tolerate something ◆ *He would brook no interference.*
WORD HISTORY from Old English *brucan*

broom *NOUN* **brooms**
1 a brush with a long handle, for sweeping floors
2 a shrub with yellow, white, or pink flowers
WORD HISTORY from Old English *brom* 'broom plant', because brushes used to be made from its twigs

broomstick *NOUN* **broomsticks**
a long thick handle of a broom, which in stories witches use to ride on

Bros *ABBREVIATION*
Brothers

broth *NOUN* **broths**
a kind of thin soup
WORD HISTORY an Old English word

brothel *NOUN* **brothels**
a house in which women work as prostitutes
WORD HISTORY from an earlier meaning of 'a worthless person', from Old English *brothen* 'ruined, degenerate'

brother *NOUN* **brothers**
1 a son of the same parents as another person
2 a man who is a fellow member of a trade union, Christian Church, or other association
3 a member of a religious order of men
▷ **brotherly** *ADJECTIVE*
WORD HISTORY from Old English *brothor*
WORD FAMILY A related adjective is fraternal.

brotherhood *NOUN* **brotherhoods**
1 friendliness and companionship between men, or between people in general
2 a society or association of men

brother-in-law *NOUN* **brothers-in-law**
the brother of a married person's husband or wife; the husband of a person's sister

brought *past tense and past participle of* **bring**

brouhaha (*say* **broo**-ha-ha) *NOUN*
a noisy uproar or commotion

brow *NOUN* **brows**
1 an eyebrow
2 your forehead
3 the top of a hill

brown *NOUN* **browns**
a colour between orange and black, like the colour of dark wood

brown *ADJECTIVE*
1 of the colour brown
2 dark-skinned or suntanned
3 brown bread and rolls are made with wholemeal flour

brown *VERB* **browns, browning, browned**
1 to make something brown, especially by cooking it
2 to become brown
to be browned off (*informal*) is to be fed up or annoyed
WORD HISTORY from Old English *brun*

brownie *NOUN* **brownies**
1 a rich chocolate cake baked in a tray and cut into squares
2 a helpful goblin

Brownie *NOUN* **Brownies**
a member of a junior branch of the Guides, for girls between about 7 and 10

brownie points *PLURAL NOUN*
(*informal*) credit or recognition for doing something good

browse *VERB* **browses, browsing, browsed**
1 to look through a book, or examine items for sale, in a casual way
2 (*ICT*) to search files on a network or on the Internet
3 animals browse when they feed on grass or leaves
WORD HISTORY from an Old French word meaning 'young shoot'

browser *NOUN* **browsers**
(*ICT*) a program for displaying HTML files, used to search and view websites

bruise *NOUN* **bruises**
1 a dark mark made on the skin by a blow or by pressure
2 a similar mark on a fruit or vegetable

bruise *VERB* **bruises, bruising, bruised**
1 to cause a bruise or bruises to appear on a person's skin
2 to develop a bruise or bruises ◆ *I bruise easily.*
WORD HISTORY from Old English *brysan* 'to crush or injure'

brunch *NOUN*
(*informal*) a late-morning meal combining breakfast and lunch
WORD HISTORY from *breakfast* and *lunch*

brunette *NOUN* **brunettes**
a woman with dark brown hair
WORD HISTORY from French *brun* 'brown'

brunt *NOUN*
the main impact of something bad ◆ *They bore the brunt of the attack.*

brush *NOUN* **brushes**
1 an implement with bristles set in a solid base, used for cleaning, smoothing, or painting things, or for smoothing your hair
2 an act of using a brush ◆ *Give it a good brush.*
3 a brief unpleasant encounter
4 a fox's bushy tail

brush *VERB* **brushes, brushing, brushed**
1 to clean something or make something tidy with a brush

My coat was brushed every day till it shone like a rook's wing. — *Anna Sewell, Black Beauty*

2 to touch someone or something lightly in passing
to brush something aside is to dismiss it casually or rudely

The doctor brushed my mother's apologies aside with a laugh. — *Christy Brown, My Left foot*

to brush someone off is to reject them in an abrupt way
to brush something up to brush up a subject is to revise your knowledge of it
WORD HISTORY from Old French *broisse*

brush-off *NOUN* **brush-offs**
a rude or abrupt rejection

brusque (*say* bruusk) *ADJECTIVE*
abrupt and offhand in manner
▷ **brusquely** *ADVERB*
▷ **brusqueness** *NOUN*
WORD HISTORY via French from Italian *brusco* 'sour'

Brussels sprouts *PLURAL NOUN*
the edible buds of a kind of cabbage, which grow thickly on its stem
WORD HISTORY so called because they were first grown near Brussels, the capital of Belgium

brutal *ADJECTIVE*
cruel and violent ◆ *a brutal attack*
▷ **brutally** *ADVERB*
▷ **brutality** *NOUN*

brutalize *VERB* **brutalizes, brutalizing, brutalized**
to make someone brutal or inhumane by treating them in a cruel or violent way ◆ *They have been brutalized by the constant struggle to survive.*
▷ **brutalization** *NOUN*
USAGE NOTE This word can also be spelled brutalise.

brute *NOUN* **brutes**
1 a brutal person
2 an animal in contrast to a human being
3 (*informal*) something that is very difficult or unpleasant to do
▷ **brutish** *ADJECTIVE*
WORD HISTORY from Latin *brutus* 'stupid'

brute *ADJECTIVE*
brute force or strength is purely physical, in contrast to mental effort

B.Sc. *ABBREVIATION*
Bachelor of Science

BSE *ABBREVIATION*
bovine spongiform encephalopathy; a fatal disease of cattle that affects the nervous system and makes the cow stagger about. BSE is sometimes known as 'mad cow disease'.

bubble *NOUN* **bubbles**
1 a thin film of liquid filled with air or gas
2 a small ball of air in a fizzy drink or enclosed in glass
3 a transparent dome-shaped cover

bubble *VERB* **bubbles, bubbling, bubbled**
1 to form bubbles or rise to the surface in bubbles
2 to make gurgling sounds like bubbles rising in liquid
3 to be bubbling with an emotion is to be very lively or excited because of it

bubble and squeak *NOUN*
cooked cabbage and potato that is chopped, mixed, and fried

bubblegum *NOUN*
chewing gum that can be blown into large bubbles

bubble wrap *NOUN*
plastic packaging which contains small air pockets to protect its contents from damage

bubbly *ADJECTIVE* **bubblier, bubbliest**
1 full of bubbles
2 cheerful and excited

bubbly *NOUN*
(*informal*) champagne or sparkling wine

bubonic plague *NOUN*
a contagious disease, transmitted by rat fleas, which produces swellings in the groin or armpit

WORD HISTORY from Latin *bubo* 'a swelling'

buccaneer *NOUN* **buccaneers**
1 a pirate
2 someone who behaves ruthlessly in business or politics

▷ **buccaneering** *ADJECTIVE*

WORD HISTORY originally a name for European hunters in the Caribbean, from French *boucanier*

buck❶ *NOUN* **bucks**
a male deer, rabbit, or hare

buck *VERB* **bucks, bucking, bucked**
1 a horse bucks when it jumps with its back arched
2 to buck a trend or fashion is to resist or oppose it

to buck up (*informal*)
1 is to become more cheerful
2 is to hurry up

buck❷ *NOUN*
to pass the buck (*informal*) is to give the responsibility for something to another person when you should have it yourself

WORD HISTORY from *buck*, a word used in poker meaning 'an article placed as a reminder before the person whose turn it is to deal'

buck❸ *NOUN* **bucks**
(*informal*) a word used North America and Australia meaning a dollar

bucket *NOUN* **buckets**
a round open container with a handle, for carrying liquids or solids

bucket *VERB* **buckets, bucketing, bucketed**
rain is bucketing, or bucketing down, when it is raining heavily

bucketful *NOUN* **bucketfuls**
an amount of something that can be held in a bucket

buckets *PLURAL NOUN*
(*informal*) large quantities of rain or tears
◆ *I cried buckets at the end of the film.*

buckle❶ *NOUN* **buckles**
a device with a hinged prong, through which a belt or strap is threaded to fasten it

buckle *VERB* **buckles, buckling, buckled**
to fasten something with a buckle, especially a belt or strap

to buckle down to something is to start working hard at it

WORD HISTORY from Latin *buccula* 'cheek-strap of a helmet'

buckle❷ *VERB* **buckles, buckling, buckled**
something that gives support buckles when it bends or warps and gives way

WORD HISTORY from French *boucler* 'to bulge'

buckler *NOUN* **bucklers**
a small round shield with a handle

buckram *NOUN*
stiffened cotton or linen, used to bind books

buckshot *NOUN*
coarse lead shot, used for hunting animals or birds

bucolic (*say* bew-**kol**-ik) *ADJECTIVE*
to do with country life

WORD HISTORY from Greek *boukolos* 'herdsman'

bud *NOUN* **buds**
a flower or leaf before it opens

bud *VERB* **buds, budding, budded**
to produce buds

Buddhism (*say* **buud**-izm) *NOUN*
(*Religion*) a religion that began in Asia and follows the teachings of the Indian philosopher Gautama Buddha, who lived in the 5th century BC

▷ **Buddhist** *NOUN*

WORD HISTORY from Sanskrit *buddha* 'enlightened one'

budding *ADJECTIVE*
beginning to develop ◆ *a budding poet*

buddy *NOUN* **buddies**
(*informal*) a friend

budge *VERB* **budges, budging, budged**
1 something that won't budge cannot be moved or shifted
2 someone who won't budge refuses to move their position, or to alter their opinions

budgerigar *NOUN* **budgerigars**
an Australian parakeet, often kept as a pet
WORD HISTORY from Australian Aboriginal *budgeri* 'good' and *gar* 'cockatoo'

budget *NOUN* **budgets**
1 a plan for spending money in a given period
2 an amount of money set aside for a purpose ◆ *I have a budget of £30 for their present.*
the Budget a regular statement made by the Chancellor of the Exchequer about plans for government spending and taxes
▷ **budgetary** *ADJECTIVE*

budget *VERB* **budgets, budgeting, budgeted**
to budget for something is to include its cost in your spending plan ◆ *I didn't budget for staying in a hotel.*
WORD HISTORY from Old French *bougette* 'bag, purse', because the Chancellor was said to open his purse to reveal his financial plans

budget *ADJECTIVE*
inexpensive ◆ *budget seats*

budgie *NOUN* **budgies**
(*informal*) a budgerigar

buff❶ *NOUN* **buffs**
someone who is interested in and knows a lot about a particular subject ◆ *a film buff*
WORD HISTORY so called after volunteer fire-fighters in New York who used to wear buff-coloured uniforms

buff❷ *NOUN*
in the buff (*informal*) wearing no clothes; naked
WORD HISTORY from *buff leather* 'leather of buffalo hide'

buff *VERB* **buffs, buffing, buffed**
to polish something with soft material

buff *ADJECTIVE*
of a dull yellow colour

buffalo *NOUN* **buffalo** or **buffaloes**
a large ox. Different kinds are found in Asia, Africa, and North America (where they are also called *bison*).
WORD HISTORY from Portuguese *bufalo*

buffer❶ *NOUN* **buffers**
1 something that reduces an impact or shock
2 one of a pair of shock-absorbing pads on either end of a train or at the end of a railway track
3 (*ICT*) a temporary storage area for text or data

buffer❷ *NOUN* **buffers**
(*informal*) an elderly person (usually said as an insult)

buffer state *NOUN* **buffer states**
a small country between two powerful ones, thought to reduce the chance of these two attacking each other

buffet (*say* **buu**-fay) *NOUN* **buffets**
1 a room or counter selling light meals or snacks
2 a meal where guests serve themselves
WORD HISTORY a French word meaning 'stool'

buffet (*say* **buf**-it) *VERB* **buffets, buffeting, buffeted**
to hit or knock something repeatedly ◆ *Strong winds buffeted the aircraft.*
WORD HISTORY from Old French *buffe* 'a blow'

buffet car *NOUN* **buffet cars**
a railway carriage which serves snacks and light meals

buffoon *NOUN* **buffoons**
a person who acts like a fool
▷ **buffoonery** *NOUN*
WORD HISTORY from Latin *buffo* 'clown'

bug *NOUN* **bugs**
1 a tiny insect
2 a secret hidden microphone
3 (*ICT*) an error in a computer program that prevents it working properly
4 (*informal*) a germ or virus
5 (*informal*) an enthusiasm for something ◆ *We've caught the skateboarding bug.*

bug *VERB* **bugs, bugging, bugged**
1 to fit a room with a secret hidden microphone
2 (*informal*) to pester or annoy someone ◆ *Stop bugging me!*

bugbear *NOUN* **bugbears**
something you fear or dislike
WORD HISTORY from an old word *bug* 'evil spirit'

bug-eyed *ADJECTIVE*
having bulging eyes

buggy *NOUN* **buggies**
1 a light collapsible pushchair for young children
2 a small open-topped vehicle used on beaches or golf courses
3 (*old use*) a light carriage pulled by a horse

bugle *NOUN* **bugles**
a brass instrument like a small trumpet, used for sounding military signals
▷ **bugler** *NOUN*

build *VERB* **builds, building, built**
1 to make something by putting parts together

One day Hrothgar made up his mind to build a great hall with some of the spoils he had won in war. — *Robert Nye, Beowulf*

2 to develop something gradually ◆ *We first need to build trust.*
3 to accumulate or increase ◆ *Traffic has been building all morning.*
to build something in is to incorporate it in a structure or plan
to build on something is to base future plans on something you have done or learned
to build up is to grow or increase
to build someone up
1 is to praise them a great deal to other people
2 food builds someone up when it makes them stronger or healthier
to build something up is to establish it gradually
▷ **built-in** ADJECTIVE
▷ **built-up** ADJECTIVE
build NOUN **builds**
the shape of someone's body ◆ *She is of slender build.*
builder NOUN **builders**
someone whose trade is constructing buildings
building NOUN **buildings**
1 a structure with a roof and walls, such as a house or office block
2 the constructing of houses and other structures
building society NOUN **building societies**
an organization that accepts deposits and lends money to people who want to buy houses
built *past tense and past participle of* **build**
bulb NOUN **bulbs**
1 a thick rounded part of a plant from which a stem grows up and roots grow down
2 a rounded part of something ◆ *the bulb of a thermometer*
3 a glass globe that produces electric light
▷ **bulbous** ADJECTIVE
WORD HISTORY from Greek *bolbos* 'onion'
bulgar wheat NOUN
a cereal food made from whole wheat that has been boiled and then dried
WORD HISTORY from Turkish *bulgur* 'bruised grain'
bulge NOUN **bulges**
a rounded swelling; an outward curve
bulge VERB **bulges, bulging, bulged**
to swell or protrude outwards in a curve
WORD HISTORY from Latin *bulga* 'bag'
bulimia (*say* buh-**lim**-ia) NOUN
an illness that makes someone alternately overeat and fast, often making themselves vomit after eating
▷ **bulimic** ADJECTIVE
WORD HISTORY from a Greek word meaning 'hunger of an ox'

bulk NOUN **bulks**
1 the size of something, especially when it is large

He came to stand near her, also looking out at the misty horizon of the sea, the stars, the dark bulk of the mountain above them. — *Ursula Le Guin, Tehanu*

2 the bulk of something is the greater part or the majority of it ◆ *The bulk of the population voted for it.*
in bulk in large amounts
bulk VERB **bulks, bulking, bulked**
to bulk something out is to increase it in size or thickness
bulkhead NOUN **bulkheads**
a partition between separate compartments in a ship, aircraft, or vehicle
bulky ADJECTIVE **bulkier, bulkiest**
taking up a lot of space; large and awkward
▷ **bulkiness** NOUN
bull① NOUN **bulls**
1 a fully grown male of any animal of the ox family
2 a male seal, whale, or elephant
WORD HISTORY from Old Norse *boli*
bull② NOUN **bulls**
an official order issued by the Pope
WORD HISTORY from Latin *bulla* 'seal, sealed letter'
bulldog NOUN **bulldogs**
a powerful dog with a short thick neck
WORD HISTORY so called because it was used for attacking tethered bulls in the sport of 'bull-baiting'
bulldoze VERB **bulldozes, bulldozing, bulldozed**
1 to clear an area with a bulldozer
2 to bulldoze someone into doing something is to force them to do it
bulldozer NOUN **bulldozers**
a powerful tractor with a wide metal blade or scoop in front, used for shifting soil or clearing ground
bullet NOUN **bullets**
a small piece of shaped metal shot from a rifle or revolver
WORD HISTORY from French *boulet* 'little ball'
bulletin NOUN **bulletins**
1 a short announcement of news on television or radio
2 a regular newsletter or report
bulletin board NOUN **bulletin boards**
(*ICT*) an area on a network or the Internet where people interested in a special topic or activity can read and exchange information

bullet point *NOUN* **bullet points**
(*ICT*) a short piece of information with a small black blob in front of it, usually one in a displayed list in a printed or word-processed document

bulletproof *ADJECTIVE*
able to keep out bullets

bullfighting *NOUN*
the baiting and killing of bulls for public entertainment, as in Spain
▷ **bullfighter** *NOUN*

bullfinch *NOUN* **bullfinches**
a bird with a strong beak and a pinkish breast

bullfrog *NOUN* **bullfrogs**
a large frog with a loud deep croak

bullion *NOUN*
bars of solid gold or silver
WORD HISTORY from Old French *bouillon* 'a mint'

bullock *NOUN* **bullocks**
a young castrated bull
WORD HISTORY from Old English *bulloc* 'young bull'

bullseye *NOUN* **bullseyes**
1 the centre of a target
2 a hard round peppermint sweet

bull terrier *NOUN* **bull terriers**
a dog originally produced by crossing a bulldog and a terrier

bully *NOUN*
a person who tries to hurt or frighten people who are weaker
bully for you! (*informal*) good for you! well done! (often said sarcastically when you mean 'so what?')
WORD HISTORY the original meaning of the word was 'sweetheart', but it later developed into 'a fine person' and then 'a loud and aggressive person'

bully *VERB* **bullies, bullying, bullied**
to use strength or power to hurt or frighten a weaker person ◆ *They had bullied me into taking more exercise and beginning a strict diet.*

bulrush *NOUN* **bulrushes**
a tall plant which grows in marshes, with a thick velvety head

bulwark (*say* **buul**-werk) *NOUN* **bulwarks**
1 a wall of earth built as a defence
2 something that acts as a protection or defence
3 a wall of earth built as a defence; a protection

bulwarks *PLURAL NOUN*
a ship's side above the level of the deck

bum[1] *NOUN* **bums**
(*informal*) your buttocks; your bottom

bum[2] *NOUN* **bums** (*American*)
(*informal*) a tramp

bum bag *NOUN* **bum bags**
(*informal*) a pouch to hold money and valuable items, worn on a belt around your waist

bumble *VERB* **bumbles, bumbling, bumbled**
1 to move or act in a clumsy way
2 to ramble when speaking

bumblebee *NOUN* **bumblebees**
a large hairy bee with a loud hum

bump *VERB* **bumps, bumping, bumped**
1 to knock against something
2 to move along with jolts
to bump into someone (*informal*) is to meet them by chance
to bump someone off (*informal*) is to kill them
to bump something up (*informal*) is to increase a figure or price

bump *NOUN* **bumps**
1 a bumping sound, knock, or movement
2 a swelling or lump

bumper[1] *NOUN* **bumpers**
a bar along the front or back of a motor vehicle to reduce the impact of a collision

bumper[2] *ADJECTIVE*
unusually large or plentiful ◆ *a bumper crop*

bumpkin *NOUN* **bumpkins**
a country person with awkward manners

bumptious (*say* **bump**-shus) *ADJECTIVE*
loud and conceited
▷ **bumptiousness** *NOUN*
WORD HISTORY from *bump* and *fractious*

bumpy[1] *ADJECTIVE* **bumpier, bumpiest**
1 a bumpy road or surface is uneven and full of bumps
2 a bumpy journey is one where you travel over lots of bumps
▷ **bumpily** *ADVERB*

bun *NOUN* **buns**
1 a small sweet cake or roll
2 hair twisted into a round bunch at the back of your head

bunch *NOUN* **bunches**
1 a cluster of fruit joined on a stem
2 a number of things joined or fastened together
3 (*informal*) a group of people

bunch *VERB* **bunches, bunching, bunched**
to gather or tie things into a bunch

bundle *NOUN* **bundles**
1 a number of things tied or wrapped together
2 (*informal*) a large amount of money

bundle *VERB* **bundles, bundling, bundled**
1 to wrap or tie things into a bundle
2 to put something away hastily and untidily ◆ *She bundled the letters into a drawer.*
3 to bundle someone into a room or vehicle is to push them hurriedly or carelessly into it

to bundle up to bundle up, or bundle yourself up, is to put on warm clothes, especially a hat and scarf
to bundle something up is to wrap or tie it into a bundle

bun fight *NOUN* **bun fights** (*informal*)
1 a grand tea party
2 a noisy argument

bung *NOUN* **bungs**
a stopper for closing a hole in a barrel or jar

bung *VERB* **bungs, bunging, bunged**
(*informal*) to throw or toss something carelessly ◆ *Bung it in the washing machine.*
to be bunged up (*informal*) is to be completely blocked

bungalow *NOUN* **bungalows**
a house with only one storey
WORD HISTORY from Hindi *bangla* 'of Bengal'

bungee jumping *NOUN*
the sport of jumping from a height with a long piece of elastic (called a *bungee*) tied to your legs to stop you from hitting the ground

bungle *VERB* **bungles, bungling, bungled**
to make a mess of doing something

bungle *NOUN* **bungles**
a mistake or failure

bunion *NOUN* **bunions**
a swelling at the side of the joint where your big toe joins your foot

bunk❶ *NOUN* **bunks**
a single bed built on a shelf or in a recess

bunk❷ *NOUN*
to do a bunk (*informal*) is to run away

bunk *VERB* **bunks, bunking, bunked**
to bunk off (*informal*) is to sneak away from somewhere you are supposed to be, especially school

bunk❸ *NOUN*
(*informal*) nonsense; rubbish
WORD HISTORY a short form of *bunkum*

bunk beds *PLURAL NOUN*
a pair of single beds mounted one above the other as a unit

bunker *NOUN* **bunkers**
1 an outdoor container for storing coal
2 a sandy hollow built as an obstacle on a golf course
3 an underground shelter for use in wartime

bunkum *NOUN*
(*informal*) nonsense; rubbish
WORD HISTORY from Buncombe County in North Carolina, mentioned in a political speech given there

bunny *NOUN* **bunnies**
(*informal*) a child's name for a rabbit
WORD HISTORY from a dialect word *bun* 'rabbit'

Bunsen burner *NOUN* **Bunsen burners**
a small gas burner used in laboratories
WORD HISTORY named after the German chemist, Robert *Bunsen* (1811–99), who popularized it

bunting❶ *NOUN* **buntings**
a small bird related to the finches

bunting❷ *NOUN*
strips of small flags hung up to decorate streets and buildings

buoy (*say* boi) *NOUN* **buoys**
a floating object anchored to mark a channel or underwater rocks

buoy *VERB* **buoys, buoying, buoyed**
to keep something afloat
to buoy someone up is to encourage them or keep their spirits up

buoyant (*say* **boi**-ant) *ADJECTIVE*
1 able to float
2 light-hearted; cheerful ◆ *He was in a buoyant mood.*
▷ **buoyancy** *NOUN*

burble *VERB* **burbles, burbling, burbled**
1 to make a gentle murmuring sound
2 to speak in a confused way; to ramble

burden *NOUN* **burdens**
1 a heavy load that you have to carry
2 something troublesome that you have to put up with
▷ **burdensome** *ADJECTIVE*

burden *VERB* **burdens, burdening, burdened**
1 to load someone heavily ◆ *She staggered in, burdened with shopping.*
2 to cause someone worry or trouble ◆ *I'm sorry to burden you with my troubles.*

bureau (*say* bewr-oh) *NOUN* **bureaux**
1 a writing desk with drawers and a hinged flap to use as a writing surface
2 an office or department ◆ *an information bureau*
WORD HISTORY a French word meaning 'desk'

bureaucracy (*say* bewr-**ok**-ra-see) *NOUN*
the use of too many rules and forms by officials, especially in government departments

bureaucrat (*say* **bewr**-ok-rat) *NOUN* **bureaucrats**
an official who works in a government department

bureaucratic (*say* bewr-ok-**rat**-ik) *ADJECTIVE*
a bureaucratic rule or system is one that uses too many forms and applies rules rigidly

burgeon (*say* **ber**-jon) *VERB* **burgeons, burgeoning, burgeoned**
to begin to grow rapidly ◆ *the country's burgeoning tourist industry*
WORD HISTORY from Old French *bourgeonner* 'to put out buds'

burger *NOUN* **burgers**
1 a piece of minced beef formed into a flat round shape, eaten grilled
2 a similar item of food made with other meat or vegetables

WORD HISTORY short for *hamburger*, named after the city of *Hamburg* in northern Germany

burglar *NOUN* **burglars**
a person who breaks into a building in order to steal things
▷ **burglary** *NOUN*

burgle *VERB* **burgles, burgling, burgled**
to burgle a person or place is to break into their house or office and steal things

burgundy *NOUN* **burgundies**
a rich red or white wine from Burgundy in central France

burial *NOUN* **burials**
the act or ritual of burying of a dead body

burkha (*say* ber-ka) *NOUN* **burkhas**
a loose robe covering the whole body including the head, worn in public by some Muslim women

burlesque (*say* ber-lesk) *NOUN* **burlesques**
a comical imitation which makes fun of something

WORD HISTORY via French from Italian *burla* 'joke'

burly *ADJECTIVE* **burlier, burliest**
having a strong heavy body
▷ **burliness** *NOUN*

burn ❶ *VERB* **burns, burning, burned** or **burnt**
1 to blaze or glow with fire; to be on fire
2 to damage or destroy something by fire, heat, or acid

Warlords and brigands roam the countryside burning and pillaging at will. — *Michael Morpurgo, Arthur, High King of Britain*

3 to spoil food by cooking it for too long
4 to feel very hot
5 your skin burns when it becomes red and painful from too much sunlight
6 someone burns with an emotion when they feel it intensely

to burn your boats or **bridges** is to do something that makes it impossible to go back to the situation you were in before
to burn the midnight oil is to work late into the night
to have money to burn is to have so much money that you can afford to waste some of it

USAGE NOTE Take care to use *burnt* (not *burned*) when you are using the word as an adjective, as in *burnt remains*. If you are using it as the past tense of *burn*, you can use either *burned* or *burnt*.

burn *NOUN* **burns**
1 a mark or injury made by burning
2 the firing of a spacecraft's rockets

WORD HISTORY from Old English *birnan*

burn ❷ *NOUN* **burns**
a Scottish word for a small stream

WORD HISTORY from Old English *burna*

burner *NOUN* **burners**
the part of a lamp or cooker that gives out the flame

burning *ADJECTIVE*
1 a burning desire or ambition is one that is very intense
2 a burning issue or question is one that is very topical and important

burnish *VERB* **burnishes, burnishing, burnished**
to polish a surface by rubbing

WORD HISTORY from Old French *burnir*

burnt *past tense and past participle of* **burn ❶**

burp *NOUN* **burps**
a belch

burp *VERB* **burps, burping, burped**
1 to belch
2 to make a baby bring up wind from its stomach after feeding

burr ❶ *NOUN* **burrs**
1 a whirring sound
2 the strong pronunciation of the letter 'r', as in some regional accents

burr ❷ *NOUN* **burrs**
a plant's seed case or flower that clings to hair or clothes

burrow *NOUN* **burrows**
a hole or tunnel dug by a rabbit or fox as a place to live

burrow *VERB* **burrows, burrowing, burrowed**
1 to dig a burrow
2 to push your way through or into something
3 to search by rummaging ◆ *She burrowed in her handbag.*

WORD HISTORY from an old spelling of *borough*

bursar *NOUN* **bursars**
1 a person who manages the finances and other business of a school or college
2 a student who has a bursary

WORD HISTORY from Latin *bursa* 'bag'

bursary *NOUN* **bursaries**
a grant given to a student

burst *VERB* **bursts, bursting, burst**
1 to break or force something apart suddenly or violently
2 to come apart or tear open suddenly ◆ *One of my tyres has burst.*
3 a door bursts open when it opens very suddenly or violently

a b c d e f g h i j k l m n o p q r s t u v w x y z

4 someone bursts into a room or building when they go in suddenly in a rush
to burst into flame is to catch fire
to burst into song is to start singing
to burst into tears is to start to cry suddenly
to burst out laughing is to start laughing noisily
to be bursting to do something is to be very anxious or desperate to do it
to be bursting with something is to be full of it

burst *NOUN* **bursts**
1 a split caused by something bursting
2 a short outbreak of something violent or noisy ◆ *a burst of gunfire*

bury *VERB* **buries, burying, buried**
1 to place a dead body in the earth, a tomb, or the sea

Golda's family performed the traditional rites and buried the body near some small acacia bushes. — *Doris Pilkington, Rabbit Proof Fence*

2 to put something underground
3 to hide something from sight
to bury the hatchet is to agree to stop quarrelling or fighting
to bury yourself in something is to involve yourself deeply in it

bus *NOUN* **buses**
1 a large vehicle for passengers to travel in, often as part of a public transport system
2 (*ICT*) a device which connects pieces of equipment to the main processor

WORD HISTORY short for an earlier word *omnibus* 'bus', from a Latin word meaning 'for everyone'

bus *VERB* **buses, busing, bused**
to take passengers somewhere in a bus

busby *NOUN* **busbies**
a tall fur cap worn by some army regiments on ceremonial occasions

bush *NOUN* **bushes**
1 a shrub
2 wild uncultivated land, especially in Africa and Australia

bushel *NOUN* **bushels**
a measure for grain and fruit equal to 8 gallons (36.4 litres)

bushman *NOUN* **bushmen**
a person who lives or travels in the Australian or African bush

bush telegraph *NOUN*
a way in which news or gossip is passed on unofficially

bushveld *NOUN*
an area of wild or uncultivated country in South Africa

bushy *ADJECTIVE* **bushier, bushiest**
1 bushy eyebrows are thick and hairy
2 bushy ground is covered with bushes

busily *ADVERB*
in a busy way

business (*say* biz-niss) *NOUN* **businesses**
1 the activity of buying and selling things; trade

Your father and I have been friendly rivals in business for some time now. — *J. B. Priestley, An Inspector Calls*

2 a shop or firm
3 a person's concern or responsibilities
4 an affair or subject ◆ *I'm tired of the whole business.*

WORD HISTORY from Old English *bisignis* 'busyness'

businesslike *ADJECTIVE*
practical and well organized

businessman or **businesswoman** *NOUN* **businessmen** or **businesswomen**
a man or woman who works in business, especially at a senior level

busker *NOUN* **buskers**
a person who plays music in the street for money
▷ **busking** *NOUN*

WORD HISTORY from an old word *busk* 'to be a pedlar'

busman's holiday *NOUN*
leisure time spent doing the same thing that you do at work

bust❶ *NOUN* **busts**
1 a sculpture of a person's head, shoulders, and chest
2 a woman's breasts or chest

WORD HISTORY from Latin *bustum* 'tomb'

bust❷ *VERB* **busts, busting, bust** (*informal*)
1 to break or burst something
2 to arrest someone in a police raid

bust *ADJECTIVE* (*informal*)
1 broken or damaged
2 a company goes bust when it becomes bankrupt

bustard *NOUN* **bustards**
a large bird that can run very fast

bustier (*say* bus-ti-ay) *NOUN* **bustiers**
a tight-fitting woman's top without straps

WORD HISTORY a French word

bustle❶ *VERB* **bustles, bustling, bustled**
to hurry in a busy or excited way

The little man ... was in a terrific hurry. He was bustling along the pavement, sidestepping the other pedestrians. — *Roald Dahl, The Umbrella Man*

bustle *NOUN*
hurried or excited activity

a b c d e f g h i j k l m n o p q r s t u v w x y z

bustle❷ *NOUN* **bustles**
padding used to puff out the top of a long skirt at the back

bust-up *NOUN* **bust-ups**
(*informal*) a serious quarrel

busy *ADJECTIVE* **busier, busiest**
1 having a lot to do; occupied

Nobody seemed to be paying me much attention—too busy chatting loudly.— *Keith Gray, Malarkey*

2 full of activity
3 a busy telephone line or number is one that is engaged
4 a busy picture or design has too many distracting details in it
▷ **busily** *ADVERB*
▷ **busyness** *NOUN*

busy *VERB* **busies, busying, busied**
to busy yourself is to do things to keep yourself occupied
WORD HISTORY from Old English *bisig*

busybody *NOUN* **busybodies**
a person who meddles or interferes

but *CONJUNCTION*
however; nevertheless

but *PREPOSITION*
except; other than ◆ *I could see no one but a few friends.*
but for if it wasn't for ◆ *I'd have drowned but for you.*

but *ADVERB*
only; no more than ◆ *We can but hope.*

but *NOUN* **buts**
an objection ◆ *You're coming, and no buts.*

butane (*say* bew-tayn) *NOUN*
a liquid gas produced from petroleum, used as a fuel

butch *ADJECTIVE*
(*informal*) masculine in appearance or behaviour

butcher *NOUN* **butchers**
1 a person who cuts up and sells meat in a shop
2 a person who kills cruelly or needlessly

butcher *VERB* **butchers, butchering, butchered**
1 to slaughter or cut up an animal for meat
2 to kill cruelly or needlessly

butchery *NOUN*
1 a butcher's trade
2 unnecessary or brutal killing

butler *NOUN* **butlers**
the chief male servant in a private house
WORD HISTORY from Old French *bouteillier* 'bottler'

butt❶ *NOUN* **butts**
1 the thicker end of a weapon or tool
2 the stub of a cigar or cigarette
3 (*American*) (*informal*) your buttocks; your bottom
WORD HISTORY from Dutch *bot* 'stumpy'

butt❷ *NOUN* **butts**
a large cask or barrel
WORD HISTORY from Latin *buttis* 'cask'

butt❸ *NOUN* **butts**
someone who is a target for ridicule or teasing ◆ *He was the butt of their jokes.*
WORD HISTORY from Old French *but* 'goal'

butt❹ *VERB* **butts, butting, butted**
1 an animal butts something when it pushes or hits it with its head and horns
2 to push or shove a part of your body forwards
3 something that butts against another thing is next to it with the sides or edges touching
to butt in is to interrupt or interfere

butt *NOUN* **butts**
a rough push with your head
WORD HISTORY from Old French *buter* 'to hit'

butter *NOUN*
a soft fatty food made by churning cream
▷ **buttery** *ADJECTIVE*
WORD HISTORY from Old English *butere*

butter *VERB* **butters, buttering, buttered**
to spread something with butter

buttercup *NOUN* **buttercups**
a wild plant with bright yellow cup-shaped flowers

butter-fingers *NOUN*
a clumsy person who often drops things

butterfly *NOUN* **butterflies**
1 an insect with four wings, often brightly coloured, and two feelers
2 a swimming stroke in which both arms are lifted forwards at the same time
to have butterflies in your stomach (*informal*) is to have a fluttering feeling in your stomach because you feel nervous

buttermilk *NOUN*
the liquid that is left after butter has been churned from milk

butterscotch *NOUN*
a kind of hard toffee

buttock *NOUN* **buttocks**
either of the two fleshy rounded parts of your bottom, or of an animal's rump
WORD HISTORY from Old English *buttoc*

button *NOUN* **buttons**
1 a knob or disc sewn on clothes as a fastening or ornament
2 a small knob pressed to work an electronic device

a b c d e f g h i j k l m n o p q r s t u v w x y z

3 a small image on a computer screen that can be clicked to perform a function

button *VERB* **buttons, buttoning, buttoned**
to fasten a piece of clothing with a button or buttons

buttonhole *NOUN* **buttonholes**
1 a slit through which a button passes to fasten clothes
2 a flower worn in the buttonhole of a coat lapel

buttonhole *VERB* **buttonholes, buttonholing, buttonholed**
to come up to someone and talk to them for a long time

buttress *NOUN* **buttresses**
a support built against a wall

buttress *VERB* **buttresses, buttressing, buttressed**
1 to support a building or wall with buttresses
2 to support or strengthen something

buxom *ADJECTIVE*
an old-fashioned word to describe a woman with a full figure

WORD HISTORY from Old English *bugan* 'to bend'. The word originally meant 'obedient or obliging', and later 'healthily plump'.

buy *VERB* **buys, buying, bought**
1 to get something by paying for it
2 to get something by effort or sacrifice ◆ *This victory was dearly bought.*
3 (*informal*) to believe or accept the truth of something ◆ *Do you really expect me to buy that?*

to have bought it (*informal*) is to have been killed
to buy someone out is to pay them to give up their share in something
to buy time is to delay so that you have more time to improve your position

buy *NOUN* **buys**
something that is bought ◆ *That suit was a good buy.*

WORD HISTORY from Old English *bycgan*

buyer *NOUN* **buyers**
1 a person who buys something
2 an agent who buys stock for a large shop

buzz *NOUN* **buzzes**
1 a vibrating humming sound
2 (*informal*) to get a buzz from something is to find it exciting

buzz *VERB* **buzzes, buzzing, buzzed**
1 to make a buzz or humming sound
2 to be busy ◆ *The room was buzzing with activity.*
3 to signal with a buzzer
4 to threaten an aircraft by deliberately flying close to it

to buzz off (*informal*) is to go away

buzzard *NOUN* **buzzards**
a kind of hawk

WORD HISTORY from Latin *buteo* 'falcon'

buzzer *NOUN* **buzzers**
a device that makes a buzzing sound as a signal

by *PREPOSITION*
1 used to indicate closeness to something ◆ *The house is by the bottom of the steps.*
2 used to show the direction or route something takes ◆ *Someone had come in by the back door.*
3 used to show the time before which something happens ◆ *By early afternoon they had reached the city.*
4 used to show manner or method ◆ *Anna went to school by boat.*
5 used to indicate a cause or subject ◆ *He had always been fascinated by anything that had to do with bees.*
6 used to indicate distance or amount ◆ *He reached the house before them by about an hour.*

by the way used to introduce an additional or less important fact or piece of information ◆ *By the way, they said they might be late.*
by yourself alone; without help

by *ADVERB*
past ◆ *Lots of taxis came by but they all had passengers in them.*

by and by soon; later on
by and large on the whole
to put something by is to keep it in reserve for future use

bye *NOUN* **byes**
1 a run scored in cricket when the ball goes past the batsman without being touched
2 having no opponent for one round in a tournament and so going on to the next round as if you had won

bye-bye *EXCLAMATION*
(*informal*) a word for goodbye

by-election *NOUN* **by-elections**
an election to replace a Member of Parliament who has died or resigned

WORD HISTORY from *by-* meaning 'extra', because it is an extra election between general elections

byeline *NOUN* **byelines**
the goal line of a football pitch

bygone *ADJECTIVE*
belonging to the past

to let bygones be bygones is to forgive and forget past offences

by-law *NOUN* **by-laws**
a law that applies only to a particular town or district

WORD HISTORY from Old Norse *byjarlagu* 'town law'

byline *NOUN* **bylines**
a line in a newspaper naming the writer of an article

bypass *NOUN* **bypasses**
1 a road which takes traffic round a city or congested area
2 a channel that allows something to flow when the main route is blocked
3 an operation to make an alternative passage to help the circulation of the blood

bypass *VERB* **bypasses, bypassing, bypassed**
1 to avoid something by means of a bypass
2 to ignore a rule or procedure in order to act quickly

by-product *NOUN* **by-products**
a product that is produced during the making of something else

byre (*rhymes with* fire) *NOUN* **byres**
a cowshed
WORD HISTORY an Old English word

byroad *NOUN* **byroads**
a minor road

bystander *NOUN* **bystanders**
a person standing near but taking no part when something happens

byte *NOUN* **bytes**
(*ICT*) a fixed number of bits (= binary digits) in a computer, often representing a single character
WORD HISTORY an invented word based on *bit* and *bite*

byway *NOUN* **byways**
a minor road or path

byword *NOUN* **bywords**
1 a person or thing spoken of as a famous example of something ◆ *The hotel had become a byword for luxury and comfort.*
2 a word or phrase that sums up a person's principles ◆ *Punctuality is my byword.*
WORD HISTORY from Old English *biwyrde* 'proverb'

Byzantine (*say* bi-**zan**-tyn) *ADJECTIVE*
1 to do with Byzantium or the Eastern Roman Empire
2 a Byzantine plan or plot is devious or underhand
WORD HISTORY from *Byzantium*, the city later called Constantinople and now Istanbul

Cc

cab *NOUN* **cabs**
1 a taxi
2 the driver's compartment at the front of a lorry, bus, or train

cabaret (*say* kab-er-ay) *NOUN* **cabarets**
an entertainment in a restaurant or nightclub for guests who sit at tables

cabbage *NOUN* **cabbages**
a vegetable with thick green or purple leaves

caber *NOUN* **cabers**
a tree trunk used in the Scottish Highland sport of 'tossing the caber'

cabin *NOUN* **cabins**
1 a small wooden hut or shelter
2 a private sleeping room on a ship
3 the part of an aircraft where the passengers sit
4 a driver's cab

Cabinet *NOUN*
a group of chief ministers, chosen by the Prime Minister, who meet to decide government policy

cabinet *NOUN* **cabinets**
a cupboard with drawers or shelves for storing things

cable *NOUN* **cables**
1 a thick rope of fibre or wire
2 a covered group of wires laid underground for transmitting electrical signals

cable car *NOUN* **cable cars**
a small cabin suspended on a moving cable, used for carrying people up and down a mountainside

cable television *NOUN*
a broadcasting service with signals transmitted by cable to subscribers

cacao (*say* ka-**kay**-oh) *NOUN* **cacaos**
a tropical tree with a seed from which cocoa and chocolate are made

cache (*say* kash) *NOUN* **caches**
a hidden store of valuable things

cackle *NOUN* **cackles**
1 a loud silly laugh
2 noisy chatter
3 the loud clucking noise a hen makes
▷ **cackle** *VERB*

cacophony (*say* kak-**off**-on-ee) *NOUN* **cacophonies**
a harsh mixture of loud unpleasant sounds
▷ **cacophonous** *ADJECTIVE*

cactus *NOUN* **cacti**
a thick fleshy plant with prickles but no leaves, growing in a hot dry climate

cad *NOUN* **cads**
a dishonourable man

cadaver (*say* kad-**av**-er) *NOUN*
(*formal*) a dead body

cadaverous *ADJECTIVE*
pale and thin, like a dead body

caddie *NOUN* **caddies**
a person who carries a golfer's clubs during a game

caddy *NOUN* **caddies**
a small container for tea

cadence (*say* **kay**-denss) *NOUN* **cadences**
1 the rise and fall of the voice in speaking
2 the final notes of a musical phrase

cadenza (*say* ka-**den**-za) *NOUN* **cadenzas**
an elaborate passage for a solo instrument or singer in a longer piece of music

cadet *NOUN* **cadets**
a young trainee in the armed forces or the police

cadge *VERB* **cadges, cadging, cadged**
(*informal*) to ask for or get something you are not really entitled to

WORD HISTORY from a dialect word meaning 'to carry about'

cadmium *NOUN*
a metal that looks like tin

Caesarean section (*say* siz-**air**-ee-an) *NOUN*
a surgical operation for taking a baby out of the mother's womb by cutting through the wall of the abdomen

WORD HISTORY so called because the Roman dictator Julius *Caesar* is said to have been born in this way

caesura (*say* siz-**yoor**-a) *NOUN*
a short pause in a line of verse

cafe (*say* **kaf**-ay) *NOUN* **cafes**
a small restaurant selling light meals and drinks

SPELLING NOTE Some words with a hard **c**- sound begin with **ch**- (e.g. character)

cafeteria (*say* kaf-it-**eer**-ee-a) *NOUN* **cafeterias**
a self-service restaurant

cafetière (*say* kaf-it-i-**air**) *NOUN* **cafetières**
a coffee pot with a plunger that you push down to force the grounds to the bottom before you pour the coffee

caffeine (*say* **kaf**-een) *NOUN*
a stimulant substance found in tea and coffee

caftan *NOUN* **caftans**
another spelling of **kaftan**

cage *NOUN* **cages**
a structure of bars or wires, used for keeping animals or birds

cagoule (*say* kag-**ool**) *NOUN* **cagoules**
a lightweight waterproof jacket with a hood

cairn *NOUN* **cairns**
a mound of loose stones set up as a landmark or monument

cajole *VERB* **cajoles, cajoling, cajoled**
to persuade someone to do something by flattering them

cake *NOUN* **cakes**
1 an item of sweet baked food made from a mixture of flour, fat, eggs, sugar, etc.
2 a shaped or hardened mass, e.g. of soap

caked *ADJECTIVE*
covered with dried mud etc.

calamine *NOUN*
a pink powder used to make a soothing lotion for the skin

calamity *NOUN* **calamities**
an event that causes great damage or distress
▷ **calamitous** *ADJECTIVE*

calcium *NOUN*
a chemical substance found in teeth, bones, and lime

calcium carbonate *NOUN*
a white compound found as chalk, limestone, and marble

calculate *VERB* **calculates, calculating, calculated**
to work something out by using mathematics
▷ **calculable** *ADJECTIVE*
▷ **calculation** *NOUN*

calculated *ADJECTIVE*
a calculated remark or action is one that you intend to have a particular effect

calculating *ADJECTIVE*
planning things carefully so that you get what you want

calculator *NOUN* **calculators**
a small electronic device for making mathematical calculations

calculus *NOUN*
mathematics for working out problems about rates of change

WORD HISTORY from Latin *calculus* 'a small stone', formerly used on an abacus

calendar *NOUN* **calendars**
1 a chart or set of pages showing the days, weeks, and months of the year
2 a list of special days or events

WORD HISTORY from Latin *kalendae*, the name of the first day of the month

calf[1] *NOUN* **calves**
a young cow or bull, or the young of some other mammals, e.g. a whale or seal

calf[2] *NOUN* **calves**
the fleshy back part of the back of the leg below the knee

calibrate (*say* **kal**-i-brayt) *VERB* **calibrates, calibrating, calibrated**
to mark a gauge or instrument with a scale of measurements
▷ **calibration** *NOUN*

calibre (*say* **kal**-ib-er) *NOUN* **calibres**
1 the diameter of the inside of a tube or gun barrel, or of a bullet or shell
2 ability or quality ◆ *Barbados has been waiting for a hotel of this calibre for a very long time.*

calico *NOUN*
a kind of plain white cotton cloth

WORD HISTORY named after *Calicut*, a town in India from which the cloth was exported

calipers *PLURAL NOUN*
compasses for measuring the width of tubes or of round objects

caliph (*say* **kal**-if *or* **kay**-lif) *NOUN* **caliphs**
the former title of the ruler in certain Muslim countries

WORD HISTORY from Arabic *khalifa* 'successor of Muhammad'

call *VERB* **calls, calling, called**
1 to shout or speak loudly to attract someone's attention or to get them to come to you
2 to telephone someone
3 to name a person or thing ◆ *Why did you call your dog Alfred?*
4 to call on someone is to visit them for a short time

to call a person's bluff is to challenge a person to do what they threatened, when you think they are bluffing
to call for something is to require it ◆ *This news calls for a celebration.*
to call something off is to cancel or postpone it
to call someone up is to summon them to join the armed forces
▷ **caller** *NOUN*

call *NOUN* **calls**
1 a shout or cry to attract someone's attention
2 a short visit
3 an act of telephoning someone
4 a request for someone to come

calligram *NOUN* **calligrams**
a poem in which the form of the writing relates to the content of the poem, e.g. a poem about growth shown with the letters getting larger

calligraphy (*say* kal-**ig**-raf-ee) *NOUN*
the art of fine handwriting
WORD HISTORY from Greek *kalos* 'beautiful' and *graphia* 'writing'

calling *NOUN* **callings**
1 an occupation; a profession or trade
2 a strong feeling that you should follow a particular occupation; a vocation

callipers *PLURAL NOUN*
another spelling of **calipers**

callous (*say* **kal**-us) *ADJECTIVE*
hard-hearted and cruel
▷ **callously** *ADVERB*
▷ **callousness** *NOUN*

callow *ADJECTIVE*
immature and inexperienced
▷ **callowly** *ADVERB*
▷ **callowness** *NOUN*

callus *NOUN* **calluses**
an area of skin that has become thick and hard from being continually pressed or rubbed
WORD HISTORY from Latin *callum* 'hard skin'

calm *ADJECTIVE*
1 not excited or agitated
2 quiet and still; not windy
▷ **calmly** *ADVERB*
▷ **calmness** *NOUN*

calm *VERB* **calms, calming, calmed**
to make or become calm
WORD HISTORY from Greek *kauma* 'hot time of the day' (when people rested)

calorie *NOUN* **calories**
a unit for measuring an amount of heat or the energy produced by food
▷ **calorific** *ADJECTIVE*
WORD HISTORY from Latin *calor* 'heat'

calumny (*say* **kal**-um-nee) *NOUN* **calumnies**
a false statement that damages a person's reputation

calve *VERB* **calves, calving, calved**
to give birth to a calf

calypso *NOUN* **calypsos**
a West Indian song on a topical theme, made up as the singer goes along

calyx (*say* **kay**-liks) *NOUN* **calyces**
a ring of leaves (called *sepals*) forming the outer case of a bud
WORD HISTORY from Greek *kalyx* 'drinking goblet', because of the shape

camaraderie (*say* kam-er-**ah**-der-ee) *NOUN*
trust and comradeship between friends

camber *NOUN* **cambers**
a slight curved shape on a road or other horizontal surface

camcorder *NOUN* **camcorders**
a portable combined video camera and sound recorder

camel *NOUN* **camels**
a large animal with a long neck and either one or two humps on its back, used in desert countries for riding on and for carrying goods

camellia (*say* ka-**mee**-lia) *NOUN* **camellias**
a kind of evergreen flowering shrub with bright flowers
WORD HISTORY named after Joseph *Camellus*, a botanist

cameo (*say* **kam**-ee-oh) *NOUN* **cameos**
1 a small hard piece of stone carved with a raised design in its upper layer
2 a short descriptive piece of writing
3 a short part in a play or film, played by a well-known actor

camera *NOUN* **cameras**
a device for taking photographs, films, or television pictures
in camera in a judge's private room

camera obscura *NOUN*
1 a darkened box with a lens or small opening for projecting the image of an external object on to a screen inside
2 a small round building with a rotating angled mirror at the top of the roof, projecting an image of the landscape on to a surface inside

camomile *NOUN*
another spelling of **chamomile**

camouflage (*say* **kam**-off-lahzh) *NOUN*
1 a way of making military equipment look like part of its surroundings by painting it in special colours
2 the ability of an animal to make its appearance blend in with its surroundings, for protection

camouflage *VERB* **camouflages, camouflaging, camouflaged**
to disguise with camouflage

camp *NOUN* **camps**
1 a number of tents or huts set up together for people to live in for a short time
2 the supporters of a particular party or group

camp *VERB* **camps, camping, camped**
to live in a tent while on holiday

campaign *NOUN* **campaigns**
1 a series of military operations in one area or with one purpose
2 a planned series of actions to arouse interest in something ◆ *an election campaign*

campaign *VERB* **campaigns, campaigning, campaigned**
to take part in a campaign ◆ *Those opposed to the hunt had pledged to continue campaigning for an outright ban.*
▷ **campaigner** *NOUN*

camper *NOUN* **campers**
someone living in a camp on holiday

camphor *NOUN*
a strong-smelling white substance used in medicine and mothballs and in making plastics

campsite *NOUN* **campsites**
a place where a camp can be set up

campus *NOUN* **campuses**
the grounds and buildings of a university or college

can❶ *AUXILIARY VERB* *past tense* **could**
1 to be able to ◆ *She can speak three languages.*
2 to be allowed to ◆ *You can go now.*
WORD HISTORY from Old English *cunnan* 'to know'

can❷ *NOUN* **cans**
1 a sealed tin in which food or drink is preserved
2 a metal or plastic container for liquids
a can of worms is a complicated situation that will be difficult to manage

can *VERB* **cans, canning, canned**
to can food is to preserve it in sealed cans
WORD HISTORY from Old English *canne* 'container for liquids'

canal *NOUN* **canals**
1 an artificial water channel cut through land for boats to sail along or for irrigating land
2 a tube through which food or air passes in a plant or animal body

canary *NOUN* **canaries**
a small yellow singing bird, originally from the Canary Islands off the north-west coast of Africa

cancan *NOUN* **cancans**
a lively high-kicking dance performed by women on a stage

cancel *VERB* **cancels, cancelling, cancelled**
1 to say that something planned will not be done or will not take place
2 to stop an order or instruction for something
3 to mark a stamp or ticket etc. so that it cannot be used again
to cancel something out is to have an equal and opposite effect to something else ◆ *Their profits last year were cancelled out by tax rises.*
▷ **cancellation** *NOUN*

cancer *NOUN* **cancers**
1 a disease in which an uncontrolled growth of abnormal cells forms in the body
2 a harmful tumour
▷ **cancerous** *ADJECTIVE*
WORD HISTORY a Latin word meaning 'crab', because the swollen veins around the area of the cancer were thought to resemble the legs of a crab

candelabrum (*say* kan-dil-**ahb**-rum) *NOUN* **candelabra**
a candlestick with several branches for holding candles

candid *ADJECTIVE*
frank and honest
▷ **candidly** *ADVERB*

candidate *NOUN* **candidates**
1 a person who wants to be elected or chosen for a particular job or position
2 a person taking an examination
▷ **candidacy** *NOUN*
▷ **candidature** *NOUN*
WORD HISTORY from Latin *candidus* 'white' (because Roman candidates for office wore a white toga)

candied *ADJECTIVE*
candied fruit is fruit preserved in sugar

candle *NOUN* **candles**
a stick of wax with a wick running through the centre, producing a light when the wick burns

candlelight *NOUN*
the light from a candle

candlestick *NOUN* **candlesticks**
a holder or support for a candle

candour (*say* kan-der) *NOUN*
the quality of being frank and honest

candy *NOUN* **candies**
(*American*) sweets or a sweet

candyfloss *NOUN* **candyflosses**
a fluffy mass of thin strands of spun sugar wrapped round a stick

cane *NOUN* **canes**
1 the hollow stem of a reed or tall grass
2 a long thin stick

cane *VERB* **canes, caning, caned**
to beat someone with a long thin stick as a punishment

canine (*say* **kayn**-yn) *ADJECTIVE*
to do with dogs

canine *NOUN* **canines**
1 a dog
2 a pointed tooth at the front of the mouth

canister *NOUN* **canisters**
a round container

canker *NOUN*
a disease that rots the wood of trees and plants or causes ulcers and sores on animals

cannabis *NOUN*
hemp smoked as a drug

cannibal *NOUN* **cannibals**
1 a person who eats human flesh
2 an animal that eats the flesh of animals of its own species

▷ **cannibalism** *NOUN*

WORD HISTORY from Spanish *Canibales*, the name given to the original inhabitants of the Caribbean islands, who were thought by the Spanish to eat people

cannibalize *VERB* **cannibalizes, cannibalizing, cannibalized**
to cannibalize a machine or vehicle is to take it apart to get spare parts for others

▷ **cannibalization** *NOUN*

USAGE NOTE This word can also be spelled cannibalise.

cannon *NOUN* **cannon**
a large heavy gun formerly used in warfare

cannon *VERB* **cannons, cannoning, cannoned**
to cannon into something is to collide with it clumsily or heavily

USAGE NOTE Take care not to confuse this word with *canon*.

cannonball *NOUN* **cannonballs**
a large solid ball fired from a cannon

cannot
can not

canny *ADJECTIVE* **cannier, canniest**
shrewd

▷ **cannily** *ADVERB*

canoe *NOUN* **canoes**
a narrow lightweight boat, moved forwards with paddles

canoe *VERB* **canoes, canoeing, canoed**
to travel in a canoe

▷ **canoeist** *NOUN*

canon *NOUN* **canons**
1 a general rule or principle
2 a clergyman of a cathedral

USAGE NOTE Take care not to confuse this word with *cannon*.

canonize *VERB* **canonizes, canonizing, canonized**
to declare officially that a person who has died is a saint

▷ **canonization** *NOUN*

USAGE NOTE This word can also be spelled canonise.

canopy *NOUN* **canopies**
1 a hanging cover forming a shelter above a throne or bed
2 a natural covering, e.g. of leaves and branches

Beneath the dark canopy of leaves and smoke the fire laid hold on the forest and began to gnaw.
— *William Golding, Lord of the Flies*

3 the part of a parachute that spreads in the air

cant❶ *VERB*
to slope or tilt

cant❷ *NOUN*
1 insincere talk about moral behaviour
2 the jargon of a particular group or profession

can't
short for *cannot*

cantaloupe *NOUN* **cantaloupes**
a small round orange-coloured melon

WORD HISTORY from *Cantaluppi*, a place near Rome where the fruit was first grown in Europe

cantankerous *ADJECTIVE*
bad-tempered and uncooperative

I hated the new donkey on sight. He was a big, strong beast, carrying his nose high and with a cantankerous set to his ears. — *Alison Prince, Oranges and Murder*

cantata (*say* kant-**ah**-ta) *NOUN* **cantatas**
a musical composition for singers, usually with a chorus and orchestra

canteen *NOUN* **canteens**
1 a restaurant for workers in a factory or office
2 a case containing a set of cutlery
3 a small water flask carried by a soldier or camper

canter *NOUN*
a gentle gallop by a horse

canter *VERB* **canters, cantering, cantered**
to move or ride at a gentle gallop

Hrun's warhorse cantered through a creaking archway and reared up by its master, its mane streaming in the gale. — *Terry Pratchett, The Colour of Magic*

WORD HISTORY short for *Canterbury gallop*, the gentle pace at which pilgrims were said to travel to Canterbury in the Middle Ages

canticle *NOUN* **canticles**
a song or chant with words taken from the Bible

cantilever *NOUN* **cantilevers**
a beam or girder fixed at only one end and used to support a bridge

canton *NOUN* **cantons**
each of several districts into which a country, especially Switzerland, is divided

canvas *NOUN* **canvases**
1 a kind of strong coarse cloth
2 an oil painting on canvas

WORD HISTORY from Latin *cannabis* 'hemp', because canvas was made from hemp fibres

a b c d e f g h i j k l m n o p q r s t u v w x y z

SPELLING NOTE Some words with a hard **c-** sound begin with **ch-** (e.g. character)

canvass *VERB* **canvasses, canvassing, canvassed**
to visit people to ask them for their support in an election
▷ **canvasser** *NOUN*

canyon *NOUN* **canyons**
a deep valley, usually with a river running through it

cap *NOUN* **caps**
1 a soft flat or close-fitting hat with a peak
2 a special headdress, e.g. that worn by a nurse
3 a cap awarded to members of a sports team
4 a cover or top like a cap
5 an upper limit to money that can be spent or borrowed
6 a tiny explosive device that bangs when fired in a toy pistol

cap *VERB* **caps, capping, capped**
1 to put a cap or cover on something
2 to award a cap to a member of a sports team
3 to do better than something ◆ *It would certainly cap everything we've been doing if you did find a black hole.*
4 to set a limit on something, e.g. spending

capable *ADJECTIVE*
able to do something
▷ **capably** *ADVERB*
▷ **capability** *NOUN*

capacious (*say* ka-pay-shus) *ADJECTIVE*
having a lot of space; able to hold a large amount

capacity *NOUN* **capacities**
1 the amount that something can hold
2 ability or capability
3 the position that someone occupies ◆ *Melina Mercouri once came here in her capacity as Greek Minister for the Arts.*

cape❶ *NOUN* **capes**
a short cloak

cape❷ *NOUN* **capes**
a piece of high land that sticks out into the sea

caper❶ *VERB* **capers, capering, capered**
to jump about playfully

caper *NOUN* **capers**
1 jumping about playfully
2 (*informal*) an adventure or prank

caper❷ *NOUN* **capers**
the pickled bud of a prickly shrub, used in cooking

capillary (*say* ka-**pil**-er-ee) *NOUN* **capillaries**
a very fine blood vessel that connect veins and arteries

capillary *ADJECTIVE*
to do with a narrow tube or blood vessel; capillary action is the force which acts on a liquid in a narrow tube to push it up or down

capital *NOUN* **capitals**
1 the capital, or capital city, of a country is its most important city, usually where the government is based
2 a capital, or capital letter, is a large letter that you use at the start of a name or sentence
3 capital is money or property that is used or invested to produce more wealth
4 a capital is the ornamental shaped top part of a pillar

capital *ADJECTIVE*
(*old use*) very good; excellent

capitalism (*say* **kap**-it-al-izm) *NOUN*
a system in which a country's trade and industry are controlled by private owners for profit, and not by the state (SEE ALSO **communism, socialism**)

capitalist (*say* **kap**-it-al-ist) *NOUN* **capitalists**
1 a rich person who has a lot of their wealth invested
2 a person who supports the system of capitalism

capitalize (*say* **kap**-it-al-yz) *VERB* **capitalizes, capitalizing, capitalized**
1 to capitalize on something is to use it to your own advantage ◆ *It was important to capitalize on the goodwill that existed in the country.*
2 to write or print as a capital letter
3 to change something into money or property
4 to provide something with capital
▷ **capitalization** *NOUN*

USAGE NOTE This word can also be spelled capitalise.

capital punishment *NOUN*
punishment by being put to death, e.g. by hanging or beheading

capitulate *VERB* **capitulates, capitulating, capitulated**
to admit that you are defeated and surrender
▷ **capitulation** *NOUN*

cappuccino (*say* ka-poo-**chee**-noh) *NOUN* **cappuccinos**
milky coffee made frothy by putting steam through it under pressure

WORD HISTORY an Italian word: named after the *Capuchin* monks who wore coffee-coloured habits

caprice (*say* ka-**preess**) *NOUN* **caprices**
a sudden impulsive whim or change of behaviour

capricious (*say* ka-**prish**-us) *ADJECTIVE*
deciding or changing your mind in an impulsive way
▷ **capriciously** *ADVERB*

capsize *VERB* **capsizes, capsizing, capsized**
a boat capsizes when it overturns in the water

capstan *NOUN* **capstans**
a thick revolving post round which a rope or cable can be wound

capsule *NOUN* **capsules**
1 a hollow gelatin case containing a dose of medicine for swallowing
2 the seed case of a plant, which splits open when ripe
3 a compartment of a spacecraft that can be separated from the main part

captain *NOUN* **captains**
1 the person in command of a ship or aircraft
2 the leader of a sports team
3 an army officer ranking next below a major, or a naval officer ranking next below a commodore
▷ **captaincy** *NOUN*

captain *VERB* **captains, captaining, captained**
to be the captain of a sports team

caption *NOUN* **captions**
1 the words printed next to a picture, giving its title or description

> It was one of those pictures which are so contrived that the eyes follow you about when you move. BIG BROTHER IS WATCHING YOU, the caption beneath it ran. — *George Orwell, Nineteen Eighty-four*

2 a short title or heading in a newspaper or magazine

captious (*say* kap-shus) *ADJECTIVE*
liking to point out small mistakes or faults

captivate *VERB* **captivates, captivating, captivated**
to charm or delight someone
▷ **captivation** *NOUN*

captive *NOUN* **captives**
someone who has been taken prisoner

captive *ADJECTIVE*
taken prisoner; unable to escape
▷ **captivity** *NOUN*

captor *NOUN* **captors**
someone who has captured a person or animal

capture *VERB* **captures, capturing, captured**
1 to take someone prisoner
2 to take a place with an army
3 (*ICT*) to put data in a form that can be stored in a computer

capture *NOUN*
the act of capturing someone or something

car *NOUN* **cars**
1 a vehicle with an engine, designed to carry a small number of people
2 a railway carriage

carafe (*say* ka-**raf**) *NOUN* **carafes**
a glass bottle used for serving wine or water

caramel *NOUN* **caramels**
1 a soft toffee made with sugar and butter
2 sugar heated until it turns brown, used for colouring and flavouring food

carapace (*say* ka-ra-payss) *NOUN* **carapaces**
the hard shell on the back of a tortoise or crustacean

carat *NOUN* **carats**
1 a unit of weight for precious stones and pearls
2 a measure of the purity of gold

caravan *NOUN* **caravans**
1 a vehicle towed by a car and used for living in
2 (*History*) a group of people travelling together across desert country
▷ **caravanning** *NOUN*

caraway *NOUN*
a plant with spicy seeds used for flavouring food

carbohydrate *NOUN* **carbohydrates**
a compound of carbon, oxygen, and hydrogen (e.g. sugar or starch) found in food and a source of energy

carbolic *NOUN*
a kind of disinfectant

carbon *NOUN* **carbons**
an element that is present in all living things and that occurs in its pure form as diamond and graphite

carbonate *NOUN* **carbonates**
a compound that gives off carbon dioxide when mixed with acid

carbonated *ADJECTIVE*
a carbonated drink has carbon dioxide added to make it fizzy

carbon dating *NOUN*
a process of dating organic objects by measuring the amount of radiocarbon present in it

carbon dioxide *NOUN*
a gas formed when things burn, or breathed out by humans and animals

carboniferous *ADJECTIVE*
producing coal

carbuncle *NOUN* **carbuncles**
1 a large boil or abscess in the skin
2 a bright red gem

carburettor *NOUN* **carburettors**
a device in an engine for mixing the fuel and air in the right proportions

carcass *NOUN* **carcasses**
the dead body of an animal

carcinogen *NOUN* **carcinogens**
a substance that can cause cancer

SPELLING NOTE Some words with a hard **c-** sound begin with **ch-** (e.g. character)

card *NOUN* **cards**
1 thick stiff paper or thin cardboard
2 a small piece of stiff paper for writing or printing messages or greetings on
3 a small oblong piece of plastic with machine-readable information, issued to a customer by a bank for drawing out money and making payments
4 a playing card used in a game (called *cards*)
to be on the cards is to be possible or likely
to put your cards on the table is to be completely open in saying what you intend to do.

cardboard *NOUN*
a thin board made of layers of paper or wood fibre

cardiac (*say* **kard**-ee-ak) *ADJECTIVE*
to do with the heart

cardigan *NOUN* **cardigans**
a knitted sweater shaped like a jacket, with buttons down the front
WORD HISTORY named after the Earl of *Cardigan*, a commander in the Crimean War whose soldiers were the first to wear cardigans

cardinal *NOUN* **cardinals**
a senior priest in the Roman Catholic Church, who votes in elections for the Pope

cardinal *ADJECTIVE*
chief or most important ◆ *What happens next is a cardinal moment in 5th-century Greek history.*
WORD HISTORY from Latin *cardo cardin-* 'hinge', because cardinals were regarded as 'pivots' of church life

cardinal number *NOUN* **cardinal numbers**
a number for expressing a quantity (one, two, three, etc.) (SEE ALSO **ordinal number**)

cardinal point *NOUN* **cardinal points**
each of the four main points of the compass (North, South, East, West)

cardiology *NOUN*
the study of the heart and its diseases
▷ **cardiological** *ADJECTIVE*
▷ **cardiologist** *NOUN*

care *NOUN* **cares**
1 serious attention and thought ◆ *Plan your holiday with care.*
2 caution to avoid damage or loss ◆ *Glass—handle with care*
3 protection or supervision ◆ *Leave the child in my care.*
4 worry or anxiety ◆ *She was free from care.*
to take care is to be especially careful
to take care of someone is to look after them
to take care of something is to deal with it

care *VERB* **cares, caring, cared**
1 to be interested or concerned
2 to feel affection

I also said that I cared about dogs because they were faithful and honest, and some dogs were cleverer and more interesting than some people. *— Mark Haddon, The Curious Incident of the Dog in the Night-Time*

3 to care for someone is to be fond of them or to look after them

career *NOUN* **careers**
the series of jobs that someone has as they make progress in their occupation

career *VERB* **careers, careering, careered**
rush along wildly

The beast was careering through the tunnels, crashing, bellowing, thundering through the maze. *— Alan Gibbons, Shadow of the Minotaur*

carefree *ADJECTIVE*
having no worries or responsibilities

careful *ADJECTIVE*
1 giving serious thought and attention to something
2 avoiding damage or danger etc.; cautious
▷ **carefully** *ADVERB*

careless *ADJECTIVE*
not taking enough care to avoid mistakes or harm
▷ **carelessly** *ADVERB*
▷ **carelessness** *NOUN*

caress *NOUN* **caresses**
a gentle loving touch

caress *VERB* **caresses, caressing, caressed**
to touch lovingly

caret *NOUN* **carets**
a mark (^) showing where something is to be inserted in writing or printing

caretaker *NOUN* **caretakers**
a person employed to look after a large building

cargo *NOUN* **cargoes**
goods carried in a ship or aircraft

Caribbean *ADJECTIVE*
to do with or from the Caribbean Sea, a part of the Atlantic Ocean east of Central America

caribou (*say* **ka**-rib-oo) *NOUN* **caribou**
a North American reindeer
WORD HISTORY from a Native American word meaning 'snow-shoveller' (because the caribou scrapes away the snow to feed on the grass underneath)

caricature *NOUN* **caricatures**
an amusing or exaggerated picture or description of a person

caries (*say* **kair**-eez) *NOUN* **caries**
decay in a tooth or bone

carmine *ADJECTIVE, NOUN*
a deep red colour

carnage *NOUN*
the killing of large numbers of people

carnal *ADJECTIVE*
to do with the body and its sexual needs and activities

carnation *NOUN* **carnations**
a garden flower with a sweet smell

carnival *NOUN* **carnivals**
a festival with music, dancing, and processions

WORD HISTORY from Latin *carnis* 'of the flesh' (because a carnival was originally held as part of the festivities before Lent, when people gave up meat until Easter)

carnivore (*say* kar-ni-vor) *NOUN*
an animal that feeds on the flesh of other animals (SEE ALSO **herbivore, omnivore**)

carnivorous (*say* kar-**niv**-er-us) *ADJECTIVE*
a carnivorous animal feeds on the flesh of other animals (SEE ALSO **herbivorous, omnivorous**)

carol *NOUN* **carols**
a hymn sung at Christmas time
▷ **caroller** *NOUN*
▷ **carolling** *NOUN*

carouse *VERB* **carouses, carousing, caroused**
to drink and enjoy yourself with other people

WORD HISTORY originally in the phrase *drink carouse*, from German *gar aus trinken* 'drink to the bottom of the glass'

carousel (*say* ka-roo-**sel**) *NOUN* **carousels**
1 a merry-go-round at a fair
2 a device with a rotating belt for passengers to collect their baggage at an airport

carp❶ *NOUN* **carp**
an edible freshwater fish

carp❷ *VERB* **carps, carping, carped**
to keep complaining or finding fault

car park *NOUN* **car parks**
an area where cars may be parked

carpenter *NOUN* **carpenters**
a person who makes objects and structures out of wood
▷ **carpentry** *NOUN*

carpet *NOUN* **carpets**
a thick soft covering for a floor
▷ **carpeted** *ADJECTIVE*
▷ **carpeting** *NOUN*

carport *NOUN* **carports**
a shelter with a roof and open sides for a car

carriage *NOUN* **carriages**
1 one of the separate parts of a train, where passengers sit
2 a passenger vehicle pulled by horses
3 the process of carrying goods from one place to another, or the cost of this ◆ *Carriage is extra.*
4 a moving part carrying or holding something in a machine

carriageway *NOUN* **carriageways**
the part of a road on which vehicles travel

carrier *NOUN* **carriers**
a person or thing that carries or holds something

carrier bag *NOUN* **carrier bags**
a plastic or paper bag with handles

carrier pigeon *NOUN* **carrier pigeons**
a pigeon used to carry messages

carrion *NOUN*
the decaying flesh of a dead animal

carrot *NOUN* **carrots**
a plant with a thick orange-coloured root used as a vegetable

carry *VERB* **carries, carrying, carried**
1 to take something from one place to another
2 to support the weight of something
3 to take an amount into the next column when adding figures
4 sound carries when it can be heard a long way away
5 to carry a proposal at a meeting is to get it approved by most of the people there

to be carried away is to be very excited
to carry on is to continue or keep doing something
to carry out a plan is to put it into practice

WORD FAMILY Something you can carry is portable.

cart *NOUN* **carts**
an open vehicle for carrying loads

cart *VERB* **carts, carting, carted**
1 (*informal*) to carry something heavy or tiring ◆ *I've been carting these books around all morning.*
2 to carry something in a cart

carte blanche (*say* kart **blahnsh**) *NOUN*
freedom to act as you think best

cartel (*say* kar-**tel**) *NOUN* **cartels**
(*Economics*) an association of manufacturers or suppliers formed to maintain high prices and limit competition

carthorse *NOUN* **carthorses**
a large strong horse used for pulling heavy loads

cartilage *NOUN*
tough white flexible tissue attached to a bone

cartography *NOUN*
the art of drawing maps
▷ **cartographer** *NOUN*
▷ **cartographic** *ADJECTIVE*

carton *NOUN* **cartons**
a light cardboard or plastic container

a b c d e f g h i j k l m n o p q r s t u v w x y z

SPELLING NOTE Some words with a hard **c-** sound begin with **ch-** (e.g. character)

cartoon *NOUN* **cartoons**
1 a humorous drawing in a newspaper or magazine
2 a series of drawings that tell a story
3 an animated film made from a sequence of drawings
▷ **cartoonist** *NOUN*
WORD HISTORY from Italian *cartone* 'cardboard'; the original meaning was 'a drawing on stiff paper'

cartridge *NOUN* **cartridges**
1 a case containing the explosive for a bullet or shell
2 a container holding film for a camera, ink for a pen or printer etc.

cartwheel *NOUN* **cartwheels**
a sideways handstand performed by balancing on each hand in turn with arms and legs spread like the spokes of a wheel

carve *VERB* **carves, carving, carved**
1 to make an object or design by cutting a hard material such as wood or stone
2 to cut cooked meat into slices

carvery *NOUN* **carveries**
a restaurant that serves carved meats

cascade *NOUN* **cascades**
a small gentle waterfall

cascade *VERB* **cascades, cascading, cascaded**
to pour down in large amounts

case[1] *NOUN* **cases**
1 a container or covering
2 a suitcase
WORD HISTORY from Latin *capsa* 'box'

case[2] *NOUN* **cases**
1 an instance of something existing or occurring ◆ *In every case we found that someone had cheated.*
2 an incident that the police are investigating or that is being decided in a law trial ◆ *a murder case*
3 a set of facts or arguments put forward to support an idea or proposition ◆ *She put forward a good case for equality.*
4 the form of a word that shows how it is related to other words. *Fred's* is the possessive case of *Fred*; *him* is the objective case of *he*.

in any case whatever happens; anyway
in case to allow for the possibility of something happening
WORD HISTORY from Latin *casus* 'a fall', 'an occasion'

casement *NOUN* **casements**
a window that opens on hinges at its side like a door

cash *NOUN*
1 money in coin or notes
2 immediate payment for goods

cash *VERB* **cashes, cashing, cashed**
to change a cheque or money order for cash
WORD HISTORY from Latin *capsa* 'box'; the original meaning was 'a box for cash'

cash card *NOUN* **cash cards**
a plastic card used to draw money from a cash dispenser

cash dispenser *NOUN* **cash dispensers**
a machine, usually outside a bank or building society, from which people can draw out cash by using a cash card

cashew *NOUN* **cashews**
a kind of small nut shaped like a kidney

cash flow *NOUN*
the amount of money coming into a business as income and being spent by it

cashier *NOUN* **cashiers**
a person who takes in and pays out money in a bank or takes payments in a shop

cashmere *NOUN*
a very fine soft wool originally made from a breed of goat in the Himalayas
WORD HISTORY from *Kashmir* in Asia, where it was first produced

cashpoint *NOUN* **cashpoints**
a cash dispenser

cash register *NOUN* **cash registers**
a machine that records and stores the money received in a shop

casing *NOUN* **casings**
a protective case or covering

casino *NOUN* **casinos**
a public building or room for gambling

cask *NOUN* **casks**
a large barrel for storing alcoholic liquid

casket *NOUN* **caskets**
a small ornamental box for jewellery and other valuable items

cassava *NOUN*
a tropical plant with starchy roots that are an important source of food in tropical countries

casserole *NOUN* **casseroles**
1 a covered dish in which food is cooked and served
2 a kind of stew cooked in a casserole

cassette *NOUN* **cassettes**
a sealed plastic case containing film, recording tape, etc., ready to be inserted in a camera or player

cassock *NOUN* **cassocks**
a long piece of clothing worn by clergy and members of a church choir

cast *VERB* **casts, casting, cast**
1 to throw something with force
2 to shed something or throw it off

3 to make a light or shadow appear on a surface

The oil-burning torches had been lit and the flames cast flickering shadows across the square. — *Anthony Horowitz, Scorpia*

4 to direct your eyes or thoughts
5 to cast a vote is to record a vote in an election
6 to make something of metal or plaster in a mould
7 to choose performers for a play or film

to cast about or around is to look or search over a large area

The dæmon seemed suspicious, and cast around as if she'd sensed an intruder. — *Philip Pullman, Northern Lights*

cast *NOUN* **casts**
1 a shape made by pouring liquid metal or plaster into a mould
2 the performers in a play or film
3 the appearance or character of something

We stood, our shadows lengthening in the last rays of the sun, the dust beneath our feet taking on a golden cast. — *Celia Rees, Witch Child*

castanets *PLURAL NOUN*
two pieces of wood or ivory held in one hand and clicked together with the fingers as an accompaniment to Spanish dancing

WORD HISTORY from Spanish *castañetas* 'little chestnuts'

castaway *NOUN* **castaways**
a person who has been shipwrecked in a deserted place

caste *NOUN* **castes**
(in India) each of the social classes into which Hindus are born

WORD HISTORY from Spanish or Portuguese *casta* 'lineage', from *castus* 'pure'

caster sugar *NOUN*
finely ground white sugar

castigate *VERB* **castigates, castigating, castigated**
to punish or rebuke someone severely
▷ **castigation** *NOUN*

casting vote *NOUN* **casting votes**
the vote that decides which group wins when the votes on each side are equal

cast iron *NOUN*
a hard alloy of iron made by casting it in a mould

castle *NOUN* **castles**
1 (*History*) a large fortified building in medieval times
2 a piece in chess, also called a *rook*

castles in the air daydreams or wild hopes

castor *NOUN* **castors**
a small wheel on the leg of a table or other piece of furniture

castor oil *NOUN*
oil from the seeds of a tropical African plant, used as a laxative

castor sugar *NOUN* another spelling of **caster sugar**

castrate *VERB* **castrates, castrating, castrated**
to castrate a male animal is to remove its testicles so that it cannot mate (SEE ALSO **spay**)
▷ **castration** *NOUN*

casual *ADJECTIVE*
1 happening by chance and not planned ◆ *They had got to know each other from casual meetings in the street.*
2 not carefully done or thought out ◆ *He made a few casual remarks and left.*
3 relaxed and not bothered by something ◆ *Emily tried to sound casual.*
4 casual clothes are those suitable for informal occasions
5 casual work is work that is not permanent
▷ **casually** *ADVERB*

casualty *NOUN* **casualties**
1 a person who is killed or injured in war or in an accident
2 a person or thing that is badly affected by some event or situation
3 a casualty department in a hospital

casualty department *NOUN* **casualty departments**
the department of a hospital that deals with emergency patients

cat *NOUN* **cats**
1 a small furry domestic animal
2 a wild animal of the same family as a domestic cat, e.g. a lion, tiger, or leopard

to let the cat out of the bag is to reveal a secret by mistake

WORD FAMILY A related adjective is feline.

cataclysm (*say* kat-a-klizm) *NOUN* **cataclysms**
a violent upheaval or disaster

cataclysmic (*say* kat-a-**klizm**-ik) *ADJECTIVE*
violent and disastrous

catacombs (*say* **kat**-a-koomz) *PLURAL NOUN*
underground passages with compartments for tombs

catafalque (*say* **kat**-a-falk) *NOUN* **catafalques**
a decorated wooden framework for a coffin at a ceremonial funeral

catalogue *NOUN* **catalogues**
1 a list of items arranged in order
2 a book or pamphlet listing the things that can be bought at a shop
3 a list of all the books in a library or all the objects in a museum, with information on where to find them
4 a succession of bad or unpleasant things, e.g. disasters or failures

SPELLING NOTE Some words with a hard **c-** sound begin with **ch-** (e.g. character)

catalogue *VERB* **catalogues, cataloguing, catalogued**
to list a collection of items in a catalogue

catalyst (*say* kat-a-list) *NOUN* **catalysts**
1 something that starts or speeds up a chemical reaction
2 a person or thing that brings about a change
WORD HISTORY from Greek *lysis* 'loosening'

catalytic converter *NOUN*
a device fitted to a car's exhaust system, with a catalyst for converting the exhaust gases into less polluting ones

catamaran *NOUN* **catamarans**
a boat with twin parallel hulls

catapult *NOUN* **catapults**
1 a forked stick with elastic fastened to each prong, used for shooting small stones
2 an ancient military weapon for hurling small stones
3 a device for launching a glider from the ground or an aircraft from the deck of a ship

catapult *VERB* **catapults, catapulting, catapulted**
to hurl or rush violently

cataract *NOUN* **cataracts**
1 a large waterfall or rush of water
2 a cloudy area that forms in the eye and causes blurred vision
WORD HISTORY from Greek *kataraktes* 'rushing down'

catarrh (*say* ka-tar) *NOUN*
excessive mucus in the nose or throat

catastrophe (*say* ka-tass-trof-ee) *NOUN* **catastrophes**
a sudden great disaster
▷ **catastrophic** (*say* kat-a-**strof**-ik) *ADJECTIVE*
▷ **catastrophically** *ADVERB*
WORD HISTORY from Greek *katastrophe* 'overturning'

catch *VERB* **catches, catching, caught**
1 to seize and take hold of something moving
2 to capture a person or animal
3 to overtake
4 to be in time to get on a bus or train or to see a person
5 to become infected with an illness
6 to hear what someone says
7 to discover someone doing something wrong ◆ *She was caught smoking in the playground.*
8 to make or become snagged or entangled ◆ *I caught my dress on a nail.*
9 to hit or strike ◆ *The blow caught him on the nose.*
to catch fire is to start burning
to catch it (*informal*) is to be scolded or punished
to catch on
1 (*informal*) is to become popular
2 (*informal*) someone catches on when they begin to understand something
to catch someone out is to discover that they have made a mistake

catch *NOUN* **catches**
1 the act of catching something
2 something caught or worth catching
3 a hidden difficulty
4 a device for fastening a door, window, or container
5 a disease is catching when it is infectious

catchment area *NOUN* **catchment areas**
1 the area from which a hospital takes patients or a school takes pupils
2 the whole area from which water drains into a river or reservoir

catchphrase *NOUN* **catchphrases**
a well-known sentence or phrase

catchy *ADJECTIVE*
a catchy tune is pleasant and easy to remember

catechism (*say* kat-ik-izm) *NOUN* **catechisms**
(*Religion*) a book of questions and answers that explain the basic beliefs of a religion

categorical (*say* kat-ig-o-rik-al) *ADJECTIVE*
completely clear and definite ◆ *a categorical refusal*
▷ **categorically** *ADVERB*

category *NOUN* **categories**
a set of people or things classified as belonging to the same group or type

cater *VERB* **caters, catering, catered**
1 to cater for people is to provide them with food on a social occasion
2 to cater for something is to provide what is needed for it ◆ *New buildings should cater for the needs of the disabled.*
▷ **caterer** *NOUN*
▷ **catering** *NOUN*

caterpillar *NOUN* **caterpillars**
a creature like a worm with tiny legs, which turns into a butterfly or moth
WORD HISTORY from Old French *chatepelose* 'hairy cat'

cathedral *NOUN* **cathedrals**
(*Religion*) the most important church of a district called a diocese, usually under the control of a bishop
WORD HISTORY from Greek *kathedra* 'seat'

Catherine wheel *NOUN*
a firework in the form of a coil that spins round when lit
WORD HISTORY named after St Catherine of Alexandria (thought to have lived in the 4th century), who was martyred on a spiked wheel

catheter *NOUN* **catheters**
a flexible tube inserted through a narrow opening into the bladder for removing fluid

cathode *NOUN* **cathodes**
the electrode by which electric current leaves a device (SEE ALSO **anode**)

cathode ray tube *NOUN*
a tube used in televisions and computers, in which a beam of electrons from a cathode produces an image on a fluorescent screen

Catholic *ADJECTIVE*
belonging to the Roman Catholic Church
▷ **Catholicism** *NOUN*

Catholic *NOUN* **Catholics**
a Roman Catholic

catholic *ADJECTIVE*
including a wide range of things ◆ *Her taste in literature is catholic.*
WORD HISTORY from Greek *katholikos* 'universal'

catkin *NOUN*
a spike of small soft flowers on trees such as hazel and willow

catnap *NOUN* **catnaps**
a short sleep during the day

Catseye *NOUN* **Catseyes**
(*trademark*) each of a line of reflecting studs marking the centre or edge of a road

cattle *PLURAL NOUN*
animals with horns and hoofs, kept by farmers for their milk and beef

catty *ADJECTIVE* **cattier, cattiest**
unpleasant and spiteful

catwalk *NOUN* **catwalks**
a long narrow platform that models walk along at a fashion show

caucus *NOUN* **caucuses**
a small influential group within a political party

cauldron *NOUN* **cauldrons**
a large deep pot for boiling things in

cauliflower *NOUN* **cauliflowers**
a cabbage with a large head of white flowers
WORD HISTORY from French *chou fleuri* 'flowered cabbage'

cause *NOUN* **causes**
1 a person or thing that makes something happen or produces an effect

Mother died eight years ago, from perfectly natural causes. — *Dodie Smith, I Capture the Castle*

2 a good or sound reason ◆ *There is no cause for worry.*
3 a purpose for which people work; an organization or charity

cause *VERB* **causes, causing, caused**
to be the cause of something or make it happen

Football teams are extraordinarily inventive in the ways they find to cause their supporters sorrow. — *Nick Hornby, Fever Pitch*

causeway *NOUN* **causeways**
a raised road across low or marshy ground

caustic *ADJECTIVE*
1 able to burn or wear things away by chemical action
2 severely critical or sarcastic
▷ **caustically** *ADVERB*
WORD HISTORY from Greek *kaustikos* 'able to burn'

cauterize *VERB* **cauterizes, cauterizing, cauterized**
to cauterize a wound is to burn the surface of the flesh round it to destroy the infection and stop any bleeding
USAGE NOTE This word can also be spelled cauterise.

caution *NOUN* **cautions**
1 caution is care you take to avoid difficulty or danger
2 a caution is a warning

caution *VERB* **cautions, cautioning, cautioned**
to give someone a warning

cautionary *ADJECTIVE*
giving or serving as a warning

cautious *ADJECTIVE*
taking care to avoid difficulty or danger
▷ **cautiously** *ADVERB*

cavalcade *NOUN* **cavalcades**
a procession of vehicles or people on horseback

Cavalier *NOUN* **Cavaliers**
a supporter of King Charles I in the English Civil War (1642–9)

cavalry *NOUN*
soldiers who fight on horseback or in armoured vehicles (SEE ALSO **infantry**)

cave *NOUN* **caves**
a large hollow place in the side of a hill or cliff, or underground

cave *VERB* **caves, caving, caved**
to cave in
1 is to collapse or fall inwards
2 is to give in to an argument or demand

caveat (*say* kav-ee-at) *NOUN* **caveats**
a warning or reservation about something that is generally satisfactory
WORD HISTORY a Latin word meaning 'let a person beware'

caveman *NOUN* **cavemen**
a person living in a cave in prehistoric times

cavern *NOUN* **caverns**
a large cave

cavernous *ADJECTIVE*
a cavernous room or space is a huge empty one

SPELLING NOTE Some words with a hard **c-** sound begin with **ch-** (e.g. character)

caviar or **caviare** (*say* kav-ee-ar) *NOUN*
the pickled roe of sturgeon or other large fish

cavil *VERB* **cavils, cavilling, cavilled**
to raise minor objections

caving *NOUN*
the activity of exploring caves

cavity *NOUN* **cavities**
a hollow or hole

cavort (*say* ka-**vort**) *VERB* **cavorts, cavorting, cavorted**
to jump or run about excitedly

caw *NOUN* **caws**
the harsh cry of a crow or other large bird

CBE *ABBREVIATION*
Companion of the Order of the British Empire

cc *ABBREVIATION*
cubic centimetre(s)

CD *ABBREVIATION*
compact disc

CD-ROM *ABBREVIATION*
(*ICT*) compact disc read-only memory; a compact disc on which large amounts of data can be stored and then displayed on a computer screen

CDT *ABBREVIATION*
craft, design, and technology

cease *VERB* **ceases, ceasing, ceased**
to stop or end ◆ *The mill was eventually forced to cease operations.*

ceasefire *NOUN* **ceasefires**
a period in a conflict when fighting stops for a time

ceaseless *ADJECTIVE*
not stopping; going on continuously

cedar *NOUN* **cedars**
an evergreen tree with hard fragrant wood
▷ **cedarwood** *NOUN*

cede (*say* seed) *VERB* **cedes, ceding, ceded**
to give up your rights to something; to surrender something you own ◆ *They had to cede some of their territory.*

WORD FAMILY *Cede* comes from the Latin word *cedere* meaning 'to go' or 'to yield'. Other words to do with going and yielding and having the same origin include *accede, concede, intercede, precede, recede,* and *secede.*

cedilla (*say* sid-**il**-a) *NOUN* **cedillas**
a mark under *c* in certain languages to show that it is pronounced as *s*, e.g. in *façade*

WORD HISTORY a Spanish word meaning 'little *z*'

ceilidh (*say* **kay**-lee) *NOUN* **ceilidhs**
a party for Scottish or Irish folk music and dancing

WORD HISTORY from Scottish and Irish Gaelic words, from *céile* 'companion'

ceiling *NOUN* **ceilings**
1 the flat surface at the top of a room
2 a top limit set on prices, wages, or spending

celandine *NOUN* **celandines**
a small wild plant with yellow flowers

WORD HISTORY from Greek *khelidon* 'swallow' (because the plant flowers at the time the swallows arrive in the early spring)

celebrate *VERB* **celebrates, celebrating, celebrated**
1 to do something special or enjoyable to show that a day or event is important
2 (*Religion*) to perform a religious ceremony
▷ **celebrant** *NOUN*
▷ **celebration** *NOUN*

celebrated *ADJECTIVE*
a celebrated person or event is very well known and famous

celebration *NOUN* **celebrations**
1 an act of celebration
2 an occasion that celebrates something

celebrity *NOUN* **celebrities**
1 a celebrity is a famous person
2 celebrity is fame or being famous

celery *NOUN*
a vegetable with crisp white or green stalks

celestial (*say* sil-**est**-ee-al) *ADJECTIVE*
1 to do with the sky
2 to do with heaven; divine
3 celestial body is a literary term for a star or planet

celibate (*say* **sel**-ib-at) *ADJECTIVE*
remaining unmarried or not having sex, especially for religious reasons
▷ **celibacy** *NOUN*

cell *NOUN* **cells**
1 a small room where a prisoner is locked up
2 a small room in a monastery or convent
3 a microscopic unit of living matter
4 a compartment of a honeycomb
5 a device for producing electric current chemically
6 a small group or unit in an organization etc.

cellar *NOUN* **cellars**
an underground room

cello (*say* **chel**-oh) *NOUN* **cellos**
a musical instrument like a large violin, played upright between the knees of the player
▷ **cellist** *NOUN*

USAGE NOTE The formal name is *violoncello*, and *cello* is a shortening of it.

Cellophane *NOUN*
(*trademark*) a thin transparent wrapping material

cellular *ADJECTIVE*
1 to do with or containing cells
2 with an open mesh ◆ *cellular blankets*
3 a cellular telephone uses a network of radio stations to allow messages to be sent over a wide area

celluloid *NOUN*
a kind of plastic

cellulose *NOUN*
tissue that forms the main part of all plants and trees

Celsius (*say* **sel**-see-us) *ADJECTIVE*
measuring temperature on a scale using 100 degrees, where water freezes at 0° and boils at 100°

WORD HISTORY named after A. *Celsius*, the Swedish astronomer who devised it

Celtic (*say* **kel**-tik) *ADJECTIVE*
to do with the languages or inhabitants of ancient Britain and France before the Romans came, or of their descendants, e.g. Irish, Welsh, Gaelic

cement *NOUN*
1 a mixture of lime and clay used in building to join bricks together
2 a strong glue

cement *VERB* **cements, cementing, cemented**
1 to build something with cement
2 to strengthen or join something firmly

cemetery (*say* **sem**-et-ree) *NOUN* **cemeteries**
a place where dead people are buried

cenotaph (*say* **sen**-o-taf) *NOUN* **cenotaphs**
a monument or war memorial dedicated to soldiers who are buried in other places

WORD HISTORY from Greek *kenos taphos* 'empty tomb'

censer *NOUN* **censers**
a container in which incense is burnt

censor *NOUN* **censors**
a person who examines films, books, letters, etc. and removes or bans parts that are unacceptable
▷ **censor** *VERB*
▷ **censorship** *NOUN*

censor *VERB* **censors, censoring, censored**
to ban or remove uncacceptable parts of a book, film, letter, etc.

USAGE NOTE Take care not to confuse this word with *censure*.

WORD HISTORY A Latin name for the Roman magistrate who had the power to ban unsuitable people from ceremonies, from *censere* 'to judge'

censorious (*say* sen-**sor**-ee-us) *ADJECTIVE*
criticizing something strongly

censure (*say* **sen**-sher) *NOUN*
strong criticism or disapproval of something

censure *VERB* **censures, censuring, censured**
to criticize or disapprove of someone or something openly

USAGE NOTE Take care not to confuse this word with *censor*.

census *NOUN* **censuses**
an official count or survey of the population of a country or area

cent *NOUN* **cents**
a coin worth one-hundredth of a dollar

centaur (*say* **sen**-tor) *NOUN* **centaurs**
in Greek mythology, a creature with a man's head, upper body, and arms and the lower body and legs of a horse

A centaur was standing over him, not Ronan or Bane; this one looked younger; he had white-blond hair and a palomino body. — *J. K. Rowling, Harry Potter and the Philosopher's Stone*

centenarian (*say* sent-in-**air**-ee-an) *NOUN* **centenarians**
a person who is 100 years old or more

centenary (*say* sen-**teen**-er-ee) *NOUN* **centenaries**
the hundredth anniversary of an important event ◆ *The centenary of Voltaire's death fell in 1878.*
▷ **centennial** (*say* sen-**ten**-ee-al) *ADJECTIVE*

centigrade *ADJECTIVE*
relating to a scale of a hundred degrees; Celsius

centilitre *NOUN* **centilitres**
one-hundredth of a litre

centimetre *NOUN* **centimetres**
one-hundredth of a metre

centipede *NOUN* **centipedes**
a small crawling creature with a long body and many legs

central *ADJECTIVE*
1 to do with or at the centre
2 most important
▷ **centrally** *ADVERB*

central heating *NOUN*
a system of heating a building from one source by circulating hot water or hot air or steam in pipes or by linked radiators

centralize *VERB* **centralizes, centralizing, centralized**
to bring under the control of a central authority ◆ *The university plans to centralize its catering services.*
▷ **centralization** *NOUN*

USAGE NOTE This word can also be spelled centralise.

SPELLING NOTE Some words with a hard **c**- sound begin with **ch**- (e.g. character)

centre *NOUN* **centres**
1 the middle point or part
2 an important place
3 a building or place for a special purpose, e.g. a shopping centre or a sports centre

USAGE NOTE The American spelling of this word is center.

centre *VERB* **centres, centring, centred**
to place something at the centre
to centre on or centre around something is to have it as its main subject or concern

centre forward *NOUN* **centre forwards**
the player in the middle of the forward line in football or hockey

centre of gravity *NOUN* **centres of gravity**
the point in an object around which its mass is perfectly balanced

centrifugal *ADJECTIVE*
moving away from the centre; using centrifugal force

centrifugal force *NOUN*
a force that makes a thing that is travelling round a central point fly outwards off its circular path

centurion (*say* sent-yoor-ee-on) *NOUN* **centurions**
an officer in the ancient Roman army, originally commanding a hundred men

century *NOUN* **centuries**
1 a period of one hundred years
2 a hundred runs scored by a batsman in an innings at cricket

cephalopod (*say* sef-al-o-pod) *NOUN* **cephalopods**
a mollusc (such as an octopus or squid) that has a head with a ring of tentacles round the mouth

ceramic *ADJECTIVE*
to do with or made of pottery

ceramics *PLURAL NOUN*
pottery-making

cereal *NOUN* **cereals**
1 a grass producing seeds which are used as food, e.g. wheat, barley, or rice
2 a breakfast food made from these seeds

USAGE NOTE Take care not to confuse this word with *serial*.

WORD HISTORY from *Ceres*, the Roman goddess of farming

cerebral (*say* se-rib-ral) *ADJECTIVE*
to do with the brain

cerebral palsy *NOUN*
a condition caused by brain damage before birth that makes a person suffer from spasms of the muscles and jerky movements

ceremonial *ADJECTIVE*
to do with or used in a ceremony; formal
▷ **ceremonially** *ADVERB*

ceremonious *ADJECTIVE*
full of ceremony; elaborately performed

ceremony *NOUN* **ceremonies**
1 a ceremony is a formal religious or public occasion celebrating an important event
2 ceremony is the set of formal actions carried out on an important occasion, e.g. at a wedding or a funeral

certain *ADJECTIVE*
sure; without doubt
a certain person or thing a person or thing that is known but not named

certainly *ADVERB*
1 for certain
2 yes

certainty *NOUN* **certainties**
1 something that is sure to happen
2 being sure

certificate *NOUN* **certificates**
an official written or printed statement giving information about a person etc. ◆ *a birth certificate*

certify *VERB* **certifies, certifying, certified**
to declare formally that something is true
▷ **certification** *NOUN*

cervix *NOUN* **cervices** (*say* ser-vis-ees)
the entrance to the womb
▷ **cervical** *ADJECTIVE*

cessation *NOUN*
the stopping or ending of something

cesspit or **cesspool** *NOUN* **cesspits** or **cesspools**
a covered pit where liquid waste or sewage is stored temporarily

CFC *ABBREVIATION*
chlorofluorocarbon; a gas containing chlorine and fluorine that is thought to be harmful to the ozone layer in the Earth's atmosphere

chafe *VERB* **chafes, chafing, chafed**
1 to make something sore or become sore by rubbing
2 to chafe at something is to be irritated by it or impatient because of it ◆ *We chafed at the delay.*

chaff❶ *NOUN*
husks of corn, separated from the seed

chaff❷ *VERB*
to tease someone

chaffinch *NOUN* **chaffinches**
a kind of finch

chagrin (*say* shag-rin) *NOUN*
a feeling of being annoyed or disappointed

chain *NOUN* **chains**
1 a row of metal rings fastened together
2 a connected series of things ◆ *To the south lies the great mountain chain of the Alps.* ◆ *According to the myth, Paris began a chain of events that led to the Trojan War.*
3 a number of shops, hotels, or other businesses owned by the same company and located in different places

chain *VERB* **chains, chaining, chained**
to fasten or restrain someone or something with a chain or chains

chain letter *NOUN* **chain letters**
a letter that you are asked to copy and send to several other people, who are supposed to do the same

chain reaction *NOUN* **chain reactions**
a series of happenings in which each causes the next

chain store *NOUN* **chain stores**
one of a number of similar shops owned by the same firm

chair *NOUN* **chairs**
1 a movable seat, with a back, for one person
2 the person in charge at a meeting

chair *VERB* **chairs, chairing, chaired**
to chair a meeting is to be in charge of it and run it

The meeting was being chaired by an elderly man in the robes of a Cardinal. — *Philip Pullman, The Subtle Knife*

chairman *NOUN* **chairmen**
the person who is in charge of a meeting
▷ **chairmanship** *NOUN*

USAGE NOTE The word *chairman* can be used of a man or of a woman, but *chairperson* is now often used instead.

chairperson *NOUN* **chairpersons**
a chairman

chalet (*say* **shal**-ay) *NOUN* **chalets**
1 a Swiss hut or cottage
2 a hut in a holiday camp etc.

chalice *NOUN* **chalices**
a large goblet for holding wine, especially one from which the Communion wine is drunk in Christian services

chalk *NOUN* **chalks**
1 a soft white or coloured stick used for writing on blackboards or for drawing
2 soft white limestone
▷ **chalky** *ADJECTIVE*

challenge *NOUN* **challenges**
1 a task or activity that is new and exciting but also difficult
2 a call to someone to take part in a contest or to show their ability or strength

challenge *VERB* **challenges, challenging, challenged**
1 to make a challenge to someone
2 to be a challenge to someone
3 to question whether something is true or correct
▷ **challenger** *NOUN*
▷ **challenging** *ADJECTIVE*

chamber *NOUN* **chambers**
1 (*old use*) a room
2 a hall used for meetings of a parliament etc.; the members of the group using it
3 a compartment in machinery etc.

chamberlain *NOUN* **chamberlains**
an official who manages the household of a sovereign or great noble

chambermaid *NOUN* **chambermaids**
a woman employed to clean bedrooms at a hotel etc.

chamber music *NOUN*
classical music for a small group of players

chamber pot *NOUN* **chamber pots**
a bowl kept in a bedroom and used as a toilet

chameleon (*say* kam-**ee**-lee-on) *NOUN* **chameleons**
a small lizard that can change its colour to that of its surroundings

chamois *NOUN* **chamois**
1 (*say* **sham**-wa) a small wild antelope living in the mountains
2 (*say* **sham**-ee) a piece of soft yellow leather used for washing and polishing things

chamomile (*say* **kam**-o-myl) *NOUN*
a plant with sweet-smelling daisy-like flowers

champ *VERB* **champs, champing, champed**
to eat food noisily

champagne (*say* sham-**payn**) *NOUN*
a bubbly white wine from the region of Champagne in France

champion *NOUN* **champions**
1 a person or thing that has defeated all the others in a sport or competition etc.
2 someone who supports a cause by fighting, speaking, etc.
▷ **championship** *NOUN*

champion *VERB* **champions, championing, championed**
to support a cause by fighting or speaking for it

chance *NOUN* **chances**
1 an opportunity or possibility ◆ *We have one more chance to sort this out.*
2 the way things happen without being planned ◆ *He met Isabella by chance in front of the house.*
to take a chance is to risk something

SPELLING NOTE Some words with a hard **c-** sound begin with **ch-** (e.g. character)

chance *VERB* **chances, chancing, chanced**
1 to happen by chance ◆ *He chanced to be staying in Vienna at the same time as her.*
2 to risk ◆ *We decided to chance a walk in the hills, despite the prospect of rain.*

chancel *NOUN* **chancels**
the part of a church nearest to the altar

chancellor *NOUN* **chancellors**
1 an important government or legal official
2 the chief minister of the government in some European countries

Chancellor of the Exchequer *NOUN*
the government minister in charge of a country's finances and taxes

chancy *ADJECTIVE*
uncertain or risky

chandelier (*say* shan-di-**leer**) *NOUN* **chandeliers**
a large hanging light with branches for several light bulbs or candles

change *VERB* **changes, changing, changed**
1 to make something different or become different
2 to exchange one thing for another
3 to change clothes is to put on different ones
4 to change trains or buses is to get off one and on another
5 to change money is to give smaller units, or money in another currency, for a particular amount

change *NOUN* **changes**
1 the process of changing; a difference in doing something
2 coins or notes of small values
3 money given back to the payer when the price is less than the amount handed over
4 a fresh set of clothes
5 a variation in a person's routine or habit ◆ *It was nice to win for a change.*

changeable *ADJECTIVE*
likely to change; changing frequently ◆ *She experiences changeable moods and panic attacks.*

changeling *NOUN* **changelings**
a child who is believed to have been substituted secretly for another, especially by fairies

channel *NOUN* **channels**
1 a stretch of water connecting two seas
2 a broadcasting wavelength
3 a way for water to flow along
4 the part of a river or sea that is deep enough for ships

channel *VERB* **channels, channelling, channelled**
1 make a channel in something
2 direct something through a channel or other route

chant *NOUN* **chants**
1 a tune to which words with no regular rhythm are fitted, especially one used in church music
2 a rhythmic call or shout

chant *VERB* **chants, chanting, chanted**
1 to sing a chant
2 to call out words in a rhythm

chaos (*say* **kay**-oss) *NOUN*
great disorder
▷ **chaotic** *ADJECTIVE*
▷ **chaotically** *ADVERB*

chap *NOUN* **chaps**
(*informal*) a man

chapatti (*say* cha-**pat**-ee) *NOUN* **chapattis**
a flat cake of unleavened bread, used in Indian cookery

chapel *NOUN* **chapels**
1 (*Religion*) a small building or room used for Christian worship
2 a section of a large church, with its own altar

chaperone (*say* **shap**-er-ohn) *NOUN* **chaperones**
an older woman in charge of a young one on social occasions
▷ **chaperone** *VERB*

chaplain *NOUN* **chaplains**
a member of the clergy who regularly works in a college, hospital, prison, regiment, etc.

chapped *ADJECTIVE*
with skin split or cracked from cold etc.

chapter *NOUN* **chapters**
1 a division of a book
2 the clergy of a cathedral or members of a monastery

char[1] *VERB* **chars, charring, charred**
to make something black or become black by burning

char[2] *NOUN* **chars**
a charwoman

character *NOUN* **characters**
1 all the special features and qualities that give a distinct identity to a particular person or thing
2 to have character is to be especially interesting or attractive
3 (*Drama*) a person appearing in a story, film, or play
4 a letter of the alphabet or other written symbol

characteristic *NOUN* **characteristics**
a quality that forms part of a person's or thing's character

characteristic *ADJECTIVE*
typical of a person or thing
▷ **characteristically** *ADVERB*

characterize *VERB* **characterizes, characterizing, characterized**
1 to be a characteristic of
2 to describe the character of
▷ **characterization** *NOUN*

USAGE NOTE This word can also be spelled characterise.

charade (*say* sha-**rahd**) *NOUN* **charades**
1 a scene in a game (called **charades**), in which the other players try to guess a word from players acting the scene
2 a pretence

charcoal *NOUN*
(*Art*) a black substance made by burning wood slowly, used for fuel and as a medium for drawing

charge *NOUN* **charges**
1 the price asked for something
2 an accusation that someone has committed a crime
3 a rushing attack
4 the amount of explosive needed to fire a gun etc.
5 electricity in something
6 a person or thing in someone's care

in charge in control; deciding what will happen to a person or thing

charge *VERB* **charges, charging, charged**
1 to ask a particular price for something
2 to accuse someone of committing a crime
3 to rush forward in an attack
4 to give an electric charge to something
5 to entrust someone with a responsibility or task

charger *NOUN* **chargers**
(*old use*) a cavalry horse

chariot *NOUN* **chariots**
a horse-drawn vehicle with two wheels, used in ancient times for fighting, racing, etc.
▷ **charioteer** *NOUN*

charisma (*say* ka-**riz**-ma) *NOUN*
the special quality that makes a person attractive or influential

charismatic (*say* ka-riz-**mat**-ik) *ADJECTIVE*
having charisma

charity *NOUN* **charities**
1 an organization set up to help people who are poor, ill, or disabled or have suffered a disaster
2 giving money or help etc. to the needy
3 kindness and sympathy towards others; being unwilling to think badly of people
▷ **charitable** *ADJECTIVE*
▷ **charitably** *ADVERB*

charlatan (*say* **shar**-la-tan) *NOUN* **charlatans**
a person who falsely claims to be an expert

charm *NOUN* **charms**
1 the power to please or delight people; attractiveness
2 a magic spell
3 a small object believed to bring good luck
4 an ornament worn on a bracelet etc.

charm *VERB* **charms, charming, charmed**
1 to give pleasure or delight to people
2 to put a spell on someone
▷ **charmer** *NOUN*

charnel house *NOUN* **charnel houses**
in the past, a place where the bodies or bones of dead people were kept

chart *NOUN* **charts**
1 a map for people sailing ships or flying aircraft
2 an outline map showing special information
◆ *a chart of ancient sites in the area*
3 a diagram, list, or table giving information in an orderly way

the charts a published list of the best-selling pop records

chart *VERB* **charts, charting, charted**
to make a chart or map of something

charter *NOUN* **charters**
1 an official document giving someone certain rights etc.
2 chartering an aircraft, ship, or vehicle

charter *VERB* **charters, chartering, chartered**
1 to hire an aircraft, ship, or vehicle
2 to give a charter to someone

chartered accountant *NOUN* **chartered accountants**
an accountant who is qualified according to the rules of a professional association that has a royal charter

charwoman *NOUN* **charwomen**
(*old use*) a woman employed as a cleaner

chary (*say* **chair**-ee) *ADJECTIVE*
cautious about doing or giving something

chase *VERB* **chases, chasing, chased**
to go quickly after a person or thing in order to capture or catch them up or drive them away
▷ **chase** *NOUN*

chasm (*say* kazm) *NOUN* **chasms**
a deep opening in the ground

chassis (*say* **shas**-ee) *NOUN* **chassis**
the framework under a car etc., on which other parts are mounted

chaste *ADJECTIVE*
not having sex at all, or only with the person you are married to

chasten (*say* **chay**-sen) *VERB* **chastens, chastening, chastened**
to make someone realize that they have behaved badly or done something wrong

a b c d e f g h i j k l m n o p q r s t u v w x y z

chastise *VERB* **chastises, chastising, chastised**
to punish or scold someone severely
▷ **chastisement** *NOUN*

chastity (*say* chas-ti-ti) *NOUN*
the state of being chaste, especially by not having sex

chat *NOUN* **chats**
a friendly conversation

chat *VERB* **chats, chatting, chatted**
to have a chat

chateau (*say* shat-oh) *NOUN* **chateaux**
a castle or large country house in France

chattel *NOUN* **chattels**
(*old use*) something you own that can be moved from place to place, as distinct from a house or land

chatter *VERB* **chatters, chattering, chattered**
1 to talk quickly about unimportant things; to keep on talking

No one speaks to a stranger at a funeral: they just chatter idly. — *Geraldine McCaughrean, The Kite Rider*

2 your teeth chatter when they make a rattling sound because you are cold or frightened
▷ **chatterer** *NOUN*

chatter *NOUN*
chattering talk or sound

chatterbox *NOUN* **chatterboxes**
a talkative person

chauffeur (*say* shoh-fer) *NOUN* **chauffeurs**
a person employed to drive a car

chauvinism (*say* shoh-vin-izm) *NOUN*
1 prejudiced belief that your own country is superior to any other
2 the belief of some men that men are superior to women
▷ **chauvinist** *NOUN*
▷ **chauvinistic** *ADJECTIVE*

WORD HISTORY from the name of Nicolas *Chauvin*, a French soldier in Napoleon's army, noted for his extreme patriotism

cheap *ADJECTIVE*
1 low in price; not expensive
2 of poor quality; of low value
▷ **cheaply** *ADVERB*
▷ **cheapness** *NOUN*

cheapen *VERB* **cheapens, cheapening, cheapened**
to make something less valuable or useful

cheat *VERB* **cheats, cheating, cheated**
1 to be dishonest or unfair when taking part in an exam or game
2 to trick or deceive someone so they lose something

cheat *NOUN* **cheats**
a person who cheats

check[1] *VERB* **checks, checking, checked**
1 to make sure that something is correct or in good condition

At the entrance to the Community Hall, a lady Assistant Examiner sat checking names against a list. — *William Nicholson, The Wind Singer*

2 to make something stop or go slower

check *NOUN* **checks**
1 checking something
2 stopping or slowing; a pause
3 (*American*) a bill in a restaurant
4 the situation in chess when a king may be captured

WORD HISTORY the oldest meaning is the chess meaning, which comes from Persian *shah* 'king'

check[2] *NOUN* **checks**
a pattern of squares
▷ **checked** *ADJECTIVE*

checkmate *NOUN*
a winning position in chess, in which the opponent's king is threatened and cannot be moved out of danger

WORD HISTORY from Persian *shah mat* 'the king is dead'

checkout *NOUN* **checkouts**
a place where goods are paid for in a self-service shop

check-up *NOUN* **check-ups**
a routine medical or dental examination

Cheddar *NOUN*
a kind of cheese originally made in Cheddar in Somerset

cheek *NOUN* **cheeks**
1 the side of the face below the eye
2 rude or disrespectful talk or behaviour

cheekbone *NOUN* **cheekbones**
the bone below your eye

cheeky *ADJECTIVE*
rude or disrespectful; impudent
▷ **cheekily** *ADVERB*
▷ **cheekiness** *NOUN*

cheer *NOUN* **cheers**
1 a cheer is a shout of praise or pleasure or encouragement
2 good cheer is being cheerful and enjoying yourself

cheer *VERB* **cheers, cheering, cheered**
1 to give a cheer
2 to gladden or encourage someone
to cheer up is to become more cheerful

cheerful *ADJECTIVE*
1 looking or sounding happy
2 pleasantly bright or colourful
▷ **cheerfully** *ADVERB*
▷ **cheerfulness** *NOUN*

cheerio *EXCLAMATION*
(*informal*) used when you leave someone

cheerless *ADJECTIVE*
gloomy or dreary

cheers *EXCLAMATION*
(*informal*) used to express good wishes when drinking or when you leave someone

cheery *ADJECTIVE*
bright and cheerful

cheese *NOUN* **cheeses**
a solid food made from milk

cheesecake *NOUN* **cheesecakes**
a dessert made of a mixture of sweetened curds on a layer of biscuit

cheetah *NOUN* **cheetahs**
a large spotted animal of the cat family that can run extremely fast

chef (*say* shef) *NOUN* **chefs**
the cook in a hotel or restaurant

chemical *ADJECTIVE*
to do with or produced by chemistry

chemical *NOUN* **chemicals**
a substance obtained by or used in chemistry

chemist *NOUN* **chemists**
1 a person who makes or sells medicines
2 a shop selling medicines, cosmetics, etc.
3 an expert in chemistry

chemistry *NOUN*
1 the way that substances combine and react with one another
2 the study of substances and their reactions etc.

chemotherapy *NOUN*
the treatment of disease, especially cancer, by the use of chemical substances

cheque *NOUN* **cheques**
a printed form on which you write instructions to a bank to pay out money from your account

chequered *ADJECTIVE*
marked with a pattern of squares

cherish *VERB* **cherishes, cherishing, cherished**
1 to look after a person or thing lovingly
2 to be fond of

cheroot *NOUN* **cheroots**
a cigar with both ends open

cherry *NOUN* **cherries**
a small soft round fruit with a stone

cherub *NOUN* **cherubim** or **cherubs**
an angel, often pictured as a chubby child with wings
▷ **cherubic** (*say* che-roo-bik) *ADJECTIVE*

chess *NOUN*
a game for two players with sixteen pieces each (called *chessmen*) on a board of 64 squares (a *chessboard*)

chest *NOUN* **chests**
1 the front part of the body between the neck and the waist
2 a large strong box for storing things in

chestnut *NOUN* **chestnuts**
1 a tree that produces hard brown nuts
2 the nut of this tree
3 an old joke or story

chest of drawers *NOUN* **chests of drawers**
a piece of furniture with drawers for storing clothes etc.

chevron (*say* shev-ron) *NOUN* **chevrons**
a V-shaped stripe

chew *VERB* **chews, chewing, chewed**
to grind food between the teeth
▷ **chewy** *ADJECTIVE*

chewing gum *NOUN*
a sticky flavoured type of sweet for chewing

chic (*say* sheek) *ADJECTIVE*
stylish and elegant

chicanery (*say* shik-ayn-er-ee) *NOUN*
trickery

chick *NOUN* **chicks**
a very young bird

chicken *NOUN* **chickens**
1 a young hen
2 a hen's flesh used as food

chicken *ADJECTIVE*
(*informal*) afraid to do something; cowardly

chicken *VERB* **chickens, chickening, chickened**
to chicken out (*informal*) is to refuse to take part in something because you are afraid

chickenpox *NOUN*
a disease that produces red spots on the skin

chickpea *NOUN* **chickpeas**
the yellow seed of a plant of the pea family, eaten as a vegetable

chicory *NOUN*
a plant whose leaves are used in salads

chide *VERB* **chides, chiding, chided, chidden**
to scold someone

chief *NOUN* **chiefs**
1 a leader or ruler of a people, especially of a Native American tribe
2 a person with the highest rank or authority

chief *ADJECTIVE*
most important; main
▷ **chiefly** *ADVERB*

chieftain *NOUN* **chieftains**
the chief of a tribe or clan

a b c d e f g h i j k l m n o p q r s t u v w x y z

SPELLING NOTE Some words with a hard **c-** sound begin with **ch-** (e.g. character)

chiffon (*say* shif-on) ***NOUN***
a very thin, almost transparent, fabric

chilblain ***NOUN*** **chilblains**
a sore swollen place, usually on a hand or foot, caused by cold weather

child ***NOUN*** **children**
1 a young person; a boy or girl
2 someone's son or daughter

childhood ***NOUN*** **childhoods**
the time when a person is a child

childish ***ADJECTIVE***
1 like a child; unsuitable for a grown person
2 silly and immature
▷ **childishly** ***ADVERB***

childless ***ADJECTIVE***
having no children

childlike ***ADJECTIVE***
having the good qualities associated with a child

childminder ***NOUN*** **childminders**
a person who is paid to look after children while their parents are out at work

chill ***NOUN*** **chills**
1 unpleasant coldness
2 an illness that makes you shiver

chill ***VERB*** **chills, chilling, chilled**
1 to make a person or thing cold
2 (*informal*) to chill, or chill out, is to relax and enjoy yourself

chilli ***NOUN*** **chillies**
the hot-tasting pod of a red pepper

chilli con carne (*say* kar-nay) ***NOUN***
a stew of chilli-flavoured minced beef and beans

WORD HISTORY a Spanish phrase meaning 'chilli with meat'

chilly ***ADJECTIVE***
1 rather cold

The sun hadn't cleared the ridge of mountains opposite and it was still chilly in the shadows.
— *Joe Simpson, Touching the Void*

2 unfriendly ◆ *We got a chilly reception.*
▷ **chilliness** ***NOUN***

chime ***NOUN*** **chimes**
a series of notes sounded by a set of bells each making a different musical sound

chime ***VERB*** **chimes, chiming, chimed**
to make a chime

chimney ***NOUN*** **chimneys**
a tall pipe or structure that carries smoke away from a fire

chimney pot ***NOUN*** **chimney pots**
a pipe fitted to the top of a chimney

chimney sweep ***NOUN*** **chimney sweeps**
a person who cleans soot from inside chimneys

chimpanzee ***NOUN*** **chimpanzees**
an intelligent African ape, smaller than a gorilla

chin ***NOUN*** **chins**
the lower part of the face below the mouth

china ***NOUN***
thin delicate pottery

Chinese ***ADJECTIVE***
to do with China or its people

Chinese ***NOUN*** **Chinese**
1 the language of China
2 a person from China

chink ***NOUN*** **chinks**
1 a narrow opening that lets light through, e.g. a slight gap between curtains
2 a chinking sound

chink ***VERB*** **chinks, chinking, chinked**
to make a ringing sound like glasses or coins being struck together

chintz ***NOUN***
a shiny cotton cloth used for making curtains etc.

chip ***NOUN*** **chips**
1 a thin piece cut or broken off something hard
2 a fried oblong strip of potato
3 a place where a small piece has been knocked off something
4 a small counter used in games
5 a microchip

a chip off the old block a child who is very like his or her father or mother

to have a chip on your shoulder is to feel resentful or defensive about something

chip ***VERB*** **chips, chipping, chipped**
1 to knock small pieces off something
2 to cut a potato into chips

chipboard ***NOUN***
board made from chips of wood pressed and stuck together

chipolata ***NOUN*** **chipolatas**
a small spicy sausage

chiropody (*say* ki-rop-od-ee) ***NOUN***
medical treatment of conditions affecting the feet, such as corns or verrucas
▷ **chiropodist** ***NOUN***

WORD HISTORY from Greek *cheir* 'hand' and *podos* 'of the foot' (because chiropodists originally treated both hands and feet)

chirp ***VERB*** **chirps, chirping, chirped**
to make short sharp sounds like a small bird
▷ **chirp** ***NOUN***

chirpy ***ADJECTIVE***
lively and cheerful

chisel ***NOUN*** **chisels**
a tool with a sharp end for shaping wood, stone, etc.

chisel ***VERB*** **chisels, chiselling, chiselled**
to shape or cut something with a chisel

chivalry (*say* shiv-al-ree) *NOUN*
1 the code of good behaviour and brave fighting that medieval knights used to follow
2 behaviour that is considerate and helpful, especially by men towards women
▷ **chivalrous** *ADJECTIVE*

chive *NOUN* **chives**
a small herb with leaves that taste like onions

chivvy *VERB* **chivvies, chivvying, chivvied**
to try to make someone hurry
WORD HISTORY probably from *Chevy Chase*, the scene of a skirmish which was the subject of an old ballad

chlorinate *VERB* **chlorinates, chlorinating, chlorinated**
to put chlorine into something
▷ **chlorination** *NOUN*

chlorine (*say* klor-een) *NOUN*
a greenish yellow gas used to disinfect water etc.

chloroform (*say* klo-ro-form) *NOUN*
a liquid that gives off a vapour that makes people unconscious

chlorophyll (*say* klo-ro-fil) *NOUN*
the substance that makes plants green

choc ice *NOUN* **choc ices**
a bar of ice cream covered with chocolate

chock *NOUN* **chocks**
a block or wedge used to prevent an aircraft from moving

chock-a-block *ADJECTIVE*
crammed or crowded together

chock-full *ADJECTIVE*
crammed full

chocolate *NOUN* **chocolates**
1 a solid brown food or powder made from roasted cacao seeds
2 a drink made with this powder
3 a sweet made of or covered with chocolate

choice *NOUN* **choices**
1 the opportunity to choose between things
2 the range of things from which someone can choose ◆ *The island has a wide choice of watersport centres.*
3 a person or thing that someone has chosen ◆ *A librarian? Was that her own choice of occupation?*

choice *ADJECTIVE*
1 very good or special ◆ *A few choice plants and shrubs will add interest to the garden.*
2 choice words are rude and angry ones ◆ *She had had a few choice words with him.*

choir *NOUN* **choirs**
a group of people trained to sing together
▷ **choirboy** *NOUN*
▷ **choirgirl** *NOUN*

choke *VERB* **chokes, choking, choked**
1 to cause someone to stop breathing properly
2 to be unable to breathe properly
3 to block up or clog something
4 to choke back tears is to stop yourself crying only with great difficulty

choke *NOUN* **chokes**
a device controlling the flow of air into the engine of a motor vehicle

cholera (*say* kol-er-a) *NOUN*
an infectious disease that is often fatal

cholesterol (*say* kol-est-er-ol) *NOUN*
a fatty substance that can clog the arteries

choose *VERB* **chooses, choosing, chose, chosen**
to decide which you are going to take from among a number of people or things

choosy *ADJECTIVE* **choosier, choosiest**
(*informal*) careful or fussy about what you choose

chop *VERB* **chops, chopping, chopped**
to cut or hit something with a heavy blow

chop *NOUN* **chops**
1 a small thick slice of meat, usually on a rib
2 a chopping blow

chopper *NOUN* **choppers**
1 a chopping tool; a small axe
2 (*informal*) a helicopter

choppy *ADJECTIVE* **choppier, choppiest**
the sea is choppy when it is not smooth but full of small waves

The men in the boat below looked very small indeed. It was a long, long way down to the water's choppy, whitecapped [= having patches of white foam] surface. — *Meg Cabot, Victoria and the Rogue*

▷ **choppiness** *NOUN*

chopsticks *PLURAL NOUN*
a pair of thin sticks used for lifting Chinese and Japanese food to your mouth

chop suey *NOUN* **chop sueys**
a Chinese dish of meat fried with bean sprouts and vegetables, served with rice
WORD HISTORY from Chinese *tsaap sui* 'mixed bits'

choral *ADJECTIVE*
to do with or sung by a choir or chorus

chorale (*say* kor-ahl) *NOUN* **chorales**
a choral composition using the words of a hymn

chord[1] (*say* kord) *NOUN* **chords**
1 (*Music*) a number of musical notes sounded together
2 (*Mathematics*) a straight line joining two points on a curve
USAGE NOTE Take care not to confuse this word with *cord*.

a b c d e f g h i j k l m n o p q r s t u v w x y z

SPELLING NOTE Some words with a hard **c-** sound begin with **ch-** (e.g. character)

chore (*say* chor) ***NOUN*** **chores**
a regular or dull task

> I spent the time hanging out with Inderjit and Jasbir as they went about their daily chores. — *Bali Rai, (Un)arranged Marriage*

choreography (*say* ko-ree-**og**-ra-fee) ***NOUN***
the art of writing the steps for ballets or stage dances
▷ **choreographer** ***NOUN***

chorister (*say* **ko**-rist-er) ***NOUN*** **choristers**
a member of a choir

chortle ***NOUN*** **chortles**
a loud chuckle
▷ **chortle** ***VERB***

chorus ***NOUN*** **choruses**
1 the words repeated after each verse of a song or poem
2 music sung by a group of people
3 a group singing together

chorus ***VERB*** **choruses, chorusing, chorused**
to sing or speak in chorus

chow mein (*say* chou **mayn**) ***NOUN***
a Chinese dish of fried noodles with shredded meat or shrimps etc. and vegetables

WORD HISTORY from Chinese *chao mian* 'fried noodles'

christen ***VERB*** **christens, christening, christened**
1 to baptize someone
2 to give a name or nickname to a person or thing
▷ **christening** ***NOUN***

Christian ***NOUN*** **Christians**
(*Religion*) a person who believes in Jesus Christ and his teachings

Christian ***ADJECTIVE***
to do with Christians or their beliefs
▷ **Christianity** ***NOUN***

Christian name ***NOUN*** **Christian names**
a name given to a person at their christening; a person's first name

Christmas ***NOUN*** **Christmases**
the day (25 December) when Christians commemorate the birth of Jesus Christ; the days round it

Christmas pudding ***NOUN*** **Christmas puddings**
a dark pudding containing dried fruit etc., eaten at Christmas

Christmas tree ***NOUN*** **Christmas trees**
an evergreen or artificial tree decorated at Christmas

chromatic (*say* krom-**at**-ik) ***ADJECTIVE***
1 to do with colours
2 (*Music*) a chromatic scale is a musical scale that goes up or down in semitones

chrome (*say* krohm) ***NOUN***
chromium

chromium (*say* **kroh**-mee-um) ***NOUN***
a shiny silvery metal

chromosome (*say* **kroh**-mos-ohm) ***NOUN*** **chromosomes**
a tiny thread-like part of an animal cell or plant cell, carrying genes

chronic ***ADJECTIVE***
1 a chronic disease or sickness is one that lasts for a long time
2 a chronic problem is one that affects people for a long time ◆ *The north of the city has areas of chronic unemployment.*
▷ **chronically** ***ADVERB***

WORD FAMILY *Chronic* comes from the Greek word *chronos* meaning 'time'. Other words to do with time and having the same origin include *anachronism, chronicle, chronological, chronology, chronometer*, and *synchronize*.

chronicle ***NOUN*** **chronicles**
a record of events in the order that they happened

chronological ***ADJECTIVE***
(*History*) arranged in the order that things happened
▷ **chronologically** ***ADVERB***

chronology (*say* kron-**ol**-oj-ee) ***NOUN***
(*History*) the arrangement of events in the order in which they happened, e.g. in history or geology

chronometer (*say* kron-**om**-it-er) ***NOUN*** **chronometers**
a very exact device for measuring time

chrysalis ***NOUN*** **chrysalises**
the hard cover a caterpillar makes round itself before it changes into a butterfly or moth

chrysanthemum ***NOUN*** **chrysanthemums**
a garden flower that blooms in autumn

chubby ***ADJECTIVE*** **chubbier, chubbiest**
plump
▷ **chubbiness** ***NOUN***

chuck¹ ***VERB*** **chucks, chucking, chucked**
(*informal*) to throw something carelessly

> What am I expecting now? That if I chuck a few pebbles up at the windows the family will come down and rescue me? — *Nicky Singer, Feather Boy*

chuck² ***NOUN*** **chucks**
1 the gripping part of a lathe
2 the part of a drill that holds the bit

chuckle ***NOUN*** **chuckles**
a quiet laugh

chuckle ***VERB*** **chuckles, chuckling, chuckled**
to laugh quietly

a b c d e f g h i j k l m n o p q r s t u v w x y z

chug *VERB* **chugs, chugging, chugged**
to make the sound of an engine running slowly, or to move making this sound

The vessel chugged slowly out into the deep, blue waters of the open sea. — *Doris Pilkington, Rabbit Proof Fence*

chum *NOUN* **chums**
(*informal*) a friend
▷ **chummy** *ADJECTIVE*

chunk *NOUN* **chunks**
a thick piece of something

chunky *ADJECTIVE* **chunkier, chunkiest**
thick and big

The phone was a fairly chunky black thing that had probably gone out of fashion within a couple of months. — *Keith Gray, Malarkey*

chupatty (*say* chu-pat-ee) *NOUN* **chupatties**
another spelling of **chapatti**

church *NOUN* **churches**
1 (*Religion*) a building where Christians go to worship
2 to go to church is to attend a religious service in a church
3 a particular Christian religion, e.g. the Church of England

churchyard *NOUN* **churchyards**
the ground round a church, often used as a graveyard

churlish *ADJECTIVE*
rude and bad-tempered

churn *NOUN* **churns**
1 a large can in which milk is carried from a farm
2 a machine in which milk is beaten to make butter

churn *VERB* **churns, churning, churned**
1 to stir or swirl vigorously
2 your stomach churns when you feel very nervous and excited

Alex sat hunched up in the back of the low-flying C-130 military aircraft, his stomach churning behind his knees. — *Anthony Horowitz, Stormbreaker*

3 to make butter in a churn
to churn things out is to produce them without much care and in large quantities

chute (*say* shoot) *NOUN* **chutes**
a steep channel for people or things to slide down

chutney *NOUN* **chutneys**
a strong-tasting mixture of fruit, peppers, etc., eaten with meat

CID *ABBREVIATION*
Criminal Investigation Department

cider *NOUN* **ciders**
an alcoholic drink made from apples

cigar *NOUN* **cigars**
a roll of compressed tobacco leaves for smoking

cigarette *NOUN* **cigarettes**
a small roll of shredded tobacco in thin paper for smoking

cinder *NOUN* **cinders**
a small piece of partly burnt coal or wood

cine camera (*say* sin-ee) *NOUN* **cine cameras**
a camera used for taking moving pictures

cinema *NOUN* **cinemas**
1 a place where films are shown
2 the business or art of making films

cinnamon (*say* sin-a-mon) *NOUN*
a yellowish brown spice

cinquain *NOUN* **cinquains**
a poem of five lines with a total of 22 syllables arranged as 2, 4, 6, 8, and 2 syllables in successive lines

cipher (*say* sy-fer) *NOUN* **ciphers**
1 a kind of code
2 the symbol 0, representing nought or zero
WORD HISTORY from Arabic *sifr* 'nought'

circle *NOUN* **circles**
1 (*Mathematics*) a perfectly round flat shape or thing
2 the balcony of a cinema or theatre
3 a number of people with similar interests

circle *VERB* **circles, circling, circled**
to move round something in a circle

circuit (*say* ser-kit) *NOUN* **circuits**
1 a circular line or journey
2 a track for motor racing
3 the path of an electric current

circuitous (*say* ser-kew-it-us) *ADJECTIVE*
going a long way round; not direct

circular *ADJECTIVE*
1 shaped like a circle; round
2 moving round in a circle or back to the starting point ◆ *Meet for a circular forest walk this weekend.*
▷ **circularity** *NOUN*

circular *NOUN* **circulars**
a letter or advertisement sent to a number of people

circulate *VERB* **circulates, circulating, circulated**
1 blood circulates as it passes continuously through the body
2 people circulate when they pass from place to place or from one person to another at a gathering
3 to circulate something such as information is to send it round to a number of people

circulation *NOUN* **circulations**
1 (*Biology*) the movement of blood around the body
2 the number of copies of each issue of a newspaper or magazine that are sold or distributed

SPELLING NOTE Some words with a hard **c**- sound begin with **ch**- (e.g. character)

circumcise *VERB* **circumcises, circumcising, circumcised**
to cut off the fold of skin at the tip of the penis
▷ **circumcision** *NOUN*

circumference *NOUN* **circumferences**
(*Mathematics*) the line or distance round something, especially round a circle

circumflex accent *NOUN* **circumflex accents**
a mark over a vowel, as over *e* in *fête*

circumlocution *NOUN* **circumlocutions**
a roundabout expression, using many words where a few would do, e.g. 'at this moment in time' for 'now'

circumnavigate *VERB* **circumnavigates, circumnavigating, circumnavigated**
to sail completely round something
▷ **circumnavigation** *NOUN*

circumscribe *VERB* **circumscribes, circumscribing, circumscribed**
1 to draw a line round something
2 to limit or restrict something ◆ *The options open to planners are circumscribed by local conditions.*

circumspect *ADJECTIVE*
cautious and watchful ◆ *Mr Cubbage was very circumspect in his choice of lady friends.*
▷ **circumspection** *NOUN*

circumstance *NOUN* **circumstances**
a fact or condition connected with an event or person or action

circumstantial (*say* ser-kum-**stan**-shal) *ADJECTIVE*
circumstantial evidence consists of facts that suggest something without actually proving it

circumvent *VERB* **circumvents, circumventing, circumvented**
to find a way of avoiding something ◆ *Developers cannot circumvent regulations designed to protect our heritage.*
▷ **circumvention** *NOUN*

circus *NOUN* **circuses**
a travelling show usually performed in a tent, with clowns, acrobats, and sometimes trained animals

cirrus (*say* **si**-rus) *NOUN* **cirri**
cloud made up of light wispy streaks

cistern *NOUN* **cisterns**
a tank for storing water

citadel *NOUN* **citadels**
a fortress protecting a city

cite *VERB* **cites, citing, cited**
to quote or name something as an example ◆ *Press reports cited evidence of his links with terrorist networks.*
▷ **citation** *NOUN*

citizen *NOUN* **citizens**
(*Politics*) a person belonging to a particular city or country

citizenry *NOUN*
all the citizens

citizens' band *NOUN*
a range of special radio frequencies on which people can speak to one another over short distances

citizenship *NOUN*
the rights or duties of a citizen

citrus fruit *NOUN* **citrus fruits**
a lemon, orange, grapefruit, or other sharp-tasting fruit

city *NOUN* **cities**
a large important town, often having a cathedral
the City the oldest part of London, now a centre of commerce and finance

cityscape *NOUN* **cityscapes**
a landscape in a city

civic *ADJECTIVE*
1 to do with a city or town
2 to do with citizens

WORD HISTORY from Latin *civis* 'citizen'

civics *NOUN*
the study of the rights and duties of citizens

civil *ADJECTIVE*
1 polite and courteous
2 to do with citizens
3 to do with civilians and not the armed forces ◆ *cooperation between military and civil aviation*
▷ **civilly** *ADVERB*

civil engineering *NOUN*
the work of designing or maintaining roads, bridges, dams, etc.
▷ **civil engineer** *NOUN*

civilian *NOUN* **civilians**
a person who is not serving in the armed forces

civility *NOUN* **civilities**
kindness and politeness

civilization *NOUN* **civilizations**
1 (*History*) a society or culture at a particular time in history ◆ *the ancient civilizations of the Near East*
2 a developed or organized way of life ◆ *'Where do you get your water,' she asked, 'so far from civilization?'*

USAGE NOTE This word can also be spelled civilisation.

civilize *VERB* **civilizes, civilizing, civilized**
1 to bring culture and education to a primitive community
2 to improve a person's behaviour and manners

USAGE NOTE This word can also be spelled civilise.

civil rights *PLURAL NOUN*
the rights of citizens, especially to have freedom, equality, and the right to vote

civil service *NOUN*
officials who work for the government to run its affairs
▷ **civil servant** *NOUN*

civil war *NOUN* **civil wars**
war between groups of people of the same country

clack *NOUN* **clacks**
a short sharp sound like that of plates struck together
▷ **clack** *VERB*

clad *ADJECTIVE*
to be clad in something is to be wearing it or covered by it

> Look at him. Scrawny, like most wizards, and clad in a dark red robe. — *Terry Pratchett, The Colour of Magic*

claim *VERB* **claims, claiming, claimed**
1 ask for something to which you believe you have a right
2 declare; state something without being able to prove it
▷ **claimant** *NOUN*

claim *NOUN* **claims**
1 claiming
2 something claimed
3 a piece of ground claimed or assigned to someone for mining etc.

clairvoyant *NOUN* **clairvoyants**
a person who is said to be able to predict future events or know about things that are happening out of sight
▷ **clairvoyance** *NOUN*

clam *NOUN* **clams**
a large shellfish

clamber *VERB* **clambers, clambering, clambered**
to climb or move with difficulty, using your hands and feet

> The ghosts clambered out of the earth, pale forms paler still in the midday light. — *Philip Pullman, The Amber Spyglass*

clammy *ADJECTIVE*
damp and slimy

> Katie's throat went dry as she tried to speak. She felt clammy perspiration on her brow. — *Catherine MacPhail, Run Zan Run*

clamour *NOUN* **clamours**
1 a loud confused noise
2 an outcry; a loud protest or demand
▷ **clamorous** *ADJECTIVE*

clamour *VERB* **clamours, clamouring, clamoured**
to make a loud protest or demand

clamp *NOUN* **clamps**
a device for holding things tightly

clamp *VERB* **clamps, clamping, clamped**
1 to fix something with a clamp
2 to fix something firmly
to clamp down on something is to become stricter about it or put a stop to it

clan *NOUN* **clans**
a group sharing the same ancestor, especially in Scotland

clandestine (*say* klan-dest-in) *ADJECTIVE*
done secretly; kept secret

clang *NOUN* **clangs**
a loud ringing sound
▷ **clang** *VERB*

clank *NOUN* **clanks**
a sound like heavy pieces of metal banging together
▷ **clank** *VERB*

clap *VERB* **claps, clapping, clapped**
1 to strike the palms of the hands together loudly, especially as applause
2 to slap someone in a friendly way ◆ *He laughed and clapped me on the shoulder.*
3 to clap someone into prison or some other unpleasant place is to send them there hurriedly or with force

clap *NOUN* **claps**
1 a sudden sharp noise, especially of thunder
2 to give someone a clap is to clap your hands in applause for them
3 a friendly slap

clapper *NOUN* **clappers**
the tongue or hanging piece inside a bell that strikes against the bell to make it sound

claptrap *NOUN*
insincere or foolish talk

claret *NOUN* **clarets**
a kind of red wine

clarify *VERB* **clarifies, clarifying, clarified**
to make something clear or easier to understand
▷ **clarification** *NOUN*

clarinet *NOUN* **clarinets**
a woodwind instrument
▷ **clarinettist** *NOUN*

clarion *NOUN* **clarions**
an old type of trumpet

clarity *NOUN*
the state of being clear and easily seen or heard or understood

clash *VERB* **clashes, clashing, clashed**
1 to make a loud sound like that of cymbals banging together
2 two events clash when they happen inconveniently at the same time ▸▸

a b c d e f g h i j k l m n o p q r s t u v w x y z

3 people clash when they have a fight or argument
4 colours clash when they do not go well together
▷ **clash** *NOUN*

clasp *NOUN* **clasps**
1 a device for fastening things, with interlocking parts
2 a tight grasp

clasp *VERB* **clasps, clasping, clasped**
1 to grasp or hold someone or something tightly
2 to fasten something with a clasp

class *NOUN* **classes**
1 a group of children, students, etc. who are taught together
2 a group of similar people, animals, or things
3 people of the same social or economic level
4 a level of quality, of which first class is the highest

class *VERB* **classes, classing, classed**
to arrange things in classes or groups; to classify things

classic *ADJECTIVE*
generally agreed to be excellent or important

classic *NOUN* **classics**
a classic book, film, writer, etc.

classical *ADJECTIVE*
1 to do with ancient Greek or Roman literature or art
2 classical art or music is serious or conventional in style, and is often associated with the 18th century in Europe

classics *NOUN*
the study of ancient Greek and Latin languages and literature

classified *ADJECTIVE*
1 put into classes or groups
2 classified information is officially secret and available only to certain people

classify *VERB* **classifies, classifying, classified**
to arrange things in classes or groups
▷ **classification** *NOUN*

classmate *NOUN* **classmates**
someone in the same class at school

classroom *NOUN* **classrooms**
a room where a class of children or students is taught

clatter *VERB* **clatters, clattering, clattered**
to make a sound like hard objects rattling together

I started awake to the sound of horses' hooves clattering on cobblestones. — *Celia Rees, Witch Child*

clatter *NOUN*
a clattering noise

clause *NOUN* **clauses**
1 a single part of a treaty, law, or contract
2 (*Grammar*) a part of a sentence having its own verb

clauses

A **clause** is a part of a sentence that has its own verb. A sentence can contain one or more **main clauses**, linked by a conjunction such as *and*, *but*, *or*, or *yet*, or by a semicolon:

Ladybirds eat aphids.
We approached cautiously; the lioness was beginning to stir.
It was a bright, cold day in April, and the clocks were striking thirteen.
(George Orwell, Nineteen Eighty-Four)

A **subordinate clause** begins with a conjunction such as *because*, *if*, or *when*, and it can come before or after the main clause:

Because they eat aphids, ladybirds are useful in the garden.
I'll never speak to you again if you lose that CD.

A **relative clause** explains or describes something that has just been mentioned, and is introduced by *that, which, who, whom, whose, when,* or *where*. A relative clause can either restrict meaning:

Of all Tolkien's books, the one which I prefer is 'The Hobbit'.

or can simply add further information, in which case you put a comma before it:

The book, which Tolkien wrote for his children, was an instant success.

In the first of these two examples, but not the second, you can use *that* instead of *which*; you can also say *the one I prefer is* The Hobbit.

See also the panels on **conjunctions and connectives** and **commas**.

claustrophobia (*say* claw-stro-**foh**-bee-a) *NOUN*
an extreme fear of being inside an enclosed space
▷ **claustrophobic** *ADJECTIVE*

claw *NOUN* **claws**
1 a sharp nail on a bird's or animal's foot
2 a claw-like part or device used for grasping things

claw *VERB* **claws, clawing, clawed**
to grasp, pull, or scratch with a claw or hand

clay *NOUN*
a kind of stiff sticky earth that becomes hard when baked, used for making bricks and pottery
▷ **clayey** *ADJECTIVE*

clean *ADJECTIVE*
1 without any dirt or marks or stains
2 fresh; not yet used
3 honourable; not unfair ◆ *a clean fight*
4 not indecent
5 a clean catch is one made skilfully with no fumbling
▷ **cleanly** *ADVERB*
▷ **cleanness** *NOUN*

clean *VERB* **cleans, cleaning, cleaned**
to make something clean

clean *ADVERB*
completely ◆ *She had clean forgotten to buy any milk.* ◆ *The gales blew the roof clean off.*

cleaner *NOUN* **cleaners**
1 a person who cleans things, especially rooms etc.
2 something used for cleaning things

cleanliness (*say* **klen**-li-nis) *NOUN*
a clean state

cleanse (*say* klenz) *VERB* **cleanses, cleansing, cleansed**
1 to clean something
2 to make something pure
▷ **cleanser** *NOUN*

clear *ADJECTIVE*
1 transparent; not muddy or cloudy
2 easy to see or hear or understand; distinct
3 free from obstacles or unwanted things
4 a clear conscience is one that doesn't make you feel guilty
5 a clear period of time is one that is complete and unbroken ◆ *We will need three clear days' notice.*
▷ **clearly** *ADVERB*
▷ **clearness** *NOUN*

clear *ADVERB*
1 distinctly; clearly ◆ *We heard the message loud and clear.*
2 completely ◆ *The killers got clear away.*
3 to stay clear or stand clear of something is to avoid getting too close to it

clear *VERB* **clears, clearing, cleared**
1 to make something clear or become clear
2 to prove that someone is innocent or reliable
3 to jump over something without touching it
4 to get approval or authorization for something ◆ *Plans for the demo had to be cleared with the local police.*

to clear things away is to remove them when they are no longer needed
to clear off or out (*informal*) is to go away
to clear up
1 is to make things tidy ◆ *It helps to wash and clear up as you go.*
2 is to become better or brighter

clearance *NOUN* **clearances**
1 clearing something
2 getting rid of unwanted goods
3 the space between two things

clearing *NOUN* **clearings**
an open space in a forest

cleavage *NOUN*
the hollow between a woman's breasts

cleave❶ *VERB* **cleaves, cleaving;** *past tense* **cleaved, clove** or **cleft;** *past participle* **cleft** or **cloven**
1 to divide something by chopping it

> For the second time in an hour Harry felt as though his head had been cleaved in two. — *J. K. Rowling, Harry Potter and the Order of the Phoenix*

2 to make a way through something ◆ *Barges cleaved the sunlit surface of the river.*

cleave❷ *VERB* **cleaves, cleaving, cleaved**
(*old use*) to cling to something

cleaver *NOUN* **cleavers**
a butcher's chopping tool

clef *NOUN* **clefs**
a symbol on a stave in music, showing the pitch of the notes

cleft *past tense of* **cleave**❶

cleft *NOUN* **clefts**
a split in something

clemency *NOUN*
gentleness or mildness; mercy

clementine (*say* **klem**-en-teen) *NOUN* **clementines**
a deep orange-red tangerine

clench *VERB* **clenches, clenching, clenched**
to close your teeth or fingers tightly

clergy *NOUN*
the people who have been ordained as priests or ministers of the Christian Church
▷ **clergyman** *NOUN*
▷ **clergywoman** *NOUN*

clerical *ADJECTIVE*
1 to do with the routine work in an office, such as filing and writing letters
2 to do with the clergy

clerihew *NOUN* **clerihews**
(*Language*) a short comic or nonsense poem, typically in two rhyming couplets with lines of unequal length and referring to a famous person in the first line

WORD HISTORY named after Edmund *Clerihew* Bentley, the English writer who invented it

clerk (*say* klark) *NOUN* **clerks**
a person employed to keep records or accounts, deal with papers in an office, etc.

clever *ADJECTIVE*
1 quick at learning and understanding things
2 showing intelligence or imagination ◆ *That's a clever idea.*
▷ **cleverly** *ADVERB*
▷ **cleverness** *NOUN*

cliché (*say* **klee**-shay) *NOUN* **clichés**
(*Language*) a phrase or idea that is used so often that it has little meaning

click *VERB*
1 to make a short sharp sound
2 to press a button on a computer mouse

click *NOUN* **clicks**
a short sharp sound

client *NOUN* **clients**
a person who gets help or advice from a professional person such as a lawyer, accountant, architect, etc.; a customer

clientele (*say* klee-on-tel) *NOUN*
customers

cliff *NOUN* **cliffs**
a steep rock face, especially on a coast

cliffhanger *NOUN* **cliffhangers**
a tense and exciting ending to an episode of a story

climate *NOUN* **climates**
(*Geography*) the regular weather conditions of an area
▷ **climatic** (*say* kly-mat-ik) *ADJECTIVE*

climax *NOUN* **climaxes**
the most interesting or important point of a story, series of events, etc.

climb *VERB* **climbs, climbing, climbed**
1 to go up or over or down something
2 to go higher
3 a plant climbs when it grows upwards
to climb down is to admit that you have been wrong
▷ **climb** *NOUN*
▷ **climber** *NOUN*

clinch *VERB* **clinches, clinching, clinched**
1 to settle something definitely ◆ *The USA had been trying for a decade to clinch the deal.* ◆ *A goal two minutes from the end clinched their third successive victory.*
2 boxers clinch when they clasp each other during a fight
▷ **clinch** *NOUN*

cling *VERB* **clings, clinging, clung**
to hold on tightly

cling film *NOUN*
a thin clinging transparent film, used as a covering for food

clinic *NOUN* **clinics**
a place where people see doctors etc. for treatment or advice

clinical *ADJECTIVE*
1 to do with the medical treatment of patients
2 cool and unemotional
▷ **clinically** *ADVERB*

clink *NOUN* **clinks**
a thin sharp sound like glasses being struck together
▷ **clink** *VERB*

clip❶ *NOUN* **clips**
a fastener for keeping things together, usually worked by a spring

clip *VERB* **clips, clipping, clipped**
to fasten something with a clip

clip❷ *VERB* **clips, clipping, clipped**
1 to cut something with shears or scissors
2 (*informal*) to hit someone or something

clip *NOUN* **clips**
1 a short piece of film shown on its own
2 (*informal*) a hit on the head

clipper *NOUN* **clippers**
an old type of fast sailing ship

clippers *PLURAL NOUN*
an instrument for cutting hair

clique (*say* kleek) *NOUN* **cliques**
a small group of people who stick together and keep others out

clitoris *NOUN* **clitorises**
the small sensitive lump of flesh near the opening of a woman's vagina

cloak *NOUN* **cloaks**
a sleeveless piece of outdoor clothing that hangs loosely from the shoulders

cloak *VERB* **cloaks, cloaking, cloaked**
to cover or conceal

cloakroom *NOUN* **cloakrooms**
1 a place where people can leave coats and bags while visiting a building
2 a toilet

clobber *VERB* **clobbers, clobbering, clobbered** (*informal*)
1 to hit someone hard and repeatedly
2 to defeat an opponent completely

cloche (*say* klosh) *NOUN* **cloches**
a glass or plastic cover to protect outdoor plants

clock *NOUN* **clocks**
1 a device that shows what the time is
2 a measuring device with a dial or digital display

clock *VERB* **clocks, clocking, clocked**
to clock in or out is to register the time you arrive at work or leave work
to clock up a speed is to reach a certain speed

clockwise *ADVERB, ADJECTIVE*
moving round a circle in the same direction as a clock's hands

clockwork *NOUN*
a mechanism with a spring that has to be wound up
like clockwork very regularly

clod *NOUN* **clods**
a lump of earth or clay

clog *NOUN* **clogs**
a shoe with a wooden sole

clog *VERB* **clogs, clogging, clogged**
to block something up

My arms were aching and my skin was stinging. Dust and pollen clogged my nose and throat.
— *David Almond, Skellig*

cloister *NOUN* **cloisters**
a covered path along the side of a church or monastery etc., round a courtyard

clone *NOUN* **clones**
an animal or plant made from the cells of another animal or plant and therefore exactly like it

clone *VERB* **clones, cloning, cloned**
to produce a clone of an animal or plant

close ❶ (*say* klohss) *ADJECTIVE*
1 near
2 detailed or concentrated ◆ *Mary realized he was paying her close attention.*
3 a close fit is tight and with little space to spare
4 a close contest or fight is one in which the competitors are nearly equal
5 stuffy
▷ **closely** *ADVERB*
▷ **closeness** *NOUN*

close *ADVERB*
closely ◆ *Two people were walking close behind them.*

close *NOUN* **closes**
1 a street that is closed at one end
2 an enclosed area, especially round a cathedral

close ❷ (*say* klohz) *VERB* **closes, closing, closed**
1 to shut
2 to end a meeting or activity

to close in
1 is to get nearer someone you are chasing

Tom looked round and saw Wreyland and a couple of his boys closing in, carrying heavy clubs. — *Philip Reeve, Mortal Engines*

2 you say the days are closing in when they start to get noticeably shorter in late autumn

close *NOUN*
the close of an acitivity is when it ends ◆ *Scores were still level at the close of play.*

closet *NOUN* **closets**
(*American*) a cupboard or storeroom

closet *VERB* **closets, closeting, closeted**
to closet yourself is to shut yourself away in a private room

close-up *NOUN* **close-ups**
a photograph or piece of film taken at close range

closure *NOUN* **closures**
the process of closing something

clot *NOUN* **clots**
1 a small mass of blood, cream, etc. that has become solid
2 (*informal*) a stupid person

clot *VERB* **clots, clotting, clotted**
to form clots

cloth *NOUN* **cloths**
1 woven material or felt
2 a piece of this material
3 a tablecloth

clothe *VERB* **clothes, clothing, clothed**
to put clothes on someone

clothes *PLURAL NOUN*
things worn to cover the body

clothing *NOUN*
clothes

clotted cream *NOUN*
cream thickened by being scalded

cloud *NOUN* **clouds**
1 a mass of condensed water vapour floating in the sky
2 a mass of smoke, dust, etc. in the air

cloud *VERB* **clouds, clouding, clouded**
to cloud over is to become cloudy

cloudburst *NOUN* **cloudbursts**
a sudden heavy rainstorm

cloudless *ADJECTIVE*
without clouds

cloudy *ADJECTIVE* **cloudier, cloudiest**
1 full of clouds
2 a cloudy liquid is not clear or transparent
▷ **cloudiness** *NOUN*

clout *VERB* **clouts, clouting, clouted**
(*informal*) to hit someone roughly
▷ **clout** *NOUN*

clove ❶ *NOUN* **cloves**
the dried bud of a tropical tree, used as a spice

clove ❷ *NOUN* **cloves**
one of the small bulbs in a compound bulb, e.g. of garlic

clove ❸ *past tense of* **cleave** ❶

cloven *past participle of* **cleave** ❶
cloven hoof a hoof that is divided, like those of cows and sheep

clover *NOUN*
a small plant usually with three leaves on each stalk
in clover in ease and luxury

clown *NOUN* **clowns**
1 a performer who does amusing tricks and actions, especially in a circus
2 a person who does silly things

clown *VERB* **clowns, clowning, clowned**
to fool about and do silly things

cloying *ADJECTIVE*
sickeningly sweet

cloze test *NOUN* **cloze tests**
a test in which you have to read a passage and put in words that have been removed from it, to show that you understand it

SPELLING NOTE Some words with a hard **c-** sound begin with **ch-** (e.g. character)

a b c d e f g h i j k l m n o p q r s t u v w x y z

club *NOUN* **clubs**
1 a heavy stick used as a weapon
2 a stick with a shaped head used to hit the ball in golf
3 a group of people who meet because they are interested in the same thing; the building where they meet
4 a playing card with black clover leaves on it

club *VERB* **clubs, clubbing, clubbed**
to hit someone hard with a heavy stick
to club together is to join with other people in order to pay for something ◆ *Some friends have clubbed together to buy an old van.*

cluck *VERB* **clucks, clucking, clucked**
to make the throaty noise of a hen
▷ **cluck** *NOUN*

clue *NOUN* **clues**
something that helps a person to solve a puzzle or a mystery
not to have a clue (*informal*) is to be stupid or helpless

WORD HISTORY originally a ball of thread: in Greek legend, the warrior Theseus had to go into a maze (the Labyrinth); as he went in he unwound a ball of thread, and found his way out by winding it up again

clump *NOUN* **clumps**
1 a cluster or mass of things or people

Magda automatically stands wherever there's a clump of likely looking boys. — *Jacqueline Wilson, Girls Out Late*

2 a clumping sound

clump *VERB* **clumps, clumping, clumped**
1 to form a cluster or mass
2 to walk with a heavy tread

clumsy *ADJECTIVE* **clumsier, clumsiest**
1 heavy and ungraceful; likely to knock things over or drop things
2 not skilful or tactful ◆ *His clumsy handling of the affair damaged the reputation of his office.*
▷ **clumsily** *ADVERB*
▷ **clumsiness** *NOUN*

cluster *NOUN* **clusters**
a small close group

cluster *VERB* **clusters, clustering, clustered**
to form a cluster

clutch[1] *VERB* **clutches, clutching, clutched**
to grasp something tightly

We moved off quietly sideways, in the direction the water was coming from, clutching our unlit candles and trying to keep out of sight. — *Diana Wynne Jones, The Merlin Conspiracy*

clutch *NOUN* **clutches**
1 a tight grasp
2 a device for connecting and disconnecting the engine of a motor vehicle from its gears

clutch[2] *NOUN* **clutches**
a group of eggs laid at the same time

clutter *NOUN*
a lot of things lying about untidily

clutter *VERB* **clutters, cluttering, cluttered**
to fill a place with clutter ◆ *Bottles of make-up cluttered the small bathroom.*

Co. *ABBREVIATION*
Company

c/o *ABBREVIATION*
care of

coach *NOUN* **coaches**
1 a bus used for long journeys
2 a carriage of a railway train
3 a large horse-drawn carriage with four wheels
4 an instructor who gives training in sports
5 a teacher who gives private tuition in a subject

coach *VERB* **coaches, coaching, coached**
to train someone in a sport or give someone private tuition

coagulate *VERB* **coagulates, coagulating, coagulated**
to change from liquid to semi-solid; to clot
▷ **coagulation** *NOUN*

coal *NOUN*
a hard black mineral substance used for burning to supply heat; a piece of this
▷ **coalfield** *NOUN*

coalesce (*say* koh-a-less) *VERB* **coalesces, coalescing, coalesced**
to combine and form one whole thing
▷ **coalescence** *NOUN*

coalition *NOUN* **coalitions**
a temporary alliance, especially of two or more political parties in order to form a government

coarse *ADJECTIVE*
1 not smooth or delicate; rough
2 composed of large particles; not fine
3 rude or vulgar
▷ **coarsely** *ADVERB*
▷ **coarseness** *NOUN*

coarsen *VERB* **coarsens, coarsening, coarsened**
to make something coarse or become coarse

coast *NOUN* **coasts**
the seashore or the land close to it
the coast is clear there is no chance of being seen or hindered
▷ **coastal** *ADJECTIVE*

coast *VERB* **coasts, coasting, coasted**
to ride downhill without using power

coastguard *NOUN* **coastguards**
a person whose job is to keep watch on the coast, detect or prevent smuggling, etc.

coastline *NOUN* **coastlines**
the shape or outline of a coast

coat *NOUN* **coats**
1 a piece of clothing with sleeves, worn over other clothes
2 the hair or fur on an animal's body
3 a coating of paint or other liquid that dries

coat *VERB* **coats, coating, coated**
to cover something with a coating

coating *NOUN* **coatings**
a covering layer

coat of arms *NOUN* **coats of arms**
a design on a shield, used as an emblem by a family, city, etc.

coax *VERB* **coaxes, coaxing, coaxed**
to persuade someone gently or patiently ◆ *It was not easy to coax them into speaking about their ordeal.*

cob *NOUN* **cobs**
1 the central part of an ear of maize, on which the corn grows
2 a sturdy horse for riding
3 a male swan (SEE ALSO **pen**❸)

cobalt *NOUN*
a hard silvery white metal

WORD HISTORY from German *Kobalt* 'demon' (because it was believed to harm the silver ore with which it was found)

cobble *VERB* **cobbles, cobbling, cobbled**
to cobble something together is to make it quickly and without much care

cobbler *NOUN* **cobblers**
someone who mends shoes

cobbles *PLURAL NOUN*
cobbles are a surface of cobblestones on a road or street
▷ **cobbled** *ADJECTIVE*

cobblestone *NOUN* **cobblestones**
a small smooth rounded stone sometimes used in large numbers to pave roads in towns

cobra (*say* **koh**-bra) *NOUN* **cobras**
a poisonous snake that can rear up

WORD HISTORY from Portuguese *cobra de capello* 'snake with a hood'

cobweb *NOUN* **cobwebs**
the thin sticky net made by a spider to trap insects

cocaine *NOUN*
a drug made from the leaves of a tropical plant called *coca*

cock *NOUN* **cocks**
1 a male chicken or other bird
2 a lever in a gun

cock *VERB* **cocks, cocking, cocked**
1 to make a gun ready to fire by raising the cock
2 an animal cocks its ears when it turns them stiffly upwards to listen, and you cock your head when you turn it to listen

Nanny sat with her head cocked to one side, as though listening to a voice only she could hear.
— *Terry Pratchett, Wyrd Sisters*

cockatoo *NOUN* **cockatoos**
a crested parrot

cockcrow *NOUN*
(*literary*) dawn, when the cock crows

cocked hat *NOUN* **cocked hats**
a triangular hat worn with some uniforms

cockerel *NOUN* **cockerels**
a young male chicken

cocker spaniel *NOUN* **cocker spaniels**
a kind of small spaniel

cock-eyed *ADJECTIVE* (*informal*)
1 crooked; not straight
2 odd or absurd

cockle *NOUN* **cockles**
an edible shellfish

cockney *NOUN* **cockneys**
1 a person born in the East End of London
2 the dialect or accent of cockneys

WORD HISTORY originally a small misshapen egg, believed to be a cock's egg (because country people believed townspeople were feeble)

cockpit *NOUN* **cockpits**
the compartment where the pilot of an aircraft sits

cockroach *NOUN* **cockroaches**
a dark brown beetle-like insect, often found in dirty houses

cocksure *ADJECTIVE*
too confident

cocktail *NOUN* **cocktails**
1 a mixed alcoholic drink
2 a dish consisting of small pieces of shellfish or mixed fruit

WORD HISTORY originally a racehorse that was not a thoroughbred (because carthorses had their tails cut so that they stood up like a cock's tail)

cocky *ADJECTIVE* **cockier, cockiest**
(*informal*) too self-confident and cheeky
▷ **cockiness** *NOUN*

cocoa *NOUN* **cocoas**
1 a hot drink made from a powder of crushed cacao seeds
2 this powder

coconut *NOUN* **coconuts**
1 a large round nut that grows on a kind of palm tree
2 its white lining, used in sweets and cookery

a b c d e f g h i j k l m n o p q r s t u v w x y z

cocoon *NOUN* **cocoons**
1 the covering round a chrysalis
2 a protective wrapping

cocoon *VERB* **cocoons, cocooning, cocooned**
to protect something by wrapping it carefully

cod *NOUN* **cod**
a large edible sea fish

coddle *VERB* **coddles, coddling, coddled**
to cherish and protect someone carefully

code *NOUN* **codes**
1 a word or phrase used to represent a message in order to keep its meaning secret
2 a set of secret or special signs used in sending messages
3 a set of numbers used for an area in making telephone calls
4 a set of laws or rules to follow, especially the Highway Code

code *VERB* **codes, coding, coded**
to put a message into code

codicil *NOUN* **codicils**
an addition to a will

codify *VERB* **codifies, codifying, codified**
to organize laws or rules into a code or system
▷ **codification** *NOUN*

coeducation *NOUN*
educating boys and girls together
▷ **coeducational** *ADJECTIVE*

coefficient *NOUN* **coefficients**
a number by which another number is multiplied; a factor

coelacanth (*say* see-le-kanth) *NOUN*
a large bony sea fish with fleshy fins, known only from fossils until one was found alive in 1938

coerce (*say* koh-erss) *VERB* **coerces, coercing, coerced**
to make someone do something by using threats or force
▷ **coercion** *NOUN*

coexist *VERB* **coexists, coexisting, coexisted**
to exist together or at the same time
▷ **coexistence** *NOUN*
▷ **coexistent** *ADJECTIVE*

coffee *NOUN* **coffees**
1 a hot drink made from the roasted ground seeds (*coffee beans*) of a tropical plant
2 these seeds
WORD HISTORY from Arabic *kahwa*

coffer *NOUN* **coffers**
1 a large strong box for holding money and valuables
2 the coffers are the funds or financial resources of an organization

coffin *NOUN* **coffins**
a long box in which a body is buried or cremated

cog *NOUN* **cogs**
one of a number of tooth-like parts round the edge of a wheel, fitting into and pushing those on another wheel

cogent (*say* koh-jent) *ADJECTIVE*
a cogent argument is strong and convincing

cogitate *VERB* **cogitates, cogitating, cogitated**
to think deeply about something
▷ **cogitation** *NOUN*

cognac (*say* kon-yak) *NOUN* **cognacs**
brandy, especially from Cognac in France

cogwheel *NOUN* **cogwheels**
a wheel with cogs

cohere *VERB* **coheres, cohering, cohered**
things cohere when they stick to each other in a mass
▷ **cohesion** *NOUN*
▷ **cohesive** *ADJECTIVE*

coherent (*say* koh-heer-ent) *ADJECTIVE*
clear, reasonable, and making sense
▷ **coherently** *ADVERB*

cohort *NOUN* **cohorts**
a group of people working together
WORD HISTORY from Latin *cohors*, originally a unit in the ancient Roman army, one tenth of a legion

coil *NOUN* **coils**
something wound into a spiral

coil *VERB* **coils, coiling, coiled**
to wind something into a coil

coin *NOUN* **coins**
a piece of metal, usually round, used as money
WORD FAMILY The two sides of a coin are the obverse (also called *heads*) and reverse (also called *tails*).

coin *VERB* **coins, coining, coined**
1 to manufacture coins
2 to invent a word or phrase

coinage *NOUN* **coinages**
1 coins; a system of money
2 a new word or phrase

coincide *VERB* **coincides, coinciding, coincided**
1 to happen at the same time or be in the same place as someone or something else ◆ *The book's publication coincides with a major exhibition in London.*
2 to be the same by chance ◆ *For once our opinions coincided.*

coincidence *NOUN* **coincidences**
the happening of similar events at the same time by chance

coke *NOUN*
the solid fuel left when gas and tar have been extracted from coal

col ***NOUN*** **cols**
a low part between peaks and ridges in mountains or hills

colander ***NOUN*** **colanders**
a bowl-shaped container with holes in it, used for straining water from vegetables etc. after cooking

cold ***ADJECTIVE***
1 having or at a low temperature; not warm
2 not friendly or loving; not enthusiastic

to get cold feet is to have doubts about doing something bold or ambitious

to give someone the cold shoulder is to be deliberately unfriendly

▷ **coldly** ***ADVERB***
▷ **coldness** ***NOUN***

cold ***NOUN*** **colds**
1 lack of warmth; low temperature; cold weather
2 an infectious illness that makes your nose run, your throat sore, etc.

cold-blooded ***ADJECTIVE***
1 having a body temperature that changes according to the surroundings (SEE ALSO **warm-blooded**)
2 callous; deliberately cruel

cold-hearted ***ADJECTIVE***
unkind; not showing affection (SEE ALSO **warm-hearted**)

cold war ***NOUN***
a situation where nations are enemies without actually fighting

colic ***NOUN***
pain in a baby's stomach

collaborate ***VERB*** **collaborates, collaborating, collaborated**
1 people collaborate when they work together on a job
2 a person collaborates with an enemy when they cooperate with them

▷ **collaboration** ***NOUN***
▷ **collaborator** ***NOUN***

collage (*say* kol-**ah***zh*) ***NOUN*** **collages**
(*Art*) a picture made by fixing small objects to a surface

collapse ***VERB*** **collapses, collapsing, collapsed**
1 to break or fall to pieces; fall in
2 to become very weak or ill
3 to fold up

collapse ***NOUN*** **collapses**
1 the process of collapsing
2 a failure or breakdown

collapsible ***ADJECTIVE***
able to be folded up ◆ *She had a collapsible pushchair that tended to collapse when it was occupied.*

collar ***NOUN*** **collars**
1 the part of a piece of clothing that goes round your neck
2 a band that goes round the neck of a dog, cat, horse, etc.

collar ***VERB*** **collars, collaring, collared**
(*informal*) to seize or catch someone

collarbone ***NOUN*** **collarbones**
the bone joining the breastbone and shoulder blade

collate ***VERB*** **collates, collating, collated**
to collect and arrange pieces of information in an organized way

▷ **collation** ***NOUN***

collateral ***ADJECTIVE***
additional but less important

collateral ***NOUN***
money or property that is used as a guarantee that a loan will be repaid

colleague ***NOUN*** **colleagues**
a person you work with

collect❶ (*say* kol-**ekt**) ***VERB*** **collects, collecting, collected**
1 to bring people or things together from various places
2 to systematically get together examples of something interesting as a hobby, e.g. stamps or CDs
3 to ask for money or contributions etc. from people
4 to go to fetch someone or something from a place where they have been left or where they are expected to be
5 people collect when they come together to meet

▷ **collector** ***NOUN***

collect❷ (*say* **kol**-ekt) ***NOUN*** **collects**
a short prayer

collection ***NOUN*** **collections**
1 the process of collecting
2 (*Art*) a number of things someone has collected, for example art works
3 money collected for a charity or other purpose

collective ***ADJECTIVE***
to do with all the people in a group ◆ *the collective interests of the community*

▷ **collectively** ***ADVERB***

collective noun ***NOUN*** **collective nouns**
a noun that is singular in form but refers to many individuals taken as a unit, e.g. *army*, *government*

SPELLING NOTE Some words with a hard **c-** sound begin with **ch-** (e.g. character)

college *NOUN* **colleges**
a place where people can continue learning something after they have left school

collide *VERB* **collides, colliding, collided**
to crash into something

The men had a frantic distracted look, and kept colliding with each other on the narrow platform. — *William Nicholson, Firesong*

collie *NOUN* **collies**
a dog with a long pointed face

colliery *NOUN* **collieries**
a coal mine and its buildings

collision *NOUN* **collisions**
the act of crashing into something

colloquial (*say* col-**oh**-kwee-al) *ADJECTIVE*
(*Language*) suitable for conversation but not for formal speech or writing
▷ **colloquially** *ADVERB*
▷ **colloquialism** *NOUN*

collusion *NOUN*
a secret agreement between two or more people who are trying to deceive or cheat someone

cologne (*say* kol-**ohn**) *NOUN*
eau de Cologne or a similar liquid

colon ❶ *NOUN* **colons**
(*Language*) a punctuation mark (:), often used to introduce lists or an explanation

colons

You use a **colon** to introduce an example or explanation within a sentence. The part of a sentence after a colon should illustrate, explain, or expand on what comes before it.

Colons can come before a single comment or description:

These words were scratched in blood: 'Do not return without the gold.'
It wasn't much of a holiday: two weeks of constant rain in a leaky tent.

They can also introduce a list of people or items, or a range of options:

The following players are injured: Figo, Sanchez, and Ronaldo.
What would you like on your sandwich: mayonnaise, butter, or margarine?

In this literary example, colons separate pairs of clauses, where the second clause completes the information given in the first:

To Kirsty the cruelty of the sea held no mercy.
It was not merely deadly: it was ravenous. It was not merely ravenous: it was uncaring.
(Neil Gunn, Morning Tide)

colon ❷ *NOUN* **colons**
the largest part of the intestine

colonel (*say* **ker**-nel) *NOUN* **colonels**
an army officer in charge of a regiment

colonial *ADJECTIVE*
(*History*) to do with a colony

colonialism *NOUN*
(*History*) the policy of acquiring and keeping colonies

colonize *VERB* **colonizes, colonizing, colonized**
(*History*) to establish a colony in a country
▷ **colonist** *NOUN*
▷ **colonization** *NOUN*

USAGE NOTE This word can also be spelled colonise.

colonnade *NOUN* **colonnades**
a row of columns

colony *NOUN* **colonies**
1 (*History*) an area of land that the people of another country settle in and control
2 the people of a colony
3 a group of people or animals of the same kind living close together

coloration *NOUN*
colouring

colossal *ADJECTIVE*
extremely large; enormous

colossus *NOUN* **colossi**
1 a huge statue
2 a person of great importance

WORD HISTORY named after an ancient bronze statue of Apollo at Rhodes, called the *Colossus of Rhodes*

colour *NOUN* **colours**
1 the effect produced by waves of light of a particular wavelength
2 the use of various colours, not only black and white
3 the colour of someone's skin
4 (*Art*) a substance used to colour things, for example in painting
5 the special flag of a ship or regiment

colour *VERB* **colours, colouring, coloured**
1 to put colour on something; to paint or stain a surface
2 to blush
3 to influence what someone says or believes

colour-blind *ADJECTIVE*
unable to see the difference between certain colours

coloured *ADJECTIVE*
1 having colour
2 having a dark skin

USAGE NOTE The word *coloured*, used to describe people, is often considered to be insulting. It is better to use *black*.

colourful *ADJECTIVE*
1 full of colour
2 lively; with vivid details

colouring *NOUN*
shade or complexion

colourless *ADJECTIVE*
without colour

a b c d e f g h i j k l m n o p q r s t u v w x y z

colt *NOUN* **colts**
a young male horse

column (*say* **kol**-um) *NOUN* **columns**
1 a pillar
2 a tall narrow length of something rising upwards, e.g. of smoke
3 a division down the length of a page
4 a regular article or feature in a newspaper or magazine

columnist (*say* **kol**-um-nist) *NOUN*
a journalist who writes regularly for one newspaper or magazine

coma (*say* **koh**-ma) *NOUN* **comas**
a state of deep unconsciousness, especially in someone who is ill or injured

comb *NOUN* **combs**
1 a strip of wood or plastic having a row of thin teeth, used to tidy hair or hold it in place
2 something used like this, e.g. to separate strands of wool
3 the red crest on a chicken's head
4 a honeycomb

comb *VERB* **combs, combing, combed**
1 to tidy your hair with a comb
2 to search a place thoroughly

combat *NOUN*
1 a combat is a fight between armies or individual soldiers
2 combat is the process of fighting

combat *VERB* **combats, combating, combated**
to combat something bad or unpleasant is to resist it strongly or try to stop it

combatant (*say* **kom**-ba-tant) *NOUN* **combatants**
someone who takes part in a fight

combination *NOUN* **combinations**
1 the process of combining things
2 a number of people or things that are combined
3 a series of numbers or letters used to open a combination lock

combination lock *NOUN* **combination locks**
a lock that is opened by setting a dial or dials to positions shown by numbers or letters

combine (*say* komb-**yn**) *VERB* **combines, combining, combined**
to join or mix together

combine (*say* **komb**-yn) *NOUN* **combines**
a group of people or firms combining in business

combine harvester *NOUN* **combine harvesters**
a machine that both reaps and threshes grain

combustible *ADJECTIVE*
able to be set on fire and burn

combustion *NOUN*
(*Science*) the process of burning, a chemical process in which substances combine with oxygen in air and produce heat

come *VERB* **comes, coming, came, come**
1 to move towards a place near the person speaking ◆ *Come here!*
2 to arrive at or reach a place or condition or result ◆ *They came to a city.* ◆ *We came to a decision.*
3 to happen ◆ *How did you come to lose it?*
4 to occur or be present ◆ *It comes on the next page.*
5 to result ◆ *That's what comes of being careless.*

to come by something is to obtain it
to come in for something is to receive a share of it
to come to is to become conscious again
to come to an amount is to add up to it
to come to pass is to happen

comedian *NOUN* **comedians**
someone who entertains people by making them laugh

comedy *NOUN* **comedies**
1 a play or film etc. that makes people laugh
2 humour

comely *ADJECTIVE*
(*old use*) handsome or good-looking

comet *NOUN* **comets**
an object moving across the sky with a bright tail of light

comfort *NOUN* **comforts**
1 a comfortable feeling or condition
2 soothing someone who is unhappy or in pain
3 a person or thing that gives comfort

comfort *VERB* **comforts, comforting, comforted**
to make a person less unhappy; to soothe someone

comfortable *ADJECTIVE*
1 at ease; free from worry or pain
2 comfortable clothes fit well and are pleasant to wear

▷ **comfortably** *ADVERB*

comfy *ADJECTIVE*
(*informal*) comfortable and pleasant

comic *ADJECTIVE*
making people laugh

▷ **comical** *ADJECTIVE*
▷ **comically** *ADVERB*

comic *NOUN* **comics**
1 a paper full of comic strips
2 a comedian

comic strip *NOUN* **comic strips**
a series of drawings telling a story, especially a funny one

SPELLING NOTE Some words with a hard **c-** sound begin with **ch-** (e.g. character)

comma *NOUN* **commas**
(*Language*) a punctuation mark (,) used to mark a pause in a sentence or to separate items in a list

commas

Commas are used:
- to mark a pause in a sentence, especially to separate a subordinate clause from the main clause:
When the howling stopped, we ventured out from the cave.
- to separate items in a list or series:
I've packed a bikini, flippers, snorkel, and a periscope.
- in pairs before and after the name of someone who is being introduced or described:
The guitarist, Jimi Hendrix, once lived here.
- to mark a pause in a compound sentence:
The film is rated 15, but it's not that scary.

Notice the difference commas can make to the meaning of a sentence:
The robot, who spoke 93 languages, was famous for telling jokes.
(The robot was famous for telling jokes, and happened to speak 93 languages as well.)
The robot who spoke 93 languages was famous for telling jokes.
(Only the robot who spoke 93 languages was famous for his jokes; the robots who spoke 92 or 94 languages were not.)

command *NOUN* **commands**
1 a statement telling someone to do something; an order
2 to be in command of someone is to have authority or control over them
3 a command of a subject or language is a good knowledge of it and an ability to use it well ◆ *A good command of at least one European language is essential.*

command *VERB* **commands, commanding, commanded**
1 to give a command to someone; to order someone
2 to have authority over a person or group of people
3 to command something like attention or respect is to deserve it and receive it
▷ **commander** *NOUN*

commandant (*say* kom-an-dant) *NOUN* **commandants**
a military officer in charge of a fortress etc.

commandeer *VERB* **commandeers, commandeering, commandeered**
to take or seize something for military use, especially during a war

commandment *NOUN* **commandments**
(*Religion*) a sacred command, especially one of the Ten Commandments given to Moses

commando *NOUN* **commandos**
a soldier trained for making dangerous raids

commemorate *VERB* **commemorates, commemorating, commemorated**
to be a celebration or reminder of some past event or person
▷ **commemoration** *NOUN*
▷ **commemorative** *ADJECTIVE*

commence *VERB* **commences, commencing, commenced**
(*formal*) to begin
▷ **commencement** *NOUN*

commend *VERB* **commends, commending, commended**
1 to praise ◆ *He was commended for telling the truth.*
2 (*formal*) to entrust ◆ *They commended him to our care.*
▷ **commendation** *NOUN*

commendable *ADJECTIVE*
deserving praise; praiseworthy

comment *NOUN* **comments**
an opinion given about an event etc. or to explain something

comment *VERB* **comments, commenting, commented**
to make a comment

commentary *NOUN* **commentaries**
1 a description of an event by someone who is watching it, especially for radio or television
2 a set of comments that explain special features or difficulties in a published work

commentate *VERB* **commentates, commentating, commentated**
to give a radio or television commentary
▷ **commentator** *NOUN*

commerce *NOUN*
trade and the services that assist it, e.g. banking and insurance

commercial *ADJECTIVE*
1 to do with commerce
2 a commercial radio or television station is one paid for by advertising
3 a commercial business or operation is one that is making a profit
▷ **commercially** *ADVERB*

commercial *NOUN* **commercials**
a broadcast advertisement

commercialized *ADJECTIVE*
developed in order to make more money from visitors and customers ◆ *Here you can find unspoilt surroundings away from the more commercialized resort areas.*
▷ **commercialization** *NOUN*

USAGE NOTE This word can also be spelled commercialised.

commiserate *VERB* **commiserates, commiserating, commiserated**
to sympathize with someone
▷ **commiseration** *NOUN*

commission *NOUN* **commissions**
1 a task formally given to someone, e.g. to paint a portrait
2 an appointment to be an officer in the armed forces
3 a group of people given authority to do or investigate something
4 payment to someone for selling your goods etc.
out of commission not in working order

commission *VERB* **commissions, commissioning, commissioned**
to give someone a task or assignment

commissionaire *NOUN* **commissionaires**
an attendant in uniform at the entrance to a theatre or other large building

commissioner *NOUN* **commissioners**
1 an official appointed by commission
2 a member of a commission

commit *VERB* **commits, committing, committed**
1 to do something bad or wrong ◆ *The offences were committed over a six-year period.*
2 to commit time or money is to make it available for a particular purpose ◆ *Don't commit all your spare time to helping him.*
3 to commit yourself to something is to promise to do it or to devote all your energy to doing it ◆ *The Opposition have committed themselves to abolishing the Act.*
4 to commit a person to a place or person is to send them into special care or custody ◆ *The Council committed him to the Tower on suspicion of high treason.*

committal *NOUN* **committals**
1 the process of committing a person to prison or special care
2 the ceremony of giving over a body for burial or cremation

committee *NOUN* **committees**
a group of people appointed to deal with something

commode *NOUN* **commodes**
a box or chair into which a chamber pot is fitted

commodious *ADJECTIVE*
having plenty of space

The rent is forty pounds a year, which seems little for a commodious castle, but we have only a few acres of land. — *Dodie Smith, I Capture the Castle*

commodity *NOUN* **commodities**
a useful thing; a product

commodore *NOUN* **commodores**
1 a naval officer ranking next below a rear admiral
2 the commander of part of a fleet

common *ADJECTIVE*
1 ordinary or usual; occurring frequently ◆ *Noise is a common problem in large cities.* ◆ *a common weed of the daisy family*
2 affecting most people ◆ *The enemies agreed to sink their differences for the common good.*
3 a common interest or opinion is one that most people share
4 vulgar
in common shared by two or more people or things

My dad actually has a lot in common with Captain Picard. You know, he's white and bald and has to rule over a small populace. — *Meg Cabot, The Princess Diaries*

▷ **commonly** *ADVERB*
▷ **commonness** *NOUN*

common *NOUN* **commons**
a piece of land that everyone can use

commoner *NOUN* **commoners**
a member of the ordinary people, not of the nobility

commonplace *ADJECTIVE*
ordinary; usual

common room *NOUN* **common rooms**
a room for students or teachers at a school or college to use when they are not involved in lessons

common sense *NOUN*
normal good sense in thinking or behaviour

commonwealth *NOUN*
1 a group of countries cooperating together
2 a country made up of an association of states
the Commonwealth
1 an association of Britain and various other countries that used to be part of the British Empire, including Canada, Australia, and New Zealand
2 the republic set up in Britain by Oliver Cromwell, lasting from 1649 to 1660

commotion *NOUN*
a noisy disturbance or excitement

communal (*say* **kom**-yoo-nal) *ADJECTIVE*
shared by several people
▷ **communally** *ADVERB*

commune❶ (*say* **kom**-yoon) *NOUN* **communes**
1 a group of people living together and sharing everything
2 a district of local government in France and some other countries

commune❷ (*say* ko-**mewn**) *VERB* **communes, communing, communed**
several people commune when they talk together

communicant *NOUN* **communicants**
(*Religion*) a person who receives Holy Communion

communicate *VERB* **communicates, communicating, communicated**
1 to pass news or information to other people
2 rooms communicate when there is a door leading from one to the other

communication *NOUN* **communications**
1 communication is the process of communicating
2 a communication is something communicated, e.g. a message
3 communications are the links between people and places, e.g. roads, railways, telephones, and the Internet

communicative *ADJECTIVE*
willing to talk

communion *NOUN*
religious fellowship
Communion or Holy Communion (*Religion*) the Christian ceremony in which bread and wine are blessed and given to worshippers in commemoration of the death of Christ

communiqué (*say* ko-**mew**-nik-ay) *NOUN* **communiqués**
an official message giving a report

communism *NOUN*
a political system in which property is shared by the community and the state controls the means of production (SEE ALSO **capitalism, socialism**)

communist *NOUN* **communists**
a person who believes in communism

community *NOUN* **communities**
1 the people living in one area
2 a group with similar interests or origins

commute *VERB* **commutes, commuting, commuted**
1 to travel by train, bus, or car to and from your daily work
2 to commute a punishment is to make it less severe

commuter *NOUN* **commuters**
a person who commutes to and from work

compact❶ (*say* **kom**-pakt) *NOUN* **compacts**
an agreement or contract

compact❷ (*say* kom-**pakt**) *ADJECTIVE*
1 closely or neatly packed together
2 neat and small; concise
▷ **compactly** *ADVERB*
▷ **compactness** *NOUN*

compact (*say* **kom**-pakt) *NOUN* **compacts**
a small flat container for face powder

compact *VERB* **compacts, compacting, compacted**
to join or press firmly together or into a small space

compact disc *NOUN* **compact discs**
a small plastic disc on which music, information, etc. is stored as digital signals and is read by a laser beam

companion *NOUN* **companions**
1 a person who you spend time with or travel with
2 one of a matching pair of things
▷ **companionship** *NOUN*

WORD HISTORY literally 'someone you eat bread with': from Latin *panis* 'bread'

companionable *ADJECTIVE*
friendly and sociable

company *NOUN* **companies**
1 a number of people together
2 a business firm
3 having people with you; companionship
4 visitors ◆ *We will have company tomorrow evening.*
5 a section of a battalion

comparable (*say* **kom**-per-a-bul) *ADJECTIVE*
able to be compared, similar
▷ **comparably** *ADVERB*

comparative *ADJECTIVE*
compared with something else ◆ *the comparative rarity of smoking among elderly women*
▷ **comparatively** *ADVERB*

comparative *NOUN* **comparatives**
the form of an adjective or adverb that expresses 'more', e.g. *faster* and *more difficult*

comparative and superlative forms

Comparative and **superlative** adjectives and adverbs are used to compare and contrast people, things, or actions. The comparative shows which of two things is greater or more: *Cheetahs run faster than antelopes.* The superlative shows which of three or more things is greatest or most: *Cheetahs are the fastest land animals.*

For many adjectives, and some adverbs, the comparative is formed by adding *-er* (or *-r* if the word already ends in *e*), and the superlative by adding *-est* (or *-st*) (note that some adjectives double their final letter, and those ending *-y* change to *-i*):

This bloom is bigger and paler than the others.
What's the scariest film you've ever seen?
The guests arrived sooner than expected.

For longer adjectives, and for adverbs ending in *-ly*, the comparative and superlative are formed with *more* and *most*:

Hot-air balloons are the most interesting way to travel.
Professor Smout typed more furiously than ever.

However, some common adjectives and adverbs have irregular comparatives and superlatives which in some cases are different words, e.g. *good / well* (*better, best*), *bad / badly* (*worse, worst*), and *far* (*farther, farthest* or *further, furthest*).

You will find guidance in this dictionary on irregular comparatives and superlatives.

compare *VERB* **compares, comparing, compared**
1 to compare people or things is to consider them in relation to one another in order to tell how they are similar or different
2 to form the comparative and superlative of an adjective or adverb

to compare notes is to share information
to compare with something is to be similar to it or as good as it

USAGE NOTE *Compare* can be followed by either *to* or *with*. As a general rule, you use *to* when you are showing the similarity between two things (*She compared the cottage to a huge cake*), and you use *with* when you are looking at the similarities and differences between things (*Just compare this year's results with last year's*).

comparison *NOUN* **comparisons**
the process of comparing people or things

compartment *NOUN* **compartments**
1 one of the spaces into which something is divided; a separate room or enclosed space
2 a division of a railway carriage

compass *NOUN* **compasses**
a device that shows direction, with a magnetized needle pointing to the north

compasses or **pair of compasses** a device for drawing circles, usually with two rods hinged together at one end

compassion *NOUN*
sympathetic concern for other people
▷ **compassionate** *ADJECTIVE*
▷ **compassionately** *ADVERB*

compatible *ADJECTIVE*
1 able to live or exist together without trouble
2 one thing is compatible with another when both are possible at the same time ◆ *The bruising is compatible with his having had a fall.*
3 machines and pieces of equipment are compatible when they can be used together
▷ **compatibly** *ADVERB*
▷ **compatibility** *NOUN*

compatriot (*say* kom-pat-ri-ot) *NOUN*
a person from the same country as another

compel *VERB* **compels, compelling, compelled**
to force someone to do something

compendious *ADJECTIVE*
giving much information concisely

compendium *NOUN* **compendiums** or **compendia**
1 an encyclopedia or handbook in one volume
2 a set of different board games in one box

compensate *VERB* **compensates, compensating, compensated**
1 to give a person money or some other benefit to make up for a loss or injury
2 one thing compensates for another when it balances it or counteracts it ◆ *The strength of their weapons more than compensates for the lack of a shield.*
▷ **compensation** *NOUN*
▷ **compensatory** *ADJECTIVE*

compère (*say* kom-pair) *NOUN* **compères**
a person who introduces the performers in a show or broadcast
▷ **compère** *VERB*

compete *VERB* **competes, competing, competed**
to take part in a competition

competent *ADJECTIVE*
able to do a particular thing
▷ **competently** *ADVERB*
▷ **competence** *NOUN*

competition *NOUN* **competitions**
1 a game or race or other contest in which people try to win
2 the process of competing
3 the people who compete with you
▷ **competitive** *ADJECTIVE*

competitor *NOUN* **competitors**
someone who competes; a rival

compile *VERB* **compiles, compiling, compiled**
to produce a book, record, etc. by collecting together material from various sources
▷ **compiler** *NOUN*
▷ **compilation** *NOUN*

complacent *ADJECTIVE*
smugly satisfied with the way things are, and feeling that no change or action is necessary
▷ **complacently** *ADVERB*
▷ **complacency** *NOUN*

complain *VERB* **complains, complaining, complained**
to say that you are dissatisfied or unhappy about something

complaint *NOUN* **complaints**
1 an act of complaining about something, or the statement someone makes when doing this
2 a minor illness

complement *NOUN* **complements**
1 the quantity needed to fill or complete something, e.g. the crew of a ship

> 'Right,' says Miss Raynham, doing a quick count-up. 'I make that eight. So, if we add in young Wesley Parr and Mr Niker here, I think we have a full complement.' — *Nicky Singer, Feather Boy*

2 (*Grammar*) the word or words used after verbs such as *be* and *become* to complete the sense. In *She was brave* and *He became king of England*, the complements are *brave* and *king of England*.

complement *VERB* **complements, complementing, complemented**
one thing complements another when they go well together or when one makes the other complete ◆ *Highlights give Michelle's hair a softer tone that complements her skin.* ◆ *Computers should complement other resources and not replace them.*

USAGE NOTE Take care not to confuse this word with *compliment*.

complementary *ADJECTIVE*
completing; forming a complement

USAGE NOTE Take care not to confuse this word with *complimentary*.

complementary angle *NOUN* **complementary angles**
either of two angles that add up to 90°

complementary medicine *NOUN*
alternative medicine

complete *ADJECTIVE*
1 having all its parts
2 finished
3 thorough; in every way ◆ *a complete stranger*
▷ **completely** *ADVERB*
▷ **completeness** *NOUN*

complete *VERB* **completes, completing, completed**
to make a thing complete; to add what is needed to something
▷ **completion** *NOUN*

complex *ADJECTIVE*
1 made up of many different parts
2 difficult or complicated
▷ **complexity** *NOUN*

complex *NOUN* **complexes**
1 a large set of buildings used for a particular purpose, e.g. an industrial complex or a leisure complex
2 a group of feelings or ideas that make a person behave abnormally, e.g. someone with a persecution complex believes that other people dislike them and are always trying to harm them

complexion *NOUN* **complexions**
1 the natural colour and appearance of the skin of the face
2 the way things seem ◆ *Laura found the evening taking on a completely different complexion.*

compliant *ADJECTIVE*
willing to obey
▷ **compliance** *NOUN*

complicate *VERB* **complicates, complicating, complicated**
to make a thing complex or complicated

complicated *ADJECTIVE*
1 made up of many parts

People believe in God because the world is very complicated and they think it is very unlikely that anything as complicated as a flying squirrel or the human eye or a brain could happen by chance.
— *Mark Haddon, The Curious Incident of the Dog in the Night-Time*

2 difficult to understand or do

complication *NOUN* **complications**
1 something that complicates things or adds difficulties
2 a difficult or confused situation

complicity *NOUN*
being involved in a crime etc.

compliment *NOUN* **compliments**
1 something you say to show that you approve of a person or thing
2 to pay someone a compliment is to say something good or praiseworthy about them
3 compliments are formal greetings given in a message

compliment *VERB* **compliments, complimenting, complimented**
to pay someone a compliment; to congratulate someone

USAGE NOTE Take care not to confuse this word with *complement*.

complimentary *ADJECTIVE*
1 expressing a compliment
2 given free of charge ◆ *complimentary tickets*

USAGE NOTE Take care not to confuse this word with *complementary*.

comply *VERB* **complies, complying, complied**
to comply with laws or rules is to obey them

component *NOUN* **components**
(D & T) each of the parts of which a thing is made up

compose *VERB* **composes, composing, composed**
1 to write music or poetry
2 to be composed of several things is to contain or include them ◆ *The Committee is composed of delegates from each of the member states.*
3 to arrange things in good order
4 to compose yourself is to become calm after being excited or angry

composed *ADJECTIVE*
calm and in control of your feelings or behaviour ◆ *Marcus had resumed his composed posture.*

composer *NOUN* **composers**
a person who composes music

composite (*say* **kom**-poz-it) *ADJECTIVE*
made up of a number of parts or different styles

composition *NOUN* **compositions**
1 the process of composing music or poetry
2 something composed, especially a piece of music
3 an essay or story written as a school exercise
4 the composition of a substance is the way it is made up

compost *NOUN*
1 decayed leaves and grass etc. used as a fertilizer
2 a soil-like mixture for growing seedlings, cuttings, etc.

composure *NOUN*
calmness of manner

compound❶ *ADJECTIVE*
made of two or more parts or ingredients

compound *NOUN* **compounds**
a compound substance

compound *VERB* **compounds, compounding, compounded**
to put together; to combine

compound❷ *NOUN* **compounds**
a fenced area containing buildings

compound word *NOUN*
(*Grammar*) a word or expression made from other words joined together, e.g. *football* and *newspaper*

compound words

A **compound word** is made from two or more separate words. Many compounds, like *ice cream* and *website*, are made from two nouns and can be spelled as either two words or one. Well-known compounds, like *football* and *newspaper*, are spelled as one word; but compounds made from longer words are normally spelled as two words, e.g. *bottle bank*, *market research*. Compounds can also be spelled with a hyphen, especially if there is a clash of consonants, as in *best-seller* and *cross-section*.
Compounds made from an adjective plus a noun (e.g. *long-range*) behave like adjectives and usually need a hyphen when they come before another noun, e.g. *a long-range missile* and *a steel-string guitar* (the hyphen shows that the strings are steel and not the guitar). Other compounds are made from a noun plus an adjective (e.g. *homesick*, *twenty-odd*) or from phrases (e.g. *down-to-earth*, *makeshift*, *mother-in-law*). Note that the plural of *mother-in-law* is *mothers-in-law*, because *mother* is the main noun in the compound.
See also the panel on **hyphens**.

comprehend *VERB* **comprehends, comprehending, comprehended**
1 to understand something
2 to include something

comprehensible *ADJECTIVE*
able to be understood

comprehension *NOUN*
1 (*Language*) the level of understanding of a passage or text
2 a passage with questions on it, given to language students to test their understanding

comprehensive *ADJECTIVE*
including all or many kinds of people or things

comprehensive *NOUN* **comprehensives**
a comprehensive school

comprehensive school *NOUN* **comprehensive schools**
a secondary school for all or most of the children of an area

compress (*say* kom-**press**) *VERB* **compresses, compressing, compressed**
to press together or into a smaller space
▷ **compression** *NOUN*
▷ **compressor** *NOUN*

compress (*say* **kom**-press) *NOUN* **compresses**
a soft pad or cloth pressed on the body to stop bleeding or cool inflammation etc.

comprise *VERB* **comprises, comprising, comprised**
to include or consist of

At the restaurant we have zakuski—an hors d'oeuvre comprising slices of tomato, cucumber, pickle, tinned ham, beef and pork. — *Michael Palin, Pole to Pole*

compromise (*say* **kom**-prom-yz) *NOUN* **compromises**
settling a dispute by each side accepting less than it wanted or asked for

compromise *VERB* **compromises, compromising, compromised**
1 to agree to a compromise; to accept less than you originally wanted
2 to compromise something is to make it weaker or less effective ◆ *His relationship with his father had been compromised by their inability to confide in each other.*
3 to compromise someone is to say or do something that leaves them in danger or under suspicion ◆ *He was afraid that his presence might compromise her.*

compulsion *NOUN* **compulsions**
a strong and uncontrollable desire to do something

compulsive *ADJECTIVE*
a compulsive action or habit is one arising from a strong and uncontrollable desire ◆ *the social consequences of compulsive gambling*. You can also call the person compulsive ◆ *Most compulsive gamblers are not hugely successful.*

USAGE NOTE Take care not to confuse this word with *compulsory*.

compulsory *ADJECTIVE*
something is compulsory when you have to do it and cannot choose ◆ *Regular tests are compulsory for all road vehicles.*

USAGE NOTE Take care not to confuse this word with *compulsive*.

compunction *NOUN*
a feeling of doubt or guilt about doing something ◆ *He had treated them cruelly, without compunction.*

compute *VERB* **computes, computing, computed**
to calculate
▷ **computation** *NOUN*

computer *NOUN* **computers**
(*ICT*) an electronic machine for making calculations, storing and analysing information put into it, or controlling machinery automatically

computerize *VERB* **computerizes, computerizing, computerized**
(*ICT*) to equip a place or organization with computers; to perform or produce things by means of a computer
▷ **computerization** *NOUN*

USAGE NOTE This word can also be spelled computerise.

computing *NOUN*
(*ICT*) the use of computers

comrade *NOUN* **comrades**
a companion who shares in your activities

Now, comrades, what is the nature of this life of ours? Let us face it: our lives are miserable, laborious, and short. — *George Orwell, Animal Farm*

▷ **comradeship** *NOUN*

con *VERB* **cons, conning, conned**
(*informal*) to swindle someone

concave *ADJECTIVE*
curved like the inside of a ball or circle (SEE ALSO **convex**)
▷ **concavity** *NOUN*

conceal *VERB* **conceals, concealing, concealed**
to hide someone or something or keep it secret
▷ **concealment** *NOUN*

concede *VERB* **concedes, conceding, conceded**
1 to admit that something is true ◆ *Many people are prepared to concede that some kind of animal has been seen in the loch.*
2 to give up a possession or right
3 to admit that you have been defeated

conceit *NOUN*
being too proud of yourself; vanity
▷ **conceited** *ADJECTIVE*

conceivable *ADJECTIVE*
able to be imagined or believed
▷ **conceivably** *ADVERB*

conceive *VERB* **conceives, conceiving, conceived**
1 to become pregnant; to form a baby in the womb
2 to form an idea or plan in the mind ◆ *I could hardly conceive what the place must be like in winter; it was cold enough in summer.*

concentrate *VERB* **concentrates, concentrating, concentrated**
1 to give your full attention or effort to something
2 to bring or come together in one place
3 to make a liquid etc. less dilute

concentration *NOUN* **concentrations**
1 the process of concentrating
2 the amount of a substance dissolved in each part of a liquid

concentration camp *NOUN* **concentration camps**
a prison camp where political prisoners are kept together, especially one set up by the Nazis during the Second World War

concentric *ADJECTIVE*
concentric circles have their centres in the same position

concept *NOUN* **concepts**
an idea

conception *NOUN* **conceptions**
1 the process of forming a baby in the womb
2 an idea or way of thinking about something

concern *VERB* **concerns, concerning, concerned**
1 to be important to or affect someone
2 to worry someone
3 to have as the theme or subject ◆ *The other news story concerns the surveying of Loch Ness.*

concern *NOUN* **concerns**
1 something that concerns you or worries you; a responsibility

Rushing this way and that, everyone was far too wrapped up in their own concerns to spare a thought for anyone else. — *Paul Stewart and Chris Riddell, Stormchaser*

2 fear or worry that something is wrong ◆ *Concern is growing over the safety of the missing couple.*
3 a business

concerned *ADJECTIVE*
1 worried or anxious about something
2 involved in or affected by something

concerning *PREPOSITION*
on the subject of; about ◆ *Walter needed advice on matters concerning his domestic life.*

concert *NOUN* **concerts**
a musical entertainment

concerted *ADJECTIVE*
a concerted effort is one that you make in cooperation with other people

concertina *NOUN* **concertinas**
a portable musical instrument with bellows, played by squeezing

concerto (*say* kon-**chert**-oh) *NOUN* **concertos**
a piece of music for a solo instrument and an orchestra

concession *NOUN* **concessions**
1 the process of giving up a possession or right
2 something that someone gives up
3 a reduction in price for a certain category of person
▷ **concessionary** *ADJECTIVE*

conch *NOUN* **conches**
a large shell in the form of a spiral with a flared lip

By the time Ralph finished blowing the conch the platform was crowded. — *William Golding, Lord of the Flies*

conciliate *VERB* **conciliates, conciliating, conciliated**
1 to win over an angry or hostile person by friendliness
2 to help people who disagree to come to an agreement
▷ **conciliation** *NOUN*

concise *ADJECTIVE*
brief; giving a lot of information in a few words
▷ **concisely** *ADVERB*
▷ **conciseness** *NOUN*

conclave *NOUN* **conclaves**
a private meeting

conclude *VERB* **concludes, concluding, concluded**
1 to bring or come to an end
2 to decide; to form an opinion by reasoning ◆ *The Commission concluded that poor management was a major contributory factor.*

conclusion *NOUN* **conclusions**
1 an ending
2 an opinion formed by reasoning

I've come to the shocking conclusion that I have only one long-sleeved dress and three cardigans to wear in the winter. — *Anne Frank, The Diary of a Young Girl*

conclusive *ADJECTIVE*
putting an end to all doubt
▷ **conclusively** *ADVERB*

concoct *VERB* **concocts, concocting, concocted**
1 to make something by putting ingredients together
2 to concoct an idea or story is to make it up hurriedly

Over the next few days, Lyra concocted a dozen plans and dismissed them impatiently. — *Philip Pullman, Northern Lights*

▷ **concoction** *NOUN*

concord *NOUN*
1 friendly agreement or harmony
2 (*Grammar*) agreement between words in a sentence

concordance *NOUN* **concordances**
1 agreement
2 an index of the words used in a book or an author's works

concourse *NOUN* **concourses**
an open area through which people pass, e.g. at an airport

concrete *NOUN*
cement mixed with sand and gravel, used in building

concrete *ADJECTIVE*
1 able to be touched and felt; not abstract
2 definite and useful ◆ *If he wasn't going to give her more concrete help himself, she would have to find other allies.*

concrete poem *NOUN* **concrete poems**
(*Language*) a poem in which the arrangement of the letters and words relates to the subject of the poem, e.g. a poem about falling written with the words moving down the page (SEE ALSO **shape poem**)

concur *VERB* **concurs, concurring, concurred**
to agree
▷ **concurrence** *NOUN*

concurrent *ADJECTIVE*
happening or existing at the same time

concussion *NOUN*
a temporary injury to the brain caused by a hard knock
▷ **concussed** *ADJECTIVE*

condemn *VERB* **condemns, condemning, condemned**
1 to say that you strongly disapprove of something
2 to convict or sentence a criminal to death
3 to be condemned to something unpleasant is to have to suffer it ◆ *For the people condemned to live in shanty towns, drugs are a means of survival.*
4 to condemn a building is to declare that it is not fit to be used
▷ **condemnation** *NOUN*

condensation *NOUN* (*Science*)
1 water from humid air collecting as tiny drops on a cold surface
2 the conversion of a vapour or gas to a liquid

a b c d e f g h i j k l m n o p q r s t u v w x y z

condense *VERB* **condenses, condensing, condensed**
1 to make a liquid denser or more compact
2 to express an idea in fewer words
3 to change from gas or vapour to liquid
▷ **condenser** *NOUN*

condensed milk *NOUN*
milk that has been thickened by evaporation and sweetened

condescend *VERB* **condescends, condescending, condescended**
1 to behave in a superior or haughty way towards someone
2 to allow yourself to do something that you think is unworthy of you or beneath you
▷ **condescension** *NOUN*

condiment *NOUN* **condiments**
a seasoning (e.g. salt or pepper) for food

condition *NOUN* **conditions**
1 the state or fitness of a person or thing ◆ *By now his bike was in poor condition.*
2 the situation or surroundings that affect people ◆ *measures to improve working conditions in state-owned factories*
3 something required as part of an agreement
on condition that only if; on the understanding that something will be done

condition *VERB* **conditions, conditioning, conditioned**
1 to bring something into a healthy or proper condition
2 to train someone to behave in a particular way or become used to a particular situation

conditional *ADJECTIVE*
1 containing a condition; dependent on something else
2 (*Language*) expressing a condition, typically with *if* or *unless* (as in *If you come I will be able to see you* or *Unless you come I won't be able to see you*)
▷ **conditionally** *ADVERB*

conditioner *NOUN* **conditioners**
a substance you put on your hair to keep it in good condition

condole *VERB* **condoles, condoling, condoled**
to express sympathy

condolence *NOUN* **condolences**
an expression of sympathy, especially for someone who is bereaved

condom *NOUN* **condoms**
a rubber sheath worn on the penis during sexual intercourse as a contraceptive and as a protection against disease

condone *VERB* **condones, condoning, condoned**
to condone something wrong or unpleasant is to ignore it or quietly approve of it ◆ *Union leaders would not condone the use of violence.*

condor *NOUN* **condors**
a kind of large vulture

conducive *ADJECTIVE*
helping to cause or produce something ◆ *The hard bench under her was not conducive to sound sleep.*

conduct (*say* kon-**dukt**) *VERB* **conducts, conducting, conducted**
1 to manage or direct something ◆ *He sometimes took his turn to conduct services in sign language.*
2 to lead or guide someone to a place
3 to be the conductor of an orchestra or choir
4 to allow heat, light, sound, or electricity to pass along or through something
5 to conduct yourself in a particular way is to behave in that way ◆ *They conducted themselves with great patience and dignity.*

conduct (*say* **kon**-dukt) *NOUN*
behaviour

conduction *NOUN*
the conducting of heat or electricity etc. (SEE **conduct** 4)

conductor *NOUN* **conductors**
1 a person who directs the performance of an orchestra or choir by movements of the arms
2 a person who collects the fares on a bus etc.
3 something that conducts heat or electricity etc.

conduit (*say* **kon**-dit) *NOUN* **conduits**
1 a pipe or channel for liquid
2 a tube protecting electric wire

cone *NOUN* **cones**
1 an object that is circular at one end and narrows to a point at the other end
2 an ice cream cornet
3 the dry cone-shaped fruit of a pine, fir, or cedar tree

confection *NOUN* **confections**
1 something made of various things put together
2 a specially made sweet dish of food

confectioner *NOUN* **confectioners**
someone who makes or sells sweets
▷ **confectionery** *NOUN*

confederacy *NOUN* **confederacies**
a union of states; a confederation

confederate *ADJECTIVE*
allied; joined by an agreement or treaty

confederate *NOUN* **confederates**
1 a member of a confederacy
2 an ally; an accomplice

confederation *NOUN* **confederations**
1 the process of joining in an alliance
2 a group of people, organizations, or states joined together by an agreement or treaty

confer *VERB* **confers, conferring, conferred**
1 to grant a right or privilege to someone
2 to confer with someone, or to confer, is to have a discussion before deciding something

conference *NOUN* **conferences**
a meeting for holding a discussion

confess *VERB* **confesses, confessing, confessed**
to state openly that you have done something wrong or have a weakness; to admit something

confession *NOUN* **confessions**
1 admitting that you have done wrong
2 (in the Roman Catholic Church) an act of telling a priest that you have sinned

confessional *NOUN* **confessionals**
a small room where a priest hears confessions

confessor *NOUN* **confessors**
a priest who hears confessions

confetti *NOUN*
tiny pieces of coloured paper thrown by wedding guests at the bride and bridegroom

confidant *NOUN* (**confidante** is used of a woman) **confidants** or **confidantes**
a person you confide in

confide *VERB* **confides, confiding, confided**
1 to tell someone a secret ◆ *He wanted to confide in O'Hara, to get him on their side.*
2 to entrust something to someone

confidence *NOUN* **confidences**
1 firm trust in someone
2 a feeling of being certain that you can do something well
3 something told as a secret
in confidence as a secret or private matter

confidence trick *NOUN* **confidence tricks**
swindling a person after persuading him or her to trust you

confident *ADJECTIVE*
showing or feeling confidence
▷ **confidently** *ADVERB*

confidential *ADJECTIVE*
meant to be kept secret
▷ **confidentially** *ADVERB*
▷ **confidentiality** *NOUN*

configuration *NOUN* **configurations**
1 a method of arrangement of parts etc.
2 a shape

confine *VERB* **confines, confining, confined**
1 to keep something within limits; to restrict something ◆ *At the university the lecturers usually confined their classes to one hour.*
2 to keep someone in a place and not let them leave

confined *ADJECTIVE*
a confined space is narrow or very restricted

confinement *NOUN* **confinements**
1 the process of confining or restricting
2 (*old use*) the time of giving birth to a baby

confines (*say* kon-fynz) *PLURAL NOUN*
the limits or boundaries of an area

confirm *VERB* **confirms, confirming, confirmed**
1 to show definitely that something is true or correct ◆ *New evidence confirms the risks to health caused by passive smoking.*
2 to confirm an arrangement or undertaking is to say, usually in writing, that you definitely agree to it ◆ *To confirm the booking, you will be required to sign the booking form.*
3 to make a person a full member of the Christian Church
▷ **confirmation** *NOUN*
▷ **confirmatory** *ADJECTIVE*

confiscate *VERB* **confiscates, confiscating, confiscated**
to take something away from someone as a punishment
▷ **confiscation** *NOUN*

conflagration *NOUN* **conflagrations**
a great and destructive fire

conflict (*say* **kon**-flikt) *NOUN* **conflicts**
a fight, struggle, or disagreement

conflict (*say* kon-**flikt**) *VERB* **conflicts, conflicting, conflicted**
to have a conflict; to differ or disagree

confluence *NOUN* **confluences**
the place where two rivers meet

conform *VERB* **conforms, conforming, conformed**
to keep to accepted rules, customs, or ideas
▷ **conformist** *NOUN*
▷ **conformity** *NOUN*

confound *VERB* **confounds, confounding, confounded**
to astonish or confuse someone

confront *VERB* **confronts, confronting, confronted**
1 to come or bring face to face, especially in a hostile way
2 to be present and have to be dealt with ◆ *'I understand the difficulties that confront them,' he said.*
▷ **confrontation** *NOUN*

SPELLING NOTE Some words with a hard **c-** sound begin with **ch-** (e.g. character)

confusable *ADJECTIVE*
easily confused or mistaken

confusable words

A **confusable word** is one that is sometimes misused or misspelled because it has been confused with another word that is like it in some way. Some confusable words are homophones (words pronounced the same way) that have different spellings (e.g. *stationary* and *stationery*). Others just sound similar, or have similar but distinct meanings (e.g. *tortuous* and *torturous*). Often, confusable words come in pairs, but sometimes there is a larger set of words, such as *their* / *there* / *they're*.

Some common pairs of confusable words are:
allude / elude
complement / compliment
discreet / discrete
faint / feint
flaunt / flout
fortunate / fortuitous
guerrilla / gorilla
precede / proceed
prescribe / proscribe
principal / principle
stationary / stationery
tortuous / torturous

You will find usage notes alerting you to **confusable words** in this dictionary.
See also the panel on **homographs and homophones**.

confuse *VERB* **confuses, confusing, confused**
1 to make a person puzzled or muddled
2 to mistake one thing for another
▷ **confusion** *NOUN*

congeal (*say* kon-**jeel**) *VERB* **congeals, congealing, congealed**
a liquid, e.g. blood, congeals when it becomes jelly-like, especially in cooling

congenial *ADJECTIVE*
a congenial place or situation is one that you like and feel happy in, and a congenial person is one you like as a friend or companion
▷ **congenially** *ADVERB*

congenital (*say* kon-**jen**-it-al) *ADJECTIVE*
existing in a person from birth
▷ **congenitally** *ADVERB*

congested *ADJECTIVE*
1 a congested place is crowded or blocked up with people or traffic
2 your breathing or a part of your body are congested when they become blocked with mucus
▷ **congestion** *NOUN*

conglomerate *NOUN* **conglomerates**
a large business group formed by merging several different companies

conglomeration *NOUN* **conglomerations**
a mass of different things put together

congratulate *VERB* **congratulates, congratulating, congratulated**
to tell a person that you are pleased about what they have done or experienced
▷ **congratulation** *NOUN*
▷ **congratulatory** *ADJECTIVE*

congregate *VERB* **congregates, congregating, congregated**
to assemble or come together

congregation *NOUN* **congregations**
a group of people who have come together to take part in religious worship

Congress *NOUN*
the parliament of the USA

congress *NOUN* **congresses**
a conference

WORD FAMILY *Congress* comes from the Latin word *gressus* meaning 'going'. Other words to do with going (some only loosely) and having the same origin include *digress*, *progress*, *regress*, and *transgress*.

congruent *ADJECTIVE*
1 (*Mathematics*) congruent shapes have the same shape and size
2 ideas or opinions are congruent when they agree or are compatible ◆ *Such an education policy may not be congruent with local needs.*
▷ **congruence** *NOUN*

conical *ADJECTIVE*
cone-shaped
▷ **conically** *ADVERB*

conifer (*say* **kon**-if-er) *NOUN* **conifers**
an evergreen tree with cones
▷ **coniferous** *ADJECTIVE*

conjecture *NOUN* **conjectures**
guesswork or a guess
▷ **conjecture** *VERB*
▷ **conjectural** *ADJECTIVE*

conjoined *ADJECTIVE*
conjoined twins are born with their bodies joined together (SEE ALSO **Siamese twins**)

conjugal (*say* **kon**-jug-al) *ADJECTIVE*
to do with marriage

conjugate *VERB* **conjugates, conjugating, conjugated**
to give all the different forms of a verb
▷ **conjugation** *NOUN*

conjunction *NOUN* **conjunctions**
1 (*Grammar*) a word that joins words or phrases or sentences
2 to do one thing in conjunction with another is to do them together or as part of the same

task or undertaking ◆ *Do this exercise in conjunction with one of the slimming programmes.*

conjunctions and connectives

Conjunctions are used to join words, phrases, or clauses in a sentence.

Coordinating conjunctions, such as *and, but, for, or, neither, nor*, and *yet*, join words or clauses which are of equal importance or which have the same structure:

Would you prefer tea and biscuits, or coffee and cake?
Neither Holmes nor Watson had ever seen such a diamond.

Subordinating conjunctions, such as *although, because, if, until, unless, when, where, while*, and *whereas*, are used to link a main and a dependent clause:

Mira felt brave because she had her lucky pebble.
The computer won't work unless you switch it on.

Connectives are used to link ideas in a piece of writing. They often occur at the start of a sentence and connect it with a previous sentence or paragraph. Common connectives are the words *moreover, nevertheless, finally, furthermore*, and *thus*:

Nevertheless, in this mansion of gloom I now proposed to myself a sojourn of some weeks.
(Edgar Allan Poe, The Fall of the House of Usher)

conjure *VERB* **conjures, conjuring, conjured**
to perform tricks that look like magic
to conjure something up is to produce an image or impression in your mind ◆ *The name 'Nine Elms' conjures up visions of leafy glades.*
▷ **conjuror** *NOUN*

conker *NOUN* **conkers**
the hard shiny brown nut of the horse chestnut tree, used in a game called *conkers*, in which each player has a conker threaded on a string and tries to break the other player's conker with it

WORD HISTORY from a dialect word meaning 'shell of a snail' (because the game was originally played with snail shells)

connect *VERB* **connects, connecting, connected**
1 to join things together; to link one thing with another
2 to think of things or people as being associated with each other

connection *NOUN* **connections**
1 an association or link between things or ideas ◆ *She rejected the simplistic connection between high unemployment and rioting.*
2 a point where a wire or pipe is joined to another or to a piece of equipment
3 (*ICT*) an electrical or electronic link between telephones or computers
4 a train, bus, or aircraft that you catch to continue a journey after getting off another one ◆ *We had to wait an hour for our connection to Frankfurt.*

connective *NOUN*
(*Grammar*) a word that joins words or phrases or sentences, e.g. *thus* and *moreover*: see the language panel at **conjunction**

conning tower *NOUN* **conning towers**
the part on top of a submarine, containing the periscope

connive (*say* kon-**yv**) *VERB* **connives, conniving, connived**
to connive at something wrong is to ignore it or quietly approve of it
▷ **connivance** *NOUN*

connoisseur (*say* kon-a-**ser**) *NOUN* **connoisseurs**
a person with great experience and appreciation of something ◆ *The Prince Regent was renowned as a connoisseur of elegant living and art treasures.*

conquer *VERB* **conquers, conquering, conquered**
to defeat or overcome a person, country, etc.
▷ **conqueror** *NOUN*

conquest *NOUN* **conquests**
1 a victory over someone
2 a conquered territory

cons *PLURAL NOUN* SEE **pros and cons**

conscience (*say* **kon**-shens) *NOUN* **consciences**
knowing what is right and wrong, especially in your own actions

conscientious (*say* kon-shee-**en**-shus) *ADJECTIVE*
careful and honest about doing your work properly
▷ **conscientiously** *ADVERB*

conscientious objector *NOUN* **conscientious objectors**
a person who refuses to serve in the armed forces because he or she believes it is morally wrong

conscious (*say* **kon**-shus) *ADJECTIVE*
1 awake and knowing what is happening
2 to be conscious of something is to be fully aware of it ◆ *Edward became conscious of a strong smell coming from the kitchen.* ◆ *The country's leaders remain conscious that water is a scarce commodity.*
3 a conscious decision is one you make knowingly and deliberately
▷ **consciously** *ADVERB*
▷ **consciousness** *NOUN*

conscript (*say* kon-**skript**) *VERB* **conscripts, conscripting, conscripted**
to make a person join the armed forces
▷ **conscription** *NOUN*

conscript (*say* **kon**-skript) *NOUN* **conscripts**
a person who has been conscripted

a b c d e f g h i j k l m n o p q r s t u v w x y z

consecrate *VERB* **consecrates, consecrating, consecrated**
to say officially that a building or other object is holy
▷ **consecration** *NOUN*

consecutive *ADJECTIVE*
following one after another

Ninety-two coins spun consecutively have come down heads ninety-two consecutive times. *— Tom Stoppard, Rosencrantz & Guildenstern are Dead*

▷ **consecutively** *ADVERB*

consensus *NOUN* **consensuses**
general agreement; the opinion of most people

One of West Brom's goals was by general consensus hundreds of yards offside, provoking the crowd into invading the pitch. *— Nick Hornby, Fever Pitch*

consent *NOUN*
the act of agreeing to what someone wishes; permission

consent *VERB* **consents, consenting, consented**
to say that you are willing to do or allow what someone wishes

consequence *NOUN* **consequences**
1 something that happens as the result of an event or action
2 something is of consequence when it is important, and is of little (or of no) consequence when it is trivial or unimportant

consequent *ADJECTIVE*
happening as a result
▷ **consequently** *ADVERB*

consequential *ADJECTIVE*
happening as a result

conservation *NOUN*
the process of conserving; preservation, especially of the natural environment
▷ **conservationist** *NOUN*

Conservative *NOUN* **Conservatives**
a person who supports the Conservative Party, a British political party that favours private enterprise and freedom from state control
▷ **Conservative** *ADJECTIVE*

conservative *ADJECTIVE*
1 liking traditional ways and disliking changes
2 a conservative opinion or estimate is one that is moderate or cautious, and not extreme
▷ **conservatively** *ADVERB*
▷ **conservatism** *NOUN*

conservatory *NOUN* **conservatories**
a room with a glass roof and large windows, built against an outside wall of a house with a connecting door from the house

conserve *VERB* **conserves, conserving, conserved**
to prevent something valuable from being changed, spoilt, or wasted

consider *VERB* **considers, considering, considered**
1 to think carefully about or give attention to something, especially in order to make a decision
2 to have something as an opinion; to think something ◆ *We would consider it immoral to treat animals as if they had no value in themselves.*

considerable *ADJECTIVE*
fairly great or large ◆ *The work will take a considerable amount of time.*
▷ **considerably** *ADVERB*

considerate *ADJECTIVE*
taking care not to inconvenience or hurt others
▷ **considerately** *ADVERB*

consideration *NOUN* **considerations**
1 being considerate
2 careful thought or attention
3 a fact that must be kept in mind
4 payment given as a reward
to take something into consideration is to allow for it in making a judgement or decision

considering *PREPOSITION*
taking something into consideration ◆ *The job is demanding, considering the time it takes.*

consign *VERB* **consigns, consigning, consigned**
to hand something over formally to someone

consignment *NOUN* **consignments**
1 consigning
2 a batch of goods etc. sent to someone

consist *VERB* **consists, consisting, consisted**
to be made up or composed of ◆ *The apartment consists of a living room, two bedrooms, a kitchen, and a bathroom.*

consistency *NOUN* **consistencies**
1 being consistent
2 thickness or stiffness, especially of a liquid

consistent *ADJECTIVE*
1 keeping to a regular pattern or style; not changing
2 not contradictory
▷ **consistently** *ADVERB*

consolation *NOUN* **consolations**
1 consolation is the process of consoling someone
2 a consolation is something that consoles someone

consolation prize *NOUN* **consolation prizes**
a prize given to a competitor who has just missed winning one of the main prizes

console❶ (*say* kon-**sohl**) *VERB* **consoles, consoling, consoled**
to comfort someone who is unhappy or disappointed

console❷ (*say* **kon**-sohl) *NOUN* **consoles**
1 a panel or unit containing the controls for electrical or other equipment
2 a frame containing the keyboard and stops etc. of an organ

consolidate *VERB* **consolidates, consolidating, consolidated**
1 to make or become secure and strong
2 to combine two or more organizations, funds, etc. into one
▷ **consolidation** *NOUN*

consonant *NOUN* **consonants**
(*Language*) a letter that is not a vowel (SEE ALSO **vowel**)

> **consonants**
>
> The **consonants** in the English alphabet are: *b, c, d, f, g, h, j, k, l, m, n, p, q, r, s, t, v, w, x, y,* and *z*. Although the letter *y* is a consonant in words like *yeti* and *yoga*, it can sometimes act as a vowel (e.g. in *crypt*). Unlike consonants, which are shaped using your lips, teeth, etc., vowel sounds are pronounced mainly using your vocal cords.
>
> Most of the consonant letters are found in the ancient Roman alphabet (from which the English alphabet comes). However, the letters *j, v,* and *w* are more recent additions from medieval times; before then, the letter *i* was used to represent *j* sounds, and the letter *u* was used for *v* and *w* sounds.
>
> See also the panel on **vowels**.

consort (*say* **kon**-sort) *NOUN* **consorts**
a husband or wife, especially of a queen or king

consort (*say* kon-**sort**) *VERB* **consorts, consorting, consorted**
to consort with someone is to be often in their company

consortium *NOUN* **consortia**
a combination of countries, companies, or other groups acting together

conspicuous *ADJECTIVE*
easily seen; noticeable
▷ **conspicuously** *ADVERB*
▷ **conspicuousness** *NOUN*

conspiracy *NOUN* **conspiracies**
a secret plan made by a group of people to do something illegal

conspire *VERB* **conspires, conspiring, conspired**
to take part in a conspiracy
▷ **conspirator** *NOUN*
▷ **conspiratorial** *ADJECTIVE*

constable *NOUN* **constables**
a police officer of the lowest rank

constabulary *NOUN* **constabularies**
a police force

constant *ADJECTIVE*
1 not changing; happening all the time
2 faithful or loyal
▷ **constantly** *ADVERB*
▷ **constancy** *NOUN*

constant *NOUN* **constants**
1 a thing that does not vary
2 (*Mathematics*) a number or value that does not change

constellation *NOUN* **constellations**
a group of stars

constipated *ADJECTIVE*
unable to empty the bowels easily or regularly
▷ **constipation** *NOUN*

constituency *NOUN* **constituencies**
a district represented by a Member of Parliament elected by the people who live there

constituent *NOUN* **constituents**
1 one of the parts that form a whole thing
2 someone who lives in a particular constituency
▷ **constituent** *ADJECTIVE*

constitute *VERB* **constitutes, constituting, constituted**
to make up or amount to something ◆ *Twelve monthly payments constitute the full repayment of the loan.* ◆ *His lawyer argued that the donations of money did not constitute bribery.*

constitution *NOUN* **constitutions**
1 (*Politics*) the group of laws or principles that state how a country is to be organized and governed
2 the condition of your body in terms of its general physical health ◆ *You need plenty of stamina and a sound constitution to complete this gruelling course.*
3 the process of forming or constituting something
4 the composition of something
▷ **constitutional** *ADJECTIVE*

constrain *VERB* **constrains, constraining, constrained**
to force someone to act in a certain way

constraint *NOUN* **constraints**
1 a constraint is a restriction
2 constraint is the act of constraining or compelling someone

constrict *VERB* **constricts, constricting, constricted**
to squeeze or tighten something by making it narrower
▷ **constriction** *NOUN*

a b c d e f g h i j k l m n o p q r s t u v w x y z

construct *VERB* **constructs, constructing, constructed**
to make something by placing parts together; to build something from parts
▷ **constructor** *NOUN*

construction *NOUN* **constructions**
1 the process of constructing something
2 something constructed; a building
3 two or more words put together to form a phrase or clause or sentence
4 an explanation or interpretation ◆ *His opponents put a rather different construction on the affair.*

constructive *ADJECTIVE*
helpful and positive ◆ *You will need a constructive dialogue with everyone involved if this idea is going to work.*

construe *VERB* **construes, construing, construed**
to interpret or explain something difficult

consul *NOUN* **consuls**
1 a government official appointed to live in a foreign city to help people from his or her own country who visit there
2 either of the two chief magistrates in ancient Rome
▷ **consular** *ADJECTIVE*

consulate *NOUN* **consulates**
the building where a consul works

consult *VERB* **consults, consulting, consulted**
to go to a person or book etc. for information or advice
▷ **consultation** *NOUN*

consultant *NOUN* **consultants**
a person who is qualified to give expert advice

consultative *ADJECTIVE*
a consultative process or body is one that involves consulting people ◆ *the Scottish bus passengers' consultative committee*

consume *VERB* **consumes, consuming, consumed**
1 to eat or drink something
2 to use something up ◆ *A lot of time was consumed in looking for the wrong people.*
3 fire consumes a building when it destroys the building completely
4 to be consumed by an emotion is to feel it very deeply ◆ *Alexandra was consumed by impatient curiosity.*

consumer *NOUN* **consumers**
a person who buys or uses goods or services

consummate (*say* kon-sum-ayt) *VERB* **consummates, consummating, consummated**
1 to make complete or perfect
2 to complete a marriage by having sexual intercourse
▷ **consummation** *NOUN*

consummate (*say* kon-**sum**-at) *ADJECTIVE*
highly skilled or expert

Even Butler, the consummate professional, was beginning to dread the long nights of damp and insect bites. — *Eoin Colfer, Artemis Fowl*

consumption *NOUN*
1 the process of consuming or the amount consumed
2 (*old use*) tuberculosis of the lungs

contact *NOUN* **contacts**
1 the process or state of touching
2 being in touch; communication
3 a person you can communicate with when you need information or help

contact *VERB* **contacts, contacting, contacted**
to get in touch with a person

contact lens *NOUN* **contact lenses**
a thin plastic lens placed directly on the eyeball, instead of glasses

contagion *NOUN* **contagions**
a contagious disease

contagious *ADJECTIVE*
a contagious disease is one that spreads by contact with an infected person

contain *VERB* **contains, containing, contained**
1 to include or have inside ◆ *The packet contained two smaller packets, one blue and one white.*
2 to consist of ◆ *A litre contains a hundred centilitres.*
3 to restrain or hold back a strong feeling ◆ *Ben breathed deeply to contain his anger.*

container *NOUN* **containers**
1 a box or bottle or carton designed to contain something
2 a large box-like object of standard design in which goods are transported

contaminate *VERB* **contaminates, contaminating, contaminated**
to make a thing dirty or impure or diseased; to pollute something
▷ **contamination** *NOUN*

contemplate *VERB* **contemplates, contemplating, contemplated**
1 to look at something thoughtfully
2 to consider or think about doing something ◆ *We are contemplating a trip to Paris.*
▷ **contemplation** *NOUN*
▷ **contemplative** *ADJECTIVE*

contemporary *ADJECTIVE*
1 living or happening in the same period ◆ *historians contemporary with the period they were writing about*

2 belonging to the present time ◆ *Neither of them had much interest in contemporary British politics.*
3 contemporary art, architecture, furniture, etc. is modern in style

contemporary *NOUN* **contemporaries**
a person who is about the same age as another or is living at the same time ◆ *Owen was an older contemporary of Forbes and Darwin.*

contempt *NOUN*
a feeling of despising a person or thing

contemptible *ADJECTIVE*
deserving contempt ◆ *You are a contemptible girl to tell such mischievous lies.*

contemptuous *ADJECTIVE*
feeling or showing contempt ◆ *Maisie gave him a contemptuous look and marched towards the patio.*
▷ **contemptuously** *ADVERB*

contend *VERB* **contends, contending, contended**
1 to struggle in a fight or battle or against difficulties
2 to compete in a contest
3 to declare or maintain that something is true ◆ *Both companies contend that they are the market leaders.*
4 to have something difficult to contend with is to have to cope with it or deal with it ◆ *I have all these overhanging branches to contend with.*
▷ **contender** *NOUN*

content[1] (*say* kon-**tent**) *ADJECTIVE*
happy or satisfied

content *NOUN*
a happy or satisfied feeling; contentment

content *VERB* **contents, contenting, contented**
to make a person happy or satisfied

content[2] (*say* **kon**-tent) *NOUN* or **contents** *PLURAL NOUN*
the things or the amount that something contains

contented *ADJECTIVE*
happy with what you have; satisfied
▷ **contentedly** *ADVERB*

contention *NOUN* **contentions**
1 contention is strong disagreement or arguing
2 a contention is a point of view or opinion that someone puts forward

contentment *NOUN*
a feeling of being happy or satisfied

contest (*say* **kon**-test) *NOUN* **contests**
a competition; a struggle in which rivals try to obtain something or to be the best

contest (*say* kon-**test**) *VERB* **contests, contesting, contested**
1 to try to win a competition, election, etc. ◆ *A total of seven political parties contested the October election.*
2 to dispute something or argue that it is wrong or not legal ◆ *Strikers contested the ruling as unconstitutional.*

contestant *NOUN* **contestants**
a person taking part in a contest; a competitor

context *NOUN* **contexts**
1 the words that come before and after a particular word or phrase and help to fix its meaning
2 the background to an event that helps to explain it

contiguous (*say* con-**tig**-yoo-us) *ADJECTIVE*
in contact with something or with each other; touching

continent *NOUN* **continents**
one of the main masses of land in the world. The continents are Europe, Asia, Africa, North America, South America, Australia, and Antarctica.
the Continent the mainland of Europe, not including the British Isles
▷ **continental** *ADJECTIVE*

contingency *NOUN* **contingencies**
something that may happen but cannot be known for certain

contingent *ADJECTIVE*
1 one thing is contingent on another when the first depends on the second ◆ *Resolution of the conflict is contingent on signing a ceasefire agreement.*
2 a contingent event is one that is subject to chance and may happen

contingent *NOUN* **contingents**
a group that forms part of a larger group or gathering

continual *ADJECTIVE*
happening repeatedly over a time ◆ *The goods are subject to continual changes in price.*
▷ **continually** *ADVERB*

USAGE NOTE Take care not to confuse *continual* with *continuous*. You use continual to describe something that happens repeatedly (*There have been continual interruptions*), whereas you use continuous to describe something that happens without a pause (*There is a continuous hum from the fridge*).

continuance *NOUN*
the process of continuing something or of something being continued

continue *VERB* **continues, continuing, continued**
1 to do something without stopping
2 to begin again after stopping ◆ *The game continued after a short break.*
▷ **continuation** *NOUN*

a b c d e f g h i j k l m n o p q r s t u v w x y z

SPELLING NOTE Some words with a hard **c-** sound begin with **ch-** (e.g. character)

continuo (*say* kon-**tin**-yew-o) *NOUN* **continuos**
(*Music*) an accompaniment consisting of a bass line and harmonies, played on a keyboard instrument or cello

continuous *ADJECTIVE*
going on without interruption
▷ **continuously** *ADVERB*
▷ **continuity** *NOUN*
USAGE NOTE See the note at *continual*.

contort *VERB* **contorts, contorting, contorted**
to twist or force something out of the usual shape
▷ **contortion** *NOUN*

contortionist *NOUN* **contortionists**
a person who can twist their body into unusual positions

contour *NOUN* **contours**
1 (*Geography*) a line on a map joining the points that are the same height above sea level
2 an outline

contraband *NOUN*
smuggled goods

contraception *NOUN*
the use of contraceptives to prevent pregnancy; birth control

contraceptive *NOUN* **contraceptives**
a substance or device that prevents pregnancy

contract (*say* **kon**-trakt) *NOUN* **contracts**
1 a formal agreement to do something
2 a document stating the terms of an agreement

contract (*say* kon-**trakt**) *VERB* **contracts, contracting, contracted**
1 to make or become smaller
2 to make a contract
3 to contract an illness is to be affected by it and begin to suffer from it

contraction *NOUN* **contractions**
1 the process of getting smaller or of making something smaller
2 (*Grammar*) a shortened form of a word or words. *Don't* is a contraction of *do not*.

contractor *NOUN* **contractors**
a person who makes a contract, especially to provide materials or workers for a particular job

contradict *VERB* **contradicts, contradicting, contradicted**
1 to say that something said is not true or that someone is wrong
2 to say the opposite of ◆ *There is nothing to contradict your opinion and much to support it.*
▷ **contradiction** *NOUN*
▷ **contradictory** *ADJECTIVE*

contraflow *NOUN* **contraflows**
an arrangement where road traffic is temporarily diverted to the other half of the carriageway and travels beside traffic moving in the opposite direction

contralto *NOUN* **contraltos**
(*Music*) a female singer with a low voice

contraption *NOUN* **contraptions**
a strange or unnecessarily complicated device or machine

contrary *ADJECTIVE*
1 (*say* **kon**-tra-ree) having the opposite meaning or direction; opposite
2 (*say* kon-**trair**-ee) a person is contrary when they are awkward and obstinate

contrary (*say* **kon**-tra-ree) *NOUN*
the opposite
on the contrary the opposite is true

contrast *NOUN* **contrasts**
1 a difference clearly seen when things are compared
2 something showing a clear difference compared with something else

contrast *VERB* **contrasts, contrasting, contrasted**
1 to compare two things in order to show that they are clearly different
2 to be clearly different when compared

contravene *VERB* **contravenes, contravening, contravened**
to do something that breaks a rule or the terms of an agreement
▷ **contravention** *NOUN*

contretemps (*say* **kawn**-tre-tahn) *NOUN*
a disagreement about something minor or trivial

contribute *VERB* **contributes, contributing, contributed**
1 to give money or help jointly with others
2 to write something for a newspaper or magazine etc.
3 to help to cause something ◆ *chemicals that contribute to acid rain*
▷ **contribution** *NOUN*
▷ **contributor** *NOUN*
▷ **contributory** *ADJECTIVE*

contrite *ADJECTIVE*
sorry for having done wrong

contrivance *NOUN* **contrivances**
an ingenious device

contrive *VERB* **contrives, contriving, contrived**
to plan something cleverly; to find a way of doing or making something

control *VERB* **controls, controlling, controlled**
1 to have the power to influence the actions of other people

2 to regulate or limit something
3 to operate a machine and make it work effectively
4 to control yourself is to hold your feelings in check
▷ **controller** *NOUN*

control *NOUN*
the process or right of controlling a person or thing; authority
to be in control is to have control of something
to be out of control is to be no longer able to be controlled

controls *PLURAL NOUN*
the switches and other devices used to control a machine

control tower *NOUN* **control towers**
a tall building at an airport, from which officials control the movements of air traffic

controversial *ADJECTIVE*
causing or likely to cause disagreement

controversy (*say* kon-tro-ver-see or kon-trov-er-see) *NOUN* **controversies**
a long argument or disagreement

contusion *NOUN* **contusions**
(*Medicine*) a bruise

conundrum *NOUN* **conundrums**
a riddle or difficult question

conurbation *NOUN* **conurbations**
a large urban area where towns have spread into each other

convalesce *VERB* **convalesces, convalescing, convalesced**
to be recovering from an illness
▷ **convalescence** *NOUN*
▷ **convalescent** *ADJECTIVE, NOUN*

convection *NOUN*
the passing on of heat within liquid, air, or gas by circulation of the warmed parts

convector *NOUN* **convectors**
a heater that circulates warm air by convection

convene *VERB* **convenes, convening, convened**
to bring people together for a meeting
▷ **convener** *NOUN*

convenience *NOUN* **conveniences**
1 convenience is suitability and ease of use
2 a convenience is something that is convenient
3 a convenience is also a public toilet
at your convenience whenever you find it convenient; as it suits you

convenience food *NOUN* **convenience foods**
food sold in a form that is already partly prepared and so is easy to use

convenient *ADJECTIVE*
suited to your needs; easy to use or deal with or reach
▷ **conveniently** *ADVERB*

convent *NOUN* **convents**
a place where nuns live and work

convention *NOUN* **conventions**
1 an accepted way of doing things
2 a large meeting or conference

conventional *ADJECTIVE*
1 done or doing things in the normal or accepted way; traditional
2 conventional weapons are those that are not nuclear
▷ **conventionally** *ADVERB*
▷ **conventionality** *NOUN*

converge *VERB* **converges, converging, converged**
to come towards the same point from different directions
▷ **convergence** *NOUN*
▷ **convergent** *ADJECTIVE*

conversant *ADJECTIVE*
(*formal*) to be conversant with something is to know a lot about it

conversation *NOUN* **conversations**
an informal or spontaneous talk between two or more people
▷ **conversational** *ADJECTIVE*

converse ❶ (*say* kon-verss) *VERB* **converses, conversing, conversed**
to hold a conversation

converse ❷ (*say* kon-verss) *ADJECTIVE*
opposite; contrary
▷ **conversely** *ADVERB*

converse *NOUN*
the opposite of something ◆ *The converse is also possible.*

conversion *NOUN* **conversions**
the process of converting

convert (*say* kon-vert) *VERB* **converts, converting, converted**
1 to change something from one form to another
2 to cause a person to change their principles or religious beliefs
3 to kick a goal after scoring a try at rugby football
▷ **converter** *NOUN*

convert (*say* kon-vert) *NOUN* **converts**
a person who has changed their religious or other beliefs

convertible *ADJECTIVE*
able to be converted
▷ **convertibility** *NOUN*

convertible *NOUN* **convertibles**
a car with a folding or detachable roof

a b c d e f g h i j k l m n o p q r s t u v w x y z

convex *ADJECTIVE*
curved like the outside of a ball or circle (SEE ALSO **concave**)
▷ **convexity** *NOUN*

convey *VERB* **conveys, conveying, conveyed**
1 to transport people or goods
2 to communicate a message or idea
▷ **conveyor** *NOUN*

conveyance *NOUN* **conveyances**
1 the process of conveying
2 (*formal*) a vehicle for transporting people

conveyancing *NOUN*
the legal process of transferring ownership of land or property from one person to another

conveyor belt *NOUN* **conveyor belts**
a continuous moving band for moving objects from one place to another

convict (*say* kon-**vikt**) *VERB* **convicts, convicting, convicted**
to prove or declare that a person is guilty of a crime

convict (*say* **kon**-vikt) *NOUN* **convicts**
a convicted person who is in prison

conviction *NOUN* **convictions**
1 the process of convicting someone of a crime
2 being firmly convinced of something
3 a firm opinion or belief
to carry conviction is to be convincing

convince *VERB* **convinces, convincing, convinced**
to make a person certain that something is true

convivial *ADJECTIVE*
sociable and lively

convoluted *ADJECTIVE*
1 a convoluted story is complicated and full of details
2 coiled or twisted
▷ **convolution** *NOUN*

convoy *NOUN* **convoys**
a group of ships or vehicles travelling together

convulse *VERB* **convulses, convulsing, convulsed**
to be convulsed is to experience violent movements of the body from laughing or feeling strong emotion
▷ **convulsive** *ADJECTIVE*

convulsion *NOUN* **convulsions**
1 a violent movement of the body
2 a violent upheaval

coo *VERB* **coos, cooing, cooed**
to make a soft murmuring sound like a dove
▷ **coo** *NOUN*

cook *VERB* **cooks, cooking, cooked**
1 to prepare food by mixing the ingredients and heating the mixture
2 to cook up a story or plan is to invent it

cook *NOUN* **cooks**
a person who cooks

cooker *NOUN* **cookers**
a piece of equipment for cooking food

cookery *NOUN*
the skill or practice of cooking food

cool *ADJECTIVE*
1 fairly cold; not hot or warm
2 calm or casual about something
3 not friendly or enthusiastic
4 (*informal*) impressive or fashionable

It was still kind of cool to have someone in your family robbed by a famous outlaw. — *Louis Sachar, Holes*

▷ **coolly** *ADVERB*
▷ **coolness** *NOUN*

cool *VERB* **cools, cooling, cooled**
to make or become cool
▷ **cooler** *NOUN*

coolibah *NOUN*
an Australian gum tree which yields very strong, hard wood

coop *NOUN* **coops**
a cage or area for keeping chickens, turkeys, etc.

cooped up *ADJECTIVE*
having to stay in a place which is small and uncomfortable

cooperate *VERB* **cooperates, cooperating, cooperated**
to work in a helpful way with other people
▷ **cooperation** *NOUN*
▷ **cooperative** *ADJECTIVE*

co-opt *VERB* **co-opts, co-opting, co-opted**
to invite someone to become a member of a committee or other official body

coordinate *VERB* **coordinates, coordinating, coordinated**
to organize people or things to work properly together
▷ **coordination** *NOUN*
▷ **coordinator** *NOUN*

coordinate *NOUN* **coordinates**
(*Mathematics*) each of a pair of numbers or letters used to fix the position of a point on a graph or map

coot *NOUN* **coots**
a waterbird with a horny white patch on its forehead

cop *VERB* **cops, copping, copped**
(*informal*) **to cop it** is to get into trouble or be punished

cop *NOUN* **cops**
(*informal*) a police officer

cope *VERB* **copes, coping, coped**
to manage or deal with something successfully

copier *NOUN* **copiers**
a machine for copying documents and other printed material

coping *NOUN*
the top course in a stone or brick wall, usually slanted to drain off rainwater

copious *ADJECTIVE*
plentiful; abundant
▷ **copiously** *ADVERB*

copper❶ *NOUN* **coppers**
1 a reddish-brown metal used to make electrical wiring and as a component of brass and bronze
2 a reddish brown colour
3 a coin made of copper or metal of this colour
▷ **copper** *ADJECTIVE*

WORD HISTORY via Old English from Latin *cyprium* 'Cyprus metal' (because the Romans got most of their copper from Cyprus)

copper❷ *NOUN* **coppers**
(*informal*) a police officer

copperplate *NOUN*
a style of neat round handwriting

WORD HISTORY in the past, people learning to write copied examples from books that were printed from copper plates

coppice *NOUN* **coppices**
a small group of trees

copra *NOUN*
dried coconut kernels, which produce an oil

copse *NOUN* **copses**
a small group of trees

copulate *VERB* **copulates, copulating, copulated**
to have sexual intercourse
▷ **copulation** *NOUN*

copy *NOUN* **copies**
1 a thing made to look like or be similar to another
2 something written or typed out again from its original form
3 one of a number of specimens of the same book or newspaper etc.

copy *VERB* **copies, copying, copied**
1 to make a copy of something
2 to do the same as someone else; to imitate someone

copyright *NOUN*
(*Library*) the exclusive legal right to print a book, reproduce a picture, record a piece of music, etc.

coquette (*say* ko-**ket**) *NOUN* **coquettes**
a woman who flirts
▷ **coquettish** *ADJECTIVE*

coral *NOUN*
1 a hard red, pink, or white substance formed by the skeletons of tiny sea creatures massed together
2 a pink colour

corbel *NOUN* **corbels**
a piece of stone or wood that sticks out from a roof to support a structure above it

cord *NOUN* **cords**
1 a long thin flexible strip made from twisted threads or strands
2 a piece of flex
3 a cord-like structure in the body, e.g. the spinal cord
4 corduroy

USAGE NOTE Take care not to confuse this word with *chord*.

cordial *NOUN* **cordials**
a fruit-flavoured drink

cordial *ADJECTIVE*
warm and friendly
▷ **cordially** *ADVERB*
▷ **cordiality** *NOUN*

cordon *NOUN* **cordons**
a line of police, soldiers, or vehicles placed round an area to guard or enclose it

cordon *VERB* **cordons, cordoning, cordoned**
to surround with a cordon

The whole area had been cordoned off. Police cars had moved in from every direction. — *Anthony Horowitz, Scorpia*

cordon bleu (*say* kor-dawn **bler**) *ADJECTIVE*
of the highest class in cookery

corduroy *NOUN*
a thick cotton cloth with velvety ridges

core *NOUN* **cores**
1 the part in the middle of something
2 the hard central part of an apple or pear etc., containing the seeds

corgi *NOUN* **corgis**
a small dog with short legs and upright ears

cork *NOUN* **corks**
1 cork is the lightweight bark of a kind of oak tree
2 a cork is a stopper for a bottle, made of cork or other material

cork *VERB* **corks, corking, corked**
to close a bottle or other container with a cork

corkscrew *NOUN* **corkscrews**
1 a device with a spiral metal rod, for screwing into bottle corks to remove them
2 a spiral

corm *NOUN* **corms**
an underground part of some plants, rather like a bulb

cormorant *NOUN* **cormorants**
a large black seabird

corn❶ *NOUN*
1 the seed of wheat and similar plants
2 a plant, such as wheat, grown for its grain

corn❷ *NOUN* **corns**
a small hard painful lump on the foot

cornea *NOUN* **corneas**
the transparent covering over the pupil of the eye
▷ **corneal** *ADJECTIVE*

corned beef *NOUN*
tinned beef preserved with salt

corner *NOUN* **corners**
1 the angle or area where two lines or sides or walls meet or where two streets join
2 a free hit or kick from the corner of a hockey or football field
3 a remote or distant region

corner *VERB* **corners, cornering, cornered**
1 to drive someone into a corner or other position from which it is difficult to escape
2 to corner the market is to get possession of all or most of something that people want
3 to go round a corner or a bend in the road

cornerstone *NOUN* **cornerstones**
1 a vitally important feature or quality on which other things are based ◆ *This piece of evidence became the cornerstone of their argument.*
2 a stone built into the corner at the base of a building

cornet *NOUN* **cornets**
1 a cone-shaped wafer for holding ice cream
2 (*Music*) a brass instrument like a trumpet but shorter and wider

cornflakes *PLURAL NOUN*
toasted flakes made from maize flour, eaten as a breakfast cereal

cornflour *NOUN*
a fine flour made from maize or rice, used in sauces and milk puddings

cornflower *NOUN* **cornflowers**
a plant with blue flowers that grows wild in fields of corn

cornice (*say* kor-nis) *NOUN* **cornices**
a band of ornamental moulding on walls just below a ceiling or at the top of a building

cornucopia (*say* korn-yoo-**koh**-pee-a) *NOUN*
1 a plentiful supply of good things
2 a horn-shaped container overflowing with fruit and flowers, used as a symbol of abundance

corny *ADJECTIVE* **cornier, corniest**
(*informal*) a corny joke or remark is one that is silly or repeated so often that it no longer has much effect

corollary (*say* ker-**ol**-er-ee) *NOUN* **corollaries**
a fact or idea that logically results from another ◆ *It is a pity that, as a corollary of his later greatness, his earlier poetry is rarely read.*

corona (*say* kor-**oh**-na) *NOUN* **coronas**
a circle of light round something

coronary *NOUN* **coronaries**
short for *coronary thrombosis*, a blockage of an artery carrying blood to the heart, caused by a blood clot

coronation *NOUN* **coronations**
the ceremony of crowning a king or queen

coroner *NOUN* **coroners**
an official who holds an inquiry into the cause of a death thought to be from unnatural causes

coronet *NOUN* **coronets**
a small crown

corporal❶ *NOUN* **corporals**
a soldier ranking next below a sergeant

corporal❷ *ADJECTIVE*
to do with the body

corporal punishment *NOUN*
punishment inflicted on the body, e.g. caning or spanking

corporate *ADJECTIVE*
corporate activities and responsibilities are shared by members of a group, especially in business

corporation *NOUN* **corporations**
1 a group of people elected to govern a town
2 a large business company or group of companies legally operating as one unit

corps (*say* kor) *NOUN* **corps** (*say* korz)
1 a special army unit, e.g. a medical corps
2 a large group of soldiers
3 a group of people working together

corps de ballet (*say* kor der **bal**-ay) *NOUN*
the ordinary members of a ballet company, apart from the principal performers

corpse *NOUN* **corpses**
a dead body

corpulent *ADJECTIVE*
having a bulky body; fat
▷ **corpulence** *NOUN*

corpuscle (*say* **kor**-pusl) *NOUN* **corpuscles**
one of the minute red or white cells in blood

corral (*say* kor-**ahl**) *NOUN* **corrals**
(*American*) an enclosure for horses, cattle, or other livestock on a farm or ranch

correct *ADJECTIVE*
1 true or accurate; not having any mistakes
2 correct behaviour is behaving properly or in a way that people approve of
▷ **correctly** *ADVERB*
▷ **correctness** *NOUN*

correct *VERB* **corrects, correcting, corrected**
1 to make a thing correct by altering or adjusting it
2 to mark the mistakes in something
3 to point out or punish a person's faults
▷ **correction** *NOUN*
▷ **corrective** *ADJECTIVE*

correlate *VERB* **correlates, correlating, correlated**
to compare or connect things systematically
▷ **correlation** *NOUN*

correspond *VERB* **corresponds, corresponding, corresponded**
1 to agree or match ◆ *Your story corresponds with his.*
2 to be similar or equivalent ◆ *Their assembly corresponds to our parliament.*
3 people correspond, or one person corresponds with another, when they write letters to each other

correspondence *NOUN*
1 similarity or agreement between things
2 letters, or the process of writing letters

correspondent *NOUN* **correspondents**
1 a person who writes letters to someone else
2 a journalist who gathers news and sends reports on a particular topic to a newspaper or broadcasting station

corridor *NOUN* **corridors**
a passage in a building

corroborate *VERB* **corroborates, corroborating, corroborated**
to help to confirm a statement or argument
▷ **corroboration** *NOUN*

corrode *VERB* **corrodes, corroding, corroded**
to destroy metal gradually by chemical action
▷ **corrosion** *NOUN*

corrosive *ADJECTIVE*
able to corrode something ◆ *corrosive acid*

corrugated *ADJECTIVE*
shaped into alternate ridges and grooves ◆ *corrugated iron*

corrupt *ADJECTIVE*
1 dishonest; willing to accept bribes
2 wicked or immoral
3 (*ICT*) corrupt data is data made unreliable by errors or faults

corrupt *VERB* **corrupts, corrupting, corrupted**
1 to cause someone to become dishonest or wicked
2 to spoil something or cause it to decay
▷ **corruption** *NOUN*
▷ **corruptible** *ADJECTIVE*

corsair *NOUN* **corsairs**
1 an old word for a pirate
2 a pirate ship

corset *NOUN* **corsets**
a close-fitting piece of underwear worn by women to shape or support the body

cortège (*say* kort-**ayzh**) *NOUN* **cortèges**
a funeral procession

cortex *NOUN* (*Biology*)
1 an outer layer of tissue on an organ such as a kidney or a plant stem
2 the outer grey material forming part of the brain

cosh *NOUN* **coshes**
a thick heavy stick used as a weapon

cosine *NOUN* **cosines**
(*Mathematics*) in a right-angled triangle, the ratio of the length of a side adjacent to one of the acute angles to the length of the hypotenuse (SEE ALSO **sine**)

cosmetic *NOUN* **cosmetics**
a substance put on the face to make it look more attractive, such as lipstick, mascara, or eyeshadow

cosmetic *ADJECTIVE*
1 affecting only the outward appearance of something; superficial
2 cosmetic surgery is surgery carried out to make people look more attractive

cosmic *ADJECTIVE*
to do with the universe or outer space

cosmonaut *NOUN* **cosmonauts**
a Russian astronaut

cosmopolitan *ADJECTIVE*
from many countries; containing people from many countries

cosmos (*say* **koz**-moss) *NOUN*
the universe

Cossack *NOUN* **Cossacks**
a member of a people of south Russia, famous as horsemen

cosset *VERB* **cossets, cosseting, cosseted**
to pamper someone or treat them very kindly and lovingly

cost *NOUN* **costs**
1 the amount of money needed to buy, do, or make something
2 the effort or loss needed to achieve something
at all costs or **at any cost** no matter what the cost or difficulty may be

cost *VERB* **costs, costing, cost**
1 to have a certain amount as the price or charge
2 to cause the loss of ◆ *The war cost many lives.*
3 to estimate the cost of something

USAGE NOTE The past tense and past participle in meaning 3 is *costed.*

costermonger *NOUN* **costermongers**
(*old use*) a person who sells fruit and vegetables from a barrow in the street

WORD HISTORY from old words *costard* 'large apple' and *monger* 'trader'

a b c d e f g h i j k l m n o p q r s t u v w x y z

costly *ADJECTIVE* **costlier, costliest**
1 expensive
2 causing great damage or loss
▷ **costliness** *NOUN*

cost of living *NOUN*
the level of prices for food, clothing, and housing

costume *NOUN* **costumes**
1 a set of clothes, especially for a particular purpose or of a particular place or period
2 (*Drama*) the clothes worn by an actor playing a particular role

cosy *ADJECTIVE* **cosier, cosiest**
warm and comfortable
▷ **cosily** *ADVERB*
▷ **cosiness** *NOUN*

cosy *NOUN* **cosies**
a cover placed over a teapot or boiled egg to keep it hot

cot *NOUN* **cots**
a small bed with high barred sides for a baby or young child
WORD HISTORY from Hindi *khat* 'bedstead'

cottage *NOUN* **cottages**
a small simple house, especially in the country

cottage cheese *NOUN*
soft white cheese made from curds of skimmed milk

cottage pie *NOUN* **cottage pies**
a dish of minced meat covered with mashed potato and baked

cotton *NOUN*
1 a soft white substance covering the seeds of a tropical plant; the plant itself
2 thread made from this substance
3 cloth made from cotton thread

cotton wool *NOUN*
soft fluffy wadding originally made from cotton

couch *NOUN* **couches**
1 a long soft seat like a sofa but with only one end raised
2 a sofa or settee

couch *VERB* **couches, couching, couched**
to express ideas in words of a certain kind ◆ *The questions were couched in very simple language.*

cougar (*say* koo-ger) *NOUN* **cougars**
(*American*) a puma

cough (*say* kof) *VERB* **coughs, coughing, coughed**
to send out air from the lungs with a sudden sharp sound

cough *NOUN* **coughs**
1 the act or sound of coughing
2 an illness that makes you cough

could *VERB* *past tense of* **can** ❷

couldn't
short for *could not*

council *NOUN* **councils**
a group of people chosen or elected to organize or discuss something, especially those elected to organize the affairs of a town or county
USAGE NOTE Take care not to confuse this word with *counsel*.

council house *NOUN* **council houses**
a house owned by a town council and let to tenants

councillor *NOUN* **councillors**
a member of a town or county council

council tax *NOUN* **council taxes**
a tax paid to a local authority to pay for local services, based on the estimated value of your house or flat

counsel *NOUN* **counsels**
1 advice given by a trained person
2 a barrister or group of barristers representing someone in a lawsuit
USAGE NOTE Take care not to confuse this word with *council*.

counsel *VERB* **counsels, counselling, counselled**
to give someone advice, especially important or personal advice

counsellor *NOUN* **counsellors**
a person trained to give advice on personal matters

count ❶ *VERB* **counts, counting, counted**
1 to find the total of something by using numbers
2 to say a sequence of numbers in their proper order
3 to include in a total ◆ *There was only one passenger on the bus, not counting the driver.*
4 to be important ◆ *It's what you do that counts.*
5 to regard or consider ◆ *I should count it an honour to be invited.*

to count on someone is to rely on them

count *NOUN* **counts**
1 a process of counting
2 a number reached by counting; a total
3 each of the points being considered, e.g. in accusing someone of crimes ◆ *guilty on all counts*

count ❷ *NOUN* **counts**
a foreign nobleman

countable *ADJECTIVE*
(*Language*) a countable noun can have a plural form, e.g. *houses* and *ideas* (SEE ALSO **uncountable**)

countdown *NOUN* **countdowns**
a process of counting numbers backwards to zero before an event, especially the launching of a space rocket

countenance *NOUN* **countenances**
a person's face; the expression on a person's face

countenance *VERB* **countenances, countenancing, countenanced**
to give approval to; to allow

counter ❶ *NOUN* **counters**
1 a flat surface over which customers are served in a shop, bank, or office
2 a small round playing piece used in certain board games
3 a device for counting things

counter ❷ *VERB* **counters, countering, countered**
1 to counteract something
2 to return an opponent's blow or attack

counter *ADVERB*
contrary to something ◆ *This is counter to what we really want.*

counteract *VERB* **counteracts, counteracting, counteracted**
to act against something and reduce or prevent its effects
▷ **counteraction** *NOUN*

counter-attack *VERB* **counter-attacks, counter-attacking, counter-attacked**
to attack in reponse to an enemy's attack
▷ **counter-attack** *NOUN*

counterbalance *NOUN* **counterbalances**
a weight or influence that balances another
▷ **counterbalance** *VERB*

counterfeit (*say* **kownt**-er-feet) *ADJECTIVE*
fake; not genuine

counterfeit *NOUN* **counterfeits**
a forgery or imitation

counterfeit *VERB* **counterfeits, counterfeiting, counterfeited**
to forge or make an imitation of something

counterfoil *NOUN* **counterfoils**
a section of a cheque or receipt etc. that is torn off and kept as a record

countermand *VERB* **countermands, countermanding, countermanded**
to cancel a command or instruction that someone else has given

counterpane *NOUN* **counterpanes**
a bedspread

counterpart *NOUN* **counterparts**
a person or thing that corresponds to another ◆ *Their President is the counterpart of our Prime Minister.*

counterpoint *NOUN*
(*Music*) a method of combining melodies in harmony

countersign *VERB* **countersigns, countersigning, countersigned**
to add another signature to a document to give it authority

countertenor *NOUN* **countertenors**
(*Music*) the highest male adult singing voice

counterweight *NOUN*
a counterbalancing weight or influence

countess *NOUN* **countesses**
the wife or widow of a count or earl; a female count

countless *ADJECTIVE*
too many to count

countrified *ADJECTIVE*
like the country or countryside

country *NOUN* **countries**
1 the land occupied by a nation, or the nation itself
2 all the people of a country
3 the countryside

country dance *NOUN* **country dances**
a traditional dance performed by couples facing each other in lines

countryman or **countrywoman** *NOUN* **countrymen** or **countrywomen**
1 a man or woman who lives in the countryside
2 a man or woman who comes from the same country as someone else

countryside *NOUN*
an area away from towns, with fields, woods, villages, etc.

county *NOUN* **counties**
(*Geography*) each of the main areas that a country is divided into for local government

coup (*say* koo) *NOUN* **coups**
1 (short for **coup d'état**) the sudden overthrow of a government
2 a sudden action taken to win power; a clever victory

WORD HISTORY a French word meaning 'a blow or stroke'

coup de grâce (*say* koo der **grahs**) *NOUN*
a stroke or blow that puts an end to something

WORD HISTORY a French phrase meaning 'stroke of grace'

coup d'état (*say* koo day-**tah**) *NOUN* **coups d'état**
the sudden overthrow of a government

WORD HISTORY a French phrase meaning 'blow of state'

couple *NOUN* **couples**
two people or things considered together; a pair

couple *VERB* **couples, coupling, coupled**
to fasten or link two things together

couplet *NOUN* **couplets**
(*Language*) a pair of lines in rhyming verse

coupon *NOUN* **coupons**
a piece of paper that gives you the right to receive or do something

courage *NOUN*
the ability to face danger or difficulty or pain even when you are afraid; bravery
▷ **courageous** *ADJECTIVE*

courgette (*say* koor-*zh*et) *NOUN* **courgettes**
a kind of small vegetable marrow

courier (*say* koor-ee-er) *NOUN* **couriers**
1 a messenger who takes goods or documents
2 a person employed to guide and help a group of tourists

course *NOUN* **courses**
1 the direction followed by a ship, aircraft, road, or river
2 a series of events or actions; a way of proceeding ◆ *The wisest course was to keep the place under observation.*
3 a series of lessons and exercises in a particular subject
4 a dish forming one part of a meal
5 a racecourse or golf course
6 a series of medical treatments or doses of medication
of course without a doubt; as we expected

course *VERB* **courses, coursing, coursed**
to move or flow freely ◆ *A thrill coursed through him.*

court *NOUN* **courts**
1 the household of a king or queen
2 a lawcourt; the judges and lawyers in a lawcourt
3 an enclosed area for games such as tennis or netball
4 a courtyard

court *VERB* **courts, courting, courted**
1 to try to get someone's support
2 (*old use*) to try to win someone's love

courteous (*say* ker-tee-us) *ADJECTIVE*
polite and helpful
▷ **courteously** *ADVERB*
▷ **courtesy** *NOUN*

courtier *NOUN* **courtiers**
(*old use*) a king's or queen's companion or adviser at court

courtly *ADJECTIVE*
dignified and polite

court martial *NOUN* **courts martial**
1 a court for trying members of the armed services who have broken military law
2 a trial in this court

court-martial *VERB* **court-martials, court-martialling, court-martialled**
to try a person by a court martial

courtship *NOUN*
1 (*old use*) a period of courting someone in the hope of marrying them
2 the mating ritual of some birds and animals

courtyard *NOUN* **courtyards**
a space surrounded by walls or buildings

cousin *NOUN* **cousins**
a child of your uncle or aunt

cove *NOUN* **coves**
a small bay

coven (*say* kuv-en) *NOUN* **covens**
a group of witches

covenant (*say* kuv-en-ant) *NOUN* **covenants**
a formal agreement or contract

Coventry *NOUN*
to send someone to Coventry is to refuse to speak to them

WORD HISTORY the phrase possibly arose because, during the English Civil War, Cavalier prisoners were sent to Coventry in the Midlands: the citizens supported the Roundheads, and would not speak to the Cavaliers

cover *VERB* **covers, covering, covered**
1 to place one thing over or round another; to conceal something

> Lennie covered his face with his huge paws and bleated with terror. — *John Steinbeck, Of Mice and Men*

2 to deal with or include a particular topic or subject ◆ *The book covers all aspects of outdoor photography.*
3 to travel a certain distance ◆ *They managed to cover twenty miles every day.*
4 to protect by insurance or a guarantee
5 to be enough money to pay for something ◆ *You will need to take enough to cover your hotel costs.*
to cover something up is to conceal an awkward fact or piece of information

cover *NOUN* **covers**
1 a thing used for covering something else; a lid, wrapper, envelope, etc.
2 the binding of a book
3 something that hides or shelters or protects you

coverage *NOUN*
the amount of time or space given to reporting an event in a newspaper or broadcast

coverlet *NOUN* **coverlets**
a bedspread

covert (*say* kuv-ert) *NOUN* **coverts**
an area of thick bushes in which birds and animals hide

covert *ADJECTIVE*
done secretly

cover-up *NOUN* **cover-ups**
an attempt to conceal information about something, especially a crime or mistake

covet (*say* **kuv**-it) *VERB* **covets, coveting, coveted**
to wish to have something that belongs to someone else

Crane looked up at the bedraggled corpse and coveted the new boots it was wearing.
— *G. P. Taylor, Shadowmancer*

▷ **covetous** *ADJECTIVE*

covey (*say* **kuv**-ee) *NOUN* **coveys**
a group of partridges

cow❶ *NOUN* **cows**
the fully grown female of cattle or of certain other large animals (e.g. the elephant, whale, or seal)

cow❷ *VERB* **cows, cowing, cowed**
to frighten someone into doing what you want them to

coward *NOUN* **cowards**
a person who has no courage and shows fear in a shameful way

▷ **cowardice** *NOUN*
▷ **cowardly** *ADJECTIVE*

cowboy *NOUN* **cowboys**
a man in charge of grazing cattle on a ranch in the USA

cower *VERB* **cowers, cowering, cowered**
to crouch or shrink back in fear

cowl *NOUN* **cowls**
1 a monk's hood
2 a hood-shaped covering, e.g. on a chimney

cowshed *NOUN* **cowsheds**
a shed for cattle

cowslip *NOUN* **cowslips**
a wild plant with small yellow flowers

cox *NOUN* **coxes**
a coxswain

coxswain (*say* **kok**-swayn or **kok**-sun) *NOUN* **coxswains**
1 a person who steers a rowing boat
2 a sailor with special duties

coy *ADJECTIVE*
pretending to be shy or modest

▷ **coyly** *ADVERB*
▷ **coyness** *NOUN*

crab *NOUN* **crabs**
a shellfish with ten legs, the first pair being a set of pincers

crab apple *NOUN* **crab apples**
a small sour kind of apple

crack *NOUN* **cracks**
1 a line on the surface of something where it has broken but not come completely apart
2 a narrow gap
3 a sudden sharp noise
4 a hard knock or blow ◆ *a crack on the head*
5 (*informal*) a joke; a wisecrack
6 a drug made from cocaine

crack *ADJECTIVE*
(*informal*) first-class ◆ *He is a crack shot.*

crack *VERB* **cracks, cracking, cracked**
1 to break or split with a crack
2 to make a sudden sharp noise
3 to break down ◆ *He cracked under the strain.*

to crack a joke is to tell a joke
to crack down on something (*informal*) is to stop something that is illegal or against the rules
to get cracking (*informal*) is to start to do something busily

cracker *NOUN* **crackers**
1 a paper tube that makes a sharp sound when pulled apart, releasing a small toy or novelty
2 a firework that explodes with a crack
3 a thin dry biscuit

crackle *VERB* **crackles, crackling, crackled**
to make a lot of slight cracking sounds

There is a storm on its way. The air crackles with static as I let myself softly out the front door.
— *Theresa Breslin, Whispers in the Graveyard*

▷ **crackle** *NOUN*

crackling *NOUN*
the crisp skin on roast pork

cradle *NOUN* **cradles**
1 a small cot for a baby
2 a supporting framework

cradle *VERB* **cradles, cradling, cradled**
to hold gently and protectively

craft *NOUN* **crafts**
1 an activity that needs skill, especially with the hands
2 skill in doing your work
3 cunning or trickery
4 (*plural* **craft**) a ship or boat; an aircraft or spacecraft

craftsman *NOUN* **craftsmen**
a person who is skilled in a particular craft

▷ **craftsmanship** *NOUN*

crafty *ADJECTIVE* **craftier, craftiest**
cunning or deceitful

▷ **craftily** *ADVERB*
▷ **craftiness** *NOUN*

crag *NOUN* **crags**
a steep piece of rough rock

▷ **craggy** *ADJECTIVE*
▷ **cragginess** *NOUN*

cram *VERB* **crams, cramming, crammed**
1 to push or fit something on with a lot of force

Adam reached up both hands to cram his bonnet closer down on his head. — *Mollie Hunter, The Thirteenth Member*

2 to push a lot of people or things into a room or container so that it is very full
3 to study intensively just before an examination

a b c d e f g h i j k l m n o p q r s t u v w x y z

cramp *NOUN* **cramps**
pain caused by a muscle tightening suddenly

cramp *VERB* **cramps, cramping, cramped**
to hinder the freedom or growth of someone or something

cramped *ADJECTIVE*
uncomfortably small or crowded

cranberry *NOUN* **cranberries**
a small sour red berry used for making jelly and sauce

crane *NOUN* **cranes**
1 a machine for lifting and moving heavy objects
2 a large wading bird with long legs and a long slender neck

crane *VERB* **cranes, craning, craned**
to stretch your neck to try to see something

crane fly *NOUN* **crane flies**
a flying insect with very long thin legs; a daddy-long-legs

cranium *NOUN* **craniums**
the skull

crank *NOUN* **cranks**
1 an L-shaped part used for changing the direction of movement in machinery
2 a person with strange or fanatical ideas
▷ **cranky** *ADJECTIVE*

crank *VERB* **cranks, cranking, cranked**
to move something by means of a crank

cranny *NOUN* **crannies**
a crevice

crash *NOUN* **crashes**
1 the loud noise of something breaking or colliding
2 a violent collision or fall
3 a sudden drop or failure

crash *VERB* **crashes, crashing, crashed**
1 to make or have a crash; to cause something to crash
2 to move or fall with a crash
3 a computer crashes when it stops working suddenly

crash *ADJECTIVE*
done rapidly and intensively ◆ *a crash course*

crash helmet *NOUN* **crash helmets**
a padded helmet worn by cyclists and motorcyclists to protect the head

crash-land *VERB* **crash-lands, crash-landing, crash-landed**
to land an aircraft roughly in an emergency, often causing damage
▷ **crash-landing** *NOUN*

crass *ADJECTIVE*
very stupid or insensitive

crate *NOUN* **crates**
1 a packing case made of strips of wood
2 an open container with compartments for carrying bottles

crater *NOUN* **craters**
1 the mouth of a volcano
2 a bowl-shaped cavity or hollow caused by an explosion or impact

cravat *NOUN* **cravats**
a short wide scarf worn by men round the neck and tucked into an open-necked shirt

WORD HISTORY from French *Cravate* 'Croatian' (because Croatian soldiers wore linen cravats)

crave *VERB* **craves, craving, craved**
1 to want something very strongly
2 (*old use*) to beg for something

craven *ADJECTIVE*
cowardly

craving *NOUN* **cravings**
a strong desire; a longing

crawl *VERB* **crawls, crawling, crawled**
1 to move with the body close to the ground or other surface, or on hands and knees
2 traffic is said to crawl when it moves very slowly
3 (*informal*) a place is crawling with people or things when there are a lot of them there
▷ **crawler** *NOUN*

crawl *NOUN*
1 a crawling movement
2 a very slow pace
3 an overarm swimming stroke

crayon *NOUN* **crayons**
a stick or pencil of coloured wax or chalk, used for drawing

craze *NOUN* **crazes**
a widespread but short-lived enthusiasm for something

crazed *ADJECTIVE*
driven insane

crazy *ADJECTIVE* **crazier, craziest**
1 insane
2 very foolish ◆ *a crazy idea*
▷ **crazily** *ADVERB*
▷ **craziness** *NOUN*

crazy paving *NOUN*
paving made of oddly shaped pieces of stone etc.

creak *NOUN* **creaks**
a harsh squeak like that of a stiff door hinge
▷ **creaky** *ADJECTIVE*

creak *VERB* **creaks, creaking, creaked**
to make a creak

cream *NOUN* **creams**
1 the thick fatty part of milk that rises to the top when left to stand
2 a pale yellow or off-white colour

3 a food containing cream or having its consistency ◆ *chocolate cream*
4 a soft substance ◆ *shoe cream*
5 the best of a group of people or things
▷ **creamy** *ADJECTIVE*

cream *VERB* **creams, creaming, creamed**
to make something creamy; to beat a mixture until it is soft like cream
to cream something off is to remove the best part of something

crease *NOUN* **creases**
1 a line made in something by folding, pressing, or crushing it
2 a line on a cricket pitch marking a batsman's or bowler's position

crease *VERB* **creases, creasing, creased**
to make a crease or creases in something

create *VERB* **creates, creating, created**
1 to bring something into existence; to make or produce something new or original
2 (*informal*) to grumble or make a fuss

creation *NOUN* **creations**
1 the act of creating something
2 something that has been created
3 (*Religion*) the Creation is the time when God is said to have created the world

creative *ADJECTIVE*
showing imagination and thought as well as skill ◆ *his creative use of language*
▷ **creativity** *NOUN*

creator *NOUN* **creators**
a person who creates something
the Creator a name for God

creature *NOUN* **creatures**
a living being, especially an animal

crèche (*say* kresh) *NOUN* **crèches**
a place where babies and young children are looked after while their parents are at work

credence *NOUN*
belief ◆ *Don't give it any credence.*

credentials *PLURAL NOUN*
1 documents showing a person's identity, qualifications, etc.
2 a person's past achievements that make them suitable for something

credible *ADJECTIVE*
able to be believed; convincing
▷ **credibly** *ADVERB*
▷ **credibility** *NOUN*
USAGE NOTE Take care not to confuse this word with *creditable* or *credulous*.

credit *NOUN* **credits**
1 a source of pride or honour ◆ *She is a credit to her family.*
2 praise or acknowledgement given for some achievement or good quality ◆ *I must give you credit for persistence.*
3 an arrangement trusting a person to pay for something later on
4 an amount of money in an account at a bank etc., or entered in a financial account as paid in (SEE ALSO **debit**)
5 belief or trust ◆ *I put no credit in this rumour.*
6 the credits at the end of a film or television programme are a list of the people who have helped to make it

credit *VERB* **credits, crediting, credited**
1 to believe something
2 to associate a particular quality or achievement with a person ◆ *The hero is usually credited with wholly worthy motives.*
3 to enter something as a credit in a financial account (SEE ALSO **debit**)

creditable *ADJECTIVE*
deserving praise
▷ **creditably** *ADVERB*
USAGE NOTE Take care not to confuse this word with *credible* or *credulous*.

credit card *NOUN* **credit cards**
a small plastic card authorizing a person to buy things on a special account and to be paid for later

creditor *NOUN* **creditors**
a person to whom money is owed

credulous *ADJECTIVE*
too ready to believe things; gullible
USAGE NOTE Take care not to confuse this word with *credible* or *creditable*.

creed *NOUN* **creeds**
a set or formal statement of religious beliefs

creek *NOUN* **creeks**
1 a narrow strip of water reaching into the land from a sea or lake
2 (*American and Australian*) a small stream
to be up the creek (*informal*) is to be in trouble

creep *VERB* **creeps, creeping, crept**
1 to move along close to the ground
2 to move quietly
3 to come gradually ◆ *The day of their departure crept closer.*
4 your flesh creeps when it prickles with fear or nervousness

creep *NOUN* **creeps**
1 a creeping movement
2 (*informal*) an unpleasant person, especially one who constantly tries to get other people's approval
to have or get the creeps (*informal*) is to feel slightly nervous and frightened about something

creeper *NOUN* **creepers**
a plant that grows along the ground or up a wall

creepy *ADJECTIVE* **creepier, creepiest**
(*informal*) slightly frightening and sinister

a b c d e f g h i j k l m n o p q r s t u v w x y z

SPELLING NOTE Some words with a hard **c**- sound begin with **ch**- (e.g. character)

cremate *VERB* **cremates, cremating, cremated**
to burn a dead body to ashes
▷ **cremation** *NOUN*

crematorium *NOUN* **crematoria**
a place where dead people are cremated

crème de la crème (*say* krem der la krem) *NOUN*
the very best of something

creosote *NOUN*
an oily brown liquid painted on wood to prevent it from rotting

crêpe (*say* krayp) *NOUN* **crêpes**
a thin pancake

crêpe paper *NOUN*
paper with a wrinkled surface

crescendo (*say* krish-**end**-oh) *NOUN* **crescendos**
a gradual increase in loudness

crescent *NOUN* **crescents**
1 a narrow curved shape coming to a point at each end
2 a curved street forming an arc

cress *NOUN*
a plant with hot-tasting leaves, used in salads and sandwiches

crest *NOUN* **crests**
1 a tuft of hair, skin, or feathers on the head of an animal or bird
2 the top of a hill or wave etc.
3 a design representing a family or organization, used e.g. on notepaper
▷ **crested** *ADJECTIVE*

crestfallen *ADJECTIVE*
disappointed or dejected

cretin (*say* **kret**-in) *NOUN* **cretins**
(*informal*) a stupid person
WORD HISTORY via French from Latin *Christianus* 'Christian' (as a reminder that handicapped people were Christian souls, and should be cared for)

crevasse (*say* kri-vass) *NOUN* **crevasses**
a deep open crack, especially in a glacier

crevice *NOUN* **crevices**
a narrow opening, especially in a rock or wall

crew ❶ *NOUN* **crews**
1 a group of people who work on a ship or aircraft and help to operate it
2 a group of people working together ◆ *The company has the best film crew in the business.*

crib *NOUN* **cribs**
1 a cot for a baby
2 a framework holding fodder for animals
3 a model representing the Nativity of Christ
4 (*informal*) a translation for use by students, or something that has been copied dishonestly

crib *VERB* **cribs, cribbing, cribbed**
to copy someone else's work dishonestly

cribbage *NOUN*
a card game for two players

crick *NOUN* **cricks**
painful stiffness in the neck or back

cricket ❶ *NOUN*
a game played outdoors between teams with a ball, bats, and two wickets, the object being to score runs by hitting the ball and running between the wickets
▷ **cricketer** *NOUN*
WORD HISTORY origin unknown

cricket ❷ *NOUN* **crickets**
a brown insect like a grasshopper, the male of which makes a chirping sound
WORD HISTORY from Old French *criquer* 'crackle' (imitating the sound it makes)

crime *NOUN* **crimes**
1 a crime is an action that breaks the law ◆ *According to the police it was a particularly brutal crime.*
2 crime is the activity of breaking the law ◆ *They say crime does not pay.*

criminal *NOUN* **criminals**
a person who has committed a crime
▷ **criminal** *ADJECTIVE*
▷ **criminally** *ADVERB*

criminology *NOUN*
the study of crime
▷ **criminologist** *NOUN*

crimp *VERB* **crimps, crimping, crimped**
to press into small ridges

crimson *ADJECTIVE*
deep red
▷ **crimson** *NOUN*
WORD HISTORY from Arabic *kirmiz*, the name for an insect which was used to make crimson dye

cringe *VERB* **cringes, cringing, cringed**
to shrink back in fear; to cower

crinkle *VERB* **crinkles, crinkling, crinkled**
to make or become wrinkled
▷ **crinkly** *ADJECTIVE*

crinoline *NOUN* **crinolines**
a long skirt worn over a framework that makes it stand out

cripple *NOUN* **cripples**
a person who is permanently lame
USAGE NOTE This word is now offensive to many people and you should avoid using it.

cripple *VERB* **cripples, crippling, crippled**
1 to make a person lame
2 to weaken or damage something seriously

crisis *NOUN* **crises**
an important and dangerous or difficult situation

crisp *ADJECTIVE*
1 dry enough to break with a snap
2 a piece of paper or a banknote is crisp when it is new and slightly stiff
3 the weather is crisp when it is cold and dry
4 a person's manner or way of speaking is crisp when it is brisk and sharp
▷ **crisply** *ADVERB*
▷ **crispness** *NOUN*

crisp *NOUN* **crisps**
a very thin fried slice of potato, sold in packets and eaten as a snack

criss-cross *ADJECTIVE, ADVERB*
with crossing lines

criss-cross *VERB* **criss-crosses, criss-crossing, criss-crossed**
to form a pattern of crossing lines

criterion (*say* kry-**teer**-ee-on) *NOUN* **criteria**
a standard or principle by which something is judged or decided
USAGE NOTE Note that *criteria* is a plural noun. You should say *this criterion* and *these criteria*, and not *this criteria*.

critic *NOUN* **critics**
1 a person who gives opinions about literary or artistic work
2 a person who criticizes

critical *ADJECTIVE*
1 pointing out faults or weaknesses in a person or thing
2 to do with the assessment of a literary or artistic work
3 to do with or at a crisis; very serious
▷ **critically** *ADVERB*

criticism *NOUN* **criticisms**
1 the pointing out of faults and weaknesses
2 the assessment of a literary or artistic work

criticize *VERB* **criticizes, criticizing, criticized**
to point out the faults or weaknesses of a person or thing
USAGE NOTE This word can also be spelled criticise.

croak *NOUN* **croaks**
a deep hoarse sound like that of a frog

croak *VERB* **croaks, croaking, croaked**
to make a croak

crochet (*say* **kroh**-shay) *NOUN*
a kind of needlework done by using a hooked needle to loop a thread into patterns

crochet *VERB* **crochets, crocheting, crocheted**
to make a piece of clothing or fabric with crochet

crock❶ *NOUN* **crocks**
a piece of crockery

crock❷ *NOUN* **crocks**
(*informal*) a decrepit person or thing

crockery *NOUN*
household china

crocodile *NOUN* **crocodiles**
1 a large tropical reptile with a thick skin, long tail, and huge jaws
2 a long line of schoolchildren walking in pairs
crocodile tears sorrow that is not sincere (so called because the crocodile was said to shed tears while it ate its victim)

crocus *NOUN* **crocuses**
a small plant with yellow, purple, or white flowers

croft *NOUN* **crofts**
a small rented farm in Scotland
▷ **crofter** *NOUN*

croissant (*say* **krwah**-sahn) *NOUN* **croissants**
a flaky crescent-shaped bread roll
WORD HISTORY a French word meaning 'crescent'

crone *NOUN* **crones**
a very old woman

crony *NOUN* **cronies**
a close friend or companion

My mum and some of her cronies stood in the doorway and poured saffron oil onto the step just before I left. — *Bali Rai, (Un)arranged Marriage*

crook *NOUN* **crooks**
1 a shepherd's stick with a curved end
2 a bend at the elbow of a person's arm
3 (*informal*) a thief or other criminal

crook *VERB* **crooks, crooking, crooked**
to crook a finger is to bend or curl it

crook *ADJECTIVE*
(*Australian and New Zealand*) sick or unwell

crooked *ADJECTIVE*
1 bent or twisted out of shape; not straight
2 (*informal*) criminal or dishonest

croon *VERB* **croons, crooning, crooned**
to sing softly and gently

crop *NOUN* **crops**
1 a plant grown in large quantities for food
2 a very short haircut
3 a whip with a loop instead of a lash
4 a pouch in a bird's throat, where it stores food

crop *VERB* **crops, cropping, cropped**
1 to crop a person's hair is to cut it very short
2 an animal crops the grass or plants when it bites off their tops to eat
3 to crop an area of land is to put plants in it that will produce crops
to crop up is to happen unexpectedly

cropper *NOUN*
to come a cropper (*informal*) is to fail or be defeated badly

SPELLING NOTE Some words with a hard **c-** sound begin with **ch-** (e.g. character)

croquet (*say* **kroh**-kay) ***NOUN***
a game played on a lawn, in which you drive wooden balls through a series of hoops with long-handled mallets

crosier (*say* **kroh**-zee-er) ***NOUN*** **crosiers**
a bishop's staff shaped like a shepherd's crook

cross ***NOUN*** **crosses**
1 a mark or shape made with two intersecting lines (+ or ×)
2 an upright post with another piece of wood across it, used in ancient times for crucifixion
3 **the Cross** the cross on which Christ was crucified, used as a symbol of Christianity
4 a mixture of two different things

cross ***VERB*** **crosses, crossing, crossed**
1 to go across something or to the other side of something
2 to draw a line or lines across something
3 to cross your arms or legs is to place one across the other
4 to cross yourself is to make the sign of the cross as a Christian
5 to cross animals or plants of different kinds is to produce a new animal or plant from them
to cross something out is to draw a line across a word or phrase because it is wrong or not wanted

cross ***ADJECTIVE***
annoyed or bad-tempered
▷ **crossly** ***ADVERB***
▷ **crossness** ***NOUN***

crossbar ***NOUN*** **crossbars**
a horizontal bar between two uprights

crossbow ***NOUN*** **crossbows**
a powerful bow used in medieval times, with a mechanism for pulling and releasing the string

cross-breed ***VERB*** **cross-breeds, cross-breeding, cross-bred**
to breed by mating an animal with an animal of a different kind
▷ **cross-breed** ***NOUN*** (SEE ALSO **hybrid**)

crosse ***NOUN*** **crosses**
a stick with a curved piece at one end holding a piece of net, used in lacrosse

cross-examine ***VERB*** **cross-examines, cross-examining, cross-examined**
to question a witness called by the other side in a lawcourt, to check the evidence they have already given
▷ **cross-examination** ***NOUN***

cross-eyed ***ADJECTIVE***
with eyes that look or seem to look towards the nose

crossfire ***NOUN***
lines of gunfire that cross each other

cross-hatch ***VERB*** **cross-hatches, cross-hatching, cross-hatched**
(*Art*) to shade part of a drawing with two sets of parallel lines crossing each other
▷ **cross-hatching** ***NOUN***

crossing ***NOUN*** **crossings**
a place where people can cross a road or railway

cross-legged ***ADJECTIVE, ADVERB***
to sit cross-legged is to sit with the ankles across each other and the knees bent outwards

crossover ***NOUN***
the process by which a musician in one field or style performs music in another style, such as popular or folk music

crosspiece ***NOUN*** **crosspieces**
a beam or bar placed across something else

cross-question ***VERB*** **cross-questions, cross-questioning, cross-questioned**
to question someone in detail to test answers they have already given

cross-reference ***NOUN*** **cross-references**
a note telling readers to look at another part of a book or text for more information

crossroads ***NOUN*** **crossroads**
a place where two or more roads cross one another

cross-section ***NOUN*** **cross-sections**
1 a drawing of something as if it has been cut through
2 a typical sample from a larger group

crosswind ***NOUN*** **crosswinds**
a wind blowing across the direction you are travelling in

crosswise ***ADVERB, ADJECTIVE***
with one thing crossing another; diagonally

crossword ***NOUN*** **crosswords**
a puzzle in which words have to be guessed from clues and then written into the blank squares in a grid

crotch ***NOUN*** **crotches**
1 the part between the legs where they join the upper body
2 a fork in a road, river, or tree

crotchet ***NOUN*** **crotchets**
(*Music*) a note in music (written ♩) and usually representing one beat

crotchety ***ADJECTIVE***
bad-tempered or irritable

crouch ***VERB*** **crouches, crouching, crouched**
to lower your body, with your arms and legs bent

croup (*say* kroop) ***NOUN***
a disease causing a hard cough and difficulty in breathing

crow❶ ***NOUN*** **crows**
a large black bird
as the crow flies in a straight line

crow❷ ***VERB*** **crows, crowing, crowed** or **crew**
1 a cock crows when it makes a shrill cry
2 to boast or be triumphant
▷ **crow** ***NOUN***

crowbar ***NOUN*** **crowbars**
an iron bar with a flat tip, used as a lever

crowd ***NOUN*** **crowds**
a large number of people gathered together

crowd ***VERB*** **crowds, crowding, crowded**
1 to come together in a crowd
2 to make an area or space uncomfortably full of people or things

crown ***NOUN*** **crowns**
1 an ornamental headdress worn by a king or queen
2 (often **Crown**) the king or queen ◆ *This land belongs to the Crown.*
3 the highest part ◆ *the crown of the road*
4 a former coin worth 5 shillings (25p)
Crown Prince or **Crown Princess** the heir to the throne

crown ***VERB*** **crowns, crowning, crowned**
1 to place a crown on someone's head as a symbol of royal power or victory
2 to form or cover or decorate the top of something
3 to reward something; to make a successful end to something ◆ *Our efforts were crowned with victory.*
4 (*informal*) to hit someone on the head

Crown court ***NOUN*** **Crown courts**
a lawcourt where criminal cases are tried

crow's-nest ***NOUN*** **crow's-nests**
a lookout platform high up on a ship's mast

crucial (*say* kroo-shal) ***ADJECTIVE***
most important or decisive
▷ **crucially** ***ADVERB***

crucible ***NOUN*** **crucibles**
a container in which metals or other substances may be melted or heated to very high temperatures

crucifix ***NOUN*** **crucifixes**
a model of the Christian Cross with a figure of Christ on it

crucify ***VERB*** **crucifies, crucifying, crucified**
1 to put a person to death by nailing or tying their hands and feet to a cross
2 to criticize severely
▷ **crucifixion** ***NOUN***

crude ***ADJECTIVE***
1 crude oil or other minerals are in a form not yet processed or refined
2 a crude piece of art or other work is not properly finished
3 offensively coarse or rude
▷ **crudely** ***ADVERB***
▷ **crudity** ***NOUN***

cruel ***ADJECTIVE*** **crueller, cruellest**
deliberately causing pain or suffering
▷ **cruelly** ***ADVERB***
▷ **cruelty** ***NOUN***

cruet ***NOUN*** **cruets**
a set of small containers for salt, pepper, oil, etc. for use at the table

cruise ***NOUN*** **cruises**
a voyage on a ship, taken as a holiday

cruise ***VERB*** **cruises, cruising, cruised**
1 to sail or travel at a moderate speed

> The moment dusk fell, several police cars began to cruise the quiet streets. — *Julie Bertagna, The Opposite of Chocolate*

2 to have a cruise

cruiser ***NOUN*** **cruisers**
1 a fast warship, larger than a destroyer
2 a large motor boat used for leisure

crumb ***NOUN*** **crumbs**
a tiny piece of bread, cake, or biscuit

crumble ***VERB*** **crumbles, crumbling, crumbled**
to break or fall into small fragments
▷ **crumbly** ***ADJECTIVE***

crumble ***NOUN*** **crumbles**
a pudding made with fruit cooked with a crumbly topping

crummy or **crumby** ***ADJECTIVE*** **crummier, crummiest**
(*informal*) bad or unpleasant

> They gave me this very crumby room, with nothing to look out of the window at except the other side of the hotel. — *J. D. Salinger, The Catcher in the Rye*

crumpet ***NOUN*** **crumpets**
a soft flat cake made with yeast, eaten toasted with butter

crumple ***VERB*** **crumples, crumpling, crumpled**
1 to crush something, or to become crushed, into creases
2 to lose force or effectiveness; to fail ◆ *The business venture was beginning to crumple.*

crunch ***VERB*** **crunches, crunching, crunched**
to crush something noisily, for example between your teeth

crunch ***NOUN*** **crunches**
a crunching sound
the crunch (*informal*) a crucial event or turning point
▷ **crunchy** ***ADJECTIVE***

Crusade *NOUN* **Crusades**
each of a series of military expeditions made by Christians in the Middle Ages to recover the Holy Land from the Muslims who had conquered it
▷ **Crusader** *NOUN*

crusade *NOUN* **crusades**
a campaign in favour of some social reform or change

crush *VERB* **crushes, crushing, crushed**
1 to press something so that it gets broken or harmed
2 to squeeze tightly
3 to defeat an opponent completely
4 to be crushed by a disappointment or embarrassment is to be deeply affected by it

crush *NOUN* **crushes**
1 a crowd of people pressed together
2 a drink made with crushed fruit

crust *NOUN* **crusts**
1 the hard outer layer of something, especially bread
2 the rocky outer layer of the earth

crustacean (*say* krust-ay-shon) *NOUN* **crustaceans**
an animal with a shell that lives in water, e.g. a crab, lobster, or shrimp

crusty *ADJECTIVE* **crustier, crustiest**
1 having a crisp crust
2 bad-tempered or irritable
▷ **crustiness** *NOUN*

crutch *NOUN* **crutches**
a support like a long walking stick with a crosspiece at the top, for helping a lame person to walk

cry *NOUN* **cries**
1 a loud shout or sound expressing pain, grief, joy, etc.
2 the special sound made by a bird or animal
3 a spell of crying

cry *VERB* **cries, crying, cried**
1 to shed tears; to weep
2 to call out loudly
to cry off is to withdraw suddenly from an arrangement

SYNONYMS (meaning 1) weep, shed tears, sob, howl, whimper, snivel, blubber, bawl, wail; (meaning 2) call, yell, exclaim, shout, shriek, scream, bawl

crypt *NOUN* **crypts**
a room under a church, used as a chapel or burial place

cryptic *ADJECTIVE*
having a hidden or obscure meaning
▷ **cryptically** *ADVERB*

cryptogram *NOUN* **cryptograms**
words written in code

crystal *NOUN* **crystals**
1 a transparent colourless mineral like glass
2 clear high-quality glass
3 a small solid piece of a substance, e.g. ice, with a symmetrical shape
▷ **crystalline** *ADJECTIVE*

crystallize *VERB* **crystallizes, crystallizing, crystallized**
1 to form into crystals
2 to become definite in form ◆ *The solution to the problem began to crystallize.*
▷ **crystallization** *NOUN*

USAGE NOTE This word can also be spelled crystallise.

crystallized fruit *NOUN*
fruit preserved in sugar

USAGE NOTE This can also be spelled crystallised fruit.

cub *NOUN* **cubs**
a young fox, lion, tiger, bear, or other flesh-eating animal

Cub or **Cub Scout** *NOUN* **Cubs** or **Cub Scouts**
a member of the junior branch of the Scout Association

cubbyhole *NOUN* **cubbyholes**
a small compartment

WORD HISTORY from an old word *cub* meaning 'coop' or 'hutch'

cube *NOUN* **cubes**
1 an object that has six equal square sides, like a box or dice
2 the number you get by multiplying a number by itself twice, e.g. the cube of 2 is $2\times2\times2 = 8$

cube *VERB* **cubes, cubing, cubed**
1 to multiply a number by itself twice, e.g. 3 cubed is $3\times3\times3 = 27$
2 to cut something into small cubes

cube root *NOUN* **cube roots**
the number that gives a particular number if it is multiplied by itself twice, e.g. the cube root of 125 is 5 ($5\times5\times5 = 125$)

cubic *ADJECTIVE*
having three dimensions
a cubic metre, centimetre, etc. is the volume of a cube with sides one metre, centimetre, etc. long, used as a unit of measurement for volume

cubicle *NOUN* **cubicles**
a small compartment or marked-off area of a room

cubism *NOUN*
(*Art*) a style of painting in the early 20th century which abandoned normal perspective and used simple geometric shapes and connecting planes
▷ **cubist** *NOUN, ADJECTIVE*

cuboid (*say* kew-boid) *NOUN* **cuboids**
an object with six rectangular sides

cuckoo *NOUN* **cuckoos**
a bird that makes a two-note sound that carries for a long distance, and is known for laying its eggs in the nests of other birds

cucumber *NOUN* **cucumbers**
a long green-skinned fruit eaten raw or pickled

cud *NOUN*
partly digested food that a cow or other ruminant animal brings back from its first stomach to chew again

cuddle *VERB* **cuddles, cuddling, cuddled**
to put your arms closely round someone in a loving or affectionate way
▷ **cuddly** *ADJECTIVE*

cudgel *NOUN* **cudgels**
a short thick stick used as a weapon

cudgel *VERB* **cudgels, cudgelling, cudgelled**
to beat with a cudgel

cue❶ *NOUN* **cues**
something said or done that acts as a signal for an actor or other performer to come on stage or begin speaking or performing

cue❷ *NOUN* **cues**
a long stick for striking the ball in billiards or snooker

cuff *NOUN* **cuffs**
1 the end of a sleeve that fits round the wrist
2 a slap or blow with the hand
off the cuff without rehearsal or preparation

cuff *VERB* **cuffs, cuffing, cuffed**
to hit someone roughly with the open hand

cufflink *NOUN* **cufflinks**
a fastening for a shirt cuff, passed through a hole in each side of the cuff and used instead of buttons

cuisine (*say* kwiz-een) *NOUN* **cuisines**
a style or method of cooking

cul-de-sac *NOUN* **cul-de-sacs**
a street or passage closed at one end; a dead end

WORD HISTORY a French word meaning 'bottom of a sack'

culinary *ADJECTIVE*
to do with cooking

cull *VERB* **culls, culling, culled**
1 to kill selected animals from a flock in order to reduce the population
2 to select and use a small number of things from a large quantity ◆ *Here are a few soundbites culled from her television interview.*
▷ **cull** *NOUN*

cull *NOUN* **culls**
a selective killing of animals

culminate *VERB* **culminates, culminating, culminated**
to reach a climax or highest point
▷ **culmination** *NOUN*

culpable *ADJECTIVE*
deserving blame

culprit *NOUN* **culprits**
a person who has committed a crime or done something wrong

cult *NOUN* **cults**
1 a small religious group having special beliefs and practices
2 something that is very fashionable or popular with a particular group of people

cultivate *VERB* **cultivates, cultivating, cultivated**
1 to use land to grow crops
2 to grow or develop things by looking after them
▷ **cultivation** *NOUN*
▷ **cultivator** *NOUN*

cultivated *ADJECTIVE*
having good manners and education

culture *NOUN* **cultures**
1 the appreciation and understanding of literature, art, music, and other creative achievements
2 the customs and traditions of a particular people ◆ *West Indian culture*
3 (*Science*) a quantity of bacteria or cells grown for study
▷ **cultural** *ADJECTIVE*

cultured *ADJECTIVE*
well educated

cultured pearl *NOUN* **cultured pearls**
a pearl formed by an oyster when a piece of grit is put into its shell

culvert *NOUN* **culverts**
a tunnel taking a stream or drain under a road or railway

cumbersome *ADJECTIVE*
difficult or awkward to carry or use

cumin (*say* **kum**-in) *NOUN*
a plant with spicy seeds used for flavouring food

cummerbund *NOUN* **cummerbunds**
a broad sash worn round the waist

cumulative (*say* **kyoo**-myoo-la-tiv) *ADJECTIVE*
increasing by continuous additions

cumulus (*say* **kyoo**-myoo-lus) *NOUN* **cumuli**
a type of cloud consisting of rounded heaps on a horizontal base

cunning *ADJECTIVE*
1 clever at deceiving people to get what you want
2 cleverly designed or planned; ingenious

a b c d e f g h i j k l m n o p q r s t u v w x y z

cunning *NOUN*
1 skill in deceiving people; craftiness
2 skill or ingenuity

cup *NOUN* **cups**
1 a small bowl-shaped container for drinking from
2 anything shaped like a cup
3 a trophy shaped like a cup with a stem, given as a prize in a sports competition
▷ **cupful** *NOUN* **cupfuls**

cup *VERB* **cups, cupping, cupped**
to form your hands into the curved shape of a cup

cupboard *NOUN* **cupboards**
a piece of furniture or a recess in a room, with a door and often with shelves, for storing things

cupidity (*say* kew-**pid**-it-ee) *NOUN*
greed for more money or possessions

cupola (*say* **kew**-pol-a) *NOUN* **cupolas**
a small dome on a roof or ceiling

cur *NOUN* **curs**
a scruffy or aggressive dog

curable *ADJECTIVE*
a curable illness is one that can be cured

curate *NOUN* **curates**
a member of the clergy who helps a vicar

curative (*say* **kewr**-at-iv) *ADJECTIVE*
helping to cure illness

curator (*say* kewr-**ay**-ter) *NOUN* **curators**
a person in charge of a museum or other collection

curb *VERB* **curbs, curbing, curbed**
to keep in check; to restrain ◆ *It seemed a shame to curb their enthusiasm.*

curb *NOUN* **curbs**
a restraint ◆ *Put a curb on spending.*

USAGE NOTE Take care not to confuse this word with *kerb*.

curd *NOUN* or **curds** *PLURAL NOUN*
a thick substance formed when milk turns sour

curdle *VERB* **curdles, curdling, curdled**
to form into curds or lumps
to make someone's blood curdle is to horrify or terrify them

cure *VERB* **cures, curing, cured**
1 to end someone's illness
2 to stop a bad habit or practice
3 to treat meat or fish in order to preserve it

cure *NOUN* **cures**
a treament or medication that cures a person or thing; a remedy ◆ *An effective cure has still not been found.*

curfew *NOUN* **curfews**
1 a regulation stating that people must remain indoors between specified times, usually at night
2 the time specified for the beginning of this restriction

WORD HISTORY from old French *cuevrefeu*, literally 'cover fire' (from an old law saying that all fires should be covered or put out by a certain time each evening)

curio *NOUN* **curios**
a rare or unusual object

curiosity *NOUN* **curiosities**
1 curiosity is being curious
2 a curiosity is something unusual and interesting

curious *ADJECTIVE*
1 wanting to find out about things; inquisitive
2 strange or unusual ◆ *There was a curious silence.*
▷ **curiously** *ADVERB*

curl *NOUN* **curls**
a curve or coil, e.g. of hair

curl *VERB* **curls, curling, curled**
to form into curls
to curl up is to sit or lie with your knees drawn up

curler *NOUN* **curlers**
a device for making the hair curl

curlew *NOUN* **curlews**
a wading bird with a long bill that curves downwards

curling *NOUN*
a game played on ice with large flat stones

WORD HISTORY so called because the stones are made to 'curl round' opponents' stones to get to the target

curly *ADJECTIVE*
having a lot of curls

currant *NOUN* **currants**
1 a small black dried grape used in cookery
2 a small round red, black, or white berry

WORD HISTORY from Old French *raisins de Courauntz* 'grapes from Corinth' (a city in Greece)

USAGE NOTE Take care not to confuse this word with *current*.

currency *NOUN* **currencies**
1 the form of money in general use in a particular country
2 the general use of something ◆ *Some words have no currency now.*

current *ADJECTIVE*
happening or being used now
▷ **currently** *ADVERB*

current *NOUN* **currents**
1 water or air etc. moving in one direction
2 the flow of electricity along a wire etc. or through something

USAGE NOTE Take care not to confuse this word with *currant*.

current affairs *PLURAL NOUN*
political events in the news

curriculum *NOUN* **curricula**
the subjects forming a course of study in a school or university

curriculum vitae (*say* vee-ty) *NOUN* **curricula vitae**
a brief summary of a person's education and career, for sending with a job application

curry❶ *NOUN* **curries**
a dish of meat or vegetables cooked with hot spices
▷ **curried** *ADJECTIVE*

WORD HISTORY from Tamil *kari* 'sauce'

curry❷ *VERB* **curries, currying, curried**
to curry favour is to try to win someone's approval or support by flattering them

curse *NOUN* **curses**
1 a solemn appeal for some supernatural force to harm a person or thing
2 something very harmful or unpleasant
3 an angry or offensive word or expression

curse *VERB* **curses, cursing, cursed**
1 to say offensive words; to swear
2 to use a curse against a person or thing
to be cursed with something is to suffer from it

cursor *NOUN* **cursors**
(*ICT*) a movable indicator on a computer screen, usually a flashing bar or arrow, showing the point where new data will appear

cursory *ADJECTIVE*
hasty and therefore not very thorough ◆ *She gave the table a cursory wipe.*
▷ **cursorily** *ADVERB*

curt *ADJECTIVE*
brief and hasty or rude

Except for a curt 'You girls awright back there!', the policeman didn't speak to them or tell the girls where he was taking them. — *Doris Pilkington, Rabbit Proof Fence*

▷ **curtly** *ADVERB*
▷ **curtness** *NOUN*

curtail *VERB* **curtails, curtailing, curtailed**
to reduce something or cut it short ◆ *The war curtailed his career.*
▷ **curtailment** *NOUN*

curtain *NOUN* **curtains**
1 a piece of material hung at a window or door
2 (*Drama*) a large cloth screen hung at the front of a stage and raised or lowered at the beginning and end of a performance

curtsy *NOUN* **curtsies**
a formal greeting made by women and girls by putting one foot behind the other and bending the knees

curtsy *VERB* **curtsies, curtsying, curtsied**
to make a curtsy

curvature *NOUN* **curvatures**
curving, or the amount that something curves

curve *NOUN* **curves**
a line or shape that bends gradually and smoothly from being straight
▷ **curvy** *ADJECTIVE*

curve *VERB* **curves, curving, curved**
to bend gradually and smoothly; to form a curve

cushion *NOUN* **cushions**
1 a bag of cloth filled with soft material, so that it is comfortable to sit on or lean against
2 anything soft or springy that supports something or protects it against impact
3 something that gives protection against the worst effects of something ◆ *Their savings provided a cushion against inflation.*

cushion *VERB* **cushions, cushioning, cushioned**
to protect from the effects of a knock or shock ◆ *There was nothing soft to cushion their fall.* ◆ *George broke the news to her, making no effort to cushion the blow.*

cushy *ADJECTIVE*
(*informal*) pleasant and easy ◆ *managers with cushy jobs and inflated salaries*

WORD HISTORY from Urdu *kushi* 'pleasure'

cusp *NOUN* **cusps**
1 a pointed end where two curves meet, e.g. the tips of a crescent moon
2 in Astrology, the time when one sign of the zodiac ends and the next begins

custard *NOUN* **custards**
a thick sweet yellow sauce or pudding made with milk and eggs

custodian *NOUN* **custodians**
a person who is responsible for looking after something; a keeper

custody *NOUN*
1 care and supervision of someone or something; guardianship
2 to be in custody is to be in prison awaiting trial

custom *NOUN* **customs**
1 the usual or generally accepted way of behaving or doing something
2 regular business from customers

customary *ADJECTIVE*
in accordance with custom; usual
▷ **customarily** *ADVERB*

custom-built *ADJECTIVE*
made according to a particular customer's order

customer *NOUN* **customers**
a person who buys goods or services from a shop or business

customs *PLURAL NOUN*
1 the place at a port or airport where officials inspect goods brought into the country and collect taxes and duties to be paid on them
2 taxes charged on goods brought into a country

cut *VERB* **cuts, cutting, cut**
1 to divide or separate something by using a knife, scissors, or other sharp object
2 to wound someone with a sharp object or weapon
3 to make something smaller or less, e.g. costs or prices; to remove part of something
4 to divide a pack of playing cards
5 to go through or across something
6 to switch off an engine or source of power
7 in a film, to move from one shot or scene to another
8 to make a sound recording
to be cut and dried is to have been already decided
to cut a corner is to pass round it very closely
to cut and paste is to remove text on a computer screen from one position and insert it in another position
to cut in is to interrupt

cut *NOUN* **cuts**
1 the act of cutting, or the result of cutting
2 a small wound
3 (*informal*) a share of profits
to be a cut above someone or something (*informal*) is to be noticeably superior to them

cute *ADJECTIVE* (*informal*)
1 pretty in an endearing way
2 (*American*) clever or shrewd
▷ **cutely** *ADVERB*
▷ **cuteness** *NOUN*

cuticle (*say* kew-tik-ul) *NOUN* **cuticles**
the skin at the base of a fingernail or toenail

cutlass (*say* kut-lus) *NOUN* **cutlasses**
a short sword with a broad curved blade, formerly used by sailors

cutlery *NOUN*
knives, forks, and spoons used for serving or eating food

cutlet *NOUN* **cutlets**
a thick slice of meat for cooking

cut-out *NOUN* **cut-outs**
a shape cut out of paper, cardboard, etc.

cut-price *ADJECTIVE*
for sale at a reduced price

cutter *NOUN* **cutters**
1 a person or thing that cuts
2 a small fast sailing ship

cutting *NOUN* **cuttings**
1 an open passage with straight sides cut through high ground for a road, railway, or canal to pass through
2 an article or picture cut out of a newspaper or magazine
3 a piece cut from a plant to form a new plant

cuttlefish *NOUN* **cuttlefish**
a sea creature like a squid, with ten arms and two long tentacles, which sends out a black liquid when attacked

cyanide *NOUN*
an extremely poisonous chemical

cyberspace *NOUN*
(*ICT*) the electronic environment in which people communicate through computer networks

cycle *NOUN* **cycles**
1 a bicycle or motorcycle
2 a series of events that are regularly repeated in the same order
3 (*Science*) a complete series of changes associated with a physical or organic process
4 (*Music*) a set of songs on a common theme and usually performed together

cycle *VERB* **cycles, cycling, cycled**
to ride a bicycle or tricycle
▷ **cyclist** *NOUN*

cyclic *ADJECTIVE*
repeated regularly in the same order
▷ **cyclical** *ADJECTIVE*

cyclone *NOUN* **cyclones**
a system of winds that rotates inwards round a calm central area
▷ **cyclonic** *ADJECTIVE*

cygnet (*say* sig-nit) *NOUN* **cygnets**
a young swan

cylinder *NOUN* **cylinders**
a shape with straight sides and circular ends
▷ **cylindrical** *ADJECTIVE*

cymbal *NOUN* **cymbals**
a percussion instrument consisting of a metal plate that is hit to make a ringing sound
USAGE NOTE Take care not to confuse this word with *symbol*.

cynic (*say* sin-ik) *NOUN* **cynics**
a person who believes that people's reasons for doing things are usually selfish or bad
▷ **cynical** *ADJECTIVE*
▷ **cynicism** *NOUN*

cypress *NOUN* **cypresses**
an evergreen tree with dark leaves and cones

cyst (*say* sist) *NOUN* **cysts**
an abnormal swelling in the body, containing fluid or soft matter

czar (*say* zar) *NOUN* **czars**
another spelling of **tsar**

Dd

dab *NOUN* **dabs**
1 a quick gentle touch, usually with something wet
2 a small amount of paint or other material applied to a surface

dab *VERB* **dabs, dabbing, dabbed**
to touch a surface quickly and gently

dabble *VERB* **dabbles, dabbling, dabbled**
1 to move your hands or feet around gently in water
2 to dabble in an activity is to study or work at it casually, as a hobby

dab hand *NOUN* **dab hands**
someone who is a dab hand at doing something is very good at it

dachshund (*say* daks- huund) *NOUN* **dachshunds**
a small dog with a long body and very short legs
WORD HISTORY a German word meaning 'badger dog' (because these dogs were once used to hunt badgers)

dad *NOUN* **dads**
(*informal*) a person's father

daddy *NOUN* **daddies**
(*informal*) a person's father

daddy-long-legs *NOUN* **daddy-long-legs**
a flying insect with very long thin legs; a crane fly

dado (*say* day- doh) *NOUN* **dados**
the lower part of a wall in a room which is decorated in a different style from the upper part
WORD HISTORY an Italian word meaning 'dice or cube'

daemon *NOUN* **daemons**
another spelling of **demon** (meaning 2)

daffodil *NOUN* **daffodils**
a yellow flower that grows from a bulb
WORD HISTORY from *asphodel*, the name of another plant with yellow flowers

daft *ADJECTIVE*
(*informal*) silly or stupid
WORD HISTORY from Old English *gedæfte*, which originally meant 'mild or gentle', but developed into 'compliant' and then 'stupid'

dagger *NOUN* **daggers**
a pointed knife with two sharp edges, used as a weapon
to be at daggers drawn is to be on the point of arguing or fighting with one another
to look daggers at someone is to glare angrily at them

dahlia (*say* day- lee- a) *NOUN* **dahlias**
a garden plant with brightly coloured flowers
WORD HISTORY from Andreas *Dahl* (1751–87), a Swedish botanist who discovered the plant in Mexico

Dáil (*say* doil) *NOUN*
the lower House of Parliament in the Republic of Ireland
WORD HISTORY an Irish word meaning 'assembly'

daily *ADJECTIVE*
1 a daily event happens every day
2 a daily newspaper is published every day, or every weekday

daily *ADVERB*
something that happens daily happens every day, or once a day

daily *NOUN* **dailies**
a daily newspaper

dainty *ADJECTIVE* **daintier, daintiest**
small, delicate, and pretty
▷ **daintily** *ADVERB*
▷ **daintiness** *NOUN*
WORD HISTORY via old French from Latin *dignitas* 'value, beauty'

dairy *NOUN* **dairies**
1 a place where milk, butter, and cheese are processed and sold
2 dairy products are made with or contain milk
WORD HISTORY from Old English *daege* 'bread- kneader', from which it developed to mean a female servant generally, and then a place where a dairymaid worked

dais (*say* day- iss) *NOUN* **daises**
a low platform, especially at one end of a room or hall
WORD HISTORY from Old French *deis*

daisy ***NOUN*** **daisies**
a small flower with white petals surrounding a yellow centre
WORD HISTORY from *day's eye*, because daisies open in daylight and close at night

Dalai Lama (*say* dal- y **lah**- ma) ***NOUN***
the spiritual leader of Tibetan Buddhists
WORD HISTORY from Tibetan words meaning 'ocean monk', because he is thought of as 'the ocean of compassion'

dale ***NOUN*** **dales**
a valley, especially in north England
WORD HISTORY from Old English *dæl*

dally ***VERB*** **dallies, dallying, dallied**
1 to dawdle or waste time
2 to dally with a subject is to show a casual interest in it
▷ **dalliance** ***NOUN***
WORD HISTORY from Old French *dalier* 'to chat'

Dalmatian (*say* dal- **may**- shun) ***NOUN*** **Dalmatians**
a large white dog with dark spots
WORD HISTORY from *Dalmatia*, a region of Croatia where the dog is thought to come from

dam[1] ***NOUN*** **dams**
1 a barrier built across a river to control the flow of water, or to form a reservoir
2 a barrier of branches in a stream made by a beaver to create a deep pool and lodge

dam ***VERB*** **dams, damming, dammed**
to hold water back with a dam

dam[2] ***NOUN*** **dams**
the mother of a horse or dog (SEE ALSO **sire**)
WORD HISTORY from *dame*

damage ***NOUN***
harm or injury that reduces the performance of something or spoils its appearance

damage ***VERB*** **damages, damaging, damaged**
to do harm or injury to something
WORD HISTORY from Latin *damnum* 'loss'

damages ***PLURAL NOUN***
money paid as compensation for an injury or loss

damask (*say* **dam**- ask) ***NOUN***
silk or linen material woven with a pattern that is visible on either side
WORD HISTORY from *Damascus*, the city in Syria where it was first produced

Dame ***NOUN*** **Dames**
the title of a woman who has been awarded an order of knighthood (corresponding to the title of *Sir* for a knight)

dame ***NOUN*** **dames**
1 a comic female character in pantomime, usually played by a man
2 (*American*) (*informal*) a woman
WORD HISTORY from Latin *domina* 'lady'

damn ***VERB*** **damns, damning, damned**
1 to condemn someone to eternal punishment in hell
2 to swear at someone or curse them
I'll be damned (*informal*) I am astonished
I'm damned if I know (*informal*) I certainly do not know
WORD HISTORY from Latin *damnare* 'to condemn'

damn ***EXCLAMATION***
(*informal*) said to show you are angry or annoyed

damnable ***ADJECTIVE***
(*informal*) hateful or annoying
▷ **damnably** ***ADVERB***

damnation ***NOUN***
being condemned to eternal punishment in hell

damned ***ADJECTIVE***
hateful or annoying

damp ***ADJECTIVE***
slightly wet; not quite dry
▷ **damply** ***ADVERB***
▷ **dampness** ***NOUN***

damp ***NOUN***
moisture in the air, on a surface, or throughout something

damp ***VERB*** **damps, damping, damped**
1 to make something slightly wet
2 to dampen or weaken an emotion
3 you damp a string on a musical instrument when you reduce its vibration
to damp something down to damp down a noise is to make it quieter
WORD HISTORY the word's original meaning was 'vapour', which developed into 'mist' and then 'moisture'

damp course ***NOUN*** **damp courses**
a layer of material built into a wall to prevent dampness in the ground from rising

dampen ***VERB*** **dampens, dampening, dampened**
1 to make something damp or moist
2 to dampen someone's spirits or enthusiasm is to discourage them or make them less enthusiastic

Mr Cartright shook his head. It saddened him to have to dampen enthusiasm in any educational sphere. — *Anne Fine, Flour Babies*

damper ***NOUN*** **dampers**
1 a felt pad that presses against a piano string to stop it vibrating
2 a metal plate that can be moved to control the flow of air into a fire or furnace
to put a damper on something is to reduce your enthusiasm or enjoyment of it

damsel *NOUN* **damsels**
an old-fashioned word for a young unmarried woman
WORD HISTORY from Old French *dameisele*

damson *NOUN* **damsons**
1 a small dark purple plum
2 a dark purple colour
WORD HISTORY from an earlier word *damascene plum* 'plum from Damascus' (a city in Syria)

dan *NOUN*
a degree of proficiency in judo or karate
WORD HISTORY from a Japanese word

dance *VERB* **dances, dancing, danced**
1 to move with rhythmical steps or movements, usually to music
2 to perform a particular dance ◆ *How do you dance the macarena?*

dance *NOUN* **dances**
1 a set of movements used in dancing
2 a piece of music for dancing to
3 a party or gathering where people dance
▷ **dancer** *NOUN*
WORD HISTORY from Old French
WORD FAMILY The art of writing or arranging a dance is choreography, and someone who does this is a choreographer.

dandelion *NOUN* **dandelions**
a wild plant with bright yellow flowers and jagged leaves
WORD HISTORY from a French phrase *dent-de-lion* 'tooth of a lion', because of the tooth-like shape of the jagged leaves

dandle *VERB* **dandles, dandling, dandled**
to move a baby or young child up and down on your knee

dandruff *NOUN*
tiny white flakes of dead skin on a person's scalp and hair

D and T *ABBREVIATION*
design and technology

dandy *NOUN* **dandies**
a man who likes to look very smart
WORD HISTORY from an earlier Scottish word *Jack-a-dandy*, from *Dandy*, a short form of the name *Andrew*

Dane *NOUN* **Danes**
a person who lives in, or was born in, Denmark

danger *NOUN* **dangers**
1 a situation where you could be injured or killed ◆ *Are they in any danger?*
2 a bad effect that happens as the result of doing something ◆ *the dangers of overeating*
3 a risk or possibility of something unpleasant happening ◆ *There's a danger they might be sold out.*
to be in danger of doing something is to be on the point of doing something you don't want to do ◆ *I'm in danger of losing my best friend.*
WORD HISTORY from Old French *dangier* 'power to harm'

dangerous *ADJECTIVE*
likely to kill or harm you
▷ **dangerously** *ADVERB*

dangle *VERB* **dangles, dangling, dangled**
1 to hang or swing loosely

> The speaker was an old man in a shabby coat, a cigarette dangling out of the corner of his mouth.
> — *Anthony Horowitz, Groosham Grange*

2 to hold or carry something so that it swings loosely ◆ *She dangled her legs over the side of the boat.*

Danish pastry *NOUN* **Danish pastries**
a cake of sweet yeast pastry filled or topped with fruit or icing

dank *ADJECTIVE*
unpleasantly damp, cold, or chilly
WORD HISTORY from a Scandinavian word

dapper *ADJECTIVE*
dressed neatly and smartly
WORD HISTORY from an Old German or Old Dutch word, which originally meant 'heavy or stout'

dappled *ADJECTIVE*
marked with patches of a different colour, or with patches of shade
WORD HISTORY probably from Old Norse *depill* 'spot'

dare *VERB* **dares, daring, dared**
1 to dare to do something is to be brave or bold enough to do it

> He didn't dare look up. A shadow fell across the window as the two men passed. — *Anthony Horowitz, Stormbreaker*

2 to challenge someone to do something risky or rash ◆ *I dare you to send him a Valentine.*
I dare say it is very likely

dare *NOUN* **dares**
a challenge to do something risky
WORD HISTORY from Old English *durran* 'to dare'

daredevil *NOUN* **daredevils**
a person who enjoys doing dangerous things

daren't
short for *dare not*

daring *ADJECTIVE*
1 a daring person is courageous and takes risks
2 a daring act is bold or unusual
▷ **daringly** *ADVERB*

daring *NOUN*
adventurous courage

dark *ADJECTIVE*
1 with little or no light

Night had fallen but through the window she could see the dark outline of trees. — *Tim Bowler, River Boy*

2 of a deep shade of colour closer to black than to white ◆ *dark grey* ◆ *a dark suit*
3 having dark hair
4 involving misery or suffering ◆ *the long dark years of the war*
5 mysterious or unknown ◆ *a dark secret*
6 sinister or evil ◆ *dark deeds*
to keep something dark is to keep it secret
▷ **darkly** *ADVERB*
▷ **darkness** *NOUN*

dark *NOUN*
1 absence of light ◆ *The night-vision camera allows us to film in the dark.*
2 the time when darkness has come; nightfall ◆ *We'll go out after dark.*
to be in the dark is to have no information about something
▷ **darkish** *ADJECTIVE*
WORD HISTORY from Old English *deorc*

darken *VERB* **darkens, darkening, darkened**
1 to make something dark or darker
2 to become dark or darker
never to darken someone's door is to stay away from their home because you are unwelcome

dark horse *NOUN*
someone who does surprisingly well in a race or competition, because they have unexpected abilities

darkroom *NOUN* **darkrooms**
a room for developing photographs which is kept free of light

darling *NOUN* **darlings**
someone who is loved very much

darling *ADJECTIVE*
1 dearly loved
2 (*informal*) pretty or charming
WORD HISTORY from Old English *deorling* 'little dear'

darn *VERB* **darns, darning, darned**
to mend a hole in woven or knitted material by weaving threads across it

darn *NOUN* **darns**
an area on a piece of material that has been darned
WORD HISTORY from Old English *diernan* 'to hide'

dart *NOUN* **darts**
1 a small metal-tipped object thrown in the game of darts
2 a small pointed missile thrown or fired as a weapon
3 a sudden swift movement
4 a stitched tuck in a piece of clothing to make it fit

dart *VERB* **darts, darting, darted**
1 to move suddenly and quickly

The police darted off in different directions, their rifles forward, while the white officer spoke into a radio which he held close to his face. — *Beverley Naidoo, Chain of Fire*

2 you dart a look or expression at someone when you show them it suddenly and briefly

Katie darted one quick glance behind her. She'd never get away from them. — *Catherine MacPhail, Run Zan Run*

dartboard *NOUN* **dartboards**
a circular board used as a target in the game of darts

darts *NOUN*
a game in which darts are thrown at a dartboard

dash *VERB* **dashes, dashing, dashed**
1 to run quickly; to rush
2 to throw something violently against a hard surface or edge ◆ *The storm dashed the ship against the rocks.*
3 to destroy a hope or expectation
to dash something off is to write it hurriedly and without much effort

dash *NOUN* **dashes**
1 a short quick run; a rush ◆ *We made a dash for the door.*
2 a small amount of liquid added to a mixture ◆ *Add a dash of cream.*
3 (*Language*) the punctuation mark (—) used to mark a pause or to show that letters or words are missing
4 to do something with dash is to do it with confidence and style

dashes

Dashes are used to mark a break in the flow of a sentence.
They can be used on their own, to add a final comment, question, or summary:
I have only two words to say to you—'Never again'!
Would you like your bagel split, toasted, buttered—or none of the above?
They can be used in pairs before and after an interruption in a narrative or conversation, and are more emphatic than parentheses. For example, they can show a change of subject, or a break or hesitation in thought:
Maybe I'll just say 'oh, I don't know that—I'm allergic to opera'.
or they can be used to elaborate or explain a point:
The creature was vast—over ten feet tall and was staring at my sandwich.
It was called Casa Bruja—that is, Witch House —although I never asked why.

dashboard *NOUN* **dashboards**
a panel with dials and controls in front of the driver of a vehicle

WORD HISTORY a *dashboard* was originally a board on the front of a carriage to keep out mud, which dashed against it

dashing *ADJECTIVE*
attractive in a romantic, adventurous way

dastardly *ADJECTIVE*
an old-fashioned word meaning wicked and cruel

WORD HISTORY from an earlier meaning 'dull, stupid', related to *dazed*

DAT (*say* dat) *ABBREVIATION*
digital audiotape, a magnetic tape used to make digital recordings

data (*say* day- ta) *NOUN*
1 information, or pieces of information ◆ *The project uses data from a nationwide survey.*
2 (*ICT*) information held in a computer file

USAGE NOTE This word is now usually treated as a singular form, although strictly speaking it is the plural of *datum*, a word that is hardly ever used. So you can say *this data* and *The data is accurate*, although you will sometimes come across *these data* and *The data are accurate*. The singular forms emphasize the collected nature of *data* as 'information', whereas the plural forms regard *data* as as 'pieces of information'.

WORD HISTORY a Latin word meaning 'things given', originally a technical term in philosophy

database *NOUN* **databases**
(*ICT*) a set or collection of information held in a computer

data capture *NOUN*
(*ICT*) putting data into a form that can be processed by a computer

data protection *NOUN*
(*ICT*) a system of making sure that data stored in computers, especially personal information, can only be accessed by people who are legally allowed to do so

date❶ *NOUN* **dates**
1 the day of the month or year expressed by a number or series of numbers
2 a day or year when something happened or will happen ◆ *She still doesn't know the date of her operation.*
3 (*informal*) an appointment to meet someone socially, especially at the start of a romantic relationship
4 (*informal*) a person you have a date with

to date until now ◆ *These are the best results to date.*

date *VERB* **dates, dating, dated**
1 to give a date to something from the past ◆ *Archaeologists hope to date the pots from coins that were found with them.*
2 to have existed from a particular time ◆ *It seems most likely that the painting dates from the 1630s.*
3 to show signs of becoming out of date ◆ *Some fashions date quickly.*
4 (*informal*) to go out with someone in a romantic relationship

▷ **datable** *ADJECTIVE*

WORD HISTORY from Latin *data* 'given or delivered (at a certain time)'

> ***dates***
>
> The normal way to write a **date** is to put the day first, followed by the month, then the year, e.g. *12 June 2006*. This is how you would write the date at the top of a letter. You can also use numbers for the months and the last two digits for the year, e.g. *12/06/06* or *12.06.06*.
>
> But beware: the American practice is to put the month first and then the date (as in *9/11* to refer to 11 September), so that *12 June 2006* would be *6/12/06*, which in Britain would be understood as *6 December 2006*. If there is any danger of confusion, it is better to write out the month in full.
>
> Most of the month names have shorter forms: *Jan., Feb., Mar., Apr., Jun., Jul., Aug., Sept., Oct., Nov., Dec.*, which you can use in more informal writing. (*May* is too short to have a short form, and *June* and *July* are best written in full.) Years are written as *AD 2006* and *431 BC* (or *BCE*): see the dictionary entries for **AD**, **BC**, and **BCE**.

date❷ *NOUN* **dates**
a small sweet brown fruit that grows on palm trees in North Africa and SW Asia

WORD HISTORY from Greek *daktulos* 'finger', because of the finger- like shape of its leaves

dated *ADJECTIVE*
old-fashioned; out of date

dative *NOUN*
(*Grammar*) a form of a word that is an indirect object or someone who receives something in a sentence. For example, the word *me* is in the dative in *Give me the book.*

WORD HISTORY from Latin *datum* 'something given'

daub *VERB* **daubs, daubing, daubed**
to paint or smear something clumsily

daub *NOUN* **daubs**
a thick smear of paint, glue, etc.

WORD HISTORY from Latin *dealbare* 'to whitewash or plaster', from *albus* 'white', which is also the source of our words *albino* and *album*

daughter *NOUN* **daughters**
a girl or woman as a child of her parents

WORD HISTORY from Old English *dohtor*

WORD FAMILY A related adjective is filial.

daughter-in-law *NOUN* **daughters-in-law**
the wife of your son

daunt *VERB* **daunts, daunting, daunted**
to be daunted by a person or task is to feel discouraged because you do not think you are good enough for them ◆ *I felt a bit daunted by the presence of all these clever people.*
WORD HISTORY from Latin *domitare* 'to tame'

daunting *ADJECTIVE*
a daunting task makes you feel nervous or discouraged

dauntless *ADJECTIVE*
brave and determined

Lili, I thought, would be dauntless in darkened rooms. — *Alice T. Ellis, The Clothes in the Wardrobe*

▷ **dauntlessly** *ADVERB*

dauphin (*say* daw- fin) *NOUN* **dauphins**
(*History*) the eldest son of the kings of France between 1349 and 1830
WORD HISTORY an Old French word meaning 'dolphin', because the dauphins once had a coat of arms with three dolphins in it

Davy Jones's locker *NOUN*
the bottom of the sea thought of as the grave of those who are drowned or buried at sea
WORD HISTORY from *Davy Jones*, a name given by sailors to the evil spirit of the sea

Davy lamp *NOUN* **Davy lamps**
a safety lamp used by miners
WORD HISTORY from the English chemist, Sir Humphry *Davy* (1778–1829), who invented it

dawdle *VERB* **dawdles, dawdling, dawdled**
to walk or do things slowly and lazily
▷ **dawdler** *NOUN*

dawn *NOUN* **dawns**
1 the first light of the day just before sunrise
2 the beginning of something important
◆ *There was a lot of grand talk about the dawn of a new era.*

dawn *VERB* **dawns, dawning, dawned**
1 a day dawns when it begins to grow light in the morning

Before the next day dawned their journey to Mordor was over. — *J. R. R. Tolkien, The Two Towers*

2 a fact or truth dawns on someone when they begin to realize it
▷ **dawning** *NOUN*
WORD HISTORY from an earlier word *dawing*, from *daw* 'to become day', related to *day*

day *NOUN* **days**
1 the 24 hours between midnight and the next midnight
2 the time during which the sun is above the horizon; the daytime
3 a day on which a particular event happens, e.g. a sports day
4 a period of time in the past or in a person's life
◆ *This never happened in my grandmother's day.*
to call it a day is to decide to stop doing something
day by day each day, gradually and steadily
WORD HISTORY from Old English *dæg*

daybreak *NOUN*
the first light of day; dawn

daydream *NOUN* **daydreams**
pleasant thoughts that you have during the day

daydream *VERB* **daydreams, daydreaming, daydreamed**
to have daydreams

daylight *NOUN*
1 the natural light of day; sunlight
2 dawn; the first light of day
to see daylight is to begin to understand something

daytime *NOUN*
the time of daylight

day-to-day *ADJECTIVE*
happening every day; ordinary

daze *VERB* **dazes, dazing, dazed**
to make someone stunned or bewildered
▷ **dazed** *ADJECTIVE*

daze *NOUN*
in a daze unable to think or see clearly; stunned
WORD HISTORY from Old Norse *dasathr* 'weary'

dazzle *VERB* **dazzles, dazzling, dazzled**
1 a light dazzles you when it is so bright that you cannot see clearly because of it

The brightness was still dazzling, blinding their closed eyes with blood-red light. — *William Nicholson, The Wind Singer*

2 to amaze or impress someone by a splendid display

DC *ABBREVIATION*
direct current

D-day *NOUN*
(*History*) 6 June 1944, the day on which British and American forces invaded northern France in the Second World War
WORD HISTORY the *D* is thought to be an abbreviation for *day*

deacon *NOUN* **deacons** (*Religion*)
1 a member of the clergy who ranks below a priest in Catholic, Anglican, and Orthodox Christian Churches
2 a church officer who is not a member of the clergy in some Christian Churches
WORD HISTORY from Greek *diakonos* 'servant'

deaconess *NOUN* **deaconesses**
(*Religion*) a woman who is a deacon

deactivate *VERB* **deactivates, deactivating, deactivated**
to make a machine or device stop working
◆ *He had forgotten to deactivate the alarm.*

dead *ADJECTIVE*
1 no longer alive

> I thought he was dead. He was sitting with his legs stretched out, and his head tipped back against the wall. — *David Almond, Skellig*

2 your arm or your leg goes dead when it has become numb and has no feeling for a while
3 a place is described as dead when nothing interesting ever happens there
4 a device like a telephone or radio is dead when it is not working or producing any sound
5 a dead language is one that no one uses any more
6 the *dead of night* and the *dead of winter* are the quietest or most intense parts of night and winter
7 complete or total ◆ *There was dead silence.* ◆ *The juggernaut came to a dead stop.*
8 exact or precise ◆ *The arrow hit the target in the dead centre.*

a dead loss a useless person or thing

WORD FAMILY A disease or injury that causes death is fatal, lethal, mortal, or terminal. A place where dead bodies are kept is a mortuary. A posthumous work is one that appears after the writer's death. A word element meaning 'death' is necro-.

dead *ADVERB*
1 completely; exactly ◆ *The table was dead level.*
2 (*informal*) very; extremely ◆ *He tried to sound dead casual.*

WORD HISTORY an Old English word

deaden *VERB* **deadens, deadening, deadened**
1 something deadens a pain when it makes it less intense
2 something deadens a noise when it makes it quieter

dead end *NOUN* **dead ends**
1 a road or passage with one end closed
2 a situation where there is no chance of making progress

dead heat *NOUN* **dead heats**
a race in which two or more winners finish exactly together

deadline *NOUN* **deadlines**
a time by which you have to finish something

WORD HISTORY a *deadline* was originally a line marked around an American military prison; prisoners could be shot if they crossed it

deadlock *NOUN* **deadlocks**
a situation in which no progress can be made

deadly *ADJECTIVE, ADVERB* **deadlier, deadliest**
1 likely to kill; fatal ◆ *The area is threatened by pollution from deadly chemicals.*
2 complete or total ◆ *There was a deadly hush in the room.* ◆ *Don was deadly serious.*

dead-pan *ADJECTIVE*
having a look on your face that shows no feeling or expression

deaf *ADJECTIVE*
1 wholly or partly without the sense of hearing
2 refusing to listen ◆ *The demon was deaf to reason, and longed only to kill.*

▷ **deafness** *NOUN*

WORD HISTORY an Old English word

deafen *VERB* **deafens, deafening, deafened**
1 a noise deafens you when it is so loud that you cannot hear anything else
2 a deafening noise is extremely loud

deal ❶ *VERB* **deals, dealing, dealt**
1 to give out cards for a card game
2 to hand something out to several people
3 you deal in an item when you are in the business of buying and selling it ◆ *He deals in scrap metal.*
4 you deal someone a blow or injury when you inflict it on them

to deal with something
1 to deal with a task or problem is to take responsibility for it
2 to deal with a painful or difficult situation is to cope with it
3 a book, film, or television programme deals with a topic when that is its subject

deal *NOUN* **deals**
1 a business transaction or agreement
2 treatment ◆ *Working mothers don't always get a fair deal.*
3 a player's turn to deal at cards

a big deal (*informal*) something important or significant

a good deal or a great deal a large amount

WORD HISTORY from Old English *daelan* 'to divide or share out'

deal ❷ *NOUN*
sawn fir or pine wood

WORD HISTORY from Old Dutch *dele* 'plank'

dealer *NOUN* **dealers**
1 a person or business that buys and sells goods
2 the person who deals in a game of cards

dean *NOUN* **deans**
1 (*Religion*) an important member of the clergy in a cathedral
2 the head of a university, college, or department

▷ **deanery** *NOUN*

WORD HISTORY from Latin *decanus* 'chief of a group of ten'

dear *ADJECTIVE*
1 loved very much
2 a polite greeting before the name of the recipient in a letter ◆ *Dear Mrs Grimble ...*
3 expensive; costing a lot of money

dearly *ADVERB*
very much; a lot ◆ *She loved her husband dearly.*

dearth (*say* derth) ***NOUN***
a dearth of something valuable or important is a lack of it ◆ *The year 1439 saw a great dearth of corn.*
WORD HISTORY from *dear*, because things that are scarce are expensive

death ***NOUN*** **deaths**
1 the process of dying; the end of life
2 the ending or destruction of something ◆ *It was the death of all our hopes.*
3 two people fight to the death when one or the other is killed
to be at death's door is to be nearly dying
to be the death of someone (*informal*) is to be a cause of great trouble to them
to put someone to death is to kill them deliberately
to death extremely, to the utmost limit ◆ *sick to death*
WORD HISTORY an Old English word

deathbed ***NOUN*** **deathbeds**
the bed on which a person dies or is dying

deathly ***ADJECTIVE***
1 a deathly shade or colour is extremely pale
2 a deathly silence or hush is very deep and quiet

death row ***NOUN***
an area in a prison, with cells for prisoners sentenced to death

death trap ***NOUN*** **death traps**
a dangerous place or vehicle that puts people's lives at risk

death-watch beetle ***NOUN*** **death-watch beetles**
a beetle whose larva bores holes in old wood and makes a ticking sound
WORD HISTORY so called because the sound used to be thought of as a sign of an imminent death

debacle (*say* day- **bahkl**) ***NOUN*** **debacles**
a complete failure or disaster ◆ *The election debacle had marked a turning point in his life.*
WORD HISTORY from French *débâcler* 'to unbar'

debar ***VERB*** **debars, debarring, debarred**
to ban someone from doing something, or from taking part in a contest
WORD HISTORY from French *barrer* 'to bar'

debark ***VERB*** **debarks, debarking, debarked**
to leave a ship or aircraft
▷ **debarkation** ***NOUN***
WORD HISTORY from French *débarquer*

debase ***VERB*** **debases, debasing, debased**
to reduce the quality or value of something
▷ **debasement** ***NOUN***

debatable ***ADJECTIVE***
a debatable question or issue is one that people might discuss or argue about
▷ **debatably** ***ADVERB***

debate ***NOUN*** **debates**
a formal discussion or argument

debate ***VERB*** **debates, debating, debated**
to discuss or argue about a subject or matter
▷ **debater** ***NOUN***
WORD HISTORY via Old French from Latin *battere* 'to fight'

debauchery (*say* di- **bawch**- er- i) ***NOUN***
over-indulgence in sensual or immoral pleasures
▷ **debauched** ***ADJECTIVE***
WORD HISTORY from French *débaucher* 'to turn away from your duty'

debilitating ***ADJECTIVE***
a debilitating disease or illness makes your body very weak

debility (*say* dib- **il**- it- ee) ***NOUN***
weakness of the body
WORD HISTORY via French from Latin *debilis* 'weak'

debit ***NOUN*** **debits**
an entry in an account showing how much money is owed (SEE ALSO **credit**)

debit ***VERB*** **debits, debiting, debited**
1 to enter an amount as a debit in an account
2 to remove a sum of money from an account
WORD HISTORY from Latin *debitum* 'what is owed'

debit card ***NOUN*** **debit cards**
a card which transfers money electronically from a person's bank account, used for buying things

debonair (*say* deb- on- **air**) ***ADJECTIVE***
having a carefree self-confident manner ◆ *He was in top form, witty and debonair.*
WORD HISTORY from a French phrase *de bon air* 'of good disposition'

debrief ***VERB*** **debriefs, debriefing, debriefed**
to question someone for information about a mission or task they have just completed
▷ **debriefing** ***NOUN***

debris (*say* **deb**- ree) ***NOUN***
scattered broken pieces or remains
WORD HISTORY from French *débris* 'broken down'

debt (*say* det) ***NOUN*** **debts**
the amount of money someone owes to a person or bank
to be in debt is to owe money
to be in someone's debt is to be grateful to someone who has done you a favour
WORD HISTORY related to *debit*

debtor (*say* **det**- or) ***NOUN*** **debtors**
a person who owes money to someone

debug *VERB* **debugs, debugging, debugged**
1 (*ICT*) to remove errors from a program or system
2 to remove concealed listening devices from a room

debunk *VERB* **debunks, debunking, debunked**
to show that a claim or theory, or a person's reputation, is exaggerated or false

debut (*say* **day**- bew) *NOUN* **debuts**
the first public appearance of an actor or other performer
WORD HISTORY from French *débuter* 'to begin'

decade (*say* **dek**- ayd) *NOUN* **decades**
a period of ten years
WORD HISTORY via French from Greek *deka* 'ten'

decadent (*say* **dek**- a- dent) *ADJECTIVE*
1 immoral or dishonest ◆ *Occasionally the voters lose patience and throw out decadent governments.*
2 lazily enjoying luxury and pleasure ◆ *She thought him very decadent to be still in his pyjamas at lunchtime.*
▷ **decadence** *NOUN*
▷ **decadently** *ADVERB*
WORD HISTORY related to *decay*

decaffeinated *ADJECTIVE*
decaffeinated coffee or tea has had caffeine removed from it

decagon (*say* **dek**- a- gon) *NOUN* **decagons**
a geometric figure with ten sides
▷ **decagonal** *ADJECTIVE*

decamp *VERB* **decamps, decamping, decamped**
to go away suddenly or secretly
WORD HISTORY from French *décamper*

decant (*say* dik- **ant**) *VERB* **decants, decanting, decanted**
to pour wine or other liquid gently from one container into another, in order to remove sediment
WORD HISTORY from Latin *decanthare*, from *canthus* 'lip of a jug', which came from Greek *kanthos* 'corner of your eye' because it was the same shape as a jug lip

decanter (*say* dik- **ant**- er) *NOUN* **decanters**
a stoppered glass bottle into which wine or spirit is decanted before serving

decapitate *VERB* **decapitates, decapitating, decapitated**
to cut someone's head off; to behead someone
▷ **decapitation** *NOUN*
WORD HISTORY from Latin *decapitare*, from *caput* 'head'

decathlon *NOUN* **decathlons**
an athletic contest in which each competitor takes part in ten events
▷ **decathlete** *NOUN*
WORD HISTORY from Greek *athlon* 'contest'

decay *VERB* **decays, decaying, decayed**
1 to go bad; to rot
2 to become less good or less strong ◆ *The rituals of the past have been perverted and decayed.*

decay *NOUN*
the process of decaying or rotting
WORD HISTORY from Latin *decidere* 'to fall off or away', which is also the source of our word *deciduous*

decease (*say* dis- **eess**) *NOUN*
(*formal*) a person's death
WORD HISTORY from Latin *decedere* 'to go away', from *cedere* 'to go'

deceased *ADJECTIVE*
(*formal*) a deceased person is recently dead

deceit (*say* dis- **eet**) *NOUN* **deceits**
the process of intending to make a person believe something that is not true

deceitful *ADJECTIVE*
a deceitful person or action is one that deliberately deceives people
▷ **deceitful** *ADJECTIVE*
▷ **deceitfulness** *NOUN*

deceive *VERB* **deceives, deceiving, deceived**
1 to make someone believe something that is not true
2 to give someone the wrong idea or impression ◆ *Don't let the shabby appearance of the house deceive you.*
3 to deceive yourself is to continue to believe something that is not true
▷ **deceiver** *NOUN*
WORD HISTORY from Latin *decipere* 'to ensnare or cheat'

decelerate (*say* dee- **sel**- er- ayt) *VERB* **decelerates, decelerating, decelerated**
to decrease your speed
▷ **deceleration** *NOUN*

December *NOUN*
the twelfth month of the year
WORD HISTORY from Latin *decem* 'ten', because it was the tenth month of the ancient Roman calendar

decency *NOUN*
decent behaviour

decent *ADJECTIVE*
1 respectable and honest ◆ *Violence disgusts decent people.*
2 reasonable or adequate ◆ *No one can make a decent living this way.*
3 (*informal*) kind or generous ◆ *It was decent of you to show up today.*
▷ **decently** *ADVERB*
WORD HISTORY from Latin *decere* 'to be fit'

deception *NOUN* **deceptions**
1 deceiving someone
2 something that deceives people

deceptive *ADJECTIVE*
misleading; giving a false impression ◆ *The elaborate facade of the building is deceptive.*
▷ **deceptively** *ADVERB*

decibel (*say* dess- ib- el) *NOUN* **decibels**
(*Science*) a unit for measuring the loudness of sound
WORD HISTORY originally one- tenth of the unit called a *bel*

decide *VERB* **decides, deciding, decided**
1 to make up your mind; to make a choice

Suppose you ought to do a recce around the schools and colleges, see what they have to offer before you decide. — *Alison Allen-Gray, Unique*

2 to settle a contest, question, or argument
3 to work something out or reach a conclusion

At this point, I decided it might be best to retire to my room. — *Meg Cabot, The Princess Diaries*

WORD HISTORY from Latin *decidere* 'to determine'

decided *ADJECTIVE*
1 noticeable or definite ◆ *She felt a decided reluctance to go into the house.*
2 having clear and definite opinions
▷ **decidedly** *ADVERB*

decider *NOUN* **deciders**
an extra game or contest that settles the outcome of a series of contests

deciduous (*say* dis- **id**- yoo- us) *ADJECTIVE*
a deciduous tree is one that sheds its leaves in autumn
WORD HISTORY from Latin *decidere* 'to fall off or away', from *cadere* 'to fall'

decimal *ADJECTIVE*
(*Mathematics*) decimal numbers or fractions are expressed in tens or tenths

decimal *NOUN* **decimals**
a number or fraction using decimal units
WORD HISTORY from Latin *decimus* 'tenth'

decimal currency *NOUN* **decimal currencies**
a currency in which each unit is ten or one hundred times the value of the one next below it

decimal fraction *NOUN* **decimal fractions**
(*Mathematics*) a fraction with tenths shown as numbers after a dot ($\frac{1}{3}$ is 0.3; $1\frac{1}{2}$ is 1.5)

decimalize *VERB* **decimalizes, decimalizing, decimalized**
1 to express a number as a decimal
2 to change a coinage or other counting system to a decimal one
▷ **decimalization** *NOUN*
USAGE NOTE This word can also be spelled decimalise.

decimal point *NOUN* **decimal points**
the dot in a decimal fraction

decimate (*say* dess- im- ayt) *VERB* **decimates, decimating, decimated**
1 to kill or destroy a large proportion of something ◆ *Pollution has decimated the seabird population.*
2 to reduce the strength of something drastically
▷ **decimation** *NOUN*
WORD HISTORY from Latin *decimare* 'to kill every tenth man', from the practice of putting to death one in every ten of a body of soldiers guilty of mutiny in the ancient Roman army

decipher (*say* dis- y- fer) *VERB* **deciphers, deciphering, deciphered**
1 to work out the meaning of a coded message
2 to work out the meaning of a piece of writing that is hard to read
▷ **decipherment** *NOUN*

decision *NOUN* **decisions**
1 decision is deciding or making a judgement about something
2 a decision is what someone has decided

decisive (*say* dis- y- siv) *ADJECTIVE*
1 a decisive event is one that settles or ends something
2 a decisive person is able to make decisions quickly and firmly
▷ **decisively** *ADVERB*
▷ **decisiveness** *NOUN*

deck *NOUN* **decks**
1 each floor or level on a ship or bus
2 a pack of playing cards
3 a part of a music system that contains a player for discs or tapes
to hit the deck (*informal*) is to fall to the ground or floor

deck *VERB* **decks, decking, decked**
1 a building or street is decked with flags or other decorations when it is decorated with them
2 to be decked out in smart or bright clothes is to be dressed in them
WORD HISTORY from Old Dutch *dec* 'a covering'

deckchair *NOUN* **deckchairs**
a folding chair with a wooden frame and a canvas seat, for using outdoors
WORD HISTORY so called because they were first used on the decks of passenger ships

declaim *VERB* **declaims, declaiming, declaimed**
to speak or say something impressively or dramatically
▷ **declamation** (*say* dek- la- **may**- shon) *NOUN*
▷ **declamatory** *ADJECTIVE*
WORD HISTORY from Latin *declamare* 'to cry out' from *clamare* 'to shout'

declare *VERB* **declares, declaring, declared**
1 to say something clearly and positively ◆ *He has always declared that he is innocent.*
2 to inform customs officials when you come into a country that you have goods on which you ought to pay duty
3 to end a cricket innings before all the batsmen are out
4 to declare war is to announce that you are starting a war against someone
▷ **declaration** *NOUN*
▷ **declarative** *ADJECTIVE*
▷ **declaratory** *ADVERB*

WORD HISTORY from Latin *declarare* 'to make clear', from *clarus* 'clear'

declension *NOUN* **declensions**
(*Grammar*) a listing of the various forms of a noun, adjective, or pronoun, especially in languages that have inflections

decline *VERB* **declines, declining, declined**
1 to refuse something politely ◆ *She tactfully declined all offers of help.* ◆ *He declined to comment on the matter.*
2 to become weaker or smaller ◆ *Our audience numbers are declining.*
3 to slope or move downwards
4 (*Grammar*) to give the forms of a noun, pronoun, or adjective that correspond to its cases, number, and gender

decline *NOUN* **declines**
1 a gradual decrease or loss of strength
2 a downward slope
in decline getting less or worse

WORD HISTORY from Latin *declinare* 'to turn aside', from *clinare* 'to bend'

declivity (*say* di- **kliv**- iti) *NOUN* **declivities**
a downward slope

WORD HISTORY from Latin *declivis* 'sloping down'

decode *VERB* **decodes, decoding, decoded**
1 to work out the meaning of something written in code
2 (*Language*) to convert language into words that are easier to understand
▷ **decoder** *NOUN*

decommission *VERB* **decommissions, decommissioning, decommissioned**
to take a ship or piece of equipment out of service

decompose *VERB* **decomposes, decomposing, decomposed**
to decay or rot
▷ **decomposition** *NOUN*

decompress *VERB* **decompresses, decompressing, decompressed**
1 to reduce pressure in air
2 (*ICT*) to expand compressed data to the normal size
▷ **decompression** *NOUN*

decongestant (*say* dee- kon- **jest**- ant) *NOUN* **decongestants**
a medicine used to relieve a blocked nose

decontaminate *VERB* **decontaminates, decontaminating, decontaminated**
to get rid of poisonous chemicals or radioactive material from a place, clothes, etc.
▷ **decontamination** *NOUN*

decor (*say* **day**- kor) *NOUN*
the style of furnishings and decorations used in a room

WORD HISTORY from French *décorer* 'to decorate'

decorate *VERB* **decorates, decorating, decorated**
1 to make something look more attractive or colourful by adding objects or details to it
2 to put fresh paint or wallpaper on walls
3 to give someone a medal or other award
▷ **decorator** *NOUN*

WORD HISTORY from Latin *decor* 'beauty'

decoration *NOUN* **decorations**
1 the process of decorating
2 an ornament or detail used to decorate
3 a medal or other award given as an honour

decorative (*say* **dek**- er- ativ) *ADJECTIVE*
ornamental; attractive to look at
▷ **decoratively** *ADVERB*

decorous (*say* **dek**- er- us) *ADJECTIVE*
polite and dignified

Something creamy lay among the ferny weeds. A stone. No. A shell. Suddenly Piggy was a-bubble with decorous excitement. — *William Golding, Lord of the Flies*

▷ **decorously** *ADVERB*

WORD HISTORY from Latin *decorus* 'suitable, proper'

decorum (*say* dik- **or**- um) *NOUN*
polite and dignified behaviour

WORD HISTORY related to *decorous*

decoy (*say* **dee**- koi) *NOUN* **decoys**
something used to lure a person or animal into a trap or into danger

Either this was a decoy and the real tiara was hidden elsewhere, or this was a test, and he had been lured here to take that test. — *Eoin Colfer, Artemis Fowl: The Seventh Dwarf*

decoy (*say* dik- **oi**) *VERB* **decoys, decoying, decoyed**
to lure a person or animal into a trap or danger

WORD HISTORY from Dutch *de kooi* 'the cage', originally a pond surrounded by nets to trap wild birds

decrease *VERB* **decreases, decreasing, decreased**
1 to become smaller or fewer
2 to make something smaller or fewer in number

decrease *NOUN* **decreases**
1 the process of decreasing; a reduction
2 the amount by which something decreases
WORD HISTORY from Latin *decrescere*, from *crescere* 'to grow'

decree *NOUN* **decrees**
an official order or decision

decree *VERB* **decrees, decreeing, decreed**
to order something by decree
WORD HISTORY from Latin *decretum* 'what has been decided'

decrepit (*say* dik- **rep**- it) *ADJECTIVE*
old and weak
▷ **decrepitude** *NOUN*
WORD HISTORY from Latin *decrepitus* 'creaking'

decry (*say* di- **kry**) *VERB* **decries, decrying, decried**
to say that something is unimportant
WORD HISTORY from French *décrier* 'to cry down'

dedicate *VERB* **dedicates, dedicating, dedicated**
1 to devote all your time or energy to something
2 to address a book, film, etc. to a person as a compliment, by including their name at its beginning or end
▷ **dedication** *NOUN*
WORD HISTORY from Latin *dedicare* 'to devote or consecrate'

dedicated *ADJECTIVE*
1 devoted to a task or purpose ◆ *a dedicated scientist*
2 used exclusively for a particular purpose ◆ *a dedicated phoneline*

deduce (*say* di- **dewss**) *VERB* **deduces, deducing, deduced**
to work something out by reasoning from facts that you know are true
▷ **deducible** *ADJECTIVE*
WORD HISTORY from Latin *deducere* 'to lead out', from *ducere* 'to lead'

deduct *VERB* **deducts, deducting, deducted**
to take away an amount or quantity, to subtract something
▷ **deductible** *ADJECTIVE*

deduction *NOUN* **deductions**
1 deducting; an amount that is deducted
2 deducing; a conclusion that is deduced

deed *NOUN* **deeds**
1 something that someone has done; an act
2 a legal document, especially one giving ownership or rights to something
WORD HISTORY from Old English *ded*, related to our word *do*

deed poll *NOUN*
a deed made by one party only, especially one that formally changes a person's name

deem *VERB* **deems, deeming, deemed**
(*formal*) to consider or judge something to be an honour, success, etc.
WORD HISTORY from Old English *deman*, related to our word *doom*

deep *ADJECTIVE*
1 going a long way down or back or in

Three deep parallel grooves of skin appeared upon George's rather low sloping forehead. — *Roald Dahl, Vengeance Is Mine Inc.*

2 measured from top to bottom or front to back ◆ *a hole two metres deep*
3 intense or strong ◆ *deep feelings*
4 a deep colour is dark and intense
5 a deep sleep is profound
6 a deep voice or sound is low-pitched, not shrill
7 to be deep in an activity is to be fully absorbed by it ◆ *deep in thought*
8 difficult to understand, obscure ◆ *That's too deep for me.*

to go off the deep end (*informal*) is to give way to emotion or anger
in deep water (*informal*) in trouble or difficulty
to be thrown in at the deep end (*informal*) is to be faced with a difficult situation in which you have little experience
▷ **deepness** *NOUN*

deep *ADVERB*
1 far down or in ◆ *We'll have to dig deep to get to the bottom layer.*
2 strongly, intensely ◆ *Feelings were running deep.*

deep *NOUN*
the deep (*literary*) the deep sea; the ocean
WORD HISTORY from Old English *deop*, related to our words *dip* and *dive*

deepen *VERB* **deepens, deepening, deepened**
1 to become deep or deeper
2 to make something deep or deeper

deep freeze *NOUN* **deep freezes**
a freezer

deep-fry *VERB* **deep-fries, deep-fried, deep-frying**
to fry food in fat that covers it

deeply *ADVERB*
1 very much ◆ *I deeply regret sending that email.*
2 very, extremely

Dark and deeply mysterious, the Deepwoods is a harsh and perilous place for those who call it home. — *Paul Stewart and Chris Riddell, Beyond the Deep Woods*

3 in a deep voice

deep-seated *ADJECTIVE*
a deep-seated feeling is one that you have felt deeply for some time

deep space *NOUN*
the far distant regions beyond our solar system; outer space

deer *NOUN* **deer**
a fast-running graceful animal, the male of which usually has antlers

WORD HISTORY from Old English *deor* which originally meant any animal (Old English had a different word for a deer, which is the origin of our word *hart*). The modern meaning had replaced 'animal' by the 15th century.

deerstalker *NOUN* **deerstalkers**
a soft cloth cap with one peak in front and another at the back

WORD HISTORY so called because it was originally worn by deer- hunters

deface *VERB* **defaces, defacing, defaced**
to spoil or damage the surface of something by marking it
▷ **defacement** *NOUN*

de facto (*say* dee **fak**- toh) *ADJECTIVE*
existing in fact, whether by right or not ◆ *The software sold in such numbers that it became the de facto standard.*

WORD HISTORY a Latin phrase meaning 'of fact'

defame *VERB* **defames, defaming, defamed**
to attack or damage a person's good reputation
▷ **defamation** (*say* def- a- **may**- shon) *NOUN*
▷ **defamatory** (*say* dif- **am**- a- ter- ee) *ADJECTIVE*

WORD HISTORY from Latin *diffamare*, from *fama* 'fame, reputation'

default *VERB* **defaults, defaulting, defaulted**
1 you default on an agreement if you fail to do what you have agreed to do
2 you default on a loan if you fail to pay it back
▷ **defaulter** *NOUN*

default *NOUN* **defaults**
1 failure to do something, especially to pay back a loan
2 (*ICT*) a pre-selected option adopted by a computer program when no alternative is specified

by default because there is no opposition or positive action ◆ *The other team didn't arrive in time, so we won by default.*

WORD HISTORY from Old French *defaut*, from *defaillir* 'to fail'

defeat *VERB* **defeats, defeating, defeated**
1 to win a victory over someone
2 to prevent something from being achieved ◆ *Surely, this defeats the object of the exercise.*
3 to baffle someone or be too difficult for them ◆ *The problem completely defeated me.*

defeat *NOUN* **defeats**
1 defeating someone
2 being defeated; a lost game or battle

WORD HISTORY from Latin *disfacere* 'to undo or destroy'

defeatist *NOUN* **defeatists**
a person who expects to fail or accepts failure too easily

defeatist *ADJECTIVE*
expecting to fail or be defeated
▷ **defeatism** *NOUN*

defecate (*say* **dee**- fik- ayt) *VERB* **defecates, defecating, defecated**
to get rid of faeces from your body
▷ **defecation** *NOUN*

defect (*say* dif- **ekt** or **dee**- fekt) *NOUN* **defects**
a flaw or deficiency

defect (*say* dif- **ekt**) *VERB* **defects, defecting, defected**
to abandon your country or cause in favour of another one
▷ **defection** *NOUN*
▷ **defector** *NOUN*

WORD HISTORY from Latin *deficere* 'to fail, leave, or undo'

defective *ADJECTIVE*
having defects; incomplete
▷ **defectively** *ADVERB*
▷ **defectiveness** *NOUN*

defence *NOUN* **defences**
1 the act of defending a place from attack, or the ability to do this
2 (*Politics*) a country's defences are the means it has to defend itself against attack
3 something that defends or protects against attack
4 the defendant's case in a lawsuit
5 the lawyers representing an accused person
6 the players in a defending position in a game

USAGE NOTE The American spelling of this word is defense.

defenceless *ADJECTIVE*
having no defences; unable to defend yourself

defend *VERB* **defends, defending, defended**
1 to protect someone or something against an attack or accusation
2 to try to preserve or retain a title or honour ◆ *The world champion is defending her title.*
3 to try to justify something ◆ *How can you defend such behaviour?*
4 to represent the defendant in a lawsuit
▷ **defender** *NOUN*

WORD HISTORY from Latin *defendere* 'to ward off'

defendant *NOUN* **defendants**
a person accused of something in a lawcourt (SEE ALSO **plaintiff**)

a b c d e f g h i j k l m n o p q r s t u v w x y z

defensible *ADJECTIVE*
able to be defended
▷ **defensibility** *NOUN*

defensive *ADJECTIVE*
1 used or done for defence; protective
2 anxious about being criticized ◆ *There's no need to be so defensive.*
on the defensive ready to defend yourself against criticism
▷ **defensively** *ADVERB*

defer❶ *VERB* **defers, deferring, deferred**
to put something off to a later time, to postpone something
▷ **deferment** *NOUN*
▷ **deferral** *NOUN*
WORD HISTORY from Latin *differre*, which meant both 'to carry apart' and 'to delay' and is also the source of our word *differ*

defer❷ *VERB* **defers, deferring, deferred**
to give way to a person's wishes, judgement, or authority ◆ *I defer to your superior knowledge.*
WORD HISTORY from Latin *deferre* 'to grant'

deference (*say* **def**- er- ens) *NOUN*
polite respect
in deference to out of respect for

deferential (*say* def- er- **en**- shal) *ADJECTIVE*
showing polite respect
▷ **deferentially** *ADVERB*

defiance *NOUN*
open disobedience, bold resistance
WORD HISTORY from Old French *defier* 'to defy'

defiant *ADJECTIVE*
defying; openly disobedient
▷ **defiantly** *ADVERB*
WORD HISTORY from Old French *defier* 'to defy'

deficiency *NOUN* **deficiencies**
1 a lack or shortage
2 a defect or failing

deficient (*say* di- **fish**- ent) *ADJECTIVE*
1 insufficient or inadequate
2 to be deficient in a quality or ingredient is not to have enough of it ◆ *Their diet is deficient in protein.*
▷ **deficiently** *ADVERB*

deficit (*say* **def**- iss- it) *NOUN* **deficits**
1 the amount by which a total is smaller than what is required
2 the amount by which spending is greater than income
WORD HISTORY a Latin word meaning 'it is lacking', from *deficere* 'to fail'

defile *VERB* **defiles, defiling, defiled**
to make something dirty or impure; to pollute something
▷ **defilement** *NOUN*
WORD HISTORY from an old word *defoul* 'to trample down', from Old French *defouler*

define *VERB* **defines, defining, defined**
1 to give the meaning of a word or phrase
2 to state or explain the scope of something ◆ *Customers' rights are defined by law.*
3 to show clearly the outline of something
▷ **definable** *ADJECTIVE*
WORD HISTORY from Latin *finis* 'limit'

definite *ADJECTIVE*
1 clearly stated; exact ◆ *Let's fix a definite time.*
2 certain or settled ◆ *Is it definite that we are to move?*
WORD HISTORY from Latin *definitus* 'defined'

definite article *NOUN* **definite articles**
the word 'the'

definite and indefinite articles

The word *the* is called the **definite article**. It comes before a noun or noun phrase when referring to people or things which are specific and definite:
That is the cave where the dragon sleeps.
Jupiter is the largest gas planet.
The words *a* and *an* are **indefinite articles** and are used before a singular noun or noun phrase when referring to people or things in a general or indefinite way:
I saw a cave and a dragon in my dream.
Jupiter is a gas planet.
A is used before words which begin with a consonant (*a beetle*, *a text*), and *an* before those which begin with a vowel (*an ant*, *an email*). Abbreviations take either *a* or *an* depending on whether they begin with the *sound* of a consonant or a vowel: *a CD*, but *an MP3 player*; *an IQ test*, but *a UFO*.
See also the panel on **determiners**.

definitely *ADVERB*
without doubt; certainly

A giant Egyptian sarcophagus popped open in the deepest of the shadows, revealing two figures who were most definitely not mummies.
— Eoin Colfer, Artemis Fowl: The Seventh Dwarf

definition *NOUN* **definitions**
1 a statement of what a word or phrase means or of what a thing is
2 clearness of outline, especially of a photographic image ◆ *The face lacks definition.*

definitive (*say* dif- **in**- it- iv) *ADJECTIVE*
1 finally settling something; conclusive ◆ *a definitive answer*
2 the most authoritative of its kind; not able to be bettered ◆ *He wrote the definitive history of French cinema.*

deflate *VERB* **deflates, deflating, deflated**
1 to let air or gas out of an inflated tyre, balloon, etc.
2 to make someone feel less proud or less confident
3 to reduce the amount of money in circulation in a country's economy
▷ **deflation** *NOUN*
▷ **deflationary** *ADJECTIVE*

a b c d e f g h i j k l m n o p q r s t u v w x y z

deflect *VERB* **deflects, deflecting, deflected**
1 to make a moving object turn in its path
2 to make a remark or criticism miss its target ◆ *The article was meant to deflect criticism away from the government.*
▷ **deflection** *NOUN*
▷ **deflector** *NOUN*

WORD HISTORY from Latin *deflectere* 'to bend away', from *flectere* 'to bend'

deforest *VERB* **deforests, deforesting, deforested**
to clear away the trees from an area
▷ **deforestation** *NOUN*

deform *VERB* **deforms, deforming, deformed**
to spoil the shape or appearance of something
▷ **deformation** *NOUN*

WORD HISTORY from Latin *deformare*, from *forma* 'shape, form'

deformed *ADJECTIVE*
badly or abnormally shaped

deformity *NOUN* **deformities**
1 being deformed
2 something that is deformed or misshapen

defraud *VERB* **defrauds, defrauding, defrauded**
to get money from someone by fraud

WORD HISTORY from Latin *defraudare* from *fraudere* 'to cheat'

defray *VERB* **defrays, defraying, defrayed**
to provide money to pay costs or expenses
▷ **defrayal** *NOUN*

WORD HISTORY from French *défrayer*, from *frais* 'costs, expenses'

defrost *VERB* **defrosts, defrosting, defrosted**
1 to thaw out something frozen
2 to remove the ice and frost from a refrigerator or windscreen

deft *ADJECTIVE*
skilful and quick ◆ *a deft hand*
▷ **deftly** *ADVERB*
▷ **deftness** *NOUN*

WORD HISTORY from an old spelling of *daft*

defunct *ADJECTIVE*
no longer in use or existing ◆ *The building was once a cinema but it's now defunct.*

WORD HISTORY from Latin *defunctus* 'finished'

defuse *VERB* **defuses, defusing, defused**
1 to remove the fuse from a bomb so that it cannot explode
2 to make a situation less dangerous or tense ◆ *Her joke defused the situation and we all relaxed.*

defy *VERB* **defies, defying, defied**
1 to resist something openly; to refuse to obey something
2 to challenge a person to do something you believe cannot be done ◆ *I defy you to prove this.*
3 to prevent something being done ◆ *The cupboard defied all efforts to open it.*

WORD HISTORY from Old French *defier*, from Latin *fidus* 'faithful'; the original meaning was 'to be disloyal'

degauss *VERB* **degausses, degaussing, degaussed**
to demagnetize a computer screen or other object

WORD HISTORY from the German physicist, Johann Karl Friedrich *Gauss* (1777–1855)

degenerate (*say* di- **jen**- er- ayt) *VERB* **degenerates, degenerating, degenerated**
to become worse or lower in standard
▷ **degeneracy** *NOUN*
▷ **degeneration** *NOUN*

degenerate (*say* di- **jen**- er- it) *ADJECTIVE*
having become immoral or bad

degenerate (*say* di- **jen**- er- it) *NOUN* **degenerates**
someone who behaves in a bad or immoral way

WORD HISTORY from Latin *degeneratus* 'no longer of its kind'

degradable *ADJECTIVE*
able to be broken down by chemical or biological processes

degrade *VERB* **degrades, degrading, degraded**
1 to humiliate or dishonour someone
2 to cause a chemical substance to break down or decompose
▷ **degradation** (*say* deg- ra- **day**- shon) *NOUN*

WORD HISTORY from Latin *degradare*, from *gradus* 'grade' or 'step'

degree *NOUN* **degrees**
1 a unit for measuring temperature
2 (*Mathematics*) a unit for measuring angles, shown by the symbol °, e.g. 45°
3 extent, amount ◆ *to some degree* ◆ *a high degree of skill*
4 an academic award given to someone who has successfully finished a course at a college or university

WORD HISTORY from Old French *degre*, from Latin *gradus* 'grade' or 'step'

dehumanize *VERB* **dehumanizes, dehumanizing, dehumanized**
to take away human qualities from someone; to brutalize someone

USAGE NOTE This word can also be spelled dehumanise.

a b c d e f g h i j k l m n o p q r s t u v w x y z

dehydrated *ADJECTIVE*
1 someone who is dehydrated has lost a lot of water from their body
2 a dehydrated substance has had all its moisture removed
▷ **dehydration** *NOUN*
WORD HISTORY from Greek *hydor* 'water'

de-ice *VERB* **de-ices, de-icing, de-iced**
to remove ice from a windscreen or other surface

deify (*say* **dee**- i- fy or **day**- i- fy) *VERB* **deifies, deifying, deified**
to make a god of someone; to treat someone as a god
▷ **deification** *NOUN*

deign (*say* dayn) *VERB* **deigns, deigning, deigned**
to do something that you think is below your dignity ◆ *I didn't deign to reply.*
WORD HISTORY from Latin *dignare* 'to deem worthy'

deity (*say* **dee**- it- ee or **day**- it- ee) *NOUN* **deities**
1 a god or goddess ◆ *ancient Egyptian deities*
2 divine status or nature; divinity
WORD HISTORY from Old French *deite*, from Latin *deus* 'god'

déjà vu (*say* day- *zha* **vew**) *NOUN*
a feeling that you have already experienced what is happening now
WORD HISTORY a French phrase meaning 'already seen'

dejected *ADJECTIVE*
sad or depressed
▷ **dejectedly** *ADVERB*
▷ **dejection** *NOUN*
WORD HISTORY from Latin *dejicere* 'to throw down', from *jacere* 'to throw'

delay *VERB* **delays, delaying, delayed**
1 to make someone or something late
2 to postpone something until later
3 to hesitate or linger ◆ *Don't delay!*

delay *NOUN* **delays**
1 delaying
2 the amount of time by which something is delayed ◆ *a two-hour delay*
WORD HISTORY from Old French *delayer*

delectable *ADJECTIVE*
delightful or delicious
▷ **delectably** *ADVERB*
WORD HISTORY from Latin *delectare* 'to please', which is also the source of our word *delight*

delectation *NOUN*
(*formal*) pleasure or delight ◆ *an evening of song for your delectation*

delegate (*say* **del**- ig- at) *NOUN* **delegates**
a person who represents others and acts on their instructions

delegate (*say* **del**- ig- ayt) *VERB* **delegates, delegating, delegated**
1 to entrust a task, power, or responsibility to someone else ◆ *I'm going to delegate this job to my assistant.*
2 to appoint someone as a representative ◆ *We delegated Rob to meet the visitors.*
WORD HISTORY from Latin *delegare* 'to entrust'

delegation (*say* del- ig- **ay**- shon) *NOUN* **delegations**
1 a group of delegates ◆ *the delegation from South Africa*
2 delegating

delete (*say* dil- **eet**) *VERB* **deletes, deleting, deleted**
1 to strike out something written or printed
2 (*ICT*) to remove data or files stored on a computer
▷ **deletion** *NOUN*
WORD HISTORY from Latin *delere* 'to blot out'

deleterious (*say* del- i- **teer**- i- us) *ADJECTIVE*
causing harm or damage
WORD HISTORY from Greek *dēlētērios* 'harmful'

deliberate (*say* dil- **ib**- er- it) *ADJECTIVE*
1 done on purpose; intentional
2 slow and careful; unhurried ◆ *She entered the room with deliberate steps.*
▷ **deliberately** *ADVERB*

deliberate (*say* dil- **ib**- er- ayt) *VERB* **deliberates, deliberating, deliberated**
to think over or discuss something carefully before reaching a decision
WORD HISTORY from Latin *deliberare*, 'to weigh carefully', from *librare* 'to weigh'

deliberation *NOUN*
1 long and careful consideration or discussion
2 careful slowness

deliberative *ADJECTIVE*
a deliberative group or body is one that is formed to consider or discuss issues.

delicacy *NOUN* **delicacies**
1 tact and sensitivity ◆ *We must handle the matter with the utmost delicacy.*
2 a delicious, often rare or expensive, food ◆ *Truffles are considered a delicacy.*

delicate *ADJECTIVE*
1 of fine quality or craftsmanship ◆ *delicate embroidery*
2 fragile and easily damaged
3 a delicate colour or flavour is pleasant and subtle ◆ *a delicate shade of pink*
4 someone who is delicate, or whose health is delicate, becomes ill easily
5 a delicate situation is one that needs tact and careful handling
6 skilful and sensitive ◆ *a delicate touch*
▷ **delicately** *ADVERB*
▷ **delicateness** *NOUN*
WORD HISTORY from Latin *delicatus* 'delightful'

a b c d e f g h i j k l m n o p q r s t u v w x y z

delicatessen (*say* del- i- ka- **tess**- en) ***NOUN*** **delicatessens**
a shop that sells cooked meats, cheeses, salads, etc.
WORD HISTORY a German word meaning 'delicacies to eat'

delicious ***ADJECTIVE***
tasting or smelling very pleasant
▷ **deliciously** ***ADVERB***
WORD HISTORY an Old French word, from Latin *delicia* 'delight or pleasure'

delight ***VERB*** **delights, delighting, delighted**
1 to please someone greatly
2 you delight in doing something when you take great pleasure in doing it

delight ***NOUN*** **delights**
1 great pleasure
2 something that gives great pleasure ◆ *Writing this book has been a real delight.*
WORD HISTORY from Old French *delit*, from Latin *delectare* 'to please'

delightful ***ADJECTIVE***
giving delight; very pleasant or pleasing
▷ **delightfully** ***ADVERB***

delimit (*say* dee- **lim**- it) ***VERB*** **delimits, delimiting, delimited**
to fix the limits or boundaries of something
▷ **delimitation** ***NOUN***

delineate (*say* di- **lin**- i- ayt) ***VERB*** **delineates, delineating, delineated**
to show something by drawing or describing it
▷ **delineation** ***NOUN***
WORD HISTORY from Latin *delineare* 'to outline'

delinquent (*say* dil- **ing**- kwent) ***ADJECTIVE*** **delinquents**
1 a delinquent person is guilty of committing minor crimes
2 you are delinquent in a task or duty if you fail to perform it
▷ **delinquency** ***NOUN***

delinquent ***NOUN*** **delinquents**
a delinquent person, especially a young person who breaks the law
WORD HISTORY from Latin *delinquere* 'to offend'

delirious (*say* di- **li**- ri- us) ***ADJECTIVE***
1 suffering from delirium
2 extremely excited or enthusiastic
▷ **deliriously** ***ADVERB***

delirium (*say* di- **li**- ri- um) ***NOUN***
1 a state of mental confusion and agitation during a feverish illness
2 wild excitement
WORD HISTORY a Latin word meaning 'deranged'

deliver ***VERB*** **delivers, delivering, delivered**
1 to take letters or goods to the person or place they are addressed to
2 to give a speech or lecture
3 to help with the birth of a baby
4 to aim or strike a blow or an attack
5 to provide something you have promised ◆ *But will the government deliver on its election pledges?*
6 to rescue someone; to set someone free
▷ **deliverer** ***NOUN***
WORD HISTORY from Old French *delivrer*, from Latin *liberare* 'to set free'

deliverance ***NOUN***
being rescued or set free

delivery ***NOUN*** **deliveries**
1 delivering letters or goods ◆ *Your order is ready for delivery.*
2 a regular distribution of letters or goods ◆ *We have two deliveries a day.*
3 the manner of delivering a speech ◆ *a clipped delivery*
4 giving birth to a baby ◆ *She had a difficult delivery.*
5 a ball bowled in cricket

dell ***NOUN*** **dells**
a small valley with trees
WORD HISTORY an Old English word related to *dale*

delphinium ***NOUN*** **delphiniums**
a garden plant with tall spikes of blue flowers
WORD HISTORY from Greek *delphinion*, related to our word *dolphin*

delta ***NOUN*** **deltas**
1 the fourth letter of the Greek alphabet, Δ or δ, equivalent to Roman *D*, *d*
2 a triangular area at the mouth of a river where it spreads into branches
WORD HISTORY a river *delta* is so called because its triangular shape is like that of the capital Greek letter delta, Δ

delude (*say* di- **lood**) ***VERB*** **deludes, deluding, deluded**
to deceive or mislead someone
WORD HISTORY from Latin *deludere* 'to play unfairly', from *ludere* 'to play'

deluge (*say* **del**- yooj) ***NOUN*** **deluges**
1 a large flood
2 a heavy fall of rain
3 a large number of comments, questions, etc. that come in a rush

deluge ***VERB*** **deluges, deluging, deluged**
1 to flood a place or region
2 to be deluged with comments, questions, etc. is to be overwhelmed by a great number of them ◆ *The company was deluged with complaints.*
WORD HISTORY an Old French word, from Latin *diluere* 'to wash away', which is also the source of our word *dilute*

delusion ***NOUN*** **delusions**
something you believe or think wrongly

de luxe *ADJECTIVE*
of very high quality; luxurious
WORD HISTORY a French phrase meaning 'of luxury'

delve *VERB* **delves, delving, delved**
1 to delve into a subject is to study it closely ♦ *I've been delving into the local history of the area where I live.*
2 to delve into a bag or container is to reach into it and search for something
WORD HISTORY from Old English *delfan* 'to dig'

demagnetize *VERB* **demagnetizes, demagnetizing, demagnetized**
to remove the magnetic properties from something
▷ **demagnetization** *NOUN*
USAGE NOTE This word can also be spelled demagnetise.

demagogue (*say* **dem**- a- gog) *NOUN* **demagogues**
a political leader who wins people's support by appealing to their emotions rather than their reasoning
▷ **demagogic** *ADJECTIVE*
WORD HISTORY from Greek *demos* 'people' and *agogos* 'leading'

demand *VERB* **demands, demanding, demanded**
1 to ask for something firmly or forcefully
2 a task that demands a particular skill or quality needs it to be successful ♦ *This work demands great skill.*

demand *NOUN* **demands**
1 a firm or forceful request
2 a desire to have or buy something ♦ *There is an increased demand for online shopping.*
3 something that is done on demand is done as soon as it is asked for or required ♦ *payable on demand*
to be in demand is to be wanted or needed
WORD HISTORY from Latin *demandare* 'to entrust completely', from *mandare* 'to order or entrust'

demanding *ADJECTIVE*
1 a demanding job or task is one that needs skill or effort
2 a demanding child needs a lot of attention from a parent or carer

demarcation (*say* dee- mar- **kay**- shon) *NOUN*
marking the boundary or limits of something
WORD HISTORY from Spanish *demarcación*

demean *VERB* **demeans, demeaning, demeaned**
to lower a person's dignity ♦ *I wouldn't demean myself by asking them for money.*
WORD HISTORY from *mean* in the sense 'poor or inferior'

demeanour (*say* dim- **een**- er) *NOUN* **demeanours**
the way a person behaves
WORD HISTORY from Old French *demener* 'to lead'

demented *ADJECTIVE*
driven mad; crazy

dementia (*say* di- **men**- sha) *NOUN*
a mental disorder that is characterized by memory loss and personality changes
WORD HISTORY from Latin *demens* 'out of your mind'

demerara (*say* dem- er- **air**- a) *NOUN*
brown raw cane sugar
WORD HISTORY from *Demerara* in Guyana, South America, where it was first produced

demerit (*say* di- **mer**- it) *NOUN* **demerits**
a fault or defect

demigod *NOUN* **demigods**
a partly divine being

demilitarize *VERB* **demilitarizes, demilitarizing, demilitarized**
to remove all military forces from an area
▷ **demilitarization** *NOUN*
USAGE NOTE This word can also be spelled demilitarise.

demise (*say* dim- **yz**) *NOUN*
1 the end or failure of something
2 a old-fashioned word for death
WORD HISTORY from Old French *desmettre* 'to dismiss'

demisemiquaver *NOUN* **demisemiquavers**
a musical note which lasts half as long as a semiquaver

demist *VERB* **demists, demisting, demisted**
to clear a windscreen or other surface of misty condensation

demo (*say* **dem**- oh) *NOUN* **demos** (*informal*)
1 a demonstration to show how a new product works
2 a public demonstration or march

demo *VERB* **demos, demoing, demoed**
(*informal*) to give a demonstration of a new product

democracy *NOUN* **democracies**
1 government of a country by representatives elected by all the people
2 a country governed in this way
WORD HISTORY from Greek *dēmos* 'people' and *-kratia* 'rule'

democrat *NOUN* **democrats**
1 a person who supports democracy
2 a *Democrat* is a member of the Democratic Party, one of the two main political parties in the USA

a b c d e f g h i j k l m n o p q r s t u v w x y z

democratic *ADJECTIVE* **democrats**
1 supporting or ruled by democracy
2 produced with equal participation from all ◆ *We've reached a democratic decision.*
▷ **democratically** *ADVERB*

demographics *PLURAL NOUN*
statistics relating to people and where they live
WORD HISTORY from Greek *dēmos* 'people' and *graphein* 'to write or draw'

demolish *VERB* **demolishes, demolishing, demolished**
1 to pull or knock down a building
2 to destroy an argument or theory completely
3 (*informal*) to eat food hungrily
▷ **demolition** *NOUN*
WORD HISTORY from Latin *demoliri*, from *moles* 'mass', which is also the source of our word *molecule*

demon *NOUN* **demons**
1 a devil or evil spirit
2 (also **daemon**) a person's spirit or genius
3 a forceful or skilful person ◆ *She's a demon on the squash court.*
▷ **demonic** (*say* dim- **on**- ik) *ADJECTIVE*
WORD HISTORY from Greek *daimōn* 'a spirit'

demonize *VERB* **demonizes, demonizing, demonized**
to portray someone as being evil or dangerous
USAGE NOTE This word can also be spelled demonise.

demonstrable (*say* **dem**- on- strab- ul) *ADJECTIVE*
able to be shown or proved
▷ **demonstrably** *ADVERB*

demonstrate *VERB* **demonstrates, demonstrating, demonstrated**
1 to show evidence of something; to prove something ◆ *This demonstrates how easy it is to set up a website.*
2 to show someone how to do something or how something works
3 to take part in a public demonstration
▷ **demonstrator** *NOUN*
WORD HISTORY from Latin *demonstrare*, from *monstrum* 'omen', which is also the source of our word *monster*

demonstration *NOUN* **demonstrations**
1 demonstrating; showing how to do or work something
2 an organized public gathering or march held to show support for, or to protest against, something

demonstrative (*say* dim- **on**- strat- iv) *ADJECTIVE*
1 showing or proving something
2 a demonstrative person shows their feelings or affections openly
3 (*Grammar*) pointing out the person or thing referred to. *This, that, these*, and *those* are demonstrative adjectives and pronouns
▷ **demonstratively** *ADVERB*
▷ **demonstrativeness** *NOUN*

demoralize *VERB* **demoralizes, demoralizing, demoralized**
to weaken someone's confidence or morale
▷ **demoralization** *NOUN*
USAGE NOTE This word can also be spelled demoralise.

demote *VERB* **demotes, demoting, demoted**
to give someone a less senior position or rank
▷ **demotion** *NOUN*

demur (*say* dim- **er**) *VERB* **demurs, demurring, demurred**
to object to something ◆ *They demurred at working on Sundays.*
WORD HISTORY from Latin *demorari* 'to delay'

demure *ADJECTIVE*
shy and modest
▷ **demurely** *ADVERB*
▷ **demureness** *NOUN*

demystify *VERB* **demystifies, demystifying, demystified**
to make a subject easier to understand
▷ **demystification** *NOUN*

den *NOUN* **dens**
1 a wild animal's lair
2 a person's private room
3 a place where something illegal happens ◆ *a gambling den*
WORD HISTORY from Old English *denn*

denarius (*say* di- **nair**- i- us) *NOUN* **denarii**
an ancient Roman silver coin
WORD HISTORY a Latin word meaning 'containing ten', because the coin was originally worth the equivalent of ten asses

deniable *ADJECTIVE*
able to be denied

denial *NOUN* **denials**
1 denying or refusing something
2 a statement that a thing is not true

denier (*say* **den**- yer) *NOUN* **deniers**
a unit for measuring the fineness of silk, rayon, or nylon thread, especially when used to make tights or stockings
WORD HISTORY an Old French word, from Latin *denarius* 'containing ten'

denigrate *VERB* **denigrates, denigrating, denigrated**
to damage the reputation of someone or something
▷ **denigration** *NOUN*
WORD HISTORY from Latin *denigrare* 'to blacken', from *niger* 'black'

denim *NOUN*
a strong cotton cloth, often dyed with indigo, used to make jeans and hard-wearing clothes
WORD HISTORY from a French phrase *serge de Nîmes*, 'serge from Nîmes' (a town in southern France)

denizen (*say* **den**- iz- en) *NOUN* **denizens**
an inhabitant ◆ *Monkeys are denizens of the jungle.*
WORD HISTORY from Old French *deinz* 'within'

denomination *NOUN* **denominations**
1 a person's name or title
2 a branch of a Church or religion
3 a unit of money ◆ *coins of small denomination*
WORD HISTORY from Latin *denominare* 'to name completely', from *nominare* 'to name'

denominator *NOUN* **denominators**
(*Mathematics*) the number below the line in a fraction, showing how many parts the whole is divided into, e.g. 4 in $\frac{1}{4}$ (SEE ALSO **numerator**)

denote *VERB* **denotes, denoting, denoted**
to mean or indicate something ◆ *In road signs, P denotes a car park.*
▷ **denotation** *NOUN*
WORD HISTORY from Latin *denotare* 'to mark completely', from *notare* 'to mark'

dénouement (*say* day- **noo**- mahn) *NOUN* **dénouements**
the final outcome of a plot or story, which is revealed at the end
WORD HISTORY a French word meaning 'unravelling'

denounce *VERB* **denounces, denouncing, denounced**
1 to speak strongly against someone or something
2 to give information against someone ◆ *They denounced him as a spy.*
▷ **denunciation** *NOUN*
WORD HISTORY from Latin *denuntiare*, from *nuntiare* 'to announce'

dense *ADJECTIVE*
1 dense fog or cloud is thick and not easy to see through
2 a dense crowd of people is packed closely together
3 (*informal*) stupid; unable to understand things
▷ **densely** *ADVERB*
WORD HISTORY from Latin *densus*

density *NOUN* **densities**
1 thickness or compactness
2 (*Science*) the relation of mass to volume

dent *NOUN* **dents**
a hollow left in a surface where something has pressed or hit it

dent *VERB* **dents, denting, dented**
1 to make a dent in something
2 to lessen a person's confidence, enthusiasm, etc.
WORD HISTORY from an earlier spelling of *dint*

dental *ADJECTIVE*
to do with your teeth or with dentistry
WORD HISTORY from Latin *dentis* 'of a tooth'

dental surgeon *NOUN* **dental surgeons**
a dentist

dentist *NOUN* **dentists**
a person who is qualified to treat people's teeth and gums
▷ **dentistry** *NOUN*

dentures *PLURAL NOUN*
a set of false teeth
WORD HISTORY from French *denture*

denude *VERB* **denudes, denuding, denuded**
1 to make something bare or naked
2 someone or something is denuded of a possession if it is taken or stripped away from them ◆ *The trees were denuded of their leaves.*
▷ **denudation** *NOUN*
WORD HISTORY from Latin *denudare* 'to strip away', from *nudare* 'to bare'

denunciation *NOUN* **denunciations**
denouncing someone or something

deny *VERB* **denies, denying, denied**
1 to say that something is not true ◆ *Do you deny it?*
2 to refuse to allow or accept something ◆ *I couldn't deny her request.*
3 you deny someone something if you refuse to give it to them ◆ *She doesn't deny her children anything.*
to deny yourself is to go without pleasures
WORD HISTORY from Latin *denegare*, from *negare* 'to say no'

deodorant (*say* dee- **oh**- der- ant) *NOUN* **deodorants**
a substance that removes or conceals unwanted smells
WORD HISTORY from Latin *odor* 'smell'

deodorize *VERB* **deodorizes, deodorizing, deodorized**
to remove unwanted smells
▷ **deodorization** *NOUN*
USAGE NOTE This word can also be spelled deodorise.

depart *VERB* **departs, departing, departed**
1 to go away; to leave
2 a train or bus departs when it begins a journey
3 to depart from a set course or procedure is to stop following it
WORD HISTORY from French *départir* 'to separate'

department *NOUN* **departments**
one section of a large organization or shop
◆ *the hardware department*
WORD HISTORY from French *département* 'division'

departmental *ADJECTIVE*
to do with a department
▷ **departmentally** *ADVERB*

department store *NOUN* **department stores**
a large shop with several departments which sell separate kinds of goods

departure *NOUN* **departures**
1 departing, going away
2 a new course of action or thought ◆ *His new film shows a radical departure in style.*

depend *VERB* **depends, depending, depended**
to depend on someone or something
1 is to rely on someone or something ◆ *We depend on your help.*
2 is to be determined by something ◆ *It all depends on the weather.*
WORD HISTORY from Latin *dependere* 'to hang down', from *pendere* 'to hang'

dependable *ADJECTIVE*
able to be relied on
▷ **dependably** *ADVERB*
▷ **dependability** *NOUN*

dependant *NOUN* **dependants**
a person who depends on someone else, especially financially
USAGE NOTE Take care to spell this noun with the ending *-ant*, and to spell the adjective with the ending *-ent*.

dependence *NOUN*
the state of being dependent on someone

dependency *NOUN* **dependencies**
a country or province that is controlled by another

dependent *ADJECTIVE*
1 relying on someone else for financial support ◆ *two dependent children*
2 to be dependent on something is to need it or be unable to do without it
USAGE NOTE See the note at *dependant*.

depict *VERB* **depicts, depicting, depicted**
1 to show something in the form of a picture
2 to describe something in words
▷ **depiction** *NOUN*
WORD HISTORY from Latin *depingere*, from *pingere* 'to paint'

depilatory (*say* di- **pil**- a- ter- i) *ADJECTIVE*
a depilatory cream is used to remove unwanted hair from your body
WORD HISTORY from Latin *pilus* 'hair'

deplete (*say* dip- **leet**) *VERB* **depletes, depleting, depleted**
to reduce the supply of something by using up large amounts ◆ *Fish stocks are severely depleted.*
▷ **depletion** *NOUN*
WORD HISTORY from Latin *deplere* 'to empty out'

deplorable *ADJECTIVE*
extremely bad or regrettable
▷ **deplorably** *ADVERB*

deplore *VERB* **deplores, deploring, deplored**
to feel or show strong disapproval of something ◆ *We deplore racism in any form.*
WORD HISTORY from Latin *deplorare* 'to lament', from *plorare* 'to cry or weep'

deploy *VERB* **deploys, deploying, deployed**
1 to place troops or weapons in position so that they are ready to be used
2 to use something effectively ◆ *He deployed his arguments well.*
▷ **deployment** *NOUN*
WORD HISTORY from French *déployer*

depopulate *VERB* **depopulates, depopulating, depopulated**
to reduce the population of a place
▷ **depopulation** *NOUN*

deport *VERB* **deports, deporting, deported**
to send an unwanted foreign person out of a country
▷ **deportation** *NOUN*
▷ **deportee** *NOUN*
WORD HISTORY from Latin *deportare* 'to carry off', from *portare* 'to carry'

deportment *NOUN*
a person's way of standing and walking
WORD HISTORY from an Old French word

depose *VERB* **deposes, deposing, deposed**
to remove a person or government from power
WORD HISTORY from Old French *deposer* 'to put down'

deposit *NOUN* **deposits**
1 a sum of money paid into a bank or other account
2 a sum of money paid as a first instalment
3 a layer of solid matter in or on the earth ◆ *New deposits of copper were found.*

deposit *VERB* **deposits, depositing, deposited**
1 to put something down ◆ *She deposited the books on the desk.*
2 to pay money as a deposit
3 to store or entrust something for safe keeping
4 to leave a layer of solid matter ◆ *Floods deposited mud on the land.*
▷ **depositor** *NOUN*
WORD HISTORY from Latin *depositum*, from *deponere* 'to put down'

deposition *NOUN* **depositions**
1 a written piece of evidence, given under oath
2 deposing someone from power or office

depot (*say* **dep**- oh) *NOUN* **depots**
1 a place where things are stored
2 a place where buses or trains are kept and repaired
3 a headquarters

WORD HISTORY via French from Latin *depositum*, which is also the source of our word *deposit*

depraved *ADJECTIVE*
of bad character or morals; corrupt
▷ **depravity** *NOUN*

WORD HISTORY from Latin *depravare* 'to corrupt', from *pravus* 'perverse, wrong'

deprecate (*say* **dep**- rik- ayt) *VERB* **deprecates, deprecating, deprecated**
to say that you disapprove of something
▷ **deprecation** *NOUN*
▷ **deprecatory** (*say* **dep**- ri- kay- ter- i) *ADJECTIVE*

WORD HISTORY from Latin *deprecari* 'to keep away misfortune by prayer'

depreciate (*say* dip- **ree**- shee- ayt) *VERB* **depreciates, depreciating, depreciated**
1 to make something lower in value over a period of time
2 to become lower in value over time
▷ **depreciation** *NOUN*

WORD HISTORY from Latin *depreciare* from *pretium* 'price'

depredation (*say* dep- rid- **ay**- shon) *NOUN* **depredations**
plundering or damaging something

WORD HISTORY from Latin *depraedari*, 'to plunder completely', from *praedari* 'to plunder'

depress *VERB* **depresses, depressing, depressed**
1 to make someone sad or dejected
2 to lower the value of something ◆ *The stock market is depressed.*
3 to press something down ◆ *Depress the lever.*
▷ **depressive** *ADJECTIVE*

WORD HISTORY from Latin *depressum* 'pressed down'

depressing *ADJECTIVE*
making you feel sad or dejected
▷ **depressingly** *ADVERB*

depression *NOUN* **depressions**
1 a feeling of great sadness or hopelessness, often with physical symptoms
2 a long period when trade is very slack because no one can afford to buy things, with widespread unemployment
3 a sunken place or hollow on a surface
4 an area of low air pressure which may bring rain
5 pressing something down
▷ **depressive** *ADJECTIVE*

deprive *VERB* **deprives, depriving, deprived**
you deprive someone of something if you take or keep it away from them

Being deprived of sight, Frodo found his hearing and other senses sharpened. — *J. R. R. Tolkien, The Fellowship of the Ring*

▷ **deprival** *NOUN*
▷ **deprivation** *NOUN*

WORD HISTORY from Latin *deprivare*, from *privare* 'to rob'

deprived *ADJECTIVE*
suffering from poverty or neglect ◆ *a deprived area*

depth *NOUN* **depths**
1 how deep something is; the distance from the top down, or from the front to the back
2 deep learning or thought or feeling ◆ *The poem has great depth.*
3 intensity of colour or darkness
4 lowness of pitch in a voice or sound
5 the lowest or most central part of something ◆ *the depths of the country*

in depth carefully and thoroughly
out of your depth
1 in water that is too deep to stand in
2 trying to do something that is too difficult for you

deputation *NOUN* **deputations**
a group of people sent as representatives of others

depute (*say* dip- **yoot**) *VERB* **deputes, deputing, deputed**
1 to appoint a person to do something ◆ *We deputed John to take the message.*
2 to assign or delegate a task to someone

WORD HISTORY from Old French *deputer*

deputize *VERB* **deputizes, deputizing, deputized**
to act as someone's deputy

USAGE NOTE This word can also be spelled deputise.

deputy *NOUN* **deputies**
a person appointed to act as a substitute for another

WORD HISTORY from French *député* 'deputed'

derail *VERB* **derails, derailing, derailed**
to make a train leave the tracks
▷ **derailment** *NOUN*

derailleur (*say* di- **ray**- ler) *NOUN* **derailleurs**
a device for changing gears on a bicycle which moves the chain from one gear wheel to another

WORD HISTORY from French *dérailler* 'to derail'

deranged *ADJECTIVE*
insane; wild and out of control
▷ **derangement** *NOUN*
WORD HISTORY from French *rang* 'rank'

derby (*say* **dar**- bi) *NOUN* **derbies**
1 a sports match between two teams from the same city or area
2 **the Derby** is an annual flat horse race, run on Epsom Downs in Surrey
WORD HISTORY from the Earl of *Derby*, who founded the Epsom Derby in 1780

deregulate *VERB* **deregulates, deregulating, deregulated**
to free something from regulations or controls
▷ **deregulation** *NOUN*

derelict (*say* **derri**- likt) *ADJECTIVE*
abandoned and left to fall into ruin
▷ **dereliction** *NOUN*
WORD HISTORY from Latin *derelinquere* 'to abandon completely', from *relinquere* 'to leave behind'

deride *VERB* **derides, deriding, derided**
to laugh at someone or something with contempt or scorn
WORD HISTORY from Latin *deridere* 'to laugh down', from *ridere* 'to laugh'

de rigueur (*say* der rig- **er**) *ADJECTIVE*
proper; required by custom or etiquette
WORD HISTORY a French phrase meaning 'of strictness'

derision *NOUN*
scorn or ridicule
▷ **derisive** (*say* dir- **y**- siv) *ADJECTIVE*
▷ **derisively** *ADVERB*

derisory *ADJECTIVE*
1 scornful; expressing contempt
2 so small that it is ridiculous ◆ *a derisory offer*

derivation *NOUN* **derivations**
1 the process of obtaining something from a source
2 (*Language*) the origin of a word from another language or from another word

derivative *ADJECTIVE*
derived from a source; not original

derivative *NOUN* **derivatives**
a thing that is derived from another

derive *VERB* **derives, deriving, derived**
1 to obtain something from a source ◆ *She derived great enjoyment from music.*
2 to originate from a language or from another word ◆ *Some English words are derived from Latin words.*
WORD HISTORY from Latin *derivare* 'to divert a channel of water', from *rivus* 'stream'

dermatitis *NOUN*
a disease that causes inflammation of the skin
WORD HISTORY from Greek *derma* 'skin'

dermatology *NOUN*
the study of the skin and its diseases
WORD FAMILY Someone who studies dermatology is a dermatologist.

dermis *NOUN*
the layer of skin below the epidermis
WORD HISTORY a Latin word, from Greek *derma* 'skin'

derogatory (*say* di- **rog**- at- er- ee) *ADJECTIVE*
scornful or disparaging
WORD HISTORY from Latin *derogare* 'to make smaller'

derrick *NOUN* **derricks**
1 a kind of crane with a pivoting arm
2 a tall framework which holds the machinery used for drilling an oil well
WORD HISTORY from an earlier meaning of 'gallows', because *Derrick* was the surname of a hangman in London around 1600

derv *NOUN*
diesel fuel for lorries and other vehicles
WORD HISTORY from the initials of '*d*iesel- *e*ngined *r*oad *v*ehicle'

dervish *NOUN* **dervishes**
a member of a Muslim religious order who vow to live a life of poverty
WORD HISTORY from Persian *darvish* 'poor'

descant *NOUN* **descants**
a tune sung or played in accompaniment to the main tune
WORD HISTORY from late Latin *discantus* 'refrain', from *cantus* 'song'

descend *VERB* **descends, descending, descended**
1 to go or come down
2 to slope or lead downwards ◆ *The path descended into a valley.*
3 you descend on someone when you surprise them with a sudden visit ◆ *I hope you don't mind us descending on you like this.*
4 to be descended from a person or family is to be related to them by birth in a direct line
WORD HISTORY from Old French *descendre*

descendant *NOUN* **descendants**
a person's descendant is someone who is descended from them by birth

descender *NOUN* **descenders**
(*Language*) a letter with a downward stroke that goes below the normal level of writing or printing, e.g. *g*, *j*, and *p*

descent *NOUN* **descents**
1 descending
2 a downward slope
3 a person's family origin ◆ *She is of French descent.*

a b c d e f g h i j k l m n o p q r s t u v w x y z

describe *VERB* **describes, describing, described**

1 to say what someone or something is like ◆ *How would you describe the painting?*

2 to give an account of events ◆ *Can you describe what happened?*

3 to draw or move in a particular shape ◆ *The orbit of the Earth around the Sun describes an ellipse.*

WORD HISTORY from Latin *describere* 'to write down', from *scribere* 'to write'

description *NOUN* **description**

1 the process of describing something or someone

2 an account or picture in words

3 a kind or class of something ◆ *There's no food left of any description.*

descriptive *ADJECTIVE*

giving a description; full of details

▷ **descriptively** *ADVERB*

desecrate (*say* dess- ik- rayt) *VERB* **desecrates, desecrating, desecrated**

to treat a sacred thing without respect

▷ **desecration** *NOUN*

▷ **desecrator** *NOUN*

desert (*say* dez- ert) *NOUN* **deserts**

(*Geography*) a large area of dry land, often covered with sand

desert (*say* diz- ert) *VERB* **deserts, deserting, deserted**

1 to leave a person or place without intending to return

2 to leave service in the armed forces without permission

▷ **deserter** *NOUN*

▷ **desertion** *NOUN*

WORD HISTORY from Latin *desertus* 'abandoned'

deserted *ADJECTIVE*

empty or abandoned

The bush slept: motionless: silent: apparently deserted. Drugged to immobility by the heat of the midday sun. — *James Vance Marshall, Walkabout*

desert island *NOUN* **desert islands**

an uninhabited island

deserts (*say* diz- erts) *PLURAL NOUN*

what a person deserves ◆ *He got his deserts.*

deserve *VERB* **deserves, deserving, deserved**

to have a right to something; to be worthy of something or someone

▷ **deservedly** *ADVERB*

WORD HISTORY from Latin *deservire* 'to serve someone well'

desiccated *ADJECTIVE*

desiccated coconut or other food has had all its moisture removed in order to preserve it

USAGE NOTE Take care to spell this word with one *s* and two *c*s.

WORD HISTORY from Latin *desiccare* 'to dry completely', from *siccus* 'dry'

design *NOUN* **designs**

1 lines and shapes that form a decoration; a pattern

Dr Fian chanted the next line of his litany, his wand tracing a design again as he chanted. — *Mollie Hunter, The Thirteenth Member*

2 (*D & T*) a drawing that shows how something is to be made

3 the way something is made or arranged ◆ *The design of the room was unusual.*

4 a plan or scheme in the mind

by design on purpose

to have designs on something is to plan to get hold of it

design *VERB* **designs, designing, designed**

1 to draw a design or plan for something

2 to plan or intend something for a special purpose ◆ *The course is designed for beginners.*

WORD HISTORY from Latin *designare* 'to mark out', from *signum* 'mark'

designate *VERB* **designates, designating, designated**

1 to give a name or title to something ◆ *It has been designated an area of outstanding natural beauty.*

2 to mark or point something out clearly ◆ *The river was designated as the western boundary.*

3 to appoint someone to a position ◆ *She designated me as her successor.*

▷ **designation** *NOUN*

designate *ADJECTIVE*

appointed to a job but not yet doing it ◆ *the bishop designate*

designer *NOUN* **designers**

1 someone who designs clothes or room furnishings

2 designer clothes are clothes made by a famous fashion designer

desirable *ADJECTIVE*

1 a desirable object is one that people want to own

2 a desirable action is one that is advisable to do

▷ **desirability** *NOUN*

▷ **desirably** *ADVERB*

desire *NOUN* **desires**

1 a feeling of wanting something very much

2 a request or wish ◆ *He expressed a desire to rest.*

▷ **desirous** *ADJECTIVE*

desire *VERB* **desires, desiring, desired**

to want something very much

WORD HISTORY from Latin *desiderare*

desist (*say* diz- **ist**) ***VERB*** **desists, desisting, desisted**
to stop doing something
WORD HISTORY from Latin *desistere*

desk ***NOUN*** **desks**
1 a piece of furniture with a flat top and often drawers, used when writing or doing work
2 a counter at which a cashier or receptionist sits
3 the section of a news organization dealing with specified topics ◆ *the sports desk*
WORD HISTORY from late Latin *desca*, from Latin *discus*, which originally meant 'disc' and later, because of the circular shape, 'plate or tray' and then 'table'

desktop ***NOUN*** **desktops**
a computer designed to be used on a desk

desktop publishing ***NOUN***
the production of books and magazines by using a computer and printer

desolate ***ADJECTIVE***
1 lonely and sad
2 uninhabited or barren
▷ **desolation** ***NOUN***
WORD HISTORY from Latin *desolare* 'to abandon', from *solus* 'alone', which is also the source of our word *solitary*

despair ***NOUN***
a feeling of hopelessness

despair ***VERB*** **despairs, despairing, despaired**
to lose all hope ◆ *I despaired of ever seeing her again.*
▷ **despairing** ***ADJECTIVE***
▷ **despairingly** ***ADVERB***
WORD HISTORY from Latin *desperare* 'to stop hoping', from *sperare* 'to hope'

despatch ***VERB*** **despatches, despatching, despatched**
another spelling of **dispatch**
▷ **despatch** ***NOUN***

desperado (*say* dess- per- **ah**- doh) ***NOUN*** **desperadoes**
a reckless criminal
WORD HISTORY coined in the 17th century and influenced by the Spanish word *desesperado* 'desperate'

desperate ***ADJECTIVE***
1 extremely serious or hopeless ◆ *a desperate situation*
2 you are desperate to get or do something, or are desperate for something, when you need or want it very much ◆ *They are desperate to get tickets.* ◆ *We were desperate for news.*
3 reckless and ready to do anything
▷ **desperately** ***ADVERB***
▷ **desperation** ***NOUN***

despicable ***ADJECTIVE***
deserving to be hated; contemptible
▷ **despicably** ***ADVERB***
WORD HISTORY from late Latin *despicari* 'to look down on'

despise ***VERB*** **despises, despising, despised**
to think someone or something is inferior or worthless
WORD HISTORY from Latin *despicere* 'to look down on' from *specere* 'to look', which is also the source of our word *spectacle*

despite ***PREPOSITION***
in spite of, notwithstanding

Despite many threats, Granny Weatherwax had never turned anyone into a frog. — *Terry Pratchett, Witches Abroad*

despondent ***ADJECTIVE***
sad or gloomy
▷ **despondently** ***ADVERB***
▷ **despondency** ***NOUN***
WORD HISTORY from Latin *despondere* 'to give up or resign'

despot (*say* **dess**- pot) ***NOUN*** **despots**
a ruler who has unrestricted power; a tyrant
▷ **despotism** ***NOUN***
WORD HISTORY from Greek *despotes* 'master'

despotic (*say* dis- **pot**- ik) ***ADJECTIVE***
exercising power in a cruel or oppressive way
▷ **despotically** ***ADVERB***

dessert (*say* diz- **ert**) ***NOUN*** **desserts**
fruit or a sweet food served as the last course of a meal
WORD HISTORY from French *desservir* 'to clear the table'

dessertspoon ***NOUN*** **dessertspoons**
a medium-sized spoon used for eating puddings, or as a measure for cooking

destination ***NOUN*** **destinations**
the place to which a person or thing is going or being sent

destined ***ADJECTIVE***
you are destined for something, or destined to do something, when you are chosen or set apart for that purpose, as if by fate

destiny ***NOUN*** **destinies**
what will happen or has happened to a person or thing, thought of as determined in advance by fate
WORD HISTORY from Latin *destinare* 'to fix or settle'

a b c d e f g h i j k l m n o p q r s t u v w x y z

destitute *ADJECTIVE*
1 living in extreme poverty
2 a place is destitute of something if it is lacking in it ◆ *On the horizon, the land was destitute of trees.*
▷ **destitution** *NOUN*
WORD HISTORY from Latin *destitutus* 'left in the lurch'

destroy *VERB* **destroys, destroying, destroyed**
1 to damage something so badly that it is completely spoiled
2 to put an end to something ◆ *It destroyed our chances.*
3 to kill an animal by humane means
WORD HISTORY via Old French from Latin *destruere* 'to unbuild', from *struere* 'to build', which is also the source of our word *structure*

destroyer *NOUN* **destroyers**
a small fast warship

destruction *NOUN*
1 the process of destroying or being destroyed
2 a cause of destruction or ruin ◆ *Greed was his destruction.*
▷ **destructive** *ADJECTIVE*

desultory (*say* dess- ul- ter- ee) *ADJECTIVE*
half-hearted, without enthusiasm or a definite plan
▷ **desultorily** *ADVERB*
WORD HISTORY from Latin *desultorius* 'like an acrobat', because acrobats leap about

detach *VERB* **detaches, detaching, detached**
to unfasten or separate something
▷ **detachable** *ADJECTIVE*

detached *ADJECTIVE*
1 separated; not connected
2 a detached house does not share any walls with another house
3 not emotionally involved in what is happening ◆ *As a journalist, I need to remain detached.*

detachment *NOUN* **detachments**
1 detaching or being detached
2 a small group of soldiers sent away from a larger group for a special duty

detail *NOUN* **details**
1 a very small part of a design, plan, or decoration
2 a small piece of information
3 a small group of soldiers or police officers given a special duty
in detail describing or dealing with everything fully
▷ **detailed** *ADJECTIVE*
WORD HISTORY from French *tailler* 'to cut in pieces'

detail *VERB* **details, detailing, detailed**
to give the details of something; to describe something fully

detain *VERB* **detains, detaining, detained**
1 to keep someone waiting
2 to keep someone at a police station or prison
WORD HISTORY via Old French from Latin *detinere* 'to hold back', from *tenere* 'to hold'

detainee *NOUN* **detainees**
a person who is officially detained or kept in custody

detect *VERB* **detects, detecting, detected**
to discover something
▷ **detection** *NOUN*
▷ **detector** *NOUN*
WORD HISTORY from Latin *detegere* 'to uncover', from *tegere* 'to cover'

detective *NOUN* **detectives**
a police officer or other person who investigates crimes

detective story *NOUN* **detective stories**
a story that describes a crime and its investigation

detention *NOUN* **detentions**
1 detaining or being detained
2 being made to stay late in school as a punishment

deter *VERB* **deters, deterring, deterred**
to discourage or prevent someone from doing something from fear of the consequences
WORD HISTORY from Latin *deterrere* 'to frighten away' from *terrere* 'to frighten'

detergent *NOUN* **detergents**
a chemical substance used for cleaning or washing things
WORD HISTORY from Latin *detergere* 'to wipe away' from *tergere* 'to wipe'

deteriorate (*say* dit- eer- ee- er- ayt) *VERB* **deteriorates, deteriorating, deteriorated**
to become worse
▷ **deterioration** *NOUN*
WORD HISTORY from Latin *deterior* 'worse'

determination *NOUN*
1 the firm intention to achieve what you have decided to achieve
2 determining or deciding something

determine *VERB* **determines, determining, determined**
1 you determine to do something when you decide definitely to do it ◆ *He determined to go.*
2 to cause or influence something ◆ *Where you live can determine your state of health.*
3 to find out or calculate something ◆ *Can you determine the height of the mountain?*
WORD HISTORY from Latin *determinare* 'to set the limits of', from *terminus* 'limit'

determined ***ADJECTIVE***
full of determination; with your mind firmly made up

Christopher scuffed one shoe against the other. He was determined not to surrender. — *Anne Fine, Madame Doubtfire*

▷ **determinedly** ***ADVERB***

determiner ***NOUN*** **determiners**
(*Grammar*) a word that gives information about a noun, for example *a*, *the*, *this*, *every*, *some*

determiners

Nouns often have a **determiner** in front of them. The most common determiners are the words *the*, *a*, or *an*, which are known as the **definite article** (*the*) and the **indefinite article** (*a* or *an*). The following words are also determiners when they come before a noun:
- *this*, *that*, *these*, and *those* (known as **demonstratives**), e.g. *this weekend*, *those boots*;
- *my*, *your*, *his*, *her*, *its*, *our*, and *their* (known as **possessives**), e.g. *That's my idea; It's your problem*;
- *what*, *which*, and *whose* (known as **interrogatives**), e.g. *What flavours do you have? Which team won?*

Other determiners, such as *all*, *another*, *any*, *both*, *each*, *every*, *few*, *many*, *some*, and *several*, are used to express quantity, e.g. *Both socks are missing; Few people have seen a yeti*. Note that *any* and *some* can refer to either a number of separate things (*any coins*, *some biscuits*), or to an amount of something (*any money*, *some cake*).
Numbers can also be determiners when they come before a noun, e.g. *one slice*, *thirty euros*, as can the words *next* and *last*, e.g. *next season*, *last summer*.
See also the panels on **definite and indefinite articles** and **possessives**.

deterrent ***NOUN*** **deterrents**
something that may deter people, such as a nuclear weapon that deters other countries from making war on one that has it

▷ **deterrence** ***NOUN***

detest ***VERB*** **detests, detesting, detested**
to dislike someone or something very much

Peter Watson was always the enemy. Ernie and Raymond detested him because he was nearly everything that they were not. — *Roald Dahl, The Swan*

▷ **detestable** ***ADJECTIVE***
▷ **detestably** ***ADVERB***
▷ **detestation** ***NOUN***

WORD HISTORY from an earlier meaning 'to curse', from Latin *detestari* 'to denounce', from *testis* 'witness'

detonate (*say* **det**- on- ayt) ***VERB*** **detonates, detonating, detonated**
1 a bomb or missile detonates when it explodes
2 to detonate an explosive device is to make it explode

▷ **detonation** ***NOUN***
▷ **detonator** ***NOUN***

WORD HISTORY from Latin *detonare* 'to thunder down' from *tonare* 'to thunder'

detour (*say* **dee**- toor) ***NOUN*** **detours**
a roundabout route instead of the normal one

WORD HISTORY from French *détour*, from *détourner* 'to turn away'

detoxify ***VERB*** **detoxifies, detoxifying, detoxified**
to rid your body of harmful substances, such as alcohol or caffeine

▷ **detoxification** ***NOUN***

USAGE NOTE The noun is sometimes shortened to *detox* in informal use.

detract ***VERB*** **detracts, detracting, detracted**
something detracts from a feeling or experience when it lessens or diminishes it
◆ *Not even the rain could detract from our pleasure.*

▷ **detraction** ***NOUN***

WORD HISTORY from Latin *detrahere* 'to pull away', from *trahere* 'to pull'

detriment (*say* **det**- rim- ent) ***NOUN***
something is to the detriment of a person or their well-being if it is harmful or damaging to them ◆ *She worked long hours, to the detriment of her health.*

WORD HISTORY from Latin *detrimentum* 'worn away'

detrimental (*say* det- rim- **en**- tal) ***ADJECTIVE***
harmful or disadvantageous

▷ **detrimentally** ***ADVERB***

detritus (*say* di- **try**- tus) ***NOUN***
rubbish or debris

WORD HISTORY a Latin word, related to *detriment*

de trop (*say* der **troh**) ***ADJECTIVE***
not wanted; unwelcome

WORD HISTORY a French phrase meaning 'too much'

deuce ***NOUN*** **deuces**
a score in tennis where both sides have 40 points and must gain two consecutive points to win

WORD HISTORY from Old French *deus* 'two'

devalue ***VERB*** **devalues, devaluing, devalued**
1 to reduce the value of something
2 to reduce the value of a country's currency in relation to other currencies or to gold

▷ **devaluation** ***NOUN***

devastate *VERB* **devastates, devastating, devastated**
1 to ruin or cause great destruction to something
2 to overwhelm someone with shock or grief
▷ **devastating** *ADJECTIVE*
▷ **devastation** *NOUN*

WORD HISTORY from Latin *devastare* 'to lay waste completely' from *vastus* 'waste'

develop *VERB* **develops, developing, developed**
1 to create or improve something gradually

One really useful skill you can develop is 'getting the feel' of when an answer is right. — *Kjartan Poskitt, Murderous Maths*

2 to become bigger or better
3 to come gradually into existence ◆ *A storm was developing on the horizon.*
4 to begin to show or suffer from something ◆ *They developed bad habits.*
5 to use an area of land for building houses, shops, or factories
6 to treat photographic film with chemicals so that pictures appear
▷ **developer** *NOUN*

WORD HISTORY from French *développer*

developing country *NOUN* **developing countries**
a poor country that is building up its industry and trying to improve its living conditions

development *NOUN* **developments**
1 developing or being developed
2 a recent event that changes a situation
3 an area of land with new buildings on it

deviant (*say* **dee**- vee- ant) *ADJECTIVE*
deviant behaviour is contrary to what is accepted as normal or usual

deviate (*say* **dee**- vee- ayt) *VERB* **deviates, deviating, deviated**
1 to turn aside from a path or course
2 to differ from normal behaviour or practice
▷ **deviation** *NOUN*

WORD HISTORY from Latin *deviare*, from *via* 'way'

device *NOUN* **devices**
1 a thing that is made or used for a particular purpose
2 a design used as an emblem or signature

He signed the postcard with his private device: an elongated cat, supposed to be a tom. It signified Tom Long. — *Philippa Pearce, Tom's Midnight Garden*

to leave someone to their own devices is to leave them to do as they wish

WORD HISTORY related to *devise*

devil *NOUN* **devils**
1 an evil spirit
2 in Jewish and Christian belief, **the Devil** is the supreme spirit of evil and enemy of God
3 a wicked, cruel, or annoying person
4 (*informal*) a person ◆ *You lucky devil!*

WORD HISTORY Old English *deofol*, via Latin from Greek *diabolos* which originally meant 'slanderer' or 'someone who throws things across' and is related to our word *ballistic*

devilish *ADJECTIVE*
extremely cruel or cunning

devilment *NOUN*
wicked or mischievous behaviour

devil's advocate *NOUN*
a person who tests a theory by putting forward possible objections to it

devious (*say* **dee**- vee- us) *ADJECTIVE*
1 a devious route is roundabout and not direct
2 a devious person or plan is underhand and cunning
▷ **deviously** *ADVERB*
▷ **deviousness** *NOUN*

devise *VERB* **devises, devising, devised**
to invent or plan something

WORD HISTORY from Old French *deviser*

devoid *ADJECTIVE*
a person or thing that is devoid of something is lacking in it ◆ *His work is devoid of merit.*

WORD HISTORY from Old French *voider* 'to make void'

devolution *NOUN*
the process of handing over power from central government to local or regional government

devolve *VERB* **devolves, devolving, devolved**
1 to hand over power from central government to local or regional government
2 a task or power devolves on a deputy or successor when it is passed on to them

WORD HISTORY from Latin *devolvere* 'to roll down'

devote *VERB* **devotes, devoting, devoted**
to give something completely for a particular activity or purpose ◆ *He devoted all his time to sport.*

WORD HISTORY from Latin *devovere* 'to dedicate with a vow'

devoted *ADJECTIVE*
very loving or loyal
▷ **devotedly** *ADVERB*

devotee (*say* dev- o- **tee**) *NOUN* **devotees**
a person who is devoted to something; an enthusiast

devotion *NOUN*
1 great love or loyalty
2 religious worship

devour *VERB* **devours, devouring, devoured**
1 to eat food hungrily or greedily

After they had devoured the nuts and drunk the lemonade they discussed who would write what for the Gazette. — *Michelle Magorian, Goodnight Mister Tom*

2 to destroy something completely
3 to look at, or listen to, something eagerly ◆ *They sat quietly, devouring the story.*

WORD HISTORY from Latin *devorare* 'to swallow down', from *vorare* 'to swallow'

devout *ADJECTIVE*
earnestly religious or sincere
▷ **devoutly** *ADVERB*
▷ **devoutness** *NOUN*

WORD HISTORY related to *devote*

dew *NOUN*
tiny drops of water that form during the night on the ground or outside surfaces

WORD HISTORY from Old English *deaw*

dewdrop *NOUN* **dewdrops**
a drop of dew

dewy *ADJECTIVE* **dewier, dewiest**
covered with dew; moist

dewy-eyed
1 feeling sentimental or nostalgic
2 childishly innocent ◆ *dewy-eyed optimism*

dexterity (*say* deks- **terri**- tee) *NOUN*
skill in handling things
▷ **dexterous** *ADJECTIVE*

WORD HISTORY from Latin *dexter* which meant both 'skilful' and 'on the right-hand side', because the right hand was thought of as the stronger hand

dhal *NOUN*
an Indian dish of cooked lentils

WORD HISTORY from Hindi *dal*, with the same meaning

dharma *NOUN*
in Hinduism, the eternal law of the cosmos

WORD HISTORY a Sanskrit word meaning 'decree'

dhoti *NOUN* **dhotis**
a loincloth worn by male Hindus

WORD HISTORY from a Hindi word

diabetes (*say* dy- a- **bee**- teez) *NOUN*
a disease in which there is too much sugar in a person's blood

diabetic (*say* dy- a- **bet**- ik) *ADJECTIVE*
to do with, or suffering from, diabetes

diabetic *NOUN* **diabetics**
a person who suffers from diabetes

WORD HISTORY via Latin from Greek *diabētēs* 'siphon'

diabolical *ADJECTIVE*
1 like a devil; very wicked
2 very clever or annoying ◆ *a diabolical crossword puzzle*

WORD HISTORY from Latin *diabolus*

diabolo (*say* di- **a**- bol- o) *NOUN* **diabolos**
a game in which a top is spun on a string between two sticks

WORD HISTORY an Italian word meaning 'devil'

diadem (*say* **dy**- a- dem) *NOUN* **diadems**
a crown or headband worn by a royal person

WORD HISTORY from Greek *diadēma*, from *diadein* 'to bind around'

diagnose *VERB* **diagnoses, diagnosing, diagnosed**
to find out what disease a person has or what is wrong ◆ *Typhoid fever was diagnosed in six patients.*

WORD HISTORY from Greek *gignōskein* 'to know'

diagnosis (*say* diy- ag- **noh**- sis) *NOUN* **diagnoses**
the naming of a disease or other condition after observing its signs and symptoms
▷ **diagnostic** *ADJECTIVE*

diagonal (*say* dy- **ag**- on- al) *ADJECTIVE*
slanting, crossing from corner to corner
▷ **diagonally** *ADVERB*

diagonal *NOUN* **diagonals**
a straight line joining opposite corners

WORD HISTORY from Greek *gōnia* 'angle'

diagram *NOUN* **diagrams**
a drawing or picture that shows the parts of something or how it works
▷ **diagramatic** *ADJECTIVE*
▷ **diagramatically** *ADVERB*

dial *NOUN* **dials**
1 a disc marked with a series of letters or numbers, used for measuring something
2 a disc on a radio set which is turned to choose a wavelength
3 the face of a clock or watch

dial *VERB* **dials, dialling, dialled**
to telephone a person or place by selecting the numbers on a telephone dial or keypad

WORD HISTORY from Latin *diale* 'clock-face', from *dies* 'day'

dialect *NOUN* **dialects**
(*Language*) the words and pronunciations used by people in one district but not in the rest of a country

WORD HISTORY from Greek *dialektos* 'way of speaking'

dialogue *NOUN* **dialogues**
1 the words spoken by characters in a play, film, or story
2 (*Language*) a spoken or printed conversation

USAGE NOTE In Computing, it is usual to use the American spelling *dialog*; e.g. *dialog box*.

WORD HISTORY from Greek *dialogos*

dialysis (*say* dy- **al**- iss- iss) *NOUN*
a way of removing harmful substances from a person's blood by passing it through a machine
WORD HISTORY from Greek *dialusis* 'loosening', from *luein* 'to loosen'

diameter (*say* dy- **am**- it- er) *NOUN* **diameters**
1 (*Mathematics*) a line drawn straight across a circle or sphere and passing through its centre
2 the length of this line
WORD HISTORY from Greek *diametros* 'measuring across'

diametrical *ADJECTIVE*
something that is the diametrical opposite of another thing is its complete opposite
▷ **diametrically** *ADVERB*

diamond *NOUN* **diamonds**
1 a very hard precious stone formed from pure crystallized carbon
2 a shape with four equal sides and four angles that are not right angles
3 a playing card of the suit marked with red diamond shapes
WORD HISTORY from Old French *diamant*, from Greek *adamas* 'unbreakable', which is also the source of our word *adamant*

diamond jubilee *NOUN* **diamond jubilees**
the 60th anniversary of an event

diamond wedding *NOUN* **diamond weddings**
a couple's 60th wedding anniversary

diaper *NOUN* **diapers**
(*American*) a baby's nappy
WORD HISTORY from Greek *diaspros* 'made of white cloth'

diaphanous (*say* dy- **af**- an- us) *ADJECTIVE*
diaphanous fabric is thin, light, and almost transparent
WORD HISTORY from Greek *phainein* 'to show'

diaphragm (*say* **dy**- a- fram) *NOUN* **diaphragms**
1 a muscular layer inside your body that separates your chest from your abdomen and is used in breathing
2 a dome-shaped contraceptive cap which fits over the neck of the womb
3 a device for varying the aperture of a camera lens
WORD HISTORY from Greek *phragma* 'fence'

diarist *NOUN* **diarists**
a person who keeps a diary

diarrhoea (*say* dy- a- **ree**- a) *NOUN*
frequent and watery emptying of the bowels
WORD HISTORY from Greek *rhoia* 'a flow'

diary *NOUN* **diaries**
a book in which someone writes down what happens each day
WORD HISTORY from Latin *dies* 'day'

diaspora (*say* dy- **ass**- per- a) *NOUN* **diasporas**
the movement and dispersal of a people from their native country
WORD HISTORY from Greek *diaspeirein* 'to disperse', from *sperein* 'to sow or scatter' which is also the source of our word *sperm*

diatribe (*say* **dy**- a- tryb) *NOUN* **diatribes**
a strong verbal attack
WORD HISTORY via French from Greek *diatribē* 'discourse, discussion'. A *diatribe* was originally a learned discourse; it developed its modern, more negative, meaning in the 19th century.

dice *NOUN*
a small cube marked with dots (1 to 6) on its sides, used in games
USAGE NOTE *Dice* was originally the plural of *die*, but now it is often used as a singular, with the plural *dice*. The old singular *die* is now mainly used in the phrase *the die is cast*.

dice *VERB* **dices, dicing, diced**
1 to cut meat, vegetables, etc. into small cubes for cooking
2 to play gambling games using dice

dicey (*say* **dy**- see) *ADJECTIVE* **dicier, diciest**
(*informal*) risky or unreliable
WORD HISTORY so called because of the risks involved in gambling with dice

dichotomy (*say* dy- **kot**- o- mi) *NOUN* **dichotomies**
a separation into two contrasting or opposing parts ◆ *a dichotomy between his public and private lives*
WORD HISTORY from Greek *dikhotomia* 'cutting in two', from *temnein* 'to cut'

dictate *VERB* **dictates, dictating, dictated**
1 to speak or read something aloud for someone else to write down
2 to state or order something with authority ◆ *We are in a strong enough position to dictate terms.*
3 to give orders in a bossy way
▷ **dictation** *NOUN*
WORD HISTORY from Latin *dictare* 'to keep saying'

dictates (*say* **dik**- tayts) *PLURAL NOUN*
rules or principles that must be obeyed ◆ *the dictates of fashion*

dictator *NOUN* **dictators**
1 a ruler who has unlimited power
2 a domineering person
▷ **dictatorship** *NOUN*

dictatorial *ADJECTIVE*
exercising power in a cruel or oppressive way

diction *NOUN*
1 a person's way of speaking words ◆ *clear diction*
2 a writer's choice of words
WORD HISTORY from Latin *dictio* 'saying, word'

dictionary *NOUN* **dictionaries**
a book that lists words in alphabetical order, and explains what they mean or gives their equivalents in another language
WORD HISTORY from Latin *dictio* 'word'
WORD FAMILY Writing or editing dictionaries is lexicography, and someone who does this is a lexicographer.

did *past tense of* **do**

didactic (*say* dy- **dak**- tik) *ADJECTIVE*
a didactic piece of writing or speech is meant to teach something or make a point
▷ **didactically** *ADVERB*
WORD HISTORY from Greek *didaktikos* 'teaching'

diddle *VERB* **diddles, diddling, diddled**
(*informal*) to cheat or swindle someone

didn't
short for *did not*

die❶ *VERB* **dies, dying, died**
1 to stop living or existing
2 a machines dies when it stops working ◆ *The engine sputtered and died.*
3 a fire or flame dies when it goes out
to be dying for something or **to do something** (*informal*) is to want to have it, or to do it, very much ◆ *I'm dying for a drink.* ◆ *We are all dying to see you again.*
to die away a sound dies away when it becomes fainter
to die down a noise, disturbance, or pain dies down when it becomes quieter or less intense
to die out a species dies out when it becomes gradually extinct

die❷ *NOUN*
a dice: see the note at *dice*
WORD HISTORY from Old French *de*, from Latin *dare* 'to give or play'

die❸ *NOUN* **dies**
a device that stamps a design on coins or medals, or that cuts or moulds metal

diehard *NOUN* **diehards**
a person who obstinately refuses to give up old ideas or policies
WORD HISTORY from the phrase *die hard* meaning 'to die painfully'

diesel (*say* **dee**- zel) *NOUN* **diesels**
1 an engine that works by burning oil in compressed air
2 fuel for this kind of engine
WORD HISTORY from Rudolf *Diesel* (1858–1913), the German engineer who invented it

diet❶ *NOUN* **diets**
1 the sort of foods usually eaten by a person or animal ◆ *a vegetarian diet*
2 special meals that a person eats in order to be healthy or to reduce weight
▷ **dietary** *ADJECTIVE*

diet *VERB* **diets, dieting, dieted**
to keep to a diet, especially in order to control your weight
WORD HISTORY from Greek *diaita* 'way of life'

diet❷ *NOUN* **diets**
the parliament of certain countries, such as Japan
WORD HISTORY from Latin *dieta* 'day's business'

dietitian (*say* dy- it- **ish**- an) *NOUN* **dietitians**
an expert in diet and nutrition

differ *VERB* **differs, differing, differed**
1 two things differ when they are different from each other ◆ *The two accounts differ in some important details.*
2 to disagree in opinion
WORD HISTORY from Latin *differre* 'to carry apart', from *ferre* 'to carry'

difference *NOUN* **differences**
1 being different
2 the way in which things differ ◆ *There's a big difference between reading about China and actually going there.*
3 the remainder left after one number is subtracted from another ◆ *The difference between 8 and 3 is 5.*
4 a disagreement

different *ADJECTIVE*
1 unlike; not the same as another or others
2 not the same as before or as usual ◆ *Your hair looks different today.*
3 separate or distinct

> 'Now,' I said, 'we have two different people both loathing Lionel Pantaloon's guts this morning.'
> — *Roald Dahl, Vengeance Is Mine Inc.*

4 unusual or novel ◆ *The garden wasn't very interesting or different.*
▷ **differently** *ADVERB*
USAGE NOTE It is better to use *different from* rather than *different to* in written or formal language. The phrase *different than* is used in American English but not in standard British English.

differential *NOUN* **differentials**
1 a difference in wages between one group of workers and another
2 a differential gear

differential gear *NOUN* **differential gears**
a system of gears that makes a vehicle's driving wheels revolve at different speeds when going round corners

differentiate *VERB* **differentiates, differentiating, differentiated**
1 a feature that differentiates one thing from another is what makes them different from each other
2 to recognize differences between things; to distinguish things ◆ *We do not differentiate between them.*
▷ **differentiation** *NOUN*

difficult *ADJECTIVE*
1 needing a lot of effort or skill; not easy

The Duchessa regained her composure with some difficulty and began a story so improbable that Arianna found it difficult to take in. — *Mary Hoffman, Stravaganza: City of Masks*

2 full of problems or hardships ◆ *Things are a bit difficult just now.*
3 a difficult person is not easy to please or satisfy

WORD HISTORY from Latin *difficilis* 'not easy', from *facilis* 'easy'

difficulty *NOUN* **difficulties**
1 being difficult
2 something that causes a problem
3 a difficult state of affairs, trouble ◆ *They are in financial difficulties.*

diffident (*say* **dif**- id- ent) *ADJECTIVE*
shy and not self-confident; hesitating to put yourself or your ideas forward
▷ **diffidently** *ADVERB*
▷ **diffidence** *NOUN*

WORD HISTORY from Latin *diffidere* 'to distrust', from *fidere* 'to trust'; the original meaning of the word was 'distrustful'

diffract *VERB* **diffracts, diffracting, diffracted**
to break up a beam of light
▷ **diffraction** *NOUN*

WORD HISTORY from Latin *diffringere* 'to break apart', from *frangere* 'to break'

diffuse (*say* dif- **yooz**) *VERB* **diffuses, diffusing, diffused**
1 to spread something widely or thinly ◆ *The Internet is being used to diffuse knowledge.*
2 a liquid or gas diffuses when it slowly mixes with another liquid or gas
▷ **diffusion** *NOUN*

diffuse (*say* dif- **yooss**) *ADJECTIVE*
1 spread widely; not concentrated
2 using many words; not concise
▷ **diffusely** *ADVERB*
▷ **diffuseness** *NOUN*

WORD HISTORY from Latin *diffusus* 'spread out', from *fundere* 'to pour'

dig *VERB* **digs, digging, dug**
1 to break up and move soil using a tool or machine
2 to make a hole or tunnel by moving soil
3 to get something from the ground by digging ◆ *I spent the morning digging potatoes.*
4 to look for or find something by investigating ◆ *We dug up some facts.*
5 to poke or jab something sharply ◆ *Its claws dug into my hand.*

to dig in
1 an army digs in when it takes up a defensive position
2 (*informal*) you dig in when you start to eat a meal or food

to dig something up
1 you dig up a plant or other object when you remove it from the ground by digging
2 you dig up a fact or information when you discover it by investigating

to dig your heels in is to be stubborn and refuse to give way

dig *NOUN* **digs**
1 a piece of digging, especially an archaeological excavation
2 a thrust or poke ◆ *a dig in the ribs*
3 an unpleasant remark
▷ **digger** *NOUN*

digest (*say* dy- **jest**) *VERB* **digests, digesting, digested**
1 (*Biology*) your stomach digests food when it softens and breaks it down so that it can be absorbed into your body
2 to take information into your mind and think it over
▷ **digestible** *ADJECTIVE*

digest (*say* **dy**- jest) *NOUN* **digests**
a summary of news or information

WORD HISTORY from Latin *digerere* 'to distribute or dissolve'

digestion *NOUN*
1 (*Biology*) the process of digesting food
2 a person's ability to digest food

digestive *ADJECTIVE*
to do with digestion ◆ *the digestive system*

digestive *NOUN* **digestives**
a digestive biscuit

digestive biscuit *NOUN* **digestive biscuits**
a wholemeal biscuit

WORD HISTORY so called because it is supposed to be easy to digest

digit (*say* **dij**- it) *NOUN* **digits**
1 (*Mathematics*) any of the numbers from 0 to 9
2 a finger or toe

WORD HISTORY from Latin *digitus* 'finger or toe'

digital *ADJECTIVE*
1 to do with or using fingers
2 a digital watch or clock shows the time with a row of figures
3 a digital image or sound is represented as a series of binary digits
4 a digital camera or recorder records digital sound and images
▷ **digitally** *ADVERB*

a b c d e f g h i j k l m n o p q r s t u v w x y z

digitize *VERB* **digitizes, digitizing, digitized**
to convert information to a digital form, so that it can be used on a computer
▷ **digitization** *NOUN*

USAGE NOTE This word can also be spelled digitise.

dignified *ADJECTIVE*
having or showing dignity

dignitary *NOUN* **dignitaries**
an important official

dignity *NOUN*
1 a calm and serious or respectful way of behaving
2 being worthy of respect or honour ◆ *the dignity of labour*
beneath your dignity not considered worthy enough for you to do

WORD HISTORY from Latin *dignus* 'worthy'

digraph *NOUN* **digraphs**
(*Language*) a group of two letters forming one sound, e.g. *th* and *ey*

digress *VERB* **digresses, digressing, digressed**
to stray from the main subject
▷ **digression** *NOUN*
▷ **digressive** *ADJECTIVE*

WORD HISTORY from Latin *digredi* 'to step aside', from *gradus* 'step'

dike *NOUN* **dikes**
another spelling of **dyke**

diktat *NOUN* **diktats**
an order that must be obeyed

WORD HISTORY a German word, related to our word *dictate*

dilapidated *ADJECTIVE*
falling to pieces; in disrepair
▷ **dilapidation** *NOUN*

WORD HISTORY from Latin *dilapidare* 'to demolish or squander', from *lapis* 'stone'

dilate *VERB* **dilates, dilating, dilated**
1 to make something wider or larger
2 to become wider or larger
▷ **dilation** *NOUN*

WORD HISTORY from Latin *dilatare* 'to spread widely', from *latus* 'wide'

dilatory (*say* **dil**- at- er- ee) *ADJECTIVE*
slow in doing something; not prompt

WORD HISTORY from Latin *dilator* 'someone who delays'

dilemma (*say* dil- **em**- a) *NOUN* **dilemmas**
a situation where someone has to choose between two or more possible actions, either of which would bring difficulties

WORD HISTORY a Greek word meaning 'double proposal'

USAGE NOTE Take care not to use *dilemma* to mean simply a problem or difficult situation. A *dilemma* always involves choosing between two or more things.

dilettante (*say* di- li- **tan**- ti) *NOUN* **dilettantes**
someone who dabbles in a subject for enjoyment rather than serious study

WORD HISTORY an Italian word meaning 'lover of the arts', which was also the first meaning in English; from Italian *dilettare* 'to delight'

diligent (*say* **dil**- ij- ent) *ADJECTIVE*
1 hard-working; conscientious
2 done with care and effort ◆ *a diligent search*
▷ **diligently** *ADVERB*
▷ **diligence** *NOUN*

WORD HISTORY from Latin *diligens* 'careful, conscientious'

dill *NOUN*
a herb with feathery leaves and spicy seeds which are used to flavour pickles

WORD HISTORY from Old English *dile*

dilly-dally *VERB* **dilly-dallies, dilly-dallying, dilly-dallied**
(*informal*) to dawdle or hesitate

dilute *VERB* **dilutes, diluting, diluted**
1 to make a liquid weaker by adding water or other liquid to it
2 to weaken or reduce the force of something
▷ **dilution** *NOUN*

dilute *ADJECTIVE*
a dilute liquid is diluted

WORD HISTORY from Latin *diluere* 'to wash away'

dim *ADJECTIVE* **dimmer, dimmest**
1 not bright or clear; only faintly lit
2 indistinct, not vivid ◆ *I have only a dim memory of him.*
3 (*informal*) stupid; not intelligent
to take a dim view of something is to disapprove of it
▷ **dimly** *ADVERB*
▷ **dimness** *NOUN*

dim *VERB* **dims, dimming, dimmed**
1 to make something dim
2 to become dim ◆ *As the music started, the lights in the cinema dimmed.*
▷ **dimmer** *NOUN*

dimension *NOUN* **dimensions**
1 a measurement such as length, width, area, or volume ◆ *What are the dimensions of the room?*
2 the dimensions of something are the size or extent of it
3 an aspect or feature ◆ *It adds a new dimension to the team.*
▷ **dimensional** *ADJECTIVE*

WORD HISTORY from Latin *dimensio* 'measuring out'

diminish *VERB* **diminishes, diminishing, diminished**
1 to make something smaller or less
2 to become smaller or less
▷ **diminution** *NOUN*

diminutive (*say* dim- **in**- yoo- tiv) ***ADJECTIVE***
very small
▷ **diminutively** ***ADVERB***
WORD HISTORY from Latin *diminuere* 'to lessen'

dimple ***NOUN*** **dimples**
1 a small natural hollow on the skin of a person's cheek or chin
2 a small hollow or dip in a surface
▷ **dimpled** ***ADJECTIVE***

dim sum ***NOUN***
a Chinese dish of small steamed or fried savoury dumplings
WORD HISTORY from Chinese (Cantonese) *tim sam* 'small heart'

din ***NOUN***
a loud annoying noise
WORD HISTORY from Old English *dyne*

dine ***VERB*** **dines, dining, dined**
(*formal*) to have dinner
▷ **diner** ***NOUN***
WORD HISTORY from Old French *disner*

diner ***NOUN*** **diners**
1 a person who is dining
2 (*American*) a small inexpensive restaurant

dinghy (*say* **ding**- ee) ***NOUN*** **dinghies**
a small open boat driven by oars or sails
WORD HISTORY from Hindi *dingi* 'a small river boat'

dingo ***NOUN*** **dingoes**
an Australian wild dog
WORD HISTORY from an Australian Aboriginal word

dingy (*say* **din**- jee) ***ADJECTIVE*** **dingier, dingiest**
looking gloomy and drab ◆ *The room was all dark and dingy inside.*
▷ **dingily** ***ADVERB***
▷ **dinginess** ***NOUN***

dinky ***ADJECTIVE*** **dinkier, dinkiest**
attractively small and neat

There were dinky little bottles of shampoo and bath foam so we had the bath brimming with bubbles. — *Jacqueline Wilson, Lola Rose*

WORD HISTORY from a Scots and northern English dialect word *dink* 'neat or trim'

dinner ***NOUN*** **dinners**
1 the main meal of the day, either at midday or in the evening
2 a formal evening meal in honour of something

dinosaur (*say* **dy**- noss- or) ***NOUN*** **dinosaurs**
1 a prehistoric reptile, often of enormous size
2 a person or organization that has become out of date
WORD HISTORY from Greek *deinos* 'terrible' and *sauros* 'lizard'

dint ***NOUN*** **dints**
by dint of by means of; using
WORD HISTORY from Old English *dynt* 'stroke, blow'

diocese (*say* **dy**- oss- iss) ***NOUN*** **dioceses**
a district under the care of a bishop in the Christian Church
▷ **diocesan** (*say* dy- **oss**- iss- an) ***ADJECTIVE***
WORD HISTORY from Latin *dioecesis* 'governor's jurisdiction'

dioxide ***NOUN***
(*Science*) an oxide with two atoms of oxygen to one of another element ◆ *carbon dioxide*

dip ***VERB*** **dips, dipping, dipped**
1 to lower something into liquid
2 to lower or move something downwards ◆ *dip the wing tips*
3 to lower the beam of a vehicle's headlights
4 to move or slope downwards ◆ *The sun dipped below the horizon.* ◆ *The road dips after the bend.*
5 to become lower or smaller ◆ *Attendances have dipped this month.*
6 to dip into something is to use a little of it ◆ *He had to dip into his savings when he lost his job.*

dip ***NOUN*** **dips**
1 dipping
2 a downward slope
3 a quick swim
4 a creamy mixture into which pieces of food are dipped before eating
5 a disinfectant liquid for washing sheep

diphtheria (*say* dif- **theer**- ee- a) ***NOUN***
a serious disease that causes inflammation in the throat
WORD HISTORY from Greek *diphthera* 'leather, hide', because the disease causes tough skin to form on the throat

diphthong (*say* **dif**- thong) ***NOUN*** **diphthongs**
(*Language*) a compound vowel sound made up of two sounds; for example, *oi* in *point* or *ou* in *loud*
WORD HISTORY from Latin *diphthongus* 'two sounds', from Greek *phthongos* 'sound'

diplodocus (*say* di- **plod**- o- kus) ***NOUN*** **diplodocuses**
a large dinosaur with a long slender neck and tail, which fed on plants
WORD HISTORY from Greek *diplous* 'double' and *dokos* 'wooden beam', because of its enormous size

diploma ***NOUN*** **diplomas**
a certificate awarded by a college or university to a person who has successfully completed a course of study
WORD HISTORY a Latin word for an official letter given to travellers, saying who they were; from a Greek word meaning 'folded paper'

diplomacy *NOUN*
1 the work of making agreements with other countries
2 skill in dealing with people and gently persuading them to agree to things; tact

diplomat *NOUN* **diplomats**
1 a person who represents their country officially abroad
2 a tactful person

diplomatic *ADJECTIVE*
1 to do with diplomats or diplomacy
2 tactful; careful not to offend people

▷ **diplomatically** *ADVERB*

WORD HISTORY from an original meaning 'to do with official documents', from *diploma*

dipper *NOUN* **dippers**
1 a kind of bird that dives for its food
2 a ladle or scoop

dire *ADJECTIVE*
1 extremely serious or urgent ◆ *There is a dire need for more aid in the area.*
2 (*informal*) of poor quality ◆ *It was a dire performance.*

to be in dire straits is to be in deep trouble or difficulty

WORD HISTORY from Latin *dirus* 'fearful, threatening'

direct *ADJECTIVE*
1 a direct road or journey goes from one place to another without changing direction
2 direct contact or communication is between two people or groups with no one in between
3 a direct person or manner is very frank and goes straight to the point
4 something that is the direct opposite of another thing is its complete opposite

▷ **directness** *NOUN*

direct *ADVERB*
by a direct route ◆ *We flew there direct.*

direct *VERB* **directs, directing, directed**
1 to tell or show someone the way
2 to guide or aim something in a certain direction
3 to control or manage someone or something ◆ *There was no one to direct the workmen.*
4 you direct someone to do something when you order them to do it

WORD HISTORY from Latin *directus* 'kept straight'

direct current *NOUN*
electric current flowing only in one direction

direct debit *NOUN*
an arrangement with a bank which allows bills to be paid directly from your account

direction *NOUN* **directions**
1 the line along which something moves or faces
2 directing or managing people

▷ **directional** *ADJECTIVE*

directions *PLURAL NOUN*
information on how to use or do something or how to get somewhere

directive *NOUN* **directives**
an official command

directly *ADVERB, CONJUNCTION*
1 by a direct route ◆ *You can instruct your bank to make payments directly from your account.*
2 immediately ◆ *I want you to come directly.*
3 as soon as ◆ *I went directly I knew.*

direct object *NOUN* **direct objects**
(*Grammar*) the word that receives the action of the verb. In *she hit him*, *him* is the direct object.

director *NOUN* **directors**
1 a person who is in charge of something, especially one of a group of people managing a company
2 (*Drama*) a person who decides how a film, programme, or play should be made or performed

▷ **directorial** *ADJECTIVE*

directory *NOUN* **directories**
1 a book containing a list of people with their telephone numbers, addresses, and other information
2 (*ICT*) a file containing a group of other files

WORD HISTORY from Latin *directorius* 'guiding'

direct speech *NOUN*
(*Grammar*) someone's words written down exactly in the way they were said, with speech marks as in *'I'm leaving,' she said.*

direct and indirect speech

Direct speech shows exactly what a person or character says. The spoken words—and any punctuation that goes with them, such as full stops, exclamation marks, or question marks—are enclosed in quotation marks:

'Wait! Can you at least tell me your name?' I shouted at the retreating figure.

Any description of who is speaking (e.g. *she said, I exclaimed*) is separated from the spoken words by a comma or commas:

'We are planning', said a NASA spokesperson, 'to send a manned expedition to Mars.'

Indirect speech is also called **reported speech.** It describes or reports what a person or character says without using their exact words. You do not use quotation marks in indirect speech and the tense of the verb (*were* in this example) follows that of the reporting verb (*said* in the example):

A NASA spokesperson said that they were planning to send a manned expedition to Mars.

You can also leave out the word *that* at the beginning of the reported speech:

A NASA spokesperson said they were planning to send a manned expedition to Mars.

See also the panels on **question marks** and **quotation marks.**

dirge *NOUN* **dirges**
a slow sad song
WORD HISTORY from Latin *dirige* 'guide', the first word of a song used in the Roman Catholic service for a dead person

dirigible (*say* **di**- rij- ib- al) *NOUN* **dirigibles**
a balloon or airship that can be steered
WORD HISTORY from Latin *dirigere* 'to direct or guide'

dirk *NOUN* **dirks**
a kind of dagger

dirt *NOUN*
1 an unclean substance
2 loose earth or soil
3 (*informal*) unpleasant or unkind remarks
WORD HISTORY from Old Norse *drit* 'excrement'

dirty *ADJECTIVE* **dirtier, dirtiest**
1 covered with an unclean substance; not clean
2 making someone become dirty ◆ *a dirty job*
3 unfair; dishonourable ◆ *a dirty trick*
4 indecent; obscene ◆ *a dirty magazine*
5 a dirty bomb or weapon produces a large amount of radioactive fallout
▷ **dirtily** *ADVERB*
▷ **dirtiness** *NOUN*

disability *NOUN* **disabilities**
a physical or mental condition that restricts someone's movements, senses, or activities

disable *VERB* **disables, disabling, disabled**
to stop something from working properly
▷ **disablement** *NOUN*

disabled *ADJECTIVE*
unable to use part of your body properly because of illness or injury

disabuse *VERB* **disabuses, disabusing, disabused**
you disabuse someone of a belief or idea when you show them that it is not true

disadvantage *NOUN* **disadvantages**
something that hinders or is unhelpful
▷ **disadvantaged** *ADJECTIVE*
▷ **disadvantageous** *ADJECTIVE*

disagree *VERB* **disagrees, disagreeing, disagreed**
1 to have or express a different opinion from someone
2 two people or groups disagree when they have different opinions about something

to disagree with someone
1 is to have a different opinion from them
2 food disagrees with you if it makes you feel ill
▷ **disagreement** *NOUN*
WORD HISTORY from Old French *desagreer*

disagreeable *ADJECTIVE*
1 unpleasant
2 a disagreeable person is unfriendly and bad-tempered
▷ **disagreeably** *ADVERB*

disallow *VERB* **disallows, disallowing, disallowed**
to refuse to accept something as valid ◆ *The goal was disallowed.*

disappear *VERB* **disappears, disappearing, disappeared**
1 to stop being visible; to vanish

The helicopter disappeared in a huge fireball, then plunged down. — *Anthony Horowitz, Point Blanc*

2 to stop existing
▷ **disappearance** *NOUN*

disappoint *VERB* **disappoints, disappointing, disappointed**
to fail to do what someone hoped for or expected
▷ **disappointment** *NOUN*
WORD HISTORY from an earlier meaning 'to dismiss someone from an important position'

disapprove *VERB* **disapproves, disapproving, disapproved**
to have an unfavourable opinion of someone or something
▷ **disapproval** *NOUN*

disarm *VERB* **disarms, disarming, disarmed**
1 to reduce the size of armed forces
2 to take away someone's weapons
3 to overcome someone's doubts or suspicions
WORD HISTORY from Old French *desarmer*

disarmament *NOUN*
reduction of a country's armed forces or weapons

disarray *NOUN*
disorder; untidiness

disassemble *VERB* **disassembles, disassembling, disassembled**
(*D & T*) to take something apart or into pieces
▷ **disassembly** *NOUN*

disaster *NOUN* **disasters**
1 a very bad accident or misfortune
2 a complete failure
▷ **disastrous** *ADJECTIVE*
▷ **disastrously** *ADVERB*
WORD HISTORY meaning literally 'unlucky star', from Latin *astrum* 'star'

disavow *VERB* **disavows, disavowing, disavowed**
to deny any knowledge of or responsibility for something
▷ **disavowal** *NOUN*

disband *VERB* **disbands, disbanding, disbanded**
a group or organization disbands when it breaks up

disbelief *NOUN*
refusal or unwillingness to believe something

disbelieve *VERB* **disbelieves, disbelieving, disbelieved**
to refuse or be unable to believe something
▷ **disbeliever** *NOUN*

disburse *VERB* **disburses, disbursing, disbursed**
to pay out money
▷ **disbursal** *NOUN*
▷ **disbursement** *NOUN*

WORD HISTORY from French *bourse* 'purse'

disc *NOUN* **discs**
1 a flat circular shape or object
2 a CD or DVD
3 a layer of cartilage between vertebrae in your spine

WORD HISTORY from Latin *discus* 'disc'

USAGE NOTE In Computing, it is usual to use the American spelling *disk*.

discard *VERB* **discards, discarding, discarded**
to get rid of something because it is useless or unwanted

WORD HISTORY from an earlier meaning 'to throw out an unwanted playing card from a hand'

discern (*say* dis- **sern**) *VERB* **discerns, discerning, discerned**
to see or recognize something clearly
▷ **discernible** *ADJECTIVE*

WORD HISTORY from Latin *discernere* 'to separate off'

discerning *ADJECTIVE*
perceptive; showing good judgement
▷ **discernment** *NOUN*

discharge *VERB* **discharges, discharging, discharged**
1 to discharge someone from a hospital or other institution is to release or dismiss them
2 to send something out

The Martians are able to discharge enormous clouds of a black and poisonous vapour by means of rockets. — *H. G. Wells, The War of the Worlds*

3 to discharge a debt or promise is to pay it off or do what has been agreed

discharge *NOUN* **discharges**
1 discharging
2 something that is discharged

WORD HISTORY from Latin *discarricare* 'to unload'

disciple *NOUN* **disciples**
1 a follower or pupil of a leader, or of a religion or philosophy
2 (*Religion*) any of the original followers of Jesus Christ

WORD HISTORY from Latin *discipulus* 'learner'

disciplinarian *NOUN* **disciplinarians**
a person who believes in strict discipline

discipline *NOUN* **disciplines**
1 training that produces orderly and obedient behaviour
2 self-control; obedience
3 a discipline is a subject for study
▷ **disciplinary** (*say* **dis**- ip- lin- er- ee) *ADJECTIVE*

discipline *VERB* **disciplines, disciplining, disciplined**
1 to train someone to be orderly and obedient
2 to punish someone

WORD HISTORY from Latin *disciplina* 'training'

disc jockey *NOUN* **disc jockeys**
a person who introduces and plays records on the radio or at a disco

disclaim *VERB* **disclaims, disclaiming, disclaimed**
to disclaim responsibility for, or knowledge of, something is to say that it has nothing to do with you
▷ **disclaimer** *NOUN*

WORD HISTORY from Old French *desclamer*

disclose *VERB* **discloses, disclosing, disclosed**
you disclose a fact or information when you reveal it or make it known
▷ **disclosure** *NOUN*

WORD HISTORY from Old French *desclore* 'to open up'

disco *NOUN* **discos**
(*informal*) a party or club where people dance to pop music

WORD HISTORY short for *discotheque*

discolour *VERB* **discolours, discolouring, discoloured**
to spoil or change the colour of something
▷ **discoloration** *NOUN*

WORD HISTORY from Latin *discolorare* from *colorare* 'to colour'

discomfit *VERB* **discomfits, discomfiting, discomfited**
to make someone feel uneasy; to disconcert someone
▷ **discomfiture** *NOUN*

WORD HISTORY from Old French *desconfit* 'defeated'

discomfort *NOUN*
1 slight pain
2 uneasiness or embarrassment

disconcert (*say* dis- kon- **sert**) *VERB* **disconcerts, disconcerting, disconcerted**
to make someone feel uneasy

It was disconcerting, having no idea of the time. He could have slept for a few hours or all night. — *Anthony Horowitz, Scorpia*

WORD HISTORY from French *desconcerter*

disconnect *VERB* **disconnects, disconnecting, disconnected**
1 to break a connection in a power supply
2 to break a telephone connection
▷ **disconnection** *NOUN*

disconnected *ADJECTIVE*
not joined together in a logical way or order ◆ *a disconnected narrative*

disconsolate (*say* dis- **kon**- sol- at) *ADJECTIVE*
unhappy at the loss of something
▷ **disconsolately** *ADVERB*

WORD HISTORY from Latin *disconsolatus* 'comfortless'

discontent *NOUN*
lack of contentment; dissatisfaction
▷ **discontented** *ADJECTIVE*
▷ **discontentment** *NOUN*

discontinue *VERB* **discontinues, discontinuing, discontinued**
1 to stop doing something
2 to stop producing a product for sale ◆ *That design has been discontinued.*

discord *NOUN* **discords**
1 disagreement; quarrelling
2 a combination of musical notes which produces a harsh or unpleasant sound
▷ **discordance** *NOUN*
▷ **discordant** *ADJECTIVE*

WORD HISTORY from Latin *discordia*, from *cordis* 'of the heart'

discotheque (*say* **dis**- ko- tek) *NOUN* **discotheques**
a disco

WORD HISTORY from French *discothèque* 'record- library'

discount *NOUN* **discounts**
an amount by which a price is reduced

discount *VERB* **discounts, discounting, discounted**
1 to ignore or disregard something ◆ *We cannot discount the possibility.*
2 to reduce something in price

discourage *VERB* **discourages, discouraging, discouraged**
1 to take away someone's enthusiasm or confidence
2 to try to persuade someone not to do something; to put someone off ◆ *The new software is designed to discourage spammers.*
3 to show disapproval of something ◆ *Smoking is discouraged.*
▷ **discouragement** *NOUN*

WORD HISTORY from Old French *descouragier*

discourse *NOUN* **discourses**
a formal speech or piece of writing about something

discourse *VERB* **discourses, discoursing, discoursed**
to speak or write at length about something

WORD HISTORY from Latin *discursus* 'running to and fro'

discourteous *ADJECTIVE*
not courteous or polite; rude
▷ **discourteously** *ADVERB*
▷ **discourtesy** *NOUN*

discover *VERB* **discovers, discovering, discovered**
1 to find or find out something, especially by searching
2 to be the first person to find something ◆ *Herschel discovered the planet Uranus.*
▷ **discoverer** *NOUN*

WORD HISTORY from Latin *discooperire* 'to uncover'

discovery *NOUN* **discoveries**
1 discovering or being discovered
2 something that is discovered

discredit *VERB* **discredits, discrediting, discredited**
1 to cause an idea or theory to be doubted
2 to damage someone's reputation
▷ **discreditable** *ADJECTIVE*

discredit *NOUN*
damage to someone's reputation

discreet *ADJECTIVE*
1 not giving away secret information ◆ *I'll make a few discreet enquiries.*
2 not showy
▷ **discreetly** *ADVERB*

USAGE NOTE Take care not to confuse this word with *discrete*, which means 'separate or distinct'.

WORD HISTORY from Latin *discernere* 'to be discerning'

discrepancy (*say* dis- **krep**- an- see) *NOUN* **discrepancies**
lack of agreement between things which should be the same ◆ *There are several discrepancies in the two accounts.*

WORD HISTORY from Latin *discrepantia* 'discord'

discrete *ADJECTIVE*
separate; distinct from each other

USAGE NOTE Take care not to confuse this word with *discreet*, which means 'not giving away secret information'.

WORD HISTORY from Latin *discretus* 'separated'

discretion (*say* dis- **kresh**- on) *NOUN*
1 being discreet; keeping secrets ◆ *I hope I can count on your discretion.*
2 freedom to decide things and take action according to your own judgement ◆ *You can use your discretion.*

discriminate *VERB* **discriminates, discriminating, discriminated**
1 to notice and understand the differences between things
2 to treat people differently or unfairly, usually because of their race, sex, age, or religion
▷ **discrimination** *NOUN*
▷ **discriminatory** *ADJECTIVE*
WORD HISTORY from Latin *discrimen* 'separator'

discus *NOUN* **discuses**
a thick heavy disc thrown in athletic contests
WORD HISTORY via Latin from Greek *diskos*

discuss *VERB* **discusses, discussing, discussed**
1 to examine a subject in speech or writing
2 to have a conversation in order to decide something ◆ *Let's discuss it later.*
▷ **discussion** *NOUN*
WORD HISTORY from Latin *discutere* 'to dash to pieces'

disdain *NOUN*
scorn or contempt
▷ **disdainful** *ADJECTIVE*
▷ **disdainfully** *ADVERB*

disdain *VERB* **disdains, disdaining, disdained**
1 to regard or treat someone or something with disdain
2 to refuse to do something because of disdain ◆ *She disdained to reply.*

disease *NOUN* **diseases**
an unhealthy condition; an illness in your body or mind
▷ **diseased** *ADJECTIVE*
WORD FAMILY The study of the causes and effects of disease is pathology.

disembark *VERB* **disembarks, disembarking, disembarked**
to get off a ship or aircraft
▷ **disembarkation** *NOUN*

disembodied *ADJECTIVE*
1 a disembodied soul or spirit is separated or freed from its body
2 a disembodied voice comes from an invisible or unknown source

disembowel *VERB* **disembowels, disembowelling, disembowelled**
to take out the bowels or inside parts of something

disenchanted *ADJECTIVE*
you are disenchanted with something if you no longer believe that it is worthwhile

disengage *VERB* **disengages, disengaging, disengaged**
to disconnect or detach something
▷ **disengagement** *NOUN*

disentangle *VERB* **disentangles, disentangling, disentangled**
1 to take the knots or tangles out of something; to untangle
2 to free something from difficulty or confusion
▷ **disentanglement** *NOUN*

disfavour *NOUN*
disapproval or dislike

disfigure *VERB* **disfigures, disfiguring, disfigured**
to spoil the appearance of a person or thing
▷ **disfigurement** *NOUN*
WORD HISTORY via Old French from Latin *figura* 'a shape'

disgorge *VERB* **disgorges, disgorging, disgorged**
to pour or send something out ◆ *The pipe disgorged its contents.*
WORD HISTORY from French *gorge* 'throat'

disgrace *NOUN*
1 shame; loss of approval or respect
2 something that is shameful or unacceptable ◆ *The bus service is a disgrace.*

disgrace *VERB* **disgraces, disgracing, disgraced**
to bring disgrace on someone
WORD HISTORY via French from Latin *gratia* 'grace'

disgraceful *ADJECTIVE*
shameful or unacceptable
▷ **disgracefully** *ADVERB*

disgruntled *ADJECTIVE*
discontented or resentful
WORD HISTORY from an old word *gruntle* 'to grunt softly'

disguise *VERB* **disguises, disguising, disguised**
1 to make a person or thing look different in order to deceive people
2 to conceal a feeling or emotion ◆ *She could not disguise her amazement.*

disguise *NOUN* **disguises**
something worn or used for disguising your identity

disgust *NOUN*
a feeling that something is very unpleasant or disgraceful

disgust *VERB* **disgusts, disgusting, disgusted**
to cause disgust in someone
▷ **disgusted** *ADJECTIVE*
WORD HISTORY via French or Italian from Latin *gustare* 'to taste', related to our word *gusto*

disgusting *ADJECTIVE*
causing disgust; extremely unpleasant ◆ *I couldn't eat the food. It looked disgusting.*

dish *NOUN* **dishes**
1 a plate or bowl for food
2 a meal of food ◆ *They specialize in vegetarian dishes.*
3 a bowl-shaped aerial for receiving satellite communications

dish *VERB* **dishes, dishing, dished**
to dish something out is to give it out in portions to several people

WORD HISTORY from Old English *disc*

dishcloth *NOUN* **dishcloths**
a cloth for washing dishes

dishearten *VERB* **disheartens, disheartening, disheartened**
to cause someone to lose hope or confidence
▷ **disheartening** *ADJECTIVE*

dishevelled (*say* dish- ev- eld) *ADJECTIVE*
ruffled and untidy in appearance
▷ **dishevelment** *NOUN*

WORD HISTORY from Old French *chevel* 'hair'

dishonest *ADJECTIVE*
not honest
▷ **dishonestly** *ADVERB*
▷ **dishonesty** *NOUN*

dishonour *NOUN*
loss of honour or respect; disgrace
▷ **dishonourable** *ADJECTIVE*
▷ **dishonourably** *ADVERB*

dishonour *VERB* **dishonours, dishonouring, dishonoured**
to bring dishonour or disgrace to someone

dishwasher *NOUN* **dishwashers**
a machine for washing dishes automatically

disillusion *VERB* **disillusions, disillusioning, disillusioned**
you disillusion someone if you show them that something they like to think is true is wrong or mistaken
▷ **disillusionment** *NOUN*

disincentive *NOUN* **disincentives**
something that discourages an action or effort

disinclination *NOUN*
unwillingness to do something

disinclined *ADJECTIVE*
you are disinclined to do something if you are unwilling to do it

disinfect *VERB* **disinfects, disinfecting, disinfected**
to destroy the germs in something
▷ **disinfection** *NOUN*

disinfectant *NOUN* **disinfectants**
a substance used for disinfecting things

disingenuous *ADJECTIVE*
not frank or sincere, especially because you pretend to know less about something than you really do
▷ **disingenuously** *ADVERB*

disinherit *VERB* **disinherits, disinheriting, disinherited**
to deprive a person of the right to inherit something

disintegrate *VERB* **disintegrates, disintegrating, disintegrated**
1 to break up into small parts or pieces
2 to weaken and fall apart ◆ *Their relationship disintegrated under the strain.*
▷ **disintegration** *NOUN*

disinter *VERB* **disinters, disinterring, disinterred**
to dig up something that is buried

disinterested *ADJECTIVE*
not influenced by the hope of gaining something yourself; impartial ◆ *She gave us some disinterested advice.*

USAGE NOTE Take care not to use this word to mean 'not interested' or 'bored'. If this is what you mean, use *uninterested.*

disjointed *ADJECTIVE*
disjointed speaking or writing is not well joined together and is difficult to understand

WORD HISTORY from Old French *disjoindre*

disk *NOUN* **disks**
1 the American spelling of **disc**
2 (*ICT*) a computer storage device consisting of magnetically coated plates

dislike *NOUN* **dislikes**
1 a feeling of not liking someone or something
2 something that you do not like ◆ *She listed her likes and dislikes.*

dislike *VERB* **dislikes, disliking, disliked**
to not like someone or something

dislocate *VERB* **dislocates, dislocating, dislocated**
a bone is dislocated when it moves or is forced from its proper position in one of your joints
▷ **dislocation** *NOUN*

WORD HISTORY from Latin *dislocare*, from *locare* 'to place'

dislodge *VERB* **dislodges, dislodging, dislodged**
to move or force something from its place

disloyal *ADJECTIVE*
not loyal
▷ **disloyally** *ADVERB*
▷ **disloyalty** *NOUN*

dismal ***ADJECTIVE***
1 gloomy or dreary
2 of poor quality; feeble ◆ *a dismal performance by the home team*
▷ **dismally** ***ADVERB***

WORD HISTORY from Latin *dies mali* 'unlucky days'

dismantle ***VERB*** **dismantles, dismantling, dismantled**
to take something to pieces

WORD HISTORY from Old French *manteler* 'to fortify'

dismay ***NOUN***
a feeling of surprise and discouragement
▷ **dismayed** ***ADJECTIVE***

dismember ***VERB*** **dismembers, dismembering, dismembered**
to tear or cut the limbs from a body

WORD HISTORY from Old French *desmembrer*

dismiss ***VERB*** **dismisses, dismissing, dismissed**
1 to send someone away
2 to tell someone that you will no longer employ them
3 to put something out of your thoughts because it is not worth thinking about
4 to get a batsman or cricket side out
▷ **dismissal** ***NOUN***

WORD HISTORY from Latin *dismissum* 'sent away'

dismissive ***ADJECTIVE***
you are dismissive of something if you feel or say that it is not worth considering
▷ **dismissively** ***ADVERB***

dismount ***VERB*** **dismounts, dismounting, dismounted**
to get off a bicycle or horse

disobedient ***ADJECTIVE***
not obedient
▷ **disobediently** ***ADVERB***
▷ **disobedience** ***NOUN***

disobey ***VERB*** **disobeys, disobeying, disobeyed**
1 to refuse to obey someone
2 to refuse to follow a rule or order

disobliging ***ADJECTIVE***
refusing to help or cooperate with someone

disorder ***NOUN*** **disorders**
1 disorder is untidiness or lack of order
2 a disorder is a disturbance
3 a disorder is also an illness
▷ **disorderly** ***ADJECTIVE***

disorganized ***ADJECTIVE***
muddled and badly organized
▷ **disorganization** ***NOUN***

USAGE NOTE This word can also be spelled disorganised.

disoriented or **disorientated** ***ADJECTIVE***
feeling confused because you have lost your bearings

disown ***VERB*** **disowns, disowning, disowned**
you disown someone if you refuse to acknowledge that they have any connection with you

disparage (*say* dis- **pa**- rij) ***VERB*** **disparages, disparaging, disparaged**
to disparage or be disparaging about something is to criticize it or say that it is unimportant
▷ **disparagement** ***NOUN***

WORD HISTORY from Old French *parage* 'equality in rank'

disparate (*say* **dis**- per- at) ***ADJECTIVE***
different in kind

WORD HISTORY from Latin *disparare* 'to separate'

disparity (*say* dis- **pa**- ri- ti) ***NOUN*** **disparities**
difference or inequality

WORD HISTORY from Latin *disparitas* 'inequality', from *paritas* 'equality'

dispassionate ***ADJECTIVE***
not emotional; calm and impartial
▷ **dispassionately** ***ADVERB***

dispatch ***VERB*** **dispatches, dispatching, dispatched**
1 to send someone or something off to a destination
2 to kill a person or animal

dispatch ***NOUN*** **dispatches**
1 dispatching
2 a report or message sent
3 to do something with dispatch is to do it promptly and efficiently

dispatch box ***NOUN*** **dispatch boxes**
1 a container for carrying official documents
2 the **Dispatch Box** is a box in the House of Commons where ministers stand to speak

dispatch rider ***NOUN*** **dispatch riders**
a messenger who travels by motorcycle

dispel ***VERB*** **dispels, dispelling, dispelled**
1 to drive or clear something away ◆ *Wind dispels fog.*
2 to get rid of a fear or doubt

WORD HISTORY from Latin *dispellere* 'to drive away'

dispensary ***NOUN*** **dispensaries**
a place where medicines are dispensed

dispensation ***NOUN***
1 dispensing or distributing something
2 exemption from a rule or duty

dispense *VERB* **dispenses, dispensing, dispensed**
1 to distribute something to a number of people
2 a machine dispenses money or goods when it gives them out to customers
3 to prepare and give out medicines according to prescriptions
to dispense with something is to do without it
▷ **dispenser** *NOUN*
WORD HISTORY from Latin *dispensare* 'to weigh out'

disperse *VERB* **disperses, dispersing, dispersed**
1 to scatter something over a wide area
2 a crowd disperses when it breaks up and the people move away in different directions
3 you disperse a crowd when you force it to break up
▷ **dispersal** *NOUN*
▷ **dispersion** *NOUN*
WORD HISTORY from Latin *dispersum* 'scattered'

dispiriting *ADJECTIVE*
making you feel depressed and discouraged

displace *VERB* **displaces, displacing, displaced**
1 to shift something from its usual place
2 to take the place of a person or thing
▷ **displacement** *NOUN*

display *VERB* **displays, displaying, displayed**
1 to show or arrange something so that it can be seen
2 to show a particular quality or emotion ◆ *They displayed great courage.*

display *NOUN* **displays**
1 the process of displaying something
2 (*Art*) a collection of items displayed, e.g. in a museum or gallery
3 an electronic device for visually presenting data
WORD HISTORY from Latin *displicare* 'to unfold'

displease *VERB* **displeases, displeasing, displeased**
to annoy or offend someone
▷ **displeasure** *NOUN*

disposable *ADJECTIVE*
disposable goods are designed to be thrown away after they have been used ◆ *disposable camera*

disposable *NOUN* **disposables**
a disposable item

disposal *NOUN*
getting rid of something
at your disposal for you to use; ready for you

dispose *VERB* **disposes, disposing, disposed**
1 to make someone willing or ready to do something ◆ *I didn't feel disposed to drive all that way in the rain.*
2 to dispose of something is to get rid of it
3 to place something in position; to arrange something
to be disposed to do something is to feel ready or willing to do it
to be well disposed to someone is to feel friendly towards them

disposition *NOUN* **dispositions**
1 a person's nature or qualities ◆ *She has a cheerful disposition.*
2 setting in order; arrangement

disproportionate *ADJECTIVE*
out of proportion; too large or too small
▷ **disproportionately** *ADVERB*

disprove *VERB* **disproves, disproving, disproved**
to show that a belief or theory is not true

disputation *NOUN* **disputations**
a debate or argument

dispute *VERB* **disputes, disputing, disputed**
1 to argue or debate
2 to quarrel
3 to question or object to a claim

dispute *NOUN* **disputes**
1 an argument or debate
2 a quarrel
in dispute being argued about
WORD HISTORY from Latin *disputare* 'to argue out'

disqualify *VERB* **disqualifies, disqualifying, disqualified**
to bar someone from a competition because they have broken the rules or are not properly qualified to take part
▷ **disqualification** *NOUN*

disquiet *NOUN*
anxiety or worry
▷ **disquieting** *ADJECTIVE*

disregard *VERB* **disregards, disregarding, disregarded**
to pay no attention to someone or something

disregard *NOUN*
lack of attention to someone or something

disrepair *NOUN*
a poor condition caused by not doing repairs ◆ *The house was in a state of disrepair.*

disreputable *ADJECTIVE*
not respectable in character

disrepute *NOUN*
bad reputation ◆ *He has been charged with bringing the game into disrepute.*

disrespect *NOUN*
lack of respect; rudeness
▷ **disrespectful** *ADJECTIVE*
▷ **disrespectfully** *ADVERB*

disrupt *VERB* **disrupts, disrupting, disrupted**
to throw something into disorder; to interrupt the flow of something ◆ *Severe flooding is disrupting traffic.*
▷ **disruption** *NOUN*
WORD HISTORY from Latin *disruptum* 'broken apart'

disruptive *ADJECTIVE*
causing disruption
▷ **disruptively** *ADVERB*

dissatisfied *ADJECTIVE*
not satisfied or pleased
▷ **dissatisfaction** *NOUN*

dissect (*say* dis- **sekt**) *VERB* **dissects, dissecting, dissected**
to cut something up in order to examine it internally
▷ **dissection** *NOUN*
WORD HISTORY from Latin *dissectum* 'cut apart'

dissemble *VERB* **dissembles, dissembling, dissembled**
to conceal your true feelings
WORD HISTORY from Latin *dissimulare* 'to disguise or conceal'

disseminate *VERB* **disseminates, disseminating, disseminated**
to spread ideas or information widely
▷ **dissemination** *NOUN*
WORD HISTORY from Latin *disseminare* 'to sow or scatter about'

dissent *NOUN*
disagreement; the act of stating a different opinion

dissent *VERB* **dissents, dissenting, dissented**
to have or state a different opinion; to disagree
WORD HISTORY from Latin *dissentire* 'to feel differently'

dissertation *NOUN* **dissertations**
a long essay on an academic subject, written as part of a university degree
WORD HISTORY from Latin *dissertare* 'to examine or discuss'

disservice *NOUN*
a harmful action done by someone who is trying to help

dissident *NOUN* **dissidents**
a person who disagrees, especially someone who opposes the government of their country
▷ **dissident** *ADJECTIVE*
▷ **dissidence** *NOUN*
WORD HISTORY from Latin *dissidere* 'to sit by yourself'

dissimilar *ADJECTIVE*
not similar; unlike
▷ **dissimilarity** *NOUN*

dissipate *VERB* **dissipates, dissipating, dissipated**
1 to disappear or scatter ◆ *The fog gradually dissipated.*
2 to waste or squander something
WORD HISTORY from Latin *dissipatus* 'scattered'

dissipated *ADJECTIVE*
indulging in vices; living immorally
▷ **dissipation** *NOUN*

dissociate *VERB* **dissociates, dissociating, dissociated**
1 you dissociate one thing from another when you separate them in your thoughts
2 you dissociate yourself from a person or group when you say that you do not support or agree with them
▷ **dissociation** *NOUN*

dissolute *ADJECTIVE*
having an immoral way of life
WORD HISTORY from Latin *dissolutus* 'loosened'

dissolution *NOUN* **dissolutions**
1 putting an end to a marriage or partnership
2 the formal ending of a parliament or assembly

dissolve *VERB* **dissolves, dissolving, dissolved**
1 to mix something with a liquid so that it becomes part of the liquid
2 to break up and become mixed with liquid ◆ *Wait for the tablet to dissolve.*
3 to weaken or fade and then disappear ◆ *By the time I saw him again, my anger had dissolved.*
4 to put an end to a marriage or partnership
5 to end a parliament or assembly formally
WORD HISTORY from Latin *dissolvere* 'to loosen apart'
WORD FAMILY A substance that can be dissolved in liquid is soluble.

dissonance *NOUN* **dissonances**
(*Music*) a lack of harmony
▷ **dissonant** *ADJECTIVE*

dissuade *VERB* **dissuades, dissuading, dissuaded**
to persuade somebody not to do something
▷ **dissuasion** *NOUN*
▷ **dissuasive** *ADJECTIVE*
WORD HISTORY from Latin *dissuadere* 'to advise against'

distaff *NOUN* **distaffs**
a stick for holding raw wool for spinning into yarn
on the distaff side on the woman's side of a family
WORD HISTORY from an Old English word

distance *NOUN* **distances**
1 the amount of space between one point and another
2 being far away in space or time
in the distance far away but visible

distance *VERB* **distances, distancing, distanced**
to distance yourself from someone or something is to show that you do not support or agree with them

distant *ADJECTIVE*
1 far away in space or time ◆ *a distant planet*
2 not friendly; not sociable
3 not closely related ◆ *Jamal and Layla were distant cousins.*
▷ **distantly** *ADVERB*
WORD HISTORY from Latin *distans* 'standing apart'

distaste *NOUN*
a dislike of something

distasteful *ADJECTIVE*
unpleasant or offensive
▷ **distastefully** *ADVERB*

distemper *NOUN*
1 a disease of dogs and certain other animals which causes coughing
2 paint made from powdered pigment mixed with glue
WORD HISTORY from Latin *distemperare* 'to soak'

distend *VERB* **distends, distending, distended**
to make something swell outwards because of pressure from inside
▷ **distension** *NOUN*
WORD HISTORY from Latin *distendere* 'to stretch apart'

distil *VERB* **distils, distilling, distilled**
1 to purify a liquid by boiling it and condensing the vapour
2 to make whisky or other spirits in this way
▷ **distillation** *NOUN*
WORD HISTORY from Latin *distillare* 'to drip apart'

distillery *NOUN* **distilleries**
a place where whisky or other alcoholic spirit is made
▷ **distiller** *NOUN*

distinct *ADJECTIVE*
1 easily heard or seen; noticeable
2 clearly separate or different
▷ **distinctness** *NOUN*
WORD HISTORY from Latin *distinctus* 'separated'
USAGE NOTE See the note at *distinctive*.

distinction *NOUN* **distinctions**
1 a difference between things ◆ *According to Einstein, the distinction between the past, present, and future is only an illusion.*
2 excellence or honour ◆ *It has the distinction of being the oldest building in the city.*
3 an award for excellence; a high mark in an examination

distinctive *ADJECTIVE*
a distinctive feature or characteristic distinguishes one thing from another or others ◆ *Geraniums have a very distinctive smell.*
▷ **distinctively** *ADVERB*
▷ **distinctiveness** *NOUN*
USAGE NOTE Take care not to confuse this word with *distinct*. A distinct mark is a clear mark; whereas a distinctive mark is one that is not found anywhere else.

distinctly *ADVERB*
1 noticeably, clearly ◆ *I can see Mars distinctly through my binoculars.*
2 particularly, definitely

Hugh Pylum-Haight was becoming distinctly twitchy, waiting upstairs in the complete silence of the great hall. — *Debi Gliori, Pure Dead Wicked*

distinguish *VERB* **distinguishes, distinguishing, distinguished**
1 to make or notice differences between things
2 to see or hear something clearly
3 you distinguish yourself when you do something that brings you honour or respect ◆ *She distinguished herself by her bravery.*
▷ **distinguishable** *ADJECTIVE*
WORD HISTORY from Latin *distinguere* 'to separate'

distinguished *ADJECTIVE*
1 excellent and famous
2 dignified in appearance

distort *VERB* **distorts, distorting, distorted**
1 to pull or twist something out of its normal shape
2 to give a false account or impression of something ◆ *This film deliberately distorts the truth.*
3 to change the quality of a sound, usually by electronic means
▷ **distortion** *NOUN*
WORD HISTORY from Latin *distortum* 'completely twisted'

distract *VERB* **distracts, distracting, distracted**
to take a person's attention away from something
WORD HISTORY from Latin *distractum* 'pulled apart'

distracted *ADJECTIVE*
greatly upset by worry or distress; distraught

distraction *NOUN* **distractions**
1 something that distracts a person's attention
2 an amusement or entertainment
3 great worry or distress
4 to do something to distraction is to go on doing it until you cannot stand it any longer

distraught (*say* dis- **trawt**) *ADJECTIVE*
greatly upset by worry or distress

distress ***NOUN*** **distresses**
great sorrow, pain, or trouble
in distress in danger and requiring help

distress ***VERB*** **distresses, distressing, distressed**
1 to cause distress to someone
2 to give artificial marks of wear to leather, furniture, etc.

distribute ***VERB*** **distributes, distributing, distributed**
1 to deal or share something out
2 to spread or scatter something
▷ **distribution** ***NOUN***
▷ **distributor** ***NOUN***
WORD HISTORY from Latin *distributum* 'assigned separately'

district ***NOUN*** **districts**
part of a town or country
WORD HISTORY from a French word

distrust ***NOUN***
lack of trust; suspicion
▷ **distrustful** ***ADJECTIVE***

distrust ***VERB*** **distrusts, distrusting, distrusted**
to have no trust in someone or something

disturb ***VERB*** **disturbs, disturbing, disturbed**
1 to spoil someone's peace, rest, or privacy ◆ *Sorry, I didn't mean to disturb you.*
2 to cause someone to worry ◆ *What you are about to read may disturb you.*
3 to move something from its position
▷ **disturbance** ***NOUN***
WORD HISTORY from Latin *disturbare* 'to disturb or upset thoroughly'

disuse ***NOUN***
the state of being no longer used

disused ***ADJECTIVE***
no longer used

ditch ***NOUN*** **ditches**
a trench dug to hold water or carry it away, or to serve as a boundary

ditch ***VERB*** **ditches, ditching, ditched**
1 (*informal*) to abandon or discard something
2 to bring an aircraft down in a forced landing on the sea
WORD HISTORY from an Old English word

dither ***VERB*** **dithers, dithering, dithered**
to hesitate indecisively

dither ***NOUN***
in a dither hesitating indecisively

ditto ***NOUN***
used in a list of items with the meaning 'the same again'
WORD HISTORY from Italian *detto* 'said'

ditto marks ***PLURAL NOUN***
two small marks (resembling apostrophes) placed under an item in a list to show that it should be repeated

ditty ***NOUN*** **ditties**
a short simple song
WORD HISTORY from Old French *dite* 'composition'

divan ***NOUN*** **divans**
a bed or couch without a raised back or sides
WORD HISTORY from a Persian word meaning 'cushioned bench'

dive ***VERB*** **dives, diving, dived**
1 to go under water, especially head first
2 to move downwards quickly
3 to swim under water using breathing equipment
4 to run or jump suddenly into a vehicle, room, etc. ◆ *They ran down the road and dived into a taxi.*

dive ***NOUN*** **dives**
1 an act of diving
2 a sudden downward movement or fall
WORD HISTORY from an Old English word

diver ***NOUN*** **divers**
1 someone who dives
2 a person who works under water in a special suit with an air supply
3 a bird that dives for its food

diverge ***VERB*** **diverges, diverging, diverged**
1 a path diverges when it turns off in a different direction
2 to diverge from a fact or truth is to depart from it
▷ **divergent** ***ADJECTIVE***
▷ **divergence** ***NOUN***
WORD HISTORY from Latin *vergere* 'to slope'

divers (*say* **dy**- verz) ***ADJECTIVE***
(*formal*) various or several
WORD HISTORY from Latin *diversus* 'diverted'

diverse (*say* dy- **verss**) ***ADJECTIVE***
varied; of several different kinds
▷ **diversity** ***NOUN***
WORD HISTORY from another spelling of *divers*

diversify ***VERB*** **diversifies, diversifying, diversified**
1 to make something varied
2 a company diversifies when it expands its range of products or services
▷ **diversification** ***NOUN***

diversion ***NOUN*** **diversions**
1 diverting something from its course
2 something intended to divert attention ◆ *You look in the room, while I create a diversion.*
3 an alternative route for traffic when a road is closed
4 a recreation or entertainment
▷ **diversionary** ***ADJECTIVE***

divert ***VERB*** **diverts, diverting, diverted**
1 to make something change its direction or path ◆ *Police will divert traffic during the carnival.*
2 to entertain or amuse someone
WORD HISTORY from Latin *vertere* 'to turn'

divest *VERB* **divests, divesting, divested**
you divest someone of power or authority when you take it away from them
WORD HISTORY from Latin *vestire* 'to clothe'

divide *VERB* **divides, dividing, divided**
1 to separate something into smaller parts; to split something up
2 to distribute something or share it out ◆ *We'll divide the prize money between us.*
3 to cause people to disagree ◆ *On this one issue, the group was divided.*
4 (*Mathematics*) to find how many times one number is contained in another ◆ *Divide six by three.*
▷ **divider** *NOUN*

divide *NOUN* **divides**
a dividing line; a gap ◆ *the divide between rich and poor*
▷ **divisible** *ADJECTIVE*
WORD HISTORY from Latin *dividere* 'to force apart or remove'

dividend *NOUN* **dividends**
1 a share of a business's profit
2 a number that is to be divided by another (SEE ALSO **divisor**)
WORD HISTORY from Latin *dividendum* 'something to be divided'

dividers *PLURAL NOUN*
a pair of compasses for measuring distances

divine *ADJECTIVE*
1 coming from a god or from God
2 like a god
3 (*informal*) to look divine is to look very beautiful or glamorous
▷ **divinely** *ADVERB*

divine *VERB* **divines, divining, divined**
1 to discover something by guessing
2 to foretell or prophesy something
▷ **divination** *NOUN*
WORD HISTORY from Latin *divus* 'god'

divinity *NOUN* **divinities**
1 being divine
2 a god or goddess
3 the study of religion

division *NOUN* **divisions**
1 (*Mathematics*) the process of dividing
2 a dividing line; a partition
3 one of the parts into which something is divided
4 a major unit of an organization ◆ *our export division*
5 the separation of Members of Parliament into two sections for counting votes
▷ **divisional** *ADJECTIVE*

divisive (*say* div- y- siv) *ADJECTIVE*
causing disagreement within a group

divisor *NOUN* **divisors**
a number by which another is to be divided (SEE ALSO **dividend**)

divorce *NOUN* **divorces**
the legal ending of a marriage

divorce *VERB* **divorces, divorcing, divorced**
1 to end a marriage to someone by divorce
2 you divorce one thing from another when you think of them separately ◆ *You can't divorce science from ethics.*
WORD HISTORY a French word, related to *divert*

divulge *VERB* **divulges, divulging, divulged**
to reveal information
▷ **divulgence** *NOUN*
WORD HISTORY from Latin *vulgare* 'to publish'

Diwali (*say* di- wah- lee) *NOUN*
a Hindu religious festival at which lamps are lit, held in October or November
WORD HISTORY from Sanskrit *dipavali* 'row of lights'

DIY *ABBREVIATION*
the activity of doing your own house repairs and improvements
WORD HISTORY an abbreviation of *do it yourself*

dizzy *ADJECTIVE* **dizzier, dizziest**
1 feeling that everything is spinning round you; giddy
2 making you feel dizzy or giddy ◆ *dizzy heights*
▷ **dizzily** *ADVERB*
▷ **dizziness** *NOUN*
WORD HISTORY from Old English *dysig* 'foolish'

DJ *ABBREVIATION*
disc jockey

djinn *NOUN* **djinn** or **djinns**
another spelling of **jinn**

DNA *ABBREVIATION*
(*Science*) deoxyribonucleic acid, a substance in chromosomes that stores genetic information

do *VERB* **does, doing, did, done**
1 to be engaged in something; to perform or deal with something

'And what, precisely, were you doing in the garden?' he asked. — Mark Haddon, *The Curious Incident of the Dog in the Night-Time*

2 to be suitable; to be enough ◆ *This dress will have to do. I don't have time to change.*
3 used with another verb to form a question or negative, or to add emphasis ◆ *Do you want to dance?* ◆ *I don't know anything about cars.* ◆ *Do give me a ring.*
4 used instead of repeating a verb that has just been used ◆ *You watch more TV than I do.*

to do away with something is to get rid of it

to do something up
1 to do up a piece of clothing is to fasten or button it
2 to do up a room or house is to repair or redecorate it
SYNONYMS (meaning 1) carry out, deal with, undertake, perform, achieve, accomplish, complete

do ***NOUN*** **dos**
(*informal*) a party or other social event
WORD HISTORY from an Old English word

docile (*say* **doh**- syl) ***ADJECTIVE***
willing to obey
▷ **docilely** ***ADVERB***
▷ **docility** ***NOUN***
WORD HISTORY from Latin *docilis* 'easily taught'

dock❶ ***NOUN*** **docks**
a part of a harbour where ships are loaded, unloaded, or repaired

dock ***VERB*** **docks, docking, docked**
1 to bring a ship into a dock
2 to come into a dock
3 when two spacecraft dock, they join together in space
WORD HISTORY from an Old German or Old Dutch word

dock❷ ***NOUN***
an enclosure for the prisoner on trial in a lawcourt
WORD HISTORY from Flemish *dok* 'cage'

dock❸ ***NOUN***
a weed with broad leaves
WORD HISTORY from an Old English word

dock❹ ***VERB*** **docks, docking, docked**
1 to cut short an animal's tail
2 to reduce or take away part of someone's wages
3 to reduce points from a score or total

docker ***NOUN*** **dockers**
a worker in a port who loads and unloads ships

docket ***NOUN*** **dockets**
a document or label listing the contents of a package

dockyard ***NOUN*** **dockyards**
an open area with docks and equipment for building or repairing ships

doctor ***NOUN*** **doctors**
1 a person who is trained to treat sick or injured people
2 a person who holds an advanced degree (called a **doctorate**) at a university ◆ *Doctor of Music*

doctor ***VERB*** **doctors, doctoring, doctored**
to tamper with or falsify something ◆ *I believe that someone has doctored the evidence.*
WORD HISTORY a Latin word meaning 'teacher'

doctrine ***NOUN*** **doctrines**
a belief held by a religious, political, or other group
▷ **doctrinal** ***ADJECTIVE***
WORD HISTORY from Latin *doctrina* 'teaching'

document ***NOUN*** **documents**
1 a written or printed paper giving information or evidence about something
2 (*ICT*) a piece of computer text or graphics that can be worked on
▷ **documentation** ***NOUN***
WORD HISTORY from Latin *documentum* 'lesson, official paper'

document ***VERB*** **documents, documenting, documented**
to provide written evidence to support or prove something

documentary ***ADJECTIVE***
1 consisting of documents ◆ *documentary evidence*
2 showing real events or situations

documentary ***NOUN*** **documentaries**
a film or television programme giving information about real events

dodder ***VERB*** **dodders, doddering, doddered**
to walk unsteadily, especially because of old age
▷ **doddery** ***ADJECTIVE***

doddle ***NOUN*** **doddles**
(*informal*) something very easy to do

dodge ***VERB*** **dodges, dodging, dodged**
to move quickly to avoid someone or something
▷ **dodger** ***NOUN***

dodge ***NOUN*** **dodges**
1 a dodging movement
2 (*informal*) a trick; a clever way of doing something

dodgem ***NOUN*** **dodgems**
a small electrically driven car at a funfair, in which each driver tries to bump some cars and dodge others
WORD HISTORY from the phrase *dodge 'em*, i.e. 'dodge them'

dodgy ***ADJECTIVE*** **dodgier, dodgiest** (*informal*)
1 awkward or tricky
2 not working properly
3 suspect or dishonest
WORD HISTORY from *dodge* meaning 'a trick'

dodo ***NOUN*** **dodos**
a large non-flying bird that used to live on the island of Mauritius but became extinct in the 18th century
WORD HISTORY from Portuguese *doudo* 'fool', because the bird had no fear of people

doe ***NOUN*** **does**
a female deer, rabbit, or hare
WORD HISTORY from an Old English word

doer *NOUN* **doers**
a person who does things, rather than just thinking or talking about them

doesn't
short for *does not*

doff *VERB* **doffs, doffing, doffed**
you doff a hat or cap when you take it off in order to greet someone or show them respect (SEE ALSO **don**)
WORD HISTORY from the phrase *do off*

dog *NOUN* **dogs**
a four-legged carnivorous animal that barks, often kept as a pet
to go to the dogs (*informal*) is to reach a very poor standard
WORD FAMILY A related adjective is canine.

dog *VERB* **dogs, dogging, dogged**
to dog someone's footsteps is to follow them closely or persistently
WORD HISTORY from an Old English word

doge (*say* dohj) *NOUN* **doges**
the elected ruler of the former republics of Venice and Genoa
WORD HISTORY from Latin *dux* 'leader'

dog-eared *ADJECTIVE*
a dog-eared book has the corners of its pages bent from constant use

dogfish *NOUN* **dogfish**
a kind of small shark

dogged (*say* dog- id) *ADJECTIVE*
determined and persistent; not giving up easily
▷ **doggedly** *ADVERB*
▷ **doggedness** *NOUN*
WORD HISTORY from *dog*

doggerel *NOUN*
bad or comic verse

doggy-paddle *NOUN*
a simple swimming stroke with short quick movements of your arms and legs

dogma *NOUN* **dogmas**
a belief or principle that a Church or other authority declares is true and must be accepted
WORD HISTORY a Greek word meaning 'opinion or decree'

dogmatic *ADJECTIVE*
expressing ideas in a very firm authoritative way
▷ **dogmatically** *ADVERB*

dogsbody *NOUN* **dogsbodies**
(*informal*) a person who is given boring or unimportant jobs to do

doh *NOUN*
a name for the keynote of a scale in music, or the note C
WORD HISTORY an Italian word

doily *NOUN* **doilies**
a small ornamental table-mat, made of paper or lace
WORD HISTORY after a Mr *Doily* or *Doyley*, who sold household linen in the 17th century

Dolby *NOUN*
(*trademark*) a stereophonic system used in sound reproduction, e.g. in cinemas and in DVD players
WORD HISTORY after the American engineer, Ray M. *Dolby* (born 1933)

doldrums *PLURAL NOUN*
to be in the doldrums is to be feeling depressed and unable to do anything
WORD HISTORY after the *Doldrums*, an ocean region near the equator where there is little or no wind

dole *VERB* **doles, doling, doled**
to dole something out is to distribute it among a group of people

dole *NOUN*
to be on the dole (*informal*) is to be receiving unemployment benefit from the state
WORD HISTORY from an Old English word

doleful *ADJECTIVE*
sad or sorrowful
▷ **dolefully** *ADVERB*
WORD HISTORY from an old word *dole* meaning 'grief'

doll *NOUN* **dolls**
a small toy model of a human figure

doll *VERB* **dolls, dolling, dolled**
to doll yourself up or **to get dolled up** (*informal*) is to dress smartly
WORD HISTORY an affectionate form of the name *Dorothy*

dollar *NOUN* **dollars**
a unit of money in the USA and some other countries
WORD HISTORY from German *Thaler* 'a silver coin'

dollop *NOUN* **dollops**
(*informal*) a lump of something soft ◆ *a dollop of cream*

dolly *NOUN* **dollies**
(*informal*) a doll

dolphin *NOUN* **dolphins**
a sea animal like a small whale with a beak-like snout
WORD HISTORY from Greek *delphin*

domain (*say* dom- ayn) *NOUN* **domains**
1 a kingdom
2 an area of knowledge or interest
3 (*ICT*) a distinct group of Internet addresses with the same suffix
WORD HISTORY from French *domaine*, related to our word *dominion*

a b c d e f g h i j k l m n o p q r s t u v w x y z

dome *NOUN* **domes**
a rounded roof with a circular base
▷ **domed** *ADJECTIVE*
WORD HISTORY via French from Italian *duomo* 'cathedral or dome'

domestic *ADJECTIVE*
1 to do with your house, home, or family ◆ *a domestic problem*
2 to do with your own country; not foreign or international ◆ *a domestic flight*
3 domestic animals are kept by people and are not wild
▷ **domestically** *ADVERB*
WORD HISTORY from Latin *domesticus*

domesticated *ADJECTIVE*
domesticated animals are trained to live with and be kept by humans

domicile (*say* **dom**- iss- syl) *NOUN* **domiciles**
(*formal*) the place where someone lives; a residence
▷ **domiciled** *ADJECTIVE*
WORD HISTORY from Latin *domus* 'home'

dominate *VERB* **dominates, dominating, dominated**
1 to control someone or something by being stronger or more powerful
2 to be the most prominent person or thing in a place or situation ◆ *The mountain dominates the whole landscape.*
▷ **dominant** *ADJECTIVE*
▷ **dominance** *NOUN*
▷ **domination** *NOUN*
WORD HISTORY from Latin *dominus* 'master'

domineer *VERB* **domineers, domineering, domineered**
to behave in a forceful or arrogant way towards others
▷ **domineering** *ADJECTIVE*

dominion *NOUN* **dominions**
1 authority to rule others; control
2 an area over which someone rules; a domain
WORD HISTORY from Latin *dominium* 'property'

domino *NOUN* **dominoes**
a small flat oblong piece of wood or plastic with dots (1 to 6) or a blank space at each end, used in the game called **dominoes**
WORD HISTORY from a French word meaning a hood worn by priests in winter

don *VERB* **dons, donning, donned**
you don a piece of clothing when you put it on (SEE ALSO **doff**)
WORD HISTORY from the phrase *do on*

donate *VERB* **donates, donating, donated**
1 to present money or a gift to a fund or institution
2 to give some of your blood, or a body organ, to a hospital for use by other patients
▷ **donation** *NOUN*
WORD HISTORY from Latin *donum* 'gift'

done *past participle of* **do**

done *ADJECTIVE*
1 socially acceptable
2 finished, completed
3 cooked thoroughly
to be done for (*informal*) is to be in serious trouble
to be done in (*informal*) is to be extremely tired or exhausted

donga *NOUN*
1 (*South African*) a dry watercourse
2 (*Australian*) a makeshift shelter

donkey *NOUN* **donkeys**
an animal that looks like a small horse with long ears and makes a braying sound
for donkey's years (*informal*) for a very long time

donor *NOUN* **donors**
1 someone who donates a gift or money
2 someone who donates blood, or a body organ, to a hospital
WORD HISTORY from Old French *doneur*

don't
short for *do not*

doodle *VERB* **doodles, doodling, doodled**
to scribble or draw while thinking about something else

doodle *NOUN* **doodles**
a drawing made by doodling
WORD HISTORY from an Old German word

doom *NOUN*
a grim fate that you cannot avoid, especially death or destruction

doom *VERB* **dooms, dooming, doomed**
to destine someone to a grim fate

Madame Zeroni warned that if he failed to do this, he and his descendants would be doomed for all of eternity. — *Louis Sachar, Holes*

WORD HISTORY from an Old English word

doomed *ADJECTIVE*
1 destined to a grim fate
2 bound to fail or be destroyed

doomsday *NOUN*
the day of the Last Judgement; the end of the world
WORD HISTORY from an earlier meaning of *doom* in the sense 'judgement'

door *NOUN* **doors**
1 a hinged, sliding, or revolving barrier, used to open or close an entrance
2 an entrance to a room or building
WORD HISTORY from an Old English word

a b c d e f g h i j k l m n o p q r s t u v w x y z

doorbell *NOUN* **doorbells**
an electric or electronic bell in a building, rung by visitors

doorstep *NOUN* **doorsteps**
the step or piece of ground just outside a door
on your doorstep nearby; very close

door-to-door *ADJECTIVE*
door-to-door selling is done at each house in turn

doorway *NOUN* **doorways**
the opening into which a door fits

dope *NOUN* **dopes** (*informal*)
1 a drug, especially one taken or given illegally
2 a stupid person

dope *VERB* **dopes, doping, doped**
(*informal*) to give a drug to a person or animal
WORD HISTORY from Dutch *doop* 'sauce'

dopey *ADJECTIVE* **dopier, dopiest** (*informal*)
1 sleepy, as if drugged
2 stupid or silly
▷ **dopily** *ADVERB*
▷ **dopiness** *NOUN*

dormant *ADJECTIVE*
1 sleeping
2 living or existing but not active; not extinct ◆ *a dormant volcano*
WORD HISTORY a French word meaning 'sleeping'

dormitory *NOUN* **dormitories**
a room for several people to sleep in, especially in a school or institution
WORD HISTORY from Latin *dormire* 'to sleep'

dormouse *NOUN* **dormice**
an animal like a large mouse that hibernates in winter

dorp *NOUN*
a small rural town or village in South Africa
WORD HISTORY a Dutch word meaning 'village'

dorsal *ADJECTIVE*
to do with, or on, the back of an animal or plant ◆ *a dorsal fin*
WORD HISTORY from Latin *dorsum* 'the back'

dosage *NOUN* **dosages**
1 the giving of medicine in doses
2 the size of a dose

dose *NOUN* **doses**
1 an amount of medicine taken at one time
2 an amount of something unpleasant ◆ *a dose of flu*

dose *VERB* **doses, dosing, dosed**
to give a dose of medicine to a person or animal
WORD HISTORY from Greek *dosis* 'something given'

dossier (*say* doss- ee- er or doss- ee- ay) **dossiers**
a set of documents containing information about a person or event
WORD HISTORY from a French word meaning 'a bundle of papers with a label on the back'

dot *NOUN* **dots**
a small round mark or spot
on the dot (*informal*) exactly on time

dot *VERB* **dots, dotting, dotted**
1 to mark something with dots
2 a scene or image is dotted with things when they are scattered randomly over it
WORD HISTORY from an Old English word

dotage (*say* doh- tij) *NOUN*
someone is in their dotage when they are old and weak

dotcom *NOUN* **dotcoms**
(*Economics*) a company that does its business on the Internet
WORD HISTORY from the ending '.com' in Internet addresses used by commercial sites

dote *VERB* **dotes, doting, doted**
to dote on someone is to be very fond of them
WORD HISTORY from Old Dutch *doten* 'to be silly'

dotty *ADJECTIVE* **dottier, dottiest**
(*informal*) slightly mad or eccentric
to be dotty about someone or **something** is to be infatuated or obsessed with them or it
▷ **dottiness** *NOUN*

double *ADJECTIVE*
1 twice as much; twice as many ◆ *a double helping*
2 having two things or parts that form a pair
3 a double bed or room is suitable for two people
4 something with a double meaning or sense has two possible meanings
▷ **doubly** *ADVERB*

double *NOUN* **doubles**
1 a double amount or thing
2 a person or thing that looks exactly like another ◆ *He's his father's double.*
3 doubles is a game of tennis or badminton between two pairs of players
at the double very fast, hurrying

double *VERB* **doubles, doubling, doubled**
1 to become twice as much or as many
2 to make something twice as much or as many
3 to bend or fold something in two
to double back is to turn and go back the same way you have come

double *ADVERB*
twice the amount or quantity ◆ *The hotel cost double what it did last year.*

double agent *NOUN* **double agents**
a spy who spies for two rival countries at the same time

double-barrelled *ADJECTIVE*
1 a double-barrelled gun has two barrels
2 a double-barrelled name has two surnames joined by a hyphen

double bass *NOUN* **double basses**
a musical instrument with strings, like a large cello

double-cross *VERB* **double-crosses, double-crossing, double-crossed**
to deceive or cheat someone who thinks you are working with them

double-decker *NOUN* **double-deckers**
a bus with two floors, one above the other

double entendre *NOUN* **double entendres**
a word or phrase with two meanings, one of which is sexual or rude

WORD HISTORY a French phrase meaning 'double understanding'

double negative *NOUN* **double negatives**
(*Grammar*) a negative statement containing two negative words

double negatives

A **negative** is a word such as *no, not, never, nobody*, and *nowhere*. You normally only need one negative word to make a negative statement or ask a negative question: *We never wanted any trouble; Won't they give you some money?* A **double negative** is when you have two negative words to make a sentence, e.g. *We never wanted no trouble; Won't they give you no money?* This use of two negatives is not acceptable in standard English and you should avoid it, especially in writing.
Note also that the words *barely, hardly*, and *scarcely* are effectively negative and should not be used with another negative:
The burial chamber was so dark, we could barely see the tomb (not *we couldn't barely see the tomb*).
Another type of double negative is more acceptable because each cancels out the other and together they produce a positive meaning. For example, to visit a place *not infrequently* is to visit it often, and a *not unpleasant* sound is one that is rather pleasant.

doublet *NOUN* **doublets**
a man's close-fitting jacket worn in the 15th–17th centuries

WORD HISTORY from an Old French word meaning 'something folded'

double take *NOUN* **double takes**
a second look at or reaction to something, because it is puzzling or unexpected

doubloon (*say* dub- **loon**) *NOUN* **doubloon**
an old Spanish gold coin

WORD HISTORY from French *doublon*

doubt *NOUN* **doubts**
a feeling of not being sure about something
◆ *Is there any remaining doubt that birds are descended from dinosaurs?*

doubt *VERB* **doubts, doubting, doubted**
1 to feel unsure or undecided about something
◆ *I never doubted his confidence in me.*
2 to think that something is unlikely to be true
◆ *I doubt that the shop will be open on Sundays.*
no doubt certainly; very probably
▷ **doubter** *NOUN*

WORD HISTORY from Latin *dubitare* 'to hesitate'

doubtful *ADJECTIVE*
1 feeling doubt; unsure
2 not certain to happen ◆ *It is doubtful whether the match will go ahead now.*
▷ **doubtfully** *ADVERB*

doubtless *ADVERB*
certainly

dough *NOUN*
1 a thick mixture of flour and water used for making bread, pastry, etc.
2 (*informal*) an amount of money
▷ **doughy** *ADJECTIVE*

WORD HISTORY from an Old English word

doughnut *NOUN* **doughnuts**
a sweet bun or ring of dough, fried and sprinkled with sugar

doughty (*say* **dow**- tee) *ADJECTIVE* **doughtier, doughtiest**
an old-fashioned word meaning brave and stout-hearted

WORD HISTORY from Old English *dohtig*

dour (*say* doo- er) *ADJECTIVE*
stern and gloomy-looking
▷ **dourly** *ADVERB*

WORD HISTORY from Scottish Gaelic *dur* 'dull, obstinate'

douse *VERB* **douses, dousing, doused**
1 to pour water over something
2 you douse a light or fire when you put it out

USAGE NOTE Take care not to confuse *douse* with *dowse*, which means 'to search for water or minerals'.

dove *NOUN* **doves**
a kind of pigeon

WORD HISTORY from an Old Norse word

dovetail *NOUN* **dovetails**
a wedge-shaped joint used to join two pieces of wood

dovetail *VERB* **dovetails, dovetailing, dovetailed**
1 to join pieces of wood with a dovetail
2 one thing dovetails with another when the two of them fit neatly together

WORD HISTORY so called because the wedge shape looks like a dove's tail

dowager *NOUN* **dowagers**
a woman who holds a title or property after her husband has died ◆ *the dowager duchess*

WORD HISTORY from Old French *douage* 'widow's share'

dowdy *ADJECTIVE* **dowdier, dowdiest**
shabby and unfashionable; not stylish
▷ **dowdily** *ADVERB*
▷ **dowdiness** *NOUN*

dowel *NOUN* **dowels**
a headless wooden or metal pin for holding together two pieces of wood or stone
▷ **dowelling** *NOUN*

down❶ *ADVERB, PREPOSITION*
1 to or in a lower place, position, or level

Adolph Knipe ... sat down in front of the typewriter that was on the table. — *Roald Dahl, The Great Automatic Grammatizator*

2 along, towards the end of a road or passage ◆ *He walked casually down the corridor, heading for the exit.*
3 you track someone or something down when you trace them to a source or place
4 you write or take down a piece of information when you put it on paper
5 you pay or put a sum of money down when you make it as a payment
6 a computer or telephone network is down when it is not connected or working properly

down to someone or something
1 a task is down to someone when it is their responsibility
2 an event or situation is down to something when it has been caused by it

down *ADJECTIVE*
feeling unhappy or depressed ◆ *You're looking a bit down today.*

down *VERB* **downs, downing, downed**
(*informal*)
1 to knock someone or something to the ground
2 to swallow a drink or medicine

WORD HISTORY from Old English *adune*

down❷ *NOUN*
very fine soft feathers or hair
▷ **downy** *ADJECTIVE*

WORD HISTORY from an Old Norse word

down❸ *NOUN* **downs**
a grass-covered hill ◆ *the South Downs*

WORD HISTORY from Old English *dun*

downbeat *ADJECTIVE*
pessimistic or gloomy

downcast *ADJECTIVE*
1 looking downwards ◆ *downcast eyes*
2 dejected; despondent

downfall *NOUN* **downfalls**
1 a fall from power or prosperity
2 a heavy fall of rain or snow

downgrade *VERB* **downgrades, downgrading, downgraded**
to reduce something to a lower grade or rank

downhill *ADVERB, ADJECTIVE*
down a slope
to go downhill is to decline in quality or deteriorate

downland *NOUN*
open countryside of gently rolling hills

download *VERB* **downloads, downloading, downloaded**
(*ICT*) to transfer data from one system to another, especially from the Internet to a personal computer

downmarket *ADVERB, ADJECTIVE*
of or towards the cheaper end of the market

downplay *VERB* **downplays, downplaying, downplayed**
to make something seem less important than it really is

downpour *NOUN* **downpours**
a heavy fall of rain

downright *ADJECTIVE*
complete, total ◆ *a downright lie*

downright *ADVERB*
thoroughly, extremely ◆ *He was downright rude on the phone.*

downside *NOUN* **downsides**
the disadvantage of a plan or situation

Down's syndrome *NOUN*
a medical condition caused by a chromosome defect that causes intellectual impairment and physical abnormalities such as short stature and a broad flattened skull

downstairs *ADVERB, ADJECTIVE*
to or on a lower floor

You'd better get dressed and come downstairs and never mind your imaginings.
— *L. M. Montgomery, Anne of Green Gables*

downstream *ADJECTIVE, ADVERB*
in the direction in which a stream flows

down-to-earth *ADJECTIVE*
sensible and practical

downturn *NOUN* **downturns**
a decline in economic or other activity

downward *ADJECTIVE*
going towards a lower point or level

downwards *ADVERB*
towards a lower point or level

dowry *NOUN* **dowries**
property or money brought by a bride to her husband when she marries him

WORD HISTORY from Old French *dowarie*, related to our word *endow*

dowse *VERB* **dowses, dowsing, dowsed**
to search for underground water or minerals with a special rod

USAGE NOTE Take care not to confuse *dowse* with *douse*, which means 'to pour water over'.

doyen (*say* doy- en) or **doyenne** (*say* doy- **en**) *NOUN* **doyens** or **doyennes**
someone who is respected in a particular field or profession

USAGE NOTE You use *doyen* for a man, and *doyenne* for a woman.

WORD HISTORY a French word

doze *VERB* **dozes, dozing, dozed**
to sleep lightly

Frodo dozed, though the pain of his wound was slowly growing. — *J. R. R. Tolkien, The Fellowship of the Ring*

doze *NOUN*
a short light sleep

dozen *NOUN* **dozens**
a set of twelve

WORD HISTORY from an Old French word

USAGE NOTE You use *two dozen, three dozen*, etc. to talk about more than one dozen; but you say *dozens of* things when you mean 'lots of' things.

dozy *ADJECTIVE* **dozier, doziest**
slightly sleepy or drowsy

DPI *ABBREVIATION*
(*ICT*) dots per inch; a measurement used to describe the resolution of a computer screen, scanner, or printer

drab *ADJECTIVE* **drabber, drabbest**
1 not colourful
2 dull or uninteresting ◆ *a drab life*
▷ **drably** *ADVERB*
▷ **drabness** *NOUN*

WORD HISTORY from an Old French word

Draconian (*say* drak- **oh**- nee- an) *ADJECTIVE*
Draconian rules or laws are very harsh or strict

WORD HISTORY from *Draco*, who established very severe laws in ancient Athens

draft *NOUN* **drafts**
1 a rough sketch or plan
2 a written order for a bank to pay out money

draft *VERB* **drafts, drafting, drafted**
1 to prepare a draft of something
2 to select someone for a special duty ◆ *She was drafted to our office in Paris.*

USAGE NOTE This is also the American spelling of *draught*

WORD HISTORY from another spelling of *draught*

drag *VERB* **drags, dragging, dragged**
1 to pull something with effort or difficulty
2 to search a river or lake with nets and hooks
3 to continue slowly in a boring manner

The morning dragged, the way it does when you feel let down or disappointed. — *Darren Shan, Cirque du Freak*

to drag your feet is to be deliberately slow or reluctant
to drag something out is to prolong it unnecessarily

drag *NOUN*
1 (*informal*) something that is tedious or a nuisance
2 women's clothes worn by men

WORD HISTORY from Old Norse *draga* 'to draw'

dragon *NOUN* **dragons**
1 a mythological monster, usually with wings and able to breathe out fire
2 a fierce person, especially a woman

WORD HISTORY from Greek *drakōn* 'serpent'

dragonfly *NOUN* **dragonflies**
an insect with a long thin body and two pairs of transparent wings

dragoon *NOUN* **dragoons**
a member of certain cavalry regiments

dragoon *VERB* **dragoons, dragooning, dragooned**
to force someone into doing something

WORD HISTORY related to *dragon*

drain *NOUN* **drains**
1 a pipe or ditch for taking away water or other liquid
2 something that takes away your strength or resources

drain *VERB* **drains, draining, drained**
1 to take away water or other liquid through a drain
2 to flow or trickle away
3 to pour off liquid in which something has been coooked ◆ *First, drain the pasta thoroughly.*
4 to take away your strength gradually ◆ *I feel drained by the whole experience.*
5 to drink the contents of a glass
▷ **drainage** *NOUN*

drainpipe *NOUN* **drainpipes**
a pipe used for carrying water or sewage from a building

drake *NOUN* **drakes**
a male duck

drama *NOUN* **dramas**
1 a play
2 writing or performing plays
3 a series of exciting or emotional events

WORD HISTORY a Greek word

dramatic *ADJECTIVE*
1 to do with drama
2 exciting and impressive; full of exciting events or scenes ◆ *The last ten minutes of the film are very dramatic.*
3 extreme, highly noticeable ◆ *Scientists have noticed a dramatic change in the Amazonian forests.*
▷ **dramatics** *PLURAL NOUN*
▷ **dramatically** *ADVERB*

dramatis personae (*say* **dram**- a- tis per- **sohn**- eye) *PLURAL NOUN*
the characters in a play

WORD HISTORY a Latin phrase meaning 'persons of the drama'

dramatist *NOUN* **dramatists**
a person who writes plays; a playwright

dramatize *VERB* **dramatizes, dramatizing, dramatized**
1 (*Drama*) to make a story into a play for the theatre or for broadcasting
2 to make an event or situation seem exciting
▷ **dramatization** *NOUN*

USAGE NOTE This word can also be spelled dramatise.

drank *past tense of* **drink**

drape *VERB* **drapes, draping, draped**
to arrange cloth or clothing loosely over something

> Next day, there was a grand funeral. Nai Nai's coffin was draped with white sheets and placed on a hearse pulled by four men. — *Adeline Yen Mah, Chinese Cinderella*

WORD HISTORY from French *drap* 'cloth'

draper *NOUN* **drapers**
an old word for a shopkeeper who sold cloth or clothes

drapery *NOUN* **draperies**
cloth arranged in loose folds

drastic *ADJECTIVE*
having a strong or violent effect
▷ **drastically** *ADVERB*

WORD HISTORY from a Greek word *drastikos*

draught (*say* drahft) *NOUN* **draughts**
1 a current of usually cold air indoors
2 a haul of fish in a net
3 the depth of water needed to float a ship
4 a swallow of liquid

WORD HISTORY from an Old Norse word

draughts *PLURAL NOUN*
a game played with 24 round pieces on a chessboard

WORD HISTORY from an earlier meaning of *draught* in the sense 'way of moving'

draughtsman *NOUN* **draughtsmen**
1 a person who makes technical drawings or plans
2 someone who is good at drawing
3 a piece used in the game of draughts

WORD HISTORY from an old spelling of *draft* 'to draw'

draughty *ADJECTIVE* **draughtier, draughtiest**
a draughty room or building is one that lets in currents of cold air
▷ **draughtiness** *NOUN*

draw *VERB* **draws, drawing, drew, drawn**
1 to produce a picture or outline by making marks on a surface
2 to pull something along or across a surface ◆ *He drew a grimy hand across his face.*
3 to pull a door or curtain shut

> Salimba retreated, drawing the door closed behind him. — *William Nicholson, The Wind Singer*

4 to take water or liquid from a well or other source
5 to take out and aim a gun, sword, or other weapon
6 to get a prize or ticket in a raffle or lottery
7 to derive information from a source ◆ *This story is drawn from first-hand accounts.*
8 to attract attention or an audience ◆ *We hope the festival will draw a large crowd.*
9 to move or come gradually

> The discordant tones of the voices and instruments drew nearer. — *Jules Verne, Around the World in Eighty Days*

10 to write out a cheque to be cashed
11 two contestants or teams draw when they both end a game or contest with the same score

to draw a blank is to get no response or result
to draw a conclusion is to form an opinion about something by thinking about the evidence
to draw in days or nights draw in when the time of daylight becomes shorter in the winter
to draw something out to draw out a discussion or argument is to make it last longer
to draw the line is to refuse to do or tolerate something
to draw to a close is to reach or approach an ending
to draw up a vehicle draws up when it comes to a halt
to draw something up to draw up a contract or plan is to prepare it in detail

draw *NOUN* **draws**
1 a game or match that ends with the scores even
2 the drawing of lots to decide the winner of a raffle or lottery
3 something that attracts an audience

to be quick on the draw is to be fast at taking out and aiming a gun

drawback *NOUN* **drawbacks**
a disadvantage

drawbridge *NOUN* **drawbridges**
a bridge over a moat, hinged at one end so that it can be raised or lowered

drawer *NOUN* **drawers**
1 a sliding box-like compartment in a piece of furniture
2 a person who draws something
3 someone who writes out a cheque

drawing *NOUN* **drawings**
1 drawing is making a picture with a pencil, pen, or crayon rather than paint
2 a drawing is a picture made in this way

drawing board *NOUN* **drawing boards**
a flat board on which paper is stretched while a drawing is made
to go back to the drawing board is to begin planning something from the start again

drawing pin *NOUN* **drawing pins**
a flat-headed pin for fastening paper to a surface

drawing room *NOUN* **drawing rooms**
a room in a house for receiving guests; a sitting room
WORD HISTORY from an earlier phrase *withdrawing room*

drawl *VERB* **drawls, drawling, drawled**
to speak very slowly, with drawn-out vowel sounds

drawl *NOUN* **drawls**
a drawling way of speaking
WORD HISTORY from Old German or Old Dutch *dralen* 'to delay'

drawn *past participle of* **draw**

drawn *ADJECTIVE*
looking strained from tiredness or worry

dray *NOUN* **drays**
a low flat cart for carrying heavy loads
WORD HISTORY related to *draw*

dread *NOUN*
great fear or worry about something that might happen

dread *VERB* **dreads, dreading, dreaded**
to fear or worry about something that might happen
▷ **dreaded** *ADJECTIVE*

dreadful *ADJECTIVE*
very bad or unpleasant ◆ *What a dreadful time they had!*
▷ **dreadfully** *ADVERB*

dreadlocks *PLURAL NOUN*
hair worn in many ringlets or plaits, especially by Rastafarians
WORD HISTORY so called because the style was copied from pictures of Ethiopian warriors

dream *NOUN* **dreams**
1 a series of pictures or events in a sleeping person's mind
2 a person's ambition or ideal
like a dream (*informal*) in the best way possible; very easily or successfully

dream *VERB* **dreams, dreaming, dreamt** or **dreamed**
1 to have a dream or dreams while sleeping
2 to have an ambition ◆ *He had always dreamt of being a chef.*
3 to think something might happen ◆ *I never dreamt she would take me seriously.*
to dream something up to dream up a plan or idea is to imagine it or invent it
▷ **dreamer** *NOUN*

dreamy *ADJECTIVE* **dreamier, dreamiest**
1 like a dream; pleasantly distracting or unreal
2 a dreamy person likes daydreaming
▷ **dreamily** *ADVERB*

dreary *ADJECTIVE* **drearier, dreariest**
1 dull or boring
2 gloomy or depressing
▷ **drearily** *ADVERB*
▷ **dreariness** *NOUN*
WORD HISTORY from an Old English word

dredge❶ *VERB* **dredges, dredging, dredged**
to drag something up from the bottom of a river or the sea
▷ **dredger** *NOUN*

dredge❷ *VERB* **dredges, dredging, dredged**
to sprinkle food with sugar or flour
▷ **dredger** *NOUN*
WORD HISTORY from an old word *dredge* 'sweetmeat'

dregs *PLURAL NOUN*
1 the last drops of liquid at the bottom of a glass, bottle, or barrel, together with any sediment
2 the worst and most useless part of something ◆ *the dregs of society*

drench *VERB* **drenches, drenching, drenched**
to make someone or something wet all through; to soak someone or something
WORD HISTORY from Old English *drencan*, related to *drink*

dress *NOUN* **dresses**
1 a woman's or girl's piece of clothing with a bodice and skirt
2 clothes; costume ◆ *fancy dress*

dress *VERB* **dresses, dressing, dressed**
1 to put your clothes on ◆ *He slipped out of bed and dressed quickly.*
2 to put clothes on someone, or on a doll or model
3 to wear clothes in a particular way or of a particular type ◆ *She always dresses well.*
4 to arrange a display in a window; to decorate something
5 to prepare a salad or certain other kinds of food for cooking or eating
6 to put a dressing on a wound
to dress up is to put on smart clothes or fancy dress
to dress something up is to make it look or seem more interesting
WORD HISTORY from French *dresser* 'to prepare'
WORD FAMILY A formal word meaning 'to do with dress or clothes' is sartorial.

a b c d e f g h i j k l m n o p q r s t u v w x y z

dressage (*say* **dress**- ahzh) *NOUN*
the training of a horse to perform various manoeuvres in order to show its obedience
WORD HISTORY a French word meaning 'training'

dresser *NOUN* **dressers**
1 someone who dresses in a particular way ◆ *He is a stylish dresser.*
2 a sideboard with shelves at the top for displaying plates

dressing *NOUN* **dressings**
1 a bandage, plaster, or ointment for a wound
2 a sauce made with oil and vinegar, for pouring over a salad
3 manure or other fertilizer for spreading on the soil

dressing gown *NOUN* **dressing gowns**
a loose garment for wearing when you are not fully dressed

dressing table *NOUN* **dressing tables**
a table or desk with a mirror and drawers, used while dressing or putting on make-up

dressmaker *NOUN* **dressmakers**
a person who makes women's clothes
▷ **dressmaking** *NOUN*

dress rehearsal *NOUN* **dress rehearsals**
the final rehearsal of a play at which the cast wear their costumes

dressy *ADJECTIVE* **dressier, dressiest**
dressy clothes are elegant or elaborate, and suitable for special occasions

drew *past tense of* **draw**

drey *NOUN* **dreys**
a squirrel's nest

dribble *VERB* **dribbles, dribbling, dribbled**
1 to let saliva trickle out of your mouth
2 liquid dribbles when it flows in drops
3 to move the ball forward in football or hockey with slight touches of your feet or stick

dribble *NOUN* **dribbles**
1 a trickle of saliva
2 dribbling a ball

dribs and drabs *PLURAL NOUN*
(*informal*) small scattered amounts

dried *past tense and past participle of* **dry**

drier *NOUN* **driers**
a device for drying wet hair or clothes

drift *VERB* **drifts, drifting, drifted**
1 to be carried gently along by water or air

> Clouds shaped mightily like whales and dragons drifted over the land by day. — *Terry Pratchett, Wyrd Sisters*

2 to move along slowly and casually
3 to move into a situation without meaning or planning to ◆ *He drifted into teaching.*

to drift apart
1 things drift apart when they move apart gradually
2 people drift apart when they become gradually less close or friendly with each other
▷ **drifter** *NOUN*

drift *NOUN* **drifts**
1 a drifting movement
2 a mass of snow or sand piled up by the wind
3 the general meaning of what someone says ◆ *I'm afraid I don't get your drift.*
4 (*South African*) a ford
WORD HISTORY an Old Norse word meaning 'snowdrift'

driftwood *NOUN*
wood floating on the sea or washed ashore by it

drill *NOUN* **drills**
1 a pointed tool for making holes
2 a machine for sinking a well in the ground
3 training or instruction by repeated exercises
4 (*informal*) a recognized procedure ◆ *You should know the drill by now.*

drill *VERB* **drills, drilling, drilled**
1 to make a hole or well with a drill
2 to teach someone to do something by making them do repeated exercises
WORD HISTORY from Dutch *drillen* 'to bore, to turn in a circle'

drily *ADVERB*
in a dry way

drink *VERB* **drinks, drinking, drank, drunk**
1 to swallow liquid
2 to drink a lot of alcoholic drinks
▷ **drinker** *NOUN*

drink *NOUN* **drinks**
1 a liquid for drinking
2 an amount of liquid swallowed
3 an alcoholic drink
WORD HISTORY from an Old English word

drip *VERB* **drips, dripping, dripped**
1 to fall in drops
2 to let a liquid fall in drops

drip *NOUN* **drips**
1 liquid falling in drops
2 the sound of liquid dripping
3 a machine in a hospital which drips a liquid or drug into a patient's veins

drip-dry *ADJECTIVE*
made of material that dries easily and does not need ironing

dripping *NOUN*
fat melted from roasted meat and allowed to set

drive *VERB* **drives, driving, drove, driven**
1 to operate a motor vehicle or a train
2 to take someone to a place in a car ◆ *Hop in and I'll drive you there.*

a b c d e f g h i j k l m n o p q r s t u v w x y z

3 to force someone to do something or go somewhere ◆ *The noise drove us all inside.*
4 to force someone into a particular state of mind

The song that has been driving me pleasurably potty recently is 'I'm Like a Bird' by Nelly Furtado. — *Nick Hornby, 31 Songs*

5 to force a nail or stake into a surface by hitting it hard
6 to hit or kick a ball hard
7 rain or snow drives down or against something when it is falling fast and hard

what someone is driving at is the point that they are trying to make

drive *NOUN* **drives**
1 a journey in a vehicle
2 a hard stroke in cricket or golf
3 the transmitting of power to machinery ◆ *four-wheel drive*
4 energy or enthusiasm
5 an organized effort to achieve something ◆ *a sales drive*
6 a track for vehicles through the grounds of a house
7 (*ICT*) a device that turns the disk on a computer while data is saved or retrieved

drive-in *ADJECTIVE*
a drive-in cinema or restaurant is one where the audience or customers stay in their cars

drivel *NOUN*
silly talk; nonsense

drivel *VERB* **drivels, drivelling, drivelled**
to talk or write drivel

WORD HISTORY from Old English *dreflian* 'to dribble'

driven *past participle of* **drive**

driver *NOUN* **drivers**
1 someone who drives a vehicle or train
2 a golf club used to hit a ball from a tee

drizzle *NOUN*
very fine rain

drizzle *VERB* **drizzles, drizzling, drizzled**
1 to rain in very fine drops
2 to trickle oil or sauce over food in a thin stream

WORD HISTORY from Old English *dreosan* 'to fall'

droll (*say* drohl) *ADJECTIVE*
amusing in an odd way
▷ **drolly** *ADVERB*

WORD HISTORY from a French word

dromedary *NOUN* **dromedaries**
a camel with one hump, bred for riding on

WORD HISTORY from Greek *dromas* 'runner'

drone *VERB* **drones, droning, droned**
1 to make a deep humming sound
2 to talk in a boring way or in a boring voice

drone *NOUN* **drones**
1 a deep humming sound
2 a continuous deep note produced by a bagpipe or other instrument
3 a male bee

drool *VERB* **drools, drooling, drooled**
to water at the mouth; to dribble

to drool over something is to show an excessive liking or desire for it

droop *VERB* **droops, drooping, drooped**
to bend or hang downwards through tiredness or weakness ◆ *The tulips were beginning to droop.*

drop *NOUN* **drops**
1 a tiny amount of a drink or liquid ◆ *There's only a drop of orange juice left.*
2 a fall or decrease ◆ *a drop in prices*
3 a vertical descent ◆ *a drop of 20 feet*
4 a small round sweet
5 a hanging ornament

drop *VERB* **drops, dropping, dropped**
1 to fall downwards
2 to crouch or lower your body towards the ground
3 to collapse with tiredness ◆ *After a day's shopping, I felt ready to drop.*
4 to let something fall

Miranda was so startled she almost dropped the eggs in her hand. — *Anne Fine, Madame Doubtfire*

5 your jaw drops when you open your mouth in surprise
6 to become lower or less

The temperature dropped quickly after dark. — *Philip Pullman, The Subtle Knife*

7 to descend steeply

From their feet the land dropped away into a shallow vale, then rose again to sombre moors inland. — *Rosemary Sutcliff, Beowulf: Dragonslayer*

8 to move behind others in position ◆ *The defending champion has dropped back to third place.*
9 to abandon or stop dealing with something ◆ *Let's just drop the subject!*
10 to leave a passenger at a destination ◆ *Can you drop me at the station?*
11 to leave someone or something out of a group or list ◆ *I've been dropped from the team.*

to drop by or **drop in** is to visit someone casually

to drop off
1 is to fall asleep
2 to drop someone or something off is to take them to a destination

to drop out is to stop taking part in a contest or course of study

to drop someone a line is to send them an informal letter or note

droplet *NOUN* **droplets**
a small drop

a b c d e f g h i j k l m n o p q r s t u v w x y z

dropout *NOUN* **dropouts**
a person who has dropped out of ordinary society or a course of study

droppings *PLURAL NOUN*
the dung of animals or birds

dross *NOUN*
1 scum on a surface
2 rubbish; worthless things or people

drought (*say* drout) *NOUN* **droughts**
a long period of dry weather

drove *past tense of* **drive**

drove *NOUN* **droves**
1 a moving herd or flock
2 droves of people are large crowds

drown *VERB* **drowns, drowning, drowned**
1 to die by suffocation under water
2 to kill someone by suffocating them under water
3 to flood or drench an area
4 to make so much noise that another sound cannot be heard

WORD HISTORY from an Old Norse word

drowse *VERB* **drowses, drowsing, drowsed**
to be sleepy or falling asleep

drowsy *ADJECTIVE* **drowsier, drowsiest**
sleepy
▷ **drowsily** *ADVERB*
▷ **drowsiness** *NOUN*

WORD HISTORY from an Old English word, related to *dreary*

drubbing *NOUN* **drubbings**
a severe defeat

WORD HISTORY from Arabic *daraba* 'beat'

drudge *NOUN* **drudges**
a person who does hard, boring, or menial work
▷ **drudgery** *NOUN*

drug *NOUN* **drugs**
1 a substance used in medicine
2 a substance that affects your senses or your mind, e.g. a narcotic or stimulant, especially one causing addiction

drug *VERB* **drugs, drugging, drugged**
to give a drug to someone, especially to make them unconscious

WORD HISTORY from Old French *drogue*

Druid (*say* droo- id) *NOUN* **Druids**
a priest of an ancient Celtic religion in Britain and France

drum *NOUN* **drums**
1 a musical instrument made of a cylinder with a skin or parchment stretched over one or both ends
2 a cylindrical object or container ◆ *an oil drum*

drum *VERB* **drums, drumming, drummed**
1 to play a drum or drums
2 to tap repeatedly on something ◆ *She drummed her fingers on the table impatiently.*
3 you drum a lesson or fact into someone when you make them remember it by constant repetition

to drum up support is to campaign for more support for a cause or plan
▷ **drummer** *NOUN*

drumstick *NOUN* **drumsticks**
1 a stick for beating a drum
2 the lower part of a cooked bird's leg

drunk *past participle of* **drink**

drunk *ADJECTIVE*
not able to control your behaviour through drinking too much alcohol

drunk *NOUN* **drunks**
a person who is drunk

drunkard *NOUN* **drunkards**
a person who is often drunk

drunken *ADJECTIVE*
1 drunk, or often drunk
2 caused by drinking alcohol ◆ *a drunken brawl*

dry *ADJECTIVE* **drier, driest**
1 without water or moisture
2 written or spoken in a dull, boring style
3 dry bread is eaten without butter or other spread
4 a dry remark or dry humour is said in a matter-of-fact or ironical way
▷ **drily** *ADVERB*
▷ **dryness** *NOUN*

dry *VERB* **dries, drying, dried**
1 to make something dry
2 to become dry

to dry out
1 something dries out when it becomes completely dry
2 (*informal*) someone dries out when they receive treatment to cure alcohol addiction

to dry up
1 you dry up when you dry washed dishes
2 a source or income or supply dries up when it gradually comes to an end

dryad *NOUN* **dryads**
a wood nymph

WORD HISTORY from Greek *drys* 'tree'

dry-cleaning *NOUN*
a method of cleaning clothes using a liquid that evaporates quickly

dry dock *NOUN* **dry docks**
a dock that can be emptied of water so that ships can float in and then be repaired

dry ice *NOUN*
solid carbon dioxide

DTP *ABBREVIATION*
desktop publishing

dual *ADJECTIVE*
composed of two parts; double
▷ **duality** *NOUN*
WORD HISTORY from Latin *duo* 'two'

dual carriageway *NOUN* **dual carriageways**
a road with a dividing strip between lanes of traffic in opposite directions

dub¹ *VERB* **dubs, dubbing, dubbed**
1 to make a man a knight by touching him on the shoulder with a sword
2 to give a person or thing a nickname
WORD HISTORY from Old French *adober* 'to equip with armour'

dub² *VERB* **dubs, dubbing, dubbed**
1 to replace the original soundtrack of a film with one in a different language ◆ *It is a Spanish film dubbed into English.*
2 to add new sounds or effects to a music recording
WORD HISTORY a short form of *double*

dubbin *NOUN*
thick grease used to soften leather and make it waterproof
WORD HISTORY from an Old French word

dubious (*say* **dew**- bee- us) *ADJECTIVE*
1 doubtful or suspicious about something ◆ *I'm dubious about their motives.*
2 not to be relied on; questionable
▷ **dubiously** *ADVERB*
WORD HISTORY from Latin *dubium* 'doubt'

ducal *ADJECTIVE*
to do with a duke

ducat (*say* **duk**- at) *NOUN* **ducats**
a former gold coin used in Europe

duchess *NOUN* **duchesses**
1 a duke's wife or widow
2 a woman whose rank is equal to that of a duke
WORD HISTORY from Latin *ducissa*

duchy *NOUN* **duchies**
the territory of a duke or duchess
WORD HISTORY from Old French *duche*

duck *NOUN* **ducks**
1 a swimming bird with a flat beak
2 the female of this kind of bird
3 a batsman's score of nought at cricket
4 a ducking movement

duck *VERB* **ducks, ducking, ducked**
1 to bend down quickly to avoid being hit or seen ◆ *He ran along the side of the house, ducking under the windows.*
2 to dip your head under water quickly
3 to push someone or something into water briefly
4 to avoid a task or duty; to dodge something
WORD HISTORY from Old English *duce*

duckling *NOUN* **ducklings**
a young duck

duct *NOUN* **ducts**
a tube or channel through which liquid, gas, air, or cables can pass
WORD HISTORY from Latin *ductus* 'leading', from *ducere* 'to lead'
WORD FAMILY A number of English words are related to *duct* because part of their original meaning comes from the Latin words *ducere* meaning 'to lead'. These include *abduct, conduct, deduct, conducive, induce, introduce, produce,* and *reduce.*

ductile *ADJECTIVE*
ductile metal is able to be drawn out into fine strands

dud *NOUN* **duds**
(*informal*) something that is useless or fails to work

dude *NOUN* **dudes**
(*American*) (*informal*) a person; a man
WORD HISTORY probably from German dialect *Dude* 'fool'

dudgeon (*say* **duj**- on) *NOUN*
in high dudgeon very resentful or indignant

due *ADJECTIVE*
1 expected; scheduled to do something or to arrive ◆ *The train is due in ten minutes.*
2 owing; needing to be paid ◆ *The rent was due on Monday.*
3 that ought to be given; rightful ◆ *Please treat the animals with due respect.*
due to as a result of; caused by
in due course at the appropriate time

due *ADVERB*
exactly ◆ *We sailed due east.*

due *NOUN* **dues**
dues money owed; fees
to give someone their due is to give them credit for what they have done well
WORD HISTORY from French *dû* 'something owed'

duel *NOUN* **duels**
a fight between two people, especially with pistols or swords
▷ **duelling** *NOUN*
▷ **duellist** *NOUN*

duel *VERB* **duels, duelling, duelled**
to fight a duel
WORD HISTORY from an Italian word

duet *NOUN* **duets**
a piece of music for two players or singers
WORD HISTORY from Italian *duo* 'two'

duff *ADJECTIVE*
(*informal*) worthless or broken

duffel bag *NOUN* **duffel bags**
a cylindrical canvas bag closed by a drawstring

duffel coat *NOUN* **duffel coats**
a thick overcoat with a hood, fastened with toggles
WORD HISTORY from *Duffel*, a town in Belgium, where the cloth for it was made

duffer *NOUN* **duffers**
(*informal*) a person who is stupid or not good at doing something

dug *past tense and past participle of* **dig**

dugout *NOUN* **dugouts**
1 an underground shelter
2 a shelter at the side of a sports field for a team's coaches and substitutes
3 a canoe made by hollowing out a tree trunk

duke *NOUN* **dukes**
a member of the highest rank of noblemen
▷ **dukedom** *NOUN*
WORD HISTORY from Latin *dux* 'leader'

dulcet (*say* **dul**- sit) *ADJECTIVE*
sweet-sounding; pleasant
WORD HISTORY from Latin *dulcis* 'sweet'

dulcimer (*say* **dul**- sim- er) *NOUN* **dulcimers**
a musical instrument with strings that are struck by two small hammers
WORD HISTORY from Old French *doulcemer*

dull *ADJECTIVE*
1 not bright or clear ◆ *dull weather*
2 not interesting or exciting; boring ◆ *a dull concert*
3 not sharp ◆ *a dull pain*
4 stupid; slow to understand
▷ **dully** *ADVERB*
▷ **dullness** *NOUN*
WORD HISTORY from Old English *dol* 'stupid'

dullard *NOUN* **dullards**
a stupid person

duly *ADVERB*
in the due or proper way; as expected ◆ *He was duly astonished to see me.*

dumb *ADJECTIVE*
1 without the ability to speak
2 silent; unable or unwilling to speak
3 (*informal*) stupid or foolish ◆ *It's a dumb idea.*
▷ **dumbly** *ADVERB*
▷ **dumbness** *NOUN*

dumb *VERB* **dumbs, dumbing, dumbed**
to dumb something down (*informal*) is to make it simpler so that more people can understand it
WORD HISTORY from an Old English word

dumbfounded *ADJECTIVE*
unable to say anything because you are so astonished
WORD HISTORY from *dumb* and *confound*

dummy *NOUN* **dummies**
1 a model of a human figure used to display clothes
2 a rubber teat for a baby to suck
3 an imitation of something
4 a pretended pass or kick in football or rugby
WORD HISTORY related to *dumb*

dump *NOUN* **dumps**
1 a place where rubbish is left or stored
2 (*informal*) a dull or unattractive place

dump *VERB* **dumps, dumping, dumped**
1 to get rid of something you do not want
2 to put something down carelessly ◆ *Dump your schoolbag and let's go.*

dumpling *NOUN* **dumplings**
a ball of dough cooked in a stew or baked with fruit inside

dumps *PLURAL NOUN*
in the dumps (*informal*) feeling depressed or unhappy
WORD HISTORY from Old Dutch *domp* 'mist, dampness'

dumpy *ADJECTIVE* **dumpier, dumpiest**
short and fat
WORD HISTORY from an old word *dump* 'dumpy person'

dunce *NOUN* **dunces**
a person who is slow at learning
WORD HISTORY from the Scottish medieval philosopher, John *Duns* Scotus, whose followers were said by their opponents to be unable to understand new ideas

dune *NOUN* **dunes**
a mound of loose sand shaped by the wind

dung *NOUN*
solid waste matter excreted by an animal

dungarees *PLURAL NOUN*
trousers with a bib held up by straps over your shoulders
WORD HISTORY from Hindi *dungri*, the cloth from which they were originally made

dungeon (*say* **dun**- jon) *NOUN* **dungeons**
an underground prison cell
WORD HISTORY from an Old French word

dunk *VERB* **dunks, dunking, dunked**
to dip something into liquid
WORD HISTORY from a German word

duo (*say* dew- oh) *NOUN* **duos**
a pair of performers, especially musicians
WORD HISTORY via Italian from Latin *duo* 'two'

duodenum (*say* dew- o- **deen**- um) *NOUN* **duodenums**
the part of the small intestine that is just below your stomach
▷ **duodenal** *ADJECTIVE*
WORD HISTORY from Latin *duodecim* 'twelve', because its length is about twelve times the breadth of a finger

dupe *VERB* **dupes, duping, duped**
to deceive or trick someone

a b c d e f g h i j k l m n o p q r s t u v w x y z

duplicate (*say* dyoop- lik- at) *NOUN* **duplicates**
1 something that is exactly the same as another thing
2 an exact copy

duplicate (*say* dyoop- lik- ayt) *VERB* **duplicates, duplicating, duplicated**
1 to make an exact copy of something
2 to repeat effort or work unnecessarily
▷ **duplication** *NOUN*
▷ **duplicator** *NOUN*
WORD HISTORY from Latin *duplex* 'double'

duplicity (*say* dew- **plis**- it- ee) *NOUN*
deceitful behaviour
▷ **duplicitous** *ADJECTIVE*

durable *ADJECTIVE*
strong and likely to last; hard-wearing
▷ **durably** *ADVERB*
▷ **durability** *NOUN*
WORD HISTORY from Latin *durare* 'to endure'

duration *NOUN*
the length of time something lasts

duress (*say* dewr- ess) *NOUN*
the use of force or threats to make someone do something against their will
WORD HISTORY from Latin *durus* 'hard'

during *PREPOSITION*
used to show that something happens while another event or action is taking place

It had snowed a little during the night, and the grass crunched frostily under my feet. — *Joe Simpson, Touching the Void*

WORD HISTORY from Latin *durans* 'lasting, enduring'

dusk *NOUN* **dusks**
the darker stage of twilight
WORD HISTORY from an Old English word

dusky *ADJECTIVE* **duskier, duskiest**
darkish in colour
▷ **duskiness** *NOUN*

dust *NOUN*
1 tiny particles of earth or other solid material
2 a cleaning to remove dust ◆ *These shelves need a dust.*

dust *VERB* **dusts, dusting, dusted**
1 to wipe away dust from a surface
2 to sprinkle something with powder

dustbin *NOUN* **dustbins**
a bin for household rubbish

duster *NOUN* **dusters**
a cloth for dusting things

dustman *NOUN* **dustmen**
a person employed to empty dustbins and take away household rubbish

dustpan *NOUN* **dustpans**
a pan into which dust is brushed from a floor

dusty *ADJECTIVE* **dustier, dustiest**
1 covered with dust
2 like dust
▷ **dustiness** *NOUN*

Dutch *ADJECTIVE*
to do with or coming from the Netherlands
to go Dutch is to share the cost of a meal equally

Dutch *NOUN*
the language of the Netherlands

dutiful *ADJECTIVE*
doing your duty; obedient
▷ **dutifully** *ADVERB*

duty *NOUN* **duties**
1 duty is what you ought to do or must do

My mother wasn't content just to say that I was not an idiot, she set out to prove it, not because of any rigid sense of duty, but out of love. — *Christy Brown, My Left Foot*

2 a duty is a task that must be done, often as part of your job
3 duty is a tax charged on imports and on certain other things
on or **off duty** actually doing (or not doing) what is your regular work
WORD HISTORY related to *due*

duty-free *ADJECTIVE*
duty-free goods are goods on which import duty is not charged

duvet (*say* doo- vay) *NOUN* **duvets**
a thick soft quilt used instead of other bedclothes
WORD HISTORY a French word meaning 'down (feathers)'

DV *ABBREVIATION*
digital video

DVD *NOUN* **DVDs**
digital videodisc, or digital versatile disc; a disc used for storing large amounts of audio or video information, especially films

dwarf *NOUN* **dwarfs** or **dwarves**
1 a very small person, animal, or plant
2 a mythological creature like a small human being, often with magical powers

dwarf *VERB* **dwarfs, dwarfing, dwarfed**
to make something seem small by contrast ◆ *The castle dwarfed the houses that stood near it.*
WORD HISTORY from an Old English word

dwell *VERB* **dwells, dwelling, dwelt**
(*formal*) to dwell in a place is to live there permanently
to dwell on something is to think or talk about it for a long time
▷ **dweller** *NOUN*
WORD HISTORY from Old English *dwellan* 'to lead astray'

dwelling *NOUN* **dwellings**
a house or other building to live in

dwindle *VERB* **dwindles, dwindling, dwindled**
to become gradually less or smaller

dye *NOUN* **dyes**
a substance used for changing the colour of cloth, hair, etc.

dye *VERB* **dyes, dyeing, dyed**
to make something a particular colour with dye ◆ *She dyed her hair green.*
▷ **dyer** *NOUN*

dying *present participle of* **die**

dyke *NOUN* **dykes**
1 a long wall or embankment to hold back water and prevent flooding
2 a ditch for draining water from land
WORD HISTORY from an Old Norse word

dynamic *ADJECTIVE*
1 a dynamic person is energetic and forceful
2 a dynamic force produces motion (SEE ALSO **static**)
▷ **dynamically** *ADVERB*
WORD HISTORY from Greek *dunamis* 'power'

dynamics *NOUN*
1 (*Science*) the scientific study of force and motion
2 (*Music*) the level of loudness with which music is performed

dynamite *NOUN*
1 a powerful explosive
2 something likely to make people very excited or angry ◆ *These latest revelations are dynamite.*

dynamo *NOUN* **dynamos**
1 a machine that makes electricity
2 (*informal*) a very energetic person
WORD HISTORY from Greek *dunamis* 'power'

dynasty (*say* **din**- a- stee) *NOUN* **dynasties**
(*History*) a line of rulers or powerful people all from the same family
▷ **dynastic** *ADJECTIVE*

dysentery (*say* **dis**- en- tree) *NOUN*
a disease causing severe diarrhoea
WORD HISTORY from Greek *dus-* 'badly' and *entera* 'bowels'

dysfunctional *ADJECTIVE*
not able to act or function normally
▷ **dysfunction** *NOUN*

dyslexia (*say* dis- **leks**- ee- a) *NOUN*
special difficulty in being able to read and spell, caused by a brain condition
▷ **dyslexic** *ADJECTIVE*
WORD HISTORY from Greek *dus-* 'badly' and *lexis* 'speech'

dyspepsia (*say* dis- **pep**- see- a) *NOUN*
indigestion
▷ **dyspeptic** *ADJECTIVE*
WORD HISTORY from Greek *dus-* 'badly' and *peptikos* 'able to digest'

dystrophy (*say* **dis**- trof- ee) *NOUN*
a hereditary disease which causes muscles to weaken gradually
WORD HISTORY from Greek *dus-* 'badly' and *-trophia* 'nourishment'

Ee

E. *ABBREVIATION*
east; eastern

each *ADJECTIVE, PRONOUN*
every one of two or more people or things ◆ *Each player gets seven cards.* ◆ *Each of us wanted to help.*

USAGE NOTE Take care to use the pronoun *each* with a singular verb and singular pronouns: ◆ *Each of the girls is bringing her own packed lunch.*

eager *ADJECTIVE*
wanting very much to do something; very keen

Lee was talking to a group of astronomers eager to learn what news he could bring them. — *Philip Pullman, The Subtle Knife*

▷ **eagerly** *ADVERB*
▷ **eagerness** *NOUN*

eagle *NOUN* **eagles**
a large bird of prey with very strong sight

ear¹ *NOUN* **ears**
1 the organ that is used for hearing and balance in humans and some animals
2 someone who has an ear for music or language has the ability to appreciate it, or to learn it easily

ear² *NOUN* **ears**
the spike of seeds at the top of a stalk of corn

earache *NOUN*
a pain in the eardrum

eardrum *NOUN* **eardrums**
a membrane in the ear that vibrates when sounds reach it

earl *NOUN* **earls**
a British nobleman ranking below a marquis and above a viscount
▷ **earldom** *NOUN*

ear lobe *NOUN* **ear lobes**
the soft fleshy part at the lower end of the ear

early *ADJECTIVE, ADVERB* **earlier, earliest**
1 before the usual or expected time
2 near the beginning of something

The organization was formed in the early eighties, during the so-called Cold War. — *Anthony Horowitz, Scorpia*

3 near the beginning of the day
4 an early night is one in which you go to bed early in the evening

an early bird is a person who gets up early in the morning or who arrives early
▷ **earliness** *NOUN*

earmark *VERB* **earmarks, earmarking, earmarked**
to put something aside for a particular purpose ◆ *The Japanese government has already earmarked $80 million for the project.*

WORD HISTORY so called from the custom of marking an animal's ear to identify it

earn *VERB* **earns, earning, earned**
1 to earn money is to receive it as an income for doing work
2 to earn praise or blame is to deserve it for what you do

earnest *ADJECTIVE*
showing serious feelings or intentions

in earnest
1 more seriously or with more determination ◆ *The Olympic squad began training in earnest last summer.*
2 meaning what you say
▷ **earnestly** *ADVERB*
▷ **earnestness** *NOUN*

earnings *PLURAL NOUN*
money earned

earphone *NOUN* **earphones**
an electrical device worn on your ear to listen to audio sounds, e.g. in an MP3 player

earplug *NOUN* **earplugs**
a device that fits in your ear to block out noise

earring *NOUN* **earrings**
a piece of jewellery worn on your ear

earshot *NOUN*
the distance within which a sound can be heard ◆ *Many parts of London are within earshot of Big Ben.*

ear-splitting *ADJECTIVE*
an ear-splitting sound is unpleasantly loud

earth *NOUN* **earths**
1 (also **Earth**) the planet that we live on
2 the ground; soil
3 the hole where a fox or badger lives
4 connection to the ground to complete an electrical circuit

earth *VERB* **earths, earthing, earthed**
to connect an electrical circuit to the ground

earthenware *NOUN*
pottery made of coarse baked clay

earthly *ADJECTIVE*
1 to do with the planet Earth

What lay before him looked at first strangely like an earthly landscape — a landscape of grey downland ridges rising and falling likes waves of the sea. — *C. S. Lewis, Out of the Silent Planet*

2 concerning life in this world, rather than spiritual life after death
3 possible, imaginable ◆ *There is no earthly chance of them winning the match.*

earthquake *NOUN* **earthquakes**
a violent movement of part of the earth's surface

earthwork *NOUN* **earthworks**
a large artificial bank of earth

earthworm *NOUN* **earthworms**
a burrowing worm that lives in the soil

earthy *ADJECTIVE* **earthier, earthiest**
1 like earth or soil in appearance or texture
2 earthy humour is crude or vulgar

earwig *NOUN* **earwigs**
a crawling insect with pincers at the end of its body

WORD HISTORY so called because it was once thought to crawl into people's ears

ease *NOUN*
1 to do something with ease is to do it without effort or trouble
2 to be or feel at ease with someone is to feel comfortable and relaxed and not intimidated when you are with them

ease *VERB* **eases, easing, eased**
1 to make something less painful, tight, or troublesome ◆ *I tried every trick to ease the pain.*
2 to ease something into a position is to move it there gently
3 pain or pressure eases when it becomes less severe

easel *NOUN* **easels**
(*Art*) a stand for supporting a painting or a blackboard

WORD HISTORY from Dutch *ezel* 'donkey', because it carried a load

easily *ADVERB*
1 without difficulty; with ease
2 by far ◆ *It was easily the most boring lesson of the morning.*
3 very likely ◆ *Household materials can easily become fire hazards.*

east *NOUN*
1 the direction where the sun rises
2 the eastern part of a country, city, or other area

the East the countries of Asia, especially China, Japan, and India, in relation to Europe and North America

east *ADJECTIVE, ADVERB*
towards or in the east; coming from the east

WORD FAMILY An easterly wind comes from the direction of the east; an eastern person, place or thing comes from, or is situated in, the east; an easterner is a person who comes from or lives in the east of a country or area; an easternmost place or point is at the most eastern point of a country or area. Another word for 'belonging to the east' is oriental, which usually refers to the peoples and cultures of the Far East.

Easter *NOUN*
the Sunday (in March or April) when Christians commemorate the resurrection of Christ; the days around this date

WORD HISTORY named after *Eastre*, an Anglo-Saxon goddess whose feast was celebrated in spring

Easter egg *NOUN* **Easter eggs**
a chocolate or hen's egg decorated and given as a gift at Easter

eastward *ADJECTIVE, ADVERB*
towards the east
▷ **eastwards** *ADVERB*

easy *ADJECTIVE* **easier, easiest**
able to be done, used, or understood without trouble
▷ **easiness** *NOUN*

easy *ADVERB*
to take it easy is to relax or calm down

easy chair *NOUN* **easy chairs**
a comfortable armchair

easygoing *ADJECTIVE*
an easygoing person or atmosphere is relaxed and tolerant

eat *VERB* **eats, eating, ate, eaten**
1 to chew and swallow something as food
2 to have a meal ◆ *When do we eat?*
3 to eat into a supply or store is to start to use it up

to eat something up
1 to eat up food is to finish it
2 to eat up savings or resources is to use them up completely

SYNONYMS (meaning 1) consume, devour, swallow; *informal* scoff, put away, tuck into, polish off

WORD FAMILY Words with eating in their meaning often end in *-vore* or *-phagous*. For example, animals that eat meat are called *carnivores*, and a *sarcophagus*, a kind of large stone coffin, was so called because it was thought to eat the flesh.

eatable *ADJECTIVE*
fit to be eaten

USAGE NOTE Note that *eatable* describes food that is fit to be eaten, whereas *edible* describes something that can be eaten and is not harmful or poisonous.

eatery *NOUN* **eateries**
(*informal*) a restaurant

eau de Cologne (*say* oh der kol- **ohn**) *NOUN*
a light perfume first made at Cologne, in Germany

eaves *PLURAL NOUN*
the overhanging edges of a roof

eavesdrop *VERB* **eavesdrops, eavesdropping, eavesdropped**
to listen secretly to a private conversation

Mrs Hooper, he noticed, was leaning dangerously far over the fence, still eavesdropping in hopes of hearing more. — *Anne Fine, Madame Doubtfire*

▷ **eavesdropper** *NOUN*

WORD HISTORY so called from the idea of someone listening outside a wall, where water drops from the eaves

ebb *NOUN* **ebbs**
the movement of the tide when it is going out, away from the land (SEE ALSO **flow** *NOUN*)
at a low ebb at a low point; very weak or depleted

ebb *VERB* **ebbs, ebbing, ebbed**
1 the tide ebbs when it flows away from the land (SEE ALSO **flow** *VERB*)
2 your strength or courage ebbs when it weakens or fades

Ebola *NOUN*
a deadly virus which causes the linings of body organs to leak blood and fluids

WORD HISTORY after the River *Ebola* in Zaire, near where the virus was first identified

ebony *NOUN*
the hard black wood of a tropical tree

ebullient (*say* i- **bul**- ient) *ADJECTIVE*
cheerful, full of high spirits

▷ **ebullience** *NOUN*

WORD HISTORY from a Latin word meaning 'bubbling' or 'boiling'

EC *ABBREVIATION*
European Community, a former name for the European Union (EU)

eccentric (*say* ik- **sen**- trik) *ADJECTIVE*
behaving strangely

▷ **eccentrically** *ADVERB*

▷ **eccentricity** *NOUN*

WORD HISTORY from a Greek word meaning 'away from the centre'

eccentric *NOUN* **eccentrics**
someone who behaves strangely; an eccentric person

ecclesiastical *ADJECTIVE*
to do with the Christian Church or clergy

WORD HISTORY from Greek *ekklesia* 'a church'

echidna (*say* i- **kid**- nu) *NOUN* **echidnas**
a spiny mammal of Australia and New Guinea, with a long snout

WORD HISTORY from a Greek word meaning 'viper'

echo *NOUN* **echoes**
a sound that is heard again as it is reflected off something

echo *VERB* **echoes, echoing, echoed**
1 to make an echo
2 to repeat a sound or saying

éclair (*say* ay- **klair**) *NOUN* **éclairs**
a finger-shaped cake of pastry with a creamy filling

eclipse *NOUN* **eclipses**
the blocking of the sun's or moon's light when the moon or the Earth is in the way

eclipse *VERB* **eclipses, eclipsing, eclipsed**
1 to block the light and cause an eclipse
2 to seem better or more important than others ◆ *Sudan is the forgotten civilization of the Nile, long eclipsed by its better known neighbour, Egypt.*

ecology (*say* ee- **kol**- o- jee) *NOUN*
the study of living things in relation to each other and to where they live

▷ **ecological** *ADJECTIVE*

▷ **ecologically** *ADVERB*

▷ **ecologist** *NOUN*

WORD HISTORY from Greek *oikos* 'a house'

e-commerce *NOUN*
business conducted electronically on the Internet

economic (*say* ee- kon- **om**- ik) *ADJECTIVE*
1 to do with economy or economics
2 making enough money; profitable

economical *ADJECTIVE*
using as little as possible

▷ **economically** *ADVERB*

economics *NOUN*
the study of how money is used and how goods and services are provided and used

▷ **economist** *NOUN*

economize *VERB* **economizes, economizing, economized**
1 to spend less money
2 to economize on fuel or another resource is to use up less of it

USAGE NOTE This word can also be spelled economise.

a b c d e f g h i j k l m n o p q r s t u v w x y z

economy *NOUN* **economies**

1 the resources of a country or region and the way it uses these to produce wealth

2 careful use of resources

3 a saving ◆ *We've been forced to make some economies this year.*

WORD HISTORY from Greek *oikonomia* 'household management', from *oikos* 'house' and *nemein* 'to manage'

ecosystem *NOUN* **ecosystems**

a group of plants and animals that interact with each other and form an ecological unit

ecstasy (*say* **ek**- sta- see) *NOUN*

1 a feeling of great delight

2 an illegal drug that makes people feel very energetic and can cause hallucinations

▷ **ecstatic** (*say* ik- **stat**- ik) *ADJECTIVE*

▷ **ecstatically** *ADVERB*

WORD HISTORY from a Greek word meaning 'standing outside yourself'

ecumenical (*say* ee- kew- **men**- i- kal) *ADJECTIVE*

to do with the unity of all the Christian Churches

WORD HISTORY from a Greek word meaning 'the inhabited world'

eczema (*say* **eks**- ma) *NOUN*

a skin disease which causes rough itching patches

WORD HISTORY a Greek word meaning 'eruption', from *zein* 'to boil'

eddy *NOUN* **eddies**

a swirling patch of water, air, or smoke

eddy *VERB* **eddies, eddying, eddied**

to swirl

edge *NOUN* **edges**

1 the part along the side or end of something

2 the sharp part of the blade of a knife or axe

3 a sharp or penetrating quality

Reverend Cornwell's voice took on the edge of command. — *Celia Rees, Witch Child*

to be on edge is to be tense and irritable

edge *VERB* **edges, edging, edged**

1 to be the edge or border of something

2 to put a border on something

3 to move something gradually

Very slowly, Thomas edged his feet along the stone floor. As he did so he could feel dankness with his bare feet. — *G. P. Taylor, Shadowmancer*

edgeways *ADVERB*

with the edge forwards or outwards

edgy *ADJECTIVE* **edgier, edgiest**

tense and irritable

▷ **edgily** *ADVERB*

▷ **edginess** *NOUN*

edible *ADJECTIVE*

suitable for eating, not poisonous ◆ *I'm not sure if those mushrooms are edible.*

USAGE NOTE See the note at *eatable*.

edict (*say* **ee**- dikt) *NOUN* **edicts**

an official command

edifice (*say* **ed**- if- iss) *NOUN* **edifices**

a large building

WORD HISTORY from Latin *aedis* 'a temple'

edify *VERB* **edifies, edifying, edified**

to be an improving influence on a person's mind

▷ **edification** *NOUN*

edit *VERB* **edits, editing, edited**

1 to be the editor of a newspaper or other publication

2 to make written material ready for publishing

3 to choose and put the parts of a film or tape recording into order

edition *NOUN* **editions**

1 the form in which something is published ◆ *a paperback edition*

2 all the copies of a book or other publication issued at the same time

3 an individual television or radio programme in a series

editor *NOUN* **editors**

1 the person in charge of a newspaper or a section of it

2 a person who edits something

editorial *ADJECTIVE*

to do with editing or editors

editorial *NOUN* **editorials**

a newspaper article giving the editor's comments on something

educate *VERB* **educates, educating, educated**

to provide a person with education

▷ **educative** *ADJECTIVE*

▷ **educator** *NOUN*

educated *ADJECTIVE*

showing a high standard of knowledge and culture, as a result of a good education

education *NOUN*

the process of training people's minds and abilities so that they acquire knowledge and develop skills

▷ **educational** *ADJECTIVE*

▷ **educationally** *ADVERB*

▷ **educationist** *NOUN*

Edwardian *ADJECTIVE*
belonging to the reign of King Edward VII (1901–10)

Edwardian *NOUN* **Edwardians**
someone who lived at this time

eel *NOUN* **eels**
a long fish that looks like a snake

eerie *ADJECTIVE* **eerier, eeriest**
strange in a frightening or mysterious way

Still the eerie silence. It seemed to go on and on and on, and as it continued, it grew deeper and more frightening. — *Tim Bowler, Starseeker*

▷ **eerily** *ADVERB*
▷ **eeriness** *NOUN*

efface *VERB* **effaces, effacing, effaced**
to wipe or rub something out
▷ **effacement** *NOUN*

effect *NOUN* **effects**
1 a change that is produced by an action or cause; a result
2 an impression that is produced by something

Nguyen was by now thoroughly spooked. Artemis generally had that effect on people. — *Eoin Colfer, Artemis Fowl*

effect *VERB* **effects, effecting, effected**
to effect a change is to make it happen

USAGE NOTE Take care not to confuse this word with *affect*.

effective *ADJECTIVE*
1 producing the effect that is wanted ◆ *an effective treatment for migraine*
2 impressive and striking ◆ *I didn't think the president's speech was very effective.*
▷ **effectively** *ADVERB*
▷ **effectiveness** *NOUN*

effectual *ADJECTIVE*
producing the result that is wanted
▷ **effectually** *ADVERB*

effeminate *ADJECTIVE*
with features or qualities that are traditionally thought to be feminine
▷ **effeminacy** *NOUN*

effervesce (*say* ef- er- **vess**) *VERB* **effervesces, effervescing, effervesced**
liquid effervesces when it fizzes or gives off bubbles of gas
▷ **effervescent** *ADJECTIVE*
▷ **effervescence** *NOUN*

WORD HISTORY from a Latin word meaning 'to come to the boil'

efficacious (*say* ef- ik- **ay**- shus) *ADJECTIVE*
able to produce the result that is wanted
▷ **efficacy** (*say* **ef**- ik- a- see) *NOUN*

efficient *ADJECTIVE*
doing work well; effective
▷ **efficiently** *ADVERB*
▷ **efficiency** *NOUN*

effigy (*say* **ef**- i- jee) *NOUN* **effigies**
a model or sculptured figure

effort *NOUN* **efforts**
1 the use of energy, or the energy used to do something

Albard fixed his mind on the hilt of the sword, and with great effort, he caused it to stir beneath the debris. — *William Nicholson, Firesong*

2 a difficult or tiring task
3 an attempt

effortless *ADJECTIVE*
done with little or no effort
▷ **effortlessly** *ADVERB*

effusive *ADJECTIVE*
showing a great deal of affection or enthusiasm
▷ **effusively** *ADVERB*
▷ **effusiveness** *NOUN*

e.g. *ABBREVIATION*
for example

WORD HISTORY short for Latin *exempli gratia* 'for the sake of an example'

egalitarian (*say* ig- al- it- **air**- ee- an) *ADJECTIVE*
an egalitarian person or belief maintains that everybody is equal and that nobody should be given special privileges
▷ **egalitarianism** *NOUN*

egg ❶ *NOUN* **eggs**
1 an oval object produced by the female of birds, fishes, reptiles, and insects, which may develop into a new individual if fertilized
2 a hen's or duck's egg used as food
3 an ovum

egg ❷ *VERB* **eggs, egging, egged**
to egg someone on is to encourage them to do something

WORD HISTORY from an Old Norse word meaning 'to sharpen'

eggplant *NOUN* **eggplants**
(*American*) an aubergine

WORD HISTORY so called because of its egg- like shape

ego (*say* **eeg**- oh) *NOUN* **egos**
a person's self or self-respect

WORD HISTORY a Latin word meaning 'I'

egocentric *ADJECTIVE*
self-centred
▷ **egocentricity** *NOUN*

egotist (*say* eg- oh- tist) ***NOUN*** **egotists**
a conceited person who is always talking about themselves
▷ **egotism** ***NOUN***
▷ **egotistic** ***ADJECTIVE***

egress ***NOUN***
a way out; an exit

egret ***NOUN*** **egrets**
a kind of heron with white plumage and long tail feathers

Egyptology
the study of the language and culture of ancient Egypt
▷ **Egyptologist** ***NOUN***

Eid (*say* eed) ***NOUN***
a Muslim festival marking the end of the fast of Ramadan

WORD HISTORY an Arabic word meaning 'festival'

eiderdown ***NOUN*** **eiderdowns**
a quilt stuffed with soft material

WORD HISTORY from an earlier meaning, the soft down of the *eider*, a kind of duck

eight ***NOUN, ADJECTIVE*** **eights**
the number 8, one more than seven
▷ **eighth** ***ADJECTIVE, NOUN***

eighteen ***NOUN, ADJECTIVE*** **eighteens**
the number 18, one more than seventeen
▷ **eighteenth** ***ADJECTIVE, NOUN***

eighty ***NOUN, ADJECTIVE*** **eighties**
the number 80, equal to eight times ten
▷ **eightieth** ***ADJECTIVE, NOUN***

eisteddfod (*say* eye- **steth**- vod) ***NOUN*** **eisteddfods or eisteddfodau**
an annual Welsh gathering of poets and musicians for competitions

WORD HISTORY a Welsh word meaning 'session'

either (*say* **eye**- *ther* or **ee**- *ther*) ***ADJECTIVE, PRONOUN***
1 one or the other of two ◆ *Either team can win.* ◆ *Either of those dates will do.*
2 both of two ◆ *People sat on either side of a long table.*

either ***ADVERB***
also; similarly ◆ *If you don't go, I won't either.*

either ***CONJUNCTION***
(used with *or*) the first of two possibilities

You've got to make up your mind now ... Either he's your father and you pay him that respect, or else you're not to come here. — *Arthur Miller, Death of a Salesman*

ejaculate ***VERB*** **ejaculates, ejaculating, ejaculated**
1 to produce semen from the penis during orgasm
2 (*formal*) to say something suddenly; to exclaim

'Did ever anyone hear the like!' ejaculated Marilla, who had listened in dumb amazement. — *L. M. Montgomery, Anne of Green Gables*

▷ **ejaculation** ***NOUN***
▷ **ejaculatory** ***ADJECTIVE***

eject ***VERB*** **ejects, ejecting, ejected**
1 to send something out forcefully
2 to force someone to leave
3 a pilot ejects when they exit from an aircraft in a special seat in an emergency
▷ **ejection** ***NOUN***
▷ **ejector** ***NOUN***

eke (*say* eek) ***VERB*** **ekes, eking, eked**
to eke something out is to make it last as long as possible by only using small amounts at a time

elaborate (*say* il- **ab**- er- at) ***ADJECTIVE***
having many parts or details; complicated
▷ **elaborately** ***ADVERB***
▷ **elaborateness** ***NOUN***

elaborate (*say* il- **ab**- er- ayt) ***VERB*** **elaborates, elaborating, elaborated**
to explain or work out a plan or design in detail
▷ **elaboration** ***NOUN***

élan (*say* ay- **lan**) ***NOUN***
enthusiastic or vigorous style

eland (*say* ee- land) ***NOUN***
a large African antelope with spiral horns

elapse ***VERB*** **elapses, elapsing, elapsed**
an amount of time elapses when it passes

elastic ***NOUN***
cord or material woven with strands of rubber so that it can stretch

elastic ***ADJECTIVE***
an elastic object can be stretched or squeezed and then return to its original length or shape
▷ **elasticity** ***NOUN***

elated ***ADJECTIVE***
feeling very pleased
▷ **elation** ***NOUN***

elbow ***NOUN*** **elbows**
the joint in the middle of your arm

elbow ***VERB*** **elbows, elbowing, elbowed**
to push someone or something with your elbow

Faster and faster Twig ran, barging through the crowds, elbowing dawdlers out of his way. — *Paul Stewart and Chris Riddell, Stormchaser*

elder[1] *ADJECTIVE*
older of two or more ◆ *my elder brother*

elder *NOUN* **elders**
1 someone who is older than you
2 an official in a church or community

The next day a group of elders from all the nine villages of Umuofia came to Okonkwo's house early in the morning. — *Chinua Achebe, Things Fall Apart*

elder[2] *NOUN* **elders**
a tree with white flowers and black berries

elderberry *NOUN* **elderberries**
the fruit of the elder tree

elderly *ADJECTIVE*
an elderly person is rather old or ageing

eldest *ADJECTIVE*
oldest

eldritch *ADJECTIVE*
uncanny, eerie

As the cauldron bubbled an eldritch voice shrieked: 'When shall we three meet again?' — *Terry Pratchett, Wyrd Sisters*

elect *VERB* **elects, electing, elected**
1 to choose someone or something by voting
2 to choose or decide to do something

elect *ADJECTIVE*
chosen by a vote but not yet in office ◆ *the president elect*

election *NOUN* **elections**
1 the process of choosing someone or something, or of being chosen
2 the process of electing representatives to a country's parliament or assembly

elector *NOUN* **electors**
someone who has the right to vote in an election
▷ **electoral** *ADJECTIVE*

electorate *NOUN* **electorates**
all those who have the right to vote in an election

electric *ADJECTIVE*
1 to do with or worked by electricity
2 full of excitement or tension ◆ *The atmosphere inside the hall was electric.*
▷ **electrical** *ADJECTIVE*
▷ **electrically** *ADVERB*

WORD HISTORY from Greek *elektron* 'amber', because it is easily given a charge of static electricity

electric chair *NOUN*
an electrified chair used for capital punishment in the USA

electrician *NOUN* **electricians**
a person whose job is to install or repair electrical equipment

electricity *NOUN*
a form of energy carried by certain particles of matter (electrons and protons), used for lighting and heating and for making machines work

electrify *VERB* **electrifies, electrifying, electrified**
1 to give an electric charge to something
2 to supply something with electric power to make it work
3 to make something very exciting and lively
▷ **electrification** *NOUN*

electrocute *VERB* **electrocutes, electrocuting, electrocuted**
to kill someone with an electric charge
▷ **electrocution** *NOUN*

electrode *NOUN* **electrodes**
a solid conductor through which electricity enters or leaves a vacuum tube

electromagnet *NOUN* **electromagnets**
a magnet worked by electricity
▷ **electromagnetic** *ADJECTIVE*

electron *NOUN* **electrons**
a particle of matter with a negative electric charge

electronic *ADJECTIVE*
1 produced or worked by a flow of electrons
2 produced by or on a computer
▷ **electronically** *ADVERB*

electronics *NOUN*
the use or study of electronic devices

elegant *ADJECTIVE*
graceful and dignified

A hundred miles ahead, the sunrise shone on Circle Park, the elegant loop of lawns and flower-beds that encircled Tier One. — *Philip Reeve, Mortal Engines*

▷ **elegantly** *ADVERB*
▷ **elegance** *NOUN*

elegiac *ADJECTIVE*
expressing sadness or sorrow

elegy (*say* **el**- ij- ee) *NOUN* **elegies**
(*Language*) a sad or sorrowful poem

element *NOUN* **elements**
1 (*Science*) each of about 100 substances that cannot be split up into simpler substances, composed of atoms that have the same number of protons
2 each of the parts that make up a whole thing
3 a basic or elementary principle ◆ *the elements of algebra* ▸▸

4 a wire or coil that gives out heat in an electric fire or cooker

5 the environment or circumstances that suit you best ◆ *Mother was in her element, organizing everything for the wedding.*

6 the elements are the forces of weather, such as rain, wind, and cold

elementary *ADJECTIVE*
dealing with the simplest stages of something; easy

> Witches never bothered with elementary road safety. — *Terry Pratchett, Wyrd Sisters*

elephant *NOUN* **elephants**
a very large land animal with a trunk, large ears, and long curved ivory tusks

WORD HISTORY from Greek *elephas* 'ivory', because of its tusks

elephantine (*say* el- if- **ant**- yn) *ADJECTIVE*

1 very large

2 clumsy and slow-moving

elevate *VERB* **elevates, elevating, elevated**
to lift or raise something to a higher position

▷ **elevation** *NOUN*

elevator *NOUN* **elevators**

1 a machine or tool used to raise things

2 (*American*) a lift in a building

> You don't raise a guy to a responsible job who whistles in the elevator! — *Arthur Miller, Death of a Salesman*

eleven *ADJECTIVE, NOUN* **elevens**
the number 11, one more than ten

eleventh *ADJECTIVE, NOUN*

1 next after tenth

2 one of eleven equal parts of a thing

at the eleventh hour at the last possible moment; just in time

elf *NOUN* **elves**
a small supernatural being with magic powers

> The hall of Elrond's house was filled with folk: Elves for the most part, though there were a few guests of other sorts. — *J. R. R. Tolkien, The Fellowship of the Ring*

elfin *ADJECTIVE*
small and delicate, like an elf

elicit (*say* ill- **iss**- it) *VERB* **elicits, eliciting, elicited**
to draw out information by reasoning or questioning

USAGE NOTE Take care not to confuse this word with *illicit*.

elide *VERB* **elides, eliding, elided**
to omit part of a word by elision

eligible (*say* **el**- ij- ib- ul) *ADJECTIVE*

1 qualified or suitable for something ◆ *You will be eligible for a provisional driving licence from your seventeenth birthday.*

2 regarded as suitable for marriage

▷ **eligibility** *NOUN*

eliminate *VERB* **eliminates, eliminating, eliminated**
to get rid of something; to discount or omit something from a group or process

> Every satellite dish in London was noted, photographed, authenticated and then eliminated from the search. — *Anthony Horowitz, Scorpia*

▷ **elimination** *NOUN*

elision (*say* il- **lizh**- on) *NOUN*
the omission of part of a word in pronouncing it, e.g. in saying *I'm* for *I am*

elite (*say* ay- **leet**) *NOUN* **elites**
a group of people given privileges which are not given to others

WORD HISTORY from an Old French word meaning 'chosen'

elitism *NOUN*
the belief that a society or system should be run by an elite

▷ **elitist** *NOUN*

elixir (*say* il- **iks**- er) *NOUN* **elixirs**
a liquid that is believed to have magic powers, such as restoring youth to someone who is old

> The Stone will transform any metal into pure gold. It also produces the Elixir of Life, which will make the drinker immortal. — *J. K. Rowling, Harry Potter and the Philosopher's Stone*

WORD HISTORY from Arabic *al-iksir* 'a substance that would cure illness and change metals into gold'

Elizabethan (*say* il- iz- a- **beeth**- an) *ADJECTIVE*
during or from the reign of Queen Elizabeth I of England (1558–1603)

Elizabethan *NOUN* **Elizabethans**
someone who lived at this time

elk *NOUN* **elks**
a large deer of northern Europe and Asia

ellipse (*say* il- **ips**) *NOUN* **ellipses**
an oval shape

ellipsis *NOUN*
(*Grammar*) the omission of a word or words from a sentence, usually so that the sentence can still be understood

a b c d e f g h i j k l m n o p q r s t u v w x y z

elliptical (*say* il- **ip**- tik- al) *ADJECTIVE*
1 shaped like an ellipse
2 an elliptical phrase or comment has some words omitted
▷ **elliptically** *ADVERB*
WORD HISTORY from Greek *elleipsis* 'fault, omission'

elm *NOUN* **elms**
a tall deciduous tree with rough leaves

elocution (*say* el- o- **kew**- shon) *NOUN*
the art of speaking clearly and correctly

elongated *ADJECTIVE*
made longer; lengthened
▷ **elongation** *NOUN*

elope *VERB* **elopes, eloping, eloped**
two people elope if they run away secretly to get married
▷ **elopement** *NOUN*

eloquent *ADJECTIVE*
1 an eloquent person speaks fluently and expresses their ideas clearly
2 an eloquent speech or piece of writing is well written and well expressed
▷ **eloquently** *ADVERB*
▷ **eloquence** *NOUN*

else *ADVERB*
1 besides; other ◆ *Nobody else could have done such a thing.*
2 otherwise; if not ◆ *I must run or else I'll miss my bus.*

elsewhere *ADVERB*
somewhere else

elucidate (*say* il- **oo**- sid- ayt) *VERB* **elucidates, elucidating, elucidated**
to make something clear by explaining it
▷ **elucidation** *NOUN*

elude (*say* il- **ood**) *VERB* **eludes, eluding, eluded**
1 to avoid being caught by someone
2 a name or fact that eludes you is too difficult for you to remember or understand
▷ **elusive** *ADJECTIVE*
USAGE NOTE Take care not to confuse this word with *allude*.

emaciated (*say* im- **ay**- see- ay- tid) *ADJECTIVE*
very thin from illness or starvation
▷ **emaciation** *NOUN*

email *NOUN* **emails**
1 (*ICT*) a system of sending messages and data from one computer to another by means of a network
2 a message sent in this way

email *VERB* **emails, emailing, emailed**
to send an email to someone

emanate (*say* **em**- an- ayt) *VERB* **emanates, emanating, emanated**
something that emanates from a place or person comes out of it or from them

emancipate (*say* im- **an**- sip- ayt) *VERB* **emancipates, emancipating, emancipated**
to set someone free from slavery or other restraints
▷ **emancipation** *NOUN*
WORD HISTORY from Latin *mancipium* 'a slave'

embalm *VERB* **embalms, embalming, embalmed**
to preserve a corpse from decay by using spices or chemicals

There is something in individual technique ... if I saw a pair that had been embalmed by different hands I should know at once. — *Evelyn Waugh, The Loved One*

▷ **embalmer** *NOUN*
▷ **embalmment** *NOUN*

embankment *NOUN* **embankments**
a long bank of earth or stone to hold back water or support a road or railway

embargo *NOUN* **embargoes**
an official ban, especially on trade with a country

embark *VERB* **embarks, embarking, embarked**
1 to go on board a ship or aircraft
2 to embark on a long or difficult journey or task is to begin it
▷ **embarkation** *NOUN*
WORD HISTORY from French *barque* 'a sailing ship'

embarrass *VERB* **embarrasses, embarrassing, embarrassed**
to make someone feel awkward or ashamed ◆ *It embarrassed them to have to discuss money at a time like that.*
▷ **embarrassment** *NOUN*

embassy *NOUN* **embassies**
1 an ambassador and his or her staff
2 the building where they work

embed *VERB* **embeds, embedding, embedded**
to fix something firmly in a solid material

embellish *VERB* **embellishes, embellishing, embellished**
to ornament something; to add details to something

Winston, in addition to his regular work, spent long periods ... altering and embellishing news items which were to be quoted in speeches. — *George Orwell, Nineteen Eighty-four*

▷ **embellishment** *NOUN*

embers *PLURAL NOUN*
small pieces of glowing coal or wood in a dying fire

embezzle *VERB* **embezzles, embezzling, embezzled**
to take money dishonestly that was left in your care
▷ **embezzlement** *NOUN*
▷ **embezzler** *NOUN*

emblazon *VERB* **emblazons, emblazoning, emblazoned**
1 to decorate something with a coat of arms
2 to decorate something with bright or eye-catching designs or words

WORD HISTORY from French *blason* 'a shield'

emblem *NOUN* **emblems**
a symbol that represents something
▷ **emblematic** *ADJECTIVE*

embody *VERB* **embodies, embodying, embodied**
1 to express principles or ideas in a visible form ◆ *At its best, the marathon embodies the true spirit of the Olympics.*
2 to include or contain something ◆ *All the information is embodied in the main text.*
▷ **embodiment** *NOUN*

emboss *VERB* **embosses, embossing, embossed**
to decorate a flat surface with a raised design

embrace *VERB* **embraces, embracing, embraced**
1 to hold someone closely in your arms
2 to include or contain something
3 to accept or adopt a cause or belief

embrace *NOUN* **embraces**
an act of embracing; a close hug

embrocation *NOUN* **embrocations**
a lotion for rubbing on parts of your body to soothe an ache or pain

embroider *VERB* **embroiders, embroidering, embroidered**
1 to decorate cloth with needlework
2 to add made-up details to a story to make it more interesting
▷ **embroidery** *NOUN*

embroil *VERB* **embroils, embroiling, embroiled**
to involve someone in an argument or quarrel

embryo (*say* **em**- bree- oh) *NOUN* **embryos**
1 a baby or young animal as it starts to grow in the womb; a young bird growing in an egg
2 anything in its earliest stages of development
▷ **embryonic** (*say* em- bree- **on**- ik) *ADJECTIVE*

emend *VERB* **emends, emending, emended**
to remove errors from a piece of writing or other work

emerald *NOUN* **emeralds**
1 a bright green precious stone
2 a bright green colour

emerge *VERB* **emerges, emerging, emerged**
1 to come out or appear

The heavy bronze doors of the Institute swung open and the paramedics emerged with a stretcher. — *Michael Hoeye, Time Stops for No Mouse*

2 a fact or piece of information emerges when it becomes known
▷ **emergence** *NOUN*
▷ **emergent** *ADJECTIVE*

emergency *NOUN* **emergencies**
a sudden serious happening needing prompt action

emery paper *NOUN*
paper with a gritty coating, often used for filing the fingernails

emetic (*say* im- **et**- ik) *NOUN* **emetics**
a medicine used to make a person vomit

emigrate *VERB* **emigrates, emigrating, emigrated**
to leave your own country and go to live in another
▷ **emigrant** *NOUN*

USAGE NOTE People are *emigrants* from the country they leave and *immigrants* in the country they move to.

emigration *NOUN*
(*History*) the process by which people from one country go and live in other countries

eminent *ADJECTIVE*
an eminent person is famous and respected
▷ **eminently** *ADVERB*
▷ **eminence** *NOUN*

emir (*say* em- **eer**) *NOUN* **emirs**
the title of a Muslim ruler
▷ **emirate** *NOUN*

WORD HISTORY from Arabic *amir* 'ruler'

emission *NOUN* **emissions**
1 the action of emitting something
2 something that is emitted, especially fumes or radiation

emit *VERB* **emits, emitting, emitted**
to send out light, heat, or sound

Ralph pursed his lips and squirted air into the shell, which emitted a low, farting noise. — *William Golding, Lord of the Flies*

emolument (*say* im- **ol**- yoo- ment) ***NOUN*** **emoluments**
(*formal*) payment for work; a salary

emotion ***NOUN*** **emotions**
a strong feeling that you have in your mind, such as love, anger, or hate
▷ **emotional** ***ADJECTIVE***
▷ **emotionally** ***ADVERB***

emotive ***ADJECTIVE***
arousing emotion or strong feelings

empathize ***VERB*** **empathizes, empathizing, empathized**
to be able to understand and share in the feelings of another person
▷ **empathy** ***NOUN***

WORD HISTORY from Greek *pathos* 'feeling'

USAGE NOTE This word can also be spelled empathise.

emperor ***NOUN*** **emperors**
a man who rules an empire

WORD HISTORY from Latin *imperator* 'commander'

emphasis (*say* **em**- fa- sis) ***NOUN*** **emphases**
1 special importance given to something
2 stress put on a word or part of a word

WORD HISTORY from Greek *phanein* 'to show'

emphasize ***VERB*** **emphasizes, emphasizing, emphasized**
to put emphasis on something

USAGE NOTE This word can also be spelled emphasise.

emphatic (*say* im- **fat**- ik) ***ADJECTIVE***
using or showing emphasis
▷ **emphatically** ***ADVERB***

empire ***NOUN*** **empires**
1 a group of countries controlled by one person or government
2 a large business organization controlled by one person or group

empirical ***ADJECTIVE***
based on observation or experiment, not on theory

employ ***VERB*** **employs, employing, employed**
1 to pay someone to work for you
2 to make use of a method or technique
▷ **employer** ***NOUN***

employee ***NOUN*** **employees**
someone who is employed in a job

employment ***NOUN***
the situation of having a paid job, or in which people have paid jobs ◆ *In the last few years the country has achieved nearly full employment.*

emporium (*say* em- **por**- ee- um) ***NOUN*** **emporias** or **emporiums**
a large shop

WORD HISTORY from Greek *emporos* 'a merchant'

empower ***VERB*** **empowers, empowering, empowered**
to give someone the power to do something; to authorize someone

empress ***NOUN*** **empresses**
1 a woman who rules an empire
2 an emperor's wife

empty ***ADJECTIVE***
1 an empty place or container has nothing in it
2 an empty seat, room, or building has nobody in it
3 an empty promise or threat is one that is not kept or not carried out
▷ **emptily** ***ADVERB***
▷ **emptiness** ***NOUN***

empty ***VERB*** **empties, emptying, emptied**
1 to remove the contents from something ◆ *It took half the morning to empty the huge bath.*
2 to become empty

It was amazing how rapidly schools emptied after the final bell, as if someone pulled the plug under a giant whirlpool. — *Carl Hiaasen, Hoot*

emu ***NOUN*** **emus**
a large Australian bird similar to an ostrich, with rough grey or brown feathers

WORD HISTORY from a Portuguese word

emulate ***VERB*** **emulates, emulating, emulated**
to emulate someone is to try to do as well as them, especially by imitating them
▷ **emulation** ***NOUN***

WORD HISTORY from Latin *aemulus* 'a rival'

emulsion ***NOUN*** **emulsions**
1 a creamy or slightly oily liquid
2 a kind of water-based paint
3 the coating on photographic film which is sensitive to light

enable ***VERB*** **enables, enabling, enabled**
to give someone the means or ability to do something

enact ***VERB*** **enacts, enacting, enacted**
1 to make a law by a formal process
2 to represent a story in a dramatic performance; to perform a play
▷ **enactment** ***NOUN***

enamel ***NOUN*** **enamels**
1 a shiny substance for coating metal
2 paint that dries hard and shiny
3 the hard shiny surface of teeth

enamel *VERB* **enamels, enamelling, enamelled**
to coat or decorate a surface with enamel

enamoured (*say* in- **am**- erd) *ADJECTIVE*
to be enamoured of someone or something is to be very fond of them or it

en bloc (*say* ahn **blok**) *ADVERB*
all at the same time; in a block
WORD HISTORY originally a French phrase

encamp *VERB* **encamps, encamping, encamped**
to settle in a camp; to make camp

encampment *NOUN* **encampments**
a camp

encapsulate *VERB* **encapsulates, encapsulating, encapsulated**
to express an idea or set of ideas concisely

encase *VERB* **encases, encasing, encased**
to enclose an object in a case

enchant *VERB* **enchants, enchanting, enchanted**
1 to put someone under a magic spell
2 to fill someone with intense delight
▷ **enchanter** *NOUN*
▷ **enchantment** *NOUN*
▷ **enchantress** *NOUN*

encircle *VERB* **encircles, encircling, encircled**
to surround someone or something

At the side of the road was a little hill, encircled by a ring of silver birch trees. Everyone in Hungry called it the fairy ring, because of the perfect circle of trees. — *Julie Bertagna, The Opposite of Chocolate*

▷ **encirclement** *NOUN*

enclave *NOUN* **enclaves**
a territory belonging to one country, which lies within the boundaries of another country
WORD HISTORY from Latin *clavis* 'key'

enclose *VERB* **encloses, enclosing, enclosed**
1 to put a wall or fence round an area; to shut something in on all sides
2 to put something into a container or wrapping

enclosure *NOUN* **enclosures**
1 the action of enclosing something
2 an enclosed area
3 an item enclosed with a letter or parcel

encompass *VERB* **encompasses, encompassing, encompassed**
1 to surround something
2 to contain or include a subject

encore (*say* **on**- kor) *NOUN* **encores**
an extra item performed at a concert after previous items have been applauded
WORD HISTORY a French word meaning 'again'

encounter *VERB* **encounters, encountering, encountered**
1 to meet or come across someone

Victoria was convinced that if there were a ruder young man in all the world, she had yet to encounter him. — *Meg Cabot, Victoria and the Rogue*

2 to experience a problem or difficulty

encounter *NOUN* **encounters**
1 an unexpected meeting
2 a battle

encourage *VERB* **encourages, encouraging, encouraged**
1 to give someone confidence or hope
2 to encourage someone to do something is to urge or try to persuade them to do it
3 to stimulate a development or process ◆ *The council has launched a poster campaign to encourage healthy eating.*
▷ **encouragement** *NOUN*

encroach *VERB* **encroaches, encroaching, encroached**
to encroach upon someone's rights or privacy is to intrude upon them or it
▷ **encroachment** *NOUN*

encrust *VERB* **encrusts, encrusting, encrusted**
to cover something with a crust or layer
▷ **encrustation** *NOUN*

encryption (*say* en- **krip**- shon) *NOUN*
(*ICT*) the process of converting confidential data into code, so that it can only be read by authorized people
▷ **encrypted** *ADJECTIVE*

encumber *VERB* **encumbers, encumbering, encumbered**
to be a burden to someone; to hamper someone
▷ **encumbrance** *NOUN*

encyclopedia *NOUN* **encyclopedias**
a book or set of books containing information about many subjects
WORD HISTORY from Greek *enkyklopaideia* 'general education'

encyclopedic *ADJECTIVE*
knowing about or giving information about many different subjects

end *NOUN* **ends**
1 the last part or extreme point of something

The end of the summer holidays came too quickly for Harry's liking. — *J. K. Rowling, Harry Potter and the Chamber of Secrets*

2 the half of a sports pitch or court defended or occupied by one team or player

3 destruction or death
4 a goal or purpose

end *VERB* **ends, ending, ended**
1 to come to an end; to cease
2 to bring something to an end; to stop something

SYNONYMS (both meanings) finish, stop, conclude, terminate, discontinue, break off

endanger *VERB* **endangers, endangering, endangered**
to cause danger to a person or a person's life

endangered species *NOUN* **endangered species**
a species in danger of extinction

endear *VERB* **endears, endearing, endeared**
to endear yourself to someone is to make them fond of you
▷ **endearing** *ADJECTIVE*

endearment *NOUN* **endearments**
a word or phrase that expresses love or affection

endeavour (*say* in- **dev**- er) *VERB* **endeavours, endeavouring, endeavoured**
to endeavour to do something is to attempt to do it

endeavour *NOUN* **endeavours**
an attempt to do something

WORD HISTORY from an earlier phrase *to put yourself in devoir* 'to do your best', from French *devoir* 'duty'

endemic (*say* en- **dem**- ik) *ADJECTIVE*
an endemic disease is often found in a certain area or group of people

ending *NOUN* **endings**
the last or final part of something

endless *ADJECTIVE*
1 never stopping

Outside the tent there was still the endless drip-drip of wet leaves on the canvas, but the storm was over. — *Philip Pullman, The Subtle Knife*

2 an endless belt or loop has the ends joined to make a continuous strip for use in machinery
▷ **endlessly** *ADVERB*

endorse *VERB* **endorses, endorsing, endorsed**
1 to endorse a cheque or document is to sign your name on its back
2 an official endorses a licence by noting in it an offence committed by its holder
3 to endorse a plan or proposal is to give your approval or support to it
▷ **endorsement** *NOUN*

WORD HISTORY from Latin *in dorsum* 'on the back'

endow *VERB* **endows, endowing, endowed**
1 to endow a scholarship or other source of funding is to provide money to establish it
2 to be endowed with a talent or feature is to possess it
▷ **endowment** *NOUN*

endure *VERB* **endures, enduring, endured**
1 to suffer or put up with difficulty or pain
2 to continue to exist; to last
▷ **endurable** *ADJECTIVE*

endurance noun
is the ability to put up with difficulty or pain for a long period

enema (*say* en- im- a) *NOUN* **enemas**
(*Medicine*) a medical procedure in which liquid is inserted into the rectum by means of a syringe

enemy *NOUN* **enemies**
1 a person who hates or seeks to harm another

There, comrades, is the answer to all our problems. It is summed up in a single word —Man. Man is the only real enemy we have. — *George Orwell, Animal Farm*

2 a country which is at war with another

energetic *ADJECTIVE*
full of energy
▷ **energetically** *ADVERB*

energize *VERB* **energizes, energizing, energized**
to give energy to someone or something

USAGE NOTE This word can also be spelled energise.

energy *NOUN* **energies**
1 strength to do things, liveliness ◆ *He says he's now well and full of energy.*
2 the ability of matter or radiation to do work
3 power obtained from fuel and other resources and used for light and heat, or to operate machinery

WORD HISTORY from Greek *ergon* 'work'

enfold *VERB* **enfolds, enfolding, enfolded**
to surround or be wrapped round something

enforce *VERB* **enforces, enforcing, enforced**
to enforce a law or rule is to compel people to obey it
▷ **enforcement** *NOUN*
▷ **enforceable** *ADJECTIVE*

enfranchise *VERB* **enfranchises, enfranchising, enfranchised**
to give people the right to vote in elections
▷ **enfranchisement** *NOUN*

WORD HISTORY from Old French *franc* 'free'

engage *VERB* **engages, engaging, engaged**
1 to engage someone's interest or attention is to attract and retain their attention
2 to be engaged in conversation with someone is to be having a conversation with them
3 to engage an enemy or opponent is to begin a battle against them ⏩

4 to engage to do something is to promise or pledge to do it
5 to engage an employee is to arrange to employ them
6 a machine or engine part engages when it moves into a position that allows it to operate or to connect with another part

engaged *ADJECTIVE*
1 someone who is engaged has promised to marry another person
2 in use; occupied

engagement *NOUN* **engagements**
1 the process of engaging something
2 a promise to marry someone
3 an arrangement to meet someone or do something
4 a battle

engaging *ADJECTIVE*
attractive or charming

engine *NOUN* **engines**
1 a machine that provides power
2 a vehicle that pulls a railway train; a locomotive

engineer *NOUN* **engineers**
an expert in engineering

engineer *VERB* **engineers, engineering, engineered**
1 to plan and construct something
2 to cause something to happen ◆ *I want you to engineer a meeting with her agent.*

engineering *NOUN*
the design and building or control of machinery or of structures such as roads and bridges

engrave *VERB* **engraves, engraving, engraved**
to carve a design or words onto a hard surface such as stone
▷ **engraver** *NOUN*
▷ **engraving** *NOUN*

engross *VERB* **engrosses, engrossing, engrossed**
you are engrossed by a task or activity when it occupies your whole attention

WORD HISTORY originally 'to buy up all of something', from French *en gros* 'wholesale'

engulf *VERB* **engulfs, engulfing, engulfed**
to flow over and cover something; to swamp something

The heavy cloud bank in the southwest had engulfed the sun and a coolness came into the air.
— *Mary O'Hara, My Friend Flicka*

enhance *VERB* **enhances, enhancing, enhanced**
to make something more attractive; to increase the value of something
▷ **enhancement** *NOUN*

enigma (*say* in- ig- ma) *NOUN* **enigmas**
something very difficult to understand; a puzzle

WORD HISTORY originally a Greek word

enigmatic (*say* en- ig- **mat**- ik) *ADJECTIVE*
mysterious and puzzling ◆ *The new CD has a more moody, introspective feel, with poetic and enigmatic lyrics.*
▷ **enigmatically** *ADVERB*

enjoy *VERB* **enjoys, enjoying, enjoyed**
to get pleasure from something
▷ **enjoyable** *ADJECTIVE*
▷ **enjoyment** *NOUN*

enlarge *VERB* **enlarges, enlarging, enlarged**
to make a photograph or other object bigger
▷ **enlargement** *NOUN*

enlighten *VERB* **enlightens, enlightening, enlightened**
to give someone more knowledge or information about something
▷ **enlightenment** *NOUN*

enlist *VERB* **enlists, enlisting, enlisted**
1 to join the armed forces
2 to enlist someone's help or support is to ask for and be given it
▷ **enlistment** *NOUN*

enliven *VERB* **enlivens, enlivening, enlivened**
to make something more lively
▷ **enlivenment** *NOUN*

en masse (*say* ahn **mass**) *ADVERB*
all together; in large numbers ◆ *The crowds turned out en masse, despite the weather.*

enmity *NOUN*
the feeling of being someone's enemy; hostility

enormity *NOUN* **enormities**
1 great wickedness ◆ *It was only then that the enormity of the crime began to hit home.*
2 great size; hugeness ◆ *The team was undaunted by the enormity of the task before them.*

USAGE NOTE For the second meaning, it is better in formal writing to use *enormousness*, or a different word such as *magnitude*, instead.

enormous *ADJECTIVE*
very large; huge
▷ **enormously** *ADVERB*
▷ **enormousness** *NOUN*

enough *ADJECTIVE, NOUN, ADVERB*
as much or as many as necessary ◆ *Chris moved close enough to the window to see out.* ◆ *They had enough food for survival, and a little more.*

en passant (*say* ahn **pas**- ahn) *ADVERB*
by the way

WORD HISTORY a French phrase meaning 'in passing'

enquire ***VERB*** **enquires, enquiring, enquired**
1 to ask for information

'How are you taking to the piratical life?' he enquired, looking up from his mortar and pestle. — *Celia Rees, Pirates!*

2 to enquire into something is to find out about it

USAGE NOTE See the note at *inquire*.

enquiry ***NOUN*** **enquiries**
1 a question
2 an investigation

enrage ***VERB*** **enrages, enraging, enraged**
to make someone very angry

enrapture ***VERB*** **enraptures, enrapturing, enraptured**
to make someone extremely happy

enrich ***VERB*** **enriches, enriching, enriched**
to make someone or something richer
▷ **enrichment** ***NOUN***

enrol ***VERB*** **enrols, enrolling, enrolled**
1 to become a member of a club or society
2 to make someone into a member

I am enrolled as member 116,747 of the Royal and Ancient Polar Bear Society and issued with card, stickers, hat, badge, certificate and a carrier bag to hold them all in. — *Michael Palin, Pole to Pole*

▷ **enrolment** ***NOUN***

en route (*say* ahn **root**) ***ADVERB***
on the way

WORD HISTORY a French phrase

ensconce ***VERB*** **ensconces, ensconcing, ensconced**
to be ensconced in a place is to be settled there comfortably

As a cold clear night came over the mountains we were cosily ensconced in our snow hole beneath the face. — *Joe Simpson, Touching the Void*

WORD HISTORY from an old word *sconce* meaning 'a shelter'

ensemble (*say* on- **sombl**) ***NOUN*** **ensembles**
1 a group of things that go together
2 a group of musicians
3 a matching outfit of clothes

enshrine ***VERB*** **enshrines, enshrining, enshrined**
to enshrine an idea or memory is to preserve it with love or respect

ensign ***NOUN*** **ensigns**
a military or naval flag

enslave ***VERB*** **enslaves, enslaving, enslaved**
to make a slave of someone; to force someone into slavery
▷ **enslavement** ***NOUN***

ensue ***VERB*** **ensues, ensuing, ensued**
something ensues when it happens afterwards or as a result of another event or action

ensure ***VERB*** **ensures, ensuring, ensured**
to make certain of something; to guarantee that something happens

I had a little surprise ... that would ensure that my birthday party was talked about and remembered for ages to come. — *Malorie Blackman, Noughts and Crosses*

USAGE NOTE Take care not to confuse this word with *insure*.

entail ***VERB*** **entails, entailing, entailed**
to entail danger, risk, or hardship is to involve it or make it necessary
▷ **entailment** ***NOUN***

entangle ***VERB*** **entangles, entangling, entangled**
two or more things are entangled when they are tangled together
▷ **entanglement** ***NOUN***

entente (*say* on- **tont**) ***NOUN*** **ententes**
an agreement or treaty between countries

enter ***VERB*** **enters, entering, entered**
1 to come or go into a room or other place
2 to note an item in a list or book
3 to key information into a computer
4 to register as a contestant in a competition

enterprise ***NOUN*** **enterprises**
1 a person's adventurous spirit
2 an undertaking or project
3 business activity ♦ *private enterprise*

enterprising ***ADJECTIVE***
an enterprising person or group is willing to undertake new or adventurous projects

entertain ***VERB*** **entertains, entertaining, entertained**
1 to amuse someone
2 to have people as guests and give them food and drink
3 to entertain a proposal or suggestion is to consider it
▷ **entertainer** ***NOUN***

entertainment ***NOUN*** **entertainments**
1 the feeling of being entertained or amused
2 something performed before an audience to amuse or interest them

enthral (*say* in- **thrawl**) ***VERB*** **enthrals, enthralling, enthralled**
to hold someone's complete attention; to fascinate someone

enthusiasm ***NOUN*** **enthusiasms**
a strong liking, interest, or excitement
▷ **enthusiast** ***NOUN***

WORD HISTORY from a Greek word meaning 'to be possessed by a god'

a b c d e f g h i j k l m n o p q r s t u v w x y z

enthusiastic *ADJECTIVE*
full of enthusiasm
▷ **enthusiastically** *ADVERB*

entice *VERB* **entices, enticing, enticed**
to entice someone to do something is to persuade them by offering something pleasant
▷ **enticement** *NOUN*

entire *ADJECTIVE*
whole or complete ◆ *The entire children's section was no more than a few scruffy paperbacks.*
▷ **entirely** *ADVERB*

entirety (*say* in- **ty**- rit- ee) *NOUN*
the whole of something
in its entirety in its complete form

entitle *VERB* **entitles, entitling, entitled**
to give someone the right to have or do something ◆ *This coupon entitles you to a free ticket.*
▷ **entitlement** *NOUN*

entitled *ADJECTIVE*
having as a title

Mrs Grace Merriweather had composed an original pageant entitled 'Maycomb County: Ad Astra Per Aspera', and I was to be a ham. — *Harper Lee, To Kill a Mockingbird*

entity *NOUN* **entities**
something that exists as a distinct and separate thing

entomb (*say* in- **toom**) *VERB* **entombs, entombing, entombed**
to place a body in a tomb
▷ **entombment** *NOUN*

entomology (*say* en- tom- **ol**- o- jee) *NOUN*
the study of insects
▷ **entomologist** *NOUN*

entourage (*say* on- toor- **ahzh**) *NOUN*
the people who accompany an important person

Really attractive people, like Lana and Josh, don't ever go anywhere alone. They always have this sort of entourage that follows them around. — *Meg Cabot, The Princess Diaries*

WORD HISTORY from French *entourer* 'to surround'

entrails *PLURAL NOUN*
the intestines of a person or animal

entrance❶ (*say* **en**- trans) *NOUN* **entrances**
1 the way into a place
2 the action of entering

A bell rang, and the big room fell quiet for the entrance of the Examiners. — *William Nicholson, The Wind Singer*

3 (*Drama*) the moment when an actor comes on stage

entrance❷ (*say* in- **trahns**) *VERB* **entrances, entrancing, entranced**
to fill someone with intense delight; to enchant someone

entrant *NOUN* **entrants**
someone who takes part in an examination or competition

entreat *VERB* **entreats, entreating, entreated**
to beg or plead with someone earnestly

entreaty *NOUN* **entreaties**
an earnest request

entrench *VERB* **entrenches, entrenching, entrenched**
1 to entrench an idea or image is to fix it firmly in your mind
2 to settle in a well-defended position
▷ **entrenchment** *NOUN*

entrust *VERB* **entrusts, entrusting, entrusted**
to entrust someone or something to another person is to place them in their care

entry *NOUN* **entries**
1 a place where people go in; an entrance
2 something entered in a list, diary, or reference book
3 something entered in a competition ◆ *Send your entries to this address.*

entwine *VERB* **entwines, entwining, entwined**
a thread or vine is entwined around something when it is wound or twisted round it

enumerate *VERB* **enumerates, enumerating, enumerated**
to count a series of items; to list things one by one

envelop (*say* en- **vel**- op) *VERB* **envelops, enveloping, enveloped**
to enclose or wrap round someone or something completely

Darkness now enveloped him like a shroud. He twisted his head round and gazed into the blackness of the forest. — *Tim Bowler, Starseeker*

envelope (*say* **en**- vel- ohp) *NOUN* **envelopes**
a paper or cardboard pocket for a letter, with a flap for sealing it

enviable *ADJECTIVE*
likely to be envied

envious *ADJECTIVE*
feeling envy
▷ **enviously** *ADVERB*

environment *NOUN* **environments**
1 the daily surroundings of a person or animal
2 the natural world of the land, sea, and air
▷ **environmental** *ADJECTIVE*

environmentalist *NOUN* **environmentalists**
a person who wishes to protect or improve the environment

environmentally friendly *ADJECTIVE*
not harmful to the environment

environs (*say* in- **vy**- ronz) *PLURAL NOUN*
the surrounding districts ◆ *They all lived in the environs of Liverpool.*

envisage (*say* in- **viz**- ij) *VERB* **envisages, envisaging, envisaged**
to picture something in your mind; to imagine something

envoy *NOUN* **envoys**
an official representative, especially one sent by one government to another
WORD HISTORY from French *envoyé* 'sent'

envy *NOUN*
1 a feeling of discontent you have when someone possesses things that you would like to have for yourself
2 something causing this feeling ◆ *My garden was soon the envy of all my friends.*

envy *VERB* **envies, envying, envied**
to feel envy towards someone

We envied the princesses and the younger princes particularly. They were allowed to stay in Windsor most of the year. — *Diana Wynne Jones, The Merlin Conspiracy*

enzyme *NOUN* **enzymes**
1 a protein which assists in digestion
2 a synthetic chemical used in household detergents
WORD HISTORY from Greek *enzymos* 'leavened'

epaulette (*say* **ep**- al- et) *NOUN* **epaulettes**
an ornamental flap on the shoulder of a uniform
WORD HISTORY a French word meaning 'little shoulder'

ephemeral (*say* if- **em**- er- al) *ADJECTIVE*
lasting only a very short time
WORD HISTORY from a Greek word meaning 'lasting a day'

epic *NOUN* **epics**
1 (*Language*) a long poem or story about heroic deeds or history
2 a long book or film dealing with a similar subject
WORD HISTORY from Greek *epos* 'song'

epic *ADJECTIVE*
on a grand or heroic scale, like an epic

epicentre *NOUN* **epicentres**
the point where an earthquake reaches the earth's surface

epidemic *NOUN* **epidemics**
an outbreak of a disease that spreads quickly among the people of an area

epidermis *NOUN*
the outer layer of the skin

epigram *NOUN* **epigrams**
a short witty saying or remark

epilepsy *NOUN*
a disease of the nervous system which causes convulsions
▷ **epileptic** *ADJECTIVE* *NOUN*

epilogue (*say* **ep**- il- og) *NOUN* **epilogues**
a short section at the end of a book or play
WORD HISTORY from Greek *logos* 'speech'

Epiphany (*say* ip- **if**- an- ee) *NOUN*
a Christian festival celebrated on 6 January, commemorating the showing of Christ to the Magi
WORD HISTORY from a Greek word meaning 'to show clearly'

episcopal (*say* ip- **iss**- kop- al) *ADJECTIVE*
1 to do with a bishop or bishops
2 an episcopal church is governed by bishops

episode *NOUN* **episodes**
1 one event in a series of happenings
2 one programme in a radio or television serial

epistle *NOUN* **epistles**
a letter, especially one forming part of the New Testament

epitaph *NOUN* **epitaphs**
words written on a tomb or describing a person who has died
WORD HISTORY from Greek *taphos* 'tomb'

epithet *NOUN* **epithets**
a word or phrase used to describe someone and often forming part of their name, e.g. 'the Great' in *Alfred the Great*

epitome (*say* ip- **it**- om- ee) *NOUN*
a person or thing that is a perfect example of something ◆ *Sprawled on the sofa, he was the epitome of relaxation.*
WORD HISTORY a Greek word meaning 'shortening'

epoch (*say* **ee**- pok) *NOUN* **epochs**
a period of time marked by particular events
WORD HISTORY a Greek word meaning 'fixed point of time'

epoch-making *ADJECTIVE*
an epoch-making event is historically very important or significant

eponym (*say* **ep**- o- nim) ***NOUN*** **eponyms**
a word or name that is derived from the name of a person

eponyms

An **eponym** is a word which is derived from a person's name, usually because that person invented the object or was associated with it. For example, *Braille*, *Biro*, *guillotine*, and *saxophone* are all named after their inventors.

The flowers *begonia*, *dahlia*, and *wisteria* are named after the botanists who discovered them, and other scientists gave their names to *fahrenheit*, *hertz*, and *watt*. Some items of food or clothing are named after famous people who enjoyed eating or wearing them: for example, *cardigan*, *wellingtons*, and *sandwich*.

Some eponyms come from mythological or fictional characters. For example, an *atlas* is named after the ancient Greek giant, *Atlas*, who was believed to hold up the sky on his shoulders and was pictured at the front of early books of maps; and the word *gargantuan* (meaning 'gigantic') comes from another giant character (*Gargantua*) created by the French writer Rabelais.

equable (*say* **ek**- wa- bul) ***ADJECTIVE***
1 an equable person or attitude is calm and not easily annoyed
2 an equable climate is moderate, neither too hot nor too cold

equal ***ADJECTIVE***
1 the same in amount, size, or value
2 someone who is equal to a task has the necessary strength, courage, or ability to do it
▷ **equally** ***ADVERB***

equal ***NOUN*** **equals**
a person or thing that is equal to another

When Thrall was a young man, a girl who was his equal in every way came to his hut. — *Kevin Crossley-Holland, Viking!*

equal ***VERB*** **equals, equalling, equalled**
1 to be the same in amount, size, or value

According to Pythagoras' theorem, if the sum of the squares of the two shorter sides equals the square of the hypotenuse then the triangle is right-angled. — *Mark Haddon, The Curious Incident of the Dog in the Night-Time*

2 to match or be as good as someone or something

equality ***NOUN***
the state of being equal

equalize ***VERB*** **equalizes, equalizing, equalized**
to make things equal

With one minute remaining in the game, Arsenal equalized, unexpectedly and bizarrely, a diving header from a rebound off the goalkeeper's knee. — *Nick Hornby, Fever Pitch*

▷ **equalization** ***NOUN***

USAGE NOTE This word can also be spelled equalise.

equalizer ***NOUN*** **equalizers**
a goal or point that makes the score equal

USAGE NOTE This word can also be spelled equaliser.

equanimity (*say* ekwa- **nim**- it- ee) ***NOUN***
calmness of mind or temper

equate ***VERB*** **equates, equating, equated**
to equate one person or thing with another is to consider them to be equal or equivalent to one another

equation ***NOUN*** **equations**
(*Mathematics*) a statement that two amounts are equal, e.g. $3 + 4 = 2 + 5$

equator ***NOUN*** **equators**
an imaginary line round the Earth at an equal distance from the North and South Poles

WORD HISTORY from the Latin words *circulus aequator diei et noctis* 'circle equalizing day and night'

equatorial (*say* ek- wa- **tor**- ee- al) ***ADJECTIVE***
to do with or near the equator

equerry (*say* **ek**- wer- ee) ***NOUN*** **equerries**
a personal attendant of a member of the British royal family

WORD HISTORY from Latin *scutarius* 'a shield- bearer'

equestrian (*say* ik- **wes**- tree- an) ***ADJECTIVE***
an equestrian event involves horse riding

equidistant (*say* ee- kwi- **dis**- tant) ***ADJECTIVE***
at an equal distance

equilateral (*say* ee- kwi- **lat**- er- al) ***ADJECTIVE***
(*Mathematics*) an equilateral triangle has all its sides equal

equilibrium (*say* ee- kwi- **lib**- ree- um) ***NOUN***
1 a balance between different forces or influences
2 a balanced state of mind

equine (*say* **ek**- wyn) ***ADJECTIVE***
an equine activity or event is one which involves horses

WORD HISTORY from Latin *equus* 'horse'

equinox (*say* **ek**- win- oks) ***NOUN*** **equinoxes**
the time of year when day and night are equal in length (about 20 March in spring, about 22 September in autumn)
▷ **equinoctial** ***ADJECTIVE***

WORD HISTORY meaning 'equal night', from Latin *nox* 'night'

equip ***VERB*** **equips, equipping, equipped**
to supply a person or team with what they need

equipment *NOUN*
the things needed for a particular purpose

Getting themselves aboard the zeppelin was hazardous for the spies, not least because of the equipment they had to carry. — *Philip Pullman, The Amber Spyglass*

equity (*say* **ek**- wit- ee) *NOUN*
fairness; justice
▷ **equitable** *ADJECTIVE*

equivalent *ADJECTIVE*
two things that are equivalent are equal in importance, meaning, or value
▷ **equivalence** *NOUN*

equivocal (*say* ik- **wiv**- ok- al) *ADJECTIVE*
an equivocal statement is not clear in meaning, because it can be interpreted in more than one way
▷ **equivocally** *ADVERB*

era (*say* **eer**- a) *NOUN* **eras**
a period of history ◆ *the era of silent films*

eradicate *VERB* **eradicates, eradicating, eradicated**
to get rid of something; to remove all traces of something
▷ **eradication** *NOUN*

WORD HISTORY from Latin *eradicare* 'to root out'

erase *VERB* **erases, erasing, erased**
1 to rub out writing or a mark on a surface

Mrs Casper turned her shoes over in her hands, licking her fingers and trying to erase the scuff marks on the heels. — *Barry Hines, A Kestrel for a Knave*

2 to wipe out a recording on magnetic tape
3 to erase a memory or thought is to forget or stop thinking about it

eraser *NOUN* **erasers**
a piece of rubber or plastic used for rubbing out writing or other marks

erasure *NOUN* **erasures**
1 the action of erasing something
2 the place where something has been erased

ere (*say* air) *PREPOSITION, CONJUNCTION*
(*literary*) before (in time)

erect *ADJECTIVE*
standing straight up

erect *VERB* **erects, erecting, erected**
to set up or build a statue, building, or other structure

erection *NOUN* **erection**
1 a building or monument
2 sexual arousal in a man or male animal

ergonomic *ADJECTIVE*
an ergonomic system or piece of equipment is designed to help people work efficiently
▷ **ergonomically** *ADVERB*

WORD HISTORY from Greek *ergon* 'work'

ermine *NOUN* **ermines**
1 a kind of weasel with brown fur that turns white in winter
2 the fur of this animal, sometimes used to trim ceremonial robes

erode *VERB* **erodes, eroding, eroded**
to wear away the surface of something over time

erosion *NOUN*
1 the action of wearing something away
2 (*Geography*) the wearing away of the earth's surface by the action of water and wind

erotic *ADJECTIVE*
arousing sexual feelings
▷ **erotically** *ADVERB*

WORD HISTORY from Greek *eros* 'sexual love'

err (*say* er) *VERB* **errs, erring, erred**
to make a mistake; to be incorrect

errand *NOUN* **errands**
a short journey to take a message or fetch goods

errant (*say* **e**- rant) *ADJECTIVE*
(*literary*) wandering; travelling in search of adventure ◆ *a knight errant*

WORD HISTORY from Latin *errare* 'to wander'

erratic (*say* ir- **at**- ik) *ADJECTIVE*
not regular or reliable
▷ **erratically** *ADVERB*

erroneous (*say* ir- **oh**- nee- us) *ADJECTIVE*
incorrect; false
▷ **erroneously** *ADVERB*

error *NOUN* **errors**
a mistake

ersatz *ADJECTIVE*
substitute or imitation ◆ *ersatz designer clothes*

WORD HISTORY a German word meaning 'replacement'

erstwhile (*say* **erst**- wyl) *ADJECTIVE*
(*formal*) former; from before ◆ *Most of their erstwhile fans thought the band had split up.*

erudite (*say* **e**- rew- dyt) *ADJECTIVE*
having or showing great knowledge or learning
▷ **eruditely** *ADVERB*
▷ **erudition** *NOUN*

erupt *VERB* **erupts, erupting, erupted**
1 to burst out
2 a volcano erupts when it shoots out lava

eruption *NOUN* **eruptions**
1 the action of erupting
2 a spot or inflammation on the skin

escalate *VERB* **escalates, escalating, escalated**
1 to become greater, more serious, or more intense ◆ *The violence soon escalated into a full-scale riot.*
2 to make something greater or more intense
▷ **escalation** *NOUN*

a b c d e f g h i j k l m n o p q r s t u v w x y z

escalator ***NOUN*** **escalators**
a staircase with an endless line of steps moving up or down
WORD HISTORY from a French word meaning 'scaling a wall with ladders'

escalope (*say* is- **kal**- op) ***NOUN*** **escalopes**
a slice of boneless meat

escapade (*say* es- ka- **payd**) ***NOUN*** **escapades**
a reckless adventure

escape ***VERB*** **escapes, escaping, escaped**
1 to get yourself free; to get out or away
2 to avoid something unpleasant ◆ *The driver was flung out of the car but escaped serious injury.*
3 a fact or name escapes you when you are unable to remember it

escape ***NOUN*** **escapes**
1 the action of escaping
2 a way to escape

escapism ***NOUN***
the desire to escape from the difficulties of life by thinking about or doing more pleasant things
▷ **escapist** ***NOUN***

escarpment ***NOUN*** **escarpments**
a steep slope at the edge of some high level ground

eschew (*say* iss- **choo**) ***VERB*** **eschews, eschewing, eschewed**
to avoid or abstain from something deliberately ◆ *The ranks of those who eschew all animal products are rapidly growing.*

escort (*say* **ess**- kort) ***NOUN*** **escorts**
a person or group accompanying a person or thing to give protection or as an honour

escort (*say* iss- **kort**) ***VERB*** **escorts, escorting, escorted**
to act as an escort to someone or something

We were met at the landing place by a file of musketeers and escorted to the fort. — *Celia Rees, Pirates!*

Eskimo ***NOUN*** **Eskimos** or **Eskimo**
a member of a people living near the Arctic coast of North America, Greenland, and Siberia
USAGE NOTE It is now more usual, and preferred by the people themselves, to use the name *Inuit* for those who live in northern Canada and Greenland, and *Yupik* for those who live in Alaska and Asia.

esoteric ***ADJECTIVE***
intended only for people with special knowledge or interest

ESP ***ABBREVIATION***
extrasensory perception, the ability to perceive things by means other than the known senses

espadrille (*say* ess- pa- **dril**) ***NOUN*** **espadrilles**
a light canvas shoe with a sole of plaited fibre

especial ***ADJECTIVE***
particular or outstanding ◆ *The website will be of especial interest to jazz fans.*

especially ***ADVERB***
specially; more than anything else

Esperanto ***NOUN***
an artificial language devised in 1887 as an international means of communication
WORD HISTORY based on the Latin word *sperare* 'to hope'

espionage (*say* **ess**- pee- on- ah*zh*) ***NOUN***
the activity of spying or using spies to obtain secret information
WORD HISTORY from French *espion* 'a spy'

esplanade ***NOUN*** **esplanades**
a flat open area where people can walk or ride, often beside the sea

espouse ***VERB*** **espouses, espousing, espoused**
to adopt or support an idea or cause ◆ *a revolutionary new book espousing the virtues of a meatless diet*
▷ **espousal** ***NOUN***

espresso ***NOUN*** **espressos**
strong black coffee made by forcing steam through ground coffee beans
WORD HISTORY an Italian word meaning 'pressed out'

esprit de corps (*say* es- pree der **kor**) ***NOUN***
loyalty to the group you belong to
WORD HISTORY a French phrase meaning 'spirit of the body'

espy ***VERB*** **espies, espying, espied**
(*literary*) to catch sight of someone or something

Esq. ***ABBREVIATION***
Esquire, a title written after a man's surname where no title is used before his name
WORD HISTORY an esquire was originally a knight's attendant; from Latin *scutarius* 'a shield- bearer'

essay (*say* **ess**- ay) ***NOUN*** **essays**
1 a short piece of non-fiction writing in prose
2 (*formal*) an attempt

essay (*say* ess- **ay**) ***VERB*** **essays, essaying, essayed**
(*formal*) to essay to do something is to attempt to do it

essence ***NOUN*** **essences**
1 the most important quality or element of something
2 a concentrated liquid

essential *ADJECTIVE*
1 an essential item, quality, or action is one that you must have or must do

A radio will be essential for keeping up to date with what's going on outside. — *David Almond, The Fire-Eaters*

2 an essential feature or aspect is an important or key feature
3 an essential oil is a natural oil extracted from a plant

essential *NOUN* **essentials**
something that you cannot do without ◆ *Remember to pack essentials like sun cream and insect repellent.*

essentially *ADVERB*
1 vitally; crucially
2 basically; in essence ◆ *The plots of both films are essentially the same.*

establish *VERB* **establishes, establishing, established**
1 to set up a business, government, or relationship on a firm basis
2 to show something to be true; to prove something ◆ *The police are yet to establish a motive behind the murder.*
▷ **established** *ADJECTIVE*

establishment *NOUN* **establishments**
1 the process of establishing something
2 a business firm or other institution
the Establishment the people in a country in positions of power and influence

estate *NOUN* **estates**
1 an area of land with a set of houses or factories on it
2 a large area of land owned by one person
3 all that a person owns when he or she dies
4 (*formal*) a condition or status ◆ *the holy estate of matrimony*

estate agent *NOUN* **estate agents**
a person whose business is selling or letting houses and land

estate car *NOUN* **estate cars**
a car with a door or doors at the back, and rear seats that can be removed or folded away

esteem *VERB* **esteems, esteeming, esteemed**
1 to think highly of someone or something
2 (*formal*) to esteem something an honour or virtue is to see it that way

esteem *NOUN*
respect and admiration

ester *NOUN* **esters**
(*Science*) a kind of organic chemical compound

estimable *ADJECTIVE*
an estimable person is worth respect and admiration

estimate (*say* ess- tim- at) *NOUN* **estimates**
1 (*Mathematics*) a calculation about the size or value of something
2 a written or printed statement of what a piece of work is likely to cost

estimate (*say* ess- tim- ayt) *VERB* **estimates, estimating, estimated**
to calculate the size, value, or cost of something
▷ **estimation** *NOUN*

estranged *ADJECTIVE*
a person's estranged husband, wife, or friend is no longer in contact with them, or on friendly terms with them
▷ **estrangement** *NOUN*

estuary (*say* ess- tew- er- ee) *NOUN* **estuaries**
(*Geography*) the mouth of a river where it reaches the sea and the tide flows in and out

WORD HISTORY from Latin *aestus* 'tide'

etc. *ABBREVIATION*
et cetera, a Latin phrase meaning 'and other similar things, and so on'

etch *VERB* **etches, etching, etched**
1 (*Art*) to engrave a picture with acid on a metal plate in order to make a print from it
2 an event or image is etched on your mind or memory when it has made a deep impression on you
▷ **etcher** *NOUN*

etching *NOUN* **etchings**
a picture printed from an etched metal plate

eternal *ADJECTIVE*
1 lasting for ever; not ending or changing
2 (*informal*) constant, too frequent ◆ *I was getting sick and tired of the eternal arguments.*
▷ **eternally** *ADVERB*

eternity *NOUN*
1 everlasting time
2 (*informal*) a very long time ◆ *The bus took an eternity to arrive.*

ether (*say* ee- ther) *NOUN*
1 a colourless liquid that evaporates easily into fumes that are used as an anaesthetic
2 (*literary*) the upper air beyond the clouds

ethereal (*say* ith- eer- ee- al) *ADJECTIVE*
light and delicate
▷ **ethereally** *ADVERB*

WORD HISTORY from a Latin word meaning 'belonging to the upper air'

ethical (*say* eth- ik- al) *ADJECTIVE*
1 to do with ethics
2 morally right; honourable
▷ **ethically** *ADVERB*

ethics (*say* eth- iks) *PLURAL NOUN*
standards of right behaviour; moral principles

WORD HISTORY from Greek *ethos* 'character'

ethnic *ADJECTIVE*
belonging to a group of people with a particular national or cultural identity
WORD HISTORY from Greek *ethnos* 'nation'

ethnic cleansing *NOUN*
the expulsion or mass killing of people from other ethnic or religious groups within a certain area

ethnology *NOUN*
the study of the characteristics and conditions of peoples of the world
▷ **ethnological** *ADJECTIVE*
▷ **ethnologist** *NOUN*

etiquette (*say* **et**- ik- et) *NOUN*
the rules of correct behaviour

It was the grossest breach of etiquette imaginable to touch another person's dæmon.
— *Philip Pullman, Northern Lights*

WORD HISTORY from a French word

etymology (*say* et- im- **ol**- oj- ee) *NOUN* **etymologies** (*Language*)
1 an account of the origin of a word and its meaning
2 the study of the origins of words
▷ **etymological** *ADJECTIVE*
WORD HISTORY from Greek *etymon* 'original word'

EU *ABBREVIATION*
European Union

eucalyptus (*say* yoo- kal- **ip**- tus) *NOUN* **eucalyptuses**
1 a kind of evergreen tree
2 a strong-smelling oil obtained from its leaves
WORD HISTORY from Greek words meaning 'well covered', because the flower is covered by a cap before it opens

Eucharist (*say* **yoo**- ker- ist) *NOUN*
the Christian sacrament in which bread and wine are consecrated and swallowed, commemorating the Last Supper of Christ and his disciples
WORD HISTORY from a Greek word meaning 'thanksgiving'

eulogize *VERB* **eulogizes, eulogizing, eulogized**
to praise a person or thing highly
USAGE NOTE This word can also be spelled eulogise.

eulogy (*say* **yoo**- loj- ee) *NOUN* **eulogies**
a speech or piece of writing in praise of a person or thing

eunuch (*say* **yoo**- nuk) *NOUN* **eunuchs**
a man who has been castrated

euphemism (*say* **yoo**- fim- izm) *NOUN* **euphemisms**
a mild word or phrase used instead of an offensive or frank one, e.g. *to pass away* instead of *to die*
▷ **euphemistic** *ADJECTIVE*
▷ **euphemistically** *ADVERB*

euphonium (*say* yoof- **oh**- nee- um) *NOUN* **euphoniums**
a large brass wind instrument

euphony (*say* **yoo**- fo- ni) *NOUN*
harmonious or pleasant sound, especially made by words
▷ **euphonious** (*say* yoo- **foh**- ni- us) *ADJECTIVE*

euphoria (*say* yoo- **for**- ee- a) *NOUN*
a feeling of general happiness
▷ **euphoric** (*say* yoo- **fo**- rik) *ADJECTIVE*

Eurasian *ADJECTIVE*
having European and Asian parents or ancestors
▷ **Eurasian** *NOUN*

eureka (*say* yoor- **eek**- a) *EXCLAMATION*
a cry of triumph at a great discovery
WORD HISTORY a Greek word meaning 'I have found it', said to have been uttered by the Greek mathematician Archimedes (3rd century BC), who was excited by his new ideas about the volume and density of matter

euro *NOUN* **euros** or **euro**
the single currency introduced in the EU in 1999

European *ADJECTIVE*
to do with Europe or its people

European *NOUN* **Europeans**
a person born in Europe or descended from people born there

eurozone *NOUN*
(*Economics*) the group of countries of the European Union that have adopted the euro

euthanasia (*say* yooth- an- **ay**- zee- a) *NOUN*
the act of causing someone to die gently and without pain, especially when they are suffering from a painful incurable disease
WORD HISTORY from Greek *eu* 'well' and *thanatos* 'death'

evacuate *VERB* **evacuates, evacuating, evacuated**
1 to move people away from a dangerous place
2 to make a container empty of air or other contents
▷ **evacuation** *NOUN*

evacuee *NOUN* **evacuees**
a person who has been evacuated

evade *VERB* **evades, evading, evaded**
to avoid a person or thing by cleverness or trickery

evaluate *VERB* **evaluates, evaluating, evaluated**
to estimate the value of something; to assess something

evaluation *NOUN* **evaluations**
1 the process of evaluating something
2 (*D & T*) an assessment of how effective a design is and how well it might work

evangelist *NOUN* **evangelists**
1 each of the writers of the four Christian Gospels (Matthew, Mark, Luke, John)
2 a person who preaches the Christian faith enthusiastically
▷ **evangelism** *NOUN*
▷ **evangelical** *ADJECTIVE*

WORD HISTORY from a Greek word meaning 'good news', related to our word *angel*

evaporate *VERB* **evaporates, evaporating, evaporated**
1 (*Science*) to change from liquid into steam or vapour
2 to cease to exist ◆ *By this time, the public's enthusiasm for the space programme had evaporated.*
▷ **evaporation** *NOUN*

evasion *NOUN* **evasions**
1 the action of evading someone or something
2 an evasive answer or excuse

evasive *ADJECTIVE*
1 an evasive action tries to avoid danger or difficulty
2 an evasive reply is not frank or straightforward and avoids answering the question
▷ **evasively** *ADVERB*
▷ **evasiveness** *NOUN*

eve *NOUN* **eves**
1 the day or evening before an important day or event ◆ *On the eve of the festival of Lupercalia the names of Roman girls were written on slips of paper and placed into jars.*
2 (*literary*) the evening

even❶ *ADJECTIVE*
1 an even surface or ground is level and smooth
2 not changing or varying, regular
3 an even temper is calm and not easily upset
4 equally balanced or matched ◆ *Up until that point it had been a surprisingly even contest of sublime boxing talent.*
5 equal in number or amount ◆ *The scores were even at full time and so extra time followed.*
6 an even number can be divided exactly by two (SEE ALSO **odd**)

to get even with someone is to take revenge on them
▷ **evenly** *ADVERB*
▷ **evenness** *NOUN*

even *VERB* **evens, evening, evened**
1 to make something even
2 two or more things even up when they become even

even *ADVERB*
1 used with a comparative adjective to indicate more or a greater degree

There are very few people, and even fewer amateur zoologists, who stumble upon a sizeable mammal previously unknown to science. — *Gavin Maxwell, Ring of Bright Water*

2 used with a negative to add emphasis ◆ *I couldn't even stand, let alone walk.*

even so although that is correct

even❷ *NOUN*
(*literary*) the evening

even-handed *ADJECTIVE*
fair and impartial

evening *NOUN* **evenings**
the part of the day between late afternoon and bedtime

evening dress formal clothing worn for social events in the evening

event *NOUN* **events**
1 something that happens, especially something important
2 a race or competition that forms part of a sports contest

eventful *ADJECTIVE*
full of happenings ◆ *It's been an eventful week in Parliament.*

eventual *ADJECTIVE*
happening at last ◆ *The organization is dedicated to finding the cause, treatment, and eventual cure for autism.*
▷ **eventually** *ADVERB*

eventuality (*say* iv- en- tew- **al**- it- ee) *NOUN* **eventualities**
something that may happen

ever *ADVERB*
1 at any time

No animal must ever live in a house, or sleep in a bed, or wear clothes, or drink alcohol, or smoke tobacco, or touch money, or engage in trade. — *George Orwell, Animal Farm*

2 at all times, always ◆ *We are told that the scientists are ever hopeful of finding signs of life.*
3 (*informal*) used in a question to add emphasis ◆ *Why ever didn't you tell us?*

evergreen *ADJECTIVE*
an evergreen tree or shrub has green leaves throughout the year

evergreen *NOUN* **evergreens**
an evergreen tree or shrub

everlasting *ADJECTIVE*
lasting for ever or for a very long time

every *ADJECTIVE*
1 each without any exceptions ◆ *The first time I saw the film, I hated every minute of it.*
2 each in a series of intervals ◆ *Take one tablet every four hours.* ▸▸

a b c d e f g h i j k l m n o p q r s t u v w x y z

3 all that is possible ◆ *We take every precaution possible to ensure your package arrives safely.*
every other every second or alternate one ◆ *The magazine is published every other Friday.*
every so often at intervals; occasionally

USAGE NOTE Take care to use a singular verb with *every*. You would say *Every one of the eggs has hatched* (not *have hatched*).

everybody *PRONOUN*
every person; everyone

everyday *ADJECTIVE*
ordinary; usual ◆ *The book describes traditional home remedies for everyday ailments.*

everyone *PRONOUN*
every person; everybody

everything *PRONOUN*
1 all things; all
2 the only or most important thing ◆ *In the end, the Party decided that winning was not everything.*

everywhere *ADVERB*
in every place

evict *VERB* **evicts, evicting, evicted**
to make people move out from where they are living
▷ **eviction** *NOUN*

evidence *NOUN*
1 anything that gives people reason to believe something
2 statements made or objects produced in a lawcourt to prove something

evident *ADJECTIVE*
obvious; clearly seen or understood ◆ *The importance of signals intelligence became evident during the war.*
▷ **evidently** *ADVERB*

evil *ADJECTIVE*
morally bad; wicked
▷ **evilly** *ADVERB*

evil *NOUN* **evils**
1 extreme wickedness
2 an evil thing

evocative (*say* i- **vok**- it- iv) *ADJECTIVE*
something is evocative of a memory or feeling when it reminds you of it
▷ **evocatively** *ADVERB*

evoke *VERB* **evokes, evoking, evoked**
to produce or inspire a memory or feelings ◆ *The photographs evoked memories of my childhood.*
▷ **evocation** *NOUN*

evolution (*say* ee- vol- **oo**- shon) *NOUN*
1 gradual change into something different
2 the development of animals and plants from earlier or simpler forms of life
▷ **evolutionary** *ADJECTIVE*

evolve *VERB* **evolves, evolving, evolved**
to develop gradually or naturally ◆ *A new exhibition shows how El Greco's style evolved throughout his life.*

ewe (*say* yoo) *NOUN* **ewes**
a female sheep

ewer (*say* **yoo**- er) *NOUN* **ewers**
a large water jug

exacerbate (*say* eks- **ass**- er- bayt) *VERB* **exacerbates, exacerbating, exacerbated**
to make a pain, disease, or other problem worse

exact *ADJECTIVE*
1 correct in every detail; precise
2 clearly stated; giving all details ◆ *The instructions on the packet are very exact.*
▷ **exactitude** *NOUN*
▷ **exactness** *NOUN*

exact *VERB* **exacts, exacting, exacted**
1 to exact payment or obedience from someone is to demand and obtain it from them
2 to exact revenge on someone is to take revenge on them, often ruthlessly
▷ **exaction** *NOUN*

exacting *ADJECTIVE*
making great demands on your ability or stamina

Yam, the king of crops, was a very exacting king. For three or four moons it demanded hard work and constant attention from cockcrow till the chickens went back to roost. — Chinua Achebe, *Things Fall Apart*

exactly *ADVERB*
1 in an exact manner; precisely
2 used to express agreement with what someone has said

exaggerate *VERB* **exaggerates, exaggerating, exaggerated**
to make something seem bigger, better, or worse than it really is
▷ **exaggeration** *NOUN*

WORD HISTORY from a Latin word meaning 'to heap up'

exalt (*say* ig- **zawlt**) *VERB* **exalts, exalting, exalted**
1 to raise someone in rank or status
2 to praise someone or something highly
▷ **exaltation** *NOUN*

WORD HISTORY from Latin *altus* 'high'

exam *NOUN* **exams**
(*informal*) an examination

examination *NOUN* **examinations**
1 a test of a person's knowledge or skill by means of oral or written questions
2 the process of examining something; an inspection ◆ *a medical examination*
3 a formal questioning of a witness or an accused person in a lawcourt

examine *VERB* **examines, examining, examined**
1 to test a person's knowledge or skill in an examination
2 to question a witness or accused person in a lawcourt
3 to look at something closely or in detail

I took my mitts and inner gloves off, and examined my fingers. Two blackened fingers on each hand, and one bluish thumb. — *Joe Simpson, Touching the Void*

▷ **examiner** *NOUN*

WORD HISTORY from a Latin word meaning 'to weigh accurately'

examinee *NOUN* **examinees**
a person who is sitting an examination

example *NOUN* **examples**
1 anything that shows what others of the same kind are like or how they work
2 a person or thing good enough to be worth imitating

for example by way of illustrating a general rule

to make an example of someone is to punish them as a warning to others

to set an example is to behave in a way that is worthy of imitation

exasperate *VERB* **exasperates, exasperating, exasperated**
to annoy someone very much

▷ **exasperation** *NOUN*

WORD HISTORY from Latin *asper* 'rough'

excavate *VERB* **excavates, excavating, excavated**
1 to make a hole or channel by digging
2 to reveal or extract something by digging
3 to carry out an archaeological investigation by digging

▷ **excavation** *NOUN*
▷ **excavator** *NOUN*

exceed *VERB* **exceeds, exceeding, exceeded**
1 to be greater or more numerous than something else; to surpass someone or something
2 to go beyond the limit of what is normal or permitted ◆ *As the Parliament had exceeded its authority, it was dissolved.*

exceedingly *ADVERB*
very; extremely

excel *VERB* **excels, excelling, excelled**
to be better at something than someone else or other people

WORD HISTORY from Latin *celsus* 'lofty'

Excellency *NOUN* **Excellencies**
the title of high officials such as ambassadors and governors

excellent *ADJECTIVE*
extremely good

▷ **excellently** *ADVERB*
▷ **excellence** *NOUN*

except *PREPOSITION*
excluding; not including

By mid-afternoon, we'd sold the whole barrow-load except for a couple of cabbages and a few leeks. — *Alison Prince, Oranges and Murder*

except *VERB* **excepts, excepting, excepted**
to be excepted, or excepted from something, is to be excluded or omitted from consideration

USAGE NOTE Take care not to confuse this word with *accept*.

excepting *PREPOSITION*
except for; apart from

exception *NOUN* **exceptions**
a person or thing that is left out or does not follow the general rule ◆ *Most of the houses had gardens, although ours was an exception.*

to take exception to someone or **something** is to raise objections to them or to it

with the exception of except for; apart from

exceptional *ADJECTIVE*
1 very unusual
2 outstandingly good ◆ *The weather has been exceptional for this time of year.*

▷ **exceptionally** *ADVERB*

excerpt (*say* **ek**- serpt) *NOUN* **excerpts**
a passage taken from a book, speech, or film

WORD HISTORY from a Latin word meaning 'plucked out'

excess *NOUN* **excesses**
too much of something ◆ *An excess of sugar in the blood stream is dangerous.*

in excess of more than

excessive *ADJECTIVE*
too much or too great

▷ **excessively** *ADVERB*

exchange *VERB* **exchanges, exchanging, exchanged**
to give something and receive something else for it

exchange *NOUN* **exchanges**
1 the action of exchanging things
2 a place where things are bought and sold, especially a **stock exchange** where stocks and shares are traded
3 a place where telephone lines are connected to each other when a call is made

exchequer *NOUN* **exchequers**
a national treasury into which taxes and other public funds are paid

WORD HISTORY from Latin *scaccarium* 'a chessboard', because the Norman kings kept their accounts by means of counters placed on a chequered tablecloth

excise❶ (*say* **eks**- yz) ***NOUN***
a tax charged on certain goods and licences
WORD HISTORY from a Dutch word meaning 'tax'

excise❷ (*say* iks- **yz**) ***VERB*** **excises, excising, excised**
to remove something by cutting it away ◆ *A laser beam is used to excise the tumour.*

excitable ***ADJECTIVE***
easily excited

excite ***VERB*** **excites, exciting, excited**
1 to make someone eager and enthusiastic about something
2 to cause a feeling or reaction ◆ *Sumo wrestling is Japan's national sport and the annual tournament excites great interest throughout the country.*
▷ **excitedly** ***ADVERB***

excitement ***NOUN*** **excitements**
a strong feeling of eagerness or pleasure

I recollect that in the excitement of the moment we did a kind of dance around the room in our pyjamas. — *Roald Dahl, Vengeance Is Mine Inc.*

exclaim ***VERB*** **exclaims, exclaiming, exclaimed**
to shout or cry out in eagerness or surprise

'This must be Jo'burg!' exclaimed Naledi, as the lorry raced along a great wide road towards tall shapes. — *Beverley Naidoo, Journey to Jo'burg*

exclamation ***NOUN*** **exclamations**
1 the action of exclaiming
2 (*Language*) a word or words cried out expressing joy, pain, or surprise

exclamation mark ***NOUN*** **exclamation marks**
(*Language*) the punctuation mark (!) placed after an exclamation

exclamation marks

You use an **exclamation mark** to indicate shouting, surprise, or excitement in direct speech:
'Stop! Don't drink! The goblet is poisoned!'
'Wow! That's a real mammoth's tooth!'
It can also be used to express surprise, alarm, or excitement in a narrative, or in a character's thoughts:
The sun was coming up. She must hurry! Soon the spell would wear off!
Swimming with sharks! That would be something to remember!

exclude ***VERB*** **excludes, excluding, excluded**
1 to keep someone or something out of a place
2 to overlook or omit something ◆ *We cannot exclude the possibility that life came to this planet from Mars.*
▷ **exclusion** ***NOUN***

exclusive ***ADJECTIVE***
1 an exclusive offer or organization is open to a limited or selected number of people
2 an exclusive report or story is one that is reported in only one source
3 to be exclusive of something is not to include it ◆ *The price is exclusive of meals.*
▷ **exclusively** ***ADVERB***
▷ **exclusiveness** ***NOUN***

excommunicate ***VERB*** **excommunicates, excommunicating, excommunicated**
to cut a person off from membership of a Church
▷ **excommunication** ***NOUN***

excrement (*say* **eks**- krim- ent) ***NOUN***
waste matter excreted from the bowels

excrescence (*say* iks- **kress**- ens) ***NOUN*** **excrescences**
1 a growth or lump on a plant or animal's body
2 an ugly addition or part of a building or other structure

excrete ***VERB*** **excretes, excreting, excreted**
to get rid of waste matter from the body
▷ **excretion** ***NOUN***
▷ **excretory** ***ADJECTIVE***

excruciating (*say* iks- **kroo**- shee- ayt- ing) ***ADJECTIVE***
extremely painful; agonizing ◆ *The woman suffered from excruciating headaches.*
▷ **excruciatingly** ***ADVERB***
WORD HISTORY from Latin *cruciatum* 'tortured'

excursion ***NOUN*** **excursions**
a short journey made for pleasure

excusable ***ADJECTIVE***
able to be excused
▷ **excusably** ***ADVERB***

excuse (*say* iks- **kewz**) ***VERB*** **excuses, excusing, excused**
1 to forgive someone, or forgive an action or deed
2 to allow someone not to do something

Inspector, I think Miss Birling ought to be excused any more of this questioning. She's nothing more to tell you. — *J. B. Priestley, An Inspector Calls*

3 to allow someone to leave a room, meeting, or table

excuse (*say* iks- **kewss**) ***NOUN*** **excuses**
a reason given to explain why something wrong has been done

execrable (*say* **eks**- ik- rab- ul) ***ADJECTIVE***
very bad or unpleasant
WORD HISTORY from a Latin word meaning 'to curse'

execute *VERB* **executes, executing, executed**
1 to put someone to death as a punishment
2 to perform an action or manoeuvre

The driver ... executed a clumsy and violent U-turn on the narrow street, lunging up over the kerbs. — *Michael Hoeye, Time Stops for No Mouse*

▷ **execution** *NOUN*

executioner *NOUN* **executioners**
an official who executes a condemned person

executive (*say* ig- **zek**- yoo- tiv) *NOUN* **executives**
a senior person with authority in a business or government organization

executive *ADJECTIVE*
having the authority to carry out plans or laws

executor (*say* ig- **zek**- yoo- ter) *NOUN* **executors**
a person appointed to carry out the instructions in someone's will

exemplary (*say* ig- **zem**- pler- ee) *ADJECTIVE*
very good; being a good example to others ◆ *an award for exemplary conduct*

exemplify *VERB* **exemplifies, exemplifying, exemplified**
to be an example of something ◆ *This painting perfectly exemplifies the naturalistic style which was so popular at the time.*

exempt *ADJECTIVE*
a person, place, or organization that is exempt from a rule or law, or from doing something, is not legally or officially required to comply with it, or to do it ◆ *In some cases the home you live in might be exempt from Council Tax altogether.*

exempt *VERB* **exempts, exempting, exempted**
to make someone or something exempt

▷ **exemption** *NOUN*

exercise *NOUN* **exercises**
1 the action of using your body to make it strong and healthy
2 a piece of work done for practice

exercise *VERB* **exercises, exercising, exercised**
1 to do exercises
2 to give exercise to an animal
3 to use ◆ *Motorists have been asked to exercise patience as there may be some delays.*

WORD HISTORY from a Latin word meaning 'to keep someone working'

exert *VERB* **exerts, exerting, exerted**
to use power, strength, or influence ◆ *In the Aztec myth, Quetzalcoatl exerts all his strength to create an enormous wind.*
to exert yourself is to make an effort

▷ **exertion** *NOUN*

exeunt (*say* **eks**- ee- unt) *VERB*
(*Drama*) a stage direction meaning 'they leave the stage'

WORD HISTORY a Latin word meaning 'they go out'

exfoliate *VERB* **exfoliates, exfoliating, exfoliated**
to remove dead skin cells from your skin, often by scrubbing

ex gratia (*say* eks **gray**- sha) *ADJECTIVE*
an ex gratia payment is given without being legally required

WORD HISTORY a Latin phrase meaning 'from favour'

exhale *VERB* **exhales, exhaling, exhaled**
1 to breathe out
2 to breathe out air, fumes, or fire

'Dear, dear,' said Professor McGonagall sardonically, as one of the dragons soared around her classroom, emitting loud bangs and exhaling flame. — *J. K. Rowling, Harry Potter and the Order of the Phoenix*

▷ **exhalation** *NOUN*

exhaust *VERB* **exhausts, exhausting, exhausted**
1 to make someone very tired
2 to use something up completely

▷ **exhaustion** *NOUN*

exhaust *NOUN* **exhausts**
1 the waste gases or steam from an engine
2 the pipe through which they are sent out

exhaustive *ADJECTIVE*
an exhaustive search or effort is as thorough and as complete as possible

▷ **exhaustively** *ADVERB*

exhibit *VERB* **exhibits, exhibiting, exhibited**
to show or display something in public

▷ **exhibitor** *NOUN*

exhibit *NOUN* **exhibits**
an object or work of art on display in a gallery or museum

exhibition *NOUN* **exhibitions**
(*Art*) a collection of things put on display for people to look at, for example at a museum or gallery

exhibitionist *NOUN* **exhibitionists**
a person who behaves in a way that is meant to attract attention

▷ **exhibitionism** *NOUN*

exhilarate (*say* ig- **zil**- er- ayt) *VERB* **exhilarates, exhilarating, exhilarated**
to be exhilarated is to feel very happy and excited

▷ **exhilaration** *NOUN*

a b c d e f g h i j k l m n o p q r s t u v w x y z

exhort (*say* ig- **zort**) ***VERB*** **exhorts, exhorting, exhorted**
to try hard to persuade someone to do something
▷ **exhortation** ***NOUN***

exhume (*say* ig- **zewm**) ***VERB*** **exhumes, exhuming, exhumed**
to dig up a body that has been buried
▷ **exhumation** ***NOUN***

exile ***VERB*** **exiles, exiling, exiled**
to banish someone from a country

exile ***NOUN*** **exiles**
1 to be in exile is to be forced to live away from your own country
2 someone who has been banished from their own country

exist ***VERB*** **exists, existing, existed**
1 to be present as part of what is real

Inside the house lived a malevolent phantom. People said he existed, but Jem and I had never seen him. — *Harper Lee, To Kill a Mockingbird*

2 to stay alive
▷ **existence** ***NOUN***
▷ **existent** ***ADJECTIVE***

exit ***NOUN*** **exits**
1 the way out of a building
2 (*Drama*) the moment when an actor leaves the stage

exit ***VERB***
an actor or performer exits when they leave the stage

WORD HISTORY a Latin word meaning 'he or she goes out'

exit poll ***NOUN*** **exit polls**
a poll of people leaving a polling station after voting, to estimate the result

exodus ***NOUN*** **exoduses**
the departure of many people ◆ *The Midsummer Festival causes a mass exodus from the city, as the locals head to the countryside.*

WORD HISTORY from Greek *exodos* 'a way out'

exonerate ***VERB*** **exonerates, exonerating, exonerated**
to exonerate someone is to say or prove that they are not to blame for something
▷ **exoneration** ***NOUN***

WORD HISTORY from Latin *onus* 'a burden'

exorbitant ***ADJECTIVE***
an exorbitant price or demand is much too high, or much too great

WORD HISTORY from Latin *orbita* 'an orbit'

exorcize ***VERB*** **exorcizes, exorcizing, exorcized**
to exorcize an evil spirit is to drive it out from a person or place
▷ **exorcism** ***NOUN***
▷ **exorcist** ***NOUN***

USAGE NOTE This word can also be spelled exorcise.

exotic ***ADJECTIVE***
1 strikingly unusual and exciting ◆ *Beyond the house were hothouses filled with exotic plants.*
2 from or in a distant part of the world ◆ *holidaying in an exotic location*
▷ **exotically** ***ADVERB***

WORD HISTORY from Greek *exo* 'outside'

expand ***VERB*** **expands, expanding, expanded**
1 to make something larger or fuller
2 to become larger or fuller
to expand on something is to describe it in more detail
▷ **expansion** ***NOUN***

expanse ***NOUN*** **expanses**
a wide area of open land, sea, or space

expansive ***ADJECTIVE***
1 covering a wide area
2 an expansive person or manner is genial and readily communicates thoughts and feelings
▷ **expansively** ***ADVERB***
▷ **expansiveness** ***NOUN***

expat ***NOUN*** **expats**
(*informal*) an expatriate

expatiate (*say* iks- **pay**- shi- ayt) ***VERB*** **expatiates, expatiating, expatiated**
to speak or write about a subject at length or in detail

expatriate (*say* eks- **pat**- ree- at) ***NOUN*** **expatriates**
a person living away from his or her own country

expect ***VERB*** **expects, expecting, expected**
1 to think or believe that something will happen ◆ *They were expecting something exciting to happen.*
2 to demand something or think that it is necessary ◆ *The Court will expect prompt payment of these fines.*

expectant ***ADJECTIVE***
1 expecting something to happen; hopeful
2 an expectant mother is a woman who is pregnant
▷ **expectantly** ***ADVERB***
▷ **expectancy** ***NOUN***

expectation ***NOUN*** **expectations**
1 a belief that something will happen
2 something you expect to happen or get

expecting ***ADJECTIVE***
(*informal*) a woman who is expecting is pregnant

expectorant ***NOUN*** **expectorants**
a medicine that makes you cough and spit out phlegm

expedient (*say* iks- **pee**- dee- ent) ***ADJECTIVE***
1 suitable or convenient
2 useful or advantageous rather than right or just
▷ **expediently** ***ADVERB***
▷ **expediency** ***NOUN***

expedient ***NOUN*** **expedients**
a convenient means of achieving something

expedite (*say* **eks**- pid- dyt) ***VERB*** **expedites, expediting, expedited**
to get something done quickly or efficiently

WORD HISTORY from a Latin word meaning 'to free someone's feet'

expedition ***NOUN*** **expeditions**
1 a journey or voyage made by a group of people for a special purpose
2 the people or vehicles making such a journey
3 (*formal*) speed or promptness
▷ **expeditionary** ***ADJECTIVE***

expeditious (*say* eks- pid- **ish**- us) ***ADJECTIVE***
quick and efficient
▷ **expeditiously** ***ADVERB***

expel ***VERB*** **expels, expelling, expelled**
1 to send or force something out ◆ *Gently squeeze the mould to expel any air bubbles.*
2 to make a person leave a school or country

The Ministry of Magic said I'd be expelled from Hogwarts if there was any more magic there!
— *J. K. Rowling, Harry Potter and the Prisoner of Azkaban*

expend ***VERB*** **expends, expending, expended**
to spend money, or use time or effort to get something done

expendable ***ADJECTIVE***
not worth keeping or preserving; suitable for sacrificing to gain an objective ◆ *The 33-year-old striker was deemed expendable at the start of the season.*

expenditure ***NOUN*** **expenditures**
1 the spending of money or other resources
2 the amount of money or resources spent

expense ***NOUN*** **expenses**
1 the cost of doing something
2 something that you have to spend money on ◆ *Moving house is always a huge expense.*
3 a person's expenses are the amounts of money they spend in doing something

at the expense of with the loss of something or damage to it ◆ *His drive to succeed in the business world often came at the expense of his health.*

expensive ***ADJECTIVE***
costing a lot of money
▷ **expensively** ***ADVERB***
▷ **expensiveness** ***NOUN***

experience ***NOUN*** **experiences**
1 skill or knowledge that a person gains over time
2 an event or activity that has an effect on you

experience ***VERB*** **experiences, experiencing, experienced**
to have something happen to you

experienced ***ADJECTIVE***
having a lot of knowledge or skill through experience

experiment ***NOUN*** **experiments**
a test or trial done to see how something works or to prove something
▷ **experimental** ***ADJECTIVE***
▷ **experimentally** ***ADVERB***

experiment ***VERB*** **experiments, experimenting, experimented**
1 to carry out an experiment
2 to try out new things
▷ **experimentation** ***NOUN***

expert ***NOUN*** **experts**
a person with great knowledge or skill in a particular subject or activity

expert ***ADJECTIVE***
someone who is expert at something has great knowledge or skill in it
▷ **expertly** ***ADVERB***
▷ **expertness** ***NOUN***

expertise (*say* eks- per- **teez**) ***NOUN***
expert knowledge or skill

expiate (*say* **eks**- pee- ayt) ***VERB*** **expiates, expiating, expiated**
to make amends for something wrong you have done; to atone for something
▷ **expiation** ***NOUN***

expire ***VERB*** **expires, expiring, expired**
1 a card, ticket, or licence expires when it is has passed the time during which it is usable or valid
2 to die
3 to breathe out air
▷ **expiration** ***NOUN***
▷ **expiry** ***NOUN***

explain ***VERB*** **explains, explaining, explained**
1 to make something plain or clear; to show the meaning of something
2 to account for something ◆ *That explains his absence.*

explanation ***NOUN*** **explanations**
1 the process of explaining something
2 a statement or fact that explains something

explanatory (*say* iks- **plan**- at- er- ee) ***ADJECTIVE***
serving or intended to explain something

expletive (*say* iks- **plee**- tiv) ***NOUN*** **expletives**
an oath or swear word

explicit (*say* iks- **pliss**- it) ***ADJECTIVE***
stated or stating something openly and exactly (SEE ALSO **implicit**)
▷ **explicitly** ***ADVERB***

explode ***VERB*** **explodes, exploding, exploded**
1 to burst or suddenly release energy with a loud noise

Goyle's potion exploded, showering the whole class. People shrieked as splashes of the Swelling Solution hit them. — *J. K. Rowling, Harry Potter and the Chamber of Secrets*

2 a person explodes with anger or laughter when they burst into it suddenly
3 to increase suddenly or quickly
4 to destroy an idea or theory by showing it to be false

WORD HISTORY from an earlier meaning 'to drive a player off the stage by clapping or hissing', from Latin *plaudere* 'to clap'

exploit (*say* **eks**- ploit) ***NOUN*** **exploits**
a brave or exciting deed

The killing of the Fire Dragon was an exploit that called for the best of their cunning. — *Robert Nye, Beowulf*

exploit (*say* iks- **ploit**) ***VERB*** **exploits, exploiting, exploited**
1 to develop a resource or talent and get benefit from it
2 to make unfair use of someone or something
▷ **exploitation** ***NOUN***

exploratory (*say* iks- **plo**- ruh- ter- ee) ***ADJECTIVE***
for the purpose of exploring

explore ***VERB*** **explores, exploring, explored**
1 to travel through a country or region in order to learn about it
2 to examine a subject or idea carefully ◆ *Students will be able to explore the possibilities of digital animation.*
▷ **exploration** ***NOUN***
▷ **explorer** ***NOUN***

explosion ***NOUN*** **explosions**
1 the action or sound of something exploding
2 a sudden great increase ◆ *a population explosion*

explosive ***ADJECTIVE***
1 able or likely to explode
2 an explosive situation is one that is likely to cause violent and dangerous reactions
▷ **explosively** ***ADVERB***

explosive ***NOUN*** **explosives**
an explosive substance

exponent ***NOUN*** **exponents**
1 someone who favours a particular theory or policy
2 (*Mathematics*) a raised number or letter placed immediately after another (e.g. 3 in 2^3) which shows how many times the first one is to be multiplied by itself

exponential ***ADJECTIVE***
an exponential number or amount is one that is indicated by an exponent

export ***VERB*** **exports, exporting, exported**
to send goods abroad to be sold
▷ **exportation** ***NOUN***
▷ **exporter** ***NOUN***

export ***NOUN*** **exports**
1 the process of exporting goods
2 something that is exported for sale

expose ***VERB*** **exposes, exposing, exposed**
1 to leave someone or something uncovered or unprotected, especially from the weather
2 to make someone or something visible; to reveal something

I could not go abroad in snow—it would settle on me and expose me. Rain, too, would make me a watery outline, a glistening surface of a man—a bubble. — *H. G. Wells, The Invisible Man*

3 to allow light to reach a photographic film so as to take a picture
4 to reveal information about a crime or the person who has committed it
5 to subject someone to a risk or danger
6 to introduce someone to an experience

I can remember the first time my son Danny was exposed to music. — *Nick Hornby, 31 Songs*

exposition ***NOUN*** **expositions**
1 an explanatory account of a plan or theory
2 a large public exhibition

expostulate ***VERB*** **expostulates, expostulating, expostulated**
to argue or protest strongly about something ◆ *The manager was on his feet immediately after the match, heatedly expostulating with the two officials on the sideline.*
▷ **expostulation** ***NOUN***

exposure ***NOUN*** **exposures**
1 the harmful effects of being exposed to cold weather without enough protection
2 the process of exposing film to the light so as to take a picture
3 a piece of film exposed in this way
4 publicity ◆ *Her autobiography will be released alongside the film in order to give it maximum exposure.*

expound ***VERB*** **expounds, expounding, expounded**
to describe or explain something in detail

express ***ADJECTIVE***
1 an express vehicle, journey, or mail is one that goes or is sent quickly
2 an express aim, motive, or instruction is one that is clearly stated

express ***NOUN*** **expresses**
a fast train or bus which makes a limited number of stops

express ***VERB*** **expresses, expressing, expressed**
1 to make a feeling or idea known by your words or gesture

Marilla sniffed, to express her contempt for Matthew's opinions concerning anything feminine, and walked off to the dairy with the pails. — *L. M. Montgomery, Anne of Green Gables*

2 to press or squeeze out juice, milk, or other liquid

expression ***NOUN*** **expressions**
1 the look on a person's face that shows their feelings

Winston ... had set his features into the expression of quiet optimism which it was advisable to wear. — *George Orwell, Nineteen Eighty-four*

2 a word or phrase
3 the action of expressing something
4 a way of speaking or of playing music so as to show your feelings

expressionism ***NOUN***
a style of painting, drama, or music that tries to express the artist's or writer's emotional feeling rather than to represent what is in the outside world
▷ **expressionist** ***NOUN, ADJECTIVE***

expressive ***ADJECTIVE***
an expressive word or gesture is full of expression and feeling

expressly ***ADVERB***
1 clearly and plainly ◆ *Mobile phones are expressly forbidden in class and in examinations.*
2 for a special purpose ◆ *The museum has a hands-on exhibition designed expressly for children.*

expulsion ***NOUN*** **expulsions**
the process of expelling someone or something, or of being expelled

expunge ***VERB*** **expunges, expunging, expunged**
to wipe something out; to erase or delete something ◆ *Clicking this button will expunge the records permanently from the database.*

expurgate ***VERB*** **expurgates, expurgating, expurgated**
to remove unsuitable or obscene material from a publication
▷ **expurgation** ***NOUN***

exquisite (*say* **eks**- kwiz- it) ***ADJECTIVE***
1 very beautiful or delicate ◆ *Each chess piece is hand-painted in exquisite detail.*
2 exquisite taste is highly refined or sensitive
▷ **exquisitely** ***ADVERB***

WORD HISTORY from a Latin word meaning 'sought out'

extant (*say* eks- **tant**) ***ADJECTIVE***
still existing ◆ *The survey of the island recorded 21 extant mammal species.*

extemporize ***VERB*** **extemporizes, extemporizing, extemporized**
to speak, produce, or do something without advance preparation
▷ **extemporization** ***NOUN***

USAGE NOTE This word can also be spelled extemporise.

WORD HISTORY from a Latin phrase *ex tempore* 'on the spur of the moment'

extend ***VERB*** **extends, extending, extended**
1 to stretch something out
2 to make something become longer or larger
3 to offer or give sympathy, help, or welcome to someone
4 to continue for a certain distance; to reach something ◆ *The boundary of the new National Park extends to the coast.*
▷ **extendible** ***ADJECTIVE***

extension ***NOUN*** **extensions**
1 the process of extending something, or of being extended
2 a section added on to a building or other structure
3 an extra period for something to be done
4 one of a set of telephones in an office or house

extensive ***ADJECTIVE***
1 covering a large area ◆ *extensive grounds*
2 large in scope, wide-ranging ◆ *an extensive search*
▷ **extensively** ***ADVERB***
▷ **extensiveness** ***NOUN***

extent ***NOUN*** **extents**
1 the area or length over which something extends
2 the amount, level, or scope of something ◆ *It is too early to gauge the full extent of the damage to property.*

extenuating ***ADJECTIVE***
extenuating circumstances provide a partial excuse and make a crime seem less great
▷ **extenuation** ***NOUN***

exterior ***ADJECTIVE***
on the outside, or coming from the outside

exterior ***NOUN*** **exteriors**
the outside, or an outside part, of something

exterminate *VERB* **exterminates, exterminating, exterminated**
to destroy or kill all the members or examples of something
▷ **extermination** *NOUN*
▷ **exterminator** *NOUN*
WORD HISTORY from an earlier meaning 'to banish', from Latin *terminus* 'boundary'

external *ADJECTIVE*
1 on or from the outside or visible part of something
2 on or for the outside of your body ◆ *Essential oils are for external use only.*
▷ **externally** *ADVERB*

extinct *ADJECTIVE*
1 an extinct animal does not exist any more
2 an extinct volcano is no longer active

extinction *NOUN*
1 the process of becoming extinct
2 the process of extinguishing something

extinguish *VERB* **extinguishes, extinguishing, extinguished**
1 to put out a fire or light
2 to put an end to a hope or dream ◆ *The team's hopes of causing a major shock were extinguished after just four minutes.*

extinguisher *NOUN* **extinguishers**
a portable device for sending out water, chemicals, or gases to extinguish a fire

extol *VERB* **extols, extolling, extolled**
to praise someone or something enthusiastically

extort *VERB* **extorts, extorting, extorted**
to obtain something by force or threats
▷ **extortion** *NOUN*

extortionate *ADJECTIVE*
an extortionate price, fee, or demand is unreasonably high or great

extra *ADJECTIVE*
additional; more than is usual

Now the clock had struck thirteen, affirming that—for this once at least—there was an extra, thirteenth hour. — *Philippa Pearce, Tom's Midnight Garden*

extra *ADVERB*
more than usually ◆ *extra strong mints*

extra *NOUN* **extras**
1 an extra person or thing
2 a person who acts as part of a crowd in a film or play

extract (*say* iks- **trakt**) *VERB* **extracts, extracting, extracted**
to take something out; to remove something ◆ *She extracted a spare set of keys from the jar on the shelf.*

extract (*say* **eks**- trakt) *NOUN* **extracts**
1 a passage taken from a longer work, such as a book, film, or piece of music
2 a substance separated or obtained from another

extraction *NOUN*
1 the process of extracting something
2 a person's family history ◆ *She is of Chinese extraction.*

extractor *NOUN* **extractors**
a device that removes unwanted smells or fumes from the air

extradite *VERB* **extradites, extraditing, extradited**
to hand over an accused person to the police of the country where the crime was committed
▷ **extradition** (*say* eks- tra- **dish**- on) *NOUN*

extraneous (*say* iks- **tray**- nee- us) *ADJECTIVE*
1 added from outside
2 not belonging to the matter in hand; irrelevant

extraordinary *ADJECTIVE*
very unusual or strange ◆ *It is the story of an extraordinary friendship between a boy and a seal.*
▷ **extraordinarily** *ADVERB*

extrapolate (*say* iks- **trap**- ol- ayt) *VERB* **extrapolates, extrapolating, extrapolated**
to draw conclusions about something based on known facts

extrasensory *ADJECTIVE*
outside the range of the known human senses

extraterrestrial *ADJECTIVE*
from beyond the earth's atmosphere; from outer space

extraterrestrial *NOUN* **extraterrestrials**
an imaginary creature from outer space

extravagant *ADJECTIVE*
spending too much money, or using too many resources
▷ **extravagantly** *ADVERB*
▷ **extravagance** *NOUN*
WORD HISTORY from Latin *extra* 'outside' and *vagans* 'wandering'

extravaganza *NOUN* **extravaganzas**
a lavish or spectacular film or show

extreme *ADJECTIVE*
1 very great or intense ◆ *I need to speak to you as a matter of extreme urgency.*
2 furthest away, outermost ◆ *The village was in the extreme north.*
3 going to great lengths in actions or opinions; not moderate
▷ **extremely** *ADVERB*

extreme *NOUN* **extremes**
1 something extreme
2 either end of something

extremist *NOUN* **extremists**
a person who holds extreme (not moderate) opinions in political or other matters
▷ **extremism** *NOUN*

extremity (*say* iks- **trem**- it- ee) *NOUN* **extremities**
1 an extreme point; the very end of something
2 an extreme need, feeling, or danger
3 your extremities are your hands and feet

extricate (*say* **eks**- trik- ayt) *VERB* **extricates, extricating, extricated**
to free someone or something from a difficult position or situation
▷ **extrication** *NOUN*

extrovert *NOUN* **extroverts**
a person who is generally friendly and likes company (SEE ALSO **introvert**)

extrude *VERB* **extrudes, extruding, extruded**
to push or squeeze something out
▷ **extrusion** *NOUN*

exuberant (*say* ig- **zew**- ber- ant) *ADJECTIVE*
an exuberant person or manner is very lively and cheerful
▷ **exuberantly** *ADVERB*
▷ **exuberance** *NOUN*

WORD HISTORY from a Latin word meaning 'to grow thickly'

exude *VERB* **exudes, exuding, exuded**
1 to give off moisture or a smell
2 to display a feeling or quality openly ◆ *Size and shape are no barrier to looking fabulous and exuding confidence.*

exult *VERB* **exults, exulting, exulted**
to show great pleasure about something
▷ **exultant** *ADJECTIVE*
▷ **exultation** *NOUN*

WORD HISTORY from a Latin word meaning 'to leap up'

eye *NOUN* **eyes**
1 the organ that is used for seeing in humans and some animals
2 the power of seeing ◆ *You have sharp eyes.*
3 the small hole in a needle
4 the centre of a storm

to cast or **run an eye over something** is to read or study it quickly
in the eyes of someone in their opinion or judgement
to keep an eye on someone or something is to to watch them or it carefully
to keep an eye out for someone or something is to watch out for them or it
to make eyes at someone is to look at them with sexual interest
to see eye to eye with someone is to agree with them, or to have the same opinion as them
to be up to the eyes in something is to be deeply involved or occupied in it
with an eye to with the aim or intention of doing something
with your eyes open knowing all the circumstances full well

eye *VERB* **eyes, eyeing, eyed**
to look at someone or something with interest, or in a particular way

The other three children murmured solemn greetings but continued to eye Victoria with suspicion. — *Meg Cabot, Victoria and the Rogue*

eyeball *NOUN* **eyeballs**
the ball-shaped part of an eye inside an eyelid

eyeball *VERB* **eyeballs, eyeballing, eyeballed**
(*informal*) to look at someone or something intently ◆ *Tension grew as locals eyeballed the strangers.*

eyebrow *NOUN* **eyebrows**
the fringe of hair that grows on your face above each eye

eye-catching *ADJECTIVE*
striking or attractive

eyeful *NOUN* **eyefuls**
(*informal*) a long close look at someone or something

eyelash *NOUN* **eyelashes**
one of the short hairs that grow on an eyelid

eyelet *NOUN* **eyelets**
a small metal ring in a piece of fabric through which a rope or cord is passed

eyelid *NOUN* **eyelids**
either of the two folds of skin that can close over an eyeball

eyeliner *NOUN*
a cosmetic applied as a line round the eyes

eyepiece *NOUN* **eyepieces**
the lens of a telescope or microscope that you put to your eye

eyeshadow *NOUN*
a cosmetic used to colour the skin round the eyes

eyesight *NOUN*
1 the ability to see
2 a range of vision ◆ *Parents can relax in the cafeteria while the children play within eyesight.*

eyesore *NOUN* **eyesores**
something that is ugly to look at

eyewash *NOUN*
1 a cleansing lotion for your eyes
2 (*informal*) nonsense; rubbish

eyewitness *NOUN* **eyewitnesses**
a person who actually saw an accident or crime

eyrie (*say* **ee**- ree) *NOUN* **eyries**
the nest of an eagle or other bird of prey

a b c d e f g h i j k l m n o p q r s t u v w x y z

Ff

fable *NOUN* **fables**
a short story, usually with animals as characters, intended to convey a moral
▷ **fabled** *ADJECTIVE*
WORD HISTORY from Latin *fabula* 'story'

fabric *NOUN* **fabrics**
1 material produced from woven or knitted fibres; cloth
2 the basic framework of something, especially the walls, floors, and roof of a building

fabricate *VERB* **fabricates, fabricating, fabricated**
1 to construct or manufacture something
2 to invent a false story or excuse
▷ **fabrication** *NOUN*

fabulous *ADJECTIVE*
1 (*informal*) wonderful; really good
2 very great

The Brazilian's ship contained fabulous riches. Bales of gossamer silks and shining satins hid still greater wealth. — *Celia Rees, Pirates!*

3 told of in fables and myths ◆ *the fabulous monster of the Labyrinth*
▷ **fabulously** *ADVERB*

facade (*say* fas- **ahd**) *NOUN* **facades**
1 the front of a building
2 an outward appearance, especially a deceptive one ◆ *He comes across as likeable and charming but it's all just a facade.*

face *NOUN* **faces**
1 the front part of a person's head
2 the expression on a person's face

Mr Bohlen glanced up at the long, melancholy face of the younger man. 'Aren't you proud, Knipe? Aren't you pleased?' — *Roald Dahl, The Great Automatic Grammatizator*

3 an aspect of something ◆ *Philip Glass has been called the acceptable face of modern classical music.*
4 the front or upper side of something
5 a flat surface on a three-dimensional shape

face *VERB* **faces, facing, faced**
1 to look or have the front towards something

They faced each other across the table, their fingers spread on the cloth, like two pianists ready to begin. — *Barry Hines, A Kestrel for a Knave*

2 to meet and have to deal with a situation, especially a difficult or dangerous one ◆ *One of the world's largest freshwater fish is facing the danger of extinction.*
3 to cover a surface with a layer of different material

faceless *ADJECTIVE*
a faceless place or expression is one without any individual interest or character

The reception was cold and faceless, white marble and mirrors, with a single potted plant tucked into the corner as an afterthought. — *Anthony Horowitz, Point Blanc*

facelift *NOUN* **facelifts**
cosmetic surgery to remove wrinkles by tightening the skin of the face

facet (*say* **fas**- it) *NOUN* **facets**
1 one of the many sides of a cut stone or jewel
2 one aspect of a situation or problem, or one part of the character of a person or place ◆ *A new photography exhibit reveals the many facets of Japan.*
WORD HISTORY from French *facette* 'small face'

facetious (*say* fas- **ee**- shus) *ADJECTIVE*
trying to be funny at an unsuitable time
▷ **facetiously** *ADVERB*

facial (*say* **fay**- shal) *ADJECTIVE*
to do with your face

facial *NOUN* **facials**
a beauty treatment applied to a person's face

facile (*say* **fas**- yl) *ADJECTIVE*
a facile solution or argument is produced easily or with little thought or care
WORD HISTORY from Latin *facilis* 'easy'

facilitate (*say* fas- **il**- it- ayt) *VERB* **facilitates, facilitating, facilitated**
to make something easy or easier to do
▷ **facilitation** *NOUN*
▷ **facilitator** *NOUN*

facility (*say* fas- **il**- it- ee) *NOUN* **facilities**
1 a building or piece of equipment used for a special purpose ◆ *The college boasts a brand new sports facility.*
2 ease or skill in doing something ◆ *She had a great facility with language and went on to learn French, Spanish, and Italian.*

facsimile (*say* fak- **sim**- il- ee) *NOUN* **facsimiles**
an exact reproduction of a document
WORD HISTORY from Latin *fac* 'to make' and *simile* 'a likeness'

fact *NOUN* **facts**
something that is known to have happened or to be true

the facts of life information about sexual reproduction

WORD FAMILY *Fact* comes from Latin *facere* 'to do or make'. Other words having the same origin include *benefactor*, *factor*, *factory*, *malefactor*, and *satisfaction*.

faction *NOUN* **factions**
a small united group within a larger one, especially in politics
▷ **factional** *ADJECTIVE*

factor *NOUN* **factors**
1 something that helps to bring about a result ◆ *What was the decisive factor in your success?*
2 (*Mathematics*) a number by which a larger number can be divided exactly ◆ *2 and 3 are factors of 6.*

factory *NOUN* **factories**
a building or group of buildings in which goods are manufactured

factotum (*say* fakt- **oh**- tum) *NOUN* **factotums**
(*formal*) a servant or assistant who does all kinds of work

WORD HISTORY from Latin *fac* 'do' and *totum* 'everything'

factual *ADJECTIVE*
based on facts; containing facts
▷ **factually** *ADVERB*

faculty *NOUN* **faculties**
1 any of the powers of the body or mind (e.g. sight, speech, understanding)
2 a department teaching a particular subject in a university or college ◆ *the faculty of music*

fad *NOUN* **fads**
1 a person's particular like or dislike
2 a temporary fashion or craze

WORD HISTORY originally a dialect word

faddy *ADJECTIVE* **faddier, faddiest**
having a lot of special likes and dislikes

fade *VERB* **fades, fading, faded**
1 to lose colour or freshness or strength
2 a sound, image, or memory fades when it becomes indistinct or blurred

to fade something in or **up** to fade in a sound or signal is to make it gradually stronger

to fade something out to fade out a sound or signal is to make it gradually weaker

fade *NOUN* **fades**
an act or sound of fading

faeces (*say* **fee**- seez) *PLURAL NOUN*
solid waste matter passed out of a person's or animal's body

WORD HISTORY the plural of Latin *faex* 'dregs'

fag *NOUN* **fags** (*informal*)
1 a tiring or boring task
2 a cigarette

fagged out *ADJECTIVE*
(*informal*) tired out; exhausted

faggot *NOUN* **faggots**
1 a meatball made with chopped liver and baked
2 a bundle of sticks bound together, used for firewood

WORD HISTORY from Greek *phakelos* 'a bundle'

Fahrenheit *ADJECTIVE*
measured on a temperature scale where water freezes at 32° and boils at 212°

WORD HISTORY named after G. D. *Fahrenheit* (1686–1736), a German scientist who invented the mercury thermometer

fail *VERB* **fails, failing, failed**
1 to try to do something but be unable to do it
2 to become weak or useless; to stop working ◆ *The day after I picked up my car, the brakes failed completely.*
3 to neglect or be unable to do something ◆ *Park rangers failed to warn visitors of the potential risks of landslides.*
4 to be unable to meet the standard needed to pass an examination
5 to judge that someone has not passed an examination

fail *NOUN* **fails**
a mark which does not pass an examination

without fail for certain; whatever happens

failing *NOUN* **failings**
a weakness or a fault

failure *NOUN* **failures**
1 the act of failing; a lack of success
2 a person or thing that has failed

faint *ADJECTIVE*
1 pale or dim; not distinct
2 feeling weak or giddy; nearly unconscious
3 weak or vague ◆ *Scientists retain a faint hope of making contact with the spacecraft.*
▷ **faintly** *ADVERB*
▷ **faintness** *NOUN*

faint *VERB* **faints, fainting, fainted**
to become unconscious for a short time

USAGE NOTE Take care not to confuse this word with *feint*.

faint-hearted *ADJECTIVE*
timid or cowardly

fair[1] *ADJECTIVE*
1 a fair contest or fight is one in which everyone is treated fairly and follows the rules
2 a fair judge or decision is impartial and just
3 fair hair or skin is light in colour, and a fair person has this colour of hair
4 (*literary*) pretty or beautiful ◆ *Mirror, mirror, on the wall, who is the fairest of them all?*
5 fair weather is fine or favourable
6 of a reasonable size, amount, or number ◆ *The return match next Saturday promises to attract a fair crowd.*
▷ **fairness** *NOUN*

SPELLING NOTE Some words pronounced **f-** begin with **ph-** (e.g. phrase)

fair *ADVERB*
to play fair is to act fairly, according to the rules
fair and square honestly; straightforwardly
fair❷ *NOUN* **fairs**
1 a group of outdoor entertainments such as rollercoasters, sideshows, and stalls
2 an exhibition or market ◆ *an international book fair*
WORD HISTORY from Latin *feriae* 'holiday'
fairground *NOUN* **fairgrounds**
an open outdoor space where a fair is held
fairly *ADVERB*
1 justly; according to the rules
2 quite or rather; up to a point ◆ *The manual is fairly easy to understand, even for a beginner.*
fairway *NOUN* **fairways**
the part of a golf course between a tee and the green, where the grass is kept short
fairy *NOUN* **fairies**
a tiny imaginary creature with supernatural powers
WORD HISTORY from an old word *fay*, from Latin *fata* 'the Fates', three goddesses who were believed to control people's lives
fairyland *NOUN* **fairylands**
the imaginary land where fairies live
fairy lights *PLURAL NOUN*
strings of small decorative coloured lights
fairy tale *NOUN* **fairy tales**
a story about fairies or other supernatural creatures
fait accompli (*say* fayt ah- **kom**- pli) *NOUN* **faits accomplis**
a thing that has already been done and cannot be changed
WORD HISTORY a French phrase meaning 'accomplished fact'
faith *NOUN* **faiths**
1 strong trust or confidence in a person or thing
2 (*Religion*) a system of religious beliefs
in good faith with honest intentions
faithful *ADJECTIVE*
1 a faithful person or animal is loyal and trustworthy
2 a faithful account or description of events is true to the facts
3 having a sexual relationship with one partner and not anyone else
Yours faithfully SEE **yours**
▷ **faithfully** *ADVERB*
▷ **faithfulness** *NOUN*
fake *NOUN* **fakes**
something that looks genuine but is not; a forgery
fake *ADJECTIVE*
1 false or forged; not genuine
2 artificial, not natural
fake *VERB* **fakes, faking, faked**
1 to make something false look real or genuine in order to deceive people
2 to fake an illness or condition is to pretend to have it, often so as to provide an excuse
▷ **faker** *NOUN*
fakir (*say* **fay**- keer) *NOUN* **fakirs**
a Muslim or Hindu religious beggar regarded as a holy man
WORD HISTORY an Arabic word meaning 'a poor man'
falafel (*say* fa- **laf**- ul) *NOUN*
a Middle Eastern dish of spiced mashed chickpeas made into balls and fried
falcon *NOUN* **falcons**
a bird of prey with long pointed wings, often used in the sport of hunting other birds or game
▷ **falconry** *NOUN*
fall *VERB* **falls, falling, fell, fallen**
1 to come or go down without being pushed or thrown

There was no wind, and the snow fell silently in large heavy flakes. — *Joe Simpson, Touching the Void*

2 a price, number, or amount falls when it decreases or becomes lower
3 an area of land falls when it drops or slopes downwards
4 a place that is being attacked falls when it is captured or overthrown
5 to die in battle
6 silence or darkness falls when it happens or arrives
7 to enter into a state, such as sleep or silence

When Sattamax was ready to speak, the rest of the crowd fell silent. — *Philip Pullman, The Amber Spyglass*

8 to occur; to have as a date ◆ *Valentine's Day falls on a Saturday this year.*
to fall back is to retreat
to fall back on a person or resource is to use them for support in an emergency
to fall for someone or something
1 to fall for a person is to be attracted by them
2 to fall for a trick or deception is to be taken in by it
to fall in love with someone is to begin to love them
to fall out with someone is to quarrel with them
to fall through a plan or scheme falls through when it fails
fall *NOUN* **falls**
1 the action of falling
2 the sound of something falling or striking a surface

From their hiding place Thomas and Kate listened to the fall of the hoofs going into the distance. — *G. P. Taylor, Shadowmancer*

3 (*American*) autumn, when leaves fall

fallacy (*say* **fal**- a- see) ***NOUN*** **fallacies**
a false or mistaken idea or belief that many people believe is true
▷ **fallacious** (*say* fal- **ay**- shus) ***ADJECTIVE***

fallback ***ADJECTIVE***
a fallback plan or position is an alternative plan or position that is adopted if the main one fails

fallible (*say* **fal**- ib- ul) ***ADJECTIVE***
liable to make mistakes; not infallible
▷ **fallibility** ***NOUN***

Fallopian tube ***NOUN*** **Fallopian tubes**
one of the two tubes in a woman's body along which the eggs travel from the ovaries to the uterus

WORD HISTORY named after Gabriele *Fallopio*, a 16th-century Italian anatomist

fallout ***NOUN***
particles of radioactive material carried in the air after a nuclear explosion

fallow ***ADJECTIVE***
fallow land is ploughed but left without crops in order to make it fertile again

WORD HISTORY from Old English *falu* 'pale brown', because of the colour of the bare earth

fallow deer ***NOUN*** **fallow deer**
a kind of light-brown deer

falls ***PLURAL NOUN***
a waterfall

false ***ADJECTIVE***
1 untrue or incorrect ◆ *Many websites have been shut down as a result of a false accusation of spamming.*
2 not genuine; artificial
3 treacherous or deceitful
▷ **falsely** ***ADVERB***
▷ **falseness** ***NOUN***
▷ **falsity** ***NOUN***

falsehood ***NOUN*** **falsehoods**
1 a lie
2 the action of telling lies

falsetto ***NOUN*** **falsettos**
a high-pitched male voice above the natural range

WORD HISTORY an Italian word meaning 'little false one'

falsify ***VERB*** **falsifies, falsifying, falsified**
to alter a document or evidence dishonestly
▷ **falsification** ***NOUN***

falter ***VERB*** **falters, faltering, faltered**
1 to hesitate when you move or speak
2 to become weaker; to begin to give way

The man tried to meet Abhorsen's gaze, but faltered and looked away at his fellows. — *Garth Nix, Sabriel*

fame ***NOUN***
1 the fact of being famous or known to many people
2 a good reputation; renown

Beowulf was only a young man, but already he had won fame on account of his goodness and daring. — *Robert Nye, Beowulf*

▷ **famed** ***ADJECTIVE***

familiar ***ADJECTIVE***
1 well known; often seen or experienced

The striking of the grandfather clock became a familiar sound to Tom, especially in the silence of those nights when everyone else was asleep. — *Philippa Pearce, Tom's Midnight Garden*

2 knowing something well ◆ *Are you familiar with the author's recent work?*
3 friendly and informal ◆ *The neighbour's cat and I are on very familiar terms.*
4 too informal, over-friendly
▷ **familiarly** ***ADVERB***
▷ **familiarity** ***NOUN***

familiar ***NOUN*** **familiars**
in stories, an animal or creature believed to be the pet of a witch or wizard

familiarize ***VERB*** **familiarizes, familiarizing, familiarized**
to make yourself familiar with something
▷ **familiarization** ***NOUN***

USAGE NOTE This word can also be spelled familiarise.

family ***NOUN*** **families**
1 parents and their children, sometimes including grandchildren and other relations
2 a group of things that are alike in some way
3 a group of related plants or animals ◆ *Lions belong to the cat family.*

family planning ***NOUN***
the use of contraceptives to control pregnancies; birth control

family tree ***NOUN*** **family trees**
a diagram showing how people in a family are related

famine ***NOUN*** **famines**
a very severe shortage of food in an area

WORD HISTORY from Latin *fames* 'hunger'

famished ***ADJECTIVE***
very hungry, starving

famous ***ADJECTIVE***
1 known to very many people
2 to be famous for an ability or attribute is to be known for doing or having it

The island of Gont, a single mountain that lifts its peak a mile above the storm-racked Northeast Sea, is a land famous for wizards. — *Ursula Le Guin, A Wizard of Earthsea*

a b c d e f g h i j k l m n o p q r s t u v w x y z

SPELLING NOTE Some words pronounced **f-** begin with **ph-** (e.g. phrase)

famously *ADVERB* (*informal*)
to get along or **on famously** is to be very friendly with one another ◆ *The families seemed to get along famously.*

fan❶ *NOUN* **fans**
a device or machine for making air move about so as to cool people or things

fan *VERB* **fans, fanning, fanned**
to send a current of air on someone or something
to fan out is to spread out in the shape of a fan

fan❷ *NOUN* **fans**
an enthusiastic admirer or supporter

fanatic *NOUN* **fanatics**
a person who is very enthusiastic or too enthusiastic about something
▷ **fanatical** *ADJECTIVE*
▷ **fanatically** *ADVERB*
▷ **fanaticism** *NOUN*
WORD HISTORY from Latin *fanaticus* 'inspired by a god'

fan belt *NOUN*
a belt used to drive the fan that cools the radiator of a motor vehicle

fanciful *ADJECTIVE*
1 a fanciful person or imagination is highly imaginative and unrealistic
2 a fanciful idea or story is imaginary or made up
3 designed in a quaint or imaginative style

The organization was called Scorpia. It was a fanciful name, they all knew it, invented by someone who had probably read too much James Bond. — *Anthony Horowitz, Scorpia*

fan club *NOUN*
an organized group of supporters or admirers

fancy *VERB* **fancies, fancying, fancied**
1 (*informal*) to wish or desire something or to do something ◆ *Do you fancy getting a bite to eat?*
2 to imagine something

I fancied I saw some black object flopping about ... but it became motionless as I looked at it, and I judged that my eye had been deceived. — *H. G. Wells, The Time Machine*

3 **to fancy yourself as something** is to wish or hope to become it ◆ *Cosimo de Medici rather fancied himself as an archaeologist.*
4 to be inclined to believe or suppose something

Ha! I fancy that I hear his step now upon the stairs. — *Sir Arthur Conan Doyle, The Adventure of the Noble Bachelor*

fancy *NOUN* **fancies**
1 a liking or desire for something ◆ *I don't know why, but I have a sudden fancy for strawberries.*
2 something that you imagine
3 (*literary*) a person's imagination

Sitting by the fire in the housekeeper's room, I approached that island in my fancy from every possible direction. — *Robert Louis Stevenson, Treasure Island*

fancy *ADJECTIVE*
decorated or elaborate; not plain ◆ *Add buttons, beads, ribbons, or fancy stitching to personalize your jeans.*

fancy dress *NOUN*
unusual costume worn for a party, often to make you look like a famous person

fanfare *NOUN* **fanfares**
a short piece of loud music played on trumpets, especially as part of a ceremony

fang *NOUN* **fangs**
a long sharp tooth, especially on a wild animal or vampire

And then, as her face contorted into a horrible shape, she bared her fangs, burying them swiftly into his neck. — *Buffy the Vampire-Slayer: The Harvest*

fanlight *NOUN* **fanlights**
a window above a door, often semicircular in shape
WORD HISTORY so called because their shape is usually like that of an open fan

fantasia (*say* fan- **tay**- zee- a) *NOUN* **fantasias**
an imaginative piece of music or writing

fantasize *VERB* **fantasizes, fantasizing, fantasized**
to imagine something pleasant or strange that you would like to happen
USAGE NOTE This word can also be spelled fantasise.

fantastic *ADJECTIVE*
1 (*informal*) excellent; really good
2 a fantastic design or idea is very imaginative or strange
▷ **fantastically** *ADVERB*
WORD HISTORY from Greek *phantazesthai* 'to imagine'

fantasy *NOUN* **fantasies**
1 something imaginary or fantastic
2 an imaginative piece of music or writing

FAQ *ABBREVIATION*
frequently asked questions

far *ADJECTIVE*
1 distant or remote ◆ *From this viewpoint, the Grand Canyon lies in the far distance.*
2 the far side or end of something is the side or end facing you or furthest away
a far cry from very different from
by far by a great amount
the Far East China, Japan, and other countries of east and south-east Asia

far *ADVERB*
1 at or to a great distance
2 much; by a great amount ◆ *A new and far more sophisticated spacecraft is about to begin a journey to explore Mercury.*
far and away by a large amount
far and wide over a large area

far *NOUN*
a place far away; a great distance

The Oracle was called Agbala, and people came from far and near to consult it. — *Chinua Achebe, Things Fall Apart*

farce *NOUN* **farces**
1 a comedy in which the humour is exaggerated
2 a situation or series of events that is ridiculous or a pretence ◆ *Last month's elections have been dismissed as a complete farce.*
▷ **farcical** *ADJECTIVE*
▷ **farcically** *ADVERB*
WORD HISTORY a French word meaning originally 'stuffing', later the name for a comic interlude between acts of a play

fare *NOUN* **fares**
1 the price charged for a passenger to travel
2 a passenger who pays a fare, especially in a taxi
3 food and drink

He was supplied with bread of a finer, whiter quality than the usual prison fare, and even regaled each Sunday with a small quantity of wine. — *Alexandre Dumas, The Count of Monte Cristo*

fare *VERB* **fares, faring, fared**
to get along; to survive or progress ◆ *The Serengeti cheetah, like many others, is not faring well.*

farewell *EXCLAMATION, NOUN* **farewells**
(*formal*) a word said when you leave someone; goodbye

far-fetched *ADJECTIVE*
a far-fetched story is one that sounds unlikely and is therefore difficult to believe

farm *NOUN* **farms**
1 an area of land and its buildings used for raising crops or rearing animals
2 a farmhouse

farm *VERB* **farms, farming, farmed**
1 to grow crops or keep animals for food etc.
2 to use land for growing crops

farmer *NOUN* **farmers**
a person who owns or manages a farm

farmhand *NOUN* **farmhands**
a hired worker on a farm

farmhouse *NOUN* **farmhouses**
the main house on a farm, used by the farmer

farmyard *NOUN* **farmyards**
the yard or area round farm buildings

farrago (*say* fa- **rah**- goh) *NOUN* **farragos**
a confused muddle of things
WORD HISTORY a Latin word meaning 'mixed fodder'

far-reaching *ADJECTIVE*
far-reaching consequences or implications are important and widespread

farrier (*say* fa- ree- er) *NOUN* **farriers**
a smith who shoes horses
▷ **farriery** *NOUN*
WORD HISTORY from Latin *ferrum* 'iron, an iron horseshoe'

farrow *NOUN* **farrows**
a litter of young pigs

Farsi *NOUN*
the modern form of the Persian language
WORD HISTORY from an Arabic word, from *Fars* 'Persia'

farther *ADVERB, ADJECTIVE*
at or to a greater distance; more distant

I could not but note that the farther north I traveled, the fewer were the great dinosaurs, though they still persisted in lesser numbers. — *Edgar Rice Burroughs, The Land that Time Forgot*

USAGE NOTE Take care to use *farther* and *farthest* only if you are talking about distance: *The Moon is farther from the Earth in winter.* You can also use *further* to talk about distance, or to mean 'additional': *Phone this number for further details.*

farthest *ADVERB, ADJECTIVE*
at or to the greatest distance; most distant
USAGE NOTE See the note at *farther*.

farthing *NOUN* **farthings**
a former British coin worth one-quarter of a penny
WORD HISTORY from Old English *feorthing* 'one-fourth'

fascinate *VERB* **fascinates, fascinating, fascinated**
a person or thing that fascinates someone is very attractive or interesting to them

The Radley Place fascinated Dill. In spite of our warnings and explanations it drew him as the moon draws water. — *Harper Lee, To Kill a Mockingbird*

▷ **fascination** *NOUN*
▷ **fascinator** *NOUN*
WORD HISTORY from Latin *fascinum* 'a spell'

Fascism (*say* **fash**- izm) *NOUN*
a system of extreme right-wing government in which people are not allowed to hold opposing political views
▷ **Fascist** *NOUN*
WORD HISTORY from Latin *fasces*, the bundle of rods with an axe through it, carried before a magistrate in ancient Rome as a symbol of his power to punish people

a b c d e f g h i j k l m n o p q r s t u v w x y z

fashion *NOUN* **fashions**
1 the popular style of dress or behaviour at a particular time
2 the business of making and selling clothes in new styles
3 a way of doing something ◆ *The castle's herb garden is still cultivated in the same fashion as it was hundreds of years ago.*
after a fashion to some extent but not very satisfactorily

fashion *VERB* **fashions, fashioning, fashioned**
to make something into a particular form or shape

fashionable *ADJECTIVE*
following the fashion of the time; popular

Puffed sleeves are so fashionable now. It would give me such a thrill, Marilla, just to wear a dress with puffed sleeves. — *L. M. Montgomery, Anne of Green Gables*

▷ **fashionably** *ADVERB*

fast❶ *ADJECTIVE*
1 moving or able to move quickly
2 done or happening quickly ◆ *Thank you for your fast response.*
3 a fast road, lane, or slope is one where vehicles or people travel at high speed
4 a clock or watch is fast if it shows a time later than the correct time
5 firmly fixed or attached

The old man made the sheet fast and jammed the tiller. — *Ernest Hemingway, The Old Man and the Sea*

6 a fast colour or dye is not likely to fade or run
▷ **fastness** *NOUN*

fast *ADVERB*
1 quickly ◆ *The larger dinosaurs probably could not run fast.*
2 to hold or stick something fast is to grasp or secure it firmly ◆ *We came to a halt as the carriage wheels stuck fast in the mud.*
fast asleep in a deep sleep

fast❷ *VERB* **fasts, fasting, fasted**
to go without food or certain kinds of food, especially for religious or medical reasons

fast *NOUN* **fasts**
a period of fasting

fasten *VERB* **fastens, fastening, fastened**
1 to fix one thing firmly to another, or fix two things together
2 to become fastened ◆ *The dress fastens with a zipper at the back.*
▷ **fastener** *NOUN*
▷ **fastening** *NOUN*

fast food *NOUN*
food that is quickly prepared in a restaurant or snack bar

fast-forward *VERB* **fast-forwards, fast-forwarding, fast-forwarded**
to wind an audio or video tape forwards at high speed to reach a point further on in the recording

fastidious *ADJECTIVE*
1 fussy and hard to please
2 very careful about small details of dress or cleanliness
▷ **fastidiously** *ADVERB*
▷ **fastidiousness** *NOUN*

WORD HISTORY from Latin *fastidium* 'loathing'

fast track *NOUN*
a quick way to achieve something or make progress

fat *NOUN* **fats**
1 a white greasy substance found in animal bodies and certain seeds
2 oil or grease used in cooking

fat *ADJECTIVE* **fatter, fattest**
1 containing a lot of fat, or covered with fat
2 a fat person or animal has a very thick round body
3 a fat book is thick and contains a lot of pages
a fat chance (*informal*) no chance at all
▷ **fatness** *NOUN*

SYNONYMS (meaning 2) plump, stout, large, overweight, rotund, podgy, obese, corpulent; (meaning 3) thick, bulky, chunky, substantial

fatal *ADJECTIVE*
1 causing or ending in death ◆ *The sting of some scorpions is painful, but not fatal, to human beings.*
2 having a very bad effect or consequence ◆ *Any mistake could prove fatal to the team's hopes of regaining their title.*
▷ **fatally** *ADVERB*

WORD HISTORY from Latin *fatalis* 'by fate'

fatalist *NOUN* **fatalists**
a person who accepts whatever happens and thinks it could not have been avoided
▷ **fatalism** *NOUN*
▷ **fatalistic** *ADJECTIVE*

WORD HISTORY from an old sense of *fatal*, meaning 'decreed by fate'

fatality (*say* fa- tal- it- ee) *NOUN* **fatalities**
a death caused by an accident, war, or other disaster

fate *NOUN* **fates**
1 an unavoidable power that is thought to make things happen
2 a person's fate is what will happen or has happened to them; destiny

WORD HISTORY from Latin *fatum* 'that which has been spoken'

fated *ADJECTIVE*
destined by fate; doomed

fateful *ADJECTIVE*
a fateful day or time is one when important but disastrous events happen
▷ **fatefully** *ADVERB*

father *NOUN* **fathers**
1 a male parent
2 the title of a priest in certain religious orders
▷ **fatherly** *ADJECTIVE*
▷ **fatherhood** *NOUN*

WORD FAMILY A related adjective is paternal.

father *VERB* **fathers, fathering, fathered**
1 to become the father of a child by making a woman pregnant
2 to father an idea or plan is to originate or invent it

father-in-law *NOUN* **fathers-in-law**
the father of a married person's husband or wife

fathom *NOUN* **fathoms**
a unit used to measure the depth of water, equal to 1.83 metres or 6 feet

fathom *VERB* **fathoms, fathoming, fathomed**
1 to measure the depth of something
2 to understand a difficult situation or problem
▷ **fathomless** *ADJECTIVE*

fatigue *NOUN*
1 tiredness caused by work or exercise; exhaustion
2 weakness in metals, caused by constant stress
3 fatigues are the non-military duties of soldiers, such as cooking and cleaning

fatigue *VERB* **fatigues, fatiguing, fatigued**
to make someone very tired

fatten *VERB* **fattens, fattening, fattened**
to feed a person or animal so as to make them fat or fatter

fatty *ADJECTIVE* **fattier, fattiest**
fatty meat or food contains a lot of fat
▷ **fattiness** *NOUN*

fatty acid *NOUN* **fatty acids**
an acid that occurs in natural oils

fatuous *ADJECTIVE*
a fatuous remark is pointless and silly
▷ **fatuity** *NOUN*
▷ **fatuously** *ADVERB*
▷ **fatuousness** *NOUN*

WORD HISTORY from Latin *fatuus* 'foolish'

fatwa *NOUN* **fatwas**
a ruling on a religious matter given by an Islamic authority

faucet *NOUN* **faucets**
(*American*) a water tap

WORD HISTORY from Old French *fausset*

fault *NOUN* **faults**
1 anything that makes a person or thing imperfect; a flaw or mistake
2 responsibility for a mistake or failure

It was nobody's fault that the rain came down in torrents the next morning, making a picnic a fantastic impossibility. — *Saki, The Brogue*

3 a break in a layer of rock, caused by movement of the earth's crust
4 an incorrect serve in tennis

at fault responsible for a mistake or failure

fault *VERB* **faults, faulting, faulted**
to find a fault in someone or something
◆ *Simon was generous. Lorna couldn't fault him on that score.*

faultless *ADJECTIVE*
without a fault; perfect
▷ **faultlessly** *ADVERB*
▷ **faultlessness** *NOUN*

faulty *ADJECTIVE*
having a fault or faults; imperfect
▷ **faultily** *ADVERB*

faun *NOUN* **fauns**
an ancient Roman god with a man's body and goat's legs, horns, and tail

WORD HISTORY from *Faunus*, the name of an ancient Roman country god, brother of Fauna

fauna *NOUN*
the animals of a certain area or period of time (SEE ALSO **flora**)

WORD HISTORY from *Fauna*, the name of an ancient Roman country goddess, sister of Faunus

faux pas (*say* foh **pah**) *NOUN* **faux pas**
an embarrassing blunder in a social setting

WORD HISTORY French words meaning 'false step'

favour *NOUN* **favours**
1 a kind or helpful act
2 approval or liking
3 friendly support shown to one person or group but not to another ◆ *without fear or favour*

to be in or out of favour is to have (or not have) support

in favour of to be in favour of an idea or cause is to approve of or support it

favour *VERB* **favours, favouring, favoured**
to approve of or support someone or something ◆ *Which solar systems could favour the development of life forms?*

favourable *ADJECTIVE*
1 helpful or advantageous

We'll have favourable winds, a quick passage, and not the least difficulty in finding the spot. — *Robert Louis Stevenson, Treasure Island*

2 pleasing or satisfactory ◆ *When I leave Korea, I will do so with a very favourable impression of the country and its people.*
▷ **favourably** *ADVERB*

a b c d e f g h i j k l m n o p q r s t u v w x y z

favourite *ADJECTIVE*
a favourite thing or person is one that you like more than others

Morning coffee was Hermux's favourite time of the day. It was when he did his best thinking. — *Michael Hoeye, Time Stops for No Mouse*

favourite *NOUN* **favourites**
1 a person or thing that you like most
2 a competitor that is generally expected to win ◆ *Spain is outright favourite to win the Cup and has been since the qualifiers started.*

favouritism *NOUN*
behaviour that favours one person or group to the disadvantage of others

fawn[1] *NOUN* **fawns**
1 a young deer
2 a light-brown colour

WORD HISTORY from an Old French word, related to our word *fetus*

fawn[2] *VERB* **fawns, fawning, fawned**
to get someone to like you by flattering or praising them too much

fax *NOUN* **faxes**
1 (also **fax machine**) a machine that sends an exact copy of a document electronically
2 a copy produced by a fax machine

fax *VERB* **faxes, faxing, faxed**
to send a copy of a document using a fax machine

WORD HISTORY a shortening of *facsimile*

FBI *ABBREVIATION*
Federal Bureau of Investigation, in the USA

fear *NOUN* **fears**
1 the unpleasant feeling you have when you are in danger or expect something unpleasant to happen
2 a danger or likelihood of something bad happening ◆ *Our tent was well secured, so there was no fear of it blowing away in the night.*

for fear of because of the risk of

fear *VERB* **fears, fearing, feared**
1 to feel fear; to be afraid of someone or something
2 to suspect or anticipate something unpleasant ◆ *I fear that I may be allergic to your cooking.*

fearful *ADJECTIVE*
1 feeling fear; afraid

Some mystery, some positive danger, overhung our father. He was very fearful of going out alone. — *Sir Arthur Conan Doyle, The Sign of Four*

2 causing fear or horror

Clayton came to his feet with a start. His blood ran cold. Never in all his life had so fearful a sound smote upon his ears. — *Edgar Rice Burroughs, Tarzan of the Apes*

3 (*informal*) very bad

▷ **fearfully** *ADVERB*

fearless *ADJECTIVE*
without fear

▷ **fearlessly** *ADVERB*
▷ **fearlessness** *NOUN*

fearsome *ADJECTIVE*
dreadful; frightening

feasible *ADJECTIVE*
1 a feasible idea or plan is one that is possible to carry out
2 a feasible story or explanation is one that is probable and can be believed

▷ **feasibly** *ADVERB*
▷ **feasibility** *NOUN*

USAGE NOTE The use of *feasible* to mean 'likely or probable' is not generally accepted and it is better to avoid it in formal or written English.

feast *NOUN* **feasts**
1 a large meal for several people, especially to celebrate something
2 an annual religious festival

feast *VERB* **feasts, feasting, feasted**
to eat a feast; to eat a large amount

to feast your eyes on something is to gaze admiringly at it

feat *NOUN* **feats**
a deed that needs a lot of skill or strength

The trek back home to Jigalong in the north-west of Western Australia ... was also one of the most incredible feats imaginable, undertaken by three Aboriginal girls in the 1930s. — *Doris Pilkington, Rabbit Proof Fence*

feather *NOUN* **feathers**
any of the flat pieces that grow from a bird's skin and cover its body

▷ **feathery** *ADJECTIVE*

feather *VERB* **feathers, feathering, feathered**
to cover or line something with feathers

featherweight *NOUN* **featherweights**
a boxer weighing between 54 and 57 kg

feature *NOUN* **features**
1 any part of the face, such as the mouth, nose, or eyes, that make it look the way it does
2 an important or noticeable part of something; a characteristic
3 a special newspaper article or programme that deals with a particular subject
4 the main film in a cinema programme

feature *VERB* **features, featuring, featured**
1 to include something as an important part ◆ *The new film features an impressive all-star cast.*
2 to be a noticeable or important part of something ◆ *Sydney's most famous landmarks are expected to feature in the latest Godzilla remake.*

February *NOUN*
the second month of the year

WORD HISTORY from *februa*, the ancient Roman feast of purification held in this month

feckless ***ADJECTIVE***
weak in character and not having much ambition
▷ **fecklessly** ***ADVERB***

WORD HISTORY from a Scots word *feck* 'effect'

fecund (*say* **feek**- und or **fek**- und) ***ADJECTIVE***
very fertile
▷ **fecundity** (*say* fi- **kund**- iti) ***NOUN***

fed *past tense* of **feed**
to be fed up (*informal*) is to feel depressed, unhappy, or bored

federal ***ADJECTIVE***
a federal government or system is one in which several states are ruled by a central government but are responsible for their own internal affairs
▷ **federalism** ***NOUN***

WORD HISTORY from Latin *foederis* 'of a treaty'

federation ***NOUN*** **federations**
a group of states under a federal government

fee ***NOUN*** **fees**
a charge paid for a professional service, or for membership of an organization

feeble ***ADJECTIVE***
weak; without strength

Stanley made a feeble attempt to punch Zigzag, then he felt a flurry of fists against his head and neck. — *Louis Sachar, Holes*

▷ **feebly** ***ADVERB***
▷ **feebleness** ***NOUN***

WORD HISTORY from Latin *flebilis* 'wept over'

feed ***VERB*** **feeds, feeding, fed**
1 to give food to a person or animal
2 to take and eat food
3 to feed data or money into a machine is to enter or insert it
4 a route, channel, or line feeds into something when it flows into or merges with it
▷ **feeder** ***NOUN***

feed ***NOUN***
food for animals or babies

feedback ***NOUN***
1 the response you get from people to something you have done
2 the harsh noise produced when some of the sound from an amplifier goes back into it

feel ***VERB*** **feels, feeling, felt**
1 to touch something to find out what it is like
2 to experience an emotion ◆ *I'll feel a lot happier after my exams are over.*
3 to have something as an opinion ◆ *We felt we couldn't leave without saying goodbye.*
4 to be affected by something ◆ *Suddenly he was feeling very cold.*
5 to produce a certain sensation ◆ *It feels really damp in here.*
6 to feel like having or doing something is to want to have or do it
7 to feel for someone is to sympathize with them

feel ***NOUN***
1 the action or experience of feeling something ◆ *Have a feel of this material.*
2 the sensation caused by feeling something ◆ *the feel of wind in your hair*
3 the atmosphere of a place or situation ◆ *a group of artists who sought to capture the feel of turn-of-the-century New York City*

feeler ***NOUN*** **feelers**
1 either of the long thin parts that stick out from an insect's or crustacean's body, used for feeling; an antenna
2 a cautious question or suggestion to test people's reactions

feelgood ***ADJECTIVE***
(*informal*) a feelgood book, film, or other work is one that makes you feel happy when you read or watch it

feeling ***NOUN*** **feelings**
1 the ability to feel things ◆ *Frostbite causes a loss of feeling in fingers, toes, ear lobes, or the tip of the nose.*
2 a person's feelings are their emotional attitudes or responses
3 an intuitive sense or belief ◆ *I had a feeling that we were being followed.*
4 an opinion or attitude ◆ *What's your feeling about moving to the city?*

feign (*say* fayn) ***VERB*** **feigns, feigning, feigned**
to feign an emotion or state is to pretend to feel or experience it ◆ *When attacked, the opossum feigns death, with closed eyes, lolling tongue and a limp, apparently lifeless body.*

feint (*say* faynt) ***NOUN*** **feints**
a pretended attack or punch meant to deceive an opponent

feint ***VERB*** **feints, feinting, feinted**
to pretend to attack or hit someone

WORD HISTORY an Old French word meaning 'feigned'

USAGE NOTE Take care not to confuse this word with *faint.*

feisty (*say* **fy**- sti) ***ADJECTIVE*** **feistier, feistiest**
a feisty person is lively and rather aggressive
▷ **feistily** ***ADVERB***
▷ **feistiness** ***NOUN***

WORD HISTORY from an old word *feist* 'a small dog'

felicitous ***ADJECTIVE***
a felicitous word or remark is well chosen and apt
▷ **felicitously** ***ADVERB***

WORD HISTORY from Latin *felix* 'happy'

a b c d e f g h i j k l m n o p q r s t u v w x y z

felicity *NOUN*
1 great happiness; good fortune

I tell you, my lambkins, ... you shall not much longer have the felicity of conspiring together. — *Alexandre Dumas, The Black Tulip*

2 to do something with felicity is to do it effortlessly or with ease

feline (*say* **feel**- yn) *ADJECTIVE*
to do with cats; cat-like
WORD HISTORY from Latin *feles* 'cat'

fell❶ *past tense of* **fall**

fell❷ *VERB* **fells, felling, felled**
1 to cut down a tree
2 to strike someone down with a hard blow

fell❸ *NOUN* **fells**
a piece of wild hilly country, especially in the north of England
WORD HISTORY from an Old Norse word meaning 'hill'

fell❹ *ADJECTIVE*
(*literary*) ruthless and cruel
at one fell swoop in a single action; all in one go
WORD HISTORY from an Old French word, related to our word *felon*

fellow *NOUN* **fellows**
1 a friend or companion; someone who belongs to the same group
2 a man or boy
3 a member of a learned society

fellow *ADJECTIVE*
of the same group or kind ◆ *Please be considerate to your fellow passengers when using your mobile phone.*

fellowship *NOUN* **fellowships**
1 good company; friendship
2 a group of friends; a society

felon (*say* **fel**- on) *NOUN* **felons**
a criminal

But it was not seemly for young English ladies, Mrs White informed her, to show such avid interest in convicted felons. — *Meg Cabot, Victoria and the Rogue*

WORD HISTORY from Latin *felo* 'an evil person'

felony (*say* **fel**- on- ee) *NOUN* **felonies**
a serious crime

felt❶ *past tense of* **feel**

felt❷ *NOUN*
a thick fabric made of wool fibres pressed together

female *ADJECTIVE*
1 of the sex that can bear offspring or produce eggs or fruit
2 a female connection or machine part is hollow in shape to receive a corresponding male part

female *NOUN* **females**
a female person, animal, or plant
WORD HISTORY from Latin *femina* 'woman'

feminine *ADJECTIVE*
1 to do with or like women
2 having qualities traditionally associated with women
3 (*Grammar*) belonging to the class (in some languages) that includes words referring to females or regarded as female
▷ **femininity** *NOUN*

feminist *NOUN* **feminists**
a person who believes that women should have the same rights and status as men
▷ **feminism** *NOUN*

femur (*say* **fee**- mer) *NOUN* **femurs** or **femora**
the thigh bone
▷ **femoral** *ADJECTIVE*
WORD HISTORY a Latin word

fen *NOUN* **fens**
an area of low-lying marshy or flooded ground

fence *NOUN* **fences**
1 a barrier, usually made of wood or metal, to enclose an area
2 a structure for a horse to jump over
3 (*informal*) a person who deals in stolen goods

fence *VERB* **fences, fencing, fenced**
1 to put a fence round or along something
2 to take part in the sport of fencing
▷ **fencer** *NOUN*
WORD HISTORY shortened from *defence*

fencing *NOUN*
1 a set of fences, or a length of fence
2 the sport of fighting with long narrow swords (called *foils*)

fend *VERB* **fends, fending, fended**
to fend for yourself is to take care of yourself
to fend off someone or something is to defend yourself against them or it
WORD HISTORY shortened from *defend*

fender *NOUN* **fenders**
1 a frame around a fireplace to stop coals from falling into the room
2 a tyre or pad on the side of a boat to protect it from knocks
3 (*American*) a bumper on a car or other vehicle

feng shui (*say* fung **shway**) *NOUN*
in Chinese thought, a set of rules about the ways buildings and the objects in them are laid out to achieve the well-being and happiness of the people who live in them
WORD HISTORY from Chinese words meaning 'wind' and 'water'

fennel *NOUN*
a herb with yellow flowers whose seeds and root are used for flavouring

feral (*say* **ferr**- al) ***ADJECTIVE***
a feral animal is wild and untamed

WORD HISTORY from Latin *fera* 'wild animal'

ferment (*say* fer- **ment**) ***VERB*** **ferments, fermenting, fermented**
to bubble and change chemically by the action of a substance such as yeast

▷ **fermentation** ***NOUN***

USAGE NOTE Take care not to confuse this word with *foment*.

ferment (*say* **fer**- ment) ***NOUN***
1 the process of fermenting
2 an excited or agitated condition

fern ***NOUN*** **ferns**
a plant with feathery leaves and no flowers

▷ **ferny** ***ADJECTIVE***

ferocious ***ADJECTIVE***
fierce or savage

Twig trembled under the ferocious gaze of the creature in front of him. — *Paul Stewart and Chris Riddell, Stormchaser*

▷ **ferociously** ***ADVERB***
▷ **ferocity** ***NOUN***

WORD HISTORY from Latin *ferox* 'fierce'

ferret ***NOUN*** **ferrets**
a small weasel-like animal sometimes used for catching rabbits and rats

▷ **ferrety** ***ADJECTIVE***

ferret ***VERB*** **ferrets, ferreting, ferreted**
1 to hunt with a ferret
2 to search or rummage about for something

Nobody seemed to be paying me much attention—too busy chatting loudly and ferreting around in their own bags for books and pens and pencils. — *Keith Gray, Malarkey*

WORD HISTORY from Latin *fur* 'thief'

ferric or **ferrous** ***ADJECTIVE***
containing iron

WORD HISTORY from Latin *ferrum* 'iron'

ferry ***NOUN*** **ferries**
a boat or ship used for carrying people or things across a short stretch of water

ferry ***VERB*** **ferries, ferrying, ferried**
to carry people or things across water or for a short distance

fertile ***ADJECTIVE***
1 fertile soil is rich and produces good crops
2 a fertile person or animal is able to produce offspring
3 a fertile brain or imagination is inventive and able to produce ideas

▷ **fertility** ***NOUN***

fertilize ***VERB*** **fertilizes, fertilizing, fertilized**
1 to add substances to the soil to make it more fertile
2 to put pollen into a plant or sperm into an egg or female animal so that it develops seed or young

▷ **fertilization** ***NOUN***

USAGE NOTE This word can also be spelled fertilise.

fertilizer ***NOUN*** **fertilizers**
chemicals or manure added to the soil to make it more fertile

USAGE NOTE This word can also be spelled fertiliser.

fervent or **fervid** ***ADJECTIVE***
showing strong and sincere feelings about something

▷ **fervently** ***ADVERB***
▷ **fervency** ***NOUN***
▷ **fervour** ***NOUN***

WORD HISTORY from Latin *fervens* 'boiling'

fester ***VERB*** **festers, festering, festered**
1 a wound festers if it becomes septic and fills with pus
2 to cause resentment for a long time ◆ *The current conflict has been festering for over 50 years.*

festival ***NOUN*** **festivals**
1 (*Religion*) a time of celebration, especially for religious reasons
2 an organized series of concerts, films, or other performances, especially one held every year

festive ***ADJECTIVE***
1 to do with a festival ◆ *During Diwali, gifts are exchanged and festive meals are prepared.*
2 suitable for a festival; joyful ◆ *The horses look very festive decked out with tinsel and baubles.*

▷ **festively** ***ADVERB***

festivity ***NOUN*** **festivities**
a festive occasion or celebration

festoon ***NOUN*** **festoons**
a chain of flowers or ribbons hung as a decoration

festoon ***VERB*** **festoons, festooning, festooned**
to decorate something with ornaments

Smoke was rising here and there among the creepers that festooned the dead or dying trees. — *William Golding, Lord of the Flies*

WORD HISTORY via French from Italian *festone* 'festive ornament'

feta (*say* **fet**- a) ***NOUN***
a salty white cheese made from goats' or sheeps' milk, originally from Greece

fetch ***VERB*** **fetches, fetching, fetched**
1 to go to find a person or thing and bring them or it back ◆ *Can you fetch a cloth from the kitchen?* ◆ *There was no time to fetch a doctor.*
2 to fetch a particular price is to be sold at that price ◆ *A photo album including a picture of A. A. Milne's son Christopher Robin fetched £3,500 at auction.*

fetching *ADJECTIVE*
attractive and appealing

Rose looks particularly fetching by firelight because she is a pinkish gold, very light and feathery. — *Dodie Smith, I Capture the Castle*

fête (*say* fayt) *NOUN* **fêtes**
an outdoor entertainment with stalls and sideshows

fête *VERB* **fêtes, fêting, fêted**
to honour a person with celebrations ◆ *After receiving their prizes, the Nobel laureates will be fêted at a banquet in the city hall.*

fetid (*say* **fet**- id) *ADJECTIVE*
smelling unpleasant

It was a difficult birth, a long hard struggle in the fetid half-darkness of that little tent. — *Celia Rees, Witch Child*

fetish *NOUN* **fetishes**
1 an object worshipped for its supposed magical powers
2 something that a person has an obsession about, especially a sexual obsession

WORD HISTORY from a Portuguese word meaning 'a charm'

fetlock *NOUN* **fetlocks**
the part of a horse's leg above and behind the hoof

WORD HISTORY from a Germanic language, related to our word *foot*

fetter *NOUN* **fetters**
a chain or shackle put round a prisoner's ankle

fetter *VERB* **fetters, fettering, fettered**
1 to put fetters on a prisoner
2 to restrict someone's freedom to do what they want

fettle *NOUN*
in fine fettle in good health

fetus (*say* **fee**- tus) *NOUN* **fetuses**
a developing embryo, especially an unborn human baby
▷ **fetal** *ADJECTIVE*

USAGE NOTE The word is also spelled foetus in general usage, though not in medical contexts.

feud (*say* fewd) *NOUN* **feuds**
a long-lasting quarrel, especially between two families

feud *VERB* **feuds, feuding, feuded**
to carry on a feud

WORD HISTORY from Germanic, related to our word *foe*

feudal (*say* **few**- dal) *ADJECTIVE*
to do with the system used in the Middle Ages in which people could farm land in exchange for work done for the owner
▷ **feudalism** *NOUN*
▷ **feudalistic** *ADJECTIVE*

fever *NOUN* **fevers**
1 an abnormally high body temperature, usually with an illness
2 excitement or agitation
▷ **fevered** *ADJECTIVE*

feverish *ADJECTIVE*
1 having a fever or high temperature
2 frantic or restless with excitement ◆ *It took six months of feverish activity to finalize the plans for the wedding.*
▷ **feverishly** *ADVERB*
▷ **feverishness** *NOUN*

few *ADJECTIVE*
not many

I'm surprised, talking to Anne afterwards, to find how few people have ever been to the South Pole. — *Michael Palin, Pole to Pole*

USAGE NOTE See the note at *less*.

few *NOUN*
a small number of people or things
quite a few or **a good few** a fairly large number

fey (*say* fay) *ADJECTIVE*
1 strange, as though from another world
2 having clairvoyant powers

fez *NOUN* **fezzes**
a high flat-topped hat with a tassel, worn by Muslim men in some countries

WORD HISTORY after *Fez*, a town in Morocco where fezzes were made

fiancé (*say* fee- **ahn**- say) *NOUN* **fiancés**
a woman's fiancé is the man to whom she is engaged to be married

WORD HISTORY a French word meaning 'betrothed'

fiancée (*say* fee- **ahn**- say) *NOUN* **fiancées**
a man's fiancée is the woman to whom he is engaged to be married

fiasco (*say* fee- as- koh) *NOUN* **fiascos**
a humiliating or embarrassing failure

WORD HISTORY from an Italian phrase *far fiasco* meaning literally 'to make a bottle', and figuratively 'to fail in a performance'

fib *NOUN* **fibs**
a lie about something unimportant

fib *VERB* **fibs, fibbing, fibbed**
to tell a fib; to lie
▷ **fibber** *NOUN*

WORD HISTORY related to *fable*

fibre *NOUN* **fibres**
1 a very thin thread
2 (*D & T*) a substance made of thin threads
3 material in certain foods that your body cannot digest but that stimulates the action of the intestines
▷ **fibrous** *ADJECTIVE*

USAGE NOTE The American spelling of this word is fiber.

fibreglass *NOUN*
1 fabric made from glass fibres
2 plastic containing glass fibres

fickle *ADJECTIVE*
a fickle person is constantly changing their mind or allegiance, and is not loyal to one person or group
▷ **fickleness** *NOUN*

fiction *NOUN* **fiction**
1 writing, such as novels and stories, that describes imaginary people and events
2 something imagined or untrue
▷ **fictional** *ADJECTIVE*

fictitious *ADJECTIVE*
imagined or untrue
▷ **fictitiously** *ADVERB*

fiddle *NOUN* **fiddles**
1 (*informal*) a violin
2 (*informal*) a swindle or cheat

fiddle *VERB* **fiddles, fiddling, fiddled**
1 (*informal*) to play the violin
2 to fidget or tinker with something, using your fingers
3 (*informal*) to alter accounts or records dishonestly
▷ **fiddler** *NOUN*

fiddly *ADJECTIVE*
1 a fiddly object is small and awkward to use
2 a fiddly task is awkward to do

fidelity *NOUN*
1 faithfulness or loyalty
2 accuracy; the exactness with which sound is reproduced

WORD HISTORY from Latin *fides* 'faith'

fidget *VERB* **fidgets, fidgeting, fidgeted**
someone who fidgets makes small restless movements because they are nervous or impatient
▷ **fidgety** *ADJECTIVE*

fidget *NOUN* **fidgets**
a person who fidgets

field *NOUN* **fields**
1 a piece of land with grass or crops growing on it
2 an area of interest or study ◆ *recent advances in the field of genetics*
3 a range or area in which things can be observed

> As soon as the moon rose above the horizon, he immediately caught her in the field of the telescope. — *Jules Verne, From the Earth to the Moon*

4 those who are taking part in a race or outdoor game

field *VERB* **fields, fielding, fielded**
1 to stop or catch the ball in cricket or other ball games
2 to field a series of questions is to respond to and deal with them effectively
3 to put a team into the field for a ball game
▷ **fielder** *NOUN*
▷ **fieldsman** *NOUN*

field events *PLURAL NOUN*
athletic sports other than track races, such as jumping and throwing events

Field Marshal *NOUN* **Field Marshals**
an army officer of the highest rank

fieldwork *NOUN*
practical work or research done in various places, not in a library, museum, or laboratory

fiend (*say* feend) *NOUN* **fiends**
1 an evil spirit or devil
2 a very wicked or cruel person
3 a person who is enthusiastic about doing or having something ◆ *She has always been a fresh-air fiend.*

fiendish *ADJECTIVE*
1 very wicked or cruel
2 a fiendish problem is extremely difficult or complicated

fierce *ADJECTIVE*
1 a fierce person, or a fierce temper, is angry and violent or cruel
2 strong or intense

> That summer the sun was a mighty furnace, with a blast so fierce it loosened the edges of things. — *Julie Bertagna, The Opposite of Chocolate*

▷ **fiercely** *ADVERB*
▷ **fierceness** *NOUN*

WORD HISTORY from Latin *ferus* 'untamed'

fiery *ADJECTIVE*
1 full of flames or heat
2 irritable; easily made angry

> Her mother was a European elf with a fiery temper. — *Eoin Colfer, Artemis Fowl*

fiesta (*say* fee- est- a) *NOUN* **fiestas**
a religious festival in Spanish-speaking countries

fife *NOUN* **fifes**
a small shrill flute played in military bands

WORD HISTORY from German *Pfeife* 'pipe'

fifteen *NOUN, ADJECTIVE* **fifteens**
1 the number 15, one more than fourteen
2 a team in rugby union football
▷ **fifteenth** *ADJECTIVE, NOUN*

fifth *ADJECTIVE, NOUN* **fifths**
1 next after fourth
2 one of five equal parts of a thing

fifth column *NOUN* **fifth columns**
an organized group working for the enemy within a country at war

fifty *NOUN, ADJECTIVE* **fifties**
the number 50, equal to five times ten
▷ **fiftieth** *ADJECTIVE, NOUN*

a b c d e f g h i j k l m n o p q r s t u v w x y z

SPELLING NOTE Some words pronounced **f-** begin with **ph-** (e.g. phrase)

fifty-fifty *ADJECTIVE, ADVERB*

1 to split or divide something (such as money) fifty-fifty is to divide it evenly between two people or groups

2 a fifty-fifty chance is an even chance of something happening or not happening

fig *NOUN* **figs**

a soft fruit with a dark purplish skin and many small seeds

fight *NOUN* **fights**

1 a physical struggle against an opponent using hands or weapons

2 an attempt to achieve or overcome something ♦ *A campaign focusing on the fight against obesity is being launched this month.*

fight *VERB* **fights, fighting, fought**

1 to have a fight with a person, animal, or group

2 to fight for or against something is to try to achieve or overcome it

▷ **fighter** *NOUN*

figment *NOUN* **figments**

a figment of your imagination is something that you only imagine and is not real

figurative *ADJECTIVE*

(*Language*) figurative language uses figures of speech, and is meant to be understood in a metaphorical rather than a literal sense

▷ **figuratively** *ADVERB*

figurative language

Figurative language uses words for the effects they create, rather than their literal meanings. It often produces vivid images and sounds in the mind of the reader or listener. In these two examples, the first description of the sea is literal and the second is figurative:

Ahead of us the sea formed a spiralling whirlpool.
Ahead of us the sea was being churned by an unseen hand, and we were being scooped like so many currants into a giant's mixing bowl.

Types of figurative language are also called *figures of speech*. The most common types are:

- **simile** and **metaphor**, which describe something by comparing or likening it to something else: *an expression as cold as ice; his eyes were pools of ice*
- **personification**, which describes something inanimate as if it were human: *the waves rocked us to sleep*
- **onomatopoeia**, in which words have sounds that seem to imitate what they describe: *the engine chugged and chuffed up the hill.*

See also the panels on **simile and metaphor** and **onomatopoeia**.

figure *NOUN* **figures**

1 the symbol of a number

2 an amount or value

3 a diagram or illustration

4 a shape

5 the shape of a person's, especially a woman's, body

> Clover was a stout motherly mare approaching middle life, who had never quite got her figure back after her fourth foal. — *George Orwell, Animal Farm*

6 a person

> The doorway was blocked by a figure hooded and draped in oilskins. — *Alan Garner, The Owl Service*

7 a representation of a person or animal in visual art

figure *VERB* **figures, figuring, figured**

to appear or feature as part of something

to figure something out is to come to understand or realize something by thinking about it

figurehead *NOUN* **figureheads**

1 a carved figure decorating the prow of a sailing ship

2 a person who is head of a country or organization but has no real power

figure of speech *NOUN* **figures of speech**

a word or phrase used for special effect and not intended literally, e.g. 'flood' in *a flood of emails*

filament *NOUN* **filaments**

a thread or thin wire, especially one in a light bulb

WORD HISTORY from Latin *filum* 'thread'

filch *VERB* **filches, filching, filched**

(*informal*) to steal something slyly

file❶ *NOUN* **files**

a metal tool with a rough surface that is rubbed on things to shape them or make them smooth

file *VERB* **files, filing, filed**

to shape or smooth an object, or the edge of your nails, with a file

file❷ *NOUN* **files**

1 a folder or box for keeping papers in order

2 a collection of data stored under one name in a computer

3 a line of people one behind the other

file *VERB* **files, filing, filed**

1 to put a piece of paper or information into a file

2 people file into or out of a place when they enter or leave it in a line

> As they filed out of the classroom, Harry saw Professor Umbridge approach the teacher's desk. — *J. K. Rowling, Harry Potter and the Order of the Phoenix*

WORD HISTORY from Latin *filum* 'thread', because a string or wire was put through papers to hold them in order

filial (*say* **fil**- ee- al) *ADJECTIVE*
(*formal*) to do with a son or daughter
WORD HISTORY from Latin *filius* 'son', or *filia* 'daughter'

filibuster *VERB* **filibusters, filibustering, filibustered**
to try to delay or prevent the passing of a law by making long speeches
▷ **filibuster** *NOUN*
WORD HISTORY from Dutch *vrijbuiter* 'pirate'

filigree *NOUN*
delicate lace-like decoration made from twisted metal wire
WORD HISTORY from Latin words *filum* 'thread' and *granum* 'grain'

filings *PLURAL NOUN*
tiny pieces of iron or other metal rubbed off by a file

fill *VERB* **fills, filling, filled**
1 to make something full, or to become full
2 to block up a hole or cavity
3 to fill a post is to appoint a person to a vacant post
to fill someone in (*informal*) is to give them the information they need
to fill something in to fill in a form is to put answers or other information into it

fill *NOUN*
to eat your fill is to eat enough to make you feel full

filler *NOUN* **fillers**
a substance used to fill a hole or gap or to make something more bulky

fillet *NOUN* **fillets**
a piece of fish or meat with the bones taken out

fillet *VERB* **fillets, filleting, filleted**
to remove the bones from fish or meat

filling *NOUN* **fillings**
1 something used to fill a hole or gap, e.g. in a tooth
2 an ingredient inside a pie, or between layers of bread to make a sandwich

filling station *NOUN* **filling stations**
a place where petrol is sold from pumps

filly *NOUN* **fillies**
a young female horse
WORD HISTORY from Old Norse *fylja*

film *NOUN* **films**
1 a story or event recorded by a camera as a series of moving images and shown in a cinema or on television, video, or DVD
2 a rolled strip or sheet of thin plastic coated with material that is sensitive to light, used for taking photographs or cinema images
3 a very thin layer or coating of a substance ◆ *Devastating scenes of marine life dying under a film of oil were broadcast around the world.*

film *VERB* **films, filming, filmed**
1 to record a story or event on film
2 to record an actor or their performance on film
WORD HISTORY from Old English *filmen* 'thin skin'

filmy *ADJECTIVE* **filmier, filmiest**
a filmy coating or material is thin and almost transparent
▷ **filminess** *NOUN*

filo (*say* **fee**- loh) *NOUN*
a paper-thin pastry that is wrapped around food in layers, used especially in Greek cooking

filter *NOUN* **filters**
1 a device for holding back dirt or other unwanted material from a liquid or gas that passes through it
2 a traffic signal which allows one lane of traffic to move or turn while other lanes are held up

filter *VERB* **filters, filtering, filtered**
1 to pass a substance through a filter
2 light filters through a window, or into a room, when it passes slowly and gently through or into it
3 a group of people filter into or out of a place when they enter or leave it gradually and separately, not as a crowd ◆ *They filtered into the hall.*
4 information filters in or out when it gradually accumulates or emerges ◆ *News began to filter out.*
5 traffic filters when a traffic signal allows it to move or turn while other lanes are held up

filth *NOUN*
disgusting dirt

filthy *ADJECTIVE* **filthier, filthiest**
1 disgustingly dirty
2 obscene or offensive
▷ **filthily** *ADVERB*
▷ **filthiness** *NOUN*

fin *NOUN* **fins**
1 a thin flat part sticking out from a fish's body, that helps it to swim
2 a flat part that sticks out from an aircraft or rocket and helps it to balance

final *ADJECTIVE*
1 coming at the end; last
2 a final word or statement is one that puts an end to an argument
▷ **finally** *ADVERB*
▷ **finality** *NOUN*

final *NOUN* **finals**
1 the last in a series of contests
2 finals are the examinations held at the end of a degree course
▷ **finalist** *NOUN*
WORD HISTORY from Latin *finis* 'end'

SPELLING NOTE Some words pronounced **f-** begin with **ph-** (e.g. phrase)

finale (*say* fin- **ah**- lee) ***NOUN*** **finales**
the final section of a piece of music or entertainment

finalize ***VERB*** **finalizes, finalizing, finalized**
to put something into its final form
▷ **finalization** ***NOUN***

USAGE NOTE This word can also be spelled finalise.

finance ***NOUN***
1 the use or management of money
2 the money used to pay for something
3 a person's or company's finances are the money and other funds they have

finance ***VERB*** **finances, financing, financed**
to provide the money for something
▷ **financier** ***NOUN***

WORD HISTORY from Old French *finer* 'to settle a debt'

financial ***ADJECTIVE***
to do with finance
▷ **financially** ***ADVERB***

finch ***NOUN*** **finches**
a small bird with a short stubby bill

find ***VERB*** **finds, finding, found**
1 to look for and get someone or something through searching
2 to come across or discover a person or situation by chance

I came down to breakfast next morning ... to find Sir Walter decoding a telegram in the midst of muffins and marmalade. — *John Buchan, The Thirty-Nine Steps*

3 to learn something by experience ◆ *They are finding the work quite exhausting at times.*
4 a judge or jury finds a person innocent or guilty when they decide and give their verdict on them

to find something out is to get or discover information about something

find ***NOUN*** **finds**
something interesting or valuable that has been found

findings ***PLURAL NOUN***
the conclusions reached from an investigation

fine❶ ***ADJECTIVE***
1 of high quality; excellent

Willy Loman never made a lot of money. His name was never in the paper. He's not the finest character that ever lived. — *Arthur Miller, Death of a Salesman*

2 fine weather is dry and clear, or sunny
3 very thin; consisting of small particles
4 to be feeling or looking fine is to be feeling or looking healthy and well
▷ **finely** ***ADVERB***
▷ **fineness** ***NOUN***

fine ***ADVERB***
1 finely ◆ *a bunch of parsley, chopped fine*
2 (*informal*) very well ◆ *A ten o'clock appointment will suit me fine.*

fine❷ ***NOUN*** **fines**
money which has to be paid as a punishment

fine ***VERB*** **fines, fining, fined**
to make someone pay a fine

WORD HISTORY from Latin *finis* 'end', which in the Middle Ages referred to the sum paid to settle a lawsuit

fine arts ***PLURAL NOUN***
painting, sculpture, and music

finery ***NOUN***
fine clothes or decorations

finesse (*say* fin- **ess**) ***NOUN***
skill and elegance in doing something

WORD HISTORY a French word meaning 'fineness'

finger ***NOUN*** **fingers**
1 each of the four parts sticking out from each hand (or five parts including the thumb)
2 an object, such as a biscuit or other food, in a narrow oblong shape

finger ***VERB*** **fingers, fingering, fingered**
to touch or feel something with your fingers

Tom looked across the clutter of tables and saw the other pirates glaring at him, fingering their knives. — *Philip Reeve, Mortal Engines*

fingernail ***NOUN*** **fingernails**
the hard covering at the end of a finger

fingerprint ***NOUN*** **fingerprints**
a mark made by the tiny ridges on your fingertip, used as a way of identifying someone

fingertip ***NOUN*** **fingertips**
the tip of your finger

to have a subject or information at your fingertips is to know all about it and be able to talk about it readily

finicky ***ADJECTIVE***
fussy about details; hard to please

finish ***VERB*** **finishes, finishing, finished**
1 to complete a task
2 to come to an end

finish ***NOUN*** **finishes**
1 the last stage of something; the end
2 a decorative coating on woodwork or another surface

finite (*say* **fy**- nyt) ***ADJECTIVE***
limited; not infinite ◆ *There is a finite supply of fossil fuels, as well as a finite supply of uranium which is used to produce nuclear power.*

finite verb *NOUN* **finite verbs**
(*Grammar*) a verb that agrees with its subject in person and number; 'was', 'went', and 'says' are finite verbs; 'going' and 'to say' are not

fiord (*say* fee- **ord**) *NOUN* **fiords**
another spelling of **fjord**

fir *NOUN* **firs**
an evergreen tree with needle-like leaves, that produces cones

fire *NOUN* **fires**
1 the flames, heat, and light produced when something burns
2 coal, wood, or other fuel burning in a grate or furnace to give heat
3 a device using electricity or gas to heat a room
4 the shooting of guns ◆ *Hold your fire!*
on fire producing flames; burning
to set fire to something is to set it alight and start it burning

fire *VERB* **fires, firing, fired**
1 to set fire to something
2 to bake pottery or bricks in a kiln
3 to shoot a gun; to send out a bullet or missile
4 (*informal*) to fire someone is to dismiss them from their job
5 to fire someone with interest or enthusiasm is to make them extremely interested or enthusiastic
to fire someone up is to make them excited and enthusiastic
▷ **firer** *NOUN*

firearm *NOUN* **firearms**
a small gun; a rifle, pistol, or revolver

fireball *NOUN* **fireballs**
a large ball of fire caused by an explosion

firebrand *NOUN* **firebrands**
a person who stirs up trouble

fire brigade *NOUN* **fire brigades**
a team of people organized to fight fires

fire drill *NOUN* **fire drills**
a rehearsal of the procedure that needs to be followed in case of a fire

fire engine *NOUN* **fire engines**
a large vehicle that carries firefighters and equipment to put out large fires

fire escape *NOUN* **fire escapes**
a special staircase by which people may escape from a burning building

fire extinguisher *NOUN* **fire extinguishers**
a metal cylinder from which water or foam can be sprayed to put out a fire

firefighter *NOUN* **firefighters**
a member of a fire brigade

firefly *NOUN* **fireflies**
a kind of beetle that gives off a glowing light

firelight *NOUN*
the light from a fire in a room
▷ **firelit** *ADJECTIVE*

fireplace *NOUN* **fireplaces**
a structure against a wall with an opening leading into a chimney, for holding a fire in a room

fireproof *ADJECTIVE*
able to withstand fire or intense heat

fireside *NOUN* **firesides**
the part of the room near a fireplace

firewall *NOUN* **firewalls**
(*ICT*) a program in a computer network that prevents other people from getting access to it

firewood *NOUN*
wood for use as fuel

firework *NOUN* **fireworks**
a device containing chemicals that burn or explode with spectacular effects and loud noises, used at celebrations

firing line *NOUN* **firing lines**
1 the front line of troops in a battle
2 a situation in which you are vulnerable to criticism or blame

firing squad *NOUN* **firing squads**
a group of soldiers given the duty of shooting a condemned person

firm *NOUN* **firms**
a business organization

> Mr Dursley was the director of a firm called Grunnings, which made drills. — *J. K. Rowling, Harry Potter and the Philosopher's Stone*

firm *ADJECTIVE*
1 not giving way when pressed; hard or solid
2 steady; not shaking or moving
3 a firm belief or position is one that is definite and not likely to change
▷ **firmly** *ADVERB*
▷ **firmness** *NOUN*

firm *ADVERB*
firmly ◆ *NASA is standing firm on its decision not to service the Hubble Space Telescope.*

firm *VERB* **firms, firming, firmed**
to firm something up to firm up a proposal or plan is to make it definite

firmament *NOUN*
(*poetic*) the sky with its clouds and stars

first *ADJECTIVE*
coming before all others in time or order or importance
▷ **firstly** *ADVERB*

first *ADVERB*
before everything else ◆ *We should have read the instructions first.*

a b c d e f g h i j k l m n o p q r s t u v w x y z

first *NOUN* **firsts**
1 a person or thing that is first
2 the first time something is done or occurs ◆ *The appointment of a woman to the cricket board is a first for New South Wales.*

first aid *NOUN*
treatment given to an injured person before full medical treatment is available

first-class *ADJECTIVE*
1 using the best class of a service ◆ *Send it by first-class post.* ◆ *He had bought a first-class ticket.*
2 of the best quality; excellent

first-footing *NOUN*
the practice of being the first person to cross someone's threshold in the New Year

first-hand *ADJECTIVE, ADVERB*
first-hand knowledge or experience is obtained directly, rather than from other people or from books

first lady *NOUN*
the wife of the US President

first minister *NOUN*
the leader of the Scottish Parliament

firth *NOUN* **firths**
an estuary or inlet of the sea on the coast of Scotland
WORD HISTORY from Old Norse *fjorthr* 'fjord'

fiscal *ADJECTIVE*
to do with public finances
WORD HISTORY from Latin *fiscus* 'treasury'

fish *NOUN* **fish** or **fishes**
1 an animal with gills and fins that lives and breathes wholly in water
2 the flesh of a fish eaten as food

fish *VERB* **fishes, fishing, fished**
1 to try to catch fish
2 to fish for something is to search or rummage around for it

> I fished inside my jacket for my fags and lighter, only to swear loudly when I found a pocket full of tobacco flakes. — *Keith Gray, Malarkey*

3 to fish for a compliment or information is to try to get it out of someone by hinting
to fish something out is to pull it out of a place where it is hidden or hard to find

fishcake *NOUN* **fishcakes**
a small fried cake of chopped fish and mashed potato

fisherman *NOUN* **fishermen**
a person who catches fish for a living or for sport

fishery *NOUN* **fisheries**
1 the part of the sea where fishing is carried on
2 the business of fishing

fish finger *NOUN* **fish fingers**
a small oblong piece of fish in batter or breadcrumbs

fishmonger *NOUN* **fishmongers**
a shopkeeper who sells fish
WORD HISTORY from an old word *monger* 'trader'

fishy *ADJECTIVE* **fishier, fishiest**
1 smelling or tasting of fish
2 (*informal*) causing doubt or suspicion ◆ *Parts of his story sound a bit fishy to me.*
▷ **fishily** *ADVERB*
▷ **fishiness** *NOUN*

fissile *ADJECTIVE*
1 likely to split
2 capable of undergoing nuclear fission

fission *NOUN*
1 the process of splitting something
2 the process of splitting the nucleus of an atom so as to release energy
WORD HISTORY from Latin *fissum* 'split'

fissure (*say* **fish**- er) *NOUN* **fissures**
a narrow opening made where something splits or separates

fist *NOUN* **fists**
a tightly closed hand with the fingers bent into the palm

fisticuffs *NOUN*
(*old use*) fighting with the fists
WORD HISTORY from *fist* and *cuff* meaning 'to slap'

fit[1] *ADJECTIVE* **fitter, fittest**
1 something that is fit for a person is suitable or good enough for them ◆ *a party dress that's fit for a princess*
2 healthy, in good physical condition ◆ *Dancing is a unique and relaxing way of keeping fit.*
3 to be fit to do something is to be ready or about to do it ◆ *The whole crowd danced till they were fit to drop.*
in a fit state in a suitable condition
to see or **think fit** is to decide or choose to do something, especially unwisely or without good reason
▷ **fitness** *NOUN*

fit *VERB* **fits, fitting, fitted**
1 an item fits when it is the right size and shape for what is required ◆ *This dress doesn't fit me any more.*
2 to put something into place ◆ *Be wary of fitting this kind of lock to any door other than an exterior door.*
3 to alter something to make it the right size and shape
4 to make someone suitable for a task or position ◆ *His credentials include a degree in sports education which fits him for his current post.*
to fit in is to get on well with a group of people
▷ **fitter** *NOUN*

fit *NOUN*
the way something fits ◆ *These jeans are a good fit.*

fit ❷ ***NOUN*** **fits**
1. a sudden illness, especially one that makes you move violently or become unconscious
2. an outburst of emotion ◆ *Legend has it that the Giant's Causeway was built by a local giant who flew into a fit of rage.*

fitful ***ADJECTIVE***
happening in short bursts; not steady
▷ **fitfully** ***ADVERB***

fitment ***NOUN*** **fitments**
a piece of fixed furniture or equipment

fitting ***ADJECTIVE***
proper or appropriate ◆ *I wanted the poem to be a fitting memorial to my brother.*

fitting ***NOUN*** **fittings**
the process of having a piece of clothing fitted ◆ *At the first fitting, the seamstress will pin your dress.*

fittings ***PLURAL NOUN***
pieces of furniture or equipment in a room or building

five ***NOUN, ADJECTIVE*** **fives**
the number 5, one more than four

fiver ***NOUN*** **fivers**
(*informal*) a five-pound note; £5

fives ***NOUN***
a game in which a ball is hit with gloved hands or a bat against the walls of a court

fix ***VERB*** **fixes, fixing, fixed**
1. to fasten or place something firmly
2. to make something permanent and unable to change
3. to decide or arrange a date or time for an event ◆ *They've finally fixed a date for the wedding.*
4. to repair something that is broken ◆ *I need to get my computer fixed.*
5. (*informal*) to affect the result of a contest or election by using dishonest methods

to fix on something is to choose or decide on it
to fix something up is to arrange or organize it
▷ **fixer** ***NOUN***

fix ***NOUN*** **fixes**
1. (*informal*) an awkward situation ◆ *By meddling in magic, the Sorcerer's Apprentice gets himself into a terrible fix.*
2. the position of a ship or aircraft determined by using a compass or radar
3. (*informal*) a dose of a narcotic drug taken by an addict

fixation ***NOUN*** **fixations**
an obsession or concentration on a single idea
▷ **fixated** ***ADJECTIVE***

fixative ***NOUN*** **fixatives**
a substance used to keep something in position or make it permanent

fixedly ***ADVERB***
to look fixedly at someone is to stare at them with a fixed expression

fixity ***NOUN***
a fixed condition; permanence

fixture ***NOUN*** **fixtures**
1. a piece of furniture or equipment that is fixed in position, such as a cupboard or washbasin
2. a sports event planned for a particular day

fizz ***VERB*** **fizzes, fizzing, fizzed**
to make a hissing or spluttering sound; to produce a lot of small bubbles

fizzle ***VERB*** **fizzles, fizzling, fizzled**
to make a slight fizzing sound
to fizzle out is to come to a disappointing end

fizzy ***ADJECTIVE*** **fizzier, fizziest**
a fizzy drink contains a lot of small bubbles
▷ **fizziness** ***NOUN***

fjord (*say* fee- **ord**) ***NOUN*** **fjords**
a long narrow inlet of the sea between high cliffs, especially in Norway

flabbergasted ***ADJECTIVE***
greatly astonished

flabby ***ADJECTIVE*** **flabbier, flabbiest**
fat and soft, not firm
▷ **flabbily** ***ADVERB***
▷ **flabbiness** ***NOUN***

flaccid (*say* **flass**- id) ***ADJECTIVE***
soft and limp
▷ **flaccidly** ***ADVERB***
▷ **flaccidity** ***NOUN***

WORD HISTORY from Latin *flaccus* 'flabby'

flag ❶ ***NOUN*** **flags**
1. a piece of cloth with a coloured pattern or shape on it, used as the emblem of a country or as a signal
2. a small piece of paper or plastic that looks like a flag

flag ***VERB*** **flags, flagging, flagged**
to droop or become weak because of tiredness
to flag someone down to flag down a person or vehicle is to signal them to stop by waving

WORD HISTORY from an old word *flag* meaning 'drooping'

flag ❷ ***NOUN*** **flags**
a flagstone

> There were cold stone flags under Tom's feet, and in his nostrils a smell of old dust that it had been nobody's business to disperse. — *Philippa Pearce, Tom's Midnight Garden*

WORD HISTORY from Old Norse *flaga* 'slab of stone'

flagon ***NOUN*** **flagons**
a large bottle or container for drink, especially wine

WORD HISTORY from Italian *flasco* 'flask'

SPELLING NOTE Some words pronounced **f-** begin with **ph-** (e.g. phrase)

flagpole or **flagstaff** *NOUN* **flagpoles** or **flagstaffs**
a pole used for flying a flag

flagrant (*say* **flay**- grant) *ADJECTIVE*
shocking in an obvious way ◆ *The decision was a flagrant abuse of their powers.*
▷ **flagrantly** *ADVERB*
▷ **flagrancy** *NOUN*
WORD HISTORY from Latin *flagrans* 'blazing'

flagship *NOUN* **flagships**
1 a ship that carries an admiral and flies the admiral's flag
2 a company's best or most important product or store

flagstone *NOUN* **flagstones**
a flat slab of stone used for paving

flail *NOUN* **flails**
an old-fashioned tool for threshing grain

flail *VERB* **flails, flailing, flailed**
to flail your arms or legs is to wave them about wildly
WORD HISTORY from Latin *flagellum* 'a whip'

flair *NOUN*
a natural ability or talent for something
◆ *a flair for languages*
WORD HISTORY a French word meaning 'power to smell things'
USAGE NOTE Take care not to confuse this word with *flare*.

flak *NOUN*
1 shells fired by anti-aircraft guns
2 strong criticism ◆ *The manager came in for a lot of flak from the press.*
WORD HISTORY from German *Fliegerabwehrkanone* 'aircraft defence cannon'

flake *NOUN* **flakes**
1 a very light thin piece of something
2 a small flat piece of falling snow
▷ **flaky** *ADJECTIVE*

flake *VERB* **flakes, flaking, flaked**
a surface layer or skin flakes when it breaks up and comes off in flakes

flambeau *NOUN* **flambeaux**
a flaming torch

I took from their sconces two flambeaux, and giving one to Fortunato bowed him through several suites of rooms to the archway that led into the vaults. — *Edgar Allan Poe, The Cask of Amontillado*

flamboyant *ADJECTIVE*
very showy in appearance or manner
WORD HISTORY a French word meaning 'blazing'

flame *NOUN* **flames**
a tongue-shaped portion of fire or burning gas

flame *VERB* **flames, flaming, flamed**
1 to produce flames
2 to become bright red

flamenco (*say* fla- **menk**- oh) *NOUN* **flamencos**
a traditional Spanish style of singing, guitar playing, and dancing that originated in Gypsy culture
WORD HISTORY a Spanish word meaning 'Flemish, like a Gypsy'

flamingo *NOUN* **flamingoes**
a wading bird with long legs, a long neck, and pinkish feathers

flammable *ADJECTIVE*
flammable material is able to be set on fire
▷ **flammability** *NOUN*
USAGE NOTE See the note at *inflammable*.

flan *NOUN* **flans**
a pastry or sponge shell with no cover over the filling

flank *NOUN* **flanks**
1 the side of an animal's body

The creature grunted, and with one swipe of a claw gouged a wound in the flank of Twoflower's horse. — *Terry Pratchett, The Colour of Magic*

2 the left or right side of an army during a battle or of a football team during a game

flank *VERB* **flanks, flanking, flanked**
to be positioned at the side of something

Polydectes sat on a raised platform flanked by his bodyguards. He lounged on his throne, only his eyes shifting. — *Alan Gibbons, Shadow of the Minotaur*

▷ **flanker** *NOUN*

flannel *NOUN* **flannels**
1 a soft cloth for washing your face
2 a soft woollen material
WORD HISTORY from Welsh *gwlanen* 'woollen'

flap *VERB* **flaps, flapping, flapped**
1 to move loosely back and forth in the wind or air
2 to make something move back and forth in the air, especially a wing
3 (*informal*) to panic or fuss about something

flap *NOUN* **flaps**
1 a part that is fixed at one edge to something else, often to cover an opening
2 the action or sound of flapping
to be in a flap (*informal*) is to fuss or panic

flapjack *NOUN* **flapjacks**
a cake made from oats and golden syrup

flare *VERB* **flares, flaring, flared**
1 to blaze with a sudden bright flame
2 to become angry suddenly
3 your nostrils flare when they become gradually wider
to flare up
1 an illness or condition flares up when it reappears or worsens suddenly
2 a dispute flares up when it suddenly starts or becomes worse

flare *NOUN* **flares**
1 a sudden bright flame or light, especially one used as a signal
2 a gradual widening towards the hem of a skirt or pair of trousers
USAGE NOTE Take care not to confuse this word with *flair*.

flash *NOUN* **flashes**
1 a sudden bright flame or light
2 a device for making a sudden bright light for taking photographs
3 a sudden display of wit, anger, or other feelings
4 a short item of news

flash *VERB* **flashes, flashing, flashed**
1 to make a flash of light
2 to appear or move suddenly and quickly ◆ *It was a perfect header which flashed past the goalkeeper in an instant.*

flashback *NOUN* **flashbacks**
an episode in a film or book that tells an earlier part of the story

flashpoint *NOUN* **flashpoints**
a place where trouble or fighting can easily arise, or a topic that can arouse argument

flashy *ADJECTIVE* **flashier, flashiest**
gaudy or showy
▷ **flashily** *ADVERB*
▷ **flashiness** *NOUN*

flask *NOUN* **flasks**
1 a bottle with a narrow neck
2 a vacuum flask

flat *ADJECTIVE* **flatter, flattest**
1 a surface is flat when it has no curves or bumps, and is smooth and level
2 spread out; lying at full length ◆ *With a spiral-bound book, the pages can lie flat when open.*
3 a flat tyre has no air inside
4 flat feet do not have the normal arch underneath
5 a flat refusal or denial is a firm one that is not open to discussion
6 a flat voice or tone is dull and monotonous
7 a drink that is flat is no longer fizzy
8 a flat battery is unable to produce any more electric current
9 (*Music*) one semitone lower than the natural note ◆ *E flat*
▷ **flatly** *ADVERB*
▷ **flatness** *NOUN*

flat *ADVERB*
1 so as to be flat ◆ *Divide the dough into four pieces and press them flat with your knuckles.*
2 (*informal*) exactly ◆ *The CD teaches you how to make friends over the telephone in 30 seconds flat.*
3 (*Music*) below the correct pitch
flat broke (*informal*) completely broke, penniless
flat out as fast, or with as much effort, as possible

flat *NOUN* **flats**
1 a set of rooms for living in, usually on one floor of a building
2 (*Music*) a note one semitone lower than the natural note, or the sign (♭) that indicates this
3 a punctured tyre

flatten *VERB* **flattens, flattening, flattened**
1 to make something flat
2 to become flat

flatter *VERB* **flatters, flattering, flattered**
1 to praise someone more than they deserve
2 to make a person or thing seem better or more attractive than they really are
▷ **flatterer** *NOUN*
▷ **flattery** *NOUN*
WORD HISTORY from Old French *flater* 'to smooth down'

flatulent *ADJECTIVE*
1 affected by gas building up in the digestive tract
2 a flatulent speech or speaker uses pompous or pretentious language
▷ **flatulence** *NOUN*
▷ **flatulently** *ADVERB*

flaunt *VERB* **flaunts, flaunting, flaunted**
to display something proudly or ostentatiously; to show something off ◆ *If you've got great nails we have everything you need to flaunt them.*
USAGE NOTE Take care not to confuse this word with *flout*.

flautist (*say* **flaw**- tist) *NOUN* **flautists**
a flute player

flavour *NOUN* **flavours**
the taste something has in the mouth

flavour *VERB* **flavours, flavouring, flavoured**
to give something a flavour; to season food
▷ **flavouring** *NOUN*

flaw *NOUN* **flaws**
something that makes a person or thing imperfect
▷ **flawed** *ADJECTIVE*

flawless *ADJECTIVE*
without a flaw; perfect
▷ **flawlessly** *ADVERB*
▷ **flawlessness** *NOUN*

flax *NOUN*
a plant that produces fibres from which linen is made and seeds from which linseed oil is obtained

flaxen *ADJECTIVE*
pale yellow in colour, like flax fibres

Doctor Kemp was a tall and slender young man, with flaxen hair and a moustache almost white.
— *H. G. Wells, The Invisible Man*

flay *VERB* **flays, flaying, flayed**
1 to strip the skin from an animal
2 to whip or beat someone

a b c d e f g h i j k l m n o p q r s t u v w x y z

flea *NOUN* **fleas**
a small jumping insect that sucks blood

flea market *NOUN* **flea markets**
a street market that sells cheap or second-hand goods

fleck *NOUN* **flecks**
1 a very small patch of colour
2 a particle; a speck ◆ *flecks of foam*
▷ **flecked** *ADJECTIVE*

fled *past tense and past participle of* **flee**

fledged *ADJECTIVE*
young birds are fledged when they have grown feathers and are able to fly

fledgeling or **fledgling** *NOUN* **fledgelings** or **fledglings**
a young bird that is just fledged

flee *VERB* **flees, fleeing, fled**
to run or hurry away from something in fear

fleece *NOUN* **fleeces**
1 the woolly hair of a sheep or similar animal
2 a soft warm fabric, or a piece of clothing made from this
▷ **fleecy** *ADJECTIVE*

fleece *VERB* **fleeces, fleecing, fleeced**
1 to shear the fleece from a sheep
2 to fleece someone is to swindle them out of some money

fleet[1] *NOUN* **fleets**
1 the ships that make up a country's navy
2 a number of commercial aircraft or vehicles owned by one company

fleet[2] *ADJECTIVE*
moving swiftly; nimble

fleeting *ADJECTIVE*
passing quickly; very brief ◆ *A witness to the crime may have caught a fleeting glimpse of the suspect in the dark.*

Flemish *ADJECTIVE*
to do with Flanders in Belgium or its people or language

Flemish *NOUN*
a language spoken in Flanders in Belgium

flesh *NOUN*
1 the soft substance of the bodies of people and animals, consisting of muscle and fat
2 a person's body as opposed to their mind or soul
3 the pulpy part of fruits and vegetables
▷ **fleshy** *ADJECTIVE*

flex *VERB* **flexes, flexing, flexed**
to bend or stretch a limb or muscle

Jud slipped his suit jacket on and flexed his shoulders, smiling at himself in profile through the mirror. — *Barry Hines, A Kestrel for a Knave*

flex *NOUN* **flexes**
flexible insulated wire for carrying electric current

WORD HISTORY from Latin *flexum* 'bent'

flexible *ADJECTIVE*
1 easy to bend or stretch without breaking
2 able to be changed or adapted ◆ *The job is also quite flexible in terms of how you manage your time.*
3 able to adapt to changing circumstances
▷ **flexibly** *ADVERB*
▷ **flexibility** *NOUN*

flexitime *NOUN*
a system that allows workers to vary their working hours

flick *NOUN* **flicks**
a quick light hit or movement

flick *VERB* **flicks, flicking, flicked**
1 to move something with a flick
2 to flick a switch is to press and activate it
3 to flick through a book, newspaper, etc., is to turn its pages quickly, without close reading

Hastily, Mr Cartright flicked through the pages of Dr Feltham's vast Science Fair memorandum. — *Anne Fine, Flour Babies*

flicker *VERB* **flickers, flickering, flickered**
1 a light or flame flickers when it shines or burns unsteadily

Simon's head-torch kept flickering from a loose or damaged connection. — *Joe Simpson, Touching the Void*

2 to move quickly to and fro

flicker *NOUN* **flickers**
1 a flickering light or movement
2 a brief occurrence or display of an emotion ◆ *a flicker of hope*

flick knife *NOUN* **flick knives**
a knife with a blade that springs out when a button is pressed

flier *NOUN* **fliers**
another spelling of **flyer**

flight *NOUN* **flights**
1 the action of flying, or the ability to fly
2 a journey in an aircraft
3 a series of stairs
4 a group of flying birds or aircraft
5 the feathers or fins on a dart or arrow
6 the action of fleeing; an escape

to put someone to flight is to force them to flee

to take flight is to run away or escape

flight deck *NOUN* **flight decks**
the cockpit of a large aircraft

flight path *NOUN* **flight paths**
the plotted course of an aircraft

flight recorder *NOUN* **flight recorders**
an electronic device in an aircraft that records technical information about its flight, and which can be used after an accident to help find the cause

flighty *ADJECTIVE* **flightier, flightiest**
silly and frivolous
▷ **flightiness** *NOUN*

flimsy *ADJECTIVE* **flimsier, flimsiest**
1 made of thin or weak material

Alison and Roger were playing with three flimsy cut out paper models of birds. — *Alan Garner, The Owl Service*

2 a flimsy excuse or flimsy evidence is insubstantial and not likely to be believed
▷ **flimsily** *ADVERB*
▷ **flimsiness** *NOUN*

flinch *VERB* **flinches, flinching, flinched**
to move or shrink back because you are afraid; to wince

flinch *NOUN* **flinches**
a sudden move backwards in fear; a wince

fling *VERB* **flings, flinging, flung**
1 to throw something violently or carelessly

Then, suddenly, Christopher scowled horribly and flung his bathing things in a wet lump on the floor. — *Anne Fine, Madame Doubtfire*

2 to fling someone into or out of a place is to force them to go or leave there suddenly ◆ *On the basis of these wild accusations, scores of innocent people were flung into prison.*

fling *NOUN* **flings**
1 a short time of enjoyment ◆ *Thousands of people jammed the streets for Mardi Gras, the final fling before the austerity of Lent.*
2 a brief romantic affair
3 a lively traditional Scottish Highland dance

flint *NOUN* **flints**
1 a very hard kind of stone
2 a piece of flint or hard metal used to produce sparks
▷ **flinty** *ADJECTIVE*

flip *VERB* **flips, flipping, flipped**
1 to turn over with a quick movement
2 to turn something over with a quick movement
3 to flip a coin is to toss it in the air so that it turns over, often as a means of making a decision according to which side lands uppermost
4 (*informal*) to become crazy or very angry

flip *NOUN* **flips**
a flipping movement

flip-flop *NOUN* **flip-flops**
a light sandal with a thong that goes between the big toe and the second toe

flippant *ADJECTIVE*
a flippant remark or attitude does not take a situation as seriously as it should
▷ **flippantly** *ADVERB*
▷ **flippancy** *NOUN*

flipper *NOUN* **flippers**
1 a limb that some sea animals such as seals, turtles, and penguins use for swimming
2 each of a pair of flat rubber attachments worn on your feet for underwater swimming

flirt *VERB* **flirts, flirting, flirted**
1 to behave as though you are sexually attracted to someone
2 to flirt with an idea is to take an interest in it without being too serious
3 to flirt with danger or death is to risk it
▷ **flirtation** *NOUN*

flirt *NOUN* **flirts**
a person who flirts

flirtatious *ADJECTIVE*
fond of flirting with people
▷ **flirtatiously** *ADVERB*
▷ **flirtatiousness** *NOUN*

flit *VERB* **flits, flitting, flitted**
1 to fly or move lightly and quickly
2 to run away secretly

flit *NOUN* **flits**
the action of flitting

flitter *VERB* **flitters, flittering, flittered**
to flit about

float *VERB* **floats, floating, floated**
1 to stay or move on the surface of a liquid or in air
2 to make something move on the surface of a liquid
3 to float an idea is to propose it and ask for other people's opinions
4 to float a business is to offer shares in it to the public for the first time
5 to float a currency is to allow it to have a variable rate of exchange
▷ **floater** *NOUN*

float *NOUN* **floats**
1 a device designed to float on water or other liquid
2 a small electric vehicle or cart, especially one used for delivering milk
3 a vehicle with a platform for carrying a display in a parade or carnival
4 a small amount of money kept for paying expenses or giving change

floating voter *NOUN* **floating voters**
a person who has not yet decided who to vote for in an election

flock① *NOUN* **flocks**
1 a number of birds that are flying or resting together
2 a number of sheep or goats that are kept together
3 a number of people in someone's charge, especially a Christian congregation

flock *VERB* **flocks, flocking, flocked**
people flock when they gather or move in a crowd, or in large numbers

flock② *NOUN* **flocks**
a tuft of wool or cotton

floe *NOUN* **floes**
a sheet of floating ice
WORD HISTORY from a Norwegian word meaning 'layer'

flog *VERB* **flogs, flogging, flogged**
1 to beat a person or animal hard with a whip or stick as a punishment
2 (*informal*) to sell something
▷ **flogging** *NOUN*

flood *NOUN* **floods**
1 a large amount of water spreading over a place that is usually dry
2 a huge number of things ◆ *She found a flood of emails on her return from holiday.*
3 the movement of the tide when it is coming in towards the land

flood *VERB* **floods, flooding, flooded**
1 a river floods when its waters overflow the banks onto the surrounding land
2 to cover or fill an area with a flood
3 to flood a market is to introduce a large quantity of an item for sale
to flood in is to arrive in large quantities

floodlight *NOUN* **floodlights**
a lamp that makes a broad bright beam to light up a stage, stadium, or important building
▷ **floodlit** *ADJECTIVE*

floor *NOUN* **floors**
1 the part of a room that people walk or stand on
2 a storey of a building; all the rooms at the same level
3 the part of a legislative assembly hall where members sit
to take the floor is to stand up to perform or make a speech
USAGE NOTE In Britain, the *ground floor* of a building is the one at street level, and the one above it is the *first floor*. In the USA, the *first floor* is the one at street level, and the one above it is the *second floor*.

floor *VERB* **floors, flooring, floored**
1 to put a floor into a building
2 to knock a person down
3 (*informal*) to baffle or astonish someone

floorboard *NOUN* **floorboards**
one of the boards forming the floor of a room

flop *VERB* **flops, flopping, flopped**
1 to fall or sit down clumsily
2 to hang or sway heavily and loosely
3 (*informal*) to be a failure

flop *NOUN* **flops**
1 a flopping movement or sound
2 (*informal*) a failure

floppy *ADJECTIVE*
hanging loosely; not firm or rigid
▷ **floppily** *ADVERB*
▷ **floppiness** *NOUN*

floppy disk *NOUN* **floppy disks**
a flexible disk containing data for use in a computer

flora *NOUN*
the plants of a particular area or period (SEE ALSO **fauna**)
WORD HISTORY from *Flora*, the ancient Roman goddess of flowers, whose name was based on Latin *flores* 'flowers'

floral *ADJECTIVE*
to do with flowers

florid (*say* **flo**- rid) *ADJECTIVE*
1 a florid complexion or skin is red and flushed
2 florid language is elaborate and ornate
▷ **floridly** *ADVERB*

florin *NOUN* **florins**
1 a former British coin worth two shillings (10p)
2 a Dutch guilder
WORD HISTORY from Italian *fiore* 'flower', also the name of an Italian coin with a picture of a lily on one side

florist *NOUN* **florists**
a shopkeeper who sells cut flowers, or a person who arranges flowers for special occasions

floss *NOUN*
1 silky thread or fibres
2 a soft medicated thread pulled between your teeth to clean them
▷ **flossy** *ADJECTIVE*

flotation *NOUN* **flotations**
1 the process of floating something
2 the process of offering shares in a company on the stock market for the first time

flotilla (*say* flot- **il**- a) *NOUN* **flotillas**
a fleet of boats or small ships
WORD HISTORY a Spanish word meaning 'little fleet'

flotsam *NOUN*
wreckage or cargo found floating after a shipwreck
flotsam and jetsam odds and ends
WORD HISTORY from an Old French word meaning 'to float'

flounce❶ *VERB* **flounces, flouncing, flounced**
to flounce into or out of a place is to enter or leave it in an impatient and annoyed manner

flounce *NOUN* **flounces**
a flouncing movement

flounce❷ *NOUN* **flounces**
a wide frill of material sewn on a skirt or dress

flounder❶ *VERB* **flounders, floundering, floundered**
1 to move clumsily and with difficulty
2 to experience setbacks or difficulties ◆ *Her singing career floundered so she tried other avenues for success.*

flounder❷ *NOUN* **flounder**
a small flat edible sea fish

flour *NOUN*
a fine powder of wheat or other grain, used in cooking
▷ **floury** *ADJECTIVE*

WORD HISTORY an old spelling of *flower*

flourish *VERB* **flourishes, flourishing, flourished**
1 plants flourish when they grow or develop strongly
2 to be successful; to prosper
3 to wave something about dramatically ◆ *A man approached us flourishing a rolled-up newspaper.*

flourish *NOUN* **flourishes**
a showy or dramatic sweeping movement, curve, or passage of music

WORD HISTORY from Latin *florere* 'to flower'

flout *VERB* **flouts, flouting, flouted**
to flout a rule or instruction is to disobey it openly and scornfully

WORD HISTORY probably from Dutch *fluiten* 'to whistle or hiss'

USAGE NOTE Take care not to confuse this word with *flaunt*.

flow *VERB* **flows, flowing, flowed**
1 a stream of water or other liquid flows when it moves along continuously and freely
2 a crowd or line of traffic flows when it moves along smoothly or continuously
3 to flow from a place is to come out from it in a stream
4 a situation or event flows from something when it is the result of it
5 hair or fabric flows when it hangs down loosely
6 the tide flows when it comes in towards the land (SEE ALSO **ebb** *VERB*)

flow *NOUN* **flows**
1 a flowing movement or mass
2 a steady continuous stream of something ◆ *a flow of ideas*
3 the movement of the tide when it is coming in towards the land (SEE ALSO **ebb** *NOUN*)

flow chart *NOUN* **flow charts**
(*D&T*) a diagram that shows how the different stages of a process or parts of a system are connected

flower *NOUN* **flowers**
1 the part of a plant from which seed and fruit develop
2 a blossom and its stem used for decoration, usually in groups

flower *VERB* **flowers, flowering, flowered**
to produce flowers; to blossom

flowerpot *NOUN* **flowerpots**
a pot in which a plant may be grown

flowery *ADJECTIVE*
1 full of flowers
2 flowery language is elaborate and full of fancy phrases

flu *NOUN*
influenza or a similar infectious disease

fluctuate *VERB* **fluctuates, fluctuating, fluctuated**
a temperature or price fluctuates when it varies by rising and falling
▷ **fluctuation** *NOUN*

WORD HISTORY from Latin *fluctus* 'a wave'

flue *NOUN* **flues**
a duct in a chimney for smoke and gases to escape

fluent (*say* **floo**- ent) *ADJECTIVE*
1 skilful at speaking clearly and without hesitating
2 able to speak a foreign language easily and well
▷ **fluently** *ADVERB*
▷ **fluency** *NOUN*

WORD HISTORY from Latin *fluens* 'flowing'

fluff *NOUN*
1 a light soft substance
2 (*informal*) a mistake, especially in speaking

fluff *VERB* **fluffs, fluffing, fluffed**
(*informal*) to make a mistake

to fluff something up to fluff up a pillow or cushion is to pat it to make it softer and rounder

fluffy *ADJECTIVE* **fluffier, fluffiest**
having a mass of soft fur or fibres
▷ **fluffiness** *NOUN*

fluid *NOUN* **fluids**
a substance that is able to flow freely as liquids and gases do

fluid *ADJECTIVE*
1 able to flow freely
2 a fluid idea or plan is not fixed and can be changed
▷ **fluidity** *NOUN*

a b c d e f g h i j k l m n o p q r s t u v w x y z

fluke❶ *NOUN* **flukes**
a success that you achieve by unexpected good luck
▷ **fluky** *ADJECTIVE*

fluke❷ *NOUN* **flukes**
1 each of the triangular halves of a whale's tail
2 a triangular piece at the end of each arm of an anchor

flummox *VERB* **flummoxes, flummoxing, flummoxed**
(*informal*) to baffle someone

fluorescent (*say* floo- er- **ess**- ent) *ADJECTIVE*
1 a fluorescent light is a very bright electric light, often used in offices
2 a fluorescent dye or colour is very bright and shines in the dark
▷ **fluorescence** *NOUN*

WORD HISTORY from *fluorspar*, a fluorescent mineral

fluoridation *NOUN*
the process of adding fluoride to drinking water in order to help prevent tooth decay

fluoride *NOUN*
a chemical substance that is thought to prevent tooth decay

flurry *NOUN* **flurries**
1 a sudden whirling gust of wind, rain, or snow
2 a short period of activity or excitement

The hospital in Bain was relatively new, built six years before when a flurry of hospital reform came sweeping up from the South. — *Garth Nix, Lirael*

WORD HISTORY from an old word *flurr* 'to throw about'

flush❶ *VERB* **flushes, flushing, flushed**
1 to become red in the face; to blush
2 to flush something out or away is to remove it with a flow of water
3 to flush something out or from your body is to get rid of it by drinking a lot of water
4 to flush a toilet is to empty and refill it with a fast flow of water
5 to flush out someone or something hidden is to uncover or expose them or it

flush *NOUN* **flushes**
1 a blush
2 a fast flow of water
3 a hand of playing cards of the same suit

in the first flush to be in the first flush of an experience or time is to be at the very start of it and feeling enthusiastic or hopeful

flush❷ *ADJECTIVE*
1 to be flush with a wall or surface is to be level with it
2 (*informal*) someone who is flush is very wealthy

fluster *VERB* **flusters, flustering, flustered**
to make someone nervous and confused

fluster *NOUN* **flusters**
to be in a fluster is to be nervous and confused

WORD HISTORY from an earlier meaning 'to make slightly drunk'

flute *NOUN* **flutes**
1 a musical instrument consisting of a long pipe with holes that are stopped by fingers or keys, which you play by blowing across a hole at one end
2 an ornamental groove on a surface or edge

WORD FAMILY A musician who plays the flute is a flautist.

flutter *VERB* **flutters, fluttering, fluttered**
1 to flap wings quickly
2 to move or flap quickly and irregularly

flutter *NOUN* **flutters**
1 a fluttering movement
2 a nervously excited condition
3 (*informal*) a small bet

flux *NOUN* **fluxes**
continual change or flow

WORD HISTORY from Latin *fluxus* 'flowing'

fly❶ *NOUN* **flies**
1 a small flying insect with two wings
2 a real or artificial fly used as bait in fishing

WORD HISTORY from Old English *flycge*

fly❷ *VERB* **flies, flying, flew, flown**
1 to move through the air by means of wings or in an aircraft
2 to go or move quickly ◆ *His hand flew to his mouth.* ◆ *The door flew open.*
3 a flag flies when it is raised and waving in the air
4 to make something fly ◆ *Open fields, parks, and beaches are great places for flying kites.*
5 a period of time flies when it passes quickly

fly *NOUN* **flies**
the front opening of a pair of trousers

WORD HISTORY from Old English *fleogan*

flyer *NOUN* **flyers**
1 a person or vehicle that flies
2 a small poster advertising an event

flying saucer *NOUN* **flying saucers**
a saucer-shaped aircraft supposed to be an alien spacecraft

flying squad *NOUN* **flying squads**
a team of police officers organized so that they can move rapidly

flyleaf *NOUN* **flyleaves**
a blank page at the beginning or end of a book

flyover *NOUN* **flyovers**
a bridge that carries one road or railway over another

flywheel *NOUN* **flywheels**
a heavy wheel used to regulate machinery

a b c d e f g h i j k l m n o p q r s t u v w x y z

FM *ABBREVIATION*
frequency modulation, a system of high-quality radio broadcasting

foal *NOUN* **foals**
a young horse

foal *VERB* **foals, foaling, foaled**
to give birth to a foal

foam *NOUN*
1 a white mass of tiny bubbles on a liquid; froth
2 a spongy kind of rubber or plastic
▷ **foamy** *ADJECTIVE*

foam *VERB* **foams, foaming, foamed**
to form bubbles or froth

fob ❶ *NOUN* **fobs**
1 a chain for a pocket watch
2 a tab on a key ring

fob ❷ *VERB* **fobs, fobbing, fobbed**
to fob someone off is to get rid of them by an excuse or a trick
to fob something off on someone is to make them take something inferior or unwanted

focal *ADJECTIVE*
to do with or at a focus

focus *NOUN* **focuses** or **foci**
1 the distance from an eye or lens at which an object appears clearest
2 the point at which rays seem to meet
3 something that is a centre of interest or attention
in focus appearing clearly
out of focus not appearing clearly

focus *VERB* **focuses, focusing, focused** or **focussed**
1 to adjust the focus of your eye or a lens so that objects appear clearly

All eyes were focussed on the stranger. This tall, young man was neither black nor white, they observed. — *Doris Pilkington, Rabbit Proof Fence*

2 to focus on something is to concentrate on it

WORD HISTORY from a Latin word meaning 'hearth', because it was the central point of a household

fodder *NOUN*
food for horses or farm animals

foe *NOUN* **foes**
(*literary*) an enemy

foetus (*say* fee- tus) *NOUN* **foetuses**
another spelling of **fetus**

fog *NOUN*
thick mist
▷ **foggy** *ADJECTIVE*

fogey *NOUN* **fogeys**
old fogey a person with old-fashioned ideas

foghorn *NOUN* **foghorns**
a loud horn for warning ships in fog

foible *NOUN* **foibles**
a slight peculiarity in someone's character or tastes

foil ❶ *NOUN* **foils**
1 a very thin sheet of metal
2 a person or thing that serves as a contrast or balance to another, and so emphasizes the other's good qualities ◆ *Dr Watson, who narrates the Sherlock Holmes stories, acts as a foil to Holmes.*

WORD HISTORY from Latin *folium* 'leaf'

foil ❷ *NOUN* **foils**
a long narrow sword used in the sport of fencing

foil ❸ *VERB* **foils, foiling, foiled**
to prevent something from being successful, or to prevent someone from doing something ◆ *He had been foiled in his attempt to escape.*

WORD HISTORY from Old French *fouler* 'to trample'

foist *VERB* **foists, foisting, foisted**
to foist something unwelcome or inferior on someone is to make them accept it

I love my family dearly, but they were rather foisted on me. — *Nick Hornby, Fever Pitch*

WORD HISTORY from an earlier meaning 'to use a loaded dice'

fold ❶ *VERB* **folds, folding, folded**
1 to bend or wrap one part of something over another part
2 (*informal*) a business folds when it fails and stops trading
3 to blend an ingredient in baking by spooning one part over another

fold *NOUN* **folds**
a line where something is folded

fold ❷ *NOUN* **folds**
an enclosure for sheep

folder *NOUN* **folders**
1 a folding cover for loose papers
2 (*ICT*) a directory containing a set of files

foliage *NOUN*
the leaves of a tree or plant

WORD HISTORY from Latin *folium* 'leaf'

folk *PLURAL NOUN*
people

folk dance *NOUN* **folk dances**
a dance in the traditional style of a country

folklore *NOUN*
old beliefs and legends

folk music *NOUN*
the traditional music of a country

folk song *NOUN* **folk songs**
a song in the traditional style of a country

follow *VERB* **follows, following, followed**
1 to go or come after someone or something
2 to do a thing after something else
3 to take a person or thing as a guide or example
4 to take an interest in the progress of events or a sport or team ▸▸

5 to understand someone or something that is being said

The children couldn't follow everything the Madam was saying in English, but her voice sounded annoyed. — *Beverley Naidoo, Journey to Jo'burg*

6 to result from something

▷ **follower** *NOUN*

following *PREPOSITION*
after, as a result of ◆ *Following the burglary, we had new locks fitted.*

folly *NOUN* **follies**
1 foolishness; a foolish action
2 an ornamental building with no practical purpose, often in a large park or garden

WORD HISTORY from French *folie* 'madness'

foment (*say* fo- **ment**) *VERB* **foments, fomenting, fomented**
to stir up trouble or difficulty deliberately
◆ *Attempts to foment civil unrest will not succeed.*

▷ **fomentation** *NOUN*

WORD HISTORY from Latin *fomentum* 'poultice'

USAGE NOTE Take care not to confuse this word with *ferment*.

fond *ADJECTIVE*
1 to be fond of someone is to feel affection for them
2 to be fond of something is to enjoy or get pleasure from it ◆ *I happen to be extremely fond of dark chocolate.*
3 a fond memory is one that you remember with affection

▷ **fondly** *ADVERB*
▷ **fondness** *NOUN*

WORD HISTORY from an old word *fon* 'a fool'

fondant *NOUN*
a thick paste made with water and flavoured sugar, used as icing or for making sweets

WORD HISTORY a French word meaning 'melting'

fondle *VERB* **fondles, fondling, fondled**
1 to touch or stroke someone or something affectionately
2 to touch someone in a sexual manner

fondue *NOUN* **fondues**
a dish in which pieces of food are dipped into a melted ingredient, especially cheese or chocolate

WORD HISTORY a French word meaning 'melted'

font *NOUN* **fonts**
1 a basin in a Christian church, used to hold water for baptism
2 a set of characters in printing

WORD HISTORY from Latin *fontis* 'of a spring'

food *NOUN* **foods**
any substance that an animal or plant can take into its body to help it to grow and be healthy

food chain *NOUN* **food chains**
a series of plants and animals each of which serves as food for the one above it in the series

food poisoning *NOUN*
illness caused by bacteria or other toxins in food

food processor *NOUN* **food processors**
an electrical device with blades for cutting or mixing food

foodstuff *NOUN* **foodstuffs**
something that can be used as food

fool *NOUN* **fools**
1 a stupid person; someone who acts unwisely
2 a jester or clown
3 a creamy pudding of crushed fruit mixed with cream or custard

a fool's paradise is happiness you achieve only by ignoring things that are awkward or difficult

fool *VERB* **fools, fooling, fooled**
to trick or deceive someone

to fool about or **around** is to behave in a joking way, or to play about

foolhardy *ADJECTIVE*
a foolhardy person or action is bold but foolish; reckless

▷ **foolhardiness** *NOUN*

WORD HISTORY from Old French *fol* 'fool' and *hardi* 'bold'

foolish *ADJECTIVE*
without good sense or judgement; unwise

▷ **foolishly** *ADVERB*
▷ **foolishness** *NOUN*

foolproof *ADJECTIVE*
easy to use, do, or carry out without mistakes

foolscap *NOUN*
a large size of paper

WORD HISTORY said to be named after a watermark which showed a *fool's cap*, a jester's cap with bells

foot *NOUN* **feet**
1 the lower part of the leg below the ankle, on which a person or animal stands and moves
2 the lowest part or end of something, e.g. of stairs or a bed
3 a measure of length, equal to 12 inches (30.48 cm)
4 a unit of rhythm in a line of poetry, e.g. each of the four divisions in *Jack / and Jill / went up / the hill*

by or **on foot** walking rather than using a car or transport

under foot on the ground; in a position to be trodden on

foot *VERB* **foots, footing, footed**
to foot a bill is to pay for it in full

footage *NOUN*
an amount of cinema or television film

foot-and-mouth disease *NOUN*
a serious contagious disease that affects cattle, sheep, and other animals

football *NOUN* **footballs**
1 a game played by two teams which try to kick a ball into their opponents' goal
2 a large inflated leather or plastic ball used in this game
▷ **footballer** *NOUN*

foothill *NOUN* **foothills**
a low hill near the bottom of a mountain or range of mountains

foothold *NOUN* **footholds**
1 a place to put your foot when climbing
2 a small but firm position from which further progress can be made

footing *NOUN*
1 the position of your feet when you are standing on something ◆ *It is very easy to lose your footing in the deeper water.*
2 the status or nature of a relationship ◆ *We have been on a friendly footing for some years.*

footlights *PLURAL NOUN*
a row of lights along the front of the floor of a stage

footling *ADJECTIVE*
trivial or insignificant ◆ *a footling amount of money*

footman *NOUN* **footmen**
a male servant who opens doors, serves at table, etc.

WORD HISTORY originally a servant who accompanied his master on foot

footnote *NOUN* **footnotes**
a note printed at the bottom of the page in a book or article

footpath *NOUN* **footpaths**
a path for pedestrians

footprint *NOUN* **footprints**
a mark made by a foot or shoe

footsore *ADJECTIVE*
having feet that are painful or sore from walking

footstep *NOUN* **footsteps**
1 a step taken in walking or running
2 the sound of a step being taken

to follow in someone's footsteps is to follow their example

footstool *NOUN* **footstools**
a stool for resting your feet on when you are sitting

footwear *NOUN*
shoes, boots, and other coverings for your feet

footwork *NOUN*
the way in which someone moves or uses their feet in dancing or sport

foppish *ADJECTIVE*
a foppish man is very fussy about his dress and appearance
▷ **foppishly** *ADVERB*
▷ **foppishness** *NOUN*

for *PREPOSITION*
1 used to show purpose or direction ◆ *This text message is for you.* ◆ *We were heading for the bus shelter.*
2 used to show the length of time that an action takes ◆ *She spoke for fifteen minutes.* ◆ *I worked there for four years.*
3 used to show how much an item costs ◆ *Where can I buy a bike for under £50?*
4 used to show cause ◆ *I don't want to get arrested for disturbing the peace.*
5 used to show defence or support ◆ *Everyone says that she stands up for her staff.* ◆ *A majority of MPs voted for the amendment.*
6 used to mean 'in spite of' ◆ *For all their abilities and skills, the Neanderthals completely disappeared about 27,000 years ago.*
7 used to show similarity or correspondence ◆ *They took me for an amateur.*

for ever for all time; always

for *CONJUNCTION*
because; having as a reason

forage *NOUN*
1 food for horses and cattle
2 the action of foraging

forage *VERB* **forages, foraging, foraged**
to go searching for something, especially food or fuel

foray *NOUN* **forays**
a sudden attack or raid

forbear *VERB* **forbears, forbearing, forbore, forborne**
1 to forbear to do something is to avoid or refrain from doing it

We forbore to light a fire or to make any unnecessary sound. — *Sir Arthur Conan Doyle, The Lost World*

2 to be patient or tolerant
▷ **forbearance** *NOUN*

forbid *VERB* **forbids, forbidding, forbade, forbidden**
1 to order someone not to do something
2 to refuse to allow something ◆ *The committee has the authority to forbid the merger of the two companies.*

forbidding *ADJECTIVE*
a forbidding person or thing looks unfriendly or daunting

a b c d e f g h i j k l m n o p q r s t u v w x y z

SPELLING NOTE Some words pronounced **f-** begin with **ph-** (e.g. phrase)

force *NOUN* **forces**
1 strength or power
2 (*Science*) an influence, which can be measured, that causes something to move
3 an organized body of soldiers, police, or workers
4 effectiveness or validity ◆ *The court ruling has no force outside the United States.*

to come into force is to become effective or legally valid
the forces a country's military forces
in force
1 legally valid
2 in great strength or numbers

force *VERB* **forces, forcing, forced**
1 to force someone to do something is to get them to do it by using force or power
2 to force yourself to do something is to make yourself do it, despite being weak or reluctant
3 to force a door or lock is to break it open by force
4 to force a plant is to make it grow or bloom earlier than is normal

to force someone's hand is to compel them to take action

WORD HISTORY from Latin *fortis* 'strong'

force-feed *VERB* **force-feeds, force-feeding, force-fed**
1 to feed someone by force and against their will
2 to impose something inferior or undesirable on someone ◆ *The public were being force-fed propaganda and misinformation.*

forceful *ADJECTIVE*
strong and vigorous
▷ **forcefully** *ADVERB*
▷ **forcefulness** *NOUN*

forceps *NOUN* **forceps**
pincers or tongs used by dentists or surgeons

forcible *ADJECTIVE*
done by force; forceful
▷ **forcibly** *ADVERB*

ford *NOUN* **fords**
a shallow place where people or animals can walk across a river

ford *VERB* **fords, fording, forded**
to cross a river at a ford

fore *ADJECTIVE*
at or towards the front

fore *NOUN*
the front part of something

to the fore to or at the front; in or to a prominent position ◆ *The recent storms have brought the issue of climate change to the fore.*

forearm[1] *NOUN* **forearms**
the arm of a person or animal from the elbow to the wrist or fingers

forearm[2] *VERB* **forearms, forearming, forearmed**
to be forearmed is to be prepared in advance against a possible threat or danger

forebears *PLURAL NOUN*
your forebears are your ancestors

foreboding *NOUN*
a feeling that trouble is coming

Harry's sense of foreboding increased; he was sure nothing Snape had to say was going to do him any good. — *J. K. Rowling, Harry Potter and the Chamber of Secrets*

forecast *VERB* **forecasts, forecasting, forecast**
to say in advance what is likely to happen; to predict something
▷ **forecaster** *NOUN*

forecast *NOUN* **forecasts**
a prediction about something likely to happen, especially a description of future weather patterns

forecastle (*say* **fohk**- sul) *NOUN* **forecastles**
the forward part of a ship below deck, formerly where the crew had their living quarters

WORD HISTORY from the words *fore* and *castle*, because originally this part was raised up like a castle to see over the deck

forecourt *NOUN* **forecourts**
an open area in front of a large building or petrol station

forefathers *PLURAL NOUN*
your forefathers are your ancestors

forefinger *NOUN* **forefingers**
the finger next to your thumb

forefoot *NOUN* **forefeet**
an animal's front foot

forefront *NOUN*
the leading place or position ◆ *at the forefront of genetic research*

foregoing *ADJECTIVE*
preceding; previously mentioned

USAGE NOTE Take care to spell this word with an 'e'. The word *forgo* (without an 'e') has a different meaning.

foregone conclusion *NOUN* **foregone conclusions**
a result that can be foreseen easily or is bound to happen

foreground *NOUN*
(*Art*) the part of a scene, picture, or view that is nearest to you (SEE ALSO **background**)

foreground *VERB* **foregrounds, foregrounding, foregrounded**
to emphasize or draw attention to something by putting it in the foreground

forehand *NOUN* **forehands**
a stroke made in tennis or other sports with the palm of the hand turned forwards

forehead (*say* **for**- hed) *NOUN* **foreheads**
the part of your face above your eyes

foreign *ADJECTIVE*
1 belonging to or in another country
2 an action or behaviour that is foreign to someone is not part of their natural behaviour or character

foreigner *NOUN* **foreigners**
a person from another country

foreleg *NOUN* **forelegs**
an animal's front leg

forelock *NOUN* **forelocks**
a lock of hair growing just above a person's forehead

foreman *NOUN* **foremen**
1 a worker in charge of a group of other workers
2 a member of a jury who is in charge of the jury's discussions and who speaks on its behalf

foremost *ADJECTIVE, ADVERB*
first in position or rank; most important

forename *NOUN* **forenames**
a person's first name

forensic (*say* fer- **en**- sik) *ADJECTIVE*
1 to do with or used in lawcourts
2 involving medical knowledge or science needed in legal matters or police investigations ◆ *forensic evidence*

WORD HISTORY from Latin *forum*, a place where courts of law were held

forerunner *NOUN* **forerunners**
a person or thing that comes before another and prepares the way ◆ *ARPANET, the forerunner of the Internet, was established in 1969.*

foresee *VERB* **foresees, foreseeing, foresaw, foreseen**
to realize or predict a future event

foreseeable *ADJECTIVE*
a foreseeable event is one that can be predicted or foreseen
for the foreseeable future for as long as can be seen or planned at the moment

foreshadow *VERB* **foreshadows, foreshadowing, foreshadowed**
to be a sign of something that is to come

foreshorten *VERB* **foreshortens, foreshortening, foreshortened**
(*Art*) to draw an object with some lines shortened to give an effect of distance or depth
▷ **foreshortening** *NOUN*

foresight *NOUN*
the ability to realize what is likely to happen in the future and be prepared for it

foreskin *NOUN* **foreskins**
the fold of skin covering the end of a penis

forest *NOUN* **forests**
trees and undergrowth covering a large area
▷ **forested** *ADJECTIVE*

WORD HISTORY from Latin *forestis* 'outside'

forestall *VERB* **forestalls, forestalling, forestalled**
to prevent someone from doing something or something from happening by speaking or acting first ◆ *The introduction aims to forestall criticism of the author as sexist or racist.*

WORD HISTORY from Old English *foresteall* 'an ambush'

forestry *NOUN*
the practice of planting forests and looking after them
▷ **forester** *NOUN*

foretaste *NOUN* **foretastes**
an experience of something that is to come in the future

foretell *VERB* **foretells, foretelling, foretold**
to tell about something in advance; to predict something

forethought *NOUN*
careful thought and planning for the future

forever *ADVERB*
1 for all time, or for a long time
2 continually or constantly ◆ *The politicians were forever arguing among themselves.*

forewarn *VERB* **forewarns, forewarning, forewarned**
to warn someone beforehand

forewoman *NOUN* **forewomen**
1 a female worker in charge of other workers
2 a female member of a jury who is in charge of the jury's discussions and who speaks on its behalf

foreword *NOUN* **forewords**
a short introduction at the beginning of a book

forfeit (*say* **for**- fit) *VERB* **forfeits, forfeiting, forfeited**
to pay or give up something as a penalty
▷ **forfeiture** *NOUN*

forfeit *NOUN* **forfeits**
something forfeited

WORD HISTORY from Old French *forfaire* 'to transgress'

forge[1] *NOUN* **forges**
a workshop where metals are heated and shaped, especially a blacksmith's workshop

a b c d e f g h i j k l m n o p q r s t u v w x y z

SPELLING NOTE Some words pronounced **f-** begin with **ph-** (e.g. phrase)

forge *VERB* **forges, forging, forged**
1 to shape metal by heating and hammering it
2 to make an imitation of a document or banknote in order to deceive or cheat people
▷ **forger** *NOUN*
▷ **forgery** *NOUN*

forge[2] *VERB* **forges, forging, forged**
to forge ahead is to move forward with strength or determination

forget *VERB* **forgets, forgetting, forgot, forgotten**
1 to fail to remember someone or something
2 to stop thinking or worrying about something
to forget yourself is to behave rudely or thoughtlessly

forgetful *ADJECTIVE*
a forgetful person frequently forgets things
▷ **forgetfully** *ADVERB*
▷ **forgetfulness** *NOUN*

forget-me-not *NOUN* **forget-me-nots**
a plant with small blue flowers
WORD HISTORY so called because in the Middle Ages the flower was worn by lovers

forgive *VERB* **forgives, forgiving, forgave, forgiven**
to forgive someone is to stop feeling angry towards them about something
▷ **forgiveness** *NOUN*

forgo *VERB* **forgoes, forgoing, forwent, forgone**
to give something up; to go without something ◆ *Being on a diet doesn't mean that you need to forgo the pleasure of eating out.*
USAGE NOTE See the note at *foregoing*.

fork *NOUN* **forks**
1 a small device with prongs for lifting food to your mouth
2 a large device with prongs used for digging or lifting things
3 a place where a road or river separates into two or more parts

fork *VERB* **forks, forking, forked**
1 to lift or dig something with a fork
2 a road or river forks when it separates into two or more branches
3 to follow one fork of a road or river
to fork out for something (*informal*) is to pay out money for it

fork-lift truck *NOUN* **fork-lift trucks**
a truck with two metal bars at the front for lifting and moving heavy loads

forlorn *ADJECTIVE*
left alone and unhappy ◆ *From a distance, the cottage looked abandoned and forlorn.*
▷ **forlornly** *ADVERB*
WORD HISTORY from an old word *lorn* meaning 'lost'

form *NOUN* **forms**
1 the shape, appearance, or condition of something
2 the figure or outline of a person or animal
3 the particular way in which something exists ◆ *Heat is a form of energy.*
4 the ability or performance of a sports competitor or artist at a particular time ◆ *The team has slipped from its peak form recently.*
5 a document with blank spaces for writing in information
6 a class in school
7 a long bench
in good form or **on form** in good or peak condition; performing well

form *VERB* **forms, forming, formed**
1 to shape or construct something; to create something ◆ *Some of us have decided to form a book club.*
2 to come into existence; to develop ◆ *Frost was forming on the windows.*

formal *ADJECTIVE*
1 strictly following the accepted rules or customs; ceremonious ◆ *a formal occasion* ◆ *formal dress*
2 behaving in a serious and stiff manner
▷ **formally** *ADVERB*
USAGE NOTE In this dictionary, words are marked *formal* when they are chiefly used in more serious writing or speaking.

formal and informal language

The choice between **formal** and **informal language** depends on the type of thing you are writing or saying, on how well you know the reader or listener, and on what effect you want to make. An email to a friend might begin with an informal *Hi Hermione* and end with *Cheers*; whereas a letter to someone you have never met would use more formal language (e.g. *Dear Miss Granger* and *Yours sincerely*). A word or phrase can have a synonym which is more formal (*precipitous* is more formal than *steep*), or more informal (*loo* is more informal than *toilet*).

Informal writing gives a feeling of closeness between the writer and the reader, whereas formal writing creates distance; for this reason, the passive voice is often used in formal language. Formal language also tends to use longer and more complex sentences. Compare these two examples, where the second is more formal:

You've got the job. Well done!
Your application has been successful. We would like to congratulate you upon your success on this occasion.

See also the panel on **active and passive**.

formaldehyde *NOUN*
a colourless gas used in solution as a preservative and disinfectant

formality *NOUN* **formalities**
1 formal behaviour
2 something done to obey a rule or custom ◆ *The signing of the contract was really just a formality.*

formalize *VERB* **formalizes, formalizing, formalized**
to make something formal or official
▷ **formalization** *NOUN*

USAGE NOTE This word can also be spelled formalise.

format *NOUN* **formats**
1 the shape and size of something, especially a book
2 the way something is arranged or organized
3 (*ICT*) the way data is organized for processing or storage by a computer

format *VERB* **formats, formatting, formatted**
(*ICT*) to organize data in the correct format, or prepare a disk for holding data

formation *NOUN* **formations**
1 the process of forming something
2 something that has been formed ◆ *a rock formation*
3 a special arrangement or pattern ◆ *flying in formation*

formative *ADJECTIVE*
having an important influence on how someone or something develops ◆ *His formative years were spent working on his father's steamboat.*

former *ADJECTIVE*
belonging to an earlier time

Thaddeus Valentine was Tom's hero: a former scavenger who had risen to become London's most famous archaeologist. — *Philip Reeve, Mortal Engines*

former *NOUN*
the former is the first of two people or things just mentioned (SEE ALSO **latter**)

formerly *ADVERB*
at an earlier time; previously

Formica (*say* for- **my**- ka) *NOUN*
(*trademark*) a hard heat-resistant plastic used for worktops and other surfaces

formidable (*say* **for**- mid- a- bul) *ADJECTIVE*
1 a formidable task or challenge is difficult to deal with or overcome
2 inspiring fear or awe ◆ *a formidable opponent*
▷ **formidably** *ADVERB*

WORD HISTORY from Latin *formidare* 'to fear'

formless *ADJECTIVE*
not having any distinct or regular form

He gave a great start of fright. A colossal and formless something was rushing across the field of his vision. — *Jack London, White Fang*

formula *NOUN* **formulae** or **formulas**
1 a set of chemical symbols showing what a substance consists of
2 (*Mathematics*) a rule or statement expressed in symbols or numbers

No one has ever worked out a simple formula for telling you whether a very big number is a prime number or what the next one will be. — *Mark Haddon, The Curious Incident of the Dog in the Night-Time*

3 a list of ingredients needed for making something
4 a fixed form of words for a speech or ceremony
5 one of the groups into which racing cars are placed according to the size of their engines, e.g. Formula One

formulate *VERB* **formulates, formulating, formulated**
to express an idea or plan clearly and exactly
▷ **formulation** *NOUN*

fornication *NOUN*
(*formal*) sexual intercourse between people who are not married to each other

WORD HISTORY from Latin *fornix* 'a brothel'

forsake *VERB* **forsakes, forsaking, forsook, forsaken**
1 (*formal*) to give up something; to leave a place ◆ *Some people are forsaking the suburbs and returning to the city.*
2 (*old use*) to abandon someone

forsythia *NOUN*
a shrub with yellow flowers which bloom in spring

WORD HISTORY named after the Scottish botanist, William *Forsyth* (1737–1804)

fort *NOUN* **forts**
a building made strong against attack

WORD HISTORY from Latin *fortis* 'strong'

forte❶ (*say* **for**- tay) *NOUN*
a person's forte is something they are particularly good at

forte❷ (*say* **for**- tay) *ADVERB*
(*Music*) to be played loudly

fortepiano *NOUN* **fortepianos**
(*Music*) an early form of piano

forth *ADVERB*
to go or travel forth is to go out or into view

Rosa availed herself of this favourable moment to come forth from her hiding place. — *Alexandre Dumas, The Black Tulip*

and so forth and so on

forthcoming *ADJECTIVE*
1 a forthcoming event is one which is due to happen soon
2 money or support that is forthcoming is made available when it is needed
3 someone who is forthcoming is willing to talk or give information

forthright *ADJECTIVE*
frank and outspoken

forthwith ***ADVERB***
immediately

fortification ***NOUN*** **fortifications**
1 the process of fortifying something
2 a wall or building constructed to make a place strong against attack

fortify ***VERB*** **fortifies, fortifying, fortified**
1 to make a place strong against attack, especially by building fortifications
2 to give someone additional strength or energy

fortissimo ***ADVERB***
(*Music*) to be played very loudly

fortitude ***NOUN***
courage in bearing pain or trouble

fortnight ***NOUN*** **fortnights**
a period of two weeks
▷ **fortnightly** ***ADVERB, ADJECTIVE***

WORD HISTORY from Old English *feowertene niht* 'fourteen nights'

fortress ***NOUN*** **fortresses**
a fortified building or town

fortuitous (*say* for- tew- it- us) ***ADJECTIVE***
happening by chance; accidental ◆ *They had lost contact with each other and so their meeting was completely fortuitous.*
▷ **fortuitously** ***ADVERB***

USAGE NOTE Take care not to use this word when you mean *fortunate*.

fortunate ***ADJECTIVE***
having or caused by good fortune; lucky
▷ **fortunately** ***ADVERB***

fortune ***NOUN*** **fortunes**
1 luck, especially good luck
2 prosperity or success
3 a large amount of money

Was Phileas Fogg rich? Undoubtedly. But those who knew him best could not imagine how he had made his fortune. — *Jules Verne, Around the World in Eighty Days*

to tell someone's fortune is to predict what will happen to them

WORD HISTORY from Latin *fortuna* 'luck'

forty ***NOUN, ADJECTIVE*** **forties**
the number 40, equal to four times ten
forty winks a short sleep; a nap
▷ **fortieth** ***ADJECTIVE, NOUN***

forum ***NOUN*** **forums**
1 the public square in an ancient Roman city
2 a meeting where a public discussion is held

WORD HISTORY a Latin word meaning literally 'out of doors'

forward ***ADJECTIVE***
1 going towards the front
2 placed in the front
3 someone who is forward behaves in a way that is too bold or assertive
▷ **forwardness** ***NOUN***

forward ***ADVERB***
forwards or ahead

forward ***NOUN*** **forwards**
a player who takes an attacking position in a football, rugby, or hockey team

forward ***VERB*** **forwards, forwarding, forwarded**
1 to send on a letter, parcel, or email to a new address
2 to help something to improve or make progress

forwards ***ADVERB***
1 to or towards the front
2 in the direction you are facing

USAGE NOTE The adverb *forward* is mainly used in American English. In British English, you would use *forwards*, except in the phrases *come forward, look forward to,* and *put forward.*

fossick ***VERB*** **fossicks, fossicking, fossicked**
(*Australian*) to search or rummage for things

Then, amongst the roots, he fossicked for resin. — *James Vance Marshall, Walkabout*

fossil ***NOUN*** **fossils**
the remains or traces of a prehistoric animal or plant that has been buried in the ground for a very long time and become hardened in rock

WORD HISTORY from Latin *fossilis* 'dug up'

fossil fuel ***NOUN*** **fossil fuels**
a natural fuel such as coal or gas formed in the geological past

fossilize ***VERB*** **fossilizes, fossilizing, fossilized**
to turn a plant or animal into a fossil
▷ **fossilization** ***NOUN***
▷ **fossilized** ***ADJECTIVE***

USAGE NOTE This word can also be spelled fossilise.

foster ***VERB*** **fosters, fostering, fostered**
1 to take care of and bring up a child who is not your own
2 to help a plan or enterprise grow and develop

WORD FAMILY A foster parent is an adult who fosters a child; a family which takes care of a foster child is a foster family; and a child who is taken care of in this way is a foster child.

foul ***ADJECTIVE***
1 disgusting; tasting or smelling unpleasant
2 foul weather is wet and stormy
3 foul language is offensive or obscene
4 a foul hit or move in a game is unfair and breaks the rules of play
5 colliding or entangled with something
foul-mouthed using offensive or obscene language
▷ **foully** ***ADVERB***
▷ **foulness** ***NOUN***

foul ***NOUN*** **fouls**
an action that breaks the rules of a game

foul *VERB* **fouls, fouling, fouled**
1 to make something foul or unpleasant
2 to commit a foul against a player in a game

foul play *NOUN*
1 unfair play in a game or sport
2 a violent crime, especially murder

found❶ *past tense of* **find**

found❷ *VERB* **founds, founding, founded**
1 to establish an organization or institution, especially by providing money
2 to be founded on something is to be based on it ◆ *This plot is founded on real historical events.*

WORD HISTORY from Latin *fundus* 'bottom'

foundation *NOUN* **foundations**
1 the solid base on which a building is built up
2 the basis for something
3 the founding of an organization or institution
4 a fund of money set aside for a charitable purpose

foundation stone *NOUN* **foundation stones**
a stone laid with a ceremony to celebrate the founding of a building

founder❶ *NOUN* **founders**
a person who founds an organization or institution

founder❷ *VERB* **founders, foundering, foundered**
1 a ship founders when it fills with water and sinks
2 a plan founders if it fails completely

foundling *NOUN* **foundlings**
a child found abandoned, whose parents are not known

foundry *NOUN* **foundries**
a factory or workshop where metal or glass is made

fount *NOUN* **founts**
1 (*poetic*) a fountain
2 a source of something good or desirable ◆ *a fount of wisdom*

fountain *NOUN* **fountains**
1 an ornamental structure in which a jet of water shoots up into the air
2 a structure providing a supply of drinking water in a public place

fountain pen *NOUN* **fountain pens**
a pen that can be filled with a supply of ink

four *NOUN, ADJECTIVE* **fours**
the number 4, next after three
on all fours on your hands and knees

fourteen *NOUN, ADJECTIVE* **fourteens**
the number 14, next after thirteen
▷ **fourteenth** *ADJECTIVE, NOUN*

fourth *ADJECTIVE*
next after third
▷ **fourthly** *ADVERB*

fourth *NOUN* **fourths**
1 the fourth person or thing
2 one of four equal parts of a thing; a quarter
3 (*Music*) an interval or chord spanning four alphabetical notes, e.g. C to F

four-wheel drive *NOUN*
a vehicle transmission system which provides power directly to all four wheels

fowl *NOUN* **fowls**
a bird, especially one kept on a farm for its eggs or meat

fox *NOUN* **foxes**
a wild animal that looks like a dog with a pointed snout, reddish fur, and a bushy tail

fox *VERB* **foxes, foxing, foxed**
(*informal*) to deceive or puzzle someone ◆ *The last question on the test really foxed me.*

foxglove *NOUN* **foxgloves**
a tall plant with purple or white flowers

WORD HISTORY so called because the flowers look like the fingers of a glove

foyer (*say* **foy**- ay) *NOUN* **foyers**
the entrance hall of a theatre, cinema, or hotel

WORD HISTORY a French word meaning 'hearth' or 'home'

fracas (*say* **frak**- ah) *NOUN*
a noisy quarrel or disturbance

fraction *NOUN* **fractions**
1 (*Mathematics*) a number that is not a whole number, e.g. $\frac{1}{2}$ or 0.5
2 a tiny part of something

We can only know about a fraction of the things that go on in the universese. — *Mark Haddon, The Curious Incident of the Dog in the Night-Time*

▷ **fractional** *ADJECTIVE*
▷ **fractionally** *ADVERB*

fractious (*say* **frak**- shus) *ADJECTIVE*
irritable or bad-tempered
▷ **fractiously** *ADVERB*
▷ **fractiousness** *NOUN*

fracture *NOUN* **fractures**
the breaking of something, especially of a bone

fracture *VERB* **fractures, fracturing, fractured**
to break something, especially a bone

WORD HISTORY from Latin *fractus* 'broken'

fragile *ADJECTIVE*
easy to break or damage
▷ **fragility** *NOUN*

a b c d e f g h i j k l m n o p q r s t u v w x y z

fragment (*say* **frag**- ment) ***NOUN*** **fragments**
1 a small piece broken off
2 a small part of something ◆ *I can only remember a fragment of the song.*
▷ **fragmentary** ***ADJECTIVE***

fragment (*say* frag- **ment**) ***VERB*** **fragments, fragmenting, fragmented**
1 to break something into fragments
2 to break up into fragments
▷ **fragmentation** ***NOUN***
▷ **fragmented** ***ADJECTIVE***

WORD HISTORY from Latin *fractus* 'broken'

fragrant ***ADJECTIVE***
having a pleasant smell
▷ **fragrance** ***NOUN***

frail ***ADJECTIVE***
not strong, physically weak

Gilly looked very frail, struggling to lift the full bucket from the well, but Adam resisted the thought of helping her. — *Mollie Hunter, The Thirteenth Member*

▷ **frailty** ***NOUN***

frame ***NOUN*** **frames**
1 a holder that fits round the outside of a picture
2 a rigid structure that supports something
3 a human or animal body

The curtains were drawn back and he could see the portly frame of Mr Speedwell standing with his back to the pane. — *Tim Bowler, Starseeker*

4 each of the single photographs that a cinema film or video is made from

a frame of mind is the way you think or feel at a particular time

frame ***VERB*** **frames, framing, framed**
1 to put a frame on or round something
2 an object is framed by something that surrounds it, or against which it stands out

Jude threw open the front door but was halted in his tracks by the presence of two police officers, framed by the darkness outside. — *Malorie Blackman, Noughts and Crosses*

3 to construct or express something in words

My head was swimming so wildly that I could not frame a coherent answer. — *John Buchan, The Thirty-Nine Steps*

4 (*informal*) to frame an innocent person is to make them seem guilty by arranging false evidence

framework ***NOUN*** **frameworks**
1 a frame supporting something
2 a basic plan or system

franc ***NOUN*** **francs**
a unit of money in Switzerland, and formerly in France and some other countries

franchise ***NOUN*** **franchises**
1 the right to vote in elections
2 a licence to sell a firm's goods or services in a certain area

frank ***ADJECTIVE***
making your thoughts and feelings clear to people; candid
▷ **frankly** ***ADVERB***
▷ **frankness** ***NOUN***

frank ***VERB*** **franks, franking, franked**
to frank a letter or parcel is to mark it to show that postage has been paid

WORD HISTORY from Latin *francus* 'free'

frankfurter ***NOUN*** **frankfurters**
a smoked sausage

WORD HISTORY from *Frankfurt*, a city in Germany where it was originally made

frankincense ***NOUN***
a sweet-smelling gum burnt as incense

WORD HISTORY from Old French *franc encens* 'finest incense'

frantic ***ADJECTIVE***
wildly agitated or excited

The men had a frantic distracted look, and kept colliding with each other on the narrow platform. — *William Nicholson, Firesong*

▷ **frantically** ***ADVERB***

fraternal (*say* fra- **tern**- al) ***ADJECTIVE***
to do with brothers; brotherly
▷ **fraternally** ***ADVERB***

WORD HISTORY from Latin *frater* 'brother'

fraternity ***NOUN*** **fraternities**
1 a brotherly feeling
2 a group of people who have the same interests or occupation

fraternize ***VERB*** **fraternizes, fraternizing, fraternized**
to fraternize with other people is to be friendly towards them and socialize with them
▷ **fraternization** ***NOUN***

USAGE NOTE This word can also be spelled fraternise.

fraud ***NOUN*** **frauds**
1 the crime of swindling people
2 a dishonest trick
3 a person who is not what they claim to be; an impostor

fraudulent (*say* **fraw**- dew- lent) ***ADJECTIVE***
involving fraud; deceitful or dishonest
▷ **fraudulently** ***ADVERB***
▷ **fraudulence** ***NOUN***

fraught *ADJECTIVE*
1 an action that is fraught with danger or hazard is very dangerous or hazardous

Every journey between your world and ours is fraught with hazards and is not to be undertaken lightly. — *Mary Hoffman, Stravaganza: City of Masks*

2 you feel fraught if you are tense or upset

WORD HISTORY from an earlier meaning 'loaded with freight'

fray❶ *NOUN* **frays**
(*literary*) a fight or conflict ◆ *With the election looming, both parties are getting ready for the fray.*

WORD HISTORY shortened from *affray*

fray❷ *VERB* **frays, fraying, frayed**
1 fabric frays when it becomes ragged so that loose threads show
2 to fray fabric is to make it ragged
3 a person's temper or nerves fray when they become strained or upset

WORD HISTORY from a French word, related to our word *friction*

freak *NOUN* **freaks**
1 a very strange or abnormal person, animal, or thing
2 a person who is obsessed with a particular thing

We had this lecturer though, he was a real Blake freak. He was on about it every day. Everythin' he said, honest, everything was related to Blake. — *Willy Russell, Educating Rita*

▷ **freakish** *ADJECTIVE*
▷ **freaky** *ADJECTIVE*
▷ **freakily** *ADVERB*

freak *VERB* **freaks, freaking, freaked**
(*informal*) to freak, or freak out, is to panic suddenly

I was so freaked out by what Mr Gianini said, I couldn't even say anything. I just sat there and felt myself turning all red. — *Meg Cabot, The Princess Diaries*

freckle *NOUN* **freckles**
a small light brown spot on the skin
▷ **freckled** *ADJECTIVE*

WORD HISTORY from an Old Norse word

free *ADJECTIVE* **freer, freest**
1 able to do what you want or go where you want; not tied up or kept as a prisoner
2 not costing anything
3 not fixed ◆ *Tape the sides to the container, leaving one end free.*
4 to be free of something is to be unaffected by it, or to not possess it ◆ *The main roads are still relatively free of snow.*
5 available; not being used or occupied
6 not having any commitments or things to do ◆ *Are you free next Saturday?*
7 to be free with money or possessions is to give out or share them generously

to be free and easy is to be relaxed or casual
to have a free hand is to have the right to act as you choose
▷ **freely** *ADVERB*

free *VERB* **frees, freeing, freed**
1 to set someone or something free
2 to remove something that is unwelcome or a burden to someone ◆ *The police report freed him from suspicion.*
3 to release or disentangle something that is caught up

freedom *NOUN* **freedoms**
1 being free; independence
2 unrestricted use of a place or facility ◆ *Students have the freedom of the library.*

freehand *ADJECTIVE*
a freehand drawing is done without a ruler or without tracing

freehold *NOUN*
the possession of land or a house as its absolute owner, not as a tenant renting from a landlord

freelance *ADJECTIVE*
self-employed and available to do work for several companies

freelance *VERB* **freelances, freelancing, freelanced**
to be self-employed and work as a freelance
▷ **freelancer** *NOUN*
▷ **freelance** *NOUN* a freelance worker

WORD HISTORY from an earlier meaning of a mercenary soldier who carried a 'free lance'

Freemason *NOUN* **Freemasons**
a member of an international order set up to promote fellowship, with elaborate secret ceremonies
▷ **Freemasonry** *NOUN*

WORD HISTORY originally, a society of stonemasons

free-range *ADJECTIVE*
1 free-range hens are not kept in small cages but are allowed to move about freely
2 free-range eggs are ones laid by these hens

freestyle *NOUN*
a sporting competition or race in which the competitors may choose from a wide range of styles or techniques

free verse *NOUN*
(*Language*) poetry that does not rhyme or have a regular rhythm

freeware *NOUN*
(*ICT*) software that can be downloaded from the Internet and used free of charge

freewheel *VERB* **freewheels, freewheeling, freewheeled**
to ride a bicycle without pedalling

a b c d e f g h i j k l m n o p q r s t u v w x y z

SPELLING NOTE Some words pronounced **f-** begin with **ph-** (e.g. phrase)

freeze *VERB* **freezes, freezing, froze, frozen**
1 to turn into ice; to become covered with ice
2 to feel extremely cold
3 to suddenly stand completely still
4 to freeze wages or prices is to keep them at a fixed level
5 (*Drama*) to pause the running of a film at a particular point, so that the action stops temporarily

freeze *NOUN* **freezes**
1 a period of freezing weather
2 the freezing of wages or prices

freezer *NOUN* **freezers**
a refrigerator in which food can be frozen quickly and stored

freezing point *NOUN* **freezing points**
the temperature at which a liquid freezes

freight (*say* frayt) *NOUN*
goods transported as cargo
WORD HISTORY from an Old Dutch word, related to our word *fraught*

freighter *NOUN* **freighters**
a ship or aircraft used for carrying cargo

French *ADJECTIVE*
to do with France or its people

French *NOUN*
the language of France, also used as a first language in some other countries

French words in English

French words have been borrowed into English since the time of the Norman Conquest in the 11th century. The Normans who settled in England (and later Scotland) spoke a dialect of Norman French, and French was spoken by people in the ruling classes throughout the Middle Ages, leading to an influx of French vocabulary into English. Some terms which were borrowed from French at an early date are *commerce, damage, honour, justice, labour, marriage, money, receive,* and *regard*. The word *tennis* is thought to come from French *tenez!*, a call meaning 'receive (the ball)'; and the tennis term *deuce* comes from French *deus* 'two'. More recent borrowings from French have kept their original spelling, such as *gateau* (which still retains its French plural form, *gateaux*) and *derailleur*. Several French phrases are also used in English in their original form, e.g. *au fait, déjà vu, en masse*, and *joie de vivre*.

French dressing *NOUN*
a salad dressing of seasoned oil and vinegar

French fries *PLURAL NOUN*
(*American*) deep-fried potato chips

French toast *NOUN*
(*American*) bread dipped in a mixture of egg and milk and fried

French window *NOUN* **French windows**
a long window that serves as a door on an outside wall

frenetic *ADJECTIVE*
fast-paced and energetic

frenzy *NOUN*
wild excitement or agitation
▷ **frenzied** *ADJECTIVE*
▷ **frenziedly** *ADVERB*
WORD HISTORY from Greek *phren* 'the mind'

frequency *NOUN* **frequencies**
1 the fact of being frequent or happening often ◆ *This is a small community, and people move around with great frequency.*
2 how often something happens ◆ *What is the frequency of buses to the city centre?*
3 (*Science*) the number of vibrations made each second by a wave of sound, radio, or light

frequent (*say* **freek**- went) *ADJECTIVE*
happening often
▷ **frequently** *ADVERB*

frequent (*say* frik- **went**) *VERB* **frequents, frequenting, frequented**
to visit a place, or be seen there, often

> There was no law, not even an unwritten law, against frequenting the Chestnut Tree Café, yet the place was somehow ill-omened. — *George Orwell, Nineteen Eighty-four*

WORD HISTORY from Latin *frequens* 'crowded'

fresco *NOUN* **frescoes** or **frescos**
a picture painted on a wall or ceiling before the plaster is dry
WORD HISTORY from Italian *affresco* 'on the fresh (plaster)'

fresh *ADJECTIVE* **fresher, freshest**
1 newly made, produced, or harvested; not stale
2 not preserved by being tinned, frozen, or salted ◆ *fresh orange juice*
3 fresh air is cool and refreshing
4 full of energy and not tired
5 fresh water is not salty
6 impudent or cheeky
▷ **freshly** *ADVERB*
▷ **freshness** *NOUN*

freshen *VERB* **freshens, freshening, freshened**
1 to make something fresh
2 to become fresh
to freshen up (*informal*) is to wash or tidy yourself quickly

freshwater *ADJECTIVE*
a freshwater fish or creature lives in a river or lake, not the sea

fret[1] *VERB* **frets, fretting, fretted**
to worry or be upset about something

> Now, chin up, don't fret. You're not the first girl in the world to be in this pickle and unfortunately you won't be the last. — *Julie Bertagna, The Opposite of Chocolate*

▷ **fretful** *ADJECTIVE*
▷ **fretfully** *ADVERB*

fret❷ *NOUN* **frets**
a bar or ridge on the fingerboard of a guitar or similar instrument

fretsaw *NOUN* **fretsaws**
a very narrow saw used for cutting patterns in thin wood
WORD HISTORY from French *frete* 'trellis'

fretwork *NOUN*
carved ornamental work in wood, done with a fretsaw

friar *NOUN* **friars**
a man who is a member of a Roman Catholic religious order and has vowed to live a life of poverty
WORD HISTORY from French *frère* 'brother'

friary *NOUN* **friaries**
a building or community of friars

friction *NOUN*
1 the action of rubbing one thing against another
2 (*Science*) the resistance that one surface or object meets when moving over another
3 bad feeling between people; quarrelling
▷ **frictional** *ADJECTIVE*
WORD HISTORY from Latin *fricare* 'to rub'

Friday *NOUN*
the day of the week following Thursday
WORD HISTORY from Old English *Frigedaeg* 'day of Frigga', a Norse goddess

fridge *NOUN* **fridges**
a refrigerator

friend *NOUN* **friends**
1 a person you like and who likes you
2 someone who helps or supports an organization such as a museum or gallery
▷ **friendless** *ADJECTIVE*

friendly *ADJECTIVE* **friendlier, friendliest**
behaving like a friend; kind and pleasant
▷ **friendliness** *NOUN*

friendly *NOUN* **friendlies**
a sports match that is not part of a formal competition

friendship *NOUN* **friendships**
friendly feelings between people; being friends

frieze (*say* freez) *NOUN* **friezes**
(*Art*) a band of sculpture or decoration round the top of a wall or building
WORD HISTORY from a Latin word referring to sculpture from Phrygia in Asia Minor (now Turkey), because Phrygia was famous for its decorative patterns

frigate *NOUN* **frigates**
a small warship

fright *NOUN* **frights**
1 sudden great fear
2 (*informal*) a person or thing that looks ridiculous ◆ *I must look an absolute fright!*

frighten *VERB* **frightens, frightening, frightened**
1 to make someone afraid
2 to become afraid ◆ *Rabbits are timid and shy and may frighten easily.*
3 to be frightened of someone or something is to fear them

frightful *ADJECTIVE*
1 horrifying, terrifying
2 (*informal*) extreme; extremely bad ◆ *Your hair is in a frightful mess.*
▷ **frightfully** *ADVERB*

frigid *ADJECTIVE*
1 extremely cold
2 unfriendly; not affectionate
▷ **frigidly** *ADVERB*
▷ **frigidity** *NOUN*

frill *NOUN* **frills**
1 a decorative gathered or pleated trimming on a dress, skirt, or curtain
2 something extra that is pleasant but unnecessary ◆ *Budget airlines have eliminated standard frills like on-board catering.*
▷ **frilled** *ADJECTIVE*
▷ **frilly** *ADJECTIVE*

fringe *NOUN* **fringes**
1 a decorative edging with many threads hanging down loosely
2 a straight line of hair hanging down over the forehead
fringe benefits are extra benefits for an employee in addition to wages or salary
on the fringe or **fringes** on the outer edge of something
▷ **fringed** *ADJECTIVE*

fringe *VERB* **fringes, fringing, fringed**
1 to decorate something with a fringe
2 to form a fringe or edge to something

frisk *VERB* **frisks, frisking, frisked**
1 to run your hands or a detecting device over a person to check for things hidden on them
2 to jump or run about playfully
WORD HISTORY from Old French *frisque* 'lively'

frisky *ADJECTIVE* **friskier, friskiest**
playful or lively
▷ **friskily** *ADVERB*
▷ **friskiness** *NOUN*

frisson (*say* free- son) *NOUN*
a thrill of excitement or fear
WORD HISTORY a French word meaning 'a shiver'

fritter❶ *NOUN* **fritters**
a slice of meat, potato, or fruit coated in batter and fried
WORD HISTORY from Latin *frictum* 'fried'

a b c d e f g h i j k l m n o p q r s t u v w x y z

SPELLING NOTE Some words pronounced **f-** begin with **ph-** (e.g. phrase)

fritter ❷ *VERB* **fritters, frittering, frittered**
to fritter something away to fritter away time or money is to spend or waste it on trivial things

WORD HISTORY from an old word *fritters* 'fragments'

frivolous *ADJECTIVE*
without a serious purpose; light-hearted when you should be serious
▷ **frivolously** *ADVERB*
▷ **frivolity** *NOUN*

frizzy *ADJECTIVE* **frizzier, frizziest**
frizzy hair has a texture of tight curls
▷ **frizziness** *NOUN*

fro *ADVERB*
to and fro backwards and forwards

frock *NOUN* **frocks**
a girl's or woman's dress

frog *NOUN* **frogs**
a small cold-blooded animal, with long hind legs for jumping, that can live both in water and on land
to have a frog in your throat is to be temporarily hoarse and unable to speak

frogman *NOUN* **frogmen**
a swimmer equipped with a rubber suit, flippers, and breathing apparatus for swimming and working underwater

frogmarch *VERB* **frogmarches, frogmarching, frogmarched**
to force someone to move forward by holding their arms from behind and pushing them

frolic *NOUN* **frolics**
a lively cheerful game or entertainment
▷ **frolicsome** *ADJECTIVE*

frolic *VERB* **frolics, frolicking, frolicked**
to play about in a lively cheerful way

WORD HISTORY from Dutch *vrolijk* 'joyously'

from *PREPOSITION*
1 used to show a starting point in space, time, or order ◆ *We are flying from Edinburgh to Paris.* ◆ *He works from 9 to 5 o'clock.* ◆ *My daughter can count from one to twenty now.*
2 used to show source or origin ◆ *You can fill the kettle from the cold water tap.*
3 used to show separation or release ◆ *Remove the battery from the camera.* ◆ *The legendary computer hacker has been released from prison.*
4 used to show difference ◆ *How do you tell one twin from the other?*
5 used to show cause ◆ *They were all suffering from exhaustion.*

frond *NOUN* **fronds**
a leaf-like part of a fern, palm tree, or other plant

WORD HISTORY from Latin *frondis* 'of a leaf'

front *NOUN* **fronts**
1 the part or side that comes first or is the most important or furthest forward
2 a road or promenade along the seashore
3 the place where fighting is happening in a war
4 a particular area of activity or concern ◆ *I've had some good news on the job front.*
5 something serving as a cover for secret or illegal activities ◆ *The website is simply a front for getting hold of your personal bank details.*
6 the leading edge of an advancing mass of cold or warm air

front *ADJECTIVE*
of the front; in front

front *VERB* **fronts, fronting, fronted**
1 to face or have the front towards something ◆ *This popular holiday hotel fronts a sandy beach.*
2 to host a television programme

frontage *NOUN*
the front side of a building, or the land in front of this

front bench *NOUN*
the seats at the front on each side of the House of Commons, where members of the cabinet and shadow cabinet sit
▷ **frontbencher** *NOUN*

frontier *NOUN* **frontiers**
the boundary between two countries or regions

frontispiece *NOUN* **frontispieces**
an illustration opposite the title page of a book

WORD HISTORY from Latin *frontispicium* 'façade'

front-runner *NOUN* **front-runners**
the contestant who seems most likely to succeed in a race, competition, or election

frost *NOUN* **frosts**
1 powdery ice that forms on things in freezing weather
2 weather with a temperature below freezing point

frost *VERB* **frosts, frosting, frosted**
1 to cover something with frost
2 (*American*) to cover a cake with icing
to frost over a surface frosts over when it becomes covered with frost

frostbite *NOUN*
harm done to the body by exposure to very cold weather
▷ **frostbitten** *ADJECTIVE*

frosted glass *NOUN*
glass made cloudy so that you cannot see clearly through it

frosting *NOUN*
(*American*) sugar icing for cakes

frosty ***ADJECTIVE*** **frostier, frostiest**
1 cold with frost
2 a frosty look or remark is unfriendly or unwelcoming
▷ **frostily** ***ADVERB***
▷ **frostiness** ***NOUN***

froth ***NOUN***
a white mass of tiny bubbles on a liquid
▷ **frothy** ***ADJECTIVE***

froth ***VERB*** **froths, frothing, frothed**
to form a froth; to go bubbly

frown ***VERB*** **frowns, frowning, frowned**
to wrinkle your forehead because you are angry or worried
to frown on or **upon something** is to disapprove of it

frown ***NOUN*** **frowns**
a frowning movement or look

frugal (*say* **froo**- gal) ***ADJECTIVE***
1 a frugal person is careful and economical with money
2 small and meagre; costing very little money ◆ *Soups can make a healthy yet frugal meal.*
▷ **frugally** ***ADVERB***
▷ **frugality** ***NOUN***

fruit ***NOUN*** **fruits** or **fruit**
1 the seed container that grows on a tree or plant and is often used as food
2 the fruits of an effort or enterprise are its eventual results or rewards ◆ *Four or five years on, we are finally seeing the fruits of our investment.*

fruit ***VERB*** **fruits, fruiting, fruited**
a tree or plant fruits when it produces fruit

fruitful ***ADJECTIVE***
producing good results ◆ *The show ended with a lively and fruitful discussion about the future of television.*
▷ **fruitfully** ***ADVERB***
▷ **fruitfulness** ***NOUN***

fruition (*say* froo- **ish**- on) ***NOUN***
something comes to fruition when you achieve it and it is successful

fruitless ***ADJECTIVE***
a fruitless attempt or effort is one that produces no results
▷ **fruitlessly** ***ADVERB***
▷ **fruitlessness** ***NOUN***

fruit machine ***NOUN*** **fruit machines**
a gambling machine worked by putting a coin in a slot

fruity ***ADJECTIVE*** **fruitier, fruitiest**
1 like or containing fruit
2 a fruity voice is deep and rich
▷ **fruitiness** ***NOUN***

frumpish or **frumpy** ***ADJECTIVE***
dressed in a dowdy and unattractive way
WORD HISTORY from an old meaning of *frump* 'a bad-tempered woman'

frustrate ***VERB*** **frustrates, frustrating, frustrated**
1 to prevent someone from doing something, and so make them annoyed and upset
2 to prevent a plan or action from being successful ◆ *The unpredictable Antarctic weather frustrated the expedition's plans.*
WORD HISTORY from Latin *frustra* 'in vain'

frustration ***NOUN***
a feeling of annoyance when you have been prevented from doing something

fry[1] ***VERB*** **fries, frying, fried**
1 to cook food in very hot fat
2 food fries when it is being cooked in very hot fat
▷ **fryer** ***NOUN***

fry[2] ***PLURAL NOUN***
very young fishes

frying pan ***NOUN*** **frying pans**
a shallow pan for frying things

FTP ***ABBREVIATION***
(*ICT*) file transfer protocol, a procedure for transfering data over a network

fuchsia (*say* **few**- sha) ***NOUN*** **fuchsias**
an ornamental plant with bright red, pink, or purple flowers that hang down
WORD HISTORY from Leonard *Fuchs* (1501–66), a German botanist

fudge ***NOUN***
a soft sweet made of milk, sugar, and butter

fudge ***VERB*** **fudges, fudging, fudged**
1 to fudge something is to put it together in a makeshift or inadequate way
2 to fudge is to avoid giving a clear answer

fuel ***NOUN*** **fuels**
1 something that is burnt to produce heat or power
2 something that causes or increases anger or other strong feelings

fuel ***VERB*** **fuels, fuelling, fuelled**
1 to supply something with fuel
2 to strengthen a feeling or belief ◆ *Their remarks fuelled suspicions that they had something to hide.*

fug ***NOUN***
(*informal*) a stuffy or smoky atmosphere in a room
▷ **fuggy** ***ADJECTIVE***
▷ **fugginess** ***NOUN***

fugitive (*say* **few**- jit- iv) ***NOUN*** **fugitives**
a person who is running away, especially from the police

fugue (*say* fewg) ***NOUN*** **fugues**
(*Music*) a piece of music in which tunes are repeated in a carefully developed pattern

fulcrum ***NOUN*** **fulcrums** or **fulcra**
the point on which a lever rests

fulfil *VERB* **fulfils, fulfilling, fulfilled**
1 to fulfil a condition or requirement is to meet or satisfy it
2 to fulfil a promise is to carry it out
3 to fulfil a prediction or prophecy is to make it come true
4 to give someone a feeling of satisfaction
▷ **fulfilment** *NOUN*

full *ADJECTIVE*
1 containing as much or as many people or things as possible ◆ *The auditorium was full ten minutes before the film was due to start.*
2 to be full of people or things is to contain many of them

Imshi took Lirael to the Robing Room, a huge room full of all the equipment, weapons and miscellaneous items the librarians needed.
— Garth Nix, Lirael

3 a full story, description, or picture is complete and comprehensive
4 at the greatest or highest level possible ◆ *The radiators are all on full.*
5 a full skirt or dress fits loosely and has many folds or pleats
in full with nothing left out; completely ◆ *They have paid in full.*
▷ **fullness** *NOUN*

full *ADVERB*
completely and directly ◆ *When I turned the corner, the wind caught me full in the face.*

full-blown *ADJECTIVE*
fully developed

full moon *NOUN* **full moons**
the moon when you can see the whole of it as a bright disc

full stop *NOUN* **full stops**
the dot used as a punctuation mark at the end of a sentence or an abbreviation

full stops

A **full stop** (also called a **period**) shows where a sentence ends, when the sentence is neither a question nor an exclamation:
Our story begins in 1914, on the eve of the First World War.
It can also be used to indicate a complete break between single words or phrases that are not complete sentences:
There was nothing left of the cake. Not a crumb. Not a particle. Nothing.
Full stops go within quotation marks in direct speech:
He said, 'I'll meet you outside the cinema.'
and within parentheses when these surround a complete sentence:
The waiter arrived with a plate of toast. (I had ordered waffles.)
A full stop is also used to mark an abbreviation (e.g. *Mon.* = Monday). This is no longer necessary for common abbreviations, like *Mr, Mrs*, and *Dr*.

full-time *ADJECTIVE, ADVERB*
for all the normal working hours of the day ◆ *a full-time job*

fully *ADVERB*
completely; to the limit

fully fledged *ADJECTIVE*
fully trained or developed

fulminate *VERB* **fulminates, fulminating, fulminated**
to protest loudly and angrily
▷ **fulmination** *NOUN*

WORD HISTORY from Latin *fulminis* 'of lightning'

fulsome *ADJECTIVE*
fulsome praise or thanks is overdone or excessive

USAGE NOTE Take care not to use *fulsome praise* to mean 'generous praise'.

fumble *VERB* **fumbles, fumbling, fumbled**
to fumble with an object is to hold or handle it clumsily

A hand thrust beyond the broken glass, fumbling with the lock and sliding the window up. *— Buffy the Vampire-Slayer: The Harvest*

fume *VERB* **fumes, fuming, fumed**
1 to give off fumes
2 to fume or be fuming is to be extremely angry

fumes *PLURAL NOUN*
strong-smelling smoke or gas

fumigate (*say* **few- mig- ayt**) *VERB* **fumigates, fumigating, fumigated**
to disinfect a place using fumes
▷ **fumigation** *NOUN*

fun *NOUN*
amusement or enjoyment
to make fun of someone or **something** is to make people laugh at them or it

function *NOUN* **functions**
1 the particular purpose or activity that a person or thing is meant for ◆ *What is the function of this button?*
2 an important social event or ceremony
3 a basic operation of a computer or calculator
4 (*Mathematics*) a variable quantity whose value depends on the value of other variable quantities ◆ *X is a function of Y and Z.*

function *VERB* **functions, functioning, functioned**
to perform a function; to work properly

functional *ADJECTIVE*
1 working properly
2 practical without being decorative or luxurious ◆ *The bathroom is small but functional.*
▷ **functionally** *ADVERB*

fund *NOUN* **funds**
1 an amount of money collected or kept for a special purpose
2 a stock or supply of something

fund *VERB* **funds, funding, funded**
to supply a person, organization, or project with money

fundamental *ADJECTIVE*
1 forming the basis or foundation of something
2 very important, essential
▷ **fundamentally** *ADVERB*

fundamentalism *NOUN*
strict observation of traditional beliefs in any religion
▷ **fundamentalist** *NOUN*

fundamentals *PLURAL NOUN*
the basic facts or principles of a subject or situation

funeral *NOUN* **funerals**
the ceremony of burying or cremating a dead person
▷ **funerary** *ADJECTIVE*

funereal (*say* few- **neer**- ee- al) *ADJECTIVE*
suitable for a funeral; gloomy or depressing

funfair *NOUN* **funfairs**
a fair consisting of amusements and sideshows

fungicide *NOUN* **fungicides**
a substance that kills fungus

fungus *NOUN* **fungi** (*say* **fung**- eye)
a plant without leaves or flowers that grows on other plants or on decayed material, such as mushrooms, toadstools, and moulds
▷ **fungal** *ADJECTIVE*

funk❶ *VERB* **funks, funking, funked**
(*old use*) to be afraid of doing something and avoid it

funk❷ *NOUN*
a style of popular music with a strong rhythm, based on jazz and blues

funky *ADJECTIVE* **funkier, funkiest** (*informal*)
1 unusually modern and stylish
2 funky music has a strong dance rhythm

funnel *NOUN* **funnels**
1 a metal chimney on a ship or steam engine
2 a tube that is wide at the top and narrow at the bottom to help you pour things into a narrow opening

funny *ADJECTIVE* **funnier, funniest**
1 that makes you laugh or smile
2 strange or odd ◆ *a funny smell*
▷ **funnily** *ADVERB*

funny bone *NOUN* **funny bones**
part of your elbow which produces a tingling feeling if you knock it

fun run *NOUN* **fun runs**
(*informal*) a sponsored run done for charity

fur *NOUN* **furs**
1 the soft hair that covers some animals
2 animal skin with the fur on it, used for clothing; fabric that looks like animal fur

furbish *VERB* **furbishes, furbishing, furbished**
to polish or clean something; to improve the appearance of something

furious *ADJECTIVE*
1 very angry

> I'm telling you, there's nothing that makes the rich so furious as being mocked and insulted in the newspapers. — *Roald Dahl, Vengeance Is Mine Inc.*

2 violent or intense ◆ *a furious debate about the true nature of evolution*
▷ **furiously** *ADVERB*

furl *VERB* **furls, furling, furled**
to roll up a sail, flag, or umbrella
WORD HISTORY from Old French *ferlier* 'to bind firmly'

furlong *NOUN* **furlongs**
a measure of distance, equal to one-eighth of a mile or 220 yards
WORD HISTORY from Old English *furlang* 'furrow long', the length of a furrow in a common field

furlough (*say* **ferl**- oh) *NOUN* **furloughs**
a time when a soldier is not on duty and is allowed to return to his or her own country

furnace *NOUN* **furnaces**
a type of large oven that produces great heat, especially for melting metals or making glass

furnish *VERB* **furnishes, furnishing, furnished**
1 to provide a room or house with furniture
2 to provide or supply someone with something

> A few sticks of driftwood furnished them with a fire that thawed down through the ice and left them to eat supper in the dark. — *Jack London, The Call of the Wild*

furnishings *PLURAL NOUN*
furniture, curtains, and fittings for a room or house

furniture *NOUN*
tables, chairs, and other movable things that you need in a house, school, or office

furore (*say* few- **ror**- ee) *NOUN*
an excited or angry uproar
WORD HISTORY from Latin *furor* 'madness'

furrow *NOUN* **furrows**
1 a long cut in the ground made by a plough or other implement
2 a groove
3 a deep wrinkle in the skin

furrow *VERB* **furrows, furrowing, furrowed**
to make furrows in something

furry *ADJECTIVE* **furrier, furriest**
like fur; covered with fur
▷ **furriness** *NOUN*

a b c d e f g h i j k l m n o p q r s t u v w x y z

SPELLING NOTE Some words pronounced **f-** begin with **ph-** (e.g. phrase)

further *ADVERB, ADJECTIVE*
1 at or to a greater distance; more distant
2 more; additional ◆ *For further details about the event, please contact the press office.*
USAGE NOTE See the note at *farther*.

further *VERB* **furthers, furthering, furthered**
to help something to progress ◆ *a great opportunity to further your career*
▷ **furtherance** *NOUN*

further education *NOUN*
education for people above school age

furthermore *ADVERB*
also; moreover

furthest *ADVERB, ADJECTIVE*
at or to the greatest distance; most distant
USAGE NOTE See the note at *farther*.

furtive *ADJECTIVE*
stealthy; trying not to be seen

He looked round him with a furtive and stealthy air, as one who dreads pursuit. Then he vanished over the hill. — *Sir Arthur Conan Doyle, The Hound of the Baskervilles*

▷ **furtively** *ADVERB*
▷ **furtiveness** *NOUN*
WORD HISTORY from Latin *furtivus* 'stolen'

fury *NOUN* **furies**
wild anger; rage

furze *NOUN*
gorse shrubs

fuse ❶ *NOUN* **fuses**
a safety device containing a short piece of wire that melts if too much electricity is passed through it

fuse *VERB* **fuses, fusing, fused**
1 an electrical device fuses when it stops working because a fuse has melted
2 to fuse things is to blend them together, especially through melting
WORD HISTORY from Latin *fusum* 'melted'

fuse ❷ *NOUN* **fuses**
a length of material that burns easily, used for setting off an explosive
WORD HISTORY from Latin *fusus* 'spindle', because originally the material was put in a tube

fuselage (*say* few- zel- ah*zh*) *NOUN* **fuselages**
the body of an aircraft
WORD HISTORY a French word meaning 'shaped like a spindle'

fusillade (*say* few- zil- ayd) *NOUN* **fusillades**
1 an outburst of rapid gunfire
2 a rapid series of questions

fusion *NOUN*
1 the action of blending or uniting things
2 the uniting of atomic nuclei, which releases energy

fuss *NOUN* **fusses**
1 unnecessary excitement or bustle
2 angry complaints about something
to make a fuss of someone is to treat them with kindness and attention

fuss *VERB* **fusses, fussing, fussed**
to be too anxious about something that is not important ◆ *He kept fussing with his hair and checking it in the mirror.*

fussy *ADJECTIVE* **fussier, fussiest**
1 worrying too much about something that is not important
2 choosing very carefully; hard to please
3 a fussy design is overly elaborate and full of unnecessary details
▷ **fussily** *ADVERB*
▷ **fussiness** *NOUN*

fusty *ADJECTIVE* **fustier, fustiest**
smelling stale or stuffy
▷ **fustiness** *NOUN*

futile (*say* few- tyl) *ADJECTIVE*
useless or pointless; having no result ◆ *There is a view that dieting is futile and that exercise is a better way.*
▷ **futility** *NOUN*
WORD HISTORY from Latin *futilis* 'leaking'

futon (*say* foo- ton) *NOUN* **futons**
a light mattress on a wooden frame, used as a couch or bed
WORD HISTORY a Japanese word

future *NOUN*
1 the time that is still to come
2 a person's future is the series of events that will happen to them later in life
3 (*Grammar*) the tense of a verb that indicates something happening in the future, expressed by using *shall*, *will*, or *be going to*

future *ADJECTIVE*
belonging or referring to the future

futuristic *ADJECTIVE*
very modern, as if belonging to the future rather than the present ◆ *An eye-catching futuristic building hosts the new arts centre.*

fuzz *NOUN*
1 something fluffy or frizzy in texture
2 (*informal*) the fuzz are the police

fuzzy *ADJECTIVE* **fuzzier, fuzziest**
1 like fuzz; covered with fuzz
2 a fuzzy picture or image is blurred and not clear
▷ **fuzzily** *ADVERB*
▷ **fuzziness** *NOUN*

fuzzy logic *NOUN*
logic in which a proposition can be applied in some cases and not others, rather than simply being true or false

Gg

gabble *VERB* **gabbles, gabbling, gabbled**
to talk very fast, so that it is difficult to be understood

gable *NOUN* **gables**
the pointed triangular part at the top of an outside wall, between two sloping roofs
▷ **gabled** *ADJECTIVE*

gad *VERB* **gads, gadding, gadded**
(*informal*) to gad about is to have a lot of fun in different places

gadget *NOUN* **gadgets**
a small tool or device

> There are all sorts of gadgets I'd like to give young Alex. I'm always working on new ideas. — *Anthony Horowitz, Scorpia*

▷ **gadgetry** *NOUN*

Gaelic (*say* gay- lik) *NOUN*
(*Language*) the Celtic languages of Scotland and Ireland

gaff *NOUN*
to blow the gaff is to reveal a plot or secret

gaffe *NOUN* **gaffes**
an obvious and embarrassing mistake

gag *NOUN* **gags**
1 a piece of cloth put into a person's mouth or tied over it to prevent them speaking
2 a joke or funny story

gag *VERB* **gags, gagging, gagged**
1 to put a gag on someone to prevent them speaking
2 to prevent someone from speaking or expressing an opinion ◆ *The Government is trying to gag its critics.*
3 to choke or retch ◆ *The stench made Benjamin and me gag.*

gaggle *NOUN* **gaggles**
1 a flock of geese
2 a random or disorganized group of people

> Behind them the dock was crowded with sightseers and aviators, and even a little gaggle of airship-spotters. — *Philip Reeve, Mortal Engines*

gaiety *NOUN*
being light-hearted and cheerful

gaily *ADVERB*
in a light-hearted and cheerful way

gain *VERB* **gains, gaining, gained**
1 to obtain or achieve something that you want or did not have before ◆ *The party gained 20 seats in the general election.* ◆ *There was nothing to be gained by arguing further.* ◆ *He gained a reputation as a practical joker.*
2 (*literary*) to reach or arrive at a place ◆ *At last we gained the shore.*
3 a clock or watch gains when it shows a time later than the correct time
to gain on someone is to come closer to them when following or chasing them

gain *NOUN* **gains**
something that you gain or obtain, especially an increase in wealth

gainful *ADJECTIVE*
a gainful activity or employment is activity or work that earns money
▷ **gainfully** *ADVERB*

gait *NOUN* **gaits**
a way of walking or running ◆ *He shuffled along with an unsteady gait.*

gaiter *NOUN* **gaiters**
a covering of leather or cloth for the lower part of the leg

gala (*say* **gah**- la) *NOUN* **galas**
1 a festival or celebration
2 a special sports competition, especially in swimming

galah (*say* ga- **lah**) *NOUN*
a small Australian cockatoo with a grey back and rosy pink head

galaxy *NOUN* **galaxies**
a system of billions of stars held together by gravity
▷ **galactic** (*say* ga- **lak**- tik) *ADJECTIVE*

WORD HISTORY originally used to refer to the Milky Way: from Greek *galaxias* 'milky'

gale *NOUN* **gales**
a very strong wind

gall (*say* gawl) *NOUN*
to have the gall to do something is to be bold or cheeky enough to do it

gall *VERB* **galls, galling, galled**
to annoy or humiliate someone ◆ *It galled him to know he was no longer needed.*

gallant (*say* **gal**- lant) *ADJECTIVE*
1 brave or heroic ◆ *The gallant army fought on.*
2 courteous towards women
▷ **gallantly** *ADVERB*
▷ **gallantry** *NOUN*

a b c d e f g h i j k l m n o p q r s t u v w x y z

SPELLING NOTE Some words with a hard **g-** sound begin with **gh-** (e.g. ghost) or **gu-** (e.g. guess)

gall bladder *NOUN* **gall bladders**
an organ attached to the liver, in which bile is stored

galleon *NOUN* **galleons**
a large Spanish sailing ship used in the 16th and 17th centuries

gallery *NOUN* **galleries**
1 a room or building for showing or selling paintings or other works of art
2 the highest balcony in a cinema or theatre
3 a long room or passage
4 a platform jutting out from the wall in a church or hall

WORD HISTORY from Italian *galleria* 'gallery' or 'church porch', perhaps from the name of *Galilee* in ancient Palestine. A church porch furthest from the altar was called a *galilee*, because Galilee was the province furthest from Jerusalem.

galley *NOUN* **galleys**
1 an ancient type of ship driven by oars
2 the kitchen in a ship or aircraft

galling (*say* **gawl**- ing) *ADJECTIVE*
annoying or humiliating

gallivant *VERB* **gallivants, gallivanting, gallivanted**
to go about in search of pleasure

gallon *NOUN* **gallons**
a unit used to measure liquids, equal to 8 pints or 4.55 litres

USAGE NOTE In America a gallon is smaller than in Britain, equal to 3.79 litres.

gallop *NOUN* **gallops**
1 the fastest pace of a horse or other four-legged animal
2 a fast ride on a horse

gallop *VERB* **gallops, galloping, galloped**
to go or ride at a gallop

gallows *NOUN* **gallows**
a framework of uprights and a crosspiece, with a noose for hanging criminals

galore *ADVERB*
in large numbers or in a large amount ◆ *There will be biscuits and cakes galore.*

galoshes *PLURAL NOUN*
a pair of waterproof shoes worn over ordinary shoes

galvanize *VERB* **galvanizes, galvanizing, galvanized**
1 to shock or stimulate someone into action
2 to coat iron with zinc to protect it from rust
▷ **galvanization** *NOUN*

USAGE NOTE This word can also be spelled galvanise.

WORD HISTORY named after an Italian scientist, Luigi *Galvani*, who discovered that muscles move because of electricity in the body

gambit *NOUN* **gambits**
1 an action or remark that someone starts with to gain an advantage
2 a kind of opening move in chess in which a player sacrifices a piece in order to gain an advantage for the other pieces

gamble *VERB* **gambles, gambling, gambled**
1 to bet on the result of a game, race, or other event
2 to take risks in the hope of gaining an advantage
▷ **gambler** *NOUN*

gamble *NOUN* **gambles**
1 a bet or chance ◆ *He was not prepared to take a gamble.*
2 a risky undertaking ◆ *The political gamble backfired.*

gambol *VERB* **gambols, gambolling, gambolled**
to jump or skip about in play

game *NOUN* **games**
1 a form of play or sport, especially one with rules
2 a section of a long game such as tennis or whist
3 (*informal*) a scheme or plan; a trick ◆ *I'm not sure what their game is.*
4 wild animals or birds hunted for sport or food
to give the game away is to reveal a secret

game *ADJECTIVE*
1 able and willing to do something ◆ *I'm game if you are.*
2 brave
▷ **gamely** *ADVERB*

gamekeeper *NOUN* **gamekeepers**
a person employed to protect game birds and animals, especially from poachers

games *PLURAL NOUN*
1 a meeting for sporting contests
2 athletics or sports as a subject taught at school

gaming *NOUN*
1 the activity of gambling
2 the activity of playing computer games

gamma *NOUN*
(*Language*) the third letter of the Greek alphabet, equivalent to Roman *G, g*

gamma rays *PLURAL NOUN*
(*Science*) very short X-rays emitted by radioactive substances

gammon *NOUN*
a kind of ham

gamut (*say* **gam**- ut) *NOUN*
the complete range or scope of anything from beginning to end ◆ *They just run the whole gamut of electronic dance music.*

WORD HISTORY originally the name for a musical scale like the modern tonic sol- fa system, in which *gamma-ut* was the name of the note below *ut* and later the name for the scale as a whole. *Gamma-ut* was eventually shortened to *gamut*

gander *NOUN* **ganders**
a male goose

gang *NOUN* **gangs**
1 a group of people who do things together
2 a group of criminals
3 a group of young people who cause trouble and fight other groups

gang *VERB* **gangs, ganging, ganged**
to gang up on someone is to form a group to fight or oppose them

gangling or **gangly** *ADJECTIVE*
tall, thin, and awkward-looking

Norbert is ... thin and gangly, his arms and legs like white string loosely knotted at the elbows and knees. — *Nicky Singer, Feather Boy*

gangplank *NOUN* **gangplanks**
a plank that can be moved into place to enable people to walk on or off a boat

gangrene (*say* **gang**- green) *NOUN*
(*Medicine*) decay of body tissue in a living person, resulting from restricted circulation or from an infection

gangster *NOUN* **gangsters**
a member of a violent criminal gang

gangway *NOUN* **gangways**
1 a passage for people to pass between rows of seats, e.g. in a theatre or aircraft
2 a movable bridge placed so that people can walk on or off a ship

gannet *NOUN* **gannets**
a large mainly white seabird which catches fish by diving into the sea

gaol (*say* jayl) *NOUN* **gaols**
another spelling of **jail**
▷ **gaol** *VERB*
▷ **gaoler** *NOUN*

gap *NOUN* **gaps**
1 a break or opening in something continuous such as a hedge or fence

The heart of flame leapt nimbly across the gap between the trees and then went swinging and flaring along the whole row of them. — *William Golding, Lord of the Flies*

2 an interval or break
3 a wide difference in ideas

gape *VERB* **gapes, gaping, gaped**
1 to stare in wonder or amazement with your mouth open
2 to be wide open

garage (*say* **ga**- rah*zh* or **ga**- rij) *NOUN* **garages**
1 a building for keeping a motor vehicle or vehicles
2 a place where petrol is sold and vehicles are repaired and serviced

garb *NOUN*
special or distinctive clothing

garbage *NOUN*
rubbish, especially household rubbish

garbed *ADJECTIVE*
dressed in a particular way ◆ *The archers are garbed in robes of pure white.*

garble *VERB* **garbles, garbling, garbled**
to give a confused account of a message or story so that it is misunderstood

WORD HISTORY from Arabic *garbala* 'to sift' (because the real facts are 'sifted out')

garden *NOUN* **gardens**
a piece of ground next to a house, for growing flowers, fruit, or vegetables, and for relaxing out of doors
▷ **gardener** *NOUN*
▷ **gardening** *NOUN*

gargantuan (*say* gar- **gan**- tew- an) *ADJECTIVE*
(*Literary*) huge; gigantic

WORD HISTORY from *Gargantua*, the name of a giant in a book written by the French writer Rabelais in the 16th century

gargle *VERB* **gargles, gargling, gargled**
to hold a liquid at the back of the mouth and breathe air through it to wash the inside of the throat
▷ **gargle** *NOUN*

gargoyle *NOUN* **gargoyles**
an ugly or comical face or figure carved on a building, especially on a waterspout

WORD HISTORY from French *gargouille* 'throat' (because the water passes through the throat of the figure)

garish (*say* **gair**- ish) *ADJECTIVE*
very bright and showy
▷ **garishly** *ADVERB*

garland *NOUN* **garlands**
a wreath of flowers worn on the head or hung as a decoration

garland *VERB* **garlands, garlanding, garlanded**
to decorate something with a garland

garlic *NOUN*
a plant with a bulb divided into smaller sections (called *cloves*), which have a strong smell and taste and are used for flavouring food

garment *NOUN* **garments**
a piece of clothing

garner *VERB* **garners, garnering, garnered**
(*formal*) to gather or collect something ◆ *I garnered information from various friends.* ◆ *The proposal failed to garner public support.*

garnet *NOUN* **garnets**
a dark red stone used as a gem

garnish *VERB* **garnishes, garnishing, garnished**
to decorate something, especially food

a b c d e f g h i j k l m n o p q r s t u v w x y z

garnish *NOUN*
something used to decorate food or give it extra flavour

garret *NOUN* **garrets**
a small dingy attic room

garrison *NOUN* **garrisons**
1 a body of troops placed in a town or fort to defend it
2 the building occupied by these troops

garrison *VERB* **garrisons, garrisoning, garrisoned**
to put a garrison in a place to defend it

garrotte (*say* ga- **rot**) *NOUN* **garrottes**
1 a metal collar for strangling a person condemned to death, formerly used in Spain
2 a cord or wire used for strangling a victim

garrotte *VERB* **garrottes, garrotting, garrotted**
to strangle someone with a garrotte

garrulous (*say* **ga**- rool- us) *ADJECTIVE*
extremely talkative
▷ **garrulousness** *NOUN*

garter *NOUN* **garters**
a band of elastic worn round the leg to hold up a sock or stocking

gas *NOUN* **gases**
1 a substance (such as oxygen or hydrogen), which can move freely and is not liquid or solid at ordinary temperatures
2 a gas that can be burned, used for lighting, heating, or cooking
3 (*American*) gasoline

gas *VERB* **gasses, gassing, gassed**
1 to kill or injure someone with gas
2 (*informal*) to chatter idly

gasbag *NOUN* **gasbags**
(*informal*) a person who talks a lot

gas chamber *NOUN* **gas chambers**
an airtight room that can be filled with poisonous gas to kill people or animals

gaseous (*say* gas- ee- us) *ADJECTIVE*
in the form of a gas

gash *NOUN* **gashes**
a long deep cut or wound

Stanley brought his fingers up the side of his neck. He felt his wet blood and a pretty big gash just below his ear. — *Louis Sachar, Holes*

gash *VERB* **gashes, gashing, gashed**
to make a gash in something

gasket *NOUN* **gaskets**
a flat ring or sheet of soft material for sealing a joint between metal surfaces in machinery

gasoline *NOUN*
(*American*) petrol

gasometer (*say* gas- **om**- it- er) *NOUN* **gasometers**
a large round tank in which gas is stored

gasp *VERB* **gasps, gasping, gasped**
1 to breathe in suddenly when you are shocked or surprised ◆ *She gasped as she stepped into the icy water.*
2 to struggle to breathe with your mouth open when you are tired or ill
3 to speak in a breathless way
▷ **gasp** *NOUN*

gassy *ADJECTIVE*
fizzy

gastric *ADJECTIVE*
(*Medicine*) to do with the stomach

gastronomy (*say* gas- **tron**- om- ee) *NOUN*
the art or practice of good eating
▷ **gastronomic** *ADJECTIVE*

gastropod *NOUN* **gastropods**
(*Biology*) an animal (e.g. a snail or slug) that moves by means of a fleshy 'foot' on its stomach

WORD HISTORY from Greek *gaster* 'stomach' and *pous, podos* 'foot'

gate *NOUN* **gates**
1 a hinged barrier, used to close an opening in a wall or fence
2 a barrier for controlling the flow of water in a dam or lock
3 an exit by which passengers board an aircraft from a terminal building
4 the number of people admitted to a sports ground for an event

gateau (*say* **gat**- oh) *NOUN* **gateaus** or **gateaux**
a large rich cream cake

gatecrash *VERB* **gatecrashes, gatecrashing, gatecrashed**
to go to a private party without being invited
▷ **gatecrasher** *NOUN*

gateway *NOUN* **gateways**
1 an opening containing a gate
2 a frame or arch built over a gate
3 (*ICT*) a device for connecting computer networks

gather *VERB* **gathers, gathering, gathered**
1 to come or bring together ◆ *Crowds had gathered along the sides of the road.*
2 to collect; to obtain or accumulate gradually ◆ *The purpose of the unit is to gather data on medical problems.*
3 to collect crops as harvest; to pick plants or produce
4 to understand or learn ◆ *I gather you know each other.*
5 to pull cloth into folds by running a thread through it

to gather speed is to move faster and faster
to gather your thoughts is to concentrate on something you have to say or think about

gathering *NOUN* **gatherings**
an assembly or meeting of people; a party

gaudy *ADJECTIVE*
very showy and bright ◆ *She wore big boots and a gaudy anorak.*
▷ **gaudily** *ADVERB*
▷ **gaudiness** *NOUN*

gauge (*say* gayj) *NOUN* **gauges**
1 an instrument that measures and displays an amount or level
2 a standard measurement
3 the distance between the rails on a railway track

gauge *VERB* **gauges, gauging, gauged**
1 to measure something
2 to estimate or form a judgement about something

gaunt *ADJECTIVE*
lean and haggard, especially from neglect or old age ◆ *His face was gaunt and unshaven.*
▷ **gauntness** *NOUN*

gauntlet❶ *NOUN* **gauntlets**
a glove with a wide cuff covering the wrist
to throw down the gauntlet is to offer a challenge

WORD HISTORY from French *gant* 'glove'

gauntlet❷ *NOUN*
to run the gauntlet is to face criticism or hostility from a lot of people

WORD HISTORY from a former military and naval punishment in which the victim was made to pass between two rows of men who struck him as he passed. The word was originally *gantlope* and is from Swedish *gatlopp* meaning 'passageway'.

gauze *NOUN*
1 thin transparent woven material
2 a very fine wire mesh
▷ **gauzy** *ADJECTIVE*

gay *ADJECTIVE*
1 homosexual, or to do with homosexual people
2 (*old use*) cheerful or bright
▷ **gayness** *NOUN*

USAGE NOTE Nowadays the most common meaning of *gay* is 'homosexual'. You can still use the older meanings 'cheerful' and 'bright' but they sound old-fashioned and are becoming much less common than alternative words such as *cheerful*, *happy*, and *carefree*.

gaze *VERB* **gazes, gazing, gazed**
to look at something steadily for a long time

gaze *NOUN* **gazes**
a long steady look

gazelle *NOUN* **gazelles** or **gazelle**
a small antelope from Africa or Asia, usually fawn and white and with curved horns

gazette *NOUN* **gazettes**
the official journal or newspaper of an organization

WORD HISTORY from Italian *gazetta de la novità* 'a halfpenny worth of news' (a *gazetta* was a Venetian coin of small value)

gazetteer (*say* gaz- it- **eer**) *NOUN* **gazetteers**
a list or index of place names

GCSE *ABBREVIATION*
General Certificate of Secondary Education

GDP *ABBREVIATION*
(*Economics*) gross domestic product, the total value of goods produced and services provided within a country during one year

gear *NOUN* **gears**
1 a toothed wheel, especially one of a set in a motor vehicle that transmits power from the engine to the road wheels
2 (*informal*) equipment or apparatus ◆ *Bring your bathing gear.*
3 (*informal*) clothing

gear *VERB* **gears, gearing, geared**
to gear one thing to another is to make them match or relate to one another
to be geared up is to be fully prepared or equipped for something ◆ *Some people are not geared up to living independently.*

gearbox *NOUN* **gearboxes**
a set of gears in a casing, fitted in a motor vehicle

Geiger counter (*say* **gy**- ger) *NOUN* **Geiger counters**
an instrument that detects and measures radioactivity

WORD HISTORY named after a German physicist, Hans *Geiger*, who helped to develop the instrument

gel *NOUN* **gels**
a jelly-like substance used for cosmetic or medicinal purposes

gel *VERB* **gels, gelling, gelled**
an idea or plan gels when it begins to take shape or to work well

gelatin or **gelatine** *NOUN*
a clear jelly-like substance made by boiling animal tissue and used to make jellies and other foods and in photographic film
▷ **gelatinous** (*say* jil- **at**- in- us) *ADJECTIVE*

geld *VERB* **gelds, gelding, gelded**
to castrate a male animal

gelding *NOUN* **geldings**
a castrated horse or other male animal

gelignite (*say* **jel**- ig- nyt) *NOUN*
a high explosive made from nitroglycerine

gem *NOUN* **gems**
1 a cut and polished precious stone
2 an outstanding person or thing

a b c d e f g h i j k l m n o p q r s t u v w x y z

gemsbok *NOUN*
a large African antelope with strong black-and-white head markings and long straight horns

gender *NOUN* **genders**
1 (*Grammar*) the group in which a noun is classed in the grammar of some languages, usually masculine, feminine, or neuter
2 the state of being male or female

gene (*say* jeen) *NOUN* **genes**
(*Biology*) the part of a living cell that controls which characteristics (such as the colour of hair or eyes) are inherited from parents

genealogy (*say* jeen- ee- **al**- o- jee) *NOUN* **genealogies**
1 a continuous line of descent from an ancestor
2 the study of family history and ancestors
▷ **genealogical** (*say* jeen- ee- a- **loj**- ik- al) *ADJECTIVE*

genera *plural of* **genus**

general *ADJECTIVE*
1 to do with or involving all or most people or things ◆ *Local authorities have a general duty to provide a range of services.* ◆ *There is general agreement on this issue.*
2 involving the main features and not details ◆ *The general idea is to cut costs.*
3 chief or principal ◆ *Is she the general manager here?*

in general or **as a general rule** in most cases; usually

general *NOUN* **generals**
a senior army officer

general election *NOUN* **general elections**
an election of MPs or other political representatives throughout the country

generality *NOUN* **generalities**
1 a general statement without exact details
2 the state of being general

generalize *VERB* **generalizes, generalizing, generalized**
to make a statement that is true in most cases
▷ **generalization** *NOUN*

USAGE NOTE This word can also be spelled generalise.

generally *ADVERB*
1 in most cases; usually ◆ *Ivy does not generally damage trees.*
2 in a general sense; without regard to details ◆ *I was speaking generally.*

general practitioner *NOUN* **general practitioners**
(*Medicine*) a community doctor who treats all kinds of diseases and is the first doctor that people see when they are ill

generate *VERB* **generates, generating, generated**
to cause something to exist or happen; to produce or create something

generation *NOUN* **generations**
1 the process of generating
2 a single stage in a family ◆ *The business had been in his family for four generations.*
3 all the people born at about the same time ◆ *The older generation of both families remained in London.*

generator *NOUN* **generators**
a machine for converting mechanical energy into electricity

generic (*say* jin- **e**- rik) *ADJECTIVE*
1 belonging to a whole class or group
2 (*Biology*) relating to a genus
▷ **generically** *ADVERB*

generous *ADJECTIVE*
1 willing to give things or share them
2 given freely; plentiful ◆ *generous donations to worthy causes*
▷ **generously** *ADVERB*
▷ **generosity** *NOUN*

genesis *NOUN*
the beginning or origin of something

genetic (*say* jin- **et**- ik) *ADJECTIVE*
(*Biology*) relating to genes, or to characteristics inherited from parents or ancestors
▷ **genetically** *ADVERB*

genetics *NOUN*
the study of genes and inherited characteristics

genial (*say* **jee**- nee- al) *ADJECTIVE*
friendly and cheerful
▷ **genially** *ADVERB*
▷ **geniality** (*say* jee- nee- **al**- it- ee) *NOUN*

genie (*say* **jee**- nee) *NOUN* **genies** or **genii** (*say* **jee**- nee- y)
in Arabian stories and folklore, a spirit with strange powers who normally lives in a lamp or bottle and can grant wishes when summoned

genital (*say* **jen**- it- al) *ADJECTIVE*
to do with the reproductive organs of a person or animal

genitals (*say* **jen**- it- alz) *PLURAL NOUN*
a person's or animal's external sexual organs

genius *NOUN* **geniuses**
1 an unusually clever person; a person with very great creativity or natural ability
2 a natural ability or cleverness ◆ *He has a genius for telling amusing stories.*

genocide (*say* **jen**- o- syd) ***NOUN***
the deliberate killing of large numbers of people from a particular nation or ethnic group

genome (*say* **jee**- nome) ***NOUN***
(*Science*) the complete set of an individual's chromosomes

genre (*say* zhan-ruh) ***NOUN*** **genres**
a particular kind or style of art or literature

gent ***NOUN*** **gents**
(*informal*) a gentleman

genteel (*say* jen- **teel**) ***ADJECTIVE***
trying to seem polite and refined
▷ **genteelly** ***ADVERB***
▷ **gentility** (*say* jen- **til**- it- ee) ***NOUN***

gentile ***NOUN*** **gentiles**
a person who is not Jewish

gentle ***ADJECTIVE***
1 mild or kind; not rough
2 not harsh or severe ◆ *She took gentle walks each day.* ◆ *A gentle breeze was blowing.*
▷ **gently** ***ADVERB***
▷ **gentleness** ***NOUN***

gentleman ***NOUN*** **gentlemen**
1 a well-mannered or honourable man
2 a man of good social position
3 (*formal*) a man

gentry ***PLURAL NOUN***
people of a good social position

genuine ***ADJECTIVE***
1 real; not faked or pretending
2 a genuine person is sincere and honest
▷ **genuinely** ***ADVERB***
▷ **genuineness** ***NOUN***

WORD HISTORY from Latin *genu* 'knee' (because in ancient Rome a father would take a baby on his knee to show that he accepted it as his, and the baby was described as *genuinus*)

genus (*say* **jee**- nus) ***NOUN*** **genera** (*say* **jen**- er- a)
(*Biology*) a group of similar animals or plants, higher than a species and lower than a family

geography (*say* jee- **og**- ra- fee) ***NOUN***
the study of the earth's physical features and climate, and of human activity relating to these
▷ **geographer** ***NOUN***
▷ **geographical** ***ADJECTIVE***
▷ **geographically** ***ADVERB***

geology (*say* jee- **ol**- o- jee) ***NOUN***
the study of the structure of the earth's crust and its layers
▷ **geological** ***ADJECTIVE***
▷ **geologically** ***ADVERB***
▷ **geologist** ***NOUN***

geometry (*say* jee- **om**- it- ree) ***NOUN***
(*Mathematics*) the branch of mathematics dealing with lines, angles, surfaces, and solids
▷ **geometric** ***ADJECTIVE***
▷ **geometrical** ***ADJECTIVE***
▷ **geometrically** ***ADVERB***

Georgian ***ADJECTIVE***
belonging to the time of the British kings George I–IV (1714–1830) or George V–VI (1910–52)

geranium ***NOUN*** **geraniums**
a garden plant with red, pink, or white flowers

gerbil (*say* **jer**- bil) ***NOUN*** **gerbils**
a small brown rodent with long hind legs, often kept as a pet

geriatric (*say* je- ree- **at**- rik) ***ADJECTIVE***
to do with the care of old people and their health

germ ***NOUN*** **germs**
1 (*Medicine*) a micro-organism, especially one that causes disease
2 a tiny living structure from which a plant or animal may develop
3 part of the seed of a cereal plant
4 a first stage from which something might develop ◆ *The germ of the idea can be found in her earlier writings.*

German ***ADJECTIVE***
to do with Germany or its people

German ***NOUN***
1 the language of Germany, also used as a first language in some other countries
2 a person from Germany

German words in English

Many very old words in English are similar to **German words**, because English and German are closely related. The earliest form of English (called Old English or Anglo-Saxon) was a Germanic language which was brought to the British Isles by peoples from Northern Germany in the 5th century. The words, *father*, *finger*, *hand*, and *king*, which all derive from Old English, are similar to their modern German equivalents.

But words have also been borrowed into English directly from German. For example, *haversack* comes from *Habersack*, an 'oat bag' used to carry food for horses; a *dachshund* is literally a 'badger dog'; *delicatessen* means 'delicacies to eat'; a *kindergarten* is literally a 'children garden'; and *waltz* comes from a German verb meaning 'to revolve'.

A less obvious borrowing from German is *dollar*, which comes from a German word for a silver coin; and the informal American term *dude* is thought to come from a German dialect word meaning 'a fool'.

Germanic ***NOUN***
1 a group of languages spoken in northern Europe and Scandinavia
2 an unrecorded language believed to be the ancestor of this group

SPELLING NOTE Some words with a hard **g-** sound begin with **gh-** (e.g. ghost) or **gu-** (e.g. guess)

German measles *NOUN*
(*Medicine*) an infectious disease causing a red rash; rubella

German shepherd dog *NOUN* **German shepherd dogs**
a large strong dog, often used in police work; an Alsatian

germicide *NOUN* **germicides**
a substance that kills harmful microorganisms

germinate *VERB* **germinates, germinating, germinated**
a seed germinates when it begins to develop and put out roots and shoots
▷ **germination** *NOUN*

gerund (*say* **je**- rund) *NOUN* **gerunds**
(*Language*) a form of a verb (in English ending in *-ing*) that functions as a noun, e.g. *telling* in *Do you mind my telling her?*

gestation (*say* jes- **tay**- shun) *NOUN*
(*Medicine*) the process of carrying a fetus in the womb between conception and birth

gesticulate (*say* jes- **tik**- yoo- layt) *VERB* **gesticulates, gesticulating, gesticulated**
to make dramatic movements with your hands and arms as a way of emphasizing what you are saying
▷ **gesticulation** *NOUN*

gesture (*say* **jes**- cher) *NOUN* **gestures**
1 a movement of the hand or head to express what a person feels or thinks
2 an action that shows good feelings or intentions towards someone ◆ *When his son was born, he thought it would be a fine gesture to name him after his friend.*

gesture *VERB* **gestures, gesturing, gestured**
to tell a person something by making a gesture

A lorry slowed down and its young driver stared out of the window. He ignored Gil but gestured to Sapphire that she could have a lift. — *Julie Bertagna, The Opposite of Chocolate*

get *VERB* **gets, getting, got**
1 to obtain or receive something ◆ *Selina didn't always get what she wanted.* ◆ *I was lucky to get a holiday job working in a supermarket.*
2 to become ◆ *I don't want to get involved in this mess.* ◆ *Don't get upset.* ◆ *Perhaps they will get married.* ◆ *Somehow the machine got damaged.*
3 to reach a place ◆ *Do you think Dad will get home today?*
4 to fetch or provide something ◆ *Shall I get you a drink?*
5 to put or move something into position ◆ *I can't get my shoe on.* ◆ *She couldn't get the string undone.*
6 to make or prepare something ◆ *She went in to get the tea.* ◆ *We could get a picnic ready.*
7 to persuade or order someone to do something ◆ *Get him to do some shopping.*
8 to catch or suffer from an illness
9 (*informal*) to understand ◆ *I don't get the third question.* ◆ *Don't get me wrong.*

to get away with something
1 is to steal it and escape with it
2 is to avoid being punished for what you have done

to get by (*informal*) is to manage with difficulty

to get on
1 is to make progress

'How is the Dictionary getting on?' said Winston, raising his voice to overcome the noise. — *George Orwell, Nineteen Eighty-four*

2 is to be friendly with somebody

to get over something is to recover from an illness, an injury, or something upsetting

to get up
1 is to stand from sitting or lying
2 is to get out of your bed in the morning

to get your own back (*informal*) is to have revenge

to have got to do something is to be obliged to do it

SYNONYMS (meaning 1) obtain, receive, acquire, come by, achieve, procure; (meaning 2) become, turn, grow; (meaning 3) arrive, reach, come to; (meaning 4) fetch, bring; (meaning 6) prepare, provide; (meaning 7) persuade, urge, compel; (meaning 8) catch, come down with, develop; (meaning 9) understand, grasp, comprehend

getaway *NOUN* **getaways**
to make a getaway is to escape after committing a crime

geyser (*say* **gee**- zer or **gy**- zer) *NOUN* **geysers**
1 a natural spring that shoots up columns of hot water
2 a gas-fired water heater in which water is heated rapidly as it passes through

ghastly *ADJECTIVE*
1 causing great horror or fear
2 (*informal*) very unpleasant or bad
3 looking pale and ill
▷ **ghastliness** *NOUN*

gherkin (*say* **ger**- kin) *NOUN* **gherkins**
a small cucumber used for pickling

ghetto (*say* **get**- oh) *NOUN* **ghettos**
an area of a city, often a slum area, where a minority group of people live

WORD HISTORY probably from Italian *getto* 'foundry' (because the first ghetto was established in 1516 in the site of a foundry in Venice)

ghetto blaster *NOUN* **ghetto blasters**
(*informal*) a large portable radio and CD player

ghost *NOUN* **ghosts**
the spirit of a dead person that is thought to appear to the living

ghosting *NOUN*
the appearance of a shadowy second image on a television or VDU screen

ghostly *ADJECTIVE*
like a ghost; eerie and unnatural
▷ **ghostliness** *NOUN*

ghoulish (*say* **gool**- ish) *ADJECTIVE*
enjoying watching or thinking about things such as death, murder, and disaster
◆ *Whenever he spoke, his mouth would form a ghoulish grin.*
▷ **ghoulishly** *ADVERB*
▷ **ghoulishness** *NOUN*

WORD HISTORY from Arabic *gul*, a name for a demon that eats dead bodies

giant *NOUN* **giants**
1 (in myths and fairy tales) a creature like a huge man

The three handsome giants looked down at him with wooden menace. Their skins were the colour of walnut husks, and under it muscles bulged like sacks of melons. — *Terry Pratchett, The Colour of Magic*

2 a man, animal, or plant that is much larger than the usual size

giant *ADJECTIVE*
of a kind that is very large in size

gibber (*say* **jib**- er) *VERB* **gibbers, gibbering, gibbered**
to speak very quickly without making sense, especially when shocked or terrified

gibberish (*say* **jib**- er- ish) *NOUN*
meaningless speech; nonsense

The massed voices of the witches wailed in response, and although the words were so much gibberish to Adam, the sound of them sent prickles of horror down his spine. — *Mollie Hunter, The Thirteenth Member*

gibbet (*say* **jib**- it) *NOUN* **gibbets**
1 a gallows
2 an upright post with an arm from which a criminal's body was hung after execution, as a warning to others

gibbon *NOUN* **gibbons**
a small ape from south-east Asia with long arms for swinging through trees

gibe *NOUN* **gibes**
another spelling of **jibe** *NOUN*

gibe *VERB* **gibes, gibing, gibed**
another spelling of **jibe** *VERB*

giblets (*say* **jib**- lits) *PLURAL NOUN*
the liver, heart, gizzard, and neck of a chicken or other fowl, which are taken out before it is cooked

giddy *ADJECTIVE* **giddier, giddiest**
1 having the feeling that everything is spinning round and that you might fall
2 causing this feeling ◆ *When I got to the top of the tower it was quite a giddy height.*
▷ **giddily** *ADVERB*
▷ **giddiness** *NOUN*

gift *NOUN* **gifts**
1 something you give to someone without payment; a present

Hrothgar gave Beowulf gifts, and the gifts were these: a banner of gold, a helmet that would not break, a sword as sharp as a flame. — *Robert Nye, Beowulf*

2 a natural talent or ability ◆ *She has a gift for music.*

gifted *ADJECTIVE*
having a special talent or ability

gig ❶ *NOUN* **gigs**
(*informal*) a live performance by a musician or other performer

gig ❷ *NOUN* **gigs**
a light two-wheeled carriage pulled by a single horse

gigabyte (*say* **gi**- ga- byt) *NOUN* **gigabytes**
(*ICT*) a unit of information equal to one thousand million bytes, or (more precisely) 2^{30} bytes

gigantic (*say* jy- **gan**- tik) *ADJECTIVE*
extremely large; huge

giggle *VERB* **giggles, giggling, giggled**
to laugh in a silly or nervous way

giggle *NOUN* **giggles**
1 a silly laugh
2 (*informal*) an amusing person or thing

gild *VERB* **gilds, gilding, gilded**
to cover something with a thin layer of gold or gold paint

gills *PLURAL NOUN*
the part of the body through which fish and certain other water animals breathe

gilt *NOUN*
a thin covering of gold or gold paint

gilt *ADJECTIVE*
covered with a thin layer of gold or gold paint; gold-coloured

gimlet *NOUN* **gimlets**
a small T-shaped tool with a screw tip for boring holes

gimmick *NOUN* **gimmicks**
something unusual or silly done or used just to attract people's attention

SPELLING NOTE Some words with a hard **g-** sound begin with **gh-** (e.g. ghost) or **gu-** (e.g. guess)

a b c d e f g h i j k l m n o p q r s t u v w x y z

gin❶ *NOUN*
a clear alcoholic drink flavoured with juniper berries

gin❷ *NOUN* **gins**
1 a kind of trap for catching animals
2 a machine for separating the fibres of the cotton plant from its seeds

ginger *NOUN*
1 the hot-tasting root of a tropical plant, or a flavouring made from this root, used especially in drinks and Eastern cooking
2 liveliness or energy
3 a light reddish-yellow colour
▷ **ginger** *ADJECTIVE*

ginger *VERB* **gingers, gingering, gingered**
to ginger something up is to make it more lively or exciting

gingerbread *NOUN*
a ginger-flavoured cake or biscuit

gingerly *ADVERB*
in a cautious or careful way

ginormous *ADJECTIVE*
(*informal*) enormous; very large
WORD HISTORY a blend of *gigantic* and *enormous*

gipsy *NOUN* **gipsies**
another spelling of **gypsy**

giraffe *NOUN* **giraffe** or **giraffes**
an African animal with long front legs and a very long neck, the world's tallest mammal

gird *VERB* **girds, girding, girded**
to fasten with a belt or band
to gird yourself or **your loins** is to get ready for action ◆ *They girded themselves for the hard journey ahead.*

girder *NOUN* **girders**
a large metal beam supporting part of a building or a bridge

girdle *NOUN* **girdles**
1 a belt or cord worn round the waist
2 a woman's elastic corset covering from the waist to the thigh

girl *NOUN* **girls**
1 a female child
2 a young woman
▷ **girlhood** *NOUN*
▷ **girlish** *ADJECTIVE*

girlfriend *NOUN* **girlfriends**
a person's regular female friend or lover

giro (*say* jy- roh) *NOUN*
a system of sending money directly from one bank account or post office account to another

girt *ADJECTIVE*
(*old use*) girded or encircled

girth *NOUN* **girths**
1 the distance round something
2 a band passing under a horse's body to hold the saddle in place

gist (*say* jist) *NOUN*
the essential points or general sense of what someone says

give *VERB* **gives, giving, gave, given**
1 to let someone have something, especially as a gift or without payment
2 to provide someone with information ◆ *He gave her his email address.*
3 to make or do something ◆ *Rosie gave him an affectionate kiss.*
4 to be flexible or springy; to bend or collapse when pressed

Harry struggled against the ropes binding him, but they didn't give. — *J. K. Rowling, Harry Potter and the Philosopher's Stone*

to give in is to yield or acknowledge that you are wrong or defeated

I begged and pleaded and nagged, and eventually my mother gave in and allowed me to travel to away games. — *Nick Hornby, Fever Pitch*

to give up is to stop trying

'Did Sir Edmund Hillary give up on the slopes of Everest?' she demands. 'Did Captain Scott turn back?' — *Theresa Breslin, Whispers in the Graveyard*

to give something up is to stop doing or using it
▷ **giver** *NOUN*

giveaway *NOUN* **giveaways**
(*informal*) something that reveals a secret

given *ADJECTIVE*
named or stated in advance ◆ *Work out how much you can do in a given time.*

gizzard *NOUN* **gizzards**
a bird's second stomach, in which food is ground up

glacé (*say* glas- ay) *ADJECTIVE*
iced with sugar; crystallized

glacial (*say* glay- shal) *ADJECTIVE*
icy; made of or produced by ice
▷ **glacially** *ADVERB*

glaciation (*say* glay- see- ay- shun) *NOUN*
the process or state of being covered with glaciers or ice sheets
▷ **glaciated** *ADJECTIVE*

glacier (*say* glas- ee- er) *NOUN* **glaciers**
a mass of ice that moves very slowly down a mountain valley

glad *ADJECTIVE*
1 pleased or happy; expressing joy
2 giving pleasure or happiness ◆ *We've heard the glad news.*
3 **to be glad of something** is to be grateful for it or pleased with it
▷ **gladly** *ADVERB*
▷ **gladness** *NOUN*

gladden *VERB* **gladdens, gladdening, gladdened**
to make a person glad

glade *NOUN* **glades**
an open space in a wood or forest

gladiator (*say* **glad**- ee- ay- ter) *NOUN* **gladiators**
a man trained to fight for public entertainment in ancient Rome

▷ **gladiatorial** (*say* glad- ee- at- **or**- ee- al) *ADJECTIVE*

glamorize *VERB* **glamorizes, glamorizing, glamorized**
to make something seem glamorous or romantic

USAGE NOTE This word can also be spelled glamorise.

glamorous *ADJECTIVE*
1 what makes something attractive or exciting
2 a person's beauty or attractiveness

glamour *NOUN*
attractiveness, romantic charm

glance *VERB* **glances, glancing, glanced**
1 to look at something briefly
2 to glance off something is to strike it at an angle and slide off it ◆ *The ball glanced off the player's bat.* ◆ *The sun was glancing off the gleaming rocks.*

▷ **glance** *NOUN*

gland *NOUN* **glands**
an organ of the body that separates substances from the blood so that they can be used or passed out of the body

▷ **glandular** *ADJECTIVE*

glandular fever *NOUN*
(*Medicine*) an infectious disease causing swelling of the lymph glands and long periods of tiredness

glare *VERB* **glares, glaring, glared**
1 to stare angrily or fiercely
2 to shine with a bright or dazzling light

▷ **glare** *NOUN*

glaring *ADJECTIVE*
a glaring error or mistake is one that is very obvious

glass *NOUN* **glasses**
1 a hard brittle substance that is usually transparent or translucent
2 a container for drinking from, made of glass
3 a mirror
4 a lens or optical instrument

▷ **glassy** *ADJECTIVE*

glasses *PLURAL NOUN*
a pair of lenses in a frame, worn over the eyes to help improve eyesight

glass fibre *NOUN*
a strong plastic material reinforced with embedded glass threads

glaucoma (*say* glaw- **koh**- ma) *NOUN*
a condition caused by increased pressure of fluid within the eyeball, causing gradual loss of sight

glaze *VERB* **glazes, glazing, glazed**
1 to fit a window or building with glass
2 to give a shiny surface to something
3 to lose brightness

glaze *NOUN* **glazes**
1 a shiny surface or coating, especially on pottery
2 a liquid such as milk or beaten egg, brushed on the surface of food to give it a shiny coating

glazier (*say* **glay**- zee- er) *NOUN* **glaziers**
a person whose job is to fit glass in windows

gleam *NOUN* **gleams**
1 a faint or flickering beam of soft light
2 a brief or faint feeling of an emotion, e.g. hope

gleam *VERB* **gleams, gleaming, gleamed**
to shine brightly

A fire gleamed among the dripping furze bushes like the madness in a weasel's eye. — *Terry Pratchett, Wyrd Sisters*

glean *VERB* **gleans, gleaning, gleaned**
1 to glean information is to gather it bit by bit
2 to pick up grain left by harvesters

▷ **gleaner** *NOUN*

glee *NOUN*
great and often mischievous delight

▷ **gleeful** *ADJECTIVE*
▷ **gleefully** *ADVERB*

glen *NOUN* **glens**
a narrow valley, especially in Scotland

glib *ADJECTIVE*
speaking or writing fluently but not sincerely or thoughtfully

▷ **glibly** *ADVERB*
▷ **glibness** *NOUN*

glide *VERB* **glides, gliding, glided**
1 to move along smoothly and continuously
2 to fly without using an engine
3 birds glide when they fly without beating their wings

▷ **glide** *NOUN*

glider *NOUN* **gliders**
an aircraft without an engine that flies by floating on warm air currents called thermals

glimmer *NOUN* **glimmers**
1 a faint light ◆ *There was a glimmer from the window over the stairs.*
2 a small sign or trace of something ◆ *A win on Saturday would offer them a glimmer of hope.*

glimmer *VERB* **glimmers, glimmering, glimmered**
to shine with a faint, flickering light

glimpse *NOUN* **glimpses**
a brief view

Willie peered gingerly outside to see if he could catch a glimpse of the strange boy from the Post Office. — *Michelle Magorian, Goodnight Mister Tom*

glimpse *VERB* **glimpses, glimpsing, glimpsed**
to see something briefly

glint *NOUN* **glints**
a brief flash of reflected light

glint *VERB* **glints, glinting, glinted**
to shine with small flashes of light

glisten (*say* glis- en) *VERB* **glistens, glistening, glistened**
to shine like something wet or polished

Always darkish in colour, Simon was burned by the sun to a deep tan that glistened with sweat. — *William Golding, Lord of the Flies*

glitch *NOUN* **glitches**
a sudden temporary malfunction or setback

glitter *VERB* **glitters, glittering, glittered**
to shine with tiny flashes of light; to sparkle

In the harbour one or two rowing boats lay still at anchor, and beyond the breakwater the starlight glittered on a calm sea. — *Philip Pullman, The Subtle Knife*

glitter *NOUN*
tiny sparkling pieces used for decoration

gloaming *NOUN*
(*poetic*) the evening twilight

gloat *VERB* **gloats, gloating, gloated**
to be pleased in a smug or unkind way about your own success or someone else's difficulties or failings

global *ADJECTIVE*
1 to do with the whole world; worldwide
2 affecting or involving the whole of a system or set of data
▷ **globally** *ADVERB*

globalization *NOUN*
the process of making ideas and institutions affect the whole world

USAGE NOTE This word can also be spelled globalisation.

global village *NOUN*
the world regarded as a single community linked by the Internet and other telecommunications

global warming *NOUN*
the increase in the temperature of the earth's atmosphere, caused by the greenhouse effect

globe *NOUN* **globes**
1 a map of the world shown on the surface of a sphere
2 something shaped like a ball or sphere
3 the world as a whole ◆ *The conference heard speakers from across the globe.*

globular (*say* glob- yoo- ler) *ADJECTIVE*
shaped like a globe

globule (*say* glob- yool) *NOUN* **globules**
a small rounded drop

gloom *NOUN*
1 deep darkness

Stone led us down the garden, tugged the door open and shone his little torch into the gloom. — *David Almond, Skellig*

2 sadness or despair

gloomy *ADJECTIVE* **gloomier, gloomiest**
1 almost dark, in a way that causes fear or depression
2 causing or feeling depression
▷ **gloomily** *ADVERB*
▷ **gloominess** *NOUN*

glorify *VERB* **glorifies, glorifying, glorified**
1 to give great praise or great honour to someone
2 to make a thing seem more splendid or attractive than it really is ◆ *a film that glorifies war*
3 a glorified thing is little better than the way it is described ◆ *Some local hospitals are run down to the level of glorified health centres.*
▷ **glorification** *NOUN*

glorious *ADJECTIVE*
splendid or magnificent
▷ **gloriously** *ADVERB*

glory *NOUN* **glories**
1 fame and honour won by great achievements
2 praise and thanksgiving offered to a deity
3 great beauty or magnificence

glory *VERB* **glories, glorying, gloried**
to glory in an achievement is to rejoice over it and take great pride in it

gloss❶ *NOUN* **glosses**
the shine on a smooth surface

gloss *VERB* **glosses, glossing, glossed**
to make a surface glossy

gloss❷ *VERB* **glosses, glossing, glossed**
to gloss over something is to mention a fault or mistake only briefly to make it seem less serious than it really is

glossary *NOUN* **glossaries**
a list of technical or difficult words with their meanings explained, added at the end of a book or text

glossy *ADJECTIVE* **glossier, glossiest**
smooth and shiny
▷ **glossily** *ADVERB*
▷ **glossiness** *NOUN*

glove *NOUN* **gloves**
a covering for the hand with separate parts for each finger and the thumb
▷ **gloved** *ADJECTIVE*

a b c d e f g h i j k l m n o p q r s t u v w x y z

glow *NOUN*
1 brightness and warmth without flames
2 a warm or cheerful feeling ◆ *There was a glow of recognition on his face.*

glow *VERB* **glows, glowing, glowed**
1 to shine gently with a soft warm light
2 to show great pleasure or pride by your expression

glower (*rhymes with* flower) *VERB* **glowers, glowering, glowered**
to stare angrily; to scowl

Daniel glowered rather unpleasantly at all of his children. — *Anne Fine, Madame Doubtfire*

glowing *ADJECTIVE*
a glowing report or tribute is very enthusiastic or favourable

glow-worm *NOUN* **glow-worms**
a kind of beetle of which the female gives out a greenish light in the tail to attract males

glucose *NOUN*
a form of sugar found in fruit juice and honey, and an important source of energy

glue *NOUN* **glues**
a sticky substance used for joining things together
▷ **gluey** *ADJECTIVE*

glue *VERB* **glues, gluing, glued**
1 to stick something with glue
2 to be glued to something is to pay close attention to it for a long period ◆ *They were glued to the screen for several hours.*

glum *ADJECTIVE*
miserable or depressed
▷ **glumly** *ADVERB*
▷ **glumness** *NOUN*

glut *NOUN* **gluts**
an over-large supply of something; a surfeit

glutamate (*say* gloo- ta- mate) *NOUN*
a substance used to bring out the flavour in food

gluten (*say* gloo- ten) *NOUN*
a sticky protein substance in flour

glutinous (*say* gloo- ti- nus) *ADJECTIVE*
like glue in texture; sticky

glutton *NOUN* **gluttons**
a person who eats too much
a glutton for punishment is a person who seems eager to take on difficult or unpleasant tasks
▷ **gluttonous** *ADJECTIVE*

gluttony *NOUN*
the habit of eating too much

glycerol (*say* glis- er- ol) or **glycerine** (*say* glis- er- een) *NOUN*
a thick sweet colourless liquid used in ointments and medicines and in explosives

GM *ABBREVIATION*
genetically modified

gm *ABBREVIATION*
gram

GMT *ABBREVIATION*
Greenwich Mean Time

gnarled (*say* narld) *ADJECTIVE*
a gnarled tree or back of the hand is twisted and knobbly with age

gnash (*say* nash) *VERB* **gnashes, gnashing, gnashed**
to grind your teeth together, especially in anger

gnat (*say* nat) *NOUN* **gnats**
a small two-winged fly that bites

gnaw (*say* naw) *VERB* **gnaws, gnawing, gnawed**
to keep on biting something so that it wears away

gnome (*say* nohm) *NOUN* **gnomes**
a kind of dwarf in fairy tales, usually living underground

GNP *ABBREVIATION*
(*Economics*) gross national product, the total value of goods produced and services provided by a country during one year, equal to the gross domestic product plus the net income from foreign investments

gnu (*say* noo) *NOUN* **gnu** or **gnus**
a large African antelope with a long head and a sloping back

GNVQ *ABBREVIATION*
General National Vocational Qualification

go *VERB* **goes, going, went, gone**
1 to move or travel from one place to another ◆ *She went downstairs.* ◆ *Where do you usually go for your holiday?*
2 to leave ◆ *I don't want you to go yet.*
3 to lead from one place to another ◆ *The road on the left goes to the coast.*
4 to become ◆ *The milk was going sour.* ◆ *Everyone went mad.* ◆ *The company has gone bust.*
5 to make a sound ◆ *A cannon went bang at one o'clock.*
6 to belong in some place or position ◆ *Large books go on the bottom shelf.*
7 to be used ◆ *All the money has gone.*
8 to be sold ◆ *The house went for the asking price.*
to go off
1 is to explode
2 is to become stale
3 is to stop liking something
to go on is to continue or resume something
to go out is to stop burning or shining ▸▸

SPELLING NOTE Some words with a hard **g-** sound begin with **gh-** (e.g. ghost) or **gu-** (e.g. guess)

a b c d e f g h i j k l m n o p q r s t u v w x y z

to go through something is to experience something unpleasant or difficult

SYNONYMS (meaning 1) move, walk, advance, proceed, progress; (meaning 2) leave, depart, go away, withdraw; (meaning 3) lead, take you, extend; (meaning 4) become, turn; (meaning 6) belong, be kept, be placed, have a place; (meaning 7) be used up, be spent, be exhausted

go *NOUN* **goes**
1 a turn or try at something ◆ *The teacher explains how to change a tyre, then you have a go.*
2 (*informal*) energy or liveliness ◆ *children with a lot of go*

to make a go of something is to be successful at it

to be on the go (*informal*) is to be active or busy

goad *NOUN* **goads**
a stick with a pointed end for prodding cattle to move onwards

goad *VERB* **goads, goading, goaded**
1 to stir or provoke someone into action ◆ *If you goad him into attacking you, you might regret it.*
2 to annoy or pester someone deliberately

go-ahead *NOUN*
permission to do something planned

goal *NOUN* **goals**
1 a pair of posts with a crossbar and sometimes a net, forming a space you have to send the ball into to score in football, hockey, and other team games
2 a successful shot at goal, scoring a point
3 something that you are trying to reach or achieve

goalkeeper *NOUN* **goalkeepers**
a player in football or hockey who stands in the goal and tries to keep the ball out

goanna (*say* goh- **an**- a) *NOUN*
(*Australian*) a kind of lizard

goat *NOUN* **goats**
a mammal with shaggy hair, horns, and a beard, often kept for its milk

goatee (*say* goh- **tee**) *NOUN* **goatees**
a short pointed beard

gobble *VERB* **gobbles, gobbling, gobbled**
to eat quickly and greedily

gobbledegook *NOUN*
(*informal*) meaningless or difficult technical language used by officials

go-between *NOUN* **go-betweens**
a person who acts as a messenger or negotiator between others

goblet *NOUN* **goblets**
a drinking glass with a long stem and a base

goblin *NOUN* **goblins**
a mischievous ugly elf-like creature in stories and folklore

The goblin was about a head shorter than Harry. He had a swarthy, clever face, a pointed beard and, Harry noticed, very long fingers and feet.
— *J. K. Rowling, Harry Potter and the Philosopher's Stone*

God *NOUN*
(*Religion*) the creator of the universe in Christian, Jewish, and Muslim belief

god *NOUN* **gods**
(*Religion*) a male being that is worshipped

godchild *NOUN* **godchildren**
a child that has a godparent

WORD FAMILY A female godchild is a god-daughter, and a male godchild is a godson.

goddess *NOUN* **goddesses**
1 (*Religion*) a female being that is worshipped
2 a beautiful and famous woman

godhead *NOUN*
the divine nature of God or a god

godly *ADJECTIVE* **godlier, godliest**
sincerely religious
▷ **godliness** *NOUN*

godparent *NOUN* **godparents**
a person at a child's christening who promises to look after the child's religious education

WORD FAMILY A female godparent is a godmother, and a male godparent is a godfather.

godsend *NOUN* **godsends**
a piece of unexpected good luck

goggle *VERB* **goggles, goggling, goggled**
to stare with wide-open eyes

goggles *PLURAL NOUN*
large glasses worn over the eyes to protect them from wind, water, dust, and other dangers

going *present participle* of **go**

to be going to do something is be ready or likely to do it

going *NOUN*
progress ◆ *Explaining the problem might be heavy going.*

good going quick progress ◆ *It was good going to get home before dark.*

go-kart *NOUN* **go-karts**
a kind of small lightweight racing car

gold *NOUN* **golds**
1 a yellow precious metal
2 a deep yellow colour
3 a gold medal, awarded as first prize

gold *ADJECTIVE*
1 made of gold
2 deep yellow in colour

golden *ADJECTIVE*
1 made of gold
2 coloured like gold
3 a golden opportunity is a very favourable one that comes only rarely

golden wedding *NOUN* **golden weddings**
a couple's fiftieth wedding anniversary

goldfinch *NOUN* **goldfinches**
a bird with yellow feathers in its wings

goldfish *NOUN* **goldfish**
a small red or orange fish kept in a pond or special bowl

gold leaf *NOUN*
gold that has been beaten into a very thin sheet

goldsmith *NOUN* **goldsmiths**
a person who makes gold jewellery

golf *NOUN*
an outdoor game played by hitting a small white ball with a club into a series of holes on a specially prepared ground (a **golf course** or **golf links**) with as few strokes as possible
▷ **golfer** *NOUN*
▷ **golfing** *NOUN*

gondola (*say* **gond**- ol- a) *NOUN* **gondolas**
a light flat-bottomed boat with high pointed ends, used on the canals in Venice

gondolier *NOUN* **gondoliers**
the person who steers a gondola with a long oar at the stern

gone *past participle of* **go**

gong *NOUN* **gongs**
a large metal disc that makes an echoing sound when it is hit

good *ADJECTIVE* **better, best**
1 having the right qualities; virtuous ◆ *These are good people.*
2 of the kind that people like or admire; enjoyable ◆ *I would have loved an evening to myself with a good book.*
3 favourable or pleasant ◆ *She was in a good mood that morning.*
4 substantial or convincing ◆ *He had good reasons for what he did.*
5 correct and accurate ◆ *They speak good English.*
6 kind ◆ *It was good of you to come.*
7 well behaved ◆ *Steven tried hard to be good.*
8 skilled or talented ◆ *She is a good swimmer.*
9 healthy; giving benefit ◆ *Exercise is good for you.*
10 thorough ◆ *Give it a good clean.*
11 large; considerable ◆ *It's a good distance from the shops.*

SYNONYMS (meaning 1) virtuous, moral, righteous, honest, upright; (meaning 2) fine, enjoyable, pleasant, satisfactory; (meaning 3) agreeable, friendly, pleasant, favourable; (meaning 4) valid, genuine, convincing, cogent; (meaning 6) kind, generous, considerate, obliging; (meaning 7) polite, obedient, well behaved, well mannered; (meaning 8) capable, able, proficient, accomplished, talented, skilled; (meaning 9) wholesome, beneficial, healthy; (meaning 10) thorough, complete

good *NOUN*
1 something good ◆ *They tried to do good to others.*
2 benefit or advantage ◆ *It's for their own good.*
for good for ever
no good useless or unsuccessful

goodbye *EXCLAMATION*
a word used when you leave someone or at the end of a phone call

> At seven-thirty we too closed the door behind us; Moortje, my cat, was the only living creature I said goodbye to. — *Anne Frank, The Diary of a Young Girl*

good-for-nothing *NOUN* **good-for-nothings**
a worthless or useless person

Good Friday *NOUN*
(*Religion*) the Friday before Easter, when Christians commemorate the Crucifixion of Christ

good-looking *ADJECTIVE*
attractive or handsome

goodness *NOUN*
1 the quality of being good
2 the good part of something

goods *PLURAL NOUN*
1 things that are bought and sold
2 merchandise or commercial products that are carried by rail or road

goodwill *NOUN*
a friendly or helpful feeling towards another person

goody *NOUN* **goodies** (*informal*)
1 a good person, especially a hero in a story
2 something tasty to eat

gooey *ADJECTIVE*
soft and sticky

goofy *ADJECTIVE*
(*informal*) having front teeth that stick out

goose *NOUN* **geese**
a large water bird with a long neck and webbed feet

gooseberry *NOUN* **gooseberries**
1 a small green fruit with a hairy skin that grows on a prickly bush
2 (*informal*) an unwanted extra person when two people want to be alone together

goose pimples or **goosebumps** *PLURAL NOUN*
skin that has turned rough with small bumps from fear or cold

a b c d e f g h i j k l m n o p q r s t u v w x y z

SPELLING NOTE Some words with a hard **g-** sound begin with **gh-** (e.g. ghost) or **gu-** (e.g. guess)

gore¹ *VERB* **gores, goring, gored**
a bull or other large animal gores a person or another animal when it wounds them with its horn or tusk

gore² *NOUN*
thickened blood from a cut or wound

gorge *NOUN* **gorges**
a narrow valley with steep sides

gorge *VERB* **gorges, gorging, gorged**
to eat greedily; to stuff with food

gorgeous *ADJECTIVE*
very attractive or beautiful
▷ **gorgeously** *ADVERB*

gorilla *NOUN* **gorillas**
a large powerful African ape, the largest of all the apes

USAGE NOTE Take care not to confuse this word with *guerrilla*, which can be pronounced in the same way.

gorse *NOUN*
a prickly bush with small yellow flowers

gory *ADJECTIVE*
1 covered with blood
2 involving a lot of blood and violence

gosh *EXCLAMATION*
a word used to express surprise

gosling *NOUN* **goslings**
a young goose

gospel *NOUN*
1 (*Religion*) the teachings of Jesus Christ
2 something you can trust to be true
the Gospels the first four books of the New Testament, telling of the life and teachings of Jesus Christ

WORD HISTORY from Old English *god spel* 'good news'

gospel music *NOUN*
a style of black American religious singing

gossamer *NOUN*
1 fine cobwebs made by small spiders
2 any fine delicate material

WORD HISTORY from *goose summer*, a period of fine weather in the autumn (when geese were eaten), when gossamer is very common

gossip *VERB* **gossips, gossiping, gossiped**
to talk a lot about other people

gossip *NOUN* **gossips**
1 talk, especially rumours, about other people
2 a person who enjoys gossiping
▷ **gossipy** *ADJECTIVE*

WORD HISTORY from Old English *godsibb* 'godfather' or 'godmother', and later 'close friend', i.e. someone to gossip with

got *past tense of* **get**
to have got something is to possess it or be carrying it ◆ *Have you got a pen with you?*
to have got to is to be obliged to do something

Gothic *NOUN*
the style of building common in the 12th–16th centuries, with pointed arches and decorative carving

gouache *NOUN*
(*Art*) a method of painting using opaque pigments ground in water and thickened with a glue-like substance

WORD HISTORY from Italian *guazzo*

gouge (*say* gowj) *VERB* **gouges, gouging, gouged**
to scoop or force something out roughly

On the left-hand wall is a rubble hole where a fireplace has been gouged out and the floor is strewn with paper, envelopes and smashed brick.
— Nicky Singer, Feather Boy

goulash (*say* goo- lash) *NOUN*
a spicy Hungarian meat stew flavoured with paprika

gourd (*say* goord) *NOUN* **gourds**
(*Biology*) the rounded hard-skinned fruit of a climbing plant

gourmet (*say* goor- may) *NOUN* **gourmets**
a person who knows about and enjoys good food and drink

gout *NOUN*
(*Medicine*) a disease that causes painful swelling in the legs and feet
▷ **gouty** *ADJECTIVE*

govern *VERB* **governs, governing, governed**
to be in charge of the public affairs of a country or region

governess *NOUN* **governesses**
a woman employed to teach children in a private household

government *NOUN* **governments**
1 (*Politics*) the group of people who are in charge of the public affairs of a country
2 the process of governing
▷ **governmental** *ADJECTIVE*

governor *NOUN* **governors**
1 an official who governs a town or region or who is sent to govern a colony
2 a member of the group of people who manage a school or other institution
3 the person in charge of a prison

gown *NOUN* **gowns**
1 a woman's long dress
2 a loose robe worn by lawyers, members of a university, etc.

GP *ABBREVIATION*
(*Medicine*) general practitioner

grab *VERB* **grabs, grabbing, grabbed**
to take hold of something firmly or suddenly

I ran upstairs and I grabbed my school bag and I put some food for Toby in it. — *Mark Haddon, The Curious Incident of the Dog in the Night-Time*

grace *NOUN*
1 beauty of posture and movement
2 courteous goodwill or favour
3 to have the grace to do something is to be kind or polite enough to do it, especially when you have done something wrong ◆ *At least she had the grace to apologize.*
4 a short prayer of thanks said before or after a meal

His, Her, or Your Grace the title of a duke, duchess, or archbishop

grace *VERB* **graces, gracing, graced**
to bring honour or dignity to something ◆ *The mayor himself graced the occasion with his presence.*

graceful *ADJECTIVE*
elegant in form or movement
▷ **gracefully** *ADVERB*
▷ **gracefulness** *NOUN*

gracious *ADJECTIVE*
generous and pleasant ◆ *I am pleased to accept your gracious offer.*
▷ **graciously** *ADVERB*
▷ **graciousness** *NOUN*

grade *NOUN* **grades**
1 a mark showing the quality of a student's work
2 a step in a scale of quality or value or rank

to make the grade is (*informal*) to be successful or good enough

grade *VERB* **grades, grading, graded**
to sort or divide something into grades

gradient (*say* **gray**- dee- ent) *NOUN* **gradients**
1 a sloping part of a road or railway line
2 the steepness of a slope: a gradient of 10% (or 1 in 10) rises one metre for every ten metres of its length

gradual *ADJECTIVE*
happening slowly but steadily
▷ **gradually** *ADVERB*

graduate (*say* **grad**- yoo- ayt) *VERB* **graduates, graduating, graduated**
1 to be awarded a university or college degree
2 to divide something into graded sections; to mark something with units of measurement
▷ **graduation** *NOUN*

graduate (*say* **grad**- yoo- at) *NOUN* **graduates**
a person who has a university or college degree

graffiti *NOUN*
words or drawings scribbled or sprayed on a wall

USAGE NOTE Strictly speaking, this word is a plural noun (the singular is *graffito*), so it should be used with a plural verb: *There are graffiti daubed on the wall.* However, the word is widely used nowadays as if it were a singular noun like *writing* and most people do not regard this as wrong: *There is graffiti daubed on the wall.* In many cases, you can't tell the difference: *The wall is daubed with graffiti.*

graft *NOUN* **grafts**
1 (*Biology*) a shoot from one plant or tree fixed into another to form a new growth
2 (*Medicine*) a piece of living tissue transplanted by a surgeon to replace what is diseased or damaged
3 (*informal*) hard work

graft *VERB* **grafts, grafting, grafted**
to insert or transplant as a graft

grain *NOUN* **grains**
1 a small hard seed or similar particle
2 cereal plants when they are growing or after being harvested
3 a very small amount ◆ *There is a grain of truth in the story.*
4 (also **graining**) the pattern of lines made by the fibres in a piece of wood or paper
▷ **grainy** *ADJECTIVE*

gram *NOUN* **grams**
a unit of mass or weight in the metric system

grammar *NOUN* **grammars** (*Language*)
1 the rules for using language correctly
2 a book about these rules

grammar school *NOUN* **grammar schools**
a secondary school for pupils with academic ability

grammatical *ADJECTIVE*
to do with grammar; following the rules of grammar
▷ **grammatically** *ADVERB*

gramophone *NOUN* **gramophones**
(*old use*) a record player

grampus *NOUN* **grampuses**
a large sea animal of the dolphin family

granadilla (*say* gran- a- **dil**- a) *NOUN*
a passion fruit

granary *NOUN* **granaries**
a storehouse for grain

grand *ADJECTIVE*
1 large and impressive ◆ *We stood before a grand Victorian building.*
2 fine or wonderful ◆ *It was rather grand to be having supper on the boat.*
3 most important or highest-ranking
▷ **grandly** *ADVERB*
▷ **grandness** *NOUN*

SPELLING NOTE Some words with a hard **g**- sound begin with **gh**- (e.g. ghost) or **gu**- (e.g. guess)

grandad ***NOUN*** **grandads**
(*informal*) a person's grandfather

grandchild ***NOUN*** **grandchildren**
the child of a person's son or daughter

WORD FAMILY A female grandchild is a granddaughter, and a male grandchild is a grandson.

grandeur (*say* **grand**- yer) ***NOUN***
grand and impressive beauty; splendour
◆ *I enjoyed the grandeur of the Rocky Mountains.*

grandfather ***NOUN*** **grandfathers**
the father of a person's father or mother

grandfather clock ***NOUN*** **grandfather clocks**
a clock in a tall wooden case

grandiose (*say* **grand**- ee- ohss) ***ADJECTIVE***
large and impressive; trying to seem impressive ◆ *These grandiose building plans were replaced by more realistic ones.*

grandma ***NOUN*** **grandmas**
(*informal*) a person's grandmother

grandmother ***NOUN*** **grandmothers**
the mother of a person's father or mother

grandpa ***NOUN*** **grandpas**
(*informal*) a person's grandfather

grandparent ***NOUN*** **grandparents**
a grandfather or grandmother

grand piano ***NOUN*** **grand pianos**
(*Music*) a large piano with the body and strings arranged horizontally and supported on three legs

grandstand ***NOUN*** **grandstands**
the main stand for spectators at a racecourse or sports ground

grand total ***NOUN***
the sum of other totals

grange ***NOUN*** **granges**
a large country house with farm buildings

granite ***NOUN***
a very hard kind of rock used for building

granny ***NOUN*** **grannies**
(*informal*) a person's grandmother

granny knot ***NOUN*** **granny knots**
a reef knot with the strings crossed the wrong way and so likely to slip

grant ***VERB*** **grants, granting, granted**
1 to give or allow someone what they have asked for ◆ *I only wish I could wave a wand and grant their wish.*
2 to admit something or agree that it is true ◆ *They're strange, I grant you, but they're exciting.*

to take something for granted
1 is to assume that it is true or will happen
2 is to be so used to having something that you no longer appreciate it

grant ***NOUN*** **grants**
a sum of money awarded for a special purpose

Granth (*say* grunt) ***NOUN***
the sacred scriptures of the Sikhs

granular ***ADJECTIVE***
like grains or granules

granulated ***ADJECTIVE***
in the form of small grains ◆ *granulated sugar*

granule ***NOUN*** **granules**
a small grain or particle

grape ***NOUN*** **grapes**
a small green or purple berry that grows in bunches on a vine, eaten as a fruit and used to make wine

grapefruit ***NOUN*** **grapefruit**
a large round yellow citrus fruit

grapevine ***NOUN*** **grapevines**
1 a vine on which grapes grow
2 a way by which news spreads unofficially, with people passing it on from one to another ◆ *I heard on the grapevine that you were coming home.*

graph ***NOUN*** **graphs**
(*Mathematics*) a diagram showing how two quantities or variables are related

WORD FAMILY *Graph* comes from the Greek word *graphein* meaning 'to write' or 'to draw'. Other words to do with writing and having the same origin include *autograph*, *graphic*, *graphite*, *photograph*, *seismograph*, and *telegraph*.

grapheme ***NOUN*** **graphemes**
(*Language*) a basic written or printed expression of a sound, for example *f* and *ph* to represent the same initial sound in *face* and *phase*

graphic ***ADJECTIVE***
1 to do with drawing or painting
2 a graphic account or description is lively and vivid

▷ **graphically** ***ADVERB***

graphics ***PLURAL NOUN***
(*ICT*) diagrams, lettering, and drawings, especially pictures that are produced by a computer

graphite ***NOUN***
a soft black form of carbon used for the lead in pencils, as a lubricant, and in nuclear reactors

graph paper ***NOUN***
paper printed with small squares, used for drawing graphs

grapnel ***NOUN*** **grapnels**
a heavy metal device with claws for hooking things

grapple ***VERB*** **grapples, grappling, grappled**
1 to grapple someone, or with someone, is to struggle or wrestle with them
2 to grapple something is to seize or hold it firmly
3 to grapple with a problem is to try hard to deal with it

grasp *VERB* **grasps, grasping, grasped**
1 to seize something and hold it firmly
2 to grasp an idea is to understand it

grasp *NOUN*
1 a firm hold

The knife dropped from the ghost's tenuous grasp and clattered to the floor. — Terry Pratchett, *Wyrd Sisters*

2 a person's understanding of something ◆ *a good grasp of computer science*

grasping *ADJECTIVE*
greedy for money or possessions

grass *NOUN* **grasses**
1 a plant with green blades and stalks that are eaten by animals
2 ground covered with grass; an area of lawn
▷ **grassy** *ADJECTIVE*

grasshopper *NOUN* **grasshoppers**
a jumping insect that makes a shrill chirping noise

grassland *NOUN* **grasslands**
a wide area covered in grass with few trees

grass roots *PLURAL NOUN*
the ordinary people in a political party or other group

grate ❶ *NOUN* **grates**
1 a metal framework that keeps fuel in a fireplace
2 a fireplace

grate ❷ *VERB* **grates, grating, grated**
1 to shred food into small pieces by rubbing it on a rough surface
2 to make an unpleasant noise by rubbing
3 to sound harshly
4 to grate on someone is to irritate them

grateful *ADJECTIVE*
feeling or showing that you want to thank someone for what they have done for you
▷ **gratefully** *ADVERB*

grater *NOUN* **graters**
a device with a jagged surface for grating food

gratify *VERB* **gratifies, gratifying, gratified**
1 to please or satisfy someone
2 to satisfy a feeling or desire
▷ **gratifying** *ADJECTIVE*
▷ **gratification** *NOUN*

grating *NOUN* **gratings**
a framework of metal bars placed across an opening

gratis (*say* **grah**- tiss) *ADVERB, ADJECTIVE*
free of charge

gratitude *NOUN*
a feeling of being grateful

gratuitous (*say* gra- **tew**- it- us) *ADJECTIVE*
done without good reason; uncalled for
▷ **gratuitously** *ADVERB*

gratuity (*say* gra- **tew**- it- ee) *NOUN* **gratuities**
money given in gratitude; a tip

grave ❶ *NOUN* **graves**
the place where a dead person is buried

grave ❷ *ADJECTIVE*
serious or solemn
▷ **gravely** *ADVERB*

grave accent (*rhymes with* starve) *NOUN* **grave accents**
(*Language*) a backward-sloping mark over a vowel, as in *vis-à-vis*

gravel *NOUN*
small stones mixed with coarse sand, used to make paths and roads
▷ **gravelled** *ADJECTIVE*
▷ **gravelly** *ADJECTIVE*

gravestone *NOUN* **gravestones**
a stone monument put over a grave

graveyard *NOUN* **graveyards**
a burial ground

gravitate *VERB* **gravitates, gravitating, gravitated**
to move or be attracted towards a person or place

gravitation *NOUN*
1 the process of gravitating
2 the force of gravity
▷ **gravitational** *ADJECTIVE*

gravity *NOUN*
1 (*Science*) the force that pulls everything towards the centre of the earth or towards another physical body
2 the importance or seriousness of a situation

gravy *NOUN*
a hot brown sauce made from meat juices

graze *VERB* **grazes, grazing, grazed**
1 animals graze when they feed on growing grass
2 to scrape your skin slightly
3 to touch something lightly in passing

graze *NOUN* **grazes**
a raw place where skin has been scraped

grease *NOUN*
1 any thick oily substance
2 melted fat
▷ **greasy** *ADJECTIVE*

grease *VERB* **greases, greasing, greased**
to put grease on something

SPELLING NOTE Some words with a hard **g-** sound begin with **gh-** (e.g. ghost) or **gu-** (e.g. guess)

great *ADJECTIVE*
1 very large ◆ *A great hill rose before them.*
2 well above average; exceptional ◆ *She is a person of great courage.*
3 very important or distinguished ◆ *a great statesman*
4 (*informal*) very good or enjoyable ◆ *We all had a great time.*
5 older or younger by one generation ◆ *a great-grandson*
▷ **greatly** *ADVERB*
▷ **greatness** *NOUN*

SYNONYMS (meaning 1) large, huge, big, enormous, massive, gigantic, colossal; (meaning 2) considerable, exceptional, outstanding, extraordinary; (meaning 3) famous, eminent, distinguished, celebrated, prominent; (meaning 4) enjoyable, excellent, marvellous, wonderful

Great Britain *NOUN*
the island made up of England, Scotland, and Wales, with the small islands close to it

USAGE NOTE See the usage note at *Britain*.

grebe (*say* greeb) *NOUN* **grebes**
a diving water bird with a long neck

greed *NOUN*
1 a strong desire for more food than you need
2 a strong selfish desire for more money or possessions than you need

greedy *ADJECTIVE* **greedier, greediest**
wanting more food, money, or other things than you need
▷ **greedily** *ADVERB*
▷ **greediness** *NOUN*

Greek *ADJECTIVE*
to do with ancient or modern Greece or its people

Greek *NOUN*
1 the language of Greece, which has ancient and modern forms
2 a person from Greece

Greek words in English

The spelling of an English word often shows that it comes from ancient **Greek**. Many words which begin with *ph-* and *ps-* are Greek in origin (e.g. *phobia*, *psychic*), as are words beginning with *ch-* which have a *k* sound (e.g. *chiropody*, *chord*, *choreography*, and *chorus*). The Greek origin of other words, like *dragon* and *planet* (from Greek words meaning respectively 'serpent' and 'wanderer') is less obvious.

English uses many prefixes and suffixes of Greek origin. The prefixes *bio-*, *eco-* , *mega-*, and *micro-* are derived from the Greek words *bios* 'life', *oikos* 'house', *megas* 'great', and *mikros* 'small', and are still being used to form new words, like *biodiversity*, *ecosystem*, *megabyte*, and *microwave*. And the Greek words *graphein* 'to write', *logia* 'study', and *patheia* 'feeling' have produced the suffixes *-graphy*, *-logy*, and *-pathy*, which feature in many English words, such as *biography*, *calligraphy*, *astrology*, *mythology*, *sympathy*, and *telepathy*.

green *NOUN* **greens**
1 the colour of grass, leaves, etc.
2 an area of grassy land

green *ADJECTIVE*
1 of the colour green
2 concerned with protecting the natural environment
3 inexperienced and likely to make mistakes
▷ **greenness** *NOUN*

green belt *NOUN* **green belts**
an area kept as open land round a city

greenery *NOUN*
green leaves or plants

greenfly *NOUN* **greenfly**
a small green insect that feeds on and damages plants

greengrocer *NOUN* **greengrocers**
a shopkeeper who sells fruit and vegetables
▷ **greengrocery** *NOUN*

greenhouse *NOUN* **greenhouses**
a glass building where plants are protected from cold

greenhouse effect *NOUN*
the warming up of the earth's surface when heat from the sun is trapped in the earth's atmosphere by gases such as carbon dioxide and methane

greenhouse gas *NOUN* **greenhouse gases**
a gas, such as carbon dioxide and methane, that is found in the earth's atmosphere and contributes to the greenhouse effect

greens *PLURAL NOUN*
green vegetables, such as cabbage and spinach

Greenwich Mean Time (*say* **gren**- ich) *NOUN*
the time on the line of longitude which passes through Greenwich in London, used as a basis for calculating time throughout the world

greet *VERB* **greets, greeting, greeted**
1 to speak to someone in a friendly way when they arrive
2 to receive something or respond to someone in a certain way

At the grand dinner, the children's entrance was greeted by a standing ovation. — William Nicholson, *The Wind Singer*

3 something interesting or unusual greets you when you notice it ◆ *A strange sight greeted our eyes.*

greeting *NOUN* **greetings**
words or actions used to greet somebody

greetings *PLURAL NOUN*
good wishes

gregarious (*say* grig- **air**- ee- us) *ADJECTIVE*
1 fond of company; sociable
2 living in flocks or communities
▷ **gregariously** *ADVERB*
▷ **gregariousness** *NOUN*

grenade (*say* grin- **ayd**) ***NOUN*** **grenades**
a small bomb thrown by hand

WORD HISTORY from Old French *pome grenate* 'pomegranate' (because the shape of the grenade was once similar to a pomegranate)

grenadier (*say* gren- ad- **eer**) ***NOUN*** **grenadiers**
a soldier armed with grenades

grey ***NOUN*** **greys**
the colour between black and white, like the colour of ashes or dark clouds
▷ **grey** ***ADJECTIVE***
▷ **greyness** ***NOUN***

greyhound ***NOUN*** **greyhounds**
a thin dog with smooth hair and long legs, used in racing

grid ***NOUN*** **grids**
1 a framework or pattern of spaced bars or lines that cross each other
2 a network of cables or wires for carrying electricity over a large area

griddle ***NOUN*** **griddles**
a round iron plate that is heated for cooking food

gridiron ***NOUN*** **gridirons**
a framework of bars for cooking on

gridlock ***NOUN*** **gridlocks**
a traffic jam that extends over several streets in various directions

grid reference ***NOUN*** **grid references**
(*Geography*) a set of numbers that allows you to describe the exact position of something on a map

grief ***NOUN***
deep sorrow, especially because a close relative or friend has died
to come to grief is to fail or suffer a disaster

grievance ***NOUN*** **grievances**
something that people are unhappy or angry about

grieve ***VERB*** **grieves, grieving, grieved**
1 to grieve is to feel very sad, especially because a close relative or friend has died
2 to grieve someone is to make them feel very sad ◆ *It grieves me to have to speak to you like this.*

grievous (*say* **gree**- vus) ***ADJECTIVE***
1 causing grief
2 very serious
▷ **grievously** ***ADVERB***

griffin ***NOUN*** **griffins**
a creature in fables, with the head and wings of an eagle and the body of a lion

grill ***NOUN*** **grills**
1 a heated element on a cooker, for sending heat downwards
2 food cooked under this
3 a grille

grill ***VERB*** **grills, grilling, grilled**
1 to cook food under a grill
2 (*informal*) to grill someone is to question them closely and intensively

grille ***NOUN*** **grilles**
a metal grating covering a window or other opening

grim ***ADJECTIVE*** **grimmer, grimmest**
1 a grim person is stern and severe
2 a grim place or situation is unpleasant or unattractive
▷ **grimly** ***ADVERB***
▷ **grimness** ***NOUN***

grimace (*say* grim- **ayss** or **grim**- as) ***NOUN*** **grimaces**
an ugly twisted expression on the face, expressing pain or disgust

grimace ***VERB*** **grimaces, grimacing, grimaced**
to make a grimace

grime ***NOUN***
dirt in a layer sticking to a surface or the skin
▷ **grimy** ***ADJECTIVE***

grin ***NOUN*** **grins**
a broad smile

grin ***VERB*** **grins, grinning, grinned**
to smile broadly

grind ***VERB*** **grinds, grinding, ground**
1 to crush something into tiny pieces or powder
2 to sharpen or smooth something by rubbing it on a rough surface
3 to grind your teeth is to rub the upper and lower teeth harshly together, often as a sign of anger or impatience
to grind to a halt is to stop abruptly

After five hours we grind to a halt, our vehicles stuck in deep fresh-fallen snow at the top of a pass. — *Michael Palin, Pole to Pole*

▷ **grinder** ***NOUN***

grindstone ***NOUN*** **grindstones**
a flat round stone that revolves, for sharpening or grinding things
to keep your nose to the grindstone is to keep working hard

grip ***VERB*** **grips, gripping, gripped**
1 to hold something firmly
2 to affect a person deeply

Kate felt the palms of her hand begin to sweat as sudden panic gripped her tightly. — *G. P. Taylor, Shadowmancer*

grip ***NOUN*** **grips**
1 a firm hold
2 a handle, especially on a sports racket or bat
3 control or power ◆ *The country was in the grip of revolution.*
to get to grips with something is to begin to deal with it successfully

SPELLING NOTE Some words with a hard **g-** sound begin with **gh-** (e.g. ghost) or **gu-** (e.g. guess)

gripe *VERB* **gripes, griping, griped**
(*informal*) to grumble or complain

gripe *NOUN* **gripes**
(*informal*) a complaint

gripping *ADJECTIVE*
a gripping story or film is very interesting and exciting

grisly *ADJECTIVE* **grislier, grisliest**
causing horror or disgust; gruesome

grist *NOUN*
corn for grinding

grist to the mill experience or knowledge that you can make use of

gristle *NOUN*
tough rubbery tissue in meat
▷ **gristly** *ADJECTIVE*

grit *NOUN*
1 small loose pieces of stone or sand
2 courage and endurance
▷ **gritty** *ADJECTIVE*
▷ **grittiness** *NOUN*

grit *VERB* **grits, gritting, gritted**
1 to spread a road or path with grit
2 to clench your teeth when in pain or trouble

to grit your teeth is to persevere bravely in the face of difficulty

grizzle *VERB* **grizzles, grizzling, grizzled**
a baby or young child grizzles when it cries or whimpers

grizzled *ADJECTIVE*
grizzled hair is streaked with grey

grizzly *ADJECTIVE*
grey-haired

grizzly bear *NOUN* **grizzly bears**
a large fierce bear of North America

groan *VERB* **groans, groaning, groaned**
1 to make a long deep sound in pain, distress, or disapproval
2 to creak loudly under a heavy load

groan *NOUN* **groans**
the sound of groaning

grocer *NOUN* **grocers**
a person who keeps a shop that sells food and household goods

WORD HISTORY originally = 'wholesaler'; from medieval Latin *grossarius* from *grossus* 'gross' (because a wholesaler buys goods *in the gross* 'in large quantities')

groceries *PLURAL NOUN*
goods that a grocer sells

grocery *NOUN* **groceries**
a grocer's shop

grog *NOUN*
a drink of rum mixed with water, formerly given to sailors in the Royal Navy

WORD HISTORY from *Old Grog*, the nickname of Admiral Vernon, who ordered that sailors should be issued with grog instead of neat rum

groggy *ADJECTIVE* **groggier, groggiest**
dizzy and unsteady, especially after illness or injury
▷ **groggily** *ADVERB*
▷ **grogginess** *NOUN*

groin *NOUN*
the hollow between your thigh and the trunk of the body

groom *NOUN* **grooms**
1 a person whose job is to look after horses
2 a bridegroom

groom *VERB* **grooms, grooming, groomed**
1 to clean and brush a horse or other animal
2 to make something, especially hair or a beard, neat and trim
3 to groom someone for a certain job or position is to prepare or train them for it

groove *NOUN* **grooves**
a long narrow furrow or channel cut in the surface of something
▷ **grooved** *ADJECTIVE*

grope *VERB* **gropes, groping, groped**
to feel about for something you cannot see

Hester groped for something she could use as a weapon and came up with a gnarled old length of wood. — *Philip Reeve, Mortal Engines*

gross (*say* grohss) *ADJECTIVE*
1 a gross person is fat and ugly
2 very obvious or shocking ◆ *gross stupidity*
3 gross behaviour or a gross act is very bad or offensive

It was the grossest breach of etiquette imaginable to touch another person's dæmon. — *Philip Pullman, Northern Lights*

4 (*informal*) disgusting
5 a gross income or other amount is the total, without anything being deducted (SEE ALSO **net**[2])
▷ **grossly** *ADVERB*
▷ **grossness** *NOUN*

gross *NOUN* **gross**
twelve dozen (144) of something

grotesque (*say* groh-**tesk**) *ADJECTIVE*
very strange and ugly
▷ **grotesquely** *ADVERB*
▷ **grotesqueness** *NOUN*

grotto *NOUN* **grottoes**
an attractive cave, usually an artificial one that is brightly decorated

ground[1] *past tense* of **grind**

ground❷ ***NOUN*** **grounds**
1 the surface of the earth
2 a piece of land used for a special purpose, e.g. a sport
3 the ground covered by a book or course is the range of topics it includes

ground ***VERB*** **grounds, grounding, grounded**
1 an aircraft is grounded when it has to remain on the ground
2 to ground a child is to forbid them to go out socially, as a punishment

'You young idiot!' he bawled. 'Pull a trick like that again and I'll ground you for a month.' — *Alan Gibbons, Shadow of the Minotaur*

3 to be grounded in a subject is to have a good basic training in it
4 an idea or story is grounded on something when it is based on it

ground control ***NOUN***
the people and machinery that control and monitor an aircraft or spacecraft from the ground

grounding ***NOUN***
basic training or instruction

groundless ***ADJECTIVE***
having no good reason or cause ◆ *Our fears proved groundless.*

grounds ***PLURAL NOUN***
1 the gardens of a large house
2 solid particles that sink to the bottom of a drink
3 good reasons or causes ◆ *There are strong grounds for suspicion.*

groundsheet ***NOUN*** **groundsheets**
a piece of waterproof material for spreading on the ground inside a tent

groundsman ***NOUN*** **groundsmen**
a person whose job is to look after a sports ground

groundwork ***NOUN***
work that lays the basis for something

ground zero ***NOUN***
the point on the earth's surface directly above or below an exploding nuclear bomb

group ***NOUN*** **groups**
1 a number of people, animals, or things that come together or belong together in some way
2 a band of musicians who play popular music

group ***VERB*** **groups, grouping, grouped**
to put together or come together in a group or groups

grouse❶ ***NOUN*** **grouse**
a bird with feathered feet, hunted as game

grouse❷ ***VERB*** **grouses, grousing, groused**
(*informal*) to grumble or complain
▷ **grouse** ***NOUN***
▷ **grouser** ***NOUN***

grove ***NOUN*** **groves**
a small wood or group of trees

grovel ***VERB*** **grovels, grovelling, grovelled**
1 to act in an excessively humble way by repeatedly apologizing or asking for favours
2 to crawl on the ground
▷ **groveller** ***NOUN***

grow ***VERB*** **grows, growing, grew, grown**
1 to become bigger or greater
2 to develop
3 to grow a plant is to put it in the ground or in a pot and look after it
4 to become ◆ *He grew very angry.*
5 something grows on you when you gradually start to like it or enjoy it
to grow up is to become an adult
▷ **grower** ***NOUN***

growl ***VERB*** **growls, growling, growled**
to make a deep angry sound in the throat

growl ***NOUN*** **growls**
the sound of growling

grown-up ***NOUN*** **grown-ups**
an adult person
▷ **grown-up** ***ADJECTIVE***

growth ***NOUN*** **growths**
1 growth is the process of growing or developing
2 a growth is something that has grown
3 a growth is also a lump or tumour that has grown on or inside a person's body

grub ***NOUN*** **grubs**
1 a grub is a tiny worm-like creature that will become an insect; a larva
2 (*informal*) grub is food

grubby ***ADJECTIVE*** **grubbier, grubbiest**
rather dirty
▷ **grubbiness** ***NOUN***

grudge ***NOUN*** **grudges**
to have or bear a grudge is to feel resentful towards someone who has done you harm

grudge ***VERB*** **grudges, grudging, grudged**
to grudge someone something is to resent having to let them have it

gruelling ***ADJECTIVE***
a gruelling task or activity is hard and exhausting

gruesome ***ADJECTIVE***
horrible or disgusting

gruff ***ADJECTIVE***
having a rough unfriendly voice or manner
▷ **gruffly** ***ADVERB***
▷ **gruffness** ***NOUN***

a b c d e f g h i j k l m n o p q r s t u v w x y z

SPELLING NOTE Some words with a hard **g-** sound begin with **gh-** (e.g. ghost) or **gu-** (e.g. guess)

grumble *VERB* **grumbles, grumbling, grumbled**
to complain in a bad-tempered way

'Christmas won't be Christmas without any presents,' grumbled Jo, lying on the rug. — *Louisa M. Alcott, Little Women*

▷ **grumble** *NOUN*
▷ **grumbler** *NOUN*

grumpy *ADJECTIVE* **grumpier, grumpiest**
bad-tempered
▷ **grumpily** *ADVERB*
▷ **grumpiness** *NOUN*

grunt *VERB* **grunts, grunting, grunted**
to make a pig's gruff snort

grunt *NOUN* **grunts**
the sound of grunting

grysbok (*say* grys- bok) *NOUN*
a small southern African antelope with small vertical horns

guarantee *NOUN* **guarantees**
1 a formal promise
2 a written promise that a product will be repaired or replaced if it proves to be faulty

guarantee *VERB* **guarantees, guaranteeing, guaranteed**
1 to make a formal promise
2 to make it certain that something will happen ◆ *Money cannot guarantee happiness.*

guarantor *NOUN* **guarantors**
a person or organization that guarantees something, e.g. payment of money or the terms of a treaty

guard *VERB* **guards, guarding, guarded**
1 to protect a place or thing from danger; to keep something safe
2 to watch over someone and prevent them from escaping
3 to guard against something is to try to prevent it

guard *NOUN* **guards**
1 a soldier or other person who guards a person or place
2 a group of soldiers or police officers acting as a guard
3 to keep someone under guard is to guard or protect them
4 a railway official in charge of a train
5 a device or screen for preventing danger or injury

to be on guard is to be alert for possible danger or difficulty

guardian *NOUN* **guardians**
1 someone who guards or protects something
2 a person who is legally in charge of a child instead of the child's parents
▷ **guardianship** *NOUN*

guerrilla (*say* ger- **il**- a) *NOUN* **guerrillas**
a member of a small unofficial army that fights by making surprise attacks

USAGE NOTE Take care not to confuse this word with *gorilla*.

guess *NOUN* **guesses**
an opinion or answer that you give without making careful calculations or without being certain

guess *VERB* **guesses, guessing, guessed**
to make a guess
▷ **guesser** *NOUN*

guesswork *NOUN*
something you do by guessing

guest *NOUN* **guests**
1 a person who is invited to visit or stay at another person's house
2 a person staying at a hotel
3 a performer invited to appear on a television show by the presenter

guest house *NOUN* **guest houses**
a kind of small hotel

guffaw *VERB* **guffaws, guffawing, guffawed**
to laugh noisily

Some of the Geats guffawed, delighted by their leader's quick wit. The Danes laughed too. — *Robert Nye, Beowulf*

▷ **guffaw** *NOUN*

guidance *NOUN*
help and advice

Guide *NOUN* **Guides**
a member of the Girl Guides Association, an organization for girls

guide *NOUN* **guides**
1 a person who shows others the way or points out interesting sights
2 a book giving information about a place or subject

guide *VERB* **guides, guiding, guided**
to show someone the way or how to do something

guidebook *NOUN* **guidebooks**
a book of information about a place for tourists or visitors

guide dog *NOUN* **guide dogs**
a dog that has been trained to lead a blind person

guidelines *PLURAL NOUN*
statements that give general advice about how something should be done

guild (*say* gild) *NOUN* **guilds**
a society of people with similar skills or interests

guile (*rhymes with* mile) *NOUN*
craftiness and deceit

a b c d e f g h i j k l m n o p q r s t u v w x y z

guillotine (*say* **gil**- ot- een) ***NOUN*** **guillotines**
1 a machine with a heavy blade for beheading criminals, used in the past in France
2 a machine used in an office for cutting paper

WORD HISTORY named after a French doctor, Joseph *Guillotin*, who suggested its use in France during the Revolution in 1789

guilt ***NOUN***
1 an unpleasant feeling when you have done wrong or are to blame for something
2 the fact that you have committed a crime or done wrong

guilty ***ADJECTIVE*** **guiltier, guiltiest**
1 to be guilty of a crime or offence is to have done it
2 feeling or showing guilt ◆ *a guilty conscience* ◆ *a guilty look*

▷ **guiltily** ***ADVERB***

guinea (*say* **gin**- ee) ***NOUN*** **guineas**
an old British gold coin worth 21 shillings (£1.05)

WORD HISTORY named after *Guinea* in West Africa (because it was originally a coin used by British traders in Africa)

guinea pig ***NOUN*** **guinea pigs**
1 a small furry animal without a tail, kept as a pet
2 a person who is used to try out something new

WORD HISTORY from *Guinea* in West Africa, probably by mistake for Guiana in South America, where the guinea pig comes from

guise (*say* guys) ***NOUN*** **guises**
a misleading appearance or pretence

guitar ***NOUN*** **guitars**
a musical instrument with six strings stretched over a hollow body, played by plucking or strumming

▷ **guitarist** ***NOUN***

gulf ***NOUN*** **gulfs**
1 a large area of the sea that is partly surrounded by land
2 a wide gap or difference between people's thoughts or opinions

gull ***NOUN*** **gulls**
a seabird with long wings; a seagull

gullet ***NOUN*** **gullets**
the tube that goes from the throat to the stomach

gullible ***ADJECTIVE***
easily deceived or persuaded to believe something

WORD HISTORY from an old word *gull* 'to fool or deceive'

gully ***NOUN*** **gullies**
1 (*Geography*) a long narrow valley or channel worn by water
2 (*Australian and New Zealand*) a valley

gulp ***VERB*** **gulps, gulping, gulped**
1 to swallow a drink hastily or greedily

A big carp rose to the surface of the pool, gulped air, and then sank mysteriously into the dark water again, leaving widening rings on the water.
— *John Steinbeck, Of Mice and Men*

2 to make a loud swallowing noise, especially because of fear

gulp ***NOUN*** **gulps**
1 the act of gulping food or drink
2 a large mouthful of liquid swallowed quickly

gum ***NOUN*** **gums**
1 the firm flesh in which your teeth are rooted
2 a sticky substance produced by some trees and shrubs, used as glue
3 a sweet made with gum or gelatine
4 chewing gum

▷ **gummy** ***ADJECTIVE***

gum ***VERB*** **gums, gumming, gummed**
to cover or stick something with gum

gumption ***NOUN***
(*informal*) common sense

gun ***NOUN*** **guns**
1 a weapon that fires shells or bullets
2 a device that forces grease or another thick substance out of a tube

gun ***VERB*** **guns, gunning, gunned**
to gun someone down is to shoot and kill them with a gun

WORD HISTORY probably from a medieval female first name *Gunnilda*, from the Swedish name *Gunnhildr*, from *gunnr* 'war'

gunboat ***NOUN*** **gunboats**
a small warship

gunfire ***NOUN***
the rapid firing of guns

gunman ***NOUN*** **gunmen**
a criminal with a gun

gunner ***NOUN*** **gunners**
a person in the armed forces who operates a large gun

gunpowder ***NOUN***
an explosive made from a powdered mixture of potassium nitrate, charcoal, and sulphur

gunshot ***NOUN*** **gunshots**
the sound of a gun being fired

gunwale (*say* **gun**- al) ***NOUN*** **gunwales**
the upper edge of the side of a boat

gurdwara ***NOUN*** **gurdwaras**
a Sikh place of worship

gurgle ***VERB*** **gurgles, gurgling, gurgled**
to make a low bubbling sound

gurgle ***NOUN*** **gurgles**
a low bubbling sound

guru ***NOUN*** **gurus**
1 a Hindu religious leader and teacher
2 an influential teacher or mentor

a b c d e f g h i j k l m n o p q r s t u v w x y z

gush *VERB* **gushes, gushing, gushed**
1 to flow suddenly and fast
2 to talk too enthusiastically or emotionally
▷ **gush** *NOUN*

gust *NOUN* **gusts**
a short sudden rush of wind
▷ **gusty** *ADJECTIVE*

gust *VERB* **gusts, gusting, gusted**
to blow in gusts

gusto *NOUN*
great enjoyment and enthusiasm

gut *NOUN* **guts**
the lower part of the digestive system; the intestine

gut *VERB* **guts, gutting, gutted**
1 to remove the guts from a dead fish or other animal
2 to remove or destroy the inside of something
◆ *A fire had gutted the building.*

guts *PLURAL NOUN*
1 the digestive system; the insides of a person or thing
2 (*informal*) courage

gutted *ADJECTIVE*
(*informal*) extremely disappointed or upset

gutter *NOUN* **gutters**
a long narrow channel at the side of a street, or along the edge of a roof, for carrying away rainwater

guttural (*say* **gut**- er- al) *ADJECTIVE*
a guttural voice is throaty and harsh-sounding

guy ❶ *NOUN* **guys**
1 (*informal*) a man or boy
2 a figure representing Guy Fawkes, burnt as part of a fireworks display on Guy Fawkes Night (5 November)

WORD HISTORY named after Guy Fawkes, leader of the Gunpowder Plot which planned to blow up Parliament on 5 November 1605

guy ❷ or **guy-rope** *NOUN* **guys** or **guy-ropes**
a rope used to hold down a tent

WORD HISTORY probably from Old German

guzzle *VERB* **guzzles, guzzling, guzzled**
to eat or drink greedily
▷ **guzzler** *NOUN*

gym (*say* jim) *NOUN* **gyms** (*informal*)
1 a gym is a gymnasium
2 gym is gymnastics

gymkhana (*say* jim- **kah**- na) *NOUN* **gymkhanas**
a series of horse-riding contests and other sports events

gymnasium *NOUN* **gymnasia** or **gymnasiums**
a place with equipment for performing physical exercises (gymnastics)

WORD HISTORY from Greek *gymnos* 'naked' (because in ancient Greece men exercised naked)

gymnast *NOUN* **gymnasts**
a person trained in gymnastics

gymnastics *PLURAL NOUN*
exercises performed to develop the muscles or to show the performer's agility
▷ **gymnastic** *ADJECTIVE*

gynaecology (*say* guy- ni- **kol**- o- ji) *NOUN*
(*Medicine*) the branch of medicine concerned with the functioning and disorders of the female reproductive system

Gypsy *NOUN* **Gypsies**
a member of a community of people, also called travellers, who live in caravans or similar vehicles and travel from place to place

WORD HISTORY from *Egyptian* (because Gypsies were originally thought to have come from Egypt)

gyrate (*say* jy- **rayt**) *VERB* **gyrates, gyrating, gyrated**
to move round in circles or spirals
▷ **gyration** *NOUN*

gyroscope (*say* **jy**- ro- skohp) *NOUN* **gyroscopes**
a device used in navigation, that keeps steady because of a heavy wheel spinning inside it

Hh

habit ***NOUN*** **habits**
1 something you do regularly or often; a settled way of behaving ◆ *He had the habit of making up nicknames for his friends.*
2 something that you find hard to stop doing ◆ *A majority of adult smokers want to give up the habit.*
3 a piece of clothing like a long dress worn by a monk or nun

habitat ***NOUN*** **habitats**
(*Geography*) a place where a particular animal or plant lives or grows naturally

habitation ***NOUN*** **habitations**
1 a habitation is a place to live in
2 habitation is living in a place

habitual ***ADJECTIVE***
a habitual action is one that you do often as a habit
▷ **habitually** ***ADVERB***

hack❶ ***VERB*** **hacks, hacking, hacked**
1 to chop or cut roughly something that is tough or tangled
2 (*ICT*) to gain illegal access to a computer system

hack❷ ***NOUN*** **hacks**
a writer who produces a lot of dull or poor work

WORD HISTORY it originally meant 'a horse for ordinary riding', from *Hackney* in London (because many horses used to be kept on Hackney Marshes)

hacker ***NOUN*** **hackers**
(*ICT*) a person who gains illegal access to a computer system, especially that of a company or government

hackles ***PLURAL NOUN***
to make someone's hackles rise is to make them angry or indignant

WORD HISTORY *hackles* are the long feathers on some birds' necks, which the bird raises when alarmed

hackneyed ***ADJECTIVE***
a hackneyed phrase or expression is one that has been used so often that it no longer has any real meaning or force

hacksaw ***NOUN*** **hacksaws**
a saw for cutting metal

had *past tense and past participle of* **have**

haddock ***NOUN*** **haddock**
a sea fish like cod but smaller, used as food

hadn't *short for* **had not**

haemoglobin (*say* heem- a- **gloh**- bin) ***NOUN***
a red protein containing iron, which carries oxygen in the blood

haemophilia (*say* heem- o- **fil**- ee- a) ***NOUN***
a condition that causes severe bleeding from even a slight cut, because it prevents the blood from clotting
▷ **haemophiliac** ***NOUN***

haemorrhage (*say* **hem**- er- ij) ***NOUN***
severe bleeding, especially inside a person's body

hag ***NOUN*** **hags**
an ugly old woman

haggard ***ADJECTIVE***
looking very tired or ill

haggis ***NOUN*** **haggises**
a Scottish dish made from sheep's offal, boiled in a skin with suet and oatmeal

haggle ***VERB*** **haggles, haggling, haggled**
to argue about a price or agreement

haiku (*say* **hy**- koo) ***NOUN*** **haiku**
(*Language*) a Japanese poem written in three lines of five, seven, and five syllables

hail❶ ***NOUN***
rain falling in frozen drops

hail ***VERB*** **hails, hailing, hailed**
it hails when rain falls in frozen drops

hail❷ ***EXCLAMATION***
(*old use*) a word used to express greeting

hail ***VERB*** **hails, hailing, hailed**
to call out to somebody
to hail from somewhere is to come from a particular place ◆ *Joan is married and hails from Newcastle.*

hailstone ***NOUN*** **hailstones**
a frozen drop of rain

hair ***NOUN*** **hairs**
1 a soft covering that grows on the heads and bodies of people and animals
2 one of the threads that make up this covering
to keep your hair on (*informal*) is to stay calm and not get angry
to split hairs is to make petty or unimportant distinctions of meaning

hairbrush ***NOUN*** **hairbrushes**
a brush for tidying and arranging the hair

hairbrush *NOUN* **hairbrushes**
a brush for tidying and arranging the hair

haircut *NOUN* **haircuts**
the act of cutting a person's hair, or the style in which it is cut

hairdresser *NOUN* **hairdressers**
a person who is trained to cut and arrange people's hair

hairpin *NOUN* **hairpins**
a U-shaped pin for keeping the hair in place

hairpin bend *NOUN* **hairpin bends**
a sharp bend in a road

hair-raising *ADJECTIVE*
very frightening

hairstyle *NOUN* **hairstyles**
a way or style of arranging the hair

hairy *ADJECTIVE* **hairier, hairiest**
1 having a lot of hair
2 (*informal*) a hairy adventure or experience is dangerous and frightening

hajj (*rhymes with* badge) *NOUN*
the pilgrimage to Mecca which all Muslims are expected to make at least once

haka (*say* **hah**- ka) *NOUN*
(*New Zealand*) a warlike Maori dance with chanting, or an imitation of this by a New Zealand sports team before a match

hake *NOUN* **hake**
a sea fish used as food

halal *NOUN*
meat prepared according to Muslim law

halcyon (*say* **hal**- see- on) *ADJECTIVE*
halcyon days are happy and peaceful days that you long for from the past

WORD HISTORY from Greek *alkyon*, a name for a mythical bird once believed to build its nest on the sea at the winter solstice, causing the wind and waves to stay magically calm

hale *ADJECTIVE*
someone who is hale and hearty is strong and healthy

half *NOUN* **halves**
one of the two equal parts or amounts into which something is or can be divided

half *ADVERB*
partly; not completely ◆ *Some of the carvings were broken or half finished.*

half-baked *ADJECTIVE*
(*informal*) not properly planned or thought out

half-brother *NOUN* **half-brothers**
a brother to whom you are related by one parent only

half-hearted *ADJECTIVE*
not very keen or enthusiastic
▷ **half-heartedly** *ADVERB*

half-life *NOUN* **half-lives**
(*Science*) the time taken for the radioactivity of a substance to fall to half its original value

half mast *NOUN*
a point halfway up a flagpole, to which a flag is lowered as a mark of respect for a person who has died

halfpenny (*say* **hayp**- nee) *NOUN* **halfpennies** or **halfpence**
a former coin worth half a penny

USAGE NOTE The plural is *halfpennies* for a number of coins and *halfpence* for a sum of money.

half-rhyme *NOUN* **half-rhymes**
(*Language*) a pair of words that rhyme partly but not completely, e.g. *bottle* and *settle*

half-sister *NOUN* **half-sisters**
a sister to whom you are related by one parent only

half-term *NOUN* **half-terms**
a short holiday in the middle of a school term

half-time *NOUN*
the point or interval halfway through a game

halfway *ADJECTIVE, ADVERB*
at a point half the distance or amount between two other points

My dad made this weird French noise he makes sometimes. It's halfway between a snort and a sigh. — *Meg Cabot, The Princess Diaries*

half-witted *ADJECTIVE*
stupid
▷ **half-wit** *NOUN*

halibut *NOUN* **halibut**
a large flat fish used as food

WORD HISTORY from *holy* and *butt*, a dialect word meaning 'flatfish' (because it was eaten on Christian holy days, when meat was forbidden)

hall *NOUN* **halls**
1 a space or passage inside the front entrance of a house or other building
2 a large room or building used for meetings, concerts, or social events
3 a large country house

hallmark *NOUN* **hallmarks**
1 an official mark made on gold, silver, and platinum to show its quality
2 a typical quality or feature by which you can recognize a person or thing

hallo *EXCLAMATION*
another spelling of **hello**

hallowed *ADJECTIVE*
honoured as being holy

Hallowe'en *NOUN*
31 October, traditionally a time when ghosts and witches are believed to appear
WORD HISTORY from *All Hallow Even*, the evening before the Christian festival of All Saints honouring all the *hallows* (saints)

hallucinate *VERB* **hallucinates, hallucinating, hallucinated**
to see things that are not really there, especially as a result of drugs or illness
▷ **hallucination** *NOUN*
▷ **hallucinatory** *ADJECTIVE*

hallway *NOUN* **hallways**
an entrance hall in a large building

halo *NOUN* **haloes**
a circle of light round something, especially round the head of a holy person in religious paintings

halt *VERB* **halts, halting, halted**
to stop, or to make someone or something stop

Jude threw open the front door but was halted in his tracks by the presence of two police officers, framed by the darkness outside. — *Malorie Blackman, Noughts and Crosses*

halt *NOUN* **halts**
1 to come to a halt is to stop or finish
2 a small stopping place on a railway

halter *NOUN* **halters**
a rope or strap put round a horse's head so that it can be led or tied

halting *ADJECTIVE*
a halting walk or movement is slow and uncertain
▷ **haltingly** *ADVERB*

halve *VERB* **halves, halving, halved**
1 to divide something into halves
2 to reduce something to half its size

ham *NOUN* **hams**
1 cured and salted meat from the leg of a pig
2 (*informal*) an actor who exaggerates feelings and actions
3 (*informal*) an amateur radio operator

hamburger *NOUN* **hamburgers**
a flat round cake of minced beef served fried, often in a bread roll
WORD HISTORY named after *Hamburg*, a city and port in Germany

hamlet *NOUN* **hamlets**
a small village

hammer *NOUN* **hammers**
a tool with a heavy metal head, used for driving nails into things

hammer *VERB* **hammers, hammering, hammered**
1 to hit something with a hammer
2 to knock loudly
3 (*informal*) to criticize or defeat someone

hammock *NOUN* **hammocks**
a bed made of a strong net or piece of cloth hung by cords

hamper❶ *NOUN* **hampers**
a large box-shaped basket with a lid

hamper❷ *VERB* **hampers, hampering, hampered**
to hinder someone, or prevent them from moving or working freely

hamster *NOUN* **hamsters**
a small furry animal with cheek pouches for carrying grain

hamstring *NOUN* **hamstrings**
any of the five tendons at the back of a person's knee

hand *NOUN* **hands**
1 the end part of the arm below the wrist
2 a pointer on a clock or dial
3 the way you write ◆ *She wrote in a clear and legible hand.*
4 a member of a ship's crew, or anyone who contributes to an effort
5 the cards held by one player in a card game

George stacked the scattered cards and began to lay out his solitaire hand. — *John Steinbeck, Of Mice and Men*

6 the side or direction of something ◆ *There were windows down the left-hand side of the building.*
7 help or assistance ◆ *I need a hand sorting out the loft.*
8 a round of applause ◆ *They got a huge hand at the end of the show.*

at hand nearby, and ready to help
by hand using your hand or hands
hands down winning easily
in good hands in the care or control of someone who can be trusted
in hand being dealt with
on hand available; ready to help
on the other hand used to introduce a different thought or point of view
out of hand out of control

hand *VERB* **hands, handing, handed**
to give or pass something to someone

Simon handed me a steaming mug as I sat on my rucksack and gazed at the whole range laid out before us. — *Joe Simpson, Touching the Void*

to hand something down is to pass it from one generation to the next

handbag *NOUN* **handbags**
a small bag for holding a purse and personal articles

handbook *NOUN* **handbooks**
a small book that gives useful facts about a subject

handcuff ***NOUN*** **handcuffs**
each of a pair of metal rings linked by a chain, for fastening a prisoner's wrists

handcuff ***VERB*** **handcuffs, handcuffing, handcuffed**
to put handcuffs on someone

handful ***NOUN*** **handfuls**
1 as much as you can hold in one hand
2 a few people or things
3 (*informal*) a difficult or awkward person or task

handicap ***NOUN*** **handicaps**
1 a disadvantage
2 a physical or mental disability
▷ **handicapped** ***ADJECTIVE***

WORD HISTORY originally the name of a gambling game in which forfeit money was put in a cap, into which players put their hands ('hand in cap'); later it was used about a type of horse race in which the better horses were given disadvantages

handicraft ***NOUN*** **handicrafts**
creative work done with the hands, e.g. woodwork or needlework

handiwork ***NOUN***
something you have made or done

handkerchief ***NOUN*** **handkerchiefs**
a small square of cloth used for blowing your nose

handle ***NOUN*** **handles**
the part of a thing by which it is held, carried, or controlled

handle ***VERB*** **handles, handling, handled**
1 to touch or feel something with your hands
2 to deal with or manage something

> Inspector, I've told you before, I don't like your tone nor the way you're handling this inquiry.
> — *J. B. Priestley, An Inspector Calls*

▷ **handler** ***NOUN***

handlebar ***NOUN*** or **handlebars** ***PLURAL NOUN***
the bar, with a handle at each end, that steers a bicycle or motorcycle

handout ***NOUN*** **handouts**
1 money given to a needy person or organization
2 a sheet of information given out during a lesson or as an advertisement

hand-picked ***ADJECTIVE***
carefully chosen

handrail ***NOUN*** **handrails**
a narrow rail for holding on to as a support

handset ***NOUN*** **handsets**
1 the part of a telephone that you speak into and listen with
2 a hand-held control device for a piece of electronic equipment

handshake ***NOUN*** **handshakes**
the act of shaking hands with someone as a greeting or sign of agreement

handsome ***ADJECTIVE***
1 attractive or good-looking
2 a handsome gift or offer is a generous one
▷ **handsomely** ***ADVERB***

hands-on ***ADJECTIVE***
involving actual experience of using equipment or doing something

handstand ***NOUN*** **handstands**
the exercise of balancing upside down on your hands

handwriting ***NOUN***
writing done by hand; a person's style of writing
▷ **handwritten** ***ADJECTIVE***

handy ***ADJECTIVE*** **handier, handiest**
1 convenient or useful
2 conveniently close or well positioned ◆ *The hotel is in a handy central location.*
3 good at using the hands
▷ **handily** ***ADVERB***
▷ **handiness** ***NOUN***

handyman ***NOUN*** **handymen**
a person who does household repairs or odd jobs

hang ***VERB*** **hangs, hanging, hung** or (in meaning 7) **hanged**
1 to fix the top or side of something to a hook or nail etc.; to be supported in this way ◆ *Coats hung from pegs along one wall.*
2 to paste wallpaper to a surface
3 to decorate with drapery or hanging ornaments etc. ◆ *The tree was hung with lights.*
4 to lean or lie over something ◆ *Her clothes hung over a chair.*
5 to hang your head is to lower it in shame or embarrassment

> I hung my head. I could see now that I wasn't going to win this argument. — *Keith Gray, Malarkey*

6 something hangs in the air or over people when it remains there in an unpleasant or threatening way ◆ *A thin layer of cloud hung over the moor.* ◆ *The threat is still hanging over them.*
7 to execute someone by hanging them from a rope that tightens round the neck

to hang about or **around** is to loiter or wait around
to hang back is to hesitate to go forward or to do something
to hang on (*informal*) is to wait for a while
to hang on to something is to hold it tightly
to hang up is to end a telephone conversation

hang ***NOUN***
to get the hang of something (*informal*) is to learn how to do it or use it

hangar ***NOUN*** **hangars**
a large building where aircraft are kept

hanger *NOUN* **hangers**
a shaped piece of wood or plastic with a hook, for hanging clothes from a rail

hang-glider *NOUN* **hang-gliders**
a frame with a stretched covering, from which you can hang and glide through the air
▷ **hang-gliding** *NOUN*

hangover *NOUN* **hangovers**
a headache and sick feeling caused by drinking too much alcohol

hang-up *NOUN* **hang-ups**
(*informal*) an emotional fear or anxiety about something

hanker *VERB* **hankers, hankering, hankered**
to hanker after something is to feel a longing for it

hanky *NOUN* **hankies**
(*informal*) a handkerchief

Hanukkah (*say* **hah**- noo- ka) *NOUN*
an eight-day Jewish festival of lights beginning in December

haphazard *ADJECTIVE*
not having any order or plan

hapless *ADJECTIVE*
(*literary*) unlucky

WORD HISTORY from an old word *hap* 'luck'

happen *VERB* **happens, happening, happened**
1 to take place; to occur

> What actually happens when you die is that your brain stops working and your body rots. — *Mark Haddon, The Curious Incident of the Dog in the Night-Time*

2 to do something by chance ◆ *I happened to be passing the house when they came out.*

happening *NOUN* **happenings**
something that happens; an event

happy *ADJECTIVE* **happier, happiest**
1 pleased or contented
2 willing to do something ◆ *Mrs Rooney was happy to stay on for a while to help out.*
3 fortunate or lucky ◆ *By a happy chance they met again in the village.*
▷ **happily** *ADVERB*
▷ **happiness** *NOUN*

SYNONYMS (meaning 1) contented, cheerful, joyful, jolly, delighted, merry, smiling; (meaning 2) pleased, glad, willing, delighted, disposed; (meaning 3) fortunate, lucky, felicitous, favourable

harangue (*say* ha- **rang**) *VERB* **harangues, haranguing, harangued**
to make a long aggressive speech to somebody
▷ **harangue** *NOUN*

harass (*say* **ha**- ras) *VERB* **harasses, harassing, harassed**
to trouble or annoy somebody continually
▷ **harassment** (*say* **ha**- ras- ment) *NOUN*

harbour *NOUN* **harbours**
a place where ships can moor for shelter

harbour *VERB* **harbours, harbouring, harboured**
1 to harbour a feeling is to feel it strongly ◆ *Kylie had started to harbour doubts about the wisdom of their journey.*
2 to harbour someone, especially a criminal, is to give them shelter secretly

hard *ADJECTIVE*
1 firm or solid; not soft
2 strong and violent ◆ *The injury had been caused by a hard blow to the head.*
3 difficult or needing a lot of effort ◆ *This year has been hard work for us.*
4 unpleasant or causing suffering ◆ *She says she has had a hard life.*
5 hard information or evidence is very specific and reliable
6 a hard person is severe or stern
7 to be hard on someone is to treat them severely
8 hard water contains minerals that prevent soap from making much lather
9 hard drugs are strong and addictive
to be hard of hearing is to be slightly deaf
to be hard up (*informal*) is to have very little money
▷ **hardness** *NOUN*

SYNONYMS (meaning 1) firm, solid, hardened, tough; (meaning 2) heavy, forceful, strong, powerful, violent; (meaning 3) arduous, strenuous, difficult, demanding; (meaning 7) strict, harsh, firm, stern, severe

hard *ADVERB*
1 with a lot of effort or force ◆ *He thought hard before he spoke.*
2 to follow hard on something is to happen immediately afterwards

hardback *NOUN* **hardbacks**
a book with stiff covers

hardboard *NOUN*
stiff board made of compressed wood pulp

hard disk *NOUN* **hard disks**
(*ICT*) a rigid metal disk for storing large amounts of data in a computer or other electronic device

harden *VERB* **hardens, hardening, hardened**
to make something hard, or to become hard
▷ **hardener** *NOUN*

hard-hearted *ADJECTIVE*
unkind or unsympathetic

hardly *ADVERB*
only just; only with difficulty

'Sorry couldn't come', scribbled on the back of your essay and thrust through the letterbox? Rita, that's hardly an apology. — *Willy Russell, Educating Rita*

USAGE NOTE Take care to avoid saying *not hardly*: you should say *She could hardly speak*, not *She couldn't hardly speak*.

hardship *NOUN* **hardships**
difficult conditions that cause discomfort or suffering ◆ *Being out of work will certainly cause hardship.*

hardware *NOUN*
1 tools and machinery
2 (*ICT*) the machinery of a computer as distinct from the programs and data (called *software*) (SEE ALSO **software**)

hard-wearing *ADJECTIVE*
able to stand a lot of wear

hardwood *NOUN* **hardwoods**
hard heavy wood from a deciduous tree, e.g. oak and teak

hardy *ADJECTIVE* **hardier, hardiest**
able to endure cold or difficult conditions
▷ **hardiness** *NOUN*

hare *NOUN* **hares**
an animal like a large rabbit, with very long hind legs

hare *VERB* **hares, haring, hared**
to hare about or hare off is to rush away at great speed

Before any of the others could stop him, he slammed the front door shut, ran to the gate and vaulted over, then hared off down the track towards the forest. — *Tim Bowler, Starseeker*

harem (*say* **har**- eem) *NOUN* **harems**
the women in a Muslim palace or house; the separate part of the building where they live

WORD HISTORY from Arabic *harim* 'forbidden' (because it was forbidden for anyone other than the head of the house to visit the harem)

hark *VERB* **harks, harking, harked**
(*literary*) to listen
to hark back to something is to return to an earlier subject

harlequin *ADJECTIVE*
having mixed colours

WORD HISTORY from *Arlecchino*, the name of a character in Italian comedies who wore brightly coloured clothes

harm *VERB* **harms, harming, harmed**
to damage or injure someone or something

harm *NOUN*
damage or injury

harmful *ADJECTIVE*
causing harm, or likely to cause harm
▷ **harmfully** *ADVERB*

harmless *ADJECTIVE*
unable or unlikely to cause harm
▷ **harmlessly** *ADVERB*

harmonic *ADJECTIVE*
(*Music*) based on or producing musical harmony

harmonica *NOUN* **harmonicas**
a small musical instrument, held against the lips and moved from side to side to produce different notes by blowing or sucking

harmonious *ADJECTIVE*
1 combining together in a pleasant, attractive, or effective way
2 sounding pleasant
3 peaceful and friendly

harmonize *VERB* **harmonizes, harmonizing, harmonized**
to combine together in an attractive or effective way
▷ **harmonization** *NOUN*

USAGE NOTE This word can also be spelled harmonise.

harmony *NOUN* **harmonies**
1 (*Music*) a pleasant combination of musical notes
2 friendly and peaceful feelings between people

harness *NOUN* **harnesses**
a set of straps put round a horse's head and neck for controlling it

harness *VERB* **harnesses, harnessing, harnessed**
1 to put a harness on a horse
2 to control and use something ◆ *It was essential to harness science and technology to improve the environment.*

harp *NOUN* **harps**
a musical instrument made of parallel strings stretched down a triangular frame and plucked with the fingers
▷ **harpist** *NOUN*

harp *VERB* **harps, harping, harped**
to harp on about something is to keep on talking about it in a tiresome way

harpoon *NOUN* **harpoons**
a spear attached to a rope, used for catching whales or large fish

harpoon *VERB* **harpoons, harpooning, harpooned**
to spear a whale or fish with a harpoon

harpsichord *NOUN* **harpsichords**
an instrument like a small grand piano, with horizontal strings that are plucked when keys are pressed

harrow *NOUN* **harrows**
a device for breaking up the soil, with teeth set in a heavy frame that is pulled over the ground

harrowing *ADJECTIVE*
very upsetting or distressing

harry *VERB* **harries, harrying, harried**
to harass or worry someone

harsh *ADJECTIVE*
1 rough and unpleasant
2 severe or cruel
▷ **harshly** *ADVERB*
▷ **harshness** *NOUN*

hart *NOUN* **harts**
an adult male deer (SEE ALSO **hind❷**)

hartebeest (*say* **har**- ti- beest) *NOUN*
a large African antelope with a long head and sloping back

harvest *NOUN* **harvests**
1 the time when farmers gather in ripened crops from the fields
2 the process of doing this, or the crop that is gathered in

harvest *VERB* **harvests, harvesting, harvested**
to harvest a crop is to gather it in when it has ripened
▷ **harvester** *NOUN*

WORD HISTORY from Old English, originally the name for the season we now call *autumn*

hash❶ *NOUN*
a mixture of small pieces of meat and vegetables, usually fried
to make a hash of something (*informal*) is to make a mess of it or bungle it

hash❷ *NOUN*
the symbol #

hashish *NOUN*
a drug made from hemp

hasn't
short for *has not*

hassle *NOUN*
(*informal*) something that is difficult or troublesome

hassle *VERB* **hassles, hassling, hassled**
(*informal*) to annoy or pester someone

haste *NOUN*
haste is doing something in a short time or too quickly
to make haste is to move or act quickly

hasten *VERB* **hastens, hastening, hastened**
to hurry

hasty *ADJECTIVE* **hastier, hastiest**
acting or done too quickly
▷ **hastily** *ADVERB*

hat *NOUN* **hats**
a covering for the head
to keep something under your hat is to keep it secret
▷ **hatless** *ADJECTIVE*

hatch❶ *NOUN* **hatches**
an opening in a floor, wall, or roof, usually with a covering

hatch❷ *VERB* **hatches, hatching, hatched**
1 a chick hatches when it breaks out of its egg and is born
2 a bird hatches its eggs when it keeps them warm until a chick comes out
3 to hatch a plot is to plan it carefully

hatch❸ *VERB* **hatches, hatching, hatched**
to shade part of a drawing with close parallel lines
▷ **hatching** *NOUN*

hatchback *NOUN* **hatchbacks**
a car with a sloping back and a rear door hinged at the top

hatchet *NOUN* **hatchets**
a small axe with a short handle
to bury the hatchet is to settle a quarrel and become friends again

hate *VERB* **hates, hating, hated**
to dislike someone or something very strongly

hate *NOUN* **hates**
1 hate is extreme dislike
2 a hate is something you dislike very much

hateful *ADJECTIVE*
extremely unkind or unpleasant; horrible
▷ **hatefully** *ADVERB*

hatred *NOUN*
hatred is extreme dislike

hatter *NOUN* **hatters**
a person who makes hats

hat-trick *NOUN* **hat-tricks**
three successive wins, goals, or other achievements

haughty (*say* **haw**- ti) *ADJECTIVE* **haughtier, haughtiest**
proud and arrogant
▷ **haughtily** *ADVERB*
▷ **haughtiness** *NOUN*

haul *VERB* **hauls, hauling, hauled**
pull or drag something with great effort

Hester reached the airship first, hauling herself aboard through its shattered flank. — *Philip Reeve, Mortal Engines*

haul *NOUN* **hauls**
1 an amount or number of things taken or obtained by effort ◆ *Police recovered a large haul of weapons.*
2 a distance to be travelled over ◆ *There was a long haul ahead.*

a b c d e f g h i j k l m n o p q r s t u v w x y z

haulage *NOUN*
the transporting of goods by road

haunches *PLURAL NOUN*
the buttocks and the top part of the thighs

haunt *VERB* **haunts, haunting, haunted**
1 a ghost is said to haunt a person or place when it appears often
2 to haunt a place is to visit it often or often be there

'I do not know this country,' said Beowulf. 'Perhaps you can tell me of other monsters who are known to haunt the fen?' — *Robert Nye, Beowulf*

3 a thought or memory haunts you when it stays for a long time in your mind
▷ **haunted** *ADJECTIVE*

haunt *NOUN* **haunts**
a place you like to visit often

haunting *ADJECTIVE*
a haunting sound or picture is a beautiful or sad one that stays in your mind
▷ **hauntingly** *ADVERB*

have *VERB* **has, having, had**
1 to possess or own something ◆ *They have a house by the lake.*
2 to contain something ◆ *The tin had money in it.*
3 to experience something ◆ *Susan had quite a surprise.*
4 to be obliged to do something ◆ *We have to finish by the end of the week.*
5 to allow something to happen ◆ *I won't have them arguing with you.*
6 to receive or accept something ◆ *Will you have a biscuit?*
7 to get something done ◆ *He was determined to have the factory closed down.*
8 (*informal*) to be had is to be cheated or deceived
to have somebody on (*informal*) is to fool them

have *AUXILIARY VERB*
used to form the past tense of verbs, e.g. *They have arrived.*

haven *NOUN* **havens**
a safe place or refuge

Every citizen of Aramanth knew how fortunate they were, to live in this rare haven of peace, plenty, and equal opportunity for all. — *William Nicholson, The Wind Singer*

haven't
short for *have not*

haversack *NOUN* **haversacks**
a strong bag carried on your back or over your shoulder

WORD HISTORY from Old German *Habersack* 'oat bag' (a bag used by the German cavalry for carrying oats for their horses)

havoc *NOUN*
great destruction or disorder
to play havoc with something is to confuse or disrupt it completely

hawk[1] *NOUN* **hawks**
a bird of prey with very strong eyesight

hawk[2] *VERB* **hawks, hawking, hawked**
to hawk goods is to carry them about and try to sell them
▷ **hawker** *NOUN*

hawthorn *NOUN* **hawthorns**
a thorny tree with white or pink blossom and dark red berries

hay *NOUN*
dried grass used as feed for animals

hay fever *NOUN*
an allergy to pollen or dust, causing irritation of the nose, throat, and eyes

haystack or **hayrick** *NOUN* **haystacks, hayricks**
a large tightly packed pile of hay in the open

haywire *ADJECTIVE*
(*informal*) erratic or out of control

WORD HISTORY from the use of wire for tying up hay bales in makeshift repairs

hazard *NOUN* **hazards**
1 a danger or risk
2 an obstacle to be overcome in a game or sport

hazard *VERB* **hazards, hazarding, hazarded**
to put at risk
to hazard a guess is to make a guess

WORD HISTORY from Persian or Turkish *zar* 'dice'

hazardous *ADJECTIVE*
dangerous or risky

Getting themselves aboard the zeppelin was hazardous for the spies, not least because of the equipment they had to carry. — *Philip Pullman, The Amber Spyglass*

haze *NOUN*
thin mist in the atmosphere, which obscures visibility

hazel *NOUN* **hazels**
1 a bush with small nuts
2 a reddish-brown colour
▷ **hazelnut** *NOUN*

hazy *ADJECTIVE* **hazier, haziest**
1 covered in haze; misty
2 vague or uncertain
▷ **hazily** *ADVERB*
▷ **haziness** *NOUN*

H-bomb *NOUN* **H-bombs**
a hydrogen bomb

he *PRONOUN*
1 the male person or animal being talked about
2 a person (male or female) ◆ *He who hesitates is lost.*

head ***NOUN*** **heads**
1 the part of the body containing the brains, eyes, and mouth
2 your brains or mind; intelligence ◆ *He had all the information in his head.*
3 a talent or ability ◆ *She has a good head for figures.*
4 heads is the side of a coin on which the head of an important person is shown (SEE ALSO **tails**)
5 each person ◆ *Rooms cost £20 a head.*
6 the top or front of something long, e.g. a nail or a line of people
7 the layer of froth at the top of a glass of beer
8 the person in charge of an organization or group of people
9 a headteacher

to come to a head is to reach a decisive moment
to keep your head is to stay calm and not panic
to lose your head is to panic
to say something off the top of your head is to say it without thinking carefully about it

head ***VERB*** **heads, heading, headed**
1 to be at the top or front of something
2 to hit a ball with your head
3 to head for a particular place is to start to go in that direction

> Less than a day later we were heading straight into an iceberg field. — *Ellen MacArthur, Taking on the World*

to head someone off is to force them to turn aside by getting in front of them
to head something off is to prevent it happening

headache ***NOUN*** **headaches**
1 a pain in the head
2 (*informal*) something that is very difficult or worrying

headdress ***NOUN*** **headdresses**
a covering or decoration for the head

header ***NOUN*** **headers**
a shot or pass made with the head in football

heading ***NOUN*** **headings**
a title or summary at the top of a piece of printing or writing

headland ***NOUN*** **headlands**
a narrow piece of high land that juts out into the sea

headlight ***NOUN*** **headlights**
a powerful light at the front of a road vehicle or railway engine

headline ***NOUN*** **headlines**
1 the heading of a report or article in a newspaper
2 the headlines are the main items of a radio or television news programme

headlong ***ADVERB, ADJECTIVE***
1 falling head first
2 in a hasty or thoughtless way

headmaster ***NOUN*** **headmasters**
a male headteacher

headmistress ***NOUN*** **headmistresses**
a female headteacher

head-on ***ADVERB, ADJECTIVE***
a head-on collision is one between vehicles moving in directly opposite directions

headphones ***PLURAL NOUN***
a pair of earphones on a band that fits over the head

headquarters ***NOUN***
the place from which an organization is controlled

> **USAGE NOTE** This word can be either singular or plural: *the headquarters is in Paris* and *the headquarters are in Paris* are both correct.

headstone ***NOUN*** **headstones**
a stone set up on a grave, with the name of the person buried there

headstrong ***ADJECTIVE***
determined to do what you want

headteacher ***NOUN*** **headteachers**
the teacher in charge of a school

headway ***NOUN***
to make headway is to make good progress

heal ***VERB*** **heals, healing, healed**
1 to make or become healthy again ◆ *His wounds began to heal.*
2 (*old use*) to heal the sick is to cure them

health ***NOUN***
1 the condition of a person's body or mind ◆ *People were concerned about the president's health.*
2 the state of being well and not ill ◆ *A balanced diet is important for health.*

health centre ***NOUN*** **health centres**
a medical practice consisting of a group of doctors and nurses

health food ***NOUN*** **health foods**
food that contains only natural substances and is thought to be good for your health

healthy ***ADJECTIVE*** **healthier, healthiest**
1 enjoying good health; not ill or unwell
2 producing good health ◆ *He was aware of the importance of a healthy lifestyle.*
3 desirable or useful

> I kept well back from the edge after that, leaving a healthy margin of fifty feet. — *Joe Simpson, Touching the Void*

▷ **healthily** ***ADVERB***
▷ **healthiness** ***NOUN***

heap ***NOUN*** **heaps**
1 an untidy pile of things
2 (*informal*) heaps of things are a lot of them ◆ *There must be heaps of things we could do.*

a b c d e f g h i j k l m n o p q r s t u v w x y z

heap *VERB* **heaps, heaping, heaped**
1 to put things in a heap
2 to heap (for example) praise or criticism on someone is to praise them or criticize them very strongly

hear *VERB* **hears, hearing, heard**
1 to take in sounds through the ears
2 to receive news or information
3 to listen to and try a case in a lawcourt
4 to hear from someone is to get a phone call, letter, or email from them

hear! hear! I agree with what someone has just said

to not hear of something to refuse to allow something ◆ *She will not hear of us leaving early.*

▷ **hearer** *NOUN*

hearing *NOUN* **hearings**
1 the ability to hear
2 an opportunity to state your view or to defend yourself
3 a trial in a lawcourt

hearsay *NOUN*
something you have heard from another person or as a rumour, without knowing whether it is true

hearse *NOUN* **hearses**
a vehicle for taking the coffin to a funeral

heart *NOUN* **hearts**
1 the muscular organ that pumps the blood round your body
2 a person's feelings or emotions; sympathy
3 enthusiasm or courage ◆ *They did not have the heart for a fight.*
4 the middle or most important part of an activity or place

> At the heart of Midwich is a triangular Green ornamented by five fine elms and a white-railed pond. — *John Wyndham, The Midwich Cuckoos*

5 a curved shape representing a heart
6 a playing card of the suit marked with red heart shapes

to break a person's heart is to make them very unhappy

to learn or know something by heart is to memorize it

to wear your heart on your sleeve is to show your affections quite openly

heartache *NOUN*
great sadness or grief

heart attack *NOUN* **heart attacks**
a sudden failure of the heart to work properly, causing pain and sometimes death

heartbreak *NOUN*
great sadness or unhappiness

heartbroken *ADJECTIVE*
very sad or unhappy

heartburn *NOUN*
a burning feeling in the chest, caused by indigestion

hearten *VERB* **heartens, heartening, heartened**
to encourage someone or make them feel confident

heart failure *NOUN*
severe failure of the heart to work properly, especially as a cause of death

heartfelt *ADJECTIVE*
felt deeply and sincerely

hearth *NOUN* **hearths**
the floor of a fireplace, or the area in front of it

heartily *ADVERB*
1 in an enthusiastic way ◆ *She thanked them heartily.*
2 to be (for example) heartily sick of something is to be completely sick of it

heartland *NOUN*
the central or most important part of a country or region

heartless *ADJECTIVE*
unkind or cruel

hearty *ADJECTIVE* **heartier, heartiest**
1 strong and healthy
2 enthusiastic and sincere ◆ *He offered his hearty congratulations.*
3 a hearty meal is large and nourishing

heat *NOUN* **heats**
1 the state of being hot
2 (*Science*) the form of energy that causes things to be hot
3 hot weather
4 strong feeling, especially anger
5 a race or contest to decide who will take part in the final

on heat a female animal is on heat when she is ready for mating

heat *VERB* **heats, heating, heated**
to make something hot, or to become hot

heater *NOUN* **heaters**
a device for heating a room or vehicle

heath *NOUN* **heaths**
an area of flat open land with low shrubs

heathen *NOUN* **heathens**
a person who does not believe in any of the world's chief religions

> **WORD HISTORY** from an Old English word related to *heath* (because heathens were often thought of as the people who lived outside cities 'on the heath')

heather *NOUN*
a plant with small purple, pink, or white flowers, often growing on heaths and moors

heatwave *NOUN* **heatwaves**
a period of unusually hot weather

heave *VERB* **heaves, heaving, heaved** or (*in meaning 5*) **hove**
1 to lift or move or throw something heavy, using a lot of effort
2 the sea heaves when it rises and falls in rough weather
3 to heave a sigh is to sigh deeply
4 your stomach heaves when you begin to feel sick
5 a ship heaves into view when it appears on the horizon, and it heaves to when it stops without mooring or anchoring

heave *NOUN* **heaves**
an act of heaving; a strong pull or shove

heaven *NOUN* **heavens**
1 the place where, in some religions, good people are thought to go when they die and where God and angels are thought to live
2 a very pleasant place or state
3 the heavens are the sky

heavenly *ADJECTIVE*
1 to do with heaven
2 a heavenly body is a star or planet in the sky
3 (*informal*) very pleasing

heavy *ADJECTIVE* **heavier, heaviest**
1 weighing a lot; difficult to lift or carry
2 great in amount or force ◆ *The weather turned sour with heavy rain.* ◆ *They inflicted a heavy penalty.*
3 strong and bulky ◆ *We propose a higher road tax for heavy vehicles.*
4 heavy work is difficult and needs a lot of effort
5 someone with a heavy heart is very sad and anxious
▷ **heavily** *ADVERB*
▷ **heaviness** *NOUN*

heavyweight *NOUN* **heavyweights**
1 a heavy person
2 a boxer of the heaviest weight
▷ **heavyweight** *ADJECTIVE*

Hebrew *NOUN*
the language of the Jews in ancient Palestine and modern Israel

heckle *VERB* **heckles, heckling, heckled**
to interrupt a speaker with rude or awkward remarks or questions
▷ **heckler** *NOUN*

hectare (*say* **hek**- tair) *NOUN* **hectares**
a unit of area equal to 10,000 square metres or nearly 2.5 acres

hectic *ADJECTIVE*
full of frantic activity
▷ **hectically** *ADVERB*

hector *VERB* **hectors, hectoring, hectored**
to talk to someone in a bullying way

WORD HISTORY named after *Hector*, a hero in the Trojan War and in Homer's *Iliad*. The name was used for any hero, and later came to mean 'a bully'.

he'd short for *he had* or *he would*

hedge *NOUN* **hedges**
a row of bushes forming a barrier or boundary

hedge *VERB* **hedges, hedging, hedged**
to avoid giving a definite answer

to hedge your bets is to avoid committing yourself when you are faced with a difficult choice

hedgehog *NOUN* **hedgehogs**
a small animal with long prickles covering its back

hedgerow *NOUN* **hedgerows**
a hedge of bushes bordering a field

heed *VERB* **heeds, heeding, heeded**
to pay attention to someone or something

heed *NOUN*
to take or pay heed is to give your attention to something

heedful *ADJECTIVE*
to be heedful of something such as advice is to listen to it

heedless *ADJECTIVE*
to be heedless of something is to take no notice of it
▷ **heedlessly** *ADVERB*

heel ❶ *NOUN* **heels**
1 the back part of the foot
2 the part of a sock or shoe that covers your heel

to be down at heel is to look untidy or dishevelled
to take to your heels is to run away

heel *VERB* **heels, heeling, heeled**
1 to repair the heel of a shoe
2 to kick a ball with your heel

heel ❷ *VERB* **heels, heeling, heeled**
a ship heels when it leans over to one side

The ship heeled and turned and we heard again the steady hiss against the side as the vessel cut through the water. — *Celia Rees, Witch Child*

hefty *ADJECTIVE* **heftier, heftiest**
large and strong
▷ **heftily** *ADVERB*

Hegira (*say* **hej**- ir- a) *NOUN*
the flight of Muhammad from Mecca in AD622, reckoned as the start of the Muslim era

heifer (*say* **hef**- er) *NOUN* **heifers**
a young cow

height *NOUN* **heights**
1 the distance or measurement from the bottom to the top of something
2 a high place
3 the highest or most intense part ◆ *We are running 26 trains per day at the height of our season.*

heighten *VERB* **heightens, heightening, heightened**
to make something higher or more intense, or to become higher or more intense

heinous (*say* **hay**- nus or **hee**- nus) *ADJECTIVE*
very bad or wicked

OK, OK, I'm late home, but it's not that heinous a crime, is it? — *Jacqueline Wilson, Girls Out Late*

heir (*say* air) *NOUN* **heirs**
someone who inherits the property or rank of a person who has died

heiress (*say* **air**- ess) *NOUN* **heiresses**
a woman who will inherit great wealth or property

heirloom (*say* **air**- loom) *NOUN* **heirlooms**
a valued possession that has been handed down in a family for several generations

helicopter *NOUN* **helicopters**
a kind of aircraft with a large horizontal propeller or rotor

heliotrope *NOUN* **heliotropes**
a plant with small fragrant purple flowers

helium (*say* **hee**- lee- um) *NOUN*
a light colourless gas used to fill balloons

helix (*say* **hee**- liks) *NOUN* **helices** (*say* **hee**- liss- eez)
a spiral

hell *NOUN*
1 a place where, in some religions, bad or evil people are thought to be punished after they die
2 a very unpleasant place or situation

he'll
short for *he will*

hellish *ADJECTIVE*
(*informal*) very difficult or unpleasant

hello *EXCLAMATION*
a word used to greet someone or attract their attention

helm *NOUN* **helms**
the handle or wheel used to steer a ship

to be at the helm is to be in charge of an organization or project

helmet *NOUN* **helmets**
a strong hat worn to protect the head

helmsman *NOUN* **helmsmen**
a person who steers a boat

help *VERB* **helps, helping, helped**
1 to do something useful for someone
2 to benefit someone or make something better or easier ◆ *Our user survey will help us to plan future events.*
3 you cannot help doing something when you cannot avoid doing it

Rincewind couldn't help noticing that the hand holding the wand was shaking. — *Terry Pratchett, The Colour of Magic*

4 to serve food or drink to someone
▷ **helper** *NOUN*

help *NOUN*
1 the act of helping someone
2 a person or thing that helps

helpful *ADJECTIVE*
giving help; useful
▷ **helpfully** *ADVERB*

helping *NOUN* **helpings**
a portion of food

helpless *ADJECTIVE*
1 unable to defend yourself or to act without help
2 helpless laughter is uncontrollable or hysterical
▷ **helplessly** *ADVERB*
▷ **helplessness** *NOUN*

helpline *NOUN* **helplines**
a telephone service giving advice on problems

helter-skelter *ADVERB*
in great haste or confusion

helter-skelter *NOUN* **helter-skelters**
a tall spiral slide at a fair

hem *NOUN* **hems**
the edge of a piece of cloth that is folded over and sewn down

hem *VERB* **hems, hemming, hemmed**
to put a hem on something

to hem someone in is to surround them and prevent them from leaving

If you are hemmed in on all sides in a patch of land there is only one chance of escape. You must stay in the patch, and let your enemies search it and not find you. — *John Buchan, The Thirty-Nine Steps*

hemisphere *NOUN* **hemispheres**
1 half a sphere
2 half the earth, divided into north and south
▷ **hemispherical** *ADJECTIVE*

hemlock *NOUN*
a poisonous plant, or the poison made from it

hemp *NOUN*
1 a plant that produces coarse fibres from which cloth and ropes are made
2 the drug cannabis, made from this plant
▷ **hempen** *ADJECTIVE*

hen *NOUN* **hens**
a female bird, especially a female fowl

hence *ADVERB*
1 as a result; therefore
2 from now on
3 (*old use*) from here

henceforth *ADVERB*
from now on

henchman *NOUN* **henchmen**
a faithful supporter

WORD HISTORY from Old English *hengest* 'a male horse': a henchman was originally a groom, then a squire or page to a person of rank

henna *NOUN*
a reddish-brown dye, especially used for colouring hair

hepatitis *NOUN*
a disease causing inflammation of the liver

heptagon *NOUN* **heptagons**
a geometric figure with seven sides
▷ **heptagonal** *ADJECTIVE*

heptathlon *NOUN* **heptathlons**
an athletic contest in which each competitor takes part in seven events

her *PRONOUN*
the form of *she* used as the object of a verb or after a preposition

her *ADJECTIVE*
belonging to her ◆ *This is her book.*

herald *NOUN* **heralds**
an official in former times who made announcements and carried messages for a king or queen

herald *VERB* **heralds, heralding, heralded**
to show that something is coming

The only time the wind blew was to herald the sudden torrential cloudburst which daily replenished the water lying in the paddy fields.
— *Geraldine McCaughrean, The Kite Rider*

heraldry *NOUN*
the study or use of coats of arms
▷ **heraldic** (*say* hir- **al**- dik) *ADJECTIVE*

herb *NOUN* **herbs**
a plant used for flavouring or for making medicine
▷ **herbal** *ADJECTIVE*

herbaceous (*say* her- **bay**- shus) *ADJECTIVE*
a herbaceous border is one containing many flowering plants

herbivore (*say* **her**- bi- vor) *NOUN*
an animal that feeds on plants and not on the flesh of other animals (SEE ALSO **carnivore, omnivore**)

herbivorous (*say* her- **biv**- er- us) *ADJECTIVE*
a herbivorous animal feeds on plants and not on the flesh of other animals (SEE ALSO **carnivorous, omnivorous**)

herculean (*say* her- kew- **lee**- an) *ADJECTIVE*
a herculean task is one that needs great strength or effort

WORD HISTORY from *Hercules*, a hero in ancient Greek legend who had to perform twelve great tasks or 'labours'

herd *NOUN* **herds**
1 a group of cattle or other animals that feed together
2 a mass of people; a mob

herd *VERB* **herds, herding, herded**
1 to move or send in a herd ◆ *The visitors were herded into two large halls.*
2 to look after a herd of animals

herdsman *NOUN* **herdsmen**
a person who looks after a herd of animals

here *ADVERB*
in or to this place
here and there in various places or directions

hereafter *ADVERB*
(*formal*) from now on; in future

hereby *ADVERB*
(*formal*) as a result of this act or statement

hereditary *ADJECTIVE*
1 a hereditary disease or characteristic is passed from one generation to the next
2 a hereditary rank is one inherited from a previous holder

heredity (*say* hir- **ed**- it- ee) *NOUN*
the process of inheriting physical or mental characteristics from parents or ancestors

heresy (*say* **he**- ri- see) *NOUN* **heresies**
a belief or opinion that disagrees with those generally accepted, especially in Christianity

heretic (*say* **he**- ri- tik) *NOUN* **heretics**
a person who believes in a heresy
▷ **heretical** (*say* hi- **ret**- ik- al) *ADJECTIVE*

heritage *NOUN*
1 the things that someone has inherited
2 a nation's heritage is the historic buildings and other valuable things that are passed from generation to generation

I would cheerfully have swapped England's entire heritage—Stonehenge, Stratford, Wordsworth, Buckingham Palace, the lot—for the ability to watch quiz shows in the morning.
— *Nick Hornby, 31 Songs*

hermaphrodite (*say* her- **maf**- ro- dyt) *NOUN* **hermaphrodites**
an animal, flower, or person that has both male and female sexual organs or characteristics

WORD HISTORY from Greek *hermaphroditos*, originally the name of the son of the gods Hermes and Aphrodite, who became joined in one body with a nymph

hermetically *ADVERB*
a container is hermetically sealed when it is completely airtight

WORD HISTORY from the name of an Egyptian priest of the time of Moses, who became known as *Hermes Trismegistus*, meaning literally 'Hermes the three- times- greatest'; he was supposed to have invented a magic seal that kept things airtight

hermit *NOUN* **hermits**
a person who lives alone and avoids other people

hernia *NOUN* **hernias**
a condition in which part of the intestine or other organ pushes through the wall of the cavity containing it

hero *NOUN* **heroes**
1 a man or boy who is admired for an achievement or for bravery

There was something very odd about Dad of all people creating games about heroes. Anybody less like a hero would be hard to imagine. — *Alan Gibbons, Shadow of the Minotaur*

2 the chief male character in a book, play, or film
▷ **heroic** *ADJECTIVE*
▷ **heroically** *ADVERB*
▷ **heroism** *NOUN*

heroin *NOUN*
a very strong drug, made from morphine

heroine *NOUN* **heroines**
1 a woman or girl who is admired for an achievement or for bravery
2 the chief female character in a book, play, or film

heron *NOUN* **herons**
a wading bird with long legs and a long neck

herring *NOUN* **herring** or **herrings**
a sea fish used as food

hers *POSSESSIVE PRONOUN*
belonging to her ◆ *The books are hers.*
USAGE NOTE It is incorrect to write *her's*, with an apostrophe.

herself *PRONOUN*
she or her and nobody else: used to refer back to the subject of a sentence (e.g. *She cut herself*) or for emphasis (e.g. *She herself has said it*)
by herself on her own; alone

hertz *NOUN* **hertz**
(*Science*) a unit of frequency of electromagnetic waves, equal to one cycle per second
WORD HISTORY named after a German scientist, H. R. *Hertz*, who discovered radio waves

he's
short for *he is* or *he has* (when followed by a participle, as in *he's taken my pen*)

hesitant *ADJECTIVE*
slow or uncertain about doing or saying something
▷ **hesitantly** *ADVERB*
▷ **hesitancy** *NOUN*

hesitate *VERB* **hesitates, hesitating, hesitated**
to be slow or uncertain in doing or saying something
▷ **hesitation** *NOUN*

hessian *NOUN*
a type of strong coarse cloth, used for making sacks
WORD HISTORY named after *Hesse*, a region of Germany where it was made

heterogeneous (*say* het- er- o- **jeen**- ee- us) *ADJECTIVE*
consisting of people or things of different kinds

heterosexual (*say* het- er- o- **sek**- shul) *ADJECTIVE*
sexually attracted to people of the opposite sex, or involving this kind of attraction; not homosexual
▷ **heterosexual** *NOUN*

hew *VERB* **hews, hewing, hewn**
to chop or cut with an axe, pick, or other heavy tool

hexagon *NOUN* **hexagons**
a geometric figure with six sides
▷ **hexagonal** *ADJECTIVE*

heyday *NOUN*
the time of a person's or thing's greatest success or prosperity

hi *EXCLAMATION*
(*informal*) a friendly greeting

hiatus (*say* hy- ay- tus) *NOUN* **hiatuses**
a gap in something that is otherwise continuous

hibernate *VERB* **hibernates, hibernating, hibernated**
an animal hibernates when it passes the winter in a state like deep sleep
▷ **hibernation** *NOUN*
WORD HISTORY from Latin *hibernus* 'wintry'

hiccup *NOUN* **hiccups**
1 a short high gulping sound made when your breath is briefly interrupted
2 a minor hitch or setback

hiccup *VERB* **hiccups, hiccuping, hiccuped**
to make a sound of hiccups

hickory *NOUN* **hickories**
a North American tree like a walnut tree

hide[1] *VERB* **hides, hiding, hid, hidden**
1 to get into a place where you cannot be seen

Raphah hid in the damp cellar of the Vicarage, among some stored apples that had been stacked in wooden trays and covered in sackcloth. — *G. P. Taylor, Shadowmancer*

2 to keep a person or thing from being seen
3 to keep a thing secret

hide❷ ***NOUN*** **hides**
an animal's skin

hide-and-seek ***NOUN***
a game in which one person looks for others who are hiding

hidebound ***ADJECTIVE***
narrow-minded and conservative

WORD HISTORY originally used of cattle that were poorly fed, so that their skin was stretched tight over their bones, and later of a tree whose bark was so tight it could not grow

hideous ***ADJECTIVE***
very ugly or unpleasant
▷ **hideously** ***ADVERB***

hideout ***NOUN*** **hideouts**
a place for hiding in

hiding ***NOUN*** **hidings**
1 to go into hiding is to go where no one can find you
2 a thrashing or beating

hierarchy (*say* **hyr**- ark- ee) ***NOUN*** **hierarchies**
an organization that ranks people according to how important they are

hieroglyphics (*say* hyr- o- **glif**- iks) ***PLURAL NOUN***
pictures or symbols used in ancient Egypt to represent words

hi-fi ***NOUN*** **hi-fis**
(*informal*) equipment for playing CDs or other recorded music

WORD HISTORY short for *high fidelity* (sound)

higgledy-piggledy ***ADVERB, ADJECTIVE***
completely jumbled up

high ***ADJECTIVE***
1 far above the ground, or reaching a long way upwards
2 having a specified measurement from top to bottom ◆ *The tower is over twenty metres high.*
3 above average level in importance, quality, or amount ◆ *Such fruits have high levels of protein.*
4 near the top of the range in a musical scale
5 meat is high when it is beginning to go bad
6 (*informal*) a person is high when they are affected by a drug
it is high time it is past the time when something should have happened

highbrow ***ADJECTIVE***
having serious or intellectual tastes

Higher ***NOUN*** **Highers**
the advanced level of the Scottish Certificate of Education

higher education ***NOUN***
education at a university or college

high fidelity ***NOUN***
reproducing recorded sound clearly and faithfully

high jump ***NOUN***
an athletic contest in which competitors jump over a high bar

highlands ***PLURAL NOUN***
areas of land with hills and mountains
▷ **highland** ***ADJECTIVE***
▷ **highlander** ***NOUN***

highlight ***NOUN*** **highlights**
1 the most interesting part of something ◆ *A highlight of the visit is the ride on a steam train.*
2 (*Art*) a light area in a painting or photograph, showing where the light falls in real life
3 highlights are light-coloured streaks in a person's hair

highlight ***VERB*** **highlights, highlighting, highlighted**
to draw special attention to something

highly ***ADVERB***
1 extremely ◆ *The architect is highly experienced and very professional.*
2 very well or favourably ◆ *Employers rate these qualifications very highly.*

highly-strung ***ADJECTIVE***
nervous and easily upset

Highness ***NOUN*** **Highnesses**
the title of a prince or princess

high-pitched ***ADJECTIVE***
high in sound

high-rise ***ADJECTIVE***
a high-rise building is tall with many storeys

high school ***NOUN*** **high schools**
a secondary school

high spirits ***PLURAL NOUN***
cheerful and lively behaviour
▷ **high-spirited** ***ADJECTIVE***

high street ***NOUN*** **high streets**
the main street of a town

high-tech ***ADJECTIVE***
using the most advanced technology, especially electronic devices and computers

highway ***NOUN*** **highways**
a main road or route for vehicles

highwayman ***NOUN*** **highwaymen**
in former times, a man on horseback who robbed travellers on highways

hijack ***VERB*** **hijacks, hijacking, hijacked**
to seize control of an aircraft or vehicle by force during a journey
▷ **hijack** ***NOUN***
▷ **hijacker** ***NOUN***

SPELLING NOTE Some words pronounced like *hit* or *hike* begin with **hy-** (e.g. hysteria, hypothetical)

hike *NOUN* **hikes**
a long walk in the country

hike *VERB* **hikes, hiking, hiked**
to go on a hike
▷ **hiker** *NOUN*

hilarious *ADJECTIVE*
very funny
▷ **hilariously** *ADVERB*
▷ **hilarity** *NOUN*

hill *NOUN* **hills**
a rounded piece of land that is higher than the ground around it

hillock *NOUN* **hillocks**
a small hill or mound

hillside *NOUN* **hillsides**
a piece of land forming the side of a hill

hilly *ADJECTIVE* **hillier, hilliest**
hilly country has a lot of hills

hilt *NOUN* **hilts**
the handle of a sword, dagger, or knife

him *PRONOUN*
the form of *he* used as the object of a verb or after a preposition

himself *PRONOUN*
he or him and nobody else: used to refer back to the subject of a sentence (e.g. *He cut himself*) or for emphasis (e.g. *He himself has told us*)
by himself on his own; alone

hind❶ *ADJECTIVE*
at the back ◆ *the hind legs*

hind❷ *NOUN* **hinds**
a female deer (SEE ALSO **hart**)

hinder *VERB* **hinders, hindering, hindered**
to get in your way or make things difficult for you

Hindi *NOUN*
one of the languages of India

hindmost *ADJECTIVE*
furthest behind

hindquarters *PLURAL NOUN*
an animal's hind legs and rear parts

hindrance *NOUN* **hindrances**
something that hinders you or gets in your way

hindsight *NOUN*
the ability to look back on an event or activity with an understanding you did not have at the time ◆ *With hindsight, we could have done the job much better.*

Hindu *NOUN* **Hindus**
(*Religion*) a person who believes in Hinduism, which is one of the religions of India
▷ **Hinduism** *NOUN*

hinge *NOUN* **hinges**
a movable joint on which a door or window or cover turns when it opens

hinge *VERB* **hinges, hinging, hinged**
1 to be hinged is to be fixed on with a hinge
2 to hinge on something is to depend on it ◆ *The plot hinges on the contrast between the two main characters.*

hint *NOUN* **hints**
1 a slight indication or suggestion
2 a useful idea or piece of advice

hint *VERB* **hints, hinting, hinted**
to make a hint

hinterland *NOUN* **hinterlands**
the district lying inland beyond a coast or port

We searched the beach and its hinterland for timber. — *David Almond, The Fire-Eaters*

hip❶ *NOUN* **hips**
the bony part at the side of the body between the waist and the thigh

hip❷ *NOUN* **hips**
the fruit of the wild rose

hippo *NOUN* **hippos**
(*informal*) a hippopotamus

hippopotamus *NOUN* **hippopotamuses**
a large African animal with a tough skin and short legs, that lives near water
WORD HISTORY from Greek *hippos* 'horse' and *potamos* 'river'

hippy *NOUN* **hippies**
(*informal*) a young person, especially in the 1960s, who joined with others to live in an unconventional way based on ideas of peace and love

hipsters *PLURAL NOUN*
trousers with the waistline at the hips rather than the waist

hire *VERB* **hires, hiring, hired**
1 to pay to have use of something for a time
2 to give someone a job
3 to hire something out is to lend it in return for payment
▷ **hirer** *NOUN*

hire *NOUN*
something is available for hire when people can hire it

hirsute (*say* **herss**- yoot) *ADJECTIVE*
(*formal*) covered in hair; hairy

his *ADJECTIVE, POSSESSIVE PRONOUN*
belonging to him ◆ *This is his book.* ◆ *The book is his.*

hiss *VERB* **hisses, hissing, hissed**
make a sound like an *s*

The yellow smoke hissed from the dragon's nostrils: that was his laughter. — *Ursula Le Guin, A Wizard of Earthsea*

▷ **hiss** *NOUN*

histogram *NOUN* **histograms**
a chart showing amounts as rectangles of varying sizes

historian *NOUN* **historians**
a person who writes or studies history

historic *ADJECTIVE*
famous or important in history; likely to be remembered ◆ *The meeting was held in the historic setting of York.* ◆ *It was a truly historic occasion.*

historical *ADJECTIVE*
1 to do with history
2 a historical event is one that actually happened

history *NOUN* **histories**
1 the events that happened in the past, or the study of these
2 a record or description of important events

hit *VERB* **hits, hitting, hit**
1 to come forcefully against a person or thing or direct a blow at them
2 a moving object hits something when it comes into violent contact with it
3 to upset someone; to affect someone or something badly ◆ *A fall in demand has hit the tourist industry.*
4 to be suddenly obvious or clear to someone ◆ *Then it hit me that she was talking about us.*
5 to hit a problem or difficulty is to have to deal with it
6 to hit a high note is to succeed in singing or playing it

to hit it off (*informal*) is to get on well with someone
to hit on something is to discover it suddenly or by chance

SYNONYMS (meaning 1) strike, smack, slap, thump, whack; (meaning 2) crash into, run into, smash into, collide with; (meaning 3) affect, hurt, harm, damage

hit *NOUN* **hits**
1 hitting; a knock or stroke
2 a shot that hits the target
3 a success

I had my birthday party on Sunday afternoon. The Rin Tin Tin film was a big hit with my classmates. — *Anne Frank, The Diary of a Young Girl*

4 a successful song, show, etc.

hit-and-miss *ADJECTIVE*
done in a random or haphazard way

hit-and-run *ADJECTIVE*
a hit-and-run driver is one who injures someone in an accident and drives off without stopping

hitch *VERB* **hitches, hitching, hitched**
1 to raise or pull with a slight jerk
2 to fasten with a loop or hook
3 to hitch-hike

We really knew so very little about hitching lifts ... but we went on waving and cars went on passing, until at length one did stop. — *Diana Wynne Jones, The Merlin Conspiracy*

hitch *NOUN* **hitches**
1 a slight difficulty causing delay
2 a hitching movement
3 a knot

hitch-hike *VERB* **hitch-hikes, hitch-hiking, hitch-hiked**
to travel by getting lifts from passing vehicles
▷ **hitch-hiker** *NOUN*

hi-tech *ADJECTIVE*
another spelling of **high-tech**

hither *ADVERB*
(*old use*) to or towards this place

hitherto *ADVERB*
until this time

HIV *ABBREVIATION*
human immunodeficiency virus; a virus that causes Aids

hive *NOUN* **hives**
1 a beehive
2 the bees living in a beehive

a hive of industry is a place where people are working busily

hoard *NOUN* **hoards**
a carefully saved store of money, food, or other things

People said there were hoards of gold and jewels in those rooms above the warehouses, and rich carpets and chandeliers and oil paintings in gold frames. — *Alison Prince, Oranges and Murder*

hoard *VERB* **hoards, hoarding, hoarded**
to store something away
▷ **hoarder** *NOUN*

USAGE NOTE Take care not to confuse this word with *horde*.

hoarding *NOUN* **hoardings**
a large board covered with advertisements

hoar frost *NOUN*
a white frost

hoarse *ADJECTIVE*
having a rough or croaking voice
▷ **hoarsely** *ADVERB*
▷ **hoarseness** *NOUN*

a b c d e f g h i j k l m n o p q r s t u v w x y z

SPELLING NOTE Some words pronounced like *hit* or *hike* begin with **hy-** (e.g. hysteria, hypothetical)

hoary *ADJECTIVE* **hoarier, hoariest**
1 hoary hair is white or grey from age
2 old and over-used ◆ *He has a vast collection of hoary old jokes.*

hoax *VERB* **hoaxes, hoaxing, hoaxed**
to play a trick on somebody

> Somebody put that fellow up to coming here and hoaxing us. There are people in this town who dislike me enough to do that. — *J. B. Priestley, An Inspector Calls*

▷ **hoax** *NOUN*
▷ **hoaxer** *NOUN*

hob *NOUN* **hobs**
a flat surface on the top of a cooker, for cooking or heating food

hobble *VERB* **hobbles, hobbling, hobbled**
to walk with difficulty, especially because of an injury

hobby *NOUN* **hobbies**
something you enjoy doing in your spare time

hobby horse *NOUN* **hobby horses**
a subject that a person likes to talk about whenever they can

hobgoblin *NOUN* **hobgoblins**
a mischievous or evil spirit

hobnob *VERB* **hobnobs, hobnobbing, hobnobbed**
(*informal*) to hobnob with people is to spend a lot of time with them

hockey *NOUN*
a team game in which players use curved sticks to drive a hard ball into the other side's goal

hoe *NOUN* **hoes**
a tool with a long handle and a thin blade, for removing weeds

hoe *VERB* **hoes, hoeing, hoed**
to scrape or dig with a hoe

hog *NOUN* **hogs**
1 a castrated male pig
2 (*informal*) a greedy person

to go the whole hog (*informal*) is to do something completely or thoroughly

hog *VERB* **hogs, hogging, hogged**
(*informal*) to take more than your fair share of something

Hogmanay *NOUN*
New Year's Eve in Scotland

hoi polloi *NOUN*
the ordinary people; the masses

WORD HISTORY from Greek, meaning 'the many'

hoist *VERB* **hoists, hoisting, hoisted**
to lift something heavy by using ropes or pulleys

hold *VERB* **holds, holding, held**
1 to have and keep something, especially in your hands
2 to contain or have space for ◆ *The container holds two gallons.*
3 to support ◆ *The bridge won't hold the weight of large vehicles.*
4 to stay the same; to continue ◆ *The fine weather is expected to hold for a few days more.*
5 to believe or consider ◆ *We will have to hold you responsible.*
6 to arrange something or cause it to take place ◆ *They held a party to celebrate their success.*
7 to keep someone somewhere or stop them getting away ◆ *The police cannot hold these men any longer without charging them.*

to hold forth is to make a long tedious speech
hold it stop; wait a minute
to hold out
1 is to refuse to give in
2 is to last or continue
to hold someone up
1 is to hinder them
2 is to stop and rob someone with force
to hold with something is to approve of it
to hold your tongue (*informal*) is to stop talking

hold *NOUN* **holds**
1 the act of holding something; a grasp
2 a place where you can put your hand or foot when climbing
3 the part of a ship where cargo is stored, below the deck

to get hold of someone is to make contact with them
to get hold of something
1 is to grasp it
2 is to obtain it

holdall *NOUN* **holdalls**
a large soft bag with handles

holder *NOUN* **holders**
a person or thing that holds something

hold-up *NOUN* **hold-ups**
1 a brief delay
2 a robbery with threats or force

hole *NOUN* **holes**
1 a hollow place; a gap or opening
2 a burrow
3 one of the small holes into which you have to hit the ball in golf
4 (*informal*) an unpleasant place

to be in a hole (*informal*) is to be in an awkward situation

▷ **holey** *ADJECTIVE*

hole *VERB* **holes, holing, holed**
1 to make a hole in something
2 in golf, to hit the ball into one of the holes

Holi *NOUN*
a Hindu festival held in the spring

holiday ***NOUN*** **holidays**
1 a day or time for enjoyment away from work or school
2 a time when you go away to enjoy yourself

WORD HISTORY originally *holy day* (because holidays were religious festivals)

holiness ***NOUN***
being holy or sacred
His Holiness the title of the pope

hollow ***ADJECTIVE***
1 having an empty space inside; not solid
2 a hollow sound is loud and echoing
3 a hollow promise is insincere
4 (*informal*) to beat someone hollow is to win by a large margin

hollow ***NOUN*** **hollows**
a hollow or sunken place

hollow ***VERB*** **hollows, hollowing, hollowed**
to make a thing hollow

holly ***NOUN***
an evergreen bush with shiny prickly leaves and red berries

hollyhock ***NOUN*** **hollyhocks**
a plant with large showy flowers on a tall stem

holocaust ***NOUN*** **holocausts**
a large-scale destruction, especially by fire or in a war
the Holocaust the mass murder of Jews by the Nazis in World War II

WORD HISTORY from Greek *holos* and *kaustos* meaning 'completely burnt'

hologram ***NOUN*** **holograms**
a type of photograph made by laser beams that produces a three-dimensional image

holster ***NOUN*** **holsters**
a leather case for carrying a pistol or revolver, worn on a belt or under the arm

holy ***ADJECTIVE*** **holier, holiest**
1 belonging or devoted to God
2 a holy person is religious and leads a pure life

homage ***NOUN*** **homages**
an act or expression of respect or admiration
◆ *He would pay homage to the Emperor.*

home ***NOUN*** **homes**
1 the place where a person lives
2 the place where a person was born or where they feel they belong
3 a place where those who need help are looked after
4 the place to be reached in a race or in certain games
to bring something home to someone is to make them realize it
to push something home is to push it as far as it will go

home ***ADJECTIVE***
1 to do with your own home or country ◆ *home industries.*
2 a home game or match is one played on a team's own ground

home ***VERB*** **homes, homing, homed**
to home in on a target or objective is to be aimed at it or seek it out

home economics ***NOUN***
the study of cookery and how to run a home

homeland ***NOUN*** **homelands**
1 a person's native country
2 (*South African*) each of ten areas in South Africa that were formerly set aside for indigenous African peoples and were partly self-governing

homeless ***ADJECTIVE***
having no home
▷ **homelessness** ***NOUN***

homely ***ADJECTIVE***
simple and ordinary
▷ **homeliness** ***NOUN***

home-made ***ADJECTIVE***
made at home, not bought from a shop

homeopathy ***NOUN***
the treatment of disease by tiny doses of drugs that in a healthy person would produce symptoms of the disease
▷ **homeopathic** ***ADJECTIVE***

home page ***NOUN*** **home pages**
an introductory page on a website

homesick ***ADJECTIVE***
upset because of being away from home
▷ **homesickness** ***NOUN***

homestead ***NOUN*** **homesteads**
a farmhouse with the land and buildings round it

homeward ***ADJECTIVE, ADVERB***
going towards home
▷ **homewards** ***ADVERB***

homework ***NOUN***
school work given to pupils to do at home

homicide ***NOUN*** **homicides**
the crime of killing another person
▷ **homicidal** ***ADJECTIVE***

homily ***NOUN*** **homilies**
a lecture about behaviour

homing ***ADJECTIVE***
1 an animal with a homing instinct is trained to return to its home
2 a homing weapon is programmed to reach its target

homogeneous (*say* hom-o-**jeen**-ee-us) ***ADJECTIVE***
formed of people or things of the same kind

homograph *NOUN* **homographs**
(*Language*) a word that is spelled like another but has a different meaning or origin, e.g. *hide* (to keep secret) and *hide* (an animal's skin)

homographs and homophones

Homographs are words which are spelled the same but have different meanings, and often different origins. Some examples are *cricket* (a sport or an insect), *mould* (fungus or a shape), and *swallow* (to gulp or a bird). Sometimes homographs are pronounced differently, like *bow* (to bend down) and *bow* (for archery), or *wind* (a gust) and *wind* (to twist).
Homophones are words which sound the same but have different spellings and meanings, such as *aisle* (in a church) and *isle* (an island), *currant* (dried fruit) and *current* (river flow), *metal* (gold, silver, etc.) and *mettle* (strength), *yolk* (of an egg) and *yoke* (a harness). And these three words are all homophones: *vain* (proud), *vane* (weathercock), and *vein* (blood vessel).
So, *dessert* (pudding) and *desert* (to abandon) are homophones, because they sound the same (but are written differently); whereas *desert* (Sahara desert) and *desert* (to abandon) are homographs because they are written the same way (but do not sound the same).
See also the panel on **confusable words**.

homonym (*say* hom- o- nim) *NOUN* **homonyms**
(*Language*) a homograph or homophone

homophone *NOUN* **homophones**
(*Language*) a word that sounds the same as another but has a different spelling, e.g. *pair* (two things) and *pear* (a fruit): see the panel on **homographs and homophones**

Homo sapiens *NOUN*
human beings regarded as a species of animal

homosexual (*say* hom- o- sek- shul) *ADJECTIVE*
attracted to people of the same sex
▷ **homosexual** *NOUN*
▷ **homosexuality** *NOUN*

honest *ADJECTIVE*
being truthful and behaving properly without cheating or stealing
▷ **honestly** *ADVERB*
▷ **honesty** *NOUN*

honey *NOUN*
a sweet sticky food made by bees

honeycomb *NOUN* **honeycombs**
a wax structure formed by rows of small six-sided sections made by bees to hold their honey and eggs

honeycombed *ADJECTIVE*
having lots of holes or tunnels

honeymoon *NOUN* **honeymoons**
a holiday spent together by a newly married couple
WORD HISTORY from *honey* and *moon* (because people believed that love is sweet like honey but fades like the moon)

honeysuckle *NOUN*
a climbing plant with fragrant yellow or pink flowers

honk *NOUN* **honks**
a short deep sound like that made by a goose or an old-fashioned car horn

honk *VERB* **honks, honking, honked**
to make a short deep sound

honorary *ADJECTIVE*
1 an honorary title is given to someone as an honour
2 an honorary job or office is one that is unpaid
USAGE NOTE Take care not to confuse this word with *honourable*.

honour *NOUN* **honours**
1 honour is great respect or reputation
2 honour is also honesty and loyalty ◆ *He was a person of honour.*
3 an honour is something a person is proud to do ◆ *It will be an honour to meet them.*
4 an honour is also an award given as a mark of respect
5 to do something in honour of someone or something is to do it out of respect for them ◆ *Memorials were set up in honour of the dead.*

honour *VERB* **honours, honouring, honoured**
1 to feel or show honour for a person
2 to keep to the terms of an agreement or promise
USAGE NOTE The American spelling of this word is honor.

honourable *ADJECTIVE*
deserving honour; honest and loyal
▷ **honourably** *ADVERB*
USAGE NOTE Take care not to confuse this word with *honorary*.

hood *NOUN* **hoods**
1 a covering of soft material for the head and neck
2 a folding roof or cover for a vehicle or piece of machinery
▷ **hooded** *ADJECTIVE*

hoodwink *VERB* **hoodwinks, hoodwinking, hoodwinked**
to deceive someone
WORD HISTORY it originally meant 'to blindfold with a hood': from *hood* and an old meaning of *wink* 'to close the eyes'

hoody or **hoodie** *NOUN* **hoodies**
a jacket or sweatshirt with a hood that goes over the head

hoof *NOUN* **hoofs** or **hooves**
the hard horny part of some animals' feet

hook *NOUN* **hooks**
a bent or curved piece of metal or plastic for hanging things on or for catching hold of something
to be let off the hook (*informal*) is to escape punishment

hook *VERB* **hooks, hooking, hooked**
1 to fasten something with a hook
2 to catch a fish with a hook
3 to hit a ball in a curving path
to be hooked on something (*informal*) is to like doing it very much or to be addicted to it

hookah *NOUN* **hookahs**
an oriental tobacco pipe with a long tube which draws the smoke through a jar of water

hooked *ADJECTIVE*
having the shape of a hook

hooligan *NOUN* **hooligans**
a rough and violent young person
▷ **hooliganism** *NOUN*

hoop *NOUN* **hoops**
a large ring used as a toy

hoopla *NOUN*
a game in which people try to throw hoops round an object, which they win as a prize if they succeed

hooray *EXCLAMATION*
another spelling of **hurray**

hoot *NOUN* **hoots**
1 the sound made by an owl or a vehicle's horn or a steam whistle
2 a cry of scorn or disapproval
3 a loud laugh
4 something funny

hoot *VERB* **hoots, hooting, hooted**
1 to make the sound of a hoot
2 (*informal*) to laugh loudly

The idea of our family ever coming by six pounds a week made us all hoot with laughter. — *Dodie Smith, I Capture the Castle*

▷ **hooter** *NOUN*

Hoover *NOUN* **Hoovers**
(*trademark*) a vacuum cleaner

hoover *VERB* **hoovers, hoovering, hoovered**
to clean a floor with a vacuum cleaner

hop ❶ *VERB* **hops, hopping, hopped**
1 to jump on one foot
2 an animal hops when it springs from all its feet at once
3 (*informal*) to hop in or out of something is to move quickly there
to hop it (*informal*) is to go away quickly or suddenly

hop *NOUN* **hops**
a hopping movement

hop ❷ *NOUN* **hops**
a climbing plant used to give beer its flavour

hope *NOUN* **hopes**
1 hope is the feeling of wanting something to happen, and thinking that it will happen
2 a hope is a person or thing that gives hope

hope *VERB* **hopes, hoping, hoped**
to feel hope; to want and expect something

hopeful *ADJECTIVE*
1 feeling hope
2 likely to be good or successful

hopefully *ADVERB*
1 in a hopeful way ◆ *She spoke hopefully about her plans for the future.*
2 it is to be hoped; I hope that ◆ *Hopefully we can all benefit from this experience.*

hopeless *ADJECTIVE*
1 without hope
2 very bad at something

I was hopeless. I couldn't tackle. I missed the ball by a mile when I jumped up to head it. — *David Almond, Skellig*

▷ **hopelessly** *ADVERB*
▷ **hopelessness** *NOUN*

hopper *NOUN* **hoppers**
a large funnel-shaped container for grain or sand

hopscotch *NOUN*
a game of hopping into squares drawn on the ground

horde *NOUN* **hordes**
a large group or crowd
USAGE NOTE Take care not to confuse this word with *hoard*.

horizon *NOUN* **horizons**
1 the line where the earth and the sky seem to meet
2 the limit of a person's experience or interests
on the horizon likely to happen or begin soon

horizontal *ADJECTIVE*
level and parallel to the horizon (SEE ALSO **vertical**)
▷ **horizontally** *ADVERB*

hormone *NOUN* **hormones**
a substance produced by glands in the body and carried by the blood to stimulate other organs in the body
▷ **hormonal** *ADJECTIVE*

horn *NOUN* **horns**
1 each of the hard growths forming a point on the head of bulls, cows, goats, and other animals
2 a musical instrument made of brass (originally of horn), consisting of a tube or coiled pipe with a wide opening at the end, played by blowing
3 a device on a motor vehicle for making a warning sound
▷ **horned** *ADJECTIVE*
▷ **horny** *ADJECTIVE*

hornet *NOUN* **hornets**
a large kind of wasp

hornpipe *NOUN* **hornpipes**
a sailors' lively dance, or the music for this

horoscope *NOUN* **horoscopes**
a forecast made by an astrologer of what is going to happen to someone in the future
WORD HISTORY from Greek *hora* 'hour (of birth)' and *skopos* 'observer'

horrendous *ADJECTIVE*
extremely unpleasant

The howling is horrendous, a terrible baying noise, blocking out all other sounds, filling us up, tipping us towards madness. — *Theresa Breslin, Whispers in the Graveyard*

horrible *ADJECTIVE*
1 causing horror
2 very unpleasant or nasty
▷ **horribly** *ADVERB*

horrid *ADJECTIVE*
very unpleasant; horrible
▷ **horridly** *ADVERB*

horrific *ADJECTIVE*
causing horror; horrifying
▷ **horrifically** *ADVERB*

horrify *VERB* **horrifies, horrifying, horrified**
1 to make someone feel very afraid or disgusted
2 to shock someone

horror *NOUN* **horrors**
1 horror is great fear or disgust
2 a horror is a person or thing causing horror

It was from the darkest of these pools that the creature with green eyes had come. It was chief of all the horrors of the fen. — *Robert Nye, Beowulf*

3 (*informal*) a badly behaved child

hors-d'oeuvre (*say* or- **dervr**) *NOUN* **hors-d'oeuvres**
food served as an appetizer at the start of a meal
WORD HISTORY from French, meaning 'outside the work' (because people eat them after their work is finished)

horse *NOUN* **horses**
1 a large four-legged animal used for riding on
2 a padded block for vaulting over in gymnastics

horseback *NOUN*
on horseback riding on a horse

horse chestnut *NOUN* **horse chestnuts**
a large tree that produces dark-brown nuts called *conkers*

horseman or **horsewoman** *NOUN* **horsemen** or **horsewomen**
a skilled rider of a horse
▷ **horsemanship** *NOUN*

horseplay *NOUN*
rough play

horsepower *NOUN*
a unit for measuring the power of an engine, equal to 746 watts

horseshoe *NOUN* **horseshoes**
a U-shaped piece of metal nailed to a horse's hoof

horticulture *NOUN*
the study or practice of cultivating gardens
▷ **horticultural** *ADJECTIVE*

hose *NOUN* **hoses**
1 (also **hosepipe**) a flexible tube for taking water to something
2 (*old use*) men's breeches, worn with a doublet (a close-fitting jacket)

hose *VERB* **hoses, hosing, hosed**
to water or spray with a hose

hosiery *NOUN*
socks, stockings, and tights sold in shops

hospice (*say* **hosp**- iss) *NOUN* **hospices**
a nursing home for people who are very ill or dying

hospitable *ADJECTIVE*
welcoming and friendly to guests and visitors
▷ **hospitably** *ADVERB*

hospital *NOUN* **hospitals**
a place providing medical and surgical treatment for people who are ill or injured
WORD HISTORY see the word history at *hostel*

hospitality *NOUN*
a friendly welcome and entertainment given to guests and visitors

host❶ *NOUN* **hosts**
1 a person who receives guests and looks after them
2 the presenter of a television or radio programme

host *VERB* **hosts, hosting, hosted**
to organize an event or be the host of it

host❷ *NOUN* **hosts**
a large number of people or things

host❸ *NOUN* **hosts**
(*Religion*) in the Christian Church, the bread consecrated at Communion

hostage *NOUN* **hostages**
a person who is held prisoner and only released if certain demands are met

hostel *NOUN* **hostels**
a building where people can stay or live
WORD HISTORY *hostel*, *hotel*, and *hospital* are all related and come from a medieval Latin word *hospitale*, meaning 'a place where guests were received'. Some of these people were sick, and over time in English the word *hospital* came to be used of a place where sick people were looked after. In French, *hostel* meant 'a place where guests were received', and *hotel* meant 'a large house'. *Hotel* used to have this meaning in English too, but now has a different meaning.

a b c d e f g h i j k l m n o p q r s t u v w x y z

hostess ***NOUN*** **hostesses**
a woman who receives guests and looks after them

hostile ***ADJECTIVE***
1 unfriendly and aggressive

If Captain Carstairs noticed Rebecca's hostile glance in Victoria's direction, he did not indicate it. — *Meg Cabot, Victoria and the Rogue*

2 opposed to something
3 belonging to an enemy ◆ *hostile aircraft.*
▷ **hostility** ***NOUN***

hot ***ADJECTIVE*** **hotter, hottest**
1 having a high temperature
2 spicy and giving a burning sensation in the mouth
3 a person with a hot temper is passionate and excitable
to be in hot water (*informal*) is to be in trouble
▷ **hotly** ***ADVERB***
▷ **hotness** ***NOUN***

hot ***VERB*** **hots, hotting, hotted**
to hot up (*informal*) is to become hotter or more exciting

hot dog ***NOUN*** **hot dogs**
a hot sausage eaten in a long bread roll

hotel ***NOUN*** **hotels**
a building where visitors and travellers pay to stay for the night and have meals
WORD HISTORY see the word history at *hostel*

hotfoot ***ADVERB***
in eager haste ◆ *He rushed hotfoot back to the house.*

hothead ***NOUN*** **hotheads**
a person who is impetuous or easily angered
▷ **hotheaded** ***ADJECTIVE***

hothouse ***NOUN*** **hothouses**
a heated greenhouse

hotplate ***NOUN*** **hotplates**
a heated surface for cooking food or keeping it hot

hotpot ***NOUN*** **hotpots**
a kind of stew

hot-water bottle ***NOUN*** **hot-water bottles**
a container that is filled with hot water and used to warm a bed

hound ***NOUN*** **hounds**
a dog used in hunting or racing

hound ***VERB*** **hounds, hounding, hounded**
to pursue or harass someone

hour ***NOUN*** **hours**
1 a period of sixty minutes, of which there are 24 in a day
2 a particular time of the day ◆ *It was strange to be still up at such a late hour.*
3 hours are a fixed period for work or some activity ◆ *Visiting hours are from 10 a.m. to 4 p.m.*

hourly ***ADVERB, ADJECTIVE***
every hour

house (*say* howss) ***NOUN*** **houses**
1 a building made for a person or group of people to live in
2 a building or establishment for a special purpose, e.g. an opera house or a storehouse
3 a building for a government assembly, or the assembly itself, e.g. the British House of Commons or the American House of Representatives
4 one of several divisions in some schools for sports competitions and other events
5 a family or dynasty, e.g. the House of Lancaster

house (*say* howz) ***VERB*** **houses, housing, housed**
to provide accommodation or room for someone or something

On the other side of the canal was an ancient church which, according to Mum's guidebook, housed the bones of a dragon killed by the spit of a saint. — *Mary Hoffman, Stravaganza: City of Masks*

houseboat ***NOUN*** **houseboats**
a boat like a small barge, for living in on a river or canal

household ***NOUN*** **households**
all the people who live together in the same house

householder ***NOUN*** **householders**
a person who owns or rents a house

housekeeper ***NOUN*** **housekeepers**
a person employed to look after a household

housekeeping ***NOUN***
1 the activity of looking after a household
2 the money for a household's food and other necessities

housewife ***NOUN*** **housewives**
a married woman who does the housekeeping for her family, and does not have a paid job

housework ***NOUN***
the regular work that has to be done in a house, such as cleaning and cooking

housing ***NOUN*** **housings**
1 buildings in which people live
2 a hard cover or casing for a piece of machinery

hove *past tense* of **heave** (when used of ships)

hovel ***NOUN*** **hovels**
a small shabby or badly built house

hover ***VERB*** **hovers, hovering, hovered**
1 a bird, insect, or aircraft hovers when it stays in one position in the air
2 a person hovers when they wait about near someone or something

hovercraft *NOUN* **hovercraft**
a vehicle that travels over the surface of land or water, supported by a current of air sent downwards from its engines

how *ADVERB*
1 in what way; by what means ◆ *How did you manage that?* ◆ *I don't know how you can say such a thing.*
2 to what extent or amount etc. ◆ *How long will the operation take?*
3 in what condition ◆ *I asked her how she was.*
4 used for emphasis ◆ *How strange you seem.*

however *ADVERB*
1 in whatever way; to whatever extent ◆ *It will be a long journey, however fast you go.*
2 all the same; nevertheless ◆ *This is, however, extremely uncertain.*

howl *NOUN* **howls**
a long loud sad-sounding cry or sound, such as that made by a dog

howl *VERB* **howls, howling, howled**
1 to make a howl
2 to weep loudly

howler *NOUN* **howlers**
(*informal*) a foolish or obvious mistake

HQ *ABBREVIATION*
headquarters

HTML *ABBREVIATION*
(*ICT*) hypertext mark-up language

HTTP *ABBREVIATION*
(*ICT*) hypertext transport (or transfer) protocol, used before the name of an Internet website that is accessed by a hypertext file

hub *NOUN* **hubs**
1 the centre part of a wheel
2 the central point of an activity or region

hubbub *NOUN*
a loud confused noise of voices

'Family Council is now in session,' declared the Elder Paw above the hubbub in the front room. — *S.F. Said, Varjak Paw*

huddle *VERB* **huddles, huddling, huddled**
1 people huddle when they crowd together, often for warmth
2 to curl up your body closely

I wanted to huddle into a ball on the old leather sofa. No, I wanted to hide behind it like a really little kid. — *Jacqueline Wilson, Lola Rose*

huddle *NOUN* **huddles**
a small group of people crowded together

hue ❶ *NOUN* **hues**
a colour or tint

hue ❷ *NOUN*
hue and cry a public outcry of alarm or protest

huff *NOUN*
in a huff offended or sulking about something
▷ **huffy** *ADJECTIVE*

huff *VERB* **huffs, huffing, huffed**
to blow out noisily

hug *VERB* **hugs, hugging, hugged**
1 to clasp someone closely in your arms
2 to keep close to a length of land ◆ *The little boat hugged the shore.*

hug *NOUN* **hugs**
to give someone a hug is to clasp them closely

huge *ADJECTIVE*
extremely large; enormous
▷ **hugely** *ADVERB*
▷ **hugeness** *NOUN*

hui *NOUN*
(*New Zealand*) a Maori gathering or conference

hulk *NOUN* **hulks**
1 the body or wreck of an old ship
2 a large clumsy person or thing
▷ **hulking** *ADJECTIVE*

hull *NOUN* **hulls**
the main framework of a ship that rests in the water

hullabaloo *NOUN* **hullabaloos**
a commotion or uproar

hullo *EXCLAMATION*
another spelling of **hello**

hum *VERB* **hums, humming, hummed**
1 to sing a tune with your lips closed
2 to make a low continuous sound like that of a bee

hum *NOUN* **hums**
a humming sound

There was a single metallic click and then the hum of machinery as a wheel turned somewhere overhead. — *Anthony Horowitz, Scorpia*

human *ADJECTIVE*
to do with human beings

human *NOUN* **humans**
a person

human being *NOUN* **human beings**
a person; a man, woman, or child

humane (*say* hew- **mayn**) *ADJECTIVE*
kind-hearted and merciful
▷ **humanely** *ADVERB*

humanism *NOUN*
the belief that people can use reason and understanding of others to live full lives, without needing religions
▷ **humanist** *NOUN*

humanitarian *ADJECTIVE*
concerned with people's welfare and the reduction of suffering
▷ **humanitarian** *NOUN*

humanity *NOUN* **humanities**
1 human beings as a whole; people
2 the condition of being human ◆ *We take pride in our humanity.*
3 compassion and understanding
4 the humanities are arts subjects such as history, literature, and music, as distinct from the sciences

humble *ADJECTIVE*
1 very modest about yourself and your importance
2 simple or unimportant ◆ *He gave his visitors a humble meal.*
▷ **humbly** *ADVERB*

WORD FAMILY The noun from humble is humility.

humble *VERB* **humbles, humbling, humbled**
to make someone feel humble or humiliated

humbug *NOUN* **humbugs**
1 insincere or dishonest talk or behaviour
2 a hard peppermint sweet

humdrum *ADJECTIVE*
dull and boring or monotonous

humid (*say* **hew**- mid) *ADJECTIVE*
humid air is warm and damp
▷ **humidity** *NOUN*

humiliate *VERB* **humiliates, humiliating, humiliated**
to make a person feel disgraced or ashamed
▷ **humiliation** *NOUN*

humility *NOUN*
the quality of being humble

hummingbird *NOUN* **hummingbirds**
a small tropical bird that makes a humming sound by beating its wings rapidly

hummock *NOUN* **hummocks**
a small hill or hump

humorist *NOUN* **humorists**
a writer of amusing stories or articles

humorous *ADJECTIVE*
full of humour; amusing

humour *NOUN*
1 being amusing; what makes people laugh
2 the ability to enjoy comical things ◆ *You need a good sense of humour.*
3 a person's mood ◆ *She is in a good humour today.*

humour *VERB* **humours, humouring, humoured**
to keep a person contented by doing what they want

hump *NOUN* **humps**
1 a rounded lump or mound
2 a rounded growth on the back of a camel or an abnormal growth forming a lump on a person's back

hump *VERB* **humps, humping, humped**
to carry something heavy with difficulty

humpback bridge *NOUN* **humpback bridges**
a small bridge that curves steeply upwards in the middle

humus (*say* **hew**- mus) *NOUN*
rich soil formed by decomposing leaves and plants

hunch① *NOUN* **hunches**
a feeling or guess about something, without knowing for certain

hunch② *VERB* **hunches, hunching, hunched**
to hunch your shoulders is to raise them so that your back is rounded

hunchback *NOUN* **hunchbacks**
(*old use*) a person with an abnormal hump on their back
▷ **hunchbacked** *ADJECTIVE*

hundred *NOUN, ADJECTIVE* **hundreds**
the number 100
▷ **hundredth** *ADJECTIVE, NOUN*

hundredweight *NOUN* **hundredweight**
a unit of weight equal to 112 pounds (about 50.8 kilograms)

hunger *NOUN*
1 the feeling that you have when you need to eat
2 a strong desire for something

hunger *VERB* **hungers, hungering, hungered**
to hunger for something is to want it very much

hunger strike *NOUN* **hunger strikes**
a protest in which a prisoner or other protester refuses to eat

hungry *ADJECTIVE* **hungrier, hungriest**
needing to eat
▷ **hungrily** *ADVERB*

hunk *NOUN* **hunks**
a large piece of something

hunker *VERB* **hunkers, hunkering, hunkered**
to squat or crouch down low

hunt *VERB* **hunts, hunting, hunted**
1 to chase and kill animals for food or as a sport
2 to search for something
▷ **hunter** *NOUN*
▷ **huntsman** *NOUN*

hunt *NOUN* **hunts**
1 the act of hunting or searching ◆ *The hunt for clues has begun.*
2 a group of hunters

hurdle *NOUN* **hurdles**
1 an upright frame forming one of a series for athletes to jump over in a race
2 a difficulty to be overcome

hurdling *NOUN*
the athletic sport of racing over hurdles
▷ **hurdler** *NOUN*

hurl *VERB* **hurls, hurling, hurled**
to throw something with great force

Christopher peeled the rumpled sleeve from his arm, and hurled the coat down on the floor. *— Anne Fine, Madame Doubtfire*

hurly-burly *NOUN*
a rough bustle of activity

hurray or **hurrah** *EXCLAMATION*
a shout of joy or approval; a cheer

hurricane *NOUN* **hurricanes**
a storm with a violent wind

hurry *VERB* **hurries, hurrying, hurried**
1 to move or do something quickly
2 to make someone be quick
▷ **hurried** *ADJECTIVE*
▷ **hurriedly** *ADVERB*

hurry *NOUN*
the act of hurrying; a need to hurry

hurt *VERB* **hurts, hurting, hurt**
1 to cause pain or injury to someone
2 to feel painful ◆ *My leg is hurting.*
3 to upset or offend someone ◆ *I didn't mean to hurt your feelings.*

hurt *NOUN*
physical or mental pain or injury

hurtful *ADJECTIVE*
a hurtful remark or action is one that upsets or offends someone
▷ **hurtfully** *ADVERB*

hurtle *VERB* **hurtles, hurtling, hurtled**
to move rapidly in a wild, barely controlled way

Mother came hurtling down the steps, her expression dour and fierce as always. *— Malorie Blackman, Noughts and Crosses*

husband *NOUN* **husbands**
the man a woman is married to

husbandry *NOUN*
1 the cultivation of crops and breeding of farm animals
2 the careful management of resources

hush *VERB* **hushes, hushing, hushed**
to become silent or quiet, or to make someone do this
to hush something up is to prevent it from becoming generally known

hush *NOUN*
a silence and lack of activity

hush-hush *ADJECTIVE*
(*informal*) highly secret or confidential

husk *NOUN* **husks**
the dry outer covering of some seeds and fruits

husky[1] *ADJECTIVE* **huskier, huskiest**
a husky voice is low-pitched and slightly hoarse
▷ **huskily** *ADVERB*
▷ **huskiness** *NOUN*

husky[2] *NOUN* **huskies**
a large powerful dog with a thick coat, used in the Arctic for pulling sledges

hustings *PLURAL NOUN*
a meeting for political speeches and campaigning just before an election

hustle *VERB* **hustles, hustling, hustled**
1 to hurry
2 to push or jostle someone roughly

hut *NOUN* **huts**
a small roughly made house or shelter

hutch *NOUN* **hutches**
a box or cage for keeping rabbits or other animals as pets

hyacinth *NOUN* **hyacinths**
a plant that grows from a bulb and produces bell-shaped fragrant flowers

WORD HISTORY from *Hyacinthus*, a youth in Greek legend who was accidentally killed by Apollo: the flower sprang from his blood

hybrid *NOUN* **hybrids**
1 a plant or animal produced by combining two different species or varieties
2 something made by combining parts or characteristics of two different things

hydra *NOUN* **hydras** or **hydrae**
a microscopic freshwater animal with a tubular body and a ring of tentacles round the mouth

WORD HISTORY named after the *Hydra* in Greek mythology, a water snake with many heads that grew again if they were cut off (because if a hydra is cut up, each section can grow into a whole animal)

hydrangea (*say* hy- **drayn**- ja) *NOUN* **hydrangeas**
a shrub with pink, blue, or white flowers growing in large clusters

hydrant *NOUN* **hydrants**
a water pipe with a nozzle that a fire hose can be attached to

hydraulic *ADJECTIVE*
worked by the force of water or other fluid under pressure

hydrochloric acid ***NOUN***
(*Science*) a strong colourless acid containing hydrogen and chlorine

hydroelectric ***ADJECTIVE***
using water power to produce electricity
▷ **hydroelectricity** ***NOUN***

hydrofoil ***NOUN*** **hydrofoils**
a boat fitted with special vanes that lift it clear of the water, enabling it to travel at speed over the surface

hydrogen ***NOUN***
a lightweight highly flammable gas that combines with oxygen to form water

hydrogen bomb ***NOUN*** **hydrogen bombs**
a very powerful bomb using energy created by the fusion of hydrogen isotopes (deuterium and tritium)

hydrolysis ***NOUN***
(*Science*) the chemical reaction of a substance with water, usually resulting in decomposition

hydrometer ***NOUN*** **hydrometers**
an instrument for measuring the density of liquids

hydrophobia ***NOUN***
extreme fear of water, as a symptom of rabies

hyena ***NOUN*** **hyenas**
a wild doglike animal that hunts in packs and makes a shrieking howl

hygiene (*say* **hy**- jeen) ***NOUN***
the practice of keeping things clean in order to remain healthy and prevent disease
▷ **hygienic** ***ADJECTIVE***
▷ **hygienically** ***ADVERB***

hymn ***NOUN*** **hymns**
(*Religion*) a religious song, usually a Christian song praising God
▷ **hymn book** ***NOUN***

hype ***NOUN***
(*informal*) extravagant publicity or advertising

hyperactive ***ADJECTIVE***
a hyperactive person is unable to relax and is always moving about or doing things

hyperbola (*say* hy- **per**- bol- a) ***NOUN*** **hyperbolas**
(*Mathematics*) the curve formed when a cone is cut by a plane that makes a larger angle with the base than the side of the cone does

hyperbole (*say* hy- **per**- bol- ee) ***NOUN*** **hyperboles**
a deliberate exaggeration that is not meant to be taken literally, e.g. 'I've got a stack of work a mile high'

hypermarket ***NOUN*** **hypermarkets**
a very large supermarket, usually outside a town

hypertext ***NOUN***
(*ICT*) a system allowing many links between related sections of text

hyphen ***NOUN*** **hyphens**
(*Language*) a short dash used to join words or parts of words together

hyphens

Hyphens connect two or more words which make up a compound noun or adjective. Sometimes, the hyphen is part of a fixed compound, like *close-up*, *free-range*, or *orang-utan*; but hyphens can join any pair or group of words to form a new compound: an *ultra-squidgy sandwich*; *that morning-after-the-night-before feeling*.

Hyphens are often useful to avoid ambiguity. Note, for example, the difference between *a cross-section of the audience* (= a typical sample) and *a cross section of the audience* (= an annoyed group). You do not need a hyphen for compound adjectives which follow a noun (*an out-of-date hairstyle* but *a hairstyle which looks out of date*), or for compounds which begin with an -ly adverb (*a well-written autobiography* but *a badly scripted film*).

Hyphens are also used in compound numbers and fractions, such as *thirty-two* and *four-fifths*, and in some place names, such as *Henley-on-Thames* and *Aix-en-Provence*.

See also the panel on **compounds**.

hyphenate ***VERB*** **hyphenates, hyphenating, hyphenated**
(*Language*) to write a word or group of words with a hyphen
▷ **hyphenation** ***NOUN***

hypnosis (*say* hip- **noh**- sis) ***NOUN***
a specially induced state like a deep sleep, in which a person can be made to follow the commands of someone else

hypnotize ***VERB*** **hypnotizes, hypnotizing, hypnotized**
to put someone in a state of hypnosis, so that their thoughts and actions may be influenced
▷ **hypnotism** ***NOUN***
▷ **hypnotic** ***ADJECTIVE***
▷ **hypnotist** ***NOUN***

USAGE NOTE This word can also be spelled hypnotise.

hypochondriac (*say* hy- po- **kon**- dree- ak) ***NOUN*** **hypochondriacs**
a person who is abnormally anxious about their health and believes they are ill even though there is nothing wrong with them
▷ **hypochondria** ***NOUN***

WORD HISTORY from Greek *hypochondrios* 'under the breastbone' (because the organs there were once thought to be the source of depression and anxiety)

hypocrisy (*say* hi- **pok**- ris- i) ***NOUN***
the pretence that you are more virtuous or have higher standards than is really the case

hypocrite (*say* **hip**- o- krit) ***NOUN*** **hypocrites**
someone who claims to be more virtuous or have higher standards than is really the case, or who criticizes others for weaknesses they also share
▷ **hypocritical** ***ADJECTIVE***

hypodermic ***ADJECTIVE***
a hypodermic needle or syringe is injected under the skin

hypotenuse (*say* hy- **pot**- i- newz) ***NOUN*** **hypotenuses**
(*Mathematics*) the longest side in a right-angled triangle, opposite the right angle

hypothermia ***NOUN***
the condition of having an abnormally low body temperature

hypothesis (*say* hy- **poth**- i- sis) ***NOUN*** **hypotheses**
a suggested explanation made on the basis of limited evidence or experiment, which tries to account for something but needs further investigation

hypothetical (*say* hy- po- **thet**- ikal) ***ADJECTIVE***
1 based on a theory or possibility
2 supposed but not necessarily real or true

hysterectomy (*say* hist- er- **ek**- tom- ee) ***NOUN*** **hysterectomies**
a surgical operation to remove the womb or part of it

hysteria ***NOUN***
wild uncontrolled emotion or excitement

WORD HISTORY from Greek *hystera* 'womb' (because people used to believe that the womb was the source of hysteria, and that only women suffered from it)

hysterical ***ADJECTIVE***
1 suffering from hysteria
2 (*informal*) extremely funny
▷ **hysterically** ***ADVERB***

hysterics (*say* hiss- **te**- riks) ***PLURAL NOUN***
1 a fit of hysteria
2 (*informal*) uncontrollable laughter

a b c d e f g h i j k l m n o p q r s t u v w x y z

Ii

I *PRONOUN*
a word used by a person to refer to himself or herself

ice *NOUN* **ices**
1 solid frozen water
2 an ice cream

ice *VERB* **ices, icing, iced**
1 to become covered with ice
2 to decorate a cake with icing

ice age *NOUN* **ice ages**
a period in the past when most of the earth's surface was covered with ice

iceberg *NOUN* **icebergs**
a large mass of ice floating in the sea with most of it under water

the tip of the iceberg a small sign or beginning of something much larger or more significant

ice cap *NOUN* **ice caps**
a permanent covering of ice and snow at the North or South Pole

ice cream *NOUN* **ice creams**
a sweet creamy frozen food made with sweetened milk fat

ice hockey *NOUN*
a form of hockey played on ice between teams of six skaters

ice lolly *NOUN* **ice lollies**
a piece of frozen juice on a stick

ice rink *NOUN* **ice rinks**
a building or enclosed area for skating

ichor (*say* eye- kaw) *NOUN*
in Greek mythology, the fluid that flowed like blood in the veins of the gods

Steam hissed from holes in the Stalker's chest and black ichor dripped from him and bubbled from the corners of his mouth. — *Philip Reeve, Mortal Engines*

icicle *NOUN* **icicles**
a hanging pointed piece of ice formed when dripping water freezes

icing *NOUN*
a sugary liquid mixture used as a coating for cakes

icon (*say* eye- kon) *NOUN* **icons**
1 a sacred painting or mosaic of a holy person, used especially in the Eastern Churches
2 a famous and highly admired person
3 (*ICT*) a small symbol or picture on a computer screen, representing a program or window that you can select

WORD HISTORY from Greek *eikon* 'image'

ICT *ABBREVIATION*
information and communication technology

icy *ADJECTIVE* **icier, iciest**
1 covered with ice
2 very cold
3 very unfriendly

Rodolfo greeted Rinaldo di Chimici with icy politeness but inwardly he was seething at the audacity of this aristocratic spy. — *Mary Hoffman, Stravaganza: City of Masks*

▷ **icily** *ADVERB*
▷ **iciness** *NOUN*

I'd
short for *I had* or *I would*

idea *NOUN* **ideas**
1 a plan or thought that you form in your mind
2 an opinion or belief
3 a feeling that something is likely

ideal *ADJECTIVE*
perfect; completely suitable
▷ **ideally** *ADVERB*

ideal *NOUN* **ideals**
1 a person who seems to be perfect
2 a high standard or principle that people try to follow

idealist *NOUN* **idealists**
a person who has high ideals and wishes to achieve them
▷ **idealistic** *ADJECTIVE*

identical *ADJECTIVE*
exactly the same

The close where Will and his mother lived was a loop of road in a modern estate, with a dozen identical houses of which theirs was the shabbiest. — *Philip Pullman, The Subtle Knife*

▷ **identically** *ADVERB*

identification *NOUN*
1 an official document, such as a passport or driving licence, that proves who someone is
2 the act of identifying someone or something

identify *VERB* **identifies, identifying, identified**
1 to recognize a person or thing as being who or what they are ▸▸

2 to treat something as being identical to something else or closely connected with it ◆ *It is important not to identify crime with poverty.*
3 to think of yourself as sharing another person's feelings or experiences ◆ *He was beginning to identify with his captors.*
▷ **identifiable** *ADJECTIVE*

identity *NOUN* **identities**
1 the fact of being who or what a person or thing is
2 the state of being the same or similar
3 a person's or group's distinctive character

ideology (*say* eye- dee- **ol**- o- jee) *NOUN* **ideologies**
a set of political beliefs and aims
▷ **ideological** *ADJECTIVE*

idiocy *NOUN* **idiocies**
stupid behaviour

idiom *NOUN* **idioms**
(*Language*) a phrase having a meaning that cannot be worked out from the meanings of the words in it, e.g. *in hot water* (in trouble), *hell for leather* (at great speed)
▷ **idiomatic** *ADJECTIVE*
▷ **idiomatically** *ADVERB*

idiosyncrasy (*say* id- ee- o- **sink**- ra- see) *NOUN* **idiosyncrasies**
a person's particular way of behaving or doing something
▷ **idiosyncratic** *ADJECTIVE*
USAGE NOTE Note that this word ends *-crasy* and not *-cracy*.
WORD HISTORY from Greek words *idios* 'personal or private', *syn* 'with', and *krasis* 'mixture': the meaning is 'a special or personal mixture (of ideas, activities, etc.)'

idiot *NOUN* **idiots**
a very silly or foolish person
▷ **idiotic** *ADJECTIVE*
▷ **idiotically** *ADVERB*
WORD HISTORY from Greek *idiotes* 'private citizen' and then 'uneducated person'

idle *ADJECTIVE*
1 doing no work; lazy
2 machinery or equipment is idle when it is not being used
3 idle thinking or talk has no real purpose or basis
▷ **idly** *ADVERB*
▷ **idleness** *NOUN*

idle *VERB* **idles, idling, idled**
1 to be idle or lazy
2 an engine idles when it is running slowly
▷ **idler** *NOUN*

idol *NOUN* **idols**
1 a statue or image that is worshipped as a god
2 a famous person who is widely admired
WORD HISTORY from Greek *eidolon* 'image'

idolatry *NOUN*
1 worship of idols
2 great admiration for someone
▷ **idolatrous** *ADJECTIVE*

idolize *VERB* **idolizes, idolizing, idolized**
to admire someone very much
▷ **idolization** *NOUN*
USAGE NOTE This word can also be spelled idolise.

idyll (*say* **id**- il) *NOUN* **idylls**
1 a beautiful or peaceful scene or situation
2 a poem describing a peaceful or romantic scene
WORD HISTORY from Greek *eidyllion* 'little picture'

idyllic (*say* id- **il**- ik) *ADJECTIVE*
beautiful and peaceful

i.e. *ABBREVIATION*
that is ◆ *her older brothers, i.e. Charlie and Alan*
WORD HISTORY short for Latin *id est* 'that is'

if *CONJUNCTION*
1 on condition that; supposing that ◆ *They will help you if you ask them.*
2 even though ◆ *I'll get this finished if I have to stay up all night.*
3 whether ◆ *They're not sure if it's ready yet.*
if only used to express a wish ◆ *If only I could come too!*

igloo *NOUN* **igloos**
an Inuit round house built of blocks of hard snow
WORD HISTORY from Inuit *iglu* 'house'

igneous *ADJECTIVE*
igneous rock is formed when hot liquid rock from a volcano cools and becomes hard
WORD HISTORY from Latin *ignis* 'fire'

ignite *VERB* **ignites, igniting, ignited**
1 to set fire to something
2 to catch fire

ignition *NOUN* **ignitions**
1 the process of igniting
2 the part of a motor engine that starts the fuel burning

ignoble *ADJECTIVE*
not honourable; shameful

ignominious *ADJECTIVE*
bringing disgrace or shame
▷ **ignominy** *NOUN*

ignoramus *NOUN* **ignoramuses**
an ignorant person
WORD HISTORY a Latin word meaning 'we do not know'

ignorant *ADJECTIVE*
1 to be ignorant is to know very little in general
2 to be ignorant of something is not to know about it
▷ **ignorantly** *ADVERB*
▷ **ignorance** *NOUN*

ignore *VERB* **ignores, ignoring, ignored**
to take no notice of a person or thing

iguana (*say* ig- **wah**- na) *NOUN* **iguanas**
a large tree-climbing tropical lizard

WORD HISTORY via Spanish from Arawak (a South American language)

ilk *NOUN*
of that ilk (*informal*) of that kind

WORD HISTORY from Old English *ilca* meaning 'same'. *Ilk* is Scottish and *of that ilk* was originally used to describe a person belonging to a place or estate having the same name as the person's name.

I'll short for *I will* or *I shall*

ill *ADJECTIVE*
1 unwell; in bad health
2 bad or harmful ◆ *There were no ill effects.*
to be ill at ease is to feel uncomfortable or embarrassed

ill *ADVERB*
badly ◆ *The animals had clearly been ill-treated.*

illegal *ADJECTIVE*
not legal; against the law
▷ **illegally** *ADVERB*
▷ **illegality** *NOUN*

illegible *ADJECTIVE*
not clear enough to read
▷ **illegibly** *ADVERB*
▷ **illegibility** *NOUN*

illegitimate *ADJECTIVE*
an illegitimate child is one born of parents who are not married to each other
▷ **illegitimacy** *NOUN*

ill-fated *ADJECTIVE*
bound to fail or have bad luck

illicit *ADJECTIVE*
forbidden by law or rules
▷ **illicitly** *ADVERB*

USAGE NOTE Take care not to confuse this word with *elicit*.

illiterate *ADJECTIVE*
unable to read or write
▷ **illiteracy** *NOUN*

illness *NOUN* **illnesses**
1 a period of being ill
2 a particular disease or form of bad health

illogical *ADJECTIVE*
not logical; not reasoning correctly
▷ **illogicality** *NOUN*
▷ **illogically** *ADVERB*

ill-omened *ADJECTIVE*
having bad omens; unlucky

ills *PLURAL NOUN*
problems and difficulties

illuminate *VERB* **illuminates, illuminating, illuminated**
1 to light something up
2 to decorate streets or a building with lights
3 to decorate a manuscript with coloured designs
▷ **illumination** *NOUN*

illuminating *ADJECTIVE*
helping to explain something or make it clear

illusion *NOUN* **illusions**
1 something that seems to be real or actually happening but is not, especially something that deceives the eye
2 (*Art*) a special effect created by deceiving the eye in a painting or drawing
to be under an illusion is to believe something wrongly

USAGE NOTE Take care not to confuse this word with *allusion*, which means 'a reference to something without naming it'.

illusionist *NOUN* **illusionists**
a person who performs tricks that deceive the eye; a conjuror

illusory *ADJECTIVE*
false but seeming to be real

illustrate *VERB* **illustrates, illustrating, illustrated**
1 to show something with pictures or examples
2 to put illustrations in a book
▷ **illustrator** *NOUN*

illustration *NOUN* **illustrations**
1 a picture in a book or magazine
2 an example that helps to explain something
3 the act of illustrating something

illustrious *ADJECTIVE*
famous and distinguished

ill will *NOUN*
unkind feelings towards a person

I'm short for **I am**

image *NOUN* **images**
1 a picture or statue of a person or thing
2 the appearance of something as seen in a mirror or through a lens etc.
3 a person or thing that is very much like another ◆ *She is the image of her grandmother.*
4 a word or phrase that describes something in an imaginative way
5 a person's public reputation

imagery *NOUN*
(*Language*) a writer's or speaker's use of words to produce pictures in the mind of the reader or hearer

imaginable *ADJECTIVE*
able to be imagined or thought about

imaginary *ADJECTIVE*
existing only in the imagination; not real

imagination *NOUN* **imaginations**
1 the ability to imagine things
2 the ability to be creative or inventive

imaginative *ADJECTIVE*
having or showing imagination

imagine *VERB* **imagines, imagining, imagined**
1 to form pictures or ideas in your mind

Those who have never seen a living Martian can scarcely imagine the strange horror of its appearance. — *H. G. Wells, The War of the Worlds*

2 to suppose or think ◆ *I don't imagine they'll be coming now.*

imam *NOUN* **imams**
a Muslim religious leader
WORD HISTORY from an Arabic word meaning 'leader'

imbalance *NOUN*
a lack of balance or proportion

imbecile (*say* imb- i- seel) *NOUN* **imbeciles**
a stupid or foolish person
▷ **imbecilic** *ADJECTIVE*
▷ **imbecility** *NOUN*

imbibe *VERB* **imbibes, imbibing, imbibed**
(*formal*) to drink alcohol

imitate *VERB* **imitates, imitating, imitated**
to copy or mimic something

Every bit of woodwork was a drab ginger colour, painted to imitate the graining of wood. — *Dodie Smith, I Capture the Castle*

▷ **imitation** *NOUN*
▷ **imitator** *NOUN*
▷ **imitative** *ADJECTIVE*

immaculate *ADJECTIVE*
1 perfectly clean or tidy
2 not having any faults or mistakes
▷ **immaculately** *ADVERB*

immaterial *ADJECTIVE*
something is immaterial when it does not matter at all ◆ *It is immaterial whether they agree or not.*

immature *ADJECTIVE*
not mature
▷ **immaturity** *NOUN*

immediate *ADJECTIVE*
1 happening or done without any delay
2 nearest in space or time; with nothing or no one between ◆ *Our immediate neighbours are a hundred yards away.* ◆ *She had been his immediate predecessor as treasurer.*
▷ **immediacy** *NOUN*

immediately *ADVERB*
at once; without any delay

immemorial *ADJECTIVE*
from time immemorial further back in time than anyone can remember

immense *ADJECTIVE*
extremely large or great
▷ **immensely** *ADVERB*
▷ **immensity** *NOUN*

immerse *VERB* **immerses, immersing, immersed**
1 to put something completely into a liquid
2 to be immersed in work or some other activity is to be concentrating fully on it
▷ **immersion** *NOUN*

immersion heater *NOUN* **immersion heaters**
an electric heating element that heats the water in a tank by being immersed in it

immigrate *VERB* **immigrates, immigrating, immigrated**
to come into a country to live there
▷ **immigrant** *NOUN*
USAGE NOTE See the note at *emigrate*.

immigration *NOUN*
the process by which people from another country come and live in this country

imminent *ADJECTIVE*
likely to happen at any moment ◆ *We had to prepare for their imminent arrival.*
▷ **imminence** *NOUN*

immobile *ADJECTIVE*
not moving or able to be moved
▷ **immobility** *NOUN*

immobilize *VERB* **immobilizes, immobilizing, immobilized**
to stop a thing from moving or working
▷ **immobilization** *NOUN*
USAGE NOTE This word can also be spelled immobilise.

immodest *ADJECTIVE*
1 not behaving or dressing decently or modestly
2 conceited or self-important

immoral *ADJECTIVE*
morally wrong
▷ **immorally** *ADVERB*
▷ **immorality** *NOUN*

immortal *ADJECTIVE*
1 living for ever; not mortal
2 famous for all time
▷ **immortal** *NOUN*
▷ **immortality** *NOUN*

immortalize *VERB* **immortalizes, immortalizing, immortalized**
to make someone famous for all time
USAGE NOTE This word can also be spelled immortalise.

immovable *ADJECTIVE*
unable to be moved
▷ **immovably** *ADVERB*

immune *ADJECTIVE*
1 to be immune to a disease is to be unlikely to catch it
2 to be immune from or against an obligation or punishment is to be exempt from it ◆ *No one was immune from persecution any more.*
3 to be immune to something is to be unlikely to be affected by it ◆ *No one is immune to his immense charm.*
▷ **immunity** *NOUN*

immune system *NOUN* **immune systems**
the body's means of resisting infection by producing antibodies

immunize *VERB* **immunizes, immunizing, immunized**
to make a person immune from a disease, e.g. by vaccination
▷ **immunization** *NOUN*
USAGE NOTE This word can also be spelled immunise.

immutable (*say* i- **mewt**- a- bul) *ADJECTIVE*
unchangeable
▷ **immutably** *ADVERB*

imp *NOUN* **imps**
1 a small devil
2 a mischievous child
▷ **impish** *ADJECTIVE*

impact *NOUN* **impacts**
1 a collision, or the force of a collision
2 an influence or effect ◆ *The development of the Internet has had a huge impact on communications.*

impair *VERB* **impairs, impairing, impaired**
to damage or weaken something ◆ *Extreme stress can impair memory.*
▷ **impairment** *NOUN*

impala (*say* im- **pah**- la) *NOUN* **impala**
a small African antelope
WORD HISTORY from a Zulu word

impale *VERB* **impales, impaling, impaled**
to pierce or fix something on a sharp pointed object

impart *VERB* **imparts, imparting, imparted**
1 to impart news or information is to tell it to someone
2 to impart a certain taste, smell, or other quality is to make something have it ◆ *The process imparts a soft surface to the leather.*

impartial *ADJECTIVE*
not favouring one side more than the other; treating everyone equally
▷ **impartially** *ADVERB*
▷ **impartiality** *NOUN*

impassable *ADJECTIVE*
not able to be travelled along or over ◆ *The road was impassable after the floods.*

impasse (*say* am- pahss) *NOUN* **impasses**
a situation in which no progress can be made; a deadlock

impassive *ADJECTIVE*
not showing any emotion ◆ *He remained impassive throughout the ordeal.*
▷ **impassively** *ADVERB*

impasto (*say* im- **past**- oh) *NOUN*
(*Art*) the technique of applying paint thickly to make it stand out from the surface of the picture

impatient *ADJECTIVE*
1 not patient or tolerant
2 eager to do something and not wanting to wait
▷ **impatiently** *ADVERB*
▷ **impatience** *NOUN*

impeach *VERB* **impeaches, impeaching, impeached**
to bring an important public figure to trial for a serious crime against their country
▷ **impeachment** *NOUN*

impeccable *ADJECTIVE*
completely good; having no faults
▷ **impeccably** *ADVERB*

impede *VERB* **impedes, impeding, impeded**
to hinder or get in the way of something or someone

impediment *NOUN* **impediments**
1 a hindrance
2 a fault or defect, e.g. in the way a person speaks

impel *VERB* **impels, impelling, impelled**
to urge or drive someone to do something ◆ *Hunger impelled them to look for shelter.*

impending *ADJECTIVE*
about to happen; imminent

impenetrable *ADJECTIVE*
1 impossible to get through
2 impossible to understand

impenitent *ADJECTIVE*
not feeling any regret or shame for something wrong you have done

imperative *ADJECTIVE*
1 (*Grammar*) expressing a command or instruction, as in *Go away!* or *Add milk to the mixture*
2 extremely important ◆ *It is imperative that these people are found.*

imperative *NOUN* **imperatives**
1 something essential or urgent
2 the form of a verb used in making commands (e.g. 'come' in *Come here!*)

imperceptible *ADJECTIVE*
too small or gradual to be noticed

a b c d e f g h i j k l m n o p q r s t u v w x y z

imperfect *ADJECTIVE*
1 not perfect
2 the imperfect tense of a verb describes continuous action in the past, e.g. *It was raining*
▷ **imperfectly** *ADVERB*
▷ **imperfection** *NOUN*

imperial *ADJECTIVE*
1 (*History*) to do with an empire or its rulers
2 imperial weights and measures are the non-metric ones formerly in use in Britain and still used for some purposes
▷ **imperially** *ADVERB*

imperialism *NOUN*
(*History*) the policy of extending a country's empire or influence by military force or colonization
▷ **imperialist** *NOUN*

imperious *ADJECTIVE*
arrogant and bossy

impermeable *ADJECTIVE*
an impermeable substance does not allow liquid to pass through it

impersonal *ADJECTIVE*
1 not affected by personal feelings; showing no emotion
2 not referring to a particular person
▷ **impersonally** *ADVERB*

impersonate *VERB* **impersonates, impersonating, impersonated**
to pretend to be another person dishonestly or for entertainment
▷ **impersonation** *NOUN*
▷ **impersonator** *NOUN*

impertinent *ADJECTIVE*
not showing someone proper respect; insolent
▷ **impertinently** *ADVERB*
▷ **impertinence** *NOUN*

imperturbable *ADJECTIVE*
not easily excited or upset
▷ **imperturbably** *ADVERB*

impervious *ADJECTIVE*
1 a substance is impervious to water, heat, etc. when water or heat cannot pass through it
2 to be impervious to attack or criticism is to be unaffected by it

impetuous *ADJECTIVE*
acting hastily without thinking

impetus *NOUN*
1 the force that makes an object start moving and that keeps it moving
2 the influence that causes something to develop more quickly ◆ *The impetus to learn is a strong human characteristic.*

impiety *NOUN*
lack of respect for God and holy things
▷ **impious** (*say* **imp**- ee- us) *ADJECTIVE*

impinge *VERB* **impinges, impinging, impinged**
to have an effect or influence on people or events ◆ *The law impinges on people's lives in all sorts of ways.*

implacable *ADJECTIVE*
1 not easily calmed or placated
2 relentless; persistent
▷ **implacably** *ADVERB*

implant *VERB* **implants, implanting, implanted**
to insert something; to fix something in
▷ **implantation** *NOUN*

implant *NOUN* **implants**
an organ or piece of tissue inserted in the body

implement *NOUN* **implements**
a tool or piece of equipment used for a special purpose

implement *VERB* **implements, implementing, implemented**
to put a plan or idea into action ◆ *The company plans to implement another round of redundancies.*
▷ **implementation** *NOUN*

implicate *VERB* **implicates, implicating, implicated**
to involve someone in a crime or wrongdoing, or to show that a person is involved ◆ *The new evidence implicates his brother.*

implication *NOUN* **implications**
1 something that is implied or can be concluded from something said
2 the act of implicating someone

implicit (*say* im- **pliss**- it) *ADJECTIVE*
1 implied but not stated directly (SEE ALSO **explicit**)
2 absolute or unquestioning ◆ *They have an implicit faith in their teachers.*
▷ **implicitly** *ADVERB*

implode *VERB* **implodes, imploding, imploded**
to burst or explode inwards

> Behind them, the fire raged. Booms and crashes filled the air as the East India Tyre Factory imploded. — *Julie Bertagna, The Opposite of Chocolate*

▷ **implosion** *NOUN*

implore *VERB* **implores, imploring, implored**
to beg someone desperately to do something

imply *VERB* **implies, implying, implied**
to suggest something without actually saying it
USAGE NOTE See the note at *infer*.

impolite *ADJECTIVE*
not polite; having bad manners

imponderable *ADJECTIVE*
not able to be judged or estimated
WORD HISTORY literally 'not able to be weighed', from Latin *pondus* 'weight'

import *VERB* **imports, importing, imported**
to bring in goods or services from another country

import *NOUN* **imports**
1 the process of importing
2 something imported
3 (*formal*) meaning or importance ◆ *It took a while for the import of this conclusion to sink in.*

important *ADJECTIVE*
1 having a great effect or value
2 having great authority or influence
▷ **importantly** *ADVERB*
▷ **importance** *NOUN*

impose *VERB* **imposes, imposing, imposed**
1 to impose a responsibility or difficulty on someone is to make them have to accept it
2 to impose a tax or charge is to make people have to pay it
3 to impose on someone is to put an unfair burden on them

imposing *ADJECTIVE*
grand and impressive

imposition *NOUN* **impositions**
1 something imposed; an unfair burden or inconvenience
2 the act of imposing something

impossible *ADJECTIVE*
1 not possible
2 (*informal*) you say that a person is impossible when they are very difficult to deal with
▷ **impossibly** *ADVERB*
▷ **impossibility** *NOUN*

impostor *NOUN* **impostors**
a person who dishonestly pretends to be someone else

impotent *ADJECTIVE*
1 powerless; unable to take action
2 a man is impotent when he is unable to have an erection or sexual intercourse
▷ **impotently** *ADVERB*
▷ **impotence** *NOUN*

impound *VERB* **impounds, impounding, impounded**
to confiscate something or take possession of it

impoverish *VERB* **impoverishes, impoverishing, impoverished**
1 to make a person poor
2 to make a thing poor in quality
▷ **impoverishment** *NOUN*

impracticable *ADJECTIVE*
not able to be done in practice

impractical *ADJECTIVE*
not practical or sensible

imprecise *ADJECTIVE*
not precise

impregnable *ADJECTIVE*
strong enough to be safe against attack

impregnate *VERB* **impregnates, impregnating, impregnated**
1 to make a female person or animal pregnant; to fertilize
2 to be impregnated with something is to be saturated or filled with it throughout
▷ **impregnation** *NOUN*

impresario *NOUN* **impresarios**
a person who organizes concerts and entertainments

impress *VERB* **impresses, impressing, impressed**
1 to make a person admire something or think it is very good
2 to impress an idea or need on someone is to make them realize its importance
3 to press a mark into something

impression *NOUN* **impressions**
1 an effect produced on the mind

Professor Dumbledore, though very old, always gave an impression of great energy. — *J. K. Rowling, Harry Potter and the Prisoner of Azkaban*

2 a vague idea
3 an imitation of a person or a sound
4 a reprint of a book

impressionable *ADJECTIVE*
easily influenced or affected

impressionism *NOUN*
a style of painting that gives the general effect of a scene without details

impressionist *NOUN* **impressionists**
1 a painter in the style of impressionism
2 an entertainer who does impressions of famous people

impressive *ADJECTIVE*
making a strong impression; seeming to be very good

imprint *NOUN* **imprints**
a mark pressed into or on something

imprison *VERB* **imprisons, imprisoning, imprisoned**
to put someone in prison
▷ **imprisonment** *NOUN*

improbable *ADJECTIVE*
unlikely
▷ **improbably** *ADVERB*
▷ **improbability** *NOUN*

impromptu *ADJECTIVE, ADVERB*
done without any rehearsal or preparation
WORD HISTORY from Latin *in promptu* 'in readiness'

improper *ADJECTIVE*
1 unsuitable or wrong
2 indecent
▷ **improperly** *ADVERB*
▷ **impropriety** (*say* im- pro- **pry**- it- ee) *NOUN*

improper fraction *NOUN* **improper fractions**
a fraction that is greater than 1, with the numerator greater than the denominator, e.g. $\frac{5}{4}$

improve *VERB* **improves, improving, improved**
to make something better, or to become better
▷ **improvement** *NOUN*

improvident *ADJECTIVE*
not providing or planning for the future

improvise *VERB* **improvises, improvising, improvised**
1 to make something quickly with whatever is available
2 (*Music, Drama*) to perform something by making it up as you go along, rather than following a score or script
▷ **improvisation** *NOUN*

imprudent *ADJECTIVE*
unwise or rash in your actions

impudent *ADJECTIVE*
cheeky or disrespectful
▷ **impudently** *ADVERB*
▷ **impudence** *NOUN*

impulse *NOUN* **impulses**
1 a sudden desire or urge to do something

> My first impulse had been to write a letter to the Prime Minister, but a little reflection convinced me that that would be useless. — *John Buchan, The Thirty-Nine Steps*

2 a push or impetus
3 (*Science*) an electrical or other force acting on something for a very short time

impulsive *ADJECTIVE*
done or acting on impulse, without much thought
▷ **impulsively** *ADVERB*
▷ **impulsiveness** *NOUN*

impunity (*say* im- **pewn**- it- ee) *NOUN*
freedom from punishment or injury

impure *ADJECTIVE*
1 not pure; mixed with something unwanted
2 morally wrong; indecent
▷ **impurity** *NOUN*

impute *VERB* **imputes, imputing, imputed**
(*formal*) to regard someone as being responsible for something; to attribute blame or credit to someone
▷ **imputation** *NOUN*

in *PREPOSITION*
1 at or inside something ◆ *I was in the kitchen.* ◆ *He fell in a ditch.*
2 within the limits of something ◆ *I will see you in an hour.*
3 consisting of ◆ *a serial in three instalments*
4 a member of ◆ *He is in the army.*
5 by means of ◆ *They were paid in gold.*
in all in total number; altogether

in *ADVERB*
1 at or to a position inside something ◆ *Get in!* ◆ *The roof fell in.*
2 at home or indoors ◆ *Is anyone in?*
3 at its destination ◆ *The train will be in soon.*
to be in for something is to be likely to suffer it
to be in on something (*informal*) is to be aware of it or sharing in it

inability *NOUN*
the state of being unable to do something

inaccessible *ADJECTIVE*
not able to be reached

inaccurate *ADJECTIVE*
not accurate

inactive *ADJECTIVE*
not active or working
▷ **inaction** *NOUN*
▷ **inactivity** *NOUN*

inadequate *ADJECTIVE*
1 not enough; not good enough
2 someone is inadequate for a task or situation when they are not able to cope with it
▷ **inadequately** *ADVERB*
▷ **inadequacy** *NOUN*

inadvertent *ADJECTIVE*
unintentional; not planned

inadvisable *ADJECTIVE*
not advisable; unwise

inalienable *ADJECTIVE*
an inalienable right is one that cannot be taken away from someone

inane *ADJECTIVE*
silly; not having any sense
▷ **inanely** *ADVERB*
▷ **inanity** *NOUN*

WORD HISTORY from Latin *inanis* 'empty'

inanimate *ADJECTIVE*
1 not living
2 showing no sign of life; lifeless

inappropriate *ADJECTIVE*
not appropriate

inarticulate *ADJECTIVE*
1 not able to speak or express yourself clearly
2 an inarticulate cry or sound is one not expressed in words

inattentive *ADJECTIVE*
not listening or paying attention
▷ **inattention** *NOUN*

inaudible *ADJECTIVE*
not loud enough to be heard
▷ **inaudibly** *ADVERB*
▷ **inaudibility** *NOUN*

inaugurate *VERB* **inaugurates, inaugurating, inaugurated**
1 to start or introduce something new and important
2 to establish a person formally in office
▷ **inaugural** *ADJECTIVE*
▷ **inauguration** *NOUN*

inauspicious *ADJECTIVE*
not auspicious; unlikely to be successful

inborn *ADJECTIVE*
an inborn ability or characteristic is one that is present in a person or animal from birth

inbred *ADJECTIVE*
1 inborn
2 produced by inbreeding

inbreeding *NOUN*
breeding from closely related individuals over many generations

incalculable *ADJECTIVE*
not able to be calculated or predicted

in camera *ADVERB*
in a judge's private room, not in public
WORD HISTORY from a Latin phrase meaning 'in the room'

incandescent *ADJECTIVE*
giving out light when heated; shining
▷ **incandescence** *NOUN*

incantation *NOUN* **incantations**
a set of words spoken as a spell or charm

incapable *ADJECTIVE*
to be incapable of doing something is to be unable to do it

incapacitate *VERB* **incapacitates, incapacitating, incapacitated**
to make a person or thing unable to do something; to disable someone

incapacity *NOUN*
inability; lack of sufficient strength or power

incarcerate *VERB* **incarcerates, incarcerating, incarcerated**
to shut in or imprison someone
▷ **incarceration** *NOUN*

incarnate *ADJECTIVE*
(usually put after a noun) having a body or human form ◆ *He looked like the devil incarnate as he stood glaring at them.*

incarnation *NOUN*
a living form of a god or abstract quality
the Incarnation (*Religion*) in Christian teaching, God's taking a human form as Jesus Christ

incautious *ADJECTIVE*
rash; ignoring risks

incendiary *ADJECTIVE*
an incendiary bomb or device is one that is designed to cause a fire

incense (*say* **in**- sens) *NOUN*
a substance that is burned to produce a sweet fragrant smell

incense (*say* in- **sens**) *VERB* **incenses, incensing, incensed**
to make a person angry

incentive *NOUN* **incentives**
something that encourages a person to do something or to work harder

inception *NOUN*
the start of an activity or institution

incessant *ADJECTIVE*
something unpleasant is incessant when it continues for a long time without a pause

The only notion Lyra had of the search for her was the incessant drone of the gas engines of airships criss-crossing the skies. — *Philip Pullman, Northern Lights*

incest *NOUN*
sexual intercourse between two people who are so closely related that they cannot marry each other
▷ **incestuous** *ADJECTIVE*

inch *NOUN* **inches**
a measure of length, one-twelfth of a foot (about $2\frac{1}{2}$ centimetres)

inch *VERB* **inches, inching, inched**
to move slowly and gradually

The jeep inched forward at a painfully slow rate, made all the more excruciating by the anticipation building in Artemis's chest. — *Eoin Colfer, Artemis Fowl*

incidence *NOUN*
the extent or frequency of something ◆ *There are new measures to reduce the incidence of food poisoning.*

incident *NOUN* **incidents**
an event, especially an unusual one or one involving danger or violence

incidental *ADJECTIVE*
happening as a less important additional part of something else ◆ *There will be several incidental benefits to the scheme as well as the main one of saving money.*

incidentally *ADVERB*
1 by the way ◆ *Incidentally, there's no food left.*
2 by chance

incinerate *VERB* **incinerates, incinerating, incinerated**
to destroy something by burning it
▷ **incineration** *NOUN*

incinerator *NOUN* **incinerators**
a device for burning rubbish

incipient (*say* in- **sip**- ee- ent) *ADJECTIVE*
just beginning ◆ *Signs of an incipient revolution brought panic to the streets.*

incise *VERB* **incises, incising, incised**
to cut or engrave something into a surface

incision *NOUN* **incisions**
a cut, especially one made in a surgical operation

incisive *ADJECTIVE*
incisive comments or remarks are clear and sharp

incisor (*say* in- **sy**- zer) *NOUN* **incisors**
each of the sharp-edged front teeth in the upper and lower jaws

incite *VERB* **incites, inciting, incited**
to urge a person to do something wrong or violent; to stir people up ◆ *Rage incited them to the most extreme action.*
▷ **incitement** *NOUN*

incivility *NOUN*
rudeness or discourtesy

inclement *ADJECTIVE*
(*formal*) the weather is inclement when it is unpleasantly cold and wet

inclination *NOUN* **inclinations**
1 a tendency
2 a liking or preference
3 a slope or slant

incline (*say* in- **klyn**) *VERB* **inclines, inclining, inclined**
1 to lean or slope
2 to bend the head or body forward, as in a nod or bow
3 to influence someone to act or think in a certain way ◆ *The urgency of the situation inclines us to advise quick action.*
4 to be inclined to do something is to tend to do it or want to do it ◆ *The ends are inclined to split.* ◆ *I'm inclined to doubt the truth of these stories.*

incline (*say* **in**- klyn) *NOUN* **inclines**
a slope

include *VERB* **includes, including, included**
to make or consider something as part of a group of things
▷ **inclusion** *NOUN*

inclusive *ADJECTIVE*
1 including everything or something specified ◆ *What is your income inclusive of tax?*
2 including the items mentioned ◆ *We shall be away from the third to the twentieth inclusive.*

incognito (*say* in- kog- **neet**- oh) *ADJECTIVE, ADVERB*
with your name or identity concealed ◆ *For the next few years he lived incognito at the homes of various friends.*

WORD HISTORY an Italian word, from Latin *cognitus* 'known'

incoherent *ADJECTIVE*
not speaking or reasoning in a way that can be understood

incombustible *ADJECTIVE*
not able to be set on fire

income *NOUN* **incomes**
money received regularly from doing work or from investments

income tax *NOUN*
a tax charged on income

incoming *ADJECTIVE*
1 an incoming message or call is one that is being received rather than sent
2 an incoming official is one who is about to take over from someone else

incomparable (*say* in- **komp**- er- a- bul) *ADJECTIVE*
without an equal; unsurpassed

incompatible *ADJECTIVE*
not able to exist or be used together

incompetent *ADJECTIVE*
not able or skilled enough to do something properly

incomplete *ADJECTIVE*
not complete

incomprehensible *ADJECTIVE*
not able to be understood
▷ **incomprehension** *NOUN*

inconceivable *ADJECTIVE*
not able to be imagined; most unlikely

inconclusive *ADJECTIVE*
not conclusive

incongruous *ADJECTIVE*
out of place or unsuitable
▷ **incongruously** *ADVERB*
▷ **incongruity** *NOUN*

inconsiderable *ADJECTIVE*
of small size or value

inconsiderate *ADJECTIVE*
not considerate towards other people

inconsistent *ADJECTIVE*
not consistent
▷ **inconsistently** *ADVERB*
▷ **inconsistency** *NOUN*

inconsolable *ADJECTIVE*
not able to be consoled or comforted; overcome with sadness

inconspicuous *ADJECTIVE*
not clearly visible or attracting attention
▷ **inconspicuously** *ADVERB*

incontinent *ADJECTIVE*
not able to control the bladder or bowels
▷ **incontinence** *NOUN*

incontrovertible *ADJECTIVE*
not able to be denied or disputed

inconvenience *NOUN* **inconveniences**
an inconvenient fact or situation ◆ *We are sorry for any inconvenience.*

inconvenience *VERB* **inconveniences, inconveniencing, inconvenienced**
to cause inconvenience or slight difficulty to someone

inconvenient *ADJECTIVE*
not convenient

incorporate *VERB* **incorporates, incorporating, incorporated**
to include something as a part of something larger
▷ **incorporation** *NOUN*

incorrect *ADJECTIVE*
not correct; wrong
▷ **incorrectly** *ADVERB*

incorrigible *ADJECTIVE*
not able to be reformed or changed ◆ *Jason is an incorrigible flirt.*

incorruptible *ADJECTIVE*
1 not able to be bribed
2 not able to decay

increase *VERB* **increases, increasing, increased**
to make something larger, or to become larger

increase *NOUN* **increases**
the process of increasing, or the amount by which something increases

increasingly *ADVERB*
more and more

incredible *ADJECTIVE*
1 impossible to believe
2 (*informal*) extremely good
▷ **incredibly** *ADVERB*
▷ **incredibility** *NOUN*

USAGE NOTE Take care not to confuse this word with *incredulous.*

incredulous *ADJECTIVE*
unwilling to believe something; doubtful that something is true
▷ **incredulously** *ADVERB*
▷ **incredulity** *NOUN*

USAGE NOTE Take care not to confuse this word with *incredible.*

increment (*say* **in**- krim- ent) *NOUN* **increments**
an increase; an added amount, especially of money
▷ **incremental** *ADJECTIVE*

incriminate *VERB* **incriminates, incriminating, incriminated**
to incriminate someone is to show, or appear to show, that they have been involved in a crime or wrongdoing
▷ **incrimination** *NOUN*

incubate *VERB* **incubates, incubating, incubated**
1 to hatch eggs by keeping them warm
2 to cause bacteria or a disease to develop
▷ **incubation** *NOUN*

incubator *NOUN* **incubators**
an enclosed apparatus for hatching eggs or a similar apparatus for protecting premature babies

incumbent *ADJECTIVE*
it is incumbent on someone to do something when it is their duty to do it ◆ *It is incumbent on us to do everything possible to ensure safety.*

incumbent *NOUN* **incumbents**
a person who holds a particular office or position

incur *VERB* **incurs, incurring, incurred**
to incur something difficult or unwelcome is to do or say something that makes it happen ◆ *Because I had to return the goods I incurred extra postal costs.*

incurable *ADJECTIVE*
not able to be cured
▷ **incurably** *ADVERB*

incurious *ADJECTIVE*
feeling or showing no curiosity about something

incursion *NOUN* **incursions**
a sudden brief raid or invasion

indebted *ADJECTIVE*
owing money or gratitude to someone

indecent *ADJECTIVE*
not decent; improper
▷ **indecently** *ADVERB*
▷ **indecency** *NOUN*

indecipherable *ADJECTIVE*
not able to be deciphered

indecision *NOUN*
the inability to make decisions; hesitation

indecisive *ADJECTIVE*
not able to make decisions quickly and effectively
▷ **indecisively** *ADVERB*

indeed *ADVERB*
1 used to strengthen a meaning ◆ *He was very fond of her indeed.*
2 really and truly; admittedly ◆ *He may be — indeed he is — a kind person.*

indefatigable (*say* in-di- **fat**-ig-a-bal) *ADJECTIVE*
not tiring easily; having a lot of stamina

indefensible *ADJECTIVE*
not able to be defended or justified ◆ *These mistakes are indefensible.*

indefinable *ADJECTIVE*
not able to be defined or described clearly

a b c d e f g h i j k l m n o p q r s t u v w x y z

indefinite *ADJECTIVE*
not definite; vague

indefinite article *NOUN* **indefinite articles**
the word 'a' or 'an': see the language panel at **definite article**

indefinitely *ADVERB*
for an indefinite or unlimited time

indelible *ADJECTIVE*
impossible to rub out or remove
▷ **indelibly** *ADVERB*

indelicate *ADJECTIVE*
1 slightly indecent
2 tactless
▷ **indelicacy** *NOUN*

indent *VERB* **indents, indenting, indented**
1 to make notches or recesses in something
2 to start a line of writing or printing further in from the margin than other lines, e.g. at the start of a new paragraph
▷ **indentation** *NOUN*

indenture *NOUN*
an agreement binding an apprentice to work for a certain employer
▷ **indentured** *ADJECTIVE*

WORD HISTORY based on *indent* (because each copy of the agreement had notches cut into it, so that the copies could be fitted together to show that they were genuine)

independence *NOUN*
1 the freedom to live your life without being dependent on someone else
2 (*History*) the freedom of a country from foreign rule and the ability to govern itself

independent *ADJECTIVE*
1 not dependent on any other person or thing for help, money, or support
2 (*History*) an independent country is one that has its own government and rules itself
3 not connected or involved with something
▷ **independently** *ADVERB*

indescribable *ADJECTIVE*
unable to be described
▷ **indescribably** *ADVERB*

indestructible *ADJECTIVE*
unable to be destroyed
▷ **indestructibility** *NOUN*

indeterminate *ADJECTIVE*
not fixed or decided exactly; left vague

index *NOUN* **indexes** or (in meaning 3) **indices**
1 an alphabetical list of things, especially at the end of a book
2 a number showing how prices or wages have changed from a previous level
3 (*Mathematics*) the raised number etc. written to the right of another (e.g. 3 in 2^3) showing how many times the first one is to be multiplied by itself

index *VERB* **indexes, indexing, indexed**
to make an index to a book; to put something into an index

index finger *NOUN* **index fingers**
the forefinger

Indian *ADJECTIVE*
1 to do with India or its people
2 to do with Native Americans
▷ **Indian** *NOUN*

USAGE NOTE The preferred term for the descendants of the original inhabitants of North and South America is *Native American. American Indian* is usually acceptable but the term *Red Indian* is now regarded as offensive and should not be used.

Indian summer *NOUN* **Indian summers**
a period of warm weather in autumn

india rubber *NOUN* **india rubbers**
a rubber

WORD HISTORY named after India, from where the rubber it was made from originally came

indicate *VERB* **indicates, indicating, indicated**
1 to point something out or make it known
2 to be a sign of something
3 a driver indicates when they use their indicators to signal which direction they are turning
▷ **indication** *NOUN*

indicative *ADJECTIVE*
giving an indication

indicative *NOUN*
the form of a verb used in making a statement (e.g. 'he said' or 'he is coming'), not in a command, question, or wish

indicator *NOUN* **indicators**
1 a thing that indicates or points to something
2 a flashing light used to signal that a motor vehicle is turning
3 (*Science*) a chemical compound (such as litmus) that changes colour in the presence of a particular substance or condition

indict (*say* ind- **yt**) *VERB* **indicts, indicting, indicted**
to charge a person with having committed a serious crime

indictment (*say* ind- **yt**- ment) *NOUN*
a formal charge or accusation of a serious crime

indie *NOUN* **indies**
a pop group or record label that does not belong to a major company

WORD HISTORY a shortening of *independent*

a b c d e f g h i j k l m n o p q r s t u v w x y z

indifferent *ADJECTIVE*
1 not caring about something; not interested
2 not very good ◆ *We had a happy time despite indifferent weather.*
▷ **indifferently** *ADVERB*
▷ **indifference** *NOUN*

indigenous (*say* in- **dij**- in- us) *ADJECTIVE*
an indigenous people, animal, or plant is one that has always grown or lived in a particular country

indigent (*say* **in**- dij- ent) *ADJECTIVE*
poor or needy

indigestible *ADJECTIVE*
difficult or impossible to digest

indigestion *NOUN*
pain or discomfort caused by difficulty in digesting food

indignant *ADJECTIVE*
angry at something you think is bad or unfair

Alex was woken by an indignant Nadia Vole knocking at his door. He had overslept. — *Anthony Horowitz, Stormbreaker*

▷ **indignantly** *ADVERB*
▷ **indignation** *NOUN*

indignity *NOUN* **indignities**
treatment that makes a person feel undignified or humiliated; an insult

indigo *NOUN*
a deep-blue colour

indirect *ADJECTIVE*
not direct
▷ **indirectly** *ADVERB*

indirect speech *NOUN*
(*Grammar*) a speaker's words given in a changed form reported by someone else, as in *She said she was leaving* (reporting the words 'I am leaving'): see the language panel at **direct speech**

indiscreet *ADJECTIVE*
1 not discreet; revealing secrets or too much information
2 not cautious; rash
▷ **indiscreetly** *ADVERB*

indiscretion *NOUN*
something indiscreet that someone does or says

indiscriminate *ADJECTIVE*
showing no discrimination; not making a careful choice
▷ **indiscriminately** *ADVERB*

indispensable *ADJECTIVE*
not able to be dispensed with; essential
▷ **indispensability** *NOUN*

indisposed *ADJECTIVE*
to be indisposed is to be slightly unwell and unable to do the things you normally do
▷ **indisposition** *NOUN*

indisputable *ADJECTIVE*
undeniable

indistinct *ADJECTIVE*
not distinct
▷ **indistinctly** *ADVERB*
▷ **indistinctness** *NOUN*

indistinguishable *ADJECTIVE*
not able to be told apart; not distinguishable

individual *ADJECTIVE*
1 of or for one person
2 single or separate ◆ *Count each individual person.*
▷ **individually** *ADVERB*

individual *NOUN* **individuals**
one person, animal, or plant

individuality *NOUN*
the things that make one person or thing different from another; distinctive identity

indivisible *ADJECTIVE*
not able to be divided or separated
▷ **indivisibly** *ADVERB*

indoctrinate *VERB* **indoctrinates, indoctrinating, indoctrinated**
to fill a person's mind with particular ideas or beliefs, so that they come to accept them without thinking
▷ **indoctrination** *NOUN*

indolent *ADJECTIVE*
lazy
▷ **indolently** *ADVERB*
▷ **indolence** *NOUN*

indomitable *ADJECTIVE*
not able to be overcome or conquered

indoor *ADJECTIVE*
indoor items or activities are used or done inside a building

indoors *ADVERB*
inside a building

indubitable (*say* in- **dew**- bit- a- bul) *ADJECTIVE*
not able to be doubted; certain
▷ **indubitably** *ADVERB*

induce *VERB* **induces, inducing, induced**
1 to persuade someone to do something
2 to produce or cause something ◆ *The hour before dusk induces a mood of solemnity.*
3 a pregnant woman, or her baby, is induced when the birth is brought on artificially with the use of drugs
▷ **induction** *NOUN*

inducement *NOUN* **inducements**
an incentive

a b c d e f g h i j k l m n o p q r s t u v w x y z

indulge *VERB* **indulges, indulging, indulged**
to allow someone to have or do whatever they want
to indulge in something is to allow yourself to have or do something that you enjoy

indulgent *ADJECTIVE*
allowing someone to have or do whatever they want; kind and lenient
▷ **indulgence** *NOUN*

industrial *ADJECTIVE*
to do with industry; working or used in industry
▷ **industrially** *ADVERB*

industrial action *NOUN*
ways for workers to protest, such as striking or working to rule

industrialist *NOUN* **industrialists**
a person who owns or manages an industrial business

industrialized *ADJECTIVE*
an industrialized country or district is one that has many industries
▷ **industrialization** *NOUN*
USAGE NOTE This word can also be spelled industrialised.

Industrial Revolution *NOUN*
the expansion of British industry by the use of machines in the late 18th and early 19th centuries

industrious *ADJECTIVE*
working hard
▷ **industriously** *ADVERB*

industry *NOUN* **industries**
1 the process of making or producing goods
2 a particular branch of this, or any business activity ♦ *the aviation industry* ♦ *the tourist industry*
3 the state of being industrious

inebriated *ADJECTIVE*
drunk

inedible *ADJECTIVE*
not edible

ineffective *ADJECTIVE*
not effective; inefficient
▷ **ineffectively** *ADVERB*

ineffectual *ADJECTIVE*
not achieving anything

inefficient *ADJECTIVE*
not efficient
▷ **inefficiently** *ADVERB*
▷ **inefficiency** *NOUN*

inelegant *ADJECTIVE*
not elegant

ineligible *ADJECTIVE*
not eligible

inept *ADJECTIVE*
lacking any skill; clumsy
▷ **ineptly** *ADVERB*
▷ **ineptitude** *NOUN*

inequality *NOUN* **inequalities**
not being equal

inequity *NOUN* **inequities**
unfairness or lack of justice
▷ **inequitable** *ADJECTIVE*

inert *ADJECTIVE*
not moving or reacting
▷ **inertly** *ADVERB*

inert gas *NOUN* **inert gases**
a gas that almost never combines with other substances

inertia (*say* in- er- sha) *NOUN*
1 being inert or slow to take action
2 (*Science*) the tendency for a moving thing to keep moving in a straight line

inescapable *ADJECTIVE*
unavoidable

inessential *ADJECTIVE*
not essential

inestimable *ADJECTIVE*
too great or precious to be able to be estimated

inevitable *ADJECTIVE*
unavoidable; sure to happen
▷ **inevitably** *ADVERB*
▷ **inevitability** *NOUN*

inexact *ADJECTIVE*
not exact

inexcusable *ADJECTIVE*
not able to be excused or justified

inexhaustible *ADJECTIVE*
so large that it is never used up completely
♦ *She seemed to have an inexhaustible supply of jokes.*

inexorable (*say* in- eks- er- a- bul) *ADJECTIVE*
1 not able to be stopped; relentless
2 not able to be persuaded by requests or entreaties
▷ **inexorably** *ADVERB*

inexpensive *ADJECTIVE*
not expensive; cheap
▷ **inexpensively** *ADVERB*

inexperience *NOUN*
lack of experience
▷ **inexperienced** *ADJECTIVE*

inexpert *ADJECTIVE*
unskilful

inexplicable *ADJECTIVE*
impossible to explain
▷ **inexplicably** *ADVERB*

in extremis (*say* eks- **treem**- iss) ***ADVERB***
at the point of death; in very great difficulties

infallible ***ADJECTIVE***
1 never wrong ◆ *The experts are not always infallible.*
2 never failing ◆ *They believed they had found an infallible cure for all sorts of ailments.*
▷ **infallibly** ***ADVERB***
▷ **infallibility** ***NOUN***

infamous (*say* **in**- fam- us) ***ADJECTIVE***
having a bad reputation; wicked
▷ **infamously** ***ADVERB***
▷ **infamy** ***NOUN***

infancy ***NOUN***
1 early childhood; babyhood
2 an early stage of development

infant ***NOUN*** **infants**
a baby or young child

infantile ***ADJECTIVE***
1 to do with young children
2 very childish

infantry ***NOUN***
soldiers who fight on foot

infatuated ***ADJECTIVE***
filled with foolish or unreasoning love
▷ **infatuation** ***NOUN***

infect ***VERB*** **infects, infecting, infected**
to pass on a disease or bacteria to a person, animal, or plant

infection ***NOUN*** **infections**
1 an infectious disease or condition
2 the process of infecting

infectious ***ADJECTIVE***
1 an infectious disease is one that can spread from one person to another through the environment. (SEE ALSO **contagious**)
2 quickly spreading to others ◆ *Her enthusiasm for work was infectious.*

infer ***VERB*** **infers, inferring, inferred**
to form an opinion or work something out from what someone says or does, even though they do not actually say it ◆ *As you may infer from my name and address, I am of Irish origin.*
▷ **inference** ***NOUN***

USAGE NOTE Take care not to confuse this word with *imply*. You should not say 'What are you inferring?' when you mean 'What are you implying (i.e. suggesting)?'.

inferior ***ADJECTIVE***
less good or less important; low or lower in position, quality, etc.
▷ **inferiority** ***NOUN***

inferior ***NOUN*** **inferiors**
a person who is lower in position or rank than someone else

infernal ***ADJECTIVE***
(*informal*) detestable or tiresome ◆ *I do think it's the most infernal cheek.*
▷ **infernally** ***ADVERB***

WORD HISTORY from Latin *infernus* 'below', used by Christians to mean 'hell'

inferno ***NOUN*** **infernos**
a raging fire

infertile ***ADJECTIVE***
1 infertile land is not able to produce crops
2 an infertile woman is not able to have children
▷ **infertility** ***NOUN***

infest ***VERB*** **infests, infesting, infested**
insects or other pests infest a place when they are numerous and troublesome there
▷ **infestation** ***NOUN***

infidel (*say* **in**- fid- el) ***NOUN*** **infidels**
(*old use*) a person who does not believe in a particular religion

WORD HISTORY from Latin *infidelis* 'unfaithful'

infidelity ***NOUN***
the state of being unfaithful to your husband, wife, or partner

infiltrate ***VERB*** **infiltrates, infiltrating, infiltrated**
to get into a place or organization gradually and without being noticed
▷ **infiltration** ***NOUN***
▷ **infiltrator** ***NOUN***

infinite ***ADJECTIVE***
1 endless; without a limit
2 too great to be measured
▷ **infinitely** ***ADVERB***

infinitesimal ***ADJECTIVE***
extremely small
▷ **infinitesimally** ***ADVERB***

infinitive ***NOUN*** **infinitives**
(*Grammar*) the form of a verb that does not change to indicate a particular tense or number or person, in English used with or without *to*, e.g. *go* in 'I will go', 'Let me go' or 'Allow me to go'

infinity ***NOUN***
(*Mathematics*) an infinite number or distance or time

infirm ***ADJECTIVE***
weak, especially from old age or illness
▷ **infirmity** ***NOUN***

infirmary ***NOUN*** **infirmaries**
1 a hospital
2 a place where sick people are cared for in a school or monastery etc.

inflame ***VERB*** **inflames, inflaming, inflamed**
1 to produce strong feelings or anger in people
2 to cause redness, heat, and swelling in a part of the body

inflammable *ADJECTIVE*
able to be set on fire
USAGE NOTE This word means the same as *flammable*. If you want to say that something is not able to be set on fire, use *non-flammable*.

inflammation *NOUN*
painful redness or swelling in a part of the body

inflammatory *ADJECTIVE*
likely to make people angry ◆ *inflammatory leaflets*

inflatable *ADJECTIVE*
able to be inflated

inflate *VERB* **inflates, inflating, inflated**
1 to fill something with air or gas so that it expands
2 to increase something too much

inflation *NOUN*
1 inflating
2 a general rise in prices and fall in the purchasing power of money
▷ **inflationary** *ADJECTIVE*

inflect *VERB* **inflects, inflecting, inflected**
1 (*Grammar*) to change the ending or form of a word to show its tense or its grammatical relation to other words, e.g. *sing* changes to *sang* or *sung*, *child* changes to *children*
2 to alter the voice in speaking

inflection *NOUN* **inflections**
(*Grammar*) an ending or form of a word used to inflect it, e.g. *-ed* in *killed* and *-es* in *bunches*

inflexible *ADJECTIVE*
not able to be bent or changed or persuaded
▷ **inflexibly** *ADVERB*
▷ **inflexibility** *NOUN*

inflexion *NOUN* **inflexions**
another spelling of **inflection**

inflict *VERB* **inflicts, inflicting, inflicted**
to make a person or people suffer something ◆ *They claimed to have inflicted casualties running into several hundreds killed.*
▷ **infliction** *NOUN*

inflow *NOUN*
flowing in; what flows in

influence *NOUN* **influences**
1 the power to affect other people or things ◆ *The layout of houses has an important influence on family behaviour.*
2 a person or thing with this power ◆ *Claudia had always been a good influence on her brother.*

influence *VERB* **influences, influencing, influenced**
to have an influence on a person or thing ◆ *The style he created strongly influenced English art for the rest of the century.*

influential *ADJECTIVE*
having great influence

influenza *NOUN*
an infectious disease that causes fever, catarrh, and pain; flu

influx *NOUN*
a flowing in, especially of people or things coming in

inform *VERB* **informs, informing, informed**
to give information to somebody
▷ **informant** *NOUN*

informal *ADJECTIVE*
not formal; casual and relaxed
▷ **informally** *ADVERB*
▷ **informality** *NOUN*
USAGE NOTE In this dictionary, words are marked *informal* when they are used in everyday speaking but not when you are writing or speaking formally: see the panel at *formal*.

information *NOUN*
facts or knowledge given to people or learned by them

information technology *NOUN*
the study and use of systems for storing, arranging, and sending information, especially computers and telecommunications

informative *ADJECTIVE*
providing useful information

informed *ADJECTIVE*
knowing about something

informer *NOUN* **informers**
a person who gives information against someone, especially to the police

infrared *ADJECTIVE*
below or beyond red in the spectrum

infrastructure *NOUN* **infrastructures**
(*Geography*) the basic services and systems that a country needs in order for its society and economy to work properly, such as buildings, roads, transport, and power supplies

infrequent *ADJECTIVE*
not frequent

infringe *VERB* **infringes, infringing, infringed**
1 to break a rule, law, or agreement
2 to limit a person's rights
▷ **infringement** *NOUN*

infuriate *VERB* **infuriates, infuriating, infuriated**
to make a person very angry

infuse *VERB* **infuses, infusing, infused**
1 to add or inspire with a feeling ◆ *She infused them all with a new purpose.*
2 to soak or steep tea or herbs etc. in a liquid to extract the flavour
▷ **infusion** *NOUN*

ingenious *ADJECTIVE*
1 clever at inventing things
2 cleverly made or done
▷ **ingeniously** *ADVERB*
▷ **ingenuity** *NOUN*

USAGE NOTE Take care not to confuse this word with *ingenuous.*

ingenuous *ADJECTIVE*
without cunning; innocent
▷ **ingenuously** *ADVERB*
▷ **ingenuousness** *NOUN*

USAGE NOTE Take care not to confuse this word with *ingenious.*

ingot *NOUN* **ingots**
a lump of gold or silver etc. that is cast in a brick shape

ingrained *ADJECTIVE*
1 ingrained feelings or habits are deeply fixed in people's minds
2 ingrained dirt marks a surface deeply

ingratiate *VERB* **ingratiates, ingratiating, ingratiated**
to ingratiate yourself is to find favour with someone by flattering them or always agreeing with them
▷ **ingratiation** *NOUN*

ingratitude *NOUN*
lack of gratitude

ingredient *NOUN* **ingredients**
1 each of the parts of a mixture
2 each of the items used in a cooking recipe

inhabit *VERB* **inhabits, inhabiting, inhabited**
to live in a place
▷ **inhabitant** *NOUN*

inhale *VERB* **inhales, inhaling, inhaled**
to breathe in
▷ **inhalation** *NOUN*

inhaler *NOUN* **inhalers**
a device for taking a drug that has to be breathed in, especially for relieving asthma

inherent (*say* in- **heer**- ent) *ADJECTIVE*
existing in something as one of its natural or permanent qualities
▷ **inherently** *ADVERB*

inherit *VERB* **inherits, inheriting, inherited**
1 to receive money, property, or a title when the previous owner dies
2 to get certain qualities or characteristics from parents or predecessors
▷ **inheritance** *NOUN*
▷ **inheritor** *NOUN*

inhibit *VERB* **inhibits, inhibiting, inhibited**
to hinder or restrain someone or something

inhibited *ADJECTIVE*
feeling embarrassed and worried about doing something or expressing your emotions
▷ **inhibition** *NOUN*

inhospitable *ADJECTIVE*
1 unfriendly to visitors
2 giving no shelter or good weather

inhuman *ADJECTIVE*
cruel; without pity or kindness
▷ **inhumanity** *NOUN*

inhumane *ADJECTIVE*
not humane

inimitable *ADJECTIVE*
impossible to imitate

iniquitous *ADJECTIVE*
very unjust
▷ **iniquity** *NOUN*

initial *NOUN* **initials**
the first letter of a word or name

initial *VERB* **initials, initialling, initialled**
to mark or sign something with the initials of your names

initial *ADJECTIVE*
at the beginning ◆ *the initial stages*
▷ **initially** *ADVERB*

initiate *VERB* **initiates, initiating, initiated**
1 to start something
2 to admit a person as a member of a society or group, often with special ceremonies
▷ **initiator** *NOUN*
▷ **initiation** *NOUN*

initiative (*say* in- **ish**- a- tiv) *NOUN*
1 the power or right to get something started
2 the ability to make decisions and take action on your own without being told what to do
to take the initiative is to take action yourself to start something happening

inject *VERB* **injects, injecting, injected**
1 to put a medicine or drug into the body by means of a hollow needle
2 to put liquid into something by means of a syringe etc.
3 to add a new quality ◆ *She tried to inject confidence into her voice.*
▷ **injection** *NOUN*

injudicious *ADJECTIVE*
unwise

injunction *NOUN* **injunctions**
a command given with authority, e.g. by a lawcourt

injure *VERB* **injures, injuring, injured**
to harm or hurt someone

injury *NOUN* **injuries**
1 the process of being injured; harm or damage
2 an act of being injured; damage done to a person's body
▷ **injurious** (*say* in- **joor**- ee- us) *ADJECTIVE*

injustice *NOUN* **injustices**
1 lack of justice
2 an unjust action or treatment

ink *NOUN* **inks**
a black or coloured liquid used in writing and printing

inkling *NOUN* **inklings**
a slight idea or suspicion ◆ *I had no inkling of what was going to happen.*

inky *ADJECTIVE*
1 stained with ink
2 black like ink

inland *ADJECTIVE, ADVERB*
in or towards the interior of a country; away from the coast

Inland Revenue *NOUN*
the government department responsible for collecting taxes and similar charges inland (not at a port)

in-laws *PLURAL NOUN*
(*informal*) relatives by marriage
WORD HISTORY from French *en loi de mariage* 'in law of marriage'

inlay *VERB* **inlays, inlaying, inlaid**
to set pieces of wood or metal into a surface to form a design

inlay *NOUN* **inlays**
a design or piece of material decorated by inlaying

inlet *NOUN* **inlets**
a strip of water reaching into the land from a sea or lake

inmate *NOUN* **inmates**
one of the occupants of a prison, hospital, or other institution

in memoriam *PREPOSITION*
in memory of

inmost *ADJECTIVE*
most inward

inn *NOUN* **inns**
a hotel or public house, especially in the country
▷ **innkeeper** *NOUN*

innards *PLURAL NOUN*
(*informal*) the internal organs of a person or animal; the inner parts of a machine

innate *ADJECTIVE*
inborn or natural

inner *ADJECTIVE*
inside; nearer to the centre
▷ **innermost** *ADJECTIVE*

innings *NOUN* **innings**
the time when a cricket team or player is batting

innocent *ADJECTIVE*
1 to be innocent of a crime or wrongdoing is not to have done it

Stanley was not a bad kid. He was innocent of the crime for which he was convicted. He'd just been in the wrong place at the wrong time. — *Louis Sachar, Holes*

2 not wicked; lacking experience of evil
3 harmless
▷ **innocence** *NOUN*
▷ **innocently** *ADVERB*

innocuous *ADJECTIVE*
harmless

innovation *NOUN* **innovations**
1 the process of introducing new things or new methods
2 a completely new process or way of doing things that has just been introduced
▷ **innovator** *NOUN*

innovative *ADJECTIVE*
new and interesting

innuendo *NOUN* **innuendoes**
indirect reference to something insulting or rude

innumerable *ADJECTIVE*
too many to be counted

inoculate *VERB* **inoculates, inoculating, inoculated**
to inject or treat someone with a vaccine or serum as a protection against a disease
▷ **inoculation** *NOUN*
USAGE NOTE Note the spelling of this word. It has one *n* and one *c*.

inoffensive *ADJECTIVE*
harmless

inordinate *ADJECTIVE*
excessive
▷ **inordinately** *ADVERB*

inorganic *ADJECTIVE*
not of living organisms; of mineral origin

in-patient *NOUN* **in-patients**
a patient who stays at a hospital for treatment

input *NOUN*
(*ICT*) something that is put into or contributes to a larger amount of something, especially data put into a computer

input *VERB* **inputs, inputting, input** or **inputted**
(*ICT*) to put data into a computer

inquest *NOUN* **inquests**
an official inquiry to find out how a person died

inquire *VERB* **inquires, inquiring, inquired**
1 to investigate something carefully
2 to ask for information

USAGE NOTE You can spell this word *inquire* or *enquire* in either of its meanings, but *inquire* is often preferred in the first meaning and *enquire* is often preferred in the second meaning.

inquiry *NOUN* **inquiries**
1 an official investigation
2 a question

inquisition *NOUN* **inquisitions**
1 a detailed investigation involving a lot of questions
2 the Inquisition was a council of the Roman Catholic Church in Spain in the Middle Ages, set up to discover and punish heretics

inquisitor *NOUN* **inquisitors**
an official who conducts a formal investigation and asks questions

inquisitive *ADJECTIVE*
always asking questions or trying to find out things
▷ **inquisitively** *ADVERB*

inroads *PLURAL NOUN*
to make inroads into or on something is to use a lot of it, or to get a lot of it (for example, a task) done

inrush *NOUN* **inrushes**
a sudden rushing in

insane *ADJECTIVE*
not sane; mad
▷ **insanely** *ADVERB*
▷ **insanity** *NOUN*

insanitary *ADJECTIVE*
unclean and likely to be harmful to health

insatiable (*say* in- **say**- sha- bul) *ADJECTIVE*
an insatiable appetite or demand is so strong that it cannot be completely satisfied

inscribe *VERB* **inscribes, inscribing, inscribed**
to write or carve words or symbols on a hard surface

inscription *NOUN* **inscriptions**
words written or carved on a monument, coin, stone, etc. or written in the front of a book

inscrutable *ADJECTIVE*
mysterious; impossible to interpret ◆ *He was wearing that inscrutable look again.*

insect *NOUN* **insects**
a small animal with six legs, no backbone, and a body divided into three parts (head, thorax, abdomen)

insecticide *NOUN* **insecticides**
a substance for killing insects

insectivorous *ADJECTIVE*
feeding on insects and other small invertebrate creatures
▷ **insectivore** *NOUN*

insecure *ADJECTIVE*
1 not secure or safe
2 lacking confidence about yourself
▷ **insecurely** *ADVERB*
▷ **insecurity** *NOUN*

inseminate *VERB* **inseminates, inseminating, inseminated**
to insert semen into the womb
▷ **insemination** *NOUN*

insensible *ADJECTIVE*
1 unconscious
2 to be insensible of something is to be unaware of it or uninterested in it ◆ *He was insensible of her needs.*

insensitive *ADJECTIVE*
not sensitive or thinking about other people's feelings
▷ **insensitively** *ADVERB*
▷ **insensitivity** *NOUN*

inseparable *ADJECTIVE*
1 not able to be separated
2 liking to be constantly together ◆ *Claire and her sister were inseparable.*
▷ **inseparably** *ADVERB*

insert (*say* in- **sert**) *VERB* **inserts, inserting, inserted**
to put a thing into something else
▷ **insertion** *NOUN*

insert (*say* **in**- sert) *NOUN* **inserts**
something put into something else, for example a leaflet in a magazine

inshore *ADVERB, ADJECTIVE*
near or nearer to the shore

inside *NOUN* **insides**
1 the inner side, surface, or part
2 (*informal*) a person's insides are their stomach and bowels

inside out with the inside turned to face outwards

inside *ADJECTIVE*
on or coming from the inside; in or nearest to the middle

inside *ADVERB, PREPOSITION*
on or to the inner side of something

I opened up my special food box. Inside was the Milky Bar and two liquorice laces and three clementines and a pink wafer biscuit and my red food colouring. — *Mark Haddon, The Curious Incident of the Dog in the Night-Time*

Rincewind knew what was inside trees: wood, sap, possibly squirrels. Not a palace. — *Terry Pratchett, The Colour of Magic*

insider *NOUN* **insiders**
a member of a certain group, especially someone with access to private information

insidious *ADJECTIVE*
causing harm gradually, without being noticed
▷ **insidiously** *ADVERB*

insight *NOUN* **insights**
1 the ability to perceive the truth about things
2 an understanding of something

insignia *NOUN* **insignia**
a badge or symbol which shows that you belong to something or hold a particular office

insignificant *ADJECTIVE*
not important or influential
▷ **insignificance** *NOUN*

insincere *ADJECTIVE*
not sincere
▷ **insincerely** *ADVERB*
▷ **insincerity** *NOUN*

insinuate *VERB* **insinuates, insinuating, insinuated**
1 to hint something unpleasant
2 to introduce a thing or yourself gradually or craftily into a place

insinuation *NOUN* **insinuations**
an unpleasant hint or suggestion that someone makes

insipid *ADJECTIVE*
1 lacking flavour
2 not lively or interesting
▷ **insipidity** *NOUN*

insist *VERB* **insists, insisting, insisted**
to be very firm in saying or asking for something ◆ *I insist on seeing the manager.*
▷ **insistent** *ADJECTIVE*
▷ **insistence** *NOUN*

in situ (*say* in **sit**-yoo) *ADVERB*
in its original place

insolent *ADJECTIVE*
very rude and disrespectful

Simon stuck out his tongue and, after a small, insolent pause, began licking the grains of spilled sugar from his wrists. — *Anne Fine, Flour Babies*

▷ **insolently** *ADVERB*
▷ **insolence** *NOUN*

insoluble *ADJECTIVE*
1 an insoluble problem or difficulty is one that is impossible to solve
2 an insoluble substance cannot be dissolved
▷ **insolubility** *NOUN*

insolvent *ADJECTIVE*
unable to pay your debts
▷ **insolvency** *NOUN*

insomnia *NOUN*
being unable to sleep
▷ **insomniac** *NOUN*

inspect *VERB* **inspects, inspecting, inspected**
to examine something carefully

Billy picked the pellet up and inspected it in his palm. It was the size of a blackbird's egg, charcoal coloured, and shining faintly as though lacquered. — *Barry Hines, A Kestrel for a Knave*

▷ **inspection** *NOUN*

inspector *NOUN* **inspectors**
1 a person whose job is to inspect or supervise things
2 a police officer ranking next above a sergeant

inspiration *NOUN* **inspirations**
1 a sudden brilliant idea
2 a person or thing that fills you with ideas or enthusiasm

inspire *VERB* **inspires, inspiring, inspired**
1 to fill a person with ideas or enthusiasm
2 to create a strong positive feeling in someone ◆ *The applause inspired us with confidence.*

instability *NOUN*
lack of stability

install *VERB* **installs, installing, installed**
1 to put something in position ready for use ◆ *They have installed a new computer system.*
2 to put a person into an important position with a ceremony ◆ *He was installed as the city's mayor.*

installation *NOUN* **installations**
1 the process of installing something
2 a piece of equipment that has been installed
3 (*Art*) an exhibit specially assembled in an art gallery

instalment *NOUN* **instalments**
1 each of a series of payments made for something over a period of time
2 each part of a television serial or of a series of publications

instance *NOUN* **instances**
an example
for instance for example

instant *ADJECTIVE*
1 happening immediately ◆ *The new museum was an instant success.*
2 instant food or drink is designed to be prepared quickly and easily
▷ **instantly** *ADVERB*

instant *NOUN* **instants**
a moment ◆ *It was done in an instant.*

instantaneous *ADJECTIVE*
happening immediately
▷ **instantaneously** *ADVERB*

instead *ADVERB*
in place of something else

instep *NOUN* **insteps**
the top of the foot between the toes and the ankle

instigate *VERB* **instigates, instigating, instigated**
to cause something violent or troublesome to happen ◆ *The rebels instigated a reign of terror in the city.*
▷ **instigation** *NOUN*
▷ **instigator** *NOUN*

instil *VERB* **instils, instilling, instilled**
to put ideas into a person's mind gradually

instinct *NOUN* **instincts**
a natural tendency or ability ◆ *Babies have a strong survival instinct.* ◆ *When she heard someone call her name, her instinct was to run.*

instinctive *ADJECTIVE*
1 prompted by instinct
2 an instinctive action or reaction is one that is natural or automatic
▷ **instinctively** *ADVERB*

institute *NOUN* **institutes**
a society or organization; the building used by this

institute *VERB* **institutes, instituting, instituted**
to establish or found something; to start an inquiry or custom etc.

institution *NOUN* **institutions**
1 an institute; a public organization, e.g. a hospital or university
2 an established habit or custom
3 instituting something
▷ **institutional** *ADJECTIVE*

instruct *VERB* **instructs, instructing, instructed**
1 to teach a person a subject or skill
2 to inform someone about something
3 to tell a person what they must do
▷ **instructor** *NOUN*

instruction *NOUN* **instructions**
1 teaching a subject or skill
2 an order or piece of information ◆ *Read the instructions carefully.*
▷ **instructional** *ADJECTIVE*

instructive *ADJECTIVE*
giving knowledge

instrument *NOUN* **instruments**
1 (*Music*) a device for producing musical sounds
2 a tool used for delicate or scientific work
3 a measuring device

instrumental *ADJECTIVE*
1 (*Music*) performed on a single musical instrument or group of instruments, without voices
2 someone is instrumental in doing something when they play an important part in it ◆ *The club was instrumental in establishing winter sports as a popular type of holiday.*

instrumentalist *NOUN* **instrumentalists**
a person who plays a musical instrument

insubordinate *ADJECTIVE*
disobedient or rebellious
▷ **insubordination** *NOUN*

insufferable *ADJECTIVE*
unbearable

insufficient *ADJECTIVE*
not sufficient

insular *ADJECTIVE*
1 to do with or like an island
2 narrow-minded

insulate *VERB* **insulates, insulating, insulated**
to cover or protect something to prevent heat, cold, or electricity from passing in or out
▷ **insulation** *NOUN*
▷ **insulator** *NOUN*

WORD HISTORY from Latin *insula* 'island'

insulin *NOUN*
a substance that controls the amount of sugar in the blood. The lack of insulin causes diabetes.

insult (*say* in-**sult**) *VERB* **insults, insulting, insulted**
to hurt a person's feelings or pride

insult (*say* **in**-sult) *NOUN* **insults**
an insulting remark or action

insuperable *ADJECTIVE*
an insuperable problem or difficulty is one that cannot be overcome

insurance *NOUN*
an agreement to compensate someone for a loss, damage, or injury etc., in return for a payment (called a *premium*) made in advance

insure *VERB* **insures, insuring, insured**
to protect something by means of insurance ◆ *Have you insured all your valuables?*

USAGE NOTE Take care not to confuse this word with *ensure*.

insurgent *NOUN* **insurgents**
someone who rebels against a ruler or government
▷ **insurgent** *ADJECTIVE*

insurmountable *ADJECTIVE*
unable to be overcome

insurrection *NOUN* **insurrections**
a rebellion

intact *ADJECTIVE*
not damaged; complete

intake *NOUN* **intakes**
1 taking something in
2 an intake of people is the number that an institution admits at one time or over a particular period

intangible *ADJECTIVE*
not able to be touched; not solid

integer *NOUN* **integers**
(*Mathematics*) a whole number (e.g. 0, 3, 19), not a fraction

integral (*say* **in**- tig- ral) *ADJECTIVE*
1 an integral part of something is an essential part that helps to make it what it is
2 whole or complete

integrate *VERB* **integrates, integrating, integrated**
1 to make parts into a whole; to combine things
2 to bring people together harmoniously into a single community
▷ **integration** *NOUN*

integrity (*say* in- **teg**- rit- ee) *NOUN*
reliability and honesty

intellect *NOUN* **intellects**
the ability to think well and use the mind

intellectual *ADJECTIVE*
1 to do with or using the intellect
2 having a good intellect and a liking for knowledge
▷ **intellectually** *ADVERB*

intellectual *NOUN* **intellectuals**
an intellectual person

intelligence *NOUN*
1 being intelligent
2 information, especially of military value; the people who collect and study this information

intelligent *ADJECTIVE*
able to learn and understand things; having or showing great mental ability
▷ **intelligently** *ADVERB*

intelligentsia *NOUN*
intellectual people regarded as a group

intelligible *ADJECTIVE*
able to be understood
▷ **intelligibly** *ADVERB*
▷ **intelligibility** *NOUN*

intend *VERB* **intends, intending, intended**
1 to have something in mind as what you want to do
2 to plan that something should be used or understood in a particular way

intense *ADJECTIVE*
1 very strong or great

> The cold grew so intense that Thomas could hardly breathe as he felt the moisture in his throat turning to ice. — *G. P. Taylor, Shadowmancer*

2 an intense person feels things very seriously and deeply
▷ **intensely** *ADVERB*
▷ **intensity** *NOUN*

intensify *VERB* **intensifies, intensifying, intensified**
to make something more intense, or to become more intense
▷ **intensification** *NOUN*

intensive *ADJECTIVE*
concentrated; using a lot of effort over a short time
▷ **intensively** *ADVERB*

intensive care *NOUN*
the medical treatment of a patient who is dangerously ill and needs constant supervision

intent *NOUN* **intents**
what someone intends; an intention

intent *ADJECTIVE*
with concentrated attention; very interested
to be intent on something is to be eager or determined about doing it
▷ **intently** *ADVERB*

intention *NOUN* **intentions**
what someone intends; a purpose or plan

intentional *ADJECTIVE*
deliberate, not accidental
▷ **intentionally** *ADVERB*

inter *VERB* **inters, interring, interred**
to bury a corpse

interact *VERB* **interacts, interacting, interacted**
to have an effect on one another
▷ **interaction** *NOUN*

interactive *ADJECTIVE*
(*ICT*) allowing information to be sent immediately in either direction between a computer system and the user

interbreed *VERB* **interbreeds, interbreeding, interbred**
animals interbreed when they breed with each other

intercede *VERB* **intercedes, interceding, interceded**
to intervene on behalf of another person or as a peacemaker
▷ **intercession** *NOUN*

intercept *VERB* **intercepts, intercepting, intercepted**
to stop or catch a person or thing that is going from one place to another
▷ **interception** *NOUN*

interchange *VERB* **interchanges, interchanging, interchanged**
1 to put each of two things into the other's place
2 to exchange things
▷ **interchangeable** *ADJECTIVE*

interchange *NOUN* **interchanges**
1 interchanging
2 a road junction where vehicles can move from one motorway etc. to another

intercom *NOUN* **intercoms**
a system of communication between rooms or compartments, operating rather like a telephone

intercourse *NOUN*
1 communication or dealings between people
2 sexual intercourse

interdependent *ADJECTIVE*
dependent on one other

interest *NOUN* **interests**
1 a feeling of wanting to know about something or help with it
2 a thing that someone is interested in or takes part in ◆ *Local history is an interest of mine.*
3 your interests are what benefits you or is useful to you
4 money paid regularly by a borrower in return for money someone has lent them or deposited with them

interest *VERB* **interests, interesting, interested**
to arouse a person's interest
▷ **interested** *ADJECTIVE*

interesting *ADJECTIVE*
arousing interest or curiosity

interface *NOUN* **interfaces**
(*ICT*) a connection between two parts of a computer system

interfere *VERB* **interferes, interfering, interfered**
1 to interfere, or interfere with something, is to take part in something that has nothing to do with you
2 to interfere with someone or something is to get in their way or obstruct them ◆ *Power lines here might interfere with approaching aircraft.*

interference *NOUN*
1 interfering
2 a crackling or distorting of a radio or television signal

interim *NOUN*
an interval of time between two events

interim *ADJECTIVE*
arranged or in force for the time being, and likely to be changed

interior *ADJECTIVE*
inner

interior *NOUN* **interiors**
1 the inside of something
2 the central or inland part of a country

interject *VERB* **interjects, interjecting, interjected**
to break in with a remark while someone else is speaking

interjection *NOUN* **interjections**
(*Grammar*) a word or words someone exclaims to express joy or pain or surprise, such as *oh!* or *ouch!*

interlock *VERB* **interlocks, interlocking, interlocked**
things interlock when they fit into each other

interloper *NOUN* **interlopers**
an intruder

interlude *NOUN* **interludes**
1 an interval
2 something happening in an interval or between other events

intermediary *NOUN* **intermediaries**
someone who tries to settle a dispute by negotiating with both sides; a mediator

intermediate *ADJECTIVE*
coming between two things in time, place, or order

interment *NOUN* **interments**
burial

USAGE NOTE Take care not to confuse this word with *internment*.

interminable *ADJECTIVE*
seeming to be endless; long and tedious
▷ **interminably** *ADVERB*

intermission *NOUN* **intermissions**
an interval between parts of a film or show

intermittent *ADJECTIVE*
happening at intervals; not continuous
▷ **intermittently** *ADVERB*

intern *VERB* **interns, interning, interned**
to imprison someone in a special camp or area, usually in wartime

internal *ADJECTIVE*
inside; within something
▷ **internally** *ADVERB*

internal-combustion engine *NOUN* **internal-combustion engines**
an engine that produces power by burning fuel inside the engine itself

internal rhyme *NOUN* **internal rhymes**
(*Language*) a rhyme involving words in the same line, e.g. *The fair breeze blew, the white foam flew* (from 'The Rime of the Ancient Mariner' by Coleridge)

international *ADJECTIVE*
to do with or belonging to more than one country; agreed between nations
▷ **internationally** *ADVERB*

international *NOUN* **internationals**
1 a sports contest between teams representing different countries
2 a sports player who represents a country

Internet *NOUN*
(*ICT*) an international computer network that allows users all over the world to communicate and exchange information

internment *NOUN*
the process of being interned in wartime

USAGE NOTE Take care not to confuse this word with *interment*.

interplanetary *ADJECTIVE*
between planets

interplay *NOUN*
the way two things have an effect on each other

interpolate *VERB* **interpolates, interpolating, interpolated**
1 to add a remark during a conversation
2 to insert words; to put terms into a mathematical series
▷ **interpolation** *NOUN*

interpose *VERB* **interposes, interposing, interposed**
to place something between two things

interpret *VERB* **interprets, interpreting, interpreted**
1 to explain what something means
2 to translate what someone says into another language as they are speaking
3 to perform music, dance, or another performing art in a way that shows your feelings about its meaning
▷ **interpretation** *NOUN*
▷ **interpreter** *NOUN*

interregnum *NOUN* **interregnums** or **interregna**
an interval between the reign of one ruler and that of his or her successor

interrogate *VERB* **interrogates, interrogating, interrogated**
to question someone closely or formally
▷ **interrogation** *NOUN*
▷ **interrogator** *NOUN*

interrogative *ADJECTIVE*
1 asking a question
2 used in expressing a question
▷ **interrogatory** *ADJECTIVE*

interrupt *VERB* **interrupts, interrupting, interrupted**
1 to break in on what someone is saying by inserting a remark
2 to prevent something from continuing
▷ **interruption** *NOUN*

intersect *VERB* **intersects, intersecting, intersected**
1 to divide a thing by passing or lying across it
2 lines or roads intersect when they cross each other
▷ **intersection** *NOUN*

intersperse *VERB* **intersperses, interspersing, interspersed**
to be interspersed with things is to have them at various points

It was a valley ... with high slopes on either side and, again, dense patches of woodland interspersed with rocky clearings. — *Tim Bowler, River Boy*

interval *NOUN* **intervals**
1 a time between two events or parts of a play or show
2 a space between two things
3 (*Music*) the difference in pitch between two sounds

at intervals with some time or distance between each one

WORD HISTORY from Latin *intervallum* 'space between ramparts'

intervene *VERB* **intervenes, intervening, intervened**
1 to come between two events ◆ *in the intervening years*
2 to interrupt a discussion or fight to try and stop it or change its result
▷ **intervention** *NOUN*

interview *NOUN* **interviews**
a formal meeting with someone to ask them questions or to obtain information

interview *VERB* **interviews, interviewing, interviewed**
to hold an interview with someone
▷ **interviewer** *NOUN*

intestine *NOUN* **intestines**
the long tube along which food passes while being absorbed by the body, between the stomach and the anus
▷ **intestinal** *ADJECTIVE*

intimate (*say* **in**- tim- at) *ADJECTIVE*
1 you are intimate with someone when you are close friends
2 intimate thoughts or secrets are private and personal
3 intimate knowledge about something is thorough and detailed
▷ **intimacy** *NOUN*
▷ **intimately** *ADVERB*

intimate (*say* **in**- tim- ayt) *VERB* **intimates, intimating, intimated**
to hint at something
▷ **intimation** *NOUN*

intimidate *VERB* **intimidates, intimidating, intimidated**
to frighten someone with threats into doing something
▷ **intimidation** *NOUN*

into *PREPOSITION*
1 used to express movement to the inside of something ◆ *He put his hand into the bag.*
2 used to express a change of condition or state ◆ *The glass shattered into tiny pieces.* ◆ *She wanted to go into teaching.*

intolerable *ADJECTIVE*
unable to be tolerated or endured
▷ **intolerably** *ADVERB*

intolerant *ADJECTIVE*
not tolerant
▷ **intolerantly** *ADVERB*
▷ **intolerance** *NOUN*

intonation *NOUN* **intonations**
1 (*Language*) the tone or pitch of the voice in speaking
2 intoning

intone *VERB* **intones, intoning, intoned**
to recite in a chanting voice

'A sailing man is lucky to have had such a dry death,' Great-Uncle Bo intoned in his croaking, bullfrog voice. — *Geraldine McCaughrean, The Kite Rider*

intoxicate *VERB* **intoxicates, intoxicating, intoxicated**
to make a person drunk or excited
▷ **intoxication** *NOUN*

intractable *ADJECTIVE*
unmanageable; difficult to deal with or control
▷ **intractability** *NOUN*

intransigent *ADJECTIVE*
stubborn
▷ **intransigence** *NOUN*

intransitive *ADJECTIVE*
(*Grammar*) an intransitive verb is one that does not have a direct object after it, e.g. *see* in *we can see* (but not in *we can see you*, which has an object (*you*) and is transitive) (SEE ALSO **transitive**)

intravenous (*say* in- tra- **veen**- us) *ADJECTIVE*
an intravenous injection is made directly into a vein

intrepid *ADJECTIVE*
fearless and brave
▷ **intrepidly** *ADVERB*

intricate *ADJECTIVE*
very complicated, with a lot of fine details
▷ **intricately** *ADVERB*
▷ **intricacy** *NOUN*

intrigue (*say* in- **treeg**) *VERB* **intrigues, intriguing, intrigued**
1 to interest someone very much ◆ *The subject intrigues me.*
2 to plot with someone in an underhand way

intrigue *NOUN* **intrigues**
1 plotting; an underhand plot
2 (*old use*) a secret love affair

intrinsic *ADJECTIVE*
being part of the essential nature or character of something ◆ *The coins have little intrinsic value.*
▷ **intrinsically** *ADVERB*

introduce *VERB* **introduces, introducing, introduced**
1 to bring an idea or practice into use
2 to make a person known to other people
3 to announce a broadcast, speaker, etc.

introduction *NOUN* **introductions**
1 introducing somebody or something
2 an explanation put at the beginning of a book or speech etc.
▷ **introductory** *ADJECTIVE*

introspective *ADJECTIVE*
examining your own thoughts and feelings
▷ **introspection** *NOUN*

introvert *NOUN* **introverts**
someone who is shy and does not like to talk openly about their own thoughts and feelings (SEE ALSO **extrovert**)
▷ **introverted** *ADJECTIVE*

intrude *VERB* **intrudes, intruding, intruded**
to come into a place or situation where you are not needed or wanted
▷ **intrusion** *NOUN*
▷ **intrusive** *ADJECTIVE*

intruder *NOUN* **intruders**
someone who enters a building to commit a crime

intuition *NOUN*
the power to know or understand things without having to think hard or without being taught
▷ **intuitive** *ADJECTIVE*
▷ **intuitively** *ADVERB*

Inuit (*say* in- yoo- it) *NOUN* **Inuit**
1 a member of a people living in northern Canada and Greenland; an Eskimo
2 the language of the Inuit

USAGE NOTE See the note at *Eskimo*.

inundate *VERB* **inundates, inundating, inundated**
to flood or overwhelm a place ◆ *The radio station was inundated with replies to their quiz question.*
▷ **inundation** *NOUN*

inure (*say* in- **yoor**) *VERB* **inures, inuring, inured**
to accustom someone to something unpleasant or unusual ◆ *My skin is pretty well inured to all kinds of weather.*

invade *VERB* **invades, invading, invaded**
1 to attack and enter a country
2 to crowd into a place ◆ *Tourists invade the Mediterranean in summer.*
▷ **invader** *NOUN*

invalid (*say* **in**- va- leed) *NOUN* **invalids**
a person who is ill or who is weakened by illness

invalid (*say* in- **val**- id) *ADJECTIVE*
not valid or true

invalidate *VERB* **invalidates, invalidating, invalidated**
to make a thing invalid
▷ **invalidation** *NOUN*

invalidity (*say* in- va- **lid**- i- tee) *NOUN*
1 the state of being an invalid
2 the state of being invalid or untrue

invaluable *ADJECTIVE*
having a value that is too great to be measured; extremely valuable

invariable *ADJECTIVE*
not variable; never changing

invariably *ADVERB*
without exception; always

invasion *NOUN* **invasions**
the act of attacking and entering a country to occupy it

invective *NOUN*
abusive words

inveigle (*say* in- **vay**- gul) *VERB* **inveigles, inveigling, inveigled**
to entice someone
▷ **inveiglement** *NOUN*

invent *VERB* **invents, inventing, invented**
1 to be the first person to make or think of a particular thing
2 to make up something imaginary or untrue ◆ *Ask the children to invent new signals for 'stop' and 'go'.* ◆ *He had to invent an excuse fairly quickly.*
▷ **invention** *NOUN*
▷ **inventor** *NOUN*

inventive *ADJECTIVE*
having good or original ideas

inventory (*say* **in**- ven- ter- ee) *NOUN* **inventories**
a detailed list of goods or furniture

WORD HISTORY from Latin *inventarium* 'a list of what is found', from *invenire* 'to find'

inverse *ADJECTIVE*
opposite or reverse
▷ **inversely** *ADVERB*

invert *VERB* **inverts, inverting, inverted**
to turn something upside down
▷ **inversion** *NOUN*

invertebrate *NOUN* **invertebrates**
(*Biology*) an animal without a backbone
▷ **invertebrate** *ADJECTIVE*

inverted commas *PLURAL NOUN*
punctuation marks " " or ' ' put round quotations and spoken words. Also called *quotation marks, speech marks.*

invest *VERB* **invests, investing, invested**
1 to use money to make a profit, e.g. by lending it in return for interest to be paid, or by buying stocks and shares or property
2 to give someone an honour, medal, or special title in a formal ceremony
▷ **investor** *NOUN*

investigate *VERB* **investigates, investigating, investigated**
to find out as much as you can about something; to make a systematic inquiry
▷ **investigation** *NOUN*
▷ **investigator** *NOUN*
▷ **investigative** *ADJECTIVE*

investiture *NOUN* **investitures**
the process or ceremony of investing someone with an honour etc.

investment *NOUN* **investments**
1 an amount of money invested
2 something in which money is invested ◆ *Property is a sound investment right now.*

inveterate *ADJECTIVE*
firmly established; habitual ◆ *He was shown to be an inveterate liar.*

invidious *ADJECTIVE*
causing resentment because of unfairness

invigilate *VERB* **invigilates, invigilating, invigilated**
to supervise candidates at an examination
▷ **invigilation** *NOUN*
▷ **invigilator** *NOUN*

invigorate *VERB* **invigorates, invigorating, invigorated**
to give a person strength or courage

invincible *ADJECTIVE*
not able to be defeated
▷ **invincibly** *ADVERB*
▷ **invincibility** *NOUN*

invisible *ADJECTIVE*
not visible; not able to be seen
▷ **invisibly** *ADVERB*
▷ **invisibility** *NOUN*

invitation *NOUN* **invitations**
1 a written or spoken request asking someone to go somewhere or to do something
2 the act of inviting someone or something

invite *VERB* **invites, inviting, invited**
1 to ask a person to come or do something
2 to be likely to cause something unpleasant to happen ◆ *You are inviting trouble.*

inviting *ADJECTIVE*
attractive or tempting

The back of the Radley house was less inviting than the front: a ramshackle porch ran the width of the house; there were two doors and two dark windows between the doors. — *Harper Lee, To Kill a Mockingbird*

▷ **invitingly** *ADVERB*

invoice *NOUN* **invoices**
a list of goods sent or work done, with the prices charged

invoke *VERB* **invokes, invoking, invoked**
1 to appeal to a law or someone's authority for help or protection
2 to call upon a god in prayer asking for help etc.
▷ **invocation** *NOUN*

involuntary *ADJECTIVE*
not deliberate; unintentional
▷ **involuntarily** *ADVERB*

involve *VERB* **involves, involving, involved**
1 to have as a result or necessary part ◆ *The exercise involved pedalling on a stationary bicycle.*
2 to make or let someone share or take part in something ◆ *I always finish the team practice with something that involves everyone.*
▷ **involvement** *NOUN*

involved *ADJECTIVE*
1 complicated
2 concerned; sharing in something

invulnerable *ADJECTIVE*
not able to be harmed

inward *ADJECTIVE*
1 on the inside
2 going or facing inwards

inward *ADVERB*
inwards

inwardly *ADVERB*
in your thoughts; privately

inwards *ADVERB*
towards the inside

iodine *NOUN*
a chemical substance used as an antiseptic

ion *NOUN* **ions**
an electrically charged particle

ionosphere (*say* eye- **on**- os- feer) *NOUN*
a region of the upper atmosphere, containing ions

iota *NOUN* **iotas**
a tiny amount of something

Whoever told you this is a completely vicious liar. There is not one iota of truth in any of it. — *Michael Hoeye, Time Stops for No Mouse*

IOU *NOUN* **IOUs**
a signed note acknowledging that you owe someone some money

IQ *ABBREVIATION*
intelligence quotient; a number showing how a person's intelligence compares with that of an average person

irascible (*say* ir- **as**- ib- ul) *ADJECTIVE*
easily becoming angry; irritable

irate (*say* eye- **rayt**) *ADJECTIVE*
angry

iridescent *ADJECTIVE*
showing rainbow-like colours
▷ **iridescence** *NOUN*

iris *NOUN* **irises**
1 the coloured part of the eyeball
2 a plant with long pointed leaves and large flowers

irk *VERB* **irks, irking, irked**
to annoy

irksome *ADJECTIVE*
annoying or tiresome

iron *NOUN* **irons**
1 a hard grey metal
2 a device with a flat base that is heated for smoothing clothes or cloth
3 a tool made of iron ◆ *a branding iron*
▷ **iron** *ADJECTIVE*

iron *VERB* **irons, ironing, ironed**
to smooth clothes or cloth with an iron
to iron something out is to deal with a difficulty or problem

Iron Age *NOUN*
the time when tools and weapons were made of iron

ironic (*say* eye- **ron**- ik) *ADJECTIVE*
using irony; full of irony
▷ **ironical** *ADJECTIVE*
▷ **ironically** *ADVERB*

ironmonger *NOUN* **ironmongers**
a shopkeeper who sells tools and other metal objects
▷ **ironmongery** *NOUN*

irons *PLURAL NOUN*
shackles or fetters

irony (*say* **eye**- ron- ee) *NOUN* **ironies**
1 irony, or an irony, is saying the opposite of what you mean in a slightly sarcastic way in order to make the point more effectively or as a joke, e.g. saying 'What a lovely day' when it is pouring with rain
2 a situation that is the opposite of what you might have expected ◆ *The irony was that their victory contained the seeds of eventual defeat.*

WORD HISTORY from Greek *eiron* 'someone who pretends not to know'

irrational *ADJECTIVE*
not rational; illogical
▷ **irrationally** *ADVERB*

irreducible *ADJECTIVE*
not able to be reduced or simplified

irrefutable (*say* ir- **ef**- yoo- ta- bul) *ADJECTIVE*
unable to be proved wrong

irregular ***ADJECTIVE***
1 not regular; uneven
2 not following the normal rules or usual custom
3 (*Mathematics*) having sides and angles that are not equal
▷ **irregularly** ***ADVERB***
▷ **irregularity** ***NOUN***

irrelevant (*say* ir- **el**- iv- ant) ***ADJECTIVE***
not relevant
▷ **irrelevantly** ***ADVERB***
▷ **irrelevance** ***NOUN***

irreparable (*say* ir- **ep**- er- a- bul) ***ADJECTIVE***
unable to be repaired or replaced
▷ **irreparably** ***ADVERB***

irreplaceable ***ADJECTIVE***
unable to be replaced

irrepressible ***ADJECTIVE***
unable to be repressed; always lively and cheerful
▷ **irrepressibly** ***ADVERB***

irreproachable ***ADJECTIVE***
blameless or faultless
▷ **irreproachably** ***ADVERB***

irresistible ***ADJECTIVE***
too strong or attractive to be resisted
▷ **irresistibly** ***ADVERB***

irresolute ***ADJECTIVE***
feeling uncertain; hesitant
▷ **irresolutely** ***ADVERB***

irrespective ***ADJECTIVE***
not taking something into account ◆ *No company, irrespective of its size, can afford to ignore these changes.*

irresponsible ***ADJECTIVE***
not showing a proper sense of responsibility; not thinking enough about the consequences of your actions
▷ **irresponsibly** ***ADVERB***
▷ **irresponsibility** ***NOUN***

irretrievable ***ADJECTIVE***
not able to be retrieved
▷ **irretrievably** ***ADVERB***

irreverent ***ADJECTIVE***
not reverent or respectful
▷ **irreverently** ***ADVERB***
▷ **irreverence** ***NOUN***

irrevocable (*say* ir- **ev**- ok- a- bul) ***ADJECTIVE***
unable to be revoked or altered
▷ **irrevocably** ***ADVERB***

irrigate ***VERB*** **irrigates, irrigating, irrigated**
to supply land with water so that crops can grow
▷ **irrigation** ***NOUN***

irritable ***ADJECTIVE***
easily annoyed; bad-tempered
▷ **irritably** ***ADVERB***
▷ **irritability** ***NOUN***

irritant ***NOUN*** **irritants**
something that causes inflammation or soreness

irritate ***VERB*** **irritates, irritating, irritated**
1 to annoy someone
2 to cause inflammation or soreness in a part of the body
▷ **irritation** ***NOUN***

irrupt ***VERB*** **irrupts, irrupting, irrupted**
to enter a place forcibly or violently
▷ **irruption** ***NOUN***

USAGE NOTE Take care not to confuse this word with *erupt*.

Islam ***NOUN***
(*Religion*) the religion of Muslims
▷ **Islamic** ***ADJECTIVE***

WORD HISTORY from an Arabic word meaning 'submission to God'

island ***NOUN*** **islands**
1 a piece of land surrounded by water
2 something that resembles an island because it is isolated or detached, e.g. a traffic island

islander ***NOUN*** **islanders**
an inhabitant of an island

isle (*rhymes with* mile) ***NOUN*** **isles**
(*poetic and in names*) an island

isn't short for **is not**

isobar (*say* **eye**- so- bar) ***NOUN*** **isobars**
a line on a map connecting places that have the same atmospheric pressure

isolate ***VERB*** **isolates, isolating, isolated**
to place a person or thing apart or alone; to separate someone or something
▷ **isolation** ***NOUN***

isosceles (*say* eye- **soss**- il- eez) ***ADJECTIVE***
(*Mathematics*) an isosceles triangle has two sides of equal length

WORD HISTORY from Greek *isos* 'equal' and *skelos* 'leg', because an isosceles triangle is regarded as having two equal legs

isotope ***NOUN*** **isotopes**
(*Science*) a form of an element that differs from other forms in the structure of its nucleus but has the same chemical properties as the other forms

WORD HISTORY from Greek *isos* 'same' and *topos* 'place' (because they appear in the same place in the table of chemical elements)

ISP ***ABBREVIATION***
(*ICT*) Internet service provider, a company providing individual users with a connection to the Internet

issue ***VERB*** **issues, issuing, issued**
1 to supply; to give out ◆ *We issued one blanket to each refugee.*
2 to send out ◆ *They issued a gale warning.*
3 to put something out for sale; to publish something
4 to come or go out; to flow out

issue *NOUN* **issues**
1 a subject for discussion or concern ◆ *There were two main issues the jury had to consider.*
2 a particular edition of a newspaper or magazine ◆ *I would like to reply to a letter printed in your July issue.*
3 the process of issuing an official document
4 (*formal*) the birth of children ◆ *He died without issue.*

to take issue with someone is to disagree with them

isthmus (*say* iss- mus) *NOUN* **isthmuses**
a narrow strip of land connecting two larger pieces of land

IT *ABBREVIATION*
information technology

it *PRONOUN*
1 used to refer to a thing already mentioned or known
2 used in statements about the weather, the time, or a distance ◆ *It has been snowing.* ◆ *It will soon be midnight.* ◆ *It is twenty miles to home.*
3 used to refer forward to a following phrase ◆ *It's a pity she was so tired.*

Italian (*say* it- **al**- ee- an) *ADJECTIVE*
to do with Italy or its people

Italian *NOUN*
1 the language of Italy, also used as a first language in some other countries
2 a person from Italy

Italian words in English

Because Italian art and music have been so important in history, many cultural terms are of Italian origin. These include, for example, names of musical instruments and musical terms, such as *cello*, *concerto*, *libretto*, *piano*, *soprano*, *staccato*, *tempo*, and *viola*; and words used in art and architecture, like *terracotta* (literally, 'baked earth') and *umber*. The word *graffiti* is also Italian and originally meant 'scratchings'.
Italian words relating to food have been borrowed into English along with the food items they describe: for example, *cappuccino*, *chipolata*, *espresso*, *macaroni*, *penne*, and *pizza*. *Cappuccino* is named after the coffee-coloured habits of Italian *Capuchin* monks.
Other words with interesting derivations are *trampoline*, which comes from an Italian word meaning 'stilts', and *umbrella*, from Italian *ombrella* meaning 'little shadow'.
Most Italian words have now become naturalized so that they use normal English plurals (*espressos*, *pizzas*, etc.). But some words, such as *concerto*, *libretto*, and *virtuoso*, can also use their original Italian plural (i.e. *concerti* or *libretti* as well as *concertos*, *librettos*, etc.).

italic (*say* it- **al**- ik) *ADJECTIVE*
printed with sloping letters (called *italics*) *like this*

itch *VERB* **itches, itching, itched**
1 to have or feel a tickling sensation in the skin that makes you want to scratch it
2 to long to do something

itch *NOUN* **itches**
1 an itching feeling
2 a longing
▷ **itchy** *ADJECTIVE*
▷ **itchiness** *NOUN*

item *NOUN* **items**
1 one thing in a list or group of things
2 one piece of news, article etc. in a newspaper or bulletin

itinerant (*say* it- **in**- er- ant) *ADJECTIVE*
travelling from place to place ◆ *A group of itinerant musicians had arrived.*

itinerary (*say* eye- **tin**- er- er- ee) *NOUN* **itineraries**
a list of places to be visited on a journey; a route

it'll *short for* **it will**

its *POSSESSIVE PRONOUN*
belonging to it ◆ *The cat was licking its paw.*
USAGE NOTE Remember not to use an apostrophe unless you mean 'it is' or 'it has' (see the next entry).

it's
1 short for *it is* ◆ *It's cold outside.*
2 short for *it has* ◆ *It's been snowing.*
USAGE NOTE Take care not to confuse this word, which has an apostrophe, with *its*, which means 'belonging to it' (see the previous entry).

itself *PRONOUN*
it and nothing else: used to refer back to the subject of a sentence (e.g. *The cat was licking itself*) or for emphasis (e.g. *The house itself is quite small*)

by itself on its own; alone

I've *short for* **I have**

ivory *NOUN*
1 the hard creamy-white substance that forms elephants' tusks
2 a creamy-white colour

ivy *NOUN* **ivies**
a climbing evergreen plant with shiny leaves

Jj

jab *VERB* **jabs, jabbing, jabbed**
1 to poke someone roughly, especially with a finger or pointed object

> I jabbed the lad nearest to me with my elbow. 'Hey, mate?' — *Keith Gray, Malarkey*

2 to poke a finger or sharp object into something

jab *NOUN* **jabs**
1 a sharp poke or blow, especially with a finger or pointed object
2 (*informal*) an injection with a syringe

WORD HISTORY originally a Scots word

jabber *VERB* **jabbers, jabbering, jabbered**
to speak quickly and not clearly; to chatter

> 'You were making groans. You were jabbering.' 'Jabbering? Me? ... I don't jabber, man. Nobody ever told me that before.' — *Harold Pinter, The Caretaker*

▷ **jabberer** *NOUN*

jabber *NOUN*
jabbering talk; chatter

jack *NOUN* **jacks**
1 a device for lifting something heavy off the ground, especially one for raising a motor vehicle in order to change a wheel or tyre
2 a playing card with a picture of a young man, which ranks below a queen in card games
3 the small white ball that players aim at in the game of bowls

jack of all trades someone who can do many different kinds of work

jack *VERB* **jacks, jacking, jacked**
to lift something with a jack

WORD HISTORY the name *Jack* was given to various tools, as though it was the name of a helper or assistant

jackal *NOUN* **jackals**
a wild animal of Africa and Asia, which is related to the dog and often hunts in packs

jackass *NOUN* **jackasses**
1 a male donkey
2 (*informal*) a stupid person

jackdaw *NOUN* **jackdaws**
a kind of small crow

WORD HISTORY from the name *Jack* and an old word *dawe*, an earlier name for the jackdaw

jacket *NOUN* **jackets**
1 a short coat, usually reaching to your hips
2 a cover to keep the heat in a water tank or boiler
3 a paper wrapper for a book
4 the skin of a potato that is baked without being peeled

jack-in-the-box *NOUN* **jack-in-the-boxes**
a toy figure that springs out of a box when the lid is lifted

jackknife *NOUN* **jackknives**
1 a large knife with a folding blade
2 a dive in which a diver first bends their body double and then straightens it

jackknife *VERB* **jackknifes, jackknifing, jackknifed**
an articulated lorry jackknifes if it skids and folds against itself in an accident

jackpot *NOUN* **jackpots**
an amount of prize money that increases until someone wins it

to hit the jackpot is to win a large prize or be very successful

WORD HISTORY a *jackpot* was originally prize money which could be won only by playing a pair of jacks or cards of higher value

jacks *PLURAL NOUN*
a game played by tossing and catching star-shaped pieces of metal or plastic

Jacobean *ADJECTIVE*
from the reign of James VI of Scotland and I of England, during the period 1603 to 1625

WORD HISTORY from *Jacobus*, the Latin form of 'James'

Jacobite *NOUN* **Jacobites**
a supporter of the exiled Stuarts after the abdication of James VII of Scotland and II of England in 1688

Jacuzzi (*say* ja- **koo**- zi) *NOUN* **Jacuzzis**
(*trademark*) a large bath in which underwater jets of water massage your body

WORD HISTORY from its Italian American inventor, Candido *Jacuzzi* (1903–86)

jade *NOUN*
a hard green stone that is carved to make ornaments and jewellery

WORD HISTORY from Spanish *piedra de ijada* 'colic stone', because it was believed to cure stomach ailments

jaded ***ADJECTIVE***
tired and no longer interested or enthusiastic

I was not jaded, nor was I exactly bored. But the zest had gone out of things. — *Jack London, The Mutiny of the Elsinore*

WORD HISTORY from an old word *jade* meaning 'a worn-out horse'

jagged (*say* **jag**- id) ***ADJECTIVE***
a jagged line or outline has an uneven edge with sharp points

Ralph shaded his eyes and followed the jagged outline of the crags up towards the mountain. — *William Golding, Lord of the Flies*

WORD HISTORY from Scots *jag* 'to prick or pierce'

jaguar ***NOUN*** **jaguars**
a large South American animal of the cat family, which has a yellowish-brown coat with black spots

jail ***NOUN*** **jails**
a prison

jail ***VERB*** **jails, jailing, jailed**
to put someone in prison
▷ **jailer** ***NOUN***

WORD HISTORY from Old French *jaiole* 'cage or prison'

jailbreak ***NOUN*** **jailbreaks**
an escape from prison

Jainism ***NOUN***
an Indian religion similar to Buddhism
▷ **Jainist** ***NOUN***

jam ***NOUN*** **jams**
1 a sweet food made of fruit boiled with sugar until it is thick
2 a lot of people, cars, or logs etc. crowded together so that movement is difficult

in a jam (*informal*) in a difficult situation

jam ***VERB*** **jams, jamming, jammed**
1 to make something fixed, or to become fixed, and difficult to move ◆ *The paper has jammed in the printer again.*
2 to crowd or squeeze into a space ◆ *The crowd jammed into the wooden pews and stretched out into the hallway.*
3 to push or drive something forcibly
4 to block a broadcast by causing interference with the transmission
5 to jam on the brakes of a vehicle is to brake hard and suddenly
6 (*informal*) musicians jam when they improvise together

jamb (*say* jam) ***NOUN*** **jambs**
a side post of a doorway or window frame

WORD HISTORY from French *jambe* 'leg'

jamboree ***NOUN*** **jamborees**
a large party or celebration

jam-packed ***ADJECTIVE***
(*informal*) extremely crowded or packed full

jangle ***VERB*** **jangles, jangling, jangled**
1 to make a loud harsh ringing sound

The bag of gold, silver and bronze jangling cheerfully in Harry's pocket was clamouring to be spent. — *J. K. Rowling, Harry Potter and the Chamber of Secrets*

2 your nerves are jangling when you feel very nervous or edgy

jangle ***NOUN*** **jangles**
a loud harsh ringing sound

janitor ***NOUN*** **janitors**
a caretaker of a school or other building

WORD HISTORY from an earlier meaning 'doorkeeper', from Latin *janua* 'door'

January ***NOUN***
the first month of the year

WORD HISTORY from *Janus*, a Roman god of gates and beginnings, because January is the beginning of the new year

Japanese ***ADJECTIVE***
to do with Japan or its people

Japanese ***NOUN*** **Japanese**
1 the language of Japan
2 a person from Japan

japonica (*say* ja- **pon**- i- ka) ***NOUN***
an ornamental variety of quince, with red flowers

WORD HISTORY a Latin word meaning 'Japanese'

jar❶ ***NOUN*** **jars**
a cylindrical container made of glass or pottery

jar❷ ***VERB*** **jars, jarring, jarred**
1 to give something an unpleasant jolt or vibration ◆ *Last year, I had a bad fall which jarred my spine and neck.*
2 two things jar, or jar with each other, when they clash or conflict
3 a sound jars, or jars on you, when you find it annoyingly harsh or shrill

jar ***NOUN*** **jars**
a sudden jolt or vibration

jargon ***NOUN***
(*Language*) words or expressions used by a profession or group that are difficult for other people to understand ◆ *scientific jargon* ◆ *Internet jargon*

WORD HISTORY from an earlier meaning 'twittering, chattering', from an Old French word *jargoun*

jasmine ***NOUN***
a shrub with fragrant yellow or white flowers

jasper ***NOUN***
a type of quartz stone, usually coloured red, yellow, or brown

jaundice ***NOUN***
a disease in which the skin becomes yellow

WORD HISTORY from French *jaune* 'yellow'

jaundiced *ADJECTIVE*
1 affected with jaundice
2 bitter and cynical

jaunt *NOUN* **jaunts**
a short trip taken for pleasure

jaunty *ADJECTIVE* **jauntier, jauntiest**
lively and cheerful ◆ *He wore the hat tilted at a jaunty angle.*
▷ **jauntily** *ADVERB*
▷ **jauntiness** *NOUN*
WORD HISTORY from an earlier meaning 'stylish, elegant', from a French word related to our word *gentle*

javelin *NOUN* **javelins**
a lightweight spear thrown in an athletics competition or as a weapon

jaw *NOUN* **jaws**
1 either of the two bones that form the framework of a person's or animal's mouth
2 the lower part of your face

jaws *PLURAL NOUN*
the gripping parts of a wrench or vice

jay *NOUN* **jays**
a noisy brightly coloured bird

jaywalker *NOUN* **jaywalkers**
a person who walks carelessly across a road without looking out for traffic
▷ **jaywalking** *NOUN*
WORD HISTORY from an American meaning of *jay* in the sense 'fool'

jazz *NOUN*
a kind of music with syncopated rhythms, usually improvised
to jazz something up is to make it more lively or interesting
▷ **jazzy** *ADJECTIVE*

jealous *ADJECTIVE*
1 unhappy or resentful because you feel that someone is your rival or is better or luckier than yourself
2 angry or upset because someone you love seems to love someone else
3 to be jealous of something you own or possess is to guard or preserve it very carefully ◆ *These birds are quite jealous of their privacy and are not easy to spot.*
▷ **jealously** *ADVERB*
▷ **jealousy** *NOUN*

jeans *PLURAL NOUN*
trousers made of denim or another strong cotton fabric
WORD HISTORY *jean* was originally a strong fabric produced in *Genoa* in Italy in the sixteenth century

jeep *NOUN* **jeeps**
(*trademark*) a small sturdy motor vehicle with four-wheel drive, especially one used in the army
WORD HISTORY from *G. P.*, an abbreviation of 'general purpose'

jeer *VERB* **jeers, jeering, jeered**
to laugh or shout at someone rudely or scornfully

'Well, sir,' said I, with a jeering tone, 'have you nothing more to say to me?' — *Robert Louis Stevenson, Kidnapped*

jeer *NOUN* **jeers**
a rude or scornful remark

jejune (*say* ji-**joon**) *ADJECTIVE*
naive and simplistic ◆ *The film's ending is so jejune that it's an insult to the audience.*
WORD HISTORY the original meaning was 'meagre, scanty', from Latin *jejunus* 'fasting'; the current meaning arose in the 19th century by confusion with the word *juvenile*

jell *VERB* **jells, jelling, jelled**
another spelling of **gel** *VERB*

jelly *NOUN* **jellies**
1 a clear, sweet or savoury food set with gelatin
2 a fruit jam that has been strained to remove seeds and pulp
3 an ointment or other substance with a soft, slippery texture
4 a jellied eel or other food is set in jelly
WORD HISTORY from Latin *gelare* 'to freeze'

jellyfish *NOUN* **jellyfish**
a sea animal with a body like jelly and stinging tentacles

jemmy *NOUN* **jemmies**
a crowbar used by burglars to force doors, windows, and drawers
WORD HISTORY from the name *Jimmy*, used in a similar way to 'Jack' for the name of a tool

jeopardize (*say* **jep**-er-dyz) *VERB*
jeopardizes, jeopardizing, jeopardized
to put someone or something in danger or at risk ◆ *There have been reports of dust storms on Mars which it is feared could jeopardize the mission.*
USAGE NOTE This word can also be spelled jeopardise.

jeopardy (*say* **jep**-er-dee) *NOUN*
in jeopardy in danger of harm or failure ◆ *The financial crisis has put the future of the football club in jeopardy.*

jerboa (*say* jer-**boh**-a) *NOUN* **jerboas**
a small rat-like animal of the North African desert

jerk *VERB* **jerks, jerking, jerked**
1 to make a sudden sharp movement
2 to pull something suddenly

jerk *NOUN* **jerks**
1 a sudden sharp movement
2 (*informal*) a stupid person

At the end of the first act we went out with all the other jerks for a cigarette. What a deal that was. — *J. D. Salinger, The Catcher in the Rye*

▷ **jerky** *ADJECTIVE*
▷ **jerkily** *ADVERB*

jerkin *NOUN* **jerkins**
a sleeveless jacket

jerry-built *ADJECTIVE*
built badly and with poor materials

jersey *NOUN* **jerseys**
1 a pullover with sleeves
2 a plain machine-knitted material used for making clothes

WORD HISTORY originally a woollen cloth made in *Jersey*, one of the Channel Islands

jest *NOUN* **jests**
a joke

jest *VERB* **jests, jesting, jested**
to make jokes

WORD HISTORY from an old word *gest* meaning 'a story'

jester *NOUN* **jesters**
a professional entertainer at a royal court in the Middle Ages

jet[1] *NOUN* **jets**
1 a stream of water, gas, or flame shot out from a narrow opening
2 a spout or nozzle from which a jet comes
3 an aircraft driven by engines that send out a high-speed jet of hot gases at the back

jet *VERB* **jets, jetting, jetted**
1 to come out, or to send something out, in a strong stream
2 (*informal*) to travel in a jet aircraft

WORD HISTORY from French *jeter* 'to throw'

jet[2] *NOUN*
1 a hard black mineral substance
2 a deep glossy black colour

WORD HISTORY from an Old French word

jet lag *NOUN*
extreme tiredness that a person feels after a long flight between different time zones

▷ **jet-lagged** *ADJECTIVE*

jetsam *NOUN*
goods thrown overboard from a ship in difficulty and washed ashore

WORD HISTORY from the word *jettison*

jettison *VERB* **jettisons, jettisoning, jettisoned**
1 to throw something overboard
2 to get rid of something you no longer want
3 to release or drop something from an aircraft or spacecraft in flight

jetty *NOUN* **jetties**
a small landing stage or pier

Jew *NOUN* **Jews**
1 a member of a people descended from the ancient Hebrews
2 someone who believes in Judaism

▷ **Jewish** *ADJECTIVE*

WORD HISTORY from Hebrew *yehudi* 'belonging to the tribe of Judah'

jewel *NOUN* **jewels**
1 a precious stone
2 an ornament containing precious stones

▷ **jewelled** *ADJECTIVE*

jeweller *NOUN* **jewellers**
a person or company who sells or makes jewellery

jewellery *NOUN*
ornaments for wearing, often made of jewels and precious metals

jib[1] *NOUN* **jibs**
1 a triangular sail stretching forward from a ship's front mast
2 the arm of a crane

jib[2] *VERB* **jibs, jibbing, jibbed**
to jib at something is to be unwilling to do or accept it ◆ *Film fans may jib at the thought of remaking this classic comedy.*

jibe *NOUN* **jibes**
a remark that is meant to mock or insult someone

jibe *VERB* **jibes, jibing, jibed**
to make jibes; to mock someone

jiffy *NOUN*
(*informal*) a brief moment

In a jiffy I had slipped over the side and curled up in ... the nearest boat, and almost at the same moment she shoved off. — *Robert Louis Stevenson, Treasure Island*

jig *NOUN* **jigs**
1 a lively traditional dance, or the music for this
2 a device that holds something in place while you work on it with tools

jig *VERB* **jigs, jigging, jigged**
to move up and down quickly and jerkily

Aunt Susan's hand was oddly small now. It shook a little; the cup jigged in the saucer. — *Penelope Lively, The House in Norham Gardens*

jiggery-pokery *NOUN*
(*informal*) trickery, underhand dealing

jiggle *VERB* **jiggles, jiggling, jiggled**
to rock or jerk something lightly

jigsaw *NOUN* **jigsaws**
1 a puzzle consisting of a picture printed on board or wood and cut into irregular pieces which have to be fitted together

Carrie's thoughts were like bits of jigsaw, whirling round in her head. Separate pieces but all fitting in, one to another. — *Nina Bawden, Carrie's War*

2 a saw used to cut curved shapes

SPELLING NOTE Some words pronounced **j-** begin with **ge-** (e.g. germ), **gi-** (e.g. ginger), or **gy-** (e.g. gyro)

jihad (*say* ji-**hahd**) *NOUN* **jihads**
a war or struggle undertaken by Muslims

jilt *VERB* **jilts, jilting, jilted**
to abandon a boyfriend or girlfriend, especially after promising to marry them

jingle *VERB* **jingles, jingling, jingled**
1 metal objects jingle when they rub together to make a tinkling or ringing sound
2 to shake metal objects together so as to make a tinkling or ringing sound

jingle *NOUN* **jingles**
1 a jingling sound
2 a short catchy verse or tune, especially one used in advertising

jingoism *NOUN*
an extremely strong and unreasonable belief that your country is superior to others
▷ **jingoistic** *ADJECTIVE*
WORD HISTORY from the phrase *by jingo!*, used in a patriotic music-hall song in the 19th century

jinn *NOUN* **jinn** or **jinns**
a supernatural being in Arabian and Muslim mythology, which can help or hinder human beings

jinx *NOUN* **jinxes**
a person or thing that is thought to bring bad luck
WORD HISTORY probably a variation of *jynx* 'wryneck', a bird used in witchcraft

jinx *VERB* **jinxes, jinxing, jinxed**
a person or thing jinxes you, or is jinxed, if it brings you bad luck ◆ *There is a legend in the theatre that Shakespeare's 'Macbeth' is jinxed.*
▷ **jinxed** *ADJECTIVE*

jitters *PLURAL NOUN*
to have the jitters (*informal*) is to feel extremely nervous
▷ **jittery** *ADJECTIVE*

job *NOUN* **jobs**
1 work that someone does regularly to earn a living
2 a piece of work to be done ◆ *The children had the job of emptying the wooden buckets.*
3 (*informal*) a difficult task ◆ *You'll have a job to get that wardrobe through the door.*
4 (*informal*) a thing; a state of affairs ◆ *It's a good job we bought our tickets early.*
5 work done to improve or repair something ◆ *a nose job*
just the job (*informal*) exactly what you want

jobcentre *NOUN* **jobcentres**
a government office with information about available jobs

jockey *NOUN* **jockeys**
a person who rides horses in horse races

jockey *VERB* **jockeys, jockeying, jockeyed**
to jockey for position people jockey for position when they compete against each other to gain an advantage

jocular *ADJECTIVE*
joking, humorous

Someone made a jocular remark which I did not catch, but which raised a general laugh. — *Jack London, The Sea-Wolf*

▷ **jocularly** *ADVERB*
▷ **jocularity** *NOUN*
WORD HISTORY from Latin *jocus* 'a joke'

jodhpurs (*say* **jod**-perz) *PLURAL NOUN*
trousers worn for horse-riding, which fit closely from the knee to the ankle
WORD HISTORY from *Jodhpur*, a city in north-west India

jog *VERB* **jogs, jogging, jogged**
1 to run or trot slowly, especially for exercise
2 to give something a slight push ◆ *The waiter jogged my elbow, sending a stream of coffee up my nose.*
to jog someone's memory is to help them to remember something
▷ **jogger** *NOUN*

jog *NOUN* **jogs**
1 a slow run or trot
2 a slight knock or push

joggle *VERB* **joggles, joggling, joggled**
to shake slightly or move jerkily

joggle *NOUN* **joggles**
a slight shake or jerk

joie de vivre (*say* zh**wah** der **veevr**) *NOUN*
a feeling of great enjoyment of life
WORD HISTORY a French phrase meaning 'joy of life'

join *VERB* **joins, joining, joined**
1 two things join when they come together
2 to put things together; to fasten or connect things

The Nautilus is composed of two hulls, one inside, the other outside, joined by T-shaped irons. — *Jules Verne, 20,000 Leagues Under the Sea*

3 to take part with others in doing something or going somewhere

The lookouts came scrambling down the slopes to join the rest of the marchers. — *William Nicholson, Firesong*

4 to become a member of a group or organization ◆ *You can join the RSPB by filling in this form.*
to join forces is to combine efforts
to join hands is to clasp each other's hands
to join up is to become a member of the armed forces

join *NOUN* **joins**
a place where things join

joiner *NOUN* **joiners**
a person whose job is to make or repair doors, window frames, and other household fittings made of wood
▷ **joinery** *NOUN*

joint ***NOUN*** **joints**
1 a place where two things are joined
2 the place where two bones fit together
3 a large piece of meat cut ready for cooking
4 (*informal*) a cannabis cigarette

joint ***ADJECTIVE***
shared or done by two or more people, groups, or countries ◆ *The film is a joint effort between the two animation studios.*
▷ **jointly** ***ADVERB***

joist ***NOUN*** **joists**
any of the long beams supporting a floor or ceiling

jojoba (*say* ho- **hoh**- ba) ***NOUN***
a desert shrub of North America which produces an oil used in cosmetics

joke ***NOUN*** **jokes**
1 something said or done to make people laugh
2 a ridiculous person or thing ◆ *With so many players injured, the match was in danger of becoming a joke.*

joke ***VERB*** **jokes, joking, joked**
1 to make jokes
2 to tease someone or not be serious

'It cannot be! Tell me that you are mistaken, or that you are but joking.' — *Edgar Rice Burroughs, At the Earth's Core*

beyond a joke or **no joke** very serious or worrying

joker ***NOUN*** **jokers**
1 someone who likes making jokes
2 an extra playing card with a jester on it, used as a wild card in some card games

jolly ***ADJECTIVE*** **jollier, jolliest**
cheerful and good-humoured

Smithers was so fat and jolly that it was hard to believe he was part of MI6 at all. — *Anthony Horowitz, Scorpia*

▷ **jollity** ***NOUN***

jolly ***ADVERB***
(*informal*) very; extremely ◆ *It was jolly late by now.*

jolly ***VERB*** **jollies, jollying, jollied** (*informal*)
to jolly someone along is to keep them in a cheerful mood

jolt ***VERB*** **jolts, jolting, jolted**
1 to shake or dislodge something with a sudden sharp movement
2 to move along jerkily

Soon the cobbles ended and the thick wheels jolted over the rutted track which was the road south. — *Celia Rees, Witch Child*

3 to give someone a shock

jolt ***NOUN*** **jolts**
1 a jolting movement
2 a shock

Lyra realized with a jolt of sickness what was happening: the man was being attacked by Spectres. — *Philip Pullman, The Subtle Knife*

jostle ***VERB*** **jostles, jostling, jostled**
to push someone roughly, especially in a crowd

WORD HISTORY from the word *joust*

jot ***VERB*** **jots, jotting, jotted**
to jot something down is to write it down quickly

jot ***NOUN*** **jots**
a very small amount ◆ *Since when has the company cared a jot about the environment?*

WORD HISTORY from Greek *iōta*, the smallest letter of the Greek alphabet

jotter ***NOUN*** **jotters**
a notepad or notebook

joule (*say* jool) ***NOUN*** **joules**
(*Science*) the SI unit of energy or work

WORD HISTORY from the British physicist, James Prescott *Joule* (1818–89)

journal ***NOUN*** **journals**
1 a newspaper or magazine
2 a diary in which someone writes about what has happened to them from day to day

WORD HISTORY from a Latin word meaning 'by day'

journalist ***NOUN*** **journalists**
a person who writes for a newspaper or magazine, or who prepares news broadcasts on radio or television
▷ **journalism** ***NOUN***
▷ **journalistic** ***ADJECTIVE***

journey ***NOUN*** **journeys**
1 the action of going from one place to another

Every journey between your world and ours is fraught with hazards and is not to be undertaken lightly. — *Mary Hoffman, Stravaganza: City of Masks*

2 the distance or time taken to travel somewhere ◆ *How long is the train journey from Edinburgh to London?*

journey ***VERB*** **journeys, journeying, journeyed**
to make a journey

WORD HISTORY from French *journée* 'a day's travel', from *jour* 'day'

joust (*say* jowst) ***VERB*** **jousts, jousting, jousted**
to fight on horseback with lances, as knights did in the Middle Ages

joust ***NOUN*** **jousts**
a jousting contest

WORD HISTORY from Old French *juster* 'to bring together'

a b c d e f g h i j k l m n o p q r s t u v w x y z

jovial *ADJECTIVE*
cheerful and good-humoured

Colonel Barclay ... was a dashing, jovial old soldier in his usual mood. — *Sir Arthur Conan Doyle, 'The Crooked Man'*

▷ **jovially** *ADVERB*
▷ **joviality** *NOUN*

WORD HISTORY from Latin *jovialis* 'to do with Jupiter', because people born under the planet's influence were said to be cheerful

jowl *NOUN* **jowls**
1 the jaw or cheek
2 loose skin on the neck

joy *NOUN* **joys**
1 a feeling of great pleasure or happiness
2 a thing that causes joy
3 satisfaction or success ◆ *Have you had any joy with selling your bike?*

joyful *ADJECTIVE*
very happy
▷ **joyfully** *ADVERB*
▷ **joyfulness** *NOUN*

joyous *ADJECTIVE*
full of joy; causing joy
▷ **joyously** *ADVERB*

joyride *NOUN* **joyrides**
a drive in a stolen car for amusement
▷ **joyrider** *NOUN*
▷ **joyriding** *NOUN*

joystick *NOUN* **joysticks**
1 the control lever of an aircraft
2 a device for moving a cursor or image on a computer screen

JP *ABBREVIATION*
Justice of the Peace

Jr *ABBREVIATION*
Junior

jubilant *ADJECTIVE*
rejoicing or triumphant

I remember how jubilant Markham was at securing a new photograph of the planet for the illustrated paper he edited in those days. — *H. G. Wells, The War of the Worlds*

▷ **jubilantly** *ADVERB*
▷ **jubilation** *NOUN*

WORD HISTORY from Latin *jubilans* 'shouting for joy'

jubilee (*say* **joo**- bil- ee) *NOUN* **jubilees**
a special anniversary, especially one celebrating 25, 50, or 60 years

WORD HISTORY from Hebrew *yobel*, a year when slaves were freed and property returned to its owners, held in ancient Israel every 50 years

USAGE NOTE A 25th anniversary is called a *silver jubilee*, a 50th anniversary is called a *golden jubilee*, and a 60th anniversary is called a *diamond jubilee*.

Judaism (*say* **joo**- day- izm) *NOUN*
(*Religion*) the religion of the Jewish people, based on the teachings of the Old Testament and the Talmud
▷ **Judaic** *ADJECTIVE*

judder *VERB* **judders, juddering, juddered**
to shake noisily or violently

judge *NOUN* **judges**
1 a person appointed to hear cases in a lawcourt and decide what should be done
2 a person who decides the winner of a contest or competition
3 someone who is good at forming opinions or making decisions about things ◆ *She prides herself on being a good judge of people.*

judge *VERB* **judges, judging, judged**
1 to act as a judge
2 to form and give an opinion
3 to estimate something

Outside the day had darkened. I judged it to be late afternoon, although tall buildings crowded out the sky. — *Celia Rees, Witch Child*

WORD HISTORY from Latin *judex* 'a judge', from *jus* 'law'

judgement *NOUN* **judgements**
1 the process of judging, or of being judged
2 the decision made by a lawcourt
3 someone's opinion
4 the ability to judge wisely
5 something considered as a punishment from God

'This is a judgement on me for something, I suppose,' said the Reverend Septimus, wearily, 'but I really cannot at the moment remember what.' — *Edith Nesbit, The Phoenix and the Carpet*

judicial *ADJECTIVE*
to do with lawcourts, judges, or judgements ◆ *Scotland has a separate legal and judicial system.*
▷ **judicially** *ADVERB*

USAGE NOTE Take care not to confuse this word with *judicious*.

judiciary (*say* joo- **dish**- er- ee) *NOUN* **judiciaries**
all the judges in a country

judicious (*say* joo- **dish**- us) *ADJECTIVE*
having or showing good sense or good judgement ◆ *Food is often improved by a judicious use of herbs and spices.*
▷ **judiciously** *ADVERB*

USAGE NOTE Take care not to confuse this word with *judicial*.

judo *NOUN*
a Japanese method of self-defence without using weapons

WORD HISTORY from Japanese words meaning 'gentle way'

jug *NOUN* **jugs**
a container for holding and pouring liquids, with a handle and a lip
WORD HISTORY a familiar form of the name *Joan* or *Jenny*

juggernaut *NOUN* **juggernauts**
a huge lorry
WORD HISTORY from Sanskrit *Jagannatha*, an image of the Hindu god Krishna which was dragged in procession on a huge wheeled vehicle

juggle *VERB* **juggles, juggling, juggled**
1 to toss and catch a number of objects skilfully for entertainment, keeping one or more in the air at any time
2 to rearrange or alter things skilfully or in order to deceive people
▷ **juggler** *NOUN*

jugular *ADJECTIVE*
to do with your throat or neck ◆ *jugular veins*
WORD HISTORY from Latin *jugulum* 'throat'

juice *NOUN* **juices**
1 the liquid from fruit, vegetables, or other food
2 a liquid produced by the body ◆ *digestive juices*

juicy *ADJECTIVE* **juicier, juiciest**
1 full of juice
2 (*informal*) a juicy story or detail is full of interest, often because it involves scandal
▷ **juicily** *ADVERB*
▷ **juiciness** *NOUN*

jukebox *NOUN* **jukeboxes**
a coin-operated machine that automatically plays a record you have selected

July *NOUN*
the seventh month of the year
WORD HISTORY from *Julius* Caesar, who was born in this month

jumble *VERB* **jumbles, jumbling, jumbled**
to mix things up into a confused mass

jumble *NOUN*
a confused mixture of things; a muddle

> The town was a jumble, with no streets, no squares, and no open spaces except where a building had fallen. — *Philip Pullman, The Subtle Knife*

jumble sale *NOUN* **jumble sales**
a sale of second-hand goods

jumbo *NOUN* **jumbos**
1 something very large of its kind
2 a jumbo jet
WORD HISTORY from the name of a very large elephant in London Zoo

jumbo jet *NOUN* **jumbo jets**
a very large jet aircraft

jumbuck *NOUN* **jumbucks**
(*Australian*) (*informal*) a sheep

jump *VERB* **jumps, jumping, jumped**
1 to move up suddenly from the ground into the air
2 to go over something by jumping
3 to pass over something; to miss out a part of something
4 to move suddenly in surprise

> Beadle jumped back in fear, lost his footing and fell from the stone to the shingle beach. — *G. P. Taylor, Shadowmancer*

5 to get into or out of a vehicle quickly ◆ *We jumped on the train just as the doors were closing.* ◆ *Jump in!*
6 to pass quickly to a different place or level
to jump at something to jump at a chance or suggestion is to seize or accept it eagerly
to jump on someone is to start criticizing them
to jump the gun is to start before you are meant to
to jump the queue is to get something without waiting for your proper turn

jump *NOUN* **jumps**
1 a jumping movement
2 an obstacle to jump over
3 a sudden increase in number or amount ◆ *There has been a sharp jump in the number of cases of measles.*

jumper *NOUN* **jumpers**
a jersey
WORD HISTORY from French *jupe* 'tunic'

jumpy *ADJECTIVE* **jumpier, jumpiest**
nervous and edgy

> Why do large numbers make you so jumpy? I can assure you that most large numbers are perfectly harmless. — *Hans Magnus Enzensberger, The Number Devil*

junction *NOUN* **junctions**
1 a join
2 a place where roads or railway lines meet

juncture *NOUN* **junctures**
1 a point of time, especially in a crisis
2 a place where things join

June *NOUN*
the sixth month of the year
WORD HISTORY named after the Roman goddess *Juno*

jungle *NOUN* **jungles**
an area of land with dense forest and vegetation, especially in the tropics
▷ **jungly** *ADJECTIVE*
WORD HISTORY from Hindi *jangal* 'forest'

junior *ADJECTIVE*
1 younger or youngest
2 for young children ◆ *a junior school*
3 lower in rank or importance

> The junior member of the trio gave a sigh, and ladled some boiling water out of the cauldron into the teapot. — *Terry Pratchett, Wyrd Sisters*

a b c d e f g h i j k l m n o p q r s t u v w x y z

SPELLING NOTE Some words pronounced **j-** begin with **ge-** (e.g. germ), **gi-** (e.g. ginger), or **gy-** (e.g. gyro)

junior *NOUN* **juniors**
a junior person
WORD HISTORY a Latin word meaning 'younger'

juniper *NOUN* **junipers**
an evergreen shrub with prickly leaves and dark purple berries

junk❶ *NOUN*
rubbish; things of no value

junk❷ *NOUN* **junks**
a flat-bottomed Chinese sailing boat

junket *NOUN*
1 a sweet food like custard, made with curdled milk
2 (*informal*) an extravagant trip, especially one made at public expense

junk food *NOUN*
food that is not nourishing

junkie *NOUN* **junkies**
(*informal*) a drug addict
WORD HISTORY from American slang *junk* meaning 'heroin'

junk mail *NOUN*
unwanted advertising material sent by post or email

Jurassic *ADJECTIVE*
to do with the second period of the Mesozoic era, a time when large reptiles were dominant and the first birds appeared

jurisdiction *NOUN*
authority; official power, especially to interpret and apply the law

juror *NOUN* **jurors**
a member of a jury

jury *NOUN* **juries**
1 a group of people appointed to give a verdict about a case in a lawcourt

A jury never looks at a defendant it has convicted, and when this jury came in, not one of them looked at Tom Robinson. — *Harper Lee, To Kill a Mockingbird*

2 a group of people appointed to judge a competition

just *ADJECTIVE*
1 a just decision or ruling is one that gives proper consideration to everyone's claims
2 a just person makes fair decisions after considering everyone's claims
3 someone who gets a just reward or just deserts gets what they deserve
▷ **justly** *ADVERB*
▷ **justness** *NOUN*

just *ADVERB*
1 exactly ◆ *It's just what I wanted!* ◆ *You phoned at just the right time.*
2 only; simply

What we call our gargoyle is really just a carved stone head high above the kitchen fireplace. — *Dodie Smith, I Capture the Castle*

3 barely; by only a small amount ◆ *Leave the parcel just inside the door.*
4 at this moment or only a little while ago

I've just set a bomb to blow this place to smithereens in ... ninety-two seconds. So I don't think we have time for a chat. — *Anthony Horowitz, Scorpia*

5 very soon ◆ *I'm just going to the shops.*
just as equally, to the same extent ◆ *It'll be just as quick to walk there.*

justice *NOUN* **justices**
1 fair treatment; fairness
2 legal proceedings ◆ *a court of justice*
3 a judge or magistrate
4 the title of a judge ◆ *Mr Justice Humphreys*
Justice of the Peace a non-professional magistrate

justify *VERB* **justifies, justifying, justified**
1 to justify an action or statement is to show that it is fair, just, or reasonable
2 (*ICT*) to justify printed text is to arrange the lines so that one or both edges are straight
▷ **justifiable** *ADJECTIVE*
▷ **justification** *NOUN*

jut *VERB* **juts, jutting, jutted**
to jut out is to stick out or protrude

jute *NOUN*
fibre from tropical plants, used for making sacks or hard-wearing rugs
WORD HISTORY from a Bengali word

juvenile *ADJECTIVE*
1 to do with or for young people
2 childish ◆ *It's a good film, although some of the jokes are a bit juvenile.*

juvenile *NOUN* **juveniles**
a young person, not old enough to be legally considered an adult
WORD HISTORY from Latin *juvenis* 'young person'

juvenile delinquent *NOUN* **juvenile delinquents**
a young person who has broken the law

juxtapose *VERB* **juxtaposes, juxtaposing, juxtaposed**
to juxtapose two or more things is to put them next to each other to compare or contrast them
▷ **juxtaposition** *NOUN*
WORD HISTORY from Latin *juxta* 'next' and *positum* 'put'

kaftan *NOUN* **kaftans**
1 a long coat-like garment worn by men in the Middle East
2 a woman's long loose dress

kale *NOUN*
a kind of cabbage with curly leaves

kaleidoscope (*say* kal- **y**- dos- kohp) *NOUN* **kaleidoscopes**
1 a toy consisting of a tube containing mirrors and small brightly coloured pieces of glass or paper which change pattern as you turn the end of the tube
2 a place or thing full of colour and variety
◆ *Hong Kong is a kaleidoscope of life, a city of diversity where East meets West.*
▷ **kaleidoscopic** *ADJECTIVE*
WORD HISTORY from Greek *kalos* 'beautiful' and *eidos* 'form' and *skopein* 'to look at'

kamikaze (*say* kam- i- **kah**- zi) *NOUN*
1 a type of Japanese suicide aircraft in the Second World War, filled with explosives, whose pilots crashed deliberately on to enemy targets
2 a kamikaze attitude or approach is one that is recklessly self-destructive
WORD HISTORY from Japanese words meaning 'divine wind'

kangaroo *NOUN* **kangaroos**
an Australian animal with strong hind legs; the female carries its young in a pouch on the front of its body (SEE ALSO **marsupial**)
WORD HISTORY an Australian Aboriginal word

kangaroo court *NOUN* **kangaroo courts**
an unofficial court formed by a group of people to settle disputes among themselves

kangha *NOUN* **kanghas**
a comb worn in the hair by Sikhs

kaolin *NOUN*
fine white clay used in making porcelain and in medicine
WORD HISTORY from Chinese *gao ling* 'high hill', because it was first found on a hill in northern China

kapok *NOUN*
a woolly substance which grows around the seeds of a tropical tree, used for stuffing cushions and soft toys

kaput *ADJECTIVE*
(*informal*) broken or useless; out of order
◆ *Your speakers must be kaput—there's no sound coming out.*
WORD HISTORY a German word

karaoke (*say* ka- ri- **oh**- ki) *NOUN*
a form of entertainment in which people sing well-known songs against a pre-recorded backing
WORD HISTORY a Japanese word meaning 'empty orchestra'

karate (*say* ka- **rah**- tee) *NOUN*
a Japanese method of self-defence in which the hands and feet are used as weapons
WORD HISTORY from Japanese words meaning 'empty hand'

karma *NOUN*
in Buddhist and Hindu belief, the sum of a person's actions in successive existences, which decides their destiny
WORD HISTORY from Sanskrit *karman* meaning 'action' or 'fate'

kasbah *NOUN* **kasbahs**
the citadel of an Arab city in North Africa, or the crowded area near this
WORD HISTORY from Arabic *kasba* 'citadel'

kauri (*say* **kow**- ree) *NOUN*
a large forest tree in New Zealand

kayak *NOUN* **kayaks**
a small canoe with a covering that fits round the canoeist's waist
WORD HISTORY an Inuit word

kazoo (*say* ka- **zoo**) *NOUN* **kazoos**
a musical instrument which produces a buzzing sound when you hum into it

KB or **Kb** *ABBREVIATION*
kilobytes

kebab *NOUN* **kebabs**
small pieces of meat or vegetables cooked on a skewer

kedgeree (*say* **kej**- e- ree) *NOUN*
a cooked dish of smoked fish, rice, and hard-boiled eggs
WORD HISTORY from Hindi *khichri*, a dish of rice and split peas

keel *NOUN* **keels**
the long piece of wood or metal along the bottom of a ship
on an even keel well balanced and steady

SPELLING NOTE Many words pronounced **k**- begin with **ca**- (e.g. cat), **co**- (e.g. cot), **cu**- (e.g. cut), or **ch**- (e.g. character)

keel *VERB* **keels, keeling, keeled**
to keel over is to fall down or overturn

> The cockroach keeled over and, with an almost inaudible splash, fell backwards into the potty. — *Debi Gliori, Pure Dead Magic*

keen ❶ *ADJECTIVE*
1 enthusiastic or eager ◆ *All the children are keen swimmers.*
2 a keen edge or keen eyesight is very sharp

> Young men with keen eyes and ready swords loped ahead of the straggling column, watching for danger. — *William Nicholson, Firesong*

3 to be keen on a person is to like them or be attracted to them
4 to be keen on a subject or activity is to like it or be interested in it
5 a keen wind is piercingly cold
▷ **keenly** *ADVERB*
▷ **keenness** *NOUN*

keen ❷ *VERB* **keens, keening, keened**
to wail in grief for a dead person

keep *VERB* **keeps, keeping, kept**
1 to have something and look after it or not get rid of it ◆ *My grandmother kept the letter all these years.*
2 to own and look after an animal
3 to remain deliberately in the same place or condition

> We moved off quietly sideways, in the direction the water was coming from, clutching our unlit candles and trying to keep out of sight. — *Diana Wynne Jones, The Merlin Conspiracy*

4 to keep something or someone (for example) warm or safe is to make sure that they continue to be warm or safe
5 to keep doing something is to do it continually or repeatedly ◆ *I keep forgetting to buy toothpaste.*
6 food or drink keeps when it lasts without going bad ◆ *How long will this milk keep?*
7 to keep a promise or secret, or to keep your word, is to respect and not break it
8 to keep a diary or journal is to make regular entries in it

to keep something down
1 to keep noise down is to stop it being too loud
2 to keep numbers or weeds down is to stop them becoming too high or widespread
3 to keep food down is to eat it without vomiting

to keep fit is to be and remain healthy, especially through exercising
to keep in with someone is to remain on good terms with them
to keep off rain or other bad weather keeps off when it fails to arrive
to keep on about something (*informal*) is to talk about it continually or repeatedly
to keep to something
1 to keep to a path or area is to stay within its bounds
2 to keep to a promise or agreement is to carry it out as stated

to keep to yourself is to avoid meeting people socially
to keep up is to make the same progress as others
to keep up something
1 to keep up a custom or tradition is to continue to practise it
2 to keep up an attack is to continue with it
3 to keep up a house or family is to maintain or look after it

to keep your hair on (*informal*) is to remain calm

keep *NOUN* **keeps**
1 a person's keep is the food, clothes, and other essential things they need to live
2 a strong tower in a castle

for keeps (*informal*) to keep for always ◆ *A CD can be yours for keeps if you answer two simple questions.*

keeper *NOUN* **keepers**
1 a person who keeps or looks after something
2 a goalkeeper or wicketkeeper
3 a person in charge of animals in a zoo

keeping *NOUN*
to be in someone's keeping is to be looked after or protected by them
in keeping with something appropriate or suitable for it ◆ *The windows are not in keeping with traditional cottage design.*
in safe keeping under protection; safe from harm

keepsake *NOUN* **keepsakes**
a gift to be kept in memory of the person who gave it

keg *NOUN* **kegs**
a small barrel

kelp *NOUN*
a large brown type of seaweed

kelvin *NOUN* **kelvins**
(*Science*) the SI unit of thermodynamic temperature

WORD HISTORY from the Scottish physicist, William Thomson (Lord *Kelvin*), 1824–1907

ken *NOUN*
beyond your ken something is beyond your ken when you can't understand it, or have no knowledge of it

ken *VERB* **kens, kenning, kenned**
(*Scottish*) to know someone or something

WORD HISTORY from Old English *cennan* 'to make known'

kendo *NOUN*
the Japanese art of fencing with two-handed bamboo swords

WORD HISTORY from Japanese words meaning 'sword way'

kennel *NOUN* **kennels**
1 a shelter for a dog
2 kennels are a place where dogs are bred or where they can be looked after while their owners are away

WORD HISTORY from Latin *canis* 'dog'

kenning *NOUN* **kennings**
(*Language*) a compound expression in Old English and Old Norse poetry, which describes something without using its name, e.g. *oar-steed* meaning 'ship'

kerb *NOUN* **kerbs**
the edge of a pavement

WORD HISTORY another spelling of *curb*

kerchief *NOUN* **kerchiefs** (*old use*)
1 a square headscarf
2 a handkerchief

WORD HISTORY from Old French words *couvre* 'cover' and *chief* 'head'

kernel *NOUN* **kernels**
1 the part inside the shell of a nut, or inside the husk of a seed
2 the central or most important part of something

'In every fairy-tale there is a kernel of truth,' said Old Parson. — *Elizabeth Goudge, The Little White Horse*

kerosene (*say* ke- ro- seen) *NOUN*
paraffin

WORD HISTORY from Greek *keros* 'wax'

kestrel *NOUN* **kestrels**
a small falcon that hunts by hovering while beating its wings rapidly

ketchup *NOUN*
a thick sauce made from tomatoes and vinegar, used as a relish

WORD HISTORY from Chinese *koechiap* 'tomato juice'

kettle *NOUN* **kettles**
a container with a spout and handle, for boiling water in

a different kettle of fish something altogether different from what has just been mentioned

kettledrum *NOUN* **kettledrums**
a drum consisting of a large metal bowl with skin or plastic over the top

key *NOUN* **keys**
1 a piece of metal shaped so that it will open a lock
2 a device for winding up a clock or clockwork toy
3 a small lever or button to be pressed by a finger, e.g. on a piano, typewriter, or computer
4 (*Music*) a system of related notes based on a particular note ◆ *the key of C major*
5 a fact or clue that explains or solves something ◆ *The key to the problem is to figure out how many possible pairs of numbers there are.*
6 a list of symbols used in a map or table

key *VERB* **keys, keying, keyed**
to key data or key in data is to type it into a computer using a keyboard

▷ **keyer** *NOUN*

keyboard *NOUN* **keyboards**
1 (*Music*) the set of keys on a piano or similar musical instrument
2 (*ICT*) the set of keys for putting data into a computer
3 an electronic musical instrument with keys arranged like a piano

keyboard *VERB* **keyboards, keyboarding, keyboarded**
to key data into a computer

▷ **keyboarder** *NOUN*

keyed-up *ADJECTIVE*
nervously tense or excited

keyhole *NOUN* **keyholes**
the hole through which a key is put into a lock

keyhole surgery *NOUN*
surgery carried out through a very small cut in the patient's body, using special instruments

keynote *NOUN* **keynotes**
1 (*Music*) the note on which a musical key is based ◆ *The keynote of C major is C.*
2 the main tone or theme of a speech or conference

keypad *NOUN* **keypads**
a small keyboard or set of buttons used to operate a telephone, calculator, or other device

keystone *NOUN* **keystones**
the central wedge-shaped stone in an arch which locks the other stones together

keystroke *NOUN* **keystrokes**
the action of pressing down an individual key on a keyboard

keyword *NOUN* **keywords**
a significant word or heading in a piece of text, especially one used for electronic searching

kg *ABBREVIATION*
kilogram

kgotla (*say* kot- la) *NOUN* **kgotlas**
(*South African*) a meeting of a tribal council or court, or the place where it is held

Word had been sent round through the chief's messengers that this unexpected kgotla would take place in the church. — *Beverley Naidoo, Chain of Fire*

a b c d e f g h i j **k** l m n o p q r s t u v w x y z

SPELLING NOTE Many words pronounced **k-** begin with **ca-** (e.g. cat), **co-** (e.g. cot), **cu-** (e.g. cut), or **ch-** (e.g. character)

khaki *NOUN*
a dull yellowish-brown colour, used for military uniforms
WORD HISTORY an Urdu word meaning 'dust-coloured'

kHz *ABBREVIATION*
kilohertz

kibbutz *NOUN* **kibbutzim**
a communal farming settlement in Israel
WORD HISTORY from Hebrew *qibbus* 'gathering'

kick *VERB* **kicks, kicking, kicked**
1 to hit or move a person or thing with your foot
2 to move your legs about vigorously
3 a gun kicks if it recoils when it is fired
to kick in a drug or stimulant kicks in when it begins to take effect
to kick off
1 is to start a football match by kicking the ball
2 (*informal*) is to start doing something
to kick someone out is to dismiss them or get rid of them
to kick the bucket (*informal*) is to die
to kick the habit (*informal*) is to succeed in giving up a bad habit
to kick up a fuss (*informal*) is to protest strongly about something
to kick yourself is to be annoyed with yourself

kick *NOUN* **kicks**
1 a kicking movement
2 the recoiling movement of a gun
3 (*informal*) a thrill or stimulating effect ◆ *I've seen the film several times but I still get a kick out of it.*
4 (*informal*) an enjoyable interest or activity ◆ *He's been on a health kick lately.*
a kick in the teeth (*informal*) is a serious setback or disappointment

kick-boxing *NOUN*
a martial art which combines boxing with elements of karate, especially kicking with bare feet
▷ **kick-boxer** *NOUN*

kick-off *NOUN* **kick-offs**
the starting time of a football match

kid *NOUN* **kids**
1 (*informal*) a child
2 a young goat
3 fine leather made from goatskin
to handle or treat someone with kid gloves is to deal with them gently or carefully

kid *VERB* **kids, kidding, kidded**
(*informal*) to tease or fool someone in fun

kiddie *NOUN* **kiddies**
(*informal*) a child

kidnap *VERB* **kidnaps, kidnapping, kidnapped**
to take someone away by force, especially in order to obtain a ransom
▷ **kidnapper** *NOUN*
WORD HISTORY from an old word *napper* 'thief'

kidney *NOUN* **kidneys**
either of the two organs in the body that remove waste products from the blood and excrete urine into the bladder

kidney bean *NOUN* **kidney beans**
a dark red bean with a curved shape like a kidney

kilim (*say* ki- **leem**) *NOUN* **kilims**
a Turkish or Middle Eastern rug or carpet woven without a pile

kill *VERB* **kills, killing, killed**
1 to make a person or thing die
2 to destroy or put an end to something
3 (*informal*) a part of your body is killing you if it is very painful ◆ *After an afternoon Christmas shopping, my feet were killing me.*
4 (*informal*) a wait or suspense is killing you if you find it hard to bear
5 to kill time, or an amount of time, is to spend it idly while waiting

Alex killed a couple of hours in the evening playing his Nintendo 64—and then felt vaguely guilty when Jack caught him at it. — *Anthony Horowitz, Stormbreaker*

to kill two birds with one stone is to achieve two purposes with one action
to kill yourself is to try too hard to do something ◆ *Don't kill yourself trying to cook a perfect meal.*
▷ **killer** *NOUN*

kill *NOUN* **kills**
1 the action of killing an animal
2 the animal or animals killed by a hunter
to be in at the kill is to be present at the end of something

killer whale *NOUN* **killer whales**
a large toothed whale with distinctive black-and-white markings

killing *NOUN* **killings**
an act of killing someone deliberately
to make a killing is to make a lot of money

kiln *NOUN* **kilns**
an oven for hardening pottery or bricks, for drying hops, or for burning lime
WORD HISTORY from Latin *culina* 'cooking stove'

kilo *NOUN* **kilos**
a kilogram

kilobyte *NOUN* **kilobytes**
(*ICT*) a unit of memory or data equal to 1,024 bytes

kilogram *NOUN* **kilograms**
a unit of mass or weight equal to 1,000 grams (about 2.2 pounds)

kilohertz *NOUN* **kilohertz**
a unit of frequency of electromagnetic waves, equal to 1,000 cycles per second

kilolitre *NOUN* **kilolitres**
a liquid measure equal to 1,000 litres

kilometre (*say* **kil**- o- meet- er or kil- **om**- it- er) *NOUN* **kilometres**
a unit of length equal to 1,000 metres (0.62 miles)

kilowatt *NOUN* **kilowatts**
a unit of electrical power equal to 1,000 watts

kilt *NOUN* **kilts**
a knee-length skirt of pleated tartan wool, traditionally worn as part of Scottish Highland dress
▷ **kilted** *ADJECTIVE*

kilter *NOUN*
out of kilter out of balance or harmony; out of step ◆ *By 1582, the Julian calendar was about 10 days out of kilter with the real world.*

kimono *NOUN* **kimonos**
a long loose Japanese robe with wide sleeves, worn with a sash
WORD HISTORY from Japanese words meaning 'wearing thing'

kin *NOUN*
a person's relatives
next of kin a person's closest relative

kind❶ *NOUN* **kinds**
a class of similar things or animals; a sort or type

> The young dragon ... was not large of his kind, maybe the length of a forty-oared ship. — *Ursula Le Guin, A Wizard of Earthsea*

in kind
1 in the same way ◆ *Galileo returned in kind the loving support he received from his daughter.*
2 payment in kind is given in the form of goods or services, not in money
kind of (*informal*) to some extent; rather ◆ *It's kind of quiet here at the weekends.*
of a kind of a similar type ◆ *Your dad and your brother are two of a kind.*
WORD HISTORY from Old English *cynd* 'nature'
USAGE NOTE You say *this* or *this kind of thing*, but when you are talking about more than one of something you say *these* or *those kinds of things*. You can also say *these* or *those kinds of thing*.

kind❷ *ADJECTIVE*
friendly and helpful; considerate towards others
▷ **kindness** *NOUN*
WORD HISTORY from Old English *gecynd* 'natural or proper'

kindergarten *NOUN* **kindergartens**
a school or class for very young children; a nursery
WORD HISTORY a German word meaning 'children's garden'

kind-hearted *ADJECTIVE*
kind and sympathetic
▷ **kind-heartedness** *NOUN*

kindle *VERB* **kindles, kindling, kindled**
1 to start a flame; to set light to something
2 to begin burning
WORD HISTORY from an Old Norse word

kindling *NOUN*
small pieces of wood used for lighting fires

kindly *ADJECTIVE* **kindlier, kindliest**
kind or friendly ◆ *He had a smile and a kindly word for everyone.*
▷ **kindliness** *NOUN*

kindly *ADVERB*
1 in a kind manner
2 used in a polite request ◆ *Kindly ignore my previous email.*

kindred *NOUN*
(*formal*) a person's family and relatives

kindred *ADJECTIVE*
(*formal*) related or similar ◆ *The Conservatory is devoted to instilling a love of music and kindred arts.*
kindred spirit someone whose tastes or attitudes are similar to your own

kinetic *ADJECTIVE*
to do with or produced by movement ◆ *kinetic energy.*
WORD HISTORY from Greek *kinetikos* 'moving'

king *NOUN* **kings**
1 a man who is the ruler of a country through inheriting the position
2 a person or thing regarded as supreme in some way ◆ *By this time, Elvis was the king of rock and roll.*
3 the most important piece in chess, which if captured loses the game
4 a playing card with a picture of a king, ranking next below an ace
▷ **kingly** *ADJECTIVE*
▷ **kingship** *NOUN*
WORD HISTORY from Old English *cyning*
USAGE NOTE You use a capital letter (*the King, King Charles*) when you are using the word as a title.

kingdom *NOUN* **kingdoms**
1 a country ruled by a king or queen
2 a division of the natural world ◆ *the animal kingdom*

kingfisher *NOUN* **kingfishers**
a small bird with blue feathers that dives to catch fish

kingpin *NOUN* **kingpins**
the most important person or thing in an organization, without which it cannot operate

king-size or **king-sized** *ADJECTIVE*
extra large

kink *NOUN* **kinks**
1 a short twist in a rope, wire, or length of hair

Nadine is so lucky. Her long liquorice-black hair falls straight past her shoulders, no kinks at all. — *Jacqueline Wilson, Girls Out Late*

2 a peculiarity

kinky *ADJECTIVE*
(*informal*) involving peculiar sexual behaviour

kinship *NOUN*
1 a family relationship
2 a feeling of closeness between people who have similar attitudes or interests

kinsman or **kinswoman** *NOUN* **kinsmen** or **kinswomen**
a family relative

kiosk *NOUN* **kiosks**
1 a public telephone booth
2 a small hut or stall which sells newspapers, magazines, and refreshments

WORD HISTORY from a Persian word meaning 'pavilion'

kip *NOUN* **kips**
(*informal*) a sleep

kip *VERB* **kips, kipping, kipped**
(*informal*) to sleep

The police down here have got used to seeing kids kipping in doorways, and mostly they leave you alone. — *Robert Swindells, Stone Cold*

kipper *NOUN* **kippers**
a herring that has been split open, salted, and dried or smoked

kirk *NOUN* **kirks**
(*Scottish*) a church

WORD HISTORY from an Old Norse word

kirpan *NOUN* **kirpans**
a symbolic sword worn by Sikh men

WORD HISTORY from a Sanskrit word meaning 'sword'

kiss *NOUN* **kisses**
the action of touching somebody with your lips as a sign of affection, or as a greeting

kiss of life
1 mouth-to-mouth resuscitation
2 something that revives a failing activity

kiss *VERB* **kisses, kissing, kissed**
1 to give someone a kiss
2 to touch something lightly

kit *NOUN* **kits**
1 equipment or clothes for a particular occupation or activity ◆ *a first-aid kit*
2 a set of parts sold ready to be fitted together

kit *VERB* **kits, kitting, kitted**
to kit someone out is to provide them with the clothing or equipment they need ◆ *We were all kitted out for a day in the hills.*

kitchen *NOUN* **kitchens**
a room in which meals are prepared and cooked

kitchenette *NOUN* **kitchenettes**
a small room or part of a room used as a kitchen

kitchen-sink *ADJECTIVE*
kitchen-sink drama deals realistically with drab or sordid subjects

kite *NOUN* **kites**
1 a toy consisting of a light framework covered with cloth or paper and flown in the wind on the end of a long piece of string

Haoyou made triangular kites and square ones, oblongs and pennons [= pennants] with swallow tails. — *Geraldine McCaughrean, The Kite Rider*

2 a large hawk

kith and kin
friends and relatives

WORD HISTORY from an Old English word *cyth* 'what or who you know', and our word *kin*

kitsch (*rhymes with* rich) *ADJECTIVE*
an object or work of art that is kitch is sentimental and lacks good taste

WORD HISTORY a German word

kitten *NOUN* **kittens**
a very young cat

WORD HISTORY from Old French *chitoun* 'small cat'

kitty *NOUN* **kitties**
1 a fund of money for use by several people
2 an amount of money that you can win in a card game

kiwi (*say* kee- wee) *NOUN* **kiwis**
1 a New Zealand bird that cannot fly
2 (*informal*) a person from New Zealand

WORD HISTORY a Maori word

kiwi fruit *NOUN* **kiwi fruits**
a fruit with thin hairy skin, green flesh, and black seeds

WORD HISTORY named after the *kiwi*, because the fruit was exported from New Zealand

kleptomania *NOUN*
an uncontrollable urge to steal things
▷ **kleptomaniac** *NOUN*

WORD HISTORY from Greek *kleptes* 'thief'

km *ABBREVIATION*
kilometre

knack *NOUN*
a skilful or effective way of doing something ◆ *There is a definite knack to eating mangoes.*

knacker *NOUN*
a person who buys and slaughters horses in order to sell the meat and hides

knackered *ADJECTIVE*
(*informal*) exhausted; worn out

knapsack *NOUN* **knapsacks**
a bag with shoulder straps, carried on your back

knave *NOUN* **knaves**
1 (*old use*) a dishonest man; a rogue
2 a jack in playing cards
▷ **knavery** *NOUN*
▷ **knavish** *ADJECTIVE*

WORD HISTORY from Old English *cnafa* 'a boy or male servant'

knead *VERB* **kneads, kneading, kneaded**
1 to work dough or clay by pressing and stretching it with your hands
2 to press or massage something with kneading movements

knee *NOUN* **knees**
1 the joint between your thigh and the lower part of your leg
2 a person's lap ◆ *My cat likes to curl up on my knee.*

knee *VERB* **knees, kneeing, kneed**
to strike someone with your knee

kneecap *NOUN* **kneecaps**
the small bone covering the front of your knee joint

knee-deep *ADJECTIVE*
1 deep enough to cover a person up to their knees
2 to be knee-deep in an activity is to be deeply involved in it

knee-jerk *ADJECTIVE*
a knee-jerk reaction is done automatically without thinking

kneel *VERB* **kneels, kneeling, knelt**
to be or move into a position where your body is supported on your knees

knell *NOUN* **knells**
the sound of a bell rung solemnly after a death or at a funeral

knickerbockers *PLURAL NOUN*
loose-fitting short trousers gathered in at the knees

WORD HISTORY from Diedrich *Knickerbocker*, the fictitious author of a book by Washington Irving which pictured people wearing these kinds of trousers

knickers *PLURAL NOUN*
underpants worn by women and girls

WORD HISTORY shortened from *knickerbockers*

knick-knack *NOUN* **knick-knacks**
a small ornament

knife *NOUN* **knives**
a cutting instrument or weapon consisting of a sharp blade set in a handle

knife *VERB* **knifes, knifing, knifed**
to stab someone with a knife

knight *NOUN* **knights**
1 a man who has been given an honorary title that allows him to put 'Sir' before his name
2 a man raised to a high military rank in medieval Europe, usually mounted and in armour
3 a chess piece with a horse's head
▷ **knighthood** *NOUN*

knight *VERB* **knights, knighting, knighted**
to make someone a knight

WORD HISTORY from Old English *cniht* 'young man'

knit *VERB* **knits, knitting, knitted** or **knit**
1 to make something by looping together wool or other yarn, using long needles or a machine
2 broken bones knit together when they join back together and heal
to knit your brow is to frown
▷ **knitter** *NOUN*

knitting needle *NOUN* **knitting needles**
each of a pair of thick needles used for knitting by hand

knob *NOUN* **knobs**
1 the round handle of a door or drawer
2 a round lump on something
3 a round button or switch on a dial or machine
4 a small round piece of something soft and firm ◆ *a knob of butter*
▷ **knobbly** *ADJECTIVE*
▷ **knobby** *ADJECTIVE*

knobkerrie (*say* **nob**- ke- ree) *NOUN*
a short stick with a knob-shaped head, used as a weapon by South African tribesmen

knock *VERB* **knocks, knocking, knocked**
1 to hit something hard so as to make a noise
2 to produce something by hitting ◆ *We'll need to knock a hole in the wall.*
3 (*informal*) to criticize someone or something ◆ *Don't knock public transport until you try it.*
to knock something back (*informal*) to knock back a drink is to consume it quickly
to knock something down (*informal*) to knock down a price is to reduce it
to knock it off (*informal*) is to stop doing something
to knock off (*informal*) is to stop working
to knock something off
1 to knock off an amount is to deduct it from a price
2 (*informal*) to knock off a piece of work is to produce it quickly ▸▸

a b c d e f g h i j **k** l m n o p q r s t u v w x y z

3 (*informal*) to knock something off is to steal it
to knock someone out is to make them unconscious, especially by a blow to their head
to knock spots off someone (*informal*) is to be far better than them at something

knock *NOUN* **knocks**
1 the act or sound of knocking
2 a slight collision; a bump

knocker *NOUN* **knockers**
a hinged metal device for knocking on a door

knock-on *ADJECTIVE*
the knock-on effect of an action is something that happens as an indirect result

knockout *NOUN* **knockouts**
1 the action of knocking someone out
2 a contest in which the loser in each round has to drop out
3 (*informal*) an extremely attractive or outstanding person or thing

knoll *NOUN* **knolls**
a small round hill; a mound

knot *NOUN* **knots**
1 a fastening made by intertwining one or more pieces of string, rope, or thread and pulling the ends tight
2 a tangle; a lump

Minerva groomed my hair for hours, combing out knots and tangles, and I did the same for her. — *Celia Rees, Pirates!*

3 a round spot on a piece of wood where a branch joined it
4 a cluster of people or things
5 a unit of speed used by ships and aircraft, equal to one nautical mile (1,852 metres or 2,025 yards) per hour

knot *VERB* **knots, knotting, knotted**
1 to tie or fasten something with a knot
2 to become tangled up

knotty *ADJECTIVE* **knottier, knottiest**
1 full of knots
2 a knotty problem is difficult or puzzling

know *VERB* **knows, knowing, knew, known**
1 to have something in your mind that you have learned or discovered

Did you know that any number doubled is even? — *Tom Stoppard, Rosencrantz & Guildenstern are Dead*

2 to recognize or be familiar with a person or place

As soon as I mentioned the name Daisy Renton, it was obvious you'd known her. You gave yourself away at once. — *J. B. Priestley, An Inspector Calls*

3 to understand or realize something

Every citizen of Aramanth knew how fortunate they were, to live in this rare haven of peace, plenty, and equal opportunity for all. — *William Nicholson, The Wind Singer*

to be known as something is to be called or named it
to be known to do something is to be heard or reported to do it
to know of someone or something is to be familiar with them or it
▷ **knowable** *ADJECTIVE*

know *NOUN*
in the know (*informal*) having inside information

know-all *NOUN* **know-alls**
a person who behaves as if they know everything

know-how *NOUN*
practical knowledge or skill for a particular job

knowing *ADJECTIVE*
a knowing look or expression shows that you know or are aware of something

knowingly *ADVERB*
1 in a knowing way
2 to do something knowingly is to do it deliberately, while fully aware of the situation
◆ *The athlete denies having knowingly taken the drug.*

knowledge *NOUN*
1 information and skills you have through experience or education
2 the state of knowing about a particular fact or situation

Titus was about to deny all knowledge of the missing handbag when Mrs Fforbes-Campbell stalked into the dining room. — *Debi Gliori, Pure Dead Wicked*

3 all that is known
to my knowledge as far as I know

knowledgeable *ADJECTIVE*
well informed
▷ **knowledgeably** *ADVERB*

knuckle *NOUN* **knuckles**
1 a joint in your finger
2 the knee joint of an animal, or the part joining the leg to the foot
to rap someone over the knuckles is to scold them

knuckle *VERB* **knuckles, knuckling, knuckled**
to knuckle down is to begin to work hard
to knuckle under is to yield or submit

koala (*say* koh- **ah**- la) *NOUN* **koalas**
an Australian animal with thick grey fur and large ears, which climbs trees and feeds on eucalyptus leaves
WORD HISTORY an Australian Aboriginal word

kohl *NOUN*
a black powder used as eye make-up

kohlrabi (*say* kohl- **rah**- bi) *NOUN*
a cabbage with an edible stem shaped like a turnip

kookaburra *NOUN* **kookaburras**
a large Australian kingfisher with a loud call

Koran (*say* kor- **ahn**) *NOUN*
the sacred book of Islam, written in Arabic, believed by Muslims to contain the words of Allah revealed to the prophet Muhammad

WORD HISTORY from Arabic *kur'an* 'reading'

korma *NOUN*
a mild Indian meat or fish curry

kosher (*say* **koh**- sher) *ADJECTIVE*
1 kosher food conforms to Jewish laws about the preparation of food
2 (*informal*) genuine and legitimate; acceptable ◆ *On some of the islands, it's not kosher to hang out washing on Sundays.*

WORD HISTORY from Hebrew *kasher* 'suitable or proper'

kowtow (*rhymes with* cow- cow) *VERB* **kowtows, kowtowing, kowtowed**
to kowtow to someone is to behave in an extremely submissive and respectful way towards them

WORD HISTORY from Chinese *ketou*, a former Chinese custom of kneeling and touching the ground with your forehead as a sign of worship or submission

kph *ABBREVIATION*
kilometres per hour

kraal (*say* krahl) *NOUN* **kraals**
a traditional African village of huts, with a fence around it

Kremlin *NOUN*
the Kremlin is the citadel in Moscow, where the Russian government meets

WORD HISTORY from Russian *kreml'* 'citadel'

krill *NOUN*
a mass of tiny shrimp-like creatures, the chief food of certain whales

WORD HISTORY from Norwegian *kril* 'fish fry'

krypton *NOUN*
an inert gas that is present in the earth's atmosphere and is used in fluorescent lamps

WORD HISTORY from Greek *kryptos* 'hidden'

kudos (*say* **kew**- doss) *NOUN*
honour and glory ◆ *Being from London seems to carry a lot of kudos here.*

WORD HISTORY a Greek word meaning 'praise'

kudu *NOUN* **kudu** or **kudus**
a striped African antelope, of which the male has long spiral horns

kung fu *NOUN*
a Chinese method of self-defence, similar to karate

WORD HISTORY from Chinese words meaning 'merit master'

Kurd *NOUN* **Kurds**
a member of an Islamic people of Kurdistan, a mountainous region of east Turkey, north Iraq, and NW Iran

▷ **Kurdish** *ADJECTIVE*

kw or **kW** *ABBREVIATION*
kilowatt

a b c d e f g h i j k l m n o p q r s t u v w x y z

Ll

L *ABBREVIATION*
learner, especially a person learning to drive a car

laager *NOUN* **laagers**
(*South African*) a camp formed by a circle of wagons

lab *NOUN* **labs**
(*informal*) a laboratory

label *NOUN* **labels**
a small piece of paper or other material attached to an item to show its name or price, or the name of its owner or recipient

label *VERB* **labels, labelling, labelled**
1 to put a label on an item
2 to label someone is to identify or describe them in a particular way ◆ *He was labelled as a troublemaker from the start.*

WORD HISTORY from an Old French word meaning 'ribbon'

labial (*say* lay- bee- al) *ADJECTIVE*
to do with your lips

WORD HISTORY from Latin *labia* 'lips'

laboratory *NOUN* **laboratories**
(*Science*) a room or building equipped for scientific experiments

laborious *ADJECTIVE*
1 needing or using a lot of hard work
2 explaining something at great length and with obvious effort ◆ *The camera comes with a rather laborious instruction manual.*

▷ **laboriously** *ADVERB*

Labour *NOUN*
the Labour Party, a British political party formed to represent the interests of working people and believing in social equality and socialism

labour *NOUN* **labours**
1 hard work
2 a task
3 workers considered as a group
4 the contractions of the womb when a baby is being born

labour *VERB* **labours, labouring, laboured**
1 to work hard at something
2 to explain or discuss something at great length and with obvious effort ◆ *I could make similar comments about the rest of the cast but don't want to labour a point.*

USAGE NOTE The American spelling of this word is labor.

WORD HISTORY from Latin *labor* 'work, trouble, or suffering'

labourer *NOUN* **labourers**
a person who does hard manual work, especially outdoors

Labrador *NOUN* **Labradors**
a large black or light-brown dog

WORD HISTORY from *Labrador*, a district in Canada, where it was bred

laburnum *NOUN* **laburnums**
a tree with hanging yellow flowers

labyrinth *NOUN* **labyrinths**
a complicated arrangement of passages or paths; a maze

Twig continued on his way through the labyrinth of tiny winding alleyways. — *Paul Stewart & Chris Riddell, Stormchaser*

WORD HISTORY from Greek, originally referring to the mythological maze in which the Minotaur lived

labyrinthine *ADJECTIVE*
a labyrinthine route or system is very complicated or confusing

lace *NOUN* **laces**
1 net-like material with a decorative pattern of holes
2 a piece of thin cord or leather for fastening footwear or clothing

lace *VERB* **laces, lacing, laced**
1 to fasten something with a lace
2 to thread a cord through something
3 to lace a drink is to add spirits to it

lacerate *VERB* **lacerates, lacerating, lacerated**
to injure flesh by cutting or tearing it

▷ **laceration** *NOUN*

lachrymal (*say* lak- rim- al) *ADJECTIVE*
to do with tears; producing tears ◆ *lachrymal ducts*

WORD HISTORY from Latin *lacrima* 'a tear'

lachrymose *ADJECTIVE*
(*formal*) tearful

Miss Wilson was a poor sickly thing, lachrymose and low-spirited, not worth the trouble of vanquishing, in short. — *Charlotte Brontë, Jane Eyre*

lack *NOUN*
the fact of being without something or not having enough of it

lack *VERB* **lacks, lacking, lacked**
to lack a quality or feature is to fail to have or show it

His earlier pictures all lacked something. They had plenty of technical skill, but the magic wasn't there. — *Tim Bowler, River Boy*

lackadaisical *ADJECTIVE*
lacking energy or determination; careless

Sir Walter was staring, for he had never seen his rather lackadaisical young friend look like that before. — *G. K. Chesterton, The Man Who Knew Too Much*

WORD HISTORY from an old phrase, *lack-a-day*, used to express grief or surprise

lackey *NOUN* **lackeys**
a servant; a person who behaves or is treated like a servant

lacking *ADJECTIVE*
not having any or enough of something ◆ *The film is completely lacking in wit and intelligence.*

laconic *ADJECTIVE*
using few words; terse

Like most men of action, he is laconic in speech, and sinks readily into his own thoughts. — *Sir Arthur Conan Doyle, The Lost World*

▷ **laconically** *ADVERB*

WORD HISTORY from Greek *Lakon* 'a native of Laconia (an area in Greece)', because the Laconians were famous for their terse speech

lacquer *NOUN*
a hard glossy varnish

▷ **lacquered** *ADJECTIVE*

lacrosse *NOUN*
a ball game played with a stick which has a net on it (called a *crosse*) to catch and throw the ball

WORD HISTORY from French *la crosse* 'the crosse'

lactate *VERB* **lactates, lactating, lactated**
a woman or female mammal lactates when she produces milk

WORD HISTORY from Latin *lac* 'milk'

lactic *ADJECTIVE*
to do with milk or made from milk

lacy *ADJECTIVE*
made of lace or like lace

lad *NOUN* **lads**
a boy or youth

ladder *NOUN* **ladders**
1 two upright pieces of wood or metal with crosspieces (called *rungs*), used for climbing up or down
2 a vertical ladder-like flaw in a pair of tights or stockings where a stitch has become undone

ladder *VERB* **ladders, laddering, laddered**
to get a ladder in a pair of tights or stockings

laden *ADJECTIVE*
1 carrying a heavy load
2 to be laden with something is to be filled with or surrounded by it

The hot night was laden with the scent of flowers and with the salt smell of the sea. — *Philip Pullman, The Subtle Knife*

WORD HISTORY from Old English *hladan* 'to load a ship'

ladle *NOUN* **ladles**
a large deep spoon with a long handle, used for lifting and pouring liquids

ladle *VERB* **ladles, ladling, ladled**
to lift and pour a liquid with a ladle

lady *NOUN* **ladies**
1 a well-mannered woman
2 a woman of good social position
3 used as a polite way of describing or addressing a woman
4 (**Lady**) the title of a noblewoman

▷ **ladyship** *NOUN*

WORD HISTORY from Old English *hlaefdige* 'person who makes the bread' (see the word history for *lord*)

ladybird *NOUN* **ladybirds**
a small flying beetle, usually red with black spots

lady-in-waiting *NOUN* **ladies-in-waiting**
a woman of good social position who attends a queen or princess

ladylike *ADJECTIVE*
ladylike behaviour is well mannered and refined, as a lady is supposed to be

'No, thank you,' said Sylvia, in as ladylike a tone as she could muster. 'I never touch chocolate.' — *Joan Aiken, The Wolves of Willoughby Chase*

lag ❶ *VERB* **lags, lagging, lagged**
to lag, or lag behind, is go too slowly and fail to keep up with others

lag *NOUN* **lags**
a delay ◆ *There may be a slight lag while you wait for the web page to download.*

lag ❷ *VERB* **lags, lagging, lagged**
to lag a pipe or boiler is to wrap it in insulating material (called *lagging*) to prevent loss of heat

lager (*say* lah- ger) *NOUN* **lagers**
a light beer

WORD HISTORY from German *Lager* 'storehouse', because the beer was kept to mature

laggard *NOUN* **laggards**
a person who lags behind

lagoon *NOUN* **lagoons**
a salt-water lake separated from the sea by sandbanks or reefs

Within the irregular arc of coral the lagoon was still as a mountain lake—blue of all shades and shadowy green and purple. — *William Golding, Lord of the Flies*

WORD HISTORY from Latin *lacuna* 'pool'

laid *past tense* of **lay**

laid-back *ADJECTIVE*
(*informal*) a laid-back person or attitude is relaxed and easy-going

lain *past participle* of **lie** ❷

lair *NOUN* **lairs**
a sheltered place where a wild animal lives

laissez-faire (*say* lay- say- **fair**) *NOUN*
a government policy of not interfering in the way private businesses operate

WORD HISTORY a French phrase meaning 'let (them) act'

laity (*say* **lay**- it- ee) *NOUN*
lay people, not the clergy

lake *NOUN* **lakes**
a large area of water entirely surrounded by land

lama *NOUN* **lamas**
a Buddhist priest or monk in Tibet and Mongolia

lamb *NOUN* **lambs**
1 a young sheep
2 meat from a lamb

lambswool *NOUN*
soft fine wool from lambs

lame *ADJECTIVE*
1 a lame animal is injured and unable to walk normally
2 a lame excuse or argument is weak and unconvincing
▷ **lamely** *ADVERB*
▷ **lameness** *NOUN*

lament *NOUN* **laments**
a statement, song, or poem expressing grief or regret

lament *VERB* **laments, lamenting, lamented**
to express grief or regret about something

'The mean thing about your getting married is that I won't be able to be your bridesmaid,' lamented Diana. — *L. M. Mongomery, Anne of the Island*

▷ **lamentation** *NOUN*
WORD HISTORY from Latin *lamentari* 'to weep'

lamentable (*say* **lam**- in- ta- bul) *ADJECTIVE*
regrettable or deplorable

laminate *VERB* **laminates, laminating, laminated**
to laminate a document is to protect it by covering it on both sides with thin layers of plastic
▷ **laminated** *ADJECTIVE*
WORD HISTORY from Latin *lamina* 'a layer'

lamp *NOUN* **lamps**
a device for producing light from electricity, gas, or oil
▷ **lamplight** *NOUN*
▷ **lampshade** *NOUN*
WORD HISTORY from Greek *lampas* 'a torch'

lamppost *NOUN* **lampposts**
a tall post with a lamp at the top, used to provide light in a street or path

lamprey *NOUN* **lampreys**
a small eel-like water animal

lance *NOUN* **lances**
a long spear

lance *VERB* **lances, lancing, lanced**
a surgeon lances a boil on someone's skin by cutting it with a surgical knife

lance corporal *NOUN* **lance corporals**
a soldier ranking between a private and a corporal

lancet *NOUN* **lancets**
1 a pointed two-edged knife used by surgeons
2 a tall narrow pointed window or arch
WORD HISTORY from French *lancette* 'a small lance'

land *NOUN* **lands**
1 the part of the earth's surface not covered by sea
2 the ground or soil; an area of country ◆ *suitable land for a wind farm*
3 the area occupied by a nation; a country

land *VERB* **lands, landing, landed**
1 to arrive on land from a ship or aircraft
2 to reach the ground after jumping or falling
3 to come down through the air and settle on something ◆ *A fly landed on his arm.*
4 to bring a fish out of the water
5 to obtain or be given a task or responsibility ◆ *She landed a top job in the city.*
6 to arrive at a certain place or position ◆ *After traipsing around town for two hours, we landed back at my flat.*
7 to present someone with a difficult task or problem ◆ *I've been landed with organizing the Christmas party this year.*

landed *ADJECTIVE*
1 a landed person or group is one that owns a lot of land
2 consisting of land ◆ *landed estates*

landing *NOUN* **landings**
1 the level area at the top of a flight of stairs
2 the action of bringing an aircraft to the ground ◆ *The pilot made a smooth landing.*
3 a place where people can get on and off a boat

landing stage *NOUN* **landing stages**
a platform on which people and goods are taken on and off a boat

landlady *NOUN* **landladies**
1 a woman who lets rooms to lodgers
2 a woman who runs a pub

landlocked *ADJECTIVE*
a landlocked area or country is surrounded by land and has no coastline

landlord *NOUN* **landlords**
1 a person who lets a house, room, or land to a tenant
2 a person who runs a pub

landlubber *NOUN* **landlubbers**
(*informal*) a person who is not used to travelling on the sea
WORD HISTORY from an old word *lubber* meaning 'an awkward, clumsy person'

landmark *NOUN* **landmarks**
1 an object that is easily seen in a landscape
2 an important event in the history or development of something ◆ *The book became a landmark in science fiction.*

landmine *NOUN* **landmines**
an explosive mine laid on or just under the surface of the ground

landowner *NOUN* **landowners**
a person who owns a large amount of land

landscape *NOUN* **landscapes**
1 (*Geography*) a view of a particular area of countryside or town
2 (*Art*) a picture of a scene in the countryside
3 (*ICT*) a page of text that is wider than it is tall

landscape gardening *NOUN*
the process of laying out a garden to imitate natural scenery

landslide *NOUN* **landslides**
1 a landslip
2 an overwhelming victory in an election ◆ *The party won the last local election by a landslide.*

landslip *NOUN* **landslips**
a huge mass of soil and rocks sliding down a slope

landward *ADJECTIVE, ADVERB*
towards the land
▷ **landwards** *ADVERB*

lane *NOUN* **lanes**
1 a narrow road, especially in the country
2 a strip of road for a single line of traffic
3 a narrow strip marked off on a race track or in a swimmimg pool, used by a single athlete or swimmer in a race

language *NOUN* **languages**
1 spoken and written communication by using words in a systematic way
2 the words used in a particular country or by a particular group of people
3 a system of signs or symbols giving information, especially in computing
WORD HISTORY from Latin *lingua* 'a tongue'

language laboratory *NOUN* **language laboratories**
a room equipped with audio equipment for learning a foreign language

languid *ADJECTIVE*
a languid person is slow and lacks energy because they are tired, weak, or lazy
▷ **languidly** *ADVERB*
▷ **languor** *NOUN*

languish *VERB* **languishes, languishing, languished**
1 to live in miserable conditions; to be neglected ◆ *He has been languishing in prison for three years.*
2 to become weak or listless; to fade out or away ◆ *As the afternoon dragged on, conversation soon languished.*
WORD HISTORY from Latin *languere* 'to be faint or weak'

lank *ADJECTIVE*
lank hair is long and limp

lanky *ADJECTIVE* **lankier, lankiest**
a lanky person is awkwardly thin and tall

Charlie was built like the twins, shorter and stockier than Percy and Ron, who were both long and lanky. — *J. K. Rowling, Harry Potter and the Goblet of Fire*

▷ **lankiness** *NOUN*

lanolin *NOUN*
a kind of waxy ointment, made of fat from sheep's wool
WORD HISTORY from the Latin words *lana* 'wool' and *oleum* 'oil'

lantern *NOUN* **lanterns**
a portable glass case for carrying a light and shielding it from the wind

lanyard *NOUN* **lanyards**
a short cord for fastening or holding something
WORD HISTORY from Old French *laniere*

lap❶ *NOUN* **laps**
1 the area formed by the top of your legs when you are sitting down with your knees together
2 the action of going once round a racetrack
3 one section of a journey; a leg

lap *VERB* **laps, lapping, lapped**
to overtake another competitor in a race to go one or more laps ahead
WORD HISTORY from Old English *laeppa*

lap ❷ *VERB* **laps, lapping, lapped**
1 a cat or other animal laps a liquid when it drinks it by scooping it up in its tongue
2 a wave laps when it makes a gentle splash against a surface

WORD HISTORY from Old English *lapian*

lapel (*say* la- **pel**) *NOUN* **lapels**
a flap folded back at the front edge of a coat or jacket

lapse *NOUN* **lapses**
1 a slight mistake or failure ◆ *A lapse of concentration let the ball into the net.*
2 an amount of time that has passed ◆ *We met again after a lapse of six months.*

lapse *VERB* **lapses, lapsing, lapsed**
1 time lapses when it passes gradually
2 a certificate or policy lapses when the period of time for which it was valid comes to an end and it is not renewed
3 to lapse into or out of consciousness is to become gradually conscious or unconscious

WORD HISTORY from Latin *lapsus* 'sliding'

laptop *NOUN* **laptops**
a portable computer for use while travelling

lapwing *NOUN* **lapwings**
a black and white bird with a crested head and a shrill cry

larceny *NOUN*
the crime of stealing other people's possessions

WORD HISTORY from Latin *latro* 'a robber'

larch *NOUN* **larches**
a tall deciduous tree that bears small cones

lard *NOUN*
a white greasy substance prepared from pig fat and used in cooking

WORD HISTORY a French word meaning 'bacon'

larder *NOUN* **larders**
a cupboard or small room for storing food

In Aunt Gwen's larder there were two cold pork chops, half a trifle, some bananas and some buns and cakes. — *Philippa Pearce, Tom's Midnight Garden*

large *ADJECTIVE*
of more than the ordinary or average size; big

at large
1 free to roam about, not captured ◆ *The escaped wolves are still at large.*
2 in general, as a whole ◆ *the country at large*

▷ **largeness** *NOUN*

WORD HISTORY from Latin *largus* 'abundant or generous'

largely *ADVERB*
to a great extent; mostly ◆ *Human activities are largely to blame for the problem of global warming.*

largesse (*say* lar- **jess**) *NOUN*
money or gifts generously given

'Scores,' the Director repeated and flung out his arms, as though he were distributing largesse. — *Aldous Huxley, Brave New World*

WORD HISTORY a French word, related to our word *large*

USAGE NOTE Take care not to confuse this word with *largeness*.

lark ❶ *NOUN* **larks**
a small sandy-brown bird; the skylark

lark ❷ *NOUN* **larks**
(*informal*) something amusing; a bit of fun

But did you do it for a lark or what? — *Edith Nesbit, The Railway Children*

lark *VERB* **larks, larking, larked**
to lark about (*informal*) is to have fun playing jokes or tricks

larkspur *NOUN*
a plant with spur-shaped blue or pink flowers

larva *NOUN* **larvae**
an insect in the first stage of its life, after it comes out of the egg

▷ **larval** *ADJECTIVE*

WORD HISTORY a Latin word meaning 'ghost or mask'

laryngitis *NOUN*
inflammation of the larynx, causing hoarseness

larynx (*say* **la**- rinks) *NOUN* **larynxes**
the part of your throat that contains the vocal cords

lasagne (*say* laz- **an**- ya) *NOUN*
pasta in the form of sheets, usually cooked with minced meat and cheese sauce

laser *NOUN* **lasers**
a device that makes a very strong narrow beam of light or other electromagnetic radiation

WORD HISTORY from the initials in the phrase '*l*ight *a*mplification by *s*timulated *e*mission of *r*adiation'

lash *NOUN* **lashes**
1 a stroke with a whip or stick
2 the cord or cord-like part of a whip
3 an eyelash

lash *VERB* **lashes, lashing, lashed**
1 to strike a person or animal with a whip
2 to lash things together is to tie them tightly with a rope or cord

to lash down rain lashes down when it is raining heavily
to lash out is to speak or hit out angrily at someone

lashings *PLURAL NOUN*
(*informal*) lashings of food or drink is a large amount or helping ◆ *Serve the pudding hot or cold, with lashings of whipped cream.*

lass or **lassie** *NOUN* **lasses** or **lassies**
a girl or young woman

lassitude *NOUN*
tiredness; lack of energy
WORD HISTORY from Latin *lassus* 'weary'

lasso *NOUN* **lassoes** or **lassos**
a rope with a sliding noose at the end, used for catching cattle

lasso *VERB* **lassoes, lassoing, lassoed**
to catch an animal with a lasso

last❶ *ADJECTIVE, ADVERB*
1 coming after all others; final

The last person to be burned as a witch in Scotland was in Dornoch, in the Highlands, in 1722. — *Theresa Breslin, Whispers in the Graveyard*

2 latest; most recent ◆ *Where did you go for your holidays last summer?*
3 least likely ◆ *He is the last person I'd have chosen for the team.*
the last straw a final thing that makes a problem unbearable

last *NOUN*
a person or thing that is last in position
at last or **at long last** finally; after much delay
to the last to the end
WORD HISTORY from Old English *latost*

last❷ *VERB* **lasts, lasting, lasted**
1 to continue to exist, live, or be usable

Mr Evans's rages were noisy while they lasted but they didn't last long. — *Nina Bawden, Carrie's War*

2 food or drink lasts when it stays fresh and in good condition ◆ *The milk won't last very long in this heat.*
3 food, fuel, or other provisions last when they are enough for your needs ◆ *We've got enough petrol to last us until the weekend.*
WORD HISTORY from Old English *laestan*

last❸ *NOUN* **lasts**
a block of wood or metal shaped like a foot, used in making and repairing shoes
WORD HISTORY from Old English *laeste*

lasting *ADJECTIVE*
able to last for a long time ◆ *a lasting effect*

lastly *ADVERB*
in the last place; finally

last post *NOUN*
a military bugle call sounded at sunset and at military funerals

last rites *PLURAL NOUN*
a Christian ceremony given to a person who is close to death

latch *NOUN* **latches**
a small bar fastening a door or gate, lifted by a lever or spring
▷ **latchkey** *NOUN*

latch *VERB* **latches, latching, latched**
to fasten a door or gate with a latch
to latch on
1 to latch on to someone is to meet and stay close to them
2 to latch on to an idea is to understand and use or apply it

late *ADJECTIVE, ADVERB*
1 after the usual or expected time
2 near the end ◆ *late in the afternoon*
3 recent ◆ *the latest news*
4 who has died recently

The duke was the son of the late King of Ruritania. — *Anthony Hope, The Prisoner of Zenda*

of late recently

lately *ADVERB*
recently

Poor Rose has been so miserable lately that a smile from her is like late afternoon sunshine after a long, wet day. — *Dodie Smith, I Capture the Castle*

latent (*say* lay- tent) *ADJECTIVE*
a latent ability or talent is one that exists but is not yet developed, active, or visible
WORD HISTORY from Latin *latens* 'lying hidden'

latent heat *NOUN*
the heat needed to change a solid into a liquid or vapour, or a liquid into a vapour, without a change in temperature

later *ADVERB*
after in time; afterwards ◆ *Two days later we set off again.*

lateral *ADJECTIVE*
1 to do with the side or sides of something
2 a lateral movement or action is one that goes sideways
▷ **laterally** *ADVERB*
WORD HISTORY from Latin *lateris* 'of a side'

lateral thinking *NOUN*
solving problems by thinking about them in an unusual and creative (and apparently illogical) way

latex *NOUN*
the milky juice of various plants and trees, especially the rubber tree

lath *NOUN* **laths**
a narrow thin strip of wood

lathe (*say* layth) *NOUN* **lathes**
a machine for holding and turning pieces of wood while they are being shaped

lather *NOUN*
a mass of froth

a b c d e f g h i j k l m n o p q r s t u v w x y z

lather *VERB* **lathers, lathering, lathered**
1 to cover something with lather
2 to form a lather

Latin *NOUN*
the language of the ancient Romans, which spread through the Roman Empire. It is no longer used but is a source of some modern European languages.
▷ **Latin** *ADJECTIVE*
WORD HISTORY from Latin *Latium*, an ancient district of Italy including Rome

Latin words in English

Most words derived from **Latin** have entered English since the revival of classical learning in the Renaissance (14th–16th centuries). Some have been borrowed as whole words, e.g. *axis*, *formula*, *forum*, *radius*; but many more have been created by using Latin words to form new compounds in English. Latin has been used for centuries to coin words for inventions, discoveries, or new ideas, e.g. *aviation*, *binoculars*, *circumnavigate*, *equinox*, *submarine*. And many words have been created on Latin models to make our language sound more formal or impressive: *imbibe*, *serenity*, and *terrestrial* are more formal than *drink*, *calm*, and *earthly*. Some Latin elements are easy to spot: words beginning *mal-* (e.g. *malevolent*, *malefactor*) often come from Latin *male* 'badly'; and words beginning *ben-* (e.g. *beneficial*, *benefactor*) often come from Latin *bene* 'well'. Several Latin phrases are used in English in their original form, e.g. *bona fide*, *in situ*, and *vice versa*.
Words are still being created from Latin. The prefixes *bi-*, *ex-*, *post-*, and *super-* all come from Latin and have been used to form many new words, such as *bimonthly*, *ex-husband*, (a woman's former husband), *post-war*, and *supernova*.

Latin America *NOUN*
the parts of Central and South America where the main language is Spanish or Portuguese
WORD HISTORY so called because these languages developed from Latin

latitude *NOUN* **latitudes**
1 (*Geography*) the distance of a place from the equator, measured in degrees
2 freedom from restrictions on what people can do or believe
WORD HISTORY from Latin *latitudo* 'breadth'

latrine (*say* la- **treen**) *NOUN* **latrines**
a toilet in a camp or barracks

latter *ADJECTIVE*
later or more recent ◆ *It happened in the latter part of the year.*

latter *NOUN*
the latter is the second of two people or things just mentioned (SEE ALSO **former**)

latterly *ADVERB*
recently; not long ago

lattice *NOUN* **lattices**
a framework of crossed strips or bars with spaces between

laud (*rhymes with* ford) *VERB* **lauds, lauding, lauded**
(*formal*) to praise someone or something
WORD HISTORY from Latin *laudare* 'to praise'

laudable *ADJECTIVE*
deserving praise

We are doing a laudable thing ..., and yet we should be hung by order of the king if we were caught. — *Victor Hugo, The Hunchback of Notre Dame*

▷ **laudably** *ADVERB*

laudatory (*say* law- dat- er- ee) *ADJECTIVE*
expressing praise

laugh *VERB* **laughs, laughing, laughed**
1 to make the sounds that show you are happy or think something is funny
2 to laugh at someone is to mock them or make fun of them
SYNONYMS (meaning 1) giggle, chuckle, chortle, snigger, titter, guffaw; *informal* scream; (meaning 2) mock, ridicule, make fun of, scoff at, deride, jeer at

laugh *NOUN* **laughs**
1 the sound of laughing
2 (*informal*) something amusing and enjoyable

laughable *ADJECTIVE*
deserving to be laughed at

laughing stock *NOUN* **laughing stocks**
a person or thing that is the object of ridicule and scorn

laughter *NOUN*
the act, sound, or manner of laughing

launch ❶ *VERB* **launches, launching, launched**
1 to send a ship from the land into the water
2 to send a rocket or spacecraft into space
3 to set a thing moving by throwing or pushing it
4 to make a new book or product available for the first time ◆ *Our new range of sports gear will be launched in the summer.*
5 to launch an attack or campaign is to start it off

launch *NOUN* **launches**
the launching of a ship or spacecraft
WORD HISTORY from an Old French word

launch ❷ *NOUN* **launches**
a large motor boat
WORD HISTORY from a Spanish word

launch pad *NOUN* **launch pads**
a platform from which a rocket is launched

launder *VERB* **launders, laundering, laundered**
to wash and iron clothes and other items

launderette *NOUN* **launderettes**
a place fitted with washing machines that people pay to use

a b c d e f g h i j k l m n o p q r s t u v w x y z

laundry *NOUN* **laundries**
1 a place where clothes and bedlinen are washed and ironed for customers
2 items set aside to be washed or sent to a laundry
WORD HISTORY from Latin *lavandaria* 'things to be washed'

laureate (*say* lor- i- at) *ADJECTIVE*
Poet Laureate a person appointed to write poems for national occasions
WORD HISTORY because a *laurel* wreath was worn in ancient times as a sign of victory

laurel *NOUN* **laurels**
an evergreen shrub with smooth shiny leaves
to rest on your laurels is to be content with your previous achievements or success

lava *NOUN*
1 molten rock that flows from a volcano
2 the solid rock formed when this cools
WORD HISTORY from Latin *lavare* 'to wash'

lavatory *NOUN* **lavatories**
1 a toilet
2 a room containing a toilet
WORD HISTORY from Latin *lavatorium* 'a basin or bath for washing'

lavender *NOUN*
1 a shrub with sweet-smelling purple flowers
2 a light purple colour

lavish *ADJECTIVE*
1 generous
2 plentiful
▷ **lavishly** *ADVERB*
▷ **lavishness** *NOUN*

lavish *VERB* **lavishes, lavishing, lavished**
to give large or generous amounts of something

There the French officers received them with open arms, and lavished upon them all the resources of their hospitality. — *Jules Verne, Five Weeks in a Balloon*

WORD HISTORY from Old French *lavasse* 'heavy rain'

law *NOUN* **laws**
1 a rule or set of rules that everyone must obey
2 the profession of being a lawyer
3 (*informal*) the police
4 a scientific statement of something that always happens ◆ *the law of gravity*
WORD FAMILY Related adjectives are legal and judicial.

law-abiding *ADJECTIVE*
obeying the law

law court *NOUN* **law courts**
a room or building in which a magistrate or a judge and jury hear evidence and decide whether someone has broken the law

lawful *ADJECTIVE*
allowed or accepted by the law
▷ **lawfully** *ADVERB*

lawless *ADJECTIVE*
1 a lawless person does not obey the law
2 a lawless country or town is one in which there are no proper laws or the laws are not enforced
▷ **lawlessly** *ADVERB*
▷ **lawlessness** *NOUN*

lawn¹ *NOUN* **lawns**
an area of closely cut grass in a garden or park.
WORD HISTORY from an Old French word

lawn² *NOUN*
very fine cotton material
WORD HISTORY probably from *Laon*, a town in France where cloth was made

lawnmower *NOUN* **lawnmowers**
a machine for cutting the grass of lawns

lawn tennis *NOUN*
tennis played on an outdoor grass or hard court

lawsuit *NOUN* **lawsuits**
a dispute or claim that is brought to a lawcourt to be settled

lawyer *NOUN* **lawyers**
a person who is qualified to give advice in matters of law

lax *ADJECTIVE*
slack; not strict enough

Lane's views on marriage seem somewhat lax. Really, if the lower orders don't set us a good example, what on earth is the use of them? — *Oscar Wilde, The Importance of Being Earnest*

▷ **laxly** *ADVERB*
▷ **laxity** *NOUN*
WORD HISTORY from Latin *laxus* 'loose'

laxative *NOUN* **laxatives**
a medicine that stimulates your bowels to empty

lay¹ *VERB* **lays, laying, laid**
1 to put something down in a particular place or way

The girl was carrying a bundle wrapped in faded cotton, which she laid at Mrs Coulter's feet. — *Philip Pullman, The Amber Spyglass*

2 to lay a table is to arrange it in preparation for a meal
3 to lay blame or responsibility on someone is to attribute it to them
4 to lay a plan or trap is to prepare it in detail
5 a bird or reptile lays an egg when it produces it from its body
to lay something in to lay in fuel, for example, is to stock up with a supply of it
to lay someone off (*informal*) is to stop employing them for a while
to lay off (*informal*) is to stop doing something
to lay something on is to supply or provide it

to lay something or someone out
1 to lay things out is to arrange or prepare them
2 (*informal*) to lay someone out is to knock them unconscious
3 to lay out a corpse is to prepare it for burial

USAGE NOTE Take care not to confuse *lay* meaning 'to put down' (which has a past tense *laid*) with *lie* meaning 'to be in a flat position' (which has a past tense *lay*). You would say: *Please lay the parcel on the floor* and *She laid it on the floor*; but *Go and lie down* and *She went and lay down.*

lay❷ *past tense* of **lie❷**

lay❸ *NOUN* **lays**
(*literary*) a poem meant to be sung; a ballad

lay❹ *ADJECTIVE*
1 not belonging to the clergy ◆ *a lay preacher*
2 not professionally qualified ◆ *lay opinion*

WORD HISTORY from Greek *laos* 'people'

layabout *NOUN* **layabouts**
a person who lazily avoids working for a living

lay-by *NOUN* **lay-bys**
a place where vehicles can stop beside a main road

layer *NOUN* **layers**
a single thickness or coating

The four of us were wrapped in so many layers of clothes it looked as if we were going off to spend the night in a refrigerator. — *Anne Frank, The Diary of a Young Girl*

layman or **laywoman** or **layperson** *NOUN* **laymen** or **laywomen** or **laypeople**
1 a man or woman who does not have specialized knowledge or training in a particular area, such as medicine or the law
2 a man or woman who is not ordained as a member of the clergy

layout *NOUN* **layouts**
an arrangement of parts of something according to a plan

laze *VERB* **lazes, lazing, lazed**
to spend time in a lazy way

lazy *ADJECTIVE* **lazier, laziest**
not wanting to work; doing little work
▷ **lazily** *ADVERB*
▷ **laziness** *NOUN*

lea *NOUN* **leas**
(*poetic*) a meadow

leach *VERB* **leaches, leaching, leached**
to remove a soluble substance from soil or rock by making water percolate through it

WORD HISTORY from Old English *leccan* 'water'

lead❶ (*say* leed) *VERB* **leads, leading, led**
1 to take or guide someone, especially by going in front
2 to be winning in a race or contest; to be ahead
3 to be in charge of a group of people
4 to be a way or route

Soon Crane was at the entrance to the hidden tunnel that led from the cliff to the Vicarage. — *G. P. Taylor, Shadowmancer*

5 to play the first card in a card game
6 to lead a particular kind of life is to live or experience it ◆ *Nowadays, I lead a fairly quiet life.*

to lead to something to lead to an event or situation is to result in or cause it

lead (*say* leed) *NOUN* **leads**
1 a leading place or part or position ◆ *The French champion cyclist took the lead on the final hill.*
2 a clue to be followed
3 a strap or cord for leading a dog or other animal
4 an electrical wire attached to something

to take a lead is to provide a good example or guidance for others to follow

lead *ADJECTIVE*
the most important of a number or group ◆ *the lead singer*

lead❷ (*say* led) *NOUN* **leads**
1 a soft heavy grey metal
2 the writing substance (graphite) in a pencil

lead *ADJECTIVE*
made of or like lead

leaden (*say* led-en) *ADJECTIVE*
1 made of lead
2 heavy and slow

My legs felt leaden trudging through the deep snow towards the end of the plateau. — *Joe Simpson, Touching the Void*

3 of the colour of lead; dark grey ◆ *leaden sky*

leader *NOUN* **leaders**
1 the person in charge of a group of people; a chief
2 the person who is winning
3 a newspaper article giving the editor's opinion
▷ **leadership** *NOUN*

leaf *NOUN* **leaves**
1 a flat usually green part of a plant, growing out from its stem, branch, or root
2 the paper forming one page of a book
3 a very thin sheet of metal ◆ *gold leaf*
4 a folding or removable section of a table or other piece of furniture

to turn over a new leaf is to make a fresh start and improve your behaviour or performance
▷ **leafy** *ADJECTIVE*
▷ **leafless** *ADJECTIVE*

leaf *VERB* **leafs, leafing, leafed**
to leaf through something to leaf through a book or pile of paper is to turn over the pages one by one

leaflet *NOUN* **leaflets**
a piece of paper printed with information

league❶ ***NOUN*** **leagues**
1 a group of teams who compete against each other for a championship
2 a group of people or nations who agree to work together

in league with someone working or plotting together

WORD HISTORY from Latin *legare* 'to bind'

league❷ ***NOUN*** **leagues**
an old measure of distance, roughly equal to 3 miles or 5 kilometres

leak ***NOUN*** **leaks**
1 a hole or crack through which liquid or gas accidentally escapes
2 the revealing of secret information

▷ **leaky** ***ADJECTIVE***

leak ***VERB*** **leaks, leaking, leaked**
1 to escape through a leak
2 to let something escape through a leak
3 to reveal secret information

▷ **leakage** ***NOUN***

lean❶ ***ADJECTIVE***
1 lean meat contains little or no fat
2 a lean person or body is thin with little or no body fat

WORD HISTORY from Old English *hlaene*

lean❷ ***VERB*** **leans, leaning, leaned** or **leant**
1 to bend your body towards or over something
2 to put something in a sloping position
3 to lean on or against something is to rest on or against it

Madame Doubtfire was leaning on the bannister of the upstairs landing, scratching a hairy leg and smoking a cheroot. — *Anne Fine, Madame Doubtfire*

4 to lean on someone is to rely or depend on them for help

WORD HISTORY from Old English *hleonian*

leaning ***NOUN*** **leanings**
a tendency or preference

leap ***VERB*** **leaps, leaping, leaped** or **leapt**
1 to jump high or a long way
2 to increase sharply in amount or value

leap ***NOUN*** **leaps**
1 a high or long jump
2 a sudden increase in amount or value

leapfrog ***NOUN***
a game in which each player jumps with legs apart over another who is bending down

leap year ***NOUN*** **leap years**
a year with an extra day in it (29 February)

WORD HISTORY probably because dates from March onwards *leap* a day of the week, so that a date which would fall on a Monday in an ordinary year will be on Tuesday in a leap year

learn ***VERB*** **learns, learning, learned** or **learnt**
1 to gain knowledge or skill through study or training

Alex had started learning karate when he was six years old. — *Anthony Horowitz, Stormbreaker*

2 to find out about something

A kindly farmer took me in, and from him I learned that I was in the Kingdom of Korva, on Anlap. — *Edgar Rice Burroughs, Carson of Venus*

USAGE NOTE Take care not to use *learn* to mean 'to teach'.

learned (*say* ler- nid) ***ADJECTIVE***
a learned person has gained a lot of knowledge through study or training

learner ***NOUN*** **learners**
a person who is learning something, especially how to drive a car

learning ***NOUN***
knowledge obtained by study

lease ***NOUN*** **leases**
an agreement to allow someone to use a building or land for a fixed period in return for payment

a new lease of life a chance to be healthy, active, or usable again

▷ **leaseholder** ***NOUN***

lease ***VERB*** **leases, leasing, leased**
to allow or obtain the use of something by lease

leash ***NOUN*** **leashes**
a dog's lead

least ***ADJECTIVE, ADVERB***
smallest in amount or degree ♦ *the least amount of time* ♦ *the least expensive bike*

at least
1 not less than what is mentioned ♦ *It will cost at least £40.*
2 anyway

When he awoke a dragon was watching him; at least, it was staring in his general direction. — *Terry Pratchett, The Colour of Magic*

not the least bit not in the slightest; not at all

It was very late, almost midnight, but I wasn't the least bit sleepy. — *Malorie Blackman, Noughts and Crosses*

least ***NOUN***
the least amount or degree ♦ *The least I could do was to offer to drive him home.*

to say the least putting it mildly

leather ***NOUN***
material made from animal skin

▷ **leathery** ***ADJECTIVE***

leave ***VERB*** **leaves, leaving, left**
1 to leave a person or place is to go away from them or it
2 to leave a group or workplace is to stop belonging to it, or stop working there ▸▸

3 to allow something to stay where it is or as it is ◆ *You left the bedroom window open.*
4 to go away without taking something ◆ *I've left my mobile phone at home.*
5 to leave an activity or task to someone else is to let them deal with it ◆ *Leave the washing-up to me.*
6 to leave a note or message is to write, record, or say it for someone to read, hear, or be told later

to leave off (*informal*) is to stop doing something
to leave something out is to omit it or not include it

leave *NOUN*
1 permission
2 official permission to be away from work, or the time for which this permission lasts ◆ *three days' leave*

leaven (*say* lev- en) *NOUN*
a substance, especially yeast, added to dough to make it rise

leaven *VERB* **leavens, leavening, leavened**
to add leaven to dough
WORD HISTORY from Latin *levare* 'to lighten or raise'

leaver *NOUN* **leavers**
a school student in their last term of school

lechery *NOUN*
excessive sexual lust
▷ **lecherous** *ADJECTIVE*

lectern *NOUN* **lecterns**
a stand to hold a Bible or other large book or notes for reading

lecture *NOUN* **lectures**
1 a talk about a subject to an audience or a class
2 a long serious warning or reprimand given to someone

lecture *VERB* **lectures, lecturing, lectured**
to give a lecture
▷ **lecturer** *NOUN*
WORD HISTORY from Latin *lectura* 'reading, or something to be read'

led *past tense of* **lead**❶

ledge *NOUN* **ledges**
a narrow shelf or strip ◆ *a window ledge* ◆ *a mountain ledge*

ledger *NOUN* **ledgers**
an account book

lee *NOUN* **lees**
the sheltered side or part of something, away from the wind

I crawled on my belly in the lee of a stone dyke till I reached the fringe of trees which surrounded the house. — *John Buchan, The Thirty-Nine Steps*

leech *NOUN* **leeches**
a small blood-sucking worm that lives in water

leek *NOUN* **leeks**
a vegetable of the onion family, with a white bulb and long green stem

leer *VERB* **leers, leering, leered**
to look at someone in a lustful or unpleasant way
▷ **leer** *NOUN*

leeward *ADJECTIVE*
on the lee side

leeway *NOUN*
extra space or time available
to make up leeway is to make up lost time, or to regain a lost position

left❶ *ADJECTIVE, ADVERB*
1 on or towards the west when you are facing north
2 supporting or believing in socialism (SEE ALSO **right**)
▷ **left-hand** *ADJECTIVE*

left *NOUN*
the left-hand side or part of something
WORD HISTORY from Old English *lyft* 'weak'

left❷ *past tense of* **leave**

left-handed *ADJECTIVE*
using the left hand in preference to the right hand

leftovers *PLURAL NOUN*
food not eaten at a meal

leg *NOUN* **legs**
1 one of the limbs on which a person or animal stands or moves
2 the part of a piece of clothing covering a leg
3 each of the supports of a chair or other piece of furniture
4 one part of a journey

We decided to stage the journey back over two legs; the first to Cape Horn, with a crew of four; then I would sail home to Europe alone. — *Ellen MacArthur, Taking on the World*

5 each of a pair of matches played between the same teams in a round of a competition

legacy *NOUN* **legacies**
1 money or possessions left to someone in a will
2 a situation or quality passed on as a result of someone or something in the past ◆ *The conflict has left a legacy of hatred and suspicion.*

legal *ADJECTIVE*
1 lawful
2 to do with the law or lawyers
▷ **legally** *ADVERB*
▷ **legality** *NOUN*
WORD HISTORY from Latin *legis* 'of a law'

legalize *VERB* **legalizes, legalizing, legalized**
to make something legal
▷ **legalization** *NOUN*

USAGE NOTE This word can also be spelled legalise.

legate *NOUN* **legates**
an official representative, especially of the Pope

legend *NOUN* **legends**
1 an old story handed down from the past, which may or may not be true (SEE ALSO **myth**)
2 a very famous person ◆ *Elvis Presley was a legend among his fans, who adored his singing and loved his movies.*

WORD HISTORY from Latin *legenda* 'things to be read'

legendary *ADJECTIVE*
1 to do with legends, or happening in legends
2 very famous or well known in the past

leggings *PLURAL NOUN*
1 tight-fitting stretchy trousers, worn by women
2 protective outer coverings for each leg from knee to ankle

legible *ADJECTIVE*
legible writing is clear enough to read
▷ **legibly** *ADVERB*
▷ **legibility** *NOUN*

WORD HISTORY from Latin *legere* 'to read'

legion *NOUN* **legions**
1 a division of the ancient Roman army
2 a group of soldiers or former soldiers

legionnaire *NOUN* **legionnaires**
a member of an association of former soldiers

legionnaires' disease *NOUN*
a serious form of pneumonia caused by bacteria

WORD HISTORY because there was an outbreak of the disease at a meeting of the American Legion of ex- servicemen in 1976

legislate *VERB* **legislates, legislating, legislated**
to make laws
▷ **legislation** *NOUN*
▷ **legislator** *NOUN*

legislative *ADJECTIVE*
a legislative body or assembly is one that has the authority to make laws

legislature *NOUN* **legislatures**
a country's parliament or law-making assembly

legitimate *ADJECTIVE*
1 lawful
2 a legitimate child is one whose parents are married to each other
▷ **legitimately** *ADVERB*
▷ **legitimacy** *NOUN*

leisure *NOUN*
time that is free from work, when you can do what you like
at leisure having leisure; not hurried
at your leisure when you have time
▷ **leisured** *ADJECTIVE*

leisurely *ADJECTIVE*
done with plenty of time; unhurried ◆ *a leisurely stroll*

lemming *NOUN* **lemmings**
a small mouse-like animal of Arctic regions that migrates in large numbers and is said to run headlong into the sea and drown

lemon *NOUN* **lemons**
1 an oval yellow citrus fruit with a sour taste
2 a pale yellow colour

WORD HISTORY related to the word *lime*

lemonade *NOUN*
a lemon-flavoured drink

lemur (*say* lee- mer) *NOUN* **lemurs**
a monkey-like animal

lend *VERB* **lends, lending, lent**
1 to lend someone an item is to give them it to use for a short time
2 a bank or financial institution lends you an amount of money that you must repay over time, usually with an additional charge (called *interest*)
3 to give or add a quality ◆ *A series of new illustrations lend humour to the book.*
to lend a hand is to give help or assistance
▷ **lender** *NOUN*

USAGE NOTE Take care not to confuse *lend* with *borrow*, which means just the opposite.

length *NOUN* **lengths**
1 how long something is
2 a piece of cloth, rope, or wire, cut from a larger piece
3 the distance of a swimming pool from one end to the other
at length
1 after a long time
2 taking a long time; in detail
to go to great lengths is to take a lot of trouble or effort over something

lengthen *VERB* **lengthens, lengthening, lengthened**
to make something longer, or to become longer

lengthways or **lengthwise** *ADVERB*
from end to end; along the longest part

lengthy *ADJECTIVE* **lengthier, lengthiest**
going on for a long time
▷ **lengthily** *ADVERB*

a b c d e f g h i j k l m n o p q r s t u v w x y z

lenient (*say* lee- nee- ent) *ADJECTIVE*
merciful; not severe
▷ **leniently** *ADVERB*
▷ **lenience** *NOUN*

WORD HISTORY from Latin *lenis* 'gentle'

lens *NOUN* **lenses**
1 a curved piece of glass or plastic used to focus things
2 the transparent part of the eye, immediately behind the pupil

WORD HISTORY from Latin *lens* 'lentil', because a lens has a shape like a lentil

Lent *NOUN*
a time of fasting and penitence observed by Christians for about six weeks before Easter
▷ **Lenten** *ADJECTIVE*

WORD HISTORY from Old English *lencten* 'the spring'

lent *past tense* of **lend**

lentil *NOUN* **lentils**
a kind of small bean

leopard (*say* lep- erd) *NOUN* **leopards**
a large spotted mammal of the cat family, also called a panther
▷ **leopardess** *NOUN*

leotard (*say* lee- o- tard) *NOUN* **leotards**
a close-fitting piece of clothing worn for dance, exercise, and gymnastics

WORD HISTORY from J. *Leotard*, the French trapeze artist who designed it

leper *NOUN* **lepers**
a person who has leprosy

lepidopterous *ADJECTIVE*
to do with the group of insects that includes butterflies and moths

WORD HISTORY from Greek *lepis* 'scale or flake' and *pteron* 'wing'

leprechaun (*say* lep- rek- awn) *NOUN* **leprechauns**
an Irish mythological creature resembling a little old man

WORD HISTORY an Irish word meaning 'a small body'

leprosy *NOUN*
an infectious disease that makes parts of the body waste away
▷ **leprous** *ADJECTIVE*

WORD HISTORY from Greek *lepros* 'scaly', because leprosy causes white scales on the skin

lesbian *NOUN* **lesbians**
a homosexual woman

WORD HISTORY from the Greek island of *Lesbos*, home of Sappho, a poetess of around 600 BC who was said to be homosexual

lesion (*say* lee- zhon) *NOUN* **lesions**
(*Medicine*) a part of an organ or tissue which has suffered damage through injury or disease

less *ADJECTIVE, ADVERB*
smaller in amount; not so much ◆ *The new computer makes less noise than the old one.* ◆ *Sometimes it is less stressful to take the bus.*

USAGE NOTE Take care not to confuse *less* and *fewer*. You should use *fewer* when you mean 'not so many', and *less* when you mean 'not so much': *Venus has fewer craters than the Earth, and also less water.*

less *NOUN*
a smaller amount

less *PREPOSITION*
minus; deducting ◆ *She earns £30,000 a year, less tax.*

lessen *VERB* **lessens, lessening, lessened**
to make something less, or to become less

lesser *ADJECTIVE*
the lesser of two things is less or not so great as the other ◆ *the lesser evil*

lesson *NOUN* **lessons**
1 an amount of teaching given at one time
2 something to be learnt by a pupil or student
3 an example or experience from which you should learn
4 a passage from the Bible read aloud as part of a Christian church service

lest *CONJUNCTION*
(*old use*) so that something should not happen ◆ *Remind us, lest we forget.*

let *VERB* **lets, letting, let**
1 to allow somebody or something to do something ◆ *Can you let me hold the puppy?*
2 to cause someone to do something ◆ *Let us know what happens.*
3 to allow someone or something to come or go or pass ◆ *Let me out!*
4 to allow someone to use a house or building in return for payment (called *rent*)

to let someone or something be is to leave them or it alone
to let someone down is to disappoint them or fail to do what you said you would
to let something down to let down a tyre or balloon is to let the air out of it
to let someone off to let someone off is to excuse them from a duty or punishment
to let something off to let off an explosive is to make it explode
to let on (*informal*) to reveal a secret
to let up (*informal*)
1 to let up is to relax or do less work
2 pressure or work lets up when it becomes less intense

lethal (*say* **lee**- thal) ***ADJECTIVE***
deadly; causing death
▷ **lethally** ***ADVERB***
WORD HISTORY from Latin *letum* 'death'

lethargy (*say* **leth**- er- jee) ***NOUN***
extreme lack of energy or vitality
▷ **lethargic** (*say* lith- **ar**- jik) ***ADJECTIVE***
▷ **lethargically** ***ADVERB***
WORD HISTORY from Greek *lēthargos* 'forgetful'

letter ***NOUN*** **letters**
1 a symbol representing a sound used in speech
2 a written message, usually sent by post
to the letter paying strict attention to every detail

letterbox ***NOUN*** **letterboxes**
1 a slot in a door, through which letters are delivered
2 a postbox

lettering ***NOUN***
letters drawn or painted

lettuce ***NOUN*** **lettuces**
a garden plant with broad crisp leaves used in salads

leukaemia (*say* lew- **kee**- mee- a) ***NOUN***
a disease in which there are too many white corpuscles in the blood
WORD HISTORY from the Greek words *leukos* 'white' and *haima* 'blood'

level ***ADJECTIVE***
1 flat or horizontal
2 two things are level when they are at the same height or position as each other

level ***NOUN*** **levels**
1 height, depth, position, or value ◆ *Fix the shelves at eye level.*
2 a level surface
3 a device that shows whether something is level
on the level (*informal*) honest; telling the truth

level ***VERB*** **levels, levelling, levelled**
1 to make something level, or to become level
2 to aim a gun or missile
3 to level a charge or accusation at someone is to direct it towards them
WORD HISTORY from Latin *libra* 'balance'

level crossing ***NOUN*** **level crossings**
a place where a road crosses a railway at the same level

lever ***NOUN*** **levers**
1 a bar that turns on a fixed point (called the *fulcrum*) in order to lift something or force something open
2 a bar used as a handle to operate machinery ◆ *a gear lever*

lever ***VERB*** **levers, levering, levered**
to lift or move something by means of a lever
WORD HISTORY from Latin *levare* 'to raise'

leverage ***NOUN***
1 the force you need when you use a lever
2 influence over a person or group

leveret ***NOUN*** **leverets**
a young hare
WORD HISTORY from French *lièvre* 'a hare'

leviathan (*say* li- **vy**- a- thon) ***NOUN***
1 a huge sea monster

The ship lay like a stranded leviathan. Men were swarming over her, scraping away at the weed and barnacles that collect below the water line and slow a ship down. — *Celia Rees, Pirates!*

2 something of enormous size and power
WORD HISTORY from the name of a sea monster in the Bible

levitate ***VERB*** **levitates, levitating, levitated**
to rise into the air and float there
▷ **levitation** ***NOUN***

levity ***NOUN***
humorous behaviour, especially at an unsuitable time
WORD HISTORY from Latin *levis* 'lightweight'

levy ***VERB*** **levies, levying, levied**
to collect a tax or other payment by the use of authority or force

levy ***NOUN*** **levies**
an amount of money paid in tax

lewd ***ADJECTIVE***
indecent or crude
▷ **lewdly** ***ADVERB***
▷ **lewdness** ***NOUN***

lexeme ***NOUN*** **lexemes**
(*Language*) a basic lexical unit of a language consisting of one word or an idiom

lexical ***ADJECTIVE***
(*Language*) to do with the words or vocabulary of a language

lexicography ***NOUN***
(*Language*) the writing of dictionaries
▷ **lexicographer** ***NOUN***
▷ **lexicographical** ***ADJECTIVE***
WORD HISTORY from Greek *lexis* 'word'

liability ***NOUN*** **liabilities**
1 the fact of being legally responsible for something
2 a debt or obligation
3 a disadvantage or handicap ◆ *Our goalkeeper is proving a liability.*

liable *ADJECTIVE*
1 likely to do or suffer something ◆ *My daughter is very liable to colds.* ◆ *That cliff looks liable to crumble.*
2 legally responsible for something

liaise (*say* lee- ayz) *VERB* **liaises, liaising, liaised**
to act as a liaison or go-between

liaison (*say* lee- ay- zon) *NOUN* **liaisons**
1 communication and cooperation between people or groups
2 a person who is a link or go-between
3 a sexual affair, especially a secretive one
WORD HISTORY from French *lier* 'to bind'

liar *NOUN* **liars**
a person who tells lies

libel (*say* ly- bel) *NOUN* **libels**
an untrue written, printed, or broadcast statement that damages a person's reputation (SEE ALSO **slander**)
▷ **libellous** *ADJECTIVE*

libel *VERB* **libels, libelling, libelled**
to make a libel against someone
WORD HISTORY from Latin *libellus* 'little book'

liberal *ADJECTIVE*
1 giving generously
2 given in large amounts

'I believe, sir, that you have instructed Monsieur Estragon to put liberal quantities of vinegar in the salad-dressing.' — *Roald Dahl, The Butler*

3 not strict; tolerant
4 a liberal political view or politician is one that supports individual freedom and moderate political and social reform
▷ **liberally** *ADVERB*
▷ **liberality** *NOUN*

liberal *NOUN* **liberals**
a person with liberal views or principles

Liberal Democrat *NOUN* **Liberal Democrats**
a member of the Liberal Democratic political party in the UK

liberalize *VERB* **liberalizes, liberalizing, liberalized**
to liberalize a law or regulation is to make it less strict
▷ **liberalization** *NOUN*
USAGE NOTE This word can also be spelled liberalise.

liberate *VERB* **liberates, liberating, liberated**
to liberate a person or animal is to set them free
▷ **liberation** *NOUN*
▷ **liberator** *NOUN*

liberty *NOUN* **liberties**
1 freedom from control or imprisonment
2 the right to do or think as you choose
to take liberties is to behave too casually or in too familiar a way
WORD HISTORY from Latin *liber* 'free'

librarian *NOUN* **librarians**
a person in charge of or working in a library
▷ **librarianship** *NOUN*

library (*say* ly- bra- ree) *NOUN* **libraries**
1 a place where books are kept for people to use or borrow
2 a collection of books, videos, CDs, or DVDs
WORD HISTORY from Latin *libraria* 'bookshop'

libretto *NOUN* **librettos**
the words of an opera or other long musical work
▷ **librettist** *NOUN*
WORD HISTORY an Italian word meaning 'little book'

lice *plural of* **louse**

licence *NOUN* **licences**
1 an official permit to do or use or own something ◆ *a driving licence*
2 special freedom to avoid the usual rules or customs
WORD HISTORY from Latin *licere* 'to be allowed'

license *VERB* **licenses, licensing, licensed**
to give a licence to a person; to authorize someone to do something ◆ *The restaurant is not licensed to sell alcohol.*

licensee *NOUN* **licensees**
a person who holds a licence, especially to sell alcohol

licentious (*say* ly- **sen**- shus) *ADJECTIVE*
licentious behaviour is sexually immoral
▷ **licentiousness** *NOUN*
WORD HISTORY from Latin *licentiosus* 'not restrained'

lichen (*say* ly- ken) *NOUN* **lichens**
a dry-looking plant that grows on rocks, walls, or trees

lick *VERB* **licks, licking, licked**
1 to move your tongue over something
2 a wave or flame licks a surface when it touches it lightly
3 (*informal*) to defeat a rival person or team

lick *NOUN* **licks**
1 the action of licking something
2 a slight application of paint to a surface
at a lick (*informal*) at a fast pace

lid *NOUN* **lids**
1 a cover for a box, pot, or jar
2 an eyelid

lido (*say* **leed**- oh) ***NOUN*** **lidos**
a public open-air swimming pool or bathing beach
WORD HISTORY from *Lido*, the name of a beach near Venice

lie❶ ***NOUN*** **lies**
a statement a person makes that they know is untrue

lie ***VERB*** **lies, lying, lied**
1 to tell a lie or lies
2 to give a false impression ◆ *The camera does not lie.*
WORD HISTORY from Old English *leogan*

lie❷ ***VERB*** **lies, lying, lay, lain**
1 to be resting or positioned flat on a surface
2 to get into a flat or resting position

The two horses had just lain down when a brood of ducklings, which had lost their mother, filed into the barn, cheeping feebly. — *George Orwell, Animal Farm*

3 to be situated ◆ *The island lies near the coast.*
4 to remain in a particular state ◆ *The machinery lay idle.*
to let something lie is to take no action regarding it
to lie behind something is to be the real reason for it ◆ *What lies behind this announcement?*
to lie down is to have a brief rest on a bed or sofa
to lie in is to stay in bed late in the morning
to lie low is to keep yourself hidden or unnoticed
to take something lying down is to accept an insult or personal attack without protest

lie ***NOUN*** **lies**
the lie of the land
1 the features of an area

Sir Harry's map had given me the lie of the land, and all I had to do was to steer a point or two west of south-west. — *John Buchan, The Thirty-Nine Steps*

2 the way a situation is developing
WORD HISTORY from Old English *licgan*
USAGE NOTE See the note at *lay*.

liege (*say* leej) ***NOUN*** **lieges**
(*History*) a person who was entitled to receive feudal service or allegiance
WORD HISTORY from an Old French word
WORD FAMILY A **liege lord** is another word for a *liege*, and a **liegeman** is a person who was bound to give feudal service or allegiance to a *liege*.

lieu (*say* lew) ***NOUN***
in lieu instead ◆ *He accepted a cheque in lieu of cash.*
WORD HISTORY a French word meaning 'place'

lieutenant (*say* lef- **ten**- ant) ***NOUN*** **lieutenants**
1 an officer in the army or navy
2 a deputy or chief assistant
WORD HISTORY from the French words *lieu* 'place' and *tenant* 'holding'

life ***NOUN*** **lives**
1 the period between birth and death, or the period that a person has been alive
2 the state of being alive and able to function and grow
3 living things ◆ *Is there life on Mars?*
4 liveliness ◆ *This is a city full of life and charm, both by day and night.*
5 a person's biography
6 the length of time that something exists or functions ◆ *These batteries have a life of two years.*
to bring something to life is to make it active, lively, or interesting
to come to life is to become active, lively, or interesting
not on your life (*informal*) certainly not

lifebelt ***NOUN*** **lifebelts**
a ring of material that will float, used to support a person's body in water

lifeblood ***NOUN***
an influence or force that gives strength and vitality to something ◆ *Email is the lifeblood of our business.*

lifeboat ***NOUN*** **lifeboats**
a boat for rescuing people at sea

lifebuoy ***NOUN*** **lifebuoys**
a device to support a person's body in water

life cycle ***NOUN*** **life cycles**
the series of changes in the life of a living thing

life expectancy ***NOUN***
the average length of time that a particular person or animal may be expected to live

life form ***NOUN*** **life forms**
any living thing ◆ *an alien life form*

lifeguard ***NOUN*** **lifeguards**
someone whose job is to rescue swimmers who are in difficulty

life jacket ***NOUN*** **life jackets**
a jacket of material that will float, used to support someone's body in water

lifeless ***ADJECTIVE***
1 without any signs of life or living things

For a moment the place was lifeless, and then two men emerged from the path and came into the opening by the green pool. — *John Steinbeck, Of Mice and Men*

2 unconscious
▷ **lifelessly** ***ADVERB***
▷ **lifelessness** ***NOUN***

lifelike *ADJECTIVE*
looking exactly like a real person or thing

lifelong *ADJECTIVE*
continuing for the whole of someone's life
◆ *a lifelong love of reading*

lifespan *NOUN* **lifespans**
the length of someone's life

lifestyle *NOUN* **lifestyles**
the way of life of a person or a group of people

lifetime *NOUN* **lifetimes**
the time for which someone is alive

lift *VERB* **lifts, lifting, lifted**
1 to raise or pick up something
2 to rise or go upwards

> The sand flowed out, and the balloon lifted gently to clear the tower by six feet or so. — *Philip Pullman, The Subtle Knife*

3 to lift a ban or restriction is to remove or abolish it
4 (*informal*) to steal something

lift *NOUN* **lifts**
1 the action of lifting something
2 a device in a building for taking people or goods from one floor or level to another
3 a ride in somebody else's vehicle ◆ *Can you give me a lift to the station?*

lift-off *NOUN* **lift-offs**
the vertical take-off of a rocket or spacecraft

ligament *NOUN* **ligaments**
a piece of the tough flexible tissue that holds your bones together
WORD HISTORY from Latin *ligare* 'to bind'

ligature *NOUN* **ligatures**
1 a thing used in tying something, especially in surgical operations
2 (*Music*) a curved line showing that two notes are to be played or sung without a break

light❶ *NOUN* **lights**
1 radiation that stimulates the sense of sight and makes things visible
2 something that provides light, especially an electric lamp
3 a flame

to bring something to light is to make it known
to come to light is to become known
in the light of something taking it into consideration ◆ *The decision needs to be reconsidered in the light of the new evidence.*

light *ADJECTIVE*
1 full of light; not dark
2 a light colour is pale and not dark ◆ *light blue*

light *VERB* **lights, lighting, lit** or **lighted**
1 to start a thing burning
2 to begin to burn
3 to provide light for something

> Night came on, and a full moon rose high over the trees into the sky, lighting the land till it lay bathed in ghostly day. — *Jack London, The Call of the Wild*

to light up
1 to put lights on, especially at dusk.
2 to make something light or bright, or to become light
WORD HISTORY from Old English *leoht*
USAGE NOTE The usual form for the past tense and past participle is *lit*: *She lit a candle, The lamps were lit.* But when the past participle is used as an adjective before a noun or pronoun, *lighted* is more usual: *She came in with a lighted candle.*

light❷ *ADJECTIVE*
1 having little weight; not heavy
2 small in amount or force ◆ *light rain*
3 a light punishment or sentence is one that is not severe
4 a light task or light work needs little effort to do it
5 cheerful, not sad ◆ *with a light heart*
6 not serious or profound ◆ *light music*
▷ **lightly** *ADVERB*
▷ **lightness** *NOUN*

light *ADVERB*
to travel light is to travel with little luggage, or while carrying only a small load

light *VERB* **lights, lighting, lit** or **lighted**
to come to rest; to settle

> Harry's eyes ... lit first upon Professor Dumbledore, sitting in his high-backed golden chair at the centre of the long staff table. — *J. K. Rowling, Harry Potter and the Order of the Phoenix*

WORD HISTORY from Old English *liht*

lighten❶ *VERB* **lightens, lightening, lightened**
to make something lighter or brighter, or to become lighter

lighten❷ *VERB* **lightens, lightening, lightened**
to make something lighter or less heavy, or to become lighter

lighter *NOUN* **lighters**
a device for lighting a cigarette, cigar, or pipe

light-hearted *ADJECTIVE*
1 cheerful and free from worry
2 not serious

lighthouse *NOUN* **lighthouses**
a tower with a bright light at the top to guide or warn ships

lighting *NOUN*
1 lamps or other sources of light for a room, building, or street
2 the light provided by lamps or other sources of light
3 (*Drama*) a set of lights in a theatre, for shining on the scene and performers on stage

lightning *NOUN*
a flash of bright light produced by natural electricity during a thunderstorm
like lightning extremely fast

lightning conductor *NOUN* **lightning conductors**
a metal rod or wire fixed on a building to divert lightning into the earth

lightweight *NOUN* **lightweights**
1 a person who is not heavy
2 someone who has little power or influence
3 a boxer weighing between 57.1 and 59 kg
▷ **lightweight** *ADJECTIVE*

light year *NOUN* **light years**
a unit of distance equal to the distance that light travels in one year (about 9.5 million million km)

like❶ *VERB* **likes, liking, liked**
1 to think a person or thing is pleasant or satisfactory
2 to enjoy doing something ◆ *Do you like swimming?*
3 to wish to do something ◆ *I'd like to learn to swim under water.*

SYNONYMS (meaning 1) be fond of, care for, be attached to, adore; *informal* fancy; (meaning 2) enjoy, care for, appreciate, be keen on; *informal* fancy

like❷ *PREPOSITION*
1 similar to; in the manner of

Juliet snored like a drunken sailor. — *Eoin Colfer, Artemis Fowl*

2 in a suitable state for ◆ *It looks like rain this morning.* ◆ *I feel like a cup of tea.*
3 such as ◆ *She's really good at things like computers.*

like *ADJECTIVE*
similar; having some or all of the qualities of another person or thing ◆ *We are of like mind about it.*

like *NOUN*
the like of a person or thing is someone or something very similar to them ◆ *The garden was full of flowers and plants that they had never seen the like of.*

likeable *ADJECTIVE*
easy to like; pleasant

likelihood *NOUN*
the fact of being likely to happen; probability

likely *ADJECTIVE* **likelier, likeliest**
1 probable; expected to happen or be true

Grundo and I realised we were likely to get locked inside the garden. We nearly panicked. — *Diana Wynne Jones, The Merlin Conspiracy*

2 expected to be suitable or successful ◆ *a likely spot for a picnic*

liken *VERB* **likens, likening, likened**
to compare one person or thing to another ◆ *The building has a distinctive shape that has been likened to a pine cone or a gherkin.*

likeness *NOUN* **likenesses**
1 a similarity in appearance; a resemblance
2 a portrait

likewise *ADVERB*
similarly; in the same way

liking *NOUN*
a feeling that you like something

Harry, Ron and Hermione had always known that Hagrid had an unfortunate liking for large and monstrous creatures. — *J. K. Rowling, Harry Potter and the Chamber of Secrets*

lilac *NOUN*
1 a bush with fragrant purple or white flowers
2 pale purple

WORD HISTORY from Persian *lilak* 'bluish'

lilt *NOUN* **lilts**
a light pleasant rhythm in a voice or tune
▷ **lilting** *ADJECTIVE*

lily *NOUN* **lilies**
a garden plant with trumpet-shaped flowers, which grows from a bulb

limb *NOUN* **limbs**
1 a leg, arm, or wing
2 a large branch of a tree
out on a limb isolated; without any support

limber *VERB* **limbers, limbering, limbered**
to limber up is do exercises in preparation for a sport or athletic activity

limbo❶ *NOUN*
in limbo in an uncertain situation where you are waiting for something to happen

We wait by the aircraft, in a curious state of mental and physical limbo. — *Michel Palin, Pole to Pole*

WORD HISTORY the name of a place formerly believed by Christians to exist on the borders of hell, where the souls of people who were not baptized waited for God's judgement

limbo❷ *NOUN*
a West Indian dance in which you bend backwards to pass under a low bar

lime❶ *NOUN*
a white chalky substance (called *calcium oxide*) used in making cement and as a fertilizer

WORD HISTORY from Old English *lim*

lime❷ *NOUN* **limes**
1 a green fruit like a small round lemon
2 a drink made from lime juice

WORD HISTORY from Arabic *lima* 'citrus fruit'

lime❸ *NOUN* **limes**
a tree with yellow flowers

WORD HISTORY from Old English *lind*

limelight *NOUN*
in the limelight receiving a lot of publicity and attention

WORD HISTORY from *lime* (calcium oxide), which gives a bright light when heated and was formerly used to light up the stage of a theatre

limerick *NOUN* **limericks**
(*Language*) a type of amusing poem with five lines

WORD HISTORY from *Limerick*, a town in the Republic of Ireland

limestone *NOUN*
a kind of rock from which lime (calcium oxide) is obtained

limit *NOUN* **limits**
1 a line, point, or level where something ends
2 the greatest amount that is allowed ◆ *the speed limit*

limit *VERB* **limits, limiting, limited**
1 to keep something within certain limits
2 to be a limit to something
▷ **limitation** *NOUN*

WORD HISTORY from Latin *limes* 'boundary'

limited *ADJECTIVE*
kept within limits; not great ◆ *There's a fairly limited choice on the menu today.*

limited company *NOUN* **limited companies**
a business company whose shareholders would have to pay only some of its debts

limousine (*say* lim- oo- **zeen**) *NOUN* **limousines**
a large luxurious car

WORD HISTORY a *limousine* was originally a kind of hooded cape worn in *Limousin*, a district in France; early versions of the car had a canvas roof, which was reminiscent of a cape

limp ❶ *VERB* **limps, limping, limped**
to walk with difficulty because of an injury to your leg or foot

limp *NOUN* **limps**
a limping walk

limp ❷ *ADJECTIVE*
1 not stiff or firm
2 without strength or energy
▷ **limply** *ADVERB*
▷ **limpness** *NOUN*

limpet *NOUN* **limpets**
a small shellfish that attaches itself firmly to rocks

limpid *ADJECTIVE*
a liquid is limpid if it is clear or transparent
▷ **limpidity** *NOUN*

linchpin *NOUN* **linchpins**
the person or thing that is vital to the success of something

line ❶ *NOUN* **lines**
1 a long thin mark on paper or another surface
2 a row or series of people or things; a row of words
3 a length of rope, string, or wire used for a special purpose ◆ *a fishing line*
4 a railway; a railway track
5 a company operating a transport service of ships, aircraft, or buses
6 a way of doing things or behaving; a type of business
7 a telephone connection
8 several generations of a family

in line
1 forming a straight line
2 under control

in line for to be in line for an award or promotion is to be likely to receive it

in line with in accordance with

out of line behaving in an unacceptable way

line *VERB* **lines, lining, lined**
to mark paper or another surface with lines

to line up people line up when they form themselves into a line or queue

to line someone or something up
1 to line up a group of people or things is to form them into a line or lines
2 to line up a performance or surprise is to have it prepared

WORD HISTORY from Latin *linea* 'linen thread'

line ❷ *VERB* **lines, lining, lined**
to cover the inside of something with a lining

WORD HISTORY from *linen*, because it was used to line things

lineage (*say* **lin**- ee- ij) *NOUN* **lineages**
ancestry; a line of descendants from an ancestor

lineal (*say* **lin**- ee- al) *ADJECTIVE*
in the direct line of descent or ancestry

linear (*say* **lin**- ee- er) *ADJECTIVE*
1 arranged in a line
2 to do with a line or length

linen *NOUN*
1 cloth made from flax
2 items that were originally made of linen, such as shirts, bedsheets, tablecloths, and napkins

WORD HISTORY from Latin *linum* 'flax'

liner *NOUN* **liners**
a large passenger ship

linesman *NOUN* **linesmen**
an official in football and other sports who rules on whether the ball has crossed a line

linger *VERB* **lingers, lingering, lingered**
to stay for a long time, as if unwilling to leave; to be slow to leave

Robbie lingered outside for a moment in the fresh air as it washed off the hillside, bringing the scent of pines and the sea. — *Nicola Morgan, Fleshmarket*

lingerie (*say* lan- *zher*- ee) ***NOUN***
women's underwear
WORD HISTORY a French word, from *linge* 'linen'

lingo ***NOUN*** **lingos** or **lingoes**
(*informal*) a foreign language
WORD HISTORY via Portuguese from Latin *lingua* 'tongue'

linguist ***NOUN*** **linguists**
an expert in languages

linguistics ***NOUN***
the study of languages
▷ **linguistic** ***ADJECTIVE***

liniment ***NOUN***
a lotion for rubbing on parts of the body that ache; embrocation
WORD HISTORY from Latin *linire* 'to smear'

lining ***NOUN*** **linings**
a layer that covers the inside of something

link ***NOUN*** **links**
1 one of the rings or loops of a chain
2 a connection or relationship

link ***VERB*** **links, linking, linked**
1 to join things together; to connect people or things
2 to be or become connected
▷ **linkage** ***NOUN***

links ***NOUN*** or ***PLURAL NOUN***
a golf course, especially one near the sea
WORD HISTORY from Old English *hlinc* 'sandy ground near the seashore'

linnet ***NOUN*** **linnets**
a kind of finch
WORD HISTORY from an Old French word; the bird was given this name because it feeds on *linseed*

lino ***NOUN***
linoleum

linocut ***NOUN*** **linocuts**
a print made from a design cut into a block of thick linoleum

linoleum ***NOUN***
a stiff shiny material used for covering floors
WORD HISTORY from the Latin words *linum* 'flax' and *oleum* 'oil', because linseed oil is used to make linoleum

linseed ***NOUN***
the seed of flax, from which oil is obtained
WORD HISTORY from Latin *linum* 'flax'

lint ***NOUN***
a soft material for covering wounds
WORD HISTORY probably from Old French *lin* 'flax', from which lint was originally made

lintel ***NOUN*** **lintels**
a horizontal piece of wood or stone above a door or other opening

lion ***NOUN*** **lions**
a large strong flesh-eating animal of the cat family found in Africa and India
▷ **lioness** ***NOUN***
WORD HISTORY from Greek *leōn*

lip ***NOUN*** **lips**
1 either of the two fleshy edges of your mouth
2 the edge of something hollow, such as a cup or crater
3 the pointed part at the top of a jug or saucepan from which you pour things

lip-read ***VERB*** **lip-reads, lip-reading, lip-read**
to understand what a person says by watching the movements of their lips, rather than by hearing them

lip-service ***NOUN***
to pay lip-service to pay lip-service to an idea or policy is to say that you approve of it but do nothing to support it

lipstick ***NOUN*** **lipsticks**
a stick of a waxy substance for colouring your lips

liquefy ***VERB*** **liquefies, liquefying, liquefied**
to make something liquid, or to become liquid
▷ **liquefaction** ***NOUN***

liqueur (*say* lik- **yoor**) ***NOUN*** **liqueurs**
a strong sweet alcoholic drink
WORD HISTORY a French word meaning 'liquor'

liquid ***NOUN*** **liquids**
(*Science*) a substance, such as water or oil, that flows freely but (unlike a gas) has a constant volume

liquid ***ADJECTIVE***
1 in the form of a liquid; flowing freely
2 a liquid asset is one that is easily converted into cash
▷ **liquidity** ***NOUN***
WORD HISTORY from Latin *liquidus* 'flowing'

liquidate ***VERB*** **liquidates, liquidating, liquidated**
1 to liquidate a business is to close it down and divide its value between its creditors
2 to liquidate a debt is to settle or pay it off
3 (*informal*) to get rid of someone, especially by killing them
▷ **liquidation** ***NOUN***
▷ **liquidator** ***NOUN***

liquidize ***VERB*** **liquidizes, liquidizing, liquidized**
to make something, especially food, into a liquid or pulp
USAGE NOTE This word can also be spelled liquidise.

liquidizer *NOUN* **liquidizers**
a piece of kitchen equipment used to reduce solid food to a liquid or pulp

USAGE NOTE This word can also be spelled liquidiser.

liquor *NOUN*
1 alcoholic drink
2 juice produced in cooking; liquid in which food has been cooked

liquorice (*say* **lick**- er- iss) *NOUN*
1 a chewy black substance used in medicine and as a sweet
2 the plant from whose root this substance is obtained

WORD HISTORY from the Greek words *glukus* 'sweet' and *rhiza* 'root'

lisp *NOUN* **lisps**
a fault in speech in which *s* and *z* are pronounced like *th*

lisp *VERB* **lisps, lisping, lisped**
to speak with a lisp

list[1] *NOUN* **lists**
a number of names, items, or figures written or printed one after another

list *VERB* **lists, listing, listed**
to make a list of people or things

list[2] *VERB* **lists, listing, listed**
a boat or ship lists if it leans over to one side

list *NOUN* **lists**
the action of leaning over to one side

listed *ADJECTIVE*
a listed building is protected from being demolished or altered because of its historical importance

listen *VERB* **listens, listening, listened**
to pay attention in order to hear something
▷ **listener** *NOUN*

listless *ADJECTIVE*
you feel listless if you are too tired to be active or enthusiastic
▷ **listlessly** *ADVERB*
▷ **listlessness** *NOUN*

WORD HISTORY from an old word *list* meaning 'desire'

lit *past tense of* **light**[1]

litany *NOUN* **litanies**
a formal prayer with fixed responses

WORD HISTORY from Greek *litaneia* 'prayer'

literacy *NOUN*
the ability to read and write

literal *ADJECTIVE*
1 the literal meaning of a word or statement is the exact or simple meaning, without being metaphorical or exaggerating
2 a literal translation is one that translates every word exactly

WORD HISTORY from Latin *littera* 'letter'

literally *ADVERB*
really; exactly as stated ◆ *The noise made me literally jump out of my seat.*

USAGE NOTE Take care not to use *literally* in ways that can sound comical or absurd, e.g. *He was literally beside himself with rage.*

literary (*say* **lit**- er- er- i) *ADJECTIVE*
to do with literature; interested in literature

literate *ADJECTIVE*
a literate person is able to read and write

literature *NOUN*
books and other writings, especially those that are widely read and thought to be well written

terms for literature

A piece of literature can be either **fiction** (a story about imaginary characters and situations) or **non-fiction** (describing real people or events). Sometimes a writer creates a **semi-fictional** work which mixes real and imaginary situations.

Prose is non-poetic writing and is usually written in sentences and paragraphs.

Drama is writing that is meant to be performed by actors; scripts for film, radio, and television are also types of drama.

A **novel** is a long piece of fiction (a story) that is divided into separate chapters.

A **biography** is a piece of non-fiction that describes the life of a person, and an **autobiography** describes the life of the author who has written it.

An **epic** is a novel, poem, or film that deals with a lot of different characters and situations over a long period of time, or at an important time in history.

A **trilogy** is a set of three books or plays by the same author that are linked by a common theme, or that follow each other in time, such as J. R. R. Tolkien's *Lord of the Rings* trilogy.

Sometimes literature belongs to a particular **genre**, such as *fantasy*, *science fiction*, *detective fiction*, or *horror*, and uses subjects and language that are suited to that genre.

See also the panel on **terms for poetry**.

lithe *ADJECTIVE*
flexible and supple

WORD HISTORY from an Old English word meaning 'gentle or meek'

litigant *NOUN* **litigants**
a person who is involved in a lawsuit

WORD HISTORY from Latin *litigare* 'to start a lawsuit'

litigation *NOUN* **litigations**
a lawsuit; the process of carrying on a lawsuit

litmus *NOUN*
a blue substance that is turned red by acids and can be turned back to blue by alkalis

WORD HISTORY from the Old Norse words *litr* 'dye' and *mosi* 'moss', because litmus is obtained from some kinds of moss

litmus paper *NOUN*
(*Science*) paper that is stained with litmus

litmus test *NOUN* **litmus tests**
a crucial or decisive test

WORD HISTORY originally in chemistry, a test using litmus

litre *NOUN* **litres**
a measure of liquid, equal to about $1\frac{3}{4}$ pints

litter *NOUN* **litters**
1 rubbish or untidy things left lying about in a public place
2 the young animals born to one mother at one time
3 absorbent material put down on a tray for a cat to urinate and defecate in indoors
4 a kind of stretcher

litter *VERB* **litters, littering, littered**
to make a place untidy with litter

People dumped their rubbish here now. Black bags littered the area—cardboard boxes lay askew on the ground. — *Catherine MacPhail, Run Zan Run*

WORD HISTORY from Old French *litière* 'bed'

little *ADJECTIVE* **less, least**
1 small in amount or size or intensity; not great or big or much

There was very little traffic now: a car every minute or so, no more than that. — *Philip Pullman, The Subtle Knife*

2 a small amount of something ◆ *Could I have a little milk, please?*
3 slightly ◆ *I'm feeling a little tired now.*

little by little gradually; by a small amount at a time

SYNONYMS (meaning 1) small, tiny, minute, wee, teeny; (meaning 2) some, a bit of; (meaning 3) rather, fairly, slightly, somewhat, a bit

little *NOUN*
a small amount

little *ADVERB*
hardly or not at all ◆ *Little did she realize what was about to happen.*

liturgy *NOUN* **liturgies**
a fixed form of public worship used in Christian churches

▷ **liturgical** *ADJECTIVE*

WORD HISTORY from Greek *leitourgia* 'worship'

live❶ (*rhymes with* give) *VERB* **lives, living, lived**
1 to have life; to be alive
2 to live in a place is to have your home there
3 to pass your life in a certain way ◆ *Emily Dickinson lived as a recluse, dedicating herself to writing poetry.*
4 to live on something is to use it as food, or to depend on it for your living

to live something down if you cannot live down a mistake or embarrassment, you cannot make people forget it

live❷ (*rhymes with* hive) *ADJECTIVE*
1 alive
2 a live wire or connection is connected to a source of electric current
3 a live television programme is broadcast while it is actually happening, not from a recording
4 a live coal is still burning

livelihood *NOUN* **livelihoods**
a way of earning money or providing enough food to support yourself

lively *ADJECTIVE* **livelier, liveliest**
full of life or action; vigorous and cheerful

▷ **liveliness** *NOUN*

liven *VERB* **livens, livening, livened**
to make something lively, or to become lively
◆ *The match livened up in the second half.*

liver *NOUN* **livers**
1 a large organ of the body, found in your abdomen, that processes digested food and purifies your blood
2 an animal's liver used as food

livery *NOUN* **liveries**
1 a uniform worn by a servant or official
2 the distinctive colours used by a railway, bus company, or airline

WORD HISTORY from an earlier meaning 'the giving of food or clothing', from Latin *librare* 'to set free or hand over'

livery stable *NOUN* **livery stables**
a place where horses are kept for their owner or where horses may be hired

livestock *NOUN*
farm animals

live wire *NOUN* **live wires**
(*informal*) a forceful energetic person

livid *ADJECTIVE*
1 bluish-grey in colour ◆ *a livid bruise*
2 (*informal*) furiously angry

WORD HISTORY from Latin *livere* 'to be bluish'

living *NOUN*
1 the fact of being alive
2 the way that a person lives ◆ *a good standard of living*
3 a way of earning money or providing enough food to support yourself

living room *NOUN* **living rooms**
a room for general use during the day

lizard *NOUN* **lizards**
a reptile with a rough or scaly skin, four legs, and a long tail

WORD HISTORY from Latin *lacertus*

llama (*say* lah-ma) *NOUN* **llamas**
a South American animal with woolly fur, like a camel but with no hump

WORD HISTORY via Spanish from Quechua (a South American language)

a b c d e f g h i j k l m n o p q r s t u v w x y z

lo *EXCLAMATION*
(*old use*) see; behold
WORD HISTORY from an Old English word

load *NOUN* **loads**
1 something carried; a burden
2 the quantity that can be carried
3 the total amount of electric current supplied
4 (*informal*) a large amount ◆ *There was just a load of rubbish on TV last night.*
loads (*informal*) a lot; plenty

It was strange being at school again. Loads had happened to me, but school stayed just the same.
— *David Almond, Skellig*

load *VERB* **loads, loading, loaded**
1 to put a load in or on something
2 to fill something heavily
3 to load dice is to weight them on one side, so that they will land in a predictable way
4 to load a gun is to put a bullet or shell into it
5 to load a camera is to put a blank film into it
6 to enter programs or data into a computer

loaf[1] *NOUN* **loaves**
a shaped mass of bread baked in one piece
to use your loaf (*informal*) is to think or use your common sense
WORD HISTORY from Old English *hlaf*

loaf[2] *VERB* **loafs, loafing, loafed**
to spend time idly; to loiter or stand about
▷ **loafer** *NOUN*
WORD HISTORY probably from German *Landläufer* 'a tramp'

loam *NOUN*
rich soil containing clay, sand, and decayed leaves
▷ **loamy** *ADJECTIVE*

loan *NOUN* **loans**
something lent, especially money
on loan being lent ◆ *This painting is on loan from the National Gallery.*

loan *VERB* **loans, loaning, loaned**
to lend something
USAGE NOTE Some people dislike the use of this verb except when it means 'to lend money', but it is now well established in standard English.

loath (*rhymes with* both) *ADJECTIVE*
unwilling to do something

Edmund was loath to start on his voyage without again seeing the king, but no one knew where Alfred now was. — *G. A. Henty, The Dragon and the Raven*

WORD HISTORY from Old English *lath* 'angry or repulsive'

loathe (*rhymes with* clothe) *VERB* **loathes, loathing, loathed**
to feel great hatred and disgust for someone or something

She'd loathed her guitar lessons as a child, had used every excuse in the book to avoid practising.
— *Keith Gray, Warehouse*

▷ **loathing** *NOUN*
WORD HISTORY from an Old English word *lathian*, related to our word *loath*

loathsome *ADJECTIVE*
deeply disgusting and repellent; repulsive
For a while we gazed at the loathsome and still glittering creature, then pushed on fearful lest we should stumble upon more of its kind.
— *H. Rider Haggard, The Ivory Child*

lob *VERB* **lobs, lobbing, lobbed**
to hit or kick a ball in a high arc, especially in playing tennis or football

lob *NOUN* **lobs**
a lobbed ball in tennis or football

lobby *NOUN* **lobbies**
1 an entrance hall
2 a large hall in the Houses of Parliament where members of the public can meet MPs
3 each of two corridors in the Houses of Parliament where MPs go to vote
4 a group of people who contact MPs and seek to influence government policy or legislation ◆ *the anti-hunting lobby*

lobby *VERB* **lobbies, lobbying, lobbied**
to try to persuade an MP or other person to support your cause, by speaking to them in person or writing letters
▷ **lobbyist** *NOUN*
WORD HISTORY related to *lodge*

lobe *NOUN* **lobes**
1 a rounded fairly flat part of a leaf or an organ of the body
2 the rounded soft part at the bottom of your ear
▷ **lobed** *ADJECTIVE*

lobster *NOUN* **lobsters**
a large shellfish with eight legs and two long claws

lobster pot *NOUN* **lobster pots**
a basket for catching lobsters

local *ADJECTIVE*
1 belonging to a particular place or a small area ◆ *your local post office*
2 a local anaesthetic affects only the part of the body where it is applied
▷ **locally** *ADVERB*

local *NOUN* **locals** (*informal*)
1 someone who lives in a particular district
2 a pub near a person's home
3 a local anaesthetic
WORD HISTORY from Latin *locus* 'a place'

local government *NOUN*
the system of administration of a town or county by people elected by those who live there

locale (*say* loh- **kahl**) *NOUN* **locales**
the scene or locality of an event or operation

locality *NOUN* **localities**
a district or location

localized *ADJECTIVE*
restricted to a particular place ◆ *localized showers*

USAGE NOTE This word can also be spelled localised.

locate *VERB* **locates, locating, located**
1 to discover where someone or something is

'I had quite a bit of trouble locating you,' the man said to me. 'What are you doing here?' — *Diana Wynne Jones, The Merlin Conspiracy*

2 to be located in a place is to be situated there ◆ *The cinema is located in the High Street.*

WORD HISTORY from Latin *locare* 'to place'

location *NOUN* **locations**
1 the place where something is situated
2 the process of discovering or fixing the place where something is
3 (*Drama*) a film is made on location when it is made in natural surroundings and not in a studio

loch *NOUN* **lochs**
a lake in Scotland

WORD HISTORY a Scottish Gaelic word

lock❶ *NOUN* **locks**
1 a fastening that is opened with a key or other device
2 a section of a canal or river fitted with gates and sluices so that boats can be raised or lowered to the level beyond each gate
3 the distance that a vehicle's front wheels can turn
4 a wrestling hold that keeps an opponent's arm or leg from moving

lock, stock, and barrel completely

lock *VERB* **locks, locking, locked**
1 to fasten or secure something by means of a lock
2 to store something away securely or inaccessibly

The pain of losing her mother was locked away in Lirael's heart, but not so deep it could not be uncovered. — *Garth Nix, Lirael*

3 to become fixed in one place; to jam

WORD HISTORY from Old English *loc*

lock❷ *NOUN* **locks**
a clump of hair

WORD HISTORY from Old English *locc*

locker *NOUN* **lockers**
a small cupboard or compartment with a lock, where things can be stowed safely

locket *NOUN* **lockets**
a small ornamental case for holding a portrait or lock of hair, worn on a chain round the neck

WORD HISTORY from Old French *locquet* 'a small latch or lock'

locks *PLURAL NOUN*
the hair on a person's head

locksmith *NOUN* **locksmiths**
a person whose job is to make and mend locks

locomotive *NOUN* **locomotives**
a railway engine

locomotive *ADJECTIVE*
to do with movement or the ability to move ◆ *locomotive power*

▷ **locomotion** *NOUN*

WORD HISTORY from the Latin words *locus* 'a place' and *motivus* 'moving'

locum *NOUN* **locums**
a doctor or member of the clergy who takes the place of another who is temporarily away

WORD HISTORY short for Latin *locum tenens* 'person holding the place'

locus (*say* **loh**- kus) *NOUN* **loci** (*say* **loh**- ky)
1 (*Mathematics*) the path traced by a moving point, or made by points placed in a certain way
2 the exact place of something

WORD HISTORY a Latin word meaning 'a place'

locust *NOUN* **locusts**
a kind of grasshopper that travels in large swarms and eats all the plants in an area

WORD HISTORY from Latin *locusta* 'locust, crustacean'

locution *NOUN*
a person's style of speech

lodestone *NOUN* **lodestones**
a kind of stone that can be used as a magnet

WORD HISTORY from an old word *lode* meaning 'way', because it was used in compasses to guide travellers

lodge *NOUN* **lodges**
1 a small house, especially at the gates of a park
2 a porter's room at the entrance to a college or other building
3 the lair of a beaver or otter

lodge *VERB* **lodges, lodging, lodged**
1 to stay somewhere as a lodger
2 to provide a person with somewhere to live temporarily
3 to become stuck or caught somewhere ◆ *The bullet lodged in his brain.*

to lodge a complaint is to make an official complaint

WORD HISTORY from Old French *loge* 'a hut', related to our word *lobby*

a b c d e f g h i j k l m n o p q r s t u v w x y z

lodger *NOUN* **lodgers**
a person who pays to live in another person's house

lodgings *PLURAL NOUN*
a room or rooms, not in a hotel, rented for living in

loft *NOUN* **lofts**
a room or storage space under the roof of a house or barn

lofty *ADJECTIVE* **loftier, loftiest**
1 very tall, towering
2 a lofty aim or ambition is a noble or admirable one
3 a lofty attitude or manner is a very arrogant one
▷ **loftily** *ADVERB*
▷ **loftiness** *NOUN*

WORD HISTORY from an earlier meaning of *loft* meaning 'sky'

log❶ *NOUN* **logs**
1 a large piece of a tree that has fallen or been cut down; a piece cut off this
2 a detailed record kept of a voyage or flight

log *VERB* **logs, logging, logged**
to enter facts in a log
to log in or **log on** (*ICT*) to log in or log on to a computer system is to key in a command to become connected to it
to log out or **log off** (*ICT*) to log out or log off from a computer system is to key in a command to become disconnected from it

log❷ *NOUN* **logs**
(*Mathematics*) a logarithm ◆ *log tables*

loganberry *NOUN* **loganberries**
a dark red fruit like a blackberry

WORD HISTORY from H. R. *Logan*, an American lawyer who was the first to grow the fruit

logarithm *NOUN* **logarithms**
(*Mathematics*) one of a series of numbers set out in tables which make it possible to do sums by adding and subtracting instead of multiplying and dividing

WORD HISTORY from the Greek words *logos* 'reckoning' and *arithmos* 'number'

logbook *NOUN* **logbooks**
1 a book in which a log of a voyage is kept
2 the registration document of a motor vehicle

log cabin *NOUN* **log cabins**
a hut built of logs

loggerheads *PLURAL NOUN*
at loggerheads disagreeing or quarrelling

WORD HISTORY from an old word *loggerhead* meaning 'a stupid person'

logic *NOUN*
1 the science of reasoning
2 a particular system or method of reasoning ◆ *I don't really understand your logic there.*
3 the principles used in designing a computer; the circuits involved in this

WORD FAMILY *Logic* comes from the Greek word *logos* meaning 'word, speech, or reason'. Other words to do with speech and reason include *dialogue*, *epilogue*, *monologue*, and *prologue*.

logical *ADJECTIVE*
1 a logical argument or conclusion is one that follows logic and is correctly reasoned
2 in accordance with what seems reasonable or natural ◆ *That was the logical thing to do.*
▷ **logically** *ADVERB*
▷ **logicality** *NOUN*

logistics *PLURAL NOUN*
the organizing and coordinating of everything involved in a large complex operation
▷ **logistic** *ADJECTIVE*
▷ **logistical** *ADJECTIVE*
▷ **logistically** *ADVERB*

logo (*say* **loh**- goh or **log**- oh) *NOUN* **logos**
a printed symbol used by a business company as its emblem

WORD HISTORY short for *logogram*, from Greek *logos* 'word' and *gramma* 'letter' or 'piece of writing'

logogram *NOUN* **logograms**
a sign or character representing a word or phrase rather than a letter or sound, used in shorthand and some ancient writing systems

loin *NOUN* **loins**
the side and back of your body between your ribs and hip bone

WORD HISTORY from an Old French word, related to our word *lumbar*

loincloth *NOUN* **loincloths**
a piece of cloth wrapped round the hips, worn by men in some hot countries as their only piece of clothing

loiter *VERB* **loiters, loitering, loitered**
to linger or stand about idly
▷ **loiterer** *NOUN*

loll *VERB* **lolls, lolling, lolled**
1 to lean lazily against something
2 to hang loosely

Lofur's red tongue lolled down dripping over his open throat. — *Philip Pullman, Northern Lights*

lollipop *NOUN* **lollipops**
a large round hard sweet on a stick

lollipop woman or **lollipop man** *NOUN* **lollipop women** or **lollipop men**
(*informal*) an official who uses a circular sign on a stick to signal traffic to stop so that children can cross a road

a b c d e f g h i j k l m n o p q r s t u v w x y z

lollop *VERB* **lollops, lolloping, lolloped**
to move with clumsy leaps or bounds

The small rabbit came closer to his companions, lolloping on long, hind legs. — *Richard Adams, Watership Down*

lolly *NOUN* **lollies** (*informal*)
1 a lollipop or an ice lolly
2 money
3 (*Australian and New Zealand*) a boiled sweet
WORD HISTORY short for *lollipop*

lone *ADJECTIVE*
solitary; on your own

lonely *ADJECTIVE* **lonelier, loneliest**
1 sad because you are on your own or have no friends
2 solitary, without companions
3 a lonely place is one that is far from inhabited places and is not often visited or used
▷ **loneliness** *NOUN*

loner *NOUN*
someone who prefers to be alone and not to be with other people

lonesome *ADJECTIVE*
lonely

long❶ *ADJECTIVE*
1 measuring a large distance from one end to the other
2 taking a lot of time or space ◆ *a long silence*
3 lasting; going far into the past or future ◆ *a long memory*
4 of a specified distance or time ◆ *The first track on the CD is six minutes long.*
SYNONYMS (meaning 2) lengthy, prolonged, extended, extensive, long-lasting

long *ADVERB*
for a long time ◆ *Have you been waiting long?*
all day or **all night long** throughout the whole day or the whole night

All night long the Martians were hammering and stirring, sleepless, indefatigable, at work upon the machines they were making ready. — *H. G. Wells, The War of the Worlds*

as long as or **so long as** provided that; on condition that
before long soon
long ago a long time before now
no longer not any more
WORD HISTORY from Old English *lang*

long❷ *VERB* **longs, longing, longed**
to long for something, or long to do something, is to feel a strong desire for it

Harpreet was the sort of best friend I'd always longed for. We sat next to each other in class and helped each other with all our work. — *Jacqueline Wilson, Lola Rose*

WORD HISTORY from Old English *langian* 'to grow long'

long-distance *ADJECTIVE*
travelling or covering a long distance
◆ *a long-distance runner*

long division *NOUN*
(*Mathematics*) the process of dividing one number by another with all the calculations written down

longevity (*say* lon-**jev**-it-ee) *NOUN*
long life
WORD HISTORY from the Latin words *longus* 'long' and *aevum* 'age'

longhand *NOUN*
ordinary writing, contrasted with shorthand, typing, or printing

longing *NOUN* **longings**
a strong desire for something or someone

longitude *NOUN* **longitudes**
(*Geography*) the distance east or west, measured in degrees, from the Greenwich meridian
WORD HISTORY from Latin *longitudo* 'length'

longitudinal *ADJECTIVE*
1 to do with longitude
2 to do with length; measured lengthways
▷ **longitudinally** *ADVERB*

long jump *NOUN*
an athletic contest in which competitors jump as far as possible along the ground in one leap

long-range *ADJECTIVE*
1 covering a long distance or range
◆ *a long-range missile*
2 relating to a period far into the future
◆ *a long-range weather forecast*

longship *NOUN* **longships**
(*History*) a long narrow Viking warship, with oars and a sail

long shot *NOUN*
a guess or venture that is unlikely to be correct or successful

long-sighted *ADJECTIVE*
a long-sighted person can see distant things clearly but not things close to them (SEE ALSO **short-sighted**)

long-standing *ADJECTIVE*
having existed for a long time
◆ *a long-standing love affair*

long-suffering *ADJECTIVE*
a long-suffering person puts up with things patiently

long-term *ADJECTIVE*
to do with or happening over a long period of time ◆ *long-term care for the elderly*

long wave *NOUN*
a radio wave of a wavelength above one kilometre and a frequency less than 300 kilohertz

long-winded *ADJECTIVE*
a long-winded person, speech, or piece of writing talks or continues at great length and is often boring

loo *NOUN* **loos**
(*informal*) a toilet

loofah *NOUN* **loofahs**
a rough sponge made from a dried gourd
WORD HISTORY from Arabic *lufa*

look *VERB* **looks, looking, looked**
1 to use your eyes; to turn your eyes in a particular direction

Tom looked across the clutter of tables and saw the other pirates glaring at him, fingering their knives. — *Philip Reeve, Mortal Engines*

2 to face in a particular direction
3 to have a certain appearance; to seem

Gilly looked very frail, struggling to lift the full bucket from the well, but Adam resisted the thought of helping her. — *Mollie Hunter, The Thirteenth Member*

to look after someone or something
1 to look after someone is to protect them or take care of them
2 to look after something is to be in charge of it
to look down on someone is to regard them with contempt
to look for someone or something is to try to find them or it
to look forward to something is to wait eagerly for it to happen
to look into something to look into a matter or situation is to investigate it
to look out is to be careful
to look something up
1 to look up a fact or information is to search for it in a reference book or other source

But sometimes it is fun not knowing what the words mean because you can look them up in a dictionary. — *Mark Haddon, The Curious Incident of the Dog in the Night-Time*

2 a situation is looking up if it is improving
to look up to someone is to admire or respect them
SYNONYMS (meaning 1) see, observe, glance, regard, survey; (meaning 3) seem, appear; (*look after*) take care of, care for, tend, attend to, mind, nurse, watch over, supervise; (*look into*) investigate, inquire into, find out about, explore, examine; (*look out*) beware, watch out, be careful, keep your eyes open; (*look up*) find, search for, research, track down

look *NOUN* **looks**
1 the act of looking; a gaze or glance

For a moment, a dreamy, faraway look came into Mr Bohlen's eyes, and he smiled. — *Roald Dahl, The Great Automatic Grammatizator*

2 an appearance or general impression ◆ *I don't like the look of this place.*
3 the expression on a person's face

look-alike *NOUN* **look-alikes**
someone who looks very like a famous person

looking glass *NOUN* **looking glasses**
(*old use*) a mirror

lookout *NOUN* **lookouts**
1 the action of looking out or watching for something ◆ *Keep a lookout for snakes.*
2 a place from which you can keep watch
3 a person whose job is to keep watch
4 (*informal*) a person's own fault or concern ◆ *If he wastes his money, that's his lookout.*

loom ❶ *NOUN* **looms**
a machine for weaving cloth

loom ❷ *VERB* **looms, looming, loomed**
to appear suddenly; to seem large or close and threatening

Finally the coast loomed ahead of her. The old country. Éiriú, the land where time began. — *Eoin Colfer, Artemis Fowl*

loony *ADJECTIVE* **loonier, looniest**
(*informal*) mad; crazy
WORD HISTORY short for *lunatic*

loop *NOUN* **loops**
1 the shape made by a curve crossing itself
2 a length of some material, such as string, ribbon, or wire, made into this shape
3 (*ICT*) a set of instructions that is carried out repeatedly until some specified condition is satisfied

loop *VERB* **loops, looping, looped**
1 to make a length of string or other material into a loop
2 to enclose something in a loop
3 to move in the shape of a loop ◆ *The ball looped high in the air.*

loophole *NOUN* **loopholes**
1 a way of avoiding a law, rule, or promise without actually breaking it
2 a narrow opening in the wall of a castle, for shooting arrows through

loose *ADJECTIVE*
1 not tight; not firmly fixed
2 not tied up or shut in ◆ *The hunt continues for a tiger loose in South Florida.*
3 not packed in a box or packet
4 a loose translation is not literal or exact
at a loose end with nothing to do
on the loose escaped or free
▷ **loosely** *ADVERB*
▷ **looseness** *NOUN*

loose *VERB* **looses, loosing, loosed**
1 to loosen something
2 to untie or release someone or something

loose-leaf *ADJECTIVE*
a loose-leaf folder has each sheet of paper separate so that it can be removed

loosen *VERB* **loosens, loosening, loosened**
to make something loose or looser, or to become loose

loot *NOUN*
stolen things; goods taken from an enemy

loot *VERB* **loots, looting, looted**
1 to rob a place or an enemy, especially in a time of war or disorder
2 to take something as loot
▷ **looter** *NOUN*
WORD HISTORY from a Hindi word

lop *VERB* **lops, lopping, lopped**
to lop a branch or twig is to cut it off from a tree or bush

lope *VERB* **lopes, loping, loped**
to run with a long bounding stride

Young men with keen eyes and ready swords loped ahead of the straggling column, watching for danger. — *William Nicholson, Firesong*

lope *NOUN* **lopes**
a loping stride or movement
WORD HISTORY from Old Norse *hlaupa* 'to leap'

lop-eared *ADJECTIVE*
with drooping ears
WORD HISTORY from an old word *lop* meaning 'to droop'

lopsided *ADJECTIVE*
with one side lower or smaller than the other
WORD HISTORY from an old word *lop* meaning 'to droop'

loquacious (*say* lok- way- shus) *ADJECTIVE*
talkative
▷ **loquacity** (*say* lok- wass- it- ee) *NOUN*
WORD HISTORY from Latin *loqui* 'to speak'

lord *NOUN* **lords**
1 a nobleman, especially one who is allowed to use the title 'Lord' in front of his name
2 a master or ruler

the Lord in Christianity, God or Christ
the Lords the House of Lords

lord *VERB* **lords, lording, lorded**
to lord it over someone to lord it over a person or group is to behave in a superior or domineering way towards them
WORD HISTORY from Old English *hlaford* 'person who keeps the bread' (see the word history for *lady*)

lordly *ADJECTIVE* **lordlier, lordliest**
1 to do with a lord
2 proud or haughty

Lord Mayor *NOUN* **Lord Mayors**
the title of the mayor of some large cities

lordship *NOUN*
a title used in speaking to or about a man of the rank of 'Lord'

lore *NOUN*
a set of traditional facts or beliefs about a particular topic or culture ◆ *werewolf and vampire lore*

lorgnette (*say* lorn- yet) *NOUN* **lorgnettes**
a pair of glasses held on a long handle
WORD HISTORY a French word, from *lorgner* 'to squint'

lorry *NOUN* **lorries**
a large strong motor vehicle for carrying heavy goods or troops

lose *VERB* **loses, losing, lost**
1 to be without something that you once had, especially because you cannot find it
2 to fail to keep or obtain something

Eva Smith lost her job with Birling and Company because the strike failed and they were determined not to have another one.
— J. B. Priestley, An Inspector Calls

3 to be defeated in a contest or argument
4 to cause the loss of something ◆ *That one mistake lost us the game.*
5 a clock or watch loses time if it shows a time that is behind the correct one
▷ **loser** *NOUN*

to lose your life is to be killed
to lose your way is not to know where you are or which is the right path

loss *NOUN* **losses**
1 the process of losing something
2 something that has been lost

to be at a loss is not to know what to do or say

lost *past tense and past participle* of **lose**

lost *ADJECTIVE*
1 when you are lost you do not know where you are, or you cannot find your way
2 missing or strayed ◆ *a lost cat*

lost cause an idea or policy that is failing
to be lost in something to be lost in a task or activity is to be engrossed in it

lot *NOUN* **lots**
1 a large number or amount ◆ *The police will ask a lot of questions.* ◆ *We don't have a lot of time.*
2 a person's lot is their share or fate
3 an item or group of items for sale at an auction
4 a piece of land

a lot very much ◆ *You are looking a lot healthier these days.*
to draw lots is to draw cards or other objects from a set in turn in order to choose or decide something by chance
the lot or **the whole lot** everything; all

loth *ADJECTIVE*
another spelling of **loath**

lotion *NOUN* **lotions**
a creamy liquid for putting on your skin
WORD HISTORY from Latin *lotio* 'washing'

lottery *NOUN* **lotteries**
a way of raising money by selling numbered tickets which are then drawn at random, with prizes being given to people who hold the selected numbers

lotto *NOUN*
a game like bingo

lotus *NOUN* **lotuses**
a kind of tropical water lily

loud *ADJECTIVE*
1 easily heard; producing a lot of noise
2 a loud colour or pattern is gaudy or garish
▷ **loudly** *ADVERB*
▷ **loudness** *NOUN*

loudspeaker *NOUN* **loudspeakers**
a device that changes electrical signals into sound, for reproducing music or voices

lounge *NOUN* **lounges**
a sitting room

lounge *VERB* **lounges, lounging, lounged**
to sit or stand in a lazy and relaxed way

Sirius was lounging in his chair at his ease, tilting it back on two legs. — *J. K. Rowling, Harry Potter and the Order of the Phoenix*

louring (*rhymes with* flowering) *ADJECTIVE*
looking dark and threatening

The next morning dawned grey and louring. Snow was falling fast out of the heavy sky, the flakes hurrying down like dirty feathers from a leaking mattress. — *Joan Aiken, The Wolves of Willoughby Chase*

louse *NOUN* **lice**
a small insect that lives as a parasite on animals or plants

lousy *ADJECTIVE* **lousier, lousiest**
1 full of lice
2 (*informal*) very bad or unpleasant

Except for one lousy F in a class that will be of no use to me whatsoever in my future life, I'm doing pretty well. — *Meg Cabot, The Princess Diaries*

lout *NOUN* **louts**
a bad-mannered man

lovable *ADJECTIVE*
easy to love

lovage (*say* **luv- ij**) *NOUN*
a herb with leaves that are used for flavouring soups and in salads

love *NOUN* **loves**
1 great liking or affection for someone or something
2 sexual affection or passion
3 a loved person; a sweetheart
4 a score of nil in tennis
for love to do something for love is to do it for pleasure, not because you will be paid
in love feeling strong love for another person
to make love is to have sexual intercourse

WORD FAMILY Words which include 'love' in their meaning often begin with *phil-*: for example, *philanthropy* is a love of other human beings.

love *VERB* **loves, loving, loved**
1 to feel love for a person
2 to like something very much

His mother assured Roy that he would love Florida. Everybody in America wants to move there, she'd said, it's so sunny and gorgeous. — *Carl Hiaasen, Hoot*

▷ **lovingly** *ADVERB*

love affair *NOUN* **love affairs**
a romantic or sexual relationship between two people in love

loveless *ADJECTIVE*
without love

lovelorn *ADJECTIVE*
pining with love, especially when abandoned by a lover

WORD HISTORY from an old word *lorn* meaning 'abandoned'

lovely *ADJECTIVE* **lovelier, loveliest**
1 beautiful
2 very pleasant or enjoyable
▷ **loveliness** *NOUN*

SYNONYMS (meaning 1) beautiful, attractive, good- looking, exquisite, pretty, enchanting, charming, delightful; (meaning 2) pleasant, enjoyable, delightful, wonderful

lover *NOUN* **lovers**
1 someone who loves something ◆ *an art lover*
2 a person with whom someone is having a sexual relationship, but to whom they are not married

lovesick *ADJECTIVE*
longing for someone you love, especially someone who does not love you

low[1] *ADJECTIVE*
1 only reaching a short way up; not high
2 below average in importance, quality, or amount ◆ *As local governments cut back, wildlife conservation is seen as a low priority.* ◆ *a very low price*
3 unhappy

And if you've never been caught begging by someone who knew you before, you can't possibly know how low it makes you feel. — *Robert Swindells, Stone Cold*

4 a low note or voice is not high-pitched
5 a low sound is quiet, not loud
▷ **lowness** *NOUN*

low *ADVERB*
at or to a low level or position ◆ *The plane was flying low.*

a b c d e f g h i j k l m n o p q r s t u v w x y z

low² *VERB* **lows, lowing, lowed**
to moo like a cow

low-down *NOUN*
(*informal*) the true facts or relevant information

lower *ADJECTIVE, ADVERB*
less high

lower *VERB* **lowers, lowering, lowered**
to make something lower, or to become lower

Demurral lowered himself down the rope ladder at the side of the waterfall and then on to the shingle beach. — *G. P. Taylor, Shadowmancer*

lower case *NOUN*
small letters, not capitals

low-key *ADJECTIVE*
restrained, not intense or emotional ◆ *The actor has a surprisingly low-key entrance in his first appearance as James Bond.*

lowlands *PLURAL NOUN*
1 low-lying country
2 the **Lowlands** are the part of Scotland which lies south and east of the Highlands
▷ **lowland** *ADJECTIVE*
▷ **lowlander** *NOUN*

lowly *ADJECTIVE* **lowlier, lowliest**
humble
▷ **lowliness** *NOUN*

loyal *ADJECTIVE*
showing strong and constant support to a person, group, or country
▷ **loyally** *ADVERB*
▷ **loyalty** *NOUN*

loyalist *NOUN* **loyalists**
a person who is loyal to the government during a revolt
▷ **loyalism** *NOUN*

lozenge *NOUN* **lozenges**
1 a small flavoured tablet, especially one containing medicine
2 a diamond shape

WORD HISTORY from Old French *losenge*

Ltd. *ABBREVIATION*
limited (used after the name of a company)

lubricant *NOUN* **lubricants**
an oily substance used to lubricate machinery

lubricate *VERB* **lubricates, lubricating, lubricated**
to oil or grease something so that it moves smoothly
▷ **lubrication** *NOUN*

WORD HISTORY from Latin *lubricus* 'slippery'

lucid *ADJECTIVE*
1 a lucid argument or piece of writing is clear and easy to understand
2 a lucid person thinks clearly and is not confused in their mind
▷ **lucidly** *ADVERB*
▷ **lucidity** *NOUN*

WORD HISTORY from Latin *lucidus* 'bright'

luck *NOUN*
1 the way things happen without being planned; chance
2 good fortune ◆ *This crystal will bring you luck.*

luckless *ADJECTIVE*
unlucky

lucky *ADJECTIVE* **luckier, luckiest**
having or bringing or resulting from good luck

Mr Boggis ... began to get the feeling that this was going to be one of his lucky days. — *Roald Dahl, Parson's Pleasure*

▷ **luckily** *ADVERB*

lucrative (*say* loo- kra- tiv) *ADJECTIVE*
profitable; earning you a lot of money

When Dad gave up his job at Compu-soft and accepted the lucrative offer from Magna-com, he'd fulfilled a lifelong dream. — *Alan Gibbons, Shadow of the Minotaur*

lucre (*say* loo- ker) *NOUN*
(*literary*) money or profit thought of as a motive for doing something

WORD HISTORY from Latin *lucrum* 'profit'

Luddite *NOUN* **Luddites**
1 (*History*) one of a group of English workers in 1811–16 who destroyed new machinery which they thought would cause unemployment
2 a person who opposes the introduction of new technology or methods

WORD HISTORY probably named after one of the original Luddites, Ned *Lud*

ludicrous *ADJECTIVE*
ridiculous or laughable
▷ **ludicrously** *ADVERB*

WORD HISTORY from Latin *ludere* 'to play or have fun'

ludo *NOUN*
a game played with dice and counters on a board

WORD HISTORY a Latin word meaning 'I play'

lug *VERB* **lugs, lugging, lugged**
to drag or carry something heavy

lug *NOUN* **lugs**
1 an ear-like part on an object, by which it may be carried or fixed
2 (*informal*) an ear

luggage *NOUN*
suitcases and bags for holding items to take on a journey
WORD HISTORY from *lug* in the sense 'to drag'

lugubrious (*say* loo- goo- bree- us) *ADJECTIVE*
gloomy or mournful
▷ **lugubriously** *ADVERB*
WORD HISTORY from Latin *lugubris* 'mourning'

lukewarm *ADJECTIVE*
1 only slightly warm; tepid
2 lukewarm applause or a lukewarm response is not very enthusiastic
WORD HISTORY from an old word *luke* meaning 'tepid'

lull *VERB* **lulls, lulling, lulled**
1 to soothe or calm someone; to send someone to sleep
2 to give someone a false feeling of being safe

lull *NOUN* **lulls**
a short period of quiet or inactivity

lullaby *NOUN* **lullabies**
a song that is sung to send a baby to sleep
WORD HISTORY from *lull* and *bye* as in *bye-byes*, a child's word for 'bed' or 'sleep'

lumbago *NOUN*
pain in the muscles of the lower back

lumbar *ADJECTIVE*
to do with the lower back area
WORD HISTORY from Latin *lumbus* 'loin'

lumber *NOUN*
1 unwanted furniture or other goods; junk
2 (*American*) timber; wood

lumber *VERB* **lumbers, lumbering, lumbered**
1 to leave someone with an unwanted or unpleasant task
2 to move in a heavy clumsy way

Alex watched as a heavy-shouldered boy with dark hair and serious acne lumbered over to the car, paused by the window and then continued on his way. — *Anthony Horowitz, Point Blanc*

lumberjack *NOUN* **lumberjacks**
a person whose job is to cut or carry timber

luminescent *ADJECTIVE*
giving out light
▷ **luminescence** *NOUN*
WORD HISTORY from Latin *lumen* 'light'

luminous *ADJECTIVE*
glowing in the dark

Suddenly there was a flash of light, and a quantity of luminous greenish smoke came out of the pit in three distinct puffs, which drove up, one after the other, straight into the still air. — *H. G. Wells, The War of the Worlds*

▷ **luminosity** *NOUN*

lump❶ *NOUN* **lumps**
1 a solid piece of something
2 a swelling
▷ **lumpy** *ADJECTIVE*

lump *VERB* **lumps, lumping, lumped**
to lump things together is to put or treat them in a group because you regard them as alike in some way

lump❷ *VERB* **lumps, lumping, lumped**
to lump it (*informal*) is to put up with a difficult or unpleasant situation
WORD HISTORY from an old word *lump* meaning 'to look sulky'

lump sum *NOUN* **lump sums**
a single payment, especially one covering a number of items

lunacy *NOUN* **lunacies**
insanity or great foolishness

lunar *ADJECTIVE*
to do with the moon
WORD HISTORY from Latin *luna* 'the moon'

lunar month *NOUN* **lunar months**
the period between new moons; four weeks

lunatic *NOUN* **lunatics**
an insane person

lunatic *ADJECTIVE*
insane, mad
WORD HISTORY from Latin *luna* 'the moon', because formerly people were thought to be affected by changes of the moon

lunch *NOUN* **lunches**
a meal eaten in the middle of the day

lunch *VERB* **lunches, lunching, lunched**
to eat lunch
WORD HISTORY short for *luncheon*

luncheon *NOUN* **luncheons**
(*formal*) lunch

lung *NOUN* **lungs**
either of the two parts of the body, in your chest, used in breathing
WORD FAMILY Related adjectives are (*technical*) bronchial and pulmonary.

lunge *VERB* **lunges, lunging, lunged**
to thrust your body forward suddenly

Suddenly Lorek lunged at Will and cuffed him hard with his left paw: so hard that Will fell half-stunned into the snow and tumbled over and over. — *Philip Pullman, The Amber Spyglass*

lunge *NOUN* **lunges**
a sudden forward movement
WORD HISTORY from French *allonger* 'to lengthen'

lupin *NOUN* **lupins**
a garden plant with tall spikes of flowers
WORD HISTORY from Latin *lupinus*

lurch❶ *VERB* **lurches, lurching, lurched**
to stagger; to lean suddenly to one side

The giant kite lurched into a gust of wind and soared upwards, drawing a gasp of relief from the crowd. — *Geraldine McCaughrean, The Kite Rider*

lurch *NOUN* **lurches**
a staggering movement
WORD HISTORY originally a word used by sailors, of unknown origin

lurch❷ *NOUN*
to leave somebody in the lurch is to abandon them when they are in difficulty

lure *VERB* **lures, luring, lured**
1 to tempt a person or animal into a trap
2 to entice someone

lure *NOUN* **lures**
something used as a bait to lure an animal into a trap

lurid (*say* lewr- id) *ADJECTIVE*
1 in very bright colours; gaudy
2 sensational and shocking ◆ *the lurid details of the murder*
▷ **luridly** *ADVERB*
▷ **luridness** *NOUN*

lurk *VERB* **lurks, lurking, lurked**
to wait where you cannot be seen

Filch, who had been lurking unnoticed in a far corner of the Hall, now approached Dumbledore, carrying a great wooden chest, encrusted with jewels. — *J. K. Rowling, Harry Potter and the Goblet of Fire*

luscious (*say* lush- us) *ADJECTIVE*
1 having a delicious rich taste
2 luxuriant, lush

Her thick and luscious hair, piled high on her head, was held in place by one small and strategically placed diamanté clip. — *Anne Fine, Madame Doubtfire*

▷ **lusciously** *ADVERB*
▷ **lusciousness** *NOUN*

lush *ADJECTIVE*
growing thickly and strongly

The girls from the edge of the desert were fascinated by the lush green pastures and bracken that grew thick and high beside the road. — *Doris Pilkington, Rabbit Proof Fence*

▷ **lushly** *ADVERB*
▷ **lushness** *NOUN*

lust *NOUN* **lusts**
powerful desire, especially sexual desire
▷ **lustful** *ADJECTIVE*

lust *VERB* **lusts, lusting, lusted**
1 to lust after a person is to feel a powerful sexual desire for them
2 to lust after a position or power is to want it very deeply
WORD HISTORY an Old English word meaning 'pleasure'

lustre *NOUN*
brightness or brilliance

The Nautilus had put on full speed. All the quiet lustre of the ice-walls was at once changed into flashes of lightning. — *Jules Verne, 20,000 Leagues Under the Sea*

▷ **lustrous** *ADJECTIVE*
WORD HISTORY from Latin *lustrare* 'to illuminate'

lusty *ADJECTIVE* **lustier, lustiest**
strong and vigorous
▷ **lustily** *ADVERB*
▷ **lustiness** *NOUN*
WORD HISTORY from an earlier meaning 'lively and cheerful', related to *lust*

lute *NOUN* **lutes**
a stringed musical instrument with a pear-shaped body and rounded back, popular in the 14th-17th centuries
WORD HISTORY via Old French from Arabic *al-'ūd*
WORD FAMILY A lutenist is a musician who plays the lute.

luxuriant *ADJECTIVE*
growing abundantly
USAGE NOTE Take care not to confuse this word with *luxurious*.

luxuriate *VERB* **luxuriates, luxuriating, luxuriated**
to luxuriate in something is to enjoy it as a luxury ◆ *We've been luxuriating in the warm sunshine.*

luxurious *ADJECTIVE*
full of luxury; expensive and comfortable
▷ **luxuriously** *ADVERB*
USAGE NOTE Take care not to confuse this word with *luxuriant*.

luxury *NOUN* **luxuries**
1 something expensive that you enjoy but do not really need
2 expensive and comfortable surroundings

Sara's comfortable sitting room seemed a bower of luxury to the scullery maid, though it was, in fact, merely a nice, bright little room. — *Frances Hodgson Burnett, A Little Princess*

WORD HISTORY from Latin *luxus* 'plenty'

lychee (*say* ly- chi) *NOUN* **lychees**
a small fruit with a sweet white scented pulp and a large stone in a thin brown shell, originally grown in China

lychgate *NOUN* **lychgates**
a churchyard gate with a roof over it
WORD HISTORY from Old English *lic* 'corpse', because the coffin-bearers would shelter there until it was time to enter the church

Lycra *NOUN*
(*trademark*) a thin stretchy material used especially for sports clothing

lying *present participle of* **lie❶** and **lie❷**

lymph (*say* limf) *NOUN*
a colourless fluid from the flesh or organs of the body, containing white blood cells
▷ **lymphatic** *ADJECTIVE*
WORD HISTORY from Latin *lympha* 'water'

lynch *VERB* **lynches, lynching, lynched**
a group of people lynch someone if they execute them without a proper trial, especially by hanging them
WORD HISTORY after William *Lynch*, an American judge who allowed this kind of punishment in about 1780

lynx *NOUN* **lynxes**
a wild animal like a very large cat with thick fur and very sharp sight
WORD HISTORY from Greek *lunx*

lyre *NOUN* **lyres**
an ancient musical instrument like a small harp
WORD HISTORY from Greek *lura*

lyric (*say* **li**- rik) *NOUN* **lyrics**
1 a short poem that expresses the poet's feelings
2 (*Music*) lyrics are the words of a popular song
WORD HISTORY from Greek *lurikos* 'to be sung to the lyre'

lyrical *ADJECTIVE*
1 like a song
2 expressing poetic feelings
3 expressing yourself enthusiastically
▷ **lyrically** *ADVERB*

a b c d e f g h i j k l m n o p q r s t u v w x y z

Mm

MA *ABBREVIATION*
Master of Arts

ma *NOUN*
(*informal*) a person's mother

ma'am (*say* mam) *NOUN*
a polite form of address to a woman, short for *madam*

mac *NOUN* **macs**
(*informal*) a raincoat
WORD HISTORY short for *mackintosh*

macabre (*say* mak- **ah**br) *ADJECTIVE*
a macabre scene or idea is strange and horrible because it is connected with death or injury

macadam *NOUN*
layers of broken stone rolled flat to make a firm road surface
▷ **macadamized** or **macadamised** *ADJECTIVE*
WORD HISTORY named after a Scottish engineer, J. *McAdam*, who first made roads in this way

macaroni *NOUN*
pasta in the form of short narrow tubes

macaroon *NOUN* **macaroons**
a small sweet cake or biscuit made with ground almonds

macaw (*say* ma- **kaw**) *NOUN* **macaws**
a brightly coloured parrot from Central and South America

mace *NOUN* **maces**
an ornamental staff carried or placed in front of an official

mach number (*say* mahk) *NOUN*
the ratio of the speed of a moving object to the speed of sound. Mach one is the speed of sound, mach two is twice the speed of sound, and so on.
WORD HISTORY named after the Austrian scientist Ernst *Mach* (1838–1916)

machete (*say* mash- **et**- ee) *NOUN* **machetes**
a broad heavy knife used as a tool or weapon
WORD HISTORY a Spanish word, from *macho* 'hammer'

machiavellian (*say* mak- ee- a- **vel**- ee- an) *ADJECTIVE*
very cunning or deceitful in your dealings
WORD HISTORY named after an Italian statesman, Niccolo dei *Machiavelli* (1469–1527), who wrote a political book that recommended unscrupulous methods

machinations (*say* mash- in- ay- shonz) *PLURAL NOUN*
clever schemes or plots

machine *NOUN* **machines**
a device with parts that work together to perform a particular task
WORD FAMILY A related adjective is mechanical.

machine *VERB* **machines, machining, machined**
(*D & T*) to make something with a machine

machine gun *NOUN* **machine guns**
an automatic gun that fires bullets rapidly and continuously

machine-readable *ADJECTIVE*
(*ICT*) machine-readable data is in a form that a computer can process

machinery *NOUN*
1 machines, or the moving parts of a machine
2 an organized system for doing something ◆ *There is an elaborate machinery of consultation and negotiation.*

macho (*say* **mach**- oh) *ADJECTIVE*
showing off masculine strength

mackerel *NOUN* **mackerel**
a sea fish used as food

mackintosh *NOUN* **mackintoshes**
a raincoat
WORD HISTORY named after C. *Macintosh*, the Scottish inventor of a waterproof material used for making coats

mad *ADJECTIVE* **madder, maddest**
1 having something wrong with the mind; insane
2 extremely foolish
3 to be mad about something is to be very enthusiastic about it
4 (*informal*) very excited or annoyed
like mad (*informal*) with great speed, energy, or enthusiasm
▷ **madness** *NOUN*

madam *NOUN*
a word used when speaking politely to a woman ◆ *Can I help you, madam?*

madcap *ADJECTIVE*
foolish and rash ◆ *Think before you embark on any more madcap escapades.*

mad cow disease *NOUN*
a name for BSE

madden *VERB* **maddens, maddening, maddened**
to make a person mad or angry
▷ **maddening** *ADJECTIVE*

madly *ADVERB*
extremely; very much ◆ *She was madly in love with him.*

madman *NOUN* **madmen**
someone who is mad

madonna *NOUN* **madonnas**
a picture or statue of the Virgin Mary

madrigal *NOUN* **madrigals**
an unaccompanied song for several voices singing different parts together

maelstrom (*say* **mayl**- strom) *NOUN* **maelstroms**
1 a large whirlpool
2 a state of great confusion

WORD HISTORY originally the name of a whirlpool off the Norwegian coast, from Dutch *malen* 'whirl' and *stroom* 'stream'

maestro (*say* **my**- stroh) *NOUN* **maestros**
a master, especially a musician

mafia *NOUN*
1 a large organization of criminals in Italy, Sicily, and the USA
2 any group of people who act together in a sinister way

magazine *NOUN* **magazines**
1 a paper-covered publication that is published at regular intervals, with articles, stories, or features by several writers
2 the part of a gun that holds the cartridges
3 a store for weapons and ammunition or for explosives
4 a device that holds film for a camera or slides for a projector

WORD HISTORY from Arabic *makhazin* 'storehouses', the original meaning in English. It then came to mean 'a store for weapons and ammunition' and later the part of a gun.

magenta (*say* ma- **jen**- ta) *NOUN*
a colour between bright red and purple

WORD HISTORY named after *Magenta*, a town in north Italy where Napoleon III of France won a battle in 1859, the year in which the dye was first developed

maggot *NOUN* **maggots**
the larva of some kinds of fly
▷ **maggoty** *ADJECTIVE*

Magi (*say* **mayj**- eye) *PLURAL NOUN*
the three wise men from the East who brought offerings to the infant Jesus at Bethlehem

WORD HISTORY from Old Persian *magus* originally meaning 'priest' and later 'astrologer' or 'wizard'

magic *NOUN*
1 the art of making apparently impossible things happen by a mysterious or supernatural power
2 mysterious tricks performed for entertainment
3 a mysterious and enchanting quality that a particular place or time has ◆ *reconstructing the magic of past decades*
▷ **magic** *ADJECTIVE*

magical
1 to do with magic, or using magic
2 wonderful or marvellous ◆ *You'll sit on palm-fringed beaches watching magical sunsets.*
▷ **magically** *ADVERB*

magician *NOUN* **magicians**
1 a person who does magic tricks
2 a wizard

magisterial *ADJECTIVE*
1 to do with a magistrate
2 having or showing authority; masterful

magistrate *NOUN* **magistrates**
an official who hears and judges minor cases in a local law court
▷ **magistracy** *NOUN*

magma *NOUN*
a molten substance under the earth's crust

magnanimous (*say* mag- **nan**- im- us) *ADJECTIVE*
generous and forgiving; not mean or petty
▷ **magnanimously** *ADVERB*
▷ **magnanimity** *NOUN*

magnate *NOUN* **magnates**
a wealthy influential person, especially in business

magnesia *NOUN*
a white powder that is a compound of magnesium, used in medicine

magnesium *NOUN*
a silvery-white metal that burns with a very bright flame

magnet *NOUN* **magnets**
a piece of iron or steel that can attract iron and that points north and south when it is hung up

WORD HISTORY from Greek *magnes lithos*, literally 'stone of Magnesia', an ancient city in Asia Minor (modern Turkey) where many minerals were mined, including stones which attracted iron

magnetic *ADJECTIVE*
1 having or using the powers of a magnet
2 having the power to attract people ◆ *The part suited his magnetic acting style.*
▷ **magnetically** *ADVERB*

magnetic tape *NOUN* **magnetic tapes**
a plastic strip coated with a magnetic substance for recording sound or pictures or storing computer data

magnetism *NOUN*
1 the properties and effects of magnetic substances
2 great personal charm and attraction

magnetize *VERB* **magnetizes, magnetizing, magnetized**
1 to make a substance into a magnet
2 to attract or fascinate someone strongly
▷ **magnetization** *NOUN*

USAGE NOTE This word can also be spelled magnetise.

magneto (*say* mag- **neet**- oh) *NOUN* **magnetos**
a small electric generator using magnets

magnificent *ADJECTIVE*
1 grand or splendid
2 very good; excellent
▷ **magnificently** *ADVERB*
▷ **magnificence** *NOUN*

magnify *VERB* **magnifies, magnifying, magnified**
1 to make something look bigger than it really is, as a lens or microscope does
2 to exaggerate something
▷ **magnification** *NOUN*
▷ **magnifier** *NOUN*

magnifying glass *NOUN* **magnifying glasses**
a lens that magnifies things

magnitude *NOUN* **magnitudes**
1 size or extent
2 great importance

magnolia *NOUN* **magnolias**
a tree with large white or pale-pink flowers

WORD HISTORY named after a 17th-century French botanist, P. *Magnol*

magnum *NOUN* **magnums**
a large wine bottle of about twice the standard size (about 1.5 litres)

magpie *NOUN* **magpies**
a large bird with a long tail and black and white feathers, related to the crow

WORD HISTORY originally called *pie*: the name *Mag* (short for *Margaret*) was added later, rather like Jenny Wren and other familiar names for birds

maharajah *NOUN* **maharajahs**
the title of certain Indian princes

mah-jong *NOUN*
a Chinese game for four people, played with pieces called *tiles*

mahogany *NOUN*
a hard brown wood

maid *NOUN* **maids**
1 a female servant in a house
2 (*old use*) a girl

maiden *NOUN* **maidens**
(*old use*) a girl
▷ **maidenhood** *NOUN*

maiden *ADJECTIVE*
1 a maiden aunt is one who is not married
2 a ship's maiden voyage is its first voyage after being built

maiden name *NOUN* **maiden names**
a woman's family name before she marries

maiden over *NOUN* **maiden overs**
a cricket over in which no runs are scored

maidservant *NOUN* **maidservants**
(*old use*) a female servant in a house

mail❶ *NOUN*
letters and parcels sent by post

mail *VERB* **mails, mailing, mailed**
to send something by post

mail❷ *NOUN*
armour made of metal rings joined together

mailing list *NOUN* **mailing lists**
a list of names and addresses of people to whom an organization sends information from time to time

mail order *NOUN*
a system for buying and selling goods by post

maim *VERB* **maims, maiming, maimed**
to injure a person so that part of their body is made useless

main *ADJECTIVE*
largest or most important

main *NOUN*
1 the main pipe or cable in a public system carrying water, gas, or (usually called **mains**) electricity
2 (*old use*) the seas ◆ *Drake sailed the Spanish main.*

in the main for the most part; on the whole

main clause *NOUN* **main clauses**
a clause containing a verb, which makes complete sense by itself and can be used as a complete sentence (SEE ALSO **subordinate clause**)

mainframe *NOUN* **mainframes**
a large powerful computer that many users can access at the same time

mainland *NOUN*
the main part of a country or continent, without the islands round it

mainly *ADVERB*
1 chiefly or principally
2 almost completely
3 usually or typically

mainmast *NOUN* **mainmasts**
the tallest and most important mast on a ship

mainstay *NOUN*
the chief support or main part

mainstream *NOUN*
the most widely accepted ideas or activities ◆ *Music should be part of the mainstream of education.*

maintain *VERB* **maintains, maintaining, maintained**
1 to cause something to continue; to keep something in existence
2 to keep a thing in good condition
3 to provide money for a person to live on
4 to state that something is true

maintenance *NOUN*
1 the process of maintaining or keeping something in good condition
2 money for food and clothing
3 money to be paid by a husband or wife to the other partner after a divorce

maisonette *NOUN* **maisonettes**
1 a small house
2 part of a house used as a separate dwelling

maize *NOUN*
a tall kind of corn with large seeds on cobs
WORD HISTORY via French and Spanish from Taino (a South American language)

majestic *ADJECTIVE*
1 stately and dignified
2 very impressive
▷ **majestically** *ADVERB*

majesty *NOUN* **majesties**
1 the title of a king or queen
2 a majestic state

major *ADJECTIVE*
1 serious or important ◆ *Her husband had to go into hospital for a major operation.*
2 greater or more important ◆ *Lack of money was a major part of the difficulty.*
3 (*Music*) of the musical scale that has a semitone after the 3rd and 7th notes (SEE ALSO **minor**)

major *NOUN* **majors**
an army officer ranking next above a captain

majority *NOUN* **majorities**
1 the greatest part of a group of people or things ◆ *The majority of manufacturing firms are small businesses.* (SEE ALSO **minority**)
2 the amount by which the winner in an election beats the loser ◆ *The candidate was elected with a majority of 3,000.*
3 the age at which a person becomes an adult according to the law, now usually 18

make *VERB* **makes, making, made**
1 to bring something into existence, especially by putting things together
2 to cause or compel

> Drawing makes you look at the world more closely. It helps you to see what you're looking at more clearly. — *David Almond, Skellig*

3 to gain or earn ◆ *They make a handsome profit on these deals.*
4 to achieve or reach

> That day they made forty miles, the trail being packed; but the next day, and for many days to follow, they broke their own trail, worked harder, and made poorer time. — *Jack London, The Call of the Wild*

5 to succeed in being or acting as something

> I think I would make a very good astronaut. To be a good astronaut you have to be intelligent and I'm intelligent. — *Mark Haddon, The Curious Incident of the Dog in the Night-Time*

6 to reckon ◆ *I make it nearly midnight.*
7 to result in or add up to ◆ *10 and 20 make 30.*
8 to perform an action or attempt ◆ *I'll try to make a better effort.*
9 to make a bed is to tidy it and arrange the sheets and blankets for use
10 to cause to be successful or happy ◆ *Her visit made my day.*

to make do is to manage with something that is not what you really want
to make for a place is to go resolutely towards it
to make love
1 is to have sexual intercourse
2 (*old use*) is to try to win someone's love
to make off is to go away quickly
to make something out
1 is to manage to see, hear, or understand something
2 is to claim or pretend that something is true
to make up
1 is to be friendly again after a disagreement
2 is to put on make-up
to make something up
1 is to build something or put something together
2 is to invent a story or excuse
to make up for something is to compensate for it
to make up your mind is to decide about something

make *NOUN* **makes**
a brand of goods; something made by a particular firm

make-believe *NOUN*
the action of pretending or imagining things

make-over *NOUN* **make-overs**
changes in your make-up, hairstyle, and the way you dress to make you look and feel more attractive

maker *NOUN* **makers**
the person or firm that has made something

makeshift *ADJECTIVE*
improvised or used because you have nothing better

Makeshift stalls sold vegetables and dried meat, kitchen implements, blankets and harness, books of prophecies and maps. — *William Nicholson, Firesong*

make-up *NOUN*
1 cosmetics for the face
2 the way something is made up
3 a person's character

maladjusted *ADJECTIVE*
unable to fit in or cope with other people or your own circumstances

maladministration *NOUN*
(*formal*) bad administration, especially of business affairs

malady *NOUN* **maladies**
an illness or disease

malapropism *NOUN* **malapropisms**
a comical confusion of words, e.g. using *hooligan* instead of *hurricane*

WORD HISTORY named after Mrs *Malaprop*, a character who made mistakes of this kind in a play *The Rivals* by R. B. Sheridan, produced in London in 1775

malaria *NOUN*
a feverish disease spread by mosquitoes
▷ **malarial** *ADJECTIVE*

WORD HISTORY from Italian *mala aria* 'bad air': it was once thought that the bad air around marshes caused the disease

malcontent *NOUN* **malcontents**
a discontented person who is likely to make trouble

male *ADJECTIVE*
1 belonging to the sex that reproduces by fertilizing egg cells produced by the female ◆ *A male ferret can be either a hob or a jack.*
2 consisting of men ◆ *a male voice choir*

male *NOUN* **males**
a male person, animal, or plant

male chauvinist *NOUN* **male chauvinists**
a man who thinks that women are not as good as men

malefactor (*say* **mal**- if- ak- ter) *NOUN* **malefactors**
a criminal or wrongdoer

malevolent (*say* ma- **lev**- ol- ent) *ADJECTIVE*
wishing to harm people

Inside the house lived a malevolent phantom. People said he existed, but Jem and I had never seen him. — *Harper Lee, To Kill a Mockingbird*

▷ **malevolently** *ADVERB*
▷ **malevolence** *NOUN*

malformed *ADJECTIVE*
faultily formed

malfunction *NOUN* **malfunctions**
faulty functioning ◆ *A bug in the software caused a computer malfunction.*

malfunction *VERB* **malfunctions, malfunctioning, malfunctioned**
to fail to work properly

malice *NOUN*
a desire to harm other people; spite ◆ *They were given the wrong information, through ignorance or malice.*
▷ **malicious** *ADJECTIVE*
▷ **maliciously** *ADVERB*

malign (*say* mal- y'n) *ADJECTIVE*
1 harmful and sinister ◆ *She was under some malign spell.*
2 showing malice ◆ *Their malign intentions were clear.*
▷ **malignity** (*say* mal- **ig**- nit- ee) *NOUN*

malign *VERB* **maligns, maligning, maligned**
to say unpleasant and untrue things about someone or something ◆ *There are people all too ready to malign the whole project.*

malignant *ADJECTIVE*
1 a tumour is malignant when it is growing uncontrollably
2 full of malice
▷ **malignantly** *ADVERB*
▷ **malignancy** *NOUN*

malinger *VERB* **malingers, malingering, malingered**
to pretend to be ill in order to avoid work
▷ **malingerer** *NOUN*

mall (*say* mal or mawl) *NOUN* **malls**
a shopping area closed to traffic

mallard *NOUN* **mallard** or **mallards**
a kind of wild duck of North America, Europe, and parts of Asia

malleable *ADJECTIVE*
1 able to be pressed or hammered into shape
2 easy to influence; adaptable
▷ **malleability** *NOUN*

mallet *NOUN* **mallets**
1 a large hammer, usually made of wood
2 an implement with a long handle, used in croquet or polo for striking the ball

WORD HISTORY from Latin *malleus* 'a hammer'

malnutrition *NOUN*
bad health caused by not having enough food or not having the right kind of food
▷ **malnourished** *ADJECTIVE*

malpractice *NOUN*
wrongdoing by a professional person such as a doctor or lawyer

a b c d e f g h i j k l m n o p q r s t u v w x y z

malt *NOUN*
dried barley used in brewing, making vinegar, etc.
▷ **malted** *ADJECTIVE*

maltreat *VERB* **maltreats, maltreating, maltreated**
to ill-treat someone
▷ **maltreatment** *NOUN*

mama or **mamma** *NOUN*
(*old use*) mother

mamba *NOUN*
a large poisonous African snake

mammal *NOUN* **mammals**
(*Biology*) any animal of which the female gives birth to live babies which are fed with milk from her own body
▷ **mammalian** (*say* mam- **ay**- lee- an) *ADJECTIVE*

mammary *ADJECTIVE*
(*Biology*) relating to the human female breasts or the milk-producing organs of other mammals

mammoth *NOUN* **mammoths**
an extinct elephant with a hairy skin and curved tusks

mammoth *ADJECTIVE*
very large; huge

man *NOUN* **men**
1 a grown-up male human being
2 an individual person
3 people in general ◆ *Man cannot live by bread alone.*
4 a piece used in chess or some other board game

WORD FAMILY Related adjectives are male, masculine, and virile.

man *VERB* **mans, manning, manned**
to provide a place or machine with the people to run or operate it ◆ *Volunteers will man the helplines.*

manacle *NOUN* **manacles**
a fetter or handcuff

manacle *VERB* **manacles, manacling, manacled**
to put manacles on someone

manage *VERB* **manages, managing, managed**
1 to be able to cope with something difficult

> There was no electric light upstairs and they had to manage with the candle Carrie was holding.
> — *Nina Bawden, Carrie's War*

2 to be in charge of a business or part of it, or a group of people
▷ **manageable** *ADJECTIVE*

management *NOUN*
1 the process of managing
2 managers; the people in charge

manager *NOUN* **managers**
a person who manages something
▷ **managerial** (*say* man- a- **jeer**- ee- al) *ADJECTIVE*

manageress *NOUN* **manageresses**
a woman manager, especially of a shop or hotel

mandarin *NOUN* **mandarins**
1 an important official
2 a kind of small orange

WORD HISTORY via Portuguese and Malay (a language spoken in Malaysia) from Sanskrit

mandate *NOUN* **mandates**
authority given to someone to carry out a certain task or policy

mandatory *ADJECTIVE*
obligatory or compulsory

mandible *NOUN* **mandibles**
1 a jaw, especially the lower one
2 either part of a bird's beak or the similar part in insects etc.
(SEE ALSO **maxilla**)

mandolin *NOUN* **mandolins**
a musical instrument rather like a guitar

mane *NOUN* **manes**
the long hair on a horse's or lion's neck

manful *ADJECTIVE*
brave or determined
▷ **manfully** *ADVERB*

manganese *NOUN*
a hard brittle metal

mange *NOUN*
a skin disease of dogs etc.

manger *NOUN* **mangers**
a trough in a stable for horses or cattle to feed from

mangle *VERB* **mangles, mangling, mangled**
to damage something by crushing or cutting it roughly

mango *NOUN* **mangoes**
a tropical fruit with yellow pulp

mangold *NOUN* **mangolds**
a large beet used as cattle food

mangrove *NOUN* **mangroves**
a tropical tree growing in mud and swamps, with many tangled roots above the ground

mangy *ADJECTIVE*
1 having mange
2 scruffy or dirty

manhandle *VERB* **manhandles, manhandling, manhandled**
to treat or push a person or thing roughly

manhole *NOUN* **manholes**
a space or opening, usually with a cover, by which a person can get into a sewer or boiler etc. to inspect or repair it

manhood *NOUN*
1 the condition of being a man
2 manly qualities

mania *NOUN* **manias**
1 violent madness
2 a great enthusiasm for something

maniac *NOUN* **maniacs**
a person with mania

manic *ADJECTIVE*
suffering from mania

manicure *NOUN* **manicures**
care and treatment of the hands and nails

manicure *VERB* **manicures, manicuring, manicured**
to give a manicure to the hands and nails
▷ **manicurist** *NOUN*

manifest *ADJECTIVE*
clear and obvious
▷ **manifestly** *ADVERB*

manifest *VERB* **manifests, manifesting, manifested**
to manifest a feeling or sign is to show it clearly
▷ **manifestation** *NOUN*

manifesto *NOUN* **manifestos**
a public statement of a group's or person's policy or principles

manifold *ADJECTIVE*
of many kinds; very varied

manikin *NOUN* **manikins**
1 a very small person
2 a small model of the human body, with arms and legs that can be moved

manipulate *VERB* **manipulates, manipulating, manipulated**
1 to handle or arrange something skilfully
2 to get someone to do what you want by treating them cleverly
▷ **manipulation** *NOUN*
▷ **manipulator** *NOUN*

mankind *NOUN*
human beings in general

manly *ADJECTIVE*
1 suitable for a man
2 brave and strong
▷ **manliness** *NOUN*

manner *NOUN*
1 the way something happens or is done
2 a person's way of behaving
all manner of many different kinds of things

mannerism *NOUN* **mannerisms**
a person's own particular gesture or way of speaking

manners *PLURAL NOUN*
how a person behaves with other people; politeness

mannish *ADJECTIVE*
a woman is mannish when she is like a man

manoeuvre (*say* man- **oo**- ver) *NOUN* **manoeuvres**
a difficult or skilful or cunning action

manoeuvre *VERB* **manoeuvres, manoeuvring, manoeuvred**
to move carefully and skilfully
▷ **manoeuvrable** *ADJECTIVE*

man-of-war *NOUN* **men-of-war**
a warship

manor *NOUN* **manors**
1 a manor house
2 the land belonging to a manor house
▷ **manorial** *ADJECTIVE*

manor house *NOUN* **manor houses**
a large important house in the country

manpower *NOUN*
the number of people who are working or needed or available for work on something

manse *NOUN* **manses**
a church minister's house, especially in Scotland

mansion *NOUN* **mansions**
a large stately house

manslaughter *NOUN*
killing a person unlawfully but without meaning to

mantelpiece *NOUN* **mantelpieces**
a shelf above a fireplace

mantilla *NOUN* **mantillas**
a lace veil worn by Spanish women over the hair and shoulders

mantle *NOUN* **mantles**
1 a cloak
2 a covering

Across the road behind a rampart of ancient elms lay Brookfield, russet under its autumn mantle of creeper. — *James Hilton, Goodbye, Mr. Chips*

mantra *NOUN* **mantras**
a word or phrase that is constantly repeated to help people meditate, originally in Hinduism and Buddhism

It is a magical chant, a secret mantra, and the words are blurred together, deliberately fast, so that no human can take them away. — *Julie Hearn, The Merrybegot*

WORD HISTORY a Sanskrit word meaning 'thought'

manual *ADJECTIVE*
done or used with the hands
▷ **manually** *ADVERB*

manual *NOUN* **manuals**
a handbook

manufacture *VERB* **manufactures, manufacturing, manufactured**
to make things to be sold
▷ **manufacture** *NOUN*
▷ **manufacturer** *NOUN*

manure *NOUN*
fertilizer, especially dung

manuscript *NOUN* **manuscripts**
something written or typed but not printed

Manx *ADJECTIVE*
to do with the Isle of Man

many *ADJECTIVE* **more, most**
great in number; numerous ◆ *Many people will be coming.*

many *NOUN*
many people or things ◆ *We looked for shells and found many.*

Maori (*rhymes with* flowery) *NOUN* **Maoris**
1 a member of the aboriginal people of New Zealand
2 their language

map *NOUN* **maps**
a diagram of part or all of the earth's surface or of the sky

WORD FAMILY A related adjective is (*technical*) cartographic.

map *VERB* **maps, mapping, mapped**
to make a map of an area

to map something out is to plan the details of something

maple *NOUN* **maples**
a tree with broad leaves

maple syrup *NOUN*
a sweet substance made from the sap of some kinds of maple

mar *VERB* **mars, marring, marred**
to spoil something

marabou (*say* **ma**- ra- boo) *NOUN*
a large African stork with a huge bill and large neck pouch

maraca *NOUN* **maracas**
(*Music*) each of a pair of hollowed club-shaped devices containing beans or small stones, held in the hands and shaken as a percussion instrument

WORD HISTORY from Portuguese *maracá*

marathon *NOUN* **marathons**
a long-distance running race, especially one covering 26 miles 385 yards (42.195 km)

WORD HISTORY named after *Marathon* in Greece, where the Athenians defeated a Persian army in 490 BC. There is a story that after the battle a runner named Pheidippides ran from Marathon to Athens (a distance of a little over 26 miles) with news of the victory, but this story may not be true because the only account close to the time says that he ran from Athens to Sparta (a much longer distance) before the battle to ask for help. When the Olympic Games were revived in Athens in 1896, a new long-distance road race called the *marathon* was introduced, based on the later version of the story.

marauding *ADJECTIVE*
going about in search of plunder or prey

▷ **marauder** *NOUN*

marble *NOUN* **marbles**
1 a small glass ball used in games
2 a kind of limestone polished and used in sculpture or building

March *NOUN*
the third month of the year

WORD HISTORY from Latin *Martius mensis* 'the month of Mars' (the Roman god of war)

march *VERB* **marches, marching, marched**
1 to walk with strong regular steps
2 to make somebody walk somewhere ◆ *She marched them into her office.*

▷ **marcher** *NOUN*

march *NOUN* **marches**
1 a spell of marching; a journey by marching
2 music suitable for marching to

marchioness *NOUN* **marchionesses**
the wife or widow of a marquis

mare *NOUN* **mares**
a female horse or donkey

margarine (*say* mar- ja- **reen** or mar- ga- **reen**) *NOUN*
a substance used like butter, made from animal or vegetable fats

marge *NOUN*
(*informal*) margarine

margin *NOUN* **margins**
1 an edge or border
2 the blank space between the edge of a page and the writing or pictures on it
3 the difference between two scores or prices etc. ◆ *The independent candidate won by a small margin.*

WORD HISTORY from Latin *margo* 'edge'

marginal *ADJECTIVE*
1 very slight ◆ *The difference is only marginal.*
2 a marginal note or comment is one written in the margin of a book

▷ **marginally** *ADVERB*

marginal seat *NOUN* **marginal seats**
a constituency in which an MP was elected with only a small majority and may be defeated in the next election

marigold *NOUN* **marigolds**
a yellow or orange garden flower

WORD HISTORY From *Mary* (probably the Virgin Mary), added to the word *gold* which was the name in Old English for the flower

marijuana (*say* ma- ri- **hwah**- na) *NOUN*
a drug made from hemp

WORD HISTORY an American Spanish word

marina *NOUN* **marinas**
a harbour for yachts, motor boats, etc.

The sides of the marina were lined with people, many of them waving little Kingfisher flags.
— *Ellen MacArthur, Taking on the World*

marinade *NOUN* **marinades**
a flavoured liquid in which meat or fish is soaked before being cooked

marinate *VERB* **marinates, marinating, marinated**
to soak meat or fish in a marinade

marine (*say* ma- **reen**) *ADJECTIVE*
to do with the sea; living in the sea

marine *NOUN* **marines**
a member of the troops who are trained to serve at sea as well as on land

WORD HISTORY from Latin *mare* 'sea'

mariner (*say* **ma**- rin- er) *NOUN* **mariners**
a sailor

marionette *NOUN* **marionettes**
a puppet worked by strings or wires

marital *ADJECTIVE*
to do with marriage

WORD HISTORY from Latin *maritus* 'husband'

maritime *ADJECTIVE*
1 to do with the sea or ships
2 found near the sea

marjoram *NOUN*
a herb with a mild flavour, used in cooking

mark *NOUN* **marks**
1 a spot, dot, line, or stain etc. on something
2 a number or letter put on a piece of work to show how good it is
3 a distinguishing feature
4 a sign or symbol ◆ *The next day's race was cancelled as a mark of respect.*
5 a target

on your marks! an instruction to runners to get ready to begin a race

to be up to the mark is to reach the normal or expected standard

mark *VERB* **marks, marking, marked**
1 to put a mark on something
2 to give a mark to a piece of work
3 to mark what someone says is to listen attentively to them ◆ *They'll regret it, you mark my words.*
4 to keep close to an opposing player in football etc.

to mark time
1 is to march on the spot without moving forward
2 is to occupy your time without making any progress

▷ **marker** *NOUN*

marked *ADJECTIVE*
a marked change or improvement is one that is very significant or noticeable

▷ **markedly** *ADVERB*

market *NOUN* **markets**
1 a place where things are bought and sold, usually from stalls in the open air
2 a market for a product or service is a demand from the public for it ◆ *The market for video recorders has declined considerably.*

to be on the market is to be available to buy

market *VERB* **markets, marketing, marketed**
to offer things for sale

▷ **marketable** *ADJECTIVE*

marketing *NOUN*
the branch of business concerned with advertising and selling products

marketplace *NOUN* **marketplaces**
the place in a town where a market is held or used to be held

market research *NOUN*
the study of what people need or want to buy

marksman *NOUN* **marksmen**
an expert in shooting at a target

▷ **marksmanship** *NOUN*

mark-up *NOUN*
(*ICT*) a set of codes given to parts of a text to identify or classify them in some way

marmalade *NOUN*
jam made from oranges, lemons, or other citrus fruit

WORD HISTORY via French from Portuguese *marmelo* 'quince' (from which marmalade was first made)

marmoset *NOUN* **marmosets**
a kind of small monkey

maroon ❶ *VERB* **maroons, marooning, marooned**
to abandon or isolate somebody in a deserted place; to strand

maroon ❷ *NOUN*
dark red

marquee (*say* mar- **kee**) *NOUN* **marquees**
a large tent used for a party or exhibition etc.

marquis *NOUN* **marquises**
a nobleman ranking next above an earl

marriage *NOUN* **marriages**
1 the state of being married
2 a wedding

WORD FAMILY Related adjectives are bridal, marital, matrimonial, and nuptial.

marrow *NOUN* **marrows**
1 a large gourd eaten as a vegetable
2 the soft substance inside bones

marry *VERB* **marries, marrying, married**
1 to become a person's husband or wife
2 to join two people as husband and wife; to be in charge of a marriage ceremony

marsh *NOUN* **marshes**
a low-lying area of very wet ground
▷ **marshy** *ADJECTIVE*

marshal *NOUN* **marshals**
1 an official who supervises a contest or ceremony
2 an army officer of very high rank

marshal *VERB* **marshals, marshalling, marshalled**
1 to arrange things neatly
2 to usher or escort people

marshmallow *NOUN* **marshmallows**
a soft spongy sweet, usually pink or white
WORD HISTORY called this because it was originally made from the root of the marsh mallow, a pink flower that grows in marshes

marsupial (*say* mar- **soo**- pee- al) *NOUN* **marsupials**
an animal such as a kangaroo or wallaby. The female has a pouch on the front of its body in which its babies are carried.
WORD HISTORY from Greek *marsupion* 'pouch'

martial *ADJECTIVE*
to do with war; warlike
WORD HISTORY from Latin *martialis* 'belonging to Mars' (the Roman god of war)

martial arts *PLURAL NOUN*
fighting sports, such as judo and karate

martial law *NOUN*
government of a country by the armed forces during a crisis

Martian *NOUN* **Martians**
in stories, someone who comes from the planet Mars

Martian *ADJECTIVE*
to do with the planet Mars

martin *NOUN* **martins**
a bird rather like a swallow
WORD HISTORY probably called this after St Martin of Tours, a patron saint of France who gave half his cloak to a beggar, because the bird's markings look like a torn cloak

martinet *NOUN* **martinets**
a very strict person
WORD HISTORY named after a 17th- century French army officer, Jean *Martinet*, who imposed harsh discipline on his troops

martyr *NOUN* **martyrs**
a person who is killed or made to suffer because of their beliefs, especially religious beliefs
▷ **martyrdom** *NOUN*

martyr *VERB* **martyrs, martyring, martyred**
to kill someone or make them suffer as a martyr
WORD HISTORY from Greek *marturos* 'witness', because early Christian martyrs were regarded as witnesses to their faith

marvel *NOUN* **marvels**
a wonderful thing

marvel *VERB* **marvels, marvelling, marvelled**
to be filled with wonder

marvellous *ADJECTIVE*
extremely good; wonderful

Marxism *NOUN*
the Communist theories of the German writer Karl Marx (1818–83)
▷ **Marxist** *NOUN* & *ADJECTIVE*

marzipan *NOUN*
a soft sweet food made of ground almonds, eggs, and sugar

mascara *NOUN*
a cosmetic for darkening the eyelashes

mascot *NOUN* **mascots**
a person, animal, or thing that is believed to bring good luck

masculine *ADJECTIVE*
1 to do with men
2 typical of or suitable for men
3 (in some languages) belonging to the class of words which includes the words referring to men, such as *garçon* and *livre* in French
▷ **masculinity** *NOUN*

mash *VERB* **mashes, mashing, mashed**
to crush something into a soft mass

mash *NOUN* **mashes**
1 a soft mixture of cooked grain or bran etc.
2 (*informal*) mashed potatoes

mask *NOUN* **masks**
a covering worn over the face to disguise or protect it

mask *VERB* **masks, masking, masked**
1 to cover with a mask
2 to disguise or conceal

masochist (*say* **mas**- ok- ist) *NOUN* **masochists**
a person who enjoys things that seem painful or humiliating
▷ **masochistic** *ADJECTIVE*
▷ **masochism** *NOUN*
WORD HISTORY named after a 19th- century Austrian novelist, Leopold von *Sacher-Masoch*, who wrote about masochism

Mason ***NOUN*** **Masons**
a Freemason
▷ **Masonic** (*say* ma- **sonn**- ik) ***ADJECTIVE***

mason ***NOUN*** **masons**
a person who builds or works with stone

masonry ***NOUN***
1 the stone parts of a building; stonework
2 a mason's work

masquerade ***NOUN*** **masquerades**
a pretence

masquerade ***VERB*** **masquerades, masquerading, masqueraded**
to pretend to be something ◆ *He masqueraded as a police officer.*

Mass ***NOUN*** **Masses**
the Communion service in a Roman Catholic church

mass ***NOUN*** **masses**
1 a large amount
2 a heap or other collection of matter

I lit my candle-end and stuck it on the melted mass in the candlestick. — *Dodie Smith, I Capture the Castle*

3 (*Science*) the quantity of physical matter that a thing contains
the masses the ordinary people

mass ***ADJECTIVE***
involving a large number of people ◆ *The troubles led to a mass exodus of refugees.*

mass ***VERB*** **masses, massing, massed**
to collect things into a mass

massacre ***NOUN*** **massacres**
the deliberate and brutal killing of a large number of people

massacre ***VERB*** **massacres, massacring, massacred**
to kill a large number of people deliberately

massage (*say* **mas**- ahzh) ***VERB*** **massages, massaging, massaged**
to rub and press the body to make it less stiff or less painful
▷ **massage** ***NOUN***
▷ **masseur** ***NOUN***
▷ **masseuse** ***NOUN***

massive ***ADJECTIVE***
large and heavy; huge

Your body received massive injuries; it takes time to come to any acceptance of the new situation. — *Brian Clark, Whose Life is it Anyway?*

mass media ***PLURAL NOUN***
the main media of news information, especially newspapers and broadcasting

mass production ***NOUN***
manufacturing goods in large quantities
▷ **mass-produced** ***ADJECTIVE***

mast ***NOUN*** **masts**
a tall pole that holds up a ship's sails or a flag or an aerial

master ***NOUN*** **masters**
1 a man who is in charge of something
2 a male teacher
3 a great artist, composer, sportsman, etc.
4 something from which copies are made
5 (*old use*) a title put before a boy's name

master ***VERB*** **masters, mastering, mastered**
1 to learn a subject or a skill thoroughly
2 to overcome a person or group of people; to bring them under control

masterful ***ADJECTIVE***
having control; domineering
▷ **masterfully** ***ADVERB***

master key ***NOUN*** **master keys**
a key that will open several different locks

masterly ***ADJECTIVE***
very skilful

mastermind ***NOUN*** **masterminds**
1 a very clever person
2 the person who plans and organizes a scheme or crime

mastermind ***VERB*** **masterminds, masterminding, masterminded**
to plan and organize a scheme or crime

Master of Arts ***NOUN*** **Masters of Arts**
a person who has taken the next degree after Bachelor of Arts

master of ceremonies ***NOUN*** **masters of ceremonies**
a person who introduces the speakers at a formal event, or the entertainers at a variety show

Master of Science ***NOUN*** **Masters of Science**
a person who has taken the next degree after Bachelor of Science

masterpiece ***NOUN*** **masterpieces**
1 an excellent piece of work
2 a person's best piece of work

mastery ***NOUN***
complete control or thorough knowledge or skill in something

masticate ***VERB*** **masticates, masticating, masticated**
(*formal*) to chew food

Magrat gave an imploring look to Nanny Ogg, who was masticating an apple and studying the stage with the glare of a research scientist. — *Terry Pratchett, Wyrd Sisters*

▷ **mastication** ***NOUN***

a b c d e f g h i j k l m n o p q r s t u v w x y z

mastiff *NOUN* **mastiffs**
a large kind of dog

masturbate *VERB* **masturbates, masturbating, masturbated**
to get sexual pleasure by rubbing your genitals
▷ **masturbation** *NOUN*

mat *NOUN* **mats**
1 a small carpet
2 a doormat
3 a small piece of material put on a table to protect the surface

matador *NOUN* **matadors**
a bullfighter who fights on foot

match ❶ *NOUN* **matches**
a small thin stick with a head made of a substance that gives a flame when rubbed on something rough
▷ **matchbox** *NOUN*
▷ **matchstick** *NOUN*

match ❷ *NOUN* **matches**
1 a game or contest between two teams or players
2 one person or thing that matches another
3 a marriage

match *VERB* **matches, matching, matched**
1 to be equal or similar to another person or thing
2 to put teams or players to compete against each other
3 to find something that is similar or corresponding

matchboard *NOUN* **matchboards**
a piece of board that fits into a groove in a similar piece

mate ❶ *NOUN* **mates**
1 a companion or friend
2 each of a mated pair of birds or animals
3 an officer on a merchant ship

mate *VERB* **mates, mating, mated**
1 to come together or bring two together in order to breed
2 to put things together as a pair or because they correspond

mate ❷ *NOUN, VERB*
(in chess) checkmate

material *NOUN* **materials**
1 anything used for making something else
2 cloth or fabric

material *ADJECTIVE*
1 to do with possessions, money, and other physical things rather than the mind ◆ *We enjoy our material comforts.*
2 important or relevant ◆ *The changes made little material difference.*

materialism *NOUN*
the belief that possessions are very important
▷ **materialist** *NOUN*
▷ **materialistic** *ADJECTIVE*

materialize *VERB* **materializes, materializing, materialized**
1 to become visible; to appear
2 to become a fact; to happen

It snowed steadily through the night but the feared storm did not materialise. — *Joe Simpson, Touching the Void*

▷ **materialization** *NOUN*

USAGE NOTE This word can also be spelled materialise.

maternal *ADJECTIVE*
to do with a mother
▷ **maternally** *ADVERB*

WORD HISTORY from Latin *mater* 'mother'

maternity *NOUN*
1 the state of being a mother; motherhood
2 the time when a woman is having a baby or has recently had a baby

matey *ADJECTIVE*
(*informal*) friendly and sociable

mathematics *NOUN*
the study of numbers, measurements, and shapes
▷ **mathematical** *ADJECTIVE*
▷ **mathematically** *ADVERB*
▷ **mathematician** *NOUN*

WORD HISTORY from Greek *mathema* 'learning' or 'science'

maths *NOUN*
mathematics

matilda *NOUN*
(*Australian and New Zealand*) a bundle formerly carried by a man in the bush

matinée *NOUN* **matinées**
an afternoon performance at a theatre or cinema

matins *NOUN*
the church service of morning prayer

matriarch (*say* may- tree- ark) *NOUN* **matriarchs**
a woman who is head of a family or tribe (SEE ALSO **patriarch**)
▷ **matriarchal** *ADJECTIVE*
▷ **matriarchy** *NOUN*

matrimony *NOUN*
the ceremony of marriage
▷ **matrimonial** *ADJECTIVE*

matrix (*say* may- triks) *NOUN* **matrices** (*say* may- tri- seez)
1 (*Mathematics*) a set of quantities arranged in rows and columns
2 a mould or framework in which something is made or allowed to develop

matron *NOUN* **matrons**
1 a mature married woman
2 a woman in charge of nursing in a school etc. or (formerly) of the nursing staff in a hospital
▷ **matronly** *ADJECTIVE*

matt *ADJECTIVE*
a matt colour or paint is slightly dull and not shiny

matted *ADJECTIVE*
tangled into a mass

This girl's hair was matted, her face smudged with dirt. She was wearing a red shirt and trousers much too big for her. — *Catherine MacPhail, Run Zan Run*

matter *NOUN* **matters**
1 something you can touch or see, not spirit or mind or qualities etc.
2 a physical substance ◆ *Peat consists mainly of vegetable matter.*
3 things of a certain kind ◆ *printed matter*
4 something you can think about or do ◆ *This is a serious matter.*
5 a quantity ◆ *in a matter of minutes*

as a matter of course as the natural or expected thing; routinely ◆ *I always lock my bike as a matter of course.*
as a matter of fact in fact
no matter it does not matter
what is the matter? what is wrong?

matter *VERB* **matters, mattering, mattered**
to be important

matter-of-fact *ADJECTIVE*
1 keeping strictly to the facts ◆ *It is a clear, matter-of-fact treatment of the subject.*
2 sensible and unemotional ◆ *His voice was calm and matter-of-fact.*

matting *NOUN*
rough material for covering floors

mattress *NOUN* **mattresses**
soft or springy material in a fabric covering, used on or as a bed

mature *ADJECTIVE*
1 fully grown or developed
2 adult; grown-up
▷ **maturely** *ADVERB*
▷ **maturity** *NOUN*

mature *VERB* **matures, maturing, matured**
to make mature, or to become mature

maudlin *ADJECTIVE*
sentimental in a silly or tearful way

WORD HISTORY from an old pronunciation of St Mary Magdalen (because pictures usually show her weeping)

maul *VERB* **mauls, mauling, mauled**
to injure someone by violent handling or clawing

mausoleum (*say* maw- sol- **ee**- um) *NOUN* **mausoleums**
a magnificent tomb

WORD HISTORY named after the tomb of *Mausolus*, a king in the 4th century BC in Asia Minor (modern Turkey)

mauve (*say* mohv) *NOUN*
pale purple

maverick *NOUN* **mavericks**
a person who belongs to a group but often disagrees with its beliefs or acts on his or her own

WORD HISTORY originally an unbranded calf: named after an American rancher, S. A. *Maverick*, who did not brand his cattle

maw *NOUN* **maws**
the jaws, mouth, or stomach of a hungry or fierce animal

mawkish *ADJECTIVE*
feeble and sentimental

maxilla *NOUN* **maxillae** (*say* **mak**- si- lee)
the upper jaw; a similar part in a bird or insect etc. (SEE ALSO **mandible**)

maxim *NOUN* **maxims**
a short saying giving a general truth or rule of behaviour, e.g. 'Waste not, want not'

WORD HISTORY from Latin *maxima propositio* 'greatest statement'

maximize *VERB* **maximizes, maximizing, maximized**
to make something as great, large, or effective as possible

USAGE NOTE This word can also be spelled maximise.

maximum *NOUN* **maxima** or **maximums**
the greatest possible number or amount (SEE ALSO **minimum**)

maximum *ADJECTIVE*
greatest or most

May *NOUN*
the fifth month of the year

WORD HISTORY from Latin *Maius mensis* 'the month of Maia' (the Roman goddess associated with growing)

may ❶ *AUXILIARY VERB* **may, might**
used to express
1 permission (*You may go now*)
2 possibility (*It may be true*)
3 wish (*Long may she reign*)
4 uncertainty (*whoever it may be*)

may ❷ *NOUN*
hawthorn blossom

WORD HISTORY called this because the hawthorn blooms in the month of May

maybe *ADVERB*
perhaps; possibly

mayday *NOUN* **maydays**
an international radio signal calling for help
WORD HISTORY from French *m'aider* 'help me'

mayfly *NOUN* **mayflies**
an insect that lives for only a short time, in spring

mayhem *NOUN*
violent confusion or damage ♦ *They did not want hooligans everywhere causing mayhem.*

mayn't
short for *may not*

mayonnaise *NOUN*
a creamy sauce made from eggs, oil, vinegar, etc., eaten with salad
WORD HISTORY a French word, named after Mahón on Minorca, which the French had just captured when mayonnaise was invented

mayor *NOUN* **mayors**
the person in charge of the council in a town or city
▷ **mayoral** *ADJECTIVE*
▷ **mayoress** *NOUN*

maypole *NOUN* **maypoles**
a decorated pole round which people dance on 1 May

maze *NOUN* **mazes**
a network of paths, especially one designed as a puzzle in which to try and find your way

Mb *ABBREVIATION*
megabyte(s)

MBE *ABBREVIATION*
Member of the Order of the British Empire

MC *ABBREVIATION*
master of ceremonies

MD *ABBREVIATION*
Doctor of Medicine

ME *NOUN*
long-lasting fever, weakness, and pain in the muscles following a viral infection
WORD HISTORY an abbreviation of the scientific name *myalgic encephalomyelitis*

me *PRONOUN*
the form of *I* used as the object of a verb or after a preposition

mead *NOUN*
an alcoholic drink made from honey and water

meadow (*say* med- oh) *NOUN* **meadows**
a field of grass

meagre *ADJECTIVE*
scanty in amount; barely enough ♦ *They had to manage on meagre resources.*

meal❶ *NOUN* **meals**
food served and eaten at one sitting

meal❷ *NOUN*
coarsely ground grain
▷ **mealy** *ADJECTIVE*

mealie *NOUN*
(*South African*) a maize plant or cob

First they passed the field where the mealie stalks, looking grey and parched, had managed to push their way through hard clods of earth.
— *Beverley Naidoo, Chain of Fire*

mealtime *NOUN* **mealtimes**
a regular time for having a meal

mealy-mouthed *ADJECTIVE*
too polite or timid to say what you really mean

mean❶ *VERB* **means, meaning, meant** (*say* ment)
1 to have as an equivalent or explanation ♦ *I'm not sure what this word means.*
2 to have something as a purpose; to intend something

I ran all the way to the castle and dashed up the kitchen stairs meaning to lock myself in my room. — *Dodie Smith, I Capture the Castle*

3 to show that something is likely ♦ *The cold weather could mean snow.*
4 to have something as a result ♦ *This means I'll have to leave extra early.*

mean❷ *ADJECTIVE* **meaner, meanest**
1 not generous; miserly
2 unkind or spiteful ♦ *Sending him away was a mean thing to do.*
3 poor in quality or appearance ♦ *They lived in a mean little hovel.*
no mean feat a fine achievement
▷ **meanly** *ADVERB*
▷ **meanness** *NOUN*

mean❸ *NOUN* **means**
a point or number midway between two extremes; the average of a set of numbers

mean *ADJECTIVE*
midway between two points; average

meander (*say* mee- an- der) *VERB* **meanders, meandering, meandered**
to take a winding course; to wander

The river in this countryside meandered in huge glistening curves, taking twenty miles to cover five. — *Terry Pratchett, Witches Abroad*

▷ **meander** *NOUN*
WORD HISTORY named after the *Meander*, an ancient river in Asia Minor (modern Turkey: the river is now called Menderes)

a b c d e f g h i j k l m n o p q r s t u v w x y z

meaning *NOUN* **meanings**
what something means
▷ **meaningful** *ADJECTIVE*
▷ **meaningless** *ADJECTIVE*
WORD FAMILY A related adjective is semantic.

means *NOUN*
a way of achieving something or producing a result ◆ *Use any means you can.*
by all means certainly; of course
by means of by this method; using this
by no means not at all

means *PLURAL NOUN*
money or other wealth
to live beyond your means is to spend more than you can afford

means test *NOUN* **means tests**
an inquiry into how much money or income a person has, in order to decide whether they are entitled to get help from public funds

meantime *NOUN*
in the meantime the time between two events or while something else is happening

meanwhile *ADVERB*
in the time between two events or while something else is happening

measles *NOUN*
an infectious disease that causes small red spots on the skin

measly *ADJECTIVE*
(*informal*) not adequate or generous

measure *VERB* **measures, measuring, measured**
1 (*Mathematics*) to find the size, amount, or extent of something by comparing it with a fixed unit or with an object of known size

Harry suddenly realised that the tape measure, which was measuring between his nostrils, was doing this on its own. — *J. K. Rowling, Harry Potter and the Philosopher's Stone*

2 to be a certain size ◆ *The room measures 4 metres by 5.*
▷ **measurable** *ADJECTIVE*

measure *NOUN* **measures**
1 a unit used for measuring
2 a device used in measuring
3 the size or quantity of something
4 something done for a particular purpose ◆ *The local authority will take measures to improve the library service.*

measurement *NOUN* **measurements**
1 the process of measuring something
2 a size or amount found by measuring

meat *NOUN*
animal flesh used as food
▷ **meaty** *ADJECTIVE*

mecca *NOUN*
a place which attracts people with a particular interest
WORD HISTORY from *Mecca* in Saudi Arabia, a holy city and place of pilgrimage for Muslims

mechanic *NOUN* **mechanics**
a person who maintains or repairs machinery

mechanical *ADJECTIVE*
1 to do with machines
2 produced or worked by machines
3 done or doing things without thought
▷ **mechanically** *ADVERB*
WORD HISTORY from Greek *mechane* 'machine'

mechanics *NOUN*
1 the study of movement and force
2 the study or use of machines

mechanism *NOUN* **mechanisms**
1 the moving parts of a machine
2 the way a machine works
3 the process by which something is done

mechanized *ADJECTIVE*
equipped with machines
▷ **mechanization** *NOUN*
USAGE NOTE This word can also be spelled mechanised.

medal *NOUN* **medals**
a piece of metal shaped like a coin, star, or cross, given to a person for bravery or for achieving something
WORD FAMILY The two sides of a medal are the obverse and reverse.

medallion *NOUN* **medallions**
a large medal, usually worn round the neck as an ornament

medallist *NOUN* **medallists**
a winner of a medal

meddle *VERB* **meddles, meddling, meddled**
1 to interfere
2 to tinker with something
▷ **meddler** *NOUN*
▷ **meddlesome** *ADJECTIVE*

media *plural of* **medium** *NOUN*
the media newspapers, radio, and television, which convey information and ideas to the public

medial *ADJECTIVE*
situated in the middle

median *ADJECTIVE*
situated in the middle or passing through the middle

median *NOUN* **medians**
1 a median point or line
2 (*Mathematics*) the middle number in a set of numbers that have been arranged in order. The median of 2, 3, 5, 8, 9, 14, and 15 is 8.
3 a straight line passing from a point of a triangle to the centre of the opposite side

mediate *VERB* **mediates, mediating, mediated**
to negotiate between the opposing sides in a dispute
▷ **mediation** *NOUN*
▷ **mediator** *NOUN*

medical *ADJECTIVE*
to do with the treatment of disease
▷ **medically** *ADVERB*
WORD HISTORY from Latin *medicus* 'doctor'

medicated *ADJECTIVE*
treated with a medicinal substance

medication *NOUN*
1 a medicine
2 treatment using medicine

medicine *NOUN* **medicines**
1 a substance, usually swallowed, used to try to cure a disease
2 the study and treatment of diseases
▷ **medicinal** (*say* med- **iss**- in- al) *ADJECTIVE*
▷ **medicinally** *ADVERB*
WORD FAMILY A related adjective is pharmaceutical.

medieval (*say* med- ee- **ee**- val) *ADJECTIVE*
belonging to or to do with the Middle Ages

mediocre (*say* mee- dee- **oh**- ker) *ADJECTIVE*
not very good; of only medium quality
▷ **mediocrity** *NOUN*

meditate *VERB* **meditates, meditating, meditated**
to think deeply and quietly
▷ **meditation** *NOUN*
▷ **meditative** *ADJECTIVE*

Mediterranean *ADJECTIVE*
to do with the Mediterranean Sea (which lies between Europe and Africa) or the countries round it
WORD HISTORY from Latin *Mare Mediterraneum* 'sea in the middle of land', from *medius* 'middle' and *terra* 'land'

medium *ADJECTIVE*
neither large nor small; moderate

medium *NOUN* **media** or (in meaning 2) **mediums**
1 a thing in which something exists or moves or is expressed ◆ *Air is the medium in which sound travels..* ◆ *Television is used as a medium for advertising.* (See **media**)
2 a person who claims to be able to communicate with the dead

Soon the relations would traipse in again from town and countryside to hear what the medium had to say about Pei's 'troubled spirit'. — *Geraldine McCaughrean, The Kite Rider*

medium wave *NOUN*
a radio wave of a frequency between 300 kilohertz and 3 megahertz

medley *NOUN* **medleys**
1 an assortment or mixture of things
2 a collection of songs or tunes played as a continuous piece

meek *ADJECTIVE* **meeker, meekest**
quiet and obedient
▷ **meekly** *ADVERB*
▷ **meekness** *NOUN*

meerkat *NOUN* **meerkats**
a small southern African mongoose

meet❶ *VERB* **meets, meeting, met**
1 to come together from different places ◆ *We can meet in the centre of town.*
2 to get to know someone ◆ *I met her at a party.*
3 to come into contact; to touch
4 to go to find someone when they arrive ◆ *Text me and I'll meet your train.*
5 to meet the cost of something is to pay it
6 to meet a need or obligation is to fulfil it

meet *NOUN* **meets**
a gathering of riders and hounds for a hunt

meet❷ *ADJECTIVE*
(*old use*) proper or suitable

meeting *NOUN* **meetings**
1 coming together
2 a number of people who have come together for a discussion, contest, etc.

megabyte *NOUN* **megabytes**
(*ICT*) a unit of information roughly equal to one million bytes

megalomania *NOUN*
an exaggerated idea of your own importance
▷ **megalomaniac** *NOUN*

megaphone *NOUN* **megaphones**
a funnel-shaped device for amplifying a person's voice

melamine *NOUN*
a strong kind of plastic

melancholy *ADJECTIVE*
sad; gloomy

melancholy *NOUN*
sadness or depression
WORD HISTORY from Greek *melas* 'black' and *chole* 'bile' (because black bile in the body was once thought to cause melancholy)

mêlée (*say* **mel**- ay) *NOUN* **mêlées**
1 a confused fight
2 a muddle

mellow *ADJECTIVE* **mellower, mellowest**
1 not harsh; soft and rich in flavour, colour, or sound
2 kinder and more sympathetic with age
▷ **mellowness** *NOUN*

a b c d e f g h i j k l m n o p q r s t u v w x y z

mellow *VERB* **mellows, mellowing, mellowed**
1 to make something softer or less harsh, or to become this

Something like a reluctant smile, rather rusty from long disuse, mellowed Marilla's grim expression. — *L. M. Montgomery, Anne of Green Gables*

2 a person mellows when they become more kindly with age

melodic *ADJECTIVE*
having or producing melody

melodious *ADJECTIVE*
like a melody; pleasant to listen to

melodrama *NOUN* **melodramas**
a play full of dramatic excitement and strong emotion
▷ **melodramatic** *ADJECTIVE*

melody *NOUN* **melodies**
(*Music*) a tune, especially a pleasing tune

melon *NOUN* **melons**
a large sweet fruit with a yellow or green skin

melt *VERB* **melts, melting, melted**
1 to make something liquid by heating it, or to become liquid
2 a crowd or other group melts away when it disappears or disperses slowly
3 to become more loving or gentle

melting pot *NOUN* **melting pots**
a place where people of many different races and cultures live and influence each other

member *NOUN* **members**
1 a person or thing that belongs to a particular society or group

Breakfast was, on the whole, a leisurely and silent meal, for no member of the family was very talkative at that hour. — *Gerald Durrell, My Family and Other Animals*

2 a part of something
▷ **membership** *NOUN*

Member of Parliament *NOUN* **Members of Parliament**
a person elected to represent the people of an area in Parliament

membrane *NOUN* **membranes**
a thin skin or similar covering
▷ **membranous** *ADJECTIVE*

memento *NOUN* **mementoes**
a souvenir

memo (*say* **mem**- oh) *NOUN* **memos**
a memorandum

memoir (*say* **mem**- wahr) *NOUN* **memoirs**
a biography, especially one written by someone who knew the person

memoirs *PLURAL NOUN*
an autobiography

memorable *ADJECTIVE*
1 worth remembering
2 easy to remember
▷ **memorably** *ADVERB*

memorandum *NOUN* **memoranda** or **memorandums**
1 a note to remind yourself of something
2 a note from one person to another in the same firm

memorial *NOUN* **memorials**
a statue or other structure put up to remind people of a person or event
▷ **memorial** *ADJECTIVE*

memorize *VERB* **memorizes, memorizing, memorized**
to learn something so that you can remember it in future

USAGE NOTE This word can also be spelled memorise.

memory *NOUN* **memories**
1 the ability to remember things
2 a memory is something that you remember from the past

Preoccupied by the thought of going into hiding, I stuck the craziest things in the satchel, but I'm not sorry. Memories mean more to me than dresses. — *Anne Frank, The Diary of a Young Girl*

3 (*ICT*) the part of a computer where information is stored

in memory of someone in honour of a person or event remembered

menace *NOUN* **menaces**
1 a threat or danger
2 a troublesome person or thing

menace *VERB* **menaces, menacing, menaced**
to threaten someone with harm or danger

Rabbits avoid close woodland, where the ground is shady, damp and grassless and they feel menaced by the undergrowth. — *Richard Adams, Watership Down*

menagerie *NOUN* **menageries**
a small zoo

mend *VERB* **mends, mending, mended**
1 to repair something broken
2 to make something better, or to become better; to improve
▷ **mender** *NOUN*

mend *NOUN* **mends**
a repair

on the mend getting better after an illness

mendacious (*say* men- **day**- shus) *ADJECTIVE*
(*formal*) untruthful; telling lies
▷ **mendaciously** *ADVERB*
▷ **mendacity** *NOUN*

menial (*say* **meen**- ee- al) *ADJECTIVE*
menial work is work that needs little skill or thought

menial ***NOUN*** **menials**
a person who does menial work; a servant

meningitis ***NOUN***
a disease causing inflammation of the membranes (called *meninges*) round the brain and spinal cord

menopause ***NOUN***
the time of life when a woman gradually stops menstruating

menstruate ***VERB*** **menstruates, menstruating, menstruated**
a woman menstruates when she bleeds from the womb about once a month, as women normally do from their teens until middle age
▷ **menstruation** ***NOUN***
▷ **menstrual** ***ADJECTIVE***

mental ***ADJECTIVE***
1 to do with or in the mind
2 (*informal*) crazy or mad
▷ **mentally** ***ADVERB***
WORD HISTORY from Latin *mentis* 'of the mind'

mentality ***NOUN*** **mentalities**
a person's mental ability or attitude

menthol ***NOUN***
a solid white peppermint-flavoured substance

mention ***VERB*** **mentions, mentioning, mentioned**
to speak or write about a person or thing briefly; to refer to a person or thing

mention ***NOUN*** **mentions**
an example of mentioning someone or something

Hermux wasn't hungry. But the mention of biscuits got his attention. — *Michael Hoeye, Time Stops for No Mouse*

mentor ***NOUN*** **mentors**
an experienced and trusted adviser
WORD HISTORY named after *Mentor* in Homer's *Odyssey*, who advised Odysseus' son Telemachus

menu (*say* **men**- yoo) ***NOUN*** **menus**
1 a list of the food available in a restaurant or served at a meal
2 (*ICT*) a list of options or commands shown on a computer screen, from which the user can select an action

MEP ***ABBREVIATION***
Member of the European Parliament

mercantile ***ADJECTIVE***
to do with trade or trading

mercenary ***ADJECTIVE***
working only for money or some other reward

mercenary ***NOUN*** **mercenaries**
a soldier hired to serve in a foreign army

merchandise ***NOUN***
goods for sale

merchant ***NOUN*** **merchants**
a person involved in trade

merchant bank ***NOUN*** **merchant banks**
a bank that gives loans and advice to businesses

merchant navy ***NOUN***
the ships and sailors that carry goods for trade

merciful ***ADJECTIVE***
showing mercy
▷ **mercifully** ***ADVERB***

merciless ***ADJECTIVE***
showing no mercy; cruel
▷ **mercilessly** ***ADVERB***

mercurial ***ADJECTIVE***
1 having sudden changes of mood
2 to do with mercury

mercury ***NOUN***
a heavy silvery metal that is usually liquid, used in thermometers
▷ **mercuric** ***ADJECTIVE***

mercy ***NOUN*** **mercies**
1 kindness or pity shown in not punishing a wrongdoer severely or not harming a defeated enemy etc.
2 something to be thankful for
to be at the mercy of someone or something is to be completely in their power

mere❶ ***ADJECTIVE***
not more than ◆ *The job was finished in a mere fortnight.*

mere❷ ***NOUN*** **meres**
(*poetic*) a lake

merely ***ADVERB***
only; simply

My companion still said nothing, merely smiled beneath her veil and put one gloved finger to her lips. — *Celia Rees, Witch Child*

merest ***ADJECTIVE***
very small or slight ◆ *The weather was warm with the merest hint of a breeze.*

merge ***VERB*** **merges, merging, merged**
to combine or blend

merger ***NOUN*** **mergers**
the combining of two business companies into one

meridian ***NOUN*** **meridians**
a line on a map or globe from the North Pole to the South Pole. The meridian that passes through Greenwich is shown on maps as 0° longitude.

The Nautilus was steadily pursuing its southerly course, following the fiftieth meridian with considerable speed. — *Jules Verne, 20,000 Leagues Under the Sea*

meringue (*say* mer- **ang**) ***NOUN*** **meringues**
a crisp cake of sweet food made from egg white and sugar

merino ***NOUN*** **merinos**
a kind of sheep with fine soft wool

merit ***NOUN*** **merits**
1 a quality that deserves praise
2 good quality; excellence
▷ **meritorious** ***ADJECTIVE***

merit ***VERB*** **merits, meriting, merited**
to deserve something

mermaid ***NOUN*** **mermaids**
a mythical sea creature with a woman's body but with a fish's tail instead of legs
▷ **merman** ***NOUN***

merry ***ADJECTIVE*** **merrier, merriest**
cheerful and lively
▷ **merrily** ***ADVERB***
▷ **merriment** ***NOUN***

merry-go-round ***NOUN*** **merry-go-rounds**
a roundabout at a fair

mesh ***NOUN*** **meshes**
1 the open spaces in a net, sieve, or other criss-cross structure
2 material made like a net

mesh ***VERB*** **meshes, meshing, meshed**
gears mesh when they engage or fit together

mesmerize ***VERB*** **mesmerizes, mesmerizing, mesmerized**
1 (*old use*) to hypnotize someone
2 to fascinate or hold a person's attention completely
▷ **mesmerism** ***NOUN***
▷ **mesmeric** ***ADJECTIVE***

USAGE NOTE This word can also be spelled mesmerise.

WORD HISTORY named after an Austrian doctor, F. A. *Mesmer*, who was an early user of techniques that developed into hypnotism

mess ***NOUN*** **messes**
1 a dirty or untidy condition or thing
2 a difficult or confused situation
3 (in the armed forces) a dining room
to make a mess of something is to bungle it

mess ***VERB*** **messes, messing, messed**
to mess about is to behave stupidly or idly
to mess something up
1 is to make something dirty or untidy
2 is to bungle or ruin something
to mess with something (*informal*) is to interfere or tinker with it

message ***NOUN*** **messages**
1 a piece of information etc. sent from one person to another
2 the main theme or moral of a book, film, etc.

messenger ***NOUN*** **messengers**
a person who carries a message

Messiah (*say* mis- **y**- a) ***NOUN*** **Messiahs**
1 the saviour expected by the Jews
2 Jesus Christ, who Christians believe was this saviour
▷ **Messianic** ***ADJECTIVE***

WORD HISTORY from Hebrew *mashiah* 'anointed'

Messrs *plural* of **Mr**

messy ***ADJECTIVE*** **messier, messiest**
1 dirty and untidy
2 (*informal*) difficult and complicated

Tom's parents were going through a messy divorce, and they had packed him off to get him out of the way. — *Anthony Horowitz, Scorpia*

▷ **messily** ***ADVERB***
▷ **messiness** ***NOUN***

metabolism (*say* mit- **ab**- ol- izm) ***NOUN***
the process by which food is built up into living material in an animal or plant, or used to supply it with energy
▷ **metabolic** ***ADJECTIVE***

metabolize ***VERB*** **metabolizes, metabolizing, metabolized**
food metabolizes when it undergoes metabolism

USAGE NOTE This word can also be spelled metabolise.

metal ***NOUN*** **metals**
a chemical substance, usually hard, that conducts heat and electricity and melts when it is heated. Gold, silver, copper, iron, and uranium are metals.
▷ **metallic** ***ADJECTIVE***

metalanguage ***NOUN***
(*Language*) a set of terms used for describing or analysing a language, including *sentence*, *verb*, *voice*, etc.

metallurgy (*say* mit- **al**- er- jee) ***NOUN***
1 the study of metals
2 the craft of making and using metals
▷ **metallurgical** ***ADJECTIVE***
▷ **metallurgist** ***NOUN***

metamorphic ***ADJECTIVE***
metamorphic rock is rock that has been formed or changed by heat or pressure, e.g. marble

metamorphosis (*say* met- a- **mor**- fo- sis) ***NOUN*** **metamorphoses** (*say* met- a- **mor**- fo- seez)
1 a complete change made by some living things, such as a caterpillar changing into a butterfly
2 a change of form or character

metaphor ***NOUN*** **metaphors**
(*Language*) the use of a word or phrase to represent someone or something that is like it in some way, e.g. 'He was a little monkey' and 'Her heart leapt for joy': see the panel at **simile**
▷ **metaphorical** ***ADJECTIVE***
▷ **metaphorically** ***ADVERB***

mete ***VERB*** **metes, meting, meted**
to mete something out is to allot or dispense punishment or something else unpleasant

meteor (*say* meet- ee- er) ***NOUN*** **meteors**
a piece of rock or metal that moves through space and burns up when it enters the earth's atmosphere
WORD HISTORY from Greek *meteoros* 'high in the air'

meteoric (*say* meet- ee- o- rik) ***ADJECTIVE***
1 to do with meteors
2 like a meteor in brilliance or sudden appearance ◆ *Her meteoric rise from dancer to actress was complete.*

meteorite ***NOUN*** **meteorites**
the remains of a meteor that has landed on the earth

meteorology ***NOUN***
the study of the conditions of the atmosphere, especially in order to forecast the weather
▷ **meteorological** ***ADJECTIVE***
▷ **meteorologist** ***NOUN***

meter ***NOUN*** **meters**
a device for measuring the amount of something, especially the amount of something used
USAGE NOTE Take care not to confuse this word with *metre*.

meter ***VERB*** **meters, metering, metered**
to measure something with a meter

methane (*say* mee- thayn) ***NOUN***
an inflammable gas produced by decaying matter

method ***NOUN*** **methods**
1 a procedure or way of doing something
2 (*Science*) the way in which a scientific experiment is performed
3 methodical behaviour; orderliness

methodical ***ADJECTIVE***
doing things in an orderly or systematic way
▷ **methodically** ***ADVERB***

Methodist ***NOUN*** **Methodists**
a member of a Christian religious group started by John and Charles Wesley in the 18th century
▷ **Methodism** ***NOUN***

meths ***NOUN***
(*informal*) methylated spirit

methylated spirit or **spirits** ***NOUN***
a liquid fuel made from alcohol

meticulous ***ADJECTIVE***
very careful and precise
▷ **meticulously** ***ADVERB***

metonymy (*say* mi- ton- i- mi) ***NOUN***
(*Language*) the use of a word or expression (called a *metonym*) used to stand for something it is closely associated with, e.g. *Washington* for 'the American government'

metre ***NOUN*** **metres**
1 a unit of length in the metric system, about $39\frac{1}{2}$ inches
2 rhythm in poetry
WORD HISTORY from Greek *metron* 'a measure'
USAGE NOTE Take care not to confuse this word with *meter*.

metric ***ADJECTIVE***
1 to do with the metric system
2 to do with metre in poetry
▷ **metrically** ***ADVERB***

metrical ***ADJECTIVE***
a metrical piece of writing has a rhythmic metre, not like prose

metrication ***NOUN***
changing to the metric system

metric system ***NOUN***
a measuring system based on decimal units (the metre, litre, and gram)

metric ton ***NOUN*** **metric tons**
1,000 kilograms

metronome ***NOUN*** **metronomes**
a device that makes a regular clicking noise to help a person keep in time when practising music

metropolis ***NOUN*** **metropolises**
the chief city of a country or region

metropolitan ***ADJECTIVE***
1 to do with a metropolis
2 to do with a city and its suburbs

mettle ***NOUN***
courage or strength of character
to be on your mettle is to be ready to show courage or ability
▷ **mettlesome** ***ADJECTIVE***

mew ***VERB*** **mews, mewing, mewed**
to make a cat's cry
▷ **mew** ***NOUN***

mews ***NOUN*** **mews**
a row of houses in a small street or square, converted from former stables
WORD HISTORY first used of royal stables in London, built on the site of hawks' cages (called *mews*)

miaow (*say* mee- ow) ***VERB, NOUN***
to mew

miasma (*say* mee- az- ma) ***NOUN*** **miasmas**
unpleasant or unhealthy air

mica ***NOUN***
a mineral substance used to make electrical insulators

mice *plural* of **mouse**

microbe ***NOUN*** **microbes**
a microorganism

microchip ***NOUN*** **microchips**
a very small piece of silicon etc. made to work like a complex wired electric circuit

microcomputer ***NOUN*** **microcomputers**
a small computer with a microprocessor as its central processing unit

microcosm ***NOUN*** **microcosms**
a world in miniature; something regarded as resembling something else on a very small scale

WORD HISTORY from Greek *mikros kosmos* 'little world'

microfiche ***NOUN*** **microfiches**
a piece of film on which pages of information are photographed in greatly reduced size

microfilm ***NOUN***
a length of film on which written or printed material is photographed in greatly reduced size

micron ***NOUN*** **microns**
a unit of measurement equal to one millionth of a metre

microorganism ***NOUN*** **microorganisms**
a microscopic creature, e.g. a bacterium or virus

microphone ***NOUN*** **microphones**
an electrical device that picks up sound waves for recording, amplifying, or broadcasting

microprocessor ***NOUN*** **microprocessors**
the central processing unit of a computer, consisting of one or more microchips

microscope ***NOUN*** **microscopes**
an instrument with lenses that magnify tiny objects or details

microscopic ***ADJECTIVE***
1 extremely small; too small to be seen without the aid of a microscope
2 to do with a microscope

microwave ***NOUN*** **microwaves**
1 a very short electromagnetic wave
2 a microwave oven

microwave ***VERB*** **microwaves, microwaving, microwaved**
to cook food in a microwave oven

microwave oven ***NOUN*** **microwave ovens**
an oven that uses microwaves to heat or cook food very quickly

mid ***ADJECTIVE***
1 in the middle of ◆ *By mid-January he received another letter.*
2 being the middle part of a period ◆ *The institution was set up in the mid nineties.*

mid-air ***NOUN***
the area above ground level; the open sky

midday ***NOUN***
the middle of the day; noon

middle ***NOUN*** **middles**
1 the place or part of something that is at the same distance from all its sides or edges or from both its ends
2 someone's waist

to be in the middle of something is to be occupied with a process or activity ◆ *She was in the middle of eating her dinner.*

middle ***ADJECTIVE***
1 placed or happening in the middle
2 moderate in size or rank etc.

middle-aged ***ADJECTIVE***
aged between about 40 and 60
▷ **middle age** ***NOUN***

Middle Ages ***PLURAL NOUN***
the period in history from about AD 1000 to 1400

middle class or **classes** ***NOUN***
the class of people between the upper class and the working class, including business and professional people such as teachers, doctors, and lawyers
▷ **middle-class** ***ADJECTIVE***

Middle East ***NOUN***
the countries from Egypt to Iran inclusive

Middle English ***NOUN***
the English language from about 1150 to 1500

middleman ***NOUN*** **middlemen**
1 a trader who buys from a producer and sells to a consumer
2 a go-between or intermediary

middle school ***NOUN*** **middle schools**
a school for children aged from about 9 to 13

middling ***ADJECTIVE***
of medium size or quality

midge ***NOUN*** **midges**
a small insect like a gnat

midget ***NOUN*** **midgets**
an extremely small person or thing
▷ **midget** ***ADJECTIVE***

midland ***ADJECTIVE***
1 to do with the middle part of a country
2 to do with the Midlands

Midlands ***PLURAL NOUN***
the central part of England

midnight ***NOUN***
twelve o'clock at night

midriff *NOUN* **midriffs**
the front part of the body just above the waist
WORD HISTORY from *mid* and Old English *hrif* 'stomach'

midshipman *NOUN* **midshipmen**
a sailor ranking next above a cadet

midst *NOUN*
in the midst of in the middle of or surrounded by
in our midst among us

midsummer *NOUN*
the middle of summer, about 21 June in the northern hemisphere

Midsummer's Day *NOUN*
24 June

midway *ADVERB*
halfway between two points

midwife *NOUN* **midwives**
a person trained to look after a woman who is giving birth to a baby
▷ **midwifery** (*say* **mid**- wif- ri) *NOUN*

midwinter *NOUN*
the middle of winter, about 21 December in the northern hemisphere

mien (*say* meen) *NOUN*
a person's manner and expression

might❶ *NOUN*
great strength or power
with all your might using all your strength and determination

Snape threw Harry from him with all his might. Harry fell hard on to the dungeon floor.
— *J. K. Rowling, Harry Potter and the Order of the Phoenix*

might❷ *AUXILIARY VERB*
1 the past tense of **may**❶ ◆ *We told her she might go.*
2 used to express possibility ◆ *It might be true.*

mightn't
short for *might not*

mighty *ADJECTIVE* **mightier, mightiest**
very large or powerful

On a dais at the far end of the room, a mighty throne reared up high. It was made of granite for strength and massiveness. — *Philip Pullman, Northern Lights*

▷ **mightily** *ADVERB*
▷ **mightiness** *NOUN*

migraine (*say* **mee**- grayn or **my**- grayn) *NOUN* **migraines**
a severe kind of headache

migrant *NOUN* **migrants**
a person or animal that migrates or has migrated

migrate *VERB* **migrates, migrating, migrated**
1 people migrate when they leave one place or country and settle in another
2 birds and animals migrate when they move periodically from one area to another
▷ **migration** *NOUN*
▷ **migratory** *ADJECTIVE*

mike *NOUN* **mikes**
(*informal*) a microphone

mild *ADJECTIVE* **milder, mildest**
1 not harsh or severe
2 gentle and kind
3 not strongly flavoured
4 mild weather is quite warm and pleasant
▷ **mildly** *ADVERB*
▷ **mildness** *NOUN*

mildew *NOUN*
a tiny fungus that forms a white coating on things kept in damp conditions
▷ **mildewed** *ADJECTIVE*

mile *NOUN* **miles**
a measure of distance equal to 1,760 yards (about 1.6 kilometres)

mileage *NOUN* **mileages**
1 the number of miles travelled
2 (*informal*) benefit or advantage

milestone *NOUN* **milestones**
1 a stone of a kind that used to be fixed beside a road to mark the distance between towns
2 an important event in life or history

milieu (*say* **meel**- yer) *NOUN* **milieus** or **milieux**
environment or surroundings

militant *ADJECTIVE*
1 eager to fight
2 forceful or aggressive ◆ *They seemed determined to force a militant confrontation.*
▷ **militant** *NOUN*
▷ **militancy** *NOUN*

militarism *NOUN*
belief in the use of military strength and methods
▷ **militarist** *NOUN*
▷ **militaristic** *ADJECTIVE*

military *ADJECTIVE*
to do with soldiers or the armed forces
the military a country's armed forces
WORD HISTORY from Latin *miles* 'soldier'

militate *VERB* **militates, militating, militated**
to be a strong influence against something; to make something difficult or unlikely
◆ *Several factors militated against the success of the rebellion.*
USAGE NOTE Take care not to confuse this word with *mitigate*.

militia (*say* mil- **ish**- a) ***NOUN*** **militias**
a military force, especially one raised from civilians

milk ***NOUN***
1 a white liquid that female mammals produce in their bodies to feed their babies
2 the milk of cows, used as food by human beings
3 a milky liquid, e.g. that in a coconut

WORD FAMILY Related adjectives are milky and (*technical*) lactic.

milk ***VERB*** **milks, milking, milked**
to get the milk from a cow or other animal

milkman ***NOUN*** **milkmen**
a man who delivers milk to customers' houses

milkshake ***NOUN*** **milkshakes**
a cold frothy drink made from milk whisked with sweet fruit flavouring

milk tooth ***NOUN*** **milk teeth**
one of the first set of teeth of a child or animal, which will be replaced by adult teeth

milky ***ADJECTIVE*** **milkier, milkiest**
smooth or white like milk

Milky Way ***NOUN***
the broad band of stars formed by our galaxy

mill ***NOUN*** **mills**
1 machinery for grinding corn to make flour; a building containing this machinery
2 a machine for grinding coffee, pepper, etc. into powder or granules
3 a factory for processing paper or other materials

mill ***VERB*** **mills, milling, milled**
1 to grind or crush in a mill
2 to cut markings round the edge of a coin
3 to mill about or mill around is to move in a confused crowd ◆ *Tourists were milling about everywhere.*

▷ **miller** ***NOUN***

millennium ***NOUN*** **millenniums**
a period of 1,000 years

millet ***NOUN***
a kind of cereal with tiny seeds

milliner ***NOUN*** **milliners**
a person who makes or sells women's hats

▷ **millinery** ***NOUN***

WORD HISTORY originally 'a person from Milan', an Italian city where fashionable accessories and hats were made

million ***NOUN*** **millions**
one thousand thousand (1,000,000)

▷ **millionth** ***ADJECTIVE*** & ***NOUN***

millionaire ***NOUN*** **millionaires**
a person who has at least a million pounds or dollars; an extremely rich person

millipede ***NOUN*** **millipedes**
a small crawling creature like a centipede, with many legs

millstone ***NOUN*** **millstones**
either of a pair of large circular stones between which corn is ground

a millstone around someone's neck a heavy responsibility or burden

milometer ***NOUN*** **milometers**
an instrument for measuring how far a vehicle has travelled

mime ***NOUN*** **mimes**
acting with movements of the body, not using words

mime ***VERB*** **mimes, miming, mimed**
to use mime to act or express something

'Let me think.' Mrs Hath proceeded, rather ostentatiously, to mime the act of thinking, lips pursed, finger stroking brow. — *William Nicholson, The Wind Singer*

mimic ***VERB*** **mimics, mimicking, mimicked**
to imitate someone, especially as entertainment

▷ **mimicry** ***NOUN***

mimic ***NOUN*** **mimics**
a person who mimics others

mimosa ***NOUN*** **mimosas**
a tropical tree or shrub with small ball-shaped flowers

minaret ***NOUN*** **minarets**
the tall tower of a mosque

WORD HISTORY from Arabic *manara* 'lighthouse'

mince ***VERB*** **minces, mincing, minced**
1 to cut meat or other food into very small pieces in a machine
2 to walk in an affected way with short quick steps

Mollie, the foolish, pretty white mare who drew Mr Jones's trap, came mincing daintily in, chewing at a lump of sugar. — *George Orwell, Animal Farm*

not to mince words or matters is to speak bluntly

▷ **mincer** ***NOUN***

mince ***NOUN***
minced meat

mincemeat ***NOUN***
a sweet mixture of currants, raisins, apple, etc. used in pies

mince pie ***NOUN*** **mince pies**
a pie containing mincemeat

mind *NOUN* **minds**
1 the ability to think, feel, understand, and remember, originating in the brain
2 a person's thoughts, opinion, or intention
3 a great mind is a person with great intelligence, especially a famous one

He has puzzled the greatest medical minds and sent many of them gibbering to their own hospitals. — *Eoin Colfer, Artemis Fowl*

to be in two minds is to be unable to decide about something
to be out of your mind is to be insane or very foolish

WORD FAMILY A related adjective is mental.

mind *VERB* **minds, minding, minded**
1 to mind a person or animal is to look after it for a while
2 to be careful about something ◆ *Do mind the broken glass.*
3 to be sad or upset about something; to object to something ◆ *People don't mind waiting so much if they know the reason.*
▷ **minder** *NOUN*

mindful *ADJECTIVE*
taking thought or care

I leaped up the stairs two at a time, mindful of the wet footprints, wary of slipping. — *Keith Gray, Malarkey*

mindless *ADJECTIVE*
done without thinking; stupid or pointless

mine❶ *POSSESSIVE PRONOUN*
belonging to me

mine❷ *NOUN* **mines**
1 a place where coal, metal, precious stones, etc. are dug out of the ground
2 an explosive placed in or on the ground or in the sea etc. to destroy people or things that come close to it

mine *VERB* **mines, mining, mined**
1 to dig materials from a mine
2 to lay explosive mines in a place

minefield *NOUN* **minefields**
1 an area where explosive mines have been laid
2 something with hidden dangers or problems

miner *NOUN* **miners**
a person who works in a mine

mineral *NOUN* **minerals**
1 a hard inorganic substance found in the ground
2 a cold fizzy non-alcoholic drink

mineralogy (*say* min- er- **al**- o- jee) *NOUN*
the study of minerals
▷ **mineralogist** *NOUN*

mineral water *NOUN*
water from a natural spring, containing mineral salts or gases

minestrone (*say* mi- ni- **stroh**- nee) *NOUN*
an Italian soup containing vegetables and pasta

WORD HISTORY an Italian word, from *ministrare* 'to serve up a dish'

mingle *VERB* **mingles, mingling, mingled**
to mix or blend

It had been raining, and thick mud mingled with the horse-dung in the streets. — *Alison Prince, Oranges and Murder*

mingy *ADJECTIVE* **mingier, mingiest**
(*informal*) not generous; mean

miniature *ADJECTIVE*
1 very small
2 copying something on a very small scale

miniature *NOUN* **miniatures**
1 a very small portrait
2 a small-scale model

minibus *NOUN* **minibuses**
a small bus, seating about ten people

minim *NOUN* **minims**
(*Music*) a note in music (written ...), lasting twice as long as a crotchet

minimal *ADJECTIVE*
very little; as little as possible

minimize *VERB* **minimizes, minimizing, minimized**
to make something as small as possible

USAGE NOTE This word can also be spelled minimise.

minimum *NOUN* **minima** or **minimums**
the lowest possible number or amount (SEE ALSO **maximum**)

minimum *ADJECTIVE*
least or smallest

minion *NOUN* **minions**
a very humble or obedient assistant or servant

minister *NOUN* **ministers**
1 a person in charge of a government department
2 a member of the clergy
▷ **ministerial** *ADJECTIVE*

minister *VERB* **ministers, ministering, ministered**
to attend to people's needs

ministry *NOUN* **ministries**
1 a government department dealing with a particular range of affairs
2 the work of the clergy

mink *NOUN* **mink** or **minks**
1 an animal rather like a stoat
2 this animal's valuable brown fur, or a coat made from it

minnow *NOUN* **minnows**
a tiny freshwater fish

a b c d e f g h i j k l m n o p q r s t u v w x y z

minor *ADJECTIVE*
1 not very important, especially when compared to something else

Do you think a minor problem like my life falling to pieces is going to mess up my piano playing?
— *Tim Bowler, Starseeker*

2 (*Music*) to do with the musical scale that has a semitone after the second note (SEE ALSO **major**)

minor *NOUN* **minors**
a person under the age of legal responsibility

minority *NOUN* **minorities**
1 the smallest part of a group of people or things
2 a small group that is different from others (SEE ALSO **majority**)

minstrel *NOUN* **minstrels**
a travelling singer and musician in the Middle Ages

mint❶ *NOUN* **mints**
1 a plant with fragrant leaves that are used for flavouring things
2 peppermint or a sweet flavoured with this

mint❷ *NOUN* **mints**
the place where a country's coins are made
in mint condition in perfect condition, as if newly made

mint *VERB* **mints, minting, minted**
to make coins by stamping metal

WORD HISTORY from Latin *moneta* 'coins', 'a mint'

minuet *NOUN* **minuets**
a slow stately dance

minus *PREPOSITION*
(*Mathematics*) with the next number or thing subtracted ◆ *Ten minus four equals six (10 - 4 = 6).*

minus *ADJECTIVE*
(*Mathematics*) less than zero ◆ *The temperature fell to minus ten degrees.* (-10°)

minuscule *ADJECTIVE*
extremely small

USAGE NOTE This word is derived from Latin *minuscula littera* meaning 'smaller letter'. It should not be spelled miniscule.

minute❶ (*say* **min**- it) *NOUN* **minutes**
1 one-sixtieth of an hour
2 a very short time; a moment
3 one-sixtieth of a degree (used in measuring angles)

minute❷ (*say* my- **newt**) *ADJECTIVE*
very small or detailed
▷ **minutely** *ADVERB*

minutes *PLURAL NOUN*
a written summary of what was said at a meeting

minx *NOUN* **minxes**
(*old use*) a cheeky or mischievous girl

miracle *NOUN* **miracles**
1 (*Religion*) something believed to have a supernatural or divine cause
2 something good and wonderful or unexpected that happens
▷ **miraculous** *ADJECTIVE*
▷ **miraculously** *ADVERB*

mirage (*say* **mi**- rahzh) *NOUN* **mirages**
an illusion; something that seems to be there but is not, especially when a stretch of water seems to appear in a desert

mire *NOUN*
1 a swamp
2 deep mud

mirror *NOUN* **mirrors**
a device or surface of reflecting material, usually glass

mirror *VERB* **mirrors, mirroring, mirrored**
to reflect in or like a mirror

mirth *NOUN*
merriment or laughter
▷ **mirthful** *ADJECTIVE*
▷ **mirthless** *ADJECTIVE*

misadventure *NOUN* **misadventures**
a piece of bad luck

misanthropy *NOUN*
dislike of people in general
▷ **misanthrope** *NOUN*
▷ **misanthropic** *ADJECTIVE*

WORD HISTORY from Greek *misos* 'hatred' and *anthropos* 'human being'

misapprehend *VERB* **misapprehends, misapprehending, misapprehended**
to misunderstand something
▷ **misapprehension** *NOUN*

misappropriate *VERB* **misappropriates, misappropriating, misappropriated**
to take something dishonestly
▷ **misappropriation** *NOUN*

misbehave *VERB* **misbehaves, misbehaving, misbehaved**
to behave badly
▷ **misbehaviour** *NOUN*

miscalculate *VERB* **miscalculates, miscalculating, miscalculated**
to calculate something incorrectly
▷ **miscalculation** *NOUN*

miscarriage *NOUN* **miscarriages**
1 the birth of a baby before it has developed enough to live
2 a miscarriage of justice occurs when a law court or a legal process fails to achieve the right result

miscarry *VERB* **miscarries, miscarrying, miscarried**
1 to have a miscarriage
2 a plan or idea miscarries when it goes wrong

miscellaneous (*say* mis- el- **ay**- nee- us) *ADJECTIVE*
of various kinds; mixed

miscellany (*say* mis- **el**- an- ee) *NOUN* **miscellanies**
a collection or mixture of different things

mischance *NOUN*
misfortune; bad luck

mischief *NOUN*
1 naughty or troublesome behaviour
2 trouble caused by this

WORD HISTORY from Old French *meschever* 'to come to a bad end'

mischievous *ADJECTIVE*
behaving badly and causing trouble or harm
▷ **mischievously** *ADVERB*

misconception *NOUN* **misconceptions**
a wrong or mistaken idea

misconduct *NOUN*
bad behaviour by someone in a responsible position

misconstrue *VERB* **misconstrues, misconstruing, misconstrued**
to understand or interpret something wrongly
▷ **misconstruction** *NOUN*

miscreant (*say* **mis**- kree- ant) *NOUN* **miscreants**
a wrongdoer or criminal

misdeed *NOUN* **misdeeds**
a wrong or improper action

misdemeanour *NOUN* **misdemeanours**
an action which is wrong or illegal but not serious; a petty crime

miser *NOUN* **misers**
a person who hoards money and spends as little as possible
▷ **miserly** *ADJECTIVE*
▷ **miserliness** *NOUN*

miserable *ADJECTIVE*
1 full of misery; very unhappy, poor, or uncomfortable
2 disagreeable or unpleasant ◆ *It was a cold miserable place.*
▷ **miserably** *ADVERB*

misery *NOUN* **miseries**
1 great unhappiness or discomfort or suffering, especially lasting for a long time
2 (*informal*) a person who is always unhappy or complaining

misfire *VERB* **misfires, misfiring, misfired**
1 an engine misfires when it fails to fire or start
2 a plan or remark misfires when it goes wrong or has the wrong effect

misfit *NOUN* **misfits**
a person who does not fit in well with other people or with their surroundings

misfortune *NOUN* **misfortunes**
1 bad luck
2 an unlucky event or accident

misgiving *NOUN* **misgivings**
a feeling of doubt or slight fear or mistrust

WORD HISTORY from an old word *misgive* 'to cause someone doubts or bad feelings'

misguided *ADJECTIVE*
showing bad reasoning or judgement

mishap (*say* **mis**- hap) *NOUN* **mishaps**
an unlucky accident

misinterpret *VERB* **misinterprets, misinterpreting, misinterpreted**
to interpret something incorrectly
▷ **misinterpretation** *NOUN*

misjudge *VERB* **misjudges, misjudging, misjudged**
to judge something wrongly; to form a wrong opinion or estimate
▷ **misjudgement** *NOUN*

mislay *VERB* **mislays, mislaying, mislaid**
to lose something for a time because you cannot remember where you put it

mislead *VERB* **misleads, misleading, misled**
to give somebody a wrong idea or impression deliberately

mismanagement *NOUN*
bad management

misnomer *NOUN* **misnomers**
an unsuitable name; a word or phrase that does not suit the person or thing it describes

misogynist (*say* mis- **oj**- in- ist) *NOUN* **misogynists**
a person who hates women
▷ **misogyny** *NOUN*

misplaced *ADJECTIVE*
1 put in the wrong place ◆ *There were several misplaced books.*
2 inappropriate or unjustified ◆ *His confidence proved to be misplaced.*
▷ **misplacement** *NOUN*

misprint *NOUN* **misprints**
a mistake in printing

mispronounce *VERB* **mispronounces, mispronouncing, mispronounced**
to pronounce a word or name incorrectly
▷ **mispronunciation** *NOUN*

misquote ***VERB*** **misquotes, misquoting, misquoted**
to quote someone or something incorrectly
▷ **misquotation** ***NOUN***

misread ***VERB*** **misreads, misreading, misread** (*say* mis- **red**)
to read or interpret something incorrectly

misrepresent ***VERB*** **misrepresents, misrepresenting, misrepresented**
to represent someone or something in a false or misleading way
▷ **misrepresentation** ***NOUN***

misrule ***NOUN***
bad government

Miss ***NOUN*** **Misses**
a title put before a girl's or unmarried woman's name

miss ***VERB*** **misses, missing, missed**
1 to fail to hit, reach, catch, see, hear, or find something
2 to be sad because someone or something is not with you
3 to notice that something has gone
to miss something out is to omit it
to miss out on something is not to get the benefit or enjoyment from something that others have had

miss ***NOUN*** **misses**
an instance of missing something
to give something a miss (*informal*) is to decide not to do it or have it on a particular occasion

> Rita. Don't you think that for tonight we could give the class a miss? — *Willy Russell, Educating Rita*

misshapen ***ADJECTIVE***
distorted or badly shaped

missile ***NOUN*** **missiles**
1 a weapon that is remotely guided to its target
2 an object that is thrown at someone or something

missing ***ADJECTIVE***
1 lost; not in the proper place
2 not present; absent

mission ***NOUN*** **missions**
1 an important job that somebody is sent to do or feels he or she must do
2 a place or building where missionaries work
3 a military or scientific expedition

missionary ***NOUN*** **missionaries**
a person who is sent to another country to spread a religious faith

misspell ***VERB*** **misspells, misspelling, misspelled** or **misspelt**
to spell a word wrongly

mist ***NOUN*** **mists**
1 damp cloudy air near the ground
2 condensed water vapour on a window, mirror, etc.

mist ***VERB*** **mists, misting, misted**
to become covered with mist

mistake ***NOUN*** **mistakes**
1 something done wrongly
2 an incorrect opinion

mistake ***VERB*** **mistakes, mistaking, mistook, mistaken**
1 to misunderstand someone or something ◆ *I hope he did not mistake my intentions.*
2 to choose or identify a person or thing wrongly ◆ *She initially mistook him for a police officer as he was wearing a police-style anorak.*

mistaken ***ADJECTIVE***
1 not correct
2 having an incorrect opinion

mister ***NOUN***
(*informal*) a form of address to a man

mistime ***VERB*** **mistimes, mistiming, mistimed**
to do or say something at a wrong time

mistletoe ***NOUN***
a plant with white berries that grows as a parasite on trees

mistreat ***VERB*** **mistreats, mistreating, mistreated**
to treat a person or thing badly

mistress ***NOUN*** **mistresses**
1 a woman who is in charge or has authority
2 a woman schoolteacher
3 the woman owner of a dog or other animal
4 a woman who is a man's lover but not his wife

mistrust ***VERB*** **mistrusts, mistrusting, mistrusted**
to have no trust in somebody or something
▷ **mistrust** ***NOUN***

misty ***ADJECTIVE*** **mistier, mistiest**
1 having a lot of mist or covered in mist
2 not clear or distinct
▷ **mistily** ***ADVERB***
▷ **mistiness** ***NOUN***

misunderstand ***VERB*** **misunderstands, misunderstanding, misunderstood**
to get a wrong idea or impression of something
▷ **misunderstanding** ***NOUN***

misuse (*say* mis- **yooz**) ***VERB*** **misuses, misusing, misused**
1 to use something incorrectly or badly
2 to treat someone badly
▷ **misuse** (*say* mis- **yooss**) ***NOUN***

mite *NOUN* **mites**
1 a tiny spider-like creature that lives on plants, animals, carpets, etc.
2 a small child

mitigate *VERB* **mitigates, mitigating, mitigated**
1 to make a thing less intense or less severe ◆ *The rainforest will help to mitigate the worst effects of global warming.*
2 mitigating circumstances are facts or situations that partially excuse a wrong
▷ **mitigation** *NOUN*

USAGE NOTE Take care not to confuse this word with *militate*.

mitre *NOUN* **mitres**
1 the tall tapering hat worn by a bishop
2 a joint of two pieces of wood or cloth with their ends tapered so that together they form a right angle

mitre *VERB* **mitres, mitring, mitred**
to join pieces of wood or cloth with a mitre

mitten *NOUN* **mittens**
a kind of glove without separate parts for the fingers

mix *VERB* **mixes, mixing, mixed**
1 to put different things together so that the substances etc. are no longer distinct; to blend or combine
2 someone mixes when they get together with other people socially

to mix things up
1 is to mix them together thoroughly
2 is to confuse them in your mind
▷ **mixer** *NOUN*

mix *NOUN* **mixes**
a mixture

mixed *ADJECTIVE*
1 containing two or more kinds of things or people

> The people in the theatre were a mixed bunch. Some were dressed stylishly, others in tracksuits. — *Darren Shan, Cirque du Freak*

2 for both sexes ◆ *mixed doubles*

mixed farming *NOUN*
farming of both crops and animals

mixture *NOUN* **mixtures**
something made of different things mixed together

mix-up *NOUN* **mix-ups**
a confusion or misunderstanding

mnemonic (*say* nim- **on**- ik) *NOUN* **mnemonics**
(*Language*) a verse or saying that helps you to remember something

WORD HISTORY from Greek *mneme* 'memory'

moan *VERB* **moans, moaning, moaned**
1 to make a long low sound of pain or suffering
2 (*informal*) to grumble

> When he came down from his bath, Dad started moaning that there was no bread and there were no eggs. — *David Almond, Skellig*

▷ **moan** *NOUN*

moat *NOUN* **moats**
a deep wide ditch round a castle, usually filled with water

mob *NOUN* **mobs**
a large disorderly crowd

mob *VERB* **mobs, mobbing, mobbed**
to crowd round a person or place

> Broadway was mobbed and messy. It was Sunday, and only about twelve o'clock, but it was mobbed anyway. Everybody was on their way to the movies. — *J. D. Salinger, The Catcher in the Rye*

WORD HISTORY from Latin *mobile vulgus* 'excitable crowd'

mobile *ADJECTIVE*
able to move or be moved or carried easily
▷ **mobility** *NOUN*

mobile *NOUN* **mobiles**
1 a decoration for hanging up so that its parts move in currents of air
2 a mobile phone

mobile phone *NOUN* **mobile phones**
a portable telephone that uses a cellular radio system

mobilize *VERB* **mobilizes, mobilizing, mobilized**
to assemble people or things for a particular purpose, especially for war
▷ **mobilization** *NOUN*

USAGE NOTE This word can also be spelled mobilise.

moccasin *NOUN* **moccasins**
a soft leather shoe

mock *VERB* **mocks, mocking, mocked**
1 to make fun of a person or thing
2 to imitate someone or something to make people laugh

mock *ADJECTIVE*
1 pretended and not real ◆ *'Still here?' he asked in mock surprise.*
2 a mock exam is one done as a practice before the real one

mockery *NOUN*
1 ridicule or contempt
2 a ridiculous imitation

mock-up *NOUN* **mock-ups**
a model of something, made in order to test or study it

modal verb *NOUN* **modal verbs**
(*Grammar*) a verb such as *can*, *may*, or *will* that is used with another verb to express possibility, permission, intention, etc.

mode *NOUN* **modes**
1 the way a thing is done
2 what is fashionable

model *NOUN* **models**
1 a copy of an object, usually on a smaller scale
2 a particular design
3 a person who poses for an artist or displays clothes by wearing them
4 a person or thing that is worth copying

model *VERB* **models, modelling, modelled**
1 to make a model of something; to make something out of wood or clay
2 to design or plan something using another thing as an example
3 to work as an artist's model or a fashion model

WORD HISTORY from Latin *modulus* 'a small measure'

modem (*say* **moh**- dem) *NOUN* **modems**
(*ICT*) a device that links a computer to a telephone line for transmitting data

moderate (*say* **mod**- er- at) *ADJECTIVE*
1 not extreme or intense ◆ *The region has moderate rainfall in the autumn months.*
2 a moderate opinion or point of view is one that is not extreme or unreasonable
▷ **moderately** *ADVERB*

moderate (*say* **mod**- er- ayt) *VERB* **moderates, moderating, moderated**
to make moderate, or become moderate

moderation *NOUN*
being moderate
in moderation in moderate amounts

modern *ADJECTIVE*
1 belonging to the present or recent times
2 in fashion now
▷ **modernity** *NOUN*

modernize *VERB* **modernizes, modernizing, modernized**
to make a thing more modern
▷ **modernization** *NOUN*

USAGE NOTE This word can also be spelled modernise.

modest *ADJECTIVE*
1 not vain or boastful
2 moderate in size or amount ◆ *He made a modest income from his garage business.*
3 not showy or splendid
4 behaving or dressing decently or decorously
▷ **modestly** *ADVERB*
▷ **modesty** *NOUN*

modicum *NOUN*
a small amount

modify *VERB* **modifies, modifying, modified**
1 to change something slightly
2 to describe a word or limit its meaning, as adjectives and adverbs do
▷ **modification** *NOUN*

modulate *VERB* **modulates, modulating, modulated**
1 to adjust or regulate something
2 to vary in pitch or tone etc.
3 to alter an electronic wave to allow signals to be sent
▷ **modulation** *NOUN*

module *NOUN* **modules**
1 an independent part of a spacecraft, building, etc.
2 (*ICT*) a part of a computer system that performs a specific task
3 a unit or section of a course of study
▷ **modular** *ADJECTIVE*

modus operandi (*say* moh- dus op- er- **and**- ee) *NOUN*
a particular method of working

WORD HISTORY a Latin phrase meaning 'way of working'

mogul (*say* **moh**- gul) *NOUN* **moguls**
(*informal*) an important or influential person

WORD HISTORY named after the Moguls, the ruling dynasty in northern India in the 16th–19th centuries

mohair *NOUN*
fine silky wool from an angora goat

moist *ADJECTIVE*
slightly wet
▷ **moistness** *NOUN*

moisten *VERB* **moistens, moistening, moistened**
to make something moist

moisture *NOUN*
water in tiny drops in the air or on a surface

moisturizer *NOUN*
a cream used to make the skin less dry

USAGE NOTE This word can also be spelled moisturiser.

molar *NOUN* **molars**
any of the wide teeth at the back of the jaw, used in chewing

molasses *NOUN*
dark syrup from raw sugar

mole❶ *NOUN* **moles**
1 a small furry animal that burrows under the ground
2 a spy working within an organization and passing information to another organization or country

mole❷ *NOUN* **moles**
a small dark spot on the skin

molecule *NOUN* **molecules**
the smallest part into which a substance can be divided without changing its chemical nature; a group of atoms
▷ **molecular** (*say* mo- **lek**- yoo- ler) *ADJECTIVE*

molehill *NOUN* **molehills**
a small pile of earth thrown up by a burrowing mole

molest *VERB* **molests, molesting, molested**
1 to annoy or pester someone
2 to attack or abuse someone sexually
▷ **molestation** *NOUN*

mollify *VERB* **mollifies, mollifying, mollified**
to make a person less angry

mollusc *NOUN* **molluscs**
any of a group of animals including snails, slugs, and mussels, with soft bodies, no backbones, and, in some cases, external shells

molten *ADJECTIVE*
melted; made liquid by great heat

moment *NOUN* **moments**
1 a very short time
2 a particular point in time ◆ *I'll call you the moment they arrive.*

momentary *ADJECTIVE*
lasting for only a moment

There was a momentary stillness. Then chairs began to creak and shoes to scrape upon the carpet. — *H. G. Wells, The Time Machine*

▷ **momentarily** *ADVERB*

momentous (*say* mo- **ment**- us) *ADJECTIVE*
very important

momentum *NOUN*
1 the ability something has to keep developing or increasing
2 the ability an object has to keep moving as a result of the speed it already has
3 (*Science*) the quantity of motion of a moving object, measured as its mass multiplied by its velocity

monarch *NOUN* **monarchs**
a king, queen, emperor, or empress ruling a country

monarchy *NOUN* **monarchies**
1 a country ruled by a monarch
2 (*Politics*) government by a monarch
▷ **monarchist** *NOUN*

monastery *NOUN* **monasteries**
a building where monks live and work
▷ **monastic** *ADJECTIVE*

WORD HISTORY from Greek *monazein* 'to live alone', from *monos* 'alone'

Monday *NOUN*
the day of the week following Sunday

WORD HISTORY from Old English *monandaeg* 'day of the moon'

monetary *ADJECTIVE*
to do with money

money *NOUN*
1 coins and banknotes
2 wealth or riches

WORD FAMILY Related adjectives are monetary and pecuniary.

mongoose *NOUN* **mongooses**
a small tropical animal rather like a stoat, that can kill snakes

WORD HISTORY from Marathi (a southern Indian language) *mangus*

mongrel (*say* **mung**- rel) *NOUN* **mongrels**
a dog of mixed breeds

monitor *NOUN* **monitors**
1 a device for watching or testing how something is working
2 (*ICT*) a screen that displays data and images produced by a computer
3 a pupil who is given a special responsibility in a school

monitor *VERB* **monitors, monitoring, monitored**
to watch or test how something is working

monk *NOUN* **monks**
a member of a community of men who live according to the rules of a religious organization (SEE ALSO **nun**)

WORD FAMILY A related adjective is monastic.

monkey *NOUN* **monkeys**
1 an animal with long arms, hands with thumbs, and often a tail
2 a mischievous person, especially a child

monochrome *ADJECTIVE*
done in one colour or in black and white

monocle *NOUN* **monocles**
a lens worn over one eye, like half of a pair of glasses

monogamy *NOUN*
the practice of being married to only one person during that person's lifetime (SEE ALSO **polygamy**)
▷ **monogamous** *ADJECTIVE*

monogram *NOUN* **monograms**
a design made up of a letter or letters, especially a person's initials
▷ **monogrammed** *ADJECTIVE*

monograph *NOUN* **monographs**
a scholarly book or article on one particular subject

monolith *NOUN* **monoliths**
a large single upright block of stone

monolithic *ADJECTIVE*
1 to do with or like a monolith
2 huge and difficult to move or change

monologue *NOUN* **monologues**
(*Drama*) a long speech by one person

monoplane ***NOUN*** **monoplanes**
a type of aeroplane with only one set of wings

monopolize ***VERB*** **monopolizes, monopolizing, monopolized**
to take the whole of something for yourself ◆ *I must not monopolize your attention when so many people want to meet you.*
▷ **monopolization** ***NOUN***

USAGE NOTE This word can also be spelled monopolise.

monopoly ***NOUN*** **monopolies**
1 the exclusive right or opportunity to sell a commodity or supply a service
2 complete possession, control, or use of something by one group

monorail ***NOUN*** **monorails**
a railway that uses a single rail, not a pair of rails

monosyllable ***NOUN*** **monosyllables**
a word with only one syllable
▷ **monosyllabic** ***ADJECTIVE***

monotone ***NOUN***
a level unchanging tone of voice in speaking or singing

monotonous ***ADJECTIVE***
dull and tedious because it does not change

The sky became quite grey and, along with it, the whole countryside seemed to lose its colour and assume the same monotonous tone. — *Norton Juster, The Phantom Tollbooth*

▷ **monotonously** ***ADVERB***
▷ **monotony** ***NOUN***

monoxide ***NOUN*** **monoxides**
an oxide with one atom of oxygen

monsoon ***NOUN*** **monsoons**
1 a strong wind in and near the Indian Ocean, bringing heavy rain in summer
2 the rainy season brought by this wind

WORD HISTORY via Dutch from Arabic *mawsim* 'season'

monster ***NOUN*** **monsters**
1 a large frightening creature
2 a huge thing
3 a wicked or cruel person

monster ***ADJECTIVE***
very large; huge

monstrosity ***NOUN*** **monstrosities**
a monstrous thing

monstrous ***ADJECTIVE***
1 like a monster; huge
2 very shocking or outrageous

montage (*say* **mon**- tah*zh*) ***NOUN***
a picture, film, or other work of art made by putting together separate pieces or pieces from other works

WORD HISTORY a French word, from *monter* 'to mount'

month ***NOUN*** **months**
each of the twelve parts into which a year is divided

WORD HISTORY from Old English; related to *moon* (because time was measured by the changes in the moon's appearance)

monthly ***ADJECTIVE, ADVERB***
happening or done once a month

monument ***NOUN*** **monuments**
a statue, building, or column etc. put up as a memorial of some person or event

monumental ***ADJECTIVE***
1 built as a monument
2 very large or important

moo ***VERB*** **moos, mooing, mooed**
to make the low deep sound of a cow
▷ **moo** ***NOUN***

mood ***NOUN*** **moods**
the way someone feels ◆ *She was in a more cheerful mood the next day.*

moody ***ADJECTIVE*** **moodier, moodiest**
1 gloomy or sullen
2 having sudden changes of mood for no apparent reason
▷ **moodily** ***ADVERB***
▷ **moodiness** ***NOUN***

moon ***NOUN*** **moons**
1 the natural satellite of the earth that can be seen in the sky at night
2 a satellite of any planet

WORD FAMILY A related adjective is lunar.

moon ***VERB*** **moons, mooning, mooned**
to act or go about in a dreamy or listless way

I mooned in front of the mirror, experimenting with ways of doing my hair. — *Jacqueline Wilson, Lola Rose*

moonbeam ***NOUN*** **moonbeams**
a ray of moonlight

moonlight ***NOUN***
the light from the moon
▷ **moonlit** ***ADJECTIVE***

moonscape ***NOUN*** **moonscapes**
a landscape on the moon

Moor ***NOUN*** **Moors**
a member of a Muslim people of north-west Africa
▷ **Moorish** ***ADJECTIVE***

moor ❶ ***NOUN*** **moors**
an area of rough land covered with heather, bracken, and bushes
▷ **moorland** ***NOUN***

moor ❷ ***VERB*** **moors, mooring, moored**
to fasten a boat to a fixed object by means of a cable

moorhen ***NOUN*** **moorhens**
a small waterbird

mooring *NOUN* **moorings**
a place where a boat can be moored

moose *NOUN* **moose**
a North American elk
WORD HISTORY from Abnaki (a Native American language) *mos*

moot *ADJECTIVE*
a moot point a question that is undecided or debatable

mop *NOUN* **mops**
1 a bunch or pad of soft material fastened on the end of a stick, used for cleaning floors etc.
2 a thick mass of hair

mop *VERB* **mops, mopping, mopped**
to clean or wipe something with a mop or sponge
to mop something up
1 is to wipe or soak up liquid
2 is to deal with the last parts of a difficult or dangerous operation ◆ *The police were busy mopping up a crowd of drug smugglers.*

mope *VERB* **mopes, moping, moped**
to be sad

moped (*say* **moh**- ped) *NOUN* **mopeds**
a kind of small motorcycle that can be pedalled

moraine *NOUN* **moraines**
a mass of stones and earth etc. carried down by a glacier

moral *ADJECTIVE*
1 connected with what is right and wrong in behaviour
2 good or virtuous
moral support help in the form of encouragement
▷ **morally** *ADVERB*
▷ **morality** *NOUN*

moral *NOUN* **morals**
a lesson in right behaviour taught by a story or event

morale (*say* mor- **ahl**) *NOUN*
the level of confidence and good spirits in a person or group of people ◆ *It's important to keep up morale in the ranks.*

moralize *VERB* **moralizes, moralizing, moralized**
to talk or write about right and wrong behaviour
▷ **moralist** *NOUN*
USAGE NOTE This word can also be spelled moralise.

morals *PLURAL NOUN*
standards of behaviour

morass (*say* mo- **rass**) *NOUN* **morasses**
1 a marsh or bog
2 a confused mass

moratorium *NOUN* **moratoriums**
a temporary ban

morbid *ADJECTIVE*
1 thinking about gloomy or unpleasant things
2 (*Medicine*) unhealthy or indicating disease ◆ *The X-ray had revealed a morbid growth.*
▷ **morbidly** *ADVERB*
▷ **morbidity** *NOUN*

more *ADJECTIVE* (comparative of **much** and **many**)
greater in amount or degree

more *NOUN*
a greater amount

more *ADVERB*
1 to a greater extent ◆ *She'd never seen anything more beautiful.*
2 again or on further occasions ◆ *I don't want to do it any more.*
more or less
1 approximately
2 nearly or practically

moreover *ADVERB*
besides; in addition to what has been said

Mormon *NOUN* **Mormons**
a member of a religious group founded in the USA

morn *NOUN*
(*poetic*) the morning

morning *NOUN* **mornings**
the early part of the day, before noon or before lunchtime

morocco *NOUN*
a kind of leather originally made in Morocco in North Africa from goatskins

moron *NOUN* **morons**
(*informal*) a very stupid person
▷ **moronic** *ADJECTIVE*

morose (*say* mo- **rohss**) *ADJECTIVE*
bad-tempered and miserable
▷ **morosely** *ADVERB*
▷ **moroseness** *NOUN*

morpheme *NOUN* **morphemes**
(*Language*) a unit of language that cannot be divided further, e.g. *go* and *-ing* in the word *going*

morphine (*say* **mor**- feen) *NOUN*
a drug made from opium, used to lessen pain
WORD HISTORY named after *Morpheus*, the Roman god of dreams

morris dance *NOUN* **morris dances**
a traditional English dance performed in costume by men with ribbons and bells
WORD HISTORY originally *Moorish dance* (because it was thought to have come from the Moors of north-west Africa)

morrow *NOUN*
(*poetic*) the following day

Morse code *NOUN*
a signalling code using short and long sounds or flashes of light (dots and dashes) to represent letters
WORD HISTORY named after its American inventor, Samuel F. B. *Morse*

morsel *NOUN* **morsels**
a small piece of food

At long last, when the last morsels of pumpkin tart had melted from the golden platters, Dumbledore gave the word that it was time for them all to go to bed. — *J. K. Rowling, Harry Potter and the Prisoner of Azkaban*

mortal *ADJECTIVE*
1 mortal beings are those that die eventually
2 a mortal blow or wound or illness is one that causes death
3 mortal enemies are bitter enemies who do not ever become reconciled
▷ **mortally** *ADVERB*

mortal *NOUN* **mortals**
a human being, as compared to a god or immortal spirit
WORD HISTORY from Latin *mortis* 'of death'

mortality *NOUN*
1 the state of being mortal and bound to die
2 the number of people who die in a particular period of time ◆ *Declining mortality rates meant people lived longer.*

mortar *NOUN* **mortars**
1 a mixture of sand, cement, and water used in building to stick bricks together
2 a hard bowl in which substances are pounded with a pestle
3 a short cannon for firing shells at a high angle

mortarboard *NOUN* **mortarboards**
an academic cap with a stiff square top
WORD HISTORY called this because it looks like the board used by builders to hold mortar

mortgage (*say* **mor**- gij) *NOUN* **mortgages**
an arrangement to borrow money to buy a house, with the house as security for the loan

mortgage *VERB* **mortgages, mortgaging, mortgaged**
to take out a loan to buy a house, with the house as security

mortify *VERB* **mortifies, mortifying, mortified**
to humiliate someone or make them feel very ashamed
▷ **mortification** *NOUN*

mortise *NOUN* **mortises**
a slot made in a piece of wood or other material for another piece to be joined to it (SEE ALSO **tenon**)

mortise lock *NOUN* **mortise locks**
a lock set into a door

mortuary *NOUN* **mortuaries**
a place where dead bodies are kept before being buried or cremated

mosaic (*say* mo- **zay**- ik) *NOUN* **mosaics**
a picture or design made from small coloured pieces of stone or glass

mosque (*say* mosk) *NOUN* **mosques**
(*Religion*) a building where Muslims worship

mosquito *NOUN* **mosquitoes**
a kind of gnat that sucks blood

moss *NOUN* **mosses**
a plant that grows in damp places and has no flowers
▷ **mossy** *ADJECTIVE*

most *ADJECTIVE* (superlative of **much** and **many**)
greatest in amount or degree ◆ *Most people enjoy this kind of humour.*

most *NOUN*
the greatest amount ◆ *Most of the sounds we are surrounded by are not musical sounds.*

most *ADVERB*
1 to the greatest extent; more than any other ◆ *It seemed the most natural thing in the world.*
2 very or extremely ◆ *The scene was a most beautiful one.*

mostly *ADVERB*
mainly; in most ways

MOT *NOUN* **MOTs**
in Britain, a compulsory annual test of motor vehicles of more than a specified age
WORD HISTORY from the initial letters of *Ministry of Transport*, the government department that introduced the test

motel (*say* mo- **tel**) *NOUN* **motels**
a hotel providing accommodation for motorists and their cars

motet (*say* mo- **tet**) *NOUN* **motets**
a short piece of sacred choral music

moth *NOUN* **moths**
an insect rather like a butterfly, that usually flies at night

mother *NOUN* **mothers**
a female parent
▷ **motherhood** *NOUN*
WORD FAMILY A related adjective is maternal.

mother *VERB* **mothers, mothering, mothered**
to look after someone in a motherly way

motherboard *NOUN* **motherboards**
(*ICT*) a circuit board containing the main components of a microcomputer or other device, with connections for slotting in other circuit boards

Mothering Sunday *NOUN*
Mother's Day

mother-in-law *NOUN* **mothers-in-law**
the mother of a married person's husband or wife

motherly *ADJECTIVE*
kind and gentle like a mother
▷ **motherliness** *NOUN*

mother-of-pearl *NOUN*
a pearly substance lining the shells of mussels etc.

Mother's Day *NOUN*
the fourth Sunday in Lent, when many people give cards or presents to their mothers

motif (*say* moh- **teef**) *NOUN* **motifs**
a repeated design or theme

motion *NOUN* **motions**
1 a way of moving; movement
2 a formal statement to be discussed and voted on at a meeting

WORD FAMILY Related adjectives are dynamic and kinetic.

motion *VERB* **motions, motioning, motioned**
to signal to someone with a gesture

Beatrice parked the bicycle and motioned for Roy to follow her through the hole in the fence. — *Carl Hiaasen, Hoot*

motionless *ADJECTIVE*
not moving

motivate *VERB* **motivates, motivating, motivated**
1 to give a person a motive or reason to do something ◆ *The need to pay the bills motivates us all.*
2 to stimulate someone's interest or enthusiasm ◆ *A cheering crowd motivates the players.*
▷ **motivation** *NOUN*

motive *NOUN* **motives**
what makes a person do something ◆ *It was clearly a murder but the motive was unclear.*

motive *ADJECTIVE*
producing movement ◆ *He patented the first engine that used steam as its motive power.*

motley *ADJECTIVE*
1 multicoloured
2 made up of various sorts of things

WORD HISTORY *the motley* was originally the costume of a court jester

motor *NOUN* **motors**
a machine providing power to drive machinery etc.; an engine

motor *VERB* **motors, motoring, motored**
to go or take someone in a car

motorbike *NOUN* **motorbikes**
a motorcycle

motorcade *NOUN* **motorcades**
a procession of cars

motorcycle *NOUN* **motorcycles**
a two-wheeled road vehicle with an engine
▷ **motorcyclist** *NOUN*

motorist *NOUN* **motorists**
a person who drives a car

motorized *ADJECTIVE*
equipped with a motor or with motor vehicles

USAGE NOTE This word can also be spelled motorised.

motor neuron disease *NOUN*
a disease of the nerves that control movement, so that the muscles get weaker and weaker until the person dies

motorway *NOUN* **motorways**
a wide road for fast long-distance traffic

mottled *ADJECTIVE*
marked with spots or patches of colour

motto *NOUN* **mottoes**
1 a short saying that captures a belief or ideal ◆ *Their motto should be 'If in doubt, chuck it out'.*
2 a short verse or riddle found inside a cracker

WORD HISTORY an Italian word meaning 'witty remark'

mould ❶ *NOUN* **moulds**
a hollow container of a particular shape, in which a liquid or soft substance is put to set into this shape

mould *VERB* **moulds, moulding, moulded**
to make something have a particular shape or character

mould ❷ *NOUN*
a fine furry growth of very small fungi
▷ **mouldy** *ADJECTIVE*

moulder *VERB* **moulders, mouldering, mouldered**
to rot away or decay into dust

moult *VERB* **moults, moulting, moulted**
to shed feathers, hair, or skin etc. while a new growth forms

mound *NOUN* **mounds**
1 a pile of earth or stones etc.
2 a small hill

mount *VERB* **mounts, mounting, mounted**
1 to climb or go up; to ascend

The teachers mounted the stage and sat on hard chairs facing us. Many of them had their black gowns on. — *David Almond, The Fire-Eaters*

2 to climb on to a horse or bicycle
3 to increase in amount ◆ *The costs are starting to mount.*
4 to mount a picture or photograph is to fix it in a frame or album
5 to organize something ◆ *The gallery is mounting an exhibition of recent work by young sculptors.*

mount *NOUN* **mounts**
1 (usually in names) a mountain
2 something on which an object is mounted
3 a horse for riding

mountain *NOUN* **mountains**
1 a very high hill
2 a large heap or pile or quantity
▷ **mountainous** *ADJECTIVE*

mountaineer *NOUN* **mountaineers**
a person who climbs mountains
▷ **mountaineering** *NOUN*

mounted *ADJECTIVE*
serving on horseback ♦ *mounted police*

mourn *VERB* **mourns, mourning, mourned**
to be sad when someone has died or something has been lost or damaged

Nadine spends the next five minutes mourning her broken nail. — *Jacqueline Wilson, Girls Out Late*

▷ **mourner** *NOUN*

mournful *ADJECTIVE*
sad and sorrowful
▷ **mournfully** *ADVERB*

mouse *NOUN* **mice**
1 a small animal with a long thin tail and a pointed nose
2 (*ICT*) (*plural* **mouses** or **mice**) a small device which you move around on a mat to control the movements of a cursor on a VDU screen

mousetrap *NOUN* **mousetraps**
a trap for catching and killing mice

moussaka *NOUN*
a dish of minced meat, aubergine, etc., with a cheese sauce

mousse (*say* mooss) *NOUN* **mousses**
1 a creamy pudding flavoured with fruit or chocolate
2 a frothy creamy substance put on the hair so that it can be styled more easily

moustache (*say* mus- **tahsh**) *NOUN* **moustaches**
hair allowed to grow on a man's upper lip

mousy *ADJECTIVE* **mousier, mousiest**
1 mousy hair is a dull light brown in colour
2 a mousy person is timid and feeble

mouth *NOUN* **mouths**
1 the opening through which food is taken into the body
2 the place where a river enters the sea
3 an opening or outlet
▷ **mouthful** *NOUN*

mouth *VERB* **mouths, mouthing, mouthed**
to form words carefully with your lips, especially without saying them aloud

I mouthed the words, 'Say nothing,' then cautiously peered around the corner, to see what Mr Crepsley was up to. — *Darren Shan, Tunnels of Blood*

mouth organ *NOUN* **mouth organs**
a small musical instrument that you play by blowing and sucking while passing it along your lips

mouthpiece *NOUN* **mouthpieces**
the part of a musical instrument or other device that you put to your mouth

mouth-to-mouth *ADJECTIVE*
mouth-to-mouth resuscitation is a method of blowing into someone's lungs through their mouth to start their breathing again after an illness or accident

movable *ADJECTIVE*
able to be moved

move *VERB* **moves, moving, moved**
1 to take or go from one place to another; to change a person's or thing's position
2 to move someone is to affect their feelings, especially of sorrow or pity
3 to put forward a formal statement (called a *motion*) to be discussed and voted on at a meeting
▷ **mover** *NOUN*

SYNONYMS (meaning 1) go, walk, march, proceed, advance, stroll; (meaning 2) touch, affect, impress, disturb, agitate

move *NOUN* **moves**
1 a movement or action
2 a player's turn to move a piece in a game such as chess

to get a move on (*informal*) is to hurry or act promptly
on the move moving or making progress

movement *NOUN* **movements**
1 the action of moving or being moved
2 a group of people working together to achieve something
3 a person's movements are what they were doing and where they were going over a particular period
4 (*Music*) one of the main divisions of a symphony or other long musical work

WORD FAMILY Related adjectives (in meaning 1) are dynamic and kinetic.

movie *NOUN* **movies**
(*American*) (*informal*) a cinema film

moving *ADJECTIVE*
making someone feel strong emotion, especially sorrow or pity

mow *VERB* **mows, mowing, mowed, mown**
to cut down grass or cereal crops
to mow someone down is to knock them down and kill them
▷ **mower** *NOUN*

mozzarella *NOUN*
a kind of Italian cheese used in cooking, originally made from buffalo's milk

MP *ABBREVIATION*
Member of Parliament

MP3 *NOUN*
(*ICT*) a method of compressing sound into a very small file, used to download audio files from the Internet

Mr (*say* **mist**- er) *NOUN* **Messrs**
a title put before a man's name

Mrs (*say* **mis**- iz) *NOUN* **Mrs**
a title put before a married woman's name

MS *ABBREVIATION*
multiple sclerosis

Ms (*say* **miz**) *NOUN*
a title put before a woman's name

USAGE NOTE You put *Ms* before the name of a woman if she does not wish to be called 'Miss' or 'Mrs', or if you do not know whether she is married.

M.Sc. *ABBREVIATION*
Master of Science

MSP *ABBREVIATION*
Member of the Scottish Parliament

Mt *ABBREVIATION*
mount or mountain

much *ADJECTIVE* **more, most**
existing in a large amount ◆ *There is much work to do.*

much *NOUN*
a large amount of something

much *ADVERB*
1 greatly or considerably ◆ *It would have been much easier to do nothing.*
2 approximately ◆ *These are much the same.*

muck *NOUN*
1 farmyard manure
2 (*informal*) dirt or filth
3 (*informal*) a mess
▷ **mucky** *ADJECTIVE*

muck *VERB*
to muck about (*informal*) is to mess about
to muck something out is to clean out the place where an animal is kept
to muck something up (*informal*)
1 is to make it dirty
2 is to spoil it or make a mess of it

mucous (*say* **mew**- kus) *ADJECTIVE*
1 like mucus
2 a mucous membrane is a tissue covered with mucus and lining a body cavity

mucus (*say* **mew**- kus) *NOUN*
the moist sticky substance on the inner surface of the throat etc.

mud *NOUN*
wet soft earth
▷ **muddy** *ADJECTIVE*
▷ **muddiness** *NOUN*

muddle *VERB* **muddles, muddling, muddled**
1 to jumble or mix things up
2 to confuse things in your mind
▷ **muddler** *NOUN*

muddle *NOUN* **muddles**
a muddled condition or thing; confusion or disorder

mudguard *NOUN* **mudguards**
a curved cover over the top part of the wheel of a bicycle etc. to protect the rider from the mud and water thrown up by the wheel

muesli (*say* **mooz**- lee) *NOUN*
a breakfast food made of mixed cereals, dried fruit, and nuts

muezzin (*say* moo- **ez**- een) *NOUN* **muezzins**
a Muslim crier who calls the hours of prayer from a minaret

WORD HISTORY from Arabic *mu'addin* 'calling to prayer'

muff[1] *NOUN* **muffs**
a short tube-shaped piece of warm material into which the hands are pushed from opposite ends

muff[2] *VERB* **muffs, muffing, muffed**
(*informal*) to bungle something

muffin *NOUN* **muffins**
1 a flat bun eaten toasted and buttered
2 a small sponge cake, usually containing fruit, chocolate chips, etc.

muffle *VERB* **muffles, muffling, muffled**
1 to cover or wrap something to protect it or keep it warm
2 to deaden the sound of something ◆ *The mist and the rain muffled the sounds of the world outside.*

muffler *NOUN* **mufflers**
a warm scarf

mufti *NOUN*
ordinary clothes worn by someone who usually wears a uniform

mug *NOUN* **mugs**
1 a kind of large straight-sided cup
2 (*informal*) a fool; a person who is easily deceived
3 (*informal*) a person's face

mug *VERB* **mugs, mugging, mugged**
to attack and rob someone in the street
▷ **mugger** *NOUN*

muggy *ADJECTIVE* **muggier, muggiest**
muggy weather is unpleasantly warm and damp
▷ **mugginess** *NOUN*

mulberry *NOUN* **mulberries**
a purple or white fruit rather like a blackberry

a b c d e f g h i j k l m n o p q r s t u v w x y z

mule *NOUN* **mules**
an animal that is the offspring of a donkey and a mare, known for being stubborn
▷ **mulish** *ADJECTIVE*

mulga *NOUN*
a small Australian acacia shrub with greyish foliage, grown for its wood

mull *VERB* **mulls, mulling, mulled**
to mull something over is to think about it carefully

mulled *ADJECTIVE*
mulled wine or beer is heated with sugar and spices and drunk hot

mullet *NOUN* **mullet**
a kind of fish used as food

multicultural *ADJECTIVE*
made up of people of many different races, religions, and cultures

multifarious (*say* mul- ti- **fair**- ee- us) *ADJECTIVE*
of many kinds; very varied

multilateral *ADJECTIVE*
a multilateral agreement or treaty is made between three or more people or organizations or countries

multimedia *ADJECTIVE*
(*ICT*) using more than one medium of communication

multimedia *NOUN*
(*ICT*) a computer program with sound and video pictures linked to a text

multimillionaire *NOUN* **multimillionaires**
a person with a fortune of several million pounds or dollars

multinational *NOUN* **multinationals**
a large business company which works in several countries

multiple *ADJECTIVE*
having many parts or elements

multiple *NOUN* **multiples**
a number that contains another number (called a *factor*) an exact amount of times with no remainder ◆ *10 and 15 are multiples of 5.*

multiple sclerosis *NOUN*
a disease of the nervous system which makes a person unable to control their movements, and may affect their sight

multiplex *NOUN* **multiplexes**
a large cinema complex that has many screens

multiplication *NOUN*
1 (*Mathematics*) the process of multiplying one number by another
2 a large or steady increase in the number of people or things

multiplicity *NOUN*
a great variety or large number

multiply *VERB* **multiplies, multiplying, multiplied**
1 (*Mathematics*) to add a number to itself a given quantity of times ◆ *Five multiplied by four equals twenty* ($5 \times 4 = 20$).
2 to make things many, or to become many; to increase
▷ **multiplier** *NOUN*

multiracial *ADJECTIVE*
consisting of people of many different races

multitude *NOUN* **multitudes**
a great number of people or things
▷ **multitudinous** *ADJECTIVE*

mum❶ *NOUN* **mums**
(*informal*) a person's mother

mum❷ *ADJECTIVE*
(*informal*) to stay or keep mum is to say nothing

mumble *VERB* **mumbles, mumbling, mumbled**
to speak indistinctly so that you are not easy to hear
▷ **mumble** *NOUN*
▷ **mumbler** *NOUN*

mumbo-jumbo *NOUN*
talk or ceremony that has no real meaning

mummify *VERB* **mummifies, mummifying, mummified**
in ancient Egypt, to preserve a corpse as a mummy

mummy❶ *NOUN* **mummies**
(*informal*) a person's mother

mummy❷ *NOUN* **mummies**
in ancient Egypt, a corpse wrapped in cloth and treated with oils and preservatives before burial so that it does not decay

mumps *NOUN*
an infectious disease that makes the neck swell painfully

munch *VERB* **munches, munching, munched**
to chew vigorously

mundane *ADJECTIVE*
1 ordinary, not exciting
2 concerned with practical matters, not ideals

municipal (*say* mew- **nis**- ip- al) *ADJECTIVE*
to do with a town or city

municipality *NOUN* **municipalities**
a town or city that has its own local government

a b c d e f g h i j k l m n o p q r s t u v w x y z

munificent *ADJECTIVE*
(*formal*) extremely generous
▷ **munificently** *ADVERB*
▷ **munificence** *NOUN*

munitions *PLURAL NOUN*
military weapons, ammunition, and equipment

mural *NOUN* **murals**
a picture painted on a wall

mural *ADJECTIVE*
on or to do with a wall

murder *VERB* **murders, murdering, murdered**
to kill a person unlawfully and deliberately
▷ **murderer** *NOUN*
▷ **murderess** *NOUN*

murder *NOUN* **murders**
the murdering of somebody
▷ **murderous** *ADJECTIVE*

murk *NOUN*
darkness or fog that makes it hard to see

We will need something to light this murk if we are to see what we are doing. — *Celia Rees, Witch Child*

murky *ADJECTIVE* **murkier, murkiest**
dark and gloomy
▷ **murkiness** *NOUN*

murmur *VERB* **murmurs, murmuring, murmured**
1 to make a low continuous sound
2 to speak in a soft voice

murmur *NOUN* **murmurs**
a sound of soft voices

A murmur rose up from the people round the fire. Such a thing had never happened before. — *William Nicholson, Firesong*

muscle *NOUN* **muscles**
1 a band or bundle of fibrous tissue that can contract and relax and so produce movement in parts of the body
2 the power of muscles; strength

WORD HISTORY from Latin *musculus* 'little mouse', because a flexed muscle was thought to have the shape of a mouse hiding under a mat

muscular *ADJECTIVE*
1 to do with the muscles
2 having well-developed muscles
▷ **muscularity** *NOUN*

muse *VERB* **muses, musing, mused**
to think deeply about something; to ponder or meditate

museum *NOUN* **museums**
a place where interesting, old, or valuable objects are displayed for people to see

WORD HISTORY from Greek *mouseion* 'place of the Muses' (goddesses of the arts and sciences)

mush *NOUN*
soft pulp
▷ **mushy** *ADJECTIVE*

mushroom *NOUN* **mushrooms**
an edible fungus with a stem and a dome-shaped top

mushroom *VERB* **mushrooms, mushrooming, mushroomed**
to grow or appear suddenly in large numbers
◆ *The meadow began to mushroom with huts and tents.*

music *NOUN*
1 a pattern of pleasant or interesting sounds made by instruments or by the voice
2 printed or written symbols which stand for musical sounds

WORD HISTORY from Greek *mousike tekhne* 'art of the Muses'

musical *ADJECTIVE*
1 to do with music
2 producing music
3 good at music or interested in it
▷ **musically** *ADVERB*

musical *NOUN* **musicals**
a play or film containing a lot of songs

musician *NOUN* **musicians**
someone who plays a musical instrument

musk *NOUN*
a strong-smelling substance used in perfumes
▷ **musky** *ADJECTIVE*

musket *NOUN* **muskets**
a kind of gun with a long barrel, formerly used by soldiers

musketeer *NOUN* **musketeers**
a soldier armed with a musket

Muslim *NOUN* **Muslims**
(*Religion*) a person who follows the religious teachings of Muhammad (who lived in about 570–632), set out in the Koran

muslin *NOUN*
very thin cotton cloth

WORD HISTORY named after Mosul, a city in Iraq where it was first made

mussel *NOUN* **mussels**
a shellfish with a black shell

WORD HISTORY from Old English from Latin *musculus* 'little mouse': the word was originally the same as *muscle* and spelled the same way: the shellfish, like the human muscle, was thought to have the shape of a little mouse

must *AUXILIARY VERB*
used to express
1 necessity or obligation (*You must go*)
2 certainty (*You must be joking!*)

a b c d e f g h i j k l m n o p q r s t u v w x y z

mustang *NOUN* **mustangs**
a wild horse of the United States of America and Mexico

WORD HISTORY from Spanish *mestengo* 'stray animal', from Latin *mixta* 'mixed' : the word originally referred to stray cattle, but in Mexican Spanish it was used of stray horses

mustard *NOUN*
a yellow paste or powder used to give food a hot taste

muster *VERB* **musters, mustering, mustered**
to assemble or gather together

muster *NOUN* **musters**
an assembly of people or things

to pass muster is to be up to the required standard

mustn't
short for *must not*

musty *ADJECTIVE* **mustier, mustiest**
smelling or tasting mouldy or stale
▷ **mustiness** *NOUN*

mutable (*say* mew- ta- bul) *ADJECTIVE*
able or likely to change
▷ **mutability** *NOUN*

mutate *VERB* **mutates, mutating, mutated**
to experience mutation, or subject something to mutation

mutation *NOUN* **mutations**
a change in the form of a living creature because of changes in its genes
▷ **mutant** *NOUN*

mute *ADJECTIVE*
1 silent; not speaking or able to speak
2 a mute letter is one that is not pronounced, e.g. the *k* in *knife*
▷ **mutely** *ADVERB*
▷ **muteness** *NOUN*

mute *NOUN* **mutes**
1 a person who cannot speak
2 a device fitted to a musical instrument to deaden its sound

mute *VERB* **mutes, muting, muted**
to make a thing quieter or less intense
▷ **muted** *ADJECTIVE*

mutilate *VERB* **mutilates, mutilating, mutilated**
to damage something by breaking or cutting off part of it
▷ **mutilation** *NOUN*

mutineer *NOUN* **mutineers**
a person who mutinies

mutiny *NOUN* **mutinies**
rebellion against authority, especially refusal by members of the armed forces to obey orders
▷ **mutinous** *ADJECTIVE*
▷ **mutinously** *ADVERB*

mutiny *VERB* **mutinies, mutinying, mutinied**
to take part in a mutiny

mutter *VERB* **mutters, muttering, muttered**
1 to speak in a low voice
2 to grumble
▷ **mutter** *NOUN*

mutton *NOUN*
meat from a sheep

mutual (*say* mew- tew- al) *ADJECTIVE*
1 given or done to each other ◆ *We depend on one another for mutual support.*
2 shared by two or more people ◆ *They visited Claire, who was a mutual friend.*
▷ **mutually** *ADVERB*

muzzle *NOUN* **muzzles**
1 an animal's nose and mouth
2 a cover put over an animal's nose and mouth so that it cannot bite
3 the open end of a gun

muzzle *VERB* **muzzles, muzzling, muzzled**
1 to put a muzzle on an animal
2 to silence someone; to prevent a person from expressing opinions

muzzy *ADJECTIVE*
blurred or confused

my *ADJECTIVE*
belonging to me

myriad (*say* mi- ri- ad) *NOUN*
a huge number of people or things

Yes! the open sea, with but a few scattered pieces of ice and moving icebergs, a long stretch of sea; a world of birds in the air, and myriads of fishes under those waters. — *Jules Verne, 20,000 Leagues Under the Sea*

▷ **myriad** *ADJECTIVE*

myrrh (*say* mer) *NOUN*
a substance used in perfumes and incense and medicine

myrtle *NOUN* **myrtles**
an evergreen shrub with dark leaves and white flowers

myself *PRONOUN*
I or me and nobody else : used to refer back to the subject of a sentence (e.g. *I have hurt myself*) or for emphasis (e.g. *I myself will not be coming*)

by myself on my own; alone

mysterious *ADJECTIVE*
full of mystery; puzzling
▷ **mysteriously** *ADVERB*

mystery *NOUN* **mysteries**
something that cannot be explained or understood; something puzzling

mystic *ADJECTIVE*
1 having a spiritual meaning
2 mysterious and filling people with wonder
▷ **mystical** *ADJECTIVE*
▷ **mystically** *ADVERB*
▷ **mysticism** *NOUN*

mystic *NOUN* **mystics**
a person who seeks to obtain spiritual contact with God by deep religious meditation

mystify *VERB* **mystifies, mystifying, mystified**
to puzzle or bewilder someone
▷ **mystification** *NOUN*

mystique (*say* mis- **teek**) *NOUN*
an air of mystery or secret power

myth (*say* mith) *NOUN* **myths**
1 an old story containing ideas about ancient times or about supernatural beings (SEE ALSO **legend**)
2 an untrue story or belief

mythical *ADJECTIVE*
1 imaginary; found only in myths
2 to do with myths

mythology *NOUN*
myths or the study of myths
▷ **mythological** *ADJECTIVE*

myxomatosis (*say* miks- om- at- **oh**- sis) *NOUN*
a disease that kills rabbits

Nn

N. *ABBREVIATION*
1 north
2 northern

nab *VERB* **nabs, nabbing, nabbed** (*informal*)
1 to catch or arrest someone
2 to seize or grab something

nadir (*say* nay- deer) *NOUN*
1 the part of the sky that is directly below someone looking at it
2 the lowest point

WORD HISTORY from Arabic *nazir* (*as-samt*) 'opposite (the zenith)'

nag❶ *VERB* **nags, nagging, nagged**
1 to pester someone by constantly criticizing, complaining, or asking for things

I begged and pleaded and nagged, and eventually my mother gave in and allowed me to travel to away games. — *Nick Hornby, Fever Pitch*

2 a nagging pain or doubt is one that keeps on hurting or bothering you

nag❷ *NOUN* **nags**
(*informal*) a horse

nail *NOUN* **nails**
1 the hard covering over the end of a finger or toe
2 a small sharp piece of metal hammered in to fasten pieces of wood together

nail *VERB* **nails, nailing, nailed**
1 to fasten something with a nail or nails
2 (*informal*) to catch or arrest someone

naive or **naïve** (*say* ny- eev) *ADJECTIVE*
showing a lack of experience or good judgement; innocent and trusting ◆ *Like most young recruits, we were hopelessly naive about the realities of combat and army life.*
▷ **naively** *ADVERB*
▷ **naivety** *NOUN*

naked *ADJECTIVE*
1 without any clothes or coverings on

Piggy rose dripping from the water and stood naked, cleaning his glasses with a sock. — *William Golding, Lord of the Flies*

2 obvious; not hidden ◆ *the naked truth*
▷ **nakedly** *ADVERB*
▷ **nakedness** *NOUN*

naked eye *NOUN*
to look at something with your naked eye is to look at it without the help of a telescope, binoculars, or microscope

name *NOUN* **names**
1 the word or words by which a person, animal, place, or thing is known
2 a person's reputation

I go ... Trailing white plumes of freedom, garlanded With my good name. — *Edmond Rostand, Cyrano de Bergerac*

name *VERB* **names, naming, named**
1 to give a name to a person or thing
2 to state the name or names of a person or thing
3 to name a price or condition is to say what price or condition you will accept

to name the day is to decide when an event, especially a wedding, is to take place or happen

nameless *ADJECTIVE*
1 without a name
2 with name undisclosed; anonymous ◆ *The sources, who wished to remain nameless, said the party would run in the elections.*

namely *ADVERB*
that is to say

Every ordinary number, be it fourteen or fourteen billion, may be followed by one and only one number, namely, that number plus one. — *Hans Magnus Enzensberger, The Number Devil*

namesake *NOUN* **namesakes**
a person or thing with the same name as another

nan❶ *NOUN*
a type of flat leavened Indian bread

WORD HISTORY an Urdu and Persian word

nan❷ *NOUN*
(*informal*) a person's grandmother

nanny *NOUN* **nannies**
1 a person (usually a woman) who looks after young children
2 (*informal*) a person's grandmother

WORD HISTORY a pet form of the name *Ann*

nanny goat *NOUN* **nanny goats**
a female goat (SEE ALSO **billy goat**)

nap❶ *NOUN* **naps**
a short sleep

to catch someone napping is to find them unprepared for something or not alert

nap❷ *NOUN*
short raised fibres on the surface of cloth or leather

SPELLING NOTE Some words pronounced **n-** begin with **gn-** (e.g. gnaw), **kn-** (e.g. knee), or **pn-** (e.g. pneumatic)

napalm (*say* **nay**- pahm) *NOUN*
a substance made of petrol, used in some incendiary bombs
WORD HISTORY from the chemicals *naphtha* and *palmitic acid*, from which it is made

nape *NOUN* **napes**
the back part of your neck

napkin *NOUN* **napkins**
1 a piece of cloth or paper used at meals to protect your clothes or for wiping your lips or fingers
2 (*old use*) a nappy
WORD HISTORY from French *nappe* 'tablecloth'

nappy *NOUN* **nappies**
a piece of cloth or other fabric put round a baby's bottom

narcissistic *ADJECTIVE*
extremely vain
▷ **narcissism** *NOUN*
WORD HISTORY from *Narcissus*, a youth in Greek legend who fell in love with his own reflection and was turned into a flower

narcissus *NOUN* **narcissi**
a garden flower like a daffodil

narcotic *ADJECTIVE*
a narcotic drug or effect makes you sleepy or unconscious

narcotic *NOUN* **narcotics**
a narcotic drug
WORD HISTORY from Greek *narke* 'numbness'

narrate *VERB* **narrates, narrating, narrated**
to tell a story or give an account of something
▷ **narration** *NOUN*
▷ **narrator** *NOUN*
WORD HISTORY from Latin *narrare* 'to relate'

narrative *NOUN* **narratives**
(*Language*) a spoken or written account of something

narrow *ADJECTIVE*
1 not wide or broad
2 uncomfortably close; with only a small margin of error or safety

'You have had a narrow escape,' he said. 'There is a sword-thrust just below your collar-bone.' — *G. A. Henty, A March on London*

▷ **narrowly** *ADVERB*
▷ **narrowness** *NOUN*

narrow *VERB* **narrows, narrowing, narrowed**
to make something narrower, or to become narrower

Victoria narrowed her eyes at the odious Captain Carstairs. — *Meg Cabot, Victoria and the Rogue*

Today, the way narrowed. The broad road we took out of Salem has diminished to a track. — *Celia Rees, Witch Child*

narrow-minded *ADJECTIVE*
unwilling to accept other people's beliefs and ways

narwhal (*say* **nar**- wul) *NOUN* **narwhals**
a small Arctic whale, the male of which has a long tusk with a spiral groove
WORD HISTORY via Dutch from Old Norse *nar* 'corpse', because the colour of the whale's skin resembled that of a corpse

nasal *ADJECTIVE*
1 to do with your nose
2 a nasal sound or voice sounds as if your breath is coming out through your nose
▷ **nasally** *ADVERB*
WORD HISTORY from Latin *nasus* 'nose'

nasturtium (*say* na- **ster**- shum) *NOUN* **nasturtiums**
a garden plant with round leaves and red, yellow, or orange flowers
WORD HISTORY from Latin *nasus* 'nose' and *torquere* 'to twist', because of its sharp smell

nasty *ADJECTIVE* **nastier, nastiest**
1 horrid or unpleasant

Harry saw the edge of Snape's sallow face turn a nasty brick colour, the vein in his temple pulsing more rapidly. — *J. K. Rowling, Harry Potter and the Goblet of Fire*

2 cruel or unkind
▷ **nastily** *ADVERB*
▷ **nastiness** *NOUN*

natal (*say* **nay**- tal) *ADJECTIVE*
1 to do with birth
2 from or since birth
WORD HISTORY from Latin *natus* 'born'

nation *NOUN* **nations**
a large community of people most of whom have the same ancestors, language, history, and customs, and who usually live in the same part of the world under one government
WORD HISTORY from Latin *natio* 'birth or race'

national *ADJECTIVE*
to do with or belonging to a nation or country
◆ *the national flag* ◆ *a national holiday*
▷ **nationally** *ADVERB*

national *NOUN* **nationals**
a citizen of a particular country

national anthem *NOUN* **national anthems**
a nation's official song, which is played or sung on important occasions

national curriculum *NOUN*
the subjects that must be taught by state schools in England and Wales

a b c d e f g h i j k l m n o p q r s t u v w x y z

nationalist *NOUN* **nationalists**
1 a person who is very patriotic
2 a person who wants their country to be independent and not to form part of another country
▷ **nationalism** *NOUN*
▷ **nationalistic** *ADJECTIVE*

nationality *NOUN* **nationalities**
the condition of belonging to a particular nation ◆ *What is your nationality?*

nationalize *VERB* **nationalizes, nationalizing, nationalized**
to put an industry or business under state ownership or control
▷ **nationalization** *NOUN*

USAGE NOTE This word can also be spelled nationalise.

national park *NOUN* **national parks**
an area of natural beauty which is protected by the government and which the public may visit

nationwide *ADJECTIVE, ADVERB*
over the whole of a country ◆ *A nationwide appeal has raised over a million pounds.*

native *NOUN* **natives**
a person born in a particular place ◆ *Taliesin was a late sixth-century poet who was perhaps a native of Wales.*

native *ADJECTIVE*
1 a person's native country or city is the place where they were born
2 grown or originating in a particular place ◆ *The tomato is native to the Americas and was initially cultivated by the Aztecs.*
3 belonging to a person by nature; natural, innate ◆ *We hear speech from the moment we are born, and speaking is a native skill for humans.*

WORD HISTORY from Latin *nativus* 'natural or innate'

Native American *NOUN* **Native Americans**
a member of any of the indigenous peoples of North and South America and the Caribbean Islands

Native American *ADJECTIVE*
relating to the indigenous peoples of North and South America and the Caribbean Islands

nativity *NOUN* **nativities**
a person's birth

the Nativity (*Religion*) the birth of Jesus Christ

natter *VERB* **natters, nattering, nattered**
(*informal*) to chat informally; to chatter

natty *ADJECTIVE* **nattier, nattiest**
(*informal*) neat and trim; dapper

'Hey, are you shivering? You shouldn't be cold in that natty furry jacket.' — *Jacqueline Wilson, Lola Rose*

▷ **nattily** *ADVERB*

natural *ADJECTIVE*
1 produced or done by nature, not by people or machines
2 normal; not surprising ◆ *It is only natural to be a bit nervous about a race.*
3 having a quality or ability that you were born with

Next door was always twitching her curtains. She was a natural spy. She'd love to gang up with the enemy. — *Anne Fine, Flour Babies*

4 (*Music*) a natural note is neither sharp nor flat
▷ **naturally** *ADVERB*
▷ **naturalness** *NOUN*

natural *NOUN* **naturals**
1 to be a natural at something is to have the right character and ability to do it well
2 (*Music*) a natural note; a sign (♮) that shows this

natural gas *NOUN*
gas found underground or under the sea, and not made from coal

natural history *NOUN*
the study of plants and animals

naturalist *NOUN* **naturalists**
an expert in natural history

naturalize *VERB* **naturalizes, naturalizing, naturalized**
1 to give a person full rights as a citizen of a country although they were not born there
2 to cause a plant or animal to grow or live naturally in a country that is not its own
▷ **naturalization** *NOUN*

USAGE NOTE This word can also be spelled naturalise.

natural science *NOUN*
the study of physics, chemistry, and biology

natural selection *NOUN*
Charles Darwin's theory that only the plants and animals best suited to their surroundings will survive and breed

nature *NOUN* **natures**
1 everything in the world that was not made by people
2 the qualities and characteristics of a person or thing

Elsewhere immense research into the nature, habits, and constitution of the triffid went on. — *John Wyndham, The Day of the Triffids*

3 a kind or sort of thing ◆ *At Hallowe'en, we'd dress up as witches and vampires or things of that nature.*

nature reserve *NOUN* **nature reserves**
an area of land which is managed in a way that preserves the wild animals and plants that live there

a b c d e f g h i j k l m n o p q r s t u v w x y z

nature trail *NOUN* **nature trails**
a path in a country area with signs giving information about the plants and animals that live there

naturist *NOUN* **naturists**
a nudist
▷ **naturism** *NOUN*

naught *NOUN*
(*old use*) nothing

Geordie snarled, 'Ye know what the Prince is. He's a trickster, a liar & he cares for naught save the crown.' — *Frances Mary Hendry, My Story: The '45 Rising*

to come to naught is to fail or be unsuccessful

WORD HISTORY from Old English *nawiht* 'no thing'

naughty *ADJECTIVE* **naughtier, naughtiest**
1 badly behaved or disobedient
2 slightly rude or indecent ◆ *In 1818 Thomas Bowdler edited the naughty bits out of Shakespeare, much to the amusement of contemporary critics.*
▷ **naughtily** *ADVERB*
▷ **naughtiness** *NOUN*

WORD HISTORY from an earlier meaning 'poor', from *naught*

nausea (*say* naw- zee- a) *NOUN*
a feeling of sickness or disgust
▷ **nauseous** *ADJECTIVE*
▷ **nauseating** *ADJECTIVE*
▷ **nauseatingly** *ADVERB*

WORD HISTORY from Greek *nausia* 'seasickness', from *naus* 'a ship'

nautical *ADJECTIVE*
to do with ships or sailors

WORD FAMILY *Nautical* comes from the Greek word *nautēs* meaning 'sailor'. Other words having the same origin include *astronaut* and *cosmonaut*.

nautical mile *NOUN* **nautical miles**
a measure of distance used at sea, equal to 2,025 yards (1.852 kilometres)

nautilus (*say* naw- til- us) *NOUN* **nautiluses**
a mollusc with a spiral shell divided into compartments

The library was shaped like a nautilus shell, a continuous tunnel that wound down into the mountain in an ever-tightening spiral. — *Garth Nix, Lirael*

WORD HISTORY from Greek *nautilos* 'sailor, nautilus'

naval *ADJECTIVE*
to do with a navy

WORD HISTORY from Latin *navis* 'ship'

nave *NOUN* **naves**
the main part of a church apart from the chancel, aisles, and transepts

WORD HISTORY from Latin *navis* 'ship', because the form of a church was compared to that of a ship

navel *NOUN* **navels**
the small hollow in the centre of a person's abdomen, where the umbilical cord was attached before birth

navigable *ADJECTIVE*
a navigable river or channel is suitable for boats or ships to sail in
▷ **navigability** *NOUN*

navigate *VERB* **navigates, navigating, navigated**
1 to sail in or through a river, sea, or channel ◆ *The ship navigated the Suez Canal.*
2 to make sure that a ship, aircraft, or vehicle is going in the right direction
3 (*ICT*) to access various parts of an Internet website
▷ **navigation** *NOUN*
▷ **navigator** *NOUN*

WORD HISTORY from Latin *navis* 'ship' and *agere* 'to drive'

navvy *NOUN* **navvies**
(*History*) a labourer digging a road, railway, or canal

WORD HISTORY a short form of *navigator* meaning 'someone who constructs a navigation, or canal'

navy *NOUN* **navies**
1 a country's warships and the people trained to use them
2 (also **navy blue**) a very dark blue, the colour of naval uniform

WORD HISTORY from Old French *navie* 'a ship or fleet', related to our word *naval*

nawab (*say* na- wahb) *NOUN* **nawabs**
the title of a governor or nobleman in India at the time of the Mogul empire in the 16th to 19th centuries

WORD HISTORY from Urdu *nawwab*, from Arabic

nay *ADVERB*
(*old use*) no (used to introduce something extra and even more significant)

'Well, then, to save my son, I will sacrifice my life, nay, even my fortune.' — *Alexandre Dumas, The Count of Monte Cristo*

WORD HISTORY from Old Norse *nei*

Nazi (*say* nah- tsee) *NOUN* **Nazis**
a member of the National Socialist Party in Germany under Adolf Hitler from about 1930 to 1945, having Fascist beliefs
▷ **Nazism** *NOUN*

WORD HISTORY from the German pronunciation of *Nationalsozialist*

NB *ABBREVIATION*
take note that (used to draw attention to an instruction or piece of information)

WORD HISTORY from Latin *nota bene* 'note well'

NCO *ABBREVIATION*
non-commissioned officer

NE *ABBREVIATION*
1 north-east
2 north-eastern

Neanderthal (*say* nee- **an**- der- tahl) *NOUN*
an early type of human who lived in Europe during the Stone Age

WORD HISTORY from *Neanderthal*, an area in Germany where fossil remains have been found

near *ADVERB, ADJECTIVE*
not far away in place or time ◆ *The other side of the river looked quite near.* ◆ *The time for leaving was getting near.*

near *PREPOSITION*
not far away from ◆ *The number 32 bus stops near our house.*

near *VERB* **nears, nearing, neared**
to come near to a place or point

We were nearing the second crossroads, where deep gullies lined both sides of the road and the dense forest crept to the very edges of high, jagged, clay-walled banks. — *Mildred D. Taylor, Roll of Thunder, Hear My Cry*

nearby *ADJECTIVE, ADVERB*
near; not far away

Unferth, the son of Ecglaf, was standing nearby. — *Robert Nye, Beowulf*

nearly *ADVERB*
almost; not quite ◆ *I've nearly finished knitting the sleeves on my jumper.*

neat *ADJECTIVE* **neater, neatest**
1 simple and clean and tidy
2 clever or skilful
3 neat whisky or other alcohol is drunk without anything added

▷ **neatly** *ADVERB*
▷ **neatness** *NOUN*

WORD HISTORY from Latin *nitidus* 'clean, shining'

neaten *VERB* **neatens, neatening, neatened**
to make something neat

nebula *NOUN* **nebulae**
a bright or dark patch in the sky, caused by a distant galaxy or a cloud of dust or gas

WORD HISTORY a Latin word meaning 'mist'

nebulous *ADJECTIVE*
unclear or vague

The day of Loretta's arrival, a nebulous plan began shaping itself in Mrs. Hemingway's brain. — *Jack London, A Wicked Woman*

WORD HISTORY from *nebula*

necessary *ADJECTIVE*
needed for something; essential

Is it absolutely necessary that you should be in New York on the 11th, before nine o'clock in the evening? — *Jules Verne, Around the World in Eighty Days*

▷ **necessarily** *ADVERB*

necessitate *VERB* **necessitates, necessitating, necessitated**
to make something necessary

necessity *NOUN* **necessities**
1 need; great importance ◆ *the necessity of buying food and clothing*
2 something necessary

neck *NOUN* **necks**
1 the part of a person's or animal's body that joins the head to the shoulders
2 the part of a piece of clothing round your neck
3 a narrow part of a bottle or other object

neck and neck almost exactly together in a race or contest

necklace or **necklet** *NOUN* **necklaces** or **necklets**
an ornament worn round the neck

necktie *NOUN* **neckties**
a strip of material worn passing under the collar of a shirt and knotted in front

necromancy *NOUN*
the supposed practice of communicating with the dead in order to predict future events

▷ **necromancer** *NOUN*
▷ **necromantic** *ADJECTIVE*

WORD HISTORY from Greek *nekros* 'corpse' and *manteia* 'divination'

nectar *NOUN*
1 a sweet liquid collected by bees from flowers
2 a delicious drink of any kind

WORD HISTORY from Greek *nektar*, a liquid which was drunk by the gods

nectarine *NOUN* **nectarines**
a kind of peach with a thin, smooth skin

nectary *NOUN* **nectaries**
the nectar-producing part of a plant

née (*say* nay) *ADJECTIVE*
born, used to indicate a married woman's maiden name ◆ *Mrs Smith, née Jones*

WORD HISTORY a French word meaning 'born'

need *VERB* **needs, needing, needed**
1 to be without something you should have; to have to have a person or thing with you or available
2 used before another verb to indicate that something must be done

'There's nothing broken,' he said. 'You don't need to fuss over me.' — *Tim Bowler, Starseeker*

a b c d e f g h i j k l m n o p q r s t u v w x y z

SPELLING NOTE Some words pronounced **n-** begin with **gn-** (e.g. gnaw), **kn-** (e.g. knee), or **pn-** (e.g. pneumatic)

need *NOUN* **needs**
1 something needed; a necessary thing
2 a situation where something is necessary

There was no need to starve, so she ate the stew and mashed potatoes with relish. — *Philip Pullman, Northern Lights*

3 great poverty or hardship
▷ **needless** *ADJECTIVE*
▷ **needlessly** *ADVERB*

needle *NOUN* **needles**
1 a very thin pointed piece of steel used in sewing
2 either of a pair of metal, plastic, or bamboo rods using in knitting
3 a thin spike on a tree or plant
4 the pointer of a meter or compass

needlework *NOUN*
sewing or embroidery

needn't
short for *need not*

needy *ADJECTIVE* **needier, neediest**
very poor; lacking things necessary for life
▷ **neediness** *NOUN*

ne'er *ADVERB*
(*poetic*) never; not ever or not again

'So be it,' the count said solemnly. 'My blessing on you both should I ne'er see you again.' — *G. A. Henty, The Lion of the North*

nefarious (*say* nif- **air**- ee- us) *ADJECTIVE*
bad or wicked

And all would have been well, had not Curly Jim conceived a nefarious scheme ..., first to get Marcus O'Brien drunk, and next, to buy his mine from him. — *Jack London, The Passing of Marcus O'Brien*

WORD HISTORY from Latin *nefas* 'wickedness'

negate *VERB* **negates, negating, negated**
1 to make something ineffective
2 to disprove or deny something
▷ **negation** *NOUN*

WORD HISTORY from Latin *negare* 'to deny'

negative *ADJECTIVE*
1 a negative statement or reply is one that means 'no'
2 a negative person or attitude looks only at the bad aspects of a situation
3 a negative test result indicates that there is no sign of what is being tested for
4 (*Mathematics*) a negative number or quantity is less than zero; minus (SEE ALSO **positive**)
5 (*Science*) to do with the kind of electric charge carried by electrons
▷ **negatively** *ADVERB*

USAGE NOTE The opposite of a *negative* answer is an *affirmative* one; for all other meanings, the opposite of *negative* is *positive.*

negative *NOUN* **negatives**
1 a negative answer or statement
2 a negative quality or quantity
3 a photograph or film in which the dark parts appear light and the light parts appear dark, from which a positive print (with the dark and light or colours correct) can be made (SEE ALSO **positive**)

neglect *VERB* **neglects, neglecting, neglected**
1 to fail to look after or pay attention to a person or thing
2 to fail or forget to do something ◆ *Dudley had neglected to tell Elizabeth that he was already married.*

neglect *NOUN*
the state of neglecting or being neglected
▷ **neglectful** *ADJECTIVE*

WORD HISTORY from Latin *nec* 'not' and *legere* 'to choose'

negligence *NOUN*
lack of proper care or attention; carelessness
▷ **negligent** *ADJECTIVE*
▷ **negligently** *ADVERB*

negligible *ADJECTIVE*
not big enough or important enough to be worth bothering about ◆ *The gravity of the Moon has a negligible effect on our bodies.*

WORD HISTORY from French *négliger* 'to neglect'

negotiable *ADJECTIVE*
a negotiable term or payment is able to be changed after being discussed

negotiate *VERB* **negotiates, negotiating, negotiated**
1 to bargain or discuss with others in order to reach an agreement
2 to negotiate a treaty or agreement is to arrange it after discussion
3 to get over or past an obstacle or difficulty

The beasts tiptoed in single file, negotiating the gorse-lined path that led from the loch shore to the meadow. — *Debi Gliori, Pure Dead Wicked*

▷ **negotiation** *NOUN*
▷ **negotiator** *NOUN*

WORD HISTORY from Latin *negotium* 'business'

Negro *NOUN* **Negroes**
a member of a dark-skinned people originating in Africa

WORD HISTORY from Latin *niger* 'black'

USAGE NOTE This word is considered to be old- fashioned and offensive. *Black* is the term that is generally preferred.

neigh *VERB* **neighs, neighing, neighed**
a horse neighs when it makes a high-pitched cry

neigh ***NOUN*** **neighs**
the high-pitched cry of a horse

neighbour ***NOUN*** **neighbours**
a person's neighbour is someone who lives next door to, or near, them
▷ **neighbouring** ***ADJECTIVE***

WORD HISTORY from Old English *neahgebur* 'near dweller'

neighbourhood ***NOUN*** **neighbourhoods**
1 the surrounding district or area

The neighbourhood of the inn looked pretty lonely at that time of day, for the boat had just gone north with passengers. — *Robert Louis Stevenson, Kidnapped*

2 a part of a town where people live

neighbourly ***ADJECTIVE***
a neighbourly person is friendly and helpful to people who live near them

neither (*say* **ny**- *ther* or **nee**- *ther*) ***ADJECTIVE, PRONOUN***
not either

Neither of the boys had read the book of Sir John de Mandeville, so they did not know that a griffin was eight times larger than a lion. — *T. H. White, The Once and Future King*

USAGE NOTE Take care to use a singular verb with *neither*, unless one of the subjects is plural. For example, you would say *Neither of them likes it*, but *Neither he nor his children like it*.

neither ***ADVERB, CONJUNCTION***
neither ... nor not one thing and not the other

The face of Elrond was ageless, neither old nor young. — *J. R. R. Tolkien, The Fellowship of the Ring*

nemesis (*say* **nem**- i- sis) ***NOUN***
a punishment that someone deserves because they have been too proud

WORD HISTORY from *Nemesis*, goddess of retribution in Greek mythology

neolithic (*say* nee- o- **lith**- ik) ***ADJECTIVE***
belonging to the later part of the Stone Age

WORD HISTORY from the Greek words *neos* 'new' and *lithos* 'stone'

neon ***NOUN***
a gas that glows when electricity passes through it, used in glass tubes to make illuminated signs

WORD HISTORY from Greek *neos* 'new'

nephew ***NOUN*** **nephews**
the son of a person's brother or sister

WORD HISTORY from Latin *nepos* 'nephew'

nepotism (*say* **nep**- ot- izm) ***NOUN***
showing favouritism to relatives in appointing them to jobs
▷ **nepotistic** ***ADJECTIVE***

WORD HISTORY from Latin *nepos* 'nephew'

nerve ***NOUN*** **nerves**
1 any of the fibres in your body that carry messages to and from your brain, so that parts of your body can feel and move
2 a person's nerve is their ability to stay calm and act in a dangerous situation
3 cheek or impudence ◆ *They've got a nerve!*
4 nerves are a state of nervousness or anxiety ◆ *I suffer from nerves before exams.*
to get on someone's nerves is to irritate them

nerve ***VERB*** **nerves, nerving, nerved**
to give strength or courage to someone

WORD HISTORY from Latin *nervus* 'sinew'

nerve centre ***NOUN*** **nerve centres**
1 a cluster of neurons
2 the place from which a system or organization is controlled

nerve-racking ***ADJECTIVE***
making you feel anxious or stressed

It was a nerve-racking drive, from Shorings Bank to West 52nd Street, because the gorilla was not in complete control of the lorry. — *Georgia Byng, Molly Moon's Incredible Book of Hypnotism*

nervous ***ADJECTIVE***
1 easily upset or agitated; excitable
2 slightly afraid; timid
3 to do with your nerves
▷ **nervously** ***ADVERB***
▷ **nervousness** ***NOUN***

nervous breakdown ***NOUN*** **nervous breakdowns**
a state of severe depression and anxiety, making it difficult to cope with life

nervous system ***NOUN*** **nervous systems**
the system, consisting of the brain, spinal cord, and nerves, which sends electrical messages from one part of your body to another

nervy ***ADJECTIVE*** **nervier, nerviest**
(*informal*) nervous or anxious

nest ***NOUN*** **nests**
1 a structure or place in which a bird lays its eggs and feeds its young
2 a place where some small creatures, especially mice and wasps, live
3 a set of tables or other items designed to fit inside each other for storage

nest ***VERB*** **nests, nesting, nested**
1 to have or make a nest
2 to fit inside something

nest egg ***NOUN*** **nest eggs**
a sum of money saved up for future use

WORD HISTORY from an earlier meaning 'an egg left in the nest to encourage a hen to lay more'

nestle ***VERB*** **nestles, nestling, nestled**
to curl up comfortably

WORD HISTORY from Old English *nestlian* 'to nest'

a b c d e f g h i j k l m n o p q r s t u v w x y z

SPELLING NOTE Some words pronounced **n-** begin with **gn-** (e.g. gnaw), **kn-** (e.g. knee), or **pn-** (e.g. pneumatic)

nestling *NOUN* **nestlings**
a bird that is too young to leave its nest

net❶ *NOUN* **nets**
1 material made of pieces of thread, cord, or wire joined together in a criss-cross pattern with holes between
2 something made of this
the Net (*informal*) the Internet

net *VERB* **nets, netting, netted**
1 to catch a fish or animal with a net
2 to cover something with a net

net❷ *ADJECTIVE*
a net figure or amount is what remains when nothing more is to be deducted ◆ *The net weight, without the box, is 100 grams.* (SEE ALSO **gross**)

net *VERB* **nets, netting, netted**
to obtain or produce a certain amount as net profit

WORD HISTORY from French *net* 'neat'

netball *NOUN*
a game in which two teams try to throw a ball into a high net hanging from a ring

nether *ADJECTIVE*
low down; lower

There was a quality of intelligence in his forehead and eyes, and a certain tremulousness in his nether lip that decided me. — *H. G. Wells, 'The Diamond Maker'*

▷ **nethermost** *ADJECTIVE*

WORD HISTORY from Old English *neothera*

netting *NOUN*
a piece of net

nettle *NOUN* **nettles**
a wild plant with leaves that sting when they are touched

nettle *VERB* **nettles, nettling, nettled**
to annoy or provoke someone

Jess looked and listened, feeling somewhat nettled that no one had asked about Grandpa. — *Tim Bowler, River Boy*

network *NOUN* **networks**
1 a net-like arrangement or pattern of intersecting lines or parts ◆ *the railway network*
2 an organization with many connecting parts that work together ◆ *a spy network*
3 a group of radio or television stations which broadcast the same programmes
4 (*ICT*) a set of computers which are linked to each other

neuralgia (*say* newr- al- ja) *NOUN*
pain along a nerve, especially in your face or head

WORD HISTORY from Greek *neuron* 'nerve' and *algos* 'pain'

neurology *NOUN*
the study of nerves and their diseases
▷ **neurological** *ADJECTIVE*
▷ **neurologist** *NOUN*

WORD HISTORY from Greek *neuron* 'nerve'

neuron or **neurone** *NOUN* **neurons** or **neurones**
a cell that is part of the nervous system and sends impulses to and from your brain

neurotic (*say* newr- ot- ik) *ADJECTIVE*
a neurotic person is always very worried about something
▷ **neurotically** *ADVERB*

WORD HISTORY from Greek *neuron* 'nerve'

neuter *ADJECTIVE*
1 neither masculine nor feminine
2 in some languages, a neuter word belongs to a class which is neither masculine nor feminine; for example in German *das Fenster*, meaning 'the window'

neuter *VERB* **neuters, neutering, neutered**
to remove an animal's sexual organs so that it cannot breed

WORD HISTORY a Latin word meaning 'neither'

neutral *ADJECTIVE*
1 a neutral person or country does not support either side in a war or quarrel
2 not very distinctive ◆ *a neutral colour such as grey*
3 neither acid nor alkaline
▷ **neutrally** *ADVERB*
▷ **neutrality** *NOUN*

neutral *NOUN* **neutrals**
1 a neutral person or country
2 a gear that is not connected to the driving parts of an engine

neutralize *VERB* **neutralizes, neutralizing, neutralized**
1 to stop something from having any effect
2 to make a substance chemically neutral
▷ **neutralization** *NOUN*

USAGE NOTE This word can also be spelled neutralise.

neutron *NOUN* **neutrons**
a particle of matter with no electric charge

never *ADVERB*
1 at no time; not ever
2 not at all

Witches never bothered with elementary road safety. — *Terry Pratchett, Wyrd Sisters*

WORD HISTORY from Old English *naefre* 'not ever'

nevertheless *ADVERB*
in spite of this; although this is a fact

new *ADJECTIVE*
not existing before; just made, invented, discovered, or received
▷ **newly** *ADVERB*
▷ **newness** *NOUN*
SYNONYMS fresh, original, novel, innovative; modern, up-to-date, recent

new *ADVERB*
newly or recently ◆ *new-laid eggs*

New Age *ADJECTIVE*
to do with a way of living and thinking that includes belief in astrology and alternative medicine, and concern for environmental and spiritual matters rather than possessions

newcomer *NOUN* **newcomers**
a person who has arrived recently

newel *NOUN* **newels**
the upright post to which the handrail of a stair is fixed, or that forms the centre pillar of a winding stair

newfangled *ADJECTIVE*
a newfangled device or method is disliked because it is new and unfamiliar

'Well, Mr. Prendergast, I am against these newfangled steamboats—I suppose every true sailor is.' — *G. A. Henty, The Treasure of the Incas*

WORD HISTORY from *new* and Middle English *fang* 'to seize'

newly *ADVERB*
1 in the recent past ◆ *a newly discovered comet*
2 in a new way

new moon *NOUN* **new moons**
the moon at the beginning of its cycle, when only a thin crescent can be seen

news *NOUN*
1 information about recent events or a broadcast report of this
2 a piece of new information ◆ *That's news to me.*

newsagent *NOUN* **newsagents**
a shopkeeper who sells newspapers

newsflash *NOUN* **newsflashes**
a short news broadcast which interrupts a programme because something important has happened

newsgroup *NOUN* **newsgroups**
a place on the Internet where people discuss a particular subject and exchange information about it

newsletter *NOUN* **newsletters**
a short, informal report sent regularly to members of an organization

newspaper *NOUN* **newspapers**
1 a daily or weekly publication on large sheets of paper, containing news reports, reviews, and articles
2 the sheets of paper forming a newspaper

newsy *ADJECTIVE*
(*informal*) full of news

newt *NOUN* **newts**
a small animal rather like a lizard, that lives near or in water
WORD HISTORY from an Old English word; the original spelling was *an ewt*

newton *NOUN* **newtons**
a unit for measuring force
WORD HISTORY from the English scientist, Sir Isaac *Newton* (1642–1727)

New Year's Day *NOUN*
the first day of the year, 1 January

next *ADJECTIVE*
nearest; coming immediately after ◆ *over the next few days* ◆ *the next chapter*

next *ADVERB*
1 in the next place
2 on the next occasion ◆ *What happens next?*

next door *ADVERB, ADJECTIVE*
in the next house or room

nib *NOUN* **nibs**
the pointed metal part of a pen
WORD HISTORY from Old English *nebb* 'beak, bill'

nibble *VERB* **nibbles, nibbling, nibbled**
to eat something by taking a lot of small or gentle bites

nice *ADJECTIVE* **nicer, nicest**
1 a nice person is pleasant or kind
2 a nice experience is one you enjoy
3 precise or subtle ◆ *a nice distinction*
▷ **nicely** *ADVERB*
▷ **niceness** *NOUN*
SYNONYMS (meaning 1) pleasant, likeable, agreeable, genial; (meaning 2) enjoyable, marvellous, wonderful
WORD HISTORY from an earlier meaning 'stupid', from Latin *nescius* 'ignorant'

nicety (*say* ny-sit-ee) *NOUN* **niceties**
1 a small detail or difference
2 precision or accuracy

niche (*say* nich or neesh) *NOUN* **niches**
1 a small recess, especially in a wall
2 a suitable place or position ◆ *I have finally found my niche in life as a martial arts instructor.*
WORD HISTORY an Old French word, from *nichier* 'to make a nest'

nick *NOUN* **nicks**
1 a small cut or notch
2 (*informal*) a police station or prison
in good nick (*informal*) in good condition
in the nick of time only just in time

nick *VERB* **nicks, nicking, nicked**
1 to make a nick in something
2 (*informal*) to steal something
3 (*informal*) to arrest someone

SPELLING NOTE Some words pronounced **n-** begin with **gn-** (e.g. gnaw), **kn-** (e.g. knee), or **pn-** (e.g. pneumatic)

nickel *NOUN* **nickels**
1 a silvery-white metal
2 (*American*) a 5-cent coin

WORD HISTORY from German *Kupfernickel*, meaning the copper- coloured ore from which nickel was produced

nickname *NOUN* **nicknames**
a name given to a person instead of his or her real name

WORD HISTORY originally *an eke-name*, from Middle English *eke* 'addition' and *name*

nicotine *NOUN*
a poisonous oily liquid found in tobacco

WORD HISTORY from the French diplomat Jean *Nicot* (born 1530), who introduced tobacco into France in 1560

niece *NOUN* **nieces**
the daughter of a person's brother or sister

niggardly *ADJECTIVE*
mean or stingy

It had not been our way to build great fires; we were, indeed, by the captain's orders, somewhat niggardly of firewood. — *Robert Louis Stevenson, Treasure Island*

▷ **niggardliness** *NOUN*

WORD HISTORY from Middle English *nig* 'a mean person'

niggle *VERB* **niggles, niggling, niggled**
1 to fuss over details or very small faults
2 a thought or idea niggles you when it is always present at the back of your mind

▷ **niggling** *ADJECTIVE*

nigh *ADVERB, PREPOSITION*
(*poetic*) near; nearly

'With these and the brothers of the abbey, in all, as I reckon, nigh four hundred men, he will to-morrow march to join Algar.' — *G. A. Henty, The Dragon and the Raven*

WORD HISTORY from Old English *nēah*, related to our words *near* and *next*

night *NOUN* **nights**
1 the dark hours between sunset and sunrise
2 a particular night or evening ◆ *the first night of the play*

WORD FAMILY A related adjective, meaning 'happening or active at night', is nocturnal.

nightcap *NOUN* **nightcaps**
1 (*old use*) a knitted cap worn in bed
2 a drink, especially an alcoholic one, which you have before going to bed

nightclub *NOUN* **nightclubs**
a place that is open at night where people go to drink and dance

nightdress *NOUN* **nightdresses**
a loose dress that girls or women wear in bed

nightfall *NOUN*
the coming of darkness at the end of the day

nightie *NOUN* **nighties**
(*informal*) a nightdress

nightingale *NOUN* **nightingales**
a small brown bird that sings sweetly

WORD HISTORY from Old English *nihtegala* 'night- singer', because the bird often sings until late in the evening

nightlife *NOUN*
the places of entertainment that you can go to at night ◆ *a popular resort with plenty of nightlife*

nightly *ADJECTIVE, ADVERB*
happening every night

nightmare *NOUN* **nightmares**
1 a frightening dream
2 an unpleasant experience ◆ *School was a nightmare because I was unbelievably shy, and terrible at sports.*

▷ **nightmarish** *ADJECTIVE*

WORD HISTORY from Middle English *mare* 'an evil spirit'

nihilism *NOUN*
the rejection of all religious and moral principles

▷ **nihilist** *NOUN*
▷ **nihilistic** *ADJECTIVE*

WORD HISTORY from Latin *nihil* 'nothing'

nil *NOUN*
nothing or nought

WORD HISTORY from Latin *nihil* 'nothing'

nimble *ADJECTIVE*
able to move quickly; agile

▷ **nimbly** *ADVERB*

nincompoop *NOUN* **nincompoops**
(*informal*) a foolish person; an idiot

nine *NOUN, ADJECTIVE* **nines**
the number 9, one more than eight

ninepins *NOUN*
the game of skittles played with nine objects

nineteen *NOUN, ADJECTIVE*
the number 19, one more than eighteen

▷ **nineteenth** *ADJECTIVE, NOUN*

ninety *NOUN, ADJECTIVE* **nineties**
the number 90, equal to nine times ten

▷ **ninetieth** *ADJECTIVE, NOUN*

ninny *NOUN* **ninnies**
(*informal*) a foolish person

ninth *ADJECTIVE, NOUN*
1 next after eighth
2 one of nine equal parts of a thing

nip *VERB* **nips, nipping, nipped**
1 to pinch or bite someone quickly
2 (*informal*) to go or move quickly ◆ *I'll just nip along to the shops.*

nip *NOUN* **nips**
1 a quick pinch or bite
2 sharp coldness ◆ *There's a nip in the air tonight.*
3 a small drink of a spirit ◆ *a nip of brandy*

nipper *NOUN* **nippers**
(*informal*) a young child

nippers *PLURAL NOUN*
(*informal*) a pair of pincers

nipple *NOUN* **nipples**
the small part that sticks out at the front of a person's breast, from which babies suck milk

nippy *ADJECTIVE* **nippier, nippiest** (*informal*)
1 quick or nimble
2 rather cold

nirvana *NOUN*
in Buddhism and Hinduism, the highest state of knowledge and understanding, achieved by meditation
WORD HISTORY from a Sanskrit word meaning 'to be extinguished'

nit *NOUN* **nits** (*informal*)
1 a parasitic insect or its egg, found in people's hair
2 a stupid or foolish person

nit-picking *NOUN*
(*informal*) the act of pointing out very small faults

nitrate *NOUN* **nitrates**
1 a chemical compound containing nitrogen
2 potassium or sodium nitrate, used as a fertilizer

nitric acid (*say* **ny**- trik) *NOUN*
a very strong colourless acid containing nitrogen

nitrogen (*say* **ny**- tro- jen) *NOUN*
a gas that makes up about four-fifths of the air
WORD HISTORY from *nitre*, a substance once thought to be a vital part of the air

nitroglycerine (*say* ny- tro- **glis**- er- een) *NOUN*
an explosive yellow liquid made from glycerol and used in dynamite

nitwit *NOUN* **nitwits**
(*informal*) a stupid person

no *ADJECTIVE*
not any

Liz Finch, our student teacher, is bland, harmless and has no known habits. — *Nicky Singer, Feather Boy*

no *ADVERB*
1 used to deny or refuse something ◆ *'Is this your copy of The Hobbit?' 'No.'*
2 not at all ◆ *The new drama series is no more realistic than the last one.*

No. or **no.** *ABBREVIATION* **Nos.** or **nos.**
number (followed by a numeral, as in *No. 10*)
WORD HISTORY from Latin *numero* 'by number'

nobility *NOUN*
1 the state of being noble
2 the aristocracy

noble *ADJECTIVE* **nobler, noblest**
1 of high social rank; aristocratic
2 having a very good character or qualities ◆ *a noble statesman*
3 stately or impressive

I found very noble specimens of the magnificent silver fir, the tallest about two hundred and forty feet high. — *John Muir, My First Summer in the Sierra*

▷ **nobly** *ADVERB*

noble *NOUN* **nobles**
a person of high social rank
▷ **nobleman** *NOUN*
▷ **noblewoman** *NOUN*

nobody *PRONOUN*
no person; no one

nobody *NOUN* **nobodies**
(*informal*) an unimportant person

nock *VERB* **nocks, nocking, nocked**
to nock an arrow is to place it on a bowstring ready to be fired

They ran back on silent feet, arrows already nocked to their bowstrings, and stopped suddenly. — *Philip Pullman, The Subtle Knife*

nocturnal *ADJECTIVE*
1 happening at night
2 a nocturnal animal is active at night
WORD HISTORY from Latin *noctis* 'of night'

nocturne *NOUN* **nocturnes**
a piece of music with the quiet dreamy feeling of night

nod *VERB* **nods, nodding, nodded**
1 to move your head up and down to show you agree with someone, or to greet them
2 to let your head fall forward in drowsiness; to be drowsy
▷ **nod** *NOUN*

node *NOUN* **nodes**
a small round swelling
WORD HISTORY from Latin *nodus* 'a knot'

nodule *NOUN* **nodules**
a small node

a b c d e f g h i j k l m n o p q r s t u v w x y z

SPELLING NOTE Some words pronounced **n-** begin with **gn-** (e.g. gnaw), **kn-** (e.g. knee), or **pn-** (e.g. pneumatic)

noise *NOUN* **noises**
a loud and unpleasant sound
WORD HISTORY from a French word meaning 'uproar'; related to our words *nausea* and *nautical*

noisome (*say* **noi**- sum) *ADJECTIVE*
smelling unpleasant; harmful
WORD HISTORY from *annoy*

noisy *ADJECTIVE* **noisier, noisiest**
making a lot of noise
▷ **noisily** *ADVERB*
▷ **noiseless** *ADJECTIVE*

nomad *NOUN* **nomads**
a member of a tribe that moves from place to place looking for pasture for their animals
▷ **nomadic** *ADJECTIVE*
WORD HISTORY from Greek *nomas* 'roaming'

no man's land *NOUN*
an area that does not belong to anybody, especially the land between opposing armies

nom de plume *NOUN* **noms de plume**
a special name used by a writer; a pseudonym
WORD HISTORY a French phrase meaning 'pen- name' (although this phrase is not used in French)

nominal *ADJECTIVE*
1 existing in name only ◆ *He is the nominal ruler, but the real power is held by the generals.*
2 a nominal figure or amount is small or insignificant

As a matter of fact, I was going to suggest that we'd lower your rent, make it just a nominal sum, I mean until you get fixed up. — *Harold Pinter, The Caretaker*

3 (*Grammar*) relating to a noun or nouns
▷ **nominally** *ADVERB*
WORD HISTORY from Latin *nomen* 'a name'

nominate *VERB* **nominates, nominating, nominated**
to propose someone as a candidate in an election, or to be appointed to a post
▷ **nomination** *NOUN*
▷ **nominator** *NOUN*
WORD HISTORY from Latin *nominare* 'to name'

nominee *NOUN* **nominees**
a person who is nominated

nonagenarian *NOUN* **nonagenarians**
a person aged between 90 and 99
WORD HISTORY from Latin *nonageni* '90 each'

nonchalant (*say* **non**- shal- ant) *ADJECTIVE*
calm and casual; showing no anxiety or excitement

Hermux ... checked himself hurriedly in the mirror. He tried to look breezy and nonchalant. But he only succeeded in looking disoriented. — *Michael Hoeye, Time Stops for No Mouse*

▷ **nonchalantly** *ADVERB*
▷ **nonchalance** *NOUN*
WORD HISTORY from French *chalant* 'being concerned'

non-commissioned officer *NOUN* **non-commissioned officers**
a member of the armed forces, such as a corporal or sergeant, who has not been commissioned as an officer but has been promoted from the ranks of ordinary soldiers

non-committal *ADJECTIVE*
not committing yourself; not showing what you think

Nonconformist *NOUN* **Nonconformists**
a member of a Protestant Church (e.g. Baptist, Methodist) that does not conform to all the customs of the Church of England

nondescript *ADJECTIVE*
having no special or distinctive qualities and therefore difficult to describe

none *PRONOUN*
1 not any ◆ *I usually get a few valentine cards, but this year I got none.*
2 no one; nobody

None can say what the gods have in store for us, it may be victory or it may be destruction. — *H. Rider Haggard, Montezuma's Daughter*

USAGE NOTE It is better to use a singular verb with *none*, rather than a plural. For example, *None of them is here* is better than *None of them are here*, although the second example is not wrong.

none *ADVERB*
none other no other person
none the wiser no better informed than before
none the worse not badly affected by something ◆ *They are none the worse for their experience.*
none too not very, not at all ◆ *Shrek rightly assumes that his father-in-law will be none too pleased that his daughter has married a big, green ogre.*
WORD HISTORY from Old English *nan* 'not one'

nonentity (*say* non- **en**- tit- ee) *NOUN* **nonentities**
an unimportant person

nonetheless *ADVERB*
in spite of this; although this is a fact

non-European *ADJECTIVE*
not belonging to or coming from Europe

non-European words in English

European explorers and settlers often used the local names for animals and plants they found outside Europe. Thus English includes words like *chocolate*, *raccoon*, *squash* (the vegetable), and *toboggan*, borrowed from Native American languages in North and South America; and *billabong*, *dingo*, *kangaroo*, *kiwi*, *koala*, and *wombat*, derived from the Aboriginal and Maori languages of Australia and New Zealand. Later, British colonial ties with the Indian subcontinent led to English importing the words *bungalow* and *shampoo* from Hindi, and *gymkhana*, *khaki*, and *pyjamas* from Urdu. Words from Indian languages continue to enter English, especially cultural terms relating to food, fashion, and music, such as *balti*, *bindi*, and *bhangra*.
Words from other languages are often borrowed along with the cultural items they describe. Japanese culture has given us *bonsai*, *karate*, *kimono*, and *origami*, as well as *kamikaze* and, more recently, *karaoke*. *Anorak*, *parka*, and *kayak* have all been borrowed from Inuit, as well as the more obvious *igloo*; and *ukulele* is a Hawaiian word meaning literally 'jumping flea'.
See also the panel on **Arabic words in English**.

non-existent *ADJECTIVE*
not existing; unreal

non-fiction *NOUN*
writings that are not fiction; books about real people and things and true events

non-flammable *ADJECTIVE*
not able to be set on fire

nonplussed *ADJECTIVE*
puzzled or confused
WORD HISTORY from Latin *non plus* 'not further'

nonsense *NOUN*
1 words put together in a way that does not mean anything
2 stupid ideas or behaviour
▷ **nonsensical** (*say* non- **sens**- ik- al) *ADJECTIVE*

non sequitur (*say* non **sek**- wit- er) *NOUN* **non sequiturs**
a conclusion that does not follow from the evidence given
WORD HISTORY a Latin phrase meaning 'it does not follow'

non-stop *ADJECTIVE, ADVERB*
1 not stopping ◆ *They talked non-stop for hours.*
2 a non-stop journey or vehicle does not stop at intermediate stations

noodles *PLURAL NOUN*
pasta made in narrow strips, used in soups and stir-fries
WORD HISTORY from German *Nudel*

nook *NOUN* **nooks**
a sheltered corner; a recess

noon *NOUN*
twelve o'clock midday

no one *NOUN*
no person; nobody

noose *NOUN* **nooses**
a loop in a rope that gets smaller when the rope is pulled

nor *CONJUNCTION*
and not

The cat did not speak aloud, nor did Bowman answer him aloud. But they understood each other well. — *William Nicholson, Firesong*

norm *NOUN* **norms**
1 a standard or average type, amount, or level
2 normal or expected behaviour ◆ *social norms*
WORD HISTORY from Latin *norma* 'a pattern or rule'

normal *ADJECTIVE*
1 usual or ordinary

The cat didn't move. It just gave him a stern look. Was this normal cat behaviour, Mr Dursley wondered. — *J. K. Rowling, Harry Potter and the Philosopher's Stone*

2 natural and healthy; not suffering from an illness
▷ **normally** *ADVERB*
▷ **normality** *NOUN*

Norman *NOUN* **Normans**
a member of the people of Normandy in northern France, who conquered England in 1066
▷ **Norman** *ADJECTIVE*
WORD HISTORY from Old Norse *northmathr* 'man from the north', because the Normans were partly descended from the Vikings

north *NOUN*
1 the direction to the left of a person who faces east
2 the northern part of a country, city, or other area

north *ADJECTIVE, ADVERB*
towards or in the north; coming from the north
WORD FAMILY A northerly wind comes from the direction of the north; a northern person, place, or thing comes from, or is situated in, the north; a northerner is a person who comes from or lives in the north of a country or area; the northernmost place or point is at the most northern point of a country or area.

north-east *NOUN, ADJECTIVE, ADVERB*
midway between north and east
▷ **north-easterly** *ADJECTIVE*
▷ **north-eastern** *ADJECTIVE*

northward *ADJECTIVE, ADVERB*
towards the north
▷ **northwards** *ADVERB*

SPELLING NOTE Some words pronounced **n-** begin with **gn-** (e.g. gnaw), **kn-** (e.g. knee), or **pn-** (e.g. pneumatic)

north-west *NOUN, ADJECTIVE, ADVERB*
midway between north and west
▷ **north-westerly** *ADJECTIVE*
▷ **north-western** *ADJECTIVE*

Nos. or **nos.** *plural of* **No.** or **no.**

nose *NOUN* **noses**
1 the part of a person's or animal's face that is used for breathing and for smelling
2 the front end or part

WORD FAMILY A related adjective is nasal.

nose *VERB* **noses, nosing, nosed**
1 to push your nose into or near something

The dragon turned its immense head and in a completely animal gesture nosed and sniffed at the man's body. — *Ursula Le Guin, Tehanu*

2 to go forward cautiously

The tractor nosed back and forth over the ground, leaving a smooth black wave of soil behind it. — *Roald Dahl, 'The Mildenhall Treasure'*

nosebag *NOUN* **nosebags**
a bag containing fodder, for hanging on a horse's head

nosedive *NOUN* **nosedives**
a steep downward dive, especially by an aircraft

nosedive *VERB* **nosedives, nosediving, nosedived**
to make a nosedive; to descend steeply

nosegay *NOUN* **nosegays**
a small bunch of flowers

WORD HISTORY from *nose* and Middle English *gay* 'an ornament'

nostalgia (*say* nos- **tal**- ja) *NOUN*
sentimental remembering or longing for the past
▷ **nostalgic** *ADJECTIVE*
▷ **nostalgically** *ADVERB*

WORD HISTORY from an earlier meaning 'homesickness', from Greek *nostos* 'return home' and *algos* 'pain'

nostril *NOUN* **nostrils**
either of the two openings in the nose

WORD HISTORY from Old English *nosthryl* 'nose- hole'

nosy *ADJECTIVE* **nosier, nosiest**
(*informal*) too curious about other people's business
▷ **nosily** *ADVERB*
▷ **nosiness** *NOUN*

WORD HISTORY from the idea of *sticking your nose into something* meaning 'being inquisitive'

not *ADVERB*
used to express the opposite or absence of a thing or action ◆ *Try not to waste paper.* ◆ *There was not a single tree for five miles in any direction.*

notable *ADJECTIVE*
worth noticing; remarkable ◆ *My family displays a notable lack of interest in current affairs and politics.*
▷ **notably** *ADVERB*
▷ **notability** *NOUN*

notation *NOUN* **notations**
a system of symbols representing numbers, quantities, or musical notes

notch *NOUN* **notches**
a small V-shape cut into a surface

notch *VERB* **notches, notching, notched**
to cut a notch or notches in a surface

to notch something up to notch up a figure or score is to achieve or score it

note *NOUN* **notes**
1 something written down as a reminder or as a comment or explanation
2 a short letter
3 a banknote
4 a single sound in music
5 any of the keys on a piano or other keyboard instrument
6 a sound or quality that indicates something ◆ *Anna thought that she detected a note of resignation in his voice.*
7 notice or attention ◆ *Please take note that the museum is closed to the public on Mondays.*

note *VERB* **notes, noting, noted**
1 to make a note about something; to write something down

Every satellite dish in London was noted, photographed, authenticated and then eliminated from the search. — *Anthony Horowitz, Scorpia*

2 to notice or pay attention to someone ◆ *Note the instructions on the label.*

WORD HISTORY from Latin *nota* 'a mark'

notebook *NOUN* **notebooks**
a book with blank pages on which to write notes

noted *ADJECTIVE*
famous, especially for a particular reason ◆ *Woolgoolga is a quiet holiday resort noted for its large Sikh population.*

notepaper *NOUN*
paper for writing letters

nothing *NOUN*
1 no thing; not anything
2 no amount; nought

for nothing
1 without payment, free
2 without a result

nothing *ADVERB*
1 not at all
2 in no way ◆ *The band's new CD is nothing like as good as their debut album.*

notice *NOUN* **notices**
1 something written or printed and displayed for people to see
2 attention

Someone was blowing a whistle and waving their arms, but no one was taking much notice. — *Philip Pullman, Northern Lights*

3 warning that something is going to happen
4 a formal announcement that you are about to end an agreement or leave a job at a specified time ◆ *You will need to give a month's notice.*

notice *VERB* **notices, noticing, noticed**
to see or become aware of something

Thomas noticed that Rueben had five fingers and a thumb on his right hand. — *G. P. Taylor, Shadowmancer*

WORD HISTORY from Latin *notus* 'known'

noticeable *ADJECTIVE*
easily seen or noticed
▷ **noticeably** *ADVERB*

noticeboard *NOUN* **noticeboards**
a board on which notices may be displayed

notifiable *ADJECTIVE*
that must be reported ◆ *Measles, mumps, and rubella are all notifiable diseases.*

notify *VERB* **notifies, notifying, notified**
to notify someone of or about an incident or situation is to report it formally or officially to them ◆ *A passer-by had notified the police of an unattended shopping bag in the city centre.*
▷ **notification** *NOUN*

WORD HISTORY from Latin *notificare* 'to make known'

notion *NOUN* **notions**
an idea, especially one that is vague or incorrect

'The Welsh have strange notions,' said my father. 'But not as strange as the people who live in Greece and Italy.' — *Kevin Crossley-Holland, The Seeing Stone*

WORD HISTORY from Latin *notio* 'getting to know'

notional *ADJECTIVE*
a notional idea or amount is guessed and not definite ◆ *These are notional figures only, used for the purpose of illustration.*
▷ **notionally** *ADVERB*

notorious *ADJECTIVE*
a notorious person or place is well known for something bad
▷ **notoriously** *ADVERB*
▷ **notoriety** (*say* noh- ter- **y**- it- ee) *NOUN*

notwithstanding *PREPOSITION*
in spite of

During that time, notwithstanding the researches they had made, no human being had been discovered. — *Jules Verne, The Mysterious Island*

nougat (*say* **noo**- gah) *NOUN*
a chewy sweet made from nuts, sugar or honey, and egg white

WORD HISTORY a French word

nought (*say* nawt) *NOUN* **noughts**
the figure 0

WORD HISTORY from Old English *nowiht* 'not anything'

noun *NOUN* **nouns**
(*Grammar*) a word that stands for a person, place, or thing

WORD HISTORY from Latin *nomen* 'name'

WORD FAMILY A related adjective is (*technical*) nominal.

nouns

Nouns are used to name people, places, or things and tell you who or what a sentence is about.
Common nouns describe a whole group or category of people or things: for example, *dancer, lizard, sandwich, television*. They can be divided into **concrete nouns**, which stand for physical objects (e.g. *baby, penguin, telescope*), and **abstract nouns**, which stand for ideas (e.g. *beauty, horror, mystery*).
Proper nouns give the name of a specific person, place, or thing: for example *Shakespeare, Antarctica, Hallowe'en*. Proper nouns always begin with a capital letter; common nouns only begin with a capital when they start a sentence: *Penguins are non-flying birds that live in Antarctica.*
See also the panels on **proper nouns** and **singular and plural forms**.

nourish *VERB* **nourishes, nourishing, nourished**
to keep a person, animal, or plant alive and well by means of food

Greymuzzle returned to the duck pond with only seaweed and shellfish to nourish herself and her cub. — *Henry Wiliamson, Tarka the Otter*

▷ **nourishing** *ADJECTIVE*
▷ **nourishment** *NOUN*

nouveau riche (*say* noo- voh **reesh**) *NOUN* **nouveaux riches**
a person who has only recently become rich

WORD HISTORY a French phrase meaning 'new rich'

nova (*say* **noh**- va) *NOUN* **novae** (*say* **noh**- vee) or **novas**
a star that suddenly becomes much brighter for a short time

WORD HISTORY a Latin word meaning 'new'

novel *NOUN* **novels**
a story of fiction that fills a whole book

novel *ADJECTIVE*
of a new and unusual kind ◆ *a novel sensation*

WORD HISTORY from Latin *novus* 'new'

novelist *NOUN* **novelists**
a person who writes novels

SPELLING NOTE Some words pronounced **n-** begin with **gn-** (e.g. gnaw), **kn-** (e.g. knee), or **pn-** (e.g. pneumatic)

novelty *NOUN* **novelties**

1 newness and originality

The mountain had lost its excitement, its novelty, and I wanted to get off it as soon as possible. — *Joe Simpson, Touching the Void*

2 something new and unusual

3 a cheap toy or ornament

November *NOUN*

the eleventh month of the year

WORD HISTORY from Latin *novem* 'nine', because it was the ninth month of the ancient Roman calendar

novice *NOUN* **novices**

1 a beginner

2 a person who is preparing to be a monk or nun

now *ADVERB*

1 at this time

My biggest concern right now was that the librarian, Mrs Wright, could recognize me. — *Keith Gray, Malarkey*

2 by this time

3 immediately ◆ *I've got to hang up now.*

4 I wonder, or I am telling you

Well, Inspector, I don't see that it's any concern of yours how I choose to run my business. Is it now? — *J. B. Priestley, An Inspector Calls*

now and again or **now and then** sometimes; occasionally

now *CONJUNCTION*

as a result of or at the same time as something

The man in yellow overalls seemed to stand a little taller, now that his 'boss' was with him. — *Beverley Naidoo, Chain of Fire*

now *NOUN*

this moment

I'm twenty-six. I should have had a baby by now; everyone expects it. — *Willy Russell, Educating Rita*

nowadays *ADVERB*

at the present time, as contrasted with years ago

nowhere *ADVERB*

not anywhere

nowhere *NOUN*

no place ◆ *There was nowhere to shelter from the rain.*

noxious *ADJECTIVE*

unpleasant and harmful

WORD HISTORY from Latin *noxius* 'harmful'

nozzle *NOUN* **nozzles**

the spout of a hose, pipe, or tube

WORD HISTORY meaning literally 'a little nose'

nuance (*say* new- ahns) *NOUN* **nuances**

a slight difference or shade of meaning

WORD HISTORY a French word, from *nuer* 'to shade', from Latin *nubes* 'a cloud'

nub *NOUN* **nubs**

1 a small knob or lump

Belch scratched the nub of flesh on his crown where the implant had been inserted. — *Eoin Colfer, The Wish List*

2 the central point of a problem

nuclear *ADJECTIVE*

1 to do with a nucleus, especially of an atom

2 using the energy that is created by reactions in the nuclei of atoms ◆ *nuclear power*

nucleus *NOUN* **nuclei**

1 the part in the centre of something, round which other things are grouped

2 the central part of an atom or of a seed or a biological cell

WORD HISTORY a Latin word meaning 'kernel'

nude *ADJECTIVE*

not wearing any clothes; naked

▷ **nudity** *NOUN*

nude *NOUN* **nudes**

a painting or sculpture representing a naked human figure

in the nude not wearing any clothes

WORD HISTORY from Latin *nudus* 'bare'

nudge *VERB* **nudges, nudging, nudged**

1 to poke a person gently with your elbow

'Look.' Ben nudged Sorrel. 'See that castle over there?' — *Cornelia Funke, Dragon Rider*

2 to push something slightly or gradually

nudge *NOUN* **nudges**

a slight push or poke

nudist *NOUN* **nudists**

a person who believes that going naked is enjoyable and good for your health

▷ **nudism** *NOUN*

nugget *NOUN* **nuggets**

1 a rough lump of gold or platinum found in the earth

2 a small but valuable fact

nuisance *NOUN* **nuisances**

an annoying person or thing

WORD HISTORY from French *nuire* 'to hurt someone'

null *ADJECTIVE*

null and void an agreement which is null and void is not legally valid

WORD HISTORY from Latin *nullus* 'none'

nullify *VERB* **nullifies, nullifying, nullified**

to make a thing no longer valid; to cancel an agreement or arrangement

▷ **nullification** *NOUN*

numb *ADJECTIVE*
unable to feel or move
▷ **numbly** *ADVERB*
▷ **numbness** *NOUN*

numb *VERB* **numbs, numbing, numbed**
to make someone, or part of someone, numb

number *NOUN* **numbers**
1 a symbol or word indicating how many; a numeral or figure
2 a numeral given to a thing to identify it ◆ *a telephone number*
3 a quantity of people or things

The orphans were four in number; the two eldest were boys, and the youngest were girls. — *Captain Marryat, The Children of the New Forest*

4 one issue of a magazine or newspaper
5 a song or piece of music

Anyway, we danced about four numbers, and then I turned off the radio. — *J. D. Salinger, The Catcher in the Rye*

USAGE NOTE The phrase *a number of*, meaning 'several', should be used with a plural verb: *There are a number of reasons why people choose to be vegetarians; A number of residents report seeing UFOs in the sky.*

number *VERB* **numbers, numbering, numbered**
1 to mark items with numbers
2 to count items
3 to amount to a given figure ◆ *The crowd numbered 10,000.*

numberless *ADJECTIVE*
too many to count

It was a whole menagerie of rare and curious beasts in a wondrous hot-house, where numberless birds with plumage of a thousand hues gleamed and fluttered in the sunshine. — *Jules Verne, Five Weeks in a Balloon*

numeral *NOUN* **numerals**
a symbol that represents a certain number; a figure
WORD HISTORY from Latin *numerus* 'number'

numerate (*say* **new**- mer- at) *ADJECTIVE*
having a good basic knowledge of mathematics
▷ **numeracy** *NOUN*

numerator *NOUN* **numerators**
(*Mathematics*) the number above the line in a fraction, showing how many parts are to be taken, e.g. 2 in $\frac{2}{3}$ (SEE ALSO **denominator**)
WORD HISTORY from Latin *numerare* 'to number'

numerical (*say* new- **mer**- ik- al) *ADJECTIVE*
to do with or consisting of numbers ◆ *in numerical order*
▷ **numerically** *ADVERB*

numerous *ADJECTIVE*
1 many; lots of ◆ *Doug is the author of two books and numerous articles published in magazines and newspapers.*

numismatics (*say* new- miz- **mat**- iks) *NOUN*
the study of coins
▷ **numismatist** *NOUN*
WORD HISTORY from Latin *nomisma* 'coin'

nun *NOUN* **nuns**
a member of a community of women who live according to the rules of a religious organization (SEE ALSO **monk**)
WORD HISTORY via Old English from Latin *nonna*, feminine of *nonnus* 'monk'

nunnery *NOUN* **nunneries**
a convent

nuptial *ADJECTIVE*
to do with marriage or a wedding
WORD HISTORY from Latin *nuptiae* 'a wedding'

nuptials *PLURAL NOUN*
a wedding

nurse *NOUN* **nurses**
1 a person trained to look after people who are ill or injured
2 a woman employed to look after young children

nurse *VERB* **nurses, nursing, nursed**
1 to look after someone who is ill or injured
2 to feed a baby at the breast
3 to nurse a grudge or other bad feeling against someone is to continue feeling it for a long time
4 to hold something carefully in your hands

Rincewind the wizard ... was sitting in the darkest corner nursing a mug of very small beer. — *Terry Pratchett, The Colour of Magic*

nursemaid *NOUN* **nursemaids**
a young woman employed to look after young children

nursery *NOUN* **nurseries**
1 a place where young children are looked after or play
2 a place where young plants are grown and usually for sale

nursery rhyme *NOUN* **nursery rhymes**
a simple rhyme or song of the kind that young children like

nursery school *NOUN* **nursery schools**
a school for children below primary school age

nursing home *NOUN* **nursing homes**
a small hospital or home for invalids

nurture *VERB* **nurtures, nurturing, nurtured**
1 to train and educate a child; to bring up a child
2 to cherish an idea or hope

SPELLING NOTE Some words pronounced **n-** begin with **gn-** (e.g. gnaw), **kn-** (e.g. knee), or **pn-** (e.g. pneumatic)

a b c d e f g h i j k l m n o p q r s t u v w x y z

nurture *NOUN*
1 upbringing and education
2 the process of nourishing
WORD HISTORY from Old French *nourture* 'nourishment'

nut *NOUN* **nuts**
1 a fruit with a hard shell
2 a kernel
3 a small piece of metal with a hole in the middle, for screwing onto a bolt
4 (*informal*) your head
5 (*informal*) a mad or eccentric person
▷ **nutty** *ADJECTIVE*

nutcrackers *PLURAL NOUN*
pincers for cracking nuts

nutmeg *NOUN*
the hard seed of a tropical tree, grated and used in cooking
WORD HISTORY from Latin *nux muscata* 'spicy nut'

nutrient (*say* **new**- tree- ent) *NOUN* **nutrients**
(*Biology*) a nourishing substance
▷ **nutrient** *ADJECTIVE*
WORD HISTORY from Latin *nutrire* 'to nourish'

nutriment (*say* **new**- trim- ent) *NOUN*
nourishing food

nutrition (*say* new- **trish**- on) *NOUN*
1 the process of nourishing
2 the study of what nourishes people
▷ **nutritional** *ADJECTIVE*
▷ **nutritionally** *ADVERB*

nutritious (*say* new- **trish**- us) *ADJECTIVE*
nourishing; giving good nourishment
▷ **nutritiousness** *NOUN*

nuts *ADJECTIVE*
(*informal*) mad or eccentric

nutshell *NOUN* **nutshells**
the shell of a nut
in a nutshell stated very briefly

nuzzle *VERB* **nuzzles, nuzzling, nuzzled**
an animal nuzzles you when it rubs you gently with its nose

NVQ *ABBREVIATION*
National Vocational Qualification

NW *ABBREVIATION*
1 north-west
2 north-western

nylon *NOUN*
a synthetic, strong, lightweight cloth or fibre

nymph (*say* nimf) *NOUN* **nymphs**
1 in Classical mythology, a female spirit who lived in the sea or woods
2 the immature form of insects such as the dragonfly
WORD HISTORY from Greek *nymphē*

NZ *ABBREVIATION*
New Zealand

Oo

O *EXCLAMATION*
oh

oaf *NOUN* **oafs**
a stupid or clumsy man

▷ **oafish** *ADJECTIVE*

WORD HISTORY from an Old Norse word meaning 'elf'

oak *NOUN* **oaks**
a large deciduous tree with irregularly shaped leaves and seeds called *acorns*

OAP *ABBREVIATION*
old-age pensioner

oar *NOUN* **oars**
a pole with a flat blade at one end, used for rowing a boat

to put or stick your oar in is to give an opinion about something without being asked

oasis (*say* oh- **ay**- sis) *NOUN* **oases**
1 a fertile place in a desert, with a spring or well of water
2 a place of relief or refuge; a haven

Druimfiaclach is a tiny oasis in a wilderness of mountain and peat-bog, and it is a full four miles from the nearest roadside dwelling. — *Gavin Maxwell, Ring of Bright Water*

WORD HISTORY from a Greek word

oatcake *NOUN* **oatcakes**
a thin biscuit made of oatmeal

oath *NOUN* **oaths**
1 a solemn promise to do something or that something is true, sometimes appealing to God as witness
2 a swear word

on or under oath having sworn to tell the truth in a lawcourt

oatmeal *NOUN*
ground oats, used to make porridge or in baking

oats *PLURAL NOUN*
a hardy cereal plant grown in cool climates

obdurate *ADJECTIVE*
stubbornly refusing to change your mind

I was loath to lose so much time; but the fellow was obdurate, and so I accompanied them. — *Edgar Rice Burroughs, The Land That Time Forgot*

▷ **obdurately** *ADVERB*
▷ **obduracy** *NOUN*

OBE *ABBREVIATION*
Order of the British Empire

obedient *ADJECTIVE*
doing what you are told; willing to obey

▷ **obediently** *ADVERB*
▷ **obedience** *NOUN*

obeisance (*say* o- **bay**- sans) *NOUN* **obeisances**
1 an attitude of great respect or deference

Not the least obeisance made he; not a minute stopped or stayed he; But, with the mien of lord or lady, perched above my chamber door. — *Edgar Allan Poe, The Raven*

2 a deep bow or curtsy showing respect

▷ **obeisant** *ADJECTIVE*

WORD HISTORY from Old French *obeissant* 'obeying'

obelisk *NOUN* **obelisks**
a tall pillar set up as a monument or landmark

WORD HISTORY from Greek *obeliskos* 'small pillar'

obese (*say* o- **beess**) *ADJECTIVE*
very fat; overweight

▷ **obesity** (*say* o- **beess**- it- ee) *NOUN*

WORD HISTORY from Latin *obesus* 'having overeaten'

obey *VERB* **obeys, obeying, obeyed**
1 to do what you are told to do; to be obedient
2 to behave in accordance with a scientific law or rule ◆ *Astronomers noticed that the planet's orbit did not seem to obey the laws of physics.*

WORD HISTORY from Latin *ob* 'towards, against' and *audire* 'to listen or hear'

obituary *NOUN* **obituaries**
an announcement in a newspaper of a person's death, often with a short account of their life

WORD HISTORY from Latin *obitus* 'death'

object (*say* **ob**- jikt) *NOUN* **objects**
1 something solid that can be seen or touched
2 a purpose or intention
3 a person or thing to which some action or feeling is directed ◆ *Soon after its invention, the television became an object of desire.*
4 (*Grammar*) a noun or its equivalent that is affected by the action of a transitive verb or by a preposition: *him* is the object in *The tarantula bit him* and in *We all looked at him*

no object not an obstacle or problem ◆ *Money is no object.*

object (*say* ob- **jekt**) *VERB* **objects, objecting, objected**
to object, or object to something, is to say that you are not in favour of it, or do not agree ◆ *Residents have objected to the plans for a multi-storey carpark.*
▷ **objector** *NOUN*
WORD HISTORY from Latin *ob* 'against' and *-jectum* 'thrown'

objection *NOUN* **objections**
1 the action of objecting to something
2 a reason for objecting

objectionable *ADJECTIVE*
an objectional person, belief, or action is one that other people find unpleasant or nasty
▷ **objectionably** *ADVERB*

objective *NOUN* **objectives**
what you are trying to reach or do; an aim

Our next objective was to be the unclimbed South Ridge of Cerro Yantauri, only a short walk across the river bed from our tents. — *Joe Simpson, Touching the Void*

objective *ADJECTIVE*
1 not influenced by personal feelings or opinions

'But you told me not to have a view. You told me to be objective, to consult recognized authorities.' — *Willy Russell, Educating Rita*

2 having real existence outside your mind ◆ *Dreams have no objective existence.*
(SEE ALSO **subjective**)
▷ **objectively** *ADVERB*
▷ **objectivity** *NOUN*

objet d'art (*say* ob- *zhay* **dar**) *NOUN* **objets d'art**
a small artistic object
WORD HISTORY a French phrase meaning 'object of art'

obligation *NOUN* **obligations**
1 the fact of being obliged to do something
2 what you are obliged to do; a duty
under an obligation owing gratitude to someone who has helped you

obligatory (*say* ob- **lig**- a- ter- ee) *ADJECTIVE*
compulsory, not optional ◆ *Attendance at lectures and tutorials is obligatory.*

oblige *VERB* **obliges, obliging, obliged**
1 to force or compel someone to do something

Very few of the books required in the various courses are printed for the blind, and I am obliged to have them spelled into my hand. — *Helen Keller, The Story of My Life*

2 to help someone by performing a service or favour ◆ *Can you oblige me with a loan?*
to be obliged to someone is to feel gratitude to someone who has helped you
WORD HISTORY from Latin *obligare* 'to tie or bind to'

obliging *ADJECTIVE*
an obliging person or action is polite and helpful

oblique (*say* ob- **leek**) *ADJECTIVE*
1 not parallel or at right angles; slanting
2 an oblique answer or statement is not clear or obvious in meaning
▷ **obliquely** *ADVERB*
WORD HISTORY from Latin *obliquus*

obliterate *VERB* **obliterates, obliterating, obliterated**
to destroy and remove all traces of something; to blot something out

The new snow, which had obliterated both their footprints and those of the wolves, made a crisp carpet beneath their feet. — *Joan Aiken, The Wolves of Willoughby Chase*

▷ **obliteration** *NOUN*
WORD HISTORY from Latin *oblitterare* 'to cross out, to remove letters', from *littera* 'letter'

oblivion *NOUN*
1 the fact or state of being forgotten ◆ *Many books on bestseller lists are later consigned to oblivion.*
2 the state of being unconscious

oblivious *ADJECTIVE*
completely unaware of what is happening around you

I scowled at Mother but she was oblivious—as always. To her, my dirty looks were like water off a duck's feathers. — *Malorie Blackman, Noughts and Crosses*

WORD HISTORY from Latin *oblivisci* 'to forget'

oblong *NOUN* **oblongs**
a rectangular shape that is longer than it is wide

oblong *ADJECTIVE*
in the shape of an oblong
WORD HISTORY from Latin *oblongus* 'fairly long'

obnoxious *ADJECTIVE*
very unpleasant; objectionable
WORD HISTORY from a Latin word meaning 'vulnerable to harm', from *noxa* 'harm'

oboe *NOUN* **oboes**
a woodwind instrument of treble pitch
▷ **oboist** *NOUN*
WORD HISTORY from French *hautbois*, from *haut* 'high' and *bois* 'wood'; *hautboy* was an early word for an oboe

obscene (*say* ob- **seen**) *ADJECTIVE*
indecent in a very offensive way
▷ **obscenely** *ADVERB*
WORD HISTORY from Latin *obscaenus* 'ill- omened or abominable'

obscenity *NOUN* **obscenities**
1 the action or fact of being obscene
2 an obscene action or expression

obscure *ADJECTIVE*
1 difficult to see or to understand; not clear ◆ *The film is full of obscure references to Japanese cinema.*
2 not well known

Betty Bloemendaal ... lives on an obscure street in West Amsterdam, and none of us knows where it is. — *Anne Frank, The Diary of a Young Girl*

▷ **obscurely** *ADVERB*
▷ **obscurity** *NOUN*

obscure *VERB* **obscures, obscuring, obscured**
to make something obscure; to darken or conceal something

Lirael squinted, her sight obscured by goggles and the snow that covered nearly all her face. — *Garth Nix, Lirael*

WORD HISTORY from Latin *obscurus* 'dark'

obsequious (*say* ob- **seek**- wee- us) *ADJECTIVE*
showing too much respect or too willing to obey or serve someone; servile
▷ **obsequiously** *ADVERB*
▷ **obsequiousness** *NOUN*

WORD HISTORY from Latin *obsequi* 'to follow towards'

observance *NOUN*
the action of obeying or keeping a law, custom, or religious festival

observant *ADJECTIVE*
quick at observing or noticing things
▷ **observantly** *ADVERB*

observation *NOUN* **observations**
1 the action of observing or watching
2 a comment or remark

observatory *NOUN* **observatories**
a building with a telescope and other instruments for observing the stars or weather

observe *VERB* **observes, observing, observed**
1 to see and notice someone or something; to watch something carefully
2 to observe a rule, law, or promise is to comply with it or fulfil it
3 to keep or celebrate a custom or religious festival
4 to make a remark

'But,' observed Herbert, 'there's nothing to prove that this bottle has been floating long in the sea.' — *Jules Verne, The Mysterious Island*

▷ **observer** *NOUN*

WORD HISTORY from Latin *ob* 'towards' and *servare* 'to watch or keep'

obsess *VERB* **obsesses, obsessing, obsessed**
to be obsessed with something is to be continually thinking about it ◆ *Selina is obsessed with shoes and buys a new pair every month.*

WORD HISTORY from Latin *obsessum* 'haunted or besieged'

obsession *NOUN* **obsession**
1 the fact or state of being obsessed with something
2 a persistent idea that dominates a person's thoughts
▷ **obsessional** *ADJECTIVE*

obsessive *ADJECTIVE*
causing or showing obsession
▷ **obsessively** *ADVERB*

obsidian *NOUN*
a dark glassy kind of hardened lava or volcanic rock

obsolescent *ADJECTIVE*
becoming obsolete; going out of use or fashion
▷ **obsolescence** *NOUN*

obsolete *ADJECTIVE*
not used any more; out of date

WORD HISTORY from Latin *obsoletus* 'worn out'

obstacle *NOUN* **obstacles**
something that stands in the way or obstructs progress

WORD HISTORY from Latin *ob* 'in the way' and *stare* 'to stand'

obstetrics *NOUN*
the branch of medicine and surgery that deals with childbirth
▷ **obstetric** *ADJECTIVE*
▷ **obstetrician** *NOUN*

WORD HISTORY from Latin *obstetrix* 'midwife', literally 'woman who is present'

obstinate *ADJECTIVE*
1 stubbornly refusing to change your mind, not easily persuaded
2 an obstinate problem or stain is difficult to overcome or remove
▷ **obstinately** *ADVERB*
▷ **obstinacy** *NOUN*

WORD HISTORY from Latin *obstinare* 'to persist'

obstreperous (*say* ob- **strep**- er- us) *ADJECTIVE*
noisy and argumentative
▷ **obstreperously** *ADVERB*

WORD HISTORY from Latin *obstreperus* 'noisy', from *strepere* 'to make a noise'

obstruct *VERB* **obstructs, obstructing, obstructed**
to stop someone or something from getting past; to hinder the progress of something
▷ **obstructive** *ADJECTIVE*
▷ **obstructively** *ADVERB*

WORD HISTORY from Latin *ob* 'against' and *structum* 'built'

obstruction *NOUN* **obstructions**
1 the action of obstructing or fact of being obstructed
2 something that obstructs or hinders progress

obtain *VERB* **obtains, obtaining, obtained**
1 to get or be given something
2 (*formal*) a law or custom obtains when it applies or is in use
▷ **obtainable** *ADJECTIVE*
WORD HISTORY from Latin *obtinere* 'to take hold of'

obtrude *VERB* **obtrudes, obtruding, obtruded**
to force yourself or your ideas on someone; to be obtrusive

Not a leaf stirred; not a sound obtruded upon great Nature's meditation. — *Mark Twain, The Adventures of Tom Sawyer*

▷ **obtrusion** *NOUN*
WORD HISTORY from Latin *obtrudere* 'to push or thrust against'

obtrusive *ADJECTIVE*
unpleasantly noticeable ◆ *Didn't you find the music obtrusive?*
▷ **obtrusively** *ADVERB*
▷ **obtrusiveness** *NOUN*

obtuse *ADJECTIVE*
1 slow to understand something

Holmes rose and tossed the end of his cigarette into the grate. 'I have been very obtuse, Watson,' said he. — *Sir Arthur Conan Doyle, 'The Adventure of the Solitary Cyclist'*

2 not sharp or pointed; blunt
▷ **obtusely** *ADVERB*
▷ **obtuseness** *NOUN*
WORD HISTORY from Latin *ob* 'towards' and *tusum* 'blunted'

obtuse angle *NOUN* **obtuse angles**
(*Mathematics*) an angle of more than 90° but less than 180° (SEE ALSO **acute angle**)

If a corner is murderously sharp then it's an acute angle, and if it's not sharp enough, it's an obtuse angle. — *Kjartan Poskitt, Murderous Maths*

obverse *NOUN*
the side of a coin or medal showing the head or chief design (SEE ALSO **reverse**)
WORD HISTORY from Latin *ob* 'towards' and *versum* 'turned'

obviate *VERB* **obviates, obviating, obviated**
to make something unnecessary ◆ *Ploughing the soil destroys weeds and obviates the need for chemical herbicides.*
WORD HISTORY from Latin *obviare* 'to prevent'

obvious *ADJECTIVE*
easy to see, recognize, or understand

It was a very obvious hiding-place, so obvious that it offered a bare chance of safety ... because the hunters might well have searched it already. — *Rosemary Sutcliff, The Eagle of the Ninth*

▷ **obviously** *ADVERB*
WORD HISTORY from a Latin phrase *ob viam* 'in the way'

ocarina (*say* ok- a- **ree**- na) *NOUN* **ocarinas**
a small wind instrument with holes for the fingers, usually in the shape of a bird

Hey, if Dr Scott could drill some holes in my head, you could blow in my ear and play me like an ocarina. — *Brian Clark, Whose Life is it Anyway?*

WORD HISTORY an Italian word, from *oca* 'goose', because of its shape

occasion *NOUN* **occasions**
1 the time when something happens
2 a special event or happening
3 a suitable time or opportunity

Never having had occasion to use the door, Tom had no idea how it might be secured at night. — *Philippa Pearce, Tom's Midnight Garden*

on occasion from time to time

occasion *VERB* **occasions, occasioning, occasioned**
(*formal*) to cause something to happen
WORD HISTORY from Latin *occidere* 'to go down or set'

occasional *ADJECTIVE*
1 happening from time to time but not regularly or frequently

In Thul there was only an occasional bus driving down the main road of the village to the highway, and very rarely a single, dusty car. — *Anita Desai, The Village by the Sea*

2 occasional poetry or music is written or performed for a special occasion
▷ **occasionally** *ADVERB*

Occident (*say* **ok**- sid- ent) *NOUN*
(*literary*) the countries of the West, especially those of Europe and America (SEE ALSO **Orient**)
▷ **occidental** *ADJECTIVE*
WORD HISTORY from a Latin word meaning 'sunset'

occult *ADJECTIVE*
to do with the supernatural or magic
WORD HISTORY from Latin *occultum* 'hidden'

occupant *NOUN* **occupants**
someone who occupies a place

The only occupants of the carriage were an old shepherd and his dog. — *John Buchan, The Thirty-Nine Steps*

▷ **occupancy** *NOUN*

occupation *NOUN* **occupations**
1 a person's job or profession
2 something you do to pass your time
3 the action of capturing a country by military force

occupational *ADJECTIVE*
1 an occupational disease is caused by a person's job
2 an occupational risk or hazard is accepted as a consequence of a certain job

occupational therapy *NOUN*
creative work designed to help people to recover from certain illnesses
▷ **occupational therapist** *NOUN*

occupy *VERB* **occupies, occupying, occupied**
1 to live or work in a place; to inhabit somewhere
2 to fill a space or position

The Royal & General occupied a tall, antique-looking building with a Union Jack fluttering from a pole about fifteen floors up. — *Anthony Horowitz, Stormbreaker*

3 an activity occupies you when it keeps you busy
4 to capture a country by force and place troops there
5 to enter and stay in a building as a form of protest
▷ **occupier** *NOUN*

WORD HISTORY from Latin *occupare* 'to seize'

occur *VERB* **occurs, occurring, occurred**
1 to happen or take place

The great age of polar exploration occurred in the decades before the First World War. — *Paul Dowswell, True Polar Adventures*

2 to be found to exist in some places or conditions ◆ *These types of forest only occur in small and isolated patches.*
3 an idea occurs to you when it comes into your mind

WORD HISTORY from Latin *occurrere* 'to go to meet'

occurrence *NOUN* **occurrences**
1 the action or fact of occurring
2 something that happens; an incident or event

ocean *NOUN* **oceans**
the seas that surround the continents of the earth, especially one of the large named areas of this ◆ *the Pacific Ocean*
▷ **oceanic** *ADJECTIVE*

WORD HISTORY from *Oceanus*, the river that the ancient Greeks thought surrounded the world

oceanography *NOUN*
the scientific study of the sea
▷ **oceanographer** *NOUN*

ocelot (*say* **oss- il- ot**) *NOUN* **ocelots**
a leopard-like animal of Central and South America

WORD HISTORY via French from a Nahuatl (Central American) word meaning 'jaguar'

ochre (*say* **oh- ker**) *NOUN*
1 a yellow, red, or brownish mineral used as a pigment
2 pale brownish yellow

WORD HISTORY via French from Greek *ochros* 'pale yellow'

o'clock *ADVERB*
used to specify the hour when telling the time ◆ *The programme starts at eight o'clock.*

WORD HISTORY short for *of the clock*

octagon *NOUN* **octagons**
a geometric figure with eight sides and eight angles
▷ **octagonal** *ADJECTIVE*

WORD HISTORY from Greek *oktō* 'eight' and *gonia* 'angle'

octave *NOUN* **octaves**
(*Music*) the interval of eight steps between one musical note and the next note of the same name above or below it

WORD HISTORY from Latin *octavus* 'eighth'

octet *NOUN* **octets**
(*Music*) a group of eight instruments or singers

October *NOUN*
the tenth month of the year

WORD HISTORY from Latin *octo* 'eight', because it was the eighth month of the ancient Roman calendar

octogenarian *NOUN* **octogenarians**
a person aged between 80 and 89

WORD HISTORY from Latin *octogeni* '80 each'

octopus *NOUN* **octopuses**
a sea creature with eight long tentacles and a soft body

WORD HISTORY from Greek *oktō* 'eight' and *pous* 'foot'

ocular *ADJECTIVE*
to do with your eyes or vision

WORD HISTORY from Latin *oculus* 'eye'

oculist *NOUN* **oculists**
a doctor who specializes in diseases and defects of the eyes

odd *ADJECTIVE*
1 strange or unusual
2 an odd number cannot be divided exactly by 2 (SEE ALSO **even**)
3 part of a pair or set when the other ones are missing ◆ *I've got one odd sock.* ▸▸

4 occasional; not regular

I loved those old houses and the way the streets were so narrow, with the odd tree or shrub planted into the pavement. — *Bali Rai, (Un)arranged Marriage*

5 (*informal*) or so; thereabouts

'So what do you say? Eight hundred odd for this room or three thousand down for the whole upper storey.' — *Harold Pinter, The Caretaker*

odd one out a person or thing differing in some way from the others in a group or set

▷ **oddly** *ADVERB*

▷ **oddness** *NOUN*

oddball *NOUN* **oddballs**
(*informal*) a strange or eccentric person

oddity *NOUN* **oddities**
a strange person or thing

oddments *PLURAL NOUN*
scraps or pieces left over from a larger piece or set

odds *PLURAL NOUN*
1 the chances that a certain thing will happen
2 the proportion of money that you will win if a bet is successful ♦ *When the odds are 10 to 1, you will win £10 if you bet £1.*

to be at odds with someone is to disagree or conflict with them

odds and ends *PLURAL NOUN*
miscellaneous items or pieces left over

ode *NOUN* **odes**
(*Language*) a poem expressing noble feelings, often addressed to a person or thing or celebrating an event

WORD HISTORY from Greek *ōidē* 'a song'

odious (*say* **oh**- dee- us) *ADJECTIVE*
extremely unpleasant; hateful

Victoria narrowed her eyes at the odious Captain Carstairs. Really; but he was exceedingly full of himself! — *Meg Cabot, Victoria and the Rogue*

▷ **odiously** *ADVERB*

▷ **odiousness** *NOUN*

odium (*say* **oh**- dee- um) *NOUN*
general hatred or disgust felt towards someone or something

WORD HISTORY a Latin word meaning 'hatred'

odour *NOUN* **odours**
a smell, especially an unpleasant one

There was a little fog or smoke-wreath in the air, with an odour of burning weeds. — *J. Meade Falkner, Moonfleet*

▷ **odorous** *ADJECTIVE*

▷ **odourless** *ADJECTIVE*

USAGE NOTE The American spelling of this word is odor.

WORD HISTORY from Latin *odor* 'a smell'

odyssey (*say* **od**- iss- ee) *NOUN* **odysseys**
a long adventurous journey

WORD HISTORY from the *Odyssey*, a Greek epic poem telling of the wanderings of Odysseus on his journey home from Troy

o'er *PREPOSITION, ADVERB*
(*poetic*) over; above

oesophagus (*say* ee- **sof**- a- gus) *NOUN* **oesophagi**
the tube leading from the throat to the stomach; the gullet

WORD HISTORY from Greek *oisophagos*

oestrogen (*say* **ees**- tro- jen) *NOUN*
a hormone which develops and maintains female sexual and physical characteristics

WORD HISTORY from Latin *oestrus* 'frenzy', from a Greek word meaning 'gadfly'

of *PREPOSITION*
1 belonging to; originating from or created by ♦ *the mother of the cub* ♦ *the poems of Robert Burns*
2 concerning; about

Tom hadn't told the pirate mayor of his adventures aboard Airhaven. — *Philip Reeve, Mortal Engines*

3 made from; comprising or including ♦ *lifesize statues of marble* ♦ *a breakfast of porridge and toast*
4 directed towards; for ♦ *She admitted to a love of low-budget horror films.*
5 in a particular direction from ♦ *five miles east of here*

off *PREPOSITION*
1 not on; away or down from ♦ *The storm blew some tiles off our roof.*
2 not taking or wanting ♦ *The new puppy is off its food.*
3 deducted from ♦ *£5 off normal price*
4 a short distance from

The balloon was higher than us by about thirty metres, and drifting off our starboard bow. — *Kenneth Oppel, Airborn*

off *ADVERB*
1 away; at or to a distance ♦ *She drove off without even a backward glance.* ♦ *The elections are still six months off.*
2 not on or attached; separate ♦ *I can't get the lid off this jar.*
3 disconnected; not working or happening ♦ *Can you turn the TV off?*
4 not happening; cancelled ♦ *The match is off because of snow.*
5 to the end; completely ♦ *I'll be able to finish off this essay tonight.*
6 as regards money or supplies ♦ *How are you off for cash?*
7 food that is off is beginning to go bad

offal *NOUN*
the organs of an animal, such as liver and kidneys, sold as food

WORD HISTORY originally meaning 'waste products', from *off* and *fall*

offbeat *ADJECTIVE*
(*informal*) unconventional or unusual

off-colour *ADJECTIVE*
slightly unwell

offence *NOUN* **offences**
1 an illegal or prohibited action

The girls could not take off their panama hats because this was not far from the school gates and hatlessness was an offence. — *Muriel Spark, The Prime of Miss Jean Brodie*

2 a feeling of annoyance or resentment
to give offence is to hurt someone's feelings
to take offence is to be upset by something said or done

USAGE NOTE The American spelling of this word is offense.

offend *VERB* **offends, offending, offended**
1 to cause offence to someone; to hurt someone's feelings
2 to do wrong or commit a crime
▷ **offender** *NOUN*

WORD HISTORY from Latin *offendere* 'to strike'

offensive *ADJECTIVE*
1 causing offence; insulting
2 an offensive smell is unpleasant or disgusting
3 an offensive weapon is one used for attacking
▷ **offensively** *ADVERB*
▷ **offensiveness** *NOUN*

offensive *NOUN* **offensives**
a forceful attack or campaign
to be on the offensive is to be ready to act aggressively

offer *VERB* **offers, offering, offered**
1 to present something so that people can accept it if they want to

Okonkwo brought out his snuff-bottle and offered it to Ogbuefi Ezenwa, who sat next to him. — *Chinua Achebe, Things Fall Apart*

2 to say that you are willing to do or give something, or to pay a certain amount ◆ *Thanks for offering to help sell tickets.*

offer *NOUN* **offers**
1 the action of offering something
2 an amount of money offered
3 a specially reduced price

offering *NOUN* **offerings**
something that is offered

offhand *ADJECTIVE*
an offhand manner is rather casual and rude, without thought or consideration

offhand *ADVERB*
without previous thought or preparation ◆ *I can't think of anyone offhand who would be suitable.*
▷ **offhanded** *ADJECTIVE*
▷ **offhandedly** *ADVERB*

office *NOUN* **offices**
1 a room or building used for business, especially for clerical work; the people who work there
2 a job or position

The three female servants held the offices of cook, attendant upon Miss Villiers, and housemaid. — *Captain Marryat, The Children of the New Forest*

to be in office is to hold an official position

WORD HISTORY from Latin *officium* 'a service or duty'

officer *NOUN* **officers**
1 a person who is in charge of others, especially in the armed forces
2 an official
3 a member of the police force

official *ADJECTIVE*
1 done or said by someone with authority
2 an official duty or task is done as part of your job or position
▷ **officially** *ADVERB*
▷ **officialdom** *NOUN*

USAGE NOTE Take care not to confuse this word with *officious*.

official *NOUN* **officials**
a person who holds a position of authority

officiate *VERB* **officiates, officiating, officiated**
to be in charge of a meeting or event

WORD HISTORY from Latin *officiare* 'to hold a service'

officious *ADJECTIVE*
too ready to give orders; bossy
▷ **officiously** *ADVERB*

WORD HISTORY from Latin *officiosus* 'ready to do your duty'

USAGE NOTE Take care not to confuse this word with *official*.

offing *NOUN*
in the offing likely to happen soon

WORD HISTORY the *offing* was originally the more distant part of the sea that could be seen from the shore, and so a ship that was *in the offing* would be arriving soon

off-licence *NOUN* **off-licences**
a shop with a licence to sell alcoholic drinks to be drunk away from the shop

off-putting *ADJECTIVE*
making you less keen on something; disconcerting ◆ *There was rather an off-putting smell coming from the hotel kitchen.*

off-road *ADJECTIVE*
an off-road vehicle can be driven on rough ground, away from public roads

offset *VERB* **offsets, offsetting, offset**
to cancel out or make up for something

Offsetting all the difficulties and wasted hours was the fact that the weather held. — *Mary O'Hara, My Friend Flicka*

offshoot *NOUN* **offshoots**
1 a side shoot on a plant
2 a by-product

offshore *ADJECTIVE*
1 in the sea some distance from the shore
2 an offshore wind blows from the land towards the sea

offside *ADJECTIVE, ADVERB*
a player in football or other sports is offside when they are in a position where the rules do not allow them to play the ball

offspring *NOUN* **offspring**
a person's child or children; the young of an animal

offstage *ADJECTIVE, ADVERB*
(*Drama*) in a theatre, not on the stage and not visible to the audience

oft *ADVERB*
(*old use*) often; many times

As the manner of journeying over the moor has been described oft enough already, I will say no more. — *R. D. Blackmore, Lorna Doone*

often *ADVERB*
many times; in many cases

ogle *VERB* **ogles, ogling, ogled**
to stare at someone whom you find attractive

Sir William was ogling me at kirk, but I ignored him. — *Frances Mary Hendry, My Story: The '45 Rising*

ogre *NOUN* **ogres**
1 a cruel giant in fairy tales and legends
2 a terrifying person
▷ **ogress** *NOUN*

WORD HISTORY from a French word

oh *EXCLAMATION*
1 a cry of pain, surprise, or delight
2 used for emphasis ◆ *Oh yes I will!*

ohm *NOUN* **ohms**
a unit of electrical resistance

WORD HISTORY after the German physicist, G. S. *Ohm* (1787–1854), who studied electric currents

OHMS *ABBREVIATION*
On Her (or His) Majesty's Service

oil *NOUN* **oils**
1 a thick slippery liquid that will not dissolve in water
2 a kind of petroleum used as fuel
3 oil paint

oil *VERB* **oils, oiling, oiled**
to put oil on something, especially to make it work smoothly

WORD HISTORY from Latin *oleum* 'olive oil'

WORD FAMILY A related adjective, meaning 'oily or greasy', is oleaginous.

oilfield *NOUN* **oilfields**
an area where oil is found in the ground or under the sea

oil paint *NOUN* **oil paints**
paint made with oil

oil painting *NOUN* **oil paintings**
a painting done with oil paints

oil rig *NOUN* **oil rigs**
a structure with equipment for drilling for oil

oilskin *NOUN* **oilskins**
cloth made waterproof by treatment with oil

oil well *NOUN* **oil wells**
a hole drilled in the ground or under the sea to get oil

oily *ADJECTIVE* **oilier, oiliest**
1 containing or like oil; covered or soaked with oil
2 behaving in an insincerely polite way
▷ **oiliness** *NOUN*

ointment *NOUN* **ointments**
a cream or slippery paste for putting on sore skin and cuts

WORD HISTORY from Old French *oignement*

OK or **okay** *ADVERB, ADJECTIVE*
(*informal*) all right

SYNONYMS all right, satisfactory, fine, in order, acceptable, adequate

OK or **okay** *VERB* **OK's, okays, OK'ed, okayed, OK'ing, okaying**
(*informal*) to give your approval or agreement to something ◆ *Has the President okayed the changes to his speech?*

SYNONYMS agree to, approve, authorize, consent to, endorse, accept, ratify

WORD HISTORY perhaps from the initials of *oll* (or *orl*) *korrect*, a humorous spelling of *all correct*, first used in the USA in 1839

okapi (*say* oh-**kah**-pi) *NOUN* **okapis**
an animal of Central Africa, like a giraffe but with a shorter neck and a striped body

okra (*say* **oh**-kra or **ok**-ra) *NOUN*
a tropical plant with seed pods that are used as a vegetable

old *ADJECTIVE*
1 having lived or existed for a long time

Hwel didn't consider himself old. His father had still been digging three tons of ore a day at the age of two hundred. — *Terry Pratchett, Wyrd Sisters*

2 made or built long ago; not recent or modern
3 known, used, or established for a long time ◆ *She's an old friend of mine from primary school.*

4 of a particular age ◆ *I'm fourteen years old.*
5 former or original ◆ *Stephen is applying for his old job again.*
6 (*informal*) used for emphasis

'I've sat through as many boring old child health clinics and grisly play groups in church halls as she has, I assure you.' — *Anne Fine, Madame Doubtfire*

of old long ago; in the distant past
▷ **oldish** *ADJECTIVE*
▷ **oldness** *NOUN*

SYNONYMS (meaning 1) elderly, aged; (meaning 2) ancient, antiquated, antique, vintage

WORD HISTORY from Old English *ald*

old age *NOUN*
the period of a person's life from about 65 or 70 onwards

olden *ADJECTIVE*
of former times

In the olden days people had several different methods of recording numbers. — *Kjartan Poskitt, Murderous Maths*

Old English *NOUN*
the English language from about 700 to 1150, also called **Anglo-Saxon**

old-fashioned *ADJECTIVE*
of the kind that was usual a long time ago; no longer fashionable

Old Norse *NOUN*
the language spoken by the Vikings, the ancestor of modern Scandinavian languages

oleaginous (*say* oh- li- **aj**- in- us) *ADJECTIVE*
oily or greasy

WORD HISTORY from Latin *oleum* 'oil'

oleander (*say* oh- li- **an**- der) *NOUN*
a poisonous Mediterranean shrub with red, white, or pink flowers

olfactory *ADJECTIVE*
to do with your sense of smell

WORD HISTORY from Latin *olfacere* 'to smell'

oligarchy *NOUN* **oligarchies**
a country ruled by a small group of people
▷ **oligarch** *NOUN*
▷ **oligarchic** *ADJECTIVE*

WORD HISTORY from Greek *oligoi* 'few' and *arkhein* 'to rule'

olive *NOUN* **olives**
1 an evergreen tree with a small bitter fruit
2 this fruit, from which an oil (*olive oil*) is made
3 a shade of green like an unripe olive

olive branch *NOUN* **olive branches**
something you do or offer that shows you want to make peace

WORD HISTORY from a story in the Bible, where the dove brings Noah an olive branch as a sign that God is no longer angry with mankind

Olympic Games or **Olympics** *PLURAL NOUN*
a series of international sports contests held every four years in a different part of the world
▷ **Olympic** *ADJECTIVE*

WORD HISTORY from *Olympia*, a city in Greece where games were held in ancient times

ombudsman *NOUN* **ombudsmen**
an official whose job is to investigate complaints against government organizations

WORD HISTORY a Swedish word meaning 'legal representative'

omega (*say* **oh**- meg- a) *NOUN*
the last letter of the Greek alphabet, equivalent to Roman *o*

WORD HISTORY from Greek *o mega* 'big O'

omelette *NOUN* **omelettes**
a dish made of beaten eggs cooked in a frying pan, served folded and sometimes with a filling

WORD HISTORY from a French word

omen *NOUN* **omens**
an event regarded as a sign of what is going to happen

WORD HISTORY from a Latin word, which is also the source of our words *abominate* and *abominable*

ominous *ADJECTIVE*
making you think that something bad is going to happen

The ominous sound of a human voice came to Tarka, and a houndlike taint which raised the hair of his neck. — *Henry Williamson, Tarka the Otter*

▷ **ominously** *ADVERB*

WORD HISTORY from Latin *ominosus* 'acting as an omen'

omission *NOUN* **omissions**
1 the action of omitting something
2 something that has been omitted or not done

omit *VERB* **omits, omitting, omitted**
1 to miss something out
2 to fail to do something

WORD HISTORY from Latin *ob* 'away' and *mittere* 'to send or let go'

omnibus *NOUN* **omnibuses**
1 a book containing several stories or books that were previously published separately
2 a single edition of several radio or television programmes previously broadcast separately
3 (*old use*) a bus

WORD HISTORY a Latin word meaning 'for everybody'

omnipotent *ADJECTIVE*
having unlimited power or very great power
▷ **omnipotence** *NOUN*

WORD HISTORY from Latin *omnis* 'all' and *potens* 'potent, able'

omnipresent *ADJECTIVE*
present everywhere

omniscient (*say* om- **niss**- ee- ent) *ADJECTIVE*
knowing everything
▷ **omniscience** *NOUN*
WORD HISTORY from Latin *omnis* 'all' and *sciens* 'knowing'

omnivore (*say* **om**- ni- vor) *NOUN*
an animal that feeds on both plants and the flesh of other animals (SEE ALSO **carnivore, herbivore**)

omnivorous (*say* om- **niv**- er- us) *ADJECTIVE*
an omnivorous animal feeds on both plants and the flesh of other animals (SEE ALSO **carnivorous, herbivorous**)
WORD HISTORY from Latin *omnis* 'all' and *vorare* 'to devour'

on *PREPOSITION*
1 supported by, attached to, or covering something ◆ *Two Persian cats were curled up on the sofa.* ◆ *There was no sign on the door.*
2 close to; in the area or direction of ◆ *The hotel is right on the coast.* ◆ *Slowly and stealthily the jaguar advanced on its prey.*
3 during a particular day or time ◆ *The film is only showing on Valentine's Day.*
4 while doing something

'Yes,' said Tom bluntly, on opening the front door. 'What d'you want?' — *Michelle Magorian, Goodnight Mister Tom*

5 by reason of, because of ◆ *Two men were arrested on suspicion.*
6 by means of ◆ *Giant pandas live mostly on a diet of bamboo.*
7 concerning; about ◆ *I'm looking for a book on Viking history.*
8 in a state of; using or showing ◆ *My pet parrot was on its best behaviour that day.*
9 doing or taking part in something ◆ *We're going on a tour of the city tomorrow.*
10 paid for by ◆ *Lunch is on me today.*

on *ADVERB*
1 so as to be on something ◆ *Make sure you put the lid on tightly.* ◆ *It was so cold I put on two cardigans and a scarf.*
2 further forward ◆ *The elephants were moving on towards the river.*
3 working; in action ◆ *Is the central heating on?*
4 due to take place, not cancelled ◆ *Despite all the rain, the match is still on.*
on and off occasionally; not all the time

once *ADVERB*
1 for one time or on one occasion only
2 at an earlier time; formerly ◆ *The building had once been a hospital.*

once *NOUN*
one time ◆ *Once is enough.*
at once
1 immediately; without waiting
2 at the same time
once and for all finally, now and for the last time
once in a while from time to time, not often

once *CONJUNCTION*
as soon as ◆ *Once everyone had arrived we could begin.*

once-over *NOUN*
(*informal*) a rapid inspection or search ◆ *I'd better give the tyres the once-over.*

oncoming *ADJECTIVE*
an oncoming vehicle or traffic is approaching or coming towards you

one *ADJECTIVE*
1 single; alone
2 individual or united

one *NOUN*
1 the smallest whole number, 1
2 a person or thing alone
one another each other

one *PRONOUN*
1 a person or thing previously mentioned ◆ *There are lots of films on but I can't find one I want to see.*
2 a person; any person ◆ *One likes to help in any way one can.*
▷ **oneself** *PRONOUN*
WORD FAMILY Words which include 'one' in their meaning often begin with *mono-* or *uni-*: for example, a *monoplane* is 'a type of aeroplane with only one set of wings', and a *unicycle* is 'a cycle with a single wheel'.

one-off *ADJECTIVE*
done or happening only once, not repeated

onerous (*say* **ohn**- er- us or **on**- er- us) *ADJECTIVE*
an onerous task is difficult to bear or do
WORD HISTORY from Latin *onus* 'burden'

one-sided *ADJECTIVE*
1 in a one-sided contest or conversation, one side or person is much stronger or does a lot more than the other
2 a one-sided account gives only one point of view in an unfair way

one-way *ADJECTIVE*
allowing traffic to travel in one direction only

ongoing *ADJECTIVE*
continuing to exist or be in progress ◆ *It's part of an ongoing project.*

onion *NOUN* **onions**
a vegetable with an edible rounded bulb that has a strong smell and flavour
▷ **oniony** *ADJECTIVE*
WORD HISTORY from Old French *oignon*

online *ADJECTIVE, ADVERB*
connected to a computer, or to the Internet

onlooker *NOUN* **onlookers**
a spectator

a b c d e f g h i j k l m n o p q r s t u v w x y z

only *ADJECTIVE*
1 being the one person or thing of a kind; sole ◆ *I was the only person to volunteer to wash the dishes.*
2 an only child is a child who has no brothers or sisters

only *ADVERB*
1 no more than; and that is all

Because I was a half-vampire I aged at only a fifth the rate of humans. — *Darren Shan, Tunnels of Blood*

2 nothing other than; solely

A unicorn is a magic animal, and only a maiden can catch it. — *T. H. White, The Once and Future King*

3 no longer ago than ◆ *I saw her only yesterday.*

only *CONJUNCTION*
except that; however ◆ *He often makes promises, only he never keeps them.*

onomatopoeia (*say* on- om- at- o- **pee**- a) *NOUN*
(*Language*) the formation of words that imitate or suggest what they stand for, e.g. *cuckoo, plop, sizzle*
▷ **onomatopoeic** *ADJECTIVE*

WORD HISTORY from Greek *onoma* 'name' and *poiein* 'to make'

onomatopoeia

Onomatopoeia is the effect produced when the sound of a word seems to imitate what it describes. Words for animal noises are often onomatopoeic, like *baa, bark, caw, cheep, chirp, growl, meow,* and *mew*; so are words describing loud noises, or sounds made by machines, like *bang, beep, buzz, clang,* and *whirr*. The sound or movement of water, steam, or wind can be evoked with onomatopoeic words like *gurgle, hiss, murmur, rustle,* or *wheeze*; and the idea of speed can be conveyed with *whizz* or *whoosh*.
Writers sometimes use onomatopoeia together with alliteration to create poetic effects, as in the swishing sound evoked by 'the silken, sad, uncertain rustling of the curtain' in Edgar Allan Poe's poem, 'The Raven'. See also the panel on **alliteration**.

onrush *NOUN*
a surging rush forward

onset *NOUN*
1 the beginning of something unwelcome or unpleasant ◆ *the onset of winter*
2 (*Language*) the first part of a syllable, e.g. *d* in *dog* (SEE ALSO **rime**)

onshore *ADJECTIVE*
1 situated or occurring on land
2 an onshore wind blows from the sea towards the land

onside *ADJECTIVE, ADVERB*
1 not offside in football or other sports
2 supporting a common plan or message

onslaught *NOUN* **onslaughts**
a fierce attack

WORD HISTORY from Old Dutch *aan* 'on' and *slag* 'a blow'

onstage *ADJECTIVE, ADVERB*
(*Drama*) in a theatre, on the stage and visible to the audience

onto *PREPOSITION*
to a position on

USAGE NOTE Take care not to use *onto* where *on* is an adverb. For example, you would say, *We walked on to the river* (continued walking until we reached it), but *We walked onto the escalator.*

onus (*say* **oh**- nus) *NOUN*
the duty or responsibility of doing something ◆ *The onus is on the prosecution to prove he did it.*

WORD HISTORY a Latin word meaning 'a burden'

onward *ADVERB, ADJECTIVE*
going forward; further on
▷ **onwards** *ADVERB*

onyx *NOUN*
a stone rather like marble, with different colours in layers

WORD HISTORY from Greek *onux*

oodles *PLURAL NOUN*
(*informal*) a great quantity; plenty

ooze *VERB* **oozes, oozing, oozed**
1 to flow or trickle out of something slowly
2 a wound, crack, or other opening oozes when liquid seeps or trickles out of it

Deep, ragged burns covered most of his body. They were chalky white and oozed clear liquid. — *Christopher Paolini, Eragon*

3 to express or display something freely

All three men oozed wealth. — *Nicola Morgan, Fleshmarket*

ooze *NOUN*
mud at the bottom of a river or sea

WORD HISTORY from an Old English word meaning 'juice or sap'

opal *NOUN* **opals**
a quartz-like stone with a rainbow sheen, often used as a gem

WORD HISTORY via French or Latin from Sanskrit *upala* 'precious stone'

opalescent *ADJECTIVE*
having a rainbow sheen like an opal
▷ **opalescence** *NOUN*

opaque (*say* o- **payk**) *ADJECTIVE*
1 not able to be seen through; not transparent or translucent
2 an opaque message or meaning is unclear and difficult to understand

WORD HISTORY from Latin *opacus* 'shady or dark'

open *ADJECTIVE*
1 allowing people or things to go in and out; not closed or fastened
2 not covered or blocked up

> Lowrie McCall ... was spasming weakly on the lino, blood pumping from his open wound. — *Eoin Colfer, The Wish List*

3 spread out; unfolded or unwrapped
4 letting in visitors or customers
5 open country has wide empty spaces or gaps
6 an open competition or championship has no restrictions on who can enter
7 a course of action is open to you when it is possible or feasible
8 honest and frank; not secret or secretive ◆ *The letter was very open about the risks of the expedition.*
9 you have an open mind when you have not yet decided or made up your mind about something
10 to be open to suggestions or comments is to be willing or likely to receive them
11 to be open to attack or criticism is to be vulnerable or susceptible to it

in the open
1 outside; out of doors
2 not secret

in the open air not inside a house or building
▷ **open-air** *ADJECTIVE*
▷ **openness** *NOUN*

open *VERB* **opens, opening, opened**
1 to make something open or more open
2 to become open or more open
3 to open a meeting or discussion is to begin it
4 a film, play, or exhibition opens when it becomes available for public viewing
5 to give access to somewhere ◆ *The French windows open on to a beautiful garden.*
▷ **opener** *NOUN*

open-and-shut *ADJECTIVE*
(*informal*) an open-and-shut case is straightforward and easy to solve

opencast *ADJECTIVE*
an opencast mine is worked by removing layers of earth from the surface, not underground

open day *NOUN* **open days**
a day when the public may visit a place that is not normally open to them

open-ended *ADJECTIVE*
an open-ended ticket has no fixed limit or end-date

opening *NOUN* **openings**
1 a space or gap; a place where something opens
2 the beginning of something
3 an event to mark the start of a public exhibition
4 an opportunity, especially for a job or position ◆ *I hear there's an opening for a trainee florist.*

openly *ADVERB*
without secrecy

open-minded *ADJECTIVE*
ready to listen to other people's ideas and opinions; not having fixed ideas

opera❶ *NOUN* **operas**
1 a drama in which the words are sung to a musical accompaniment
2 dramatic works of this kind
▷ **operatic** *ADJECTIVE*

WORD HISTORY the plural of Latin *opus* 'work'

opera❷ *plural* of **opus**

operate *VERB* **operates, operating, operated**
1 to make a machine work
2 to be in action; to work

> In the next ten years computers will operate thousands of times faster than they do now! — *Michael Cox, The Incredible Internet*

3 to perform a surgical operation on somebody
▷ **operable** *ADJECTIVE*

WORD HISTORY from Latin *operari* 'to work'

operation *NOUN* **operations**
1 a piece of work or method of working
2 something done to the body by a surgeon to take away or repair a part of it
3 a planned military activity
4 (*Mathematics, ICT*) a process in which a number or expression is altered according to set rules

in operation working or in use ◆ *When does the new system come into operation?*
▷ **operational** *ADJECTIVE*

operating system *NOUN* **operating systems**
(*ICT*) the software that controls a computer's basic functions

operative *ADJECTIVE*
1 working or functioning
2 to do with surgical operations

operator *NOUN* **operators**
1 a person who works something, especially a telephone switchboard or exchange
2 (*Mathematics, ICT*) a symbol or word used in an operation, for example ×, ÷, +

operetta *NOUN* **operettas**
a short opera on a light or humorous theme

WORD HISTORY an Italian word meaning 'little opera'

ophthalmic (*say* off- **thal**- mik) *ADJECTIVE*
to do with or for your eyes

WORD HISTORY from Greek *ophthalmos* 'eye'

ophthalmic optician *NOUN* **ophthalmic opticians**
a person who is qualified to examine a person's eyes and to prescribe glasses and contact lenses

opinion *NOUN* **opinions**
what you think of something; a belief or judgement

I am not asking for a guarantee on oath. I am simply asking for your professional opinion. Do you believe I will ever walk again? — *Brian Clark, Whose Life is it Anyway?*

WORD HISTORY from Latin *opinari* 'to believe'

opinionated *ADJECTIVE*
having strong opinions and holding them whatever anybody says

opinion poll *NOUN* **opinion polls**
an estimate of what people think, made by questioning a sample of them

opium *NOUN*
a narcotic drug made from the juice of certain poppies, sometimes used in medicine as a sedative

WORD HISTORY from Greek *opion* 'poppy juice'

opossum *NOUN* **opossums**
a small furry American or Australian marsupial that lives in trees

WORD HISTORY from a word from a Native American language meaning 'white dog'

opponent *NOUN* **opponents**
a person or group opposing another in a contest or war

WORD HISTORY from Latin *opponere* 'to set against'

opportune *ADJECTIVE*
1 an opportune time is convenient or suitable for a purpose
2 done or happening at a convenient or appropriate time ◆ *The silence was broken by the opportune arrival of the post.*

▷ **opportunely** *ADVERB*

WORD HISTORY from Latin *ob* 'towards, against' and *portus* 'harbour', originally used of wind blowing a ship towards a harbour

opportunist *NOUN* **opportunists**
a person who is quick to seize opportunities

▷ **opportunism** *NOUN*
▷ **opportunistic** *ADJECTIVE*

opportunity *NOUN* **opportunities**
a good chance to do a particular thing ◆ *He would never lose an opportunity of speaking to her.*

oppose *VERB* **opposes, opposing, opposed**
1 to argue or fight against someone or something; to resist something
2 to place something, or to be, in opposition to something else

as opposed to in contrast with
to be opposed to something is to be strongly against it

opposite *ADJECTIVE*
1 placed on the other or further side; facing ◆ *on the opposite side of the road*
2 moving away from or towards each other ◆ *The trains were travelling in opposite directions.*
3 completely different ◆ *the opposite end of the price range*

the opposite sex women in relation to men, or men in relation to women

opposite *NOUN* **opposites**
an opposite person or thing

opposite *ADVERB, PREPOSITION*
in an opposite place, position, or direction to a person or thing ◆ *I'll sit opposite.* ◆ *Our new house is just opposite the shops.*

WORD HISTORY from Latin *oppositus* 'set or placed against'

opposition *NOUN*
1 the action of opposing something; resistance
2 the people who oppose something

the Opposition the chief political party opposing the one that is in power

oppress *VERB* **oppresses, oppressing, oppressed**
1 to govern or treat somebody cruelly or unjustly
2 to weigh somebody down with worry or sadness

▷ **oppression** *NOUN*
▷ **oppressor** *NOUN*

WORD HISTORY from Latin *ob* 'towards, against' and *pressus* 'pressed'

oppressive *ADJECTIVE*
1 an oppressive government or regime is cruel or harsh
2 worrying and difficult to bear

The silence of the forest was more oppressive than the heat, and at this hour of the day there was not even the whine of insects. — *William Golding, Lord of the Flies*

3 oppressive weather is unpleasantly hot and humid

opprobrium (*say* op- **roh**- bree- um) *NOUN*
harsh criticism or scorn

▷ **opprobrious** *ADJECTIVE*

WORD HISTORY a Latin word meaning 'infamy'

opt *VERB* **opts, opting, opted**
to choose ◆ *Diana opted for the ice cream for pudding.*

to opt out is to decide not to take part in something

WORD HISTORY from Latin *optare* 'to wish for'

optic *ADJECTIVE*
to do with your eyes or sight

WORD HISTORY from Greek *optos* 'seen'

optical *ADJECTIVE*
to do with sight; aiding sight ◆ *optical instruments*

▷ **optically** *ADVERB*

optical illusion *NOUN* **optical illusions**
a deceptive appearance that makes you think you see something that is not really there

optician *NOUN* **opticians**
a person qualified to prescribe and dispense glasses and contact lenses, and to detect eye diseases

optics *NOUN*
the study of sight and of light as connected with this

optimal *ADJECTIVE*
best; most favourable ◆ *This chart shows your optimal weight according to your age and height.*
▷ **optimally** *ADVERB*

optimist *NOUN* **optimists**
a person who takes a positive or hopeful view, or who expects things to turn out well (SEE ALSO **pessimist**)
▷ **optimism** *NOUN*
▷ **optimistic** *ADJECTIVE*
▷ **optimistically** *ADVERB*

optimize *VERB* **optimizes, optimizing, optimized**
to make the best possible use of something
USAGE NOTE this word can also be spelled optimise.

optimum *ADJECTIVE*
best; most favourable

optimum *NOUN*
the best or most favourable conditions or amount
WORD HISTORY a Latin word meaning 'best thing'

option *NOUN* **options**
1 the right or power to choose something
2 something chosen or that may be chosen

optional *ADJECTIVE*
that you can choose, not compulsory
▷ **optionally** *ADVERB*

opulent *ADJECTIVE*
1 wealthy or luxurious ◆ *The wedding took place in the opulent surroundings of the hotel ballroom.*
2 plentiful or abundant
▷ **opulently** *ADVERB*
▷ **opulence** *NOUN*
WORD HISTORY from Latin *opes* 'wealth'

opus (*say* **oh**- pus) *NOUN* **opuses** or **opera**
1 a musical composition numbered as one of a composer's works ◆ *Beethoven's string quartet, opus 74.*
2 any artistic work
WORD HISTORY a Latin word meaning 'work'

or *CONJUNCTION*
used to show that there is a choice or an alternative ◆ *Would you like chocolate or cinnamon on your cappuccino?*

oracle *NOUN* **oracles**
1 a shrine where the ancient Greeks consulted one of their gods for advice or a prophecy
2 a wise or knowledgeable adviser
▷ **oracular** (*say* or- **ak**- yoo- ler) *ADJECTIVE*
WORD HISTORY from Latin *orare* 'to speak'

oral *ADJECTIVE*
1 spoken; not written
2 to do with or using your mouth
▷ **orally** *ADVERB*

oral *NOUN* **orals**
a spoken examination or test
WORD HISTORY from Latin *oris* 'of the mouth'
USAGE NOTE Take care not to confuse this word with *aural*.

orange *NOUN* **oranges**
1 a round juicy citrus fruit with reddish-yellow peel
2 a reddish-yellow colour

orange *ADJECTIVE*
reddish-yellow in colour, like an orange
WORD HISTORY via French, Arabic, and Persian from Sanskrit

orang-utan *NOUN* **orang-utans**
a large ape of Borneo and Sumatra
WORD HISTORY from Malay (a language spoken in Malaysia) *orang hutan* 'man of the forest'

oration *NOUN* **orations**
a long formal speech
WORD HISTORY from Latin *orare* 'to speak'
WORD FAMILY *Oration* comes from the Latin words *orare* meaning 'to speak' and *oratio* meaning 'speech'. Other words to do with speaking include *oracle*, *oral*, *orator*, and *peroration*.

orator *NOUN* **orators**
a person who is good at making speeches in public
▷ **oratorical** *ADJECTIVE*

oratorio *NOUN* **oratorios**
(*Music*) a piece of music for voices and an orchestra, usually on a religious subject
WORD HISTORY an Italian word, related to our word *oration*

oratory *NOUN*
1 the art of making speeches in public
2 eloquent speech

orb *NOUN* **orbs**
a sphere or globe
WORD HISTORY from Latin *orbis* 'a circle'

orbit *NOUN* **orbits**
1 the curved path taken by something moving round a planet, moon, or star
2 the range of someone's influence or control
▷ **orbital** *ADJECTIVE*

orbit *VERB* **orbits, orbiting, orbited**
to move in an orbit round something

The Moon orbits around Earth once every 28 days but not quite in a perfect circle. — *Kjartan Poskitt, The Gobsmacking Galaxy*

orchard *NOUN* **orchards**
a piece of ground planted with fruit trees

WORD HISTORY from Old English *ortgeard*, from Latin *hortus* 'a garden' and *yard*

orchestra *NOUN* **orchestras**
(*Music*) a large group of people playing various musical instruments together

▷ **orchestral** *ADJECTIVE*

WORD HISTORY a Greek word, referring to the space where the chorus danced during a play

orchestrate *VERB* **orchestrates, orchestrating, orchestrated**
1 to compose or arrange music for an orchestra
2 to coordinate things deliberately ◆ *a carefully orchestrated publicity campaign*

▷ **orchestration** *NOUN*

orchid *NOUN* **orchids**
a kind of plant with brightly coloured, often unevenly shaped, flowers

ordain *VERB* **ordains, ordaining, ordained**
1 to ordain someone is to make them a member of the clergy in the Christian Church
2 to declare or order something by law

ordeal *NOUN* **ordeals**
a difficult or horrific experience

The passengers' first ordeal was a winter storm that pounded the iron ship for ten days and nights. — *Henry Brook, True Sea Stories*

order *NOUN* **orders**
1 a command

As the sun climbed over the horizon ... Raka gave the order for the battle horns to be sounded. — *William Nicholson, The Wind Singer*

2 a request for something to be supplied
3 the way things are arranged ◆ *in alphabetical order*
4 a neat arrangement; a proper arrangement or condition ◆ *All the parts are in working order.*
5 obedience to rules or laws ◆ *law and order*
6 a kind or sort ◆ *Two search and rescue dogs were given awards for courage of the highest order.*
7 a group of monks or nuns who live by certain religious rules

in order that or **in order to** for the purpose of

order *VERB* **orders, ordering, ordered**
1 to command someone or a group of people
2 to ask for something to be supplied
3 to put something into order; to arrange things neatly

WORD HISTORY from Latin *ordo* 'a row, series, or arrangement'

orderly *ADJECTIVE*
1 arranged neatly or well; methodical
2 well behaved and obedient

▷ **orderliness** *NOUN*

orderly *NOUN* **orderlies**
1 a soldier whose job is to assist an officer
2 an assistant in a hospital

ordinal number *NOUN* **ordinal numbers**
a number that shows a thing's position in a series, for example, first, fifth, twentieth (SEE ALSO **cardinal number**)

WORD HISTORY from Latin *ordinalis* 'showing the order'

ordinance *NOUN* **ordinances**
(*formal*) a command or decree

WORD HISTORY from Latin *ordinare* 'to put in order'

ordinary *ADJECTIVE*
normal or usual; not special

It was an ordinary-looking dagger, with a double-sided blade of dull metal about eight inches long. — *Philip Pullman, The Subtle Knife*

out of the ordinary unusual

▷ **ordinarily** *ADVERB*

WORD HISTORY from Latin *ordinarius* 'orderly or usual'

ordination *NOUN* **ordinations**
the process of ordaining someone, or of being ordained, as a member of the Christian clergy

ordnance *NOUN*
weapons and other military equipment

WORD HISTORY from Old French *ordenance*

Ordnance Survey *NOUN*
an official survey organization that makes detailed maps of the British Isles

WORD HISTORY from *ordnance*, because the maps were originally made for the army

ore *NOUN* **ores**
rock with metal or other useful substances in it ◆ *iron ore*

oregano (*say* o- ri- **gah**- noh) *NOUN*
the dried leaves of wild marjoram used as a herb in cooking

WORD HISTORY via Spanish from a Greek word

organ *NOUN* **organs**
1 a musical instrument from which sounds are produced by air forced through pipes, played by keys and pedals
2 a part of the body with a particular function ◆ *the digestive organs*

WORD HISTORY from Greek *organon* 'a tool'

organdie *NOUN*
a kind of thin fabric, usually stiffened

organic *ADJECTIVE*
1 to do with or formed from living things ◆ *organic matter*
2 organic food or farming is grown without, or does not use, chemical fertilizers or pesticides
3 to do with the organs of your body ◆ *organic diseases*
▷ **organically** *ADVERB*

organism *NOUN* **organisms**
(*Biology*) a living thing; an individual animal or plant

organist *NOUN* **organists**
a person who plays the organ

organization *NOUN* **organizations**
1 an organized group of people, such as a business, charity, or government department
2 the process of organizing something
▷ **organizational** *ADJECTIVE*
USAGE NOTE This word can also be spelled organisation.

organize *VERB* **organizes, organizing, organized**
1 to plan and prepare something ◆ *We're organizing a picnic for next weekend.*
2 to form people into a group to work together
3 to put things in order
▷ **organizer** *NOUN*
USAGE NOTE This word can also be spelled organise.

orgasm *NOUN* **orgasms**
the climax of sexual excitement
▷ **orgasmic** *ADJECTIVE*
WORD HISTORY from Greek *orgasmos*

orgy *NOUN* **orgies**
1 a wild party that involves a lot of drinking and sex
2 an extravagant activity ◆ *Every year, there is an orgy of spending around Christmas.*
▷ **orgiastic** *ADJECTIVE*
WORD HISTORY from Latin *orgia* 'secret rites', held in honour of Bacchus, the Greek and Roman god of wine

Orient *NOUN*
(*literary*) the countries of the East, especially east Asia (SEE ALSO **Occident**)
WORD HISTORY from a Latin word meaning 'sunrise'

orient *VERB* **orients, orienting, oriented**
to orientate something

oriental *ADJECTIVE*
(*old use*) to do with the countries east of the Mediterranean Sea, especially China and Japan

orientate *VERB* **orientates, orientating, orientated**
1 to place something or face in a certain direction
2 to orientate yourself is to get your bearings
▷ **orientation** *NOUN*
WORD HISTORY originally meaning 'to turn to face the east', related to *Orient*

orienteering *NOUN*
the sport of finding your way across rough country with a map and compass
WORD HISTORY from Swedish *orientering* 'orientating'

orifice (*say* o- rif- iss) *NOUN* **orifices**
an opening in your body
WORD HISTORY from Latin *oris* 'of the mouth'

origami (*say* o- rig- **ah**- mee) *NOUN*
the Japanese art of folding paper into decorative shapes
WORD HISTORY from Japanese *ori* 'fold' and *kami* 'paper'

origin *NOUN* **origins**
1 the start of something; the point or cause from which something began
2 a person's family background ◆ *a man of humble origins*
3 the point where two or more axes on a graph meet
WORD HISTORY from Latin *oriri* 'to rise'

original *ADJECTIVE*
1 existing from the start; earliest ◆ *the original inhabitants*
2 new in its design; not a copy
3 producing new ideas; inventive
▷ **originally** *ADVERB*
▷ **originality** *NOUN*

original *NOUN* **originals**
a document, painting, or other work which was the first one made and is not a copy

originate *VERB* **originates, originating, originated**
1 to cause something to begin; to create something
2 to have its origin; to begin ◆ *The lute originated in the Middle East.*
▷ **origination** *NOUN*
▷ **originator** *NOUN*

ornament *NOUN* **ornaments**
an object displayed or worn as a decoration

ornament *VERB* **ornaments, ornamenting, ornamented**
to decorate a place with beautiful things
▷ **ornamentation** *NOUN*
WORD HISTORY from Latin *ornare* 'to adorn'

ornamental *ADJECTIVE*
used as an ornament; decorative rather than useful

ornate *ADJECTIVE*
elaborately decorated
▷ **ornately** *ADVERB*

ornithology *NOUN*
the study of birds
▷ **ornithologist** *NOUN*
▷ **ornithological** *ADJECTIVE*
WORD HISTORY from Greek *ornithos* 'of a bird'

orphan *NOUN* **orphans**
a child whose parents are dead
▷ **orphaned** *ADJECTIVE*
WORD HISTORY from Greek *orphanos* 'bereaved'

orphanage *NOUN* **orphanages**
a home for orphans

orthodontics *NOUN*
the treatment of irregularities in the teeth and jaws
▷ **orthodontic** *ADJECTIVE*
▷ **orthodontist** *NOUN*
WORD HISTORY from Greek *orthos* 'straight' and *odontos* 'of a tooth'

orthodox *ADJECTIVE*
1 holding beliefs that are correct or generally accepted
2 conventional or normal
▷ **orthodoxy** *NOUN*
WORD HISTORY from Greek *orthos* 'straight' and *doxa* 'opinion'

Orthodox Church *NOUN*
the Christian Churches of eastern Europe

orthography *NOUN*
the spelling system of a language
▷ **orthographic** *ADJECTIVE*

orthopaedics (*say* orth- o- **pee**- diks) *NOUN*
the treatment of deformities and injuries to bones and muscles
▷ **orthopaedic** *ADJECTIVE*
WORD HISTORY from Greek *orthos* 'straight' and *paideia* 'rearing of children', because the treatment was originally of children

OS *ABBREVIATION*
(*ICT*) operating system

oscillate *VERB* **oscillates, oscillating, oscillated**
1 to move to and fro like a pendulum; to vibrate
2 to waver or vary
▷ **oscillation** *NOUN*
▷ **oscillator** *NOUN*
WORD HISTORY from Latin *oscillare* 'to swing'

osier (*say* **oh**- zee- er) *NOUN* **osiers**
a willow with flexible twigs used in making baskets

osmosis *NOUN*
the passing of fluid through a porous partition into another more concentrated fluid
WORD HISTORY from Greek *osmos* 'a push'

ossify *VERB* **ossifies, ossifying, ossified**
1 to change into bone; to become hard like bone
2 to stop developing
▷ **ossification** *NOUN*
WORD HISTORY from Latin *os* 'bone'

ostensible *ADJECTIVE*
apparently true, but actually concealing the true reason ◆ *Their ostensible reason for travelling was to visit friends.*
▷ **ostensibly** *ADVERB*
WORD HISTORY from Latin *ostendere* 'to show'

ostentatious *ADJECTIVE*
making a showy display of something to impress people
▷ **ostentatiously** *ADVERB*
▷ **ostentation** *NOUN*

osteopath *NOUN* **osteopaths**
a person who treats certain diseases and abnormalities by manipulating a patient's bones and muscles
▷ **osteopathy** *NOUN*
▷ **osteopathic** *ADJECTIVE*
WORD HISTORY from Greek *osteon* 'bone' and *patheia* 'feeling or suffering'

ostinato (*say* ost- i- **nah**- toh) *NOUN* **ostinatos**
(*Music*) a continually repeated phrase or rhythm
WORD HISTORY an Italian word meaning 'obstinate'

ostler (*say* oss- ler) *NOUN* **ostlers**
(*History*) a person who looked after the horses of people staying at an inn

The ostler entered the hall, slow, shuffling, hissing gently, a perpetual habit of his whether grooming a horse or not. — *Mervyn Peake, Gormenghast*

WORD HISTORY from Old French *hostelier* 'innkeeper'

ostracize *VERB* **ostracizes, ostracizing, ostracized**
to exclude someone from your group and completely ignore them
▷ **ostracism** *NOUN*
USAGE NOTE This word can also be spelled ostracise.
WORD HISTORY from Greek *ostrakon* 'piece of pottery', because people voted to banish someone by writing their name on this

ostrich *NOUN* **ostriches**
a large African bird with long legs that can run very fast but cannot fly. It is said to bury its head in the sand when pursued, in the belief that it cannot be seen then.

other *ADJECTIVE*
1 different, not the same

Christmas Day began like any other day: baths, breakfast, three lessons, then lunch. — *Anthony Horowitz, Groosham Grange*

2 additional or remaining ◆ *There is no other exit.* ◆ *The airport is on the other side of the city.*

the other day (*informal*) a few days ago; recently

other *NOUN, PRONOUN* **others**
the other person or thing ◆ *The others have already left.*

otherwise *ADVERB*
1 if things happen differently; or else ◆ *Write it down, otherwise you'll forget.*
2 in other ways; in other respects ◆ *There was a mark on the cover, but otherwise the book looked like new.*
3 differently; in another way ◆ *We could not do otherwise than agree to the truce.*

otter *NOUN* **otters**
a fish-eating animal with webbed feet, a flat tail, and thick brown fur, living near water

WORD HISTORY from Old English *otr*

ottoman *NOUN* **ottomans**
1 a long padded seat
2 a storage box with a padded top

WORD HISTORY from *Ottomanus*, the Latin name of the family who ruled Turkey from the 14th to the 20th century (because the ottoman originated in Turkey)

ought *AUXILIARY VERB*
expressing duty, rightness, advisability, or strong probability ◆ *We ought to offer to help.* ◆ *You ought to take more exercise.* ◆ *At this speed, we ought to be there by noon.*

WORD HISTORY from Old English *ahte* 'owed'

oughtn't
short for *ought not*

I said to Sophie: 'What now? Oughtn't we to try to get as far away as we can before it's light?' — *John Wyndham, The Chrysalids*

ounce *NOUN* **ounces**
1 a unit of weight equal to one-sixteenth of a pound (about 28 grams)
2 a tiny amount; a drop, a morsel

With the absolute last ounce of strength in his legs, Stefan struggled to his knees. — *Eoin Colfer, The Supernaturalist*

our *ADJECTIVE*
belonging to us

ours *POSSESSIVE PRONOUN*
something belonging to us ◆ *These seats are ours.*

USAGE NOTE It is incorrect to write *our's*, with an apostrophe.

ourselves *PRONOUN*
we or us and nobody else: used to refer back to the subject of a sentence (e.g. *We blame ourselves*) and for emphasis (e.g. *We made all the costumes ourselves*)

by ourselves on our own; alone

oust *VERB* **ousts, ousting, ousted**
to drive someone out from a place, position, or office ◆ *During the war, many people were ousted from their homes.*

WORD HISTORY from Old French *ouster* 'to take away'

out *ADVERB*
1 away from or not in a particular place, position, or state; not at home ◆ *Your mum phoned last night when you were out.*
2 into the open; into existence or sight ◆ *The sun has come out at last.*
3 no longer burning or shining ◆ *Don't let the campfire go out.*
4 in error ◆ *The estimate was £100 out.*
5 to or at an end; completely ◆ *Tomorrow's concert is sold out.* ◆ *You look utterly worn out.*
6 without restraint; boldly or loudly ◆ *You have always encouraged me to speak out, so I did.*
7 not possible or not worth considering ◆ *I'm afraid skateboarding is out until the snow clears.*
8 no longer batting in cricket

to be out to do something is to be seeking or wanting to do it

to be out of something is to have no more of it left

out of date
1 old-fashioned
2 no longer valid

out of doors in the open air

out of the way remote or distant

out-and-out *ADJECTIVE*
thorough or complete ◆ *The holiday was an out-and-out disaster.*

outback *NOUN*
the remote inland districts of Australia

outboard motor *NOUN* **outboard motors**
a motor fitted to the outside of a boat's stern

outbreak *NOUN* **outbreaks**
the start of a disease or war or anger

Then, the outbreak of the First World War in 1914 transformed the science of aeronautics. — *Paul Dowswell, True Polar Adventures*

outburst *NOUN* **outbursts**
a sudden bursting out of anger or laughter

outcast *NOUN* **outcasts**
a person who has been rejected by family, friends, or society

outcome *NOUN* **outcomes**
the result of what happens or has happened

outcrop *NOUN* **outcrops**
a piece of rock from a lower level that sticks out on the surface of the ground

outcry *NOUN* **outcries**
a strong protest ◆ *The proposal caused an immediate public outcry.*

outdated *ADJECTIVE*
out of date

outdistance *VERB* **outdistances, outdistancing, outdistanced**
to get far ahead of someone in a race

outdo *VERB* **outdoes, outdoing, outdid, outdone**
to do better than another person

outdoor *ADJECTIVE*
done or used outdoors

outdoors *ADVERB*
in the open air

outer *ADJECTIVE*
outside or external; nearer to the outside
▷ **outermost** *ADJECTIVE*

outer space *NOUN*
the universe beyond the earth's atmosphere

outfit *NOUN* **outfits**
1 a set of clothes worn together
2 a set of equipment
3 (*informal*) a team or organization

outflow *NOUN* **outflows**
1 the action of flowing out; what flows out
2 a pipe for liquid flowing out

outgoing *ADJECTIVE*
1 soon to leave or retire from office ◆ *the outgoing director of the festival*
2 sociable and friendly

outgoings *PLURAL NOUN*
what you have to spend; expenditure

outgrow *VERB* **outgrows, outgrowing, outgrew, outgrown**
1 to grow out of clothes or habits
2 to grow faster or larger than another person or thing

outgrowth *NOUN* **outgrowths**
something that grows out of another thing ◆ *Feathers are outgrowths on a bird's skin.*

outhouse *NOUN* **outhouses**
a small building, such as a shed or barn, that belongs to a house but is separate from it

outing *NOUN* **outings**
a journey for pleasure

outlandish *ADJECTIVE*
looking or sounding strange or foreign

Hari ... saw Mrs de Silva standing there, dressed in an outlandish costume unlike anything worn by the women in Thul. — *Anita Desai, The Village by the Sea*

WORD HISTORY from Old English *utland* 'a foreign land'

outlast *VERB* **outlasts, outlasting, outlasted**
to last longer than something else

outlaw *NOUN* **outlaws**
a person who is punished by being excluded from legal rights and the protection of the law, especially a robber or bandit

outlaw *VERB* **outlaws, outlawing, outlawed**
1 to make a person an outlaw
2 to declare something to be illegal; to forbid something

'They don't allow freak shows any more,' I told him. 'Wolf-men and snake-boys were outlawed years ago. Mr Dalton said so.' — *Darren Shan, Cirque du Freak*

outlay *NOUN* **outlays**
the amount of money spent on something

outlet *NOUN* **outlets**
1 a way for something to get out
2 a way of expressing strong feelings
3 a place from which goods are sold or distributed

outline *NOUN* **outlines**
1 a line round the outside of something, showing its boundary or shape

The moon was almost complete, its outline well defined, except for the blur on the waxing curve. — *Barry Hines, A Kestrel for a Knave*

2 a summary

outline *VERB* **outlines, outlining, outlined**
1 to make an outline of something
2 to summarize something

outlive *VERB* **outlives, outliving, outlived**
to live or last longer than another person

outlook *NOUN* **outlooks**
1 a view on which people look out ◆ *a pleasant outlook over the lake*
2 a person's mental attitude to something

Major's speech had given to the more intelligent animals on the farm a completely new outlook on life. — *George Orwell, Animal Farm*

3 future prospects ◆ *The outlook is bleak.*

outlying *ADJECTIVE*
far from the centre; remote ◆ *A regular bus service is available into the city centre and outlying districts.*

outmanoeuvre *VERB* **outmanoeuvres, outmanoeuvring, outmanoeuvred**
to use skill or cunning to gain an advantage over someone

outmoded *ADJECTIVE*
out of date; old-fashioned

outnumber *VERB* **outnumbers, outnumbering, outnumbered**
to be more numerous than another group

outpace *VERB* **outpaces, outpacing, outpaced**
to go faster than someone or something else

outpatient *NOUN* **outpatients**
a person who visits a hospital for treatment but does not stay there

outpost *NOUN* **outposts**
a distant settlement

output *NOUN* **outputs**
1 the amount produced
2 (*ICT*) the information or results produced by a computer

output *VERB* **outputs, outputting, output** or **outputted**
1 to produce information or results
2 (*ICT*) to produce data from a computer system

outrage *NOUN* **outrages**
1 something that shocks people by being very wicked or cruel
2 great anger or indignation
▷ **outrageous** *ADJECTIVE*
▷ **outrageously** *ADVERB*

outrage *VERB* **outrages, outraging, outraged**
to shock and anger people greatly

WORD HISTORY from Old French *outrer* 'to go beyond, to exaggerate', influenced by *rage*

outrider *NOUN* **outriders**
a person riding on a motorcycle as an escort or guard

outrigger *NOUN* **outriggers**
a framework attached to the side of a seagoing canoe to prevent it from capsizing

outright *ADVERB*
1 completely; not gradually

Once in my life I would like to own something outright before it's broken! — *Arthur Miller, Death of a Salesman*

2 frankly ◆ *You have to tell him outright to stop phoning you at work.*

outright *ADJECTIVE*
thorough or complete

In his enthusiasm, Dr Feltham failed to catch Mr Cartright's tone of outright scorn. — *Anne Fine, Flour Babies*

outrun *VERB* **outruns, outrunning, outran, outrun**
to run faster or further than someone else

outset *NOUN*
the beginning of something ◆ *The mission to Mars was seriously flawed from the outset.*

outshine *VERB* **outshines, outshining, outshone**
1 to shine more brightly than something else
2 to be much better than someone or something else

outside *NOUN* **outsides**
the outer side, surface, or part of something
at the outside at the most

The man who entered was young, some two-and-twenty at the outside. — *Sir Arthur Conan Doyle, The Five Orange Pips*

outside *ADJECTIVE*
1 on, near, or coming from the outside
2 an outside chance is remote or slight
3 an outside interest is not connected with your work or studies
4 an outside player in football or hockey is positioned nearest to the edge of the field

outside *ADVERB*
on, at, or to the outside; outdoors ◆ *Please leave your trainers outside.* ◆ *It's freezing cold outside!*

outside *PREPOSITION*
1 on the outer side of; at or to the outside of ◆ *We could hear giggling and laughter outside the room.*
2 beyond the limits or scope of something ◆ *He has no interests outside his work.*

outside broadcast *NOUN* **outside broadcasts**
a broadcast made on location and not in a studio

outsider *NOUN* **outsiders**
1 a person who does not belong to a certain group
2 a horse or person thought to have no chance of winning a race or competition

outsize *ADJECTIVE*
much larger than average

outskirts *PLURAL NOUN*
the outer parts or districts, especially of a town

outspoken *ADJECTIVE*
speaking or spoken very frankly

outspread *ADJECTIVE*
spread out

outstanding *ADJECTIVE*
1 extremely good or distinguished

We can have cheese rolls for lunch, Link old son. They do an outstanding cheese roll here. — *Robert Swindells, Stone Cold*

2 an outstanding debt or bill is not yet paid or dealt with

outstretched *ADJECTIVE*
stretched out

outstrip *VERB* **outstrips, outstripping, outstripped**
1 to run faster or further than someone else
2 to achieve more, or be more successful, than someone else

WORD HISTORY from *out* and Middle English *strypen* 'to move quickly'

out-take *NOUN* **out-takes**
a scene cut from the final version of a film or television programme

outvote *VERB* **outvotes, outvoting, outvoted**
to defeat someone by a majority of votes

outward *ADJECTIVE*
1 going outwards
2 on the outside
▷ **outwardly** *ADVERB*
▷ **outwards** *ADVERB*

outweigh *VERB* **outweighs, outweighing, outweighed**
to be greater in weight or importance than something else

outwit *VERB* **outwits, outwitting, outwitted**
to deceive somebody by being crafty

Robert ... laughed to think he had outwitted the number devil. — *Hans Magnus Enzensberger, The Number Devil*

ova *plural of* **ovum**

oval *ADJECTIVE*
shaped like a 0, rounded and longer than it is broad

oval *NOUN* **ovals**
a rounded symmetrical shape longer than it is broad

WORD HISTORY from Latin *ovum* 'egg'

ovary *NOUN* **ovaries**
1 either of the two organs in which ova or egg cells are produced in a woman's or female animal's body
2 part of the pistil in a plant, from which fruit is formed

ovation *NOUN* **ovations**
enthusiastic applause

WORD HISTORY from Latin *ovare* 'to rejoice'

oven *NOUN* **ovens**
a closed space in which things are cooked or heated

over *PREPOSITION*
1 above; higher than ◆ *Black rain clouds were hovering over the town.*
2 across the top of; on or to the other side of ◆ *It's just a short walk over the bridge.*
3 more than

Mr Flay had been sitting for over an hour at the entrance to his cave. — *Mervyn Peake, Gormenghast*

4 concerning ◆ *My aunt and uncle were always quarrelling over money.*
5 in superiority or preference to ◆ *The Athenians won a great victory over the Persians at Marathon.*
6 so as to visit or examine all parts ◆ *Let's go over the plan again.*
7 during a period of time

Over the following couple of weeks I slowly got to know all the members of my family. — *Bali Rai, (Un)arranged Marriage*

over *ADVERB*
1 out and down from the top or edge; from an upright position ◆ *The car rolled to the edge of the cliff and went over.* ◆ *The vase was too full and tipped over.*
2 so that a different side shows ◆ *Turn the omelette over to cook the other side.*
3 at or to a place; across ◆ *You can swim over to the other side of the bay.*
4 remaining; still available ◆ *There is nothing left over from my birthday money.*
5 all through; thoroughly ◆ *Do you need more time to think it over?*
6 at an end

Lessons for the day were over, and they were sitting before the schoolroom fire, enjoying the time they liked best. — *Frances Hodgson Burnett, A Little Princess*

over and over many times; repeatedly

over *NOUN* **overs**
a series of six balls bowled in cricket

overact *VERB* **overacts, overacting, overacted**
to act your part in an exaggerated manner

overactive *ADJECTIVE*
excessively active

Lilly says I have an overactive imagination and a pathological need to invent drama in my life. — *Meg Cabot, The Princess Diaries*

overall *ADJECTIVE*
including everything; total ◆ *What will be the overall cost of the repairs?*

overall *ADVERB*
taken as a whole

overall *NOUN* **overalls**
a type of coat worn over other clothes to protect them when working

overalls *PLURAL NOUN*
a piece of clothing, like a shirt and trousers combined, worn over other clothes to protect them

overarm *ADJECTIVE, ADVERB*
you bowl or throw overarm with your arm lifted above shoulder level and coming down in front of your body

overawe *VERB* **overawes, overawing, overawed**
to overcome or inhibit someone with awe

a b c d e f g h i j k l m n o p q r s t u v w x y z

overbalance *VERB* **overbalances, overbalancing, overbalanced**
to lose balance and fall over

overbearing *ADJECTIVE*
domineering or overpowering

overblown *ADJECTIVE*
1 exaggerated or pretentious
2 an overblown flower is too fully open and past its best

overboard *ADVERB*
from a ship into the water ◆ *A crew member dived overboard to rescue the exhausted man.*
to go overboard (*informal*) is to be too enthusiastic or to do too much

overcast *ADJECTIVE*
overcast sky or cloudy weather

overcoat *NOUN* **overcoats**
a warm outdoor coat

overcome *VERB* **overcomes, overcoming, overcame, overcome**
1 to win a victory over an opponent; to defeat someone
2 to have a strong physical or emotional effect on someone and make them helpless ◆ *One of the firefighters was overcome by gas fumes.*
3 to find a way of dealing with a problem or difficulty

Sorrel overcame her seasickness by eating the delicious leaves she had picked in the valley where the djinn lived. — *Cornelia Funke, Dragon Rider*

overcrowded *ADJECTIVE*
an overcrowded place or vehicle has too many people crammed into it
▷ **overcrowding** *NOUN*

overdo *VERB* **overdoes, overdoing, overdid, overdone**
1 do something too much
2 to cook food for too long
to overdo it or things is to exhaust yourself; to work too hard

overdose *NOUN* **overdoses**
too large a dose of a drug

overdose *VERB* **overdoses, overdosing, overdosed**
to take an overdose

overdraft *NOUN* **overdrafts**
the amount by which a bank account is overdrawn

overdraw *VERB* **overdraws, overdrawing, overdrew, overdrawn**
to draw more money from a bank account than the amount you have in it
▷ **overdrawn** *ADJECTIVE*

overdrive *NOUN*
a mechanism providing an extra gear above the normal top gear in a vehicle

overdue *ADJECTIVE*
late; not paid or arrived by the proper time

overestimate *VERB* **overestimates, overestimating, overestimated**
to estimate something too highly

overflow *VERB* **overflows, overflowing, overflowed**
to flow over the edge or limits of something

overflow *NOUN*
1 an amount of something that overflows
2 an outlet for excess liquid

overgrown *ADJECTIVE*
covered with weeds or unwanted plants
▷ **overgrowth** *NOUN*

overhang *VERB* **overhangs, overhanging, overhung**
to jut out over something

The cliffs overhung fragrant little dells where mushrooms and larkspur and strawberry plants pushed up through the loam and pine needles. — *Mary O'Hara, My Friend Flicka*

overhang *NOUN*
a part of a building or structure that juts out

overhaul *VERB* **overhauls, overhauling, overhauled**
1 to examine something thoroughly and repair or improve it if necessary
2 to overtake someone or something

overhaul *NOUN*
an examination and repair of something

overhead *ADJECTIVE, ADVERB*
1 above the level of your head
2 in the sky

The glare of the exploding plane, right overhead, did queer things to Chas's eyes. — *Robert Westall, The Machine Gunners*

overheads *PLURAL NOUN*
the expenses of running a business (e.g. rent, heating, cleaning) that are not directly related to production

overhear *VERB* **overhears, overhearing, overheard**
to hear something accidentally or without the speaker intending you to hear it

overjoyed *ADJECTIVE*
filled with great joy

overkill *NOUN*
(*informal*) excessive use or treatment of something ◆ *The movie suffers from an overkill of special effects.*

overland *ADJECTIVE, ADVERB*
travelling over the land, not by sea or air

overlap *VERB* **overlaps, overlapping, overlapped**
1 to lie across part of something
2 events overlap when they happen partly at the same time

overlap *NOUN*
an overlapping part or amount

overlay *VERB* **overlays, overlaying, overlaid**
to cover something with a layer; to lie on top of something

overlay *NOUN* **overlays**
a thing laid over another

overleaf *ADVERB*
on the other side of the page ◆ *See the diagram overleaf.*

overlie *VERB* **overlies, overlying, overlay, overlain**
to lie over something

overload *VERB* **overloads, overloading, overloaded**
to put too great a load on someone or something

overlook *VERB* **overlooks, overlooking, overlooked**
1 to fail to notice or consider something
2 to deliberately ignore something; to allow an offence to go unpunished
3 to have a view of a place from above

overlord *NOUN* **overlords**
a supreme lord

overly *ADVERB*
too; excessively ◆ *Would you say Cyrano is overly sensitive about his nose?*

overnight *ADJECTIVE, ADVERB*
of or during a night ◆ *an overnight stop in Rome*

overpower *VERB* **overpowers, overpowering, overpowered**
to defeat someone by greater strength or numbers

overpowering *ADJECTIVE*
very strong or intense; overwhelming ◆ *The air was filled with the overpowering scent of honeysuckle.*

overrate *VERB* **overrates, overrating, overrated**
to have too high an opinion of someone or something

overreach *VERB* **overreaches, overreaching, overreached**
to overreach yourself is to fail through being too ambitious

override *VERB* **overrides, overriding, overrode, overridden**
1 to overrule someone or something
2 to be more important than something else ◆ *Safety overrides all other considerations.*
3 to interrupt the operation of an automatic mechanism
▷ **overriding** *ADJECTIVE*

overripe *ADJECTIVE*
too ripe

overrule *VERB* **overrules, overruling, overruled**
to reject or disallow a suggestion or decision by using your authority

overrun *VERB* **overruns, overrunning, overran, overrun**
1 to spread over and occupy a place in large numbers ◆ *The attic is overrun with mice.*
2 to go on for longer than it should ◆ *The programme overran by ten minutes.*

overseas *ADVERB*
across or beyond the sea; abroad

oversee *VERB* **oversees, overseeing, oversaw, overseen**
to watch over or supervise people working
▷ **overseer** *NOUN*

overshadow *VERB* **overshadows, overshadowing, overshadowed**
1 to cast a shadow over something

> The whole garden was overshadowed by a large magnolia tree, the glossy dark green leaves of which cast a deep shadow. — *Gerald Durrell, My Family and Other Animals*

2 to make a person or thing seem unimportant in comparison

overshoot *VERB* **overshoots, overshooting, overshot**
to go beyond a target or limit ◆ *The spacecraft had overshot the landing site and almost ran out of fuel.*

oversight *NOUN* **oversights**
a mistake made by not noticing something

oversleep *VERB* **oversleeps, oversleeping, overslept**
to sleep for longer than you intended

overspill *NOUN*
1 an amount of something that spills over or overflows
2 the extra population of a town, who take homes in nearby districts

overstate *VERB* **overstates, overstating, overstated**
to exaggerate how important something is ◆ *Perhaps we have overstated the danger of the situation.*

overstep *VERB* **oversteps, overstepping, overstepped**
to go beyond a limit

overt *ADJECTIVE*
done or shown openly ◆ *The overt hostility between the guests on the talk show was unmistakable.*
▷ **overtly** *ADVERB*

WORD HISTORY from an Old French word meaning 'open'

overtake *VERB* **overtakes, overtaking, overtook, overtaken**
1 to pass a moving vehicle or person
2 to catch up with someone

overtax *VERB* **overtaxes, overtaxing, overtaxed**
1 to tax someone too heavily
2 to put too heavy a burden or strain on someone

overthrow *VERB* **overthrows, overthrowing, overthrew, overthrown**
to remove a ruler or government from power by force

The dragon was dead, and the goblins overthrown, and their hearts looked forward after winter to a spring of joy. — *J. R. R. Tolkien, The Hobbit*

overthrow *NOUN* **overthrows**
1 the action of overthrowing a ruler or government; a downfall or defeat
2 the action of throwing a ball too far

overtime *NOUN*
1 time spent working outside the normal hours
2 payment for this

overtone *NOUN* **overtones**
1 an additional or subtle quality or implication ◆ *There were overtones of malice in his comments.*
2 (*Music*) any of the tones above the lowest in a harmonic series

overture *NOUN* **overtures**
a piece of music written as an introduction to an opera or ballet
to make overtures is to begin negotiations or start a relationship

WORD HISTORY from an Old French word meaning 'opening'

overturn *VERB* **overturns, overturning, overturned**
1 to turn over or upside down, or to make something do this
2 to reverse a legal decision

overuse *VERB* **overuses, overusing, overused**
to use something too much

overuse *NOUN*
excessive use of something

overview *NOUN*
a general review or summary

overweight *ADJECTIVE*
1 too heavy
2 too fat

overwhelm *VERB* **overwhelms, overwhelming, overwhelmed**
1 to bury or drown someone or something beneath a huge mass
2 to defeat someone completely, especially by force of numbers
3 to have a strong emotional effect on someone ◆ *We were overwhelmed by the generosity of the local people.*

▷ **overwhelming** *ADJECTIVE*

WORD HISTORY from *over* and Middle English *whelm* 'to turn upside down'

overwork *VERB* **overworks, overworking, overworked**
1 to work too hard, or to make someone work too hard

My driver was my owner, and it was his interest to treat me well and not overwork me. — *Anna Sewell, Black Beauty*

2 to use something too often or too much ◆ *'Nice' is an overworked word.*

overwrought *ADJECTIVE*
very upset and nervous or worried

ovoid *ADJECTIVE*
having the shape of an egg

ovulate *VERB* **ovulates, ovulating, ovulated**
to produce an ovum from an ovary

ovum (*say* **oh**- vum) *NOUN* **ova**
a female cell that can develop into a new individual when it is fertilized

WORD HISTORY a Latin word meaning 'egg'

owe *VERB* **owes, owing, owed**
1 to have a duty to pay or give something to someone, especially money
2 to have something because of the action of another person or thing ◆ *They owed their lives to the bravery of the firefighters.*
owing to because of; caused by

Was it owing to your influence, as the most prominent member of the committee, that help was refused the girl? — *J. B. Priestley, An Inspector Calls*

owl *NOUN* **owls**
a bird of prey with a large head, large eyes, and a hooked beak, usually flying at night

own *ADJECTIVE*
belonging to yourself or itself
to come into your own is to have the opportunity to show your qualities or abilities
to get your own back (*informal*) is to get revenge
to hold your own is to succeed in holding your position against competition or attack
on your own alone; by yourself

own *VERB* **owns, owning, owned**
1 to possess something; to have something as your property
2 (*formal*) to acknowledge or admit something ◆ *I own that I made a mistake.*
to own up is to admit that you have done something wrong or foolish

a b c d e f g h i j k l m n o p q r s t u v w x y z

owner ***NOUN*** **owners**
the person who owns something
▷ **ownership** ***NOUN***

own goal ***NOUN*** **own goals**
a goal scored by a member of a team against their own side

ox ***NOUN*** **oxen**
a large animal kept for its meat and for pulling carts

oxide ***NOUN*** **oxides**
a compound of oxygen and one other element

oxidize ***VERB*** **oxidizes, oxidizing, oxidized**
1 to combine, or to cause a substance to combine, with oxygen
2 to coat something with an oxide
▷ **oxidation** ***NOUN***

USAGE NOTE This word can also be spelled oxidise.

oxtail ***NOUN*** **oxtails**
the tail of an ox, used to make soup or stew

oxygen ***NOUN***
(*Biology*) a colourless odourless tasteless gas that exists in the air and is essential for living things

oxymoron (*say* ok- si- **mor**- on) ***NOUN*** **oxymorons**
a combination of words which seem to contradict one another, e.g. *bitter-sweet*, *living death*

WORD HISTORY from Greek *oxumoros* 'pointedly foolish'

oyster ***NOUN*** **oysters**
a kind of edible shellfish whose shell sometimes contains a pearl

WORD HISTORY via Old French from Latin *ostrea*

ozone ***NOUN***
a form of oxygen with a sharp smell

WORD HISTORY from Greek *ozein* 'to smell'

ozone layer ***NOUN***
a layer of ozone high in the atmosphere, which protects the earth from harmful amounts of the sun's radiation

Pp

a b c d e f g h i j k l m n o p q r s t u v w x y z

p *ABBREVIATION*
penny or pence

p. *ABBREVIATION* **pp.**
page or pages

pa *NOUN*
(*informal*) a person's father

pace *NOUN* **paces**
1 one step taken in walking or running
2 the rate or speed at which something happens

Down by the Galata Bridge, close by the old spice markets, the pace of Istanbul life is at its most frenetic. — *Michael Palin, Pole to Pole*

pace *VERB* **paces, pacing, paced**
1 to walk with slow or deliberate steps, especially when worried or preoccupied

I paced furiously around the hotel room, hands clenched into fists, cursing angrily. — *Darren Shan, Tunnels of Blood*

2 to pace out a distance is to measure it in paces

pacemaker *NOUN* **pacemakers**
1 a person who sets the pace for others in a race
2 an electrical device for keeping the heart beating

pacific (*say* pa- **sif**- ik) *ADJECTIVE*
peaceful; making or loving peace
▷ **pacifically** *ADVERB*

pacifist (*say* **pas**- if- ist) *NOUN* **pacifists**
a person who believes that war is unjustified and should always be avoided
▷ **pacifism** *NOUN*

pacify *VERB* **pacifies, pacifying, pacified**
1 to calm a person down
2 to bring peace to a country or warring sides
▷ **pacification** *NOUN*

pack *NOUN* **packs**
1 a bundle or collection of things wrapped or tied together
2 a set of playing cards (usually 52)
3 a bag carried on your back
4 a large amount ◆ *Clearly they had told a pack of lies.*
5 a group of wild animals that hunt together, especially hounds or wolves
6 an organized group of Brownies or Cub Scouts

pack *VERB* **packs, packing, packed**
1 to put things into a suitcase, bag, or container for travel or storage
2 a room or space is packed when it is crowded with people
to pack something in (*informal*) is to stop doing it
to pack someone off (*informal*) is to send them away abruptly
to send someone packing (*informal*) is to dismiss them angrily

package *NOUN* **packages**
1 a parcel or packet
2 a number of terms or proposals offered or agreed together
▷ **packaging** *NOUN*

package holiday *NOUN* **package holidays**
a holiday with all the travel and accommodation arranged and included in the price

packet *NOUN* **packets**
a small parcel

pack ice *NOUN*
a mass of pieces of ice floating in the sea

pact *NOUN* **pacts**
an agreement or treaty

pad[1] *NOUN* **pads**
1 a piece of soft thick material
2 a piece of soft material worn to protect the legs in cricket and other games
3 a set of sheets of paper fastened together at one edge
4 the soft fleshy part under an animal's foot or the end of a finger or toe
5 a flat surface from which rockets are launched or where helicopters take off and land

pad *VERB* **pads, padding, padded**
to put a pad on or in something
to pad something out is to make a book, speech, etc. longer than it needs to be

pad[2] *VERB* **pads, padding, padded**
to walk softly

Towflower padded over to the corner, poking gingerly at the stones in case there was a secret panel. — *Terry Pratchett, The Colour of Magic*

padding *NOUN*
material used to pad things

paddle❶ *VERB* **paddles, paddling, paddled**
to walk about in shallow water
▷ **paddle** *NOUN*

paddle❷ *NOUN* **paddles**
1 a short oar with a broad blade
2 something shaped like a paddle

paddle *VERB* **paddles, paddling, paddled**
to move a boat along with a paddle or paddles; to row gently

paddock *NOUN* **paddocks**
1 a small field where horses are kept
2 (*Australian and New Zealand*) a field or plot of land enclosed by fencing or defined by natural boundaries
WORD HISTORY from a dialect word *parrock*, of unknown origin

paddy *NOUN* **paddies**
(also **paddy field**) a field where rice is grown
WORD HISTORY from Malay (a language spoken in Malaysia) *padi* 'rice'

padlock *NOUN* **padlocks**
a detachable lock with a metal loop that passes through a ring or chain

padlock *VERB* **padlocks, padlocking, padlocked**
to lock something with a padlock

padre (*say* **pah**- dray) *NOUN* **padres**
(*informal*) a chaplain in the armed forces
WORD HISTORY a word meaning 'father' in Italian, Spanish, and Portuguese

paean (*say* **pee**- an) *NOUN* **paeans**
a song of praise or triumph
WORD HISTORY from a Greek word meaning 'hymn'

paediatrics (*say* peed- ee- **at**- riks) *NOUN*
the study of children's diseases
▷ **paediatric** *ADJECTIVE*
▷ **paediatrician** *NOUN*
WORD HISTORY from Greek *paidos* 'of a child' and *iatros* 'doctor'

pagan (*say* **pay**- gan) *NOUN* **pagans**
a person who does not believe in one of the main religions of the world
▷ **pagan** *ADJECTIVE*
WORD HISTORY from Latin *paganus* 'a person from the country', from *pagus* 'a village or country district'. Later *paganus* came to mean 'a civilian (as distinct from a soldier)', and in Christian Latin it referred to someone who was not a soldier of Christ, i.e. a heathen.

page❶ *NOUN* **pages**
a piece of paper that is part of a book or newspaper, or one side of this

page❷ *NOUN* **pages**
1 a boy or man employed to go on errands or be an attendant
2 a young boy attending a bride at a wedding

pageant *NOUN* **pageants**
1 a play or entertainment about historical events and people
2 a procession of people in costume as an entertainment
▷ **pageantry** *NOUN*

pager *NOUN* **pagers**
a small radio device which bleeps or vibrates to let the user know that someone wants to contact them or that it has received a short text message

pagoda (*say* pag- **oh**- da) *NOUN* **pagodas**
a Buddhist or Hindu temple having a tower with several tiers
WORD HISTORY via Portuguese from Persian *butkada* 'temple of idols'

paid *past tense* of **pay**
to put paid to something (*informal*) is to put an end to what someone is doing or hoping for

pail *NOUN* **pails**
a bucket

pain *NOUN* **pains**
1 an unpleasant feeling caused by injury or disease
2 suffering in the mind
on or under pain of with the threat of
to take pains is to make a careful effort over something
▷ **painful** *ADJECTIVE*
▷ **painfully** *ADVERB*
▷ **painless** *ADJECTIVE*

pain *VERB* **pains, paining, pained**
to cause suffering or distress to someone
WORD HISTORY from Latin *poena* 'punishment'

painkiller *NOUN* **painkillers**
a medicine or drug that relieves pain

painstaking *ADJECTIVE*
very careful and thorough

paint *NOUN* **paints**
a liquid substance put on something to colour it

paint *VERB* **paints, painting, painted**
1 to put paint on something
2 to make a picture with paints
▷ **painter** *NOUN*
▷ **painting** *NOUN*

paintbox *NOUN* **paintboxes**
a box of dry paints for painting pictures

paintbrush *NOUN* **paintbrushes**
a brush for putting paint on a surface

pair *NOUN* **pairs**
1 a set of two things or people; a couple
2 something made of two joined parts, e.g. a pair of scissors or a pair of trousers

pair *VERB* **pairs, pairing, paired**
to put two things together as a pair
to pair off or **up** is to form a couple

pal *NOUN* **pals**
(*informal*) a friend
WORD HISTORY a Romany word meaning 'brother'

palace *NOUN* **palaces**
a grand building where a king, queen, president, or other important person lives
WORD HISTORY from *Palatium*, the name of a hill in ancient Rome where the house of the emperor Augustus stood

palaeolithic (*say* pal- ee- o- **lith**- ik) *ADJECTIVE*
belonging to the early part of the Stone Age

palaeontology (*say* pal- ee- on- **tol**- o- jee) *NOUN*
the study of fossils

palatable *ADJECTIVE*
tasting pleasant

palate *NOUN* **palates**
1 the roof of your mouth
2 a person's sense of taste
USAGE NOTE Take care not to confuse this word with *palette* or *pallet*.

palatial (*say* pa- **lay**- shal) *ADJECTIVE*
grand and spacious like a palace

pale¹ *ADJECTIVE*
1 having little colour; almost white ◆ *She looked terrible, pale and yawning.*
2 not bright in colour or light ◆ *The walls of the room were pale green.*
▷ **palely** *ADVERB*
▷ **paleness** *NOUN*
WORD HISTORY from Latin *pallidus* 'pallid'

pale² *NOUN* **pales**
beyond the pale beyond the limits of acceptable behaviour
WORD HISTORY an old word meaning 'a boundary', from Latin *palus* 'a stake or fence post'

palette *NOUN* **palettes**
(*Art*) a board on which an artist mixes colours ready for use
USAGE NOTE Take care not to confuse this word with *palate* or *pallet*.

palindrome *NOUN* **palindromes**
(*Language*) a word or phrase that reads the same forwards and backwards, e.g. *radar* or *Madam, I'm Adam*

palindromes

A **palindrome** is a word or group of words which reads the same both forwards and backwards (discounting any spaces and punctuation). So *eye*, *mum*, and *tenet* are all palindromes, and so is the phrase *never odd or even*. Sometimes a palindrome can form a complete sentence: for example, *Don't nod; Madam, I'm Adam*; and *Was it a cat I saw?* Numbers and dates can also be palindromes. The year 2002 was a palindrome, as were the dates *10/11/01*, *20/11/02*, and *30/11/03*.

paling *NOUN* **palings**
a fence made of wooden posts or railings; one of its posts

palisade *NOUN* **palisades**
a fence of pointed sticks or boards

At the top of the cliff, the path passed through a high rampart, now partly tumbled down, topped by the remains of a stout palisade. — *Celia Rees, Pirates!*

pall¹ (*say* pawl) *NOUN* **palls**
1 a cloth spread over a coffin
2 a dark cloud of dust or smoke

pall² (*say* pawl) *VERB* **palls, palling, palled**
to become uninteresting or tedious to someone after a time ◆ *The thrill of flouting grandfather's wishes was beginning to pall.*

pallbearer *NOUN* **pallbearers**
a person helping to carry the coffin at a funeral

pallet *NOUN* **pallets**
1 a mattress stuffed with straw
2 a hard narrow bed
3 a large platform for carrying goods that are being stacked, especially one that can be lifted by a forklift truck
USAGE NOTE Take care not to confuse this word with *palate* or *palette*.

palliative *NOUN* **palliatives**
something that reduces pain or suffering without dealing with the cause
▷ **palliative** *ADJECTIVE*

pallid *ADJECTIVE*
pale, especially because of illness

The woman nodded, the thin line of pallid skin around the mask giving no hint of expression, as if the face behind it were as frozen as the metal. — *Garth Nix, Lirael*

pallor *NOUN*
paleness in a person's face, especially because of illness

palm *NOUN* **palms**
1 the inner part of the hand, between the fingers and the wrist
2 a palm tree

palm *VERB* **palms, palming, palmed**
to pick something up secretly and hide it in the palm of your hand
to palm someone off is to deceive them into accepting something
WORD HISTORY from Latin *palma*. It was applied to the palm tree because its leaves looked like an outstretched hand, although this meaning of the word is older in English.
USAGE NOTE You palm someone off *with* something, or palm something off *on* someone.

palmistry *NOUN*
fortune-telling by looking at the creases in the palm of a person's hand
▷ **palmist** *NOUN*

Palm Sunday *NOUN*
the Sunday before Easter, on which Christians commemorate Christ's entry into Jerusalem, when the people spread palm leaves in his path

palmtop *NOUN* **palmtops**
a small light computer that can be held in one hand

palm tree *NOUN* **palm trees**
a tropical tree with large leaves and no branches

palomino (*say* pal- o- **mee**- no) *NOUN* **palominos**
a pale golden or tan-coloured horse with a white mane and tail

palpable *ADJECTIVE*
1 able to be touched or felt
2 plain to see or realize ◆ *They sometimes stooped to making public statements that were palpable nonsense.*
▷ **palpably** *ADVERB*

palpitate *VERB* **palpitates, palpitating, palpitated**
1 the heart palpitates when it beats hard and quickly
2 a person palpitates when they quiver with fear or excitement
▷ **palpitation** *NOUN*

palsy (*say* **pawl**- zee) *NOUN*
(*old use*) paralysis with tremors

paltry (*say* **pol**- tree) *ADJECTIVE*
very little in amount or value ◆ *Much of her paltry income goes on the rent.*

pampas *NOUN*
wide grassy plains in South America

WORD HISTORY via Spanish from Quechua (a South American language)

pampas grass *NOUN*
a tall grass with long feathery flowers

pamper *VERB* **pampers, pampering, pampered**
to treat or look after someone very kindly and indulgently

pamphlet *NOUN* **pamphlets**
a small leaflet or booklet giving information on a subject

WORD HISTORY from *Pamphilet*, the name of a 12th- century Latin love poem

pan *NOUN* **pans**
1 a wide container with a flat base, used for cooking
2 something having this shape
3 the bowl of a lavatory

pan *VERB* **pans, panning, panned**
(*informal*) to criticize someone or something harshly
to pan out is have a particular result or outcome

panacea (*say* pan- a- **see**- a) *NOUN* **panaceas**
a cure for all kinds of diseases or troubles

panache (*say* pan- **ash**) *NOUN*
a confident and dashing manner

WORD HISTORY via French and Italian from Latin *pinnaculum* 'little feather': it originally referred to a plume of feathers on a helmet or headdress

panama *NOUN* **panamas**
a hat made of a fine straw-like material

WORD HISTORY from *Panama* in Central America (because the hats were originally made from the leaves of a plant which grows there)

pancake *NOUN* **pancakes**
a thin round cake of batter fried on both sides

Pancake Day *NOUN*
Shrove Tuesday, when pancakes are eaten

pancreas (*say* **pan**- kree- as) *NOUN*
a gland near the stomach, producing insulin and digestive juices

panda *NOUN* **pandas**
1 a large black-and-white animal like a bear, found in China
2 a mammal of the Himalayas, like a raccoon with thick reddish-brown fur and a bushy tail

panda car *NOUN* **panda cars**
a police patrol car, originally white with black stripes on the doors

pandemonium *NOUN*
uproar and complete confusion

Up on the command deck, Raka prowled the observation window, in the midst of a pandemonium of shouting voices. — *William Nicholson, The Wind Singer*

WORD HISTORY from *Pandemonium*, John Milton's name for the capital of hell in his poem *Paradise Lost*, from *pan-* 'everything' and *demon*

pander *VERB* **panders, pandering, pandered**
to pander to someone is to indulge them by giving them whatever they want

WORD HISTORY from *Pandare*, a character in Chaucer's poem *Troilus and Criseyde* who acted as go- between for two lovers

pane *NOUN* **panes**
a sheet of glass in a window

panegyric (*say* pan- i- **ji**- rik) *NOUN* **panegyrics**
a speech or piece of writing praising a person or thing

panel *NOUN* **panels**
1 a long flat piece of wood, metal, or other material forming a part of a door, wall, piece of furniture, piece of clothing, etc.
2 a flat board on which controls or instruments are fixed
3 a group of people chosen to discuss or decide something
▷ **panelled** *ADJECTIVE*
▷ **panelling** *NOUN*

panel game *NOUN* **panel games**
a television or radio quiz played by a panel of people

pang *NOUN* **pangs**
a sudden sharp pain

panic *NOUN*
sudden uncontrollable fear
▷ **panic-stricken** *ADJECTIVE*
▷ **panicky** *ADJECTIVE*

panic *VERB* **panics, panicking, panicked**
to fill someone with panic, or to be filled with panic
WORD HISTORY from the name of *Pan*, an ancient Greek god famous for causing sudden fear

pannier *NOUN* **panniers**
a large bag or basket hung on one side of a bicycle, motorcycle, or horse

panoply *NOUN* **panoplies**
an impressive display or collection of things

panorama *NOUN* **panoramas**
a view or picture of a wide area
▷ **panoramic** *ADJECTIVE*
WORD HISTORY from Greek *pan* 'all' and *horama* 'view'. The word was coined in the 18th century by an Irish artist called Robert Barker, who used it to describe scenes he painted in rooms in a London building which was also called *Panorama*.

pansy *NOUN* **pansies**
a small brightly coloured garden flower with velvety petals

pant *VERB* **pants, panting, panted**
to take short quick breaths, usually after running or working hard

pantaloons *PLURAL NOUN*
wide trousers, gathered at the ankle
WORD HISTORY named after *Pantalone*, a character in old Italian comedies ('commedia dell 'arte') who wore these

pantechnicon *NOUN* **pantechnicons**
a large van used for carrying furniture
WORD HISTORY originally the name of a large art and craft gallery in London, which was later used for storing furniture: from Greek *pan* 'all' and *techne* 'art'

panther *NOUN* **panthers**
a leopard, especially a black one

panties *PLURAL NOUN*
(*informal*) short knickers worn by women and girls

pantile *NOUN* **pantiles**
a curved tile for a roof

pantomime *NOUN* **pantomimes**
a musical entertainment, usually based on a fairy tale and performed at Christmas

pantry *NOUN* **pantries**
a small room for storing food and crockery
WORD HISTORY from Old French *paneterie* 'bread store', from *paneter* 'a baker'

pants *PLURAL NOUN*
1 underpants or knickers
2 (*American*) trousers

pap *NOUN*
1 soft food suitable for babies
2 (*South African*) porridge made from maize

Naledi sat down to eat a little cold pap. Her last proper meal had been the night before and she was hungry. — *Beverley Naidoo, Chain of Fire*

3 trivial entertainment; nonsense

papa *NOUN*
(*old use*) a person's father

papacy (*say* **pay**- pa- see) *NOUN* **papacies**
the position of the pope

papal (*say* **pay**- pul) *ADJECTIVE*
to do with the pope

paper *NOUN* **papers**
1 material made in thin sheets from wood, rags, etc. and used for writing or printing or drawing on or for wrapping things
2 a newspaper
3 a set of examination questions
4 an official document

paper *VERB* **papers, papering, papered**
to cover a wall or room with wallpaper

paperback *NOUN* **paperbacks**
a book with a thin flexible cover

paperweight *NOUN* **paperweights**
a small heavy object used for holding down loose papers

paperwork *NOUN*
all the writing and record-keeping that someone has to do as part of their job

papier mâché (*say* pap- yay **mash**- ay) *NOUN*
paper made into pulp and moulded to make models, ornaments, etc.
WORD HISTORY a French term, meaning literally 'chewed paper'

papoose *NOUN* **papooses**
a bag for carrying a baby, worn on the back
WORD HISTORY from an Algonquian (North American) word

paprika (*say* **pap**- rik- a) *NOUN*
a powdered spice made from red pepper

papyrus (*say* pap- y- rus) ***NOUN*** **papyri**
1 a kind of paper made from the stems of a plant like a reed, used in ancient Egypt
2 a document written on this paper

par ***NOUN***
the number of strokes in golf that a good player should normally take for a particular hole or course
to feel below par is to feel unwell or unfit
on a par with equal to in amount or quality

parable ***NOUN*** **parables**
(*Religion*) a story told to teach people something, especially one of those told by Jesus Christ

parabola (*say* pa- **rab**- ol- a) ***NOUN*** **parabolas**
a curve like the path of an object thrown into the air and falling down again
▷ **parabolic** ***ADJECTIVE***

parachute ***NOUN*** **parachutes**
a cloth canopy which fills with air to allow a person or heavy object to descend slowly to the ground from an aircraft

parachute ***VERB*** **parachutes, parachuting, parachuted**
to descend or drop something by means of a parachute
▷ **parachutist** ***NOUN***

parade ***NOUN*** **parades**
1 a procession that displays people or things
2 an assembly of troops for inspection, drill, etc.; a ground for this
3 a public square, promenade, or row of shops

parade ***VERB*** **parades, parading, paraded**
1 to move in a parade
2 to assemble people for a parade

paradise ***NOUN***
1 heaven; a heavenly place
2 the Garden of Eden

WORD HISTORY from Avestan (an ancient Iranian language) *pairidaeza* 'a park or garden'

paradox ***NOUN*** **paradoxes**
a statement that seems to contradict itself but which contains a truth, e.g. 'More haste, less speed'
▷ **paradoxical** ***ADJECTIVE***
▷ **paradoxically** ***ADVERB***

paraffin ***NOUN***
a kind of oil used as fuel

WORD HISTORY via German from Latin *parum* 'hardly' and *affinis* 'related' (because paraffin does not combine readily with other substances)

paragliding ***NOUN***
the sport of being towed through the air while being supported by a wide parachute

paragon ***NOUN*** **paragons**
a person or thing that seems to be perfect

paragraph ***NOUN*** **paragraphs**
(*Language*) one or more sentences on a single subject, forming a section of a piece of writing and beginning on a new line

> ***paragraphs***
>
> A long piece of prose writing, such as a chapter of a book, an essay, or a long email, is often divided into **paragraphs**. A paragraph includes several sentences that are linked by a common theme or refer to the same period of time. The second and later paragraphs in a piece of writing begin on a new line.
>
> The *topic sentence* (usually the first sentence in the paragraph) tells you what the rest of the paragraph is about.
>
> In poetry, the equivalent of a paragraph is called a *verse* or *stanza*.

parakeet ***NOUN*** **parakeets**
a kind of small parrot

parallax ***NOUN***
an apparent change in the position of an object when you look at it from different points

parallel ***ADJECTIVE***
1 (*Mathematics*) parallel lines run side by side and the same distance apart from each other for their whole length, like railway lines

> Three deep parallel grooves of skin appeared upon George's rather low sloping forehead.
> — *Roald Dahl, Vengeance Is Mine Inc*

2 similar or corresponding ◆ *Parallel situations have arisen in different countries.*
▷ **parallelism** ***NOUN***

parallel ***NOUN*** **parallels**
1 something similar or corresponding
2 to draw a parallel between two things is to compare them and point out their similarities
3 a line that is parallel to another
4 a line of latitude

parallel ***VERB*** **parallels, paralleling, paralleled**
to find or be a parallel to something

USAGE NOTE Take care with the spelling of this word: one 'r', two 'l's, then one 'l'.

parallelogram ***NOUN*** **parallelograms**
(*Mathematics*) a four-sided figure with its opposite sides equal and parallel

paralyse ***VERB*** **paralyses, paralysing, paralysed**
1 to cause paralysis in a person or a part of the body
2 to be paralysed with fear or emotion is to be so affected by it that you cannot act

paralysis ***NOUN***
being unable to move, especially because of a disease or an injury to the nerves
▷ **paralytic** (*say* pa- ra- **lit**- ik) ***ADJECTIVE***

a b c d e f g h i j k l m n o p q r s t u v w x y z

paramedic *NOUN* **paramedics**
a person who is trained to do medical work, especially emergency first aid, but is not a fully qualified doctor

parameter (*say* pa- **ram**- it- er) *NOUN* **parameters**
a quantity, quality, or factor that is variable and affects other things by its changes

USAGE NOTE Take care not to confuse this word with *perimeter*.

paramilitary *ADJECTIVE*
organized like a military force but not part of the armed services

paramount *ADJECTIVE*
more important than anything else ◆ *The highest levels of service are paramount.*

paranoia *NOUN*
1 a mental illness in which a person has delusions or suspects and distrusts people
2 an unjustified suspicion and mistrust of others

paranoid *ADJECTIVE*
suffering from paranoia

Foaly was a paranoid centaur, convinced that human intelligence agencies were monitoring his transport and surveillance network. — *Eoin Colfer, Artemis Fowl*

paranormal *ADJECTIVE*
beyond what is normal and can be rationally explained; supernatural

parapet *NOUN* **parapets**
a low wall along the edge of a roof, bridge, or balcony

paraphernalia *NOUN*
various pieces of equipment or belongings

WORD HISTORY originally the personal belongings a woman could keep after her marriage (as opposed to her dowry, which went to her husband): from Greek *para-* 'beside' and *pherne* 'dowry'

paraphrase *VERB* **paraphrases, paraphrasing, paraphrased**
to give the meaning of something by using different words
▷ **paraphrase** *NOUN*

paraplegia *NOUN*
paralysis of the lower half of the body
▷ **paraplegic** *NOUN, ADJECTIVE*

parasite *NOUN* **parasites**
an animal or plant that lives in or on another organism and gets nourishment from it
▷ **parasitic** *ADJECTIVE*

WORD HISTORY from Greek *parasitos* 'a guest at a meal', from *para-* 'beside' and *sitos* 'food'

parasol *NOUN* **parasols**
a lightweight umbrella used to keep off the heat of the sun

paratroops *PLURAL NOUN*
troops trained to be dropped from aircraft by parachute
▷ **paratrooper** *NOUN*

parboil *VERB* **parboils, parboiling, parboiled**
to boil food until it is partly cooked

parcel *NOUN* **parcels**
something wrapped up to be sent by post or carried

parcel *VERB* **parcels, parcelling, parcelled**
1 to wrap something up as a parcel
2 to parcel something out is to divide it and give shares to those involved

parched *ADJECTIVE*
very dry or (*informal*) thirsty

parchment *NOUN* **parchments**
a kind of heavy paper, originally made from animal skins

WORD HISTORY from the city of Pergamum, now in Turkey, where parchment was made in ancient times

pardon *NOUN*
the act of forgiving an offence or error or of cancelling a punishment
I beg your pardon used as a polite apology or to ask someone to say something again

pardon *VERB* **pardons, pardoning, pardoned**
1 to forgive or excuse somebody
2 to cancel a person's punishment
pardon me used as a polite apology
▷ **pardonable** *ADJECTIVE*

pare (*sounds like* pair) *VERB* **pares, paring, pared**
1 to trim something by cutting away the edges
2 to pare something down is to reduce it gradually

parent *NOUN* **parents**
1 a father or mother; an animal or plant that has produced others of its kind
2 a parent company or organization is one that owns or controls other companies or organizations
▷ **parenthood** *NOUN*
▷ **parenting** *NOUN*
▷ **parental** (*say* pa- **rent**- al) *ADJECTIVE*

parentage *NOUN*
a person's parents and ancestors

parenthesis (*say* pa- **ren**- thi- sis) *NOUN* **parentheses**
(*Language*)
1 something extra that is inserted in a sentence, usually between brackets or dashes
2 either of the pair of brackets (like these) used to mark off words from the rest of a sentence
▷ **parenthetical** *ADJECTIVE*

par excellence (*say* par eks- el- **ahns**) *ADVERB*
more than all the others; to the greatest degree

WORD HISTORY French words meaning 'because of special excellence'

pariah (*say* pa- **ry**- a) *NOUN* **pariahs**
an outcast

WORD HISTORY from a Tamil (Indian language) word meaning 'drummer': pariahs were originally members of the lowest social class in India who were drummers accompanying religious processions (without being allowed to take part in the religious ceremony proper)

parish *NOUN* **parishes**
a district with its own church

▷ **parishioner** *NOUN*

WORD HISTORY from Greek *paroikia* 'neighbourhood'

WORD FAMILY A related adjective is parochial.

parity *NOUN*
the state of being equal or equivalent

park *NOUN* **parks**
1 a large garden or recreation ground for public use
2 an area of grassland or woodland belonging to a country house

park *VERB* **parks, parking, parked**
to leave a vehicle somewhere for a time

parka *NOUN* **parkas**
a warm jacket with a hood attached

Parkinson's disease *NOUN*
a disease that makes the arms and legs shake and the muscles become stiff

WORD HISTORY named after an English physician, James *Parkinson* (1755–1824), who first described it

parley *VERB* **parleys, parleying, parleyed**
to hold a discussion with someone, especially an opponent in a dispute

▷ **parley** *NOUN*

parliament *NOUN* **parliaments**
(*Politics*) the assembly of representatives and politicians that makes a country's laws

▷ **parliamentary** *ADJECTIVE*

parlour *NOUN* **parlours**
(*old use*) a sitting room

WORD HISTORY originally a room in a monastery where the monks were allowed to talk: from French *parler* 'to speak'

parochial (*say* per- **oh**- kee- al) *ADJECTIVE*
1 to do with a church parish
2 having a narrow point of view; only interested in local matters

parody *NOUN* **parodies**
(*Language, Drama, Music*) an exaggerated imitation of the style of a particular writer, artist, composer, or performer

parody *VERB* **parodies, parodying, parodied**
to be a parody of a person or thing, or to make a parody of them

parole *NOUN*
a prisoner is on parole when they are released before the end of their sentence on the condition that they behave well

parole *VERB* **paroles, paroling, paroled**
to release a prisoner on parole

paroxysm (*say* **pa**- roks- izm) *NOUN* **paroxysms**
a sudden outburst of laughter, crying, or strong feeling

The baby was reduced to paroxysms of mirth. It squirmed energetically in its backpack.
— *Anne Fine, Flour Babies*

parquet (*say* **par**- kay) *NOUN*
wooden blocks arranged in a pattern to make a floor

parrot *NOUN* **parrots**
a brightly coloured tropical bird, some kinds of which can be trained to mimic human speech

parry *VERB* **parries, parrying, parried**
1 to turn aside an opponent's weapon or blow by using your own to block it
2 to avoid an awkward question skilfully

parse *VERB* **parses, parsing, parsed**
to analyse the grammatical form and parts of a sentence

parsimonious *ADJECTIVE*
very sparing in the use of something; mean or ungenerous

▷ **parsimony** *NOUN*

parsley *NOUN*
a plant with crinkled green leaves used to flavour and decorate food

parsnip *NOUN* **parsnips**
a plant with a pointed pale-yellow root used as a vegetable

parson *NOUN* **parsons**
a member of the clergy, especially a rector or vicar

parsonage *NOUN* **parsonages**
a church house provided for a parson

part *NOUN* **parts**
1 some but not all of a thing or number of things; anything that belongs to something bigger
2 the character played by an actor or actress
3 the words spoken by a character in a play
4 to play a part in something is to be involved in it or influence it
5 one side in an agreement or in a dispute or quarrel

to take something in good part is to accept it without being upset or offended

to take part is to join in an activity

a b c d e f g h i j k l m n o p q r s t u v w x y z

part *VERB* **parts, parting, parted**
to separate or divide

Before long, I saw a couple of policemen parade past down there, parting the crowd like butter. — *Diana Wynne Jones, The Merlin Conspiracy*

to part with something is to give it away or get rid of it

partake *VERB* **partakes, partaking, partook, partaken**
to partake of food is to eat or drink it

part exchange *NOUN*
a method of paying for something by giving something you already own as part of the price

partial *ADJECTIVE*
1 not complete or total ◆ *The exhibition was only a partial success.*
2 favouring one side more than the other; biased or unfair

to be partial to something is to like it or like doing it
▷ **partially** *ADVERB*
▷ **partiality** *NOUN*

participate *VERB* **participates, participating, participated**
to take part in something or have a share in it
▷ **participant** *NOUN*
▷ **participation** *NOUN*
▷ **participator** *NOUN*

participle *NOUN* **participles**
(*Grammar*) a word formed from a verb (e.g. *gone, going; guided, guiding*) and used with an auxiliary verb to form certain tenses (e.g. *It has gone. It is going*) or the passive (e.g. *We were guided to our seats*), or as an adjective (e.g. *a guided missile; a guiding light*). The **past participle** (e.g. *gone, guided*) describes a completed action or past condition. The **present participle** (e.g. *going, guiding*) describes a continuing action or condition.

particle *NOUN* **particles**
1 a very small piece or amount
2 (*Science*) a basic constituent of the physical world, e.g. an electron or proton

particoloured *ADJECTIVE*
partly of one colour and partly of another; variegated

particular *ADJECTIVE*
1 to do with this one and no other; individual ◆ *I got to know the habits of one particular animal.* ◆ *Particular industries are no longer located in particular regions.*
2 special or exceptional ◆ *She took particular care with her make-up.*
3 a person is particular about something when they are fussy and want it to be exactly right

'If Mrs Bartholomew's particular about her clock, why doesn't she have it upstairs with her?' Tom asked. — *Philippa Pearce, Tom's Midnight Garden*

▷ **particularly** *ADVERB*
▷ **particularity** *NOUN*

particular *NOUN* **particulars**
a detail or single fact ◆ *They had no particulars of the allegations made against them.*

in particular
1 especially ◆ *We enjoyed one part of the show in particular.*
2 special ◆ *He had nothing in particular to gain.*

parting *NOUN* **partings**
1 the act of leaving or separating
2 a line where hair is combed away in different directions

parting shot *NOUN* **parting shots**
a sharp remark made by a person who is just leaving

> **USAGE NOTE** This is also sometimes called a *Parthian shot*, after the horsemen of Parthia (an ancient kingdom in what is now Iran), who were famous for shooting arrows at the enemy while retreating.

partisan *NOUN* **partisans**
1 a strong supporter of a party or group
2 a member of an armed group fighting secretly against an occupying force

partisan *ADJECTIVE*
strongly supporting a particular cause

partition *NOUN* **partitions**
1 a thin wall that divides a room or space
2 the process of dividing a country or territory into separate parts

partition *VERB* **partitions, partitioning, partitioned**
1 to divide something into separate parts
2 to divide a room or space with a partition

partly *ADVERB*
to some extent but not completely

I am writing this journal partly to practise my newly acquired speed-writing and partly to teach myself how to write a novel. — *Dodie Smith, I Capture the Castle*

partner *NOUN* **partners**
1 each of a pair of people who do something together, such as dancing or playing a game
2 a person who jointly owns a business with one or more other people
3 each member of a married couple or of a couple living together
▷ **partnership** *NOUN*

partner ***VERB*** **partners, partnering, partnered**
to be a person's partner

part of speech ***NOUN*** **parts of speech**
(*Grammar*) a word class, any of the groups into which words are divided to show their role in a sentence (noun, verb, adjective, adverb, pronoun, conjunction, preposition, and exclamation): see the panel at **word class**

partook *past tense of* **partake**

partridge ***NOUN*** **partridges**
a game bird with brown feathers

part song ***NOUN*** **part songs**
a song with voice parts for several performers

part-time ***ADJECTIVE, ADVERB***
working for only some of the normal working day or week
▷ **part-timer** ***NOUN***

party ***NOUN*** **parties**
1 a gathering of people to enjoy themselves
2 a group working or travelling together
3 an organized group of people with similar political beliefs
4 a person who is involved in a legal agreement or dispute

Pascal ***NOUN***
(*ICT*) a computer language, used mainly in training
WORD HISTORY named after the French mathematician and philosopher Blaise *Pascal* (1623–62)

pas de deux (*say* pah der der) ***NOUN*** **pas de deux**
a dance for two people, usually in a ballet
WORD HISTORY French words meaning 'a step of two'

pass ***VERB*** **passes, passing, passed**
1 to go or move in a certain direction
2 to go past something

In the bus on the way to school next morning we passed 4 red cars in a row which meant that it was a Good Day. — *Mark Haddon, The Curious Incident of the Dog in the Night-Time*

3 time passes when it happens and is over

Alex glanced at his watch. About three minutes had passed since Crawley had left the office, and he had said he would be back in five. — *Anthony Horowitz, Stormbreaker*

4 to move something in a certain direction ◆ *You have to pass the string through this little hole.*
5 to give or transfer something to another person
6 in ball games, to kick or throw the ball to another player of your own side
7 to be successful in a test or examination
8 to pass a law is to go through the process of bringing it into force
9 to occupy time
10 to come to an end
11 to pass a remark or comment is to make it
12 (in a game, quiz, etc.) to let your turn go by or choose not to answer

to pass out
1 is to faint
2 is to complete a military training

pass ***NOUN*** **passes**
1 the process of passing something
2 a success in an examination
3 in ball games, the action of kicking or throwing the ball to another player on the same side
4 a permit to go in or out of a place
5 a route through a gap in a range of mountains

to come to a pretty pass is to reach a bad or regrettable state of affairs

passable ***ADJECTIVE***
1 able to be passed
2 satisfactory but not especially good

Her clothes weren't exactly school ruling, but were passable as Brook colours—enough to keep most of the teachers from complaining anyway. — *Keith Gray, Malarkey*

▷ **passably** ***ADVERB***

passage ***NOUN*** **passages**
1 a way through something; a corridor
2 a journey by sea or air along a particular route
3 a short section from a piece of writing or music
4 the process of going by or passing ◆ *The house deteriorated with the passage of time.*
▷ **passageway** ***NOUN***

passé (*say* pas- say) ***ADJECTIVE***
no longer fashionable

passenger ***NOUN*** **passengers**
a person other than the driver or crew who travels in a car, train, ship, or aircraft

passer-by ***NOUN*** **passers-by**
a person who happens to be going past something

passion ***NOUN*** **passions**
1 strong emotion
2 a great enthusiasm ◆ *a passion for reading*

the Passion the sufferings of Jesus Christ at the Crucifixion

passionate ***ADJECTIVE***
full of passion
▷ **passionately** ***ADVERB***

passion fruit ***NOUN***
a climbing plant found in warm regions, with a complex flower whose parts are said to suggest things associated with Christ's Crucifixion

passive *ADJECTIVE*
1 not resisting or fighting against something
2 acted upon and not active
3 (*Grammar*) a form that verbs taking an object can have, in which the person or thing affected by the action of the verb becomes the subject and the performer of the action can be expressed with *by* (as in *The mystery was solved by our neighbour*): see the language panel at **active** (SEE ALSO **active**)
▷ **passively** *ADVERB*
▷ **passiveness** *NOUN*
▷ **passivity** *NOUN*

passive smoking *NOUN*
the action of breathing in other people's cigarette smoke, thought of as a health risk

Passover *NOUN*
a Jewish religious festival commemorating the freeing of the Jews from slavery in Egypt
WORD HISTORY from *pass over* (because according to the Bible God 'passed over', i.e. spared, the Jews when he killed the eldest sons of the Egyptians)

passport *NOUN* **passports**
an official document that entitles the person holding it to travel abroad

password *NOUN* **passwords**
1 a secret word or phrase needed to be admitted to a place
2 (*ICT*) a secret set of letters you key in to gain access to certain computer files

past *ADJECTIVE*
relating to time gone by ◆ *She had been away for the past three weeks.*

past *NOUN*
the time gone by

past *PREPOSITION*
beyond a certain place or after a certain time
past it (*informal*) too old to be of any use

pasta *NOUN*
an Italian food consisting of a dried paste made from flour in various shapes such as macaroni, spaghetti, and lasagne which are cooked in boiling water

paste *NOUN* **pastes**
1 a soft, moist, and sticky substance
2 a glue, especially for paper
3 a soft edible mixture
4 a hard glassy substance used to make imitation jewellery

paste *VERB* **pastes, pasting, pasted**
1 to stick something to a surface by using paste
2 to coat something with paste

pastel *NOUN* **pastels** (*Art*)
1 a crayon that is like chalk
2 a light delicate colour

pastern *NOUN* **pasterns**
the part of a horse's foot between the fetlock and the hoof

pasteurize *VERB* **pasteurizes, pasteurizing, pasteurized**
to purify milk by heating it and then cooling it
USAGE NOTE This word can also be spelled pasteurise.
WORD HISTORY named after a French scientist, Louis *Pasteur*, who invented the process

pastille *NOUN* **pastilles**
a small flavoured sweet for sucking

pastime *NOUN* **pastimes**
something you do to make time pass pleasantly; a hobby or game

pastor *NOUN* **pastors**
a member of the clergy who is in charge of a church or congregation

pastoral *ADJECTIVE*
1 to do with country life
2 to do with a pastor or a pastor's duties

pastry *NOUN* **pastries**
1 dough made with flour, fat, and water, rolled flat and baked
2 something made of pastry

pasture *NOUN* **pastures**
land covered with grass that cattle, sheep, or horses can eat

pasture *VERB* **pastures, pasturing, pastured**
to put animals to graze in a pasture

pasty❶ (*say* **pas**- tee) *NOUN* **pasties**
a folded pastry case with a filling of seasoned meat and vegetables

pasty❷ (*say* **pay**- stee) *ADJECTIVE*
looking pale and unhealthy

pat *VERB* **pats, patting, patted**
to tap something gently with the open hand or with something flat

'Did you bring the sandwiches?' I interrupted, patting the bulging pockets of Mum's anorak. 'I'm really hungry.' — *Anne Fine, Goggle-Eyes*

pat *NOUN* **pats**
1 a patting movement or sound
2 a small piece of butter or other soft substance
a pat on the back an expression of praise or encouragement

patch *NOUN* **patches**
1 a piece of material put over a hole or damaged place
2 an area that is different from its surroundings
3 a piece of ground ◆ *He went to work on his vegetable patch.*
4 a small area or piece of something ◆ *There were patches of fog on the motorway.*
not a patch on (*informal*) not nearly as good as

patch *VERB* **patches, patching, patched**
to put a patch on something
to patch something up
1 is to repair something roughly
2 is to settle a quarrel

patchwork *NOUN*
1 needlework in which small pieces of different cloth are sewn edge to edge
2 a collection of different things making up a whole

Looking up, Alex saw a fantastic patchwork of crumbling plaster, wooden shutters, ornate railings, window boxes and terraces with Italian women leaning out to chat with their neighbours. — *Anthony Horowitz, Scorpia*

patchy *ADJECTIVE*
occurring in patches; uneven
▷ **patchily** *ADVERB*
▷ **patchiness** *NOUN*

pate *NOUN* **pates**
(*old use*) the top of a person's head

pâté (*say* **pat**- ay) *NOUN* **pâtés**
paste made of meat or fish

patent (*say* **pat**- ent or **pay**- tent) *NOUN* **patents**
the official right given to an inventor to make or sell an invention and to prevent other people from copying it

patent (*say* **pay**- tent) *ADJECTIVE*
1 very clear or obvious
2 protected by a patent

patent *VERB* **patents, patenting, patented**
to obtain a patent for something

WORD HISTORY from Latin *patens* 'lying open': originally (in *letters patent*), an open letter from a monarch or government recording a contract or granting a right

patentee (*say* pay- ten- **tee** or pat- en- **tee**) *NOUN* **patentees**
a person who holds a patent

patent leather *NOUN*
glossy leather used for shoes, belts, and handbags

patently *ADVERB*
clearly or obviously ◆ *The story was patently absurd.*

paternal *ADJECTIVE*
to do with a father
▷ **paternally** *ADVERB*

WORD HISTORY from Latin *pater* 'father'

paternity *NOUN*
1 the state of being a father; fatherhood
2 the state of being the father of a particular baby

path *NOUN* **paths**
1 a narrow way along which people or animals can walk
2 a line along which a person or thing moves
3 a course of action

pathetic *ADJECTIVE*
1 making you feel pity or sympathy
2 (*informal*) miserably inadequate or useless
◆ *She was tired of their pathetic excuses.*
▷ **pathetically** *ADVERB*

pathological *ADJECTIVE*
1 to do with pathology or disease
2 (*informal*) compulsive or obsessive

All her life, Mrs Foster had had an almost pathological fear of missing a train, a plane, a boat, or even a theatre curtain. — *Roald Dahl, The Way up to Heaven*

pathology *NOUN*
the study of diseases of the body
▷ **pathologist** *NOUN*

pathos (*say* **pay**- thoss) *NOUN*
a quality of making people feel pity or sympathy

WORD FAMILY *Pathos* is from a Greek word *pathos* meaning 'suffering' or 'feeling'. Other words to do with suffering and feeling and having the same origin include *antipathy*, *apathy*, *empathize*, *homeopathy*, *osteopath*, *pathetic*, *pathology*, *sympathy*, and *telepathy*.

patience *NOUN*
1 the quality of being patient
2 a card game for one person

patient *ADJECTIVE*
able to wait for a long time or put up with trouble or inconvenience without becoming angry or upset
▷ **patiently** *ADVERB*

patient *NOUN* **patients**
a person who is receiving treatment from a doctor or dentist

patio *NOUN* **patios**
a paved area beside a house

WORD HISTORY a Spanish word meaning 'courtyard'

patois (*say* **pat**- wa) *NOUN*
(*Language*) the dialect of the common people of a region, which differs from the standard language of the country

patriarch (*say* **pay**- tree- ark) *NOUN* **patriarchs**
1 a man who is head of a family or tribe (SEE ALSO **matriarch**)
2 a bishop of high rank in the Orthodox Christian Churches
▷ **patriarchal** *ADJECTIVE*

patrician *NOUN* **patricians**
an ancient Roman noble (SEE ALSO **plebeian**)

patrician *ADJECTIVE*
from a noble family; aristocratic

patriot (*say* pay- tree- ot or pat- ree- ot) ***NOUN*** **patriots**
a person who actively supports their country and defends it loyally
▷ **patriotic** ***ADJECTIVE***
▷ **patriotically** ***ADVERB***
▷ **patriotism** ***NOUN***

patrol ***VERB*** **patrols, patrolling, patrolled**
to walk or travel regularly over an area in order to guard it and see that all is well

patrol ***NOUN*** **patrols**
1 a patrolling group of people, ships, aircraft, etc.
2 a group of Scouts or Guides
on patrol patrolling an area

patron (*say* pay- tron) ***NOUN*** **patrons**
1 someone who supports a person or cause with money or encouragement
2 a regular customer
▷ **patronage** (*say* pat- ron- ij) ***NOUN***

patronize (*say* pat- ron- yz) ***VERB*** **patronizes, patronizing, patronized**
1 to be a regular customer of a particular shop, restaurant, or organization
2 to talk to someone in a way that shows you think they are stupid or inferior to you
USAGE NOTE This word can also be spelled patronise.

patron saint ***NOUN*** **patron saints**
a saint who is thought to protect a particular place or activity

patter[1] ***NOUN***
a series of light tapping sounds

patter ***VERB*** **patters, pattering, pattered**
1 to move with light steps ◆ *She pattered to the bathroom to take a shower.*
2 to make light tapping sounds ◆ *Outside the rain pattered lightly on the window.*

patter[2] ***NOUN***
the rapid continuous talk of a comedian, conjuror, salesperson, etc.
WORD HISTORY originally 'to recite a prayer': from Latin *pater noster* 'Our Father', the first words of a Christian prayer

pattern ***NOUN*** **patterns**
1 a repeated arrangement of lines, shapes, or colours ◆ *Several small huts stood in a roughly circular pattern.*
2 a plan or outline you copy or use as a guide in order to make something, for example a dress
3 the regular way in which something happens ◆ *There was a predictable pattern to his movements round the country.*
4 an excellent example or model
▷ **patterned** ***ADJECTIVE***

patty ***NOUN*** **patties**
a small pie or pasty

paucity ***NOUN***
(*formal*) smallness of number or quantity; scarcity

paunch ***NOUN*** **paunches**
a large rounded stomach

pauper ***NOUN*** **paupers**
a person who is very poor

pause ***NOUN*** **pauses**
a temporary stop in speaking or doing something

pause ***VERB*** **pauses, pausing, paused**
1 to stop speaking or doing something for a short time

Granny Weatherwax paused with a second scone halfway to her mouth. — *Terry Pratchett, Wyrd Sisters*

2 to stop a device or machine temporarily, e.g. a CD player

pave ***VERB*** **paves, paving, paved**
to lay a hard surface on a road, path, or other area
to pave the way is to prepare for something

pavement ***NOUN*** **pavements**
a paved path along the side of a street

pavilion ***NOUN*** **pavilions**
1 a building at a sports ground for use by players and spectators
2 an ornamental building or shelter used for dances, concerts, or exhibitions

paw ***NOUN*** **paws**
the foot of an animal that has claws

paw ***VERB*** **paws, pawing, pawed**
to touch or scrape something with a hand or foot

Still the beast stood in the archway, pawing at the floor. It was bigger than a man. — *Alan Gibbons, Shadow of the Minotaur*

pawn[1] ***NOUN*** **pawns**
1 a chess piece, one of eight on each side, of the smallest size and value
2 a person whose actions are controlled by another person or other people

pawn[2] ***VERB*** **pawns, pawning, pawned**
to leave something with a pawnbroker as security for a loan

pawnbroker ***NOUN*** **pawnbrokers**
a shopkeeper who lends money to people in return for objects that they leave as security
▷ **pawnshop** ***NOUN***

pawpaw ***NOUN*** **pawpaws**
an orange-coloured tropical fruit used as food
WORD HISTORY via Spanish and Portuguese from Carib, a South American language

pay ***VERB*** **pays, paying, paid**
1 to give money in return for goods or services
2 to give what is owed

3 to be profitable or worthwhile

The shovel sank a few inches into the packed earth. He smiled. For once in his life it paid to be overweight. — *Louis Sachar, Holes*

4 to pay someone a compliment is to praise them
5 to pay attention is to watch and listen closely
6 to pay a penalty is to suffer it
7 to let out a rope by loosening it gradually

to pay off is to be worthwhile or have good results ♦ *His intensive training had paid off handsomely.*

to pay something off is to pay in full what you owe

to pay up is to pay the full amount you owe

▷ **payer** *NOUN*

pay *NOUN*
salary or wages

payable *ADJECTIVE*
money is payable when you have to pay it, e.g. to settle a bill

payee *NOUN* **payees**
a person to whom money is paid or is to be paid

paymaster *NOUN* **paymasters**
an official who pays troops or workmen etc.

payment *NOUN* **payments**
1 the act of paying
2 an amount of money paid

payphone *NOUN* **payphones**
a public telephone operated by coins or a card

PC *ABBREVIATION*
1 personal computer
2 police constable
3 political correctness; politically correct

PE *ABBREVIATION*
physical education

pea *NOUN* **peas**
the small round green seed of a climbing plant, growing inside a pod and used as a vegetable; the plant bearing these pods

peace *NOUN*
1 a time when there is no war, violence, or disorder
2 quietness and calm

WORD FAMILY A related adjective is pacific.

peaceable *ADJECTIVE*
fond of peace; not quarrelsome or warlike

▷ **peaceably** *ADVERB*

peaceful *ADJECTIVE*
quiet and calm

▷ **peacefully** *ADVERB*

▷ **peacefulness** *NOUN*

peach *NOUN* **peaches**
1 a round soft juicy fruit with a pinkish or yellowish skin and a large stone
2 (*informal*) a very fine example of a thing ♦ *On this peach of a day the hills looked magnificent.*

peacock *NOUN* **peacocks**
a large male bird with a long brightly coloured tail that it can spread out like a fan

▷ **peahen** *NOUN*

peak *NOUN* **peaks**
1 a pointed top, especially of a mountain
2 the highest or most intense part of something ♦ *The birth rate reached its peak in the 1960s.*
3 something is in peak condition when it is at its best
4 the part of a cap that sticks out in front

▷ **peaked** *ADJECTIVE*

peak *VERB* **peaks, peaking, peaked**
to reach the highest point or value

peaky *ADJECTIVE*
looking pale and ill

'You're looking peaky, dear,' said Mrs Rider. 'Tired. Working you hard at school, are they?' — *Penelope Lively, The House in Norham Gardens*

peal *NOUN* **peals**
1 the loud ringing of a bell or set of bells
2 a loud burst of thunder or laughter

peal *VERB* **peals, pealing, pealed**
bells peal when they ring loudly

peanut *NOUN* **peanuts**
a small round nut that grows in a pod in the ground

peanut butter *NOUN*
roasted peanuts crushed into a paste

pear *NOUN* **pears**
a juicy fruit that is narrow near the stalk and more rounded at the tip

pearl *NOUN* **pearls**
a small shiny white ball found in the shells of some oysters and used as a jewel

▷ **pearly** *ADJECTIVE*

pearl barley *NOUN*
grains of barley made small by grinding

peasant *NOUN* **peasants**
a person who belongs to a farming community that is poor or low in social status

▷ **peasantry** *NOUN*

WORD HISTORY from Latin *paganus* 'villager': related to *pagan*

peat *NOUN*
rotted plant material that can be dug out of the ground and used as fuel or in gardening

▷ **peaty** *ADJECTIVE*

pebble *NOUN* **pebbles**
a small round stone

▷ **pebbly** *ADJECTIVE*

peccadillo *NOUN* **peccadilloes**
a small and unimportant fault or offence

WORD HISTORY a Spanish word meaning 'little sin'

peck *VERB* **pecks, pecking, pecked**
1 to bite at something quickly with the beak

Ailsa giggled at the chicken that pecked around her feet. — *David Almond, The Fire-Eaters*

2 to kiss someone lightly on the cheek

peck *NOUN* **pecks**
1 a quick bite by a bird
2 a light kiss on the cheek

pecking order *NOUN*
the order by which people exercise authority over others and are themselves subject to authority

WORD HISTORY called this from the way hens behave

peckish *ADJECTIVE*
(*informal*) slightly hungry

pectin *NOUN*
a substance found in ripe fruits, used to make jam set firmly

WORD HISTORY from Greek *pektos* meaning 'fixed or set'

pectoral *ADJECTIVE*
in the chest or breast

peculiar *ADJECTIVE*
1 strange or unusual

It was on the corner of the street that he noticed the first sign of something peculiar — a cat reading a map. — *J. K. Rowling, Harry Potter and the Philosopher's Stone*

2 belonging to a particular person, place, or thing; restricted ◆ *He had a look that is peculiar to ageing men.*
3 special or exceptional ◆ *This was a point of peculiar concern to us.*
▷ **peculiarly** *ADVERB*

peculiarity *NOUN* **peculiarities**
a strange feature or habit

Our father had a few peculiarities: one was, he never ate desserts; another was that he liked to walk. — *Harper Lee, To Kill a Mockingbird*

pecuniary *ADJECTIVE*
(*formal*) to do with money

WORD HISTORY from Latin *pecunia* 'money', from *pecu* 'flock of sheep' (because in early times a person's wealth was measured by how many sheep or cattle they owned)

pedagogue (*say* **ped- a- gog**) *NOUN* **pedagogues**
a teacher, especially one who teaches in a strict or exact way

WORD HISTORY from Greek *paidagogos* 'a slave who took a boy to school', from *paidos* 'of a boy' and *agogos* 'guide'

pedal *NOUN* **pedals**
a lever pressed by the foot to operate a bicycle, car, or machine, or in certain musical instruments

pedal *VERB* **pedals, pedalling, pedalled**
to use a pedal; to move or work something, especially a bicycle, by means of pedals

WORD FAMILY *Pedal* comes from the Latin words *pedes* meaning 'feet' and *pedis* meaning 'of a foot'. Other words to do with the feet or walking and having the same origin include *biped*, *centipede*, *millipede*, *pedestrian*, and *quadruped*. The word *expedite* comes from a Latin word meaning 'to free the feet', and *impede* comes from a Latin word with the opposite meaning 'to tie up the feet'.

pedant *NOUN* **pedants**
a pedantic person

pedantic *ADJECTIVE*
too concerned with minor details or with sticking strictly to formal rules
▷ **pedantically** *ADVERB*

peddle *VERB* **peddles, peddling, peddled**
1 to go from house to house selling goods

We walked on past the smoked haddock stall and the woman who sold sweets and a haggard-looking man who was peddling ink and paper. — *Alison Prince, Oranges and Murder*

2 to sell illegal drugs
3 to try to get people to accept an idea or way of life

pedestal *NOUN* **pedestals**
the raised base on which a statue or pillar etc. stands
to put someone on a pedestal is to admire them a lot or too much

pedestrian *NOUN* **pedestrians**
a person who is walking

pedestrian *ADJECTIVE*
ordinary and dull

pedestrian crossing *NOUN* **pedestrian crossings**
a place marked out for pedestrians to cross the road

pedigree *NOUN* **pedigrees**
a list of a person's or animal's ancestors, especially to show how well an animal has been bred

WORD HISTORY from Old French *pe de grue* 'foot of a crane' (the bird, because the lines on a family tree made a pattern that looked like this)

pediment *NOUN* **pediments**
a wide triangular part at the top of a classical building, often with a portico below

pedlar *NOUN* **pedlars**
a person who goes from house to house selling small things

WORD HISTORY from Middle English *ped* 'a hamper or basket' (which a pedlar used for carrying goods)

peek *VERB* **peeks, peeking, peeked**
to have a quick or sly look at something
▷ **peek** *NOUN*

peel *NOUN* **peels**
the skin of certain fruits and vegetables

peel *VERB* **peels, peeling, peeled**
1 to remove the peel or covering from something
2 to come off in strips or layers
3 to lose a covering or skin

peelings *PLURAL NOUN*
strips of skin peeled from vegetables or fruit

peep *VERB* **peeps, peeping, peeped**
1 to look quickly or secretly
2 to look through a narrow opening

In the corner of the sofa there was a cushion, and in the velvet which covered it there was a hole, and out of the hole peeped a tiny head with a pair of frightened eyes in it. — *Frances Hodgson Burnett, The Secret Garden*

3 to come slowly or briefly into view ◆ *The afternoon sun was peeping through the little window.*
▷ **peep** *NOUN*
▷ **peephole** *NOUN*

peer❶ *VERB* **peers, peering, peered**
to look at something closely or with difficulty

Across the road a plump, middle-aged woman with greying auburn hair was peering out of a window. — *Michelle Magorian, Goodnight Mister Tom*

peer❷ *NOUN* **peers**
1 a member of the nobility, such as a duke or an earl
2 someone who is equal to another in rank, ability, or age
▷ **peeress** *NOUN*

peerage *NOUN* **peerages**
1 the rank of a peer
2 peers collectively

peer group *NOUN* **peer groups**
a group of people of roughly the same age or status

peerless *ADJECTIVE*
without an equal; better than the others

peer pressure *NOUN*
the pressure to do what others in your peer group do

peeved *ADJECTIVE*
(*informal*) slightly annoyed or irritated

peevish *ADJECTIVE*
irritable or bad-tempered

peewit *NOUN* **peewits**
a lapwing

peg *NOUN* **pegs**
a piece of wood or metal or plastic used for fastening things together or for hanging things on

peg *VERB* **pegs, pegging, pegged**
1 to fix something with pegs
2 to keep wages or prices at a fixed level

pejorative (*say* pi- **jo**- ra- tiv) *ADJECTIVE*
showing disapproval; insulting or derogatory

Pekinese or **Pekingese** *NOUN* **Pekinese** or **Pekingese**
a small kind of dog with short legs, a flat face, and long silky hair

WORD HISTORY from *Peking*, the old name of Beijing, the capital of China (where the breed came from)

pelican *NOUN* **pelicans**
a large bird with a pouch in its long beak for storing fish

pelican crossing *NOUN* **pelican crossings**
a place where pedestrians can cross a street safely by operating lights that signal traffic to stop

WORD HISTORY from *pe(destrian) li(ght) con(trolled)*

pellet *NOUN* **pellets**
a tiny ball of metal, food, paper, etc.

pell-mell *ADVERB, ADJECTIVE*
in a confused or hasty way

pelmet *NOUN* **pelmets**
an ornamental strip of wood or material above a window, used to conceal a curtain rail

pelt❶ *VERB* **pelts, pelting, pelted**
1 to hurl things at someone
2 to run fast
3 to rain very hard
at full pelt as fast as possible

pelt❷ *NOUN* **pelts**
an animal skin, especially with the fur still on it

pelvis *NOUN* **pelvises**
the round framework of bones at the lower end of the spine
▷ **pelvic** *ADJECTIVE*

pen❶ *NOUN* **pens**
an instrument with a point for writing with ink

WORD HISTORY from Latin *penna* 'feather' (because a pen was originally a sharpened quill)

pen❷ *NOUN* **pens**
an enclosure for cattle, sheep, pigs, or other farm animals

pen *VERB* **pens, penning, penned**
to shut animals into a pen or other enclosed space

a b c d e f g h i j k l m n o p q r s t u v w x y z

pen③ *NOUN* **pens**
a female swan (SEE ALSO **cob**)

penal (*say* peen- al) *ADJECTIVE*
to do with the punishment of criminals, especially in prisons

penalize *VERB* **penalizes, penalizing, penalized**
to punish someone or impose a penalty on them
▷ **penalization** *NOUN*

USAGE NOTE This word can also be spelled penalise.

penalty *NOUN* **penalties**
1 a punishment
2 a point or advantage given to one side in a game when a member of the other side has broken a rule, e.g. a free kick at goal in football

penance *NOUN*
a punishment that you willingly suffer to show that you regret something wrong that you have done

pence *PLURAL NOUN* SEE **penny**

penchant (*say* pon- shon) *NOUN*
a special liking or inclination a person has ◆ *She has a penchant for quoting Shakespeare.*

pencil *NOUN* **pencils**
1 an instrument for drawing or writing, made of a thin stick of graphite or coloured substance enclosed in a cylinder of wood or metal
2 a fine paintbrush

pencil *VERB* **pencils, pencilling, pencilled**
to write, draw, or mark with a pencil

WORD HISTORY from Latin *penicillum* 'little tail' and then 'paintbrush' (because some animals' tails have a tuft at the end like a brush)

pendant *NOUN* **pendants**
an ornament worn hanging on a cord or chain round the neck

pendent *ADJECTIVE*
hanging down

pending *ADJECTIVE*
1 waiting to be decided or settled
2 about to happen

pending *PREPOSITION*
while waiting for; until ◆ *He was released on bail, pending an appeal.*

pendulous *ADJECTIVE*
hanging down

pendulum *NOUN* **pendulums**
a weight hung so that it can swing from side to side, especially in the works of a clock

penetrable *ADJECTIVE*
able to be penetrated

penetrate *VERB* **penetrates, penetrating, penetrated**
to make or find a way through or into something; to pierce something
▷ **penetration** *NOUN*
▷ **penetrative** *ADJECTIVE*

penetrating *ADJECTIVE*
1 showing great insight
2 clearly heard above other sounds

penfriend *NOUN* **penfriends**
a friend you write to regularly, usually without meeting them

penguin *NOUN* **penguins**
a seabird that cannot fly but uses its wings as flippers for swimming

penicillin *NOUN*
an antibiotic obtained from the spores of a mould

WORD HISTORY from Latin *penicillum* 'little tail' (because the parts of the mould that carry the spores are shaped like tufts)

peninsula *NOUN* **peninsulas**
a piece of land that is almost surrounded by water
▷ **peninsular** *ADJECTIVE*

WORD HISTORY from Latin *paene* 'almost' and *insula* 'island'

penis (*say* peen- iss) *NOUN* **penises**
the part of the body with which a male urinates and has sexual intercourse

WORD HISTORY a Latin word meaning 'tail'

penitence *NOUN*
regret for having done wrong
▷ **penitent** *ADJECTIVE*
▷ **penitently** *ADVERB*

penknife *NOUN* **penknives**
a small folding knife

WORD HISTORY called this because it was originally used for sharpening quill pens

pen name *NOUN* **pen names**
a name used by an author instead of their real name

pennant *NOUN* **pennants**
a long pointed flag

penne (*say* pen- ay) *PLURAL NOUN*
pasta in the form of short wide tubes

WORD HISTORY an Italian word meaning 'quills'

penniless *ADJECTIVE*
having no money; very poor

penny *NOUN* **pennies** for separate coins, **pence** for a sum of money
1 a British coin worth $\frac{1}{100}$ of a pound
2 a former coin worth $\frac{1}{240}$ of a pound

pension *NOUN* **pensions**
an income consisting of regular payments made to someone who is retired, widowed, or disabled

a b c d e f g h i j k l m n o p q r s t u v w x y z

pension *VERB* **pensions, pensioning, pensioned**
to pension someone off is to make them retire from employment and pay them a pension

pensioner *NOUN* **pensioners**
a person who receives a pension

pensive *ADJECTIVE*
deep in thought

The worthy baron seemed pensive; more than pensive: melancholy. He sat on his bed, half-naked, his legs dangling. — *Alexandre Dumas, The Man in the Iron Mask*

▷ **pensively** *ADVERB*

pentagon *NOUN* **pentagons**
a flat shape with five sides and five angles

the Pentagon a five-sided building near Washington DC, the headquarters of the leaders of the American armed forces

▷ **pentagonal** (*say* pen- **tag**- on- al) *ADJECTIVE*

pentameter (*say* pen- **tam**- i- ter) *NOUN* **pentameters**
a line of verse with five rhythmic beats

pentathlon *NOUN* **pentathlons**
an athletic contest consisting of five events

Pentecost *NOUN*
1 the Jewish harvest festival, fifty days after Passover
2 Whit Sunday

WORD HISTORY from Greek *pentekoste* 'fiftieth (day)'

penthouse *NOUN* **penthouses**
a flat at the top of a tall building, usually luxuriously furnished

pent-up *ADJECTIVE*
pent-up feelings are held back or suppressed, causing them to become stronger ◆ *The answer was like a rifle shot, full of pent-up rage.*

penultimate *ADJECTIVE*
last but one

penumbra *NOUN* **penumbras** or **penumbrae**
an area that is partly in shadow, especially part of the earth or moon during an eclipse

WORD HISTORY from Latin *paene* 'almost' and *umbra* 'shade'

penurious (*say* pin- **yoor**- ee- us) *ADJECTIVE* (*formal*)
1 extremely poor
2 mean or ungenerous

penury (*say* **pen**- yoor- ee) *NOUN*
(*formal*) great poverty

peony *NOUN* **peonies**
a plant with large round red, pink, or white flowers

WORD HISTORY named after *Paion*, physician of the Greek gods (because the plant was once used in medicines)

people *PLURAL NOUN*
human beings in general

people *NOUN* **peoples**
a particular community or nation

WORD FAMILY A related adjective is ethnic.

people *VERB* **peoples, peopling, peopled**
to fill a place with people; to populate a place

pep *NOUN*
(*informal*) vigour or energy

pepper *NOUN* **peppers**
1 a hot-tasting powder used to flavour food
2 a bright green, red, or yellow vegetable

▷ **peppery** *ADJECTIVE*

pepper *VERB* **peppers, peppering, peppered**
1 to sprinkle something with pepper
2 to pelt an area with many small objects

peppercorn *NOUN* **peppercorns**
the dried black berry from which pepper is made

peppermint *NOUN* **peppermints**
1 a kind of mint used for flavouring
2 a sweet flavoured with this mint

pepperoni *NOUN*
beef and pork sausage seasoned with pepper

pep talk *NOUN* **pep talks**
(*informal*) a talk given to someone to encourage them or give them confidence

peptide *NOUN* **peptides**
(*Science*) a compound consisting of two or more amino acids linked in a chain

per *PREPOSITION*
for each ◆ *You are given two meals per day.*

per annum *ADVERB*
for each year; yearly

WORD HISTORY Latin words meaning 'for each year'

per capita (*say* **kap**- it- a) *ADVERB, ADJECTIVE*
for each person

WORD HISTORY Latin words meaning 'by heads'

perceive *VERB* **perceives, perceiving, perceived**
to see, notice, or understand something

per cent *ADVERB*
for or in every hundred

WORD HISTORY from Latin *per centum* meaning 'for each hundred'

percentage *NOUN* **percentages**
(*Mathematics*) an amount or rate expressed as a proportion of 100

perceptible *ADJECTIVE*
able to be seen or noticed

▷ **perceptibly** *ADVERB*

▷ **perceptibility** *NOUN*

perception *NOUN* **perceptions**
1 the ability to notice or understand something
2 the process of receiving information through the senses, especially sight

perceptive *ADJECTIVE*
quick to notice or understand things

perch ❶ *NOUN* **perches**
1 a place where a bird sits or rests
2 a seat high up

perch *VERB* **perches, perching, perched**
1 to rest on a perch, or place something on a perch
2 to sit on the edge of something or somewhere high or narrow

I perched on the deck in the evening mist practising sea shanties on my tin whistle. — *Ellen MacArthur, Taking on the World*

perch ❷ *NOUN* **perch**
an edible freshwater fish

percipient *ADJECTIVE*
(*formal*) quick to notice or understand things; perceptive
▷ **percipience** *NOUN*

percolate *VERB* **percolates, percolating, percolated**
to filter through a porous surface or substance
▷ **percolation** *NOUN*

percolator *NOUN* **percolators**
a pot for making coffee, in which boiling water percolates through coffee grounds

percussion *NOUN*
1 (*Music*) musical instruments played by being struck or shaken, such as drums and maracas
2 the act of striking one thing with force against another
▷ **percussive** *ADJECTIVE*

peregrine *NOUN* **peregrines**
a kind of falcon

WORD HISTORY from Latin *peregrinus* 'travelling' (because the young birds were taken by falconers not from their nests but while they were travelling from their breeding places)

peremptory *ADJECTIVE*
giving commands and expecting to be obeyed at once

perennial *ADJECTIVE*
lasting for many years; recurring constantly
▷ **perennially** *ADVERB*

perennial *NOUN* **perennials**
a plant that lives for many years

perfect (*say* **per**- fikt) *ADJECTIVE*
1 so good that it cannot be made any better
2 complete or utter ◆ *Another delay would be a perfect nuisance.*
3 (*Grammar*) the perfect tense of a verb describes a completed action in relation to the present, e.g. *They have gone*
▷ **perfectly** *ADVERB*

perfect (*say* per- **fekt**) *VERB* **perfects, perfecting, perfected**
to make a thing perfect

After covering ten yards I had managed to perfect my hobbling technique. — *Joe Simpson, Touching the Void*

perfection *NOUN*
a perfect state or achievement

perfectionist *NOUN* **perfectionists**
a person who is only satisfied if something is done perfectly
▷ **perfectionism** *NOUN*

perfidious *ADJECTIVE*
treacherous or disloyal
▷ **perfidiously** *ADVERB*
▷ **perfidy** *NOUN*

perforate *VERB* **perforates, perforating, perforated**
1 to make tiny holes in something, especially so that it can be torn off easily
2 to pierce a surface
▷ **perforated** *ADJECTIVE*
▷ **perforation** *NOUN*

perform *VERB* **performs, performing, performed**
1 to carry out a form of entertainment in front of an audience ◆ *The play will be performed in the large hall.*
2 to do or carry out something important or difficult ◆ *They will need to perform miracles to get the work finished in time.*
▷ **performer** *NOUN*

performance *NOUN* **performances**
1 (*Drama, Music*) a form of entertainment presented to an audience
2 the way in which someone does something, or the standard they reach

perfume *NOUN* **perfumes**
1 a pleasant smell
2 a liquid for giving something a pleasant smell; a scent
▷ **perfumery** *NOUN*

perfume *VERB* **perfumes, perfuming, perfumed**
to give a sweet smell to something

WORD HISTORY originally used of pleasant-smelling smoke from something burning: via French from Italian *parfumare* 'to smoke through'

perfunctory *ADJECTIVE*
done without much care or interest

I arrived at George's villa out of breath, bursting with suppressed excitement, gave a perfunctory knock at the door and dashed in. — *Gerald Durrell, My Family and Other Animals*

▷ **perfunctorily** *ADVERB*

pergola *NOUN* **pergolas**
an arch formed by climbing plants growing over trellis-work

perhaps *ADVERB*
it may be; possibly

peril *NOUN* **perils**
a situation of great immediate danger
at your peril at your own risk
▷ **perilous** *ADJECTIVE*
▷ **perilously** *ADVERB*

perimeter *NOUN* **perimeters**
1 (*Mathematics*) the outer edge or boundary of an area or flat object
2 the distance round the edge

USAGE NOTE Take care not to confuse this word with *parameter*.

period *NOUN* **periods**
1 a length of time
2 the time allowed for a lesson in school
3 the time when a woman menstruates
4 a full stop in punctuation

periodic *ADJECTIVE*
occurring at regular intervals
▷ **periodically** *ADVERB*

periodical *NOUN* **periodicals**
a magazine published at regular intervals

periodic table *NOUN*
a table in which the chemical elements are arranged in order of increasing atomic number

peripatetic *ADJECTIVE*
going from place to place

peripheral *ADJECTIVE*
1 of minor importance
2 at the edge or boundary

periphery (*say* per- **if**- er- ee) *NOUN* **peripheries**
the part at the edge or boundary

periphrasis (*say* per- **if**- ra- sis) *NOUN* **periphrases**
a roundabout way of saying something; a circumlocution

periscope *NOUN* **periscopes**
a device with a tube and mirrors with which a person in a trench or submarine etc. can see things that are otherwise out of sight

perish *VERB* **perishes, perishing, perished**
1 to die; to be destroyed
2 to rot or disintegrate ◆ *The rubber seal had perished and caused a leak.*
▷ **perishable** *ADJECTIVE*

perished *ADJECTIVE*
(*informal*) feeling very cold

perishing *ADJECTIVE*
(*informal*) freezing cold

periwinkle❶ *NOUN* **periwinkles**
a trailing plant with blue or white flowers

periwinkle❷ *NOUN* **periwinkles**
a winkle

perjure *VERB* **perjures, perjuring, perjured**
to perjure yourself is to commit perjury

perjury *NOUN*
the act of telling a lie while you are on oath to speak the truth, especially in a lawcourt

perk❶ *VERB* **perks, perking, perked**
to perk up is to become more cheerful

perk❷ *NOUN* **perks**
(*informal*) an extra benefit given to an employee ◆ *Travel was one of the perks of her new job.*

perky *ADJECTIVE* **perkier, perkiest**
lively and cheerful
▷ **perkily** *ADVERB*

perm *NOUN* **perms**
treatment of the hair to give it long-lasting waves or curls

WORD HISTORY short for *permanent wave*

perm *VERB* **perms, perming, permed**
to give hair a perm

permafrost *NOUN*
a permanently frozen layer of soil in polar regions

permanent *ADJECTIVE*
lasting for always or for a very long time
▷ **permanently** *ADVERB*
▷ **permanence** *NOUN*

permeable *ADJECTIVE*
able to be permeated by fluids etc.
▷ **permeability** *NOUN*

permeate *VERB* **permeates, permeating, permeated**
to spread into every part of something; to pervade an area ◆ *The smell of leather permeated the air.*
▷ **permeation** *NOUN*

permissible *ADJECTIVE*
permitted or allowable

permission *NOUN*
the right to do something, given by someone in authority; authorization

Doctor, I didn't give you permission to stick that needle in me. Why did you do it? — *Brian Clark, Whose Life is it Anyway?*

permissive ***ADJECTIVE***
allowing people to behave as they wish; tolerant or liberal

permit (*say* per- **mit**) ***VERB*** **permits, permitting, permitted**
to give someone permission or consent or a chance to do something; to allow something

permit (*say* **per-** mit) ***NOUN*** **permits**
written or printed permission to do a particular thing or have access to a particular place

permutation ***NOUN*** **permutations**
1 a way in which a set or number of things can be arranged
2 (*Mathematics*) the action of changing the order of a sequence

pernicious ***ADJECTIVE***
extremely harmful

peroration ***NOUN*** **perorations**
an elaborate ending to a speech

peroxide ***NOUN***
a chemical used for bleaching hair

perpendicular ***ADJECTIVE***
(*Mathematics*) at an angle of 90° to a line or surface; upright, vertical

perpetrate ***VERB*** **perpetrates, perpetrating, perpetrated**
to commit a crime or serious error
▷ **perpetration** ***NOUN***
▷ **perpetrator** ***NOUN***

perpetual ***ADJECTIVE***
lasting for a long time; occurring repeatedly, continual
▷ **perpetually** ***ADVERB***

perpetuate ***VERB*** **perpetuates, perpetuating, perpetuated**
to cause something to continue or be remembered for a long time ◆ *The monument will perpetuate the memory of those who died in the war.*
▷ **perpetuation** ***NOUN***

perpetuity ***NOUN***
the state of lasting for ever
in perpetuity for ever

perplex ***VERB*** **perplexes, perplexing, perplexed**
to bewilder or puzzle somebody
▷ **perplexity** ***NOUN***

perquisite (*say* **per-** kwiz- it) ***NOUN*** **perquisites**
(*formal*) something extra given to an employee; a perk

perry ***NOUN***
a drink like cider, made from pears

persecute ***VERB*** **persecutes, persecuting, persecuted**
1 to treat someone cruelly because of their beliefs
2 to keep on harassing or annoying someone
▷ **persecution** ***NOUN***
▷ **persecutor** ***NOUN***

persevere ***VERB*** **perseveres, persevering, persevered**
to go on doing something even though it is difficult or likely to fail
▷ **perseverance** ***NOUN***

persist ***VERB*** **persists, persisting, persisted**
1 to persist in doing something is to continue to do it firmly or obstinately
2 a custom or situation persists when it continues to exist for a long time

persistent ***ADJECTIVE***
1 continuing or constant

The drums were still beating, persistent and unchanging. — *Chinua Achebe, Things Fall Apart*

2 determined or obstinate
▷ **persistently** ***ADVERB***
▷ **persistence** ***NOUN***

person ***NOUN*** **people** or **persons**
1 a human being; a man, woman, or child
2 (*Grammar*) any of the three groups of personal pronouns and forms taken by verbs. The **first person** (*I, me, we, us*) refers to the person or people speaking; the **second person** (*you*) refers to the person or people spoken to; the **third person** (*he, him, she, her, it, they, them*) refers to the person or thing or the people or things spoken about.
in person being actually present oneself ◆ *I want to talk to him in person.*

WORD HISTORY from Latin *persona* originally 'an actor's mask' and 'a character in a play'

personable ***ADJECTIVE***
pleasing in appearance and behaviour

personage ***NOUN*** **personages**
an important or well-known person

personal ***ADJECTIVE***
1 to do with, belonging to, or done by, a particular person ◆ *He was a member of the King's personal bodyguard.*
2 intended for a particular person and no one else; private ◆ *Each complaint is followed up with a personal letter.*
3 criticizing a person's appearance, character, or private affairs ◆ *He tried to get a reaction by making personal insults.*

USAGE NOTE Take care not to confuse this word with *personnel*.

personal computer ***NOUN*** **personal computers**
a small computer designed to be used by a single user

personality *NOUN* **personalities**
1 a person's character ◆ *It was hard sometimes to keep the lid on his bubbly personality.*
2 a well-known person ◆ *They asked several national personalities to support the scheme in public.*

personally *ADVERB*
1 in person; being actually there ◆ *She always greeted visitors to the house personally.*
2 as far as I am concerned ◆ *Personally, I would advise you to stay.*

personify *VERB* **personifies, personifying, personified**
to represent a quality or idea etc. as if it were a person
▷ **personification** *NOUN*

personnel *NOUN*
the people employed by a firm or other large organization

USAGE NOTE Take care not to confuse this word with *personal*.

perspective *NOUN* **perspectives**
1 (*Art*) the impression of depth and space in a two-dimensional picture or scene
2 a person's particular opinion or point of view about something
3 a good understanding of how important different things are ◆ *It is important to put these difficulties into perspective.*

Perspex *NOUN*
(*trademark*) a tough transparent plastic used instead of glass

perspicacious *ADJECTIVE*
quick to notice or understand things
▷ **perspicacity** *NOUN*

perspire *VERB* **perspires, perspiring, perspired**
to sweat
▷ **perspiration** *NOUN*

persuade *VERB* **persuades, persuading, persuaded**
to make someone believe or agree to do something
▷ **persuasion** *NOUN*
▷ **persuasive** *ADJECTIVE*

pert *ADJECTIVE*
cheeky in a lively and attractive way
▷ **pertly** *ADVERB*
▷ **pertness** *NOUN*

pertain *VERB* **pertains, pertaining, pertained**
(*formal*) to be relevant to something ◆ *There are wider social factors pertaining to the historical role of women.*

WORD HISTORY from Latin *pertinere* 'to belong'

pertinacious *ADJECTIVE*
(*formal*) persistent and determined
▷ **pertinaciously** *ADVERB*
▷ **pertinacity** *NOUN*

pertinent *ADJECTIVE*
relevant to what you are talking about
▷ **pertinently** *ADVERB*
▷ **pertinence** *NOUN*

perturb *VERB* **perturbs, perturbing, perturbed**
to worry someone
▷ **perturbation** *NOUN*

peruse (*say* per- **ooz**) *VERB* **peruses, perusing, perused**
to read something carefully
▷ **perusal** *NOUN*

pervade *VERB* **pervades, pervading, pervaded**
to spread all through something
▷ **pervasive** *ADJECTIVE*

perverse *ADJECTIVE*
obstinately doing something unreasonable or unacceptable
▷ **perversely** *ADVERB*
▷ **perversity** *NOUN*

pervert (*say* per- **vert**) *VERB* **perverts, perverting, perverted**
1 to turn something from the right course of action ◆ *They were accused of conspiracy to pervert the course of justice.*
2 to make a person behave in a wrong or unacceptable way
▷ **perversion** *NOUN*

pervert (*say* **per**- vert) *NOUN* **perverts**
a person whose sexual behaviour is thought to be unnatural or unacceptable

Pesach *NOUN*
the Passover festival

pessimist *NOUN* **pessimists**
a person who expects that things will turn out badly (SEE ALSO **optimist**)
▷ **pessimism** *NOUN*
▷ **pessimistic** *ADJECTIVE*
▷ **pessimistically** *ADVERB*

pest *NOUN* **pests**
1 a destructive insect or animal, such as some insects or rodents
2 (*informal*) an annoying person or thing

pester *VERB* **pesters, pestering, pestered**
to keep annoying someone by frequent questions or requests

WORD HISTORY from French *empestrer* 'to infect with plague'

pesticide *NOUN* **pesticides**
a substance for killing harmful insects and other pests

a b c d e f g h i j k l m n o p q r s t u v w x y z

pestilence *NOUN* **pestilences**
a deadly epidemic

pestilential *ADJECTIVE*
troublesome or harmful

pestle *NOUN* **pestles**
a tool with a heavy rounded end for pounding substances in a mortar

pet *NOUN* **pets**
1 a tame animal kept for companionship and pleasure
2 a person treated as a favourite

pet *ADJECTIVE*
favourite or particular ◆ *My pet hate has always been woodwork.*

pet *VERB* **pets, petting, petted**
to treat or fondle someone affectionately

petal *NOUN* **petals**
one of the separate coloured outer parts of a flower

peter *VERB* **peters, petering, petered**
to peter out is to become gradually less and come to an end

petition *NOUN* **petitions**
a formal request for something, especially a written one signed by many people

petition *VERB* **petitions, petitioning, petitioned**
to request something by a petition
▷ **petitioner** *NOUN*

petrel *NOUN* **petrels**
a kind of seabird
WORD HISTORY perhaps named after St Peter, who tried to walk on the water (because the bird flies just over the waves with its legs dangling)

petrify *VERB* **petrifies, petrifying, petrified**
1 to make someone so terrified that they cannot move
2 to turn something to stone
▷ **petrifaction** *NOUN*

petrochemical *NOUN* **petrochemicals**
a chemical substance obtained from petroleum or natural gas

petrol *NOUN*
a liquid made from petroleum, used as fuel for engines

petroleum *NOUN*
an oil found underground that is refined to make fuel (e.g. petrol or paraffin) or for use in dry-cleaning etc.

petticoat *NOUN* **petticoats**
a woman's or girl's dress-length piece of underwear worn under a skirt or dress

pettifogging *ADJECTIVE*
paying too much attention to unimportant details
WORD HISTORY from an old slang word *pettifogger* 'a lawyer who dealt with trivial cases'

petting *NOUN*
affectionate touching or fondling

pettish *ADJECTIVE*
irritable or bad-tempered; peevish

petty *ADJECTIVE* **pettier, pettiest**
1 unimportant or trivial ◆ *Many felt that their schools were too strict in imposing petty regulations.*
2 mean and small-minded
▷ **pettily** *ADVERB*
▷ **pettiness** *NOUN*

petty cash *NOUN*
cash kept by an office for small payments

petty officer *NOUN* **petty officers**
a non-commissioned officer in the navy

petulant *ADJECTIVE*
childishly irritable or bad-tempered; peevish
▷ **petulantly** *ADVERB*
▷ **petulance** *NOUN*

petunia *NOUN* **petunias**
a garden plant with funnel-shaped flowers

pew *NOUN* **pews**
a long wooden seat, usually fixed in rows, in a church

pewter *NOUN*
a grey alloy of tin and lead

pH *NOUN*
a measure of the acidity or alkalinity of a solution. Pure water has a pH of 7, acids have a pH between 0 and 7, and alkalis have a pH between 7 and 14.
WORD HISTORY from the initial letter of German *Potenz* 'power', and H, the symbol for hydrogen

phalanx *NOUN* **phalanxes**
a number of people or soldiers in a close formation

phantasm *NOUN* **phantasms**
a phantom

phantom *NOUN* **phantoms**
1 a ghost
2 something that does not really exist

Pharaoh (*say* **fair**- oh) *NOUN* **Pharaohs**
the title of a king in ancient Egypt

pharmaceutical (*say* far- ma- **syoo**- tik- al) *ADJECTIVE*
to do with medicinal drugs or with pharmacy ◆ *The company markets pharmaceutical products throughout the world.*

pharmacist *NOUN* **pharmacists**
a person who is trained to prepare and sell medicines

pharmacology *NOUN*
the study of medicinal drugs
▷ **pharmacological** *ADJECTIVE*
▷ **pharmacologist** *NOUN*
WORD HISTORY from Greek *pharmakon* 'drug'

pharmacy *NOUN* **pharmacies**
1 a place where medicines and medicinal drugs are prepared or sold
2 the science or practice of preparing medicines

pharynx (*say* **fa**- rinks) *NOUN* **pharynges**
the cavity at the back of the mouth and nose

phase *NOUN* **phases**
a stage in the progress or development of something

I have always liked the process of commuting; every phase of the little journey is a pleasure to me. — *Roald Dahl, Galloping Foxley*

phase *VERB* **phases, phasing, phased**
1 to do something in stages and not all at once ◆ *The skills improvement programme will be phased over a number of years.*
2 to phase something in or out is to introduce it or withdraw it gradually ◆ *It made sense to phase out nuclear power and phase in renewable forms of energy.*

Ph.D. *ABBREVIATION*
Doctor of Philosophy; a university degree awarded to someone who has done advanced research in their subject

pheasant (*say* **fez**- ant) *NOUN* **pheasants**
a game bird with a long tail

phenomenal *ADJECTIVE*
amazing or remarkable
▷ **phenomenally** *ADVERB*

phenomenon *NOUN* **phenomena**
a remarkable or interesting event or fact

Another curious scientific phenomenon is the fact that the fingernails grow after death, as does the beard. — *Tom Stoppard, Rosencrantz and Guildenstern are Dead*

USAGE NOTE Note that *phenomena* is a plural noun. It is incorrect to say 'this phenomena' or 'these phenomenas'.

phial *NOUN* **phials**
a small glass bottle

philander *VERB* **philanders, philandering, philandered**
a man philanders when he has many casual affairs with women
▷ **philanderer** *NOUN*

philanthropy *NOUN*
concern for your fellow human beings, especially as shown by kind and generous acts that benefit large numbers of people
▷ **philanthropist** *NOUN*
▷ **philanthropic** *ADJECTIVE*

philately (*say* fil- **at**- il- ee) *NOUN*
the collection and study of postage stamps
▷ **philatelist** *NOUN*

philharmonic *ADJECTIVE*
devoted to music (used chiefly in names of orchestras)

philistine (*say* **fil**- ist- yn) *NOUN* **philistines**
a person who dislikes or is indifferent to culture and the arts

WORD HISTORY from the Philistines in the Bible, who were enemies of the Israelites

philology *NOUN*
the study of words and their history
▷ **philological** *ADJECTIVE*
▷ **philologist** *NOUN*

philosopher *NOUN* **philosophers**
an expert in philosophy

philosophical *ADJECTIVE*
1 to do with philosophy
2 calm and unbothered after a misfortune or disappointment ◆ *People were more philosophical about these hardships in wartime.*
▷ **philosophically** *ADVERB*

philosophy *NOUN* **philosophies**
1 the study of the nature of knowledge and existence
2 a set of ideas or principles or beliefs

WORD HISTORY from Greek *philein* 'to love' and *sophia* 'wisdom'

philtre (*say* **fil**- ter) *NOUN* **philtres**
a love potion

phlegm (*say* **flem**) *NOUN*
thick mucus that forms in the throat and lungs when you have a bad cold

WORD HISTORY from Greek, from *phlegein* 'to burn'

phlegmatic (*say* fleg- **mat**- ik) *ADJECTIVE*
not easily excited or worried
▷ **phlegmatically** *ADVERB*

WORD HISTORY the same origin as *phlegm* (because too much phlegm in the body was believed to make you sluggish)

phobia (*say* **foh**- bee- a) *NOUN* **phobias**
an extreme or abnormal fear of something

WORD HISTORY from Greek *phobos* 'fear'

phoenix (*say* **feen**- iks) *NOUN* **phoenixes**
a mythical bird that was said to burn itself to death in a fire every five or six centuries and be born again from the ashes

phone *NOUN* **phones**
a telephone

phone *VERB* **phones, phoning, phoned**
to make a telephone call

phonecard *NOUN* **phonecards**
a plastic card that you can use to work some public telephones instead of money

phone-in *NOUN* **phone-ins**
a radio or television programme during which people telephone the studio and take part in a discussion

phoneme *NOUN* **phonemes**
(*Language*) a distinct unit of sound that distinguishes one word from another, e.g. *p*, *b*, *d*, and *t* in *pad*, *pat*, *bad*, and *bat*

phonetic (*say* fon- **et**- ik) *ADJECTIVE*
1 to do with speech sounds
2 representing speech sounds
▷ **phonetically** *ADVERB*

WORD HISTORY from Greek *phonein* 'to speak'

phoney *ADJECTIVE*
(*informal*) sham; not genuine

phonic *ADJECTIVE*
to do with speech sounds

phonics *NOUN*
a method of teaching reading by relating sounds to letters of the alphabet

phosphate *NOUN* **phosphates**
a substance containing phosphorus, especially an artificial fertilizer

phosphorescent (*say* fos- fer- **ess**- ent) *ADJECTIVE*
glowing in the dark; luminous
▷ **phosphorescence** *NOUN*

phosphorus *NOUN*
a chemical substance that glows in the dark

photo *NOUN* **photos**
(*informal*) a photograph

photocopy *NOUN* **photocopies**
a copy of a document or page made by photographing it on special paper

photocopy *VERB* **photocopies, photocopying, photocopied**
to make a photocopy of a document or page
▷ **photocopier** *NOUN*

photoelectric *ADJECTIVE*
using the electrical effects of light

photogenic *ADJECTIVE*
looking attractive in photographs

photograph *NOUN* **photographs**
a picture made by the effect of light or other radiation on film or special paper, using a camera

photograph *VERB* **photographs, photographing, photographed**
to take a photograph of a person or thing
▷ **photographer** *NOUN*

photography *NOUN*
taking photographs
▷ **photographic** *ADJECTIVE*

photosynthesis *NOUN*
the process by which green plants use sunlight to turn carbon dioxide and water into complex substances, giving off oxygen

phrase *NOUN* **phrases**
1 (*Grammar*) a group of words that form a unit in a sentence or clause, e.g. *in his bedroom* in the sentence *Harry was in his bedroom*
2 a short section of a tune

phrase *VERB* **phrases, phrasing, phrased**
1 to put something into words
2 to divide music into phrases

phrase book *NOUN* **phrase books**
a book which lists useful words and expressions in a foreign language, with their translations

phraseology (*say* fray- zee- **ol**- o- jee) *NOUN* **phraseologies**
the way something is worded or expressed

physical *ADJECTIVE*
1 to do with the body rather than the mind or feelings
2 to do with things that you can touch or see
3 to do with physics
▷ **physically** *ADVERB*

physical education or **physical training** *NOUN*
exercises and sports done to keep the body healthy

physician *NOUN* **physicians**
a doctor, especially one who is not a surgeon

physicist (*say* **fiz**- i- sist) *NOUN* **physicists**
someone who studies or is expert in physics

physics (*say* **fiz**- iks) *NOUN*
the study of the properties of matter and energy (e.g. heat, light, sound, and movement)

WORD HISTORY from Greek *physikos* 'natural'

physiognomy (*say* fiz- ee- **on**- o- mee) *NOUN* **physiognomies**
the features of a person's face

physiology (*say* fiz- ee- **ol**- o- jee) *NOUN*
the study of the body and its parts and how they function
▷ **physiological** *ADJECTIVE*
▷ **physiologist** *NOUN*

physiotherapy (*say* fiz- ee- o- **the**- ra- pee) *NOUN*
the treatment of a disease or injury by physical methods such as massage and exercise
▷ **physiotherapist** *NOUN*

physique (*say* fiz- **eek**) *NOUN* **physiques**
a person's build

pi *NOUN*
the symbol (π) of the ratio of the circumference of a circle to its diameter. The value of pi is approximately 3.14159.

pianist *NOUN* **pianists**
a person who plays the piano

piano *NOUN* **pianos**
a large musical instrument with a keyboard and a wooden case containing metal strings which are struck by hammers when keys are pressed

WORD HISTORY short for *pianoforte*, from Italian *piano* 'soft' and *forte* 'loud' (because it can produce soft notes and loud notes)

picaresque (*say* pik- er- **esk**) *ADJECTIVE*
picaresque fiction is about the adventures of a rough but likeable hero in a series of episodes

WORD HISTORY via French from Spanish *picaro* 'rogue'

piccolo *NOUN* **piccolos**
a small high-pitched flute

WORD HISTORY an Italian word meaning 'small'

pick❶ *VERB* **picks, picking, picked**
1 to pull a flower or fruit away from its plant
2 to choose something or someone with care
3 to pull bits off or out of something
4 to open a lock by using something pointed, not with a key

to pick a quarrel is to provoke it deliberately with somebody
to pick holes in something is to find fault with it
to pick on someone is to single them out for criticism or unkind treatment

What does he keep picking on me for anyway? He should know by now that I don't know the quadratic formula from a hole in the ground.
— *Meg Cabot, The Princess Diaries*

to pick someone's pocket is to steal from it
to pick up is to recover or improve
to pick someone up is to take them into a vehicle
to pick something up
1 is to lift or take it up
2 is to collect it from somewhere
3 is to learn or acquire something
4 is to manage to hear something

pick *NOUN*
1 a free choice ◆ *When the others had gone we had the pick of the left-over food.*
2 the best of a group

pick❷ *NOUN* **picks**
1 a pickaxe
2 a plectrum

pickaxe *NOUN* **pickaxes**
a heavy pointed tool with a long handle, used for breaking up hard ground etc.

picket *NOUN* **pickets**
1 a striker or group of strikers who try to persuade other people not to go into a place of work during a strike
2 a pointed post as part of a fence

picket *VERB* **pickets, picketing, picketed**
to stand outside a place of work to try to persuade other people not to go in during a strike

pickle *NOUN* **pickles**
1 a strong-tasting food made of pickled vegetables
2 (*informal*) a mess

pickle *VERB* **pickles, pickling, pickled**
to preserve food in vinegar or salt water

pick-me-up *NOUN* **pick-me-ups**
(*informal*) something that makes you feel more energetic or cheerful

pickpocket *NOUN* **pickpockets**
a thief who steals from people's pockets or bags

pickup *NOUN* **pickups**
1 an open truck for carrying small loads
2 a device that converts sound vibrations into electrical signals to be amplified, e.g. on an electric guitar or record player

picnic *NOUN* **picnics**
a meal eaten in the open air away from home

picnic *VERB* **picnics, picnicking, picnicked**
to have a picnic
▷ **picnicker** *NOUN*

picosecond (*say* **pee**- koh) *NOUN*
one million millionth of a second

Pict *NOUN* **Picts**
a member of an ancient people of north Britain
▷ **Pictish** *ADJECTIVE*

pictorial *ADJECTIVE*
with or using pictures
▷ **pictorially** *ADVERB*

picture *NOUN* **pictures**
1 a representation of a person or thing made by painting, drawing, or photography
2 a film at the cinema
3 how something seems; an impression

to be in the picture (*informal*) is to have all the information about something

picture *VERB* **pictures, picturing, pictured**
1 to show someone or something in a picture
2 to imagine a person or thing

picturesque *ADJECTIVE*
1 pretty and attractive to look at ◆ *People on the whole preferred a modern bungalow to a picturesque cottage.*
2 picturesque language or description is vivid and expressive
▷ **picturesquely** *ADVERB*

pidgin *NOUN* **pidgins**
a simplified form of a language used by people who do not speak the same language

WORD HISTORY from the Chinese pronunciation of *business* (because the word was used by traders)

a b c d e f g h i j k l m n o p q r s t u v w x y z

pie *NOUN* **pies**
a baked dish of meat, fish, or fruit covered with pastry

WORD HISTORY perhaps from *magpie* (because the contents of a pie look like the bits and pieces a magpie collects in its nest)

piebald *ADJECTIVE*
a piebald animal has patches of black and white

piece *NOUN* **pieces**
1 a part or portion of something; a fragment
2 a separate example of something done or created, such as prose or music
3 one of the objects used to play a game on a board
4 a coin of a certain value ◆ *He had dropped a fifty-pence piece.*
in one piece not harmed or damaged
piece by piece gradually; one bit at a time

piece *VERB* **pieces, piecing, pieced**
to put pieces together to make something

pièce de résistance (*say* pee- ess der ray- zees- **tahns**) *NOUN* **pièces de résistance**
the most important item

WORD HISTORY French words meaning 'piece (i.e. means) of resistance'

piecemeal *ADJECTIVE, ADVERB*
done or made one piece at a time

pie chart *NOUN* **pie charts**
a type of graph in the form of a circle divided into sectors to represent the way in which an amount is divided up

pier *NOUN* **piers**
1 a long structure built out into the sea for people to walk on, for small boats to moor at, or as a place of entertainment
2 a pillar supporting a bridge or arch

pierce *VERB* **pierces, piercing, pierced**
to make a hole through something; to penetrate a surface

piercing *ADJECTIVE*
1 very loud and high-pitched ◆ *The dog let out a piercing howl.*
2 penetrating; very strong ◆ *He gave her a piercing look.*

piety *NOUN*
the quality of being religious and devout; piousness

piffle *NOUN*
(*informal*) nonsense; rubbish

pig *NOUN* **pigs**
1 a fat animal with short legs and a blunt snout, kept for its meat
2 (*informal*) someone greedy, dirty, or unpleasant
▷ **piggy** *ADJECTIVE, NOUN*

pigeon[1] *NOUN* **pigeons**
a bird with a fat body and a small head

WORD HISTORY from Old French *pijon* 'young bird'

pigeon[2] *NOUN*
(*informal*) a person's business or responsibility ◆ *Bill regarded the library as his pigeon.*

pigeonhole *NOUN* **pigeonholes**
a small compartment for holding letters, messages, or papers, for someone to collect

pigeonhole *VERB* **pigeonholes, pigeonholing, pigeonholed**
to decide that a person belongs to a particular category ◆ *For many years he was pigeonholed as a children's writer.*

piggery *NOUN* **piggeries**
a place where pigs are bred or kept

piggyback *NOUN* **piggybacks**
a ride on somebody else's back or shoulders

piggy bank *NOUN* **piggy banks**
a money box made in the shape of a hollow pig

pig-headed *ADJECTIVE*
stubborn or obstinate

pig iron *NOUN*
iron that has been processed in a smelting furnace

WORD HISTORY called this because the layout of the blocks of iron reminded people of piglets feeding

piglet *NOUN* **piglets**
a young pig

pigment *NOUN* **pigments**
1 a substance that colours skin or other tissue in animals and plants
2 a substance that gives colour to paint, inks, and dyes
▷ **pigmented** *ADJECTIVE*
▷ **pigmentation** *NOUN*

pigsty *NOUN* **pigsties**
1 a partly covered pen for pigs
2 a filthy room or house

pigtail *NOUN* **pigtails**
a plait of hair worn hanging at the back of the head

pike *NOUN* **pikes**
1 a heavy spear
2 (*plural* **pike**) a large freshwater fish

pilau (*say* pi- **low**) *NOUN*
an Indian dish of spiced rice with meat and vegetables

WORD HISTORY from Turkish *pilav*

pilchard *NOUN* **pilchards**
a small sea fish

pile[1] *NOUN* **piles**
1 a number of things on top of one another
2 (*informal*) a large quantity; a lot of money
3 a large impressive building

pile *VERB* **piles, piling, piled**
to put things into a pile; to make a pile

pile[2] *NOUN* **piles**
a heavy beam made of metal, concrete, or timber driven into the ground to support a structure

pile[3] *NOUN*
a raised surface on fabric, made of upright threads

pile-up *NOUN* **pile-ups**
a road accident that involves a number of vehicles

pilfer *VERB* **pilfers, pilfering, pilfered**
to steal things of little value
▷ **pilferer** *NOUN*

pilgrim *NOUN* **pilgrims**
(*Religion*) a person who travels to a holy place for religious reasons
▷ **pilgrimage** *NOUN*

pill *NOUN* **pills**
a small solid piece of medicine for swallowing
the Pill a contraceptive pill

pillage *VERB* **pillages, pillaging, pillaged**
to carry off goods using force, especially in a war; to plunder a place
▷ **pillage** *NOUN*

pillar *NOUN* **pillars**
a tall stone or wooden post

pillar box *NOUN* **pillar boxes**
a postbox standing in a street

pillion *NOUN* **pillions**
a seat behind the driver on a motorcycle

WORD HISTORY from Scottish Gaelic *pillean* 'a small cushion'

pillory *NOUN* **pillories**
a wooden framework with holes for a person's head and hands, in which offenders were formerly made to stand and be ridiculed by the public as a punishment

pillory *VERB* **pillories, pillorying, pilloried**
to pillory someone is to expose them to public ridicule and scorn

pillow *NOUN* **pillows**
a cushion for a person's head to rest on, especially in bed

pillowcase or **pillowslip** *NOUN* **pillowcases** or **pillowslips**
a cloth cover for a pillow

pilot *NOUN* **pilots**
1 a person who works the controls for flying an aircraft
2 a person qualified to steer a ship in and out of a port or through a difficult stretch of water
3 a guide

pilot *VERB* **pilots, piloting, piloted**
1 to be pilot of an aircraft or ship
2 to guide or steer someone

pilot *ADJECTIVE*
testing on a small scale how something will work ◆ *The coaching programme is being run as a pilot scheme in three countries.*

pilot light *NOUN* **pilot lights**
1 a small flame that lights a larger burner on a gas cooker or boiler
2 an electric indicator light

pimp *NOUN* **pimps**
a man who finds clients for prostitutes and lives off their earnings

pimpernel (*say* **pimp**- er- nel) *NOUN* **pimpernels**
a plant with small red, blue, or white flowers that close in cloudy weather

pimple *NOUN* **pimples**
a small round raised spot on the skin
▷ **pimply** *ADJECTIVE*

PIN *ABBREVIATION*
personal identification number, a number that you need to key in when you use a cash machine or bank card

USAGE NOTE Strictly speaking you should not say *PIN number* because the word *number* is already included in *PIN*.

pin *NOUN* **pins**
1 a short thin piece of metal with a sharp point and a rounded head, used to fasten pieces of material together
2 a pointed device for fixing or marking something
pins and needles a tingling feeling in the skin

pin *VERB* **pins, pinning, pinned**
1 to fasten something with a pin or pins
2 to hold someone firmly so that they cannot move
3 to pin the blame for something on someone is to hold them responsible or to blame for it

pinafore *NOUN* **pinafores**
an apron like a dress without sleeves, worn over clothes to keep them clean

WORD HISTORY from *pin* and *afore* 'in front' (because originally the bib of the apron was pinned to the front of the dress)

pinball *NOUN*
a game in which you shoot small metal balls across a special table and score points when they strike special pins

pincer *NOUN* **pincers**
the claw of a shellfish such as a lobster

a b c d e f g h i j k l m n o p q r s t u v w x y z

pincer movement *NOUN* **pincer movements**
an attack in which two forces converge on an enemy from different directions

pincers *PLURAL NOUN*
a tool with two parts that are pressed together for gripping and holding things

pinch *VERB* **pinches, pinching, pinched**
1 to squeeze something tightly or painfully between two things, especially between the finger and thumb
2 (*informal*) to steal something

pinch *NOUN* **pinches**
1 a pinching movement
2 a small amount of something that can be held between the tips of the thumb and forefinger, especially of salt

at a pinch in time of difficulty; if necessary
to feel the pinch is to be short of money

pincushion *NOUN* **pincushions**
a small pad into which you stick pins to keep them ready for use

pine❶ *NOUN* **pines**
an evergreen tree with needle-shaped leaves

pine❷ *VERB* **pines, pining, pined**
1 to feel an intense longing for somebody or something
2 to become weak through longing for somebody or something

pineapple *NOUN* **pineapples**
a large tropical fruit with a tough prickly skin and yellow flesh

ping *NOUN* **pings**
a short sharp ringing sound

ping *VERB* **pings, pinging, pinged**
to make a sharp ringing sound

ping-pong *NOUN*
(*informal*) table tennis

WORD HISTORY so called from the sound of the bats hitting the ball

pinion❶ *NOUN* **pinions**
a bird's wing, especially the outer end

pinion *VERB* **pinions, pinioning, pinioned**
1 to clip a bird's wings to prevent it from flying
2 to hold or fasten someone's arms or legs in order to prevent them from moving

My grandmother ... was held, arms pinioned behind her, and pushed to the foot of the ladder which leant against the gallows tree. — *Celia Rees, Witch Child*

WORD HISTORY from Latin *pinna* 'arrow' or 'feather'

pinion❷ *NOUN* **pinions**
a small cogwheel that fits into another or into a rod (called a *rack*)

WORD HISTORY from Latin *pinus* 'pine tree' (because the wheel's teeth reminded people of a pine cone)

pink❶ *ADJECTIVE*
pale red
▷ **pinkness** *NOUN*

pink *NOUN* **pinks**
1 a pink colour
2 a garden plant with fragrant flowers, often pink or white

pink❷ *VERB* **pinks, pinking, pinked**
1 to pierce something slightly
2 to cut a zigzag edge on cloth

pinnacle *NOUN* **pinnacles**
1 a pointed ornament on a roof
2 a high pointed piece of rock
3 the highest point of something ◆ *Winning an Olympic gold medal was the pinnacle of her career.*

pinpoint *ADJECTIVE*
exact or precise ◆ *The aircraft has to be navigated with pinpoint accuracy.*

pinpoint *VERB* **pinpoints, pinpointing, pinpointed**
to find or identify something precisely

pinprick *NOUN* **pinpricks**
a small annoyance

pinstripe *NOUN* **pinstripes**
one of the very narrow stripes that form a pattern in cloth
▷ **pinstriped** *ADJECTIVE*

pint *NOUN* **pints**
a measure for liquids, equal to one-eighth of a gallon

pin-up *NOUN* **pin-ups**
(*informal*) a picture of an attractive or famous person for pinning on a wall

pioneer *NOUN* **pioneers**
one of the first people to go to a place or do or investigate something

WORD HISTORY from French *pionnier* 'foot soldier', later one of the troops who went ahead of the army to prepare roads

pioneer *VERB* **pioneers, pioneering, pioneered**
to be one of the first people to go to a place or do something

pious *ADJECTIVE*
very religious; devout
▷ **piously** *ADVERB*
▷ **piousness** *NOUN*

pip *NOUN* **pips**
1 a small hard seed of an apple, pear, orange, or other fruit
2 one of the stars on the shoulder of an army officer's uniform
3 each of a series of short high-pitched sounds emitted as a signal

pip *VERB* **pips, pipping, pipped**
(*informal*) to defeat someone by a small amount

pipe *NOUN* **pipes**
1 a tube through which water, gas, oil, etc. can flow from one place to another
2 a short narrow tube with a bowl at one end for burning tobacco for smoking
3 a tube forming a musical instrument or part of one
the pipes a set of bagpipes

pipe *VERB* **pipes, piping, piped**
1 to send something along pipes
2 to transmit music or other sound by wire or cable
3 to play music on a pipe or the bagpipes
4 to decorate a cake with thin lines of icing, cream, etc.
to pipe down (*informal*) is to be quiet
to pipe up is to begin to say something

pipe dream *NOUN* **pipe dreams**
an impossible wish

pipeline *NOUN* **pipelines**
a pipe for carrying oil, gas, etc. over long distances
in the pipeline in the process of being made or organized

piper *NOUN* **pipers**
a person who plays a pipe or bagpipes

pipette (*say* pip- et) *NOUN* **pipettes**
a small glass tube used in a laboratory, usually filled by suction

piping *NOUN*
1 pipes; a length of pipe
2 a decorative line of icing, cream, etc. on a cake or other dish
3 a long narrow pipe-like fold decorating clothing, upholstery, etc.

piping *ADJECTIVE*
1 shrill ◆ *She heard the piping voice of a little girl.*
2 food is piping hot when it is very hot and ready to eat

pipit *NOUN* **pipits**
a small songbird

pippin *NOUN* **pippins**
a kind of apple

piquant (*say* pee- kant) *ADJECTIVE*
1 pleasantly sharp and appetizing
2 pleasantly stimulating
▷ **piquancy** *NOUN*

pique (*say* peek) *NOUN*
a feeling of hurt pride

pique *VERB* **piques, piquing, piqued**
to be piqued is to feel irritated or annoyed

piranha *NOUN* **piranhas**
a South American freshwater fish that has sharp teeth and eats flesh
WORD HISTORY via Portuguese from Tupi (a South American language)

pirate *NOUN* **pirates**
1 a person on a ship who attacks and robs other ships at sea
2 someone who publishes or broadcasts copyright material without authorization
▷ **piratical** *ADJECTIVE*
▷ **piracy** *NOUN*

pirouette (*say* pir- oo- et) *NOUN* **pirouettes**
a spinning movement of the body made while balanced on the point of the toe or on one foot

I jump. A huge pirouette in the air ... to land, with a degree of grace, at Catherine's feet. — *Nicky Singer, Feather Boy*

pirouette *VERB* **pirouettes, pirouetting, pirouetted**
to perform a pirouette

pistachio *NOUN* **pistachios**
a nut with an edible green kernel

piste (*say* peest) *NOUN*
a ski track of tight dense snow

pistil *NOUN* **pistils**
the part of a flower that produces the seed, consisting of the ovary, style, and stigma

pistol *NOUN* **pistols**
a small handgun

piston *NOUN* **pistons**
a disc or cylinder that fits inside a tube in which it moves up and down as part of an engine or pump

pit *NOUN* **pits**
1 a deep hole in the ground
2 a hollow
3 a coal mine
4 the part of a race circuit where racing cars are refuelled and repaired during a race

pit *VERB* **pits, pitting, pitted**
1 a piece of ground or other surface is pitted when it is covered with a lot of small holes
2 people are pitted against one another when they are competing with one another or are in conflict
to pit your wits against someone is to compete with them in a test of knowledge or intelligence

pit bull terrier *NOUN* **pit bull terriers**
a small strong and fierce breed of dog

pitch ❶ *NOUN* **pitches**
1 a piece of ground marked out for cricket, football, or another game
2 (*Music*) the highness or lowness of a voice or a musical note
3 intensity or strength ◆ *The rush in London reached fever pitch.*
4 the steepness of a slope, especially of a roof

a b c d e f g h i j k l m n o p q r s t u v w x y z

SPELLING NOTE Some words pronounced like *pin* or *pine* begin with **py-** (e.g. pyjamas, pylon)

pitch *VERB* **pitches, pitching, pitched**
1 to throw or fling something
2 to set up a tent or camp
3 to fall heavily forward
4 a ship pitches when it moves violently up and down on a rough sea
5 to set something at a particular level ◆ *Prices are pitched at an affordable level.*
6 a ball bowled in cricket pitches when it strikes the ground

to pitch in (*informal*) is to start working or doing something vigorously

pitch❷ *NOUN*
a black sticky substance rather like tar

pitch-black or **pitch-dark** *NOUN*
completely black or dark

pitchblende *NOUN*
a mineral ore (uranium oxide) from which radium is obtained

pitched battle *NOUN* **pitched battles**
a battle between armies in prepared positions

pitcher *NOUN* **pitchers**
a large jug

pitchfork *NOUN* **pitchforks**
a large fork with two prongs, used for lifting hay

pitchfork *VERB* **pitchforks, pitchforking, pitchforked**
1 to lift something with a pitchfork
2 to put a person somewhere suddenly

piteous *ADJECTIVE*
deserving pity
▷ **piteously** *ADVERB*

pitfall *NOUN* **pitfalls**
an unsuspected danger or difficulty

pith *NOUN*
the spongy substance in the stems of certain plants or lining the rind of oranges or other fruits

pithy *ADJECTIVE*
1 like pith; containing much pith
2 short and full of meaning ◆ *A pithy summary tells you what is in the article.*

pitiable *ADJECTIVE*
deserving pity; pitiful

pitiful *ADJECTIVE*
deserving pity; pathetic
▷ **pitifully** *ADVERB*

pitiless *ADJECTIVE*
showing no pity; harsh or cruel
▷ **pitilessly** *ADVERB*

pitta *NOUN*
a kind of flat thick bread with a hollow inside, originally from Greece and the Middle East
WORD HISTORY from a modern Greek word meaning 'cake or pie'

pittance *NOUN*
a very small allowance of money
WORD HISTORY from Latin *pietas* 'pity': originally it was a 'pious gift' (one given to a church)

pity *NOUN*
1 the feeling of being sorry because someone is suffering or in difficulty
2 a cause for regret ◆ *It's a pity you weren't able to stay on any longer.*

to take pity on someone is to feel sorry for them and try to help them

pity *VERB* **pities, pitying, pitied**
to feel pity for someone

pivot *NOUN* **pivots**
a point or part on which something turns or balances
▷ **pivotal** *ADJECTIVE*

pivot *VERB* **pivots, pivoting, pivoted**
to turn on a pivot, or place something to turn on a pivot

pixel (*say* **piks**- el) *NOUN* **pixels**
each of the tiny dots on a computer display screen from which the image is formed
WORD HISTORY short for *picture element*

pixie *NOUN* **pixies**
an elf or small fairy with pointed ears and a pointed hat

pizza (*say* **peets**- a) *NOUN* **pizzas**
an Italian food made from a flat round base of dough baked with a savoury topping
WORD HISTORY an Italian word meaning 'pie'

pizzicato (*say* pits- i- **kah**- toh) *ADJECTIVE, ADVERB*
(*Music*) plucking the strings of a musical instrument that is normally played with a bow
WORD HISTORY an Italian word meaning 'pinched' or 'twisted'

placard *NOUN* **placards**
a poster or notice carried in public, e.g. at a demonstration

placate *VERB* **placates, placating, placated**
to make someone feel calmer and less angry
▷ **placatory** *ADJECTIVE*

place *NOUN* **places**
1 a particular part of space, especially where something belongs; an area or position
2 a city, town, or village having a name
3 a seat ◆ *There were two empty places at the table.*
4 a job; employment
5 a home or other special building

They had coffee from condensed-milk cans at an early morning place that served fishermen.
— *Ernest Hemingway, The Old Man and the Sea*

6 a role or function ◆ *He did not think it was his place to argue with them.*
7 a point in a series of things ◆ *Why call a search in the first place?*

to be in place is to be in the correct place or position

in place of instead of

to be out of place
1 is to be in the wrong position
2 is to be inappropriate or unsuitable

to take place is to happen

place names

Many **place names** come from the languages of the people who first settled there, and because of this you can often date a place from its name.

Place names which end in *-borough* or *-burgh* (e.g. *Scarborough* and *Edinburgh*) derive from the Old English word *burg*, meaning 'city'; those ending in *-ton* are based on Old English *tun* 'town'; and *-shire* names incorporate Old English *scir*, meaning 'office' or 'authority'.

Place names which end in *-caster* or *-chester* (e.g. *Doncaster* and *Manchester*) come from Roman names which incorporated the Latin word *castra* meaning 'fort' or 'camp'. Other place names have Celtic origins: *Dublin* comes from Irish words meaning 'black pool', *Glasgow* comes from Gaelic words meaning 'green hollow', and *Cardiff* includes the Welsh word *caer* meaning 'fort' or 'castle'. The endings *-by* meaning 'farmstead' , *-ness* 'cape', and *-wick* 'bay' are all Norse in origin and feature in place names such as *Whitby*, *Skegness*, and *Lerwick*.

Names modelled on British place names have been adopted in other English-speaking countries: for example, *Dunedin* in New Zealand comes from an old Gaelic name for *Edinburgh*, and *Kingston* in Jamaica is an English version of an older French name *Port Royal* ('King's Port').

place *VERB* **places, placing, placed**
to put something in a particular place

placebo (*say* **plas-** ee- boh) *NOUN* **placebos**
a harmless substance given as if it were a medicine, usually to reassure a patient

WORD HISTORY a Latin word meaning 'I (= the pill) shall be pleasing', i.e. 'I shall satisfy'

placement *NOUN* **placements**
the action of placing something in a position

placenta *NOUN*
a piece of body tissue that forms in the womb during pregnancy and supplies the fetus with nourishment

placid *ADJECTIVE*
calm and peaceful; not easily made anxious or upset
▷ **placidly** *ADVERB*
▷ **placidity** *NOUN*

plagiarize (*say* **play-** jeer- yz) *VERB* **plagiarizes, plagiarizing, plagiarized**
to take someone else's writings or ideas and use them as if they were your own
▷ **plagiarism** *NOUN*
▷ **plagiarist** *NOUN*

USAGE NOTE This word can also be spelled plagiarise.

WORD HISTORY from Latin *plagiarius* 'kidnapper' from *plagium* 'kidnapping'

plague *NOUN* **plagues**
1 a dangerous illness that spreads very quickly
2 a huge invasion of insects or other pests

plague *VERB* **plagues, plaguing, plagued**
to pester or annoy someone

Will was passionately curious about his father, and he used to plague his mother with questions, most of which she couldn't answer. — *Philip Pullman, The Subtle Knife*

plaice *NOUN* **plaice**
a flat edible sea fish

WORD HISTORY from Greek *platys* 'broad'

plaid (*say* plad) *NOUN*
cloth with a tartan or similar pattern

WORD HISTORY from Scottish Gaelic *plaide* 'blanket'

plain *ADJECTIVE*
1 simple; not decorated or elaborate
2 not very attractive or beautiful
3 easy to see or hear or understand

It was plain that there was not a great deal of strength in Mistress Mary's arms and legs when she first began to skip. — *Frances Hodgson Burnett, The Secret Garden*

4 frank and straightforward
5 a plain knitting stitch is made by putting the needle through the front of the stitch from left to right (SEE ALSO **purl**)
▷ **plainly** *ADVERB*
▷ **plainness** *NOUN*

plain *NOUN* **plains**
a large area of flat country

USAGE NOTE Take care not to confuse this word with *plane*.

plain clothes *PLURAL NOUN*
civilian clothes worn instead of a uniform, e.g. by police

plaintiff *NOUN* **plaintiffs**
a person who brings a complaint against another person in a lawcourt (SEE ALSO **defendant**)

plaintive *ADJECTIVE*
sounding sad and mournful ◆ *He left them, knowing they were safe despite their plaintive cries.*

WORD HISTORY from French *plaintif* 'grieving or complaining'

plait (*say* plat) *VERB* **plaits, plaiting, plaited**
to weave three or more strands of hair or rope to form one length

a b c d e f g h i j k l m n o p q r s t u v w x y z

plait *NOUN* **plaits**
a length of hair or rope that has been plaited

plan *NOUN* **plans**
1 a way of doing something thought out in advance

I decided that my best plan would be to wait for a really sunny day and then use my glasses to focus the sunlight on a piece of my clothing and start a fire. — *Mark Haddon, The Curious Incident of the Dog in the Night-Time*

2 a drawing showing the arrangement of the parts of something
3 a map of a town or district

plan *VERB* **plans, planning, planned**
to make a plan for something
▷ **planner** *NOUN*

plane❶ *NOUN* **planes**
1 an aeroplane
2 a tool for making wood smooth by scraping its surface
3 a flat or level surface

plane *VERB* **planes, planing, planed**
to smooth wood with a plane

plane *ADJECTIVE*
a plane surface is flat and level

USAGE NOTE Take care not to confuse this word with *plain*.

plane❷ *NOUN* **planes**
a tall tree with broad leaves

planet *NOUN* **planets**
one of the bodies that move in an orbit round the sun. The main planets of the solar system are Mercury, Venus, Earth, Mars, Jupiter, Saturn, Uranus, Neptune, and Pluto.
▷ **planetary** *ADJECTIVE*

WORD HISTORY from Greek *planetes* 'wanderer' (because planets seem to move in relation to the stars)

plank *NOUN* **planks**
a long flat piece of wood

plankton *NOUN*
microscopic plants and animals that float in the sea, lakes, or fresh water

plant *NOUN* **plants**
1 a living thing that cannot move, makes its food from chemical substances, and usually has a stem, leaves, and roots. Flowers, trees, and shrubs are plants.
2 a small plant that is not a tree or shrub
3 a factory or its equipment
4 (*informal*) something deliberately placed to incriminate someone

plant *VERB* **plants, planting, planted**
1 to put something in soil for growing
2 to fix something firmly in place
3 to place something where it will be found, usually to incriminate someone
▷ **planter** *NOUN*

plantation *NOUN* **plantations**
1 a large area of land where crops such as cotton, tobacco, or tea are planted
2 a group of planted trees

plaque (*say* plak) *NOUN* **plaques**
1 a flat piece of metal or porcelain fixed on a wall as an ornament or memorial
2 a sticky film that forms on teeth and gums, where bacteria can live

plasma *NOUN*
the colourless liquid part of blood, carrying the corpuscles

plaster *NOUN* **plasters**
1 a small covering put over the skin around a cut or wound to protect it
2 a soft mixture of lime, sand, and water etc. for covering walls and ceilings
3 (also **plaster of Paris**) a white paste used for making moulds or for casts to put round a broken leg or arm

WORD HISTORY *plaster of Paris* is called this because the substance it is made from originally came from Paris in France

plaster *VERB* **plasters, plastering, plastered**
1 to cover a wall or other surface with plaster
2 to cover something thickly
3 to display or publish something widely ◆ *The story was plastered all over the newspapers.*

plastic *NOUN* **plastics**
a strong light synthetic substance that can be moulded into a permanent shape

plastic *ADJECTIVE*
1 made of plastic
2 soft and easy to mould
▷ **plasticity** *NOUN*

WORD HISTORY from Greek *plastos* 'moulded or formed'

plastic surgery *NOUN*
surgery to repair deformed or injured parts of the body
▷ **plastic surgeon** *NOUN*

plate *NOUN* **plates**
1 an almost flat usually circular object from which food is eaten or served
2 a thin flat sheet of metal, glass, or other hard material
3 a printed illustration or photograph in a book
▷ **plateful** *NOUN*

plate *VERB* **plates, plating, plated**
1 to coat metal with a thin layer of gold, silver, tin, etc.
2 to cover something with sheets of metal

plateau (*say* **plat**- oh) *NOUN* **plateaux** or **plateaus** (*say* **plat**- ohz)
a flat area of high land

platelet *NOUN* **platelets**
(*Medicine*) a small colourless disc found in the blood and involved in clotting

platform *NOUN* **platforms**
1 a flat raised area along the side of a line at a railway station, where passengers get on and off trains
2 a flat surface that is above the level of the ground or floor, especially one from which a speaker addresses an audience
3 the policies that a political party puts forward when there is an election

platinum *NOUN*
a valuable silver-coloured metal that does not tarnish

platitude *NOUN* **platitudes**
a trite or insincere remark that people often use
▷ **platitudinous** *ADJECTIVE*

platoon *NOUN* **platoons**
a small group of soldiers

platter *NOUN* **platters**
a flat dish or plate

platypus *NOUN* **platypuses**
an Australian animal with a beak like a duck's, that lays eggs like a bird but is a mammal and suckles its young
WORD HISTORY from Greek *platys* 'broad' and *pous* 'foot'

plaudits *PLURAL NOUN*
applause; expressions of approval
WORD HISTORY from Latin *plaudite* 'applaud' (called out by actors in ancient Rome at the end of a play)

plausible *ADJECTIVE*
seeming to be honest or worth believing but perhaps deceptive

Very simple was my explanation, and plausible enough—as most wrong theories are! — *H. G. Wells, The Time Machine*

▷ **plausibly** *ADVERB*
▷ **plausibility** *NOUN*

play *VERB* **plays, playing, played**
1 to take part in a game, sport, or other amusement
2 to make music or sound with a musical instrument, radio or CD player, or other device
3 to perform a part in a play or film
to play about or around is to have fun or be mischievous
to play something down is to give people the impression that it is not important
to play up (*informal*) is to tease or annoy someone
▷ **player** *NOUN*

play *NOUN* **plays**
1 a story acted on a stage or on radio or television
2 the activity of playing or having fun
a play on words a pun

playa (*say* **plah**-ya) *NOUN* **playas**
a piece of flat dried-out land at the bottom of a sunken area in a desert
WORD HISTORY a Spanish word meaning 'beach'

playback *NOUN*
the process of playing back something that has been recorded

playful *ADJECTIVE*
1 wanting to play; full of fun
2 done in fun; not serious
▷ **playfully** *ADVERB*
▷ **playfulness** *NOUN*

playground *NOUN* **playgrounds**
a piece of ground for children to play on

playgroup *NOUN* **playgroups**
a group of very young children who play together regularly, supervised by adults

playing card *NOUN* **playing cards**
each of a set of cards (usually 52) used for playing games

playing field *NOUN* **playing fields**
a field used for outdoor games

playmate *NOUN* **playmates**
a friend that a child plays with

play-off *NOUN* **play-offs**
an extra match that is played to decide a draw or tie

plaything *NOUN* **playthings**
1 a toy
2 someone a person has fun with and treats as unimportant

playwright *NOUN* **playwrights**
(*Drama*) a person who writes plays; a dramatist

PLC or **plc** *ABBREVIATION*
public limited company

plea *NOUN* **pleas**
1 an earnest request or appeal
2 a formal statement of 'guilty' or 'not guilty' made in a lawcourt by a person accused of a crime

plead *VERB* **pleads, pleading, pleaded**
1 to beg someone to do something
2 to state formally in a lawcourt that you are guilty or not guilty of a crime
3 to give something as an excuse

As soon as they were back home in London and had unpacked, Lucien pleaded tiredness and the need for an early night. — *Mary Hoffman, Stravaganza: City of Masks*

pleasant *ADJECTIVE*
pleasing; giving pleasure
▷ **pleasantly** *ADVERB*
▷ **pleasantness** *NOUN*

pleasantry *NOUN* **pleasantries**
a casual friendly or good-humoured remark

please *VERB* **pleases, pleasing, pleased**
1 to make a person feel satisfied or glad
2 used to make a request or an order polite
3 to do as you please is to act in whatever way you think is suitable

pleasurable *ADJECTIVE*
causing pleasure; enjoyable

pleasure *NOUN* **pleasures**
1 a feeling of satisfaction or gladness; enjoyment
2 a pleasure is something that pleases you

pleat *NOUN* **pleats**
a flat fold made by doubling cloth upon itself
▷ **pleated** *ADJECTIVE*

plebeian (*say* plib- **ee**- an) *NOUN* **plebeians**
a member of the common people, especially in ancient Rome (SEE ALSO **patrician**)
▷ **plebeian** *ADJECTIVE*

plebiscite (*say* **pleb**- iss- it) *NOUN* **plebiscites**
a referendum

plectrum *NOUN* **plectra**
a small piece of metal, plastic, or bone for plucking the strings of a musical instrument

pledge *NOUN* **pledges**
1 a solemn promise
2 a thing handed over as security for a loan or contract

pledge *VERB* **pledges, pledging, pledged**
1 to promise solemnly to do or give something
2 to hand something over as security

plenary (*say* **pleen**- er- ee) *ADJECTIVE*
a plenary meeting or session is one attended by all the people involved

plenipotentiary (*say* plen- i- pot- **en**- sher- ee) *ADJECTIVE*
a plenipotentiary ambassador or other official has full authority to make decisions on behalf of a government
▷ **plenipotentiary** *NOUN*

plentiful *ADJECTIVE*
quite enough in amount; abundant
▷ **plentifully** *ADVERB*

plenty *NOUN*
quite enough; as much as is needed or wanted

plenty *ADVERB*
(*informal*) quite or fully ◆ *A staff of 120 is plenty large enough.*

plethora *NOUN*
too large an amount of something

pleurisy (*say* **ploor**- i- see) *NOUN*
inflammation of the membranes round the lungs

pliable *ADJECTIVE*
1 easy to bend; flexible
2 easy to influence or control
▷ **pliability** *NOUN*

pliant *ADJECTIVE*
flexible or pliable

pliers *PLURAL NOUN*
pincers that have jaws with flat surfaces for gripping things

plight❶ *NOUN* **plights**
a dangerous or difficult situation

plight❷ *VERB* **plights, plighting, plighted**
(*old use*) to pledge devotion or loyalty

plimsoll *NOUN* **plimsolls**
a canvas sports shoe with a rubber sole

WORD HISTORY from *Plimsoll line* (because the thin sole of the shoe reminded people of a Plimsoll line)

Plimsoll line *NOUN* **Plimsoll lines**
a mark on a ship's side showing how deeply it is allowed to go down in the water when loaded

WORD HISTORY named after an English politician, Samuel *Plimsoll*, who in the 1870s protested about ships being overloaded

plinth *NOUN* **plinths**
a block or slab forming the base of a column or a support for a statue or vase

plod *VERB* **plods, plodding, plodded**
1 to walk slowly and heavily
2 to work slowly but steadily
▷ **plodder** *NOUN*

plonk *NOUN*
(*informal*) cheap inferior wine

plonk *VERB* **plonks, plonking, plonked**
(*informal*)
1 to put something down clumsily or heavily
2 to plonk yourself down is to sit down heavily, typically when you are tired

Lydia ... plonked herself down in front of the television, and scowled at the blank screen.
— Anne Fine, Madame Doubtfire

WORD HISTORY originally Australian: probably from French (*vin*) *blanc* 'white (wine)'

plop *NOUN* **plops**
the sound of something dropping into water

plop *VERB* **plops, plopping, plopped**
to drop or fall with a plop

plot *NOUN* **plots**
1 a secret plan
2 the story in a play, novel, or film
3 a small piece of land

plot *VERB* **plots, plotting, plotted**
1 to make a secret plan
2 to plot a route or set of figures is to mark them on a chart or graph

plough *NOUN* **ploughs**
a farming implement for turning the soil over, in preparation for planting seeds

plough *VERB* **ploughs, ploughing, ploughed**
1 to turn over soil with a plough
2 to plough through a long piece of work or reading is to finish it with a lot of effort
to plough something back is to reinvest profits in the business that produced them
▷ **ploughman** *NOUN*

ploughshare *NOUN* **ploughshares**
the cutting blade of a plough

plover (*say* **pluv**- er) *NOUN* **plovers**
a kind of wading bird with a short bill

ploy *NOUN* **ploys**
a cunning manoeuvre to gain an advantage; a ruse
WORD HISTORY originally Scots in the meaning 'pastime': origin unknown

pluck *VERB* **plucks, plucking, plucked**
1 to pick a flower or fruit
2 to pull the feathers off a bird
3 to pull something up or out
4 to pull a string (e.g. on a guitar) and let it go again
to pluck up courage is find the courage or nerve to do something difficult or frightening

pluck *NOUN*
courage or spirit

plucky *ADJECTIVE* **pluckier, pluckiest**
brave or spirited
▷ **pluckily** *ADVERB*

plug *NOUN* **plugs**
1 something used to stop up a hole
2 a device that fits into a socket to connect wires to a supply of electricity
3 (*informal*) a piece of publicity for something

plug *VERB* **plugs, plugging, plugged**
1 to stop up a hole
2 (*informal*) to publicize something
to plug something in is to put the plug of a device into an electrical socket

plughole *NOUN* **plugholes**
a hole at the bottom of a bath or sink, through which waste water drains away

plum *NOUN* **plums**
1 a soft juicy fruit with a pointed stone in the middle
2 a reddish purple colour
3 (*informal*) a plum job or role is a very good one that many people would like

plumage (*say* **ploom**- ij) *NOUN* **plumages**
a bird's feathers

plumb *VERB* **plumbs, plumbing, plumbed**
1 to measure how deep something is
2 to plumb a mystery or problem is to investigate it and solve it
3 to fit a room or building with a plumbing system

plumb *ADJECTIVE*
a plumb surface is exactly upright or vertical

plumb *ADVERB*
(*informal*) exactly; precisely ◆ *The new building is plumb in the centre of town.*

plumber *NOUN* **plumbers**
a person who fits and mends plumbing

plumbing *NOUN*
1 the water pipes, water tanks, and drainage pipes in a building
2 the work of a plumber
WORD HISTORY from Latin *plumbum* 'lead' (because water pipes used to be made of lead)

plumb line *NOUN* **plumb lines**
a cord with a weight on the end, used to find how deep something is or whether a wall or other surface is vertical

plume *NOUN* **plumes**
1 a large feather
2 a plume of smoke or dust or fire is a thin column of it that rises in the air
▷ **plumed** *ADJECTIVE*

plummet *NOUN* **plummets**
a plumb line or the weight on its end

plummet *VERB* **plummets, plummeting, plummeted**
1 to drop downwards quickly
2 a price or other amount plummets when it decreases rapidly

plump[1] *ADJECTIVE*
slightly fat; rounded
▷ **plumpness** *NOUN*

plump *VERB* **plumps, plumping, plumped**
to plump up a cushion or pillow is to shake it to give it a rounded shape

plump[2] *VERB* **plumps, plumping, plumped**
to plump for something (*informal*) is to choose it

plunder *VERB* **plunders, plundering, plundered**
to rob a person or place using force, especially during a war or riot

The ship was thoroughly plundered. Every single useful thing was taken off her. — *Celia Rees, Pirates!*

▷ **plunderer** *NOUN*

plunder *NOUN*
1 the act of plundering
2 goods that have been plundered

plunge *VERB* **plunges, plunging, plunged**
1 to go or push forcefully into something; to dive
2 to fall or go downwards suddenly

The helicopter disappeared in a huge fireball, then plunged down. It was still burning when it hit the ground. — *Anthony Horowitz, Point Blanc*

3 to plunge into an activity is to begin it with energy or enthusiasm
4 to put someone suddenly and deeply into a particular state, usually an unpleasant one ◆ *The strife of the barons plunged the country into anarchy.*

plunge *NOUN* **plunges**
a sudden fall or dive
to take the plunge (*informal*) is to start decisively on a bold course of action

plunger *NOUN* **plungers**
a rubber cup on a handle used for clearing blocked pipes

plural *NOUN* **plurals**
(*Grammar*) the form of a word used when it stands for more than one person or thing, e.g. the words *tables* and *children* (SEE ALSO **singular**)
▷ **plural** *ADJECTIVE*
▷ **plurality** *NOUN*

plural forms

Most words in English form their plurals by adding -s or -es (*ants, branches*). However, some types of words have more unusual **plural forms:**

- words which have the same form in the singular and plural, e.g. *aircraft, deer, fish, sheep, series,* and *species*: *There are thousands of species of jellyfish.*
- words which have irregular plurals: *child, children; goose, geese; louse, lice; mouse, mice; ox, oxen; tooth, teeth.*
- words of Greek and Latin origin which retain a Greek or Latin plural form:
  -a, -ae, e.g. *antenna, antennae; formula, formulae*
  -ex, -ices, e.g. *index, indices; vortex, vortices*
  -is, -es, e.g. *axis, axes; basis, bases; thesis, theses*
  -ix, -ices, e.g. *appendix, appendices*
  -on, -a, e.g. *phenomenon, phenomena*
  -um, -a, e.g. *medium, media*
  -us, -i, e.g. *radius, radii; sarcophagus, sarcophagi*
  -yx, -yces, e.g. *calyx, calyces*
  Sometimes the use of a Latin or Greek plural is optional, e.g. *plectrums* or *plectra, radiuses* or *radii;* it can also depend on meaning, e.g. the form *appendixes* is used for parts of the body, but *appendices* for sections of a book.
- words from other languages which retain their original plurals, e.g. *gateau, gateaux.*

See also the panel on **singular and plural forms.**

plus *PREPOSITION*
used to indicate a number or thing added ◆ *The bill came to over a thousand dollars plus tax.*

plus *ADJECTIVE*
1 used to show a grade slightly higher than normal, e.g. B plus
2 used before a number to show that it is more than zero ◆ *a temperature between minus five and plus five degrees*

plush *NOUN*
a thick velvety cloth used in furnishings
▷ **plushy** *ADJECTIVE*

plutocrat *NOUN* **plutocrats**
a person who is powerful because of their wealth

plutonium *NOUN*
a radioactive substance used in nuclear weapons and reactors
WORD HISTORY named after the planet *Pluto*

ply¹ *NOUN* **plies**
1 a thickness or layer of wood or cloth etc.
2 a strand in yarn

ply² *VERB* **plies, plying, plied**
1 to ply a trade is to work at it as your regular job
2 to ply someone with something, especially food, is to keep offering it to them
3 a bus or other vehicle or boat plies between two points when it goes regularly back and forth between them
4 to ply for hire is to drive or wait about looking for custom

plywood *NOUN*
strong thin board made of layers of wood glued together

PM *ABBREVIATION*
Prime Minister

p.m. *ABBREVIATION*
after 12 o'clock midday
WORD HISTORY short for Latin *post meridiem* 'after noon'

pneumatic (*say* new- **mat**- ik) *ADJECTIVE*
filled with or worked by compressed air
▷ **pneumatically** *ADVERB*
WORD HISTORY from Greek *pneuma* 'wind'

pneumonia (*say* new- **moh**- nee- a) *NOUN*
a serious illness caused by inflammation of one or both lungs

PO *ABBREVIATION*
1 Post Office
2 postal order

poach *VERB* **poaches, poaching, poached**
1 to cook an egg without its shell in or over boiling water
2 to cook fish or fruit in a small amount of liquid
3 to steal game or fish on someone else's land
4 to poach people or ideas is to take them unfairly from someone else ◆ *The new company poached most of its engineers from rival firms.*
▷ **poacher** *NOUN*

pocket *NOUN* **pockets**
1 a small bag-shaped part, especially in a piece of clothing
2 a person's supply of money ◆ *These prices won't hurt your pocket too much.*
3 an isolated part or area ◆ *Away from these pockets of excitement, business was relatively quiet.*
to be out of pocket is to have spent more money than you have gained
▷ **pocketful** *NOUN*

pocket *VERB* **pockets, pocketing, pocketed**
to put something into a pocket

pocket money *NOUN*
money given to a child to spend

pockmark *NOUN* **pockmarks**
a scar or mark left on the skin by a disease
▷ **pockmarked** *ADJECTIVE*

pod *NOUN* **pods**
a long seed container of the kind found on a pea or bean plant

podgy *ADJECTIVE* **podgier, podgiest**
short and slightly fat

You're not fat, sweetheart. You're just going through a little podgy stage. — *Jacqueline Wilson, Clean Break*

podium (*say* **poh**- dee- um) *NOUN* **podiums** or **podia**
a small platform on which a music conductor or someone making a speech stands

podzol *NOUN*
an infertile soil found in cold regions, in which minerals have been washed below the surface
WORD HISTORY from Russian *pod* 'under' and *zola* 'ashes'

poem *NOUN* **poems**
a piece of writing arranged in short lines, usually with a particular rhythm and sometimes with rhymes

poet *NOUN* **poets**
a person who writes poetry
▷ **poetess** *NOUN*

poetry *NOUN*
poems or the writing of poems
▷ **poetic** *ADJECTIVE*
▷ **poetical** *ADJECTIVE*
▷ **poetically** *ADVERB*

terms for poetry

The most common type of rhyme in poetry is **end-rhyme**, which occurs at the end of two or more lines:

At midnight, in the month of June,
I stand beneath the mystic moon.
(from Edgar Allan Poe, The Sleeper)

Internal rhyme occurs in the middle of a line:

In mist or cloud, on mast or shroud
(from S. T. Coleridge, The Rime of the Ancient Mariner)

The **metre** of a line of poetry is its pattern of stressed or accented syllables, e.g. *Double, double, toil and trouble.* **Blank verse** is a particular type of metre with lines of five accents; it was often used by Shakespeare. A poem written in **free verse** does not use a regular metre or rhyming pattern.

A **narrative poem** tells a story, whereas a **lyrical poem** expresses the poet's feelings. A **shape poem** or **concrete poem** creates an effect by the way it is set out on the page. Long poems are often divided into groups of lines called **verses** or **stanzas**.

Some types of poem have strict rules. A **sonnet** must always have fourteen lines, and a **limerick** must have five. **Syllabic poems** (such as *haiku*) contain a set number of syllables in each line, often in exact patterns.

pogrom *NOUN* **pogroms**
an organized massacre

After the pogroms in 1938 my two uncles (my mother's brothers) fled Germany, finding safe refuge in North America. — *Anne Frank, The Diary of a Young Girl*

WORD HISTORY a Russian word meaning 'destruction'

poignant (*say* **poin**- yant) *ADJECTIVE*
causing sadness and strong feelings
◆ *Poignant pictures recall wartime memories.*
▷ **poignancy** *NOUN*

point *NOUN* **points**
1 the narrow or sharp end of something
2 a particular place or time

It was at this point that two dozen forgotten roasting chestnuts exploded in a fusillade of what sounded remarkably like machine-gun fire. — *Debi Gliori, Pure Dead Magic*

3 a detail, feature, or characteristic ◆ *Here are some useful points for you to consider.* ◆ *The place certainly has some good points.*
4 the point is the important or essential idea being discussed ◆ *What you are saying is beside the point.*
5 purpose or value

What was the point in stealing a wallet if you didn't take the cash? — *Keith Gray, Malarkey*

6 the dot in a decimal fraction
7 an electrical socket
8 a device for changing a train from one track to another

point *VERB* **points, pointing, pointed**
1 to show where something is, especially by holding out a finger or hand towards it
2 to aim or direct something, especially a weapon, at someone or something
3 to fill in the parts between bricks with mortar or cement

to point something out is to show it or make it known to someone

point-blank *ADJECTIVE*
1 aimed or fired from close to the target
2 direct and straightforward ◆ *Their request met with a point-blank refusal.*

point-blank *ADVERB*
directly; without any qualification ◆ *He refused point-blank to let us in.*
WORD HISTORY from to *point* and *blank* 'the white spot in the centre of a target'

point duty *NOUN*
the activity of a police officer stationed at a road junction to control the movement of traffic

pointed *ADJECTIVE*
1 with a point at the end
2 a pointed remark is one clearly directed at a particular person
▷ **pointedly** *ADVERB*

pointer *NOUN* **pointers**
1 a stick, rod, or mark used to point at something
2 a dog that points with its muzzle towards birds that it scents
3 an indication or hint

pointless *ADJECTIVE*
without a point; with no purpose
▷ **pointlessly** *ADVERB*

point of view *NOUN* **points of view**
a way of looking at something or thinking about it; a standpoint

poise *NOUN*
1 a dignified self-confident manner
2 balance or equilibrium

poise *VERB* **poises, poising, poised**
to balance something or hold it in a suspended position

His mother was standing in her underslip [= petticoat], a lipstick poised at her mouth, watching the doorway through the mirror.
— *Barry Hines, A Kestrel for a Knave*

poised *ADJECTIVE*
1 dignified and self-confident
2 to be poised to do something is to be ready to do it

poison *NOUN* **poisons**
a substance that can harm or kill a living thing if swallowed or absorbed into the body

WORD FAMILY Related adjectives are poisonous and toxic.

poison *VERB* **poisons, poisoning, poisoned**
1 to give poison to someone; to kill somebody with poison
2 to put poison in something
3 to poison someone's mind against a person or thing is to make someone think badly of them
▷ **poisoner** *NOUN*

poke❶ *VERB* **pokes, poking, poked**
1 to prod or jab
2 to push out or forward; to stick out
3 to poke about somewhere is to search in a casual way

to poke fun at someone or something is to ridicule them

poke *NOUN* **pokes**
a poking movement; a prod

poke❷ *NOUN*
to buy a pig in a poke is to buy something without knowing anything about it beforehand

poker❶ *NOUN* **pokers**
a stiff metal rod for poking a fire

poker❷ *NOUN*
a card game in which players bet on who has the best cards

WORD HISTORY probably from German *pochen* 'to brag'

poky *ADJECTIVE* **pokier, pokiest**
a poky room or space is small and cramped

polar *ADJECTIVE*
1 to do with or near the North Pole or South Pole
2 to do with either pole of a magnet
▷ **polarity** *NOUN*

polar bear *NOUN* **polar bears**
a white bear living in Arctic regions

polarize *VERB* **polarizes, polarizing, polarized**
1 (*Science*) to keep vibrations of light waves to a single direction
2 to divide into two groups having opposite feelings or opinions
▷ **polarization** *NOUN*

USAGE NOTE This word can also be spelled polarise.

Polaroid *NOUN*
(*trademark*) a type of plastic, used in sunglasses, which reduces the brightness of light passing through it

Polaroid camera *NOUN* **Polaroid cameras**
(*trademark*) a camera that takes a picture and produces the finished photograph a few seconds later

pole❶ *NOUN* **poles**
a long slender rounded piece of wood or metal

pole❷ *NOUN* **poles**
1 a point on the earth's surface that is furthest north (**North Pole**) or furthest south (**South Pole**)
2 either of the ends of a magnet
3 either terminal of an electric cell or battery

polecat *NOUN* **polecats**
an animal of the weasel family with an unpleasant smell

polemic (*say* pol- **em**- ik) *NOUN* **polemics**
an attack in words against someone's opinion or actions
▷ **polemical** *ADJECTIVE*

pole star *NOUN*
the star above the North Pole

pole vault *NOUN*
an athletic contest in which competitors jump over a high bar with the help of a long flexible pole

police *NOUN*
a force of officials whose job is to catch criminals and make sure that the law is kept
▷ **policeman** *NOUN*
▷ **policewoman** *NOUN*

police *VERB* **polices, policing, policed**
to keep order in a place by means of police

police officer *NOUN* **police officers**
a member of the police

policy❶ *NOUN* **policies**
the aims or plan of action of a person or group

policy❷ *NOUN* **policies**
a document stating the terms of a contract of insurance

polio *NOUN*
a disease that can cause paralysis

WORD HISTORY in full *poliomyelitis*, from Greek *polios* 'grey' and *myelos* 'marrow'

polish *VERB* **polishes, polishing, polished**
1 to make a thing smooth and shiny by rubbing
2 to make a thing better by making corrections and alterations
to polish something off is to finish it quickly
▷ **polisher** *NOUN*

polish *NOUN* **polishes**
1 a substance used in polishing
2 a shine on a surface
3 a refined or elegant manner

polite *ADJECTIVE*
having good manners; respectful
▷ **politely** *ADVERB*
▷ **politeness** *NOUN*

politic (*say* **pol**- it- ik) *ADJECTIVE*
prudent or wise

political *ADJECTIVE*
connected with the governing of a country or region
▷ **politically** *ADVERB*

political correctness *NOUN*
language and behaviour that avoid discrimination and insensitivity towards certain groups of people, especially minorities
▷ **politically correct** *ADJECTIVE*

politician *NOUN* **politicians**
a person who is involved in politics, especially as a holder of a public office

politics *NOUN*
political matters; the business of governing a country or region

polka *NOUN* **polkas**
a lively dance for couples

poll (*sounds like* pole) *NOUN* **polls**
1 the process of voting at an election, or the votes cast
2 an opinion poll
3 (*old use*) the head

poll *VERB* **polls, polling, polled**
1 to vote at an election
2 to receive a stated number of votes in an election

WORD HISTORY probably from an Old Dutch word *polle* meaning 'head' (because votes used to be counted by making those voting 'yes' stand apart from those voting 'no', and then counting the heads in the two groups)

pollarded *ADJECTIVE*
a tree is pollarded when its top and branches are cut short so that young shoots start to grow thickly there

pollen *NOUN*
powder produced by the anthers of flowers, containing male cells for fertilizing other flowers

pollen count *NOUN* **pollen counts**
a measurement of the amount of pollen in the air, given as information for people who are allergic to pollen

pollinate *VERB* **pollinates, pollinating, pollinated**
to fertilize a plant with pollen
▷ **pollination** *NOUN*

polling station *NOUN* **polling stations**
a place where people go to vote in an election

pollster *NOUN* **pollsters**
a person who conducts an opinion poll

poll tax *NOUN* **poll taxes**
a tax that every adult has to pay regardless of income

pollutant *NOUN* **pollutants**
something that pollutes

pollute *VERB* **pollutes, polluting, polluted**
to make air or water impure or poisoned

pollution *NOUN*
(*Geography*) the process of polluting the earth or atmosphere with dangerous or poisonous substances

polo *NOUN*
a game like hockey, with players on horseback using long-handled mallets to strike the ball

WORD HISTORY a Tibetan word meaning 'ball'

polo neck *NOUN* **polo necks**
a high round turned-over collar
▷ **polo-necked** *ADJECTIVE*

poltergeist *NOUN* **poltergeists**
a ghost or spirit that throws things about noisily

Peeves was the school poltergeist, a grinning, airborne menace who lived to cause havoc and distress. — *J. K. Rowling, Harry Potter and the Chamber of Secrets*

WORD HISTORY from German *poltern* 'to make a disturbance' and *Geist* 'a spirit or ghost'

polyanthus *NOUN* **polyanthuses**
a kind of cultivated primrose

polychromatic or **polychrome** *ADJECTIVE*
having many colours

polyester *NOUN*
(*D & T*) a synthetic material, used to make clothing

polygamy (*say* pol- **ig**- a- mee) *NOUN*
the practice of having more than one wife or husband at the same time (SEE ALSO **monogamy**)
▷ **polygamous** *ADJECTIVE*
▷ **polygamist** *NOUN*

polyglot *ADJECTIVE*
knowing or using several languages

polygon *NOUN* **polygons**
a flat shape with many sides, such as a hexagon or octagon
▷ **polygonal** *ADJECTIVE*

polyhedron *NOUN* **polyhedrons**
a solid shape with many sides

polymer *NOUN* **polymers**
(*Science*) a substance with a molecule structure consisting of many simple molecules combined

polyp (*say* pol- ip) *NOUN* **polyps**
1 a tiny creature with a tube-shaped body
2 a small abnormal growth

polysaccharide (*say* pol- i- **sak**- a- ryd) *NOUN* **polysaccharides**
(*Science*) a carbohydrate that can be broken down into two or more simple sugars

polystyrene *NOUN*
a kind of plastic used as insulating or packing material

polytechnic *NOUN* **polytechnics**
a name used before 1992 for a college teaching subjects at degree level or below

USAGE NOTE Since 1992 polytechnics in Britain have been allowed to call themselves universities.

polytheism (*say* **pol**- i- thee- izm) *NOUN*
belief in more than one god
▷ **polytheist** *NOUN*

polythene *NOUN*
a lightweight plastic used to make bags or wrappings

polyunsaturated *ADJECTIVE*
(*Science*) a polyunsaturated fat or oil is not linked with the formation of cholesterol in the blood

polyurethane (*say* pol- i- **yure**- a- thayn) *NOUN*
a kind of synthetic resin or plastic

pomegranate *NOUN* **pomegranates**
a tropical fruit with many seeds

pommel *NOUN* **pommels**
1 a knob on the handle of a sword
2 the raised part at the front of a saddle

pomp *NOUN*
the ceremonial splendour that is traditional on important public occasions

pompom or **pompon** *NOUN* **pompoms** or **pompons**
a ball of coloured threads used as a decoration

pompous *ADJECTIVE*
excessively grand and self-important

I gotta show some of those pompous, self-important executives over there that Hap Loman can make the grade. — *Arthur Miller, Death of a Salesman*

▷ **pompously** *ADVERB*
▷ **pomposity** *NOUN*

pond *NOUN* **ponds**
a small area of still water surrounded by land

ponder *VERB* **ponders, pondering, pondered**
to think deeply and seriously

That night, Molly shivered as she lay on the ground pondering on the day's events. — *Doris Pilkington, Rabbit Proof Fence*

ponderous *ADJECTIVE*
1 heavy and awkward
2 a ponderous style of speaking or writing is laborious and dull
▷ **ponderously** *ADVERB*

pong *NOUN* **pongs**
(*informal*) a strong unpleasant smell

pong *VERB* **pongs, ponging, ponged**
(*informal*) to have an unpleasant smell

pontiff *NOUN* **pontiffs**
the Pope

WORD HISTORY from Latin *pontifex* 'chief priest'

pontifical *ADJECTIVE*
1 to do with a pontiff or pope
2 speaking or writing pompously
▷ **pontifically** *ADVERB*

pontificate *VERB* **pontificates, pontificating, pontificated**
to give your opinions in a pompous way
▷ **pontification** *NOUN*

pontoon ❶ *NOUN* **pontoons**
a boat or float used to support a bridge over a river

pontoon ❷ *NOUN*
a card game in which players try to get cards whose value totals 21

pony *NOUN* **ponies**
a small horse

ponytail *NOUN* **ponytails**
a bunch of long hair tied at the back of the head

pony-trekking *NOUN*
the activity of travelling across country on a pony for pleasure
▷ **pony-trekker** *NOUN*

poodle *NOUN* **poodles**
a dog with thick curly hair that is usually clipped

pooh *EXCLAMATION*
a word used to express disgust or contempt

pool❶ *NOUN* **pools**
1 a small area of still water; a pond
2 a small shallow patch of liquid on a surface
3 a swimming pool

pool❷ *NOUN* **pools**
1 the fund of money staked in a gambling game
2 a group of things shared by several people
3 a game resembling billiards
the pools a form of gambling based on the results of football matches

pool *VERB* **pools, pooling, pooled**
to put money or things together for sharing

poop *NOUN* **poops**
the stern of a ship

poor *ADJECTIVE*
1 having very little money or other resources
2 not good; inadequate
3 unfortunate; deserving pity

> Everyone knew that poor Hanno Hath hadn't been promoted for three years now. — *William Nicholson, The Wind Singer*

▷ **poorness** *NOUN*

poorly *ADVERB*
in a poor way

poorly *ADJECTIVE*
slightly ill or unwell

pop❶ *NOUN* **pops**
1 a small explosive sound
2 (*informal*) a fizzy drink

pop *VERB* **pops, popping, popped**
1 to make a pop
2 (*informal*) to go quickly or put something somewhere quickly

> We popped into a couple of record stores, not really staying for longer than a few minutes in each. — *Bali Rai, (Un)arranged Marriage*

> Mum popped her head round the door. 'Are you two ready for something to eat?' — *Alan Gibbons, Shadow of the Minotaur*

pop❷ *NOUN*
modern popular music

popcorn *NOUN*
maize heated to burst and form fluffy balls

pope *NOUN* **popes**
the leader of the Roman Catholic Church

USAGE NOTE You use a capital letter (*the Pope, Pope Benedict*) when you are using the word as a title.

WORD FAMILY Related adjectives are papal and pontifical.

pop-eyed *ADJECTIVE*
(*informal*) with bulging eyes

popgun *NOUN* **popguns**
a toy gun that shoots a cork or pellet with a popping sound

poplar *NOUN* **poplars**
a tall slender tree

poplin *NOUN*
a plain woven cotton material

poppadam or **poppadom** *NOUN* **poppadams** or **poppadoms**
a thin crisp biscuit made of lentil flour, eaten with Indian food

WORD HISTORY from Tamil *pappadam*

poppy *NOUN* **poppies**
a plant with large red flowers

populace *NOUN*
the general public

popular *ADJECTIVE*
1 liked or enjoyed by many people
2 a popular belief or opinion is one held or believed by many people
3 intended for the general public
▷ **popularly** *ADVERB*
▷ **popularity** *NOUN*

popularize *VERB* **popularizes, popularizing, popularized**
to make a thing generally liked or known
▷ **popularization** *NOUN*

USAGE NOTE This word can also be spelled popularise.

populate *VERB* **populates, populating, populated**
to supply a place with a population; to inhabit a country

population *NOUN* **populations**
the people who live in a district or country, or the total number of these people

porcelain *NOUN*
the finest kind of china

porch *NOUN* **porches**
a shelter outside the entrance to a building

porcupine *NOUN* **porcupines**
a small animal covered with long prickles

WORD HISTORY from Old French *porc espin* 'spiny pig'

pore❶ *NOUN* **pores**
a tiny opening on the skin through which moisture can pass in or out

a b c d e f g h i j k l m n o p q r s t u v w x y z

pore❷ *VERB* **pores, poring, pored**
to pore over something is to study it closely
USAGE NOTE Take care not to confuse this word with *pour*.

pork *NOUN*
meat from a pig

pornography (*say* porn- **og**- ra- fee) *NOUN*
pictures or writings that are meant to stimulate sexual excitement
▷ **pornographic** *ADJECTIVE*

porous *ADJECTIVE*
allowing liquid or air to pass through
▷ **porosity** *NOUN*

porphyry (*say* **por**- fir- ee) *NOUN*
a kind of rock containing crystals of minerals

porpoise (*say* **por**- pus) *NOUN* **porpoises**
a sea animal like a small whale

porridge *NOUN*
a food made by boiling oatmeal to a thick paste

port❶ *NOUN* **ports**
1 a harbour, or a city or town built around a harbour
2 the left-hand side of a ship or aircraft when you are facing forward (SEE ALSO **starboard**)

port❷ *NOUN*
a strong red Portuguese wine
WORD HISTORY from the city of *Oporto* in Portugal

portable *ADJECTIVE*
able to be carried easily
WORD FAMILY *Portable* comes from the Latin word *portare* meaning 'to carry'. Other words to do with carrying and having the same origin include *deport*, *export*, *import*, *porter*, *report*, *support*, and *transport*.

portal *NOUN* **portals**
a doorway or gateway

portcullis *NOUN* **portcullises**
a strong heavy vertical grating that can be lowered to block the gateway to a castle
WORD HISTORY from Old French *porte coleice* 'sliding door'

portend *VERB* **portends, portending, portended**
to be a sign or warning of something unpleasant or harmful

portent *NOUN* **portents**
an omen; a sign that something will happen

It was a winter of portents. Comets sparkled against the chilled skies at night. Clouds shaped mightily like whales and dragons drifted over the land by day. — *Terry Pratchett, Wyrd Sisters*

▷ **portentous** *ADJECTIVE*

porter *NOUN* **porters**
1 a person whose job is to carry luggage or other goods
2 a person whose job is to look after the entrance to a large building

portfolio *NOUN* **portfolios**
1 a case for holding documents or drawings
2 a government minister's special responsibility
3 (*D & T*) a set of pieces of artwork or designs

porthole *NOUN* **portholes**
a small window in the side of a ship or aircraft

portico *NOUN* **porticoes**
a roof supported on columns, usually forming a porch to a building

portion *NOUN* **portions**
a part or share given to somebody

portion *VERB* **portions, portioning, portioned**
to divide something into portions

portly *ADJECTIVE* **portlier, portliest**
rather fat
▷ **portliness** *NOUN*

portmanteau (*say* port- **mant**- oh) *NOUN* **portmanteaus**
a large travelling bag that opens into two equal parts
WORD HISTORY from French *porter* 'to carry' and *manteau* 'coat'

portmanteau word *NOUN* **portmanteau words**
(*Language*) a word made from the sounds and meanings of two others, e.g. *motel* (from *mo*tor + ho*tel*)

portrait *NOUN* **portraits**
1 (*Art*) a picture or photograph of a person or animal
2 (*ICT*) a page of text that is taller than it is wide
3 a description in words or on film

portray *VERB* **portrays, portraying, portrayed**
1 to make a picture of a person or scene
2 to portray a person or thing in a particular way is to describe or show them in that way
◆ *Wilde portrays a romantic young man who killed his wife in passion and then paid the ultimate penalty.*
▷ **portrayal** *NOUN*

Portuguese *ADJECTIVE*
to do with Portugal or its people

Portuguese *NOUN* **Portuguese**
1 the language of Portugal, also used as a first language in some other countries
2 a person from Portugal

pose *NOUN* **poses**
1 a position or posture of the body taken for a portrait or photograph
2 a way of behaving that someone adopts to give a particular impression

pose *VERB* **poses, posing, posed**
1 to take up a pose
2 to put someone into a pose
3 to pose as a person is to pretend to be that person
4 to put forward or present ◆ *Drug abuse poses a serious threat to the fabric of our society.*

WORD FAMILY *Pose* comes from the Latin word *ponere* meaning 'to place' or 'to put'. Other words to do with placing and putting (some only loosely) and having the same origin include *compose*, *depose*, *dispose*, *expose*, *interpose*, *propose*, *position*, *positive*, *purpose*, *suppose*, and *transpose*.

poser *NOUN* **posers**
1 a puzzling question or problem
2 a person who behaves in an affected way in order to impress other people

posh *ADJECTIVE* (*informal*)
1 very smart; high-class

Mum stopped outside this immensely posh French cake and coffee shop. 'Let's live dangerously,' she said, and went inside.
— Jacqueline Wilson, Lola Rose

2 typical of the upper classes ◆ *I heard a rather posh voice say 'Excuse me'.*

WORD HISTORY origin unknown: it is often thought to come from the first letters of the phrase *port out, starboard home*, which referred to the side of the ship where the most comfortable cabins were (because they were away from the heat of the sun) on the route between Britain and India; but this story is not the true origin

position *NOUN* **positions**
1 the place where something is or should be
2 the way a person or thing is placed or arranged ◆ *Hold your back in a straight upright position.*
3 a situation or condition ◆ *We were in no position to argue.*
4 a piece of paid employment; a job

▷ **positional** *ADJECTIVE*

position *VERB* **positions, positioning, positioned**
to place a person or thing in a certain position

positive *ADJECTIVE*
1 definite or certain ◆ *Are you positive the tank was full?* ◆ *I can only offer you a theory, since positive proof is impossible.*
2 a positive statement or reply is one that means 'yes'
3 a positive person or attitude looks at the best or most hopeful aspects of a situation
4 a positive test result indicates that there is a sign of what is being tested for
5 (*Mathematics*) a positive number or quantity is greater than zero; plus (SEE ALSO **negative**)
6 (*Science*) to do with the kind of electric charge that lacks electrons
7 (*Grammar*) the positive form of an adjective or adverb is its simple form, e.g. *fast* as distinct from *faster* (the comparative form) and *fastest* (the superlative form)

▷ **positively** *ADVERB*

USAGE NOTE The opposite of meaning 1 is *uncertain*; for meanings 2–6, the opposite of *positive* is *negative*.

positive *NOUN* **positives**
a photograph or film in which the light and dark parts or colours appear as in the original scene or subject (SEE ALSO **negative**)

positron *NOUN* **positrons**
(*Science*) a particle of matter with a positive electric charge

posse (*say* poss- ee) *NOUN* **posses**
a group of people recruited to help a sheriff

WORD HISTORY from Latin *posse comitatus* 'force of the county'

possess *VERB* **possesses, possessing, possessed**
1 to have or own something as your property
2 to control someone's thoughts or behaviour ◆ *What possessed his aunt to make such a crazy will?*

▷ **possessor** *NOUN*

possessed *ADJECTIVE*
seeming to be controlled by strong emotion or an evil spirit ◆ *He ran down the street like a man possessed.*

possession *NOUN* **possessions**
1 something that a person possesses or owns
2 the right or state of owning something

possessive *ADJECTIVE*
1 wanting to possess and keep things for yourself
2 (*Grammar*) a possessive word, e.g. *his* or *ours*, shows what or whom something belongs to

possessives

Possessive adjectives and **possessive pronouns** show to whom, or to what, something belongs or is connected.

The **possessive adjectives** are *my*, *your*, *his*, *her*, *its*, *our*, and *their*:
Is it okay to wear my trainers?
Our fate was in their hands.

The **possessive pronouns** are: *mine*, *yours*, *his*, *hers*, *ours*, and *theirs*:
Is that last slice of pizza mine or yours?
Theirs was the fastest finishing time.

Possessive pronouns can also be used after *of*:
That song is an old favourite of mine.

Note that there is no apostrophe in the possessive pronouns *hers*, *ours*, *yours*, and *theirs*, or in the possessive adjective *its*: *The shark opened its jaws.*

See also the panel on **determiners**.

possibility *NOUN* **possibilities**
1 the state of being possible
2 something that may happen or be the case

possible *ADJECTIVE*
able to exist, happen, be done, or be used

possibly *ADVERB*
1 in any way; at all ◆ *I decided I could not possibly accept the money.*
2 perhaps; maybe

possum *NOUN* **possums**
an Australian marsupial animal living in trees

post① *NOUN* **posts**
1 an upright piece of wood, concrete, or metal etc. set in the ground
2 the starting point or finishing point of a race

post *VERB* **posts, posting, posted**
to put up a notice or poster to announce something

post② *NOUN*
1 an official system of regularly collecting and delivering letters, packets, and parcels
2 letters and parcels sent or delivered

post *VERB* **posts, posting, posted**
1 to put a letter or package into a postbox for collection
2 to keep someone posted is to give them regular information about something

post③ *NOUN* **posts**
1 a position of paid employment; a job
2 the place where a sentry or other official is on duty
3 a place occupied by soldiers or traders

post *VERB* **posts, posting, posted**
to place someone on duty

postage *NOUN*
the charge for sending something by post

postage stamp *NOUN* **postage stamps**
a stamp for fixing to letters and packets for posting, showing the amount paid

postal *ADJECTIVE*
to do with or by the post

postal order *NOUN* **postal orders**
an order for payment of a certain amount, bought from a post office for sending by post and redeemable for the stated value

postbox *NOUN* **postboxes**
a box into which letters are put for collection

postcard *NOUN* **postcards**
a card for sending messages by post without an envelope

postcode *NOUN* **postcodes**
a group of letters and numbers included in an address to help in sorting the post

poster *NOUN* **posters**
a large sheet of paper announcing or advertising something, for display in a public place

posterior *ADJECTIVE*
at or near the back (SEE ALSO **anterior**)

posterior *NOUN* **posteriors**
(*formal*) a person's bottom

posterity *NOUN*
future generations of people ◆ *The names of those who died are recorded on a plaque for posterity.*

postern *NOUN* **posterns**
a small entrance at the back or side of a fortress etc.

postgraduate *ADJECTIVE*
to do with studies carried on after taking a first university degree

postgraduate *NOUN* **postgraduates**
a person who continues studying or doing research after taking a first university degree

post-haste *ADVERB*
with great speed or haste

posthumous (*say* poss- tew- mus) *ADJECTIVE*
coming or happening after a person's death ◆ *Her last novel was a posthumous publication.*
▷ **posthumously** *ADVERB*

postilion (*say* poss- **til**- yon) *NOUN* **postilions**
a person riding one of the horses pulling a carriage

postman *NOUN* **postmen**
a person who delivers or collects post

postmark *NOUN* **postmarks**
an official mark put on something sent by post to show where and when it was posted

post-mortem *NOUN* **post-mortems**
an examination of a dead body to discover the cause of death

WORD HISTORY Latin words meaning 'after death'

post-natal (*say* pohst- **nay**- tal) *ADJECTIVE*
(*Medicine*) to do with the period after childbirth

post office *NOUN* **post offices**
1 a building or room where postal services are provided
2 the national organization responsible for postal services

postpone *VERB* **postpones, postponing, postponed**
to arrange something for a later time or date than originally intended ◆ *They have had to postpone their wedding.*
▷ **postponement** *NOUN*

postscript *NOUN* **postscripts**
1 an extra remark added at the end of a letter after the writer's signature
2 additional words added after the main part of a book

postulant *NOUN* **postulants**
a person who applies to be admitted to an order of monks or nuns

postulate *VERB* **postulates, postulating, postulated**
to assume that something is true and use it in reasoning
▷ **postulation** *NOUN*

postulate *NOUN* **postulates**
an idea or argument that has been postulated

posture *NOUN* **postures**
a particular position of the body, or the way in which a person stands, sits, or walks

post-war *ADJECTIVE*
happening in the period after a war

posy *NOUN* **posies**
a small bunch of flowers

pot❶ *NOUN* **pots**
1 a deep usually round container
2 (*informal*) to have pots of something, especially money, is to have a lot of it
to go to pot (*informal*) is to lose quality or be ruined
to take pot luck (*informal*) is to take whatever happens to be available

pot *VERB* **pots, potting, potted**
to put something into a pot

pot❷ *NOUN*
(*informal*) the drug cannabis
WORD HISTORY short for Mexican Spanish *potiguaya* 'cannabis leaves'

potash *NOUN*
potassium carbonate
WORD HISTORY from Dutch *potasch* 'pot ash' (because it was first obtained from vegetable ashes washed in a pot)

potassium *NOUN*
a soft silvery-white metal substance that is essential for living things

potato *NOUN* **potatoes**
a starchy white tuber growing underground, cooked and eaten as a vegetable
WORD HISTORY via Spanish from Taino (a South American language)

potent (*say* **poh**- tent) *ADJECTIVE*
having great power or effect
▷ **potency** *NOUN*

potentate (*say* **poh**- ten- tayt) *NOUN* **potentates**
a powerful monarch or ruler

potential (*say* po- **ten**- shal) *ADJECTIVE*
capable of happening or developing into something ◆ *They were already marked out as potential leaders.*
▷ **potentially** *ADVERB*
▷ **potentiality** *NOUN*

potential *NOUN*
1 the ability of a person or thing to develop in the future
2 (*Science*) the voltage between two points

pothole *NOUN* **potholes**
1 a deep natural hole in the ground
2 a hole in the surface of a road, caused by wear

potholing *NOUN*
the pastime of exploring underground potholes
▷ **potholer** *NOUN*

potion *NOUN* **potions**
a liquid for drinking for its healing or magical properties

pot-pourri (*say* **poh**- poor- ee) *NOUN* **pot-pourris**
a scented mixture of dried petals and spices
WORD HISTORY French words meaning 'rotten pot'

pot shot *NOUN* **pot shots**
a shot aimed casually or at random

potted *ADJECTIVE*
1 a potted account or story is one that has been shortened or abridged
2 potted food is preserved in a pot

potter❶ *NOUN* **potters**
a person who makes pottery

potter❷ *VERB* **potters, pottering, pottered**
to potter about is to work or move about in a gentle or leisurely way

pottery *NOUN* **potteries**
1 cups, plates, and ornaments made of baked clay
2 the craft of making these things
3 a place where a potter works

potty❶ *ADJECTIVE*
(*informal*) eccentric or foolish

potty❷ *NOUN* **potties**
(*informal*) a small bowl used by a young child instead of a toilet

pouch *NOUN* **pouches**
1 a small bag
2 a fold of skin in which a kangaroo or other marsupial animal keeps its young
3 something shaped like a bag

pouffe (*say* poof) *NOUN* **pouffes**
a low padded stool

poultice *NOUN* **poultices**
a soft hot dressing put on a sore or inflamed place

poultry *NOUN*
chickens, geese, turkeys, and other birds kept for their eggs and meat

pounce *VERB* **pounces, pouncing, pounced**
to jump or swoop down quickly on something
▷ **pounce** *NOUN*

pound❶ *NOUN* **pounds**
1 a unit of money, in Britain equal to 100 pence
2 a unit of weight equal to 16 ounces or about 454 grams

pound❷ *NOUN* **pounds**
1 a place where stray animals are taken
2 a public enclosure for vehicles officially removed

pound[3] *VERB* **pounds, pounding, pounded**
1 to hit something repeatedly ◆ *He pounded at the door, and Mandy went to answer it.*
2 to run or go heavily ◆ *The rest of the herd pounded close behind.*
3 your heart pounds when it beats very fast and hard

poundage *NOUN*
a payment or charge based on each pound (of money) in a transaction

pour *VERB* **pours, pouring, poured**
1 to flow or make something flow
2 to rain heavily
3 to come or go in large amounts

Bright sunlight was still pouring through the open hatch. — *Cornelia Funke, Dragon Rider*

▷ **pourer** *NOUN*

USAGE NOTE Take care not to confuse this word with *pore*.

pout *VERB* **pouts, pouting, pouted**
to push out your lips when you are annoyed or sulking
▷ **pout** *NOUN*

poverty *NOUN*
1 the state of being poor
2 a lack or scarcity

POW *ABBREVIATION*
prisoner of war

powder *NOUN* **powders**
1 a mass of fine dry particles of something
2 a medicine or cosmetic made as a powder
3 short for *gunpowder*
▷ **powdery** *ADJECTIVE*

powder *VERB* **powders, powdering, powdered**
1 to put powder on something
2 to make something into powder

powder room *NOUN* **powder rooms**
a women's toilet in a public building

power *NOUN* **powers**
1 strength or energy
2 the ability to do something ◆ *She lost the power of sight at a young age.*
3 political authority or control ◆ *It was in his power to help these people.*
4 a powerful country, person, or organization
5 mechanical or electrical energy; the supply of electricity
6 (*Science*) the rate of doing work, measured in watts or horsepower
7 (*Mathematics*) the product of a number multiplied by itself a given number of times ◆ *The third power of* $5 = 5 \times 5 \times 5 = 125$.
▷ **powered** *ADJECTIVE*
▷ **powerless** *ADJECTIVE*

power *VERB* **powers, powering, powered**
to provide with power

The pressure elevators were powered by gaseous columns vented from the earth's core. — *Eoin Colfer, Artemis Fowl*

powerboat *NOUN* **powerboats**
a fast powerful motor boat

powerful *ADJECTIVE*
having great power, strength, or influence
▷ **powerfully** *ADVERB*

powerhouse *NOUN* **powerhouses**
1 a person with great strength and energy
2 a power station

power station *NOUN* **power stations**
a building where electricity is produced

pp. *ABBREVIATION*
pages

practicable *ADJECTIVE*
able to be done

USAGE NOTE Take care not to confuse this word with *practical*.

practical *ADJECTIVE*
1 a practical person is able to do or make useful things
2 a practical idea or thing is one that is likely to be useful in everyday life ◆ *What she needs is some practical help in the garden.*
3 practical experience of something involves actually doing it and not just knowing about it
▷ **practicality** *NOUN*

USAGE NOTE Take care not to confuse this word with *practicable*.

practical *NOUN* **practicals**
a lesson or examination in which you actually do or make something rather than reading or writing about it

practical joke *NOUN* **practical jokes**
a trick played on somebody

practically *ADVERB*
1 in a practical way
2 almost, nearly ◆ *The work was practically complete.*

practice *NOUN* **practices**
1 the activity of doing something repeatedly in order to become better at it
2 the process of actually doing something ◆ *The car's specification looked good, but there was no knowing what it might be like in practice.*
3 the professional business of a doctor, dentist, lawyer, etc.
4 a habit or custom ◆ *It used to be normal practice to repaint the bridge every year.*

to be out of practice is to be no longer so skilful at something because you have not practised it recently

USAGE NOTE Note that the noun is spelled practice and the verb is spelled practise.

practise *VERB* **practises, practising, practised**
1 to do something repeatedly in order to become better at it
2 to do something actively or habitually

Hathorne asks Tituba if she had ever practised witchcraft in her own country. — *Chris Priestley, Witch Hunt*

3 to work as a doctor, lawyer, or other professional person

USAGE NOTE See the note at *practice.*

practised *ADJECTIVE*
experienced or expert

practitioner *NOUN* **practitioners**
a professional worker, especially a doctor

pragmatic *ADJECTIVE*
practical and sensible ◆ *The choice of holiday venue was limited by pragmatic considerations.*
▷ **pragmatically** *ADVERB*
▷ **pragmatism** *NOUN*
▷ **pragmatist** *NOUN*

prairie *NOUN* **prairies**
a large area of flat grass-covered land in North America

praise *VERB* **praises, praising, praised**
1 to say that somebody or something is very good
2 to honour God or another divine being in words

praise *NOUN* **praises**
words that praise somebody or something

praiseworthy *ADJECTIVE*
deserving praise; commendable

pram *NOUN* **prams**
a four-wheeled carriage for a baby, pushed by a person walking

prana (*say* **prah**- na) *NOUN*
in Hinduism, breath as the life-giving force

prance *VERB* **prances, prancing, pranced**
to move about in a lively or happy way

prank *NOUN* **pranks**
a trick played for mischief; a practical joke
▷ **prankster** *NOUN*

prattle *VERB* **prattles, prattling, prattled**
to chatter like a young child
▷ **prattle** *NOUN*

prawn *NOUN* **prawns**
an edible shellfish like a large shrimp

pray *VERB* **prays, praying, prayed**
1 (*Religion*) to talk to God to give thanks or ask for help
2 to ask earnestly for something
3 (*formal*) please ◆ *Pray tell me your name.*

prayer *NOUN* **prayers**
(*Religion*) the act of praying; words used in praying

preach *VERB* **preaches, preaching, preached**
to give a religious or moral talk
▷ **preacher** *NOUN*

preamble *NOUN* **preambles**
the introduction to a speech or book or document etc.

pre-arranged *ADJECTIVE*
arranged beforehand
▷ **pre-arrangement** *NOUN*

precarious (*say* pri- **kair**- ee- us) *ADJECTIVE*
not very safe or secure
▷ **precariously** *ADVERB*

precaution *NOUN* **precautions**
something done to prevent future trouble or danger
▷ **precautionary** *ADJECTIVE*

precede *VERB* **precedes, preceding, preceded**
to come or go before something else or someone else

USAGE NOTE Take care not to confuse this word with *proceed.*

precedence (*say* **press**- i- dens) *NOUN*
the right of something to be put first because it is more important
to take precedence is to go first or have priority

precedent (*say* **press**- i- dent) *NOUN* **precedents**
a previous case that is used as an example or guide to be followed

precept (*say* **pree**- sept) *NOUN* **precepts**
a rule for action or conduct; an instruction

precinct (*say* **pree**- sinkt) *NOUN* **precincts**
1 in a town, a pedestrian precinct or shopping precinct is an area where traffic is not allowed
2 the area round a place, especially round a cathedral

precious *ADJECTIVE*
1 very valuable
2 greatly loved
▷ **preciousness** *NOUN*

precious *ADVERB*
(*informal*) very ◆ *We had precious little idea of how to go about it.*

precipice *NOUN* **precipices**
a very steep place, such as the face of a cliff

precipitate *VERB* **precipitates, precipitating, precipitated**
1 to make something happen suddenly or soon ◆ *The experiment precipitates an interesting question.*
2 to throw or send something down; to make something fall ◆ *A shove in the back precipitated him into the room.*
3 to cause a solid substance to separate chemically from a solution

a b c d e f g h i j k l m n o p q r s t u v w x y z

precipitate *NOUN* **precipitates**
a substance precipitated from a solution

precipitate *ADJECTIVE*
hurried or hasty ◆ *She wanted to avoid making too precipitate a decision.*

precipitation *NOUN*
the amount of rain, snow, or hail that falls during a period of time

precipitous *ADJECTIVE*
like a precipice; steep
▷ **precipitously** *ADVERB*

précis (*say* **pray**- see) *NOUN* **précis** (*say* **pray**- seez)
a summary

precise *ADJECTIVE*
exact; clearly stated
▷ **precisely** *ADVERB*
▷ **precision** *NOUN*

preclude *VERB* **precludes, precluding, precluded**
to prevent something from happening

precocious (*say* prik- **oh**- shus) *ADJECTIVE*
a precocious child is very advanced or developed for their age
▷ **precociously** *ADVERB*
▷ **precocity** *NOUN*

preconceived *ADJECTIVE*
a preconceived idea is one you have before you know all the facts that might affect it
▷ **preconception** *NOUN*

precursor *NOUN* **precursors**
something that was an earlier form of something that came later; a forerunner

predator (*say* **pred**- a- ter) *NOUN* **predators**
(*Biology*) an animal that hunts or preys upon others
▷ **predatory** *ADJECTIVE*

predecessor (*say* **pree**- dis- ess- er) *NOUN* **predecessors**
an earlier person or thing, e.g. an ancestor or the former holder of a job

predestine *VERB* **predestines, predestining, predestined**
to determine something beforehand
▷ **predestination** *NOUN*

predicament (*say* prid- **ik**- a- ment) *NOUN* **predicaments**
a difficult or unpleasant situation

predicate *NOUN* **predicates**
(*Grammar*) the part of a sentence that says something about the subject, e.g. 'was poisoned' in *The drink was poisoned*

predicative (*say* prid- **ik**- a- tiv) *ADJECTIVE*
(*Grammar*) a predicative adjective is one that forms part of the predicate, e.g. 'clever' in *The girl is clever* (SEE ALSO **attributive**)
▷ **predicatively** *ADVERB*

predict *VERB* **predicts, predicting, predicted**
to say what will happen in the future; to foretell or prophesy a future event
▷ **prediction** *NOUN*

predictable *ADJECTIVE*
1 able to be predicted
2 always the same; showing no imagination
▷ **predictably** *ADVERB*

predispose *VERB* **predisposes, predisposing, predisposed**
to influence you in advance so that you are likely to do something or be in favour of something ◆ *The authorities are predisposed to leave things as they are.*
▷ **predisposition** *NOUN*

predominate *VERB* **predominates, predominating, predominated**
to be the largest or most important or most powerful
▷ **predominant** *ADJECTIVE*
▷ **predominance** *NOUN*

pre-eminent *ADJECTIVE*
better than all others; outstanding
▷ **pre-eminently** *ADVERB*
▷ **pre-eminence** *NOUN*

pre-empt *VERB* **pre-empts, pre-empting, pre-empted**
to take action to prevent or block something; to forestall something

pre-emptive *ADJECTIVE*
a pre-emptive action or attack is one designed to prevent an action or attack from someone else

preen *VERB* **preens, preening, preened**
1 a bird preens its feathers when it smooths them with its beak
2 to preen yourself is to smarten your appearance

prefab *NOUN* **prefabs**
(*informal*) a prefabricated building

prefabricated *ADJECTIVE*
made in sections ready to be assembled on a site
▷ **prefabrication** *NOUN*

preface (*say* **pref**- as) *NOUN* **prefaces**
an introduction at the beginning of a book or speech

preface *VERB* **prefaces, prefacing, prefaced**
to introduce a speech or event with particular words or actions ◆ *The author has prefaced each chapter with a short quotation.*

prefect *NOUN* **prefects**
1 a senior pupil in a school, given authority to help to keep order
2 a regional official in France, Japan, and other countries

prefer (*say* pri- **fer**) ***VERB*** **prefers, preferring, preferred**
1 to like one person or thing more than another
2 (*formal*) to prefer charges is to charge someone with an offence

preferable (*say* **pref**- er- a- bul) ***ADJECTIVE***
liked better; more desirable
▷ **preferably** ***ADVERB***

preference (*say* **pref**- er- ens) ***NOUN*** **preferences**
1 something you prefer
2 to give preference to someone or something is to favour them over others

preferential (*say* pref- er- **en**- shal) ***ADJECTIVE***
better than for other people or most people
◆ *Staff are able to buy goods at preferential rates.*

preferment ***NOUN***
promotion or appointment to an office or job

prefix ***NOUN*** **prefixes**
(*Grammar*) a word or syllable joined to the front of a word to change or add to its meaning, as in *dis*advantage, *over*active, *un*healthy

prefixes and suffixes

Prefixes and **suffixes** are groups of letters that are not themselves words, but can be combined with other words to change their meaning and form new words. Prefixes are added at the beginning of other words (e.g. *anti*clockwise, *in*definite, *re*birth), and suffixes at the end (e.g. read*able*, green*ish*, pictur*esque*).

Some prefixes and suffixes make words that are closely related to the original word. For example, *in-*, and *un-* often make words opposite in meaning (e.g. *ineffective*, *unnatural*,); *re-* often indicates a repeated action (e.g. *rebuild*, *remake*); and suffixes such as *-ly*, *-ity*, *-ness*, and *-y*, are used to form derivatives which belong to a new word class (e.g. *naturally*, *normality*, *softness*). *In-* sometimes changes to *il-* (e.g. *illegible*), *im-* (e.g. *impossible*), or *ir-* (e.g. *irresponsible*), depending on the letter that follows. Other prefixes and suffixes (many of them based on Greek or Latin words) contain their own meaning, which they combine with that of the words they join; for example, *eco*system, *inter*face, *multi*cultural, *super*market, *trans*atlantic, *ultra*violet.

You sometimes need a hyphen after a prefix to make a special meaning clear (e.g. to *re-mark* an exam, to distinguish it from the word *remark*), or when the word after the prefix begins with a capital letter (e.g. *anti-British*, *pre-Victorian*). Words like *free* and *friendly* can be added to the ends of other words to form compounds (e.g. *dairy-free*, *user-friendly*). These are not true suffixes but separate words in their own right.

A list of common **prefixes and suffixes** is given at the back of this dictionary.

See also the panels on **Greek words in English** and **Latin words in English**.

pregnant ***ADJECTIVE***
1 a woman is pregnant when she has a baby developing in the womb
2 a pregnant pause or silence is one full of meaning or significance
▷ **pregnancy** ***NOUN***

prehensile ***ADJECTIVE***
an animal's foot or tail is called prehensile when it is able to grasp things

prehistoric ***ADJECTIVE***
belonging to a time before written records of events were made
▷ **prehistory** ***NOUN***

prejudice ***NOUN*** **prejudices**
an unfavourable opinion or dislike formed without examining the facts fairly
▷ **prejudiced** ***ADJECTIVE***

prelate (*say* **prel**- at) ***NOUN*** **prelates**
an important member of the clergy

preliminary ***ADJECTIVE***
coming before an important action or event and preparing for it

prelude ***NOUN*** **preludes**
1 a thing that introduces or leads up to something else
2 a short piece of music, especially one that introduces a longer piece

premature ***ADJECTIVE***
too early; coming before the usual or proper time
▷ **prematurely** ***ADVERB***

premeditated ***ADJECTIVE***
a premeditated act or crime is one that has been planned beforehand

premenstrual ***ADEJCTIVE***
to do with the time immediately before a woman's menstruation

premier (*say* **prem**- ee- er) ***ADJECTIVE***
first in importance, order, or time

premier ***NOUN*** **premiers**
a prime minister or other head of government

premiere (*say* prem- **yair**) ***NOUN*** **premieres**
the first public performance of a play or film

premise or **premiss** (*say* **prem**- iss) ***NOUN*** **premises** or **premisses**
a statement used as the basis for a piece of reasoning

premises ***PLURAL NOUN***
a building and the grounds around it

premium ***NOUN*** **premiums**
1 an amount or instalment paid to an insurance company
2 an extra charge or payment

at a premium
1 in demand but scarce
2 above the normal price

WORD HISTORY from Latin *praemium* 'reward'

Premium Bond *NOUN* **Premium Bonds**
a savings certificate that gives the person who holds it a chance to win a money prize

premonition *NOUN* **premonitions**
a feeling that something bad or unwelcome is about to happen

preoccupied *ADJECTIVE*
thinking all the time about one particular thing and unable to think about anything else
▷ **preoccupation** *NOUN*

preparation *NOUN* **preparations**
1 the process of getting something ready
2 something done in order to get ready for an event or activity
3 something prepared, especially medicine or food

preparatory *ADJECTIVE*
preparing for something

preparatory school *NOUN* **preparatory schools**
a school that prepares pupils for a higher school

prepare *VERB* **prepares, preparing, prepared**
1 to get ready, or to make something ready
2 to be prepared to do something is to be ready and willing to undertake it

preponderate *VERB* **preponderates, preponderating, preponderated**
to be greater than others in number or importance
▷ **preponderance** *NOUN*
▷ **preponderant** *ADJECTIVE*

preposition *NOUN* **prepositions**
(*Grammar*) a word used with a noun or pronoun to show place, position, time, or means, e.g. *at* home, *in* the hall, *on* Sunday, *by* train

> ***prepositions***
>
> **Prepositions** show how a noun or pronoun relates to the other words in a sentence or clause. They can show:
>
> - the position or direction of a person or thing:
>   *The spider scurried along the wall, across the carpet, through the doorway, down the stairs, past the cat, up the curtain, out of the window, and into the garden.*
> - the time something happens or lasts:
>   *Can you come to my house on Tuesday around five o'clock? We were in Athens in August, during the Olympics.*
> - the connection between people or things:
>   *Inspector McBride was always grumbling about something.*
>   *Does this dress go better with the red shoes or the brown?*
>
> You also use prepositions with verbs to form special meanings, e.g. *deal with*, *look after*, and *run into*.

prepossessing *ADJECTIVE*
attractive and welcome ◆ *Less prepossessing were three bluebottles on the table ready to dive on my dinner.*

preposterous *ADJECTIVE*
completely absurd or ridiculous

prep school *NOUN* **prep schools**
a preparatory school

prerequisite *NOUN* **prerequisites**
something required as a condition or in preparation for something else ◆ *Knowledge of one foreign language is a prerequisite of being taken on for this work.*
▷ **prerequisite** *ADJECTIVE*

prerogative *NOUN* **prerogatives**
a right or privilege that belongs to one person or group

Presbyterian (*say* prez- bit- **eer**- ee- an) *NOUN* **Presbyterians**
a member of a Christian Church governed by elders who are all of equal rank, especially the national Church of Scotland

WORD HISTORY from Greek *presbyteros* 'an elder'

presbytery *NOUN* **presbyteries**
the house of a Roman Catholic priest

pre-school *ADJECTIVE*
to do with the time before a child is old enough to go to school

prescribe *VERB* **prescribes, prescribing, prescribed**
1 to advise a person to use a particular medicine or treatment
2 to say what should be done

USAGE NOTE Take care not to confuse this word with *proscribe*.

prescription *NOUN* **prescriptions**
1 a doctor's written order for a medicine, or the medicine itself
2 the process of prescribing
3 an authoritative recommendation

prescriptive *ADJECTIVE*
laying down rules

presence *NOUN*
1 the state of being present in a place ◆ *Their presence made things rather awkward for a time.*
2 a person's impressive appearance or manner

presence of mind *NOUN*
the ability to act quickly and sensibly in an emergency

present[1] *ADJECTIVE*
1 there in a particular place ◆ *The work was recorded with an audience present.*
2 belonging or referring to what is happening now; existing now ◆ *We are not happy with the present state of affairs.*

a b c d e f g h i j k l m n o **p** q r s t u v w x y z

present *NOUN*
1 the present is the time now
2 something is happening at present when it is happening now

present❷ *NOUN* **presents**
something given or received as a gift

present (*say* priz- **ent**) *VERB* **presents, presenting, presented**
1 to give something, especially formally or with a ceremony
2 to introduce someone to another person; to introduce a radio or television programme to an audience
3 to put on a play or other entertainment
4 to show or reveal something ◆ *The outside of the building presents a drab appearance.*
5 to cause or provide something ◆ *The birds move quickly, and this presents a challenge.*
▷ **presenter** *NOUN*

presentable *ADJECTIVE*
fit to be presented to other people; looking good

presentation *NOUN* **presentations**
1 the act of presenting something
2 the way in which work is written or printed, and the general impression it gives to people who read it
3 (*D & T*) a talk with illustrations and charts showing work you have been doing or plan to do

presentiment *NOUN* **presentiments**
a feeling that something bad is about to happen; a foreboding

presently *ADVERB*
1 soon, after a while

> Presently I came to a bridge, below which a clear, slow stream flowed between snowy beds of water buttercups. — *John Buchan, The Thirty-Nine Steps*

2 at the present time; now ◆ *The vehicles are presently housed in an old aircraft hangar.*

preservative *NOUN* **preservatives**
a substance added to food to preserve it

preserve *VERB* **preserves, preserving, preserved**
to keep something safe or in good condition
▷ **preserver** *NOUN*
▷ **preservation** *NOUN*

preserve *NOUN* **preserves**
1 jam made with preserved fruit
2 an activity that belongs to a particular person or group ◆ *Gardening is sometimes considered the preserve of the middle-aged and elderly.*

preset (*say* pree- **set**) *VERB* **presets, presetting, preset**
to set a device, e.g. a telephone or radio, so that you can easily choose a particular function at any time

preset (*say* **pree**- set) *NOUN* **presets**
a function of a device that has been preset

preside *VERB* **presides, presiding, presided**
to be in charge of a meeting or other formal event

president *NOUN* **presidents**
1 the person in charge of a club, society, council, or educational institution
2 the elected head of a state that is a republic
▷ **presidency** *NOUN*
▷ **presidential** *ADJECTIVE*

USAGE NOTE You use a capital letter (*the President, President Smith*) when you are using the word as a title.

press *VERB* **presses, pressing, pressed**
1 to put weight or force steadily on something; to squeeze something
2 to make something by pressing
3 to make clothes smooth by ironing them
4 to gather round in a crowd

> Many knights press round the great slab of marble, eager to be the first to try to draw the sword from the stone. — *Kevin Crossley-Holland, The Seeing Stone*

5 to urge someone or make demands of them ◆ *We need to press them for an answer.*

press *NOUN* **presses**
1 a device for pressing things
2 a machine for printing on paper
3 a firm that prints or publishes books or magazines
4 the press is the business of newspapers and journalists

press conference *NOUN* **press conferences**
a meeting held by a public figure or organization with a group of journalists to make an announcement or give information and answer questions

press-gang *NOUN* **press-gangs**
(*History*) a group of men employed to force people to serve in the army or navy

pressing *ADJECTIVE*
needing immediate action; urgent ◆ *We have a pressing need for volunteers.*

press-up *NOUN* **press-ups**
an exercise in which you lie face downwards and press down with your hands to lift your body

pressure *NOUN* **pressures**
1 the action of continuous pressing
2 the force with which something presses
3 (*Science*) the force of the atmosphere on the earth's surface
4 an influence that persuades or compels you to do something

a b c d e f g h i j k l m n o p q r s t u v w x y z

pressure cooker *NOUN* **pressure cookers**
a large airtight pan used for cooking food quickly under steam pressure

pressure group *NOUN* **pressure groups**
an organized group that tries to influence public policy on a particular issue

pressurize *VERB* **pressurizes, pressurizing, pressurized**
1 to keep a compartment at a constant air pressure
2 to try to force a person to do something
▷ **pressurization** *NOUN*
USAGE NOTE This word can also be spelled pressurise.

prestige (*say* pres- **teej**) *NOUN*
great respect and reputation gained from achievements
▷ **prestigious** *ADJECTIVE*
WORD HISTORY from Latin *praestigiae* 'conjuring tricks'. The original meaning of *prestige* was 'trickery' or 'deception', and the modern meaning probably arose from the idea of tricks being clever and impressive.

presumably *ADVERB*
as you may reasonably suppose ◆ *Presumably the library will have a copy of the book.*

presume *VERB* **presumes, presuming, presumed**
1 to suppose something or assume it to be true ◆ *I presume you had a reason for saying those things?*
2 to take the liberty of doing something; to venture something ◆ *I wouldn't presume to judge them.*
▷ **presumption** *NOUN*

presumptive *ADJECTIVE*
presumed when there is no further information

presumptuous *ADJECTIVE*
too bold or confident

> 'You remember how I said I was going to adopt you, so you could live with me always, until you grew up into a man? I have been too presumptuous. It's not destined to be that way.'
> — *Rachel Anderson, Warlands*

▷ **presumptuously** *ADVERB*

presuppose *VERB* **presupposes, presupposing, presupposed**
1 to suppose or assume something beforehand
2 to require something as a condition before a certain thing can happen
▷ **presupposition** *NOUN*

pretence *NOUN* **pretences**
an attempt to pretend that something is true
by or under false pretences pretending to be something or someone you are not, in order to deceive people ◆ *He had got a permit under false pretences.*
USAGE NOTE The American spelling of this word is pretense.

pretend *VERB* **pretends, pretending, pretended**
1 to behave as if something is true or real when you know that it is not, either in play or to deceive people
2 to claim or maintain that something is the case ◆ *We will not pretend that this is going to be easy.*

pretender *NOUN* **pretenders**
a person who claims a throne or title ◆ *He had paid a visit in 1873 to the Bourbon pretender to the French throne.*

pretension *NOUN* **pretensions**
1 a doubtful or unrealistic claim ◆ *I don't think the group have any pretensions to be pop stars.*
2 pretentious or showy behaviour ◆ *They named their house, with absurd pretension, 'The White House'.*

pretentious *ADJECTIVE*
1 trying to impress by claiming greater importance or merit than is actually the case
2 showy or ostentatious
▷ **pretentiously** *ADVERB*
▷ **pretentiousness** *NOUN*

pretext *NOUN* **pretexts**
a false or unconvincing reason put forward to justify an action

pretty *ADJECTIVE* **prettier, prettiest**
attractive in a delicate way
▷ **prettily** *ADVERB*
▷ **prettiness** *NOUN*

pretty *ADVERB*
(*informal*) quite; fairly ◆ *I enjoyed the work and did it pretty well.*

pretzel *NOUN* **pretzels**
a crisp biscuit in the shape of a stick or knot and flavoured with salt

prevail *VERB* **prevails, prevailing, prevailed**
1 to be successful or victorious
2 a prevailing wind is the one blowing in an area for most of the time

prevalent (*say* **prev**- a- lent) *ADJECTIVE*
most frequent or common; widespread
▷ **prevalence** *NOUN*

prevaricate *VERB* **prevaricates, prevaricating, prevaricated**
to say something that is evasive or misleading though not untrue
▷ **prevarication** *NOUN*

prevent *VERB* **prevents, preventing, prevented**
1 to stop something from happening
2 to stop a person from doing something
▷ **preventable** *ADJECTIVE*
▷ **prevention** *NOUN*
▷ **preventive** or **preventative** *ADJECTIVE*

preview *NOUN* **previews**
1 a showing of a film, play, or other performance before it is shown to the general public
2 (*ICT*) a computer option that allows you to see on the screen how a piece of text or graphics will appear when it is printed

previous *ADJECTIVE*
existing or coming at an earlier time; preceding
▷ **previously** *ADVERB*

pre-war *ADJECTIVE*
happening in the period before a war

prey (*sounds like* pray) *NOUN*
an animal that is hunted or killed by another animal for food

prey *VERB* **preys, preying, preyed**
1 an animal preys on another when it hunts it for food
2 something preys on your mind when it worries you constantly

price *NOUN* **prices**
1 the amount of money for which something is bought or sold
2 something that must be done or experienced in order to achieve something or as a result of something ◆ *Resignation was the price demanded for even a minor mistake.*

price *VERB* **prices, pricing, priced**
to set the price of something

priceless *ADJECTIVE*
1 too valuable to be priced

The gift I got that afternoon was priceless, like world peace or an end to Third World poverty, something that couldn't be bought for a million pounds. — *Nick Hornby, Fever Pitch*

2 (*informal*) very amusing

pricey *ADJECTIVE*
(*informal*) costing a lot of money; expensive

The boy's fleece jacket, two sizes too big and pricey by the look of it, was soaked and hanging shapelessly on him. — *Keith Gray, Warehouse*

prick *VERB* **pricks, pricking, pricked**
1 to make a tiny hole in something
2 to hurt somebody with a pin or other sharp point

to prick up your ears is to start listening when something attracts your attention

prick *NOUN* **pricks**
the act or sensation of pricking

prickle *NOUN* **prickles**
1 a small thorn
2 a sharp spine on the skin of an animal (e.g. a hedgehog) or the surface of a plant
3 a feeling that something is pricking you

prickle *VERB* **prickles, prickling, prickled**
to feel or cause a pricking feeling

I could feel the sweat prickle my forehead under the bandages. I knew now that something fearful and horrible was happening. — *John Wyndham, The Day of the Triffids*

prickly *ADJECTIVE*
1 causing a pricking feeling; thorny
2 irritable or bad-tempered

pride *NOUN* **prides**
1 a feeling of deep pleasure or satisfaction when you have done something well
2 something that makes you feel proud
3 dignity or self-respect
4 too high an opinion of yourself
5 a group of lions

pride of place the most important or most honoured position

pride *VERB* **prides, priding, prided**
to pride yourself on something is to be proud of something, especially an achievement

The governor prides himself on being a good judge of port. I don't pretend to know much about it. — *J. B. Priestley, An Inspector Calls*

priest *NOUN* **priests**
1 a member of the clergy in certain Christian Churches
2 an official who performs ceremonies in a non-Christian religion
▷ **priesthood** *NOUN*
▷ **priestly** *ADJECTIVE*

WORD FAMILY A related adjective is clerical.

priestess *NOUN* **priestesses**
a female priest in a non-Christian religion

prig *NOUN* **prigs**
a self-righteous person
▷ **priggish** *ADJECTIVE*

prim *ADJECTIVE* **primmer, primmest**
formal and correct in manner; disliking anything rude or improper
▷ **primly** *ADVERB*
▷ **primness** *NOUN*

primacy (*say* **pry**- ma- see) *NOUN*
the right or state of being first or most important

prima donna (*say* **preem**- a) ***NOUN*** **prima donnas**
the chief female singer in an opera company
WORD HISTORY Italian words meaning 'first lady'

prima facie (*say* pry- ma **fay**- shee) ***ADVERB, ADJECTIVE***
at first sight; judging by the first impression
WORD HISTORY Latin words meaning 'on first appearance'

primarily (*say* **pry**- mer- il- ee) ***ADVERB***
most importantly; mainly ◆ *History is after all primarily about people.*

primary ***ADJECTIVE***
first or most important (SEE ALSO **secondary**)

primary colour ***NOUN*** **primary colours**
each of the colours from which all others can be made by mixing (red, yellow, and blue for paint; red, green, and violet for light)

primary school ***NOUN*** **primary schools**
a school for the first stage of a child's education

primate (*say* **pry**- mayt) ***NOUN*** **primates**
1 an animal of the group that includes human beings, apes, and monkeys
2 an archbishop

prime ***ADJECTIVE***
1 chief; most important ◆ *Rapid conquest of the country was the prime objective.*
2 belonging to the best quality

prime ***NOUN***
a person's or thing's prime is the time when they are at their best

prime ***VERB*** **primes, priming, primed**
1 to prepare something for use or action
2 to put a coat of liquid on something to prepare it for painting
3 to equip a person with information

prime minister ***NOUN*** **prime ministers**
the head of an elected government

prime number ***NOUN*** **prime numbers**
a number (e.g. 2, 3, 5, 7, 11) that can be divided exactly only by itself and one

primer ***NOUN*** **primers**
1 a liquid for priming a surface
2 an elementary textbook

primeval (*say* pry- **mee**- val) ***ADJECTIVE***
belonging to the earliest times of the world

primitive ***ADJECTIVE***
1 at an early stage of civilization
2 at an early stage of development; not complicated or sophisticated

primogeniture ***NOUN***
being a first-born child; the custom by which an eldest son inherits all his parents' property

primordial ***ADJECTIVE***
belonging to the earliest times of the world; primeval

primrose ***NOUN*** **primroses**
a pale-yellow flower that blooms in spring

prince ***NOUN*** **princes**
1 the son of a king or queen
2 a man or boy in a royal family
▷ **princely** ***ADJECTIVE***
USAGE NOTE You use a capital letter (*the Prince, Prince William*) when you are using the word as a title.

princess ***NOUN*** **princesses**
1 the daughter of a king or queen
2 a woman or girl in a royal family
3 the wife of a prince
USAGE NOTE You use a capital letter (*the Princess, Princess Anne*) when you are using the word as a title.

principal ***ADJECTIVE***
chief; most important
▷ **principally** ***ADVERB***

principal ***NOUN*** **principals**
the head of a college or school
WORD HISTORY from Latin *principalis* 'first or chief'
USAGE NOTE Take care not to confuse this word with *principle*.

principality ***NOUN*** **principalities**
a country ruled by a prince

principle ***NOUN*** **principles**
1 a general truth, belief, or rule ◆ *It was against their principles to use violence.*
2 the principles of a subject or theory are the rules and methods that make it what it is ◆ *He learned the basic principles of grammar at a language class.*
3 a rule of conduct ◆ *Governments have to live up to principles of social justice.*
in principle in general, not in details
on principle because of your principles of behaviour
WORD HISTORY from Latin *principium* 'a source'
USAGE NOTE Take care not to confuse this word with *principal*.

print ***VERB*** **prints, printing, printed**
1 to put words or pictures on paper by a mechanical process
2 to write with letters that are not joined together
3 to press a mark or design on a surface
4 to make a picture from the negative of a photograph

print ***NOUN*** **prints**
1 printed lettering or words
2 a mark made by something pressing on a surface
3 a printed picture, photograph, or design

in or out of print a book is in print when it is available from the publisher, and out of print when it is no longer available

printed circuit *NOUN* **printed circuits**
an electric circuit made by pressing thin metal strips on to a board

printer *NOUN* **printers**
1 a person who prints books or newspapers
2 a machine that prints on paper from data in a computer

printout *NOUN* **printouts**
information produced in printed form by a computer

prion *NOUN* **prions**
(*Medicine*) a microscopic protein particle thought to be the cause of BSE and other brain diseases

WORD HISTORY from the first letters of *protein* and *infectious*

prior *ADJECTIVE*
1 a prior arrangement or engagement is one that you have made earlier
2 a prior duty or obligation is one that is more important than the others

prior *NOUN* **priors**
a monk who is the head of a religious house or order
▷ **prioress** *NOUN*

prioritize *VERB* **prioritizes, prioritizing, prioritized**
to put tasks in order of importance, so that you can deal with the most important first

USAGE NOTE This word can also be spelled prioritise.

priority *NOUN* **priorities**
1 the right to go or act first; precedence ◆ *Traffic coming from the right has priority.*
2 the level of importance or urgency you give to something ◆ *Self-protection always has a high priority.*
3 something considered more important than other things ◆ *Completing his education was his priority.*

priory *NOUN* **priories**
a religious house governed by a prior or prioress

prise *VERB* **prises, prising, prised**
to force something out or open gently

prism (*say* prizm) *NOUN* **prisms**
1 (*Mathematics*) a solid shape with ends that are triangles or polygons which are equal and parallel
2 a glass prism that breaks up light into the colours of the rainbow
▷ **prismatic** *ADJECTIVE*

prison *NOUN* **prisons**
a place where criminals are confined as a punishment

prisoner *NOUN* **prisoners**
1 a person confined in a prison
2 a captive in a war or battle

prisoner of war *NOUN* **prisoners of war**
a person captured and imprisoned by the enemy in a war

pristine *ADJECTIVE*
in its original condition; unspoilt

private *ADJECTIVE*
1 private property belongs to a particular person or group and no one else
2 private talks or affairs are confidential or shared by a few people
3 a private place is somewhere quiet and secluded
4 a private citizen is someone who does not hold a public office
5 something such as education or health is private when it is not run or directly controlled by the state

in private where only particular people can see or hear; not in public
▷ **privately** *ADVERB*
▷ **privacy** (*say* **priv**- a- see) *NOUN*

private *NOUN* **privates**
a soldier of the lowest rank

WORD HISTORY from Latin *privus* 'single or individual'

privation *NOUN* **privations**
loss or lack of something; lack of necessities

privatize *VERB* **privatizes, privatizing, privatized**
to transfer the running of a business or industry from the state to private owners
▷ **privatization** *NOUN*

USAGE NOTE This word can also be spelled privatise.

privet *NOUN* **privets**
an evergreen shrub with small leaves, used to make hedges

privilege *NOUN* **privileges**
a special right or advantage given to one person or group
▷ **privileged** *ADJECTIVE*

privy *ADJECTIVE* (*old use*)
1 secret and private
2 to be privy to a secret idea or plan is to know about it or be involved in it

privy *NOUN* **privies**
(*old use*) an outside toilet

Privy Council *NOUN*
a group of distinguished people who advise the sovereign

prize *NOUN* **prizes**
1 an award given to the winner of a game or competition, or in recognition of an achievement
2 something of great value that is worth trying to obtain
3 something taken from an enemy

prize *VERB* **prizes, prizing, prized**
to value something highly

pro *NOUN* **pros**
(*informal*) a professional

probability *NOUN* **probabilities**
1 likelihood
2 something that is likely to happen or be true

probable *ADJECTIVE*
likely to happen or be true
▷ **probably** *ADVERB*

probate *NOUN*
the official process of proving that a person's will is valid

probation *NOUN*
1 the testing of a person's character and abilities in a new job or role
2 the release of an offender from detention, subject to good behaviour and under the supervision of a probation officer
▷ **probationary** *ADJECTIVE*

probationer *NOUN* **probationers**
a person at an early stage of training or under probation in a job or role

probe *NOUN* **probes**
1 a long thin instrument used to look closely at something such as a wound
2 an unmanned spacecraft used for exploring
3 an investigation

probe *VERB* **probes, probing, probed**
1 to explore or look at something with a probe
2 to investigate something

WORD HISTORY from Latin *proba* 'proof'

probity (*say* **proh**- bit- ee) *NOUN*
(*formal*) honesty or integrity

problem *NOUN* **problems**
1 something difficult to deal with or understand
2 something that has to be done or answered

The number devil started doing the problem in his head, but his face turned bright red again and swelled up like a balloon. — *Hans Magnus Enzensberger, The Number Devil*

▷ **problematic** or **problematical** *ADJECTIVE*

WORD HISTORY from Greek *proballein* 'to throw forward' (because a problem is something that is 'thrown forward' for someone to deal with)

proboscis (*say* pro- **boss**- iss) *NOUN* **proboscises**
1 an animal's long flexible snout
2 an insect's long mouthpart

procedure *NOUN* **procedures**
an orderly way of doing something

I glanced down at my own shoes powdered red and, raising my right foot, rubbed it against the back of my left leg, then reversed the procedure. — *Mildred D. Taylor, Roll of Thunder, Hear My Cry*

proceed *VERB* **proceeds, proceeding, proceeded**
1 to make progress; to continue ◆ *As work proceeded, the outline of the building took shape.*
2 to go on to do something ◆ *He proceeded to declare a state of military alert.*

USAGE NOTE Take care not to confuse this word with *precede*.

proceedings *PLURAL NOUN*
1 a series of events or activities that follow a set procedure
2 a lawsuit

proceeds *PLURAL NOUN*
the money made from a sale or event

process[1] (*say* **proh**- sess) *NOUN* **processes**
1 a series of actions for making or doing something
2 to be in the process of something is to be engaged in doing it

process *VERB* **processes, processing, processed**
to put something through a manufacturing or other process

process[2] (*say* pro- sess) *VERB* **processes, processing, processed**
to go in procession

procession *NOUN* **processions**
a number of people or vehicles etc. moving steadily forward following each other

processor *NOUN* **processors**
1 a machine that processes things
2 (*ICT*) the part of a computer that controls its operations

proclaim *VERB* **proclaims, proclaiming, proclaimed**
to announce something officially or publicly
▷ **proclamation** *NOUN*

procrastinate *VERB* **procrastinates, procrastinating, procrastinated**
to put off doing something
▷ **procrastination** *NOUN*
▷ **procrastinator** *NOUN*

procreate *VERB* **procreates, procreating, procreated**
to produce offspring by the natural process of reproduction
▷ **procreation** *NOUN*

procure *VERB* **procures, procuring, procured**
to obtain or acquire something
▷ **procurement** *NOUN*

prod *VERB* **prods, prodding, prodded**
1 to poke something or someone
2 to stimulate someone into action
▷ **prod** *NOUN*

prodigal *ADJECTIVE*
wasteful or extravagant
▷ **prodigally** *ADVERB*
▷ **prodigality** *NOUN*

prodigious *ADJECTIVE*
remarkably large or impressive
▷ **prodigiously** *ADVERB*

prodigy *NOUN* **prodigies**
1 a young person with exceptional abilities
2 a wonderful thing

produce *VERB* **produces, producing, produced**
1 to make or create something; to bring something into existence
2 to bring something out so that it can be seen
3 to organize the performance of a play, making of a film, etc.
4 (*Mathematics*) in geometry, to produce a line, e.g. the side of a triangle, is to continue it further
▷ **producer** *NOUN*

produce (*say* **prod**- yooss) *NOUN*
things that have been produced or grown, especially by farmers

product *NOUN* **products**
1 something produced
2 (*Mathematics*) the result of multiplying two numbers (SEE ALSO **quotient**)

production *NOUN* **productions**
1 (*D & T*) the process of making or creating something, especially in large quantities
2 the amount of goods produced by a company or country ◆ *Oil production had declined by 9 per cent.*
3 (*Drama*) a version of a play, opera, or film and the way it is staged or performed

productive *ADJECTIVE*
1 producing a lot of things
2 producing good results; useful
▷ **productivity** *NOUN*

profane *ADJECTIVE*
showing disrespect for religion; blasphemous
▷ **profanely** *ADVERB*

profane *VERB* **profanes, profaning, profaned**
to treat something, especially religion, with disrespect

profanity *NOUN* **profanities**
words or language that show disrespect for religion

profess *VERB* **professes, professing, professed**
1 to declare or express something ◆ *The country always professed a policy of neutrality.*
2 to claim to have or do something ◆ *They thrived on the publicity which they professed to loathe.*
▷ **professedly** *ADVERB*

profession *NOUN* **professions**
1 an occupation that needs special education and training, such as medicine or law
2 a declaration ◆ *We were not willing to question their professions of loyalty.*

professional *ADJECTIVE*
1 to do with a profession
2 doing a certain kind of work as a full-time job for payment, not as an amateur
3 done with a high standard of skill
▷ **professional** *NOUN*
▷ **professionally** *ADVERB*

professor *NOUN* **professors**
a university teacher of the highest rank
▷ **professorship** *NOUN*

proffer *VERB* **proffers, proffering, proffered**
to offer something

proficient *ADJECTIVE*
doing something properly because of training or practice; skilled
▷ **proficiency** *NOUN*

profile *NOUN* **profiles**
1 a side view of a person's face
2 a short description of a person's character or career
to keep a low profile is to try to avoid being noticed

profit *NOUN* **profits**
1 the extra money obtained by selling something for more than it cost to buy or make
2 an advantage gained by doing something
▷ **profitable** *ADJECTIVE*
▷ **profitably** *NOUN*

profit *VERB* **profits, profiting, profited**
to gain an advantage or benefit from something

profiteer *NOUN* **profiteers**
a person who makes a great profit unfairly
▷ **profiteering** *NOUN*

profligate *ADJECTIVE*
wasteful and extravagant
▷ **profligacy** *NOUN*

profound *ADJECTIVE*
1 very deep or intense ◆ *The farming industry was going through a period of profound change.*
2 showing or needing great knowledge, understanding, or thought ◆ *He is a man of immense talents and profound insights.*
▷ **profoundly** *ADVERB*
▷ **profundity** *NOUN*

profuse *ADJECTIVE*
lavish or plentiful
▷ **profusely** *ADVERB*
▷ **profuseness** *NOUN*
▷ **profusion** *NOUN*

progenitor *NOUN* **progenitors**
an ancestor

progeny (*say* **proj**- in- ee) *NOUN*
offspring or descendants

prognosis (*say* prog- **noh**- sis) *NOUN* **prognoses**
a forecast or prediction, especially about a disease
▷ **prognostication** *NOUN*

program *NOUN* **programs**
(*ICT*) a series of coded instructions for a computer to carry out

program *VERB* **programs, programming, programmed**
(*ICT*) to put instructions into a computer by means of a program
▷ **programmer** *NOUN*

programme *NOUN* **programmes**
1 a list of planned events
2 a leaflet or pamphlet giving details of a play, concert, football match, or other entertainment
3 a show, play, talk, etc. broadcast on radio or television

WORD HISTORY from Greek *programma* 'a public notice', from *pro* 'before' and *graphein* 'to write'

progress (*say* **proh**- gress) *NOUN*
1 forward movement; an advance
2 a development or improvement
3 something is in progress when it is happening

From the window of the tram it looked like a street festival was in progress. — *Michael Hoeye, Time Stops for No Mouse*

progress (*say* pro- **gress**) *VERB* **progresses, progressing, progressed**
1 to move forward
2 to develop or improve a plan or activity
▷ **progression** *NOUN*

progressive *ADJECTIVE*
1 moving forward or developing
2 in favour of political or social reforms
3 a progressive disease is one that becomes gradually more severe

prohibit *VERB* **prohibits, prohibiting, prohibited**
to forbid or ban something
▷ **prohibition** *NOUN*

prohibitive *ADJECTIVE*
1 restricting or preventing
2 prices or costs are prohibitive when they are too high for most people to be able to afford

project (*say* **proj**- ekt) *NOUN* **projects**
1 a plan or scheme
2 the task of finding out as much as you can about something and writing about it

project (*say* pro- **jekt**) *VERB* **projects, projecting, projected**
1 to stick out
2 to show a picture on a screen
3 to give people a particular idea or impression ◆ *He had always been able to project an appealing public image .*
▷ **projection** *NOUN*

projectile *NOUN* **projectiles**
a missile

projectionist *NOUN* **projectionists**
a person who works a projector

projector *NOUN* **projectors**
a machine for showing films or photographs on a screen

proletariat (*say* proh- lit- **air**- ee- at) *NOUN*
working people

proliferate *VERB* **proliferates, proliferating, proliferated**
to increase rapidly in numbers
▷ **proliferation** *NOUN*

prolific *ADJECTIVE*
producing a lot of work ◆ *She is a prolific author and writes regularly for newspapers.*
▷ **prolifically** *ADVERB*

prologue (*say* **proh**- log) *NOUN* **prologues**
1 an introduction to a poem or play
2 an event that leads to another

prolong *VERB* **prolongs, prolonging, prolonged**
to make a thing longer or make it last for a longer time
▷ **prolongation** *NOUN*

prom *NOUN* **proms** (*informal*)
1 a promenade
2 a promenade concert
3 (*American*) a formal dance at a college or high school

promenade (*say* prom- in- **ahd**) *NOUN* **promenades**
1 a place suitable for walking, especially beside the seashore
2 a leisurely walk

promenade *VERB* **promenades, promenading, promenaded**
to take a leisurely walk

promenade concert *NOUN* **promenade concerts**
a concert where part of the audience stands in an area without seating

prominent *ADJECTIVE*
1 easily seen; conspicuous ◆ *The house stood in a prominent position.*
2 sticking out

> The Director ... had a long chin and big rather prominent teeth, just covered, when he was not talking, by his full, floridly curved lips. — *Aldous Huxley, Brave New World*

3 important or famous
▷ **prominently** *ADVERB*
▷ **prominence** *NOUN*

promiscuous *ADJECTIVE*
1 having many casual sexual relationships
2 indiscriminate or casual
▷ **promiscuously** *ADVERB*
▷ **promiscuity** *NOUN*

promise *NOUN* **promises**
1 a definite assurance about what you will do or what will happen
2 an indication of future success or good results

> The School on Roke is where boys who show promise in sorcery are sent from all the Inner Lands of Earthsea to learn the highest arts of magic. — *Ursula Le Guin, The Farthest Shore*

promise *VERB* **promises, promising, promised**
to make a promise

promising *ADJECTIVE*
likely to be good or successful

promontory *NOUN* **promontories**
a piece of high land that sticks out into a sea or lake

promote *VERB* **promotes, promoting, promoted**
1 to move a person to a higher rank or position
2 to help the progress of something
3 to publicize or advertise a product in order to sell it
▷ **promoter** *NOUN*
▷ **promotion** *NOUN*

prompt *ADJECTIVE*
1 done or given quickly, without delay ◆ *The victims all received prompt medical attention.*
2 punctual; on time
▷ **promptly** *ADVERB*
▷ **promptness** *NOUN*

prompt *ADVERB*
exactly at the stated time ◆ *The show starts at 7.30 prompt.*

prompt *NOUN* **prompts**
something said or done to remind someone ◆ *He went ahead without any prompt from us.*

prompt *VERB* **prompts, prompting, prompted**
1 to cause or encourage a person to do something
2 to remind an actor or speaker of words when they have forgotten them
▷ **prompter** *NOUN*

promulgate *VERB* **promulgates, promulgating, promulgated**
1 to make something known to the public
2 to put a law or decree into effect
▷ **promulgation** *NOUN*

prone *ADJECTIVE*
1 to be prone to something is to be likely to do it or be affected by it ◆ *He is prone to jump to conclusions.*
2 lying flat, face downwards (SEE ALSO **supine**)

prong *NOUN* **prongs**
one of the spikes on a fork
▷ **pronged** *ADJECTIVE*

pronoun *NOUN* **pronouns**
(*Grammar*) a word used instead of a noun, e.g. *I, you, them, this, those,* and *which*

pronouns

Pronouns are used to replace a noun or noun phrase in a sentence or clause, and help to avoid having to repeat words. There are several types of pronoun:

- **personal pronouns** replace the name of a person or thing. *I, you, he, she, it, we,* and *they* are used when the pronoun is the subject of the clause; *me, you, him, her, it, us,* and *them*, are used when the pronoun is the object: *Zoe and Bill are coming to the concert. She's got a ticket, but he hasn't. The guards were following us and we were unable to shake them off.*
- **reflexive pronouns** (*myself, yourself, himself, herself, itself, ourselves, yourselves,* and *themselves*) refer back to the subject of a clause: *Most baby birds are unable to feed themselves. I wanted to see for myself what all the fuss was about.*
- **relative pronouns** (*what, who, whom, whose, which,* and *that*) introduce a clause which describes or limits the subject, e.g. *the artist who painted this portrait; the song that I love.*
- **interrogative pronouns** (*what, who, whom, whose*) are used to form questions e.g. *What is happening? Who wants some ice cream?*
- **demonstrative pronouns** (*this, that, these,* and *those*) indicate a particular person or thing, or a particular time or situation, e.g. *These are my glasses, and those are yours; This has been a hectic week.* (Note, however, that in the sentence *These glasses are mine, and those glasses are yours*, the words *these* and *those* are adjectives and determiners, not pronouns.)

See also the panels on **determiners** and **possessives**.

pronounce *VERB* **pronounces, pronouncing, pronounced**
1 to say a sound or word in a particular way
2 to declare something formally

> They stayed with Mr Wilderness for three days, until he pronounced Sylvia better and fit to travel. — *Joan Aiken, The Wolves of Willoughby Chase*

pronounced *ADJECTIVE*
very noticeable ◆ *Barney walked with a pronounced limp.*

pronouncement *NOUN* **pronouncements**
a declaration

a b c d e f g h i j k l m n o p q r s t u v w x y z

pronunciation *NOUN* **pronunciations**
the way a word is pronounced

USAGE NOTE Note the spelling of this word: it should not be written or spoken as 'pronounciation'.

pronunciation

Many English words are pronounced the way they look. In other words, their spelling tells you how to say them: for example, *kidnap*, *nostril*, and *thump*. However, some individual letters and letter combinations can be pronounced in more than one way: the letter *c* sounds like *s* in *city* but like *k* in *cabbage*; and the combination *-ough* is pronounced differently in the words *bough*, *cough*, *rough*, and *through*. Sometimes, the **pronunciation** of a word changes over time, leading to a mismatch between its spelling and the way it is said: both the *k* and the *gh* in *knight*, which are now 'silent', were once pronounced. The pronunciation of a word can also vary according to the variety of English being spoken. In American English, for example, the word *clerk* rhymes with *murk* and not, as in British English, with *mark*.
You will find guidance in this dictionary on words that are pronounced in ways that are not clear from their spelling.
See also the panel on **spelling**.

proof *NOUN* **proofs**
1 a fact or thing that shows something is true
2 a trial version of a piece of printing made for checking before other copies are printed

proof *ADJECTIVE*
able to resist something or not to be affected by it ◆ *Oliver was proof against Emma's attempts to frighten him.* ◆ *The pills were in a tamper-proof bottle.*

proofread *VERB* **proofreads, proofreading, proofread**
to read a printer's proofs for errors

prop❶ *NOUN* **props**
a support, especially one made of a long piece of wood or metal

prop *VERB* **props, propping, propped**
to support something by leaning it against something else

prop❷ *NOUN* **props**
an object or piece of furniture used on a theatre stage or in a film

propaganda *NOUN*
(*Politics*) biased or misleading publicity intended to convince people of a political cause or point of view

WORD HISTORY an Italian word, from Latin *congregatio de propaganda fide* 'congregation for propagating (i.e. spreading) the faith', a committee of Roman Catholic cardinals set up in 1622 to spread the Catholic faith round the world

propagate *VERB* **propagates, propagating, propagated**
1 to breed or reproduce
2 to spread an idea or belief to a large number of people
▷ **propagation** *NOUN*
▷ **propagator** *NOUN*

propel *VERB* **propels, propelling, propelled**
to push something forward

WORD FAMILY *Propel* comes from the Latin word *pellere* meaning 'to drive'. Other words to do with driving (some only loosely) and having the same origin include *compel*, *dispel*, *expel*, *impel*, and *repel*.

propellant *NOUN* **propellants**
a fuel or other substance that propels things

propeller *NOUN* **propellers**
a device with blades that spin round to drive an aircraft or ship

propensity *NOUN* **propensities**
a tendency or inclination

proper *ADJECTIVE*
1 suitable or right ◆ *The room had a few boxes to sit on but no proper furniture.*
2 decent or respectable ◆ *It would not be proper to take more money.*
3 (*informal*) complete or thorough ◆ *The delay proved to be a proper nuisance.*
▷ **properly** *ADVERB*

proper fraction *NOUN* **proper fractions**
a fraction that is less than 1, with the numerator less than the denominator, e.g. $\frac{5}{8}$

proper noun *NOUN* **proper nouns**
the name of an individual person or thing, e.g. *London, Spain, Gareth*, usually written with a capital first letter

proper nouns

A **proper noun** is the name of a particular person, place, or thing, as distinct from a **common noun** which can refer to many people, places, or things. Proper nouns always begin with a capital letter.
Proper nouns include:
- personal names and titles (e.g. *Alexander*, *Einstein*, *the Queen*)
- place names and names of geographical features (e.g. *Johannesburg*, *Saturn*, *the Grand Canyon*)
- the names of organizations and religions (e.g. *the World Bank*, *Buddhism*)
- the days of the week, months of the year, and festivals (e.g. *Tuesday*, *April*, *Diwali*, *Easter*, *Hogmanay*, *Ramadan*)

If a proper noun consists of more than one word, then each part (except for the definite article) begins with a capital letter, e.g. *Captain Nemo*, *Mount Kilimanjaro*, *the Milky Way*.

property *NOUN* **properties**
1 a thing or things that a person owns
2 a building with the land belonging to it

The Grange was the most expensive property in Upper Dinton, a beautiful old house, set apart from the rest of the village. — *Tim Bowler, Starseeker*

3 the quality or characteristic that a substance has

prophecy *NOUN* **prophecies**
1 a statement that prophesies something
2 the action of prophesying

prophesy *VERB* **prophesies, prophesying, prophesied**
to say what will happen in the future; to foretell an event

prophet *NOUN* **prophets**
1 a person who makes prophecies
2 (*Religion*) a religious teacher who is believed to be inspired by God
the Prophet a name for Muhammad, the founder of the Muslim faith
▷ **prophetess** *NOUN*

WORD HISTORY from Greek *prophetes* 'someone who speaks for someone else', from *pro* 'on behalf of' and *phetes* 'a speaker'

prophetic *ADJECTIVE*
saying or showing what will happen in the future

propinquity *NOUN*
(*formal*) the state of being close or nearby

propitiate (*say* pro- **pish**- ee- ayt) *VERB* **propitiates, propitiating, propitiated**
to win a person's favour or forgiveness
▷ **propitiation** *NOUN*
▷ **propitiatory** *ADJECTIVE*

propitious (*say* pro- **pish**- us) *ADJECTIVE*
favourable; providing a good opportunity

proponent (*say* prop- **oh**- nent) *NOUN* **proponents**
a person who supports a proposal or idea

proportion *NOUN* **proportions**
1 a part or share of a whole thing
2 a ratio
3 the correct relationship in size, amount, or importance between two things
4 the proportions of a large object are its size or scale ◆ *They came to a building of huge proportions.*

proportional or **proportionate** *ADJECTIVE*
in proportion; according to a ratio
▷ **proportionally** *ADVERB*
▷ **proportionately** *ADVERB*

proportional representation *NOUN*
a system in which each political party has a number of Members of Parliament in proportion to the number of votes for all its candidates

propose *VERB* **proposes, proposing, proposed**
1 to suggest an idea or plan
2 to plan or intend to do something
3 to ask a person to marry you
▷ **proposal** *NOUN*

proposition *NOUN* **propositions**
1 a suggestion or offer
2 a statement
3 (*informal*) an undertaking or problem ◆ *A biography of an artist is a tricky proposition for a writer.*

propound *VERB* **propounds, propounding, propounded**
to put forward an idea for consideration

proprietary (*say* pro- **pry**- it- er- ee) *ADJECTIVE*
1 a proprietary medicine or product is one made or sold by a particular firm
2 to do with an owner or ownership

proprietor *NOUN* **proprietors**
the owner of a shop or business
▷ **proprietress** *NOUN*

propriety (*say* pro- **pry**- it- ee) *NOUN* **proprieties**
1 correctness of behaviour or morals
2 correct behaviour

propulsion *NOUN*
the action of propelling or driving something

prorogue (*say* pro- **rohg**) *VERB* **prorogues, proroguing, prorogued**
to stop the meetings of a parliament temporarily without dissolving it
▷ **prorogation** *NOUN*

prosaic *ADJECTIVE*
plain or dull and ordinary
▷ **prosaically** *ADVERB*

pros and cons *PLURAL NOUN*
reasons for and against doing or accepting something

proscribe *VERB* **proscribes, proscribing, proscribed**
to forbid something by law

USAGE NOTE Take care not to confuse this word with *prescribe*.

prose *NOUN*
(*Language*) writing or speech that is not in verse

prosecute *VERB* **prosecutes, prosecuting, prosecuted**
1 to make someone go to a lawcourt to be tried for a crime
2 (*formal*) to continue with something; to pursue an activity
▷ **prosecution** *NOUN*
▷ **prosecutor** *NOUN*

proselyte *NOUN* **proselytes**
a person who has been converted from one religion, opinion, etc. to another, especially to Judaism

a b c d e f g h i j k l m n o p q r s t u v w x y z

proselytize *VERB* **proselytizes, proselytizing, proselytized**
to convert people from one religion or opinion to another

USAGE NOTE This word can also be spelled proselytise.

prosody (*say* **pross**- od- ee) *NOUN*
the study of verse and its structure

prospect *NOUN* **prospects**
1 a possibility or expectation of something ◆ *There is little prospect of them changing their minds.*
2 a wide view

prospect (*say* pro- **spekt**) *VERB* **prospects, prospecting, prospected**
to explore an area in search of gold or some other mineral
▷ **prospector** *NOUN*

prospective *ADJECTIVE*
expected to be or to happen; possible ◆ *Prospective owners were expected to put down large deposits on their houses.*

prospectus *NOUN* **prospectuses**
a booklet describing and advertising a school, business company, etc.

prosper *VERB* **prospers, prospering, prospered**
to be successful

prosperous *ADJECTIVE*
successful or rich
▷ **prosperity** *NOUN*

prostate *NOUN*
(*Medicine*) a gland round the neck of the bladder in males, which releases semen

prostitute *NOUN* **prostitutes**
a person, usually a woman, who takes part in sexual acts for payment
▷ **prostitution** *NOUN*

prostrate *ADJECTIVE*
lying face downwards

prostrate *VERB* **prostrates, prostrating, prostrated**
to prostrate yourself is to lie flat on the ground face down, especially as an act of submission
▷ **prostration** *NOUN*

protagonist *NOUN* **protagonists**
1 the main character in a play
2 a prominent figure in a real situation

protect *VERB* **protects, protecting, protected**
to keep someone safe from harm or injury
▷ **protection** *NOUN*
▷ **protective** *ADJECTIVE*
▷ **protector** *NOUN*

protectorate *NOUN* **protectorates**
a country that is under the official protection of a stronger country

protégé (*say* **prot**- ezh- ay) *NOUN* **protégés**
someone who is helped and supported by an older or more experienced person

protein *NOUN* **proteins**
a substance that is found in all living things and is an essential part of the food of animals

pro tem *ADVERB*
(*informal*) for the time being

WORD HISTORY short for Latin *pro tempore*, which has the same meaning

protest (*say* **proh**- test) *NOUN* **protests**
a statement or action showing that you disapprove of something

protest (*say* pro- **test**) *VERB* **protests, protesting, protested**
1 to make a protest
2 to declare something firmly ◆ *They had always protested their innocence.*
▷ **protestation** *NOUN*

WORD HISTORY from Latin *pro-* 'before' and *testari* 'to say on oath'

Protestant *NOUN* **Protestants**
a member of any of the western Christian Churches separated from the Roman Catholic Church

WORD HISTORY called this because in the 16th century many people protested (declared firmly) their opposition to the Catholic Church

protocol *NOUN*
the correct or official procedure for behaving in certain formal situations

proton *NOUN* **protons**
a particle of matter with a positive electric charge

prototype *NOUN* **prototypes**
the first model of something, from which others are copied or developed

protract *VERB* **protracts, protracting, protracted**
to make something last longer than usual; to prolong an event or activity
▷ **protracted** *ADJECTIVE*
▷ **protraction** *NOUN*

protractor *NOUN* **protractors**
a device for measuring angles, usually a semicircle marked off in degrees

protrude *VERB* **protrudes, protruding, protruded**
to stick out from a surface
▷ **protrusion** *NOUN*

protuberance *NOUN* **protuberances**
a part that bulges out from a surface

protuberant *ADJECTIVE*
bulging out from a surface

proud *ADJECTIVE*
1 to be proud of someone or of yourself is to be pleased when you or they have done well
2 a proud occasion or moment is one that makes you feel proud about someone or something
3 full of self-respect and independence ◆ *He was too proud to ask his family for help.*
4 having too high an opinion of yourself
to do someone proud is to look after them and treat them well
▷ **proudly** *ADVERB*

prove *VERB* **proves, proving, proved**
1 to show that something is true
2 something proves to be (for example) suitable or correct when it becomes clear after a time that it is suitable or correct ◆ *The programme proved not at all suitable for young children.*
▷ **provable** *ADJECTIVE*

proven (*say* **proh**- ven) *ADJECTIVE*
proved or established ◆ *Taking exercise is of proven value as part of this treatment.*

proverb *NOUN* **proverbs**
(*Language*) a short well-known saying, e.g. *Many hands make light work*

proverbs

A **proverb** is a short saying which offers a piece of advice, often as a warning or a consolation, or which states a general truth. Most proverbs are very old and have become so familar that they can even be understood from a shortened form (e.g. *a bird in the hand* or *too many cooks*).
Here are some well-known proverbs and their meanings:
absence makes the heart grow fonder (people like each other more after they have been apart)
a bird in the hand is worth two in the bush (keeping what you already have is better than risking it to try to get something better)
birds of a feather flock together (people of similar types enjoy each other's company)
don't count your chickens until they're hatched (don't take something for granted until it happens)
every cloud has a silver lining (some good always comes out of a bad experience)
too many cooks spoil the broth (things don't work well if too many people are involved)

proverbial *ADJECTIVE*
1 referred to in a proverb or idiom
2 well known or familiar

provide *VERB* **provides, providing, provided**
1 to make something available; to supply something
2 to provide for something that might happen is to prepare for it
▷ **provider** *NOUN*

provided *CONJUNCTION*
on condition that; only if ◆ *He was good in crises provided they didn't happen too often.*

providence *NOUN*
1 the quality of being careful and providing for the future
2 the care and protection given by God or nature

provident *ADJECTIVE*
wisely providing for the future; thrifty

providential *ADJECTIVE*
happening very luckily
▷ **providentially** *ADVERB*

providing *CONJUNCTION*
on condition that; only if

province *NOUN* **provinces**
1 a section of a country
2 the area of a person's special knowledge or responsibility
3 the provinces of a country are the parts outside its capital city

provincial (*say* pro- **vin**- shul) *ADJECTIVE*
1 to do with the provinces
2 culturally limited or narrow-minded

provision *NOUN* **provisions**
1 the process of providing something
2 a statement or requirement forming part of a treaty or other legal document

provisional *ADJECTIVE*
arranged or agreed on for the time being but possibly to be changed later
▷ **provisionally** *ADVERB*

provisions *PLURAL NOUN*
supplies of food and drink

proviso (*say* prov- y- zoh) *NOUN* **provisos**
a condition that is insisted on in advance

provocative *ADJECTIVE*
1 a provocative remark or action is likely to make someone angry
2 intended to arouse sexual desire
▷ **provocatively** *ADVERB*

provoke *VERB* **provokes, provoking, provoked**
1 to make a person angry
2 to cause or give rise to something
▷ **provocation** *NOUN*

provost *NOUN* **provosts**
a Scottish official with authority similar to a mayor in England and Wales

prow *NOUN* **prows**
the front end of a ship

prowess *NOUN*
great ability or daring

prowl *VERB* **prowls, prowling, prowled**
to move about quietly or cautiously, like a hunter

prowl *NOUN*
1 an animal goes on the prowl when it hunts other animals
2 a person is on the prowl when they are moving about secretively looking for something
▷ **prowler** *NOUN*

proximity *NOUN*
nearness in position or time

proxy *NOUN* **proxies**
a person authorized to represent or act for another person, for example in voting

prude *NOUN* **prudes**
a person who is easily shocked
▷ **prudish** *ADJECTIVE*
▷ **prudery** *NOUN*

prudent *ADJECTIVE*
careful, not rash or reckless
▷ **prudently** *ADVERB*
▷ **prudence** *NOUN*
▷ **prudential** *ADJECTIVE*

prune❶ *NOUN* **prunes**
a dried plum

prune❷ *VERB* **prunes, pruning, pruned**
to cut off unwanted parts of a tree or bush

pry *VERB* **pries, prying, pried**
to look into or ask about someone else's affairs when they do not concern you

PS *ABBREVIATION*
postscript, used when you add something at the end of a letter

psalm (*say* sahm) *NOUN* **psalms**
a religious song, especially one from the Book of Psalms in the Bible
▷ **psalmist** *NOUN*

pseudonym *NOUN* **pseudonyms**
a special name used by a writer

PSHE *ABBREVIATION*
personal, social, and health education

psychedelic *ADJECTIVE*
having bright strong colours and patterns

psychiatrist (*say* sy- **ky**- a- trist) *NOUN* **psychiatrists**
a doctor who treats mental illnesses
▷ **psychiatry** *NOUN*
▷ **psychiatric** *ADJECTIVE*

psychic (*say* sy- kik) *ADJECTIVE*
1 to do with the supernatural
2 appearing to have supernatural powers, especially in being able to predict the future
3 to do with the mind or soul
▷ **psychical** *ADJECTIVE*

psychoanalysis *NOUN*
investigation of a person's mental processes, especially in psychotherapy
▷ **psychoanalyst** *NOUN*
WORD HISTORY from Greek *psyche* 'life or soul'

psychology *NOUN*
the study of the mind and how it works
▷ **psychological** *ADJECTIVE*
▷ **psychologist** *NOUN*

psychotherapy *NOUN*
treatment of mental illness by psychological methods
▷ **psychotherapist** *NOUN*

psychosomatic *ADJECTIVE*
(*Medicine*) a psychosomatic illness is one with physical symptoms made worse by stress or other psychological factors

PT *ABBREVIATION*
physical training

PTA *ABBREVIATION*
parent–teacher association, an organization that arranges discussions between teachers and parents about school business

ptarmigan (*say* tar- mig- an) *NOUN* **ptarmigans**
a bird of the grouse family

pterodactyl (*say* te- ro- **dak**- til) *NOUN* **pterodactyls**
an extinct flying reptile
WORD HISTORY from Greek *pteron* 'wing' and *daktylos* 'finger' (because one of the 'fingers' on its front leg was enlarged to support its wing)

PTO *ABBREVIATION*
please turn over (put at the end of a page of writing when there is more writing on the next page)

pub *NOUN* **pubs**
a building licensed to serve alcoholic drinks to the public
WORD HISTORY short for *public house*

puberty (*say* **pew**- ber- tee) *NOUN*
the time when a young person is developing physically into an adult

pubic (*say* **pew**- bik) *ADJECTIVE*
to do with the lower front part of the abdomen

public *ADJECTIVE*
belonging to or known by everyone; not private
▷ **publicly** *ADVERB*

public *NOUN*
people in general
in public openly; not in private

publican *NOUN* **publicans**
the person in charge of a pub

publication *NOUN* **publications**
1 the process or activity of publishing
2 a publication is a published book, newspaper, or magazine

public house ***NOUN*** **public houses**
(*formal*) a pub

publicity ***NOUN***
1 information in newspapers or other public media promoting a product, service, or event
2 public attention about something

publicize ***VERB*** **publicizes, publicizing, publicized**
to bring something to people's attention; to advertise something publicly

USAGE NOTE This word can also be spelled publicise.

public school ***NOUN*** **public schools**
1 in Britain, a private secondary school that charges fees
2 in Scotland and the USA, a school run by a local authority or by the state

publish ***VERB*** **publishes, publishing, published**
1 to have something printed and sold to the public
2 to announce something in public
▷ **publisher** ***NOUN***

puce ***NOUN***
a dark red or brownish-purple colour

I told Uncle Andrew about the whispers in kirk & he turned puce & snapped the stem of his pipe in anger! — *Frances Mary Hendry, My Story: The '45 Rising*

WORD HISTORY from French *couleur puce* 'colour of a flea'

puck ***NOUN*** **pucks**
a hard rubber disc used in ice hockey

pucker ***VERB*** **puckers, puckering, puckered**
to wrinkle

The aunts looked at each other, and then at Clare, their faces puckered with incomprehension. — *Penelope Lively, The House in Norham Gardens*

pudding ***NOUN*** **puddings**
1 the sweet course of a meal
2 a food made in a soft mass, especially in a mixture of flour and other ingredients

puddle ***NOUN*** **puddles**
a shallow patch of liquid, especially of rainwater on a road

pudgy ***ADJECTIVE***
short and fat

puerile (*say* pew- er- yl) ***ADJECTIVE***
silly and childish
▷ **puerility** ***NOUN***

puff ***NOUN*** **puffs**
1 a short blowing of breath, wind, smoke, steam, or other vapour
2 a soft pad for putting powder on the skin
3 a cake of very light pastry filled with cream

puff ***VERB*** **puffs, puffing, puffed**
1 to blow out puffs of smoke or steam
2 to pant or breathe with difficulty
3 to inflate or swell something

puff adder ***NOUN*** **puff adders**
a large poisonous African snake that puffs out the upper part of its body when threatened

puffin ***NOUN*** **puffins**
a seabird with a large striped beak

puffy ***ADJECTIVE***
puffed out or swollen
▷ **puffiness** ***NOUN***

pug ***NOUN*** **pugs**
a small dog like a bulldog, with a flat nose and a deeply wrinkled face

pugilist (*say* pew- jil- ist) ***NOUN*** **pugilists**
a boxer

pugnacious ***ADJECTIVE***
wanting to fight; aggressive
▷ **pugnaciously** ***ADVERB***
▷ **pugnacity** ***NOUN***

puke ***VERB*** **pukes, puking, puked**
(*informal*) to vomit

pull ***VERB*** **pulls, pulling, pulled**
1 to use force to make a thing come towards you or after you
2 to pull something up or out is to remove it from where it is fixed or growing

to pull a face is to make a strange or rude expression

to pull in
1 a vehicle or driver pulls in when they move to the side of the road and stop
2 a train pulls in when it arrives and stops at a station

to pull somebody's leg is to tease them

to pull something off is to be successful and achieve it

to pull out
1 a vehicle or driver pulls out when they move out into the road from the side
2 a train pulls out when it leaves a station

to pull through is to recover from an illness

to pull up a vehicle or driver pulls up when they stop abruptly

to pull yourself together is to make an effort to be calm again after being upset or distressed

pull ***NOUN*** **pulls**
1 an action of pulling, or the force of pulling
2 something has a pull when it is pleasant and attracts you

pullet ***NOUN*** **pullets**
a young hen

pulley ***NOUN*** **pulleys**
a wheel with a rope, chain, or belt over it, used for lifting or moving heavy objects

pullover *NOUN* **pullovers**
a knitted piece of clothing put on over the head and covering the top half of the body

pulmonary (*say* pul- mon- er- ee) *ADJECTIVE*
(*Medicine*) to do with the lungs

pulp *NOUN*
1 the soft moist part of fruit
2 any soft moist mass
▷ **pulpy** *ADJECTIVE*

pulpit *NOUN* **pulpits**
a small enclosed platform for the preacher in a church or chapel

pulsate *VERB* **pulsates, pulsating, pulsated**
to expand and contract rhythmically; to vibrate

Through the warm air fireflies drifted, pulsating briefly like pink pearls against the dark undergrowth. — *Gerald Durrell, A Zoo in My Luggage*

▷ **pulsation** *NOUN*

pulse❶ *NOUN* **pulses**
1 the rhythmical movement of the arteries as blood is pumped through them by the beating of the heart
2 a throb

pulse *VERB* **pulses, pulsing, pulsed**
to throb or pulsate

WORD HISTORY from Latin *pulsum* 'driven, beaten', from *pellere* 'to beat'

pulse❷ *NOUN* **pulses**
the edible seed of peas, beans, lentils, etc.

WORD HISTORY from Latin *puls* 'thick mixture of food'

pulverize *VERB* **pulverizes, pulverizing, pulverized**
to crush something into powder
▷ **pulverization** *NOUN*

USAGE NOTE This word can also be spelled pulverise.

puma (*say* pew- ma) *NOUN* **pumas**
a large brown animal of western America, also called a cougar or mountain lion

WORD HISTORY via Spanish from Quechua (a South American language)

pumice *NOUN*
a kind of porous stone used for rubbing stains from the skin or as powder for polishing hard surfaces

pummel *VERB* **pummels, pummelling, pummelled**
to keep on hitting something

pump❶ *NOUN* **pumps**
a device that pushes air or liquid into or out of something, or along pipes

pump *VERB* **pumps, pumping, pumped**
1 to move air or liquid with a pump
2 (*informal*) to question someone to get information
to pump something up is to fill it with air using a pump

pump❷ *NOUN* **pumps**
a canvas sports shoe with a rubber sole

pumpkin *NOUN* **pumpkins**
a large round fruit with a hard orange skin

pun *NOUN* **puns**
(*Language*) a joking use of a word sounding the same as another or having more than one meaning, e.g. 'When is coffee like earth? — When it is ground.'

punch❶ *VERB* **punches, punching, punched**
1 to hit someone with your fist

'Oh, yes!' I ran across the grass, punching the air with my fist. 'What a goal!' — *Narinder Dhami, Bend It Like Beckham*

2 to make a hole in something

punch *NOUN* **punches**
1 a hit with a fist
2 a device or machine for making holes in paper, metal, leather, or other materials
3 vigour or effectiveness ◆ *The criticisms lacked punch.*

punch❷ *NOUN*
a drink made by mixing wine or spirits and fruit juice in a bowl

WORD HISTORY from Sanskrit *pañca* 'five' (because there are five ingredients in the traditional recipe: spirits, fruit juice, water, sugar, and spice)

punchline *NOUN* **punchlines**
words that give the climax of a joke or story

punch-up *NOUN* **punch-ups**
(*informal*) a fight

punctilious *ADJECTIVE*
very careful about correct behaviour and detail
▷ **punctiliously** *ADVERB*
▷ **punctiliousness** *NOUN*

punctual *ADJECTIVE*
doing things exactly at the time arranged; not late
▷ **punctually** *ADVERB*
▷ **punctuality** *NOUN*

punctuate *VERB* **punctuates, punctuating, punctuated**
1 (*Language*) to put punctuation marks into a piece of writing
2 **to be punctuated with something** is to have it at intervals ◆ *His remarks were punctuated with occasional jokes.*

punctuation *NOUN*
(*Language*) marks such as commas, full stops, and brackets put into a piece of writing to make it easier to read

> ***punctuation***
>
> **Punctuation** is the use of special marks to make a piece of writing easier to read and understand. **Punctuation marks** show divisions and connections between sentences, clauses, or individual words: for example, a *full stop* (.) marks the end of a sentence; a *comma* (,) separates clauses or items in a list; a *question mark* (?) indicates a question; and *quotation marks* (' ' or " ") show direct speech (the actual words someone speaks). Other types of punctuation are the use of *capital letters* at the start of a sentence or proper noun, and the use of an *apostrophe* to show possession (*the cat's bowl*) or to indicate a missing letter (*don't, I've*). *Bullet points* (•) can be used to display separate items in a list.
>
> Punctuation can completely change the meaning of a piece of writing. Compare, for example, the meaning of these two sentences:
>
> *There was nothing to eat that we could see.*
> *There was nothing to eat: that we could see.*
>
> See also the panels for individual punctuation marks: **apostrophes**, **brackets**, **colons**, **commas**, **dashes**, **exclamation marks**, **full stops**, **hyphens**, **question marks**, **quotation marks**, and **semicolons**.

puncture *NOUN* **punctures**
a small hole made by something sharp, especially in a tyre

puncture *VERB* **punctures, puncturing, punctured**
to make a puncture in something

pundit *NOUN* **pundits**
a person who is an authority on something

pungent (*say* **pun**- jent) *ADJECTIVE*
1 having a strong taste or smell
2 pungent remarks are sharp and effective
▷ **pungently** *ADVERB*
▷ **pungency** *NOUN*

punish *VERB* **punishes, punishing, punished**
to make a person suffer because they have done something wrong
▷ **punishable** *ADJECTIVE*

punishment *NOUN* **punishments**
something someone suffers because they have done something wrong

WORD FAMILY Related adjectives are penal and punitive.

punitive (*say* **pew**- nit- iv) *ADJECTIVE*
a punitive action or measure is intended to be a punishment

punk *NOUN* **punks**
1 (also **punk rock**) a loud aggressive style of rock music
2 a person who likes this music

punnet *NOUN* **punnets**
a small light container for strawberries or other soft fruit

punt¹ *NOUN* **punts**
a flat-bottomed boat, usually moved by pushing a pole against the bottom of a river while standing in the punt

punt *VERB* **punts, punting, punted**
to move a punt with a pole

punt² *VERB* **punts, punting, punted**
to kick a ball after dropping it from your hands and before it touches the ground

punt³ *VERB* **punts, punting, punted**
(*informal*) to gamble; to bet on a horse race
▷ **punt** *NOUN*

punter *NOUN* **punters**
1 a person who lays a bet
2 (*informal*) a customer

> Here I am sitting in this doorway which is now my bedroom, hoping some kind punter will give me a bit of small change so I can eat. — *Robert Swindells, Stone Cold*

puny (*say* **pew**- nee) *ADJECTIVE*
small or undersized; feeble

> I shouted, but the sound echoed in the blackness, mocking my puny effort. — *Joe Simpson, Touching the Void*

pup *NOUN* **pups**
1 a puppy
2 a young seal

pupa (*say* **pew**- pa) *NOUN* **pupae**
a chrysalis

pupate (*say* pew- **payt**) *VERB* **pupates, pupating, pupated**
an insect pupates when it becomes a pupa
▷ **pupation** *NOUN*

pupil *NOUN* **pupils**
1 someone who is being taught by a teacher, especially at school
2 the opening in the centre of the eye

WORD HISTORY from Latin *pupilla* 'little girl or doll' (because the use in meaning 2 refers to the tiny images of people and things that can be seen in the eye)

puppet *NOUN* **puppets**
1 a kind of doll that can be made to move by fitting it over your hand or working it by strings or wires
2 a person whose actions are controlled by someone else
▷ **puppetry** *NOUN*

puppy *NOUN* **puppies**
a young dog

purchase *VERB* **purchases, purchasing, purchased**
(*formal*) to buy something
▷ **purchaser** *NOUN*

purchase *NOUN* **purchases**
1 something someone has bought
2 the act of buying something
3 a firm hold or grip

Tock emerged from the loch, his scales dripping and his claws scrabbling for purchase on the seaweedy pebbles. — *Debi Gliori, Pure Dead Wicked*

purdah *NOUN*
the Muslim or Hindu custom of keeping women from the sight of men or strangers
WORD HISTORY from Persian or Urdu *parda* 'veil or curtain'

pure *ADJECTIVE*
1 a pure substance is not mixed with anything else
2 pure water or other liquid is clean and clear
3 free from evil or sin
4 mere; nothing but ◆ *What he said was pure nonsense.*
▷ **purely** *ADVERB*
▷ **pureness** *NOUN*

purée (*say* pewr- ay) *NOUN* **purées**
fruit or vegetables made into pulp
WORD HISTORY a French word meaning 'squeezed'

purgative *NOUN* **purgatives**
a strong laxative

purgatory *NOUN*
1 a state of temporary suffering
2 in Roman Catholic belief, a place in which souls are purified by punishment before they can enter heaven

purge *VERB* **purges, purging, purged**
to get rid of unwanted people or things

purge *NOUN* **purges**
1 the process of purging
2 a purgative

purify *VERB* **purifies, purifying, purified**
to make something pure
▷ **purification** *NOUN*
▷ **purifier** *NOUN*

purist *NOUN* **purists**
a person who likes things to be exactly correct, especially in the use of language

Puritan *NOUN* **Puritans**
a Protestant in the 16th and 17th centuries who wanted simpler religious ceremonies and strict moral behaviour

puritan *NOUN* **puritans**
a person with strict morals
▷ **puritanical** *ADJECTIVE*

purity *NOUN*
the state of being pure

purl❶ *NOUN* **purls**
a knitting stitch made by putting the needle through the front of the stitch from right to left (SEE ALSO **plain**)

purl❷ *VERB* **purls, purling, purled**
(*poetic*) a stream purls when it ripples with murmuring sounds

purloin *VERB* **purloins, purloining, purloined**
(*formal*) to take something without permission

I search the airing cupboard for something dark and plain and end up purloining a dark grey V-necked school sweater belonging to my little brother. — *Jacqueline Wilson, Girls Out Late*

purple *NOUN*
a deep reddish blue colour

purport (*say* per- **port**) *VERB* **purports, purporting, purported**
to claim to be something or someone ◆ *She may not be the person she purports to be.*
▷ **purportedly** *ADVERB*

purport (*say* **per-** port) *NOUN*
the general meaning or intention of something said or written

purpose *NOUN* **purposes**
1 what you intend to do; a plan or aim
2 determination
3 to do something on purpose is to do it intentionally
▷ **purposeful** *ADJECTIVE*
▷ **purposefully** *ADVERB*

purposely *ADVERB*
on purpose

purr *VERB* **purrs, purring, purred**
to make the low murmuring sound that a cat does when it is pleased
▷ **purr** *NOUN*

purse *NOUN* **purses**
a small pouch for carrying money

purse *VERB* **purses, pursing, pursed**
to draw your lips tightly together, typically in disapproval or annoyance

purser *NOUN* **pursers**
a ship's officer who keeps the accounts, especially the head steward on a passenger ship

pursuance *NOUN*
(*formal*) the performance or process of carrying something out ◆ *The State has to act in pursuance of its obligations under international law.*

pursue *VERB* **pursues, pursuing, pursued**
1 to chase someone in order to catch them
2 to continue with something; to work at an activity
▷ **pursuer** *NOUN*

pursuit *NOUN* **pursuits**
1 the act of pursuing
2 a pursuit is a regular activity

purvey ***VERB*** **purveys, purveying, purveyed**
(*formal*) to supply food and provisions as a trade
▷ **purveyor** ***NOUN***

pus ***NOUN***
a thick yellowish substance produced in inflamed or infected tissue, e.g. in an abscess or boil

push ***VERB*** **pushes, pushing, pushed**
1 to make a thing go away from you by using force on it
2 to move yourself by using force ◆ *Someone tried to push in front of her.* ◆ *Dave pushed his way into the room.*
3 to try to force someone to do or use something; to urge someone
to push off (*informal*) is to go away

push ***NOUN*** **pushes**
a pushing movement or effort
at a push if necessary but only with difficulty
to get the push (*informal*) is to be dismissed from a job

pushchair ***NOUN*** **pushchairs**
a folding chair on wheels, for pushing a child along

pusher ***NOUN*** **pushers**
a person who sells illegal drugs

pushover ***NOUN***
(*informal*) something that is easy to do, or someone it is easy to persuade

pushy ***ADJECTIVE***
unpleasantly self-confident or ambitious

pusillanimous (*say* pew- zil- **an**- im- us) ***ADJECTIVE***
timid or cowardly

puss ***NOUN*** **pusses**
(*informal*) a cat

pussy ***NOUN*** **pussies**
(*informal*) a cat

pussyfoot ***VERB*** **pussyfoots, pussyfooting, pussyfooted**
to act cautiously and timidly

pussy willow ***NOUN*** **pussy willows**
a willow with furry catkins

pustule ***NOUN*** **pustules**
(*Medicine*) a pimple containing pus

put ***VERB*** **puts, putting, put**
1 to move a person or thing to a place or position ◆ *She put the phone down.*
2 to make a person or thing do or experience something or be in a certain condition ◆ *Go and put the heating on.* ◆ *The news put him in a better mood.*
3 to express something in words ◆ *You must put your request in writing.* ◆ *I wasn't quite sure how to put it to them.*
4 to impose something ◆ *The government is sure to put a tax on it.*
to be hard put to do something is to find it difficult to do
to put someone off is to dissuade or discourage someone
to put something off is to postpone it to a later time
to put out a fire or **light** is to stop it from burning or shining
to put someone out is to annoy or inconvenience them
to put someone up is to give them a place to sleep for the night
to put something up
1 is to build or erect it
2 is to raise the price of something
3 to put up money is to provide for a special purpose
to put up with something is to endure or tolerate it

SYNONYMS (meaning 1) place, set, leave, stand, position; (meaning 3) express, word, phrase, formulate, couch; (meaning 4) impose, levy, inflict, apply (to); (*put someone off*) deter, discourage, disconcert, unnerve, distract; (*put something off*) postpone, defer, delay, hold over, shelve, reschedule; (*put someone out*) offend, annoy, anger, irritate, affront, insult; (*put someone up*) accommodate, house, give a room to, take in; (*put something up*) erect, build, construct, assemble; (*put up with something*) tolerate, endure, stand for, accept, take, bear, stomach

putrefy (*say* **pew**- trif- eye) ***VERB*** **putrefies, putrefying, putrefied**
to decay or rot
▷ **putrefaction** ***NOUN***

putrid (*say* **pew**- trid) ***ADJECTIVE***
1 decaying or rotting
2 smelling bad

putt ***VERB*** **putts, putting, putted**
to hit a golf ball gently towards the hole
▷ **putt** ***NOUN***
▷ **putter** ***NOUN***

putty ***NOUN***
a soft paste that sets hard, used for fitting the glass into a window frame

puzzle ***NOUN*** **puzzles**
1 a difficult question or problem
2 a game or toy that sets a problem to solve or a difficult task to complete

puzzle ***VERB*** **puzzles, puzzling, puzzled**
1 to give someone a problem so that they have to think hard
2 to think patiently about how to solve something
▷ **puzzlement** ***NOUN***

PVC *ABBREVIATION*
polyvinyl chloride, a tough plastic used to make clothing, pipes, flooring, etc.

WORD HISTORY the initial letters of *polyvinyl chloride*, a polymer of vinyl, from which it is made

pygmy (*say* **pig**- mee) *NOUN* **pygmies**
1 a very small person or thing
2 a member of certain unusually short peoples of equatorial Africa

WORD HISTORY from Greek *pygme* 'a fist', used as a measure of length equal to the distance from the elbow to the knuckle; the adjective *pygmaios* was used to refer to a very small or short person

pyjamas *PLURAL NOUN*
a loose jacket and trousers worn in bed

USAGE NOTE The American spelling of this word is pajamas.

WORD HISTORY from Persian or Urdu *pay* 'leg' and *jamah* 'clothing': the word originally meant long loose trousers

pylon *NOUN* **pylons**
a tall framework made of strips of steel, supporting electric cables

WORD HISTORY a Greek word meaning 'a grand gateway', which the modern pylon resembles in shape at its lower end

pyramid *NOUN* **pyramids**
1 a structure with a square base and with sloping sides that meet in a point at the top
2 an ancient Egyptian royal tomb having this shape

▷ **pyramidal** (*say* pir- **am**- id- al) *ADJECTIVE*

pyre *NOUN* **pyres**
a pile of wood for burning a dead body as part of a funeral ceremony

python *NOUN* **pythons**
a large snake that kills its prey by coiling round and crushing it

WORD HISTORY from *Python*, the name of a huge serpent killed by Apollo in Greek legend

a b c d e f g h i j k l m n o p q r s t u v w x y z

Qq

QC *ABBREVIATION*
Queen's Counsel

QED *ABBREVIATION*
quod erat demonstrandum (Latin, which was the thing that had to be proved)

quack❶ *VERB* **quacks, quacking, quacked**
to make the harsh cry of a duck
▷ **quack** *NOUN*

quack❷ *NOUN* **quacks**
a person who falsely claims to have medical skill or have remedies to cure diseases

quad (*say* kwod) *NOUN* **quads**
1 a quadrangle
2 a quadruplet

quadrangle *NOUN* **quadrangles**
a rectangular courtyard with large buildings round it

quadrant *NOUN* **quadrants**
a quarter of a circle

quadratic equation *NOUN* **quadratic equations**
(*Mathematics*) an equation that involves quantities or variables raised to the power of two, but no higher than two

quadriceps *NOUN* **quadriceps**
the large muscle at the front of the thigh

quadrilateral *NOUN* **quadrilaterals**
(*Mathematics*) a flat geometric shape with four sides

quadruped *NOUN* **quadrupeds**
an animal with four feet

quadruple *ADJECTIVE*
1 four times as much or as many
2 having four parts

quadruple *VERB* **quadruples, quadrupling, quadrupled**
1 to become four times as much or as many
2 to make something four times as much or as many

quadruplet *NOUN* **quadruplets**
each of four children born to the same mother at one time

quadruplicate *NOUN* **quadruplicates**
each of four things that are exactly alike

quaff (*say* kwof) *VERB* **quaffs, quaffing, quaffed**
to drink something heartily or quickly

quagmire *NOUN* **quagmires**
a bog or marsh

quail❶ *NOUN* **quail** or **quails**
a bird related to the partridge

quail❷ *VERB* **quails, quailing, quailed**
to feel or show fear

A man in pyjamas on a raw morning does not feel at his bravest, and Dickson quailed under the expectation of assault. —*John Buchan, Huntingtower*

quaint *ADJECTIVE*
attractively odd or old-fashioned
▷ **quaintly** *ADVERB*
▷ **quaintness** *NOUN*

quake *VERB* **quakes, quaking, quaked**
to tremble; to shake with fear

Quaker *NOUN* **Quakers**
a member of a religious group called the Society of Friends, founded by George Fox in the 17th century

WORD HISTORY probably from Fox's instruction that people should 'tremble at the name of the Lord'

qualification *NOUN* **qualifications**
1 a skill or ability that makes you suitable for a job
2 an exam that you have passed or a course of study that you have completed
3 a statement or remark that reduces the effect of another statement or remark or makes it less extreme

qualify *VERB* **qualifies, qualifying, qualified**
1 to become able to do something through having certain qualities or training, or by passing an exam, or to make someone able to do this
2 to make a remark or statement less extreme; to limit the meaning of something
3 (*Grammar*) an adjective qualifies a noun when it describes it or adds meaning to it
▷ **qualified** *ADJECTIVE*

quality *NOUN* **qualities**
1 the extent to which something is good or bad
2 a characteristic; something that is special in a person or thing

qualm (*say* kwahm) *NOUN* **qualms**
a misgiving or scruple

quandary *NOUN* **quandaries**
a difficult situation leaving you uncertain what to do

quantity ***NOUN*** **quantities**
1 the amount of something there is, or the number of things there are
2 a large amount

quantum ***NOUN*** **quanta**
a quantity or amount

quantum leap or **quantum jump** ***NOUN*** **quantum leaps** or **quantum jumps**
a sudden large increase or advance

quarantine ***NOUN***
the act of keeping a person or animal isolated in case they have a disease which could spread to others

WORD HISTORY from Italian *quaranta* 'forty' (because the original period of isolation was 40 days)

quarrel ***NOUN*** **quarrels**
an angry disagreement

quarrel ***VERB*** **quarrels, quarrelling, quarrelled**
to have a quarrel
▷ **quarrelsome** ***ADJECTIVE***

quarry❶ ***NOUN*** **quarries**
an open place where stone or slate is dug or cut out of the ground

quarry ***VERB*** **quarries, quarrying, quarried**
to dig or cut from a quarry

WORD HISTORY via Old French from Latin *quadrum* 'a square' (because stones from a quarry were cut into regular shapes for use in building)

quarry❷ ***NOUN*** **quarries**
an animal or person that is being hunted or pursued

WORD HISTORY via Old French *cuiree* 'entrails' (given to the hounds after a kill in hunting) from Latin *cor* 'heart'

quart ***NOUN*** **quarts**
two pints; a quarter of a gallon

quarter ***NOUN*** **quarters**
1 each of four equal parts into which a thing is or can be divided
2 a period of three months, one-fourth of a year
3 a district or region

Where am I? Tell the truth—I can bear it. In what quarter of the globe Have I descended like a meteorite? — *Edmond Rostand, Cyrano de Bergerac*

at close quarters very close together
to give no quarter is to show no mercy

quarter ***VERB*** **quarters, quartering, quartered**
1 to divide something into quarters
2 to put soldiers into lodgings

quarterdeck ***NOUN*** **quarterdecks**
the part of a ship's upper deck nearest the stern, usually reserved for the officers

quarter-final ***NOUN*** **quarter-finals**
each of the matches or rounds before a semi-final, in which there are eight contestants or teams
▷ **quarter-finalist** ***ADJECTIVE***

quarterly ***ADJECTIVE, ADVERB***
happening or produced once in every three months

quarterly ***NOUN*** **quarterlies**
a quarterly magazine

quarters ***PLURAL NOUN***
rooms or lodgings

quartet ***NOUN*** **quartets**
1 a group of four musicians
2 a piece of music for four musicians
3 a set of four people or things

quartz ***NOUN***
a hard mineral, often in crystal form

quasar ***NOUN*** **quasars**
(*Science*) a distant object looking like a star, giving out powerful electromagnetic radiation

WORD HISTORY a shortening of *quasi-stellar* meaning 'like a star'

quash ***VERB*** **quashes, quashing, quashed**
to cancel or annul a decision or verdict

quatrain ***NOUN*** **quatrains**
a stanza with four lines

quaver ***VERB*** **quavers, quavering, quavered**
to tremble or quiver

quaver ***NOUN*** **quavers**
1 a quavering sound
2 (*Music*) a note in music (written ♪) lasting half as long as a crotchet

quay (*say* kee) ***NOUN*** **quays**
a landing place where ships can be tied up for loading and unloading; a wharf
▷ **quayside** ***NOUN***

queasy ***ADJECTIVE***
feeling slightly sick
▷ **queasily** ***ADVERB***
▷ **queasiness** ***NOUN***

queen ***NOUN*** **queens**
1 a woman who is the ruler of a country through inheriting the position
2 the wife of a king
3 a female bee or ant that produces eggs
4 the most powerful piece in chess
5 a playing card with a picture of a queen on it, ranking next below a king

USAGE NOTE You use a capital letter (*the Queen, Queen Elizabeth*) when you are using the word as a title.

WORD FAMILY Related adjectives are queenly, meaning 'like a queen', royal, and regal, a more formal word meaning 'to do with a queen or king'.

queen mother ***NOUN*** **queen mothers**
a king's widow who is the mother of the present king or queen

Queen's Counsel ***NOUN*** **Queen's Counsels**
a senior barrister

queer ***ADJECTIVE***
1 strange or eccentric
2 slightly ill or faint

Well, when I picked up the top plate, I came over all queer. A sort of tingling in my hands, and everything went muzzy. — *Alan Garner, The Owl Service*

▷ **queerly** ***ADVERB***
▷ **queerness** ***NOUN***

queer ***VERB*** **queers, queering, queered**
to queer a person's pitch is to spoil their chances before they have begun

quell ***VERB*** **quells, quelling, quelled**
1 to crush a rebellion by force
2 to stop a feeling, especially of fear or anger

quench ***VERB*** **quenches, quenching, quenched**
1 to satisfy your thirst by drinking
2 to put out a fire or flame

querulous (*say* **kwe**- rew- lus) ***ADJECTIVE***
constantly complaining
▷ **querulously** ***ADVERB***

query (*say* **kweer**- ee) ***NOUN*** **queries**
a question that expresses doubt or uncertainty

query ***VERB*** **queries, querying, queried**
to question whether something is true or correct

quest ***NOUN*** **quests**
a long search for something ◆ *The quest for peace has taken a step forward.*

question ***NOUN*** **questions**
1 a sentence asking for information or a reply
2 a matter to be considered or dealt with ◆ *It is simply a question of finding the right person.*
in question being discussed or disputed ◆ *Much of the land in question is unsuitable for cereal growing.*
open to question in doubt; causing uncertainty
out of the question impossible; not allowed

WORD FAMILY A related word, meaning 'asking a question', is interrogative.

question ***VERB*** **questions, questioning, questioned**
1 to ask someone questions
2 to say that you are doubtful about something
▷ **questioner** ***NOUN***

questionable ***ADJECTIVE***
causing doubt; not certainly true or honest or advisable

question mark ***NOUN*** **question marks**
(*Language*) a punctuation mark (?) placed after a question

question marks

Question marks are used to mark a sentence that is a question:
Are there wild animals in this wood?
You also use them to indicate a query in direct speech, or in the thought of a character or narrator:
'Detective Vijay? Are you there?'
Did the label say one spoonful or ten? If only she could remember.
Note that question marks are not needed in indirect speech:
The patient opened his eyes and asked me what day of the week it was.
Question marks usually come at the end of a sentence. However, in informal writing, they can be put after single words in the middle of a sentence, where there are a series of short questions:
Did you see its eyes? Were they green? yellow? opaque?
See also the panel on **direct and indirect speech**.

questionnaire ***NOUN*** **questionnaires**
a written set of questions asked to provide information for a survey

queue (*say* kew) ***NOUN*** **queues**
a line of people or vehicles waiting for something

queue ***VERB*** **queues, queueing, queued**
to form a queue, or wait in a queue

WORD HISTORY a French word meaning 'tail' (which a queue of people was thought to resemble)

quibble ***NOUN*** **quibbles**
a trivial complaint or objection

quibble ***VERB*** **quibbles, quibbling, quibbled**
to make trivial complaints or objections

quiche (*say* keesh) ***NOUN*** **quiches**
an open tart with a savoury filling

quick ***ADJECTIVE***
1 taking only a short time to do something
2 done in a short time
3 able to notice or learn or think quickly
▷ **quickly** ***ADVERB***
▷ **quickness** ***NOUN***

quicken ***VERB*** **quickens, quickening, quickened**
1 to become quicker, or to make something quicker

Ransom quickened his pace. So did the dragon. He stopped; so did it. — *C. S. Lewis, Perelandra*

2 to stimulate an activity; to make it livelier or or to become livelier

quicksand ***NOUN*** **quicksands**
an area of loose wet deep sand that sucks in anything resting or falling on top of it

quicksilver ***NOUN***
liquid mercury

quick-witted ***ADJECTIVE***
able to think and act quickly

a b c d e f g h i j k l m n o p q r s t u v w x y z

quid *NOUN* **quid**
(*informal*) a pound of money; £1

quid pro quo (*say* kwoh) *NOUN* **quid pro quos**
something given or done in return for something

WORD HISTORY Latin words meaning 'something for something'

quiescent (*say* kwee- **ess**- ent) *ADJECTIVE*
inactive or quiet
▷ **quiescence** *NOUN*

quiet *ADJECTIVE*
1 silent; not saying anything
2 with little sound; not loud or noisy
3 calm and peaceful; without disturbance
4 quiet colours are soft and not bright
▷ **quietly** *ADVERB*
▷ **quietness** *NOUN*

quiet *NOUN*
a quiet state

quieten *VERB* **quietens, quietening, quietened**
to become quiet, or to make a person or thing quiet

quiff *NOUN* **quiffs**
an upright tuft of hair

quill *NOUN* **quills**
1 a large feather
2 a pen made from a large feather
3 one of the spines on a hedgehog

quilt *NOUN* **quilts**
a padded bedcover

quilt *VERB* **quilts, quilting, quilted**
to line material with padding and fix it with lines of stitching

quin *NOUN* **quins**
a quintuplet

quince *NOUN* **quinces**
a hard pear-shaped fruit used for making jam

quincentenary *NOUN* **quincentenaries**
the 500th anniversary of something

quinine (*say* kwin- **een**) *NOUN*
a bitter-tasting medicine used to cure malaria

quintessence *NOUN*
1 the most essential part of something
2 a perfect example of a quality
▷ **quintessential** *ADJECTIVE*

WORD HISTORY from Latin *quinta essentia* 'the fifth essence' (after earth, air, fire, and water, which the alchemists thought everything contained)

quintet *NOUN* **quintets**
1 a group of five musicians
2 a piece of music for five musicians

quintuplet *NOUN* **quintuplets**
each of five children born to the same mother at one time

quip *NOUN* **quips**
a witty remark

quirk *NOUN* **quirks**
1 a peculiarity of a person's behaviour
2 a trick of fate
▷ **quirky** *ADJECTIVE*

quit *VERB* **quits, quitting, quitted** or **quit**
1 to leave or abandon a place or job
2 (*informal*) to stop doing something
▷ **quitter** *NOUN*

quite *ADVERB*
1 completely or entirely ◆ *It is quite obvious what happened.* ◆ *The news was quite a surprise to them.*
2 somewhat; to some extent ◆ *She quite likes the challenge.*

quits *ADJECTIVE*
people are quits when they are on equal terms again after one of them has had an advantange over the other
to call it quits (*informal*) is to stop doing something

quiver[1] *NOUN* **quivers**
a container for arrows

quiver[2] *VERB* **quivers, quivering, quivered**
to tremble

Hugh's mortal body was quivering like a leaf. Cold shivers rayed over his skin, under his hair, made his teeth click. — *Neil Gunn, Morning Tide*

▷ **quiver** *NOUN*

quixotic (*say* kwiks- **ot**- ik) *ADJECTIVE*
having imaginative or idealistic ideas that are not practical
▷ **quixotically** *ADVERB*

WORD HISTORY named after Don *Quixote*, hero of a 17th- century Spanish story by Cervantes

quiz *NOUN* **quizzes**
a series of questions, especially as an entertainment or competition

quiz *VERB* **quizzes, quizzing, quizzed**
to question someone closely

WORD HISTORY origin unknown: it originally meant 'an odd person' and was used as a verb meaning 'to make fun of'. It may have been a nonsense word, later associated with *inquisitive* (which has a related meaning).

quizzical *ADJECTIVE*
1 in a questioning way
2 gently amused
▷ **quizzically** *ADVERB*

quoit (*say* koit) *NOUN* **quoits**
a ring thrown at a peg in the game of **quoits**

quorum *NOUN*
the smallest number of people needed to make a meeting of a committee etc. valid

quota *NOUN* **quotas**
1 a fixed share that must be given or received or done
2 a limited amount

quotation *NOUN* **quotations**
1 an instance of quoting
2 something quoted
3 a statement of the price of something

quotation marks ***PLURAL NOUN***
inverted commas, used to mark a quotation

> ***quotation marks***
>
> **Quotation marks** occur in pairs and can surround a single word or phrase, or a longer piece of text. They are used:
> - in direct speech to show which words are being spoken: *'Look!' said a voice behind me. 'Look at the sky!'*
> - to highlight a word to which you are referring: *The words 'turn back' were scratched on the door.*
> - to show you are being ironic or sarcastic (for example, by using a cliché or slang): *Disneyland wasn't my idea of a place to 'chill' on holiday.*
> - to enclose direct quotations from a speech, book, play, or film: *Casablanca contains the famous line, 'Here's looking at you, kid'.*
>
> Pairs of quotation marks can be single ('...') or double (" ..."), but are never mixed. You can, however, use a pair of double quotes within a pair of single quotes:
> *'When I say, "Action", start the gladiator scene again.'*
> Quotation marks are also known as **speech marks**, **inverted commas**, or simply, **quotes**.
> See also the panel on **direct and indirect speech**.

quote ***VERB*** **quotes, quoting, quoted**
1 to repeat words that were first written or spoken by someone else
2 to mention something as proof
3 to state the price of goods or services that you can supply

quote ***NOUN*** **quotes**
a quotation

quoth ***VERB***
(*old use*) said ◆ *'My Lord,' quoth he.*

quotient (*say* **kwoh**- shent) ***NOUN*** **quotients**
(*Mathematics*) the result of dividing one number by another (SEE ALSO **product**)
WORD HISTORY from Latin *quotiens* 'how many times?'

a b c d e f g h i j k l m n o p q r s t u v w x y z

Rr

rabbi (*say* **rab**- eye) ***NOUN*** **rabbis**
a Jewish religious leader
▷ **rabbinic** ***ADJECTIVE***
▷ **rabbinical** ***ADJECTIVE***
WORD HISTORY a Hebrew word meaning 'my master'

rabbit ***NOUN*** **rabbits**
a burrowing animal with long ears and a short furry tail

rabble ***NOUN*** **rabbles**
a disorderly crowd or mob

rabid (*say* **rab**- id) ***ADJECTIVE***
1 extreme or fanatical ◆ *a rabid anarchist.*
2 suffering from rabies
▷ **rabidity** ***NOUN***
▷ **rabidly** ***ADVERB***

rabies (*say* **ray**- beez) ***NOUN***
a fatal disease that affects dogs, bats, and other mammals and can be passed to humans by the bite of an infected animal
WORD HISTORY from Latin *rabere* 'to be mad'

raccoon ***NOUN*** **raccoons** or **raccoon**
a North American animal with a bushy striped tail, sharp snout, and greyish-brown fur
WORD HISTORY from an Algonquian (Native American) word

race❶ ***NOUN*** **races**
1 a sports contest in which the fastest competitor wins
2 a competition to be the first to reach a particular place or to do something ◆ *From the late 1950s, the US and Russia were in a race to reach the Moon.*
3 a strong fast current of water

race ***VERB*** **races, racing, raced**
1 to compete in a race
2 to move or go very fast ◆ *The patient's heart was racing at 200 beats per minute.*
▷ **racer** ***NOUN***

race❷ ***NOUN*** **races**
1 a very large group of people thought to have the same ancestors and with physical characteristics (e.g. colour of skin and hair, shape of eyes and nose) that differ from those of other groups
2 racial origin ◆ *The committee deals with complaints of discrimination on the grounds of race or ethnic origin.*
the human race human beings collectively

racecourse ***NOUN*** **racecourses**
a ground or track where horse races are run

racehorse ***NOUN*** **racehorses**
a horse bred or kept for racing

race relations ***NOUN***
relationships between people of different races in the same country

racetrack ***NOUN*** **racetracks**
a track for horse or vehicle races

racial (*say* **ray**- shul) ***ADJECTIVE***
to do with a particular race or based on race
▷ **racially** ***ADVERB***

racism (*say* **ray**- sizm) ***NOUN***
1 discrimination against or hostility towards people of other races
2 the belief that there are characteristics, abilities, or qualities specific to each race
▷ **racist** ***NOUN, ADJECTIVE***

rack❶ ***NOUN*** **racks**
1 a framework used as a shelf or container
2 a bar or rail with cogs into which the cogs of a gear or wheel fit
3 (*historical*) an instrument of torture on which people were tied and stretched

rack ***VERB*** **racks, racking, racked**
to be racked with physical or mental pain is to be tormented by it

Our bodies were covered with scratches and bruises, and our heads racked with pain.
— *H. G. Wells, The First Men in the Moon*

to rack your brains is to think hard, especially when you are trying to remember something
WORD HISTORY from an Old German or Old Dutch word

rack❷ ***NOUN***
to go to rack and ruin is to gradually get worse due to neglect
WORD HISTORY from an Old English word meaning 'destruction': related to *wreck*

rack❸ ***NOUN***
a joint of lamb or other meat including the front ribs
WORD HISTORY origin unknown

racket❶ ***NOUN*** **rackets**
a bat with strings stretched across a frame, used in tennis, badminton, and squash
WORD HISTORY from Arabic *rahat* 'palm of your hand'

racket❷ *NOUN* **rackets**
1 a loud noise or din
2 (*informal*) a dishonest or illegal business ◆ *Two men have been jailed for running a pirate video racket.*

racketeer *NOUN* **racketeers**
a person involved in a dishonest or illegal business
▷ **racketeering** *NOUN*

raconteur (*say* rak- on- **ter**) *NOUN* **raconteurs**
a person who tells anecdotes well
WORD HISTORY a French word

racoon *NOUN* **racoons** or **racoon**
another spelling of **raccoon**

racquet *NOUN* **racquets**
another spelling of **racket**❶

racy *ADJECTIVE* **racier, raciest**
lively and slightly shocking in style ◆ *The author gives a racy account of her life in the Swinging 60s.*
▷ **racily** *ADVERB*
▷ **raciness** *NOUN*

radar *NOUN*
a system or apparatus used to detect the position or movement of objects by sending out short radio waves which are reflected back off the object
WORD HISTORY from the initial letters of *ra*dio *d*etection *a*nd *r*anging

radar trap *NOUN* **radar traps**
a system using radar to detect vehicles travelling faster than the speed limit

radial *ADJECTIVE*
1 to do with rays or radii
2 having spokes or lines that radiate from a central point
▷ **radially** *ADVERB*

radiant *ADJECTIVE*
1 radiating light or heat
2 radiant heat is transmitted by radiation
3 a radiant smile or expression is very bright and happy
▷ **radiantly** *ADVERB*
▷ **radiance** *NOUN*

radiate *VERB* **radiates, radiating, radiated**
1 to send out light, heat, or other energy in rays
2 to give out a strong feeling or quality ◆ *The photograph shows a woman who radiates confidence and pride.*
3 to spread out from a central point like the spokes of a wheel

radiation *NOUN*
1 light, heat, or other energy radiated
2 the energy or particles sent out by a radioactive substance
3 the process of radiating light, heat, or other energy

radiator *NOUN* **radiators**
1 a device that gives out heat, especially a metal case that is heated electrically or through which steam or hot water flows
2 a device that cools the engine of a motor vehicle or aircraft

radical *ADJECTIVE*
1 going to the root or foundation of something; basic and thorough ◆ *A leading environmentalist has called for a radical rethink on climate change.*
2 a radical politician or belief is one that proposes major reforms
▷ **radicalism** *NOUN*
▷ **radically** *ADVERB*

radical *NOUN* **radicals**
a person who wants to make major reforms
WORD HISTORY from Latin *radicis* 'of a root'

radicchio (*say* ra- **dee**- ki- oh) *NOUN*
a kind of chicory with dark red leaves
WORD HISTORY an Italian word meaning 'chicory'

radio *NOUN* **radios**
1 the process of sending and receiving sound or pictures by means of electromagnetic waves
2 an apparatus for receiving radio programmes or for sending or receiving radio messages
3 sound broadcasting

radio *ADJECTIVE*
1 operated by radio
2 broadcast on radio

radio *VERB* **radios, radioing, radioed**
to send a message to someone by radio

radioactive *ADJECTIVE*
having atoms that break up spontaneously and send out radiation which produces electrical and chemical effects and penetrates things
▷ **radioactivity** *NOUN*

radio beacon *NOUN* **radio beacons**
an instrument that sends out radio signals, which aircraft use to find their way

radiocarbon *NOUN*
a radioactive form of carbon that is present in organic materials and is used in carbon dating

radiography *NOUN*
the production of X-ray photographs
▷ **radiographer** *NOUN*

radiology *NOUN*
the study of X-rays and similar radiation, especially in treating diseases
▷ **radiologist** *NOUN*

radio telescope *NOUN* **radio telescopes**
an instrument that can detect radio waves from space

radiotherapy *NOUN*
the use of X-rays or other forms of radiation to treat diseases such as cancer

radish *NOUN* **radishes**
a red-skinned root vegetable with a spicy taste that is eaten raw in salads
WORD HISTORY from Latin *radix* 'a root'

radium *NOUN*
a radioactive substance found in pitchblende, often used in radiotherapy
WORD HISTORY from Latin *radius* 'a spoke or ray'

radius *NOUN* **radii** or **radiuses**
1 (*Mathematics*) a straight line from the centre of a circle or sphere to the circumference; the length of this line
2 a range or distance from a central point ◆ *The health centre caters to residents within a radius of 20 to 25 km.*
WORD HISTORY a Latin word meaning 'a spoke or ray'

radon *NOUN*
a radioactive gas used in radiotherapy

RAF *ABBREVIATION*
Royal Air Force

raffia *NOUN*
soft fibre from the leaves of a kind of palm tree, used for making mats and baskets
WORD HISTORY from a word from Malagasy (the language of Madagascar)

raffish *ADJECTIVE*
unconventional in a cheerful or light-hearted way
▷ **raffishly** *ADVERB*
▷ **raffishness** *NOUN*
WORD HISTORY from *riff-raff*

raffle *NOUN* **raffles**
a kind of lottery, usually to raise money for a charity

raffle *VERB* **raffles, raffling, raffled**
to offer something as a prize in a raffle

raft *NOUN* **rafts**
1 a flat floating structure made of wood or other materials, used as a boat
2 a coordinated series of plans or policies ◆ *The Environment Minister has announced a raft of new programmes to protect threatened species.*

rafter *NOUN* **rafters**
any of the long sloping pieces of wood that hold up a roof

rag ❶ *NOUN* **rags**
1 an old or torn piece of cloth
2 (*informal*) a newspaper of low quality
3 rags are old and torn clothes

rag ❷ *NOUN* **rags**
a series of entertainments and activities held by students to collect money for charity

rag *VERB* **rags, ragging, ragged**
(*informal*) to tease or play jokes on someone

rag ❸ *NOUN* **rags**
a piece of ragtime music

raga *NOUN* **ragas**
a pattern of notes used as a basis for improvisation in Indian music
WORD HISTORY a Sanskrit word meaning 'colour or tone'

ragbag *NOUN*
1 a bag in which scraps of fabric are kept for future use
2 a miscellaneous collection

rage *NOUN* **rages**
great or violent anger

> Mary went and sat on the hearth-rug, pale with rage. She did not cry, but ground her teeth.
> — *Frances Hodgson Burnett, The Secret Garden*

all the rage very popular or fashionable for a time

rage *VERB* **rages, raging, raged**
1 to be very angry
2 a storm or fire rages when it continues fiercely or violently

ragged *ADJECTIVE*
1 torn or frayed
2 wearing torn clothes
3 irregular or uneven ◆ *For both teams, the play was a bit ragged at the start of the second half.*
WORD HISTORY from Old Norse *roggvathr* 'tufted'

raglan *ADJECTIVE*
a raglan sleeve is joined to a piece of clothing by sloping seams
WORD HISTORY from Lord *Raglan*, British military commander (1788-1855), who wore a coat with this kind of sleeve

ragtime *NOUN*
a form of jazz music played especially on the piano
WORD HISTORY perhaps from *ragged time*

ragwort *NOUN*
a wild plant with yellow flowers and ragged leaves

raid *NOUN* **raids**
1 a sudden attack
2 a surprise visit by police to arrest people or seize illegal goods

raid *VERB* **raids, raiding, raided**
1 to make a raid on a place
2 to sneak into a place in order to take something ◆ *Who's been raiding the fridge?*
▷ **raider** *NOUN*
WORD HISTORY originally a Scots word, from Old English *rād* 'road, riding'

rail ❶ *NOUN* **rails**
1 a level or sloping bar for hanging things on or forming part of a fence or banisters
2 a long metal bar forming part of a railway track

by rail on a train

to go off the rails (*informal*) is to start behaving oddly or out of control

WORD HISTORY from an Old French word meaning 'iron rod', related to *rule*

rail *VERB* **rails, railing, railed**

to rail something off to rail off an area is to enclose it with a rail for protection

rail² *VERB* **rails, railing, railed**

to rail at a person or thing is to complain strongly about them ◆ *He delivered a passionate speech railing against the evils of globalisation.*

WORD HISTORY via French from Portuguese

railing or **railings** *PLURAL NOUN*

a fence made of upright metal bars

railroad *NOUN*

(*American*) a railway

railroad *VERB* **railroads, railroading, railroaded**

to rush or force someone into doing something hasty or unwelcome ◆ *We are being railroaded into paying for a building we don't need.*

railway *NOUN*

1 the parallel metal bars that trains travel on
2 a system of transport using rails

raiment *NOUN*

(*old use*) clothes; clothing

WORD HISTORY from *array*

rain *NOUN*

drops of water that fall from the sky

rain *VERB* **rains, raining, rained**

to fall as rain or like rain

to be rained off an event is rained off when it it cancelled or postponed because of rain

to rain blows on someone is to hit them rapidly many times

rainbow *NOUN* **rainbows**

an arch of all the colours of the spectrum formed in the sky when the sun shines through rain

WORD HISTORY from Old English *regnboga*

raincoat *NOUN* **raincoats**

a waterproof coat

raindrop *NOUN* **raindrops**

a single drop of rain

rainfall *NOUN*

the amount of rain that falls in a particular place or time

rainforest *NOUN* **rainforests**

a dense tropical forest in an area of very heavy rainfall

rainy *ADJECTIVE*

having a lot of rainfall

to save something for a rainy day is to save money for a time when you may need it

raise *VERB* **raises, raising, raised**

1 to move something to a higher place or an upright position
2 to increase the amount or level of something ◆ *Use the remote control to raise or lower the volume.*
3 to collect an amount of money; to manage to obtain something ◆ *The event raised £2000 for the tsunami appeal.*
4 to bring up a child or family
5 to raise an issue or suggestion is to put it forward for consideration
6 to raise a doubt or other feeling is to cause it to be felt
7 to raise an army is to gather it together ready for action
8 to bring a siege, blockade, or embargo to an end

to raise the alarm is to give a warning of imminent danger

to raise the dead is to bring back to life those who have died

to raise your glass to someone is to drink a toast to them

to raise a laugh or smile is to make someone laugh or smile

to raise your voice is to speak more loudly

raisin *NOUN* **raisins**

a partially dried grape

WORD HISTORY from a French word meaning 'grape'

raison d'être (*say* ray- zawn **detr**) *NOUN* **raisons d'être**

the reason or purpose for a thing's existence

WORD HISTORY a French phrase meaning 'reason for being'

raita (*say* **ry**- ta) *NOUN*

an Indian side dish of yoghurt mixed with cucumber, garlic, and mint

WORD HISTORY from a Hindi word

Raj (*say* rahj) *NOUN*

the period of Indian history when the country was ruled by Britain

WORD HISTORY a Hindi word meaning 'reign'

raja or **rajah** *NOUN* **rajas** or **rajahs**

(*History*) an Indian king or prince (SEE ALSO **rani**)

WORD HISTORY a Hindi word, from Sanskrit *rājan* 'king'

rake¹ *NOUN* **rakes**

a gardening tool with a row of short spikes fixed to a long handle

rake *VERB* **rakes, raking, raked**

1 to gather or smooth something with a rake
2 to search through something ◆ *He's been raking through all our old photographs.*

to rake it in (*informal*) is to make a lot of money

to rake something up is to remind people of an incident or topic that is best forgotten

SPELLING NOTE Some words pronounced **r-** begin with **rh-** or **wr-**

a b c d e f g h i j k l m n o p q r s t u v w x y z

rake ❷ *NOUN* **rakes**
a man who lives an irresponsible and immoral life
WORD HISTORY from an old word *rakehell*

rakish (*say* ray- kish) *ADJECTIVE*
jaunty and dashing in appearance ◆ *Fred Astaire famously wore his top hat tilted at a jaunty, almost rakish angle.*
▷ **rakishly** *ADVERB*
▷ **rakishness** *NOUN*

rally *NOUN* **rallies**
1 a large public meeting to support a cause or make a protest
2 a race for cars or motorcycles over public roads or rough country
3 a series of strokes in tennis before a point is scored
4 a recovery of your energy or spirits

rally *VERB* **rallies, rallying, rallied**
1 to bring people together, or to come together, for a united effort ◆ *Campaigners are trying to rally support for a nationwide referendum.*
2 to summon up or revive something

Odin knew he must rally his own strength and summon the gods to council. — *Kevin Crossley-Holland, Viking!*

3 to revive; to recover your strength
4 share prices rally when they increase again after a fall

RAM *ABBREVIATION*
(*ICT*) random- access memory, with contents that can be retrieved or stored directly without having to read through items already stored

ram *NOUN* **rams**
1 a male sheep
2 a device for ramming things

ram *VERB* **rams, ramming, rammed**
to push one thing hard against another

The next thing Alex knew, the heel of Wolf's palm had rammed into his chest, pushing him back with astonishing force. — *Anthony Horowitz, Stormbreaker*

Ramadan *NOUN*
the ninth month of the Muslim year, when Muslims fast between sunrise and sunset
WORD HISTORY an Arabic word, from *ramida* 'to be parched'

ramble *NOUN* **rambles**
a walk in the countryside taken for pleasure

ramble *VERB* **rambles, rambling, rambled**
1 to go for a ramble; to wander
2 to talk or write in a disorganized way, without keeping to the subject
▷ **rambler** *NOUN*

rambling *ADJECTIVE*
1 a rambling speech or piece of writing is confused or disorganized and wanders from one subject to another
2 extending or growing in various directions irregularly

We live in a charming, rambling house ... on the outskirts of Stoneleigh. — *Pamela Oldfield, My Story: Victorian Workhouse*

ramekin (*say* ram- i- kin) *NOUN* **ramekins**
a small dish for baking and serving an individual portion of food
WORD HISTORY via French from Old Dutch *rameken* 'little cream'

ramifications *PLURAL NOUN*
1 the many effects of a plan or action ◆ *The proposed legal reforms may have far-reaching ramifications.*
2 the branches of a structure
WORD HISTORY from Latin *ramificare* 'to branch out'

ramp *NOUN* **ramps**
a slope joining two different levels
WORD HISTORY from French *ramper* 'to climb'

rampage *VERB* **rampages, rampaging, rampaged**
to rush about wildly or destructively

The Castle soldiers rampaged out after the Highlanders had left—searching for arms, they claim, but really just smashing & plundering. — *Frances Mary Hendry, My Story: The '45 Rising*

rampage *NOUN*
on the rampage rushing about wildly

rampant *ADJECTIVE*
growing or spreading uncontrollably ◆ *Disease was rampant in the poorer districts.*
lion rampant a picture on a coat of arms of a lion standing upright on a hind leg

rampart *NOUN* **ramparts**
a wide bank of earth built as a fortification or a wall on top of this

On the highest rampart of the fortress was a tower of adamant. — *Philip Pullman, The Amber Spyglass*

WORD HISTORY from French *remparer* 'to fortify'

ramrod *NOUN* **ramrods**
a straight rod formerly used for ramming an explosive into a gun

ramshackle *ADJECTIVE*
a ramshackle building or other structure is badly made and rickety
WORD HISTORY from an old word *ransackle* meaning 'to ransack'

ranch *NOUN* **ranches**
a large farm in North America where cattle or other animals are bred
▷ **rancher** *NOUN*
WORD HISTORY from Spanish *rancho* 'a group of people eating together'

a b c d e f g h i j k l m n o p q r s t u v w x y z

rancid *ADJECTIVE*
smelling or tasting unpleasant like stale fat
WORD HISTORY from Latin *rancidus* 'stinking'

rancour (*say* **rank**- er) *NOUN*
bitter resentment or ill will
▷ **rancorous** *ADJECTIVE*
▷ **rancorously** *ADVERB*
WORD HISTORY from an Old French word, related to *rancid*

R & B *ABBREVIATION*
rhythm and blues

R & D *ABBREVIATION*
research and development

random *NOUN*
at random using no particular order or method ◆ *The names of the contestants were chosen at random.*

random *ADJECTIVE*
done, made, or selected at random

range *NOUN* **ranges**
1 a set of different things of the same type ◆ *Our students come from a wide range of backgrounds.* ◆ *The company is launching its new range of skiwear.*
2 the limits between which something varies ◆ *the age range 15 to 18*
3 the distance that a gun can shoot, an aircraft can travel, or that a sound can be heard
4 a place with targets for shooting practice
5 a line or series of mountains or hills
6 an open area of land or sea for animals to graze or hunt

The giant whales had migrated four months earlier from their Antarctic feeding range to mate, calve, and rear their young in two large, calm bays. — *Witi Ihimaera, The Whale Rider*

7 a kitchen fireplace with one or more ovens

range *VERB* **ranges, ranging, ranged**
1 to exist between two limits; to extend ◆ *Prices ranged from £1 to £50.*
2 to arrange items in an order

Piggy took off his shoes and socks, ranged them carefully on the ledge, and tested the water with one toe. — *William Golding, Lord of the Flies*

3 to move over a wide area; to wander

The wolves were now more open in their pursuit, ... ranging along on either side, their red tongues lolling out. — *Jack London, White Fang*

Ranger *NOUN* **Rangers**
a senior Guide

ranger *NOUN* **rangers**
someone who looks after or patrols a park or forest

rani or **ranee** (*say* **rah**- nee) *NOUN* **ranis** or **ranees**
(*History*) an Indian queen or princess; a raja's wife or widow (SEE ALSO **raja**)
WORD HISTORY from a Hindi word

rank❶ *NOUN* **ranks**
1 a line of people or things

A groan ran through the ranks of the dragons. — *Cornelia Funke, Dragon Rider*

2 a place where taxis stand to await customers
3 a position in a series of different levels ◆ *My judo instructor holds the rank of black belt.*
to close ranks is to support one another when criticized or in the wrong
to pull rank is to use your superior position or status to get what you want

rank *VERB* **ranks, ranking, ranked**
1 to put things in order according to their rank
2 to rank among a particular group or list is to be included in it ◆ *The garden ranks among the greatest landscape parks in Europe.*
WORD HISTORY via old French from a Germanic word

rank❷ *ADJECTIVE* **ranker, rankest**
1 rank growth or vegetation is too thick and coarse
2 smelling very unpleasant
3 unmistakably bad; utter, complete

What are you, anyway? A beginner! A rank amateur! And you want to teach me my trade? — *Hans Magnus Enzensberger, The Number Devil*

▷ **rankly** *ADVERB*
▷ **rankness** *NOUN*
WORD HISTORY from Old English *ranc* 'proud, rebellious, sturdy'

rank and file *NOUN*
the ordinary people or soldiers, not the leaders
WORD HISTORY referring to the 'ranks' and 'files' into which privates and non-commissioned officers form on parade

rankle *VERB* **rankles, rankling, rankled**
to cause lasting annoyance or resentment

Dan's insult continued to rankle in her soul. — *L. M. Mongomery, Rainbow Valley*

WORD HISTORY from Old French *rancle* 'festering sore'

ransack *VERB* **ransacks, ransacking, ransacked**
1 to search a place thoroughly or roughly
2 to rob or pillage a place

For half an hour they ransacked the mill. I could hear them kicking over the barrels and pulling up the rotten planking. — *John Buchan, The Thirty-Nine Steps*

WORD HISTORY from Old Norse *rannsaka*

SPELLING NOTE Some words pronounced **r-** begin with **rh-** or **wr-**

ransom *NOUN* **ransoms**
money that has to be paid for a prisoner to be set free
to hold someone to ransom is to hold them captive and demand ransom

ransom *VERB* **ransoms, ransoming, ransomed**
1 to free someone by paying a ransom
2 to get a ransom for someone
WORD HISTORY from an Old French word, related to *redeem*

rant *VERB* **rants, ranting, ranted**
to speak or shout loudly and wildly

rant *NOUN*
a spell of ranting
WORD HISTORY from Dutch *ranten* 'to talk nonsense'

rap *VERB* **raps, rapping, rapped**
1 to strike something quickly and sharply
2 to knock or strike lightly

While I nodded, nearly napping, suddenly there came a tapping, As of someone gently rapping, rapping at my chamber door. — *Edgar Allan Poe, The Raven*

3 (*informal*) to reprimand someone
4 to speak words rhythmically to a backing of rock music
▷ **rapper** *NOUN*

rap *NOUN* **raps**
1 a quick sharp knock or blow
2 (*American*) (*informal*) a criminal charge
3 words recited rhythmically to a backing of rock music; a type of popular music in which this is done
to take the rap for something (*informal*) is to take the blame or punishment for it

rapacious (*say* ra- **pay**- shus) *ADJECTIVE*
greedy and grasping, especially for money
▷ **rapaciously** *ADVERB*
▷ **rapacity** *NOUN*
WORD HISTORY from Latin *rapax* 'grasping'

rape❶ *NOUN* **rapes**
the act of forcing someone to have sexual intercourse unwillingly

rape *VERB* **rapes, raping, raped**
to force someone to have sexual intercourse
▷ **rapist** *NOUN*
WORD HISTORY from Latin *rapere* 'to take by force'

rape❷ *NOUN*
a plant with bright yellow flowers, grown as food for sheep and for its seed from which oil is obtained
WORD HISTORY from Latin *rapum* 'turnip', to which it is related

rapid *ADJECTIVE*
moving very quickly; swift
▷ **rapidly** *ADVERB*
▷ **rapidity** *NOUN*
WORD HISTORY from Latin *rapidus* 'seizing', from *rapere* 'to take by force'

rapids *PLURAL NOUN*
part of a river where the water flows very quickly

rapier *NOUN* **rapiers**
a thin lightweight sword
WORD HISTORY from French *râpe* 'grater', because the perforated hilt looks like a grater

rapport (*say* rap- **or**) *NOUN*
a friendly and understanding relationship between people ◆ *The comedian quickly established a good rapport with the audience.*
WORD HISTORY a French word

rapt *ADJECTIVE*
very intent and absorbed; enraptured

The dress rehearsal took place before a rapt audience of the ladies from the kitchens, the caretaker and his wife, and anyone else with nothing better to do. — *Penelope Lively, The House in Norham Gardens*

▷ **raptly** *ADVERB*
WORD HISTORY from Latin *raptum* 'seized'

rapture *NOUN*
very great joy or delight
▷ **rapturous** *ADJECTIVE*
▷ **rapturously** *ADVERB*
WORD HISTORY from an Old French word, related to *rapt*

rare❶ *ADJECTIVE* **rarer, rarest**
1 unusual; not often found or happening

On rare occasions Nono was given a few oranges or vegetables when the farm produced more than was needed. — *Beverley Naidoo, Chain of Fire*

2 rare air is thin and below normal pressure
▷ **rarely** *ADVERB*
▷ **rareness** *NOUN*
WORD HISTORY from Latin *rarus*

rare❷ *ADJECTIVE*
meat is rare when it is lightly cooked so that the inside is still red
WORD HISTORY from an old word *rear* meaning 'half- cooked'

rarefied *ADJECTIVE*
1 rarified air is rare or thin
2 a rarified atmosphere is one remote from everyday life ◆ *The family moved from London's East End to the rarefied atmosphere of Cambridge.*

a b c d e f g h i j k l m n o p q r s t u v w x y z

rarity *NOUN* **rarities**
1 the state of being rare
2 something uncommon; a thing valued because it is rare

The birth of a child had become a comparative rarity, and only one marriage in ten yielded any offspring. — *J. G. Ballard, The Drowned World*

rascal *NOUN* **rascals**
a dishonest or mischievous person; a rogue
▷ **rascally** *ADJECTIVE*
WORD HISTORY from Old French *rascaille* 'rabble'

rash ❶ *ADJECTIVE*
a rash action, decision, or promise is done or made without thinking of the possible consequences

By the time Hallowe'en arrived, Harry was regretting his rash promise to go to the Deathday Party. — *J. K. Rowling, Harry Potter and the Chamber of Secrets*

▷ **rashly** *ADVERB*
▷ **rashness** *NOUN*
WORD HISTORY probably from an Old English word meaning 'quick'

rash ❷ *NOUN* **rashes**
1 an outbreak of spots or patches on the skin
2 a number of unwelcome events happening in a short time ◆ *A late winter storm has caused a rash of accidents in and around the city.*
WORD HISTORY probably from an Old French word meaning 'a sore'

rasher *NOUN* **rashers**
a slice of bacon

rasp *NOUN* **rasps**
1 a file with sharp points on its surface
2 a rough grating sound

rasp *VERB* **rasps, rasping, rasped**
1 to scrape something roughly
2 to make a rough grating sound or effect

raspberry *NOUN* **raspberries**
an edible soft red fruit

Rastafarian *NOUN* **Rastafarians**
a member of a religious group that originated in Jamaica and which reveres Haile Selassie, the former emperor of Ethiopia, as God
WORD HISTORY from *Ras Tafari* (*ras* meaning 'chief'), the name by which Haile Selassie was known

rat *NOUN* **rats**
1 an animal like a large mouse
2 an unpleasant or treacherous person

rat *VERB* **rats, ratting, ratted**
to rat on someone (*informal*) to betray or inform on someone
WORD HISTORY from Old English *ræt*

ratatouille (*say* rat- a- **too**- i) *NOUN*
a vegetable dish consisting of onions, courgettes, tomatoes, and peppers, stewed in oil
WORD HISTORY a French dialect word

ratchet *NOUN* **ratchets**
a row of notches on a bar or wheel in which a device catches to prevent it running backwards
WORD HISTORY from French *rochet*

rate *NOUN* **rates**
1 a measure obtained by expressing the quantity or amount of one thing with respect to another

Because I was a half-vampire I aged at only a fifth the rate of humans. — *Darren Shan, Tunnels of Blood*

2 speed of movement or change ◆ *The bus chugged uphill at a painfully slow rate.*
3 a fixed charge, cost, or value ◆ *Postage rates are due to go up in the New Year.*
at any rate anyway; whatever else is true

rate *VERB* **rates, rating, rated**
1 to put a value on something
2 to regard or be regarded in a certain way

The witches sat in careful silence. This was not going to rate among the hundred most exciting coven meetings of all time. — *Terry Pratchett, Wyrd Sisters*

WORD HISTORY from Latin *ratum* 'reckoned'

rates *PLURAL NOUN*
a local tax paid by owners of commercial land and buildings

rather *ADVERB*
1 slightly or somewhat ◆ *I've had rather too much to eat.* ◆ *They were met at the door by a rather grumpy housekeeper.*
2 preferably or more willingly ◆ *I would rather wait till tomorrow.*
3 more exactly; instead of

'Dr Torrance is an eminent psychiatrist, rather than a schoolmaster,' Bernard explained. — *John Wyndham, The Midwich Cuckoos*

4 (*informal*) definitely; yes ◆ *'Would you like to see my latest invention?' 'Rather!'*

ratify *VERB* **ratifies, ratifying, ratified**
to ratify a treaty or other agreement is to confirm or agree to it officially
▷ **ratification** *NOUN*
WORD HISTORY from Latin *ratus* 'fixed or established'

rating *NOUN* **ratings**
1 the way something is rated; the value of something
2 a sailor who is not an officer

ratio (*say* **ray**- shee- oh) *NOUN* **ratios**
1 (*Mathematics*) the relationship between two numbers, given by the quotient ◆ *The ratio of 2 to 10* $= 2{:}10 = \frac{2}{10} = \frac{1}{5}$.
2 proportion ◆ *Mix flour and butter in the ratio of two to one.* (two measures of flour to one measure of butter)
WORD HISTORY a Latin word meaning *ratus* 'reasoning, reckoning'

abcdefghijklmnopqrstuvwxyz

SPELLING NOTE Some words pronounced **r**- begin with **rh**- or **wr**-

ration *NOUN* **rations**
1 a fixed quantity of something, especially food, allowed to one person
2 rations are a fixed daily amount of food supplied to a soldier or member of an expedition

ration *VERB* **rations, rationing, rationed**
to share something out in fixed amounts

After that Tom was rationed to ten minutes reading in bed; and he had to promise not to switch the bedroom light on again after it had been switched off. — *Philippa Pearce, Tom's Midnight Garden*

rational *ADJECTIVE*
1 reasonable or sane

Can't you understand that Mr Harrison is suffering from depression? He is incapable of making a rational decision about his life and death. — *Brian Clark, Whose Life is it Anyway?*

2 able to reason

In a fit of enthusiastic madness I created a rational creature and was bound towards him to assure, as far as was in my power, his happiness and well-being. — *Mary Shelley, Frankenstein*

▷ **rationally** *ADVERB*
▷ **rationality** *NOUN*

rationale (*say* rash- on- **ahl**) *NOUN*
a fundamental reason, the logical basis of something

rationalize *VERB* **rationalizes, rationalizing, rationalized**
1 to make something logical and consistent ◆ *Attempts to rationalize English spelling have failed.*
2 to justify something by inventing a reasonable explanation for it ◆ *Some UFO sightings cannot be rationalized away so easily.*
3 to make a company or industry more efficient by reorganizing it

▷ **rationalization** *NOUN*

USAGE NOTE This word can also be spelled rationalise.

rat race *NOUN*
(*informal*) a continuous struggle for success in a career or business

rattle *VERB* **rattles, rattling, rattled**
1 to make a series of short sharp hard sounds
2 to rattle someone is to make them feel nervous or flustered
3 to move or travel with a rattling noise

The mule cart rattled noisily over the jigsaw of stones and summer-dried mud of the roadway. — *Mollie Hunter, The Thirteenth Member*

to rattle something off to rattle off a speech or recital is to read it through rapidly

rattle *NOUN* **rattles**
1 a rattling sound
2 a device or baby's toy that rattles

rattlesnake *NOUN* **rattlesnakes**
a poisonous American snake with a tail that rattles

rattling *ADJECTIVE*
a rattling pace or speed is vigorous and brisk

ratty *ADJECTIVE* **rattier, rattiest**
(*informal*) angry or irritable

WORD HISTORY from *rat*

raucous (*say* **raw**- kus) *ADJECTIVE*
making a loud and harsh noise

The children ... were cavorting to raucous music with a thunderous pulsating beat. — *Michael Morpurgo, The Dancing Bear*

WORD HISTORY from Latin *raucus* 'hoarse'

ravage *VERB* **ravages, ravaging, ravaged**
to do great damage to something; to devastate a place or thing

On the following day the army landed and ravaged the surrounding country and returned to the ships with much booty. — *G. A. Henty, The Dragon and the Raven*

ravages *PLURAL NOUN*
damaging effects ◆ *the ravages of war*

rave *VERB* **raves, raving, raved**
1 to talk wildly or angrily or madly
2 to rave about something is to talk very enthusiastically about it

to be raving mad (*informal*) is to be completely mad or crazy

rave *NOUN* **raves** (*informal*)
1 a very enthusiastic review
2 a large party or event with dancing to loud fast electronic music

raven *NOUN* **ravens**
a large black bird, related to the crow

WORD HISTORY from Old English *hræfn*

ravenous *ADJECTIVE*
very hungry; starving

Buck was ravenous. The pound and a half of sun-dried salmon, which was his ration for each day, seemed to go nowhere. — *Jack London, The Call of the Wild*

▷ **ravenously** *ADVERB*

WORD HISTORY from French *raviner* 'to rush or ravage'

ravine (*say* ra- **veen**) *NOUN* **ravines**
a deep narrow gorge or valley

WORD HISTORY a French word meaning 'a rush of water', because a ravine is cut by rushing water

ravings *PLURAL NOUN*
wild talk that makes no sense

ravioli *NOUN*
an Italian dish of small squares of pasta filled with meat or cheese

ravish *VERB* **ravishes, ravishing, ravished**
1 (*old use*) to rape someone
2 to fill someone with delight; to enrapture someone
▷ **ravishment** *NOUN*

WORD HISTORY from Old French *ravir*, related to *rape*

ravishing *ADJECTIVE*
extremely beautiful or attractive
▷ **ravishingly** *ADVERB*

raw *ADJECTIVE*
1 not cooked
2 in its natural state; not yet processed
3 new to a job or position; not having much experience ◆ *It was a large, inexperienced army filled with conscripts and raw recruits.*
4 a raw wound is stripped of skin and has the underlying flesh exposed
5 raw weather is cold and damp
a raw deal unfair treatment
in the raw in its true state, without a softening or refining influence
▷ **rawness** *NOUN*

raw material *NOUN* **raw materials**
the basic material from which a product is made

ray❶ *NOUN* **rays**
1 a thin line of light, heat, or other radiation
2 each of a set of lines or parts extending from a centre
3 a trace of something ◆ *This ancient herbal remedy may offer a ray of hope for eczema sufferers.*

WORD HISTORY from Latin *radius* 'ray'

ray *VERB* **rays, raying, rayed**
to spread out from a central point

ray❷ *NOUN* **ray** or **rays**
a large sea fish with a flat body and a long tail, related to the shark

WORD HISTORY from Latin *raia*

rayon *NOUN*
a synthetic fibre or cloth made from cellulose

WORD HISTORY a made- up word, probably based on French *rayon* 'a ray of light', because of its shiny surface

raze *VERB* **razes, razing, razed**
to raze a building or town to the ground is to destroy it completely

WORD HISTORY from Latin *rasum* 'scraped'

razor *NOUN* **razors**
an instrument with a sharp blade or cutters, used to shave hair from the face or body

WORD HISTORY from *raze*

razzmatazz *NOUN*
(*informal*) showy publicity or display

RC *ABBREVIATION*
Roman Catholic

reach *VERB* **reaches, reaching, reached**
1 to go as far as a place or point
2 to succeed in achieving something

Airship technology had reached levels that even the Ancients had never dreamed of. — *Philip Reeve, Mortal Engines*

3 to extend in time ◆ *The family reaches back for ten generations.*
4 to stretch out your hand to get or touch something
5 to make contact with someone ◆ *You can reach me on my mobile.*
▷ **reachable** *ADJECTIVE*

reach *NOUN* **reaches**
1 the distance a person or thing can reach
2 a distance you can easily travel ◆ *We've rented a cottage within reach of the sea.*
3 a straight stretch of a river or canal

reaches *PLURAL NOUN*
an area or level of a particular place

At its lower reaches, the Twilight Woods give way to the Mire. — *Paul Stewart and Chris Riddell, Beyond the Deep Woods*

react *VERB* **reacts, reacting, reacted**
1 to respond to something; to have a reaction
2 to undergo a chemical change

WORD HISTORY from Latin *agere* 'to act or do'

reaction *NOUN* **reactions**
1 an effect or feeling produced in one person or thing by another ◆ *My immediate reaction was one of shock.*
2 a chemical change caused when substances act upon each other
3 a response by the body to a drug or other substance ◆ *an allergic reaction*
4 your reactions are your ability to respond quickly to an event or situation

reactionary *ADJECTIVE*
opposed to change or reform

reactionary *NOUN* **reactionaries**
a person who is opposed to progress or reform

reactor *NOUN* **reactors**
an apparatus for producing nuclear power in a controlled way

read (*sounds like* red) *VERB* **reads, reading, read**
1 to look at something written or printed and understand it or say it aloud
2 a computer reads data when it copies, searches, or extracts it
3 to indicate or register a number or amount ◆ *The thermometer reads 20° Celsius.*
4 to study a subject at university
▷ **readable** *ADJECTIVE*

reader *NOUN* **readers**
1 a person who reads
2 a book that helps you learn to read

readership ***NOUN*** **readerships**
the readers of a newspaper or magazine; the number of these

readily (*say* red- il- ee) ***ADVERB***
1 keenly or willingly
2 easily; without any difficulty ◆ *Many different shapes of pasta are now readily available in supermarkets.*

reading ***NOUN*** **readings**
1 the action of reading books or literature
2 the figure shown on a meter, gauge, or other instrument
3 a gathering of people at which something is read aloud ◆ *The bookshop plans to host a poetry reading every month.*

ready ***ADJECTIVE*** **readier, readiest**
1 fully prepared to do something; completed and able to be used ◆ *Are you ready to go?* ◆ *When will tea be ready?*
2 willing to do something
3 sharp and lively ◆ *Cassandra was a woman of ready wit, famed for her impromptu verses and stories.*
at the ready ready for use or action
▷ **readiness** ***NOUN***

ready ***VERB*** **readies, readying, readied**
to get ready; to prepare yourself

ready ***ADVERB***
beforehand, previously ◆ *There has been an increasing demand for gourmet ready-cooked meals.*

ready-made ***ADJECTIVE***
1 ready-made food is sold ready to be served, sometimes after being heated up
2 a ready-made excuse or opinion is one that belongs to a familiar pattern and is not original

reagent (*say* ree- ay- jent) ***NOUN*** **reagents**
a substance used in a chemical reaction, especially to detect another substance

real ***ADJECTIVE***
1 existing or true; not imaginary ◆ *I remember everything that happened in my dream, it seemed so real.*
2 genuine; not an imitation ◆ *This painting is a copy: the real Mona Lisa is in the Louvre.*
WORD HISTORY from Latin *res* 'a thing'

real estate ***NOUN***
(*American*) property consisting of land and buildings

realism ***NOUN***
the fact of seeing or showing things as they really are
▷ **realist** ***NOUN***

realistic ***ADJECTIVE***
1 true to life ◆ *The computer animation is filled with crisp and realistic images.*
2 seeing things as they really are
▷ **realistically** ***ADVERB***

reality ***NOUN*** **realities**
1 what is real; the truth

> I have plenty of dreams, but the reality is that we'll have to stay here until the war is over. — *Anne Frank, The Diary of a Young Girl*

2 something real ◆ *The dream of colonizing Mars could become a reality in the next millennium.*

realize ***VERB*** **realizes, realizing, realized**
1 to be fully aware of something; to accept something as true ◆ *I realize that you are not interested in stamp collecting.*
2 to make a hope or plan happen ◆ *Sarah will realize her greatest ambition when she competes in the Olympics.*
3 to obtain money in exchange for something by selling it
▷ **realization** ***NOUN***
USAGE NOTE This word can also be spelled realise.

really ***ADVERB***
1 truly or in fact

> What we call our gargoyle is really just a carved stone head high above the kitchen fireplace. — *Dodie Smith, I Capture the Castle*

2 extremely; very ◆ *The last question was really tricky.*
3 an expression of interest, surprise, doubt, or protest ◆ *'My little brother hates ice cream.' 'Really?'*

realm (*say* relm) ***NOUN*** **realms**
1 a kingdom

> By that time the dwarves had gone on again, a long, long, way on into the dark tunnels of the goblins' realm. — *J. R. R. Tolkien, The Hobbit*

2 an area of knowledge or interest ◆ *the realms of science fiction*
WORD HISTORY from an Old French word, related to *regiment*

ream ***NOUN*** **reams**
a quantity of paper (about 500 sheets) of the same size
WORD HISTORY via French fromArabic *rizma* 'a bundle'

reams ***PLURAL NOUN***
a large quantity of writing or other information ◆ *Almost every company these days collects reams of data about its customers.*

reap ***VERB*** **reaps, reaping, reaped**
1 to cut down and gather corn when it is ripe
2 to gain something as the result of your actions ◆ *The athletes are now reaping the benefits of months of hard training.*
▷ **reaper** ***NOUN***
WORD HISTORY from Old English *ripan*

reappear ***VERB*** **reappears, reappearing, reappeared**
to appear again

reappraise *VERB* **reappraises, reappraising, reappraised**
to think about or examine something again
▷ **reappraisal** *NOUN*

rear❶ *NOUN*
1 the back part of something
2 (*informal*) the buttocks of a person or animal
to bring up the rear is to come last in a line or race

rear *ADJECTIVE*
placed at the back of something
WORD HISTORY from Latin *retro-* 'back'

rear❷ *VERB* **rears, rearing, reared**
1 to bring up young children or animals
2 to rise

The hill whose sides we were now assaulting reared up in an almost perfect cone. — *Gerald Durrell, A Zoo in My Luggage*

3 an animal rears or rears up when it raises itself upright on its hind legs
4 to build or set something up

They reared the ladder against the wall in the yard, and Roger climbed up while Gwyn stood on the bottom rung. — *Alan Garner, The Owl Service*

rearguard *NOUN* **rearguards**
troops protecting the rear of an army
to fight a rearguard action is to go on defending or resisting something even though you are losing

rearrange *VERB* **rearranges, rearranging, rearranged**
to arrange things in a different way or order

By ten o'clock, Miss Crocker has rearranged our seating and written our names on her seating chart. — *Mildred D. Taylor, Roll of Thunder, Hear My Cry*

▷ **rearrangement** *NOUN*

reason *NOUN* **reasons**
1 a cause or explanation of something ◆ *What is the reason for the delay?*
2 reasoning; common sense ◆ *The film depicts Stalin as a stubborn leader who never listens to reason.*
USAGE NOTE Try to avoid using *the reason … is because*. It is better to say *The reason we can't come is that we both have flu* (not 'The reason we can't come is because we both have flu').

reason *VERB* **reasons, reasoning, reasoned**
1 to use your ability to think and draw conclusions
2 to try to persuade someone by giving reasons ◆ *Some players tried to reason with the referee, but the goal was still disallowed.*
WORD HISTORY from an Old French word, related to *ratio*

reasonable *ADJECTIVE*
1 ready to use or listen to reason; sensible or logical
2 fair or moderate; not expensive ◆ *The restaurant offers superb food at reasonable prices.*
3 acceptable or fairly good

If you are looking around the sky with a reasonable telescope, most stars and planets look rather similar. — *Kjartan Poskitt, The Gobsmacking Galaxy*

▷ **reasonably** *ADVERB*

reassure *VERB* **reassures, reassuring, reassured**
to restore someone's confidence by removing doubts and fears
▷ **reassurance** *NOUN*

rebate *NOUN* **rebates**
a reduction in the amount to be paid; a partial refund
WORD HISTORY from French *abattre* 'to beat down, to abate'

rebel (*say* rib- **el**) *VERB* **rebels, rebelling, rebelled**
1 (*History*) to resist an established government or ruler
2 to resist authority, control, or convention

rebel (*say* **reb**- el) *NOUN* **rebels**
(*History*) someone who rebels against the government, or against accepted standards of behaviour
WORD HISTORY from Latin *bellum* 'war', because the word originally meant a defeated enemy who began to fight again

rebellion *NOUN* **rebellions**
1 the action of rebelling against authority
2 (*History*) an organized armed resistance to the government; a revolt

rebellious *ADJECTIVE*
a rebellious person is often rebelling against authority, or is not easily controlled

rebirth *NOUN*
a return to life or activity; a revival of something ◆ *The European Renaissance witnessed a rebirth of interest in classical learning.*

reboot *VERB* **reboots, rebooting, rebooted**
to boot a computer system again

rebound *VERB* **rebounds, rebounding, rebounded**
to bounce back after hitting something

rebound *NOUN*
on the rebound to hit a ball on the rebound is to hit it when it has bounced up or back

rebuff *NOUN* **rebuffs**
an unkind refusal; a snub

rebuff *VERB* **rebuffs, rebuffing, rebuffed**
to give someone a rebuff
WORD HISTORY from Italian *buffo* 'a gust or puff'

rebuild *VERB* **rebuilds, rebuilding, rebuilt**
to build something again after it has been destroyed

a b c d e f g h i j k l m n o p q r s t u v w x y z

rebuke *VERB* **rebukes, rebuking, rebuked**
to speak severely to a person who has done wrong

Dr Feltham couldn't help rebuking his colleague for his unprofessional way of speaking. — *Anne Fine, Flour Babies*

rebuke *NOUN* **rebukes**
a sharp or severe criticism

WORD HISTORY from an earlier meaning 'to force back', from Old French *buker* 'to hit'

rebut *VERB* **rebuts, rebutting, rebutted**
to claim or prove that a criticism or accusation is not true
▷ **rebuttal** *NOUN*

WORD HISTORY from Old French *boter* 'to butt'

recalcitrant *ADJECTIVE*
disobedient or uncooperative
▷ **recalcitrance** *NOUN*

WORD HISTORY from Latin *recalcitrare* 'to kick back'

recall *VERB* **recalls, recalling, recalled**
1 to bring something back into your mind; to remember something
2 to ask a person to come back
3 to ask for an item to be returned

recall *NOUN*
1 the ability to remember; the act of remembering something
2 an order for a person to return, or for an item to be returned

recant *VERB* **recants, recanting, recanted**
to state formally and publicly that you no longer believe something
▷ **recantation** *NOUN*

WORD HISTORY from Latin *recantare* meaning literally 'to sing back'

recap *VERB* **recaps, recapping, recapped**
(*informal*) to recapitulate

recap *NOUN*
a recapitulation

recapitulate *VERB* **recapitulates, recapitulating, recapitulated**
to state again the main points of a plan or discussion

recapitulation *NOUN*
a restatement of the main points of a plan or discussion

WORD HISTORY from Latin *capitulare* 'to arrange under headings'

recapture *VERB* **recaptures, recapturing, recaptured**
1 to capture a person or place again
2 to bring or get back a mood or feeling

recapture *NOUN*
the action of recapturing someone or something

recce (*say* **rek**- ee) *NOUN*
(*informal*) a search or exploration

WORD HISTORY short for *reconnaissance*

recede *VERB* **recedes, receding, receded**
1 to move back or further away

As I watched, the planet seemed to grow larger and smaller and to advance and recede, but that was simply that my eye was tired. — *H. G. Wells, The War of the Worlds*

2 pain recedes when it becomes less severe
3 hair recedes when it stops growing at the temples and above the forehead

WORD HISTORY from Latin *recedere* 'to go back'

receipt (*say* ris- **eet**) *NOUN* **receipts**
1 a written statement that money has been paid or something has been received
2 the action of receiving something, or of being received ◆ *on receipt of your letter*

receive *VERB* **receives, receiving, received**
1 to take or get something that is given or sent to you
2 to experience or be treated with something ◆ *One man received injuries to his hands and face.*
3 to react to something in a particular way ◆ *We received the news of her sudden death with sadness.* ◆ *I received the news of your appointment with great delight.*
4 to greet a guest or visitor

WORD HISTORY from Latin *recipere* 'to take back'

receiver *NOUN* **receivers**
1 a person or thing that receives something
2 a person who buys and sells stolen goods
3 an official who takes charge of a bankrupt person's property
4 a radio or television set that receives broadcasts
5 the part of a telephone that receives the sound and is held to a person's ear

recent *ADJECTIVE*
happening or made or done a short time ago ◆ *The newsletter gives details of our most recent events and activities.* ◆ *Please enclose a recent photograph with your application.*
▷ **recently** *ADVERB*

WORD HISTORY from Latin *recens*

receptacle *NOUN* **receptacles**
an object which holds or contains what is put into it

reception *NOUN* **receptions**
1 the way a person or thing is received
2 a formal party to receive guests
3 a place in a hotel or office where visitors are greeted and registered
4 the first class in an infant school
5 the quality of television or radio signals ◆ *We have quite poor reception because of the surrounding hills.*

receptionist *NOUN* **receptionists**
a person whose job is to greet and deal with visitors, clients, or patients

receptive *ADJECTIVE*
a receptive person is quick or willing to receive ideas
▷ **receptiveness** *NOUN*
▷ **receptivity** *NOUN*

recess (*say* ris- **ess**) *NOUN* **recesses**
1 a small hollow or alcove set back from a wall or other surface
2 recesses are the hidden or secret parts of something
3 a time when work or business is stopped for a while ◆ *Parliament is in recess for the summer.*

recession *NOUN* **recessions**
1 a temporary decline in a country's trade or prosperity
2 the action of receding from a point or level

recharge *VERB* **recharges, recharging, recharged**
1 to reload a gun with ammunition
2 to put an electric charge in a used battery so that it will work again
3 to regain your strength or energy after a period of exertion
▷ **rechargeable** *ADJECTIVE*

recherché (*say* ri- **shair**- shay) *ADJECTIVE*
rare, exotic, or obscure
WORD HISTORY a French word meaning 'carefully sought out'

recipe (*say* **ress**- ip- ee) *NOUN* **recipes**
1 a set of instructions for preparing or cooking a dish
2 a course of action likely to lead to something ◆ *a recipe for disaster*
WORD HISTORY a Latin word meaning 'take', which was used at the beginning of a list of ingredients

recipient *NOUN* **recipients**
a person who receives something

reciprocal (*say* ris- **ip**- rok- al) *ADJECTIVE*
1 affecting each of two people, groups, or countries equally; mutual ◆ *The UK has a reciprocal agreement with several countries regarding emergency healthcare.*
2 given or done in return ◆ *After last year's trip to China, we are looking forward to a reciprocal visit from a school in Beijing.*
▷ **reciprocally** *ADVERB*
▷ **reciprocity** *NOUN*

reciprocal *NOUN* **reciprocals**
(*Mathematics*) a reversed fraction, ◆ $\frac{3}{2}$ *is the reciprocal of* $\frac{2}{3}$.
WORD HISTORY from Latin *reciprocus* 'moving backwards and forwards'

reciprocate *VERB* **reciprocates, reciprocating, reciprocated**
to return a feeling or gesture to someone who gives it to you; to do the same thing in return ◆ *Daphne did not reciprocate Apollo's love and fled to the mountains, where she was transformed into a laurel tree.*
▷ **reciprocation** *NOUN*

recital *NOUN* **recitals**
1 the action of reciting something
2 a musical entertainment given by one performer or group

recite *VERB* **recites, reciting, recited**
to repeat a poem or passage aloud from memory, especially before an audience

Miss Brodie was reciting poetry to the class at a quarter to four, to raise their minds before they went home. — *Muriel Spark, The Prime of Miss Jean Brodie*

▷ **recitation** *NOUN*
WORD HISTORY from Latin *recitare* 'to read aloud'

reckless *ADJECTIVE*
rash; ignoring risk or danger ◆ *Though climbing without a guide was considered reckless, Mallory paid no attention, and returned to the Alps again and again.*
▷ **recklessly** *ADVERB*
▷ **recklessness** *NOUN*
WORD HISTORY from an old word *reck* meaning 'to heed or care'

reckon *VERB* **reckons, reckoning, reckoned**
1 (*informal*) to have something as an opinion; to think or believe something

Do you reckon we should have used a thicker rope? This one nearly broke last time he used it. — *Tim Bowler, Starseeker*

2 to calculate an amount or total
to reckon on something is to rely or base your plans on it ◆ *The festival organizers were reckoning on the support of the local council.*
to reckon with something is to think about or deal with it ◆ *We didn't reckon with the rail strike when we planned our journey.*
someone to be reckoned with is someone who must not be underestimated
WORD HISTORY from an Old English word meaning 'to tell or explain'

reclaim *VERB* **reclaims, reclaiming, reclaimed**
1 to take action in order to get something back
2 to reclaim flooded or waste land is to make it able to be used again
▷ **reclamation** *NOUN*

recline *VERB* **reclines, reclining, reclined**
1 to lean or lie back
2 a seat reclines when the back part of it is tilted backwards
WORD HISTORY from Latin *reclinare* 'to bend or lean back'

SPELLING NOTE Some words pronounced **r-** begin with **rh-** or **wr-**

recluse *NOUN* **recluses**
a person who lives alone and avoids mixing with people
▷ **reclusive** *ADJECTIVE*
▷ **reclusiveness** *NOUN*
WORD HISTORY from Latin *recludere* 'to shut again'

recognize *VERB* **recognizes, recognizing, recognized**
1 to know who someone is or what something is because you have seen that person or thing before
2 to realize or admit the nature of something ◆ *Ancient humans recognized that the Sun's light and warmth were necessary for their survival.*
3 to show appreciation of someone's ability or service, especially by giving them an award
4 to acknowledge or accept something formally as genuine, valid, or lawful ◆ *France has recognized the island's new government.*
▷ **recognition** *NOUN*
▷ **recognizable** *ADJECTIVE*
▷ **recognizably** *ADVERB*
WORD HISTORY from Latin *recognoscere* 'to know again'
USAGE NOTE This word can also be spelled recognise.

recoil *VERB* **recoils, recoiling, recoiled**
1 to move back suddenly in shock or disgust
2 a gun recoils when it jerks backwards when it is fired

recollect *VERB* **recollects, recollecting, recollected**
to remember someone or something
▷ **recollection** *NOUN*
WORD HISTORY from Latin *recolligere* 'to collect again'

recommence *VERB* **recommences, recommencing, recommenced**
to start, or make something start, again
▷ **recommencement** *NOUN*

recommend *VERB* **recommends, recommending, recommended**
1 to say that a person or thing is suitable for a job or task
2 to advise someone to do something
3 to make something acceptable or desirable ◆ *This plan has much to recommend it.*
▷ **recommendation** *NOUN*
WORD HISTORY from Latin *commendare* 'to commend'

recompense *VERB* **recompenses, recompensing, recompensed**
1 to repay or reward someone
2 to compensate someone for a loss or injury

recompense *NOUN*
compensation or reward for something
WORD HISTORY from Latin *compensare* 'to balance out'

reconcile *VERB* **reconciles, reconciling, reconciled**
1 to make people who have quarrelled become friendly again
2 to get someone to accept an unwelcome fact or situation ◆ *It took me a while to reconcile myself to wearing glasses.*
3 to reconcile a fact or statement with another is to make them agree or be compatible
▷ **reconcilable** *ADJECTIVE*
▷ **reconciliation** *NOUN*
WORD HISTORY from Latin *reconciliare*

recondite (*say* **rek**- on- dyt) *ADJECTIVE*
a recondite subject is one that is understood only by specialists or experts
WORD HISTORY from Latin *recondere* 'to hide away'

recondition *VERB* **reconditions, reconditioning, reconditioned**
to overhaul and repair something

reconnaissance (*say* rik- **on**- i- sans) *NOUN*
1 an exploration of an area, especially in order to gather information about it for military purposes
2 a preliminary survey
WORD HISTORY a French word meaning 'recognition'

reconnoitre *VERB* **reconnoitres, reconnoitring, reconnoitred**
to make a reconnaissance of an area
WORD HISTORY an Old French word meaning 'to recognize'

reconsider *VERB* **reconsiders, reconsidering, reconsidered**
to consider something again and perhaps change your previous decision
▷ **reconsideration** *NOUN*

reconstitute *VERB* **reconstitutes, reconstituting, reconstituted**
1 to form something again, especially in a different way
2 to reconstitute dried food is to make it edible again by adding water

reconstruct *VERB* **reconstructs, reconstructing, reconstructed**
1 to construct or build something again
2 to create or act out past events again ◆ *Police officers have reconstructed the scene in order to determine the cause of the accident.*
▷ **reconstruction** *NOUN*

record (*say* **rek**- ord) *NOUN* **records**
1 information kept in a permanent form, e.g. written or printed
2 a disc on which sound has been recorded
3 the best performance in a sport or other activity, or the most remarkable event of its kind ◆ *Pelé holds the world record for the number of goals scored in international football.*

4 facts known about the history or past performance of a person, group, or institution ◆ *All applicants must have a proven record of teaching.* ◆ *The club has an excellent record in coaching world-class tennis players.*

for the record so that the true facts are recorded or known

off the record stated unofficially or not for publication or broadcast

on record preserved in written records

to put or set the record straight is to correct a mistaken belief

record *ADJECTIVE*
best, highest, or most extreme recorded up to now ◆ *We are expecting record temperatures for this time of year.*

record (*say* rik-**ord**) *VERB* **records, recording, recorded**
1 to put something down in writing or other permanent form
2 to store sounds or scenes (e.g. television pictures) on a disc or magnetic tape so that you can play or show them later

WORD HISTORY an Old French word meaning 'remembrance'

recorder *NOUN* **recorders**
1 a kind of flute held downwards from the player's mouth
2 a person or thing that records something

recount¹ (*say* ri- **kownt**) *VERB* **recounts, recounting, recounted**
to give an account of an experience or event

Ayrton then in a few words recounted what had happened, or, at least, as much as he knew. — *Jules Verne, The Mysterious Island*

WORD HISTORY from Old French *reconter* 'to tell'

recount² (*say* ree- **kownt**) *VERB* **recounts, recounting, recounted**
to count something again

recount (*say* **ree**- kownt) *NOUN* **recounts**
the process of counting something again, especially the votes in an election or referendum

recoup (*say* ri- **koop**) *VERB* **recoups, recouping, recouped**
to recover the cost of an investment, or of a loss

WORD HISTORY from Old French

USAGE NOTE Take care not to confuse this word with *recuperate*, which has a different meaning.

recourse *NOUN*
a source of help or support

to have recourse to someone or something is to turn to them or it for help

WORD HISTORY from Old French *recours*

recover *VERB* **recovers, recovering, recovered**
1 to get something back again after losing it; to regain something
2 to get well again after being ill or weak
▷ **recoverable** *ADJECTIVE*

recovery *NOUN* **recoveries**
1 a return to a state of health or strength
2 the action or process of recovering something ◆ *There is to be a substantial reward for the recovery of the stolen painting.*

recreate *VERB* **recreates, recreating, recreated**
to create something again; to reconstruct something ◆ *Archaeologists have been able to recreate the likenesses of ancient people from their remains.*

recreation *NOUN* **recreations**
1 the process of refreshing or entertaining yourself after work by some enjoyable activity
2 a game or hobby that is an enjoyable activity
▷ **recreational** *ADJECTIVE*

recrimination *NOUN* **recriminations**
an accusation made against a person who has criticized or blamed you

WORD HISTORY from Latin *criminare* 'to accuse'

recruit *NOUN* **recruits**
1 a person who has just joined the armed forces
2 a new member of a society, company, or other group

recruit *VERB* **recruits, recruiting, recruited**
1 to enlist or enrol someone as a recruit
2 to persuade someone to do or help with something
▷ **recruitment** *NOUN*

WORD HISTORY from French *recroître* 'to increase again'

rectangle *NOUN* **rectangles**
a geometric figure with four sides and four right angles, especially one with adjacent sides of unequal length
▷ **rectangular** *ADJECTIVE*

WORD FAMILY *Rectangle* comes from the Latin word *rectus* meaning 'straight' or 'right'. Other words to do with being straight or right and having the same origin include *correct, direct, erect, rectify, rectitude*, and *rectum*.

rectify *VERB* **rectifies, rectifying, rectified**
to correct an error; to put something right
▷ **rectifiable** *ADJECTIVE*
▷ **rectification** *NOUN*

rectilinear *ADJECTIVE*
a rectilinear figure is bounded by straight lines

rectitude *NOUN*
morally correct behaviour

rector *NOUN* **rectors**
1 a member of the Church of England clergy in charge of a parish
2 the head of certain universities, colleges, schools, and religious institutions
3 the students' elected representative on the governing body of a Scottish university

WORD HISTORY a Latin word meaning 'ruler'

rectum *NOUN* **rectums** or **recta**
the last part of the large intestine, ending at the anus

WORD HISTORY a Latin word meaning 'straight (intestine)'

recumbent *ADJECTIVE*
1 lying down, reclining
2 a recumbent bicycle is designed to be ridden in a reclined position with your back supported and your feet out in front

WORD HISTORY from Latin *recumbere* 'to lie back'

recuperate *VERB* **recuperates, recuperating, recuperated**
to get better after an illness, accident, or exhaustion

After my birth mother was sent to recuperate for some weeks and I was kept in the hospital while she was away. — *Christy Brown, My Left Foot*

▷ **recuperation** *NOUN*
▷ **recuperative** *ADJECTIVE*

WORD HISTORY from Latin *recuperare* 'to regain'

recur *VERB* **recurs, recurring, recurred**
1 to happen again; to keep on happening
2 a thought recurs when it comes back to your mind

▷ **recurrent** *ADJECTIVE*
▷ **recurrence** *NOUN*

WORD HISTORY from Latin *recurrere* 'to run back'

recurring decimal *NOUN* **recurring decimals**
(*Mathematics*) a decimal fraction in which a digit or group of digits is repeated indefinitely, e.g. 0.666 …

recycle *VERB* **recycles, recycling, recycled**
to convert waste material into a form in which it can be used again

red *ADJECTIVE* **redder, reddest**
1 the colour of blood
2 red hair or fur is of a reddish brown colour
3 a red face is flushed with embarrassment or anger
4 (*informal*) communist or socialist

▷ **redness** *NOUN*

red *NOUN*
1 a red colour
2 (*informal*) a communist or socialist

in the red (*informal*) in debt

to see red is to become suddenly angry

red deer *NOUN* **red deer**
a kind of large deer with a reddish brown coat, found in Europe and Asia

redden *VERB* **reddens, reddening, reddened**
1 to make something red, or to become red
2 to blush

reddish *ADJECTIVE*
fairly red

red dwarf *NOUN* **red dwarfs** or **red dwarves**
a small faint cool star

redeem *VERB* **redeems, redeeming, redeemed**
1 to make up for faults or deficiencies
2 to buy something back or pay off a debt
3 to save a person from damnation, as in some religions

a redeeming feature a positive feature that makes up for other faults

to redeem yourself is to make up for doing badly in the past

▷ **redeemer** *NOUN*
▷ **redemption** *NOUN*

WORD HISTORY from Latin *redimere* 'to buy back'

redeploy *VERB* **redeploys, redeploying, redeployed**
to deploy something, especially troops, again or differently

▷ **redeployment** *NOUN*

redevelop *VERB* **redevelops, redeveloping, redeveloped**
to develop a place or area in a different way

▷ **redeveloper** *NOUN*
▷ **redevelopment** *NOUN*

red giant *NOUN* **red giants**
a very large cool star

red-handed *ADJECTIVE*

to catch someone red-handed is to catch them in the act of doing something wrong

WORD HISTORY called this because someone who had just committed a murder or some other violent act would have red blood on their hands

redhead *NOUN* **redheads**
a person with red or reddish hair

red herring *NOUN* **red herrings**
something that draws attention away from the main subject; a misleading clue

WORD HISTORY called this because a 'red herring' (i.e. a kipper) put the hounds off the scent when it was dragged across the path of the fox being hunted

red-hot *ADJECTIVE*
very hot; so hot that it has turned red

Red Indian *NOUN* **Red Indians**
(*old use*) a Native American from North America

USAGE NOTE This term is now regarded as offensive and should not be used. The preferred term is *Native American*. See the note at *Indian*.

redirect *VERB* **redirects, redirecting, redirected**
to send or direct someone or something to a different place
▷ **redirection** *NOUN*

rediscover *VERB* **rediscovers, rediscovering, rediscovered**
to discover something again
▷ **rediscovery** *NOUN*

redistribute *VERB* **redistributes, redistributing, redistributed**
to distribute something again or differently
▷ **redistribution** *NOUN*

red-letter day *NOUN* **red-letter days**
a special or memorable day

WORD HISTORY from the practice of highlighting a festival in red on a calendar

red-light district *NOUN*
an area in a city where there are many prostitutes, strip clubs, etc.

red meat *NOUN*
meat such as beef, lamb, or mutton, which is red when raw

redo *VERB* **redoes, redoing, redid, redone**
to do something again or differently

redolent (*say* **red**- ol- ent) *ADJECTIVE*
1 smelling or tasting strongly of something ◆ *The soup was redolent of fresh tomatoes and basil.*
2 strongly suggesting or reminding you of something ◆ *His music is redolent of his Russian homeland.*
▷ **redolence** *NOUN*

WORD HISTORY from Latin *redolere* 'to smell strongly'

redouble *VERB* **redoubles, redoubling, redoubled**
to redouble an attempt or effort is to make it greater or more intense

redoubtable *ADJECTIVE*
formidable, especially as an opponent

WORD HISTORY from French *redouter* ' to fear'

redound *VERB* **redounds, redounding, redounded**
(*formal*) to cause someone credit or honour

Now this affair made a noise at the time, and redounded so much to my credit that I was deeply grieved at it, because deserving none.
— *R. D. Blackmore, Lorna Doone*

WORD HISTORY from Latin *redundare* ' to overflow'

redress *VERB* **redresses, redressing, redressed**
to remedy or set something right
to redress the balance is to make things equal again

redress *NOUN*
1 the action of redressing something
2 compensation for damage, injury, or loss

WORD HISTORY from Old French *redresser*

red tape *NOUN*
the use of too many rules and forms in official business

WORD HISTORY because bundles of official papers are tied up with red or pink tape

reduce *VERB* **reduces, reducing, reduced**
1 to make something smaller or less
2 to become smaller or less
3 to force someone into an undesirable state or condition ◆ *He was reduced to borrowing from his parents.* ◆ *The ending of the film reduced most of the audience to tears.*
4 to reduce a sauce is to boil it until it becomes thicker and more concentrated
▷ **reduction** *NOUN*

WORD HISTORY from Latin *reducere* 'to bring back'

redundant *ADJECTIVE*
1 no longer needed or useful; superfluous
2 a worker is redundant when they are dismissed because they are no longer needed for a particular job
▷ **redundancy** *NOUN*

reed *NOUN* **reeds**
1 a tall plant that grows in water or marshy ground
2 a thin strip that vibrates to make the sound in a clarinet, saxophone, or oboe

reedy *ADJECTIVE* **reedier, reediest**
1 full of reeds
2 a reedy voice or sound has a thin high tone like a reed instrument
▷ **reediness** *NOUN*

reef❶ *NOUN* **reefs**
a ridge of rock, coral, or sand near the surface of the sea

WORD HISTORY via Old German or Old Dutch from an Old Norse word

reef❷ *NOUN* **reefs**
each of several strips at the top or bottom of a sail that can be drawn in to reduce the area of sail exposed to the wind

reef *VERB* **reefs, reefing, reefed**
to shorten a sail by drawing in a reef or reefs

WORD HISTORY via Dutch from an Old Norse word

reef knot *NOUN* **reef knots**
a symmetrical double knot that is very secure

a b c d e f g h i j k l m n o p q r s t u v w x y z

reek *VERB* **reeks, reeking, reeked**
1 to smell strongly or unpleasantly
2 to suggest something unwelcome or sinister ◆ *This refusal to release the document to the public reeks of a cover-up.*

reek *NOUN* **reels**
a strong unpleasant smell

The mixture of smells seemed stronger at night — a yeasty reek of flour and the fragrances of tea and spices. — *Alison Prince, Oranges and Murder*

WORD HISTORY from an Old English word meaning 'to give off smoke'

reel *NOUN* **reels**
1 a small cylinder on which cotton, thread, or photographic film is wound
2 a lively Scottish or Irish traditional dance, or the music for this

reel *VERB* **reels, reeling, reeled**
1 to wind something on to or off a reel
2 to stagger
3 to feel giddy or confused ◆ *The city is still reeling from the shock of the recent scandal.*

to reel something off is to say or recite it quickly

re-elect *VERB* **re-elects, re-electing, re-elected**
to elect a person, group, or political party again
▷ **re-election** *NOUN*

re-enter *VERB* **re-enters, re-entering, re-entered**
to enter a place or contest again
▷ **re-entry** *NOUN*

re-examine *VERB* **re-examines, re-examining, re-examined**
to examine someone or something again
▷ **re-examination** *NOUN*

ref *NOUN* **refs**
(*informal*) a sports referee

refectory *NOUN* **refectories**
the dining room of a college, monastery, or similar institution

WORD HISTORY from Latin *refectum* 'refreshed'

refer *VERB* **refers, referring, referred**
1 to refer to a person or topic is to mention or speak about them or it
2 to refer to a person as something is to describe them in this way

My father has sometimes been referred to as the prime minister of Thembuland. — *Nelson Mandela, Long Walk to Freedom*

3 a word or phrase refers to someone or something it denotes or describes ◆ *What does 'the Red Planet' refer to?*
4 to refer to a book or other source is to look in it for information
5 a doctor refers a patient to a specialist when they pass on their case for treatment
▷ **referral** *NOUN*

WORD HISTORY from Latin *referre* 'to bring or carry back'

referee *NOUN* **referees**
1 someone appointed to see that people keep to the rules of a game
2 a person willing to testify about the character or ability of someone applying for a job

referee *VERB* **referees, refereeing, refereed**
to act as a referee

WORD HISTORY meaning literally 'someone who is referred to'

reference *NOUN* **references**
1 the action of referring to something ◆ *The report made no reference to recent events.*
2 a direction to a book, page, or file where information can be found
3 a letter from a previous employer describing someone's abilities and qualities

in or with reference to concerning; about

reference book *NOUN* **reference books**
a book giving information for reference but not designed to be read straight through

reference library *NOUN* **reference libraries**
a library where books can be consulted but not taken away

referendum *NOUN* **referendums** or **referenda**
a vote on a particular question by all the people of a country

WORD HISTORY a Latin word meaning 'referring'

refill *VERB* **refills, refilling, refilled**
to fill a glass or other container again

refill *NOUN* **refills**
1 the action of refilling a glass or other container
2 something used for refilling, especially a cartridge for an ink pen

refine *VERB* **refines, refining, refined**
1 to remove impurities or defects from a substance
2 to improve something, especially by making small changes

WORD HISTORY from an old word *fine* meaning 'to make pure'

refined *ADJECTIVE*
1 purified or processed
2 cultured; having good taste or good manners

refinement *NOUN* **refinements**
1 the process of refining something, or of being refined
2 elegance of behaviour or manners
3 an improvement added to something

refinery *NOUN* **refineries**
a factory for refining a raw material, such as oil or sugar

reflect *VERB* **reflects, reflecting, reflected**
1 to send back light, heat, or sound from a surface
2 a mirror or other surface reflects an object when it shows an image of it
3 to think deeply or carefully about something
4 to be a sign of something or make it apparent ◆ *Brazil's passion for football is reflected in the number and size of stadiums all over the country.*
5 to bring about a good or bad impression of something ◆ *A poorly designed website can reflect badly upon your business.*

WORD HISTORY from Latin *reflectere* 'to bend back'

reflection *NOUN* **reflections**
1 reflection is the process of reflecting light
2 reflection is also a spell of thinking about something
3 a reflection is an image seen in a mirror or other reflecting surface
4 (*Mathematics*) the process of inverting a line or flat figure

reflective *ADJECTIVE*
1 reflecting light, heat, or sound
2 thoughtful or pensive
▷ **reflectively** *ADVERB*
▷ **reflectiveness** *NOUN*

reflector *NOUN* **reflectors**
something which reflects light, heat, or sound, especially a panel on the back of a bicycle or vehicle which reflects the lights of vehicles behind it

reflex *NOUN* **reflexes**
a movement or action done without any conscious thought

reflex angle *NOUN* **reflex angles**
an angle of more than 180°

reflexive pronoun *NOUN* **reflexive pronouns**
(*Grammar*) any of the pronouns *myself, herself, himself*, etc. (as in *She watched herself in the mirror*), which refer back to the subject of the verb

reflexive verb *NOUN* **reflexive verbs**
(*Grammar*) a verb for which the subject and the object are the same person or thing, as in *He cut himself shaving*, or *The cat washed itself*

reflexology *NOUN*
a method of massaging certain points on the feet, hands, and head, used to treat illness and relieve tension
▷ **reflexologist** *NOUN*

reform *VERB* **reforms, reforming, reformed**
1 to make changes in something in order to improve it
2 to give up a criminal or immoral lifestyle, or make someone do this
▷ **reformer** *NOUN*
▷ **reformative** *ADJECTIVE*
▷ **reformatory** *ADJECTIVE*

reform *NOUN* **reforms**
1 the process of reforming something, or of being reformed
2 a change made in order to improve something

WORD HISTORY from Latin *reformare* 'to form again'

reformat *VERB* **reformats, reformatting, reformatted**
1 to give a new format to something
2 (*ICT*) to format a computer disk or drive again

reformation *NOUN*
the process of reforming something, or of being reformed

the Reformation a religious movement in Europe in the 16th century intended to reform certain teachings and practices of the Roman Catholic Church, which resulted in the establishment of the Reformed or Protestant Churches

refract *VERB* **refracts, refracting, refracted**
to bend a ray of light at the point where it enters water or glass at an angle
▷ **refraction** *NOUN*
▷ **refractor** *NOUN*
▷ **refractive** *ADJECTIVE*

WORD HISTORY from Latin *refractus* 'broken off', from *frangere* 'to break'

refractory *ADJECTIVE*
1 difficult to control; stubborn
2 a refractory substance is resistant to heat and is hard to fuse or melt

refrain[1] *VERB* **refrains, refraining, refrained**
to stop yourself from doing something ◆ *Please refrain from talking in the corridor.*

WORD HISTORY from Latin *refrenare* 'to bridle'

refrain[2] *NOUN* **refrains**
the chorus of a song

refresh *VERB* **refreshes, refreshing, refreshed**
1 to give new strength or energy to a tired person or animal by food, drink, or rest
2 to refresh someone's drink is to refill or replenish it

to refresh someone's memory is to remind them of something by going over previous information

refresher course *NOUN* **refresher courses**
a training course to bring people's knowledge up to date

refreshing *ADJECTIVE*
1 that restores your strength or energy ◆ *a refreshing sleep*
2 pleasantly different or unusual ◆ *I found the book a refreshing change from the usual science-fiction novel.*

refreshment *NOUN* **refreshments**
1 the giving of fresh strength or energy
2 food and drink ◆ *Would you like some refreshment?*

refreshments *PLURAL NOUN*
drinks and snacks provided at an event

refrigerate *VERB* **refrigerates, refrigerating, refrigerated**
to make food or drink extremely cold, especially in order to preserve and keep it fresh
▷ **refrigeration** *NOUN*
WORD HISTORY from Latin *refrigerare* 'to chill again', from *frigus* 'cold'

refrigerator *NOUN* **refrigerators**
a cabinet in which food or drink is stored at a very low temperature

refuel *VERB* **refuels, refuelling, refuelled**
to supply a ship or aircraft with more fuel

refuge *NOUN* **refuges**
a place where a person is safe from pursuit or danger
to take refuge is to go somewhere or do something so that you are protected
WORD HISTORY from Latin *refugium*, from *fugere* 'to flee'

refugee *NOUN* **refugees**
someone who has had to leave their home or country and seek refuge elsewhere, e.g. because of war or persecution or famine

refund *VERB* **refunds, refunding, refunded**
to pay back money received or expenses that you have paid out

refund *NOUN* **refunds**
money that is paid back to you
WORD HISTORY from Latin *refundere* 'to pour back'

refurbish *VERB* **refurbishes, refurbishing, refurbished**
to freshen something up; to redecorate and repair a room or building

refusal *NOUN* **refusals**
the action of refusing something, or of being refused

refuse (*say* ri- **fewz**) *VERB* **refuses, refusing, refused**
1 to say that you are unwilling to do or give or accept something
2 a machine or vehicle refuses to start or work when it is not starting or working properly

refuse (*say* **ref**- yooss) *NOUN*
waste material; rubbish

refute *VERB* **refutes, refuting, refuted**
to prove that a person, opinion, or statement is wrong
▷ **refutation** *NOUN*
WORD HISTORY from Latin *refutare* 'to repel'
USAGE NOTE It is best to avoid using *refute* as if it meant 'to deny' or 'to repudiate'.

regain *VERB* **regains, regaining, regained**
1 to get something back after losing it

Sabriel regained consciousness slowly, her brain fumbling for connections to her senses. — *Garth Nix, Sabriel*

2 to reach a place again ◆ *It was dusk by the time we regained the shelter of the woods.*

regal (*say* **ree**- gal) *ADJECTIVE*
1 by or to do with a monarch
2 dignified and splendid; fit for a king or queen

'I've been imagining ... the wedding and everything—Diana dressed in snowy garments, with a veil, and looking as beautiful and regal as a queen. — *L. M. Montgomery, Anne of Green Gables*

WORD HISTORY from Latin *regis* 'of a king'

regale (*say* ri- **gayl**) *VERB* **regales, regaling, regaled**
to amuse or entertain someone with a story or conversation

Simon came over to the cooking rock and regaled us with a vivid dream. — *Joe Simpson, Touching the Void*

WORD HISTORY from French *régaler*

regalia (*say* ri- **gayl**- i- a) *PLURAL NOUN*
the emblems of royalty or rank, such as a crown and sceptre ◆ *The Scottish regalia are kept in Edinburgh Castle.*

regard *VERB* **regards, regarding, regarded**
1 to think of someone or something in a certain way; to consider someone or something to be

Among the Ibo the art of conversation is regarded very highly, and proverbs are the palm-oil with which words are eaten. — *Chinua Achebe, Things Fall Apart*

2 to look or gaze at someone or something

regard *NOUN*
1 consideration or heed

Figures of reptiles and beasts were painted without regard to any uniform scheme here and there upon the walls. — *Edgar Rice Burroughs, Out of Time's Abyss*

2 respect ◆ *Zoe's family had always had a great regard for history.*
3 a gaze
as regards or **in regard to** concerning; to do with ◆ *The butler was innocent as regards the first charge.*
WORD HISTORY from French *garder* 'to guard'

regarding *PREPOSITION*
concerning, about ◆ *The laws regarding copyright are quite clear.*

regardless *ADVERB*
without considering something; in spite of something ◆ *I'm booking myself a holiday next year, regardless of the cost.*

regards *PLURAL NOUN*
kind wishes sent in a message ◆ *Give your family my regards.*

regatta *NOUN* **regattas**
a meeting for boat or yacht races

WORD HISTORY from an Italian word meaning 'a fight or contest'

regency *NOUN* **regencies**
1 the fact of being a regent
2 a period when a country is ruled by a regent
the Regency (*History*) the period 1811–20 in Great Britain, when George, Prince of Wales, acted as regent

regenerate *VERB* **regenerates, regenerating, regenerated**
to give new life or strength to something
▷ **regeneration** *NOUN*

WORD HISTORY from Latin *regenerare* 'to create again'

regent *NOUN* **regents**
a person appointed to rule a country while the monarch is too young or unable to rule
Prince Regent the title of a prince who is acting as regent

WORD HISTORY from Latin *regens* 'ruling'

reggae (*say* **reg**- ay) *NOUN*
a West Indian style of popular music with a strongly accented subsidiary beat

regime (*say* ray- **zheem**) *NOUN* **regimes**
a system of government or organization ◆ *an authoritarian regime*

regiment *NOUN* **regiments**
an army unit, usually divided into battalions or companies
▷ **regimental** *ADJECTIVE*

regiment *VERB* **regiments, regimenting, regimented**
to organize people, work, or data rigidly into groups or into a pattern

WORD HISTORY from Latin *regimentum* 'rule, governing'

region *NOUN* **regions**
an area; a part of a country or of the world

Bree was the chief village of the Bree-land, a small inhabited region, like an island in the empty lands round about. — *J. R. R. Tolkien, The Fellowship of the Ring*

in the region of near, approximately ◆ *The cost will be in the region of £100.*
▷ **regional** *ADJECTIVE*
▷ **regionally** *ADVERB*

WORD HISTORY from Latin *regio* 'boundary'

register *NOUN* **registers**
1 an official list of names or items
2 a book which records information about the attendance of pupils or students
3 the range of a voice or musical instrument

register *VERB* **registers, registering, registered**
1 to list names or items in a register

Every airship has to register its flight plan before departing. — *Kenneth Oppel, Airborn*

2 an instrument registers a figure or level when it indicates or displays it
3 to make an impression on someone's mind ◆ *It did not register with me at first that there was anything unusual about the room.*
4 to express an emotion on your face or by gesture ◆ *Although he said nothing, the boy's eyes registered his disappointment.*
5 to register a letter or parcel is to pay extra for it to be sent with special care
▷ **registration** *NOUN*

WORD HISTORY from Latin *regesta* 'things recorded'

register office *NOUN* **register offices**
an office where marriages are performed and records of births, marriages, and deaths are kept

registrar *NOUN* **registrars**
1 an official whose job is to keep written records or registers
2 a doctor undergoing hospital training to be a specialist
3 the chief administrative officer in a university

registration number *NOUN* **registration numbers**
a series of letters and numbers identifying a motor vehicle

registry *NOUN* **registries**
a place where registers are kept

registry office *NOUN* **registry offices**
a register office

regress *VERB* **regresses, regressing, regressed**
to go back to an earlier or less advanced form, state, or way of behaving
▷ **regression** *NOUN*
▷ **regressive** *ADJECTIVE*

WORD HISTORY from Latin *regressus* 'gone backwards'

regret *NOUN* **regrets**
a feeling of sorrow or disappointment about something that has happened or been done
▷ **regretful** *ADJECTIVE*
▷ **regretfully** *ADVERB*

regret *VERB* **regrets, regretting, regretted**
to feel regret about something
▷ **regrettable** *ADJECTIVE*
▷ **regrettably** *ADVERB*

WORD HISTORY from Old French *regreter* 'to mourn for the dead'

a b c d e f g h i j k l m n o p q r s t u v w x y z

regular *ADJECTIVE*
1 always happening or doing something at certain times

The kid was … someone who girls laughed at and who got bullied on a regular basis. — *Keith Gray, Warehouse*

2 even or symmetrical

The walls of the tunnel by the entrance were smooth and regular, built from huge blocks of stone. — *Alan Gibbons, Shadow of the Minotaur*

3 normal, standard, or correct ◆ *the regular procedure*
4 belonging to a country's permanent armed forces ◆ *a regular soldier*
5 (*Mathematics*) having equal angles and sides
▷ **regularly** *ADVERB*
▷ **regularity** *NOUN*

WORD HISTORY from Latin *regula* 'a rule'

regulate *VERB* **regulates, regulating, regulated**
1 to control something, especially by rules
2 to make a machine work at a certain speed
▷ **regulator** *NOUN*

regulation *NOUN*
1 the action of regulating something
2 a rule or law

regurgitate *VERB* **regurgitates, regurgitating, regurgitated**
1 to bring swallowed food up again into the mouth
2 to repeat information without really thinking about or understanding it
▷ **regurgitation** *NOUN*

WORD HISTORY from Latin *regurgitare* 'to flood back', related to *gorge*

rehabilitate *VERB* **rehabilitates, rehabilitating, rehabilitated**
to restore someone to a normal life or health after a period of imprisonment, addiction, or illness
▷ **rehabilitation** *NOUN*

rehash *VERB* **rehashes, rehashing, rehashed**
(*informal*) to use old ideas or material again with no great change or improvement

rehash *NOUN*
something made of rehashed material

rehearse *VERB* **rehearses, rehearsing, rehearsed**
(*Drama*) to practise a performance or recital before performing it in front of an audience

rehearsal *NOUN* **rehearsals**
(*Drama*) the practice of a performance before the first actual performance

reign *VERB* **reigns, reigning, reigned**
1 (*History*) to rule a country as king or queen
2 to prevail or dominate ◆ *Confusion reigned in the capital.*

reign *NOUN*
(*History*) the period of time when a particular king or queen reigns

WORD HISTORY from Latin *regnum* 'royal authority'

reigning *ADJECTIVE*
currently holding a particular title ◆ *the reigning Olympic champion*

reimburse *VERB* **reimburses, reimbursing, reimbursed**
to repay money that has been spent ◆ *Your travelling expenses will be reimbursed.*
▷ **reimbursement** *NOUN*

WORD HISTORY from an old word *imburse* meaning 'to pay'

rein *NOUN* **reins**
1 a strap used to guide a horse
2 a harness used to guide a very young child when walking

reincarnation *NOUN*
the belief that after death the soul is born again in another body

reindeer *NOUN* **reindeer**
a kind of deer that lives in Arctic regions

WORD HISTORY from an Old Norse word

reinforce *VERB* **reinforces, reinforcing, reinforced**
1 to strengthen something by adding extra people or supports
2 to emphasize or strengthen an idea, belief, or feeling ◆ *Games like these can reinforce the idea that exercise is enjoyable.* ◆ *Their words only served to reinforce my sense of despair.*

reinforced concrete *NOUN*
concrete containing metal bars or wires to strengthen it

reinforcement *NOUN* **reinforcements**
1 the action of reinforcing something
2 something that reinforces

reinforcements *PLURAL NOUN*
extra troops or ships sent to strengthen a military force

reinstate *VERB* **reinstates, reinstating, reinstated**
to restore a person or thing to a previous position
▷ **reinstatement** *NOUN*

reiterate *VERB* **reiterates, reiterating, reiterated**
to say something again or repeatedly
▷ **reiteration** *NOUN*

reject (*say* ri- **jekt**) *VERB* **rejects, rejecting, rejected**
1 to refuse to accept a person or thing
2 to throw away or discard something
▷ **rejection** *NOUN*

reject (*say* ree- jekt) ***NOUN*** **rejects**
a person or thing that is rejected, especially because of being faulty or poorly made
WORD HISTORY from Latin *rejectum* 'thrown back'

rejig ***VERB*** **rejigs, rejigging, rejigged**
(*informal*) to rearrange or reorganize something ◆ *I've rejigged my website to make it easier to navigate.*

rejoice ***VERB*** **rejoices, rejoicing, rejoiced**
to feel or show great joy
WORD HISTORY from Old French *rejoir*

rejoin ***VERB*** **rejoins, rejoining, rejoined**
1 to join a person or group again
2 to join things together again

rejoinder ***NOUN*** **rejoinders**
a sharp or witty reply
WORD HISTORY from an Old French word

rejuvenate ***VERB*** **rejuvenates, rejuvenating, rejuvenated**
to make a person seem young again
▷ **rejuvenation** ***NOUN***
WORD HISTORY from Latin *juvenis* 'young'

relapse ***VERB*** **relapses, relapsing, relapsed**
1 to return to a previous condition ◆ *Having given an account of his adventure, Jake relapsed into silence.*
2 a sick or injured person relapses when they become worse after a period of improvement

> The next day the doctors were back; Tom had relapsed. — *Mark Twain, The Adventures of Tom Sawyer*

relapse ***NOUN*** **relapses**
the fact of relapsing, especially after partial recovery from illness
WORD HISTORY from Latin *relapsum* 'slipped back'

relate ***VERB*** **relates, relating, related**
1 to tell a story or give an account of something ◆ *The book relates the history of the city since Roman times.*
2 to establish a link between one thing and another ◆ *I can't relate this scene to the rest of the film.*
3 one thing relates to another when there is a link or connection between them
4 to relate to a person or animal is to understand them and get on well with them
WORD HISTORY from French *relater* 'to report', from Latin *referre* 'to bring back'

related ***ADJECTIVE***
1 belonging to the same family by birth or marriage
2 connected, linked

relation ***NOUN*** **relations**
1 a relative
2 the way one thing is related to another ◆ *The last track on the CD bears no obvious relation to the others.*
3 the action of telling a story or giving an account
4 a person's or country's relations are their dealings with others ◆ *the country's foreign relations*
in relation to in connection with

relationship ***NOUN*** **relationships**
1 the way in which people or things are connected or related to one another
2 the way in which people or groups think of and behave towards each other
3 an emotional or sexual association between two people

relative ***NOUN*** **relatives**
a person who is related to another by birth or marriage

relative ***ADJECTIVE***
connected or compared with something; compared with the average ◆ *That night we slept in the relative warmth and safety of the cave.*
relative pronoun see the language panel at **pronoun**
▷ **relatively** ***ADVERB***

relative clause ***NOUN*** **relative clauses**
(*Language*) a subordinate clause introduced by *who, whom, whose, which,* or *that*: see the language panel at **clause**

relative density ***NOUN*** **relative densities**
the ratio of the density of a substance to that of a standard substance (usually water for liquids and solids and air for gases)

relax ***VERB*** **relaxes, relaxing, relaxed**
1 to stop working; to rest
2 to become less anxious or worried
3 to make a rule less strict or severe
4 to make a limb or muscle less stiff or tense

> After a while Willie's shoulders relaxed and the gripping sensation in his stomach subsided a little. — *Michelle Magorian, Goodnight Mister Tom*

▷ **relaxed** ***ADJECTIVE***
▷ **relaxation** ***NOUN***
WORD HISTORY from Latin *relaxare* 'to loosen'

relay (*say* ri- lay) ***VERB*** **relays, relaying, relayed**
1 to pass on news
2 to transmit a message or broadcast

relay (*say* ree- lay) ***NOUN*** **relays**
1 a fresh group taking the place of another ◆ *The emergency services worked in relays to search for survivors.*
2 a relay race
3 a device for relaying a broadcast

relay race ***NOUN*** **relay races**
a race between teams in which each person covers part of the distance

a b c d e f g h i j k l m n o p q r s t u v w x y z

release *VERB* **releases, releasing, released**
1 to set something free; to unfasten something
2 to let something fall, fly, or go out
3 to make information or details available
4 to put a record on sale, or to open a film for public viewing

release *NOUN* **releases**
1 the action of releasing something, or the process of being released
2 something released, such as a new film or record
3 a device that unfastens something

WORD HISTORY from Old French *relesser*, related to *relax*

relegate *VERB* **relegates, relegating, relegated**
1 to put something into a less important place
2 to put a sports team into a lower division of a league

▷ **relegation** *NOUN*

WORD HISTORY from Latin *relegatum* 'sent away'

relent *VERB* **relents, relenting, relented**
to become less severe or more merciful

WORD HISTORY from Latin *lentare* 'to bend or soften'

relentless *ADJECTIVE*
not stopping or relenting; pitiless ◆ *Darwin saw nature in general as characterized by the relentless struggle for survival.*

▷ **relentlessly** *ADVERB*

relevant *ADJECTIVE*
related to what is being discussed or dealt with

▷ **relevance** *NOUN*

WORD HISTORY from Latin *relevare* 'to raise up'

reliable *ADJECTIVE*
able to be relied on; trustworthy

▷ **reliably** *ADVERB*
▷ **reliability** *NOUN*

reliance *NOUN*
the fact of relying or depending on someone or something

▷ **reliant** *ADJECTIVE*

relic *NOUN* **relics**
something that has survived from an earlier time

WORD HISTORY from Latin *reliquus* 'remaining'

relief *NOUN* **reliefs**
1 the ending or lessening of pain, trouble, or boredom
2 something that gives relief or help
3 help given to people in need ◆ *The UN has set up a relief fund for the victims of the earthquake.*
4 a person who takes over a turn of duty when another finishes
5 a sculpture or other design that stands out from a flat surface

relief map *NOUN* **relief maps**
a map that shows hills and valleys by shading or moulding

relieve *VERB* **relieves, relieving, relieved**
1 to remove or lessen pain, anxiety, or difficulty
2 to take over a turn of duty from someone
3 to relieve someone of something is to take it from them

to relieve yourself is to use the toilet

WORD HISTORY from Latin *relevare* 'to raise again'

religion *NOUN* **religions**
1 belief in the existence of a superhuman controlling power, especially of God or gods, usually expressed in worship
2 a particular system of beliefs and worship

WORD HISTORY from Latin *religio* 'reverence'

religious *ADJECTIVE*
1 to do with religion
2 believing firmly in a religion and taking part in its customs

▷ **religiously** *ADVERB*
▷ **religiosity** *NOUN*

relinquish *VERB* **relinquishes, relinquishing, relinquished**
to give something up; to let something go

▷ **relinquishment** *NOUN*

WORD HISTORY from Latin *relinquere* 'to leave behind'

relish *NOUN* **relishes**
1 great enjoyment, especially of food
2 pleasure at anticipating something ◆ *The team are looking forward with relish to the return match.*
3 a sauce or pickle that adds flavour to plainer food

relish *VERB* **relishes, relishing, relished**
1 to enjoy something greatly
2 to look forward to something with pleasure ◆ *I don't relish the prospect of driving home in this weather.*

WORD HISTORY from Old French *reles* 'remainder'

relive *VERB* **relives, reliving, relived**
to remember an experience very vividly, as though it was happening again

relocate *VERB* **relocates, relocating, relocated**
to move or be moved to a new place or home

reluctant *ADJECTIVE*
unwilling; not keen

▷ **reluctantly** *ADVERB*
▷ **reluctance** *NOUN*

WORD HISTORY from Latin *luctatus* 'struggling'

rely *VERB* **relies, relying, relied**
1 to rely on someone is to trust them to help or support you ◆ *You can rely on me not to tell anyone.*

2 to rely on something is to need it for a particular purpose

Anybody who doesn't rely on calculators all the time always looks cool. — *Kjartan Poskitt, Murderous Maths*

WORD HISTORY from Old French *relier* 'to bind together'

REM (*say* rem) ***ABBREVIATION***
rapid eye movement, referring to the jerky eye movements made while someone is dreaming during sleep

remain ***VERB*** **remains, remaining, remained**
1 to be left after other parts have gone or been dealt with ◆ *One big problem remained.*
2 to continue to be in the same place or condition; to stay ◆ *Fortunately the place remains a favourite resort for travellers.*

WORD HISTORY from Latin *remanere*, from *manere* 'to stay'

remainder ***NOUN***
1 the remaining part of people or things
2 (*Mathematics*) the number left after subtraction or division

remainder ***VERB*** **remainders, remaindering, remaindered**
a publisher remainders a book when they dispose of unsold copies at a reduced price

remains ***PLURAL NOUN***
1 all that is left over after other parts have been removed or destroyed

Behind the church the crumbling remains of an abbey dominated the skyline. — *G. P. Taylor, Shadowmancer*

2 ancient ruins or objects; relics
3 a person's body after death

remake (*say* ree-**mayk**) ***VERB*** **remakes, remaking, remade**
to make something again or differently

remake (*say* **ree**-mayk) ***NOUN*** **remakes**
something made again, especially a new version of a film

remand ***VERB*** **remands, remanding, remanded**
to remand a prisoner is to send them back into custody while further evidence is being gathered

on remand in custody or on bail while waiting for a trial

WORD HISTORY from Latin *mandare* 'to entrust or command'

remark ***NOUN*** **remarks**
something said; a comment

remark ***VERB*** **remarks, remarking, remarked**
1 to make a remark; to say something
2 to notice something

WORD HISTORY from French *remarquer* 'to note again'

remarkable ***ADJECTIVE***
unusual or extraordinary

One morning in April of that year, I read in the newspaper about a remarkable find of Roman silver. — *Roald Dahl, The Mildenhall Treasure*

▷ **remarkably** ***ADVERB***

remedial ***ADJECTIVE***
1 helping to cure an illness or deficiency
2 to do with the teaching of children with learning difficulties

remedy ***NOUN*** **remedies**
something that cures or relieves a disease, or that puts a matter right

remedy ***VERB*** **remedies, remedying, remedied**
to provide a remedy for something; to put a matter right

WORD HISTORY from Latin *remedium* 'medicine'

remember ***VERB*** **remembers, remembering, remembered**
1 to keep something in your mind ◆ *Please remember to switch off the lights.*
2 to bring something back into your mind

'I remember lemons,' said Winston. 'They were quite common in the 'fifties. They were so sour that it set your teeth on edge even to smell them.' — *George Orwell, Nineteen Eighty-four*

3 to remember someone to another person is to send their greetings to them ◆ *Please remember me to your mother.*

WORD HISTORY from Latin *memor* 'mindful, remembering'

remembrance ***NOUN***
the process of remembering something, or the fact of being remembered

Remembrance Sunday the Sunday nearest to 11 November, when those killed in the First and Second World Wars are commemorated

remind ***VERB*** **reminds, reminding, reminded**
1 to help or make a person remember something ◆ *Remind me to buy some stamps.*
2 to make a person think of something because of being similar

The lake was so full of holes and mounds that it reminded Stanley of pictures he'd seen of the moon. — *Louis Sachar, Holes*

reminder ***NOUN*** **reminders**
1 a thing that reminds you of something
2 a letter sent to remind you to pay a bill

WORD HISTORY from an old use of *mind* meaning 'to put into someone's mind, to mention'

reminisce (*say* rem-in-**iss**) ***VERB*** **reminisces, reminiscing, reminisced**
to think or talk about things that you remember

WORD HISTORY from Latin *reminisci* 'to remember'

reminiscence *NOUN*
1 the action of thinking or talking about past events and experiences
2 a spoken or written account of what you remember ◆ *Her letters are full of reminiscences of her voyages.*

reminiscent *ADJECTIVE*
1 tending to remind you of something

On the drive, the tyres of the car had imprinted two patterned bands, reminiscent of markings on a snake's back. — *Barry Hines, A Kestrel for a Knave*

2 inclined to reminisce
▷ **reminiscently** *ADVERB*

remiss *ADJECTIVE*
negligent; careless about doing what you ought to do ◆ *It was very remiss of me not to reply to your email.*

remission *NOUN*
1 a period during which a serious illness improves for a time
2 the reduction of a prison sentence, especially for good behaviour while in prison
3 the action of remitting something

remit (*say* ri- **mit**) *VERB* **remits, remitting, remitted**
1 to reduce or cancel a punishment or debt
2 to send money in payment to a person or place
3 to forgive a person's sins

remit (*say* **ree**- mit) *NOUN* **remits**
a task or area of activity officially given to a person, group, or project ◆ *The remit of the Inquiry is to report to Ministers, not to publish its own findings.*
WORD HISTORY from Latin *remittere* 'to send back'

remittance *NOUN* **remittances**
1 the action of sending money
2 an amount of money sent

remix *VERB* **remixes, remixing, remixed**
to produce a different version of a musical recording by changing the balance of the separate tracks

remix *NOUN* **remixes**
a remixed recording

remnant *NOUN* **remnants**
a part or piece left over from something

Round his neck was knotted the remnant of what had once been a silk bandanna. — *John Buchan, Huntingtower*

remonstrate *VERB* **remonstrates, remonstrating, remonstrated**
to remonstrate is to protest to someone about something

'I am mortal,' Scrooge remonstrated, 'and liable to fall.' — *Charles Dickens, A Christmas Carol*

▷ **remonstrance** *NOUN*
WORD HISTORY from Latin *monstrare* 'to show'

remorse *NOUN*
deep regret for having done wrong
▷ **remorseful** *ADJECTIVE*
▷ **remorsefully** *ADVERB*
WORD HISTORY from Latin *morsum* 'bitten'

remorseless *ADJECTIVE*
unpleasantly persistent or relentless
▷ **remorselessly** *ADVERB*

remote *ADJECTIVE*
1 far away in place or time
2 isolated or inaccessible
3 a remote chance, possibility, or idea is faint or slight
▷ **remotely** *ADVERB*
▷ **remoteness** *NOUN*
WORD HISTORY from Latin *remotum* 'removed'

remote control *NOUN* **remote controls**
1 the action of controlling something from a distance, usually by electricity or radio
2 a device for doing this

removable *ADJECTIVE*
able to be removed

removal *NOUN*
1 the action of removing or moving something
2 the transfer of furniture and goods when moving house

remove *VERB* **removes, removing, removed**
1 to take something away or off

Professore Flense-Filleto removed his surgeon's gloves with an audible snap. — *Debi Gliori, Pure Dead Magic*

2 to get rid of something ◆ *A dab of lemon juice should remove the stain.*

remove *NOUN* **removes**
a distance or degree away from something ◆ *The only surviving copy of the manuscript is at several removes from the original text.*
WORD HISTORY from Latin *movere* 'to move'

remunerate *VERB* **remunerates, remunerating, remunerated**
to pay or reward someone for work or a service
▷ **remuneration** *NOUN*
▷ **remunerative** *ADJECTIVE*
WORD HISTORY from Latin *remunerari* 'to reward', from *munus* 'gift'

renaissance (*say* ren- **ay**- sans) *NOUN*
a revival of something
the Renaissance the revival of classical styles of art and literature in Europe in the 14th–16th centuries
WORD HISTORY a French word meaning 'rebirth'

renal (*say* **reen**- al) *ADJECTIVE*
to do with your kidneys
WORD HISTORY from Latin *renes* 'kidneys'

rename *VERB* **renames, renaming, renamed**
to give a new name to a person or thing

rend ***VERB*** **rends, rending, rent**
(*literary*) to rip or tear something

WORD HISTORY from an Old English word

render ***VERB*** **renders, rendering, rendered**
1 to cause a person or thing to become something

This was a dreadful time, rendered the more dreadful by the gloom of the weather and the country. — *Robert Louis Stevenson, Kidnapped*

2 to represent or perform something ◆ *The artist has rendered her features with great delicacy.*
3 to give something, especially in return or exchange or as something due ◆ *a reward for services rendered*
4 to translate something ◆ *Underneath, the inscription has been rendered into English.*
5 to melt down fat

rendezvous (*say* **rond**- ay- voo) ***NOUN*** **rendezvous** (*say* **rond**- ay- vooz)
1 a meeting with someone at an agreed time and place
2 a place arranged for this

rendezvous ***VERB*** **rendezvousing, rendezvoused**
to meet at an agreed time and place

WORD HISTORY from a French phrase *rendez-vous* 'present yourselves'

rendition ***NOUN*** **renditions**
the way a piece of music, a poem, or a dramatic role is performed

renegade (*say* **ren**- ig- ayd) ***NOUN*** **renegades**
a person who deserts a group or cause and joins another

WORD HISTORY from Latin *negare* 'to deny'

renege (*say* ri- **nayg**) ***VERB*** **reneges, reneging, reneged**
to renege on your word, or on a promise or agreement, is to break it

renew ***VERB*** **renews, renewing, renewed**
1 to restore something to its original condition
2 to replace or refresh a supply of something

'The only difficulty,' continued Captain Nemo, 'is that of remaining several days without renewing our provision of air.' — *Jules Verne, 20,000 Leagues Under the Sea*

3 to arrange for a passport, card, or licence to be valid for a further period
4 to begin or make or give something again ◆ *The government is making renewed efforts to combat software piracy.*

▷ **renewal** ***NOUN***

renewable ***ADJECTIVE***
a renewable form of energy is one that can never be used up, or which can be renewed, such as power from the sun, wind, or waves

renga ***NOUN***
(*Language*) a type of Japanese poetry consisting of linked verses often composed by different poets

rennet ***NOUN***
a substance used to curdle milk in making cheese

renounce ***VERB*** **renounces, renouncing, renounced**
to give up or reject something

▷ **renunciation** ***NOUN***

WORD HISTORY from Latin *renuntiare* 'to report'

renovate ***VERB*** **renovates, renovating, renovated**
to repair a thing and make it look new

▷ **renovation** ***NOUN***

WORD HISTORY from Latin *renovare*, from *novus* 'new'

renown ***NOUN***
great fame

That night the Lord of O was a guest of the school, himself a sorcerer of renown. — *Ursula Le Guin, A Wizard of Earthsea*

WORD HISTORY from Old French *renon*, from *nomer* 'to name'

renowned ***ADJECTIVE***
famous or celebrated ◆ *Jersey is renowned for its zoo.*

rent❶ ***NOUN*** **rents**
a regular payment for the use of something, especially a house that belongs to another person

rent ***VERB*** **rents, renting, rented**
to have or allow the use of something in return for rent

rent❷ *past tense of* **rend**

rent❸ ***NOUN*** **rents**
a torn place; a split

rental ***NOUN***
1 an amount of money paid as rent
2 the action or process of renting something

reorganize ***VERB*** **reorganizes, reorganizing, reorganized**
to change the way in which something is organized

▷ **reorganization** ***NOUN***

USAGE NOTE This word can also be spelled reorganise.

rep ***NOUN*** **reps**
(*informal*) a business firm's travelling representative

repair❶ ***VERB*** **repairs, repairing, repaired**
to put something into good condition after it has been damaged or broken

▷ **repairable** ***ADJECTIVE***
▷ **repairer** ***NOUN***

a
b
c
d
e
f
g
h
i
j
k
l
m
n
o
p
q
r
s
t
u
v
w
x
y
z

repair *NOUN* **repairs**
1 the process of repairing something
2 a place where something has been mended ◆ *The repair to the dress is hardly visible.*

in good or **bad repair** in good or poor condition; well or badly maintained

WORD HISTORY from Latin *reparare* 'to get ready again'

repair ❷ *VERB* **repairs, repairing, repaired**
(*formal*) to repair to a place is to go there

reparation *NOUN* **reparations**
(*formal*) the action of making amends, or for paying for damage or loss

to make reparations is to make amends or compensate for something

reparations *PLURAL NOUN*
compensation for war damage paid by the defeated nation

repartee *NOUN*
witty replies and remarks

WORD HISTORY from French *repartir* 'to answer back'

repast *NOUN* **repasts**
(*formal*) a large meal or feast

WORD HISTORY via Old French from Latin *pascere* 'to feed'

repatriate *VERB* **repatriates, repatriating, repatriated**
to repatriate someone is to send them back to their own country

▷ **repatriation** *NOUN*

WORD HISTORY from Latin *repatriare* 'to go back home', from *patria* 'native country'

repay *VERB* **repays, repaying, repaid**
1 to pay back money borrowed or owed
2 to return a favour or kindness
3 to do something for, or give something to, a person in return ◆ *How can we ever repay you for your kindness?*

▷ **repayable** *ADJECTIVE*
▷ **repayment** *NOUN*

repeal *VERB* **repeals, repealing, repealed**
a government or ruler repeals a law when it abolishes or cancels it

▷ **repeal** *NOUN*

WORD HISTORY from Old French *rapeler* 'to appeal again'

repeat *VERB* **repeats, repeating, repeated**
1 to say or do the same thing again
2 to tell another person about something told to you

▷ **repeatedly** *ADVERB*

repeat *NOUN* **repeats**
1 the action of repeating something
2 something that is repeated, especially a television programme

WORD HISTORY from Latin *repetere* 'to seek again'

repel *VERB* **repels, repelling, repelled**
1 to drive an opponent back or away
2 an object or surface repels a substance when it prevents it from mixing or penetrating
3 to push something away by means of a physical force (SEE ALSO **attract**)
4 someone repels you when you find them disgusting or offensive

WORD HISTORY from Latin *repellere* 'to drive back'

repellent *ADJECTIVE*
1 causing disgust or distaste
2 not able to be penetrated by a specified substance ◆ *All parts of the tent are water-repellent.*

repellent *NOUN* **repellents**
a substance that repels something ◆ *an insect repellent*

▷ **repellence** *NOUN*

repent *VERB* **repents, repenting, repented**
to be sorry for what you have done or failed to do

▷ **repentance** *NOUN*
▷ **repentant** *ADJECTIVE*

repercussion *NOUN* **repercussions**
a consequence of an event or action

repertoire (*say* **rep- er- twahr**) *NOUN*
a stock of songs, plays, jokes etc. that a person or company knows and can perform

WORD HISTORY from a French word, related to *repertory*

repertory *NOUN* **repertories**
a repertoire

WORD HISTORY from Latin *repertorium* 'a list or catalogue'

repertory company *NOUN* **repertory companies**
a theatrical company that gives performances of various plays for short periods

repetition *NOUN* **repetitions**
1 the action of repeating something
2 something repeated

▷ **repetitious** *ADJECTIVE*
▷ **repetitiously** *ADVERB*

repetitive *ADJECTIVE*
full of repetitions

▷ **repetitively** *ADVERB*

rephrase *VERB* **rephrases, rephrasing, rephrased**
to express something in a different way

replace *VERB* **replaces, replacing, replaced**
1 to put a thing back in its place
2 to take the place of another person or thing
3 to put a new or different thing in place of something

▷ **replacement** *NOUN*

replay ***NOUN*** **replays**
1 a sports match played again after a draw
2 the playing or showing again of a recording

replay ***VERB*** **replays, replaying, replayed**
1 to play a match again
2 to play back a recording

replenish ***VERB*** **replenishes, replenishing, replenished**
1 to fill up a supply that has been depleted

Harry ... went to the apothecary to replenish his store of Potions' ingredients. — *J. K. Rowling, Harry Potter and the Prisoner of Azkaban*

2 to fill someone with energy or food that they need

▷ **replenishment** ***NOUN***

WORD HISTORY from Latin *plenus* 'full'

replete ***ADJECTIVE***
1 well stocked or supplied

It was a house ... replete with every modern convenience. — *Edith Nesbit, The Wouldbegoods*

2 feeling full after eating

▷ **repletion** ***NOUN***

WORD HISTORY from Latin *repletum* 'filled again'

replica ***NOUN*** **replicas**
an exact copy or reproduction of something

Little Elsa fitted her name, for she was a replica of her mother at the same age. — *Joy Adamson, Born Free*

WORD HISTORY from an Italian word

replicate ***VERB*** **replicates, replicating, replicated**
1 to make or be an exact copy of something
2 to reproduce itself ◆ *A computer virus is a program that is able to replicate.*

WORD HISTORY from Latin *replicare* 'to fold back'

reply ***NOUN*** **replies**
1 an answer to a question
2 a spoken or written message in response to a previous one

reply ***VERB*** **replies, replying, replied**
to give a reply to a person or message; to answer someone or something

report ***VERB*** **reports, reporting, reported**
1 to give an account of something you have seen, done, or studied
2 to give information about something or make something known ◆ *Do you have much progress to report?*
3 to make a formal complaint or accusation ◆ *I wish to report a break-in.*
4 to report for work or duty is to tell somebody that you have arrived or are ready to start
5 to present yourself somewhere when you arrive ◆ *Visitors are asked to report to reception.*
6 to report to a manager or supervisor is to be responsible to them in your work

report ***NOUN*** **reports**
1 a description or account of something you have seen, done, or studied
2 an account of a news story for publication or broadcasting
3 a regular statement about a pupil's or employee's work and behaviour
4 an explosive sound like that made by a gun

Here he was interrupted by a loud report, and a cannon ball came tearing through the trees and pitched in the sand not a hundred yards from where we two were talking. — *Robert Louis Stevenson, Treasure Island*

WORD HISTORY from Latin *reportare* 'to carry back'

reportage (*say* rep- or- **tahj**) ***NOUN***
the reporting of news by journalists

reportedly ***ADVERB***
according to reports

reported speech ***NOUN***
indirect speech

reporter ***NOUN*** **reporters**
a person whose job is to collect and report news for a newspaper, radio, or television programme

repose ***NOUN***
calm, rest, or sleep

repose ***VERB*** **reposes, reposing, reposed**
to rest or lie somewhere

On the table reposed a nut cake which she had baked that morning. — *L. M. Montgomery, Anne of Avonlea*

WORD HISTORY from Latin *pausare* 'to pause'

repository ***NOUN*** **repositories**
a place where things are stored

repossess ***VERB*** **repossesses, repossessing, repossessed**
to take back an item because it has not been paid for

reprehend ***VERB*** **reprehends, reprehending, reprehended**
to blame or criticize someone

WORD HISTORY from Latin *reprehendere*, meaning literally 'to seize again'

reprehensible ***ADJECTIVE***
extremely bad and deserving blame or criticism

▷ **reprehensibly** ***ADVERB***

represent ***VERB*** **represents, representing, represented**
1 to help someone by speaking or doing something on their behalf
2 to symbolize or stand for something ◆ *In Roman numerals, v represents 5.*
3 to be an example or equivalent of something
4 to show a person or thing in a picture, play, or story
5 to describe a person or thing in a particular way

▷ **representation** ***NOUN***

WORD HISTORY from Latin *praesentare* 'to present or show'

a b c d e f g h i j k l m n o p q r s t u v w x y z

representative *NOUN* **representatives**
a person or thing that represents another or others

representative *ADJECTIVE*
1 representing others
2 typical of a group

repress *VERB* **represses, repressing, repressed**
1 to keep something down; to control something by force
2 to restrain or suppress someone
▷ **repression** *NOUN*
▷ **repressive** *ADJECTIVE*

reprieve *NOUN* **reprieves**
postponement or cancellation of a punishment, especially the death penalty

reprieve *VERB* **reprieves, reprieving, reprieved**
to give a reprieve to someone
WORD HISTORY from an old word *repry* 'to take back to prison'

reprimand *NOUN* **reprimands**
a rebuke, especially a formal or official one

reprimand *VERB* **reprimands, reprimanding, reprimanded**
to give someone a reprimand

reprisal *NOUN* **reprisals**
an act of revenge

reproach *VERB* **reproaches, reproaching, reproached**
to tell someone you are upset and disappointed by something they have done
▷ **reproach** *NOUN*
▷ **reproachful** *ADJECTIVE*
▷ **reproachfully** *ADVERB*
WORD HISTORY from Old French *reprochier*

reproduce *VERB* **reproduces, reproducing, reproduced**
1 to cause something to be seen or heard or happen again
2 to make a copy of something
3 (*Biology*) to produce offspring

reproduction *NOUN*
1 a copy of something, especially a work of art
2 the process of producing offspring

reproductive *ADJECTIVE*
to do with reproduction ◆ *the reproductive system*

reprove *VERB* **reproves, reproving, reproved**
to rebuke or reproach someone
▷ **reproof** *NOUN*
WORD HISTORY from Latin *reprobare* 'to disapprove'

reptile *NOUN* **reptiles**
a cold-blooded animal that has a backbone and very short legs or no legs at all, e.g. a snake, lizard, crocodile, or tortoise
WORD HISTORY from Latin *reptilis* 'crawling'

republic *NOUN* **republics**
(*Politics*) a country in which the supreme power is held by the people and their elected representatives, and which has an elected or nominated president rather than a monarch
▷ **republican** *ADJECTIVE*
WORD HISTORY from Latin *res publica* 'public affairs'

Republican *NOUN* **Republicans**
a supporter of the Republican Party, one of the two main political parties in the USA

repudiate *VERB* **repudiates, repudiating, repudiated**
to reject or deny a suggestion or accusation
▷ **repudiation** *NOUN*
WORD HISTORY from Latin *repudiare* 'to divorce'

repugnant *ADJECTIVE*
distasteful or objectionable; very unpleasant or disgusting

The longer he thought about it, the more repugnant became the thought of taking human life needlessly. — *Edgar Rice Burroughs, The Return of Tarzan*

▷ **repugnance** *NOUN*
WORD HISTORY from Latin *repugnare* 'to fight back'

repulse *VERB* **repulses, repulsing, repulsed**
1 to drive back an attacking force
2 to reject an offer or help firmly

repulsion *NOUN*
1 the action of repulsing or repelling something
2 the ability to repel something by physical force
3 a feeling of strong distaste or disgust

repulsive *ADJECTIVE*
1 disgusting or revolting
2 able to repel things by physical force
▷ **repulsively** *ADVERB*
▷ **repulsiveness** *NOUN*

reputable (*say* rep- yoo- ta- bul) *ADJECTIVE*
having a good reputation; respected ◆ *I only buy software from reputable companies.*
▷ **reputably** *ADVERB*

reputation *NOUN* **reputations**
1 the opinion that is generally held about a person or thing
2 public recognition for your abilities or achievements
WORD HISTORY from Latin *reputare* 'to consider'

repute *NOUN*
reputation ◆ *a team of scientists of international repute*

reputed *ADJECTIVE*
said or thought to be something ◆ *This is reputed to be the best hotel in the area.*
▷ **reputedly** *ADVERB*

request *VERB* **requests, requesting, requested**
1 to ask for a thing
2 to ask a person to do something

request *NOUN* **requests**
1 the process of asking, or of being asked, for something

'The Glass Master made the mask at the request of the Duchessa,' said Arianna, munching on a radish. — *Mary Hoffman, Stravaganza City of Masks*

2 a thing asked for ◆ *Does the prisoner have any last requests?*

WORD HISTORY from an Old French word, related to *require*

requiem (*say* **rek**- wee- em) *NOUN* **requiems**
1 a special Mass said for someone who has died
2 a musical setting for this

WORD HISTORY a Latin word meaning 'rest'

require *VERB* **requires, requiring, required**
1 to need or depend on something
2 to demand that someone does something; to oblige someone to do something ◆ *All applicants are required to fill in a short questionnaire.*
3 to wish to have something ◆ *Will you require any refreshments?*

WORD HISTORY from Latin *requirere* 'to seek in return', from *quaerere* 'to seek'

requirement *NOUN* **requirements**
something that is required; a need

requisite (*say* **rek**- wiz- it) *ADJECTIVE*
required or needed for some purpose ◆ *You can pick up the requisite form at your local Post Office.*

requisite *NOUN* **requisites**
a thing needed for some purpose

requisition *VERB* **requisitions, requisitioning, requisitioned**
to take something over for official use ◆ *In 1940 the building was requisitioned by the Army and was used as a military bakery.*

rerun *VERB* **reruns, rerunning, reran**
1 to run a race or other event again
2 to broadcast a television programme or film again

rerun *NOUN* **reruns**
1 a race or other event that is run again
2 a repeat of a television programme or film

rescind (*say* ri- **sind**) *VERB* **rescinds, rescinding, rescinded**
to repeal or cancel a law or rule
▷ **rescission** *NOUN*

WORD HISTORY from Latin *rescindere* 'to cut back'

rescue *VERB* **rescues, rescuing, rescued**
to save a person or thing from danger or harm; to free someone from captivity
▷ **rescuer** *NOUN*

rescue *NOUN* **rescues**
the action of rescuing a person or thing, or the process of being rescued

WORD HISTORY from Old French *rescoure*

research (*say* ri- **serch** or **ree**- serch) *NOUN*
careful study and investigation, especially in order to discover new facts or information

USAGE NOTE The first pronunciation is the one traditionally used in British English. However, the US pronunciation, with the stress on the first syllable, is also now commonly used in British English.

research (*say* ri- **serch**) *VERB* **researches, researching, researched**
to carry out research into something
▷ **researcher** *NOUN*

WORD HISTORY from Old French *recerche* 'careful search'

resemblance *NOUN* **resemblances**
likeness or similarity

You know, believe it or not, you've got a funny kind of resemblance to a bloke I once knew in Shoreditch. — *Harold Pinter, The Caretaker*

resemble *VERB* **resembles, resembling, resembled**
to look like or have features in common with another person or thing

resent *VERB* **resents, resenting, resented**
to feel bitter and indignant about something; to feel insulted by something said or done

Sir Ector regarded the forest as his forest, and resented the intrusion of the royal hounds — as if his own would not do just as well! — *T. H. White, The Once and Future King*

▷ **resentment** *NOUN*

WORD HISTORY from Latin *sentire* 'to feel'

resentful *ADJECTIVE*
feeling bitter and indignant about something
▷ **resentfully** *ADVERB*

reservation *NOUN* **reservations**
1 the action of reserving something
2 a reserved seat, table, or room ◆ *We booked our hotel reservations on the Internet.*
3 an area of land set aside for the exclusive use of North American Indians or Australian Aboriginals
4 a doubt or feeling of unease
5 a limit on how far you agree with something; a doubt or condition ◆ *I can recommend her for the job without reservation.*
6 a strip of land between the carriageways of a road

a b c d e f g h i j k l m n o p q r s t u v w x y z

reserve *VERB* **reserves, reserving, reserved**
to keep or order something for a particular person or a use in the future

to reserve judgement is to leave your decision until you have had time to consider it properly

reserve *NOUN* **reserves**
1 a person or thing kept ready to be used if necessary
2 an extra player chosen in case a substitute is needed in a team
3 an area of land kept for a special purpose ◆ *a nature reserve*
4 shyness; being reserved

in reserve in a state of being unused but available

WORD HISTORY from Latin *reservare* 'to keep back'

reserved *ADJECTIVE*
1 kept for someone's use ◆ *This table is reserved.*
2 a reserved person is shy and unwilling to show their feelings

reservoir (*say* **rez**- er- vwar) *NOUN* **reservoirs**
1 a natural or artificial lake that is a source of water supply
2 a container for a supply of fuel or other liquid

WORD HISTORY from French *réservoir*

reshuffle *VERB* **reshuffles, reshuffling, reshuffled**
1 to rearrange the posts or responsibilities of a group of people, especially government ministers
2 to shuffle cards again

reshuffle *NOUN* **reshuffles**
the process of reshuffling something, especially a rearrangement of posts in a governnment or cabinet

reside *VERB* **resides, residing, resided**
to live in a particular place; to dwell

WORD HISTORY from Latin *residere* 'to stay behind', from *sedere* 'to sit'

residence *NOUN* **residences**
1 a place where a person lives
2 the fact of living in a place

Under the eaves of the villa itself the swallows had taken up residence. — *Gerald Durrell, My Family and Other Animals*

3 a writer, musician, or other artist in residence is appointed to work in a specified place for a period of time

resident *NOUN* **residents**
1 a person living or residing in a particular place
2 a person staying overnight in a hotel

resident *ADJECTIVE*
living or residing in a particular place; in residence

▷ **residency** *NOUN*

residential *ADJECTIVE*
1 a residential area is one that contains or is suitable for private houses
2 a residential course or home is one that provides accommodation

residue *NOUN* **residues**
what is left over; the remainder

▷ **residual** *ADJECTIVE*
▷ **residually** *ADVERB*

WORD HISTORY from Latin *residuus* 'remaining'

resign *VERB* **resigns, resigning, resigned**
to give up your job or position

to be resigned or resign yourself to something is to accept that you must put up with a difficult situation

WORD HISTORY from Latin *resignare* 'to unseal'

resignation *NOUN* **resignations**
1 acceptance of a difficult situation without complaining
2 the fact of resigning from a job or position
3 a letter stating that you wish to resign

resilient *ADJECTIVE*
1 a resilient material springs back into shape after being bent or stretched
2 a resilient person is able to recover quickly from illness or trouble

▷ **resilience** *NOUN*
▷ **resiliently** *ADVERB*

WORD HISTORY from Latin *resilire* 'to jump back'

resin *NOUN* **resins**
1 a sticky substance that oozes from certain plants, especially fir and pine trees
2 a similar substance made synthetically, used in making paints and varnishes

▷ **resinous** *ADJECTIVE*

WORD HISTORY from Latin *resina*

resist *VERB* **resists, resisting, resisted**
1 to fight or act to prevent something from happening
2 to oppose or refuse to accept a plan or proposal ◆ *Campaigners are urging residents to resist the plan to flood the whole valley.*
3 to stop yourself yielding to something although you are tempted by it ◆ *I find it difficult to resist homemade chocolate cake.*

WORD HISTORY from Latin *resistere* 'to stand against'

resistance *NOUN*
1 the act of resisting something, or the ability to resist ◆ *Resistance is futile.*
2 the ability of a substance to hinder the flow of electricity
3 the ability of your body to resist a virus or disease, or to be unaffected by a drug or poison

I had built up a considerable resistance to triffid poison since my first sting in the garden. — *John Wyndham, The Day of the Triffids*

▷ **resistant** *ADJECTIVE*

resistor *NOUN* **resistors**
a device that increases the resistance to an electric current

resit *VERB* **resits, resitting, resat**
to sit an examination again after a previous failure

resit *NOUN* **resits**
an examination that you sit again

resolute *ADJECTIVE*
showing great determination
▷ **resolutely** *ADVERB*

resolution *NOUN* **resolutions**
1 the quality of being resolute; great determination
2 a personal pledge to do something, especially one made at New Year
3 a formal decision made by a committee
4 the solving of a problem
5 the degree to which a photograph or image on a screen can reproduce fine detail

resolve *VERB* **resolves, resolving, resolved**
1 to decide something firmly or formally
2 to solve or settle a problem
3 to overcome doubts or disagreements
4 (*Music*) to convert a discord into a pleasing chord

resolve *NOUN*
1 something you have decided to do; a resolution
2 great determination

WORD HISTORY from Latin *resolvere* 'to loosen up'

resonant *ADJECTIVE*
1 resounding or echoing
2 suggesting or bringing to mind a feeling or memory
▷ **resonance** *NOUN*

resonate *VERB* **resonates, resonating, resonated**
to be resonant; to resound
▷ **resonator** *NOUN*

WORD HISTORY from Latin *resonare* 'to resound', from *sonare* 'to sound'

resort *VERB* **resorts, resorting, resorted**
to turn to and make use of a course of action, especially one that you would normally avoid ◆ *My sister resorted to bribing me with the promise of ice cream.* ◆ *As the debate went on, some participants resorted to name-calling.*

resort *NOUN* **resorts**
1 a place where people go for relaxation or holidays
2 the fact of resorting to some measure or action ◆ *It may be possible to treat the patient without resort to surgery.*

the last resort something to be tried when everything else has failed

WORD HISTORY from Old French *resortir* 'to come back'

resound *VERB* **resounds, resounding, resounded**
1 to fill a place with sound; to echo
2 a place resounds when it is filled with, or echoes with, a particular sound

At that moment, the air suddenly resounded with a deafening CRACK! — *Paul Stewart and Chris Riddell, Stormchaser*

resounding *ADJECTIVE*
1 loud and echoing
2 a resounding success or victory is very great; outstanding

resource *NOUN* **resources**
1 something that can be used to achieve a purpose
2 a teaching aid

resource *VERB* **resources, resourcing, resourced**
to provide money or other resources for a plan or enterprise

WORD HISTORY from an Old French word meaning 'to rise again'

resources *PLURAL NOUN*
1 a source of wealth to a country ◆ *The country's natural resources include coal and oil.*
2 available assets, especially money ◆ *By pooling their resources, islanders were able to convert the hall into a community cinema.*
3 a person's natural qualities and abilities

resourceful *ADJECTIVE*
clever at finding ways of doing things
▷ **resourcefully** *ADVERB*
▷ **resourcefulness** *NOUN*

respect *NOUN* **respects**
1 admiration for the good qualities or achievements of a person or group
2 politeness or consideration

We children were supposed to show our respect and bow whenever we ran past Japanese soldiers. — *Adeline Yen Mah, Chinese Cinderella*

3 a detail or aspect

I did everything Phillis said, disobeying her in only one respect. I would not get rid of the rubies. — *Celia Rees, Pirates!*

with respect to with reference to; regarding

respect *VERB* **respects, respecting, respected**
to have respect for a person or thing

WORD HISTORY from Latin *respicere* 'to look back at, to consider'

respectable *ADJECTIVE*
1 honest and decent; of good social standing
2 a respectable score or mark is fairly good and is adequate or acceptable
▷ **respectably** *ADVERB*
▷ **respectability** *NOUN*

SPELLING NOTE Some words pronounced **r-** begin with **rh-** or **wr-**

a b c d e f g h i j k l m n o p q r s t u v w x y z

respectful *ADJECTIVE*
showing respect
▷ **respectfully** *ADVERB*

respecting *PREPOSITION*
concerning; regarding

respective *ADJECTIVE*
belonging to each one of several

After school the next day Alem and Robert went to their respective homes to eat and change their clothes. — *Benjamin Zephaniah, Refugee Boy*

respectively *ADVERB*
in the same order as the people or things already mentioned ◆ *The British and American relay teams finished first and second respectively.*

respiration *NOUN*
(*Biology*) the process of breathing
▷ **respiratory** *ADJECTIVE*

WORD HISTORY from Latin *respirare* 'to breathe out'

respirator *NOUN* **respirators**
1 a device that fits over a person's nose and mouth to purify air before it is breathed
2 an apparatus for giving artificial respiration

respire *VERB* **respires, respiring, respired**
(*Biology*) to breathe

respite *NOUN* **respites**
a short period of rest or relief from something difficult or unpleasant ◆ *Weather forecasters are predicting no respite from the heatwave in the coming days.*

WORD HISTORY from an Old French word

resplendent *ADJECTIVE*
impressively bright and colourful

Rebecca, resplendent in another gown she'd borrowed from Victoria, looked more beautiful than ever. — *Meg Cabot, Victoria and the Rogue*

▷ **resplendence** *NOUN*
▷ **resplendently** *ADVERB*

WORD HISTORY from Latin *resplendere* 'to shine brightly'

respond *VERB* **responds, responding, responded**
1 to reply
2 to act in answer to, or because of, something; to react ◆ *The British public have responded marvellously to our appeal.*
3 to show a favourable reaction to something ◆ *The disease did not respond to treatment.*

WORD HISTORY from Latin *respondere* 'to promise back'

respondent *NOUN* **respondents**
1 someone who responds to a questionnaire or advertisement
2 the defendant in a lawsuit, especially in a divorce case

response *NOUN* **responses**
1 a reply or answer
2 a reaction to something ◆ *There has been an enthusiastic response to World Book Day across the country.*

responsibility *NOUN* **responsibilities**
1 the fact of being responsible for a person or thing
2 the opportunity to work independently and take your own decisions ◆ *I'm looking for a job with more responsibility.*
3 something for which a person is responsible ◆ *It is your responsibility to check that the details on the form are correct.*

responsible *ADJECTIVE*
1 legally or morally obliged to take care of something or to carry out a duty, and having to take the blame if something goes wrong
2 reliable and trustworthy
3 a responsible job or position involves important duties or decisions

'You don't raise a guy to a responsible job who whistles in the elevator!' — *Arthur Miller, Death of a Salesman*

4 causing something ◆ *The San Francisco earthquake was responsible for the death of around 7000 people.*
▷ **responsibly** *ADVERB*

responsive *ADJECTIVE*
responding well or quickly to something
▷ **responsiveness** *NOUN*

rest❶ *NOUN* **rests**
1 a time of sleep or freedom from work as a way of regaining strength
2 a support, especially on a piece of furniture to support part of your body ◆ *The chair comes with detachable foot and head rests.*
3 (*Music*) an interval of silence between notes

rest *VERB* **rests, resting, rested**
1 to have a rest; to be still
2 to allow a part of your body to rest ◆ *Sit down and rest your feet for a moment.*
3 to lean or place something so it is supported, or to be supported

Mina's mother rested a wooden board on her knees. She smiled and put a pomegranate on the board. — *David Almond, Skellig*

4 to let a matter rest is to leave it without further investigation

rest❷ *NOUN*
the rest the remaining part; the others

rest *VERB* **rests, resting, rested**
a matter rests with someone when it is left to them to deal with ◆ *It rests with you to send out the invitations.*

to rest assured is to be confident or certain about something ◆ *You can rest assured, the play will be a success.*

restaurant *NOUN* **restaurants**
a place where food is prepared and served to paying customers

WORD HISTORY a French word meaning literally 'restoring'

restaurateur (*say* res- ter- a- **tur**) *NOUN* **restaurateurs**
a person who owns or manages a restaurant

USAGE NOTE Note the spelling of this word, which does not have an 'n' (unlike the word *restaurant*).

rested *ADJECTIVE*
you feel rested when you have been refreshed by a period of rest

restful *ADJECTIVE*
giving rest or a feeling of rest ◆ *We had a very restful holiday in the Highlands this year.*
▷ **restfully** *ADVERB*
▷ **restfulness** *NOUN*

restitution *NOUN*
1 the process of restoring something to its proper owner or its original state
2 compensation for injury or damage

WORD HISTORY from Latin *restituere* 'to restore'

restive *ADJECTIVE*
to feel restive is to be restless or impatient because of delay, anxiety, or boredom
▷ **restively** *ADVERB*
▷ **restiveness** *NOUN*

WORD HISTORY from an earlier meaning 'refusing to move', used to describe a horse

restless *ADJECTIVE*
1 unable to keep still; restive
2 without rest or sleep ◆ *a restless night*
▷ **restlessly** *ADVERB*
▷ **restlessness** *NOUN*

restoration *NOUN*
the process of restoring something, or of being restored
the Restoration (*History*) the re-establishment of the monarchy in Britain in 1660 when Charles II became king

restorative *ADJECTIVE*
tending to restore health or strength

restorative *NOUN*
a restorative food, drink, or medicine

restore *VERB* **restores, restoring, restored**
1 to put something back to its original place or condition

Artemis Fowl had devised a plan to restore his family's fortune. — *Eoin Colfer, Artemis Fowl*

2 to clean and repair a work of art or building so that it looks as good as it did originally

restrain *VERB* **restrains, restraining, restrained**
to hold a person or thing back; to keep a person or animal under control
▷ **restraint** *NOUN*

WORD HISTORY from Latin *restringere* 'to tie up firmly, to confine'

restrict *VERB* **restricts, restricting, restricted**
to keep someone or something within certain limits ◆ *Their freedom was severely restricted by these laws.*
▷ **restriction** *NOUN*
▷ **restrictive** *ADJECTIVE*

result *NOUN* **results**
1 something produced by an activity or operation; an effect or consequence
2 the score or situation at the end of a game, competition, or race
3 a satisfactory outcome, such as a victory
4 the answer to a sum or calculation

result *VERB* **results, resulting, resulted**
1 to happen as a result
2 to result in something is to have it as a particular result

In the 16th century, a long voyage at sea usually resulted in the deaths of at least half the men.
— *Henry Brook, True Sea Stories*

▷ **resultant** *ADJECTIVE*

resume *VERB* **resumes, resuming, resumed**
1 to begin an activity or operation again after stopping for a while
2 to take something again; to occupy a place or position again ◆ *After the interval we resumed our seats.*
▷ **resumption** *NOUN*

WORD HISTORY from Latin *resumere* 'to take up again'

résumé (*say* **rez**- yoo- may) *NOUN* **résumés**
1 a summary
2 (*American and Australian*) a curriculum vitae

WORD HISTORY a French word meaning 'summed up'

resurgence *NOUN* **resurgences**
a rise or revival of something ◆ *A new series of children's books has led to a resurgence of interest in Latin.*

WORD HISTORY from Latin *resurgens* 'rising again'

resurrect *VERB* **resurrects, resurrecting, resurrected**
1 to bring something back into use or existence ◆ *This year, we will be resurrecting the tradition of holding an annual summer ceilidh.*
2 to revive someone's fortune or career

resurrection *NOUN*
1 the process of coming back to life after being dead
2 the revival of something after disuse
the Resurrection in the Christian religion, the resurrection of Jesus Christ three days after his death

resuscitate *VERB* **resuscitates, resuscitating, resuscitated**
to revive someone from unconsciousness or apparent death
▷ **resuscitation** *NOUN*
WORD HISTORY from Latin *resuscitare* 'to raise again'

retail *VERB* **retails, retailing, retailed**
1 to sell goods, or to be sold as goods, to the general public
2 to recount or relate the details of something
▷ **retailer** *NOUN*

retail *NOUN*
the selling of goods to the general public (SEE ALSO **wholesale**)
WORD HISTORY from an Old French word *retaille* 'a piece cut off', because retail items were sold in small amounts

retain *VERB* **retains, retaining, retained**
1 to continue to have something; to keep something in your possession or memory
2 to hold something in place
WORD HISTORY from Latin *retinere* 'to hold back'

retainer *NOUN* **retainers**
1 a sum of money regularly paid to someone so that they will work for you when needed
2 a servant who has worked for a person or family for a long time

retake *VERB* **retakes, retaking, retook, retaken**
to take a test or examination again

retake *NOUN* **retakes**
1 a test or examination taken again
2 a scene filmed again

retaliate *VERB* **retaliates, retaliating, retaliated**
to repay an injury or insult with a similar one; to attack someone in return for a similar attack

The white settlers used muskets, swords and guns against the Nyungar people, who retaliated with spears. — *Doris Pilkington, Rabbit Proof Fence*

▷ **retaliation** *NOUN*
▷ **retaliatory** (*say* ri- **tal**- ya- ter- i) *ADJECTIVE*
WORD HISTORY from Latin *retaliare* 'to pay back in kind'

retard *VERB* **retards, retarding, retarded**
to slow down or delay the progress or development of something

The wind, obstinately remaining in the north-west, blew a gale, and retarded the steamer. — *Jules Verne, Around the World in Eighty Days*

▷ **retarded** *ADJECTIVE*
▷ **retardation** *NOUN*
WORD HISTORY from Latin *retardere*, from *tardus* 'slow'

retch *VERB* **retches, retching, retched**
to strain your throat as if being sick
WORD HISTORY from an Old English word
USAGE NOTE Take care not to confuse this word with *wretch*, which has a different meaning.

retell *VERB* **retells, retelling, retold**
to tell a story or account of something again

retention *NOUN*
the action of retaining or keeping something

retentive *ADJECTIVE*
someone with a retentive mind or memory is able to retain information and remember things easily
▷ **retentiveness** *NOUN*

rethink *VERB* **rethinks, rethinking, rethought**
to think about a course of action again; to plan something again and differently

rethink *NOUN*
an instance of rethinking

reticent (*say* **ret**- i- sent) *ADJECTIVE*
a reticent person or manner is discreet and does not reveal thoughts or feelings
▷ **reticence** *NOUN*
▷ **reticently** *ADVERB*
WORD HISTORY from Latin *reticere* 'to keep silent'

retina *NOUN* **retinas** or **retinae**
a layer of membrane at the back of the eyeball, which is sensitive to light
WORD HISTORY from Latin *rete* 'net', because of the network of blood vessels

retinue (*say* **ret**- in- yoo) *NOUN* **retinues**
a group of attendants accompanying an important person

The Prince, with a splendid retinue of officers and men, marched into Exeter. — *Charles Dickens, A Child's History of England*

WORD HISTORY from Old French *retenue* 'restrained, in someone's service'

retire *VERB* **retires, retiring, retired**
1 to give up your job or career when you reach a certain age, usually 60 or 65
2 a sports player retires when they stop playing competitively
3 to retreat or withdraw

4 to go to bed or to your private room

At this point, I decided it might be best to retire to my room. — *Meg Cabot, The Princess Diaries*

▷ **retirement** *NOUN*

WORD HISTORY from French *retirer* 'to retreat', from *tirer* 'to draw'

retiring *ADJECTIVE*
shy; avoiding company

retort *NOUN* **retorts**
1 a quick, witty, or angry reply
2 a glass bottle with a long downward-bent neck, used in distilling liquids
3 a container or furnace used in making gas or steel

retort *VERB* **retorts, retorting, retorted**
to make a quick, witty, or angry reply

'I will do as I like,' retorted the queen sulkily. — *George MacDonald, The Princess and the Goblin*

WORD HISTORY from Latin *retortum* 'twisted again', from *torquere* 'to twist'

retrace *VERB* **retraces, retracing, retraced**
1 to go back over the route that you have just taken ◆ *We retraced our steps, looking for the glove I had lost.*
2 to trace something back to the source or beginning
▷ **retraceable** *ADJECTIVE*

retract *VERB* **retracts, retracting, retracted**
1 to pull something back or in ◆ *The cheetah is the only cat which cannot retract its claws.*
2 to withdraw a statement or accusation
3 to go back on an agreement or promise
▷ **retraction** *NOUN*
▷ **retractable** *ADJECTIVE*
▷ **retractile** *ADJECTIVE*

WORD HISTORY from Latin *retractum* 'pulled back', from *trahere* 'to pull'

retrain *VERB* **retrains, retraining, retrained**
to teach or learn new skills for a different job

retreat *VERB* **retreats, retreating, retreated**
to go back after being defeated or to avoid danger or difficulty; to withdraw

The creature scrambled to its feet and retreated into the thick undergrowth where the horses couldn't follow. — *Stuart Hill, The Cry of the Icemark*

retreat *NOUN* **retreats**
1 the action of retreating
2 a quiet or secluded place
3 a period of withdrawal from worldly activities for prayer or meditation

retrench *VERB* **retrenches, retrenching, retrenched**
to reduce your costs or spending ◆ *The company has been forced to retrench this year.*
▷ **retrenchment** *NOUN*

WORD HISTORY from French *retrancher* 'to recut', related to *trench* and *truncate*

retrial *NOUN* **retrials**
a second or further trial

retribution *NOUN* **retributions**
a deserved punishment

WORD HISTORY from Latin *retribuere* 'to hand back', from *tribuere* 'to assign'

retrieve *VERB* **retrieves, retrieving, retrieved**
1 to bring or get something back
2 to find or extract information stored in a computer
3 to rescue or save a situation; to restore something to a flourishing state ◆ *The accountant discovered the error and was able to retrieve the situation.*
▷ **retrievable** *ADJECTIVE*
▷ **retrieval** *NOUN*

WORD HISTORY from Old French *retrover* 'to find again'

retriever *NOUN* **retrievers**
a kind of dog originally trained to retrieve game

retro *ADJECTIVE*
(*informal*) an object that is retro in design or appearance is based on the style of a previous period ◆ *I love the retro look of these platform shoes.*

retrograde *ADJECTIVE*
1 going backwards
2 becoming less good

WORD HISTORY from Latin *retrogradus* 'going backwards', from *gradus* 'a step'

retrogress *VERB* **retrogresses, retrogressing, retrogressed**
to go back to an earlier and worse condition
▷ **retrogression** *NOUN*
▷ **retrogressive** *ADJECTIVE*

retrospect *NOUN*
in retrospect when you look back at what has happened ◆ *In retrospect, it was a good idea to bring both cars.*

retrospective *ADJECTIVE*
1 looking back on the past ◆ *This is the first retrospective exhibition of Andy Warhol's work to be seen in Japan.*
2 applying to the past as well as the future ◆ *The pay rises have been made retrospective.*
▷ **retrospection** *NOUN*
▷ **retrospectively** *ADJECTIVE*

return *VERB* **returns, returning, returned**
1 to come back or go back
2 to bring, give, put, or send something back
3 to elect someone as a Member of Parliament ◆ *In 1908, Churchill was returned as MP for Dundee.*

a b c d e f g h i j k l m n o p q r s t u v w x y z

SPELLING NOTE Some words pronounced **r-** begin with **rh-** or **wr-**

return *NOUN* **returns**
1 the action of returning, or of returning something

The return of Mr Bilbo Baggins created quite a disturbance, both under the Hill and over the Hill, and across the Water. — *J. R. R. Tolkien, The Hobbit*

2 something that has been returned, such as an unwanted ticket to a performance
3 profit ◆ *How can I get a better return on my savings?*
4 a return ticket

return match *NOUN* **return matches**
a second match played between the same teams

return ticket *NOUN* **return tickets**
a ticket for a journey to a place and back again

reunify *VERB* **reunifies, reunifying, reunified**
to make a divided country into one country again
▷ **reunification** *NOUN*

reunion *NOUN* **reunions**
1 the process of reuniting people or things, or of being reunited
2 a meeting of people who have not met for some time, such as former school pupils or students from the same class or year

reunite *VERB* **reunites, reuniting, reunited**
to come together or bring people together after a period of separation

reuse (*say* ree- **yooz**) *VERB* **reuses, reusing, reused**
to use something again
▷ **reusable** *ADJECTIVE*

reuse (*say* ree- **yooss**) *NOUN*
the action of using something, or the process of being used, again

Rev. or **Revd.** *ABBREVIATION*
Reverend

rev *VERB* **revs, revving, revved**
(*informal*) to make an engine run quickly, especially when starting

rev *NOUN* **revs**
(*informal*) a revolution of an engine
WORD HISTORY short for *revolution*

revamp *VERB* **revamps, revamping, revamped**
to improve the appearance or structure of something

revamp *NOUN*
an improved version of something
WORD HISTORY from an earlier meaning 'to put a new upper part on a shoe'

reveal *VERB* **reveals, revealing, revealed**
1 to uncover and allow something to be seen
2 to make something known ◆ *Police have not yet revealed the identity of the victim.*
WORD HISTORY from Latin *revelare* 'to unveil'

revealing *ADJECTIVE*
1 a revealing act or statement gives interesting or significant information, often unintentionally
2 revealing clothing allows a lot of someone's body to be seen

reveille (*say* riv- **al**- ee) *NOUN* **reveilles**
a military waking signal sounded on a bugle or drums
WORD HISTORY from French *réveillez* 'wake up!'

revel *VERB* **revels, revelling, revelled**
1 to revel in an action or situation is to take great delight in it
2 to celebrate or enjoy yourself with others in a lively or noisy style
▷ **reveller** *NOUN*
WORD HISTORY from an Old French word, related to *rebel*

revelation *NOUN* **revelations**
1 the action of revealing something; disclosure
2 something revealed, especially a surprising fact or experience ◆ *Learning to use a computer has been a revelation to my grandmother.*
▷ **revelatory** *ADJECTIVE*

revelry *NOUN* **revelries**
1 the action of revelling
2 lively and noisy celebration

revels *PLURAL NOUN*
lively and noisy celebrations

revenge *NOUN*
the action of harming somebody in return for harm that they have done to you

revenge *VERB* **revenges, revenging, revenged**
to get satisfaction for harm done by inflicting revenge ◆ *The ghost calls upon Hamlet to revenge his father's murder.*
WORD HISTORY from an Old French word, related to *vindicate*

revenue *NOUN* **revenues**
1 a country's income from taxes and other sources, used for paying public expenses
2 a company's income
WORD HISTORY from an Old French word meaning 'returned'

reverberate *VERB* **reverberates, reverberating, reverberated**
1 a sound reverberates when it is repeated as an echo; to resound
2 an event or situation reverberates when it continues to have serious effects
▷ **reverberation** *NOUN*
▷ **reverberative** *ADJECTIVE*
WORD HISTORY from Latin *reverberare* 'to beat or whip again'

revere (*say* riv- **eer**) ***VERB*** **reveres, revering, revered**
to revere someone is to respect or admire them deeply

WORD HISTORY from Latin *vereri* 'to fear or be in awe of someone'

reverence ***NOUN***
1 a feeling of awe and deep respect or admiration
2 a title given to a member of the clergy, especially a priest in Ireland

Reverend ***NOUN***
a title or form of address to members of the clergy ◆ *the Reverend Mary Johnson*

WORD HISTORY from Latin *reverendus* 'someone to be revered'

USAGE NOTE Take care not to confuse this word with *reverent.*

reverent ***ADJECTIVE***
feeling or showing reverence
▷ **reverently** ***ADVERB***
▷ **reverential** ***ADJECTIVE***

USAGE NOTE Take care not to confuse this word with *Reverend.*

reverie (*say* rev- er- ee) ***NOUN*** **reveries**
a daydream; a state of daydreaming

WORD HISTORY from a French word, from *rêver* 'to dream'

reversal ***NOUN*** **reversals**
1 a change to an opposite direction, position, or course of action
2 a piece of bad luck or misfortune

reverse ***ADJECTIVE***
1 facing or moving in the opposite direction
2 opposite in character or order ◆ *I will read out the names of the winners in reverse order.*

reverse ***NOUN*** **reverses**
1 the opposite or contrary of something
2 the reverse side or face of something ◆ *Please put your address on the reverse of the cheque.*
3 a piece of misfortune; a setback
4 the reverse gear of a vehicle
5 the side of a coin or medal showing the second or less important design (SEE ALSO **obverse**)

in reverse the opposite way round

reverse ***VERB*** **reverses, reversing, reversed**
1 to turn in the opposite direction or order
2 to turn something inside out or upside down
3 to move backwards
4 to cancel a decision or decree

to reverse the charges is to charge the cost of a phone call to the person receiving it instead of to the caller
▷ **reversible** ***ADJECTIVE***

reverse gear ***NOUN***
a gear that allows a vehicle to be driven backwards

revert ***VERB*** **reverts, reverting, reverted**
1 to return to a previous state, practice, or belief
2 to return to a subject in talk or thought
▷ **reversion** ***NOUN***

WORD HISTORY from Latin *revertere* 'to turn back'

review ***NOUN*** **reviews**
1 a re-examination or reconsideration of something
2 a general survey of past events or of a subject
3 a published description and opinion of a book, film, or play

review ***VERB*** **reviews, reviewing, reviewed**
1 to write a review of a book, film, or play
2 to reconsider a matter or decision
3 to inspect or survey something
▷ **reviewer** ***NOUN***

USAGE NOTE Take care not to confuse this word with *revue.*

revile ***VERB*** **reviles, reviling, reviled**
to criticize someone angrily in abusive language ◆ *The director's work has been both praised and reviled by critics.*
▷ **revilement** ***NOUN***

WORD HISTORY from Old French *reviler*, related to *vile*

revise ***VERB*** **revises, revising, revised**
1 to go over work that you have already learnt in preparation for an examination
2 to examine something again and correct any faults in it
3 to change or amend an opinion or belief ◆ *After rereading the play, I have revised my opinion of it.*
▷ **revision** ***NOUN***

WORD HISTORY from Latin *revisere* 'to examine again'

revisit ***VERB*** **revisits, revisiting, revisited**
1 to pay another visit to a place
2 to examine and reconsider a matter or decision

revitalize ***VERB*** **revitalizes, revitalizing, revitalized**
to put new strength or vitality into something

USAGE NOTE This word can also be spelled revitalise.

revival ***NOUN*** **revivals**
1 an improvement in the condition or strength of something
2 a renewal of interest or fashion
3 an evangelical Christian meeting

revive ***VERB*** **revives, reviving, revived**
1 to come or bring something back to life, strength, activity, or use

> As they ate, the children's spirits revived, and they began to be curious about where exactly they were. — *William Nicholson, The Wind Singer*

2 to restore interest in or the popularity of something

WORD HISTORY from Latin *vivere* 'to live'

SPELLING NOTE Some words pronounced **r-** begin with **rh-** or **wr-**

a b c d e f g h i j k l m n o p q r s t u v w x y z

revoke *VERB* **revokes, revoking, revoked**
to withdraw or cancel a decree, licence, or right
WORD HISTORY from Latin *revocare* 'to call back'

revolt *VERB* **revolts, revolting, revolted**
1 to disgust someone ◆ *The smell of stale smoke in the room revolted me.*
2 (*History*) to take part in a rebellion

revolt *NOUN* **revolts**
1 (*History*) a rebellion against a government or other authority
2 a refusal to obey or conform

revolting *ADJECTIVE*
causing disgust; horrible

revolution *NOUN* **revolutions**
1 (*History*) a rebellion that overthrows the government, especially by force
2 a complete or drastic change ◆ *a revolution in the treatment of burns*
3 the action of turning or moving around an axis; a single complete turn of a wheel or engine

revolutionary *ADJECTIVE*
1 involving a great change ◆ *a revolutionary method of harnassing the sun's energy*
2 to do with a political revolution

revolutionize *VERB* **revolutionizes, revolutionizing, revolutionized**
to make a great change in something ◆ *The Internet has revolutionized the way we shop.*
USAGE NOTE This word can also be spelled revolutionise.

revolve *VERB* **revolves, revolving, revolved**
1 to turn or cause something to turn round
2 to treat something as the most important point or element ◆ *Zoe's life revolves around her new Dalmatian puppy.*
WORD HISTORY from Latin *revolvere* 'to roll back'

revolver *NOUN* **revolvers**
a pistol with a revolving mechanism that can be fired several times without reloading

revue *NOUN* **revues**
an entertainment consisting of songs and sketches, often about current events
WORD HISTORY a French word meaning *review*
USAGE NOTE Take care not to confuse this word with *review*.

revulsion *NOUN*
1 strong disgust ◆ *Though spiders produce feelings of revulsion in many people, only a few species are dangerous to humans.*
2 a sudden violent change of feeling
WORD HISTORY from Latin *revulsum* 'pulled back'

reward *NOUN* **rewards**
1 something given in return for a good deed, or an achievement or success
2 a sum of money offered for help in catching a criminal or finding lost property

reward *VERB* **rewards, rewarding, rewarded**
to give a reward to someone
WORD HISTORY from an earlier meaning 'to consider, to take notice', related to *regard*

rewarding *ADJECTIVE*
a rewarding job or experience gives you a sense of satisfaction and achievement

rewind *VERB* **rewinds, rewinding, rewound**
to wind a cassette or videotape back to or towards the beginning

reword *VERB* **rewords, rewording, reworded**
to put something into different words

rewrite *VERB* **rewrites, rewriting, rewrote, rewritten**
to write something again or differently

rhapsodize *VERB* **rhapsodizes, rhapsodizing, rhapsodized**
to talk or write about something in an extremely enthusiastic way
USAGE NOTE This word can also be spelled rhapsodise.

rhapsody (*say* **rap**- so- dee) *NOUN* **rhapsodies**
1 an extremely enthusiastic and emotional statement
2 (*Music*) a romantic composition written in an irregular form
WORD HISTORY from Greek *rhapsōidos* 'someone who stitches songs together'

rhebok (*say* **ree**- bok) *NOUN* **rheboks**
a small South African antelope with a woolly brownish-grey coat, a long slender neck, and short straight horns

rhesus monkey *NOUN* **rhesus monkeys**
a kind of small monkey from Northern India

rhesus factor *NOUN*
a substance found in the red blood cells of many humans and some other primates, first found in the rhesus monkey

rhetoric (*say* **ret**- er- ik) *NOUN*
1 the art of using words impressively, especially in public speaking
2 language used for its impressive effect, but often lacking sincerity or meaningful content
▷ **rhetorical** *ADJECTIVE*
▷ **rhetorically** *ADVERB*
WORD HISTORY from Greek *rhētōr* 'orator'

rhetorical question *NOUN* **rhetorical questions**
(*Language*) a question asked for dramatic effect and not intended to get an answer, e.g. 'Who cares?' (= nobody cares)

rheumatism *NOUN*
a disease that causes pain and stiffness in joints and muscles
▷ **rheumatic** *ADJECTIVE*
▷ **rheumatoid** *ADJECTIVE*

WORD HISTORY from Greek *rheuma*, literally 'stream', a substance in the body which was once believed to cause rheumatism

rhinestone *NOUN* **rhinestones**
an imitation diamond

rhino *NOUN* **rhino** or **rhinos**
(*informal*) a rhinoceros

rhinoceros *NOUN* **rhinoceros** or **rhinoceroses**
a large thick-skinned animal of Africa and south Asia with a horn or two horns on its nose

WORD HISTORY from Greek *rhinos* 'of the nose' and *keras* 'horn'

rhizome *NOUN* **rhizomes**
a thick underground stem which produces roots and new plants

WORD HISTORY from Greek *rhiza* 'root'

rhododendron *NOUN* **rhododendrons**
an evergreen shrub with large clusters of trumpet-shaped flowers

WORD HISTORY from Greek *rhodon* 'rose' and *dendron* 'tree'

rhomboid *NOUN* **rhombuses**
a four-sided geometric figure with adjacent sides that are not equal

rhomboid *ADJECTIVE*
shaped like a rhombus

rhombus *NOUN* **rhombuses**
(*Mathematics*) a geometric figure with four equal sides but no right angles, shaped like the diamond on playing cards

WORD HISTORY from Greek *rhombos*

rhubarb *NOUN*
a garden plant with thick reddish stalks that can be cooked and eaten as fruit

WORD HISTORY from Latin *rheubarbarum*

rhyme *NOUN* **rhymes**
1 (*Language*) a similar sound in the endings of words, e.g. *bat/fat/mat, batter/fatter/matter*
2 a poem with rhymes
3 a word that rhymes with another

without rhyme or reason not making any sense

rhyme *VERB* **rhymes, rhyming, rhymed**
(*Language*)
1 to form a rhyme
2 to have rhymes

WORD HISTORY from an Old French word, related to *rhythm*; originally used of a kind of rhythmic verse which usually rhymed

rhyming slang *NOUN*
a type of slang based on words or phrases that rhyme with the word in question, often with the rhyming part omitted, e.g. *butcher's* (*hook*) meaning 'look'

rhythm *NOUN* **rhythms**
1 (*Language, Music*) the regular pattern of beats or stresses in a piece of speech or music
2 a regularly recurring sequence of movements or events

As the journey progressed, Ousland established a rhythm: one and a half hours walking, then a rest for food and water. — *Paul Dowswell, True Polar Adventures*

▷ **rhythmic** *ADJECTIVE*
▷ **rhythmical** *ADJECTIVE*
▷ **rhythmically** *ADVERB*

WORD HISTORY from Greek *rhuthmos*

rib *NOUN* **ribs**
1 each of the curved bones round the chest of a person or animal
2 a curved part that looks like a rib or supports something ◆ *the ribs of an umbrella*
3 a type of knitting stitch used for collars and cuffs
▷ **ribbed** *ADJECTIVE*

ribald (*say* **rib**- uld) *ADJECTIVE*
humorous in a rude or disrespectful way
▷ **ribaldry** *NOUN*

riband *NOUN* **ribands**
(*old use*) a ribbon

WORD HISTORY from an Old French word

ribbon *NOUN* **ribbons**
1 a narrow strip of silk or nylon used for decoration or for tying something
2 a long narrow strip of inked material used in a typewriter or printer

WORD HISTORY another spelling of *riband*

ribcage *NOUN*
the framework of ribs round the chest

rice *NOUN*
a cereal plant grown in flooded fields in hot countries, or its seeds

WORD HISTORY from Greek *oruza*

rich *ADJECTIVE*
1 having a lot of money or property; wealthy
2 having a large supply of something ◆ *The North Sea is rich in oil deposits.*
3 expensive or luxurious; made of costly materials
4 a rich colour, sound, or smell is pleasantly deep or strong
5 rich food contains a lot of fat, butter, or eggs
▷ **richness** *NOUN*

riches *PLURAL NOUN*
great wealth

a b c d e f g h i j k l m n o p q r s t u v w x y z

SPELLING NOTE Some words pronounced **r**- begin with **rh**- or **wr**-

richly *ADVERB*
1 in a rich or luxurious way
2 fully or thoroughly ◆ *This award is richly deserved.*

Richter scale *NOUN*
a scale (from 0-10) used to show the force of an earthquake
WORD HISTORY named after an American scientist, Charles Francis *Richter* (1900-85), who studied earthquakes

rick❶ *NOUN* **ricks**
a built stack of hay, corn, or straw
WORD HISTORY from an Old English word

rick❷ *VERB* **ricks, ricking, ricked**
to sprain or strain your neck or back slightly
WORD HISTORY origin unknown

rickets *NOUN*
a childhood disease caused by lack of vitamin D, causing softening and deformity of the bones

rickety *ADJECTIVE*
poorly made and likely to fall down or apart

Mother's convinced that Father is taking us to live in a rickety cottage far from the village. — *Sue Reid, My Story: Mill Girl*

WORD HISTORY from *rickets*

rickshaw *NOUN* **rickshaws**
a two-wheeled carriage pulled by one or more people, used in the Far East
WORD HISTORY from Japanese *jin-riki-sha* 'person- power- vehicle'

ricochet (*say* **rik**- osh- ay) *VERB* **ricochets, ricocheting, ricocheted**
to bounce off a surface; to rebound

In this metal box the bullet would ricochet round like a demented bee, till it found somebody's flesh. — *Robert Westall, The Machine Gunners*

ricochet *NOUN*
a shot or hit that ricochets
WORD HISTORY from an Old French word

ricotta *NOUN*
a kind of soft Italian cheese made from sheep's milk

rid *VERB* **rids, ridding, rid**
to free a person or place from something unwanted ◆ *According to the legend, the Pied Piper rid the town of rats.*
to be rid of someone or something is to be finished with, or free of, a person or task
to get rid of someone or something is to send someone away, or to dispose of an item
WORD HISTORY from Old Norse *rythja*

riddle❶ *NOUN* **riddles**
1 a puzzling question, designed to test your ingenuity
2 a puzzling or unexplained situation or event ◆ *Science is unlocking the riddle of how the Universe was formed.*
WORD HISTORY from Old English *raedels*

riddle❷ *NOUN* **riddles**
a coarse sieve for gravel or ashes

riddle *VERB* **riddles, riddling, riddled**
1 to pass gravel or ashes through a riddle
2 to pierce or mark a surface with many holes

Much of Antarctica's icy surface is riddled with crevasses. — *Paul Dowswell, True Polar Adventures*

3 someone is riddled with a disease when it permeates or covers their body
WORD HISTORY from Old English *hridder*

ride *VERB* **rides, riding, rode, ridden**
1 to sit on a horse, bicycle, or motorcycle and control it as it carries you along
2 to travel as a passenger in a car, bus, train, etc.
to ride high is to be successful
to ride on something is to depend on it ◆ *There's a lot of money riding on this decision.*
to ride out something to ride out a storm or difficult situation is to come safely through it
to ride the waves is to float on or be supported by the sea
to ride up a piece of clothing rides up when it works upwards when worn

ride *NOUN* **rides**
1 a journey or lift in a vehicle
2 a roundabout, roller coaster, etc. on which people ride at a fair or amusement park
a rough or easy ride a difficult or easy time
to take someone for a ride (*informal*) is to deceive or swindle them

rider *NOUN* **riders**
1 a person who rides a horse, bicycle, or motorcycle
2 an extra clause added to a document or statement

ridge *NOUN* **ridges**
1 a narrow raised strip; a line where two upward-sloping surfaces meet
2 a long narrow hilltop or mountain range
▷ **ridged** *ADJECTIVE*
WORD HISTORY from Old English *hrycg* 'spine, crest'

ridicule *VERB* **ridicules, ridiculing, ridiculed**
to make fun of a person or thing

ridicule *NOUN*
words or behaviour intended to make a person or thing appear ridiculous
WORD HISTORY from Latin *ridere* 'to laugh'

ridiculous *ADJECTIVE*
1 something ridiculous is so silly or foolish that it makes people laugh or despise it
2 not worth serious consideration; preposterous ◆ *The idea of leaving them without any money seemed ridiculous.*
▷ **ridiculously** *ADVERB*

rife *ADJECTIVE*
1 widespread; happening frequently ◆ *In the days of Dick Turpin, highway robbery was rife.*
2 full of something ◆ *Rumours were rife that the ship had met with a terrible disaster on its homeward voyage.*

riff *NOUN* **riffs**
(*Music*) a short repeated phrase in popular music or jazz

riff-raff *NOUN*
the rabble; disreputable people
WORD HISTORY from Old French *rif et raf* 'everybody or everything'

rifle❶ *NOUN* **rifles**
a long gun with spiral grooves (called *rifling*) inside the barrel that make the bullet spin and so travel more accurately
WORD HISTORY from French *rifler* 'to scratch'

rifle❷ *VERB* **rifles, rifling, rifled**
to search and rob a place where something is stored ◆ *It looks as if someone has been rifling through my desk.*
WORD HISTORY from Old French *rifler* 'to plunder'

rift *NOUN* **rifts**
1 a crack, split, or break in something
2 a disagreement that separates friends or breaks up the unity of a group

rift valley *NOUN* **rift valleys**
a steep-sided valley formed where the land has sunk

rig❶ *VERB* **rigs, rigging, rigged**
to provide a ship with ropes, spars, sails, etc.
to rig someone out to provide someone with clothes or equipment
to rig something up is to set up a structure quickly or out of makeshift materials

> It's all right, thanks; I'm quite comfortable in there. I've rigged up a sort of little table beside the bed. — *R. C. Sherriff, Journey's End*

rig *NOUN* **rigs**
1 a framework supporting the machinery for drilling an oil well
2 the way a ship's masts and sails etc. are arranged
3 (*informal*) an outfit of clothes

rig❷ *VERB* **rigs, rigging, rigged**
to arrange the result of an election or contest dishonestly

rigging *NOUN*
the ropes etc. that support a ship's mast and sails

right *ADJECTIVE*
1 on or towards the side which is to the east when you are facing north
2 proper, correct, or true

> Lyra checked the alethiometer: keep going it said; this is the right direction. — *Philip Pullman, The Subtle Knife*

3 morally good; fair or just ◆ *I don't feel it's right to read other people's email.*
4 perfect; exactly suitable

> Everyone agreed that the day was just right for the picnic to Hanging Rock—a shimmering morning warm and still. — *Joan Lindsay, Picnic at Hanging Rock*

5 holding conservative political views; not in favour of socialist reforms (SEE ALSO **left**)
6 real; properly so called ◆ *You've made a right old mess of things.*
▷ **right-hand** *ADJECTIVE*
▷ **rightness** *NOUN*

right *ADVERB*
1 on or towards the right ◆ *Turn right at the traffic lights.*
2 straight; directly ◆ *Go right on.*
3 all the way, completely ◆ *We went right round the town centre.*
4 exactly; precisely ◆ *The Cyclops had one enormous eye right in the middle of its forehead.*
5 correctly or appropriately ◆ *They haven't spelled my name right in the programme.*
6 (*informal*) immediately ◆ *I'll be right back.*
right away immediately; without delay

right *NOUN* **rights**
1 the right-hand side or part of something
2 what is morally good or fair or just
3 something that people are allowed to do or have ◆ *People over 18 have the right to vote in elections.*
by rights if things were fair or correct ◆ *By rights that prize should have been mine.*
in the right having justice or truth on your side
in your own right as a result of your own claims, qualifications, or efforts

right *VERB* **rights, righting, righted**
1 to restore something to a correct or upright position ◆ *The crew managed to right the boat.*
2 to put a matter right; to correct a fault or error ◆ *She was an idealist who sought to right the wrongs of society.*
WORD HISTORY from Old English *riht*

right angle *NOUN*
an angle of 90°

righteous *ADJECTIVE*
doing what is morally right; virtuous
▷ **righteously** *ADVERB*
▷ **righteousness** *NOUN*

SPELLING NOTE Some words pronounced **r-** begin with **rh-** or **wr-**

rightful *ADJECTIVE*
deserved or proper

'This boy you see before you is Arthur Pendragon, and he is the rightful High King of Britain.' — *Michael Morpurgo, Arthur, High King of Britain*

▷ **rightfully** *ADVERB*

right-handed *ADJECTIVE*
1 a right-handed person uses their right hand in preference to their left
2 designed to be used or operated with your right hand

▷ **right-handedness** *NOUN*

right-hand man *NOUN* **right-hand men**
a trusted and impartial assistant

rightly *ADVERB*
1 correctly, properly

Hrothgar was not able to remember rightly what happened then, nor exactly how he managed to escape with his life. — *Robert Nye, Beowulf*

2 with good cause; justifiably ◆ *The players were rightly disappointed with their own performance in the final.*

right-minded *ADJECTIVE*
having ideas and opinions which are sensible and morally good

right of way *NOUN* **rights of way**
1 a public path across private land
2 the right of one vehicle to pass or cross a junction before another

right wing *NOUN*
the section of a political party or system supporting more conservative or traditional policies

▷ **right-wing** *ADJECTIVE*
▷ **right-winger** *NOUN*

WORD HISTORY from the arrangement in the French National Assembly of 1789, where conservatives sat on the right side and revolutionaries on the left

rigid *ADJECTIVE*
1 not able to bend or be forced out of shape
2 strict and inflexible ◆ *There are no rigid rules about the best way to write a short story.*

▷ **rigidly** *ADVERB*
▷ **rigidity** (*say* ri- **jid**- iti) *NOUN*

WORD HISTORY from Latin *rigere* 'to be stiff'

rigmarole *NOUN* **rigmaroles**
1 a long rambling statement

Your rigmarole would have detained a saint / Entering Paradise—decidedly / You must not fail to write that book some day! — *Edmond Rostand, Cyrano de Bergerac*

2 a complicated procedure

WORD HISTORY from an old word *ragman* meaning 'a legal document'

rigor mortis (*say* ry- ger **mor**- tis) *NOUN*
stiffening of the body after death

WORD HISTORY a Latin phrase meaning 'stiffness of death'

rigorous *ADJECTIVE*
1 strict or severe ◆ *The dogs follow a rigorous diet and exercise regime to keep them in perfect condition.*
2 careful and thorough ◆ *Sherlock Holmes was aways rigorous in his methods of detection.*

▷ **rigorously** *ADVERB*

rigour *NOUN* **rigours**
1 strictness or severity
2 strict precision ◆ *The report lacks the rigour a legal mind might have brought to it.*
3 harshness of weather or conditions ◆ *The expedition was unprepared for the rigours of a Siberian winter.*

WORD HISTORY from Latin *rigor* 'stiffness'

rile *VERB* **riles, riling, riled**
(*informal*) to annoy or irritate someone

I love horses, and it riles me to see them badly used. — *Anna Sewell, Black Beauty*

rill *NOUN* **rills**
a small shallow stream over rocks

rim *NOUN* **rims**
the outer edge of a cup, wheel, or other round object

WORD HISTORY from Old English *rima* 'a border, a coast'

rime ❶ *NOUN*
a coating of frost

▷ **rimy** *ADJECTIVE*

WORD HISTORY from Old English *hrim*

rime ❷ *NOUN*
(*Language*) the part of a syllable that includes the vowel and final consonant, e.g. *og* in *dog*, or the whole of words of one syllable beginning in a vowel, e.g. *eel* (SEE ALSO **onset**)

rimmed *ADJECTIVE*
having an edge or border

rind *NOUN*
a tough outer layer or skin on bacon, cheese, fruit, etc.

rinderpest *NOUN*
an infectious viral disease of cattle, with a fever and dysentery

ring ❶ *NOUN* **rings**
1 the outline of a circle
2 something shaped like this, a circular band
3 a thin circular piece of metal worn on a finger
4 a flat circular device forming part of a gas or electric hob
5 the space where a circus performs
6 a square area in which a boxing match or wrestling match takes place

7 (*informal*) a group of people acting together, especially in some illegal activity ◆ *a drugs ring*

to run rings round someone is to outwit them easily

ring *VERB* **rings, ringing, ringed**
to put a ring round something; to encircle something

WORD HISTORY from Old English *hring*

ring❷ *VERB* **rings, ringing, rang, rung**
1 to sound as a bell, or to cause a bell to sound
2 to make a loud clear sound like that of a bell
3 to be filled with sound ◆ *The auditorium rang with applause.*
4 your ears ring when they are filled with a buzzing or humming sound
5 to telephone someone ◆ *Please ring me as soon as you get this message.*

to ring a bell (*informal*) is to arouse a vague memory, or to sound faintly familiar
to ring the changes is to vary things
to ring true is to sound as though it is true

▷ **ringer** *NOUN*

ring *NOUN* **rings**
1 the act of ringing a bell
2 a ringing sound or tone
3 a hint or indication of truth or some other quality

The parson's words had the ring of truth in them to me, and I never doubted that he was right. — *J. Meade Falkner, Moonfleet*

to give someone a ring (*informal*) is to telephone them

WORD HISTORY from Old English *hringan*

ringleader *NOUN* **ringleaders**
a person who leads others in rebellion, mischief, crime, etc.

ringlet *NOUN* **ringlets**
a tube-shaped curl of hair

ringmaster *NOUN* **ringmasters**
the person in charge of a performance in a circus ring

ring road *NOUN* **ring roads**
a road that runs around the edge of a town so that traffic does not have to go through the centre

ringtone *NOUN* **ringtones**
the special sounds a mobile phone makes when it receives a call

ringworm *NOUN*
a fungal skin infection that causes itchy circular patches, especially on the scalp

rink *NOUN* **rinks**
a place made for skating on ice

WORD HISTORY originally a Scots word, perhaps from Old French *renc* 'rank'

rinse *VERB* **rinses, rinsing, rinsed**
1 to wash something lightly
2 to wash an item in clean water to remove soap or dirt

rinse *NOUN* **rinses**
1 the action of rinsing
2 an antiseptic solution for cleaning your mouth
3 a liquid for colouring hair

riot *NOUN* **riots**
1 a wild and violent disturbance by a crowd of people
2 a profuse or wild display of something

to read the Riot Act is to give someone a severe reprimand or warning
to run riot
1 is to behave in an unruly way
2 is to grow or spread in an uncontrolled way

riot *VERB* **riots, rioting, rioted**
to take part in a riot

A Jacobite mob rioted in the Lawnmarket early on, shouting, 'Surrender! Open the gates! The True King home again!' & threw cobbles at windows. — *Frances Mary Hendry, My Story: The '45 Rising*

▷ **rioter** *NOUN*

WORD HISTORY from Old French *rioter* 'to quarrel'

riot gear *NOUN*
protective clothing and equipment worn or carried by police or soldiers dealing with riots

riotous *ADJECTIVE*
1 disorderly or unruly
2 boisterous or unrestrained ◆ *Sounds of riotous laughter were coming from the party downstairs.*

▷ **riotously** *ADVERB*

RIP *ABBREVIATION*
rest in peace, often used as an inscription on a grave

WORD HISTORY from the Latin phrase *requiescat* (or *requiescant*) *in pace*

rip *VERB* **rips, ripping, ripped**
1 to tear something apart roughly
2 to become torn
3 to rush along

to rip someone off (*informal*) is to swindle or charge them too much
to rip something up is to tear it into small pieces

rip *NOUN*
a rough tear or split

ripcord *NOUN*
a cord that is pulled to release a parachute from its pack

ripe *ADJECTIVE* **riper, ripest**
1 a ripe fruit, grain, vegetable is ready to be harvested or eaten
2 a ripe cheese is fully matured ▸▸

a b c d e f g h i j k l m n o p q r s t u v w x y z

3 ready, prepared or able to undergo something ◆ *My horoscope tells me the time is ripe for a change of career.*
a ripe old age a great age
▷ **ripely** *ADVERB*
▷ **ripeness** *NOUN*

ripen *VERB* **ripens, ripening, ripened**
to make something ripe, or to become ripe

rip-off *NOUN* **rip-offs**
(*informal*) a fraud or swindle

riposte (*say* rip- **ost**) *NOUN* **ripostes**
1 a quick clever reply ◆ *I tried to come up with a witty riposte, but all I could think of was, 'So what?'*
2 a quick return thrust in fencing
WORD HISTORY from Italian *risposta* 'response'

ripple *NOUN* **ripples**
1 a small wave or series of waves
2 something resembling this in appearance or movement

Nick felt every muscle in his shoulders and neck suddenly relax, as a ripple of relief passed through on its way to his toes. — *Garth Nix, The Creature in the Case*

3 a gentle sound that rises and falls ◆ *A ripple of laughter passed through the crowd.*

ripple *VERB* **ripples, rippling, rippled**
to form or cause ripples

rip-roaring *ADJECTIVE*
full of energy; wildly noisy

rise *VERB* **rise, rising, rose, risen**
1 to come or go upwards; to grow or extend upwards
2 to increase in amount, number, or intensity
3 to get up from lying, sitting, or kneeling
4 to get out of bed
5 to rebel against a government or other authority
6 dough or batter rises in cooking when it swells up by the action of yeast
7 a river rises at the point at which it begins its course
8 wind rises when it begins to blow more strongly
to rise to the occasion is to cope well with a challenging situation

rise *NOUN* **rises**
1 the action of rising; an upward movement
2 an increase in amount, number, or intensity
3 an increase in wages or salary
4 an upward slope
to give rise to something is to cause it to happen
on the rise increasing or prospering
to take a rise out of someone is to tease someone in order to make them angry or annoyed

riser *NOUN* **risers**
1 a person, animal, or thing that rises ◆ *Grey squirrels are early risers and leave their nests at the first light of day.*
2 a vertical piece between treads of a staircase

rising *NOUN* **risings**
a revolt against a government or other authority

risk *NOUN* **risks**
1 a chance of danger or loss
2 a person or thing representing a source of risk; a hazard ◆ *These candles are a fire risk.*

risk *VERB* **risks, risking, risked**
1 to take the chance of damaging or losing something ◆ *Bilbo risked his life to save the dwarfs from the clutches of evil.*
2 to run the risk of something unpleasant happening ◆ *You risk injuring your knees and ankles if you have the wrong type of footwear.*

risky *ADJECTIVE* **riskier, riskiest**
involving risk; hazardous
▷ **riskily** *ADVERB*
▷ **riskiness** *NOUN*

risotto *NOUN*
an Italian dish of rice cooked with vegetables and meat or seafood
WORD HISTORY an Italian word, from *riso* 'rice'

risqué (*say* **risk**- ay) *ADJECTIVE*
slightly rude or indecent
WORD HISTORY a French word

rissole *NOUN* **rissoles**
a cake of minced meat coated with breadcrumbs and fried

rite *NOUN* **rites**
a religious or other solemn ceremony
WORD HISTORY from Latin *ritus* 'religious ceremony'

ritual *NOUN* **rituals**
1 the series of actions used in a religious or other ceremony
2 a procedure that is regularly followed ◆ *I look forward to the ritual of writing up my diary every evening.*
▷ **ritualistic** *ADJECTIVE*

ritual *ADJECTIVE*
to do with or done as a ritual
▷ **ritually** *ADVERB*

rival *NOUN* **rivals**
a person or thing that competes with another or tries to do the same thing

Your father and I have been friendly rivals in business for some time now. — *J. B. Priestley, An Inspector Calls*

▷ **rivalry** *NOUN*

rival *VERB* **rivals, rivalling, rivalled**
to be a rival of a person or thing
WORD HISTORY from Latin *rivalis* 'someone using the same stream', from *rivus* 'stream'

riven (*say* riv- en) ***ADJECTIVE***
split or torn apart

The sycamore was riven and burnt by lightning, yet sap still gave it a few leaves for summer.
— Henry Williamson, Tarka the Otter

WORD HISTORY from an Old Norse word

river ***NOUN*** **rivers**
a large stream of water flowing in a natural channel
WORD HISTORY from Latin *ripa* 'river bank'

rivet ***NOUN*** **rivets**
a strong nail or bolt for holding pieces of metal together. The end opposite the head is flattened to form another head when it is in place.

rivet ***VERB*** **rivets, riveting, riveted**
1 to fasten something with rivets
2 to be riveted is to be unable to move because of fear, amazement, or excitement
3 something or someone rivets you when they fascinate you or absorb your attention
▷ **riveting** ***ADJECTIVE***
WORD HISTORY from Old French *river* 'to fix or clinch'

rivulet ***NOUN*** **rivulets**
a small stream
WORD HISTORY from Latin *rivus* 'stream'

RM ***ABBREVIATION***
Royal Marines

RN ***ABBREVIATION***
Royal Navy

roach ***NOUN*** **roach**
a small freshwater fish
WORD HISTORY from Old French *roche*

road ***NOUN*** **roads**
1 a level way with a hard surface made for traffic to travel on
2 a way of finding or achieving something ◆ *A week after her operation, my aunt is now on the road to recovery.*

roadblock ***NOUN*** **roadblocks**
a barrier across a road, set up by the police or army to stop and check vehicles

roadholding ***NOUN***
the ability of a vehicle to remain stable and under control, especially when cornering

road pricing ***NOUN***
the practice of charging motorists for the use of roads, with charges increasing on busy roads and at busy times

road rage ***NOUN***
aggressive or violent behaviour by a driver towards other drivers

roadside ***NOUN***
the strip of land beside a road

roadway ***NOUN***
the middle part of the road, used by traffic

roadworks ***PLURAL NOUN***
construction or repair of roads

roadworthy ***ADJECTIVE***
safe to be used on roads

roam ***VERB*** **roams, roaming, roamed**
to wander widely

roam ***NOUN***
a spell of wandering

roan ***ADJECTIVE***
a roan horse has a brown or black coat sprinkled with white or grey hairs

roar ***NOUN*** **roars**
1 a long deep loud sound, like that made by a lion
2 loud laughter

roar ***VERB*** **roars, roaring, roared**
1 to give a roar
2 to laugh loudly

roaring ***ADJECTIVE***
(*informal*) unmistakable, emphatic ◆ *The concert was a roaring success and we plan to repeat it next month.*
to do a roaring trade is to do very good business

roast ***VERB*** **roasts, roasting, roasted**
1 to cook meat or vegetables in an hot oven or by exposing them to high heat
2 to undergo roasting ◆ *Leave the potatoes roasting while you prepare the other vegetables.*
3 to be roasting is to feel very hot

roast ***ADJECTIVE***
cooked by roasting ◆ *roast beef*

roast ***NOUN*** **roasts**
1 meat for roasting
2 roast meat

rob ***VERB*** **robs, robbing, robbed**
1 to steal items from a person or place; to commit robbery
2 to deprive someone of something they need or deserve ◆ *Many Democrats felt they were robbed of victory in the presidential election.*
▷ **robber** ***NOUN***
▷ **robbery** ***NOUN***
WORD HISTORY from Old French *robe* 'booty'

robe ***NOUN*** **robes**
a long loose piece of clothing, especially one worn in ceremonies

robe ***VERB*** **robes, robing, robed**
to dress someone or yourself in a robe

robin ***NOUN*** **robins**
a small brown European bird with a red breast
WORD HISTORY from an Old French word meaning 'Robert'

SPELLING NOTE Some words pronounced **r**- begin with **rh**- or **wr**-

robot (*say* **roh**- bot) ***NOUN*** **robots**
1 a machine that looks or acts like a person
2 a machine programmed to perform specific tasks
3 a person who seems to work or act like a machine
4 (*South African*) a set of traffic lights

WORD HISTORY from Czech *robota* 'forced labour'; the word *robot* was first used in a play by Karel Čapek in 1920

robotics (*say* roh- **bot**- iks) ***NOUN***
the study of the design, construction, and use of robots
▷ **robotic** ***ADJECTIVE***
▷ **robotically** ***ADVERB***

robust ***ADJECTIVE***
1 strong and vigorous
2 sturdily built
▷ **robustly** ***ADVERB***
▷ **robustness** ***NOUN***

WORD HISTORY from Latin *robur* 'strength, an oak tree'

rock❶ ***NOUN*** **rocks**
1 a large stone or boulder
2 the hard part of the earth's crust, under the soil
3 a hard sweet made in cylindrical sticks, usually flavoured with peppermint

on the rocks (*informal*) experiencing difficulties and likely to fail
rock solid completely firm or stable

WORD HISTORY from Old French *rocque*

rock❷ ***VERB*** **rocks, rocking, rocked**
1 to move gently backwards and forwards or from side to side
2 to shake someone or something violently ◆ *A terrible explosion rocked the city to its foundations.*
3 to disturb, shock, or undermine someone or something ◆ *Recent scandals in the industry have rocked the confidence of many investors.*

to rock the boat (*informal*) is to do something that upsets the plans or progress of your group

rock ***NOUN***
1 a rocking movement
2 rock music

WORD HISTORY from Old English *roccian*

rock and roll or **rock 'n' roll** ***NOUN***
a kind of popular dance music with a strong beat, originating in the 1950s

rock-bottom ***ADJECTIVE***
at the lowest level ◆ *This year's sale features rock-bottom prices.*

rock bottom ***NOUN***
the lowest possible level ◆ *The film depicts a journalist whose career has reached rock bottom.*

rock cake ***NOUN*** **rock cakes**
a small fruit cake with a flat base and a hard rough surface

rocker ***NOUN*** **rockers**
1 a thing that rocks something or is rocked
2 a rocking chair

off your rocker (*informal*) mad or crazy

rockery ***NOUN*** **rockeries**
a mound or bank in a garden, where plants are made to grow between large rocks

rocket❶ ***NOUN*** **rockets**
1 a firework that shoots high into the air
2 a structure that is propelled into the air by burning gases, used to send up a missile or a spacecraft
▷ **rocketry** ***NOUN***

rocket ***VERB*** **rockets, rocketing, rocketed**
1 to move with great speed
2 to increase or rise rapidly ◆ *House prices in the area have rocketed in the last six months.*

WORD HISTORY from Italian *rocchetto* 'small distaff', because of the shape

rocket❷ ***NOUN***
a Mediterranean plant of the cabbage family, eaten in salads

WORD HISTORY from French *roquette*

rocking chair ***NOUN*** **rocking chairs**
a chair mounted on rockers or with springs that can be rocked by a person sitting in it

rocking horse ***NOUN*** **rocking horses**
a model of a horse mounted on rockers or springs that can be rocked by a child sitting on it

rock music ***NOUN***
a kind of popular modern music usually with a strong beat

rock pool ***NOUN*** **rock pools**
a pool of water among rocks on a shoreline

rock salt ***NOUN***
common salt as it is found naturally in the earth

rocky❶ ***ADJECTIVE*** **rockier, rockiest**
1 like or made of rock
2 full of rocks ◆ *The rocky landscape of east Harris can look like the surface of the Moon.*

rocky❷ ***ADJECTIVE*** **rockier, rockiest**
unsteady or unstable
▷ **rockily** ***ADVERB***
▷ **rockiness** ***NOUN***

rod ***NOUN*** **rods**
1 a long thin stick or bar
2 a stick with a line attached for fishing

rodent ***NOUN*** **rodents**
an animal that has large front teeth for gnawing, such as a rat, mouse, or squirrel

WORD HISTORY from Latin *rodens* 'gnawing'

rodeo (*say* **roh**- dee- oh) *NOUN* **rodeos**
a display of cowboys' skill in riding and handling horses, roping calves, etc.
WORD HISTORY a Spanish word, from *rodear* 'go round'

roe❶ *NOUN*
a mass of eggs or reproductive cells in a fish's body
WORD HISTORY from an Old German or Old Dutch word

roe❷ *NOUN* **roes** or **roe**
a kind of small deer of Europe and Asia
WORD HISTORY from an Old English word

roebuck *NOUN* **roebucks**
a male roe deer

rogue *NOUN* **rogues**
1 a dishonest or unprincipled person
2 a mischievous but likeable person
3 a wild animal driven away from the herd or living apart from it ◆ *a rogue elephant*
▷ **roguery** *NOUN*

roguish *ADJECTIVE*
playful and mischievous
▷ **roguishly** *ADVERB*
▷ **roguishness** *NOUN*

roil *VERB* **roils, roiling, roiled**
1 to make a liquid cloudy by stirring up sediment, or to become cloudy in this way
2 to swirl or stir about

Dreams roiled in Eragon's mind, breeding and living by their own laws. — *Christopher Paolini, Eragon*

roister *VERB* **roisters, roistering, roistered**
to enjoy yourself in a noisy or boisterous way
▷ **roisterer** *NOUN*
WORD HISTORY from Old French *rustre* 'ruffian'

role *NOUN* **roles**
1 (*Drama*) an actor's part in a play or film
2 an identity that someone assumes in life
3 the purpose or function of a person or thing ◆ *What exactly is your role in the project?* ◆ *The school is keen to increase the role of ICT in the classroom.*
WORD HISTORY from French *rôle* 'roll', originally the roll of paper on which an actor's part was written

role model *NOUN* **role models**
a person looked to by others as an example of how to behave

roll *VERB* **rolls, rolling, rolled**
1 to move along by turning over and over, like a ball or wheel
2 to form something into the shape of a cylinder or ball
3 to flatten something by pushing a roller over it ◆ *Roll out the pastry into a large circle.*
4 a ship or boat rolls when it rocks or sways from side to side
5 land is rolling when it goes gently up and down like waves for a long way
6 to pass steadily

Four years rolled by and I was now five, and still as helpless as a new-born baby. — *Christy Brown, My Left Foot*

7 to move or extend in an undulating way ◆ *To the east, the hills roll down to the clear waters of the bay.*
8 thunder rolls when it rumbles or makes a long vibrating sound
to be rolled into one is to be combined in one person or thing
to be rolling in it or **in money** (*informal*) is to be very rich
to roll in (*informal*)
1 to arrive in great numbers or quantities ◆ *Offers of help soon started to roll in.*
2 to arrive casually at a later time than expected
to roll up (*informal*) is to arrive

roll *NOUN* **rolls**
1 a cylinder made by rolling something up
2 a small individual portion of bread baked in a rounded shape
3 a fold or undulation ◆ *rolls of fat*
4 an official list or register of names
5 a long vibrating sound, especially of thunder or of drums being played ◆ *A clash of cymbals and a drum roll announced the beginning of the Chinese New Year celebration.*
on a roll (*informal*) having a spell of good luck or success
WORD HISTORY from Latin *rotula* 'little wheel'

roll-call *NOUN* **roll-calls**
the calling of a list of names to check that everyone is present

roller *NOUN* **rollers**
1 a cylinder used for flattening or spreading things, or on which something is wound
2 a long swelling sea wave

Rollerblade *NOUN* **Rollerblades**
(*trademark*) a boot like an ice-skating boot, with a line of wheels in place of the skate, for rolling smoothly on hard ground
▷ **rollerblading** *NOUN*

roller coaster *NOUN* **roller coasters**
a type of railway ride in fairgrounds and amusement parks with a series of alternate steep descents and ascents

roller skate *NOUN* **roller skates**
a boot or metal frame fitted under a shoe, with small wheels on it so the wearer can roll smoothly over the ground
▷ **roller-skating** *NOUN*

rollicking *ADJECTIVE*
boisterous and full of fun
WORD HISTORY from *romp* and *frolic*

rolling pin *NOUN*
a heavy cylinder for rolling out pastry or dough

rolling stock *NOUN*
the railway engines, carriages, and wagons used on a railway

roly-poly *NOUN* **roly-polies**
a pudding of suet pastry spread with jam, rolled up, and steamed or baked

ROM *ABBREVIATION*
read-only memory, a type of computer memory with contents that can be searched or copied but not changed

Roman *ADJECTIVE*
to do with ancient or modern Rome or its people

Roman *NOUN* **Romans**
an inhabitant of ancient or modern Rome

Roman alphabet *NOUN*
the alphabet in which most European languages are written

Roman candle *NOUN* **Roman candles**
a tubular firework that sends out coloured sparks

Roman Catholic *ADJECTIVE*
belonging to or to do with the Christian Church that acknowledges the Pope as its head
▷ **Roman Catholicism** *NOUN*

Roman Catholic *NOUN* **Roman Catholics**
a member of this Church

romance (*say* ro- **manss**) *NOUN* **romances**
1 tender feelings, experiences, and qualities connected with love
2 a love affair
3 a fictional love story
4 a quality or feeling of mystery, excitement, and remoteness from everyday life ◆ *the romance of ocean cruises*
5 a medieval story about the adventures of heroes

romance *VERB* **romances, romancing, romanced**
1 to romance someone is to treat them in a romantic way while courting them
2 to exaggerate or distort the truth in an imaginative way
WORD HISTORY from Old French *romanz*

Romance language *NOUN*
any of the group of European languages descended from Latin, such as French, Italian and Spanish

Roman numerals *PLURAL NOUN*
the letters representing numbers in the Roman system (I = 1, V = 5, X = 10, L = 50, C = 100, D = 500, M = 1,000) (SEE ALSO **arabic numerals**)

romantic *ADJECTIVE*
1 to do with or characterized by love or romance
2 sentimental or idealistic; not realistic or practical
▷ **romantically** *ADVERB*

romantic *NOUN* **romantics**
a person with romantic beliefs or attitudes

romanticize *VERB* **romanticizes, romanticizing, romanticized**
to describe or think about something in an idealized or unrealistic way
USAGE NOTE This word can also be spelled romanticise.

Romany *NOUN* **Romanies**
1 a member of a nomadic people thought to originate in India, now living in travelling communities throughout the world
2 the Indic language spoken by these people
WORD HISTORY from Romany *rom* 'man'

romp *VERB* **romps, romping, romped**
to play about together in a rough and lively way, as children do

Belle, our dog, my other companion, was old and lazy, and liked to sleep by the open fire rather than to romp with me. — *Helen Keller, The Story of My Life*

to romp home or in to win a race or competition easily

romp *NOUN* **romps**
a spell of romping

rompers *PLURAL NOUN*
a piece of clothing for a baby or young child, covering their body and legs

rondo *NOUN* **rondos**
a piece of music with a theme that recurs several times
WORD HISTORY an Italian word, from French *rondeau* 'circle'

roof *NOUN* **roofs**
1 the part that covers the top of a building, shelter, or vehicle
2 the top inside surface of something ◆ *the roof of your mouth*
to go through the roof (*informal*) the price of something goes through the roof when it becomes extremely high
to hit the roof (*informal*) is to suddenly become very angry

roof *VERB* **roofs, roofing, roofed**
1 to cover something with a roof
2 to be the roof of something

roof garden *NOUN* **roof gardens**
a garden on the flat roof of a building

roofing *NOUN*
material used to construct the roof of a building

roof rack *NOUN* **roof racks**
a framework for carrying luggage on top of a vehicle

rook❶ *NOUN* **rooks**
a black crow that nests in colonies

rook *VERB* **rooks, rooking, rooked**
(*informal*) to swindle or overcharge someone
WORD HISTORY from Old English *hroc*

rook❷ *NOUN* **rooks**
a chess piece shaped like a castle
WORD HISTORY from Arabic *rukk*

rookery *NOUN* **rookeries**
1 a colony of rooks; a place where rooks nest
2 a colony or breeding place of penguins or seals

room *NOUN* **rooms**
1 a part of a building with its own walls and ceiling
2 the people present in a room ◆ *The whole room fell silent.*
3 enough space ◆ *There's room in the attic for another couple of boxes.*
4 opportunity or scope for something ◆ *Although the new software is impressive, there is still some room for improvement.*
▷ **roomful** *NOUN* **roomfuls**

room-mate *NOUN* **room-mates**
a person sharing a room with another

room service *NOUN*
a hotel service providing food and drink to guests in their rooms

room temperature *NOUN*
a comfortable surrounding temperature, about 20°C

roomy *ADJECTIVE* **roomier, roomiest**
containing plenty of room; spacious

roost *VERB* **roosts, roosting, roosted**
birds roost when they perch or settle for sleep
to rule the roost is to be the dominant person in a group or household

roost *NOUN* **roosts**
a place where birds roost

rooster *NOUN* **roosters**
(*American*) a male domestic fowl; a cockerel

root❶ *NOUN* **roots**
1 that part of a plant that grows under the ground and absorbs water and nourishment from the soil
2 a person's roots are their family origins, or their sense of belonging to a place where they or their family live or used to live ◆ *Although I've lived in London for many years, my roots are in Jamaica.*
3 a source or basis of something ◆ *We are trying to get to the root of the problem.*
4 (*Mathematics*) a number that when multiplied by itself one or more times produces a given number ◆ *3 is the square root of 9* ◆ *2 is the cube root of 8*
5 (*Language*) a word from which other forms are made by adding prefixes and suffixes, e.g. *happy* is the root of *unhappy* and *happiness*
at root fundamentally
to take root
1 to grow roots
2 to become established

root *VERB* **roots, rooting, rooted**
1 to take root, or to cause something to take root
2 someone is rooted in a place when they are standing still and unmoving

> Ivy stood rooted to the spot, too terrified, surprised, shocked, to move at all. — *Catherine MacPhail, Run Zan Run*

3 something is rooted in a place when it is firmly or deeply established there ◆ *The tradition of open air theatre is deeply rooted in British culture.*
to root something out is to find and get rid of something unwanted
WORD HISTORY from an Old Norse word

root❷ *VERB* **roots, rooting, rooted**
1 a pig or other animal roots when it turns up ground in search of food
2 to rummage or poke about in search for something

> Mrs McLachlan ... rooted in a battered handbag and produced a crumpled newspaper advert and a pair of reading glasses. — *Debi Gliori, Pure Dead Magic*

to root for someone to root for a person or team is to support them enthusiastically
WORD HISTORY from an Old English word

rootless *ADJECTIVE*
1 having no root or roots
2 a rootless person has no family or other connections with a community
▷ **rootlessness** *NOUN*

rope *NOUN* **ropes**
a strong thick cord made of twisted strands of fibre
to show someone the ropes is to show them how to do something

rope *VERB* **ropes, roping, roped**
to fasten something with a rope
to rope someone in is to persuade them to take part in something

ropy *ADJECTIVE* **ropier, ropiest**
1 a ropy substance forms long sticky threads
2 (*informal*) poor in quality or health
▷ **ropiness** *NOUN*

rosary *NOUN* **rosaries**
1 a set series of prayers used in the Roman Catholic Church
2 a string of beads for keeping count of a set of prayers in some other religions
WORD HISTORY from Latin *rosarium* 'rose garden'

a b c d e f g h i j k l m n o p q r s t u v w x y z

rose❶ *NOUN* **roses**
1 a prickly bush or shrub with ornamental usually fragrant flowers
2 a flower from this bush or shrub
3 a deep pink colour
4 a sprinkling nozzle with many holes, such as on a watering can or hosepipe

rose *ADJECTIVE*
deep pink in colour
WORD HISTORY via Old English from Latin *rosa*

rose❷ *past tense of* **rise**

rosé *NOUN*
a light pink wine
WORD HISTORY a French word meaning 'pink'

rosebud *NOUN* **rosebuds**
the bud of a rose

rosemary *NOUN*
an evergreen shrub with fragrant leaves, used as a herb in cooking
WORD HISTORY from Latin *ros marinus* 'dew of the sea', because it grows near coasts and has blossom which looks like dew

rosette *NOUN* **rosettes**
a large circular badge or ornament, made of ribbon
WORD HISTORY a French word meaning 'little rose'

rose water *NOUN*
a fragrant liquid perfumed with roses

rose window *NOUN*
a circular window in a church, with a pattern of tracery

rosewood *NOUN*
a fragrant close-grained wood used for making furniture

Rosh Hashana or **Rosh Hashanah** *NOUN*
the Jewish New Year festival
WORD HISTORY a Hebrew phrase meaning 'head of the year'

rosin (*say* roz- in) *NOUN*
a kind of resin, often rubbed on the bows of stringed instruments to stop them sliding over the strings

roster *NOUN* **rosters**
a list of people showing their turns to be on duty

roster *VERB* **rosters, rostering, rostered**
to place a person or name on a roster
WORD HISTORY from Dutch *rooster* 'list'

rostrum *NOUN* **rostra**
a platform for one person, used especially when giving a speech or conducting an orchestra
WORD HISTORY a Latin word meaning 'beak, prow of a warship', because in ancient Rome rostra were decorated with the prows of captured enemy ships

rosy *ADJECTIVE* **rosier, rosiest**
1 rose-coloured; deep pink
2 a rosy view or prospect is hopeful or cheerful ◆ *At the start of the year, things were looking rosy for United.*
▷ **rosily** *ADVERB*
▷ **rosiness** *NOUN*

rot *VERB* **rots, rotting, rotted**
to go soft or bad and become useless; to decay

rot *NOUN*
1 the process of rotting; decay
2 a process of becoming worse in standard or condition ◆ *Isn't there anything we can do to stop the rot?*
3 (*informal*) nonsense, rubbish

rota (*say* roh- ta) *NOUN* **rotas**
a list of people to do things or of things to be done in turn
WORD HISTORY a Latin word meaning 'wheel'

rotate *VERB* **rotates, rotating, rotated**
1 to go round like a wheel; to revolve
2 to arrange or deal with something in a set sequence
3 to take turns at doing something, to be used in turn ◆ *The kitchen teams rotate every three weeks in the summer.*
▷ **rotation** *NOUN*
▷ **rotary** *ADJECTIVE*
▷ **rotatory** *ADJECTIVE*

rote *NOUN*
by rote from memory or by routine, without full understanding of the meaning ◆ *I remember learning this speech from Macbeth by rote.*

rotor *NOUN* **rotors**
1 a rotating part of a machine
2 a propeller blade on a helicopter

rotten *ADJECTIVE*
1 rotted or decayed, so as to break or fall apart easily

> Most of the wood was so rotten that when they pulled it broke up into a shower of fragments and woodlice and decay. — *William Golding, Lord of the Flies*

2 morally corrupt
3 (*informal*) very bad or unpleasant ◆ *We had rotten weather on our holiday, so we stayed indoors most of the time.*
▷ **rottenness** *NOUN*

rotten *ADVERB*
(*informal*) very much ◆ *Your grandparents spoil you rotten.*

rottweiler *NOUN* **rottweilers**
a breed of large black German dog, sometimes used as a guard dog
WORD HISTORY a German word, from *Rottweil*, a town in Germany where the dog was bred

rotund (*say* ro- **tund**) ***ADJECTIVE***
rounded or plump

He was a large man, very rotund of belly and helpless looking. — *Jack London, The Valley of the Moon*

▷ **rotundity** ***NOUN***

WORD HISTORY from Latin *rotundus* 'round'

rotunda ***NOUN*** **rotundas**
a circular domed building or hall

WORD HISTORY from Italian *rotonda (camera)* 'round (chamber)'

rouble (*say* **roo**- bul) ***NOUN*** **roubles**
the unit of money in Russia and some other countries

roué (*say* **roo**- ay) ***NOUN*** **roués**
a debauched man

WORD HISTORY a French word meaning 'broken on a wheel', referring to a type of torture thought to be deserved by such a person

rouge (*say* roozh) ***NOUN***
a reddish cosmetic for colouring the cheeks

rouge ***VERB*** **rouges, rouging, rouged**
to colour your cheeks with rouge

WORD HISTORY a French word meaning 'red'

rough ***ADJECTIVE*** **rougher, roughest**
1 having an uneven or irregular surface; not level or smooth
2 not gentle, restrained, or careful; violent ◆ *The prisoner was forced to move forward with a rough shove in the back.*
3 rough sea or weather is wild and stormy
4 difficult and unpleasant ◆ *My husband's had a rough time at work recently.*
5 a rough version or draft of something is not finished in detail
6 not exact

I merely suggest that the position of the sun, if it is out, would give you a rough idea of the time. — *Tom Stoppard, Rosencrantz & Guildenstern are Dead*

rough and ready crude or hastily put together, but effective or adequate
to sleep rough is to sleep out of doors, not in a proper bed
▷ **roughness** ***NOUN***

rough ***NOUN***
1 a ruffian or hooligan
2 the area of longer grass around the fairway and green on a golf course
3 a rough drawing or design
in the rough in a natural or unfinished state
rough and tumble disorderly fighting or rough play

rough ***VERB*** **roughs, roughing, roughed**
to rough it is to do without ordinary comforts
to rough something out to rough out an idea or plan is to draw or describe it roughly
to rough someone up (*informal*) is to beat someone up

roughage ***NOUN***
fibre in food, which helps digestion

roughen ***VERB*** **roughens, roughening, roughened**
to make something rough, or to become rough

roughly ***ADVERB***
1 in a rough manner
2 approximately ◆ *The nearest petrol station is roughly five miles from here.*

roughneck ***NOUN*** **roughnecks**
1 a worker on an oil rig
2 (*informal*) a rough uncouth person

roughshod ***ADVERB***
to ride roughshod over someone is to treat them inconsiderately or arrogantly

WORD HISTORY from an earlier meaning, a *roughshod* horse had shoes with the nail heads left sticking out to prevent slipping

roulette (*say* roo- **let**) ***NOUN***
a gambling game where players bet on where the ball on a revolving wheel will come to rest

WORD HISTORY a French word meaning 'little wheel'

round ***ADJECTIVE***
1 having a curved shape or outline; shaped like a circle, ball, or cylinder
2 a round number is expressed to the nearest whole number or the nearest ten, hundred, etc.

Fractions are numbers that are not nice round numbers. — *Kjartan Poskitt, Murderous Maths*

3 full or complete ◆ *a round dozen*
in round figures approximately; without giving exact units
▷ **roundness** ***NOUN***

round ***ADVERB***
1 in a circle or curve; surrounding something ◆ *Go round to the back of the house.*
2 in every direction or to every person ◆ *Could you hand round the sandwiches?*
3 so as to face in a different direction ◆ *If you turn your chair round, you'll get a better view.*
4 from place to place ◆ *Our guests were happy to wander round for a while.*
5 to someone's house or place of work ◆ *Come round after lunch.*
to come round is to become conscious again
round about
1 near by
2 roughly; approximately

round ***PREPOSITION***
1 on all sides of something; circling or enclosing ◆ *They've put a new net round the tennis court.*
2 at points on or near the circumference of something ◆ *There were eight chairs set round the table.*
3 in a curve, circle, or orbit at an even distance from something

Uranus takes 84 Earth years to travel right round the sun once. — *Kjartan Poskitt, The Gobsmacking Galaxy*

SPELLING NOTE Some words pronounced **r-** begin with **rh-** or **wr-**

4 to or around all parts of a place ◆ *After tea, I'll show you round the house.*
5 on or to the further side of a place ◆ *The post box is just round the corner.*
6 in the general area; around

Red Jack lived somewhere round here, people said, in a place called Black Raven Alley. — *Alison Prince, Oranges and Murder*

round the clock continuously throughout day and night

round *NOUN* **rounds**
1 a series of visits made by a doctor, postman, or other person as part of their duties
2 one section or stage in a competition ◆ *The final round of judging at Crufts will be held on Sunday.*
3 a recurring course or series, or one event in a series ◆ *The daily round of village life has changed little here.*
4 a shot or volley of shots from a gun; ammunition for this
5 the playing of all the holes on a golf course once
6 a whole slice of bread; a sandwich made with two slices of bread
7 a song in which people sing the same words but start at different times
8 a set of drinks bought for all the members of a group

to do or go the rounds a story or piece of news does the rounds when it is passed round among a lot of people

round *VERB* **rounds, rounding, rounded**
1 to make something round, or to become round
2 to travel or go round something

Two figures were rounding a corner and were approaching through the gloom. — *Nicola Morgan, Fleshmarket*

to round something off
1 to round off an event or occasion is to complete it in a pleasant way ◆ *Let's round the evening off with some music.*
2 to round off an edge or corner is to make it smooth and not sharp

to round on someone is to attack them suddenly

to round something or someone up
1 to round up people or animals is to gather them together
2 to round up a figure is to make it into a round number

roundabout *NOUN* **roundabouts**
1 a road junction with a circular structure round which traffic has to pass in the same direction
2 a circular revolving ride in a playground or a merry-go-round at a funfair

roundabout *ADJECTIVE*
indirect; not using the shortest way of going or of saying or doing something ◆ *This is a rather roundabout way of saying thank you.*

rounders *NOUN*
a team game played with bat and ball, in which players have to run round a circuit of bases

Roundhead *NOUN* **Roundheads**
(*History*) a supporter of the Parliamentary party in the English Civil War (1642-9)

WORD HISTORY so called because they wore their hair cut short at a time when long hair was in fashion for men

roundly *ADVERB*
1 thoroughly or severely ◆ *We were roundly told off for being late.*
2 in a rounded shape

round robin *NOUN* **round robins**
1 a statement or petition signed by a number of people, often with signatures written in a circle to conceal who signed first
2 a competition in which each player or team plays in turn against every other one

round-shouldered *ADJECTIVE*
with the shoulders bent forward, so that the back is rounded

round-the-clock *ADJECTIVE*
lasting or happening all day and all night

round trip *NOUN* **round trips**
a trip to one or more places and back to where you started

round-up *NOUN* **round-ups**
1 a gathering up of cattle or people ◆ *a police round-up of suspects*
2 a summary ◆ *a round-up of the news*

roundworm *NOUN* **roundworms**
a kind of worm that lives as a parasite in the intestines of animals and birds

rouse *VERB* **rouses, rousing, roused**
1 to wake someone, or to wake up from a sleep or reverie
2 to cause someone to become active or excited

rousing *ADJECTIVE*
1 a rousing speech is one that excites or stirs an audience
2 a rousing cheer is loud and emphatic

rout (*rhymes with* shout) ❶ *VERB* **routs, routing, routed**
to defeat an enemy completely and force them to retreat

rout *NOUN* **routs**
utter defeat; a disorderly retreat of defeated troops

WORD HISTORY via Old French from Latin *rumpere* 'to break'

route (*sounds like* root) *NOUN* **routes**
the way taken to get from a starting point to a destination

route *VERB* **routes, routing, routed**
to send someone or something by a certain route

router (*say* roo- ter) *NOUN* **routers**
(*ICT*) a device which sends data to different parts of a computer network

routine (*say* roo- **teen**) *NOUN* **routines**
1 a regular way of doing things; a series of acts performed regularly in the same way

Human beings are great adaptors, and by lunchtime life in the environs of Arthur's house had settled into a steady routine. — *Douglas Adams, The Hitch Hiker's Guide to the Galaxy*

2 a set sequence in a performance, especially in a comedy act
3 (*ICT*) a sequence of instructions to a computer

routine *ADJECTIVE*
1 performed as part of a regular procedure ◆ *a routine inspection*
2 in accordance with routine, not varying
▷ **routinely** *ADVERB*

rove *VERB* **roves, roving, roved**
to roam or wander
▷ **rover** *NOUN*

roving *ADJECTIVE*
travelling for your work, with no fixed base ◆ *our roving reporter*

row❶ (*rhymes with* go) *NOUN* **rows**
a line of people or things
WORD HISTORY from Old English *raw*

row❷ (*rhymes with* go) *VERB* **rows, rowing, rowed**
1 to make a boat move by using oars
2 to take part in the sport of rowing
▷ **rower** *NOUN*
▷ **rowing boat** *NOUN*
WORD HISTORY from Old English *rowan*

row❸ (*rhymes with* cow) *NOUN* **rows**
1 a loud noise or uproar
2 a noisy quarrel or argument
3 a scolding

row *VERB* **rows, rowing, rowed**
to quarrel or argue noisily
WORD HISTORY origin unknown

rowan (*say* **roh**- an) *NOUN* **rowans**
a tree that bears hanging bunches of red berries
WORD HISTORY from a Scandinavian word

rowdy *ADJECTIVE* **rowdier, rowdiest**
noisy and disorderly

This is not a church meeting, this is a public meeting; no sitting in stiff obedience today. This is an altogether more rowdy affair. — *Chris Priestley, Witch Hunt*

▷ **rowdily** *ADVERB*
▷ **rowdiness** *NOUN*
WORD HISTORY originally an American word

rowlock (*say* rol- ok) *NOUN* **rowlocks**
a device on the side of a boat for keeping an oar in place
WORD HISTORY from an earlier word *oarlock*, with *row* replacing *oar*

royal *ADJECTIVE*
to do with, or suitable for, a king or queen
▷ **royally** *ADVERB*

royal *NOUN* **royals**
(*informal*) a member of the royal family
WORD HISTORY from an Old French word, related to *regal*

royalist *NOUN* **royalists**
1 a person who favours the idea of a monarchy
2 (*History*) a **Royalist** was a supporter of the monarchy in the English Civil War (1642–9)

royalty *NOUN*
1 the fact of being royal
2 a royal person or royal people ◆ *There will be royalty present.*
3 a payment made to an author or composer for each copy of a book sold or for each public performance of a work

RSVP *ABBREVIATION*
please reply (often written at the end of an invitation)
WORD HISTORY short for a French phrase *répondez s'il vous plaît*

rub *VERB* **rubs, rubbing, rubbed**
1 to press something against a surface and move it back and forth ◆ *Try not to rub your eyes.* ◆ *Rub some garlic over the chicken before you pop it in the oven.*
2 to polish, clean, or dry something by rubbing
3 to keep moving against a surface and make it sore or worn ◆ *These new shoes are rubbing my heels.*

to rub something down is to dry, smooth, or clean it by rubbing
to rub it in (*informal*) is to emphasize or remind someone constantly of an unpleasant or embarrassing fact
to rub off
1 a mark or stain rubs off when it is removed by rubbing
2 success or luck rubs off when it is transferred from one person to another ◆ *I wish some of your good luck would rub off on me.*
to rub something out to rub out a pencil mark is to remove it using a rubber
to rub shoulders with someone is to associate or come into contact with them
to rub someone up the wrong way is to irritate them by your actions

rub *NOUN* **rubs**
the act or process of rubbing

rubber *NOUN* **rubbers**
1 a tough elastic substance, made from the sap of a tropical tree or manufactured synthetically, used for making tyres, balls, hoses, etc.
2 a piece of rubber for erasing pencil or ink marks
▷ **rubbery** *ADJECTIVE*

rubber plant *NOUN* **rubber plants**
a tall evergreen plant with tough shiny leaves, often grown as a house plant

rubber stamp *NOUN* **rubber stamps**
a small device with lettering or a design on it, which is inked and used to mark paper

rubber-stamp *VERB* **rubber-stamps, rubber-stamping, rubber-stamped**
to give official approval to a decision without thinking about it

rubber tree *NOUN* **rubber trees**
a tropical tree from which rubber is obtained

rubbish *NOUN*
1 waste material to be thrown away
2 something that is worthless or stupid ◆ *I don't want to hear any more rubbish about selling the house.*

rubbish *ADJECTIVE*
(*informal*) very poor in quality
▷ **rubbishy** *ADVERB*

rubbish *VERB* **rubbishes, rubbishing, rubbished**
(*informal*) to criticize something severely or dismiss it as worthless

Rubbishing our children's tastes is one of the few pleasures remaining to us as we become old.
— *Nick Hornby, 31 Songs*

WORD HISTORY from Old French *rubbous*

rubble *NOUN*
broken pieces of brick or stone

rubella *NOUN*
an infectious disease which causes a red rash, and which can damage a baby if the mother catches it early in pregnancy

WORD HISTORY from Latin *rubellus* 'reddish'

rubric *NOUN*
a set of instructions at the beginning of an official document or an examination paper

WORD HISTORY from Latin *rubeus* 'red', because rubrics used to be written in red ink

ruby *NOUN* **rubies**
1 a type of red gemstone
2 a deep red colour

WORD HISTORY from Latin *rubeus* 'red'

ruby wedding *NOUN*
the 40th anniversary of a wedding

ruche (*say* roosh) *NOUN* **ruches**
a frill or pleat of fabric
▷ **ruched** *ADJECTIVE*

ruck❶ *NOUN* **rucks**
1 a tightly packed crowd of people
2 a loose rugby scrum with the ball on the ground

WORD HISTORY probably from a Scandinavian word

ruck❷ *NOUN* **rucks**
a crease or wrinkle

ruck *VERB* **rucks, rucking, rucked**
a garment or material rucks or rucks up when it forms creases or wrinkles

WORD HISTORY from Old Norse *hrukka*

rucksack *NOUN* **rucksacks**
a bag with straps for carrying on your back; a backpack

WORD HISTORY from a German word meaning 'back sack'

ructions *PLURAL NOUN*
(*informal*) angry protests or arguments ◆ *The controversial film caused ructions when it was previewed at the festival.*

rudder *NOUN* **rudders**
a hinged upright piece at the back of a ship or aircraft, used for steering

ruddy *ADJECTIVE* **ruddier, ruddiest**
a ruddy complexion is red and healthy-looking
▷ **ruddily** *ADVERB*
▷ **ruddiness** *NOUN*

WORD HISTORY from Old English *rudig*

rude *ADJECTIVE* **ruder, rudest**
1 impolite, bad-mannered
2 indecent or improper
3 roughly made; crude ◆ *a rude shelter*
4 rude health is vigorous and hearty

a rude awakening an unexpected shocking or unpleasant experience
▷ **rudely** *ADVERB*
▷ **rudeness** *NOUN*

WORD HISTORY from Latin *rudis* 'raw, wild'

rudimentary *ADJECTIVE*
1 to do with rudiments; elementary
2 not fully developed ◆ *Penguins have rudimentary wings.*

rudiments (*say* **rood**- i- ments) *PLURAL NOUN*
the elementary principles of a subject ◆ *This book covers the rudiments of chess.*

rue❶ *VERB*
to regret something and wish it had not happened ◆ *You'll live to rue the day you betrayed your friends.*

WORD HISTORY from an Old English word

rue❷ *NOUN*
a shrub with bitter leaves used in herbal medicine

WORD HISTORY via Old French and Latin from a Greek word

rueful *ADJECTIVE*
showing sad regret ◆ *She gave a rueful smile.*
▷ **ruefully** *ADVERB*

ruff *NOUN* **ruffs**
1 a starched pleated frill worn round the neck in the 16th century
2 a collar-like ring of feathers or fur round a bird's or animal's neck
3 a bird of the sandpiper family
WORD HISTORY another spelling of *rough*

ruffian *NOUN* **ruffians**
a violent lawless person
▷ **ruffianly** *ADJECTIVE*

ruffle *VERB* **ruffles, ruffling, ruffled**
1 to disturb the smoothness or evenness of something
2 a bird ruffles its feathers by making them stand upright to show anger or to make a display
3 to upset or annoy someone
▷ **ruffled** *ADJECTIVE*

ruffle *NOUN* **ruffles**
a gathered ornamental frill

rug *NOUN* **rugs**
1 a small carpet or thick mat for the floor
2 a piece of thick fabric used as a blanket

rugby or **rugby football** *NOUN*
a kind of football game using an oval ball that players may carry or kick
WORD HISTORY named after *Rugby* School in Warwickshire, where it was first played

rugby league *NOUN*
a form of rugby played in teams of 13 players

rugby union *NOUN*
a form of rugby played in teams of 15 players

rugged *ADJECTIVE*
1 a rugged landscape has an uneven surface or outline; craggy
2 showing toughness and determination; sturdy
▷ **ruggedly** *ADVERB*
▷ **ruggedness** *NOUN*

rugger *NOUN*
(*informal*) rugby football

ruin *NOUN* **ruins**
1 severe damage or destruction to something
2 complete loss of a person's resources or prospects
3 a building that has fallen down or been badly damaged
to be in ruins is to have failed completely ◆ *The team's hopes for a gold medal are now in ruins.*

ruin *VERB* **ruins, ruining, ruined**
1 to damage or spoil something so severely that it is useless
2 to make someone bankrupt
▷ **ruination** *NOUN*
WORD HISTORY from Latin *ruere* 'to fall'

ruinous *ADJECTIVE*
1 causing ruin
2 in ruins; ruined
▷ **ruinously** *ADVERB*

rule *NOUN* **rules**
1 a statement of what you must or should do in a certain set of circumstances or in playing a game
2 control or government ◆ *East Timor was under Portuguese rule until 1975.*
3 the customary or normal way of doing things ◆ *By the 4th century BC, carefully planned cities had become the rule in ancient Greece.*
4 a carpenter's ruler
as a rule usually; more often than not

'As a rule,' said Holmes, 'the more bizarre a thing is the less mysterious it proves to be.' — *Sir Arthur Conan Doyle, The Red-Headed League*

rule *VERB* **rules, ruling, ruled**
1 to govern or reign
2 to give a decision as judge or other authority ◆ *The referee ruled that it was a foul.*
3 to draw a straight line with a ruler or other straight edge
to rule something out is to exclude it as a possibility
WORD HISTORY via French from Latin *regula* 'a rule'

ruler *NOUN* **rulers**
1 a person who governs
2 a strip of wood, metal, or plastic with straight edges, used for measuring and drawing straight lines

ruling *NOUN* **rulings**
a judgement

rum *NOUN*
a strong alcoholic drink made from sugar or molasses

rumba *NOUN*
a lively ballroom dance of Cuban origin, or music for this

rumble *VERB* **rumbles, rumbling, rumbled**
1 to make a deep heavy continuous sound like thunder

I was just wiping the sauce off my mouth after lunch when I heard cartwheels rumbling in the lane outside. — *David Almond, The Fire-Eaters*

2 your stomach rumbles when it makes a noise because you are hungry
3 (*informal*) to be rumbled is to be found out or discovered doing something wrong
to rumble on a dispute or argument rumbles on when it keeps going for a long time

rumble *NOUN* **rumbles**
a rumbling sound
WORD HISTORY probably from Old Dutch *rommelen*

a b c d e f g h i j k l m n o p q r s t u v w x y z

rumble strip *NOUN* **rumble strips**
a series of raised strips on a road that warns drivers of the edge of the roadway, or tells them to slow down, by making vehicles vibrate

rumbustious *ADJECTIVE*
boisterous or unruly
WORD HISTORY probably from an old word *robustious* 'boisterous or robust'

ruminant *NOUN* **ruminants**
an animal that chews the cud, such as cattle, sheep, deer, etc.

ruminant *ADJECTIVE*
to do with ruminants
WORD HISTORY from Latin *ruminari* 'to chew over again'

ruminate *VERB* **ruminates, ruminating, ruminated**
1 to chew the cud
2 to meditate or ponder

Here he had not been long, ruminating on his new love, when Juliet appeared above at a window. — *Charles & Mary Lamb, Tales From Shakespeare*

▷ **rumination** *NOUN*
▷ **ruminative** *ADJECTIVE*

rummage *VERB* **rummages, rummaging, rummaged**
to search for something by turning things over or moving them about in an untidy way

Harry rummaged once more in his trunk, extracted his money bag and shoved some silver into Stan's hand. — *J. K. Rowling, Harry Potter and the Prisoner of Azkaban*

rummage *NOUN*
a search of this kind
WORD HISTORY from Old French *arrumage* 'stowing of a cargo in a ship's hold', from Dutch *ruim* 'space'

rummy *NOUN*
a card game in which players try to form sets or sequences of cards

rumour *NOUN* **rumours**
information that spreads to a lot of people but may not be true

These were dangerous days. There were rumours of bandit gangs that preyed on travellers. — *William Nicholson, Firesong*

rumour *VERB* **rumours, rumouring, rumoured**
to be rumoured is to be spread as a rumour
WORD HISTORY from Latin *rumor* 'noise'

rump *NOUN* **rumps**
1 the hind part of an animal
2 a person's buttocks

rumple *VERB* **rumples, rumpling, rumpled**
to make something look untidy or dishevelled; to crumple something

In the distance I could see an area where the rocks had been pushed up and rumpled, like bedclothes, by some ancient volcanic upheaval. — *Gerald Durrell, A Zoo in My Luggage*

WORD HISTORY from a Dutch word

rump steak *NOUN* **rump steaks**
a piece of meat from the rump of a cow

rumpus *NOUN* **rumpuses**
(*informal*) an uproar; an angry protest

Now there's quite a rumpus at the hall-door, and then a fully-armed knight rides into the court, holding up a woman's dress. — *Kevin Crossley-Holland, The Seeing Stone*

run *VERB* **runs, running, ran, run**
1 to move with quick steps so that both or all feet leave the ground at each stride
2 to pass over or through something, or to make something do this ◆ *She ran her fingers through her hair.*
3 to go or travel smoothly or swiftly
4 to flow; to produce mucus or other liquid

Mumpo started to cry. When he cried, his nose ran, and it was even harder to be sympathetic to him, because his upper-lip was shiny with nose-dribble. — *William Nicholson, The Wind Singer*

5 to work or function ◆ *The engine is running smoothly now.*
6 to manage or organize an institution or event

'You're wasted running that hospital,' Gerald Faulkner told Mum.... 'You ought to be running British Telecom. Or Great Britain! Or the World!' — *Anne Fine, Goggle-Eyes*

7 to compete in a race or contest; to stand in an election ◆ *My sister is running for president of the Students' Union.*
8 to extend in distance or time ◆ *The room runs for the full length of the house.*
9 to pass or make something pass into a specified condition ◆ *Supplies of petrol are running low on the island.*
10 to recur as a characteristic ◆ *Musical ability runs in the family.*
11 to publish a story in a newspaper or magazine
12 (*ICT*) to cause a computer program to operate
13 to go or take someone in a vehicle ◆ *I'll run you to the station.*
14 to own and use a motor vehicle
15 to run a temperature is to be suffering from a high temperature

to run across someone is to happen to meet or find them
to run a risk is to take a chance
to run away is to leave a place secretly or quickly
run away with something or someone
1 to run away with a prize or competition is to win it easily

2 your imagination runs away with you when it is no longer under your control
3 to run away with someone is to elope with them

to run down
1 something runs down when it stops gradually or declines
2 (*informal*) to run someone down is to say unkind or unfair things about them

to run for it (*informal*) is to try to escape by running away

run in (*informal*)
1 to run someone in is to arrest and take them into custody
2 to run in a new car, pair of shoes, etc. is to use them gently at first

to run into something or **someone**
1 to run into something is to collide with it
2 to run into someone is to happen to meet them

to run on is to continue for longer than expected

to run out a licence or permit runs out when it is no longer valid

to run someone out to run out a batsman in cricket is to knock over their wicket

to run out of something is to have used up your stock of it

to run someone over is to knock them down with a moving vehicle

to run through something is to examine, repeat, or rehearse it quickly

to run something up
1 to run up a bill or score is to allow it to mount up
2 to run up a garment or other item is to sew it quickly

to run up against something is to experience or meet a difficulty or problem

SYNONYMS (meaning 1) sprint, race, jog, tear, dash, rush, hasten, speed, streak, bolt; (meaning 4) stream, trickle, flow, pour, spill, gush; (meaning 5) function, work, operate, perform; (*run out*) expire, cease, terminate

run *NOUN* **runs**
1 the action of running; a time spent running ◆ *I usually go for a run on Sunday mornings.*
2 a point scored in cricket or baseball
3 a continuous series of events ◆ *We've had a run of good luck recently.*
4 a general demand for goods ◆ *There has been a run on bread this morning.*
5 an enclosure for animals ◆ *a chicken run*
6 a series of damaged stitches in a pair of tights or stockings
7 a track ◆ *a ski run*
8 permission to make unrestricted use of something ◆ *You can have the run of the house while we're away.*

on the run running away, especially from the police

WORD HISTORY from Old English *rinnan*

runaway *NOUN* **runaways**
someone who has run away

runaway *ADJECTIVE*
1 having run away or out of control
2 a runaway victory is one that you win easily

rundown *ADJECTIVE*
1 tired and in bad health
2 in bad condition; dilapidated

rune *NOUN* **runes**
any of the letters in an alphabet used by early Germanic peoples

▷ **runic** *ADJECTIVE*

WORD HISTORY from an Old Norse word meaning 'magic sign'

rung[1] *NOUN* **rungs**
one of the crossbars on a ladder

WORD HISTORY from Old English *hrung*

rung[2] *past participle* of **ring**[2]

runner *NOUN* **runners**
1 a person or animal that runs, especially in a race
2 a stem that grows away from a plant and roots itself
3 a groove, rod, or roller for a thing to move on; each of the long strips under a sledge
4 a long narrow strip of carpet or covering

runner bean *NOUN* **runner beans**
a kind of climbing bean with long green pods which are eaten

runner-up *NOUN* **runners-up**
someone who comes second in a competition

running *present participle* of **run**

in or **out of the running** with a good chance, or no chance, of winning

to make the running is to set the pace

running *ADJECTIVE*
continuous or consecutive; without an interval ◆ *It rained for four days running.*

runny *ADJECTIVE* **runnier, runniest**
1 flowing like liquid; watery ◆ *runny honey*
2 a runny nose produces a flow of mucus

run-of-the-mill *ADJECTIVE*
ordinary; not special

runt *NOUN* **runts**
an undersized animal, especially the smallest in a litter

runtime *NOUN*
(*ICT*) the length of time a computer program takes to run

runway *NOUN* **runways**
a long hard surface on which aircraft take off and land

rupee *NOUN* **rupees**
the unit of money in India, Pakistan, and certain other countries

WORD HISTORY via Hindi from a Sanskrit word *rupya* 'wrought silver'

rupture *VERB* **ruptures, rupturing, ruptured**
1 to break or burst suddenly, or cause something to do this
2 to disturb a friendship or other relationship

rupture *NOUN* **ruptures**
a break or breach

WORD FAMILY *Rupture* comes from the Latin word *ruptum* meaning 'broken' or 'burst'. Other words to do with breaking or bursting and having the same origin include *corrupt, disrupt, erupt, irrupt,* and *interrupt.*

rural *ADJECTIVE*
(*Geography*) to do with or belonging to the countryside

WORD HISTORY from Latin *ruris* 'of the country'

ruse (*say* rooz) *NOUN* **ruses**
a deception or trick

WORD HISTORY from Old French *ruser* 'to use trickery'

rush ❶ *VERB* **rushes, rushing, rushed**
1 to go or move quickly ◆ *We rushed here as soon as we heard the news.*
2 to transport someone or something quickly ◆ *The survivors were rushed to hospital.*
3 to do something with speed or haste
4 to make someone hurry ◆ *Don't rush me —I need to think about it.*
5 to dash towards someone suddenly to attack or capture them

rush *NOUN* **rushes**
1 an instance of rushing; a hurry
2 a sudden movement forwards

The shark came in in a rush and the old man hit him as he shut his jaws. — *Ernest Hemingway, The Old Man and the Sea*

3 a sudden great demand for something

WORD HISTORY from Old French *ruser* 'to drive back'

rush ❷ *NOUN* **rushes**
a plant with a thin stem that grows in marshy places

WORD HISTORY from Old English *risc*

rushes *PLURAL NOUN*
the first prints of a cinema film before it is cut and edited

rush hour *NOUN* **rush hours**
the time when traffic is busiest

rusk *NOUN* **rusks**
a kind of hard, dry biscuit, especially for feeding babies

WORD HISTORY from Spanish or Portuguese *rosca* 'coil or roll of bread'

russet *NOUN*
1 a reddish-brown colour

The trees were laden with russet and were glowing gold in the autumn sun. — *Sue Reid, My Story: Mill Girl*

2 an apple with a reddish rough skin

WORD HISTORY from Latin *russus* 'red'

Russian *ADJECTIVE*
to do with Russia or its people

Russian *NOUN* **Russians**
1 a person from Russia
2 the language of Russia

rust *NOUN*
1 a red or brown substance that forms on iron or steel exposed to damp and corrodes it
2 a reddish-brown colour

rust *VERB* **rusts, rusting, rusted**
to make something rusty, or to become rusty

rustic *ADJECTIVE*
1 to do with life in the countryside; rural
2 a rustic structure or piece of furniture is made of rough timber or branches

rustle *VERB* **rustles, rustling, rustled**
1 to make a sound like paper being crumpled
2 (*American*) to steal horses or cattle

to rustle something up (*informal*) is to prepare or produce it quickly

▷ **rustler** *NOUN*

rustle *NOUN* **rustles**
a rustling sound

There was a rustle, as if the wind had moved in the last few leaves of the nine-hundred-year-old oak. — *T. H. White, The Once and Future King*

rusty *ADJECTIVE* **rustier, rustiest**
1 coated with rust
2 weakened by lack of use or practice ◆ *My French is a bit rusty these days.*

▷ **rustiness** *NOUN*

rut ❶ *NOUN* **ruts**
1 a deep track made by wheels in soft ground
2 a settled and usually dull way of life ◆ *Hazel felt she was getting into a rut and decided to take up snowboarding.*

▷ **rutted** *ADJECTIVE*

WORD HISTORY probably related to *route*

rut ❷ *VERB*
male deer and other mammals rut when they fight each other for females during the mating season

WORD HISTORY from Latin *rugire* 'to roar'

ruthless *ADJECTIVE*
having no pity or compassion; merciless

▷ **ruthlessly** *ADVERB*
▷ **ruthlessness** *NOUN*

WORD HISTORY from an old word *ruth* meaning 'pity'

rye *NOUN*
1 a kind of cereal used for making flour or as food for cattle
2 a kind of whisky made from rye

Ss

S. *ABBREVIATION*
1 south
2 southern

sabbath *NOUN* **sabbaths**
a weekly day for rest and prayer, Saturday for Jews, Sunday for Christians

WORD HISTORY from Hebrew *shabat* 'rest'

sabbatical (*say* sa- **bat**- ikal) *NOUN* **sabbaticals**
a period of paid leave granted to a university teacher for study or travel

sable *NOUN*
1 a kind of dark fur
2 (*poetic*) dark or black

sabotage *NOUN*
deliberate damage or disruption to machinery or equipment, especially to hinder an enemy or large organization

sabotage *VERB* **sabotages, sabotaging, sabotaged**
to damage or disrupt equipment or a process by an act of sabotage

WORD HISTORY from French *saboter* 'to make a noise with wooden clogs (*sabots*)', as 19th- century French factory workers did on their way to work. The sound became associated with clumsiness and later with doing deliberate damage to machinery and equipment.

saboteur *NOUN* **saboteurs**
a person who commits sabotage

sabre *NOUN* **sabres**
1 a heavy sword with a curved blade
2 a light fencing sword

sac *NOUN* **sacs**
a bag-shaped part in an animal or plant

saccharin (*say* **sak**- er- in) *NOUN*
a sweet-tasting synthetic substance used as a substitute for sugar

saccharine (*say* **sak**- er- een) *ADJECTIVE*
excessively sweet or sentimental ◆ *He began by rattling off a handful of saccharine songs.*

sachet (*say* **sash**- ay) *NOUN* **sachets**
a small sealed packet or bag containing a small amount of shampoo, sugar, or other soft substances

sack❶ *NOUN* **sacks**
a large bag made of strong material
to get the sack (*informal*) is to be dismissed from a job
▷ **sackful** *NOUN* **sackfuls**
▷ **sacking** *NOUN*

sack *VERB* **sacks, sacking, sacked**
(*informal*) to dismiss someone from a job

sack❷ *VERB* **sacks, sacking, sacked**
(*old use*) to plunder and destroy a captured town
▷ **sack** *NOUN*

sacrament *NOUN* **sacraments**
an important Christian religious ceremony such as baptism or Holy Communion

sacred *ADJECTIVE*
holy; to do with God or a god

sacred cow *NOUN* **sacred cows**
an idea or institution which its supports regard as above criticism

WORD HISTORY from the Hindu practice of regarding the cow as a holy animal

sacrifice *NOUN* **sacrifices**
1 the act of giving something that will please a god, especially an offering of a killed animal
2 the act of giving up a thing of value, to benefit someone else
3 a thing sacrificed
▷ **sacrificial** *ADJECTIVE*

sacrifice *VERB* **sacrifices, sacrificing, sacrificed**
to offer something or give it up as a sacrifice

sacrilege (*say* **sak**- ril- ij) *NOUN*
disrespect or damage to something sacred or valuable
▷ **sacrilegious** *ADJECTIVE*

sacrosanct *ADJECTIVE*
too sacred or respected to be harmed or interfered with

sad *ADJECTIVE* **sadder, saddest**
1 unhappy; feeling sorrow
2 showing or causing sorrow
▷ **sadly** *ADVERB*
▷ **sadness** *NOUN*

SYNONYMS (meaning 1) unhappy, sorrowful, dejected, downcast, despondent, downhearted, depressed, miserable, glum; (meaning 2) distressing, depressing, upsetting, grave, tragic, unfortunate

sadden *VERB* **saddens, saddening, saddened**
to make a person sad

SPELLING NOTE Some words pronounced **s-** begin with **ce-** (e.g. cent), **ci-** (e.g. city), or **cy-** (e.g. cymbal)

saddle *NOUN* **saddles**
1 a seat for putting on the back of a horse or other animal
2 the seat of a bicycle
3 a ridge of high land between two peaks

They climbed steadily to the mountain saddle, and came dropping down on the seaward side. — *Rosemary Sutcliff, The Eagle of the Ninth*

saddle *VERB* **saddles, saddling, saddled**
to put a saddle on a horse or other animal for riding
to saddle someone with something is to burden them with a task or problem

sadhu *NOUN*
(*Religion*) a holy man or sage in Hinduism or Jainism

sadist (*say* say- dist) *NOUN* **sadists**
a person who gets sexual or general pleasure from hurting or humiliating other people
▷ **sadism** *NOUN*
▷ **sadistic** *ADJECTIVE*

WORD HISTORY named after a French novelist, the Marquis de *Sade* (1740–1814), noted for the cruelties in his stories

s.a.e. *ABBREVIATION*
stamped addressed envelope

safari *NOUN* **safaris**
an expedition to watch or hunt wild animals

WORD HISTORY from Kiswahili (an African language), from Arabic *safara* 'to travel'

safari park *NOUN* **safari parks**
a park where wild animals are kept in large enclosures to be seen by visitors driving through

safe *ADJECTIVE*
1 free from or protected from danger
2 offering safety or protection ◆ *She was now in the safe hands of the doctors.*
3 not dangerous ◆ *Make sure you drive at a safe speed.*
▷ **safely** *ADVERB*
▷ **safeness** *NOUN*
▷ **safety** *NOUN*

safe *NOUN* **safes**
a strong cupboard or box in which valuables can be locked safely

safeguard *NOUN* **safeguards**
a measure taken to protect or prevent something

safeguard *VERB* **safeguards, safeguarding, safeguarded**
to protect someone or something

safe house *NOUN* **safe houses**
a house in a place kept secret, used by spies or criminals or for concealing witnesses who might be in danger

safe sex *NOUN*
sexual activity in which precautions are taken, such as using a condom, to prevent the spread of Aids or other infections

safety pin *NOUN* **safety pins**
a U-shaped pin with a clip fastening over the point

saffron *NOUN*
1 a deep yellow spice used for flavouring and colouring food, made from the dried stigmas of a crocus
2 the crocus that yields this spice

sag *VERB* **sags, sagging, sagged**
1 to sink down or bulge in the middle under weight or pressure or from lack of strength

The timbers holding the roof were rotten and the roof was sagging in. — *David Almond, Skellig*

2 to hang down loosely; to droop

A stout man, with a red sweater that sagged generously at the neck, came out and signed the book for the driver. — *Jack London, The Call of the Wild*

▷ **sag** *NOUN*

saga (*say* sah- ga) *NOUN* **sagas**
a long story with many episodes or adventures

sagacious (*say* sa- gay- shus) *ADJECTIVE*
shrewd and wise
▷ **sagaciously** *ADVERB*
▷ **sagacity** *NOUN*

sage[1] *NOUN*
a kind of herb used in cooking and formerly used in medicine

sage[2] *ADJECTIVE*
wise and experienced
▷ **sagely** *ADVERB*

sage *NOUN* **sages**
a wise and respected person

sago *NOUN*
a starchy white food used to make puddings

said *past tense of* **say**

sail *NOUN* **sails**
1 a large piece of strong cloth attached to a mast to catch the wind and make a ship or boat move
2 a short voyage
3 an arm of a windmill
to set sail is to start on a voyage by ship

sail *VERB* **sails, sailing, sailed**
1 to travel in a ship or boat
2 to start a voyage by sea ◆ *The boat will sail on the early morning tide.*
3 to control a ship or boat
4 to move quickly and smoothly
▷ **sailing ship** *NOUN*

sailboard *NOUN* **sailboards**
a flat board with a mast and sail, used in windsurfing

sailor *NOUN* **sailors**
a person who sails; a member of a ship's crew or of a navy

saint *NOUN* **saints**
a holy or very good person
▷ **saintly** *ADVERB*
▷ **saintliness** *NOUN*

sake *NOUN*
for the sake of something in order to get or achieve something ◆ *He took more exercise for the sake of his health.*
for someone's sake so as to help or please them ◆ *We hope for their sake that everything goes well.*

salad *NOUN* **salads**
a mixture of vegetables eaten raw or cold

salamander *NOUN* **salamanders**
a lizard-like amphibian formerly thought to live in fire

salami *NOUN*
a spiced sausage, originally made in Italy

salary *NOUN* **salaries**
a regular wage, usually for a year's work, paid in monthly instalments
▷ **salaried** *ADJECTIVE*

WORD HISTORY from Latin *salarium* 'salt money', money given to Roman soldiers to buy salt (an essential part of nutrition)

sale *NOUN* **sales**
1 the act of selling
2 a time when things are sold at reduced prices
for sale or **on sale** available for buying

salesperson *NOUN* **salespersons**
a person employed to sell goods
▷ **salesman** *NOUN* **salesmen**
▷ **saleswoman** *NOUN* **saleswomen**

salient (*say* say- lee- ent) *ADJECTIVE*
1 a salient characteristic or feature is one that is especially noticeable or important
2 jutting out; projecting

WORD HISTORY from Latin *saliens* 'leaping', originally used to describe animals on heraldic coats of arms

saline *ADJECTIVE*
containing salt

saliva *NOUN*
the natural liquid in a person's or animal's mouth
▷ **salivary** *ADJECTIVE*

salivate (*say* sal- iv- ayt) *VERB* **salivates, salivating, salivated**
to form saliva, especially a large amount
▷ **salivation** *NOUN*

sallow *ADJECTIVE*
sallow skin is slightly yellow
▷ **sallowness** *NOUN*

sally *NOUN* **sallies**
1 a sudden rush forward
2 an excursion
3 a lively or witty remark

sally *VERB* **sallies, sallying, sallied**
to make a sortie; to set forth

salmon (*say* **sam**- on) *NOUN* **salmon**
a large edible fish with pink flesh

salmonella (*say* sal- mon- **el**- a) *NOUN*
a bacterium that can cause food poisoning

WORD HISTORY named after an American scientist, Daniel E *Salmon*, who studied the causes of disease

salon *NOUN* **salons**
1 a large elegant room
2 a room or shop where customers go for hair or beauty treatment

saloon *NOUN* **saloons**
1 a car with a hard roof and a separate boot
2 a place where alcoholic drinks are bought and drunk, especially a comfortable bar in a pub

salsa *NOUN* **salsas**
1 a hot spicy sauce
2 a kind of modern Latin American dance music; a dance to this

salt *NOUN* **salts**
1 sodium chloride, the white substance that gives sea water its taste and is used for flavouring food
2 a chemical compound of a metal and an acid
▷ **salty** *ADJECTIVE*

salt *VERB* **salts, salting, salted**
to flavour or preserve food with salt

salt cellar *NOUN* **salt cellars**
a small dish or perforated pot holding salt for use at meals

saltire *NOUN*
a diagonal cross dividing a shield or flag into four triangular sections

salts *PLURAL NOUN*
a substance that looks like salt, especially a laxative

salubrious *ADJECTIVE*
healthy and pleasant
▷ **salubrity** *NOUN*

salutary *ADJECTIVE*
beneficial; having a good effect ◆ *The incidents were a salutary reminder of how dangerous these places can be.*

salutation *NOUN* **salutations**
a greeting

Miss Slighcarp advanced and made her salutations to her employers. — *Joan Aiken, The Wolves of Willoughby Chase*

a b c d e f g h i j k l m n o p q r s t u v w x y z

SPELLING NOTE Some words pronounced **s-** begin with **ce-** (e.g. cent), **ci-** (e.g. city), or **cy-** (e.g. cymbal)

salute *VERB* **salutes, saluting, saluted**
1 to raise your right hand to your head as a sign of respect
2 to greet someone
3 to say that you respect or admire something

salute *NOUN* **salutes**
1 the act of saluting
2 the firing of guns as a sign of greeting or respect

The loud boom that had startled the Nyungar people was a salute from an eighteen-pounder cannon by the soldiers as they raised the British flag. — *Doris Pilkington, Rabbit Proof Fence*

salvage *VERB* **salvages, salvaging, salvaged**
to save or rescue something such as a damaged ship's cargo so that it can be used again
▷ **salvage** *NOUN*

salvation *NOUN*
1 the act of saving from loss or damage
2 (*Religion*) in Christian teaching, the act of saving the soul from sin and its consequences

salve *NOUN* **salves**
1 a soothing ointment
2 something that soothes

salve *VERB* **salves, salving, salved**
to soothe a person's conscience or wounded pride

salver *NOUN* **salvers**
a small tray, usually of metal

salvo *NOUN* **salvoes** or **salvos**
a volley of shots or of applause

WORD HISTORY from Italian *salva* 'salutation'

same *ADJECTIVE*
1 of one kind; exactly alike or equal
2 not changing or different
▷ **sameness** *NOUN*

samosa *NOUN* **samosas**
a triangular fried pastry case filled with spicy meat or vegetables

WORD HISTORY a Persian and Urdu word

samovar *NOUN* **samovars**
a Russian tea urn

WORD HISTORY a Russian word meaning 'self- boiler'

sampan *NOUN* **sampans**
a small flat-bottomed boat used in China

WORD HISTORY from Chinese *sanpan*, from *san* 'three' and *pan* 'boards'

sample *NOUN* **samples**
a small amount that shows what something is like; a specimen

sample *VERB* **samples, sampling, sampled**
to take a sample of something, or try a part of it

sampler *NOUN* **samplers**
a piece of embroidery worked in various stitches to show skill in needlework

samsara *NOUN*
(*Religion*) in Hinduism and Buddhism, the cycle of life, death, and rebirth that the soul experiences

samurai (*say* sam- oor- eye) *NOUN* **samurai**
a member of an ancient Japanese warrior caste

sanatorium *NOUN* **sanatoriums** or **sanatoria**
a hospital for treating chronic diseases or convalescents

sanctify *VERB* **sanctifies, sanctifying, sanctified**
to make a place holy or sacred
▷ **sanctification** *NOUN*

WORD FAMILY *Sanctify* comes from the Latin word *sanctus* meaning 'holy'. Other words connected with being holy and having the same origin include *sacrosanct, sanctimonious, sanctity*, and *sanctuary*; but *sanction* has a different origin.

sanctimonious *ADJECTIVE*
making a show of being virtuous or devout

sanction *NOUN* **sanctions**
1 action taken against a nation that is considered to have broken an international law
2 a penalty for disobeying a law
3 permission or authorization

sanction *VERB* **sanctions, sanctioning, sanctioned**
to permit or authorize something

WORD HISTORY from Latin *sanctio*, from *sancire* 'to give approval'

sanctity *NOUN*
being sacred; holiness

sanctuary *NOUN* **sanctuaries**
1 a safe place or refuge where people can be protected
2 an area where wildlife is protected
3 a sacred place; the part of a church where the altar stands

sanctum *NOUN* **sanctums**
a person's private room

sand *NOUN*
tiny particles of rock that cover the ground on beaches, river beds, and deserts

sand *VERB* **sands, sanding, sanded**
to smooth or polish a hard surface with sandpaper or some other rough material
▷ **sander** *NOUN*

sandal *NOUN* **sandals**
a lightweight shoe with straps over the foot
▷ **sandalled** *ADJECTIVE*

sandalwood *NOUN*
a scented wood from a tropical tree

sandbag *NOUN* **sandbags**
a bag filled with sand, used to build defences

sandbank *NOUN* **sandbanks**
a bank of sand under water

sandblast *VERB* **sandblasts, sandblasting, sandblasted**
to clean a surface with a jet of sand under pressure

sandpaper *NOUN*
strong paper coated with sand or a similar substance, rubbed on rough surfaces to make them smooth

sands *PLURAL NOUN*
a beach or sandy area

sandstone *NOUN*
rock formed from compressed sand

sandwich *NOUN* **sandwiches**
two or more slices of bread with a filling (e.g. of cheese or meat) between them

sandwich *VERB* **sandwiches, sandwiching, sandwiched**
to put one person or thing tightly between two others

Now Sapphire, who had been trapped indoors all day, found herself sandwiched on the sofa between two tipsy and determined women.
— *Julie Bertagna, The Opposite of Chocolate*

WORD HISTORY named after the Earl of *Sandwich* (1718–92), who enjoyed gambling and ordered food in this form so that he could continue to gamble while he ate

sandwich board *NOUN*
a linked pair of boards bearing advertisements, hung over a person's shoulders

sandwich course *NOUN* **sandwich courses**
a college or university course which includes periods in industry or business

sandy *ADJECTIVE*
1 like sand
2 covered with sand
3 yellowish-red ◆ *sandy hair*
▷ **sandiness** *NOUN*

sane *ADJECTIVE*
1 having a healthy mind; not mad
2 sensible or reasonable
▷ **sanely** *ADVERB*

WORD FAMILY *Sane* comes from the Latin word *sanus* meaning 'healthy'. Other words connected with being healthy and having the same origin include *insane*, *sanitary*, and *sanity*.

sanguine (*say* sang-gwin) *ADJECTIVE*
hopeful; cheerful and optimistic

WORD HISTORY from Latin *sanguis* 'blood' (because good blood was believed to be the cause of cheerfulness)

sanitary *ADJECTIVE*
1 free from germs and dirt; hygienic
2 to do with sanitation

sanitary towel *NOUN* **sanitary towels**
an absorbent pad worn by a woman to absorb blood during menstruation

sanitation *NOUN*
arrangements for drainage and the disposal of sewage

sanitize *VERB* **sanitizes, sanitizing, sanitized**
to disinfect something and make it hygienic

USAGE NOTE This word can also be spelled sanitise.

sanity *NOUN*
a sane state; sensible behaviour

Sanskrit *NOUN*
the ancient and sacred language of the Hindus in India

sap *NOUN*
the liquid inside a plant, carrying food to all its parts

sap *VERB* **saps, sapping, sapped**
to take away a person's strength gradually

sapling *NOUN* **saplings**
a young tree

sapphire *NOUN* **sapphires**
a bright-blue jewel

Saracen *NOUN* **Saracens**
an Arab or Muslim of the time of the Crusades

sarcasm *NOUN*
the use of irony or cutting remarks to express disapproval or contempt

WORD HISTORY from Greek *sarkazein* 'to tear the flesh' (the original image which later became toned down into the idea of remarks being 'sharp' and 'cutting')

sarcastic *ADJECTIVE*
using sarcasm
▷ **sarcastically** *ADVERB*

sarcophagus *NOUN* **sarcophagi**
a stone coffin, often decorated with carvings

WORD HISTORY from Greek *sarkos* 'of flesh' and *-phagos* 'eating' (because it was thought that the stone from which ancient coffins were made caused the bodies inside to decay)

sardine *NOUN* **sardines**
a small sea fish, usually sold in tins, packed tightly in oil

sardonic *ADJECTIVE*
funny in a grim or sarcastic way
▷ **sardonically** *ADVERB*

sari *NOUN* **saris**
a length of cloth worn wrapped round the body as a dress, especially by Indian women and girls

WORD HISTORY a Hindi word

sarong *NOUN* **sarongs**
a strip of cloth worn like a kilt by men and women of Malaya and Java
WORD HISTORY a Malay word meaning 'sheath' (Malay is a language spoken in Malaysia)

sartorial *ADJECTIVE*
to do with clothes

sash *NOUN* **sashes**
a strip of cloth worn round the waist or over one shoulder

sashay *VERB* **sashays, sashaying, sashayed**
to walk in a showy way, with exaggerated hip and shoulder movements
WORD HISTORY from the name of an American dance in which partners circle each other by taking sideways steps

sash window *NOUN* **sash windows**
a window that slides up and down

SAT *ABBREVIATION*
standard assessment task

satanic (*say* sa- **tan**- ik) *ADJECTIVE*
to do with or like Satan, the Devil in Jewish and Christian teaching

satchel *NOUN* **satchels**
a bag worn on the shoulder or the back, especially for carrying books to and from school
WORD HISTORY from Latin *saccellus* 'little sack'

sate *VERB* **sates, sating, sated**
to satisfy someone fully; to satiate someone

satellite *NOUN* **satellites**
1 a spacecraft put in orbit round a planet to collect information or transmit communications signals
2 a moon moving in an orbit round a planet
3 a country that is under the influence of a more powerful neighbouring country
WORD HISTORY from Latin *satelles* 'a guard' (because astronomers compared the moons of Jupiter to guards or attendants of an important person)

satellite dish *NOUN* **satellite dishes**
a bowl-shaped aerial for receiving broadcasting signals transmitted by satellite

satellite television *NOUN*
television broadcasting in which the signals are transmitted by means of a communications satellite

satiate (*say* say- shee- ayt) *VERB* **satiates, satiating, satiated**
to satisfy an appetite or desire completely

satiety (*say* sat- y- it- ee) *NOUN*
being or feeling satiated

satin *NOUN*
a silky material that is shiny on one side
▷ **satiny** *ADJECTIVE*
WORD HISTORY via Old French from Arabic *zaytuni* 'to do with Tsinkiang' (the name of a Chinese port where silk was produced)

satire *NOUN* **satires**
1 humour or exaggeration used to show what is bad or weak about a person or thing, especially the government and other important institutions
2 a play, poem, or other piece of writing that does this
▷ **satirical** *ADJECTIVE*
▷ **satirically** *ADVERB*
▷ **satirist** *NOUN*

satirize *VERB* **satirizes, satirizing, satirized**
to use satire to mock or show the faults in a government or other institution
USAGE NOTE This word can also be spelled satirise.

satisfaction *NOUN*
1 the process of satisfying someone
2 the state of being satisfied and pleased because something has satisfed you
3 something that satisfies a need or wish

satisfactory *ADJECTIVE*
good enough; sufficient
▷ **satisfactorily** *ADVERB*

satisfy *VERB* **satisfies, satisfying, satisfied**
1 to give someone what they need or want
2 to make someone feel certain; to convince someone ◆ *The authorities were satisfied that no crime had been committed.*
3 to satisfy a requirement is to achieve or fulfil it

satsuma *NOUN* **satsumas**
a kind of mandarin orange originally grown in Japan
WORD HISTORY named after *Satsuma*, a province of Japan

saturate *VERB* **saturates, saturating, saturated**
1 to make a thing thoroughly wet
2 to make something take in as much as possible of a substance
3 to supply a market with goods beyond the demand for them
▷ **saturation** *NOUN*

Saturday *NOUN*
the day of the week following Friday
WORD HISTORY from Old English *Saeternesdaeg* 'day of Saturn', a Roman god

saturnine *ADJECTIVE*
looking gloomy and forbidding ◆ *She had never seen a man with so saturnine and yet so handsome a face.*
WORD HISTORY called this because people born under the influence of the planet Saturn were believed to be gloomy

satyr (*say* sat- er) ***NOUN*** **satyrs**
in Greek mythology, a woodland god with a man's body and a goat's ears, tail, and legs

sauce ***NOUN*** **sauces**
1 a thick liquid served with food to add flavour
2 (*informal*) being cheeky; impudence

WORD HISTORY related to *salt*: via Old French from Latin *salsus* 'salted'

saucepan ***NOUN*** **saucepans**
a metal cooking pan with a handle at the side

saucer ***NOUN*** **saucers**
a small shallow object on which a cup or bowl is placed

saucy ***ADJECTIVE*** **saucier, sauciest**
cheeky or impudent
▷ **saucily** ***ADVERB***
▷ **sauciness** ***NOUN***

sauerkraut (*say* sowr- krowt) ***NOUN***
chopped and pickled cabbage, originally made in Germany

WORD HISTORY from German *sauer* 'sour' and *Kraut* 'cabbage'

sauna ***NOUN*** **saunas**
a room or compartment filled with steam, used as a kind of bath

WORD HISTORY a Finnish word

saunter ***VERB*** **saunters, sauntering, sauntered**
to walk slowly and casually
▷ **saunter** ***NOUN***

sausage ***NOUN*** **sausages**
a tube of skin or plastic stuffed with minced meat and other filling

savage ***ADJECTIVE***
wild and fierce; cruel
▷ **savagely** ***ADVERB***
▷ **savageness** ***NOUN***
▷ **savagery** ***NOUN***

savage ***NOUN*** **savages**
1 a savage person
2 (*old use*) a member of a people thought of as primitive or uncivilized

savage ***VERB*** **savages, savaging, savaged**
to attack a person or animal fiercely and wound them badly

WORD HISTORY from Latin *silvaticus* (later *salvaticus*) 'of the woods' and then 'wild' (because people who lived in the woods were regarded as wild and unruly)

savannah or **savanna** ***NOUN*** **savannahs** or **savannas**
a grassy plain in a hot country, with few or no trees

WORD HISTORY via Spanish from Taino (a South American language)

save ***VERB*** **saves, saving, saved**
1 to keep someone or something safe; to free a person or thing from danger or harm
2 to keep something, especially money, so that it can be used later
3 to save time is to do something in less time than usual or expected
4 (*ICT*) to keep data by storing it in the computer's memory or on a disk
5 to prevent an opponent from scoring in a game
▷ **saver** ***NOUN***

WORD FAMILY *Save* comes from the Latin word *salvus* meaning 'safe'. Other words connected with safety having the same origin include *safe*, *salvage*, *salvation*, and *saviour*, and *solid* is also related to these words.

save ***NOUN***
an act of preventing an opponent from scoring in a game

save ***PREPOSITION***
except

I could see nothing of the moonlight save that here and there the high branches made a tangled filigree against the starry sky. — *Sir Arthur Conan Doyle, The Lost World*

savings ***PLURAL NOUN***
money saved

saviour ***NOUN*** **saviours**
a person who saves someone
the or **our Saviour** in Christianity, Jesus Christ

savour ***NOUN*** **savours**
the taste or smell of something

savour ***VERB*** **savours, savouring, savoured**
1 to enjoy the taste or smell of something
2 to have a certain taste or smell

savoury ***ADJECTIVE***
1 tasty but not sweet
2 having an appetizing taste or smell

savoury ***NOUN*** **savouries**
a savoury dish

saw❶ ***NOUN*** **saws**
a tool with a zigzag edge for cutting wood, metal, or other hard material

saw ***VERB*** **saws, sawing, sawed, sawn**
1 to cut something with a saw
2 to move to and fro as a saw does

saw❷ *past tense of* **see**❶

sawdust ***NOUN***
powder that comes from wood cut by a saw

sawmill ***NOUN*** **sawmills**
a mill where timber is cut by machinery

Saxon ***NOUN*** **Saxons**
1 a member of a people who came from Europe and occupied parts of England in the 5th–6th centuries
2 an Anglo-Saxon

a b c d e f g h i j k l m n o p q r s t u v w x y z

saxophone *NOUN* **saxophones**
a brass wind instrument with a reed in the mouthpiece
▷ **saxophonist** *NOUN*

WORD HISTORY named after a Belgian instrument maker, Adolphe *Sax*, who invented the instrument in the 19th century, although it did not become widely used until the 20th century

say *VERB* **says, saying, said**
1 to speak or express something in words
2 to give an opinion

SYNONYMS speak, utter, voice, articulate, enunciate; observe, remark, declare, state

say *NOUN*
to have a say is to be permitted to decide or help decide something

saying *NOUN* **sayings**
a well-known phrase or proverb or other statement

scab *NOUN* **scabs**
a hard crust that forms over a cut or graze while it is healing
▷ **scabby** *ADJECTIVE*

scabbard *NOUN* **scabbards**
the sheath of a sword or dagger

scabies (*say* skay- beez) *NOUN*
a contagious skin disease with severe itching, caused by a parasite

scaffold *NOUN* **scaffolds**
a platform on which criminals are executed

scaffolding *NOUN*
a temporary structure of poles and planks attached to the side of a building to provide platforms while repairing or cleaning it

scald *VERB* **scalds, scalding, scalded**
1 to burn yourself with very hot liquid or steam
2 to heat a liquid until it is nearly boiling
▷ **scald** *NOUN*

scale❶ *NOUN* **scales**
1 a series of units, degrees, or other values for measuring something
2 (*Music*) a series of musical notes going up or down in a fixed pattern
3 the scale of a map or drawing is its proportion or ratio to real life, e.g. one centimetre to the kilometre
4 the relative size or importance of something ◆ *Buildings were erected on a large scale.*

to scale with the parts in the same proportions as those of an original ◆ *The plans have been drawn to scale.*

scale *VERB* **scales, scaling, scaled**
to climb something steep and tall

to scale something down or **up** is to reduce or increase it at a fixed rate, or in proportion to something else

WORD HISTORY from Latin *scala* 'ladder'

scale❷ *NOUN* **scales**
1 each of the thin overlapping parts on the outside of fish and reptiles; a thin flake or part like this
2 a hard substance formed in a kettle or boiler by hard water, or on teeth

scale *VERB* **scales, scaling, scaled**
to remove the scales or scale from something

scale model *NOUN* **scale models**
a model of an object, made to scale

scalene (*say* skay- leen) *ADJECTIVE*
a scalene triangle has unequal sides

scales *PLURAL NOUN*
a device for weighing things

scallop *NOUN* **scallops**
1 a shellfish with two hinged fan-shaped shells
2 each curve in an ornamental wavy border
▷ **scalloped** *ADJECTIVE*

scalp *NOUN* **scalps**
the skin on the top of the head

scalp *VERB* **scalps, scalping, scalped**
to cut or tear the scalp from a person or animal

scalpel *NOUN* **scalpels**
a small knife with a thin, sharp blade, used by a surgeon or artist

scaly *ADJECTIVE* **scalier, scaliest**
covered in scales or scale

scam *NOUN* **scams**
(*informal*) a dishonest scheme or swindle

scamp *NOUN* **scamps**
a rascal or mischievous child

I suppose Giles has been a scamp. But I don't think he's been wicked. Just not very bright that's all.
— *Alan Bennett, Talking Heads*

scamper *VERB* **scampers, scampering, scampered**
to run quickly, lightly, or playfully
▷ **scamper** *NOUN*

scampi *PLURAL NOUN*
large prawns

scan *VERB* **scans, scanning, scanned**
1 to look at every part of something

From my vantage-ground I could scan the whole moor right away to the railway line and to the south of it where green fields took the place of heather. — *John Buchan, The Thirty-Nine Steps*

2 to glance at something
3 (*Language*) to scan poetry is to count the beats in each line; poetry scans when it is correct in rhythm
4 to sweep a radar or electronic beam over an area to examine it or in search of something
5 (*ICT*) to use a scanner to read data from printed text or graphics into a computer

scan *NOUN* **scans**
1 the process of scanning
2 an examination using a scanner ◆ *His doctor sent him to the hospital for a brain scan.*

scandal *NOUN* **scandals**
1 something shameful or disgraceful
2 gossip about people's faults and wrongdoing
▷ **scandalous** *ADJECTIVE*

WORD HISTORY via Old French from Greek *skandalon* 'a trap'

scandalize *VERB* **scandalizes, scandalizing, scandalized**
to shock a person by something considered shameful or disgraceful

USAGE NOTE This word can also be spelled scandalise.

scandalmonger *NOUN* **scandalmongers**
a person who invents or spreads scandal

Scandinavian *ADJECTIVE*
to do with or coming from the countries of Scandinavia (Norway, Sweden, and Denmark, and sometimes also Finland and Iceland)
▷ **Scandinavian** *NOUN*

scanner *NOUN* **scanners**
1 a machine that examines things by means of light or other rays
2 (*ICT*) a machine that converts printed text or graphics into a form that can be put into a computer

scansion *NOUN*
the scanning of verse

scant *ADJECTIVE*
barely enough or adequate ◆ *It is an argument that pays scant attention to the facts.*

scanty *ADJECTIVE* **scantier, scantiest**
small in amount or extent; meagre ◆ *The available information was fairly scanty.*
▷ **scantily** *ADVERB*
▷ **scantiness** *NOUN*

scapegoat *NOUN* **scapegoats**
a person who is made to bear the blame or punishment for what others have done

WORD HISTORY from *goat* and *escape* (because in the Bible the ancient Jews sent a goat into the desert after the priest had symbolically laid the people's sins upon it)

scar❶ *NOUN* **scars**
1 the mark left by a cut or burn after it has healed
2 a lasting effect left by an unpleasant experience

scar *VERB* **scars, scarring, scarred**
to make a scar or scars on skin

scar❷ *NOUN* **scars**
a steep craggy place

scarab *NOUN* **scarabs**
an ancient Egyptian ornament or symbol carved in the shape of a beetle

scarce *ADJECTIVE* **scarcer, scarcest**
1 not enough to supply people
2 rare; not often found

to make yourself scarce (*informal*) is to go away or keep out of the way
▷ **scarcity** *NOUN*

scarcely *ADVERB*
only just; only with difficulty ◆ *She could scarcely walk.*

scare *VERB* **scares, scaring, scared**
to frighten a person or animal

scare *NOUN* **scares**
1 a frightening event or situation
2 a sudden widespread sense of alarm about something ◆ *There had been another health scare over additives in children's food.*

scarecrow *NOUN* **scarecrows**
a figure of a person dressed in old clothes, set up to frighten birds away from crops

scaremonger *NOUN* **scaremongers**
a person who spreads scare stories

scare story *NOUN* **scare stories**
an inaccurate or exaggerated account of something which makes people worry unnecessarily

scarf *NOUN* **scarves**
a strip of material worn round the neck or head

scarlet *ADJECTIVE* *NOUN*
bright red

scarlet fever *NOUN*
an infectious fever producing a scarlet rash

scarp *NOUN* **scarps**
a steep slope on a hill

scarper *VERB* **scarpers, scarpering, scarpered**
(*informal*) to run away or leave hurriedly, especially to avoid being caught or discovered

WORD HISTORY probably from Italian *scappare* 'to escape', influenced by rhyming slang *Scapa Flow* (a naval base in the Orkney Islands) = 'go'

scary *ADJECTIVE*
(*informal*) alarming or frightening

scathing (*say* **skayth**- ing) *ADJECTIVE*
severely criticizing a person or thing

Geordie's scathing about Prince Charles: 'Fine & fancy, all frills & lace, & did ye see the powder on his face? More like a lady than a man!' — *Frances Mary Hendry, My Story: The '45 Rising*

WORD HISTORY from Old Norse *skatha* 'to injure or damage'

a b c d e f g h i j k l m n o p q r s t u v w x y z

scatter *VERB* **scatters, scattering, scattered**
1 to throw or send things in all directions
2 to run or leave quickly in all directions

scatterbrain *NOUN* **scatterbrains**
a careless forgetful person
▷ **scatterbrained** *ADJECTIVE*

scatter diagram *NOUN*
a graph that shows the relationship between two variables by plotting their values along two axes, causing a scattering or clustering of the resulting points

scavenge *VERB* **scavenges, scavenging, scavenged**
1 to search in rubbish for useful things
2 a bird or animal scavenges when it searches for decaying flesh as food

scavenger *NOUN* **scavengers**
a person or animal that scavenges

They were hateful sharks, bad-smelling, scavengers as well as killers, and when they were hungry they would bite at an oar or the rudder of a boat. — *Ernest Hemingway, The Old Man and the Sea*

scenario *NOUN* **scenarios**
1 (*Drama*) a summary of the plot of a play or story
2 an imagined or possible series of events or circumstances

scene *NOUN* **scenes**
1 the place where something has happened ◆ *Police officers had arrived at the scene of the crash.*
2 (*Drama*) a part of a play or film that happens in a particular place
3 a view as seen by a spectator
4 an angry or noisy outburst ◆ *At all costs she wanted to avoid causing a scene.*
5 stage scenery
6 an area of activity ◆ *musicians involved in the local folk scene*

WORD HISTORY from Greek *skene* meaning 'tent' and later 'stage' (because plays used to be performed in tents)

scenery *NOUN*
1 the natural features of a landscape
2 things put on a stage to make it look like a place

scenic *ADJECTIVE*
having fine natural scenery ◆ *a scenic tour round the Alps*

scent *NOUN* **scents**
1 a pleasant smell

Steam and scents from the hot-dog stalls and popcorn-makers drifted across us. — *David Almond, The Fire-Eaters*

2 a liquid perfume
3 an animal's smell that other animals can detect

scent *VERB* **scents, scenting, scented**
1 to discover something by its scent; to detect something
2 to put scent on or in something; to make something fragrant
▷ **scented** *ADJECTIVE*

sceptic (*say* **skep**- tik) *NOUN* **sceptics**
a sceptical person

sceptical (*say* **skep**- tik- al) *ADJECTIVE*
inclined to question things; not believing easily
▷ **sceptically** *ADVERB*
▷ **scepticism** *NOUN*

sceptre *NOUN* **sceptres**
a rod carried by a king or queen as a symbol of power

schedule (*say* **shed**- yool) *NOUN* **schedules**
a programme or timetable of planned events or work
on schedule on time according to a plan

schedule *VERB* **schedules, scheduling, scheduled**
1 to put a task or activity into a schedule
2 to arrange something for a certain time

WORD HISTORY from Latin *scedula* 'little piece of paper'

schematic (*say* skee- **mat**- ik) *ADJECTIVE*
in the form of a diagram or chart

scheme *NOUN* **schemes**
a plan of action

scheme *VERB* **schemes, scheming, schemed**
to make plans; to plot
▷ **schemer** *NOUN*

scherzo (*say* **skairts**- oh) *NOUN* **scherzos**
a lively piece of music, often a movement in a longer composition

WORD HISTORY an Italian word meaning 'joke'

schism (*say* sizm) *NOUN* **schisms**
the splitting of a group into two opposing sections when they disagree about something important

schizophrenia (*say* skit- so- **free**- nee- a) *NOUN*
a kind of mental illness in which a person cannot relate thoughts and feelings to reality
▷ **schizophrenic** *ADJECTIVE, NOUN*

WORD HISTORY from Greek *schizein* 'to split' and *phren* 'the mind'

schnitzel (*say* **shnit**- sel) *NOUN* **schnitzels**
a piece of veal or other pale meat, coated in breadcrumbs and fried

WORD HISTORY a German word meaning 'slice'

scholar *NOUN* **scholars**
1 a person who has studied a subject thoroughly
2 a person who has been awarded a scholarship
▷ **scholarly** *ADJECTIVE*

scholarship *NOUN* **scholarships**
1 a grant of money given to someone to help pay for their education
2 the knowledge or methods used by scholars; advanced study

scholastic *ADJECTIVE*
to do with schools or education; academic

school❶ *NOUN* **schools**
1 a place where teaching is done, especially of pupils aged 5-18
2 the pupils in a school
3 the time when teaching takes place in a school ◆ *There was no school the next day.*
4 a group of people who have the same ideas or beliefs or use the same methods or styles

school *VERB* **schools, schooling, schooled**
to teach or train a person or animal

school❷ *NOUN* **schools**
a large group of fish or sea mammals such as whales or dolphins

schoolchild *NOUN* **schoolchildren**
a child who goes to school
▷ **schoolboy** *NOUN*
▷ **schoolgirl** *NOUN*

schooling *NOUN*
education at a school

schoolteacher *NOUN* **schoolteachers**
a person who teaches in a school

WORD FAMILY Older words that are not used so much now are *schoolmaster* for a male teacher and *schoolmistress* for a female teacher.

schooner (*say* **skoon**- er) *NOUN* **schooners**
1 a sailing ship with two or more masts
2 a tall glass for serving sherry

sciatica (*say* sy- **at**- ik- a) *NOUN*
pain in the sciatic nerve (a large nerve in the hip and thigh)

science *NOUN*
1 the study of the physical world by means of observation and experiment
2 a branch of this, such as chemistry, physics, or biology

WORD HISTORY from Latin *scientia* 'knowledge'

science fiction *NOUN*
stories about imaginary scientific discoveries or space travel and life on other planets, often set in the future

science park *NOUN* **science parks**
an area set up for industries using science or for organizations doing scientific research

scientific *ADJECTIVE*
1 to do with science or scientists
2 studying things systematically and testing ideas carefully
▷ **scientifically** *ADVERB*

scientist *NOUN* **scientists**
1 an expert in science
2 someone who uses scientific methods

scimitar (*say* **sim**- it- ar) *NOUN* **scimitars**
a curved oriental sword

scintillating *ADJECTIVE*
1 lively and witty ◆ *We had a scintillating conversation.*
2 outstanding or brilliant ◆ *The defence was in scintillating form.*
▷ **scintillation** *NOUN*

WORD HISTORY from Latin *scintilla* 'a spark'

scion (*say* **sy**- on) *NOUN* **scions**
a descendant, especially of a noble family

scissors *PLURAL NOUN*
a cutting instrument used with one hand, with two blades pivoted so that they can close against each other

sclerosis (*say* skleer- **oh**- sis) *NOUN*
(*Medicine*) an abnormal hardening of the arteries or other body tissue

scoff❶ *VERB* **scoffs, scoffing, scoffed**
to scoff at someone or something is to jeer or speak contemptuously about them

> He was full of speculation that night about the condition of Mars, and scoffed at the vulgar idea of its having inhabitants who were signalling us.
> — *H. G. Wells, The War of the Worlds*

▷ **scoffer** *NOUN*

scoff❷ *VERB* **scoffs, scoffing, scoffed**
(*informal*) to eat something completely or greedily

scold *VERB* **scolds, scolding, scolded**
to speak angrily to someone because they have done wrong
▷ **scolding** *NOUN*

scone (*say* skon or skohn) *NOUN* **scones**
a soft flat cake, usually eaten with butter

scoop *NOUN* **scoops**
1 a kind of deep spoon for serving ice cream or similar substances
2 a deep shovel for lifting grain, sugar, or liquids
3 a scooping movement
4 an important piece of news published by only one newspaper

scoop *VERB* **scoops, scooping, scooped**
1 to lift or hollow something out with a scoop
2 to lift someone or something with a broad sweeping movement

scoot *VERB* **scoots, scooting, scooted**
1 to propel a bicycle or scooter by sitting or standing on it and pushing it along with one foot
2 (*informal*) to run or go away quickly

scooter *NOUN* **scooters**
1 a kind of motorcycle with small wheels
2 a board with wheels and a long handle, which you ride on by scooting

SPELLING NOTE Some words pronounced **s-** begin with **ce-** (e.g. cent), **ci-** (e.g. city), or **cy-** (e.g. cymbal)

a b c d e f g h i j k l m n o p q r s t u v w x y z

scope *NOUN*
1 opportunity or possibility for something
◆ *Everyone has some scope for doing their job better.*
2 the range or extent of a subject

scorch *VERB* **scorches, scorching, scorched**
to make something go brown by burning it slightly

scorching *ADJECTIVE*
(*informal*) very hot

score *NOUN* **scores** or, in sense 2, **score**
1 the number of points or goals made in a game; a result
2 (*old use*) a score of something is twenty of them
3 (*Music*) a written or printed version of a piece of music

on that score for that reason, because of that
◆ *They were not unduly worried on that score.*

score *VERB* **scores, scoring, scored**
1 to win a point or goal in a game
2 keep a count of the score
3 mark with lines or cuts
4 write out a musical score

▷ **scorer** *NOUN*

scores *PLURAL NOUN*
many; a large number

scorn *NOUN*
openly expressed disapproval or contempt

'Ha,' Jacob Carstairs said with a certain amount of scorn. 'We'll see about that.' — *Meg Cabot, Victoria and the Rogue*

▷ **scornful** *ADJECTIVE*
▷ **scornfully** *ADVERB*

scorn *VERB* **scorns, scorning, scorned**
1 to treat someone with contempt
2 to refuse something with contempt

scorpion *NOUN* **scorpions**
an animal that looks like a tiny lobster, with a poisonous sting

Scot *NOUN* **Scots**
a person who comes from Scotland

scotch❶ *NOUN*
whisky made in Scotland

scotch❷ *VERB* **scotches, scotching, scotched**
to put an end to an idea or rumour

Scotch egg *NOUN* **Scotch eggs**
a hard-boiled egg enclosed in sausage meat and fried

Scotch terrier *NOUN* **Scotch terriers**
a breed of terrier with rough hair

scot-free *ADJECTIVE*
without harm or punishment

WORD HISTORY originally not having to pay a *scot* (a form of tax), from Old Norse *skot* 'a shot'

Scots *ADJECTIVE*
from or belonging to Scotland

USAGE NOTE See the note at *Scottish*.

Scottish *ADJECTIVE*
to do with or belonging to Scotland

USAGE NOTE *Scottish* is the most widely used word for describing things to do with Scotland: *Scottish education, Scottish mountains. Scots* is less common and is mainly used to describe people: *a Scots girl. Scotch* is only used in fixed expressions like *Scotch egg* and *Scotch terrier*.

scoundrel *NOUN* **scoundrels**
a wicked or dishonest person

scour❶ *VERB* **scours, scouring, scoured**
1 to rub something until it is clean and bright
2 to clear a channel or pipe by the force of water flowing through it

▷ **scourer** *NOUN*

scour❷ *VERB* **scours, scouring, scoured**
to search a place thoroughly

scourge (*say* skerj) *NOUN* **scourges**
1 a whip for flogging people
2 something that inflicts suffering or punishment

Scout *NOUN* **Scouts**
a member of the Scout Association, an organization for boys

scout *NOUN* **scouts**
someone sent out to collect information

scout *VERB* **scouts, scouting, scouted**
1 to act as a scout
2 to search an area thoroughly

WORD HISTORY via Old French *escouter* 'to listen' from Latin *auscultare*

scowl *NOUN* **scowls**
an angry frown

scowl *VERB* **scowls, scowling, scowled**
to frown angrily

Scrabble *NOUN*
(*trademark*) a game played on a board, in which words are built up from single letters

scrabble *VERB* **scrabbles, scrabbling, scrabbled**
1 to scratch or claw at something with the hands or feet
2 to grope or struggle to get something

scraggy *ADJECTIVE*
thin and bony

scram *VERB*
(*informal*) to go away

scramble *VERB* **scrambles, scrambling, scrambled**
1 to move quickly and awkwardly

Lyra and the others scrambled over the curved roof of one of the tunnels, and found themselves in a strange moonscape of regular hummocks and hollows. — *Philip Pullman, Northern Lights*

2 to struggle to do or get something
3 military aircraft or their crew scramble when they take off quickly to go into action

4 to cook eggs by mixing them up and heating them in a pan
5 to mix things together
6 to alter a radio or telephone signal so that it cannot be used without a decoding device
▷ **scrambler** *NOUN*

scramble *NOUN* **scrambles**
1 a climb or walk over rough ground
2 a struggle to do or get something
3 a motorcycle race over rough country

scrap❶ *NOUN* **scraps**
1 a small piece
2 rubbish; waste material, especially metal that is suitable for reprocessing

scrap *VERB* **scraps, scrapping, scrapped**
to get rid of something that is useless or unwanted

scrap❷ *NOUN* **scraps**
(*informal*) a minor fight or quarrel

scrap *VERB* **scraps, scrapping, scrapped**
(*informal*) to fight or quarrel

scrape *VERB* **scrapes, scraping, scraped**
1 to clean or smooth or damage something by passing something hard over it
2 to make a harsh sound by rubbing against a rough or hard surface
3 to remove something by scraping ◆ *Before going in he scraped the mud off his shoes.*
4 to get something by great effort or care ◆ *They might scrape together enough money to pay some of the bills.*
to scrape through is to succeed or pass an examination by only a small margin
▷ **scraper** *NOUN*

scrape *NOUN* **scrapes**
1 a scraping movement or sound

I heard the faint scrape of the back door opening downstairs. Will was going out into the garden. — *Jacqueline Wilson, Midnight*

2 a mark made by scraping
3 to get into a scrape is to be in an awkward situation because of mischief or foolishness

scrappy *ADJECTIVE*
1 made of scraps or bits or disconnected things
2 carelessly done
▷ **scrappiness** *NOUN*

scratch *VERB* **scratches, scratching, scratched**
1 to mark or cut the surface of a thing with something sharp
2 to rub the skin with fingernails or claws because it itches
3 to make a scraping noise

All around Harry quills were scratching on parchment like scurrying, burrowing rats. — *J. K. Rowling, Harry Potter and the Order of the Phoenix*

4 to withdraw from a race or competition

scratch *NOUN* **scratches**
1 a mark made by scratching
2 the action of scratching
to start from scratch is to start from the beginning or with nothing prepared
to be up to scratch is to have reached the proper standard
▷ **scratchy** *ADJECTIVE*

scratch card *NOUN* **scratch cards**
a card you buy as part of a lottery and scratch off part of the surface to see whether you have won a prize

scrawl *NOUN* **scrawls**
untidy handwriting

scrawl *VERB* **scrawls, scrawling, scrawled**
to write untidily

scrawny *ADJECTIVE*
thin and scraggy

I went back the way we'd come, past the cab rank where the scrawny horses dozed on their feet between the shafts. — *Alison Prince, Oranges and Murder*

scream *NOUN* **screams**
1 a loud cry of pain, fear, anger, or excitement
2 a loud piercing sound
3 (*informal*) a very amusing person or thing

scream *VERB* **screams, screaming, screamed**
to let out a scream

scree *NOUN*
a mass of loose stones on the side of a mountain

screech *NOUN* **screeches**
a harsh high-pitched scream or sound

screech *VERB* **screeches, screeching, screeched**
to make a screech

screed *NOUN* **screeds**
a very long piece of writing

screen *NOUN* **screens**
1 a movable panel used to hide, protect, or divide something
2 a surface on which films or television pictures are shown
3 a computer's VDU, on which data can be seen
4 a vehicle's windscreen

screen *VERB* **screens, screening, screened**
1 to carry out tests on someone to find out if they have a disease
2 to protect, hide, or divide something with a screen
3 to show a film or television pictures on a screen
4 to check whether a person is suitable for a job

screenplay *NOUN* **screenplays**
the script of a film, with instructions to the actors and scene directions

SPELLING NOTE Some words pronounced **s-** begin with **ce-** (e.g. cent), **ci-** (e.g. city), or **cy-** (e.g. cymbal)

screw *NOUN* **screws**
1 a metal pin with a spiral ridge (the *thread*) round it, holding things together by being twisted in
2 a twisting movement
3 something twisted
4 a propeller, especially for a ship or motor boat

screw *VERB* **screws, screwing, screwed**
1 to fasten with a screw or screws
2 to fit or turn something by twisting

WORD HISTORY via Old French from Latin *scrofa* 'female pig' (because the pattern of a screw resembles a pig's curly tail)

screwdriver *NOUN* **screwdrivers**
a tool for turning screws

scribble *VERB* **scribbles, scribbling, scribbled**
1 to write something quickly or untidily
2 to make meaningless marks
▷ **scribble** *NOUN*

WORD FAMILY *Scribble* comes from the Latin word *scribere* meaning 'to write'. Other words connected with writing (some only loosely) and having the same origin include *ascribe, conscript, describe, inscribe, prescribe, proscribe, postscript, scribe, script, scripture, subscribe, superscript,* and *transcribe.*

scribe *NOUN* **scribes**
1 a person who made copies of writings before printing was invented
2 (in biblical times) a professional religious scholar
▷ **scribal** *ADJECTIVE*

scrimmage *NOUN* **scrimmages**
a confused struggle

scrimp *VERB* **scrimps, scrimping, scrimped**
to economize or be thrifty ◆ *to scrimp and save*

script *NOUN* **scripts**
1 handwriting as distinct from printed text
2 (*Drama*) the text of a play, film, or broadcast

scripture *NOUN* **scriptures**
1 sacred writings
2 (*Religion*) the Christian writings in the Bible

scroll *NOUN* **scrolls**
1 a roll of paper or parchment used for writing on
2 a spiral design

scroll *VERB* **scrolls, scrolling, scrolled**
to move the display on a computer screen up or down to show what comes before or after it

scrotum (*say* **skroh**-tum) *NOUN* **scrota** or **scrotums**
the pouch of skin behind the penis, containing the testicles
▷ **scrotal** *ADJECTIVE*

scrounge *VERB* **scrounges, scrounging, scrounged**
to get something in an underhand way without paying for it
▷ **scrounger** *NOUN*

scrub[1] *VERB* **scrubs, scrubbing, scrubbed**
1 to rub a surface with a hard brush, especially to clean something
2 (*informal*) to cancel an arrangement
▷ **scrub** *NOUN*

scrub[2] *NOUN*
1 low trees and bushes
2 land covered with these

scrubby *ADJECTIVE*
small and shabby

scruff *NOUN*
the back of the neck

scruffy *ADJECTIVE*
shabby and untidy
▷ **scruffily** *ADVERB*
▷ **scruffiness** *NOUN*

scrum *NOUN* **scrums**
1 (also **scrummage**) a group of players from each side in rugby football who push against each other and try to heel out the ball which is thrown between them
2 a crowd pushing against each other

scrumptious *ADJECTIVE*
(*informal*) good to eat; delicious

scrunch *VERB* **scrunches, scrunching, scrunched**
1 to make a loud crunching noise
2 to crush or crumple something

scrunchy or **scrunchie** *NOUN* **scrunchies**
a band of elastic covered in fabric, used to tie up your hair

scruple *NOUN* **scruples**
a feeling of doubt or hesitation when your conscience tells you that an action would be wrong

scruple *VERB* **scruples, scrupling, scrupled**
to have scruples or a conscience about something ◆ *He would not scruple to take all their money if he could.*

scrupulous *ADJECTIVE*
1 very careful and conscientious
2 strictly honest or honourable
▷ **scrupulously** *ADVERB*

scrutinize *VERB* **scrutinizes, scrutinizing, scrutinized**
to look at something or examine it carefully

D'Artagnan halted at the threshold and scrutinized his wistful friend. —*Alexandre Dumas, The Man in the Iron Mask*

USAGE NOTE This word can also be spelled scrutinise.

scrutiny *NOUN*
a careful look at or examination of something

SCSI *ABBREVIATION*
(*ICT*) small computer system interface

scuba diving *NOUN*
swimming underwater using a tank of air strapped to your back

WORD HISTORY from the initials of *self-contained underwater breathing apparatus*

scud *VERB* **scuds, scudding, scudded**
to move quickly and lightly; to skim along

A mild breeze shook the leaves and a few dark clouds scudded across the sky. — *Michelle Magorian, Goodnight Mister Tom*

scuff *VERB* **scuffs, scuffing, scuffed**
1 to drag your feet while walking
2 to scrape something with your foot; to mark or damage something by doing this

scuffle *NOUN* **scuffles**
a confused fight or struggle

scuffle *VERB* **scuffles, scuffling, scuffled**
1 to take part in a scuffle
2 to move in a hurried or shuffling way

scull *NOUN* **sculls**
a small or lightweight oar

scull *VERB* **sculls, sculling, sculled**
to row with sculls

scullery *NOUN* **sculleries**
a small kitchen or room for washing dishes and doing other household work

sculpt *VERB* **sculpts, sculpting, sculpted**
to carve; to make sculptures

sculptor *NOUN* **sculptors**
a person who makes sculptures

sculpture *NOUN* **sculptures**
1 making shapes by carving wood or stone or casting metal
2 a shape made in this way

scuplture *VERB* **sculptures, sculptured, sculpturing**
to make a scultpure

scum *NOUN*
1 froth or dirt on top of a liquid
2 worthless people

scupper *NOUN* **scuppers**
an opening in a ship's side to let water drain away

scupper *VERB* **scuppers, scuppering, scuppered**
1 to sink a ship deliberately
2 (*informal*) to scupper a plan is to make it fail

scurf *NOUN*
flakes of dry skin

▷ **scurfy** *ADJECTIVE*

scurrilous *ADJECTIVE*
rude, insulting, and probably untrue ◆ *There had been a series of scurrilous accusations and counter-accusations.*

▷ **scurrilously** *ADVERB*

scurry *VERB* **scurries, scurrying, scurried**
to run with short steps; to hurry along

scurvy *NOUN*
a disease caused by lack of vitamin C in food

scut *NOUN* **scuts**
the short tail of a rabbit, hare, or deer

scutter *VERB* **scutters, scuttering, scuttered**
to scurry

scuttle❶ *NOUN* **scuttles**
a bucket or container for coal in a house

scuttle❷ *VERB* **scuttles, scuttling, scuttled**
to scurry; to hurry away

scuttle❸ *NOUN* **scuttles**
a small opening with a lid in a ship's deck or side

scuttle *VERB* **scuttles, scuttling, scuttled**
to sink a ship deliberately by letting water into it

scythe *NOUN* **scythes**
a tool with a long curved blade for cutting grass or corn

scythe *VERB* **scythes, scything, scythed**
to cut grass or other plants with a scythe

SE *ABBREVIATION*
1 south-east
2 south-eastern

sea *NOUN* **seas**
1 the salt water that covers most of the earth's surface; a part of this
2 a large lake
3 a large area of something ◆ *Inside the room was a sea of eager faces.*

at sea
1 travelling on the sea
2 completely confused and not knowing what to do

sea anemone *NOUN* **sea anemones**
a sea creature with short tentacles round its mouth

seaboard *NOUN* **seaboards**
a coastline or coastal region

sea breeze *NOUN* **sea breezes**
a breeze blowing from the sea onto the land

sea change *NOUN* **sea changes**
a dramatic change

seafaring *ADJECTIVE, NOUN*
working or travelling on the sea

▷ **seafarer** *NOUN*

seafood *NOUN*
fish or shellfish from the sea eaten as food

a b c d e f g h i j k l m n o p q r s t u v w x y z

SPELLING NOTE Some words pronounced **s-** begin with **ce-** (e.g. cent), **ci-** (e.g. city), or **cy-** (e.g. cymbal)

seagull ***NOUN*** **seagulls**
a seabird with long wings

sea horse ***NOUN*** **sea horses**
a small fish that swims upright, with a head rather like a horse's head

seal❶ ***NOUN*** **seals**
a sea mammal with thick fur or bristles, that breeds on land

seal❷ ***NOUN*** **seals**
1 a piece of metal with an engraved design for pressing on a soft substance to leave an impression
2 this impression, especially one made on a piece of wax
3 something designed to close an opening and prevent air or liquid from passing through
4 a small decorative sticker

seal ***VERB*** **seals, sealing, sealed**
1 to close something by sticking two parts together
2 to close securely; to stop up
3 to press a seal on something
4 someone's fate is sealed when they are unable to escape something harmful or unpleasant

to seal something off is to close the entrances to an area to prevent people reaching it

sea level ***NOUN***
the level of the sea halfway between high and low tide

sealing wax ***NOUN***
a substance that is soft when heated but hardens when cooled, used for sealing documents or for marking with a seal

sea lion ***NOUN*** **sea lions**
a kind of large seal that lives in the Pacific Ocean

seam ***NOUN*** **seams**
1 the line where two edges of fabric or wood or other material join
2 a layer of coal in the ground

seaman ***NOUN*** **seamen**
a sailor, especially one who is not an officer

seamanship ***NOUN***
skill in seafaring

seamy ***ADJECTIVE***
seamy side the less attractive side or part ◆ *He seemed to know a lot about the seamy side of life.*

WORD HISTORY originally, the 'wrong' side of a piece of sewing, where the rough edges of the seams show

seance (*say* say- ahns) ***NOUN*** **seances**
a meeting at which people try to make contact with the spirits of dead people

seaplane ***NOUN*** **seaplanes**
an aeroplane that can land on and take off from water

seaport ***NOUN*** **seaports**
a port on the coast

sear ***VERB*** **sears, searing, seared**
to scorch or burn the surface of something

search ***VERB*** **searches, searching, searched**
1 to look carefully in a place in order to find something
2 to examine the clothes and body of a person to see if something is hidden there
▷ **search** ***NOUN***
▷ **searcher** ***NOUN***

search engine ***NOUN*** **search engines**
(*ICT*) a program that searches for computer data, especially on the Internet

searching ***ADJECTIVE***
searching inquiries or questions are thorough and detailed

searchlight ***NOUN*** **searchlights**
a light with a strong beam that can be turned in any direction

search party ***NOUN*** **search parties**
a group of people organized to search for a missing person or thing

search warrant ***NOUN*** **search warrants**
an official document giving the police permission to search private property

searing ***ADJECTIVE***
a searing pain is sharp and burning

seascape ***NOUN*** **seascapes**
a picture or view of the sea

seasick ***ADJECTIVE***
sick because of the movement of a ship
▷ **seasickness** ***NOUN***

seaside ***NOUN***
a place by the sea where people go for holidays

season ***NOUN*** **seasons**
1 each of the four main parts of the year (spring, summer, autumn, winter)
2 the period of the year when a particular activity takes place ◆ *The club was promoted last season.*
3 fruit or other produce is in season when it is available and ready for eating

season ***VERB*** **seasons, seasoning, seasoned**
1 to give extra flavour to food by adding salt, pepper, herbs, or spices
2 to dry and treat timber to make it ready for use

WORD HISTORY from Latin *satio* meaning 'sowing' and later 'time for sowing seed'

seasonable ***ADJECTIVE***
suitable for the time of year ◆ *a choir singing seasonable carols*
▷ **seasonably** ***ADVERB***

USAGE NOTE Take care not to confuse this word with *seasonal.*

seasonal *ADJECTIVE*
1 lasting for a season; to do with a season
2 seasonal work or activity is done at a particular time of year
▷ **seasonally** *ADVERB*

USAGE NOTE Take care not to confuse this word with *seasonable*.

seasoning *NOUN* **seasonings**
a substance used to season food

season ticket *NOUN* **season tickets**
a ticket that can be used as often as you like throughout a period of time

seat *NOUN* **seats**
1 a thing made or used for sitting on
2 a place in an elected council, parliament, or committee
3 the buttocks; the part of a skirt or trousers covering these
4 the place where something is based or located ◆ *The city is the capital of the country but not the seat of government.*

seat *VERB* **seats, seating, seated**
1 to place someone in or on a seat
2 to have seats for a particular number of people

seat belt *NOUN* **seat belts**
a strap to hold a person securely in a seat

seating *NOUN*
1 the seats in a place
2 the arrangement of seats

sea urchin *NOUN* **sea urchins**
a sea animal with a spherical shell covered in sharp spikes

seaward *ADJECTIVE ADVERB*
towards the sea
▷ **seawards** *ADVERB*

seaweed *NOUN*
a plant or plants that grow in the sea
▷ **seaweedy** *ADJECTIVE*

seaworthy *ADJECTIVE*
a ship is seaworthy when it is fit for a sea voyage
▷ **seaworthiness** *NOUN*

sebum *NOUN*
the natural oil produced by glands (*sebaceous glands*) in the skin to lubricate the skin and hair

secateurs *PLURAL NOUN*
clippers held in the hand for pruning plants

secede (*say* sis- **seed**) *VERB* **secedes, seceding, seceded**
to withdraw from being a member of a political or religious organization
▷ **secession** *NOUN*

secluded *ADJECTIVE*
a secluded place is quiet and sheltered from view
▷ **seclusion** *NOUN*

second❶ *ADJECTIVE*
next or another after the first

to have second thoughts is to wonder whether a decision you have made was the right one

second *NOUN* **seconds**
1 a person or thing that is second
2 an attendant of a fighter in a boxing match or duel
3 one-sixtieth of a minute of time or of a degree used in measuring angles
4 (*informal*) a short time ◆ *Can you wait a second while I do this?*

second *VERB* **seconds, seconding, seconded**
1 to assist someone
2 to support a proposal that someone else has put forward
▷ **seconder** *NOUN*

WORD FAMILY *Second* comes from the Latin word *secundus*, which has the same meaning and is itself derived from *sequi* meaning 'to follow'. Other words connected with following (some only loosely) and having the same origin include *sequel* and *sequence, ensue, prosecute, sect* (a following forming a separate group), *set*, and *suit*.

second❷ (*say* sik- **ond**) *VERB* **seconds, seconding, seconded**
to transfer a person temporarily to another job or department
▷ **secondment** *NOUN*

WORD HISTORY from French *en second* 'in the second rank' (because officers seconded to another company served under officers who belonged to that company)

secondary *ADJECTIVE*
1 less important than something else (SEE ALSO **primary**)
2 coming after or from something

secondary colour *NOUN* **secondary colours**
a colour made by mixing two primary colours

secondary school *NOUN* **secondary schools**
a school for children of more than about 11 years old

second-hand *ADJECTIVE*
1 bought or used after someone else has owned it
2 selling used goods

secondly *ADVERB*
in the second place; as the second one

second nature *NOUN*
behaviour that has become automatic or a habit

second-rate *ADJECTIVE*
inferior; not very good

seconds *PLURAL NOUN*
1 goods that are not of the best quality, sold at a reduced price
2 a second helping of food at a meal

SPELLING NOTE Some words pronounced **s-** begin with **ce-** (e.g. cent), **ci-** (e.g. city), or **cy-** (e.g. cymbal)

second sight *NOUN*
the ability to foresee the future

secrecy *NOUN*
being secret; keeping things secret

secret *ADJECTIVE*
1 that must not be told or shown to other people
2 not known by everybody
3 working secretly
▷ **secretly** *ADVERB*

secret *NOUN* **secrets**
1 something secret
2 something useful that is not widely known

The great secret of algebra is that a letter always means the same number all the way through. — *Kjartan Poskitt, Murderous Maths*

secret agent *NOUN* **secret agents**
a spy acting for a country

secretariat *NOUN* **secretariats**
an administrative department of a large organization such as the United Nations

secretary (*say* **sek**- rit- ree) *NOUN* **secretaries**
1 a person whose job is to help with letters, answer the telephone, and make business arrangements for a person or organization
2 the chief assistant of a government minister or ambassador
▷ **secretarial** *ADJECTIVE*

WORD HISTORY from Latin *secretarius* 'an officer or servant allowed to know your secrets'

secrete (*say* sik- **reet**) *VERB* **secretes, secreting, secreted**
1 to hide something
2 to produce a substance in the body
▷ **secretion** *NOUN*

secretive (*say* **seek**- rit- iv) *ADJECTIVE*
liking or trying to keep things secret
▷ **secretively** *ADVERB*
▷ **secretiveness** *NOUN*

secret police *NOUN*
a police force which works in secret for political purposes, not to deal with crime

secret service *NOUN*
a government department responsible for espionage

sect *NOUN* **sects**
a group of people whose beliefs differ from those of others in the same religion

sectarian (*say* sekt- **air**- ee- an) *ADJECTIVE*
belonging to or supporting a sect

section *NOUN* **sections**
1 a distinct part that something is divided into

Unfortunately, Hunstanton Library did not have a large section on Witchcraft. — *Anthony Horowitz, Groosham Grange*

2 a cross-section

sectional *ADJECTIVE*
1 made in sections that can be put together and taken apart
2 concerned with only one group within a community

sector *NOUN* **sectors**
1 one part of an area
2 a part of something ◆ *Twice as many workers are now in the private sector as in the public sector.*
3 (*Mathematics*) a section of a circle between two lines drawn from its centre to its circumference

secular *ADJECTIVE*
to do with worldly affairs, not spiritual or religious matters

secure *ADJECTIVE*
1 safe against danger or attack
2 well fixed; not likely to slip or fall
3 certain or reliable
▷ **securely** *ADVERB*

secure *VERB* **secures, securing, secured**
1 to make a thing secure
2 to fasten something firmly
3 to succeed in obtaining or achieving something ◆ *a campaign to secure a change in the law*

security *NOUN* **securities**
1 the state of being secure; safety
2 precautions taken to prevent theft, spying, terrorism, or other criminal activity
3 something given as a guarantee that a promise will be kept or a debt repaid
4 investments such as stocks and shares

security guard *NOUN* **security guards**
a person employed to guard a building or its contents against theft and vandalism

security risk *NOUN* **security risks**
a person or situation thought likely to threaten the security of a country

sedan chair *NOUN* **sedan chairs**
an enclosed chair for one person, mounted on two horizontal poles and carried by two men, used in the 17th-18th centuries

sedate *ADJECTIVE*
calm and dignified
▷ **sedately** *ADVERB*
▷ **sedateness** *NOUN*

sedate *VERB* **sedates, sedating, sedated**
to give a sedative to someone
▷ **sedation** *NOUN*

sedative (*say* **sed**- a- tiv) *NOUN* **sedatives**
a medicine that makes a person calm

sedentary (*say* **sed**- en- ter- ee) *ADJECTIVE*
a sedentary way of life or work involves a lot of sitting down and little physical exercise

Seder *NOUN* **Seders**
(in Judaism) a ritual and a ceremonial meal to mark the beginning of Passover

sedge *NOUN*
a grass-like plant growing in marshes or near water

sediment *NOUN*
fine particles of solid matter that float in liquid or sink to the bottom of it

sedimentary *ADJECTIVE*
sedimentary rocks are formed from particles that have settled on a surface

sedition *NOUN*
speeches or actions intended to make people rebel against the authority of the state
▷ **seditious** *ADJECTIVE*

seduce *VERB* **seduces, seducing, seduced**
1 to persuade a person to have sexual intercourse
2 to attract or lead astray by offering temptations
▷ **seducer** *NOUN*
▷ **seduction** *NOUN*

seductive *ADJECTIVE*
1 sexually attractive
2 temptingly attractive

sedulous *ADJECTIVE*
diligent and persevering
▷ **sedulously** *ADVERB*

see❶ *VERB* **sees, seeing, saw, seen**
1 to perceive someone or something with the eyes
2 to meet someone regularly as a boyfriend or girlfriend
3 to consult a professional person
4 to understand something ◆ *I see what you mean.*
5 to regard something in a particular way ◆ *We see this as a criticism of the government.*
6 to consider a possibility ◆ *Will you see if you can help?*
7 to make sure of something ◆ *See that you leave in good time.*
8 to check or discover something ◆ *See who that is outside.*
9 to escort someone ◆ *I'll see you on to the train.*
to see through something is to be aware of its true nature and not be deceived by it
to see to something is to make sure it is done

see❷ *NOUN* **sees**
a district over which a bishop or archbishop has authority

seed *NOUN* **seeds** or **seed**
1 a fertilized part of a plant, capable of growing into a new plant
2 (*old use*) descendants
3 a seeded player

seed *VERB* **seeds, seeding, seeded**
1 to plant or sprinkle seeds in something
2 to name the best players and arrange for them not to play against each other in the early rounds of a tournament

seedling *NOUN* **seedlings**
a very young plant growing from a seed

seedy *ADJECTIVE* **seedier, seediest**
1 full of seeds
2 shabby and disreputable

The first place I come to is Vinney's. ...It's a seedy fish-and-chip shop with a cracked lino floor and chipped formica on the one table inside. — *Nicky Singer, Feather Boy*

▷ **seediness** *NOUN*

seeing *CONJUNCTION*
considering ◆ *Seeing there was to be no more entertainment, the crowd began to disperse.*

seek *VERB* **seeks, seeking, sought**
1 to search for something or someone
2 to try to do or obtain something

seem *VERB* **seems, seeming, seemed**
to give the impression of being something
▷ **seemingly** *ADVERB*

seemly *ADJECTIVE*
(*old use*) seemly talk or behaviour is proper or suitable
▷ **seemliness** *NOUN*

seep *VERB* **seeps, seeping, seeped**
to ooze slowly out or through something
▷ **seepage** *NOUN*

seer *NOUN* **seers**
a person who is supposed to see into the future; a prophet

see-saw *NOUN* **see-saws**
a plank balanced in the middle so that two people can sit, one on each end, and make it go up and down

WORD HISTORY from an old rhyme which imitated the rhythm of a saw going to and fro, later used by children on a see-saw

seethe *VERB* **seethes, seething, seethed**
1 to bubble and surge like water boiling
2 to be very angry or excited

Jamie saw a mysterious boy with darting, distrustful eyes who looked frail on the outside, but was seething on the inside. — *Rachel Anderson, Warlands*

segment *NOUN* **segments**
a part that is cut off or separates naturally from other parts
▷ **segmented** *ADJECTIVE*

segregate *VERB* **segregates, segregating, segregated**
1 to separate people of different races or religions
2 to isolate a person or thing
▷ **segregation** *NOUN*

WORD HISTORY from Latin *segregare* 'to separate from the flock', from *gregis* 'of a flock'

SPELLING NOTE Some words pronounced **s-** begin with **ce-** (e.g. cent), **ci-** (e.g. city), or **cy-** (e.g. cymbal)

seismic (*say* sy- zmik) *ADJECTIVE*
to do with earthquakes or other vibrations of the earth
WORD HISTORY from Greek *seismos* 'earthquake'

seismograph (*say* sy- zmo- grahf) *NOUN* **seismographs**
an instrument for measuring the strength of earthquakes

seize *VERB* **seizes, seizing, seized**
1 to take hold of a person or thing suddenly or forcibly
2 to take possession of something by force or by legal authority
3 to seize a chance or opportunity is to make use of it decisively
4 to have a sudden effect on someone ◆ *Fear seized them.*
5 a machine seizes, or seizes up, when it becomes jammed because of excessive friction or overheating

seizure *NOUN* **seizures**
1 the process of seizing something
2 a sudden fit, as in epilepsy or a heart attack

seldom *ADVERB*
rarely; not often

select *VERB* **selects, selecting, selected**
to choose a person or thing carefully
▷ **selector** *NOUN*

select *ADJECTIVE*
1 carefully chosen ◆ *a select band of friends*
2 a select club or organization is one that is exclusive and chooses its members carefully

selection *NOUN* **selections**
1 the process of selecting or choosing
2 a person or thing selected
3 a group selected from a larger group
4 a range of goods from which to choose

selective *ADJECTIVE*
choosing or chosen carefully
▷ **selectively** *ADVERB*
▷ **selectivity** *NOUN*

selenium *NOUN*
(*Science*) a chemical element that is a semiconductor and has various uses in electronics
WORD HISTORY from Greek *selene* 'moon'

self *NOUN* **selves**
1 a person as an individual
2 a person's particular nature ◆ *Her friend reminded her of her own former self.*

self-addressed *ADJECTIVE*
addressed to yourself

self-assured *ADJECTIVE*
confident of your abilities

self-catering *NOUN*
catering for yourself, instead of having meals provided

self-centred *ADJECTIVE*
preoccupied with your own affairs; selfish

self-confident *ADJECTIVE*
confident of your own abilities

self-conscious *ADJECTIVE*
embarrassed or unnatural because you know that people are watching you

self-contained *ADJECTIVE*
accommodation is self-contained when it is complete in itself and contains all the necessary facilities

self-control *NOUN*
the ability to control your own behaviour
▷ **self-controlled** *ADJECTIVE*

self-defence *NOUN*
the act or art of defending yourself

self-denial *NOUN*
deliberately going without things you would like to have

self-determination *NOUN*
a country's right to rule itself and choose its own government

self-employed *ADJECTIVE*
working independently and not for an employer

self-esteem *NOUN*
your own opinion of yourself and your own worth

self-evident *ADJECTIVE*
obvious and not needing proof or explanation

self-important *ADJECTIVE*
having a high opinion of yourself; haughty and pompous

self-indulgent *ADJECTIVE*
enjoying your own pleasures and comforts

self-interest *NOUN*
your own personal advantage

selfish *ADJECTIVE*
doing what you want and not thinking of other people; keeping things for yourself
▷ **selfishly** *ADVERB*
▷ **selfishness** *NOUN*

selfless *ADJECTIVE*
considerate of other people; not selfish

self-made *ADJECTIVE*
rich or successful because of your own efforts

self-pity *NOUN*
too much sorrow and pity for yourself and your own problems

self-portrait *NOUN* **self-portraits**
a portrait in which the artist is the subject

self-possessed *ADJECTIVE*
calm and dignified

a b c d e f g h i j k l m n o p q r s t u v w x y z

self-raising *ADJECTIVE*
self-raising flour is used to make cakes and puddings rise without needing to add baking powder

self-reliance *NOUN*
reliance on one's own abilities and resources

self-respect *NOUN*
your own proper respect for yourself

self-righteous *ADJECTIVE*
smugly sure that you are thinking or behaving rightly

selfsame *ADJECTIVE*
the very same

self-satisfied *ADJECTIVE*
very pleased with yourself

self-seeking *ADJECTIVE*
selfishly trying to benefit yourself

self-service *ADJECTIVE*
where customers help themselves to things and pay a cashier for what they have taken

self-sufficient *ADJECTIVE*
able to produce or provide what you need without help from others

self-supporting *ADJECTIVE*
earning enough to keep yourself without needing money from others

self-taught *ADJECTIVE*
taught by yourself and not by a teacher

self-willed *ADJECTIVE*
obstinately doing what you want; stubborn

sell *VERB* **sells, selling, sold**
1 to give something in exchange for money
2 to have something available for people to buy
3 to be on sale at a certain price
to sell out is to sell all the stock of something
to sell someone out (*informal*) is to betray them
▷ **seller** *NOUN*

sell *NOUN*
the manner of selling something
a hard sell selling by putting pressure on someone to buy
a soft sell selling by persuasion or gentle means

sell-by date *NOUN* **sell-by dates**
a date marked on packaging showing the date by which the contents must be sold

sell-out *NOUN* **sell-outs**
an entertainment, sports match, or other event for which all the tickets have been sold

selvage *NOUN* **selvages**
an edge of cloth woven so that it does not unravel

selves *plural* of **self**

semantic *ADJECTIVE*
(*Language*) to do with meaning in language

semaphore *NOUN*
a system of signalling by holding flags out with your arms in positions that indicate letters of the alphabet

semblance *NOUN*
an outward appearance or apparent likeness

semen (*say* **seem**- en) *NOUN*
a white liquid produced by males and containing sperm

semi *NOUN* **semis**
(*informal*) a semi-detached house

semibreve *NOUN* **semibreves**
(*Music*) the longest musical note normally used (written 𝅝), lasting four times as long as a crotchet

semicircle *NOUN* **semicircles**
half a circle
▷ **semicircular** *ADJECTIVE*

semicolon *NOUN* **semicolons**
(*Language*) a punctuation mark (;) used to mark a break that is stronger than one marked by a comma

semicolons

You use a **semicolon** to mark a break in a sentence that is longer, or more important, than a break made with a comma:

Castle Thule was desolate; no one had lived there for three centuries or more.
I know you don't eat meat, fish, or eggs; but what about cheese?

Semicolons can separate a series of connected clauses introduced by a colon:

There were three clues: there was mud on the carpet; the door had been forced; and the air in the room smelled of fish.

A single semicolon can also separate two contrasting or balancing clauses:

Before us lay a cliff of sheer ice; behind, a dizzying drop.
You bring cups and plates; I'll bring juice and sandwiches.

semiconductor *NOUN* **semiconductors**
a substance that can conduct electricity but not as well as most metals do

semi-detached *ADJECTIVE*
a semi-detached house is joined to another house on one side only

semifinal *NOUN* **semifinals**
a match or round whose winner will take part in the final

seminar *NOUN* **seminars**
a meeting for advanced discussion and research on a subject

seminary *NOUN* **seminaries**
a training college for priests or rabbis

semiquaver *NOUN* **semiquavers**
(*Music*) a note (𝅘𝅥𝅯) equal in length to one quarter of a crotchet

SPELLING NOTE Some words pronounced **s-** begin with **ce-** (e.g. cent), **ci-** (e.g. city), or **cy-** (e.g. cymbal)

semi-skilled *ADJECTIVE*
having or needing some training but not extensive training

semi-skimmed milk *NOUN*
milk that has had some of the cream removed

Semitic (*say* sim- **it**- ik) *ADJECTIVE*
to do with the Semites, the group of people that includes the Jews and Arabs
▷ **Semite** (*say* see- myt) *NOUN*

semitone *NOUN* **semitones**
(*Music*) half a tone

semolina *NOUN*
hard round grains of wheat used to make milk puddings and pasta

senate *NOUN* **senates**
1 the governing council in ancient Rome
2 the upper house of the parliament of the United States, France, and certain other countries
▷ **senator** *NOUN*

send *VERB* **sends, sending, sent**
1 to make a person or thing go or be taken somewhere
2 to affect someone in a certain way ◆ *The noise was sending them crazy.*
to send for someone or something is to ask for a person to come or for something to be brought to you
to send something or someone up (*informal*) is to make fun of them by imitating them in an exaggerated way
▷ **sender** *NOUN*

senile (*say* **seen**- yl) *ADJECTIVE*
weak or confused and forgetful because of old age
▷ **senility** *NOUN*

senior *ADJECTIVE*
1 older than someone else
2 higher in rank
▷ **seniority** *NOUN*

senior *NOUN* **seniors**
1 a person who is older or higher in rank than you are
2 a member of a senior school

senior citizen *NOUN* **senior citizens**
an elderly person, especially a pensioner

senna *NOUN*
the dried pods or leaves of a tropical tree, used as a laxative

sensation *NOUN* **sensations**
1 a distinct physical feeling
2 a widespread interest or excitement, or a person or event that causes this ◆ *The book created a sensation when it was published.* ◆ *She was a sensation, the talk of the evening.*

sensational *ADJECTIVE*
1 causing or trying to cause great excitement or public interest
2 (*informal*) very good; wonderful
▷ **sensationally** *ADVERB*

sensationalism *NOUN*
the deliberate use of dramatic words or styles to arouse excitement
▷ **sensationalist** *NOUN*

sense *NOUN* **senses**
1 the ability to see, hear, smell, touch, or taste things
2 the ability to feel or appreciate something ◆ *You'll need a good sense of humour.*
3 the power to think or make wise decisions ◆ *Fortunately she had the sense to keep a copy of the letter.*
4 a sense of a word or phrase is the meaning it has
to be out of your senses is to think or behave in a foolish or crazy way
to come to your senses is to start thinking or behaving sensibly after being foolish
to make sense
1 is to have a meaning you can understand
2 is to be a sensible idea

sense *VERB* **senses, sensing, sensed**
1 to feel; to get an impression

> I didn't know what I'd do if the vampire wasn't here, but somehow I sensed he would be. — *Darren Shan, Cirque du Freak*

2 a device senses something when it detects or records it

senseless *ADJECTIVE*
1 not showing good sense; foolish
2 unconscious; having no sensation

sensibility *NOUN* **sensibilities**
sensitiveness or delicate feeling ◆ *The remarks might offend their religious sensibilities.*
USAGE NOTE Note that this word does not mean 'being sensible' or 'having good sense'.

sensible *ADJECTIVE*
wise; having or showing good sense
▷ **sensibly** *ADVERB*

sensitive *ADJECTIVE*
1 a sensitive person is easily hurt or offended
2 a person is sensitive to other people's feelings when they are careful not to offend them
3 receiving impressions quickly and easily
4 to be sensitive to a physical property is to be affected by something
5 a sensitive subject or matter is one that needs to be dealt with tactfully
▷ **sensitively** *ADVERB*
▷ **sensitivity** *NOUN*

sensitize *VERB* **sensitizes, sensitizing, sensitized**
to make a thing sensitive to something
USAGE NOTE This word can also be spelled sensitise.

sensor *NOUN* **sensors**
(*ICT*) a device or instrument for detecting a physical property such as light, heat, or sound

a b c d e f g h i j k l m n o p q r s t u v w x y z

sensory *ADJECTIVE*
1 to do with the senses
2 a sensory nerve or organ is one that receives physical sensations

sensual *ADJECTIVE*
1 to do with physical pleasure
2 liking or suggesting physical or sexual pleasures

sensuous *ADJECTIVE*
giving pleasure to the senses, especially by being beautiful or delicate

sentence *NOUN* **sentences**
1 (*Grammar*) a group of words that express a complete thought and form a statement, question, exclamation, or command

'My life is a perfect graveyard of buried hopes.' That's a sentence I read in a book once, and I say it over to comfort myself whenever I'm disappointed in anything. — *L. M. Montgomery, Anne of Green Gables*

2 the punishment announced to a convicted person in a law court

sentences

A **sentence** is a group of words that typically contains a main verb. It begins with a capital letter and ends in a full stop or question mark or exclamation mark. It can contain a single clause, or several clauses joined by conjunctions or punctuation:
Bats are nocturnal creatures.
Desert animals are often nocturnal because it is cooler for hunting at night.
If a sentence is a statement, it ends with a full stop:
There was nothing to do but wait for the ice to thaw.
A sentence which is a question ends with a question mark, and one which is an exclamation or command ends with an exclamation mark:
When would the ice begin to thaw?
Come and see the ice beginning to thaw!
A single verb can form a sentence, especially if it is a command, like *Help!* or *Stop!* Sometimes, short sentences can be formed without a verb; for example, in direct speech:
'Where are you, Lieutenant?' 'Over here!'
or in literary passages, to create a stylistic effect:
In every direction lay the expanse of outer space. Vast. Empty. Desolate.
See also the panel on **clauses**.

sentence *VERB* **sentences, sentencing, sentenced**
to tell a convicted person their punishment in a law court

WORD HISTORY from Latin *sententia* 'feeling' and later 'opinion' or 'judgement', then 'a meaning expressed in words'

sententious *ADJECTIVE*
giving moral advice in a pompous way

sentient *ADJECTIVE*
able to feel and perceive things

sentiment *NOUN* **sentiments**
1 an opinion
2 sentimentality

WORD FAMILY *Sentiment* comes from the Latin word *sentire* meaning 'to feel'. Other words connected with feeling (some only loosely) and having the same origin include *assent, consent, dissent, resent, sensation, sense, sensitive*, and *sentient*.

sentimental *ADJECTIVE*
showing or arousing tenderness or romantic feeling or foolish emotion
▷ **sentimentally** *ADVERB*
▷ **sentimentality** *NOUN*

sentinel *NOUN* **sentinels**
a guard or sentry

sentry *NOUN* **sentries**
a soldier guarding something

sepal (*say* **sep**- ul) *NOUN* **sepals**
each of the leaves forming the calyx of a bud

separable *ADJECTIVE*
able to be separated

separate (*say* **sep**- er- at) *ADJECTIVE*
1 not joined to anything
2 not shared
▷ **separately** *ADVERB*

separate (*say* **sep**- er- ayt) *VERB* **separates, separating, separated**
1 to make or keep people or things separate; to divide them
2 to become separate
3 to stop living together as a couple
▷ **separation** *NOUN*
▷ **separator** *NOUN*

sepia *NOUN*
reddish-brown, like the colour of early photographs

sepsis *NOUN*
a septic condition

September *NOUN*
the ninth month of the year

WORD HISTORY from Latin *septem* 'seven' (because it was the seventh month of the ancient Roman calendar)

septet *NOUN* **septets**
1 a group of seven musicians
2 a piece of music for seven musicians

septic *ADJECTIVE*
infected with harmful bacteria that cause pus to form

septicaemia (*say* sep- ti- **see**- mia) *NOUN*
(*Medicine*) blood poisoning caused by bacteria

sepulchral (*say* sep- **ul**- kral) *ADJECTIVE*
1 to do with a sepulchre
2 a sepulchral voice sounds deep and hollow

SPELLING NOTE Some words pronounced **s-** begin with **ce-** (e.g. cent), **ci-** (e.g. city), or **cy-** (e.g. cymbal)

sepulchre (*say* **sep**- ul- ker) ***NOUN*** **sepulchres**
a tomb

sequel ***NOUN*** **sequels**
1 a book, film, or broadcast that continues the story of an earlier one or develops its themes
2 something that follows or results from an earlier event

sequence ***NOUN*** **sequences**
1 the following of one thing after another; the order in which things happen
2 a series of things

sequestrate ***VERB*** **sequestrates, sequestrating, sequestrated**
to confiscate property until the owner pays a debt or obeys a court order
▷ **sequestration** ***NOUN***

sequin ***NOUN*** **sequins**
a small bright disc sewn on to clothes for decoration
▷ **sequinned** ***ADJECTIVE***

WORD HISTORY via French and Italian from Arabic *sikka* 'a coin'

seraph ***NOUN*** **seraphim** or **seraphs**
a kind of angel

seraphic (*say* ser- **af**- ik) ***ADJECTIVE***
a seraphic smile or look is very pure and beautiful
▷ **seraphically** ***ADVERB***

serenade ***NOUN*** **serenades**
a song or tune of a kind played by a man under his lover's window

serenade ***VERB*** **serenades, serenading, serenaded**
to sing or play a serenade to someone

serendipity ***NOUN***
the ability to make pleasant or interesting discoveries by accident
▷ **serendipitous** ***ADJECTIVE***

WORD HISTORY invented by an 18th- century writer, Horace Walpole, from the title of a story *The Three Princes of Serendip* (who had this ability)

serene ***ADJECTIVE***
calm and peaceful
▷ **serenely** ***ADVERB***
▷ **serenity** (*say* ser- **en**- iti) ***NOUN***

serf ***NOUN*** **serfs**
(*History*) a farm labourer who worked for a landowner, and who was not allowed to leave
▷ **serfdom** ***NOUN***

serge ***NOUN***
a kind of strong woven fabric

sergeant (*say* **sar**- jent) ***NOUN*** **sergeants**
a soldier or policeman who is in charge of others

sergeant major ***NOUN*** **sergeant majors**
a soldier who is one rank higher than a sergeant

serial ***NOUN*** **serials**
a story, or film, or broadcast that is presented in separate parts

USAGE NOTE Take care not to confuse this word with *cereal.*

serialize ***VERB*** **serializes, serializing, serialized**
to produce a story or film as a serial
▷ **serialization** ***NOUN***

USAGE NOTE This word can also be spelled serialise.

serial killer ***NOUN*** **serial killers**
a person who commits a series of murders

serial number ***NOUN*** **serial numbers**
a number printed on an object by the manufacturers to distinguish it from other identical objects

series ***NOUN*** **series**
1 a number of things following or connected with each other
2 a number of games or matches between the same competitors
3 a number of separate radio or television programmes with the same characters or on the same subject

serious ***ADJECTIVE***
1 a person or look is serious when they are solemn and thoughtful, and not smiling
2 a serious matter is one that needs careful thought and is important
3 sincere; not casual or light-hearted ◆ *Is that meant to be a serious answer?*
4 a serious illness, problem, or incident is one that causes anxiety, and is not trivial
▷ **seriously** ***ADVERB***
▷ **seriousness** ***NOUN***

sermon ***NOUN*** **sermons**
a talk given by a preacher, especially as part of a religious service

serpent ***NOUN*** **serpents**
a snake

serpentine ***ADJECTIVE***
twisting and curving like a snake

serrated ***ADJECTIVE***
having a notched edge

serried ***ADJECTIVE***
arranged in rows close together

serum (*say* **seer**- um) ***NOUN*** **sera** or **serums**
1 the thin pale-yellow liquid that remains from blood when the rest has clotted
2 this fluid used medically, usually for the antibodies it contains

servant ***NOUN*** **servants**
a person whose job is to work or serve in someone else's house

serve *VERB* **serves, serving, served**
1 to work for a person or organization or country
2 to sell things to people in a shop
3 to give out food to people at a meal
4 to spend time doing or suffering something ◆ *At the time he was serving a sentence for armed robbery.*
5 be suitable or useful for a particular purpose

When we reached the house we climbed the long, sloping lawn to the porch and went into Mama and Papa's room, which also served as the living area. — *Mildred D. Taylor, Roll of Thunder, Hear My Cry*

6 to start play in tennis or similar games by hitting the ball

to serve someone right is to be what they deserve

WORD FAMILY *Serve* comes from the Latin word *servire*, which in turn comes from *servus* meaning 'slave'. Other words connected with serving and having the same origin include *servant, service, servile*, and *conserve, deserve*, and *preserve*.

serve *NOUN* **serves**
an act of serving in tennis or similar games

server *NOUN* **servers**
1 a person or thing that serves
2 (*ICT*) a computer or program that controls or supplies information to several computers connected to a network

service *NOUN* **services**
1 the activity of working for a person or organization or country
2 something that helps people or supplies what they want ◆ *There is no bus service to the village any more.*
3 a country's army, navy, or air force
4 a religious ceremony
5 the process of providing people with goods, food, or other needs ◆ *The restaurant was praised for its service.*
6 a set of dishes and plates for a meal
7 the servicing of a vehicle or machine
8 the action of serving in tennis or badminton

service *VERB* **services, servicing, serviced**
1 to repair or keep a vehicle or machine in working order
2 to supply with services

serviceable *ADJECTIVE*
usable; suitable for ordinary use or wear

service area *NOUN* **service areas**
an area beside a road or motorway where motorists can buy petrol and other services

service charge *NOUN* **service charges**
1 an amount added to a restaurant or hotel bill to reward the waiters and waitresses for their service
2 money paid to the landlord of a block of flats for services used by all the flats, e.g. central heating or cleaning the stairs

service industry *NOUN* **service industries**
an industry which sells service, not goods

serviceman *NOUN* **servicemen**
a man serving in the armed forces

service road *NOUN* **service roads**
a road beside a main road, for use by vehicles needing local access

services *PLURAL NOUN*
an area beside a motorway where petrol and oil, food, and other services are available to travellers

service station *NOUN* **service stations**
a place beside a road, where petrol and oil and other services are available

servicewoman *NOUN* **servicewomen**
a woman serving in the armed forces

serviette *NOUN* **serviettes**
a piece of cloth or paper used to keep your clothes or hands clean at a meal

servile *ADJECTIVE*
like a slave; too willing to serve or obey others
▷ **servility** *NOUN*

serving *NOUN* **servings**
a helping of food

servitude *NOUN*
the condition of being obliged to work for someone else and having no independence; slavery

sesame *NOUN*
an African plant whose seeds can be eaten or used to make an edible oil

session *NOUN* **sessions**
1 a meeting or series of meetings ◆ *The council held its first session on 14 December.*
2 a time spent doing a particular thing ◆ *He had pulled a hamstring during a training session.*

set *VERB* **sets, setting, set**
1 to set something somewhere is to put it into position ◆ *It took four large men to set the statue on its base.*
2 to set a date or time is to arrange or decide when something will happen
3 to put something into its proper place or fitting

Annie was a big woman with little black eyes set like currants in a round bun of a face. — *Celia Rees, Witch Child*

4 to set a device is to make it ready to work
5 something soft or runny, such as jelly, sets when it becomes firm or hard
6 to set someone a task or exercise is to give it to them to do
7 to put someone or something into a particular condition ◆ *Thieves set a stolen car alight in a nearby field.*
8 the sun sets when it disappears below the horizon ⏩

a b c d e f g h i j k l m n o p q r s t u v w x y z

to set about something is to start doing it
to set about someone (*informal*) is to attack them
to set off is to begin a journey
to set something off
1 is to start something happening
2 is to cause something to explode
to set out
1 is to begin a journey
2 display or make known
to set something out is to display or make known
to set to
1 is to begin doing something vigorously
2 is to begin fighting or arguing
to set something up
1 is to place it in position
2 is to arrange or establish something ◆ *Police set up barricades to halt the marchers.*

set *NOUN* **sets**
1 a group of people or things that belong together
2 a radio or television receiver
3 (*Mathematics*) a collection of things that have a common property
4 the scenery or stage for a play or film
5 a group of games in a tennis match
6 a badger's burrow

set *ADJECTIVE*
1 fixed or arranged in advance ◆ *The evening meal is served at a set time.*
2 ready or prepared to do something
to be set on something is to be determined about doing something

set-aside *NOUN*
the policy of paying farmers not to use some of their land because too much food is being produced

setback *NOUN* **setbacks**
something that stops progress or slows it down

set book *NOUN* **set books**
a book that must be studied for a literature examination

set square *NOUN* **set squares**
a flat device shaped like a right-angled triangle, used to draw lines in precise directions

settee *NOUN* **settees**
a long soft seat with a back and arms

setter *NOUN* **setters**
a dog of a long-haired breed that can be trained to stand rigid when it scents game

set theory *NOUN*
the branch of mathematics that deals with sets and the relations between them

setting *NOUN* **settings**
1 the way or place in which something is set
2 music for the words of a song, hymn, or other sung piece
3 a set of cutlery or crockery for one person at a meal

settle❶ *VERB* **settles, settling, settled**
1 to arrange something; to decide or solve something ◆ *One crucial detail settles the matter.*
2 to sit or come to rest

> And at last the locusts did descend. They settled on every tree and on every blade of grass; they settled on the roofs and covered the bare ground.
> — *Chinua Achebe, Things Fall Apart*

3 to settle or settle down is to become calm or comfortable
4 to go and live in another place
5 to sink; to come to rest on something ◆ *Snow had settled on the lane outside.*
6 to settle a bill or debt is to pay it in full

settle❷ *NOUN* **settles**
a long wooden seat with a high back and arms

settlement *NOUN* **settlements**
1 the process of settling something
2 the way something is settled
3 (*Geography*) a small number of people or houses established in a new area

settler *NOUN* **settlers**
one of the first people to settle in a new country; a pioneer or colonist

set-up *NOUN*
(*informal*) the way something is organized or arranged

seven *NOUN, ADJECTIVE* **sevens**
the number 7
▷ **seventh** *ADJECTIVE, NOUN*

seventeen *NOUN, ADJECTIVE*
the number 17
▷ **seventeenth** *ADJECTIVE, NOUN*

seventy *NOUN, ADJECTIVE* **seventies**
the number 70
▷ **seventieth** *ADJECTIVE, NOUN*

sever *VERB* **severs, severing, severed**
to cut or break something off
▷ **severance** *NOUN*

several *ADJECTIVE, NOUN*
more than two but not many

severally *ADVERB*
separately; one by one

severance *NOUN*
the process of ending a connection or relationship

severe *ADJECTIVE*
1 a severe person is strict and harsh
2 intense or forceful ◆ *He suffered from severe pains in his legs.*

a b c d e f g h i j k l m n o p q r s t u v w x y z

3 a severe style of clothing or furnishing is very plain or simple
▷ **severely** *ADVERB*
▷ **severity** *NOUN*

sew *VERB* **sews, sewing, sewed, sewn** or **sewed**
1 to join things together by using a needle and thread
2 to work with a needle and thread or with a sewing machine

USAGE NOTE Take care not to confuse this word with *sow*.

sewage (*say* soo- ij) *NOUN*
liquid waste matter carried away in drains

sewer (*say* soo- er) *NOUN* **sewers**
a large underground drain for carrying away sewage

sewing machine *NOUN* **sewing machines**
a machine for sewing things

sex *NOUN* **sexes**
1 each of the two groups (*male* and *female*) into which living things are placed according to their functions in the process of reproduction
2 the instinct that causes members of the two sexes to be attracted to one another
3 sexual intercourse

sexism *NOUN*
discrimination against people of a particular sex, especially women
▷ **sexist** *ADJECTIVE, NOUN*

sextant *NOUN* **sextants**
an instrument for measuring the angle of the sun and stars, used for finding your position when navigating

WORD HISTORY from Latin *sextus* 'sixth' (because early sextants consisted of an arc of one-sixth of a circle)

sextet *NOUN* **sextets**
1 a group of six musicians
2 a piece of music for six musicians

sexton *NOUN* **sextons**
a person whose job is to take care of a church and churchyard

sextuplet *NOUN* **sextuplets**
each of six children born to the same mother at one time

sexual *ADJECTIVE*
1 to do with sex or the sexes
2 sexual reproduction happens by the fusion of male and female cells
▷ **sexually** *ADVERB*
▷ **sexuality** *NOUN*

sexual harassment *NOUN*
annoying or upsetting someone, especially a woman, by touching her or making obscene remarks or gestures

sexual intercourse *NOUN*
the physical act in which a man puts his erect penis into a woman's vagina and sends semen into her womb

sexy *ADJECTIVE* **sexier, sexiest** (*informal*)
1 sexually attractive
2 concerned with sex

SF *ABBREVIATION*
science fiction

shabby *ADJECTIVE* **shabbier, shabbiest**
1 in a poor or worn-out condition; dilapidated

The village was a shabby place: a huddle of wooden buildings, with paddocks containing reindeer, and dogs that barked as he approached.
— *Philip Pullman, The Amber Spyglass*

2 poorly dressed
3 unfair or dishonourable ◆ *It was a shabby way to treat an old friend.*
▷ **shabbily** *ADVERB*
▷ **shabbiness** *NOUN*

shack *NOUN* **shacks**
a roughly-built hut

shackle *NOUN* **shackles**
an iron ring for fastening a prisoner's wrist or ankle to something

shackle *VERB* **shackles, shackling, shackled**
1 to put shackles on a prisoner
2 to be shackled by something is to be restricted or limited by it ◆ *They felt shackled by tradition.*

shade *NOUN* **shades**
1 slight darkness produced where something blocks the sun's light
2 a device that reduces or shuts out bright light
3 a colour; how light or dark a colour is
4 a slight difference in a range of meaning or opinion ◆ *a newspaper for all shades of political opinion*
5 (*poetic*) a ghost

shade *VERB* **shades, shading, shaded**
1 to shelter or protect something from bright light

Ralph shaded his eyes and followed the jagged outline of the crags up towards the mountain.
— *William Golding, Lord of the Flies*

2 to make part of a drawing darker than the rest
3 to move gradually from one state or quality to another ◆ *Slowly the wonder shaded into puzzlement.*
▷ **shading** *NOUN*

shadow *NOUN* **shadows**
1 the dark shape that falls on a surface when something is between the surface and a light
2 an area of shade
3 a slight trace ◆ *There was not a shadow of doubt about who their visitor had been.*
▷ **shadowy** *ADJECTIVE*

SPELLING NOTE Some words pronounced **s-** begin with **ce-** (e.g. cent), **ci-** (e.g. city), or **cy-** (e.g. cymbal)

shadow *VERB* **shadows, shadowing, shadowed**
1 to cast a shadow on something
2 to follow a person secretly

Shadow Cabinet *NOUN*
members of the Opposition in Parliament who each have responsibility for a particular area of policy

shady *ADJECTIVE* **shadier, shadiest**
1 in the shade, or providing shade ◆ *They came to a shady spot by the river.*
2 a shady deal or transaction is disreputable and not completely honest

shaft *NOUN* **shafts**
1 a long slender rod or straight part of something, e.g. an arrow
2 a ray of light

There was a small clearing, and a shaft of sunlight, and opposite him, between two trees, a deer. — Susan Hill, *I'm the King of the Castle*

3 a deep narrow hole in the ground

shaggy *ADJECTIVE* **shaggier, shaggiest**
1 having long rough hair or fibre
2 rough, thick, and untidy

shah *NOUN* **shahs**
the title of the former ruler of Iran

shake *VERB* **shakes, shaking, shook, shaken**
1 to move quickly up and down or from side to side, or to make something do this
2 to shock or upset someone
3 to tremble or be unsteady ◆ *He was shaking with rage.*
to shake hands is to clasp hands as a greeting or parting or as a sign of agreement
▷ **shaker** *NOUN*

shake *NOUN* **shakes**
1 an act of shaking; a shaking movement
2 (*informal*) a milkshake
in two shakes very soon

shake-up *NOUN* **shake-ups**
(*informal*) a radical reorganization or set of changes

shaky *ADJECTIVE* **shakier, shakiest**
1 unsteady or wobbly
2 uncertain or unreliable ◆ *The team recovered after a shaky start.*
▷ **shakily** *ADVERB*

shale *NOUN*
a kind of stone that splits easily into layers

shall *AUXILIARY VERB*
1 used with *I* and *we* to refer to the future ◆ *I shall come with you.*
2 used with *I* and *we* in questions when making a suggestion or offer or asking for advice ◆ *Shall I close the window?*
3 (*old use*) used with words other than *I* and *we* in promises or to express determination ◆ *You shall go to the ball.*

shallot *NOUN* **shallots**
a kind of small onion
WORD HISTORY via Old French from Latin *Ascalonia caepa* 'onion of Ascalon' (a port in ancient Palestine)

shallow *ADJECTIVE* **shallower, shallowest**
1 not deep

The river was shallow here, barely up to her knees, and the bed, though stony and uneven, was easy underfoot and not too slippery. — Tim Bowler, *River Boy*

2 superficial and weak ◆ *Their thinking was shallow and muddled.*
▷ **shallowness** *NOUN*

shallows *PLURAL NOUN*
a shallow part of a stretch of water

sham *NOUN* **shams**
something that is not genuine; a pretence
▷ **sham** *ADJECTIVE*

sham *VERB* **shams, shamming, shammed**
to pretend or fake something

shamble *VERB* **shambles, shambling, shambled**
to walk or run in a lazy or awkward way

shambles *NOUN*
a scene of great disorder or bloodshed
WORD HISTORY from an old word *shamble* 'a slaughterhouse or meat market'

shambolic (*say* sham- **bol**- ik) *ADJECTIVE*
(*informal*) chaotic or disorganized

shame *NOUN*
1 a feeling of great sorrow or guilt because you have done wrong
2 dishonour or disgrace
3 something you regret; a pity ◆ *It's a shame you have to go so soon.*
▷ **shameful** *ADJECTIVE*
▷ **shamefully** *ADVERB*

shame *VERB* **shames, shaming, shamed**
to make a person feel ashamed

shamefaced *ADJECTIVE*
looking ashamed

shameless *ADJECTIVE*
not feeling or looking ashamed
▷ **shamelessly** *ADVERB*

shampoo *NOUN* **shampoos**
1 a liquid substance for washing the hair
2 a substance for cleaning a carpet or furnishings or for washing a car
3 a wash with shampoo

shampoo *VERB* **shampoos, shampooing, shampooed**
to wash or clean with a shampoo
WORD HISTORY originally 'to massage', from Hindi *champo* 'to press'

shamrock *NOUN* **shamrocks**
a plant rather like clover, the national emblem of Ireland

shandy *NOUN* **shandies**
a mixture of beer and lemonade or some other soft drink

shank *NOUN* **shanks**
1 the leg, especially the part from knee to ankle
2 a long narrow part of something

shan't
short for *shall not*

shanty❶ *NOUN* **shanties**
a shack

shanty❷ *NOUN* **shanties**
a sailors' song with a chorus

shanty town *NOUN* **shanty towns**
a settlement consisting of shanties

shape *NOUN* **shapes**
1 a thing's outline; the appearance an outline produces
2 to be in shape is to be fit and in good form or condition
3 the general pattern or condition of something ◆ *the changing shape of family relationships*

shape *VERB* **shapes, shaping, shaped**
1 to make something into a particular shape
2 to shape or shape up is to develop ◆ *How does he think he's shaping up as a guitarist?*

shapeless *ADJECTIVE*
having no definite shape

shapely *ADJECTIVE* **shapelier, shapeliest**
having an attractive shape

shape poem *NOUN* **shape poems**
(*Language*) a poem arranged on the page in a layout that reflects the subject of the poem. (SEE ALSO **concrete poem**)

share *NOUN* **shares**
1 a part given to one person or thing out of something that is being divided
2 each of the equal parts forming a business company's capital, giving the person who holds it the right to receive a portion (a *dividend*) of the company's profits

share *VERB* **shares, sharing, shared**
1 to give portions of something to two or more people
2 to have use of something jointly with others ◆ *They shared a room in the centre of the city.*

shareholder *NOUN* **shareholders**
a person who owns shares in a company

shareware *NOUN*
computer software which is given away or which you can use free of charge

sharia (*say* sha- **ree**- a) *NOUN*
(*Religion*) the sacred law of Islam based on the teachings of the Koran

shark❶ *NOUN* **sharks**
a large sea fish with sharp teeth

shark❷ *NOUN* **sharks**
a person who exploits or cheats people

sharp *ADJECTIVE*
1 with an edge or point that can cut or make holes
2 quick at noticing or learning things
3 steep or pointed; not gradual ◆ *The bus approached a sharp bend.*
4 forceful or severe ◆ *She felt a sharp blow to her arm.* ◆ *The stairs and landing were rarely cleaned, in sharp contrast with the office and shop.*
5 a sharp sound or cry is loud and shrill
6 slightly sour
7 (*Music*) one semitone higher than the natural note ◆ *F sharp*

▷ **sharply** *ADVERB*
▷ **sharpness** *NOUN*

sharp *ADVERB*
1 to turn sharp right of left is to go round a sharp bend
2 punctually or precisely ◆ *Let's meet at eight o'clock sharp.*
3 (*Music*) above the correct pitch ◆ *Someone was singing sharp.*

sharp *NOUN* **sharps**
(*Music*) a note one semitone higher than the natural note; the sign (♯) that indicates this

sharpen *VERB* **sharpens, sharpening, sharpened**
to make something sharp, or to become sharp

▷ **sharpener** *NOUN*

sharp practice *NOUN*
dishonest or barely honest dealings in business

sharpshooter *NOUN* **sharpshooters**
a skilled marksman

shatter *VERB* **shatters, shattering, shattered**
1 to break violently into small pieces, or to make something do this
2 to destroy something

From upstairs, an earsplitting scream shattered the subterranean calm of the dungeon. — *Debi Gliori, Pure Dead Magic*

3 to upset someone very much ◆ *The bad experience had shattered him.*

shave *VERB* **shaves, shaving, shaved**
1 to scrape growing hair off the skin
2 to cut or scrape a thin slice off something

▷ **shaver** *NOUN*

shave *NOUN* **shaves**
the act of shaving the face

a close shave (*informal*) a narrow escape from danger or failure

shaven *ADJECTIVE*
a shaven head has had the hair shaved off

shavings *PLURAL NOUN*
thin strips shaved off a piece of wood or metal

a b c d e f g h i j k l m n o p q r s t u v w x y z

shawl *NOUN* **shawls**
a large piece of material worn round the shoulders or head or wrapped round a baby

she *PRONOUN*
the female person or animal being talked about

sheaf *NOUN* **sheaves**
1 a bundle of cornstalks tied together
2 a bundle of papers or other objects held together

shear *VERB* **shears, shearing, sheared, sheared** or, in sense 1, **shorn**
1 to cut or trim something; to cut the wool off a sheep
2 to break because of a sideways or twisting force ◆ *The bolts holding the rim had all sheared.*
▷ **shearer** *NOUN*

USAGE NOTE Take care not to confuse this word with *sheer*.

shears *PLURAL NOUN*
a cutting tool shaped like a very large pair of scissors and worked with both hands

sheath *NOUN* **sheaths**
1 a cover for the blade of a knife or sword
2 a close-fitting cover
3 a condom

sheathe *VERB* **sheathes, sheathing, sheathed**
1 to put something into a sheath
2 to put a close covering on something

shebeen *NOUN*
an illegal establishment or private house selling alcoholic liquor, especially in Ireland, Scotland, and South Africa

shed❶ *NOUN* **sheds**
a simply-made building used for storing things or sheltering animals, or as a workshop

shed❷ *VERB* **sheds, shedding, shed**
1 to let something fall or flow ◆ *Snakes can shed their skin and start a new life.* ◆ *The tears he shed were tears of joy.*
2 to dismiss or get rid of people or things ◆ *Two firms are to shed 700 jobs.*

she'd
short for *she had* or *she would*

sheen *NOUN*
a shine or gloss

sheep *NOUN* **sheep**
an animal that eats grass and has a thick fleecy coat, kept in flocks for its wool and its meat

sheepdog *NOUN* **sheepdogs**
a dog trained to guard and herd sheep

sheepish *ADJECTIVE*
1 shy or bashful
2 embarrassed or shamefaced
▷ **sheepishly** *ADVERB*
▷ **sheepishness** *NOUN*

sheepshank *NOUN* **sheepshanks**
a knot used to shorten a rope

sheer❶ *ADJECTIVE*
1 complete or thorough ◆ *The sheer size of the thing amazed him.*
2 vertical, with almost no slope

On the far side of the terrace, the mountain fell away in a sheer precipice. — *Garth Nix, Lirael*

3 sheer material is very thin and transparent

sheer❷ *VERB* **sheers, sheering, sheered**
to swerve; to move sharply away

USAGE NOTE Take care not to confuse this word with *shear*.

sheet❶ *NOUN* **sheets**
1 a large piece of lightweight material used on a bed in pairs for a person to sleep between
2 a whole flat piece of paper, glass, or metal
3 a wide unbroken surface area, especially of water, ice, or flame

sheet❷ *NOUN* **sheets**
a rope or chain fastening a sail

sheet lightning *NOUN*
lightning that is reflected in the clouds and spread across the sky

sheikh (*say* shayk) *NOUN* **sheikhs**
the leader of an Arab tribe or village

shelf *NOUN* **shelves**
1 a flat piece of wood, metal, or rigid material fixed to a wall or in a piece of furniture so that things can be placed on it
2 a flat level surface that sticks out; a ledge

shelf life *NOUN* **shelf lives**
the length of time something can be kept in a shop before it becomes too old to sell

shell *NOUN* **shells**
1 the hard outer covering of an egg, nut, or seed or of an animal such as a snail, crab, or tortoise
2 the walls or framework of a building, ship, or other large structure
3 a metal case filled with explosive, fired from a large gun

shell *VERB* **shells, shelling, shelled**
1 to take something out of its shell
2 to fire explosive shells at something

to shell out (*informal*) is to pay out money

she'll
short for *she will*

shellfish *NOUN* **shellfish**
a sea animal that has a shell

shell shock *NOUN*
a nervous illness caused by lengthy exposure to battle conditions

shell suit *NOUN* **shell suits**
a casual suit consisting of a loose jacket and trousers with a soft lining

shelter *NOUN* **shelters**
1 a building or structure that protects people from the weather, or from something unpleasant or harmful
2 to take shelter from something is to find protection from it

shelter *VERB* **shelters, sheltering, sheltered**
1 to provide someone with shelter
2 to protect someone
3 to find a shelter ◆ *We stopped and sheltered in a farmer's barn for the night.*

shelve *VERB* **shelves, shelving, shelved**
1 to put things on a shelf or shelves
2 to fit a wall or cupboard with shelves
3 to shelve a plan or decision is to postpone it or reject it for the time being
4 to slope ◆ *Beyond the rocks the seabed shelves steeply.*

shemozzle (*say* shi-**mozl**) *NOUN* **shemozzles**
(*informal*) a rumpus or loud brawl
WORD HISTORY from Yiddish *shlimazel* 'bad luck'

shepherd *NOUN* **shepherds**
a person whose job is to look after sheep

shepherd *VERB* **shepherds, shepherding, shepherded**
to guide or direct people

shepherd's pie *NOUN* **shepherd's pies**
a dish of minced beef or lamb under a layer of mashed potato

sherbet *NOUN* **sherberts**
a fizzy sweet powder or drink
WORD HISTORY from Arabic *sharbat* 'drinks', from *shariba* 'to drink' (the *shr* sound is said to be an imitation of the sound of drinking)

sheriff *NOUN* **sheriffs**
the chief law officer of a county, whose duties vary in different countries

sherry *NOUN* **sherries**
a kind of strong wine
WORD HISTORY named after Jerez de la Frontera, a town in Spain where it was first made

she's
short for *she is* or *she has* (when followed by a participle, as in *she's taken my pen*)

Shetland pony *NOUN* **Shetland ponies**
a kind of small, strong, shaggy pony, originally from the Shetland Isles

shield *NOUN* **shields**
1 a broad piece of armour carried by straps or a handle to protect the body in fighting
2 a model of a triangular shield used as a trophy
3 a protection

shield *VERB* **shields, shielding, shielded**
to protect someone from harm or from being discovered

shift *VERB* **shifts, shifting, shifted**
1 to move, or make something move
2 an opinion or situation shifts when it changes slightly
to shift for yourself is to manage without help from other people

shift *NOUN* **shifts**
1 a change of position or condition
2 a group of workers who start work as another group finishes; the time when they work
3 a straight dress with no waist

shifty *ADJECTIVE*
evasive, not straightforward; untrustworthy
▷ **shiftily** *ADVERB*
▷ **shiftiness** *NOUN*

Shiite (*say* **shee**-eyt) *NOUN* **Shiites**
(*Religion*) a member of one of the two main branches of Islam, based on the teachings of Muhammad and his son-in-law, Ali (SEE ALSO **Sunni**)

shilling *NOUN* **shillings**
a former British coin, equal to 5p

shilly-shally *VERB* **shilly-shallies, shilly-shallying, shilly-shallied**
to be hesitant and indecisive

shimmer *VERB* **shimmers, shimmering, shimmered**
to shine with a quivering light
▷ **shimmer** *NOUN*

shin *NOUN* **shins**
the front of the leg between the knee and the ankle

shin *VERB* **shins, shinning, shinned**
to climb something vertical by using the arms and legs, not on a ladder

shindig *NOUN* **shindigs**
(*informal*) a noisy party

shine *VERB* **shines, shining, shone,** *in sense 3* **shined**
1 to give out or reflect light; to be bright
2 to shine in something is to be very good at it
3 to aim a light ◆ *Philip shone the torch towards the path.*
4 to polish shoes or a surface

shine *NOUN*
1 a bright quality on a surface
2 the act of polishing

shingle *NOUN*
pebbles on a beach

shingles *NOUN*
a disease caused by the chicken pox virus, producing a painful rash

Shinto *NOUN*
(*Religion*) a Japanese religion which includes the worship of ancestors and nature
WORD HISTORY from Japanese, from Chinese *shen dao* 'way of the gods'

shiny *ADJECTIVE* **shinier, shiniest**
shining or glossy

ship *NOUN* **ships**
a large boat, especially one that goes to sea

ship *VERB* **ships, shipping, shipped**
to transport goods by ship or by other means

shipment *NOUN* **shipments**
1 the process of shipping goods
2 an amount of goods shipped

shipping *NOUN*
1 all the ships of a country
2 the process of transporting goods by ship

shipshape *ADJECTIVE*
in good order; tidy

shipwreck *NOUN* **shipwrecks**
1 the wrecking of a ship by storm or accident
2 a wrecked ship
▷ **shipwrecked** *ADJECTIVE*

shipyard *NOUN* **shipyards**
a place where ships are built or repaired

shire *NOUN* **shires**
a county
the Shires the country areas of (especially central) England, away from the cities

shire horse *NOUN* **shire horses**
a kind of large, strong horse used for ploughing or pulling carts

shirk *VERB* **shirks, shirking, shirked**
to avoid work or a duty selfishly or unfairly
▷ **shirker** *NOUN*

shirt *NOUN* **shirts**
a piece of clothing for the top half of the body, made of light material and with a collar and sleeves
in your shirtsleeves not wearing a jacket over your shirt

shirty *ADJECTIVE*
(*informal*) annoyed or bad-tempered

shiver *VERB* **shivers, shivering, shivered**
to tremble with cold or fear
▷ **shiver** *NOUN*
▷ **shivery** *ADJECTIVE*

shoal❶ *NOUN* **shoals**
a large number of fish swimming together

shoal❷ *NOUN* **shoals**
1 a shallow place
2 an underwater sandbank

shock❶ *NOUN* **shocks**
1 a sudden unpleasant surprise
2 an acute medical condition with fall of blood pressure and weakness, caused by pain or injury, or by sudden emotional stress
3 the effect of a violent shake or knock
4 an effect caused by electric current passing through the body

shock *VERB* **shocks, shocking, shocked**
1 to give someone a shock; to surprise or upset someone very much
2 to seem very improper or scandalous to a person

shock❷ *NOUN* **shocks**
a bushy mass of hair

shock absorber *NOUN* **shock absorbers**
a device for absorbing jolts and vibrations in a vehicle

shocking *ADJECTIVE*
1 causing indignation or disgust
2 (*informal*) very bad ◆ *The project proved to be a shocking waste of money.*

shock troops *PLURAL NOUN*
troops specially trained to make violent assaults

shock wave *NOUN* **shock waves**
a sharp change in pressure in the air around an explosion or an object moving very quickly

shod *past tense of* **shoe**

shoddy *ADJECTIVE* **shoddier, shoddiest**
of poor quality; badly made or done ◆ *We will not tolerate shoddy service, inefficiency, or waste.*
▷ **shoddily** *ADVERB*
▷ **shoddiness** *NOUN*

shoe *NOUN* **shoes**
1 a strong covering for the foot
2 a horseshoe
3 something shaped or used like a shoe
to be in somebody's shoes is to be in their situation

shoe *VERB* **shoes, shoeing, shod**
to fit with a shoe or shoes

shoehorn *NOUN* **shoehorns**
a curved piece of stiff material for easing your heel into the back of a shoe

shoelace *NOUN* **shoelaces**
a cord for lacing up and fastening a shoe

shoestring *NOUN* **shoestrings**
on a shoestring with very limited resources ◆ *Having started on a shoestring, the paper built up a circulation of 40,000.*

shogun *NOUN* **shoguns**
a hereditary commander in feudal Japan

shoo *EXCLAMATION*
a word used to frighten animals away

shoo *VERB* **shoos, shooing, shooed**
to frighten or drive away an animal or person

shoot *VERB* **shoots, shooting, shot**
1 to fire a gun or missile
2 to hurt or kill a person or animal by shooting
3 to shoot past or by is to go past at great speed
4 to kick or hit a ball at a goal
5 a plant shoots when it puts out buds or shoots
6 to slide the bolt of a door into or out of its fastening
7 to film or photograph something ◆ *The film was shot on location in India.*
8 to shoot someone a glance is to look at them sharply

shoot *NOUN* **shoots**
1 a young branch or new growth of a plant
2 an expedition for shooting animals

shooting star *NOUN* **shooting stars**
a meteor

shop *NOUN* **shops**
1 a building or room where goods or services are on sale to the public
2 a workshop

to talk shop is to talk tediously about your own work or job

shop *VERB* **shops, shopping, shopped**
1 to go and buy things at shops
2 (*informal*) to shop someone is to inform on them to the authorities

to shop around is to look around for the best bargain

▷ **shopper** *NOUN*

WORD HISTORY from Old French, originally 'a shed or stall', and also (in slang) 'a prison' (and so to shop someone was to put them in prison)

shopfitter *NOUN* **shopfitters**
a person whose job is to fit the counters, shelves, and other equipment in shops

shop floor *NOUN*
1 the workers in a factory, not the managers
2 the place where they work

shopkeeper *NOUN* **shopkeepers**
a person who owns or manages a shop

shoplifter *NOUN* **shoplifters**
a person who steals goods from a shop after entering as a customer

▷ **shoplifting** *NOUN*

shopping *NOUN*
1 buying goods in shops
2 the goods bought

shop-soiled *ADJECTIVE*
dirty, faded, or slightly damaged through being displayed or handled in a shop

shop steward *NOUN* **shop stewards**
a trade-union official who represents a body of fellow workers

shop window *NOUN* **shop windows**
a window in a shop where goods are displayed

shore❶ *NOUN* **shores**
the land along the edge of a sea or of a lake

shore❷ *VERB* **shores, shoring, shored**
to prop something up with a piece of wood or other support

shorn *past participle* of **shear**

short *ADJECTIVE*
1 not long; occupying a small distance or time ◆ *It is only a short walk to the station.*
2 a short person is not tall
3 not much or enough of something ◆ *Water was short after a long dry spell.*
4 to be short of something you need is not to have very much of it
5 curt or bad-tempered
6 short pastry is rich and crumbly because it contains a lot of fat

for short as an abbreviation ◆ *Nicola is called Nicky for short.*

in short in a few words

short for an abbreviation of ◆ *Nicky is short for Nicola.*

short of without going to the length of

> This is the most exciting thing that can happen in a school corridor, short of giraffes fighting.
> — *Jonathan Neale, The Laughter of Heroes*

to stop short or **be taken short** is to be suddenly surprised by something

▷ **shortness** *NOUN*

SYNONYMS (meaning 1) small, little, brief, concise; (meaning 2) small, little, petite, stocky; (meaning 3) low, meagre, scant, deficient, inadequate, insufficient; (meaning 5) curt, abrupt, sharp, blunt, brusque, impatient, bad-tempered, rude

shortage *NOUN* **shortages**
lack or scarcity of something; insufficiency

shortbread or **shortcake** *NOUN*
a rich sweet biscuit, made with butter

short circuit *NOUN* **short circuits**
a fault in an electrical circuit in which current flows along a shorter route than the normal one

short-circuit *VERB* **short-circuits, short-circuiting, short-circuited**
to cause a short circuit

shortcoming *NOUN* **shortcomings**
a fault or failure to reach a good standard

short cut *NOUN* **short cuts**
a route or method that is quicker than the usual one

shorten *VERB* **shortens, shortening, shortened**
to make something shorter, or to become shorter

shortfall *NOUN* **shortfalls**
a shortage; an amount that is lower than is needed or expected

a b c d e f g h i j k l m n o p q r s t u v w x y z

SPELLING NOTE Some words pronounced **s-** begin with **ce-** (e.g. cent), **ci-** (e.g. city), or **cy-** (e.g. cymbal)

shorthand *NOUN*
a set of special signs for writing words down as quickly as people say them

short-handed *ADJECTIVE*
not having enough workers or helpers

shortlist *NOUN* **shortlists**
a list of the most suitable people or things, from which a final choice will be made

shortlist *VERB* **shortlists, shortlisting, shortlisted**
to put someone on a shortlist

short-lived *ADJECTIVE*
lasting only a short time

shortly *ADVERB*
1 in a short time; soon ◆ *The bus should be here shortly.*
2 in a few words
3 rudely or curtly

shorts *PLURAL NOUN*
trousers with legs that do not reach to the knee

short shrift *NOUN*
to give someone short shrift is to treat them curtly or unkindly

WORD HISTORY originally a short time allowed for someone to confess to a priest before being executed: from an old word *shrive* meaning 'to hear a person's confession and give absolution'

short-sighted *ADJECTIVE*
1 a short-sighted person is unable to see things clearly when they are further away (SEE ALSO **long-sighted**)
2 lacking imagination or foresight

short-staffed *ADJECTIVE*
not having enough workers or staff

short-tempered *ADJECTIVE*
easily made angry

short-term *ADJECTIVE*
to do with or happening over a short period of time

short wave *NOUN*
a radio wave of a wavelength between 10 and 100 metres and a frequency of about 3 to 30 megahertz

shot❶ *past tense of* **shoot**

shot❷ *NOUN* **shots**
1 the firing of a gun or missile, or the sound this makes
2 something fired from a gun; lead pellets for firing from small guns
3 a person judged by skill in shooting ◆ *He has always been a poor shot.*
4 a heavy metal ball thrown as a sport
5 a stroke in tennis, cricket, billiards, or other games
6 a photograph; a filmed scene
7 (*informal*) to have a shot at something is to try to do it
8 an injection of a drug or vaccine

shotgun *NOUN* **shotguns**
a gun for firing small shot at close range

shot put *NOUN*
an athletic contest in which competitors throw a heavy metal ball
▷ **shot putter** *NOUN*

should *AUXILIARY VERB*
1 used to say what someone ought to do ◆ *They should have asked us.*
2 used to say what someone expects ◆ *We should be there before dark.*
3 used with an *if*-clause to say what might happen ◆ *If you should happen to see them, tell them to wait.*
4 used with *I* and *we* to make a polite statement (*We should like to come with you.*) or suggestion (*I should leave them alone now.*)

USAGE NOTE In meaning 4 you can use *would* instead of *should*, especially to avoid possible confusion with meaning 1.

shoulder *NOUN* **shoulders**
the part of the body between the neck and the arm, foreleg, or wing

shoulder *VERB* **shoulders, shouldering, shouldered**
1 to take something on your shoulder
2 to push something with your shoulder

Holly shouldered her way into the throng. 'Coming through,' she grunted. 'Police business.'
— Eoin Colfer, Artemis Fowl

3 to accept responsibility or blame for something

shoulder blade *NOUN* **shoulder blades**
either of the two large flat bones at the top of your back

shouldn't
short for *should not*

shout *NOUN* **shouts**
a loud cry or call

shout *VERB* **shouts, shouting, shouted**
to give a shout; to speak or call loudly

shove *VERB* **shoves, shoving, shoved**
to push someone or something roughly
to shove off (*informal*) is to go away

shove *NOUN* **shoves**
a rough push

shovel *NOUN* **shovels**
a tool like a spade with the sides turned up, used for lifting coal, earth, snow, or other bulky things

shovel *VERB* **shovels, shovelling, shovelled**
1 to move or clear things with a shovel
2 to scoop or push something roughly ◆ *Dave was shovelling pasta into his face.*

a b c d e f g h i j k l m n o p q r s t u v w x y z

show *VERB* **shows, showing, showed, shown**
1 to allow or cause something to be seen ◆ *Show me what you bought this morning.*
2 to make a person understand something; to explain or demonstrate something ◆ *You must show me how I do it.*
3 to guide someone to a place ◆ *An attendant showed him to the right office.*
4 to treat someone in a certain way ◆ *She showed them great kindness.*
5 to be visible ◆ *With luck the marks won't show.*
to show off is to try to impress people

Nothing in the world is quite as adorably lovely as a robin when he shows off — and they are nearly always doing it. — Frances Hodgson Burnett, *The Secret Garden*

to show something off is to display something proudly
to show up
1 is to be clearly visible
2 (*informal*) is to arrive

show *NOUN* **shows**
1 a display or exhibition
2 an entertainment
3 (*informal*) something that happens or is done ◆ *He was far too busy running the show in a club championship match.*

show business *NOUN*
the entertainment industry; the theatre, films, radio, and television

showcase *NOUN* **showcases**
a glass case for displaying articles in a shop, museum, or gallery

showdown *NOUN* **showdowns**
a final test or confrontation

shower *NOUN* **showers**
1 a brief fall of rain or snow
2 a lot of small things coming or falling like rain
3 a device or cabinet for spraying water to wash a person's body; a wash in this

shower *VERB* **showers, showering, showered**
1 to fall in a shower, or send things in a shower
2 to wash under a shower

showery *ADJECTIVE*
raining often in showers

show house *NOUN* **show houses**
a furnished and decorated house on a new estate that can be shown to people who are thinking of buying a house there

showjumping *NOUN*
a competition in which riders make their horses jump over fences and other obstacles, with penalty points for errors
▷ **showjumper** *NOUN*

showman *NOUN* **showmen**
1 a person who presents entertainments
2 someone who is good at entertaining
▷ **showmanship** *NOUN*

show-off *NOUN* **show-offs**
(*informal*) a person who tries to impress people boastfully

showpiece *NOUN* **showpieces**
a fine example of something for people to see and admire

showroom *NOUN* **showrooms**
a large room where goods are displayed for people to look at

showy *ADJECTIVE* **showier, showiest**
likely to attract attention; brightly or highly decorated
▷ **showily** *ADVERB*
▷ **showiness** *NOUN*

shrapnel *NOUN*
pieces of metal scattered from an exploding shell

WORD HISTORY named after General Henry *Shrapnel*, a British officer who invented it during the wars with Napoleon in about 1806

shred *NOUN* **shreds**
1 a tiny piece torn or cut off something
2 a small amount ◆ *Not a shred of evidence was ever produced to support any of these allegations.*

shred *VERB* **shreds, shredding, shredded**
to cut something into shreds
▷ **shredder** *NOUN*

shrew *NOUN* **shrews**
1 a small mouse-like animal
2 (*old use*) a bad-tempered woman who is constantly scolding people
▷ **shrewish** *ADJECTIVE*

WORD HISTORY from Old English

shrewd *ADJECTIVE*
having common sense and good judgement; clever
▷ **shrewdly** *ADVERB*
▷ **shrewdness** *NOUN*

WORD HISTORY from an old sense of *shrew* meaning 'a spiteful or cunning person'

shriek *NOUN* **shrieks**
a shrill cry or scream

shriek *VERB* **shrieks, shrieking, shrieked**
to give a shriek

shrill *ADJECTIVE*
sounding very high and piercing
▷ **shrilly** *ADVERB*
▷ **shrillness** *NOUN*

shrimp *NOUN* **shrimps**
a small shellfish, pink when boiled

shrimping *NOUN*
fishing for shrimps

shrine *NOUN* **shrines**
(*Religion*) an altar, chapel, or other sacred place

WORD HISTORY originally a container for holy relics: via Old English from Latin *scrinium* 'a case or chest'

a b c d e f g h i j k l m n o p q r s t u v w x y z

shrink *VERB* **shrinks, shrinking, shrank, shrunk**
1 to become smaller, or to make something smaller
2 to shrink back is to move back to avoid something
3 to shrink from something is to avoid doing it because of fear, conscience, embarrassment, or other feelings
▷ **shrinkage** *NOUN*

shrink wrap *NOUN*
clinging transparent plastic film used as wrapping

shrivel *VERB* **shrivels, shrivelling, shrivelled**
to become dry and wrinkled, or to make something like this

shroud *NOUN* **shrouds**
1 a cloth in which a dead body is wrapped
2 each of a set of ropes supporting a ship's mast

shroud *VERB* **shrouds, shrouding, shrouded**
1 to wrap something in a shroud
2 to be shrouded in mist or cloud is to be covered or partly hidden by it

Shrove Tuesday *NOUN*
the day before Lent, when pancakes are eaten, originally to use up fat before the fast

WORD HISTORY from the past tense of *shrive* to hear a person's confession (because it was the custom to go to confession on this day)

shrub *NOUN* **shrubs**
a woody plant smaller than a tree; a bush
▷ **shrubby** *ADJECTIVE*

shrubbery *NOUN* **shrubberies**
an area planted with shrubs

shrug *VERB* **shrugs, shrugging, shrugged**
to raise your shoulders as a sign that you do not know or care about something
to shrug something off is to treat it as unimportant

shrug *NOUN* **shrugs**
a gesture of shrugging the shoulders

shrunken *ADJECTIVE*
having shrunk; small and shrivelled

shudder *VERB* **shudders, shuddering, shuddered**
1 to shiver violently with horror, fear, or cold
2 to make a strong shaking movement

shudder *NOUN* **shudders**
a strong shivering or shaking movement

shuffle *VERB* **shuffles, shuffling, shuffled**
1 to walk without lifting the feet from the ground
2 to slide playing cards over each other to get them into random order
3 to shift or rearrange something

shuffle *NOUN* **shuffles**
1 an act of shuffling things
2 a shuffling walk or movement

shun *VERB* **shuns, shunning, shunned**
to keep away from something or someone deliberately

Magrat shunned the traditional pointed hat, as worn by the other witches. — *Terry Pratchett, Wyrd Sisters*

shunt *VERB* **shunts, shunting, shunted**
1 to move a train or wagons on to another track
2 to divert something or someone to a less important place or position
▷ **shunter** *NOUN*

shunt *NOUN* **shunts**
an act of shunting or diverting something

shut *VERB* **shuts, shutting, shut**
1 to move a door, lid, or cover so that it blocks an opening; to become closed, or to make something closed
2 to bring or fold together the parts of something, e.g. a book
to shut down is to stop business
to shut something down is to switch off a machine or stop it working
to shut up (*informal*) is to stop talking or making a noise

shutdown *NOUN* **shutdowns**
1 the closing of a factory or business
2 (*ICT*) the action of switching off a computer or other machine

shutter *NOUN* **shutters**
1 a panel or screen that can be closed over a window
2 the device in a camera that opens and closes to let light fall on the film
▷ **shuttered** *ADJECTIVE*

shuttle *NOUN* **shuttles**
1 a holder carrying the weft thread across a loom in weaving
2 a train, bus, or aircraft that makes frequent short journeys between two points
3 a space shuttle

shuttle *VERB* **shuttles, shuttling, shuttled**
to move or travel continuously backwards and forwards over a distance

shuttlecock *NOUN* **shuttlecocks**
a small rounded piece of cork or plastic with a crown of feathers, struck to and fro by players in badminton

shy ❶ *ADJECTIVE* **shyer, shyest**
afraid to meet or talk to other people; timid
▷ **shyly** *ADVERB*
▷ **shyness** *NOUN*

shy *VERB* **shies, shying, shied**
to jump or move suddenly in alarm

shy ❷ *VERB* **shies, shying, shied**
to throw a stone or other object

shy *NOUN* **shies**
an act of throwing

SI *NOUN*
an internationally recognized system of metric units of measurement, including the metre and kilogram

WORD HISTORY short for French *Système International d'Unités* 'International System of Units'

Siamese *ADJECTIVE*
to do with or belonging to Siam (now called Thailand) or its people
▷ **Siamese** *NOUN*

Siamese cat *NOUN* **Siamese cats**
a cat with short pale fur with darker face, ears, tail, and feet

Siamese twins *PLURAL NOUN*
twins who are born with their bodies joined together

WORD HISTORY named after two twins Chang and Eng born in 1811 in Siam (now Thailand), who were joined near the waist

USAGE NOTE It is now better to use the term *conjoined twins.*

sibilant *ADJECTIVE*
a sibilant sound is one that makes a hiss

sibilant *NOUN* **sibilants**
a speech sound that sounds like hissing, e.g. *s, sh*

sibling *NOUN* **siblings**
a brother or sister

WORD HISTORY from Old English *sib* 'related by birth, a blood relative' and *-ling* meaning 'small'

sibyl *NOUN* **sibyls**
a prophetess in ancient Greece or Rome

sick *ADJECTIVE*
1 physically or mentally unwell; ill
2 vomiting or likely to vomit
3 distressed or disgusted
4 making fun of death, disability, or misfortune in an unpleasant way

to be sick of something is to be tired of it or fed up with it

I am heartily sick and tired of meal porridge and oatcakes. Sick, sick, sick! — *Sue Reid, My Story: Mill Girl*

sicken *VERB* **sickens, sickening, sickened**
1 to begin to be ill
2 to make someone feel very upset or disgusted ◆ *The public is becoming sickened by these pictures of violence and death.*
▷ **sickening** *ADJECTIVE*

sickle *NOUN* **sickles**
a tool with a narrow curved blade, used for cutting crops or grass

sickly *ADJECTIVE*
1 often ill; unhealthy ◆ *He was a lame and sickly child.*
2 making people feel sick ◆ *A sickly smell clung to his clothes and hair.*
3 weak ◆ *He looked at her with a sickly grin.*

sickness *NOUN* **sicknesses**
1 illness or a disease
2 nausea or vomiting

side *NOUN* **sides**
1 a surface, especially one joining the top and bottom of something
2 a line that forms part of the boundary of a triangle, square, or other flat figure
3 either of the two halves into which something can be divided by a line down its centre
4 the part near the edge and away from the centre
5 the place or region next to a person or thing ◆ *He went and stood at her side.*
6 one aspect or view of something ◆ *There is another side to the problem.*
7 each of two groups or teams who oppose each other

on the side as a sideline
side by side next to each other
to take sides is to support one person or group in a dispute or disagreement and not the other

WORD FAMILY A related adjective is lateral.

side *ADJECTIVE*
1 at or on a side ◆ *a side entrance*
2 incidental or not important ◆ *a side issue*

side *VERB* **sides, siding, sided**
to side with someone is to support them in an argument

sideboard *NOUN* **sideboards**
a long piece of furniture with a flat top and with drawers and cupboards for crockery and cutlery

sideburns *PLURAL NOUN*
the strips of hair growing on each side of a man's face in front of his ears

sidecar *NOUN* **sidecars**
a small compartment for a passenger, fixed to the side of a motorcycle

side effect *NOUN* **side effects**
an effect, especially an unpleasant one, that a medicine has on you as well as the effect intended

sidelight *NOUN* **sidelights**
1 a light at the side of a vehicle or ship
2 light from one side

sideline *NOUN* **sidelines**
1 something done in addition to your main work or activity
2 each of the lines on the two long sides of a sports pitch

sidelong *ADJECTIVE*
towards one side; sideways ◆ *He cast a sidelong glance through the window.*

sidereal (*say* sid- **eer**- ee- al) *ADJECTIVE*
to do with or measured by the stars

a b c d e f g h i j k l m n o p q r s t u v w x y z

SPELLING NOTE Some words pronounced like *sit* begin with **sy-** (e.g. syllabus)

sideshow *NOUN* **sideshows**
1 a small entertainment forming part of a large one, e.g. at a fair
2 a minor incident or diversion

sidestep *VERB* **sidesteps, sidestepping, sidestepped**
1 to avoid dealing with a question or difficulty
2 to avoid someone or something by stepping sideways

sidetrack *VERB* **sidetracks, sidetracking, sidetracked**
to take someone's attention away from the main subject or problem

sidewalk *NOUN* **sidewalks**
(*American*) a pavement

sideways *ADVERB, ADJECTIVE*
1 to or from one side ◆ *The bird moved sideways on its perch and hunched its shoulders.*
2 with one side facing forwards ◆ *She was sitting sideways on the horse.*

siding *NOUN* **sidings**
a short railway line by the side of a main line

sidle *VERB* **sidles, sidling, sidled**
to walk in a shy or nervous manner

siege *NOUN* **sieges**
(*History*) the surrounding of a place with military forces in order to capture it or force it to surrender

to lay siege to a place is to begin a siege of it

sienna *NOUN*
a kind of clay used in making brownish paints

WORD HISTORY named after *Siena*, a town in central Italy, south of Florence

sierra *NOUN* **sierras**
a range of mountains with sharp peaks, in Spain or parts of America

WORD HISTORY a Spanish word, from Latin *serra* 'a saw' (because the peaks look like the teeth of a saw)

siesta (*say* see- est- a) *NOUN* **siestas**
an afternoon rest, especially in a hot country

WORD HISTORY from Latin *sexta hora* 'sixth hour', i.e. midday, the usual time for a siesta

sieve (*say* siv) *NOUN* **sieves**
a device made of mesh or perforated metal or plastic, used to separate the smaller or soft parts of something from the larger or hard parts

sieve *VERB* **sieves, sieving, sieved**
to put something through a sieve

sift *VERB* **sifts, sifting, sifted**
1 to sieve something
2 to examine and analyse facts or evidence in detail

▷ **sifter** *NOUN*

sigh *NOUN* **sighs**
a sound made by breathing out heavily to show an emotion such as relief or disappointment

sigh *VERB* **sighs, sighing, sighed**
to make a sigh

> Nadine raises her eyebrows at Magda, and they both sigh, irritated at me for giving away our age.
> — *Jacqueline Wilson, Girls Out Late*

sight *NOUN* **sights**
1 the ability to see
2 to catch sight of someone or something is to see them suddenly or briefly
3 a thing that can be seen or is worth seeing
4 an ugly or ridiculous-looking person or thing ◆ *He must have looked a sight with his bare legs and old sandals.*
5 a device looked through to help aim a gun or optical instrument

at sight or **on sight** as soon as a person or thing has been seen

in sight
1 visible or present ◆ *There was not a celebrity in sight.*
2 about to occur; imminent ◆ *No end to their problems was in sight.*

WORD FAMILY Related adjectives are optic, optical, and visual.

USAGE NOTE Take care not to confuse this word with *site*.

sight *VERB* **sights, sighting, sighted**
1 to see or observe something
2 to aim a gun or telescope

sighted *ADJECTIVE*
able to see; not blind

sightless *ADJECTIVE*
unable to see; blind

sight-reading *NOUN*
playing or singing music at sight, without preparation

sightseeing *NOUN*
the activity of visiting interesting places in a tourist location

▷ **sightseer** *NOUN*

sign *NOUN* **signs**
1 something that shows that a thing exists or is going to happen

> If there is a hurricane you always see the signs of it in the sky for days ahead, if you are at sea.
> — *Ernest Hemingway, The Old Man and the Sea*

2 a notice or mark that gives information or an instruction, such as a road sign
3 an action or movement giving information or an instruction
4 any of the twelve divisions of the zodiac, represented by a symbol

sign *VERB* **signs, signing, signed**
1 to make a sign or signal to someone

Grigory signed to them both to sit down at the table and put bread and salt in front of them, and a bowl of apples. — *Gillian Cross, Calling a Dead Man*

2 to write your signature on a contract or agreement to authorize it or show that you accept it
3 to use signing
to sign on
1 is to accept employment or membership
2 is to sign a form to say that you are unemployed and want to claim benefit

signal *NOUN* **signals**
1 a device, gesture, or sound that gives information or a command
2 a message made up of such things
3 a sequence of electrical impulses or radio waves

signal *VERB* **signals, signalling, signalled**
to make a signal to somebody
▷ **signaller** *NOUN*

signal *ADJECTIVE*
remarkable or striking ◆ *Their victory was a signal triumph.*
▷ **signally** *ADVERB*

signal box *NOUN* **signal boxes**
a building from which railway signals, points, and other track equipment are controlled

signalman *NOUN* **signalmen**
a person who controls railway signals

signatory *NOUN* **signatories**
a person who signs an agreement or contract

signature *NOUN* **signatures**
1 the form in which a person writes their own name
2 (*Music*) a set of sharps and flats after the clef in a score, showing the key the music is written in (the *key signature*), or the sign, often a fraction such as $\frac{4}{4}$ (the *time signature*), showing the number of beats in the bar and their rhythm

signature tune *NOUN* **signature tunes**
a special tune used to announce a particular programme or performer on television or radio

signet ring *NOUN* **signet rings**
a ring with a person's initials or a design engraved on it

significant *ADJECTIVE*
1 having a meaning; full of meaning
2 important, substantial ◆ *You can make a significant saving in the fare by travelling overnight.*
▷ **significantly** *ADVERB*
▷ **significance** *NOUN*

signification *NOUN*
(*formal*) the underlying meaning of words or events

signify *VERB* **signifies, signifying, signified**
1 to be a sign or symbol of something; to mean something
2 to indicate something ◆ *He signified his approval with a nod.*
3 to be important; to matter

signing or **sign language** *NOUN*
a system of visual gestures and signs used by deaf people and by people wishing to communicate with them

signpost *NOUN* **signposts**
a sign beside a road, showing the names, distances, and directions of places ahead

Sikh (*say* seek) *NOUN* **Sikhs**
(*Religion*) a member of a religion founded in northern India, believing in one God and accepting some Hindu and some Islamic beliefs
▷ **Sikhism** *NOUN*

WORD HISTORY from Sanskrit *sisya* 'disciple'

silage *NOUN*
fodder made from green crops stored in a silo

silence *NOUN* **silences**
1 absence of sound
2 a situation in which no one is speaking
in silence without speaking or making a sound

silence *VERB* **silences, silencing, silenced**
to make a person or thing silent

silencer *NOUN* **silencers**
a device for reducing the sound made by a device, especially a gun or a vehicle exhaust system

silent *ADJECTIVE*
1 without any sound

The world was so silent that Ben could hear Sorrel munching a mushroom behind him. — *Cornelia Funke, Dragon Rider*

2 not speaking
▷ **silently** *ADVERB*

silhouette (*say* sil- oo- **et**) *NOUN* **silhouettes**
1 a dark shadow seen against a light background
2 a portrait of a person in profile, showing the shape and outline only in solid black

silhouette *VERB* **silhouettes, silhouetting, silhouetted**
to show an outline as a silhouette

The old warehouse ... was silhouetted against the lights from the town, and reminded Katie of something out of a horror movie. — *Catherine MacPhail, Run Zan Run*

WORD HISTORY named after a French politician and writer, Étienne de *Silhouette*; when he was finance minister paper cut-outs of people's profiles became a popular and cheap form of making portraits

silica *NOUN*
a hard white mineral that is a compound of silicon, used to make glass

silicon *NOUN*
a substance found in many rocks, used in making transistors and electric circuits

silicon chip *NOUN* **silicon chips**
(*ICT*) a microchip made of silicon

silicone *NOUN*
a compound of silicon used in paints, varnish, and lubricants

silk *NOUN* **silks**
1 a fine soft thread or cloth made from the fibre produced by silkworms for making their cocoons
2 a length of silk thread used for embroidery
▷ **silken** *ADJECTIVE*
▷ **silky** *ADJECTIVE*

silkworm *NOUN* **silkworms**
the caterpillar of a kind of moth, which feeds on mulberry leaves and spins itself a cocoon

sill *NOUN* **sills**
a strip of stone, wood, or metal underneath a window or door

silly *ADJECTIVE* **sillier, silliest**
foolish or unwise
▷ **silliness** *NOUN*

WORD HISTORY from Old English *saelig* 'happy, blessed by God', and later 'innocent, helpless'

silo (*say* sy- loh) *NOUN* **silos**
1 a pit or tower for storing green crops (see **silage**) or grain or cement
2 an underground place for storing a missile ready for firing

silt *NOUN*
sediment laid down by a river or the sea

silt *VERB* **silts, silting, silted**
to silt up is to become blocked with silt

silver *NOUN*
1 a shiny white precious metal
2 the colour of silver
3 coins or objects made of silver or silver-coloured metal
4 a silver medal, usually given as second prize
▷ **silvery** *ADJECTIVE*

silver *ADJECTIVE*
1 made of silver
2 coloured like silver

silver *VERB* **silvers, silvering, silvered**
to make something silvery, or to become silvery

silver wedding *NOUN* **silver weddings**
a couple's twenty-fifth wedding anniversary

SIM card *NOUN* **SIM cards**
a card in a mobile phone, which holds a record of its number and stores other information

WORD HISTORY short for *s*ubscriber *i*dentification *m*odule

simian *ADJECTIVE*
(*formal*) like a monkey

similar *ADJECTIVE*
1 nearly the same as another person or thing; of the same kind
2 (*Mathematics*) similar triangles and other shapes have the same shape but not the same size
▷ **similarly** *ADVERB*
▷ **similarity** *NOUN*

simile (*say* sim- il- ee) *NOUN* **similes**
(*Grammar*) a comparison of one thing with another, especially one following a set form, e.g. *as brave as a lion* and *to sleep like a log*

simile and metaphor

A **simile** is a way of comparing a person or thing to something else, using a comparison word such as *like* or *as*:

Alex felt himself pinned down, like an insect under a microscope.
(*Anthony Horowitz, Stormbreaker*)

There are many fixed similes that people often use: (as) *brave as a lion*, (as) *dry as dust*, (as) *fit as a fiddle*. (You can say *as brave as a lion* or just *brave as a lion*, and so on.)

A **metaphor** describes a person or thing as if they were something else, without using a comparison word:

Above him ... the balloon was returning to the sky, a dark tear-drop that was quickly swallowed into the bulky belly of the clouds.
(*Philip Reeve, Mortal Engines*)

The following description uses *both* simile and metaphor for maximum effect:

The building looked like a fiery ghost, with great bursts of flame coming from the windows, and oceans of smoke pouring from great gaping holes in the walls.
(*Lemony Snicket, A Series of Unfortunate Events*)

simmer *VERB* **simmers, simmering, simmered**
to boil gently

Soups and stews simmered in huge cauldrons and terracotta bowls were filled with potatoes roasted in olive oil and sprinkled with sea salt and spikes of rosemary. — *Mary Hoffman, Stravaganza City of Masks*

to simmer down is to become calm again after being excited or angry

simper *VERB* **simpers, simpering, simpered**
to smile in a silly affected way
▷ **simper** *NOUN*

simple *ADJECTIVE* **simpler, simplest**
1 easy to answer or solve
2 not complicated or elaborate
3 plain, not showy
4 without much sense or intelligence
▷ **simplicity** *NOUN*

simple-minded *ADJECTIVE*
naive or foolish

> The more simple-minded number devils use computers. They keep them running for months at a stretch. — *Hans Magnus Enzensberger, The Number Devil*

simpleton *NOUN* **simpletons**
(*old use*) a foolish person

simplify *VERB* **simplifies, simplifying, simplified**
to make a thing simple or easy to understand
▷ **simplification** *NOUN*

simply *ADVERB*
1 in a simple way ◆ *I'll try to explain it simply.*
2 without doubt; completely ◆ *This is simply wonderful.*
3 only or merely ◆ *It's simply a matter of waiting.*

simulate *VERB* **simulates, simulating, simulated**
1 to reproduce the appearance or conditions of something; to imitate a process
2 to simulate a feeling is to pretend to have it
▷ **simulation** *NOUN*

simulator *NOUN* **simulators**
a machine or device for simulating actual conditions or events, often used for training

simultaneous (*say* sim- ul- **tay**- nee- us) *ADJECTIVE*
happening at the same time
▷ **simultaneously** *ADVERB*

sin *NOUN* **sins**
1 the breaking of a religious or moral law
2 a very bad action

sin *VERB* **sins, sinning, sinned**
to commit a sin
▷ **sinner** *NOUN*

since *CONJUNCTION*
1 from the time when ◆ *What have you been doing since we last met?*
2 because ◆ *Since you refuse to come I'll have to go on my own.*

since *PREPOSITION*
from a certain time ◆ *We've been here since early this morning.*

since *ADVERB*
between then and now ◆ *He went off and hasn't been seen since.*

sincere *ADJECTIVE*
without pretence; truly felt or meant
Yours sincerely see **yours**
▷ **sincerely** *ADVERB*
▷ **sincerity** *NOUN*

sine *NOUN* **sines**
(*Mathematics*) in a right-angled triangle, the ratio of the length of a side opposite one of the acute angles to the length of the hypotenuse (SEE ALSO **cosine**)

sinecure (*say* sy- nik- yoor) *NOUN* **sinecures**
a paid job that requires no work
WORD HISTORY from Latin *sine cura* 'without care'

sinew *NOUN* **sinews**
strong tissue that connects a muscle to a bone

sinewy *ADJECTIVE*
slim, muscular, and strong

sinful *ADJECTIVE*
1 guilty of sin
2 bad or wicked
▷ **sinfully** *ADVERB*
▷ **sinfulness** *NOUN*

sing *VERB* **sings, singing, sang, sung**
1 to make musical sounds with the voice
2 to perform a song
▷ **singer** *NOUN*

singe (*say* sinj) *VERB* **singes, singeing, singed**
to burn something slightly

single *ADJECTIVE*
1 one only; not double or multiple
2 suitable for one person
3 distinct or separate

> Billions of emails are sent, and millions of people around the world log on to the Internet every single day! — *Michael Cox, The Incredible Internet*

4 not married
5 a single ticket or journey goes to a place but not back again

single *NOUN* **singles**
1 a single person or thing
2 a single ticket
3 a record with one short piece of music on each side
singles a game of tennis between two players

single *VERB* **singles, singling, singled**
to single someone or something out is to pick them out or distinguish them from other people or things

single file *NOUN*
in single file in a line; one behind the other

single-handed *ADJECTIVE*
without help

single-minded *ADJECTIVE*
with your mind set on one purpose only

single parent *NOUN* **single parents**
a person bringing up a child or children without a partner

singles bar *NOUN* **singles bars**
a bar where unmarried people go to drink and meet each other

singlet *NOUN* **singlets**
a man's vest or similar piece of clothing worn under or instead of a shirt

singly *ADVERB*
in ones; one by one

a b c d e f g h i j k l m n o p q r s t u v w x y z

SPELLING NOTE Some words pronounced like *sit* begin with **sy-** (e.g. syllabus)

singsong *ADJECTIVE*
a singsong voice is monotonous in tone or rhythm

singsong *NOUN* **singsongs**
1 informal singing by a gathering of people
2 a singsong tone

singular *NOUN* **singulars**
(*Grammar*) the form of a noun or verb used when it stands for only one person or thing, e.g. *table* and *child* (SEE ALSO **plural**)

singular and plural forms

Many nouns have both a **singular form** (referring to one person or thing, like *book* and *child*) and a **plural form** (referring to more than one, like *books* and *children*). These are known as **countable nouns.** However, some nouns are **uncountable** and have only a singular form, because they name things which cannot be counted individually (*anger*, *beauty*, *childhood*, *money*). Some nouns, such as *cheese*, *fish*, and *wine*, are normally used in the singular, but can also have a plural form when they mean types of things, e.g. *a platter of French cheeses*. These are sometimes called **mass nouns.**

On the other hand, some words, like *scissors* and *trousers*, are always plural and have no singular form. Others are plural in form, but behave like singulars and go with a singular verb. This type includes words ending in *-ics* which describe areas of knowledge or expertise, like *aeronautics*, *gymnastics*, *mathematics*, and *robotics*: *Robotics has become a popular career choice*. But these nouns can be plural when they are referring to physical things rather than a subject of study: *The acoustics of the hall were perfect for recording*.

See also the panel on **plural forms.**

singular *ADJECTIVE*
1 to do with the singular
2 uncommon or extraordinary ◆ *a person of singular talents*
▷ **singularly** *ADVERB*
▷ **singularity** *NOUN*

sinister *ADJECTIVE*
1 looking or seeming evil or harmful

There was something weird and sinister about the place. Despite all the loveliness and the luxury, there was a whiff of danger that hung and drifted in the air like poisonous gas. — *Roald Dahl, The Boy Who Talked with Animals*

2 wicked or malicious

WORD HISTORY from Latin *sinister* 'on the left' (because people thought the left side of the body was unlucky)

sink *VERB* **sinks, sinking, sank, sunk**
1 to fall under the surface of water or to the bottom of an amount of water, or to cause something to do this
2 to go or fall slowly downwards

Miranda was deeply, deeply shaken. She sank towards the floor, like a doll without stuffing. — *Anne Fine, Madame Doubtfire*

3 to push something sharp deeply into something
4 to dig or drill a hole or well
5 to invest money in something
to sink in is to become understood

sink *NOUN* **sinks**
a fixed basin with a drainpipe and usually a tap or taps to supply water

sinuous *ADJECTIVE*
with many bends or curves

sinus (*say* sy- nus) *NOUN* **sinuses**
a hollow part in the bones of the skull, connected with the nose

sip *VERB* **sips, sipping, sipped**
to drink liquid in small mouthfuls

'Went to the zoo did you, dear?' Aunty Rose said and sipped her tea, her little finger cocked in the air. — *Michael Morpurgo, Tom's Sausage Lion*

▷ **sip** *NOUN*

siphon *NOUN* **siphons**
1 a pipe or tube in the form of an upside-down U, arranged so that liquid is forced up it and down to a lower level
2 a bottle containing soda water which is released through a tube

siphon *VERB* **siphons, siphoning, siphoned**
to draw out liquid through a siphon

sir *NOUN*
1 a word used when speaking or writing politely to a man
2 the title given to a knight or baronet and used before their name

USAGE NOTE You use a capital letter (*Dear Sir*, *Sir Galahad*) when you are using the word as a title.

sire *NOUN* **sires**
1 the male parent of a horse or dog (SEE ALSO **dam❷**)
2 a word formerly used when speaking to a king

sire *VERB* **sires, siring, sired**
to be the sire of a horse or dog

siren *NOUN* **sirens**
1 a device that makes a long loud sound as a signal
2 a dangerously attractive woman

WORD HISTORY named after women in Greek legend called *Sirens*, who sang so sweetly that they lured sailors to shipwreck on the rocks

sirloin *NOUN*
beef from the upper part of the loin

sirocco *NOUN* **siroccos**
a hot dry wind that reaches Italy from Africa

WORD HISTORY from Italian *scirocco*, from Arabic *Shaluk* 'east wind'

sisal (*say* sy- sal) *NOUN*
fibre from a tropical plant, used for making ropes

WORD HISTORY named after *Sisal*, a port in Mexico from which it was exported

sissy *NOUN* **sissies**
a timid or cowardly person

sister *NOUN* **sisters**
1 a daughter of the same parents as another person
2 a female friend or associate
3 a member of a religious order of women; a nun
4 a senior hospital nurse, especially one in charge of a ward

▷ **sisterly** *ADJECTIVE*

sisterhood *NOUN* **sisterhoods**
1 companionship and mutual support between women
2 a society or association of women

sister-in-law *NOUN* **sisters-in-law**
1 the sister of a married person's husband or wife
2 the wife of a person's brother

sit *VERB* **sits, sitting, sat**
1 to rest with your body supported on the buttocks; to occupy a seat
2 to seat someone; to cause someone to sit in a place
3 a bird sits when it stays on the nest to hatch eggs
4 to be a candidate for an examination
5 to be situated or stay in a certain place
6 a parliament or lawcourt sits when it has assembled for business

sitar *NOUN* **sitars**
an Indian musical instrument like a guitar

WORD HISTORY from Hindi, from Persian and Urdu *sih* 'three' and *tar* 'string'

sitcom *NOUN* **sitcoms**
(*informal*) a situation comedy

site *NOUN* **sites**
the place where something happens or happened or is built or positioned

USAGE NOTE Take care not to confuse this word with *sight*.

site *VERB* **sites, siting, sited**
to provide a building or organization with a site; to locate something

sit-in *NOUN* **sit-ins**
a protest in which people sit down or occupy a public place and refuse to move

sitter *NOUN* **sitters**
1 a person who poses for a portrait
2 a person who looks after children, pets, or a house while the owners are away

sitting *NOUN* **sittings**
1 the time when people are served a meal
2 the time when a parliament or committee is conducting business

sitting room *NOUN* **sitting rooms**
a room with comfortable chairs for sitting in

sitting tenant *NOUN* **sitting tenants**
a tenant who is entitled to stay in a rented place if there is a change of owner

situated *ADJECTIVE*
in a particular place or situation

The Nautical School was situated in the old lock-keeper's cottage next to the lock pit. — *Ellen MacArthur, Taking on the World*

situation *NOUN* **situations**
1 a position, with its surroundings
2 a state of affairs at a particular time ◆ *We will have to watch this situation very carefully.*
3 a job

situation comedy *NOUN* **situation comedies**
a comedy series on radio or television, based on the way characters react to unusual or comic situations

six *NOUN, ADJECTIVE* **sixes**
the number 6

at sixes and sevens in disorder or disagreement

▷ **sixth** *ADJECTIVE, NOUN*

sixth form *NOUN* **sixth forms**
a form for students aged 16–18 in a secondary school

sixth sense *NOUN*
the ability to know something by instinct rather than by using any of the five senses; intuition

sixteen *NOUN, ADJECTIVE*
the number 16

▷ **sixteenth** *ADJECTIVE, NOUN*

sixty *NOUN, ADJECTIVE* **sixties**
the number 60

▷ **sixtieth** *ADJECTIVE, NOUN*

size❶ *NOUN* **sizes**
1 the measurements or extent of something
2 any of the series of standard measurements in which certain things are made

size *VERB* **sizes, sizing, sized**
to arrange things according to their size

to size something up
1 is to estimate the size of something
2 is to form an opinion or judgement about a person or thing

WORD HISTORY originally, a law fixing the amount of a tax: from Old French *assise* 'law' or 'court session'

size❷ *NOUN*
a gluey substance used to glaze paper, stiffen cloth, or prepare plaster for decoration

size *VERB* **sizes, sizing, sized**
to treat something with size

sizeable *ADJECTIVE*
large or fairly large

a b c d e f g h i j k l m n o p q r s t u v w x y z

SPELLING NOTE Some words pronounced like *sit* begin with **sy-** (e.g. syllabus)

sizzle *VERB* **sizzles, sizzling, sizzled**
to make a crackling or hissing sound

skate[1] *NOUN* **skates**
1 a boot with a steel blade attached to the sole, used for sliding smoothly over ice
2 a roller skate

skate *VERB* **skates, skating, skated**
to move or ride on skates
▷ **skater** *NOUN*

skate[2] *NOUN* **skate**
a large flat edible sea fish

skateboard *NOUN* **skateboards**
a small board with wheels, used for standing and riding on as a sport
▷ **skateboarder, skateboarding** *NOUNS*

skein *NOUN* **skeins**
a coil of yarn or thread

skeleton *NOUN* **skeletons**
1 the framework of bones of the body
2 the shell or other hard part of a crab or other crustacean
3 a framework of a building or other structure
▷ **skeletal** *ADJECTIVE*

sketch *NOUN* **sketches**
1 (*Art*) a rough drawing or painting
2 a short account of something
3 a short amusing play

sketch *VERB* **sketches, sketching, sketched**
to make a sketch

sketchy *ADJECTIVE*
rough and not detailed or careful

skew *ADJECTIVE*
askew or slanting

skew *VERB* **skews, skewing, skewed**
to make a thing askew

skewer *NOUN* **skewers**
a long pin pushed through meat to hold it together while it is being cooked

skewer *VERB* **skewers, skewering, skewered**
to fix or pierce something with a skewer or pin

ski (*say* skee) *NOUN* **skis**
each of a pair of long narrow strips of wood, metal, or plastic fixed under the feet for moving quickly over snow

ski *VERB* **skis, skiing, skied**
to move or ride on skis
▷ **skier** *NOUN*

skid *VERB* **skids, skidding, skidded**
to slide accidentally and out of control

skid *NOUN* **skids**
1 a skidding movement
2 a runner on a helicopter, for use in landing

ski jump *NOUN* **ski jumps**
a steep slope with a sharp drop where it levels out at the bottom, for skiers to jump off as a sport

skilful *ADJECTIVE*
having or showing great skill
▷ **skilfully** *ADVERB*

skill *NOUN* **skills**
the ability to do something well

skilled *ADJECTIVE*
1 skilful; highly trained or experienced
2 skilled work needs particular skills or special training

skim *VERB* **skims, skimming, skimmed**
1 to remove something from the surface of a liquid; to take the cream off milk
2 to move quickly over a surface or through the air
3 to read something quickly

skimmed milk *NOUN*
milk that has had the cream removed

skimp *VERB* **skimps, skimping, skimped**
to skimp on something is to supply or use less than is needed

skimpy *ADJECTIVE* **skimpier, skimpiest**
scanty or too small

skin *NOUN* **skins**
1 the flexible outer covering of a person's or animal's body
2 an outer layer or covering, e.g. of a fruit
3 a skin-like film formed on the surface of a liquid

skin *VERB* **skins, skinning, skinned**
to take the skin off something

skin diving *NOUN*
swimming under water with flippers and breathing apparatus but without a diving suit
▷ **skin diver** *NOUN*

skinflint *NOUN* **skinflints**
a miserly person

skinhead *NOUN* **skinheads**
a youth with very closely cropped hair

skinny *ADJECTIVE* **skinnier, skinniest**
very thin

skip[1] *VERB* **skips, skipping, skipped**
1 to move along lightly, especially by hopping on each foot in turn
2 to jump with a skipping rope
3 to go quickly from one subject to another
4 to leave out or ignore part of something, e.g. in reading

skip *NOUN* **skips**
a skipping movement

skip[2] *NOUN* **skips**
a large open-topped container for taking away bulky refuse

skipper *NOUN* **skippers**
(*informal*) the captain of a ship or team

skipping rope *NOUN* **skipping ropes**
a rope, usually with a handle at each end, that is swung over your head and under your feet as you jump

skirmish *NOUN* **skirmishes**
(*informal*) a minor fight or conflict

skirmish *VERB* **skirmishes, skirmishing, skirmished**
to fight

skirt *NOUN* **skirts**
1 a piece of clothing for a woman or girl that hangs down from the waist
2 the part of a dress below the waist

skirt *VERB* **skirts, skirting, skirted**
to go round the edge of something

skirting or **skirting board** *NOUN* **skirtings** or **skirting boards**
a narrow board round the wall of a room, close to the floor

skit *NOUN* **skits**
a satirical or witty sketch or parody

skittish *ADJECTIVE*
frisky; lively and excitable

skittle *NOUN* **skittles**
a wooden bottle-shaped object that people try to knock down by bowling a ball in the game called **skittles**

skive *VERB* **skives, skiving, skived**
(*informal*) to dodge work
▷ **skiver** *NOUN*

skulk *VERB* **skulks, skulking, skulked**
to loiter stealthily

skull *NOUN* **skulls**
the framework of bones of the head

skullcap *NOUN* **skullcaps**
a small close-fitting cap worn on the top of the head

skunk *NOUN* **skunks**
a North American animal with black and white fur that can spray a bad-smelling fluid

sky *NOUN* **skies**
the space above the earth, appearing blue in daylight on fine days

skydiving *NOUN*
the sport of jumping from an aeroplane and performing manoeuvres before opening your parachute
▷ **skydiver** *NOUN*

skylark *NOUN* **skylarks**
a lark that sings while it hovers high in the air

skylight *NOUN* **skylights**
a window in a roof

skyline *NOUN* **skylines**
the outline of land or buildings seen against the sky

skyscraper *NOUN* **skyscrapers**
a very tall building

slab *NOUN* **slabs**
a thick flat piece

slack *ADJECTIVE*
1 not pulled or held tight; loose
2 not busy; not working hard
▷ **slackly** *ADVERB*
▷ **slackness** *NOUN*

slack *NOUN*
the loose part of a rope or line

slack *VERB* **slacks, slacking, slacked**
to avoid work; to be lazy
▷ **slacker** *NOUN*

slacken *VERB* **slackens, slackening, slackened**
to become slack, or to make something slack

slacks *PLURAL NOUN*
trousers for informal occasions

slag *NOUN*
waste material separated from metal in smelting

slag heap *NOUN* **slag heaps**
a mound of waste matter from a mine or industrial site

slain *past participle* of **slay**

slake *VERB* **slakes, slaking, slaked**
to quench your thirst

slalom *NOUN* **slaloms**
a ski race down a zigzag course

WORD HISTORY from Norwegian *sla* 'sloping' and *låm* 'track'

slam *VERB* **slams, slamming, slammed**
1 to shut loudly
2 to hit something violently
▷ **slam** *NOUN*

slander *NOUN* **slanders**
a spoken statement that damages a person's reputation and is untrue (SEE ALSO **libel**)
▷ **slanderous** *ADJECTIVE*

slander *VERB* **slanders, slandering, slandered**
to make a slander against someone
▷ **slanderer** *NOUN*

slang *NOUN*
(*Language*) words that are used very informally to add vividness or humour to what is said, especially those used only by a particular group of people
▷ **slangy** *ADJECTIVE*

slanging match *NOUN* **slanging matches**
a noisy quarrel, with people shouting insults at each other

slant *VERB* **slants, slanting, slanted**
1 to slope
2 to present news or information from a particular point of view

SPELLING NOTE Some words pronounced **s-** begin with **ce-** (e.g. cent), **ci-** (e.g. city), or **cy-** (e.g. cymbal)

slap *VERB* **slaps, slapping, slapped**
1 to hit someone or something with the palm of the hand or with something flat
2 to put something down forcefully or carelessly ◆ *The man slapped his passport on the table.*
3 to slap paint on a surface is to put it on quickly and clumsily
▷ **slap** *NOUN*

slapdash *ADJECTIVE*
hasty and careless

slapstick *NOUN*
comic acts in which people hit each other, throw things at each other, and tumble about
WORD HISTORY originally the name of a device consisting of two pieces of wood joined together at one end and used by clowns to make a slapping noise

slash *VERB* **slashes, slashing, slashed**
1 to make large cuts in something
2 to cut or strike something with a long sweeping movement
3 to slash prices or costs is to reduce them by a large amount

slash *NOUN* **slashes**
1 a slashing cut
2 a slanting line (/) used in writing and printing

slat *NOUN* **slats**
each of the thin strips of wood or metal or plastic arranged so that they overlap and form a screen, e.g. in a venetian blind

slate *NOUN* **slates**
1 a kind of grey rock that is easily split into flat plates
2 a piece of this rock used in covering a roof or (formerly) for writing on
▷ **slaty** *ADJECTIVE*

slate *VERB* **slates, slating, slated**
1 to cover a roof with slates
2 (*informal*) to criticize someone or something harshly

slattern *NOUN* **slatterns**
(*old use*) a slovenly woman
▷ **slatternly** *ADJECTIVE*

slaughter *VERB* **slaughters, slaughtering, slaughtered**
1 to kill an animal for food
2 to kill people or animals ruthlessly or in great numbers
▷ **slaughter** *NOUN*

slaughterhouse *NOUN* **slaughterhouses**
a place where animals are killed for food

slave *NOUN* **slaves**
a person who is owned by another and obliged to work for him or her without being paid
▷ **slavery** *NOUN*
WORD FAMILY A related adjective is servile.

slave *VERB* **slaves, slaving, slaved**
to work very hard, especially in poor conditions

I counted seven women slaving over the large tubs where the clothes are washed, their reddened faces shiny with sweat. — Pamela Oldfield, *My Story: Victorian Workhouse*

slave-driver *NOUN* **slave-drivers**
a person who makes others work very hard

slaver (*say* **slav**- er or **slay**- ver) *VERB* **slavers, slavering, slavered**
to have saliva flowing from the mouth

slavish *ADJECTIVE*
1 like a slave
2 showing no independence or originality

slay *VERB* **slays, slaying, slew, slain**
(*literary*) to kill people, especially in large numbers

sled *NOUN* **sleds**
(*American*) a sledge

sledge *NOUN* **sledges**
a vehicle for travelling over snow, with strips of metal or wood instead of wheels
▷ **sledging** *NOUN*

sledgehammer *NOUN* **sledgehammers**
a very large heavy hammer

sleek *ADJECTIVE*
smooth and shiny

sleep *NOUN*
the condition or time of rest in which the eyes are closed, the body relaxed, and the mind unconscious
to go to sleep you say that a part of the body goes to sleep when it becomes numb
to put an animal to sleep is to kill it painlessly, e.g. with an injection of a drug

sleep *VERB* **sleeps, sleeping, slept**
1 to have a sleep
2 to sleep with someone is to have sexual intercourse with them

sleeper *NOUN* **sleepers**
1 someone who is asleep
2 each of the wooden or concrete beams on which the rails of a railway rest
3 a railway carriage with beds or berths for passengers to sleep in; a place in this

sleeping bag *NOUN* **sleeping bags**
a padded bag to sleep in, especially when camping

sleepless *ADJECTIVE*
unable to sleep

sleepover *NOUN* **sleepovers**
a night spent away from home, after a party

sleepwalk *VERB* **sleepwalks, sleepwalking, sleepwalked**
to walk about while asleep
▷ **sleepwalker** *NOUN*

sleepy *ADJECTIVE*
1 feeling a need or wish to sleep
2 a sleepy place is quiet and lacking activity
▷ **sleepily** *ADVERB*
▷ **sleepiness** *NOUN*

sleet *NOUN*
a mixture of rain and snow or hail

sleeve *NOUN* **sleeves**
1 the part of a piece of clothing that covers the arm
2 the cover of a record
up your sleeve hidden but ready for you to use

sleeveless *ADJECTIVE*
without sleeves

sleigh (*sounds like* slay) *NOUN* **sleighs**
a sledge, especially a large one pulled by horses
▷ **sleighing** *NOUN*

sleight of hand (*say* slyt) *NOUN* **sleights of hand**
skill in using the hands, especially to do conjuring tricks

slender *ADJECTIVE*
1 slim and graceful
2 a slender hope or chance is a slight or small one
▷ **slenderness** *NOUN*

sleuth (*say* slooth) *NOUN* **sleuths**
a detective

slew ❶
VERB **slews, slewing, slewed**
to turn or slide violently

The truck revolved a half-turn, slewing off the highway in a cascade of sparks. — *Eoin Colfer, The Supernaturalist*

slew ❷ *past tense of* **slay**

slice *NOUN* **slices**
1 a thin piece cut off something
2 a portion

slice *VERB* **slices, slicing, sliced**
1 to cut something into slices
2 to cut something from a larger piece
3 to cut something cleanly

slick *ADJECTIVE*
1 done or doing things quickly and cleverly
2 a slick surface is smooth and slippery

slick *NOUN* **slicks**
1 a large patch of oil floating on water
2 a slippery place

slide *VERB* **slides, sliding, slid**
1 to move smoothly on a surface, or to cause something to do this
2 to move quietly or secretly ◆ *She slid into the water and swam to the opposite side.*

slide *NOUN* **slides**
1 a sliding movement
2 a smooth surface or structure on which people or things can slide
3 a photograph that can be projected on a screen
4 a small glass plate on which things are placed to be examined under a microscope
5 a fastener to keep hair tidy

slight *ADJECTIVE*
very small; not serious or important
▷ **slightly** *ADVERB*
▷ **slightness** *NOUN*

slight *VERB* **slights, slighting, slighted**
to insult a person by treating them without respect
▷ **slight** *NOUN*

slim *ADJECTIVE* **slimmer, slimmest**
1 thin and graceful
2 a slim chance or hope is a slight or small one
▷ **slimness** *NOUN*

slim *VERB* **slims, slimming, slimmed**
to try to make yourself thinner, especially by dieting
▷ **slimmer** *NOUN*

slime *NOUN*
unpleasant wet slippery stuff

slimy *ADJECTIVE* **slimier, slimiest**
covered in slime, or set and sticky like slime

Deep down here by the dark water lived old Gollum, a small slimy creature. — *J. R. R. Tolkien, The Hobbit*

▷ **sliminess** *NOUN*

sling *NOUN* **slings**
1 a loop or band placed round something, e.g. a broken arm, to support or lift it
2 a looped strap used to throw a stone or other small object

sling *VERB* **slings, slinging, slung**
1 to hang something up or support it with a sling or so that it hangs loosely
2 (*informal*) to throw something carelessly

slink *VERB* **slinks, slinking, slunk**
to move in a stealthy or guilty way

Varjak slunk towards the wall, willing himself to disappear. I'm a shadow, he told himself. No one can see me. I'm invisible. — *S.F. Said, Varjak Paw*

▷ **slinky** *ADJECTIVE*

slip *VERB* **slips, slipping, slipped**
1 to slide accidentally; to lose your balance by sliding
2 to go quickly and quietly somewhere

Slipping into the house, Naledi took the letter quietly from the tin without Nono or Mmangwane noticing. — *Beverley Naidoo, Journey to Jo'burg*

3 to move something or put it somewhere quickly and quietly ◆ *Wayne slipped the* ▸▸

SPELLING NOTE Some words pronounced **s-** begin with **ce-** (e.g. cent), **ci-** (e.g. city), or **cy-** (e.g. cymbal)

a b c d e f g h i j k l m n o p q r s t u v w x y z

letter into his pocket. ◆ She slipped her arms into her dressing gown.

4 an animal slips its leash when it escapes from being tied up

5 something slips your memory when you forget it for a while

to slip up is to make a minor mistake

slip *NOUN* **slips**

1 an accidental slide or fall

2 a minor or careless mistake

3 a small piece of paper for writing on or with printed information

4 a short petticoat

to give someone the slip is to escape from them or avoid them

slipper *NOUN* **slippers**

a soft comfortable shoe to wear indoors

slippery *ADJECTIVE*

smooth or wet so that it is difficult to stand on or hold

▷ **slipperiness** *NOUN*

slip road *NOUN* **slip roads**

a road by which you enter or leave a motorway

slipshod *ADJECTIVE*

careless; not systematic

WORD HISTORY originally 'wearing slippers or badly fitting shoes', from *slip* and *shod* meaning 'wearing shoes'

slipstream *NOUN* **slipstreams**

a current of air driven backward as an aircraft or vehicle is propelled forward

slit *NOUN* **slits**

a narrow straight cut or opening

slit *VERB* **slits, slitting, slit**

to make a slit or slits in something

slither *VERB* **slithers, slithering, slithered**

to slip or slide unsteadily

The lane was all potholes and the wheels kept slipping and we rocked and slithered on the cold damp coal. — *David Almond, The Fire-Eaters*

sliver (*say* sliv- er) *NOUN* **slivers**

a thin strip of something hard or brittle, especially wood or glass

slob *NOUN* **slobs**

(*informal*) a careless, untidy, lazy person

slobber *VERB* **slobbers, slobbering, slobbered**

to slaver or dribble

sloe *NOUN* **sloes**

the small dark plum-like fruit of blackthorn

slog *VERB* **slogs, slogging, slogged**

1 to hit someone or something hard

2 to work or walk hard and steadily

▷ **slog** *NOUN*

▷ **slogger** *NOUN*

slogan *NOUN* **slogans**

a short snappy phrase used in advertising or to promote a political cause

WORD HISTORY from Scottish Gaelic *sluagh-ghairm* 'battle cry', used many times in the writings of Sir Walter Scott

sloop *NOUN* **sloops**

a small sailing ship with one mast

slop *VERB* **slops, slopping, slopped**

to spill liquid over the edge of its container

I turned off the stove and gingerly slopped the water into three large mugs. — *Joe Simpson, Touching the Void*

slope *VERB* **slopes, sloping, sloped**

to lie or turn at an angle; to slant

to slope off (*informal*) is to go away furtively

slope *NOUN* **slopes**

1 a sloping surface

2 the amount by which something slopes

sloppy *ADJECTIVE* **sloppier, sloppiest**

1 liquid and splashing easily

2 careless or slipshod

3 weakly sentimental

▷ **sloppily** *ADVERB*

▷ **sloppiness** *NOUN*

slops *PLURAL NOUN*

1 slopped liquid

2 liquid waste matter

slosh *VERB* (*informal*) **sloshes, sloshing, sloshed**

1 to splash or slop

Mum banged down the dinner pan. Pasta sloshed over the sides and onto the table. — *Malorie Blackman, Noughts and Crosses*

2 to pour liquid carelessly

3 to hit someone or something

slot *NOUN* **slots**

a narrow opening to put things in

▷ **slotted** *ADJECTIVE*

slot *VERB* **slots, slotting, slotted**

to put something into a place where it fits

sloth (*rhymes with* both) *NOUN*

1 reluctance to work; laziness

2 (*plural* **sloths**) a South American animal that lives in trees and moves very slowly

▷ **slothful** *ADJECTIVE*

slot machine *NOUN* **slot machines**

a machine worked by putting a coin in the slot

slouch *VERB* **slouches, slouching, slouched**

to stand, sit, or move in a lazy awkward way, not with an upright posture

▷ **slouch** *NOUN*

slough[1] (*rhymes with* cow) *NOUN* **sloughs**

a swamp or marshy place

slough② (*say* sluf) ***VERB*** **sloughs, sloughing, sloughed**
an animal, especially a snake, sloughs its skin when it sheds it periodically

slovenly (*say* **sluv**- en- lee) ***ADJECTIVE***
careless or untidy
▷ **slovenliness** ***NOUN***

slow ***ADJECTIVE***
1 not quick; taking more time than is usual
2 a clock or watch is slow if it shows a time earlier than the correct time
3 not clever; not able to understand quickly or easily
▷ **slowly** ***ADVERB***
▷ **slowness** ***NOUN***

slow ***ADVERB***
slowly; at a slow rate ◆ *go slow*

slow ***VERB*** **slows, slowing, slowed**
to go more slowly, or to cause someone to go more slowly

slow motion ***NOUN***
movement in a film or on television which has been slowed down

slow-worm ***NOUN*** **slow-worms**
a small European legless lizard that looks like a snake, and gives birth to live young

sludge ***NOUN***
thick mud

The frog showed darkly in the dim surface mirror which reflected the grey sludge of the pond's bed. — *Henry Williamson, Tarka the Otter*

slug ***NOUN*** **slugs**
1 a small slimy animal like a snail without a shell
2 a pellet for firing from a gun

sluggard ***NOUN*** **sluggards**
a slow or lazy person

sluggish ***ADJECTIVE***
slow-moving; not alert or lively

sluice (*say* slooss) ***NOUN*** **sluices**
1 a sluice gate
2 a channel carrying off water

sluice ***VERB*** **sluices, sluicing, sluiced**
to wash something with a flow of water

sluice gate ***NOUN*** **sluice gates**
a sliding barrier for controlling a flow of water

slum ***NOUN*** **slums**
an area of dirty overcrowded houses

slumber ***VERB*** **slumbers, slumbering, slumbered**
to sleep peacefully
▷ **slumber** ***NOUN***
▷ **slumberer** ***NOUN***
▷ **slumberous** or **slumbrous** ***ADJECTIVE***

slump ***VERB*** **slumps, slumping, slumped**
to fall heavily or suddenly

slump ***NOUN*** **slumps**
a sudden large fall in prices or trade

slur ***VERB*** **slurs, slurring, slurred**
1 to pronounce words indistinctly by running the sounds together
2 (*Music*) to mark notes with a slur

slur ***NOUN*** **slurs**
1 a slurred sound
2 something that harms a person's reputation
3 (*Music*) a curved line placed over notes in music to show that they are to be sung or played smoothly without a break

slurp ***VERB*** **slurps, slurping, slurped**
to eat or drink with a loud sucking sound
▷ **slurp** ***NOUN***

slurry ***NOUN***
a semi-liquid mixture of water and cement, clay, or manure

slush ***NOUN***
1 partly melted snow on the ground
2 very sentimental talk or writing
▷ **slushy** ***ADJECTIVE***

sly ***ADJECTIVE*** **slyer, slyest**
1 unpleasantly cunning or secret
2 a sly smile or look is mischievous and knowing
▷ **slyly** ***ADVERB***
▷ **slyness** ***NOUN***

smack① ***NOUN*** **smacks**
1 a hard slap
2 a loud sharp sound of something hitting a hard surface
3 a loud kiss
4 (*informal*) a hard hit or blow

smack ***VERB*** **smacks, smacking, smacked**
1 to slap someone
2 to hit something hard
to smack your lips is to close them and then part them noisily in enjoyment

smack ***ADVERB***
(*informal*) forcefully or directly ◆ *Suddenly they were both there smack in front of me.*

smack② ***NOUN*** **smacks**
a slight flavour of something; a trace

smack ***VERB*** **smacks, smacking, smacked**
to smack of something is to have a slight flavour or trace of it ◆ *The whole thing smacks of a cover-up.*

smack③ ***NOUN*** **smacks**
a small sailing boat used for fishing

small ***ADJECTIVE***
1 not large; less than the usual size
2 not important or significant ◆ *We will need to make some small changes.*
the small of the back the smallest part of the back, at the waist
▷ **smallness** ***NOUN***

SYNONYMS (meaning 1) little, tiny, minute, compact, diminutive, minuscule; (meaning 2) minor, trivial, unimportant, negligible

smallholding *NOUN* **smallholdings**
a small area of land used for farming
▷ **smallholder** *NOUN*

small hours *PLURAL NOUN*
the early hours of the morning, after midnight

small-minded *ADJECTIVE*
selfish; petty

smallpox *NOUN*
a serious contagious disease that causes a fever and produces spots that leave permanent scars on the skin

small print *NOUN*
the details of a contract, especially if in very small letters or difficult to understand

small talk *NOUN*
conversation about unimportant things

smarmy *ADJECTIVE*
(*informal*) trying to win someone's favour by flattering them or being polite in an exaggerated way

smart *ADJECTIVE*
1 neat and elegant; dressed well
2 clever or shrewd
3 forceful; brisk ◆ *Sean drove off at a smart pace.*
▷ **smartly** *ADVERB*
▷ **smartness** *NOUN*

smart *VERB* **smarts, smarting, smarted**
to feel a stinging pain
▷ **smart** *NOUN*

smart card *NOUN* **smart cards**
a card like a credit card with a microprocessor built in, which stores information or enables you to draw or spend money from your bank account

smarten *VERB* **smartens, smartening, smartened**
to become smarter, or to make someone smarter

smash *VERB* **smashes, smashing, smashed**
1 to break something violently into pieces
2 to hit something or move with great force
3 to strike the ball forcefully downwards in tennis and other games
4 to destroy or defeat an opponent or enemy completely

smash *NOUN* **smashes**
1 the action or sound of smashing
2 a collision between vehicles
3 (*informal*) a smash hit

smash hit *NOUN* **smash hits**
(*informal*) a very successful song or entertainment

smashing *ADJECTIVE*
(*informal*) excellent or beautiful
▷ **smasher** *NOUN*

smattering *NOUN*
a slight knowledge of a subject or a foreign language

> I don't have French but what I do have is a smattering of Spanish, the legacy of several non-package holidays on the Costa del Sol. — *Alan Bennett, Talking Heads*

smear *VERB* **smears, smearing, smeared**
1 to rub something greasy or sticky or dirty on a surface
2 to try to damage someone's reputation
▷ **smeary** *ADJECTIVE*

smear *NOUN* **smears**
1 the process of smearing; something smeared
2 material smeared on a slide to be examined under a microscope
3 a smear test

smear campaign *NOUN* **smear campaigns**
an organized attempt to damage a person's reputation by spreading rumours about them

smear test *NOUN* **smear tests**
the taking and examination of a sample of the cervix lining, to check for faulty cells which may cause cancer

smell *VERB* **smells, smelling, smelt** or **smelled**
1 to be aware of something by means of the sense organs of the nose ◆ *I could smell burning from the kitchen.*
2 to give out a smell

> The police car smelt of hot plastic and aftershave and take-away chips. — *Mark Haddon, The Curious Incident of the Dog in the Night-Time*

smell *NOUN* **smells**
1 something you can smell; a quality in something that makes people able to smell it
2 an unpleasant quality of this kind
3 the ability to smell things
▷ **smelly** *ADJECTIVE*

smelt *VERB* **smelts, smelting, smelted**
to melt ore to get the metal it contains

smile *NOUN* **smiles**
an expression on the face that shows pleasure or amusement, with the lips stretched and turning upwards at the ends

smile *VERB* **smiles, smiling, smiled**
to give a smile

smirch *VERB* **smirches, smirching, smirched**
1 to soil something
2 to disgrace or dishonour a reputation
▷ **smirch** *NOUN*

smirk *NOUN* **smirks**
a self-satisfied smile

smirk *VERB* **smirks, smirking, smirked**
to give a smirk

smite *VERB* **smites, smiting, smote, smitten**
(*old use*) to strike something or someone with a hard blow

smith *NOUN* **smiths**
1 a person who makes things out of metal
2 a blacksmith

smithereens *PLURAL NOUN*
small pieces from something that is badly broken

Eight cauldrons fell off a shelf; they crashed onto the hall floor and smashed into smithereens.
— Kevin Crossley-Holland, Viking!

smithy *NOUN* **smithies**
a blacksmith's workshop

smitten *past participle* of **smite**
to be smitten with something is to be suddenly affected by a disease or desire

smock *NOUN* **smocks**
1 an overall shaped like a long loose shirt
2 a loose top worn by a pregnant woman

smock *VERB* **smocks, smocking, smocked**
to stitch material into close gathers with embroidery
▷ **smocking** *NOUN*

smog *NOUN*
a mixture of smoke and fog

smoke *NOUN*
1 the mixture of gas and solid particles given off by a burning substance
2 a spell of smoking tobacco
▷ **smoky** *ADJECTIVE*

smoke *VERB* **smokes, smoking, smoked**
1 to give out smoke
2 to draw the smoke of tobacco or of a drug into your mouth and breathe it out again
3 to preserve meat or fish by treating it with smoke
▷ **smoker** *NOUN*

smokeless *ADJECTIVE*
without producing smoke

smokescreen *NOUN* **smokescreens**
1 a mass of smoke used to hide the movement of troops
2 something that conceals what is happening

smooth *ADJECTIVE*
1 having a surface without any lumps, wrinkles, or roughness
2 moving without bumps or jolts
3 not harsh ◆ *a smooth flavour*
4 without problems or difficulties
▷ **smoothly** *ADVERB*
▷ **smoothness** *NOUN*

smooth *VERB* **smooths, smoothing, smoothed**
to make something smooth

Officer Delinko picked himself up off the ground and smoothed the front of his uniform. *— Carl Hiaasen, Hoot*

smote *past tense* of **smite**

smother *VERB* **smothers, smothering, smothered**
1 to suffocate someone
2 to put out a fire by covering it
3 to cover a thing thickly with something soft, wet, or sticky ◆ *His hair was smothered in grease.*
4 to restrain or conceal something ◆ *Two ginger-headed girls were trying to smother their giggles.*

smoulder *VERB* **smoulders, smouldering, smouldered**
1 to burn slowly without a flame
2 to feel an emotion strongly without showing it ◆ *He was still smouldering with anger.*

smudge *NOUN* **smudges**
a dirty mark made by rubbing something
▷ **smudgy** *ADJECTIVE*

smudge *VERB* **smudges, smudging, smudged**
to make a smudge on something, or to become smudged

smug *ADJECTIVE*
self-satisfied; too pleased with your own good fortune or abilities
▷ **smugly** *ADVERB*
▷ **smugness** *NOUN*

smuggle *VERB* **smuggles, smuggling, smuggled**
1 to bring something into a country secretly or illegally
2 to take something somewhere secretively

Pattern had smuggled one or two books and Bonnie's paintbox from the attic out to the cart with the food and clothes. *— Joan Aiken, The Wolves of Willoughby Chase*

▷ **smuggler** *NOUN*

smut *NOUN* **smuts**
1 a small piece of soot or dirt
2 indecent talk or pictures
▷ **smutty** *ADJECTIVE*

snack *NOUN* **snacks**
1 a small meal
2 food eaten between meals

snack bar *NOUN* **snack bars**
a small cafe where snacks are sold

snag *NOUN* **snags**
1 an unexpected difficulty
2 a sharp or jagged part sticking out from something
3 a tear in material that has been caught on something sharp

a b c d e f g h i j k l m n o p q r s t u v w x y z

snail ***NOUN*** **snails**
a small animal with a soft body and a shell

snail mail ***NOUN***
(*informal*) the ordinary post, as distinct from email

snail's pace ***NOUN***
a very slow pace

snake ***NOUN*** **snakes**
a reptile with a long narrow body and no legs
▷ **snaky** ***ADJECTIVE***

snake ***VERB*** **snakes, snaking, snaked**
to move with a winding or twisting motion

Kezzie had gazed back at the carriages snaking behind the engines across the vast gorge at Stoney Creek Bridge. — *Theresa Breslin, Kezzie*

snap ***VERB*** **snaps, snapping, snapped**
1 to break suddenly or with a sharp sound, or to make something do this
2 to bite something suddenly or quickly
3 to say something quickly and angrily
4 to take something or move quickly
5 to take a snapshot of something
to snap your fingers is to make a sharp snapping sound with your thumb and a finger, especially to call attention

snap ***NOUN*** **snaps**
1 the action or sound of snapping
2 a snapshot
3 a card game in which players shout 'snap!' when they see two cards of the same type

snap ***ADJECTIVE***
a snap reply or decision is one that you make very quickly or suddenly

snapdragon ***NOUN*** **snapdragons**
a plant with flowers that have a mouth-like opening

snappy ***ADJECTIVE***
1 snapping at people
2 quick and lively
▷ **snappily** ***ADVERB***

snapshot ***NOUN*** **snapshots**
an informal photograph that you take quickly

snare ***NOUN*** **snares**
1 a trap for catching birds or animals
2 something that attracts someone but is a trap or a danger

snare ***VERB*** **snares, snaring, snared**
to catch an animal in a snare

snarl❶ ***VERB*** **snarls, snarling, snarled**
1 to growl angrily
2 to speak in a bad-tempered way
▷ **snarl** ***NOUN***

snarl❷ ***VERB*** **snarls, snarling, snarled**
to become tangled or jammed, or cause something to do this ◆ *Drivers were swearing as they got snarled up in the midday traffic.*

snatch ***VERB*** **snatches, snatching, snatched**
to seize something; to take something quickly, eagerly, or by force

snatch ***NOUN*** **snatches**
1 an act of snatching something
2 a short and incomplete part of a song or conversation

sneak ***VERB*** **sneaks, sneaking, sneaked**
1 to move quietly and secretly
2 (*informal*) to take something furtively from somewhere ◆ *She sneaked a look at the man from across the room.*
3 (*informal*) to tell tales; to inform on someone

sneak ***NOUN*** **sneaks**
(*informal*) someone who tells tales

sneaky ***ADJECTIVE***
dishonest or deceitful
▷ **sneakily** ***ADVERB***

sneer ***VERB*** **sneers, sneering, sneered**
to speak or behave in a scornful way
▷ **sneer** ***NOUN***

sneeze ***VERB*** **sneezes, sneezing, sneezed**
to send out air suddenly and uncontrollably through the nose and mouth in order to get rid of something irritating the nostrils
not to be sneezed at (*informal*) worth considering or having
▷ **sneeze** ***NOUN***

snide ***ADJECTIVE***
sneering in a sly way

sniff ***VERB*** **sniffs, sniffing, sniffed**
1 to make a sound by drawing in air through the nose
2 to smell something
▷ **sniff** ***NOUN***
▷ **sniffer** ***NOUN***

sniffer dog ***NOUN*** **sniffer dogs**
(*informal*) a dog trained to find drugs or explosives by smell

sniffle ***VERB*** **sniffles, sniffling, sniffled**
1 to sniff slightly
2 to keep on sniffing
▷ **sniffle** ***NOUN***

snigger ***VERB*** **sniggers, sniggering, sniggered**
to giggle slyly
▷ **snigger** ***NOUN***

snip ***VERB*** **snips, snipping, snipped**
to cut something with scissors or shears in small quick cuts
▷ **snip** ***NOUN***

snipe ***NOUN*** **snipe**
a marsh bird with a long beak

snipe ***VERB*** **snipes, sniping, sniped**
1 to shoot at people from a hiding place
2 to attack someone with sly critical remarks
▷ **sniper** ***NOUN***

snippet *NOUN* **snippets**
a small piece of news or information

snivel *VERB* **snivels, snivelling, snivelled**
to cry or complain in a whining way

snob *NOUN* **snobs**
a person who despises those who have not got wealth, power, or particular tastes or interests

The bartender ... was a big snob. He didn't talk to you at all hardly unless you were a big shot or a celebrity or something. — *J. D. Salinger, The Catcher in the Rye*

▷ **snobbery** *NOUN*
▷ **snobbish** *ADJECTIVE*

WORD HISTORY origin uncertain: probably from an earlier dialect meaning 'shoemaker' and then (in Cambridge) a person from the town (i.e. not a member of the university, a vulgar person who aspired to be superior); the theory that it comes from Latin *s(ine) nob(ilitate)* meaning 'without nobility' is probably just an invention

snooker *NOUN*
a game played with cues and 21 balls on a special cloth-covered table

snoop *VERB* **snoops, snooping, snooped**
to pry; to ask or look around secretly
▷ **snooper** *NOUN*

snooty *ADJECTIVE*
(*informal*) haughty and contemptuous

snooze *NOUN* **snoozes**
(*informal*) a short sleep

snooze *VERB* **snoozes, snoozing, snoozed**
to have a short sleep

snore *VERB* **snores, snoring, snored**
to breathe noisily while sleeping
▷ **snore** *NOUN*

snorkel *NOUN* **snorkels**
a tube through which a person swimming under water can take in air
▷ **snorkelling** *NOUN*

snort *VERB* **snorts, snorting, snorted**
to make a rough sound by breathing forcefully through the nose
▷ **snort** *NOUN*

snout *NOUN* **snouts**
an animal's projecting nose and jaws

snow *NOUN*
frozen drops of water that fall from the sky in small white flakes

snow *VERB* **snows, snowing, snowed**
to come down as snow
to be snowed under is to be overwhelmed with a mass of letters or work

snowball *NOUN* **snowballs**
snow pressed into a ball for throwing
▷ **snowballing** *NOUN*

snowball *VERB* **snowballs, snowballing, snowballed**
to grow quickly in size or intensity

snow-blindness *NOUN*
temporary blindness caused by the glare of light reflected by snow

snowdrift *NOUN* **snowdrifts**
a large heap or bank of snow piled up by the wind

snowdrop *NOUN* **snowdrops**
a small white flower that blooms in early spring

snowflake *NOUN* **snowflakes**
a flake of snow

snowline *NOUN*
the level above which snow never melts

snowman *NOUN* **snowmen**
a figure made of snow

snowplough *NOUN* **snowploughs**
a vehicle or device for clearing roads of snow

snowshoe *NOUN* **snowshoes**
a frame rather like a tennis racket for walking on soft snow

snowstorm *NOUN* **snowstorms**
a storm in which snow falls

snow white *ADJECTIVE*
pure white

snowy *ADJECTIVE*
1 with snow falling ◆ *The weather remained snowy for several days.*
2 covered with snow ◆ *a land of snowy slopes and dark green forests*
3 pure white ◆ *There was a big brass bed with its snowy white sheets.*

snub *VERB* **snubs, snubbing, snubbed**
to treat someone in a scornful or unfriendly way

snub *NOUN* **snubs**
scornful or unfriendly treatment

snub-nosed *ADJECTIVE*
having a short turned-up nose

snuff❶ *NOUN*
powdered tobacco for taking into the nose by sniffing

snuff❷ *VERB* **snuffs, snuffing, snuffed**
to put out a candle by covering or pinching the flame
▷ **snuffer** *NOUN*

snuffle *VERB* **snuffles, snuffling, snuffled**
to sniff noisily
▷ **snuffle** *NOUN*

snug *ADJECTIVE* **snugger, snuggest**
1 warm and cosy
2 fitting closely or tightly
▷ **snugly** *ADVERB*
▷ **snugness** *NOUN*

SPELLING NOTE Some words pronounced **s-** begin with **ce-** (e.g. cent), **ci-** (e.g. city), or **cy-** (e.g. cymbal)

snuggle *VERB* **snuggles, snuggling, snuggled**
to curl up in a warm comfortable place

Back at the dormitory the girls were trying to snuggle down in their cold, uninviting beds. — *Doris Pilkington, Rabbit Proof Fence*

so *ADVERB*
1 in this way; to such an extent ◆ *How could this be so difficult?* ◆ *We have so little information.*
2 very; extremely ◆ *We had to wait so long.*
3 also; too ◆ *I want a drink, and so does my dog.*
and so on and other similar things
or so or about that number
so as to in order to
so far up to now
so long! (*informal*) goodbye
so what? (*informal*) that is not important

so *CONJUNCTION*
for that reason ◆ *We didn't have much money, so we decided to walk.*

soak *VERB* **soaks, soaking, soaked**
to make a person or thing very wet
to soak something up is to take in a liquid in the way that a sponge does
▷ **soak** *NOUN*

so-and-so *NOUN* **so-and-sos**
a person or thing that need not be named

soap *NOUN* **soaps**
1 a substance used with water for washing and cleaning things
2 a soap opera
▷ **soapy** *ADJECTIVE*

soap *VERB* **soaps, soaping, soaped**
to put soap on something

soap opera *NOUN* **soap operas**
a television serial about the everyday lives of a group of people

WORD HISTORY so called because in America in the 1930s they were sponsored by soap manufacturers

soar *VERB* **soars, soaring, soared**
1 to rise high in the air
2 to increase rapidly to a high level

sob *VERB* **sobs, sobbing, sobbed**
to make a gasping sound when crying
▷ **sob** *NOUN*

sober *ADJECTIVE*
1 not drunk
2 serious and calm
3 a sober colour is dark or pale and not bright or showy
▷ **soberly** *ADVERB*
▷ **sobriety** (*say* so- **bry**- it- ee) *NOUN*

sober *VERB* **sobers, sobering, sobered**
to become sober again, or to make someone sober

sob story *NOUN* **sob stories**
an account of someone's experiences, told to get your help or sympathy ◆ *I always was a sucker for a sob story.*

so-called *ADJECTIVE*
named in what may be the wrong way

The so-called Picnic Grounds at the base of the Hanging Rock were entered through a sagging wooden gate, now closed. — *Joan Lindsay, Picnic at Hanging Rock*

soccer *NOUN*
Association football, the form of the game in which the ball may not be handled in play except by the goalkeepers

WORD HISTORY short for *Association football*, the official name from the late 19th century

sociable *ADJECTIVE*
liking to be with other people; friendly
▷ **sociably** *ADVERB*
▷ **sociability** *NOUN*

social *ADJECTIVE*
1 living in a community, not alone ◆ *ants, bees, and other social insects*
2 to do with life in a community ◆ *The role of social relations is important.*
3 liking to be with other people
▷ **socially** *ADVERB*

socialism *NOUN*
a political system in which wealth is shared equally between people, and the main industries and trade are controlled by the state (SEE ALSO **capitalism, communism**)

socialist *NOUN* **socialists**
a person who believes in socialism

socialize *VERB* **socializes, socializing, socialized**
to meet other people socially

USAGE NOTE This word can also be spelled socialise.

social science *NOUN* **social sciences**
the study of human society and social relationships

social security *NOUN*
money and other assistance provided by the government for those in need through being unemployed, ill, or disabled

social services *PLURAL NOUN*
welfare services provided by the government, including schools, hospitals, and pensions

social worker *NOUN* **social workers**
a person trained to help people with social problems
▷ **social work** *NOUN*

society *NOUN* **societies**
1 a community; people living together in a group or nation ◆ *We live in a multicultural society.*
2 a group of people organized for a particular purpose ◆ *They joined a local dramatic society.*
3 company or companionship ◆ *She enjoys the society of her friends.*

sociology (*say* soh- see- **ol**- o- jee) *NOUN*
the study of human society and social behaviour
▷ **sociological** *ADJECTIVE*
▷ **sociologist** *NOUN*

sock❶ *NOUN* **socks**
a piece of clothing that covers your foot and the lower part of your leg

sock❷ *VERB* **socks, socking, socked**
(*informal*) to hit someone hard; to punch someone
▷ **sock** *NOUN*

socket *NOUN* **sockets**
1 a hollow into which something fits
2 a device into which an electric plug or bulb is put to make a connection

sod *NOUN* **sods**
a piece of turf

soda *NOUN*
1 a substance made from sodium, such as baking soda
2 soda water

soda water *NOUN*
water made fizzy with carbon dioxide, used in drinks

sodden *ADJECTIVE*
made very wet

sodium *NOUN*
a soft white metal

sodium bicarbonate *NOUN*
a soluble white powder used in fire extinguishers and fizzy drinks, and to make cakes rise; baking soda

sodium carbonate *NOUN*
white powder or crystals used to clean things; washing soda

sofa *NOUN* **sofas**
a long soft seat with a back and arms
WORD HISTORY from Arabic *suffa* 'a long stone bench'

soft *ADJECTIVE*
1 not hard or firm; easily pressed
2 smooth, not rough or stiff
3 a soft colour is pale and gentle
4 a soft sound is gentle and not loud
5 soft drugs are of a kind that are not likely to be addictive
▷ **softly** *ADVERB*
▷ **softness** *NOUN*

soft drink *NOUN* **soft drinks**
a cold drink that is not alcoholic

soften *VERB* **softens, softening, softened**
to become soft or softer, or to make something soft or softer
▷ **softener** *NOUN*

soft furnishings *PLURAL NOUN*
cushions, curtains, rugs, chair coverings, and other cloth items used as furnishings

soft-hearted *ADJECTIVE*
sympathetic and easily moved

software *NOUN*
(*ICT*) computer programs and data, which are not part of the machinery of a computer (SEE ALSO **hardware**)

soft water *NOUN*
water that is free of minerals that prevent soap from making much lather

softwood *NOUN* **softwoods**
wood from pine trees or other conifers, which is easy to saw

soggy *ADJECTIVE* **soggier, soggiest**
very wet and heavy
WORD HISTORY from dialect a dialect word *sog* 'swamp'

soil❶ *NOUN* **soils**
1 the loose earth in which plants grow
2 the territory of a particular nation ◆ *They were Scots invading English soil.*
WORD HISTORY via Old French from Latin *solium* 'seat', confused with *solum* 'ground'

soil❷ *VERB* **soils, soiling, soiled**
to make something dirty
WORD HISTORY from Old French *soiller*, from Latin *sucula* 'little pig'

sojourn (*say* soj- ern) *VERB* **sojourns, sojourning, sojourned**
to stay at a place temporarily

sojourn *NOUN* **sojourns**
a temporary stay at a place

This is the story of a five-year sojourn that I and my family made on the Greek island of Corfu.
— Gerald Durrell, My Family and Other Animals

solace (*say* sol- as) *VERB* **solaces, solacing, solaced**
to comfort someone who is unhappy or disappointed
▷ **solace** *NOUN*

solar *ADJECTIVE*
from or to do with the sun

solar panel *NOUN* **solar panels**
a panel designed to catch the sun's rays and use their energy for heating or to make electricity

a b c d e f g h i j k l m n o p q r **s** t u v w x y z

solar power *NOUN*
electricity or other forms of power derived from the sun's rays

solar system *NOUN*
the sun and the planets that revolve round it

solder *NOUN*
a soft alloy that is melted to join pieces of metal together

solder *VERB* **solders, soldering, soldered**
to join something with solder

soldier *NOUN* **soldiers**
a member of an army

WORD HISTORY via Old French *souldier* 'one who received a *soulde* (a type of coin)' in pay, from Latin *solidus* a type of gold coin in ancient Rome

sole ❶ *NOUN* **soles**
1 the bottom surface of a foot or shoe
2 a flat edible sea fish

sole *VERB* **soles, soling, soled**
to put a new sole on a shoe

sole ❷ *ADJECTIVE*
single; only ◆ *Their sole interests in life are lettuce, bread, and little things that wriggle.*
▷ **solely** *ADVERB*

WORD FAMILY This word *sole* comes from the Latin word *solus* meaning 'alone'. Other words connected with being alone and having the same origin include *desolate, soliloquy, solitary, solitude*, and *solo*.

solemn (*say* **sol**- em) *ADJECTIVE*
1 not smiling or cheerful

I picked up the faded picture and saw a solemn young man and woman, both dressed in old-fashioned Chinese robes. — *Adeline Yen Mah, Chinese Cinderella*

2 dignified or formal
▷ **solemnly** *ADVERB*
▷ **solemnity** *NOUN*

solemnize (*say* **sol**- em- nyz) *VERB* **solemnizes, solemnizing, solemnized**
1 to celebrate a festival
2 to perform a marriage ceremony
▷ **solemnization** *NOUN*

USAGE NOTE This word can also be spelled solemnise.

solenoid *NOUN* **solenoids**
a coil of wire that becomes magnetic when an electric current is passed through it

sol-fa *NOUN*
a system of syllables (*doh, ray, me fah, so, la, te*) used to represent the notes of the musical scale

WORD HISTORY *sol* was an earlier spelling of *soh*; the names of the notes came from syllables of a Latin hymn

solicit *VERB* **solicits, soliciting, solicited**
1 to ask for something or try to obtain it ◆ *He had been soliciting their help for many weeks.*
2 to approach someone and offer services as a prostitute
▷ **solicitation** *NOUN*

solicitor *NOUN* **solicitors**
a lawyer who advises clients, prepares legal documents, and represents clients in the lower courts

solicitous *ADJECTIVE*
anxious and concerned about a person's comfort and welfare
▷ **solicitously** *ADVERB*
▷ **solicitude** *NOUN*

solid *ADJECTIVE*
1 not hollow; with no space inside
2 keeping its shape; not liquid or gas
3 continuous ◆ *We had to wait for two solid hours.*
4 firm or strongly made; not flimsy ◆ *The house was built on solid foundations.*
5 showing solidarity; unanimous
▷ **solidly** *ADVERB*
▷ **solidity** *NOUN*

solid *NOUN* **solids**
1 a solid thing
2 a shape that has three dimensions (length, width, and height or depth)

WORD HISTORY from Latin *solidus*, related to *salvus* safe

solidarity *NOUN*
1 the state of being solid
2 unity and support between people sharing opinions and interests

solidify *VERB* **solidifies, solidifying, solidified**
to become solid, or to make something solid

solids *PLURAL NOUN*
solid food; food that is not liquid

soliloquize *VERB* **soliloquizes, soliloquizing, soliloquized**
to make a soliloquy

USAGE NOTE This word can also be spelled soliloquise.

soliloquy (*say* sol- **il**- ok- wee) *NOUN* **soliloquies**
a dramatic speech in which a person speaks their inner thoughts aloud when alone or without addressing anyone

solitaire *NOUN* **solitaires**
1 a game for one person, in which marbles are moved on a special board until only one is left
2 a diamond or other precious stone set by itself

solitary *ADJECTIVE*
1 alone or lonely ◆ *It must have felt solitary in that old house at night.*
2 single; by itself ◆ *A solitary starling was perched on the roof.*

solitary confinement *NOUN*
a form of punishment in which a prisoner is kept alone in a cell and not allowed to see other people

solitude *NOUN*
a state of being solitary or alone

solo *NOUN* **solos**
something sung, played, danced, or done by one person
▷ **solo** *ADJECTIVE, ADVERB*
▷ **soloist** *NOUN*

solstice (*say* **sol**- stiss) *NOUN* **solstices**
each of two times in each year when the sun is at its furthest point north or south of the equator. The summer solstice occurs about 21 June and the winter solstice about 22 December

WORD HISTORY from Latin *sol* 'sun' and *sistere* 'to stand still'

soluble *ADJECTIVE*
1 able to be dissolved
2 able to be solved
▷ **solubility** *NOUN*

solution *NOUN* **solutions**
1 the answer to a problem or puzzle
2 (*Science*) a liquid in which something is dissolved

solve *VERB* **solves, solving, solved**
to find the answer to a problem or puzzle

solvent *ADJECTIVE*
1 having enough money to pay all your debts
2 able to dissolve another substance
▷ **solvency** *NOUN*

solvent *NOUN* **solvents**
a liquid used for dissolving something

sombre *ADJECTIVE*
dark and gloomy

sombrero (*say* som- **brair**- oh) *NOUN* **sombreros**
a hat with a very wide brim

some *ADJECTIVE*
1 a few; a little ◆ *He put some cans of drink in the fridge.* ◆ *This answer caused some confusion.*
2 unknown or not identified ◆ *Some person was staring at him.* ◆ *For some reason the lights didn't work.*
3 about; as much as ◆ *It cost us some five hundred pounds.*

some *PRONOUN*
a certain number or amount that is less than the whole ◆ *Some had mouths like elephants' trunks.* ◆ *I've spent some of the time reading.*

somebody *PRONOUN*
1 some person; someone
2 an important or impressive person

somehow *ADVERB*
in some way, or for some reason ◆ *Somehow I knew the door would be locked.*

someone *PRONOUN*
some person; somebody

somersault *NOUN* **somersaults**
a movement in which you turn head over heels before landing on your feet

somersault *VERB* **somersaults, somersaulting, somersaulted**
to perform a somersault

something *NOUN*
some thing; a thing which you cannot or do not want to name

sometime *ADVERB*
at some point in time ◆ *I was woken up by a noise sometime in the small hours.*

sometimes *ADVERB*
on some occasions but not always ◆ *At night we sometimes hear the dogs barking.*

somewhat *ADVERB*
to some extent

Stanley felt somewhat dazed as the guard unlocked his handcuffs and led him off the bus.
— *Louis Sachar, Holes*

somewhere *ADVERB*
in or to some place

somnambulist *NOUN* **somnambulists**
a sleepwalker

somnolent *ADJECTIVE*
sleepy or drowsy
▷ **somnolence** *NOUN*

son *NOUN* **sons**
a boy or man as a child of his parents

sonar *NOUN*
a device for finding objects under water by the reflection of sound waves

WORD HISTORY from *so*und *na*vigation and *r*anging

sonata *NOUN* **sonatas**
a piece of music for one instrument or two, in several movements

song *NOUN* **songs**
1 a tune for singing
2 the act of singing ◆ *From time to time somebody would burst into song.*
a song and dance (*informal*) a great fuss
for a song bought or sold very cheaply

songbird *NOUN* **songbirds**
a bird that sings sweetly

sonic *ADJECTIVE*
to do with sound or sound waves

WORD FAMILY *Sonic* comes from the Latin word *sonus* meaning 'a sound'. Other sounding words having the same origin include *consonant* (= sounding together), *sound* (via French), and *unison* (sounding as one).

a b c d e f g h i j k l m n o p q r s t u v w x y z

SPELLING NOTE Some words pronounced **s-** begin with **ce-** (e.g. cent), **ci-** (e.g. city), or **cy-** (e.g. cymbal)

sonic boom *NOUN* **sonic booms**
a loud noise caused by the shock wave of an aircraft travelling faster than the speed of sound

son-in-law *NOUN* **sons-in-law**
a daughter's husband

sonnet *NOUN* **sonnets**
(*Language*) a kind of poem with 14 lines

sonorous (*say* **sonn**- er- us) *ADJECTIVE*
giving a loud deep sound; resonant ◆ *the sonorous booming of the sea*

soon *ADVERB*
1 in a short time from now
2 not long after something
as soon as much or as willingly ◆ *I'd just as soon go to bed.*
as soon as at the moment that
sooner or later at some time in the future

soot *NOUN*
the black powder left by smoke in a chimney or on a building
▷ **sooty** *ADJECTIVE*

soothe *VERB* **soothes, soothing, soothed**
1 to calm or comfort someone
2 to ease pain or distress
▷ **soothing** *ADJECTIVE*
▷ **soothingly** *ADVERB*

soothsayer *NOUN* **soothsayers**
a prophet

sop *NOUN* **sops**
1 a piece of bread dipped in liquid before being eaten or cooked
2 something unimportant given to pacify or bribe a troublesome person

sop *VERB* **sops, sopping, sopped**
to sop up liquid is to soak it up with a sponge

sophisticated *ADJECTIVE*
1 a sophisticated person has refined or cultured tastes and is experienced about life
2 complicated or advanced ◆ *A more sophisticated computer system is needed.*
▷ **sophistication** *NOUN*

sophistry (*say* **sof**- ist- ree) *NOUN* **sophistries**
a piece of reasoning that is clever but false or misleading

soporific *ADJECTIVE*
causing sleep or drowsiness

sopping *ADJECTIVE*
very wet; drenched

soppy *ADJECTIVE*
1 very wet
2 (*informal*) sentimental in a silly way

soprano *NOUN* **sopranos**
(*Music*) a high singing voice, especially of a woman

sorcerer *NOUN* **sorcerers**
a person who can perform magic
▷ **sorceress** *NOUN*

sorcery *NOUN*
magic or witchcraft

sordid *ADJECTIVE*
1 dirty and nasty
2 dishonourable; selfish and mercenary ◆ *The sordid details of his life came to light during the investigation.*
▷ **sordidly** *ADVERB*
▷ **sordidness** *NOUN*

sore *ADJECTIVE*
1 painful or smarting
2 (*informal*) annoyed or offended
3 serious or distressing ◆ *It was a sore point with their parents that Alice and Henry went out so much.*
▷ **soreness** *NOUN*

sore *NOUN* **sores**
a sore place on the body

sorely *ADVERB*
seriously; very ◆ *Medical supplies are sorely needed.*

sorrel❶ *NOUN*
a herb with sharp-tasting leaves

sorrel❷ *NOUN* **sorrels**
a reddish-brown horse

sorrow *NOUN* **sorrows**
1 unhappiness or regret caused by loss or disappointment
2 something that causes unhappiness
▷ **sorrowful** *ADJECTIVE*
▷ **sorrowfully** *ADVERB*

sorrow *VERB* **sorrows, sorrowing, sorrowed**
to feel sorrow; to grieve

sorry *ADJECTIVE* **sorrier, sorriest**
1 feeling regret ◆ *I'm sorry to be so late.*
2 to be sorry for someone is to feel pity or sympathy for them
3 wretched or unattractive ◆ *After the party the house was a sorry sight.*

sort *NOUN* **sorts**
1 a group of things or people that are similar; a kind or variety
2 a particular type of person or thing

> The girl worked things out quietly, sensibly — she wasn't the sort to get into a panic. — *James Vance Marshall, Walkabout*

out of sorts slightly unwell or depressed
sort of (*informal*) rather; to some extent ◆ *I sort of half believe them, I suppose.*

sort *VERB* **sorts, sorting, sorted**
1 to arrange things in groups according to their size and type
2 (*ICT*) to use a computer program to organize data in a file in a special way, e.g. in alphabetical order
to sort something out is to deal with a problem or difficulty and solve it
▷ **sorter** *NOUN*

sortie *NOUN* **sorties**
1 an attack by troops coming out of a besieged place
2 an attacking expedition by a military aircraft

SOS *NOUN* **SOSs**
an urgent appeal for help

WORD HISTORY the international Morse code signal of extreme distress, chosen because the letters in code are easy to recognize, but often said to stand for 'Save Our Souls'

sought *past tense of* **seek**

soul *NOUN* **souls**
1 the invisible part of a person that is believed to go on living after the body has died
2 a person's mind and emotions
3 a person when described in some way ◆ *Harry was a cheerful soul.* ◆ *There was not a soul to be seen.*

soul-destroying *ADJECTIVE*
very monotonous or depressing

soulful *ADJECTIVE*
having or showing deep feeling
▷ **soulfully** *ADVERB*

soul music *NOUN*
a kind of music combining elements of rhythm and blues and gospel music

sound¹ *NOUN* **sounds**
1 vibrations that travel through the air and can be detected by the ear; the sensation they produce
2 sound reproduced in a film or recording
3 the impression you get from a little information about someone or something ◆ *They liked the sound of the house in the Lakes.*

sound *VERB* **sounds, sounding, sounded**
1 to produce a sound, or to make something produce a sound
2 to give a particular impression when heard ◆ *He sounded tense and edgy.*
3 to test something by noting the sounds you can hear from it

WORD FAMILY Related adjectives are acoustic, aural, phonetic and phonic (to do with speech sounds), and sonic.

sound² *VERB* **sounds, sounding, sounded**
to test the depth of water beneath a ship
to sound someone out is to try to find out what they think or feel about something

sound³ *ADJECTIVE*
1 in good condition; not damaged
2 healthy; not diseased
3 reasonable or correct ◆ *Her suggestions are sound.*
4 reliable or secure ◆ *We want to be sure of a sound investment.*
5 thorough or deep ◆ *What he needed was a long sound sleep.*
▷ **soundly** *ADVERB*
▷ **soundness** *NOUN*

sound⁴ *NOUN* **sounds**
a narrow stretch of water connecting two seas; a strait

sound barrier *NOUN*
the resistance of the air to objects moving at speeds near the speed of sound

sound bite *NOUN* **sound bites**
a short extract from a speech or statement broadcast on radio or television because it seems to sum up the person's opinion in a few words

sound effects *PLURAL NOUN*
sounds produced artificially to make a play, film, or broadcast seem more realistic

sound system *NOUN*
a set of equipment for reproducing and amplifying sound

soundtrack *NOUN* **soundtracks**
the sound that goes with a cinema film

soup *NOUN* **soups**
a liquid dish made from meat, fish, or vegetables
in the soup (*informal*) in trouble

sour *ADJECTIVE*
1 tasting sharp like unripe fruit
2 sour milk or dairy products are stale and unpleasant
3 angry and resentful
▷ **sourly** *ADVERB*
▷ **sourness** *NOUN*

sour *VERB* **sours, souring, soured**
to become sour, or to make something sour

source *NOUN* **sources**
1 the person, place, or thing from which something comes

The fire was the only source of light in the room; it was casting long, spidery shadows upon the walls. — *J. K. Rowling, Harry Potter and the Goblet of Fire*

2 the starting point of a river

sour grapes *PLURAL NOUN*
a tendency to belittle or disparage something you would like but cannot have

WORD HISTORY from a fable in which a fox says that the grapes he cannot reach are probably sour

souse *VERB* **souses, sousing, soused**
1 to soak or drench something
2 to soak fish in pickle

south *NOUN*
1 the direction to the right of a person who faces east
2 the southern part of a country, city, or other area

a b c d e f g h i j k l m n o p q r s t u v w x y z

south *ADJECTIVE, ADVERB*
towards or in the south; coming from the south

WORD FAMILY A southerly wind comes from the direction of the south; a southern person, place or thing comes from, or is situated in, the south; a southerner is a person who comes from or lives in the south of a country or area; a southernmost place or point is at the most southern point of a country or area.

south-east *NOUN, ADJECTIVE, ADVERB*
midway between south and east
▷ **south-easterly** *ADJECTIVE*
▷ **south-eastern** *ADJECTIVE*

southward *ADJECTIVE, ADVERB*
towards the south
▷ **southwards** *ADVERB*

south-west *NOUN, ADJECTIVE, ADVERB*
midway between south and west
▷ **south-westerly** *ADJECTIVE*
▷ **south-western** *ADJECTIVE*

souvenir (*say* soo- ven- eer) *NOUN* **souvenirs**
something that you keep to remind you of a person, place, or event

sou'wester *NOUN* **sou'westers**
a waterproof hat with a wide flap at the back

sovereign *NOUN* **sovereigns**
1 a king or queen who is the ruler of a country; a monarch
2 an old British gold coin, originally worth £1

sovereign *ADJECTIVE*
1 sovereign power is supreme
2 a sovereign state is independent and runs its own affairs

sovereignty *NOUN*
the power a country has to govern itself and make its own laws

sow❶ (*rhymes with* go) *VERB* **sows, sowing, sowed, sown** or **sowed**
1 to put seeds into the ground so that they will grow into plants
2 to cause feelings or ideas to develop ◆ *Their words sowed fear in our minds.*
▷ **sower** *NOUN*

USAGE NOTE Take care not to confuse this word with *sew*.

sow❷ (*rhymes with* cow) *NOUN* **sows**
a female pig

soya bean *NOUN* **soya beans**
a kind of bean from which edible oil and flour are made

soy sauce or **soya sauce** *NOUN*
a Chinese or Japanese sauce made from fermented soya beans

spa *NOUN* **spas**
a health resort where there is a spring of water containing mineral salts

WORD HISTORY from *Spa*, a town in Belgium famous for its mineral springs

space *NOUN* **spaces**
1 the whole area outside the earth, where the stars and planets are
2 an area or volume ◆ *The bed took up too much space.*
3 an empty area; a gap
4 an interval of time ◆ *The package arrived within the space of two days.*

space *VERB* **spaces, spacing, spaced**
to space things, or space them out, is to arrange them with spaces between

spacecraft *NOUN* **spacecraft**
a vehicle for travelling in outer space

spaceman *NOUN* **spacemen**
a male astronaut

spaceship *NOUN* **spaceships**
a spacecraft, especially one carrying people

space shuttle *NOUN* **space shuttles**
a spacecraft for repeated use to and from outer space

space station *NOUN* **space stations**
a satellite which orbits the earth and is used as a base by scientists and astronauts

space suit *NOUN* **space suits**
a protective suit which enables an astronaut to survive in space

space walk *NOUN* **space walks**
moving about or walking by an astronaut outside the spacecraft

spacewoman *NOUN* **spacewomen**
a female astronaut

spacious *ADJECTIVE*
providing a lot of space; roomy
▷ **spaciousness** *NOUN*

spade❶ *NOUN* **spades**
a tool with a long handle and a wide blade for digging

spade❷ *NOUN* **spades**
a playing card with black shapes like upside-down hearts on it, each with a short stem

spadework *NOUN*
hard or uninteresting work done to prepare for an activity or project

spaghetti *NOUN*
pasta made in long thin sticks, which soften into strings when cooked

WORD HISTORY an Italian word meaning 'little strings'

spam ***NOUN***
1 (*trademark*) tinned meat made mainly from ham
2 (*ICT*) unwanted messages sent on the Internet to a large number of users

span ***NOUN*** **spans**
1 the length from end to end or across something
2 the part between two uprights of an arch or bridge
3 the length of a period of time
4 the distance from the tip of the thumb to the tip of the little finger when the hand is spread out

span ***VERB*** **spans, spanning, spanned**
to reach from one side or end to the other ◆ *An ancient archway spans the path.*

spangle ***NOUN*** **spangles**
a small piece of glittering material
▷ **spangled** ***ADJECTIVE***

spaniel ***NOUN*** **spaniels**
a kind of dog with long ears and silky fur

Spanish ***ADJECTIVE***
to do with Spain or its people

Spanish ***NOUN***
the language of Spain, also used as a first language in some other countries

Spanish words in English

Many words of **Spanish** origin which are used in English relate to aspects of Spanish culture. The musical and religious traditions of Spain have given us *castanets* (from a Spanish word meaning 'chestnuts'), *fiesta*, and *flamenco* (which meant, originally, 'Flemish'); and *tango* was borrowed directly from Latin American Spanish. Several words for Spanish food are now familiar in English, such as *tortilla* (literally 'little cake') and *tapas* (from a Spanish word meaning 'cover' or 'lid'). Another area of borrowing is for geographical terms, such as *canyon*, *savannah*, *sierra* (which came via Spanish from a Latin word meaning 'a saw'), and *tornado*.

The Spanish exploration of the Americas also meant that several words from South American languages entered English via Spanish: for example, *avocado*, *potato*, *puma*, *tobacco*, and *tomato*.

spank ***VERB*** **spanks, spanking, spanked**
to smack a person several times on the bottom as a punishment

spanking ***ADJECTIVE***
brisk and lively ◆ *The horse tossed its head and went off at a spanking pace.*

spanner ***NOUN*** **spanners**
a tool for gripping and turning a nut or bolt

spar¹ ***NOUN*** **spars**
a strong pole used for a mast or boom on a ship

spar² ***VERB*** **spars, sparring, sparred**
1 to practise boxing or fighting

> Daily I sparred with sword and spear against Father, against Kay, against anyone who would teach me more. — *Michael Morpurgo, Arthur, High King of Britain*

2 to quarrel or argue

spare ***VERB*** **spares, sparing, spared**
1 to afford to give or do without something ◆ *Can you spare five pounds?* ◆ *I couldn't spare the time to go and see them that evening.*
2 to be merciful towards someone; to refrain from hurting or harming a person or thing
3 to avoid making a person suffer something ◆ *I'll spare you any further worry.*
4 to use or treat something economically ◆ *No expense was spared to make the house look smart.*
to spare left over without being needed ◆ *We finished with just a few minutes to spare.*

spare ***ADJECTIVE***
1 not used but kept ready in case it is needed; extra
2 thin or lean
to go spare (*informal*) is to become very angry
▷ **sparely** ***ADVERB***
▷ **spareness** ***NOUN***

spare time ***NOUN***
time not needed for work

sparing (*say* **spair**- ing) ***ADJECTIVE***
careful or economical; not wasteful
▷ **sparingly** ***ADVERB***

spark ***NOUN*** **sparks**
1 a tiny glowing particle
2 a flash produced electrically
3 a trace ◆ *There was hardly a spark of enthusiasm in any of them.*

spark ***VERB*** **sparks, sparking, sparked**
to give off a spark or sparks

sparking plug ***NOUN*** **sparking plugs**
a spark plug

sparkle ***VERB*** **sparkles, sparkling, sparkled**
1 to shine with tiny flashes of light
2 to show brilliant wit or liveliness
▷ **sparkle** ***NOUN***

sparkler ***NOUN*** **sparklers**
a hand-held firework that gives off sparks

sparkling wine ***NOUN*** **sparkling wines**
a bubbly wine

spark plug ***NOUN*** **spark plugs**
a device that makes a spark to ignite the fuel in an engine

sparrow ***NOUN*** **sparrows**
a small brown bird

sparse ***ADJECTIVE***
thinly scattered; not numerous
▷ **sparsely** ***ADVERB***
▷ **sparseness** ***NOUN***

a b c d e f g h i j k l m n o p q r s t u v w x y z

spartan *ADJECTIVE*
simple and without comfort or luxuries
WORD HISTORY named after the people of *Sparta* in ancient Greece, who were famous for their hardiness

spasm *NOUN* **spasms**
1 a sudden involuntary movement of a muscle
2 a sudden brief spell of activity

spasmodic *ADJECTIVE*
1 happening or done at irregular intervals
2 to do with or caused by a spasm
▷ **spasmodically** *ADVERB*

spastic *NOUN* **spastics**
a person suffering from spasms of the muscles and jerky movements, especially caused by cerebral palsy
▷ **spastic** *ADJECTIVE*
USAGE NOTE This word can be offensive to some people. It is better to use *person with cerebral palsy* instead.

spat❶ *past tense of* **spit❶**

spat❷ *NOUN* **spats**
a short gaiter

spate *NOUN* **spates**
1 a lot of things or events coming one after another ◆ *There has been a spate of thefts recently.*
2 a sudden flood in a river

spathe (*rhymes with* bathe) *NOUN* **spathes**
a large petal-like part of a flower, round a central spike

spatial *ADJECTIVE*
to do with space

spatter *VERB* **spatters, spattering, spattered**
1 to scatter something wet in small drops
2 to splash something or someone
▷ **spatter** *NOUN*

spatula *NOUN* **spatulas**
a tool like a knife with a broad blunt flexible blade, used for spreading or mixing things

spawn *NOUN*
1 the eggs of fish, frogs, toads, or shellfish
2 the thread-like matter from which fungi grow

spawn *VERB* **spawns, spawning, spawned**
1 to produce spawn
2 to be produced from spawn
3 to produce something in large numbers

spay *VERB* **spays, spaying, spayed**
to sterilize a female animal by removing the ovaries (SEE ALSO **castrate**)

speak *VERB* **speaks, speaking, spoke, spoken**
1 to say something; to talk
2 to talk or be able to talk in a foreign language
to speak up is to speak more loudly or assertively

speaker *NOUN* **speakers**
1 a person who is speaking
2 someone who makes a speech
3 a loudspeaker
the Speaker the person who controls the debates in the House of Commons or a similar assembly

spear *NOUN* **spears**
a weapon for throwing or stabbing, with a long shaft and a pointed tip

spear *VERB* **spears, spearing, speared**
to pierce something with a spear or with something pointed

spearhead *VERB* **spearheads, spearheading, spearheaded**
to lead an attacking or advancing force

spearmint *NOUN*
mint used in cookery and for flavouring chewing gum

special *ADJECTIVE*
1 not ordinary or usual; exceptional
2 meant for a particular person or purpose ◆ *The pegs require special tools to fit them properly.*

special effects *PLURAL NOUN*
illusions created for films or television by using props, trick photography, or computer images

specialist *NOUN* **specialists**
an expert in a particular subject

speciality *NOUN* **specialities**
1 something in which a person specializes
2 a special product, especially a food

specialize *VERB* **specializes, specializing, specialized**
to give particular attention or study to one subject or thing
▷ **specialization** *NOUN*
USAGE NOTE This word can also be spelled specialise.

specially *ADVERB*
1 in a special way
2 for a special purpose

How do you drink with such a nose? You ought to have a cup made specially. — Edmond Rostand, *Cyrano de Bergerac*

special needs *PLURAL NOUN*
educational requirements resulting from learning difficulties, physical disability, or emotional and behavioural difficulties

species (*say* spee- shiz) *NOUN* **species**
1 a group of animals or plants that are very similar
2 a kind or sort ◆ *a species of sledge*

specific *ADJECTIVE*
definite or precise; to do with a particular thing ◆ *The project called for specific tasks to be completed.*
▷ **specifically** *ADVERB*

specification *NOUN* **specifications**
(*D & T*) a detailed description of how to make or do something

specific gravity *NOUN* **specific gravities**
relative density

specify *VERB* **specifies, specifying, specified**
to name or list things precisely ◆ *The contract specifies how many hours you have to work.*
▷ **specification** *NOUN*

specimen *NOUN* **specimens**
1 a sample
2 an example ◆ *They sat under a fine specimen of a walnut tree.*

specious (*say* **spee**- shus) *ADJECTIVE*
a specious argument or specious reasoning seems good but lacks real value

speck *NOUN* **specks**
a small spot or particle

speckle *NOUN* **speckles**
a small spot or mark
▷ **speckled** *ADJECTIVE*

specs *PLURAL NOUN*
(*informal*) spectacles

spectacle *NOUN* **spectacles**
1 an impressive sight or display
2 a ridiculous sight

WORD FAMILY *Spectacle* comes from the Latin word *specere* meaning 'to look'. Other looking words having the same origin include *inspector*, *spectator*, *special* (originally = 'of a particular appearance'), *speculate* (originally = 'to keep watch'), and *expect* (literally 'to look out for something').

spectacles *PLURAL NOUN*
a pair of glasses
▷ **spectacled** *ADJECTIVE*

spectacular *ADJECTIVE*
impressive or striking

spectator *NOUN* **spectators**
a person who watches a game, show, or other event

spectre *NOUN* **spectres**
a ghost
▷ **spectral** *ADJECTIVE*

spectrum *NOUN* **spectra**
1 the bands of colours seen in a rainbow
2 (*Art*) a range of colours used in painting
3 a wide range of ideas or opinions

speculate *VERB* **speculates, speculating, speculated**
1 to form opinions without having any definite evidence
2 to invest in stocks or property in the hope of making a profit but with the risk of loss
▷ **speculation** *NOUN*
▷ **speculator** *NOUN*
▷ **speculative** *ADJECTIVE*

sped *past tense of* **speed**

speech *NOUN* **speeches**
1 the action or power of speaking
2 a talk to an audience
3 (*Drama*) a group of lines spoken by a character in a play

speechless *ADJECTIVE*
too surprised or emotional to be able to say anything
▷ **speechlessly** *ADVERB*

speech marks *PLURAL NOUN*
(*Grammar*) punctuation marks used to show direct speech. Also called *inverted commas.*

speed *NOUN* **speeds**
1 a measure of the time in which something moves or happens
2 quickness or swiftness
at speed rapidly; quickly

speed *VERB* **speeds, speeding, sped** (in senses 2 and 3 **speeded**)
1 to go quickly
2 to drive faster than a legal limit
3 to speed up is to become quicker, and to speed something up is to make it move or happen faster
▷ **speeding** *NOUN*

speedboat *NOUN* **speedboats**
a fast motor boat

speed camera *NOUN* **speed cameras**
a camera by the side of a road which automatically takes pictures of vehicles that break the speed limit

speed hump *NOUN* **speed humps**
a ridge built across a road to make vehicles slow down

speed limit *NOUN* **speed limits**
the maximum speed at which vehicles may legally travel on a particular road

speedometer *NOUN* **speedometers**
a device in a vehicle, showing its speed

speedway *NOUN* **speedways**
a track for motorcycle racing

speedwell *NOUN* **speedwells**
a wild plant with small blue flowers

speedy *ADJECTIVE* **speedier, speediest**
quick or swift
▷ **speedily** *ADVERB*

speleology (*say* spel- ee- **ol**- o- jee) *NOUN*
the exploration and study of caves

spell❶ *NOUN* **spells**
a saying or action supposed to have magical power

spell❷ *NOUN* **spells**
1 a period of time
2 a period of a certain work or activity

a b c d e f g h i j k l m n o p q r s t u v w x y z

SPELLING NOTE Some words pronounced **s**- begin with **ce**- (e.g. cent), **ci**- (e.g. city), or **cy**- (e.g. cymbal)

spell ❸ *VERB* **spells, spelling, spelled** or **spelt**
1 to put letters in the right order to make a word or words
2 to form a word
3 to have as a result ◆ *The new housing spells excellent news for the community.*
▷ **speller** *NOUN*

spellbound *ADJECTIVE*
entranced as if by a magic spell

spellchecker or **spellcheck** *NOUN* **spellcheckers** or **spellchecks**
(*ICT*) a computer program that checks the spelling of words in a text file and reports any errors or corrects them automatically

spelling *NOUN*
the way a word is spelled

> ***spelling***
>
> In English there is often more than one way to represent the same sound. For example, the sound 'f' can be spelled either *f* or *ph* (words spelled *ph* are usually of Greek origin); and the sound 'oo' can be represented by *oo*, *ew* (as in *chew*), *ue* (as in *clue*), *ui* (as in *suit*), or *ough* (as in *through*).
> Some words have changed their pronunciation over time, so that their **spelling** no longer matches the way they are spoken: for example, words with a silent letter, like *gnome*, *knight*, *mnemonic*, *rhubarb*, and *thumb*; and words in which a letter is now often missed in pronunciation, like *cemetery*, *extraordinary*, *February*, *handkerchief*, *jewellery*, *library*, and *temperature*. The words *diphthong* and *minuscule* are sometimes mispronounced (*dip-* and *mini-*) and are therefore spelled incorrectly.
> The following words can also cause problems in spelling: *eighth*, *gauge*, *niece*, *seize*, *weird*, and words with double letters such as *accommodate*, *exaggerate*, *necessary*, *occasion*, and *success*. Note also the spellings of the following words, which are not obvious from the way you say them: *berserk*, *catarrh*, *diarrhoea*, *dinghy*, *jeopardize*, *length*, *meringue*, *posthumous*, and *silhouette*.
> Many verbs can end in either *-ize* or *-ise* (e.g. *finalize* or *finalise*). However, *advertise*, *exercise*, *revise*, *supervise*, *televise*, and some other words ending in *-cise* and *-vise* are always spelled with s.
> See also the panels on **American spelling** and **pronunciation**.

spend *VERB* **spends, spending, spent**
1 to use money to pay for things
2 to use up time in doing something ◆ *David spent long summer days at the local swimming pool.*
3 to pass time doing something ◆ *She decided to live there, where they had spent many happy holidays.*

spendthrift *NOUN* **spendthrifts**
a person who spends money extravagantly and wastefully

sperm *NOUN* **sperms** or **sperm**
1 male semen
2 a spermatozoon

spermatozoon (*say* sper- ma- toh- **zoe**- on) *NOUN* **spermatozoa**
the male cell that fuses with an ovum to produce offspring

spew *VERB* **spews, spewing, spewed**
1 to vomit
2 to send out something unpleasant in a stream ◆ *Four great chimneys spewed out their fumes into the grey clouds.*

sphere *NOUN* **spheres**
1 a perfectly round solid shape; the shape of a ball
2 a field of activity or interest
▷ **spherical** *ADJECTIVE*

spheroid *NOUN* **spheroids**
a solid which is sphere-like but not perfectly spherical

sphinx *NOUN* **sphinxes**
a stone statue with the body of a lion and a human head, especially the huge one (almost 5,000 years old) in Egypt

spice *NOUN* **spices**
1 a strong-tasting substance used to flavour food, often made from dried parts of plants
2 something that adds interest or excitement
▷ **spicy** *ADJECTIVE*

spice *VERB* **spices, spicing, spiced**
1 to flavour food with spices
2 to make something more interesting or exciting

spick and span *ADJECTIVE*
neat and clean

spider *NOUN* **spiders**
a small animal with eight legs that spins webs to catch insects on which it feeds

WORD FAMILY A related word (*technical*) is arachnid.

spidery *ADJECTIVE*
having long thin lines and sharp angles, like a spider's legs

spike *NOUN* **spikes**
a pointed piece of metal; a sharp point
▷ **spiky** *ADJECTIVE*

spike *VERB* **spikes, spiking, spiked**
1 to put spikes on something
2 to pierce with a spike
to spike someone's guns is to spoil their plans

spill *VERB* **spills, spilling, spilt** or **spilled**
1 to let something fall out of a container, especially by accident
2 to tumble or flow freely

> Light spilled into the shaft as smoke wafted out of it. — *Garth Nix, The Creature in the Case*

3 to reveal confidential or personal information
▷ **spillage** *NOUN*

spill *NOUN* **spills**
1 spilling; something spilt
2 a fall from a horse or bicycle

spin *VERB* **spins, spinning, spun**
1 to turn round and round quickly
2 to make raw wool or cotton into threads by pulling and twisting its fibres
3 a spider or silkworm spins a web or cocoon when it forms one with threads from its body

to spin a yarn is to tell a long fanciful story
to spin something out is to make it last as long as possible

spin *NOUN* **spins**
1 a spinning movement
2 a short outing in a car
3 a favourable bias or slant given to a news story

spinach *NOUN*
a vegetable with dark green leaves

spinal *ADJECTIVE*
to do with the spine

spinal cord *NOUN* **spinal cords**
the thick cord of nerves enclosed in the spine, that carries impulses to and from the brain

spindle *NOUN* **spindles**
1 a thin rod on which thread is wound
2 a pin or bar that turns round or on which something turns

spindly *ADJECTIVE*
thin and long or tall

spin doctor *NOUN* **spin doctors**
a person whose job is to make information or events seem favourable to an employer, usually a politician or political party

spin-drier *NOUN* **spin-driers**
a machine in which washed clothes are spun round and round to dry them

spindrift *NOUN*
spray blown along the surface of the sea

spine *NOUN* **spines**
1 the line of bones down the middle of the back
2 a thorn or prickle
3 the back part of a book where the pages are joined together

WORD FAMILY Related technical words are vertebra and vertebrate.

spine-chilling *ADJECTIVE*
frightening and exciting

spineless *ADJECTIVE*
1 without a backbone
2 lacking in determination or strength of character

spinet (*say* spi- **net**) *NOUN* **spinets**
a small harpsichord

spinney *NOUN* **spinneys**
a small wood or thicket

spinning wheel *NOUN* **spinning wheels**
a household device for spinning fibre into thread

spin-off *NOUN* **spin-offs**
something extra produced while making something else

spinster *NOUN* **spinsters**
a woman who has not married

WORD HISTORY from an earlier meaning 'one who spins' (because many unmarried women used to earn their living by spinning, which could be done at home)

spiny *ADJECTIVE*
covered with spines; prickly

spiral *ADJECTIVE*
going round and round a central point and becoming gradually closer to it or further from it; twisting continually round a central line or cylinder
▷ **spirally** *ADVERB*

spiral *NOUN* **spirals**
a spiral line or course

spiral *VERB* **spirals, spiralling, spiralled**
1 to move in a spiral
2 to increase or decrease continuously and quickly

spire *NOUN* **spires**
a tall pointed part on top of a church tower

spirit *NOUN* **spirits**
1 (*Religion*) the part of a person that is thought to survive death; a person's soul
2 a person's mood or mind and feelings ◆ *I had never seen her in such high spirits.*
3 a ghost or a supernatural being
4 courage or liveliness ◆ *Alice responded with spirit.*
5 a kind of quality in something

Humphrey had not that spirit of chivalry possessed by Edward. He was a younger son, and had to earn, in a way, his own fortune. — *Captain Marryat, The Children of the New Forest*

6 a strong distilled alcoholic drink

spirit *VERB* **spirits, spiriting, spirited**
to spirit someone or something away is to carry them off quickly and secretly

WORD FAMILY *Spirit* comes from the Latin word *spirare* meaning 'to breathe'. Other words connected with breathing (some only loosely) and having the same origin include *aspire, conspire, inspire, perspire, respiration, spiritual,* and *transpire.*

spirited *ADJECTIVE*
brave; self-confident and lively

spirit level *NOUN* **spirit levels**
a device consisting of a tube of liquid with an air bubble in it, used to find out whether something is level

spiritual *ADJECTIVE*
1 to do with the human soul; not physical
2 (*Religion*) to do with religion
▷ **spiritually** *ADVERB*
▷ **spirituality** *NOUN*

spiritual *NOUN* **spirituals**
a religious folk song, originally sung by black Christians in America

spiritualism *NOUN*
the belief that the spirits of dead people communicate with living people
▷ **spiritualist** *NOUN*

spit ❶ *VERB* **spits, spitting, spat** or **spit**
1 to send out drops of liquid forcibly from the mouth
2 to fall lightly as rain

spit *NOUN*
saliva or spittle

spit ❷ *NOUN* **spits**
1 a long thin metal spike put through meat to hold it while it is being roasted
2 a narrow strip of land sticking out into the sea

spite *NOUN*
a desire to hurt or annoy somebody
in spite of not being prevented by ◆ *The project is succeeding in spite of setbacks.*

spite *VERB* **spites, spiting, spited**
to hurt or annoy somebody from spite

spiteful *ADJECTIVE*
a spiteful person or act tries to hurt or annoy someone
▷ **spitefully** *ADVERB*

spitfire *NOUN* **spitfires**
a fiery-tempered person

spitting image *NOUN*
an exact likeness

spittle *NOUN*
saliva, especially when it is spat out

spittoon *NOUN* **spittoons**
a receptacle for people to spit into

splash *VERB* **splashes, splashing, splashed**
1 to make liquid fly about in drops
2 liquid splashes when it flies about in drops
3 to make something or someone wet by splashing

splash *NOUN* **splashes**
1 the action or sound or mark of splashing
2 a bright patch of colour or light
to make a splash is to attract a lot of attention

splatter *VERB* **splatters, splattering, splattered**
to splash noisily

splay *VERB* **splays, splaying, splayed**
to spread or slope apart

spleen *NOUN* **spleens**
an organ of the body, close to the stomach, that helps to keep the blood in good condition
to vent your spleen on someone is to be bad-tempered or spiteful towards them

splendid *ADJECTIVE*
1 magnificent; full of splendour
2 excellent; very fine
▷ **splendidly** *ADVERB*

splendour *NOUN*
a brilliant display or appearance

splice *VERB* **splices, splicing, spliced**
1 to join pieces of rope or line by twisting their strands together
2 to join pieces of film, tape, or wood by overlapping the ends

splint *NOUN* **splints**
a straight piece of rigid material tied to a broken arm or leg to hold it firm

splint *VERB* **splints, splinting, splinted**
to hold something with a splint

splinter *NOUN* **splinters**
a thin sharp piece of hard material such as wood or glass broken off a larger piece

splinter *VERB* **splinters, splintering, splintered**
to break into splinters

splinter group *NOUN* **splinter groups**
a group of people that has broken away from a larger group or movement

split *VERB* **splits, splitting, split**
1 to break apart, especially along the length of something
2 to divide something into parts

People decided to split the day into two halves called 'before meridian' and 'after meridian', but irritatingly for us they did it in Latin. — *Kjartan Poskitt, Murderous Maths*

3 to divide something among a group
to split up
1 is to end a marriage or other relationship
2 is to go off in different directions

split *NOUN* **splits**
1 the splitting or dividing of something
2 a place where something has split
the splits an acrobatic position in which the legs are stretched widely in opposite directions

split second *NOUN*
a very brief moment of time; an instant

split-second *ADJECTIVE*
1 very quick
2 very precise

splodge *NOUN* **splodges**
a dirty mark or stain

splurge *VERB* **splurges, splurging, splurged**
(*informal*) to spend a lot of money on something extravagant

splutter *VERB* **splutters, spluttering, spluttered**
1 to make a quick series of spitting sounds
2 to speak quickly but not clearly
▷ **splutter** *NOUN*

spoil *VERB* **spoils, spoiling, spoilt** or **spoiled**
1 to damage something and make it useless or unsatisfactory
2 to make someone selfish by always letting them have what they want
3 to treat someone kindly or indulgently

spoils *PLURAL NOUN*
plunder taken by the victor in war

spoilsport *NOUN* **spoilsports**
a person who spoils other people's enjoyment of things

spoke ❶ *NOUN* **spokes**
each of the bars or rods that go from the centre of a wheel to its rim

spoke ❷ *past tense of* **speak**

spokesman *NOUN* **spokesmen**
a spokesperson, especially a man

spokesperson *NOUN* **spokespersons**
a person who speaks on behalf of a group of people

spokeswoman *NOUN* **spokeswomen**
a female spokesperson

spoliation *NOUN*
the act of pillaging or plundering

sponge *NOUN* **sponges**
1 a sea creature with a soft porous body
2 the skeleton of this creature, or a piece of a similar substance, used for washing or padding things
3 a soft lightweight cake or pudding
▷ **spongy** *ADJECTIVE*

sponge *VERB* **sponges, sponging, sponged**
1 to wipe or wash something with a sponge
2 to sponge off people is to get money or food from them without giving anything in return
▷ **sponger** *NOUN*

sponsor *NOUN* **sponsors**
1 a person or organization that provides money for an arts or sports event or for a broadcast in return for advertising
2 someone who gives money to a charity in return for something achieved by another person
▷ **sponsorship** *NOUN*

sponsor *VERB* **sponsors, sponsoring, sponsored**
to be a sponsor for a person or thing

spontaneous (*say* spon- **tay**- nee- us) *ADJECTIVE*
happening or done naturally; not forced or suggested by someone else

That last evening, there was a spontaneous party outside the café, brought on, I think, by relief that the film was finished. — *Michael Morpurgo, The Dancing Bear*

▷ **spontaneously** *ADVERB*
▷ **spontaneity** *NOUN*

spoof *NOUN* **spoofs**
1 an amusing imitation; a parody
2 a joke or hoax

WORD HISTORY originally a card game invented and named by an English comedian, Arthur Roberts (1852–1933)

spook *NOUN* **spooks**
(*informal*) a ghost

spooky *ADJECTIVE* **spookier, spookiest**
(*informal*) ghostly or weird
▷ **spookiness** *NOUN*

spool *NOUN* **spools**
a rod or cylinder on which something is wound

spoon *NOUN* **spoons**
a small device with a rounded bowl on a handle, used for lifting things to the mouth or for stirring or measuring things
▷ **spoonful** *NOUN* **spoonfuls**

spoon *VERB* **spoons, spooning, spooned**
to take or lift something with a spoon

I spooned pasta and mince into my mouth, smiling as I chewed. — *Malorie Blackman, Noughts and Crosses*

WORD HISTORY from Old English *spon*, originally 'a chip of wood'

spoonerism *NOUN* **spoonerisms**
an expression in which the initial letters of two words are accidentally swapped, e.g. by saying *the town drain* instead of *the down train*

WORD HISTORY named after the Reverend William *Spooner* (1844–1930), who often made slips of this kind

spoon-feed *VERB* **spoon-feeds, spoon-feeding, spoon-fed**
1 to feed a baby or invalid with a spoon
2 to provide someone with so much help or information that they do not need to make any effort

spoor *NOUN*
the track left by an animal

WORD HISTORY an Afrikaans word, from Dutch *spor*

sporadic *ADJECTIVE*
happening or found at irregular intervals; scattered
▷ **sporadically** *ADVERB*

spore *NOUN* **spores**
a tiny reproductive cell of a plant such as a fungus or fern

sporran *NOUN* **sporrans**
a pouch worn in front of a kilt

WORD HISTORY via Scottish Gaelic from Latin *bursa* 'purse'

sport *NOUN* **sports**
1 a sport is an athletic activity or game, especially outdoors
2 sport is games of this kind
3 (*informal*) a sport is someone who behaves well when they are defeated or teased

sport *VERB* **sports, sporting, sported**
1 to play; to amuse yourself
2 to wear something conspicuously

sporting *ADJECTIVE*
1 connected with sport; interested in sport
2 behaving fairly and generously

sporting chance *NOUN* **sporting chances**
a reasonable chance of success

sports car *NOUN* **sports cars**
an open low-built fast car

sports jacket *NOUN* **sports jackets**
a man's jacket for informal wear (not part of a suit)

sportsman *NOUN* **sportsmen**
1 a man who takes part in sport
2 a person who shows sportsmanship

sportsmanship *NOUN*
sporting behaviour; behaving fairly and generously to rivals

sportswoman *NOUN* **sportswomen**
1 a woman who takes part in sport
2 a woman who shows sportsmanship

spot *NOUN* **spots**
1 a small round mark
2 a pimple
3 a small amount ◆ *We had a spot of trouble.*
4 a place described in some way

> I strolled away from the vans and tents and found a secluded spot around the side of the old mill. — *Darren Shan, Tunnels of Blood*

5 a drop of rain

on the spot
1 without delay; immediately ◆ *She paid for it on the spot and took it home.*
2 to put someone on the spot is to make them have to take action

spot on (*informal*) exactly right or accurate

spot *VERB* **spots, spotting, spotted**
1 to mark something with spots
2 to notice or recognize someone
3 to watch for things of a special kind and take note of them, as a hobby

▷ **spotter** *NOUN*

spot check *NOUN* **spot checks**
a check, usually without warning, on one of a group of people or things

spotless *ADJECTIVE*
perfectly clean

spotlight *NOUN* **spotlights**
1 a strong light that can shine on one small area
2 to be in the spotlight is to get a lot of public attention

spotty *ADJECTIVE*
marked with spots

spouse *NOUN* **spouses**
a person's husband or wife

spout *NOUN* **spouts**
1 a pipe or similar opening from which liquid can pour
2 a jet of liquid

spout *VERB* **spouts, spouting, spouted**
1 to come out as a jet of liquid
2 (*informal*) to speak for a long time

sprain *VERB* **sprains, spraining, sprained**
to injure a joint by twisting it

▷ **sprain** *NOUN*

sprat *NOUN* **sprats**
a small edible fish

sprawl *VERB* **sprawls, sprawling, sprawled**
1 to sit or lie with the arms and legs spread out loosely
2 to spread out loosely or untidily

> I jumped full at the man, overturning the stool and sending him sprawling. — *John Wyndham, The Chrysalids*

▷ **sprawl** *NOUN*

spray[1] *VERB* **sprays, spraying, sprayed**
to scatter tiny drops of liquid over something

spray *NOUN* **sprays**
1 tiny drops of liquid sent through the air
2 a device for spraying liquid
3 a liquid for spraying

spray[2] *NOUN* **sprays**
1 a single shoot with its leaves and flowers
2 a small bunch of flowers

spread *VERB* **spreads, spreading, spread**
1 to open or stretch something out to its full size ◆ *He spread the map on the table.*
2 to make something cover a surface ◆ *We can spread butter on our bread.*
3 to become longer or wider ◆ *A blush spread over his face.*
4 to become more widely known or distributed, or to cause something to do this ◆ *People were accused of spreading rumours.* ◆ *The story spread rapidly.*

spread *NOUN* **spreads**
1 the action or result of spreading
2 a thing's breadth or extent
3 a paste for spreading on bread
4 (*informal*) a large or grand meal

spreadeagled *ADJECTIVE*
with arms and legs stretched out

WORD HISTORY originally *spread eagle*, a picture of an eagle with legs and wings stretched out, used as an emblem on a sign or shield

spreadsheet *NOUN* **spreadsheets**
(*ICT*) a computer program for handling figures and other information, displayed in a table

spree *NOUN* **sprees**
a period of fun doing something you like

sprig ***NOUN*** **sprigs**
a small branch or shoot

sprightly ***ADJECTIVE*** **sprightlier, sprightliest**
lively and full of energy

spring ***VERB*** **springs, springing, sprang, sprung**
1 to jump or move quickly or suddenly ◆ *She sprang to her feet and went to look in the mirror.*
2 to originate, arise, or grow ◆ *Weeds were springing up everywhere.* ◆ *Their love of skiing and the mountains had sprung from their father.*
3 to spring a surprise is to do something completely unexpected

spring ***NOUN*** **springs**
1 a springy coil or bent piece of metal
2 a springing movement
3 a place where water comes up naturally from the ground
4 the season when most plants begin to grow

springboard ***NOUN*** **springboards**
a springy board from which people jump in diving and gymnastics

springbok ***NOUN*** **springboks** or **springbok**
a South African gazelle

WORD HISTORY an Afrikaans word, from Dutch *springen* 'to spring' and *bok* 'buck, antelope'

spring-clean ***VERB*** **spring-cleans, spring-cleaning, spring-cleaned**
to clean a house thoroughly in springtime

spring onion ***NOUN*** **spring onions**
a small onion with a long green stem, eaten raw in salads

spring roll ***NOUN*** **spring rolls**
a Chinese pancake filled with vegetables and (sometimes) meat, and fried until crisp

springtime ***NOUN***
the season of spring

springy ***ADJECTIVE*** **springier, springiest**
able to spring back easily after being bent or squeezed
▷ **springiness** ***NOUN***

sprinkle ***VERB*** **sprinkles, sprinkling, sprinkled**
to make tiny drops or pieces fall on something
▷ **sprinkler** ***NOUN***

sprinkling ***NOUN*** **sprinklings**
a few here and there; a small amount

sprint ***VERB*** **sprints, sprinting, sprinted**
to run very fast for a short distance

> The lad in black was only a step ahead of Robbie, ... sprinting across the patchy lawn to the next fence, head down all the way. — *Keith Gray, Warehouse*

▷ **sprint** ***NOUN***
▷ **sprinter** ***NOUN***

sprite ***NOUN*** **sprites**
an elf, fairy, or goblin

sprocket ***NOUN*** **sprockets**
each of the row of teeth round a wheel, fitting into links on a chain

sprout ***VERB*** **sprouts, sprouting, sprouted**
to start to grow; to put out shoots

sprout ***NOUN*** **sprouts**
1 a shoot of a plant
2 a Brussels sprout

spruce ❶ ***NOUN*** **spruces**
a kind of fir tree

WORD HISTORY from *Pruce*, the old name for Prussia in central Europe, where it was grown

spruce ❷ ***ADJECTIVE***
neat and trim; smart

spruce ***VERB*** **spruces, sprucing, spruced**
to smarten something or someone

WORD HISTORY probably from *spruce leather*, leather from Pruce (the old name for Prussia)

spry ***ADJECTIVE*** **spryer, spryest**
lively

spud ***NOUN*** **spuds**
(*informal*) a potato

spume ***NOUN***
froth or foam

spur ***NOUN*** **spurs**
1 a sharp device worn on the heel of a rider's boot to urge a horse to go faster
2 something shaped like a spur, such as a hard spike on the back of a cock's leg or a thin spike on a flower
3 a stimulus or incentive
4 a ridge that sticks out from a mountain
on the spur of the moment on an impulse; without planning or preparation

spur ***VERB*** **spurs, spurring, spurred**
to urge someone on; to encourage someone

spurious ***ADJECTIVE***
not genuine

spurn ***VERB*** **spurns, spurning, spurned**
to reject someone or something scornfully

spurt ***VERB*** **spurts, spurting, spurted**
1 to gush out

> I suddenly found tears spurting down my face. I put my head in my hands, scared they'd call me a baby. — *Jacqueline Wilson, Clean Break*

2 to increase your speed suddenly

spurt ***NOUN*** **spurts**
1 a sudden gush
2 a sudden increase in speed or effort

sputter ***VERB*** **sputters, sputtering, sputtered**
to splutter
▷ **sputter** ***NOUN***

SPELLING NOTE Some words pronounced **s-** begin with **ce-** (e.g. cent), **ci-** (e.g. city), or **cy-** (e.g. cymbal)

sputum *NOUN*
saliva or phlegm

spy *NOUN* **spies**
a person who works for one country or organization to collect and report secret information about another

spy *VERB* **spies, spying, spied**
1 to be a spy
2 to spy on someone is to watch them secretly and see what they do
3 to spy something is to see or notice it

spyware *NOUN*
(*ICT*) software that is secretly planted on a computer over the Internet and enables another user to get information remotely from that computer

squabble *VERB* **squabbles, squabbling, squabbled**
to quarrel or bicker
▷ **squabble** *NOUN*

squad *NOUN* **squads**
a small group of people working or being trained together

squadron *NOUN* **squadrons**
part of an army, navy, or air force

squalid *ADJECTIVE*
dirty and unpleasant
▷ **squalidly** *ADVERB*

squall *NOUN* **squalls**
1 a sudden storm or gust of wind

The wind had been very changeable, with squalls of rain during the day, but now it came on sharp, driving sleet. — *Anna Sewell, Black Beauty*

2 a baby's loud cry
▷ **squally** *ADVERB*

squall *VERB* **squalls, squalling, squalled**
a baby squalls when it cries loudly

squalor *NOUN*
dirty and unpleasant conditions ◆ *An elderly woman and her son were living in squalor.*

squander *VERB* **squanders, squandering, squandered**
to spend money or time wastefully

square *NOUN* **squares**
1 a flat shape with four equal sides and four right angles
2 an area in a town or city, surrounded by buildings
3 (*Mathematics*) the result of multiplying a number by itself ◆ *16 is the square of 4* (4×4=16)

square *ADJECTIVE*
1 having the shape of a square
2 a square shape is one that forms a right angle
3 to be all square is to have an equal or even score or to be on equal terms
4 used to give the length of each side of a square shape or object ◆ *a room four metres square*
5 used to give a measurement of an area ◆ *an area of 100 square metres*
▷ **squareness** *NOUN*

square *VERB* **squares, squaring, squared**
1 to make a thing square
2 to multiply a number by itself ◆ *4 squared is 16*
3 to match something; to be consistent with something ◆ *Their version of what happened doesn't quite square with ours.*
4 to settle or pay a bill or debt

square deal *NOUN* **square deals**
a deal or arrangement that is honest and fair

squarely *ADVERB*
directly or exactly

Phileas Fogg was seated squarely in his armchair, his feet close together like those of a grenadier on parade, his hands resting on his knees, his body straight, his head erect. — *Jules Verne, Around the World in Eighty Days*

square meal *NOUN* **square meals**
a good satisfying meal

square root *NOUN* **square roots**
the number that gives a particular number if it is multiplied by itself ◆ *4 is the square root of 16*

squash[1] *VERB* **squashes, squashing, squashed**
1 to press something so that it becomes flat or out of shape
2 to force something into a small space; to pack something tightly
3 to suppress or quash information

squash *NOUN* **squashes**
1 a crowded condition
2 a fruit-flavoured soft drink
3 a game played with rackets and a soft ball in a special indoor court

squash[2] *NOUN* **squashes**
a kind of gourd used as a vegetable

squat *VERB* **squats, squatting, squatted**
1 to sit on your heels; to crouch
2 to live in an unoccupied building without permission
▷ **squat** *NOUN*
▷ **squatter** *NOUN*

squat *ADJECTIVE*
short and fat

squaw *NOUN* **squaws**
a North American Indian woman or wife

USAGE NOTE This word is now considered to be offensive.

squawk *VERB* **squawks, squawking, squawked**
to make a loud harsh cry
▷ **squawk** *NOUN*

a b c d e f g h i j k l m n o p q r s t u v w x y z

squeak *VERB* **squeaks, squeaking, squeaked**
to make a short high-pitched cry or sound
▷ **squeak** *NOUN*
▷ **squeaky** *ADJECTIVE*
▷ **squeakily** *ADVERB*

squeal *VERB* **squeals, squealing, squealed**
to make a long shrill cry or sound
▷ **squeal** *NOUN*

squeamish *ADJECTIVE*
easily disgusted or shocked
▷ **squeamishness** *NOUN*

squeeze *VERB* **squeezes, squeezing, squeezed**
1 to press something from opposite sides
2 to force your way into or through a narrow or confined place
▷ **squeezer** *NOUN*

squeeze *NOUN* **squeezes**
1 the action of squeezing
2 a drop of liquid squeezed out ◆ *Add some olive oil and a squeeze of lemon.*
3 a time when money is difficult to get or borrow

squelch *VERB* **squelches, squelching, squelched**
to make a sound like someone treading in thick mud
▷ **squelch** *NOUN*
▷ **squelchy** *ADJECTIVE*

squib *NOUN* **squibs**
a small firework that hisses and then explodes

squid *NOUN* **squids**
a sea animal with eight short tentacles and two long ones

squidgy *ADJECTIVE*
(*informal*) soft and slightly wet

squiggle *NOUN* **squiggles**
a short curly line

The signature was an illegible squiggle that appeared to be in Arabic script. — *Hans Magnus Enzensberger, The Number Devil*

squint *VERB* **squints, squinting, squinted**
1 to be cross-eyed
2 to peer; to look with half-shut eyes at something
▷ **squint** *NOUN*

squire *NOUN* **squires**
1 the man who owns most of the land in a country parish or district
2 a young nobleman in the Middle Ages who served a knight

squirm *VERB* **squirms, squirming, squirmed**
to wriggle about when you feel embarrassed or awkward

squirrel *NOUN* **squirrels**
a small animal with a bushy tail and red or grey fur, living in trees

WORD HISTORY from Greek *skiouros*, from *skia* 'shadow' and *oura* 'tail' (because its long bushy tail cast a shadow over its body and kept it cool)

squirt *VERB* **squirts, squirting, squirted**
to send liquid out in a jet
▷ **squirt** *NOUN*

St. or **St** *ABBREVIATION*
1 Saint
2 Street

stab *VERB* **stabs, stabbing, stabbed**
to pierce or wound someone with something sharp

stab *NOUN* **stabs**
1 the action of stabbing
2 a sharp pain or sensation ◆ *He felt a sudden stab of guilt.*
3 (*informal*) to have a stab at something is to try doing it

stability *NOUN*
the state or being stable or steady

stabilize *VERB* **stabilizes, stabilizing, stabilized**
to make something stable, or to become stable
▷ **stabilization** *NOUN*

USAGE NOTE This word can also be spelled stabilise.

stabilizer *NOUN* **stabilizers**
a device for keeping a vehicle or ship steady

USAGE NOTE This word can also be spelled stabiliser.

stable❶ *ADJECTIVE*
1 steady and firmly fixed or balanced
2 not likely to change or end suddenly ◆ *Children benefit from stable relationships within the family unit.*
3 sensible and dependable
▷ **stably** *ADVERB*

stable❷ *NOUN* **stables**
a building where horses are kept

stable *VERB* **stables, stabling, stabled**
to keep a horse in a stable

staccato *ADVERB, ADJECTIVE*
(*Music*) played with each note short and separate

WORD HISTORY an Italian word, from *distaccare* 'to detach'

stack *NOUN* **stacks**
1 a neat pile
2 a haystack
3 (*informal*) a large amount of something
4 a single tall chimney; a group of small chimneys

stack *VERB* **stacks, stacking, stacked**
to pile things up

stadium *NOUN* **stadiums**
a sports ground surrounded by seats for spectators

WORD HISTORY via Latin from Greek *stadion* 'stade', a unit of length equal to about 200 metres: it became the word for a running track because the one at Olympia in southern Greece was exactly one stade long

staff *NOUN* **staffs** or, in sense 4, **staves**
1 the people who work in an office or shop or other organization
2 the teachers in a school or college
3 a stick or pole used as a weapon or support or as a symbol of authority
4 a set of five horizontal lines on which music is written

staff *VERB* **staffs, staffing, staffed**
to provide a place or organization with a staff of people ◆ *The centre is staffed by a small team of unpaid workers.*

stag *NOUN* **stags**
a male deer

stage *NOUN* **stages**
1 (*Drama*) a platform for performances in a theatre or hall
2 a point or part of a process or journey
3 the stage is the profession of acting or working in the theatre

stage *VERB* **stages, staging, staged**
1 to present a performance on a stage
2 to organize and present something in public ◆ *Last night police staged a reconstruction of the incident.*

stagecoach *NOUN* **stagecoaches**
a horse-drawn coach that formerly ran regularly from one point to another along the same route

WORD HISTORY so called because it made its journey in stages, picking up passengers at points along the route

stage fright *NOUN*
fear or nervousness before or while performing to an audience

stage-manage *VERB* **stage-manages, stage-managing, stage-managed**
1 to be stage manager of a performance
2 to organize and control an event so that it has a particular effect

stage manager *NOUN* **stage managers**
the person in charge of the scenery, lighting, and other technical workings for a stage performance

stage-struck *ADJECTIVE*
loving the theatre and wishing to be an actor

stagger *VERB* **staggers, staggering, staggered**
1 to walk unsteadily

Seeing the visitors staggering towards the house with their bags, Hari went to help. — *Anita Desai, The Village by the Sea*

2 to be staggered by something is to be very surprised or shocked by it
3 to organize holidays or other commitments so that they do not all happen at the same time

▷ **stagger** *NOUN*
▷ **staggering** *ADJECTIVE*

stagnant *ADJECTIVE*
1 not flowing
2 activity is stagnant when there is not much of it happening

stagnate *VERB* **stagnates, stagnating, stagnated**
1 to be stagnant
2 to be dull through lack of activity or variety

▷ **stagnation** *NOUN*

staid *ADJECTIVE*
steady and serious in manner; sedate

stain *NOUN* **stains**
1 a dirty mark on something
2 a blemish on someone's character or past record
3 a liquid used for staining things

stain *VERB* **stains, staining, stained**
1 to make a stain on something

Autumn came and they picked bilberries on the mountain: tiny, purple fruit that stained their teeth and their clothes. — *Nina Bawden, Carrie's War*

2 to colour something with a liquid that sinks into the surface

stained glass *NOUN*
pieces of coloured glass held together in a lead framework to make a picture or pattern

stainless *ADJECTIVE*
without a stain

stainless steel *NOUN*
steel that does not rust easily

stair *NOUN* **stairs**
each of the fixed steps in a series that lead from one level or floor to another in a building

staircase *NOUN* **staircases**
a set of stairs

stairway *NOUN* **stairways**
a staircase

stairwell *NOUN* **stairwells**
the space going up through a building, which contains the stairs

stake ***NOUN*** **stakes**
1 a thick pointed stick to be driven into the ground
2 the post to which people used to be tied for execution by being burnt alive
3 an amount of money bet on something
4 an investment that gives a person a share or interest in a business or activity

at stake being risked

stake ***VERB*** **stakes, staking, staked**
1 to fasten, support, or mark something out with stakes
2 to bet or risk money on an event

to stake a claim is to claim or obtain a right to something

stalactite ***NOUN*** **stalactites**
a stony spike hanging like an icicle from the roof of a cave

WORD HISTORY from Greek *stalaktos* 'dripping'

stalagmite ***NOUN*** **stalagmites**
a stony spike standing like a pillar on the floor of a cave

WORD HISTORY from Greek *stalagma* 'a drop'

stale ***ADJECTIVE***
1 no longer fresh
2 bored and lacking new ideas because you have been doing something for too long

▷ **staleness** ***NOUN***

stalemate ***NOUN***
1 a drawn position in chess when a player cannot make a move without putting the king in check
2 a deadlock; a situation in which neither side in an argument will give way

stalk❶ ***NOUN*** **stalks**
a stem of a plant or fruit

stalk❷ ***VERB*** **stalks, stalking, stalked**
to track or hunt a person or animal stealthily

But the beast was in there too, and it was close behind. Phoenix could hear it shifting through the darkness, stalking him. — *Alan Gibbons, Shadow of the Minotaur*

stall ***NOUN*** **stalls**
1 a table or counter from which things are sold
2 a place for one animal in a stable or shed

stall ***VERB*** **stalls, stalling, stalled**
1 an engine or vehicle stalls when it fails and stops from lack of power
2 to delay things or avoid giving an answer to give yourself more time

stallion ***NOUN*** **stallions**
a male horse

stalls ***PLURAL NOUN***
the seats in the lowest level of a theatre

stalwart ***ADJECTIVE***
strong and determined

The crowd scattered as if by magic as two stalwart figures, armed with truncheons, came at a smart pace along the street. — *Kathleen Fidler, The Desperate Journey*

stamen ***NOUN*** **stamens**
the part of a flower bearing pollen

stamina ***NOUN***
strength and ability to endure pain or hard effort over a long time

stammer ***VERB*** **stammers, stammering, stammered**
to keep repeating the same syllables when you speak

▷ **stammer** ***NOUN***

stamp ***NOUN*** **stamps**
1 a small piece of gummed paper with a special design on it; a postage stamp
2 a small device for pressing words or marks on something; the words or marks made by this
3 a distinctive characteristic ◆ *Parliament is expected to give its stamp of approval to the decision.*

stamp ***VERB*** **stamps, stamping, stamped**
1 to bang your foot heavily on the ground
2 to walk with loud heavy steps
3 to fix a postage stamp on a letter or packet
4 to press a mark or design on something

to stamp something out is to put an end to a bad or unwelcome practice or activity

stampede ***NOUN*** **stampedes**
a sudden rush by animals or people

stampede ***VERB*** **stampedes, stampeding, stampeded**
to rush fast and wildly

stance ***NOUN*** **stances**
1 the way a person or animal stands
2 a person's attitude to something

stanchion ***NOUN*** **stanchions**
an upright bar or post forming a support

stand ***VERB*** **stands, standing, stood**
1 to be on your feet without moving; to rise to your feet
2 to be upright, or to place something in an upright position
3 an offer or arrangement stands when it stays the same
4 to stand for parliament or an election is to be a candidate in an election
5 to tolerate or endure something ◆ *How can you stand the noise?*
6 to stand someone something is to buy it for them ◆ *Let me stand you a drink.*

it stands to reason it is reasonable or obvious

to stand by is to be ready for action ▸▸

to stand for something
1 is to mean or represent it ◆ *The sign '&' stands for 'and'.* ◆ *Socialist parties stand for the redistribution of wealth.*
2 is to tolerate something
to stand in for someone is to take their place
to stand out is to be clear or obvious
to stand up for someone is to support or defend them
to stand up to someone is to refuse to be threatened by them

stand *NOUN* **stands**
1 something made for putting things on
2 a stall where things are sold or displayed
3 a building with a roof and rows of seats for spectators at a racecourse or sports ground
4 a standing position
to make a stand is to resist attack or criticism, or to maintain a point of view

standard *NOUN* **standards**
1 the level of quality that something reaches ◆ *A high standard of workmanship had been achieved.*
2 a thing used to measure or judge people or work by
3 a special or official flag
4 an upright support

standard *ADJECTIVE*
1 of the usual or average quality or kind ◆ *Patients were asked to eat a standard diet and record their meal and sleep periods.* ◆ *Power steering is standard on these models.*
2 regarded as the best and widely used ◆ *This is the standard book on the subject.*

standard assessment task *NOUN*
a standard test given to schoolchildren to assess their progress in one of the subjects of the national curriculum (SEE ALSO **SAT**)

Standard English *NOUN*
(*Language*) the form of English widely accepted as the normal and correct form. It is taught in schools and spoken and written by educated people.

standardize *VERB* **standardizes, standardizing, standardized**
to make things be of a standard size or quality
▷ **standardization** *NOUN*

USAGE NOTE This word can also be spelled standardise.

standard lamp *NOUN* **standard lamps**
a lamp on an upright support that stands on the floor

standard of living *NOUN*
the level of comfort and wealth that a country or a person has

standby *NOUN* **standbys**
1 something or someone kept to be used if needed
2 a system by which tickets for a play or an air flight can be bought cheaply at the last minute if there are any seats left
to be on standby is to be ready to be used if needed

stand-in *NOUN* **stand-ins**
a deputy or substitute

standing *NOUN*
1 a person's status or reputation ◆ *His standing in the opinion polls has plummeted.*
2 the period for which something has existed ◆ *The army began to award medals to soldiers of twenty years' standing.*

standing order *NOUN* **standing orders**
an instruction to a bank to make regular payments, or to a trader to supply something regularly

stand-offish *ADJECTIVE*
cold and formal; not friendly

standpipe *NOUN* **standpipes**
a pipe connected directly to a water supply, especially one set up in the street to provide water in an emergency

standpoint *NOUN* **standpoints**
a way of looking at something or thinking about it; a point of view

standstill *NOUN*
a stop; an end to movement or activity

The traffic in west London had come to a standstill. It would take days to clear up the damage. — *Anthony Horowitz, Scorpia*

stanza *NOUN* **stanzas**
(*Language*) a verse of poetry

staple[1] *NOUN* **staples**
1 a small piece of metal pushed through papers and clenched to fasten them together
2 a U-shaped nail
▷ **stapler** *NOUN*

staple *VERB* **staples, stapling, stapled**
to fix with a staple

staple[2] *ADJECTIVE*
a staple diet is the main or usual one

staple *NOUN* **staples**
a staple food or product

star *NOUN* **stars**
1 a large mass of burning gas that is seen as a bright speck of light in the sky at night
2 a shape with a number of points or rays sticking out from it; an asterisk
3 an object or mark of this shape showing rank or quality according to the number of them used
4 a famous performer; one of the chief performers in a play, film, or show

star *VERB* **stars, starring, starred**
1 to be one of the main performers in a film or show
2 to have someone as a main performer
3 to mark something with an asterisk or star symbol

WORD FAMILY Related adjectives are astral and stellar.

starboard *NOUN*
the right-hand side of a ship or aircraft when you are facing forward (SEE ALSO **port1**)

WORD HISTORY from Old English *steorbord* 'rudder side' (because early sailing ships were steered with a paddle mounted on the right hand side)

starch *NOUN* **starches**
1 a white carbohydrate in cereals and potatoes
2 this or a similar substance used to stiffen clothes
▷ **starchy** *ADJECTIVE*

starch *VERB* **starches, starching, starched**
to stiffen something with starch

stardom *NOUN*
being a star performer

stare *VERB* **stares, staring, stared**
to look at something intensely
▷ **stare** *NOUN*

starfish *NOUN* **starfish** or **starfishes**
a sea animal shaped like a star with five points

stark *ADJECTIVE*
1 complete or unmistakable ◆ *The stark truth is that the unemployment figures are unacceptable.*
2 desolate and bare ◆ *Single-track roads meander through stark valleys.*
▷ **starkly** *ADVERB*
▷ **starkness** *NOUN*

stark *ADVERB*
completely; entirely ◆ *From a distance it probably looked as if we were all stark naked.*

starlight *NOUN*
light from the stars

starling *NOUN* **starlings**
a noisy black bird with speckled feathers

starry *ADJECTIVE*
full of stars

starry-eyed *ADJECTIVE*
made happy by foolish dreams or unrealistic hopes

start *VERB* **starts, starting, started**
1 to begin something, or to make it begin
2 to make an engine or machine begin running
3 to begin a journey
4 to make a sudden movement because of pain or surprise
▷ **starter** *NOUN*

start *NOUN* **starts**
1 the beginning of a process or activity ◆ *They've made a good start.*
2 the place where a race starts
3 an advantage that is given to someone in relation to others ◆ *They had a few minutes' start on us but we still got here first.*
4 a sudden movement ◆ *She woke with a start.*

startle *VERB* **startles, startling, startled**
to surprise or alarm someone

start-up *NOUN*
(*ICT*) the process of starting a computer and opening programs

starve *VERB* **starves, starving, starved**
1 to suffer or die from lack of food, or to cause someone to do this
2 to deprive someone of something they need
▷ **starvation** *NOUN*

starving *ADJECTIVE*
(*informal*) very hungry

stash *VERB* **stashes, stashing, stashed**
(*informal*) to store something safely in a secret place

state *NOUN* **states**
1 the quality of a person's or thing's characteristics or circumstances; condition
2 an organized community under one government or forming part of a republic
3 a country's government ◆ *The state cannot be expected to fund all these activities.*
4 (*informal*) to get into a state is to become excited or upset about something
in state in a grand style; with grand ceremony

state *VERB* **states, stating, stated**
to express something in spoken or written words

WORD FAMILY *State* comes from the Latin word *stare* meaning 'to stand'. Other words to do with standing (some only loosely) and having the same origin include *ecstasy* (literally, standing outside yourself), *estate, static, stately, station, statistic,* and *statute.*

stately *ADJECTIVE* **statelier, stateliest**
dignified, imposing, or grand
▷ **stateliness** *NOUN*

stately home *NOUN* **stately homes**
a large and magnificent house belonging to an aristocratic family

statement *NOUN* **statements**
1 words stating something, e.g. evidence provided by a witness or accused person
2 a formal account of facts ◆ *Later a statement was issued by the Royal Palace.*
3 a printed report showing the transaction and current balance of a bank account or other dealings

state school *NOUN* **state schools**
a school which is funded by the government and which does not charge fees to pupils

statesman *NOUN* **statesmen**
a person, especially a man, who is important or skilled in governing a country
▷ **statesmanship** *NOUN*

stateswoman *NOUN* **stateswomen**
a woman who is important or skilled in governing a country

a b c d e f g h i j k l m n o p q r s t u v w x y z

SPELLING NOTE Some words pronounced **s-** begin with **ce-** (e.g. cent), **ci-** (e.g. city), or **cy-** (e.g. cymbal)

static *ADJECTIVE*
not moving or changing

static electricity *NOUN*
electricity that is present in something, not flowing as current

station *NOUN* **stations**
1 a stopping place for trains or buses with platforms and buildings for passengers and goods
2 a building equipped for people who serve the public or for certain activities ◆ *The country has increased the number of nuclear power stations.*
3 a broadcasting company with its own frequency
4 a place where a person or thing stands or is stationed; a position
5 (*Australia and New Zealand*) a large sheep or cattle farm

station *VERB* **stations, stationing, stationed**
to put someone or something in a certain place for a purpose ◆ *Troops were stationed here during the occupation of the island.*

stationary *ADJECTIVE*
a vehicle or other moving thing is stationary when it is not moving
USAGE NOTE Take care not to confuse this word with *stationery*.

stationer *NOUN* **stationers**
a shopkeeper who sells stationery
WORD HISTORY from Latin *stationarius* 'tradesman' (usually a bookseller) who had a shop or stand (as opposed to one who travelled about selling goods)

stationery *NOUN*
paper, envelopes, and other articles used in writing or typing
USAGE NOTE Take care not to confuse this word with *stationary*.

statistic *NOUN* **statistics**
a piece of information expressed as a number ◆ *A single statistic does not provide enough evidence.* ◆ *The statistics show a small increase in violent crimes in the area.*
▷ **statistical** *ADJECTIVE*
▷ **statistically** *ADVERB*

statistician (*say* stat- is- **tish**- an) *NOUN* **statisticians**
an expert in statistics

statistics *NOUN*
the study of information based on the numbers of things
WORD HISTORY from Latin *statisticus* 'of the state or nation' (because it originally referred to information and numerical data about the state)

statuary *NOUN*
statues collectively

statue *NOUN* **statues**
a stone or metal figure, usually of life-size or larger, of a person or animal

statuesque (*say* stat- yoo- **esk**) *ADJECTIVE*
like a statue in stillness or dignity

statuette *NOUN* **statuettes**
a small statue

stature *NOUN*
1 the natural height of the body
2 greatness gained by ability or achievement

status (*say* **stay**- tus) *NOUN* **statuses**
1 a person's or thing's position or rank in relation to others
2 high rank or prestige

status quo (*say* stay- tus **kwoh**) *NOUN*
the state of affairs as it was before a change
WORD HISTORY Latin words meaning 'the state in which'

status symbol *NOUN* **status symbols**
something that you own because it shows off your wealth or position in society, rather than because you like it or need it

statute *NOUN* **statutes**
a law passed by a parliament
▷ **statutory** *ADJECTIVE*

staunch *ADJECTIVE*
firm and loyal

The Putnam family are staunch Puritans and are engaged in a bitter power struggle with other local landowners. — *Chris Priestley, Witch Hunt*

▷ **staunchly** *ADVERB*

stave *NOUN* **staves**
1 each of the curved strips of wood forming the side of a cask or tub
2 a set of five horizontal lines on which music is written

stave *VERB* **staves, staving, staved** or **stove**
to dent something or break a hole in it
to stave something off is to prevent something unpleasant from happening

stay❶ *VERB* **stays, staying, stayed**
1 to continue to be in the same place or condition; to remain
2 to spend time in a place as a visitor ◆ *On our way to Austria we stayed overnight in Paris.*
3 to keep something or someone back or in control ◆ *Only one thing stayed her hand.*
4 to show endurance in a race or task
to stay put (*informal*) is to remain in place and not move away

stay *NOUN* **stays**
1 a brief time spent somewhere
2 a postponement, especially of a legal sentence or execution

stay❷ *NOUN* **stays**
a support, especially a rope or wire holding up a mast or pole

stead *NOUN*
in a person's or thing's stead instead of this person or thing

Mama had a letter for Mrs Noye, so asked me to take it to the workhouse in her stead. — *Pamela Oldfield, My Story: Victorian Workhouse*

to stand someone in good stead is to be very useful to them

steadfast *ADJECTIVE*
1 firm and persistent ◆ *She had such steadfast determination in her voice.*
2 reliable and loyal ◆ *He was a generous and steadfast friend.*

steady *ADJECTIVE* **steadier, steadiest**
1 not shaking or moving; firm
2 regular; continuing the same ◆ *The traffic moved at a slow but steady pace.*
▷ **steadily** *ADVERB*
▷ **steadiness** *NOUN*

steady *VERB* **steadies, steadying, steadied**
to make something steady, or to become steady

steak *NOUN* **steaks**
a thick slice of meat (especially beef) or fish

steal *VERB* **steals, stealing, stole, stolen**
1 to take and keep something that does not belong to you; to take something secretly or dishonestly
2 to move secretly or without being noticed

Two men stole from the margins, as white as ghosts. Truly they seemed like some kind of apparition. — *Celia Rees, Witch Child*

stealthy (*say* **stel**- thee) *ADJECTIVE* **stealthier, stealthiest**
quiet and secret, so as not to be noticed
▷ **stealth** *NOUN*
▷ **stealthily** *ADVERB*
▷ **stealthiness** *NOUN*

steam *NOUN*
the gas or vapour that comes from boiling water; this used to drive machinery
to run out of steam is to lose energy
▷ **steamy** *ADJECTIVE*

steam *VERB* **steams, steaming, steamed**
1 to give off steam
2 to move by the power of steam
3 to cook or treat food with steam
to steam up is to become covered with mist or condensation

steam engine *NOUN* **steam engines**
an engine driven by steam

steamer *NOUN* **steamers**
1 a ship powered by steam
2 a container in which food is steamed

steamroller *NOUN* **steamrollers**
a heavy vehicle with a large roller used to flatten surfaces when making roads

steamship *NOUN* **steamships**
a ship powered by steam

steed *NOUN* **steeds**
(*poetic*) a horse

steel *NOUN* **steels**
1 a strong metal made from iron and carbon
2 a steel rod for sharpening knives

steel *VERB* **steels, steeling, steeled**
to steel yourself is to find courage to face something difficult

steel band *NOUN* **steel bands**
a West Indian band of musicians with instruments usually made from oil drums

steel wool *NOUN*
a mass of fine, sharp steel threads used for cleaning a surface or rubbing it smooth

steely *ADJECTIVE*
1 like or to do with steel
2 cold, hard, and severe ◆ *His eyes narrowed into a steely glare.*

steep ❶ *ADJECTIVE*
1 sloping very sharply, not gradually
2 (*informal*) a steep charge or price is unreasonably high
▷ **steeply** *ADVERB*
▷ **steepness** *NOUN*

steep ❷ *VERB* **steeps, steeping, steeped**
to soak something thoroughly
to be steeped in something is to be deeply involved in it or familiar with it ◆ *The place was steeped in history.*

steepen *VERB* **steepens, steepening, steepened**
to become steeper

steeple *NOUN* **steeples**
a church tower with a spire on top

steeplechase *NOUN* **steeplechases**
a race across country or over hedges or fences

WORD HISTORY so called because the race originally finished at a distant church steeple which was always in view

steeplejack *NOUN* **steeplejacks**
a person who climbs tall chimneys or steeples to do repairs

steer ❶ *VERB* **steers, steering, steered**
to make a car, ship, or bicycle move in the direction you want; to guide something
to steer clear of something is to take care to avoid it

steer ❷ *NOUN* **steers**
a young castrated bull kept for its beef

steering wheel *NOUN* **steering wheels**
a wheel for steering a vehicle

steersman *NOUN* **steersmen**
a person who steers a boat or ship

a b c d e f g h i j k l m n o p q r s t u v w x y z

stegosaurus *NOUN* **stegosauruses**
a large dinosaur with bony plates along its back, which fed on plants
WORD HISTORY from Greek *stegē* 'roof' and *sauros* 'lizard'

stellar *ADJECTIVE*
to do with a star or stars

stem❶ *NOUN* **stems**
1 the main central part of a tree, shrub, or plant
2 a thin part on which a leaf, flower, or fruit is supported
3 a thin upright part, e.g. the thin part of a wine glass between the bowl and the foot
4 (*Grammar*) the main part of a verb or other word, to which endings are attached
from stem to stern from one end to the other of something (originally, of a ship)

stem *VERB* **stems, stemming, stemmed**
to stem from something is to arise from it or have it as a cause or source

stem❷ *VERB* **stems, stemming, stemmed**
to stop the flow of something

stench *NOUN* **stenches**
a very unpleasant smell

stencil *NOUN* **stencils**
a piece of card, metal, or plastic with pieces cut out of it, used to produce a picture or design

stencil *VERB* **stencils, stencilling, stencilled**
to produce or decorate something with a stencil

stentorian *ADJECTIVE*
a stentorian voice is very loud and clear
WORD HISTORY from the name of *Stentor*, a herald in Homer's *Iliad* (a poem about the siege of Troy) who was said to be able to shout as loud as fifty men

step *NOUN* **steps**
1 a movement made by lifting the foot and setting it down
2 the sound of a person putting down their foot when walking or running
3 a level surface for placing the foot on in climbing up or down
4 each of a series of things done in some process or action ◆ *Keeping your room clear of clutter is the first step.*
to be in step
1 is to march or dance in time with others
2 is to agree about something
to watch your step is to be careful or cautious

step *VERB* **steps, stepping, stepped**
to tread or walk
to step in is to interfere or intervene
to step on it (*informal*) is to hurry
to step up something is to increase or intensify it

stepbrother *NOUN* **stepbrothers**
the son of one of your parents from an earlier or later marriage

stepchild *NOUN* **stepchildren**
a child that a person's husband or wife has from an earlier marriage
▷ **stepdaughter** *NOUN*
▷ **stepson** *NOUN*

stepfather *NOUN* **stepfathers**
a man who is married to your mother but was not your natural father

stepladder *NOUN* **stepladders**
a folding ladder with flat treads

stepmother *NOUN* **stepmothers**
a woman who is married to your father but was not your natural mother

steppe *NOUN* **steppes**
a grassy plain with few trees, especially in Russia

stepping stone *NOUN* **stepping stones**
1 each of a line of stones put into a shallow stream so that people can walk across
2 a way of achieving something, or a stage in achieving it

steps *PLURAL NOUN*
a stepladder

stepsister *NOUN* **stepsisters**
the daughter of one of your parents from an earlier or later marriage

stereo *ADJECTIVE*
short for *stereophonic*

stereo *NOUN* **stereos**
1 stereophonic sound or recording
2 a stereophonic CD player or record player

stereophonic *ADJECTIVE*
using sound that comes from two different directions to give a natural effect
WORD HISTORY from Greek *stereos* solid, three-dimensional

stereoscopic *ADJECTIVE*
giving the effect of being three-dimensional, e.g. in photographs

stereotype *NOUN* **stereotypes**
a fixed image or idea of a type of person or thing that is widely held ◆ *The village fits the Hollywood stereotype of a sleepy little town.*

stereotype *VERB* **stereotypes, stereotyping, stereotyped**
to regard someone as a stereotype ◆ *The city is too easily stereotyped as a bleak industrial wasteland.*
WORD HISTORY originally a kind of printing block, from Greek *stereos* 'solid, three-dimensional' (because the block always produced the same words, like the fixed idea in the modern meaning)

sterile ***ADJECTIVE***
1 not fertile; barren
2 free from germs
▷ **sterility** ***NOUN***

sterilize ***VERB*** **sterilizes, sterilizing, sterilized**
1 to make a thing free from germs, e.g. by heating it
2 to make a person or animal unable to reproduce
▷ **sterilization** ***NOUN***
▷ **sterilizer** ***NOUN***

USAGE NOTE This word can also be spelled sterilise.

sterling ***NOUN***
British money

sterling ***ADJECTIVE***
1 genuine; reaching a set standard ◆ *sterling silver*
2 excellent; of great worth ◆ *They have done sterling work in the area of international relations.*

stern❶ ***ADJECTIVE***
strict and severe, not lenient or kindly
▷ **sternly** ***ADVERB***
▷ **sternness** ***NOUN***

stern❷ ***NOUN*** **sterns**
the back part of a ship

steroid ***NOUN*** **steroids**
a substance of a kind that includes certain hormones and other natural secretions

stethoscope ***NOUN*** **stethoscopes**
a device used for listening to sounds in a person's body, e.g. heartbeats and breathing

WORD HISTORY from Greek *stethos* 'breast' and *skopein* 'to look at'

stew ***VERB*** **stews, stewing, stewed**
to cook food slowly in liquid

stew ***NOUN*** **stews**
a dish of stewed food, especially meat and vegetables
in a stew (*informal*) very worried or agitated

steward ***NOUN*** **stewards**
1 a man whose job is to look after the passengers on a ship or aircraft
2 an official who keeps order or looks after the arrangements at a large public event

stewardess ***NOUN*** **stewardesses**
a woman whose job is to look after the passengers on a ship or aircraft

stick❶ ***NOUN*** **sticks**
1 a long thin piece of wood
2 a walking stick
3 the implement used to hit the ball in hockey, polo, or other games
4 a long thin piece of something ◆ *Most of us would rather eat a chocolate bar than a stick of celery.*

stick❷ ***VERB*** **sticks, sticking, stuck**
1 to push a thing forward or into something ◆ *She stuck her chin in the air and glared.* ◆ *The men were sticking tent pegs in the ground.*
2 to fix something by glue or as if by glue ◆ *He'd stuck a plaster on his wounded knee.*
3 to become fixed and unable to move ◆ *The window keeps sticking.*
4 (*informal*) to endure or tolerate something unpleasant ◆ *I couldn't stick all that shouting.*
to stick out
1 is to come out from a surface, or to stand out from the surrounding area
2 is to be very noticeable
to stick to something
1 is to remain faithful to a promise or agreement
2 to stick to a story or account is to insist on it and not change it
to stick together
1 is to stay together
2 is to support one another
to stick up for someone (*informal*) is to support or defend them
to be stuck with something (*informal*) is to be unable to avoid something unwelcome

sticker ***NOUN*** **stickers**
an adhesive label or sign for sticking to something

sticking plaster ***NOUN*** **sticking plasters**
a strip of adhesive material for covering cuts

stick insect ***NOUN*** **stick insects**
an insect with a long thin body and legs, which looks like a twig

stickleback ***NOUN*** **sticklebacks**
a small fish with sharp spines on its back

stickler ***NOUN*** **sticklers**
a person who insists on something ◆ *Molly's a stickler for punctuality.*

sticky ***ADJECTIVE*** **stickier, stickiest**
1 able or likely to stick to things
2 sticky weather is hot and humid, causing perspiration

> The air in the room was hot and sticky and agitation could be heard in people's voices.
> — *Beverley Naidoo, Chain of Fire*

3 (*informal*) a sticky situation is difficult or awkward
to come to a sticky end is to be ruined or killed
▷ **stickily** ***ADVERB***
▷ **stickiness** ***NOUN***

stiff ***ADJECTIVE***
1 not bending or moving or changing shape easily ◆ *She closed the stiff cover of her folder.* ◆ *The window was stiff and wouldn't open.*
2 not able to move or bend the body easily ◆ *I woke up stiff as a poker.*
3 thick and hard to stir

a b c d e f g h i j k l m n o p q r s t u v w x y z

4 severe or difficult ◆ *The task would be a stiff test of their stamina.*
5 formal in manner; not friendly
6 a stiff drink is a strong alcoholic one
▷ **stiffly** ADVERB
▷ **stiffness** NOUN

stiffen VERB **stiffens, stiffening, stiffened**
to become stiff, or to make something stiff
▷ **stiffener** NOUN

stifle VERB **stifles, stifling, stifled**
1 to suffocate somone
2 to suppress something

Dickon laughed so that he was obliged to stifle the sound by putting his arm over his mouth.
— *Frances Hodgson Burnett, The Secret Garden*

stigma NOUN **stigmas**
1 a mark of disgrace; a stain on a reputation
2 the part of a pistil that receives the pollen in pollination

stigmatize VERB **stigmatizes, stigmatizing, stigmatized**
to brand someone or something as disgraceful

USAGE NOTE This word can also be spelled stigmatise.

stile NOUN **stiles**
an arrangement of steps or bars for people to climb over a fence

stiletto NOUN **stilettos**
a dagger with a narrow blade

stiletto heel NOUN **stiletto heels**
a high pointed shoe heel

still❶ ADJECTIVE
1 not moving ◆ *He remained still for several minutes.*
2 silent; not disturbed by wind or sounds ◆ *It was a still night.*
3 a still drink is not fizzy
▷ **stillness** NOUN

still ADVERB
1 up to this or that time ◆ *The light was still on.*
2 in a greater amount or degree ◆ *You can do still better if you try.*
3 nevertheless; all the same ◆ *It might be hard to get tickets. Still, let's try.*

still VERB **stills, stilling, stilled**
to become still, or to make something still

still NOUN **stills**
a photograph of a scene from a cinema film

still❷ NOUN **stills**
an apparatus for distilling alcohol or other liquid

stillborn ADJECTIVE
born dead

still life NOUN **still lifes**
a painting of lifeless things such as ornaments and fruit

stilted ADJECTIVE
stiffly formal

stilts PLURAL NOUN
1 a pair of poles with supports for the feet so that the user can walk high above the ground
2 posts for supporting a building or other structure above marshy ground

stimulant NOUN **stimulants**
something that stimulates

stimulate VERB **stimulates, stimulating, stimulated**
1 to make someone excited or enthusiastic
2 to cause something to begin or develop ◆ *The television programme stimulated a lot of interest in the project.*
▷ **stimulation** NOUN

stimulus NOUN **stimuli**
something that stimulates or produces a reaction

sting NOUN **stings**
1 a sharp-pointed part of an animal or plant, often containing a poison, that can cause a wound
2 a painful wound caused by this part

sting VERB **stings, stinging, stung**
1 to wound or hurt someone with a sting
2 to feel a sharp pain
3 to make someone feel upset or hurt
4 (*informal*) to cheat someone by charging them too much; to swindle someone

stingray NOUN **stingrays**
a fish with a flat body, fins like wings, and a poisonous spine in its tail

stingy (*say* **stin**- jee) ADJECTIVE **stingier, stingiest**
mean, not generous; giving or given in small amounts
▷ **stingily** ADVERB
▷ **stinginess** NOUN

stink NOUN **stinks**
1 an unpleasant smell
2 (*informal*) an unpleasant fuss or protest

stink VERB **stinks, stinking, stank** or **stunk**
to have an unpleasant smell

stint NOUN **stints**
1 a fixed or regular amount of work to be done ◆ *He went off to do his weekly stint of shopping.*
2 limitation of a supply or effort ◆ *They were spending money without stint.*

stint VERB **stints, stinting, stinted**
to stint on something is to be sparing or mean with it and not use much

stipend (*say* **sty**- pend) NOUN **stipends**
a salary, especially one paid to a clergyman

stipple VERB **stipples, stippling, stippled**
to paint, draw, or engrave a design in small dots

stipulate *VERB* **stipulates, stipulating, stipulated**
to insist on something as part of an agreement
▷ **stipulation** *NOUN*

stir *VERB* **stirs, stirring, stirred**
1 to mix a liquid or soft mixture by moving a spoon or other utensil round and round in it
2 to move slightly; to start to move

Out in the black fen something stirred. It was cruel and slimy and its eyes shone green. — *Robert Nye, Beowulf*

3 to excite or stimulate a feeling or activity
▷ **stirring** *ADJECTIVE*

stir *NOUN*
1 the action of stirring
2 to cause a stir is to arouse excitement or active interest

stir-fry *VERB* **stir-fries, stir-frying, stir-fried**
to cook by frying quickly over a high heat while stirring and tossing
▷ **stir-fry** *NOUN*

stirrup *NOUN* **stirrups**
a metal part that hangs from each side of a horse's saddle and supports the rider's foot

stitch *NOUN* **stitches**
1 a loop of thread made in sewing or knitting
2 a method or style of arranging the threads ◆ *an embroidery stitch*
3 a sudden sharp pain in the side of the body, caused by running

stitch *VERB* **stitches, stitching, stitched**
to sew or fasten something with stitches

stoat *NOUN* **stoats**
a kind of weasel also called an ermine

stock *NOUN* **stocks**
1 a number of things kept ready to be sold or used
2 farm animals; livestock
3 a line of ancestors ◆ *people of German stock*
4 a number of shares in a company's capital
5 liquid made by stewing meat, fish, or vegetables
6 the main stem of a tree or plant
7 the base, holder, or handle of an implement or weapon
8 a garden flower with a sweet smell
to take stock is to make an overall assessment of a situation

stock *VERB* **stocks, stocking, stocked**
1 to keep goods in stock
2 to provide a place with a stock of something
to stock up is to buy a supply of goods

stockade *NOUN* **stockades**
a fence made of stakes

stockbroker *NOUN* **stockbrokers**
a broker who deals in stocks and shares

stock car *NOUN* **stock cars**
an ordinary car strengthened for use in races where deliberate bumping is allowed

stock exchange *NOUN* **stock exchanges**
a country's central place for buying and selling stocks and shares

stocking *NOUN* **stockings**
a piece of clothing covering the foot and part or all of the leg

stockist *NOUN* **stockists**
a shopkeeper who stocks a certain kind of goods

stock market *NOUN* **stock markets**
1 a stock exchange
2 the buying and selling of stocks and shares

stockpile *NOUN* **stockpiles**
a large stock of things kept in reserve

stockpile *VERB* **stockpiles, stockpiling, stockpiled**
to store things in reserve

stocks *PLURAL NOUN*
a wooden framework with holes for a seated person's legs, used like the pillory

stock-still *ADJECTIVE*
quite still

stocktaking *NOUN*
the counting, listing, and checking of the amount of stock held by a shop or business

stocky *ADJECTIVE* **stockier, stockiest**
a stocky person is short and solidly built

stodge *NOUN*
stodgy food

stodgy *ADJECTIVE* **stodgier, stodgiest**
1 stodgy food is heavy and indigestible
2 dull and boring
▷ **stodginess** *NOUN*

stoep (*say* stoop) *NOUN*
(*South African*) a veranda on a terrace in front of a house.

stoical (*say* stoh- ik- al) *ADJECTIVE*
bearing pain or hardship calmly without complaining
▷ **stoically** *ADVERB*
▷ **stoicism** *NOUN*

WORD HISTORY named after ancient Greek philosophers called *Stoics*, from Greek *stoa* 'porch' (because Zeno, the first of the Stoics, taught in a sort of porch in ancient Athens)

stoke *VERB* **stokes, stoking, stoked**
to put fuel in a furnace or on a fire
▷ **stoker** *NOUN*

stole ❶ *NOUN* **stoles**
a wide piece of material worn round the shoulders by women

stole ❷ *past tense* of **steal**

a b c d e f g h i j k l m n o p q r s t u v w x y z

stolid *ADJECTIVE*
not showing much emotion or excitement

The sergeant was standing in the middle of the floor with the stolid air of one who is awaiting a word of command. — *Terry Pratchett, Wyrd Sisters*

▷ **stolidly** *ADVERB*
▷ **stolidity** *NOUN*

stomach *NOUN* **stomachs**
1 the part of the body where food starts to be digested
2 the abdomen

stomach *VERB* **stomachs, stomaching, stomached**
to endure or tolerate something unpleasant

stone *NOUN* **stones**
1 a piece of rock
2 stones or rock as material, e.g. for building
3 a jewel
4 the hard case round the kernel of a plum, cherry, peach, and other fruit
5 a unit of weight equal to 14 pounds (6.35 kg) ◆ *He weighs ten stone.*

stone *VERB* **stones, stoning, stoned**
1 to throw stones at somebody in order to hurt or kill them
2 to remove the stones from fruit

Stone Age *NOUN*
the earliest period of human history, when tools and weapons were made of stone

stone circle *NOUN* **stone circles**
a circle of large stones or boulders, put up in prehistoric times

stone-cold *ADJECTIVE*
extremely cold

stoned *ADJECTIVE*
(*informal*) under the influence of drugs or alcohol

stone-deaf *ADJECTIVE*
completely deaf

stoneware *NOUN*
a kind of pottery with a hard shiny surface

stony *ADJECTIVE*
1 full of stones
2 like stone; hard
3 unfriendly and not answering ◆ *They listened to him in stony silence.*

stooge *NOUN* **stooges** (*informal*)
1 a comedian's assistant, used as a target for jokes
2 an assistant who does dull or routine work

stool *NOUN* **stools**
1 a movable seat without arms or a back
2 a footstool
3 a lump of faeces

stoop *VERB* **stoops, stooping, stooped**
1 to bend your body forwards and down

The door to the cottage was so small that a grown man would have to stoop to gain entry. — *G. P. Taylor, Shadowmancer*

2 to stoop to something dishonest or shameful is to be willing to do it

▷ **stoop** *NOUN*

stop *VERB* **stops, stopping, stopped**
1 to come to an end, or bring something to an end; to no longer do something
2 to be no longer moving or working ◆ *A van had stopped at the traffic lights.*
3 to prevent or obstruct something
4 to stay in a place for a short time
5 to fill a hole, especially in a tooth

stop *NOUN* **stops**
1 the act of stopping; a pause or end
2 a place where a bus or train regularly stops
3 a punctuation mark, especially a full stop
4 a lever or knob that controls pitch in a wind instrument or allows organ pipes to sound

stopcock *NOUN* **stopcocks**
a valve controlling the flow of liquid or gas in a pipe

stopgap *NOUN* **stopgaps**
a temporary substitute

stoppage *NOUN* **stoppages**
1 an interruption in the work of a factory or business
2 a blockage
3 an amount taken off someone's wages

stopper *NOUN* **stoppers**
a plug for closing a bottle or sealing a hole

stop press *NOUN*
late news put into a newspaper after printing has started

WORD HISTORY so called because the printing presses are stopped to allow the late news to be added

stopwatch *NOUN* **stopwatches**
a watch that can be started and stopped, used for timing races

storage *NOUN*
the process of storing things

storage heater *NOUN* **storage heaters**
an electric heater that gives out heat that it has stored

store *NOUN* **stores**
1 a supply of things kept for future use
2 a place where things are kept until they are needed
3 a shop, especially a large one

in store likely to happen; imminent ◆ *Whatever was in store for them, they would survive.*

to set store by something is to value it very much

store *VERB* **stores, storing, stored**
to keep things until they are needed

storey *NOUN* **storeys**
one whole floor of a building
USAGE NOTE Take care not to confuse this word with *story*.

stork *NOUN* **storks**
a large bird with long legs and a long beak

storm *NOUN* **storms**
1 a weather disturbance with very strong wind and usually rain, thunder and lightning, or snow
2 a violent attack or outburst, especially of protest or disagreement

a storm in a teacup a lot of fuss over something unimportant

storm *VERB* **storms, storming, stormed**
1 to move or behave violently or angrily

Withel stormed across the floor, his face a mask of rage. — *Terry Pratchett, The Colour of Magic*

2 to attack a place suddenly and capture it

stormy *ADJECTIVE* **stormier, stormiest**
1 having a storm, or a lot of storms
2 a stormy scene or argument is angry or violent

story *NOUN* **stories**
1 an account of a real or imaginary event
2 the plot of a novel, play, or film
3 (*informal*) to tell stories is to be untruthful
USAGE NOTE Take care not to confuse this word with *storey*.

storyboard *NOUN* **storyboards**
(*Language*) a sequence of pictures or drawings showing the plan or plot of a video or other visual text

storyline *NOUN* **storylines**
the plot of a story, play, film, etc.

stout *ADJECTIVE*
1 rather fat
2 thick and strong ◆ *Make sure you wear a pair of stout shoes.*
3 brave and determined ◆ *He was always a stout defender of human rights.*
▷ **stoutly** *ADVERB*
▷ **stoutness** *NOUN*

stout *NOUN*
a kind of dark beer

stove ❶ *NOUN* **stoves**
1 a device containing an oven or ovens
2 a device for heating a room

stove ❷ *past tense of* **stave**

stow *VERB* **stows, stowing, stowed**
to pack or store something away

to stow away is to hide on a ship or aircraft so as to travel without paying
▷ **stowage** *NOUN*

stowaway *NOUN* **stowaways**
someone who stows away on a ship or aircraft

straddle *VERB* **straddles, straddling, straddled**
1 to sit or stand astride something
2 to be built across something ◆ *The village straddles the coast road.*

straggle *VERB* **straggles, straggling, straggled**
1 to grow or spread in an untidy way
2 to lag behind; to wander off on your own
▷ **straggler** *NOUN*
▷ **straggly** *ADJECTIVE*

straight *ADJECTIVE*
1 going continuously in one direction; not curving or bending
2 level, horizontal, or upright
3 tidy; in proper order
4 a straight answer is honest and direct

to get something straight is to make sure you understand it correctly

Let me get it straight. Your father was king. You were his only son. Your father dies. You are of age. Your uncle becomes king. — *Tom Stoppard, Rosencrantz & Guildenstern are Dead*

▷ **straightness** *NOUN*

straight *ADVERB*
1 in a straight line or manner
2 directly; without delay ◆ *Jo ran straight up to her room.*
USAGE NOTE Take care not to confuse this word with *strait*.

straightaway or **straight away** *ADVERB*
immediately; without delay

straighten *VERB* **straightens, straightening, straightened**
to make something straight, or to become straight

straightforward *ADJECTIVE*
1 easy; not complicated
2 honest and frank

strain ❶ *VERB* **strains, straining, strained**
1 to injure or weaken something by stretching or working it too hard
2 to stretch something tightly
3 to make a great effort
4 to put something through a sieve or filter to separate liquid from solid matter

strain *NOUN* **strains**
1 the process or force of straining
2 an injury caused by straining
3 something that uses up strength, patience, or resources ◆ *She had to give up work, which put a financial strain on the family.* ◆ *Leaving the children behind caused a huge emotional strain.*
4 a state of exhaustion
5 a part of a tune

strain ❷ *NOUN* **strains**
1 a distinct breed or variety of an animal, plant, or other organism
2 an inherited characteristic ◆ *There's a strong artistic strain in the family.*

strainer *NOUN* **strainers**
a device for straining liquids

strait *ADJECTIVE*
(*old use*) narrow or restricted

strait *NOUN* **straits**
a narrow stretch of water connecting two seas; a sound
USAGE NOTE Take care not to confuse this word with *straight*.

straitened *ADJECTIVE*
in straitened circumstances short of money

straitjacket *NOUN* **straitjackets**
a strong piece of clothing put round a violent person to tie their arms

strait-laced *ADJECTIVE*
very prim and proper

straits *PLURAL NOUN*
1 a strait or sound
2 to be in dire or difficult straits is to be in great difficulty or danger

strand ❶ *NOUN* **strands**
1 each of the threads or wires twisted together to form a rope, yarn, or cable
2 a single thread or hair
3 a particular element of an idea, theme, or story

strand ❷ *NOUN* **strands**
a shore

stranded *ADJECTIVE*
1 a boat or ship is stranded when it is left on sand or rocks in shallow water
2 a person is stranded when they are left in a difficult or helpless position

strange *ADJECTIVE*
1 unusual or surprising
2 not known or seen or experienced before
▷ **strangely** *ADVERB*
▷ **strangeness** *NOUN*

stranger *NOUN* **strangers**
1 a person you do not know
2 a person who is in an unfamiliar place

strangle *VERB* **strangles, strangling, strangled**
1 to kill someone by squeezing their throat to prevent them breathing
2 to restrict something so that it does not develop
▷ **strangler** *NOUN*

strangulate *VERB* **strangulates, strangulating, strangulated**
to squeeze something so that nothing can pass through
▷ **strangulation** *NOUN*

strap *NOUN* **straps**
a strip of leather, cloth, or other flexible material used for fastening things or holding them in place

strap *VERB* **straps, strapping, strapped**
to fasten or bind something with a strap or straps

strapping *ADJECTIVE*
tall and healthy-looking

strata *plural of* **stratum**

stratagem *NOUN* **stratagems**
a cunning method of achieving something; a plan or trick

strategic *ADJECTIVE*
1 to do with strategy
2 a strategic move or action is one that gives you an advantage
▷ **strategically** *ADVERB*

strategist *NOUN* **strategists**
an expert in strategy

strategy *NOUN* **strategies**
1 a plan or policy designed to achieve something
2 the planning of a war or campaign (SEE ALSO **tactics**)
WORD HISTORY from Greek *strategos* 'a general'

stratified *ADJECTIVE*
arranged in strata
▷ **stratification** *NOUN*

stratosphere *NOUN*
a layer of the atmosphere between about 10 and 60 kilometres above the earth's surface

stratum (*say* **strah**- tum or **stray**- tum) *NOUN* **strata**
a layer or level
USAGE NOTE The word *strata* is a plural. It is incorrect to say 'a strata' or 'this strata'; correct use is *this stratum* or *these strata.*

straw *NOUN* **straws**
1 dry cut stalks of corn
2 a narrow tube for drinking through

strawberry *NOUN* **strawberries**
a small red juicy fruit, with its seeds on the outside
WORD HISTORY perhaps called this because straw is put around the plants to keep slugs away, or because the long thin roots of the plants look like straw

stray *VERB* **strays, straying, strayed**
to leave a group or proper place and wander; to become lost

a b c d e f g h i j k l m n o p q r s t u v w x y z

stray ***ADJECTIVE***
1 a stray animal is one that has strayed and is wandering around lost
2 something stray has been found on its own, separated from the others

▷ **stray** ***NOUN***

streak ***NOUN*** **streaks**
1 a long thin line or mark
2 a trace

Oh, yeah, my father lived many years in Alaska. He was an adventurous man. We've got quite a little streak of self-reliance in our family. — *Arthur Miller, Death of a Salesman*

3 a spell of success or good fortune ◆ *They were definitely on a winning streak.*

▷ **streaky** ***ADJECTIVE***

streak ***VERB*** **streaks, streaking, streaked**
1 to mark with streaks
2 to move very quickly
3 to run naked in a public place for fun or to get attention

▷ **streaker** ***NOUN***

streaky bacon ***NOUN***
bacon with alternate strips of lean and fat

stream ***NOUN*** **streams**
1 water flowing in a channel; a brook or small river
2 a flow of liquid or of things or people
3 a group in which children of similar ability are placed in a school

stream ***VERB*** **streams, streaming, streamed**
1 to move in or like a stream
2 to produce a stream of liquid
3 to arrange schoolchildren in streams according to their ability

streamer ***NOUN*** **streamers**
a long narrow ribbon or strip of paper

streamline ***VERB*** **streamlines, streamlining, streamlined**
1 to give something a smooth shape that helps it to move easily through air or water
2 to organize something so that it works more efficiently

▷ **streamlined** ***ADJECTIVE***

street ***NOUN*** **streets**
a road with houses beside it in a city or village

WORD HISTORY via Old English from Latin *strata via* 'paved road', from *strata* 'laid down'

strength ***NOUN*** **strengths**
1 how strong a person or thing is; being strong
2 an ability or good quality ◆ *The artist's main strength was in large-scale landscapes.*

strengthen ***VERB*** **strengthens, strengthening, strengthened**
to make something stronger, or to become stronger

strenuous ***ADJECTIVE***
needing or using great effort

The long days and strenuous work stripped Eragon's body of excess fat. — *Christopher Paolini, Eragon*

▷ **strenuously** ***ADVERB***

streptococcus (*say* strep- toh- **kok**- us) ***NOUN*** **streptococci**
any of a group of bacteria that cause serious infection

WORD HISTORY from Greek *streptos* 'twisted' and *kokkos* 'berry'

stress ***NOUN*** **stresses**
1 a force that acts on something, e.g. by pressing, pulling, or twisting it; strain
2 emphasis, especially the extra force with which you pronounce part of a word or phrase
3 distress caused by having too many problems or too much to do

stress ***VERB*** **stresses, stressing, stressed**
1 to pronounce part of a word or phrase with extra emphasis
2 to emphasize a point or idea
3 to cause stress to someone

stretch ***VERB*** **stretches, stretching, stretched**
1 to pull something or be pulled so that it becomes longer or wider or larger
2 to extend or be continuous ◆ *The beach stretches for three kilometres.*
3 to push out your arms and legs as far as you can
4 a problem or task stretches someone when it makes them use all their ability or intelligence

to stretch out is to lie down with your arms and legs at full length

stretch ***NOUN*** **stretches**
1 the action of stretching
2 a continuous period of time or area of land or water

stretcher ***NOUN*** **stretchers**
a framework for carrying a sick or injured person

strew ***VERB*** **strews, strewing, strewed, strewn** or **strewed**
to scatter things over a surface

striated (*say* stry- ay- tid) ***ADJECTIVE***
marked with lines or ridges

▷ **striation** ***NOUN***

stricken ***ADJECTIVE***
overcome or strongly affected by an illness or unpleasant feeling such as fear or grief

strict ***ADJECTIVE***
1 demanding obedience and good behaviour
2 complete or exact ◆ *She left strict instructions on how to find her.*

▷ **strictly** ***ADVERB***
▷ **strictness** ***NOUN***

a b c d e f g h i j k l m n o p q r s t u v w x y z

stricture *NOUN* **strictures**
 1 a stern critical remark
 2 a rule restricting behaviour

stride *VERB* **strides, striding, strode, stridden**
 to walk with long steps

stride *NOUN* **strides**
 1 a long step when walking or running
 2 a step that helps to make progress
to get into your stride is to settle into a steady rate of working
to take something in your stride is to cope with something without difficulty

strident (*say* **stry**- dent) *ADJECTIVE*
 loud and harsh

> A duck quacked loudly, and when its strident alarm was finished, the air held only the slight sounds of snowflakes sinking on the roof of the shed. — *Henry Williamson, Tarka the Otter*

▷ **stridently** *ADVERB*
▷ **stridency** *NOUN*

strife *NOUN*
 conflict; fighting or quarrelling

strike *VERB* **strikes, striking, struck**
 1 to hit someone or something

> The first two cruisers struck each other head on, their great blades interlocking, mangling each other. — *William Nicholson, The Wind Singer*

 2 to attack or afflict people suddenly ◆ *Then disaster struck.*
 3 to make an impression on someone's mind ◆ *It struck me as a sensible and fair system.*
 4 to light a match by rubbing it against a rough surface
 5 to refuse to work as a protest against pay or conditions
 6 to produce coins or medals by pressing or stamping metal
 7 to sound

> It was a bright cold day in April, and the clocks were striking thirteen. — *George Orwell, Nineteen Eighty-four*

 8 to find gold, minerals, or oil by digging or drilling
 9 to go in a certain direction ◆ *The little army then struck south.*
to strike something off or out is to cross it out
to strike up a band strikes up when it starts to play music
to strike something up is to start a friendship or conversation

strike *NOUN* **strikes**
 1 a hit
 2 a military attack, especially by air
 3 refusing to work as a way of making a protest
 4 a sudden discovery of gold, minerals, or oil
on strike workers are on strike when they are striking

striker *NOUN* **strikers**
 1 a person or thing that strikes something
 2 a worker who is on strike
 3 a football player whose function is to try to score goals

striking *ADJECTIVE*
 1 impressive or attractive
 2 obvious or noticeable
▷ **strikingly** *ADVERB*

string *NOUN* **strings**
 1 thin cord made of twisted threads, used to fasten or tie things; a piece of this or similar material
 2 a piece of wire or cord stretched and vibrated to produce sounds in a musical instrument
 3 a line or series of things of the same kind

string *VERB* **strings, stringing, strung**
 1 to fit or fasten something with string
 2 to thread things on a string
 3 to remove the tough fibre from beans
to string someone along is to mislead them over a period of time
to string something out
 1 is to spread it in a line
 2 is to make something last a long time
▷ **stringed** *ADJECTIVE*

stringent (*say* **strin**- jent) *ADJECTIVE*
 strict and precise ◆ *There are stringent rules governing air pollution.*
▷ **stringently** *ADVERB*
▷ **stringency** *NOUN*

strings *PLURAL NOUN*
 the stringed instruments of an orchestra

stringy *ADJECTIVE*
 1 like string
 2 containing tough fibres

strip❶ *VERB* **strips, stripping, stripped**
 1 to take a covering or layer off something
 2 to undress
 3 to deprive a person of something

strip *NOUN*
 the distinctive clothes worn by a sports team while playing

strip❷ *NOUN* **strips**
 a long narrow piece or area

strip cartoon *NOUN* **strip cartoons**
 a series of drawings telling a story

strip club *NOUN* **strip clubs**
 a place where striptease is performed

stripe *NOUN* **stripes**
 1 a long narrow band of colour
 2 a strip of cloth worn on the sleeve of a uniform to show the wearer's rank
▷ **striped** *ADJECTIVE*
▷ **stripy** *ADJECTIVE*

strip light *NOUN* **strip lights**
 a fluorescent lamp in the form of a tube

stripling *NOUN* **striplings**
a youth

stripper *NOUN* **strippers**
1 a tool or solvent used for stripping paint
2 a person who performs striptease

striptease *NOUN* **stripteases**
an entertainment in which a person slowly undresses

strive *VERB* **strives, striving, strove, striven**
1 to try hard to do something
2 to carry on a conflict

strobe *NOUN* **strobes**
(short for **stroboscope**) a light that flashes on and off rapidly and continuously

WORD HISTORY from Greek *strobos* 'whirling'

stroke❶ *NOUN* **strokes**
1 a hit
2 a movement; a style of swimming
3 an action or effort

As I was crossing the street I had a stroke of inspiration about who might have killed Wellington. — *Mark Haddon, The Curious Incident of the Dog in the Night-Time*

4 the sound made by a clock striking
5 a sudden illness that often causes paralysis

stroke❷ *VERB* **strokes, stroking, stroked**
to move your hand gently along something
▷ **stroke** *NOUN*

stroll *VERB* **strolls, strolling, strolled**
to walk in a leisurely way
▷ **stroll** *NOUN*
▷ **stroller** *NOUN*

strong *ADJECTIVE*
1 having great power, energy, or effect
2 not easy to break, damage, or defeat
3 intense or powerful ◆ *She has a strong sense of duty.*
4 having a lot of flavour or smell
5 having a certain number of members ◆ *The king raised an army 5,000 strong.*
▷ **strongly** *ADVERB*

SYNONYMS (meaning 1) tough, powerful, brawny, strapping; (meaning 2) sturdy, robust, durable, firm, secure; (meaning 3) keen, eager, deep, intense, dedicated, passionate, fervent, zealous

strong *ADVERB*
to be going strong is to be making good progress

stronghold *NOUN* **strongholds**
1 a fortified place
2 an area of strong support for a cause or political group ◆ *Rochester Castle was an important royal stronghold for hundreds of years.*

strong point *NOUN* **strong points**
a strength; something that you are very good at

strongroom *NOUN* **strongrooms**
a room designed to protect valuable things from fire and theft

strontium *NOUN*
a soft silvery metal

WORD HISTORY named after *Strontian* in the Scottish highlands, where it was discovered

strove *past tense of* **strive**

structure *NOUN* **structures**
1 something that has been constructed or built
2 the way something is constructed or organized
▷ **structural** *ADJECTIVE*
▷ **structurally** *ADVERB*

structure *VERB* **structures, structuring, structured**
to organize or arrange something into a system or pattern

struggle *VERB* **struggles, struggling, struggled**
1 to move your arms and legs and wriggle fiercely in trying to get free
2 to make strong efforts to do something
3 to try to overcome an opponent or difficulty

struggle *NOUN* **struggles**
the action of struggling; a hard fight or great effort

strum *VERB* **strums, strumming, strummed**
to sound a guitar by running your fingers across its strings

strut *VERB* **struts, strutting, strutted**
to walk proudly or stiffly

French policemen strutted about looking important and barking out orders in their own language. — *Adeline Yen Mah, Chinese Cinderella*

strut *NOUN* **struts**
1 a bar of wood or metal strengthening a framework
2 a strutting walk

strychnine (*say* **strik**- neen) *NOUN*
a bitter poisonous substance

stub *NOUN* **stubs**
1 a short stump left when the rest has been used or worn down
2 a counterfoil of a cheque or ticket

stub *VERB* **stubs, stubbing, stubbed**
1 to bump your toe painfully
2 **to stub out a cigarette** is to stop it burning by pressing it against something hard

stubble *NOUN*
1 the short stalks of corn left in the ground after the harvest is cut
2 short hairs growing after shaving

a b c d e f g h i j k l m n o p q r s t u v w x y z

stubborn *ADJECTIVE*
1 determined not to change your ideas or ways; obstinate
2 difficult to remove or deal with ◆ *Remove stubborn marks by scrubbing with a stiff brush.*
▷ **stubbornly** *ADVERB*
▷ **stubbornness** *NOUN*

stubby *ADJECTIVE*
short and thick

stucco *NOUN*
plaster or cement used for coating walls and ceilings, often moulded into decorations
▷ **stuccoed** *ADJECTIVE*

stuck *past tense and past participle of* **stick**

stuck *ADJECTIVE*
unable to move or make progress

stuck-up *ADJECTIVE*
(*informal*) conceited or snobbish

stud❶ *NOUN* **studs**
1 a small curved lump or knob
2 a device like a button on a stalk, used to fasten a detachable collar to a shirt

stud *VERB* **studs, studding, studded**
1 to set or decorate something with studs or other decorations ◆ *The frame is studded with pearls and precious stones.*
2 to scatter or sprinkle something ◆ *The road was studded with trees on each side.*

stud❷ *NOUN* **studs**
1 a number of horses kept for breeding; the place where they are kept
2 a stallion

student *NOUN* **students**
a person who studies a subject, especially at a college or university

studied *ADJECTIVE*
not natural or spontaneous but done with deliberate effort ◆ *She made a studied gesture of looking at her watch.*

studio *NOUN* **studios**
1 the room where an artist or photographer works
2 a place where cinema films are made
3 a room from which radio or television broadcasts are made or recorded

studious *ADJECTIVE*
spending a lot of time studying or reading
▷ **studiously** *ADVERB*
▷ **studiousness** *NOUN*

study *VERB* **studies, studying, studied**
1 to spend time learning about something
2 to look at something carefully

study *NOUN* **studies**
1 the process of studying
2 a subject studied; a piece of research
3 a room used for studying or writing
4 a piece of music for playing as an exercise
5 a drawing done for practice or in preparation for another work

WORD HISTORY from Latin *studium* 'enthusiasm', from *studere* 'to apply yourself eagerly to a task'

stuff *NOUN*
1 a substance or material
2 miscellaneous things

Our living-room and all the other rooms were so full of stuff that I can't find the words to describe it. — *Anne Frank, The Diary of a Young Girl*

stuff *VERB* **stuffs, stuffing, stuffed**
1 to fill something tightly
2 to fill something with stuffing
3 to push something roughly into a place ◆ *He stuffed his hands deep into his pockets.*
4 (*informal*) to eat greedily

stuffing *NOUN*
1 material used to fill the inside of something; padding
2 a savoury mixture put into meat or poultry before cooking

stuffy *ADJECTIVE* **stuffier, stuffiest**
1 badly ventilated; without fresh air
2 having blocked breathing passages
3 formal and boring
▷ **stuffily** *ADVERB*
▷ **stuffiness** *NOUN*

stultify *VERB* **stultifies, stultifying, stultified**
to prevent something from being effective ◆ *To feel guilty is to stultify your own freedom.*
▷ **stultification** *NOUN*

stumble *VERB* **stumbles, stumbling, stumbled**
1 to trip and lose your balance
2 to speak or do something hesitantly or uncertainly
3 to stumble across something or on something is to find it by chance

There are very few people, and even fewer amateur zoologists, who stumble upon a sizeable mammal previously unknown to science. — *Gavin Maxwell, Ring of Bright Water*

▷ **stumble** *NOUN*

stumbling block *NOUN* **stumbling blocks**
an obstacle; something that causes difficulty or hesitation

stump *NOUN* **stumps**
1 the bottom of a tree trunk left in the ground when the rest has fallen or been cut down
2 something left when the main part is cut off or worn down
3 each of the three upright sticks of a wicket in cricket

stump *VERB* **stumps, stumping, stumped**
1 in cricket, to put a batsman out by knocking the bails off the stumps while the batsman is out of the crease
2 to be too difficult or puzzling for somebody
3 to walk stiffly or noisily

to stump up (*informal*) is to produce the money needed to pay for something

stumpy *ADJECTIVE*
short and thick
▷ **stumpiness** *NOUN*

stun *VERB* **stuns, stunning, stunned**
1 to knock a person unconscious
2 to shock someone or make a deep impression on them ◆ *When the castle came into view, I was stunned by its beauty.*

stunning *ADJECTIVE*
extremely beautiful or attractive
▷ **stunningly** *ADVERB*

stunt ❶ *VERB*
to prevent something from growing or developing normally

stunt ❷ *NOUN* **stunts**
1 something daring done as a performance or as part of the action of a film
2 something unusual done to attract attention ◆ *Was their much reported romance just a publicity stunt?*

stupefy *VERB* **stupefies, stupefying, stupefied**
to make a person dazed

During the first weeks of her grief Sara felt as if she were too stupefied to talk. — *Frances Hodgson Burnett, A Little Princess*

▷ **stupefaction** *NOUN*

stupendous *ADJECTIVE*
amazing or tremendous
▷ **stupendously** *ADVERB*

stupid *ADJECTIVE*
1 not clever or thoughtful
2 without reason or common sense
▷ **stupidly** *ADVERB*
▷ **stupidity** *NOUN*

stupor (*say* stew- per) *NOUN* **stupors**
a dazed condition

sturdy *ADJECTIVE* **sturdier, sturdiest**
strong and vigorous or solid
▷ **sturdily** *ADVERB*
▷ **sturdiness** *NOUN*

sturgeon *NOUN* **sturgeon**
a large edible fish

stutter *VERB* **stutters, stuttering, stuttered**
to stammer
▷ **stutter** *NOUN*

sty ❶ *NOUN* **sties**
a pigsty

sty ❷ or **stye** *NOUN* **sties** or **styes**
a sore swelling on an eyelid

style *NOUN* **styles**
1 the way something is done, made, said, or written
2 fashion or elegance
3 the part of a pistil that supports the stigma in a plant
▷ **stylistic** *ADJECTIVE*

style *VERB* **styles, styling, styled**
to design or arrange something, especially in a fashionable style
▷ **stylist** *NOUN*

stylish *ADJECTIVE*
in a fashionable style

stylus *NOUN* **styluses** or **styli**
the device like a needle that travels in the grooves of a record to produce the sound

suave (*say* swahv) *ADJECTIVE*
polite in a charming and confident way
▷ **suavely** *ADVERB*
▷ **suavity** *NOUN*

WORD HISTORY from Latin *suavis* 'sweet, pleasant'

sub *NOUN* **subs** (*informal*)
1 a submarine
2 a subscription
3 a substitute

subaltern *NOUN* **subalterns**
an army officer ranking below a captain

subaqua *ADJECTIVE*
to do with underwater sports, such as diving

subatomic *ADJECTIVE*
1 smaller than an atom
2 forming part of an atom

subconscious *ADJECTIVE*
to do with mental processes of which we are not fully aware but which influence our actions
▷ **subconscious** *NOUN*

subcontinent *NOUN* **subcontinents**
a large mass of land not large enough to be called a continent

subcontract *VERB* **subcontracts, subcontracting, subcontracted**
to hire another company as a subcontractor

subcontractor *NOUN* **subcontractors**
a person or company hired by another company to do a particular part of their work

subdivide *VERB* **subdivides, subdividing, subdivided**
to divide something again or into smaller parts
▷ **subdivision** *NOUN*

subdue *VERB* **subdues, subduing, subdued**
1 to overcome a person or people or bring them under control
2 to make someone quieter or gentler
▷ **subdued** *ADJECTIVE*

subject (*say* sub- jekt) *NOUN* **subjects**
1 the person or thing being talked or written about or dealt with
2 something that is studied
3 (*Grammar*) the word or words naming who or what does the action of a verb, e.g. *Rajiv* in *Rajiv opened the window*
4 someone who is ruled by a monarch or government

a b c d e f g h i j k l m n o p q r s t u v w x y z

subject (*say* **sub**- jekt) *ADJECTIVE*
1 ruled by a monarch or government; not independent
2 to be subject to something is to be likely to experience it or be affected by it ◆ *For years he was subject to bouts of depression.* ◆ *Ferry schedules are subject to weather conditions.*

subject (*say* sub- **jekt**) *VERB* **subjects, subjecting, subjected**
1 to subject someone to something difficult or unpleasant is to make them undergo something
2 to bring a country under your control
▷ **subjection** *NOUN*

subjective *ADJECTIVE*
1 existing in a person's mind and not produced by things outside it
2 based on a person's own tastes, feelings, or opinions
(SEE ALSO **objective**)

sub judice (*say* **joo**- di- see) *ADJECTIVE*
being decided by a judge or lawcourt and therefore not able to be discussed publicly
WORD HISTORY Latin words meaning 'under a judge'

subjugate *VERB* **subjugates, subjugating, subjugated**
to bring a country under your control; to conquer it
▷ **subjugation** *NOUN*

subjunctive *NOUN* **subjunctives**
the form of a verb used to indicate what is imagined or wished or possible. There are only a few cases where it is commonly used in English, e.g. '*were*' in *if I were you* and '*save*' in *God save the Queen!*

sublet *VERB* **sublets, subletting, sublet**
to let to another person a house or other property that is let to you by a landlord

sublime *ADJECTIVE*
1 noble or impressive ◆ *The air was filled with sublime music.*
2 extreme; not caring about the consequences ◆ *He treated his friends with sublime indifference.*

submarine *ADJECTIVE*
under the sea ◆ *The Company laid a thousand miles of submarine cables.*

submarine *NOUN* **submarines**
a ship that can travel under water

submerge *VERB* **submerges, submerging, submerged**
to go under under water, or to put something under water
▷ **submergence** *NOUN*
▷ **submersion** *NOUN*

submission *NOUN* **submissions**
1 submitting to someone
2 something submitted or offered for consideration

submissive *ADJECTIVE*
willing to obey

submit *VERB* **submits, submitting, submitted**
1 to let someone have authority over you; to surrender
2 to put an idea or proposal forward for consideration or trial

subnormal *ADJECTIVE*
below normal

subordinate *ADJECTIVE*
1 less important
2 lower in rank

subordinate *NOUN* **subordinates**
a person working under someone's authority or control

subordinate *VERB* **subordinates, subordinating, subordinated**
to treat one person or thing as being less important than another
▷ **subordination** *NOUN*

subordinate clause *NOUN* **subordinate clauses**
a clause which adds details to the main clause of the sentence, but cannot be used as a sentence by itself

suborn *VERB* **suborns, suborning, suborned**
to bribe or incite someone secretly

sub-plot *NOUN* **sub-plots**
a second plot, running alongside the main one, in a novel, film, or play

subpoena (*say* sub- **peen**- a) *NOUN* **subpoenas**
an official document ordering a person to appear in a lawcourt

subpoena *VERB* **subpoenas, subpoenaing, subpoenaed**
to summon someone by a subpoena
WORD HISTORY from Latin *sub poena* 'under a penalty' (for not obeying the order to appear)

sub-post office *NOUN* **sub-post offices**
a small local post office, often in a shop, which offers fewer services than a main post office

subscribe *VERB* **subscribes, subscribing, subscribed**
1 to make a regular payment for membership of a society or to receive a magazine or other service
2 to contribute money to a project or charity
3 to subscribe to a view or theory is to say that you agree with it

subscriber *NOUN* **subscribers**
1 someone who subscribes to something
2 someone who pays for a phone connection

subscription *NOUN* **subscriptions**
money paid to subscribe to something

subsequent *ADJECTIVE*
coming after in time or order; later
▷ **subsequently** *ADVERB*

subservient *ADJECTIVE*
prepared to obey others without question
▷ **subservience** *NOUN*

subset *NOUN* **subsets**
a group or set forming part of a larger group or set

subside *VERB* **subsides, subsiding, subsided**
1 a building subsides when it starts to sink into the ground
2 a feeling or activity subsides when it become less intense or quieter ◆ *The pains in his head subsided.*

subsidence (*say* sub- **sy**- dens or sub- **sid**- ens) *NOUN*
the gradual sinking or caving in of an area of land

subsidiary *ADJECTIVE*
1 less important; secondary
2 a subsidiary business or company is one under the control of another
▷ **subsidiary** *NOUN*

subsidize *VERB* **subsidizes, subsidizing, subsidized**
to pay a subsidy to a person or organization
USAGE NOTE This word can also be spelled subsidise.

subsidy *NOUN* **subsidies**
money paid to an industry that needs support, or to keep down the price at which its goods or services are sold to the public

subsist *VERB* **subsists, subsisting, subsisted**
to exist; to keep yourself alive ◆ *Old people often have to subsist on very small incomes.*
▷ **subsistence** *NOUN*

subsoil *NOUN*
soil lying just below the surface layer

subsonic *ADJECTIVE*
not as fast as the speed of sound (SEE ALSO **supersonic**)

substance *NOUN* **substances**
1 matter of a particular kind
2 the main or essential part of something ◆ *The substance of the myth is based on actual events.*

sub-standard *ADJECTIVE*
below the normal or required standard

substantial *ADJECTIVE*
1 of great size, value, or importance
2 solidly built

substantially *ADVERB*
1 mostly; in all important respects ◆ *The rules of the games are substantially the same.*
2 by a large amount ◆ *We have made substantially more money this year.*

substantiate *VERB* **substantiates, substantiating, substantiated**
to produce evidence to prove something
▷ **substantiation** *NOUN*

substation *NOUN* **substations**
a subsidiary station for distributing electric current

substitute *NOUN* **substitutes**
a person or thing that acts or is used instead of another

substitute *VERB* **substitutes, substituting, substituted**
to use a person or thing as a substitute
▷ **substitution** *NOUN*

subterfuge *NOUN* **subterfuges**
a deception

subterranean *ADJECTIVE*
under the ground

subtitle *NOUN* **subtitles**
1 a secondary or additional title
2 words shown on the screen during a film, e.g. to translate a foreign language

subtle (*say* **sut**- el) *ADJECTIVE*
1 faint or delicate ◆ *The walls were painted in subtle colours.*
2 slight and difficult to detect or describe ◆ *The differences between these points of view are quite subtle.*
3 ingenious but not immediately obvious ◆ *It was all intended as a subtle joke.*
▷ **subtly** *ADVERB*
▷ **subtlety** *NOUN*

subtotal *NOUN* **subtotals**
the total of part of a group of figures

subtract *VERB* **subtracts, subtracting, subtracted**
1 to deduct a number or amount
2 (*Mathematics*) to take away a part, quantity, or number from a greater one

subtraction *NOUN*
(*Mathematics*) the process of subtracting one number from another

subtropical *ADJECTIVE*
of regions that border on the tropics

suburb *NOUN* **suburbs**
a district with houses that is outside the central part of a city
▷ **suburban** *ADJECTIVE*

suburbia *NOUN*
the suburbs of a city as a social group

subvert *VERB* **subverts, subverting, subverted**
to undermine or weaken the authority or power of an organization or system
▷ **subversion** *NOUN*
▷ **subversive** *ADJECTIVE*

subway *NOUN* **subways**
1 an underground passage for pedestrians
2 (*American*) an underground railway

a b c d e f g h i j k l m n o p q r s t u v w x y z

succeed *VERB* **succeeds, succeeding, succeeded**
1 to do or get what you wanted or intended
2 to come after another person or thing ◆ *He succeeded his brother as head of department last year.*
3 to become the next holder of an office, especially the monarchy ◆ *This was the situation when Mary succeeded to the throne.*

success *NOUN* **successes**
1 doing or getting what you wanted or intended
2 a person or thing that does well

successful *ADJECTIVE*
having success, or being a success
▷ **successfully** *ADVERB*

succession *NOUN* **successions**
1 a series of people or things
2 the process of following in order
3 succeeding to the throne; the right of doing this
in succession one after another

successive *ADJECTIVE*
following one after another ◆ *The house had been extended and modernized by successive owners.*
▷ **successively** *ADVERB*

successor *NOUN* **successors**
a person or thing that succeeds another

succinct (*say* suk- **sinkt**) *ADJECTIVE*
concise; expressed briefly
▷ **succinctly** *ADVERB*

Succoth (*say* **suuk**- oht) *NOUN*
the Jewish autumn festival of thanksgiving (the Feast of Tabernacles)

succour (*say* **suk**- er) *NOUN*
help given in time of need

succour *VERB* **succours, succouring, succoured**
to offer help to someone in need

succulent *ADJECTIVE*
1 juicy and tasty
2 succulent plants have thick juicy leaves or stems

succumb (*say* suk- **um**) *VERB* **succumbs, succumbing, succumbed**
to give way to something overpowering

such *ADJECTIVE*
1 of the same kind; similar ◆ *Such a thing had never happened before.*
2 of the kind described ◆ *There's no such person.*
3 so great or intense

No other adult I know would have used such a long and complicated word when talking to me.
— *Theresa Breslin, Whispers in the Graveyard*

such as for example

such-and-such *NOUN*
something particular but not named ◆ *One day they say such-and-such and the next day they've changed their minds.*

suchlike *ADJECTIVE*
of that kind

suck *VERB* **sucks, sucking, sucked**
1 to take in liquid or air through almost-closed lips
2 to squeeze something in your mouth by using your tongue
3 to draw something in ◆ *The mud had sucked him in up to his waist.*
to suck up to someone (*informal*) is to flatter them in the hope of winning their favour
▷ **suck** *NOUN*

sucker *NOUN* **suckers**
1 a rubber or plastic cup that sticks to a surface by suction
2 an organ that enables an animal to cling to a surface by suction
3 a shoot springing from a root or underground stem
4 (*informal*) a person who is easily deceived

suckle *VERB* **suckles, suckling, suckled**
to feed on milk at the mother's breast or udder

suction *NOUN*
1 the process of sucking
2 the process of producing a vacuum so that things are sucked into the empty space

sudden *ADJECTIVE*
happening or done quickly or without warning
▷ **suddenly** *ADVERB*
▷ **suddenness** *NOUN*

sudoku (*say* soo- **doh**- koo) *NOUN*
a puzzle in which a grid of 81 squares, some of which have numbers already filled in, has to be completed so that the numbers 1 to 9 appear only once in each of the 9 rows and 9 columns and in each block of 3 rows by 3 columns

WORD HISTORY from Japanese *su doku* 'single number'

suds *PLURAL NOUN*
froth on soapy water

sue *VERB* **sues, suing, sued**
to start a lawsuit against someone to claim money from them

suede (*say* swayd) *NOUN*
leather with one side rubbed to make it velvety

WORD HISTORY from French *gants de Suède* 'gloves from Sweden' (where the leather originally came from)

suet ***NOUN***
hard fat from cattle and sheep, used in cooking

suffer ***VERB*** **suffers, suffering, suffered**
1 to feel pain or sadness
2 to experience something bad or harmful ◆ *His grandmother had suffered a stroke that morning.*
3 to become worse or be badly affected ◆ *He had been unwell and his game had suffered.*
4 (*old use*) to allow or tolerate something
▷ **sufferer** ***NOUN***
▷ **suffering** ***NOUN***

sufferance ***NOUN***
on sufferance allowed but only reluctantly

suffice ***VERB*** **suffices, sufficing, sufficed**
to be enough for someone's needs

sufficient ***ADJECTIVE***
enough; adequate
▷ **sufficiently** ***ADVERB***
▷ **sufficiency** ***NOUN***

suffix ***NOUN*** **suffixes**
(*Grammar*) a letter or set of letters joined to the end of a word to make another word (e.g. in forget*ful*, lion*ess*, rust*y*) or a form of a verb (e.g. sing*ing*, wait*ed*): see the panel at *prefix*

suffocate ***VERB*** **suffocates, suffocating, suffocated**
1 to make it difficult or impossible for someone to breathe
2 to suffer or die because breathing is prevented
▷ **suffocation** ***NOUN***

suffrage ***NOUN***
the right to vote in political elections

suffragette ***NOUN*** **suffragettes**
a woman who campaigned in the early 20th century for women to have the right to vote

suffuse ***VERB*** **suffuses, suffusing, suffused**
to spread through or over something

> The sky was pale in the south-east, and the air was suffused with a grey mist. — *Philip Pullman, Northern Lights*

sugar ***NOUN***
a sweet food obtained from the juices of various plants, such as sugar cane or sugar beet
▷ **sugary** ***ADJECTIVE***

WORD HISTORY via Old French from Sanskrit *sharkara* 'grit' or 'gravel' (because sugar is like this in consistency)

sugar ***VERB*** **sugars, sugaring, sugared**
to add sugar to food or drink

suggest ***VERB*** **suggests, suggesting, suggested**
1 to put forward an idea or plan for someone to consider
2 to cause an idea or possibility to come into the mind
▷ **suggestive** ***ADJECTIVE***

suggestion ***NOUN*** **suggestions**
1 an idea or possibility that you can consider
2 a sign or indication

> Mrs Stitch turned her face of clay, in which only the eyes gave a suggestion of welcome, towards her visitor. — *Evelyn Waugh, Scoop*

3 the process of suggesting

suggestible ***ADJECTIVE***
easily influenced by people's suggestions

suicide ***NOUN*** **suicides**
1 the act of killing yourself deliberately
2 a person who commits suicide
▷ **suicidal** ***ADJECTIVE***

suit ***NOUN*** **suits**
1 a matching jacket and trousers, or a jacket and skirt, that are meant to be worn together
2 a set of clothing for a particular activity
3 any of the four sets of cards (clubs, hearts, diamonds, spades) in a pack of playing cards
4 a lawsuit

USAGE NOTE Take care not to confuse this word with *suite*.

suit ***VERB*** **suits, suiting, suited**
1 to be suitable or convenient for a person or thing
2 to make a person look attractive

suitable ***ADJECTIVE***
satisfactory or right for a particular person, purpose, or occasion
▷ **suitably** ***ADVERB***
▷ **suitability** ***NOUN***

suitcase ***NOUN*** **suitcases**
a rectangular container for carrying clothes, usually with a hinged lid and a handle

suite (*sounds like* sweet) ***NOUN*** **suites**
1 a set of furniture
2 a set of rooms
3 a set of short pieces of music

USAGE NOTE Take care not to confuse this word with *suit*.

suitor ***NOUN*** **suitors**
a man who is courting a woman

sulk ***VERB*** **sulks, sulking, sulked**
to be silent and bad-tempered because you are not pleased
▷ **sulk** ***NOUN***
▷ **sulky** ***ADJECTIVE***
▷ **sulkily** ***ADVERB***
▷ **sulkiness** ***NOUN***

sullen ***ADJECTIVE***
sulking and gloomy

> The old man's flat face and dark eyes showed nothing, but his voice was sullen with displeasure. — *J. R. R. Tolkien, The Return of the King*

▷ **sullenly** ***ADVERB***
▷ **sullenness** ***NOUN***

a b c d e f g h i j k l m n o p q r s t u v w x y z

sully *VERB* **sullies, sullying, sullied**
to soil or stain something; to blemish something ◆ *These discoveries about his past had sullied his reputation.*

sulphur *NOUN*
a yellow chemical used in industry and in medicine
▷ **sulphurous** *ADJECTIVE*

sulphuric acid *NOUN*
a strong colourless acid containing sulphur

sultan *NOUN* **sultans**
the ruler of certain Muslim countries

sultana *NOUN* **sultanas**
a raisin without seeds

sultry *ADJECTIVE*
1 sultry weather is hot and humid
2 a sultry look or smile suggests passion or sexual desire
▷ **sultriness** *NOUN*

sum *NOUN* **sums**
1 a total
2 a problem in arithmetic
3 an amount of money

sum *VERB* **sums, summing, summed**
to sum something up is to give a summary at the end of a talk or article

summarize *VERB* **summarizes, summarizing, summarized**
to make a summary of something
USAGE NOTE This word can also be spelled summarise.

summary *NOUN* **summaries**
a statement of the main points of something said or written

summary *ADJECTIVE*
1 brief or concise
2 a summary decision or punishment is one done hastily, without delay
▷ **summarily** *ADVERB*

summer *NOUN* **summers**
the warm season between spring and autumn
▷ **summery** *ADJECTIVE*

summer house *NOUN* **summer houses**
a small building providing shade in a garden or park

summit *NOUN* **summits**
1 the top of a mountain or hill
2 a meeting between the leaders of powerful countries

summon *VERB* **summons, summoning, summoned**
1 to order someone to come or appear
2 to call people together
to summon up strength or courage is to gather together your strength or courage in order to do something

summons *NOUN* **summonses**
a command to appear in a lawcourt

sumo *NOUN*
a form of Japanese heavyweight wrestling

sump *NOUN* **sumps**
a metal case that holds oil round an engine

sumptuous *ADJECTIVE*
splendid and expensive-looking
▷ **sumptuously** *ADVERB*

sun *NOUN* **suns**
1 the star round which the earth travels
2 light and warmth from the sun
3 any star in the universe round which planets travel
WORD FAMILY A related adjective is solar.

sun *VERB* **suns, sunning, sunned**
to sun yourself is to sit or lie in the sun

sunbathe *VERB* **sunbathes, sunbathing, sunbathed**
to expose your body to the sun, especially to get a tan

sunbeam *NOUN* **sunbeams**
a ray of the sun

sunbed *NOUN* **sunbeds**
a bench that you lie on under a sunlamp

sunblock *NOUN*
a cream or lotion for protecting the skin from sunburn

sunburn *NOUN*
redness of the skin caused by the sun
▷ **sunburnt** *ADJECTIVE*

sundae (*say* **sun**- day) *NOUN* **sundaes**
a dish of ice cream with additions such as fruit, nuts, cream, and syrup
WORD HISTORY from *Sunday* (because sundaes were originally sold on a Sunday, possibly to use up ice cream not sold during the week)

Sunday *NOUN*
the first day of the week, observed by Christians as a day of rest and worship
WORD HISTORY from Old English *sunnandaeg* 'day of the sun'

sunder *VERB* **sunders, sundering, sundered**
(*poetic*) to break or tear something apart

sundial *NOUN* **sundials**
a device that shows the time by a shadow on a dial

sundown *NOUN*
(*American*) dusk or sunset

sundries *PLURAL NOUN*
various small things

sundry *ADJECTIVE*
various or several
all and sundry all people; everyone

sunflower *NOUN* **sunflowers**
a very tall flower with golden petals round a dark centre

WORD HISTORY called this because the flower head turns towards the sun

sunglasses *PLURAL NOUN*
dark glasses to protect your eyes from strong sunlight

sunken *ADJECTIVE*
sunk deeply into a surface

Macavity's a ginger cat, he's very tall and thin; You would know him if you saw him, for his eyes are sunken in. — *T. S. Eliot, Old Possum's Book of Practical Cats*

sunlamp *NOUN* **sunlamps**
a lamp which uses ultraviolet light to give people an artificial tan

sunlight *NOUN*
light from the sun
▷ **sunlit** *ADJECTIVE*

Sunni *NOUN* **Sunnis**
(*Religion*) a member of one of the two main branches of Islam; about 80% of Muslims are Sunnis (SEE ALSO **Shiite**)

sunny *ADJECTIVE* **sunnier, sunniest**
1 full of sunshine
2 happy and cheerful
▷ **sunnily** *ADVERB*

sunrise *NOUN* **sunrises**
the rising of the sun; dawn

sunscreen *NOUN*
a cream or lotion for protecting the skin from sunburn

sunset *NOUN* **sunsets**
the setting of the sun

sunshade *NOUN* **sunshades**
a parasol or other device to protect people from the sun

sunshine *NOUN*
sunlight with no cloud between the sun and the earth

sunspot *NOUN* **sunspots**
1 a dark place on the sun's surface
2 a sunny place

sunstroke *NOUN*
illness caused by being in the sun too long

suntan *NOUN* **suntans**
a brown colour of the skin caused by the sun
▷ **suntanned** *ADJECTIVE*

sun visor *NOUN* **sun visors**
a flap at the top of a vehicle's windscreen that shields your eyes from the sun

sup *VERB* **sups, supping, supped**
to drink liquid in sips or spoonfuls

super *ADJECTIVE*
(*informal*) excellent or superb

superannuation *NOUN*
regular payments made by an employee towards a pension

superb *ADJECTIVE*
magnificent or excellent
▷ **superbly** *ADVERB*

supercilious *ADJECTIVE*
haughty and scornful
▷ **superciliously** *ADVERB*

WORD HISTORY from Latin *supercilium* 'eyebrow', because raising the eyebrows is a sign of this attitude

superficial *ADJECTIVE*
1 on the surface ◆ *He survived the accident with only superficial injuries.*
2 not deep or thorough ◆ *Her knowledge of the language is fairly superficial.*
▷ **superficially** *ADVERB*
▷ **superficiality** *NOUN*

superfluous *ADJECTIVE*
more than is needed
▷ **superfluity** *NOUN*

superglue *NOUN*
a kind of strong glue that sticks very quickly

superhuman *ADJECTIVE*
1 beyond ordinary human ability
2 higher than human; divine

superimpose *VERB* **superimposes, superimposing, superimposed**
to place one thing on top of another
▷ **superimposition** *NOUN*

superintend *VERB* **superintends, superintending, superintended**
to supervise someone

superintendent *NOUN* **superintendents**
1 a supervisor
2 a police officer above the rank of inspector

superior *ADJECTIVE*
1 higher in position or rank
2 better than another person or thing
3 showing conceit
▷ **superiority** *NOUN*

superior *NOUN* **superiors**
a person or thing that is superior to another

superlative *ADJECTIVE*
of the highest degree or quality
▷ **superlatively** *ADVERB*

a b c d e f g h i j k l m n o p q r s t u v w x y z

superlative *NOUN* **superlatives**
the form of an adjective or adverb that expresses 'most', e.g. *fastest* and *most difficult*: see the language panel at **comparative**

superman *NOUN* **supermen**
a man with superhuman powers

supermarket *NOUN* **supermarkets**
a large self-service shop that sells food and other goods

supermodel *NOUN* **supermodels**
a highly successful and glamorous fashion model

supernatural *ADJECTIVE*
not belonging to the natural world nor having a natural explanation
▷ **supernatural** *NOUN*

supernova *NOUN* **supernovae**
a star that suddenly becomes much brighter because of an internal explosion

superpower *NOUN* **superpowers**
one of the most powerful nations of the world, such as the USA

superscript *ADJECTIVE*
a superscript letter, figure, or symbol is written or printed above the line

supersede *VERB* **supersedes, superseding, superseded**
to take the place of something ◆ *Steam locomotives were superseded by diesel.*

USAGE NOTE Note that this word ends *-sede* and not *-cede*.

supersonic *ADJECTIVE*
faster than the speed of sound (SEE ALSO **subsonic**)

superstition *NOUN* **superstitions**
a belief or action that is not based on reason or evidence, e.g. the belief that it is unlucky to walk under a ladder
▷ **superstitious** *ADJECTIVE*

superstore *NOUN* **superstores**
a very large supermarket selling a wide range of goods

superstructure *NOUN* **superstructures**
1 a structure that rests on something else
2 a building as distinct from its foundations

supertanker *NOUN* **supertankers**
a very large tanker

supervise *VERB* **supervises, supervising, supervised**
to be in charge of a person or thing and inspect what is done
▷ **supervision** *NOUN*
▷ **supervisor** *NOUN*
▷ **supervisory** *ADJECTIVE*

superwoman *NOUN* **superwomen**
a woman who is expected to cope with many things at once

supine (*say* **soop**- yn) *ADJECTIVE*
1 lying face upwards (SEE ALSO **prone**)
2 not taking action

supper *NOUN* **suppers**
a meal eaten in the evening

supplant *VERB* **supplants, supplanting, supplanted**
to take the place of a person or thing that has been ousted

supple *ADJECTIVE*
bending easily; flexible
▷ **supplely** *ADVERB*
▷ **suppleness** *NOUN*

supplement *NOUN* **supplements**
1 something added as an extra
2 an extra section added to a book or newspaper
▷ **supplementary** *ADJECTIVE*

supplement *VERB* **supplements, supplementing, supplemented**
to add to something

The wealthier families in our village supplemented their diets with tea, coffee and sugar. — *Nelson Mandela, Long Walk to Freedom*

suppliant (*say* **sup**- lee- ant) or **supplicant** *NOUN* **suppliants** or **supplicants**
a person who asks humbly for something

supplicate *VERB* **supplicates, supplicating, supplicated**
to ask or beg humbly for something
▷ **supplication** *NOUN*

supply *VERB* **supplies, supplying, supplied**
to sell or provide what is needed or wanted
▷ **supplier** *NOUN*

supply *NOUN* **supplies**
1 an amount of something that is available for use when needed
2 the action of supplying something

supply teacher *NOUN* **supply teachers**
a teacher who takes over when a regular teacher is absent

support *VERB* **supports, supporting, supported**
1 to keep something from falling or sinking; to hold something up
2 to give strength, help, or encouragement to someone
3 to provide children or other people with the necessities of life ◆ *They have a family to support.*
▷ **supporter** *NOUN*
▷ **supportive** *ADJECTIVE*

support *NOUN* **supports**
1 the action of supporting
2 a person or thing that supports

suppose *VERB* **supposes, supposing, supposed**
1 to think that something is likely to happen or be true
2 to assume something; to consider something as a suggestion ◆ *Suppose I agree — what then?*
3 to be supposed to do something is to have it as a duty or obligation

These stairs led up to the roof so students weren't supposed to use them. — *Keith Gray, Malarkey*

▷ **supposition** *NOUN*

supposedly *ADVERB*
so people suppose or think ◆ *The ceasefire had supposedly come into force at midnight.*

suppress *VERB* **suppresses, suppressing, suppressed**
1 to put an end to something forcibly or by authority
2 to keep something from being known or seen
▷ **suppression** *NOUN*
▷ **suppressor** *NOUN*

supremacy (*say* soo- **prem**- asi) *NOUN*
highest authority or power

supreme *ADJECTIVE*
1 most important or highest in rank
2 very great ◆ *With a supreme effort, she managed to keep calm.*
▷ **supremely** *ADVERB*

surcharge *NOUN* **surcharges**
an extra charge

sure *ADJECTIVE*
1 completely confident that you are right; feeling no doubt
2 certain to happen or do something
3 reliable; undoubtedly true
for sure definitely; certainly
to make sure
1 is to find out exactly
2 is to make something happen or be true ◆ *Make sure you have everything you need before you start.*
▷ **sureness** *NOUN*

sure *ADVERB*
(*informal*) surely; certainly
sure enough in fact; and so it turned out to be

surely *ADVERB*
1 in a sure way; certainly or securely
2 it must be true; I feel sure ◆ *Surely there must be some other way of doing this.*

surety *NOUN* **sureties**
1 a guarantee
2 a person who promises to pay a debt or fulfil a contract or agreement if another person fails to do so

surf *NOUN*
the white foam of waves breaking on a rock or shore

surf *VERB* **surfs, surfing, surfed**
1 to go surfing
2 to browse through the Internet

surface *NOUN* **surfaces**
1 the outside of something
2 any of the sides of an object, especially the top part
3 an outward appearance ◆ *On the surface he was a generous man.*

surface *VERB* **surfaces, surfacing, surfaced**
1 to put a surface on a road, path, or other area
2 to come up to the surface from under water

surface mail *NOUN*
letters and packages carried by sea or over land, not by air

surfboard *NOUN* **surfboards**
a board used in surfing

surfeit (*say* **ser**- fit) *NOUN*
too much of something
▷ **surfeited** *ADJECTIVE*

surfing *NOUN*
balancing yourself on a board that is carried to the shore on the waves
▷ **surfer** *NOUN*

surge *VERB* **surges, surging, surged**
1 to move forwards or upwards like waves
2 to increase suddenly and powerfully
▷ **surge** *NOUN*

surgeon *NOUN* **surgeons**
a doctor who treats disease or injury by cutting or repairing the parts of the body that have been affected

WORD HISTORY from Greek *kheirourgos* 'one who works with the hands', from *kheir* 'hand' (because surgeons use their hands rather than prescribing drugs and medicines as other doctors do)

surgery *NOUN* **surgeries**
1 the work of a surgeon
2 the place where a doctor or dentist regularly gives advice and treatment to patients
3 the time when patients can visit a doctor or dentist
▷ **surgical** *ADJECTIVE*
▷ **surgically** *ADVERB*

surly *ADJECTIVE* **surlier, surliest**
bad-tempered and unfriendly
▷ **surliness** *NOUN*

a b c d e f g h i j k l m n o p q r s t u v w x y z

SPELLING NOTE Some words pronounced **s**- begin with **ce**- (e.g. cent), **ci**- (e.g. city), or **cy**- (e.g. cymbal)

surmise *VERB* **surmises, surmising, surmised**
to guess or suspect something
▷ **surmise** *NOUN*

surmount *VERB* **surmounts, surmounting, surmounted**
1 to overcome a difficulty
2 to get over an obstacle
3 to be positioned on top of something ◆ *The tombstone is surmounted by a sculpture of a winged angel.*

surname *NOUN* **surnames**
the name held by all members of a family

surpass *VERB* **surpasses, surpassing, surpassed**
to do or be better than all others; to excel over others

surplus *NOUN* **surpluses**
an amount left over after spending or using all that was needed
▷ **surplus** *ADJECTIVE*

surprise *NOUN* **surprises**
1 something unexpected
2 the feeling caused by something that was not expected
take someone by surprise happen to someone unexpectedly

surprise *VERB* **surprises, surprising, surprised**
1 to be a surprise; to make someone feel surprise
2 to meet or discover somebody or something unexpectedly

Once we surprised a crocodile sunning itself on a rock. — *Joy Adamson, Born Free*

▷ **surprised** *ADJECTIVE*
▷ **surprising** *ADJECTIVE*
▷ **surprisingly** *ADVERB*

surreal *ADJECTIVE*
1 strange and bizarre
2 having the qualities of surrealism

surrealism *NOUN*
a style of art and literature that shows or describes strange objects and scenes like those seen in dreams and fantasies
▷ **surrealist** *NOUN*
▷ **surrealistic** *ADJECTIVE*

surrender *VERB* **surrenders, surrendering, surrendered**
1 to stop fighting and give yourself up to an enemy
2 to hand something over to another person, especially when compelled to do so
▷ **surrender** *NOUN*

surreptitious (*say* su- rep- **tish**- us) *ADJECTIVE*
stealthy, furtive

Framed in the staffroom window, Mr Cartright was blowing the smoke of his last surreptitious cigarette. — *Anne Fine, Flour Babies*

▷ **surreptitiously** *ADVERB*

surrogate (*say* **su**- rog- at) *NOUN* **surrogates**
a deputy or substitute
▷ **surrogacy** *NOUN*

surrogate mother *NOUN* **surrogate mothers**
a woman who agrees to conceive and give birth to a baby for a woman who cannot do so herself, using a fertilized egg of the other woman or sperm from the other woman's partner

surround *VERB* **surrounds, surrounding, surrounded**
to come or be all round a person or thing

surroundings *PLURAL NOUN*
the conditions or area around a person or thing

surveillance (*say* ser- **vay**- lans) *NOUN*
a close watch kept on a person or thing

survey (*say* **ser**- vay) *NOUN* **surveys**
1 a general look at something
2 a technical inspection of an area or building

survey (*say* ser- **vay**) *VERB* **surveys, surveying, surveyed**
to make a survey of something; to inspect something
▷ **surveyor** *NOUN*

survival *NOUN* **survivals**
1 the act of surviving; the likelihood of surviving
2 something that has survived from an earlier time

survive *VERB* **survives, surviving, survived**
1 to stay alive; to continue to exist
2 to remain alive after an accident or disaster
3 to continue living after someone has died
▷ **survivor** *NOUN*

susceptible (*say* sus- **ept**- ib- ul) *ADJECTIVE*
to be susceptible to something is to be likely to be affected by it
▷ **susceptibility** *NOUN*

suspect (*say* sus- **pekt**) *VERB* **suspects, suspecting, suspected**
1 to think that a person is not to be trusted or has committed a crime; to distrust someone
2 to have a feeling that something is likely or possible

Roger slept badly and suspects he has a sprained wrist following yesterday's excursion. — *Michael Palin, Pole to Pole*

suspect (*say* **sus**- pekt) ***NOUN*** **suspects**
a person who is suspected of a crime or offence

▷ **suspect** ***ADJECTIVE***

suspend ***VERB*** **suspends, suspending, suspended**
1 to hang something up
2 to postpone something or halt it temporarily
3 to remove a person from a job or position for a time
4 to keep something from falling or sinking in air or liquid

WORD FAMILY *Suspend* comes from the Latin word *pendere* meaning 'to hang'. Other words to do with hanging (some only loosely) and having the same origin include *depend* (literally, to hang from), *impending* (literally, hanging towards), *pendant*, and *propensity*. There is another Latin word *pendere* meaning 'to weigh' or 'to pay', and this is the source of some other English words such as *dispense*, *expend*, *pension*, and *stipend*.

suspender ***NOUN*** **suspenders**
a fastener to hold up a sock or stocking by its top

suspense ***NOUN***
an anxious or uncertain feeling while waiting for something to happen or become known

suspension ***NOUN***
1 the act of suspending something
2 the system of springs and shock absorbers in a vehicle that lessens the effect of rough road surfaces
3 a liquid containing small pieces of solid material which do not dissolve

suspension bridge ***NOUN*** **suspension bridges**
a bridge supported by cables

suspicion ***NOUN*** **suspicions**
1 suspecting or being suspected; distrust
2 a slight belief

suspicious ***ADJECTIVE***
1 distrusting people or things

She is a suspicious person, my mother. She is especially suspicious of two things — strange men and boiled eggs. — *Roald Dahl, The Umbrella Man*

2 making you distrust or suspect something

▷ **suspiciously** ***ADVERB***

sustain ***VERB*** **sustains, sustaining, sustained**
1 to keep someone alive
2 to keep something happening
3 to undergo or suffer something harmful or unpleasant
4 to support or uphold something

▷ **sustainable** ***ADJECTIVE***

susurration (*say* sus- oo- **ray**- shon) ***NOUN***
(*literary*) the sound of whispering or rustling

sustenance ***NOUN***
food and drink; nourishment

suture (*say* **soo**- cher) ***NOUN*** **sutures**
surgical stitching of a cut

suzerainty (*say* **soo**- zer- en- tee) ***NOUN***
1 the partial control of a weaker country by a stronger one
2 the power of an overlord in feudal times

svelte ***ADJECTIVE***
slim and graceful

SW ***ABBREVIATION***
1 south-west
2 south-western

swab (*say* swob) ***NOUN*** **swabs**
1 a mop or pad for cleaning or wiping something; a small pad for cleaning a wound
2 a specimen of fluid from the body taken on a swab for testing

swab ***VERB*** **swabs, swabbing, swabbed**
to clean or wipe something with a swab

swagger ***VERB*** **swaggers, swaggering, swaggered**
to walk or behave in a conceited way; to strut

▷ **swagger** ***NOUN***

swagman ***NOUN***
(*Australian and New Zealand*) a man who travels round carrying a bundle of his possessions

swain ***NOUN*** **swains**
1 (*old use*) a country lad
2 (*poetic*) a young lover or suitor

swallow[1] ***VERB*** **swallows, swallowing, swallowed**
1 to make something go down your throat
2 to believe something that ought not to be believed

to swallow something or **someone up** is to absorb or overwhelm them ◆ *The last of the straggling soldiers were swallowed up by the forest.*

swallow[2] ***NOUN*** **swallows**
a small bird with a forked tail and pointed wings

swamp ***NOUN*** **swamps**
a marsh

▷ **swampy** ***ADJECTIVE***

swamp ***VERB*** **swamps, swamping, swamped**
1 to flood a place or area
2 to overwhelm someone with a great mass or number of things

swan ***NOUN*** **swans**
a large usually white swimming bird with a long neck

swank ***VERB*** **swanks, swanking, swanked**
(*informal*) to boast or swagger; to show off

a b c d e f g h i j k l m n o p q r s t u v w x y z

swank *NOUN*
(*informal*) showing yourself or your possessions off in a conceited way

swanky *ADJECTIVE* **swankier, swankiest**
very luxurious or expensive

In case you don't live in New York, the Wicker Bar is in this sort of swanky hotel, the Seton Hotel. — *J. D. Salinger, The Catcher in the Rye*

swansong *NOUN* **swansongs**
a person's last performance or work

WORD HISTORY called this from the old belief that a swan sang sweetly when it was about to die

swap *VERB* **swaps, swapping, swapped**
(*informal*) to exchange one thing for another
▷ **swap** *NOUN*

WORD HISTORY formerly 'to seal a bargain by slapping each other's hands' (imitating the sound)

swarm *NOUN* **swarms**
a large number of insects flying or moving about together

swarm *VERB* **swarms, swarming, swarmed**
1 to gather or move in a swarm
2 to be crowded with people or moving things

The room was swarming with people now and Father grasped my hand and told me to hold on tight. — *Sue Reid, My Story: Mill Girl*

swarthy *ADJECTIVE*
having a dark complexion
▷ **swarthiness** *NOUN*

swashbuckling *ADJECTIVE*
enjoying or describing daring adventures and fighting

swastika *NOUN* **swastikas**
an ancient symbol formed by a cross with its ends bent at right angles, adopted by the Nazis as their sign

WORD HISTORY from Sanskrit *svasti* 'well- being'

swat *VERB* **swats, swatting, swatted**
to hit or crush a fly or other insect
▷ **swatter** *NOUN*

swathe❶ (*say* swayth) *NOUN* **swathes**
1 a broad strip or area of land
2 a line of cut corn or grass

to cut a swathe through something is to pass through an area causing destruction

swathe❷ (*say* swayth) *VERB* **swathes, swathing, swathed**
to wrap something in layers of bandages, paper, or clothes

sway *VERB* **sways, swaying, swayed**
1 to move or swing gently from side to side
2 to influence or affect someone
▷ **sway** *NOUN*

swear *VERB* **swears, swearing, swore, sworn**
1 to make a solemn promise ◆ *I swore to get even.*
2 to make a person take an oath ◆ *They swore us to secrecy.*
3 to use curses or coarse words in anger or surprise

to swear by something is to have great confidence in it and always recommend it

swear word *NOUN* **swear words**
a word considered rude or shocking, often used by someone who is angry

sweat (*say* swet) *NOUN*
moisture given off by the body through the pores of the skin; perspiration
▷ **sweaty** *ADJECTIVE*

sweat *VERB* **sweats, sweating, sweated**
to give off sweat; to perspire

sweater *NOUN* **sweaters**
a jersey or pullover

sweatshirt *NOUN* **sweatshirts**
a thick cotton jersey worn for sports or casual wear

swede *NOUN* **swedes**
a large kind of turnip with purple skin and yellow flesh

WORD HISTORY short for *Swedish turnip* (because it originally came from Sweden)

sweep *VERB* **sweeps, sweeping, swept**
1 to clean or clear an area with a broom or brush
2 to sweep something away is to move or remove it quickly or forcibly ◆ *The floods swept away dozens of cars.* ◆ *The country's social relationships had been swept away by the war.*
3 to go smoothly and quickly ◆ *The guest speaker swept into the room.*
4 to move quickly over an area ◆ *Forest fires were sweeping the area.*
▷ **sweeper** *NOUN*

sweep *NOUN* **sweeps**
1 an act of sweeping
2 a sweeping movement
3 a chimney sweep
4 a sweepstake

sweeping *ADJECTIVE*
general or wide-ranging

sweepstake *NOUN* **sweepstakes**
a form of gambling on sporting events in which all the money staked is divided among the winners

WORD HISTORY called this because the winner 'sweeps up' all the other players' stakes

sweet *ADJECTIVE*
1 tasting as if it contains sugar; not bitter
2 very pleasant
3 charming or delightful

a sweet tooth a liking for sweet things
▷ **sweetly** *ADVERB*
▷ **sweetness** *NOUN*

sweet ***NOUN*** **sweets**
1 a small shaped piece of sweet food made with sugar or chocolate
2 a pudding; the sweet course in a meal
3 a loved person

sweetbread ***NOUN*** **sweetbreads**
an animal's pancreas used as food

sweetcorn ***NOUN***
the juicy yellow seeds of maize

sweeten ***VERB*** **sweetens, sweetening, sweetened**
to make sweet, or to become sweet
▷ **sweetener** ***NOUN***

sweetheart ***NOUN*** **sweethearts**
a person you love very much

sweetmeat ***NOUN*** **sweetmeats**
(*old use*) a sweet

sweet pea ***NOUN*** **sweet peas**
a climbing plant with fragrant flowers

sweet potato ***NOUN*** **sweet potatoes**
a root vegetable with reddish skin and sweet yellow flesh

swell ***VERB*** **swells, swelling, swelled, swollen** or **swelled**
1 to become larger, or to make something larger
2 to increase in amount, volume, or force

swell ***NOUN*** **swells**
1 the process of swelling
2 the rise and fall of the sea's surface

swell ***ADJECTIVE***
(*American*) (*informal*) very good

swelling ***NOUN*** **swellings**
a swollen place

swelter ***VERB*** **swelters, sweltering, sweltered**
to feel uncomfortably hot
▷ **sweltering** ***ADJECTIVE***

swerve ***VERB*** **swerves, swerving, swerved**
to turn to one side suddenly
▷ **swerve** ***NOUN***

swift ***ADJECTIVE***
quick or rapid
▷ **swiftly** ***ADVERB***
▷ **swiftness** ***NOUN***

swift ***NOUN*** **swifts**
a small bird rather like a swallow

swig ***VERB*** **swigs, swigging, swigged**
(*informal*) to drink quickly, taking large mouthfuls
▷ **swig** ***NOUN***

swill ***VERB*** **swills, swilling, swilled**
to pour water over or through something; to wash or rinse something

swill ***NOUN***
1 the process of swilling
2 a sloppy mixture of waste food given to pigs

swim ***VERB*** **swims, swimming, swam, swum**
1 to move the body through the water
2 to cross a stretch of water by swimming
3 to float
4 to be covered with or full of liquid ◆ *The floor was swimming in water.*
5 to feel dizzy ◆ *He felt sick and his head swam.*
▷ **swimmer** ***NOUN***

swim ***NOUN*** **swims**
a spell of swimming

swimming bath ***NOUN*** **swimming baths**
a public swimming pool

swimming costume ***NOUN*** **swimming costumes**
the clothing a woman wears to go swimming; a bikini or swimsuit

swimming pool ***NOUN*** **swimming pools**
an artificial pool for swimming in

swimming trunks ***PLURAL NOUN***
shorts which a man wears to go swimming

swimsuit ***NOUN*** **swimsuits**
a one-piece swimming costume

swindle ***VERB*** **swindles, swindling, swindled**
to cheat a person of money or possessions, especially in business
▷ **swindle** ***NOUN***
▷ **swindler** ***NOUN***

swine ***NOUN*** **swine**
1 a pig
2 (*informal*) a very unpleasant or awkward person or thing

swing ***VERB*** **swings, swinging, swung**
1 to move back and forth while hanging
2 to move or turn in a curve
3 to change from one opinion or mood to another

swing ***NOUN*** **swings**
1 a swinging movement
2 a seat hung on chains or ropes so that it can be moved backwards and forwards
3 the amount by which votes or opinions change from one side to another
4 a kind of jazz music

in full swing full of activity; working fully

swingeing (*say* **swin**-jing) ***ADJECTIVE***
1 a swingeing blow is very hard and powerful
2 huge in amount

a b c d e f g h i j k l m n o p q r s t u v w x y z

swipe *VERB* **swipes, swiping, swiped**
1 to hit someone or something with a swinging blow
2 (*informal*) to steal something
3 to pass a credit card through an electronic reading device when making a payment
▷ **swipe** *NOUN*

swirl *VERB* **swirls, swirling, swirled**
to move round quickly in circles
▷ **swirl** *NOUN*

swish *VERB* **swishes, swishing, swished**
to move with a hissing or rushing sound

Ivy and her cohorts ignored her in the corridors at school, swishing past her as if she didn't exist.
— *Catherine MacPhail, Run Zan Run*

▷ **swish** *NOUN*

swish *ADJECTIVE*
(*informal*) smart and fashionable

Swiss roll *NOUN* **Swiss rolls**
a thin sponge cake spread with jam or cream and rolled up

switch *NOUN* **switches**
1 a device that is pressed or turned to start or stop something working, especially by electricity
2 a change of opinion, policy, or methods
3 a mechanism for moving the points on a railway track
4 a flexible rod or whip

switch *VERB* **switches, switching, switched**
1 to turn something on or off by means of a switch
2 to change something suddenly
3 to replace one thing with another

switchback *NOUN* **switchbacks**
a railway at a fair, with steep slopes up and down alternately

switchboard *NOUN* **switchboards**
1 an apparatus for making telephone connections or operating electric circuits
2 the staff operating a switchboard

swivel *VERB* **swivels, swivelling, swivelled**
to turn round smoothly

swivel *NOUN* **swivels**
a device joining two things so that one can revolve without turning the other

swollen *past participle of* **swell**

swoon *VERB* **swoons, swooning, swooned**
(*old use*) to faint
▷ **swoon** *NOUN*

swoop *VERB* **swoops, swooping, swooped**
1 to dive or come down with a rushing movement
2 to make a sudden attack or raid
▷ **swoop** *NOUN*

swop *VERB* **swops, swopping, swopped**
another spelling of *swap*
▷ **swop** *NOUN*

sword (*say* sord) *NOUN* **swords**
a weapon with a long pointed blade fixed in a handle or hilt
▷ **swordsman** *NOUN*

swordfish *NOUN* **swordfish**
a large sea fish with a long sword-like upper jaw

sworn *ADJECTIVE*
1 sworn evidence or testimony is given under oath
2 sworn enemies are determined to remain enemies

swot *VERB* **swots, swotting, swotted**
(*informal*) to study hard
▷ **swot** *NOUN*

sycamore *NOUN* **sycamores**
a tall tree with winged seeds, often grown for its timber

sycophant (*say* **sik**- o- fant) *NOUN* **sycophants**
a person who tries to win people's favour by flattering them
▷ **sycophantic** *ADJECTIVE*
▷ **sycophantically** *ADVERB*
▷ **sycophancy** *NOUN*

WORD HISTORY from Greek *sukophantes* 'showing figs', from *sukon* 'fig' (probably because it referred to making a rude sign, i.e. treating people with contempt by informing on them and winning favour with the authorities)

syllable *NOUN* **syllables**
(*Language*) a part of a word that forms a unit when you say it. 'Dog' has one syllable, and 'croc-o-dile' has three syllables.
▷ **syllabic** *ADJECTIVE*

syllabus *NOUN* **syllabuses**
the subjects or topics to be taught in a course of study

sylph *NOUN* **sylphs**
a slender girl or woman

symbol *NOUN* **symbols**
1 a thing used as a sign to represent something
2 a mark or sign that has a special meaning (e.g. +, -, and × in mathematics)

USAGE NOTE Take care not to confuse this word with *cymbal*.

symbolic *ADJECTIVE*
acting as a symbol of something
▷ **symbolical** *ADJECTIVE*
▷ **symbolically** *ADVERB*

symbolism *NOUN*
the use of symbols to represent things

symbolize *VERB* **symbolizes, symbolizing, symbolized**
to be a symbol of something

USAGE NOTE This word can also be spelled symbolise.

a b c d e f g h i j k l m n o p q r s t u v w x y z

symmetrical ***ADJECTIVE***
(*Mathematics*) able to be divided into two halves which are exactly the same but the opposite way round
▷ **symmetrically** ***ADVERB***

symmetry ***NOUN***
(*Mathematics*) the quality of being symmetrical or well-proportioned

sympathize ***VERB*** **sympathizes, sympathizing, sympathized**
to show or feel sympathy
▷ **sympathizer** ***NOUN***
USAGE NOTE This word can also be spelled sympathise.

sympathy ***NOUN*** **sympathies**
1 the sharing or understanding of other people's feelings or opinions
2 a feeling of pity or tenderness towards someone who is hurt, sad, or in trouble
▷ **sympathetic** ***ADJECTIVE***
▷ **sympathetically** ***ADVERB***

symphony ***NOUN*** **symphonies**
a long piece of music for an orchestra, usually in several sections or movements
▷ **symphonic** ***ADJECTIVE***

symptom ***NOUN*** **symptoms**
a sign that a disease or condition exists
▷ **symptomatic** ***ADJECTIVE***

synagogue (*say* **sin**- a- gog) ***NOUN*** **synagogues**
(*Religion*) a place where Jews meet for worship
WORD HISTORY from Greek *synagoge* 'assembly'

synchronize (*say* **sink**- ron- yz) ***VERB*** **synchronizes, synchronizing, synchronized**
1 to make things happen at the same time
2 to make watches or clocks show the same time
3 to happen at the same time
▷ **synchronization** ***NOUN***
USAGE NOTE This word can also be spelled synchronise.

syncopation (*say* sink- o- **pay**- shun) ***NOUN***
(*Music*) the practice of changing the strength of beats in a piece of music
▷ **syncopated** ***ADJECTIVE***

syndicate ***NOUN*** **syndicates**
1 a group of people or firms who work together in business
2 a group of people who buy something together, or who gamble together, sharing the cost and any gains

syndrome ***NOUN*** **syndromes**
1 a set of symptoms
2 a set of opinions or behaviour that are characteristic of a particular condition

synod (*say* **sin**- od) ***NOUN*** **synods**
a council of senior members of the clergy

synonym (*say* **sin**- o- nim) ***NOUN*** **synonyms**
(*Language*) a word that means the same or almost the same as another word
▷ **synonymous** (*say* sin- **on**- im- us) ***ADJECTIVE***

synonyms and antonyms

A **synonym** is a word which has the same meaning as, or a very similar meaning to, another word. For example, *unhappy*, *miserable*, *sorrowful*, and *glum* are all synonyms of the word *sad*.

An **antonym** is a word which has the opposite meaning to another word. For example, *visible* is an antonym of *invisible*; and *timid*, *cowardly*, and *spineless* are antonyms of *brave*. Note that some words which look like opposites (e.g. *valuable/invaluable*, *different/indifferent*) are not true antonyms, because they do not have opposite meanings.

A *thesaurus* is a kind of dictionary which lists synonyms and antonyms of words. You can use a thesaurus to help you find alternatives for words in your writing. For example, instead of repeating the adjective *creepy*, you could vary it with synonyms like *eerie*, *weird*, *uncanny*, *spooky*, or *spine-chilling*.

You will find synonyms of over-used words (such as *great* and *nice*) listed in this dictionary.

synopsis (*say* sin- **op**- sis) ***NOUN*** **synopses**
(*Language*) a summary of a story or book

syntax (*say* **sin**- taks) ***NOUN***
(*Grammar*) the ways in which you can organize words to form phrases or sentences
▷ **syntactic** ***ADJECTIVE***
▷ **syntactically** ***ADVERB***

synthesis (*say* **sin**- thi- sis) ***NOUN*** **syntheses**
combining different things to make something

synthesize (*say* **sin**- thi- syz) ***VERB*** **synthesizes, synthesizing, synthesized**
to make something by combining parts
USAGE NOTE This word can also be spelled synthesise.

synthesizer ***NOUN*** **synthesizers**
an electronic musical instrument that can make a large variety of sounds
USAGE NOTE This word can also be spelled synthesiser.

synthetic ***ADJECTIVE***
artificially made; not natural
▷ **synthetically** ***ADVERB***

syringe ***NOUN*** **syringes**
a device for sucking in a liquid and squirting it out
WORD HISTORY from Greek *syrinx* 'a pipe or tube'

syrup ***NOUN***
a thick sweet liquid
▷ **syrupy** ***ADJECTIVE***
WORD HISTORY from Arabic *sharab* 'a drink'

system ***NOUN*** **systems**
1 a set of parts, things, or ideas that are organized to work together
2 a way of doing something

systematic ***ADJECTIVE***
methodical; carefully planned
▷ **systematically** ***ADVERB***

a b c d e f g h i j k l m n o p q r s t u v w x y z

Tt

tab *NOUN* **tabs**
a small flap or strip that sticks out
to keep a tab or **tabs on someone** (*informal*) is to watch or monitor them closely

tabard *NOUN* **tabards**
a kind of tunic worn by a herald, open at the sides and decorated with a coat of arms

tabby *NOUN* **tabbies**
a grey or brown cat with dark stripes
WORD HISTORY from an earlier meaning 'a kind of striped material', named after *al-Attabiyya*, a district of Baghdad, where it was made

tabernacle *NOUN* **tabernacles**
(in the Bible) the portable shrine used by the ancient Jews during their wanderings in the desert
WORD HISTORY from Latin *tabernaculum* 'tent or shed'

tabla *NOUN*
a pair of small Indian drums played with the hands
WORD HISTORY from Arabic *tabl* 'drum'

table *NOUN* **tables**
1 a piece of furniture with a flat top supported on legs
2 a list of facts or figures arranged in order
3 a list of the results of multiplying a number by other numbers ◆ *My little sister is learning her three times table.*
on the table put forward for consideration or discussion
to turn the tables is to reverse a situation and put yourself at an advantage in relation to someone else

table *VERB* **tables, tabling, tabled**
to table a proposal or document is to put it forward for discussion at a meeting
WORD HISTORY from Latin *tabula* 'plank, tablet, or list'

tableau (*say* tab- loh) *NOUN* **tableaux** (*say* tab- lohz)
a dramatic or attractive scene, especially one posed on a stage by a group of people who do not speak or move
WORD HISTORY a French word meaning 'little table'

tablecloth *NOUN* **tablecloths**
a cloth for covering a table, especially at meals

table d'hôte (*say* tahbl **doht**) *NOUN*
a restaurant meal served at a fixed price (SEE ALSO **à la carte**)
WORD HISTORY a French phrase meaning 'host's table'

tablespoon *NOUN* **tablespoons**
a large spoon for serving food
▷ **tablespoonful** *NOUN* **tablespoonfuls**

tablet *NOUN* **tablets**
1 a pill of medicine
2 a solid piece of soap
3 a flat piece of stone, wood, or other material, with words carved or written on it
4 (*Scottish*) a hard sweet made from butter, sugar, and condensed milk, and formed into bars
WORD HISTORY from an Old French word meaning 'small table or slab'

table tennis *NOUN*
a game played on a table divided by a net, over which you hit a small ball with bats

tabloid *NOUN* **tabloids**
a newspaper with pages that are half the size of broadsheet newspapers, usually popular in style with many photographs and large headlines
WORD HISTORY originally, the trademark of a kind of compressed pill, later applied to these newspapers because of their condensed size

taboo *ADJECTIVE*
a taboo action, word, or subject is not to be done, spoken, or talked about

taboo *NOUN* **taboos**
a strict rule or custom in a society that prohibits a particular action

Will had no idea of the taboo in Lyra's world preventing one person from touching another's dæmon. — *Philip Pullman, The Subtle Knife*

WORD HISTORY from Tongan *tabu* 'sacred'

tabor (*say* tay- ber) *NOUN* **tabors**
a small drum

tabular *ADJECTIVE*
tabular information is arranged in a table or in columns

tabulate *VERB* **tabulates, tabulating, tabulated**
to arrange information or figures in a table or list
▷ **tabulation** *NOUN*

tabulator *NOUN* **tabulators**
a device on a typewriter or computer that automatically sets the positions for columns

tachograph (*say* tak- o- grahf) *NOUN* **tachographs**
a device that automatically records the speed and travelling time of a motor vehicle in which it is fitted

WORD HISTORY from Greek *tachos* 'speed' and *graphein* 'to write or draw'

tacit (*say* tas- it) *ADJECTIVE*
tacit agreement or approval is implied or understood without being put into words
▷ **tacitly** *ADVERB*

WORD HISTORY from Latin *tacitus* 'not speaking'

taciturn (*say* tas- i- tern) *ADJECTIVE*
a taciturn person or statement is reserved and communicates very little
▷ **taciturnity** (*say* tas- i- **tern**- iti) *NOUN*

tack❶ *NOUN* **tacks**
1 a short nail with a flat top
2 a tacking stitch
3 the direction taken when tacking in sailing
4 a course of action or policy ◆ *Detectives investigating the murder now realize that they have been on the wrong tack.*

tack *VERB* **tacks, tacking, tacked**
1 to nail down a carpet or other object with tacks
2 to sew material together with long stitches to hold it in place temporarily
3 to sail a zigzag course to take advantage of what wind there is

to tack something on is to add it as an extra

> Marilla was as fond of morals as the Duchess in Wonderland, and was firmly convinced that one should be tacked on to every remark made to a child who was being brought up.
> — *L. M. Montgomery, Anne of Green Gables*

WORD HISTORY from Old French *tache* 'a clasp or large nail'

tack❷ *NOUN*
riding equipment including harness, saddles, etc.

WORD HISTORY from *tackle* in the sense 'equipment'

tackle *VERB* **tackles, tackling, tackled**
1 to try to deal with a problem or task that must be faced
2 to talk to someone about a difficult or awkward matter
3 to try to get the ball from someone else in a game of football, rugby, or hockey

tackle *NOUN* **tackles**
1 equipment, especially for fishing
2 a set of ropes and pulleys
3 the act of tackling someone in football, rugby, or hockey

tacky❶ *ADJECTIVE* **tackier, tackiest**
sticky; not quite dry ◆ *The paint is still tacky.*
▷ **tackiness** *NOUN*

WORD HISTORY from *tack* in the sense 'a nail or fastening'

tacky❷ *ADJECTIVE* **tackier, tackiest**
(*informal*) showing poor taste or style; cheaply made

> The pub ... was really tacky inside: tatty seats, card tables and a pool table in the corner. — *Bali Rai, (Un)arranged Marriage*

▷ **tackiness** *NOUN*

WORD HISTORY from an earlier (American) meaning 'a worthless horse'

tact *NOUN*
skill in dealing with people sensitively and not offending them

WORD HISTORY from Latin *tactus* 'sense of touch'

tactful *ADJECTIVE*
having or showing tact ◆ *It wasn't very tactful to ask my mother if she'd put on weight.*
▷ **tactfully** *ADVERB*

tactical *ADJECTIVE*
1 to do with tactics
2 you use a tactical vote to prevent a strong candidate from winning rather than to support your preferred candidate
▷ **tactically** *ADVERB*

tactics *PLURAL NOUN*
1 the organization and deployment of military forces in battle, or of players in a team game. (SEE ALSO **strategy**)
2 the methods you use to achieve something or gain an advantage
▷ **tactician** *NOUN*

WORD HISTORY from Greek *taktika* 'things arranged'

USAGE NOTE Note that *tactics* refers to arrangements made for a particular objective, whereas *strategy* refers to a broader plan or policy.

tactile *ADJECTIVE*
1 to do with your sense of touch
2 a tactile substance is pleasant to feel or touch

tactless *ADJECTIVE*
having or showing a lack of tact
▷ **tactlessly** *ADVERB*
▷ **tactlessness** *NOUN*

a b c d e f g h i j k l m n o p q r s t u v w x y z

tadpole *NOUN* **tadpoles**
a young frog or toad that has developed from the egg and lives entirely in water
WORD HISTORY from *toad* and an old word *poll* meaning 'head'

tae kwon do (*say* ty kwon **doh**) *NOUN*
a Korean martial art which incorporates kicking moves
WORD HISTORY from Korean words meaning 'art of hand and foot fighting'

taffeta *NOUN*
a stiff silky material, often used for dresses
WORD HISTORY from Persian *taftan* 'to shine'

tag❶ *NOUN* **tags**
1 a label tied on or stuck into something
2 a metal or plastic point at the end of a shoelace

tag *VERB* **tags, tagging, tagged**
1 to label an object with a tag
2 to attach or add something as an extra ◆ *Some special features have been tagged on to the film for the DVD version.*
to tag along (*informal*) is to go along with another person or group, especially without being asked ◆ *Do you mind if I tag along with you and your friends?*

tag❷ *NOUN*
a children's game in which one person chases the rest, and anyone who is caught becomes the next chaser

tagliatelle (*say* tahl- yah- **tel**- i) *PLURAL NOUN*
pasta in ribbon-shaped strips
WORD HISTORY from Italian *tagliare* 'to cut'

t'ai chi or **t'ai chi ch'uan** (*say* tiy- chee- **chwahn**) *NOUN*
a Chinese martial art and system of exercises
WORD HISTORY from Chinese words meaning 'great ultimate boxing'

tail *NOUN* **tails**
1 the part that sticks out from the rear end of the body of a bird, fish, or animal
2 the part at the end or rear of something
to be on someone's tail (*informal*) is to be following them closely
with your tail between your legs (*informal*) feeling dejected or humiliated

tail *VERB* **tails, tailing, tailed**
1 to remove stalks from fruit or vegetables ◆ *Top and tail the green beans before plunging them in boiling water.*
2 (*informal*) to follow someone closely ◆ *Inspector MacBride had been tailing the suspect for three days.*
to tail away or **off** is to become fewer, smaller, or slighter; to cease gradually

tailback *NOUN* **tailbacks**
a long line of traffic stretching back from an obstruction

tailless *ADJECTIVE*
not having a tail

tail light *NOUN* **tail lights**
a red light at the back of a vehicle or bicycle

tailor *NOUN* **tailors**
a person who makes men's clothes

tailor *VERB* **tailors, tailoring, tailored**
1 to make or fit clothes
2 to adapt or make something for a special purpose ◆ *This part of the library is tailored to the needs of young children.*
WORD HISTORY from Old French *tailleur*, from Latin *taliare* 'to cut'

tailor-made *ADJECTIVE*
specially made or suited for a purpose

tails *PLURAL NOUN*
1 a man's formal jacket with two long pieces hanging down at the back
2 the side of a coin without the head on it, turned upwards after being tossed (SEE ALSO **head**)

tailspin *NOUN*
a spiral dive made by an aircraft with the tail making wider circles than the front

tailwind *NOUN*
a wind blowing from behind a vehicle or aircraft, in the direction of its travel

taint *NOUN* **taints**
a trace of a bad quality or condition that spoils something

taint *VERB* **taints, tainting, tainted**
to spoil something with a taint ◆ *The election was tainted with the suspicion of fraud and vote rigging.*
WORD HISTORY from an early French word meaning 'coloured or dyed', related to our word *tinge*

take *VERB* **takes, taking, took, taken**
1 to get something into your hands or possession or control ◆ *You take the other end of the rope.* ◆ *The Vikings took many prisoners in their raids on the coasts of Europe.*
2 carry or convey ◆ *How much money are you taking on holiday?* ◆ *I'll take the parcels to the post office tomorrow.*
3 to make use of something; to drive or travel in a vehicle ◆ *Let's take a taxi.*
4 to indulge in or undertake something ◆ *I'm taking a long holiday this summer.* ◆ *We'll take a break for lunch at one o'clock.*
5 to take an exam is to sit it
6 to study or teach a subject ◆ *Who takes you for music?*
7 to make an effort ◆ *Thanks for taking the trouble to see me.*

8 to experience a feeling ◆ *Some viewers may take offence at the programme.*
9 to accept or endure something ◆ *You shouldn't take any risks with fire.*
10 to require something

It will take a long time to repair the damage of apartheid. — *Beverley Naidoo, Journey to Jo'burg*

11 to write down a note or letter ◆ *Did you take any notes during the class?*
12 to use a camera to make a photograph
13 to subtract one number from another ◆ *Take 16 from 100.*
14 to assume that something is true

I take it that the injection is one of a series of measures to keep me alive. — *Brian Clark, Whose Life is it Anyway?*

15 to believe someone to be a particular person or thing, or to have a certain nature

A lad who Marcus took to be the Chieftain's brother ducked out from the firelit doorway and came running to meet them. — *Rosemary Sutcliff, The Eagle of the Ninth*

16 a fire takes when it starts to burn fully

to take after someone to take after a parent or other relative is to resemble them

to take someone in
1 (*informal*) is to deceive them
2 is to give them accommodation for the night

to take something in
1 is to understand or accept a piece of information

The Duchessa ... began a story so improbable that Arianna found it difficult to take in. — *Mary Hoffman, Stravaganza City of Masks*

to take leave of someone is to say goodbye to them

to take off
1 an aircraft takes off when it leaves the ground and becomes airborne
2 to start to run or move quickly
3 (*informal*) to become popular or fashionable

More than a thousand years after Diophantus died, algebra started to really take off in Italy. — *Kjartan Poskitt, Murderous Maths*

to take on (*informal*) is to become very upset ◆ *Please don't take on so!*

to take someone on
1 to take on an employee is to give them a job
2 to take on an opponent is to play or fight against them

to take something over is to take control of a business or activity

to take place is to happen or occur

to take to something
1 is to develop a liking or ability for it

'How are you taking to the piratical life?' he enquired, looking up from his mortar and pestle. — *Celia Rees, Pirates!*

2 to take to the air, sea, sky, etc. is to choose to go there

to take something up
1 to take up a hobby or interest is to start pursuing it
2 to take up space or time is to occupy it
3 to take up an offer is to accept it

▷ **taker** *NOUN*

takeaway *NOUN* **takeaways**
1 a place that sells cooked meals for customers to take away
2 a cooked meal bought from this place

take-off *NOUN* **take-offs**
the act of an aircraft leaving the ground and becoming airborne

takeover *NOUN* **takeovers**
the taking control of one business company by another

takings *PLURAL NOUN*
money received for goods or services

talcum powder *NOUN*
a scented powder put on the skin to make it feel smooth and dry

WORD HISTORY from *talc*, a soft mineral used to make this powder

tale *NOUN* **tales**
1 a story or narrative

Though mine is but a simple, personal tale of my childhood, please do not underestimate the power of such stories. — *Adeline Yen Mah, Chinese Cinderella*

2 an untrue story; a lie

talent *NOUN* **talents**
a special or very great ability

▷ **talented** *ADJECTIVE*

WORD HISTORY from Greek *talanton* 'sum of money'

talisman *NOUN* **talismans**
an object that is supposed to bring good luck

She swung the chain over him, out of his reach. 'Is this your talisman, wizard? Is it precious to you?' — *Ursula Le Guin, The Tombs of Atuan*

▷ **talismanic** *ADJECTIVE*

WORD HISTORY from Greek *telesma* 'consecrated object'

talk *VERB* **talks, talking, talked**
1 to speak; to have a conversation
2 to speak in a particular language ◆ *My aunties talk Urdu to each other at home.*
3 to talk someone into doing something is to persuade them to do it by what you say
4 to give away information ◆ *Do you think he'll talk?*
5 (*informal*) to be concerned with something ◆ *For this kind of film, we are talking big budgets.* ▸▸

a b c d e f g h i j k l m n o p q r s t u v w x y z

to talk down to someone is to speak to them using simple language in a condescending way

▷ **talker** *NOUN*

talk *NOUN* **talks**

1 a conversation or discussion

2 an informal lecture

3 rumour or gossip

There was talk of an evening curfew, but most of that came from those who had no teenagers to be grounded within their walls. — *Julie Bertagna, The Opposite of Chocolate*

talkative *ADJECTIVE*

talking a lot

tall *ADJECTIVE*

1 higher than the average ◆ *My brother is quite tall for his age.*

2 measured from the bottom to the top ◆ *Giant redwoods can grow up to 110 metres tall.*

▷ **tallness** *NOUN*

tallow *NOUN*

animal fat used to make candles, soap, lubricants, etc.

tall story *NOUN* **tall stories**

(*informal*) a story that is hard to believe

tally *NOUN* **tallies**

the total amount of a debt or score

tally *VERB* **tallies, tallying, tallied**

one thing tallies with another when they correspond or agree with each other ◆ *The stories of the two witnesses did not tally.*

WORD HISTORY from Latin *talea* 'twig or cutting'

Talmud *NOUN*

the collection of writings that contain Jewish religious law

WORD HISTORY a Hebrew word meaning 'instruction'

talon *NOUN* **talons**

a claw, especially of a bird of prey

WORD HISTORY from Latin *talus* 'ankle bone or heel'

tamarind *NOUN*

1 a tropical tree which produces a fruit with an edible sour pulp

2 the fruit of this tree

WORD HISTORY from Arabic *tamr-hindi* 'Indian date'

tambourine *NOUN* **tambourines**

a circular musical instrument with metal discs round it, tapped or shaken to make it jingle

WORD HISTORY a French word meaning 'little drum', from *tambour* 'drum'

tame *ADJECTIVE*

1 a tame animal is gentle and not afraid of people; not wild or dangerous

2 not exciting; dull ◆ *That horror film was a bit tame for my taste.*

▷ **tamely** *ADVERB*

▷ **tameness** *NOUN*

tame *VERB* **tames, taming, tamed**

1 to make an animal become tame

2 to bring something under control

Then I attack my hair with a bristle brush, trying to tame it into submission. It's as if my entire body is trying to get out of control. — *Jacqueline Wilson, Girls Out Late*

▷ **tamer** *NOUN*

WORD HISTORY from Old English *tam*

Tamil *NOUN* **Tamils**

1 a member of a people of southern India and Sri Lanka

2 the language of this people

tam-o'-shanter *NOUN* **tam-o'-shanters**

a round Scottish cap with a bobble in the middle

WORD HISTORY named after *Tam o' Shanter*, the hero of a poem by the Scottish poet, Robert Burns (1759–1796)

tamp *VERB* **tamps, tamping, tamped**

to pack or ram material down tightly

tamper *VERB* **tampers, tampering, tampered**

to tamper with something is to meddle or interfere with it

WORD HISTORY another form of *temper*

tampon *NOUN* **tampons**

a plug of absorbent material that a woman inserts into her vagina to absorb blood during her menstrual period

WORD HISTORY from a French word meaning 'plug'

tan *NOUN* **tans**

1 a light brown colour

2 brown colour in skin that has been exposed to sun

Always darkish in colour, Simon was burned by the sun to a deep tan that glistened with sweat. — *William Golding, Lord of the Flies*

tan *VERB* **tans, tanning, tanned**

1 to turn your skin brown, or to become brown, by exposing your skin to the sun

2 to turn an animal hide into leather by treating it with chemicals

3 (*informal*) to beat someone as a punishment

tan *ADJECTIVE*

light brown in colour

tandem *NOUN* **tandems**

a bicycle for two riders, one behind the other

in tandem two people or things act in tandem when they do so together, or at the same time

'Indeed,' muttered Signora Strega-Borgia, raising her coffee cup and her eyebrows in tandem. — *Debi Gliori, Pure Dead Wicked*

WORD HISTORY a Latin word meaning 'at length'

tandoori *NOUN*
a style of Indian cooking in which food is cooked in a clay oven (called a **tandoor**)

WORD HISTORY via Urdu from Arabic *tannur* 'oven'

tang *NOUN* **tangs**
a strong flavour or smell

The house was redolent with the scent of herbs and the sharp tang of garlic and onions. — *Gerald Durrell, My Family and Other Animals*

▷ **tangy** *ADJECTIVE*

tangent *NOUN* **tangents**
1 a straight line that touches the outside of a curve or circle but does not cross it
2 (*Mathematics*) the ratio of the length of the side opposite the right angle (in a right-angled triangle) to the side opposite the other acute angle

to go off at a tangent is to move away suddenly from a subject or line of thought being considered

WORD HISTORY from Latin *tangens* 'touching'

tangential *ADJECTIVE*
1 of or along a tangent
2 not directly related or relevant to a subject being considered ◆ *The first chapter descibes events which are tangential to the main story.*

▷ **tangentially** *ADVERB*

tangerine *NOUN* **tangerines**
1 a kind of small orange with a loose skin
2 a reddish orange colour

WORD HISTORY from the city of *Tangier* in Morocco, from where the fruit was exported

tangible *ADJECTIVE*
1 able to be touched
2 clear and definite, real ◆ *The creation of jobs is one of the tangible benefits of this project.*

▷ **tangibly** *ADVERB*

WORD HISTORY from Latin *tangere* 'to touch'

tangle *VERB* **tangles, tangling, tangled**
1 to twist strands, or to become twisted, into a confused mass
2 (*informal*) to tangle with someone is to fight or argue with them

It was seldom worth tangling with wizards, they so rarely had any treasure worth speaking of. — *Terry Pratchett, The Colour of Magic*

tangle *NOUN* **tangles**
a twisted, confused mass of strands, such as of hair, wires, or vegetation

tango *NOUN* **tangos**
a Latin American ballroom dance which incorporates gliding steps and sudden pauses

tango *VERB* **tangoes, tangoing, tangoed**
to dance the tango

WORD HISTORY an American Spanish word, perhaps from an African language

tank *NOUN* **tanks**
1 a large container for a liquid or gas
2 a heavy armoured vehicle used in war

tanka *NOUN* **tankas**
(*Language*) a Japanese poem written in five lines and a total of 31 syllables, giving a complete picture of an event or mood

tankard *NOUN* **tankards**
a tall drinking mug with one handle, usually of silver or pewter and often with a lid

tanker *NOUN* **tankers**
1 a large ship for carrying oil
2 a large lorry for carrying petrol or other liquid in bulk

tanner *NOUN* **tanners**
a person who tans animal hides into leather

tannery *NOUN* **tanneries**
a place where animal hides are tanned into leather

tannin *NOUN*
a substance obtained from the bark or fruit of various trees, and also found in tea, used in tanning and dyeing things

tantalize *VERB* **tantalizes, tantalizing, tantalized**
to tease or torment someone by showing them something they want but cannot reach

USAGE NOTE This word can also be spelled tantalise.

WORD HISTORY from *Tantalus* in Greek mythology, who was punished by being made to stand near water and fruit which moved away when he tried to reach them

tantamount *ADJECTIVE*
to be tantamount to something is to be equivalent to, or virtually the same as, it ◆ *Both teams felt that a draw would be tantamount to a defeat.*

WORD HISTORY from an Italian phrase *tanto montare* 'to amount to so much'

tantrum *NOUN* **tantrums**
an outburst of bad temper or frustration, especially by a young child

Taoiseach (*say* tee- shak) *NOUN*
the title of the prime minister of the Republic of Ireland

tap ❶ *NOUN* **taps**
a device for letting out liquid or gas in a controlled flow ▸▸

a b c d e f g h i j k l m n o p q r s t u v w x y z

on tap
1 liquid or gas that is on tap is ready to be drawn off by a tap
2 (*informal*) information or a supply that is on tap is readily available

tap *VERB* **taps, tapping, tapped**
1 to take liquid or gas out of a container, especially through a tap
2 to obtain supplies or information from a source
3 fix a device to a telephone line so that you can overhear conversations on it

WORD HISTORY from an Old English word meaning 'stopper for a cask'

tap[2] *NOUN* **taps**
1 a quick light hit; the sound of this
2 a spell of tap-dancing

tap *VERB* **taps, tapping, tapped**
1 to hit a person or thing quickly and lightly
2 to make a light rapping sound

Hearing Miranda's heels tapping up the garden path the next evening, Madame Doubtfire paused in her watering. — *Anne Fine, Madame Doubtfire*

WORD HISTORY from an Old French word

tapas (*say* **tap**- ass) *NOUN*
Spanish savoury snacks served with drinks at a bar

WORD HISTORY from a Spanish word meaning 'cover or lid', because they were served on a small dish placed over a drink

tap dance *NOUN* **tap dances**
a dance performed wearing shoes with metal caps, in which an elaborate rhythm is tapped with the toes and heels
▷ **tap dancer** *NOUN*
▷ **tap dancing** *NOUN*

tape *NOUN* **tapes**
1 a narrow strip of cloth, paper, plastic, etc.
2 a narrow plastic strip coated with a magnetic substance and used for making recordings
3 a tape recording
4 a tape measure

tape *VERB* **tapes, taping, taped**
1 to fix, cover, or surround something with tape
2 to record something on magnetic tape

to have something taped (*informal*) is to understand it or be able to deal with it

tape deck *NOUN* **tape decks**
the part of a sound system on which music recorded on tape can be played

tape measure *NOUN* **tape measures**
a long strip marked in centimetres or inches for measuring things

taper *NOUN* **tapers**
a very thin candle, often used to light another candle or a fire

taper *VERB* **tapers, tapering, tapered**
to make something narrower, or to become gradually narrower

to taper off is to lessen or cease gradually, or to make something do this

WORD HISTORY via Old English from Latin *papyrus*, because the pith of the papyrus plant was used to make candle wicks

tape recorder *NOUN* **tape recorders**
a machine for recording music or sound on magnetic tape and playing it back
▷ **tape recording** *NOUN*

tapestry *NOUN* **tapestries**
a piece of heavy fabric woven with pictures or patterns, used as a wall hanging or for upholstery

WORD HISTORY from French *tapis* 'carpet'

tapeworm *NOUN* **tapeworms**
a long flat worm that can live as a parasite in the intestines of humans and animals

tapioca *NOUN*
a starchy substance in hard white grains obtained from cassava, used for making puddings

WORD HISTORY from Tupi (a South American language)

tapir (*say* **tay**- per) *NOUN* **tapirs**
a pig-like animal with a long flexible snout, found in Central and South America

WORD HISTORY via Spanish or Portuguese from Tupi (a South American language)

tar *NOUN*
a thick black liquid made from coal or wood, used in making roads and for preserving timber

tar *VERB* **tars, tarring, tarred**
to coat a road or other surface with tar

to be tarred with the same brush is to be thought of as having the same faults as someone else

taramasalata (*say* ta- ra- mah- sa- **lah**- ta) *NOUN*
a soft paste made from the roe of certain fish, mixed with olive oil and seasoning

WORD HISTORY from modern Greek words meaning 'roe salad'

tarantula *NOUN* **tarantulas**
1 a large black spider of southern Europe
2 a large hairy tropical spider with a poisonous bite

WORD HISTORY from *Taranto* in southern Italy, because the spider's bite was thought to cause *tarantism*, a psychological illness once common in southern Italy

tardy *ADJECTIVE* **tardier, tardiest**
slow to act or respond
▷ **tardily** *ADVERB*
▷ **tardiness** *NOUN*

WORD HISTORY from Latin *tardus* 'slow'

target *NOUN* **targets**

1 something aimed at; a place, object, or amount that you try to hit or reach

A week and a half from the Pole and the good news is that we are almost exactly on our target of thirty degrees East. — *Michael Palin, Pole to Pole*

2 a person or thing that is being criticized

target *VERB* **targets, targeting, targeted**

to aim at someone or something; to have someone or something as your target

target *ADJECTIVE*

aimed at as a target

'So tell me,' Dad continued, 'as a fourteen-year-old, you're a member of our target audience. Will it sell?' — *Alan Gibbons, Shadow of the Minotaur*

WORD HISTORY from Old English *targa*

tariff *NOUN* **tariffs**

1 a list of fixed prices or charges

2 a tax or duty to be paid on imports or exports

WORD HISTORY via French and Italian from Arabic *arrafa* 'to notify'

tarmac *NOUN*

1 (*trademark*) a material used for making a hard surface on roads, paths, playgrounds, etc.

2 an area surfaced with tarmacadam, especially on an airfield

tarn *NOUN* **tarns**

a small mountain lake

WORD HISTORY from Old Norse *tjorn*

tarnish *VERB* **tarnishes, tarnishing, tarnished**

1 to make a metal surface less shiny, or to become less shiny

2 to spoil or damage something, especially someone's reputation

▷ **tarnish** *NOUN*

WORD HISTORY from French *terne* 'dark, dull'

tarot cards (*rhymes with* barrow) *PLURAL NOUN*

a special pack of 78 cards used for fortune-telling

WORD HISTORY via French from Italian *tarocchi*

tarpaulin *NOUN* **tarpaulins**

a large sheet of waterproof canvas

WORD HISTORY from *tar* and *pall* in the sense 'a covering'

tarragon *NOUN*

a plant with leaves that are used for flavouring salads and in cooking

WORD HISTORY from late Latin *tragonia*, perhaps from Greek *drakōn* 'dragon'

tarry[1] (*say* tar- ee) *ADJECTIVE*

covered with or like tar

tarry[2] (*say* ta- ree) *VERB* **tarries, tarrying, tarried**

(*old use*) to stay for a while longer; to linger

Here now for seven days they tarried, for the time was at hand for another parting which they were loth to make. — *J. R. R. Tolkien, The Return of the King*

tart[1] *NOUN* **tarts**

an open pastry case with a sweet or savoury filling

WORD HISTORY from Latin *tarta*

tart[2] *ADJECTIVE*

1 sharp or sour in taste

2 sharp in manner; sarcastic

▷ **tartly** *ADVERB*

▷ **tartness** *NOUN*

WORD HISTORY from Old English *teart* 'harsh, severe'

tart[3] *ADJECTIVE*

(*informal*) a prostitute

WORD HISTORY originally a term of affection, probably a shortening of *sweetheart*

tartan *NOUN*

a woollen cloth woven in a pattern of coloured stripes crossing at right angles, especially one associated with a particular Scottish clan

WORD HISTORY from an Old French word *tertaine* for a kind of material

Tartar *NOUN* **Tartars**

a member of a group of Central Asian peoples including Mongols and Turks

tartar[1] *NOUN* **tartars**

a person who is fierce or difficult to deal with

WORD HISTORY from the *Tartar* warriors from central Asia in the 13th century

tartar[2] *NOUN*

a hard chalky deposit that forms on teeth and causes decay

WORD HISTORY origin unknown

tartlet *NOUN* **tartlets**

a small pastry tart

task *NOUN* **tasks**

a piece of work to be done

to take someone to task is to scold or rebuke them

task force *NOUN* **task forces**

a group of people specially organized for a particular task

taskmaster *NOUN* **taskmasters**

a hard taskmaster is someone who gives other people a lot of work to do

tassel *NOUN* **tassels**

a bundle of threads tied together at the top and used to decorate something

▷ **tasselled** *ADJECTIVE*

WORD HISTORY from an Old French word meaning 'clasp'

taste *NOUN* **tastes**
1 the feeling caused in your tongue by something placed on it

Tarka licked a frog and liked the taste of it; ... but he did not eat it. — *Henry Williamson, Tarka the Otter*

2 the ability to taste things
3 the ability to enjoy beautiful things or to choose what is suitable ◆ *The cottage had been decorated with taste and simple furnishings.*
4 a liking or fondness for something ◆ *I've developed a taste for jazz.*
5 a very small amount of food or drink
6 a slight experience of something ◆ *Visitors to the museum get a taste of what life was like for Roman soldiers living in Britain.*

taste *VERB* **tastes, tasting, tasted**
1 to discover or test the flavour of something by putting it in your mouth
2 to be able to perceive flavours
3 to have a certain flavour ◆ *Your homemade lemonade tastes delicious.*
4 to experience something

But I quitted France five years ago, and, wishing to taste the sweets of domestic life, took service as a valet here in England. — *Jules Verne, Around the World in Eighty Days*

tasteful *ADJECTIVE*
showing good taste
▷ **tastefully** *ADVERB*
▷ **tastefulness** *NOUN*

tasteless *ADJECTIVE*
1 having no flavour
2 showing poor taste
▷ **tastelessly** *ADVERB*
▷ **tastelessness** *NOUN*

tasty *ADJECTIVE* **tastier, tastiest**
having a strong pleasant taste

The new year must begin with tasty, fresh yams and not the shrivelled and fibrous crop of the previous year. — *Chinua Achebe, Things Fall Apart*

▷ **tastily** *ADVERB*
▷ **tastiness** *NOUN*

tat *NOUN*
(*informal*) tawdry or tasteless things
WORD HISTORY probably from *tatty*

tattered *ADJECTIVE*
badly torn; ragged

Hari could see the tattered fronds of the dusty palm trees over his head and even one or two of the brightest stars. — *Anita Desai, The Village by the Sea*

tatters *PLURAL NOUN*
torn pieces of cloth, paper, etc.
in tatters
1 torn to pieces
2 badly damaged; beyond repair

tatting *NOUN*
a kind of handmade lace

tattle *NOUN*
idle chatter; gossip

tattle *VERB* **tattles, tattling, tattled**
to chatter idly; to gossip
WORD HISTORY from an early Flemish word *tatelen*

tattoo[1] *VERB* **tattoos, tattooing, tattooed**
to mark the skin with a picture or pattern by puncturing it with a needle and inserting a dye

tattoo *NOUN* **tattoos**
a tattooed picture or pattern
WORD HISTORY from a Polynesian language

tattoo[2] *NOUN* **tattoos**
1 an entertainment consisting of military displays, music, and marching
2 a drumming or tapping sound
WORD HISTORY from a Dutch expression *taptoe!* meaning 'close the tap (of the cask)', said at closing time in a tavern; later applied to a military bugle call at the end of the day

tatty *ADJECTIVE* (*informal*)
1 ragged; shabby and untidy
2 cheap and gaudy
▷ **tattily** *ADVERB*
▷ **tattiness** *NOUN*
WORD HISTORY from Old English *taettec* 'a rag'

taunt *VERB* **taunts, taunting, taunted**
to jeer at or tease someone with scornful remarks or criticism

taunt *NOUN* **taunts**
a taunting remark
WORD HISTORY from a French phrase *tant pour tant* 'tit for tat'

taut *ADJECTIVE*
stretched tightly; not slack

At the centre of Undertown is a great iron ring, to which a long and heavy chain—now taut, now slack—extends up into the sky. — *Paul Stewart and Chris Riddell, Beyond the Deep Woods*

▷ **tautly** *ADVERB*
▷ **tautness** *NOUN*
WORD HISTORY probably from *tough*

tauten *VERB* **tautens, tautening, tautened**
to make something taut, or to become taut

tautology *NOUN* **tautologies**
(*Language*) repetiton of the same thing in different words, e.g. *You can get the book free for nothing* (where *free* and *for nothing* mean the same)
WORD HISTORY from Greek *tauto* 'the same' and *logos* 'word'

tavern *NOUN* **taverns**
(*old use*) an inn or public house
WORD HISTORY from Latin *taberna* 'hut'

tawdry *ADJECTIVE*
cheap and gaudy
▷ **tawdrily** *ADVERB*
▷ **tawdriness** *NOUN*
WORD HISTORY from *St Audrey's lace*, cheap finery formerly sold at St Audrey's fair at Ely

tawny *ADJECTIVE*
brownish-yellow
WORD HISTORY from an Old French word related to *tan*

tax *NOUN* **taxes**
1 money that people or business firms have to pay to the government, to be used for public purposes
2 a strain or burden ◆ *Running a marathon is a tax on the strength and stamina of any athlete.*

tax *VERB* **taxes, taxing, taxed**
1 to put a tax on something
2 to charge someone a tax
3 to pay the tax on something ◆ *I have taxed the car up to June.*
4 to put a strain or burden on someone or something
5 to accuse someone in a challenging or reproving way ◆ *The politician was taxed with not giving a direct answer to the question.*
▷ **taxable** *ADJECTIVE*
▷ **taxation** *NOUN*
WORD HISTORY from Latin *taxare* 'to calculate'

taxi *NOUN* **taxis**
a car that carries passengers for payment, usually with a meter to record the fare to be paid
▷ **taxicab** *NOUN*

taxi *VERB* **taxies, taxiing, taxied**
an aircraft taxies when it moves along the ground or water, especially before or after flying
WORD HISTORY short for *taximeter cab*

taxidermist *NOUN* **taxidermists**
a person who prepares and stuffs the skins of animals in a lifelike form
▷ **taxidermy** *NOUN*
WORD HISTORY from Greek *taxis* 'arrangement' and *derma* 'skin'

taxpayer *NOUN* **taxpayers**
a person who pays tax, especially income tax

TB *ABBREVIATION*
tuberculosis

tea *NOUN* **teas**
1 a drink made by pouring hot water on the dried leaves of an evergreen shrub (the *tea plant*) grown in parts of south and east Asia
2 these dried leaves
3 a drink made with the leaves of other plants *camomile tea*
4 a meal at which tea is served, especially a light meal in the afternoon or early evening

It's a funny time, three o'clock, too late for lunch but a bit early for tea. — *Alan Bennett, Talking Heads*

WORD HISTORY via Dutch from Chinese *te*

tea bag *NOUN* **tea bags**
a small bag holding about a teaspoonful of tea

teacake *NOUN* **teacakes**
a kind of bun usually served toasted and buttered

teach *VERB* **teaches, teaching, taught**
1 to give a person knowledge or skill; to train someone
2 to give lessons, especially in a particular subject
3 to show someone what to do or avoid ◆ *That will teach me not to meddle!*

teachable *ADJECTIVE*
able to be taught

teacher *NOUN* **teachers**
a person who teaches others, especially in a school

teaching *NOUN* **teachings**
things that are taught ◆ *the teachings of Buddha*

tea cloth *NOUN* **tea cloths**
a tea towel

tea cosy *NOUN* **tea cosies**
a cover placed over a teapot to keep the tea hot

teacup *NOUN* **teacups**
a cup from which tea or other hot liquids are drunk

teak *NOUN*
the hard strong wood of an evergreen Asian tree

teal *NOUN* **teal**
a kind of duck

team *NOUN* **teams**
1 a set of players forming one side in certain games and sports
2 a set of people working together
3 two or more animals harnessed to pull a vehicle or a plough

team *VERB* **teams, teaming, teamed**
to put or join people or animals together in a team

team spirit *NOUN*
willingness to act for the good of the group you belong to

teamwork *NOUN*
the ability of a team or group to work well together

teapot *NOUN* **teapots**
a pot with a lid and a handle, for making and pouring tea

tear❶ (*say* teer) *NOUN* **tears**
a drop of clear salty water that comes from your eyes when you cry
in tears crying continuously
WORD HISTORY from Old English *taeher*
WORD FAMILY A related adjective, meaning 'to do with, or producing, tears', is lachrymal.

tear❷ (*say* tair) *VERB* **tears, tearing, tore, torn**
1 to pull something apart, away, or into pieces
2 to become torn ◆ *Newspaper tears easily.*
3 to run or travel hurriedly ◆ *I've just seen my neighbour tearing along the road.*
to be in a tearing hurry is to be in an extreme hurry
to tear into someone is to criticize them harshly
to tear your hair out (*informal*) is to feel extremely frustrated or desperate

tear *NOUN* **tears**
a split made by tearing
WORD HISTORY from Old English *teran*

tearaway (*say* **tair**- a- way) *NOUN* **tearaways**
someone who behaves wildly or recklessly

teardrop (*say* **teer**- drop) *NOUN* **teardrops**
a single tear

tearful (*say* **teer**- ful) *ADJECTIVE*
upset and starting to cry

Signora Strega-Borgia bid the children a tearful farewell and set off to complete her degree in advanced witchcraft. — *Debi Gliori, Pure Dead Magic*

▷ **tearfully** *ADVERB*

tear gas (*say* teer) *NOUN*
a gas that makes people's eyes water painfully, used especially for riot control

tease *VERB* **teases, teasing, teased**
1 to provoke or make fun of someone in a playful or unkind way

Stanley ... didn't have any friends at home. He was overweight and the kids at his middle school often teased him about his size. — *Louis Sachar, Holes*

2 to pick threads apart into separate strands

tease *NOUN* **teases**
a person who likes teasing others
WORD HISTORY from Old English *tæsan*

teasel *NOUN* **teasels**
a plant with bristly heads formerly used to brush up the surface of cloth
WORD HISTORY from *tease* in the sense 'to pick threads apart'

teaser *NOUN* **teasers**
(*informal*) a difficult problem or puzzle

teaspoon *NOUN* **teaspoons**
a small spoon for stirring tea or measuring small amounts
▷ **teaspoonful** *NOUN*

teat *NOUN* **teats**
1 a nipple through which a baby sucks milk
2 the cap of a baby's feeding bottle

tea towel *NOUN* **tea towels**
a cloth for drying washed dishes and cutlery

tech (*say* tek) *NOUN* **techs**
(*informal*) a technical college

technical *ADJECTIVE*
1 to do with technology
2 to do with a particular subject and its methods ◆ *The glossary lists all the technical terms used in chess.*
3 using language that only experts can understand
WORD HISTORY from Greek *tekhnikos* 'skilful'

technical college *NOUN* **technical colleges**
a college providing courses in technical and practical subjects

technicality *NOUN* **technicalities**
1 being technical
2 a technical word, phrase, or detail

technically *ADVERB*
according to the strict facts or rules

technician *NOUN* **technicians**
a person whose job is to look after scientific equipment and do practical work in a laboratory

technique *NOUN* **techniques**
a method of doing or performing something, especially in an art or science

technology *NOUN* **technologies**
the study of machinery, engineering, and how things work
▷ **technological** *ADJECTIVE*
▷ **technologically** *ADVERB*
▷ **technologist** *NOUN*
WORD HISTORY from Greek *tekhnē* 'craft, skill'

tectonics *NOUN*
the scientific study of the earth's crust and structural features
WORD HISTORY from Greek *tektōn* 'carpenter'

teddy bear *NOUN* **teddy bears**
a soft furry toy bear
WORD HISTORY named after US President Theodore (*Teddy*) Roosevelt (1858-1919), who liked hunting bears

tedious *ADJECTIVE*
annoyingly slow or long; boring
▷ **tediously** *ADVERB*
▷ **tediousness** *NOUN*
WORD HISTORY from Latin *taedium* 'tiredness'

tedium *NOUN*
a dull or boring time or experience

tee *NOUN* **tees**
1 the flat area from which golfers strike the ball at the start of play for each hole
2 a small piece of wood or plastic on which a golf ball is placed for being struck
WORD HISTORY originally a Scots word; origin unknown

teem ❶ *VERB* **teems, teeming, teemed**
a place teems with people or things when it is full of them

The seas around us teem with fish and the captain has ordered boats ashore to find fresh water.
— *Celia Rees, Witch Child*

WORD HISTORY from an Old English word

teem ❷ *VERB* **teems, teeming, teemed**
to rain very hard; to pour
WORD HISTORY from an Old Norse word

teenage *ADJECTIVE*
to do with teenagers

teenager *NOUN* **teenagers**
a person in his or her teens

teens *PLURAL NOUN*
the time of life between 13 and 19 years of age

teeny *ADJECTIVE* **teenier, teeniest**
(*informal*) very small; tiny

tee-shirt *NOUN* **tee-shirts**
a T-shirt

teeter *VERB* **teeters, teetering, teetered**
to stand or move unsteadily

Zaphod felt he was teetering on the edge of madness and wondered if he shouldn't just jump over and have done with it. — *Douglas Adams, The Restaurant at the End of the Universe*

teethe *VERB* **teethes, teething, teethed**
a baby is teething when its first teeth are beginning to grow through its gums
teething troubles short-term problems that arise in the early stages of an activity

teetotal *ADJECTIVE*
a teetotal person never drinks alcohol
▷ **teetotaller** *NOUN*

TEFL *ABBREVIATION*
teaching of English as a foreign language

Teflon *NOUN*
(*trademark*) a type of plastic used as a non-stick coating for cooking pans and utensils
WORD HISTORY from poly*tetrafl*uoroethylene, its scientific name

telecommunications *PLURAL NOUN*
communications over a long distance, e.g. by telephone, telegraph, radio, or television

telegram *NOUN* **telegrams**
a message sent by telegraph

telegraph *NOUN*
a way of sending messages by using electric current along wires or by radio
▷ **telegraphic** *ADJECTIVE*
▷ **telegraphy** *NOUN*

telepathy (*say* til- **ep**- ath- ee) *NOUN*
communication of thoughts from one person's mind to another without speaking, writing, or gestures
▷ **telepath** *NOUN*
▷ **telepathic** *ADJECTIVE*
WORD HISTORY from Greek *tēle* 'far off' and *pathos* 'feeling'

telephone *NOUN* **telephones**
a device or system which uses electric wires or radio to enable one person to speak to another who is some distance away

telephone *VERB* **telephones, telephoning, telephoned**
to speak to someone on the telephone
WORD HISTORY from Greek *tēle* 'far off' and *phone* 'sound, voice'

telephonist (*say* til- **ef**- on- ist) *NOUN* **telephonists**
a person who operates a telephone switchboard

telescope *NOUN* **telescopes**
an instrument which uses lenses to magnify distant objects
▷ **telescopic** *ADJECTIVE*

telescope *VERB* **telescopes, telescoping, telescoped**
1 to make something shorter, or to become shorter, by sliding overlapping sections into each other
2 to compress or condense something so that it takes less space or time
WORD HISTORY from Greek *tēle* 'far off' and *skopein* 'to look at'

teletext *NOUN*
a system for displaying news and information on a television screen

televise *VERB* **televises, televising, televised**
to broadcast an event or programme by television

a b c d e f g h i j k l m n o p q r s t u v w x y z

television *NOUN* **televisions**
1 a system using radio waves to reproduce a view of scenes or events on a screen
2 an apparatus for receiving these pictures
3 televised programmes
▷ **televisual** *ADJECTIVE*

telex *NOUN* **telexes**
1 a system for sending printed messages by telegraphy
2 a message sent by this system

telex *VERB* **telexes, telexing, telexed**
to send someone a message by telex

WORD HISTORY from *teleprinter* (the machine used) and *exchange*

tell *VERB* **tells, telling, told**
1 to make a thing known to someone, especially by words

It was obvious to everyone from the moment they sat down that Zach was bursting to tell them something. — *Michelle Magorian, Goodnight Mister Tom*

2 to speak or say something

'Where am I? Tell the truth—I can bear it. In what quarter of the globe Have I descended like a meteorite?' — *Edmond Rostand, Cyrano de Bergerac*

3 to order someone to do something ◆ *Tell the prisoners to wait outside.*
4 to reveal a secret ◆ *Promise you won't tell.*
5 to decide or distinguish something ◆ *How can you tell the difference between the twins?*
6 to produce an effect, especially a negative one ◆ *The strain was beginning to tell on us all.*

all told in all, all together ◆ *All told, we identified 45 different species of birds.*
to tell someone off (*informal*) is to reprimand them
to tell tales is to report something bad that someone else has done

telling *ADJECTIVE*
a telling action or statement is very powerful in meaning or effect

telltale *NOUN* **telltales**
a person who tells tales

telltale *ADJECTIVE*
revealing or indicating something unusual or suspicious ◆ *Suddenly, we saw a telltale flash of light on the horizon.*

telly *NOUN* **tellies**
(*informal*) a television set

temerity (*say* tim- erri- tee) *NOUN*
rashness or boldness

WORD HISTORY from Latin *temere* 'rashly'

temp *NOUN* **temps**
(*informal*) a secretary or other worker who works for short periods of time in different companies

temp *VERB* **temps, temping, temped**
(*informal*) to work as a temp

temper *NOUN* **tempers**
1 a person's mood

For Rebecca, Victoria had discovered..., had a volatile temper, and was somewhat prone to dramatics. — *Meg Cabot, Victoria and the Rogue*

2 an angry mood ◆ *The Greek god, Poseidon, was believed to cause earthquakes when he was in a temper.*

to lose your temper is to lose your calmness and become angry

temper *VERB* **tempers, tempering, tempered**
1 to harden or strengthen metal by heating and cooling it
2 to moderate or soften the effects of something

Artemis ... still retained a childlike belief in magic, tempered by an adult determination to exploit it. — *Eoin Colfer, Artemis Fowl*

WORD HISTORY via Old English from Latin *temperare* 'to mix'

tempera *NOUN*
(*Art*) a method of painting with powdered colours mixed with egg or size, used in Europe chiefly in the 12th–15th centuries

temperament *NOUN* **temperaments**
a person's nature as shown in the way they usually behave

Humphrey was of a much more subdued and philosophical temperament, not perhaps so well calculated to lead as to advise. — *Captain Marryat, The Children of the New Forest*

temperamental *ADJECTIVE*
1 likely to become excitable or moody suddenly
2 to do with a person's temperament
▷ **temperamentally** *ADVERB*

temperance *NOUN*
1 moderation or self-restraint
2 drinking little or no alcohol

temperate *ADJECTIVE*
a temperate climate is neither extremely hot nor extremely cold

WORD HISTORY from an earlier meaning 'not affected by strong emotions', from *temper*

temperature *NOUN* **temperatures**
1 (*Science*) a measure of how hot or cold a person or thing is
2 an abnormally high body temperature

tempest *NOUN* **tempests**
a violent storm

WORD HISTORY from Latin *tempestas* 'weather'

tempestuous *ADJECTIVE*
1 very stormy
2 full of strong feeling or emotion
▷ **tempestuously** *ADVERB*
▷ **tempestuousness** *NOUN*

template *NOUN* **templates**
a thin sheet of shaped metal, plastic, or card, used as a guide for cutting or shaping things
WORD HISTORY from an earlier spelling *templet*, from *temple*, a device in a loom for keeping the cloth stretched

temple ① *NOUN* **temples**
(*Religion*) a building where a god or goddess is worshipped in various religions
WORD HISTORY from Latin *templum* 'consecrated place'

temple ② *NOUN* **temples**
the part of your head between your forehead and your ear
WORD HISTORY from Latin *tempora* 'sides of the head'

tempo *NOUN* **tempos** or **tempi**
1 the speed or rhythm of something
2 (*Music*) the speed at which a piece of music is played

The player changes tempo, the notes of the flute leaping and gliding, leaping and gliding like invisible fish. — *Julie Hearn, The Merrybegot*

WORD HISTORY an Italian word, from Latin *tempus* 'time'

temporal *ADJECTIVE*
1 to do with the passing of time
2 to do with worldly affairs; secular

temporary *ADJECTIVE*
lasting for a limited time only; not permanent
▷ **temporarily** (*say* **tem**- per- er- il- ee) *ADVERB*
WORD HISTORY from Latin *tempus* 'time'

temporize *VERB* **temporizes, temporizing, temporized**
to avoid giving a definite answer, in order to postpone something ◆ *The President was accused of temporizing on major issues.*
USAGE NOTE This word can also be spelled temporise.

tempt *VERB* **tempts, tempting, tempted**
1 to try to persuade or attract someone, especially into doing something wrong or unwise
2 to be tempted to do something new or different is to be curious about it and inclined to try it ◆ *It is not unusual to be tempted to try diving while on holiday.*
▷ **temptation** *NOUN*
▷ **tempter** *NOUN*
▷ **temptress** *NOUN*
WORD HISTORY from Latin *temptare* 'to test'

ten *NOUN, ADJECTIVE* **tens**
the number 10, one more than nine
WORD FAMILY A related adjective, meaning 'to do with tens or tenths', is decimal.

tenable *ADJECTIVE*
1 a job or position is tenable for the length of time that someone can hold it ◆ *This post is tenable for one year only.*
2 a tenable belief or theory is one that can be upheld or defended

tenacious (*say* ten- **ay**- shus) *ADJECTIVE*
1 holding or clinging firmly to something
2 obstinate and persistent ◆ *Many people exhibit a tenacious belief in the existence of UFOs.*
▷ **tenaciously** *ADVERB*
▷ **tenacity** *NOUN*
WORD HISTORY from Latin *tenere* 'to hold'
WORD FAMILY *Tenacious* comes from the Latin word *tenere* meaning 'to hold'. Other words to do with holding (some only loosely) and having the same origin include *contain, detain, maintain, retain, sustain, tenant*, and *tenet*.

tenant *NOUN* **tenants**
a person who rents a house, building, or land
▷ **tenancy** *NOUN*

tend ① *VERB* **tends, tending, tended**
to be inclined or likely to be or do something

Bigger asteroids tend to be round but smaller ones can be all sorts of funny shapes. — *Kjartan Poskitt, The Gobsmacking Galaxy*

WORD HISTORY from *tender* in the sense 'to offer'

tend ② *VERB* **tends, tending, tended**
1 to look after something in your care, such as a group of animals or a garden

Lorna was in her favourite place, the little garden which she tended with such care and diligence. — *R. D. Blackmore, Lorna Doone*

2 to nurse a sick person, or a wound or injury
3 to watch over and maintain a fire
WORD HISTORY from *attend*

tendency *NOUN* **tendencies**
the way a person or thing is likely to behave ◆ *My sister has a tendency to giggle.*

tender ① *ADJECTIVE*
1 easy to chew; not tough or hard
2 easily hurt or damaged; sensitive or delicate ◆ *Tender plants should be brought indoors for the winter.*
3 a tender area or part of your body is painful when touched
4 a tender word or gesture is gentle and loving
at a tender age (*humorous*) young and inexperienced
▷ **tenderly** *ADVERB*
▷ **tenderness** *NOUN*
WORD HISTORY from Latin *tener* 'soft'

tender ② *VERB* **tenders, tendering, tendered**
to offer something formally ◆ *The disgraced MP was eventually forced to tender his resignation.*

a b c d e f g h i j k l m n o p q r s t u v w x y z

tender ***NOUN*** **tenders**

a formal offer to supply goods or carry out work at a stated price ◆ *The council is asking for tenders to build a new sports centre.*

legal tender kinds of money that are legal for making payments ◆ *Are pound notes still legal tender?*

WORD FAMILY This word *tender* comes from the Latin word *tendere* meaning 'to stretch or hold out'. Other words to do with stretching or holding out (some only loosely) include *attend, contend, distend, extend, tendon, tense, tensile*, and *tension*.

tender❸ ***NOUN*** **tenders**

1 a truck attached to a steam locomotive to carry its coal and water

2 a small boat which carries goods or passengers to and from a larger one

WORD HISTORY from *tend* in the sense 'to look after'

tendon ***NOUN*** **tendons**

a strong strip of tissue that joins muscle to bone

tendril ***NOUN*** **tendrils**

1 a thread-like part by which a climbing plant clings to a support

2 a thin curl of hair or fibre

WORD HISTORY from a French word, related to *tender*

tenement ***NOUN*** **tenements**

1 (in Scotland and the USA) a separate residence in a house or block of flats

2 a large house or building divided into separate flats or rooms

tenet (*say* **ten**- it) ***NOUN*** **tenets**

a firm belief held by a person or group

WORD HISTORY a Latin word meaning 'he or she holds'

tenner ***NOUN*** **tenners**

(*informal*) a ten-pound note; £10

tennis ***NOUN***

a game played with rackets and a ball on a court with a net across the middle

WORD HISTORY from French *tenez!* 'receive (the ball)', which was called by the person serving

tenon ***NOUN*** **tenons**

a piece of wood or other material shaped to fit into a slot made in another piece (SEE ALSO **mortise**)

tenor ***NOUN*** **tenors**

1 (*Music*) the highest ordinary adult male singing voice

2 a musical instrument with approximately the range of a tenor voice ◆ *a tenor saxophone*

3 the tenor of a speech or argument is its general meaning or drift

tenpin bowling ***NOUN***

a game in which players roll hard balls down a track at a group of ten skittles, trying to knock them over

tense❶ ***NOUN*** **tenses**

(*Grammar*) the form of a verb that shows whether something happens in the past, present, or future

WORD HISTORY from Latin *tempus* 'time'

tenses

The **tense** of a verb tells you when the action of the verb takes place.

The **simple present tense** describes something that is continuous or repeated:

Titan is Saturn's biggest moon.
I loathe asparagus.
Do you prefer reading sci-fi or fantasy?

The **simple past tense** describes something that happened in the past:

The Apollo 11 mission landed on the Moon in 1969.
Did you watch 'Doctor Who' last night?

The **present continuous tense** describes an action happening now, and the **past continuous** describes something that was in progress at some time in the past:

I am still reading the first chapter.
When war broke out, my grandparents were living in Austria.

The **past perfect tense** describes an action that was completed at some time in the past:

The party had finished by the time I arrived.

The **future tense** describes something that will, or may, happen in the future:

I'll send you my email address.
Will your sister mind if I borrow her hairdryer?

The **future perfect tense** describes something that will, or may, happen by a specific time in the future:

By tomorrow I will have finished all my work.

See also the panel on **verbs**.

tense❷ ***ADJECTIVE***

1 tightly stretched

2 nervous or worried and unable to relax

3 filled with tension; making people tense ◆ *The atmosphere in the courtroom was so tense you could hear the clock ticking.*

▷ **tensely** ***ADVERB***

▷ **tenseness** ***NOUN***

tense ***VERB*** **tenses, tensing, tensed**

to make something tense, or to become tense

> The hawk tensed and stood up straight, and stared past the monastery into the distance.
> — *Barry Hines, A Kestrel for a Knave*

WORD HISTORY from Latin *tensus* 'stretched'

tensile ***ADJECTIVE***

1 to do with tension

2 able to be stretched

tension ***NOUN*** **tensions**

1 (*D & T*) the process of stretching or being stretched, or the degree to which something is stretched

2 a feeling of anxiety or nervousness about something that is just about to happen

3 voltage ◆ *high-tension cables*

tent *NOUN* **tents**
a temporary shelter made of canvas or other material

tentacle *NOUN* **tentacles**
a long flexible part of the body of a snail, octopus, etc., used for feeling or grasping things or for moving

tentative *ADJECTIVE*
a tentative suggestion or approach is cautious and trying something out
▷ **tentatively** *ADVERB*

tenterhooks *PLURAL NOUN*
to be on tenterhooks is to be tense and anxious about something that is going to happen
WORD HISTORY from *tenter*, a machine with hooks for stretching cloth to dry

tenth *ADJECTIVE, NOUN*
1 next after ninth
2 one of ten equal parts of a thing

tenuous *ADJECTIVE*
1 a tenuous thread or fibre is very thin
2 a tenuous connection is very slight
▷ **tenuously** *ADVERB*
▷ **tenuousness** *NOUN*
WORD HISTORY from Latin *tenuis* 'thin'

tenure (*say* **ten**- yoor) *NOUN* **tenures**
1 the holding of a job or official position
2 the ownership of land or property

tepee or **tipi** (*say* **tee**- pee) *NOUN* **tepees**
1 a conical tent built around long poles which meet at the top
2 a traditional dwelling in this design, covered with animal hide, formerly used by Native Americans of the Plains
WORD HISTORY from a Native American word

tepid *ADJECTIVE*
tepid food or liquid is only slightly warm; lukewarm

tercentenary *NOUN* **tercentenaries**
a 300th anniversary

term *NOUN* **terms**
1 the period of weeks when a school or college is open
2 a definite period ◆ *Members are appointed to serve on the committee for a term of three years.*
3 a word or expression ◆ *The website provides a glossary of technical terms.*

term *VERB* **terms, terming, termed**
to name something; to call something by a certain term ◆ *Mountain-biking and snowboarding are sometimes termed 'extreme sports'.*

termagant *NOUN* **termagants**
a bad-tempered bullying woman
WORD HISTORY named after *Tervagant*, a fierce god in medieval plays

terminable *ADJECTIVE*
able to be terminated

terminal *NOUN* **terminals**
1 the place where something ends; a terminus
2 a building where air passengers arrive or depart
3 a place where a wire is connected in an electric circuit or battery
4 (*ICT*) a monitor and keyboard used for putting data into a computer, or for receiving it

terminal *ADJECTIVE*
1 to do with or at the end or boundary of something
2 a terminal illness is one that is incurable and fatal
▷ **terminally** *ADVERB*

terminate *VERB* **terminates, terminating, terminated**
to end; to stop finally
▷ **termination** *NOUN*

terminology *NOUN* **terminologies**
the technical terms of a subject
▷ **terminological** *ADJECTIVE*

terminus *NOUN* **termini**
1 the end of something
2 the last station on a railway or bus route

termite *NOUN* **termites**
a small insect that is very destructive to timber

terms *PLURAL NOUN*
1 a relationship between people ◆ *Are you still on friendly terms with your neighbours?*
2 conditions offered or accepted, especially in a treaty or contract
to come to terms with something is to become reconciled to a difficult or unwelcome situation

tern *NOUN* **terns**
a seabird with long wings

ternary *ADJECTIVE*
1 consisting of three parts
2 (*Music*) ternary form is a musical structure in which a subject is repeated, with a second subject in a related key played between the two parts
WORD HISTORY from Latin *terni* 'three each'

terrace *NOUN* **terraces**
1 a level area on a slope or hillside
2 a paved area beside a house
3 a row of houses forming a continuous block
▷ **terraced** *ADJECTIVE*

terracotta *NOUN*
1 a kind of pottery made with a brownish-red clay
2 a brownish-red colour
WORD HISTORY an Italian word meaning 'baked earth'

terra firma *NOUN*
dry land; the ground
WORD HISTORY a Latin phrase meaning 'firm land'

terrain *NOUN* **terrains**
a stretch of land ◆ *Mars has one of the most interesting and varied terrains of all the planets.*
WORD FAMILY *Terrain* comes from the Latin word *terra* meaning 'earth'. Other words to do with earth and having the same origin include *inter*, *subterranean*, *terrestrial*, and *territory*.

terrapin *NOUN* **terrapins**
an edible freshwater turtle of North America
WORD HISTORY from a Native American word

terrarium *NOUN* **terrariums**
a sealed transparent globe or other container for growing plants
WORD HISTORY from Latin *terra* 'earth' and *aquarium*

terrestrial *ADJECTIVE*
1 to do with the earth or land
2 a terrestrial planet (such as Earth and Mars) is composed primarily of rock and metal, rather than of gases
3 terrestrial television is broadcast by aerials on the ground rather than by satellite

terrible *ADJECTIVE*
very bad; awful

terribly *ADVERB*
1 very badly ◆ *My knee hurts terribly.*
2 (*informal*) very; extremely ◆ *I'm terribly sorry.*

terrier *NOUN* **terriers**
a kind of small lively dog
WORD HISTORY from Old French *chien terrier* 'earth- dog', because they were used to dig out foxes from their earths

terrific *ADJECTIVE* (*informal*)
1 very great ◆ *There was a terrific splash as the whale dived back into the water.*
2 very good; excellent
▷ **terrifically** *ADVERB*
WORD HISTORY from Latin *terrificus* 'frightening'

terrify *VERB* **terrifies, terrifying, terrified**
to make someone very afraid

In ancient times people used to be terrified by solar eclipses. — *Kjartan Poskitt, The Gobsmacking Galaxy*

territorial *ADJECTIVE*
1 to do with or belonging to a country's territory ◆ *This is one of the largest territorial divisions in southern Africa.*
2 a territorial animal or bird guards and defends an area of land it believes to be its own

territory *NOUN* **territories**
an area of land, especially one that belongs to a country or person

terror *NOUN* **terrors**
1 very great fear
2 a terrifying person or thing
WORD HISTORY from Latin *terrere* 'to frighten'

terrorist *NOUN* **terrorists**
a person who uses violence for political purposes
▷ **terrorism** *NOUN*

terrorize *VERB* **terrorizes, terrorizing, terrorized**
to fill someone with terror; to frighten someone with violent threats
▷ **terrorization** *NOUN*
USAGE NOTE This word can also be spelled terrorise.

terse *ADJECTIVE*
using few words; concise or curt
▷ **tersely** *ADVERB*
▷ **terseness** *NOUN*
WORD HISTORY from Latin *tersus* 'wiped, polished'

tertiary (*say* ter- sher- ee) *ADJECTIVE*
to do with the third stage of something; coming after secondary
WORD HISTORY from Latin *tertius* 'third'

tessellate *VERB* **tessellates, tessellating, tessellated**
to decorate something with small shapes to make a mosaic pattern
▷ **tessellation** *NOUN*
WORD HISTORY from Latin *tessella* 'a small piece of wood, bone, or glass, used as a token or in a mosaic'

test *NOUN* **tests**
1 a short examination
2 a way of discovering the qualities, abilities, or presence of a person or thing ◆ *Tests for pollution and water contamination are to be carried out on the site.*
3 a test match

test *VERB* **tests, testing, tested**
to carry out a test on a person or thing

Cosmo tested the ground like a swimmer testing Arctic waters. — *Eoin Colfer, The Supernaturalist*

▷ **tester** *NOUN*

testament *NOUN* **testaments**
1 a written statement
2 either of the two main parts of the Christian Bible, the *Old Testament* or the *New Testament*
WORD HISTORY from Latin *testis* 'a witness'

testator *NOUN* **testators**
a person who has made a will

testicle *NOUN* **testicles**
either of the two glands that produce sperm in male mammals, contained in the scrotum behind the penis
WORD HISTORY from Latin *testiculus*, from *testis* 'witness (to virility)'

a b c d e f g h i j k l m n o p q r s t u v w x y z

testify *VERB* **testifies, testifying, testified**
1 to give evidence; to swear that something is true
2 to be evidence or proof of something

testimonial *NOUN* **testimonials**
1 a letter describing someone's abilities, character, etc.
2 a gift presented to someone as a mark of respect

testimony *NOUN* **testimonies**
evidence; what someone testifies

test match *NOUN* **test matches**
a cricket or rugby match between teams from different countries

testosterone (*say* test- **ost**- er- ohn) *NOUN*
a male sex hormone

test tube *NOUN* **test tubes**
a tube of thin glass with one end closed, used for scientific experiments

test-tube baby *NOUN* **test-tube babies**
a baby that develops from an egg that has been fertilized outside the mother's body and then placed back in the womb

testy *ADJECTIVE*
easily annoyed; irritable
▷ **testily** *ADVERB*

WORD HISTORY from an earlier meaning 'headstrong', from Latin *testa* 'pot' or (humorously) 'head'

tetanus *NOUN*
a disease that makes the muscles become stiff, caused by bacteria

WORD HISTORY from Greek *tetanos* 'a spasm'

tetchy *ADJECTIVE*
easily annoyed; irritable
▷ **tetchily** *ADVERB*

tête-à-tête (*say* tet- ah- **tet**) *NOUN* **tête-à-têtes**
a private conversation, especially between two people

WORD HISTORY a French phrase meaning 'head to head'

tether *VERB* **tethers, tethering, tethered**
to tie an animal so that it cannot move far

tether *NOUN* **tethers**
a rope for tethering an animal
to be at the end of your tether is to be unable to endure something any more

tetrahedron *NOUN* **tetrahedrons**
a solid with four triangular faces forming a pyramid

WORD HISTORY from Greek *tetra* 'four' and *hedra* 'a base'

Teutonic *ADJECTIVE*
to do with the Teutons, an ancient Germanic people, or their languages

text *NOUN* **texts**
1 the words of something written or printed
2 (*informal*) a text message
3 a passage from the Bible used as the subject of a sermon in a Christian church

text *VERB* **texts, texting, texted**
(*informal*) to send someone a text message

textbook *NOUN* **textbooks**
a book that teaches you about a subject

textiles *PLURAL NOUN*
kinds of cloth; fabrics

text message *NOUN* **text messages**
a written message sent on a mobile phone

texture *NOUN* **textures**
the way that the surface of something feels

thalidomide *NOUN*
a medicinal drug that was found (in 1961) to cause babies to be born with deformed arms and legs

than *CONJUNCTION*
compared with another person or thing ◆ *I'm two inches taller than you.* ◆ *The surface of Venus is hotter than that of Mercury.*

thank *VERB* **thanks, thanking, thanked**
to tell someone that you are grateful to them
thank you an expression of thanks

thankful *ADJECTIVE*
1 showing thanks; grateful
2 pleased and relieved ◆ *We were thankful that the money arrived in time.*

thankfully *ADVERB*
1 in a grateful way
2 fortunately; luckily ◆ *Thankfully, the concert was short.*

thankless *ADJECTIVE*
a thankless task is one that you are unlikely to get thanked or rewarded for doing

thanks *PLURAL NOUN*
1 statements of gratitude
2 (*informal*) thank you
thanks to as a result of; because of ◆ *Thanks to your cooking, the meal was a great success.*

thanksgiving *NOUN*
1 an expression of gratitude, especially to God
2 **Thanksgiving** is an American festival in late November, which commemorates the first harvest feast by Pilgrim settlers in the 17th century

that *DETERMINER, PRONOUN* **those**
the one there ◆ *That book is from the library.* ◆ *Whose bike is that outside?* ◆ *That is your seat there.*

that *ADVERB*
to such an extent ◆ *The cable won't stretch that far; you need a longer one.*

that *RELATIVE PRONOUN*
which, who, or whom ◆ *This is the CD that I wanted.* ◆ *The people that live upstairs are really noisy.*

that *CONJUNCTION*
used to introduce a wish, reason, or result ◆ *I hope that you are well.* ◆ *The crossword was so hard that I couldn't finish it.*

thatch *NOUN*
straw or reeds used to make a roof

thatch *VERB* **thatches, thatching, thatched**
to make a roof with thatch
▷ **thatcher** *NOUN*

WORD HISTORY from an Old English word, related to *deck* and *protect*

thaw *VERB* **thaws, thawing, thawed**
to melt; to become liquid after being frozen

thaw *NOUN* **thaws**
a period of warm weather that thaws ice and snow

WORD HISTORY from an Old English word

the *DETERMINER* (called the *definite article*)
a particular one; that or those

theatre *NOUN* **theatres**
1 a building where plays or other shows are performed to an audience
2 the writing, acting, and producing of plays
3 an operating theatre is a room where surgical operations are performed

USAGE NOTE The American spelling of this word is theater.

WORD HISTORY from Greek *theatron* 'place for seeing things'

WORD FAMILY A related adjective, meaning 'to do with the theatre or acting', is thespian.

theatrical *ADJECTIVE*
1 to do with plays or acting
2 theatrical behaviour is exaggerated and done for showy effect
▷ **theatrically** *ADVERB*

theatricals *PLURAL NOUN*
performances of plays

thee *PRONOUN*
(*old use*) you (referring to one person and used as the object of a verb or after a preposition)

'God save thee, ancient Mariner! From the fiends, that plague thee thus!' — *Samuel Taylor Coleridge, The Rime of the Ancient Mariner*

theft *NOUN* **thefts**
the act of stealing something

their *ADJECTIVE*
1 belonging to them ◆ *Two of the children brought their pets to school.*
2 (*informal*) belonging to a person ◆ *Did somebody leave their coat on the bus?*

USAGE NOTE Take care not to confuse this word with *there* or *they're*.

theirs *POSSESSIVE PRONOUN*
belonging to them ◆ *Which car is theirs?*

USAGE NOTE It is incorrect to write *their's* with an apostrophe.

them *PRONOUN*
the form of *they* used as the object of a verb or after a preposition ◆ *'Where are the tickets?' 'I forgot to bring them.'.* ◆ *Suddenly, the crew realised that the storm was heading straight towards them.*

theme *NOUN* **themes**
1 the subject of a speech, piece of writing, discussion, etc.
2 a melody that is repeated throughout a piece of music
3 a piece of music played at the beginning or end of a film or television programme

WORD HISTORY from Greek *thema* 'a proposition'

theme park *NOUN* **theme parks**
an amusement park with rides and attractions based on a particular subject

theme tune *NOUN* **theme tunes**
a special tune always used to announce a particular programme or performer

themselves *PRONOUN*
they or them and nobody else: used to refer back to the subject of a sentence (e.g. *They blame themselves*) and for emphasis (e.g. *My grandparents built this house themselves*)
by themselves on their own; alone

then *ADVERB*
1 at that time ◆ *I was a lot younger then.*
2 after that; next ◆ *Put your hands behind your head, then stand up slowly.*
3 in that case ◆ *If that isn't your sock, then it must be mine.*

thence *ADVERB*
from that place

I took the path along the down ... and thence most certainly saw a light moving to and fro about the church. — *J. Meade Falkner, Moonfleet*

theology *NOUN*
the study of religion
▷ **theological** *ADJECTIVE*
▷ **theologian** *NOUN*

WORD HISTORY from Greek *theos* 'a god' and *logia* 'study'

theorem *NOUN* **theorems**
a mathematical statement that can be proved by reasoning

WORD HISTORY from Greek *theōrēma* 'theory'

theoretical *ADJECTIVE*
based on theory, not on practice or experience
▷ **theoretically** *ADVERB*

theorize *VERB* **theorizes, theorizing, theorized**
to form a theory or theories
USAGE NOTE This word can also be spelled theorise.

theory *NOUN* **theories**
1 an idea or set of ideas put forward to explain something
2 the principles of a subject rather than its practice
in theory according to what should happen rather than what may in fact happen
WORD HISTORY from Greek *theōria* 'thinking, contemplation'

therapeutic (*say* therra- **pew**- tik) *ADJECTIVE*
helping to relieve or cure a disease or illness ◆ *Sunshine can have a therapeutic effect.*

therapy *NOUN* **therapies**
a way of treating a physical or mental illness, especially without using surgery or artificial medicines
▷ **therapist** *NOUN*
WORD HISTORY from Greek *therapeia* 'healing'

there *ADVERB*
1 in or to that place
2 used to call attention to something (*There's a good dog!*) or to introduce a sentence in which the verb comes before its subject (*There are nine planets in the Solar System.*)
USAGE NOTE Take care not to confuse this word with *their* or *they're*.

thereabouts *ADVERB*
near there

thereafter *ADVERB*
from then or there onwards

thereby *ADVERB*
by that means; because of that

therefore *ADVERB*
for that reason

therm *NOUN* **therms**
(*Science*) a unit for measuring heat, especially from gas
WORD HISTORY from Greek *thermē* 'heat'

thermal *ADJECTIVE*
1 to do with heat; worked by heat
2 thermal clothing is designed to retain body heat
3 a thermal pool or bath is naturally heated by hot springs

thermodynamics *NOUN*
the science dealing with the relation between heat and other forms of energy

thermometer *NOUN* **thermometers**
(*Science*) a device for measuring temperature

Thermos *NOUN* **Thermoses**
(*trademark*) a kind of vacuum flask

thermostat *NOUN* **thermostats**
a piece of equipment that automatically keeps the temperature of a room or piece of equipment steady
▷ **thermostatic** *ADJECTIVE*
▷ **thermostatically** *ADVERB*

thesaurus (*say* thi- **sor**- us) *NOUN* **thesauruses** or **thesauri**
a kind of dictionary that lists words in groups that have similar meanings
WORD HISTORY from Greek *thēsauros* 'storehouse, treasury'

these *plural of* **this**

thesis *NOUN* **theses**
1 a theory that someone has put forward
2 a long essay written by a candidate for a university degree
WORD HISTORY from a Greek word meaning 'placing' or 'a proposition'

thespian *ADJECTIVE*
to do with the theatre or acting

thespian *NOUN* **thespians**
an actor or actress
WORD HISTORY named after the Greek tragic dramatist, *Thespis* (6th century BC)

they *PRONOUN*
1 the people or things being talked about
2 people in general ◆ *They say that tarantulas only bite when they are provoked.*
3 he or she; a person ◆ *Anyone can enter the competition if they want.*

they'd short for *they had* or *they would*

they'll
short for *they will*

they're
short for *they are*
USAGE NOTE Take care not to confuse this word with *their* or *there*.

they've
short for *they have*

thick *ADJECTIVE*
1 with opposite surfaces far apart; broad or wide ◆ *This rope isn't thick enough to bear my weight.*
2 measuring from one side to the other ◆ *The walls of the pyramid are more than 10 metres thick.*
3 thick smoke, fog, or mist is dense and hard to see or move through
4 densely covered, packed, or filled ◆ *The air was thick with smoke.*
5 a thick liquid or mixture is fairly stiff in consistency and does not flow easily
6 (*informal*) stupid
▷ **thickly** *ADVERB*
▷ **thickness** *NOUN*

thicken *VERB* **thickens, thickening, thickened**
to make something thicker, or to become thicker

thicket *NOUN* **thickets**
a number of shrubs and small trees growing close together

thickset *ADJECTIVE*
1 having a stocky or burly body

Haoyou flung himself at the man — a brute as thickset and sturdy as a bollard, with a round, neck-less, bollard head. — *Geraldine McCaughrean, The Kite Rider*

2 with parts placed or growing close together

thief *NOUN* **thieves**
a person who steals things
▷ **thievish** *ADJECTIVE*
▷ **thievery** *NOUN*
▷ **thieving** *NOUN*

WORD HISTORY from Old English *thēof*

thigh *NOUN* **thighs**
the part of the leg between the hip and the knee

thimble *NOUN* **thimbles**
a small metal or plastic cap worn on the end of the finger to push the needle in sewing

WORD HISTORY from an Old English word, related to *thumb*

thin *ADJECTIVE* **thinner, thinnest**
1 not thick or fat
2 a thin excuse or argument is feeble and unconvincing
▷ **thinly** *ADVERB*
▷ **thinness** *NOUN*

SYNONYMS ('not thick') fine, light, flimsy, wispy; ('not fat') slim, slender, lean, slight, skinny; (meaning 2) feeble, tenuous, unconvincing, implausible

thin *VERB* **thins, thinning, thinned**
to make something less thick, or to become less thick
to thin out a crowd thins out when it disperses and becomes less dense
to thin something out to thin out plants is to plant them less densely to allow them to grow

thine *ADJECTIVE, POSSESSIVE PRONOUN*
(*old use*) yours (referring to one person)

'How do they call thee in thine own country, stranger?' — *H. Rider Haggard, She*

thing *NOUN* **things**
an object; something which can be seen, touched, or thought about

WORD HISTORY from Old English *thing* 'assembly', and so 'matter to discuss'

things *PLURAL NOUN*
1 personal belongings ◆ *You can leave your things in the cloakroom.*
2 events or circumstances ◆ *How are things?* ◆ *Things have been a lot better since we moved house.*

think *VERB* **thinks, thinking, thought**
1 to use your mind; to form connected ideas
2 to have something as an idea or opinion

Some people think the Milky Way is a long line of stars, but it isn't. — *Mark Haddon, The Curious Incident of the Dog in the Night-Time*

3 to think of doing something is to intend or plan to do it ◆ *I'm thinking of buying an electric guitar.*
▷ **thinker** *NOUN*

think *NOUN*
a period spent thinking about something ◆ *Before you start to write, have a think about what you want to say in the letter.*

third *ADJECTIVE*
next after second
▷ **thirdly** *ADVERB*

third *NOUN* **thirds**
1 the third person or thing
2 one of three equal parts of something

Third World *NOUN*
the poorest and underdeveloped countries of Asia, Africa, and South America

WORD HISTORY originally called 'third' because they were not considered to be politically connected with the USA and its allies (the *First World*) or with the Communist countries led by Russia (the *Second World*)

thirst *NOUN*
1 a feeling of dryness in your mouth and throat that makes you want to drink
2 a strong desire to do or experience something ◆ *New Zealand is a great destination for those with a thirst for adventure.*
▷ **thirsty** *ADJECTIVE*
▷ **thirstily** *ADVERB*

thirst *VERB* **thirsts, thirsting, thirsted**
to have a strong desire for something

thirteen *NOUN, ADJECTIVE*
the number 13, one more than twelve
▷ **thirteenth** *ADJECTIVE, NOUN*

thirty *NOUN* **thirties** *ADJECTIVE*
the number 30
▷ **thirtieth** *ADJECTIVE, NOUN*

this *DETERMINER, PRONOUN* **these**
the one here ◆ *I'd like to order this book, please.* ◆ *Is this your bus stop?*

this *ADVERB*
to such an extent ◆ *I'm not used to getting up this early.*

thistle *NOUN* **thistles**
a prickly wild plant with purple, white, or yellow flowers
WORD HISTORY from an Old English word

thistledown *NOUN*
the very light fluff on thistle seeds

thither *ADVERB*
(*old use*) to that place
I resolved to travel thither by land, following the edge of the shore. — *Daniel Defoe, Robinson Crusoe*

thong *NOUN* **thongs**
1 a narrow strip of leather used for fastening things
2 a type of sandal with strips worn between the toes
3 a style of underpants with a narrow strip of material at the back
WORD HISTORY from an Old English word

thorax *NOUN* **thoraxes**
the part of the body between the head or neck and the abdomen
▷ **thoracic** *ADJECTIVE*
WORD HISTORY a Greek word meaning 'breastplate'

thorn *NOUN* **thorns**
1 a small pointed growth on the stem of a plant
2 a thorny tree or shrub
WORD HISTORY from an Old English word

thorny *ADJECTIVE* **thornier, thorniest**
1 having many thorns; prickly
2 a thorny problem or issue is complicated and difficult to resolve

thorough *ADJECTIVE*
1 done or doing things carefully and in detail
We take it in turns, once a fortnight, my brother and me, to give the place a thorough going over. — *Harold Pinter, The Caretaker*
2 complete; utter ◆ *The High Street is a thorough mess with all the roadworks just now.*
▷ **thoroughly** *ADVERB*
▷ **thoroughness** *NOUN*
WORD HISTORY another spelling of *through*

thoroughbred *ADJECTIVE*
bred of pure or pedigree stock

thoroughbred *NOUN* **thoroughbreds**
an animal of pure or pedigree stock

thoroughfare *NOUN* **thoroughfares**
a public road or path that is open at both ends
WORD HISTORY from an old sense of *thorough* 'through' and *fare* 'to progress'

those *plural* of **that**

thou *PRONOUN*
(*old use*) you (referring to one person)
'Fear not to speak the truth, my child; thou hast nought to fear from Wulfric de Talbot.' — *Edith Nesbit, Five Children and It*

though *CONJUNCTION*
in spite of the fact that; even if ◆ *Though the volcano has not erupted since 1944, it is far from extinct.*

though *ADVERB*
however; in site of that ◆ *I do think, though, that you'd enjoy the book more than the film.*

thought❶ *NOUN* **thoughts**
1 something that you think; an idea or opinion
2 the process of thinking ◆ *The old woman was deep in thought and I didn't want to disturb her.*

thought❷ *past tense* of **think**

thoughtful *ADJECTIVE*
1 thinking a lot
2 showing thought for other people's needs; considerate
▷ **thoughtfully** *ADVERB*
▷ **thoughtfulness** *NOUN*

thoughtless *ADJECTIVE*
1 careless; not thinking of what may happen
2 not thinking of others; inconsiderate
▷ **thoughtlessly** *ADVERB*
▷ **thoughtlessness** *NOUN*

thousand *NOUN* **thousands** *ADJECTIVE*
the number 1,000
▷ **thousandth** *ADJECTIVE, NOUN*
USAGE NOTE Take care to use the singular form, *thousand*, with words like *few* and *several*, e.g ◆ *Several thousand people were injured.* ◆ *A new kitchen may cost a few thousand pounds..*

thrall *NOUN*
to be in thrall to someone (*History*) is to be in bondage or slavery to them
WORD HISTORY from an Old Norse word, related to *enthrall*

thrash *VERB* **thrashes, thrashing, thrashed**
1 to beat someone with a stick or whip
2 to defeat an opponent or opposing team thoroughly
3 to move about, or move a part of your body, violently ◆ *If a shark feels threatened, it will let you know by swimming from side to side and thrashing its tail.*
to thrash something out is to discuss a matter thoroughly
WORD HISTORY another spelling of *thresh*

thread *NOUN* **threads**
1 a thin length of any substance
2 a length of spun cotton, wool, or nylon used for making cloth or in sewing or knitting
3 the spiral ridge round a screw
4 a theme or idea running through a story or argument ◆ *Somewhere along the way, I lost the thread of the conversation.*
5 one of a series of connected messages from an Internet discussion group

thread *VERB* **threads, threading, threaded**
1 to put a thread through the eye of a needle

Have you ever tried to thread a needle? Fact: no matter how wide the eye of the needle is, the cotton is always wider. — *Nicky Singer, Feather Boy*

2 to pass a strip of film etc. through or round something
3 to put beads on a thread

threadbare *ADJECTIVE*
a threadbare piece of fabric, clothing, or furniture has its surface worn away so that the threads show

threat *NOUN* **threats**
1 a warning that you will punish, hurt, or harm a person or thing
2 a sign of something undesirable
3 a person or thing causing danger

threaten *VERB* **threatens, threatening, threatened**
1 to make a threat or threats against someone
2 to be a threat or danger to someone or something ◆ *Food and water problems are threatening the future of developing countries.*
3 bad weather threatens when it looks as if it will occur soon

It was a cold late-November night. There hadn't been any snow yet, but it was threatening. — *Darren Shan, Tunnels of Blood*

three *NOUN* **threes** *ADJECTIVE*
the number 3, one more than two

three-dimensional *ADJECTIVE*
a three-dimensional object or image has three dimensions (length, width, and height or depth)

threefold *ADJECTIVE, ADVERB*
times three; involving three ◆ *a threefold answer*

thresh *VERB* **threshes, threshing, threshed**
to beat corn in order to separate the grain from the husks
WORD HISTORY from an Old English word

threshold *NOUN* **thresholds**
1 a slab of stone or board etc. forming the bottom of a doorway; the entrance
2 the point at which something begins to happen or change

Arthur was a young man, just on the threshold of life. — *T. H. White, The Once and Future King*

thrice *ADVERB*
(*old use*) three times

thrift *NOUN*
1 careful spending or management of money or resources
2 a plant with pink flowers
▷ **thrifty** *ADJECTIVE*
▷ **thriftily** *ADVERB*
WORD HISTORY from an Old Norse word meaning 'prosperity, thriving'

thrill *NOUN* **thrills**
a feeling of excitement

thrill *VERB* **thrills, thrilling, thrilled**
to have or give a feeling of excitement
▷ **thrilling** *ADJECTIVE*
WORD HISTORY from an Old English word meaning 'to go through', related to *nostril*

thriller *NOUN* **thrillers**
an exciting story, play, or film, usually about crime

thrive *VERB* **thrives, thriving, throve, thrived or thriven**
to grow strongly; to prosper or be successful
WORD HISTORY from an Old Norse word meaning 'to grasp or seize'

throat *NOUN* **throats**
1 the tube in a person's or animal's neck that takes food and drink down into the body
2 the front of the neck

throaty *ADJECTIVE*
1 a throaty sound is produced deep in the throat
2 hoarse; husky
▷ **throatily** *ADVERB*

throb *VERB* **throbs, throbbing, throbbed**
to beat or vibrate with a strong rhythm

I hesitated for some time, and then...with a heart that throbbed violently, I scrambled to the top of the mound in which I had been buried so long. — *H. G. Wells, The War of the Worlds*

throb *NOUN* **throbs**
a throbbing movement, sensation, or rhythm

throes *PLURAL NOUN*
severe pangs of pain

With the ship creaking and groaning behind him, like a huge, beleaguered animal in its death throes, Shackleton called his men together. — *Paul Dowswell, True Polar Adventures*

in the throes of something in the middle of something difficult or taxing ◆ *Many of the students are in the throes of mid-term exams.*

thrombosis *NOUN*
the formation of a clot of blood in the body
WORD HISTORY from Greek *thrombos* 'a lump or clot'

throne *NOUN* **thrones**
1 a special chair for a king, queen, or bishop at ceremonies
2 the position of being king or queen ◆ *the heir to the throne*
WORD HISTORY from Greek *thronos* 'a high seat'

throng *NOUN* **throngs**
a crowd of people
throng *VERB* **throngs, thronging, thronged**
1 to gather or move in a crowd
2 a place is thronged with people or things when it is filled or crowded with them
WORD HISTORY from an Old English word
throttle *NOUN* **throttles**
a device that controls the flow of fuel to an engine; an accelerator
throttle *VERB* **throttles, throttling, throttled**
to strangle someone
to throttle back or down is to reduce the speed of an engine by partially closing the throttle
through *PREPOSITION*
1 from one end or side to the other end or side of ◆ *You have to climb through the tunnel to get to the caves above.* ◆ *The moon was just visible peeking through the clouds.*
2 during, throughout ◆ *There will be celebrations all through the day.*
3 by means of; because of ◆ *Many fires are started through carelessness.*
4 at the end of; having finished successfully ◆ *We must be through the worst of the winter by now.*
through *ADVERB*
1 through something ◆ *The entrance to the crypt was narrow but we managed to squeeze through.*
2 with a telephone connection made ◆ *I'll put you through to the help desk.*
3 finished; ready ◆ *Are you through with your email yet?*
through *ADJECTIVE*
1 a through route or path leads directly from one place to another
2 a through train or journey goes directly all the way to a destination
throughout *PREPOSITION, ADVERB*
all the way through; from beginning to end
throve *past tense of* **thrive**
throw *VERB* **throws, throwing, threw, thrown**
1 to send a person or thing through the air
2 to put something in a place carelessly or hastily ◆ *When we got home, we threw all our clothes straight into the washing machine.*
3 to move part of your body quickly ◆ *In reply to the question, the witch threw back her head and laughed.*
4 to put someone in a certain condition ◆ *The announcement threw the party into instant confusion.*
5 to confuse or upset someone ◆ *The interviewer's first question threw him for a minute.*
6 to move a switch or lever in order to activate it
7 to shape a pot on a potter's wheel
8 to hold a party
to throw something away
1 is to get rid of a useless or unwanted item
2 is to waste a chance or opportunity
to throw up (*informal*) is to vomit
to throw yourself into something is to start doing it with energy or enthusiasm
▷ **thrower** *NOUN*
throw *NOUN* **throws**
a throwing movement; an act of throwing
thrum *VERB* **thrums, thrumming, thrummed**
to sound monotonously; to strum
thrum *NOUN* **thrums**
a thrumming sound
thrush❶ *NOUN* **thrushes**
a songbird with a speckled breast
WORD HISTORY from an Old English word
thrush❷ *NOUN*
an infection causing tiny white patches in the mouth and throat
WORD HISTORY origin unknown
thrust *VERB* **thrusts, thrusting, thrust**
1 to push something suddenly and forcibly
2 to drive or force a way forward
3 to force something unwelcome on someone ◆ *Fans were angry at having the new manager thrust upon them.*
4 to stretch or extend dramatically ◆ *These giant trees thrust above the dense canopy layer of the rainforest.*
thrust *NOUN* **thrusts**
a hard push
thud *NOUN* **thuds**
the dull sound of a heavy knock or fall
thud *VERB* **thuds, thudding, thudded**
to make a thud; to fall with a thud
thug *NOUN* **thugs**
a rough and violent person
▷ **thuggery** *NOUN*
WORD HISTORY from Hindi *thag* 'thief, swindler'
thumb *NOUN* **thumbs**
the short thick finger set apart from the other four
to be under someone's thumb is to be completely under their control or influence
thumb *VERB* **thumbs, thumbing, thumbed**
to turn the pages of a book or magazine quickly with your thumb
to thumb a lift is to signal with your thumb for a vehicle to give you a lift
WORD HISTORY from an Old English word
thumbnail *ADJECTIVE*
1 a thumbnail description or account is brief and gives only the main facts
2 (*ICT*) a thumbnail image is a reduced version of a larger digital image

thumbnail *NOUN* **thumbnails**
1 the nail on your thumb
2 (*ICT*) a thumbnail image

thumbscrew *NOUN* **thumbscrews**
(*History*) an instrument of torture for squeezing the thumb

thump *VERB* **thumps, thumping, thumped**
1 to hit or knock something heavily

The friar thumped the pulpit with both his fists. 'God wills it!' he shouted. — *Kevin Crossley-Holland, The Seeing Stone*

2 to punch someone or something
3 to make a heavy dull sound; to thud
4 your heart thumps when it beats strongly

thump *NOUN* **thumps**
a thumping action or sound

thunder *NOUN*
1 the loud rumbling noise that is heard with lightning
2 a similar noise, e.g. a loud outburst of applause or gunfire, or the rumble of animals' hooves
▷ **thundery** *ADJECTIVE*

thunder *VERB* **thunders, thundering, thundered**
1 to make a noise like thunder
2 to speak loudly

'Get up, and clear out!' thundered Dan, in a rage. — *Louisa May Alcott, Little Men*

thunderbolt *NOUN* **thunderbolts**
a lightning flash thought of as a destructive missile

thunderous *ADJECTIVE*
extremely loud ◆ *There was thunderous applause as the winners were announced.*

thunderstorm *NOUN* **thunderstorms**
a storm with thunder and lightning

thunderstruck *ADJECTIVE*
amazed or shocked

Thursday *NOUN*
the day of the week following Wednesday
WORD HISTORY from Old English *thuresdaeg* 'day of thunder', named after Thor, the Norse god of thunder

thus *ADVERB*
1 in this way ◆ *Van Gogh always signed his paintings thus.*
2 for this reason; therefore

thwart *VERB* **thwarts, thwarting, thwarted**
to frustrate a plan or attempt; to prevent someone from achieving something
WORD HISTORY from an Old Norse word meaning 'going across'

thwart *NOUN* **thwarts**
a crosspiece forming a seat for a rower in a boat

thy *ADJECTIVE*
(*old use*) your (referring to one person)

'Abhorred monster! Fiend that thou art! The tortures of hell are too mild a vengeance for thy crimes.' — *Mary Shelley, Frankenstein*

thyme (*sounds like* time) *NOUN*
a herb with fragrant leaves
WORD HISTORY from Greek *thumon*

thyroid gland *NOUN* **thyroid glands**
a large gland at the front of the neck
WORD HISTORY from Greek *thureos* 'a shield', because of the shape of the gland

thyself *PRONOUN*
(*old use*) yourself (referring to one person)

tiara (*say* tee- ar- a) *NOUN* **tiaras**
a woman's jewelled crescent-shaped ornament worn like a crown
WORD HISTORY from a Greek word

tibia *NOUN*
the bone on the inner side of your leg between the knee and the ankle
WORD HISTORY from a Latin word meaning 'shin bone' or 'pipe'

tic *NOUN* **tics**
an unintentional twitch of a muscle, especially of the face

tick ❶ *NOUN* **ticks**
1 a written mark (✔) put next to something to show that it is correct or has been checked
2 a regular clicking sound, especially that made by a clock or watch
3 (*informal*) a moment ◆ *I'll be back in a tick.*

tick *VERB* **ticks, ticking, ticked**
1 to put a tick next to something
2 to make the sound of a tick
3 something that makes you tick makes you behave or think in a certain way

to tick someone off (*informal*) is to reprimand them

to tick over
1 an engine ticks over when it runs slowly without being connected
2 an activity ticks over when it continues in a routine way
WORD HISTORY probably from German or Dutch

tick ❷ *NOUN* **ticks**
a bloodsucking insect
WORD HISTORY from an Old English word

ticket *NOUN* **tickets**
1 a printed piece of paper or card that allows a person to travel on a bus or train, see a show, etc.
2 a label showing the price of an item for sale

tickle *VERB* **tickles, tickling, tickled**
1 to touch a person's skin lightly so that it tingles and makes them laugh
2 a part of your body tickles when you feel a slight tingling or itching there
3 to amuse or please someone

ticklish *ADJECTIVE*
1 a ticklish person is likely to laugh or wriggle when tickled
2 a ticklish problem or situation is difficult or awkward

tidal *ADJECTIVE*
to do with or affected by tides

tidal wave *NOUN* **tidal waves**
a huge sea wave

tiddler *NOUN* **tiddlers**
(*informal*) a very small fish

tiddlywinks *NOUN*
a game played by flicking a small counter (called a **tiddlywink**) into a cup by pressing on its edge with another counter

tide *NOUN* **tides**
1 the regular rise and fall in the level of the sea, which usually happens twice a day
2 (*old use*) a time or season ◆ *Christmas-tide*

tide *VERB* **tides, tiding, tided**
to tide someone over is to provide them with what is needed for a short time

tidings *PLURAL NOUN*
(*literary*) news or information

In no region had the messengers discovered any signs or tidings of the Riders or other servants of the Enemy. — *J. R. R. Tolkien, The Fellowship of the Ring*

tidy *ADJECTIVE* **tidier, tidiest**
with everything in its right place; neat and orderly
a tidy sum (*informal*) a fairly large amount of money ◆ *It'll cost a tidy sum to get the roof repaired.*
▷ **tidily** *ADVERB*
▷ **tidiness** *NOUN*

tidy *VERB* **tidies, tidying, tidied**
to make a place tidy

WORD HISTORY from an earlier meaning 'at the right time or season', from *tide*

tidy *NOUN* **tidies**
the action of tidying a place ◆ *I'll give the house a quick tidy before they arrive.*

tie *VERB* **ties, tying, tied**
1 to fasten something with string, ribbon, etc.
2 to arrange something into a knot or bow
3 to tie with another competitor is to make the same score as them
to be tied up is to be busy

tie *NOUN* **ties**
1 a strip of material worn passing under the collar of a shirt and knotted in front
2 a result when two or more competitors have equal scores
3 one of the matches in a competition
4 a close connection or bond ◆ *The visiting president spoke of the historical ties between the two countries.*

tie-break or **tie-breaker** *NOUN* **tie-breaks** or **tie-breakers**
a way to decide the winner when competitors have tied, e.g. an additional question in a quiz or an additional game at the end of a set in tennis

tier (*say* teer) *NOUN* **tiers**
each of a series of rows or levels placed one above the other
▷ **tiered** *ADJECTIVE*

tiff *NOUN* **tiffs**
a minor quarrel or argument

tiger *NOUN* **tigers**
a large wild animal of the cat family, with yellow and black stripes

WORD HISTORY from Greek *tigris*

tight *ADJECTIVE*
1 fitting very closely
2 firmly fastened
3 fully stretched; tense
4 in short supply ◆ *Money is tight at the moment.*
5 mean or stingy ◆ *He is very tight with his money.*
6 tight regulation or security is severe or strict
7 (*informal*) slightly drunk
▷ **tightly** *ADVERB*
▷ **tightness** *NOUN*

tight *ADVERB*
tightly or firmly ◆ *Please hold tight to the handrail.*

tighten *VERB* **tightens, tightening, tightened**
to make something tighter, or to become tighter

tightrope *NOUN* **tightropes**
a tightly stretched rope high above the ground, on which acrobats perform

tights *PLURAL NOUN*
a piece of clothing that fits tightly over the feet, legs, and lower part of the body

tigress *NOUN* **tigresses**
a female tiger

tile *NOUN* **tiles**
a thin square piece of baked clay or other hard material, used in rows for covering roofs, walls, or floors
▷ **tiled** *ADJECTIVE*

till❶ *PREPOSITION, CONJUNCTION*
until; to the point when

It was dawn by three in the morning, and twilight lingered till nine at night. — *Jack London, The Call of the Wild*

WORD HISTORY from Old English *til* 'to'

USAGE NOTE It is better to use *until*, rather than *till*, at the start of a sentence (e.g. *Until today, I had never eaten a mango.*) or when you are speaking or writing formally.

till❷ *NOUN* **tills**
a drawer or box for money in a shop; a cash register

WORD HISTORY origin unknown

till❸ *VERB* **tills, tilling, tilled**
to plough land to prepare it for cultivating

WORD HISTORY from Old English *tilian* 'to try'

tiller *NOUN* **tillers**
a handle used to turn a boat's rudder

tilt *VERB* **tilts, tilting, tilted**
to move, or move something, into a sloping position

tilt *NOUN*
a sloping position

at full tilt at full speed or force

timber *NOUN* **timbers**
1 wood for building or making things
2 a wooden beam

WORD HISTORY from an Old English word meaning 'a building'

timbered *ADJECTIVE*
a timbered building is made of wood or has a wooden framework

timbre (*say* tambr) *NOUN* **timbres**
(*Music*) the quality of a voice or musical sound

I was about to shout 'Go away!' when the quite unmistakable timbre of Mrs Lupey's voice came effortlessly through the thick wooden panels of the door. — *Anne Fine, Goggle-Eyes*

WORD HISTORY a French word, related to *timpani*

time *NOUN* **times**
1 all the years of the past, present, and future; the continuous existence of the universe
2 a particular point or portion of time ◆ *It was time to build a fire.*
3 a point of time stated in hours and minutes ◆ *The time is exactly eleven o'clock.*
4 an occasion ◆ *Is this the first time you've been to Prague?*
5 a period suitable or available for something ◆ *We didn't have time to visit the Louvre.* ◆ *There will be time for questions at the end of the lecture.*
6 a system of measuring time ◆ *Greenwich Mean Time*
7 (*Music*) rhythm depending on the number and stress of beats in the bar

at times or **from time to time** sometimes; occasionally

in time
1 not late
2 after a while; eventually

on time prompt or punctual

time *VERB* **times, timing, timed**
1 to measure how long something takes ◆ *Can you time me swimming two lengths of the pool?*
2 to arrange when something is to happen ◆ *The protest march was timed to coincide with the President's visit.*

WORD FAMILY A related adjective, meaning 'to do with time', is temporal.

timeless *ADJECTIVE*
not affected by the passage of time; eternal ◆ *'The Great Gatsby' is now regarded as a timeless classic.*

time limit *NOUN* **time limits**
a fixed amount of time within which something must be done

timely *ADJECTIVE*
a timely event or warning happens at a suitable or useful time

time-out *NOUN*
a rest period or break, especially from a stressful activity

timepiece *NOUN* **timepieces**
(*formal*) a clock or watch

timer *NOUN* **timers**
1 a device for timing things
2 a device for activating something at a preset time

times *PLURAL NOUN*
(*Mathematics*) multiplied by ◆ *Five times three is 15* ($5 \times 3 = 15$).

time scale *NOUN* **time scales**
the length of time that something takes or that you need in order to do something

time share *NOUN*
an arrangement by which several people own a holiday home and have the right to use it at agreed times each year

timetable *NOUN* **timetables**
a list showing the times when things will happen, e.g. when buses or trains will arrive and depart, or when school lessons will take place

timetable *VERB* **timetables, timetabling, timetabled**
to schedule an event or events in a timetable

time zone *NOUN* **time zones**
a region between two lines of longitude, in which a common standard time is used

timid *ADJECTIVE*
easily frightened

As she was not at all a timid child and always did what she wanted to do, Mary went to the green door and turned the handle. — *Frances Hodgson Burnett, The Secret Garden*

▷ **timidly** *ADVERB*
▷ **timidity** *NOUN*

WORD HISTORY from Latin *timidus* 'nervous'

timing *NOUN*
1 the choice of time to do something ◆ *It was unbelievably bad timing to launch both festivals on the same day.*
2 the time when something happens

timorous *ADJECTIVE*
nervous and afraid

He appeared anxious, timorous, ashamed, and his eyes were constantly fixed on the ground. — *Jules Verne, The Mysterious Island*

▷ **timorously** *ADVERB*
▷ **timorousness** *NOUN*

WORD HISTORY from Latin *timor* 'fear'

timpani (*say* **timp**- an- ee) *PLURAL NOUN*
a set of large kettledrums

WORD HISTORY an Italian word, from Latin *tympanum* 'drum'

tin *NOUN* **tins**
1 a silvery-white metal
2 a metal container for food

tin *VERB* **tins, tinning, tinned**
to seal food in a tin to preserve it

tincture *NOUN* **tinctures**
1 a solution of medicine in alcohol
2 a slight trace of something

WORD HISTORY from Latin *tinctura* 'dyeing'

tinder *NOUN*
any dry substance that catches fire easily

tine *NOUN* **tines**
a point or prong of a fork, comb, or antler

WORD HISTORY from an Old English word

tinge *VERB* **tinges, tingeing, tinged**
1 to colour something slightly
2 to be tinged with a feeling or quality is to have a slight amount of it added

The noise of the waterfall and the smell of the sea filled Beadle with a sense of excitement tinged with trepidation. — *G. P. Taylor, Shadowmancer*

tinge *NOUN* **tinges**
1 a slight amount of a colour
2 a slight additional feeling or quality

tingle *VERB* **tingles, tingling, tingled**
to have a slight pricking or stinging feeling

tingle *NOUN* **tingles**
a tingling feeling

tinker *NOUN* **tinkers**
(*old use*) a travelling person who makes a living mending pots and pans etc.

tinker *VERB* **tinkers, tinkering, tinkered**
to tinker with an object or task is to work at it casually, trying to improve or mend it

tinkle *VERB* **tinkles, tinkling, tinkled**
to make a gentle ringing sound

tinkle *NOUN* **tinkles**
a tinkling sound

tinny *ADJECTIVE*
1 like tin
2 a tinny sound is unpleasantly thin and high-pitched

tinsel *NOUN*
strips of glittering material used for decoration, especially on Christmas trees

WORD HISTORY from an Old French word meaning 'a spark', related to *scintillate*

tint *NOUN* **tints**
a shade of colour, especially a pale one

tint *VERB* **tints, tinting, tinted**
to colour something slightly ◆ *The warm light of the sun tinted the tops of the trees with a golden glow.*

WORD HISTORY from Latin *tingere* 'to dye or stain'

tintinnabulation *NOUN*
a ringing or tinkling sound, especially of bells

WORD HISTORY from Latin *tintinnabulum* 'tinkling bell'

tiny *ADJECTIVE* **tinier, tiniest**
extremely small

tip❶ *NOUN* **tips**
the part right at the top or end of something

tip *VERB* **tips, tipping, tipped**
to put a tip on something

tip❷ *NOUN* **tips**
1 a small present of money given to someone who has helped you
2 a small but useful piece of advice; a hint
3 a slight push

tip *VERB* **tips, tipping, tipped**
1 to give a person a tip
2 to name someone as a likely winner ◆ *Which team would you tip to win the championship?*

to tip someone off (*informal*) is to give them a warning or special information about something

▷ **tipper** *NOUN*

tip❸ *VERB* **tips, tipping, tipped**
1 to tilt or topple
2 to empty rubbish somewhere

tip *NOUN* **tips**
1 the action of tipping something
2 a place where rubbish is tipped

tip-off *NOUN* **tip-offs**
(*informal*) a warning or special piece of information given to someone

tipple *VERB* **tipples, tippling, tippled**
to drink alcohol
▷ **tippler** *NOUN*

tipple *NOUN* **tipples**
(*informal*) a spell of drinking alcoholic drinks

tipsy *ADJECTIVE*
(*informal*) slightly drunk
▷ **tipsily** *ADVERB*
▷ **tipsiness** *NOUN*

tiptoe *VERB* **tiptoes, tiptoeing, tiptoed**
to walk on your toes very quietly or carefully

> I tiptoed closer to the drawing room. Who was Dad talking to? I could only hear their voices.
> — *Malorie Blackman, Noughts and Crosses*

on tiptoe walking or standing on your toes

tiptop *ADJECTIVE*
(*informal*) excellent; very best ◆ *Show dogs must be kept in tiptop condition.*

tirade (*say* ty- **rayd**) *NOUN* **tirades**
a long angry or violent speech

tire *VERB* **tires, tiring, tired**
to make someone tired, or to become tired
▷ **tiring** *ADJECTIVE*

tired *ADJECTIVE*
feeling that you need to sleep or rest
to be tired of something is to have had enough of it ◆ *I'm tired of waiting around all day.*

tireless *ADJECTIVE*
having a lot of energy; not tiring easily

tiresome *ADJECTIVE*
continually annoying or irritating

tissue *NOUN* **tissues**
1 tissue paper
2 a paper handkerchief
3 the substance forming any part of the body of an animal or plant ◆ *bone tissue*

WORD HISTORY from an Old French word meaning 'woven', related to *textile*

tissue paper *NOUN*
very thin soft paper used for wrapping and packing things

tit❶ *NOUN* **tits**
a kind of small bird

tit❷ *NOUN*
tit for tat something equal given in return; retaliation

WORD HISTORY from an earlier phrase *tip for tap*

titanic (*say* ty- **tan**- ik) *ADJECTIVE*
huge; enormous ◆ *The central theme of Star Wars is the titanic struggle between good and evil.*

WORD HISTORY from the *Titans*, gigantic gods and goddesses in ancient Greek mythology

titanium *NOUN*
a strong silver-grey metal used to make light alloys that do not corrode easily

titbit *NOUN* **titbits**
a nice little piece of something, e.g. of food, gossip, or information

WORD HISTORY from a dialect word *tid* meaning 'tender' and *bit* in the sense 'a piece'

tithe *NOUN* **tithes**
(*History*) one-tenth of a year's output from a farm etc., formerly paid as tax to support the clergy and church

WORD HISTORY from Old English *teotha* 'tenth'

titillate *VERB* **titillates, titillating, titillated**
to stimulate or excite someone, especially in a sexual way
▷ **titillation** *NOUN*

WORD HISTORY from Latin *titillare* 'to tickle'

USAGE NOTE Take care not to confuse this word with *titivate.*

titivate *VERB* **titivates, titivating, titivated**
to put the finishing touches to something; to smarten something up ◆ *The plan is to titivate the whole layout of the magazine.*
▷ **titivation** *NOUN*

USAGE NOTE Take care not to confuse this word with *titillate.*

title *NOUN* **titles**
1 the name of a book, film, song, etc.
2 a word used to show a person's rank or position, e.g. *Mrs, Dr, Lady, Professor*
3 a championship in sport ◆ *the world heavyweight title*
4 a legal right to something

titled *ADJECTIVE*
a titled person has a title as a noble

titter *VERB* **titters, tittering, tittered**
to laugh quietly or furtively

titter *NOUN* **titters**
a quiet or furtive laugh

tittle-tattle *NOUN*
idle chatter or gossip

titular *ADJECTIVE*
holding a title without any real power or authority

TNT *ABBREVIATION*
trinitrotoluene, a powerful explosive

to *PREPOSITION*
1 used to show direction towards a place or position ◆ *The librarian pointed to the 'No Smoking' sign.* ◆ *Whales migrate to warmer waters to give birth and mate.* ◆ *They are filming a documentary about Hitler's rise to power.*
2 used to show the limit of a defined amount ◆ *The museum is open from 10 to 4 on Sundays.* ◆ *A banana plant can grow from five to thirty-five feet in as little as one year.*

a b c d e f g h i j k l m n o p q r s t u v w x y z

3 used for comparison ◆ *The home team won by six goals to three.*

4 used to show a person or thing affected by an action or feeling ◆ *Give the tickets to me.* ◆ *The staff here are always polite to their customers.*

5 used before a verb to form an infinitive, to show purpose, or alone when the verb is understood ◆ *I have to leave soon.* ◆ *He does that to annoy us.* ◆ *I meant to post the letter, but then forgot to.*

to *ADVERB*

1 to or in the proper or closed position or condition

Just then, the door on the kitchen stairs swung to, so that we were in darkness except for the pale square at the window. — *Dodie Smith, I Capture the Castle*

2 into a state of activity ◆ *We set to and scrubbed the decks.*

to and fro backwards and forwards

toad *NOUN* **toads**

a frog-like animal that lives mainly on land

toad-in-the-hole *NOUN*

a dish of sausages baked in batter

toadstool *NOUN* **toadstools**

a fungus (usually poisonous) with a round top on a stalk

toady *VERB* **toadies, toadying, toadied**

to flatter someone to make them want to help you

toady *NOUN* **toadies**

a flatterer

WORD HISTORY short for *toad-eater*, because quack healers used to have assistants who ate toads and were then supposedly cured

toast *VERB* **toasts, toasting, toasted**

1 to heat bread etc. to make it brown and crisp

2 to warm something in front of a fire or grill

3 to drink in honour of someone

toast *NOUN* **toasts**

1 toasted bread

2 a drink in honour of someone or something; the person or thing honoured in this way ◆ *For a while, the Wright Brothers were the toast of two continents.*

WORD HISTORY from Latin *tostum* 'dried up'

toaster *NOUN* **toasters**

an electrical device for toasting bread etc.

tobacco *NOUN*

the dried leaves of certain plants prepared for smoking in cigarettes, cigars, or pipes, or for making snuff

WORD HISTORY from Spanish *tabaco*, perhaps from a Carib word

tobacconist *NOUN* **tobacconists**

a shopkeeper who sells cigarettes, cigars, etc.

toboggan *NOUN* **toboggans**

a small sledge used for sliding downhill

▷ **tobogganing** *NOUN*

WORD HISTORY via Canadian French from a Native American word

today *NOUN*

this present day ◆ *Today is the first day of spring.*

today *ADVERB*

on this day ◆ *Are you going in to work today?*

toddle *VERB* **toddles, toddling, toddled**

1 a young child toddles when it walks with short unsteady steps

2 to walk or go somewhere casually

I tidied the room, did one or two jobs, and then toddled along to the library. — *Alan Bennett, Talking Heads*

toddler *NOUN* **toddlers**

a young child who has only recently started to walk

toddy *NOUN* **toddies**

a sweetened drink made with spirits and hot water

WORD HISTORY from Sanskrit *tadi*, a tree with a sugary sap that was made into an alcoholic drink

to-do *NOUN* **to-dos**

a fuss or commotion

toe *NOUN* **toes**

1 any of the separate parts (five in humans) at the end of each foot

2 the part of a shoe, sock, or stocking that covers the toes

on your toes alert and ready to act

WORD HISTORY from an Old English word

toffee *NOUN* **toffees**

a sticky sweet made from heated butter and sugar

toga (*say* **toh**-ga) *NOUN* **togas**

(*History*) a long loose piece of clothing worn by men in ancient Rome

WORD HISTORY a Latin word, from *tegere* 'to cover'

together *ADVERB*

with another person or thing; with or against each other ◆ *My flatmates and I are going on holiday together this year.* ◆ *The eye contains many tiny cells that are packed tightly together.*

toggle *NOUN* **toggles**

a short piece of wood or metal etc. used like a button

WORD HISTORY originally a sailors' word; origin unknown

toil *VERB* **toils, toiling, toiled**
1 to work hard
2 to move slowly and with difficulty

The village carpenter had fixed up a bench upon which panting grown-ups could sit and rest themselves after they had toiled up the hill. — *Elizabeth Goudge, The Little White Horse*

▷ **toiler** *NOUN*

toil *NOUN*
hard work

toilet *NOUN* **toilets**
1 a bowl-like object, connected by pipes to a drain, which you use to get rid of urine and faeces
2 a room containing a toilet
3 the process of washing, dressing, and tidying yourself

WORD HISTORY from French *toilette* 'cloth'

token *NOUN* **tokens**
1 a piece of metal or plastic that can be used instead of money
2 a voucher or coupon that can be exchanged for goods
3 a sign or signal of something

Before a Cat will condescend To treat you as a trusted friend, Some little token of esteem Is needed, like a dish of cream. — *T. S. Eliot, Old Possum's Book of Practical Cats*

tolerable *ADJECTIVE*
able to be tolerated
▷ **tolerably** *ADVERB*

tolerant *ADJECTIVE*
willing to accept or tolerate other people's behaviour and opinions even if you do not agree with them
▷ **tolerantly** *ADVERB*
▷ **tolerance** *NOUN*

tolerate *VERB* **tolerates, tolerating, tolerated**
1 to allow something even if you do not approve of it
2 to bear or put up with something unpleasant
▷ **toleration** *NOUN*

WORD HISTORY from Latin *tolerare* 'to endure'

toll ❶ (*rhymes with* hole) *NOUN* **tolls**
1 a charge made for using a road, bridge, etc.
2 an amount of loss or damage ◆ *The death toll from the tsunami disaster is rising.*

to take its toll something takes its toll when it damages or has a bad effect on you

Exhaustion and pain were taking their toll now and he had to fight the yearning just to curl up at the foot of one of the hedgerows. — *Tim Bowler, Starseeker*

WORD HISTORY via Old English and Latin from Greek *telos* 'a tax'

toll ❷ (*rhymes with* hole) *VERB* **tolls, tolling, tolled**
to ring a bell slowly
▷ **toll** *NOUN*

WORD HISTORY probably from an Old English word

tollbooth *NOUN* **tollbooths**
(*History*) a Scottish town hall or town prison

tom or **tomcat** *NOUN* **toms** or **tomcats**
a male cat

WORD HISTORY short for *Thomas*

tomahawk *NOUN* **tomahawks**
a light axe formerly used as a tool or weapon by Native Americans

WORD HISTORY from Algonquin, a Native American language

tomato *NOUN* **tomatoes**
a soft round red or yellow fruit eaten as a vegetable

WORD HISTORY via French, Spanish, or Portuguese from Nahuatl (a Central American language)

tomb (*say* toom) *NOUN* **tombs**
1 an underground place where a dead person is buried
2 a monument built over a burial place

tombola *NOUN* **tombolas**
a game played at a fête or fair, in which tickets are drawn from a revolving drum to win prizes

WORD HISTORY from Italian *tombolare* 'to tumble', because the tickets tumble in the drum

tomboy *NOUN* **tomboys**
a girl who dresses or behaves in a boyish way

tombstone *NOUN* **tombstones**
a memorial stone set up over a grave

tome *NOUN* **tomes**
a large heavy book

WORD HISTORY from Greek *tomos* 'roll of papyrus'

tommy gun *NOUN* **tommy guns**
a small machine gun

WORD HISTORY from the name of its American inventor, J. T. *Thompson* (died 1940)

tomorrow *NOUN, ADVERB*
the day after today

tom-tom *NOUN* **tom-toms**
a drum beaten with the hands

WORD HISTORY from Hindi *tam tam*, imitating the sound

ton *NOUN* **tons**
1 a unit of weight equal to 2,240 pounds or about 1,016 kilograms
2 (*informal*) a large amount ◆ *There's tons of space in the attic.*
3 (*informal*) a speed of 100 miles per hour

WORD HISTORY another spelling of *tun*

tonal *ADJECTIVE*
tonal music is written using the normal keys and harmony
▷ **tonally** *ADVERB*
▷ **tonality** *NOUN*

tone *NOUN* **tones**
1 a sound in music or of the voice

'You both look done in,' said Horyse, speaking in the kindly, slow tone he used on shell-shocked soldiers. — *Garth Nix, Sabriel*

2 (*Music*) each of the five larger intervals between notes in a scale (the smaller intervals are **semitones**)
3 a shade of a colour
4 the quality or character of something ◆ *The joke was in poor taste and lowered the tone of the evening.*

tone *VERB* **tones, toning, toned**
1 to give a particular tone or quality to something
2 to be harmonious in colour
to tone something down is to make it quieter or less bright or less harsh

WORD HISTORY from Greek *tonos* 'tension'

tone-deaf *ADJECTIVE*
not able to tell the difference between different musical notes

toner *NOUN*
1 a liquid put on the skin to improve its condition
2 a substance used to produce tones in printing or photocopying

tongs *PLURAL NOUN*
a tool with two arms joined at one end, used to pick up or hold things

tongue *NOUN* **tongues**
1 the long soft muscular part that moves about inside the mouth
2 a language
3 the leather flap on a shoe or boot underneath the laces
4 a pointed flame

tongue-tied *ADJECTIVE*
too shy to speak

tongue-twister *NOUN* **tongue-twisters**
something that is difficult to say quickly and correctly, e.g. 'Mrs Smith's Fish Sauce Shop'

tonic *NOUN* **tonics**
1 a medicine that makes a person healthier or stronger
2 anything that makes a person more energetic or cheerful
3 tonic water
4 (*Music*) the first note in a scale, providing the keynote in a piece

tonic *ADJECTIVE*
1 having the effect of a tonic
2 (*Music*) relating to the tonic

tonic water *NOUN*
a fizzy mineral water with a bitter taste, often mixed with gin

tonight *NOUN, ADVERB*
this evening or night

tonnage *NOUN*
the amount a ship or ships can carry, expressed in tons

tonne *NOUN* **tonnes**
a metric ton (1,000 kilograms)

tonsil *NOUN* **tonsils**
either of two small masses of soft tissue at the sides of your throat

WORD HISTORY from Latin *tonsillae* 'tonsils'

tonsillitis *NOUN*
inflammation of the tonsils

too *ADVERB*
1 also; in addition ◆ *Buy a bun for yourself, too.*
2 more than is wanted or allowed etc. ◆ *It's too hot to sit outside today.*

tool *NOUN* **tools**
1 a device that helps you to do a particular job ◆ *A saw is a tool for cutting wood or metal.*
2 a thing used for a particular purpose

The Internet is the fastest-growing communication and information tool ever invented in the history of the world. — *Michael Cox, The Incredible Internet*

toolbar *NOUN* **toolbars**
(*ICT*) a row of icons on a computer screen that you can select with the mouse or cursor to open a program or perform some other function

toot *NOUN* **toots**
a short sound produced by a horn

toot *VERB* **toots, tooting, tooted**
to make a toot

tooth *NOUN* **teeth**
1 one of the hard white bony parts that are rooted in the gums, used for biting and chewing things
2 one of a row of sharp parts on a saw or other tool
to fight tooth and nail is to fight very fiercely
▷ **toothed** *ADJECTIVE*

WORD HISTORY from an Old English word

WORD FAMILY A related adjective, meaning 'to do with teeth', is dental.

toothache *NOUN*
pain in your teeth or gums

toothbrush *NOUN* **toothbrushes**
a long-handled brush for cleaning your teeth

toothpaste *NOUN* **toothpastes**
a paste for cleaning your teeth

toothpick *NOUN* **toothpicks**
a small pointed piece of wood or plastic for removing bits of food from between your teeth

toothy *ADJECTIVE*
1 having large or prominent teeth
2 a toothy smile is very full and shows lots of teeth

top❶ *NOUN* **tops**
1 the highest part of something
2 the upper surface
3 the covering or stopper of a bottle, jar, etc.
4 a piece of clothing for the upper part of the body

on top of something in addition to something

top *ADJECTIVE*
1 highest or best ◆ *What was the top score in the darts competition?*
2 important or senior ◆ *The restaurant counts many top celebrities amongst its clientele.*

top *VERB* **tops, topping, topped**
1 to put a top on something
2 to be or arrive at the top of something ◆ *Spain topped the list of holiday destinations last year.*
3 to remove the top of something ◆ *Top and tail the gooseberries to get rid of any tough bits.*

to top something up is to refill a container or supply

WORD HISTORY from an Old English word

top❷ *NOUN* **tops**
a toy that can be made to spin on its point

WORD HISTORY origin unknown

topaz *NOUN* **topazes**
a kind of gem, often yellow

WORD HISTORY from a Greek word

top hat *NOUN* **top hats**
a man's tall stiff black or grey hat worn with formal clothes

top-heavy *ADJECTIVE*
too heavy at the top and likely to overbalance

topiary *NOUN*
the art of clipping shrubs or trees into ornamental shapes

WORD HISTORY from Latin *topiarius* 'ornamental gardener'

topic *NOUN* **topics**
a subject to write, learn, or talk about

The main topic of conversation at breakfast was the admission of Alem to the school. — *Benjamin Zephaniah, Refugee Boy*

WORD HISTORY from Greek *topos* 'a place'

topical *ADJECTIVE*
connected with things that are happening now ◆ *The magazine features topical news stories from all over Asia.*
▷ **topically** *ADVERB*
▷ **topicality** *NOUN*

WORD HISTORY from an earlier meaning 'covering a particular place or topic'

topless *ADJECTIVE*
not wearing any clothes on the top half of the body

topmost *ADJECTIVE*
highest or tallest

On the topmost branch of a gum tree that overhung the gully, there alighted a bird. — *James Vance Marshall, Walkabout*

topography (*say* top- **og**- ra- fee) *NOUN* **topographies**
the position of the rivers, mountains, roads, buildings, etc. in a place
▷ **topographical** *ADJECTIVE*

topping *NOUN* **toppings**
food that is put on the top of a cake, dessert, pizza, etc.

topple *VERB* **topples, toppling, toppled**
1 to fall over; to totter and fall
2 to make something fall over
3 to overthrow a ruler or regime

top secret *ADJECTIVE*
extremely secret ◆ *This information is top secret.*

topsy-turvy *ADVERB, ADJECTIVE*
upside down; muddled

tor *NOUN* **tors**
a hill or rocky peak, especially in Devon and Cornwall

Torah (*say* taw- ra) *NOUN*
(*Religion*) in Judaism, the law of God as revealed to Moses and recorded in the first five books of the Bible

torch *NOUN* **torches**
1 a small electric lamp that you can carry in your hand
2 a stick with burning material on the end, used as a light

toreador (*say* torree- a- dor) *NOUN* **toreadors**
a bullfighter

WORD HISTORY from Spanish *toro* 'a bull'

torment *VERB* **torments, tormenting, tormented**
1 to make someone suffer greatly
2 to tease or keep annoying someone
▷ **tormentor** *NOUN*

torment *NOUN* **torments**
great suffering or anguish

torn *past participle* of **tear**❷

tornado (*say* tor- **nay**- doh) *NOUN* **tornadoes**
a violent storm or whirlwind

WORD HISTORY from Spanish *tronada* 'a thunderstorm'

torpedo *NOUN* **torpedoes**
a long tube-shaped missile that can be fired under water to destroy ships

torpedo *VERB* **torpedoes, torpedoing, torpedoed**
to attack or destroy a ship with a torpedo
WORD HISTORY from a Latin word meaning 'stiffness, numbness', used to refer to a large sea fish which could give an electric shock and cause numbness

torpid *ADJECTIVE*
slow-moving; not lively
▷ **torpidly** *ADVERB*
▷ **torpidity** *NOUN*
▷ **torpor** *NOUN*
WORD HISTORY from Latin *torpidus* 'numb'

torrent *NOUN* **torrents**
1 a rushing stream; a great flow
2 a heavy downpour of rain

Rain fell as it had never fallen before. For days and nights together it poured down in violent torrents, and washed away the yam heaps.
— *Chinua Achebe, Things Fall Apart*

torrential *ADJECTIVE*
torrential rain is rain that pours down violently

torrid *ADJECTIVE*
1 very hot and dry
2 emotional and passionate
WORD HISTORY from Latin *torridus* 'parched'

torsion *NOUN*
the action of twisting, especially twisting one end of a thing while the other is held in a fixed position

torso *NOUN* **torsos**
the trunk of the human body
WORD HISTORY an Italian word meaning 'stump'

tortilla *NOUN* **tortillas**
in Mexican cookery, a flat cake made from flour or maize, often stuffed
WORD HISTORY a Spanish word meaning 'little cake'

tortoise *NOUN* **tortoises**
a slow-moving animal with a shell over its body
WORD HISTORY from Latin *tortuca*

tortoiseshell (*say* **tort- a- shell**) *NOUN* **tortoiseshells**
1 the mottled brown and yellow shell of certain turtles, used for making combs etc.
2 a cat or butterfly with mottled brown colouring

tortuous *ADJECTIVE*
1 a tortuous route or path is full of twists and turns
2 tortuous reasoning or logic is complicated and not easy to follow
▷ **tortuosity** *NOUN*
USAGE NOTE Take care not to confuse this word with *torturous*, which has a different meaning.
WORD HISTORY from Latin *torquere* 'to twist'

torture *VERB* **tortures, torturing, tortured**
1 to inflict great physical pain on someone, especially to make them do something against their will
2 to cause someone great emotional pain or worry
▷ **torturer** *NOUN*

torture *NOUN*
the action of torturing someone, or the process of being tortured

torturous *ADJECTIVE*
like torture; agonizing ◆ *There followed a torturous wait for news of survivors.*
USAGE NOTE Take care not to confuse this word with *tortuous*, which has a different meaning.

Tory *NOUN* **Tories**
a member of the British Conservative Party
▷ **Tory** *ADJECTIVE*
WORD HISTORY originally used of Irish outlaws in the 17th century, from Irish *toraidhe* 'an outlaw'

tosh *NOUN*
(*informal*) nonsense; rubbish

toss *VERB* **tosses, tossing, tossed**
1 to throw something, especially up into the air
2 to spin a coin to decide something according to which side of it is upwards after it falls
3 to move restlessly or unevenly from side to side

toss *NOUN* **tosses**
an act of tossing a coin or other object

toss-up *NOUN* **toss-ups**
1 the tossing of a coin
2 an even chance ◆ *It was a toss-up between Shrek and Monsters, Inc. to win the Oscar.*

tot[1] *NOUN* **tots**
1 a small child
2 (*informal*) a small amount of spirits ◆ *Sailors used to be given a tot of rum on special occasions.*
WORD HISTORY originally a dialect word

tot[2] *VERB* **tots, totting, totted**
to tot something up (*informal*) is to add up figures or amounts
WORD HISTORY from *total*

total *ADJECTIVE*
1 including everything ◆ *The last column shows the total amount to pay.*
2 complete; utter ◆ *That was a total waste of time.*
▷ **totally** *ADVERB*

total *NOUN* **totals**
the amount you get by adding everything together

total *VERB* **totals, totalling, totalled**
1 to add up figures to make a total
2 to amount to something ◆ *The cost of the damage totalled £5,000.*
3 (*informal*) to destroy or wreck something

WORD HISTORY from Latin *totum* 'the whole'

totalitarian *ADJECTIVE*
using a form of government where people are not allowed to form rival political parties

totality *NOUN*
the whole of something

tote *VERB* **totes, toting, toted**
(*informal*) to carry something, especially luggage or belongings

Quarter past eleven I got up and toted my stuff across to the station. — Robert Swindells, Stone Cold

totem pole *NOUN* **totem poles**
a pole carved or painted by Native Americans with the symbols (*totems*) of their tribes or families

WORD HISTORY from Ojibwa, a Native American language

totter *VERB* **totters, tottering, tottered**
to walk unsteadily; to wobble
▷ **tottery** *ADJECTIVE*

toucan (*say* too- kan) *NOUN* **toucans**
a tropical American bird with a huge beak

WORD HISTORY via French and Portuguese from Tupi (a South American language)

touch *VERB* **touches, touching, touched**
1 to put your hand or fingers on something lightly
2 two things touch when they join together so that there is no space between
3 to come into contact with something or hit it gently
4 to move or meddle with something ◆ *Don't touch the computer until I get back.*
5 to reach a particular point ◆ *The thermometer touched 30° Celsius.*
6 to affect someone's feelings, e.g. by making them feel sympathy ◆ *All those present were deeply touched by the moving ceremony.*

touch and go uncertain or risky
to touch down
1 an aircraft or spacecraft touches down when it lands
2 a rugby player touches down when they touch the ball on the ground behind the goal line

to touch on something is to mention or discuss a subject briefly
to touch something up is to improve it by making small additions or changes

touch *NOUN* **touches**
1 the action of touching
2 the ability to feel things by touching them
3 a small amount; a small thing done ◆ *The florist is just adding the finishing touches to the bouquet.*
4 a special skill or style of workmanship ◆ *It's good to see that the former champion hasn't lost her touch.*
5 communication with someone ◆ *I've been out of touch with my old schoolfriends for years.*
6 the part of a sports field outside the playing area

WORD FAMILY A related adjective, meaning 'to do with the sense of touch', is tactile.

touchdown *NOUN* **touchdowns**
the action of touching down

touché (*say* too- shay) *EXCLAMATION*
used to acknowledge a true or clever point made against you in an argument

WORD HISTORY a French word meaning 'touched', originally referring to a hit in fencing

touching *ADJECTIVE*
causing you to feel pity or sympathy ◆ *The artist has depicted a touching scene of mother and sleeping child.*

touchline *NOUN* **touchlines**
one of the lines that mark the side of a sports pitch

touchstone *NOUN* **touchstones**
a test by which the quality of something is judged

WORD HISTORY formerly, a kind of stone against which gold and silver were rubbed to test their purity

touchy *ADJECTIVE* **touchier, touchiest**
irritable and easily offended

Harry remembered how touchy Myrtle had always been about being dead, but none of the other ghosts he knew made such a fuss about it. — J. K. Rowling, Harry Potter and the Goblet of Fire

▷ **touchily** *ADVERB*
▷ **touchiness** *NOUN*

tough *ADJECTIVE*
1 strong; difficult to break or damage
2 firm or severe
3 a tough person is able to stand hardship and is not easily hurt
4 tough food is difficult to chew
5 a tough problem or decision is difficult or tricky
▷ **toughly** *ADVERB*
▷ **toughness** *NOUN*

toughen *VERB* **toughens, toughening, toughened**
to make someone or something tough, or to become tough

to toughen someone up is to make them tough or hardy

toupee (*say* too- pay) ***NOUN*** **toupees**
a small piece of artificial hair worn to cover a bald spot

tour ***NOUN*** **tours**
a journey visiting several places

tour ***VERB*** **tours, touring, toured**
to make a tour

tourism ***NOUN***
the industry of providing services for people on holiday in a place

tourist ***NOUN*** **tourists**
a person who visits a place for pleasure, especially when on holiday

tournament ***NOUN*** **tournaments**
1 a series of games or contests
2 (*History*) a sporting contest between knights with jousting and other types of combat

tourniquet (*say* toor- nik- ay) ***NOUN*** **tourniquets**
a strip of material pulled tightly round an arm or leg to stop bleeding from an artery

WORD HISTORY from a French word

tousle (*say* towz- el) ***VERB*** **tousles, tousling, tousled**
to ruffle someone's hair

WORD HISTORY probably from an Old English word meaning 'to pull or shake'

tout (*rhymes with* scout) ***VERB*** **touts, touting, touted**
to try to sell something or get business

Traders in mysteries touted their books, showing pictures of the days of fear and wonder to come. — *William Nicholson, Firesong*

tout ***NOUN*** **touts**
a person who sells tickets for a sports match, concert, etc. at more than the original price

tow❶ (*rhymes with* go) ***VERB*** **tows, towing, towed**
to pull a vehicle or heavy object along behind you

tow ***NOUN***
an act of towing

on tow being towed

WORD HISTORY from Old English *togian*

tow❷ (*rhymes with* go) ***NOUN***
short light-coloured fibres of flax or hemp

WORD HISTORY from Old English *tow*

towards or **toward** ***PREPOSITION***
1 in the direction of ◆ *The crew were silent, staring towards the land.*
2 in relation to; regarding ◆ *Steinbeck didn't feel kindly towards the American middle class of his day.*
3 as a contribution to ◆ *We're putting the prize money towards a holiday.*
4 near; close to ◆ *It was getting on towards midnight when the messenger arrived.*

towel ***NOUN*** **towels**
a piece of absorbent cloth for drying things
▷ **towelling** ***NOUN***

tower ***NOUN*** **towers**
a tall narrow building, either standing by itself or forming part of a church or other building

tower ***VERB*** **towers, towering, towered**
1 to be very high; to be taller than the surroundings

The man was a human tree in height, towering high above Papa's six feet two inches. — *Mildred D. Taylor, Roll of Thunder, Hear My Cry*

2 to be more significant or important than others around you ◆ *Einstein towers above all other scientists of the twentieth century.*

town ***NOUN*** **towns**
a place with many houses, shops, offices, and other buildings

WORD HISTORY from Old English *tun* 'enclosure'

WORD FAMILY Related adjectives, meaning 'to do with a town or city', are municipal and urban.

town hall ***NOUN*** **town halls**
a building with offices for the local council and usually a hall for public events

township ***NOUN*** **townships**
1 a small town in South Africa with a predominantly black population
2 (*History*) in South Africa under apartheid, a town set aside for black people to live

towpath ***NOUN*** **towpaths**
a path beside a canal or river, originally for use when a horse was towing a barge

toxic ***ADJECTIVE***
poisonous; caused by or containing poison ◆ *Household toxic waste is a major source of pollution.*
▷ **toxicity** ***NOUN***

WORD HISTORY from Greek *toxikon pharmakon* 'poison for arrows', from *toxon* 'a bow'

toxicology ***NOUN***
the study of poisons
▷ **toxicologist** ***NOUN***

toxin ***NOUN*** **toxins**
a poisonous substance, especially one formed in the body by germs

toy ***NOUN*** **toys**
a thing to play with, especially one designed for a child

toy ***ADJECTIVE***
1 made as a toy
2 a toy dog is one belonging to a miniature breed kept as a pet

toy ***VERB*** **toys, toying, toyed**
to toy with something is to play with it or treat it casually

toyshop ***NOUN*** **toyshops**
a shop that sells toys

trace❶ ***NOUN*** **traces**

1 a mark left by a person or thing; a sign ◆ *There were traces of fingerprints on the mirror.*

2 a very small amount

trace ***VERB*** **traces, tracing, traced**

1 to copy a line or image by drawing over it on transparent paper

2 to form a pattern or image

Syme had fallen silent for a moment, and with the handle of his spoon was tracing patterns in the puddle of stew. — *George Orwell, Nineteen Eighty-four*

3 to find a person or thing after following tracks or other evidence ◆ *Police are still trying to trace the victim's family.*

▷ **tracer** ***NOUN***

WORD HISTORY from an Old French word, related to *tract*

trace❷ ***NOUN*** **traces**

each of the two straps or ropes by which a horse pulls a cart

to kick over the traces is to become disobedient or reckless

WORD HISTORY from an Old French word, related to *traction*

traceable ***ADJECTIVE***

able to be traced

tracery ***NOUN***

a decorative pattern of holes in stone, e.g. in a church window

track ***NOUN*** **tracks**

1 a mark or marks left by a moving person or thing

2 a rough path made by being used

3 a road or area of ground specially prepared for racing

4 a set of rails for trains or trams

5 one of the songs or pieces of music on a CD, tape, or record

6 a continuous band round the wheels of a tank or tractor etc.

to keep or lose track of something to keep or fail to keep yourself aware of something or informed about it

to make tracks (*informal*) is to leave or go away

track ***VERB*** **tracks, tracking, tracked**

1 to follow the tracks left by a person or animal

2 to follow or observe something as it moves

to track someone down is to find them by searching

▷ **tracker** ***NOUN***

track events ***PLURAL NOUN***

athletic contests on a running track, as opposed to field events

track record ***NOUN*** **track records**

a person's past achievements

track suit ***NOUN*** **track suits**

a warm loose suit of the kind worn by athletes before and after contests or for jogging

tract❶ ***NOUN*** **tracts**

1 an area of land

I had crossed a marshy tract full of willows, bulrushes, and odd, outlandish, swampy trees. — *Robert Louis Stevenson, Treasure Island*

2 a series of connected parts along which something passes ◆ *the digestive tract*

WORD FAMILY *Tract* comes from the Latin word *tractus* meaning 'drawing or draught' or *tractum* 'pulled'. Other words to do with drawing or pulling (some only loosely) and having the same origin include *attract, contract, detract, distract, subtract, traction,* and *tractor*.

tract❷ ***NOUN*** **tracts**

a pamphlet containing a short essay, especially about religion

traction ***NOUN***

1 the action of pulling a load

2 the ability of a vehicle to grip the ground ◆ *The wheels were losing traction in the snow.*

3 a medical treatment in which an injured limb is pulled gently for a long time by means of weights and pulleys

traction engine ***NOUN*** **traction engines**

a steam or diesel engine for pulling a heavy load along a road or across a field

tractor ***NOUN*** **tractors**

a motor vehicle for pulling farm machinery or other heavy loads

trade ***NOUN*** **trades**

1 the action of buying, selling, or exchanging goods

2 business of a particular kind; the people working in this

3 an occupation, especially a skilled craft

trade ***VERB*** **trades, trading, traded**

1 to buy or sell goods

2 to swop or exhange things

The next morning, Roy traded seats on the school bus to be closer to the front door. — *Carl Hiaasen, Hoot*

to trade something in is to give it as part of the payment for something new ◆ *I traded in my old mobile phone for a new one.*

▷ **trader** ***NOUN***

trademark ***NOUN*** **trademarks**

a symbol or name that a firm has registered to distinguish its products from those of other firms, and which no other firm is allowed to use for a similar product

tradesman ***NOUN*** **tradesmen**

a person employed in trade, especially one who sells or delivers goods

trade union ***NOUN*** **trade unions**

a group of workers organized to help and protect workers in their own trade or industry

tradition *NOUN* **traditions**
1 the passing down of beliefs or customs from one generation to another
2 something passed on in this way

WORD HISTORY from Latin *tradere* 'to hand on, deliver, or betray'

traditional *ADJECTIVE*
1 to do with tradition
2 holding traditional beliefs or customs

Numbers, dates, in fact mathematics of any kind, have little or no relevance in our traditional Aboriginal society. — *Doris Pilkington, Rabbit Proof Fence*

▷ **traditionally** *ADVERB*

traffic *NOUN*
1 vehicles, ships, or aircraft moving along a route
2 trading or dealing in drugs or other illegal goods

traffic *VERB* **traffics, trafficking, trafficked**
to trade in something illegal, especially drugs

▷ **trafficker** *NOUN*

traffic lights *PLURAL NOUN*
a set of coloured lights used as a signal to control traffic at road junctions or roadworks

traffic warden *NOUN* **traffic wardens**
an official who monitors the parking of vehicles and reports on those parked illegally

tragedian (*say* tra- **jee**- dee- an) *NOUN* **tragedians**
1 a person who writes tragedies
2 an actor in tragedies

tragedy *NOUN* **tragedies**
1 a play with unhappy events or a sad ending

You're familiar with the tragedies of antiquity, are you? The great homicidal classics? — *Tom Stoppard, Rosencrantz & Guildenstern are Dead*

2 a very sad or distressing event

WORD HISTORY from a Greek word meaning literally 'goat's song'

tragic *ADJECTIVE*
1 very sad or distressing
2 to do with tragedies ◆ *a great tragic actor*

▷ **tragically** *ADVERB*

trail *NOUN* **trails**
1 a track, scent, or other sign left where a person or animal has passed
2 a path or track for walking through the countryside or a forest

trail *VERB* **trails, trailing, trailed**
1 to follow the trail of a person or animal; to track a person or animal
2 to drag or be dragged along behind

Natalie ... trailed her feet along the floor so stubbornly, she left tracks even on the hardy shop carpet. — *Anne Fine, Madame Doubtfire*

3 to follow someone slowly or wearily
4 to hang down or float loosely
5 to become fainter ◆ *The voice at the other end of the phone trailed away.*

WORD HISTORY from Latin *tragula* 'a net for dragging a river'

trailer *NOUN* **trailers**
1 a truck or other container pulled along by a vehicle
2 a short piece from a film or television programme, shown in advance to advertise it

train *NOUN* **trains**
1 a railway engine which pulls a line of carriages or trucks that are linked together
2 a number of people or animals, especially camels, moving in a line
3 a series of things or events ◆ *This action set in motion the train of events that led to the outbreak of the Civil War.*
4 part of a long dress or robe that trails on the ground at the back

train *VERB* **trains, training, trained**
1 to give someone instruction or practice so that they become skilled
2 to practise, especially for a sporting event ◆ *The team is training hard for the Olympics.*
3 to make a plant grow in a particular direction ◆ *Tomatoes can be trained to grow up a pole or trellis.*
4 to train a gun, camera, telescope, etc. on something is to point or aim it in that direction

trainee *NOUN* **trainees**
a person who is being trained

trainer *NOUN* **trainers**
1 a person who trains people or animals
2 a soft rubber-soled shoe of the kind worn for running or by athletes etc. while exercising

traipse *VERB* **traipses, traipsing, traipsed**
to walk wearily; to trudge a long distance

trait (*say* tray *or* trayt) *NOUN* **traits**
one of a person's characteristics

traitor *NOUN* **traitors**
a person who betrays their country or friends

▷ **traitorous** *ADJECTIVE*

trajectory *NOUN* **trajectories**
the path taken by a moving object such as a bullet or rocket

tram *NOUN* **trams**
a public passenger vehicle which runs on rails in the road

tramlines *PLURAL NOUN*
1 rails for a tram
2 the pair of parallel lines at the side of a tennis court

tramp *NOUN* **tramps**
1 a person without a home or job who walks from place to place
2 a long walk
3 the sound of heavy footsteps

tramp *VERB* **tramps, tramping, tramped**
1 to walk with heavy footsteps.
2 to walk for a long distance

I'd tramped the narrow little streets of Soho and the boulevards of South Kensington from early morning. — *Robert Swindells, Stone Cold*

trample *VERB* **tramples, trampling, trampled**
to tread heavily on something; to crush something by treading on it

trampoline *NOUN* **trampolines**
a large piece of canvas joined to a frame by springs, used by gymnasts for jumping on
WORD HISTORY from Italian *trampolino*, from *trampoli* 'stilts'

trance *NOUN* **trances**
a dreamy or unconscious state rather like sleep

tranquil *ADJECTIVE*
calm and quiet

It was a tranquil summer dawn, the day the travellers departed, and the air was still. — *William Nicholson, The Wind Singer*

▷ **tranquilly** *ADVERB*
▷ **tranquillity** *NOUN*
WORD HISTORY from Latin *tranquillus*

tranquillize *VERB* **tranquillizes, tranquillizing, tranquillized**
a drug or medicine tranquillizes someone when it makes them feel calm
▷ **tranquillizer** *NOUN*
USAGE NOTE This word can also be spelled tranquillise.

transact *VERB* **transacts, transacting, transacted**
to carry out business
▷ **transaction** *NOUN*
WORD HISTORY from Latin *trans* 'across' and *agere* 'to do'

transatlantic *ADJECTIVE*
across or on the other side of the Atlantic Ocean

transcend *VERB* **transcends, transcending, transcended**
to go beyond superficial differences or limits; to surpass something ◆ *Great music transcends its time and speaks to listeners across the ages.*
WORD HISTORY from Latin *trans* 'across' and *scandere* 'to climb'

transcribe *VERB* **transcribes, transcribing, transcribed**
to copy or write something out
▷ **transcription** *NOUN*
WORD HISTORY from Latin *trans* 'across' and *scribere* 'to write'

transcript *NOUN* **transcripts**
a written copy

transept *NOUN* **transepts**
the part that is at right angles to the nave in a cross-shaped church
WORD HISTORY from Latin *trans* 'across' and *septum* 'a partition'

transfer *VERB* **transfers, transferring, transferred**
1 to move a person or thing to another place
2 to hand over a power or responsibility to someone else
▷ **transferable** *ADJECTIVE*
▷ **transference** *NOUN*

transfer *NOUN* **transfers**
1 the action of transferring a person or thing
2 a picture or design that can be transferred onto another surface
WORD HISTORY from Latin *trans* 'across' and *ferre* 'to carry'

transfigure *VERB* **transfigures, transfiguring, transfigured**
to change the appearance of something greatly
▷ **transfiguration** *NOUN*

transfix *VERB* **transfixes, transfixing, transfixed**
1 to make a person or animal unable to move because of fear or surprise
2 to capture someone's attention and interest completely
3 to pierce and fix an object with a spear or other point

transform *VERB* **transforms, transforming, transformed**
to change the form, appearance, or character of a person or thing ◆ *Snow fell during the night and we woke to find the countryside transformed.*
▷ **transformation** *NOUN*

transformer *NOUN* **transformers**
a device used to change the voltage of an electric current

transfuse *VERB* **transfuses, transfusing, transfused**
to put blood taken from one person into another person

transfusion *NOUN* **transfusions**
a medical procedure whereby blood is taken from one person and put into another person

transgress *VERB* **transgresses, transgressing, transgressed**
1 to break a rule or law
2 (*old use*) to commit a sin
▷ **transgression** *NOUN*
WORD HISTORY from Latin *trans* 'across' and *gressus* 'gone'

transient *ADJECTIVE*
not lasting or staying for long ◆ *This area of the city has a transient population of students and young families.*
▷ **transience** *NOUN*

a b c d e f g h i j k l m n o p q r s t u v w x y z

transistor *NOUN* **transistors**
1 a tiny semiconductor device that controls a flow of electricity
2 (in full **transister radio**) a portable radio that uses circuits with transistors
▷ **transistorized** or **transistorised** *ADJECTIVE*
WORD HISTORY from *transfer* and *resistor*

transit *NOUN*
the process of travelling from one place to another ♦ *The goods were damaged in transit.*

transition *NOUN* **transitions**
the process of changing from one condition or form to another
▷ **transitional** *ADJECTIVE*

transitive *ADJECTIVE*
(*Grammar*) a transitive verb is used with a direct object after it, e.g. *change* in *I must change my shoes* (but not in *The weather has changed*) (SEE ALSO **intransitive**)
▷ **transitively** *ADVERB*
WORD HISTORY from Latin *transitivus* 'passing over'

transitory *ADJECTIVE*
existing for a time but not lasting ♦ *The symbol of a clock on a gravestone represents the transitory nature of human existence.*

translate *VERB* **translates, translating, translated**
to put something into another language
▷ **translatable** *ADJECTIVE*
▷ **translation** *NOUN*
▷ **translator** *NOUN*

transliterate *VERB* **transliterates, transliterating, transliterated**
to write a word in the letters of a different alphabet or language
▷ **transliteration** *NOUN*

translucent (*say* tranz-**loo**-sent) *ADJECTIVE*
a translucent surface or object allows light to shine through but is not transparent

transmission *NOUN* **transmissions**
1 the action of transmitting something
2 a broadcast
3 the gears by which power is transmitted from the engine to the wheels of a vehicle

transmit *VERB* **transmits, transmitting, transmitted**
1 to send a message or information from one person or place to another
2 to pass on a disease or infection from one person to another
3 to send out a signal or broadcast
▷ **transmitter** *NOUN*

transmute *VERB* **transmutes, transmuting, transmuted**
to change something from one form or substance into another ♦ *Medieval alchemists experimented with methods to transmute base metals into gold.*
▷ **transmutation** *NOUN*
WORD HISTORY from Latin *trans* 'across' and *mutare* 'to change'

transom *NOUN* **transoms**
1 a horizontal bar of wood or stone dividing a window or separating a door from a window above it
2 a small window above a door

transparency *NOUN* **transparencies**
1 the fact of being transparent
2 a transparent photograph that can be projected onto a screen

transparent *ADJECTIVE*
1 able to be seen through
2 clear and obvious ♦ *The rules of the game are far from transparent.*

transpire *VERB* **transpires, transpiring, transpired**
1 to become known; to turn out ♦ *Years later, it transpired that the newspaper had invented the whole story.*
2 to happen ♦ *The police need to know what transpired on the night of the murder.*
3 a plant transpires when it gives off watery vapour from its leaves etc.
▷ **transpiration** *NOUN*
WORD HISTORY from Latin *trans* 'across' and *spirare* 'to breathe'

transplant *VERB* **transplants, transplanting, transplanted**
1 to remove a plant and put it to grow somewhere else
2 to transfer an organ from the body of one person or animal to another
▷ **transplantation** *NOUN*

transplant *NOUN* **transplants**
1 the process of transplanting
2 a plant or organ that is transplanted

transport *VERB* **transports, transporting, transported**
1 to take a person, animal, or thing from one place to another, especially in a vehicle
2 to be transported is to feel carried away by an extreme emotion
▷ **transportation** *NOUN*
▷ **transporter** *NOUN*

transport *NOUN*
1 the process or means of transporting people, animals, or things ♦ *Vienna has an excellent system of public transport.* ▸▸

2 a feeling of being carried away by a strong emotion

'PEEVES!' Filch roared, flinging down his quill in a transport of rage. 'I'll have you this time, I'll have you!' — *J. K. Rowling, Harry Potter and the Chamber of Secrets*

transpose *VERB* **transposes, transposing, transposed**
1 to change the position or order of something
2 (*Music*) to put a piece of music into a different key
▷ **transposition** *NOUN*

transsexual *NOUN* **transsexuals**
a person who feels emotionally and psychologically that they belong to the sex opposite to their own

transverse *ADJECTIVE*
lying across something
▷ **transversely** *ADVERB*

transvestite *NOUN* **transvestites**
a person who likes wearing clothes intended for someone of the opposite sex
WORD HISTORY from Latin *trans* 'across' and *vestire* 'to dress'

trap *NOUN* **traps**
1 a device for catching and holding animals
2 a plan or trick for capturing, detecting, or cheating someone
3 a two-wheeled carriage pulled by a horse
4 a bend in a pipe, filled with water to prevent gases from rising up from a drain

trap *VERB* **traps, trapping, trapped**
1 to catch or hold a person or animal in a trap
2 to prevent someone from escaping, or from avoiding an unpleasant situation ◆ *The driver was trapped in the wreckage for six hours.*

trapdoor *NOUN* **trapdoors**
a small door in a floor, ceiling, or roof

trapeze *NOUN* **trapezes**
a bar hanging from two ropes as a swing for acrobats

trapezium *NOUN* **trapeziums** or **trapezia**
a quadrilateral in which two opposite sides are parallel and the other two are not
WORD HISTORY from Greek *trapeza* 'a table'

trapezoid *NOUN* **trapezoids**
a quadrilateral in which no sides are parallel

trapper *NOUN* **trappers**
someone who traps wild animals, especially for their fur

trappings *PLURAL NOUN*
1 the clothes or possessions that show your rank or position
2 an ornamental harness for a horse

trash *NOUN*
rubbish or nonsense
▷ **trashy** *ADJECTIVE*

trauma (*say* traw- ma) *NOUN* **traumas**
1 a shock following a stressful event that produces a lasting effect on a person's mind
2 a very unpleasant or distressing experience
▷ **traumatic** *ADJECTIVE*
WORD HISTORY a Greek word meaning 'a wound'

traumatize *VERB* **traumatizes, traumatizing, traumatized**
to shock or distress someone in a way that produces a lasting effect on their mind
USAGE NOTE This word can also be spelled traumatise.

travail *NOUN*
(*old use*) hard or laborious work

travail *VERB* **travails, travailing, travailed**
to do hard or laborious work

travel *VERB* **travels, travelling, travelled**
to move from place to place; to go on a journey

travel *NOUN*
the action of moving from place to place; journeying

to go on your travels is to go on a long or regular journey

travel agent *NOUN* **travel agents**
a person or company whose job is to arrange travel and holidays for people

traveller *NOUN* **travellers**
1 a person who is travelling or who often travels
2 a gypsy, or a person who does not settle in one place

traveller's cheque *NOUN* **traveller's cheques**
a cheque for a fixed amount of money that is sold by banks and that can be exchanged for money in foreign countries

traverse *VERB* **traverses, traversing, traversed**
to go or travel across something, especially as part of a journey or expedition

On the ninth day after leaving Yokohama, Phileas Fogg had traversed exactly one half of the terrestrial globe. — *Jules Verne, Around the World in Eighty Days*

▷ **traversal** *NOUN*

travesty *NOUN* **travesties**
a bad or ridiculous form of something ◆ *The trial was denounced as a travesty of justice.*
WORD HISTORY from French *travesti* 'having changed clothes, disguised', from Latin *vestire* 'to clothe'

trawl *VERB* **trawls, trawling, trawled**
to fish by dragging a large net along the seabed

trawler *NOUN* **trawlers**
a boat used in trawling

tray *NOUN* **trays**
1 a flat piece of wood, metal, or plastic, usually with raised edges, for carrying cups, plates, food, etc.
2 an open container for holding documents in an office

treacherous *ADJECTIVE*
1 betraying someone; disloyal
2 dangerous or unreliable ◆ *It's been snowing all day and the roads are treacherous.*
▷ **treacherously** *ADVERB*
▷ **treachery** *NOUN*
WORD HISTORY from Old French *trechier* 'to trick or deceive'

treacle *NOUN*
a thick sticky liquid produced when sugar is purified
▷ **treacly** *ADJECTIVE*
WORD HISTORY from an earlier meaning 'ointment for an animal bite', from Greek *therion* 'wild or poisonous animal'

tread *VERB* **treads, treading, trod, trodden**
1 to walk or step
2 to tread on something is to put your foot on it

The voice of the Invisible Man was heard for the first time, yelling out sharply, as the policeman trod on his foot. — *H. G. Wells, The Invisible Man*

tread *NOUN* **treads**
1 a sound or way of walking
2 the top surface of a stair; the part you put your foot on
3 the part of a tyre that touches the ground

treadle *NOUN* **treadles**
a lever that you press with your foot to turn a wheel that works a machine

treadmill *NOUN* **treadmills**
a wide mill wheel turned by the weight of people or animals treading on steps fixed round its edge
to be on a treadmill is to be doing monotonous routine work

treason *NOUN*
the act of betraying your country
▷ **treasonable** *ADJECTIVE*
▷ **treasonous** *ADJECTIVE*

treasure *NOUN* **treasures**
1 a store of precious metals or jewels
2 a precious thing or person

treasure *VERB* **treasures, treasuring, treasured**
to value greatly something that you own or have experienced ◆ *We will treasure our memories of this trip.*

treasure hunt *NOUN* **treasure hunts**
a game in which people try to find a hidden object

treasurer *NOUN* **treasurers**
a person in charge of the money of a club, society, or institution

treasure trove *NOUN*
gold, silver, or other precious items found hidden and with no known owner

treasury *NOUN* **treasuries**
a place where money and valuables are kept
the Treasury the government department in charge of a country's income

treat *VERB* **treats, treating, treated**
1 to behave in a certain way towards a person or thing

Nadine isn't quite as crazy, although last year she went out with this total creep called Liam who treated her like dirt. — *Jacqueline Wilson, Girls Out Late*

2 to deal with a subject ◆ *The article treats a complex issue in a superficial manner.*
3 to give medical care in order to cure a person or animal
4 to put something through a chemical or other process ◆ *The fabric has been treated to make it waterproof.*
5 to pay for someone else's food, drink, or entertainment ◆ *I'll treat you to an ice cream.*

treat *NOUN* **treats**
1 something special that you enjoy
2 the process of treating someone to food, drink, or entertainment ◆ *Let's eat out tonight. It'll be my treat.*

treatise *NOUN* **treatises**
a book or long essay on a particular subject

treatment *NOUN* **treatments**
1 the process or manner of dealing with a person, animal, or thing
2 medical care

treaty *NOUN* **treaties**
a formal agreement between two or more countries

treble *ADJECTIVE*
three times as much or as many

treble *NOUN* **trebles**
1 a treble amount
2 a person with a high-pitched or soprano voice

treble *VERB* **trebles, trebling, trebled**
to make something, or to become, three times as much or as many

tree *NOUN* **trees**
a tall plant with a single very thick hard stem or trunk that is usually without branches for some distance above the ground
WORD FAMILY A related adjective, meaning 'to do with, or living in, trees', is arboreal.

trefoil *NOUN*
a plant with three small leaves (e.g. clover)
WORD HISTORY from Latin *tres* 'three' and *folium* 'leaf'

trek *NOUN* **treks**
a long walk or journey

trek *VERB* **treks, trekking, trekked**
to go on a long walk or journey
Days passed quickly as they continued to trek along the Spine, searching for the mountain pass. — *Christopher Paolini, Eragon*
WORD HISTORY from Dutch *trekken* 'to pull'

trellis *NOUN* **trellises**
a framework with crossing bars of wood or metal to support climbing plants

tremble *VERB* **trembles, trembling, trembled**
to shake gently, especially with fear

tremble *NOUN* **trembles**
a gentle shaking movement, especially caused by fear

tremendous *ADJECTIVE*
1 very large; huge
2 very good; excellent
▷ **tremendously** *ADVERB*
WORD HISTORY from Latin *tremendus* 'making someone tremble'

tremor *NOUN* **tremors**
1 a shaking or trembling movement
2 a slight earthquake

tremulous *ADJECTIVE*
trembling from nervousness or weakness
▷ **tremulously** *ADVERB*

trench *NOUN* **trenches**
a long narrow hole cut in the ground

trench *VERB* **trenches, trenching, trenched**
to dig a trench or trenches
WORD HISTORY from an Old French word, related to *truncate*

trenchant *ADJECTIVE*
very perceptive and acute; penetrating ◆ *The programme included a trenchant analysis of the Thatcher years.*
WORD HISTORY from an Old French word meaning 'cutting'

trend *NOUN* **trends**
the general direction in which something is going ◆ *Despite the recent trend towards global warming, the earth might be nearing another Ice Age.*

trendy *ADJECTIVE*
(*informal*) fashionable; following the latest trends
▷ **trendily** *ADVERB*
▷ **trendiness** *NOUN*

trepidation *NOUN*
fear and anxiety; nervousness
WORD HISTORY from Latin *trepidare* 'to be afraid'

trespass *VERB* **trespasses, trespassing, trespassed**
1 to go on someone's land or property unlawfully
2 (*old use*) to do wrong; to sin
▷ **trespasser** *NOUN*

trespass *NOUN* **trespasses**
(*old use*) wrongdoing; sin
WORD HISTORY from Old French *trespasser* 'to go beyond'

tress *NOUN* **tresses**
a lock of hair

trestle *NOUN* **trestles**
each of a set of supports on which a board is rested to form a table (called a **trestle table**)
WORD HISTORY from a Latin word meaning 'a beam'

trews *PLURAL NOUN*
close-fitting tartan trousers

triad (*say* **try**- ad) *NOUN* **triads**
1 a group or set of three things
2 (*Music*) a chord of three notes, made up of a given note with the third and fifth above it
3 a Chinese secret organization involved in crime
WORD HISTORY via French from Greek *trias* 'group of three'

trial *NOUN* **trials**
1 the process of examining the evidence in a lawcourt to decide whether a person is guilty of a crime
2 the process of testing something to see how good it is
3 a test of qualities or ability
4 an annoying person or thing; a hardship

on trial
1 being tried in a law court
2 being tested

trial and error trying out different methods of doing something until you find one that works

triangle *NOUN* **triangles**
1 (*Mathematics*) a flat shape with three sides and three angles
2 a percussion instrument made from a metal rod bent into a triangle
▷ **triangular** *ADJECTIVE*

tribal *ADJECTIVE*
belonging to or associated with a tribe
▷ **tribally** *ADVERB*

tribe *NOUN* **tribes**
1 a group of families living in one area as a community, ruled by a chief

The Thembu tribe reaches back for twenty generations to King Zwide. — *Nelson Mandela, Long Walk to Freedom*

2 a set of people

tribesman or **tribeswoman** *NOUN* **tribesmen** or **tribeswomen**
a male or female member of a tribe

tribulation *NOUN* **tribulations**
great trouble or hardship
WORD HISTORY from Latin *tribulare* 'to press or oppress'

tribunal (*say* try- **bew**- nal) *NOUN* **tribunals**
a committee appointed to hear evidence and give judgements when there is a dispute
WORD HISTORY from Latin *tribunale* 'tribune's seat'

tribune *NOUN* **tribunes**
(*History*) an official chosen by the people in ancient Rome

tributary *NOUN* **tributaries**
a river or stream that flows into a larger one or into a lake

tribute *NOUN* **tributes**
1 something said, done, or given to show respect or admiration ◆ *The exhibition is a tribute to the early pioneers of photography.*
2 payment that one country or ruler was formerly obliged to pay to a more powerful one
WORD HISTORY from Latin *tribuere* 'to assign, grant, or share'

trice *NOUN* (*old use*)
in a trice in a moment
WORD HISTORY from Old Dutch *trisen* 'to pull quickly, tug'

triceps (*say* **try**- seps) *NOUN* **triceps**
the large muscle at the back of your upper arm
WORD HISTORY a Latin word meaning 'three- headed', because the muscle is attached at three points

triceratops (*say* try- **serr**- a- tops) *NOUN*
a large dinosaur with a huge head and three horns, which fed on plants
WORD HISTORY from Greek *trikeratos* 'three- horned' and *ōps* 'face'

trick *NOUN* **tricks**
1 a crafty or deceitful action; a practical joke
2 a skilful action, especially one done for entertainment ◆ *My uncle used to do conjuring tricks for us every Christmas.*
3 the cards picked up by the winner after one round of a card game such as whist
to do the trick (*informal*) is to achieve the result that is wanted

trick *VERB* **tricks, tricking, tricked**
to deceive or cheat someone by a trick
to trick something out is to decorate it

trickery *NOUN*
the use of tricks; deception

trickle *VERB* **trickles, trickling, trickled**
to flow or move slowly

trickle *NOUN* **trickles**
a slow movement or flow

trickster *NOUN* **tricksters**
a person who tricks or cheats people

tricky *ADJECTIVE* **trickier, trickiest**
1 difficult; needing skill

A mid-air rescue would surely be tricky. But it was Skyways Law to help another vessel in distress. — *Kenneth Oppel, Airborn*

2 cunning or deceitful
▷ **trickiness** *NOUN*

tricolour (*say* **trik**- ol- er) *NOUN* **tricolours**
a flag with three coloured stripes, e.g. the national flag of France or Ireland

tricycle *NOUN* **tricycles**
a vehicle like a bicycle but with three wheels

trident *NOUN* **tridents**
a three-pronged spear, carried by Neptune and Britannia as a symbol of their power over the sea
WORD HISTORY from Latin *tridens*, from *dens* 'a tooth'

triennial (*say* try- **en**- ee- al) *ADJECTIVE*
a triennial event happens every third year

trier *NOUN* **triers**
a person who tries hard

trifle *NOUN* **trifles**
1 a pudding made of sponge cake covered in custard, fruit, and cream
2 a very small amount
3 something that has very little importance or value
a trifle (*informal*) a little bit; slightly

Lucy's heart beat a trifle more audibly to the stethoscope, and her lungs had a perceptible movement. — *Bram Stoker, Dracula*

trifle *VERB* **trifles, trifling, trifled**
to treat a person or thing without seriousness or respect ◆ *One look at her face and we knew that this was not a woman to be trifled with.*

trifling *ADJECTIVE*
small in value or importance

trigger *NOUN* **triggers**
a lever that is pulled to fire a gun

a b c d e f g h i j k l m n o p q r s t u v w x y z

trigger *VERB* **triggers, triggering, triggered**
to trigger something off is to start it happening
WORD HISTORY from Dutch *trekker* 'puller'

trigonometry (*say* trig- on- **om**- it- ree) *NOUN*
the calculation of distances and angles by using triangles
WORD HISTORY from Greek *trigonon* 'triangle'

trigraph *NOUN* **trigraphs**
(*Language*) a group of three letters forming one sound, e.g. *igh* in *high*

trilateral *ADJECTIVE*
having three sides

trilby *NOUN* **trilbies**
a man's soft felt hat
WORD HISTORY named after *Trilby* O'Ferrall, the heroine of a popular book and play, who wore a similar hat

trill *VERB* **trills, trilling, trilled**
to make a quivering musical sound

The air was still and clean, and the trilling of larks carried far over the fields of hay, which stretched away on both sides of the path. — *Barry Hines, A Kestrel for a Knave*

trill *NOUN* **trills**
a quivering musical sound

trillion *NOUN* **trillions**
1 a million million
2 (*old use*) a million million million

trilogy *NOUN* **trilogies**
a group of three stories, poems, or plays etc. about the same people or things ◆ *'The Return of the King' is the third novel of the 'Lord of the Rings' trilogy.*

trim *ADJECTIVE*
neat and orderly
▷ **trimly** *ADVERB*
▷ **trimness** *NOUN*

trim *VERB* **trims, trimming, trimmed**
1 to cut the edges or unwanted parts off something
2 to decorate a hat or piece of clothing by adding lace, ribbons, etc.
3 to arrange sails to suit the wind

trim *NOUN* **trims**
1 the action of cutting or trimming something ◆ *My hair badly needs a trim.*
2 lace, ribbons, etc. used to decorate something
in good trim in good condition; fit

Trinity *NOUN*
in Christian belief, God regarded as three persons (Father, Son, and Holy Spirit)

trinket *NOUN* **trinkets**
a small ornament or piece of jewellery

Unferth played with a silver trinket. He kept pouring the little chain through his fingers, its links making a tinkling sound. — *Robert Nye, Beowulf*

trio *NOUN* **trios**
1 a group of three people or things
2 a group of three musicians or singers
3 a piece of music for three musicians

trip *VERB* **trips, tripping, tripped**
1 to catch your foot on something and fall; to make someone do this
2 to move with quick light steps
3 to operate a switch
4 (*informal*) to suffer hallucinations after taking a drug
to trip up
1 is to stumble
2 is to make a minor mistake
to trip someone up is to make them stumble or make a mistake

trip *NOUN* **trips**
1 a journey or outing
2 the action of tripping; a stumble
3 (*informal*) hallucinations caused by taking a drug

tripartite *ADJECTIVE*
1 having three parts
2 a tripartite discussion or agreement involves three people or groups

tripe *NOUN*
1 part of an ox's stomach used as food
2 (*informal*) rubbish; nonsense
WORD HISTORY from an Old French word meaning 'animal entrails'

triple *ADJECTIVE*
1 consisting of three parts
2 a triple agreement or alliance involves three people or groups
3 three times as much or as many
▷ **triply** *ADVERB*

triple *VERB* **triples, tripling, tripled**
to make something, or to become, three times as much or as many

triple jump *NOUN*
an athletic contest in which competitors try to jump as far as possible by doing a hop, step, and jump

triplet *NOUN* **triplets**
each of three children or animals born to the same mother at one time

triplicate *NOUN*
in triplicate as three identical copies
WORD HISTORY from Latin *triplicare* 'to triple', from *plicare* 'to fold'

tripod (*say* **try**- pod) ***NOUN*** **tripods**
a stand with three legs, used especially to support a camera or telescope

WORD HISTORY from Greek *tripous* 'three- footed', from *pous* 'foot'

tripper ***NOUN*** **trippers**
a person who is making a pleasure trip

trireme (*say* **try**- reem) ***NOUN*** **triremes**
(*History*) an ancient Greek or Roman warship with three banks of oars

WORD HISTORY from Latin *triremis*, from *remus* 'an oar'

trisect ***VERB*** **trisects, trisecting, trisected**
to divide something into three equal parts
▷ **trisection** ***NOUN***

trite (*rhymes with* kite) ***ADJECTIVE***
a trite remark is one that has been worn out by overuse; hackneyed

triumph ***NOUN*** **triumphs**
1 a great success or victory; a feeling of joy at this ◆ *The race was a personal triumph for the British athlete, who ran her best time this season.*
2 a celebration of a victory

triumph ***VERB*** **triumphs, triumphing, triumphed**
1 to be successful or victorious
2 to rejoice in success or victory

triumphal ***ADJECTIVE***
celebrating a great success or victory ◆ *A triumphal arch stood in the main square.*

triumphant ***ADJECTIVE***
1 victorious in a battle or contest
2 rejoicing over a victory or success
▷ **triumphantly** ***ADVERB***

triumvirate ***NOUN*** **triumvirates**
a ruling group of three people

WORD HISTORY from Latin *trium virorum* 'of three men'

trivet ***NOUN*** **trivets**
an iron stand for a pot or kettle, placed over a fire

trivia ***PLURAL NOUN***
unimportant details or pieces of information ◆ *The website features pop quizzes and bits of celebrity trivia.*

trivial ***ADJECTIVE***
small in value or importance
▷ **trivially** ***ADVERB***
▷ **triviality** ***NOUN***

WORD HISTORY from Latin *trivialis* meaning originally 'at a crossroads', and then 'commonplace'

troglodyte ***NOUN*** **troglodytes**
(*History*) a person living in a cave in ancient times

WORD HISTORY from Greek *trōglē* 'hole'

troll (*rhymes with* hole) ***NOUN*** **trolls**
a supernatural creature in Scandinavian mythology, either a giant or a friendly but mischievous dwarf

WORD HISTORY from an Old Norse word

trolley ***NOUN*** **trolleys**
1 a small table on wheels or castors
2 a small cart or truck
3 a basket on wheels, used in supermarkets

trolleybus ***NOUN*** **trolleybuses**
a bus powered by electricity from an overhead wire to which it is connected

trombone ***NOUN*** **trombones**
a large brass musical instrument with a sliding tube

WORD HISTORY from Italian *tromba* 'a trumpet'

troop ***NOUN*** **troops**
1 an organized group of soldiers, Scouts, etc.
2 a number of people moving along together

A troop of newly arrived students, very young, pink and callow, followed nervously, rather abjectly, at the Director's heels. — *Aldous Huxley, Brave New World*

USAGE NOTE Take care not to confuse this word with *troupe*.

troop ***VERB*** **troops, trooping, trooped**
to move along as a group or in large numbers ◆ *After the ceremony, the relatives all trooped into the living- room in search of cake.*

WORD HISTORY from Latin *troppus* 'a herd'

trooper ***NOUN*** **troopers**
a soldier in the cavalry or in an armoured unit

troops ***PLURAL NOUN***
soldiers or other armed forces

trophy ***NOUN*** **trophies**
1 an ornamental cup, plate, or statue given as a prize for winning a competition
2 something taken in war or hunting as a souvenir of success

tropic ***NOUN*** **tropics**
a line of latitude about $23\frac{1}{2}$° north of the equator (**tropic of Cancer**) or $23\frac{1}{2}$° south of the equator (**tropic of Capricorn**)

the tropics the hot regions between these two latitudes

WORD HISTORY from Greek *trope* 'turning', because the sun seems to turn back when it reaches these points

tropical ***ADJECTIVE***
to do with, or found in, the tropics ◆ *All manner of flora and fauna flourish in this tropical habitat.*

troposphere ***NOUN***
the layer of the atmosphere extending about 10 kilometres upwards from the earth's surface

trot *VERB* **trots, trotting, trotted**
1 a horse trots when it moves faster than when walking but more slowly than when cantering
2 to run gently with short steps

The two boys trotted down the beach and, turning at the water's edge, looked back at the pink mountain. — *William Golding, Lord of the Flies*

to trot something out (*informal*) is to produce a predictable or worn excuse or argument ◆ *At the press conference, the minister trotted out the usual denials.*

trot *NOUN*
a trotting run
on the trot (*informal*) one after the other without a break ◆ *I've been working for eight hours on the trot.*

troth (*rhymes with* both) *NOUN*
(*old use*) loyalty; a solemn promise
WORD HISTORY another spelling of *truth*

trotter *NOUN* **trotters**
a pig's foot used for food

troubadour (*say* **troo**- bad- oor) *NOUN* **troubadours**
(*History*) a poet and singer in southern France in the 11th-13th centuries
WORD HISTORY from Old French *trover* 'to write in verse'

trouble *NOUN* **troubles**
1 difficulty, inconvenience, or distress
2 a cause of any of these
to take trouble is to take great care in doing something

trouble *VERB* **troubles, troubling, troubled**
1 to cause trouble to someone
2 to give yourself trouble or inconvenience; to bother ◆ *Don't trouble yourself to get up.*

troubled *ADJECTIVE*
feeling trouble or distress; disturbed

It was a troubled sleep with dreams of wolves and black rings and mirrors with no reflections. — *Anthony Horowitz, Groosham Grange*

troublemaker *NOUN* **troublemakers**
someone who causes trouble or makes a disturbance

troublesome *ADJECTIVE*
causing trouble or annoyance

trough (*say* trof) *NOUN* **troughs**
1 a long narrow open container, especially one holding water or food for animals
2 a channel for liquid
3 the low part between two waves or ridges
4 a long region of low air pressure

trounce *VERB* **trounces, trouncing, trounced**
to defeat an opponent or team decisively

troupe (*sounds like* troop) *NOUN* **troupes**
a company of actors or other performers
USAGE NOTE Take care not to confuse this word with *troop*.

trousers *PLURAL NOUN*
a piece of clothing worn over the lower half of the body, with a separate part for each leg
WORD HISTORY from an Irish or Scottish Gaelic word

trousseau (*say* **troo**- soh) *NOUN* **trousseaus** or **trousseaux**
a bride's collection of clothes and accessories for her married life
WORD HISTORY from a French word meaning 'a bundle'

trout *NOUN* **trout**
a freshwater fish that is caught as a sport and for food

trowel *NOUN* **trowels**
1 a small garden tool with a curved blade for lifting plants or scooping things
2 a small tool with a flat blade for spreading mortar etc.
WORD HISTORY from Latin *trulla* 'scoop'

troy weight *NOUN*
a system of weights used for precious metals and gems, in which 1 pound = 12 ounces
WORD HISTORY said to be from a weight used at *Troyes* in France

truant *NOUN* **truants**
a child who stays away from school without permission
to play truant is to stay away from school without permission
▷ **truancy** *NOUN*
WORD HISTORY from an Old French word meaning 'criminal'

truce *NOUN* **truces**
an agreement between rivals or enemies to stop fighting for a while

When the gods made a truce, and settled terms for a lasting peace, every single god and goddess spat into a great jar. — *Kevin Crossley-Holland, Viking!*

truck¹ *NOUN* **trucks**
1 an open container on wheels for transporting loads; an open railway wagon
2 (*American*) a large goods vehicle; a lorry
3 an axle with wheels attached, fitted under a skateboard

truck² *NOUN*
to have no truck with something is to refuse to have anything to do with it

truculent (*say* **truk**- yoo- lent) *ADJECTIVE*
defiant and aggressive
▷ **truculently** *ADVERB*
▷ **truculence** *NOUN*
WORD HISTORY from Latin *truculentus* 'wild, fierce'

trudge *VERB* **trudges, trudging, trudged**
to walk slowly and wearily

true *ADJECTIVE* **truer, truest**
1 a true story or account represents what has really happened or exists
2 genuine or proper; not false
3 accurate or exact
4 loyal or faithful ◆ *She had proved to be a true friend at this difficult time.*
to come true a dream or prediction that comes true actually happens as hoped or predicted
▷ **trueness** *NOUN*

truffle *NOUN* **truffles**
1 a soft sweet made with chocolate
2 a fungus that grows underground and is valued as food because of its rich flavour

truism *NOUN* **truisms**
a hackneyed statement or cliché that is obviously true but doesn't mean very much, e.g. 'Money isn't everything'

truly *ADVERB*
1 in a truthful way
2 sincerely or genuinely ◆ *We are truly sorry for all the trouble we have caused.*
3 (*old use*) loyally or faithfully
Yours truly see **yours**

trump[1] *NOUN* **trumps**
a playing card of a suit that ranks above the others for one game

trump *VERB* **trumps, trumping, trumped**
to beat a card by playing a trump
to trump something up an excuse or accusation that is trumped up has been invented or exaggerated
WORD HISTORY from *triumph*

trump[2] *NOUN* **trumps**
(*old use*) a blast of a trumpet
WORD HISTORY from Old French *trompe* 'trumpet'

trumpet *NOUN* **trumpets**
1 a brass instrument with a narrow tube that widens near the end
2 something shaped like this

trumpet *VERB* **trumpets, trumpeting, trumpeted**
1 to blow a trumpet
2 an elephant trumpets when it makes a loud sound with its trunk
3 to shout, announce, or promote a success or achievement loudly
▷ **trumpeter** *NOUN*

truncate *VERB* **truncates, truncating, truncated**
to shorten something by cutting off its beginning or end ◆ *The football coverage was truncated because of an extended news programme.*
▷ **truncation** *NOUN*
WORD HISTORY from Latin *truncare* 'to maim'

truncheon *NOUN* **truncheons**
a short thick stick carried as a weapon, especially by police

trundle *VERB* **trundles, trundling, trundled**
to roll something along, or to roll along, heavily
WORD HISTORY from an old word *trendle* 'to revolve'

trunk *NOUN* **trunks**
1 the main stem of a tree
2 an elephant's long flexible nose
3 a large box with a hinged lid for transporting or storing clothes and belongings
4 the human body except for the head, arms, and legs

trunk call *NOUN* **trunk calls**
(*old use*) a long-distance telephone call

trunk road *NOUN* **trunk roads**
an important main road
WORD HISTORY from the idea that it was a 'trunk' from which smaller roads branched off

trunks *PLURAL NOUN*
shorts worn by men and boys for swimming, boxing, etc.

truss *NOUN* **trusses**
1 a framework of beams or bars supporting a roof or bridge
2 a bundle of hay or straw
3 a type of padded belt worn to support a hernia

truss *VERB* **trusses, trussing, trussed**
1 to tie up a person or thing securely
2 to support a roof or bridge with trusses

trust *VERB* **trusts, trusting, trusted**
1 to believe that a person or thing is good, truthful, or reliable
2 to trust someone with something is to let them have it or use it, confident that they will look after it
3 to hope or expect that something is the case ◆ *I trust that you have fully recovered from your ordeal.*
to trust to something is to rely on it ◆ *We had no map or compass, trusting to luck to find our way on the moors.*

trust *NOUN* **trusts**
1 the belief that a person or thing can be trusted
2 responsibility; the fact of being trusted ◆ *a position of trust*
3 a legal arrangement in which money is entrusted to a person with instructions about how to use it
▷ **trustful** *ADJECTIVE*
▷ **trustfully** *ADVERB*

trustee *NOUN* **trustees**
a person who looks after money entrusted to them

a b c d e f g h i j k l m n o p q r s t u v w x y z

trustworthy *ADJECTIVE*
able to be trusted; reliable
▷ **trustworthiness** *NOUN*

trusty *ADJECTIVE*
(*humorous*) trustworthy or reliable ◆ *I never travel anywhere without my trusty umbrella.*

truth *NOUN* **truths**
1 a true fact or statement
2 the quality of being true

truthful *ADJECTIVE*
1 a truthful person always tells the truth
2 a truthful statement or account is true and accurate
▷ **truthfully** *ADVERB*
▷ **truthfulness** *NOUN*

try *VERB* **tries, trying, tried**
1 to make an effort to do something; to attempt something
2 to test something by using or doing it ◆ *Try walking to work for a change.*
3 to examine the evidence in a lawcourt to decide whether a person is guilty of a crime
4 to be a strain on something ◆ *Very small print can try your eyes.*

to try something on
1 is to try on clothes to see if they fit
2 (*informal*) is to ask for or claim something unacceptable

to try something out is to use it to see if it works

try *NOUN* **tries**
1 an attempt
2 in rugby, an act of touching the ball down behind the opposing goal line in order to score points

trying *ADJECTIVE*
putting a strain on your patience; annoying

The first week of my life as a cab horse was very trying. — *Anna Sewell, Black Beauty*

tsar (*say* zar) *NOUN* **tsars**
(*History*) the title of an emperor of Russia before the Revolution of 1917

WORD HISTORY a Russian word, from the Latin name *Caesar*

tsetse fly (*say* tet- see) *NOUN* **tsetse flies**
a tropical African fly which has a bite that can cause sleeping sickness in humans

WORD HISTORY from Setswana (a language spoken in southern Africa)

T-shirt *NOUN* **T-shirts**
a short-sleeved shirt shaped like a T

T-square *NOUN* **T-squares**
a T-shaped instrument for measuring or drawing right angles

tsunami *NOUN* **tsunamis**
a huge sea wave caused by an underwater earthquake

WORD HISTORY a Japanese word meaning 'harbour wave'

tub *NOUN* **tubs**
a round open container holding liquid, ice cream, soil for plants, etc.

tuba (*say* tew- ba) *NOUN* **tubas**
a large brass wind instrument with a deep tone

WORD HISTORY from a Latin word meaning 'war trumpet'

tubby *ADJECTIVE* **tubbier, tubbiest**
short and fat
▷ **tubbiness** *NOUN*

tube *NOUN* **tubes**
1 a long hollow piece of metal, plastic, rubber, glass, etc., especially for liquids or gases to pass along
2 a container made of flexible material with a screw cap ◆ *a tube of toothpaste*
3 the underground railway in London

tuber *NOUN* **tubers**
a short thick rounded root (e.g. of a dahlia) or underground stem (e.g. of a potato) that produces buds from which new plants will grow

WORD HISTORY a Latin word meaning 'a swelling'

tuberculosis *NOUN*
a disease affecting humans and animals, which causes small swellings in parts of the body, especially in the lungs
▷ **tubercular** *ADJECTIVE*

WORD HISTORY from Latin *tuberculum* 'little swelling'

tubular *ADJECTIVE*
shaped like a tube

TUC *ABBREVIATION*
Trades Union Congress

tuck *VERB* **tucks, tucking, tucked**
1 to push a loose edge into something so that it is hidden or held in place
2 to put something away in a small space ◆ *I quickly tucked the note into my back pocket.*

to tuck in (*informal*) is to eat heartily

to tuck someone in or up is to make them comfortable in bed by folding the edges of the bedclothes tightly

tuck *NOUN* **tucks**
1 a flat fold stitched in a piece of clothing
2 (*informal*) food, especially sweets, cakes, and biscuits for children

tucker *NOUN*
(*Australian and New Zealand*) (*informal*) things to eat; food

Tudor *ADJECTIVE*
to do with the royal family of England from Henry VII to Elizabeth I (1485–1603)
▷ **Tudor** *NOUN*

Tuesday *NOUN*
the day of the week following Monday
WORD HISTORY from Old English *Tiwesdaeg* 'day of Tiw, a Norse god'

tuft *NOUN* **tufts**
a bunch of threads, grass, hair, or feathers growing or placed close together

The aunts were sitting on either side of the fire, in the leather armchairs that leaked tufts of some strange stuffing on to the carpet. — *Penelope Lively, The House in Norham Gardens*

▷ **tufted** *ADJECTIVE*

tug *VERB* **tugs, tugging, tugged**
1 to pull something hard or suddenly
2 to tow a ship

tug *NOUN* **tugs**
1 a hard or sudden pull
2 a small powerful boat used for towing others

tug of war *NOUN*
a contest between two teams pulling a rope from opposite ends

tui *NOUN*
a New Zealand songbird with a glossy dark plumage and tufts of white feathers at the throat

tuition *NOUN*
teaching, especially when given to one person or a small group

tulip *NOUN* **tulips**
a large cup-shaped flower on a tall stem growing from a bulb
WORD HISTORY from Persian *dulband* 'turban', because of the shape of the flower

tulle (*say* tewl) *NOUN*
a very fine silky net material used for veils, wedding dresses, etc.
WORD HISTORY named after *Tulle*, a town in France, where it was first made

tumble *VERB* **tumbles, tumbling, tumbled**
1 to fall or roll over suddenly or clumsily
2 to move or rush in a hasty careless way ◆ *After supper we all tumbled into bed.*
3 to fall suddenly in value or amount ◆ *House prices have tumbled.*
to tumble to something (*informal*) is to realize suddenly what it means

tumble *NOUN* **tumbles**
a sudden fall or drop

tumbledown *ADJECTIVE*
falling into ruins

I came upon a small clearing and a tumbledown cabin. Nobody had been there for years and years. — *Jack London, The Night-Born*

tumble-drier *NOUN* **tumble-driers**
a machine that dries washing by turning it over many times in heated air

tumbler *NOUN* **tumblers**
1 a drinking glass with no stem or handle
2 a part of a lock that is lifted when a key is turned to open it
3 an acrobat

tumbrel or **tumbril** *NOUN* **tumbrels** or **tumbrils**
(*History*) an open cart used to carry condemned prisoners to the guillotine during the French Revolution

tumescent *ADJECTIVE*
swollen or swelling
▷ **tumescence** *NOUN*

tummy *NOUN* **tummies**
(*informal*) your stomach

tumour (*say* tew- mer) *NOUN* **tumours**
an abnormal lump growing on or in the body
WORD HISTORY from Latin *tumere* 'to swell'

tumult (*say* tew- mult) *NOUN*
an uproar; a state of noisy confusion and agitation

tumultuous (*say* tew- **mul**- tew- us) *ADJECTIVE*
noisy and excited

tun *NOUN* **tuns**
a large cask or barrel

tuna (*say* tew- na) *NOUN* **tuna**
a large edible sea fish with pink flesh

tundra *NOUN*
the vast level Arctic regions of Europe, Asia, and America where there are no trees and the subsoil is always frozen
WORD HISTORY from a Lappish word (the language spoken in Lapland)

tune *NOUN* **tunes**
a short piece of music; a pleasant series of musical notes
in tune at the correct musical pitch
▷ **tuneful** *ADJECTIVE*

tune *VERB* **tunes, tuning, tuned**
1 to put a musical instrument in tune
2 to adjust a radio or television set to receive a certain channel
3 to adjust an engine so that it runs smoothly
to tune up an orchestra tunes up when it brings its instruments to the correct pitch
▷ **tuner** *NOUN*
WORD HISTORY from another spelling of *tone*

tungsten *NOUN*
a grey metal used to make a kind of steel
WORD HISTORY from Swedish *tung* 'heavy' and *sten* 'stone'

tunic *NOUN* **tunics**
1 a jacket worn as part of a uniform
2 a piece of clothing reaching from the shoulders to the hips or knees

tuning fork *NOUN* **tuning forks**
(*Music*) a steel device with two prongs, which when struck vibrates to produce a note of fixed pitch (usually middle C)

tunnel *NOUN* **tunnels**
an underground passage

tunnel *VERB* **tunnels, tunnelling, tunnelled**
to make a tunnel
WORD HISTORY from an Old French word meaning 'barrel'

tunny *NOUN* **tunnies**
a tuna fish

turban *NOUN* **turbans**
a man's headdress made by wrapping a strip of cloth round a cap, worn especially by Muslims and Sikhs
WORD HISTORY from Persian *dulband*, related to our word *tulip*

turbid *ADJECTIVE*
turbid water is muddy and not clear
▷ **turbidly** *ADVERB*
▷ **turbidity** *NOUN*
WORD HISTORY from Latin *turba* 'crowd, disturbance'

turbine *NOUN* **turbines**
a machine or motor driven by a flow of water, steam, or gas
WORD HISTORY from Latin *turbo* 'whirlwind, spinning top'

turbojet *NOUN* **turbojets**
a jet engine or aircraft with turbines

turbot *NOUN* **turbot**
a large flat edible sea fish

turbulence *NOUN*
violent and uneven movement of air or water ◆ *Please keep your seat belts fastened as we are experiencing some turbulence.*

turbulent *ADJECTIVE*
1 moving violently and unevenly; involving turbulence ◆ *Weather conditions along the coast can be turbulent at times.*
2 involving much change and disagreement and sometimes violence ◆ *Many treasures were looted or destroyed during the turbulent years of the revolution.*
▷ **turbulently** *ADVERB*

tureen *NOUN* **tureens**
a deep dish with a lid, from which soup is served at the table
WORD HISTORY from French *terrine* 'earthenware pot'

turf *NOUN* **turfs** or **turves**
1 short grass and the earth round its roots
2 a piece of this cut from the ground

turf *VERB* **turfs, turfing, turfed**
to cover ground with turf

to turf something out (*informal*) is to throw it out

turgid (*say* **ter**- jid) *ADJECTIVE*
1 swollen and thick
2 a turgid speech or piece of writing is pompous and boring
WORD HISTORY from Latin *turgere* 'to swell'

turkey *NOUN* **turkeys**
a large game bird kept for its meat
WORD HISTORY originally the name of a different bird which was imported from Turkey

Turkish bath *NOUN*
a kind of bath in which the whole body is exposed to hot air or steam to induce sweating, followed by washing

Turkish delight *NOUN*
a sweet made from flavoured gelatine coated in powdered sugar

turmeric *NOUN*
a bright yellow powder from the plant of the ginger family, used for flavouring and colouring food

turmoil *NOUN*
1 physical agitation

> The whole sea was in turmoil, great black waves rearing out of it and storming towards the shore.
> — *Anita Desai, The Village by the Sea*

2 a feeling of emotional confusion and distress

turn *VERB* **turns, turning, turned**
1 to move or make something move round a point or axis
2 to take a new direction ◆ *Turn left at the lights.*
3 to change in nature, form, or appearance ◆ *The boy's face was quickly turning an unpleasant shade of green.*
4 to make something change; to convert something ◆ *The building had been turned into a cinema complex.*
5 to pass a certain time or age ◆ *The clock chimed to tell us it had turned midnight.* ◆ *My sister turned eighteen last week.*
6 to shape an object on a lathe
7 leaves turn when they change colour in the autumn
8 milk turns if it becomes sour

to turn something down
1 is to fold down a page corner, bed sheet, etc.
2 is to reduce a volume, flow, or temperature
3 is to reject an offer or opportunity ◆ *I was offered a job teaching English abroad but I turned it down.*

to turn someone off (*informal*) is to make them less interested in something

to turn something off to turn something off is to switch it off
to turn out
1 to happen in the end ◆ *Let's wait and see how things turn out.*
2 to prove to be ◆ *The phonecall turned out to be a hoax.*
to turn someone out is to expel or send them away
to turn something out to turn out a cupboard, drawer, or pocket, is to take out its contents to tidy it
to turn something over is to think carefully about it
to turn something round to turn round a failing enterprise or business is to make it profitable or successful
to turn to someone is to go to them for help or advice
to turn to something to turn to a task or piece of work is to start doing it
to turn up is to appear or arrive
to turn something up to turn up a volume, flow, or temperature is to increase it
turn *NOUN* **turns**
1 the action of turning; a turning movement
2 a change; the point where something turns
3 an opportunity or duty that comes to each person in succession ◆ *Whose turn is it to play?*
4 a short performance in an entertainment
5 (*informal*) an attack of illness; a nervous shock ◆ *The sight of the submarine gliding towards us gave us a nasty turn.*
a good turn a helpful action
in turn in succession; one after another
WORD HISTORY from Greek *tornos* 'a lathe'

turncoat *NOUN* **turncoats**
a person who changes their principles or beliefs

turning *NOUN* **turnings**
a place where one road meets another, forming a corner

turning point *NOUN* **turning points**
a point where an important change takes place ◆ *The Battle of Stalingrad was a major turning point of World War II.*

turnip *NOUN* **turnips**
a plant with a large round white root used as a vegetable
WORD HISTORY from Latin *napus*

turnout *NOUN* **turnouts**
the number of people who attend a meeting, vote at an election, etc. ◆ *Despite the rain, there was a pretty good turnout.*

turnover *NOUN* **turnovers**
1 the amount of money received by a firm selling things
2 the rate at which goods are sold or workers leave and are replaced
3 a small pie made by folding pastry over fruit, jam, etc.

turnpike *NOUN* **turnpikes**
(*History*) a road on which a toll was charged

turnstile *NOUN* **turnstiles**
a revolving gate that lets one person in at a time

turntable *NOUN* **turntables**
a circular revolving platform or support, e.g. for the record in a record player

turpentine *NOUN*
a kind of oil used for thinning paint, cleaning paintbrushes, etc.

turpitude *NOUN*
(*formal*) wicked behaviour or actions

As for the moral turpitude that man unveiled to me ..., I cannot, even in memory, dwell on it without a start of horror. — *Robert Louis Stevenson, Dr. Jekyll and Mr. Hyde*

WORD HISTORY from Latin *turpis* 'shameful'

turps *NOUN*
(*informal*) turpentine

turquoise *NOUN* **turquoises**
1 a sky-blue or greenish-blue colour
2 a bright blue precious stone
WORD HISTORY from French *pierre turquoise* 'Turkish stone'

turret *NOUN* **turrets**
1 a small tower on a castle or other building
2 a revolving structure containing a gun
▷ **turreted** *ADJECTIVE*

turtle *NOUN* **turtles**
a sea animal that looks like a tortoise
to turn turtle a boat turns turtle if it turns upside down in the water
WORD HISTORY probably from French *tortue* 'turtle'

turtle dove *NOUN* **turtle doves**
a wild dove

turtleneck *NOUN* **turtlenecks**
a knitted top with a high round close-fitting neck

tusk *NOUN* **tusks**
a long pointed tooth that sticks out from the mouth of an elephant, walrus, narwhal, etc.
WORD HISTORY from Old English *tux*

tussle *NOUN* **tussles**
a struggle or conflict over something
tussle *VERB* **tussles, tussling, tussled**
to take part in a tussle

tussock *NOUN* **tussocks**
a tuft or clump of grass

tut *VERB* **tuts, tutting, tutted**
to show that you are annoyed or disapprove of something

a b c d e f g h i j k l m n o p q r s t u v w x y z

tutelage (*say* tew- til- ij) *NOUN*
1 guardianship or protection of someone or something
2 instruction or tuition

tutor *NOUN* **tutors**
1 a private teacher, especially of one pupil or a small group
2 a teacher of students in a college or university

tutor *VERB* **tutors, tutoring, tutored**
to act as a tutor to someone

For three months after I had drawn the sword from the stone I stayed in London, and Merlin tutored me day and night in the arts of kingship. — *Michael Morpurgo, Arthur, High King of Britain*

WORD HISTORY a Latin word meaning 'a guardian'

tutorial *NOUN* **tutorials**
a meeting in which students discuss a subject with their tutor

tutu (*say* too- too) *NOUN* **tutus**
a ballet dancer's short stiff frilled skirt

TV *ABBREVIATION*
television

twaddle *NOUN*
(*informal*) nonsense

twain *NOUN, ADJECTIVE*
(*old use*) two

'My heart is sore,' he said at last; 'your words split my heart in twain.' — *H. Rider Haggard, King Solomon's Mines*

WORD HISTORY from Old English *twegen* 'two'

twang *NOUN* **twangs**
1 a sharp sound like that of a wire when plucked
2 a nasal tone in a person's voice

twang *VERB* **twangs, twanging, twanged**
1 to make a sharp sound like that of a wire when plucked
2 to play a guitar or other stringed instrument by plucking its strings

tweak *VERB* **tweaks, tweaking, tweaked**
to pinch and twist or pull something sharply

tweak *NOUN* **tweaks**
a tweaking movement

twee *ADJECTIVE*
affectedly quaint or pretty ◆ *I think flowery wallpaper would look too twee.*

tweed *NOUN*
thick woollen twill, often woven of mixed colours

WORD HISTORY from Scots word *tweel* 'twill', which was misread as *tweed* by being confused with the River Tweed

tweeds *PLURAL NOUN*
clothes made of tweed

tweet *NOUN* **tweets**
the chirping sound made by a small bird

tweezers *PLURAL NOUN*
small pincers for picking up or pulling very small things

WORD HISTORY from an old word *tweeze* 'a case of surgical instruments (including tweezers)'

twelve *NOUN, ADJECTIVE*
the number 12, one more than eleven

▷ **twelfth** *ADJECTIVE, NOUN*

twenty *NOUN* **twenties** *ADJECTIVE*
the number 20, one more than nineteen

▷ **twentieth** *ADJECTIVE, NOUN*

twice *ADVERB*
1 two times; on two occasions
2 double the amount

twiddle *VERB* **twiddles, twiddling, twiddled**
to play or fidget with something repeatedly; to fiddle with something ◆ *I spent ages twiddling with the TV aerial to get a better picture.*

to twiddle your thumbs is to sit around with nothing to do

▷ **twiddly** *ADJECTIVE*

twiddle *NOUN* **twiddles**
a twiddling movement

twig❶ *NOUN* **twigs**
a small shoot on a branch or stem of a tree or shrub

WORD HISTORY from an Old English word

twig❷ *VERB* **twigs, twigging, twigged**
(*informal*) to realize what something means

WORD HISTORY origin unknown

twilight *NOUN*
dim light from the sky just after sunset or just before sunrise

WORD HISTORY from Old English *twi* 'two' (in the sense 'between') and *light*

twill *NOUN*
material woven so that there is a pattern of diagonal lines

WORD HISTORY from Old English *twi* 'twice, double' and Latin *licium* 'thread'

twin *NOUN* **twins**
1 either of two children or animals born to the same mother at one time
2 either of two things that are exactly alike

twin *VERB* **twins, twinning, twinned**
1 to put things together as a pair
2 if a town is twinned with a town in a different country, the two towns exchange visits and organize cultural events together

twine *NOUN*
strong thin string

twine *VERB* **twines, twining, twined**
to twist or wind one thing round another

twinge *NOUN* **twinges**
a sudden pain or unpleasant feeling

twinge *VERB* **twinges, twinging, twinged**
to feel a sudden pain or twinge

My ankle twinged every so often and I winced. It felt as though I'd sprained it slightly. — *Narinder Dhami, Bend It Like Beckham*

twinkle *VERB* **twinkles, twinkling, twinkled**
to shine with tiny flashes of light; to sparkle

twinkle *NOUN* **twinkles**
a tiny flash of light

twirl *VERB* **twirls, twirling, twirled**
1 to twist something round quickly

'This method,' said Gilbert, proudly twirling his whiskers, 'is my own invention.' — *Cornelia Funke, Dragon Rider*

2 to turn around in a circle

twirl *NOUN* **twirls**
a twirling movement

twist *VERB* **twists, twisting, twisted**
1 to turn the ends of something in opposite directions
2 a road, path, or river, twists when its route turns alternately from side to side
3 to bend something out of its proper shape ◆ *The front of the vehicle was twisted beyond repair.*
4 to pass threads or strands round something or round each other
5 to twist what someone says is to distort its meaning
6 (*informal*) to swindle someone

▷ **twister** *NOUN*

twist *NOUN* **twists**
1 a twisting movement or action
2 a strange or unexpected development in a story or series of events ◆ *The film has a twist at the end—but I'm not telling you what it is!*

▷ **twisty** *ADJECTIVE*

twit *NOUN* **twits**
(*informal*) a silly or foolish person

twitch *VERB* **twitches, twitching, twitched**
to move something, or to move, with a slight jerk

A tiny green grasshopper with a long, melancholy face sat twitching his hind legs nervously. — *Gerald Durrell, My Family and Other Animals*

twitch *NOUN* **twitches**
a twitching movement

twitchy *ADJECTIVE*
very anxious or nervous

Hugh Pylum-Haight was becoming distinctly twitchy, waiting upstairs in the complete silence of the great hall. — *Debi Gliori, Pure Dead Wicked*

▷ **twitchily** *ADVERB*
▷ **twitchiness** *NOUN*

twitter *VERB* **twitters, twittering, twittered**
to make quick chirping sounds

twitter *NOUN* **twitters**
a twittering sound

two *NOUN* **twos** *ADJECTIVE*
the number 2, one more than one
to be in two minds is to be undecided about something

WORD FAMILY Related adjectives, meaning 'composed of two parts', are binary and dual.

two-faced *ADJECTIVE*
insincere or deceitful

twofold *ADJECTIVE, ADVERB*
times two; involving two ◆ *a twofold answer*

two-time *VERB* **two-times, two-timing, two-timed**
(*informal*) to two-time a partner is to be unfaithful to them

tycoon *NOUN* **tycoons**
a rich and influential business person

WORD HISTORY from Japanese *taikun* 'great prince'

tying *present participle of* **tie**

Tynwald (*say* **tin**- wold) *NOUN*
the parliament of the Isle of Man

WORD HISTORY from Old Norse words meaning 'place of assembly'

type *NOUN* **types**
1 a kind or sort ◆ *What type of music do you play?*
2 letters, figures, or symbols designed for use in printing

type *VERB* **types, typing, typed**
to write something using a typewriter or word-processor

WORD HISTORY from Greek *tupos* 'impression'

typecast *VERB* **typecasts, typecasting, typecast**
an actor is typecast when they are always given the same kind of role to play ◆ *After the success of his first film, the actor was in danger of being typecast as a villain.*

typescript *NOUN* **typescripts**
a typed copy of a text or document

typewriter *NOUN* **typewriters**
a machine with keys that are pressed to print letters, figures, or symbols on a piece of paper

▷ **typewritten** *ADJECTIVE*

typhoid fever *NOUN*
a serious infectious disease with fever, caused by harmful bacteria in food or water

typhoon *NOUN* **typhoons**
a violent hurricane in the western Pacific or East Asian seas
WORD HISTORY from Chinese *tai fung* 'great wind'

typhus *NOUN*
an infectious disease causing fever, weakness, and a rash
WORD HISTORY from Greek *tuphos* 'vapour'

typical *ADJECTIVE*
1 having the usual characteristics or qualities of a particular type of person or thing

It was a typical Venetian palace, pink and white, its narrow windows built into a fantastic embroidery of pillars, arches and balustrades. — *Anthony Horowitz, Scorpia*

2 usual in a particular person or thing ◆ *The battle scenes are filmed with the director's typical attention to detail.*
▷ **typically** *ADVERB*

typify (*say* **tip**- if- eye) *VERB* **typifies, typifying, typified**
to be a typical example of something ◆ *He typifies the popular image of a football manager.*

typist *NOUN* **typists**
a person who types letters and documents, especially in an office

typography (*say* ty- **pog**- ra- fee) *NOUN*
the style or appearance of the letters, figures, and symbols in printed material
▷ **typographical** *ADJECTIVE*

tyrannize (*say* **tirr**- an- yz) *VERB* **tyrannizes, tyrannizing, tyrannized**
to rule over people cruelly and unjustly; to behave like a tyrant ◆ *The Pol Pot regime tyrannized its own people.*
USAGE NOTE This word can also be spelled tyrannise.

tyrannosaurus *NOUN* **tyrannosauruses**
a huge flesh-eating dinosaur that walked upright on its large hind legs
WORD HISTORY from Greek *tyrannos* 'ruler' and *sauros* 'lizard'

tyranny (*say* **tirr**- an- ee) *NOUN* **tyrannies**
1 government by a tyrant
2 the way a tyrant behaves towards people

Is it not crystal clear, then, comrades, that all the evils of this life of ours spring from the tyranny of human beings? — *George Orwell, Animal Farm*

▷ **tyrannical** *ADJECTIVE*
▷ **tyrannous** *ADJECTIVE*

tyrant (*say* **ty**- rant) *NOUN* **tyrants**
a person who rules cruelly and unjustly; someone who insists on being obeyed

tyre *NOUN* **tyres**
a covering of rubber fitted round a wheel to make it grip the road and run more smoothly
USAGE NOTE The American spelling of this word is tire.

tyro *NOUN* **tyros**
a beginner or novice
WORD HISTORY from Latin *tiro* 'a recruit'

Uu

ubiquitous (*say* yoo- **bik**- wit- us) ***ADJECTIVE***
(*formal*) existing or found everywhere ◆ *A ubiquitous veil of secrecy covered all military matters.*
▷ **ubiquity** ***NOUN***
WORD HISTORY from Latin *ubique* 'everywhere'

U-boat ***NOUN*** **U-boats**
a German submarine of the First or Second World War
WORD HISTORY short for German *Unterseeboot* 'undersea boat'

udder ***NOUN*** **udders**
the bag-like part of a cow, ewe, female goat, or other hoofed animal, from which milk is taken

UFO ***ABBREVIATION***
unidentified flying object

ugly ***ADJECTIVE*** **uglier, ugliest**
1 unpleasant to look at; not beautiful
2 hostile and threatening ◆ *The language they use is ugly and violent.*
▷ **ugliness** ***NOUN***
WORD HISTORY from Old Norse *uggligr* 'frightening'

UHF ***ABBREVIATION***
ultra-high frequency (between 300 and 3000 megahertz)

UHT ***ABBREVIATION***
ultra heat-treated; used to describe milk that has been treated at a very high temperature so that it will keep for a long time

UK ***ABBREVIATION***
United Kingdom

ukulele (*say* yoo- ku- **lay**- lee) ***NOUN*** **ukuleles**
a small guitar with four strings
WORD HISTORY from Hawaiian, literally 'jumping flea'

ulcer ***NOUN*** **ulcers**
a sore on the inside or outside of the body
▷ **ulcerated** ***ADJECTIVE***
▷ **ulceration** ***NOUN***

ulterior ***ADJECTIVE***
beyond what is obvious or stated ◆ *Could there be an ulterior motive behind his request?*

ultimate ***ADJECTIVE***
furthest or most extreme in a series of things ◆ *The ultimate insult had been thrown at him.*
▷ **ultimately** ***ADVERB***

ultimatum (*say* ul- tim- **ay**- tum) ***NOUN*** **ultimatums**
a final demand or statement that unless something is done by a certain time action will be taken or war will be declared

ultramarine ***NOUN***
a deep bright blue
WORD HISTORY from Latin *ultra* 'beyond' and *mare* 'sea' (because it was originally imported 'across the sea' from the East)

ultrasonic ***ADJECTIVE***
(*Science*) sound is ultrasonic when it is beyond the range of human hearing

ultrasound ***NOUN***
(*Science*) sound with an ultrasonic frequency, used in medical examinations of internal parts of the body, especially a fetus

ultraviolet ***ADJECTIVE***
(*Science*) ultraviolet light rays are beyond the violet end of the spectrum and so not visible to the human eye

umber ***NOUN***
a kind of brown pigment
WORD HISTORY from Italian *terra di ombra* 'earth of shadow', or *terra di Ombra* 'earth of Umbria' (a region in central Italy)

umbilical (*say* um- **bil**- ik- al) ***ADJECTIVE***
to do with the navel

umbilical cord ***NOUN*** **umbilical cords**
the tube through which a baby receives nourishment before it is born, connecting its body with the mother's womb

umbrage ***NOUN***
to take umbrage is to be offended or feel resentment

Victoria had no choice but to take umbrage at this unfair assessment of her character.
— Meg Cabot, Victoria and the Rogue

WORD HISTORY originally 'shadow or shade': from Latin *umbra* 'shadow'

a b c d e f g h i j k l m n o p q r s t u v w x y z

umbrella *NOUN* **umbrellas**
1 a circular piece of material stretched over a folding frame with a central stick used as a handle, or a central pole, which you open to protect yourself from rain or sun
2 a general protection

WORD HISTORY from Italian *ombrella* 'a little shadow', from Latin *umbra* 'shadow' (because the first umbrellas were used as protection against the sun rather than to keep off the rain)

umlaut *NOUN* **umlauts**
a mark (¨) placed over a vowel in German to indicate a change in its pronunciation

umpire *NOUN* **umpires**
a referee in cricket, tennis, and some other games

umpire *VERB* **umpires, umpiring, umpired**
to act as an umpire

WORD HISTORY originally *numpire (a numpire* becoming *an umpire)* from French *nomper* 'not equal', i.e. neutral and impartial

umpteen *ADJECTIVE*
very many; too many to count

There are umpteen other odd people who were famous mathematicians. — *Kjartan Poskitt, Murderous Maths*

▷ **umpteenth** *ADJECTIVE*

UN *ABBREVIATION*
United Nations

unable *ADJECTIVE*
not able to do something

unaccountable *ADJECTIVE*
1 unable to be explained ◆ *For some unaccountable reason she had stopped in the middle of the road.*
2 not having to explain or account for what you do

▷ **unaccountably** *ADVERB*

unadulterated *ADJECTIVE*
pure; not mixed with things that are less good

unaided *ADJECTIVE*
without any help

unanimous (*say* yoo- **nan**- im- us) *ADJECTIVE*
a unanimous decision or view is one agreed by everyone involved

▷ **unanimously** *ADVERB*
▷ **unanimity** (*say* yoo- nan- **im**- it- ee) *NOUN*

unappealing *ADJECTIVE*
not very attractive or interesting

unassuming *ADJECTIVE*
modest; not arrogant or pretentious

unavailing *ADJECTIVE*
having no effect; achieving nothing

Edward now began to talk incoherently, and attempted to rise from the bed, but his efforts were unavailing—he was too weak. — *Captain Marryat, The Children of the New Forest*

unavoidable *ADJECTIVE*
not able to be avoided

unaware *ADJECTIVE*
not aware; not knowing about something

unawares *ADVERB*
to take or catch someone unawares is to surprise them ◆ *His response caught her completely unawares.*

unbalanced *ADJECTIVE*
1 not balanced
2 mentally disturbed or deranged

unbearable *ADJECTIVE*
not able to be endured

▷ **unbearably** *ADVERB*

unbeatable *ADJECTIVE*
1 too strong or good to be defeated or surpassed
2 extremely good

unbeaten *ADJECTIVE*
not defeated or surpassed

unbecoming *ADJECTIVE*
1 not making a person look attractive
2 not suitable or fitting

unbeknown *ADJECTIVE*
unbeknown to someone without their knowing

unbelievable *ADJECTIVE*
too unlikely or absurd to be believed; incredible

▷ **unbelievably** *ADVERB*

unbend *VERB* **unbends, unbending, unbent**
1 to change from a bent position; to straighten up
2 to relax and become friendly

unbiased *ADJECTIVE*
not biased; impartial

unbidden *ADJECTIVE*
without having been asked or invited

unblock *VERB* **unblocks, unblocking, unblocked**
to remove an obstruction from something

unborn *ADJECTIVE*
not yet born

unbridled *ADJECTIVE*
not controlled or restrained ◆ *He has an unbridled enthusiasm for politics.*

unbroken *ADJECTIVE*
not broken or interrupted

unburden *VERB* **unburdens, unburdening, unburdened**
1 to remove a burden from the person carrying it
2 to unburden yourself is to tell someone your secrets or problems so that you feel better

uncalled for *ADJECTIVE*
not justified or necessary ◆ *I considered his remarks not only uncalled for but offensive.*

uncanny *ADJECTIVE* **uncannier, uncanniest**
strange or mysterious

Luke stared at him. There was something uncanny about the way the old man seemed to see inside his head. — *Tim Bowler, Starseeker*

▷ **uncannily** *ADVERB*
▷ **uncanniness** *NOUN*

WORD HISTORY from an old sense of *canny* 'knowing' or 'able to be known'

unceremonious *ADJECTIVE*
1 without formality or ceremony
2 offhand or abrupt ◆ *He said goodbye with an unceremonious nod of his head.*

uncertain *ADJECTIVE*
1 not known certainly
2 not sure or confident about something
3 not reliable or secure ◆ *The country faces an uncertain future.*

in no uncertain terms clearly and forcefully
▷ **uncertainly** *ADVERB*
▷ **uncertainty** *NOUN*

unchanging *ADJECTIVE*
staying the same

uncharitable *ADJECTIVE*
making unkind judgements about people or actions
▷ **uncharitably** *ADVERB*

uncle *NOUN* **uncles**
the brother of your father or mother; your aunt's husband

unclothed *ADJECTIVE*
not wearing any clothes; naked

uncomfortable *ADJECTIVE*
1 not comfortable
2 uneasy or awkward about something
▷ **uncomfortably** *ADVERB*

uncommon *ADJECTIVE*
not common; unusual

uncompromising (*say* un- **komp**- ro- my- zing) *ADJECTIVE*
not allowing a compromise; inflexible

unconcerned *ADJECTIVE*
not caring about something; not worried

unconditional *ADJECTIVE*
without any conditions; complete or absolute ◆ *They would accept nothing short of unconditional surrender.*
▷ **unconditionally** *ADVERB*

unconscionable (*say* un- **kon**- shon- abl) *ADJECTIVE*
unreasonable or excessive

unconscious *ADJECTIVE*
1 not conscious or aware of your environment
2 not aware of things
3 done without realizing it ◆ *He gave an unconscious smile.*
▷ **unconsciously** *ADVERB*
▷ **unconsciousness** *NOUN*

unconstitutional *ADJECTIVE*
not conforming with the rules or procedures of a political constitution

uncontrollable *ADJECTIVE*
unable to be controlled or stopped
▷ **uncontrollably** *ADVERB*

uncooperative *ADJECTIVE*
not cooperative

uncountable *ADJECTIVE*
(*Language*) an uncountable noun does not normally have a plural form, e.g. *happiness* and *petrol* (SEE ALSO **countable**)

uncouple *VERB* **uncouples, uncoupling, uncoupled**
to disconnect one thing from another

uncouth (*say* un- **kooth**) *ADJECTIVE*
rude and rough in manner

WORD HISTORY from Old English *cuth* 'known'

uncover *VERB* **uncovers, uncovering, uncovered**
1 to remove the covering from something

Nono's hand uncovered her face but remained pressed into the sagging furrows of her cheek. — *Beverley Naidoo, Chain of Fire*

2 to reveal or expose something suspicious or wrong ◆ *He had uncovered a massive international conspiracy.*

unction *NOUN*
1 the action or ceremony of anointing with oil
2 a falsely or exaggeratedly polite manner

unctuous (*say* **unk**- tew- us) *ADJECTIVE*
having a smarmy manner; polite in an exaggerated way
▷ **unctuously** *ADVERB*
▷ **unctuousness** *NOUN*

undecided *ADJECTIVE*
1 not yet settled; not certain
2 not having made up your mind yet

undeniable *ADJECTIVE*
impossible to deny; undoubtedly true
▷ **undeniably** *ADVERB*

under *PREPOSITION*
1 below or beneath ◆ *The man who died was pinned under the front wheels.*
2 less than ◆ *The scheme would pay for itself in under two years.*
3 governed or controlled by ◆ *The country prospered under the new regime.*
4 in the process of; undergoing ◆ *The car was under repair at the time.*
5 making use of ◆ *She wrote under the name of 'George Eliot'.*
6 according to the rules of ◆ *This is prohibited under the recent trade agreement.*

under way in motion or in progress

under *ADVERB*
in or to a lower place or level or condition; below the surface of something ◆ *He jumped into the water and lowered his head under.*

underarm *ADJECTIVE, ADVERB*
an underarm throw or stroke is made by moving the hand and arm forward and upwards

undercarriage *NOUN* **undercarriages**
a structure underneath an aircraft, containing the wheels that support the aircraft on the ground

underclothes *PLURAL NOUN*
clothes worn next to the skin, under indoor clothing
▷ **underclothing** *NOUN*

undercover *ADJECTIVE*
done or doing things secretly ◆ *The case arises from an undercover police operation.*

undercurrent *NOUN* **undercurrents**
1 a current that is below the surface or below another current
2 an underlying feeling or influence ◆ *She could sense an undercurrent of tension in the room.*

undercut *VERB* **undercuts, undercutting, undercut**
to sell something for a lower price than someone else sells it

underdeveloped *ADJECTIVE*
1 not fully developed or grown
2 an underdeveloped country is poor and lacks modern industrial development

underdog *NOUN* **underdogs**
a competitor or team that is given little chance of success in a fight or contest

underdone *ADJECTIVE*
not thoroughly done; undercooked

underestimate *VERB* **underestimates, underestimating, underestimated**
to make too low an estimate of a person or thing

underfoot *ADVERB*
on the ground; under your feet

undergarment *NOUN* **undergarments**
a piece of underwear

undergo *VERB* **undergoes, undergoing, underwent, undergone**
to experience or endure something; to be subjected to something demanding or unpleasant ◆ *The dogs undergo a four-month training period.*

undergraduate *NOUN* **undergraduates**
a student at a university who has not yet taken a degree

underground *ADJECTIVE, ADVERB*
1 under the ground
2 done or working in secret

underground *NOUN*
a railway that runs through tunnels under the ground

undergrowth *NOUN*
bushes and other plants growing closely, especially under trees

underhand *ADJECTIVE*
done or doing things in a sly or secret way

underlie *VERB* **underlies, underlying, underlay, underlain**
1 to be the basis or explanation of something
2 to be or lie under something

underline *VERB* **underlines, underlining, underlined**
1 to draw a line under a word or phrase to emphasize it or draw attention to it
2 to emphasize something

underling *NOUN* **underlings**
a closely controlled subordinate having a minor role

underlying *ADJECTIVE*
an underlying reason or factor is one that helps to explain or account for something ◆ *Both these allergic conditions have the same underlying cause.*

undermine *VERB* **undermines, undermining, undermined**
to weaken something gradually

underneath *PREPOSITION, ADVERB*
below or beneath

underpants *PLURAL NOUN*
a piece of men's underwear covering the lower part of the body, worn under trousers

underpass *NOUN* **underpasses**
a road that passes underneath another road or a railway

underpay *VERB* **underpays, underpaying, underpaid**
to pay someone too little

underprivileged *ADJECTIVE*
not having the advantages some other people have, especially in having less than the normal standard of living or rights in a community

underrate *VERB* **underrates, underrating, underrated**
to have too low an opinion of a person or thing

undersell *VERB* **undersells, underselling, undersold**
to sell something at a lower price than another person

undersigned *ADJECTIVE*
in the wording of a document or contract, the undersigned are those who have signed their names at the bottom

undersized *ADJECTIVE*
of less than the normal size

understand *VERB* **understands, understanding, understood**
1 to know what something means or how it works or why it exists

Mrs Coulter understood some of the language of these mountain people, but it would never do to let them know how much. — *Philip Pullman, The Amber Spyglass*

2 to know and tolerate a person's ways
3 to have been told something, or to have reason to think it is true

I understood you were an experienced first-class professional interior and exterior decorator. — *Harold Pinter, The Caretaker*

4 to take something for granted ◆ *You can stay as long as you like, that's understood.*

understandable *ADJECTIVE*
1 able to be understood
2 reasonable or natural ◆ *It was quite understandable that they should want more information.*
▷ **understandably** *ADVERB*

understanding *NOUN*
1 the power to understand or think; comprehension or intellect
2 perception of facts or circumstances ◆ *These statistics help our understanding of population movements.*
3 sympathy or tolerance ◆ *At a time like this they need everyone's understanding.*
4 agreement in opinion or feeling ◆ *We are looking for a better understanding between different sections of the community.*

understanding *ADJECTIVE*
sympathetic and helpful

understatement *NOUN* **understatements**
an incomplete or restrained statement of facts or truth ◆ *To say I am not happy is an understatement: I am furious.*

understudy *NOUN* **understudies**
an actor who learns a part in order to be able to play it if the usual actor is ill or absent

understudy *VERB* **understudies, understudying, understudied**
to be an understudy for an actor or part

undertake *VERB* **undertakes, undertaking, undertook, undertaken**
1 to agree or promise to do something
2 to take on a task or responsibility

undertaker *NOUN* **undertakers**
a person whose job is to arrange funerals and burials or cremations

undertaking *NOUN* **undertakings**
1 a job or task that is being undertaken
2 a promise or guarantee
3 the business of an undertaker

undertone *NOUN* **undertones**
1 to speak in undertones is to speak quietly and softly
2 the underlying quality or impression that words or ideas convey ◆ *'You'd better cooperate, then,' he added with a sinister undertone in his voice.*

undertow *NOUN*
a current below that of the surface of the sea and moving in the opposite direction

underwater *ADJECTIVE, ADVERB*
placed, used, or done beneath the surface of water

underwear *NOUN*
clothes worn next to the skin, under indoor clothing

underweight *ADJECTIVE*
not heavy enough

underwent *past tense of* **undergo**

underworld *NOUN*
1 the people who are regularly involved in crime
2 in myths and legends, a place under the earth where the spirits of the dead go

underwrite *VERB* **underwrites, underwriting, underwrote, underwritten**
to guarantee to finance something, or to pay for any loss or damage
▷ **underwriter** *NOUN*

WORD HISTORY called this because underwriters used to sign their names below the names of the other people in the agreement

undesirable *ADJECTIVE*
not desirable; objectionable
▷ **undesirably** *ADVERB*

undetected *ADJECTIVE*
not detected or discovered

For a while my body went undetected, so I lay there, listening to the sounds of the night. — *Darren Shan, Cirque du Freak*

undeveloped *ADJECTIVE*
not yet developed

undignified *ADJECTIVE*
not dignified

undo *VERB* **undoes, undoing, undid, undone**
1 to unfasten or unwrap something
2 to cancel or wipe out the effect or value of something ◆ *One careless mistake can undo the work of years.*

undoing *NOUN*
be someone's undoing be the cause of their ruin or failure

undoubted *ADJECTIVE*
certain; not regarded as doubtful ◆ *The project had been an undoubted success.*
▷ **undoubtedly** *ADVERB*

undress *VERB* **undresses, undressing, undressed**
to take your clothes off

undue *ADJECTIVE*
excessive; too great ◆ *He was anxious to complete the work without undue haste.*

undulate *VERB* **undulates, undulating, undulated**
to move like a wave or waves; to have a wavy appearance

Ford pressed a large red button at the bottom of the screen and words began to undulate across it. — *Douglas Adams, The Hitch-Hiker's Guide to the Galaxy*

▷ **undulation** *NOUN*

unduly *ADVERB*
excessively; more than is reasonable

undying *ADJECTIVE*
an undying feeling or emotion lasts for always

unearth *VERB* **unearths, unearthing, unearthed**
1 to dig something up; to uncover something by digging
2 to find something by searching

unearthly *ADJECTIVE*
1 unnaturally strange and frightening

Many years back, there had come from the vault so horrible and unearthly a cry, that parson and people got up and fled from the church. — *J. Meade Falkner, Moonfleet*

2 (*informal*) very awkward or inconvenient ◆ *I used to have a job which involved getting up at some unearthly hour.*

uneasy *ADJECTIVE*
1 worried or anxious ◆ *I was uneasy about leaving them.*
2 causing anxiety or embarrassment ◆ *An uneasy silence followed.*
▷ **uneasily** *ADVERB*
▷ **uneasiness** *NOUN*

uneatable *ADJECTIVE*
food is uneatable when it is not fit to be eaten

uneconomic *ADJECTIVE*
not profitable or using resources well

uneducated *ADJECTIVE*
poorly educated; ignorant

unemployed *ADJECTIVE*
not having a job though available for work
▷ **unemployment** *NOUN*

unending *ADJECTIVE*
not coming to an end; endless

unenviable *ADJECTIVE*
difficult or unpleasant
▷ **unenviably** *ADVERB*

unequal *ADJECTIVE*
1 not equal in amount, size, or value
2 not giving the same opportunities to everyone ◆ *Socialism aims to correct the unequal distribution of wealth.*
▷ **unequalled** *ADJECTIVE*
▷ **unequally** *ADVERB*

unequivocal *ADJECTIVE*
not leaving any doubt; completely clear ◆ *The government declared its unequivocal opposition to the proposal.*

unerring (*say* un- **er**- ing) *ADJECTIVE*
making no mistake ◆ *He hit the target with unerring accuracy.*

unethical *ADJECTIVE*
not ethical; unscrupulous in business dealings
▷ **unethically** *ADVERB*

uneven *ADJECTIVE*
1 not level or regular ◆ *Her breath was coming in short uneven gasps.*
2 not equally balanced ◆ *The match proved to be an uneven contest.*
▷ **unevenly** *ADVERB*
▷ **unevenness** *NOUN*

unexceptionable *ADJECTIVE*
not in any way objectionable but not new or interesting

USAGE NOTE Take care not to confuse this word with *unexceptional*.

unexceptional *ADJECTIVE*
not exceptional; quite ordinary

USAGE NOTE Take care not to confuse this word with *unexceptionable*.

unexpected *ADJECTIVE*
not expected; coming as a surprise

In going downstairs the first time I found an unexpected difficulty because I could not see my feet; indeed I stumbled twice. — *H. G. Wells, The Invisible Man*

▷ **unexpectedly** *ADVERB*
▷ **unexpectedness** *NOUN*

unfair *ADJECTIVE*
not fair; unjust
▷ **unfairly** *ADVERB*
▷ **unfairness** *NOUN*

unfaithful *ADJECTIVE*
1 not faithful or loyal
2 not sexually loyal to one partner

unfamiliar *ADJECTIVE*
not familiar
▷ **unfamiliarity** *NOUN*

unfasten *VERB* **unfastens, unfastening, unfastened**
to open the fastenings of something

unfavourable *ADJECTIVE*
not favourable
▷ **unfavourably** *ADVERB*

unfeeling *ADJECTIVE*
not caring about other people's feelings; unsympathetic

unfit *ADJECTIVE*
1 not suitable
2 not in perfect health because you do not take enough exercise

unflappable *ADJECTIVE*
(*informal*) remaining calm in a crisis

unfold *VERB* **unfolds, unfolding, unfolded**
1 to open or spread out
2 information or a story unfolds when it becomes known slowly and in increasing detail

unforeseen *ADJECTIVE*
not foreseen or expected

unforgettable *ADJECTIVE*
so enjoyable or exciting that it is not likely to be forgotten

unforgivable *ADJECTIVE*
too serious or hurtful to be forgiven

unfortunate *ADJECTIVE*
1 having bad luck; unlucky
2 unsuitable or regrettable ◆ *Calling him a 'liar' was an unfortunate choice of word.*
▷ **unfortunately** *ADVERB*

unfounded *ADJECTIVE*
not based on facts

unfreeze *VERB* **unfreezes, unfreezing, unfroze, unfrozen**
to thaw, or to cause something to thaw

unfriendly *ADJECTIVE*
not friendly
▷ **unfriendliness** *NOUN*

unfrock *VERB* **unfrocks, unfrocking, unfrocked**
to dismiss a person from being a priest

unfurl *VERB* **unfurls, unfurling, unfurled**
to unroll or spread out ◆ *A single protester attempted to unfurl a banner in the square.*

unfurnished *ADJECTIVE*
an unfurnished house or flat is one that does not yet have any furniture

ungainly *ADJECTIVE*
awkward or clumsy in appearance or movement
▷ **ungainliness** *NOUN*

ungodly *ADJECTIVE*
1 not religious
2 (*informal*) outrageous; very inconvenient ◆ *He wasn't expecting anyone to call at such an ungodly time of the day.*
▷ **ungodliness** *NOUN*

ungovernable *ADJECTIVE*
impossible to control

ungracious *ADJECTIVE*
not kindly or courteous
▷ **ungraciously** *ADVERB*

ungrateful *ADJECTIVE*
not feeling or showing gratitude
▷ **ungratefully** *ADVERB*

unguarded *ADJECTIVE*
1 without a guard or protection ◆ *Should we leave the spaceship unguarded?*
2 without thought or caution; indiscreet ◆ *He let the information slip out in an unguarded moment.*

unguent (*say* **ung**- went) *NOUN* **unguents**
an ointment or lubricant

unhappy *ADJECTIVE*
1 not happy; sad
2 not pleased or satisfied ◆ *Let us know if you are unhappy with the advice you receive.*
3 unfortunate or unsuitable ◆ *Both of them being there at the same time was an unhappy coincidence.*
▷ **unhappily** *ADVERB*
▷ **unhappiness** *NOUN*

unhealthy *ADJECTIVE*
not healthy
▷ **unhealthiness** *NOUN*

unheard-of *ADJECTIVE*
never known or done before; extraordinary

unhinged *ADJECTIVE*
mentally unbalanced

Really, if you thought about things too much, Mr Cartright decided, you could go quite unhinged, teaching 4C. — *Anne Fine, Flour Babies*

unholy *ADJECTIVE*
1 wicked or sinful
2 (*informal*) very great; dreadful ◆ *There would be an unholy row if they found out.*

unicorn *NOUN* **unicorns**
a mythical animal that is like a horse with one long straight horn growing from its forehead

unicycle *NOUN* **unicycles**
a cycle with a single wheel, used by acrobats

uniform *NOUN* **uniforms**
special clothes showing that the wearer is a member of a particular school, sports club, or other organization

uniform *ADJECTIVE*
always the same; not varying

I descended into a uniform whiteness, snow and cloud merging into one. — *Joe Simpson, Touching the Void*

▷ **uniformed** *ADJECTIVE*
▷ **uniformly** *ADVERB*
▷ **uniformity** *NOUN*

unify *VERB* **unifies, unifying, unified**
to make a number of things into one thing; to unite things
▷ **unification** *NOUN*

unilateral *ADJECTIVE*
done by one person or group or country and not by the others that are also involved ◆ *The school had to make a unilateral decision in the matter.*

uninhabitable *ADJECTIVE*
unfit to live in

uninhabited *ADJECTIVE*
with nobody living there

uninhibited *ADJECTIVE*
having no inhibitions; not restrained

uninterested *ADJECTIVE*
not interested; showing or feeling no concern

USAGE NOTE See the note at *disinterested*.

union *NOUN* **unions**
1 the joining of things together; a united thing
2 a society or organization, especially a trade union

unionist *NOUN* **unionists**
1 a member of a trade union
2 a person who wishes to unite one country with another

Union Jack *NOUN* **Union Jacks**
the flag of the United Kingdom

unique (*say* yoo- **neek**) *ADJECTIVE*
being the only one of its kind; unlike any other ◆ *This is a unique opportunity to do something new and exciting.*
▷ **uniquely** *ADVERB*

unisex *ADJECTIVE*
suitable or designed for both men and women

unison *NOUN*
in unison
1 (*Music*) to sing in unison is to sing the same tune or notes
2 to act or speak in unison is to be agreed about something

unit *NOUN* **units**
1 an amount used as a standard in measuring or counting things ◆ *The metric units of length include metre, centimetre, and millimetre.*
2 a group of soldiers forming part of a larger military organization
3 a group of people doing particular work or serving a particular role, e.g. a political party's policy unit
4 a manufactured device or piece of furniture or equipment that is regarded as a single thing but forms part of a larger group or whole, for example a sink unit or a desk unit
5 a self-contained building or department of a larger organization, for example an intensive-care unit in a hospital
6 (*Mathematics*) any whole number less than 10

WORD FAMILY *Unit* comes from the Latin word *unus* meaning 'one' or 'single'. Other words having the same origin include *inch* (via Old English), *reunion, unanimous, unicorn, uniform, unique, unison, unite, unity.*

unite *VERB* **unites, uniting, united**
to join together; to become one thing, or to make things one

United Kingdom *NOUN*
Great Britain and Northern Ireland

USAGE NOTE See the note at *Britain*.

unity *NOUN*
1 the state of being united or in agreement
2 something whole that is made up of parts
3 (*Mathematics*) the number one

universal *ADJECTIVE*
to do with or including or done by everyone or everything

HTML is the universal language of the Web and is used by people who put text, sound and pictures on web pages. — *Michael Cox, The Incredible Internet*

▷ **universally** *ADVERB*

universe *NOUN*
everything that exists, including the earth and living things and all the stars and planets

university *NOUN* **universities**
a place where people go to study at an advanced level after leaving school

WORD HISTORY from Latin *universitas* 'the universe' and later 'a community or group of people' (i.e. the teachers and students)

unjust *ADJECTIVE*
not fair or just

unkempt *ADJECTIVE*
looking untidy or neglected

WORD HISTORY from an old word *kempt* meaning 'combed'

unkind *ADJECTIVE*
not kind; harsh
▷ **unkindly** *ADVERB*
▷ **unkindness** *NOUN*

unknown *ADJECTIVE*
not known or familiar

unlawful *ADJECTIVE*
not allowed by the law or rules

unleaded *ADJECTIVE*
unleaded petrol has no added lead

unleash *VERB* **unleashes, unleashing, unleashed**
1 to set a dog free from a leash
2 to let a strong feeling or force be released

unleavened (*say* un- **lev**- end) *ADJECTIVE*
unleavened bread is made without yeast or other substances that would make it rise

unless *CONJUNCTION*
except when; if ... not ◆ *We will send you a book each month unless you tell us not to.*

unlike *PREPOSITION*
not like; as distinct from

Clare's great-grandmother, unlike her daughters, Aunt Anne and Aunt Susan, had been a lady of fashion. — *Penelope Lively, The House in Norham Gardens*

unlike *ADJECTIVE*
not alike; different

unlikely *ADJECTIVE* **unlikelier, unlikeliest**
not likely to happen or be true

unlimited *ADJECTIVE*
not limited; very great or very many

unload *VERB* **unloads, unloading, unloaded**
to remove the load of things carried by a ship, aircraft, or vehicle

unlock *VERB* **unlocks, unlocking, unlocked**
to open something by undoing a lock

unlucky *ADJECTIVE*
not lucky; having or bringing bad luck

In this neighbourhood to meet a lawyer or a priest on the street is unlucky. We're only thought of in connection with disasters. — *Arthur Miller, A View from the Bridge*

▷ **unluckily** *ADVERB*

unmanageable *ADJECTIVE*
unable to be managed

unmarried *ADJECTIVE*
not married; single

unmask *VERB* **unmasks, unmasking, unmasked**
1 to remove a person's mask
2 to reveal what a person or thing is really like

unmentionable *ADJECTIVE*
too bad or embarrassing to be spoken about

unmistakable *ADJECTIVE*
not able to be mistaken for another person or thing

▷ **unmistakably** *ADVERB*

unmitigated *ADJECTIVE*
absolute or unqualified ◆ *Her singing was an unmitigated joy.*

unnatural *ADJECTIVE*
not natural or normal

▷ **unnaturally** *ADVERB*

unnecessary *ADJECTIVE*
not necessary; more than is necessary

unnerve *VERB* **unnerves, unnerving, unnerved**
to make someone lose courage or determination

It was an awesome thing to sleep in that ill-fated camp; and yet it was even more unnerving to do so in the jungle. — *Sir Arthur Conan Doyle, The Lost World*

unnoticed *ADJECTIVE*
not noticed or seen

They had slipped into the school unnoticed and whispered a trembling 'goodnight' in the corridor. — *Anthony Horowitz, Groosham Grange*

unoccupied *ADJECTIVE*
a building or room is unoccupied when nobody is using it or living in it

unofficial *ADJECTIVE*
not officially authorized or accepted

▷ **unofficially** *ADVERB*

unorthodox *ADJECTIVE*
not typical or generally accepted ◆ *We had to put up with some unorthodox meals at times.*

unpack *VERB* **unpacks, unpacking, unpacked**
to take things out of a suitcase or container

unpaid *ADJECTIVE*
1 not yet paid
2 not receiving payment for work you do

unpalatable *ADJECTIVE*
1 not pleasant to eat or drink
2 difficult to accept or tolerate

unparalleled *ADJECTIVE*
having no parallel or equal

unpick *VERB* **unpicks, unpicking, unpicked**
to undo the stitching of something

unpleasant *ADJECTIVE*
not pleasant; nasty

▷ **unpleasantly** *ADVERB*
▷ **unpleasantness** *NOUN*

unpopular *ADJECTIVE*
not liked or popular

unprecedented (*say* un- **press**- id- en- tid) *ADJECTIVE*
that has never happened or been done before

unpredictable *ADJECTIVE*
not able to be predicted; likely to change

unprejudiced *ADJECTIVE*
without prejudice; impartial

unprepared *ADJECTIVE*
1 not ready or equipped to deal with something
2 not prepared beforehand

unprepossessing *ADJECTIVE*
not very attractive; unappealing

unprincipled *ADJECTIVE*
not having good moral principles; unscrupulous

unprintable *ADJECTIVE*
too rude or indecent to be printed

unprofessional *ADJECTIVE*
not professional; not worthy of a member of a profession

unprofitable *ADJECTIVE*
not producing a profit or advantage
▷ **unprofitably** *ADVERB*

unqualified *ADJECTIVE*
1 not officially qualified to do something
2 complete; not limited in any way ◆ *They have our unqualified support.*

unquestionable *ADJECTIVE*
too clear or definite to be questioned or doubted
▷ **unquestionably** *ADVERB*

unravel *VERB* **unravels, unravelling, unravelled**
1 to disentangle things
2 to undo something that is knitted
3 to look into a problem or mystery and solve it

unready *ADJECTIVE*
not ready; hesitating

WORD HISTORY In modern use the word is simply understood as the prefix *un-* meaning 'not' and *ready*. Historically, in the title of the English king *Ethelred the Unready*, the word means 'lacking good advice or wisdom'.

unreal *ADJECTIVE*
not real; existing in the imagination only
▷ **unreality** *NOUN*

unreasonable *ADJECTIVE*
1 not reasonable
2 excessive or unjust
▷ **unreasonably** *ADVERB*

unreel *VERB* **unreels, unreeling, unreeled**
to unwind a thread or line from a reel

unrelieved *ADJECTIVE*
constant; without any change or relief ◆ *In those days, some children spent their days at school in unrelieved misery.*

unremitting *ADJECTIVE*
never stopping or relaxing; persistent

unrepeatable *ADJECTIVE*
1 too rude or offensive to be said again ◆ *He muttered something unrepeatable under his breath.*
2 too good to be repeated or happen again ◆ *They were having an unrepeatable run of good luck.*

unrequited (*say* un- ri- **kwy**- tid) *ADJECTIVE*
unrequited love is not returned or rewarded

unreserved *ADJECTIVE*
1 not reserved
2 without restriction; complete ◆ *He issued an unreserved apology for the error.*
▷ **unreservedly** *ADVERB*

unrest *NOUN*
trouble or rioting by people who are dissatisfied or have a grievance

unripe *ADJECTIVE*
not yet ripe

unrivalled *ADJECTIVE*
having no equal; better than all others

unroll *VERB* **unrolls, unrolling, unrolled**
to open something that has been rolled up

unruly *ADJECTIVE*
difficult to control; disorderly
▷ **unruliness** *NOUN*

unsavoury *ADJECTIVE*
unpleasant or disgusting

unscathed *ADJECTIVE*
not harmed or injured

WORD HISTORY from an old word *scathe* 'to harm or injure'

unscrew *VERB* **unscrews, unscrewing, unscrewed**
to remove or loosen something by taking out screws or twisting a lid or cap

unscrupulous *ADJECTIVE*
having no scruples about doing wrong

unseat *VERB* **unseats, unseating, unseated**
1 to cause someone to fall from the saddle of a seat or bicycle
2 to remove someone from a position of authority

unseemly *ADJECTIVE*
not proper or suitable; indecent

unseen *ADJECTIVE*
not seen; invisible

unseen *NOUN* **unseens**
a passage for translation without previous preparation

unselfish *ADJECTIVE*
not selfish; considerate

unsettle *VERB* **unsettles, unsettling, unsettled**
to make someone feel uneasy or anxious

Martha has had a visit from her sister, which always unsettles her. — *Celia Rees, Witch Child*

▷ **unsettling** *ADJECTIVE*

unsettled *ADJECTIVE*
1 not settled or calm
2 weather is unsettled when it is likely to change

unshakeable *ADJECTIVE*
not able to be shaken or changed; strong and firm ◆ *She had an unshakeable faith in other people.*

unshaven *ADJECTIVE*
not recently shaved

unsightly *ADJECTIVE*
not pleasant to look at; ugly
▷ **unsightliness** *NOUN*

unskilled *ADJECTIVE*
not having or not needing special skill or training

unsociable *ADJECTIVE*
not sociable or friendly

unsocial *ADJECTIVE*
1 not social
2 unsocial hours are time spent working when most people are free

unsolicited *ADJECTIVE*
not asked for

unsound *ADJECTIVE*
1 not reliable; not based on sound evidence or reasoning
2 not firm or strong
3 not healthy

unspeakable *ADJECTIVE*
too bad or horrid to be described

unstable *ADJECTIVE*
not stable; likely to change or become unbalanced

unsteady *ADJECTIVE*
not steady; unstable or wobbly

unstinting *ADJECTIVE*
giving or given generously

unstuck *ADJECTIVE*
to come unstuck
1 is to stop sticking to something
2 (*informal*) is to fail or go wrong

unsuccessful *ADJECTIVE*
not successful; failed

unsuitable *ADJECTIVE*
not suitable or appropriate

unsung *ADJECTIVE*
(*formal*) not famous or praised but deserving to be

unsure *ADJECTIVE*
not confident or certain

untangle *VERB* **untangles, untangling, untangled**
1 to take the knots or tangles out of something; to disentangle
2 to free something from difficulty or confusion

untenable *ADJECTIVE*
not able to be justified or defended

unthinkable *ADJECTIVE*
too bad or too unlikely to be worth considering

unthinking *ADJECTIVE*
thoughtless; not thinking of other people

untidy *ADJECTIVE* **untidier, untidiest**
not tidy or properly arranged
▷ **untidily** *ADVERB*
▷ **untidiness** *NOUN*

untie *VERB* **unties, untying, untied**
1 to undo something that has been tied
2 to release someone who has been tied up

until *PREPOSITION, CONJUNCTION*
up to a particular time or event
USAGE NOTE See the note at *till.*

untimely *ADJECTIVE*
happening too soon or at an unsuitable time

unto *PREPOSITION*
(*old use*) to or towards

untold *ADJECTIVE*
too much or too many to be counted

untoward *ADJECTIVE*
unfortunate and unexpected ◆ *Let's hope nothing untoward happens while we are away.*

untraceable *ADJECTIVE*
not able to be traced or found

untrue *ADJECTIVE*
not true; false

untruth *NOUN* **untruths**
an untrue statement; a lie
▷ **untruthful** *ADJECTIVE*
▷ **untruthfully** *ADVERB*

unused *ADJECTIVE*
1 (*say* un-yoozd) not yet used
2 (*say* un-yoost) to be unused to something or to doing something is to be unfamiliar with it

unusual *ADJECTIVE*
not usual; strange or exceptional
▷ **unusually** *ADVERB*

unutterable *ADJECTIVE*
too great or terrible to be described

unveil *VERB* **unveils, unveiling, unveiled**
1 to remove a veil or covering from something
2 to reveal something new that has been kept hidden or secret

unwanted *ADJECTIVE*
not wanted

unwarranted *ADJECTIVE*
not justified or called for

unwary *ADJECTIVE*
not cautious or careful about danger
▷ **unwarily** *ADVERB*
▷ **unwariness** *NOUN*

unwelcome *ADJECTIVE*
not welcome or wanted

unwell *ADJECTIVE*
not in good health

unwholesome *ADJECTIVE*
1 harmful to your health
2 unhealthy-looking

unwieldy *ADJECTIVE*
difficult to move or control because of its size, shape, or weight
▷ **unwieldiness** *NOUN*

unwilling *ADJECTIVE*
not willing; reluctant
▷ **unwillingly** *ADVERB*

unwind *VERB* **unwinds, unwinding, unwound**
1 to unroll something
2 (*informal*) to relax after a time of work or strain

unwise *ADJECTIVE*
not wise; foolish
▷ **unwisely** *ADVERB*

unwitting *ADJECTIVE*
1 not intended ◆ *He had made an unwitting gaffe at a dinner party.*
2 not aware of all the facts ◆ *He became an unwitting accomplice in a woman's murder of her husband.*
▷ **unwittingly** *ADVERB*

unwonted (*say* un- **wohn**- tid) *ADJECTIVE*
not customary or usual

There was an air of unwonted bustle in the house, as though someone had lately arrived or was expected to arrive at any moment. — *Rosemary Sutcliff, The Eagle of the Ninth*

▷ **unwontedly** *ADVERB*

unworkable *ADJECTIVE*
an unworkable idea or scheme is one that is not practical or able to be carried out

unworn *ADJECTIVE*
not yet worn

unworthy *ADJECTIVE*
not worthy or deserving

unwrap *VERB* **unwraps, unwrapping, unwrapped**
to open something that is wrapped

up *ADVERB*
1 to or in a higher place or position or level ◆ *The lift was going up at the time.* ◆ *Taxes are bound to go up after the election.*
2 so as to be upright ◆ *Everyone stood up to applaud.*
3 out of bed after a period of sleep ◆ *It's nearly time to get up.*
4 completely or finally ◆ *She drank up her tea and left.*
5 finished; over ◆ *Tomorrow our three weeks will be up.*
6 (*informal*) happening ◆ *Something is up.*

to be up against something or someone
1 is to be close to them
2 (*informal*) is to be faced with a difficulty or danger

ups and downs constantly changing good and bad luck

up to
1 until; as far as
2 to be up to something is to be busy doing it
3 to be up to a task is to be capable of doing it
4 a choice or obligation is up to someone when they can choose whether to do it ◆ *It's up to us to tell them.*

up to date
1 modern or fashionable
2 aware of or providing the most recent information

USAGE NOTE Use hyphens when *up to date* is used as an adjective before a noun, e.g. *up-to-date information* (but *The information is up to date*).

up *PREPOSITION*
towards a higher place or position along ◆ *A lot of sludge came up the plughole.* ◆ *The postman was coming up the road.*

up-and-coming *ADJECTIVE*
(*informal*) likely to become successful

upbraid *VERB* **upbraids, upbraiding, upbraided**
(*formal*) to scold or reproach someone

upbringing *NOUN*
the way a child is brought up and educated

update *VERB* **updates, updating, updated**
1 to make something more modern
2 to provide someone with the latest information about something
▷ **update** *NOUN*

upgrade *VERB* **upgrades, upgrading, upgraded**
1 to improve a machine by installing new or better parts in it
2 (*ICT*) to improve a piece of software by installing a newer version
3 to raise a person or their job to a higher rank
▷ **upgrade** *NOUN*

upheaval *NOUN* **upheavals**
a sudden violent change or disturbance

uphill *ADVERB*
towards the top of a slope

uphill *ADJECTIVE*
1 going up a slope
2 sloping upwards
3 difficult ◆ *He faces an uphill struggle to be fit in time.*

uphold *VERB* **upholds, upholding, upheld**
to support or maintain a decision, opinion, or belief

upholster *VERB* **upholsters, upholstering, upholstered**
to put a soft padded covering on furniture
▷ **upholstery** *NOUN*

upkeep *NOUN*
the process of keeping something in good condition, or the cost of this

uplands *PLURAL NOUN*
the higher parts of a country or region
▷ **upland** *ADJECTIVE*

uplifting *ADJECTIVE*
making you feel more happy or cheerful

upon *PREPOSITION*
(*formal*) on or on to

upper *ADJECTIVE*
higher in place or rank

upper case *NOUN*
capital letters

upper class *NOUN* **upper classes**
the highest class in society, especially the aristocracy
▷ **upper-class** *ADJECTIVE*

uppermost *ADJECTIVE*
highest in place or importance ◆ *The high maintenance costs were uppermost in their minds.*

uppermost *ADVERB*
on or to the top or the highest place ◆ *Lay the curtains out with the linings uppermost.*

upright *ADJECTIVE*
1 vertical or erect

Westside stretched before them like a box of upright dominoes, with only building graphics and neon signs to distinguish between skyscrapers. — *Eoin Colfer, The Supernaturalist*

2 strictly honest or honourable

upright *NOUN* **uprights**
a post or rod placed upright, especially as a support

uprising *NOUN* **uprisings**
a rebellion or revolt

uproar *NOUN*
an outburst of noise or excitement or anger

Suddenly there was a great uproar from the baboons across the river and in came Elsa dripping wet. — *Joy Adamson, Born Free*

WORD HISTORY from Dutch *oproer* 'an uprising or rebellion': there was originally no connection with the English word *roar*, but later this word influenced the meaning of *uproar*

uproarious *ADJECTIVE*
very noisy, or causing a lot of noise

uproot *VERB* **uproots, uprooting, uprooted**
1 to remove a plant and its roots from the ground
2 to make someone leave the place where he or she has lived for a long time

upset *VERB* **upsets, upsetting, upset**
1 to overturn something; to knock something over
2 to make a person unhappy or distressed ◆ *What upset him was hearing the door being locked.*
3 to disturb the normal working of something; to disrupt an activity ◆ *This news has upset all our plans.*

upset *ADJECTIVE*
1 unhappy or distressed
2 slightly ill ◆ *He had an upset stomach.*

upset *NOUN* **upsets**
1 a slight illness ◆ *He wasn't sure whether it was a hangover or a stomach upset.*
2 an unexpected bad result or setback ◆ *The general election that year produced the political upset of the century.*

upshot *NOUN* **upshots**
the eventual outcome

WORD HISTORY originally 'the final shot in an archery contest'

upside down *ADVERB, ADJECTIVE*
1 with the upper part underneath instead of on top
2 in great disorder; very untidy

upstairs *ADVERB, ADJECTIVE*
to or on a higher floor

upstanding *NOUN*
honest and respectable

I'll show you all the towns. America is full of beautiful towns and fine, upstanding people. — *Arthur Miller, Death of a Salesman*

upstart *NOUN* **upstarts**
a person who has risen suddenly to a high position, especially one who then behaves arrogantly

upstream *ADJECTIVE, ADVERB*
in the direction from which a stream flows

uptake *NOUN*
quick or slow on the uptake quick (or slow) to understand

uptight *ADJECTIVE*
(*informal*) tense and nervous or annoyed

upward *ADJECTIVE, ADVERB*
going towards what is higher
▷ **upwards** *ADVERB*

uranium *NOUN*
a heavy radioactive grey metal used as a source of nuclear energy

WORD HISTORY named after the planet *Uranus*, which had been discovered in 1781, eight years before the discovery of uranium

urban *ADJECTIVE*
(*Geography*) to do with a town or city

a b c d e f g h i j k l m n o p q r s t u v w x y z

urbane *ADJECTIVE*
having smoothly polite manners
▷ **urbanely** *ADVERB*
▷ **urbanity** *NOUN*

urbanize *VERB* **urbanizes, urbanizing, urbanized**
to make a place more urban
▷ **urbanization** *NOUN*

USAGE NOTE This word can also be spelled urbanise.

urchin *NOUN* **urchins**
1 a rough and poorly dressed young boy
2 a sea urchin

Urdu (*say* **oor**- doo) *NOUN*
a language related to Hindi, spoken in northern India and Pakistan

urge *VERB* **urges, urging, urged**
1 to try to persuade a person to do something
2 to drive people or animals onward

James pointed away down the road where the second gypsy was urging his horse along as fast as it would go. — *Kathleen Fidler, The Desperate Journey*

3 to recommend or advise a course of action

urge *NOUN* **urges**
a strong desire or wish

urgent *ADJECTIVE*
needing to be done or dealt with immediately
▷ **urgently** *ADVERB*
▷ **urgency** *NOUN*

urinal (*say* yoor- **ry**- nal) *NOUN* **urinals**
a bowl or trough fixed to the wall in a men's public toilet, for men to urinate into

urinate (*say* **yoor**- in- ayt) *VERB* **urinates, urinating, urinated**
to pass urine out of your body
▷ **urination** *NOUN*

urine (*say* **yoor**- in) *NOUN*
waste liquid that collects in the bladder and is passed out of the body
▷ **urinary** *ADJECTIVE*

urn *NOUN* **urns**
1 a large metal container with a tap, for heating water to make tea or coffee
2 a tall container shaped like a vase with a base, for holding the ashes of a cremated person

US *ABBREVIATION*
United States (of America)

us *PRONOUN*
the form of *we* used when it is the object of a verb or after a preposition

USA *ABBREVIATION*
United States of America

usable *ADJECTIVE*
suitable or good enough to be used

usage *NOUN* **usages**
1 the process of using something, or the way it is used
2 the way words are used in a language ◆ *British English usage sometimes differs from American.*

use (*say* yooz) *VERB* **uses, using, used**
to perform an action or job with something

Every bit of the waste cotton is swept up and gets used and often the big machines are still moving as we clean. — *Sue Reid, My Story: Mill Girl*

used to
1 was or were in the habit of doing ◆ *We used to go by train.*
2 accustomed to or familiar with

Most people at the Museum were used to Katherine and Dog by now, and nobody paid very much attention. — *Philip Reeve, Mortal Engines*

to use something up is to use all of something

use (*say* yooss) *NOUN* **uses**
1 the action of using something; the process of being used ◆ *We need a more efficient use of resources.*
2 the purpose for which something is used ◆ *I think I know a good use for all this old equipment.*
3 the quality of being useful ◆ *The heating system will be no use without good insulation.*

used *ADJECTIVE*
not new; second-hand

useful *ADJECTIVE*
able to be used a lot or to do something that needs doing
▷ **usefully** *ADVERB*
▷ **usefulness** *NOUN*

useless *ADJECTIVE*
not useful; producing no effect
▷ **uselessly** *ADVERB*
▷ **uselessness** *NOUN*

user *NOUN* **users**
a person who uses something

user-friendly *ADJECTIVE*
designed to be easy to use

user-name *NOUN*
(*ICT*) the name a user uses to log on to a computer system

usher *NOUN* **ushers**
a person who shows people to their seats in a cinema, theatre, or church

usher *VERB* **ushers, ushering, ushered**
to lead someone in or out; to escort someone as an usher

'Here we are!' Crawley smiled and ushered Alex out into a long corridor. — *Anthony Horowitz, Stormbreaker*

WORD HISTORY originally an attendant at the door to a building, from Latin *ostiarius* 'doorkeeper', from *ostium* 'door'

usherette *NOUN* **usherettes**
a woman who shows people to their seats in a cinema or theatre

a b c d e f g h i j k l m n o p q r s t u v w x y z

USSR *ABBREVIATION*
the former Union of Soviet Socialist Republics

usual *ADJECTIVE*
occurring or done always or most of the time
▷ **usually** *ADVERB*

usurp (*say* yoo- **zerp**) *VERB* **usurps, usurping, usurped**
to take a right or position of power from someone wrongfully or by force
▷ **usurpation** *NOUN*
▷ **usurper** *NOUN*

usury (*say* yoo- *zher*- ee) *NOUN*
the lending of money at an excessively high rate of interest
▷ **usurer** *NOUN*

utensil (*say* yoo- **ten**- sil) *NOUN* **utensils**
a tool, device, or container, especially one for use in the house

uterus (*say* yoo- ter- us) *NOUN* **uteruses**
the womb

utilitarian *ADJECTIVE*
designed to be useful rather than decorative or luxurious; practical

utility *NOUN* **utilities**
1 the quality of being useful
2 an organization that supplies water, gas, electricity, or other services to the community

utilize *VERB* **utilizes, utilizing, utilized**
to use something; to find a use for something
▷ **utilization** *NOUN*

USAGE NOTE This word can also be spelled utilise.

utmost *ADJECTIVE*
extreme or greatest
to do your utmost is to do the most that you are able to

Utopia (*say* yoo- **toh**- pee- a) *NOUN* **Utopias**
an imaginary place or state of things where everything is perfect
▷ **Utopian** *ADJECTIVE*

WORD HISTORY the title of a book by the 16th- century statesman and scholar Sir Thomas More, in which he describes an ideal society: from Greek *ou* 'not' and *topos* 'a place'

utter❶ *VERB* **utters, uttering, uttered**
to say or speak words or sounds; to make a sound with your mouth

The prisoner uttered a muffled cry, turning whiter than the sheet he was hiding under.
— *Alexandre Dumas, The Man in the Iron Mask*

▷ **utterance** *NOUN*

utter❷ *ADJECTIVE*
complete or absolute

In the meanwhile, the dwarves sat in darkness, and utter silence fell about them. — *J. R. R. Tolkien, The Hobbit*

▷ **utterly** *ADVERB*

uttermost *ADJECTIVE, NOUN*
extreme or greatest; utmost

U-turn *NOUN* **U-turns**
1 a U-shaped turn made in a vehicle so that it then travels in the opposite direction
2 a complete change of policy

Vv

a b c d e f g h i j k l m n o p q r s t u v w x y z

vacancy ***NOUN*** **vacancies**
1 a position or job that has not been filled
2 an available room in a hotel or guest house

vacant ***ADJECTIVE***
1 empty; not filled or occupied
2 without expression; blank

It was a big stuffed doll, a manikin with a vacant stupid human face. — *Philip Pullman, Northern Lights*

▷ **vacantly** ***ADVERB***

WORD FAMILY *Vacant* comes from Latin words *vacare* meaning 'to be empty' and *vacuus* meaning 'empty'. Other words connected with emptiness and having the same origin include *evacuate, vacate, vacation, vacuous*, and *vacuum*.

vacate ***VERB*** **vacates, vacating, vacated**
to leave or give up a place or position

vacation (*say* vak- **ay**- shon) ***NOUN*** **vacations**
a holiday period, especially between the terms in universities and law courts

vaccinate (*say* **vak**- sin- ayt) ***VERB*** **vaccinates, vaccinating, vaccinated**
to inoculate someone with a vaccine
▷ **vaccination** ***NOUN***

vaccine (*say* **vak**- seen) ***NOUN*** **vaccines**
a substance used to give someone immunity against a disease

WORD HISTORY from Latin *vacca* 'cow' (because serum from cows was used to protect people from the disease smallpox)

vacillate (*say* **vass**- il- ayt) ***VERB*** **vacillates, vacillating, vacillated**
to keep changing your mind; to waver
▷ **vacillation** ***NOUN***

vacuous (*say* **vak**- yoo- us) ***ADJECTIVE***
1 empty-headed; unintelligent
2 a vacuous look or stare is one without any expression
▷ **vacuously** ***ADVERB***
▷ **vacuousness** ***NOUN***
▷ **vacuity** ***NOUN***

vacuum ***NOUN*** **vacuums**
1 a completely empty space; a space without any air in it
2 (*informal*) a vacuum cleaner

vacuum ***VERB*** **vacuums, vacuuming, vacuumed**
to clean a room or area with a vacuum cleaner

vacuum cleaner ***NOUN*** **vacuum cleaners**
an electrical device that sucks up dust and dirt from floors and other surfaces

vacuum flask ***NOUN*** **vacuum flasks**
a container with double walls that have a vacuum between them, used for keeping liquids hot or cold

vagabond ***NOUN*** **vagabonds**
a person with no settled home or regular work; a vagrant

vagary (*say* **vay**- ger- ee) ***NOUN*** **vagaries**
an impulsive change or whim ◆ *Thanks to the vagaries of international politics, Ethiopia received only a small slice of the aid cake.*

vagina (*say* va- **jy**- na) ***NOUN*** **vaginas**
the passage that leads from the vulva to the womb

vagrant (*say* **vay**- grant) ***NOUN*** **vagrants**
a person with no settled home or regular work; a tramp
▷ **vagrancy** ***NOUN***

vague ***ADJECTIVE***
1 not definite or clear
2 not thinking clearly or precisely
▷ **vaguely** ***ADVERB***
▷ **vagueness** ***NOUN***

vain ***ADJECTIVE***
1 conceited, especially about your appearance
2 useless or unsuccessful ◆ *We moved through the water in the vain hope of seeing one of the otters that were said to live there.*

in vain with no result; uselessly ◆ *I looked in vain for the path that was marked on the map.*
▷ **vainly** ***ADVERB***

USAGE NOTE Take care not to confuse this word with *vane* or *vein*.

valance ***NOUN*** **valances**
a short curtain round the frame of a bed or above a window

vale ***NOUN*** **vales**
(*literary*) a valley

valediction (*say* val- id- **ik**- shon) ***NOUN*** **valedictions**
a farewell greeting
▷ **valedictory** ***ADJECTIVE***

valency ***NOUN*** **valencies**
(*Science*) the power of an atom to combine with other atoms, measured by the number of hydrogen atoms it is capable of combining with

valentine ***NOUN*** **valentines**
1 a card sent on St Valentine's day (14 February) to a person someone loves or is attracted to
2 the person who receives the card

valet (*say* **val**- ay or **val**- it) ***NOUN*** **valets**
a servant who takes care of a man's clothes and appearance

valetudinarian ***NOUN*** **valetudinarians**
a person who is excessively concerned about keeping healthy

valiant ***ADJECTIVE***
brave or courageous
▷ **valiantly** ***ADVERB***

valid ***ADJECTIVE***
1 a valid document or contract is one that is legally able to be used or accepted
2 reasoning is valid when it is sound and logical
▷ **validity** ***NOUN***

valley ***NOUN*** **valleys**
1 a long low area between hills
2 an area through which a river flows

valour ***NOUN***
bravery, especially in battle
▷ **valorous** ***ADJECTIVE***

valuable ***ADJECTIVE***
worth a lot of money; of great value
▷ **valuably** ***ADVERB***

valuables ***PLURAL NOUN***
valuable things

value ***NOUN*** **values**
1 the amount of money that is considered to be the equivalent of something, or for which it can be exchanged
2 the usefulness or importance of something
◆ *The task was to persuade pupils of the value of learning a language.*
3 (*Mathematics*) the number or quantity represented by a figure or term

value ***VERB*** **values, valuing, valued**
1 to think that something is valuable or important
2 to estimate the value of something
▷ **valuation** ***NOUN***
▷ **valuer** ***NOUN***

valueless ***ADJECTIVE***
having no value

valve ***NOUN*** **valves**
1 a device for controlling the flow of gas or liquid through a pipe or tube
2 a structure in the heart or in a blood vessel allowing blood to flow in one direction only
3 a device that controls the flow of electricity in old televisions and radios
4 each piece of the shell of an oyster

vamp ***NOUN*** **vamps**
(*informal*) an attractive woman who tries to seduce men

vampire ***NOUN*** **vampires**
in folklore, a dead person or creature that is supposed to leave its grave at night and suck blood from living people

van❶ ***NOUN*** **vans**
1 a covered vehicle for carrying goods
2 a railway carriage for luggage or goods, or for the use of the guard

van❷ ***NOUN***
the vanguard or forefront

vandal ***NOUN*** **vandals**
a person who deliberately breaks or damages things, especially public property
▷ **vandalism** ***NOUN***

WORD HISTORY named after the *Vandals*, a Germanic tribe who invaded the Roman Empire in the 5th century, destroying many books and works of art

vandalize ***VERB*** **vandalizes, vandalizing, vandalized**
to destroy or damage property deliberately

USAGE NOTE This word can also be spelled vandalise.

vane ***NOUN*** **vanes**
1 a weathervane
2 the blade of a propeller, sail of a windmill, or other device that acts on wind or water or is moved by them

USAGE NOTE Take care not to confuse this word with *vain* or *vein*.

vanguard ***NOUN***
1 the leading part of an army or fleet
2 the first people to adopt a fashion or idea

vanilla ***NOUN***
a flavouring obtained from the pods of a tropical plant

vanish ***VERB*** **vanishes, vanishing, vanished**
to disappear completely

> Snape stepped forward, waved his wand and the snake vanished in a small puff of black smoke.
> — *J. K. Rowling, Harry Potter and the Chamber of Secrets*

vanishing point ***NOUN***
(*Art*) the point at which parallel lines in a picture appear to meet and vanish because of the perspective

vanity ***NOUN***
conceit; the state of being vain

vanquish ***VERB*** **vanquishes, vanquishing, vanquished**
to defeat an opponent completely

vantage point ***NOUN*** **vantage points**
a place from which you have a good view of something

vapid ***ADJECTIVE***
not lively or interesting; dull

vaporize ***VERB*** **vaporizes, vaporizing, vaporized**
to change something into vapour, or to become vapour
▷ **vaporization** ***NOUN***
▷ **vaporizer** ***NOUN***

USAGE NOTE This word can also be spelled vaporise.

vapour *NOUN* **vapours**
a visible gas to which some substances can be converted by heat; steam or mist

USAGE NOTE The American spelling of this word is vapor.

variable *ADJECTIVE*
likely to vary; changeable
▷ **variably** *ADVERB*
▷ **variability** *NOUN*

variable *NOUN* **variables**
something that varies or can vary; a variable quantity

variance *NOUN*
the amount by which things differ
at variance differing or conflicting

variant *ADJECTIVE*
differing from something ◆ *There are several variant spellings of the name 'Shakespeare'.*
▷ **variant** *NOUN*

variation *NOUN* **variations**
1 varying; the amount by which something varies
2 a different form of something

varicose *ADJECTIVE*
varicose veins are permanently swollen

varied *ADJECTIVE*
of different sorts; full of variety

variegated (*say* **vair**- ig- ay- tid) *ADJECTIVE*
with patches of different colours
▷ **variegation** *NOUN*

variety *ADJECTIVE* **varieties**
1 a quantity of different kinds of things
2 the quality of not always being the same; variation
3 a particular kind of something, e.g. a plant or animal
4 an entertainment that includes short performances of various kinds
5 (*Language*) a particular form of a language

varieties of English

A **variety of English** is a form of the language that is associated with a particular place or culture. A variety can differ from standard British English in different ways: words can be pronounced or spelled differently, they can take different forms, and there can be some words that only exist in that variety. Here are a few examples, although each variety of English has many more features:
Australian English includes many diminutives like *arvo* (afternoon), *barbie* (barbecue), and *brekkie* (breakfast). **Indian English** includes many words that have now become part of standard English, such as *bhaji*, *chapatti*, and *sari*. In **Jamaican English**, the words *bear* and *beer*, and *fair* and *fear* are pronounced the same. **Scottish English** has many words that are not shared with standard English, such as *furth of* (beyond), *pinkie* (little finger), *short leet* (a shortlist) and *outwith* (outside). In **South African English**, the word *robot* has an additional meaning of 'traffic light'.
See also the panels on **American spelling** and **pronunciation**.

various *ADJECTIVE*
1 of several kinds; unlike one another ◆ *We did it for various reasons.*
2 several; individual and separate ◆ *Various people came late.*
▷ **variously** *ADVERB*

varnish *NOUN* **varnishes**
a liquid that dries to form a hard shiny usually transparent coating

varnish *VERB* **varnishes, varnishing, varnished**
to coat something with varnish

vary *VERB* **varies, varying, varied**
1 to make something different, or to become different; to change
2 to be different

vascular *ADJECTIVE*
the vascular system in animals and plants is the tubes and other vessels for circulating blood, sap, or water

vase *NOUN* **vases**
an open usually tall container used for holding cut flowers or as an ornament

Vaseline *NOUN*
(*trademark*) petroleum jelly for use as an ointment

WORD HISTORY from German *Wasser* 'water' and Greek *elaion* 'oil'

vassal *NOUN* **vassals**
a humble servant or subordinate

vast *ADJECTIVE*
very great, especially in area

Antarctica is a vast continent, twice the size of Australia. — *Paul Dowswell, True Polar Adventures*

▷ **vastly** *ADVERB*
▷ **vastness** *NOUN*

VAT *ABBREVIATION*
value added tax; a tax on goods and services

vat *NOUN* **vats**
a very large container for holding liquid

vaudeville (*say* **vawd**- vil) *NOUN*
a kind of variety entertainment popular in the early 20th century, with a mixture of music and comedy acts

WORD HISTORY from French *Vau de Vire*, name of a place in France where a 15th- century songwriter Olivier Basselin was born

vault *VERB* **vaults, vaulting, vaulted**
to jump over something, especially while supporting yourself on your hands or with the help of a pole

vault *NOUN* **vaults**
1 a vaulting jump
2 an arched roof
3 an underground room used to store things
4 a room for storing money or valuables
5 a burial chamber

vaulted *ADJECTIVE*
having an arched roof

vaulting horse *NOUN* **vaulting horses**
a padded wooden block for vaulting over in gymnastics

vaunt *VERB* **vaunts, vaunting, vaunted**
to boast something
▷ **vaunt** *NOUN*

VCR *ABBREVIATION*
video cassette recorder

VDU *ABBREVIATION*
(*ICT*) a visual display unit, a monitor for a computer

veal *NOUN*
calf's flesh used as food

vector *NOUN* **vectors**
(*Mathematics*) a quantity that has size and direction, such as velocity (which is speed in a certain direction)
▷ **vectorial** *ADJECTIVE*

Veda (*say* vay- da or vee- da) *NOUN*
the most ancient and sacred literature of the Hindus
▷ **Vedic** *ADJECTIVE*

WORD HISTORY a Sanskrit word meaning 'sacred knowledge'

veer *VERB* **veers, veering, veered**
to change direction; to swerve

A kestrel flew out of the monastery wall and veered away across the fields behind the farm. — *Barry Hines, A Kestrel for a Knave*

vegan *NOUN* **vegans**
a person who does not eat or use any animal products

vegetable *NOUN* **vegetables**
a plant that can be used as food

vegetarian *NOUN* **vegetarians**
a person who does not eat meat
▷ **vegetarianism** *NOUN*

vegetate *VERB* **vegetates, vegetating, vegetated**
to live a dull or inactive life

vegetation *NOUN*
plants that are growing

vehement (*say* vee- im- ent) *ADJECTIVE*
showing strong feeling ◆ *There was vehement opposition to the plan.*
▷ **vehemently** *ADVERB*
▷ **vehemence** *NOUN*

vehicle *NOUN* **vehicles**
a means of transporting people or goods, especially on land

veil *NOUN* **veils**
a piece of thin material worn to cover the face or head
to draw a veil over something is to avoid or stop discussing it

veil *VERB* **veils, veiling, veiled**
1 to cover something with a veil
2 a veiled threat or menace is one that is partly hidden or disguised

vein *NOUN* **veins**
1 any of the tubes that carry blood from all parts of the body to the heart (SEE ALSO **artery**)
2 a line or streak running through on a leaf, rock, insect's wing, or other material
3 a long deposit of mineral or ore in the middle of a rock
4 the mood or manner in which someone thinks or speaks

USAGE NOTE Take care not to confuse this word with *vain* or *vane*.

veld (*say* velt) *NOUN*
an area of open grassland in South Africa

From an early age, I spent most of my free time in the veld playing and fighting with the other boys of the village. — *Nelson Mandela, Long Walk to Freedom*

WORD HISTORY an Afrikaans word, from Dutch *veld* 'field'

vellum *NOUN*
smooth parchment or writing paper

velocity *NOUN* **velocities**
speed in a given direction

velour (*say* vil- **oor**) *NOUN*
a thick velvety material

velvet *NOUN*
a woven material with very short soft furry fibres on one side
▷ **velvety** *ADJECTIVE*

venal (*say* **veen**- al) *ADJECTIVE*
able or willing to take bribes or act dishonestly
▷ **venality** *NOUN*

vend *VERB* **vends, vending, vended**
to offer something for sale

vendetta *NOUN* **vendettas**
a long-lasting bitter quarrel; a feud

vending machine *NOUN* **vending machines**
a slot machine for obtaining drinks, chocolate, cigarettes, or other small items

vendor *NOUN* **vendors**
(*formal*) someone who is selling something, especially a house

veneer *NOUN* **veneers**
1 a thin layer of good wood covering the surface of a cheaper wood
2 an outward show of some good quality ♦ *His veneer of good humour vanished instantly.*

venerable *ADJECTIVE*
worthy of respect or honour, especially because of great age

venerate *VERB* **venerates, venerating, venerated**
to honour someone with great respect or reverence
▷ **veneration** *NOUN*

venereal (*say* vin- **eer**- ee- al) *ADJECTIVE*
to do with sexual intercourse

venereal disease *NOUN* **venereal diseases**
a disease passed on by sexual intercourse

venetian blind *NOUN* **venetian blinds**
a window blind consisting of horizontal strips that can be adjusted to let light in or shut it out

vengeance *NOUN*
retaliation in revenge against someone who has done you harm
with a vengeance with great force or intensity

Whatever else of Rome the British had not taken to, they seemed to have taken to the Games with a vengeance, Marcus thought. — *Rosemary Sutcliff, The Eagle of the Ninth*

vengeful *ADJECTIVE*
seeking vengeance
▷ **vengefully** *ADVERB*
▷ **vengefulness** *NOUN*

venial (*say* **veen**- ee- al) *ADJECTIVE*
venial sins or faults are pardonable and not serious

venison *NOUN*
deer's flesh as food

Venn diagram *NOUN* **Venn diagrams**
(*Mathematics*) a diagram in which circles are used to show the relationships between different sets of things

WORD HISTORY named after an English mathematician, John *Venn* (1834–1923)

venom *NOUN*
1 the poisonous fluid produced by animals such as snakes and scorpions
2 strong bitterness or spitefulness
▷ **venomous** *ADJECTIVE*

vent *NOUN* **vents**
an opening that lets out smoke, gas, or liquid from a space
to give vent to feelings is to express your feelings openly

vent *VERB* **vents, venting, vented**
1 to make a vent in something
2 to give vent to feelings

Here on the dump she could cry and scream and vent her anger. There was no one to hear her. — *Catherine MacPhail, Run Zan Run*

ventilate *VERB* **ventilates, ventilating, ventilated**
to let air move freely in and out of a room or building
▷ **ventilation** *NOUN*
▷ **ventilator** *NOUN*

ventral *ADJECTIVE*
on or to do with the abdomen or underside of an animal or plant

ventriloquist *NOUN* **ventriloquists**
an entertainer who makes their voice sound as if it comes from another source
▷ **ventriloquism** *NOUN*

WORD HISTORY from Latin *venter* 'belly' and *loqui* 'to speak' (from the ancient belief that people who were possessed by an evil spirit spoke from their stomachs)

venture *NOUN* **ventures**
something adventurous or risky that you decide to do

venture *VERB* **ventures, venturing, ventured**
to dare or be bold enough to do or say something or to go somewhere

'What's the matter?' asked Sorrel sarcastically, venturing so close to the edge of the chasm that her furry toes were over empty space. 'Don't you like mountains?' — *Cornelia Funke, Dragon Rider*

venturesome *ADJECTIVE*
ready to take risks; daring

venue (*say* **ven**- yoo) *NOUN* **venues**
the place where a special event such as a meeting, sports match, or concert is held

veracity (*say* ver- as- it- ee) *NOUN*
(*formal*) truth or being truthful
▷ **veracious** (*say* ver- ay- shus) *ADJECTIVE*

veranda *NOUN* **verandas**
a terrace with a roof along the side of a house

verb ***NOUN*** **verbs**
(*Grammar*) a word that refers to an action or state, e.g. *bring, came, sing, were*

WORD FAMILY *Verb* comes from the Latin word *verbum* meaning 'word'. Other words connected with 'word' and having the same origin include *adverb, proverb, verbal, verbatim,* and *verbose.*

verbs

A **verb** can describe an action or process (e.g. *dive, chew, heal, thaw*), a feeling (e.g. *think, know, believe*), or a state (e.g. *be, remain*). A sentence usually contains at least one verb.

Verbs change their form according to which person (*I, you, he, she, it, we,* or *they*) and tense (past, present, or future) they are in. **Regular verbs** change their endings in predictable ways, e.g. by adding *-s* or *-ed*: *I shout, she shouts, we shouted*, etc. **Irregular verbs** have more varied forms, especially in the past tense: *we swim, we swam, we have swum; I am, we were, they have been.*

An **auxiliary verb** is used to form the tenses of another verb, for example *have* in *I have just received this email*, and *will* in *They will never find us here*. The auxiliary verbs *can, will, shall, may,* and *must* are also called **modal verbs**; they are used to express a wish, need, ability, or permission to do something. A **phrasal verb** includes a preposition or adverb, for example *drop in, chill out,* and *wrap up.*

Note the forms of the following verbs, which are sometimes misspelled: *abandons, abandoning, abandoned; occurs, occurring, occurred.* You will find guidance in this dictionary on the various forms of individual verbs.

See also the panel on **tenses**.

verbal ***ADJECTIVE***
1 to do with words, or in the form of words
2 spoken and not written
3 to do with a verb
▷ **verbally** ***ADVERB***

verbatim (*say* ver- **bay**- tim) ***ADVERB, ADJECTIVE***
in exactly the same words as were originally used ◆ *She was quoting verbatim from a speech made the previous year.*

verbose ***ADJECTIVE***
using more words than are needed
▷ **verbosely** ***ADVERB***
▷ **verbosity** (*say* ver- **boss**- it- ee) ***NOUN***

verdant ***ADJECTIVE***
verdant grass or fields are fresh and green

verdict ***NOUN*** **verdicts**
a judgement or decision made after considering something, especially that made by a jury

verdigris (*say* **verd**- i- grees) ***NOUN***
green rust on copper or brass

WORD HISTORY from French *vert-de-gris* literally 'green of Greece'

verdure ***NOUN***
green vegetation; its greenness

verge ***NOUN*** **verges**
1 a strip of grass along the edge of a road or path
2 to be on the verge of something is to be close to doing it

verge ***VERB*** **verges, verging, verged**
to verge on something is to border on it or be close to it

verger ***NOUN*** **vergers**
a person who is caretaker and attendant in a church

verify ***VERB*** **verifies, verifying, verified**
to check or show that something is true or correct
▷ **verifiable** ***ADJECTIVE***
▷ **verification** ***NOUN***

verisimilitude ***NOUN***
an appearance of being true or lifelike

veritable ***ADJECTIVE***
real; rightly named ◆ *She was a veritable mine of useful information.*
▷ **veritably** ***ADVERB***

verity ***NOUN*** **verities**
(*formal*) a truth principle or belief

vermicelli (*say* verm- i- **chel**- ee) ***NOUN***
pasta made in long thin threads

vermilion ***NOUN, ADJECTIVE***
bright red

vermin ***PLURAL NOUN***
animals or insects that damage crops or food or carry disease, such as rats and fleas
▷ **verminous** ***ADJECTIVE***

vernacular (*say* ver- **nak**- yoo- ler) ***NOUN*** **vernaculars**
the language of a country or district, as distinct from an official or formal language

vernal ***ADJECTIVE***
to do with the season of spring

verruca (*say* ver- **oo**- ka) ***NOUN*** **verrucas**
a kind of wart on the sole of the foot

versatile ***ADJECTIVE***
able to do or be used for many different things
▷ **versatility** ***NOUN***

verse ***NOUN*** **verses**
1 writing arranged in short lines, usually with a particular rhythm and often with rhymes; poetry
2 a group of lines forming a unit in a poem or song
3 each of the short numbered sections of a chapter in the Bible

versed ***ADJECTIVE***
to be versed in something is to be experienced or skilled in it

version *NOUN* **versions**
1 a particular person's account of something that happened
2 a translation or modern edition of a book or text
3 a special or different form of something

WORD FAMILY *Version* comes from the Latin words *vertere* meaning 'to turn' and *versum* meaning 'turned or transformed'. These include *adverse, averse, avert, controversy, convert, divert, invert, introvert, perverse, pervert, reverse, revert, subvert, vertebra,* and *vertigo.*

versus *PREPOSITION*
against; competing with ◆ *It will be Germany versus France in the final.* ◆ *The choice is one of speed versus accuracy.*

vertebra *NOUN* **vertebrae**
each of the bones that form the backbone

vertebrate *NOUN* **vertebrates**
(*Biology*) an animal that has a backbone (SEE ALSO **invertebrate**)
▷ **vertebrate** *ADJECTIVE*

vertex *NOUN* **vertices** (*say* ver- tis- eez)
(*Mathematics*) the highest point of a cone or triangle, or other figure

vertical *ADJECTIVE*
at right angles to something horizontal; upright (SEE ALSO **horizontal**)
▷ **vertically** *ADVERB*

vertigo *NOUN*
a feeling of dizziness and loss of balance, especially when you are very high up

verve *NOUN*
enthusiasm and liveliness

very *ADVERB*
1 to a great amount or intensity; extremely ◆ *It has been very warm lately.*
2 used to emphasize something ◆ *It was the very next house.*

SYNONYMS extremely, highly, deeply, exceedingly, acutely, truly

very *ADJECTIVE*
1 exact or actual ◆ *It was the very thing we wanted.*
2 at an extreme point ◆ *Go to the very end of the street.*

vespers *PLURAL NOUN*
a church service held in the evening

vessel *NOUN* **vessels**
1 a ship or boat
2 a container, especially for liquid
3 a tube carrying blood or other liquid in the body of an animal or plant

vest *NOUN* **vests**
a piece of underwear covering the trunk of the body

vest *VERB* **vests, vesting, vested**
to give something as a right ◆ *In those days a lot of power was vested in the head of the household.*

vested interest *NOUN* **vested interests**
a strong reason that someone wants something, usually because they get some benefit from it

vestibule *NOUN* **vestibules**
1 an entrance hall or lobby
2 a church porch

vestige *NOUN* **vestiges**
a trace; a very small amount, especially of something that formerly existed
▷ **vestigial** *ADJECTIVE*

vestment *NOUN* **vestments**
a ceremonial garment, especially one worn by clergy or choir at a service

vestry *NOUN* **vestries**
a room in a church where vestments are kept and where clergy and choir put these on

vet *NOUN* **vets**
a person trained to give medical and surgical treatment to animals

vet *VERB* **vets, vetting, vetted**
to make a careful check of a person or thing, especially of someone's background before employing them

Everyone who worked in Roscoe's private office had been hand-picked and thoroughly vetted. It was impossible to see him without an appointment. — *Anthony Horowitz, Point Blanc*

vetch *NOUN*
a plant of the pea family

veteran *NOUN* **veterans**
a person who has long experience, especially in the armed forces

veteran car *NOUN* **veteran cars**
a car made before 1916

veterinary (*say* vet- rin- ree) *ADJECTIVE*
to do with the medical and surgical treatment of animals

veto (*say* vee- toh) *NOUN* **vetoes**
1 a refusal to let something happen
2 the right to prohibit something

veto *VERB* **vetoes, vetoing, vetoed**
to refuse or prohibit something

vex *VERB* **vexes, vexing, vexed**
to annoy somebody or cause them worry
▷ **vexation** *NOUN*
▷ **vexatious** *ADJECTIVE*

vexed question *NOUN* **vexed questions**
a problem that is difficult or much discussed

VHF *ABBREVIATION*
very high frequency

via (*say* vy- a) ***PREPOSITION***
1 through; by way of ◆ *The train went to Venice via Paris.* ◆ *He sneaked in via the back door.*
2 by means of

viable ***ADJECTIVE***
able to work or exist successfully ◆ *The plan must be viable and realistic.*
▷ **viability** ***NOUN***

viaduct ***NOUN*** **viaducts**
a long bridge, usually with many arches, carrying a road or railway over a valley or low ground

vial ***NOUN*** **vials**
a small glass bottle

viands (*say* vy- andz) ***PLURAL NOUN***
(*old use*) items of food

vibrant ***ADJECTIVE***
full of energy; lively

vibraphone ***NOUN*** **vibraphones**
a musical instrument like a xylophone with metal bars under which there are tiny electric fans making a vibrating effect

vibrate ***VERB*** **vibrates, vibrating, vibrated**
1 to shake very quickly to and fro
2 to make a throbbing sound
▷ **vibration** ***NOUN***

vicar ***NOUN*** **vicars**
a member of the Church of England clergy who is in charge of a parish

WORD HISTORY from Latin *vicarius* 'a substitute or deputy' (because originally a vicar looked after a parish for an absent parson or rector, or for a monastery)

vicarage ***NOUN*** **vicarages**
the house of a vicar

vicarious (*say* vik- **air**- ee- us) ***ADJECTIVE***
experienced through the feelings or actions of someone else ◆ *A good novel invites you to enjoy a vicarious experience outside your own life.*

vice ❶ ***NOUN*** **vices**
1 evil or wickedness
2 an evil or bad habit; a bad fault

vice ❷ ***NOUN*** **vices**
a device for gripping something and holding it firmly while you work on it

viceroy ***NOUN*** **viceroys**
(*History*) an official governing a colony on behalf of the king or queen of the ruling power

vice versa ***ADVERB***
the other way round ◆ *You can move money online from your main account to a reserve account and vice versa.*

WORD HISTORY Latin words meaning 'the position being reversed'

vicinity ***NOUN***
the area near or round a place ◆ *Two other men were found in the vicinity of the crime.*

vicious ***ADJECTIVE***
1 cruel and aggressive
2 severe or violent

Nine days after Eragon's return, a vicious blizzard blew out of the mountains and settled over the valley. — *Christopher Paolini, Eragon*

▷ **viciously** ***ADVERB***
▷ **viciousness** ***NOUN***

vicious circle ***NOUN*** **vicious circles**
a situation in which a problem produces an effect which in turn makes the problem worse

vicissitude (*say* viss- iss- i- tewd) ***NOUN*** **vicissitudes**
a change of circumstances or fortune

victim ***NOUN*** **victims**
a person who is injured, killed, or robbed as a result of a crime or misfortune

victimize ***VERB*** **victimizes, victimizing, victimized**
to single someone out for harsh or unfair treatment
▷ **victimization** ***NOUN***

USAGE NOTE This word can also be spelled victimise.

victor ***NOUN*** **victors**
the winner

Victorian ***ADJECTIVE***
belonging to the time of Queen Victoria (1837–1901)
▷ **Victorian** ***NOUN***

victory ***NOUN*** **victories**
success won against an opponent in a battle, contest, or game
▷ **victorious** ***ADJECTIVE***

victualler (*say* **vit**- ler) ***NOUN*** **victuallers**
a person who supplies food and drink

victuals (*say* vit- alz) ***PLURAL NOUN***
(*old use*) food and drink

video ***NOUN*** **videos**
1 the recording on tape of pictures and sound
2 a video recorder or cassette
3 a television programme or a film recorded on a video cassette

video ***VERB*** **videos, videoing, videoed**
to record pictures and sound on videotape

video game ***NOUN*** **video games**
a game in which you press electronic controls to move images on a screen

video recorder or **video cassette recorder** ***NOUN*** **video recorders** or **video cassette recorders**
a device for recording television programmes on videotape and for playing video cassettes

videotape ***NOUN*** **videotapes**
magnetic tape suitable for recording television programmes

vie ***VERB*** **vies, vying, vied**
to compete; to carry on a rivalry

Touchstone looked at her, sadness and exhaustion vying for first place in his gaze. — *Garth Nix, Sabriel*

view ***NOUN*** **views**
1 what can be seen from one place, especially a beautiful or interesting scene

From our road we had a view of the whole of Steeple Honey as we descended the hill. — *John Wyndham, The Day of the Triffids*

2 sight or range of vision ◆ *At the end of the road, the house came into view.*
3 an opinion ◆ *The old man tried to explain his views on the matter.*

in view of because of
on view displayed for inspection
with a view to with the hope or intention of

view ***VERB*** **views, viewing, viewed**
1 to look at something
2 to consider or regard someone or something in a particular way ◆ *She viewed him with deep suspicion.*

viewer ***NOUN*** **viewers**
someone who views something, especially a television programme

viewpoint ***NOUN*** **viewpoints**
1 an opinion or point of view
2 a place giving a good view

vigil (*say* **vij**- il) ***NOUN*** **vigils**
a period of staying awake to keep watch or to pray

vigilant (*say* **vij**- il- ant) ***ADJECTIVE***
keeping careful watch for danger or difficulties
▷ **vigilantly** ***ADVERB***
▷ **vigilance** ***NOUN***

vigilante (*say* vij- il- **an**- tee) ***NOUN*** **vigilantes**
a member of a group who organize themselves, without authority, to try to prevent crime and disorder in their community

vigorous ***ADJECTIVE***
full of strength and energy
▷ **vigorously** ***ADVERB***

vigour ***NOUN***
strength and energy

USAGE NOTE The American spelling of this word is vigor.

Viking ***NOUN*** **Vikings**
a Scandinavian trader and pirate in the 8th–11th centuries

vile ***ADJECTIVE***
1 extremely disgusting

Supper was dry bread, and dried smoked fish, which tasted vile. — *Ursula Le Guin, The Tombs of Atuan*

2 very bad or wicked
▷ **vilely** ***ADVERB***
▷ **vileness** ***NOUN***

vilify (*say* **vil**- if- eye) ***VERB*** **vilifies, vilifying, vilified**
to say unpleasant things about a person or thing
▷ **vilification** ***NOUN***

villa ***NOUN*** **villas**
a house, especially a holiday home abroad

village ***NOUN*** **villages**
a group of houses and other buildings in a country district, smaller than a town and usually having a church
▷ **villager** ***NOUN***

villain ***NOUN*** **villains**
a wicked person or a criminal
▷ **villainous** ***ADJECTIVE***
▷ **villainy** ***NOUN***

villein (*say* **vil**- an or **vil**- ayn) ***NOUN*** **villeins**
(*History*) a tenant in feudal times

vim ***NOUN***
(*informal*) vigour or energy

vindicate ***VERB*** **vindicates, vindicating, vindicated**
1 to clear a person of blame or suspicion
2 to prove something to be true or worthwhile
▷ **vindication** ***NOUN***

vindictive ***ADJECTIVE***
showing a desire for revenge; spiteful
▷ **vindictively** ***ADVERB***
▷ **vindictiveness** ***NOUN***

vine ***NOUN*** **vines**
a climbing or trailing plant whose fruit is the grape

vinegar ***NOUN***
a sour liquid used to flavour food or in pickling

vineyard (*say* **vin**- yard) ***NOUN*** **vineyards**
a plantation of vines producing grapes for making wine

vintage ***NOUN*** **vintages**
1 the harvest of a season's grapes; the wine made from this
2 the period from which something comes

vintage car ***NOUN*** **vintage cars**
a car made between 1917 and 1930

vinyl ***NOUN***
a kind of plastic

viola[1] (*say* vee- **oh**- la) *NOUN* **violas**
a musical instrument like a violin but slightly larger and with a lower pitch

viola[2] (*say* vy- ol- a) *NOUN* **violas**
a plant of the kind that includes violets and pansies

violate *VERB* **violates, violating, violated**
1 to break a promise or agreement
2 to treat a person or place with disrespect and violence
▷ **violation** *NOUN*
▷ **violator** *NOUN*

violence *NOUN*
1 physical force that does harm or damage
2 strength or intensity ◆ *The wind blew up with sudden violence.*

violent *ADJECTIVE*
1 using or involving violence
2 strong or intense ◆ *The decision provoked violent demonstrations.*
▷ **violently** *ADVERB*

violet *NOUN* **violets**
1 a small plant that often has purple flowers
2 a purple colour

violin *NOUN* **violins**
a musical instrument with four strings, played with a bow
▷ **violinist** *NOUN*

VIP *ABBREVIATION*
very important person

viper *NOUN* **vipers**
a small poisonous snake

virago (*say* vir- **ah**- goh) *NOUN* **viragos**
a fierce or bullying woman

virgin *NOUN* **virgins**
a person, especially a girl or woman, who has never had sexual intercourse
▷ **virginal** *ADJECTIVE*
▷ **virginity** *NOUN*

virgin *ADJECTIVE*
not yet touched or used ◆ *The travellers were passing through virgin territory.*

virginals *PLURAL NOUN*
an instrument rather like a harpsichord, used in the 16th–17th centuries
WORD HISTORY from Latin *virginalis* 'to do with virgins' (because it was often played by young women)

virile (*say* **vir**- yl) *ADJECTIVE*
having masculine strength or vigour, especially sexually
▷ **virility** *NOUN*

virology *NOUN*
(*Medicine*) the study of viruses
▷ **virological** *ADJECTIVE*
▷ **virologist** *NOUN*

virtual *ADJECTIVE*
1 being something in effect though not strictly in fact ◆ *There has been a virtual elimination of many infectious diseases over the past century.*
2 (*ICT*) existing as a computer image and not physically
3 (*Science*) to do with the points at which light rays would meet if extended backwards

virtually *ADVERB*
nearly or almost

virtual reality *NOUN*
an image or environment produced by a computer, which a user can interact with using a keyboard or other input device

virtue *NOUN* **virtues**
1 moral goodness, or a particular form of this ◆ *Patience is a virtue.*
2 a good quality or advantage ◆ *The great virtue of the book is the clear way it explains things.*
by virtue of because of

virtuous *ADJECTIVE*
having or showing moral goodness
▷ **virtuously** *ADVERB*

virtuoso (*say* ver- tew- **oh**- soh) *NOUN* **virtuosos or virtuosi**
a person with outstanding skill, especially in singing or playing music
▷ **virtuosity** *NOUN*

virulent (*say* **vir**- oo- lent) *ADJECTIVE*
1 strongly poisonous or harmful ◆ *The community suffered from a virulent attack of cholera.*
2 bitterly hostile ◆ *He was a virulent critic of these methods.*
▷ **virulence** *NOUN*

virus *NOUN* **viruses**
1 a very tiny living thing, smaller than a bacterium, that can cause disease
2 a disease caused by a virus
3 (*ICT*) a hidden set of instructions in a computer program that is designed to destroy data or do other damage to a system

visa (*say* **vee**- za) *NOUN* **visas**
an official mark put on a person's passport by officials of a foreign country to show that the holder has permission to enter the country

visage (*say* **viz**- ij) *NOUN* **visages**
a person's face

vis-à-vis (*say* veez- ah- **vee**) *ADVERB, PREPOSITION*
1 in a position facing one another; opposite to
2 as compared with
WORD HISTORY French words meaning 'face to face'

viscera (*say* **vis**- er- a) *PLURAL NOUN*
the intestines and other internal organs of the body

viscid (*say* vis- id) ADJECTIVE
thick and gluey
▷ **viscidity** NOUN

viscose (*say* vis- kohs) NOUN
fabric made from viscous cellulose

viscount (*say* vy- kownt) NOUN **viscounts**
a nobleman ranking below an earl and above a baron
▷ **viscountess** NOUN

viscous (*say* visk- us) ADJECTIVE
thick and gluey, not pouring easily
▷ **viscosity** NOUN

visibility NOUN
the distance you can see clearly ◆ *In the mist visibility was reduced to ten metres.*

visible ADJECTIVE
able to be seen or noticed ◆ *The tornado was clearly visible from satellites.*
▷ **visibly** ADVERB

USAGE NOTE Take care not to confuse this word with *visual.*

vision NOUN **visions**
1 the ability to see; sight
2 something seen in a person's imagination or in a dream
3 foresight and wisdom in planning things
4 a person or thing that is beautiful to see

WORD FAMILY *Vision* comes from Latin words *videre* meaning 'to see' and *visum* meaning 'seen'. Other words to do with seeing and having the same origin include *advice, advise, envisage, improvise, provide, supervise, survey, televise, video, view, visa, visage, visible,* and *visual.*

visionary ADJECTIVE
extremely imaginative or fanciful

visionary NOUN **visionaries**
a person with extremely imaginative ideas and plans

visit VERB **visits, visiting, visited**
1 to go to see a person or place
2 to stay somewhere for a while
▷ **visitor** NOUN

visit NOUN **visits**
1 going to see a person or place
2 a short stay somewhere

visitant NOUN **visitants**
1 a visitor, especially a supernatural one
2 a bird that is a visitor to an area while migrating

visitation NOUN **visitations**
an official visit, especially to inspect something

visor (*say* vy- zer) NOUN **visors**
1 the part of a helmet that covers the face
2 a shield to protect the eyes from bright light or sunshine

vista NOUN **vistas**
a long view

visual ADJECTIVE
to do with or used in seeing; to do with sight
▷ **visually** ADVERB

USAGE NOTE Take care not to confuse this word with *visible.*

visual aid NOUN **visual aids**
a picture, slide, or film used as an aid in teaching

visual display unit NOUN **visual display units**
a device that looks like a television screen and displays data being received from a computer or fed into it

visualize VERB **visualizes, visualizing, visualized**
to form a mental picture of something
▷ **visualization** NOUN

USAGE NOTE This word can also be spelled visualise.

vital ADJECTIVE
1 a vital function or activity is one that is necessary for life to continue, such as breathing
2 essential; very important ◆ *It is vital to seek medical help as soon as possible.*
▷ **vitally** ADVERB

vitality NOUN
liveliness or energy

vitamin (*say* vit- a- min or vy- ta- min) NOUN **vitamins**
any of a number of substances that are present in various foods and are essential to keep people and animals healthy

WORD HISTORY from Latin *vita* 'life' and *amine* a kind of chemical related to amino acids, which vitamins were once thought to contain

vitiate (*say* vish- ee- ayt) VERB **vitiates, vitiating, vitiated**
(*formal*) to spoil or damage something and make it less effective
▷ **vitiation** NOUN

vitreous (*say* vit- ree- us) ADJECTIVE
like glass in being hard, transparent, or brittle

vitriol (*say* vit- ree- ol) NOUN
1 sulphuric acid or one of its compounds
2 savage criticism
▷ **vitriolic** ADJECTIVE

vituperation NOUN
abusive words

viva (*say* vy- va) NOUN **vivas**
a spoken examination, usually for an academic qualification

vivacious (*say* viv- **ay**- shus) ***ADJECTIVE***
happy and lively

Theo looked very handsome in his black dress suit and Myra Levant very vivacious in red and black. — *Pamela Oldfield, My Story: Victorian Workhouse*

▷ **vivaciously** ***ADVERB***
▷ **vivacity** ***NOUN***

viva voce (*say* vy- va **voh**- chee) ***ADJECTIVE, ADVERB***
a viva voce examination is spoken and not written
▷ **viva voce** ***NOUN***

WORD HISTORY Latin words meaning 'with the living voice'

vivid ***ADJECTIVE***
1 bright and strong or clear ◆ *The chairs and other furniture were painted in vivid colours.* ◆ *The scene is described in vivid detail.*
2 active and lively ◆ *I always said she had a vivid imagination.*
▷ **vividly** ***ADVERB***
▷ **vividness** ***NOUN***

WORD FAMILY *Vivid* comes from the Latin words *vivere* meaning 'to live' and *vivus* meaning 'alive'. Other words having the same origin include *revive, survive, vivacious*, and *vivisection*.

vivisection ***NOUN***
the practice of carrying out surgical experiments on live animals

vixen ***NOUN*** **vixens**
a female fox

vizier (*say* viz- **eer**) ***NOUN*** **viziers**
(*History*) an important official in certain Muslim countries

WORD HISTORY from Arabic *wazir* 'chief counsellor'

vocabulary ***NOUN*** **vocabularies**
1 all the words used in a particular subject or language

Do you know that Newspeak is the only language in the world whose vocabulary gets smaller every year? — *George Orwell, Nineteen Eighty-four*

2 the words known to an individual person ◆ *You need a large vocabulary to describe these events properly.*
3 a list of words with their meanings

vocal ***ADJECTIVE***
to do with or using the voice
▷ **vocally** ***ADVERB***

WORD FAMILY *Vocal* comes from the Latin words *vocare* meaning 'to call, speak, or summon' or *vocis* meaning 'of the voice'. Other words having the same origin include *advocate, evoke, invoke, provoke, revoke, vocabulary, vocation*, and *vociferous*.

vocal cords ***PLURAL NOUN***
two strap-like membranes in the throat that can be made to vibrate and produce sounds

vocalist ***NOUN*** **vocalists**
a singer, especially in a pop group

vocation ***NOUN*** **vocations**
1 a person's job or occupation
2 a strong desire to do a particular kind of work, or a feeling of being called by God to do something

vocational ***ADJECTIVE***
teaching you the skills you need for a particular job or profession ◆ *There is a need to increase vocational opportunities for young people.*

vociferous (*say* vo- **sif**- er- us) ***ADJECTIVE***
noisily and forcefully expressing your views

vodka ***NOUN*** **vodkas**
a strong alcoholic drink very popular in Russia

vogue ***NOUN*** **vogues**
a current fashion
in vogue popular; in fashion

voice ***NOUN*** **voices**
1 sounds formed by the vocal cords and uttered by the mouth, especially in speaking or singing ◆ *She continued in a clear voice.*
2 to lose your voice is to be unable to speak or sing
3 an opinion or the person expressing it ◆ *There was not a single dissenting voice.*
4 the right to express an opinion or desire ◆ *I have no voice in this matter.*
5 (*Grammar*) the form of a verb that makes it active or passive

voice ***VERB*** **voices, voicing, voiced**
to express something in words ◆ *It was time to voice their concerns openly.*

voice-over ***NOUN*** **voice-overs**
a piece of narration in a film or television broadcast without the speaker being shown on the screen

void ***ADJECTIVE***
1 not legally valid or binding
2 completely empty
3 lacking something ◆ *a remark void of all humour*

void ***NOUN*** **voids**
an empty space or hole

The river here is broad and swollen, and roars as it hurls itself down into the swirling, misty void below. — *Paul Stewart and Chris Riddell, Beyond the Deep Woods*

voile (*say* voil) ***NOUN***
a very thin almost transparent material

volatile (*say* **vol**- a- tyl) ***ADJECTIVE***
1 a volatile liquid evaporates rapidly
2 changing quickly from one mood or interest to another
▷ **volatility** ***NOUN***

volcano *NOUN* **volcanoes**
a mountain with an opening at the top from which lava, ashes, and hot gases from below the earth's crust are or have been thrown out
▷ **volcanic** *ADJECTIVE*
WORD HISTORY an Italian word, from *Volcanus*, the ancient Roman god of fire

vole *NOUN* **voles**
a small animal rather like a rat

volition *NOUN*
to do something of your own volition is to choose to do it

volley *NOUN* **volleys**
1 a number of bullets, shells, or arrows fired together
2 the action of hitting back the ball in tennis or football before it touches the ground

volley *VERB* **volleys, volleying, volleyed**
to send or hit something in a volley or volleys

volleyball *NOUN*
a game in which two teams hit a large ball to and fro over a net with their hands

volt *NOUN* **volts**
a unit for measuring electric force
WORD HISTORY named after an Italian scientist, Alessandro *Volta* (1745–1827), who discovered how to produce electricity by a chemical reaction

voltage *NOUN* **voltages**
electric force measured in volts

volte-face (*say* volt- **fahs**) *NOUN*
a complete change in your attitude towards something

voluble *ADJECTIVE*
talking very much
▷ **volubly** *ADVERB*
▷ **volubility** *NOUN*

volume *NOUN* **volumes**
1 an amount or quantity of something ◆ *The volume of trade has increased in the last year.*
2 (*Mathematics*) the amount of space filled by something
3 the strength or power of sound produced by a radio, televison, or other equipment
4 a book, especially one of a set
WORD HISTORY from Latin *volumen* 'a roll' (because ancient books were made in a rolled form)

voluminous (*say* vol- **yoo**- min- us) *ADJECTIVE*
1 bulky; large and full
2 able to hold a lot

voluntary *ADJECTIVE*
1 done or doing something willingly, not because you are forced to do it
2 voluntary work is work you do willingly and without being paid for it
▷ **voluntarily** *ADVERB*

voluntary *NOUN* **voluntaries**
an organ solo, often improvised, played before or after a church service

volunteer *VERB* **volunteers, volunteering, volunteered**
1 to offer to do something of your own accord, without being asked or forced to

> Mrs Miller threw her puffy arm into the air and volunteered to run a canteen for any troops that might pass through. — *Michelle Magorian, Goodnight Mister Tom*

2 to provide or offer something willingly or freely ◆ *He volunteered his own opinion.*

volunteer *NOUN* **volunteers**
a person who volunteers to do something, e.g. to serve in the armed forces

voluptuous *ADJECTIVE*
1 giving a luxurious feeling ◆ *The room was adorned with voluptuous furnishings.*
2 a woman is voluptuous when she has an attractively curved figure

vomit *VERB* **vomits, vomiting, vomited**
to bring up food from the stomach and out through the mouth; to be sick
▷ **vomit** *NOUN*

voodoo *NOUN*
a form of witchcraft and magical rites, especially in the West Indies
WORD HISTORY via American French from a West African language

voracious (*say* vor- **ay**- shus) *ADJECTIVE*
greedy; devouring things eagerly
▷ **voraciously** *ADVERB*
▷ **voracity** *NOUN*

vortex *NOUN* **vortices**
a whirlpool or whirlwind

vote *VERB* **votes, voting, voted**
to make a choice between several people or things by marking a paper or by putting up your hand
▷ **voter** *NOUN*

vote *NOUN* **votes**
1 the action of voting
2 the right to vote

votive *ADJECTIVE*
a votive offering is one you make to fulfil a vow

vouch *VERB* **vouches, vouching, vouched**
to vouch for something is to guarantee that it is true or genuine

voucher *NOUN* **vouchers**
a piece of paper that can be exchanged for certain goods or services; a receipt

a b c d e f g h i j k l m n o p q r s t u v w x y z

vouchsafe *VERB* **vouchsafes, vouchsafing, vouchsafed**
(*formal*) to grant or admit something in a gracious or condescending way ◆ *They did not vouchsafe how much damage had been done.*

vow *NOUN* **vows**
a solemn promise, especially to God or a saint

vow *VERB* **vows, vowing, vowed**
to make a vow

vowel *NOUN* **vowels**
(*Language*) any of the letters which represent sounds in which breath comes out freely (SEE ALSO **consonant**)

> ***vowels***
>
> The **vowels** in the English alphabet are: *a, e, i, o,* and *u*. The letter *y* also acts as a vowel in some words, e.g. *crypt, pyramid,* and *syrup.*
> In the ancient Roman alphabet (from which the English alphabet is derived), the letter *u* could represent either the sound of *u*, or (before a vowel) the sound of *w*; you can still find this pronunciation of *u* in words like *quest* and *suave.*
> Vowel sounds are pronounced using mainly your vocal cords, whereas most consonants (*b, c, d, f,* and so on) are shaped using your lips, teeth, tongue, and throat.
> See also the panel on **consonants**.

voyage *NOUN* **voyages**
a long journey on water or in space

voyage *VERB* **voyages, voyaging, voyaged**
to make a voyage
▷ **voyager** *NOUN*

vulcanize *VERB* **vulcanizes, vulcanizing, vulcanized**
to treat rubber with sulphur to strengthen it
▷ **vulcanization** *NOUN*

USAGE NOTE This word can also be spelled vulcanise.

WORD HISTORY from *Volcanus*, the ancient Roman god of fire (because the rubber has to be made very hot)

vulgar *ADJECTIVE*
rude; without good manners
▷ **vulgarly** *ADVERB*
▷ **vulgarity** *NOUN*

WORD HISTORY from Latin *vulgaris*, from *vulgus* 'the common or ordinary people'

vulgar fraction *NOUN* **vulgar fractions**
a fraction shown by numbers above and below a line (e.g. $\frac{2}{3}$, $\frac{5}{8}$), not a decimal fraction

WORD HISTORY from Latin *vulgaris* 'common or ordinary' (because vulgar fractions were used in ordinary calculations)

vulnerable *ADJECTIVE*
able to be hurt or harmed or attacked
▷ **vulnerability** *NOUN*

vulture *NOUN* **vultures**
a large bird that feeds on dead animals

vulva *NOUN* **vulvas**
the outer parts of the female genitals

vying *present participle of* **vie**

Ww

wacky *ADJECTIVE* **wackier, wackiest**
(*informal*) crazy or silly
▷ **wackiness** *NOUN*

wad (*say* wod) *NOUN* **wads**
a pad or bundle of soft material or banknotes, papers, etc.

wad *VERB* **wads, wadding, wadded**
to pad, line, or stuff something with soft material

waddle (*say* wod- ul) *VERB* **waddles, waddling, waddled**
to walk with short steps, swaying from side to side

waddle *NOUN* **waddles**
a waddling movement or walk

wade *VERB* **wades, wading, waded**
1 to walk through water or mud etc.
2 to read through something with effort because it is dull, difficult, or long
▷ **wader** *NOUN*

wadi (*say* wod- i) *NOUN* **wadis**
a rocky river bed in North Africa that is dry except in the rainy season
WORD HISTORY from an Arabic word

wafer *NOUN* **wafers**
a kind of thin biscuit

wafer-thin *ADJECTIVE*
very thin

waffle ❶ (*say* wof- ul) *NOUN* **waffles**
a small cake made of batter and eaten hot

waffle ❷ (*say* wof- ul) *NOUN*
(*informal*) vague wordy talk or writing

waffle *VERB* **waffles, waffling, waffled**
to talk or write in a vague, wordy style
WORD HISTORY from an old word *waff* 'to bark or yelp'

waft (*say* woft) *VERB* **wafts, wafting, wafted**
to float, or to carry something, gently through the air or over water

On Hallowe'en morning they woke to the delicious smell of baking pumpkin wafting through the corridors. — *J. K. Rowling, Harry Potter and the Philosopher's Stone*

wag ❶ *VERB* **wags, wagging, wagged**
1 an animal's tail wags when it moves quickly to and fro
2 to move something quickly to and fro
3 someone's tongue wags when they are gossiping or spreading rumours

wag *NOUN* **wags**
a wagging movement
WORD HISTORY from an Old English word meaning 'to sway'

wag ❷ *NOUN* **wags**
a person who makes jokes; a wit
WORD HISTORY from an old word *waghalter* 'someone likely to be hanged'

wage *NOUN* or **wages** *PLURAL NOUN*
a regular payment to someone in return for their work

wage *VERB* **wages, waging, waged**
to carry on a war or campaign

wager (*say* way- jer) *NOUN* **wagers**
(*formal*) a bet

wager *VERB* **wagers, wagering, wagered**
(*formal*) to make a bet

'I'll wager that the black dress shows a corresponding mark to this.' — *Sir Arthur Conan Doyle, 'The Adventure of the Abbey Grange'*

waggish *ADJECTIVE*
like a wag; witty, humorous
▷ **waggishness** *NOUN*

waggle *VERB* **waggles, waggling, waggled**
to move, or move something, quickly to and fro
▷ **waggle** *NOUN*

waggle *NOUN* **waggles**
a waggling movement

wagon *NOUN* **wagons**
1 a cart with four wheels, pulled by a horse or an ox
2 an open railway truck, e.g. for coal
WORD HISTORY from Dutch *wagen*

wagtail *NOUN* **wagtails**
a small bird with a long tail that moves up and down constantly when the bird is standing

waif *NOUN* **waifs**
a homeless and helpless person, especially a child
WORD HISTORY from an Old French word

wail *VERB* **wails, wailing, wailed**
to make a long sad cry or sound

wail *NOUN* **wails**
a wailing cry or sound
WORD HISTORY from an Old Norse word

wain *NOUN* **wains**
(*old use*) a farm wagon
WORD HISTORY from an Old English word

a b c d e f g h i j k l m n o p q r s t u v w x y z

wainscot or **wainscoting** *NOUN*
wooden panelling on the wall of a room

waist *NOUN* **waists**
the narrow part in the middle of your body

USAGE NOTE Take care not to confuse this word with *waste*.

waistcoat *NOUN* **waistcoats**
a short close-fitting jacket without sleeves, worn over a shirt and under a jacket

waistline *NOUN* **waistlines**
1 the amount you measure around your waist
2 the narrowest part of a piece of clothing, fitting at or just above or below the waist

wait *VERB* **waits, waiting, waited**
1 to stay somewhere or delay doing something for a specified time or until something happens
2 to be left to be dealt with later ◆ *That question will have to wait until our next meeting.*
3 to wait on people at a meal

to wait on someone
1 is to hand food and drink to them at a meal
2 is to fetch and carry for them as an attendant

wait *NOUN*
an act or period of waiting ◆ *It's a long wait until the next train home.*

waiter *NOUN* **waiters**
a man who serves people with food and drink in a restaurant

waiting list *NOUN* **waiting lists**
a list of people waiting for something to become available

waiting room *NOUN* **waiting rooms**
a room provided for people who are waiting for something

waitress *NOUN* **waitresses**
a woman who serves people with food and drink in a restaurant

waive *VERB* **waives, waiving, waived**
1 to waive a right or claim is to refrain from using or insisting upon it
2 to waive a fee or expense is to refrain from charging it

USAGE NOTE Take care not to confuse this word with *wave*.

waiver *NOUN* **waivers**
the waiving of a right, claim, or fee; a document recording this

wake[1] *VERB* **wakes, waking, woke, woken**
to stop sleeping, or to make someone stop sleeping ◆ *I woke to the unfamiliar sound of seagulls outside my bedroom.* ◆ *You'll wake the neighbours with all that racket!*

to wake up
1 is to wake or awaken
2 is to become alert, or to make someone alert

to wake up to something is to become aware of a fact or situation

wake *NOUN* **wakes**
a watch by a corpse before burial, or a party held after a funeral

WORD HISTORY from an Old English word

wake[2] *NOUN* **wakes**
1 the track left on the water by a moving ship
2 currents of air left behind a moving aircraft.

in the wake of following or coming after

WORD HISTORY probably from an Old Norse word

wakeful *ADJECTIVE*
1 unable to sleep
2 a wakeful night is one when you get little sleep

waken *VERB* **wakens, wakening, wakened**
to wake or make someone wake from sleep

walk *VERB* **walks, walking, walked**
to move along on your feet at an ordinary speed

to walk all over someone (*informal*)
1 is to treat them badly or with disrespect
2 is to defeat them easily

to walk off with something (*informal*)
1 is to win a prize or award easily
2 is to steal something

to walk out on someone is to abandon or desert them

▷ **walker** *NOUN*

SYNONYMS go on foot, travel on foot; stroll, amble, saunter, stride, pace, trudge

walk *NOUN* **walks**
1 a journey on foot
2 a manner or style of walking
3 a path or route for walking

There was a laurel-hedged walk which curved round the secret garden and ended at a gate which opened into a wood, in the park. — *Frances Hodgson Burnett, The Secret Garden*

walkabout *NOUN* **walkabouts**
1 an informal stroll among a crowd by an important visitor
2 a journey on foot in the bush made by an Australian Aboriginal

In the bush boy's tribe every male who reached the age of thirteen or fourteen had to perform a walkabout — a selective test which ... ensured that only the fittest survived to father children. — *James Vance Marshall, Walkabout*

walkie-talkie *NOUN* **walkie-talkies**
(*informal*) a small portable radio transmitter and receiver

walking stick *NOUN* **walking sticks**
a stick used as a support while walking

walk of life *NOUN* **walks of life**
a person's occupation or social position

walkout *NOUN* **walkouts**
a sudden angry departure, especially as a protest or strike

a b c d e f g h i j k l m n o p q r s t u v w x y z

walkover *NOUN* **walkovers**
an easy victory

wall *NOUN* **walls**
1 a continuous upright structure, forming one of the sides of a building or room, or supporting something or enclosing an area
2 something that serves as a block or barrier ◆ *a wall of fire* ◆ *a wall of silence*
3 the tissue surrounding an organ of the body ◆ *the stomach wall*
to drive someone up the wall (*informal*) is to irritate them greatly
to go to the wall (*informal*) is to fail as a business

wall *VERB* **walls, walling, walled**
to wall something up is to block or surround it with a wall

wallaby *NOUN* **wallabies**
an Australian marsupial animal like a small kangaroo
WORD HISTORY from an Australian Aboriginal language

walled *ADJECTIVE*
enclosed with a wall ◆ *a walled garden*

wall-eyed *ADJECTIVE*
having eyes that show an abnormal amount of white, especially because of a squint

wallet *NOUN* **wallets**
a small flat folding case for holding banknotes, credit cards, documents, etc.

wallflower *NOUN* **wallflowers**
1 a garden plant with fragrant flowers, often found growing on old walls
2 a shy person who no one talks to or dances with at a party

wallop *VERB* **wallops, walloping, walloped**
(*informal*) to strike or hit someone or something very hard

wallop *NOUN* **wallops**
a heavy blow or punch

wallow *VERB* **wallows, wallowing, wallowed**
1 to roll about in water or mud
2 to get, or seem to get, pleasure by being surrounded by something ◆ *Zelda preferred to stay at home, wallowing in her own misery.*

wallow *NOUN* **wallows**
1 the act of wallowing
2 an area of mud or shallow water where mammals go to wallow
WORD HISTORY from Old English *walwian* 'to roll about'

wallpaper *NOUN* **wallpapers**
paper used to cover the inside walls of rooms

wallpaper *VERB* **wallpapers, wallpapering, wallpapered**
to put wallpaper on the walls of a room

wall-to-wall *ADJECTIVE*
1 covering the whole floor of a room
2 (*informal*) extensive, plentiful ◆ *TV channels are giving wall-to-wall coverage of the election.*

wally *NOUN* **wallies**
(*informal*) a stupid person

It's all right for you. You don't mind going around acting like a major wally. Nobody's going to laugh at you, are they? — *Anne Fine, Flour Babies*

walnut *NOUN* **walnuts**
1 an edible nut with a wrinkled surface
2 the wood from the tree that bears this nut, used for making furniture

walrus *NOUN* **walruses**
a large Arctic sea animal related to the seal, with two long tusks

waltz *NOUN* **waltzes**
a ballroom dance for couples, with three beats to a bar

waltz *VERB* **waltzes, waltzing, waltzed**
to dance a waltz
to waltz in (*informal*) is to enter a place in a very casual, confident way
WORD HISTORY from German *walzen* 'to revolve'

wan (*say* wonn) *ADJECTIVE*
1 pale from being ill or tired
2 a wan smile is faint and strained
▷ **wanly** *ADVERB*
▷ **wanness** *NOUN*
WORD HISTORY from Old English *wann* 'dark'

wand *NOUN* **wands**
1 a thin stick carried in the hand, used by someone performing magic

Dr Fian chanted the next line of his litany, his wand tracing a design again as he chanted. — *Mollie Hunter, The Thirteenth Member*

2 an electronic device for passing over a bar code

wander *VERB* **wanders, wandering, wandered**
1 to go about without trying to reach a particular place
2 to leave the right path or direction; to stray
3 to be distracted or digress ◆ *He let his attention wander.*
▷ **wanderer** *NOUN*

wander *NOUN*
a wandering journey

wanderlust *NOUN*
a strong desire to travel
WORD HISTORY from a German word

wane *VERB* **wanes, waning, waned**
1 the moon wanes when its area of brightness becomes gradually smaller after being full (SEE ALSO **wax** ❷)
2 to become less, smaller, or weaker

At the churchyard wall my courage had waned somewhat: it seemed a shameless thing to come to rifle Blackbeard's treasure just in the very place and hour that Blackbeard loved. — *J. Meade Falkner, Moonfleet*

wane *NOUN*
on the wane becoming less or weaker
WORD HISTORY from Old English *wanian* 'to reduce'

wangle *VERB* **wangles, wangling, wangled**
(*informal*) to get or arrange something by trickery, or clever planning or persuasion ◆ *He's managed to wangle himself a free trip to Florida.*

want *VERB* **wants, wanting, wanted**
1 to have a desire or wish for something
2 to wish to speak to or see someone ◆ *That was your secretary on the phone. You are wanted upstairs.*
3 (*informal*) to require or need something ◆ *This pencil wants sharpening.* ◆ *You want to be more careful where you tread.*
to want for something is to lack a certain quality or resource ◆ *Despite its size, this laptop doesn't want for computing power.*

want *NOUN* **wants**
1 a desire or wish to have something
2 a lack or need of something

I must admit that for all their charm and beauty these five wild geese displayed, in some matters, a truly astonishing want of intellect, a plain stupidity, indeed. — *Gavin Maxwell, Ring of Bright Water*

3 being poor and lacking the necessities of life ◆ *Many families here are living in great want.*

wanted *ADJECTIVE*
a wanted person is a suspected criminal whom the police wish to find or arrest

wanting *ADJECTIVE*
lacking in what is needed or usual; deficient ◆ *The outside of the building was completely wanting in elegance and style.*

wanton (*say* wonn- ton) *ADJECTIVE*
1 done deliberately without any provocation or motive ◆ *Everywhere, there is evidence of the wanton destruction of crops and farmland.*
2 sexually immoral or promiscuous
▷ **wantonly** *ADVERB*
▷ **wantonness** *NOUN*
WORD HISTORY from an Old English word

WAP *ABBREVIATION*
(*ICT*) Wireless Application Protocol, a means of connecting a mobile phone to the Internet

war *NOUN* **wars**
1 fighting between nations or groups, especially using armed forces
2 a serious struggle or effort against crime, disease, poverty, etc.
at war taking part in a war

warble *VERB* **warbles, warbling, warbled**
to sing with a gentle trilling note

warble *NOUN* **warbles**
a warbling song or sound

warbler *NOUN* **warblers**
a kind of small songbird

war crime *NOUN* **war crimes**
a crime committed during a war that breaks international rules of war
▷ **war criminal** *NOUN*

ward *NOUN* **wards**
1 a room with beds for patients in a hospital
2 a child looked after by a guardian
3 an area electing a councillor to represent it

ward *VERB* **wards, warding, warded**
to ward something off is to keep away something bad or unwanted

warden *NOUN* **wardens**
1 an official who is in charge of a hostel, college, etc., or who supervises something
2 (*American*) a prison governor
WORD HISTORY from an Old French word, related to *guardian*

warder *NOUN* **warders**
(*old use*) an official in charge of prisoners in a prison

wardrobe *NOUN* **wardrobes**
1 a cupboard to hang clothes in
2 a stock of clothes or costumes
WORD HISTORY from Old French *warder* 'to guard' and *robe*

ware *NOUN* **wares**
1 used in compound words to specify goods made from a particular material, or from a particular factory or area ◆ *copperware* ◆ *Delftware*
2 wares are goods offered for sale
WORD HISTORY from an Old English word

warehouse *NOUN* **warehouses**
a large building where goods are stored

warfare *NOUN*
1 the action of fighting a war
2 a style of fighting ◆ *guerrilla warfare*

wargame *NOUN* **wargames**
a game in which models representing troops are moved about on a map or model of a battlefield
▷ **wargaming** *NOUN*

a b c d e f g h i j k l m n o p q r s t u v w x y z

warhead *NOUN* **warheads**
the explosive head of a missile or torpedo

warlike *ADJECTIVE*
1 fond of making war; aggressive
2 threatening or suggesting war ◆ *The two countries had been making warlike noises for years before any fighting began.*

warlock *NOUN* **warlocks**
a man who practises witchcraft
WORD HISTORY from Old English *wær-loga* 'a traitor'

warlord *NOUN* **warlords**
a powerful military commander in charge of a region

warm *ADJECTIVE*
1 fairly hot; not cold or cool
2 keeping your body warm ◆ *Remember to bring warm clothing for the hillwalk.*
3 a warm greeting or welcome is friendly or enthusiastic
4 a warm colour suggests warmth, such as red or orange
5 close to the right answer, or to something hidden, in a game or quiz ◆ *Am I getting warm, yet?*
▷ **warmly** *ADVERB*
▷ **warmness** *NOUN*
▷ **warmth** *NOUN*

warm *VERB* **warms, warming, warmed**
to make something warm, or to become warm
to warm to someone or something
1 is to become friendly towards someone
2 is to become animated about or interested in a subject

I have had a long talk with the Count. I asked him a few questions on Transylvania history, and he warmed up to the subject wonderfully. — *Bram Stoker, Dracula*

to warm up
1 is to become warm or reach the right temperature
2 is to do light physical exercises in preparation for sports etc.
to warm something up is to reheat food or drink

warm-blooded *ADJECTIVE*
a warm-blooded animal has blood that remains warm permanently (SEE ALSO **cold-blooded**)

warm-hearted *ADJECTIVE*
sympathetic and kind (SEE ALSO **cold-hearted**)

warmonger *NOUN* **warmongers**
a person who seeks to bring about war
▷ **warmongering** *NOUN*

warm-up *NOUN* **warm-ups**
1 a series of light physical exercises done in preparation for sports etc.
2 a short performance to put an audience into a receptive mood before the main act

warn *VERB* **warns, warning, warned**
to tell someone about a danger or difficulty that may affect them; to advise someone to avoid or refrain from something

The rattlesnake didn't chase after him. It had rattled its tail to warn him to stay away. — *Louis Sachar, Holes*

to warn someone off is to tell them to keep away or to avoid something

warning *NOUN* **warnings**
1 advice to avoid or refrain from something

The Radley Place fascinated Dill. In spite of our warnings and explanations it drew him as the moon draws water. — *Harper Lee, To Kill a Mockingbird*

2 something that serves to warn ◆ *The blizzard came upon us with no warning.*
3 advice to someone that they will be punished if they continue doing something ◆ *The traffic warden let me off with a warning this time.*

warp (*say* worp) *VERB* **warps, warping, warped**
1 to become bent or twisted out of shape, usually because of heat or damp; to bend or twist something in this way
2 to distort or badly influence a person's ideas or judgement

warp *NOUN*
1 the state of being warped or twisted
2 the lengthwise threads in weaving, crossed by the weft
WORD HISTORY from an Old English word

warpath *NOUN*
on the warpath angry and getting ready for a fight or argument

warrant *NOUN* **warrants**
1 written authorization to do something ◆ *The police have a warrant for his arrest.*
2 a document entitling the holder to receive certain goods or services

warrant *VERB* **warrants, warranting, warranted**
1 to justify a behaviour or action ◆ *Nothing can warrant such rudeness.*
2 to guarantee or bet that something will happen ◆ *We have not seen the last of that creature, I warrant you.*
WORD HISTORY from an Old French word, related to *guarantee*

warranty *NOUN* **warranties**
a written guarantee issued by a manufacturer

warren *NOUN* **warrens**
1 a piece of ground where there are many burrows in which rabbits live and breed.
2 a building or place with many winding passages

Those who do make their way across the Mire find themselves in a warren of ramshackle hovels and run-down slums which straddle the oozing Edgewater River. — *Paul Stewart and Chris Riddell, Beyond the Deep Woods*

WORD HISTORY from Old French *garenne* 'a game park'

warring *ADJECTIVE*
involved in a war or dispute

warrior *NOUN* **warriors**
a person who fights in battle; a soldier

warship *NOUN* **warships**
a ship equipped with weapons and used in war

wart *NOUN* **warts**
a small hard lump on the skin, caused by a virus

warts and all including all faults or unattractive features

WORD HISTORY from an Old English word

warthog *NOUN* **warthogs**
an African wild pig with two large tusks and wart-like growths on its face

wartime *NOUN*
a time of war

wary (*say* **wair**- ee) *ADJECTIVE*
cautious about possible danger or difficulty

I leaped up the stairs two at a time, mindful of the wet footprints, wary of slipping. — *Keith Gray, Malarkey*

▷ **warily** *ADVERB*
▷ **wariness** *NOUN*

WORD HISTORY from an Old English word

wash *VERB* **washes, washing, washed**
1 to clean something with water or other liquid
2 to be washable ◆ *Cotton washes easily.*
3 to flow against or over something ◆ *At high tide, the sea washes the base of the cliffs.*
4 to carry something along in water ◆ *The waves were so high, they nearly washed the crew overboard.*
5 (*informal*) to seem convincing or genuine ◆ *I'm afraid that excuse won't wash any more.*

to wash your hands of something is to refuse to take responsibility for it

to be washed out (*informal*) an event is washed out if it is abandoned because of rain

wash *NOUN* **washes**
1 the action of washing, or the process of being washed
2 a quantity of clothes etc. for washing
3 the disturbed water or air behind a moving ship or aircraft
4 a thin coating of paint or colour

to come out in the wash (*informal*) is to be eliminated or corrected over time

washable *ADJECTIVE*
able to be washed without becoming damaged

washbasin *NOUN* **washbasins**
a small sink for washing your hands etc.

washed out *ADJECTIVE*
1 faded by washing; faded-looking
2 pale and tired

washed-up *ADJECTIVE*
no longer effective or successful

washer *NOUN* **washers**
1 a small ring of rubber or metal etc. placed between two surfaces (e.g. under a bolt or screw) to fit them tightly together
2 a washing machine

washing *NOUN*
clothes etc. being washed

washing machine *NOUN* **washing machines**
a machine for washing clothes etc.

washing soda *NOUN*
sodium carbonate, used for washing and cleaning

washing-up *NOUN*
the process of washing dishes and cutlery etc. after a meal; the dishes etc. that are to be washed

wash-out *NOUN* **wash-outs**
(*informal*) a complete failure

washroom *NOUN* **washrooms**
(*American*) a bathroom or toilet

wasn't
short for *was not*

wasp *NOUN* **wasps**
a stinging insect with black and yellow stripes round its body

WORD HISTORY from an Old English word

waspish *ADJECTIVE*
a waspish person or remark is sharp or irritable

▷ **waspishness** *NOUN*

wassail (*say* **woss**- al) *VERB* **wassails, wassailing, wassailed**
(*old use*) to make merry and drink a lot of alcohol

▷ **wassailing** *NOUN*

WORD HISTORY from Old Norse *ves heill* 'to be in good health'

wastage *NOUN*
loss of something by waste

a b c d e f g h i j k l m n o p q r s t u v w x y z

waste *VERB* **wastes, wasting, wasted**
1 to use something in an extravagant way or without getting adequate results ◆ *It's not worth wasting your time trying to get that car to start.*
2 to fail to use an opportunity
to waste away is to become gradually weaker or thinner

waste *ADJECTIVE*
1 a waste material or product is left over or thrown away because it is not wanted
2 waste ground or land is not used, cultivated, or built on
to lay waste to a place is to destroy the buildings and crops of an area

waste *NOUN* **wastes**
1 the action of wasting something or not using it effectively ◆ *That haircut was a complete waste of money.*
2 waste material or food; waste products
3 an area of barren uninhabited land ◆ *The train rumbled through the wastes of Siberia on its way to Moscow.*

WORD HISTORY from Latin *vastus* 'empty'

USAGE NOTE Take care not to confuse this word with *waist*.

wasteful *ADJECTIVE*
using more than is needed; producing waste
▷ **wastefully** *ADVERB*
▷ **wastefulness** *NOUN*

wasteland *NOUN* **wastelands**
a barren or empty area of land

waster *NOUN* **wasters**
1 a wasteful person
2 (*informal*) a person who does nothing useful

wastrel (*say* way- strel) *NOUN* **wastrels**
(*old use*) a person who wastes their life and does nothing useful

watch *VERB* **watches, watching, watched**
1 to look at someone or something for some time
2 to be on guard or ready for something to happen ◆ *Watch for the traffic lights to turn green.*
3 to pay careful attention to something ◆ *Watch where you put your feet.*
4 to safeguard or take care of something ◆ *It was the children's job to watch the goats.*
to watch out is to be careful or on your guard
to watch over someone is to guard or look after them
to watch your step is to be careful not to stumble or fall or do something wrong
▷ **watcher** *NOUN*

watch *NOUN* **watches**
1 a device like a small clock, usually worn on your wrist
2 the action of watching
3 a turn of being on duty

watchdog *NOUN* **watchdogs**
1 a dog kept to guard property
2 a person or committee whose job is to make sure that companies do not do anything harmful or illegal

watchful *ADJECTIVE*
watching closely; alert
▷ **watchfully** *ADVERB*
▷ **watchfulness** *NOUN*

watchmaker *NOUN* **watchmakers**
a person who makes and repairs watches

watchman *NOUN* **watchmen**
a person employed to look after an empty building at night

watchword *NOUN* **watchwords**
a word or phrase that sums up a group's policy; a slogan ◆ *Our watchword is 'safety first'.*

water *NOUN* **waters**
1 a colourless odourless tasteless liquid that is a compound of hydrogen and oxygen
2 a lake or sea
3 the tide ◆ *at high water*
to pass water is to urinate

water *VERB* **waters, watering, watered**
1 to supply an animal or plant with water
2 your eyes water when they start to produce tears
3 a sight or smell makes your mouth water when it makes you want to eat
to water something down
1 is to dilute liquid
2 is to make a statement or argument less strong

water cannon *NOUN* **water cannons**
a device for shooting a powerful jet of water to disperse a crowd

water closet *NOUN* **water closets**
(*old use*) a toilet with a pan that is flushed by water

watercolour *NOUN* **watercolours**
1 paint made with pigment and water (not oil)
2 a painting done with this kind of paint
▷ **watercolourist** *NOUN*

watercress *NOUN*
a kind of cress that grows in water, with strong-tasting leaves that are used in salads

waterfall *NOUN* **waterfalls**
a place where a river or stream flows over the edge of a cliff or large rock

waterfront *NOUN*
the part of a town that borders on a river, lake, or sea

waterhole or **watering hole** *NOUN* **waterholes** or **watering holes**
a hollow in which water collects, where animals go to drink water

a
b
c
d
e
f
g
h
i
j
k
l
m
n
o
p
q
r
s
t
u
v
w
x
y
z

watering can *NOUN* **watering cans**
a container with a long spout, for watering plants

water lily *NOUN* **water lilies**
a plant that grows in water, with broad floating leaves and large flowers

waterlogged *ADJECTIVE*
completely soaked or swamped in water

watermark *NOUN* **watermarks**
1 a mark showing how high a river or tide rises or how low it falls
2 a manufacturer's design in some kinds of paper, visible when the paper is held against light

watermelon *NOUN* **watermelons**
a melon with a smooth green skin, red pulp, and black seeds

watermill *NOUN* **watermills**
a mill worked by a waterwheel

water polo *NOUN*
a game played by teams of swimmers with a ball like a football

waterproof *ADJECTIVE*
that keeps out rain or water

waterproof *NOUN* **waterproofs**
a waterproof coat or jacket

waterproof *VERB* **waterproofs, waterproofing, waterproofed**
to make something waterproof

water rat *NOUN*
a rat-like rodent that lives beside a lake or stream

watershed *NOUN* **watersheds**
1 a turning point in the course of events
2 a line of high land from which streams flow down on each side
3 the time after which programmes that are thought to be unsuitable for children are broadcast on television

WORD HISTORY from *water* and Old English *scead* 'a division or parting'

waterskis *PLURAL NOUN*
a pair of flat boards worn in the sport of **waterskiing**, skimming over the surface of water while being towed by a motor boat
▷ **waterskier** *NOUN*

waterski *VERB* **waterskis, waterskiing, waterskied**
to take part in waterskiing

waterspout *NOUN* **waterspouts**
a column of water formed when a whirlwind draws up a whirling mass of water from the sea

water table *NOUN* **water tables**
the level below which the ground is saturated with water

watertight *ADJECTIVE*
1 made or fastened so that water cannot get in or out
2 a watertight excuse or argument is put together so carefully that it cannot be disputed or proved to be untrue

waterway *NOUN* **waterways**
a river or canal that ships can travel on

waterwheel *NOUN* **waterwheels**
a large wheel turned by a flow of water, used to work machinery

waterworks *PLURAL NOUN*
a place with pumping machinery etc. for supplying water to a district

watery *ADJECTIVE*
1 like water
2 full of water or tears
3 made weak or thin by too much water

watt *NOUN* **watts**
a unit of electric power, equivalent to one joule per second

WORD HISTORY named after the Scottish engineer, James *Watt* (1736-1819)

wattage *NOUN* **wattages**
electric power measured in watts

wattle❶ *NOUN* **wattles**
1 sticks and twigs woven together to make a fence or wall
2 an Australian acacia tree with long branches and golden flowers

WORD HISTORY from Old English *watul*

wattle❷ *NOUN* **wattles**
a red fold of skin hanging from the throat of turkeys and some other birds

WORD HISTORY origin unknown

wave *NOUN* **waves**
1 a ridge moving along the surface of the sea, or breaking on the shore.
2 a curling piece of hair
3 (*Science*) the wave-like movement by which heat, light, sound, or electricity travels
4 an advancing group of people, especially attackers
5 a sudden increase in or occurrence of something ◆ *The most recent wave of arrests began in September.*
6 the action of waving your hand

wave *VERB* **waves, waving, waved**
1 to move your hand to and fro as a greeting or signal
2 to signal or express something in this way ◆ *We stood on the platform, waving goodbye.*
3 to move loosely to and fro or up and down, or to move something in this way

'What did you say I should do with this?' asked Giles, waving a green chilli at me as I chopped vegetables. — *Alison Allen-Gray, Unique*

4 to make something wavy ▸▸

a b c d e f g h i j k l m n o p q r s t u v w x y z

5 to be wavy

to wave something aside is to dismiss an objection as unimportant or irrelevant

USAGE NOTE Take care not to confuse this word with *waive*.

waveband *NOUN* **wavebands**
the wavelengths between certain limits

wavelength *NOUN* **wavelengths**
1 the distance between corresponding points on a sound wave or electromagnetic wave
2 the size of a radio wave that a particular radio station uses to broadcast its programmes

wavelet *NOUN* **wavelets**
a small wave

waver *VERB* **wavers, wavering, wavered**
1 to be unsteady; to move unsteadily
2 to begin to give way or weaken ◆ *As the enemy approached, the courage of the front line began to waver.*
3 to hesitate; to be uncertain

WORD HISTORY from Old Norse *vafra* 'to flicker'

wavy *ADJECTIVE*
full of waves or curves
▷ **wavily** *ADVERB*
▷ **waviness** *NOUN*

wax[1] *NOUN* **waxes**
1 a soft substance that melts easily, used to make candles, crayons, and polish
2 a dark yellow substance produced by bees; beeswax
3 a yellow wax-like substance secreted in the ears
▷ **waxy** *ADJECTIVE*

wax *VERB* **waxes, waxing, waxed**
to coat or polish something with wax

WORD HISTORY from Old English *waex*

wax[2] *VERB* **waxes, waxing, waxed**
1 the moon waxes when its area of brightness becomes gradually larger until it is full (SEE ALSO **wane**)
2 (*literary*) to become stronger or more important

to wax lyrical is to speak or write poetically about something

WORD HISTORY from Old English *waexan*

waxen *ADJECTIVE*
1 made of wax
2 pale or smooth like wax

waxwork *NOUN* **waxworks**
a lifelike model of a person made in wax

way *NOUN* **ways**
1 how something is done; a method or style of doing something ◆ *This is the best way to make scrambled eggs.*
2 a manner ◆ *The elderly nurse spoke to the child in a kindly way.*
3 a talent or skill ◆ *My girlfriend has a way with computers.*
4 the route over which a person or thing is moving or would naturally move ◆ *Don't get in the way of stampeding wildebeest.*
5 a route or direction ◆ *Can you tell me the way to the station?*
6 advance in some direction, progress ◆ *Please make your way to the entrance.*
7 a distance to be travelled ◆ *It's a long way to the summit from here.*
8 a particular aspect of something ◆ *It's a good plan in some ways, but not in others.*
9 a condition or state ◆ *By now, things were in a bad way.*

by the way incidentally; as an extra fact

by way of
1 via; passing through ◆ *We are flying by way of Amsterdam.*
2 as a substitute for or a form of ◆ *The receptionist grunted by way of greeting.*

to get or **have your own way** is to manage to get or do what you want

to give way
1 is to collapse
2 to allow other traffic to go first
3 to yield to someone else's wishes or demands

to go out of your way is to make a special effort to do something

to go your way to happen in a way that is favourable to you

in a way to a certain extent; in some respects

in no way not at all

in the way forming an obstacle or hindrance

in the way of as a type or example of ◆ *There wasn't much in the way of real food in the fridge.*

to look the other way is to ignore a person or situation deliberately

no way (*informal*) that is impossible

on the way
1 about to arrive or happen
2 on the road or direction you are travelling

out of the way
1 distant or remote
2 dealt with or finished

under way in motion or in progress

way *ADVERB*
(*informal*) far, to a great extent ◆ *That shot was way off the target.* ◆ *The building costs are already way over budget.*

wayfarer *NOUN* **wayfarers**
a traveller, especially someone who is walking

waylay *VERB* **waylays, waylaying, waylaid**
to lie in wait for a person or people, especially in order to talk to them or rob them

All went well that day, and no sight or sound had they of the enemy waiting to waylay them.
— *J. R. R. Tolkien, The Return of the King*

way-out *ADJECTIVE*
(*informal*) unconventional in style

wayside *NOUN*
to fall by the wayside is fail to continue or be part of something

wayward *ADJECTIVE*
self-willed and unpredictable, not obedient or easily controlled

WC *ABBREVIATION*
water closet (a toilet)

we *PRONOUN*
a word used by someone to refer to themself and one or more other people, or when speaking on behalf of a group, institution, country, etc.

weak *ADJECTIVE*
1 having little power, energy, or effect
2 easy to break, damage, or defeat
3 not great in intensity
▷ **weakness** *NOUN*

weaken *VERB* **weakens, weakening, weakened**
to make something weaker, or to become weaker

weakling *NOUN* **weaklings**
a weak person or animal

weakly *ADVERB*
in a weak manner

weakly *ADJECTIVE*
sickly; not strong

weal *NOUN* **weals**
a ridge raised on the flesh by a cane or whip
WORD HISTORY from Old English *walu* 'a ridge'

wealth *NOUN*
1 a lot of money or property; riches
2 a large quantity ◆ *There is a wealth of information about comets on NASA's website.*

wealthy *ADJECTIVE* **wealthier, wealthiest**
having wealth; rich

There was a wealthy man in Okonkwo's village who had three huge barns, nine wives and thirty children. — *Chinua Achebe, Things Fall Apart*

▷ **wealthiness** *NOUN*

wean *VERB* **weans, weaning, weaned**
to get a baby used to taking food other than milk
to wean someone off to wean someone off a habit is to make them give it up gradually
WORD HISTORY from an Old English word

weapon *NOUN* **weapons**
something used to harm or kill people in a battle or fight
▷ **weaponry** *NOUN*

wear *VERB* **wears, wearing, wore, worn**
1 to have clothes, jewellery, etc. on your body
2 to have a certain look or expression ◆ *Scarlet was already at breakfast, wearing her habitual scowl.*
3 to damage something by rubbing or using it often; to become damaged in this way ◆ *The carpet has worn thin.*
4 to withstand continued use ◆ *This fabric wears well wash after wash.*
5 (*informal*) to accept or tolerate something ◆ *The public won't wear these excuses for much longer.*
to wear someone down is to get them to concede or agree to something through persistence
to wear off
1 is to be removed by wear or use
2 is to become less intense
to wear on is to pass gradually ◆ *The party got louder as the night wore on.*
to wear out is to become useless or damaged from continuous use
to wear someone out is to exhaust them
to wear thin is to gradually become less effective or be used up
▷ **wearable** *ADJECTIVE*
▷ **wearer** *NOUN*

wear *NOUN*
1 what you wear; clothes ◆ *casual wear*
2 damage resulting from continuous use
3 capacity to withstand being used ◆ *There's a lot of wear left in that jacket.*
wear and tear wear or damage from continuous use

wearisome *ADJECTIVE*
causing weariness; tiring

weary *ADJECTIVE* **wearier, weariest**
1 worn out and tired
2 a weary task is one that makes you tired
▷ **wearily** *ADVERB*
▷ **weariness** *NOUN*

weary *VERB* **wearies, wearying, wearied**
to make someone weary, or to become weary

weasel *NOUN* **weasels**
a small fierce animal with a slender body and reddish-brown fur
WORD HISTORY from an Old English word

weather *NOUN*
the rain, snow, wind, sunshine etc. at a particular time or place
under the weather feeling ill or depressed

weather *VERB* **weathers, weathering, weathered**
1 to expose something to the effects of the weather
2 to come through a storm, or through a difficult experience, successfully

weathercock or **weathervane** *NOUN* **weathercocks** or **weathervanes**
a pointer, often shaped like a cockerel, that turns in the wind and shows from which direction it is blowing

a b c d e f g h i j k l m n o p q r s t u v w x y z

weave *VERB* **weaves, weaving, wove, woven**
1 to make fabric or baskets etc. by crossing threads or strips under and over each other
2 to put a story together ◆ *The author has woven a thrilling tale of wartime espionage.*
3 (past tense also **weaved**) to move from side to side to get round things in the way ◆ *Cyclists weaved around pedestrians.*
to get weaving (*informal*) is to set to work energetically
▷ **weaver** *NOUN*

weave *NOUN* **weaves**
a style of weaving ◆ *A loose-weave fabric is perfect for keeping cool in the summer.*

web *NOUN* **webs**
1 a cobweb
2 a complicated or interlinked structure; a network ◆ *The unsuspecting couple were soon tangled up in a web of lies and deception.*
the Web the World Wide Web; the Internet
WORD HISTORY from Old English *webb* 'a piece of woven cloth'

webbed or **web-footed** *ADJECTIVE*
having toes joined by pieces of skin, as ducks and frogs do

webcast *NOUN* **webcasts**
a sound or video broadcast that is transmitted over the Internet

weblog *NOUN* **weblogs**
(*ICT*) a personal website on which you can post your own messages and make links to other websites

web page *NOUN* **web pages**
a document forming part of a website

website *NOUN* **websites**
a location on the World Wide Web, giving information about a subject, organization, etc.

wed *VERB* **weds, wedding, wedded**
1 to marry
2 to unite two different things
to be wedded to something is to be unwilling to abandon an activity or opinion

wedding *NOUN* **weddings**
the ceremony and celebration when a couple get married
WORD FAMILY A related adjective is nuptial.

wedge *NOUN* **wedges**
1 a piece of wood or metal etc. that is thick at one end and thin at the other, pushed between things to force them apart or prevent something from moving
2 a wedge-shaped object, such as a slice of cheese or cake

wedge *VERB* **wedges, wedging, wedged**
1 to keep something in place with a wedge
2 to pack people or things tightly together ◆ *Ten of us were wedged in the lift.*

wedlock *NOUN*
being married; matrimony
WORD HISTORY from Old English *wedlac* 'marriage vow'

Wednesday *NOUN*
the day of the week following Tuesday
WORD HISTORY from Old English *Wodnesdaeg* 'day of Woden or Odin, the chief Norse god'

wee *ADJECTIVE* **weer, weest**
(*Scottish*) little; small

Sometimes being wee and skinny is a bonus. I'm round behind him and into the kitchen before he knows it. — *Theresa Breslin, Whispers in the Graveyard*

weed *NOUN* **weeds**
a wild plant that grows where it is not wanted

weed *VERB* **weeds, weeding, weeded**
to remove weeds from the ground
to weed something out is to remove something inferior or undesirable
WORD HISTORY from Old English *weod*

weedy *ADJECTIVE* **weedier, weediest**
1 full of weeds
2 a weedy person is thin and puny

week *NOUN* **weeks**
1 a period of seven days, especially from Sunday to the following Saturday
2 the five days other than Saturday and Sunday ◆ *We tend to stay at home in the evenings during the week.*
WORD HISTORY from Old English *wice*

weekday *NOUN* **weekdays**
a day other than Saturday or Sunday

weekend *NOUN* **weekends**
Saturday and Sunday

weekly *ADJECTIVE, ADVERB*
happening or done once a week

The aunts, travelling in Italy in 1921, had written weekly to their parents. — *Penelope Lively, The House in Norham Gardens*

weeny *ADJECTIVE*
(*informal*) tiny

weep *VERB* **weeps, weeping, wept**
1 to shed tears; to cry
2 to seep or ooze moisture
▷ **weep** *NOUN*
▷ **weepy** *ADJECTIVE*

weep *NOUN* **weeps**
a spell of weeping; a cry
WORD HISTORY from Old English *wepan*

weeping willow *NOUN* **weeping willows**
a willow tree with drooping branches

weevil *NOUN* **weevils**
a kind of small beetle that feeds on tree bark, grain, and nuts
WORD HISTORY from Old English *wifel* 'a beetle'

weft *NOUN*
the threads on a loom that are woven across the warp

weigh *VERB* **weighs, weighing, weighed**
1 to measure the weight of something
2 to have a certain weight ◆ *An adult black rhino can weigh as much as a ton.*
3 to be important or have influence ◆ *The forensic evidence weighed heavily with the jury.*
to weigh anchor is to raise the anchor and start a voyage
to weigh someone down is to depress or trouble them
to weigh in (*informal*) is to contribute a comment to a discussion
to weigh on someone is to be a burden to them
to weigh something up is to assess the nature or importance of something

weight *NOUN* **weights**
1 how heavy something is; the amount that something weighs
2 a piece of metal of known weight, especially one used on scales to weigh things
3 a heavy object
4 importance or influence
to carry weight is to be influential
to throw your weight about (*informal*) is to use your influence aggressively
▷ **weighty** *ADJECTIVE*
▷ **weightless** *ADJECTIVE*
▷ **weightlessness** *NOUN*

weight *VERB* **weights, weighting, weighted**
1 to attach a weight to something
2 to arrange something in a way that gives someone an advantage or creates a bias ◆ *The test was weighted in favour of candidates with scientific knowledge.*

weightlifting *NOUN*
the athletic sport of lifting heavy weights
▷ **weightlifter** *NOUN*

weir (*say* weer) *NOUN* **weirs**
a small dam across a river or canal to control the flow of water

weird *ADJECTIVE*
strange and uncanny or bizarre
▷ **weirdly** *ADVERB*
▷ **weirdness** *NOUN*
WORD HISTORY from Old English *wyrd* 'fate, destiny'
USAGE NOTE Note that the 'e' comes before the 'i', not the other way round.

weirdo (*say* **weer**- doh) *NOUN* **weirdos**
(*informal*) a strange or eccentric person

welcome *NOUN* **welcomes**
a greeting or reception, especially a kindly one

welcome *ADJECTIVE*
1 a welcome guest is one that is received with pleasure
2 a welcome change or relief is pleasing because it is much needed or wanted
3 to be welcome to do something is to be allowed or invited to do it ◆ *You are welcome to stay for as long as you like.*

welcome *VERB* **welcomes, welcoming, welcomed**
1 to welcome someone is to show that you are pleased when they arrive
2 to be glad to receive or hear of something ◆ *All of us welcomed the chance to go ashore and stretch our legs.*
to make someone welcome is to make them feel welcome
you're welcome a polite phrase replying to thanks for something

weld *VERB* **welds, welding, welded**
1 to join pieces of metal or plastic by heating and pressing or hammering them together
2 to combine people or things into a whole
▷ **welder** *NOUN*

weld *NOUN* **welds**
a joint made by welding
WORD HISTORY from an old word *well* 'to melt'

welfare *NOUN*
people's health, happiness, and comfort

welfare state *NOUN*
a system in which a country's government provides money to pay for health care, social services, benefits, etc.

well❶ *NOUN* **wells**
1 a deep shaft dug to bring up water or oil from underground
2 an enclosed space in the middle of a building containing a staircase or lift
3 (*old use*) a natural spring used as a source of water
4 a plentiful supply or source of something ◆ *The new manager has a well of talent at his disposal.*

well *VERB* **wells, welling, welled**
to rise or flow up ◆ *You could see the tears welling up in Cordelia's eyes.*
WORD HISTORY from Old English *wella* 'spring of water'

well❷ *ADVERB* **better, best**
1 in a good or suitable way

Alicia, of course, did everything well, whether it was maths, magic or horse-riding. — *Diana Wynne Jones, The Merlin Conspiracy*

2 thoroughly; to a great or large extent ◆ *Make sure the meat is well cooked.* ◆ *Farms in this part of the country are spread well apart.* ◆ *Her father must be well into his eighties by now.*
3 probably or reasonably ◆ *This may well be the last time we'll see each other.*
well off
1 fairly rich
2 in a good situation

well *ADJECTIVE*
1 in good health ◆ *One of the puppies has not been well since his injection.*
2 satisfactory; fine ◆ *I returned at five o'clock to discover that all was not well at home.*

WORD HISTORY from Old English *wel* 'prosperously'

well-being *NOUN*
good health, happiness, and comfort

wellies *PLURAL NOUN*
(*informal*) wellington boots

wellington boots or **wellingtons** *PLURAL NOUN*
rubber or plastic waterproof boots covering most of the legs

WORD HISTORY named after the first Duke of *Wellington* (1769-1852), who wore long leather boots

well known *ADJECTIVE*
1 known to many people
2 known thoroughly

well mannered *ADJECTIVE*
having good manners; well behaved

well meaning *ADJECTIVE*
having good intentions, though not always with a good effect

wellnigh *ADVERB*
almost; nearly ◆ *It's wellnigh impossible to get a parking space at this time of day.*

well off *ADJECTIVE*
1 fairly rich
2 in a satisfactory or good situation

well read *ADJECTIVE*
having read a lot of good books

well-to-do *ADJECTIVE*
fairly rich

This hobbit was a very well-to-do hobbit, and his name was Baggins. — *J. R. R. Tolkien, The Hobbit*

well worn *ADJECTIVE*
1 much worn by use
2 a well worn phrase or idea has been overused and is no longer interesting or significant

welsh *VERB* **welshes, welshing, welshed**
to welsh on something is to fail to honour a debt or obligation ◆ *You're not going to welsh on our agreement, are you?*
▷ **welsher** *NOUN*

welt *NOUN* **welts**
1 a strip or border
2 a weal; the mark of a heavy blow

welter *VERB* **welters, weltering, weltered**
a ship welters when it is tossed to and fro by waves

welter *NOUN*
a confused mixture; a jumble

The screen responded as quickly as thought itself, and out of the welter of lines and flashes a series of pictures formed with perfect clarity. — *Philip Pullman, The Subtle Knife*

wen *NOUN* **wens**
a large but harmless tumour on the head or neck

wench *NOUN* **wenches**
(*old use*) a girl or young woman

WORD HISTORY from Old English *wencel* 'child'

wend *VERB* **wends, wending, wended**
to wend your way is to go somewhere slowly or by an indirect route

WORD HISTORY from Old English *wendan* 'to turn or depart'

weren't
short for *were not*

werewolf *NOUN* **werewolves**
in legends and stories, a person who changes into a wolf when the moon is full

WORD HISTORY from Old English *wer* 'man' and *wolf*

west *NOUN*
1 the direction where the sun sets, opposite east
2 the western part of a country, city, etc.
the West the countries of Europe and North America in relation to the rest of the world

west *ADJECTIVE, ADVERB*
towards or in the west; coming from the west
to go west (*informal*) is to be destroyed, lost, or killed

WORD FAMILY a westerly wind comes from the direction of the west; a western person, place or thing comes from, or is situated in, the west; a westerner is a person who comes from or lives in the west of a country or area; a westernmost place or point is at the most western point of a country or area. Another word for 'belonging to the west' is occidental.

western *NOUN* **westerns**
a film or story dealing with cowboys in western North America

westernize *VERB* **westernizes, westernizing, westernized**
to bring a person, country, etc. under the influence of ideas, customs, and institutions from Europe and North America
▷ **westernization** *NOUN*

USAGE NOTE This word can also be spelled westernise.

westernmost *ADJECTIVE*
furthest west

westward *ADJECTIVE, ADVERB*
in or towards the west

westwards *ADVERB*
towards the west

wet *ADJECTIVE* **wetter, wettest**
1 soaked or covered in water or other liquid
2 not yet dry ◆ *Don't touch the wall — the paint is still wet.*
3 affected by rain ◆ *It's too wet to play outside today.*
4 (*informal*) weak or feeble

wet behind the ears immature or inexperienced
▷ **wetness** *NOUN*

wet *VERB* **wets, wetting, wet** or **wetted**
to make something wet

I picked up the brush between my toes, wetted it in my mouth, then rubbed it on one of the paint squares—the bright blue one which I liked best. — *Christy Brown, My Left Foot*

wet *NOUN* **wets**
1 rainy weather
2 (*informal*) a feeble or ineffectual person

wet blanket *NOUN*
a gloomy person who prevents other people from enjoying themselves

wetlands *PLURAL NOUN*
swampy or marshy land

wet nurse *NOUN* **wet nurses**
a woman employed to suckle another woman's child

wet suit *NOUN* **wet suits**
a close-fitting rubber suit, worn by skin divers and windsurfers to keep them warm and dry

whack *VERB* **whacks, whacking, whacked**
(*informal*) to hit someone or something hard

whack *NOUN* **whacks**
1 a hard or heavy blow
2 (*informal*) an attempt ◆ *I've never played baseball, but I'll have a whack at it.*
3 (*informal*) a share or contribution; an amount of money

I was in my fourth year of earning a decent whack from writing, and for the first time in my life I had savings. — *Nick Hornby, 31 Songs*

whacked *ADJECTIVE* (*informal*)
1 tired out; exhausted
2 (*American*) under the influence of drugs

whacking *ADJECTIVE*
(*informal*) very large; huge

whale *NOUN* **whales**
a very large sea mammal with a horizontal tail fin and a blowhole on top of the head for breathing

to have a whale of a time (*informal*) is to enjoy yourself very much

whalebone *NOUN*
a springy substance from the upper jaw of some kinds of whale, formerly used to make stays in corsets

whaler *NOUN* **whalers**
a person or ship that hunts whales

whaling *NOUN*
hunting whales

wharf (*say* worf) *NOUN* **wharves** or **wharfs**
a quay where ships are loaded and unloaded

WORD HISTORY from Old English *hwearf*

what *ADJECTIVE*
1 used to ask the amount, number, or kind of something ◆ *What kind of music do you like?*
2 which of several ◆ *What size of shoe do you take?* ◆ *What part of town do you live in?*
3 the or any that; whatever ◆ *Just give us what food you can spare.*

what a used to intensify an adjective or noun ◆ *What an idiot!* ◆ *What a weird thing to say!*

what *PRONOUN*
1 what thing or things ◆ *What is your all-time favourite film?* ◆ *What should I wear tonight?*
2 the thing that

Of course they'd all seen what dwarf molars could do to a goblin head. Not a pretty sight. — *Eoin Colfer, Artemis Fowl*

and what not and other similar things
what is more as an additional point, moreover
what's what (*informal*) which things are important or useful
what with on account of ◆ *What with moving house and everything, we've been really busy.*

what *ADVERB*
to what extent or degree ◆ *What does it matter if they disagree with you?*

whatever *PRONOUN*
1 anything or everything ◆ *You can play whatever you like.*
2 no matter what ◆ *Whatever happens, don't let go of the rope.*

whatever *ADJECTIVE*
of any kind or amount ◆ *Buy whatever equipment you need.* ◆ *There is no doubt whatever that the dog saved his life.*

whatnot *NOUN*
other things of the same kind ◆ *The cupboard was stuffed full of broomsticks, cauldrons, and whatnot.*

whatsoever *ADJECTIVE*
at all; whatever ◆ *There is no chance whatsoever.*

wheat *NOUN*
a cereal plant from which flour is made
▷ **wheaten** *ADJECTIVE*

WORD HISTORY from an Old English word

wheaten *ADJECTIVE*
made from wheat flour

wheatmeal *NOUN*
flour made from wheat from which some of the bran and germ has been removed

Wheatstone bridge *NOUN*
(*Science*) a device for measuring an unknown resistance by combining it in a circuit with known resistances and equalizing the potential at two points

wheedle *VERB* **wheedles, wheedling, wheedled**
to persuade someone to do something by coaxing or flattering them

wheel *NOUN* **wheels**
1 a circular object that revolves on a shaft or axle that passes through its centre
2 a steering wheel
3 a horizontal revolving disc on which clay is made into a pot

wheel *VERB* **wheels, wheeling, wheeled**
1 to push a bicycle or trolley etc. along on its wheels
2 to move or fly in a wide circle or curve

Squawking, squeaking, screeching, the flock wheeled this way and that as if to the command of some unseen choreographer. — *Paul Stewart and Chris Riddell, Stormchaser*

to wheel and deal is to be involved in business or political activities in an unscrupulous or dishonest way
to wheel round is to turn round quickly to face another way

wheelbarrow *NOUN* **wheelbarrows**
a small cart with one wheel at the front and legs at the back, pushed by handles

wheelchair *NOUN* **wheelchairs**
a chair on wheels, used by a person who cannot walk

wheel clamp *NOUN* **wheel clamps**
a device that can be locked around a vehicle's wheel to stop it from moving, used especially on cars that have been parked illegally

wheelie *NOUN* **wheelies**
(*informal*) the stunt of riding a bicycle or motorcycle for a short distance with the front wheel off the ground

wheelie bin *NOUN* **wheelie bins**
a large dustbin on wheels

wheeze *VERB* **wheezes, wheezing, wheezed**
to make a hoarse whistling sound as you breathe
▷ **wheezy** *ADJECTIVE*

wheeze *NOUN* **wheezes**
1 the sound of wheezing
2 (*informal*) a clever or amusing scheme or plan

whelk *NOUN* **whelks**
a shellfish that looks like a snail
WORD HISTORY from Old English *wioloc*

whelp *NOUN* **whelps**
a young dog; a pup

whelp *VERB* **whelps, whelping, whelped**
to give birth to a whelp or whelps
WORD HISTORY from Old English *hwelp*

when *ADVERB*
used to ask at what time, or on what date or occasion, something will happen ◆ *When does the film start?* ◆ *When are they getting married?* ◆ *When will you ever listen to me?*

when *CONJUNCTION*
1 at the time that ◆ *The audience fell silent as the pianist walked on-stage.*
2 although; considering that ◆ *Why are you going canoeing when you can't swim?*

whence *ADVERB, CONJUNCTION* (*formal*)
1 from where, from what place or source
2 to the place from which ◆ *The wolves lost interest in the hunt and returned whence they came.*

whenever *ADVERB, CONJUNCTION*
at whatever time; every time ◆ *Whenever I eat pepper, it makes me sneeze.*

whensoever *ADVERB, CONJUNCTION*
(*formal*) whenever

where *ADVERB, CONJUNCTION*
1 in or to what place ◆ *Where have you hidden the map?* ◆ *Where would you like to go for lunch?*
2 in or at or to the place in which ◆ *The expedition had reached a point where no travellers had been before.*

where *PRONOUN*
1 what or which place ◆ *Where did you say you were born?* ◆ *Where would be a good spot for a picnic?*
2 the place that ◆ *This is where I belong.*

whereabouts *ADVERB*
in or near what place ◆ *Whereabouts did you park the car?*

whereabouts *PLURAL NOUN*
the place where something is

A reward had been offered for information about my whereabouts and that of the slaves who had abducted me. — *Celia Rees, Pirates!*

whereas *CONJUNCTION*
but in contrast ◆ *My sister hates spicy food, whereas I absolutely love it.*

whereby *ADVERB*
by which; by means of which ◆ *the process whereby people get the information they need.*

wherefore *ADVERB*
(*old use*) why; for what reason

'Wherefore should'st thou tarry here calling to thy love, seeing she comes not to thy call?' — *Oscar Wilde, The Fisherman and his Soul*

whereof *ADVERB, CONJUNCTION*
(*formal*) of what or which

Then when the lake was drained dry, the people whereof I speak built a mighty city on its bed. — *H. Rider Haggard, She*

whereupon *CONJUNCTION*
after which; and then

You come here recommending yourself as an interior decorator, whereupon I take you on, and what happens? — *Harold Pinter, The Caretaker*

wherever *ADVERB, CONJUNCTION*
1 at or to whatever place ◆ *The geese must be fenced in, or they will wander wherever they want.*
2 in every place that; in every case when ◆ *The Red Cross and Red Crescent provide medical help wherever it is needed.*

whet *VERB* **whets, whetting, whetted**
to sharpen a blade or edge by rubbing it against a stone etc.
to whet your appetite is to make you feel hungry

WORD HISTORY from Old English *hwettan* 'to sharpen'

whether *CONJUNCTION*
used to express a doubt or choice between two possibilities ◆ *I didn't know whether I could trust him.* ◆ *Sean couldn't decide whether to apply for the job or not.*

whetstone *NOUN* **whetstones**
a shaped stone for sharpening tools

whey (*sounds like* way) *NOUN*
the watery liquid left when milk forms curds

WORD HISTORY from an Old English word

which *ADJECTIVE, PRONOUN*
what particular one or ones of a set of things or people ◆ *Which way did they go?* ◆ *Which seats are reserved?* ◆ *Which of you is the fossil expert?*

which *RELATIVE PRONOUN*
the person or thing referred to ◆ *The photograph, which is now faded, shows my great grandmother's wedding.*

USAGE NOTE You use *which* when it begins a clause giving incidental information that you could leave out: ◆ *The book, which is now out of print, was a bestseller in its day.* You use *that* or *which* when it begins a clause that defines or identifies something and cannot be left out: ◆ *The book which I'm looking for is now out of print.*

whichever *ADJECTIVE, PRONOUN*
any which; that or those which ◆ *Choose whichever colour you want.* ◆ *You can have tea or coffee, whichever you like.*

whiff *NOUN* **whiffs**
1 a puff of smoke etc.
2 a slight smell or trace of something

Now, in late September, the whiff of woody decay filled the air and the squelchy carpet of leaves gave off a heady malty smell. — *James Riordan, The Prisoner*

Whig *NOUN* **Whigs**
(*History*) a member of a political party in the 17th–19th centuries, opposed to the Tories

WORD HISTORY from *whiggamore*, originally a name for Scottish Covenanters in the 17th century

while *CONJUNCTION*
1 during the time that; as long as ◆ *Start to make the icing while the cake is cooling.* ◆ *I learnt Spanish while I was in New Mexico.*
2 although; even though ◆ *While I can see your point, I still think it's a bad plan.*
3 on the other hand; whereas ◆ *This bike has eighteen gears, while that one has just twelve.*

while *NOUN*
1 a period of time ◆ *We haven't emailed each other for a while.* ◆ *I saw your friend just a short while ago.*
worth while or **worth your while** worth the time or effort spent

while *VERB* **whiles, whiling, whiled**
to while away time is to pass it in a leisurely manner ◆ *We whiled away the afternoon looking at old photographs.*

whilst *CONJUNCTION*
during the time that; while

whim *NOUN* **whims**
a sudden desire or change of mind ◆ *We turned off the motorway on a whim and explored some of the countryside.*

whimper *VERB* **whimpers, whimpering, whimpered**
to cry or whine softly

whimper *NOUN* **whimpers**
a whimpering sound

whimsical *ADJECTIVE*
quaint and playful ◆ *The artist is known for his witty and whimsical portraits of everyday people and celebrities.*
▷ **whimsically** *ADVERB*
▷ **whimsicality** *NOUN*

whimsy *NOUN* **whimsies**
1 playful or fanciful humour
2 a whim

whine *VERB* **whines, whining, whined**
1 to make a long high miserable cry or a shrill sound
2 to complain in a petty or feeble way
▷ **whiner** *NOUN*
▷ **whiny** *ADJECTIVE*

whine *NOUN* **whines**
a whining cry, sound, or complaint

WORD HISTORY from an Old English word meaning 'to whistle through the air'

whinge *VERB* **whinges, whinging** or **whingeing, whinged**
to grumble persistently

whinge *NOUN* **whinges**
(*informal*) an act of grumbling

WORD HISTORY from Old English *hwinsian*

whinny *VERB* **whinnies, whinnying, whinnied**
a horse whinnies when it neighs gently or happily

whinny *NOUN* **whinnies**
a gentle neigh

whip *NOUN* **whips**
1 a cord or strip of leather fixed to a handle, used for urging an animal on or for striking a person as a punishment
2 an official of a political party with authority to maintain discipline among its members
3 a pudding made of whipped cream and fruit or flavouring

whip *VERB* **whips, whipping, whipped**
1 to hit a person or animal with a whip
2 to move, or to make something move, with a whip-like movement

A strong wind tore through the trees whipping the branches fiercely to one side while the rain swept across their faces. — *Michelle Magorian, Goodnight Mister Tom*

3 to beat cream until it becomes thick, or eggs until they become frothy
4 (*informal*) to steal something

to whip something out is to take out and present a weapon, piece of paper, etc. suddenly

to whip something up
1 is to make or prepare something quickly
2 is to stimulate or rouse interest or support
3 is to excite or stir a crowd or audience

whiplash *NOUN*
1 the lash of a whip
2 injury caused by a severe jerk to the head, especially in a motor accident

whippersnapper *NOUN* **whippersnappers**
(*old use*) a young and inexperienced person who behaves in a presumptuous way

whippet *NOUN* **whippets**
a small dog rather like a greyhound, used for racing

whip-round *NOUN*
an appeal for contributions of money from a group of people

whirl *VERB* **whirls, whirling, whirled**
1 to turn around or spin very quickly, or to make something do this
2 your head or mind whirls when it seems to spin round because it is so full of ideas, information, etc.

whirl *NOUN* **whirls**
1 a quick turn or spin
2 frantic or bustling activity

For the best part of six months, Webb was a celebrity around London and his life was a whirl of regimental dinners, award ceremonies and interviews. — *Henry Brook, True Sea Stories*

to give something a whirl (*informal*) is to try it out

whirlpool *NOUN* **whirlpools**
a whirling current of water, often drawing floating objects towards its centre

whirlwind *NOUN* **whirlwinds**
a strong wind that whirls round a central point

whirlwind *ADJECTIVE*
very rapid or fast-paced ◆ *The band has recently returned from a whirlwind tour of the United States.*

whirr *VERB* **whirrs, whirring, whirred**
to make a continuous buzzing or vibrating sound

whirr *NOUN* **whirrs**
a whirring sound

whisk *VERB* **whisks, whisking, whisked**
1 to take or drive someone away rapidly ◆ *The director was whisked away in a limousine after the performance.*
2 to take or remove something quickly and lightly ◆ *The waiter whisked away our glasses before we had finished.* ◆ *I barely had time to whisk the crumbs off the table.*
3 to beat eggs etc. until they are frothy

whisk *NOUN* **whisks**
1 a kitchen tool used for whisking eggs, cream, or sauces
2 a whisking movement

whisker *NOUN* **whiskers**
1 a long hair-like bristle growing near the mouth of a cat and certain other animals
2 (*informal*) a very small amount or distance of something ◆ *The judo team came within a whisker of qualifying for the finals.*

▷ **whiskery** *ADJECTIVE*

whiskers *PLURAL NOUN*
the hair growing on a man's face, especially on his cheeks

whiskey *NOUN* **whiskeys**
Irish whisky

whisky *NOUN* **whiskies**
1 an alcoholic spirit distilled from malted grain, especially barley
2 a drink of whisky

WORD HISTORY from Scottish Gaelic *uisge beatha* 'water of life'

whisper *VERB* **whispers, whispering, whispered**
1 to speak softly, using the breath but not the vocal cords
2 to talk privately or secretly; to spread a rumour ◆ *It is whispered that they had an affair a few years ago.*
▷ **whisperer** *NOUN*

whisper *NOUN* **whispers**
1 a whispering tone of voice
2 a rumour
3 a slight trace of something

WORD HISTORY from Old English *hwisprian*

whist *NOUN*
a card game usually for two pairs of players

whistle *VERB* **whistles, whistling, whistled**
1 to make a shrill or musical sound, especially by blowing through a narrow opening in your lips
2 to speed past with a whistling sound

Arrows thick as the rain came whistling over the battlements, and fell clinking and glancing on the stones. — *J. R. R. Tolkien, The Two Towers*

to whistle in the dark is to try to keep your spirits up in the face of danger or difficulty
▷ **whistler** *NOUN*

whistle *NOUN* **whistles**
1 a whistling sound
2 a device that makes a shrill sound when blown, used for giving a signal
3 a high-pitched musical instrument played like a recorder

to blow the whistle on someone or something (*informal*) is to give information about a wrongdoer or wrongdoing

whistle-stop *ADJECTIVE*
very fast and with only brief pauses ◆ *The visitors were taken on a whistle-stop tour of the Lake District.*

whit *NOUN*
the least possible amount ◆ *I've had this cold for a week and I'm not feeling a whit better.*

WORD HISTORY from an old word *wight* meaning 'an amount'

white *NOUN* **whites**
1 the very lightest colour, like snow or salt
2 a person with light-coloured skin
3 the transparent substance (called *albumen*) round the yolk of an egg, which turns white when cooked
4 the white part of the eyeball, round the iris

white *ADJECTIVE*
1 of the colour white
2 having light-coloured skin
3 very pale from the effects of illness, fear, or worry
4 white coffee or tea is made with milk
5 white wine is made from pale grapes or skinned black grapes
▷ **whiteness** *NOUN*

white admiral *NOUN* **white admirals**
a butterfly with dark brown wings that have a broad white band on them

whitebait *NOUN* **whitebait**
a small edible silvery-white fish

WORD HISTORY from *white* and *bait*, because it was used as bait to catch larger fish

white dwarf *NOUN* **white dwarfs** or **white dwarves**
a small dense star about the size of a planet

white elephant *NOUN* **white elephants**
a useless or unwanted possession, especially one that is expensive to keep

white-hot *ADJECTIVE*
extremely hot; so hot that heated metal looks white

white lie *NOUN* **white lies**
a harmless or trivial lie that you tell in order to avoid hurting someone's feelings

white meat *NOUN*
poultry, veal, rabbit, and pork

whiten *VERB* **whitens, whitening, whitened**
to make something whiter, or to become whiter

Sir John stared at the boy speechlessly while his knuckles whitened. — *John Wyndham, The Midwich Cuckoos*

White Paper *NOUN* **White Papers**
a report issued by the government to give information on a subject

white spirit *NOUN*
a colourless liquid made from petroleum, used as a paint thinner and solvent

whitewash *NOUN*
1 a white liquid containing lime or powdered chalk, used for painting walls and ceilings
2 the action of concealing mistakes or other unpleasant facts so that someone will not be punished

whitewash *VERB* **whitewashes, whitewashing, whitewashed**
1 to paint a wall with whitewash
2 to clear someone's reputation by concealing their mistakes or faults

whither *ADVERB, CONJUNCTION*
(*old use*) to what place

This gentleman treated me with kindness, and desired I would let him know what place I came from last, and whither I was bound. — *Jonathan Swift, Gulliver's Travels*

WORD HISTORY from Old English *hwider*

whiting *NOUN* **whiting**
a small edible sea fish with white flesh

Whitsun *NOUN*
Whit Sunday and the days close to it

Whit Sunday
the seventh Sunday after Easter

WORD HISTORY from Old English *hwit* 'white', because people used to be baptized on that day and wore white clothes

whittle *VERB* **whittles, whittling, whittled**
to trim or shape wood by trimming thin slices off the surface
to whittle something down is to reduce its size or cost by removing some parts or aspects

WORD HISTORY from an Old English word meaning 'to cut'

whizz or **whiz** *VERB* **whizzes, whizzing, whizzed**
1 to move very quickly; to speed

In the time that it takes you to read this sentence a million email messages will have whizzed around the world. — *Michael Cox, The Incredible Internet*

2 to whistle through the air

whizz *NOUN* **whizzes**
a whizzing sound

whizz-kid *NOUN* **whizz-kids**
(*informal*) an exceptionally brilliant or successful young person

who *PRONOUN*
1 which person or people ◆ *Who wants to come to my birthday party?*
2 the particular person or people ◆ *Is that the actress who played Catwoman?* ◆ *Here is a list of people who have agreed to give sponsorship.*

USAGE NOTE See the note at *whom*.

whoa *EXCLAMATION*
a command to a horse to stop or stand still

whodunnit *NOUN* **whodunnits**
(*informal*) a story or film about a murder and the attempt to identify the murderer

whoever *PRONOUN*
1 any or every person who
2 no matter who

whole *ADJECTIVE*
1 complete
2 not injured or broken

whole *NOUN*
1 the full amount
2 a complete thing
3 in one piece ◆ *The snake swallowed the bird whole.*
as a whole in general
on the whole considering everything; mainly

wholefood *NOUN* **wholefoods**
food that has been processed as little as possible

wholehearted *ADJECTIVE*
wholehearted approval or support is given without doubts or reservations

wholemeal *ADJECTIVE*
made from the whole grain of wheat

whole number *NOUN* **whole numbers**
(*Mathematics*) a number without fractions

wholesale *NOUN*
the business of selling goods in large quantities to be resold by others (SEE ALSO **retail**)
▷ **wholesaler** *NOUN*

wholesale *ADJECTIVE, ADVERB*
1 on a large scale; including everybody or everything ◆ *As a result of wholesale slaughter in the last century, the bison nearly became extinct.*
2 in the wholesale trade

wholesome *ADJECTIVE*
good for your health; healthy ◆ *His doctor has prescribed a wholesome diet of whole grains, vegetables, and fresh fruits.*
▷ **wholesomeness** *NOUN*

WORD HISTORY from an old meaning of *whole* 'healthy'

wholly *ADVERB*
completely or entirely ◆ *I'm not wholly convinced that a windsurfing holiday is a good idea.*

whom *PRONOUN*
the form of *who* used when it is the object of a verb or comes after a preposition ◆ *Mr Blackadder, whom I think you know, is our new member of Parliament.* ◆ *To whom were you referring when you said 'a well-known author'?*

USAGE NOTE *Whom* can sound rather formal. In modern English, especially in speech and less formal writing, it often sounds more natural to use *who*, as in *the ghost who you heard last night* (or simply *the ghost you heard last night*) and *Who were you referring to?*

whomever *PRONOUN*
(*formal*) the form of *whoever* used when it is the object of a verb or comes after a preposition

whomsoever *PRONOUN*
(*formal*) the form of *whosoever* used when it is the object of a verb or comes after a preposition

whoop (*say* woop) *NOUN* **whoops**
a loud cry of excitement

whoop *VERB* **whoops, whooping, whooped**
to give a whoop

whoopee *EXCLAMATION*
a cry of joy

whooping cough (*say* **hoop**- ing) *NOUN*
an infectious disease that causes spasms of coughing and gasping for breath

whoosh *VERB* **whooshes, whooshing, whooshed**
to move very quickly; to whiz

A late-night taxi bringing home a fare whooshed by, throwing up spray. — *Keith Gray, Warehouse*

whopper *NOUN* **whoppers** (*informal*)
1 something very large
2 a blatant lie
WORD HISTORY from an old word *wap* 'to strike or beat'

whopping *ADJECTIVE*
(*informal*) very large or remarkable ◆ *There's a whopping great hole in the ceiling!*

whore (*say* hor) *NOUN* **whores**
a prostitute or promiscuous woman
WORD HISTORY from an Old English word

whorl *NOUN* **whorls**
1 a coil or curved shape
2 a complete circle formed by ridges in a fingerprint
3 a ring of leaves or petals
WORD HISTORY another spelling of *whirl*

who's
short for *who is* or *who has*

whose *PRONOUN*
belonging to what person or persons; of whom; of which ◆ *Whose snotty handkerchief is this?* ◆ *Whose was the best performance overall?*
USAGE NOTE Take care not to confuse the word *whose* with the contraction *who's.*

why *ADVERB*
1 for what reason or purpose ◆ *Why didn't you tell us you were a werewolf?*
2 on account of which ◆ *Can you give me one good reason why I should stay?* ◆ *Our heating has broken down and that's why it's so cold.*

wick *NOUN* **wicks**
1 the string that goes through the middle of a candle and is lit
2 the strip of material that you light in a lamp or heater that uses oil

wicked *ADJECTIVE*
1 morally bad or cruel
2 scheming or mischievous ◆ *'After you,' said the gatekeeper, standing aside with a wicked grin.*
3 (*informal*) excellent; very good
▷ **wickedly** *ADVERB*
▷ **wickedness** *NOUN*
WORD HISTORY from Old English *wicca* 'witch'

wicker *NOUN*
thin canes or twigs woven together to make baskets, fences, or furniture
▷ **wickerwork** *NOUN*

wicket *NOUN* **wickets**
1 a set of three stumps and two bails used in cricket
2 the strip of ground between the two wickets
3 the action of getting a batsman out in cricket
4 a small door or gate used to save opening a much larger one

wicketkeeper *NOUN* **wicketkeepers**
the fielder in cricket who stands behind the batsman's wicket

wide *ADJECTIVE*
1 measuring a lot from side to side; not narrow
2 measuring from side to side ◆ *This cloth is one metre wide.*
3 covering a great range; extensive ◆ *Dr Azwan has a wide knowledge of ancient Egyptian art.*
4 open to the full extent ◆ *The stricken deer stared at us with wide eyes.*
5 a shot or hit is wide if it misses the target
wide of the mark
1 a long way from the target
2 not correct or accurate ◆ *His first guess was wide of the mark.*
▷ **wideness** *NOUN*

wide *ADVERB*
1 to the full extent; far apart

'Can a vampire come back as a ghost?' I asked, eyes wide. — *Darren Shan, Cirque du Freak*

2 missing the target ◆ *The penalty shot went just wide.*
far and wide over a large area
wide awake fully awake

wide-angle *ADJECTIVE*
a wide-angle camera lens has a wider field of vision than a standard lens

widely *ADVERB*
commonly; among many people ◆ *This year's show is widely expected to be the biggest yet.*

widen *VERB* **widens, widening, widened**
to make something wider, or to become wider

From the North Sea a keen wind blew over the shallows of Loch Fleet, where the river mouth widened. — *Kathleen Fidler, The Desperate Journey*

widescreen *ADJECTIVE*
a widescreen film or television has a format that is unusually wide in relation to its height

widespread *ADJECTIVE*
existing in many places or over a wide area ◆ *In some parts of the world there is still a widespread belief in witches.*

widow *NOUN* **widows**
a woman whose husband has died and who has not married again
▷ **widowhood** *NOUN*

widowed *ADJECTIVE*
made a widow or widower

widower *NOUN* **widowers**
a man whose wife has died and who has not married again

width *NOUN* **widths**
1 the distance or measurement of something from side to side
2 a piece of material at its full extent from side to side
3 a wide range or extent ◆ *The strength of the encyclopedia lies in its width of coverage, rather than its depth.*

wield *VERB* **wields, wielding, wielded**
1 to hold and use a weapon or tool
2 to exercise power or influence
WORD HISTORY from Old English *wieldan* 'to govern or subdue'

wife *NOUN* **wives**
the woman to whom a man is married
▷ **wifely** *ADJECTIVE*
WORD HISTORY from Old English *wif* 'woman'

wig *NOUN* **wigs**
a covering made of real or artificial hair, worn on the head
WORD HISTORY from an earlier word *periwig*, from Old French *perruque*

wigeon *NOUN* **wigeon**
a kind of wild duck

wiggle *VERB* **wiggles, wiggling, wiggled**
to move repeatedly from side to side, or to make something do this
▷ **wiggly** *ADJECTIVE*

wiggle *NOUN* **wiggles**
a wiggling movement

wigwam *NOUN* **wigwams**
a hut or tent made by fastening skins or mats over a framework of poles, formerly used by some Native American peoples
WORD HISTORY from a Native American word meaning 'their house'

wild *ADJECTIVE*
1 living or growing in its natural state; not domesticated, tame, or cultivated
2 not civilized; barbarous ◆ *In the 2nd century AD these wild tribes fought a deadly war against Rome.*
3 not controlled or restrained ◆ *There were wild celebrations in the city that night.*
4 stormy or windy ◆ *Global warming may lead to rising sea levels and wilder weather.*
5 very foolish or unreasonable ◆ *The theory that dinosaurs were wiped out by an asteroid started out as just a 'wild idea'.*
6 a wild guess is unplanned or haphazard
to run wild is to grow or live without being disciplined or restrained
▷ **wildly** *ADVERB*
▷ **wildness** *NOUN*

wild *NOUN* **wilds**
1 the wild is the natural environment in which animals and plants exist ◆ *Several companies now run trips to see polar bears in the wild.*
2 the wilds are remote areas far from towns and cities

wild card *NOUN* **wild cards**
1 a playing card that can have any value chosen by the player holding it in a game
2 (*ICT*) an asterisk or other symbol used to match any character or sequence of characters in a text search

wildebeest *NOUN* **wildebeest**
a gnu
WORD HISTORY an Afrikaans word meaning 'wild beast'

wilderness *NOUN* **wildernesses**
a wild uncultivated area; a desert
WORD HISTORY from Old English *wild deor* 'wild deer'

wildfire *NOUN*
to spread like wildfire is to spread or become known over a large area very fast

wild goose chase *NOUN*
a hopeless or pointless search for something

wildlife *NOUN*
wild animals in their natural setting

Wild West *NOUN*
(*History*) the western states of the USA during the period when they were lawless frontier districts

wile *NOUN* **wiles**
a piece of deception; a trick

wilful *ADJECTIVE*
1 a wilful person is obstinately determined to do what they want
2 a wilful action or crime is carried out deliberately
▷ **wilfully** *ADVERB*
▷ **wilfulness** *NOUN*

will❶ *AUXILIARY VERB*
1 used to express the future tense ◆ *It will be daylight in a few hours.* ◆ *Someday, people will go to the Moon for their holidays.*
2 used in questions, especially requests ◆ *Will you please keep the noise down?*
3 used to express a promise, intention, or obligation ◆ *I will never let you down.*
WORD HISTORY from Old English *wyllan*

will❷ *NOUN* **wills**
1 the mental power to decide and control what you do
2 a desire; a chosen decision ◆ *The prisoner signed the document against his will.*
3 a written statement of how a person's possessions are to be disposed of after their death
at will whenever you like ◆ *If you keep your entry ticket, you can come and go at will.*
to have a will of your own is to be stubbornly determined in character
with the best will in the world however good your intentions are
with a will with determination ◆ *The assistants set to work with a will.*

a b c d e f g h i j k l m n o p q r s t u v w x y z

will *VERB* **wills, willing, willed**
1 to use your will power to try to influence a person's actions, or bring about an outcome ◆ *It felt like the whole stadium was willing the home team to score.*
2 to bequeath something in a will ◆ *The castle was willed to the National Trust in 1969.*
WORD HISTORY from Old English *willa*

willing *ADJECTIVE*
ready and happy to do what is wanted
▷ **willingly** *ADVERB*
▷ **willingness** *NOUN*

will-o'-the-wisp *NOUN* **will-o'-the-wisps**
1 a flickering spot of light seen on marshy ground
2 an elusive person or hope
WORD HISTORY from *Will*, short for *William*, and an old meaning of *wisp* 'a small bundle of straw burned as a torch'

willow *NOUN* **willows**
a tree or shrub with flexible branches, usually growing near water

willowy *ADJECTIVE*
tall and slender

The door was opened by Elain, Horst's wife, a small, willowy woman with refined features and silky blond hair pinned into a bun. — *Christopher Paolini, Eragon*

will power *NOUN*
strength of mind to control what you do

willy-nilly *ADVERB*
1 whether you want to or not
2 without planning; haphazardly ◆ *Check that the website is legitimate before downloading files willy-nilly.*
WORD HISTORY from *will I, nill I* 'I am willing, I am unwilling'

wilt *VERB* **wilts, wilting, wilted**
1 a flower or plant wilts when it loses freshness and droops
2 to lose your strength or energy ◆ *The midday heat was making us all start to wilt.*

wily (*say* wy- lee) *ADJECTIVE*
cunning or crafty
▷ **wiliness** *NOUN*

wimp *NOUN* **wimps**
(*informal*) a weak or timid person
▷ **wimpish** *ADJECTIVE*
▷ **wimpy** *ADJECTIVE*

wimple *NOUN* **wimples**
a piece of cloth folded round the head and neck, worn by women in the Middle Ages and still worn by some nuns

win *VERB* **wins, winning, won**
1 to defeat your opponents in a battle, game, or contest
2 to get a prize or award by a victory or by using effort or skill
3 to gain something as a result of effort or perseverance ◆ *After a few weeks following the wild otters, the camera crew gradually won their trust.*
to win someone over is to gain their favour or support

win *NOUN* **wins**
a victory in a game or contest

wince *VERB* **winces, wincing, winced**
to make a slight movement because of pain, distress, or embarrassment

David ... tiptoed down the corridor, wincing every time he stepped on a creaking floorboard. — *Anthony Horowitz, Groosham Grange*

wince *NOUN* **winces**
a wincing movement
WORD HISTORY from an Old French word meaning 'to turn aside'

winch *NOUN* **winches**
a device for lifting or pulling things, using a rope or cable that winds on to a revolving drum or wheel

winch *VERB* **winches, winching, winched**
to lift or pull something with a winch

Katherine watched from her bedroom window as the ground-crew winched the airship down and the excited Engineers clustered closer. — *Philip Reeve, Mortal Engines*

wind[1] (*rhymes with* tinned) *NOUN* **winds**
1 a current of air
2 gas in the stomach or intestines that makes you feel uncomfortable
3 breath used for a purpose, e.g. for running or speaking
4 the wind instruments of an orchestra
to put the wind up someone (*informal*) is to frighten or alarm them
to get wind of something is to hear a rumour about it
to take the wind out of someone's sails is to frustrate them by anticipating what they will say or do

wind *VERB* **winds, winding, winded**
1 to make someone short of breath ◆ *We stopped at the summit, winded from the steep climb.*
2 to make a baby bring up wind by patting its back
WORD HISTORY from an Old English word

wind[2] (*rhymes with* find) *VERB* **winds, winding, wound**

1 to go or turn something in twists, curves, or circles

The trail wound, taking us round outcrops of rock, slanting down the sides of gullies to cross small streams. — *John Wyndham, The Chrysalids*

2 to wrap or encircle something ◆ *Carefully, Megan wound a bandage round her daughter's finger.*

3 to haul, hoist, or move something by turning a handle or windlass ◆ *I can't wind the car window down.*

4 to wind, or wind up, a clock or watch is to set or keep it going by turning a key or handle

to wind down

1 is to gradually lose power

2 is to relax

to wind something down is to bring it to an end

to wind up (*informal*) is to end up in a place or condition ◆ *Six months later, he wound up in jail.*

to wind someone up (*informal*) is to tease them or play a trick on them

to wind something up to wind up a business is to close it down

▷ **winder** *NOUN*

WORD HISTORY from an Old English word meaning 'to go rapidly'

windbag *NOUN* **windbags**

(*informal*) a person who talks too much

windbreak *NOUN* **windbreaks**

a screen or row of trees shielding something from the full force of the wind

windfall *NOUN* **windfalls**

1 a piece of unexpected good luck, especially a sum of money

2 a fruit blown off a tree by the wind

wind farm *NOUN* **wind farms**

a group of windmills or wind turbines for generating electricity

wind instrument *NOUN* **wind instruments**

a musical instrument played by blowing, such as a trumpet or flute

windlass *NOUN* **windlasses**

a machine for pulling or lifting things (e.g. a bucket from a well), with a rope or cable that is wound round an axle by turning a handle

WORD HISTORY from Old Norse *vindlass* 'winding- pole'

windmill *NOUN* **windmills**

1 a mill worked by the wind turning its sails

2 a toy consisting of a stick with curved vanes that turn in the wind

window *NOUN* **windows**

1 an opening in a wall or roof to let in light and air, usually filled with glass

2 a space behind the window of a shop where goods are displayed

3 (*ICT*) a framed area on a computer screen for running an application or displaying data

4 an interval or opportunity to do something; an available time ◆ *Can we meet tomorrow? I've got a window at ten o'clock.*

WORD HISTORY from Old Norse *vind* 'wind, air' and *auga* 'eye'

window box *NOUN* **window boxes**

a long narrow box fixed outside a window, for growing plants and flowers

window-dressing *NOUN*

1 the displaying of goods attractively in a shop window

2 presentation of facts in a way that creates a more favourable impression

window-shopping *NOUN*

the action of looking at items in shop windows without buying anything

windpipe *NOUN* **windpipes**

the tube by which air passes from the throat to the lungs

windscreen *NOUN* **windscreens**

the glass in the window at the front of a motor vehicle

windsurfing *NOUN*

the sport of surfing on a board that has a sail fixed to it

▷ **windsurfer** *NOUN*

windswept *ADJECTIVE*

exposed to strong winds ◆ *The standing stones lay in the middle of a bleak and windswept moor.*

windward *ADJECTIVE*

the windward side of a ship or building faces the wind

windward *NOUN*

the windward side

windy *ADJECTIVE*

1 with strong winds ◆ *It's too windy to put the washing outside today.*

2 exposed to strong winds; windswept

wine *NOUN* **wines**

1 an alcoholic drink made from fermented grape juice

2 a fermented drink made from other fruits or plants ◆ *elderberry wine*

3 a dark red colour

wing *NOUN* **wings**

1 one of the pair of parts of a bird, bat, or insect, that it uses for flying

2 one of the pair of long flat parts that stick out from the side of an aircraft and support it while it flies

3 a part of a large building that extends from the main part
4 the part of a motor vehicle's body above a wheel
5 a player whose place is at one of the far ends of the forward line in football or hockey etc.
6 (*Politics*) a section of a political party, with more extreme opinions than the others
7 (*Drama*) the wings are the sides of a theatre stage out of sight of the audience

on the wing flying in the air
to spread your wings is to become more independent and try something new
to take wing is to fly away
under your wing under your protection

wing *VERB* **wings, winging, winged**
1 a bird wings its way when it flies quickly
2 to wound someone in the arm or shoulder

winged *ADJECTIVE*
having wings

wingless *ADJECTIVE*
without wings

wingspan *NOUN*
the length between the two wing tips of an aircraft or bird

wink *VERB* **winks, winking, winked**
1 to close and open your eye quickly, especially as a signal to someone
2 a light winks when it flickers or twinkles

wink *NOUN* **winks**
1 the action of winking
2 a very short period of sleep ◆ *I didn't sleep a wink last night.*

winkle *NOUN* **winkles**
a kind of edible shellfish

winkle *VERB* **winkles, winkling, winkled**
to winkle something out is to extract or obtain information with difficulty
WORD HISTORY short for *periwinkle*

winner *NOUN* **winners**
1 a person, team, or animal that wins a contest
2 something very successful ◆ *The new CD is sure to be a winner with fans of country music.*

winning *ADJECTIVE*
a winning manner or expression is charming and attractive

winnings *PLURAL NOUN*
money won by gambling

winnow *VERB* **winnows, winnowing, winnowed**
to toss or fan grain so that the loose dry outer part is blown away
WORD HISTORY from an Old English word

winsome *ADJECTIVE*
charming and attractive
WORD HISTORY from Old English *wynn* 'a pleasure'

winter *NOUN* **winters**
the coldest season of the year, between autumn and spring
▷ **wintry** *ADJECTIVE*

winter *VERB* **winters, wintering, wintered**
to spend the winter somewhere ◆ *British swallows winter in South Africa and won't return until April or May.*

wipe *VERB* **wipes, wiping, wiped**
1 to dry or clean the surface of something by rubbing a cloth, sponge, etc. over it
2 to remove something by wiping ◆ *Izzy searched for a tissue to wipe away her tears.*
3 to erase data from a tape, computer disk, etc. ◆ *I've accidentally wiped our holiday video.*

to wipe something out is to cancel or destroy it completely

wipe *NOUN* **wipes**
the action of wiping something

wiper *NOUN* **wipers**
a device for wiping something, especially on a vehicle's windscreen

wire *NOUN* **wires**
1 a strand or thin flexible rod of metal
2 a piece of wire used to carry electric current
3 a fence made from wire
4 a telegram

wire *VERB* **wires, wiring, wired**
1 to fasten or strengthen something with wire
2 to fit or connect something with wires to carry electric current

wireless *NOUN* **wirelesses**
1 (*old use*) a radio
2 (*ICT*) a link between components by means of radio signals rather than wire or cable connections

wiring *NOUN*
the system of wires carrying electricity in a building or in a device

wiry *ADJECTIVE*
1 like wire
2 lean and strong

wisdom *NOUN*
the fact of being wise; soundness of judgement and good sense

wisdom tooth *NOUN* **wisdom teeth**
a molar tooth that may grow at the back of the jaw of a person aged about 20 or more

wise *ADJECTIVE*
1 judging well and showing good sense
2 knowing or understanding many things
to be none the wiser (*informal*)
3 is to know no more than you did before
is to be unaware of what has happened
▷ **wisely** *ADVERB*
WORD HISTORY from Old English *wis*

wisecrack *NOUN* **wisecracks**
(*informal*) a witty or clever remark

a b c d e f g h i j k l m n o p q r s t u v w x y z

wish *VERB* **wishes, wishing, wished**
1 to feel or say that you would like to have or do something or would like something to happen
2 to say that you hope someone will get something ◆ *Wish me luck!*

wish *NOUN* **wishes**
1 something you wish for; a desire
2 the action of wishing ◆ *Close your eyes and make a wish.*

wishbone *NOUN* **wishbones**
a forked bone between the neck and breast of a chicken or other bird

wishful thinking *NOUN*
belief in something because you wish it were true, not belief based on facts

wishy-washy *ADJECTIVE*
(*informal*) weak or feeble in colour or character

wisp *NOUN* **wisps**
1 a small thin bunch or strand of hair, straw, etc.
2 a thin streak of smoke or cloud

wispy *ADJECTIVE*
very thin and fine, like a wisp

The ants were still there; their wispy antennae weaving from side to side. — *James Vance Marshall, Walkabout*

wisteria (*say* wis- **teer**- ee- a) *NOUN*
a climbing plant with hanging blue, purple, or white flowers

WORD HISTORY named after an American anatomist, Caspar *Wistar* (1761- 1818)

wistful *ADJECTIVE*
sadly longing for something
▷ **wistfully** *ADVERB*
▷ **wistfulness** *NOUN*

WORD HISTORY from an old word *wistly* 'intently'

wit *NOUN* **wits**
1 intelligence or understanding ◆ *No one had the wit to see what was needed.*
2 a clever kind of humour
3 a witty person

at your wits' end not knowing what to do
to keep your wits about you is to stay alert

witch *NOUN* **witches**
a person, especially a woman, who practises witchcraft

WORD HISTORY from Old English *wicca*

witchcraft *NOUN*
the use of magic, especially for evil purposes

witch doctor *NOUN* **witch doctors**
a magician who belongs to a tribe and is believed to use magic to heal people

witch hazel *NOUN*
1 a North American shrub with yellow flowers
2 a lotion made from the leaves and bark of this plant

witch-hunt *NOUN* **witch-hunts**
a campaign to find and punish people who hold views that are considered to be unacceptable or dangerous

with *PREPOSITION*
used to indicate
1 being in the company or care of someone ◆ *Why don't you come with me to New York?* ◆ *Is that dog with you?*
2 employed by or a member of ◆ *I've been with the World Bank for two years now.*
3 understanding or following a person or argument ◆ *Are you with me, or shall I go over the main points again?*
4 having or wearing ◆ *This scarf belongs to the man with the pony tail over there.*
5 using; by means of ◆ *Beat the mixture with a wooden spoon until it is smooth.*
6 because of ◆ *Zach began to unwrap the parcel, his hands trembling with excitement.*
7 feeling or showing ◆ *It is with great sadness that we bring you the following news.*
8 towards or concerning ◆ *Voters were angry with the government for ignoring their views.*
9 in opposition to; against ◆ *There's no point in arguing with the traffic warden.*

to be with child (*old use*) is to be pregnant
with it (*informal*) up to date or fashionable

withal *ADVERB*
(*old use*) in addition; moreover

withdraw *VERB* **withdraws, withdrawing, withdrew, withdrawn**
1 to pull or take something back or away ◆ *Very slowly, the boy withdrew the knife from the wound.*
2 to cancel a promise or offer, or to retract a statement ◆ *If we don't respond soon, the company will withdraw their offer.*
3 to withdraw from a meeting or discussion is to stop taking part in it
4 to leave a place; to retreat ◆ *Troops have started to withdraw from the disputed area.*

withdrawal *NOUN* **withdrawals**
1 the action of withdrawing something
2 an amount of money taken out of an account
3 the process of stopping taking drugs to which you are addicted, often with unpleasant reactions

withdrawn *ADJECTIVE*
very shy or reserved

wither *VERB* **withers, withering, withered**
1 to become dried up and shrivelled
2 to fade away or fall into decline

WORD HISTORY another spelling of *weather*

withering *ADJECTIVE*
a withering look or remark is scornful or sarcastic

withers *PLURAL NOUN*
the ridge between a horse's shoulder blades

withhold *VERB* **withholds, withholding, withheld**
1 to refuse to give or allow information or permission
2 to hold something back; to restrain something ◆ *We could not withhold our laughter for much longer.*

within *PREPOSITION, ADVERB*
inside; not beyond something

without *PREPOSITION*
1 not having ◆ *The castaways had been without food for six days.*
2 free from ◆ *The animals here have evolved without fear of humans and other predators.*
3 (*old use*) outside

The great beasts roared and fought without the walls, clawed and battered at the door. — *Edgar Rice Burroughs, Pellucidar*

without *ADVERB*
(*old use*) outside

withstand *VERB* **withstands, withstanding, withstood**
to endure something successfully; to resist something

witness *NOUN* **witnesses**
1 a person who sees or hears something happen ◆ *Police are appealing for witnesses to the accident to come forward.*
2 a person who gives evidence in a lawcourt

witness *VERB* **witnesses, witnessing, witnessed**
1 to be a witness of something
2 to sign a document to confirm that it is genuine
3 to be the place or period in which something takes place ◆ *The 1980s witnessed a revolution in the printing industry.*

witter *VERB* **witters, wittering, wittered**
to speak at annoying length about trivial matters ◆ *Do stop wittering about your lost umbrella.*

witticism *NOUN* **witticisms**
a witty remark

wittingly *ADVERB*
intentionally; deliberately

witty *ADJECTIVE* **wittier, wittiest**
clever and amusing; full of wit
▷ **wittily** *ADVERB*
▷ **wittiness** *NOUN*

wizard *NOUN* **wizards**
1 a male witch; a magician
2 a person with amazing abilities ◆ *a wizard with computers*
▷ **wizardry** *NOUN*
▷ **wizarding** *NOUN*

WORD HISTORY from an earlier meaning of *wise* 'a wise person'

wizened (*say* wiz- end) *ADJECTIVE*
shrunken or wrinkled from age

A little, wizened woman, evidently a slave, bent over the raised hearth, stirring the evening stew in a bronze cauldron. — *Rosemary Sutcliff, The Eagle of the Ninth*

WORD HISTORY from an old word *wizen* 'to shrivel'

woad *NOUN*
a kind of blue dye formerly obtained from a plant of the mustard family

WORD HISTORY from an Old English word

wobble *VERB* **wobbles, wobbling, wobbled**
1 to move unsteadily from side to side
2 to make something move unsteadily; to rock something
3 a voice or sound wobbles when it wavers or shakes

wobble *NOUN* **wobbles**
a wobbling movement or sound
▷ **wobbly** *ADJECTIVE*

wodge *NOUN* **wodges**
(*informal*) a large piece or amount

woe *NOUN* **woes**
1 great sorrow or distress
2 trouble or misfortune

WORD HISTORY from an Old English word

woebegone *ADJECTIVE*
looking unhappy

WORD HISTORY from *woe* and an old word *bego* 'to attack or surround'

woeful *ADJECTIVE*
1 full of woe; sorrowful
2 deplorable; disgraceful ◆ *At the heart of the problem has been a woeful lack of funding.*
▷ **woefully** *ADVERB*

wok *NOUN* **woks**
a Chinese cooking pan shaped like a large bowl

wold *NOUN* **wolds**
an area of open upland country

WORD HISTORY from Old English *wald*

wolf *NOUN* **wolves**
a fierce wild animal of the dog family, which often hunts in packs

to cry wolf is to raise false alarms so often that a real cry for help is ignored

a wolf in sheep's clothing a person who appears friendly or harmless but is really an enemy

wolf *VERB* **wolfs, wolfing, wolfed**
to eat food quickly and greedily

wolverine *NOUN* **wolverines**
a large animal of the weasel family, common in the north of North America

woman *NOUN* **women**
an adult female human being
▷ **womanhood** *NOUN*
WORD HISTORY from an Old English word

womanizer *NOUN* **womanizers**
a man who has sexual affairs with many women
USAGE NOTE This word can also be spelled womaniser.

womankind *NOUN*
women collectively

womanly *ADJECTIVE*
having qualities that are thought to be typical of women
▷ **womanliness** *NOUN*

womb (*say* woom) *NOUN* **wombs**
the hollow organ in a female's body where babies develop before they are born; the uterus
WORD HISTORY from an Old English word

wombat *NOUN* **wombats**
an Australian animal rather like a small bear
WORD HISTORY from an Aboriginal word

wonder *NOUN* **wonders**
1 a feeling of surprise and admiration or curiosity
2 something that causes this feeling; a marvel ◆ *The lighthouse at Alexandria in Egypt was one of the wonders of the ancient world.*
no wonder it is not surprising
to work or do wonders is to have a very good effect

wonder *VERB* **wonders, wondering, wondered**
1 to try to form an opinion or decision about something

Have you ever wondered what you'd do if you won the lottery? — *Jacqueline Wilson, Lola Rose*

2 to feel wonder or doubt

wonderful *ADJECTIVE*
marvellous or excellent
▷ **wonderfully** *ADVERB*

wonderment *NOUN*
a feeling of wonder

wondrous *ADJECTIVE*
(*literary*) wonderful; marvellous

He was wondrous to look upon, the whale rider. The water streamed away from him and he opened his mouth to gasp in the cold air. — *Witi Ihimaera, The Whale Rider*

▷ **wondrously** *ADVERB*

wont (*say* wohnt) *ADJECTIVE*
(*old use*) accustomed; used to doing something ◆ *Pandora was watching with her eyes closed as cats are wont to do.*

wont *NOUN*
a habit or custom ◆ *My parents arrived an hour early, as was their wont.*
WORD HISTORY from an Old English word

won't
short for *will not*

woo *VERB* **woos, wooing, wooed** (*old use*)
1 to try to win the love of a woman
2 to seek someone's favour or support
▷ **wooer** *NOUN*
WORD HISTORY from an Old English word

wood *NOUN* **woods**
1 the tough fibrous substance that the trunk and branches of trees are made of
2 this substance cut for use as timber or fuel
3 many trees growing close together
not to see the wood for the trees is to fail to get a clear view of the main issue because of distracting details
out of the wood or woods clear of danger or difficulty

woodcock *NOUN* **woodcock**
a kind of game bird with a long bill, related to the snipe

woodcut *NOUN* **woodcuts**
an engraving made on wood; a print made from this

wooded *ADJECTIVE*
covered with growing trees

wooden *ADJECTIVE*
1 made of wood
2 stiff and showing no expression or liveliness ◆ *While the story was good, the acting was wooden and spoiled the film.*
▷ **woodenly** *ADVERB*

woodland *NOUN* **woodlands**
wooded country

woodlouse *NOUN* **woodlice**
a small wingless creature with seven pairs of legs, which lives in rotten wood or damp soil

woodpecker *NOUN* **woodpeckers**
a bird that taps tree trunks with its beak to find insects

woodwind *NOUN*
wind instruments that are usually made of wood, e.g. the clarinet and oboe

woodwork *NOUN*
1 the art of making things out of wood
2 articles made out of wood

woodworm *NOUN* **woodworms**
1 the larva of a kind of beetle that bores into wooden furniture
2 the damage done to wood by this larva

woody *ADJECTIVE*
1 like wood; consisting of wood
2 full of trees

woof *NOUN* **woofs**
the gruff bark of a dog

woof *VERB* **woofs, woofing, woofed**
to bark gruffly

woofer *NOUN* **woofers**
a loudspeaker for reproducing low frequencies

wool *NOUN* **wools**
1 the thick soft hair of sheep and goats etc.
2 thread or cloth made from this

to pull the wool over someone's eyes is to deceive them

WORD HISTORY from Old English *wull*

woollen *ADJECTIVE*
made of wool

woollens *PLURAL NOUN*
woollen clothes

woolly *ADJECTIVE*
1 covered with wool or wool-like hair
2 like wool; woollen
3 a woolly idea or woolly thinking is vague or confused

▷ **woolliness** *NOUN*

woolly *NOUN* **woollies**
(*informal*) a woollen piece of clothing, especially a pullover

woozy *ADJECTIVE*
(*informal*) dizzy or dazed

word *NOUN* **words**
1 a single unit of speech or writing which has a meaning
2 a brief conversation ◆ *Can I have a word with you?*
3 a remark or statement ◆ *The accused didn't utter a word in his own defence.*
4 a promise ◆ *She is the kind of person who always keeps her word and I knew I could rely on her.*
5 a command or spoken signal ◆ *Run when I give the word.*
6 a message; information ◆ *It took three weeks for word of the disaster to reach the port.*

by word of mouth in spoken not written words
to have words is to quarrel
in a word briefly; concisely
word for word in exactly the same words

word *VERB* **words, wording, worded**
to express something in words ◆ *Be sure to word the question carefully.*

WORD FAMILY Related adjectives are lexical and verbal.

word class *NOUN* **word classes**
(*Grammar*) any of the groups into which words are divided to show their role in a sentence (also called *part of speech*)

word classes

The **word classes** of English are the different types of words you use in making sentences. Each word class has a special job to do: for example, a noun names things and a verb tells you what someone or something is doing. The names of the main word classes are: *noun, verb, adjective, adverb, pronoun, conjunction, preposition*, and *exclamation* (also sometimes called *interjection*). Word classes are also called **parts of speech**.

Many words belong to more than one word class. For example, the word *back* can be a noun (*a sore back*), an adjective (*the back seat*), an adverb (*to fall back*), or a verb (*to back a plan*), depending on how it is used in a sentence. Sometimes, words form new word classes as their meanings develop over time. For example, the verb *to access* (as in *accessing data*) has developed from the noun *access* ('the right to use or look at something').

See also the panels for **adjectives, adverbs, conjunctions, determiners, nouns, prepositions, pronouns, and verbs.**

wording *NOUN*
the way something is worded

word of honour *NOUN*
a solemn promise

word-perfect *ADJECTIVE*
having memorized every word perfectly ◆ *I'm rehearsing like mad, so I'll be word-perfect at the audition.*

word processor *NOUN* **word processors**
a type of computer or computer program used for editing and printing letters and documents

wordy *ADJECTIVE*
using too many words; not concise

wore *past tense of* **wear**

work *NOUN* **works**
1 physical or mental effort made in order to do or make something ◆ *Getting the gold medal has been worth all the training and hard work.*
2 (*Science*) the result of applying a force to move an object
3 a job; employment
4 something done or produced by work ◆ *The design is the work of a team of international architects.*
5 a published or exhibited piece of writing, painting, music, etc.

at work busy working
to have your work cut out is to be faced with a hard task
out of work having no work; unable to find paid employment

work *VERB* **works, working, worked**
1 to do work
2 to have a job; to be employed ◆ *Van Gogh worked as an art dealer, a teacher and a missionary before becoming a painter.*
3 to act or operate correctly or successfully

I don't really smell, do I? Has my deodorant stopped working? — *Jacqueline Wilson, Girls Out Late*

4 to make a machine etc. function; to operate something ◆ *I can't work this new vacuum cleaner.*
5 to shape or press a mixture, clay, or dough

I worked the clay again, drew it into the shape of a snake, pushed it all together again and made the shape of a human head. — *David Almond, Skellig*

6 to move gradually into a particular position ◆ *Over time, the door hinges had begun to work loose.*

to work something in is to try to include it
to work on someone is to use your influence on them
to work out
1 is to do physical exercise
2 is to have a particular result
3 to work something out is to find an answer by thinking or calculating
to work someone over (*informal*) is to beat them up
to work something up is to develop it from a raw or rough stage
to work up to something is to progress gradually to something more difficult or advanced

workable *ADJECTIVE*
that can be used or will work

worker *NOUN* **workers**
1 a person who works
2 a member of the working class
3 a bee or ant that does the work in a hive or colony but does not produce eggs

workflow *NOUN*
(*ICT*) the sequence of operations in a system

workforce *NOUN* **workforces**
the number of people who work in a particular factory, industry, country, etc.

workhouse *NOUN* **workhouses**
(*History*) a public institution where people unable to support themselves were housed in return for work

working class *NOUN* **working classes**
the class of people who work for wages, especially in manual or industrial work

workload *NOUN*
the amount of work to be done

workman *NOUN* **workmen**
a man employed to do manual labour; a worker

workmanlike *ADJECTIVE*
efficient or competent but not outstanding

workmanship *NOUN*
the degree of skill shown in making or producing something

workmate *NOUN* **workmates**
a person with whom you work

work of art *NOUN* **works of art**
a fine painting, sculpture, or composition etc.

workout *NOUN* **workouts**
a session of physical exercise or training

workplace *NOUN* **workplaces**
a place where people work

works *PLURAL NOUN*
1 the moving parts of a machine
2 a factory or industrial site

worksheet *NOUN* **worksheets**
a sheet of paper with a set of questions about a subject for students, often used with a textbook

workshop *NOUN* **workshops**
1 a place where things are made or mended
2 a meeting to discuss or learn about a subject and take part in activities relating to it

work-shy *ADJECTIVE*
avoiding work; lazy

world *NOUN* **worlds**
1 the earth with all its countries and peoples
2 all the people on the earth; everyone ◆ *It seemed as if the entire world was against their marriage.*
3 a planet ◆ *The meteors had travelled here from another world.*
4 a region or section of the earth ◆ *the English-speaking world*
5 the people or things belonging to a certain place, time, or sphere of activity

Nearly everyone in the wizarding world thought Sirius a dangerous murderer and a great Voldemort supporter. — *J. K. Rowling, Harry Potter and the Order of the Phoenix*

to do someone the world of good is to have a very good effect on them
to think the world of someone is to have the highest possible opinion of them

worldly *ADJECTIVE*
1 to do with life on earth, not spiritual
2 interested only in money, pleasure, etc.
3 experienced about people and life
▷ **worldliness** *NOUN*

worldwide *ADJECTIVE, ADVERB*
extending throughout the whole world

World Wide Web *NOUN*
(*ICT*) an information system that connects related sites and documents which can be accessed using the Internet

worm *NOUN* **worms**
1 an animal with a long small soft rounded or flat body and no backbone or limbs
2 an unimportant or unpleasant person
▷ **wormy** *ADJECTIVE*

worm *VERB* **worms, worming, wormed**
1 to move along by wriggling or crawling

I felt a homely affection for the warm security of the tent, and reluctantly wormed out of my bag to face the prospect of lighting the stove. — *Joe Simpson, Touching the Void*

2 to rid an animal of parasitic worms
to worm something out of someone is to get information from them by constant and clever questioning

wormwood *NOUN*
a woody plant with a bitter taste

worn *past participle* of **wear**

worn-out *ADJECTIVE*
1 tired and exhausted
2 damaged by too much use

worried *ADJECTIVE*
feeling or showing worry

worry *VERB* **worries, worrying, worried**
1 to be troublesome to someone; to make someone feel slightly afraid
2 to feel anxious
3 an animal worries its prey when it holds it in its teeth and shakes it
4 a dog worries sheep if it chases and attacks them
▷ **worrier** *NOUN*

worry *NOUN* **worries**
1 the condition of worrying; being uneasy
2 something that makes a person worry

worse *ADJECTIVE, ADVERB*
more bad or more badly; less good or less well
the worse for wear damaged by use
worse off less fortunate or well off

worse *NOUN*
something worse ◆ *The storm isn't over yet. I fear there may be worse to come.*
WORD HISTORY from an Old English word, related to *war*

worsen *VERB* **worsens, worsening, worsened**
to make something worse, or to become worse

worship *VERB* **worships, worshipping, worshipped**
1 (*Religion*) to give praise or respect to God or a god
2 to love or respect a person or thing greatly
▷ **worshipper** *NOUN*

worship *NOUN* **worships**
1 (*Religion*) the act of worshipping
2 (*Religion*) a religious act or ceremony of worshipping
3 a title of respect for a mayor or certain magistrates ◆ *Her Worship the Mayor of Cape Town.*
WORD HISTORY from Old English *weorth* 'worth'

worshipful *ADJECTIVE*
used in titles, meaning 'honourable' ◆ *the Worshipful Company of Goldsmiths*

worst *ADJECTIVE, ADVERB*
most bad or most badly; least good or least well

worst *NOUN*
the worst part, event, situation, etc. ◆ *When news of the hurricane reached us, we were prepared for the worst.*
at worst in the worst possible case
to get or **have the worst of it** is to suffer the most

worsted *NOUN*
a kind of woollen material made from fine smooth yarn
WORD HISTORY named after *Worstead*, a place in Norfolk, where it was made

worth *ADJECTIVE*
1 having a certain value ◆ *A first-edition of the book would be worth over £100.*
2 deserving something; good or important enough for something ◆ *The house doesn't look worth the asking price to me.* ◆ *The arts section of the paper is usually worth reading.*

worth *NOUN*
1 value or usefulness
2 the amount that a certain sum will buy ◆ *five pounds' worth of stamps*
WORD HISTORY from Old English *weorth*

worthless *ADJECTIVE*
having no value; useless
▷ **worthlessness** *NOUN*

worthwhile *ADJECTIVE*
1 a worthwhile task is important enough to spend time or effort on
2 a worthwhile cause is good enough to deserve money or support

worthy *ADJECTIVE*
1 a worthy person or cause deserves respect or support
2 to be worthy of something is to deserve it ◆ *This is a local charity that is worthy of our support.*
▷ **worthiness** *NOUN*

would *AUXILIARY VERB*
1 used as the past tense of *will* ◆ *The guide said he would meet us here.*
2 used in questions and polite requests ◆ *Would you like another doughnut?*
3 used to make a polite statement ◆ *I would like to apply for a part in the chorus.*
4 used in conditional clauses ◆ *If you hadn't reminded me, I would have forgotten to bring the bottle opener.*
5 used to give advice ◆ *I would phone the doctor straight away if I were you.*
6 used to express something to be expected ◆ *The DVD would go wrong, just before the best part of the film!*

would-be *ADJECTIVE*
wanting or pretending to be ◆ *a would-be comedian*

wouldn't
short for *would not*

wound❶ (*say* woond) *NOUN* **wounds**
1 an injury done by a cut, stab, or hit
2 a hurt to a person's feelings

wound *VERB* **wounds, wounding, wounded**
1 to cause a wound to a person or animal
2 to hurt a person's feelings ◆ *Privately, the President was deeply wounded by the attacks on his integrity.*

wound❷ (*say* wownd) *past tense* of **wind❷**

wove❷ *past tense* of **weave❶**

wow *VERB* **wows, wowing, wowed**
(*informal*) to impress or excite someone greatly

WPC *ABBREVIATION*
woman police constable

wpm *ABBREVIATION*
words per minute

wrack *NOUN*
a coarse brown seaweed thrown up on the shore or growing there
WORD HISTORY from an old word *wrack* meaning 'shipwreck'

wraith *NOUN* **wraiths**
a ghost
WORD HISTORY originally a Scots word; origin unknown

wrangle *VERB* **wrangles, wrangling, wrangled**
to have a noisy argument or quarrel
▷ **wrangler** *NOUN*

wrangle *NOUN* **wrangles**
a noisy argument or quarrel

wrap *VERB* **wraps, wrapping, wrapped**
1 to put paper or cloth etc. round something as a covering
2 (*ICT*) to make text carry over to a new line automatically; to be carried over in this way
to be wrapped up in something is to be deeply occupied by or involved in it
to wrap up is to put on warm clothes

wrap *NOUN* **wraps**
1 a shawl, coat, or cloak worn for warmth
2 a flour tortilla rolled around a filling and eaten as a sandwich
under wraps kept secret

wrapper *NOUN* **wrappers**
a piece of paper or cloth etc. wrapped round something

wrapping *NOUN*
material used to wrap something

wrath (*rhymes with* cloth) *NOUN*
extreme anger
▷ **wrathful** *ADJECTIVE*
▷ **wrathfully** *ADVERB*
WORD HISTORY from an Old English word

wreak (*sounds like* reek) *VERB* **wreaks, wreaking, wreaked**
to inflict damage; to cause destruction or chaos ◆ *Fog wreaked havoc with the flow of traffic.*
WORD HISTORY from Old English *wrecan* 'to avenge'
USAGE NOTE Note that the past form of *wreak* is *wreaked* and not *wrought*. The adjective *wrought* is used to describe metal that has been shaped by hammering or rolling.

wreath (*say* reeth) *NOUN* **wreaths**
1 flowers or leaves fastened into a circle ◆ *a holly wreath*
2 a curving line of mist or smoke
WORD HISTORY from Old English *writhan* 'to writhe'

wreathe (*say* reeth) *VERB* **wreathes, wreathing, wreathed**
1 to surround or decorate something with a wreath
2 to wind round something ◆ *The snake wreathed itself round the branch.*
3 smoke or mist wreathes when it moves in a curving line

wreck *VERB* **wrecks, wrecking, wrecked**
to damage or ruin something so badly that it cannot be used again
▷ **wrecker** *NOUN*

wreck *NOUN* **wrecks**
1 a ship that has been destroyed by a storm or accidental damage
2 the remains of a badly damaged vehicle, building, etc.
3 a person whose physical or mental health has been badly damaged ◆ *Mr Parsons was a nervous wreck by the end of the evening.*
4 the wrecking of something

wreckage *NOUN*
the pieces of a wreck

wren *NOUN* **wrens**
a small usually brown songbird

wrench *VERB* **wrenches, wrenching, wrenched**
to twist or pull something violently

The lobster had lost so many claws that, after nine had been wrenched off, its brain refused to grow any more. — *Henry Williamson, Tarka the Otter*

wrench *NOUN* **wrenches**
1 a wrenching movement
2 pain caused by parting ◆ *Leaving their home in Russia was a great wrench for my grandparents.*
3 an adjustable tool rather like a spanner, used for gripping and turning nuts or bolts

wrest *VERB* **wrests, wresting, wrested**
1 to take something away using force or effort ◆ *Leary sprang like a tiger and wrested the musket out of the prisoner's hand.*
2 to obtain something with effort or difficulty ◆ *All attempts to wrest an apology from the government have so far met with silence.*

WORD HISTORY from an Old English word

wrestle *VERB* **wrestles, wrestling, wrestled**
1 to fight by grasping your opponent and trying to throw them to the ground
2 to struggle with a problem or difficulty ◆ *The islands have been wrestling with the issue of population decline for 40 years.*
▷ **wrestler** *NOUN*

wrestle *NOUN* **wrestles**
1 a wrestling match
2 a hard struggle

wretch *NOUN* **wretches**
1 a very unfortunate or miserable person
2 a hated or despicable person

wretched *ADJECTIVE*
1 miserable or unhappy
2 of poor quality; unsatisfactory
3 used to express anger or annoyance ◆ *This wretched car won't start.*
▷ **wretchedly** *ADVERB*
▷ **wretchedness** *NOUN*

wriggle *VERB* **wriggles, wriggling, wriggled**
to move with short twisting movements
to wriggle out of something is to avoid an obligation or responsibility
▷ **wriggly** *ADJECTIVE*

wriggle *NOUN* **wriggles**
a wriggling movement

wring *VERB* **wrings, wringing, wrung**
1 to twist and squeeze something to get water or moisture out
2 to squeeze your hand or hands together in anguish or distress
3 to obtain something by a great effort ◆ *Protesters have wrung a promise from city councillors that they will hold a further inquiry.*
wringing wet so wet that water can be squeezed out of it

wring *NOUN* **wrings**
a wringing movement; a squeeze or twist

wringer *NOUN* **wringers**
a device with a pair of rollers for squeezing water out of washed clothes

wrinkle *NOUN* **wrinkles**
1 a small furrow or ridge in the skin
2 a small crease in something

wrinkle *VERB* **wrinkles, wrinkling, wrinkled**
1 to make wrinkles in something
2 to form wrinkles
▷ **wrinkly** *ADJECTIVE*

wrist *NOUN* **wrists**
the joint that connects your hand and forearm

wristwatch *NOUN* **wristwatches**
a watch for wearing on your wrist

writ (*say* rit) *NOUN* **writs**
a formal written command issued by a law court or other legal authority
Holy Writ the Bible

WORD HISTORY from an Old English word

write *VERB* **writes, writing, wrote, written**
1 to put letters, words, or other symbols on paper or another surface
2 to be the author or composer of something ◆ *Who wrote the screenplay for that film?*
3 to write and send a letter ◆ *I promise that I'll write once a week.*
4 (*ICT*) to enter data into a computer memory or storage device
to write something off
1 is to think it is lost or useless
2 is to deduct it as an expense on a tax statement
to write to someone is to send them a letter
to write something up is to write an account of an event
▷ **writer** *NOUN*

writhe *VERB* **writhes, writhing, writhed**
1 to twist your body because of pain
2 to suffer because of shame or embarrassment
3 to twist about; to wriggle

writing *NOUN* **writings**
something you write; the way you write

wrong *ADJECTIVE*
1 incorrect; not true

The only clock that can't show the wrong time is a sundial. — *Kjartan Poskitt, Murderous Maths*

2 not fair or morally right ◆ *A majority of those questioned agreed that it is wrong to hunt an animal for sport.*
3 not working properly ◆ *There's something wrong with the back wheel of your bike.*
to get the wrong end of the stick is to misunderstand a remark or situation
▷ **wrongly** *ADVERB*

wrong *ADVERB*
in the wrong way ◆ *I must have typed your name in wrong.*

wrong *NOUN* **wrongs**
something morally wrong; an injustice
in the wrong having done or said something wrong

wrong *VERB* **wrongs, wronging, wronged**
to do wrong to someone; to treat someone unfairly

wrongdoer *NOUN* **wrongdoers**
a person who does wrong
▷ **wrongdoing** *NOUN*

wrongful *ADJECTIVE*
unfair or unjust; illegal ◆ *The office manager sued for wrongful dismissal and the case went to court.*
▷ **wrongfully** *ADVERB*

wrought *ADJECTIVE*
wrought iron or other metal is worked by being beaten out or shaped by hammering or rolling
WORD HISTORY the old past participle of *work*
USAGE NOTE See the note at *wreak.*

wry *ADJECTIVE* **wryer, wryest**
1 a wry look or comment is slightly mocking or sarcastic
2 twisted or bent out of shape
▷ **wryly** *ADVERB*
▷ **wryness** *NOUN*

WWW *ABBREVIATION*
(*ICT*) World Wide Web

a b c d e f g h i j k l m n o p q r s t u v w x y z

Xx

xenophobia (*say* zen- o- **foh**- bee- a) ***NOUN***
strong dislike or distrust of foreigners
▷ **xenophobe** ***NOUN***
▷ **xenophobic** ***ADJECTIVE***
WORD HISTORY from Greek *xenos* 'foreigner' and *phobia*

Xerox (*say* **zeer**- oks) ***NOUN*** **Xeroxes**
(*trademark*) a photocopy made by a special process

xerox ***VERB*** **xeroxes, xeroxing, xeroxed**
to make a photocopy of something
WORD HISTORY from Greek *xeros* 'dry', because the process does not use liquid chemicals, as earlier photocopiers

Xmas ***NOUN***
(*informal*) Christmas
WORD HISTORY the X represents the Greek letter *chi*, the first letter of *Christos* 'Christ'

X-ray ***NOUN*** **X-rays**
a photograph or examination of the inside of something, especially a part of the body, made by a kind of radiation that can penetrate solid things

X-ray ***VERB*** **X-rays, X-raying, X-rayed**
to make an X-ray of something

xylem (*say* **zy**- lem) ***NOUN***
(*Biology*) the tissue in plants which conducts water and nutrients upwards from the root and helps to form the woody element in the stem

xylophone (*say* **zy**- lo- fohn) ***NOUN*** **xylophones**
a musical instrument made of wooden bars of different lengths that you hit with small hammers
WORD HISTORY from Greek *xulon* 'wood' and *phōnē* 'sound'

Yy

yacht (*say* yot) ***NOUN*** **yachts**
1 a sailing boat used for racing or cruising
2 a private ship
▷ **yachting** ***NOUN***
WORD HISTORY from Dutch *jaghtschip* 'a fast pirate ship'

yachtsman or **yachtswoman** ***NOUN*** **yachtsmen** or **yachtswomen**
a man or woman who sails yachts

yak ***NOUN*** **yaks**
a large long-haired ox, found in central Asia
WORD HISTORY from a Tibetan word

yam ***NOUN*** **yams**
1 the edible starchy tuber of a tropical plant
2 (*American*) a sweet potato

Yank ***NOUN*** **Yanks**
(*informal*) a Yankee

yank ***VERB*** **yanks, yanking, yanked**
(*informal*) to pull something with a sudden sharp tug

yank ***NOUN*** **yanks**
a sudden sharp tug

Yankee ***NOUN*** **Yankees**
an American, especially of the northern USA
WORD HISTORY probably from Dutch *Janke* 'Johnny'

yap ***VERB*** **yaps, yapping, yapped**
1 to bark in a noisy shrill way
2 (*informal*) to talk at length in an annoying way

yap ***NOUN*** **yaps**
a shrill bark

yard ❶ ***NOUN*** **yards**
1 a measure of length, 36 inches or about 91 centimetres
2 a long pole stretched out from a mast to support a sail
WORD HISTORY from Old English *gerd*

yard ❷ ***NOUN*** **yards**
an enclosed area beside a building or used for a certain kind of work ◆ *a timber yard*
WORD HISTORY from Old English *geard*

yardstick ***NOUN*** **yardsticks**
a standard by which something is measured

yarn ***NOUN*** **yarns**
1 thread spun by twisting fibres together, used in knitting etc.
2 (*informal*) a tale or story

yarrow ***NOUN***
a wild plant with strong-smelling flowers

yashmak ***NOUN*** **yashmaks**
a veil concealing all of the face except for the eyes, worn by some Muslim women in public
WORD HISTORY from an Arabic word

yawl ***NOUN*** **yawls**
a kind of sailing boat or fishing boat

yawn ***VERB*** **yawns, yawning, yawned**
1 to open your mouth wide and breathe in deeply when feeling sleepy or bored
2 a pit or chasm yawns when it stretches wide before you

In the centre yawned the circular pit from whose jaws I had escaped. — *Edgar Allan Poe, 'The Pit and the Pendulum'*

yawn ***NOUN*** **yawns**
an act of yawning

ye ***PRONOUN***
(*old use*) you (referring to two or more people)

yea (*say* yay) ***ADVERB***
(*old use*) yes
WORD HISTORY from an Old English word

yeah (*say* yair) ***ADVERB***
(*informal*) yes

year ***NOUN*** **years**
1 the time the earth takes to go right round the sun, about $365\frac{1}{4}$ days
2 the time from 1 January to 31 December
3 any period of twelve months
4 a group of students of roughly the same age ◆ *Is she in your year?*
▷ **yearly** ***ADJECTIVE, ADVERB***
WORD FAMILY A related adjective is annual.

yearling ***NOUN*** **yearlings**
an animal between one and two years old

yearn ***VERB*** **yearns, yearning, yearned**
to long for something ◆ *When Bellerophon was still a boy, he had yearned to ride the magic horse Pegasus.*

yeast ***NOUN***
a substance that causes alcohol and carbon dioxide to form as it develops, used in making beer and wine and in baking bread
▷ **yeasty** ***ADJECTIVE***

yell ***VERB*** **yells, yelling, yelled**
to give a loud cry; to shout

yell *NOUN* **yells**
a loud cry; a shout

yellow *NOUN* **yellows**
the colour of egg yolks and ripe lemons

yellow *ADJECTIVE*
1 of yellow colour
2 (*informal*) lacking courage; cowardly
▷ **yellowish** *ADJECTIVE*
▷ **yellowness** *NOUN*

yellow *VERB* **yellows, yellowing, yellowed**
to become yellow, especially with age ◆ *An ancient volume lay open on the desk, its pages yellowed and its ink faded.*
WORD HISTORY from Old English *geolu*

yellow fever *NOUN*
a tropical disease which causes fever and jaundice

yellowhammer *NOUN* **yellowhammers**
a kind of bunting, the male of which has a yellow head, neck, and breast

yelp *VERB* **yelps, yelping, yelped**
to give a shrill bark or cry

yelp *NOUN* **yelps**
a shrill bark or cry
WORD HISTORY from Old English *gielpan* 'to boast'

yen ❶ *NOUN* **yen**
the unit of money in Japan
WORD HISTORY from a Japanese word meaning 'round'

yen ❷ *NOUN* **yens**
a longing for something ◆ *I've always had a yen to go to Canada.*
WORD HISTORY from a Chinese dialect word

yeoman (*say* yoh- man) *NOUN* **yeomen**
(*History*) a man who owned and farmed a small estate
▷ **yeomanry** *NOUN*
WORD HISTORY probably from *young* and *man*

Yeoman of the Guard *NOUN* **Yeomen of the Guard**
a member of the ceremonial bodyguard of the British monarch, who wear Tudor dress as uniform

yes *ADVERB*
1 used to agree to or give a positive reply to something
2 used as an answer meaning 'I am here'

yes *NOUN* **yesses**
a positive reply or decision ◆ *If you don't reply, I'll take that as a 'yes'.*

yes-man *NOUN* **yes-men**
a person who always agrees with their superiors

yesterday *NOUN*
1 the day before today
2 the recent past

yesterday *ADVERB*
1 on the day before today
2 in the recent past
WORD HISTORY from an old word *yester* and *day*

yesteryear *NOUN* (*literary*)
1 last year
2 the recent past

yet *ADVERB*
1 by this time; so far ◆ *Have you checked your email yet?*
2 up to this time and continuing, still ◆ *There's life in this old engine yet.*
3 before the matter is done with; eventually

'Honestly, Mrs Hadley,' said Meggie McGregor, wiping her eyes. 'That sense of humour of yours will be the death of me yet!' — *Malorie Blackman, Noughts and Crosses*

4 in addition; even ◆ *The airship climbed yet higher, until it disappeared from view.* ◆ *There was a crash as yet another wave pounded against the pier.*

yet *CONJUNCTION*
nevertheless; but in spite of that ◆ *We've never met before, yet I feel that I know you.*

yeti *NOUN* **yetis**
a large animal said to exist in the Himalayas, also known as the *Abominable Snowman*

'Look, if someone had told me we were coming here to hunt a yeti, I'd have been expecting great ape, I'd have been expecting something like orang-utan.' — *Philip Gross, The Lastling*

WORD HISTORY from a Tibetan word

yew *NOUN* **yews**
an evergreen tree with dark green needle-like leaves and red berries

Yiddish *NOUN*
a language used by Jews of central and eastern Europe, based on a German dialect and with words from Hebrew and various modern languages
WORD HISTORY from a German word meaning 'Jewish'

yield *VERB* **yields, yielding, yielded**
1 to give in or surrender
2 to agree to do what is asked or ordered; to give way ◆ *The Count yielded to persuasion and decided not to venture out that night.*
3 to allow other traffic to have right of way
4 to produce as a natural product or profit ◆ *How much milk does your herd yield?* ◆ *On average, the shares yield 5% per annum.*
5 to produce when searched; to be found to contain

The rest of the containers, when examined, yielded nothing more exciting than three common toads, a small green viper and four weaver-birds [= a type of finch] which I did not want. — *Gerald Durrell, A Zoo in My Luggage*

a b c d e f g h i j k l m n o p q r s t u v w x y z

yield *NOUN* **yields**
the amount yielded or produced ◆ *What is the yield of wheat per acre?*
WORD HISTORY from an Old English word meaning 'to pay'

yob *NOUN* **yobs**
(*informal*) a bad-mannered or aggressive young man; a lout
▷ **yobbish** *ADJECTIVE*
WORD HISTORY from *boy*, written backwards

yodel *VERB* **yodels, yodelling, yodelled**
to sing or call with the voice alternating rapidly between a very high pitch and its normal pitch
▷ **yodeller** *NOUN*
WORD HISTORY from a German word

yoga (*say* **yoh**- ga) *NOUN*
a Hindu system of meditation and self-control; a system of physical exercises based on this
WORD HISTORY from a Sanskrit word meaning 'union'

yoghurt or **yogurt** (*say* **yog**- ert) *NOUN*
milk thickened by the action of certain bacteria, giving it a sharp taste
WORD HISTORY from a Turkish word

yoke *NOUN* **yokes**
1 a curved piece of wood put across the necks of animals pulling a cart or plough
2 a shaped piece of wood fitted across a person's shoulders, with a pail or load hung at each end
3 something thought of as oppressive or burdensome ◆ *India threw off the yoke of British rule on 15 August, 1947.*
4 a close-fitting upper part of a piece of clothing, from which the rest hangs

yoke *VERB* **yokes, yoking, yoked**
to harness or join things by means of a yoke
USAGE NOTE Take care not to confuse this word with *yolk*.

yokel (*say* **yoh**- kel) *NOUN* **yokels**
a simple and unsophisticated country person

yolk (*rhymes with* coke) *NOUN* **yolks**
the round yellow part inside an egg
WORD HISTORY from Old English *geolu* 'yellow'
USAGE NOTE Take care not to confuse this word with *yoke*.

Yom Kippur (*say* yom kip- **oor**) *NOUN*
the Day of Atonement, a solemn Jewish religious festival, a day of fasting and repentance

yon *ADJECTIVE, ADVERB*
(*literary*) over there; yonder
WORD HISTORY from an Old English word

yonder *ADJECTIVE, ADVERB*
(*old use*) over there

yonks *PLURAL NOUN*
(*informal*) a long time; ages ◆ *I haven't seen my cousins in Australia for yonks.*
WORD HISTORY may be short for *donkey's years*

yore *NOUN*
of yore (*literary*) of long ago ◆ *in days of yore.*
WORD HISTORY from an Old English word

Yorkshire pudding *NOUN* **Yorkshire puddings**
a baked batter pudding eaten with roast beef

Yorkshire terrier *NOUN* **Yorkshire terriers**
a small long-haired terrier

you *PRONOUN*
1 the person or people being spoken to ◆ *Can I help you?* ◆ *I think you should both leave now.*
2 anyone or everyone; one ◆ *You wouldn't know that we are twins.* ◆ *You never know when you might need a compass.*

you'd
short for *you had* or *you would*

you'll
short for *you will*

young *ADJECTIVE*
1 having lived or existed for only a short time; not old
2 not far advanced in time ◆ *The night is still young.*
WORD FAMILY a related adjective is juvenile.

young *PLURAL NOUN*
children or young animals or birds

The four young were almost fully fledged, and they fitted the nest as snugly as a completed jig-saw. — *Barry Hines, A Kestrel for a Knave*

youngster *NOUN* **youngsters**
a child or young person

your *ADJECTIVE*
belonging to you ◆ *Take your books.*
USAGE NOTE Take care not to confuse this word with *you're*.

you're
short for *you are* ◆ *You're late again.*
USAGE NOTE Take care not to confuse this word with *your*.

yours *POSSESSIVE PRONOUN*
belonging to you ◆ *Is this book yours?* ◆ *Yours is the seat at the window.*
Yours faithfully a more formal ending to a business letter
Yours sincerely a less formal ending to a business letter, also used in personal correspondence
Yours truly
1 a fairly formal ending to a business letter
2 (*informal*) the person speaking ◆ *Yours truly was left to do the dishes.*
USAGE NOTE It is incorrect to write *your's*, with an apostrophe.

yourself *PRONOUN* **yourselves**
you and nobody else: used to refer back to the subject of a sentence (e.g. *You've cut yourself*) and for emphasis (e.g. *You told me so yourself*)
by yourself or **by yourselves** on your own; alone

youth *NOUN* **youths**
1 the time when you are young; the period between childhood and adulthood
2 the vigour or lack of experience etc. characteristic of being young ◆ *The new players will bring an injection of youth and enthusiasm to the team.*
3 a young man
4 young people
WORD HISTORY from Old English *geoguth*

youth club *NOUN* **youth clubs**
a club providing leisure activities for young people

youthful *ADJECTIVE*
1 young; looking or seeming young
2 characteristic of young people ◆ *Mozart's early sonatas are full of youthful brilliance and warmth.*
▷ **youthfulness** *NOUN*

youth hostel *NOUN* **youth hostels**
a place where young people can stay cheaply when they are hiking or on holiday

you've short for *you have*

yowl *VERB* **yowls, yowling, yowled**
to wail or howl loudly
yowl *NOUN* **yowls**
a loud wailing cry or howl

yo-yo *NOUN* **yo-yos**
a round wooden or plastic toy that moves up and down on a string that you hold
yo-yo *VERB* **yo-yoes, yo-yoing, yo-yoed**
to move up and down repeatedly

yuan *NOUN* **yuan**
the unit of money in China
WORD HISTORY from a Chinese word meaning 'round'

yucca *NOUN*
a tall plant with white bell-like flowers and stiff spiky leaves

Yule or **Yuletide** *NOUN*
(*old use*) the Christmas festival
WORD HISTORY from an Old English word

yummy *ADJECTIVE* **yummier, yummiest**
(*informal*) good to eat; delicious

Those yummy dumplings were stuffed with pork, chives and spring onions and were absolutely delicious! — *Adeline Yen Mah, Chinese Cinderella*

yuppie *NOUN* **yuppies**
(*informal*) a young middle-class person with a well-paid professional job
WORD HISTORY from the initial letters of *young urban professional*

Zz

zany ***ADJECTIVE*** **zanier, zaniest**
funny in a weird or crazy way
▷ **zaniness** ***NOUN***

WORD HISTORY from Italian *zanni* 'a type of clown'

zap ***VERB*** **zaps, zapping, zapped** (*informal*)
1 to attack or destroy something forcefully
2 to use a remote control to change television channels quickly
▷ **zapper** ***NOUN***

zeal ***NOUN***
enthusiasm or keenness

zealot (*say* **zel**- ot) ***NOUN*** **zealots**
a zealous person; a fanatic

zealous ***ADJECTIVE***
fanatically keen or enthusiastic
▷ **zealously** ***ADVERB***

zebra (*say* **zeb**- ra) ***NOUN*** **zebras**
an African animal of the horse family, with black and white stripes all over its body

zebra crossing ***NOUN*** **zebra crossings**
a place for pedestrians to cross a road safely, marked with broad white stripes

zebu (*say* **zee**- bew) ***NOUN*** **zebus**
an ox with a humped back, found in India, East Asia, and Africa

Zen ***NOUN***
a form of Buddhism which emphasizes the value of meditation and intuition

WORD HISTORY from a Japanese word meaning 'meditation'

zenith ***NOUN***
1 the part of the sky directly above someone looking at it
2 the highest point ◆ *The power of the Roman Empire was then at its zenith.*

WORD HISTORY from Arabic *samt ar-ra's* 'path over the head'

Zeppelin (*say* **zep**- er- lin) ***NOUN***
a large German airship of the early 20th century

WORD HISTORY named after Count von *Zeppelin*, an army officer who built these airships

zephyr (*say* **zef**- er) ***NOUN*** **zephyrs**
a soft gentle wind

WORD HISTORY from Greek *Zephyros*, god of the west wind

zero ***NOUN*** **zeros**
1 nought; the figure 0
2 the point marked 0 on a thermometer or other scale

WORD HISTORY from Arabic *sifr* 'cipher, nought'

zero ***VERB*** **zeroes, zeroing, zeroed**
to zero in on something is to focus your aim or attention on it

zero hour ***NOUN***
the time when something is planned to start

zest ***NOUN***
1 great enjoyment or interest
2 the coloured part of orange or lemon peel
▷ **zestful** ***ADJECTIVE***
▷ **zestfully** ***ADVERB***

zigzag ***NOUN*** **zigzags**
a line or route that turns sharply from side to side

zigzag ***VERB*** **zigzags, zigzagging, zigzagged**
to move in a zigzag

zillion ***NOUN***
(*informal*) an extremely large number ◆ *There were about a zillion people in front of me in the queue.*

Zimmer frame ***NOUN*** **Zimmer frames**
(*trademark*) a frame that a lame or frail person uses as a support in walking

zinc ***NOUN***
a white metal

zing ***VERB*** **zings, zinging, zinged**
(*informal*) to be vibrant ◆ *Even in gloomy weather, the colours in this garden really zing.*
▷ **zingy** ***ADJECTIVE***

zip ***NOUN*** **zips**
1 a fastener consisting of two strips of material, each with rows of small teeth that interlock when a sliding tab brings them together
2 liveliness or vigour

zip ***VERB*** **zips, zipping, zipped**
1 to fasten or close something with a zip
2 to move quickly with a sharp sound

zip code ***NOUN***
(*American*) a type of postcode used in the USA

WORD HISTORY from the initial letters of *zone improvement plan*

zipper ***NOUN*** **zippers**
(*American*) a zip fastener

zippy ***ADJECTIVE*** **zippier, zippiest**
lively and vigorous
▷ **zippiness** ***NOUN***

zither ***NOUN*** **zithers**
a musical instrument with many strings stretched over a shallow box-like body
WORD HISTORY from Greek *kithara*, a type of harp

zodiac (*say* **zoh**- dee- ak) ***NOUN***
a strip of sky where the sun, moon, and main planets are found, divided into twelve equal parts (called **signs of the zodiac**), each named after a constellation
▷ **zodiacal** ***ADJECTIVE***
WORD HISTORY from Greek *zōidion* 'image of an animal'

zombie ***NOUN*** **zombies**
1 (*informal*) a person who seems to be doing things without thinking, usually because they are very tired
2 in voodoo, a corpse said to have been brought back to life by witchcraft
WORD HISTORY from a West African word

zone ***NOUN*** **zones**
an area of a special kind or for a particular purpose ◆ *a pedestrian zone* ◆ *a nuclear-free zone*
WORD HISTORY from a Greek word meaning 'girdle'

zoo ***NOUN*** **zoos**
a place where wild animals are kept so that people can look at or study them
WORD HISTORY short for *zoological gardens*

zoology (*say* zoh- **ol**- o- jee) ***NOUN***
the scientific study of animals
▷ **zoological** ***ADJECTIVE***
▷ **zoologist** ***NOUN***
WORD HISTORY from Greek *zoion* 'animal'

zoom ***VERB*** **zooms, zooming, zoomed**
1 to move or travel very quickly

> It wasn't stars she was seeing at all — just the light of stars zooming like fury to get to the earth but taking forever because it was so far to go.
> — *Katherine Paterson, The Same Stuff as Stars*

2 to rise or increase rapidly ◆ *House prices in the area have started to zoom.*
3 to use a zoom lens
to zoom in or **out** is to use a zoom lens to focus further in or out

zoom ***NOUN***
the action of a camera zooming

zoom lens ***NOUN*** **zoom lenses**
a camera lens that can be adjusted to focus on things that are close up or far away

zucchini ***NOUN*** **zucchini** or **zucchinis**
(*American*) a courgette
WORD HISTORY an Italian word

Zulu ***NOUN*** **Zulus**
1 a member of a South African people
2 the Bantu language of this people

Appendices

Prefixes and suffixes

Some common prefixes

A prefix is a group of letters joined to the beginning of a word to change its meaning, or already forming part of the word, for example *re-* in *recapture* (= to capture again), *un-* in *unknown* (= not known), and *com-* in *communicate* (= make contact with). You can use some of the prefixes to make special words that are not included in this dictionary. Here are some examples of the more common English prefixes:

prefix	**meaning**	**example**
an-	not, without	analgesic
anti-	against	anti-British
arch-	chief	archbishop
auto-	self	automatic
co-	together	coeducation
com-, con-	together, with	communicate
contra-	against	contraflow
cyber-	to do with the Internet	cyberspace
de-	undoing or taking away	de-ice
dis-	not	dishonest
dis-	taking away	disconnect
eco-	to do with the ecology and the environment	ecosystem
em-, en-	in, into	embark, entrust
ex-	that used to be, former	ex-president
extra-	beyond, outside	extraordinary, extraterrestrial
fore-	before, in front of	forefinger, foregoing
giga-	times 10^9 or (*in ICT*) 2^{30}	gigabyte
in- (*also* il-, im-, ir- *before certain letters*)	not	incorrect, illegal, impossible, irrelevant
inter-	between	international
mega-	times 10^6 or (*in ICT*) 2^{20}	megabyte
mis-	wrong	misbehave
mono-	one, single	monorail
multi-	many	multicultural
non-	not	non-existent
over-	too much	overdo
poly-	many	polygon
post-	after	post-war
pre-	before	prehistoric, pre-Victorian
pro-	supporting	pro-British
re-	again	recapture
semi-	half	semicircle
sub-	below	submarine
super-	over, beyond	superstore
tele-	at a distance	telecommunications
trans-	across	transport, transatlantic
ultra-	beyond	ultrasonic
un-	not, the opposite of	unknown, undo
under-	not enough	underdone

Some common suffixes

A suffix is a group of letters joined to the end of a word to change its meaning, or already forming part of the word, for example *-able* in *eatable* (= able to be eaten), *-er* in *maker* (= a person or machine makes something), and *-ness* in *happiness* (= the state of being happy). You can use some of the suffixes to make special words that are not included in this dictionary, and you can also make words with more than one suffix, e.g. *childishness* and *senselessly*. Here are some examples of the more common English suffixes:

suffix	**meaning**	**example**
-able (*also -ible, -uble*)	able to be	eatable, possible, soluble
-ant, -ent	someone who does something	attendant, superintendent
-dom	used to make nouns to do with condition or rank	officialdom
-ee	someone who is affected	employee, refugee
-er	a person or thing that does something	maker, opener
-er	more	faster
-esque	in the style of	picturesque
-ess	a female person or animal	lioness, actress
-est	most	fastest
-fold	times, involving two	twofold
-ful	full of	
-hood	used to make nouns to do with	beautiful, cupful
	state or condition	childhood, motherhood
-ic	belonging to, associated with	Islamic, terrific
-ish	rather like, somewhat	childish, greenish
-ism	used to make nouns to do with systems and beliefs	capitalism, Hinduism
-ist	someone who does something or believes something	dentist, sexist
-itis	used to make nouns for illnesses involving inflammation	appendicitis
-ize *or* -ise	used to make verbs	criticize, televise
-less	not having, without	senseless
-let	small	booklet
-ly	used to make adverbs and adjectives	bravely, leisurely
-ment	used to make nouns	amusement
-ness	used to make nouns	kindness, happiness
-oid	like or resembling	celluloid
-or	a person or thing that does something	sailor, escalator
-ous	used to make adjectives	dangerous
-ship	used to make nouns	friendship, citizenship
-some	full of	loathsome
-tion	used to make nouns	abbreviation, ignition, completion
-ty	used to make nouns	beauty
-ward (*also -wards*)	in a particular direction	homeward, northwards

Chief languages of the world *(spoken by over 6m people)*

language	where it is spoken
Afrikaans	southern Africa
Albanian	Albania
Amharic	Ethiopia
Arabic	northern Africa and the Middle East
Armenian	Armenia and nearby areas
Assamese	India and Bangladesh
Awadhi	India, Nepal
Azerbaijani	Azerbaijan, Russia, Iraq
Belorussian	Belarus, Poland
Bengali	Bangladesh, India
Bhojpuri	India, Nepal
Bihari	India, Nepal, and nearby areas
Braj Bhasha	India
Bulgarian	Bulgaria and nearby areas
Burmese	Myanmar
Catalan	north-east Spain, France
Cebuano	Philippines
Chattisgarhi	India
Chinese	China
Czech	Czech Republic
Danish	Denmark
Dutch	The Netherlands, Belgium, Suriname
English	UK, USA, Canada, Ireland, Australia, New Zealand, South Africa, (and worldwide as a second language)
Farsi (Persian)	Iran and nearby areas
Finnish	Finland
French	France, Canada, Belgium, Switzerland, Monaco, (and widespread as a second language)
German	Germany, Austria, Switzerland, eastern Europe, (and widespread as a second language)
Greek	Greece, Cyprus, Turkey
Gujarati	India, Pakistan
Hausa	Nigeria, Niger, and nearby areas
Hebrew	Israel, Europe, USA
Hindi	India, parts of Africa
Hungarian	Hungary, Romania
Icelandic	Iceland
Igbo	Nigeria
Indonesian	Indonesia
Italian	Italy, Switzerland, San Marino
Japanese	Japan, USA, Brazil
Javanese	Indonesia
Kannada (Kanarese)	India
Kazakh	Kazakhstan, Russia, China
Khmer (Cambodian)	south-east Asia

language	where it is spoken
Korean	North and South Korea, Japan
Kurdish	Iraq, Iran, Turkey
Lanna	Thailand, Laos
Lingala	central Africa
Magahi	India
Maithili	India, Nepal
Malagasy	Madagascar
Malay	Indonesia, Malaysia, Singapore, and nearby areas
Malayalam	India
Marathi	India
Marwari	India, Pakistan
Nepali	Nepal, India, Bhutan
Norwegian	Norway
Occitan	France
Oriya	India, Bangladesh
Oromo	Ethiopia, Kenya
Panjabi	Pakistan, India
Pashto	Afghanistan, Pakistan, Arabia
Persian (*see* Farsi)	
Polish	Poland and nearby areas
Portuguese	Portugal, Brazil
Quechua	Peru, Bolivia, Ecuador
Romanian	Romania, Moldova
Russian	Russia and nearby areas
Rwanda	central Africa
Serbian	Balkans
Sinhalese	Sri Lanka
Siraiki	Pakistan, India
Slovak	Slovak Republic and nearby areas
Spanish	Spain, North, Central, and South America
Sunda	Indonesia
Swahili	central Africa
Swedish	Sweden, Finland
Tagalog	Philippines
Tamil	India, Sri Lanka, Vietnam
Telugu	India, south-east Asia
Thai	Thailand
Turkish	Turkey
Ukrainian	Ukraine and nearby areas
Urdu	India, Pakistan
Uzbek	Uzbekistan and nearby areas
Vietnamese	Vietnam, Cambodia, Laos
Yiddish	Israel, USA, Russia
Yoruba	Nigeria, Benin
Zulu	South Africa

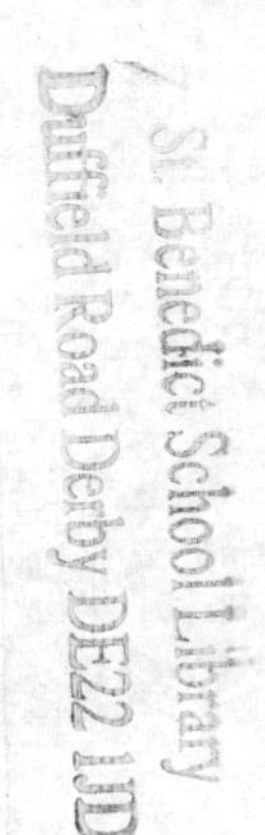

Oxford Children's Dictionaries

Age 4+

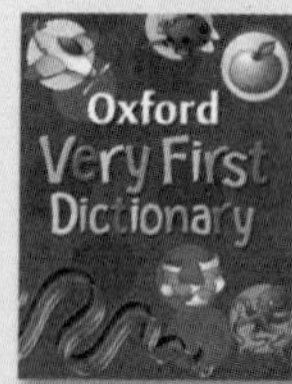

Age 5+

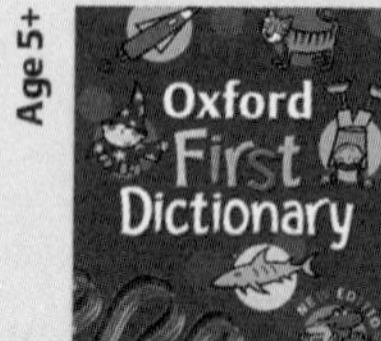

Age 7+

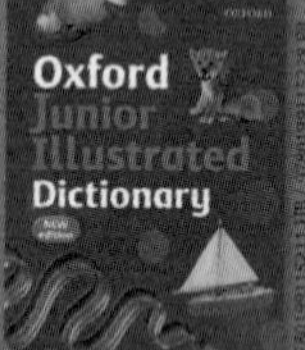

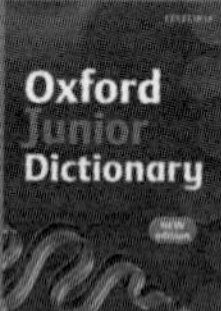

Age 8+

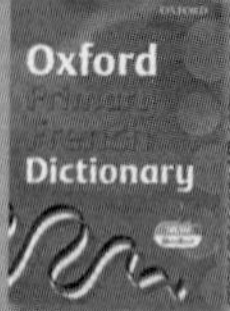

Age 10+

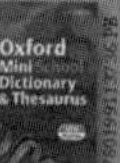

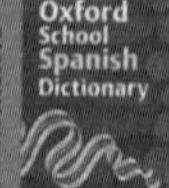

Age 14+

Think Dictionaries. Think Oxford.

www.oup.com